Walford's Guide to Reference Material

WALFORD'S GUIDE TO REFERENCE MATERIAL

SEVENTH EDITION • VOLUME 3

Generalia, Language and Literature, The Arts

EDITED BY

ANTHONY CHALCRAFT BA MA ALA
College Librarian, University College of Ripon and York St John

RAY PRYTHERCH MA MPhil ALA
Information Consultant

and

STEPHEN WILLIS BA DipLib ALA
Principal Officer, South District, Manchester City Libraries

LIBRARY ASSOCIATION PUBLISHING
LONDON

Published by
Library Association Publishing
7 Ridgmount Street
London WC1E 7AE

Library Association Publishing is wholly owned by The Library Association.

First published 1959
Supplement 1963
Second edition 1970
Third edition 1977
Fourth edition 1987
Fifth edition 1991
Sixth edition 1995
This seventh edition 1998

British Library Cataloguing in Publication Data
A catalogue record for this book is available from
The British Library

ISBN 1-85604-300-2

Computer production software and typesetting by LIBPAC (Computer Services) Ltd, Whittle le Woods, Lancs.
Printed and made in Great Britain by Bookcraft (Bath) Ltd, Midsomer Norton, Somerset.

Contents

Introduction

From its first edition the purpose of *Walford* has been to identify and evaluate the widest possible range of reference materials. In addition to the expected bibliographies, indexes, dictionaries, encyclopaedias, directories, etc., a number of important textbooks and manuals of general practice are included. While the majority of items are reference 'books', *Walford* is a guide to reference 'material'. Thus periodical articles, microforms, online, CD-ROM and Internet sources are all represented. The objective is for *Walford* to provide a 'one-stop' source of information on all types of reference material, regardless of form. Targeted users include librarians developing and revising reference collections, staff on enquiry desks needing advice on further sources when local stock has been checked, research workers in the preliminary stages of projects, and students of library and information studies.

To be of manageable proportions a guide such as this must inevitably be selective. Most major reference tools are included, whenever originally published, provided they remain useful. Geographic scope is international, but with an emphasis on English-language material. A special effort has been made to ensure that the output of small and specialist publishers is not neglected.

Entries in *Walford* follow a subject arrangement based on the Universal Decimal Classification International Medium Edition of 1985 (BS1000M). Subject access for users unfamiliar with UDC can be gained either by checking the contents page to find the relevant section and then browsing through the entries, which are subdivided by form, place, etc., or by using the subject index. The first level of subheading within each broad subject class is typographically highlighted by the use of rules (see sample entry overleaf).

Terms in the subject index are generated by the classification numbers given to the entries. Each entry has been allocated a running serial number in the text to provide easy access from both the subject and author/title indexes. There is an index of online, Internet and database services. Full instruction on the structure and use of the indexes can be found in their introductions.

Individual entries in *Walford* are wherever possible based on examination of the actual item and include full bibliographical details, ISBN, ISSN and, if in print, the price when it can be ascertained. Brief critical annotations are provided in most cases, giving summary publishing history, outline of contents, comparison with other works, especially notable features and a brief general assessment of overall value, often illustrated by quotations from or references to reviews. The example overleaf shows the general layout of entries.

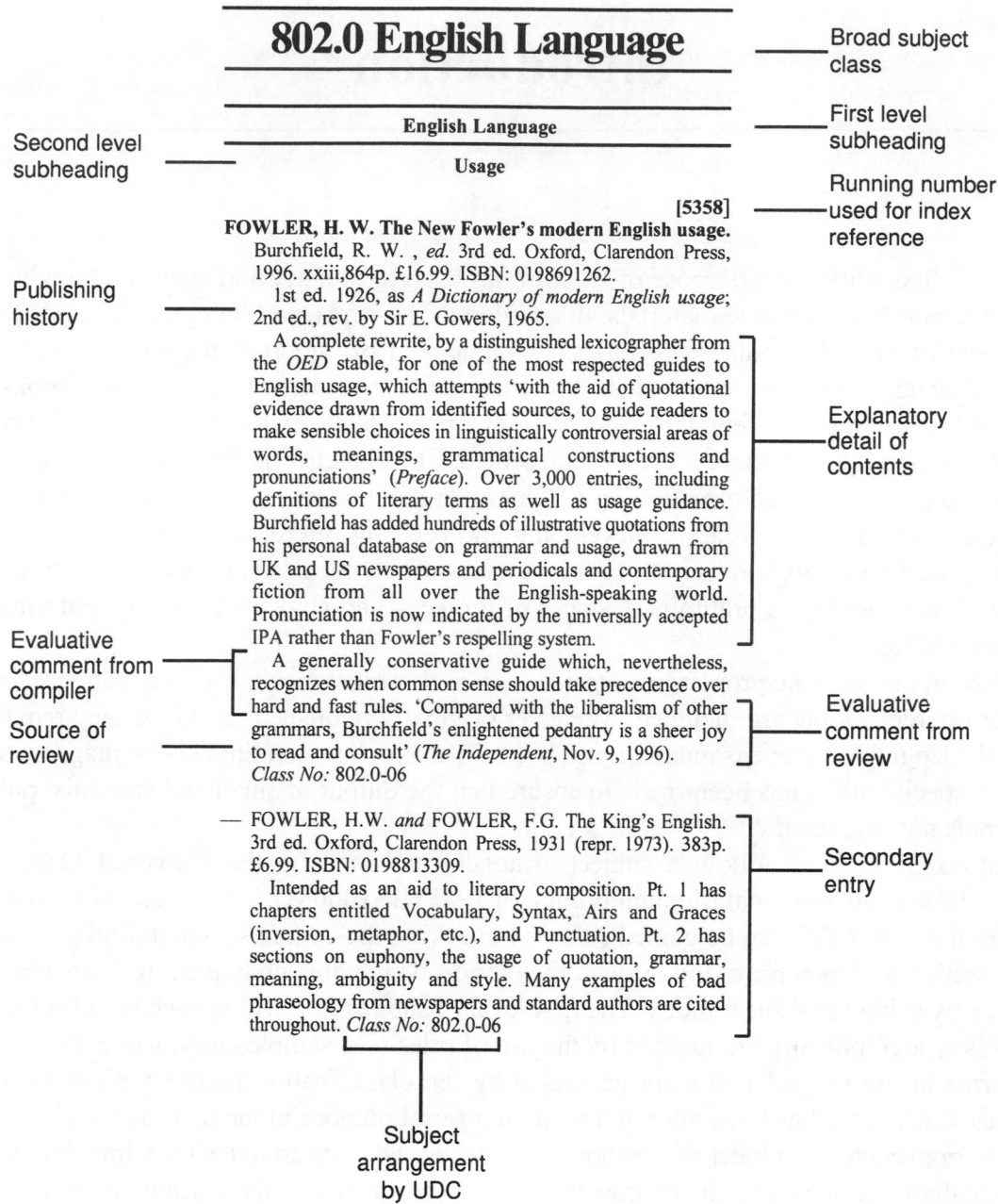

802.0 English Language

Broad subject class

English Language

First level subheading

Second level subheading

Usage

Running number used for index reference

[5358]

FOWLER, H. W. The New Fowler's modern English usage. Burchfield, R. W. , *ed.* 3rd ed. Oxford, Clarendon Press, 1996. xxiii,864p. £16.99. ISBN: 0198691262.

Publishing history

1st ed. 1926, as *A Dictionary of modern English usage*; 2nd ed., rev. by Sir E. Gowers, 1965.

A complete rewrite, by a distinguished lexicographer from the *OED* stable, for one of the most respected guides to English usage, which attempts 'with the aid of quotational evidence drawn from identified sources, to guide readers to make sensible choices in linguistically controversial areas of words, meanings, grammatical constructions and pronunciations' (*Preface*). Over 3,000 entries, including definitions of literary terms as well as usage guidance. Burchfield has added hundreds of illustrative quotations from his personal database on grammar and usage, drawn from UK and US newspapers and periodicals and contemporary fiction from all over the English-speaking world. Pronunciation is now indicated by the universally accepted IPA rather than Fowler's respelling system.

Explanatory detail of contents

Evaluative comment from compiler

A generally conservative guide which, nevertheless, recognizes when common sense should take precedence over hard and fast rules. 'Compared with the liberalism of other grammars, Burchfield's enlightened pedantry is a sheer joy to read and consult' (*The Independent*, Nov. 9, 1996).
Class No: 802.0-06

Source of review

Evaluative comment from review

— FOWLER, H.W. *and* FOWLER, F.G. The King's English. 3rd ed. Oxford, Clarendon Press, 1931 (repr. 1973). 383p. £6.99. ISBN: 0198813309.

Intended as an aid to literary composition. Pt. 1 has chapters entitled Vocabulary, Syntax, Airs and Graces (inversion, metaphor, etc.), and Punctuation. Pt. 2 has sections on euphony, the usage of quotation, grammar, meaning, ambiguity and style. Many examples of bad phraseology from newspapers and standard authors are cited throughout. *Class No:* 802.0-06

Secondary entry

Subject arrangement by UDC

Work on this volume overall was completed in mid-1998. Although no cut-off date for new material was specified, the aim has been to include as many 1997 publications as possible, together with some items published early in 1998. Intimation of planned new and revised editions is also given where possible.

This volume particularly reflects the proliferation of significant World Wide Web sites and online, CD-ROM and Internet-accessible versions of printed sources in all subject areas.

In all sections out-of-date or superseded materials have been deleted.

In section 0 Generalities there are over 350 new items, with every existing entry checked and, if necessary, revised. A special effort has been made to include a selection of significant World Wide Web sites. The major classes, particularly 015 National Bibliographies, 02 Librarianship and Information Science, 05 Periodicals and 07 Journalism have received particular attention.

In section 7 The Arts there are almost 400 new entries and over 750 amendments have been made to previous entries. Entries for Films and Videos have been a particular focus for attention in this edition. Web sites have been added throughout the section.

In section 8 Language and Literature there are well over 400 new entries and hundreds more have been updated.

This volume is the work of three compilers: Anthony Chalcraft was responsible for class 0 Generalities; Ray Prytherch was responsible for class 7 The Arts and Stephen Willis was responsible for Class 8 Language and Literature. The whole project was overseen by Kathryn Beecroft of Library Association Publishing. Joan Bibby ably constructed a thesaurus based on the UDC classification scheme. Martin Harrison of LIBPAC Computer Services automated the data capture, indexing and typesetting.

Anthony Chalcraft would like to thank Jane Thurlow for proof-reading and Chris Taylor of the National Library of Scotland for advice on French language material. Ray Prytherch would like to thank Priscilla Schlicke for advice and assistance. Stephen Willis would like to thank the staff of Waterstones bookshop in Manchester for allowing extensive access to their language and literature sections. The compilers are indebted to John Walford for his continuing interest in this work and his contributions in the form of advice and notes on new material.

Libraries consulted

(a) *General libraries*

The British Library:

- Humanities Reading Room;
- Librarianship Information Sciences Service – LISS
- Document Supply Centre (Boston Spa)
- National Sound Archive
- Science Reference and Information Service
- Social Policy Information Service.

National Library of Scotland.

(b) *Academic libraries*

College of Ripon and York St John; University of Cambridge; University of Leeds; University of Liverpool; University of Manchester; Manchester Metropolitan University;

University of Sheffield; University of York; University of London (School of Oriental and African Studies, School of Slavonic and East European Studies, University College Library, University Library); UMIST.

(c) *Public libraries*
Birmingham, Chicago, Leeds, Liverpool, Manchester, New York, Sheffield, Westminster, York.

(d) *Special libraries*
British Architectural Library, Goethe Institute (Manchester), London Library, National Art Library.

Anthony Chalcraft
Ray Prytherch
Stephen Willis

Abbreviations

Listed below are the chief bibliographical abbreviations used in the *Guide*. Generally accepted abbreviations such as Co., Corpn. *e.g.*, *i.e.*, Inc., Ltd. and *q.v.* are not included.

AG [German] – Aktiengesellschaft: Co.
ALA – American Library Association
Abt. [German] – Abteiling: part
ampl. [Italian] – ampliata: enlarged
    [Spanish] – ampliado: enlarged
Aufl. [German] – Auflage: edition
augm. [French] – augmenté: enlarged
aum. [Portuguese] – aumentada: enlarged
    [Spanish] – aumentado: enlarged
Ausg. [German] – Ausgabe: printing, edition

BS – British Standard
Bd [German] – Band: volume
BFr – Belgian francs
bearb. [German] – bearbeitet: compiled, edited
Belg. – Belgian

c – copyright date
C. Cd. Cmd. Cmnd. – Command papers
ch. – chapter(s)
chron. – chronology
col. – colour, coloured
cols. – columns
comp. – compiler
corr. – corrected
    [French] – corrigé: corrected
    [Spanish] – corregido: corrected
    [Portuguese] – corrigida: corrected

DFI – Dutch florins
Dan. – Danish
diagrs. – diagrams
distr. – distributed
DM [German] – Deutschmark
druk [Dutch] – edition

ea. – each
ed. – edition, editor(s)
    [Italian] – edizione
    [Spanish] – edición
    [French] – édition
    [Portuguese] – ediçáo: edition
enl. – enlarged
erw., erweit. [German] – erweiterte: enlarged
exp. – expanded

FID – Fédération Internationale de Documentation
facsim(s) – facsimile(s)
fasc(s) – fascicule(s)
fig. – figures
fldg. – folding
FFr – French francs
front. – frontispiece

ganz. [German] – gänzlich: complete
glav.red. [Russian] – glavnyi redaktor: editor-in-chief
Gld. [Dutch] – guilders
GmbH [German] – Gesellschaft mit beschränkter Haftung: Ltd
Gosud. [Russian] – Gosudarstvo: State

HMSO – Her Majesty's Stationery Office
Hft [German] – Heft: part number
hrsg. [German] – herausgegeben: edited, published

illus. – illustrations, illustrated
imp. [French] – imprimé, imprimerie: printed, printing firm
izd. [Russian] – izdanie: edition
    [Serbo-Croat] – izdanje: edition
Izdat. [Russian] – Izdatel': publisher

Jahrg. [German] – Jahrgang: annual publication

kiad. [Hungarian] – kiadás: edition
Kr [Danish, Norwegian, Swedish] – kroner

L. [Italian] – lire
l. – leaves
Lfg. [German] – Lieferung: number, part

m. fl. [Danish] – med flere: and others

n.d. – no date
neubearb. [German]: – neubearbeitet: revised
no. – number
Nor. – Norwegian
nouv. [French] – nouvelle: new (edition)
n.p. – no place of publication
Nr [Danish, German] – Nummer: number
n.s. – new series
NV [Dutch] – naamloze vennootschap: limited company

o.p. – out of print
omarb. [Swedish] – omarbetad: revised
opl. [Danish] – oplag: edition

p. – page(s)
pl. – plate(s)
port. – portrait(s)
pt(s) – part(s)
pub. – publisher
pubn. – publication

réd. [French] – rédigé: edited, compiled
repr. – reprinted
rev. – revised, revision
[French] – révisé: revised
[Portuguese] – revistada: revised

riv. [Italian] – riveduto: revised
R. [South Africa] – rands
Rs – rupees

Sch – Austrian schillings
ser. – series
sér. [French] – série: series
SFr – Swiss francs
supp. – supplementary, supplement(s)
Sw. – Swiss
Swed. – Swedish

t. [French] – tome(s): volume(s)
T. [German] – Teil(e): part(s)

u. [German] – und: and
UDC – Universal Decimal Classification
udg. [Danish] – udgave: edition
uit. [Dutch] – uitgaaf: publication
uitg. [Dutch] – uitgegeven: published
umgearb. [German] – umbearbeitete: revised
Univ. – University
unveränd. [German] – unverändert: unaltered
uppl. [Swedish] – upplaga: edition
utg. [Norwegian] – utgave: edition

v. – volume(s)
v. p. – various pagings
VEB [German] – Volkseigener Betrieb: People's Concern
verand. [German] – verandert: revised
verb. [German] – verbesserte: improved
verm [German] – vermehrte: enlarged
vyd. [Czech] – vydání: edition
[Slovak] – vydanie: edition

wyd. [Polish] – wydanie: edition

001 Knowledge

Intellectual Work

Index Production

[1]
BONURA, L. The Art of indexing. New York, Wiley, 1994. xxii,233p. tables. £24.95;$26.95. (*Wiley technical communications library*.) ISBN: 0471014494.

Aimed mainly at writers/editors of technical reports. 25 chaps. (*e.g.* Selecting topics, Automating the process, Editing the index) with crisp, structured text offering a step-by-step approach. Bibliography (p.165-72) and glossary; 'Sample indexes' and 'Sample index style guide'.
Class No: 001.815

[2]
COLLISON, R.L. Indexes and indexing: a guide to the indexing of books, and collections of books, periodicals, music, recordings, films and other materials, with a reference section and suggestions for further reading. 4th rev. ed. London, Benn, New York, DeGraff, 1972. 232p. ISBN: 0510457223.

First published 1953.

3 parts: The indexing of books - Wider indexing (other material) - Reference section (including 'Twenty basic rules for indexers' and 'The indexer's reference library'). 'An examination for indexers', followed by outline answers. Analytical index. Remains a standard guide.
Class No: 001.815

[3]
KNIGHT, G.N. Indexing, the art of: a guide to the indexing of books and periodicals. London, Allen & Unwin, 1979. 218p. 1 facsim. ISBN: 0040290026.

13 chapters. 1. Introductory - 2. The Mechanics - 3. Headings and subheadings - 4. Proper name headings - 5. Subject headings - 6. References and cross-references - 7. Alphabetical arrangement - 8. The Indexing of periodicals - 9. Newspaper indexing - 10. Cumulative indexing - 11. Editing the index - 12. The Correction of proofs - 13. Humour in indexing. Appendices: The Society of Indexers; The American Society of Indexers; The Wheatley medal; The Carey award. Index (p.203-18). *Class No:* 001.815

[4]
LANCASTER, F.W. Indexing and abstracting in theory and practice. London, Library Association and Graduate School of Library Science, University of Illinois, 1991. xiv,328p. illus. £40;$39.50. ISBN: 1856040046.

2nd ed. forthcoming 1998 (ISBN: 1856042685).

Concentrates 'on indexing and abstracting as practised by published indexing and abstracting services (in paper or electronic format)' (Preface p.ix). 15 main chapters with 98 'exhibits', or examples, plus 2 further chapters of exercises. Good bibliography (p.293-313). Primarily a textbook, but 'aimed more at those with a serious interest in this subject than at the beginner, who will find some of the material difficult' (*Library Association record*, v.93(10), October 1991, p.690). *Class No:* 001.815

[5]
MULVANY, N.C. Indexing books. Chicago, Univ. of Chicago Press, 1994. xiii,320p. illus. £23.95; $29.95. (*Chicago guides to writing, editing and publishing*.) ISBN: 0226550141.

Practical, non-technical guide in 10 chapters; 1. Introduction ... 4. Structure of entries ... 8. Format and layout of the index ... 10. Tools for indexing (mainly computer methods). 6 appendices (p.281-94) including 'Resources for indexers', a list of associations, organizations, software suppliers, etc. Bibliography (p.95-99); index. 'Comprehensive and attractive' (*Journal of documentation*, v.50(4), December 1994, p.349) and an alternative to the older works by Collison and Knight (above). *Class No:* 001.815

[6]
SOCIETY OF INDEXERS. Indexers available. London, Society of Indexers, 1982-. Annual. ISSN: 02664860.

1996 v. (57p.) lists *c.*220 members giving address, subjects covered, type of materials indexed, other skills, indexes compiled, clients, etc. Subject, other skills and materials index. *Class No:* 001.815

Bibliographies

[7]
WELLISCH, H.H. Indexing and abstracting: an international bibliography. Santa Barbara, Ca. and Oxford, ABC-Clio, 1980. xxi,308p. ISBN: 0874363004.

Published in cooperation with the American Society of Indexers and The Society of Indexers (UK).

2,383 numbered entries by topic *e.g.* Indexing systems (subdivided Coordinate, PRECIS etc.); Index production; Name indexes; Indexing around the world (subdivided by country). Comprehensive coverage of pre-1950 material, slightly more selective for recent items, excluding, for example, thesauri. Extensive, well-written introduction (p.xi-xix). Author and subject indexes. The major bibliography in the field and a model of its kind. Continued by:-
Class No: 001.815(01)

[8]
—WELLISCH, H.H. Indexing and abstracting, 1977-1981: an international bibliography. Santa Barbara, Ca. and Oxford, ABC-Clio, 1984. xix,276p. ISBN: 0874363985.

Adds 1,426 items published 1977-81, plus 220 missed from the earlier volume.

Continued, initially by Wellisch, in a series of articles in *The Indexer* under the title 'Indexing and abstracting: a current-awareness bibliography', then 'Indexing: a current awareness bibliography'. Latest appears in v.20(3), 1997.
Class No: 001.815(01)

Encyclopaedias & Dictionaries

[9]
BUCHANAN, B. A Glossary of indexing terms. London, Bingley, 1976. 144p. illus. ISBN: 0851572081.

More than 500 entries A-Z, initials filed at the beginning of the sequence, but recognized acronyms filed as words. Mostly basic definitions with examples, but some fuller definitions provided where necessary. Cross-referenced. Sources listed p.9. *Class No:* 001.815(03)

[10]
WELLISCH, H.H. Indexing from A to Z. 2nd rev. & enl. ed. New York, Wilson, 1995. xxix,569p. illus. £36;$40. ISBN: 082420882x.

'(A)imed at a broad range of audiences, from people with no or little experience in indexing to professional indexers' (p.xxiii). *c.*100 entries: Abbreviations... Corporate names... Grouped order... Nonprint materials... Specificity... Zen and the art of indexing. Bibliography (p.503-23); index. This ed. revised to take account of ISO 999. '(A)t once an encyclopaedic reference source and the distilled personal testimony of a master teacher and indexer' (*Journal of documentation*, v.53(1), January 1997, p.95).
Class No: 001.815(03)

Standards

[11]
BRITISH STANDARDS INSTITUTION. Information and documentation. Guidelines for the content, organization and presentation of indexes. London, B.S.I., 1996. 54p. £75. (*BSISO 999.*) ISBN: 058026517x.

Replaces *Recommendations for preparing indexes to books, periodicals and other documents* 2nd rev. ed. 1988 (17p. (BS 3700)), first published 1964.
Class No: 001.815(083.74)

Research Methods

[12]
BARZUN, J. *and* **GRAFF, H.F. The Modern researcher.** 5th ed. Fort Worth, Harcourt Brace Jovanovich, 1992. xvii,409p. illus., diags, tables £17;$24.95. ISBN: 0155625136.

First published 1957; 4th ed 1985.

Extensive, authoritative guide most valuable to graduate level scholars in the humanities and social sciences. 15 well written, practical chaps., *e.g.* Finding the facts; Handling ideas; The Rules of citing; Modes of presentation. Includes useful tables *e.g.* The Proofreader's marks. Relatively weak on electronic information sources. Indexed.

6th ed. forthcoming 1998 ($28. ISBN: 0155055291).
Class No: 001.891

[13]
BEASLEY, D. How to use a research library. New York, Oxford Univ. Press, 1988. xi,164p. $10.95. ISBN: 019504245x.

4 chapters: 1. General approach to the research library - 2. Catalogs and how to use them - 3. Tools of research (bibliographies, online searching, etc.) - 4. Research in depth (including detail for individual subject areas). Examples based on the New York Public Library. Quick reference section, with information under headings such as 'Publications in microform', 'Librarians and how to deal with them', precedes the main text. Brief bibliography; index. Not as wide ranging or readable as Mann (below).
Class No: 001.891

[14]
BERRY, R. The Research project: how to write it. 3rd rev. ed. London, Routledge, 1994. v,116p. illus., diags. £8.99;$14.95. ISBN: 0415110904.

Earlier eds. as *How to write a research paper*, 1966 and 1986.

A concise guide 'designed to be relevant to students at all levels of higher education' (Introduction p.1). Contents: 1. The choice of subject: using the library - 2. Preparing a bibliography - 3. Taking notes - 4. Composing the paper - 5. The final version - 6. Specimen paper (well-annotated, p.61-98) - 7. Some errors to avoid - 8. Publication in a learned journal. Appendix on non-sexist language. Written from a British perspective and useful as an alternative to the many US published guides. Unfortunately, updating in this ed. is less than thorough, especially in respect of electronic information sources. *Class No:* 001.891

[15]
BOOTH, W.C., ***and others*. The Craft of research.** Chicago, Univ. of Chicago Press, 1995. xii,294p. £19.95;$25. (*Chicago guides to writing, editing and publishing*.) ISBN: 0226065839.

Also published in pbck. (£10.25;$25).

Intended for student researchers. 15 well structured chaps. with topical subdivisions (*e.g.* Bibliographical trails, Building a complete argument, Creating a revisable draft). 'An Appendix on finding sources' (p.271-88) lists bibliographies, writing manuals, etc., by subject area. Index.
Class No: 001.891

[16]
GATES, J.K. Guide to the use of libraries and information services. 7th ed. New York, McGraw-Hill, 1994. xii,304p. £18.99;$23. ISBN: 0070230005.

First published 1962; 6th ed. 1989.

25 chapters in 5 main sections: 1. The Library - 2. The Organization and arrangement of library materials - 3. General information sources (dictionaries, indexes, government publications, etc.) - 4. Information sources in subject fields (by main Dewey classes) - 5. Using library resources for a research paper. Subject and title indexes. 'The American bias is not serious since the subject coverage and major reference titles dealt with are universal' (*Reference reviews*, v.8(8), 1994, p.10). *Class No:* 001.891

[17]
HOFFMAN, A. Research for writers. 5th ed. London, A. & C. Black, 1996. xvii,222p. £11.99;$20.95. ISBN: 0713642696.

First published 1975 as *Research: a handbook for writers and journalists*, with 2nd ed. 1979. Then issued under current title, previous ed. 1992.

Aimed especially at freelance writers and journalists. Gives fuller coverage of specific areas of research than many similar guides (*e.g.* 5. Research for fiction writers and dramatists; 6. Biography and autobiography; 7. Family and local history). Appendices: I. Selective list of major sources in the United Kingdom (*e.g.* The Copyright libraries); II. Reference books for the writer. Index. '(P)acked with good advice, it is practical and reasonably comprehensive' (*Reference reviews*, v.10(5), 1996, p.4). *Class No:* 001.891

[18]

LEEDY, P.D. Practical research: planning and design. 6th ed. Upper Saddle River, N.J., Merrill, 1997. xvi,304p. illus., diags., tables. £23.95;$45. ISBN: 0132414074.

First published 1974; 5th ed. 1992.

Well planned text for the student at undergraduate or postgraduate level. Takes a broad spectrum approach, covering all subject disciplines. 12 chaps. in 5 main sections, presentation under headings such as 'The Library and its resources as a tool of research' and 'Data collection and ethical standards'. Further reading at intervals in text. Indexed. *Class No:* 001.891

[19]

MANN, T. A Guide to library research methods. New York and Oxford, Oxford Univ. Press, 1990. xiv,199p. illus. $11.95 ISBN: 0195049446.

Paperback ed. First published in hardback 1987 ($30. ISBN: 0195049438).

Contents: Initial overview - Encyclopedias - Subject headings and the card catalog - Systematic browsing and the use of the classification scheme - Subject headings and indexes to journals - Keyword searches - Citation searches - Higher level overviews: review articles - Published bibliographies - Computer searches - Locating material in other libraries - Talking to people - Hidden treasures: reference sources. A readable guide, of value as an introduction to research methods at all levels. The author is a librarian in the Main Reading Room of the Library of Congress. *Class No:* 001.891

Bibliographies

[20]

BAUSELL, R.B. Advanced research methodology: an annotated guide to sources. Metuchen, N.J., Scarecrow Press, 1991. viii,903p. £76.05;$87.50. ISBN: 0810823551.

Cites 401 books and 2,259 periodical articles under topical headings (*e.g.* Sampling, Qualitative research methods, Construct validity, Cluster analysis), each with brief introduction. *c.*50-150 word annotations; author and subject indexes, the latter too brief. The 'emphasis seems to be on social science research and clinical trials' (*Choice*, v.29(6), February 1992, p.870). *Class No:* 001.891(01)

Fallacies

[21]

WARD, P. A Dictionary of common fallacies. 2nd ed. Cambridge, Oleander Press, 1980. 2v. (viii,303p.; xii,313p.). ISBN: 0900891653.

First published in 1v. 1978. Reprinted New York, Prometheus, 1989. (636p. $63.95. ISBN: 0879755113).

Each v. has entries, A-Z, covering commonly held beliefs and sayings (*e.g.* that Aethelred was 'unready', 'The earth is flat' and 'History repeats itself'), as well as phenomena (*e.g.* Ectoplasm). Keywords are used for entry, which may be the name of a person. Each v. has a bibliography of authorities and an index. *Class No:* 001.98

[22]

—ACKERMANN, A.S.E. Popular fallacies: a book of common errors explained and corrected, with copious references to authorities. 4th ed. London, Old Westminster Press, 1950. xv,843p.

Reprinted, Detroit, Omnigraphics, 1990 ($74. ISBN: 1558882103). *Class No:* 001.98

Information Technology

Abbreviations & Symbols

[23]

The SITA collection: selected information technology acronyms. Huggins-Shastri, J.H., *comp. & ed.* Farnborough, Multi-Facet(UK) 1992. vii,226p. ISBN: 0951935305.

Spiralbound.

Expand 3,500 acronyms, abbreviations and mnemonics. Intended for those closely involved with information technology on a daily basis. *Class No:* 002:60(003)

[24]

SOUTH, D.W. The Computer and information science and technology abbreviations and acronyms dictionary. Boca Raton, CRC Press, 1994. vii,302p. £45;$41.95. ISBN: 0849324440.

From the same publisher as De Sola's *Abbreviations dictionary* (*q.v.*). Intended to serve the needs of both the specialist and layperson. About 9,000 entries A-Z: appendix (p.250-302) contains miscellaneous supplementary matter (*e.g.* Chronology of computing and information technology; Selected high level languages). *Class No:* 002:60(003)

Bibliographies

[25]

Information sources in information technology. Haynes, D., *ed.* London, Bowker-Saur, 1990. xiv,350p. £47;$80. (*Guides to information sources.*) ISBN: 0408032855.

Discursive treatment in 2 pts. I. 'Information sources by subject' has 8 chapters dealing with the topics considered to make up information technology (*e.g.* Input technologies; Software, computer languages and operating systems; Transmission of information). II. 'Sources of information' comprises 11 chapters on forms of information (*e.g.* Machine-readable sources; Trade statistics and market information; Periodicals and conferences). Index (p.335-50). Rather chaotically organized. Part II contains much discussion of general sources with little apparent direct relevance to information technology. *Class No:* 002:60(01)

Encyclopaedias & Dictionaries

[26]

CAWKELL, A.E. Encyclopaedic dictionary of information technology and systems. London, Bowker-Saur, 1993. vi,339p. illus., diags. £59;$95. ISBN: 1857390369.

Defines about 5,000 terms with the needs of librarians and information workers especially in mind. Mostly short entries of 50-100 words, some simply expanding acronyms. Occasional longer entries *e.g.* 'Desktop publishing'. Includes entries for organizations and people *e.g.* *'Faraday, Michael'*, *c.*75 words. Well cross-referenced, but no bibliography,

.... *(contd.)*
appendices or index. '(D)escriptive and anecdotal definitions are often insufficient and arbitrary' (*Choice*, v.32(2), October 1994, p.257). *Class No:* 002:60(03)

[27]
COLLIN, S.M.H. Dictionary of information technology. Greasby, L. *and* Greene, T., *eds.* 2nd ed. Teddington, Peter Collin Publishing, 1996. 383p. ISBN: 0948549882.
First published 1987.
12,500 main headwords in clear two column layout. Covers all fields of computing and terms from radio, television, film and cinematography, print media, multimedia, Internet and email. Comments expand many definitions, occasional boxed quotations from journals/ magazines. *Class No:* 002:60(03)

[28]
GUNTON, T. A Dictionary of information technology and computer science. 2nd ed. Oxford, NCC Blackwell, 1993. vii,343p. illus. £25;$44.95. ISBN: 1855543273.
First published 1991.
'(C)ontains a comprehensive range of terms which are simple to understand and placed in well-considered context' (*Aslib information*, v.19(4), April 1991, p.143, on the 1st ed.). Definitions of 20-150 words. This ed. adds several hundred new entries. *Class No:* 002:60(03)

[29]
WATTERS, C. Dictionary of information science and technology. San Diego, Academic Press, 1992. vii,300p. diags., tables. £25;$29. ISBN: 012738510x.
Concise definitions of 4-8 lines for *c.*1,000 terms. Many illustrations and diagrams. Each entry followed by key into 'Subject outline' section (p.253-71) grouping terms by subject. Entries also cite one or more works providing further information; list of references (p.273-300). '(S)ome of the writing is awkward', (but) 'a reasonable tertiary source, good especially for quick reference' (*American reference books annual*, v.24, 1993, p.260).
Class No: 002:60(03)

Polyglot

[30]
Elsevier's dictionary of information technology: in English, German and French. Hoepelman, J.P., *and others comps.* Amsterdam, Elsevier, 1997. xiii,406p. $158. ISBN: 0444884106.
First substantial multilingual information technology dictionary. Over 4,500 English terms with definition and synonyms and translations into German and French. Fully cross-referenced. *Class No:* 002:60(03)=00

German

[31]
Routledge German dictionary of information technology. [Wörterbuch Informationstechnologie Deutsch-Englisch/ Englisch-Deutsch.] Seeberger, U., *ed.* London, Routledge, 1996. xxiv,436p. £80;$125. ISBN: 0415086469.
Approx. 25,000 entries in each language. Covers 'not only terminology used in computing, data transfer and telecommunications, but also developments in enabling fields such as mathematics, electronics and optics and optronics. Developing areas such as on-line services and client-server systems are also covered' (*Preface*, p.ix). Entries include

.... *(contd.)*
supplementary information on context and subject area labels. Also available on CD-ROM (£95. ISBN: 0415139635). *Class No:* 002:60(03)=30

French

[32]
PYPER, T.R. French dictionary of information technology: French-English, English-French. London, Routledge, 1989. v,282p. (French section); 293p. (English section). £50;$92.50. ISBN: 0415002443.
30,000 entries in each language. Wide coverage of terms from telecommunications, electronics, computer science and related diciplines. Includes abbreviations, compound words and phrases. Warmly received, 'remarkably well done' (*Reference reviews*, v.3(4), December 1989, p.175). A more recent, but less substantial, work is:-
Class No: 002:60(03)=40

[33]
—COLLIN, S.M.H. Computing and information technology French dictionary: French-English, English-French. Laurendeau-Collin, F. *and* Mouget, B., *eds.* Rev. ed. Teddington, Peter Collin, 1996. 494p. ISBN: 0948549653.
First published 1991. *Class No:* 002:60(03)=40

Spanish

[34]
VOLLNHALS, O.J. Dictionary of information technology: English-Spanish, Spanish-English. [Diccionario de tecnologia de la informacion: inglés-español, español-inglés.] [Barcelona], Herda, 1997. 489,480p. ISBN: 8425420148.
Class No: 002:60(03)=60

Handbooks & Manuals

[35]
World information technology manual. Cawkell, A.E., *ed.* Amsterdam, Elsevier, 1991. 2v. illus. £72.72 per v. ISBN: 0444893148.
V.1 *Computers, telecommunications and information processing*; v.2 *Systems and services*. Rev. & enl. ed. of *Handbook of information technology and office systems* (1986).
43 well referenced chaps. (*e.g.* 3. Principles of digital computing; 13. Expert systems and artificial intelligence; 24. Desktop publishing; 32. Copyright and patents), most by Cawkell, some in v.2 by guest writers. Fairly comprehensive coverage with plentiful, but poor quality illus. List of acronyms and abbreviations, glossary and subject index in both v. *Class No:* 002:60(035)

Online Information Systems

[36]
ARMSTRONG, C.J. *and* **HARTLEY, R.J. Keyguide to information sources in online and CD-ROM database searching.** 2nd ed. London, Mansell, 1997. xxviii,307p. £65;$20. ISBN: 0720122074.
Guide to the literature, reference aids and organizational sources of information about online and CD-ROM searching. In 3 main sections. I. 'Survey of information sources ...', contains 3 introductory chapters identifying and evaluating the literature. Confined to general material, items such as host manuals and guides to individual databases excluded. II. 'Bibliography' (p.67-271), has 658 briefly annotated entries

....*(contd.)*
in topical sections (*e.g.* CD-ROM networking, Subject searching - business, Training). III. 'Directory of organizations' (p.273-86), has addresses for 180 online hosts, CD-ROM publishers, advisory and membership bodies, etc. Index (p.287-307); glossary. The first such guide in the field, well-organized and presented.
Class No: 002.0

[37]

Information industry directory: an international guide to organizations, systems and services involved in the production and distribution of information in electronic form. Detroit, Gale, 1971-. Annual. $560. ISSN: 10516239.

Issued as 2 v. set. Present title from 11th ed. 1991, formerly *Encyclopedia of information systems and services.* Annual or more frequent publication since 1987. Until 10th ed. issued in separate US and international volumes. Also available on diskette and magnetic tape.

Coverage includes databases and their producers, CD-ROM and related products and services, Internet and other networks and gateways, online vendors, bulletin board systems, library networks and management systems, information storage and retrieval firms, associations, research organizations, publishers and consultants. 9,378 entries of variable length in 19th ed. (1997) (*e.g.* 'CINAHL Information Systems' 1 col., 'Information Access Company' 8½p., 'United Kingdom Online User Group' ½ col.), with main headings: email, Internet access, related organizations, staff, description, scope, input, holdings, computer-based products and services and intended market/availability. Often lengthy descriptions of individual database products. 8 main indexes: Master name and keyword; Database; Publication/ microform; Software; Function/service (26 categories); Personal name; Geographic; Subject. US based entries predominate, but coverage extends to 74 countries, UK well represented. The most comprehensive source in the field, enhanced by the thorough indexing. *Class No:* 002.0

Databases

Worldwide

[38]

Books and periodicals online: a directory of online publications. Nobari, N., *ed.* Washington, D.C., Library Technology Alliance, 1987-. Annual. $325. ISSN: 0951838x.

Publisher and title varies. From 1993 incorporates *Directory of periodicals online: indexed, abstracted and fulltext* previously published in 3 series by Info Globe.

Designed to indicate whether a particular publication is available online or on CD-ROM, and if so for what time period and whether as fulltext or in abstract/indexed format. Sources include newsletters, newspapers, popular and trade periodicals, association publications, government documents and conference proceedings. 1997 ed. (2v.) covers over 80,000 publications, main listing by title with separate sections for databases and producers/vendors and an index of former titles. Also available on CD-ROM. Limited information on databases, vendors etc., is also Internet accessible from the company WWW site at http://www.periodicals.net/. *Class No:* 002.0(003.4)(100)

[39]

Database directory. White Plains, N.Y., Knowledge Industry, 1984-95. Annual. 022.00/00 07496680

Appears to have ceased publication. Last full ed. for 1993/94; supplement for 1994/95 (1995. 87p.).

Formed the main rival to the *Gale directory of databases* (below) covering *c.*2,000 databases accessible in North America. Comprehensive and accurate entries arranged A-Z by name with vendor, producer, database alternate name and subject indexes. *Class No:* 002.0(003.4)(100)

[40]

Fulltext sources online: for periodicals, newspapers, newsletters, newswires & TV/radio transcripts. Needham, Mass., BiblioData, 1989-. Semi-annual. $116 per issue. ISSN: 10408258.

Each ed. cumulative replacing all earlier issues.

Lists titles A-Z indicating online service, database, dates of coverage, frequency of updating and approximate time lag between print publication and appearance online. International coverage, over 200 non-English language titles included. 'Fulltext means that complete articles are found online. It does not mean that a periodical is found cover-to-cover in the database' (p.iii, v.9(1), 1997). Separate listing 'Journals with free archives available on the Internet'. Subject and geographic indexes. Also available online through DataStar and on diskette, both updated quarterly.
Class No: 002.0(003.4)(100)

[41]

Gale directory of databases. V.1. Online databases. Detroit, Gale, 1993-. Semi-annual. $239. ISSN: 10668934.

Merges Gale's *Computer-readable databases* (1976-92) and Cuadra/Gale's *Directory of online databases* (1979-92). Each semi-annual fully updated and revised completely replacing the previous issue. For companion v., *Gale directory of databases. V.2. CD-ROM, diskette, magnetic tape...*, see separate entry.

July 1997 issue (xxix,1443p.) has 5,889 entries A-Z by database name. Information includes producer, contact name, alternate/former name(s), database type (*e.g.* bibliographic, directory, full-text), content, subject coverage (both 50-100 words), language, geographic coverage, year first available, time span, update frequency, availability (hosts) and alternate electronic formats. Separate lists of database producers and online services. Geographic (country), subject (1,200 headings), and master (databases, producers, online services) indexes. Also searchable online through a variety of hosts including Dialog (file 230) as part of *Gale directory of online, portable and Internet databases*. A CD-ROM version is also available from SilverPlatter (semi-annual updating). Access is also possible through Gale's subscription Internet service GaleNet. The best of the online database directories, especially valuable for its international coverage and regular updating.
Class No: 002.0(003.4)(100)

[42]

O'LEARY, M. The Online 100. Wilton, Conn., Pemberton Press, 1995. xx,223p. $22.95. ISBN: 0910965145.

Cover subtitle: *Online magazines field guide to the 100 most important online databases.*

1-2 page evaluative reviews for 100 databases grouped in 10 broad subject categories (*e.g.* Business; Life sciences and medicine; General reference/multidisciplinary). Additional databases added to each section as 'Honourable mentions'. Appendices: 'Sample records' and 'Principal databanks'; index. *Class No:* 002.0(003.4)(100)

[43]

World database series. Armstrong, C.J., *ed.* London, Bowker Saur, 1993-96. 12v.

Comprises: *World databases in agriculture* (1995. £158. ISBN: 1857390431); *World databases in biosciences and pharmacology* (1996. £195. ISBN: 1857390687); *World databases in chemistry* (1995. £150. ISBN: 1857391012); *World databases in company information* (1996. £195. ISBN: 1857391950); *World databases in geography and geology* (1995. £125. ISBN: 185739111X); *World databases in humanities* (1996. £145. ISBN: 1857390482); *World databases in industry* (1994. £105. ISBN: 1857391853); *World databases in management* (1994. £100. ISBN: 185739190X); *World databases in medicine* (1993. 2v. £178. ISBN: 0862916135); *World databases in patents* (1995. £95. ISBN: 1857391063); *World databases in physics and mathematics* (1995. £125. ISBN: 1857390385); *World databases in social sciences* (1995. £148. ISBN: 1857391160)

The most exhaustive and complete inventory of databases ever produced. Covers databases in any language and any electronic form including CD-ROM, diskette, magnetic tape and Internet. Each volume provides evaluative and comparative reviews in subject sections. Entries comprise 'master record' providing full information with subsidiary records giving basic detail on each implementation (*e.g.* versions from different hosts, CD-ROMs, etc). List of hosts/ producers with addresses and indexes (usually subject, producer and database name) in each volume. Also available online through Datastar (file WDBS). Database descriptions surpass those available in other sources such as the *Gale directory of databases* (above), but, with the online industry rapidly changing, the printed volumes will become obsolete unless frequently updated. *Class No:* 002.0(003.4)(100)

Scandinavia

[44]

Nordguide. Nordiska databaser. Esbo, NORDINFO, 1986-. Biennial. ISSN: 03587045.

English subtitle: *Nordic databases*. Title *Nordiska databaser: register över databaser producerade i de nordiska länderna* until 1992.

Covers publicly available databases produced in a Nordic country or available through a Nordic online service. Includes some CD-ROMs. Over 700 databases recorded 1996. Also available through the Internet as a free service with search and browse (subject, database type and country) options at http://info.rbt.no/norguide/norguide.html.
Class No: 002.0(003.4)(48)

Canada

[45]

Information in Canada: a directory of electronic and support resources. Ottawa, Canadian Library Association, 1995. vii,372p. ISBN: 0888022735.

Major section (p.105-354) gives basic information on 800 electronic databases selected for their Canadian content, origin or significance. Further sections on consultants, library based online services, freenets and library automation software. Indexed. *Class No:* 002.0(003.4)(71)

Bibliographies

[46]

HAWKINS, D.T. Online information retrieval bibliography, 1964-1982. Medford, N.J., Learned Information, 1983. 311p.

Replaces *Online information retrieval bibliography, 1965-1976* issued as a supplement to *Online review* v.1(1), 1975 and *Online information retrieval bibliography, 1964-1979* (1980).

Continued by *Online information retrieval bibliography, 1983-1986* (Medford, N.J., Learned Information, 1987, 300p.) and *Online information retrieval bibliography, 1987-1989* (Medford, N.J., Learned Information, 1990. 355p. ISBN: 0938734466). *Class No:* 002.0(01)

Handbooks & Manuals

[47]

CONVEY, J. Online information retrieval: an introductory manual to principles and practice. 4th ed. London, Library Association Publishing, 1992. viii,310p. £40. ISBN: 1856040119.

First published 1977; eds. 1-2 as *Online information retrieval systems*. 3rd ed. with present title 1989.

In 2 pts. Pt.1 comprises 10 chapters on general aspects including the online industry, CD-ROM, hardware and software, principles of searching and future developments. Pt.2 (p.109-251) covers the basic commands and features of 7 major hosts (Dialog, ESA/IRS, BLAISE-Line, National Library of Medicine (BLAISE-Link), Orbit, PFDS Online, Datastar). References (p.252-61) and appended lists of sources of information and databases. Index. UK orientated, but neglects new developments such as JANET and BIDS. '(N)ot recommend(ed for) practitioners and end users' (*Program*, v.27(4), October, 1993, p.445).
Class No: 002.0(035)

[48]

HARTLEY, R.J., *and others*. **Online searching principles and practice.** London, Bowker-Saur, 1990. xviii,387p. illus., tables. £30;$50. ISBN: 0408022906.

Offers 'a broad introduction to online searching and is aimed at anyone who wants to learn about online services and how to use them' (Preface p.ix). 13 chapters: 3. Database structures ... 6. Search strategies; 7. Online sources (databases described in subject sections) ... 11. Videotext and teletext systems; 12. Online public access catalogues. Examples drawn from a range of host services.

Successor edition announced for 1998 under the title *Information seeking in the online age* (*c.*£35. ISBN: 1857392604). *Class No:* 002.0(035)

[49]

Manual of online search strategies. Armstrong, C.J. *and* Large, J.A., *eds.* 2nd ed. Aldershot, Ashgate, 1992. xv,699p. tables, diags. ISBN: 1857420071.

'Offered as a guide to database selection and a navigational aid through the twists and turns of the retrieval maze' (p.xiv). 16 chaps., 13 subject based (*e.g.* 3. Patents; 8. Engineering; 12. Law; 15. Humanities). Initial chap. on database evaluation and selection; other chaps. on citation indexing and quick reference searching. Frequent use of examples, drawn from a wide range of databases. Appended 'Selective list of directories, bibliographies and reference works'. Comprehensively indexed. '(T)argetted at online searchers who already have some knowledge of command

....(*contd.*)
languages ... required to venture into new less familiar territory' (*Online notes*, September 1992, p.17).
Class No: 002.0(035)

[50]

The Online manual: a practical guide to business databases. Oxford, Learned Information, 1992-. Annual. £225. ISBN: 0631189319.

Publisher varies.

6th ed. (1997. xiii,863p. ISBN: 1900871351) has main section (p.269-863) listing 35,000 periodicals, newspapers and other sources indicating databases providing coverage. Also includes brief details of 1,500 databases and 29 online hosts. Wider coverage than the subtitle suggests, many of the databases having a general as well as business application.
Class No: 002.0(035)

[51]

UNITED KINGDOM ONLINE USER GROUP. UKOLUG quick guide to online commands. Webber, S., *and others comps*. 4th ed. London, UK Online User Group, 1994. 119p. ISBN: 1870254066.

First published 1987; 3rd ed. 1991.

Covers commands from the 19 hosts including BLAISE-Line, Data-Star, Dialog, ESA-IRS, NEXIS, ORBIT, Questel, STN International and Wilsonline. *Class No:* 002.0(035)

Reviews & Abstracts

[52]

Online & CD-ROM review. Medford, N.J., Learned Information, 1977-. Bi-monthly. ISSN: 13532642.

Current title from 1993; previously *Online review*.

In addition to refereed papers, notes and news, each issue includes the sections 'New CD-ROMs in brief' and 'New database products'. The latter, intended to complement the *Gale directory of databases* (*q.v.*), is in business and law, science and technology and social sciences and humanities sections, each appearing on a semi-annual basis.
Class No: 002.0(048)

Thesauri

[53]

CHAN, L.M. *and* **POLLARD, R. Thesauri used in online databases:** an analytical guide. New York, Greenwood Press, 1988. xvi,268p. £49.50;$59.95. ISBN: 0313257884.

122 thesauri identified and described A-Z. Includes thesauri that appear as separate publications, those which form parts of user guides and subject headings lists. Out of print items excluded. Indexed by title, personal name, organization, subject and database. *Class No:* 002.0:025.43

CD-ROMs

[54]

CD-ROM finder: the world of CD-ROM products for information seekers. Medford, N.J., Learned Information, 1986-. Irregular. $69.50.

Eds. 1-4 published as *The Optical publishing directory*.

The 6th ed. (1995. xv,764p. ISBN: 0938734865) lists 2,309 CD-ROMs by title giving publisher, description with content summary, system requirements and market data (availability of trials, distributors, price, etc.). Applications (subject), company/product and company (includes addresses) indexes. Full detail for most CD-ROMs included, but contains a considerable number of 'home entertainment' titles and cannot rival the major listings such as *CD-ROMs in print* (below) in the number of discs covered.
Class No: 002.00

[55]

CD-ROM information products: the evaluative guide. Armstrong, C.J. *and* Large, J.A., *eds*. Aldershot, Information Automation/Ashgate, 1990-93. 4v.

Title varies slightly. Format also varies: v.1-3 issued as annuals; v.4 published in 4 pts.

V.2 (xv,408p.) covers 23 CD-ROMs including *Catalogue of UK official publications, Kompass* and *Periodicals abstracts on disc*. Thorough, well-written reviews with facsimile screens, full information on software and hardware requirements, etc. Apart from publication in 4 separate pts., final v. retains similar pattern: v.4(3) has 4-8 page reviews of *Biomedical engineering citation index, Consumer reports on disc, Health reference center* and *Index to theses*.
Class No: 002.00

[56]

CD-ROMs in print: an international guide to CD-ROM, CD-I, 3DO, MMCD, CD32, multimedia and electronic products. Detroit, Gale, 1987-. Annual. $145. ISSN: 08918198.

Subtitle varies. Published by Mecklermedia until 1994, CD-ROM version also issued.

The 1998 ed. (xi,1450p.) has entries for more than 13,000 commercially available CD-ROMs A-Z by title (p.1-1006). Information given includes 10-50 word description, audience level, dates of coverage, language, previous/alternate titles, technical specifications, price, update frequency, US and international distributors, ISBN/ISSN and other media equivalents (print, online, etc.). Includes out-of-print and defunct titles. Separate section with basic details of over 4,000 companies involved in the CD-ROM market (p.1007-196). Comprehensive indexing by activity (company), country/US state, audience level, subject (2,400 headings), etc. Good international coverage, the main competitor to *The Multimedia and CD-ROM directory* (below).
Class No: 002.00

[57]

DEWEY, P.R. 303 CD-ROMs to use in your library: descriptions, evaluations and practical advice. Chicago, American Library Association, 1996. xxii,238p. $30. ISBN: 0838906664.

Arranged in 31 subject sections (Almanacs ... Business and industry ... Newspaper and periodical indexes and full text ... Sociology ... Utilities) each with brief introduction. CD-ROM descriptions, up to one page in length, include occasional citations to reviews and other evaluative material. Appendices (*e.g.* 'Vendor name and address list'), bibliography and index. *Class No:* 002.00

[58]

ENSOR, P. CD-ROM research collections: an evaluative guide to bibliographic and full-text CD-ROM databases. Westport, Conn., Meckler, 1991. ix,302p. (*Supplements to computers in libraries*.) ISBN: 0887367798.

Covers 114 periodically updated CD-ROM databases. Numeric and directory CD-ROMs excluded. Entries, A-Z, average 2½p. with the heading scope and content often accounting for half the length. Further information includes publisher, price, arrangement and control, search software and capabilities and print/online/other media counterparts. Broad term subject and publisher/producer indexes. Now

....*(contd.)*
dated, but still useful covering many of the major CD-ROM databases in greater depth than listings such as *CD-ROMs in print* (above). *Class No:* 002.00

[59]
Gale directory of databases. V.2. CD-ROM, diskette, magnetic tape, handheld and batch access database products. Detroit, Gale, 1993-. Semi-annual. $159. ISSN: 10668934.

Published under title *Directory of portable databases* (ISSN: 10458352) by Cuadra/Gale 1990-92. Present title from merger of Gale and Cuadra directories. Companion v. to *Gale directory of databases. V.1. Online databases* (*q.v.*).

5,563 entries (3,202 for CD-ROMs) in July 1997 issue (xxix,1422p.). Entries, giving similar detail to the online database v., in separate CD-ROM, diskette, magnetic tape, etc. sections. Lists of database producers and vendors/distributors. Geographic, subject and master indexes. A reliable source with full data on the products included, but fewer entries than either the *The Multimedia and CD-ROM directory* (below) or *CD-ROMs in print* (above).

Also searchable online through a variety of hosts including Dialog (file 230) as part of *Gale directory of online, portable and Internet databases*. A CD-ROM version is available from SilverPlatter (semi-annual updating). Access is also possible through Gale's subscription Internet service GaleNet. *Class No:* 002.00

[60]
KRANTZ, L. CD-ROMs rated: a guide to the best and worst CD-ROMs and multimedia titles. New York, McGraw-Hill, 1994. 302p. illus. $19.95. ISBN: 0079120520.

Reviews (50-150 words) and rates through scoring system *c.*500 CD-ROMs aimed at the home market. Topical arrangement; various appendices and index. Accompanying CD-ROM offers product demonstrations from 30 publishers. *Class No:* 002.00

[61]
The Multimedia and CD-ROM directory. 1997-. London, TFPL Multimedia, 1997-. Annual.

Combines TFPL's *The CD-ROM directory*, published annually from 1987 (1st ed. as *The International directory of information products on CD-ROM*), with *The Multimedia directory*.

17th ed. (1997) published in 2 vols. V.2 *Titles* (1588p. £175. ISBN: 0333676750) has entries for 19,000 discs A-Z. Detail includes publisher, subject, data type, language, description (10-40 words), system requirements and price. Separate list of publishers with contact details and major titles; subject index and glossary. V.1 *Marketplace* (893p. £145. ISBN: 0333681053) has information on 13,500 companies A-Z (p.117-786) listing activities, products, etc. Country, product name and product type indexes. Also issued on CD-ROM updated twice yearly (£225). Internet access is planned. *WhitakerROM* is a further CD-ROM version using Whitaker's Bookbank software. Now the largest directory of CD-ROM titles, supplemented by comprehensive market information. *Class No:* 002.00

[62]
NATIONAL LIBRARY OF SCOTLAND. Guide to CD-ROMs in Scottish university and research libraries. Edinburgh, National Library of Scotland, 1995. v,27p. ISBN: 1872116183.

Covers 13 academic and 2 public libraries, plus NLS. Entries for 179 titles A-Z with subject descriptor. Indexed by subject and holding library. *Class No:* 002.00

[63]
SORROW, B.H. *and* **LUMPKIN, B.S. CD-ROM for librarians and educators:** a guide to over 800 instructional programs. 2nd ed. Jefferson, N.C., McFarland, 1996. v,405p. illus. £40.50;$45. ISBN: 0786401761.

First published 1993.

Aims 'to present a dependable annotated collection of CD-ROM resources ... selected because of their versatility both for the classroom and for independent individualized learning' (Preface). Arranged in subject groupings Aerospace/aviation ... Stories, annotations descriptive. Glossary (p.371-79), bibliography and index.
Class No: 002.00

[64]
Union list of CD-ROMs in London libraries. Shields, W., *comp.* 2nd ed. London, Joseph Clarke, 1996. ISBN: 1872185096.

First published 1993.

Gives 1,408 locations for 447 CD-ROMs in 140 libraries.
Class No: 002.00

Bibliographies

[65]
LANGLOIS, J. CD-ROM 1992: an annotated bibliography of resources. Westport, Conn., Meckler, 1992. xi, 298p. ISBN: 0887368611.

Annotated listing of 1,391 items, all but 31 periodical articles, published 1980-91. Material included concerns CD-ROM in relation to libraries. Broad topic arrangement (no less than 415 entries under 'General') with subject index (p.283-94).

An earlier work, A.M. Elshami's *CD-ROM: an annotated bibliography* (Englewood, Colo., Libraries Unlimited, 1988. xiv,138p. ISBN: 0872877027), has 725 entries.
Class No: 002.00(01)

Indexes

[66]
CD-ROM book index: an international guide to full-text books on CD-ROM. Niles, A., *ed.* Medford, N.J., Learned Information, 1995. vii,207p. $39.50. ISBN: 0938734989.

'(T)he purpose of this index is to provide an author and title index for full-text books available on CD-ROM as well as a contents listing for each CD-ROM title' (*Introduction*, p.vii). Listing of CD-ROM titles and contents, followed by author and title indexes to books; publisher index.
Class No: 002.00(014)

Scripts, Symbols, etc.

Transliteration

[67]
BRITISH STANDARDS INSTITUTION. Transliteration of Cyrillic and Greek characters. London, B.S.I., 1958. 24p. £48.70. (*BS:2979.*)

Section 1: British traditional-type system, Table A Cyrillic-to-English transliteration, Table B English-to-Cyrillic; Section 2: International system for modern Cyrillic, Table C Cyrillic-to-Latin, Tables D and E for Church Slavonic and Rumanian Cyrillic, Table F back-transliteration (Latin-to-Cyrillic, for tables C, D and E); Section 3: rule-of-

....(contd.)
thumb system for Greek, without regard to phonetic peculiarities of Ancient or Modern Greek, in line with international practice.

Other British Standards concerning transliteration are: *Transliteration of Arabic characters* (BS 4280:1968. £26.90. ISBN: 058000508); *Specifications for the romanization of Japanese* (BS 4812:1972. £21. ISBN: 0580073454); *Guide to the romanization of Chinese* (BS 7014:1989. £26.90. ISBN: 0580168190), giving description and comparison of existing systems especially Wades-Giles and Pinyin; *Guide to the romanization of Korean* (PD 6505:1982. £63.60. ISBN: 0580127362). *Class No:* 003.034

[68]

WELLISCH, H.H. The Conversion of scripts: its nature, history and utilization. New York, Wiley, 1978. xviii,509p. (*Information sciences series.*) ISBN: 0471016209.

Chapters: Writing Systems, scripts and conversion of scripts: classification, typology and definition - The adaptation of scripts to various languages - The historical development of script conversions - The major scripts and their conversion schemes - The requirements of script conversion - Script conversion in bibliographic control systems. Appended: The international phonetic alphabet; General principles of conversion of systems of writing. Bibliography (p.441-61); index. A thoroughly documented, scholarly work. *Class No:* 003.034

[69]

WELLISCH, H.H. Transcription and transliteration: an annotated bibliography on conversion of scripts. Silver Springs, Md., Institute of Modern Languages, 1975. xxiv,133p. ISBN: 0884991490.

'The criterion for inclusion of an item was that at least one of the languages or scripts dealt with is spoken or used today' (Introduction p.ix). Excludes literature on purely phonetic transcription, articles in newspapers and brief periodical notes. 745 numbered entries in 12 sections by language or topic, with an 18 item addenda. Author/title and subject indexes. *Class No:* 003.034

Abbreviations

Databases

[70]

World Wide Web acronym and abbreviation server. Cork, University College Cork. World Wide Web resource.

URL: http://www.ucc.ie/info/net/acronyms/acro.html. Date reviewed 22nd April 1998.

Appears to contain in excess of 20,000 entries. Supports 'Search for an acronym' and 'Search for words in expansion' options. Failed enquiries posted to file 'Acronyms already sought'. 'The strength is obvious in new amendments arriving constantly from all over the world; the weakness is that in relying on such submissions of information, rather than using active central editing to seek information, there is a risk of unevenness' (*Reference reviews*, v.9(7), 1995, p.9) *Class No:* 003.083(003.4)

Bibliographies

[71]

Abbreviations, acronyms, ciphers and signs. Brewer, A.M., *ed.* Detroit, Gale, 1981. xii,323p. $98. ISBN: 0810305291.

A 'reference source for identifying books in all languages which concern themselves with short forms of communication' (Introduction p.vii). Reproduces Library of Congress cards for over 900 works which have the words abbreviations(s), acronym(s), cipher(s) or sign(s) in the title. All eds. of a work included. Arranged by Library of Congress classification with a keyword index.
Class No: 003.083(01)

Encyclopaedias & Dictionaries

[72]

Acronyms, initialisms & abbreviations dictionary: a guide to acronyms, abbreviations, contractions, alphabetic symbols, and similar condensed appellations. Detroit, Gale, 1960-. Annual. ISSN: 02704404.

First published 1960 as *Acronyms dictionary*, then issued on an irregular basis. Now published annually in 3v., each available for separate purchase.

V.1 of 23rd ed. (1997, issued in 3pts.) contains well over 500,000 acronyms, etc., 15,000 included for the first time. 'Most entries in AIAD are specifically identified with the United States. Thousands of British and Canadian items are also found. ... No attempt is made to list acronyms of local businesses or associations, local units of government or other terms in limited use. Obsolete terms are retained for historical interest' (Preface p.ix). The remaining components of the 3 v. set are *Reverse acronyms, initialisms & abbreviations dictionary* (publ. as v.3, also in 3 pts.), presenting the same terms as in v.1, but arranged alphabetically by complete word or phrase with the acronym as the definition, and *Acronyms, initialisms & abbreviations dictionary supplement* (v.2), issued between main editions and usually containing c.10-12,000 new entries.
Class No: 003.083(03)

[73]

—International acronyms, initialisms & abbreviations dictionary: a guide to over 169,000 international acronyms, initialisms, abbreviations, alphabetic symbols, contractions and similar condensed appellations in all fields. 4th ed. Detroit, Gale, 1997-.

Similar format to *Acronyms, initialisms & abbreviations dictionary*. Main v. by acronym, etc. (xx,1374p. £173;$190. ISBN: 0810374374); second v., *Reverse international acronyms, initialisms & abbreviations dictionary* (awaited early 1998).

First published 1985; 3rd ed. 1993-94.

Entries for English and non-English acronyms used internationally and in specific regions or countries. Excludes US, British and Canadian terms listed in *Acronyms, initialisms & abbreviations dictionary* unless of international significance. About 48,000 new terms in this ed. Full entries give expansion in foreign language, English translation, identification of country of origin (150 countries represented) and source code. *Class No:* 003.083(03)

[74]

The Barnhart abbreviation dictionary. Barnhart, R.K., *ed.* New York, Wiley, 1995. xxi,434p. £27.50;$34.95. ISBN: 0471571466.

Based on files collected for other Barnhart dictionaries. 60,000 entries with one or more definitions plus explanation of context, variant spellings, pronunciation guide, etc. as appropriate. Includes a valuable reverse list (p.283-434), a feature not found in most other single volume abbreviation dictionaries. A 'handy reference guide for small or medium-sized libraries' (*American reference books annual*, v.27, 1996, p.3). *Class No:* 003.083(03)

[75]
Buttress's world guide to abbreviations of organisations. Pitman, L.M., *ed.* 11th ed. London, Blackie Academic & Professional, 1997. 1149p. £130;$170. ISBN: 0751400238.

First published 1954; 10th ed. 1993.

Over 68,000 entries, more than 9,000 new or revised since the previous ed. Scope extends across the whole range of human activity, including commerce, industry, education, law, politics, public administration, religion, recreation, technology and medicine. Omits strictly local organizations. Especially strong on the EC and member states; this ed. expands treatment of Eastern Europe and strengthens coverage of British and American organizations. Features include cross-referencing between acronyms of identical organizations in different languages (*e.g.* NATO=OTAN), bracketed addition of acronyms of parent bodies to entries for subsidiary organizations and cross-referencing from names which have changed since the previous ed. Cannot rival Wennrich (*q.v.*) in number of entries, but an otherwise excellent, regularly revised, source. *Class No:* 003.083(03)

[76]
DE SOLA, R., *and others*. Abbreviations dictionary. 9th ed. Boca Raton, CRC Press, 1995. xvii,1347p. £49.95;$89.95. ISBN: 0849389445.

First published 1958; 8th ed. 1992.

Nearly 270,000 entries in the 8th ed. (1992. xx,1300p. ISBN: 0849342473). Main body of the dictionary (p.1-943) includes abbreviations, acronyms, appellations, computer jargon, contractions, initialisms, nicknames and slang. Some entries add brief definitions (*e.g.* 'Bib Nar: Biblioteka Narodowa (Polish National Library in Warsaw)'). 57 supplementary sections (p.944-1300) Airlines of the world ... Zodiacal signs. Includes some general reference information (*e.g.* Superlatives (p.1254-84) 'Afghanistan's highest peak'... 'Zimbabwe's largest city'). Probably the best of the single vol. abbreviations dictionaries; 'belongs in the reference collections of most, if not all, libraries' (*American reference books annual*, v.27, 1996, p.3).
Class No: 003.083(03)

[77]
Elsevier's dictionary of acronyms, initialisms, abbreviations and symbols. Benedetto Mattia, F., *ed. & comp.* Amsterdam, Elsevier, 1997. xvi,646p. ISBN: 0444825894.

Expands 14,000 acronyms, etc., with the emphasis on scientific and technological subjects. Some entries with brief explanations and further information. Various appendices including acronyms/initialisms of colleges and universities, airport and airline codes and chemical symbols; list of sources and references (p.633-39). Includes some unique entries, but not to be preferred to similar scale works such as *The Oxford dictionary of abbreviations* unless a slant to technical topics is required. *Class No:* 003.083(03)

[78]
International encyclopedia of abbreviations and acronyms of organizations. [Internationale Enzyklopädie der Abkürzungen und Akronyme von Organisationen.] Wennrich, P. *and* Spiller, P., *eds.* 3rd rev. & enl. ed. München, Saur, 1990-94. 10v. $2,000. (*Handbook of technical documentation and bibliography, v.9.*) ISBN: 3598221606.

V.1-6 *Abbreviations and acronyms*; v.7-10 *Organizations and institutions* (reverse sequence). First published 1968 as *Internationales Verzeichnis von Abkürzungen von Verbänden Behörden und Organisationen.* 2nd ed. in 3v. 1970-72 as *Internationales Wörterbuch der Abkürzungen von Organisationen.*

....*(contd.)*

Expands more than 500,000 abbreviations and acronyms for a wide range of organizations, including associations, companies, confederations, clubs, government offices, political parties, trade unions, universities, and other teaching and research establishments. 'Where it was deemed appropriate, technical abbreviations which do not necessarily refer to an organization or an institution have also been included' (Preface p.vii, v.1). Limited to languages using the Roman alphabet. Includes common vernacular abbreviations in general use and historical abbreviations. Entries, in one A-Z sequence, give expansion with code indicating the area or sphere (*e.g.* country, language, etc.) in which the abbreviation is used. More entries than most rival dictionaries and especially good on European abbreviations. Unless updated regularly will, however, be unable to compete on currency with the Gale set or frequently published single v. sources such as Buttress.
Class No: 003.083(03)

[79]
NTC's dictionary of acronyms and abbreviations. Kleinedler, S.R., *comp and* Spears, R.A., *ed.*. Lincolnwood, Ill., National Textbook Co., 1993. viii,311p. £11.95;$16.95. ISBN: 0844251607.

Limited to 2,100 shortened words commonly encountered in American English. Good definitions and explanations of 2-8 lines; sources and examples provided for some entries.
Class No: 003.083(03)

[80]
The Oxford dictionary of abbreviations. Oxford, Clarendon Press, 1992. ix,397p. ISBN: 0198691726.

Paperback ed. in print, £6.99;$10.95 (ISBN: 0192800035).

Main listing (p.1-381) emphasises abbreviations, acronyms and initialisms of English speaking countries, with a selection from foreign languages. Entries add field labels and brief explanations where necessary; translations for foreign abbreviations. Separate appendix of symbols (p.383-97) includes alphabets, musical notation, hallmarks, accents and diacritics, international and British vehicle registration marks and UK postcodes. Best suited to smaller libraries and home or office use; 'does not appear to offer much additional information when compared with other works devoted to abbreviations' (*Choice*, v.30(7), March 1993, p.1118).
Class No: 003.083(03)

[81]
PAXTON, J. The Everyman dictionary of abbreviations. 2nd ed. with revisions & suppl. London, Dent, 1992. 395p. ISBN: 0460030345.

First published 1974; various revisions as *The Penguin dictionary of abbreviations*, including 2nd ed. 1986.

About 27,000 entries with over 37,000 definitions. 'Supplement (1992)' (p.387-95). Abbreviation followed by definition and English translation if foreign. Occasional entries with brief explanatory note or subject reference (*e.g.* chem (chemistry)). Cross-referenced. Some unique entries; British slant. *Class No:* 003.083(03)

[82]
PICKERING, D. Dictionary of abbreviations. London, Cassell, 1996. viii,340p. £18.99;$19.95. ISBN: 0304346128.

Earlier abbreviations dictionary from Cassell's as *Cassell's dictionary of abbreviations* (1st ed. 1966; 2nd ed. 1972).

Comprises 40,000 abbreviations collected under 20,000 headword headings. Includes acronyms, initialisms and

....(*contd.*)
colloquialisms. Coverage intended to be 'ambitiously international', but distinct British slant. Appendices (p.333-40) include Russian alphabet, chemical symbols and signs of the zodiac. *Class No:* 003.083(03)

[83]

—Chambers dictionary of abbreviations. Edmonds, D., *ed.* Edinburgh, Chambers, 1995. xi,228p. £12.99. ISBN: 0550183043.

Also available in pbck. (£5.99. ISBN: 0550183051).

Another recent British published dictionary. Expands 10,000 abbreviations 'selected to meet the needs of ordinary people in the home, school and office. Special attention has been paid to sporting and commercial terms, to medical abbreviations ... to basic computing terms and to acronyms of major business, governmental and international organisations' (*Preface* p.vii). In addition to standard A-Z sequence features 20 'Panels' (insert boxes) grouping abbreviations by special subject area.
Class No: 003.083(03)

[84]

Pugh's dictionary of acronyms and abbreviations: abbreviations in management, technology and information science. Pugh, E., *comp.* London, Library Association, 1987. v,366p. ISBN: 0853655375.

1st ed. 1968; 2nd expanded ed. 1970, supplements 1974 and 1976; cumulated ed. with additional entries 1981. Available from Books on Demand ($106.10. ISBN: 0608024740).

More than 18,000 entries stating country of origin or organization as considered necessary. Librarianship and information receives particular emphasis. Lacks full introduction or clear statement of selection criteria.
Class No: 003.083(03)

[85]

WALL, C.E. Abbreviations: the comprehensive dictionary of abbreviations and letter symbols for the computer era. Ann Arbor, Pierian Press, 1984. 2v. ISBN: 087650179x, v.1; 0876501838, v.2.

V.1 *Abbreviation to word*; v.2 *Word to abbreviation.*

'(N)ot a dictionary of acronyms and abbreviations. This publication emphasizes short forms of words'. Main source of entries 'primary documents designed for data processing purposes'. Seen by the author as a 'gathering effort requisite to the identification of proposed standardized abbreviated forms' (Introduction, p.v-vi). *c.*70,000 entries. Criticized for not giving source and context of each abbreviation by *Wilson library bulletin* (v.59(6), February 1985, p.420).
Class No: 003.083(03)

Germany

[86]

GERMANY, FEDERAL REPUBLIC OF. Auswärtiges Amt. Sprachendienst. **Deutsche Einrichtungen: Bezeichnungen, Abkürzungen, Akronyme.** [German institutions: designations, abbreviations, acronyms.] Berlin, De Gruyter, 1990. viii,119p. £19.45:DM48. (*Termonologische Schriftenreihe, Bd. 3.*) ISBN: 3110120879.

Companion v. *Internationale Organisationen: Bezeichnungen...* (*q.v.*).

Contains in up to 10 languages the designations of German authorities, associations, foundations, etc., together with their respective abbreviations. Includes references to parent body and brief explanation of organizations function (in German). Keyword, abbreviation and hierarchical indexes.
Class No: 003.083(03)(430)

Africa

[87]

HALL, D.E. African acronyms and abbreviations: a handbook. London, Mansell, 1996. xi,364p. £65;$120. ISBN: 0720122759.

'The primary purpose of this dictionary is to elucidate abbreviations relating to African studies' (Introduction, p.ix). Based on authority files maintained by Hall in connection with *International African bibliography*. Coverage includes political parties, educational establishments, businesses and international aid organizations. About 20,000 entries, country of origin given where known.
Class No: 003.083(03)(6)

South Africa

[88]

South African acronyms and abbreviations of organizations. [Suid-Afrkaanse akronieme en afkortings van organisasies.] 2nd ed. Johannesburg, Johannesburg Public Library, 1990. 87p. ISBN: 0620152737.

First published 1984.

Basic list expanding 4,500 acronyms and abbreviations.
Class No: 003.083(03)(680)

Canada

[89]

The Canadian dictionary of abbreviations. Dobroslavić, T., *comp.* Toronto, ECW Press, 1994. 396p. £65.95;Can$70. ISBN: 1550221965.

Earlier version as *Abbreviations: a Canadian handbook* (Vancouver, First Avenue Press, 1985. 173p. ISBN: 0920557007).

Listing of English and French abbreviations, initialisms and acronyms commonly used in Canada. About 18,000 entries. Includes general abbreviations and initialisms/acronyms of international organizations of which Canada is a member. *Class No:* 003.083(03)(71)

Latin America

[90]

Siglas latinoamericanas. 3.ed. Santiago de Chile, Naciones Unidas Comisión Económica para América Latina y el Caribe, 1992. 379p.

First published 1978.

Expands acronyms for *c.*6,000 organizations active in Latin American countries. Full name index (p.225-379).
Class No: 003.083(03)(729.99)

Australia

[91]

COPPEL, W.G. Dictionary of abbreviations and acronyms: 37,000 of the most commonly used, and not-so-commonly used abbreviations. Melbourne, Wilkinson Books, 1993. 442p. Aus$24.95. ISBN: 1863501290.

Includes many abbreviations and acronyms peculiar to Australia. *Class No:* 003.083(03)(94)

[92]

JONES, D.J. The Australian dictionary of acronyms and abbreviations. 4th ed. Canberra, Australian Library and Information Association, 1995 472p. Aus$49.95. ISBN: 0868045217.

First published 1977; 3rd ed. 1990.

Around 47,000 entries, nearly double number in previous ed. Australian emphasis, but international abbreviations included. *Class No:* 003.083(03)(94)

German

[93]

Lexikon der Abkürzungen: über 50,000 Abkürzungen, Kurzwörter, Zeichen und Symbole. Koblischke, H., *hrsg*. Gütersloh, Bertelsmann, 1994. 552p. plates. DM54. ISBN: 3570016048.

Replaces *Grosse Abkürzungsbuch* (1980).

Two col. format, abbreviations in bold type language, subject and explanation given as necessary. Includes non-German abbreviations. Appended sections for signs and symbols, Roman numerals, etc. *Class No:* 003.083(03)=30

French

[94]

FAUDOUS, J-C. Dictionnaire des abréviations courantes de la langue française. Paris, La Maison du Dictionnaire, 1990. 255p. FFr150. ISBN: 2856080383.

Standardized list of abbreviations for French language words and terms.

A further source for initialisms is Bouscau-Faure, J-P. *Dictionnaire général des sigles* (Paris, Dalloz, 1995. vii,775p. FFr146. ISBN: 2247020062).
Class No: 003.083(03)=40

[95]

MURITH, J. Dictionnaire des abréviations et acronymes: scientifiques, techniques, médicaux, économiques, juridiques. [Dictionary of scientific, technical, medical, economic, legal abbreviations & acronyms.] 2nd ed. Paris, Technique et Documentation-Lavoisier, 1992. 949p. FFr950. ISBN: 2852066815.

First published 1984. Succeeded *Dictionnaire des sigles et abréviations* 1982.

Expands French and English abbreviations in one alphabetical sequence. *c.*102,000 entries, many more than in the 1st ed. No definitions. Organizations largely excluded, covered in companion volume (below).
Class No: 003.083(03)=40

[96]

—MURITH, J. *and* BOCABEILLE, J-M. Dictionnaire des sigles: scientifiques, techniques et économiques. [A Dictionary of initials: scientific, technical and commercial organisations.] 2nd ed. Paris, Technique et Documentation-Lavoisier, 1987. 471p. FFr600. ISBN: 2852063840.

1st ed. 1982.

Expands 26,000 initialisms, entries including organization address. International in scope. Good coverage of learned societies and research organizations.
Class No: 003.083(03)=40

Russian

[97]

BERNSHTEIN, L.B. Novyĭ slovar' sokrashcheniĭ russkogo iāzyka: okolo 32,000 sokrashcheniĭ sostaviteli. Moskva, ETS, 1995. 668p. ISBN: 5864550477.

Earlier versions as *Slovar' sokrashcheniĭ russkogo iāzyka*, first published 1963, 3rd ed. 1983.

32,000 entries in 2 col format. Brief expansions only.
Class No: 003.083(03)=82

[98]

ZALUCKY, H.K. Compressed Russian: Russian-English dictionary of acronyms, semiacronyms and other abbreviations used in contemporary standard Russian: with their pronunciation and explicit correlates in Russian and equivalents in English. Amsterdam, Elsevier, 1991. xvi,890p. £116.45;$221. ISBN: 0444987282.

About 40,000 entries. Elsevier have also published Schultz, E. *Dictionary of Russian abbreviations* (1986. ISBN: 0444995544). *Class No:* 003.083(03)=82

Alphabets

[99]

CAMPBELL, G.L. Handbook of scripts and alphabets. London, Routledge, 1997. vii,132p. tables. £11.99;$12.95. ISBN: 0415137152.

Scripts and alphabets for 39 languages Arabic ... Tibetan. Based on tables in the same author's *Compendium of the world's langauges* (*q.v.*). *Class No:* 003.23

[100]

DIRINGER, D. The Alphabet: a key to the history of mankind. Regensburger, R., *rev. & ed.* 3rd ed. London, Hutchinson, 1968. 2v. illus., plates. ISBN: 0090676416.

First published 1948.

V.1, pt.1: Non-alphabetic systems of writing; pt.2: Alphabetic scripts. V.2: Plates (sectionalized, as in v.1). General bibliography and analytical index to both volumes in v.1. 'The Greek alphabet and its offshoots' (v.1, p.356-85) is supported by 51 plates (in v.2) and 8 sectional bibliographies (totalling 5½p.). The standard work of reference on the subject, although the *Times literary supplement*, (no.3520, 14th August 1969, p.901) finds many items in the bibliography irrelevant and some of the illustrations too small. *Class No:* 003.23

[101]

GLEICHEN EDWARD, Lord *and* **REYNOLDS, J.H. Alphabets of foreign languages.** [New ed.]. London, Stanford for the Permanent Committee on Geographical Names for British Official Use, 1956. xvi,82p.

First published 1921. This edition is the 2nd ed. (1933), reprinted with incorporation of the supplement of 1938 and certain revisions by M. Aurousseau.

78 languages are covered in 11 groups. In the case of Polish (p.46-47), notes are given on stress, letters not used, accented letters, with a list of Polish letters with RGS II letters (*i.e.* letters based on rules for the spelling of geographical names for official use) alongside, and notes on pronunciation. Sometimes (*e.g.* for Gaelic), a short vocabulary is provided. *Class No:* 003.23

Runes

[102]

ARNTZ, H. Bibliographie der Runenkunde, mit Unterstutzung des Archäologischen Instituts des Deutschen Reiches. Leipzig, Harrassowitz, 1937. xiv,[1],293p.

4,131 numbered entries, (plus numerous interpolations) covering material on runic inscriptions used by the Scandinavians, Frisians and Anglo-Saxons. Author list (p.1-248); keyword title list for anonyma; supplement. 5 indexes: 1. Zeitschriften und [bio]-bibliographische Hilfsmittel (p.265-76) - 2. Verzeichnis der Rezensenten - 3. Namenverzeichnis (ausser Rezensenten) - 4. Verzeichnis der genannten Schriften - 5. Werke über bestimmte Denkmälergruppen. *Class No:* 003.345

[103]

Bibliographie der Runeninschriften nach Fundorten ... Krause, W., *hrsg*. Göttingen, Vandenhoeck und Ruprecht, 1961-73. 2v. (*Abhandlungen der Akademie der Wissenschaften in Göttingen. Philogisch-Historische Klasse ..., 3 Folge, Nr.48,80.*) ISBN: 3525823525, v.2.

V.1 *Die Runeninschriften der Britische Inseln;* v.2 *Die Runeninschriften des europäischen Kontinents.*

V.1 is a bibliography of *c*4,000 books and periodicals on Runic inscriptions in the British Isles, arranged by places A-Z. Appendix: Die angeblichen Runeninschriften von Nordamerika (p.136-66). In the index entry words are grouped by 11 types of rune (*e.g.* Norwegian).
Class No: 003.345

Standards

[104]

AMERICAN NATIONAL STANDARDS INSTITUTE. Catalog of American national standards. New York, American National Standards Institute, 19??-. Annual. ISSN: 10437002.

Title varies.

Lists over 11,000 standards available through ANSI. Entries include designation, title and price. Supplemented by the monthly *ANSI reporter*. Version also available through the Internet at http://web.ansi.org/public/catalog/cat-top.html. *Class No:* 006

[105]

ASSOCIATION FRANÇAISE DE NORMALISATION. Catalogue des normes françaises. Paris, Association française de normalisation, 193?-. Annual. ISSN: 0374096x.

Title varies.

Catalogue of the French equivalent of BSI. Arranged by broad subject headings. Also available on CD-ROM and online as *Noriane* (FIZ Technik and Questel). Internet access at http://www.afnor.fr. *Class No:* 006

[106]

BRITISH STANDARDS INSTITUTION. BSI standards catalogue. London, British Standards Institution, 1984-. Annual. £36. ISSN: 09530339.

Continues *British Standards yearbook*, 1937-83 (ISSN: 00682578).

The 1998 ed. (xiv,1081p.) lists over 15,000 BSI publications, most with brief descriptions. Arranged in numerical order within series: General series (prefix BS, p.26-502) ... Automobile series - Aerospace series - Marine series ... Drafts for development, etc. International Standards corespondence index; detailed subject index

....(contd.)

(p.869-1072). 'Library sets of British Standards in the United Kingdom' (p.1073-77). Searchable online through FIZ Technik as *BSI Standardline*. File, updated monthly, includes historical data on standards withdrawn or lapsed since the end of 1985. A CD-ROM version (monthly updating, £145) is also available.

The monthly *BSI catalogue news* (£115) is a cumulative listing of changes, etc. *Class No:* 006

[107]

DEUSTCHES INSTITUT FÜR NORMUNG. DIN Katalog für Technische Regeln. Berlin, Beuth, 1926-. Annual. DM190. ISSN: 09451080.

Title and format varies. Currently issued in 2 v.

Contains information on German standards, draft standards and technical rules. Updated by supplements. Searchable online through DataStar and FIZ Technik. Data from the catalogue is also available from the DIN WWW site at http://www.din.de. *Class No:* 006

[108]

FALLONE, E. *and* **CAMPBELL, J. Information on standards:** a guide to sources. London, British Library/ Edinburgh, National Library of Scotland, 1998. ix,120p. (*Information in focus.*) ISBN: 0712308326.

7 chaps: 1. The Process of making standards - 2. International standards - 3. Regional standards - 4. National standards - 5. Sources of standards information (p.17-48, briefly annotated entries for catalogues, newsletters, handbooks, directories, CD-ROMs, etc.) - 6. Accessing standards and standards information (UK libraries with collections of British (BSI) and other standards) - 7. Purchasing standards. Appended directories of international, regional and national standards organizations. Glossary of acronyms/abbreviations (p.105-12), short bibliography and index. Brief, but the only recent guide to standards information. *Class No:* 006

[109]

INTERNATIONAL STANDARDS ORGANIZATION. ISO catalogue. Genève, International Standards Organization, 197?-. Annual. ISSN: 1023327x.

1997 ed. (1096p.) lists 10,745 ISO standards and other publications. Classified arrangement (p.41-404) with standard no., title, brief bibliographical details and price code. Separate lists of standards withdrawn, and in numerical and technical committee order. Alphabetical index (p.507-1096). Also available through the Internet at http://www.iso.ch. Updated by the quarterly *ISO catalogue supplement* (ISSN: 10185968). *Class No:* 006

[110]

—INTERNATIONAL STANDARDS ORGANIZATION. KWIC index of international standards. Genève, International Standards Organization, 1983-. Biennial (iregular).

The 6th ed. (xvii,758p., last published?) 'contains the permuted titles of all documents resulting from the standardizing activities of ISO, IEC and 26 other international organizations (*e.g.* International Bureau of Weights and Measures, International Dairy Federation, International Maritime Organization). The documents include international standards, international recommendations, international conventions, technical annexes to international conventions and international codes of practice' (p.iii).
Class No: 006

[111]

Perinorm London, British Standards Institute in assoc. with AFNOR and DIN, 1989-. CD-ROM database.

Available in two versions: *Perinorm Europe* or *Perinorm international*, both updated monthly.

The European version contains bibliographic data on over 300,000 standards including those from the national bodies in Austria, Belgium, Czech Republic, France, Germany, Netherlands, Switzerland, Turkey and UK. The international version adds data from the US, Japan and Australia. Both versions include international standards. Searching across all records in English, French or German, up to 13 seachable fields. *Class No:* 006

[112]

Standards infobase. Ascot, ILI Infodisk, 199?-. Computer database.

Available either on CD-ROM as *Standards infodisk* (quarterly updating, £1445) or through the Internet on a subscription basis.

Contains detailed information from official sources on 350,000 national, international and military standards. Includes data from ANSI, BSI, DIN and IEEE. Most records contain summaries of up to 200 words, some have table of contents detail. *Class No:* 006

The Humanities

[113]

BLAZEK, R. *and* **AVERSA, E.S. The Humanities: a selective guide to information sources.** 4th ed. Englewood, Colo., Libraries Unlimited, 1994. xix,504p. £48.95;$55. ISBN: 1563081679.

First published 1974; 3rd ed. 1988. Also available in pbck. (£37.95;£42. ISBN: 1563081687).

Covers philosophy, religion, mythology and folklore, visual arts, performing arts and language and literature. Comparative and evaluative notes on 1,200 sources (25% increase on previous ed.) in even numbered chapters. Briefer odd numbered chapters give general information on sources, techniques, etc. Author/title index to the source chapters; subject index. Relatively weak on a few areas, *e.g.* foreign literature, and biased towards works published in the US. Otherwise a useful introduction to research in the humanities, this ed. impressively up-to-date with a good proportion of 1993 and 1994 titles. *Class No:* 009

Databases

[114]

ARMSTRONG, C.J. *and* **FENTON, R.R. World databases in humanities.** London, Bowker Saur, 1996. xiii,1060p. £145;$250. (*World database series.*) ISBN: 1857390482.

Part of the ongoing *World database series* (*q.v.*).

Covers humanities in the broadest sense. 2,055 'master' records in 13 chaps. (1. Humanities (general) ... 7. Literature ... 10. History archaeology ... 13. Patents - humanities. Full descriptions, each database implementation recorded. Indexed by personal name, title, subject, producer and database name. The entire *World database series* is also available online through DataStar (WDBS).
Class No: 009(003.4)

Internet

[115]

HUMBUL: humanities bulletin board. Oxford, Oxford University Computing Service. World Wide Web Resource.

URL: http://users.ox.ac.uk/umbul/. Date reviewed 18th June 1998.

'Gateway' to scholarly humanities Internet sites. Main links under subject based headings (Anthropology ... Film, dance and media studies ... Libraries ... Philosophy ... Visual arts); site search engine. Also provides a limited 'Conference diary' listing forthcoming humanities events.
Class No: 009(003.41)

Indexes

[116]

The American humanities index. Troy, N.Y., Whitson, 1975-. Annual. $275. ISSN: 03610144.

Issued quarterly with annual cumulations 1975-87.

Indexes 'creative, critical and scholarly journals in the arts and humanities'. Concentrates on peripheral titles not covered elsewhere and should not be confused with Wilson's *Humanities index* (*q.v.*). Author and subject entries in one alphabetical sequence, the latter in upper case. Includes review articles. About 400 titles indexed 1996.
Class No: 009(014)

[117]

Arts and humanities citation index. 1976-. Philadelphia, Institute for Scientific Information, 1978-. Semi-annual. $6,490. ISSN: 01628445.

Companion publication to *Science citation index* and *Social sciences citation index.* Each semi-annual issue in 3v.: v.1 Citation index. Guide to lists of source publications; v.2 Source index. Corporate index; v.3 Permuterm subject index.

Covers archaeology, architecture, art, Asian studies, classics, dance, film, TV and radio, folklore, history, language and linguistics, literature, music, philosophy, theatre, theology and religious studies. 6,100 journals indexed, approx. 1,000 fully, 5,100 selectively. The source index comprises an author index giving full reference, author's address (where available), language, selected key terms (where not obvious from the title) and brief bibliographical descriptions of all works cited in footnotes or bibliographies. The citation index is an alphabetical list by author of the cited items; the permuterm subject index covers every significant English word in the title of source items; the corporate index has geographic and organization sections. Wide coverage, but small type, difficult for the uninitiated to use and expensive. Searchable online from 1980, updated weekly, through Dialog (File 439), Data-Star and OCLC. In the UK higher education institutions have the option of connection throught the BIDS service. Internet access through ISI also available. The CD-ROM version, containing records 1990 to date, is updated triannually. Twenty year (1975-94) and ten year (1980-89) cumulated discs also available. *Class No:* 009(014)

[118]

—Current contents: arts and humanities. Philadelphia, Institute for Scientific Information, 1979-. Fortnightly. $442. ISSN: 01633155.

Each issue reproduces the tables of contents of the main periodicals indexed in *Arts & humanities citation index*. Subject arrangement in 8 groups, with title keyword and author indexes, the latter giving abbreviated addresses. Records 1990 to date are available though the online vendors

.... (contd.)
Data-Star, Dialog (File 440) and OVID as part of the *Current contents search* database. ISI and SilverPlatter also provide an Internet accessible version for records 1994 to date. CD-ROM discs of *Current contents* are available from OVID. *Class No:* 009(014)

[119]
British humanities index. 1962-. East Grinstead, Bowker Saur, 1963-. Quarterly, with separate annual cumulation. £480. ISSN: 00070815.

Published by Library Association Publishing until January/March 1990. Issued in 3 quarters with an annual cumulation until 1968. Continues in part *Subject index to periodicals* (*q.v.*).

Humanities interpreted broadly to include the arts, music, philosophy, religion. literature, economics, politics, history and society. *c.*300 British periodicals and newspapers indexed under subject headings A-Z, with brief *c.*50 word abstracts. Detailed subject, author and source (titles covered) indexes. Records 1985 to date also available on CD-ROM as *BHI Plus* (Quarterly updating. £850. ISSN: 09668772).
Class No: 009(014)

[120]
Humanities index. New York, Wilson, 1974-. Quarterly, with annual cumulation. ISSN: 00955981.

One of two indexes superseding *Social sciences and humanities index.*

Cover to cover indexing of 400 English language periodicals in the fields of archaeology and classical studies, area studies, folklore, history, language and literature, performing arts, philosophy, religion and theology. Includes numerous British titles *e.g. Antiquity, British journal of aesthetics, History, Mind, Past and present.* Arranged in standard Wilson format, subject and author entries in one alphabet. Separate list of book reviews. Records 1984 to date searchable online through Wilsonline. Also available from Wilson and SilverPlatter as a monthly or quarterly updated CD-ROM service (£1,188 SilverPlatter, also Internet access £1,307). The new Internet/CD-ROM database *Humanities abstracts* (*q.v.*) is an enhanced version of *Humanities index*. *Class No:* 009(014)

[121]
IDIOM: in-depth indexing of monographs on CD-ROM. Cambridge, Chadwyck-Healey, 1995-. CD-ROM database. ISSN: 1081308x.

Currently issued on separate *Undergraduate* (£1,995) and *History* (£1,675) discs, both updated annually.

IDIOM undergraduate contains indexes and table of contents listings from over 5,000 humanities and social sciences monographs published 1984-94. Titles included based on annual lists of outstanding academic books in *Choice* (*q.v.*). Browse and search features, over 1,000,000 index terms. '(C)overage is highly selective and American biased ... (but) unique in providing electronic subject access to specific pages within major academic texts ... could become a valuable additional tool in the librarian's armoury' (*Refer*, v.12(1), Winter 1996, p.19). *Class No:* 009(014)

Reviews & Abstracts

[122]
Combined retrospective index to book reviews in humanities journals, 1802-1974. Farber, E.I., *eds.* Woodbridge, Conn., Research Publications, 1982-84. 10v.

V.1-9 Authors; v.10 Titles. Companion set to *Combined retrospective index to book reviews in scholarly journals 1886-1974* (*q.v.*).

Indexes *c.*500,000 reviews with the emphasis on literary, philosophy and music journals. *Class No:* 009(048)

[123]
An Index to book reviews in the humanities. Williamstown, Mich., Philip Thomson, 1960-91. Annual. ISSN: 00735892.

Published quarterly 1960-62, with annual cumulations, that for 1960 not issued until 1978. Ceased publication with issue for 1990.

Indexed reviews in *c.*475 periodicals. From 1971 included all reviews (formerly selective) in the periodicals indexed, except those for children's literature. *Class No:* 009(048)

Black Races

[124]
Blacks in the humanities, 1750-1984: a selected annotated bibliography. Joyce, D.F., *comp.* Westport, Conn., Greenwood Press, 1986. xix,209p. £40.50;$45. (*Bibliographies and indexes in Afro-American and African studies, no.13.*) ISBN: 0313246432.

A 'guide to major published and unpublished sources in English about the contributions of Black Americans in eleven disciplines of the humanities' (Introduction p.xi). Includes a chapter on the humanities in general. Subject and name index. *Class No:* 009(=96)

Research Projects

[125]
Current research in Britain. The Humanities. London, Cartermill in assoc. with the British Library, 1985-. Annual.

Published annually. Companion volumes *Biological sciences, Physical sciences* and *Social sciences.* Often referred to as *CRIB. Current research in Britain* replaces *Research in British universities, polytechnics and colleges (RBUPC).*

12th ed. (1997. xiii,386p. ISBN: 1860672310) contains details of research projects ongoing in universities, colleges of higher education, museums and other institutions. For each project gives name(s) of researcher(s), description of topic, start and estimated conclusion dates, sponsoring bodies (if any) and proposed form of publication. Good currency, compiled from information collected January-May 1997. Name (researchers and projects), study area and keyword indexes. Also available as part of the CD-ROM database *CRIB on CD-ROM*, updated annually, £575.
Class No: 009:061:061.62.005

01 Bibliography & Bibliographies

Bibliography

[126]
BERGER, S.E. The Design of bibliographies: observations, references and examples. London, Mansell, 1991. x,198p. ISBN: 0720120772.

Published in the US by Greenwood Press ($85. ISBN: 0313284253).

Practical manual intended 'to help bibliographers and publishers' (Preface p.viii). Main contents: 1. Introduction - 2. Book design - 3. Bibliographies: their content and shape - 4. Computers and desk top publishing - Bibliography (274 extensively annotated items). Lengthy appendix of facsimile examples (p.103-89) with commentary; drawn from wide range of sources, but confusing arrangement. Further appendix 'Legibility'. Index. A 'thoroughly researched and finely written book' (*Library Association record*, v.94(7), July 1992, p.466). *Class No:* 01.0

[127]
ESDAILE, A. Esdaile's manual of bibliography. Stokes, R., *rev. & ed.* 5th rev. ed. Metuchen, N.J., Scarecrow, 1981. x,397p. illus., plates. £35;$35. ISBN: 0810814625.

First published 1931; 4th ed. 1967.

Sets out to teach the first elements of bibliography. 10 chapters: 1. The nature of bibliography - 2. The parts of a book -3. Landmarks in the development of the book - 4. Papyrus, parchment, vellum, paper - 5. Typography - 6. Composition and press work -7. Illustration - 8. Binding - 9. The collation of books - 10. The description of books. References at chapter ends. Glossary (p.382-90). Index. An established and authoritative text. *Class No:* 01.0

[128]
GASKELL, P. A New introduction to bibliography. Oxford, Clarendon Press, 1972. xxii,438p. illus. ISBN: 0198181507.

Reprinted with corrections 1974. Intended as a successor to R.A. McKerrow's classic *Introduction to bibliography for library students* (1927). Further reprint by St Paul's Bibliographies 1995 (£19.95. ISBN: 187304030X).

Contents: Introduction - Book production: the hand-press period, 1500-1800 - Book production: the machine-press period, 1800-1950 - Bibliographical applications (*e.g.* bibliographical descriptions; textual bibliography). Reference bibliography, (p.392-412, running commentary; includes periodicals). Detailed index. Well produced. *Class No:* 01.0

[129]
KRUMMEL, D.W. Bibliographies: their aims and methods. London, Mansell, 1984. x,192p. £50;$27.50. ISBN: 0720116872.

Describes the ideal practices and features of bibliographical compilation, with theoretical background, in 7 chapters: 1. Introduction - 2. Scope - 3. Citation style - 4. Annotation - 5. Organization - 6. Collecting entries - 7. Presentation. Bibliographical commentaries scattered throughout the text; major bibliography of 110 items on bibliographic compilation 1883-1983 (p.161-81). 3

....*(contd.)*

appendices, including list of 65 American and 17 German bibliographies given awards for graphic excellence. A 'well organized, readable compendium on all aspects of bibliography' (*International journal of reviews in library and information science,* v.2(2), 1986, p.57). For both the compiler and student. *Class No:* 01.0

[130]
ROBINSON, A.M.L. Systematic bibliography: a practical guide to the work of compilation. 4th rev. ed. London, Bingley, 1979. 135p. illus., facsims. $38.50. ISBN: 0851572898.

First published 1963; 3rd ed. 1971.

Aimed at students and others inexperienced in bibliographical compilation, but also of wider application. 5 sections: 1. The meaning of bibliography and its varied forms - 2. The collection of material and the mechanics of compilation - 3. Arrangement - 4. Layout - 5. The application of computers to systematic bibliography (by M. Lodder). Recommended books (p.97-101). 20 bibliographical examples (p.107-30). Index. *Class No:* 01.0

Bibliographies

[131]
BIBLIOGRAPHICAL SOCIETY. Index to selected bibliographical journals 1933-70. Oxford, Oxford University Press, 1982. vii,316p. £32. ISBN: 019721777x.

An author and subject index in one integrated sequence to articles published in the following journals: *Bibliotheck; Book collector; Book handbook; Edinburgh Bibliographical Society transactions; Records of the Glasgow Bibliographical Society; Journal of the Printing Historical Society; The Library; Oxford Bibliographical Society proceedings and papers; Papers of the Bibliographical Society of America; Studies in bibliography; Transactions of the Cambridge Bibliographical Society.* Continues and widens the coverage provided by Cole (below). *Class No:* 01.0(01)

[132]
—COLE, G.W. An Index to bibliographical papers published by the Bibliographical Society and the Library Association, London, 1877-1932. Chicago, University of Chicago Press, for Bibliographical Society of America, 1933. ix,262p.

Author and subject entries in one A-Z sequence. *Class No:* 01.0(01)

[133]
—FEATHER, J. An Index to selected bibliographical journals, 1971-1985. Oxford, Oxford Bibliographical Society, 1991. [iv],134p. (*Oxford Bibliographical Society occasional publication, no.23.*) ISBN: 0901420476.

Intended as a continuation of the Bibliographical Society's 1933-70 index (above). Six titles covered: *Bibliotheck; Book collector; Journal of the Printing Historical Society; The Library; Publishing history; Transactions of the Cambridge Bibliographical Society.* '(W)ill certainly be welcomed by all bibliographers, but it has a decidedly makeshift quality' (*The Papers of the Bibliographical Society of America,* v.85(1), March 1991, p.88). *Class No:* 01.0(01)

[134]

HARVARD UNIVERSITY. Library. **Bibliography and bibliography periodicals.** Cambridge, Mass., Harvard Univ. Press, 1966. vii,1066p. (*Widener Library shelflist, no. 7.*)

About 18,000 entries in 4 sequences: 1. Classified listing for bibliography: books (B) - 2. Classified listing for bibliography: periodicals (BP) - 3. A-Z listing by author - 4. Chronological listing by date of publication of monographs. *Class No:* 01.0(01)

[135]

'A Selective checklist of bibliographical scholarship' in (*Studies in bibliography*, v.3-27, 1951-74).

Studies in bibliography published annually, 1949-.

Primary investigations dealing with printing and publishing history, bibliographical treatment of authors and critical or textual studies. In 2 pts: Incunabula and early Renaissance; Later Renaissance to the present. Deals mainly with English and American literature. Not published since v.27, 1974, (p.246-319), which listed continuously numbered entries 4592-5204. *Class No:* 01.0(01)

Great Britain

[136]

HOWARD-HILL, T.H. British bibliography and textual criticism: a bibliography. Oxford, Clarendon Press, 1979. 2v. (*Index to British literary bibliography, IV, V.*) ISBN: 0198181639.

Comprises parts IV and V of the *Index to British literary bibliography* (*q.v.*). Records 'writings in English published from 1890 which discuss bibliographical aspects of works printed from 1475 to the present day, and the circumstances of production and distribution of books in Britain during that period' (Introduction p.xv). Contents of v.IV (xxvi,732p.): Bibliography and textual criticism - General and periodical bibliography - Regional bibliography - Book production and distribution (p.175-613) - Forms, genres and subjects. V.V (viii,488p.) covers individual authors A-Z. Indexed in v.VI of the series, *British literary bibliography and textual criticism 1890-1969, an index* (1980. £110. ISBN: 0198181809). Updated by:- *Class No:* 01.0(01)(410)

[137]

—HOWARD-HILL, T.H. British literary bibliography 1970-1979: a bibliography. Oxford, Clarendon Press, 1992. xix,912p. £110. (*Index to British literary bibliography, VII.*) ISBN: 0198181833.

6,633 items in sections: General bibliographies of and guides to British literature: Bibliography and textual criticism (p.7-31); General and period bibliography; Book production and distribution (p.105-252); Forms, genres and subjects (p.253-354); Authors (p.355-712). Index.
Class No: 01.0(01)(410)

Glossaries

[138]

STOKES, R. A Bibliographical companion. Metuchen, N.J., Scarecrow Press, 1989. x,298p. £26.55;$32.50. ISBN: 0810821753.

A glossary of bibliographical terms intended for the student rather than the experienced bibliographer. Fills the gap between Carter's *ABC for book collectors* (*q.v.*), with its emphasis on book collecting, and Glaister's *Glossary of the book,* with its concentration on book production. Around 600 well-written entries averaging 300 words in length. Omits entries for prominent bibliographies. Exhaustively cross-referenced. *Class No:* 01.0(038.1)

Reviews & Abstracts

[139]

Index to reviews of bibliographical publications: an international annual. 1976-1985. Troy, N.Y., Whitson, 1978-1991. Annual. ISSN: 01614029.

Publisher varies, initially G.K. Hall.

Reviews included 'must treat international and general bibliographical subjects or those relating specifically to British or American literature or language, or to literature in English worldwide'. Final v. indexed 905 reviews drawn from *c.*350 publications. Broad category arrangement with subject, title and scholar indexes. *Class No:* 01.0(048)

Standards

[140]

BRITISH STANDARDS INSTITUTION. Recommendations for references to published materials. London, B.S.I., 1989. 24p. £50. (*BS:1629.*) ISBN: 0580162036.

Replaces BS5195: Pt. 1: 1975, BS5195: Pt. 2: 1977 and BS6098: 1981.

Covers references to all kinds of published material including monographs, serials, patents, maps, computer software, databases, music, sound recordings and photographs. *Class No:* 01.0(083.74)

[141]

—BRITISH STANDARDS INSTITUTION. Recommendations for citing publications by bibliographical references. 2nd ed. London, B.S.I., 1990. 8p. £26. (*BS:5605.*) ISBN: 0580189724.

First published 1978.

Methods for the name and date (Harvard) and numeric systems. *Class No:* 01.0(083.74)

Bibliometrics

[142]

DIODATO, V.P. Dictionary of bibliometrics. New York, Haworth Press, 1994. xiii,185p. tables, diags. £26.95;$29.25. ISBN: 1560248521.

225 definitions with references, ranging from a few lines to several pages. *c.*200 item bibliography; name index. A 'highly original publication ... (that) explains what is meant by each of the technical terms in simple layman's language' (*Library Association record*, v.97(1), January 1995, p.52).
Class No: 01.004

[143]

SELLEN, M.K. Bibliometrics: an annotated bibliogrpahy, 1970-1990. New York, G.K. Hall/Maxwell Macmillan, 1993. xiv,169p. $40. ISBN: 0816119546.

Offers international, but very selective, coverage of bibliometrics applied to all subject areas. Classified arrangement with annotations of 20-100 words; author and subject indexes. *Class No:* 01.004

Bibliographies

Bibliographies of Bibliographies

[144]

ARNIM, M. Internationale Personalbibliographie 1800-1943. 2. verb. und stark verm. Aufl. Leipzig (later Stuttgart), Hiersemann, 1944-52. 2v.

First published 1936 covering the period 1550-1935 (25,000 entries).

Continued by: Bd.III. *1944-1959 und Nachträge zur 2. Auflage...* Fortgeführt von D. Bock und F. Hodes, (1963. xi,659p.); *1944-1975 Fortgefüjrte Auflage von Band III (1949-1959) mit Nachträgen zur zweiten Auflage von Band I/ II (1800-1943),* A-Hyppä, Lfg. 1-9, (1978-81); *Zweite völlig neubearbeitete Auflage von Band III (Berichtszeit 1944-1959) in drei bis zum Jeweiligen Erschneinungsjahr Ergänztenn Banden III-V,* Jakob-Ryzmkowski, Lfg. 10-18 (1981-84); *Schluslieferung mit Titelbogen zu Band V,* Sad-Zywczynski, Lfg. 19-24, (1985-87). All 5 v. in print (DM2760. ISBN: 3777250023 (set)).

An index to bibliographies of specific scholars and authors. International in scope, but with a marked German emphasis. Valuable for its concentration on bibliographies contained in books (*e.g.* Kürschner), bio-bibliographies (*e.g.* Poggendorf; Goedeke), periodical articles, festschriften etc. Because of omissions from the 2nd ed., the 1st ed. should still be used. *Class No:* 011/015(009)

[145]

BESTERMAN, T. A World bibliography of bibliographies and of bibliographical catalogues, calendars, abstracts, digests, indexes and the like. 4th ed., rev. and greatly enl. throughout. Lausanne, Societas Bibliographica, 1965-66. 4v. and index. $417.50 ISBN: 0874712947.

First published 1939-40 (2v.); 3rd ed. 1955-56 (4v.).

Records over 117,000 separately collated volumes of bibliographies in more than 40 languages, published up to 1963 or 1964. Arranged by subjects A-Z under more than 16,000 headings. Excludes general library catalogues, but admits patent abridgements and lists of manuscripts. Cited material not described, but the estimated number of items listed in each volume is normally stated as an 'alternative to critical annotation'. Occasional bibliographical notes (*e.g.* number of copies printed). The entries under 'Education' (v.2, cols. 1825-1914) have 32 sub-headings; one of these 'Teaching of specific subjects' deals with 45 subjects A-Z. Author, editor, etc. and anonymous title index. A monumental compilation by a single bibliographer, which is unlikely to be surpassed. Note must, however, be made of the objectionable style of entry of authors' names, with forenames preceding surnames (all in capitals), a feature which does not make for rapid location. Further points are the absence of publishers from entries and the lack of full coverage for Oriental and Slavic items.

The publishers Rowman & Littlefield produced various subject bibliographies based on reprints of sections of the 4th ed of Besterman. Examples include *Education: a bibliography of bibliographies* (1971. 306p.) and *A World bibliography of African bibliographies* (1971. 241cols. $42. ISBN: 0874712947). *Class No:* 011/015(009)

[146]

—A World bibliography of bibliographies 1964-1974: a list of works represented by Library of Congress printed catalog cards: a decennial supplement to Theodore Besterman, *A World bibliography of bibliographies.* Toomey, A.F., *comp.* Totowa, N.J., Rowmann & Littlefield, 1977. 2v. ISBN: 0874719992.

18,000 titles under 6,000 headings based on Library of Congress subject headings (8th ed.). Includes reprints of pre-1964 titles and continuation volumes. All are separately published titles, apart from some offprints. Excludes film catalogues and periodical indexes. Additional information to that given on the cards for many entries (*e.g.* references to earlier eds. or related publications). 1,400 references; author/title index. *Class No:* 011/015(009)

[147]

Bibliographic index: a cumulative bibliography of bibliographies. 1937-. New York, Wilson, 1938-. 3pa., final issue bound cumulation. ISSN: 00061255.

Annual cumulations since 1969: earlier cumulations 1937/42, 1943/46, 1947/50, 1951/55, 1956/59, 1960/62, 1963/65 and 1966/68.

Subject list of bibliographies published separately or appearing as part of books, pamphlets and periodicals. Unless relating to a particular person or very specialized topic, bibliographies included must contain 50 or more citations. Concentrates on English language material, although Germanic and Romance languages are also represented. Particularly strong on bibliographies appearing in periodicals, 2,800 titles examined on a regular basis. No author index. Also available online through Wilsonline, Ovid and OCLC for records 1984 to date.
Class No: 011/015(009)

[148]

Bibliographische Berichte. [Bibliographical bulletin.] Frankfurt am Main, Klostermann, 1959-89. Annual. ISSN: 00061506.

Previously (1957-58) as 'Bibliographische Beihefte' in *Zeitschrift für Bibliothekswesen und Bibliographie.* Frequency varies: quarterly 1959-62; semi-annual 1963-69; annual from 1970 until cessation with issue for 1988.

Listed recent bibliographies, including those 'hidden' in books and periodicals. International in scope, English and German items evenly matched. UDC classified arrangement, about 4,000 entries in final volumes. *Gesamtregister/ Cumulated subject index* for 1969-87 published as Bd. 30 1988, replacing earlier cumulations.
Class No: 011/015(009)

[149]

BOHATTA, H. *and* **HODES, F. Internationale Bibliographie der Bibliographien.** Ein Nachschlagewerk, unter Mitelwerkung von W. Funke. Frankfurt am Main, Klostermann, 1950. [iv],652p.

A bibliography of *c.*18,000 bibliographies (whether published separately or appearing as parts of books or periodicals), systematically arranged. International coverage, author bibliographies omitted. Very occasional brief annotations; unattractive layout. Subject and author indexes.
Class No: 011/015(009)

[150]

Checklist of bibliographies appearing in the *Bulletin of bibliography*, 1897-1987. Caldwell-Wood, N. *and* Ward, P.W., *eds.* Westport, Conn., Meckler, 1989. xiii,144p. £71.50;$79.50. ISBN: 0887362370.

Brings together entries from two previous compilations: *Cumulative index (1897-1975) to the Bulletin of bibliography and magazine notes* comp. E.C. Jones & M.L. Pollard (1977) and *Cumulative index (1976-1980) to the Bulletin of bibliography* (1981).

In 2 sections: author/subject index to bibliographies and articles; author/title index to book reviews. Brief book notices and news notes excluded. *Class No:* 011/015(009)

[151]

COURTNEY, W.P.A. A Register of national bibliography: with a selection of the chief bibliographical books and articles printed in other countries... London, Constable, 1905. 2v. Supplement 1912.

Reprinted New York, Franklin, 1968. 3v. in 2.

About 25,000 items, arranged under subjects A-Z in two main sequences (v.1-2; suppt.), plus appendices. The original aim was a register of English bibliographies; this was, in the event expanded. Excludes sale catalogues, bibliographies of manuscripts and charts and catalogues of 'free libraries' in England. Includes bibliographies and lists 'hidden' in books and periodical articles. Many cross-references and handy brief appended notes. Two detailed indexes, in very small type, of authors, places, subjects etc. *Class No:* 011/015(009)

[152]

SCHNEIDER, G. Handbuch der Bibliographie. 4. gänzl. veränd. und stark verm. Aufl. Leipzig, Hiersemann, 1930. ix,674p.

First published 1930. Reprinted 1969 (Hiersemann. DM180. ISBN: 3777269026), designated '5. Aufl.', but with the text unchanged.

About 5,000 entries, many with evaluative annotations. 15 sections concentrating on universal and general bibliographies, major library catalogues, lists of theses and incunabula, etc., plus some general reference material (*e.g.* encyclopedias; biographical dictionaries). Title and keyword indexes.

Still prized for its 199p. classic discussion of theoretical and historical bibliography in 1st-3rd eds.; translated by R.R. Shaw as *Theory and history of bibliography* (New York, Columbia Univ. Press, 1934) (reprinted New York, Scarecrow Press, 1961). The 4th ed. carries only a 'Geschichte der Bibliographie' (p.1-35), apart from the annotated entries. *Class No:* 011/015(009)

[153]

—PETZHOLDT, J. Bibliotheca bibliographica. Leipzig, Engelmann, 1866. 939p.

Reprinted, Nieuwkoop, De Graaf, 1961.

Still used as a source for pre-1866 bibliographies, both general and subject. Similar number of entries to Stein (below); scholarly annotations. Author and subject index. *Class No:* 011/015(009)

[154]

—STEIN, H. Manuel de bibliographie générale. Paris, Picard, 1897. xx,895p.

Reprinted, New York, Kraus, 1961.

About 5,500 entries in 17 sections (15 concerned with special subjects), some annotations. Subject index only. Three lengthy appendices: an A-Z list of towns having printing presses before 1800; list of lists of periodicals; list

....(contd.)

of printed catalogues of major libraries. Supplements in *Le Biographie moderne,* 1871-1931, edited by H. Stein. *Class No:* 011/015(009)

Ireland

[155]

EAGER, A.R. A Guide to Irish bibliographical material: a bibliography of Irish bibliographies and sources of information. 2nd rev. and enl. ed. London, Library Association; Westport, Conn., Greenwood Press, 1980. xv,502p. $105. ISBN: 0853659311, UK; 0313223432, US.

1st ed. 1964.

Primarily devoted to material relating to Ireland, although 'general bibliographies printed in Ireland, but which are not Irish in character' are included (Introduction p.ix). Arranged by Dewey DC without class-marks, items numbered serially to 9,517. Index. *Class No:* 011/015(009)(415)

Germany

[156]

Bibliographie der Bibliographien: BB Jahresverzeichnis selbständig und unselbständig erschienener Bibliographien. 1990/91-95. Deutschen Bibliothek, *hrsg.* Frankfurt am Main, Buchhändler-Vereinigung, 1992-96. Annual. ISSN: 03014614.

Continues *Bibliographie der Bibliographien: monatliches Verzeichnis* (below). Ceased publication with v. for 1995.

Much the same scope and format as its predecessor. 1993 issue (1994. 236p.) has 3,590 entries in classified arrangement with subject keyword indexes. *Class No:* 011/015(009)(430)

[157]

—Bibliographie der Bibliographien: monatliches Verzeichnis. Deutsche Bücherei, *bearb.* Leipzig, VEB Verlag für Buch- und Bibliothekswesen, 1966-90. Monthly.

As *Bibliographie der deutschen Bibliographien* 1966-71.

Included West German material and selected German language publications from other countries. Bibliographies appearing in books and periodicals indexed as well as those separately published. Keyword indexes cumulated annually.

Coverage for 1954-65 provided by *Bibliographie der deutschen Bibliographien: Jahresverzeichnis der selbständig erschienenen...* (1957-69). The Deutsche Bücherei also produced *Bibliographie der versteckten Bibliographien aus deutschsprachigen Büchern und Zeitschriften der Jahre 1930-1953* (1956. 371p.) containing *c.*13,000 entries. Does not cover separately published bibliographies. *Class No:* 011/015(009)(430)

Poland

[158]

Bibliografia bibliografii polskich. 1981-. [Bibliography of Polish bibliographies.] Warszawa, Biblioteka Narodowa, 1988-. Annual. ISSN: 08606579.

Continues Cz.1 of *Bibliografia bibliografii i nauki o ksiazce* 1937/44-1980 (1955-88). Cz.2 of this title continued by *Polska bibliografia bibliologiczna* (*q.v.*).

1993 v. (1996. 185p.) has 1,826 entries in classified arrangement with alphabetical and subject indexes.

Bibliografia bibliografii polskich 1961-1970 (Bieńkowa, M.B. & Eychlerowa, B. Warszawa, Biblioteka Narodowa, 1992. xxxii,772p. ISBN: 8370091091), containing 9,691 entries, continues a work by H. Sawoniak under the same

....*(contd.)*
title covering 1951-1960 (Wrocław, Zakład Narodowy im. Ossolińskich, 1967. xxviii,484p.). Coverage to 1950 is provided in Sawoniak's updating of Hahn's *Bibliografia bibliografij polskich do 1950 roku* (1966. xxiv,587p.)
Class No: 011/015(009)(438)

Spain

[159]

FOULCHÉ-DELBOSC, R. *and* **BARRAU-DIHIGO, L. Manuel de l'hispanisant.** New York, Hispanic Society of America, 1920-25. 2v.

Reprinted New York, Kraus, 1959.

A manual of Spanish bibliography: V.1, *Répertoires*: 1. Généralités - 2. Typo-bibliographies - 3. Biographies et bio-bibliographies - 4. Bibliographies monographiques - 5. Archives, bibliothèques et musées - 6. Collections dispersées. Additions. V.2, *Collections* (a check list, p.vii-x, followed by contents-listing of printed collections and series and an author index). *Class No:* 011/015(009)(460)

RSFSR

[160]

Bibliografiīa rossiĭskoĭ bibliografii. 1939-. Moskva, Izd-vo 'Kniznaīa palata', 1941-. Annual. ISSN: 02043866.

Present title from 1992, previously *Bibliografiīa sovetskoĭ bibliografii* (ISSN: 02016346); 1940-45 not issued.

Includes substantive bibliographies appended to books and periodical articles as well as those separately published. Now classified by UDC with index of authors, etc. Lengthy prefatory surveys provide commentary on many of the items.
Class No: 011/015(009)(470)

Scandinavia

[161]

Guide to Nordic bibliography. Munch-Petersen, E., *ed.* Copenhagen, Nordic Council of Ministers, 1984. 235p. ISBN: 8773030805.

Annotated guide to national bibliographies and major subject bibliographies of the 5 Nordic states. Includes national bibliographies of serials, theses, government publications, maps and atlases, articles, audio-visual materials and films. Also covers directories of publishers, booksellers, societies, libraries and other related institutions. 856 entries in 3 sections: national bibliographies arranged by country; bibliographies of specific authors or works arranged alphabetically; subject bibliographies arranged by UDC classification. Preceded by general introduction and bibliographic essay for each country. A thorough, well-organized work; an essential source of reference for Scandinavian bibliographic material.

Updated by supplements for 1983-1986 (1988. 146p. ISBN: 8755215483) and 1987-1990 (1992. x,105p. ISBN: 8755219721) both containing new and revised entries.
Class No: 011/015(009)(48)

Finland

[162]

GRÖNROOS, H. Finlands bibliografiska litteratur: kommenterad förteckning. Ekenäs, Ekenäs Tryckeri, 1975. 388p. illus.

Expands and updates the same author's Finnish language (French introduction and table of contents) *Suomen bibliografisen Kirjallisuuden opas*, (1965).

....*(contd.)*
1,498 numbered, briefly annotated entries, covering general bibliographies, Finland in foreign literature and foreign countries in Finnish literature, subject bibliographies and bibliographies of individuals. Subject indexes in Swedish and Finnish; index of persons with individual bibliographies (arranged by professions); indexes of compilers and titles of anonymous bibliographies. *Class No:* 011/015(009)(480)

Sweden

[163]

OLSSON, A. *and* **SCHNEIDLER-LARSSON, A. Svenska bibliografier.** Stockholm, Svenska Bibliotekariesamfundet, 1986. 115p. (*Svenska Bibliotekariesamfundets skriftserie, 6.*)

Bibliography of Swedish language bibliographies and a few foreign language bibliographies published in Sweden. 1,009 numbered entries mostly unannotated, arranged according to the Swedish Library Association classification scheme. Author, title and subject indexes.
Class No: 011/015(009)(485)

India

[164]

JAIN, M.K. Indiana: a bibliography of bibliographical sources. New Delhi, Concept Publishing Company, 1989. x,292p. (*Concepts in communication, informatics and librarianship, 4.*) ISBN: 8170222303.

With D.R. Kalia, the same author was also responsible for *A Bibliography of Indian bibliographies* (1975).

Coverage includes library catalogues, documentation lists, abstracts, dissertation lists and serial catalogues. 1,827 entries, some annotated, under detailed subject headings. English language material only, includes items published abroad. *Class No:* 011/015(009)(540)

South Africa

[165]

MUSIKER, R. *and* **MUSIKER, N. South African bibliography** a survey of bibliographies and bibliographical works. 3rd ed. London, Mansell, 1996. xvii,142p. £45;$70. ISBN: 0720122252.

First published 1970 with suppl. 1977; 2nd ed. 1980.

8 chapters in discursive format covering retrospective and current national bibliographies, subject bibliographies, periodical and newspaper indexes and lists, theses and research, official publications, archives and manuscripts and bibliography in South Africa. 869 items covered, full citations following main section. Appendices 'Chronology of principle bibliographical developments 1821-1995' and 'Southern African bibliographic databases on CD-ROM'; index (p.124-42). 'Its scope is not paralleled elsewhere' (*South African journal of library and information science*, v.65(2), June 1997, p.138). *Class No:* 011/015(009)(680)

Canada

[166]

Bibliography of Canadian bibliographies. [Bibliographie des bibliographies canadiennes.] Ingles, E.B., *ed. & comp.* 3rd updated and rev. ed. Toronto, Univ. of Toronto Press, 1994. xliii,1178p. Can$150. ISBN: 0802028373.

First published 1960; 3 supplements 1961-65. 2nd ed. 1972.

7,375 entries for items published to mid 1993. Covers bibliographies 'relating in subject to Canada' (p.ix).

.... *(contd.)*
Bibliographies published in Canada but not pertaining to Canada, included in previous eds., now excluded. 'Hidden' bibliographies and those in electronic format omitted. Arranged in subjects sections, most entries with a brief descriptive note and library location, usually National Library of Canada. Author, title and English and French subject indexes. '(M)eticulous ... (e)ssential for all Canadiana collections at every level' (*Choice*, v.33(1), September 1995, p.84). *Class No:* 011/015(009)(71)

Latin America

[167]

GROPP, A.E. A Bibliography of Latin American bibliographies. Metuchen, N.J., Scarecrow Press, 1968. ix,515p.

Updates C.K. Jones's *A Bibliography of Latin American bibliographies* (2nd ed. rev. and enl. Washington, Government Printing Office, 1942. 311p.).

About 7,000 entries arranged by subject sub-divided by country. 80 sources are cited. Detailed index.

A supplement for 1965-69 (1971. 277p.) adds a further 1,416 entries (for later supplements see next entry).

A further work by Gropp, *A Bibliography of Latin American bibliographies published in periodicals* (Scarecrow Press, 1976. 2v. (lxxii,1031p.) ISBN: 0810808382), has 9,715 entries. Most are for the years 1929-65, but with a few earlier items. Both bibliographic articles and bibliographies appended to articles are covered.
Class No: 011/015(009)(729.99)

[168]

—A Bibliography of Latin American and Caribbean bibliographies, 1985-1989: social sciences and humanities. Loroña, L.V., *ed.* Metuchen, N.J., Scarecrow Press, 1993. xiv,314p. £35.55;$39.50. ISBN: 0810827026.

The latest (5th) supplement to Gropp containing 1,867 entries in subject/country arrangement with subject and author indexes. Annual updates are provided by *Bibliography of Latin American and Caribbean bibliographies* (Seminar on the Acquisition of Latin American Library Materials (SALALM) Secretariat, 1986-. ISSN: 08843902).

Earlier supplements, all published by Scarecrow Press, issued as follows: *A Bibliography of Latin American bibliographies: v.1 social sciences and humanities.* Cordeiro, D.R. *comp.* 1979 (viii,272p. £26.55;$29.50. ISBN: 0810811707 (covers monographs 1969-74 and periodicals 1966-74)); *A Bibliography of Latin American bibliographies, 1975-1979: social sciences and humanities.* Piedracueva, H. *ed.* 1982 (xiii,313p. £31.50;$35. ISBN: 0810815249): *A Bibliography of Latin American bibliographies, 1980-1984: social sciences and humanities.* Loroña, L.V. *ed.* 1987 (xiv,223p. £26.55;$29.50. ISBN: 0810819414). *Class No:* 011/015(009)(729.99)

Brazil

[169]

BASSECHES, B. A Bibliography of Brazilian bibliographies. [Una Bibliografia das bibliografias brasileiras.] Detroit, Blaine Ethridge, 1978. 185p. ISBN: 0879170646.

2,500 items, listed A-Z with subject and author indexes. Preface in English and Portuguese.
Class No: 011/015(009)(81)

Australia

[170]

BORCHARDT, D.H. Australian bibliography: a guide to printed sources of information. 3rd ed. Rushcutters Bay, N.S.W., Pergamon Press (Australia), 1976. xvi,270p.illus.,facsims.,port. ISBN: 0080205518.

First published 1963.

10 chapters of narrative discussion, including: 3. General bibliographies; 4/6. Subject bibliographies (social sciences, humanities, pure and applied sciences); 7. Bibliographies of geographic regions ... 10. The bibliographical scene. Final chapter (p.201-64) lists the 638 works refered to in the text by author A-Z. Non-analytical subject index.
Class No: 011/015(009)(94)

Translations

[171]

Index translationum: répertoire international des traductions. Paris, Unesco, 1932-. Annual. FFr490 (CD-ROM). ISSN: 00736074.

English subtitle *International bibliography of translations.* 1932-40 issued quarterly, numbered as a separate series. Last appeared as a printed index with v.39 for 1986 (1992. xii,1323p.). CD-ROM database, cumulating the printed indexes since 1979, continues coverage.

Printed vols. list translations by country of publication (A-Z, French form of name), then by the 10 major UDC classes. Author index. Detail for each translation includes author, title, name of translator, imprint and collation, language in which originally written and original title (italics). The standard source for non-technical translations, 800,000 records on the CD-ROM. *Class No:* 013

[172]

—Cumulative index to English translations 1948-1968. Boston, Mass., G.K. Hall, 1973. 2v. ISBN: 0816110425.

44,000 entries for book translations made in 7 predominantly English speaking countries (Australia, Canada, Eire, New Zealand, South Africa, UK and US), as listed in *Index translationum*, v.1-21 (new series), 1948-68. Most items listed translations into English, but some translations into other languages included. *Index translationum* entries reproduced without editing; many typographical errors, lacks cross-references. *Class No:* 013

[173]

Transdex index: index to FBIS publications. Ann Arbor, University Microfilms International, 1975-. Monthly (printed issues), with annual cumulation on microfiche. ISSN: 10416714.

Title varies slightly; preceded by *Bibliography-index to current US JPRS translations* (1962-70) and *Transdex bibliography and index to the United States Joint Publications Research Service (JPRS) translations* (1971-74).

'(P)rovides access to non-US originated materials selected and translated by the Foreign Broadcast Information Service of the US government'. Documents translated taken from newspapers, journals, speeches and broadcasts. Social and political topics covered in addition to science and technology. Each issue contains series, publications (complete citation), keyword frequency, keyword and personal name indexes. *Class No:* 013

Periodicals

[174]
Journals in translation. 5th ed. Boston Spa, British Library Document Supply Centre; Delft, International Translations Centre, 1991. viii,286p. ISBN: 0712320733.

First published 1976. 4th ed. 1988.

List of journals A-Z (p.1-146, 1,352 titles) giving translated title, original title, date translation began, frequency, additional details, publisher of translation and whether held by BLDSC or SRIS. Indexed by title keyword and original title. Key to publishes/distributors with addresses. Includes both cover-to-cover translations and journals carrying translations of selected articles. Omits journals published simultaneously in two or more languages. Nearly all translations are into English. *Class No:* 013(051)

Canada

[175]
Canadian translations. 1984/85-. [Traductions canadiennes.] Ottawa, National Library of Canada, 1987-. Annual. ISSN: 08352291.

Ceased as printed publication 1994; diskette version (launched 1991) continues.

UDC list of translations published in Canada catalogued by the National Library of Canada. Indexed by author and title. Vast majority of translations French/English or English/French. *Class No:* 013(71)

German

[176]
BIHL, L. *and* **EPTING, K. Bibliographie französischer Übersetzungen aus dem Deutschen** 1487-1944. [Bibliographie de traductions françaises d'auteurs de langue allemande.] Tübingen, Max Niemeyer, 1987. 2v. DM476. ISBN: 3484105720.

Bd. 1 *Periode I-IV (1487-1870)*; Bd. 2 *Periode VI-VII (1871-1944).* Preface etc., in German with French translation.

Lists French translations of German works. 12,289 entries in chronological, then subject, sections. Indexes of authors/translators, anonymous editions and publishers by place. *Class No:* 013=30

[177]
Deutsche Nationalbibliographie. Reihe G. Fremdsprachige Germanica und Übersetzungen deutschsprachiger Werke. Frankfurt am Main, Buchhändler-Vereinigung, 1992-. Quarterly. DM712. ISSN: 0939057x.

A sub-series of the German national bibliography formed from the merger of *Bibliographie der Übersetzungen deutschprachiger Werke*, published by the Deutschen Bucherei at Leipzig from 1954 (ISSN: 00061409), and *Bibliographie Fremdsprachiger Germanica.*

Continues the coverage of works originally published in German but translated into other languages provided by *Bibliographie der Übersetzungen deustschsprachiger Werke.* *Class No:* 013=30

[178]
Gesamtverzeichnis der Übersetzungen deutschsprachiger Werke: Berichtszeitraum 1954-1990. Gornzy, W., *hrsg.* München, K.G. Saur, 1992-. DM5400. ISBN: 3598225369.

'Bibliography of translations of German-language publications'. Covers translations into 93 languages; language and name indexes. *Class No:* 013=30

[179]
Translations from the German: English, 1948-1964. Monnig, R., *ed.* 2nd rev. ed. Göttingen, Vandenhoeck & Ruprecht, 1968. 509p.

Entries are drawn from *Cumulative book index* (*q.v.*), British, Swiss, Austrian and German national bibliographies and *Index translationum*. Includes all major subject areas. Author index.

Further coverage is available in *Bibliography of German publications in English translation 1971-76* (Frankfurt am Main, Buchhändler-Vereinigung, 1978). *Class No:* 013=30

French

[180]
FROMM, H. Bibliographie deutscher Übersetzungen aus dem Französischen, 1700-1948. Baden-Baden, Verlag für Kunst und Wissenschaft, 1950-53. 6v.

A comprehensive retrospective bibliography of German translations of French monographs and of articles in certain scientific, medical and technical journals. Section 'A' lists items under the original authors and titles, A-Z; 'B' lists the German translators and their translations; 'C' lists German series, anthologies, etc. containing only translations from French. Indexes of translators and of French and German titles. *Class No:* 013=40

Disguised Imprints in Books

[181]
BRUNET, G. Imprimeurs imaginaires et libraires supposés: étude bibliographique, suivie de recherches sur quelques ouvrages imprimés avec des indications fictives de lieux ou avec des dates singulières. Paris, Tross, 1866. 290p.

Reprinted New York, Franklin, 1963. ISBN: 0833704044.

French language works (p.13-202); works in other languages (p.203-69). Some entries include notes, attributions etc. *Class No:* 014

[182]
WELLER, E. Die Falschen und fingirten Druckorte. Repertorium der seit erfindung der Buchdruckerkunst unter falscher Firma erschienenen deutschen, lateinischen und französischen Schriften. 2. verm. und verb. Aufl. Leipzig, Engelmann, 1864. 2v. Suppt. 1867.

First published 1858. Reprinted Hildesheim, Olms, 1960.

Chronological lists of (v.1) German and Latin works (1510-1862) and (v.2) French works (1530-1863) published with disguised imprints. Under each year arrangement is A-Z by authors or anonymous titles. Author index. *Class No:* 014

Large Type Books

[183]
The Complete directory of large print books and serials. New York, Bowker, 1970-. Annual. £150;$180. ISSN: 00001120.

Title and frequency varies: until 1987 published as *Large type books in print.*

Lists books and serials available from US publishers printed in 14 point type or larger. Entries, by subject in general reading, textbook and children's sections. Newspapers and periodicals listed separately. Title and author indexes. About 11,000 titles listed in recent volumes. Also available on CD-ROM as part of *Books in print* and *Whitaker/Bowker global BookBank* (*qq.v.*) *Class No:* 014:362.41

Unfinished Books

[184]

CORNS, A.R. *and* **SPARKE, A. A Bibliography of unfinished books in the English language:** with annotations. London, Quaritch, 1915. xvi,255p.

Original ed. limited to 300 copies. Reprinted New York, Franklin, 1969. ISBN: 0833706829.

Lists over 2,000 works, based largely on the British Museum catalogue; not restricted to pure literature, and useful to library cataloguers. Much of the information has been copied into Krieg (below). *Class No:* 014.0

[185]

KRIEG, M.O. Mehr nicht erschienen: ein Verzeichnis unvollendet gebliebener Druckwerke. Bad Bocklet, Wien, Krieg, 1954-58. 2v. (*Bibliotheca bibliographica.*)

A-Z author and anonymous title list of 24,000 works, publication of which was apparently never completed. Mainly derived from other lists (sources are cited). *Class No:* 014.0

[186]

—SEEMAN, O. Kumulierender Nachtrag zu Krieg: MNE. Zweite, Verb. und. verm. Aufl. Wien, Krieg, 1993. 200p. ISBN: 3920566386.

Supplements the original work correcting many of the inaccuracies. *Class No:* 014.0

Anonyma & Pseudonyma

Bibliographies

[187]

TAYLOR, A. *and* **MOSHER, F.J. The Bibliographical history of anonyma and pseudonyma.** Chicago, Univ. of Chicago Press for the Newberry Library, 1951. ix,289p.

5 narrative chapters: Homonyms - Latinized - Pseudepigraphia - Anonyma and pseudonyma (p.80-196) - Confusing titles and fictitious facts of publication. 'Bibliography of anonyma and pseudonyma' follows (p.207-79); *c.*350 annotated entries. Supported by 'A classified guide to dictionaries and other lists of anonyma and pseudonyma' (p.280-84). *Class No:* 014.1(01)

Worldwide

[188]

CUSHING, W. Anonyms: a dictionary of revealed authorship. Cambridge, Mass., Cushing; London, Sampson Low, 1890. 2v.(829p.).

Reprinted Hildesheim, Olms, 1969. ($210. ISBN: 0685677788).

Still an important dictionary of anonymous authors. *Class No:* 014.1(100)

[189]

CUSHING, W. Initials and pseudonyms: a dictionary of literary disguises. New York, T. Crowell, 1885-88. 2v.

Reprinted Hildesheim, Olms, 1969. ($225. ISBN:0685664570).

Over 18,500 pseudonyms and initials used by 12,500, mainly English language, writers. Each v. in 2 sequences: initials or pseudonyms, with real names; real names, giving pseudonyms or initials. 51 claimants to the title of 'Junius' in 11p. Authors revealed include Tom Paine, Matthew Arnold and Jonathan Swift. *Class No:* 014.1(100)

[190]

Handbook of pseudonyms and personal nicknames. Sharp, H.S., *comp.* Metuchen, N.J., Scarecrow Press, 1972-82. 2v. plus 2 supplements in 3v.

Original work published 1972 in 2v. (1104p. ISBN: 0810804603). First supplement, 1975, 2v. (1395p. £67.50;$79.50. ISBN: 0810808072). Second supplement, 1982 (289p. £26.55;$35. ISBN: 0810815397).

The original volumes list *c.*15,000 real names and *c.*25,000 nicknames and/or pseudonyms with birth and death dates and brief descriptions. Mostly for the western world, living persons included. The First supplement adds a further *c.*18,000 real names and *c.*30,000 nicknames and/or pseudonyms. The much smaller Second supplement adds another *c.*7,000 and *c.*10,000 entries respectively. The only serious rival to the Gale set (below). *Class No:* 014.1(100)

[191]

Pseudonyms and nicknames dictionary: a guide to 80,000 aliases, assumed names, code names, cognomens, cover names, epithets, initialisms, nicknames, noms de guerre, noms de plume, pen names, pseudonyms, sobriquets and stage names of 55,000 contemporary and historical persons, including the subjects' real names, basic biographical information and citations from which the entries were compiled. Mossman, J., *ed.* 3rd ed. Detroit, Gale, 1987. 2v. £205;$239. ISBN: 0810305410.

1st ed. 1980. 2nd ed. 1982.

Predominant categories are authors and entertainers. Others include athletes, criminals, journalists, military leaders, and politicians. One A-Z sequence with main entries giving real names, dates, identification codes (8 maximum), nationality, occupation and assumed name(s) and assumed name entries referring to main entries. List of *c.*275 bibliographical sources including who's whos and subject encyclopedias, but not the British Library or Library of Congress catalogues. Coverage increased by 32% in this edition making this one of the largest works of its kind. Only derivatives of given names, initials that replace names and middle names used as pseudonyms are excluded. Many entries are for very obscure and difficult to trace people.

Supplement *New pseudonyms and nicknames* (1988. 306p. ISBN: 0810305485), provides coverage of 9,000 additional pseudonyms and nicknames. *Class No:* 014.1(100)

[192]

ROOM, A. Dictionary of pseudonyms. 3rd ed. Jefferson, N.C., McFarland, 1998. viii,404p. ISBN: 078640423x.

First published as *Naming names: stories of pseudonyms and name changes...* (London, Routledge and Kegan Paul, 1981); 2nd ed. as *Dictionary of pseudonyms and their origins...* (London, St. James Press, 1989).

Main section (p.64-383) comprises A-Z list of about 10,000 pseudonyms (double previous ed.) giving real name, dates, country of origin, profession and 10-100 word notes. 7 introductory chapters; 5 appendices, including 'Pseudonyms used by Voltaire', 'Pseudonyms used by Daniel Defoe' and 'Writers with multiple pen names'. Bibliography (p.399-404). *Class No:* 014.1(100)

[193]

WELLER, E. Lexicon pseudonymorum. Wörterbuch der Pseudonymen aller Zeiten und Völker... 2.Aufl. Regensburg, Coppenrath, 1886. x,627p.

First published 1856; 3 suppts. 1857-67. Reprinted Hildesheim, Olms, 1963 (ISBN: 3893492445).

A-Z list of 32,000 pseudonyms. International in scope. Sources are not cited; no index of real names. *Class No:* 014.1(100)

English

[194]

ATKINSON, F. Dictionary of literary pseudonyms: a selection of popular modern writers in English. 4th ed. London, Library Association; Chicago, American Library Association, 1987. xi,299p. ISBN: 0851574017, UK; 0838920454, US.

1st ed. 1975. 3rd ed. 1982.

Arranged in 2 A-Z sequences, real names with pseudonyms and the reverse. This ed. adds 2,000 names making 6,000 in total. An 'invaluable addition to the bibliographic or reference collection' (*Aslib current awareness bulletin,* V.4(4), April 1987, p.34).

Class No: 014.1(100)=20

[195]

CARTY, T.J. A Dictionary of literary pseudonyms in the English language. London, Mansell 1995. xiv,624p. £30;$75. ISBN: 1884964133.

Published in the US by Fitzroy Dearbon (ISBN: 1884964133).

Part I lists 12,000 pseudonyms and gives the writers' real names. Part II lists 7,500 real names, with birth and death dates, nationality, brief description and list of pseudonyms with some (but not all) works where they have been used. Many journalists, essayists and nonfiction writers included as well as literary authors. Select bibliography (p.xiii-xiv). Superior to Atkinson (above). 'Although this dictionary cannot stand alone as a reliable source of literary pseudonyms, it does include some unique entries' (*Reference books bulletin* in *Booklist,* v.91(19/20), June 1995, p.1821).

Class No: 014.1(100)=20

[196]

HALKETT, S. *and* **LAING, J. Dictionary of anonymous and pseudonymous English literature.** Kennedy, J., *and others.* New ed. Edinburgh, Oliver and Boyd, 1926-62. 9v.

First published 1882-88 in 4v. V.1-7 reprinted New York, Haskell, 1971. ISBN: 0838312454. $490.

The main work (v.1-7, published 1926-34) is arranged A-Z by title. Entries (*c.*70,000) indicate size, pagination, place, date, and authors' names, and sometimes give authorities for its attributions, although usually in such general terms as 'B.M. Catalogue'. V.6 includes the first supplement; v.7 has indexes of pseudonyms and real names, plus a short second suppt.

V.8-9 (17,000 entries) list new material, 1900-50, plus corrigenda, and cover a rather wider field than English literature. Arranged as in the main work; index of authors and index of initials, pseudonyma, etc., in both volumes.

V.1 of a 3rd ed. was published 1980 (*A Dictionary of anonymous and pseudonymous publications in the English language,* Horden, J. ed., Longman, ISBN: 0582555213) covering 1475-1640. No further volumes are now planned.

Class No: 014.1(100)=20

Germany

[197]

EYMER, W. Eymers Pseudonymen-Lexikon: Realnamen und Pseudonyme in der deutschen Literatur. Bonn, Kirschbaum, 1997. xv,672p. DM68. ISBN: 3781213994.

T.1, Realnamen mit der verwendeten Pseudonymen, lists *c.*18,000 German authors, including non-fiction writers, with birth and death dates, pseudonyms used, literary genre and references to sources. T.2, Pseudonyme mit Verweisen auf die Realnamen, (p.403-69) is an pseudonym index. Superior to Weigand (below) and more entries than the Holzmann and

....*(contd.)*

Bohatta's 1906 *Deutsches Pseudonymen-Lexikon* (below). However, neither of these works are completely superseded as both contain pseudonyms Eymer overlooks.

Class No: 014.1(430)

[198]

HOLZMANN, M. *and* **BOHATTA, H. Deutsches Anonymen-Lexikon.** Weimar, Gesellschaft der Bibliophilen, 1902-28. 7v.

Reprinted Hildesheim, Olms, 1961. (ISBN: 3487001500).

The standard key to German anonymous literature Eymer (above). V.1-4: 1501-1850; v.5: 1851-1908; v.6: addenda and corrigenda, 1501-1910; v.7: addenda and corrigenda, 1501-1925. About 83,000 entries; each sequence in A-Z title order; author's name plus source of information. No author indexes.

The companion work is the same author's *Deutsches Pseudonymen-Lexikon* (Wein, Schutz, 1906. xxiv,323p. Reprinted Hildesheim, Olms, 1961. ISBN: 3487092115)

Class No: 014.1(430)

[199]

Namenschlüssel zu Pseudonymen, Doppelnamen und Namensabwandlungen. 4. Ausg. Hildesheim, Olms, 1965-68. 2v.

V.1 reprint of *Namenschlüssel die Verweisungen der Berliner Titeldrucke zu Pseudonymen, Doppelnamen und Namensabwandlungen* 3.Ausg. (Berlin, 1941). V.2 in print DM184 (ISBN: 348701808X). *Class No:* 014.1(430)

[200]

WEIGAND, J. Pseudonyme ein Lexikon: Decknamen der Autoren deutschsprachiger erzählender Literatur. 2. verb und erw. Aufl. Baden-Baden, Nomos, 1994. 421p. DM68. ISBN: 3789035262.

First published 1991.

Real name-pseudonym list (p.17-350) for 4,000 authors, mainly of post-1945 popular literature. Pseudonym-real name listing (p.353-421). Expands and improves original ed., but still many omissions and errors.

Class No: 014.1(430)

Czechoslovakia

[201]

VOPRAVIL, J. Slovník pseudonymů v české a slovenské literatuře. Praha, Státni pedagogické nakladatelstvi, 1973. 1540p.

Pseudonym-real name list (p.35-344), followed by list of authors and their pseudonyms with short biographical notes (p.347-1475). About 30,000 pseudonyms covered. Bibliography (p.17-27) includes non-Czech works.

Class No: 014.1(437)

Hungary

[202]

GULYÁS, P. Magya irói álnév lexikon: a magyarországi irók álnevei és egyéb jegyei. Budapest Akadémiai Kiadó, 1978. 706p.

First published 1956. Added Latin title page.

List of pseudonyms and initialisms for Hungarian writers. Separate list of anonyms.

Supplement and update by K. Debreczeni, 1992. (Budapest, Petófi Irodalmi Múzeum. 688p. ISBN: 9637412328). *Class No:* 014.1(439)

France

[203]
QUÉRARD, J.M. Les Supercheries littéraires dévoilées... . 2.éd. Paris, Daffis, 1869-79. 7v.

V.4-7 *Dictionnaire des ouvrages anonymes* by A.A. Barbier and P. Billard. 3.éd. V.1-3 reprinted Maisonneuve & Larose, 1964; v.4-7 reprinted Hildesheim, Olms, 1963.

The standard key to French pseudonymous and anonymous literature. Quérard identifies *c.*20,000 pseudonyms; Barbier *c.*50,000 anonymous works, with index of real names of authors, both pseudonymous and anonymous. Sources of information are only occasionally cited. *Class No:* 014.1(44)

[204]
—BRUNET, G. Dictionnaire des ouvrages anonymes ... Supplément à la dernière édition de ces deux ouvrages. Paris, Féchoz, 1889. cxxvip.,432 col.

Includes 3,500 further identifications.
Class No: 014.1(44)

[205]
RATIER, E. Encyclopédie des pseudonymes. Paris, Faits & documents, 1993-94. 2v.

V.2 (FFr220. ISBN: 2909769100) revises H.Coston's 3v. *Dictionnaire des pseudonymes* (1965-80) and his *Nouveau dictionnaire des pseudonymes* (1985). V.1 (FFr150. ISBN: 2909769011) covers 6,500 names from show business, the media, arts amd politics. Coston's original 3v. set listed 14,000 pseudonyms. Index of real names in both v. Sources not cited. *Class No:* 014.1(44)

Italy

[206]
FRATTAROLO, R. Dizionario degli scrittori italiani contemporanei pseudonimi (1900-1975), con un repertorio delle bibliografie nazional di opere anonime e pseudonime. Ravena, Longo, 1975. 325p. L.40,000.

1st ed. 1955 as *Anonim e pseudonimi: repertorio delle bibliografie nazionale*.

Dictionary entries A-Z by pseudonym: lengthy biographical/bibliographical treatment. International bibliography of dictionaries of anonymous and pseudonymous literature, arranged by language (79 titles). List of works consulted (p.285-314). Reverse index from real name to pseudonym. *Class No:* 014.1(450)

[207]
MELZI, G. Dizionario di opere anonime e pseudonime di scrittori italiani, o come che sia aventi relazione all'Italia. Milano, Pirola, 1848-1859. 3v.

Supplemented by Passano, G.B. *Dizionario di opere anonime e pseudonime in supplemento a quello di G. Melzi*. Ancona, Morelli, 1887. xi, 517p. and Rocco, E. *Anonimi e pseudonimi italiani: supplemento al Melzi e al Passano*. Napoli, Chiurazzi, 1888. 16p.

With supplements covers 16th to 19th centuries.
Class No: 014.1(450)

Spain

[208]
RODERGAS I CALMELL, J. Els pseudònims usats a Catalunya (recull de 3,800). Barcelona, Editorial Millà, 1951. xv, 408p.

Entries consist of pseudonyms (A-Z), real names, titles of works and, usually, brief biographical data. Index of real names. *Class No:* 014.1(460)

[209]
ROGERS, P.P. *and* **LAPUENTE, F.A. Diccionario de seudónimos literarios españoles,** con algunas iniciales. Madrid, Gredos, 1977. 608p. (*Biblioteca románica hispánica, 5.*) ISBN: 8424913515.

Lists *c.*12,000 pseudonyms A-Z giving proper name and citing one or more works for which the pseudonym was used. Select bibliography (p.495-502). Index to proper names. *Class No:* 014.1(460)

[210]
—PONCE DE LEON FREYRE, F. *and* ZAMORA LUCAS, F. 1500 seudónimos modernos de la literatura española (1900-1942). Madrid, Instituto Nacional de Libro Español, 1942. 126p.

Reprinted Liechtenstein, Kraus, 1978 (ISBN: 0815538206).

1,500 numbered entries under pseudonym giving real name, title of work and date. Author index.
Class No: 014.1(460)

Portugal

[211]
FONSECA, M.A.F. da. Subsidios para um dicionario de pseudonymos, iniciaes e obras anonymas de escriptores portuguezes ... . Lisboa, Academia Real das Sciencias, 1896. 298p.

The standard key to Portuguese pseudonyms until the publication of Lapa's work (below). *Class No:* 014.1(469)

[212]
VIDIGAL, M.T. Dicionário de pseudónimos de Albino Lapa. Lisbon, Imprensa Nacional Casa da Moeda, 1980. 171p.

Pseudonym - real name list with titles for which pseudonyms used. 4,178 numbered entries, some with author birth and death dates. *Class No:* 014.1(469)

RSFSR

[213]
MASANOV, I.F. Slovar' psevdonimov russkikh pisatelei, uchenykh i obshchestvennykh deyatelei. Moskva, Vsesoyuznaya Knizhnaya Palata, 1956-60. 4v.

First published 1941-49 (3v. in 2).

Dictionary of pseudonyms of Russian writers, scholars and public figures. V.1-3 list pseudonyms, plus real names; v.4 lists the real names. *Class No:* 014.1(470)

[214]
Russkie anonimnye i podpisannye psevdonimami proizvedeniia pechati; 1801-1926: bibliograficheskii ukazatel'. Leningrad, Publichnaia Biblioteka, 1977-79. 3v.

Title listing of works published anonymously or pseudonymously with name of author and source of attribution. Does not overlap with Masanov.
Class No: 014.1(470)

Finland

[215]
Kirjallisia salanimiä ja nimimerkkejä. Ellilä, E.J., *comp.* 2nd ed. Helsinki, Suomalaisen kirjallisuuden seura, 1966. 134p.

1st ed. 1952.

Lists 1261 pseudonyms mostly from 20th century literature. *Class No:* 014.1(480)

Norway

[216]
PETTERSEN, H. Norsk anonym- og pseudonym-lexikon. Christiana, Steenske Forlag, 1924. [viii],690,[35]p.

About 15,000 entries under title. Indexes of pseudonyms and names. Brief biographical notes. No sources cited.
Class No: 014.1(481)

[217]
—KOLSTAD, S. Norsk anonym- og pseudonym-leksikon. Oslo, Kunnskapsforlaget, 1981. 287p. ISBN: 8257301582.

Continues Pettersen. In two parts: publications listed by pseudonym giving real name; anonymous publications listed by title or author. Name index. *Class No:* 014.1(481)

Sweden

[218]
BYGDEN, L. Svenskt anonym- och pseudonym-lexikon. Uppsala, Svenska Litteratursällskapet, 1898-1915. 2v. (*Skrifter utg. av Svenska Litteratursällskapet, 17.*)

Reprinted Stockholm, Rediviva, 1974. 2v. in 1.

Anonymous and pseudonymous works (*c.*15,000) are arranged in one A-Z title sequence with a lengthy supplement. Index of pseudonyms and real authors.

Corrections and additions in *Rättelser och tillägg samt person- och pseudonymregister till 'Svensk anonym- och pseudonym-lexikon' af Leonard Bygden* (Stockholm, Rediviva, 1979. [8],127p. (Suecica rediviva, 79). ISBN: 9171201149). *Class No:* 014.1(485)

[219]
—ANDERSSON, P. Pseudonym-register. Lund, Bibliotekstjänst, 1967. 184p.

Pseudonym-real name list, mainly of twentieth century writers. *Class No:* 014.1(485)

Denmark

[220]
EHRENCRON-MÜLLER, H. Anonym- og pseudonym-lexikon for Danmark og Island til 1920 og Norge til 1814. Copenhagen, Hagerup, 1940. [v],392p.

Anonyms (*c.*10,000), p.1-283; pseudonyms (*c.*1,500), (p.287-356). Author index. No sources cited. Danish pseudonyms 1920-1950 are cross-referenced to proper-name in *Dansk skonlitteraert forfatterleksikon* (q.v.).
Class No: 014.1(489)

Netherlands

[221]
DOORNINCK, J.I. van. Vermomde en naamlooze schrijvers opgespoord op het gebied der Nederlandsche en Vlaamsche letteren. 2. uitg. Leiden, Brill, 1883-85. 2v.

First published 1866-70 as *Bibliotheek van Nederlandsche anonymen en pseudonymen*. Reprinted Amsterdam, B.M. Israel (ISBN: 9060780558).

V.1 contains pseudonyms, anagrams and initials; v.2 anonyms. About 8,000 entries in all. No author indexes. Gives sources. Supplemented by: *Class No:* 014.1(492)

[222]
—HAZEU, W. Het Literair pseudoniemen boek. Antwerpen, W. Hazeu, 1987. 319p. illus. ISBN: 9070876582.

Real name-pseudonym and pseudonym-real name lists for 4,300 Dutch and Flemish authors since 1880. Extensive introductory matter and essays on selected authors (p.1-90).
Class No: 014.1(492)

[223]
—KEMPENAER, A. de. Vermomde Nederlandsche en Vlaamsche schrijvers. Leiden, Sijthoff, 1928. vi,690p.

About 10,000 pseudonyma, initials, mottoes, etc., used by Dutch and Flemish writers 1885-1928. Omits anonyms. Gives sources. Author index. *Class No:* 014.1(492)

Belgium

[224]
DELECOURT, J.V. Bibliographie nationale. Dictionnaire des anonymes et pseudonymes (xve siècle-1900). Mis en ordre et enrichi par G. Delecourt. Brussels, Académie Royale de Belgique, 1960. V.1 (vii,1281,10p.).

No further volumes published. Original ed. as *Essai d'un dictionnaire des ouvrages anonymes et pseudonymes imprimés en Belgique au XIXe siècle et principalement depuis 1830* (Brussels, Heussner, 1863. iii, 550p.).

The revised and updated dictionary consists of title entries with author index. *Class No:* 014.1(493)

Greece

[225]
DELOPOULOS, K. Neollenika philologika pseudonyma, 1800-1981: 1789 syngrapheis, 3065 pseudonyma. 2nd ed. Athenai, Hellenika Logotechniko Kai Historiko Archeio, 1983. 336p.

1st ed. 1969.

Pseudonym-real name and real name-pseudonym lists. Bibliography of works consulted (p.325-36).
Class No: 014.1(495)

Bulgaria

[226]
BOGDANOV, I. Rechnik na bŭlgarskite psevdonimi: pisateli, nauchni, rabotnitsi, prevodachi, karikaturisti, publitsisti zhurnalisti. 3. izd. Sofiia, 'D-r Petŭr Beron', 1989. 528p.

First published 1961; 2nd ed. 1978.

List of pseudonyms with further detail on anonymous books signed with initials, symbols, etc. Real name index.
Class No: 014.1(497.2)

China

[227]
Modern Chinese authors: a list of pseudonyms. Shu, A.C.W., *comp.* East Lansing, Asian Studies Center, Michigan State University, 1969. xi, 108 [1]p.

Around 2,000 entries. Bibliography (p.100).
Class No: 014.1(510)

India

[228]
CHATTERJEE, A. Dictionary of Indian pseudonyms. Calcutta, Mukherjee Book House, 1977. 170p. (*India reference series, 3.*)

Supplement 1980. 34p.

Main work lists 3,500 pseudonyms from all Indian languages including English. Gives real name, date of birth (if known) and language of writing. *Class No:* 014.1(540)

[229]

—Dictionary of pseudonmys (sic) in Indian literature. Goli, N.K., *ed.* Delhi, Delhi Library Association, 1973. x, 163p. (*English series, no. 7.*)

Pseudonym-original name and original name-pseudonym sequences for *c.*2,500 authors from all Indian languages. *Class No:* 014.1(540)

South Africa

[230]

Bibliography of anonymous and pseudonymous works from "A South African bibliography to the year 1925". Smit, D.E., *comp.* Cape Town, South African Library, 1983. x, 126p. . R.25. ISBN: 0869680374.

A-Z title listing of anonymous and pseudonymous works most of which appeared in *A South African bibliography to the year 1925* (*q.v.*). Index of authors' real names: index of anonyms and pseudonyms. *Class No:* 014.1(680)

Canada

[231]

AMTMANN, B. Contributions to a dictionary of Canadian pseudonyms and anonymous works relating to Canada. [Contributions à un dictionnaire des pseudonymes canadiens et des ouvrages anonymes relatifs au Canada.] Montreal, The Author, 1973. 144p.

Partially complied from catalogues published by Amtmann over the period 1950-1972. Contribution to a dictionary only; no claim to comprehensiveness. Sources of attribution not indicated. Addenda (p.137-44). *Class No:* 014.1(71)

[232]

A Dictionary of known pseudonyms, initial sets and maiden names found in selected English-Canadian magazines, newspapers and books of the nineteenth century. Vincent, J.B., *comp.* Kingston, Ont., Loyal Colonies Press, 1993. vi,224p. ISBN: 0920832105.

Largely based on 190 intellectual and cultural magazines. Directory of pseudonyms (p.1-111); Directory of surnames (p.113-211). *Class No:* 014.1(71)

[233]

VINET, B. Pseudonymes québécois. Quebec, Éditions Garneau, 1974. xiv, 361p.

Pseudonym-real name list with real name index providing detailed coverage of French Canadian writing. Adds extensively to an earlier work by Audet and Malchelosse (1936). Sources consulted (p.351-61). *Class No:* 014.1(71)

Mexico

[234]

RUIZ CASTANEDA, M.C. Catálogo de seudónimos, anagramas, iniciales y otros alias usados por escritores mexicanos y extranjeros que han publicado en México. Mexico City, Universidad Nacional Autónoma de Mexico, 1985. lxxi, 290p. (*Instituto de Investigaciones Bibliográficas instrumenta bibliographica, 6.*) ISBN: 9688375071.

Pseudonym-real name and real name-pseudonym list in one sequence. List of sources (p.279-90). *Class No:* 014.1(72)

Latin America

[235]

MEDINA, J.T. Diccionario de anónimos y seudónimos hispanoamericanos. Buenos Aires, Imprenta de la Universidad, 1925. 2v.

Reprinted Detroit, Ethridge, 1973. 2v. in 1, ISBN: 08791702630.

About 3,400 works, entered under titles A-Z; indexes of initials, pseudonyms and anonyms. Corrections and additions are provided by Victorica, R. *Errores y omisiones del 'Diccionario de anónimos y seudónimos hispanoamericanos* ... ' (Buenos Aires, Viau & Zona, 1928. 338p.) and the same author's *Nueva epanortosis* ... (Buenos Aires, Rosso, 1929. 207p.), both also reprinted Ethridge, 1973. *Class No:* 014.1(729.99)

[236]

SAENZ, G. Diccionario de seudónimos y escritores Iberoamericanos. Miami, Fla., Ediciones Universal, 1991. 405p. (*Coleccion diccionarios.*) ISBN: 0897295978.

Pseudonym-real name sequence (p.9-100), followed by a list of Latin American writers with brief biographical detail and pseudonyms used. Bibliography (p.389-405). *Class No:* 014.1(729.99)

Australia

[237]

CRITTENDEN, V. Pseudonyms used by Australian writers: nineteenth-century. Canberra, Mulini Press, 1996. 60p. tables. Aus$20. ISBN: 0949910627.

In tabulated form: 'List arranged by pseudonym' (p.1-29); 'List arranged by author' (p.31-59). Does not provide comprehensive coverage, but nearly 1,000 pseudonyms identified including those used by contributors to magazines. *Class No:* 014.1(94)

National Bibliographies

Bibliographies

[238]

BELL, B.L. An Annotated guide to current national bibliographies. 2nd completely rev. ed. K.G. Saur, München, 1998. xxvii,487p. (*UBCIM publications: new series, v.18.*) ISBN: 3598113765.

First published by Chadwyck-Healey 1986.

Lists and meticulously describes national bibliographies by country A-Z. Entries under heads: title, compiler, scope and coverage, contents, cataloguing rules and classification schemes used, entry information, arrangement, indexes, notes and comments, latest issue examined/currency, automation, format and services available, current legal deposit laws, available from, selected articles and verifier. Confined to official national bibliographies or equivalents, commercial or 'in print' listings excluded. Regional bibliographies treated in separate section. Extensive bibliography on national bibliography (p.446-483). *Class No:* 015(01)

[239]

Bibliographical services throughout the world. 1950/59-1975/79. Paris, UNESCO, 1961-83. 5v.

5 v. issued as follows: 1950/59, by R.L. Collison (1961. 228p.); 1960/64 and 1965/69, by P. Avicenne (1969. 240p.; 1972. 302p.); 1970/74 and 1975/79, by M. Beaudiquez (1977. 419p. ISBN: 9231013947; 1983. 488p. ISBN: 9231019821). Further supplements by Beaudiquez for 1980, 1981/82 and 1983/84 (1982. 103p.; 1985. 319p.; 1987.

.... *(contd.)*
267p.).

Similar content and format in each v. 1975/79 in 2 parts: 'Developments of bibliographical services during the period 1975-1979' (p.31-70) and 'Bibliographical activities in the various countries' (121 states Afghanistan-Zambia). Now largely of historical interest. *Class No:* 015(01)

[240]

Bibliographie der nationalen Bibliographien. [A World bibliography of national bibliographies.] Domay, F., *comp.* Stuttgart, Hiersemann, 1987. xviii,557p. DM620. (*Hiersemanns bibliographische Handbücher, Bd.6.*) ISBN: 3777287091.

German language work which complements Bell (above) by also covering retrospective bibliography, bibliography of bibliographies and, to a limited extent, bibliographies of serials, newspapers and theses. Arranged by country within regional sections. Detailed entries for each title including description of contents, scope and publishing history. Name and title index (p.514-57). Generally comprehensive, but excludes commercial lists and some countries with well-developed bibliographic control systems such as New Zealand. *Class No:* 015(01)

[241]

Inventaire général des bibliographies nationales rétrospectives. [Retrospective national bibliographies an international directory.] Beaudiquez, M., *ed.* München, Saur, 1986. 189p. (*IFLA publications, 35.*) ISBN: 3598203993.

Arranged by country A-Z. For each provides brief introduction describing publishing and bibliographic situation followed by chronological listing of bibliographies. Entries give type of bibliography, full bibliographic citation and annotation indicating sources, scope, compilation mode and types of documents listed. Author and anonymous title index. Most entries in English, a few in French and German. Does not cover former Soviet Bloc countries. 'Fills a basic gap in the ability to gain access to retrospective bibliographic material' (*American reference books annual*, v.18, 1987, p.5). *Class No:* 015(01)

Developing Countries

[242]

GORMAN, G.E. *and* **MILLS, J.J. Guide to current national bibliographies in the Third World.** 2nd ed. London, Zell, 1987. xx,372p. £51. ISBN: 0905450345.

First published 1983.

Covers 98 national bibliographies or substitute services plus 12 regional bibliographies. Entries give bibliographic citation, history, scope and contents and a detailed analysis taking the form of a critical assessment of factors such as coverage of country's publishing output, currency, presentation, etc. Introductory chapter including summary of developments since previous ed. Title index. 'A valuable working tool' (*Reference reviews*, v.2(1), 1988, p.7). *Class No:* 015(01)(4/9-77)

Commonwealth

[243]

Commonwealth retrospective national bibliographies: an annotated directory. International Federation of Library Associations and Institutions. International Office for Universal Bibliographic Control. 2nd ed. London, Commonwealth Secretariat, 1981. i,128p. £7.50. ISBN: 0850922054.

.... *(contd.)*
1st ed. 1977.

Now dated. The companion work, *Commonwealth national bibliographies: an annotated directory* (2nd ed. 1981. 69p. ISBN: 0850922240), is now superseded by the revised ed. of Bell (above). *Class No:* 015(01)(41-44)

RSFSR

[244]

SEMENOVKER, B.A. Retrospektivnaia gosudarstvennaia bibliografiia SSSR: spravocnik. Moskva, Izd-va 'Knizhnaia palata', 1990. 303p. ISBN: 5700002566.

Contains detailed entries for the retrospective bibliographies of the former Soviet Union, including the autonomous republics. Indexed. An older and less adequate English language source is Whitby, T.J. & Lorkovié, T. *Introduction to Soviet national bibliography* (Littleton, Colo., Libraries Unlimited, 1979. 229p. ISBN: 0872871282). *Class No:* 015(01)(470)

Latin America

[245]

NILGES, A. National bibliographien Lateinamerika. Köln, Greven, 1983. viii,160p. tables. DM24. (*Kölner Arbeiten zum Bibliotheks und Dokumentationswesen, 4.*) ISBN: 3774305579.

Introductory chapters on the book world and bibliographic control in Latin America followed by country sections. Each has detailed data on the current national bibliography and major retrospective bibliographies. Further section on regional bibliographies. Bibliography (p.153-160). Compares well with the coverage given to Latin America in general guides to national bibliographies. *Class No:* 015(01)(729.99)

Worldwide

[246]

World bibliographies on CD-ROM. München, K.G. Saur, 1997-. CD-ROM databases.

Comprises 5 editions: *English bibliography to 1901* (£1475. ISBN: 3598403747), 2.3 million records; *English bibliography 1901-1945* (£1475. ISBN: 3598403755), 2.4 million records; *French bibliography 15th century to 1997* (£1475. ISBN: 3598403739), 1.7 million records; *Italian bibliography 15th century to 1997* (£1475. ISBN: 3598403763), 626,000 records; *Spanish bibliography 15th century to 1995*, (£1410. ISBN: 359840283X), 1 million records. Discs to be updated approx. every two years. Further discs covering Portuguese, Russian, Asian languages, printed music and maps and atlases envisaged.

Data drawn from holdings of participants in the Research Libraries Information Network (RLIN). Records MARC based, search criteria include keyword, Dewey and LC classification, publication type and author/title acronym key. *Class No:* 015(100)

English

[247]

BookFind CD-ROM. Twickenham, Book Data, 1991-. CD-ROM database.

Available in 4 main services: *BookWise-CD*, containing UK database with title descriptions (monthly or bi-monthly updating, £1,025 and £675); *BookWise-world*, (2 discs) adding Baker & Taylor and other records to provide international coverage of English language titles (monthly or

....*(contd.)*
bi-monthly updating, £1,395 and £750); *Compact-world*, offering the same records as *BookWise-world* , but without the full title descriptions (monthly or bi-monthly updating, £1,185 and £750); *Premier-CD*, (2 discs) providing similar international coverage to *BookWise-world*, but with a range of enhanced features (monthly or bi-monthly updating, £1,695 or £1,000). A specialist database, *BookFind medical & health care*, and an out-of-print listing, *Archive BookFind*, are also available.

In print database of new English language books. *Premier-CD* contains 2.3 million records, *BookWise-CD* just over 1 million. Many entries include a detailed contents listing and description, in addition to standard bibliographical and order information such as imprint, ISBN and price. All data elements searchable, other features include readership level indicators and 2,000 plus subject classifications. BookFind's main advantage over its chief rival *Whitaker Bookbank global (Global books in print)* lies in the descriptive annotations/contents listings. *Class No:* 015(100)=20

[248]

Books in English. London, British Library Bibliographic Services, 1971-. 6 pa. £525. ISSN: 00452572.

Microfiche service produced every two months, each issue cumulative, with a final annual cumulation. Further cumulations available for 1971-80 (£535) and 1981-92 (£535, replaces earlier cumulation for 1981-85).

Computer produced from records for English language titles created by the British Library and Library of Congress. Entries, in one alphabetical sequence of authors, editors, compilers, titles and series, catalogued according to AACR2 with Dewey class nos. and Library of Congress subject data. About 100,000 records added annually. 1971-80 cumulation contains more than 1,100,000 records, 1981-92 over 1,250,000. Useful for bibliographical checking and as a cataloguing aid. *Class No:* 015(100)=20

[249]

BookScope. Woodbridge, Conn., Primary Source Media, 1995-. CD-ROM database. £675. ISSN: 10826165.

Discs updated monthly. Subsets available as *BookScope business* and *BookScope medical*.

Provides infomation for English-language books published since 1989. *c.*400,000 records based on the data resources of Blackwell's North America. In addition to standard bibliographical detail, ISBN and price, many records include table of contents listings and summaries. Also contains a limited number of reviews. Cannot compete in comprehensiveness with the other major English-language book listings and the 'material included is overwhelmingly of North American origin' (*Managing information*, v.3(7/8), July/August 1996, p.52). *Class No:* 015(100)=20

[250]

International books in print: English-language titles published in Africa, Asia, Australia, Canada, Continental Europe, Latin America, New Zealand, Oceania and the Republic of Ireland. München, Saur, 1979-. Annual (initially irregular). $695. ISSN: 01709348.

16th ed. (1997) published in 2 pts. in 4 vols: Pt.1 *Author title list*; Pt.2 *Subject guide* (first published 1983).

Covers currently available English language titles published outside the US and UK. The 16th ed. lists *c.*270,000 books available from 7,000 publishers. Includes works of fiction, and some non-book materials with the exception of microfilms. Excludes publications under 32p., school textbooks, musical scores and maps. List of publishers/distributors in both pts. Subject section, arranged

....*(contd.)*
by broad Dewey class numbers, includes a 'Country index' and 'Index of persons as subjects'. Available as a CD-ROM database, updated annually £995. *International books in print* records are also a component of *Whitaker BookBank global* (below). A useful one-stop source, but far from comprehensive. Other in print listings (*e.g. Indian books in print* (*qq.v.*)) give fuller coverage for individual countries. *Class No:* 015(100)=20

[251]

Whitaker's BookBank global. London, Whitaker, 1993-. CD-ROM database. ISSN: 13515179.

Two services available: *Compact* (single disc), offering short records and more limited searching facilities; *Premium* (two discs to be used simultaneously), providing full records, greater searching capabilities and additional data from D.W. Thorpe and Bowker, including some descriptive annotations. Monthly updating for both services, *Compact* £1,660, *Premium* £1,795.

Combines *Whitaker's books in print* (*q.v.*) (CD-ROM version *BookBank*) and Bowker's *Books in print* (*q.v.*) records in one database. Also adds Australian/New Zealand data from D.W. Thorpe, plus other English language titles, including those appearing in *International books in print* (above). Well over 2,000,000 records in total, the fullest listing of in-print books available. Search software same as that employed on the *BookBank* database, offering menu and command driven options. The CD-ROM combines two distinct databases whose data retains different structures. The result is some inconsistencies in search options (*e.g.* Library of Congress based subject headings for Bowker records, but not for Whitaker's) and duplicate records.

The database is also available as a CD-ROM from Bowker under the title *Global books in print on disc* (monthly updating, £1,695). This is a one disc product and uses the same software as other Bowker CD-ROMs such as *Books in print Plus*. *Class No:* 015(100)=20

Hebrew

[252]

INSTITUTE OF HEBREW BIBLIOGRAPHY. The Bibliography of the Hebrew book 1473-1960: a bibliography of all printed Hebrew language books before 1960. Jerusalem, Electronic Publishing International, 1994. CD-ROM database.

Based on the catalogue of the Jewish National and University Library, Jerusalem. Records for about 85,000 titles. Hebrew and English search interfaces.
Class No: 015(100)=924

Great Britain

[253]

DUFF, E.G. Fifteenth century English books: a bibliography of books and documents published in England and of books for the English market printed abroad. London, Oxford University Press for the Bibliographical Society, 1917. ix,136p. 53 facsims.

Reprinted Books on Demand ($37.50. ISBN: 0317093134).

431 entries, arranged A-Z by author, or title, in the case of anonymous works. Fairly full bibliographical descriptions are given. Locations for copies in the British Museum (Library), John Rylands Library, the Bodleian, Cambridge University and other British libraries are indicated. Typographical (chronological) index. *Class No:* 015(410)

[254]

The English short title catalogue. Univ. of California, Riverside and The British Library in partnership with the American Antiquarian Society. Computer database.

Available online through RLIN via Zephyr or Eureka WWW interface.

Contains records for all letterpress printed material published to 1801 in the British Isles or British colonies, plus items in English published elsewhere. Developed from *Eighteenth century short title catalogue* (*q.v.*) to include entries from Pollard and Redgrave for the period 1475-1640 and Wing for 1641-1700. File contained 420,000 records June 1998, updated daily. A CD-ROM version is also available from Primary Source Media. *Class No:* 015(410)

[255]

LOWNDES, W.T. The Bibliographer's manual of English literature, containing an account of rare, curious, and useful books, published in or relating to Great Britain and Ireland from the invention of printing: with bibliographical and critical notices, collations of the rarer articles, and the prices at which they have been sold. Bohn, H.G., *ed.* New ed. rev., corrected & enl. London, Bell, 1857-64. 6v. in 11 pts.

Reprinted Detroit, Gale, 1968 in 7v. First published 1834.

A-Z author list; 55,000 entries. V.6 by Bohn, lists the publications of learned societies, private presses and publications in series. Uneven and sometimes untrustworthy, but frequently useful. *Class No:* 015(410)

[256]

UNIVERSITÄT GÖTTINGEN. Bibliothek. **A Catalogue of English books printed before 1801 held by the University Library at Göttingen.** Fabian, B., *ed and* Jefcoate, G. *and* Kloth, K., *comps..* Hildesheim, Olms, 1987-88. 7v. £116.40 per v. ISBN: 3487078872, pt.1 A-G.

In 3 parts: Part I. Books printed before 1701. 2v. Part II. Books printed between 1701-1800. 4v. Part III. Indices. 1v.

Catalogue of perhaps the largest collection of early English books outside the English-speaking world. Detailed entries for items in English printed anywhere in the world. Also includes books by English-speaking authors in other languages and translations of works by English-speaking authors, categories not covered by *ESTC*. A useful additional source especially for the eighteenth century. A 'startling number (*ESTC* entries) rely on Göttingen copies in the first place' (*Times Literary Supplement*, no.4462, 7 October 1988, p.1132). *Class No:* 015(410)

[257]

WATT, R. Bibliotheca Britannica; or, A general index to British and foreign literature. Edinburgh, Constable, 1824. 4v.

Reprinted Routledge, 1995. (4v. in boxed set. £650. ISBN: 0415137063).

Estimated to include more than 200,000 books, periodicals and pamphlets. V.1-2 arranged A-Z by author, with very brief biographical information, and usually title, date, size and number of vols.; v.3-4 form an alphabetical subject index that includes anonyma. Many hundreds of bibliographical sources are listed in v.3 under the heading 'Bibliography'. Objectionable typography but useful for obscure 17th and 18th century works, and rather more accurate than Lowndes (*q.v.*). *Class No:* 015(410)

[258]

WILES, R.M. Serial publications in England before 1750. Cambridge, Cambridge Univ. Press, 1957. xv,391p.

7 chapter discussion of books issued in installments. Includes: Appendix B. Short-title catalogue of books published in fascicules before 1750 (p.267-356); Appendix C. Names and addresses of booksellers, printers and others who had some share in the production and distribution of number books before 1750. Bibliography (p.367-70).
Class No: 015(410)

16th & 17th Centuries

[259]

ALLISON, A.F. *and* **ROGERS, D.M. The Contemporary printed literature of the English counter-reformation** between 1558 and 1640. Aldershot, Scolar, 1989-94. 2v. ISBN: 1859280609.

V.1 *Works in languages other than English* (xxviii,291p. £75;$129.95); v.2 *Works in English: with addenda and corrigenda to volume 1* (xxxv,250p. £75;$121.95). V.2 effectively replaces the same author's *A Catalogue of Catholic books in English printed abroad or secretly in England...* . (Bognor Regis, Arundel Press, 1956. xiii,187p.).

V.1 covers works, mainly in Latin, published abroad by English Catholics. 1,619 entries in modified author arrangement with subject section (p.189-221) and indexes. V.2 has 932 entries. Indexes; addenda and corrigenda (p.247-50). *Class No:* 015(410)"15/16"

[260]

ALLISON, A.F. *and* **GOLDSMITH, V.F. Titles of English books (and of foreign books printed in England):** an alphabetical finding-list by title of books published under the author's name, pseudonym or initials. Folkestone, Dawson, 1976-77. 2v. £35. ISBN: 0712907378.

V.1 1475-1640; v.2 1641-1700.

A supplementary index to Pollard and Redgrave and to Wing. Books entered in the original bibliographies by title excluded. Spelling (other than proper names) modernized. '(N)ot as complete as it should be', ... random checking 'revealed at least one title omitted from each page' (*Times literary supplement*, no.3889, 24th September 1976, p.1221). *Class No:* 015(410)"15/16"

[261]

CAMBRIDGE UNIVERSITY. Library. **Early English printed books in the University Library Cambridge** (1475 to 1640). Sayle, C.E., *comp.* Cambridge, Univ. Press, 1900-07. 4v.

Reprinted 1971 (New York, Johnson Reprint Corp. ISBN: 0384072216).

V.I, pt.1: Incunabula (A. England; B. Abroad); pt.2: 1501-1640. London (to F. Kingston); v.II: 1501-1640. London (concluded); English provincial presses; v.III: 1501-1640. Scottish, Irish and foreign presses; with addenda; v.IV: Indexes (books; printers, stationers etc.; engravers, printers, etc.; towns; portraits; music; bibliographies; books; supplementary index).

8,083 numbered entries, arranged in 'Proctor order' (i.e. chronologically by places of printing and then by presses). V.I, pt.1 (comprising 143 items) is superseded by *A Catalogue of the. fifteenth-century printed books in the University Library, Cambridge* (*q.v.*), while V.I-III are largely replaced by Pollard and Redgrave (below).
Class No: 015(410)"15/16"

[262]

COMPANY OF STATIONERS OF LONDON. A Transcript of the registers of the Company of Stationers of London, 1554-1640 ... Arber, E., *ed.* London, Arber, 1875-77 (v.1-4); Birmingham, Arber, 1894 (v.5). 5v.

Reprinted Peter Smith, 1967 (ISBN: 0844614491).

4,691 items in chronological order, with a gap 1570-76; no indexes. The manuscript registers continue to 1912, but they are incomplete and of little value. Many of the entries in the original registers were inaccurate, and they are now largely superseded by Pollard and Redgrave (below).
Class No: 015(410)"15/16"

[263]

—A Companion to Arber: being a calendar of documents in Edward Arber's Transcript of the register of the Company of Stationers of London, 1554-1640, with text and calendar of supplementary documents. Greg, W.W. Oxford, Clarendon Press, 1967. vii,451p.

Reprinted Peter Smith (ISBN: 0685734110).

A calendar of documents (p.3-112) used by Arber as illustrative material in his *Transcript.* The 92 supplementary documents are followed by a detailed analytical index (p.359-451). *Class No:* 015(410)"15/16"

[264]

GUILDHALL LIBRARY (London). **A List of books printed in the British Isles and of English books printed abroad before 1701 in the Guildhall Library.** London, Corporation of London, 1966-67. 2pts. £2.50 each. ISBN: 0900422114, v.1.

Pt.1 A-K; pt.2 L-Z, with addenda and concordance. 6,564 entries. *Class No:* 015(410)"15/16"

[265]

JOHN RYLANDS LIBRARY. Manchester. **Catalogue of books in the John Rylands Library, printed in England,** Scotland and of books in English printed abroad to the end of the year 1640. Duff, E.G., *comp.* Manchester, Cornish, 1895. iii,147p.

Gives author, title, size, publisher, place, date. Index of printers and publishers. *Class No:* 015(410)"15/16"

[266]

POLLARD, A.W. *and* **REDGRAVE, G.R. A Short-title catalogue of books printed in England, Scotland and Ireland: and of English books printed abroad 1475-1640.** Pantzer, K.F., *and others comps.* 2nd ed. London, Bibliographical Society, 1976-1991. 3v. £360;$750. ISBN: 0197217907.

Begun by W.A. Jackson and F.S. Ferguson, completed by K.F. Pantzer. V.1 A-H (1986. iii,620p.); v.2 I-Z (1976. xi,494p.); v.3 *A printers and publishers index, other indexes and appendices, cumulative addenda and corrigenda, with a chronological index.* (1991. xix,405p.). First published 1926 in 1v., reprinted 1950.

An author list of *c.*37,000 items (1st ed. 26,500) including books in other British languages and books in which English is on a par with other languagues. Excludes works by English authors printed outside England which are not in English. Entries follow the format of the 1st ed., but with more expansive transcriptions of titles and fuller notes and cross-references. 'S.T.C.' numbering system retained unchanged, many interpolations for new and moved items. Nearly 500 library locations (1st ed. 148); 'up to five on each side [of the Atlantic] have been listed with a view to geographical distribution' (Locations). V.1 contains a detailed introduction (p.xix-xliii). V.3 provides comprehensive indexing, etc. Contents: Index 1. Printers

.... *(contd.)*
and publishers, A-Z (p.1-193), with supplementary lists (*e.g.* Patrons/publishers; Patentees) and 6 appendices; Index 2. Places other than London (subdivided British Isles and Colonies; The Continent; Fictitious places); Index 3. Selected London indexes; Index 4. Anomalous imprints; Cumulative addenda and corrigenda (p.261-318); Concordances: Bosanquet, Duff, Gregg; Chronological index (p.325-405). The primary source for bibliographical information on early English books and a model catalogue of its kind. Records are also included in the database *The English short title catalogue* (*q.v.*).
Class No: 015(410)"15/16"

[267]

—Early English books 1475-1640 selected from Pollard and Redgrave's short-title catalogue: cross index to reels 1-1885. Ann Arbor, University Microfilms International, 1985. 163p.

S.T.C. no. to reel no. index of UMI's *Early English books,* a project to microfilm items recorded in S.T.C. 27,000 titles microfilmed to 1985.
Class No: 015(410)"15/16"

[268]

—RAMAGE, D. A Finding-list of English books to 1640 in libraries in the British Isles (excluding the national libraries and the libraries of Oxford and Cambridge) ... Durham, Council of the Durham Colleges, 1958. xvi,101p.

Gives locations for 1 to 35 copies of 14,000 books in 144 British libraries. Based on the 1st ed. of S.T.C., using S.T.C. nos. *Class No:* 015(410)"15/16"

[269]

SHAABER, M.A. Checklist of works of British authors printed abroad, in languages other than English, to 1641. New York, The Bibliographical Society of America, 1975. xx,168p. $15. ISBN: 0914930052.

Works covered are those by writers born in the British Isles, including those who spent much of their lives abroad, and writers born elsewhere who spent considerable parts of their lives in the British Isles. *c.*5,000 short entires with locations in British, European and North American libraries. Sources (p.vii-xiv). *Class No:* 015(410)"15/16"

[270]

A Short-title catalogue arranged geographically, of books printed and distributed by printers, publishers and booksellers in the English provincial towns and in Scotland and Ireland up to and including the year 1700. Clough, E.A., *comps.* London, Library Association, 1969. [3],119p. ISBN: 0853650918.

'This is a short-title catalogue of those books which bear an imprint indicating that they were printed, published or distributed in the United Kingdom, other than in London, before 1701' (Preface). Arranged by towns Aberdeen ... York, chronological sub-arrangement. Excludes books listed in Aldis (1904) (*q.v.*), Dix (1898) and Madan (1895-1931), covering Scotland, Dublin and Oxford respectively.
Class No: 015(410)"15/16"

16th Century

[271]

BIBLIOGRAPHICAL SOCIETY. Hand-lists of books printed by London printers, 1501-1556. Duff, E.G., *and others.* London, the Society, 1913. 4pts. in 1v. illus.

Issued in 4 pts. as *Hand-lists of English printers, 1501-1556* (1895-1913); pagination for each printer is separate, so that they may be bound chronologically or alphabetically.

.... (contd.)
Handy for details of addresses, devices, etc., but lacks author and title indexes; locations are given for a few libraries. *Class No:* 015(410)"15"

17th Century

[272]
BRITISH MUSEUM. Department of Printed Books. **Catalogue of the pamphlets, books, newspapers, and manuscripts relating to the Civil War,** the Commonwealth and Restoration, collected by George Thomason, 1640-1661. London, British Museum, 1908. 2v.

A remarkably full collection (22,255 items, including 7,216 newspapers and 97 manuscripts) usually known as the Thomason Tracts. Chronological order, with author and subject index. Newspapers 1641-63 in v.2, (p.371-440). The pamphlets and books are included in Wing (*q.v.*).
Class No: 015(410)"16"

[273]
CLANCY, T.H. English Catholic books 1641-1700: a bibliography. Rev. ed. Aldershot, Scolar Press, 1996. xviii,215p. £39.50;$6795. ISBN: 1859283292.

First published Chicago, Loyola Univ. Press, 1974.

Continues Allison and Rogers (*q.v.*) covering 'books written by Catholics and published in the Roman Catholic interest' (p.vii). Includes books in Irish, Scots and Welsh. 1,333 entries (1,139 in original ed.) by author with full bibliographical detail, plus library locations and Wing no. Occasional entries with note on author or literary context. Printer/bookseller, translator/editor, dedication and proper name indexes. *Class No:* 015(410)"16"

[274]
COMPANY OF STATIONERS OF LONDON. A Transcript of the registers of the Worshipful Company of Stationers, from 1640-1708 A.D. Eyre, G.E.B., *ed and* Plomer, H.R., *transcriber..* London, [Roxburghe Club], 1913-14. 3v.

Continues the Stationers' Company *Transcript ... 1554-1640* (*q.v.*). Lists about 10,000 items.
Class No: 015(410)"16"

[275]
Printing for Parliament, 1641-1700. Lambert, S., *ed.* London, List & Index Society, 1984. xii,323p. (*List & Index Society special series, v.20.*)

Main listing (p.1-221); alphabetical check list of titles in Wing S.T.C. arrangement (p.222-323), also including National Union Catalog no. Makes reference to all papers known to have been printed, whether or not copies were found. *Class No:* 015(410)"16"

[276]
Short-title catalogue of books printed in England, Scotland, Ireland, Wales and British America and of English books printed in other countries 1641-1700. Wing, D.G., *comp.* 2nd rev. & enl. ed. New York, Index Committee of the Modern Language Association of America, 1972-88. 3v. $400 per v.

V.1: A1-E2926 (1972. xx,622p. $225. ISBN: 0873520440); v.2: E2927-01000 (1982. xvii,690p. $400. ISBN: 0873520459); v.3: P1-Z28 (1988. xxvii,766p. $400. ISBN: 0873520467). Revised and updated version of v.1 issued 1994 (Morrison, J.J. & Nelson, C.W. *eds.* xli,954p. ISBN: 0873526619).

First published in 3v. 1945-51. Various independent supplements were published to the 1st ed. These included Morrison, P.G. *Index of printers, publishers, and*

.... (contd.)
booksellers in Donald Wing's 'Short-title catalogue' ... (Charlottesville, Bibliographical Society of the Univ. of Virginia, 1955. 217p); Hiscock, W.G. *The Christ Church holdings in Wing's 'Short-title catalogue, 1641-1700'* ... ([Oxford], Christ Church, 1965); Wolf, E. *A Checklist of books in the Library Company of Philadelphia in and supplementary to Wing's 'Short-title catalogue, 1641-1700'* (Philadelphia, 1959. viii,106p.).

Continues Pollard and Redgrave's *Short title catalogue ... 1475-1600* (above). About 120,000 entries (up from 50,000 in 1st ed.) structured on the basis of author, short title, edition statement, imprint, date, format and occasionally pagination. Excludes works by English authors printed in other languages and serially published items (now covered by *British newspapers and periodicals 1641-1700*). Up to 5 UK and 5 North American locations given for each item; overall number of library locations drastically increased in this ed. to well over 500. V.1 as originally published differs from v.2-3 in that 7-8% of the numbers from the 1st ed. ('Wing nos.') were reassigned. This practice was widely criticised and not continued in v.2 which contains 'A list of changes in entry numbering from the first to the second edition of volume 1 of the Wing short-title catalogue' (p.669-90). 1994 replacement of v.1 makes extensive revisions and amendments and adds new entries and locations. Overall, this ed. is a great improvement over the 1st which contained many omissions and errors. Searchable online as part of *The English short title catalogue* (*q.v.*). A Windows based CD-ROM is also available from Chadwyck-Healey (£995). Electronic versions have the advantage of additional search paths such as title keyword and publication date.
Class No: 015(410)"16"

[277]
—Early English books, 1641-1700: a cumulative index to units 1-60 of the microfilm collection. Ann Arbor, University Microfilms International, 1990. 9v. $750. ISBN: 0835709191.

V.1-2: Author index; v.3-5: Title index; v.6-8: Subject index; v.9: Wing number and reel/position indexes.

Index to the 42,500 titles in Units 1-60 of UMI's *Early English books, 1641-1700* a microfilm collection of books and other materials selected from Wing. Full AACR2 standard entries in author, title and subject sequences; latter arranged by Library of Congress headings.
Class No: 015(410)"16"

[278]
The Term catalogues, A.D. 1668-1709, with a number for Easter term, 1711 A.D. Arber, E., *ed.* London, Arber, 1903-06. 3v.

Reprinted 1965 (New York, Johnson Reprint).

About 20,000 items. A reprint of the contemporary book trade lists; includes sizes and publishers. Each volume has indexes of titles, authors, printers and subjects. Includes many items not listed in the registers of the Stationers' Company. *Class No:* 015(410)"16"

18th & 19th Centuries

[279]
The London catalogue of books.

The generic title for a series of overlapping catalogues (designated by Besterman as 'The Bent, British, Complete, English, General, Hodgson, London, Low, Modern London, New London catalogues') covering the period 1700 to 1855. The first of these is *The London catalogue of books that have*

....(contd.)
been printed in Great Britain since the year MDCC [by W. Bent], listing *c.*8,500 books for the period 1700-1773. T. Besterman's *A World bibliography of bibliographies* (4th ed. 1965-66) has a chronological listing of these catalogues under 'English literature', cols. 1986-90.
Class No: 015(410)"17/18"

18th Century

[280]

Eighteenth-century British books: an author union catalogue: extracted from the British Museum general catalogue of printed books, the catalogues of the Bodleian Library and of the University Library, Cambridge. Robinson, F.J.G., *and other comps*. Folkestone, Dawson, 1981-82. 5v. ISBN: 0712910239.

A project of the Newcastle University Programme for Historical Biobibliography.

Similar geographical scope to *ESTC* (below) covering all works wholly or partly in English, or printed in Great Britain, North America or other British colonies. Arrangement of entries A-Z with some British Museum headings (e.g. Bible, England). '(A)stonishingly short' bibliographical detail (*The Library*, Sixth series, v.IV(4), December 1982, p.453), but entries do include Dewey class nos., as in *Eighteenth-century British books: a subject catalogue*. Estimated to cover 70% of all eighteenth century imprints, excluding music, maps and other ephemeral printing. No substitute for *ESTC* and overall a poor quality production, '(E)rror and muddle have been created as well as transmitted, and three perfectly servicable library catalogues have come out of the computer much less useful than the originals' (*Book collector*, v.30(3), Autumn 1981, p.416). *Class No:* 015(410)"17"

[281]

—Eighteenth-century British books: an index to the foreign and provincial imprints in the author union catalogue. Robinson, F.J.G., *and others comps*. Newcastle-upon-Tyne, Avero (Eighteenth Century) Publications, 1982. x,320p. 9 maps in pocket. £250. ISBN: 0907977006.

Arranged by town then chronologically in main sections: Imprints of countries; English imprints; Irish imprints ...; Anonymous and satirical imprints, etc.
Class No: 015(410)"17"

[282]

—Eighteenth-century British books: a subject catalogue: extracted from the British Museum general catalogue of printed books. Averley, G., *and others comps*. Folkestone, Dawson, 1979. 4v. ISBN: 0712908692.

V.I *Generalities, philosophy, religion*; v.II *Social sciences, pure sciences, technology, the arts*; v.III *Language, literature*; v.IV *Geography and history*.

Unlike the author catalogue, confined to the holdings of the British Library. Broad Dewey classified arrangement, some long sequences subdivided by publication date.
Class No: 015(410)"17"

[283]

Eighteenth century short title catalogue. London, British Library. Computer database.

Available online via BLAISE-Line, file updated monthly, and on CD-ROM (£1,650). Known as 'ESTC'

An ongoing project to produce records for all letterpress printed material published 1701-1800 in the British Isles and British colonies, plus that published elsewhere in English or in a British language (*e.g.* Welsh, Irish, etc.). Wide range of

....(contd.)
publications covered, including handbills and circulars, songs and ballads, sale catalogues, etc., but with newspaper and periodical parts and certain other materials excluded. Records derived from more than 1,000 libraries worldwide, compilation from editorial offices at the British Library and the University of Louisiana, Baton Rouge. Entries, based on AACR and lengthier than the title implies, include library locations and Research Publications reel no. (see next entry) where applicable. Searchable by author, title, imprint, year, country, etc. No direct subject searching, but the notes field may contain a subject statement. Over 375,000 records early 1998. Also forms the core of the wider RLIN database *The English short-title catalogue* (*q.v.*). *Class No:* 015(410)"17"

[284]

—The Eighteenth century: a guide to the microfilm collection. Woodbridge, Conn., Research Publication, 1984-.

Author, title and subject indexes (latter 8 broad headings only) to Research Publication's *The Eighteenth century*, a microfilm collection based on *ESTC*. 14 bound volumes published to 1997, covering units 1-198 of the collection.
Class No: 015(410)"17"

[285]

—The Eighteenth century short title catalogue 1990: microfiche edition. Boston Spa, British Library, 1990. Microfiche.

Comprises 221 fiche (author/title catalogue, date of publication index, place of publication index, supplementary indexes etc.). Accompanied by a 30p. pamphlet. Earlier ed. in 113 fiche, 1983.

Based on entries input to *ESTC*. About 284,000 records (150,000 1983), with over 1,000,000 locations in 1,000 libraries worldwide. *Class No:* 015(410)"17"

[286]

English Catholic books 1701-1800: a bibliography. Blom, F., *and others comps*. Aldershot, Scolar Press, 1996. xl,356p. £59.50;$99.50. ISBN: 1859281486.

Continues Clancy's *English Catholic books 1641-1700* (*q.v.*). 2,690 entries by author/anonymous title with ESTC no., location symbols (max. 25) and occasional notes. Title, printer/publisher/bookseller, and proper name indexes. '(I)ncludes some Continental holdings to which ESTC has not yet penetrated, and identifies many private collections' (*The Library*, v.19(2), June 1997, p.160).
Class No: 015(410)"17"

19th & 20th Centuries

[287]

The English catalogue of books ... 1801-1968. London, Publishers' Circular, 1864-1969.

Publisher varies: Sampson Low, 1864-1901.

Basically compiled from weekly lists in the *Publishers' circular* (1837-1959) and thereafter *British books* (monthly, 1959-66; incorporated into *The Publisher* 1967-70). Initial volume covering 1835-62 published 1864. Subsequent cumulated volumes issued on an irregular basis, with a period of quinquennial publication 1901-35. Later volumes cover 1936/41, 1942/47, 1948/52, 1952/55, 1956/59, 1960/62 and 1963/65. A retrospective volume extending coverage back to 1801 was published 1914. In its day less comprehensive, particularly for provincial presses, than *Whitaker's cumulative book list* (now *Whitaker's book list* (*q.v.*)).

The preliminary volume for 1801-36, and 20v. of cumulations (1835/62 - 1963/65) reprinted New York, Kraus Reprint. *Class No:* 015(410)"18/19"

19th Century

[288]

Nineteenth century short title catalogue: extracted from the catalogues of the Bodleian Library, the British Library, Harvard University Library, the Library of Congress, the Library of Trinity College Dublin, the National Library of Scotland and the university libraries of Cambridge and Newcastle. Newcastle-upon-Tyne, Avero, 1984-. Price varies, later print vols. £240 each. ISBN: 0907977103, (Phase I).

Known as 'NSTC'. Published in 3 series. Series I. Phase I. 1801-1815 (1984-85. 6v.). Series II. Phase I. 1816-1870. (1986-95. 56v.). CD-ROM version of Series I & II issued 1996 containing 663,000 records. Series III. 1871-1919 on CD-ROM only. Third cumulative disc, with over 127,000 records A-Bz, issued October 1997. Completion scheduled for 2002.

An immense project which 'aims to provide an increasingly complete listing of books printed between 1801 and 1918 in order of authors, subjects, places of imprint, titles and date of publication. British books are taken to include all books published in Britain, its colonies and the United States of America; all books in English wherever published and all translations from English' (Introduction, Series II). Based on library catalogues, Series I excludes the Library of Congress and Harvard University Library. Entries are in form and order of the British Museum (Library) catalogue (GK3), with alternative headings in parentheses and cross-references as necessary. Author statements include epithet and lifespan. Subject indexing based on Dewey, each entry including up to 3 class nos. Many headings are very broad, making searching an impractical proposition. CD-ROM searchable through 14 indexes including author epithet, series title, date of publication, place of publication, printer/publisher, keyword and library location. An admirable project, but some items are entered twice and use of the classification scheme is inconsistent. *Class No:* 015(410)“18”

Contemporary

[289]

British national bibliography. Boston Spa, The British Library National Bibliographic Service, 1950-. Weekly, etc. £595 (full service). ISSN: 00071544.

Known as 'BNB'. Cumulated indexes 1950/54, 1955/59, 1960/64, 1965/67, 1968/70, 1971/73; cumulated subject catalogues 1951/54, 1955/59, 1960/64, 1965/67, 1968/70.

Based on items received by the Legal Deposit Office of the British Library. Excludes periodicals (other than first issues or the first issue of a changed title), music (covered by *British catalogue of music* (*q.v.*)), maps, Parliamentary papers and many publications of government departments, grey literature (covered by *British national bibliography for report literature* (*q.v.*)) and non-research level local interest material. Main listing in the form of a 'Classified subject catalogue', cataloguing by AACR2, arrangement by 21st Dewey. Cataloguing-in-publication introduced in 1977 and now used extensively. Weekly issues in two sequences: 'Recently received & forthcoming titles' and 'Name and title index', the latter including series and names as subjects. Indexes cumulate in final issue for each month with addition of subject sequence ('COMPASS' headings). Interim cumulations issued for January-April and May-August, with a final annual cumulation in 2 v. ('Subject catalogue'; 'Indexes').

BNB is also issued on microfiche (various subscription

....(contd.)

options, full fiche service £475). Two microfiche cumulations are available: 1981-92 author/title and classified subject (replaces earlier 1981-85 cumulation) containing over 500,000 records (£515); 1950-84 author/title containing 2,500,000 records (£515). *BNB* is searchable online through BLAISE-Line as *BNBMARC*, file updated weekly. The CD-ROM version, launched 1988, is a 2 disc service: backfile 1950-85 (£2,000) and current file 1986-, (monthly updating, £950). Since its inception *BNB* has been the primary source for bibliographical information on British published books. Coverage is fuller than *Whitaker's book list*, especially in respect of non-trade items. *Class No:* 015(410)“312”

[290]

Whitaker's book list. London, Whitaker, 1924-. Annual. ISSN: 0953041x.

Previously *Whitaker's cumulative book list* (ISSN: 04104229). Publication of print vol. ceased with 1993, recent coverage on microfiche (ISSN: 13593765), current status of this service uncertain. Cumulations published 1939/43, 1944/47, 1948/52, 1953/57, 1958/62, 1963/67, 1968/72 and 1973/75.

Provides a full annual record of books published in the UK available for sale. Books published overseas also included if they have an English language text and are readily obtainable through the trade. Based on the 'Publications of the week' section of *The Bookseller* (below). Entries, similar to *Whitaker's books in print*, in one A-Z sequence of authors, titles and subjects (where this forms part of the title). List of publishers and addresses. The 1993 v. (xliv,2104p.) recorded 91,735 items.

The 'Publications of the week' section in *The Bookseller* (London, Whitaker, 1858-. Weekly ISSN: 00067539) lists newly published titles. Until December 1969 listings cumulated monthly; from January 1970 to September 1992 this function was assumed by *Whitaker's books of the month* ... (below). *Class No:* 015(410)“312”

[291]

—Whitaker's books of the month and books to come: books published this month and forthcoming books. London, Whitaker, 1970-92. Monthly. ISSN: 00681350.

Ceased publication with September 1992 issue. Mainly a cumulation of the 'Publications of the week' section of *The Bookseller*, but also included forthcoming titles (denoted by star symbol). *Class No:* 015(410)“312”

[292]

Whitaker's books in print: the reference catalogue of current literature. London, Whitaker, 1874-. Annual. £410. ISSN: 09530398.

Title varies: *The Reference catalogue of current literature*, 1874-1961; *British books in print* 1965-87. From 1874-1932 issued at irregular intervals comprising publishers' catalogues bound together (A-Z by publisher), plus an index by author and title. Irregular publication continued 1936-61, but in the form of consolidated author and title lists. Annual publication under the title *British books in print* from 1967. Now issued as a 5v. set.

Lists titles published in the UK 'freely available to the general public through the book trade. English language titles published in continental Europe are also recorded. Additionally, titles published elsewhere overseas may be included provided they have English language text and are available to the trade through a sole stockholding agent based in the United Kingdom'. Arranged in one A-Z sequence of authors and titles, the former distinguished by bold type, with the addition of keyword subject entries where

.... (contd.)
the subject forms part of the title or subtitle. Entries include detail such as names of editors/revisors/translators, edition statement, number of pages, illustrations, size, binding (where not cloth) and series. Coverage extends to children's books coded for reading ability and interest. List of series and their publishers, publisher ISBN prefixes and publishers and their addresses in final v. The 1997 ed. contains details of 770,000 titles.

Whitaker's books in print is also issued monthly on microfiche (£705). A separate microfiche service, *New and forthcoming books weekly fiche*, was introduced in 1992 (£120). This includes details of *c.*50,000 forthcoming books annually, listed up to 24 months ahead of publication.

Whitaker's books in print is also searchable online through BLAISE-Line and Dialog (File 430). For the CD-ROM version see *Bookbank* (below). *Class No:* 015(410)"312"

[293]

—BookBank. London, Whitaker, 1988-. CD-ROM database.

Available as a monthly (£1220) or bi-monthly (£840) service.

Contains the full *Whitaker's books in print*, plus recently out of print and all forthcoming titles. Some records include short descriptions; supplementary file of book related products. Several enhanced versions of *BookBank are available. These include the 2,000,000 record BookBank global compact* (*q.v.*) (monthly updating, £1,660) adding English language titles published in the US, Australasia, Southern Africa and Europe, and *BookBank Global* (monthly updating, £1795) which is similar, but with improved searching facilities for advanced usage. A further CD-ROM is *BookBank OP* (quarterly updating, £345) listing over 1,000,000 out of print titles. *Class No:* 015(410)"312"

Scotland

[294]

ALDIS, H.G. A List of books printed in Scotland before 1700: including those printed furth of the realm for Scottish booksellers with brief notes on the printers and stationers. Photographically reprinted with additions including entries for books published in 1700. Edinburgh, National Library of Scotland, 1970. xxviii,189p.

Originally published Edinburgh, Edinburgh Bibliographical Society, 1904.

Records more than 4,000 items in chronological order 1505-1700. Single-line entries with locations in 18 British libraries and STC and Wing numbers. Indexes: printers, booksellers and stationers (topographical and A-Z); author and anonymous title; supplementary.

Fuller bibliographical information is available in: Dickson, R. and Edmond, J.P. *Annals of Scottish printing from ... 1507 to the beginning of the seventeenth century* (Cambridge, Macmillan and Bowes, 1890. xv,530p.). *Class No:* 015(411)

[295]

Bibliography of Scotland. 1976/77-. Edinburgh, National Library of Scotland, 1978-. Annual. ISSN: 0143571x.

Initial issues with subtitle *A Catalogue of books published in Scotland and of books published elsewhere of Scottish relevance, prepared from accessions received by the National Library of Scotland*. Print publication ceased with 1987 volume. Then issued on microfiche (looseleaf binder with introduction and index). Now also available on CD-ROM (updated annually, £95) and through the Internet (http://www.nls.uk or Telnet to library.nls.uk).

.... (contd.)
First issue of CD-ROM contains 41,000 records for material of Scottish interest published since 1988. Includes entries for major periodical articles and chapters or sections within books. Excludes general items published in Scotland covered in the printed volumes. The addition of retrospective records to the database is planned.

Older bibliographies of Scottish interest material are Sir A. Mitchell and C.G. Cash's *A Contribution to the bibliography of Scottish topography* (1917) and P.D. Hancock's *A Bibliography of works relating to Scotland 1916-1950* (1959). *Class No:* 015(411)

[296]

Books in Scotland. Edinburgh, Ramsay Head Press, 1978-. Quarterly. £9.95. ISSN: 01431285.

Published with the financial assistance of the Scottish Arts Council.

Each issue contains *c.*30 reviews of new books published in Scotland or of Scottish interest. Includes many grouped reviews. Annotated listing of new titles discontinued.
Class No: 015(411)

[297]

FERGUSON, M. *and* **MATHESON, A. Scottish Gaelic union catalogue:** a list of books printed in Scottish Gaelic from 1567 to 1973. Edinburgh, National Library of Scotland, 1984. xv,200p. illus. £10. ISBN: 0902220608.

Alphabetical main entry list of 3,038 works in Scottish Gaelic, or which contain an appreciable proportion of Scottish Gaelic. Entries provide location data for Scottish and major British libraries. Intended as a finding list rather than a bibliography, so cannot be considered to replace *Typographica Scoto-Gadelica* and *Twentieth century publications in Scottish Gaelic* (below). *Class No:* 015(411)

[298]

Leabhraichean Gàidhlig a classified catalogue of Gaelic and Gaelic related books in print. 4th ed. Glasgow, Gaelic Books Council, University of Glasgow, 1987. 60p. ISBN: 0951281003.

1st ed. 1975; 3rd ed. 1983.

Author list arranged in 19 groups including children's books, serial publications and bibliography. Entries, briefly annotated in English, include price. Index of authors and titles. List of books out of print since the 3rd ed.; list of publishers and distributors. *Class No:* 015(411)

[299]

MacLEAN, D. Typographia Scoto-Gadelica: or books printed in the Gaelic of Scotland from the year 1567 to the year 1914: with bibliographical and biographical notes. Edinburgh, Grant, 1915. x,372p.

Reprinted in a limited ed. of 250 copies, Shannon, Irish Univ. Press, 1972 (ISBN: 0716520583).

An author list, with special headings for Bibles, The Church, Periodicals, Psalms etc. Verbatim transcripts of title pages, some entries with brief notes. No indexes.
Class No: 015(411)

[300]

MACLEOD, D.J. Twentieth century publications in Scottish Gaelic. Edinburgh, Scottish Academic Press, 1980. vii,188p. ISBN: 0707302846.

Continuation of MacLean's *Typographia Scoto-Gadelica*. A 'publication is regarded as 'Gaelic' if it contains approximately 2-3 pages in that language. Sheet music, place-name studies and commercial ephemera are not included' (Introduction p.vii). Includes newspapers and

....(contd.)
periodicals. Author arrangement, names given in English. Some entries locate copies in Scottish libraries. No indexes, but comprehensively cross-referenced. *Class No:* 015(411)

Ireland

[301]
Books Ireland. Dublin, J. Addis, 1976-. 10pa. ISSN: 03766039.

Each issue contains general articles relating to publishing and the book trade, reviews of recent titles of Irish origin or interest and 'First flush' an annotated listing of new books published in Ireland. Some issues also contain an announcement section listing and briefly annotating forthcoming titles. *Class No:* 015(415)

[302]
CAMBRIDGE UNIVERSITY. Library. **Catalogue of the Bradshaw collection of Irish books** in the University Library, Cambridge. London, Quaritch, 1916. 3v.

V.1. Books printed in Dublin by known printers, 1602-1882; v.2. Books printed in Dublin without printer's name, 1642-1883 - Provincial towns - Irish authors - Books relating to Ireland, 1516-1883 - M'Ghee collection - Books added during compilation; v.3. Index.

8,743 numbered entries. *Class No:* 015(415)

[303]
Irish books in print: & Leabhair Gaeilge i gCló. 1984. Wicklow, S. & J. Cleary, 1984. 1010p. ISBN: 0947863001.

A 'catalogue of current literature from and about Ireland, North and South' (Preface). Includes British published books of Irish interest; school textbooks excluded. In 2 main pts: English language section, containing author, title and classified listings; Irish language section (p.935-96), containing author and title listings, preceded by descriptive annotations for 400 titles. List of publishers and ISBN prefixes. *Class No:* 015(415)

[304]
Irish publishing record. Dublin, National Library of Ireland, 1967-. Annual. ISSN: 05794056.

Publisher varies.

The Irish national bibliography, covering material published in the Republic and Northern Ireland selected from the databases of the National Library of Ireland, Trinity College Dublin, University College Dublin, Linen Hall Library, North Eastern Education and Library Board and Queen's University. Lists books, pamphlets, new serials, yearbooks, general interest government publications, some maps and musical scores. Arranged by Dewey classification with author and title indexes. The 1994 issue (1996. 228p.) has 1,480 entries. *Class No:* 015(415)

Wales

[305]
Llais llyfrau. [Books in Wales.] Aberystwyth, Welsh Books Council, 1964-. Quarterly. £6. ISSN: 00245437.

Includes reviews of new books published in Wales or relating to Wales. Separate English and Welsh language sections. Each issue also has an insert *Llyfrua newydd/New books* listing titles acquired by the Welsh Book Council Distribution Centre. *Class No:* 015(429)

[306]
Llyfrau Cymraeg i oedolion 1960-1982. Thomas, J., *comp.* Caernafon, Cyngor Sir Gwynedd Gwasaneth Llyfrgell, 1983. Unpaged. ISBN: 0904852350.

Unannotated author list of 3,425 books published in Welsh. Title index. *Class No:* 015(429)

[307]
Llyfryddiaeth Cymru. 1985/86-. [A Bibliography of Wales.] Aberystwyth, Llyfrgell Genedlaethol Cymru/National Library of Wales 1986-. Biennial. £40. ISSN: 09680748.

Combines *Bibliotheca Celtica* (1909-84) and *Subject index to Welsh periodicals* (*.q.v.*). Annual publication planned from 1993 volume.

Records works in Welsh or relating to Wales. 1991/92 (1995) is in separate subject and author volumes, the latter containing full bibliographic records. Foreword in Welsh and English, subject volume arranged by English (Library of Congress) headings with extensive cross-references. Also available as an option on the National Library's online catalogue. *Class No:* 015(429)

[308]
NATIONAL LIBRARY OF WALES. Libri Walliae: a catalogue of Welsh books and books printed in Wales 1546-1820. Rees, E., *comp.* Aberystwyth, National Library of Wales, 1987. 2v. (viii,923,lxxxxiip.). ISBN: 0907158196.

The most comprehensive bibliography to date listing 5,656 items. Arranged alphabetically by main entry with title, name, chronological, and book trade (Wales and outside Wales) indexes. Includes books printed in Welsh outside Wales and books in English printed in Wales. Periodicals, newspapers, ephemera and ballads (defined as poems for which tunes are provided) excluded. Also contains a substantial essay 'The Welsh book trade before 1820'. Some omissions, and the addition of library locations would have been helpful, but 'a magnificent one-woman achievement' (*The Library,* 6th series, v.10(4), December 1988, p.351-55). *Class No:* 015(429)

[309]
—CARDIFF. Free Libraries. Catalogue of printed literature in the Welsh Department. Ballinger, J. *and* Jones, J.I., *comps.* Cardiff, Free Libraries Committee, 1898. 559p.

An author catalogue, with duplicate entries under a specified number of subject headings. Reasonably complete to the end of the 19th century. *Class No:* 015(429)

[310]
—ROWLANDS, W. Cambrian bibliography: containing an account of the books printed in the Welsh language or relating to Wales, from the year 1546 to the end of the eighteenth century, with biographical notices. Evans, D., *ed. & enl.* Llanidloes, J. Pryse, 1869. xxii,762p.

A register of books, with very full bibliographical detail. Continued to 1810 by C. Ashton's *Llyfryddiaeth Gymreig o 1801 i 1810* (National Eisteddfod Association, 1908. iv,272p.). *Class No:* 015(429)

Germany

16th Century

[311]
BRITISH MUSEUM. Department of Printed Books. **Short-title catalogue of books printed in the German-speaking countries and German books printed in other countries from 1455 to 1600 now in the British Museum.** London, Trustees of the British Museum, 1962. viii,1224p. £30. ISBN: 0714102687.

....(contd.)

Author and anonymous title list of *c.*35,000 items, with abbreviated titles and references at a minimum. Long sequence of entries under 'Luther, Martin' (p.534-82). Includes a list of 'Books destroyed during the war, 1939-45'. Index of printers and publishers. *Class No:* 015(430)"15"

[312]

—BRITISH LIBRARY. Short-title catalogue of books printed in the German-speaking countries and of German books printed in other countries from 1455 to 1600 now in the British Library. Supplement. Paisey, D., *comp*. London, British Library, 1990. 141p. ISBN: 0712302077.

Lists 1,300 items added since 1962. Also includes amendments (p.71-91) and a list of books noted as destroyed in World War II subsequently replaced (p.93-96). Index of printers and publishers in the supplement. Consolidated index of places of printing. *Class No:* 015(430)"15"

[313]

Verzeichnis der im deutschen Sprachbereich erschienenen Drucke des XVI Jahrhunderts: VD 16. Bayerische Staatsbibliothek *and* Herzog August Bibliothek, *hrsg*. Stuttgart, Hiersemann, 1983-. DM8580 (Bd.1-22). ISBN: 3777283185.

Publication originally scheduled for 3 series: Abt. 1 *Verfasser, Körperschaften, Anonyma* (Authors, corporate bodies, anonyma); Abt. 2 *Herausgeber, Kommentatoren, Übersetzer* (Editors, commentators, translators); Abt. 3 *Druckorte, Drucker, Verleger* (Place of printing, printer, publisher). Abt. 1 completed in 22 v. 1995, final v. including a user's guide. Abt. 2 published 1997 in 2 v., not as a full catalogue, but as indexes (*Register der Herausgeber, Kommentatoren, Übersetzer, und literarischen Beiträger*).

Catalogue of books, including those in languages other than German, published in German speaking areas (Germany, Switzerland, Austria, Alsace) during the sixteenth century. Based on the collections of the Bavarian State Library and the Herzog August Library at Wolfenbüttel, but including entries for items at other locations and, to a limited extent, entries extracted from bibliographies. Entries in catalogue card format, contain very full information. Lengthy English language review in *Papers of The Bibliographical Society of America* (v.79(4), 1985, p.585-89). *Class No:* 015(430)"15"

[314]

—KÖHLER, H-J. Bibliographie der Flugschriften des 16. Jahrhunderts. Teil 1. Das frühe 16 Jahrhundert (1501-1530). Tübingen, Bibliotheca Academica Verlag, 1991-. DM460 per v. ISBN: 3928471015.

Descriptive listing of German Reformation pamphlets. To be completed in 6 v. Bd.3 M-S (xviii,542p.) issued 1996. *Class No:* 015(430)"15"

17th & 18th Centuries

[315]

BIRCHER, M. Deutsche Drucke des Barock 1600-1720: in der Herzog August Bibliothek, Wolfenbüttel. München, Saur, (formerly Nendeln, KTO Press), 1977-96. 46v. ISBN: 359832099x.

Comprises: Abt.A. *Bibliotheca Augusta* (1977-90. 15v.); Abt.B. *Mittlere Aufstellung* (1988-92. 20v.); Abt.C. *Helmstedter Bestände* (1983-89. 6v.); Abt.D. *Sanderbestände* (1993-96. 5v.).

....(contd.)

Catalogue of the collections of German printing of the period in the Herzog August Bibliothek.
Class No: 015(430)"16/17"

17th Century

[316]

BRITISH LIBRARY. Catalogue of books printed in the German-speaking countries and of German books printed in other countries from 1601 to 1700 now in the British Library. Paisey, D., *comp*. London, British Library, 1994. 5v. £295. ISBN: 0712303510.

V.I-v.IV A-Z; v.V Indexes.

Sequel to 1455 to 1600 short-title catalogue (above). Records over 26,000 items, the most important collection outside Germany. Includes books published in German-speaking countries in languages other than German, single-sheet material, printed music and atlases. Abbreviated, rather than short-title, entries. Comprehensively indexed by collaborators, subjects, printers and publishers (with separate sequences for false and fictitious names, names by town, etc.), places, dates, genres and titles. Online and CD-ROM versions are anticipated. '(A)n indispensable tool for researchers on the German Baroque' (*Rare books newsletter*, no.50, July 1993, p.58). *Class No:* 015(430)"16"

18th & 19th Centuries

[317]

Gesamtverzeichnis des deutschsprachigen Schrifttums (GV) 1700-1910. Geils, P. *and* Gornzy, W., *bearbs*. München, Saur, 1979-87. 160v. plus Nachträge. DM26880. ISBN: 359830000x.

Comprises photographically reproduced entries in one A-Z sequence from 3 major bibliographies (Heinsius, Hinrichs and Kayser (below)) and 175 other sources including dissertations lists and Austrian and Swiss works. About 2 million entries in total arranged by author/anonymous title. Includes periodicals, newspapers and maps. Also available in microfiche (795 fiche. DM5600. ISBN: 3598305907). Continued by *Gesamtverzeichnis des deutschsprachigen Schrifttums (GV) 1911-1965* (*q.v.*).
Class No: 015(430)"17/18"

[318]

—HEINSIUS, W. Allgemeines Bücher-Lexikon oder Vollständiges alphabetisches Verzeichnis aller von 1700 bis zu Ende 1892 erschienenen Bücher. Leipzig, Gledisch, Brockhaus, 1812-94. 19v.

Reprinted Graz, Akademische Druck-und Verlagsanstalt, 1962 (DM3370. ISBN: 3201000043).

4v. covered the period 1700-1810; thereafter volumes were usually quinquennial. An author and catchword-title list. *Class No:* 015(430)"17/18"

[319]

—HINRICHS, J.C. Fünfjahrs-Katalog ... 1851-1912. Leipzig, Hinrichs, 1857-1913. 13v.

Reprinted Graz, Akademische Druk-und Verlagsanstalt, 1964.

Five year cumulations of the half-yearly *Hinrichs' Halbjahrs-Katalog*. *Class No:* 015(430)"17/18"

[320]

—KAYSER, C.G. Vollständiges Bücherlexikon, enthaltend alle ... in Deutschland und in den angrenzeuden Ländern gredruckten Bücher ... 1750-1910. Leipzig, Tauchnitz, 1834-1911. 36v.

Reprinted Graz, Akademische Druck-und Verlagsanstalt, 1961-62 (DM6290. ISBN: 3201000051).

V.1-6 cover 1750-1832; basically an author list with a separate *Sachregister* (1838). Thereafter no index, but catchword-title entries are introduced. More carefully compiled and wider in scope than Heinsius, including some Austrian and Swiss items. *Class No:* 015(430)"17/18"

20th Century

[321]

Deutsche Bibliographie. Wöchentliches Verzeichnis. Frankfurt am Main, Buchhändler-Vereinigung, 1947-90. Weekly, etc.

National bibliography of the Federal Republic set up as a rival to the Democratic Republic's *Deutsche Nationalbibliographie (q.v.)*. Published as *Bibliographie der deutschen Bibliothek* 1947-52. Merged with the East German *Deutsche Nationalbibliographie* from 1991 to form *Deutsche Nationalbibliographie und Bibliographie des im Ausland deutschsprachigen Veröffentlichungen* (below).

Structure and scope similar to that of the current national bibliography. 3 main series from 1965: Reihe A. *Erscheinungen des Verlagsbuchhandels.* (Weekly. ISSN: 01701037); Reiche B. *Erscheinungen aussenhalb des Verlagsbuchhandels* (Weekly (semi-monthly until 1986). ISSN: 01701053); Reihe C. *Karten.* (Quarterly. ISSN: 0170107x). Cumulated by the *Halbjahres-Verzeichnis* and *Fünjahres-Verzeichnis* (below). *Class No:* 015(430)"19"

[322]

—Deutsche Bibliographie. Halbjahres-Verzeichnis. Frankfurt am Main, Buchhändler-Vereinigung, 1951-90. Semi-annual. ISSN: 05325854.

Half-yearly cumulation of *Deutsche Bibliographie. Wöchentliches Verzeichnis.* Continued by *Deutsche Nationalbibliographie... . Reihe D. Monographien und Periodika - Halbjahresverzeichnis* (below).
Class No: 015(430)"19"

[323]

—Deutsche Bibliographie. Fünfjahres-Verzeichnis. 1945/50-1981/85 Frankfurt am Main, Buchhändler-Vereinigung, 1953-89. Quinquennial. ISSN: 04188233.

Subtitle: *Verzeichnis aller im Wöchentlichen Verzeichnis und im Hochschulschriften-Verzeichnis angezeitgen deutschen und im Ausland erscheinenden deutschsprachigen Publikationen.* Effectively continued by *Deutsche Nationalbibliographie.. . Reihe E. Monographien und Periodika - Fünfjahrverzeichnis* (below).

The final cumulation of *Deustche Bibliographie*. Content varied slightly between cumulations. Last set included all entries from Reihe A, B and C of *Deutsche Bibliographie. Wöchentliches Verzeichnis.* Omissions of entries from Reihe B and other sources in some earlier cumulations partially overcome by *Gesamtverzeichnis des deutschsprachigen Schrifttums ausserhalb des Büchandels (GVB) 1966-1980 (q.v.)*. *Class No:* 015(430)"19"

[324]

Deutsche Nationalbibliographie: und Bibliographie des im Ausland erschienenen deutschsprachigen Schrifttums. Leipzig, VEB Bibliographisches Institut, 1931-90. Weekly, etc.

The Democratic Republic's German national bibliography. Merged with *Deustche bibliographie* (above) on reunification to form *Deutsche Nationalbibliographie: und Bibliographie der im Ausland erschienenen deutschsprachigen Veröffentlichungen* (below). Preceded by *Wöchentliches Verzeichnis,* 1842-1930. *Deutsche Nationalbibliographie* covered the whole of Germany until 1945. Continued to aim at comprehensive coverage of German books in the post-war period, but less complete than *Deutsche Bibliographie*.

Later issues in 3 sections: Reihe A *Neuerscheinungen des Buchhandels* (Weekly. ISSN: 03233596); Reihe B *Neuerscheinungen ausserhalb des Buchhandels* (24 issues pa. ISSN: 03233642); Reihe C *Dissertation und Habilitationsschriften* (1968-. Monthly. ISSN: 00120545). Classed arrangement with author, title and keyword indexes. Cumulated annually by *Jahresverzeichnis der Verlagschriften* until 1970 and quinquennially by *Deutsches Bücherverzeicnis* (both below). *Class No:* 015(430)"19"

[325]

—Deutsches Bücherverzeichnis. Verzeichnis der Verlagsschriften und einer Auswahl der ausserhalb des Buchhandels erschienenen Veröffentlichungen der DDR, der BRD und Westberlins sowie der deutschsprachigen Werke anderer Länder. 1911-1981/85. Leipzig, Verlag für Buch- und Bibliothekswesen, 1915-90. Quinquennial.

Title varies; publication pattern also varies slightly. First cumulation covers 1911-14 and continues the Kayser and Hinrichs cumulations (above). World War II and the immediate post-war years covered by volumes for 1941-50; quinquennial cumulations until 1966/70, then 1971/73, 1974/75, 1976/77, 1978/80 and 1981/85. More comprehensive coverage of post-war German publications in the Federal Republic's *Deutsche Bibliographie. Fünfjahres-verzeichnis* (above). *Class No:* 015(430)"19"

[326]

—Jahresverzeichnis der Verlagsschriften und einer Auswahl der ausserhalb des Buchhandels erschienenen Veröffentlichungen der DDR, der BRD und Westberlins sowie der deutschsprachigen werke anderer Länder. 1945/46-70. Leipzig, Verlag für Buch-und Bibliothekswesen, 1948-78. Annual.

Cumulated Reihe A and B of *Deutsche Nationalbibliographie.* As *Jahresverzeichnis des deutschen Schrifttums* until 1967.

Prior to 1945 cumulations were provided in the semi-annual *Halbjahrsverzeichnis der im deutschen Buchhandel erschienen Bücher ...* (1798-1944). Until 1916 published as *Hinrichs' Halbjahrs-Katalog* representing the basic list from which Hinrichs' *Fünfjahrs-Katalog (q.v.)* was compiled.
Class No: 015(430)"19"

[327]

DEUTSCHEN BIBLIOTHEK. Deutsches Exilarchiv 1933-1945: katalog der Bücher und Broschüren. Hahner, M., *red.* Stuttgart, Metzler, 1989. xix,714p. DM398. (*Sonderveröffentlichungen der Deutschen Bibliothek, no. 16.*) ISBN: 3476006573.

Main entry listing of 6,907 entries. Includes materials of all types produced by German exiles; not confined to anti-Nazi items. *Class No:* 015(430)"19"

[328]

Gesamtverzeichnis des deutschsprachigen Schrifttums ausserhalb des Buchhandels (GVB) 1966-1980. Meer, W. van der *and* Schmuck, H., *bearbs*. München, Saur, 1988-91. 45v. DM18360. ISBN: 3598316305.

V.1-28 A-Z & Nachträge; v.29-42 Sachregister; v.43-45 Autoren-und Körperschaftenregister.

Contains 453,650 entries for German language items published outside the book trade irrespective of place of publication. Most items are drawn from Reihe B of *Deutsche Bibliographie* and Reihe B of *Deutsche Nationalbibliographie*. Designed to fill the gap in the bibliographic record between *Gesamtverzeichnis des deutschprachigen Schrifttums (GV) 1911-1965* and the 1981-85 cumulation of *Deutsche Bibliographie* which includes non-book trade items. *Class No:* 015(430)"19"

[329]

Gesamtverzeichnis des deutschsprachigen Schrifttums (GV) 1911-1965. Oberschelp, R., *hrsg and* Gorzny, W., *bearb.*. München, Verlag Dokumentation, 1976-81. 150v. DM22200. ISBN: 3794056000.

V.148 lists Zeitschriften; v.150 includes brief Nachträge (p.399-411).

Consolidates into one A-Z sequence of authors, anonymous titles and series *Deutsche Bücherverzeichnis, Deutsche Nationalbibliographie* and *Deutsche Bibliographie*. Also includes entries from dissertation lists (*e.g. Jahresverzeichnis der deutschen Hochschulschriften* and *Jahresverzeichnis der Schweizerischen Hochschulschriften* (*qq.v.*)). About 2,000,000 entries, plus 500,000 cross-references. Compiled photographically, merging roman and gothic scripts. Also available in microfiche (400 fiche. DM5600. ISBN: 3598304552). *Class No:* 015(430)"19"

Contemporary

[330]

Deutsche Nationalbibliographie: und Bibliographie der im Ausland erschienenen deutschsprachigen Veröffentlichungen. Frankfurt am Main, Buchhandler-Vereinigung, 1991-. Weekly, etc. DM2340.

Merges the pre-unification national bibliographies of the Federal Republic, *Deutsche Bibliographie,* and the Democratic Republic, *Deutsche Nationalbibliographie* (above). Although the new national bibliography has the title *Deutsche Nationalbibliographie,* in structure and scope it closely resembles *Deutsche Bibliographie* and is probably best regarded as its continuation.

Deutsche Nationalbibliographie is published in a number of series. The two major listings are Reihe A. *Monographien und Periodika des Verlagsbuchhandels - Wöchentliches Verzeichnis* (Weekly. ISSN: 09390421) and Reihe B. *Monographien und Periodika ausserhalb des Verlagsbuchhandels - Wöchentliches Verzeichnis* (Weekly. ISSN: 0939043x). Other series are: Reihe C. *Karten* (Quarterly. ISSN: 09390553); Reihe D. *Monographien und Periodika. Halbjahresverzeichnis* (Semi-annual (below)); Reihe E. *Monographien und Periodika. Fünfjahresverzeichnis* (Quinquennial (below)); Reihe G. *Fremdsprachige Germanica* (Quarterly (*q.v.*)); Reihe H. *Hochschulschriften* (Monthly (*q.v.*)); Reihe M. *Musikalen und Musikschriften* (Monthly. ISSN: 09390596); Reihe N. *Vorankündigungen Monographien und Periodika (CIP)* (Weekly. ISSN: 09390634); Reihe T. *Musiktorager* (Monthly. ISSN: 09390642).

Reihe A covers books, pamphlets (over 6p.), periodicals (new and ceased), government publications, microfilms,

....*(contd.)*

electronic publications, etc. available through the book trade. Reihe B covers similar non-book trade materials. Both are main entry listings in 79 UDC based class groups. Combined indexes to A and B, giving access by author, title, subject, keyword, ISBN and publisher, issued weekly and monthly. *Deutsche Nationalbibliographie* is also available online, incorporating records from *Deutsche Bibliographie* back to 1972, as part of BIBLIODATA through STN International. A CD-ROM version *Deutsche Nationalbibliographie Aktuell CD-ROM*, containing records from Reihe A,B,C,H and N, gives coverage since 1986 on 2 discs (backfile to 1992; current file 1993-). Updated bi-monthly, available outside German-speaking countries from Chadwyck-Healey (£1,225). *Class No:* 015(430)"312"

[331]

—Deutsche Nationalbibliographie: und Bibliographie der im Ausland erschienenen deutschsprachigen Veröffentlichungen. Reihe D. Monographien und Periodika - Halbjahverzeichnis. Frankfurt am Main, Buchhandler-Vereiningung, 1991-. Semi-annual. ISSN: 09424318.

Effectively continues *Deutsche Bibliographie Halbjahres-Verzeichnis,* 1951-90 (above).

Half-yearly cumulation of the weekly listings (Reihe A and B). Published in 2 pts: Teil 1. *Alphabetisches Titelverzeichnis*, containing full bibliographic citation; Teil 2. *Schlagwort- und Stichwortregister mit Systematishcer Übersicht der Schlagwörter,* providing subject and keyword indexing. Final cumulation provided by the quinquennial *Fünfjahrverzeichnis* (below). *Class No:* 015(430)"312"

[332]

—Deutsche Nationalbibliographie: und Bibliographie des im Ausland deutschsprachigen Veröffentlichungen. Reihe E. Monographien und Periodika - Fünfjahrverzeichnis. Frankfurt am Main, Buchhändler-Vereinigung, 1992-. Quinquennial. ISSN: 09424318.

Continues the final cumulations of the German national bibliography provided by *Deutsche Bücherverzeichnis* and *Deutsche Bibliographie. Fünfjahres-Verzeichnis* (above).

Cumulates material from all sections of the weekly lists except Reihe T. Same structure as the *Halbjahresverzeichnis* (above). 1986-90 published in 26v. 1992-96. Teil 1. *Alphabetisches Titelverzeichnis* 16v. Teil 2. *Schlagwort- und Stichwortregister mit Systematischer Übersicht der Schlagwörter* 12v. *Class No:* 015(430)"312"

[333]

Verzeichnis lieferbarer Bücher. Bücherverzeichnis im Autorenalphabet kumuliert mit Titel- und Stichwortregister mit Verweisung auf den Autor. [German books in print.] Frankfurt am Main, Buchhändler-Vereinigung, 1971-. Annual. DM898. ISSN: 00678899.

The 27th ed. (1997/98. 8v.) has 748,805 entries representing the output of 14,226 publishers in Germany, Austria, Switzerland and in the German language elsewhere. Arranged in a single alphabetical sequence of authors and anonymous titles, with title and keyword entries in italics. Publisher and ISBN prefix listings in the final volume. ISBN index, *Verzeichnis lieferbarer Bücher. ISBN-Register* (DM468), published separately. Updating half yearly supplement published between editions (DM226), also with separate ISBN index.

Verzeichnis lieferbarer Bücher is available on CD-ROM as *VLB Aktuell auf CD-ROM* from Bowker (monthly updates, £1035). Same search software as other Bowker products such as *Books in print*, with English-language interface. A further CD-ROM *VVB Aktuell auf CD-ROM* (£275, updated

.... *(contd.)*

annually), lists *c*.380,000 titles out of print since 1986. Records from *Verzeichnis lieferbarer Bücher* are also freely searchable over the Internet at http://www.buchhandel.de/.
Class No: 015(430)"312"

[334]

—Verzeichnis lieferbarer Bücher. Schlagwort-Verzeichnis. [German books in print subject guide.] Frankfurt am Main, Buchhändler-Vereinigung, 1979-. Annual.

The companion subject listing, now issued as a 6 v. set.
Class No: 015(430)"312"

Luxembourg

[335]

Bibliographie luxembourgeoise 1944/45-. Luxembourg, Bibliothèque nationale Luxembourg, 1946-. Annual. Fr450. ISSN: 02531631.

Classified in 20 subject groups, periodicals and audio materials separate. Author/anonymous title and subject indexes. Includes foreign works on Luxembourg and works by Luxembourg authors published abroad. The 1994 v. (1995. 360p.) carries 2,267 entries. *Class No:* 015(435.9)

[336]

BLUM, M. Bibliographie luxembourgeoise ou Catalogue raisonné de tous les ouvrages ou travaux littéraires publiés par des Luxembourgeois ou dans le Grand-Duché actuel de Luxembourg. Nouv. éd. par C. Hury. München, Kraus, 1981. 2v.

1st ed. 1902-32.

An A-Z list of works by Luxembourg authors or those published in Luxembourg. Index of subjects related to Luxembourg. *Class No:* 015(435.9)

Austria

[337]

Österreichische Bibliographie. Reihe A: Verzeichnis der österreichischen Neuerscheinungen. 1945-. Wien, Oesterreichische Nationalbibliothek, 1946-. Semi-monthly, with quarterly and annual indexes. ISSN: 10231862.

Frequency varies, semi-monthly since 1949.

Based on legal deposit at the Österreichische Nationalbibliothek. Arranged in 25 broad subject classes, each issue has an author and title keyword index cumulated quarterly and annually. Also available in microfilm and as a semi-annually updated CD-ROM (*Verbund-CD*). From 1987 excludes periodicals and printed music now covered in annual supplements *Sonderheft Zeitschriften* and *Sonderheft praktische Musik* (ISSN: 10231870). *Reihe B: verzeichnis der österreichischen hochschulschriften* (*q.v.*) is a separate quarterly listing of dissertations, also begun in 1987.
Class No: 015(436)

Czechoslovakia

[338]

Knihopis Českých a slovenských tisku od doby nejstarsí až do konce XVIII století. Praha, Nákl Československé Akademie Věd., 1925-1967. 2v.

V.1 to 1500. V.2 1500-1800 in 9 pts.

National retrospective bibliography of Czech and Slovak books. Index to v.2 issued as *Přispěvky ke knihopisu*. Voit, P. Praha, Státni Knihovna ČSR, 1985-88 10v.
Class No: 015(437)

[339]

ŠEFLOVÁ, L. Knihy českých a slovenských autorů vydané v zahraniči v letech 1948-1978. [Books by Czech and Slovak authors published out of Czechoslovakia, in exile, 1948-1978: a bibliography.] Brno, Nakladateslství Doplněk, 1993. 313p. ISBN: 8085765136.

Expands and updates *Bibliografie literatury vydané českými a slovenskými autory v zahraniči 1948-1972*. (1978).

Includes titles by Czech and Slovak authors issued abroad regardless of language of publication. 4,527 entries by author; name and broad term subject index.
Class No: 015(437)

Czech

[340]

Česká národní bibliografie: knihy. [Czech national bibliography: books.] Praha, Národní knihovna České republiky, 1960-. Monthly. ISSN: 02108898.

Title varies, as *Bibliograficky katalog ČSSR* 1960-89 (ISSN: 03231615); present title from 1994.

UDC listing with title, name, subject and corporate body indexes in each issue. About 12,000 items recorded annually. Other components of the Czech national bibliography include *Česká národní bibliografie. Hudebniny (printed music) Česká národní bibliografie. Clánky v českých časopisech* (*q.v.*) and *Česká národni bibliografie. Disertace a autoreferáty*, (*q.v.*). The entire national bibliographic listing, with records from 1983, is also available on a quarterly updated CD-ROM and through the Internet at http://www.nkp.cz. *Class No:* 015(437.1)

[341]

—Bibliografie české knižni tvorby 1945-1960. Praha, Národni knihovna v Praze, 1973-96. 5v. ISBN: 8070501839.

V.1-4 A-Z; v.5 supplementary material and indexing.

Thoroughly produced retrospective listing.
Class No: 015(437.1)

[342]

GRUNTORÁD, J. Katalog knih českého exilu 1948-1994: libri prohibiti. Praha, Primus, 1995. 394p. ISBN: 8085625555.

3,111 entries A-Z by author, contributors listed where applicable. Name index. *Class No:* 015(437.1)

Slovakia

[343]

Slovenská národná bibliografia. Séria A: knihy. [Slovak national bibliography: books.] Martin, Matica Slovenská, 1946-. Monthly. US$78. ISSN: 02319780.

Title varies, previously *Slovenské knihy*. The inter-war years are covered by *Bibliografia slovenských knih, 1919-1938* (Martin, Matica Slovenská, 1979. 3v.).

UDC classified list of new books. Author, title and subject indexes in each issue, cumulated annually. 3,850 entries in issues for 1997. Series B-K cover periodicals, maps, dissertations, audio-visual material, printed music, official documents, etc. *Class No:* 015(437.6)

Poland

[344]

BIBLIOTEKA NARODOWA. Instytut Bibliograficzny. **Bibliografia polska 1901-1939.** Warszawa, Biblioteka Narodowa, 1986-. ISBN: 8304018993.

V.1-2 published by Państwowe Wydawnictwo Naukowe.

Author and anonymous title list intended to fill gap

.... *(contd.)*
between *Bibliografia polska XIX* (below) and current national bibliography. Includes locations in Polish libraries; v.1-2 have separate indexes. Scheduled for completion in 20 v.; 28,647 items recorded to end of v.3 *Bol-Cek* (1993).
Class No: 015(438)

[345]
ESTREICHER, K.J.T. Bibliografia polska. Kraków, Czionkami Drukarni Universytetu Jagiellońskiego, 1870-1951. 34v.

The basic retrospective bibliography published in various series: 7v. (1872-82) provide an A-Z author list of titles published 1800-1880; 4v. (1882-90) form a chronological listing 1455-1799; 23v. (1891-1951) offer an exhaustive alphabetical list through the 15th-18th centuries, some with short annotations. Continued by *Bibliografia polska XIX, stuleccia; lata 1881-1900* (Kraków, 1906-16. 4v.). Coverage of the 19th century is now being updated by *Bibliografia polska XIX* (below). *Class No:* 015(438)

[346]
—UNIWERSYTET JAGIELLOŃSKI. Bibliografia polska XIX stulecia. Wyd.2. Kraków, Państwowe Wydawnictwo Naukowe, 1959-.

First published 1906-16 in 4v. (see above). Added title page in French. Reached v.XVI *Katar-Knaus* 1991.

Author list with very full detail and locations in Polish libraries. Printed on poor quality paper. *Class No:* 015(438)

[347]
POLISH LIBRARY. (London). **Bibliography of books in Polish** or relating to Poland: published outside Poland since September 1st 1939. Zabielska, J., *comp.* London, Polish Library, 1953-85. 4v.

V.I: 1939-51. (1953. 710p.); v.II: 1952-57 and supplements to 1939-51. (1959. ii,556p.); v.III: 1958-63 and supplements to 1939-57 (1966. [3],696p.). Resumed after a 20 year gap with V.IV: 1963-1967 and supplements to 1939-1963. (Jagodzinski, Z. *ed.* 1985. xv,265p. ISBN: 0902763105).

An author catalogue with full bibliographical details, contents listed where appropriate. Includes items in languages other than Polish written or compiled by Poles and items translated or adapted from the Polish. V.IV contains 3,344 numbered entries. *Class No:* 015(438)

[348]
Przewodnik bibliograficzny: urzedowy wykaz druków wydanych w Rzeczypospolitej Polskiej... Warszawa, Biblioteka Narodowa, 1946-. Weekly. ISSN: 00332518.

Continues *Urzędowy wykaz druków,* 1928-39.

The current national bibliography. Also lists foreign publications about Poland. Classified by UDC, entries numbered consecutively. Author/title index in each issue; annual author/title and subject indexes. The issues for 1995 record 12,752 items. A CD-ROM version is also available.
Class No: 015(438)

Hungary

[349]
Magyar nemzeti bibliográfia. Könyvek bibliográfiája. Budapest, Országos Széchényi Könyvtár, 1946-. Semi-monthly. ISSN: 01336843.

Also available on floppy disc (ISSN: 12196444). Issued monthly 1947-1960. Annual print cumulation *Magyar Könyvészet* 1961/62-1991 (ISSN: 01333496). 1945-1960 covered by *Magyar Könyvészet, 1945-1960: a Magyarországon nyomtatott könyvek szakositott jegyzéke*

.... *(contd.)*
(Budapest, Országos Széchényi Könyvtár, 1965-1968. 5v.).

Covers monographs, official publications and theses. Excludes serials (in separate series *Magyar nemzeti bibliográfia. Új periodikumok* (*q.v.*)), school books and reports. Issues for 1997 contain 8,824 entries in UDC based subject groups; name, title and ISBN indexes. Also available on CD-ROM for records 1992 to date (ISSN: 12182192); recent issues Internet accessible at http://www.oszk.hu/mnbkb. *Class No:* 015(439)

[350]
—Magyar Könyvészet, 1921-1944: a Magyarországon nyomtatott könyvek szakositott jegyzéke. Budapest, Országos Széchényi Könyvtár, 1980-92. 7v. ISBN: 9632002008.

Intended to combine into a unified whole the various incomplete Hungarian bibliographies of the inter-war period. UDC classified arrangement. *Class No:* 015(439)

[351]
MAGYAR TUDOMÁNYOS AKADÉMIA. Régi magyarországi nyomtatványok. Budapest, Akadémiaikiadó, 1971-.

V.1 1473-1600 (1971, 928p.). V.2 1601-1635 (1983, 856p.).

V.2 has 763 entries (v.1 869) including extensive notes, references and locations. Reproduces title pages. 10 indexes.

The 18th and 19th centuries are covered by *Magyar Könyvészet 1712-1920.* (Budapest, Országos Széchényi Könyvtár, 1969. 13v.). Originally published 1885-1942. Supplement to v. 1-4, 1971. *Class No:* 015(439)

[352]
Short-title catalogue of Hungarian books printed before 1851 in the British Library. Arnold, G., *comp.* London, British Library, 1995. viii,354p. £50;$120. ISBN: 0712303138.

Records the best collection of Hungariana outside Hungary. Books containing a significant amount of Hungarian published outside the country included. Standard British Library short-title catalogue format; 5 indexes.
Class No: 015(439)

France

16th Century

[353]
BRITISH MUSEUM. Department of Printed Books. **Short-title catalogue of books printed in France** and of French books printed in other countries from 1470 to 1600 now in the British Museum. London, British Museum, 1924. vii,491p.

The first of the series of British Museum (now British Library) short title catalogues for all those countries of the European continent where there was a considerable output of early printing.

Reprinted British Library, 1983 (£30. ISBN: 0712300252).

Author and anonymous title list of *c.*1,200 items, including many extremely rare, although it represents only perhaps one-sixth of the publications of the period.
Class No: 015(44)"15"

[354]
—BRITISH LIBRARY. Short-title catalogue of books printed in France and of French books printed in other countries from 1470 to 1600 now in the British Library. Supplement. London, British Library, 1986. viii,291p. £50. ISBN: 0712300643.

Adds *c.*1,650 new entries. Index of printers/publishers for original v. and supplement (p.89-291).
Class No: 015(44)"15"

[355]
MOREAU, B. Inventaire chronologique des éditions parisiennes du XVIe siècle. Paris, Imprimerie Municipale, (v.1-v.2); Abbeville, Paillart (v.3-); 1972-.

V.1: 1501-1510 (1972); v.2: 1511-1520 (1977); v.3: 1521-1530 (1985); v.4: 1531-1535 (1992).

Intended to be in 10 vols. Chronological listing of books published or sold in Paris. Gives author, short title, printer, date (month and day if known), format, locations (Europe and US) and references to other bibliographies. Author, printer, etc. indexes in each vol. 1,454 items recorded in v.4. *Class No:* 015(44)"15"

[356]
Répertoire bibliographique des livres imprimés en France au seizième siècle. Baden-Baden, Koerner, 1968-1980. 30v. (*Bibliotheca bibliographica Aureliana, 25... etc.*) ISBN: 3873208997.

Fasc. 1. *Bordeaux,* (1968. 72p.); fasc. 28. *Ambroise, Avranches, Beauvais,* (1978. 167p.). Fasc. 29 contains additions and corrections; fasc. 30 comprises indexes.

Covers approximately 9,600 books published throughout France with the exception of Paris. Arranged by town, then publisher and date.

2. éd. began publication 1989, same publisher, series, etc., collective ISBN: 3873208997. Vols. published: I. *Agen - Bordeaux* (1989); II. *Bourg-en-Bresse - Douai* (1992); III. *Embrun - Metz* (1993); IV. *Moncontour - Poissy* (1994); V. *Poitiers - Romans* (1996). *Class No:* 015(44)"15"

17th Century

[357]
BRITISH MUSEUM. Department of Printed Books. **A Short-title catalogue of French books 1601-1700** in the Library of the British Museum. Goldsmith, V.F., *comp.* Folkestone, Dawsons of Pall Mall, 1973. x,690p. ISBN: 0712905758.

Published in 7 fascs. 1969-72.

Over 20,000 entries for books 'written wholly or partly in French, no matter where published' or 'in no matter what language, published or printed at any place which today forms a part of metropolitan France' (Foreword p.vii). Standard British Museum STC format, with pressmarks. Addenda and corrigenda (p.561-92). Indexes: selected titles; translators, editors and annotators; printers and publishers; places named in imprints. *Class No:* 015(44)"16"

[358]
Répertoire bibliographique des livres imprimés en France au XVII siècle. Desgraves, L., *and others eds.* Baden-Baden, Koerner, 1978-. (*Bibliotheca bibliographica Aureliana, 75... etc.*) ISBN: 3873208989.

On the same plan as the publisher's earlier series for the 16th century (above). V.XIV *Bordeaux* (1988. 427p.) has 2,744 entries. Volumes cover individual towns (*e.g.* v.V Poitiers), groups of towns, or regions (*e.g.* v.XII-XIII Normandy). Each volume individually indexed. Latest published v.XX *Saint Omer* (1996. 246p.).
Class No: 015(44)"16"

18th Century

[359]
CONLON, P.M. Le Siècle des lumières: bibliographie chronologique. Genève, Librairie Droz, 1983-. (*Histoire des idées et critique littéraire, v.213... etc.*.)

To cover 1716-89. 17v. published to 1997: v.I 1716-22; v.II 1723-29; v.III 1730-36; v.IV 1737-42; v.V 1743-47; v.VI 1748-52; v.VII 1753-56; v.VIII 1757-60: v.IX Supplément 1716-60; v.X Index des titres; v.XI-XII Index des auteurs; v.XIII 1761-63; v.XIV 1764-66; v.XV 1767-69; v.XVI 1770-72; v.XVII 1773-75.

Preceded by Conlon, P.M. *Prélude en siècle des lumières en France: répertoire chronologique de 1680 à 1715* (Genève, Droz, 1979-75. 5v.).

Based on published and unpublished library catalogues. Includes titles published in French outside France. Entries give author, short title, place, publisher/printer, date, size, pagination and locations in European libraries. (NUC no. for North America). V.1 contains just over 5,000 entries. V.9 includes works previously overlooked and revised entries. '(V)ery sharp at excavating obscure titles in French printed in all parts of the world' (*American notes and queries,* v.23(7/8), March/April 1985, p.124).
Class No: 015(44)"17"

[360]
Répertoire bibliographique des livres imprimés en France au XVIII siècle. Baden-Baden, Koerner, 1988-. ISBN: 3873208970.

A further series continuing the publisher's efforts for the 16th and 17th centuries. V.I *Agen ... Luçon* (1988. 203p.). Latest vol. issued v.VII *Artois, Flandre, Picardie* (1997. 2pts.). *Class No:* 015(44)"17"

19th & 20th Centuries

[361]
Bibliographie de la France; journal général de l'imprimerie et de la librairie. Paris, Cercle de la Librairie, 1811-1971. Weekly.

Based on legal deposit. From 1857 in 3 pts. The main part *Bibliographie officielle* covered copyright material (books, pamphlets, etc.) received and catalogued by the Bibliothèque Nationale. Arrangement by ten broad subject groups with an author and title index. 7 irregularly published supplements from later dates: A. *Périodiques nouveaux;* B. *Gravures, estampes et photographies;* C. *Musique;* D. *Thèses;* E. *Atlas, cartes et plans;* F. *Publications officielles;* G. *Catalogue des ventes publiques.* Remaining parts provided book trade news *Chronique* and a classified list of publishers' new book announcements *Annonces.* The latter cumulated in *Livres du mois,* a classified list with author index, further cumulated quarterly, *Livres du trimestre* and semi-annually, *Livres du semestre.* As from January 1972 *Bibliographie de la France* merged with *Biblio* to form *Bibliographie de la France-Biblio* (below). Later reverted to separate publication and now continuing as *Bibliographie nationale française (below).*
Class No: 015(44)"18/19"

[362]
LORENZ, O.H. Catalogue général de la librairie française, 1840-1925. Paris, Lorenz, 1867-1945. 34v.

Often referred to as 'Lorenz'. The standard key to French books of the period continuing Quérard (below). The first sequence covers 1840-65; later volumes are limited to 3, 4 or 6 years. In each case author and anonymous title entry supported by a broad subject list. Includes some theses and annuals in addition to books and pamphlets, and some

.... *(contd.)*
French language Belgian and Swiss publications. Brief biographical notes for authors; cross-references to works in earlier volumes by the same author.
Class No: 015(44)"18/19"

[363]
QUÉRARD, J.M. La France littéraire, ou Dictionnaire bibliographique des savants, historiens et gens de lettres de la France, ainsi que des littérateurs étrangers qui ont écrit en français plus particulièrement pendant les XVIIIe et XIXe siècles. Paris, Didot, 1827-64.
V.1-10, authors, A-Z; v.11-12 publ. (1854-64) contain additions and corrections and real names of authors of anonymous and pseudonymous works. Reprinted, Paris, Maisonneuve & Larose, 1964.
Lists over 150,000 items. The standard bibliography for the period covering to 1826. Continued by Quérard, J.M. and others *La Littérature française contemporaine, 1827-1849* (Paris, Daguin, 1842-57. 6v.).
Class No: 015(44)"18/19"

20th Century

[364]
Biblio: catalogue des ouvrages parus en langue française dans le monde entier. Paris, Hachette, 1933-71. Annual.
Cumulated the bibliographical section in the monthly (10pa.) periodical *Biblio*. Based on *Bibliographie de la France: Annonces* but differing from it in including French books published elsewhere in the world (*e.g.* Belgium, Switzerland, Canada). Dictionary arrangement, full bibliographical detail under author, with added title and subject entries. Continued in part by *Bibliographie de la France - Biblio* (below). *Class No:* 015(44)"19"

[365]
—Bibliographie de la France - Biblio. Paris, Cercle de la Librairie, 1972-79. Weekly.
A combination of *Bibliographie de la France* (*q.v.*) and *Biblio*, assuming the numbering and basic structure of the former. From 1976 the main section and 4 supplements *Publications en série, Publications officielles, Musique* and *Atlas, cartes et plans* reverted to the title *Bibliographie de la France* (now, *Bibliographie nationale française* (below)). The weekly trade list section continued to appear weekly, cumulating monthly (*Les Livres du mois*), quarterly, semi-monthly and annually (*Les Livres de l'année* (below)) until superseded by *Livres hebdo* and its cumulations in 1979.
Class No: 015(44)"19"

[366]
Catalogue général des ouvrages en langue française 1926-1929. Dermineur, B., *ed.* München, Saur, 1987-89. 9v. ISBN: 3598309902.
Covers the gap between Lorenz (*q.v.*) and the 1930 v. of *La Librairie française* (below). 70,000 entries: 3v. author catalogue, with supplementary 2v. title and 4v. subject listings. *Class No:* 015(44)"19"

[367]
—Catalogue général des ouvrages en langue française 1930-1933. Dermineur, B., *ed.* München, Saur, 1993-95. ISBN: 3598328613.
Similar format to the 1926-29 set; 7 v. author catalogue, with supplementary 3v. title and 5v. subject listings.
Intended to complete filling of the gap between Lorenz and *La Libraire française* by extending coverage to publication of the 1933/45 v. of the latter. *Class No:* 015(44)"19"

[368]
La Librairie française. Tables decennales: répertoire cumulatif des livres de l'anne-Biblio. 1930-1966/75. Paris, Cercle de la Librairie, 1930-79.
Initial v. as *Librairie française, catalogue général des ouvrages en vente au 1. jan 1930* (1931. 3v.). Further volumes for 1933/45 (1946. 3v.), then decennial 1946/55 (1956. 3v.), 1956/65 (1966. 4v.) and 1966/75 (1979. 6v. ISBN 2765402485).
The 1956/65 sequence devotes 2v. to authors, A-I, J-Z and 2v. to titles. Considered inferior in detail and completeness to *Bibliographie de la France* and *Biblio*.
Class No: 015(44)"19"

[369]
—Les Livres de l'année. 1933-79. Paris, Cercle de la Librairie, 1938-80. Annual.
Issues 1971-79 as *Les Livres de l'année-Biblio.* Early volumes cover 1933/38, 1946/48 and 1949/50; annual from 1950. 1939-45 not published. *Un An de nouveautés* (1980-) (*q.v.*) provides continuing coverage.
Cumulates the listings in the *Annonces* section of *Bibliographie de la France*. In turn cumulates into *La Librairie française. Tables decennales.* (above).
Class No: 015(44)"19"

Contemporary

[370]
Bibliographie nationale française: bibliographie établie par la Bibliothèque Nationale de France à partir des documents déposés au titre du dépôt légal. Paris, Bibliothèque Nationale, 1976-. Semi-monthly, etc. FFr3165.
Title varies: published as *Bibliographie de la France* until 1989. Continues the earlier series *Bibliographie de la France - Biblio* (1972-79) and *Bibliographie de la France: journal générale de l'imprimerie et de la librairie* (*qq.v.*). Publisher also varies: Éditions du Cercle de la Librarie until 1989.
Published in 5 series. The main series *Livres* (ISSN: 11423250) is now issued every 15 days (weekly until 1989), with 3 cumulative indexes on microfiche and an annual printed index. Supplementary series: I. *Publications en série* (*q.v.*) (monthly); II. *Publications officielles* (*q.v.*) (bi-monthly); III. *Musique* (3 pa., ISSN: 11423285); IV. *Atlas, cartes et plans* (semi-annual, ISSN: 11422993).
Based on legal deposit. 48,816 numbered entries in the *Livres* issues for 1997. Full cataloguing for each item with ISBN and price. Arrangement by simplified UDC classification; author, title and specific heading subject indexes in each issue, cumulated as outlined above. Available as a CD-ROM database from Chadwyck-Healey, *Bibliographie nationale française depuis 1970 sur CD-ROM.* 1,300,000 records (2 discs), English menu and search screens. Updates issued bimonthly, annual subscription £1,145. Records from *Bibliographie nationale française* are also Internet accessible as part of the Bibliothéque Nationale online catalogue, *BN-OPALE.* *Class No:* 015(44)"312"

[371]
Livres disponibles: ouvrages disponibles publiés en langue française dans le monde. Paris, Electre, 1977-. Annual. FFr3990.
English title *French books in print.* Continues *Le Catalogue de l'édition française,* published in 5 editions 1971-76.
Published as 3v. in 6 pts.: Author; Title; Subject.
The 1998 ed. lists 402,875 French language titles published anywhere in the world, including 31,501 published

....*(contd.)*

July 1996-June 1997. Full entry data in all 3 sequences: title, subtitle, author(s), edition, publisher, year, pagination, collection, ISBN and price. Subject sequence arranged by DDC classification with 14,000 term keyword index. Excludes pamphlets and limited circulation works. Directory of publishers/distributors and list of series and their publishers in each sequence. Microfiche, online (via Electre WWW site at http://www.electre.com/) and CD-ROM versions available, the latter under the title *Electre*. Electronic versions include out-of-print and multimedia titles. Records for in print French books are also freely accessible through the Internet as part of the *Alapage* service at http://www.alapage.tm.fr/. *Class No:* 015(44)"312"

[372]

Livres hebdo. Paris, Livres Hebdo, 1979-. Weekly (44 pa.). FFr2310. ISSN: 02940000.

Effectively continues the *Chronique* and *Annonces* sections of *Bibliographie de la France* (above) (cover title of earlier issues *Bibliographie de la France - Biblio*).

Resembles Whitaker's *Bookseller*. Each issue includes a section *Bibliographie de la France. Les livres de la semaine*. Cumulated in *Les Livres du mois* (Monthly. ISSN: 02940027), a DDC based subject listing, giving bibliographical detail, price, ISBN and a short (20-50 word) description. *Class No:* 015(44)"312"

[373]

—Un An de nouveautés. 1980-. Paris, Livres Hebdo, 1981-. Annual. ISSN: 02941090.

Continues coverage provided by *Les Livres de l'année* (above).

Final cumulation of the listings in *Livres hebdo* and *Les Livres du mois* (above). Interim cumulations issued as *Trois mois de nouveautés* and *Six mois de nouveautés*. The 1997 v. (855p.) has 30,293 numbered entries in Dewey based subject sections (Actualitiés, reportages, faits divers ... Zoologie) with title, author and subject indexes.
Class No: 015(44)"312"

Monaco

[374]

LAVAGNA, P. Bibliographie nationale de la Principauté de Monaco 1761-1986. Monaco, 1988. xxii,345p. FFr350.

Author list of nearly 10,000 items. Separate sequence of serial publications by title (p.337-45). No indexes. Most publications issued in Monaco are also listed in *Bibliographie national française* (*q.v*) and its predecessors.
Class No: 015(449.49)

Italy

16th Century

[375]

Biblia: biblioteca del libro italiano antico. Quondam, A., *ed.*. Milano, Editrice Bibliografica, 1996-.

New publication aiming to record works published in Italy up to 1600 as well as books published in Italian elsewhere. 20 vols. projected in 4 thematic series: La Biblioteca volgare; La Biblioteca umanistica; La Bilioteca religiosa; La Biblioteca delle professioni. Commenced publication with initial vol. of La Biblioteca volgare, *Libri di poesia* (xxii,488p. L200,000. ISBN: 887075457X), listing 5,270 titles. Largely based on secondary sources and not a substitute for other works such as *Le Edizioni italiane del XVI secolo* (below). *Class No:* 015(450)"15"

[376]

BRITISH MUSEUM. Short-title catalogue of books printed in Italy and of Italian books printed in other countries from 1465 to 1600 now in the British Museum. London, British Library, 1958. viii,992p.

Reprinted 1986 (ISBN: 071230097X).

Author list of *c.*18,000 entries (about 25% of the known books), with an appended list of 'Books destroyed during the war 1939-45'. Index of 1,300 printers and publishers, with dates and brief titles. *Class No:* 015(450)"15"

[377]

—BRITISH LIBRARY. Short-title catalogue of books printed in Italy and of Italian books printed in other countries from 1465 to 1600 in the British Library. Supplement. London, British Library, 1986. 152p. £25. ISBN: 0712300945.

1,200 books added since 1958 or omitted from original ed., plus several pages of corrigenda. Index to places in which books listed in this and earlier v. were printed. Also lists items recorded as destroyed 1939-45, since replaced.
Class No: 015(450)"15"

[378]

ISTITUTO CENTRALE PER IL CATALOGO UNICO DELLE BIBLIOTECHE ITALIANE E PER LE INFORMAZIONI BIBLIOGRAFICHE. Le Edizioni italiane del XVI secolo: censimento nazionale. Roma, ICCU, 1985-. L124,800 per v. ISBN: 8871070100.

Short entry author catalogue with locations in *c.*550 Italian libraries. Each v. includes co-author, translator and printer/publisher indexes. Latest published v.IV *Chiesa di S. Barbara-Czernius* (1996. xxiii,327p.).
Class No: 015(450)"15"

[379]

Short-title catalogue of books printed in Italy and of books in Italian printed abroad 1501-1600 held in selected North American libraries. Marshall, R.G., *ed.* Boston, Mass., G.K. Hall, 1970. 3v. ISBN: 0816108528.

*c.*15,000 entries for items in 40 North American libraries.
Class No: 015(450)"15"

17th Century

[380]

BRITISH LIBRARY. Catalogue of seventeenth century Italian books in the British Library. London, British Library, 1986. 3v. £150. ISBN: 0712300651.

V.1 A-L. V.2 M-Z. V.3 Indexes.

Follows the pattern of the 1475-1600 catalogue (*q.v.*). *c.*15,000 entries. Strong on administrative printing for the Papacy and Venice. Headings are those required by the superseded cataloguing rules of the British Museum, but with modifications for anonymous titles. Index v. in 4 sequences, giving access by publisher, printer, place of imprint and ficticious imprints. Appended list of books destroyed by enemy action 1939-1945.
Class No: 015(450)"16"

[381]

BRUNI, R.L. *and* **EVANS, D.W. Italian 17th century books in Cambridge libraries:** a short-title catalogue. [Firenze], Olschki, 1997. 589p. L140,000. (*Biblioteca di bibliografia italiana, 144.*) ISBN: 8822244737.

Lists 5,718 titles, 4,897 of which are held in the main university library. Title, name, printer, etc. indexes.
Class No: 015(450)"16"

[382]

MICHEL, S.P. *and* **MICHEL, P.H. Répertoire des ouvrages imprimés en langue italienne au XVIIe siècle** conservés dans les bibliothèques de France. Paris, Éditions du Centre National de la Recherche Scientifique, 1967-1985. 8v. FFr90 (v.1-6), FFr100 (v.7), FFr200 (v.8). ISBN: 2222009553, v.1.

Vols. 6-8 by S.P. Michel only. V.1-2 appeared in revised eds. 1972-1975. V.8 contains supplement.

Locates Italian books of the period in French libraries.

Class No: 015(450)"16"

[383]

—MICHEL, S.P. *and* MICHEL, P.H. Répertoire des ouvrages imprimés en langue italienne au XVIIe siècle. Firenze, Olschki, 1970-1979. 2v. (V.1 474p.plates. V.2 484p.plates). (*Biblioteca di bibliografia italiana, 59,87.*) ISBN: 8822228502, v.2.

V.1 A-BAZ; v.2 BE-BZ. V.2 by S.P. Michel alone.

More comprehensive than the 8v. set above. Author arrangement with biographical notes. Does not locate copies.

Class No: 015(450)"16"

19th Century

[384]

CLIO: catalogo dei libri italiani dell'Ottocento (1801-1900). [Catalogue of nineteenth century Italian books (1801-1900).] Roma, Editrice Bibliografica, 1991. 19v. (xxii,16129p.). L8,500,000. ISBN: 8870752003.

V.1-6 Author/anonymous title; v.7-12 Publisher; v.13-18 Place of publication; v.19 Index.

Records 420,898 titles, excluding most serials and government publications. Brief entries in 3 col. arrangement. Locates copies in the Biblioteca nazionale centrale at Florence, or elsewhere if not in this collection. Index v. provides access by secondary author and illustrator. More titles than Pagliani (below), but lacks subject indexing.

Class No: 015(450)"18"

[385]

PAGLIANI, A. Catálogo generale della libreria italiana... Milano, Assoc. Tip. Libr. Ital., 1901-22. 6v.

Reprinted Vaduz, Kraus, 1964.

The basic 6v. work, comprising a 3v. author and title sequence and a 3v. subject index, covers the period 1847-99, listing books and pamphlets in Italian published in Italy or other countries. 4 decennial author and title supplements, published 1912-58, extend coverage to 1940. A subject index to the 1st and 2nd suppts. was published in 4v., 1933-40. *Class No:* 015(450)"18"

20th Century

[386]

Bollettino delle pubblicazioni italiane ricevute per diritto di stampa dalla Biblioteca Nazionale Centrale di Firenze. Firenze, Biblioteca Nazionale Centrale, 1886-1957. 72v. Monthly.

The fullest Italian bibliography for the period covering all types of material (although the final section, 'Pubblicazioni minori non descritte', merely lists the number of certain publications considered too slight for individual entry). Classified in 22 subject fields, with indexes of subjects and authors, cumulated annually. Continued by *Bibliografia nazionale italiana* (*q.v.*). *Class No:* 015(450)"19"

[387]

—Catálogo cumulative 1886-1957 del Bollettino delle pubblicazioni italiane ricevute per diritto di stampa dalla Biblioteca Nazionale Centrale di Firenze. Nendeln, Kraus Reprint, 1968. 41v.

A computer-produced cumulation of the 640,000 entries in the monthly *Bollettino* (above), in one A-Z sequence. V.39 includes anonyma (congresses, conferences etc.) and a list of periodicals. V.40-1 constitute an index of secondary authors.

Class No: 015(450)"19"

Contemporary

[388]

Bibliografia nazionale italiana: nuova serie del *Bollettino delle pubblicazioni italiane ricevute per diritto di stampa.* Roma, Istituto centrale per il catalogo unico delle biblioteche italiane e per le informazioni bibliografiche, 1958-. Monthly, with annual cumulation. ISSN: 00061077.

As stated in the subtitle, continues *Bollettino delle pubblicazioni italiane.* (above).

Compiled by the Biblioteca nazionale centrale, Florence. Since 1993 main series with subtitle *Monografie*; further series for periodicals (*Periodici*) and theses (*Tesi di dottorato*) (*qq.v.*).

Main series covers monographs, pamphlets, significant official publications, maps and atlases and some audiovisual material. Excludes items of limited interest or those produced for internal use by organizations. Monthly issues in Dewey classified order, with author/title, subject and publisher indexes. The well-produced and generously set out annual cumulations (*Catalogo alfabetico annuale* ISSN: 05231876) have an alphabetical main entry arrangement, with subject and class no. indexes. Searchable online through Camera dei Deputati d'Italia, Servizio per la Documentazione. Also available on CD-ROM as *Bibliografia nazionale italiana su CD-ROM* containing records from 1958. Disc, updated quarterly and with English-language interface, marketed outside Italy by Chadwyck-Healey (£1,095). *Class No:* 015(450)"312"

[389]

Catálogo dei libri in commercio. Milano, Editrice Bibliografica, 1970-. Annual.

As *Catalogo dei libri italiani in commercio* 1970-74. Frequency varies, recent issues annual.

A catalogue of Italian books in print, issued by the Associazione Italiana Editori. Full listings in separate author, title and subject vols. Author and subject vols. include lists of publishers, ISBN prefixes and series; subject v. arranged under detailed subject headings. 1997 set records 322,008 titles available from 2,825 publishers. Also available on CD-ROM as *Archivo libri italiani su calcolatore elettronico* (*ALICE*), updated quarterly. Marketed by Bowker-Saur in UK as *Italian books in print* (£1,125), the DOS CD-ROM offers 9 search paths and includes an English interface.

Class No: 015(450)"312"

[390]

I Libri: bimestrale di bibliografia italiana. Firenze, Casalini libri, 1994-. Bimonthly. ISSN: 1122553x.

Listing of new Italian books arranged by abridged Dewey classification. Author/editor, title and series indexes in each issue, cumulated annually. More prompt than *Bibliografia nazionale italiana* (above), recording in excess of 10,000 publications each year. *Class No:* 015(450)"312"

Malta

[391]

Bibljografija nazzjonali ta' Malta. 1983-. [Malta national bibliography. 1983-.] Valetta, National Library of Malta, 1984-. Annual (irregular).

Covers works published in Malta, about Malta or by Maltese published abroad. The 1993/94 issue (1997. 103p.) has 771 entries in Dewey classified order with author/title/ series and subject indexes. *Class No:* 015(458.2)

Spain

[392]

PALAU Y DULCET, A. Manual del librero hispanoamericano: bibliografía general española e hispanoamericana desde la invención de la imprenta hasta nuestros tiempos con el valor comercial de los impresos descritos. 2. ed. corr. y aum. por el autor. Barcelona, Librería Palau; Oxford, Dolphin, 1948-1978. 28v.

A valuable and comprehensive author list of 381,827 numbered items. Coverage is of Spanish and Hispano-American publications from the beginning of printing to the mid 20th century. *Class No:* 015(460)

[393]

—PALAU CLAVERAS, A. Addenda y corrigenda o volumen complementario... . Barcelona, Editorial Palau y Dulcet, 1990-.

V.1 *A-Azzawac* (xv,648p. ISBN: 8440475150); additional material includes locations in Spanish libraries. No further vols. have appeared. *Class No:* 015(460)

[394]

—PALAU CLAVERAS, A. Indice alfabetico de titulos-materias, correcciones, conexiones y adiciones del Manuel del librero hispanoamericano de Antonio Palau y Dulcet. Empuries, Palacete Palau Dulcet; Oxford, Dolphin, 1981-1987. 7v. ISBN: 8430045722, vol. 1.

Index of titles and subjects, corrections, references and addenda. *Class No:* 015(460)

Catalan

[395]

SIMON PALMER, M. del C. Bibliografía de Cataluña: notas para su realizacion. Madrid, CSIC, 1980-82. 2v. (*Cuadernos bibliograficos, 41, 42.*) ISBN: 8400046285.

V.1 1481-1765; v.2 1766-1820).

5,644 items listed. Chronological arrangement; name, place of printing and subject indexes.
Class No: 015(460)=499

16th Century

[396]

BRITISH LIBRARY. Catalogue of books printed in Spain and of Spanish books printed elsewhere in Europe before 1601 now in the British Library. Rhodes, D.E., *comp.* 2nd ed. London, British Library, 1989. viii,294p. £50. ISBN: 071230150x.

Previous ed. 1921, reprinted as part of *Short-title catalogue of Spanish, Spanish-American and Portuguese books printed before 1601 now in the British Museum,* (London, British Museum, 1966. xv,169p.).

Retains the short-title catalogue format, about 3,300 entries. Includes references to numbers used in Norton's *A Descriptive catalogue of printing in Spain* (below). Indexes: Spanish towns; Foreign countries with Spanish printing; Printers and publishers. *Class No:* 015(460)"15"

[397]

NORTON, F.J. A Descriptive catalogue of printing in Spain and Portugal 1501-1520. Cambridge, Cambridge University Press, 1978. xxiii,581p. 1 facsim. ISBN: 0521211360.

Details of authors, translators, publishers. Index of persons other than authors. *Class No:* 015(460)"15"

17th Century

[398]

Catálogo colectivo del patrimonio bibliográfico español. Siglo XVII. Madrid, Arco, 1988-.

At head of title Dirección General del Libro y Bibliotecas. Biblioteca Nacional.

V.3, (1992. 534p. Ptas.7,930. ISBN: 8476351070) covering the letter C, brings the total number of items recorded to 4,706. Full bibliographical detail with locations in the Biblioteca Nacional and other Madrid libraries. Author, place of printing and illustrator indexes in each v.

The Internet accessible database *Catálogo colectivo del patrimonio bibliográfico español* (http://www.mcu.es.ccpb/ index.html) contains records for over 200,000 titles including those from the seventeenth-century.
Class No: 015(460)"16"

[399]

GOLDSMITH, V.F. A Short-title catalogue of Spanish and Portuguese books, 1601-1700 in the Library of the British Museum (The British Library - Reference Division). Folkestone, Dawsons of Pall Mall, 1974. vi,250p. £35. ISBN: 0712906010.

Describes pamphlets and printed documents as well as *c.*7,000 books. Includes books published in Spanish or Portuguese outside of the Iberian Peninsula. 'Although a valuable compilation, this catalogue shows signs of having been put together at great speed and with little expertise' (*Times literary supplement,* no. 3783, 4th September 1974, p.958). *Class No:* 015(460)"16"

[400]

SIMÓN DÍAZ, J. Impresos del siglo XVII: bibliografía selectiva por materias de 3,500 ediciones príncipes en lengua castellana. Madrid, Instituto Miguel de Cervantes. Consejo Superior de Investigaciones Cientificas, 1972. xvi,926p.

Classed listing of 3,500 especially significant titles: author and subject indexes. *Class No:* 015(460)"16"

18th Century

[401]

AGUILAR PIÑAL, F. Bibliografía de autores españoles del siglo XVIII. Madrid, Consejo Superior de Investigaciones Cientificas, 'Miguel de Cervantes', 1981-95. 8v. ISBN: 8400053176.

Arranged by author, entries including locations in Spanish and some overseas libraries. Name, subject, place of publication, dramatic works and printer indexes in each volume. Does not include Latin American authors.
Class No: 015(460)"17"

[402]

BRITISH LIBRARY. Short-title catalogue of eighteenth-century Spanish books in the British Library. London, British Library, 1994. 3v. plates. £150. ISBN: 0712303421.

V.I A-L; v.II M-Z; v.III Indexes.

Covers material acquired up to the end of 1992. 'The term "Spanish books" embraces all books printed in Spain, in whatever language, and all books in Spanish printed elsewhere in Europe. Books printed in Latin America have

....(contd.)
been excluded' (v.I, p.viii). About 17,500 items recorded; entries include BL shelfmarks. V.III has indexes by subject, engravers, printers and booksellers, and places.

Supplemented by Whitehead H.G. *comp. Eighteenth-century Spanish chapbooks in the British Library: a descriptive catalogue* (London, British Library 1997. xiv,145p. 30 plates. £55. ISBN: 0712345167).
Class No: 015(460)"17"

19th Century

[403]

Catálogo colectivo del patrimonio bibliográfico español. Siglo XIX. Madrid, Arco, 1989-. Ptas.7,606 per v.

Inventory of nineteenth century Spanish books. Letter A completed in 3 v. 1989, 8,003 items recorded. Includes locations in Madrid libraries. Index v. (name, title, publisher and printer) issued 1991.

The Internet accessible database *Catálogo colectivo del patrimonio bibliográfico español* (http://wwwmcu.es.ccpb/index.html) contains records for over 200,000 titles, including many from the nineteenth-century.
Class No: 015(460)"18"

20th Century

[404]

Catálogo general de la librería española, 1931-1950. Madrid, Instituto Nacional del Libro Español, 1957-65. 4v.

Arranged under authors and anonyma A-Z.

Preceded by *Catálogo general de la librería española e hispanoamericana, 1901-1930* (1932-51. 5v.), which also included Spanish language titles published in Latin America.
Class No: 015(460)"19"

[405]

El Libro español. Madrid, Instituto Nacional del Libro Español, 1958-86. Monthly, (frequency varied). ISSN: 0224273x.

Ceased with no.336/339, 1986. Formed from the merger of *Bibliografía hispánica* (1942-57. Monthly) and *Novedades editoriales españolas* (1958-63. Monthly). *Bibliografía hispánica* was preceded by *Bibliografía española* (Madrid, Asociación de la Librería, 1901-22. Annual) and its successor, *Bibliografía general española e hispano-americana* (Monthly, 1923-36; bi-monthly, 1941-42).

Booktrade/library world journal which listed new books by author, title and subject in a separate supplement. Retains some value due to the interruptions in *Bibliografía española* (below). *Class No:* 015(460)"19"

[406]

—Bibliotheca hispanica: revista de información y orientación bibliográficas. Madrid, Consejo Superior de Investigaciones Cientificas, 1943-73. Quarterly.

Later issues in 2 sections: *Letras,* covering humanities and social sciences and *Ciencias,* covering science, medicine and commerce. Entries include brief annotations of 25-100 words. Annual index. *Class No:* 015(460)"19"

Contemporary

[407]

Bibliografía española: monografías. Madrid, Biblioteca Nacional, 1958-. Monthly, with annual cumulated index. Ptas.20,000. ISSN: 1133858x.

Current title from 1993 (previously as *Bibliografía española* ISSN: 05253675). Separate supplements for non-monographic materials including *Bibliografía española: publicaciones periódicas* (*q.v.*). Publication interrupted at various times, coverage not available for 1964-66 and 1991. Annual cumulations until 1992, now replaced by annual cumulated indexes (ISSN: 11338563).

UDC classified listing with separate section for children's materials. Indexing by author, subject, title and series. Gives fairly comprehensive coverage of items published in Spain, the 1996 issues containing 43,342 titles. Also available online (monthly updating) and on CD-ROM as *Bibliografía española desde 1976 en CD-ROM* (quarterly updating, distributed by Chadwyck-Healey) with an English language interface. *Class No:* 015(460)"312"

[408]

Libros españoles en venta. Madrid, Agencia Española del ISBN, Ministerio de Cultura, 1973-. Biennial. Ptas.30,000. ISSN: 02146304.

Title varies slightly. Frequency also varies; initially irregular, then biennial or annual. Now issued in 5v.; v.1-3 *Autores-titulos; v.4-5 Materias.*

The Spanish 'books in print'. About 250,000 titles listed, including those in Catalan, Basque and Galacian. Gives only very limited coverage of Spanish language Latin American books (for these see *Libros en venta: en Américan Latina y España* (*q.v.*)). Entries, with price and ISBN, in condensed 5 col. format. Subject volumes arranged by 554 UDC classifications. List of publishers and ISBN prefixes in v.1. Updated by supplements, *e.g. Addenda 1997* (cxliii,1495p.). Also available as online and CD-ROM databases (Ptas.50,000). Updated monthly online, CD-ROM issued quarterly. *Class No:* 015(460)"312"

Catalan

[409]

Bibliografia nacional de Catalunya. 1982-. Barcelona, Departament de Cultura de la Generalitat de Catalunya, 1983-. Quarterly (some issues semi-annual). ISSN: 0212307x.

UDC classified listing of new titles published in Catalonia. Records about 7-8,000 items annually, author/title and subject indexes in each issue. Currency disappointing, the 2nd issue for 1991, listing mostly 1988 and 1989 publications, not issued until 1994.
Class No: 015(460)"312"=499

[410]

—Llibres espanyols en venda. Català. [Libros españolas en venta. Catalan.] Madrid, Agencia Española del ISBN, Ministerio de Cultura, 1972-. Annual. ISSN: 11321210.

Issued as a supplement to *Libros españolas en venta* (above). *Class No:* 015(460)"312"=499

Andorra

[411]

DIUMENJÓ I NELLO, I. *and* FONOLLEDA I PÉREZ, P.M. **Editer: catàleg dels llibres editats e Andorra.** Encamp, Comú d'Encamp, 1995. 96p. ISBN: 9992011157.

Produced with the collaboration of the Biblioteca Nacional d'Andorra.

Lists 876 publications by category; author, title and publisher indexes. *Class No:* 015(467.2)

Portugal

[412]

ACADEMIA DAS CIÊNCIAS DE LISBOA. Bibliografia geral portuguesa. Lisboa, Imprensa Nacional, 1941-83. 3v.

V.1-v.2 *Século XV* (1941-42); v.3 *Século XVI* (1983).

V.1 is devoted to 125 Portuguese incunabula and their later editions, while v.2 deals with 15th century Portuguese authors whose works were printed or otherwise distributed abroad. V.3 contains detailed descriptions of 16th century imprints. Each v. individually indexed. *Class No:* 015(469)

[413]

BIBLIOTECA NACIONAL. (PORTUGAL). Catálogo dos impressos de tipografia portuguesa do século XVI a colecção do Biblioteca Nacional. Lisboa, Biblioteca Nacional, 1990. 402p. illus. Esc2000. ISBN: 9725650743.

Introdução, organização e indices por M. A. Proença Simões.

Main entry catalogue of 928 items. Includes full descriptions and notes on copy variations. Many more entries than the corresponding British Museum catalogue (below). Author/secondary author, anonymous title, printer/publisher, date, etc., indexes. *Class No:* 015(469)

[414]

Boletim de bibliografia portuguesa. Monografias, 1935-87. Lisboa, Biblioteca Nacional, 1937-89. Quarterly (irregular). ISSN: 02533413.

Final issues in 3 series: *Monografias* (as above); *Documentos não textuais*, covering maps, plans, prints, etc.; *Publicações em série*, covering serials. Prior to 1981 issued monthly as one series under the title *Boletim de bibliografia portuguesa;* not published 1940-42 and 1952-54, issued annually until 1951.

Covered the publishing output of Portugal, as deposited at the Biblioteca Nacional, together with works produced overseas about Portugal, or by Portuguese authors. Included pamphlets and government publications. UDC classified arrangement; author, title and subject indexes.
Class No: 015(469)

[415]

BRITISH MUSEUM. Department of Printed Books. **Short-title catalogue of Portuguese books printed before 1601,** now in the British Museum. Thomas, H., *comp*. London, Trustees of the British Museum, 1940. viii,43p.

Reprinted as part of *Short-title catalogue of Spanish, Spanish-American and Portuguese books printed before 1601 now in the British Museum* (London, British Museum, 1966. xv,169p.).

An author list of *c.*300 items. Printer list, p.21-39; index of printers and booksellers, p.41-43. *Class No:* 015(469)

[416]

SILVA, I.F. da. Dicionário bibliographico portuguêz, estudos ... aplicaveis a Portugal e ao Brasil. Lisboa, Impr. Nacional, 1858-1972. 24v.

Original 7v. 1858-62; supplements v.8-20 1867-1911; v.22 A-AY 1923 (v.21 not bibliographic); *Indice alfabético* 1938; v.23 *Guia bibliografica* and v.24 *Aditamentos* both 1972.

Bio-bibliography of Portuguese books up to the 19th century. Authors, A-Z, by forenames. Nearly 70,000 items in all. *Class No:* 015(469)

Contemporary

[417]

Bibliografia nacional portuguesa em CD-ROM. Lisboa, Instituto da Biblioteca Nacional e do Livro/Base Nacional de Dados Bibliograficos, 1996-. CD-ROM database, updated semi-annually. £325. ISSN: 08733171.

Distr. by Chadwyck-Healey.

Replaces the printed *Boletim de bibliografia portuguesa* (above) providing records for books from 1980, plus theses and other academic works produced within Portuguese universities. The database *Porbase* contains records for more than 750,000 books held by Portuguese libraries, including those listed in *Bibliografia nacional portuguesa.* The database is Internet accessible at http://www.ibl.pt/english/porbase (English language version).
Class No: 015(469)"312"

[418]

Livros disponíves. Lisboa, Associação Portuguesa de Editores e Livreiros, 1985-. Biennial. ISSN: 08706093.

Initial v. as *Catálogo dos livros disponíves.* Interim updating *Actualização e addenda* issued between full editions.

Guide to Portuguese language books in print. The 1997 ed. lists 52,056 works in author, title and subject volumes, the latter arranged by UDC. Data includes bibliographical detail, physical description, price and ISBN. Subject v. also contains lists of series, publishers, booksellers etc.
Class No: 015(469)"312"

RSFSR

[419]

LIBRARY OF CONGRESS. Catalog Publication Division. **The Slavic Cyrillic union catalog of pre-1956 imprints.** Totowa, N.J., Rowmann & Littlefield, 1980. Microfiche.

174 microfiche at 48x reduction.

A successor to the *Cyrillic union catalog* (1963) and considerably expanded. About 350,000 entries, in the form of reproduced catalogue cards, for the Library of Congress and 220 other US and Canadian libraries. Includes books, pamphlets, maps, atlases, periodicals and serials in seven languages: Russian; Church Slavic; Belorussian; Ukranian; Bulgarian; Serbian; Macedonian. Arranged by main entry, with some cross-references. The *Cyrillic union catalog* was in romanized form, but in this catalogue most entries are in Cyrillic script. *Class No:* 015(470)

[420]

SOPIKOV, V.S. Opyt rossiiskoi bibliografii. Rogozhin, N., *red.* [Izd 2]. St. Petersburg, Suvorin, 1904-06. 5v.

First published 1813-21.

Now largely superseded for 18th century items. V.1 lists by title 1,737 items in ecclesiastical Cyrillic from the 15th century to the beginning of the 19th century. V.2-5 list other books in Russian to 1813. *Class No:* 015(470)

18th Century

[421]

DRAGE, C.L. Russian and Church Slavonic books 1701-1800 in United Kingdom libraries: a list with bibliographical references, locations, notes and indices. London, C.L. Drage, 1984. xviii,248p.

An author/anonymous title listing (transliterated Cyrillic) with some English annotations. Includes books printed outside Russia not covered in *Svodnyi katalog russkoi knigi grazhdanskoi pechati XVIII veka, 1725-1800* (below). 872

....(contd.)
items, 546 in the British Library, the remainder in 33 other UK locations. Title, printer and library holdings indexes.
Class No: 015(470)"17"

[422]

FESSENKO, T. Eighteenth century Russian publications in the Library of Congress: a catalog. Washington, D.C., Library of Congress, Reference Dept., Slavonic and Central European Division, 1961. xvi,157p.

Reproduces catalogue cards for 1,316 works. Author order, with title index. *Class No:* 015(470)"17"

[423]

Svodnyi katalog russkoi knigi grazhdanskoi pechati XVIII veka, 1725-1800. Kondakov, I.P., *and others*. Moskva, Izdanie Gos. Biblioteki SSSR im. Lenina, 1962-67. 5v.

A union catalogue of Russian books printed 1725-1800 in major Moscow and Leningrad libraries. Chronological arrangement with annotations and reproductions of title pages. 8,956 numbered entries v.1-v.3, 523 entries for periodicals and newspapers v.4, indexes v.5.

A supplement subtitled, *Dopolneniia, razyskivaemye izdanniia utochneniia* (Moskva, Kniga, 1975. 189p.), provides corrections and details of further acquisitions since 1967. *Class No:* 015(470)"17"

[424]

—Svodnyi katalog knig na inostrannykh iazykakh, izdannykk v Rossii v XVIII veke 1701-1800. Leningrad, 'Nauka', 1984-86. 3v.

Lists foreign-language books published in Russia during the 18th century. 3,524 numbered entries, mainly for works in French and German. Complements *Svodnyi katalog russkoi...* (above). *Class No:* 015(470)"17"

20th Century

[425]

LIBRARY OF CONGRESS. Processing Department. **Monthly index of Russian accessions.** Washington, D.C., Library of Congress, 1948-69. Monthly.

As *Monthly list of Russian accessions*, 1948-57.

Issues in 3 pts.: A. Monographic works (17 classes) - B. Periodicals (translated contents lists) - C. Subject index to monographs and periodicals. Appended list of periodicals available in cover-to-cover English translation. Separate annual monograph and periodical indexes.
Class No: 015(470)"19"

Contemporary

[426]

Knizhnaiā letopis'. Moskva, Izd-vo Kniznaiā palata, 1907-. Weekly. ISSN: 08695962.

Content and format varies: from 1993 incorporates records previously appearing in the monthly *Knizhnaiā letpois. Dopolnitel'nyi vypusk. Knigi i broshiūry*.

'Book record'. The basic component of a series of bibliographies that make up the Russian national bibliography. Based on legal deposit, encompassing books, pamphlets and government publications in all the languages of the Russian Federation. 35,285 items recorded 1996. Records now classified by UDC (previously 50 class BBK scheme (Dewey until 1940)). Quarterly index *Vspomogatel'nye ukazateli* (ISSN: 08695970) and annual publishers' series index *Ukazatel' serii* (ISSN: 02016133, previously *Ukazatel' seriinykh zdanii*). Records 1980 onwards available online. Material from *Knizhnaiā letopis'* also appears in *Rossiiskaia natsionalnaiā bibliografiiā* CD-ROM (below). *Class No:* 015(470)"312"

[427]

—Ezhegodnik knigi Rossiiskoĭ Federatsii. 1925-. Moskva, Izd-vo Knizhnaiā palata, 1927-. Annual. ISSN: 02016354.

Title and publisher varies, previously *Ezhegodnik knigi SSSR*. Not published 1930-34, 1936-40. Publication delayed in recent years, 1992 v., first under revised title, not issued until 1995.

A selected cumulation of commercially available books based on *Knizhnaia letopis'*. Now issued in 2v., v.1 covering social sciences and humanities, v.2 sciences.
Class No: 015(470)"312"

[428]

Novye knigi. Moskva, Mezhdunarodnaiā knigi, 1956-. Semi-monthly. ISSN: 01348396.

Cover subtitle *Retsenzii, abzory, annotatsiī, reklama*. Publisher and frequency varies.

Each issue lists new and forthcoming books giving full bibliographical detail price and ISBN. Subject arrangement with author index; brief descriptive annotation attached to most entries. An important tool for ordering current Russian books. *Class No:* 015(470)"312"

[429]

Rossiiskaiā natsionalnaiā bibliografiiā. [Russian national bibliography Plus.] München, K.G. Saur in assoc. with the Russian Book Chamber and Russian ISBN Agency, 1993-. CD-ROM database, irregular updating. DM3200. ISSN: 13507230.

Initial discs issued under title *Russian books in print Plus*.

1997 release (ISBN: 3598403666) contains records for 907,000 titles, data provided by the Russian Book Chamber and Russian ISBN Agency. Includes 35,000 titles published since mid-1996 and 60,000 dissertations from 1991. English and Russian interface, up to 28 search criteria including ISBN, keyword, series and price. Some records with brief descriptive annotations. *Class No:* 015(470)"312"

Estonia

[430]

Eesti rahvusbibliograafia: raamatud. [The Estonian national bibliography: books.] Tallin, Eesti Rahvusraamatukogu, 1994-. Quarterly. ISSN: 10240160.

Companion title *Eesti rahvusbibliograafia: artiklid* (ISSN: 1022517X) indexes periodical articles. The pre-independence listing of Estonian books, *Raamatukroonika* (ISSN: 02016877), covers 1946-91.

The 1996 issues list 2,601 items in UDC order with an author index in each issue. Printed music, 'art matters publications' and 'matter of short dated importance' excluded. *Class No:* 015(474.2)

[431]

Eestikeelne raamat. Annus, T.E. Tallin, 1993-.

1851-1900 (1995. 2v. ISBN: 9985500695) 1901-17 (1993. 2v. ISBN: 9985500105). At head of title pages 'Eesti Teadvste Akadeemia Raamatukogu'.

First vols. of a retrospective listing of Estonian language books. Includes sheet music, maps, annuals and pamphlets. Author arrangement, 6,847 entries 1851-1900, 8,763 1901-17. English preface; comprehensive indexing.
Class No: 015(474.2)

Latvia

[432]

Latvijas preses hronika. [The Latvian press chronicle.] Rīga, Latvijas Bibliogafijas Institūts, 1975-. Monthly. US$53. ISSN: 01309226.

Issued as *Latvijas PSR preses hronika* until 1990.

Functions as the national bibliography listing new books, pamphlets, brochures, etc. Also includes some periodical articles. UDC classified arrangement with indexes in each issue. *Class No:* 015(474.3)

Lithuania

[433]

Bibliografijos žinios: knygos. Lietuvos valstybinės bibliografijos rodyklė. [Bibliographical news: books. Lithuanian national bibliographical index.] Vilnius, Lietuvos Nacionalinė Martyna Mažvyda Biblioteka, 1992-. Monthly. ISSN: 13921738.

Current title from 1996, previously *Bibliografijos žinios: lietuvos nacionalinės bibliografijos rodyklė(ISSN: 13080308). 1957-92 covered in Spaudos metraštis: Lietuvos valstybinė bibliografine rodyklė* (ISSN: 01351354. English title *Press annals: Lithuanian state bibliographical index*).

UDC classified listing with name index. About 5,000 titles recorded annually. Other series of the Lithuanian national bibliography cover serials, *Bibliorafijos žinios: serialiniai leidiniai* (*q.v.*), articles and Lithuanica.
Class No: 015(474.5)

[434]

Knygos lietuviu kalba. Vilnius, Mintis, 1969-.

1547-1861 (1969) with *Papildymai* (1990); 1862-1904 in 2pts., A-P (1985), R-Z (1988); 1905-17 in 2v. (1977); 1918-40 in 2v. (1997. ISBN: 998641525X).

The retrospective listing. Includes titles in Lithuanian published outside the country. *Class No:* 015(474.5)

Belorussia

[435]

HALENCHANKA, T.V. Kniha Belarusi, 1517-1917: zvodny kataloh. Minsk, Vyd-va 'Belaruskaiā Savetskaiā Entsyklapediya', 1986. 614p. plates.

5,000 entries in sections for 16-18th century Cyrillic imprints, Belorussian imprints to 1917 and Russian publications to the same year. Each section indexed by author, title, subject and place. Many entries include notes on contents, etc. *Class No:* 015(476)

[436]

Knihi Belarusi. 1981-. Minsk, Natsyiānal'naiā kniznaiā palata, 1984-. Annual. ISSN: 02353393.

Now cumulates from the monthly *Letapis druku Belarusi* (1992-. ISSN: 01309218). Earlier quinquennially issued volumes give coverage back to 1956/60.

The current national listing. UDC classified arrangement with author, geographic and title indexes.
Class No: 015(476)

Ukraine

[437]

Litopys knyh. Kyïv, Knyzhkova palata Ukraïny, 1954-. Monthly. US$120. ISSN: 01309196.

UDC based listing of new books, detail including ISBN and price. Indexes in each issue. *Class No:* 015(477)

Finland

[438]

Suomen kansallisbibliografia: 1488-1700. [Finlands nationalbibliogafi: 1488-1700.] Laine, T. *and* Nyquist, R., *reds.* Helsinki, Suomolaisen Kirjallisunden Seura, 1996. 2v. ISBN: 9517179073.

Part of a projected national bibliography to 1800. V.1 contains 4,463 numbered entries by author, v.2 is an index with date and subject sequences. Full bibliographical detail for each item including notes and references.
Class No: 015(480)

[439]

Suomen kirjallisuus. 1944/48-. [The Finnish national bibliography. 1944/48-.] Helsinki, Helsingin Yliopiston Kirjasto, 1954-. Monthly, with annual cumulation. ISSN: 0355001x.

Continues *Suomalainen kirjallisuus: aakkosellinen fa aineenmukainen luettelo 1544-1877,* (Helsinki, Suomalaisen kirjallisuuden seura, 1878. 264p.) and *Suomalainen kirjallisuus 1878-1943,* (Suomalainen kirjallisuuden seura, 1880-1952. 16v.).

Annual *Vuosiluettelo* (ISSN: 03550001) has full bibliographical entries for monographs in main entry order with a classified list and subject index. Monthly similar, but in broad UDC classified arrangement. Cumulation for 1967/71 issued 1992 in 3 v., includes annuals, maps and sheet music. Also available on CD-ROM as *Fennica: Suomen kansallisbibliogafia,* updated quarterly, including records back to 1920. Records from the *Fennica* database are also Internet accessible at telnet://hyk.helsinki/fi.
Class No: 015(480)

[440]

Suomessa ilmestyneen kirjallisuuden vuosiluettelo. 1945-71. [Årskatalog över i Finland utkommen litteratur. 1945-71.] Helsinki, Kirjallisuuden Seuran Kirjapainon Oy, 1950-73. Annual.

Title varies; initially published as *Suomessa ilmestyneen kirjallisuuden aineenmukainen uutuusluettlo/Systematisk katalog över i Finland utkommen literatur.* Quarterly, 1945-48.

Three main sections (each by authors A-Z): 1. Literature in Finnish - 2. Literature in Swedish - 3. Books and periodical articles published in Finland in other languages; subject index to items in sections 1-2. *Class No:* 015(480)

Norway

[441]

Bibliotheca Norvegica. Pettersen, H., *ed.* Christiana, Cammeyer, 1899-1924. 4v. in 5.

V.1 *Norsk boglexikon 1643-1813* (books printed in Norway, 1643-1813). 1899-1908; v.2 *Norge og nordmaend i udlandets literatur* (Norway and Norwegians in foreign literature). 1908-17; v.3 *Norske forfattere for 1814* (Norwegian authors before 1814). 1911-18; v.4 *Norske forfattere after 1814* (Norwegian authors since 1814: works printed abroad), including suppts. 1-3. 1913-24.
Class No: 015(481)

[442]

Norsk bokfortegnelse. 1814/47-. [The Norwegian national bibliography.] Oslo, Universitetsbiblioteket i Oslo, 1848-. Semi-monthly, with annual cumulation. ISSN: 00291870.

Published by Norske bokhandlerforening until 1995. Decennial cumulations 1891-1920; quinquennial cumulations from 1921, last issued 1971/75 (1982. 2v.). Items omitted from later annual cumulations listed in *Norsk bokfortegnelse.*

....(contd.)
Årskatalog: tillegg 1976-1983 (1991. 618p.).

Entries now appear in the semi-monthly *Norsk bokfortegnelse: nyhetsliste* (ISSN: 08056978, until March 1994 in the monthly *Bog og samfunn*). The annual cumulation *Norsk bokfortegnelse. Årskatalog* 1952- (previously *Årskatalog over norsklittaratur*, 1903-1951), is an author main entry listing with a classified index. 1996 v. (ix,818p.) lists 6,320 items. Printed music recorded separately in *Norsk musikkfortegnelse: notetrykk* (ISSN: 08046328). *Norske bokfortegnelse* is also available in microfiche (*Norsk trykk*, published every two months cumulating throughout the year), as an online database (*NORBOK* through UBO:BOK, records 1962 to date) and on CD-ROM (as part of *Nasjonalbibliografiske data*, updated quarterly). *Class No:* 015(481)

[443]
—Norwegian scholarly books 1825-1970 complete alphabetical list from Universitetsforlaget, publishers to the Norwegian universities. Oslo, Universitetsforlaget, 1970. xx,533p.

Supplement (1978. 98p.) updates to 1977.

Author/title listing from the publishers' responsible for the bulk of Norwegian scholarly titles. Includes periodicals. No indexes in main v., author index in supplement *Katalog,* which has a classified arrangement. *Class No:* 015(481)

Sweden

[444]
COLLIJN, I. Sveriges bibliografi intill år 1600. Uppsala, Svenska Litteratursällskapet, 1927-38. 3v. illus. (*Svenska litteratursällskapet. Skrifter, 10:5-18.*)

Published in pts.

Chronologically arranged (v.1: 1478-1530; v.2: 1530-82; v.3: 1583-99). Full bibliographical notes and references, plus locations of copies. *Class No:* 015(485)

[445]
—COLLIJN, I. Sveriges bibliografi, 1600-talet. Uppsala, Almqvist, 1942-46. 2v.

Continues the earlier bibliography but is arranged by authors A-Z. Covers the 17th century. *Class No:* 015(485)

[446]
LINNSTRÖM, H. Svenskt boklexikon, 1830-65. Stockholm, Linnström, 1883-84. 2v.

Extends the coverage provided by *Svensk bok-katalog (q.v.)* Includes biographical detail for many authors.
Class No: 015(485)

[447]
Svensk bokförteckning. [The Swedish national bibliography.] Stockholm, Tidningsaktiebolaget Svensk bokhandel, 1953-. Bi-monthly, with annual cumulation. Kr2200. ISSN: 00396443.

Compiled by the Bibliographical Institute of the Royal Library. Succeeds the monthly of the same title (1913-52) and the annual *Årskatalog för svenska bokhandeln,* 1861-1952.

Based on entries in the weekly *Svensk bokhandel* (ISSN: 00396451). Excludes most government publications (*Statliga publikationer årsbibliografi q.v.*), most periodicals (*Svensk periodicaförteckning q.v.*), maps (*Svensk kartförteckning*), sheet music and foreign language works about Sweden (*Suecana extranea*). The annual cumulation (*Årskatalog*) has an alphabetical sequence giving full bibliographical detail, a classified list according to the Swedish Library Association Scheme and a subject index. Further cumulations published as *Svensk bokkatalog* (below). Records from *Svensk bokförteckning* are also included in the Royal Library's database *LIBRIS*, available on CD-ROM or through the Internet at http://www/libris.kb.se. *Class No:* 015(485)

[448]
—Svensk bok-katalog. 1866/75-. Stockholm, Tidningsaktiebolaget Svensk bokhandel, 1878-. Quinquennial or decennial. ISSN: 03477487.

Publisher and frequency varies. Decennial until 1886/95, thereafter quinuennial except for 1941/50 and 1976/85.

The latest cumulation covering 1976/85 (1994-95) is in 7v., v.1-v.6 forming an alphabetical list, v.7 a subject catalogue. *Class No:* 015(485)

[449]
Swedish imprints 1731-1833: a retrospective national bibliography. Du Rietz, R.E., *ed.* Uppsala, Dahlia Books, 1977-. ISSN: 11045388.

Prepared at the Center for Bibliographical Studies, Uppsala. Also known by the acronym 'SWIM'. An 'open-ended' bibliography published in parts: 1-15 (1977-80) 99 entries each; 16-17 (1981) 999 entries each; 18-46 (1982-97) 500 entries each.

Intended to provide comprehensive coverage of Swedish imprints of the period. Also includes imprints of Finland 1731-1809. Full bibliographical detail; entry headings and notes in English. Chronological arrangement in each part with author and publisher indexes. Cumulated index 1-35 published 1993 (replaces earlier cumulations). Separate guide *Basic information for users of SWIM* issued 1977, revised version anticipated 1997. *Class No:* 015(485)

Denmark

[450]
BRUUN, C.W. Bibliotheca Danica. Systematisk Fortegnelse over den danske Literatur fra 1482 til 1830 efter Samlingerne i det Store Kongelige Bibliothek i København. København, Gyldendal, 1877-1931. 4v.

Reprinted in 5v., (København, Rosenkilde og Bagger, 1961-63), the final v. comprising the original supplement (1914), plus a new supplement to 1962.

A classified bibliography of Danish and Scandinavian material on Denmark, Schleswig Holstein, Norway, Iceland and Greenland. Indexes (in v.4, published 1927-31) of authors, anonymous titles and subjects. *Class No:* 015(489)

[451]
—Bibliotheca Danica: supplement 1831-1840 til Bibliotheca Danica og Dansk bogfortegnelse. Ehrencron-*Müller, H., udarb.* København, Gads, 1943-48. 4pts.

Bridges the gap between the Bruun *Bibliotheca Danica* (above) and *Dansk bogfortegnelse* 1841/58-. Includes a 'Biblioteca Slesvico-Holsatica' to 1840. *Class No:* 015(489)

[452]
Dania polyglotta literature on Denmark in languages other than Danish & books of Danish interest published abroad. 1945-. Copenhagen, Royal Library, 1946-. Annual. ISSN: 00702714.

Subtitle varies. New series with present title from 1969.

A valuable bibliography covering foreign language literature about Denmark and books written, edited or illustrated by Danes published abroad. Modified Dewey arrangement with author and title index. V.28 for 1996 (1997. 179p.) has *c.*2,000 entries. Also available as a separate file of the database *REX* accessible through the Royal Library at http://www.kb.dk/natbib/.
Class No: 015(489)

[453]

—Dania polyglotta répertoire bibliographique des ouvrages, études, articles etc. en langues étrangères parus en Danemark de 1901 à 1944. Copenhagen, Bibliothèque Royale, 1947-50. 3v.

Continued by the annual *Dania polyglotta* (above).

Contents: v.1 Ouvrages; v.2 Périodiques, études et articles; v.3 Addenda, musique, index. Arranged under languages, broad subject groups and forms.
Class No: 015(489)

[454]

Dansk bogfortegnelse. [The Danish national bibliography, books.] Ballerup, Dansk BiblioteksCenter, 1851-. Monthly, with quarterly, annual and quinquennial cumulations. ISSN: 01062743.

As *Maanedlig Dansk bogfortegnelse,* 1851-1855. Publisher Gads Forlag 1856-1975. Periodic cumulations from 1841/58, quinquennial from 1915/19 (except triennial 1970-75).

Covers books, government publications, new serials/ newspapers, published dissertations, printed music, microforms and CD-ROMs. Arranged alphabetically by main entry with classified index. Monthly issues cumulated from listings in the weekly *Bogmarkedet.* Annual (*Årskatalog*) and quinquennial cumulations contain separate lists of periodicals, Greenlandic books and cartographic materials. From 1915-34 Icelandic imprints were also listed. Last printed quinquennial cumulation for 1981/85 (1987. 4v.); 1976/85 and 1986/90- on microfiche. *Dansk bogfortegnelse* is accessible online as *DanBib-Basen.* Records 1970- also available on a quarterly updated CD-ROM. *Class No:* 015(489)

[455]

NIELSEN, L.M. Dansk Bibliografi, 1482-1550, 1551-1600, med saerligt hensyn til dansk bogtrykkerkunsts Historie. København, Gyldendal, 1919-35. 2v. & index.

Separate author and title listings for 1482-1550 and 1551-1600, the latter issued in pts. 1,672 items identified; place/ printer and publisher index with each sequence. Additional index (126p.) provides author, title, date and subject access.
Class No: 015(489)

[456]

ROSENKILDE, V. *and* **BALLHAUSEN, C.J. Thesaurus librorum Danicorum** 15th and 16th century. København, Rosenkilde og Bagger, 1987. 245p. plates. ISBN: 8742304997.

Catalogues and offers extensive descriptions for 306 items in sections Theological and religious books... Statutory law books... Historical books... Belles lettres. List of literature; author and name index. Continued by:- *Class No:* 015(489)

[457]

—BALLHAUSEN, C.J. *and* JOHANSEN, P. Thesaurus librorum Danicorum 17 århundrede. København, Rosenkilde og Bagger, 1990. 357p. ISBN: 8742305489.

Catalogues and describes 745 items. Indexed.
Class No: 015(489)

Iceland

[458]

Íslensk bókaskrá. 1974-. [The Icelandic national bibliography. 1974-.] Reykjavík, Landsbókasafn Íslands, 1975-. Annual. $27. ISSN: 02541378.

Earlier listings in *Bókaskrá Bóksalafélags Íslands,* 1937-1973 and 'Íslenzkrit' in *Árbók Landsbókasafns Íslands,* 1945-1975. Icelandic works were included in the

....*(contd.)*

quinquennial vols. of *Dansk bogfortegnelse* (q.v.) 1915-1934.

The 1996 v. (1997. 206p.) has full bibliographic details in author sequence, (Icelandic persons entered under given name), with classified index by Dewey D.C. Additional sections for new serials, maps and charts. Sound recordings in separately published supplement *Íslensk hljóðritaskrá* (1980-. ISSN: 02544067).

Three quinquennial cumulations are available covering 1974-78 (1985), 1979-83 (1992) and 1984-88 (1994).
Class No: 015(491.1)

Netherlands

[459]

ABKONDE, J. van. Naamregister van de bekendste en meest in gebruik zynde Nederduitsche boeken, welke sedert het jaar 1600 tot het jaar 1761 zyn uitgekomen ... Nuoverzien, verb. en tot het jaar 1781 verm. door Renier Arrenberg. 2.druk. Rotterdam, Arrenberg, 1788. 598p.

First published 1743-56; revised 1773. Reprinted Sijthoff, 1965.

Author and anonymous title list of *c.*12,000 books published in the Netherlands, 1600-1781.

Continued (1790-1832) by: *Alphabetische naamlijst van boeken, welke sedert het jaar 1790 tot en met jaar 1832 in Noord-Nederland zijn uitgekomen* ('sGravenhage, van Clef, 1835. 755,159p. Reprinted Sijthoff, 1965).

Further continued (1833-49) by C.L. Brinkman's *Alphabetische naamlijst van boeken, plaat-en kaartwerken, die ... 1833-1849 in Nederland uitg. of herdrukt zijn* (Amsterdam, Brinkman, 1858. 792p. Reprinted Sijthoff, 1965). *Class No:* 015(492)

[460]

BRITISH LIBRARY. Catalogue of books from the Low Countries 1601-1621 in the British Library. London, British Library, 1990. xviii,842p. illus. £95. ISBN: 071230066x.

Continues the Dutch STC (below), but with much fuller cataloguing. About 3,650 entries. Appendix: 'Chronological list of news reports' (p.721-68) covers publications which formed, or are assumed to have formed, part of regularly published reports regardless of variable titles. Index of printers and publishers; general index. *Class No:* 015(492)

[461]

BRITISH MUSEUM. Department of Printed Books. **Short-title catalogue of books printed in the Netherlands** and Belgium and of Dutch and Flemish books printed in other countries from 1470 to 1600 now in the British Museum. Johnson, A.F. *and* Scholderer, V., *comps.* London, Trustees of the British Museum, 1965. viii,274p. £15. ISBN: 0714102709.

Last of the British Museum short title catalogues of books printed before 1601 to be published. Author entries for 5,000 books. 'Erasmus', (p.69-72). Index of printers and publishers (p.219-74). *Class No:* 015(492)

[462]

KONINKLIJKE BIBLIOTHEEK. Catalogus van de pamfletten-versameling berustende in de Koninklijke Bibliotheek. Knuttel, W.P.C., *comp.* 'sGravenhage, Algemeene Landsdrukkerij, 1889-1920. 9v. in 10.

Reprinted Utrecht, Hes, 1978 (ISBN: 9061940125).

Catalogue of pamphlets in the Koninklijke Bibliotheek. Chronological arrangement 1486-1853. V.1-7 (in 9) contain

....*(contd.)*
entries 1-29764, with author index in each v. V.8-9 (in 1) include supplementary entries and a subject index of items to the year 1795. *Class No:* 015(492)

[463]

KONINKLIJKE BIBLIOTHEEK. Nederlandse Bibliografie 1801-1832. Honten, Bohn Stafleu van Loghum, 1993. 3v. ISBN: 9031312177.

V.1 A-K; v.2 L-Z; v.3 Registers.

Intended to fill the gap between *The Short-title catalogue Netherlands* and *Alphabetische naamlijst van boeken ... 1833-1849* (*qq.v.*). Main entry listing similar in appearance to *Brinkman's*. Entries include locations in up to 75 Dutch libraries. Classified subject and other indexes.
Class No: 015(492)

[464]

NIJHOFF, W. *and* **KRONENBERG, M.E. Nederlandsche bibliographie van 1500 tot 1540.** s'Gravenhage, Nijhoff, etc., 1923-71. 3pts. in 8v.

4,352 entries in total, arranged by author, including items published in present day Belgium. Author, printer, location and subject indexes in pt.3. *Class No:* 015(492)

[465]

The Short-title catalogue, Netherlands 1541-1800. s'Gravenhage, Koninklijke Bibliotheek. Computer database.

Available through the Koninklijke Bibliotheek (telnet://konbib.nl:2057 or http://www.pica.nl/ (password required)), file updated bi-weekly.

Will eventually contain an estimated 300,000 records for titles published in the Netherlands or in the Dutch language abroad. Holdings of the Koninklijke Bibliotheek and several other major Dutch libraries 1540-1700 already entered. 60,000 items recorded January 1997, material published 1701-1800 now in process of being added.
Class No: 015(492)

Contemporary

[466]

Brinkman's cumulatieve catalogus van boeken: Nederlandse bibliografie betvattende de in Nederland en Vlaanderen uitgegaven of herdrukte boeken, die werden ontvangen door het Depot van Nederlandse Publikaties van de Koninklijke Bibliotheek te 'sGravenhage. Houten, Bohn Stafleu van Loghum, 1846-. Monthly, with interim (quarterly, semi-annual) and annual cumulations. ISSN: 00070165.

Title and format varies: as *Brinkman's Alphabetische lijst* until 1930.

Based on *Nederlandse bibliografie A-lijst* appearing in the weekly *Boekblad* (ISSN: 01674765). Includes Flemish titles published in Belgium and new periodicals. Author/title listing: 'Instanties en Verenigingen' (corporate body) and 'Onderwerpenregister' (subject) indexes. *Nederlandse bibliografie B lijst* (1984-. Monthly. ISSN: 01687964) is a supplementary listing of non-trade publications (*e.g.* government documents, scientific papers, privately published dissertations, etc.). A further listing, *Uitgaven in voorbereiding (CIP)* (ISSN: 09201017) announcing forthcoming titles, ceased 1996. *Brinkman's* is available (Chadwyck-Healey in UK) as a CD-ROM comprising current disc (records 1990 to date, updated quarterly) and backfile (records 1981-89). Internet access is through the Koninklijke Bibliotheek, records from *Brinkman's* forming part of the online catalogue. *Class No:* 015(492)"312"

[467]

—Brinkman's catalogus van boeken en tijdschriften: Nederlandse bibliografie betvattende de in Nederland en Vlaanderen... . Houten, Bohn Stafleu van Loghum, 1884-. Quinquennial. ISSN: 01652613.

Title and publisher varies. Initial cumulation covers 1850/82, then 1891-1900 and 1901-10. Thereafter published quinquennially. Latest cumulation for 1991/95 published in 10v. (1996): v.1-7 A-Z; v.8-9 Register (onderwerpen); v.10 Register (instantiesen verenigingen).
Class No: 015(492)"312"

Belgium

[468]

Bibliographie de Belgique. [Belgische bibliografie.] Bruxelles, Bibliothèque Royale Albert Ier, 1875-. Monthly, with annual cumulation. BFr6000. ISSN: 00061336.

The official national bibliography based on legal deposit. Also includes books by Belgian authors published abroad and books relating to Belgium obtained by the Bibliothèque Royale, categories covered 1959-1974 by the separately published *Bibliographie de Belgique. Fascicule spécial.* V.122 for 1996 carries 10,617 entries arranged by 32 broad subject groups with author, title and subject indexes.
Class No: 015(493)

[469]

Bibliographie nationale. Dictionnaire des écrivains belges et catalogue de leurs publications 1830-80. Bruxelles, Weissenbruch, 1886-1910. 4v.

About 65,000 entries for books, pamphlets, theses, maps and plans and music by Belgians published in Belgium or abroad. Gives biographical data on authors; no subject index. *Class No:* 015(493)

[470]

Bibliotheca belgica: Bibliographie générale des Pays-Bas ... Bruxelles, Culture et Civilisation, 1964-1975. 7v.

Contents: v.1-5 A-Z; v.6 Supplement; v.7 Index. Reprinted 1979. Originally published in irregular order in 3 series 1880-1964.

An author and anonymous title list that concentrates on the 15th and 16th centuries, but includes important books published after 1600. Covers works printed in Belgium and Holland, and works by Belgian and Dutch authors printed abroad. Full bibliographical descriptions with biographical notes and references. Supplement (1970) contains further entries plus indexes of authors, editors and printers. V.7 (1975) comprises detailed general index.
Class No: 015(493)

[471]

COCKX-INDESTEGE, E. *and* **GLORIEUX, G. Belgica typographica, 1541-1600:** catalogus librorum impressorum ab anno MDXLI ad annum MDC in regionibus quae nunc Regni Belgarum partes sunt. Nieuwkoop, B. de Graaf, 1968-1994. 4v.

Aims to record all items published within the present boundaries of Belgium between 1541-1600. V.1 covers the collections of the Royal Library, Brussels: 4,982 entries with indexes to collaborators, devices, illustrators, cartographers, composers and printers. V.2 covers 40 other Belgian libraries with index and supplement. V.3, based on Ghent and Louvain university libraries and the Stadsbibliothek at Antwerp, contains entries 7740-9755. V.4 is a cumulated index with six sequences including author/anonymous works, date and publisher. *Class No:* 015(493)

Switzerland

[472]

Das Schweizer Buch: Schweizerische Nationalbibliographie. [Le Livre suisse: bibliographie nationale suisse.] Bern, Schweizerischer Buchhändler und Verleger Verband 1901-. Semi-monthly (24 issues pa.). SFr400. ISSN: 0036732x.

Title varies: as *Bibliographisches Bulletin der Schweiz* 1901-42. Records included in *CD-ROM CH* and the Schweizerische Landesbibliothek online catalogue Internet accessible at http://www.wnl.ch/helveticat.

Since 1976 issued as a single list covering books, first numbers of serials, maps and non-book materials. Previously (1943-75) issued in two series: A, covering book trade publications; B, covering non-trade items, *e.g.* theses. Entries arranged in 24 broad classes with an author/title index cumulated annually. Issue 16 of each v. is a special no. devoted to music. Now records about 24,000 items annually. Quinquennial cumulations published until 1980 as:- *Class No:* 015(494)

[473]

Schweizer Bücherverzeichnis. Katalog der schweizerischen Landesbibliothek. 1948/50-1976/80. [Répertoire du livre suisse.] Zürich, Schweizerischer Buchhändler-und Verlegerverein, 1951-83. Quinquennial.

Initial v. covered 1948/50, thereafter quinquennial. Publication abandoned after 1976/80 cumulation (1983).

Cumulated *Das Schweizer Buch.* Succeeds the Schweizerische Landesbibliothek's *Katalog ... Alphabetisches Verzeichnis der bis 1900 erschienenen Druckschriften* (Bern, Francke, 1910. 2v.) and *Katalog ... Systematischer Verzeichnis der schweizerischen oder die Schweiz betreffenden Veröffentlichungen* 1901-20, 1921-30, 1931-40, 1941-47 (Bern, Huber, [1927] - 54).

Published in 2v.: v.1 an author and anonymous title catalogue; v.2 a subject catalogue, with German language subject headings and French index. *Class No:* 015(494)

Liechtenstein

[474]

Liechtensteinische Bibliographie, 1974-. Vaduz, Liechtensteinische Landesbibliothek, 1975-. Annual.

In two classified sequences: titles relating to Liechtenstein; titles produced in Liechtenstein. Author/title/keyword index. 1994 v. (1996. xiv,166p.) contains 658 entries. *Class No:* 015(494.9)

[475]

—ROECKLE, H. Liechtensteinische Bibliographie 1960-1973. Vaduz, Liechtensteinische Landesbibliothek, 1979. ix, 278p.

Retrospective volume. *Class No:* 015(494.9)

Greece

[476]

Bulletin signalétique de bibliographie hellénique. 1945-78. Athènes, Institut Français d'Athènes, 1947-85. Annual.

Ceased with v.39 for 1978. Published as *Bulletin analytique de bibliographie hellénique* 1945-80. First issue v.6 fasc.1; v.6 fasc.2-3 and v.24-27 not published.

Final v. (530p.) listed 3,471 monographs in sections for literature, science, humanities, school books and translations. Separate list of current periodicals with notes on content. Name index. *Class No:* 015(495)

[477]

Hellēnikē ethnikē bibliographia. 1989-. [Greek national bibliography.] Athēnai, Ethnikē Bibliothēkē tēs Hellados, 1990-. Annual. ISSN: 11053046.

4v. with same title covering 1972-73 and 1976-77 published 1975-79. Several earlier efforts were made to establish a regular national bibliography. One of the more sustained was *Greek bibliography*, issued quarterly by the National Printing Office 1960-68 (covers 1960-64).

A new attempt at a current national bibliography compiled by the National Library of Greece. V. for 1991 (1993. 1083p.) has 4,075 entries in classified Dewey order. Thoroughly indexed by author/series, title, subject, publisher, ISBN and year of publication. *Class No:* 015(495)

[478]

—Deltio hēllenikēs bibliograhias. [Bulletin of Greek bibliography.] Athēnai, Panellenia Homospondia Ekdoton Bibliopolon, 19— -. Quarterly. ISSN: 11054301.

Commercial listing produced by the Hellenic Federation of Publishers and Booksellers. More prompt in appearance than *Hēllenikē ethnikē bibliographia.* *Class No:* 015(495)

[479]

LEGRAND, E. Bibliographie hellénique, ou, Description raisonée des ouvrages publiés en grec par des Grecs aux XV-Se et XVI-Se siècles. Paris, Leroux, 1885-1906. 4v. illus.

Reprinted Paris, Maisonneuve, 1963.

Works published in Greek, Latin (and other languages, 1551-1600) by the Greeks, 1476-1600. 1,158 items.

Continued by *Bibliographie hellénique ... au dix-septième dix-huitème siècle* (1894-1903. 5v.) and *Bibliographie hellénique ... au dix-huitème siècle* (1918-28. 2v.).

Further supplemented by *Bibliographie ionienne: description, raisonnée des ouvrages publiés par les Grecs des Sept-Îles ... du 15. siècle à l'année 1900* (Paris, Leroux, 1910. 2v.). *Class No:* 015(495)

[480]

PAPADOPOULOS, T.I. Helleniki vivliographia 1466-1800: alphavetike kai chronologike anakatataxis. Athēnai, Akademia Athenon, 1984-1986. 2v. (*Pragmateiai tes Akademias Athenon, 48.*)

Serves to consolidate and update the works of Legrand (above). V.1 contains 6,146 entries in both the Greek and Latin alphabet with a chronological listing and printer and place of publication indexes. Includes library locations as traced by the author. V.2 contains a further 1,175 entries in chronological order with author and location indexes.

Supplemented by the same author's *Hellēniki vivliographia, 1544-1863, prosthēkes, symplērōseis* (Athēnai, Hetaireia Hellēnikou Logotechnikon kai Historiskou Archeiou, 1992. 134p. (Vivliogika ergastēri, 12). ISBN: 9602011017). *Class No:* 015(495)

Albania

[481]

Bibliografia kombëtare e librit që botohet në Republikën e Shqipërisë. Tiranë, Biblioteka Kombëtare, 1958-. Quarterly. $16. ISSN: 02505053.

Title varies, present form from 1991.

UDC based classified list. Author, title, publisher, etc. indexes in each issue, cumulated in final issue of each year. *Class No:* 015(496.5)

Yugoslavia

[482]

Bibliografija Jugoslavije: knjige, brošure i musikalije. Beograd, Jugoslovenski Bibliografsko Informacijski Institut, 1950-. Monthly. $906. ISSN: 05232201.

Frequency varies: monthly, 1950-53; semi-monthly, 1954-91 (24 issues pa.); monthly 1992- (but recent nos. issued bi-monthly). Preceded by the annual *Jugoslovenska bibliografija* covering 1945-1949.

A classified list (UDC) of books, pamphlets, maps, theses, sheet music and official publications. Author/title and subject indexes in each issue. 5,080 items listed 1997. Other components of *Bibliograija Jugoslavije* include *Serijske publikacije* and *Članci i prizoli u serijskim publikacijama* (*qq.v*). *Class No:* 015(497.1)

[483]

Katalog knjiga na jezicima jugoslovenskih narodna . Beograd, Narodna biblioteca Srbije, 1973-.

Intended as the major Yugoslav retrospective bibliography. V.1 records items published 1519-1867. Remainder of the set covers 1868-1972. Includes pamphlets, periodicals and similar material, as well as books. 14 v. issued to 1989, publication now appears to have lapsed. *Class No:* 015(497.1)

Serbia

[484]

Srpska bibliografija: knjige 1868-1944. [The Serbian national bibliography: books.] Zivanov, M., *red.* Beograd, Narodna biblioteka Srbije, 1989-. ISBN: 8670350238.

Scheduled for completion in 20 v. To be the final component of a Serbian retrospective national bibliography, other parts to cover 1494-1700, 1701-1800 and 1801-1867.

Includes books published by Serbs outside the country and books published elsewhere 'if they are intended for Serbs'. Detailed entries, with library locations, arranged by author. Co-author, editor, etc. and subject indexes in each v. 60,027 items recorded in 12 v. A-Peti 1997. *Class No:* 015(497.11)

Slovenia

[485]

Slovenska bibliografija. Knjige. 1945/47-. Ljubljana, Narodna in univerzitetna knjižniia, 1947-. Quarterly. ISSN: 03531716.

Present title and format from 1985. 1978-84 not published.

UDC classified list with author and keyword indexes separately cumulated at the end of each year. An annually updated CD-ROM was launched 1995 containing records from 1989. *Class No:* 015(497.12)

Croatia

[486]

Grada za hrvatsku retrospektivnu bibliografiju knjiga, 1835-1940. Zagreb, Nacionala i sveučilišnabiblioteka, 1982-ISBN: 867237004x.

Comprehensive main entry listing. V.12 *Krp-Lj* (1988) latest published bringing total no. of entries to 33,774. *Class No:* 015(497.13)

[487]

Hrvatska bibliografija. Niz A. Knjige. Zagreb, Nacionalna i sveučilišna knjižnica u Zagrebu, 1991-. Monthly. ISSN: 13300423.

Frequency varies, some issues combined. Earlier listings produced under a number of titles including *Bibliografija knjiga tiskanih u SR Hrvatskoj* (ISSN: 03508722).

UDC classified listing with author, title, subject and ISBN indexes. Some publication delay in recent years. The two other series of the national bibliography are *Niz B. Prilozi u časopisma i zbornicima*, indexing periodical articles, and *Niz C. Serijske publikacije*, listing serials. *Class No:* 015(497.13)

Macedonia

[488]

Makedonska bibliografija. 1. Monografski publikacii. Skopje, NUB 'St Kliment Ohridski', 1950-. Semi-annual. ISSN: 0351417x.

Subtitle and frequency varies; issued biennially until 1971.

UDC classified list. Two further series *Statii i prilozi* and *Seriski publikacii* cover articles and periodical titles respectively. *Class No:* 015(497.17)

Bulgaria

[489]

Bŭlgarski knigi 1878-1944. Bibliografski ukazatel. Sofiia, Narodna Biblioteka 'Kiril i Metodiĭ', 1978-83. 6v.

Cumulated retrospective bibliography of material published in Bulgaria. 55,851 numbered entries. V.6 includes books in foreign languages published in Bulgaria. Earlier coverage is provided by *Bŭlgarska vuzrozhdenska knizhnina: analitichen repertoar na Bŭlgarskite knigi i periodichni izdaniiā, 1806-1878.* (Sofiia, Nauka i izkustvo, 1957-59. 2v.), which lists over 20,000 items. *Class No:* 015(497.2)

[490]

Bŭlgarski knigopis: knigi, notni, graficheski i kartografski izdaniiā. Sofiiā, Narodna Biblioteka 'Kiril i Metodiĭ', 1897-. Semi-monthly, with annual cumulation. $58. ISSN: 03239616.

English subtitle: Books, music, prints, maps. Title varies: from 1974 as series 1 of the national bibliography now titled *Natšionalna bibliografiiā na Republika Bulgariiā.* Frequency varies: annual, 1897-1944; quarterly, 1945-1948; monthly, 1949-1968. Annual cumulation from 1969 (ISSN: 03239713).

A UDC classified list with separate sections for music, maps and periodicals. About 3,500-4,000 titles listed annually.

Series 2 of the national bibliography, *Bŭlgarski knigopis: sluzhebni izdaniiā i disertatšii*, also published monthly (ISSN: 03239667), covers official publications and dissertations. *Class No:* 015(497.2)

Rumania

[491]

Bibliografia naţională Românià. Cărţi, albume, hărţi. Bucureşti, Biblioteca Na1ţională a România, 1951-. Semi-monthly. Lei72,000. ISSN: 12219126.

Title and frequency varies. Initially as *Buletinul bibliografie al cărţi*, then *Bibliografia Republicii Populare Romine*. 1968-89 as *Bibliografia Republicii Socialiste România*. Current title from 1993, issues 1990-92 mainly as

....(*contd.*)

Bibliografia României.

Cărţi, albume, hărţi forms series 1 of the national bibliography covering books, pamphlets, maps/atlases and art albums. UDC based classified order with name index in each issue, cumulated annually in recent years. Other series of the national bibliography include *Publicaltii seriale* (*q.v*), *Publicaltii oficiale* (Semi-monthly. ISSN: 12215309) and *Teze de doctorat* (Annual. ISSN: 12237485).
Class No: 015(498)

[492]

BIBLIOTECA ACADEMIEI REPUBLICII SOCIALISTE ROMÂNIA. Bibliografia românească modernă 1831-1918. Bucureşti, Editura Ştiinţifică Enciclopedică/Societatea de Ştiinţe Filologice din R.S. România, 1984-.

Now produced by Biblioteca Academiei Române. To be in 3 pts. Pt.1 to contain works of Romanian authors irrespective of language and place of publication as well as other works which have appeared in Romanian. Pt.2 to contain other published material such as administrative works. Pt.3 to contain works by 'coinhabiting nationalities' and foreign authors published in Romania.

The main section (pt.1) is in author/anonymous title order; chronological, geographic, name and topic indexes to be separately published. V.4 R-Z (1996. xxi,871p ISBN: 9732905013) completes the main sequence of 73,472 entries. Exhaustive detail, entries including notes on contents and bibliographical sources, but printed on poor quality paper.
Class No: 015(498)

[493]

—BIANU, I., *and others*. Bibliografia românească veche 1508-1830. Bucureşti Atelierele Socec, 1903-43. 4v. illus.

V.1 1508-1716; v.2 1716-1808; v.3 1809-1830; v.4 Additions and corrections.

The earlier retrospective bibliography, sharing the exhaustive approach of the above. Arranged chronologically, with name and title index. *Class No:* 015(498)

China

[494]

Quan guo xin shu mu. Beijing, Depository Library of China. 1951-, Monthly. Y21.60;US$72. ISSN: 0578073x.

English title *New books catalogue of the PRC*. Frequency varies, monthly since 1977. Suspended during Cultural Revolution 1966-71.

The major listing of new titles published in China. Subject arrangement in 22 main groups. Entries include ISBN and price. A CD-ROM version of the Chinese national bibliography covering records from 1949 is scheduled to begin publication October 1998. *Class No:* 015(510)

[495]

Quarterly bulletin of Chinese bibliography. 1934-1947. Peiping, National Library of Peiping, 1937-47. Irregular.

English ed. Published in two series: 1934-37 and 1940-47.

Apart from articles, book reviews, etc., has an annotated selected list of new books published in China (in Chinese; in foreign languages; government publications).
Class No: 015(510)

Hong Kong

[496]

A Catalogue of books printed in Hong Kong. Hong Kong, Government Secretariat, 1965-97. Quarterly.

Published as Special supplement no.4 to the *Hong Kong government gazette*.

Separate English and Chinese sections, the former arranged by main entry. Author index and list of publishers. English and Chinese periodicals in 4th quarterly issue.
Class No: 015(512.317)

Korea

[497]

COURANT, M. Bibliographie coréenne. Tableau littéraire de la Corée, contenant la nomenclature des ouvrages publiés dans ce pays jusqu'en 1890, ainsi que la description et l'analyse detaillées des principaux d'entre ces ouvrages. Paris, Leroux, 1894-1901. 3v. & suppt.

V.1: *Enseignement. Études des langues. Confucianisme. Littérature*; v.2: *Moeurs et coutumes. Histoire et géographie*; v.3: *Sciences et arts. Religions. Relations extérieures: Index.*

Reprinted New York, Franklin, 1966. 4v. in 3. ISBN: 0833706926.

Annotated bibliography of 3,821 items. 30 facsimile plates. *Class No:* 015(519)

[498]

Taehan Min'guk ch'ulp'anmul ch'ongmongnok. 1963/64-. [Korean national bibliography.] Seoul, Kungnip chungang Tosŏgwan, 1965-. Annual. ISSN: 04966945.

Added title page *Korean national bibliography*. Based on the monthly listing *Nappon wŏlbo* (1972-. ISSN: 12275247. Title varies). 1945-62 covered by *Han'guk sŏmok* (Seoul, 1964).

Legal deposit based national bibliography. Arranged by form of publication, sections including government publications, general books, theses, juvenile literature, serials, audio-visual materials, etc. Title index. A CD-ROM version is also available. *Class No:* 015(519)

Japan

[499]

Japan English publications in print. 2nd ed. Tokyo, Intercontinental Marketing Corp., 1993. 446p. Yen27,000;US$270. ISBN: 490017808x.

First published 1985. Formed from the merger of *Japan English books in print* and *Japan English magazine directory*.

Lists over 10,000 books, 2,200 periodicals and 2,000 annuals from 3,500 publishers. Title arrangement, with a subject listing under 130 headings. Author/editor/translator and publisher indexes. *Class No:* 015(52)

[500]

Kokusha sōmokuroku. Tokyo, Iwanami Shoten, 1989-91. 9v. ISBN: 4000086014.

Expanded and updated version of work first published in 9v. 1963-76.

Union listing of titles written or translated by Japanese to end of the Edo era (1867). Based on reported holdings of more than 500 libraries. Title arrangement, V.9 author index. Further works listed in the same publisher's *Kotenseki sōgō mokuroku: kokusho sōmokuroku zoku-hen* (1990. 3v.).
Class No: 015(52)

[501]

—GARDNER, K.B. Descriptive catalogue of the Japanese books in the British Library printed before 1700. London, British Library/Nara-ken, Tenri Central Library, 1993. xlv,753p. 114 plates. £245. ISBN: 0712302433.

Provides detailed descriptions for 635 books, reputedly the best collection outside Japan. Subject arrangement within 3 categories: Japanese editions of Chinese classical works (89 entries); Buddhist literature (127 entries); native Japanese works (419 entries). Indexed. *Class No:* 015(52)

[502]

—HAYASHI, N. *and* KORNICKI, P. Early Japanese books in Cambridge University Library: a catalogue of the Aston, Satow and Von Siebold collections. Cambridge, Cambridge Univ. Press, 1991. xx,520p. £80;$129.95. (*University of Cambridge oriental publications, 40.*) ISBN: 0521364965.

2,569 entries in Japanese script for woodblock printing of the Edo period. With the British Library catalogue (above), one of a number of recent publications that help compensate for the inaccuracies of *Kokusha sōmokuru*. Indexed by title, author/editor/illustrator, publisher and transliterated title. *Class No:* 015(52)

[503]

Koruritsu kokkai toshokan zōsho mokuroku: Meijiki. Tokyo, Kokuritsu Kokkai Toshokan, 1994-95. 8v.

Rev. ed. of *Kokuritsu kokkai toshokan shozō Meijiki kankō tosho mokuroku*.

Lists 113,000 Japanese books published in the Meiji period (1868-1912) held by the National Diet Library. Subject arrangement with author and title indexing. A CD-ROM version is also available. *Class No:* 015(52)

[504]

Nihon shoseki sōmokuroku. Tokyo, Nihon Shoseki Shuppan Kyokai, 1977-. Annual. Yen52,530.

Functions as a Japanese books in print. Title arrangement with author and series indexes, publisher directory and statistical data. Over 500,000 titles listed 1996. *Class No:* 015(52)

[505]

Nihon zenkoku shoshi sōmokuroku. Tokyo, Kokuritsu Kokkai Toshokan, 1948-. Weekly, with quarterly and annual indexes. Yen600 per week. ISSN: 03894002.

Published as *Nōhon shūhō*, 1948-1980 (ISSN: 03853292). Added English title *Japanese national bibliography*.

Divided into two sections: government publications arranged according to agency; private publications arranged by the Nippon Decimal Classification. Separate non-classified listings for certain categories of material such as children's literature and foreign language publications. Material from public corporations and educational institutions appears in the government publications section. Quarterly index *Nihon zenkoku shoshi shubanban*. Records searchable online as part of the *J-BISC* database. A quarterly updated CD-ROM version is also available. *Class No:* 015(52)

[506]

Shuppan nenkan. Tokyo, Shuppan Nyūsusha, 1951-. Annual.

Lists new books and periodicals published on a commercial basis. Now issued in two vols., the first listing monographs by Dewey classification with separate sections for periodicals, the second providing information on the book trade. 58,310 titles recorded in the 1996 vol. *Class No:* 015(52)

Taiwan

[507]

Chung-hua min kuo ch'u pan t'u shu mu lu. Taipei, National Central Library, 1970-. Quarterly, with irregular cumulations. ISSN: 03015165.

Issued monthly 1970-91. English cover title *Chinese national bibliography*. Replaces the *Monthly list of Chinese books* 1960-1969 (ISSN: 05782007).

Based on accessions to the National Central Library. Arranged under broad subject headings with author and title indexes. Antiquarian and foreign language publications listed separately. *Class No:* 015(529)

Asia—Middle & Near East

[508]

LIBRARY OF CONGRESS. Library of Congress Office, Cairo. **Accessions list Middle East.** Cairo, Library of Congress Office, 1963-93. Bi-monthly. ISSN: 00417769.

Ceased publication 1993. Continued a similarly titled bibliography issued by the American Libraries Book Procurement Center, Cairo, 1958-63.

Publications acquired from the Arab world only excluding Djibouti, Somalia and Mauritania. From 1983 arranged by country (previously alphabetical), with subdivisions for monographs and serials. Author/title index in final annual issue; no subject index. Particularly good coverage for Egypt. *Class No:* 015(53+56)

[509]

al-Nashrah al-'Arabiyah lil-matbū'at li'ām. 1970-. [The Arab bulletin of publications.] Tunis, Arab League Educational Cultural and Scientific Organization, 1972-. Annual.

Based on national bibliographies and other listings from Arab states. Books, government publications, theses and new periodicals included. Dewey classified arrangement with author and title indexes. Coverage is strongest for North African countries. *Class No:* 015(53+56)

Asia—South & South East

[510]

LIBRARY OF CONGRESS. Library of Congress Office, New Delhi. **Accessions list South Asia.** New Delhi, Library of Congress Office, 1981-96. Monthly, (occasionally bimonthly). ISSN: 02716445.

Ceased publication with the final issue of 1996. Formed from the merger of separately published accessions lists for India (1962-79), Pakistan (1962-79), Nepal (1966-79), Bangladesh (1972-79), Sri Lanka (1973-79) and Afghanistan (1978-79). Preceded by *South Asia accessions list* (1955-60) and *Southern Asia: publications in Western languages* (1950-54).

Covered monographs, pamphlets, serials, official publications, newspapers and audio-visual materials acquired by the Library of Congress New Delhi Office. Geographic extent as for the separately published lists to 1979 (above), but Bhutan and Maldives added. From 1994, on cessation of *Accession list Southeast Asia* (*q.v.*), also included material from Burma, Cambodia, Laos, Malaysia (Chinese and Tamil only), Mongolia, Singapore (Chinese and Tamil only) and Thailand. All entries in Roman script. Annual index (authors, titles, subjects in one sequence) in final issue of each year. *Class No:* 015(54+59)

[511]

The South Asia and Burma retrospective bibliography (SABREB). Stage 1. 1556-1800. Shaw, G.W., *comp.* London, British Library, 1987. x,560p. £50. ISBN: 0712301194.

Covers books, periodicals and newspapers printed in the Indian subcontinent in both native and European languages. 1,771 entries, 1,712 for 18th century items; 1,099 of the works are in European languages, 717 in English. Chronological arrangement with name, title and subject indexes. Based on the holdings of the British Library, but includes works held elsewhere giving locations. Two further stages to SABREB are planned covering 1801-1867 and 1868-1900. *Class No:* 015(54+59)

India

[512]

Indian books in print: a bibliography of Indian books published in English language. Singh, S., *comp.* Delhi, Indian Bibliographic Bureau, 1967-. Irregular (now biennial). Rs7200. ISSN: 09711589.

Issued in 3v. V.1 Authors; v.2 Titles; v.3 Subject guide. 1st ed. covered 1955/67. Assumed current 3v. format from 1972/73.

The 1996 issue (16th ed.), lists 112,000 titles available from 3,000 Indian publishers. Confined to monographs; entries do not give ISBNs, but prices indicated where available. Subject volume, arranged by Dewey classification, includes a directory of publishers. By far the most comprehensive of a number of in print listings of English language Indian books to have appeared, and the only one to have sustained regular publication. *Class No:* 015(540)

[513]

The Indian national bibliography. Calcutta, Central Reference Library, Ministry of Human Resource Development, Dept. of Culture, 1958-. Monthly, with annual cumulation. Rs540. ISSN: 00196002.

Issued quarterly with annual cumulations to 1963. Publication variously interrupted: 1968-70 not published; monthly publication suspended 1977-83; delayed annual cumulations *e.g.* 1991 issued 1994.

Attempts comprehensive coverage of Indian publications, including items in English and Indian languages (transliterated). Classified Dewey arrangement with author/title and subject indexes. Includes new periodicals and government publications, but excludes maps, music and ephemera. *Class No:* 015(540)

[514]

National bibliography of Indian literature, 1901-1953. Kesavan, B.S., *and others eds.* New Delhi, Sahitya Akademi, 1962-90. 5v.

V.1 Assamese, Bengali, English, Gujarati; v.2 Hindi, Kannada, Kashmiri, Malayalam; v.3 Marathi, Oriya, Panjabi, Sanskrit; v.4 Sindhi, Tamil, Telugu, Urdu; v.5 Dogri, Konkani, Maithili, Manipuri, Nepali, Rajasthani.

Aims to include 'books of literary merit, and important and significant books' in the social sciences and humanities. Transliterated entries arranged by broad subjects within language sections. Annotations in English. V.5 covers titles published to 1980. *Class No:* 015(540)

Nepal

[515]

INDIA OFFICE LIBRARY AND RECORDS. Catalogue of Nepali printed books in the India Office Library. Hutt, M., *comp.* London, British Library, 1985. viii,43p. £15. ISBN: 0712300465.

Collection ranges from translations of classic Sanskrit works to contemporary Nepali literature. Discounting duplicates covers 560 items; in Library of Congress classified order with author, title and subject indexes. *Class No:* 015(541.35)

[516]

Nepalese national bibliography. 1981-. Kathmandu, Tribhuvan Univ. Central Library and Nepal Research Centre, 1983-. Annual (irregular).

Also appears in *Journal of the Nepal Research Centre* (Wiesbaden, Franz Steiner).

Confined to monographs and official publications, but includes titles by Nepalis published overseas. Dewey classified arrangement with author/title and subject indexes. Most recent issue appears to be 1984/86 published 1993. *Class No:* 015(541.35)

Sri Lanka

[517]

Sri Lanka national bibliography. Colombo, National Library of Sri Lanka, 1963-. Monthly. ISSN: 02538229.

As *Ceylon national bibliography* until 1971. Issued quarterly 1964-93.

Sinhala, Tamil and English sequences in Dewey classified order. Author/title/series and subject indexes for each language. Excludes reprints, audio-visual materials, maps and pamphlets. Well produced and up-to-date, recent issues also contain details of forthcoming publications (yellow pages). *Class No:* 015(548.7)

Pakistan

[518]

The Pakistan national bibliography: a subject catalogue of new Pakistani books... . 1947/61-. Islamabad, Dept. of Libraries, National Library of Pakistan, 1966-. Annual. ISSN: 10190678.

A retrospective issue for 1947-61 was published in 1973. 1965-67 and 1970-71 not yet published.

The 1990 issue (1994) has separate English and Urdu and other Pakistani languages sections. Both arranged according to Dewey classification, with an author/title/subject index. *Class No:* 015(549)

Bangladesh

[519]

Bangladesh national bibliography. 1972-. Dhaka, Bangladesh National Library, 1974-. Annual.

Bengali title *Bamladesa jatiya granthapanji.*

Separate sequences for English and Bengali material, both Dewey classified with author and title indexes. Covers only a fraction of the publishing output of Bangladesh. Subject to publication delays and interruptions, 1991 vol. issued 1994. *Class No:* 015(549.3)

Iran

[520]

Kitâbsinsi-'î millî-î Îrân. Tihran, Kitâbkhanah, 1963-. Irregular. ISSN: 00750522.

Title varies slightly; English subtitle *The Iranian national bibliography*. Frequency also varies, quarterly 1971-78.

Dewey classified listing with title, author and subject indexes. Some publication delays, No.72 (Summer 1992) not appearing until 1995. *Class No:* 015(55)

Turkey

[521]

Türkiye basmalari toplu kataloğu: arap harfli Türkçe eserler (1729-1928). [The Union catalogue of Turkey's printed books: Turkish publications in Arabic letters.] Ankara, Millî Kütüphane, 1990-. ISBN: 9751705517.

Aims to record books printed in Turkey between 1729 and 1928 and those Turkish books in Arabic letters printed in foreign countries and countries once under Turkish rule. Based on the holdings of 157 libraries. 10 vols. projected, v.IV (F-G) brings total no. of entries to 11,941.
Class No: 015(560)

[522]

Türkiye bibliyoğrafyasi, 1928/38-. [Turkish national bibliography.] Ankara, Millî Kütüphane, 1935-. Monthly. US$12. ISSN: 00414328.

Founded 1928 with the introduction of the Latin script in Turkey. Frequency varies: quarterly 1939-1943, monthly 1944-1948, quarterly again 1949-1982, monthly since 1982. Decennial cumulations 1928/38, 1939/48.

Approximately 7,500 entries annually in recent years, covering books, periodicals, official publications, theses, maps and audio-visual materials received on legal deposit. Dewey classified arrangement; personal/corporate author, book title, periodical title and ISBN indexes in each issue, cumulated annually. *Class No:* 015(560)

Cyprus

[523]

Kypriaké vivliographia. 1983/84-. Leukōsia, Vivliographikēs Hetaireias Kyprou, 1985. Annual (irregular).

National bibliography of the Greek half of Cyprus. Subject listing under 46 headings corresponding to Dewey; name index. Includes items by Greek Cypriots published overseas. The 1996 issue (1997. 145p.) has 830 entries.
Class No: 015(564.3)

Iraq

[524]

ABDULĪAHMAN, A.J. Fihrist al matbū'āt al-'Irāqīyah 1856-1972. Baghdād, al-Jumhurīyah al-'Irāqīyah, 1978-79. 3v.

English title *Iraqi national bibliography 1856-1972: subject catalogue of Arabic books printed in Iraq from the time printing began down to 1972 plus books by Iraqi authors published outside the country*. *Class No:* 015(567)

[525]

al-Fihris al-watanī lil-matbū'at al-'Irāqīyah. Baghdād, Maktabah al-Watanīyah, 1971-. Quarterly (irregular). ISSN: 02505290.

Title varies: Arabic title *al-Bibliyūghrāfīyah al watanīyah al-'Irāqīyah* until 1977; English title *Iraqi national bibliography*.

Format varies. Publication currently lapsed.
Class No: 015(567)

Syria

[526]

al-Bibliyūgrāfīya al-watanīyah al Sūrīyah. 1984-. Dimashq, Maktabat al-Asad, 1985-. Annual.

Added English title *The Syrian national bibliography*.

Arranged according to modified Dewey D.C. with author, title and publisher indexes. A retrospective bibliography *al-Bibliyūghrāfīyah al-watanīyah al Surīyah al-rāji'ah* began publication 1987. *Class No:* 015(569.1)

Israel

[527]

Israeli books in print 1986-. Lahar, D., *comp and* Halberstadt, C.S., *ed.*. Tel Aviv, Israel Book and Printing Center, Israel Export Institute/Jerusalem, Haberstadt Communication, 1986-. Irregular.

Initial vol. (ISBN: 9652220787) lists 1,260 non-Hebrew titles (915 English) published in Israel since 1970. No further issues traced. *Class No:* 015(569.4)

[528]

Kiryat Sefer: bibliographical quarterly of the Jewish National and University Library, Jerusalem. Jerusalem, The Jewish National and University Library, 1924-. Quarterly, with separate annual cumulated index. US$50. ISSN: 00231851.

Published as *Kirjath Sepher*, 1924-1975.

Functions as the de facto Israeli national bibliography in the absence of an official publication. 80% of the contents of each issue comprise a listing of new Israeli publications or Judaica printed abroad. Arranged under 23 broad subject groups. About 12,000 items listed annually. Heavy predominance of entries for Jewish history and literature and Judaism. *Class No:* 015(569.4)

Jordan

[529]

al-Bibliyūghrāfīyā al-waṯanīyah al-Urdunīyah. [The Jordanian national bibliography.] 'Amman, Mudīrayāt al-Maktabāt wa-al-Wathā'iq al-Waṯanīyah, 1980-. Annual (irregular). $20.

Frequency and publisher varies.

The 1996 issue (1997. vp.), produced by the Dept. of the National Library, has entries for 486 Arabic and 22 English titles in separate sequences. Both Dewey classified with author and title indexes. *Class No:* 015(569.5)

Asia—South East

[530]

LIBRARY OF CONGRESS. Library of Congress Office, Jakarta. **Accessions list Southeast Asia.** Jakarta, Library of Congress Office, 1975-93. Bimonthly. ISSN: 00962341.

Merged with *Accessions list South Asia* (*q.v. from 1994. Succeeded Accession list Indonesia, Malaysia, Singapore and Brunei*, 1964-1974.

....*(contd.)*
Listed publications acquired from Brunei, Burma, Cambodia, Indonesia, Laos, Malaysia, Philippines, Singapore, Thailand and Vietnam. Entries, all in Roman script, arranged by country then main entry. Author/title index in final issue of each year. Coverage strongest for Indonesia and Thailand. *Class No:* 015(59)

Thailand

[531]
Bannānukrom hāēng chāt Prathet Thai. 1975-. [Thai national bibliography.] Bangkok, National Library, 1978-. Quarterly. ISSN: 01251899.

Semi-annual 1975-83.

Since 1985 divided into book and periodical sections. Former classified by Dewey with author, title and cremation book indexes; periodicals listed A-Z by title. Issues include English introduction and notes. Appears subject to publication delays, no printed issues later than 1987 traced. *Class No:* 015(593)

Malaysia

[532]
Bibliografi negara Malaysia. 1967-. [Malaysian national bibliography. 1967-.] Kuala Lumpur, Perpustakaan Negara Malaysia, 1969-. Quarterly. US$200. ISSN: 01265210.

Annual 1969-1975. Printed publication ceased; now issued on CD-ROM, discs including records from 1967.

Based on legal deposit, covering material published in Bahasa Malay, English, Chinese, Tamil and east Malayan languages. Includes books, government publications, new serials, maps, and, from 1989, audio-visual materials. *Class No:* 015(595)

[533]
LIM, H.T. Penerbitan-penerbitan Malaysia: yang masih dalam pasaran pada takun 1987. Majlis Kemajuan Buku Kebangsaan Malaysia, 1988. 269p.

In print listing of 2,944 titles. *Class No:* 015(595)

[534]
PROUDFOOT, I. Early Malay printed books: a provisional account of materials published in the Singapore-Malaysia area up to 1920, noting holdings in major public collections. [Kuala Lumpur], Academy of Malay Studies and The Library, University of Malaysia, 1993. xxvi,858p. ISBN: 9679430340.

Lists just under 1,000 titles comprising over 2,000 editions. Locations noted include British Library, SOAS and Library of Congress. Entries, which give full bibliographic detail, arranged A-Z by title; indexed by persons and institutions, place of publication and languages other than Malay. *Class No:* 015(595)

Singapore

[535]
Singapore national bibliography. 1967-. Singapore, National Library, 1969-. Semi-annual. ISSN: 02186454.

Print publication (ISSN: 0129315X) ceased; now available as a semi-annually updated CD-ROM. Frequency of printed issues varied: annual 1967-77, quarterly with annual cumulation 1978-93.

Coverage includes goverenment publications and serials. Printed issues had separate sections for English (with Malay) and Chinese (with Tamil) titles, both classified by Dewey with author/title/series and subject indexes. Windows based CD-ROM provides records for English titles from 1967 and Chinese titles (image format) from 1993.
Class No: 015(595.13)

Vietnam

[536]
BIBLIOTHÈQUE NATIONALE. (FRANCE). Inventaire des livres imprimés vietnamiens 1960-79. Paris, Bibliothèque Nationale, 1987. 237p. ISBN: 2717717676.

Reproduces catalogue cards for Vietnamese language material acquired by the Bibliothèque Nationale. *c.*1,750 entries in author/anonymous title order. *Class No:* 015(597)

[537]
Thu' muc quôć gia Viêtnam. Hanoi, National Library, 1954-. Monthly with annual cumulation.

Title varies. Present title since 1974.

The current national bibliography. Classified arrangement under general subject groups. About 2,500 items recorded annually. *Class No:* 015(597)

[538]
Vietnamese holdings in the Library of Congress: a bibliography. Rony, A.K., *comp.* Washington D.C., Library of Congress, 1982. v,203p. $13. ISBN: 0844403628.

Entries for 2,902 monographs, 218 serials and 26 newspapers held in the non-legal Vietnamese language collection up to June 1979. Main entry sequence with subject, title and corporate body indexes.

A *Supplement, 1979-1985* (Rony, A.K. *comp.* Library of Congress, 1987. vii,167p. ISBN: 0844405647) contains a futher 1,927 entries, 1,795 of which are for monographs. *Class No:* 015(597)

Africa

[539]
African books in print: an index by author, title and subject. [Livres Africains disponibles.] Zell, H.M., *ed.* 4th ed. Mansell, London, 1993. 2v. £250;$400. ISBN: 1873836112.

V.1 Author/Title; v.2 Subject. First published 1975; 3rd ed. 1984.

Lists 23,186 books and pamphlets (more than 10p.) from 745 publishers in print late 1991. About 20% of titles in African languages. Coverage of North Africa relatively poor, Lusophone Africa excluded. Subject sequence organized by detailed headings. Directory of publishers in v.1. A new ed. is scheduled for late 1998. *Class No:* 015(6)

[540]
—The African book publishing record. Oxford, Hans Zell Publishers, 1975-. Quarterly. £120;$200. ISSN: 03060322.

Acts as an updating supplement to *African books in print* each quarterly issue listing *c.*400 new titles by subject, country and author. Also carries signed book reviews and news articles. 'Africana reference works: an annotated list', which appears annually, is an additional feature.
Class No: 015(6)

Tunisia

[541]

Bibliographie nationale de Tunisie. 1969-. [al-Bibliyūgrāfiyā al-qawmiyah al-Tunisiyah.] Tunis, Bibliothèque Nationale, 1970-. Quarterly, 4th issue annual cumulation. ISSN: 03301761.

Retrospective vol. 1956-68 issued 1974; 1969-73 also available in one vol. Publication currently appears suspended.

Separate Roman and Arabic script sections, both classed by UDC with additional lists of official publications, dissertations and new periodicals. Author, title, subject, publisher and printer indexes. *Class No:* 015(611)

Libya

[542]

Bibliyūghrafiyah al-Waṭaniyah al-'Arabiyah al-Libiyah. 1972-. Benghāzi, al-Markaz al-Bibliūghrāfi al-Waṭani, Dār al-Kutub al-Waṭaniyah, 1973-. Annual (irregular).

Title varies slightly. Added English title page *Libyan Arab national bibliography*. Irregular in publication, now appears to be issued on a triennial basis. First issue gave retrospective coverage in 2 pts: 1. Periodicals, 1827-1971; 2. Monographs, etc., 1951-1971.

Arabic and English listings subdivided into trade publications, official publications, periodicals, etc. Issue for 1987/89 published 1996. *Class No:* 015(612)

Egypt

[543]

Dalīl al-kitāb al-misrī. [Egyptian books in print.] Cairo, General Egyptian Book Organisation, 1972-. Irregular.

Arabic and European language sections; classified arrangement with author and title indexes. *Class No:* 015(620)

[544]

Nashrat al-ida'. [Legal deposit bulletin.] Cairo, National Library Press, 1969-. Monthly, with some annual cumulations. ISSN: 05751306.

Frequency varies; monthly with annual index from 1996.

In two sections, Arabic and English, each arranged in Dewey based subject groups. Author, title and subject indexes. Arabic works predominate. Quality and currency much improved in recent years. *Class No:* 015(620)

[545]

NUSAYR, A.I. al-Kutub al-'Arabiyah allati nushirat fi Misr fi al-qarn al-tāsi 'ashar. [Arabic books published in Egypt in the nineteenth century.] al-Qūhirah, Qism al Nashr bi-al-Jāmi'ah al-Amerikiyah bi-al-Qūhirah, 1990. xiv,403p.

About 10,000 entries in Dewey classified order. Includes an English introduction. Three companion vols. extend coverage: *al-Kutub al-'Arabiyah allati nushirat fi Misr bayna amay 1900-1925* (1983); *al-Kutub al-'Arabiyah allati nushirat fi Misr bayna amay 1926-1940* (1980); *Dalil al-matbuat al-Misriyah 1940-1956* (1975). *Class No:* 015(620)

Ethiopia

[546]

Ethiopian publications. 1963-. Addis Ababa, Institute of Ethiopian Studies, Addis Ababa Univ., 1965-. Irregular. ISSN: 00711772.

Lists Ethiopian and foreign language titles published in or relating to Ethiopia. Long publication delays, current status uncertain. *Class No:* 015(63)

Morocco

[547]

Bibliographie nationale marocaine. Monographies et périodiques.$b1961-. Rabat, Bibliothèque Générale et Archives, 1962-. Annual. ISSN: 11136405.

Title also in Arabic. Title and frequency varies; recent issues much improved in coverage and presentation.

Separate French and Arabic sections in UDC classified arrangement. The 1995 v. (1996 104,71p) lists 279 monographs and 54 periodicals in the French language section. Retrospective v. for Arabic titles 1986-1994 also issued 1995 (591p.).

Listings of new Morocan titles can also be found in the book trade journal *Le Livre Marocain: revue annuelle bibliographique, signalétique et critique* published since 1983. *Class No:* 015(64)

Algeria

[548]

al-Bibliyūghrāfiyā al-Jazā'iriyah. [Bibliographie de l'Algerie.] Alger, Bibliothèque Nationale, 1963-. Semi-annual. $20. ISSN: 05232392.

Title also in Arabic.

French and Arabic language sections, both arranged by UDC with author, collective author, collaborator and title indexes. Issue no.61 for 1993 (1995) has 88 French and 99 Arabic entries. *Class No:* 015(65)

Senegal

[549]

Bibliographie du Sénégal. Dakar, Archives du Sénégal, 1972-. Irregular. ISSN: 03789942.

Continues *Bulletin bibliographique des Archives du Sénégal*, 1964-1972.

Various formats. Combined issue no. 59/61 for 1987/1989 (1990. vp.) contains 115 entries in broad UDC classified arrangement. Author, corporate author and title indexes. Poor currency and a decreasing number of entries characterise the more recent issues. *Class No:* 015(663)

Sierra Leone

[550]

Sierra Leone publications. Freetown, Sierra Leone Library Board, 1964-. Quarterly (irregular). ISSN: 05832276.

Poorly reproduced Dewey classified list. Publication currently suspended. *Class No:* 015(664)

Gambia

[551]

The Gambia national bibliography. 1977-. Banjul, The Gambia National Library, 1978-. Annual. ISSN: 0796014x.

Current title from 1988; previously *National bibliography of the Gambia*. Issued semi-annually 1977-1982.

Dewey classified listing with author/editor/title/series and subject indexes. Prompt in appearance, the 1995 issue (1996. vi,20p.) lists *c.*40 items. *Class No:* 015(665.1)

Ghana

[552]

Ghana national bibliography. 1965-. Accra, Ghana Library Board, 1968-. Bi-monthly. $60. ISSN: 08550093.

Compiled at the George Padmore Research Library on African Affairs. Issued annually with increasing delays until 1978. From 1987 relaunched as a bi-monthly absorbing *Ghana: a current bibliography* (1967-86, also bi-monthly) and continuing its numbering. Cumulations for the period after 1978 intended. Some issues carry erroneous ISSN: 08550225.

Based on legal deposit. Main section in Dewey classified order with author/title/series and subject indexes. Also includes books, pamphlets, periodical articles, etc. about Ghana. Promptly produced, issues for 1996 contain 831 entries. *Class No:* 015(667)

Nigeria

[553]

The National bibliography of Nigeria. Lagos, National Library of Nigeria, 1973-. Monthly, with annual cumulation. ISSN: 03310507.

Previously (1950/52-1972) as *Nigerian publications* (weekly, with quarterly and annual cumulations).

Covers the publishing output of Nigeria, plus works by Nigerians or about Nigeria published abroad. On average well over 80% of items listed are in English, the remainder in Nigerian languages. The 1990 annual v. (1993. xii,150p.), is a classed listing by Dewey with author/title/series and subject indexes. New serial titles in separate section: publisher/printer list. *Class No:* 015(669)

[554]

—Nigerian publications 1950-1970. University of Ibadan Library., *comp*. Ibadan, Ibadan Univ. Pr., 1977. 433p.

Partial cumulation *Nigerian publications* the forerunner of *The National bibliography of Nigeria* (above).

Not a complete cumulation as 1971-1972, periodical titles and works published outside Nigeria are excluded. In 3 sections: Non-official publications in English; Official publications; Publications in Nigerian languages.
Class No: 015(669)

Africa—East & Equatorial

[555]

LIBRARY OF CONGRESS. Library of Congress Office, Nairobi. **Accessions list Eastern and Southern Africa.** Nairobi, Library of Congress Office, 1968-. Bi-monthly. ISSN: 10702717.

Current title from 1993; previously *Accessions list Eastern Africa* (ISSN: 0090371X). Published quarterly 1968-1971.

Publications acquired by the Library of Congress Office Nairobi from Angola, Botswana, Burundi, Djibouti, Eritrea, Ethiopia, Kenya, Lesotho, Madagascar, Malawi, Mauritius, Mozambique, Namibia, Réunion, Rwanda, Swaziland, Tanzania, Uganda, Zaire, Zambia and Zimbabwe. About 2,500 monographs catalogued each year in country then language sections. Main, added entry and title index in each issue, cumulated annually. Serials recorded in *Accessions list Eastern and Southern Africa: serials supplement* (*q.v.*).
Class No: 015(67)

Zaire

[556]

Bibliographie du Zaire. Kinshasa/Gombé, Bibilothèque Nationale du Zaire, 1971-. Annual (irregular).

Current title from 1987/88 issue (1990); previously as *Bibliographie nationale*

Classified Dewey listing with author index. Separate treatment for dissertations and audio-visual materials.
Class No: 015(675)

Uganda

[557]

Uganda national bibliography. Kampala, Makerere Univ. Library Services, 1987-. Quarterly (annual).

Dewey classified list with author/editor/title index. Books relating to Uganda published outside the country in separate sequence. *Class No:* 015(676.1)

Kenya

[558]

Kenya national bibliography. 1980-. Nairobi, Kenya National Library Service, National Reference & Bibliographic Department, 1983-. Annual.

A Dewey classified listing including foreign publications relating to Kenya and/or written by Kenyans. Increasing publication delays in recent years. 1991 v. (1996. xi,57p.), has 331 entries with an author/title index and list of publishers. *Class No:* 015(676.2)

Tanzania

[559]

Tanzania national bibliography. 1969-. Dar es Salaam, National Bibliographic Agency, Tanzania Library Services Board, 1970-. Irregular. ISSN: 0856003x.

As *Printed in Tanzania* 1969-1973. Frequency varies: annual 1969-82, monthly 1983-88; annual again 1989, now apparently triennial (1990/92 and 1993/95, latter issued 1997 (76p.)).

Dewey classified list with author/editor/title/series index. Includes reports, dissertations and first issues of serials.
Class No: 015(678)

Africa—Southern

[560]

Southern African books in print. [Suider-Afrikaanse boeke in druk.] Cape Town, Books in Print Information Services, 1993-. Annual. ISSN: 1024039x.

Continues *South African books in print* (last published 1984?). Also available on microfiche (updated semi-annually) and CD-ROM (updated quarterly). Records also available as part of Whitaker's *BookBank global compact* (*q.v.*).

The 1996 printed v. (868p.) contains 31,012 entries for books from 946 publishers. Arranged in one author/title sequence with full bibliographical detail, ISBN and price. South Africa and 'neighbouring countries' covered, 15,275 titles in English, 9,748 in Afrikaans. *Class No:* 015(68)

South Africa

[561]

MENDELSSOHN, S. A South African bibliography to the year 1925: being a revision and continuation of Sidney Mendelssohn's *South African bibliography* (1910). ['N Suid Afrikaanse bibliographie tot die jaar 1925.] South African Library, *ed.* London, Mansell, 1979. 4v. ISBN: 0720105560.

This new ed. records some 35,000 items, with 15,000 references, increasing the 1910 ed. sevenfold. Original Mendelssohn titles included in abbreviated form. Arrangement as before A-Z by author. Excludes works in African languages, periodical publications, atlases and maps, printed music, manuscripts and post 1854 government publications. Geographic coverage extends beyond South Africa, including Namibia, Botswana, Lesotho and Swaziland. Some items annotated; locations in 29 libraries. No indexes, but adequately cross-referenced.

A *Supplement*, published as v.5 (Cape Town, South African Library, 1991. xiv,476p. ISBN:086968101X), has 3,086 further entries, including 308 for revisions to citations in v.1-4. Also features volume title, subject and printer and publisher indexes and 'Additional locations for publications listed in SABIB v.1-4' (p.423-72). *Class No:* 015(680)

[562]

NIENABER, P.J. Bibliografie van Afrikaanse boeke. Johannesburg, Pevskor-Uitgewery, 1943-1981. 9v.

Each volume covers a period of years (v.1 1861-1942; v.2 1943-1948; v.3 1948-1953; v.4 1953-1958 (June); v.5 1958 (July)-1962; v.6 1963-1966; v.7 1967-1970; v.8 1971-1974; v.9 1975-1977).

V.9 (ISBN: 062802102x) has author, title and subject sequences, the former providing full entry information. *Class No:* 015(680)

[563]

Retrospective South African national bibliography for the period 1926-1958. [Retrospektiewe Suid-Afrikaanse nasionale bibliografie vir de tydperk 1926-1958.] Pretoria, State Library, 1985. 2v. ISBN: 0798912081.

V.1: xi,681p. plates; v.2: (indexes only) 384p.

Fills the gap between Mendelssohn and the current *South African national bibliography*. 18,290 items arranged by main entry. Index of titles, series, personal and corporate names, collaborators, translators, compilers, editors. Excludes African language publications. *Class No:* 015(680)

[564]

—South African catalogue of books: 4th complete ed., 1900-1950, with list of publishers and booksellers in South Africa. Coetzee, N.S., *ed.* Johannesburg, the Editor, 1952. 2v.

Previous eds. (not completely superseded) cover 1900-39, 1900-42, 1900-47. Only v.1 of a 5th ed. (*S.A. Katalogus/ Catalogue*) to cover 1950-54, was published (1954).

Author and title list of books published in South Africa in English, Afrikaans and African languages. Government publications and titles of most mission presses excluded. For English and Afrikaans works now largely superseded by the revised Mendelssohn and *Retrospective South African national bibliography*. *Class No:* 015(680)

[565]

SANB: South African national bibliography. [Suid-Afrikaanse nasionale bibliografie.] Pretoria, State Library, 1960-. Quarterly, final issue annual cumulation. R244;$160. ISSN: 00360864.

Earlier coverage in the mimeographed *Publications received in terms of Copyright Act no. 9 of 1916,* 1933-58. From 1958-1969 the South African Public Library at Cape Town issued *Africana nova: a quarterly bibliography of books currently published in and about the Republic of South Africa...* .

Based on legal deposit. Covers monographs, pamphlets, government publications, microforms, maps, technical reports and periodicals. The 1996 annual (xxii,727p.) has 5,070 entries in Dewey classified order, with title/name/ series and subject indexes. *SANB* records from 1988 are also available on the quarterly updated CD-ROM *South African studies* published by NISC. *Class No:* 015(680)

Botswana

[566]

The National bibliography of Botswana. Gaborone, Botswana National Library Service, 1969-. 3pa. (last issue annual cumulation). $6. ISSN: 00278777.

Arranged by Dewey classification with an author/title/ series index. Theses and overseas publications relating to Botswana included since 1983. *Class No:* 015(681)

Swaziland

[567]

Swaziland national bibliography. 1973/76-. Kwaluseni, University of Swaziland Library/Mbabane, Swaziland National Library Services, 1977-. Irregular. ISSN: 03787710.

The 5th issue for 1988/93 (1996. [iv],80p. $12.50) lists 762 books, annual reports, conference papers, dissertations, official publications, etc., including some items relating to Swaziland published elsewhere. Dewey classified arrangement with locations in Swaziland libraries. Author/ title index. *Class No:* 015(683.4)

Namibia

[568]

Namibian books in print: a catalogue of books from Namibia available through the book trade. Hillebrecht, W., *comp.* Windhoek, Assoc. of Namibian Publishers, 1994. 72p. ISBN: 9991672303.

Author listing of 904 numbered entries. Includes works in all Namibian languages. Co-author/title, language, subject, distributor indexes. Further eds. anticipated. *Class No:* 015(688)

Zimbabwe

[569]

Zimbabwe books in print. Harare, Zimbabwe Book Publishers' Association, 1993-. Biennial. £18.50;US$33.

The 2nd v. (1995. ix,192p. ISBN: 0797414568) lists more than 2,400 books available from over 60 publishers. Separate author and title sequences with broad term subject index. List of publishers precedes main text. Zimbabwe published titles also appear in *Southern African books in print* (*q.v.*). *Class No:* 015(689.1)

[570]
Zimbabwe national bibliography. 1979-. Harare, National Archives, 1980-. Annual (recent issues biennial). Z$40. ISSN: 00855677.

Formerly *Rhodesia national bibliography,* 1967-1978 and *List of publications deposited in the library of the National Archives,* 1961-1966.

Entries in Dewey classified order with author/title and subject indexes. The 1993/94 issue (1996. 99p.) lists 700 items. *Class No:* 015(689.1)

[571]
—HARTRIDGE, A. Rhodesia national bibliography 1890-1930. Salisbury, National Archives of Rhodesia, 1977. 50p.

Books, serials, newspapers, government publications and maps in a Dewey sequence. A further v. to fill the gap in Zimbabwean national bibliography to 1960 is planned. *Class No:* 015(689.1)

Zambia

[572]
The National bibliography of Zambia. 1970/71-. Lusaka, National Archives of Zambia, 1972-. Annual (occasionally biennial). K500. ISSN: 03771636.

Covers books, pamphlets, first issues of serials, government publications, local authority publications, proceedings, etc. Dewey classified arrangement with an author/title/series index and a list of publishers. *Class No:* 015(689.4)

[573]
Zambian books in print and ISBN publisher's directory. Mwacalimba, H. *and* Kanyengo, C., *comps.* Lusaka, Booksellers and Publishers Association of Zambia, 1995. v,282p. ISBN: 9982804006.

Author and title listings, both with full bibliographical detail, of *c.*800 titles published in Zambia. Further 'Publisher/ISBN index' and list of publishers with ISBN prefix. *Class No:* 015(689.4)

Malawi

[574]
Malawi national bibliography: list of publications deposited in the Library of the National Archives. Zomba, National Archives of Malawi, 1965-. Annual. $20. ISSN: 05423058.

Freuqency varies, biennial 1977-80. Subject to publication delays, regular issue now resumed.

In Dewey classified order with author/title and subject indexes. Cumulation for 1984-1990 (1994. v,114p) contains 597 entries and includes listings of new and ceased periodicals. *Class No:* 015(689.7)

Madagascar

[575]
Bibliographie nationale de Madagascar. 1964-. Antananarivo, Bibliothèque nationale, 1966-. Quarterly, (irregular). ISSN: 00676926.

Variant title *Rakitahirinkevi-pirenen'i Madagasikra.* Title and frequency varies: 1964-69 French title *Bibliographie annuelle de Madagascar*. Quarterly since 1987 (semi-annual from 1983), but appearance erratic.

Issues are in classified order with author, subject and series indexes. *Class No:* 015(691)

Mauritius

[576]
Bibliography of Mauritius. Port Louis, Govt. Printer, 1950-. Annual.

Issued as a bound in supplement to *Annual report of the Archives Department* (ISSN: 00765481).

The 1995 issue (1996. 32p.) has 363 entries in sections for 'private' publications, periodicals, newspapers and serials, government and semi-official publications and publications issued abroad. No indexes. *Class No:* 015(698.2)

Canada

[577]
The Canadian catalogue of books published in Canada, about Canada, as well as those written by Canadians, with imprint 1921-1949; with cumulated author index. 2nd ed. Toronto, Toronto Public Libraries, 1967. v.p.

First published in this form in 2v., 1951. Consolidates the annual of the same title published by Toronto Public Libraries 1923-50. Continued by *Canadiana* (*q.v.*).

Classed arrangement, entries for books, pamphlets and selected government publications. English language items only in this cumulation. French entries reprinted as *Notices en langue française du Canadian catalogue of books 1921-1949* (Montreal, Bibliothèque nationale du Québec, 1975. 263,199p.). *Class No:* 015(71)

[578]
—TOD, D. *and* CORDINGLEY, A. A Checklist of Canadian imprints 1900-1925. [Catalogue d'ouvrages imprimés au Canada 1900-1925.] Ottawa, Canadian Bibliographic Centre, 1950. 370l.

Brief entries for monographs only. Arranged A-Z by author; no indexes. *Class No:* 015(71)

[579]
Canadiana pre-1901 monographs. [Canadiana d'avant 1901: monographies.] Ottawa, National Library of Canada, 1980-. Microfiche. Can$140. ISSN: 11836849.

Published approx., biennially, each issue comprising a completely new cumulation. Current title from 1991; previously *Canadiana 1867-1901 monographs.* Introductory pamphlet, *Canadiana 1867-1900 monographs: Canada's national bibliography microfiche edition. An introduction* (1980. 28p. ISBN: 0662508238).

Coverage extends to pamphlets, leaflets, broadsides, atlases and printed music. Excludes most federal and provincial government publications, serials, newspapers and maps. Material relating to Canada or written by Canadians published overseas included. Over 67,000 entries in register no. order, with author/title, publication date, publisher/printer, place and subject (proper name) indexes. Locates copies in Canadian libraries. *Class No:* 015(71)

[580]
—CANADA. Public Archives. Catalogue of pamphlets in the Public Archives of Canada with an index. Casey, M., *comp.* [4th ed.]. Ottawa, Acland, 1931-32. 2v.

First published 1903.

Lists 10,072 items chronologically (v.1: 1493-1877; v.2: 1878-1931) with volume author and subject indexes. Includes pamphlets on Canada published elsewhere. *Class No:* 015(71)

[581]

—HAIGHT, W.R. Canadian catalogue of books. 1791-1897. Toronto, Haight, 1896-1904. 3v.

Reprinted Vancouver, Devlin; London, Pordes, 1958.

An incomplete listing. The main v. covers 1791-1895; supplements cover 1896-97. *Class No:* 015(71)

[582]

FLEMING, P.L. Upper Canadian imprints 1801-1841: a bibliography. Toronto, Univ. of Toronto P. in co-operation with the National Library of Canada and the Canadian Government Publishing Centre, 1988. xviii,556p. Can$125. ISBN: 0802025854.

Partially continues Tremaine (below). 1,605 entries arranged by year of publication with full bibliographical detail, extensive notes and library locations. Comprehensively indexed including by genre/subject, trades (bookbinders, printers, etc.) and place of publication. Appendices list 145 newspapers, 15 journals and copies not located. '(A) landmark in Canadian bibliography' (*The Library. Sixth series*, v.XI(3), Sept. 1989, p.285).
Class No: 015(71)

[583]

—FLEMING, P.L. Atlantic Canadian imprints 1801-1820: a bibliography. Toronto, Univ. of Toronto Press, 1991. xviii,189p. illus. Can$95. ISBN: 0802058728.

A further partial continuation of Tremaine. Full descriptive entries chronologically arranged by province. Includes serials and government publications. Short appendix lists items not located. Indexed. *Class No:* 015(71)

[584]

TREMAINE, M. A Bibliography of Canadian imprints, 1751-1800. Toronto, Toronto Univ. Press, 1952. xxvii,705p.illus.

1,204 items, arranged chronologically. Characterized by the full bibliographical description of each item whether a book, pamphlet, leaflet, broadside or handbill. Includes 'works known to have been produced, whether they are known to survive or not' (Preface p.v). Locations in Canadian, US and foreign libraries. Appendices cover printing offices, with biographical notes on printers, and manuscript sources. Detailed index. *Class No:* 015(71)

Contemporary

[585]

Canadian books in print. Toronto, Univ. of Toronto Press, 1973-. Annual (irregular).

Published in 2v: Author and title index (ISSN: 00688398); Subject index, (from 1975, ISSN: 03151999). Updating microfiche editions of author/title index issued April, July and October.

Supersedes *Canadian books in print/Catalogue des livres canadiens en librairie* (1967-72), which included French language titles.

Aims to list all English language books bearing the imprint of a Canadian publisher, or originated by Canadian subsidiaries of international publishing firms. Also covers French language titles published by predominantly English language publishers, or published outside Quebec. The 1995 ed. contains over 38,000 titles, including more than 5,000 with a 1994 imprint. Subject vol. based on Library of Congress subject headings. Publisher index in both vols.
Class No: 015(71)"312"

[586]

—Books in print Plus: Canadian edition. New Providence, N.J., Bowker, 1997-. CD-ROM database, updated monthly.

Based on the main *Books in print Plus* (*q.v.*) database. Includes 70,000 records for titles only available in Canada and addresses of 2,600 Canadian distributors.
Class No: 015(71)"312"

[587]

Canadiana: Canada's national bibliography. Ottawa, National Library of Canada, 1950-. Microfiche (monthly issues with annual cumulation). ISSN: 02253216.

Publication as a print service (ISSN: 00085391) discontinued from end of 1991. French subtitle *La Bibliographie nationale du Canada.* Succeeds *The Canadian catalogue of books published in Canada, about Canada, as well as those written by Canadians* ... (Toronto, Public Library, 1923-50. Annual).

Covers books, pamphlets, first issues of periodicals and newspapers, theses, atlases, microforms, sheet music, sound recordings, federal and provincial government publications and, since 1993, videorecordings and CD-ROMs. Arrangement has varied considerably over the years. Microfiche based on register no. order in separate Canadian and foreign imprint sections. Indexed by author/title/series, English and French subject headings (Library of Congress), ISBN/ISSN and Dewey class nos. Microfiche cumulations available for 1973-80, 1981-85, 1986-90 and 1991-95. Also available online as part of the National Library of Canada's AMICUS database system; a CD-ROM version is planned.
Class No: 015(71)"312"

Quebec

[588]

Bibliographie du Québec. Québec, Bibliothèque nationale du Québec, 1968-. Monthly, with annual index. Can$140. ISSN: 00061441.

Quarterly April 1969-January/March 1972.

Library of Congress classified listing with separate sections for serials, cartographic materials and electronic resources. Author/title and subject indexes in each issue, cumulated annually. Includes English language items published in Quebec. Also available as an online database.
Class No: 015(714)

[589]

—Les Livres disponibles de langue française. [Canadian French books in print.] Outremont, Québec, Bibliodata, 1981-. Quarterly. ISSN: 08367078.

Title varies: until 1987 as *La Liste des livres disponibles de langue française*. Also available in microfiche, 10 issues pa.

Equivalent of *Canadian books in print* (*q.v.*). Includes Canadian French language books published outside Quebec.
Class No: 015(714)

[590]

Bibliographie du Québec, 1821-1967. Québec, Bibliothèque nationale du Québec, 1980-. ISBN: 2551037166.

Issued in irregularly published volumes.

Each v. in 2pts.: pt.1 contains entries arranged by Library of Congress classification (1,000 per v. until v.20, then 3,000 or 5,000); pt.2 provides author/title, publisher, printer, place of publication, name and subject and chronological indexes. Excludes serials, government publications and maps. 26 v. published to 1996, cumulative microfiche index to v.1-22. Period before 1821 covered in Vlach (below). *Class No:* 015(714)

[591]
—DIONNE, N.E. Inventaire chronologique ... Quebec, Royal Society of Canada, 1905-12. 4v. & suppt.

V.1 lists Province of Quebec imprints in French, 1764-1905; v.3, imprints in English, 1764-1906; v.2 is a bibliography of works published elsewhere in Quebec and New France; v.4 lists maps, plans and atlases of New France and the Province of Quebec, 1508-1908.
Class No: 015(714)

[592]
Le Québec français: imprimés en français du Québec 1764-1990 à la British Library. [French Quebec: imprints in French from Quebec 1764-1990 in the British Library.] McTernan, D.J., *comp.* London, British Library/Québec, Bibliothèque nationale, 1992-93. 2v. £85 per v. ISBN: 0712302832, (v.1).

V.1 'seeks to present French Quebec's creative and artistic output as well as its conception of itself'. V.2 'deals with social and political institutions, its history, social order and geophysical features' (p.xii, v.1). Excludes maps, manuscripts, prints; includes works in English. Author order within subject groupings. Entries give BL shelfmark
Class No: 015(714)

[593]
VLACH, M. *and* **BUONO, Y. Catalogue collectif des impressions québécoises, 1764-1820.** Québec, Bibliothèque nationale, 1984. xxxiii,446p. ISBN: 2551089190.

Union catalogue of 12 Quebec libraries. 1,115 entries listed by main entry; comprehensively indexed by title, author, subject, genre, place, date, printer and provenance.
Class No: 015(714)

Mexico

[594]
Bibliografía mexicana. Mexico, Universidad Nacional Autónoma de Mexico, Biblioteca Nacional e Instituto Bibliográfico Mexicano, 1967-. Annual. US$200. ISSN: 00061069.

Now produced as a CD-ROM database, printed publication having ceased in 1989. Absorbed the irregularly published *Anuario bibliográfico* 1958-1969 in 1970. This title was preceded by *Anuario bibliográfico mexicano* issued for 1931-33 and 1940-42, intervening years not published.

Covers monographs, maps, video recordings, etc. Printed issues classified by Dewey with analytical index in which subject entries distinguished by uppercase typeface.
Class No: 015(72)

[595]
—Boletín bibliográfico mexicano. Mexico, Porrua, 1939-. Bi-monthly. US$15. ISSN: 01852027.

Includes a section *Nueva bibliografía mexicana* a classed listing including prices. *Class No:* 015(72)

[596]
—Libros de México. México, Organismo de la Cámara Nacional de la Industria Editorial Mexicana, 1985-. Quarterly. US$40. ISSN: 01862243.

Book publishing trade journal each issue of which includes a listing of *c.*750 new titles published in Mexico giving basic bibliographical data, ISBN and price. *Class No:* 015(72)

[597]
MEDINA, J.T. La Imprenta en México, 1539-1821. Santiago de Chile, the Author, 1907-12. 8v. illus., facsims.

Reprinted Amsterdam, N. Israel, 1965.

12,424 items arranged chronologically (v.1: 1539-1600 ... v.8: 1813-21).

Supplemented by F. González de Cossio's *La Imprenta en México, 1553-1820 cien adiciones...* . (1947. 205p. facsims.) and *La Imprenta en México: 510 adiciones...* . (1952. 354p. facsims.). *Class No:* 015(72)

Nicaragua

[598]
LATIN AMERICAN BIBLIOGRAPHIC FOUNDATION *and* **NICARAGUA.** Ministerio de Cultura. **Nicaraguan national bibliography, 1800-1978.** [Bibliografía nacional Nicaragüense, 1800-1978.] Redlands, Ca., Latin American Bibliographic Foundation; Managua, Biblioteca Nacional Ruebén Darío, 1986. 3v. 1911p. ISBN: 0914369016.

V.1 Monographs A-L. V.2 Monographs M-Z. V.3 Serials, indexes.

Lists 21,130 monographs and 601 serials published in or about Nicaragua, with locations in Nicaraguan or North American libraries. Author and title indexes. Subject indexes in English and Spanish. Continued by:-
Class No: 015(728.5)

[599]
—BIBLIOTECA NACIONAL 'RUEBÉN DARÍO'. Bibliografía nacional de Nicaragua. 1979/89-. Managua, Instituto Nicaragüense de Cultura, 1991-. Irregular.

The initial vol. (452p.) is a main entry listing of 4,667 items, including material about Nicaragua. Personal author, institutional and title indexes; no subject index. Further vol. for 1990/92 published 1993. *Class No:* 015(728.5)

Costa Rica

[600]
COSTA RICA. Dirección General de Bibliotecas y Biblioteca Nacional. Agencia Nacional ISBN. **Catálogo nacional ISBN:** libros publicados en Costa Rica. 1983/84-. San José, Biblioteca Nacional, 1984-. Annual (irregular).

The 1993 v. (1995. 250p.) lists over 1,000 titles in classified Dewey order (p.61-148). List of publishers with addresses precedes; author, title and ISBN indexes.

Earlier coverage of Costa Rican publications provided by *Anuario bibliográfico costarricense*, 1956-72/74 and *Boletín bibliográfico*, 1935/38-55. *Class No:* 015(728.6)

Caribbean

[601]
The Caricom bibliography. 1976-86. Georgetown, Caribbean Community Secretariat, Information and Documentation Section, 1977-89. Semi-annual, 2nd issue annual cumulation. ISSN: 02549646.

Aimed to list all material published in the 13 Caribbean Community states, (English-speaking West Indies plus Guyana and Belize). Classified arrangement by Dewey with author/title/series and subject indexes. *Class No:* 015(729)

[602]

—Bibliografía actual del Caribe. [Current Caribbean bibliography.] Rio Piedras, Puerto Rico, Biblioteca Regional del Caribe, 1951-76. Irregular, mainly annual. ISSN: 00701866.

Title also in French *Bibliographie courante de la Caraibe*. Cumulations for 1950-53 (1955), 1954-58 (1961) and 1959-61 (1968).

Covered titles published in or relating to the Caribbean held by the Biblioteca Regional del Caribe or supplied by contributing libraries. 2,702 entries in final vol.
Class No: 015(729)

Cuba

[603]

Bibliografía Cubana. 1959/62-. La Habana, Biblioteca Nacional José Marti, 1967-. Annual. ISSN: 05746086.

Frequency varies: bimonthly 1982-88 with annual index.

Main listing has sections for current Cuban books, titles relating to Cuba issued overseas and earlier material. Further listings of new periodicals and maps, music, films, etc. About 400 entries in each issue; main entry arrangement with analytical, series and overseas publisher indexes.
Class No: 015(729.1)

[604]

Bibliográfico cubano 1937-1966. Peraza Sarausa, F., *ed.* Gainesville, Fla., University of Florida Press, 1938-1967. Annual.

As *Anuario bibliográfico cubana* 1937-52. Published in Havana until 1959. The pre-revolutionary national bibliography for Cuba, Peraza Sarausa continued to produce the title in exile. Peraza Sarausa also edited the first issue of the annual *Revolutionary Cuba: a bibliographical guide*, published for 1966-68, Coral Gables, University of Miami Press, 1967-70. *Class No:* 015(729.1)

Jamaica

[605]

Jamaican national bibliography, 1968-. Kingston, National Library of Jamaica, 1969-. Quarterly, 4th issue annual cumulation. ISSN: 00752991.

Publication appears suspended since the late 1980s.

Covers books, periodicals, maps and newspapers. Includes both Jamaican publications and material about Jamaica. Classified Dewey sequence with author, title and series index. Issues also carry a selected listing of articles from Jamaican periodicals. *Class No:* 015(729.2)

[606]

—INSTITUTE OF JAMAICA. Library. Jamaican national bibliography, 1964-1974. Williams, R.I., *ed.* New York, Kraus International, 1981. 439p.

Earlier ed. covered 1964-70 (1973).

Includes works about Jamaica. Broad subject arrangement with index of authors, editors, corporate bodies and translators. List of periodicals and newspapers. Gives locations for three Jamaican libraries. *Class No:* 015(729.2)

Dominican Republic

[607]

Anuario bibliográfico dominicano. Santa Domingo, Biblioteca Nacional, 1978-84. Irregular.

Earlier volumes published under this title 1947-48. Appears to have ceased with 1980/82.

.... *(contd.)*

The v. for 1980/82 (1984) contains 2,538 entries in subject groupings A-Z. Author index. Includes many titles published before 1980. *Class No:* 015(729.3)

Barbados

[608]

National bibliography of Barbados: a subject list of works deposited with the National Library Service ... and of works of Barbadian authorship printed abroad. Bridgetown, National Library Service, 1975-. Annual. US$10. ISSN: 02567709.

Frequency varies: initially quarterly, then semi-annual.

Dewey classified listing with author, title and subject indexes. Separate 'Index of Acts, Bills and Statutory Instruments'. *c.*135 items recorded in the issue for 1994; cumulated issues for 1986-90 (1993. ix,406p.) and 1991-93 (1995. vii,165p.). *Class No:* 015(729.86)

Trinidad & Tobago

[609]

Trinidad and Tobago national bibliography. 1975-. Port of Spain, Central Library of Trinidad and Tobago and The University of the West Indies Library, 1976-. Quarterly, final issue annual cumulation. US$25.

Succeeds *Trinidad and Tobago West Indies bibliography* (1965-74). Publication pattern irregular in recent years. Cumulations for 1988/89 (1991) and 1990/91 (1993).

Classified by Dewey D.C. with an author/title/series index. 192 items listed 1990/91. *Class No:* 015(729.87)

Bermuda

[610]

Bermuda national bibliography: a list of additions to the Bermuda Library. 1983-. Hamilton, Bermuda Library Technical Services, 1984-. Quarterly, with annual cumulation. B$10. ISSN: 02550067.

Includes works about Bermuda or by Bermudians published overseas. 1996 annual (1997. iii,10p.) has *c.*75 entries classed by Dewey; author/title/series index.
Class No: 015(729.9)

Latin America

[611]

Libros en venta: en Américan Latina y España. San Juan, NISC Puerto Rico, 1964-. Biennial (Irregular). $375.

Issued as a 3v. set of author, title and subject sequences, and as a CD-ROM. Title, frequency and publisher varies: subtitle previously *en Hispanoaméricano y España*; publisher now NISC, previously Melcher with CD-ROM version from Bowker.

8th. ed. (1997) lists *c.*228,000 titles available from 10,000 publishers. Main coverage for Spanish-speaking Latin America, but includes Spain and Spanish works published elsewhere, especially the United States. Subject volume classified by Dewey under 5,000 headings. Entries inconsistent in quality often lacking basic bibliographical detail such as edition statement or publication date. The quarterly updated CD-ROM ($995) has standard NISC features with novice, advanced and expert search modes and an English interface. To be Internet accessible on NISC's BiblioLine system from 1998 ($1,195). More comprehensive coverage of works published in Spain provided by *Libros españoles en venta* (*q.v.*). *Class No:* 015(729.99)

[612]

—Fichero bibliográfico hispanoamericano: bibliografiá de todos los paises de habla española. San Juan, Puerto Rico, Melcher Ediciones, 1961-92. 11 issues pa. $75. ISSN: 00150592.

Ceased publication with March 1992 issue.

Served to update the printed version of *Libros en venta*. Arranged by the major Dewey classes, with author and title indexes. Also available in microfilm from University Microfilms International. *Class No:* 015(729.99)

USA

[613]

AMERICAN ANTIQUARIAN SOCIETY. A Dictionary catalog of American books pertaining to the 17th through 19th centuries. Westport, Conn., Greenwood, 1971. 20v. £3375;$3,750. ISBN: 0837132657.

American imprints prior to 1821, plus later first editions of American literary authors. Reproduces the catalogue cards of the Society's collection; dictionary arrangement, subject entries under Library of Congress headings.
Class No: 015(73)

[614]

Bibliography of American imprints to 1901: compiled from the database of the American Antiquarian Society and The Research Libraries Group, Inc. New York, Saur, 1993. 92v. £9,055. ISBN: 3598333404.

Contents: Part I. Main part, v.1-42; Part II. Author index, v.43-56; Part III. Subject index, v.57-71; Part IV. Place index, v.72-82; Part V. Date index, v.83-92.

Massive listing of 400,000 titles printed at presses located within the present boundaries of the US. Includes pamphlets and leaflets; excludes maps, serials and newspapers. Full MARC style entries in v.1-42 arranged by title. Fairly complete to 1820. After this date some titles omitted, the continuing series *A Checklist of American imprints* (*q.v.*) providing fuller coverage. Name index includes editors and translators, subject index based on Library of Congress headings. Place index arranged by state, date index by year then title. *Class No:* 015(73)

[615]

European Americana: a chronological guide to works printed in Europe relating to the Americas, 1493-1776. Alden, J. *and* Landis, D.C., *eds*. New York, Readex Books, 1980-. ISBN: 0918414008.

Originally intended for 8 vols. V.I: 1493-1600 (1980. $120. liii,467p.); v.II: 1601-1650 (1982. xlviii,954p. $200); v.III (1984.lxxv,682p. $340); v.V: 1701-1725 (1987. xlix,597p. $270); v.VI: 1726-1750 (1988. liii,852p. $310). Vols. IV, VII and VIII not yet published.

'(R)epresents an attempt to improve and enlarge upon material accumulated by Sabin' (V.I, Foreword p.xi). V.I has 4,300 items, ¾ not in Sabin, v.II 7,400 items, less than 1/3 in Sabin. Chronological arrangement, entries give abbreviated title, imprint, other necessary bibliographical information and locations in North American and European libraries. 3 indexes in each volume: geographical of printers and booksellers and their publications; A-Z of printers and booksellers and their geographic locations; author, title and subject. *Class No:* 015(73)

[616]

EVANS, C. American bibliography: a chronological dictionary of all books, pamphlets and periodical publications printed in the United States of America, from the genesis of printing in 1639 down to and including the year 1820, with bibliographical and biographical notes. Chicago, the Author, 1903-34. 12v.

Reprinted Magnolia, Ma., Peter Smith (ISBN: 0844611735, v.1).

Originally intended to extend to 1820, and later limited to 1800. Evans himself completed up to 1799 (letter M) when he died in 1935.

35,854 items arranged under year of publication; frequently notes locations of copies (for key to locations, see *New York Public Library bulletin,* v.40(8), August 1936, p.665-68). Each v. has author, classified subject, and printer and publisher indexes. Rounded off to 1800 by:-

V.13: *1799-1800* by C.K. Shipton (Worcester, Mass., American Antiquarian Society, 1955. xiii,349p. Reprinted Peter Smith. ISBN: 8444611743). Items 35855-39162. Titles not always recorded in full as in the previous 12v. Author and subject indexes.

V.14: *Index* by R.P. Bristol (Worcester, Mass., American Antiquarian Society, 1959. vii,450p. Reprinted Peter Smith. $30.50. ISBN: 0844611751). Cumulated author-title index, also including entries for names of people, ships, Indian tribes etc.

R.P. Bristol has also prepared an *Index of printers, publishers and booksellers indicated by Charles Evans* ... (Charlottesville, Va., Bibliographical Society of the Univ. of Virginia, 1961. iv,172p.). *Class No:* 015(73)

[617]

—BRISTOL, R.P. Supplement to Charles Evans' American bibliography. Charlottesville, Va., Univ. Press of Virginia for The Bibliographical Society of America and The Bibliographical Society of the University of Virginia, 1970. xix,636p. $50. ISBN: 0813902878.

Adds 11,262 items in chronological arrangement. An author/title and printer/publisher/bookseller index, also by Bristol, published as *Index to Supplement to Charles Evans American bibliography* (Charlottesville, Va., Univ. Press of Virginia, etc., 1971. v,191p. $30. ISBN: 0813903378).
Class No: 015(73)

[618]

—SHIPTON, C.K. *and* MOONEY, J.E. National index of American imprints through 1800: the short-title Evans. Worcester, Mass., American Antiquarian Society and Barre Publishers, 1969. 2v. $85. ISBN: 0827169086.

Primarily an index to the Readex Microprint edition of *Early American imprints.* Includes many corrections and 10,000 additions, most of which are in Bristol (above).
Class No: 015(73)

[619]

—WALSH, J. Maps contained in the publications of the American bibliography 1639-1819: an index and checklist. Metuchen, N.J., Scarecrow Press, 1988. xv,367p. £35.55;$39.50. ISBN: 0810821931.

In 3 pts.: I and II list respectively maps in Evans and the Shaw and Shoemaker bibliography; III forms the index providing access by date and place of publication, name, book and map title and geographic location.
Class No: 015(73)

[620]

SABIN, J. Dictionary of books relating to America, from its discovery to the present time. New York, Sabin, 1868-92; Bibliography Society of America, 1928-36. 29v.

Begun by Sabin, completed by W. Eames for the Bibliographical Society of America. Also known as *Bibliotheca Americana,* as given on half-title page. Reprinted Metuchen, N.J., Scarecrow Press, 1966. (29v. in 2. £292.50;$325. ISBN: 0810800330).

An author list; 106,413 numbered entries, but, counting works mentioned in notes etc., about 190,000 items. Often gives locations of copies and makes references to reviews. Includes pamphlets and periodicals. As indicated by the title, not confined to material published in the US. No subject index. Still indispensable.

The Sabin collection index on CD-ROM (1996-) is an index to Primary Source Media's ongoing *Sabin collection* microform project. *Class No:* 015(73)

[621]

—Author-title index to Joseph Sabin's 'Dictionary of books relating to America'. Molnar, J.E., *comp.* Metuchen, N.J., Scarecrow Press, 1974. 3v. ISBN: 0810806525.

Single A-Z sequence of 270,000 entries, including authors, editors, compilers, illustrators, engravers, cartographers, publishers (if the firm compiled the work), corporate bodies etc., as well as titles and series. Many cross-references; some attempt to identify pseudonyms. An essential key to the use of Sabin. *Class No:* 015(73)

[622]

THOMPSON, L.S. The New Sabin: books described by Joseph Sabin and his successors, now described again on the basis of examination of originals and fully indexed by title, subject, joint authors and institutions and agencies. Troy, N.Y., Whitson, 1974-. ISBN: 0878750495.

V.1-10 published 1974-84, $25 each.

Aims to list addenda to Sabin and amend its citations. 25,946 serially numbered entries v.1-10. The indexing, especially by subject, is the major feature of this revision. An index to v.1-5 and separate indexes to v.6-9 were superseded by a cumulative index, v.1-10, published 1986. No further volumes published since Thompson's death in 1986. *Class No:* 015(73)

19th & 20th Centuries

[623]

American book publishing record cumulative 1876-1949: an American national bibliography. New York, Bowker, 1980. 15v. ISBN: 0835212459.

V.1-10 Classified sequence; v.11 Fiction. Juvenile fiction; v.12 Non-Dewey Decimal classified titles; v.13 Author index; v.14 Title index; v.15 Subject index.

625,000 entries arranged by Dewey classification. Compiled from *A Catalog of books represented by Library of Congress printed cards* 1898-1942 plus supplement 1942-47 and *The Library of Congress author catalog, 1948-1952.* Excludes federal and other government documents etc., as with the current *American book publishing record.* *Class No:* 015(73)"18/19"

[624]

The American catalogue of books. 1876-1910. New York, Publishers' Weekly, 1880-1911. 8v. in 13.

Reprinted New York, Peter Smith, 1941. All vols. in print.

A series of trade lists of books based mainly on entries in *Publishers' weekly.* Initial list for July 1, 1876 in 2v.: Authors and titles; Subjects. Further lists: July 1, 1876-June 30, 1884; July 1, 1884-June 30, 1890; July 1, 1890-June 30, 1895; July 1, 1895-January 1, 1901; 1901-1905; 1905-1907; 1908-1910. More comprehensive and trustworthy than earlier 19th century compilations such as Roorbach. *Class No:* 015(73)"18/19"

19th Century

[625]

American bibliography: a preliminary checklist ... 1801-1819. Shaw, R.R. *and* Shoemaker, R.H., *comps.* New York, Scarecrow Press, 1958-83. 23v.

19 annual volumes for 1801-19; *Addenda. List of sources. Library symbols* (1965); *Title index* (1965); *Corrections. Author Index* (1966); *Printers, publishers and booksellers index. Geographical index* (1983. ISBN: 0810816075).

Continues Evans (*q.v.*). Compiled from secondary sources, 50,192 entries 1801-19, plus 1,768 in the addenda. *Class No:* 015(73)"18"

[626]

—A Checklist of American imprints ... 1820-. Metuchen, N.J., Scarecrow Press, 1964-.

Compiler varies; initially R.H. Shoemaker, now C. Rinderknecht. Volumes individually priced.

Issued in annual volumes as with the preceding series *American bibliography* (above), but with fuller detail and library locations. To continue through to 1875, thereby replacing Roorbach's *Bibliotheca Americana* covering 1820-60 and Kelly's *The American catalogue of books* covering 1861-65. Items numbered sequentially on a decennial basis for 1820s and 1830s. 41,633 entries 1820-29 (1964-71), with a *Title index* (1972) and an *Author index* (1973). 59,415 entries 1830-39 (1972-88), with a *Title index* (1989. 2v.) and an *Author index* (1990). From 1840 v. numbering on a annual basis; 1846 v. (1997. 588p. £66.05;$67.50. ISBN: 0810832127) lists 7,783 items. From the 1838 v. has ceased to include United States documents. *Class No:* 015(73)"18"

[627]

Bibliotheca Americana: catalogue of American publications including reprints and original works ... together with a list of periodicals published in the United States. Roorbach, O.A., *comp.* New York, Roorbach, 1852-61. 4v.

Main volume covers 1820-52. Supplementary volumes October 1852-May 1855, May 1855-March 1858, March 1858-January 1861; reprinted New York, Peter Smith ($30.50. ISBN: 0844613894).

Very incomplete, has many inaccuracies and gives few dates of publication. *Class No:* 015(73)"18"

[628]

—The American catalogue of books (original and reprints) published in the United States ... with date of publication, size, price and publisher's name... Kelly, J., *comp.* New York, Wiley, 1866-71. 2v.

Reprinted New York, Peter Smith ($39. ISBN: 0318552442).

The first volume, covering January 1861-January 1866, includes a supplement containing pamphlets, sermons and addresses of the Civil War. Both volumes contain an

....*(contd.)*
appendix of names of learned societies and other literary associations, with a list of their publications. This work and Roorbach will eventually be replaced by *A Checklist of American imprints* (above). *Class No:* 015(73)"18"

20th Century

[629]

American book publishing record cumulative 1950-1977: an American national bibliography. New York, Bowker, 1978. 15v. ISBN: 0835210944.

V.1-10 Classified sequence; v.11 Fiction. Juvenile fiction; v.12 Non-Dewey Decimal classified titles; v.13 Author index; v.14 Title index; v.15 Subject index.

900,000 entries. Includes records from Library of Congress MARC tapes 1968-77 for titles that did not appear in the previous cumulations of *American book publishing record.* V.12 includes records appearing in the *National union catalog* not assigned a Dewey class no. Some omissions from earlier cumulations and some duplication of entries resulting from the merging of computer tapes. Abbreviation of Dewey class nos. give rise to Dewey sequences of great length (*e.g.* '973', *c.*110 cols.). Nonetheless, this and the 1876-1949 cumulation represent a major bibliographical resource; a convenient alternative to the *National union catalog* (*q.v.*) for US imprints.

American book publishing record index 1876-1981: author/title/subject index on microfiche (New York, Bowker, 1982. 650 fiche. ISBN: 0835214354) indexes both the retrospective cumulations in one sequence. 1,700,000 entries. *Class No:* 015(73)"19"

Contemporary

[630]

American book publishing record. New Providence, N.J., Bowker, 1960-. Monthly, with annual cumulation. ISSN: 00027707.

Annual cumulations from 1966. Quinquennial cumulations 1960/64, 1965/69, 1970/74, 1975/79, 1980/84; 1960/64-1970/74 superseded by *American book publishing record cumulative 1950-1977* (above).

A record of books published or distributed in the US, based mainly on Library of Congress cataloguing. Excludes federal and other government documents, subscription books, dissertations (unless published), journals and most pamphlets under 49 pages. Full cataloguing records, including imprint detail, series, notes, LC class and card nos., subject tracings, ISBN and price. Arranged by Dewey classification with separate sections for adult and juvenile fiction. Author and title indexes; subject index to the classification. The 1996 annual (1997. 2v. £235;$290) has entries for 62,000 titles. The nearest equivalent to an official US national bibliography. *Class No:* 015(73)"312"

[631]

Books in print. New York, Bowker, 1948-. Annual. £430;$525. ISSN: 00680124.

Initially subtitled *An Author-title-series index to the Publishers' trade list annual.* 1997-98 issued in 9 vols: v.1-4 Authors; v.5-8 Titles; v.9 Publishers.

The 1997-98 vols. list 1,350,190 titles available from 57,600 US publishers and distributors. Includes reprints, children's fiction and school textbooks. Main exclusions are unbound material, pamphlets and booklets, books available only to members of organizations, subscription only material, books sold only to schools and music manuscripts

....*(contd.)*
and sheet music. Foreign books listed must have a sole US distributor. Brief entries include, as available, author/editor etc., title, no. of vols., edition, LC card no., series, no. of pages, grade range, date of publication, price and ISBN. V.9 includes separate listings of new and inactive/out-of-business publishers. The major source for information on current US published books.

Also available in microfiche (1982-, updated monthly (£910), quarterly (£565) or annually (£330)). *Books in print* is searchable online through Dialog (file 470), LEXIS-NEXIS and OVID (file BBIP) and as a subscription database through a number of suppliers including CARL, EBSCO, Information Access Company, OCLC and SilverPlatter. File generally updated monthly, includes records for titles declared out-of-print/out-of-stock since 1979. Various CD-ROM versions are also issued (see *Books in print Plus*, etc. below). *Class No:* 015(73)"312"

[632]

—Books in print supplement. New York, Bowker, 1973-. Annual. $265. ISSN: 00000310.

Published as an inter-edition supplement. 1997/98 issued in 3v.

Adds on average 75,000 new entries and revises a further 400,000. Author/title/subject sequences with a publisher index. *Class No:* 015(73)"312"

[633]

—Forthcoming books. New York, Bowker, 1966-. Bi-monthly. $240. ISSN: 00158119.

Subject, author and title listing of books scheduled for publication within the next 6 months, or announced but date not yet set. Separate *Subject guide to forthcoming books* no longer issued. *Class No:* 015(73)"312"

[634]

—Subject guide to books in print. New York, Bowker, 1957-. Annual. £305;$369.95 ISSN: 00000159.

1997-98 issued in 5 volumes: v.1-4 Subjects A-Z; v.5 Publishers. Thesaurus.

Lists all non-fiction works in the author/title volumes of *Books in print* under Library of Congress based subject headings. *c.*76,000 headings 1997-98 listed and cross-referenced in the subject thesaurus. Entry detail and general format as in the main *Books in print*.
Class No: 015(73)"312"

[635]

Books in print Plus. New York, Bowker, 1987-. CD-ROM database, updated monthly. £875.

Available from Bowker, Ovid and SilverPlatter.

Offers 18 search and 10 browse indexes. Includes full subject detail as in *Subject guide to books in print.* A further CD-ROM version *Books in print with book reviews plus* (updated monthly, £1,195) contains the same data with the addition of over 250,000 unabridged reviews from sources such as *Library journal, Booklist, Choice* and *School library journal*. *Books out-of print with book reviews Plus* (updated quarterly, £375) is a further CD-ROM containing records for 680,000 titles declared out-of print since 1979 (this data also freely Internet accessible after registration at http://www.reedref.com). *Global books in print Plus*, a separate CD-ROM service produced in conjunction with Whitaker (also known as *Whitaker/Bowker global Bookbank* (*q.v.*)), incorporates full data from *Books in print Plus*.

As from January 1998 database versions of *Books in print*

....*(contd.)*
include records from the Bowker products *Words on cassette* (*q.v.*) and *Complete video directory*.
Class No: 015(73)"312"

[636]
The Cumulative book index: a world list of books in the English language. New York, Wilson, 1898-. Monthly. ISSN: 0011300x.

Frequency has varied. Now monthly (except August) with paperbound cumulations within the year and, since 1969, a bound annual cumulation (now issued in 2 v.). Biennial cumulations 1957/58-1967/68; earlier cumulations for 1928/32, 1933/37, 1938/42, 1943/48, 1949/52 and 1953/56. No cumulations prior to 1928, published as a supplement to *United States catalog: books in print* ... (4 eds. 1899, 1902, 1912 and 1928).

Author, title and subjects in one A-Z sequence, arranged by Library of Congress filing rules. Since 1928 has attempted to list all books published in the English language worldwide. Excludes government documents, maps, music scores, books with less than 50 pages, editions limited to 500 or fewer copies, self-published works, local material and other ephemeral items. About ½ the entries are compiled from examination of the actual books, the remainder from US and UK MARC or other secondary sources. Directory of publishers in each issue. Records 1982 to date searchable online through Dialog, OCLC and Wilsonline, database updated twice weekly. A CD-ROM version is also available from Wilson ($1,295) and SilverPlatter, both updated quarterly.

Cumulative book index, which currently lists 50-60,000 titles annually, is mainly useful as a checking tool for English language publications of the US and to a lesser extent Canada and the UK. Very selective for other countries. Accurate and fairly prompt, but cataloguing is less full than *American book publishing record*.
Class No: 015(73)"312"

[637]
Paperbound books in print: including mass market, paper, trade and softcover titles. New Providence, N.J., Bowker, 1955-96. Semi-annual. ISSN: 00311235.

Appears to have ceased with Fall 1996 issue.

Published in 6 v. (v.1-2 Titles; v.3-4 Authors; v.5-6 Subjects), same entry format as *Books in print* (above). Retrospective coverage for paperbacks provided by Reginald, R. & Burgess, M.R. *Cumulative paperback index 1939-1959* (Detroit, Gale, 1973. xxiv,362p. ISBN: 0810310503), listing 14,000 titles from 33 publishers issued under 69 imprints. *Class No:* 015(73)"312"

[638]
Publishers' trade list annual: a buying guide to books and related products. New Providence, N.J., Bowker, 1873-. Annual. $275. ISSN: 00797855.

Collects the catalogues and booklists of US and Canadian publishers. Alphabetical arrangement with indexes of publishers (with address and ISBN prefix), subjects (publisher) and series. About 140 publishers covered 1997, many fewer than in earlier years, smaller presses featuring prominently.

Publishers' trade list annual 1903-1980 (Westport, Meckler, 1980. 5,462 fiche) is a microfiche cumulation. Separate printed index, Abbott, A. *comp.* (150p. ISBN: 093048625x). *Class No:* 015(73)"312"

Brazil

[639]
Bibliografia brasileira. 1983-. Rio de Janeiro, Biblioteca Nacional, 1984-. Quarterly (irregular). ISSN: 01023144.

Supersedes *Boletim bibliográfico* (below). An earlier publication with the same title was produced by the Instituto Nacional do Livro for the years 1938-55 and 1963-66.

Around 2,000 entries per issue in Dewey classified arrangement with author, title and subject indexes. Also available in microfiche and as an online database. A further Biblioteca Nacional product listing Brazilian imprints is the CD-ROM *ISBN*. *Class No:* 015(81)

[640]
—BBB. Boletim bibliográfico brasileiro. Rio de Janeiro, Estante Publicações, 1953-67. Irregular (approx 6 issues pa.).

An alternative to *Boletim bibliográfico* (below). Arranged in subject groups with a title index in each issue.
Class No: 015(81)

[641]
—Boletim bibliográfico. Rio de Janeiro, 1951-82. Quarterly.

Succeeded earlier series of the same title published irregularly from 1918. Subject to considerable publication delays; 1968-72 never issued. This period covered by the UDC classified *Bibliografia brasileira mensal* and its successors.

Classified arrangement with name index. Covered all types of publication including periodicals. *Class No:* 015(81)

[642]
Catalog of Brazilian acquisitions of the Library of Congress 1964-1974. Jackson, W.V., *comp.* Boston, G.K. Hall, 1977. ii-xvii,751p. $165. ISBN: 0816100330.

Reproduces catalogue cards for over 15,000 items. Subject arrangement, with author index. Introduction in English and Portuguese. Continued by:- *Class No:* 015(81)

[643]
LIBRARY OF CONGRESS. Library of Congress Office, Rio de Janeiro. **Accessions list Brazil and Uruguay.** Rio de Janeiro, Library of Congress Office, 1975-92. Bimonthly. ISSN: 0095795x.

Title and contents vary. As *Accessions list Brazil* 1975-88.

Listed about 900 titles per issue, by main entry, in separate sections for monographs, serials and special materials. No subject indexing. Cumulated list of serials published separately as *Accessions list Brazil and Uruguay: annual list of serials* (*q.v.*). *Class No:* 015(81)

[644]
SACRAMENTO BLAKE, A.V.A. do. Dicionário bibliographico brasileiro. Rio de Janeiro, Typografica Nacional, 1883-1902. 7v.

Indice alphabetico ... compilado pelo Jango Fischer. Rio de Janeiro, Imp. Nacional, 1937. vi,127p. Reprinted Leichtenstien, 1967 with *Indice* in v.7.

A bio-bibliographical dictionary arranged by first name. Index provides for surname access. *Class No:* 015(81)

[645]
—MORAES, R.B. de. Bibliografia brasileira do periodo colonial: cátalogo commentado da obras dos autores no Brasil e publicadas ante de 1808. São Paulo, 1969. xxii,437p. fascims.

Writings of persons born in Brazil before 1800. 1,200 entries. Annotated. Shortened entries from this work are included in the author's *Bibliographia brasiliana: rare books about Brazil published from 1504 to 1900 and works by*

....*(contd.)*
Brazilian authors of the colonial period (Rev. ed. Los Angeles, Univ. of California, 1983. 2v. 1114p. $150. ISBN: 0879031093). *Class No:* 015(81)

Argentina

[646]
Bibliografía Argentina. Catálogo de materiales argentinos en las bibliotecas de la Universidad de Buenos Aires. [A Union catalog of Argentine holdings in the libraries of the University of Buenos Aires.] Boston, Mass., G.K. Hall, 1980. 7v.

Serves as a retrospective national bibliography, as books published in Argentina up to 1977 and books by Argentine authors published overseas are included. Based on the holdings of 17 central and 56 departmental libraries of the University. About 110,000 author catalogue cards photographically reproduced, alphabetically arranged. *Class No:* 015(82)

[647]
Boletín bibliográfico nacional. 1937-1954/56. Buenos Aires, Biblioteca nacional, 1937-63. Irregular.

One of the more long-lived of a number of attempts to create a current national bibliography. *Class No:* 015(82)

[648]
LEVASSEUR, M. Imprimés argentins de la Bibliothèque Nationale. Paris, Bibliothèque Nationale, 1993. 467p. ISBN: 271771863x.

6,063 entries A-Z by author, with separate sections for government publications, serials, etc. Secondary author and subject indexes. *Class No:* 015(82)

[649]
Libros argentinos. 1982-. Buenos Aires, Cámara Argentina del Libro, 1984-. Irregular.

Now a quarterly updated CD-ROM service. Previously a printed listing under title *Libros argentinos ISBN*, some issues covering individual years, others covering a longer period (*e.g. Libros argentinos ISBN: producción editorial registrada 1989-1991* (1992. lxxxi,502p.)).

A register of new books published in Argentina based on legislation governing the assignment of ISBNs. The last printed v. for 1992 (1993. li,298p.) lists 7,000 titles in Dewey classified order. Author, title, publisher/ISBN prefix indexes. The CD-ROM includes records for all titles published 1982 to date still in print. *Class No:* 015(82)

[650]
—Boletín bibliográfico bimestral ISBN. Buenos Aires, Cámara Argentina del Libro, 1993-. Bimonthly. ISSN: 03279189.

A partial continuation of *Libros argentinos ISBN.* Main sequence of each issue lists new titles in Dewey classified order, giving basic bibliographical detail, price and ISBN. Separate author index. *Class No:* 015(82)

Chile

[651]
Anuario de la prensa chilena, 1877-1975. Santiago, Biblioteca Nacional, 1887-1979. Annual.

Continued by *Bibliografía chilena* (below). Retrospective volume covering 1877-85 published 1952. Suspended 1928-62: gap subsequently filled by non-cumulative quinquennial volumes published 1963-4.

Based on legal deposit. Also included books by Chilean authors published abroad or books relating to Chile. *Class No:* 015(83)

[652]
Bibliografía chilena 1976/79-. Santiago, Ministerio de Educacion Publica, Dirección de Bibliotecas, Archivos y Museos, 1981-. Annual (irregular). ISSN: 0716176x.

Continues *Anuario de la prensa chilena.* Printed vols. for 1976/79 (1981), 1980 (1982) and 1981 (1984). 1982/84 and 1985/87 (1992) issued on microfiche.

Covers books, official publications and new periodicals. Juvenile literature in a separate section. Dewey classified order: general index. *Class No:* 015(83)

[653]
Libros chilenos ISBN. Santiago, Cámara Chilena del Libro, 1989-. Irregular.

Similar coverage provided by *El Libro chileno en venta,* first published for 1950/75 (1975) and then on an approximately biennial basis to 1985/86 (1988).

Classed in print list (1989 ed. 328p. ISBN: 9567070015) giving basic bibliographical data, price and ISBN. Author and title index; list of publishers. Publication seems to have halted, last issue traced that for 1991. *Class No:* 015(83)

Bolivia

[654]
GUTTENTAG TICHAUER, W. Bio-bibliografía boliviana 1962-. La Paz, Editorial Los Amigos de Libro, 1963-. Annual. $170. ISSN: 00676578.

Title *Bibliografía boliviana* 1962-1974.

The main section of each issue is a name listing with analysis of works' contents and occasional remarks about the author, (hence publication title). Further section lists earlier works not previously covered. Title, publisher and subject indexes; cumulative indexes 1962-90 in 1991 v. The 1995 v. (1996. 299p.) has entries for 490 newly published items. *Class No:* 015(84)

Peru

[655]
Bibliografía peruano. 1943-. Lima, Biblioteca Nacional del Peru, 1945-. Triennial.

Present title from issue for 1984/86 published 1992. Earlier title *Anuario bibliográfico peruano.* This also appeared on an triennial basis *e.g.* 1973/76 (1986. 2v.), except for the initial issues which were annual then biennial.

Revamped from title change, the 1984/86 v. (xii,305p.) listing 2,118 monographs and 220 theses in separate Dewey based subject sections. Name index. As well as listing new titles the *Anuario* included bio-bibliographical listings for Peruvian authors who died during the years covered. *Class No:* 015(85)

[656]
BIBLIOTECA NACIONAL. (PERU). Catálogo de autores de la coleción peruano. [Author catalog of the Peruvian collection.] Boston, Mass., G.K. Hall, 1979. 6v. $830. ISBN: 0816102503.

V.1-v.5 Books and pamphlets. V.6 Periodicals. Maps and plans.

Photographically reproduced cards for Peruvian imprints as well as publications about Peru, 1553-1977. *Class No:* 015(85)

Colombia

[657]

Anuario bibliográfico colombiano 'Rubén Pérez Ortiz'. 1951-. Bogotá, Instituto Caro y Cuervo, Dept. de Bibliografía, 1958-. Annual or biennial. ISSN: 05231728.

1951-56 published in one volume 1958.

The 1990/91 issue, (1995. xix,565p.) is a Dewey based classified listing with separate sections for translations and new periodicals. Geographically arranged list of publishers and name index. Apparently thorough coverage, but issues are slow to appear. *Class No:* 015(86)

Ecuador

[658]

Anuario bibliográfico ecuatoriana. Cuenca, Banco Centrale del Ecuador, Centro de Investigación y Cultura, 1980-. Annual. ISSN: 02528649.

As *Ecuador bibliografía analítica* 1980-82.

Dewey main class listing with name and subject indexes. Publication currently suspended. *Class No:* 015(866)

Venezuela

[659]

Bibliografía venezolana. 1980/81-. Caracas, Instituto Antónomo Biblioteca Nacional y de Servicios de Bibliotecas, 1982-. Semi-annual. ISSN: 00061085.

Issued quarterly with annual cumulation until 1991. Replaces *Anuario bibilográfico venezolano* published for 1942-54 and 1967-77 and the quarterly *Bibliografía venezolano* published from 1970.

Library catalogue type entries arranged chronologically according to year of publication. Also available as an online database. *Class No:* 015(87)

[660]

Boletín ISBN-Venezuela. Caracas, Instituto Autónoma Biblioteca Nacional y de Servicios de Bibliotecas, 1987-. Annual.

Lists newly published Venezuelan books by major Dewey classes with author, title and subject indexes. Microfiche version also available. *Class No:* 015(87)

[661]

VILLASANA, A.R. Ensayo de un repertorio bibliográfico venezolano. Caracas, Banco Central de Venezuela, 1969-79. 6v.

Bibliography of non-technical books and pamphlets issued 1808-1950. Full entries, many with descriptive detail and notes.

Continued by the same author's *Nueva repertorio bibliográfico venezolano: años 1951-1975* (Caracas, Instituto Autónoma Biblioteca Nacional y de Servicos de Bibliotecas..., 1989-. (V.1. A-Ch ISBN: 9806016696)). *Class No:* 015(87)

Guyana

[662]

Guyanese national bibliography: a subject list of new books printed in the Republic of Guyana... . 1973-. Georgetown, National Library, 1974-. Quarterly, 4th issue annual cumulation. ISSN: 03765202.

The 1990 cumulation (1991. vii,88p. (last currently available)) is arranged by Dewey classification with an "alphabetical section" acting as an author/title/editor/series index. Also carries details of publishers and an appendix listing government publications. *Class No:* 015(88)

Paraguay

[663]

FERNÁNDEZ-CABALLERO, C.F.S. The Paraguayan bibliography: a retrospective and enumerative bibliography of printed works of Paraguayan authors. Asunción and Washington D.C., Arandú Books, 1970-83. 3v.

V.2 has imprint Amherst, Mass., Seminar on the Acquisition of Latin American Library Materials, Univ. of Massachusetts and is issued as SALALM bibliography no.3. V.3 has title *La Bibliografía paraguaya.*

Collectively the 3 v. contain nearly 7,500 entries. V.3 mainly contains items published 1975-82. *Class No:* 015(892)

[664]

KALLSEN, M. Paraguay: ... años de bibliografía. 1980/84-. Asunción, CEPUC, 1986-. Irregular. ISSN: 02577070.

The initial v., *..cinco años de bibliografía* (1986), lists 1,401 titles published in or about Paraguay. Continued by v. for individual or several years *e.g.* 1987 (1988), 1990/91 (1993). *Class No:* 015(892)

Uruguay

[665]

Anuario bibliográfico uruguayo: 1946-. Montevideo, Biblioteca Nacional, 1947-. Annual. ISSN: 03048861.

1950-67 not published.

Main section of the 1991 issue (1993. 241p.) has entries for 1,014 monographs by Library of Congress classification. Separate listings of current serials and works by foreign authors and organizations published in Uruguay. Indexes, including personal author and subject; list of publishers. 505.00/01$aA new title from the Biblioteca Nacional is *Libros uruguayos: producción editorial registrada con ISBN.* 1991/95-. (1995-). *Class No:* 015(899)

[666]

Bibliografía uruguaya. Montevideo, Biblioteca del Poder Legislativo, 1971-. Irregular. ISSN: 02517515.

Initial v. covering 1962-68 followed by a series of further issues *e.g.* 1973-77 (1983). Latest traced *Agosto 1989-Julio 1990* (1991. 311p.).

1989-90 v. contains 840 entries by title A-Z with author, subject, anonymous title and printer/publisher indexes. *Class No:* 015(899)

Indonesia

[667]

Bibliografi nasional Indonesia. [Indonesian national bibliography.] Jakarta, Perpustakaan Nasional, 1963-. Quarterly, with annual cumulation (frequency varies). ISSN: 05231639.

Formerly *Berita bulanan dari kantor bibliografi nasional Indonesia* (1953-62. Monthly). Cumulated and extended coverage of this title available in *Bibliografi nasional Indonesia: kumulasi 1945-1963* (Jakarta, P.N. Balai Pukstaka, 1965. 2v.).

Includes books, government publications, first issues of serials, research reports, conference papers, children's literature and maps. Classified Dewey arrangement with author/title and subject indexes. Currency and production standards much improved in recent years. Also available in microform. *Class No:* 015(910)

[668]

Catalogus dari buku-buku jang diterbitkan di Indonesia. 1870/1937-1954. [Catalogus van boeken en tijdschriften uit. in Ned. Oost-Indië.] Ockeleon, G., *ed.* Bandung, Gedung Buku Nasional, etc., 1940-1955. 6 v. in 7

Two vols provide separate listings of Dutch and Indonesian language titles 1870-1937; further vol. lists Dutch publications 1938-1941. Items listed in the remaining vols. cumulated in *Bibliografi nasional Indonesia: kumulasi 1945-1963* (above).

Material published during the Japanese occupation is recorded in *Katalog terbitan Indonesia selama pendudkan Jepang, 1942-1945* (Jakarta, Perpustakaan Nasional, 1983. viii,101p.). *Class No:* 015(910)

Philippines

[669]

BERNARDO, G.A. Philippine retrospective national bibliography 1523-1699. Manila, National Library of the Philippines and Ateneo de Manila University Press, 1974. xvi, 160p. (*Ateneo de Manila bibliographical series, no.3.*)

2 sections: foreign imprints p.1-106, Philippine imprints p.107-150 (218 entries). Arranged chronologically by publication date. Entries include bibliographic references. Author/subject index. *Class No:* 015(914)

[670]

JOSÉ, R.T. Impresso. Philippine imprints, 1593-1811. [Makati?], Fundación Santiago, Ayala Foundation, 1993. 312p. ISBN: 9718551158.

Chronologically arranged list of 1,088 items, building on Bernardo's work. Full entries cite bibliographical sources and locate copies. Separate listing of works of uncertain date. Bibliography (p.298-304); index of authors and translators. *Class No:* 015(914)

[671]

Philippine national bibliography. Manila, National Library of the Philippines, 1974-. Bi-monthly, with annual cumulation. ISSN: 0303190x.

Frequency varies. Preceded by *Philippine bibliography*, (1963-1972), published in 5 volumes by the University of the Philippines. Earlier coverage provided by *Copyrighted books in the Philippines: a catalog of books copyrighted from 1945-1963 by the Bureau of Public Libraries* (Manila, National Library, 1964. 255p.).

Covers books, pamphlets, first issues of serials, government publications and conference proceedings (theses and dissertations covered in *Philippine national bibliography. Part 2. Theses and dissertations* (*q.v.*). Includes works by Filipino authors or about the Philippines. The 1996 cumulation (1997. xiii,427p.) has 1,816 entries in Dewey classified order. Author/title/series and subject (LC headings) indexes; directory of publishers.
Class No: 015(914)

[672]

—LIBRARY OF CONGRESS. Philippine holdings of the Library of Congress, 1960-1987: a bibliography.
Rony, A.K., *comp.* Washington, D.C., Library of Congress, 1993. xi,702p. $46. ISBN: 0844407445.
Class No: 015(914)

New Zealand

[673]

New Zealand books in print. Wellington, D.W. Thorpe, 1957-. Annual (initially irregular). Aus$70. ISSN: 01577662.

Provides separate author and title listings of in print books published in New Zealand, about New Zealand or by New Zealand authors published overseas. Recent issues add a limited number of Pacific Islands titles. Also contains New Zealand book trade information. 24th ed. (1996. lvi,389p.) has details of trade associations, New Zealand literary awards, public libraries, booksellers, etc., plus 'New Zealand & Pacific Islands publishers, distributors and representatives'. Updated by supplement (ISSN: 11718110). CD-ROM availability as part of the *Thorpe-ROM* database with *Australian books in print*. *Class No:* 015(931)

[674]

New Zealand national bibliography. Wellington, National Library of New Zealand, 1967-. 11 pa. ISSN: 00288497.

Since June 1983 primarily a microfiche service. Monthly cumulating issues with new volume beginning in February (no issue for January), NZ$198 (NZ$270 overseas). Cumulated fiche 1983-93, NZ$292.50. Print (spiral bound) version also issued monthly, NZ$270 (NZ$810 overseas).

Replaces *Current national bibliography* and *Copyright publications* (below).

Covers works published in New Zealand, those published overseas dealing wholly or in part with New Zealand, or by authors normally resident in New Zealand. Microfiche based on register containing entries in accession order giving full bibliographic information. Separate author/title and subject listings acting as indexes; list of publishers' names and addresses. *Class No:* 015(931)

[675]

—Current national bibliography of New Zealand books and pamphlets. (in *Index to New Zealand periodicals,* 1950-1965).

Published with *Index to New Zealand periodicals.*

Author, title and subject list of titles published in New Zealand, by New Zealanders or about New Zealand.
Class No: 015(931)

[676]

—NEW ZEALAND. General Assembly Library. Copyright publications. Wellington, Government Printer, 1934-1966. Annual.

Cumulated the monthly mimeographed *Copyright list.*

Arranged by authors A-Z. Appended lists (1966 v.): "Overseas publications of New Zealand interest" - "Maps" - "New periodicals," - "Periodicals ceased publication". Index of subjects and titles. *Class No:* 015(931)

[677]

New Zealand national bibliography to the year 1960. Bagnall, A.G., *ed.* Wellington, Government Printer, 1969-1985. 5v. NZ$180. ISBN: 0477010881.

V.1 to 1889; (2 vols. 1980 xvi, 1292p.). V.2 - v.4. 1890-1960. (A-H. 1969. xvi, 604p. I-O. 1972. xi, 571p. P-Z. 1975. iv, 471p.). V.5. Supplement and index. (1985. xi, 637p.).

A project of the National Library. Approximately 29,000 main entries under author. V.1 (6,229 items) has a chronological index 1663-1889 and an index of subjects, titles, and added entries. V.2 - v.4 follow a similar plan, (government publications v.3 concentrated under New Zealand, subdivided by department), but are indexed in v.5 which also carries corrigenda and a further 2,500 entries.

....(contd.)
Locations noted include the British Library, Public Record Office, Royal Commonwealth Society and Australian libraries. *Class No:* 015(931)

Australia

[678]
Annual catalogue of Australian publications. Canberra, Commonwealth National Library, 1937-60. Annual.

Annual list of books received; a cumulation of the monthly *Books published in Australia*. Continued by *Australian national bibliography* (below).

In five sections: 1: Dictionary order (author, title and subject); 2: Books of Australian interest published overseas; 3: Official publications (omitted for 1936 and 1941-44); 4: Select list of periodicals and annuals; 5: Brief directory of publishers. *Class No:* 015(94)

[679]
Australian books: a select list of recent publications and standard works in print. Canberra, National Library of Australia, 1949-1992. Annual. ISSN: 00671738.

Ceased publication with issue for 1991 (1992). Superseded *Select list of representative works dealing with Australia, reprinted from the 'Official year book of the Commonwealth of Australia'*, 1933-48.

Designed as a current reference and reading list. Unannotated entries in subject sections each subdivided 'Standard works in print' and 'Recent publications of interest'. Author/anonymous title index. *Class No:* 015(94)

[680]
Australian books in print. Port Melbourne, D.W. Thorpe, 1956-. Annual (initially irregular). Aus$130. ISSN: 0067172x.

Lists, in separate author and title sequences, books published in Australia, by Australians published overseas, or about Australia. Additional information includes addresses of book trade and literary associations, series (Australian and foreign), overseas publishers with Australian agents and Australian publishers and distributors. A separate *Subject guide to Australian books in print* has appeared irregularly since 1986 (ISSN: 10305582, last published 1995). Updating provided by a list of new books in the monthly *Australian bookseller and publisher*. Also available as a microfiche service (monthly updates) and CD-ROM (*Thorpe-ROM*, with New Zealand titles (£327 UK)). The CD-ROM, updated monthly, includes brief descriptive annotations for titles published later than 1989. *Thorpe-ROM* records are also available from Whitaker as *Bookbank with Thorpe-ROM* (£1,402 UK) and as a component of the Whitaker/Bowker *Global bookbank* (*qq.v.*). *Class No:* 015(94)

[681]
Australian national bibliography. Canberra, National Library of Australia, 1961-1996. Monthly, with annual cumulation. ISSN: 00049816.

Ceased publication as a print service with the December 1996 issue. Records continue to be available as part of the Australian Bibliographic Network provided by the National Library of Australia. Data, comprising approx. 2,500 records each month, can be downloaded free of charge from ftp://email.nla.gov.au/pub/ANB.

Continued *Annual catalogue of Australian publications* (*q.v.*). Frequency varied: monthly 1961-66; 4 issues per month with fourth issue cumulating into a monthly 1967-80; 2 issues per month with second issue cumulating into a monthly 1981-85; monthly 1985-1996. Microfiche service

....(contd.)
also provided, cumulating annually. Further cumulation 1961-71.

List of books and pamphlets published in Australia, with a substantial Australian subject content, or written by Australians published overseas. New serials, government publications (with the exception of Acts, bills and ordinances), printed music and microforms also included. Dewey classified order with author/title/series and subject indexes. Records 1980 to 1993 also available online through OZLINE. *Class No:* 015(94)

[682]
FERGUSON, Sir J.A. Bibliography of Australia, 1784-1900. Sydney, Angus & Robertson, 1941-70. 7v. Aus$350.

V.1: 1784-1830; v.2: 1831-38; v.3: 1839-45; v.4: 1846-50 (1955); v.5-7: 1851-1900, A-G (1963), H-P (1965), Q-Z (1970).

Facsim. ed. Canberra, National Library of Australia, 1975.

'Every effort has been made to describe fully and accurately each item ... that is, every publication relating in any way to Australia printed anywhere outside Australia as well as any imprint made in Australia' (Introduction, v.1). The 'second phase', 1851-1900, occupying v.5-7 has entries under authors or anonymous titles A-Z, and is limited to printed books, pamphlets and broadsides; it excludes belles lettres, parliamentary papers, periodicals and newspapers and certain other categories. Locations are given for major Australian libraries and the British Museum (Library). *Class No:* 015(94)

[683]
—FERGUSON, Sir J.A. Bibliography of Australia: addenda 1784-1850 (Volumes I-IV). Canberra, National Library of Australia, 1986. x,706p. Aus$65. ISBN: 0642993076.

New and revised entries in chronological arrangement as before, including addenda printed in v.2-4 of the original set. Locates copies. Author, title and subject index. *Class No:* 015(94)

[684]
NATIONAL LIBRARY OF AUSTRALIA. Australian national bibliography, 1901-1950. Canberra, National Library of Australia, 1988. 4v. Aus$200. ISBN: 064210445x.

'(F)ills the gap in the national bibliographic record ... between Sir John Ferguson's *Bibliography of Australia 1784-1900* and the beginning of accurate and comprehensive coverage by the National Library of Australia's *Annual catalogue of Australian publications* in 1951' (Preface v.1,p.v). Similar in scope to Ferguson, covering books published in Australia or 'published overseas and having Australian authorship, or at least 10% Australian subject content, or an Australian setting' (Introduction V.1,p.vii). Serial and government publications excluded. 49,436 entries in v.1-2; v.3 Author/title/series index; v.4 Subject index. *Class No:* 015(94)

Papua—New Guinea

[685]
Papua New Guinea national bibliography. Waigani, National Library Service, Office of Libraries and Archives, 1981-. Semi-annual (with annual cumulation). ISSN: 02528347.

As *New Guinea bibliography*, 1969-1980 (covering all parts of the island and the Solomon Islands). Quarterly 1981-87; semi-annual since 1988 (except 1989 (annual)).

Dewey classified list with author, title, series and subject

....(*contd.*)
indexes. June 1995 issue (1996. vp.) has approx. 275 entries. Overseas publications about Papua New Guinea excluded since 1990. *Class No:* 015(954)

Polynesia

[686]
South Pacific bibliography. Suva, Pacific Information Centre, University of the South Pacific Library, 1981-. Biennial. ISSN: 02579146.

Issued annually until 1991 except for 1989/90; 1986/87 not published. Supersedes *Pacific collection accession lists* of the University of the South Pacific, 1975-1981.

Aims to cover works published in or relating to the South Pacific and the indigenous peoples of Australia, New Zealand and Hawaii. The 1994/95 v. (1996. vii,219p.) has a classified Dewey listing for monographs with author/title/series and subject indexes. Separate listing of periodicals by title. *Class No:* 015(96)

Fiji

[687]
Fiji national bibliography. 1970/78-. Suva, Library Service of Fiji, 1979-. Annual.

Publication suspended since issue for 1986.

Works published in Fiji, about Fiji, or by Fiji citizens. Last v. published (1988 vi,159p.) lists 408 monographs in Dewey Decimal sequence with author/title/series and subject indexes. Separate lists of periodicals and legal notices. Directory of publishers. *Class No:* 015(961.1)

Online Public Access Catalogues

[688]
OBI: OPACs in Britain and Ireland: a directory of library catalogues and services in Britain and Ireland. NISS. World Wide Web resource.

http://www.niss.ac.uk/reference/obi/obi.html. Date reviewed 4th August 1998. Part of the NISS WWW service.

Browsable directory in sections for UK educational institutions, educational institutions in Ireland, museums and galleries, national services, research councils, public libraries and special libraries. Entries generally provide link to catalogue and basic details of library system such as logon/logoff instructions and hours available. Some entries also contain brief information on library collections and subject strengths. Regularly updated, the key to exploiting online accessible UK library catalogues. *Class No:* 017/019/

[689]
OPAC directory: a guide to Internet-accessible online public access catalogues. Medford, N.J., Information Today, 1990-. Irregular. $70. ISSN: 10661425.

Title and publisher varies; as *Dial in* 1990-92.

1998 issue (xiv,625p. ISBN: 1573870315) has entries for 1,434 catalogues in sections for US (by state, p.1-318) and other countries (UK p.451-79, 110 entries). 'I have connected to every OPAC listed ... to verify Internet addresses, logon instructions, etc. All information was accurate as of Spring 1996' (p.xiv). Some entries include information on collections, subject strengths and library system. Geographical, subject, library name and systems index. *Class No:* 017/019/

[690]
WebCats: library OPACs. Northern Lights Internet Solutions. World Wide Web resource.

URL: http://www.lights.com/webcats/. Date reviewed 4th August 1998.

Provides links to library catalogues and Internet home pages worldwide. Browsable geographic, library type and vendor indexes. About 75 listings for the UK. Far from comprehensive and not all the links point to OPACs, but still one of the best sources for locating Internet accessible library catalogues. *Class No:* 017/019/

Library Catalogues

[691]
BAYERISCHE STAATSBIBLIOTHEK. Bayerische Staatsbibliothek Katalog 1501-1840. München, K.G. Saur, 1996. CD-ROM database. ISBN: 3598403321.

Earlier print version published as *Alphabetischer Katalog 1501-1840* in 60v., 1987-90 (ISBN: 3598308000).

Catalogue of the Bavarian State Library, the largest German collection and one of the world's greatest libraries. CD-ROM version contains records for 550,000 titles, an estimated 40% of which are not held by the British Library or Library of Congress. Maps, atlases and incunabula excluded, the latter separately catalogued in the Bayerische Staastbibliothek *Inkunabelkatalog* (*q.v.*). *Class No:* 017/019

[692]
BIBLIOTECA NACIONAL CENTRALE DI FIRENZE. Catálogo della Biblioteca Nacional Centrale di Firenze sur CD-ROM. Cambridge, Chadwyck-Healey/I.E. Informazioni Editoriali, 1996-. CD-ROM database. £800.

Issued on 2 discs: backfile containing records 1958-84 (separate purchase, £425) and current file, updated monthly.

The current file contains *c.*280,000 records. DOS or Windows interface, English menu and search options. The catalogue is also Internet accessible at telnet://sbn.bncf.firenze.sbn.it. *Class No:* 017/019

[693]
—ISTITUTO CENTRALE PER IL CATALOGO UNICO DELLE BIBLIOTECHE ITALIANE E PER LE INFORMAZIONI BIBLIOGRAFICHE. Primo catalogo collectivo delle biblioteche italiane. Roma, the Istituto, 1962-79. 9v.

9v. published cover A-Barq.

A union catalogue of books printed between 1500 and 1957 in Italian libraries. V.9 (Balo-Barq) is based on 22 libraries, including the national libraries in Florence and Rome. *Class No:* 017/019

[694]
BIBLIOTECA NACIONAL. (SPAIN). Catálogo general de libros impresos, hasta 1981. Paris, Chadwyck-Healey, 1989. 4,408 microfiche. £14,690. ISBN: 2869760221.

Updated by *Catálogo general de libros impresos 1982-1987* also published by Chadwyck-Healey. (579 microfiche. £2.050).

Together the two sets list nearly 2,000,000 books held by the Biblioteca Nacional in Madrid. Author arrangement. Separate booklet *Catalogo de autores y obra anonimas de la Biblioteca Nacional de Madrid: guía de consulta* (Chadwyck-Healey, 1990. 56p.).

The catalogues of the Biblioteca Nacional are also

....*(contd.)*
accessible through the Internet at http://www.bne.es/cat.htm. Various subfiles are available including monographs since 1831 and journals and periodicals. *Class No:* 017/019

[695]

BIBLIOTHÈQUE NATIONALE. (FRANCE). Catalogue général des livres imprimés de la Bibliothèque nationale Auteurs. Paris, Imprimerie Nationale, 1897-1981. 231v.

An author catalogue only, does not include entries for anonymous works, government and corporate authors or periodicals. Bibliographical details are fairly full; format is given but not pagination. Like the *British Library general catalogue of printed books,* it has references under entries for authors to works about them and systematically arranges entries when the literature is considerable (*e.g.* Tertullian, v.184, cols.645-700). Up to and including v.188 each v. represented the stock at date of publication resulting in uneven and incomplete coverage (microfiche supplement (below) incorporates the missing entries in one sequence). From v.189 this policy was discontinued, the remaining volumes including only works published to 1959. A primary source of information on French books and one of the great library catalogues, ranking behind only the Library of Congress and British Library catalogues. *Class No:* 017/019

[696]

—BIBLIOTHÈQUE NATIONALE. (FRANCE). Catalogue général des livres imprimés: auteurs, collectivités-auteurs, anonymes, 1960-1969. Paris, Imprimerie Nationale, 1972-78. 27v. FFr300 per v. ISBN: 2717700307.

Published in 2 series: Série 1, v.1-23 *Caractères latins et caractères grecs* (Greek characters p.684-726, v.23); Série 2, v.1 *Caractères hébraiques,* v.2-3 *Caractères cyrilliques,* v.4 *Caractères arabes.* Replaces an earlier 5 year cumulation for 1960-64 published in 12v., 1965-67.

Improves on the main catalogue by including corporate entries and title entries for collections and anonyma, plus added entries for joint authors, translators etc. A microfiche version is available from Chadwyck-Healey (430 fiche £1,500). Printed volumes for the 1970-79 supplement have only been published for non-latin characters (*e.g.* v.1 *Caractères cyrilliques; russe* (3v.); v.5 *Caractères hébraiques* (2v.)). *Class No:* 017/019

[697]

—BIBLIOTHÈQUE NATIONALE. (FRANCE). Catalogue général des livres imprimés [de la] Bibliothèque Nationale. Auteurs 1897-1959; supplement sur fiches. Paris, Chadwyck-Healey, 1986. Microfiche. £9,050. ISBN: 2869760019.

Reproduces on 2,890 microfiche 1,260,000 card records for approximately 800,000 titles acquired since 1897 which were not included in the main 231 v. printed set. Chadwyck-Healey have also produced a microfiche version of the original catalogue (1,445 fiche. £4,500) A guide to the use of both sets and the microfiche version of the 1960-69 supplement (above) is published as *Guide de l'utilisateur des catalogues des livres imprimés de la Bibliothèque Nationale* (Bernard, A. 1986. 65p. £20. ISBN: 2869760043). A further microfiche production is *Catalogue général des livres imprimés: anonymes XVIe-XVIIIe siècles.* (Paris, Bibliothèque Nationale, 1988. 12 fiche. ISBN: 2717717927) listing *c.*175,000 titles.

Recent aqcuisitions of the Bibliothèque Nationale may be searched on the online public access catalogue *Bn-Opale* using the Telnet protocol. Link available from the library's WWW pages at http://www.bnf.fr. Over 2,000,000 records searchable including all books from 1960, periodicals from 1970 and recent data from *Bibliographie national française* (*q.v.*). *Class No:* 017/019

[698]

Bodleian Library pre-1920 catalogue of printed books. Oxford, Oxford University Press, 1993. CD-ROM database £995

Contains records for over 1,000,000 titles. Windows based graphical interface offering 3 levels of searching: index (heading, title, subject, collection, incunabula, shelfmark); profiled (keyword, wildcard, etc., with further limiting option); query factory (user constructed). Disc available as a one-off purchase, no updating. For thorough reviews see *Program,* v.28(2), April 1994, p.141-53 and *The Library,* v.XVI(4), December 1994, p.327-32. *Class No:* 017/019

[699]

BRITISH LIBRARY. The British Library general catalogue of printed books to 1975. London, Saur (initially Bingley), 1981-87. 360v. $19,200. ISBN: 085157520x.

Preceded by several earlier catalogues. The first (GK1) was published as *Catalogue of printed books* (1881-1900) in 95v. with a *Supplement* (1900-5) of 13v. (both photographically reprinted Ann Arbor, Edwards, 1946-50, 58v. and 10v.). A new attempt at a catalogue *General catalogue of printed books* (GK2) began publication in 1931, but was abandoned in 1954 having covered A-Dez in 51v. The next catalogue, the monumental *General catalogue of printed books. Photolithographic edition to 1955* (GK3) (1960-66. 263v.), contained 4 million entries in 133,000 pages, recording all printed books, periodicals and newspapers, in languages other than Oriental, catalogued by the British Museum up to the end of 1955. GK3 was supplemented by a *Ten year supplement 1956-1965* (1968. 50v.), a *Five year supplement 1966-1970* (1971-72. 26v.) and a further *Five year supplement 1971-1975* (1978-79. 13v. ISBN: 0714116009). GK3 is still commonly encountered, as many libraries, largely for financial reasons, have chosen not to purchase the catalogue to 1975.

Incorporates in a single alphabetical sequence the Photolithographed ed. and its three supplements. Subsequent revisions, corrections, amendments and additions made by British Library staff are also included. Basically an author, or rather 'name' catalogue, it maintains the practices of GK3. Entries under authors list not only their works, but also (in the form of cross-references) biographical and critical works about them. Very long author sequences (*e.g.* Dickens, v.82, p.349-447) include brief indexes. Most corporate bodies are entered under the town or country in which they are located with a reference from the body name. Within many corporate headings, especially states, entries are subdivided according to type of publication (*e.g.* laws, treaties). The heading 'England' (v.96-100) is accompanied by separate title and subheading index volumes. Generic headings are widely used (*e.g.* catalogues, collections, dictionaries, encyclopaedias). Note especially the heading 'Periodical publications' (v.252-54), subdivided by place. Invaluable for British publications up to the appearance of *British national bibliography* (*q.v.*) and for its selection of major foreign publications, particularly from the nineteenth and early twentieth centuries. A 6v. *Supplement* (1987-88. $700. ISBN: 086291275x) contains 85,000 additions and amendments.

Online access to the catalogue is offered through BLAISE, (file BLC). The database, containing over 3,860,000

....(contd.)

records, was created by re-keying the 360 volumes of the printed set and has the same brief entries. Chadwyck-Healey have produced a CD-ROM version, now updated and replaced by *British Library general catalogue of printed books to 1995 on CD-ROM* (below). Records from the catalogue to 1975 are also searchable as a separate file within the British Library online public access catalogue *OPAC 97* (below). *Class No:* 017/019

[700]

—BRITISH LIBRARY. The British Library general catalogue of printed books. 1976-. London, Saur, 1983-.

Seven separate printed sets issued to date: 1976-1982 (1983. 50v. ISBN: 086291485x); 1982-1985 (1986. 26v. ISBN: 0862915406); 1986-1987 (1988. 22v. ISBN: 0862917301); 1988-1989 (1990. 28v. ISBN: 3598330502); 1990-1992 (1993. 27v. ISBN: 3598336403); 1993-1994 (1995. 27v. ISBN: 3598339402); 1995-1996 (1997. 27v. ISBN: 3598343701). Also available in microfiche: 1976-1985 (473 fiche), 1986-1987 (86 fiche), 1988-1989 (121 fiche), 1990-1992 (160 fiche) and 1993-1994 (137 fiche).

Records books and periodicals catalogued since 1975. Science and technology publications, cartography and music materials not covered comprehensively, the former restricted to items listed in *British national bibliography* (*q.v.*). Newspapers held at Colindale and items added to the collections of the British Library Information Sciences Service, National Sound Archive and Document Supply Centre also excluded. Cataloguing and headings now according to AACR2, entry arrangement by BLAISE filing rules. Access points include authors, editors, and responsible corporate bodies, persons, corporate bodies and publications as subjects, (denoted by an asterisk) and most importantly in contrast to the catalogue to 1975, all distinctive titles.

The BLAISE file *Humanities and social sciences* is the online equivalent. The database, updated weekly, is also searchable as part of the British Library's *OPAC97* (below). Records from the current catalogue are a component of *British Library general catalogue of printed books to 1995 on CD-ROM* (below). *Class No:* 017/019

[701]

BRITISH LIBRARY. British Library general catalogue of printed books to 1995 on CD-ROM. Cambridge, Chadwyck-Healey/Saztec Europe, 1997. CD-ROM database. £11,000.

Comprises 4 CD-ROM discs. Uses CARAVAN software and runs under Microsoft Windows. Replaces *British Library general catalogue of printed books to 1975 on CD-ROM*, published 1989.

Adds 1,700,000 records from the Humanities and Social Sciences file and 300,000 records from the Science Reference and Information file. Some records from the file to 1975 also re-edited. As with the online versions of the catalogue, the main advantage of the CD-ROM is the greater range of access points, the disc supporting keyword, year, place, publisher, shelfmark, language, etc. searching. *Class No:* 017/019

[702]

BRITISH LIBRARY. OPAC97: online public access catalogue. London, British Library. World Wide Web resource.

URL: http://opac97/bl.uk. Date reviewed 4th August 1998.

Online catalogue of the British Library freely accesible through the Internet. The present configuration, further version under development, supports searching of the seven

....(contd.)

files: Humanities and Social Sciences (1975-); Science Reference and Information Service; Music (1980-); Older reference material (pre 1975, corresponds to the 360v. printed catalogue (above)); Document Supply Centre books and reports (1980-, corresponds to *Books at Boston Spa* (below)); Document Supply Centre journals and serials; Document Supply Centre conferences. Searching is form based with author, organization, title phrase/keyword, subject, publisher, ISBN/ISSN and date options. Displayed records include standard bibliographical data and BL locations. *Class No:* 017/019

[703]

BRITISH LIBRARY. Document Supply Centre. **Books at Boston Spa.** Boston Spa, British Library Document Supply Centre, 198?-. Annual. Microfiche. £175. ISSN: 02686538.

Lists all Western language books published 1980 or later acquired by the Document Supply Centre. In excess of 800,000 records 1997, over 90% for English language titles. Excludes fiction and children's books. Primarily a tool for interlending purposes, entries give basic bibliographical detail and DSC stock location.

Searchable online through BLAISE as *Document Supply Centre monographs*, updated monthly. A semi-annually updated CD-ROM version, *Boston Spa books* (£325), has been available since 1992. Records are also Internet accesible as part of *OPAC97* (above). *Class No:* 017/019

[704]

BRITISH MUSEUM. Department of Printed Books. **Subject index of the modern works added to the library.** 1881-1960. London, Trustees of the British Museum, 1902-74.

Title varies slightly. Initial set for 1881-1900 published 1902-3 in 3v. (replacing 3 previous 5 year indexes covering 1880-95). Further volumes issued on a quinquennial basis: 1901-1905 (1906); 1906-1910 (1911); 1911-1915 (1918. 2v.); 1916-1920 (1922. 2v., 2nd v. covering books relating to the First World War); 1921-1925 (1927); 1926-1930 (1933. 2v.); 1931-1935 (1937. 2v.); 1936-1940 (1944. 2v.); 1941-1945 (1953); 1946-1950 (1961. 4v.); 1951-1955 (1974. 6v. ISBN: 07141034554); 1956-1960 (1965. 6v.).

A comprehensive alphabetical subject catalogue, *c.*1,260,000 entries 1881-1960. Excludes 'pure' literature and personal name headings (to be found in the *General catalogue*); biographies usually under the relevant subject. Gives author, short-title, date, place, pagination (occasionally), publishers (since 1906, if in English). Up to 1945 searching handicapped by frequent alphabetico-classed headings. More specific subject headings adopted from 1951-55 to break up long sequences. *Class No:* 017/019

[705]

—BRITISH LIBRARY. The British Library general subject catalogue 1975 to 1985. London, Saur, 1986. 75v. ISBN: 086291650x.

Also issued on microfiche as *Subject catalogue of printed books 1975-1985* comprising 437 fiche.

A major compilation on a much larger scale than the previous volumes. Modernises practice using PRECIS subject headings; extensively cross-referenced. Entries, well laid-out in 3 column format, include bibliographical detail, ISBN and BL shelf-mark. Lacks introductory notes. Continued by:- *Class No:* 017/019

[706]

—BRITISH LIBRARY. The British Library general subject catalogue 1986 to 1990. London, Saur, 1991-92. 42v. DM16,800. ISBN: 3598318103.

Microfiche version also available from the British Library as *Subject catalogue of printed books 1986-1990* (1991. 261 fiche). *Class No:* 017/019

[707]

—BRITISH LIBRARY. Subject index of modern books acquired. 1961-1975. London, British Library, 1982-86.

Published in two sets: 1961-1970 (1982. 12v. ISBN: 0904654559); 1971-1975 (1986. 14v. plus supplement. ISBN: 0712300902).

The last volumes compiled according to the traditional system begun with the 1881-1900 set. About 400,000 entries 1961-70, 470,000 1971-75. Continued by the *General subject catalogue* (above). *Class No:* 017/019

[708]

COPAC: CURL online public access catalogue. Consortium of University Research Libraries. London, Consortium of University Research Libraries, 1996-. World Wide Web resource.

URL: http://copac.ac.uk/copac/. Also accessible through Telnet at copac.ac.uk. Date reviewed 4th August 1998.

Incorporates catalogue data from the libraries of Cambridge, Edinburgh, Glasgow, Imperial College, Leeds, London, Manchester, Nottingham, Oxford, Trinity College Dublin and University College London. About 4.7 million records with 7.7 million holdings statements. 87.5% of the records are for monographs, 4% for periodicals. Data for other CURL libraries to be added. Current interface supports author/title, periodical and subject searching. Response times appear slow and the many duplicate records, especially for multi-volume works and reprints, limit effectiveness as a bibliographical resource. *Class No:* 017/019

[709]

Deutscher Gesamtkatalog. Preussischen Staatsbibliothek, *hrsg*. Berlin, Preussische Druckerei- und Verlags Aktiengesellschaft, 1931-39. 14v.

V.1-14: A-Beethordung. No more published.

V.1-8 A (1931-35), as *Gesamtkatalog der Preussichen Staatsbibliotheken* lists the holdings of 11 large Prussian libraries, plus those of the Bavarian State Library and Austrian National Library, Vienna - *c.*2500,000 items (over the whole alphabet). Includes books published up to 1930, excluding Orientalia, maps, music and dissertations. With v.9 and the letter 'B', scope was extended to cover 110 German and Austrian libraries. An author and anonymous title catalogue. If completed would have been one of the greatest bibliographies: as it stands mainly useful for a limited range of German works.

Supplemented by *Deutsche Gesamtkatalog. Neue Titel* (1892-1944) the annual cumulations of which are partly cumulated in *Berliner Titeldrucke: fünfjahrs Katalog,* 1930/34-1935/39, (1935-40), two sequences each in 8 v. *Class No:* 017/019

[710]

JOHN RYLANDS UNIVERSITY LIBRARY OF MANCHESTER. Catalogue of printed books to *c.*1978 [in the] John Rylands University Library, Manchester. Cambridge, Chadwyck Healey, 1988. Microfiche. £4,950.

Comprises 'Guardbook catalogue' of 1899 (45 fiche) and the handwritten slip catalogue recording acquisitions 1899-1978 (1,756 fiche).

Catalogue of the Deansgate Building, Rare Book Division.

....(contd.)

Approximately 550,000 author, analytical and other name entries. The nucleus of the collection is the renowned Althorp Library containing nearly 3,000 incunables including many fifteenth century books printed in Italy. The library is particularly rich in the areas of history, literature, bibliography and theology. In the latter subject, the Bible Collection includes first editions in many languages, while the Hymn Collection contains over 60,000 hymns pasted into 34 folio volumes. *Class No:* 017/019

[711]

LIBRARY OF CONGRESS. A Catalog of books represented by Library of Congress printed cards issued to July 31, 1942. Ann Arbor, Edwards, 1942-46. 167v.

Reprinted, New York, Rowman and Littlefield. ISBN 0874717248.

Reproduces photographically cards printed by the Library of Congress as part of the programme initiated at the turn of the century to maintain 'depository sets' recording its own holdings and those of a number of major research libraries. A main entry catalogue with cross-references, cards give author's full names and dates, full title, place, publisher, date, collation, edition, series, subject and added entry tracings, LC and often Dewey classification numbers, LC card number and a contents note. Pagination of 'hidden' bibliographies is also stated.

A *Supplement: cards issued August 1, 1942-December 31, 1947* (Ann Arbor, Mich., Edwards, 1948. 42v. (also reprinted Rowman & Littlefield)) provides continuing coverage. The dates (1942 and 1947) are of cards rather than books, the supplement including cards for books printed before 1 August 1942 and revised entries.

Continued by *Library of Congress author catalog: a cumulative list represented by Library of Congress printed cards, 1948-1952* (Ann Arbor, Edwards, 1953. 24v.) and thereafter in the *National union catalog* (below). The 1948-52 set includes added entries for the first time and groups films and filmstrips in the final volume.

The *Catalog of books ... to July 31, 1942* the *Supplement* and the 1948-52 volumes are now all superseded by the *National union catalog, pre-1956 imprints* (below), but can still be found in those libraries which have not acquired this cumulation. *Class No:* 017/019

[712]

—LIBRARY OF CONGRESS. National union catalog: a cumulative author list representing Library of Congress printed cards and titles reported by other libraries. Washington, D.C., Library of Congress, Card Division, 1956-82. Monthly, with quarterly and annual cumulations. ISSN: 00280348.

Continues the *Library of Congress catalog. Books: authors.* Cumulative retrospective coverage back to 1952 provided by *National union catalog: 1952-1955 imprints: an author list representing Library of Congress printed cards and titles reported by other American libraries* (Edwards, 1961. 30v.).

Five commercially published quinquennial cumulations produced as follows: 1953-1957 (Edwards, 1958. 28v.); 1958-1962 (Rowman & Littlefield, 1963. 54v.); 1963-1967 (Edwards, 1969. 72v.); 1968-1972 (Edwards, 1973. 119v. ISBN: 0318518082); 1973-1977 (Rowman & Littlefield, 1978. 150v. ISBN: 0847660222)). All cumulations include separate volumes *Music and phonorecords* and *Motion pictures and filmstrips.* No further quinquennial sets after 1977, coverage 1978-82 provided by five annual cumulations comprising 16,16,18,15 and 21 volumes

....*(contd.)*
respectively.

Ceased publication in paper 1982. Continuing coverage provided by the microfiche *National union catalog. Books.* (below).

From 1956 reported the holdings of 500 North American libraries (a figure gradually increased), in addition to the Library of Congress. Material in all languages of the Roman, Cyrillic, Greek and Hebrew alphabets included from the outset, items in Arabic and Indic alphabets and Chinese, Japanese and Korean characters included from the 1958-62 cumulation. Overall, foreign language titles probably represent nearly 50% of the total recorded. The very comprehensive acquisitions policy of the Library of Congress and the other reporting libraries, makes the *National union catalog* the most extensive printed catalogue of modern works in existence. *Class No:* 017/019

[713]

—LIBRARY OF CONGRESS. National union catalog. Books. Washington, D.C., Library of Congress, 1983-. Monthly. (Microfiche). $790. ISSN: 07347650.

Main records appear in 'Register' format in the order in which they were processed, each identified by an alpha-numeric code. Name (main and added entry), title, series and subject heading indexes, each giving brief bibliographical detail, act as a key. Indexes cumulative, with a final annual cumulation, plus additional cumulations from 1983 *e.g.* 1983-1987.

Continues to be based on records prepared by the Library of Congress and reporting North American libraries (now *c.*1,100 in number). Full Library of Congress records provided as in the paper *National union catalog*. In addition to books includes pamphlets, atlases, microform masters and monographic government publications. The introduction of series and especially title indexes, greatly increases the efficacy of the catalogue as a bibliographical tool. Complementary series include *National union catalog. Audiovisual materials (q.v.)*.

The *National union catalog* is available as an online database through a variety of online hosts including BLAISE and Dialog (file 426). The current database *LC MARC* covers English language records from 1968, French language from 1975, German, Portuguese and Spanish from 1976 and other languages from 1977. The retrospective database *REMARC* (Dialog Files 421-25) has *c.*5,500,000 entries. The Library of Congress catalogues are also Internet accessible at http://lcweb.loc.gov/catalog. Three main search options are available, word, browse and command, the latter running under Telnet using the LOCIS system.
Class No: 017/019

[714]

—National union catalog, pre-1956 imprints: a cumulative author list representing Library of Congress printed cards and titles reported by other American libraries. London, Mansell; Chicago, American Library Association, 1968-81. 754v. ISBN: 0720100038.

Compiled and edited with the co-operation of the Library of Congress and National Union Catalog Subcommittee of the Resources and Technical Services Division, American Library Association. Main sequence v.1-685; supplement v.686-754.

Replaces *A Catalog of books ... to July 31, 1942*, the *Supplement ... August 1, 1942-December 31, 1947*, *Library of Congress author catalog ... 1948-1952* and *National union catalog ... 1953-1957*. The latter set entirely replaced for printed material as works with an imprint date 1956 and

....*(contd.)*
1957 were included in the 1958-62 volumes in anticipation of this cumulation. As records for films etc. are excluded, v.24 of the 1948-52 and v.27-28 of the 1953-57 sets, which include these types of material, are not replaced.

Entries for *c.*11,000,000 works, cumulating the earlier catalogues as outlined above, plus titles reported by more than 700 contributing libraries in the US and Canada. Includes books, pamphlets, maps, atlases, microforms and music. Serials also covered, but not as comprehensively as in *Union list of serials* and *New serial titles (q.v.)*. Generally confined to works in the Latin alphabet, items in other scripts recorded only if represented by a Library of Congress printed card giving uniform transliteration (coverage of Cyrillic script works provided by *The Slavic Cyrillic union catalog of pre-1956 imprints*). The 69 supplementary volumes list further material accumulated since the editorial work began in 1967 and, in separate sequences, locations for titles in the main set that are sparsely located in the main set.

A further cumulation, effectively continuing the *National union catalog: pre-1956 imprints*, is *National union catalog, 1956 through 1967: a cumulative author list representing Library of Congress printed cards and titles reported by other American libraries* (Totowa, N.J., Rowman & Littlefield, 1970-72. 125v.). This set represents a combination of the 1958-62 (includes 1956 and 1957 imprints) and 1963-67 quinquennial cumulations of the *National union catalog*. *Class No:* 017/019

[715]

LIBRARY OF CONGRESS. The Library of Congress catalog. Books: subjects. Washington, D.C., Library of Congress, 1950-84. Quarterly, with annual and quinquennial cumulations.

Quinquennial cumulations: 1950-1954 (Edwards, 1955. 20v.); 1955-1959 (Pageant Books, 1960. 22v.); 1960-1964 (Edwards, 1965. 25v.); 1965-1969 (Edwards, 1970. 42v. $600. ISBN: 0910546053); 1970-1974 (Rowman & Littlefield, 1976. 100v. $1,740. ISBN: 087471785x).

Change of title from 1975, continuing as *Library of Congress. Subject catalog.* No further quinquennial cumulations. Ceased publication with the annual for 1982. Coverage now provided by the subject index to the microfiche *National union catalog. Books (q.v.)* and the online catalogues.

A subject index to works represented by Library of Congress printed cards. Cumulations include publications from 1945. Entries omit the notes and tracings given in the author catalogues. *Class No:* 017/019

[716]

LIBRARY OF CONGRESS. Shelflist of the Library of Congress. Arlington, Va., US Historic Documents Institute, 1968-79. 248 microfilm reels (or 3,229 microfiche from University Microfilms International).

Photoreproductions of approx. 6,800,000 cards in LC classified order for every work catalogued by the Library of Congress up to the time of filming. Two guides have been offered: Olson, N. *User's guide to the Library of Congress shelflist reference system* (US Historic Documents Institute, 1980) and Hamilton, L.K. *The Library of Congress shelflist: a user's guide to the microfiche edition* (University Microfilms International, 1979. 2v.). *Class No:* 017/019

[717]

—Cumulative title index to the Library of Congress shelflist: a combined listing of the MARC and REMARC databases through 1981. Arlington, Va., Carrollton Press, 1983. 158v. ISSN: 0840803508.

Computer produced from the MARC and REMARC databases offering title access to works catalogued by the Library of Congress 1897 to 1978. Brief entries comprising main (author) entry, edition statement, imprint, LC call number and LC card number. *Class No:* 017/019

[718]

LONDON LIBRARY. Catalogue of the London Library. [New ed.]. London, London Library, 1913-14. 2v.

Enl. ed. of catalogue issued 1903. Supplements: 1913-20 (1920); 1920-28 (1929); 1928-50 (1953).

Entries give author, title (sometimes abbreviated) and date, and note inclusion of bibliographies. Uses cataloguing rules akin to those of the British Museum. Well over 500,000 entries; the 3rd suppt. alone lists *c.*150,000v. Particularly rich in such subjects as history, philosophy and literature. *Class No:* 017/019

[719]

—LONDON LIBRARY. Subject index of the London Library. London, London Library, 1908.

Supplements: 1902-22 (1923); 1923-38 (1938); 1938-53 (1955).

Valued for its specific headings, adequate cross-references and analytical entries. No personal name entries (these are given in the *Catalogue*), but a sub-heading 'Biography' appears under many subjects. With the *Catalogue,* remains a valuable bibliographical tool, including a fair proportion of foreign material. *Class No:* 017/019

[720]

Nederlandse centrale catalogus van boeken, periodieken en congressen. s'Gravenhage, Koninklijke Bibliotheek. Computer database.

Available online through PICA.

Union catalogue of humanities and social sciences material in more than 600 Dutch university and research libraries. Over 7,000,000 records 1995. Internet access at http://www.pica.nl, password required, English-language interface available. *Class No:* 017/019

[721]

NEW YORK PUBLIC LIBRARY. Research Libraries. **Dictionary catalog of the Research Libraries of the New York Public Library** 1911-1971. New York, New York Public Library (distr. by G.K. Hall), 1979-83. 800v. ISBN: 0816103208.

The only catalogue of the great research libraries which is in full dictionary format. Reproduces about 10 million cards for book and book-like materials. Subject coverage is general but with 'no special emphasis on law, medicine and the biological sciences, pedagogy and theology' (Introduction). Entries include some indexing of the contents of periodicals, although this practice was gradually reduced as published indexes became available. The 1911 date in the title is somewhat misleading, refering to the first public availability of the catalogue. Preparation actually began in 1895, and includes holdings of the Astor, Lennox and Samuel Jones Tilden libraries which were consolidated that year to form the Research Libraries. 505.00/00$aFurther coverage is available in *Dictionary catalog of the Research Libraries: a cumulative list of authors, titles and subjects representing materials added to the collections beginning January 1, 1972.* (New York, New York Public Library,

.... (contd.)

1980. 64v.). This set based on a monthly cumulating list. Material added since 1971 is also recorded on the online catalogue *CATNYP*, freely accessible through the WWW at http://catnyp.nypl.org/. *Class No:* 017/019

[722]

Novum regestrum: cátalogo colectivo de fondo antiguo, siglos XV-XIX, de la Asociación de Bibliotecas Nacionales de Iberoamérica (ABINIA). Madrid, Biblioteca Nacional de España & Asociación de Bibliotecas Nacionales de Iberoamérica, 1994-. CD-ROM database. £1,375.

Distributed by Chadwyck-Healey.

Collective catalogue of pre-1850 Spanish and Portuguese language printed monographs held by 23 Latin American national libraries. Spanish and English search interfaces. 180,000 records on initial CD-ROM conforming to ISBD(A) or ISBD(M). *Class No:* 017/019

[723]

OCLC online union catalog. Dublin, Ohio, OCLC Online Computer Library Center. Computer database.

Available online as an OCLC FirstSearch database and through STN International. Known as *WorldCat.*

The world's largest bibliographic database, developed from a shared cataloguing system. Now contains in excess of 35,000,000 records contributed by 18,000 participating institutions in 52 countries. Also incorporates Library of Congress, CONSER and other data. Database growing at the rate of 35,000 entries weekly. Includes records for sound recordings, audio-visual materials, music scores, microforms, CD-ROMs etc., in addition to books and serials. Subscription based access through FirstSearch using either WWW or Telnet access modes. Search paths include author, title, subject, date and ISBN/ISSN. Where available the catalogue is an unrivalled bibliographical resource exceeding in size the British Library and Library of Congress databases. However, as records are contributed by OCLC participating libraries, there is, despite editorial control, an element of record duplication and error not found in databases based on the holdings of a single library. *Class No:* 017/019

[724]

ÖSTERREICHISCHEN NATIONALBIBLIOTHEK. Katalog der Österreichischen Nationalbibliothek Wien. Druckschriften 1501-1929. Hildesheim, Olms, 1982. 808 microfiche.

Reproduces cards from the typed catalogue compiled from the old handwritten catalogue over the period 1959-67. About 1,200,000 entries in short-title format. The collection is particularly rich in material relating to countries of the old Austro-Hungarian Empire and former Hapsburg possessions. *Class No:* 017/019

[725]

PEDDIE, R.A. Subject index of books published up to and including 1880. London, Grafton, 1933-48. 4v.

Reprinted London, Pordes, 1962. V.1 as *Subject index of books published before 1880.*

Supplements the British Museum *Subject index of modern works (q.v.)* by recording earlier books, but not confined to B.M. holdings. Each volume is an A-Z subject list (with more specific headings than in the B.M. index), but is compiled on no set plan, inclusion in any particular volume being quite accidental, with many titles appearing in more than one volume. Excludes personal name headings and 'pure' literature. *Class No:* 017/019

[726]
Verbundkatalog: maschinenlesbarer Katalogdaten deutscher Bibliotheken. 4. Grundwerk. Berlin, Deutsches Bibliotheksinstitut, 1994. Microfiche. DM1300. ISBN: 3870682043.

Comprises 2,044 fiche. Updated by supplement 1997 (1,777 fiche. DM1200. ISBN: 3870682191).

About 18,500,000 records based on regional and other German union catalogues. An online version is also available through the Deutsches Bibliotheksinstitut at http://www.dbilink.de/. *Class No:* 017/019

Bibliographies

[727]
COLLISON, R.L. Published library catalogues: an introduction to their contents and use. London, Mansell, 1973. viii,184p. ISBN: 072010369x.

Pt.1: Published library catalogues in various fields; pt.2: Key to published library catalogues (p.107-69), arranged under names of libraries giving full bibliographical citation (pt.1 in running commentary format). Confined to library catalogues of the English-speaking world. Includes catalogues resulting from photolitho-offset reproductions of catalogue cards (as perfected by Mansell and G.K. Hall) as well as conventional letter-press printed catalogues. Bibliography (p.171-2). Detailed subject index to pt.1. *Class No:* 017/019(01)

[728]
NELSON, B.R. A Guide to published library catalogs. Metuchen, N.J., Scarecrow Press, 1982. xvi,342p. £24.75;$27.50. ISBN: 0810814773.

Includes only modern catalogues of major collections (mostly multi-volume). Author acknowledges Collinson's *Published library catalogues* (above) and Thompson's *Checklist and union catalog of holdings of major published library catalogs in METRO libraries* (New York Metropolitan Reference and Research Library Agency, 1980). Lists in 33 subject categories, 429 catalogues mostly examined by the author. Lengthy descriptions. Indexes of subjects and libraries. *Class No:* 017/019(01)

Great Britain

[729]
Corpus of British medieval library catalogues. Sharpe, R., *general editior*. London, British Library in association with the British Academy, 1990-.

4 v. published to the end of 1997: *The Friars' libraries*, Humphreys, K.W. *ed.* (xxxv,281p. £50. ISBN: 0712300686); *Registrum Anglie des libris doctorum et anctorum veterum*, Rouse, R.H. *and others eds.* (clxix, 346p. £90. ISBN: 0712300740); *The Libraries of the Cistercians, Gilbertines and Premonstratensians*, Bell, D.N. *ed.* (xxx,340p. £75. ISBN: 0712302794); *English Benedictine libraries: the shorter catalogues*, Sharpe, R. *and others eds.* (xxx,931p. £95. ISBN: 0712303367).

'(A)ims to collect all the documents that provide evidence for the holdings, organisation and use of libraries in medieval England, Scotland and, so far as such evidence exists, Wales' (*Editorial procedures* p.ix, v.2). V.3 covers 36 libraries Beaulieu ... Welbeck, v.4 60 libraries Abbotsbury ... York. Indexes of incipts and second folios, manuscripts, authors and anonymous works. Up to 20 vols. are projected to complete the set. *Class No:* 017/019(01)(410)

[730]
DOWNS, R.B. *and* **DOWNS, E.C. British and Irish library resources:** a bibliographical guide. London, Mansell, 1981. ixv,427p. $110. ISBN: 072011604x.

Rev. and updated ed. of *British library resources* (1973).

A 'bibliographical guide to the resources for advanced study and research' (Introduction). Includes library catalogues (general and special), checklists of specialized collections, calendars of manuscripts and archives, exhibition catalogues, articles descriptive of collections, guides to individual libraries and their holdings, directories of libraries and union lists of serials. Omits annual reports, histories and administrative studies. 6,731 entries, with brief annotations, in broad Dewey classified arrangement. Author/compiler/editor and subject indexes. Minor errors and uneven indexing noted by *Library review* (v.31(4), 1982, p.285-86), but still recommended as 'a substantial addition to anyone's reference collection'. *Class No:* 017/019(01)(410)

[731]
JAYNE, S. Library catalogues of the English Renaissance. Reissue with new preface and notes. Godalming, St. Paul's Bibliographies, 1983. 240p. (*St. Paul's bibliographies, no.8.*) ISBN: 0906795176.

First published University of California Press, 1956. This ed. limited to 500 photographically reproduced copies of the original with no changes to the main text.

Inventory of the extant catalogues of English libraries 1500-1640. 2 sections: I. Institutional libraries (Oxford; Cambridge; Others); II. Private libraries. 4 appendices including 'Miscellaneous book lists 1500-1640'. Indexed (p.206-224). *Class No:* 017/019(01)(410)

[732]
Medieval libraries of Great Britain: a list of surviving books. Ker, N.R., *ed.* 2nd ed. London, Royal Historical Society, 1964. xxxii,424p. (*R.H.S. guides and handbooks, no.3.*)

First published 1941.

'Intended as a guide to medieval books and book-catalogues and to the modern catalogues in which they are described' (Preface). List of surviving books (arranged by place according to medieval ownership, p.1-218); appendix of books formerly owned by parish churches and chapels, donors, scribes and other persons before 1540 (p.225-231); glossary of words used in references to books and ownership recorded (p.225-325). Indexes: manuscripts; printed books; untraced MSS and printed books; personal names. *Class No:* 017/019(01)(410)

[733]
—Medieval libraries of Great Britain: a list of surviving books. Supplement to the second edition. Ker, N.R., *ed.* London, Royal Historical Society, 1987. xviii,149p. £15. (*R.H.S. guides and handbooks, no.15.*) ISBN: 0861931149.

Adds or occasionally reassigns 451 manuscripts and 82 printed books. Same format as original work. Includes a completely revised section for Durham, (the longest in the 1964 ed.). *Class No:* 017/019(01)(410)

[734]
Private libraries in Renaissance England: a collection and catalogue of Tudor and early Stuart booklists. Fehrenbach, R.J., *ed.* Binghamton, N.Y., Medieval & Renaissance Texts & Studies/Marlborough, Adam Matthew Publications, 1992-. (*Medieval & Renaissance texts and studies 87 ....*) ISBN: 0866981888, (v.4).

4 vol. published to 1995. V.1 contains book lists associated with four influential persons, v.2-4 contain lists

.... *(contd.)*
found in all inventories taken under the authority of the Vice-Chancellor of Oxford Univ. between 1506-1653. Indexes in each vol. *Class No:* 017/019(01)(410)

Germany

[735]

Deutsche Bibliothekskatalogue im 19. Jahrhundert: analytisches Repertorium. Kaegbein, P., *hrsg and* Schenkel, M., *bearb.*. München, K.G. Saur, 1992. 2v. DM196. (*Beitrage zur Bibliothekstheone und Bibliotheksgeschichte, Bd. 6.*)

Teil. 1. Text; Teil. 2. Register.

Covers 1815-50. Descriptions of catalogues by town Aachen ... Zweibrücken; subject and institutional indexes. *Class No:* 017/019(01)(430)

USA

[736]

DOWNS, R.B. American library resources: a bibliographical guide. Chicago, American Library Association, 1951. [11],428p.

The original 'library resources'. Includes 'printed library catalogues, union lists of books and serials, descriptions of special collections, surveys of library holdings, calendars of archives and manuscripts, selected library reports and similar works' (Introduction). 5,578 entries grouped by subject in broad Dewey order. Index of authors, subjects and libraries.

Continued by supplements: 1950-61 (1962. viii,226p.), 2,818 entries; 1961-70 (1972. viii,244p. ISBN: 0838901166), 3,421 entries and 1971-80 (1981. vii,209p. ISBN: 0838903428), 4,258 entries.

American library resources: cumulative index 1870-1970 Keller, C.D. ed. (Chicago, American Library Association, 1981. iii,87p. ISBN: 083890341x) is an author/subject index. Some of the original entries are modified. *Class No:* 017/019(01)(73)

[737]

WINANS, R.B. A Descriptive checklist of book catalogs separately printed in America, 1693-1800. Worcester, Mass., American Antiquarian Society, 1981. xxxi,207p. £34.45;$37.50. ISBN: 091229647x.

Covers catalogues from booksellers, publishers, book auctioneers, circulating libraries, social libraries, college libraries and private libraries. 286 full entries in chronological order with descriptive annotations. Further 138 entries for unlocated catalogues and 265 references to other unlocated items listed in G.L. McKay's *American book auction catalogues* (*q.v.*). Index of authors (including corporate bodies), printers, subjects and places. *Class No:* 017/019(01)(73)

[738]

—SINGERMAN, R. American library book catalogues, 1801-1875: a national bibliography. Champaign, Ill., Graduate School of Library and Information Science, Univ. of Illinois at Urbana-Champaign, 1996. ix,242p. $19.50. (*Occasional papers, 203/204.*) ISBN: 087845098x.

Lists 3,355 separately printed catalogues from public, institutional, commercial, etc., libraries. Geographic state and city arrangement, entries include bibliographical detail, references and locations. Lacks background information on libraries. Indexed by date and library type. 'Since the catalogs were produced for a local audience, and were not ordinarily distributed in the regular book trade or listed in standard bibliographies, this fills a gap' (*Choice*, v.34(4), December 1996, p.596). *Class No:* 017/019(01)(73)

Hindi

[739]

BRITISH MUSEUM. Department of Oriental Printed Books and Manuscripts. **Catalogue of the Hindi, Panjabi, Sindhi and Pushtu printed books** in the library of the British Museum. Blumhardt, J.T., *comp.* London, Trustees of the British Museum, 1893. 4 pts.

Followed by *Supplementary catalogue of Hindi books in the library of the British Museum acquired during the years 1893-1912* comp. by J.T. Blumhardt (1913. 470cols.) and *A Second supplementary catalogue of printed books in Hindi, Bihari (including Bhojpuria, Kaurmali and Maithili) and Pahari (including Nepali or Khaskura, Jaunsari, Mandeali, etc.) in the library of the British Museum*, Barnett, L.D. *and others comps.* (1957. viiip.1678cols. £45).

The British Museum (Library) has produced numerous catalogues of its holdings of printed books in the languages of the Indian sub-continent, a few of the more important of which are entered separately below. Other examples include *Catalogue of Malayalam books in the British Museum...* (1971. 587cols. £45. ISBN: 0714106232) and *Supplementary catalogue of Kannada books...* (1985. 339p. £45. ISBN: 0712300597. Also includes India Office Library and Records). *Class No:* 017/019=914.3

Persian (Farsi)

[740]

BRITISH MUSEUM. Department of Oriental Printed Books and Manuscripts. **A Catalogue of the Persian printed books** in the British Museum. Edwards, E., *comp.* London, Trustees of the British Museum, 1922. 967cols.

Includes translations of Persian books in European languages and bibliographies and writings on Persian literature. *Class No:* 017/019=915.5

[741]

—BRITISH LIBRARY. First supplementary catalogue of Persian printed books in the British Library Oriental Collections acquired 1923-1970. Meredith-*Owens, G.M., comp and* Waley, M.I., *ed.*. London, British Library, 1992.

79 microfiche in folder with preface. *Class No:* 017/019=915.5

Semitic Languages

[742]

BRITISH MUSEUM. Department of Oriental Printed Books and Manuscripts. **Catalogue of Syriac printed books and related literature** in the British Museum. Moss, C., *comp.* London, Trustees of the British Museum, 1962. viiip.,1174,206,272 cols. £40. ISBN: 0714106356.

More than 11,000 entries, including periodical articles on Syriac studies in Western languages. *Class No:* 017/019=92

Hebrew

[743]
BRITISH MUSEUM. Department of Oriental Printed Books and Manuscripts. **Catalogue of the Hebrew books in the library of the British Museum.** Zedner, J., *comp.* London, British Museum, 1867. viii,891p.

Reprinted 1964 (£30. ISBN: 0714106208).

Author catalogue. The collection 'consists of upwards of 10,100 bound volumes and comprises works in all branches of Hebrew and Rabbinical learning' (Preface p.iii). Indexes of names, titles, abbreviations and places of printing. *Class No:* 017/019=924

[744]
—BRITISH LIBRARY. Second supplementary catalogue of Hebrew printed books in the British Library 1893-1960. London, British Library, 1994. 2v. £125;$445. ISBN: 0712302417.

Prepared for publication by D.R. Smith.

The first supplement, *Catalogue of Hebrew books in the British museum acquired during the years 1868-1892* Van Straalen, S. *comp.* (London, British Museum, 1894. vii,532p. Reprinted 1968), lists 4,650 items.

Records 9,000 titles. Entries, by author, give short title in original script, transliteration, bibliographical detail and BL shelfmark. Indexes of titles in Hebrew characters and non-Hebrew titles. *Class No:* 017/019=924

[745]
—Yiddish printed books from the *British Library general catalogue*: print-out from the automated BLC file... London, British Library, 1992. Unpaged.

Basic list of 1,500 items acquired 1900 to 1975 (earlier Yiddish books catalogued with Hebrew titles (above)). *Class No:* 017/019=924

[746]
COWLEY, Sir A.E. A Concise catalogue of the Hebrew printed books in the Bodleian Library. Oxford, Clarendon Press, 1929. vii,816p.

Reprinted 1971. (ISBN: 0199153279).

Short-title entries. Based on M. Steinschneider's *Catalogus librorum Hebraeorum in Bibliotheca Bodleiana* (1852-60). *Class No:* 017/019=924

[747]
HARVARD COLLEGE LIBRARY. Catalog of the Hebrew collection of the Harvard College Library. Berlin, C., *ed.* München, K.G. Saur, 1995. 11v. $3,265. ISBN: 3598226209.

V.1-7 Author/title index; v.8-9 Subject index; v.10-11 Imprint index.

Catalogue of one of the world's leading Hebraica collections with great strength in all areas of Jewish Stuides and with the largest collection of Israeli publications outside the state of Israel' (p.ix, v.1). 112,000 romanized entries, records extracted from the Harvard *HOLLIS* database system. Includes serials, sound recordings, videotapes and scores. Imprint index is the first of its kind on this scale for Hebrew books. *Class No:* 017/019=924

Arabic

[748]
BRITISH MUSEUM. Catalogue of Arabic books in the British Museum. Ellis, A.G., *comp.* London, Trustees of the British Museum, 1894-1935. 2v. & index.

V.3 Indexes by A.S. Fulton, 1935. V.1-2 reprinted 1967, with revised shelf-marks, £30 per v. ISBN: 0714106038 (v.1).

.... *(contd.)*

Continued by *Supplementary catalogue of Arabic printed books*, Fulton, A.S. and Ellis, A.G. *comps.* (1926) and *Second supplementary catalogue of Arabic printed books,*, Fulton, A.S. and Lings, M. *comps.* (1959. £35. ISBN: 0714106062). Further updated by:- *Class No:* 017/019=927

[749]
—BRITISH LIBRARY. Third supplementary catalogue of Arabic printed books in the British Library 1958-1969. Lings, M. *and* Safadi, Y.H., *comps.* London, British Library, 1977. 4v. £250. ISBN: 0714106658.

Unlike its predecessors produced by photo-offset reproduction from the original catalogue records. V.3 Title index; v.4 Subject index. *Class No:* 017/019=927

[750]
Catalogue collectif des ouvrages en langue arabe acquis par les bibliothèques françaises 1952-1983. Haddad, G. *and* Said, M., *comps.* Paris, Saur, 1984. 4v. (*Catalogue collectif des ouvrages étrangers Bibliothéque Nationale.*)

Union catalogue of Arabic language books acquired by French libraries during the period. *Class No:* 017/019=927

[751]
—BALAGNA, J. Inventaire des livres imprimés arabes: 1514-1959. Paris, Bibliothèque Nationale, 1986. xiv,1208p. ISBN: 2717717412.

Books in Arabic script, or containing Arabic script, held by the Bibliothèque Nationale. Author (transliterated) arrangement; title index.

Holdings after 1959 recorded in supplementary volumes to main Bibliothèque Nationale *Catalogue général des livres imprimés... (q.v.).* *Class No:* 017/019=927

[752]
HARVARD UNIVERSITY. Library. **Catalog of the Arabic collection.** Abdulrazak, F., *ed.* Boston, Mass., G.K. Hall, 1983. 6v. $1,900. ISBN: 0816115079.

1st ed. published 1968 as *Catalogue of Arabic, Persian and Ottoman Turkish books.*

Catalogue of one of the largest Arabic collections in the West. Coverage includes all aspects of Arabic language and literature throughout the Islamic period, material on the modern Middle East and Islamic theology. About 90,000 cards reproduced in 3 sections: main listing in dictionary format; alphabetical listing of specialist, topical subject headings; alphabetical listing of serial holdings. *Class No:* 017/019=927

Caucasian Languages

[753]
BRITISH LIBRARY. Catalogue of early Armenian books 1512-1850. Nersessian, V., *comp.* London, British Library, 1980. 172p. plates. £50. ISBN: 0904654354.

691 numbered entries for items in the British Library and the Bodleian Library. Entries, arranged chronologically, include shelfmarks and descriptive annotations. Index (p.161-72). Essay 'Armenian printing 1512-1800' (p.9-44) precedes the catalogue. *Class No:* 017/019=946

[754]

BRITISH MUSEUM. Catalogue of Georgian and other Caucasian printed books in the British Museum. Lang, D.M., *comp.* London, Trustees of the British Museum, 1962. 430cols.

Also includes a selection of grammars, dictionaries and bibliographies, as well as a number of texts and monographs, relating to the Caucasian languages and literatures. *Class No:* 017/019=946

Oriental

[755]

INDIA OFFICE LIBRARY AND RECORDS. Catalogue of the Library of the India Office. Volume 2. [Oriental languages]. London, India Office Library and Records, 1900-57.

Pt.1 *Sanskrit books.* Rev. ed. (first published 1897) 4v. (A-G (1938); H-Krsna-lilamrta (1951); Krsna-lilamrta-R (1953); S-Z (1957)). Pt.2 *Hindustani books* (1920). Pt.3 *Hindi, Panjabi, Pushtu and Sindhi books* (1902). Pt.4 *Bengali, Oriya and Assamese books* (1905). Pt.5 *Marahti and Gujarati books* (1908). Pt.6 *Persian books* (1937).

Various updating and supplementary volumes include *Catalogue of the Punjabi printed books added to the India Office Library 1902-1964* Gaur, G. *comp.* (London, 1975. xi,404p. £19. ISBN: 090335912x) and *Catalogue of Urdu printed books in the India Office Library 1820-1920* 2nd ed. Quraishi, S.A. *comp.* (London, 1991. xv,280p. ISBN: 0712302107). *Class No:* 017/019=95

[756]

LIBRARY OF CONGRESS. Far Eastern languages catalog. Boston, Mass., G.K. Hall, 1972. 22v. ISBN: 081610980x.

339,000 card dictionary catalogue. About 55,000 works in Chinese, 55,000 in Japanese and 11,000 in Korean. Some English translations included. *Class No:* 017/019=95

16th & 17th Centuries

[757]

McLEOD, S.G., *and others*. The Cathedral libraries catalogue: books printed before 1701 in the libraries of the Anglican cathedrals of England and Wales. Vol. 1. Books printed in the British Isles, and British America and English books printed elsewhere. James, K.I. *and* Shaw, D.J., *eds.* London, British Library with The Bibliographical Society, 1984. xxi,442p. £30. ISBN: 0712300384.

Limited ed. of 500 copies.

The result of a project originally begun in 1944. Covers 37 cathedrals, 31 English, 5 Welsh, 1 Manx; Westminster Abbey and Christ Church Cathedral, Oxford notable exclusions. Entries in several sequences; to 1640 by STC no.; 1641-1700 by Wing no.; books to 1640 not in STC; books 1641-1700 not in Wing; periodicals 1641-1700. All locations given for each item included; York has the largest number of entries. Despite some discrepancies caused by lengthy compilation, forms 'a valuable research tool' (*Book collector,* v.35(4), Winter 1986, p.527-30), complementing STC and Wing (*qq.v.*).

V.2, to cover books not printed or published in Britain or English, announced for 1998 (ISBN: 0712306544). *Class No:* 017/019"15/16"

16th Century

[758]

CAMBRIDGE UNIVERSITY. Library. **Catalogue of books printed on the continent of Europe, 1501-1600 in Cambridge libraries.** Adams, H.M., *comp.* Cambridge, Cambridge Univ. Press, 1967. 2v. $500. ISBN: 0521069513.

An author list of *c.*30,000 items, numbered under each letter of the alphabet. Abridged titles; full imprints; signature collations. Locations in 35 libraries (British Museum, Cambridge Univ. Library, Fitzwilliam Museum, Whipple Museum, plus college and departmental libraries). V.2 includes index of printers (name; date; works printed) and index of places, with names of printers. Well produced. *Class No:* 017/019"15"

[759]

Index Aureliensis: catalogus librorum sedecimo saeculo impressorum. Genève, Foundation Index Aurelienis, 1965-. (*Bibliotheca bibliographica Aureliana, 11, etc.*) ISBN: 3873200007.

Main listing *Prima pars* issued at irregular intervals, 11 v. covering A-Des published to 1996. *Tertia pars* forming printer and place indexes began to appear 1983. A cumulative dictionary of printers and publishers so far identified issued 1992 as *Tertia pars. T.II. Clavis: typographorum librariorumque seaculi sedecimi* (479p.).

International listing of 16th century books. Arranged by main entry with short titles and basic bibliographical detail. Gives selected locations in over 500 libraries worldwide including the British Library, Cambridge University and the Bodleian. *Class No:* 017/019"15"

[760]

NATIONAL LIBRARY OF SCOTLAND. A Short-title catalogue of foreign books printed up to 1600: books printed or published outside the British Isles now in the National Library of Scotland and the Library of the Faculty of Advocates, Edinburgh. Edinburgh, HMSO, 1970. viii,546p. ISBN: 0114904723.

About 7,000 entries. Follows the lines of the British Library's short-title catalogues of foreign books for the same period. Index of places with printers and publishers. *Class No:* 017/019"15"

Book-auction & Book Sales Catalogues

---

[761]

American book prices current. 1894/95-. New York, Bancroft-Parkman, 1895-. Annual. Price varies. ISSN: 00919357.

Publisher varies.

Generally regarded as the most reliable of the Anglo-American series of book-auction records. Since 1958 has included records for a limited number of auctions held outside the US. V.102 September 1995-August 1996 (1996. xxiii,1015p.) covers *c.*220 sales, including a number in the UK, plus others in Australia, Germany, Italy and the Netherlands. Currently arranged in 2 main pts: I. Autographs and manuscripts; II. Books (atlases, books, broadsides, maps and charts). List of auction houses, consignors and season's sales precedes. Entries arranged alphabetically by author, detail verified rather than merely transcribed. Minimum sale price now $50. No indexes to individual volumes, but separate quinquennial indexes from 1941. Earlier indexes cover 1914-22, 1923-32 and 1933-40.

....(*contd.*)
Recent indexes issued on a quadrennial basis, (1991-95. 1996. 2v. $495 ISBN: 0914022318). Records 1975 to date also available online through Bancroft-Parkman as *Bookline utopia* (monthly updating) and on CD-ROM ($2100.95). *Class No:* 018.3

[762]

Annual register of book values. Cole, M., *ed.* York, The Clique, 1987-. Annual. £22 per. v.

Present title from 1993, previously *International rare book prices.* Published in 6 subject volumes: *Arts and architecture* (ISSN: 09687505), including the book arts; *Children's books*; *Literature* (ISSN: 09687556), emphasising 19th and early 20th century titles; *Modern first editions* (ISSN: 09687521), post-1900, limited overlap with *Literature*; *Science and medicine* (ISSN: 0968753X), including natural history and agriculture; *Voyages, travel and exploration* (ISSN: 09687548), including topography and local history. Each v. available for separate purchase.

Book prices recorded selected from sale catalogues of British and US dealers, with emphasis 'placed on books falling within the lower to middle ranges of the pricing scale'. Confined to English language titles. *c.*32,000 titles recorded across series annually. Indexes a larger proportion of British dealers' catalogues than US published rivals such as *Bookman's price index*. *Class No:* 018.3

[763]

L'Argus du livre de collection. 1982/Juillet 1984-. Paris, Éditions du Cercle de la Librairie, 1985-. Annual. FFr995. ISSN: 12667080.

First issue has title *L'Argus du livre ancien et moderne.* Replaces O. Matterlin's *Catalogue bibliographique des ventes publiques* covering 1964/65-1980/83 (initial issues with title *La Cote internationale des livres et manuscrits*).

Mainly confined to French sales, although some in Belgium and London are also covered. July 1995-July 1996 v. (1997. xxxvi,818p.) records sale prices for 9,998 items, arranged by main entry, minimum price FFr550. Chronological list of sales (p.ix-xii); indexed by publisher, illustrator, binder, provenance and subject (broad classes). *Class No:* 018.3

[764]

Book-auction records: a priced and annotated annual record of international book auctions. 1902/12-. Folkestone, Dawson, 1924-. Annual. £77. ISSN: 00680095.

Title varies slightly. Publisher has also varied, originally Karslake, then Stevens & Stiles. Published quarterly until 1940.

Now in 2 pts: I. Printed books and atlases; II. Printed maps, charts and plans. Records for books in alphabetical order of author, except for certain large categories *e.g.* Atlases, Bibles, Hymnals. Fairly full bibliographical detail for each entry, with notes on binding, imperfections etc., plus sale information, including name of auction house, date of sale, lot no., buyer's name where available and price achieved. V.93 for the 1995 season (1997. xv,552p.), has records for *c.*260 sales mainly in Great Britain, but also in North America, Europe and elsewhere. Includes only lots which realised £85 or over.

V.1-24 (1902-26/27) has articles on bibliographical subjects (indexed in *Subject index to periodicals*) and until 1939 there was a list of 'points' distinguishing editions.

Cumulative indexes issued as follows: 1902-12, 1912-23, 1924-33, 1934-43, 1944-48, 1948-58, 1958-63, 1963-68, 1968-72 (£100. ISBN: 0712908293), 1979-83 (£250. ISBN: 0712910532), 1984-89 (£350. ISBN: 0712910530) and 1989-1994 (ISBN: 0712910689). *Class No:* 018.3

[765]

—Book-prices current: a record of the prices at which books have been sold at auction. December 1886-1956/58. London, various publishers, 1888-1959. Annual (irregular).

Entries heavily abbreviated; prices indicated. V.1-27: 1886-1913, arranged by date of sale, thereafter by authors, A-Z. Rather less detailed than *Book-auction records.* A 3v. index covers 1887-96, 1897-1906 and 1907-16. *Class No:* 018.3

[766]

Book prices: used and rare. Zempel, E.N. *and* Verkler, L.A., *eds.* Peoria, Ill., Spoon River Press, 1993-. Annual. $72.

Based on the catalogues of 160 dealers. About 30,000 entries in each v. for books 'most likely to be bought and sold in daily operations of a general used book store'. An attractively priced alternative to *Bookman's price index* (below), but not as thorough or well-produced. *Class No:* 018.3

[767]

Bookman's price index: a guide to the value of rare and other out-of-print books. McGrath, A.F., *ed.* Detroit, Gale, 1964-. Semi-annual. $199. ISSN: 00680141.

Initially published annually.

The third current major English language book sale price guide, but based on dealers' catalogues rather than actual auction prices. Records for around 25,000 books in each issue with the focus on literature and history. 150-200 dealers covered including some from UK. Main section arranged by author gives title, imprint, edition, size, illustrations, binding, condition, availability and prices. Separate section for association copies, books in fine bindings and books decorated with fore-edge paintings. Series of cumulative indexes recently published (v.1-6, v.7-12, v.13-19, v.20-26, v.27-36 and v.37-46) priced at $255 each. *Class No:* 018.3

[768]

Jahrbuch der Auktionspreise für Bücher, Handschriften und Autographen: Ergebnisse der Auktionen in Deutschland, den Niederlanden, Österreich und der Schweiz. 1950-. Stuttgart, Hauswedell, 1951-. Annual. DM560. ISSN: 00752193.

Minor variations in title. Continues *Jahrbuch der Bücherpreise. Ergebnisse der Versteigerungen in Deutschland, Tschechoslowakei, Ungarn.* 1907-40.

Main entry listing in separate sections for books, manuscripts and autographs. Lower price limit currently DM250. Bd.46 1995 (1996. xxviii,804p.) has 30,000 entries drawn from 70 catalogues covering 66 sales. Decennial indexes 1950-79, quinquennial indexes 1980-94. Also available online as *JAP-Datenbank*. *Class No:* 018.3

[769]

Sale catalogues of libraries of eminent persons. Munby, A.N.L., *gen. ed.* London, Mansell and Sotheby Parke-Bernet Publications, 1971-75. 12v.

Poets and men of letters v.1-3, 5-7, 9. Architects v.4. Politicians v.8. Antiquaries v.10. Scientists v.11. Actors v.12.

Each catalogue is a facsimile, preceded by a scholarly introduction from the volume editor. V.10 comprises the Grosse, Hearne, Stukeley, Thoresby and Vertue sales catalogues. Sales catalogues included in other volumes

....*(contd.)*
include Walter Scott and Macaulay (v.1), Wren (v.4), Ruskin and Swinburne (v.6), Burke and Wilkes (v.8), Wordsworth (v.9) and Garrick (v.12). *Class No:* 018.3

Bibliographies

[770]
BLÉCHET, F. Les Ventes publiques de livres en France 1630-1750: répertoire des catalogues conservés à la Bibliothèque nationale. Oxford, Voltaire Foundation at the Taylor Institution, 1991. 156p. facsims. £20. ISBN: 072940420x.

Chronologically arranged listing with brief details of seller, place of sale, producer of catalogue, conditions of sale and size and nature of collection. Indexed. Lengthy introduction (p.15-53). *Class No:* 018.3(01)

[771]
BLOGIE, J. Répertoire de catalogues de ventes de livres imprimés. Brussels, F. Tulkens, 1982-.

V.I. *Catalogues belges appartenant à la Bibliothèque royale Albert 1er.* (1982. ix,890cols.); v.II. *Catalogues français appartenant à la Bibliothèque royale Albert 1er.* (1985. vi,985cols.); V.III. *Catalogues britanniques appartenant à la Bibliothèque royale Albert 1er.* (1988. vi,1018cols.); v.IV. *Catalogues neérlandais appartenant à la Bibliothèque royale Albert 1er.* (1992. vii,569cols.); v.V. *Catalogues allemands appartenant à la Bibliothèque royale Albert 1er* (1997.vii,1158cols.)

Covers the comprehensive collection of the Belgian Royal Library. Each volume is in 2 sections: auction catalogues arranged chronologically; dealers' catalogues by dealer. Extensive data provided for auction catalogues including date, place, subjects, material other than printed books, authors/editors of preface, indication of price and buyers. Name index and subject index to auction catalogues in each volume. V.III has *c.*3,000 entries for auction catalogues 1694-1980 and *c.*9,000 entries for dealers' catalogues. Final v. to include other countries, catalogues acquired since 1980 and a cumulated index. *Class No:* 018.3(01)

[772]
British book sale catalogues 1676-1800: a union list. Munby, A.N.L. *and* Coral, L., *comps. & eds.* London, Mansell, 1977. xxv,146p. ISBN: 0720107032.

Adds to the British Museum list (below) 'catalogues contained in collections in England, Scotland, Ireland, France, Germany and the United States, plus catalogues acquired by the British Museum since the publication of the original list' (Introduction p.xxii). Not limited to auction catalogues, but also listing retail sale catalogues. Arranged chronologically, details include consignor's name, brief title, name of auctioneer/bookseller, location and whether included in other published bibliographies. Locations in *c.*100 British and US libraries and the Bibliothèque Nationale (Paris). Indexes of consignors, and auctioneers and booksellers, but not subjects. *Class No:* 018.3(01)

[773]
BRITISH MUSEUM. Department of Printed Books. **List of catalogues of English book sales 1676-1900** now in the British Museum. London, Trustees of the British Museum, 1915. xv,523p.

Reprinted, Detroit, Gale, 1968.

Chronological list of 8,000 catalogues. Supplementary list of sale catalogues in the Department of Manuscripts (p.441-47). Index (p.449-523). *Class No:* 018.3(01)

[774]
McKAY, G.L. American book auction catalogues, 1713-1934: a union list. New York, New York Public Library, 1934. xxxii,540p. facsims. Supplement no.1-2 1946-48.

Reprinted, with additions, from *Bulletin of the New York Public Library* 1935, 1936, 1946, 1948. Includes: 'History of book auctions in America', by C.S. Brigham (p.1-37); 'Principal works consulted' (p.xvi); 'List of American book auction houses' (p.xvii-xxxii); Index of owners (p.497-540). *Class No:* 018.3(01)

02 Librarianship & Information Studies

Librarianship & Information Studies

Abbreviations & Symbols

[775]

Acronyms and abbreviations in library and information work: a reference handbook of British usage. Montgomery, A.C., *comp. and ed.* London, Library Association, 1990. 250p. £25. ISBN: 0853659893.

1st ed. 1975; 3rd ed. 1986. Prelim. ed. in *Library and information bulletin*, no.22, (1973), p.1-35.

Expands over 7,000 acronyms and abbreviations used in the English language literature of librarianship and information work. Selective coverage of related areas such as archives and museums, book trade, education and computer and micrographic technology. Entries include country of origin if not clear from the expansion. Adequately cross-referenced between name changes etc. The established source for British librarians and information workers.
Class No: 02.0(003)

[776]

Dictionary of acronyms and abbreviations: library, information and computer terms. Tayyeb, R. *and* Chandna, K., *comps*. Rev. ed. Ottawa, Canadian Library Association, 1993. vi,251p. ISBN: 0888022662.

Earlier eds. 1979 and 1985 under title *A Dictionary of acronyms and abbreviations in library and information science*.

Expands, rather than defines, acronyms and abbreviations largely derived from American and Canadian library science periodical literature. Coverage of computer science and technology greatly expanded in this ed. Considerable overlap with other sources, especially Montgomery and Sawoniak.
Class No: 02.0(003)

[777]

SAWONIAK, H. *and* **WITT, M. New international dictionary of acronyms in library and information science** and related fields. 3rd. rev & enl. ed. München, Saur, 1994. xi,522p. £120;$145. ISBN: 3598111711.

1st ed. 1988; 2nd ed. 1992. Earlier version published Wroclaw, 1976.

Includes publishing, printing, archives, journalism, reprography and some aspects of computer science. 35,000 entries in total, 1,500 new to this ed. International in scope, especially strong on acronyms from Central and Eastern Europe, Asia, Africa and Latin America. Acronyms expanded in language of acronym, but English translations given for lesser known languages. By far the most comprehensive of the library and information science acronym and abbreviation dictionaries. *Class No:* 02.0(003)

Internet

[778]

Internet library for librarians. Sha, V.T., *comp.* Cranberry Twp., Pa., InfoWorks Technology Company, 1994-. World Wide Web resource.

URL: http://www.itccompany.com/inforetriever. Date reviewed 7th July 1998.

'(D)esigned to provide a one-stop shopping center for librarians to locate Internet resources related to their profession' (*Home page*). Main access from comprehensive table of contents listing in sections for Ready reference, Librarianship and Accessories subdivided into numerous headings (*e.g.* Acquisition of foreign materials, Language dictionaries, Library planning, Descriptive cataloguing). Each heading includes brief introduction with further summary descriptions for many sites under individual links. Keyword searching also available. Probably the most comprehensive of a number of WWW sites offering links to library and information related material on the Internet.
Class No: 02.0(003.41)

[779]

Library-orientated lists and electronic serials. Houston, Univ. of Houston Libraries. World Wide Web resource.

URL: http://info.lib.uh.edu/liblists/liblists.htm. Date reviewed 7th July 1998.

Provides links to discussion lists, distribution lists and electronic serials of interest to library and information professionals. For each list includes subscription information and addresses and links to associated World Wide Web sites. Title and subject indexes and site search form.
Class No: 02.0(003.41)

[780]

Pick: quality Internet resources in library and information science. Aberystwyth, Thomas Parry Library, Univ. of Wales Aberystwyth. World Wide Web resource.

URL http://www.aber.uk/plwww/e/. Date reviewed 7th July 1998.

Aims to provide links to authoritative, current and in-depth Internet sites relevant to library and information science students and researchers. Contents listing under specific headings (*e.g.* Public libraries, OPACs and Web pages, Collection development policies, Resources for technical services, LIS education, Citation style, Researching LIS on the Internet); further subject browse, classmark browse (DDC) and keyword search options. *Class No:* 02.0(003.41)

Bibliographies of Bibliographies

[781]

SAWONIAK, H. Miedzynarodowa bibliografia bibliografii z zakresu informacji naukowej, bibliotekoznawstwa i dziedzin pokrewnych: 1945-1978. [International bibliography of bibliographies in library and information sciences and related fields: 1945-1978.] Wrocław, Zaklad narodowy imiena Ossolińskich, 1985. lxxiv,700p. ISBN: 8304019280.

Polish language bibliography of library and information science bibliographic material with an English language

....(contd.)
introduction. Includes bibliographies published as parts of books, as journal articles or as serials. Wide subject coverage, extending to the book trade, publishing, history of the book, paper-making, printing history, reprographics, journalism, archives, alphabets and writing and, very selectively, computer science. 6,566 entries some with short annotations arranged in 44 subject classes. Author/title and subject index. Abridged English-language subject index (p.685-700). Further list of 121 more important bibliographies published after 1978 as an appendix.

Listed as forthcoming by K.G. Saur 1997, *International bibliography of bibliographies in library and information sciences and related fields, 1979-1990* (ISBN: 3598111452). *Class No:* 02.0(009)

Bibliographies

[782]

BURTON, M. *and* **VOSBURGH, M.E. A Bibliography of librarianship:** classified and annotated guide to the library literature of the world (excluding Slavonic and Oriental languages). London, Library Association, 1934. iv,176p.

Reprinted Gordon Press, 1976. (ISBN: 0849014999).

Covers the literature up to the early 1930s.

Class No: 02.0(01)

[783]

CANNONS, H.G.T. Bibliography of library economy: a classified index to the professional periodical literature relating to library economy, printing, methods of publishing, copyright, bibliography, etc., from 1876 to 1920. Chicago, American Library Association, 1927. 680p.

First published 1910 with a sub-title - a classified list of articles in library periodicals in the English language.

Reprinted New York, Franklin, 1971. (ISBN: 0833704583).

Systematically arranged with subject index. Coverage continued by *Library literature* (*q.v.*). *Class No:* 02.0(01)

[784]

—BARR, L.J., *and others*. Libraries in American periodicals before 1876: a bibliography with abstracts and an index. Jefferson, McFarland, 1983. xx,426p. ISBN: 0899500668.

1,473 entries with abstracts and library locations. Items with less than 150 words reproduced verbatim. Arranged geographically with author, library type, place, libraries, librarians, donors, and other named persons or prominent events index. Extends Cannons back to the beginning for American periodicals. *Class No:* 02.0(01)

[785]

—Cannons' bibliography of library economy 1876-1920: an author index with citations. Jordan, A.H. *and* Jordan, M., *eds.* Metuchen, N.J., Scarecrow, 1976. viii,437p. ISBN: 0810809184.

Gives full citations to all items indexed in Cannons that bear an author's name. List of publications indexed.

Class No: 02.0(01)

[786]

COLUMBIA UNIVERSITY. School of Library Service. **Dictionary catalog of the Library of the School of Library Service, Columbia University.** Boston, Mass., G.K. Hall, 1962. 7v.

Reproduces approx. 127,000 cards representing 75,000 v. The collection covers pertinent literature from 1847 to 1962. Apart from the core subjects of librarianship, includes special collections on bibliographic course works, fine printing and children's historical literature and juvenile

....(contd.)
books.

Continued by *Dictionary catalog of the Library of the School of Library Service, Columbia University. First supplement* (Boston, Mass., G.K. Hall, 1976. 4v. ISBN: 0816111669) recording a further 25,000 items added to the collection up to mid 1975. *Class No:* 02.0(01)

[787]

HERRING, M.Y. Controversial issues in librarianship: an annotated bibliography 1960-1984. New York, Garland, 1987. xx,698p. (*Garland reference library of social science, v.432.*) ISBN: 0824085787.

Covers issues deemed controversial such as closing the card catalogue, charging fees and censorship. 2,513 numbered entries with brief annotations in 11 broad subject chapters. Author/name and title indexes. Some useful grouping of material, but selective, even for the topics covered. *Class No:* 02.0(01)

[788]

International bibliography of the book trade and librarianship. [Fachliteratur zum Buch- und Bibliothekswesen.] Lengenfelder, H. *and* Hausen, G., *eds.* 12th ed. München, Saur, 1981. xxix,692p. (*Handbook of international documentation and information, v.2.*) ISBN: 3598205163.

No further eds. published to date. Previous eds. cover 1973-75 (11th ed.), 1969-72 (10th ed.), etc.

9,826 entries in this ed. about 1/3 relating directly to librarianship. Confined to monograph material, including brochures and research reports. Some countries sparsely covered (81 countries in 84p., but US 94p., Europe 433p.). Author/editor and subject indexes. *Class No:* 02.0(01)

[789]

LIBRARY ASSOCIATION. Catalogue of the Library. London, Library Association, 1958. vii,519p.

Lists more than 19,000 books, pamphlets and periodicals in the L.A. Library on 1st March 1956. Dewey order with author/title index. No subject index, but an outline of the classification and a 'Subject index: select list' appear on a tinted card insert.

Supplemented in the *Library Association record* and thereafter in *Library and information bulletin* (1967-74) and *CABLIS* (1976-90).

Records for the collection of the former British Library Information Sciences Service (BLISS) (successor to the Library Association Library), available as a separate database until the removal of the collection to the new British Library at St. Pancras, are now searchable as part of the *Humanities and social sciences* file on BLAISE. The corresponding file on the British Library OPAC also provides data for the former BLISS collection.

Class No: 02.0(01)

[790]

LILLEY, D.B *and* **BADOUGH, R.M. Library and information science: a guide to information sources.** Detroit, Gale, 1982. xvi,151p. (*Gale information guide library: Books, publishing and libraries information guide series, no.5.*) ISBN: 0810315017.

In 4 pts.: 1. Recent changes that affect the literature search (*e.g.* online databases) - 2. Search strategy models - 3. Information sources by form of material (Research studies, periodicals, books, government publications) - 4. Types of information sources. Some useful information, but much needless repetition between pts.3 and 4 and several serious omissions and erroneous references. *Class No:* 02.0(01)

[791]

PRYTHERCH, R.J. Information management and library science: a guide to the literature. [3rd ed]. Aldershot, Gower, 1994. vii,323p. £45;$69.95. ISBN: 0566074672.

Rev. ed. of *Sources of information in librarianship and information science*, first published 1983, 2nd ed. 1987.

This ed. extensively remodelled. 9 narrative chaps. (*e.g.* Keeping up-to-date: current awareness ... Research activity: progress and results ... Abstracts and indexes) analyse and discuss the most important sources, including those in online and CD-ROM format. Separate 'Annotated bibliography' (p.148-267) of standard texts, reports and background reading. List of 'Key journals' (p.268-77) and 'Directory of organizations' (p.278-306). Author index to the annotated bibliography; subject and title index (excluding the bibliography). An excellent summary of the most important information sources, 'extremely valuable to hard-pressed academics, students and practising professionals who have little time to sift the proliferating mass of publications in the field' (*Reference reviews*, v.8(6), 1994, p.5). *Class No:* 02.0(01)

[792]

PURCELL, G.R. *and* **SCHLACHTER, G.A. Reference sources in library and information services:** a guide to the literature. Santa Barbara, ABC-Clio, 1984. xxvi,359p. ISBN: 0874363551.

1,193 entries in 7 chapters: Bibliography - Terminology - Encyclopedias, yearbooks, handbooks and manuals - Biographical and membership directories - Directories of libraries and archives - Sources of library statistics - Special services and operations (about 40% of total entries subdivided into 103 subject categories Academic libraries ... Women in librarianship). Entries fully annotated. International in scope, including a good range of non-US material. Author/title and geographic indexes, but the contents list provides the only subject access. More comprehensive than Prytherch (above), but now needs updating. *Class No:* 02.0(01)

Developing Countries

[793]

HUQ, A.M.A. *and* **AMAN, M.M. Librarianship and the Third World:** an annotated bibliography of selected literature on developing nations, 1960-1975. New York, Garland, 1977. xii,372p. (*Garland reference library of social sciences, v.40.*) ISBN: 0824098978.

1,475 entries, arranged geographically by country and region with an international section. A useful source for the period covered, but contains a number of errors, some items being entered twice with contradictory annotations. Partly continued by:- *Class No:* 02.0(01)(4/9-77)

[794]

—HUQ, A.M.A. World librarianship: its international and comparative dimension: an annotated bibliography, 1976-1992. Dhaka, Acadamic Publlishers, 1995. xxi,416p. maps. ISBN: 9840801341.

779 entries with lengthy annotations for material relating to the international aspects of librarianship, but with a focus on the Third World. Geographic arrangement in 8 sections; author, subject and title indexes. '(H)ighly selective in its coverage, unnecessarily discursive in its annotations and inadequately arranged and indexed' (*Australian academic and research libraries*, v.28(2), June 1997, p.178). *Class No:* 02.0(01)(4/9-77)

Poland

[795]

Polska bibliografia bibliologiczna. 1981-. [Polish bibliography of library science.] Warszawa, Biblioteka Narodowa, 1988-. Annual. ISSN: 08606560.

Continues Cz.2 of *Bibliografia bibliografii i nauki o ksiazce*. At head of title page: Biblioteka Narodowa. Instytut Bibliograficzny.

The 1993 issue (1996. 184p.) has 2,001 entries with alphabetical and subject indexes. *Class No:* 02.0(01)(438)

China

[796]

Library and information science in China: an annotated bibliography. Wei, K.T., *comp.* Westport, Conn., Greenwood, 1989. xiv,273p. £58.50;$69.50. (*Bibliographies and indexes in library and information sciences, no.3.*) ISBN: 0313255482.

991 entries, nearly all with 50-100 word annotations. Mainly English language items, but also includes material in Chinese, French, German and Japanese. Arranged in 11 topical sections with author and subject indexes. More comprehensive than Lin (*q.v.*). *Class No:* 02.0(01)(510)

India

[797]

PRASHER, R.G. Indian library literature: an annotated bibliography. Delhi, Today and Tomorrow's Printers and Publishers, 1971. xliii,504p.

Over 3,500 references, mainly post-1955, in classified order (modified Dewey). Detailed contents list, author and subject indexes. *Class No:* 02.0(01)(540)

[798]

SINGH, S. *and* **MALHAN, I.V. Indian library literature** 1971-1980: an annotated bibliographic guide. Delhi, Today and Tomorrow's Printers and Publishers, 1986. v,391p.

Continues Prasher (above) and follows a similar format. 2,371 entries including works by Indian authors contributed to foreign journals.

Three further compilations by Singh alone extend coverage: *Indian library literature 1981-1985: an annotated bibliographic guide* (New Delhi, Ess Ess Publications, 1988. xxvi,355p. ISBN: 8170000866), *Indian library and information science literature (1986-89)* (New Delhi, Ess Ess Publications, 1991. xxxiv,612p. ISBN: 8170001218) and *Indian library and information science literature, 1990-91* (New Delhi, Concept Publishing, 1994. 396p. ISBN: 817022523X). *Class No:* 02.0(01)(540)

Indexes

[799]

Library literature: an index to library and information science. 1921/32-. New York, Wilson, 1934-. Bi-monthly, with annual cumulation. ISSN: 00242373.

Published quarterly until 1968. Cumulations triennial 1933/35-1967/69, then biennial 1970/71-1976/77.

Primarily an index to periodical literature, but also covers books, pamphlets, conference proceedings, selected library science dissertations and a few electronic journals. Author and subject entries in one A-Z sequence as with other Wilson indexes. Separate list of book reviews and a 'Checklist of monographs cited'. International, but with an American bias, *c.*145 of the 234 periodicals currently indexed published in the US. Despite some shift of emphasis in recent years, still

....(contd.)
concentrates more on traditional librarianship than its main rival *Library and information science abstracts* (above). Database version, containing records December 1984 to date, searchable through CARL, Dialog, OCLC, SilverPlatter, UMI and Wilsonline. Quarterly updated CD-ROM also available from Wilson ($1,095) and SilverPlatter. *Class No:* 02.0(014)

Encyclopaedias

[800]

Encyclopedia of library and information science. Kent, A., *and others eds.* New York, Dekker, 1968-. Illus., tables, diags. £59.95;$117 per suppl.

V.1-33: A-Z; v.34-35: Indexes; v.36-45: Supplements; v.46-47: Indexes (Supplements, plus v.1-35); v.48-: Supplements.

An encyclopedia of substantial, signed articles, generally well-documented. In addition to treatment of a wide range of library and information science topics, there is coverage for individual libraries, prominent librarians, bibliographers, etc., and libraries/librarianship in individual countries and cities. As the only English language multi-volume encyclopedia in the field, this is a valuable tool much enhanced by the *c.*90,000 entry author and subject indexes in v.46-47. Coverage is, however, very uneven and unsystematic. Thus while Cambridge University Library is afforded *c.*20p. the Bodleian receives only 6p. Similarly *British technology index* is given 13p., but *British National Bibliography* only 2½p. Another major drawback is the appearance of many important articles in the individually alphabetized supplementary volumes. These articles are produced on an apparently random basis, with no particular emphasis given to new or emerging topics. Supplements, indexed in *Library literature* (*q.v.*), usually contain about 25 articles and appear set to continue indefinitely. V.61 (1998) includes 'The biological literature' 16p., 'Developments in archival theory' 18p. and 'Total quality management' 14p. *Class No:* 02.0(031)

[801]

International encyclopedia of information and library science. Feather, J. *and* Sturges, P., *eds.* London, Routledge, 1997. xxxi,492p. £85;$130. ISBN: 0415098602.

500 plus entries and 150 contributors. Based around 9 long essays of up to 8,000 words on 'central issues' *e.g* Communication, Information management, Information theory, Library institutions and systems. Further entries much shorter *e.g.* Keyword 10 lines, Dewey, Melvil 300 words, One-person library 1½p. Lacks entries on individual countries grouping information in unsatisfactory regional articles. Also weak on many technical subjects with some out of date and inaccurate data. Well cross-referenced and thoroughly indexed (p.465-92). 'Overall ... impressive and comprehensive' (*Journal of librarianship and information science*, v.29(3), September, 1997, p.167). *Class No:* 02.0(031)

[802]

World encyclopedia of library and information services. Wedgeworth, R., *ed.* 3rd ed. Chicago, American Library Association, 1993. xviiii,905p., illus., tables. $200. ISBN: 0838906095.

Earlier eds. 1980 and 1986 with title *ALA world encyclopedia of library and information services.*

An encyclopedia of lengthy articles (*e.g.* 'Classification', 5½p. 'Electronic data sources', 13p.) from 437 contributors.

....(contd.)
While arranged A-Z, articles are stated to fall into thematic categories: the library in society; the library as an institution; theory and practice of librarianship; education and research; international library information and bibliographical organizations. Includes 160 surveys of librarianship by country (*e.g.* 'Philippines', 3p., subsections on library history, national library, academic libraries, etc.) and 216 biographies (*e.g.* 'Lancaster, F. Wilfrid' 1½p.). Except for country articles has pronounced US slant, at least half the biographies being for Americans. Bibliographical references with each article, but few in number; index (p.883-905). Although 'someone looking for a ready-reference work with many articles on individual topics will be disappointed' (*College and research libraries*, v.55(2), March 1994, p.184), far more accessible and convenient than the multi-volume *Encyclopedia of library and information science* (above). *Class No:* 02.0(031)

Australia

[803]

ALIAS: Australia's library, information and archives services: an encyclopaedia of practice and practitioners. Bryan, H., *ed.* Sydney, Library Association of Australia, 1988-91. 3v. illus. ISBN: 0868040606.

Contains A-Z entries (*e.g.* 'Australian Committee on Cataloguing' 1p., 'Library education' 5p., 'Mortlock, John Andrew Tennant' 1 col.) all signed, many with appended bibliographies. Black and white illus., supplementary articles and index in v.3. Includes a large amount of general material of relevance outside Australia. Some unevenness in coverage and writing, a 'solid work ... but not first class' (*Australian academic & research libraries*, v.20(4), December 1989, p.247). *Class No:* 02.0(031)(94)

Handbooks & Manuals

[804]

WERTSMAN, V.F. The Librarian's companion: a handbook of thousands of facts and figures on libraries, librarians, books, newspapers, publishers, booksellers. 2nd ed. Westport, Conn., Greenwood Press, 1996. xvi,225p. £51.95;$65. ISBN: 0313299757.

First published 1987.

In 2 pts.: I. 'Librarian's world digest' (p.3-97) is arranged by country giving largely statistical information on the library network, publishing output/distribution, noted libraries and librarians' organizations; II. 'Librarian's special interests' has 192 brief biographical entries for librarians past and present, 125 selected quotations relating to books and libraries, references to writing that features librarians, publishers or booksellers, notes of postage stamps which have libraries or books as a theme, Latin expressions relating to the book world and sources of information on US job opportunities. Various appendices *e.g* Library bill of rights (ALA), UNESCO public library manifesto; index (p.217-25). Some unique material, but lacking in overall coherence and purpose. *Class No:* 02.0(035)

[805]

The Whole library handbook 2: current data, professional advice and curiosa about libraries and library services. Eberhart, G.M., *comp.* Chicago, American Library Association, 1995. vi,521p. illus, tables £26.95;$30. ISBN: 083890646x.

First published 1991. This ed. with 2/3 new material, original vol. not entirely replaced.

....*(contd.)*

'(A) sort of American *Whitaker's almanac* (sic) for libraries' (*Reference reviews*, v.10(2), 1996, p.4). 10 chapters: 1. Libraries - 2. People - 3. The Profession - 4. Materials - 5. Operations - 6. Special populations - 7. Public relations - 8. Technology - 9. Issues - 10. Libriana. Individual headings include 'Librarians: racial, ethnic and gender statistics', 'Selected films for young adults 1994' and 'Hostile patron situations'. Rather chaotically organized and inadequately indexed (p.515-21), but only limited overlap with other sources such as *The Bowker annual* (*q.v*).
Class No: 02.0(035)

India

[806]

Handbook of libraries, archives and information centres in India. Gupta, B.M., *and others eds.* New Delhi, Aditya Prakashan, 1985-92. 12v. in 14.

V.1-6 published by Information Industry Publications.

V.1-10 comprise collections of readings on specific subjects and organizations *e.g.* v.3 Asia-Pacific cooperative information systems, networks and programmes; v.8 Social sciences information systems and centres. V.10, Professional organizations and associations, has lengthy sections for various bodies, *e.g.* The Computer Society of India; Indian Library Association; Punjab Library Association. V.11-12 form an annotated bibliography of 5,892 items with author, publisher and subject indexes. *Class No:* 02.0(035)(540)

Dictionaries

Polyglot

[807]

Dictionarium bibliothecarii practicum ad usum internationalem in XXII linguis. [The Librarian's practical dictionary: in 22 languages.] Pipics, Z., *ed.* 7th ed. Munich, Verlag Dokumentation, 1977. 385p. ISBN: 3794041100.

First published 1963. 1st and 2nd eds. as *A Könyvtáros gyakorlati szótára* with Hungarian as base language. 3rd-5th eds. with German as the base language. 7th ed. has German title *Wörterbuch des Bibliothekars: in 22 Sprachen.*

About 770 terms in English with equivalents in 21 other languages: Bulgarian, Croatian, Czech, Danish, Dutch, Finnish, French, German, Greek, Hungarian, Italian, Latin, Norwegian, Polish, Portuguese, Rumanian, Russian, Serbian, Slovak, Spanish and Swedish. 21 language indexes.
Class No: 02.0(038)=00

[808]

Elsevier's dictionary of library science, information and documentation: in six languages English/American, French, Spanish, Italian, Dutch and German. Clason, W.E., *comp.* 2nd ed. Amsterdam, Elsevier, 1976. [10],708p. ISBN: 0444414754.

Reprinted 1992 ($350. ISBN: 082889230); CD-ROM version 1997 ($238.50. ISBN: 0444826890). First published 1973.

5,439 numbered English terms A-Z with brief definitions, followed by equivalents in the other 5 languages. French, Spanish, Italian, Dutch and German indexes refering to the numbered English language sequence. The 2nd ed., otherwise unchanged from the 1st, includes an Arabic supplement by S. Salem (p.607-708). A valuable work, but lacks a clear statement of selection criteria and includes a number of definitions best described as unusual.
Class No: 02.0(038)=00

[809]

—Dictionary of information science: in four languages: English, German, French, Russian. Bürger, E., *comp.* Amsterdam, Elsevier, 1988. 2v. $195. ISBN: 0444989048.

Covers computer science and informatics, not information science as understood in the English speaking world.
Class No: 02.0(038)=00

[810]

Terminology of documentation: a selection of 1,200 basic terms published in English, French, German, Russian and Spanish. Wersig, G. *and* Neveling, U., *comps.* Paris, The Unesco Press, 1976. 274p. ISBN: 9230012327.

Intended as an aid to standardization. Arranged by English term, with equivalents in the other languages, in classified arrangement. Alphabetical English index. Bibliography of sources (p.47-51). *Class No:* 02.0(038)=00

[811]

Vocabularium bibliothecarii. Thompson, A., *and others comps.* 2nd ed. Paris, Unesco, 1962. 627p.

1st ed. 1953; suppl. 1958.

A dictionary of library terms arranged by UDC. 2,800 English terms with French, German, Spanish and Russian equivalents. Indexes in each of the five languages. List of sources p.47-53.

An Arabic version, *Mu'jam al-mustalahāt al maktabīyah* (Cairo, 1965. 692p.), reprints this ed., but adds an Arabic introduction and index and inserts Arabic terms in the text.

Vocabularium bibliothecarii ac supplementum hungaricum (Budapest, Akadémiai Kiado, 1972) is a similar Hungarian version. *Class No:* 02.0(038)=00

English

[812]

KEENAN, S. Concise dictionary of library and information science. London, Bowker Saur, 1995. viii,214p. £25;$45. ISBN: 1857390229.

About 3,000 entries in thematic sections: Information sources - Information handling and retrieval - Computers and telecommunications (p.57-139) - Resource management - Research methodology - Publishing. Index (p.185-211) with entries under full terms and acronyms. Definitions (5-50 words) 'tend to be painfully brief. A superior resource is Ray Prytherch's 692 page *Harrod's librarians' glossary*' (*q.v.*) (*Choice*, v.34(2), October 1996, p.253).
Class No: 02.0(038)=20

[813]

STEVENSON, J. Dictionary of library and information management. Teddington, Peter Collin Publishing, 1997. [iii],189p. £9.95;$15.95. ISBN: 0948549688.

'(C)overs the basic words, with grammatical definitions, used in library organisation and management, and the language of classification and cataloguing, as well as the language of the electronic world of information management and communication' (*Preface*). About 4,500 entries, definitions up to 50 words. Various appended listings *e.g.* Major classification schemes, Proof correction marks, Basic reference titles in print or on CD-ROM (100 works, titles only). *Class No:* 02.0(038)=20

German

[814]

KEITZ, S. von *and* KEITZ, W. von. Dictionary of library and information science: English/German, German/English. [Wörterbuch Bibliotheks- und Informationswissenschaft: Englisch/Deutsch, Deutsch/Englisch.] 2nd rev. ed. Weinheim and New York, VCH, 1992. 527p. £37.50;DM105. ISBN: 3527283854.

1st ed 1989.

Covers much the same ground as Sauppe (below) having the advantage of a greater number of entries (25,000, 5,000 new to this ed.). Lacks Sauppe's subject coding and does not cite sources.

The same authors and publisher are also responsible for a French/German, German/French dictionary, *Dictionnaire des sciences de l'information, de la bibliothèque et de la documentation: français/allemand, allemand/français* (1994. DM112. ISBN: 3527292373). *Class No:* 02.0(038)=30

[815]

KNECHTGES, S. Bibliothekarisches Handwörterbuch. [Librarian's dictionary.] [2nd rev. & enl. ed.]. Köln, The British Council/Stadtbibliothek Köln, 1995. 204p. DM19.80. ISBN: 3883471879.

Title also in Russian, *Nastol'nyi slovar' bibliotekarja*. First published 1992 under the title *Praktisches Wörterbuch für Bibliothekare/Librarian's practical dictionary*.

Basic alternative to Keitz or Sauppe (above and below). Nearly 1,000 entries in three language sequences, Russian added with this ed. Further editions to include other European languages planned. *Class No:* 02.0(038)=30

[816]

SAUPPE, E. Wörterbuch des Bibliothekswesens: Unter Berücksichtigung der bibliothekarischwichtigen Terminologie des Informations- und Dokumentationswesens, des Buchwesens, der Reprographie, des Hochschulwesens und der Datenverarbeitung. Deutsch-Englisch, Englisch-Deutsch. [Dictionary of librarianship: including a selection from the terminology of information science, bibliology, reprography, higher education and data processing. German-English, English-German.] 2. durch. und erw. Aufl. München, K.G. Saur, 1996. xxiv,388p. £58;DM178. ISBN: 3598113161.

First published 1988.

Around 13,000 terms in each language section. Entries include indication of subject context of term by means of 42 coded categories. Higher education terms added in this ed. Excludes names of institutions. Based on the contents of German and English specialized glossaries, professional books and articles; list of sources (p.xvii-xx).
Class No: 02.0(038)=30

Dutch

[817]

BDI-terminologie: verklarend woordenboek van Nederlandse termen op het gebied van bibliotheek en documentaire informatie, met vertalingen in het Engels, Frans, Duits, Spaans. Swigchem, P.J. van *and* Slot, E.J., *red.* s'Gravenhage, Nederlands Biblkiotheek- en Lektuur Centrum, 1990. xlvii,493p. ISBN: 9062521231.

Definitions for about 4,500 library and documentation terms with equivalents in English, French, German and Spanish. *Class No:* 02.0(038)=393

French

[818]

SALINIÉ, F. *and* HUBERT, S. Bilingual glossary of terms in librarianship and information science. English/French: French/English. [Glossaire bilingue en bibliothéconomie et science de l'information. Anglais/Français: Français/Anglais.] London, Library Services, 1990. [4],372p.

About 5,000 terms including some from publishing and information technology, the latter denoted by an asterisk. Generous 2 column format, terms not defined. Intended to act as a quick reference tool rather than provide exhaustive coverage. *Class No:* 02.0(038)=40

Italian

[819]

VIGINI, G. Glossario di biblioteconomia e scienza dell'informazione. Milano, Editrice Bibliografica, 1985. 126p. ISBN: 8870751090.

Short definitions with English translation of many terms. Includes limited coverage of related fields such as publishing and computer science. Separate list of English terms with Italian equivalents (p.111-126). *Class No:* 02.0(038)=50

Spanish

[820]

Technical dictionary of library and information science: English/Spanish, Spanish/English. [Diccionario técnico de bibliotecología y ciencias de la información.] Ayala, M.S., *and others eds.* New York, Garland, 1993. xviii,647p. $110. (*Garland reference library of social science, v. 815.*) ISBN: 0815306555.

'(S)pecifically designed to satisfy the needs of librarians serving the Spanish-speaking population of the United States' (Preface). Despite title gives emphasis to 'everyday' terms rather than a very technical vocabulary. About 6,500 entries, definitions of 10-30 words attached. Adequately cross-referenced. 'Useful phrases' (p.653-62).
Class No: 02.0(038)=60

Russian

[821]

WALKER, G. Russian for librarians and Russian books in libraries. 2nd ed. London, Bingley, 1983. 120p. £20. ISBN: 0851573592.

1st ed. 1973.

8 sections. 1. Russian course, provides a basic grammar of Russian with exercises. Further sections on transliteration, Soviet publishing, acquisitions/interlending, cataloguing, Russian bibliographies and reference works, and other languages using the Cyrillic alphabet. Final section comprises a Russian-English library related vocabulary of 700 words. Appended lists of Russian bibliographical/library abbreviations and publishing houses.
Class No: 02.0(038)=82

Czech

[822]

MERTA, A. *and* MERTOVÁ, D. Anglicko-český slovník: knihovnictví a informatiky. [English-Czech dictionary: of library and information science practice.] Praha, Leda, 1994. 176p. ISBN: 8090166423.

Gives Czech equivalent for *c.*14,000 English terms.
Class No: 02.0(038)=850

Celtic Languages

[823]

Téarmaí leabharlainne: Gaeilge-Béarla, Béarla-Gaeilge. [Library terms: Irish-English, English-Irish.] NiDheig, I., *comp.* Dublin, Library Association of Ireland, 1989. 38p. £3.50. ISBN: 0946037108.

Includes the terminology of information.
Class No: 02.0(038)=916

Welsh

[824]

Termau llyfrgell a'r byd llyfrau. [Glossary of library and book trade terms.] Aberystwyth, Coleg Llyfrgellwyr Cymru (College of Librarianship Wales), 1978. [1],37p.

English-Welsh glossary with preface in Welsh. Over 2,500 terms. *Class No:* 02.0(038)=916.6

Oriental

[825]

YOSHIMURA, Z. Nichi-Chu-Ei taiyaku toshokan yogo jiten. [Glossary of library terms in Japanese-Chinese-English.] Tokyo, Yushodo Shuppan, 1997. vii,332p. ISBN: 4841902325.

Title also in Chinese. *Class No:* 02.0(038)=95

Chinese

[826]

LI, H. Dictionary of library and information sciences English-Chinese: Chinese-English. München, Saur, 1984. ix,327p. £35;DM98. ISBN: 3598105320.

Covers more than 1,800 terms; English term and definition left hand column, Chinese equivalent right hand column. Bilingual index using the Chinese phonetic alphabet. Brief list of acronyms. *Class No:* 02.0(038)=951

Glossaries

[827]

The ALA glossary of library and information science. Young, H., *ed.* Chicago, American Library Association, 1983. xvi,245p. ISBN: 0838903711.

Available from Books on Demand ($74.50. ISBN: 0783761562). Replaces the *ALA glossary of library terms* (1943).

Coverage and definitions reflect 'the current practices of libraries and related information agencies in the United States' (Foreword p.vii). Includes terms from related fields *e.g.* printing and publishing, graphic arts, telecommunications, educational technology. Over 4,000 entries, definitions ranging from 10-75 words. List of sources (p.xv-xvi). Definitions for some information science terms lack depth. Complements, but cannot be considered an alternative to Harrod (below). *Class No:* 02.0(038.1)

[828]

HARROD, L.M. Harrod's librarians' glossary: 9,000 terms used in information management, library science, publishing, the book trades, and archive management.
Prytherch, R.J., *comp.* 8th ed. Aldershot, Gower, 1995. xiii,692p. £75. ISBN: 0566075334.

First published 1938; 7th ed. 1990. This ed. with revised sub-title.

'The purpose of the Glossary is to explain and define terms and concepts, identify techniques and organizations, provide summaries of the activities of associations, major

....(contd.)

libraries, Governmental and other bodies.' (Preface p.vii). Improved coverage of archive work, records management, conservation and preservation, networking and computer terminology in this ed. 1,400 completely new entries, much older material dropped. Also revises 600 entries for organizations, many now giving an address. British emphasis, but international in scope with US, Australian and Japanese representatives on the 11 member advisory board. '(R)emains the preeminent source for demystifying the terminology of librarianship and its related fields' (*American reference books annual*, v.28, (1997), p.237).
Class No: 02.0(038.1)

[829]

SOPER, M.E. The Librarian's thesaurus. Chicago, American Library Association, 1990. xvi,164p. illus. £17.95;$25. ISBN: 0838905307.

Subtitle on cover *A Concise guide to library and information terms.*

Attempts to identify and explain important concepts in librarianship. Classified arrangement, terms treated at length (*e.g.* Acquisitions 1½p.; Electronic mail 2½p.). Good use of cross-references; detailed index (p.157-64).
Class No: 02.0(038.1)

Theses

[830]

FLA theses: abstracts for all theses accepted for the fellowship of the Library Association from 1964. Taylor, L.J., *comp.* London, British Library, Library Association Library, 1979. [5],90p. ISBN: 0904654206.

Subjects covered include bibliography and the book trade as well as librarianship. 297 entries in classified order. Indexes of authors and subjects. Later theses were abstracted in *CABLIS,* then *Library and information science abstracts* (*q.v.*). *Class No:* 02.0(043)

[831]

Library and information studies in the United Kingdom and Ireland 1950-1974: an index to theses. Taylor, P.J., *ed.* London, Aslib, 1976. viii,69p. ISBN: 0851420850.

Unannotated list of 659 MA, MSc, MPhil, PhD, DPhil and BLitt theses presented to 42 universities and colleges. Arranged by year; author and detailed subject indexes.
Class No: 02.0(043)

[832]

MAGNOTTI, S. Masters theses in library science, 1960-1969. Troy, N.Y., Whitson, 1975. 366p. $18. ISBN: 0878750746.

Lists *c.*2,500 theses from 31 library schools by author A-Z. Subject index.

Continued by *Masters theses in library science, 1970-1974* (Whitson, 1976. ISBN: 0878751009) listing a further 700 titles.

A further continuation under the title *Library science research, 1974-1979* (Whitson, 1983. $15. ISBN: 0878752358), has entries for 200 theses and 550 research reports accepted in place of theses. *Class No:* 02.0(043)

[833]

SCHLACHTER, G.A. *and* **THOMISON, D. Library science dissertations, 1925-1972:** an annotated bibliography. Littleton, Colo., Libraries Unlimited, 1974. 293p. tables. (*Research studies in library science, no. 12.*) ISBN: 087287074x.

Compiled from *Dissertations abstracts, Library literature, Library quarterly* etc. 660 entries, chronologically arranged, most with *c.*250 word annotations. Statistical profiles of doctoral dissertations (p.256-62). Author and subject indexes. *Class No:* 02.0(043)

[834]

—SCHLACHTER, G.A. *and* THOMISON, D. Library science dissertations, 1973-1981: an annotated bibliography. Littleton, Colo., Libraries Unlimited, 1982. 414p. ISBN: 0872872998.

Continues the 1925-72 volume. Somewhat wider scope, including interdisciplinary material judged relevant to the subject content of librarianship. 1,008 entries, annotated and arranged as before. *Class No:* 02.0(043)

Reports Literature

[835]

BRITISH LIBRARY. Research & Development Department. **Complete list of reports published by the British Library** R & D Department. Mann, M., *ed.* London, British Library Research & Development Department, 1988. v,316p. £15. (*British Library information guide, 9.*) ISBN: 0712331573.

'Contains a complete list of all British Library R & D Reports, Library and Information Research (LIR) Reports, British Library Information Guides (BLIGs), British Library Annual Research Lectures, British Library Research Papers, British Library Research Reviews and British National Bibliography Research Fund (BNBRF) Reports published to the end of 1987' (Abstract p.iv). Reports listed in numerical order within series. Includes brief abstracts. Author, title, institution and subject indexes. An 'attractive alternative to using *LISA* in order to trace British Library publications' (*Reference reviews,* 3(2), June 1989, p.54).

Continued by *Complete list of reports published by the British Library R & D Department 1988-1994* (Jones, N. *ed.* 1995. vi,258p. ISBN: 0712332928), which is similar in scope and format except that reports of centres funded by the British Library are also included. *Class No:* 02.0(047)

Reviews & Abstracts

[836]

ARBA guide to library science literature, 1970-1983. Davis, D.G. *and* Patterson, C.D., *eds.* Littleton, Co., Libraries Unlimited, 1987. xx,682p. ISBN: 0872875857.

Compilation of reviews of library science books which originally appeared in *American reference books annual* (*q.v.*). Not confined to reference material, covering library science books of all types. 1,728 entries in 56 subject sections; author/title and subject indexes. Continued by *Library and information science annual* (below).
Class No: 02.0(048)

[837]

—Library and information science annual. Littleton, Co., Libraries Unlimited, 1985-89. Annual. ISSN: 87552108.

V.1-v.2 published under the title *Library science annual.*

Aimed to review the English language literature of library and information science, with British and Australian publications included from 1987. The 1988 v. (Wynar, B.S. *ed.* xvii,325p.) had entries for 549 books, 153 periodicals and 37 doctoral dissertations. Also carried 6 general essays. Indexed by author/title and subject. *Class No:* 02.0(048)

[838]

BUBL journals: library and information science. Glasgow, BUBL Information Services, Andersonian Library, University of Strathclyde. World Wide Web resource.

URL: http:bubl.ac.uk/journals/lis/. Date reviewed 7th July 1998. Part of the *BUBL* Internet service.

Provides indexing, abstracting and very occasional full text for over 100 periodicals. Many mainstream titles (*e.g. British Library journal, Journal of information science, Journal of librarianship and information science, Serials review*) included, coverage from 1992 or later. Content browsing by title and searching of individual titles or entire file supported. Nearly 6,000 records early 1998.
Class No: 02.0(048)

[839]

Current awareness abstracts: of library and information management literature. London, Aslib, The Association for Information Management, 1984-. 10pa. £148. ISSN: 13505238.

Present title from 1993, formerly *Current awareness bulletin.* Initially a listing service, abstracts from v.7(4), April 1990.

Each issue contains *c.*175 well written indicative abstracts. The emphasis is on information technology and management, but with around 250 periodicals scanned most aspects of librarianship and information work are covered. Abstracts in classified order (26 headings); author and subject indexes. Subscribers also have access to an Internet version. Mainly valuable for promptness, abstracting many articles a few weeks after publication. *Class No:* 02.0(048)

[840]

Information science abstracts. New York, Plenum Publishing, 1966-. Monthly. $685. ISSN: 00200239.

V.1-2, 1966-67 as *Documentation abstracts;* v.3 as *Documentation and information science abstracts.* Frequency 6pa. until 1984.

8,000-9,000 abstracts annually for books, journal articles, conference proceedings, reports and patents. Coverage includes abstracting and indexing, cataloguing and classification, computer science, education, information management, information theory, library administration, technical writing and telecommunications. International in scope, but with a marked preponderance of English language material. *c.*50 core periodicals indexed/abstracted completely, others covered selectively. Improvement programme initiated 1997 to fill gaps in coverage. Abstracts, average length *c.*100-150 words, classified in 7 main sections. Author and detailed subject index in each issue, cumulated in final number of year. Appears less current than main rivals *Library and information science abstracts* (below) and *Library literature* (*q.v.*), and is not as carefully compiled. Also available as a database through Dialog (File 202) and SilverPlatter. The latter markets a CD-ROM version as *Information science abstracts Plus,* disc updated quarterly. *Class No:* 02.0(048)

[841]

Library and information science abstracts. East Grinstead, Bowker Saur, 1969-. Monthly. £435. ISSN: 00242179.

Previously published by Library Association Publishing. Issued bi-monthly 1969-82. Widely referred to as *LISA*.

Provides signed, indicative and informative *c.*100-125 word abstracts for articles on all fields of librarianship/information science and related areas such as information technology, information retrieval, technical services, bookselling and publishing. Coverage increased from 360 to 550 periodicals 1994. Also includes some books, British Library reports, conference papers and book reviews; theses excluded. Geographic spread truly international, material from 60 countries and 20 languages represented. Abstracts classified under 19 subject groupings, each subdivided. Author, alphabetical subject and source (periodicals covered with abstract nos.) indexes, cumulated annually. Cumulated indexes for 1976-80 and 1981-85. The primary indexing and abstracting source in the field, 12,325 records in the issues for 1997. Searchable online through Dialog (File 61) for abstracts 1969 to date, incorporating records from the companion publication *Current research in library and information science* (*q.v.*). Also available on CD-ROM as *LISA Plus* (quarterly updating, £925) from the publisher and SilverPlatter *Class No:* 02.0(048)

[842]

—Library science abstracts. London, Library Association, 1950-68. Quarterly.

Based on titles received by the Library Association Library. Over 200 titles regularly scanned, supplemented with reports, pamphlets and some books. Arranged by subject with annual author and names/subjects indexes. Cumulative indexes 1950-55, 1956-60, 1961-65. By its close was abstracting *c.*1,200 items pa. Succeeded by *Library and information science abstracts* (above). *Class No:* 02.0(048)

[843]

Library reference center. EBSCO Publishing. World Wide Web resource.

URL: http://www.epnet.com.lrc.html. Date reviewed 7th July 1998.

Freely accessible site providing over three years' indexing and abstracting for 30 library science periodicals. Data drawn from *EBSCO masterfile*, titles covered include *Australian library journal, Booklist, Library journal, Library quarterly* and *Library trends*. *Class No:* 02.0(048)

Germany

[844]

Dokumentationsdienst Bibliothekswessen: Informationsdienst zum Bibliothekswesen der Bundesrepublik Deutschland und des Auslands. 1982/83-. Berlin, Deutsches Bibliotheksinstitut, 1984-. Quarterly. DM120. ISSN: 0176781x.

Known by the acronym *DOBI.* Continues *Fachbibliographischer dienst Bibliothekswesen (FD),* published quarterly with annual cumulation, 1965-81. From 1992 absorbs the East German *Informationsdienst Bibliothekswesen* (ISSN: 00441457) and published jointly with the Deutsche Bücherei, Leipzig.

Subject listing of library and information science literature, at least 2/3 of which is in the German language. Most entries include abstracts; author and keyword indexes cumulated annually. Also freely available through Deutsches Bibliotheksinstitut's DBI-Link Internet service at http://dbix01.dbi-berlin.de:6100/DBI/logon.html. *Class No:* 02.0(048)(430)

Hungary

[845]

Hungarian library and information science abstracts. Budapest, National Széchényi Library, Centre for Library and Information Science, 1971-. Semi-annual. US$15. ISSN: 00468304.

Provides detailed English language abstracts of 200-400 words for books, periodical articles, reports, etc. published in Hungary. Arranged in 16 subject groups. 49 items abstracted in v.26(1), 1997. Cumulated author and subject indexes appear on irregular basis. *Class No:* 02.0(048)(439)

India

[846]

Indian library science abstracts. Calcutta; Indian Association of Special Libraries and Information Centres, 1967-. Quarterly, (recent issues combined). Rs200. ISSN: 00195790.

Annual 1967-72.

Offers short abstracts of Indian periodical articles, books and conference papers. Of limited value for tracing new material as issues seem to take 3 or 4 years to appear. V.24 (1990. 71p.) contains 403 abstracts in classified order with author and keyword index. *Class No:* 02.0(048)(540)

Australia

[847]

ALISA: Australian library and information science abstracts. Footscray, Vic., Australian Clearing House for Library and Information Science, 1982-. Annual [irregular]. Aus$60. ISSN: 08109265.

Index to library and information science literature published in Australia or produced by Australians. Sources include monographs, reports, conference papers and periodical articles; most entries with short abstracts. Also available on CD-ROM as a component database of *AUSTROM* (*q.v.*). *Class No:* 02.0(048)(94)

Periodicals

[848]

Library and information science journals and serials: an analytical guide. Bowman, M.A., *comp.* Westport, Conn. and London, Greenwood, 1985. xxiii,140p. £39.95;$49.95. (*Annotated bibliographies of serials: a subject approach, no.1.*) ISBN: 0313238073.

Annotated entries for English language titles giving foundation date, frequency, price, publisher, editor, circulation, inclusion of book reviews, where indexed/abstracted, database availability and target audience. Directory of microfilm and reprint publishers, tables of abstracts and indexes and database vendors. Geographical, publisher and classified title indexes. American bias, only 84 of the 311 titles published outside the US, and now too dated for current information. *Class No:* 02.0(051)

[849]

A Long list of electronic journals and newsletters of interest to LIS. Aberystwyth, Thomas Parry Library, University of Wales Aberystwyth. World Wide Web resource.

URL: http://www.aber.ac.uk/plwww/ej/ot2.html. Date reviewed 29th June 1998. Part of the *Pick: quality Internet resources in library and information science* (*q.v.*) site maintained by the Thomas Parry Library.

List and links to *c.* 200 'main serial publications in the field of library and information science with an Internet presence'. Arranged in broad categories (*e.g.* General, Reviewing and abstracting, Academic and public library newsletters), brief descriptions added for some titles.
Class No: 02.0(051)

Progress Reports

[850]

Advances in librarianship. Orlando, Academic Press, 1970-. Annual (Irregular). £50;$69.95. ISSN: 00652830.

Not published 1987-90.

Each issue contains 8-10 well documented, contributed essays on both general and specialist topics (*e.g.* 'Developing site licensing with particular reference to the national United Kingdom initiative' and 'Librarian-faculty partnerships in instruction' (v.20 1996)). Subject index in each issue; cumulated index to the first 10 volumes published 1980. '(A)n important barometer of the profession' (*American reference books annual*, v.24, 1993, p.262).
Class No: 02.0(055)

[851]

Annual review of information science and technology. Medford, N.J., Information Today, 1966-. Annual. $99.95. ISSN: 00664200.

Produced by the American Society for Information Science. Publisher varies.

V.31 (1996. Williams, M.E. *ed.* xv,511p.) contains 8 lengthy, scholarly reviews including 'User acceptance of information technology: theories and models', 'Cataloguing and classifying information resources on the Internet' and 'Music as information'. Each contribution extensively documented; index. Also carries keyword and author index to all previous vols. *Class No:* 02.0(055)

[852]

Librarianship and information work worldwide. Line, M.B., *and others eds.* London, Bowker-Saur, 1991-. Annual (irregular). £65;$95.

Aims to assess the most significant developments in library and information work as recorded in the literature. 1996/97 v. (1997. xiv,322p. ISBN: 1857391640) has 11 contributions: 1. The Electronic context: libraries and the World Wide Web ... 3. Academic libraries ... 7. Private sector information work ... 11. Libraries and librarianship in anglophone Africa. Contributors, mostly from the UK, seek to avoid undue emphasis on North America. References at chapter ends; subject and author index. '(H)as established itself as one of the landmarks of the professional literature' (*Library Association record*, v.98(8), August 1996, p.533).
Class No: 02.0(055)

Great Britain

[853]

British librarianship and information work 1986-1990. Bromley, D.W. *and* Allott, A., *eds*. London, Library Association Publishing, 1992-93. 2v.

V.1. *General libraries and the profession* (x,321p. £67. ISBN 1856040003); v.2 *Special libraries, materials and processes* (x,353p. £67. ISBN 1856040011).

Previous 2v. sets for 1981-85 (Bromley, D.W. & Allott, A. *eds*. 1988. £50 per v.. ISBN: 08536556x(v.1)) and 1976-80 (Taylor, L.J. *ed.* 1982. £50 per v. ISBN: 0853657637(v.1)).

Intended as a 'record of professional activity and thought'. 39 contributed chapters averaging 7,500 words written by acknowledged experts (*e.g.* 'Government information services and libraries' by S. Pantry; 'New technology in libraries' by J.E. Rowley). Other contributions include: 'National libraries', 'Public libraries', 'Local studies', 'Community information', 'Archives' (v.1); 'British and European Communities official publications', 'Music libraries', 'Indexing and abstracting' (v.2). All contributions well documented. Each v. separately indexed; repeated 10p. list of acronyms and abbreviations. 'Professional collections will be sadly incomplete without these two volumes' (*Library Association record*, v.95(6), June 1993, p.356).

British librarianship and information work continues two earlier series:- *Class No:* 02.0(055)(410)

[854]

—British librarianship and information science. 1966/70-1971/75. Whatley, H.A., *ed.* London, Library Association, 1972-77.

1966-1970 (xiv,712p. ISBN: 0853651752); 1971-1975 (xiii,379p. ISBN: 0854365993).

60 contributors to the earlier v., most sections with extensive bibliographies (*e.g.* Classification, p.41-60; 124 references). The later v. is much abridged with bibliographies correspondingly reduced (*e.g.* Classification, p.57-64; 30 references). *Class No:* 02.0(055)(410)

[855]

—Five years' work in librarianship. 1951/55-1961/65. London, Library Association, 1958-68. 3v.

Continues *The Year's work in librarianship* 1928-50. (London, Library Association, 1924-54. 17v.).

Chapter titles and coverage vary between volumes, but the overall concept and format is similar to *British librarianship and information work.* *Class No:* 02.0(055)(410)

Yearbooks & Directories

[856]

The Bowker annual: library and book trade almanac. New Providence, N.J., Bowker, 1956-. Annual. $175. ISSN: 00680540.

Title varies; first published 1950 as *American library annual.*

The 42nd ed. (1997. x,839p.) has 6 main sections: 1. Reports from the field (reports from various organizations *e.g.* National Archives and Records Administration; Association of Research Libraries) - 2. Legislation, funding, grants - 3. Library/information science education, placement and salaries (includes statistical data on placement of US LIS graduates) - 4. Research and statistics (includes data on prices of US and foreign published materials) - 5. Reference information (how to obtain an ISBN, best books of 1996, literary prizes, etc.) - 6. Directory of organizations (includes networks, consortia, etc.). Indexed by organization and

....(contd.)

subject (p.795-843). 'The preeminent almanac of the book trade and library profession ... an invaluable accumulation of wide-ranging data' (*American reference books annual*, v.28, 1997, p.238). *Class No:* 02.0(058)

[857]

CONFEDERATION OF INFORMATION COMMUNICATION INDUSTRIES. CICI directory of information products and services. 2nd ed. Harlow, Longman, 1990. viii,273p. ISBN: 0582061326.

1st ed. 1988.

Covers 1,884 organizations providing products and services in the information sector, ranging from abstracting services to telecommunications agencies. Entries by title A-Z; index of products and services (p.3-42). Also contains brief lists of relevant periodicals and directories, guides and yearbooks. Now dated, but far more comprehensive than the *Library Association directory of suppliers and services* (below) and superior to the similarly aged *Inside information* (also below). *Class No:* 02.0(058)

[858]

Inside information 1989/90: a directory of organisations, products and services in the information sector. 3rd ed. London, TPFL Publishing, 1989. 275p. £35. ISBN: 1870889142.

First published for 1986/87 (1986); 2nd ed. 1987/88 (1987).

In addition to companies supplying the library market includes library schools, special interest groups, local library cooperatives, etc. and major chambers of commerce, embassies, overseas library associations and academic and public libraries with special collections of interest. 1,054 entries A-Z including 20-150 word descriptions. Subject keyword, product name and special collection index (p.227-75). Needs updating. *Class No:* 02.0(058)

[859]

Library Association directory of suppliers and services 1994-5. McSeán, T., *comp.* 2nd ed. London, Library Association, 1994. Unpaged. £15;$30. ISBN: 1856041123.

First published 1992.

Expands the 1st ed. by 30%. In 2pts: 'Classified guide', comprising an index of organizations active in the market under topical headings Bar coding equipment and services ... Videotext services; 'Company and product list', providing name and contact address with *c.*50 word descriptions. A handy source, but coverage is very uneven. Unless expanded cannot be considered an adequate replacement for the *CICI directory* or *Inside information* (above).
Class No: 02.0(058)

Quotations

[860]

HARDING, L. A Book in the hand is worth two in the library: quotations on books and librarianship. Jefferson, N.C., McFarland, 1994. vii,119p. £19.75;$21.95. ISBN: 0899509339.

A slim v. reproducing quotations concerning books and librarianship. Tends to concentrate on frivolous remarks and pronoucements. Quotations arrayed in 10 sections (1. Libraries ... 5. Borrowing and lending ... 10. Education), each with extensive commentary. Speaker/writer and keyword/subject indexes. *Class No:* 02.0(082.2)

[861]

Quotations about libraries and librarians. The Hague, International Federation of Library Associations and Institutions. World Wide Web resource.

URL http://ifla.inist.fr/ifla/1/humour/subj.htm or http://www.nlc-bnc.ca/ifla/1/humour.subj.htm. Date reviewed 29th June 1998.

Reproduces *c.*250 quotations. Arranged in subject (Books - Borrowing - Catalogue... etc.) and author sequences.
Class No: 02.0(082.2)

Festschriften

[862]

DANTON, J.P. Index to Festschriften in librarianship. New York, Bowker, 1970. xi,461p. table. ISBN: 0835202615.

Author and subject index with cross-references to approx. 3,300 articles in 283 publications (98 German, 32 US, 6 UK). 22 countries and 14 languages represented. English language subject indexing. Prefatory matter in English, German and French. Continued by:-

Danton, J.P. and Pulis, J.F. *Index to Festschriften in librarianship, 1967-1975* (München, Saur, 1979. lxxxiv,354p. tables. ISBN: 3598070349). Same plan as the original v. Covers approx. 1,500 articles in 143 works, 104 of which were published 1967 to 1975.
Class No: 02.0(082.20)

Chronologies

[863]

SMITH, J.M. A Chronology of librarianship. Metuchen, N.J., Scarecrow Press, 1968. ix,11-263p. ISBN: 0810800241.

From 1st century A.D., but with emphasis on 19th and 20th centuries and US events. Latest date 1959. Each note is keyed to a reference source. Bibliography (p.190-210). Subject and name indexes. *Class No:* 02.0(090)

Histories

[864]

HARRIS, M.H. History of libraries in the Western world. 4th ed. Metuchen, N.J., Scarecrow Press, 1995. iii,301p. £35.55;$39.50. ISBN: 081082972x.

Reset and revised version of 3rd ed. 1976. First published 1965.

12 chaps: 1. Origins of libraries ... 5. Roman libraries ... 7. Medieval and cathedral libraries ... 9. European libraries: expansion and diversification to 1917 ... 12. Modern American libraries. Brief selected reading at chap. ends; short index (p.299-301). A selective and far from thorough account, but one of the few general histories available.
Class No: 02.0(091)

Bibliographies

[865]

ABHB annual bibliography of the history of the printed book and libraries. Koninklijke Bibliotheek. Department of Special Collections, *ed.* Dordrecht, Kluwer Academic, 1973-. Annual. Dfl370. ISSN: 03035964.

Published under the auspices of the Committee on Rare Books and Manuscripts of the International Federation of Library Associations and Institutions.

Aims 'at recording all books and articles of scholarly value which relate to the history of the printed book, to the history of the arts, crafts, techniques and equipment, and of

....(contd.)
the economic, social and cultural environment involved in its production, distribution, conservation and description' (Introduction v.24, p.vii). Classified in 12 sections: class J 'Libraries, librarianship, scholarship, institutions' divided by country. Author/anonym and geographical/personal name indexes. Cumulative subject index 1970-1986 published 1989 (209p. ISBN: 0792300394). Traditional in outlook having 'manifestly made no concession to the wide extension of bibliographical and bibliothecal studies and practices of the last 20 years' (*Reference reviews*, v.7(3), 1993, p.5). V.24 for 1993 (1996. x,509p.) contains 4,247 records selected from 1,600 periodicals. *Class No:* 02.0(091)(01)

[866]

Bibliographie der Buch- und Bibliotheksgeschichte. 1980/81-. Meyer, H., *bearb.* Bad Iburg, Bibliographischer Verlag Dr. Horst Meyer, 1982-. Annual. DM155. ISSN: 07233590.

Also known as *BBB.* International in scope, each v. has around 7,000 entries drawn from 900 periodicals. Material relating directly to library history at least 20% of total. Classified arrangement in 8 main sections, the last devoted to book reviews. Comprehensively indexed. '(N)ow something of a legend' (*Reference reviews*, v.11(4), 1997, p.11). *Class No:* 02.0(091)(01)

[867]

Cumulative library history bibliography 1990-1994. Goedeken, E., *comp.* Library History Round Table. World Wide Web resource.

URL: http://www.spertus.edu/library-history/resource.html. Date reviewed 17th March 1998.

Main bibliography originally appeared in issues of *Library History Round Table newsletter*. Twice yearly supplements continue coverage to spring 1997.

Unannotated listing of books, book chapters, articles, dissertations, etc. Latest supplement, divided into sections for the United States, non-US Western hemisphere, Europe, Asia and other continents and general topics, has *c.*175 entries. *Class No:* 02.0(091)(01)

Encyclopaedias & Dictionaries

[868]

Encyclopedia of library history. Wiegand, W.A. *and* Davis, D.G., *eds.* New York, Garland, 1994. xxxi,707p. $95. (*Garland reference library of social science, v.503.*.) ISBN: 0824057872.

Contains 300 articles from 200 international contributors. Length ranges from 200-6,000 words, most with bibliographies appended. Many articles for countries (*e.g.* 'Brazil', 2½cols.), others for types of libraries (*e.g.* 'Private libraries', 3½p.) or standard subjects (*e.g.* 'Classification', 9p.). Also covers topics of current concern (*e.g.* 'Gender issues in librarianship', 5p.). No biographical articles or illustrations. A 'meticulously edited volume which will serve as the standard reference work in library history for some time' (*Choice*, v.31(10), June 1994, p.1552). *Class No:* 02.0(091)(03)

Yearbooks & Directories

[869]

International directory of experts in library history. Kaegbein, P., *ed and* Marx, A., *comp.*. The Hague, International Federation of Library Associations and Institutions, 1992. 51p. (*IFLA professional reports, 32.*) ISBN: 9070916371.

....(contd.)
List of 210 names from 18 countries. Detail for each entrant confined to address and brief description of subject expertise. Country/name arrangement; subject and name indexes. *Class No:* 02.0(091)(058)

Great Britain

[870]

British library history: a bibliography. 1962/68-. Keeling, D.F., *ed.* Winchester, St. Paul's Bibliographies, 1972-.

6v. published to date: 1962/68 (1972. x,164p. ISBN: 0853653454); 1969/72 (1975. v,150p. ISBN: 0853654174); 1973/76 (1979. 200p. ISBN: 0853657815); 1977/80 (1983. ix,242p. £16. ISBN: 0853658056); 1981/84 (1987. x,190p. £16. ISBN: 0853658374); 1985/88 (1991. x,181p. £25. ISBN: 0906795958). 1962/68-1981/84 published by the Library Association, Library History Group.

Covers the history of libraries, librarianship and book collecting in the British Isles. In 5 sections: Librarians; Librarianship; Libraries (vast majority of entries); Reading; Study of library history. Author and subject indexes in each v. Items continuously numbered reaching 4,620 with the 1985/88v. Strong on the coverage of scattered references outside the literature of librarianship. Includes theses and obituaries. Many entries briefly annotated. '(I)ndispensable to anyone seriously interested in the role of libraries in the past' (*Library Association record*, v.94(2), February 1992, p.118). *Class No:* 02.0(091)(410)

Germany

[871]

BUZÁS, L. German library history, 800-1945. Jefferson, N.C., McFarland, 1986. vi,570p. ISBN: 0899501753.

Translation by W.D. Boyd of 3v. originally published Wiesbaden, Ludwig Reichert Verlage, 1975-78.

In 3 parts: The Middle ages; The Early modern period 1500-1800; The Modern period 1800-1945. Comprehensive, covers all aspects of libraries. Bibliography (p.483-534). A 'skillful summary' (*American notes and queries,* v.24(5/6), January/February 1986. p.87). *Class No:* 02.0(091)(430)

[872]

HERZOG AUGUST BIBLIOTHEK. Wolfenbütteler Bibliographie zur Geschichte des Buchwesens im deutschen Sprachgebiet 1840-1980 (WBB). Bd.5-Bd.6. Bibliothekswesen. Weyrauch, E., *bearb.* München, K.G. Saur, 1996. 2v.

Teil 1. xxii,478p. ISBN: 3598303289; Teil 2. xvi,473p. ISBN: 35983032973.

Vols. 5-6 of this ongoing bibliography on the history of the book trade in German-speaking countries contain 31,348 entries for material relating to libraries and librarianship. *Class No:* 02.0(091)(430)

France

[873]

Histoire des bibliothèques françaises. Jolly, C., *ed.* Paris, Promodis/Éditions du Cercle de La Librairie, 1988-92. 4v. illus.

V.1 *Les Bibliothèques médiévales du VIe siècle à 1530* (488p. FFr820. ISBN: 2903181721); v.2 *Les Bibliothèques sous l'Ancien Régime 1530-1789* (547p. FFr820. ISBN: 2903181683); v.3 *Les Bibliothèques de la Révolution et du XIXe siècle 1789-1914* (672p. FFr850. ISBN: 2765404720);

.... *(contd.)*

v.4 *Les Bibliothèques au XXe siècle 1914-1990* (793p. FFr990. ISBN: 2765405107).

V.2 (xv,547p. ISBN: 2903181683) has 38 generously illustrated contributions, mainly dealing with individual libraries and librarians. Bibliography (p.513-27); index. The similarly structured v.3 (xii,671p. ISBN: 2765404700), also has 38 contributions. The definitive account, 'conceived on a most impressive scale' (*Times literary supplement,* no.4521, November 24th-30th 1989, p.1305).
Class No: 02.0(091)(44)

USA

[874]

DAVIS, D.G. *and* **TUCKER, J.M. American library history: a comprehensive guide to the literature.** 2nd ed. Santa Barbara, ABC-Clio, 1990. xxii,471p. $125. ISBN: 0874361427.

1st ed. 1978 by M.H. Harris and D.G. Davis as *American library history: a bibliography.*

Unannotated listing of more than 7,150 entries (doubling the number in the 1st ed.) giving full coverage until the end of 1986. Includes journal articles, chapters in books, unpublished research etc. Sections: 1. Historiography and sources - 2. General studies - 3. Private libraries and reading tastes - 4. Predecessors of the public library - 5. Public libraries - 6. Academic libraries -7. School libraries - 8. State libraries - 9. Special libraries - 10. Archival enterprise - 11. Education for librarianship - 12. Library associations - 13. Special aspects of librarianship -14. Women in librarianship - 15. Bibliographies of individual librarians and library benefactors. Each section begins with an introductory essay highlighting the major sources. Author and institution index; index to the introductory essays.

The journal *Libraries & culture* contains biennial bibliographies intended to act as updating supplements (*e.g.* 'The Literature of American library history 1993-1994' in v.31(3-4), Summer/Fall 1996, p.603-44).
Class No: 02.0(091)(73)

[875]

STONE, E.W. American library development 1600-1899. New York, Wilson, 1977. xii,367p. chart. ISBN: 0824204182.

Main section comprises 20-500 word accounts of notable developments (*e.g.* '1848 Harvard slip catalogue', *c.*25 words; '1882 Third edtion of Poole's index', *c.*150 words). Arranged in 8 chronologically subdivided sections: Private, special and government libraries - Academic libraries ... Legislation - Publications - Professional activities - Buildings. Chronological chart (p.2-53); bibliography (p.333-54); index. *Class No:* 02.0(091)(73)

[876]

YOUNG, A.P. American library history: a bibliography of dissertations and theses. 3rd rev. ed. Metuchen, N.J. and London, Scarecrow Press, 1988. vii,469p. £38.25;$42.50. ISBN: 0810821389.

Earlier eds. by M.H. Harris as *A guide to research in American library history,* 1968 and 1974.

A 'work of enormous and painstaking scholarship', (*Library Association record,* v.91(2), February 1989, p.109), extending the coverage of the earlier eds. to late 1986. 964 well annotated entries for theses and dissertations, 210 unannotated entries for papers and reports. Subject and author indexes. *Class No:* 02.0(091)(73)

Biographies

[877]

DOWNS, R.B. A Dictionary of eminent librarians. Worland, Wyo., High Plains Publishing, 1990. xi,220p. $25. ISBN: 0962333352.

Variable length entries *e.g.* 'Dewey, Melvil' 5p., 'Winchell, Constance Mabel' ¾p. US librarians predominate, but reasonable number from elsewhere *e.g.* 'Ranganathan, S.R.' ½p. Several appended lists (p.191-210) including 'The British Museum's principal librarians, secretaries and keepers of departments' and 'Presidents of the American Library Association'. Indexed.
Class No: 02.0(092)

Europe

[878]

Who's who in the European information world 1997. Nordin, J.B. *and* Gili, M.B., *comps.* 3rd ed. London, TFPL Publishing in assoc. with EUSIDIC, 1996. 898p. £135. ISBN: 1870889673.

First published 1994.

Similar in scope and structure to *Who's who in the UK information world* (below). 2nd ed. (1995. 899p.) has nearly 7,000 entries, by country then name, including a reasonable number from eastern Europe. British personalities (p.572-618) limited to prominent individuals, does not duplicate UK directory. Indexed by employing organization, employing organization activity and surname. *Class No:* 02.0(092)(4)

Great Britain

[879]

MUNFORD, W.A. Who was who in British librarianship 1800-1985: a dictionary of dates with notes. London, Library Association, 1987. xi,91p. £25. ISBN: 0853659761.

Covers senior librarians who held office after 1800 and died before December 1985. *c.*2,000 entries listed alphabetically by surname giving birth and death dates, employing authorities and dates of appointment. Some entries with further annotations detailing career achievements, listing publications, etc. A 'useful starting point for further research' (*Refer,* v.4(4), Autumn 1987, p.16). *Class No:* 02.0(092)(410)

[880]

Who's who in the UK information world 1997. Nordin, J.B., *comp.* 6th ed. London, TFPL Publishing, 1996. x,584p. £92. ISBN: 1870889665.

First published 1988; 5th ed. 1995.

Questionnaire based directory of *c.*4,500 entries. Wide ranging including company and government librarians, senior public and academic library staff, lecturers in library and information science, information brokers and consultants, archivists and senior personnel from the information industry. Detail given includes email and URL, current position, qualifications, relevant memberships, training institution attended, experience, previous positions and a brief description of current responsibilities and interests. Indexed by employing organization, employing organization activity and training institution attended. A valuable source, but many prominent individuals are omitted and the length and content of entries is highly variable.
Class No: 02.0(092)(410)

Germany

[881]

HABERMANN, A., *and others*. Lexikon deutscher wissenschaftlicher Bibliothekare 1925-1980. Frankfurt am Main, Vittorio Klosterman, 1985. xxvi,417p. DM124. (*Zeitschrift für Bibliothekswessen und Bibliographie, 42.*) ISBN: 3465016645.

Information on *c.*1,500 German research librarians including academic qualifications, personal details, posts held, career achievements and bibliographical sources. Index of libraries listing persons employed. Brief biographical details of current senior German librarians can be found in *Jahrbuch der deutschen Bibliotheken* (*q.v.*).
Class No: 02.0(092)(430)

India

[882]

INDIAN LIBRARY ASSOCIATION. ILA members directory. Vashishth, C.P., *comp. and ed.* Delhi, Indian Library Association, 1987. 188p.

Lists personal and institutional members in regional sections. 2,672 entries, name and address only. Usefulness limited by lack of a name index. *Class No:* 02.0(092)(540)

Pakistan

[883]

SABZWARI, G.A. Who's who in library and information science in Pakistan. 2nd ed. Karachi, Library Promotion Bureau, 1987. xviii,368p. ports. Rs75. ISBN: 9694120691.

1st ed. 1969.

A substantial directory containing fairly full detail on those librarians covered, including qualifications, posts held, publications and honours and awards. Many portraits.
Class No: 02.0(092)(549)

USA

[884]

Dictionary of American library biography. Wynar, B.S., *and others eds.* Littleton, Colo., Libraries Unlimited, 1978. xxxix,596p. ISBN: 0872871800.

302 signed biographical sketches, from 217 contributors, for prominent librarians deceased before mid-1976. Entries, ranging in length from 1,000-6,000 words (*e.g.* W.W. Bishop, 3p.; C.A. Cutter, 5½p.; M. Dewey, 9½p.), include bibliographies.

A *Supplement to the Dictionary of American library biography*, Wiegand, W.A. *ed.* (Englewood, Colo., Libraries Unlimited, 1990. xix,184p. £27.50;$45. ISBN: 0872875865), adds 51 sketches for librarians who died before 30th June 1987. *Class No:* 02.0(092)(73)

[885]

The Directory of ethnic professionals in LIS (library and information science). Grant, G.C., *comp.* Winter Park, Fla., FOUR-G Publishers, 1991. xv,254p. $52.95. ISBN: 0962542334.

About 1,600 variable length entries, mostly for Afro-Americans. Includes some coverage of those now deceased. A—Z arrangement by name with employer and alma mater indexes. *Class No:* 02.0(092)(73)

[886]

Directory of library and information professionals. Woodbridge, Conn., Research Publications in collaboration with the American Library Association, 1988. 2v. ISBN: 089235125x.

Replaces *Who's who in library and information services* (6th ed. 1982; first published 1933 as *Who's who in library service*).

V.1 *Listings* contains biographical data on nearly 43,000 individuals. Geographic coverage extends to Canada. Information for full entries includes position, work address, previous post, education, publications, professional achievements, prizes and awards, professional memberships, expertise/subjects and consulting/freelance availability. V.2 provides full indexing. A CD-ROM version also produced. Never attained the comprehensiveness intended; no update on same basis published or planned.
Class No: 02.0(092)(73)

New Zealand

[887]

Who's who in New Zealand library and information services, 1990. Olsson, A.L., *comp.* Wellington, New Zealand Library Association, 1991. 109p. NZ$10. ISBN: 0908560273.

Continues *Who's who in New Zealand libraries*, first published 1951, 9th ed. 1986.

The last ed. of ***Who's who in New Zealand libraries*** contained 1,350 entries giving brief biographical detail, posts held, professional activities, publications, etc. Index of institutions with names of employees.
Class No: 02.0(092)(931)

Australia

[888]

Australian library and information professionals. Bundy, A.L. *and* Bundy, J., *comps. & eds.* Adelaide, Auslib Press, 1994. 134p. Aus$32. ISBN: 1875145273.

Questionnaire based. About 5,000 short entries A-Z giving qualifications, library related employment history, present position and special interests. No indexes.
Class No: 02.0(092)(94)

[889]

—Biographical dictionary of Australian librarians. Kosa, G.A., *ed.* 4th ed. Melbourne, Academia Press, 1991. xvii,252p. Aus$32.95. ISBN: 0958966834.

1st ed. 1968; 3rd ed. 1984.

Coverage limited to senior library staff. Detail includes qualifications, education, posts held, special interests and publications. *Class No:* 02.0(092)(94)

Writing & Lecturing

[890]

ENGLEBARTS, R. Librarian authors: a bibliography. Jefferson, N.C., McFarland, 1981. v,267p. £25. ISBN: 0899500072.

'(L)ists names and works of 108 men and women who were outstanding as librarians and who in addition were authors. Most of these persons are Americans' (Preface p.iii). Narrative account in 3 chronological sections (1600-1800, 1800-1950, 1950-1980). General bibliography: librarianship: librarians as authors (p.165-73); Special bibliography: individuals (p.174-266). Index.
Class No: 02.0:001.81

[891]

SCHROEDER, C.F. *and* **ROBERTSON, G.G. Guide to publishing opportunities for librarians.** New York, Haworth Press, 1995. vii,221p. $39.95. (*Haworth library and information science*.) ISBN: 1560243481.

Provides information on 168 library and information related periodicals (22 published by Haworth Press) to which librarians might submit material for publication. 'Libraries and library schools with an interest in getting research and practice published will find this work of value, though it will need supplementing to bring it up to date for UK outlets (*Reference reviews*, v.9(6), 1995, p.4).

Class No: 02.0:001.81

Research Methods

[892]

POWELL, R.R. Basic research methods for librarians. 3rd ed. Greenwich, Conn, Ablex, 1998. xii,281p., illus. £47;$73.25. (*Contemporary studies in information management, policy and services*.) ISBN: 1567503373.

First published 1985; 2nd ed. 1991.

Coverage includes research design, sampling, surveys, data collection techniques, experimental research, data analysis and writing proposals and reports. Illustrative examples in text. Bibliography (p.255-267); indexed.

Class No: 02.0:001.891

[893]

Research methods in library and information studies. Slater, M., *ed.* London, Library Association, 1990. x,182p. tables. £30. ISBN: 0853659087.

A basic guide for those undertaking research in librarianship and related fields, which is also intended as a textbook for the student. 10 contributed chapters (*e.g.* 3. Sampling techniques and recruiting respondents; 6. Data analysis and interpretation (quantitative)). Sparse bibliographical references at chapter ends. Indexed.

Class No: 02.0:001.891

Thesauri

[894]

ASIS thesaurus of information science and librarianship. Milstead, J.L., *ed.* Medford, N.J., Learned Information for the American Society for Information Science, 1994. x,139p. $34.95. (*ASIS monograph series*.) ISBN: 0938734806.

Scope limited primarily to topical subjects, related and peripheral fields (*e.g.* computer science, linguistics) covered 'as warranted'. 1,312 descriptors, 680 use references, 37 facet indicators; alphabetical (p.1-88) and hierarchical (p.89-139) displays in two column format. *Class No:* 02.0:025.43

Institutions & Associations

[895]

FANG, J.R. *and* **SONGE, A.H. World guide to library, archive and information science associations.** [3rd ed.]. München, Saur, 1990. xxvii,517p. £59;$95. (*IFLA publications 52/53*.) ISBN: 3598108141.

First preliminary ed. as *Handbook of national and international library associations* (Chicago, American Library Association, 1973). 1st standard ed. Bowker 1976; 2nd ed. 1980.

In 2 pts.: International associations, 76 entries; National associations, 511 entries arranged by country. Full data includes address, officers, staff, establishment date, activities, fields of interest, structure, sources of support,

....*(contd.)*

publications, activities and bibliography for 1981-90. Indexes: Official journals of associations; Official names of associations; Chief officers; Subject; Countries with international associations; Countries with national associations. List of acronyms (p.xiii-xxvii). Fairly comprehensive and well produced. Some specialist associations are included (*e.g.* UK entries for Agricultural Libraries in Colleges and Universities and Society of County Librarians as well as Aslib, Library Association, etc.). The earlier eds. retain some minor reference value for the bibliographies (*e.g.* 1975-80 in the 2nd ed).

Class No: 02.0:061:061.2

[896]

INTERNATIONAL FEDERATION OF LIBRARY ASSOCIATIONS AND INSTITUTIONS. IFLA directory. The Hague, IFLA, 1969-. Biennial. DFl95. ISSN: 00746002.

Details of IFLA administration and steering bodies, core pogrammes, divisions, etc., plus lists of members and publications. Index of names. Comprehensive information on IFLA is also available through the Internet at http://ifla.inist.fr/ or http://www.nlc.bnc.ca./ifla.

Class No: 02.0:061:061.2

[897]

UNESCO. Répertoire international des associations de bibliothécaires, d'archivistes et de spécialistes des sciences de l'information. [International directory of library, archives and information science associations.] 2nd ed. Paris, UNESCO, 1986. 160p.

1st ed. 1983.

392 entries in French, English or Spanish depending on the language of the country of the association. Arranged by country, (29 international associations listed first), giving address, foundation date, membership and details of activities and publications. *Class No:* 02.0:061:061.2

Great Britain

[898]

Directory of library and information organizations in the United Kingdom. Dale, P., *comp.* London, Library Association Publishing, 1993. xii,180p. £35;$60. ISBN: 1856040925.

Questionnaire based directory of 137 entries, Accountancy Library and Information Group ... Youth Libraries Group. Coverage includes policy-making and regulatory bodies, groups of professionals organized by special interest or geographic location and non library organizations whose activities have an influence on the profession. Excludes product-specific user groups, small local groups and advisory bodies with activities confined to a particular organization. Most Aslib and LA special interest groups covered. Data for each organization includes name with acronym, contact and address, activities, publications, courses, conferences, branches and membership criteria. Organization, but no subject index. Despite some errors and a number of omissions 'does fill a gap' (*Reference reviews*, v.7(5), 1993, p.6).

Forthcoming from Library Association Publishing 1998 *The LION handbook: the library and information organizations and networks handbook* (c.£29.95. ISBN: 1856041263). *Class No:* 02.0:061:061.2(410)

[899]

LIBRARY ASSOCIATION. Library Association yearbook. London, Library Association, 1891-. Annual. £37.50. ISSN: 00759066.

Title and frequency varies; annual publication since 1964.

The 1997-98 ed. (Beecroft K. *and others comps*. ix,493p.) is in 3 parts. Part I includes details of officers, LA Council, headquarters departments and staff, branches, special interest groups, medals, grants and awards and past presidents. Part II reproduces the Royal Charter and gives bye-laws, election rules, regulations for fellowship and associateship, code of professional conduct, etc. Part III (p.187-493) comprises a list of members, giving date of joining and associateship, current post and employing organization. Overseas and institutional members listed separately. Contents have varied over the years (*e.g.* 1968-73 carried a register of research in progress, the forerunner of *Current research in library and information science* (*q.v.*)). *Class No:* 02.0:061:061.2(410)

[900]

MUNFORD, W.A. A History of The Library Association 1877-1977. London, Library Association, 1976. xii,360p. illus. £35. ISBN: 0853654883.

'A Library Association centenary volume'.

Chronological account in 13 chapters. Appendices: The Royal Charter of 1898; Presidents of the Library Association; Honorary Officers of the Library Association; Honorary Fellows of the Library Association. Select bibliography; index. *Class No:* 02.0:061:061.2(410)

USA

[901]

AMERICAN LIBRARY ASSOCIATION. ALA handbook of organization. Chicago, American Library Association, 1894-. Annual. $30. ISSN: 00846406.

Title varies. Companion publication *ALA membrship directory* (ISSN: 02734605). Previously (from 1980) both publications combined as *ALA handbook of organization and membership directory*. Full information on the organizational structure of the ALA is also available from the association's WWW site at http://www.ala.org.
Class No: 02.0:061:061.2(73)

Research Projects

[902]

BRITISH LIBRARY. Research register 1995. London, British Library, 1995. 73p. ISBN: 0712304436.

Replaces *London services research register* (1993).

Describes research interests and lists publications of British Library staff. *Class No:* 02.0:061:061.62.005

[903]

Current research in library and information science. Elliott, P., *ed.* East Grinstead, Bowker-Saur, 1983-. Quarterly. £220. ISSN: 02639254.

Widely referred to as *CRLIS*. Preceded by *RADIALS bulletin* (1974-82), with earlier lists in *Library Association year book* (1968-73). The annual *Current research for the information profession* (ISSN: 02687372), published from 1985 and apparently ceased with vol. for 1991, was based on *CRLIS*.

Research defined widely, includes studies, surveys and other evaluated innovations. International in scope. Main section (Project entries sequence) arranged under 19 major subject categories. Research described in 50-300 words, supporting detail includes names of researchers, duration,

....*(contd.)*

financial support and references. Name and subject indexes, cumulated annually. Full data also available as part of the *LISA* online (Dialog, file 61) and CD-ROM database.
Class No: 02.0:061:061.62.005

[904]

SMITH, C. Directory of consultants and researchers in library and information science. London, British Library Research and Development Department, 1987. viii,182p. £19. (*British Library information guide, v.8.*) ISBN: 0712331409.

Questionnaire based directory of 262 entries. In one sequence by consultant/contact name with summaries of qualifications/expertise. Personal name, corporate name and subject indexes. 2 appendices listing further consultants who did not respond to the questionnaire or who are believed to offer services. Much needed, a 'useful handbook' (*Aslib information,* v.15(11/12), 1987, p.275).
Class No: 02.0:061:061.62.005

Education Institutions

[905]

The Education of library and information professionals: an international series. Gorman, G.E. *and* Rochester, M.K., *eds.* London, Mansell, 1996-.

Published to early 1998: *Education for librarianship in New Zealand and the Pacific Islands* Ronnie M.A. (1996. xi,228p. £50. ISBN: 0720121795); *Education for librarianship in Australia* Rochester, M.K. (1997. xvi,253p. £50. ISBN: 0720122163); *Education for librarianship in China* Wu, G. (1997. xi,250p. £40. ISBN: 0720121930); *Education for librarianship in the Nordic countries* Harbo, O. & Pors, N.O. (1998. x,197p. £50. ISBN: 0720122104). The series is projected for up to 30 titles.

Provides a detailed survey of the development and current state of professional education in each country or region. New Zealand vol. in 12 chaps., Australia in 8; both vols. have a bibliography and index. *Class No:* 02.0:061:37

[906]

World guide to library, archive and information science education. Fang, J.R., *and others eds.* 2nd rev. & enl. ed. München, K.G. Saur, 1995. xii,585p. tables. $130. (*IFLA publications, 72/73.*) ISBN: 3598217994.

First published as *International guide to library and information science education*, 1985.

Provides information on 443 institutions. For each gives general detail such as name, address, head, year founded, no. of staff and students, library and technology facilities, professional status and references (articles about institution), followed by full information on programmes of study. Entries arranged by country A-Z (UK p.431-69) with summary information on general education system. Indexed by place and institution name. Impressively thorough for most institutions, but the currency of the information presented is questionable, some of it apparently based on a questionnaire distributed in 1989. *Class No:* 02.0:061:37

[907]

World list of departments and schools of information studies, information management, information systems, etc. Wilson, T., *comp.* Sheffield, Dept. of Information Studies, Univ. of Sheffield. World Wide Web resource.

URL: http://www.shef.ac.uk/s/publications/worldlist/wlist1.html. Date reviewed 30th June 1998.

Lists and offers to links to WWW pages in sections for

....(contd.)
UK, Europe, Australia, Canada, USA and rest of the world. Regularly updated, the best of several similar Internet listings. *Class No:* 02.0:061:37

Europe

[908]

Information science in Europe: a study guide. Schröder, T.A., *ed.* Amsterdam, IOS Press, 1994. xxv,228p. £28;$42. ISBN: 9051991673.

Extended version of a special issue of the periodical *Education for information*, v.12(1), 1994.

Questionnaire based survey of institutions at university level offering courses in librarianship and information science. In 2 pts: 'Institutes of education' is a listing by country giving contact and staff details with a general description and notes on courses and publications; 'Academic subjects' is a listing of courses with a basic outline of content. Indexed by country/place and subject. *Class No:* 02.0:061:37(4)

India

[909]

AGRAWAL, S.P. Directory of LIS education in India: all-in-one compendium on library and information science study and teaching in India. New Delhi, Reliance Publishing House, 1996. 729p. ISBN: 8175100125.

'Basic bibliography' (p.50-118), a subject based listing of literature on Indian library and information science education, is followed by 'Avenues', a directory of LIS schools with full detail of syllabuses. *Class No:* 02.0:061:37(540)

Africa

[910]

Who's who in library and information science training institutions in Africa. Aina, L.O., *ed.* 2nd ed. Ibadan, Archlib and Information Services, 1995. vii,66p. ISBN: 9783141317.

First published 1991.

Questionnaire based directory of *c.*190 entries. South and Francophone Africa included in this ed. Separate list of institutions; expertise index. *Class No:* 02.0:061:37(6)

Australasia & Oceania

[911]

Directory of library schools and lecturers in librarianship in Australia and New Zealand. Reid-Smith, E.R., *comp. & ed.* 4th ed. Adelaide, Auslib Press, 1994. xii,322p. illus. Aus$38. ISBN: 1875145265.

1st ed. 1977; coverage of New Zealand and present title from 3rd ed., 1985.

In two main sections: 'Directory of responding library schools' (p.1-94) containing full information on 30 schools; 'Directory of lecturing staff' (p.95-312) with biographical and career details for *c.*140 individuals. *Class No:* 02.0:061:37(9)

Library Law

[912]

JASION, J.T. The International guide to legal deposit. Aldershot, Ashgate, 1991. ix,210p. £47.50;$69.95. ISBN: 1857420012.

Core of book (p.17-108) comprises world list of legal deposit libraries by country A-Z, list of relevant legislation (also by country) and tables indicating when deposit began, type of material deposited, etc. Further section (p.109-95) provides detailed examination of legal deposit in 27 countries, Algeria ... Virgin Islands of the United States. Useful bibliography (p.197-210). *Class No:* 021.8

Great Britain

[913]

McLEOD, I. *and* **COOLING, P. Law for librarians:** a handbook for librarians in England and Wales. London, Library Association, 1990. ix,156p. £26. ISBN: 0851574491.

Concentrates on issues of which a librarian would be expected to have legal knowledge. General introduction to the English legal system followed by chapters on key topics such as the legal context of the public library service, defamation, obscene publications, privacy and copyright. 3 appendices: citation of legal sources and judges' titles; photocopying Crown and parliamentary publications; case references. Index. A 'unique and valuable addition to the library manager's bookshelf' (*Journal of documentation*, v.47(2), June 1991, p.211). *Class No:* 021.8(410)

USA

[914]

American library laws. Ladenson, A., *ed.* Chicago, American Library Association, 1983. x,2009p. ISBN: 0838904009.

Reprint from Books on Demand ($180. ISBN: 0783759150). 4th ed. 1973.

Includes laws in effect at 31 December 1982. Federal government laws, including Library of Congress; State laws, Alabama-Wyoming (p.169-1951); Territories and dependencies (Puerto Rico, Virgin Islands). Index of subjects. *Class No:* 021.8(73)

[915]

TRYON, J.S. The Librarian's legal companion. New York, G.K. Hall/Maxwell Macmillan, 1994. xiv,168p. $40. ISBN: 0816119619.

Covers premises liability, employment discrimination and security, privacy, censorship and copyright. General index and index of cases. '(A)dmirable contribution to a sparsely studied field ... useful background or a good starting point for practicing librarians as well as for students of the discipline' (*Library quarterly*, v.65(3), July 1995, p.351). *Class No:* 021.8(73)

Library Buildings

[916]

Library buildings in the United Kingdom, 1990-1994. Harrison, D., *ed.* London, Library Services, 1995. ix,270p. illus., diags., tables, plans. £57.50. ISBN: 1870144023.

List of 421 projects (p.1-10) with size, cost and date opened. Further detailed appraisal of 96 projects based on visits of inspection. Lengthy descriptions backed by floorplans and statistical data. Refurbishment schemes included. '(A) unique record and a starting point for a dialogue between the librarian and the architect' (*Library Association record*, v.98(1), January 1996, p.40). Preceded by:- *Class No:* 022

[917]

—Library buildings 1984-1989. Harrison, K.C., *ed.* London, Library Services, 1990. x,336p. illus., diags., tables, plans. ISBN: 1870144015.

Provides thorough treatment of 121 building projects. Earlier coverage in:- *Class No:* 022

[918]

—Public library buildings, 1975-1983. Harrison, K.C., *ed.* London, Library Services, 1987. xi,228p. illus., diags., tables, plans. ISBN: 1870144007.

Produced with the assistance of the London and Home Counties Branch of the Library Association. Previous coverage provided by *Library buildings* originally a feature in *Library Association record* (1962-1964); separate issues for 1965, 1966, 1967-68, 1972, 1974 and 1976 (Ward, H. *ed.* as *New library buildings* Library Association, 269p.).

Contains detailed descriptions of around 100 buildings, with a table showing 581 projects (many conversions or extensions) reported by 129 library authorities.
Class No: 022

[919]

Planning academic and research library buildings. Leighton, P.D. *and* Weber, D.C., *eds.* 2nd ed. Chicago, American Library Association, 1986. xix,630p. illus., diags., tables. £76.50. ISBN: 0838933203.

1st ed. K.D. Metcalf, McGraw-Hill, 1965. 431p.

An updated and restructured ed. of Metcalf's seminal work. Designed for librarians and architects involved in a library building project. Coverage includes chapters on alternatives to new building, reader, collection and staff accommodation, budgeting, and legal aspects. Glossary, selected annotated bibliography and index. 'Comprehensive treatment', a 'major contribution to library building planning' (*International journal of reviews in librarianship and information science,* v.3(1), 1987, p.145), but entirely based on US experience and practice. *Class No:* 022

[920]

SWARTZBURG, S.G. *and* **BUSSEY, H. Libraries and archives: design and renovation** with a preservation perspective. Metuchen, N.J., Scarecrow Press, 1991. ix,225p. £24.75;$29.50. ISBN: 0810824205.

Pt.1 (p.3-54) is a summary history of library design with an appended bibliography. Pt.2 'A Guide to the literature' has 6 chaps. on planning, design, construction and renovation, shelving, storage, etc., environment, safety, security, etc. and preservation. Each has a short introduction followed by briefly annotated entries. Various appendices including a lists of journals and organizations. General and

....(contd.)
author indexes. The bibliographies are 'remarkable' and publication is a 'signal event' (*Library quarterly*, v.62(4), October 1992, p.460). *Class No:* 022

[921]

THOMPSON, G. Planning and design of library buildings. 3rd ed. London, Butterworth Architecture, 1989. vii,224p. illus., tables, plans. ISBN: 0408500247.

1st ed. 1973; 2nd ed. 1977. Paperback version in print (Butterworth-Heinemann, 1995. £29.99;$56.95. ISBN: 0750626372).

Intended both for students and those, including architects, involved in planning a new library building. Emphasises common factors, rather than specific types of libraries. 19 chapters covering physical conditions, lighting, security and protection, shelving, furniture etc., as well as basic planning and design procedures. Examples mainly drawn from British academic and public libraries. References (p.213-16); Bibliography (p.217-20). 'Retains its place as one of the standard works on the subject ... (but) a more comprehensive index would have aided reference to the text' (*Library Association record,* v.92(7), July 1990, p.520).
Class No: 022

Bibliographies

[922]

Planning library buildings: a select bibliography. Dahlgren, A.C. *and* Heyns, E.P., *comps.* [4th ed.]. Chicago, American Library Association, Library and Administration Association, 1995. v.63p. $15. ISBN: 0838978002.

First published 1981 as *Planning college & university library buildings: a select bibliography*; 3rd ed. 1990.

Unannotated listing of books and articles, items published before 1975 generally excluded. Topical arrangement; author index. *Class No:* 022(01)

[923]

STEPHENSON, M.S. Planning library facilities: a selected annotated bibliography. Metuchen, N.J. Scarecrow Press, 1990. ix,249p. £22.50;$28.50. ISBN: 0810822857.

Covers English language material published 1970 to mid 1988 on the planning, design and evaluation of library buildings and facilities. 800 entries; items published in the US and Canada predominate. Classified arrangement, with an author and subject index. *Class No:* 022(01)

Library Management

Bibliographies

[924]

Quality management issues: a select bibliography for library and information services managers. Garrod, P. *and* Evans, M.K., *comps.* The Hague, International Federation for Information and Documentation/London, British Library, 1995. v,46p. (*FID occasional paper, 10; British Library R&D report, 6220.*) ISBN: 9266007102.

Briefly annotated entries in topical arrangement; no indexes. *Class No:* 023(01)

Staff

[925]

JORDAN, P. *and* JONES, N. Staff management in library and information work. 3rd ed. Aldershot, Gower, 1995. xii,264p. illus., tables. £42.50. ISBN: 0566075814.

First published 1982; 2nd ed. 1987.

Established and widely used UK text. 8 chapters: 1. The Working environment - 2. Motivation and job satisfaction - 3. Workforce planning - 4. Job description and personnel specification - 5. Recruitment and selection of staff - 6. Staff appraisal - 7. Staff training and development - 8. Staff supervision and interpersonal skills training. Grouped references (p.245-60); brief index. *Class No:* 023.5

[926]

NICHOLSON, H. *and* CLEGG, S. Directory of personnel officers and trainers 1992. London, Personnel, Training and Education Group of the Library Association, 1992. 115p. ISBN: 0946852006.

Replaces LISU's *Trainers' directory* (2nd ed. 1986).

Lists personnel officers and persons responsible for training in 379 UK libraries of all types. Arranged by town; indexes of libraries, personnel officers, trainers and training co-operatives and their acronyms. *Class No:* 023.5

Women

[927]

On account of sex: an annotated bibliography on the status of women in librarianship, 1987-1992. Goetsch, L.A. *and* Watstein, S.B., *eds.* Metuchen, N.J., Scarecrow Press, 1993. xxviii,244p. tables. £29.95;$36. ISBN: 0810827018.

Edited for the Committee on the Status of Women in Librarianship, American Library Association.

About 875 entries, nearly all for US material. Chronological arrangement with author and subject indexes. Annotations very brief.

Earlier vols with same title, but both published by ALA, cover 1977-81 (Heim, K. and Phenix, K. *comps.* 1984. xl,188p. ISBN: 083892878) and 1982-86 (Phenix, K. *comp.* 1989. xv,136p. £9;$10. ISBN: 0838933750). Containing 900 and 600 entries respectively, these vols. provide a bibliographical continuation of Weibel (below).
Class No: 023.5-0055.2

[928]

The Role of women in librarianship 1876-1976: the entry, advancement and the struggle for equalization in one profession. Weibel, K., *and others eds.* London, Mansell; Phoenix, Oryx, 1979. 510p. (*Neal-Schuman professional books.*) ISBN: 0720108195, UK; 0912700017, US.

44 selections from the literature and a 1,000 item bibliography with detailed author, subject and title indexes. 'Achieves its objective of documenting the struggle' (*Library review,* v.29(1), Spring 1980, p.41-2). *Class No:* 023.5-0055.2

Library Users

Education Courses

Bibliographies

[929]

COOK, S.A., *comp.* **Instructional design for libraries: an annotated bibliography.** New York, Garland, 1986. xiv,274p. (*Garland reference library of social science, v.345.*) ISBN: 0824085752.

Selective coverage of the literature 1970-85 including journal articles and ERIC documents. 667 numbered entries; author, title and subject indexes. *Class No:* 024:377.3(01)

[930]

MALLEY, I. Education in the use of libraries and information: a bibliography. Loughborough, the Author, 1979-80. 2v. £1.50 each v.

Pt.1. Pre-1900-1954. (1),58p. ISBN: 0904641120; pt.2. 1955-1969. 55p. ISBN: 0904641155.

World-wide coverage. Pt.1 has 689 references, A-Z by author, pt.2 has 622 references, similarly arranged. Rudimentary subject indexes in both volumes. Of limited accessibility, would have been better arranged by subject or chronologically. *Class No:* 024:377.3(01)

[931]

RADER, H.B. Library orientation and information literacy 1995 (in *RSR*, v.24(4), 1996, p.77-96).

Lists and annotates 271 items. Similar bibliographies (previous title *Library orientation and instruction*) have appeared more or less annually in *RSR* since 1973.
Class No: 024:377.3(01)

Library Stock

Acquisitions & Collection Development

[932]

Collection management for the 21st century: a handbook for librarians. Gorman, G.E. *and* Miller, R.H., *eds.* Westport, Conn., Greenwood Press, 1997. xv,333p. £55.50;$75. (*Greenwood library management collection..*) ISBN: 0313299536.

General account in 15 chaps., *e.g.* The Internet and collection management in academic libraries, Collection development and performance measurement, Budgeting for information resources. Final chap. (p.287-318) provides review of the literature on collection development and management 1990-95, citing 166 items as notes. Index.

A similar work is Gorman G.E. & Howes, B.R. *Collection development for libraries* (London, Bowker, 1989. xv,432p. illus. £27.$47.50. (Topics in library and information studies). ISBN: 0408301007). *Class No:* 025.20

[933]

Directory of acquisitions librarians in the United Kingdom and Republic of Ireland. Wolfe, S., *ed.* 6th ed. Leeds, National Acquisitions Group, 1997. vi,229p. ISBN: 1870269195.

Compiled for the National Acquisitions Group. 1st ed. 1987; 5th ed. 1995, now published on a biennial basis.

Wider in scope than the title suggests. In addition to names, qualifications and job titles of staff principally

.... (contd.)
involved in acquisitions, gives expenditure on printed and audio-visual materials and automated system used. Index of libraries by name, place and automated system. A versatile source, despite the omission of many libraries and incomplete data for many others. *Class No:* 025.20

[934]
GILLESPIE, J.T. *and* **FOLCARELLI, R.J. Guides to library collection development.** Englewood, Colo., Libraries Unlimited, 1994. xii,441p. £53.50;$49.50. ISBN: 1563081733.

'The purpose of this book is to supply information on ... bibliographic sources, not only to help in the process of selecting and acquiring materials for the library collection, but also to locate additional items for readers' advisory and interlibrary loan purposes' (*Introduction*, p.xi). 1,671 annotated entries for items published 1986-93 in 15 chaps. Scope extends to some directories, handbooks and subject encyclopedias; sources relating to children and young people included. Author/title and subject indexes. *Class No:* 025.20

[935]
SPILLER, D. Book selection: principles and practice. 5th ed. London, Bingley, 1991. x,213p. £35. ISBN: 0851574645.

First published 1971; 4th ed. 1986 with subtitle 'An introduction to principles and practice'.

'(H)as become the standard work on book selection ... (c)learly written, concise and informative' (*Current awareness bulletin* (Aslib), v.8(9), November 1991, p.489). Includes sections on periodicals, fiction, audiovisual materials and databases. Further reading (p.183-208). Index. *Class No:* 025.20

Databases

[936]
AcqWeb. Leiserson, A.B., *ed.* Nashville, Tn., Vanderbilt Law Library. World Wide Web resource.

URL: http://www.library.vanderbilt.edu/law/acqs/acqs.html. Date reviewed 30th March 1998.

A 'gathering place for librarians and other professionals interested in acquisitions and collection development' (*Home page*). Links to a vast range of WWW sites under 10 main categories *e.g.* Verification tools and resources, Directory of publishers and vendors, Journals, newsletters and listserv archives. Established (began 1994), well produced and regularly updated; the best of a number of WWW sites aimed at those responsible for acquisitions and related functions. *Class No:* 025.20(003.4)

Bibliographies

[937]
Collection development and acquisitions 1970-1980: an annotated critical bibliography. Godden, I.P., *and others comps.* Metuchen, N.J., Scarecrow Press, 1982. vii,138p. £18;$20. ISBN: 0810814994.

345 entries in 7 topical sections. Author, title and subject index. *Class No:* 025.20(01)

[938]
GABRIEL, M.R. Collection development and collection evaluation: a sourcebook. Lanham, Md., Scarecrow Press, 1995. xi,421p. charts, diags. £47.25;$49.50 ISBN: 0810828774.

Provides three bibliographical essays on collection development, collection evaluation and acquisitions, each followed by extensive notes and references. 1,899 items

.... (contd.)
cited in total. Further sections offer information, with examples, on policies, guidelines and standards. Glossary (p.399-413); subject index. *Class No:* 025.20(01)

[939]
Library acquisitions 1986-1995: a select bibliography. Vickery, J., *comp.* Horsforth, National Acquisitions Group, 1996. World Wide Web resource.

URL: http:bubl.ac.uk/docs/bibliog/vickery. Date reviewed 30th March 1998. Disc version also available.

Comprises items originally listed in the 'Acquisitions update' section of the periodicals *NAG newsletter* and *Taking stock*.

893 unannotated entries in subject arrangement. Includes coverage of collection development and non-book materials. Author index. 'Acquisitions update' continues to appear in the periodical *Taking stock*, v.6(1) May 1997 listing 42 items. *Class No:* 025.20(01)

Handbooks & Manuals

[940]
Handbook on the international exchange of publications. Vanwijngaerden, F., *ed.* Paris, Unesco, 1978. 165p. £5.70. (*Unesco bibliographical manuals.*) ISBN: 9231014668.

First published 1950; 3rd ed. 1964.

Aims to provide a guide to the methodology, organization and management of the international exchange of publications. Includes a 'List of exchange centres with a national responsibility', Afghanistan ... Zimbabwe (p.107-65). *Class No:* 025.20(035)

[941]
—ALLARDYCE, A. Letters for the international exchange of publications: a guide to their composition in English, French, German, Russian and Spanish. Genzel, P., *ed.* München, Verlag Dokumentation; London, Saur, 1978. 148p. (*IFLA publications, 13.*) ISBN: 0896641139, Saur.

Intended to supplement the above. *Class No:* 025.20(035)

[942]
KIM, D.U. *and* **WILSON, C.A. Policies of publishers:** a handbook for order librarians. 1995 ed. [5th ed.]. Metuchen, N.J., Scarecrow Press, 1995. v,296p. 31.50;$35. ISBN: 0810830175.

Previous ed. 1989.

Questionnaire based guide to the policies of US publishers on distribution, discounts, returns, shipping, invoicing, back orders, etc. This ed. includes email addresses and information on electronic ordering and online catalogue access. *Class No:* 025.20(035)

[943]
WOOD, R.J. *and* **HOFFMAN, F. Library collection development policies:** a reference and writers' handbook. Lanham, Md., Scarecrow Press, 1996. xxix,467p. £40.40;$49.50. ISBN: 0810830396.

Main section (p.79-408) reproduces, in whole or in part, the collection development policies of 22 US libraries. Useful bibliography (p.445-59). Indexed.
Class No: 025.20(035)

Special Materials

[944]
STEVENS, N.D. A guide to collecting librariana. Metuchen, N.J. and London, Scarecrow Press, 1986. xii,166p. £22.50;$25. ISBN: 0810818744.

Primarily a listing of items considered to consitute librariana (p.16-89) in sections Autographs-Shopping bags and T-shirts. Further sections on acquisitions procedure and library museums. Index. Unique, but of debatable value, 'jottings around the subject rather than an orderly guide' (*Journal of documentation*, 44(2), June 1988, p.197-8).
Class No: 025.208

Conservation

[945]
CUNHA, G.M. *and* **CUNHA, D.G. Conservation of library materials:** a manual and bibliography on the care, repair and restoration of library materials. 2nd ed. Metuchen, N.J., Scarecrow Press, 1971-72. 2v. $59.50. ISBN: 0810804271.

First published 1967.

V.1 is a manual with 7 chapters on historical background, nature of library materials, the enemies of library materials, preventive care, repair and restoration, when disaster strikes, the co-operative approach to conservation, and 'In conclusion'. Appendices include a glossary, (p.302-28). 32 figures. V.2: Bibliography has 4,882 entries, often annotated, for books and periodical articles in Western languages. Arrangement reflects the order of v.1; author index. *Class No:* 025.209

[946]
—CUNHA, G.M. *and* CUNHA, D.G. Library and archives conservation: 1980's and beyond. Metuchen, N.J., Scarecrow Press, 1983. 2v. ISBN: 0810815877.

To be used in conjunction with *Conservation of library materials*. V.1, a manual as before, includes numerous appendices (p.123-88), such as Research centers and professional associations, Paper treatments and Testing for magnesium carbonate concentration. V.2, subtitled *Bibliography*, has 5,871 entries, mainly for items published in the 1970's, but including some older material omitted from the previous volume. *Class No:* 025.209

[947]
HARVEY, R. Preservation in libraries: principles, strategies and practises for librarians. London, Bowker-Saur, 1993. xvi,269p. £32;$50. (*Topics in library and information studies.*) ISBN: 0862916321.

10 chapters with individual headings such as 'Air quality', 'Dealing with acid migration', 'Establishing a microfilming programme' and 'Library materials in transit'. Select bibliography (p.229-53); index. The same author's *Preservation in libraries: a reader* (London, Bowker-Saur, 1993. xii,483p. £32;$50. ISBN: 0862916098) provides elaborative background material. *Class No:* 025.209

Bibliographies

[948]
MORROW, C.C. *and* **SCHOENLY, S.B. A Conservation bibliography for librarians,** archivists and administrators. Troy, N.Y., Whitson, 1979. vi,271p. ISBN: 087875170x.

Covers 1966 to mid-1978. 1,367 books and articles in an author list, with a separate classified sequence. Contains many non-English language items. Complements but does not replace Cunha (*q.v.*). *Class No:* 025.209(01)

[949]
A Reading guide to the preservation of library collections. Kenny, G., *ed.* London, Library Association Publishing, 1991. v,106p. £30. ISBN: 085365929x.

10 main contributions (Preservation policies ... Storage and environment ... Disaster control planning ... New technology) each briefly discussing trends and developments followed by an annotated selection of source material. Author/editor and title indexes. A handy pointer to some of the more important recent literature. *Class No:* 025.209(01)

Handbooks & Manuals

[950]
DEPEW, J.N. A Library, media and archival preservation handbook. Santa Barbara, ABC-Clio, 1991. xxv,441p. illus., tables, charts. $59.50. ISBN: 0874365430.

Well-structured book offering concise treatment of specific topics (*e.g.* Book lice, Double-fan adhesive binding) within 9 chapter framework. Illustrations and examples rather sparse. Final chapter includes list of companies and organizations (p.310-41) with subject index. Various appendices and glossary (p.423-32), expanded in *A Library, media and archival preservation glossary* (below).
Class No: 025.209(035)

[951]
SWARTZBURG, S.G. Preserving library materials: a manual. 2nd ed. Metuchen, N.J., Scarecrow Press, 1995. x,503p. £53.55;$59.50. ISBN: 0810828553.

First published 1983 as *Preserving library materials: a handbook*.

13 chaps. covering historical and philosophical perspectives, the preservation survey, collection management, book enemies, environment and preservation, emergency planning, bookbinding, paper, special materials and reformatting using microfilm and facsimilie. Extensive glossary (p.250-307) and appendices listing organizations and periodical publications. Also offers a valuable bibliography of over 1,000 briefly annotated entries. '(A)n excellent resource for those interested in learning the basics of preservation and provides the information in an easy to read and understand format' (*Special libraries*, v.86(3), Summer 1995, p.244).

A pbk. textbook version of this work, omitting the appendices and bibliography, is also available (£26.55;$29.50. ISBN: 0810829800).
Class No: 025.209(035)

Dictionaries

[952]
DEPEW, J.N. *and* **JONES, C.L. A Library, media and archival preservation glossary.** Santa Barbara, ABC-Clio, 1992. ix,192p. $59. ISBN: 0874365767.

About 1,500 definitions of 20-100 words in 9 sections following structure of the companion work *A Library, media and archival preservation handbook* (above). Not to be preferred to Roberts & Etherington (below), having a 'number of omissions and a lack of balance among subjects covered' (*Journal of academic librarianship*, v.18(2), May 1992, p.116). *Class No:* 025.209(038)

[953]

Glossary of basic archival and library conservation terms: English with equivalents in Spanish, German, Italian, French and Russian. International Council on Archives. Committee on Conservation and Restoration, *comp and* Nogueira, C.C., *ed.*. München, Saur, 1988. 151p. £29;$37.50. (*ICA handbook series, v.4.*) ISBN: 3598202768.

405 alphabetically arranged and numbered headwords in English, followed by translations into the 5 other languages. Alphabetical index in each language keyed to entry number. Draws on Roberts and Etherington (below). 'Emphasis is on paper conservation with no mention of other formats such as microfilms, fiche etc.' (*Choice*, v.27(2), October 1989, p.288-9). *Class No:* 025.209(038)

[954]

ROBERTS, M.T. *and* **ETHERINGTON, D. Bookbinding and the conservation of books:** a dictionary of descriptive terminology. Washington D.C., Library of Congress, 1982. x,296p., illus., plates. $27. ISBN: 0844403660.

'Although this dictionary is intended first and foremost for those actively involved in one or more aspects of the overall field of bookbinding and conservation ... it is perhaps no less intended for those working in related fields such as bibliography and librarianship' (Preface p.ix). About 3,000 terms defined, often at length (*e.g.* 'Caoutchone binding' *c.*200 words; 'Printing inks' 1½ cols.). Includes a few entries for historical figures (*e.g.* Caxton, William). Line drawings in text; 11 grouped plates. 373 item bibliography. *Class No:* 025.209(038)

Yearbooks & Directories

[955]

The Directory of suppliers: a comprehensive list of suppliers and services for all preservation and conservation needs in archives, museums and libraries. Weber, J., *ed.* [4th ed.]. London, Society of Archivists, 1994. 79p. £15. ISBN: 0902886495.

First published 1978.

Areas covered include conservation and bookbinding, environmental control, disaster recovery and microfilm. Main section A-Z lists companies with notes on products; index of materials, equipment, services, etc. Appendices: 'Useful addresses'; 'Training in archive conservation'. *Class No:* 025.209(058)

Information Management

[956]

FOSKETT, A.C. The Subject approach to information. 5th ed. London, Library Association, 1996. xv,576p. illus. £39.95. ISBN: 1856040488.

First published 1969; 4th ed. 1982.

The basic British text. 28 chaps. in 5 sections: 2. Features of an information retrieval system ... 11. Notation ... 18. The Universal Decimal Classification ... 23. Library of Congress subject headings ... 25. Science and technology. Includes examples, references at chap. ends. Author and subject indexes. '(S)erves as an extensive review of the subject field, a comprehensive bibliography and a dependable authoritative resource' (*Journal of*

.... (contd.)

documentation, v.53(2), March 1997, p.203). 'The key basic reference text for students of information retrieval' (*Library review*, v.46(4), 1997, p.282). *Class No:* 025.4

Cataloguing

[957]

Anglo-American cataloguing rules. Gorman, M. *and* Winkler, P., *eds*. 2nd ed. 1988 revision. London, Library Association, 1988. xxv,677p. £55. ISBN: 085365509x.

Prepared under the direction of the Joint Steering Committee for the Revision of AACR, a committee of the American Library Association, the Australian Committee on Cataloguing, the British Library, the Canadian Committee on Cataloguing, the Library Association and the Library of Congress. Published jointly by the Library Association, American Library Association and Canadian Library Association.

Originally published 1967 in separate British and North American texts. 2nd ed. 1978 in one text. This revision updates the 2nd ed., incorporating the amendments of 1981-85, and the revision of Chap. 9, Computer files, 1987.

Designed for use in general libraries of all sizes, the rules cover the description and provision of access points for any library materials commonly collected. Organized in 2 main sections. I. 'Description', contains 13 chaps., the first setting out rules of general applicability, 2-10 giving rules for specific types of material (*e.g.* 5. Music; 7. Motion pictures and videorecordings) and 11-13 covering rules of partial generality. II. 'Headings, uniform titles and references' has 6 chaps.: Choice of access points; Headings for persons; Geographic names; Headings for corporate bodies; Uniform titles; References. 4 appendices: Capitalization; Abbreviations; Numerals; Glossary. Exceptionally thorough index comp. by K.G.B. Bakewell (p.625-77). By far the most commonly used cataloguing code in English speaking countries. Also translated into 15 other languages including French, Italian, Japanese and Spanish. Updated by:

Forthcoming 1998 further revision integrating 1993 amendments (below) and changes approved up to the end of 1997 (*c.*720p. *c.*£37.50. ISBN: 1856041549). Will also include additional rules and examples for nonprint materials and revised appendix and glossary. A CD-ROM version, using FolioViews software and with customizable features, will be published simultaneously (£165. ISBN: 1856042294). *Class No:* 025.40

[958]

—AACR2 decisions & rule interpretations. Howarth, L.C., *comp*. 6th ed. Ottawa, Canadian Library Association, 1994. Looseleaf in binder. £110;$160. ISBN: 1856041522.

Published in conjunction with the American Library Association and the Library Association. 5th ed. 1991.

Consolidates the decisions and rule interpretations made by the Library of Congress, National Library of Canada, British Library and National Library of Australia. Revised to October 1994. *Class No:* 025.40

[959]

—Anglo-American cataloguing rules. Second edition. 1988 revision. Amendments to 1993. London, Library Association, 1993. Unpaged. £15. ISBN: 1856040763.

Revisions passed at Joint Steering Committee meetings 1989-92.

Drilled pages in binder designed for interleaving in text. Also contains brief list of changes and errata. Amendments are generally of a minor nature. *Class No:* 025.40

[960]

—GORMAN, M. The Concise AACR2. 1988 revision. London, Library Association, 1989. xi,161p. £21. ISBN: 0853657998.

First published 1981.

Intended 'to convey the essence and basic principles of the second edition of the *Anglo-American cataloguing rules, 1988 revision* ... without many of that comprehensive work's rules for out-of-the-way and complex materials' (General introduction p.1). Rules retained rewritten, simplified and supplied with examples. Widely used in smaller libraries instead of the full version. *Class No:* 025.40

[961]

—HUNTER, E.J. An Introduction to AACR2: a programmed guide to the second edition of the Anglo-American cataloguing rules, 1988 revision. Rev. ed. London, Bingley, 1989. 153p. £25. ISBN: 0851574572.

First published 1972; 2nd ed. 1979.

'(W)ithout question an authoritative introduction to AACR2 and rates the status of a standard work' (*Library review*, v.38(3), 1989, p.55).

Also by Hunter, *Examples illustrating AACR2 1988 revision* (2nd ed. London, Library Association Publishing, 1989. xi,235p. £25. ISBN: 0853656495) and *A Guide to the Concise AACR2 1988 revision: a programmed introduction* (London, Library Association Publishing, 1994. vi,150p. £17.50. ISBN: 1856040887). *Class No:* 025.40

[962]

—MAXWELL, M.F. *and* MAXWELL, M.F. Maxwell's handbook for AACR2: explaining and illustrating the Anglo-American cataloguing rules and the 1993 amendments. Chicago, American Library Association, 1997. xii,522p. tables, diags. £35.95. ISBN: 0838907040.

Rev. ed. of *Handbook for AACR2 1988 revision* (1989).

Arranged according to the structure of AACR2. Follows Library of Congress format with regard to optional rules. This ed. includes new chap. on cataloguing archival materials and full revision of chap. on computer files. For the working cataloguer rather than the student. Indexed. *Class No:* 025.40

[963]

BRITISH LIBRARY. Name authority list. London, British Library, 1983-. Monthly. Microfiche. £310.

Cumulative listing of all headings (personal, corporate, government and conference) used by the British Library since AACR was adopted for cataloguing in 1981. From April 1997 includes records created jointly with the Library of Congress under the Anglo-American Authority File Programme. 830,000 headings December 1997, increasing at a rate of 5,000 per month. Also available over the Internet through FTP or on magnetic tape. *Class No:* 025.40

[964]

Cataloging Service bulletin index: an index to Cataloging Service bulletin of the Library of Congress. Olson, N.B., *comp.* Lake Crystal, Minn., Soldier Creek Press, 1994. 86p.

Index nos. 1-66, Summer 1978-Fall 1994. Replaces cumulation for 1978-91. Based on the publisher's annual index (ISSN: 07393393).

The quarterly *Cataloging Service bulletin* (ISSN: 01608029, previously *Library of Congress Cataloging Service bulletin*) contains news, updates on LC cataloguing practices, LC rule interpretations, official rule revisions, etc. *Class No:* 025.40

[965]

INTERNATIONAL FEDERATION OF LIBRARY ASSOCIATIONS AND INSTITUTIONS. Committee on Cataloguing. ISBD Review Committee Working Group. **ISBD(G): general international standard bibliographic description:** annotated text. Rev. ed. München, K.G Saur, 1992. viii,36p. $20. (*UBCIM publications, new series, v.6.*) ISBN: 3598110847.

First published 1977.

Forms the basis for the specialized ISBDs. These include ISBD(A) Pre-1801 monographs, ISBD(CF) Computer files, ISBD(CM) Cartographic materials, ISBD(M) Monographs, ISBD(NBM) Non-book materials, ISBD(PM) Printed music and ISBD(S) Serials. *Class No:* 025.40

[966]

—Names of persons: national usages for entry in catalogues. International Federation of Library Associations and Institutions. Universal Bibliographic Control and International MARC Programme, *comp.* 4th rev. & enl. ed. München, K.G. Saur, 1996. xii,263p. DM178. ISBN: 3598113420.

Provisional ed. 1963; 3rd ed. 1977.

One of a number of IFLA UBC guides to selection of catalogue headings. *Class No:* 025.40

[967]

LIBRARY OF CONGRESS. Catalog Publication Division. **Name authorities.** Washington, D.C., Library of Congress Cataloging Distribution Service, 1979-. Quarterly. Microfiche. $870. ISSN: 01959093.

Issues cumulative; new cumulation begun 1997, previous cumulations for 1977-86 and 1987-96.

Covers all name headings including uniform titles and series and geographic names of political and civic jurisdictions. *Name authorities* is also searchable as part of the Library of Congress catalogues at http://www.loc.gov. The CD-ROM equivalent of the name authorities file, *CDMARC names*, is now discontinued. *Class No:* 025.40

[968]

LIBRARY OF CONGRESS. Cataloging Distribution Service. **Cataloger's desktop.** Washington, D.C., Library of Congress, Cataloging Distribution Service, 1994-. CD-ROM database; quarterly updating. $870

Contains *Library of Congress rule interpretations, Subject cataloging manual: subject headings, Subject cataloging manual: classification*, USMARC formats and all USMARC code lists. Supports table of contents viewing, index browsing and full Boolean keyword, phrase and proximity searching. Customization features include personalized notes and bookmarks. *Class No:* 025.40

Databases

[969]

International guide to MARC databases and services: national magnetic tape, online and CD-ROM services. International Federation of Library Associations and Institutions. Universal Bibliographic Control and International MARC Programme, *ed.* 3rd rev. & enl. ed. München, K.G. Saur, 1993. 307p. tables. $100;DM178. ISBN: 3598109873.

2nd ed. publ. by Deutsche Bibliothek, 1986.

Indicates which national bibliographic agencies and similar organizations offer bibliographic data in machine-readable form. Includes detail of databases and services at the planning stage. *Class No:* 025.40(003.4)

[970]

Library bibliographic networks in Europe: a LIBER directory. Dempsey, L., *ed.* 2nd ed. The Hague, NBLC, 1992. 110p. tables ISBN: 9062520898.

At head of title page 'European Research Libraries Cooperation'.

1st ed. 1988.

Covers 49 networks in 15 countries, academic and research networks (*e.g.* JANET) excluded. Data, by network A-Z, under headings: Role and organization; Membership; Hardware and software; Network environment; Operations (shared cataloguing, public access); Central files; Standards; Finance and copyright; Organizational links with other bibliographic networks; Publications (by and about). UK networks include BLCMP and CURL. No index. Select list of acronyms. *Class No:* 025.40(003.4)

Indexing

[971]

AMERICAN LIBRARY ASSOCIATION. Resources and Technical Services Division. Filing Committee. **ALA filing rules.** Chicago, American Library Association, 1980. ix,50p. £10.95;$15. ISBN: 083893255x.

Succeeds *ALA rules for filing catalog cards,* first published 1942, 2nd ed. 1968.

Based on the 'file-as-is' principle. In two parts: general rules for common situations; special rules for abbreviations, initials, numerals, terms of honour, etc. Plentiful illustrative examples. Glossary and index. *Class No:* 025.42

[972]

Cross-reference index: a guide to search terms. Atkins, T.V. *and* Ostrow, R., *eds.* 2nd ed. New York, Bowker, 1989. xi,970p. ISBN: 0832519186.

1st ed. 1974.

Comprises matrix type charts comparing selected headings from Library of Congress and Sears' subject headings, Readers' guide, New York times index, PAIS, ERIC, Psychological abstracts and the IAC databases. About 42,000 terms covered; index of terms precedes main section. *Class No:* 025.42

[973]

FOUNTAIN, J.F. Subject headings for school and public libraries: an LCSH/Sears companion. Englewood, Colo., Libraries Unlimited, 1996. xxxii,171p. £45.95;$48. ISBN: 1563083604.

First published 1993 as *Headings for children's materials.*

25,000 headings 'that might be needed to catalog a general collection used by children and readers or viewers interested in popular topics'. Headings in 2 col. format with BT, NT, etc. used to express relationships. Free-floating subdivisions precede main listing. *Class No:* 025.42

[974]

LIBRARY OF CONGRESS. Cataloging Policy and Support Service. **Library of Congress subject headings.** Washington, D.C., Library of Congress, 1908-. Annual (print; CD-ROM and microfiche quarterly). ISSN: 10489711.

First published in parts between 1908 and 1914. Present title from 8th ed. (1975). Print ed. now published annually in 4v.

Updated by weekly lists, distributed on a monthly basis. Also available in microfiche, (new cumulations quarterly. $115. ISSN: 03625243), through the Internet (http://lcweb.loc.gov, then 'Search our catalogs' option) and on CD-ROM (part of the *Classification Plus* database also including updated schedules of LC Classification (quarterly updating. $470. ISSN: 10869263)).

The 20th ed. of the printed version (1997) contains headings established through December 1996. Approx 232,000 records in dictionary format displayed in 3 columns. Relationships indicated in thesaurus style from the 11th ed. (UF, BT, NT, etc.). Much fuller than its nearest rival *Sears'* (below) and more suitable for academic libraries.
Class No: 025.42

[975]

—CHAN, L.M. Library of Congress subject headings: principles and applications. 3rd ed. Englewood, Colo., Libraries Unlimited, 1995. xiv.541p. £49.50;$45. ISBN: 1563081954.

First published 1978; 2nd ed. 1986. Also available in pbck. (£37.95;$35. ISBN: 1563081911).

'(T)he best available explanation of the history, structure and use of LC subject headings' (*American reference books annual*, v.27, 1996, p.252). *Class No:* 025.42

[976]

Sears' list of subject headings. Miller, J., *ed.* 16th ed. New York, H.W. Wilson, 1997. li,786p. ISBN: 0824209206.

1st ed. 1923. First five eds. with title *List of subject headings for small libraries*. 15th ed. 1994.

Based on Library of Congress Headings with some modifications. Mainly for school or medium-sized public libraries. From 15th ed. conforms to NISO standards for thesauri and uses labels BT, NT, etc. 16th ed. has 400 additional headings and revised suggested classification nos. based on 13th ed. of *Abridged Dewey Decimal classification*.
Class No: 025.42

[977]

SWATRIDGE, C. A List of subject headings for school and other libraries. Oxford, School Library Association, 1981. xi,148p. £7. ISBN: 0900641371.

List specially developed by Swatridge. *c.*2,500 headings with see and see also references, etc. 30 lists of standard subheadings (*e.g.* countries, periods of history, writers and orators, activities and sports). *Class No:* 025.42

Standards

[978]

BRITISH STANDARDS INSTITUTION. Recommendations for examining documents, determining their subjects and selecting indexing terms. London, B.S.I., 1984. 12p. (*BS:6529.*) *Class No:* 025.42(083.74)

Thesauri

[979]

BRITISH STANDARDS INSTITUTION. Root thesaurus. 3rd ed. Milton Keynes, British Standards Institution, 1988. 2v. ISBN: 058016991x.

V.1. *Subject display* (xix,588p.); v.2. *Alphabetical list* (iii,632p.).

First published 1981; 2nd ed. 1985.

Controlled vocabulary of 13,200 descriptors, primarily for technology, but also extending to other subjects such as administrative sciences and communications, and with general level coverage of the social sciences and humanities. V.1 uses a letter notation, v.2 indicates hierarchical relationships of terms in standard thesaurus format. *Class No:* 025.43

[980]

DAG HAMMARSKJÖLD LIBRARY. UNBIS thesaurus: trilingual list (English, French, Spanish) of terms used in subject analysis of documents and other materials relevant to United Nations programmes and activities. (English edition). 3rd ed. New York, Dag Hammarskjöld Library, United Nations, 1995. xxiii,758p. $65. (*Dag Hammarskjöld Library bibliographical series, no.40.*) ISBN: 9211005736.

First published 1981; 2nd ed. 1985.

The UNBIS (United Nations Bibliographical Information System) thesaurus is a multi-disciplinary indexing vocabulary used in the Dag Hammarskjöld Library and other parts of the UNBIS network. *Class No:* 025.43

[981]

Unesco thesaurus: a structured list of descriptors for indexing and retrieving literature in the fields of education, science, social science, culture, communication and information. Barsony, L., *comp.* [2nd ed.]. Paris, Unesco, 1995. xxxix,705p. FFr300. ISBN: 9230031003.

First published 1977.

4,261 preferred terms and 2,341 non-descriptors, French and Spanish equivalents shown in main sequence. This ed. expands coverage of development, the environment and information. Also available on CD-ROM. *Class No:* 025.43

Handbooks & Manuals

[982]

AITCHISON, J., *and others*. Thesaurus construction and use: a practical manual. 3rd ed. London, Aslib, 1997. xvi,212p. illus. £35. ISBN: 0851423906.

Earlier eds. 1972, and 1987, both with title *Thesaurus construction: a practical manual.*

Concise manual of 12 chapters, illustrated with extracts from published thesauri. Bibliography (p.187-98); index. *Class No:* 025.43(035)

Yearbooks & Directories

[983]

Thesaurus guide: analytical directory of selected vocabularies for information retrieval, 1992. Luxembourg, Office for Official Publications of the European Communities, 1993. 1033p. illus., tables. ISBN: 9282649563.

Prepared by Eurobrokers for the Commission of the European Communities. 1st ed. 1985.

Inventory of over 600 thesauri available in at least one of the official languages of the EEC, including some published in the US and Canada. Detailed descriptions under 10 subject groupings; indexes of responsible organizations and subjects. *Class No:* 025.43(058)

Standards

[984]

BRITISH STANDARDS INSTITUTION. Guide to establishment and development of monolingual thesauri. London, BSI, 1987. 32p. £66. (*BSI:5723;ISO:2788.*) ISBN: 0580161013.

Complemented by *Guide to the establishment of multilingual thesauri* (1985. 68p. £94. (BSI:6723;ISO:5964) ISBN: 0580145875). *Class No:* 025.43(083.74)

Classification Systems

[985]

BLISS, H.E. A Bibliographic classification, extended by systematic ancillary schedules for composite specification and notation. New York, H.W. Wilson. 4v. in 3.

Comprises: v.1 Systematic schedules 1-4, Classes 1-9 (anterior numerical classes), Classes A-G; v.2 Classes H-K; v.3 Classes L-Z; v.4 Indexes. Lengthy introduction in v.1 (p.3-188). V.1 and 2 published in a 2nd ed. 1952. Further volumes of the 2nd ed. published by Bowker-Saur (below). *Class No:* 025.44

[986]

—The Abridged Bliss classification: the Bibliographic classification of Henry Evelyn Bliss revised for school libraries only. London, School Library Association, 1967. xv,197p.

Reprinted with minor corrections 1970. *Class No:* 025.44

[987]

BLISS, H.E. Bliss Bibliographic Classification. Mills, J., *and others comps*. 2nd ed. London, Bowker-Saur (previously Butterworths), 1977-.

Scheduled for completion in 22 v. Following available 1997: *Introduction and auxillary schedules* (1987. £62. ISBN: 0408708212); *Class A/AL. Philosophy and logic* (1992. £50. ISBN: 1857390253); *Class AM/AX. Mathematics, probability and statistics* (1993. £45. ISBN: 1857390725); *Class H. Anthropology, human biology, health sciences* (1980. £62. ISBN: 040870828x); *Class I. Psychology and psychiatry* (1978. £28. ISBN: 0408708417); *Class J. Education* (1991. £45. ISBN: 0862912784); *Class K. Society* (1984. £45. ISBN: 0408708204); *Class P. Religion, the occult, morals and ethics* (1977. £42. ISBN: 0408708328); *Class Q. Social welfare and criminology* (1995. £45. ISBN: 1857391217); *Class S. Law* (1996. £48. ISBN: 1857390679) *Class T. Economics, management of economic enterprises* (1987. £54. ISBN: 0408708344).

Virtually a new scheme, rather than a revision of the original, though the basic framework is retained. Hardly used outside the UK, Bliss is well thought of as representing a modern consensus on the classification of subjects for bibliographic purposes and has the advantage of a relatively brief notation (principally alphabetical). With this ed. still far from complete best used on an individual basis for the classification of special collections or libraries. *Class No:* 025.44

[988]

BRITISH STANDARDS INSTITUTION. Universal Decimal Classification. English full edition. London, British Standards Institution, 1943-. (*BS:1000.*)

English language ed. of a scheme now available in 23 languages. Issued in pts., many now designated 2nd ed., each comprising schedule and subject index. Classes in humanities and social sciences tend to be available in larger class units than those in science and technology (*e.g.* 33 'Economics' (1985); 621.3 'Electrical engineering' (1989)).

....*(contd.)*
Revised at regular intervals, most schedules, especially those in class 600 which accounts for 63 of the 102 issued parts, modified since 1980 (*e.g. 65/651 + 657/659 Management and organisation of industry and commerce* (1991)). Updated by *Extensions and corrections to the UDC* (ISSN: 00145424).

UDC, produced under the auspices of the International Federation of Documentation, is an extension and modification of the Dewey Decimal Classification. Although the basic order of classes remains similar to Dewey, the scheme has developed separately and now shows many variations. It also incorporates greater synthetic facilities, by use of conventional symbols, enabling the classifier to express relationships between topics. Mainly used in special libraries, especially in science and industry, where close classification of technical materials is an important requirement. *Class No:* 025.44

[989]

—BRITISH STANDARDS INSTITUTION. Universal Decimal Classification. International medium edition. English text. 2nd ed. London, British Standards Institution, 1993. 2v. £247. (*BS:1000M.*)

Pt.1 *Systematic tables* (xxiv,914p. ISBN: 0580225534); pt.2 *Index* (iii,531p. ISBN:0580225542). First published in this form 1985-88, replacing earlier abridged eds.

Contains approx. 60,000 classifications as opposed to the 220,000 of the full ed. Includes modifications authorized in *Extensions and additions to the UDC* up to and including Series 14 no.3, September 1992. Updated by supplements, no. 3 issued 1997 (104p. ISBN: 0580225542).
Class No: 025.44

[990]

—FÉDÉRATION INTERNATIONALE DE DOCUMENTATION. Bibliographical survey of UDC editions. The Hague, Fédération Internationale de Documentation, 1982. v,73p. Dfl45. (*FID publication, 573.*) ISBN: 9266005738.

Lists 'Extensions' to UDC, published editions (full, medium, abridged, special subjects (with an index)), guides and textbooks. Index of publishers. Updated to 1980.
Class No: 025.44

[991]

—McILWANIE, I.C. Guide to the use of UDC: an introductory guide to the use and application of the Universal Decimal Classification. Rev. ed. The Hague, International Federation for Information and Documentation, 1995. 124p. £38.75. (*FID occasional paper, no. 703.*) ISBN: 926600703x. *Class No:* 025.44

[992]

DEWEY, M. Dewey Decimal Classification and relative index. Mitchell, J.S., *and others eds.* 21st ed. Albany, N.Y., Forest Press, 1996. 4v. £220;$325. ISBN: 0910608504.

V.1 Introduction. Tables; v.2-3 Schedules; v.4 Relative index. Manual. First published 1876; 20th ed. 1989.

Regularly revised by the Decimal Classification Editorial Policy Committee, which includes representatives from the LA and ALA, as well as drawing on the expertise of outside groups. Used in most countries, and in most libraries in the UK, especially public and smaller academic libraries. The 21st ed. includes revised schedules for class 350-354 Public administration, class 370 Education and class 560-590 Life sciences.

Revisions between editions are notified in the annual

....*(contd.)*
Dewey Decimal Classification: additions, notes and decisions. The classification is also available on CD-ROM as *Dewey for Windows* (annual updating). Revised discs contain additions and modifications to the schedules.
Class No: 025.44

[993]

—Abridged Dewey Decimal Classification and relative index. Mitchell, J.S., *and others eds.* 13th ed. Albany, N.Y., Forest Press, 1997. lii,1023p. £65;$90. ISBN: 0910608598.

Intended for smaller libraries with less than 20,000 titles.
Class No: 025.44

[994]

—CHAN, L.M., *and others.* Dewey Decimal Classification: a practical guide. 2nd ed. Albany, N.Y., Forest Press, 1996. xvi,246p. £27:$40. ISBN: 0910608555.

First published 1994.

13 chaps. with exercises; glossary (p.213-28) and index. '(A)n essential adjunct' (*Library Association record*, v.98(11), November 1996, p.593). *Class No:* 025.44

[995]

—Dewey Decimal Classification for school libraries. British and international edition. Smith, M.L., *ed.* Albany, N.Y., Forest Press, 1986. ix,179p. £20. ISBN: 0910608350.

Rev. ed. of *Introduction to the Dewey Decimal Classification for British schools.* (3rd ed. 1977. First published 1961).

Abridgement of the 19th ed. *Class No:* 025.44

[996]

LIBRARY OF CONGRESS. Subject Cataloging Division. Processing Department. **Library of Congress classification.** Washington, D.C., Library of Congress, 1917-.

Published in classes and subclasses in various edition states. Schedules individually indexed. Revisions now produced more frequently, recent examples include: Class H. Social sciences (1997. $36. ISBN: 0884409197); Class J. Political science (1997. $36. ISBN: 0844409006); Class PN. Literature (general) (1997. $26. ISBN: 0844409200).

Originated simply for the arrangement of the Library of Congress collection before it reached its present size, the classification has grown to be one of the most widely used in the US, and is found in a number of UK libraries, especially the 'old' universities.

Kept up-to-date by *L.C. classification. Additions and changes* (Quarterly. $105. ISSN: 00417912). The more recently updated schedules are also available as a component of the CD-ROM *Classification Plus: Library of Congress classification and Library of Congress subject headings* (Washington, D.C., Library of Congress, 1996-. Quarterly. $470. ISSN: 10869263). With issue 4 1997 the following classes are included: B-BJ, C, E-F, H, KZ, J, L, N, PN, Q, R, S, T, U-V, Z. *Class No:* 025.44

[997]

—Combined indexes to the Library of Congress Classification schedules. Olson, N.B., *comp.* Washington, D.C., United States Historical Documents Institute, 1974. 15v. ISBN: 0882220500.

Set 1: *Author-number index,* 2v. Set 2: *Biographical subject index,* 3v. Set 3: *Classified index to persons,* 3v. Set 4: *Geographial name index.* Set 5: *Subject keyword index,* 6v. *Class No:* 025.44

[998]

—IMMROTH, J.P. Immroth's guide to the Library of Congress Classification. Chan, L.M. 4th ed. Englewood, Colo., Libraries Unlimited, 1990. xiv,436p. £29;$42.50. ISBN: 0872876047.

First published 1968; 3rd ed. 1980.

5 main sections: Principles, structure and format - Notation - Tables - Individual classes (p.115-292) - Classification of special types of library materials. Bibliography (p.417-26). Index. The standard guide. *Class No:* 025.44

[999]

—Super LCCS: Gale's Library of Congress classification schedules: combined with additions and changes. Detroit, Gale, 1971-. Annual.

Brings together in one sequence the full schedules and all additions, changes and eliminations of numbers as notified in the quarterly *L.C. classification. Additions and changes* (above). Most recent ed. cumulating changes through 1997 issued in 42 v. (ISBN: £2507. ISBN: 0787613932). Vols. can be purchased individually. Also available in microfiche (£1514) and as a quarterly updated CD-ROM (£2265). *Class No:* 025.44

[1000]

SCOTT, M.L. Conversion tables: LC-Dewey, Dewey-LC. Englewood, Colo., Libraries Unlimited, 1993. viii,365p. 53.95;$60. ISBN: 1563080176.

Entries give two class nos. and brief descriptor. '(M)ust be used with caution... (t)here is no indication of what edition of the schedules are represented in the lists, how numbers were selected or what pitfalls there may be' (*American reference books annual*, v.25, 1994, p.256). *Class No:* 025.44

Bibliographies

[1001]

International classification and indexing bibliography. Dahlberg, I., *comp.* Frankfurt am Main, Indeks Verlag, 1982-85. £19.15 per v.

V.1 *Classification systems and thesauri, 1950-1982* (1982. xiv,143p. ISBN: 3886723003); v.2 *Reference tools and conferences in classification and indexing* (1984. xx,140p. ISBN: 3886723011); v.3 *Classification and indexing systems theory - structure - methodology.* (1985. xii,211p. ISBN: 388672302X).

'(C)overage is amazingly extensive, impressively far reaching' (*International journal of reviews in librarianship and information science*, v.4(2), 1988, p.62-4, on v.3). *Class No:* 025.44(01)

[1002]

—Knowledge organization literature (in *Knowledge organization*. Würzburg, Ergon-Verlag, 1993-. Quarterly).

The periodical *Knowledge organization* is a continuation of *International classification*, published quarterly from 1974. In this title the bibliography appeared regularly as 'Classification literature'.

Appears in most issues of *Knowledge organization*. V.24(4), 1997 has briefly annotated entries for about 160 items (p.262-70) with an author index. Extends *International classification and indexing bibliography* (above), offering much more detailed treatment of the field than in general library science indexing sources such as *Library and information science abstracts* (*q.v.*). *Class No:* 025.44(01)

[1003]

SATIJA, M.P. *and* **SINGH, A. Bibliography of Colon Classification** 1930-1993. New Delhi, M.D. Publications, 1994. 129p. US$50. ISBN: 8185880298.

Unnanotated entries for items relating to Ranganathan's Colon Classification many, but not all, emanating from India. *Class No:* 025.44(01)

Handbooks & Manuals

[1004]

MACELLA, R. *and* **NEWTON, R. A New manual of classification.** Aldershot, Gower, 1994. xii,287p. diags. £49.50;$69.55. ISBN: 0566075474.

Extensive reworking of W.C.B. Sayer's *A Manual of classification for librarians* (first published 1926, 5th ed., revised by A. Maltby, 1975. (ISBN: 023396603X)).

10 chapters, coverage including theory, general schemes (DDC, LC, UDC, Colon and Bibliographic Classification), special schemes, indexes, thesauri and classification, policy and administration, computers and classification, OPACs and classification and automatic classification. 'It is disappointing that a work that covers so much ground ends with a very brief five page bibliography and a rather cursory seven page index' (*Library Association record*, v.97(5), May 1995, p.281). *Class No:* 025.44(035)

Library Technical Services

[1005]

303 software programs to use in your library: descriptions, evaluations and practical advice. Dewey, P.R., *ed.* Chicago, American Library Association, 1998. xv,224p. (*101 micro series.*) ISBN: 0838907229.

Rev. ed. of *101 software packages to use in your library* (1987) and *202+ software packages to use in your library* (1992).

Brief descriptions and evaluations in sections: Accessibility for people with disabilities ... Acquisitions ... Cataloging ... Circulation systems ... Online catalogs ... Word processing and office suites. Appendices list computer periodicals, suggested reading, vendors and Internet resources. Glossary (p.209-20); index of software by name. *Class No:* 025.4900

[1006]

Directory of library automation software, systems and services. Medford, N.J., Information Today, 1993-. Biennial. $89.

Continues *Directory of information management software for libraries, information centers, record centers*, first published 1983.

1998 ed. (Cibbarelli, P.R. & Cibbarelli, S.E. *eds.* 429p. ISBN: 1573870447) contains detailed decriptions of products commercially available in North America. Information includes hardware/system requirements, components and applications, installation sites, vendor contact detail with Internet address, comments by vendors and citations to recent articles describing the product. Also provides a general bibliography of books and articles and various listings such as library automation consultants. Indexed by product name and computer hardware vendor. *Class No:* 025.4900

[1007]

The European directory of software for libraries and information centres. Wood, J., *comp.* Aldershot, Ashgate, 1993. x,251p. $73.95. ISBN: 1857420926.

Succeeds *A Directory of library and information retrieval software for microcomputers*, first published 1985, 4th ed. 1990.

Produced at the Library and Information Technology Centre, South Bank University. Contains information on *c.*275 software packages A-Z by name. Detail includes supplier, dealer/distributor, general description with some evaluative comment, operating system, special hardware requirements, price and references to reviews. Supplier, function, operating system and geographical indexes. UK produced software *c.*35% of total. Many entries with minimal data, but still 'an excellent directory, both in design and execution' (*Aslib information*, v.21(6), June 1993, p.258). *Class No:* 025.4900

[1008]

LEEVES, J. *and* **RUSSELL, R. Libsys UK:** a directory of library systems in the United Kingdom. London, Library and Information Technology Centre, South Bank University, 1995. x,291p. tables. £35. ISBN: 0951241281.

With *Library systems in Europe* (below) partially succeeds 2nd ed. of *Library systems: a buyer's guide* (1989, first published 1987).

Covers 30 integrated library management systems Adlib-Unicorn, those used exclusively in schools or for full text and information retrieval excluded. Full accounts, including some critical analysis. General Information on operating system/hardware, networking, modules available, operation and user interface, etc., followed by sections on individual functions (*e.g.* cataloguing). Introductory 'Library systems review' (p.1-24); supplier index (p.279-81).
Class No: 025.4900

[1009]

—Library systems in Europe a directory & guide. Leeves, J., *and others comps.* London, TFPL Publishing, 1994. v,401p. tables. ISBN: 1870889479.

Compiled on behalf of the Library and Information Technology Centre for the European Commission.

Covers 29 systems ABSYS ... VUBIS. Similar format and some overlap with *Libysys UK* (above), but generally more detailed and with useful tables 'Customers by type' and 'Customers by country'. *Class No:* 025.4900

Bibliographies

[1010]

An Annotated bibliography of automation in libraries. London, Aslib, 1968-80. 4v.

Series of 4 titles covering material published 1964-78. First v. as *Bibliography of library automation 1964-1967* (British National Bibliography, 1968. 107p. ISBN: 0900220007). Other vols., all published by Aslib, 1968-72 (1973. x,85p. ISBN: 0851420508), 1972-75 (1976. vii,147p. ISBN: 0851420796) and 1975-78 (1980. vi,78p. ISBN: 0851421326). 1968-72 has variant title *An Annotated bibliography of library automation.*

Nearly 2,500 entries across the series.
Class No: 025.4900(01)

[1011]

Guide to technical services resources. Johnson, P., *ed.* Chicago, American Library Association, 1994. xiv,313p. £53.95;$65. ISBN: 0838906249.

A 'first attempt at a comprehensive and practical guide to the principal information resources for technical service practitioners, educators and students' (Introduction, p.1). Well annotated entries across a very wide range of subject areas. Arrangement in 12 chapters (*e.g.* Acquisitions; Authority work; Collection management; Database management), each with introduction. Author/title and subject indexes. Most material included published after 1985; some entries for periodical articles and a few for Internet accessible resources. Superbly executed, one of the most important recent library science reference works.
Class No: 025.4900(01)

[1012]

KILPATRICK, T.L. Microcomputers and libraries: a bibliographic sourcebook. Metuchen, N.J., Scarecrow Press, 1987. xi,726p. £44.55;$49.50. ISBN: 0810819775.

Attempts to cover 'the literature of microcomputer technology as it is related to, and has influenced libraries, library services and library personnel' (*Introduction*). 1,944 annotated entries arranged by main entry in 39 subject groups. Separate listing of reviews of software and systems, books and serials adding a further 1,744 entries. Author, subject and system index. Mainly American material, but some British publications included. 505.00/01$aUpdated by *Microcomputers in libraries: a bibliographic sourcebook 1986-1989* (Metuchen, N.J., Scarecrow Press, 1990. x,1090p. £80.55;$89.50. ISBN: 0810823926) listing a further 5,407 items. *Class No:* 025.4900(01)

[1013]

Library hi tech bibliography. Ann Arbor, Pierian Press, 1986-95. Annual. ISSN: 10404333.

Continued the same publisher's *Automation in libraries: a LITA bibliography 1978-1982* (1983. ISBN: 0876501579).

Each v. provided 10-15 self-contained bibliographies on selected topics from the field of library automation. V.9 (1994) had bibliographies on 13 subjects including artificial intelligence, E-Mail, retrospective conversion and video display hazards and ergonomic issues. Title and author index in each issue. Cumulated subject index to volumes 1-5 in, *RSR*, v.17(3), 1989, p.47-50. *Class No:* 025.4900(01)

Handbooks & Manuals

[1014]

COHN, J.M., *and others.* **Planning for library automation:** a practical handbook. London, Library Association Publishing, 1998. viii.140p. tables. ISBN: 1856042952.

First published in the US 1997 by Neal—Schuman under the title *Planning automation: a how-to-do-it manual.* Revised and adapted for the UK by G. Muirhead.

Focuses on planning for an integrated system. 16 brief chaps. each with a listing of sources and readings. Index.
Class No: 025.4900(035)

Reference & Information Services

[1015]
The Burwell world directory of information brokers. Burwell, H.P., *ed.* Houston, Burwell Enterprises, 1978-. Annual (irregular). $105. ISSN: 01471678.

Title varies: prior to 1991 issued as *Directory of fee-based information services.* Data collection and distribution in Europe by TFPL, London.

Covers information brokers, document delivery firms, freelance librarians, etc., plus some public and academic libraries providing information services for a fee. US and international sections, former arranged by state, latter by country. Entries include address, contact name, subject areas, services, fee structure, language expertise and *c.*100 word descriptions. Various indexes including city, company, subjects and services. 1,776 entries in the 12th ed. (1996. xiv,796p.), international coverage much improved with 701 entries from outside US (269 UK). Also available on disk ($150) and as a freely searchable database through Burwell's WWW site at http://www.burwellinc.com. *Class No:* 025.5

[1016]
Directory of European information brokers and consultants. Crawford, M.J., *ed.* Grimsby, Effective Technology Marketing, 1986-. Annual (irregular). £65.

Eds. 1-5 as *Directory of information brokers and consultants.*

The 8th ed. (1995. v,142p. ISBN: 1874128111) has 204 entries by title, giving name, contact details, working language and 20-80 word description under heading 'expertise'. Subject expertise, information expertise, personal name and location indexes. Coverage is of organizations and individuals operating on a fee basis; services attached to larger institutions included. Despite title all but 55 of the brokers and consultants are UK based. *Class No:* 025.5

[1017]
Directory of public libraries offering information and referral services. Russo, S., *ed.* 2nd ed. Chicago, American Library Association/Public Library Association, 1994. x,146p.

Prepared for the Community Information Section of the Public Library Association. First published 1992.

State then city listing with a brief outline of services offered. Various additional listings in appendix including 'Libraries with separate I & R departments' and 'Libraries with multilingual or minority staff'. *Class No:* 025.5

Bibliographies

[1018]
MURFIN, M.E. *and* **WYNAR, L.R. Reference service an annotated bibliographic guide.** Littleton, Colo., Libraries Unlimited, 1977. 294p. ISBN: 0872871320.

Covers early history, theory and philosophy, reference teaching, reference librarians and services, reference process, sources of information, reference research, co-operation in reference, information centers, and information retrieval. 1,285 entries for articles and separates in English. Divided into 14 chapters each with a concise introduction.

A *Supplement 1976-1982* by the same authors (Libraries Unlimited, 1984. xii,353p. ISBN: 0872874028) adds a further 1,668 items. Similar scope and arrangement to the parent v., but with expanded coverage of computer applications in reference services. *Class No:* 025.5(01)

Interlending Services

[1019]
BOUCHER, V. Interlibrary loan practices handbook. 2nd ed. Chicago, American Library Association, 1997. xii,249p. illus., charts. $45. ISBN: 0838906672.

First published 1984.

'(I)ntended for those without interlibrary loan experience who seek advice on how to proceed' (*Preface* p.ix). 7 chaps. including instructions for borrowing and lending libraries, reproduction and copyright law, dissertations and international loans. Each chap. contains extensive directory material; 34 appendices including 'National interlibrary loan code for the United States 1993' and 'Guidelines for the loan of rare and unique materials'. Indexed. *Class No:* 025.6

[1020]
BRITISH LIBRARY. Document Supply Centre. **Directory of library codes:** including guidelines to the national network for interlending and document supply. Boston Spa, British Library Document Supply Centre, 1972-. Biennial (irregular).

Distributed free to registered BLDSC users.

Key to the location codes given by the Document Supply Centre. Arranged alphabetically by code with a library name index. 1997 ed. (100p. ISBN: 0712321497) also includes information on making request to BLDSC, membership and use of regional library systems, lending policies and 'A Guide to coded replies' (p.81-99) *Class No:* 025.6

[1021]
INTERNATIONAL FEDERATION OF LIBRARY ASSOCIATIONS AND INSTITUTIONS. A Guide to centres of international lending. Barwick, M.M. *and* Connolly, P.A., *comps.* 5th ed. Boston Spa, IFLA Offices for UAP and International Lending, 1995. xxiii,141p. £15. ISBN: 0712321128.

First published 1975, 4th ed. 1990. Title varies: eds 1-3 as *A Brief guide to centres of international lending and photocopying.*

Based on information gathered by questionnaire, over 190 countries represented. Directory section (A-Z by country) gives practical details (*e.g.* address, forms, payments, loan periods) required by national inter-lending services or their equivalents. Some national union catalogues also briefly noted. Prefaced (p.vii-xii) by 'International lending: principles and guidelines for procedure'. *Class No:* 025.6

[1022]
MORRIS, L.R. Interlibrary loan policies directory. 5th ed. New York, Neal-Schuman, 1995. viii,828p. $119.95. ISBN: 1555701981.

First published 1975; 4th ed. 1991.

Policies for *c.*1,400 US and a few Canadian libraries. Includes details on transmission of requests, fees and policies for different types of material. Geographic arrangement with library name index. Limited coverage, 'not comprehensive, not without errors and not as updatable as the *OCLC name address directory*' (*American reference books annual*, v.27, (1996), p.259). *Class No:* 025.6

Bibliographies

[1023]

Cumulative bibliography on interlending and document supply. Cornish, G.P., *comp.* Boston Spa, IFLA Office for International Lending, 1989. 80p. ISBN: 0712320644.

Cumulates the bibliographies which appeared in the journal *Interlending and document supply* from 1979. 1,065 entries arranged by author A-Z. Unannotated, but English translations given for foreign language titles. Subject index (p.77-80) under very broad terms. Updating bibliographies continue to appear in *Interlending and document supply* at approximately six-monthly intervals (*e.g.* no.XXXII in the series in v.25(3), 1997, p.126-32). *Class No:* 025.6(01)

026 Libraries

Libraries

Worldwide

[1024]

World guide to libraries. München, Saur, 1966-. Biennial. £340;$450. (*Handbook of international documentation and information, vol. 8.*) ISSN: 09360085.

Frequency varies: recent editions issued approx. biennially.

Also available on CD-ROM as *World guide to libraries Plus* with the addition of records from *American library directory* and *World guide to special libraries* (*q.v.*).

The 13th ed. (1998. 2v.) contains 43,654 entries for libraries in 192 countries. Largely questionnaire based. Aims to cover all general libraries with holdings of more than 30,000 volumes and special libraries with more than 10,000 volumes. Arranged by country A-Z (English form of name), then according to type of library: National libraries; General research libraries; University/college libraries; Professional school libraries/school libraries; Government libraries; Ecclesiastical libraries; Corporate business libraries; Special libraries maintained by other institutions; Public libraries. Includes separate entries for departmental libraries of universities, etc. Complete entry gives name, address and contact detail (including email and URL), year founded, name of director or head, important holdings and special collections, main departments, statistics by type of material, name of accessible databanks or hosts, inter-library participation and membership of associations. Indexed by library name. The fullest source available, but the data given for each library is limited and in many cases incomplete. Best regarded as a worldwide checklist and source of addresses. For North America and much of Europe, national and regional directories usually give fuller detail.
Class No: 026/027(100)

[1025]

—World of learning. London, Europa Publications, 1947-. Annual. ISSN: 00842117.

Includes a section on leading libraries and archives for each country, giving address and brief details (*e.g.* Italy, p.805-9 of 48th ed. (1998) *c.*165 entries).
Class No: 026/027(100)

Internet

[1026]

Libweb: library servers via WWW. Dowling, T., *comp.* Berkeley, Ca., Univ. of California Regents. World Wide Web resource.

URL: http://sunsite.Berkeley.EDU/Libweb. Date reviewed 25th May 1998.

The best of a number of WWW sites providing links to library home pages worldwide. About 2,000 libraries in 70 countries covered, links arranged in geographical sections,

.... *(contd.)*

US divided by library type. Also includes a 'Related sites' listing, keyword search engine and submission form for new or revised entries. *Class No:* 026/027(100)(003.41)

Europe

[1027]

Directory of special collections in Western Europe. Gallico, A., *ed.* London, Bowker-Saur, 1993. [vii],146p. £47;$75. ISBN: 086291616x.

IFLA Office for International Interlending inspired publication which aims to 'make known substantial collections in specific subjects which are held in larger collections' (*Introduction*). *c.*350 entries by country (Austria, Sweden, Switzerland excluded, UK 133 entries), information including library address, collection name, subject, special strengths, no. of items, types of material, special features, loan availability and catalogues. Index to institutions; subject indexes in English, French and German. Records some obscure collections, but coverage is patchy with many important omissions. *Class No:* 026/027(4)

[1028]

The European book world. Part II. Libraries. Cambridge, Anderson Rand, 1996. 4v. £320. ISBN: 187353910x.

The other two parts of *The European book world* cover publishers and the book trade.

Questionnaire based data on 55,000 libraries in 58 countries, including all the states of the former Soviet Union. Full entries comprise: contact detail, library type, year established, no. of employees, no. of qualified staff, budgets, personnel, related organizations, holdings statistics, cataloguing systems, facilities, inter-library participation and names of special collections. A-Z country then town arrangement, 8,074 entries for UK. Subject index in v.3, organization and personal name indexes in v.4. Covers a greater number of European libraries than any comparable source. *The European book world* is also available on CD-ROM (annual updates intended, £350 initial purchase). Although facilitating many more search modes than the printed set, 'the operation of the disk is behind current standards... . The program runs entirely in DOS and its screens are black and white in an old-fashioned typewriter font' (*Reference reviews*, v.11(1), 1995, p.5).
Class No: 026/027(4)

[1029]

Guide to libraries in Western Europe: national, international and government libraries. Dale, P., *ed.* 2nd ed. London, British Library Science Reference and Information Service, 1994. iv,169p. ISBN: 0712308105.

First published 1991. Issued as a companion to *Guide to libraries and information units in government departments and other organizations* (*q.v.*).

Covers 645 'libraries and information services in government departments and other 'official' organizations who perform a national role' (*Preface*). Main section, by country (sub-arranged by English library name), gives brief details including address, librarian, stock and subject

....(contd.)
coverage, availability, hours, services and publications. Further sections: National libraries - National library associations - British Council libraries. Indexed by library name, organization and subject. *Class No:* 026/027(4)

Europe—Eastern

[1030]
Guide to libraries in Central and Eastern Europe. Hughes, M. *and* Wilson, P., *comps*. London, British Library Science Reference and Information Service, 1992. [iv],82p., maps. (*Key resources series.*) ISBN: 0712307958.

Aims to cover 'those collections which would be of use to Western governments, businesses and other bodies contributing to the economic restructuring of Eastern Europe' (Introduction). 235 entries (8 for UK libraries with major Eastern European collections) for national, major academic and important special, research and government libraries. Subject and geographic indexes. Many entries contain minimal data. '(O)bviously an interim publication, but still very useful' (*Reference reviews*, v.7(3), 1993, p.9). *Class No:* 026/027(401)

[1031]
—East-West links: directory of libraries and book agents in the former Soviet Union and Central-Eastern Europe. Hogg, R. *and* Ladizesky, K., *comps*. Boston Spa, British Library Document Supply Centre, 1996. xiii,240p. ISBN: 0712321438.

First published 1994 as *Directory of libraries and book agents in the former Soviet Union and Eastern Europe*. Approx. biennial updating intended (ISSN: 13620113).

'(B)ased on addresses used by the Slavonic, Central & East European Acquisitions department at the British Library Document Supply Centre' (p.v). 1,593 entries (418 earlier ed.) giving address and other contact information only. Organization and location (town) indexes. Appendices list Cyrillic and other East European serials currently received by BLDSC. *Class No:* 026/027(401)

Great Britain

[1032]
The Aslib directory of information sources in the United Kingdom. Reynard, K.W. *and* Reynard, J.M.E., *eds*. 9th ed. London, Aslib, 1996. ix,1595p. £250. ISBN: 0851423213.

First published 1928; 8th ed. 1994. 10th ed. in preparation.

8,461 entries (8,034 8th ed.) for information disseminators of all types, ranging from major academic and public libraries (*e.g.* John Rylands University Library of Manchester; Westminster Libraries and Archives), to specialized commercial, government, research, professional and other organizations (*e.g.* Circus Society; Garden History Society; Jute Importers' Association Ltd.). Entries, arranged A-Z by name, give address with email and detail of Internet home page, acronym, type of organization, contact name, access arrangements, subject coverage (summary terms selected by organization), information services, collections (often extensive lists), printed publications and electronic and video products. Lacks other basic data (*e.g.* opening hours, stock totals). Subject index under detailed headings (p.1391-1595) and list of acronyms and abbreviations, but no other indexes. A CD-ROM version has also been published as *Information sources in the UK*. The best source for tracing

....(contd.)
information providers by subject as well as being the most comprehensive guide to UK library and related organizations available. *Class No:* 026/027(410)

[1033]
A Directory of rare book and special collections in the United Kingdom and the Republic of Ireland. Bloomfield, B.C., *ed*. 2nd ed. London, Library Association, 1997. xxiii,740p. illus. ISBN: 1856040631.

Published in association with The Rare Books Group of the Library Association. First published 1985.

Adds 50 new entries to the *c.*5,000 collections in 1,300 locations included in the 1st ed. and makes some general updating. Not comprehensive, 'there are a number of local collections in public libraries, National Trust libraries, and some society libraries that have escaped report' (p.xii). Most personal private collections also excluded. Entries, in geographic county/town arrangement give address, hours, admission conditions, research facilities, brief history and detailed description, including contents, catalogues and published references. Indexed by place, subject, collection and library (p.697-740). Extensive detail for many libraries (*e.g.* British Library, p.132-80; Nottingham University, p.484-87), but updating in this ed. is relatively modest with apparently little energy expended on locating new collections. *Class No:* 026/027(410)

[1034]
Guide to libraries and information units: in government departments and other organizations. Dale, P., *ed*. 32nd ed. London, British Library, 1996. [ii],206p. £36;$65. (*Key resource series.*) ISBN: 0712308288.

First published 1948, now issued approximately biennially. Until 29th ed. appeared under title *Guide to government department and other libraries.*

682 entries (about 150 new to this ed.) arranged alphabetically by name. Still mainly confined to government libraries, but 'also includes other selected organisations whose collections are relevant to subjects which may be of interest to government bodies, or others with similar needs'. Examples include Centre for Policy on Ageing, Lambeth Palace Library, Royal Asiatic Society and Tidy Britain Group. Data given: address (including email and URL); senior staff; stock and coverage (often lengthy descriptions); availability (admission); hours; publications. Good layout. Organization and subject indexes. *Class No:* 026/027(410)

[1035]
Guide to libraries in key UK companies. Dale, P., *comp*. London, British Library Science Reference and Information Service, 1993. viii,169p. £30. (*Key resource series.*) ISBN: 0712307966.

Companion work to *Guide to libraries and information units in government departments* (above), with similar format and detail. Very selective, covering only 196 libraries and information services providing a questionnaire response and 'which are prepared to accept serious enquiries from outside'. Organization and subject indexes; list of organizations by industry sector. A 'good idea which has not gone far enough' (*Aslib information*, v.21(4), April 1993, p.173). *Class No:* 026/027(410)

[1036]

The Libraries directory. 1985/87-. Cambridge, James Clark, 1989-. Triennial (irregular). ISSN: 09614575.

Present title from 1988/90, initial ed. as *The Libraries year book.* Revives the *Libraries, museums and art galleries yearbook,* first published 1897, last issued for 1978/79 in 1981.

The 1996/98 v. (vi,376p.) has main sections: Legal deposit libraries - Public libraries (p.18-90, by authority A-Z) - Archives & record offices - Special libraries (p.125-304, 1,646 entries, including academic libraries) - Irish public libraries - Irish archives and record offices - Irish special libraries - Library & information organizations. Carefully compiled and excellently presented in 3 col. arrangement. Data is much fuller than *Libraries in the United Kingdom and Republic of Ireland* (below). Detail on public libraries includes population served, organizational structure, branches (with addresses), special collections, loan arrangements, stock totals by category, and income and expenditure. Similar treatment for special libraries, although some omissions, especially in the academic sector. Indexed by subjects, special collections and library and institution names (p.345-76). *Class No:* 026/027(410)

[1037]

Libraries in the United Kingdom and Republic of Ireland. London, Library Association, 1960-. Annual. £32.50. ISSN: 13699687.

Now appears annually. 24th ed. (1997. vii,328p.) has sections: Public libraries in the United Kingdom, the Channel Islands and the Isle of Man (arranged by library authority) - Public libraries in the Republic of Ireland - Children's, youth and schools' library services in the United Kingdom - Libraries in academic institutions in the United Kingdom - Selected government, national and special libraries in the United Kingdom - Departments of librarianship and information science - Stop press: new unitary authorities 1998. About 2,500 libraries included. Entries give address (plus fax, email, etc.), chief librarian, other senior personnel and major branch libraries only. No information on subject strengths, hours, etc. Special libraries included 'if they are the main library or organization in their field'. More restricted coverage and less detail than *The Aslib directory* or *The Libraries directory* (above), but 'remains the best and most accurate up-to-date record of UK and Irish libraries available' (*Reference reviews*, v.11(3), 1997, p.6). *Class No:* 026/027(410)

Tables & Data Books

[1038]

LISU annual library statistics: featuring trend analysis of UK public and academic libraries. [Loughborough], Library and Information Statistics Unit, Department of Information and Library Studies, Loughborough University, 1992-. Annual. ISSN: 0967487x.

Continues *Public library statistics: a trend analysis* (annual 1985-91), but expands scope to academic and other libraries.

Each issue gives data for a 10 year period. Sections 1997 issue (x,227p., covering 1986-96): Basic statistics; Public library statistics (p.10-121); Higher education library statistics; National and special libraries; Miscellaneous statistics (book and periodical prices, book trade, library users, PLR results). Commentary accompanies most tables. Excellent presentation. *Class No:* 026/027(410)(083)

Scotland

[1039]

Scottish library and information resources. Dunsire, G., *ed.* 9th ed. Motherwell, Scottish Library Association, 1996. 198p. ISBN: 090064995x.

First published 1968; 8th ed. 1995.

Information on 375 libraries presented A-Z giving address and other contact details, name of librarian, brief notes on special collections and, for public and major academic libraries, individual branches. This ed. issued to reflect changes in public library system resulting from creation of unitary authorities in April 1996. Index of names (organizations and subsidiaries) and titles (collections). *Class No:* 026/027(411)

Ireland

[1040]

Directory of libraries and information services in Ireland. 5th ed. Dublin, The Library Association of Ireland and The Library Association (Northern Ireland Branch), 1996. [iv],294p. ISBN: 0906066115.

First published 1983 as *Directory of libraries in Ireland*; 4th ed. 1993.

Co-operative effort of the Library Association of Ireland and the Library Association Northern Ireland Branch. 311 numbered entries with address and name of librarian followed by data on hours, services, collections, stock by category, computer equipment and systems, etc. Also contains details of 33 professional associations and other library related organizations. Name (libraries, information services, special collections, associations), subject and database/software/system indexes. *Class No:* 026/027(415)

London

[1041]

Guide to libraries in London. McBurney, V., *comp.* London, British Library Science Reference and Information Service, 1995. iv,368p. illus., maps. £46;$75. (*Key resource series.*) ISBN: 0712308210.

Covers 693 libraries of all types in the 33 London boroughs. 'The main emphasis is on libraries and information services offering some access to serious enquirers ... (l)ibraries which offer no outside access ... have been excluded' (*Preface*, p.1). Entries, A-Z by organization name, include information on stock and subject coverage, availability (access conditions), transport (tube and bus routes), special facilities and publications. Libraries listed by borough (p.287-325) with location maps; organization and detailed subject indexes. '(T)here is no comparable work' (*Refer*, v.12(1), Winter 1996, p.10). *Class No:* 026/027(421)

Wales

[1042]

Directory of information sources in Wales. [Cyfeiriadur ffynonellau gwybodaeth yng Nghymru.] Hooper, D.M., *ed.* Cardiff, Welsh Development Agency in association with Information Services Group Wales, 1989. iii,83p. ISBN: 0950340677.

Replaces *Library resources in Wales and Monmouthshire* (1976), one of the regional guides issued by the Reference, Special and Information Section of the Library Association.

160 entries for public, academic and special libraries and information units. Full information including address, designation of person dealing with enquiries, subject

....(*contd.*)
coverage, special collections, services, publications, hours, restrictions on use and additional information. Subject and special collection indexes. *Class No:* 026/027(429)

Germany

[1043]
Adressbuch deutscher Bibliotheken. Deutsches Bibliotheksinstitut, *hrsg*. Berlin, Deutsches Bibliotheksinstitut, 1990-. Biennial. DM30. ISSN: 09395032.

Gives the address of well over 5,000 libraries A-Z by town. Includes special libraries with collections of more than 5,000 vols. Also available on diskette or through the Internet at DBI-Link at http://www.dbilink.de/.
Class No: 026/027(430)

[1044]
Handbuch der Bibliotheken: Deutschland, Österreich, Schweiz. 4.Aufl. München K.G. Saur, 1996. x,670p. DM178. ISBN: 3598112882.

First published 1984; 3rd ed. 1993. Title of earlier eds. *Handbuch der Bibliotheken Bundesrepublik Deutschland, Österreich Schweiz.*

7,795 numbered entries (6,113 for Germany) by town within country sections. Brief data including indication of collection size by types of material, online systems used and subject specialities. The main source for basic information on libraries in German-speaking countries. 5.Aufl. forthcoming early 1998 (DM198). *Class No:* 026/027(430)

[1045]
Handbuch der historischen Buchbestände in Deutschland. Fabian, B., *hrsg*. Hildesheim Olms-Weidmann, 1992-. ISBN: 3487101351, (v.).

'Handbook of historical book collections in Germany'. Published in regional vols. with a culmulated index. Vols. issued out of numerical sequence, 13 completed to end of 1996.

Bd.1 *Schleswig-Holstein, Hamburg, Bremen* (1996. 381p.) arranges entries in Länder sections then by town. Lengthy detail for each library including practical information, history, full description of collections by subject, extensive notes on catalogues and bibliographical references to material relating to the library. Name and subject indexes for each Länder grouping. '(O)ne of the most important bibliographical projects of our time' (*The Library*, v.XVII(3), September 1995 p.27). *Class No:* 026/027(430)

[1046]
Jahrbuch der Deutschen Bibliotheken. Verein Deutschen Bibliotheken, *hrsg*. Wiesbaden, Harrassowitz, 1902-. Biennial. DM138. ISSN: 00752223.

Previously published from Leipzig. Continued to include detail of East German libraries until 1971. From re-unification this coverage resumed replacing the East German equivalent, the triennially published *Jahrbuch der Bibliotheken, Archive und Informationseinrichtungen der Deutschen Demokratischen Republik* (ISSN: 00752215).

Jahr. 57 (1997. 670p.) provides detailed information on 703 major libraries of all types, by town A-Z (p.19-338). Entries include statistical data on holdings, names of senior personnel and lists of publications. Further information on library co-operative systems and a lengthy list of prominent librarians (p.429-644), with details of present and previous positions. Institution and abbreviation index.
Class No: 026/027(430)

[1047]
—Jahrbuch der öffentlichen Bibliotheken. Bad Honnef, Bock & Herchen, 1952-. Biennial. DM68.

Title varies: as *Handbuch der öffentlichen Bibliotheken* until 1989.

Directory of German public libraries. More comprehensive and detailed for this sector than *Jahrbuch der Deutschen Bibliotheken* (above). *Class No:* 026/027(430)

[1048]
O'BRIEN, C. A Guide to library and other archive resources in the Federal Republic of Germany. Kingston-upon-Thames, APEX Centre, Kingston Polytechnic, 1990. 21p. ISBN: 1873152094.

Brief very selective guide to 50 libraries/archives in 16 sections: General ... Economics ... Political science ... University. Entries give basic detail only concentrating on access arrangements and other practical matters. Companion French guide *A Guide to library and archive resources in France* (*q.v.*). *Class No:* 026/027(430)

[1049]
Spezialbibliotheken in Deutschland. Hauke, P., *red.* Bad Honnef, Bock & Herchen 1996-. ISBN: 3883471852, (v.1).

3 vols. published to 1997: Bd.1. *Medizin*; Bd.2. *Kunst, Kultur Museen*. Bd.3. *Parlamente, Behorden, öffentliche Verwaltung*.

Bd.1 has 348 entries arranged A-Z by town. Detail is generally brief including contact information, senior staff, special collections and publications. Institution, personal name, subject keyword and other indexing in each vol.
Class No: 026/027(430)

[1050]
Verzeichnis deutscher Informations- und Dokumentationsstellen: Bundesrepublik Deutschland und Berlin (West). Gesellschaft für Mathematik und Dataverarbeitung, *hrsg*. 5.Ausg. München, Saur, 1990. viii,518p. ISBN: 359810622x.

First published 1974; 4th ed. 1982.

613 entries in 20 subject sections. Entries give address, director, personnel, detailed data on collections/information provided, type of material held, classification system, access to online hosts etc. Subject, geographic, name and abbreviation indexes. *Class No:* 026/027(430)

[1051]
WELSCH, E.K. *and* **DANYEL, J. Archives and libraries in a new Germany.** New York, Council for European Studies, 1994. xviii,372p.

First published 1975 as *Libraries and archives in Germany*. '(H)olders of the original edition should not discard it since repeating its bibliography entirely would have made this volume unmanageable' (*Introduction*, p.i).

Aimed at humanities and social science scholars planning a research trip to Germany. Fairly detailed entries (by Länder after initial section for national archives and government libraries) include scope of collection, access conditions, facilities and publications. Bibliography focussing on works published since 1975 (p.306-50). *Class No:* 026/027(430)

Austria

[1052]
Handbuch der historischen Buchbestände in Österreich. Österreichischen Nationalbibliothek, *hrsg* *and* Lang, H.W., *bearb.*. Hildesheim OlmsWeidmann,, 1994-. DM148 (per v.)

Compiled in collaboration with, and modelled on,

.... *(contd.)*
Handbuch der historichen Buchbestände in Deutschland (above). To be complete in 4 vols., V.1-v.2 (1994-95) cover Vienna. *Class No:* 026/027(436)

[1053]
INFODOC: Bibliotheken, Informations- und Dokumentationseinrichtungen in Österreich. Austria. Bundesministerium für Wissenschaft und Forschung, *hrsg*. Graz, Wolfgang Neugebauer Verlag, 1994. 534p. OS298. ISBN: 3853760562.

Earlier versions 1983 (as *Informationsführer Bibliotheken und Dokumentationsstellen in Österreich*) and 1989.

Covers 1,414 Austrian libraries, information centres, etc. (over 700 in Vienna). Information includes librarian, library type, hours, subjects covered, special collections and publications. Good coverage of departmental libraries of academic and research institutions. Entries regionally arranged; comprehensively indexed by subject, institution, etc. (p.453-534). *Class No:* 026/027(436)

Czechoslovakia

[1054]
Adresář knihoven a informačních institucí CR. Praha, Národni knihovna CR, 1995. 292p. ISBN: 8070502169.

Replaces directory with similar title issued in 2 v. 1991.

Main section (p.9-200) lists libraries and information centres by code no. giving address and contact detail only. Comprehensive index (p.203-92). *Class No:* 026/027(437)

[1055]
BILKOVA, S. Adresář knihoven ČR. Brno, Sdružení Knihoven ČR/Moravzká Zemzká Knihovna, 1995. 154p. (*Informacni zdroje, sv. 5.*) ISBN: 8070510862.

Geographically arranged listing containing fuller detail on the libraries included than *Adresář knihoven a informačních institucí ČR* (above). Also provides biographical sketches for some principal librarians. *Class No:* 026/027(437)

Slovakia

[1056]
KIMLIČKA, S. Katalóg slovenských knižníc: fondy, služby, špecialisti. [Catalogue of Slovak libraries: holdings, services, specialists.] Bratislava, STIMUL, 1992. 128p. ISBN: 8085697033.

Directory of Slovakian research, university and college libraries. Full detail with English translation of headings. Separate listing of specialist staff with name index (p.108-28). *Class No:* 026/027(437.6)

Poland

[1057]
Guide to Polish libraries and archives. Lewanski, R.C., *comps*. Boulder, Co., East European Quarterly, (distr. by Columbia Univ. Press, New York), 1974. x,209p. $47.50. (*East European monographs, no.6.*) ISBN: 0231038968.

Covers major libraries and archives only, with the emphasis on sources in Polish history, civilization and society. Detailed entries, including descriptions of special collections and subject strengths. Arranged by town A-Z, then repository; subject index. Bibliography (p.190-95). *Class No:* 026/027(438)

[1058]
Informator o bibliotekach i ośrodkach informacji w Polsce 1996/997. Sadowska, J. *and* Stefańczyk, E. Warszawa, Biblioteka Narodowa, 1997. xii,423p. ISBN: 8370092128.

English title 'Directory of libraries and information centres in Poland 1996/1997'. Earlier ed. for 1995 (ISBN: 8370091695).

3,668 entries A-Z by town. Detail includes address, library type, holdings, catalogues, computer systems, CD-ROMs held. Indexed (p.317-423) by library and information centre name, library type, CD-ROM database and keyword. *Class No:* 026/027(438)

Hungary

[1059]
KISS, J. Libraries in Hungary. 2nd rev. & enl. ed. Budapest, Association of Hungarian Librarians and National Széchényi Library, Centre for Library Science and Methodology, 1988. 147p. illus.

Translated by D. Szekely. First ed. 1972.

Narrative description of Hungarian libraries. Chapters on types of library (public, school, special etc.), and background historical survey. Also contains information on libraries and government regulation of librarianship. Basic statistics (p.99-101). *Class No:* 026/027(439)

France

[1060]
ASSOCIATION DES BIBLIOTHÉCAIRES FRANÇAIS. Répertoire des bibliothèques spécialisées françaises. Espérou, M., *ed.* Paris, La Documentation française, 1994. 522p. FFr300. ISBN: 2900177103.

Guide to 1,085 special libraries with nationally significant collections. Both private and public sector libraries covered, including those of museums, learned societies, etc. Geographically arranged entries each with a brief description and notes on services provided. Subject and institution indexes *Class No:* 026/027(44)

[1061]
—LELEU-ROUVRAY, G. Le Fil d'Ariane: bibliothéques specialisées de Paris et de la région parisienne. Saint-Maur-des-Fosses, G. Leleu-Rouvray, 1994. xxviii,454p. FFr400. ISBN: 2950827500.

English subtitle *Special libraries in Paris and greater Paris*. Revised printing to January 1995 (FFr410. ISBN: 295082759).

Well-organised guide to 363 libraries. Entries, under *c.*150 subject headings 'Actualité et presse ... Zoologie', provide information on access arrangements, services and subject specialisms. Indexed. English language introduction and list of subject headings. *Class No:* 026/027(44)

[1062]
BAGHDADI, N. *and* **SUZUKI, N. Papyrus: répertoire des bibliothèques,** d'archives et de centres de documentation 1995-1996. 2e éd. Paris, CEP-Pilotes, 1995. x,821p. FFr660. ISBN: 2909288021.

Directory of *c.*2,500 libraries and information centres of all types throughout France (1st ed. confined to the Paris region). Generally short entries in 3 col. format giving address, access conditions, hours, scope, special collections, services, etc. Index of subject specialities (p.624-754); directory of services and suppliers; organization index. Probably the best of the recently published French library directories. *Class No:* 026/027(44)

[1063]

PARIS. Centre National d'Art et de Culture Georges Pompidou. Bibliothèque Publique d'Information. **Oriente express: répertoire des bibliothèques et centres de documentation parisiens.** Paris, Bibliothèque publique d'information au Centre Pompidou, 1985-. Irregular FFr150. (*BPI pratique 1.*) ISSN: 02461595.

Guide to libraries and documentation centres in the Paris region accessible to the public. Entries (281 in 6e. éd. (1996. 362p.)) include information on subjects covered, catalogues and services. Topic index. *Class No:* 026/027(44)

[1064]

Patrimonie des bibliothèques de France: un guide des régions. Reder, A-M., *ed.* Pais Payot, 1995. 11v. illus. FFr1,500 (set). ISBN: 2228889776.

Comprises 10 regional vols., *e.g.* VII. *Aquitaine, Languedoc-Roussillon, Midi-Pyrénées*, and general index.

A guide to the history and holdings of French libraries, mainly in the public sector. Each regional vol. covers a relatively restricted number of libraries (*e.g.* 19 in v.IX) and provides a broad description of history, notable buildings, major collections, etc. Practical details such as opening hours in appendix. More suited to the general public than the serious researcher. *Class No:* 026/027(44)

[1065]

READER, K. A Guide to library and archive resources in France. Kingston-upon-Thames, APEX Centre, Kingston Polytechnic, 1990. 26p. ISBN: 1873152086.

Brief, very selective guide in 20 subject categories Agriculture - Urban and regional planning, preceeded by a general section. *c.*70 libraries/archives covered, all in Paris and its environs. Minimal detail on subject strengths, emphasis being on practical matters such as hours, access conditions, etc. *Class No:* 026/027(44)

[1066]

WELSCH, E.K. Archives and libraries in France: with 1991 supplement. New York, Council for European Studies, 1991. xxiii,147p.

Cover title *Research resources: France: libraries and archives in France*. Reprint, with brief 23 page updating supplement, of work last issued 1979. First published 1973.

Describes *c.*60 libraries in considerable detail with the emphasis on special collections and services. No indexes. Bibliography (p.123-38); supplement also includes revised bibliographical listings. *Class No:* 026/027(44)

Italy

[1067]

Catálogo delle biblioteche d'Italia. Roma, ICCU/Milano, Editrice Bibliografico, 1993-. ISBN: 8871070305.

At head of title page 'Ministero per i Beni Culturali Ambientali, Ufficio Centrale per i Beni Librari e gli Istituti Culturali, Istituto Centrale per il Catalogo Unico delle Biblioteche Italiane e per le Informazioni Bibliografiche'. Replaces *Annuario delle biblioteche italiane* 3. ed. issued in 5 vols., 1969-81.

Abruzzo (1993. x,171p.) has entries for 317 libraries by administrative region, then town. Brief data, generally including foundation date, type of library, hours, access, services, holdings, catalogues and classification systems. Lacks detail on subject specialisms or collections.
Class No: 026/027(450)

[1068]

Guide to Italian libraries and archives. Lewanski, R.J. *and* Lewanski, R.C., *comps.* New York, Council for European Studies, 1979. ii,101p.

List of major archives and libraries by city giving history, holdings, scope and subject profile, special collections, catalogues, hours etc. Further list by 21 categories of other archives and libraries with important subject collections. Bibliography of library guides (p.93-98).
Class No: 026/027(450)

[1069]

MARRARO, F. Repertorio delle biblioteche italiane. 2. ed. Roma, Oligata Editrice 1993. 574p.

First published 1989.

Directory of *c.*13,000 libraries. Regional/provincial arrangement with further division according to library type and town. Entries provide brief information only, usually contact detail, director, no. of vols. and no. of periodicals. Larger libraries also have short annotations describing collections and history. No indexes. *Class No:* 026/027(450)

[1070]

UFFICIO CENTRALE PER I BENI LIBRARI, LE ISTITUZIONI CULTURALI E L'EDITORIA. Italian libraries: the national public libraries. Roma, Ministero per i beni culturali e ambientali, 1996. 229p. illus. ports.

Abridged English version of *Biblioteche d'Italia: le biblioteche pubbliche statali* (3. ed. 1996). Title and text also in French.

Offers detailed and often lengthy descriptions of libraries in the public State sector. Emphasis is on history, development and buildings, but information on collections, catalogues and publications is also provided.
Class No: 026/027(450)

Spain

[1071]

GIRÓN GARCÍA, A. Directorio de bibliotecas españolas. Madrid, Ministerio de Cultura, 1988. xix,529p. ISBN: 8474834953.

Brief entries for 2,950 general, 2,335 university, 2,174 special, 531 educational and 5 national libraries. Data provided on address, code number, foundation date, subject specialisms, access conditions, hours and services. Regional sections: no indexes. Updated information is available in the database *Censo de bibliotecas* (CBIB), available online through the Ministerio de Cultura. *Directorio nacional de bibliotecas españolas en CD-ROM*, available from Chadwyck-Healey (annual updating, £200), is derived from the same database and contains 9,000 records.
Class No: 026/027(460)

[1072]

—Guía de bibliotecas públicas españolas. Madrid, Fundación Germán Sánchez Ruipérez/Ediciones Pirámide, 1996. 562p. (*Biblioteca del libro, 65.*) ISBN: 8489384029.

Geographically arranged directory. Questionnaire based, lacks detail on special collections. Complements the printed *Directorio de bibliotecas españolas* (above) which does not cover public libraries. *Class No:* 026/027(460)

Portugal

[1073]

BULLER, N. Libraries and library services in Portugal. Halifax, Nova Scotia, Dalhousie University, School of Library and Information Studies, 1988. 121p. Can$16. (*Dalhousie University, School of Library and Information Studies occasional paper series, 46.*) ISBN: 0770397220.

Provides a general overview of library services in Portugal. Includes descriptions of the Biblioteca Nacional, State Archives, 9 university, 6 major public, 5 private and 8 special libraries. *Class No:* 026/027(469)

RSFSR

[1074]

Biblioteki Rossii: adresno-spravochnaia kniga. Semenova, N.A., *utv and* Firsov, V.R., *red.*. 3 e. ispr.izd. Sankt Peterburg, Rossiiskaia national'naia biblioteka, 1996. 221p.

First published 1992 as *Adresa i telefony bibliotek Rossiiskaia Federatsii*; 2nd ed. 1995.

Lists major Russian libraries and gives address, telephone number, etc. Indexed. *Class No:* 026/027(470)

[1075]

Directory of CIS libraries. Andrigal Ltd. Bibliographic Department, *comp and* Sasanova, G., *ed.*. 2nd ed. Moskva Andrigal 1994. 315p.

At head of title 'Russian Scientific News'.

Covers 2,950 scientific public and academic libraries. Entries, A-Z by Russian name, give address and English translation of title. Additional detail can include name of parent body, subjects covered and number of volumes held. *Class No:* 026/027(470)

Ukraine

[1076]

Bibliotechna Ukraina: dovidnyk. Korniienko, A.P., *red.* Kyiv, Abrys, 1996. 381p. ISBN: 5770741643.

1,186 numbered entries. Detail includes address and opening hours. *Class No:* 026/027(477)

Finland

[1077]

Suomen tieteellisten kirjastojen opas. Helsinki, Suomen Tieteellinen Kirjastoseura, 1950-. Quadrennial.

9th ed. (Linnamaa, M. & Niemelä, E. *eds.* 208p. ISBN: 951968350X) issued 1993. English title *Guide to research libraries and information services in Finland.*

Brief, but comprehensive, guide to Finish libraries. Detail includes English translation of library name. *Class No:* 026/027(480)

Norway

[1078]

Norske vitenskapelige og faglige biblioteker: en händbok. Oslo, Riksbibliotektjenesten, 1963-. Irregular.

7 utg. (Vokac, L. *red.* 457p. ISBN: 8271950967) issued 1991.

The main source for general information on Norwegian libraries, coverage including university, regional college, college of education, county and public and special libraries. Geographic, library name and Norwegian and English subject indexes. *Class No:* 026/027(481)

Sweden

[1079]

Bibliotek i Sverige. 3. rev. och. omarb. uppl. Stockholm, Tekniska litteratursällsk, 1997. 183p. illus. Kr360. (*Tekniska litteraturasällsk handbok, 24.*) ISBN: 9173900311.

First published 1988, 2nd ed. 1993; earlier eds. under title *Biblioteks- och informationsjänster i Sverige*

Standard guide to Swedish libraries and information centres. *Class No:* 026/027(485)

Denmark

[1080]

Biblioteksvejviser. København, Danmarks Biblioteksforening, 1970-. Annual. Kr335.

Published by Bibliotekscentralen, 1970-1982.

Danish library directory containing comprehensive information on Danish, Nordic and international library associations and institutions, Danish library related periodicals, the Danish national bibliography and its associated publications, foundations, research and special libraries (by subject) and public libraries (by place). English subheadings and index terms. Also available on CD-ROM and through the Internet at http://www.kb.dk.elib/guides/bv/index.htm. *Class No:* 026/027(489)

Iceland

[1081]

HILL, D.A. Icelandic libraries and archives: a selective guide for researchers. Madison, Dept. of Scandinavian Studies, Univ. of Wisconsin, 1988. 34p. (*Wisconsin introductions to Scandinavia, 5.*)

Detailed entries for 11 libraries with information on specialisms, hours, holdings, access, collections, catalogues, etc. *Class No:* 026/027(491.1)

Netherlands

[1082]

Jaarboek openbare bibliotheken. Den Haag, Nederlands Bibliotheek- en Lektuur Centrum, 1961-. Annual.

Directory of Dutch public libraries. The 1997 issue (215p. ISBN: 9054831197) lists by town (p.61-215) giving basic detail including names of senior personnel. Preliminary sections provide information on NBLC, European library associations, Dutch regional library bodies, etc. *Class No:* 026/027(492)

[1083]

NEDERLANDS BIBLIOTHEEK EN LEKTUUR CENTRUM. Nederlandse bibliotheek- en documentatiegids: adresboek van in Nederland gevestigde bibliotheken en documentatieinstellingen. Den Haag, Nederlands- Bibliotheek en Lektuur Centrum, 1984-. Irregular (recent issues biennial). DFl125.

Issue for 1996/97 [5th ed.] (1995. xxviii,396p. ISBN: 9054830808) lists 1,862 libraries and documentation centres providing a public service. Excludes elementary and secondary school collections. Arranged by town, entries include details of branches, staff, services, collections, special materials and publications. Institution, subject and publication indexes. English language preface and 'Directions for use'. *Class No:* 026/027(492)

[1084]

Research guide to libraries and archives in the Low Countries. Brogan, M. L., *comp.* New York, Greenwood P., 1991. x,546p. £76.50;$89.50. (*Bibliographies and indexes in library and information science, no. 5).*) ISBN: 0313254664.

In two sections. I. 'Field guide for research in the Low Countries' (p.11-90), is an annotated listing of national bibliographies, union catalogues, biographical dictionaries, etc. II. 'Guide to libraries and archives', has 216 entries by country (123 Netherlands) then town. Information includes address, size, general description, special collections, services, publications and further reading. Technical, scientific and medical sources and private collections excluded. A work of excellence richly deserving of the accolade 'awesome' (*Choice*, v.29(9), May 1992, p.1363). *Class No:* 026/027(492)

Switzerland

[1085]

Information Schweiz: Bibliotheken, Archive Dokumentationsstellen, Databankanbieter. [Information suisse.] Aarau, Verlag Sauerländer, 1994. 280p. SFr20. ISBN: 3794137213.

Earlier eds. as *Bibliothekstaschenbuch Schweiz*, 1988 and 1991.

Basic information for 1,177 Swiss libraries, archives, documentation centres, etc. Also covers Liechtenstein. Subject indexed. *Class No:* 026/027(494)

Greece

[1086]

Odēgos vivliatheken Ellados. Athēna, Ekdose to periodikon 'E. Vivliemporike', [1991]. 165p. illus.

Illustrated guide to Greek libraries which includes basic details such as address. Arranged by library type; no indexes. *Class No:* 026/027(495)

Yugoslavia

[1087]

A Guide to Yugoslav libraries and archives. Jovanovič, S. *and* Rojnič, M., *comps.* Columbus, Ohio, American Association for the Advancement of Slavic Studies, 1975. xiii,113p. (*Joint Committee on Eastern Europe publication series, 2.*)

A directory in 7 parts, one for each of the 6 constituent republics and one for the autonomous provinces. Each part begins with an historical introduction. Glossary of special Turkish, Arabic and Slavic terms. Dated, but the only substantial English-language guide available. *Class No:* 026/027(497.1)

Slovenia

[1088]

Razvid Knjiznic SR Slovenije. Marinko, I., *ed.* Ljubljana, Narodna in univerzitetna knjižmia, 1987. 407p. ISBN: 8672650026.

Brief details of c.1,100 Slovenian libraries arranged geographically. Indexed by type of library. *Class No:* 026/027(497.12)

Rumania

[1089]

YUSUF, N. *and* **CLINCA, G. România ghidul bibliotecilor.** Bucureşti, Asociaţia Bibliotecarilor din Bibliotecile Publice din România, 1996. 263p. ISBN: 973960160x.

On verso of title page 'Asociaţia Bibliotecarilor din Bibliotecile Publice din România, Biblioteca Naţională - Serviciul Studii si Desoltare în Biblioteconomie'. Earlier title *Ghidul bibliotecilor publice de stat din România* (Bucureşti, 1993. 278p.). *Class No:* 026/027(498)

Asia—Far East

[1090]

CARPENTER, J. Libraries and information in East Asia: a survey based on published sources. London, British Library Research and Development, 1995. iv,62p. (*British Library Research and Development report, no. 6219.*.)

Covers 14 countries, including those in Southeast Asia. Main section (p.20-45) gives brief descriptive detail on national, academic and public libraries in each state. Final section analyses trends and key issues. Short bibliography; no index. *Class No:* 026/027(51/52+57)

China

[1091]

Chung-kuo t'u shu kuan ho ch'ing pao chi kou ming lu ta ch'üan. [A Masterlist of Chinese libraries and information services.] Hsing, H. Shen-yang, Tung-pei ta hsüeh ch'u pan she, 1995. vp. ISBN: 7810069381.

Major recent listing of Chinese libraries and related organizations. Indexed. *Class No:* 026/027(510)

[1092]

Directory of Chinese libraries. Wang, E., *and others eds.* Beijing, Chinese Academic Publishers, 1982. (Distr. by Springer-Verlag). viii,426p.illus. DM148. (*World books reference guide, no.3.*) ISBN: 3540120173.

In English and Chinese. 2 main parts: 1. Selected list of libraries with foreign holdings (658 entries, with limited descriptions of collections); 2. List of libraries (2,887 entries, name and address only). Name index (transliterated). Appendix of 73 late entries to pt.1. *Class No:* 026/027(510)

Bibliographies

[1093]

LIN, S.C. *and* **LEUNG, M.C. Chinese libraries and librarianship: an annotated bibliography.** Oak Park, Ill., Chinese Cultural Service, 1986. ix,101p. $14.95. ISBN: 093725603x.

Predominantly English language works, but includes some Chinese and other foreign language publications. 550 briefly annotated entries, dating from 1936, arranged in 9 subject categories. Coverage includes library history, library legislation and administration, publishing, bibliographies and reference works. Author/title index. List of Chinese librarianship journals. *Class No:* 026/027(510)(01)

Hong Kong

[1094]

CHAN, J.L.-Y, *and others.* **Library and information centres in Hong Kong.** [Hsiang-kang tu shu kuan chi tzu hsun fu wu chung hsin.] Hong Kong, Hong Kong University Press for the Hong Kong Library Association, 1996. xix,554p. illus., plates. £63;US$99.95. (*University of Hong*

....(*contd.*)
Kong libraries publication, no.7..) ISBN: 9622094090.
Replaces *Library and information services in Hong Kong* (1988).
Information on 763 libraries (602 in 1988 ed.) including 95 in the special sector. Data includes address, person in charge, hours, services, funding, stock, loan and reader statistics and type of catalogue. Little detail on subject strengths. *Class No:* 026/027(512.317)

Korea

[1095]
LEE, P. *and* **UM, Y.A. Libraries and librarianship in Korea.** Westport, Conn., Greenwood Press, 1994. xii,172p. £49.50;$55. (*Guides to Asian librarianship*..) ISBN: 0313287430.
Confined to the Republic of Korea (South Korea). 10 chaps. covering national, academic, public, special and school libraries, bibliographic control and services, the Korean Library Association, education for librarianship and library automation. Select bibliography (p.163-67); index.
Class No: 026/027(519)

Japan

[1096]
Senmon jōhō kikan sōran. Tokyo, Senmon Toshokan Kyōgikai, 1969-. Triennial.
Earlier version 1956 as *Chosa kikan toshokan sōran*.
Regularly updated directory of Japanese special libraries, latest ed. 1997 (xi,182,802p. ISBN: 448130013X). 2,619 entries in the 1994 ed. with classified, geographical and English name indexes. Includes libraries of government bodies and learned societies. English version published as:-
Class No: 026/027(52)

[1097]
—JAPAN SPECIAL LIBRARIES ASSOCIATION. Directory of information sources in Japan 1986. Tokyo, Nichigai Associates, 1986. xiii,378p.
Previous ed. 1980.
1,778 entries in 7 sections. Data includes English and Japanese name, address, staff, budget, stock, subject and scope. Some coverage of non-library information sources. Indexes of English and romanized Japanese organization names. *Class No:* 026/027(52)

[1098]
WELCH, T.F. Libraries and librarianship in Japan. Westport, Conn., Greenwood Press, 1997. xv,215p. tables. £59.95;$75. (*Guides to Asian librarianship*..) ISBN: 0313296685.
10 chapters: 1. History of libraries - 2. The National Library - 3. Academic libraries - 4. Public libraries - 5. School libraries - 6. Special libraries - 7. Bibliographic control and services - 8. Automation - 9. Library and information science education - 10. Bibliography (p.197-210). Index. Includes paragraphs on individual libraries. A thorough, well executed survey. *Class No:* 026/027(52)

Asia—Middle & Near East

[1099]
FRANCIS, S. Libraries and information in the Near East and Central Asia. London, British Library Research and Development, 1995. vii,94p. maps. (*British Library library and information research report, no. 106*..) ISBN: 0712333010.

....(*contd.*)
Provides an overview of libraries and information services in 15 countries, including Bulgaria, Cyprus, Israel and the West Bank, and the Central Asian and Caucasus states of the former Soviet Union. Bibliography (p.86-88); index.
Class No: 026/027(53+56)

[1100]
Information and libraries in the Arab world. Wise, M. *and* Olden, A., *comps. & eds.* London, Library Association Publishing, 1994. xviii,268p. tables, map. ISBN: 1856040852.
17 chapter survey, *e.g.* 'National libraries in the Arab world', 'Egyptian university libraries', 'Public libraries in Saudi Arabia'. List of abbreviations (p.vii-xi); index.
Class No: 026/027(53+56)

[1101]
RIMA: Répertoire des bibliothèques et des organismes de documentation sur le monde arabe. 2.éd. Paris, Institut des monde arabe, 1986. 474p. ISBN: 2906062014.
1st ed. 1984.
The much expanded 2nd ed. has over 1,000 entries providing data on address, subject scope, no. of vols., access conditions etc. Covers 18 Arab states as well as libraries of centres for the study of the Arab world in 16 other countries, (17 entries for Great Britain).
Class No: 026/027(53+56)

Bibliographies

[1102]
PANTELIDIS, V.S. The Arab world: libraries and librarianship, 1960-1976: a bibliography. London, Mansell, 1979. xv,100p. £50;$70. ISBN: 0720108217.
Includes coverage of member states of the Arab League and Chad. General section, then by country, then subject and date. 1,047 entries, many multiple. Author index.
Class No: 026/027(53+56)(01)

India

[1103]
Directory of Indian public libraries: a selected list of libraries assisted by the Foundation. Barua, B.P., *ed.* Calcutta, Naya Prokash, 1986. xv,520p. £19.95. ISBN: 8185109435.
Lists only libraries assisted by the Raja Rammohun Roy Library Foundation. 6,149 entries A-Z by state with name and address. Index. *Class No:* 026/027(540)

[1104]
Directory of special and research libraries in India. Indian Association of Special Libraries and Information Centres, *comp.* 2nd ed. Calcutta, Indian Association of Special Libraries and Information Centres, 1985. 90p.
1st ed. 1962.
Alphabetical arrangement. Includes address, foundation date, subject scope, holdings total, publications and staff. Lists of libraries by location and subject. Name index to librarians. Not comprehensive, 'numerous government libraries do not appear' (*International journal of reviews in library and information science*, v.4(1), 1988, p.9).
Class No: 026/027(540)

[1105]

GUPTA, K.R. Directory of libraries in India. New Delhi, Atlantic Publishers, 1989. v,449p. Rs.400.

Generally inferior to *Indian library directory* (below) in coverage and detail. Some entries include information on subject specialisms, budgets, etc., but most limited to address. Arranged according to library type; no indexes.
Class No: 026/027(540)

[1106]

Indian library directory. Singh, J. *and* Sethi, A.R., *comps.* 4th ed. Delhi, Indian Library Association, 1985. ix,251p.

First published 1938 as *Directory of Indian libraries* (Calcutta, Indian Library Association). 3rd ed. 1951.

Much needed new ed. providing data on 1,602 Indian libraries. Arranged alphabetically in 6 sections: 1. Libraries of national importance - 2. University libraries - 3. College libraries - 4. Special libraries - 5. Government libraries - 6. Public libraries (subdivided by state). Institution and librarian's name index, with geographic state index to sections 1-5. *Class No:* 026/027(540)

Bangladesh

[1107]

Bangladesh public library directory (1972-1986). Rahman, N.N., *ed.* Dhaka, Directorate of Archives and Libraries, Bangladesh National Library, 1987. 208p.

Regionally arranged directory of nearly 200 public libraries. *Class No:* 026/027(549.3)

Turkey

[1108]

Üniversite kütüphaneleri tanitim kataloğu. [Handbook of university libraries.] Çelikoğlu, H., *comp.* [2nd ed.] Sansum, 1994. vii,255p. tables. ISBN: 9757636223.

First published 1992.

Survey based guide to Turkish university libraries, including details of staff, budgets, collections, cataloguing and classification systems, automation, publications and services. Introductory matter in English.
Class No: 026/027(560)

Asia—South East

[1109]

Directory of Southeast Asian academic and special libraries. Yee, Y-F.J., *comp.* Hong Kong, Library Marketing Services, 1992. 352p.

Intended for regular publication, ISSN: 10197516.

Selective, questionnaire based, directory of *c.*200 libraries in Brunei, Hong Kong, Indonesia, Malaysia, Philippines, Singapore and Thailand. Country, then A-Z name arrangement. Entries concentrate on practical matters such as hours, services, lending policy and equipment. Indexed; list of acronyms. *Class No:* 026/027(59)

Malaysia

[1110]

Panduan perpustakaan di Malaysia. [Directory of libraries in Malaysia.] 3rd ed. Kuala Lumpur, Perpustakaan Negara Malaysia, 1991. 565p.

First published 1978.

Contains data for all major libraries in Malaysia. Information in Malay and English. Indexed.
Class No: 026/027(595)

Singapore

[1111]

Directory of libraries in Singapore 1996. Lim-Yeo, P.P., *ed.* 6th ed. Singapore, Library Association of Singapore, 1996. vi,220p. S$50. ISBN: 9810084226.

First published 1969.

The 4th ed. (1989) is a questionnaire based directory of 96 libraries arranged A-Z by name. Detailed entries including subject coverage, historical notes and list of publications. Name and subject index. *Class No:* 026/027(595.13)

Africa

[1112]

The African book world and press directory. [Répertoire du livre et de la presse en Afrique.] Zell, H.M., *ed.* 4th ed. London, Zell, 1989. xxi,306p. £75;$135 ISBN: 0905450507.

1st ed. 1977; 3rd ed. 1983.

Aims to provide 'comprehensive, accurate and up-to-date information, in both English and French, on libraries, publishers and the retail book trade, research institutions with publishing programmes, book industry and literary associations, major periodicals and newspapers, government as well as commercial printers ...'. Data mainly collected by questionnaire. Entries for libraries largely confined to those with more than 5,000 books. Appendices include: Calendar of book trade events in Africa; Book prizes and awards; Book clubs in Africa. Subject index to special libraries.
Class No: 026/027(6)

[1113]

EDOKA, B.E. Guide to national and university libraries in Africa. Lagos, Libriservice, 1992. 174p. illus. ISBN: 9782372188.

Covers 76 libraries in country sections. Detailed entries with descriptive summary followed by data under 21 headings including head librarian, floorspace, special collections, staff, users, hours and publications. Indexed (libraries, personnel, collections, etc.).
Class No: 026/027(6)

[1114]

SITZMAN, G.L. African libraries. Metuchen, N.J. and London, Scarecrow Press, 1988. xiv,486p. illus. £51.75;$59.50. ISBN: 0810820935.

Contents: 1. Buildings and people: a photographic sampling - 2. Chronology of library and related events 1773-1984 - 3. Development of library literature, 1950-1980: a bibliographical essay - 4. Angola to Zimbabwe: a nation by nation survey - 5. Bibliography of African librarianship. South Africa and the Arab states excluded. Chap.4 includes data on major libraries, apparently culled from other directories. Chap.5 has 2,700 unannotated entries, about a third of which relate to Nigeria. Despite 'some shortcomings and many typographical errors', provides a useful overview, especially valuable for the 'mine of bibliographic citations' (*International journal of reviews in librarianship and information science,* v.4(2), 1988, p.47-8).
Class No: 026/027(6)

Bibliographies

[1115]

DAVIES, H. Libraries in West Africa: a bibliography. München, Zell, 1982. xix,170p. ISBN: 3598104405.

Earlier versions from 1972.

1,369 entries by country, preceded by a section for West Africa in general (items 1-295). Some entries briefly

.... *(contd.)*
annotated. Includes material dating back to the 1930's, cut-off date 1979. Appended select list of periodicals relating to librarianship published in West Africa. Conference index; name index. *Class No:* 026/027(6)(01)

[1116]
Libraries and information in East and Southern Africa: a bibliography. Wise, M., *comp*. Birmingham, Library Association, International & Comparative Librarianship Group, 1989. vii,200,16p. £12.50. ISBN: 0906904064.
Complements Davies *Libraries in West Africa* (above). 2,103 unannotated entries in geographic sections. Index of personal and corporate authors and subjects. Does not cover South Africa (except Bophuthatswana). About 70% of the items listed are held by the College of Librarianship Wales. *Class No:* 026/027(6)(01)

Ghana

[1117]
ALMENA, A.A. Directory of libraries in Ghana. Legon, Dept. of Library and Archival Studies, Univ. of Ghana, 1996. vi,40p.
Earlier work with same title/publisher 1974.
Class No: 026/027(667)

Nigeria

[1118]
CONFERENCE OF CHIEF EXECUTIVES OF LIBRARY BOARDS IN NIGERIA. Directory of national and state libraries in Nigeria. [Benin City], Conference of Chief Executives of Library Boards in Nigeria, 1989. 29p.
Brief information on the National Library and 21 state libraries including services and branches.
Class No: 026/027(669)

[1119]
OMONIWA, M.A. ***and*** **SALAAM, M.O. A Directory of Nigerian libraries and documentation centres.** Zaria, Kashim Ibrahim Library, Ahmadu Bella University, 1983. vi,132p.
Provides information on 124 libraries (51 academic, 31 special, 25 public and 17 legal). *Class No:* 026/027(669)

Kenya

[1120]
Subject guide to information sources in Kenya. Robins, K., *comp and* Mulaha, A.R., *ed.*. Nairobi, Kenya Library Association and National Council of Science and Technology, 1984. v, 207p.
Lists 300 libraries under broad subject headings. Standard directory information including details of special collections and services. Subject, organization and library type indexes. *Class No:* 026/027(676.2)

Tanzania

[1121]
Directory of libraries in Tanzania. Mwinyimvua, E.A., *ed.* Dar Es Salaam, Tanzania National Documentation Centre, 1984. vi, 112p.
Basic information on 171 libraries. Arranged by name of library's parent organization. Indexes to publications, (excluding annual reports), subjects, places, classification systems and personal names. *Class No:* 026/027(678)

Africa—Southern

[1122]
Directory of Southern African libraries, 1989. 5th ed. Pretoria, State Library, 1990. xiii,463p. (*Contributions to library science, no.36.*) ISBN: 0798913665.
1st ed. 1965; 4th ed. 1984.
Lists 1,377 libraries, 1,233 in South Africa (p.1-337) the remainder in 'National and neighbouring states' (p.338-82). Entries with full data include address, hours, services, special collections, expenditure, staff and details of holdings and history. South African section arranged according to library type, other section geographically Bophutatswana ... Zimbabwe. Geographical, special collection, subject specialism and library name indexes. New ed. reported as in preparation 1997. *Class No:* 026/027(68)

Botswana

[1123]
Libraries and information centres in Botswana a directory. Inganji, F., *comp.* Gaborone, University of Botswana, 1984. 208p.
Covers approximately 100 libraries. Arrangement by library type with name index. *Class No:* 026/027(681)

Namibia

[1124]
SOUTH AFRICAN INSTITUTE FOR LIBRARIANSHIP AND INFORMATION SCIENCE. SWA/Namibia Branch. **Libraries in SWA/Namibia.** [Biblioteke in SWA/Namibië.] Windhoek, SAILIS SWA/Namibia Branch, 1988. 58p. ISBN: 0869762249.
Gives information in English, Afrikaans and German on Namibian libraries of all types. A-Z arrangement by library name; no indexes. *Class No:* 026/027(688)

Zimbabwe

[1125]
Directory of libraries in Zimbabwe. Dube, S.R. *and* Douglas, R.G.S., *comps.* Harare, National Archives of Zimbabwe, 1987. iv,28p. ISBN: 0908302045.
Preceded by *Directory of Zimbabwean libraries* (1981) and *Directory of Rhodesian libraries* (1975).
243 entries arranged by library type. Indexed.
Class No: 026/027(689.1)

Malawi

[1126]
Directory of Malawi libraries. Uta, J. J., *comp.* 2nd ed. [Zomba], Univ. of Malawi Library, 1990. ii,47p. (*University of Malawi Library publications, 6.*)
1st ed. 1976.
Data for 168 libraries. Arranged by library type with a name index. *Class No:* 026/027(689.7)

Canada

[1127]
The Canadian library index. Scott, P., *comp.* Saskatoon, Northern Lights Internet Solutions. World Wide Web resource.
URL: http://www.lights.com/canlib. Date reviewed 16th March 1998. An offshoot of Scott's *WebCats* (*q.v.*) service.
Provides links to Canadian library WWW home pages and

.... *(contd.)*
connections to telnet/WWW based OPACs. Provincial arrangement; an impressive number of libraries included (*e.g.* 40 links for Manitoba). *Class No:* 026/027(71)

[1128]

Directory of libraries in Canada. [Répertoire des bibliothèques du Canada.] Toronto, Micromedia, 1985-. Annual (irregular). ISSN: 11911603.

Published as *Canadian library yearbook* until 1991. Succeeds *Canadian library handbook* issued in 3 eds. 1979/80-1983.

The 1996 issue (10th ed. [xvi],645p.) lists over 6,000 libraries and their branches, information and resource centres, archives, library associations, etc. Entries, A-Z by name, include address, librarian or equivalent, collection information, services, computer and automated systems and publications. Subject, location and personal name indexes. Introductory matter includes listings of provincial library agencies, regional library systems, library science periodicals and library schools.

Directory information on Canadian libraries is also available in a number of primarily US sources *e.g. American library directory (q.v.)*. *Class No:* 026/027(71)

[1129]

NATIONAL LIBRARY OF CANADA. Directory of special collections of research value in Canadian libraries. [Répertoire des collections spécialisées utiles à la recherche dans les bibliothèques canadiennes.] Ottawa, National Library of Canada, 1992. xi,204p. (xii,220p.). Can$32.25. ISBN: 0660573024.

Text in English and French; French text set on inverted pages.

Contains information on 245 collections in 45 university and college libraries that have at least provincial significance and are physically or bibliographically distinct from the rest of the stock. Entries (subject arrangement under 24 headings) include a brief history and description and citations to publications dealing with the collection. Title and institution listings as appendices; general index.
Class No: 026/027(71)

Mexico

[1130]

AÑORVE GUILLÉN, M.A. Directorio de bibliotecas de universidades oficiales de la República Mexicana. México, Universidad Nacional Autonoma de México/Secretaría de Educacion Pública, 1987. 252p. ISBN: 9683603394.

Regionally arranged directory of academic libraries. Entries confined to basic detail; branch and departmental libraries included. *Class No:* 026/027(72)

[1131]

MEXICO. Dirección General de Publicaciones y Bibliotecas. **Directorio de bibliotecas de la República Mexicana.** 6. ed. Mexico City, Dirección General de Publicaciones y Bibliotecas, 1979. 2v. ISBN: 9688040746.

First published 1962.

1,572 entries in the main sequence arranged geographically, followed by a further 744 entries in two annexes. Data includes address, parent institution, staff and subject coverage. Institutional, personal name, geographic and subject indexes. Up-to-date information on a limited number of Mexican libraries is available in *American library directory* (*q.v.*). *Class No:* 026/027(72)

Cuba

[1132]

ACADEMIA DE CIÊNCIAS DE CUBA. Instituto de Documentación e Información Científica y Técnica. **Directorio de organos de información** del Sistema Nacional de Información Científica y Técnica. La Habana, Instituto de Documentación e Información Científica y Técnica, 1987. 236p.

Directory of 620 information units which form part of the national organization for scientific and technical information. *Class No:* 026/027(729.1)

Jamaica

[1133]

Directory of information units in Jamaica: libraries, archives and documentation services. 2nd ed. Kingston, Jam., National Council on Libraries, Archives and Documentation Services, 1986. xvi,200p. ISBN: 9768046007.

First published 1980.

Covers libraries of all types. Most entries provide very full detail, including information on collections, services and equipment. *Class No:* 026/027(729.2)

USA

[1134]

American library directory. New York, Bowker, 1923-. Annual. $259.95. ISSN: 0065910x.

Frequency varies: annual since 1978. 1994/95 issued as a 2 v. set: v.1 *Libraries in the United States*; V.2 *Libraries in Canada and Mexico. Library networks...* .

Lists North American libraries of all types, including those in regions administered by the US. Over 37,000 entries 1997/98, 33,004 for the US (arranged by state then city), 3,919 for Canada, only 380 for Mexico. Information given varies, but includes address, names of key personnel and subject holdings and, for many entries, income and expenditure, special collections, automated systems, OPAC access and Internet home page, participation in networks, branches and publications. 9 codes indicate library type (*e.g.* C=College, L=Law). Supplementary listings in v.2 include networks, consortia and other cooperative organizations, library schools and training courses, library systems, libraries for the blind and physically handicapped, state and provincial library agencies and United States armed forces libraries overseas. Indexed by organization and personal name. Also available online (Dialog File 460) and on CD-ROM as a component of *Publishing market place reference Plus*. *Class No:* 026/027(73)

[1135]

Directory of federal libraries. Evinger, W.R., *ed.* 3rd ed. Phoenix, Oryx Press, 1997. xi,379p. £77.95;$97.50. ISBN: 1573560480.

First published 1987; 2nd ed 1992.

Libraries covered range from the Library of Congress and Smithsonian Institute to libraries of national parks and those on military bases. 2,283 entries (2,516 2nd ed.). Information varies, but includes, administrator, library type, collection size, special subjects, publications, URL and brief notes. Arranged by agency A-Z with library type, geographic, subject and, new to this ed., library name index. 'Since information about large federal libraries is available in common sources such as *American library directory*, the biggest advantage this source offers is data about obscure federal libraries' (*Choice*, v.35(3), November 1997, p.449). *Class No:* 026/027(73)

[1136]
Directory of special libraries and information centers. Detroit, Gale, 1963-. Annual. $535. ISSN: 0731633x.

First published 1963. Issued annually for many years, now seems to be appearing more frequently.

Present subtitle *A Guide to ... special libraries, research libraries, information centers, archives and data centers maintained by government agencies, business, industry, newspapers, educational institutions, nonprofit organizations and societies in the fields of science, engineering, medicine, law, art, religion, the social sciences and humanities.*

The 21st ed. (Faerber, M. & Rowe, S. *eds*. 1998. 2v. in 3) has 22,800 entries, including 2,694 for significant information centres in Canada and 3,634 for those elsewhere. Information given includes parent body, subject keywords, head librarian, founding date, no. of staff, subjects, special collections, holdings (quantitative data), services, automated operations, computerized information systems, Internet home page, publications, special catalogues, former names and principal staff. Appendices: Networks and consortia; Regional and subregional libraries for the blind and physically handicapped; Patent and trademark depository libraries; Regional government depository libraries; United Nations depository libraries; World Bank depository libraries; European Community depository libraries (US). 4,000 term subject index; geographic and personal name indexes in the separately available v.2. *Class No:* 026/027(73)

[1137]
—Subject directory of special libraries and information centers: a subject classified edition of material taken from *Directory of special libraries...* . Detroit, Gale, 1975-. Annual or biannual. $320 per v.). ISSN: 0732927x.

Published annually for many years; now appears to be issued on a more frequent basis.

Based on the parent directory arranging many, but not all, the entries by subject. Coverage and number of volumes issued has varied. The 22nd ed. (1998) is in 3v.: 1. *Business, government and law libraries* (xiv,563p. 4,131 entries); 2. *Computers, engineering and science libraries* (xv,867p. 6,237 entries); 3. *Health science libraries* (xiv,418p. 3,311 entries). *Class No:* 026/027(73)

[1138]
Subject collections: a guide to special book collections and subject emphases as reported by university, college, public and special libraries and museums in the United States and Canada. Ash, L. *and* Miller, W.G., *comps*. 7th ed. rev. & enl. New Providence, N.J., Bowker, 1993. 2v. £220;$275. ISBN: 0835231410.

First published 1958; 6th ed. 1985.

Covers 65,818 collections held by 5,882 institutions. Entries under 18,878 Library of Congress based subject headings, then by state. For each collection gives address, etc., collection size, whether catalogued and brief descriptive note. 3 col. layout, small typeface. Excludes most college and university archives and small local history and genealogy collections. No indexes. Unrivalled as a source of information on the subject collections and strengths of North American libraries. *Class No:* 026/027(73)

[1139]
—Special collections in college and university libraries. Madoc Press Inc., *comp*. New York, Macmillan, 1989. xv,639p. ISBN: 0029216516.

A 'compilation of detailed descriptive information concerning special collections, rare books and manuscripts to be found in the libraries of colleges and universities throughout the United States' (p.xiii). Collections included may represent literary interests (*e.g.* first editions of a particular author), specific periods (*e.g.* Renaissance) or faculty interests (*e.g.* Baltic studies). Generally short descriptions arranged by institution in state sections. Subject access through the 'General index' (p.547-621); separate institution index. *Class No:* 026/027(73)

Brazil

[1140]
Guia das bibliotecas públicas do Brasil. Sistema Nacional de Bibliotecas Públicas/FBN, *comp*. Rio de Janerio, O Sistema, 1995-. Biennial? ISSN: 01045857.

New guide to Brazilian public libraries; intended for regular updating. *Class No:* 026/027(81)

[1141]
Quem informa no Brasil: guia de bibliotecas, centros e serviçós de documentação e informação. Brasília, Instituto Brasileiro de Informção em Ciência e Technologia, 1987. 195p.

Lists libraries and information centres predominantly, but not exclusively, in scientific and technical disciplines. Subject arrangement with institution index (p.167-95). *Class No:* 026/027(81)

Argentina

[1142]
GONZÁLEZ, D.H. **Guía de bibliotecas y centros de documentación de la Capital Federal.** Buenos Aires, Centro de Investigaciónes Bibliotecológicas, Facultad de Filosofia y Letras, Universidad de Buenos Aires, 1994. 175p., illus., maps. (*Serie extension universitaria, 3.*)

Follows an earlier guide to libraries in the greater Buenos Aires area, *Directorio de bibliotecas y centros de documentacion de la ciudad de Buenos Aires* (Catálogo Colectivo de Bibliotecas Empresarias, 1988). *Class No:* 026/027(82)

Chile

[1143]
Bibliotecas de Chile. Santiago, Dirección de Bibliotecas, Archivos y Museos, 1985. 391p.

Earlier coverage provided by *Guia de bibliotecas y centros de documentación de Chile*, first published 1971, 3rd ed. 1979.

Regionally arranged directory of 1,037 entries. Brief boxed data giving address, days open, stock totals, classification system and subject coverage. *Class No:* 026/027(83)

Ecuador

[1144]

CARRIÓN, F. Centros de investigación y bibliotecas: directorio ecuatoriano. Quito, Ciudad, 1988. 310p.

Two part directory, the first listing research organizations, the second 194 libraries. Basic data with brief indication of subject holdings. Indexed. *Class No:* 026/027(866)

Guyana

[1145]

GUYANA LIBRARIES ASSOCIATION. Bibliographic Sub-Committee. **Directory of libraries and documentation centres in Guyana.** Georgetown, Guyana Library Association, 1990. ii,82p.

Earlier ed. as *Guide to library services in Guyana* (1978).

Questionnaire based directory of fairly lengthy entries including holdings details and an indication of subject strengths. A-Z arrangement with separate list of libraries by type. Further list of libraries from which no information received. *Class No:* 026/027(88)

Uruguay

[1146]

Directorio de servicios de información y documentación en el Uruguay. 4. ed. Montevideo, Biblioteca Nacional, 1993. 352p. ISBN: 9974550025.

At head of title page: Centro Nacional de Documentación Cientifica, Técnica y Económica. First published 1980.

328 information services A-Z by name, giving director, address, hours, type, foundation date, collection size, subjects, cataloguing and classification scheme, services, etc. Abbreviation, institution, thematic and geographical indexes. *Class No:* 026/027(899)

Australasia & Oceania

[1147]

DOWNS, R.B. Australian and New Zealand library resources. London, Mansell, 1979. 164p. ISBN: 0720109132.

Differs somewhat from *British and Irish library resources* and *American library resources* (*qq.v.*), in that the emphasis is on the description of special collections. Main section (p.29-114) consists of narrative accounts by subject (African literature ... Women), ranging from a few notes to several pages. Separate section on individual biography (26 persons only). Bibliography listing 565 guides, surveys, library catalogues etc. Index, excluding titles cited in the text. Reference value limited by narrative format and incomplete indexing. *Class No:* 026/027(9)

Indonesia

[1148]

Direktori perpustakaan jaringan informasi di Indonesia tahun 1995/1996. [Directory of information network libraries in Indonesia.] Haryanti, W.T. *and* Purawijaya, I.S., *comps.* [Jakarta], Perpustakaan Nasional, 1995. xiv,255p. ISBN: 9798289285.

Seems to supersede the irregularly published *Direktori perpustakaan Khusus dan sumber informasi di Indonesia,* [*Directory of special libraries and information sources in Indonesia*] (first issued 1966, 7th ed. 1985, publisher Indonesian Institute of Sciences), as the main source of current information on Indonesian libraries.
Class No: 026/027(910)

New Zealand

[1149]

DILSINZ: directory of information and library services in New Zealand. Szentirmay, P. *and* Szentirmay, T.C., *comps.* 6th ed. Wellington, New Zealand Library Association, 1988. 146p. NZ$10. ISBN: 0908560222.

1st ed. as *Special libraries and collections,* 1959. 5th ed. as *DISLIC: directory of special libraries and information centres in New Zealand,* 1984.

Expanded to 540 entries in this ed. Includes the National Library of New Zealand and its branches, academic libraries and major public libraries. Arranged A-Z by library name. Data presented includes hours, staff, foundation date, services, computer systems, online services, subjects, stock totals, special collections and publications. 8 indexes. A well-planned national directory, worthy of emulation.
Class No: 026/027(931)

[1150]

—Public libraries in New Zealand. Wellington, New Zealand Library and Information Association, 1980-. Irregular. ISSN: 01118072.

Latest ed. 1995 (24p. NZ$25).

Brief data by library authority. Includes branch libraries.
Class No: 026/027(931)

Australia

[1151]

Australian libraries: the essential directory. Bundy, A.L. *and* Bundy, J., *comps.* Adelaide, Auslib Press, 1988-. Irregular. Aus$34. ISSN: 10315187.

Primarily a directory of libraries, but also covers acronyms, agencies, associations, consultants, databases, directories, information brokers, journals, library publishers and library suppliers. Data for libraries taken from *Directory of Australian academic and research libraries* and *Directory of Australian public libraries* (below).
Class No: 026/027(94)

[1152]

BISKUP, P. Libraries in Australia. Wagga Wagga, Centre for Information Studies, Charles Sturt Univ., 1994. x,607p. £35;Aus$75. (*Topics in Australasian library and information studies, 9.*.) ISBN: 0949060259.

Reprinted, with changes and corrections 1995. Supersedes Biskup and Goodman's *Australian libraries* (3rd ed. Bingley, 1982).

Intended primarily for Australian library and information science students. 11 chaps. mainly covering libraries by type, 'the approach throughout ... unashamedly historical' (*Introduction*). Minimal coverage of technical developments. Notes and further reading at chap. ends; indexed. 'There is much that librarians outside Australia can learn from this text' (*Journal of librarianship and information science,* v.28(1), March 1996, p.54). *Class No:* 026/027(94)

[1153]

BUNDY, A.L. *and* **BUNDY, J. Directory of Australian academic and research libraries.** 6th ed. Adelaide, Auslib Press, 1996. 316p.

First published 1978 (early eds. as *Directory of Australian academic libraries*); 5th ed. 1992. ISSN: 10329994.

Covers university, technical and further education institutes, other providers of vocational education and training, theological colleges, state reference libraries, National Library of Australia and parliamentary libraries. Detailed entries, arranged by institution name, include information on hours, holdings, loan policies, scope and

.... *(contd.)*
subject strengths, special collections, operations and services, publications and senior staff. 'Guide to subject and named collections' (p.277-304): 'Senior staff listings' (p.305-16). *Class No:* 026/027(94)

[1154]
Directory of Australian public libraries. Bundy, A.L. *and* Bundy, J., *eds.* 4th ed. Adelaide, Auslib Press, 1995. xvi,343p. Aus$38. ISBN: 1875145109.

First published 1982.

The 3rd ed. (1991. xiii,274p.) provides basic data on bookstock, staffing, services, etc. in an A-Z sequence by library name; location index and subject guide to collection strengths. *Class No:* 026/027(94)

[1155]
Directory of special libraries in Australia. Fuller, J., *comp. & ed.* 9th ed. [Canberra], Australian Library and Information Association, Special Libraries Section, 1995. 748p. ISBN: 0868045225.

Looseleaf in a ring binder. First published 1954; 8th ed. 1991.

Basic information on over 1,400 libraries, including brief general description, address and other contact details, senior staff, headings indicating subject strengths, stock totals, network memberships, opening hours and inter-library loan terms. Arranged by name of parent body in State sections; organization/library name and detailed subject indexes. Also available on CD-ROM. *Class No:* 026/027(94)

Papua—New Guinea

[1156]
Directory of libraries in Papua New Guinea. Ikupu, W. *and* Maguire, J., *comps.* Waigani, National Library Service, 1992. 34p.

Replaces *Directory of libraries in Papua New Guinea* (Papua New Guinea Library Association, 1986. 69p.) *Class No:* 026/027(954)

Fiji

[1157]
Fiji library directory: 1991. Mamtora, J., *comp. and ed.* 5th ed. Suva, Fiji Library Association, 1991. vi,68p. ISBN: 9822050011.

1st ed. 1974; 4th ed. 1981.

Provides summary data on all libraries except those of primary schools. Arranged by institution name; indexed by place, type of library and subject. *Class No:* 026/027(961.1)

Islamic Peoples

[1158]
Directory of Islamic libraries and librarians. Khan, M.A.S., *comp.* Simi Valley Ca., Islamic Library Association, 1983. x, 108p.

In 3 sections: Muslim libraries; Islamic libraries in non-Muslim countries; Muslim librarians. The only 'non-Muslim countries' covered are India, Kenya and Nigeria, although Mozambique is curiously included in the Muslim country section. Poorly produced and lacking in substantial information on the libraries and librarians covered. *Class No:* 026/027(=95.297)

Blind People

[1159]
International directory of libraries for the blind. Kawamura, H., *ed.* 3rd ed. München, Saur, 1990. xxii,258p. $46. (*IFLA publications, 51.*) ISBN: 3598217811.

Issued under the auspices of the International Federation of Library Associations and Institutions, Section of Libraries for the Blind. First published 1984; 2nd ed. 1986.

Not confined to libraries, also including some information-related organizations (*e.g.* Scottish Braille Press; St. Dunstan's Public Relations Department). 235 libraries/organizations covered in 69 country sections. Information presented in tabular format under headings Address; Talking books/magazines; Large print; Lending policy; Catalogues; General notes. Organization and language indexes. A unique source, but the tabulated format gives a cluttered appearance which is difficult to interpret readily. *Class No:* 026/027-0056.262

Special Libraries

[1160]
Directory of special libraries and information centers. Detroit, Gale, 1963-. Annual. $535. ISSN: 0731633x.

Issued annually for many years, now seems to be appearing more frequently.

Present subtitle: *A Guide to .... special libraries, research libraries, information centers, archives and data centers maintained by government agencies, business, industry, newspapers, educational institutions, nonprofit organizations and societies in the fields of science, engineering, medicine, law, art, religion, the social sciences and humanities.*

Although still primarily a directory of US special libraries, recent issues have increased international coverage. The 21st ed. (Farber, M. & Rowe, S. *eds.* 1998. 2v. in 3) has 2,694 entries for Canada and 3,634 for other countries. Complemented by ***Subject directory of special libraries and information centers*** (*q.v.*). *Class No:* 026

[1161]
World guide to special libraries. Opitz, H. *and* Richter, E., *eds.* 3rd ed. München, Saur, 1995. 2v. £260;$325. (*Handbook of international documentation and information, v.17.*) ISBN: 3598222343.

First published 1983; 2nd ed. 1990.

Companion to *World guide to libraries* (*q.v.*), with which there is also considerable overlap. 'The term "special libraries" is understood to refer to libraries with thematically specialized holdings' (Preface p.vii). Entries range from the National Library of Medicine (Bethesda) to small specialized collections of universities *e.g.* faculty collections. 49,865 libraries included under 800 subject classifications Abrasives-Zoology. Complete entries give name (original language and English translation), address, year founded, name of director, special collections, holdings (no. of items by material type), database hosts accessed, participation in inter-library loan programmes and membership of national or international associations. Library name index in v.2 (faculty, department, etc. libraries of universities appear under the name of the university).

4th ed. forthcoming July 1998 (*c.*£295. ISBN: 3598222491). *Class No:* 026

[1162]

—Libraries, information centers and databases in science and technology: a world guide. Lengenfelder, H., *ed.* 2nd ed. München, Saur, 1988. xxxi,665p. £142;$225. ISBN: 3598107579.

First published 1984.

Narrower coverage than *World guide to special libraries,* having entries for 13,500 libraries, 200 information and documentation centres and 300 data bank producers. Geographical arrangement; indexed by institution, data bank and subject.

Further title: *Libraries, information centers and databases in biomedical sciences: a world guide* (Bartz, B. *and others eds.* München, Saur, 1991. xxiv,392p. $170. ISBN: 3598110014). *Class No:* 026

Indexes

[1163]

Special libraries: a cumulative index, 1971-1980. Coplen, R., *comp.* New York, Special Libraries Association, 1982. vii,94p. $6. ISBN: 0871113147.

'A cumulative author, title, subject and member information index to all issues of Special libraries for 1971 through 1980'.

Special libraries, published by the US Special Libraries Association, is one of the leading journals in the field. 10,000 index entries in one A-Z sequence. Further v. for 1981-86 (Post, J.A. *comp.* 1987. 40p. $6. ISBN: 0871113279) and 1987-91 (Greenberg, A.M. *comp.* 1992. 32p. $6. ISBN: 0871113953). *Class No:* 026(014)

Handbooks & Manuals

[1164]

Handbook of special librarianship and information work. Scammell, A., *ed.* 7th ed. London, Aslib, 1997. xviii,478p. tables, diags. £67.50. ISBN: 0851423981.

First published 1955; 6th ed. 1992.

20 contributed chaps. (*e.g.* Resourcing the information centre, The Internet, Records management, Managing people) each extensively referenced. Many contributions by leading authorities in the field (*e.g.* Graham Cornish on copyright). 6 futher case studies (*e.g.* Computer assisted learning at Forest Health Care); index (p.453-78). '(C)hapters are well structured and the writing is of an excellent standard' (*Managing information*, v.5(3) April 1998, p.42). *Class No:* 026(035)

Yearbooks & Directories

[1165]

The Aslib membership directory. London, Aslib, 1996-. Annual.

'Including the directory of products and services'. Replaces *Aslib membership list.*

1996 v. (248p. ISBN: 0851423620) lists corporate members A-Z (p.31-143) giving address, industry description (code), membership of special interest groups and contact. Further lists of affiliate members, etc. 'Directory of products and services' (p.171-246) arranged by category (Abstracting and indexing services ... Videos) with separate index. *Class No:* 026(058)

Tables & Data Books

[1166]

BERRIDGE, P.J. *and* **SUMISON, J. UK special library statistics:** a final report on research commissioned by British Library Research & Development August 1994. Loughborough, Library and Information Statistics Unit, Department of Information and Library Studies, Loughborough University of Technology, 1994. ii,80p. tables. £19.50. (*LISU occasional paper, no.8.*) ISBN: 0948848642.

Spiralbound.

Surveys various sources of statistical data on UK special libraries. Includes summary 'best estimate' tables based on sources analysed. *Class No:* 026(083)

Biographies

[1167]

Industrial Group index: members classified by name, employer, industry, geographic location and software used. Nunn, H., *comp.* London, Library Association Publishing, 1992. iv,396p. £26. ISBN: 1856040089.

Compiled for the Library Association Industrial Group.

Directory of *c.*1,600 personal members of the LA's Industrial Group. Questionnaire based data by surname A-Z, many entries incomplete. Comprehensively indexed. Separate list of institutional members. *Class No:* 026(092)

[1168]

Who's who in special libraries. 1980/81-. Washington, D.C., Special Libraries Association, 1980-. Annual. ISSN: 0278842x.

The 1997/98 issue (1997. 399p.) lists personal members of the SLA A-Z (p.92-284) giving employer and other basic details. Also contains SLA organizational information and a buyer's guide. Indexed. *Class No:* 026(092)

Law Libraries

[1169]

Directory of British and Irish law libraries. Fothergill, P., *ed.* 5th ed. Hebden Bridge, Legal Information Resources for the British and Irish Association of Law Libraries, 1995. viii,287p. ISBN: 1870369092.

First published 1976; 4th ed. 1992. Title varies slightly.

Entries for 512 libraries based on questionnaire replies. Arranged by town in sections: England; Wales; Scotland; Northern Ireland; Republic of Ireland; Channel Islands; Isle of Man. Data includes name and address etc., opening hours, terms of admission, contact, services available, size of legal collections, publications and membership of co-operative schemes. Indexed by name of organization, type of organization, contact name and special collections. An excellently presented, regularly updated source.
Class No: 026.072

National Libraries

[1170]

National libraries: a selection of articles on national libraries, 1986-1994. Line, M.B. *and* Line, J., *eds.* London, Aslib, 1995. vii,303p. £45. (*Aslib reader series, 10.*) ISBN: 0851423426.

Collection of 33 reprinted articles in 3 groups: General - Special aspects - National libraries in different regions of the world (19 articles, *e.g.* Myanamar National Library, The Biblioteca de Catalunya). Selected references (p.300-303). '(B)ecause these papers are mainly fragments of the ongoing

.... *(contd.)*
dialogue of insiders, this book does not provide a systematic introduction to national library issues' (*Journal of documentation*, v.52(4), December 1996, p.458).

Preceded by two earlier collections from the same editors and publisher: *National libraries* (1979. vii,328p.); *National libraries 2 1977-1985* (1987. x,398p. ISBN: 0851422039). *Class No:* 027

[1171]
National libraries of the world: an address list. Boston Spa, IFLA Programme for UAP, c/o British Library. World Wide Web resource.

URL; http://ifla.inist.fr/V1/2/p2/natlibs.htm. Date reviewed 14th April 1998.

File last updated 28th January 1997. Replaces printed listing with same title published 1988 (22p. ISBN: 0712320490).

Includes libraries claiming the function of a national library. Some entries include email address and URL. *Class No:* 027

Bibliographies

[1172]
DE BEER, J. National libraries around the world 1995-96: a review of the literature (in *Alexandria,* v.9(1), 1997, p.3-44).

Ninth bibliographical essay in a series which has appeared annually in *Alexandria* since its inception. Provides comprehensive coverage of the literature, 207 items cited in the appended list of references. *Class No:* 027(01)

Histories

[1173]
ESDAILE, A. National libraries of the world: their history, administration and public services. 2nd ed. London, Library Association, 1957. xv,413p. illus.

First published 1934 (London, Grafton) as *The World's greatest libraries. 1. National libraries of the world.* (V.2 was *Famous libraries of the world: their history, collections and administrations,* by M. Burton. 1937). 2nd ed. completely rev. by F.J. Hill.

Deals with the national libraries of 32 countries (21 of them European). Systematic description of each library under 8 headings (8. Bibliography). Remains one of the more valuable historical accounts. *Class No:* 027(091)

Biographies

[1174]
International biographical directory of national archivists, documentalists and librarians. Carroll, F.L., *ed and* Houck, S., *comp.*. Lanham, Md., Scarecrow Press, 1997. xxvii,225p. £42.75;$45. ISBN: 0810832232.

Carroll was joint editor of *Biographical directory of national librarians* (London, Mansell, 1989. xvii,134p. ISBN: 0720118751).

Provides contact detail for chief executives of national archives, national libraries or equivalents, many entries backed by variable length biographical sketches. A-Z arrangement by country with index (p.213-25). Definition of 'national' somewhat hazy, UK entry includes Bodley's Librarian as well as Chief and Deputy Chief Executive of the British Library and the Director General of BLDSC. *Class No:* 027(092)

Worldwide

French

[1175]
Les Bibliothèques nationales de la francophonie: répertoire des Bibliothèques nationales des États et gouvernements membres des sommets francophones. Fournier, C., *comp.* 2e. ed. Montreal, Bibliothèque nationale du Québec, 1997. 210p. 500.00/00 Publ. in collaboration with the Bibliothèque nationale de France. First published 1993. ISBN: 2551178215.

Detailed entries for each library arranged by county. Information includes full contact detail, principal staff, legal deposit legislation, national bibliography and international links. No indexes. *Class No:* 027(100)=40

Europe

[1176]
Gabriel: gateway to Europe's national libraries. Conference on European National Libraries. World Wide Web resource.

URL: http://minos.bl.uk/index.html. Date reviewed 16th April 1998. Available in English, French or German.

Provides links and search engine for the WWW sites of 38 European national libraries. *Class No:* 027(4)

Great Britain

[1177]
DAY, A. The British Library: a guide to its structure, publications, collections and services. London, Library Association, 1988. x,176p. ISBN: 0853656282.

Primarily a descriptive conspectus of around 550 British Library publications registered in *British Library publications 1988.* Presentation based on the Library's organizational structures as they emerged from the 1985 review, including brief accounts of departmental origins, services and activities. Lacks tables or organizational charts, but otherwise 'well presented and accurately detailed' (*Library Association record,* v.91(1), January 1989, p.46). *Class No:* 027(410)

[1178]
—DAY, A. The New British Library. London, Library Association Publishing, 1994. xiii,265p. £40. ISBN: 1856040704.

A sequel, similar in plan and style, which examines changes since 1988 with particular reference to preparations for the move to St. Pancras. A 'wonderful thorough description of all parts and series of the British Library' (*Printing Historical Society bulletin*, no.40, Winter 1995/96, p.32).

A further v., *Inside the British Library* (ISBN: 1856042804), forthcoming 1998. *Class No:* 027(410)

[1179]
ESDAILE, A. The British Museum library: a short history and survey. London, Allen and Unwin, 1946. 388p.

Reprinted Greenwood Press, 1979 (£53.95;$65. ISBN: 0313209405).

Two parts: 1. Historical (up to 1940) - 2. The collections and their catalogues (p.175-321): The printed books. The manuscripts. The oriental printed books and manuscripts. 10 appendices (9. The Natural History Museum library). Chapter notes; analytical index. *Class No:* 027(410)

[1180]

—The Library of the British Museum: retrospective essays on the Department of Printed Books. Harris, P.R., *ed.* London, British Library, 1991. xiii,305p. illus., plan. £35. ISBN: 0712302425.

'(A) useful supplement to, though not a replacement of Arundell Esdaile's *The British Museum Library*' (*The Papers of the Bibliographical Society of America*, v.85(3), Sept. 1991, p.319). 7 well written essays (The Shelving and classification of printed books ... The Acquisitions policies and funding of the Department of Printed Books, 1837-1959 ... The Private case). Chapter notes; index.

Forthcoming 1998 *A History of the British Museum library 1753-1973* (ISBN: 0712345620). *Class No:* 027(410)

[1181]

Handlist of unpublished finding aids to the London collections of the British Library. Alston, R.C., *comp.* London, British Library, 1991. [vi],188p. £15. ISBN: 0712302468.

Records *c.*1,500 lists and indexes most originally compiled as working tools. Entries, arranged according to BL Depts., give descriptive title, plus notes on physical format and location. Detailed index (p.156-88). Reveals some useful sources, but many items included now no more than historical curiosities. *Class No:* 027(410)

[1182]

Portico: the British Library's online information server. London, British Library. World Wide Web resource.

URL: http://portico.bl.uk. Date reviewed 14th April 1998.

Categories from the home page: Online (Blaise, OPAC 97, etc.) - Collections (Africa, Early Printed Collections...) - Exhibitions - Digital Library (includes images of a few major treasures such as Magna Carta) - Services (Bibliographic Sevices, Document Supply...) - Information (News ... Reader Admissions ... Locations). Site index and search facility. Now the pre-eminent source for current information on the British Library. *Class No:* 027(410)

[1183]

Treasures of the British Library. Barker, N., *comp.* London, British Library, 1996. 272p. illus., plates. £16.95. ISBN: 0712304096.

Pbck. reprint, with minor updating, of title first published 1988 (ISBN 0712301550).

Traces the history and development of the British Library in 14 chapters: 1. Sir Hans Sloane and the foundation of the British Library ... 7. Antonio Panizzi and the Department of Printed Books in the 19th century ... 13. Printed books and manuscripts in the 20th century. Sumptuously illustrated with 140 colour and 190 black and white plates. Index. Further reading. A wide ranging, serious account, 'it would be a mistake to regard *Treasures* as simply a coffee-table book' (*Library review,* v.38(3), 1989, p.49). *Class No:* 027(410)

France

[1184]

BIBLIOTHÈQUE NATIONALE. (FRANCE). Guide pratique de la Bibliothèque nationale. Nouv. ed. Paris, Bibliothèque nationale, 1990. 100p. plans. FFr55. ISBN: 2717717854.

First published 1987.

Designed for the intending user, outlining the services, collections, catalogues, user aids, etc. Individual departmental chapters (*e.g.* Département des livres; Département des manuscrits; Département de la musique). Includes floor plans. *Class No:* 027(44)

[1185]

BLASSELLE, B. Le Bibliothèque nationale. 2. éd. Paris, Presses Universitaires de France, 1993. 128p. (*Que sais-je?, 2496.*) ISBN: 2130427227.

First published 1989.

Provides useful summary information on history, organization, collections, services, etc. *Class No:* 027(44)

USA

[1186]

Library of Congress (WWW pages). Washington, D.C., Library of Congress. World Wide Web resource.

URL: http://www.loc.gov or http://lcweb.loc.gov. Date reviewed 16th April 1998.

An extensive site providing a vast range of information on the Library and the United States. Main links from the home page include: American memory (documents, photographs and sound recordings on American history) - Thomas: legislative information (US Senate and House of Representatives) - Exhibitions - Library services (Research and reference, Reading rooms...) - Research tools (Library of Congress catalogs ... Handbook of latin American studies). Site search engine provided. Also includes general information about the Library and its special programmes and a valuable collection of links under the option 'Explore the Internet'. *Class No:* 027(73)

[1187]

Special collections in the Library of Congress: a selective guide. Melville, A., *comp.* Washington D.C., Library of Congress, 1980. xv,464p. ISBN: 0844402974.

Now out of print. Contents are Internet accessible at http:lcweb.loc.gov/spcoll. File can be viewed by title or searched by subject, chronological period or custodial division.

Describes 269 special collections Abdul Hamid II ... Henrietta Yurchenco. Excludes collections composed purely of microforms or personal papers and non-music manuscript collections which fall within the scope of the *National union catalog of manuscripts* (*q.v.*). Also omits format collections *e.g.* miniature books. Appendix; 'The special collections by division'. Index. *Class No:* 027(73)

Public Libraries

[1188]

MURISON, W.J. The Public library: its origin, purpose and significance. 3rd ed. London, Bingley, 1988. x,251p. £40. ISBN: 0851574300.

1st ed. 1955, 2nd ed. 1971, both published by Harrap.

A useful general account. 12 chapters: 2. Origins of the public library movement - 3. Development of purpose in the public library ... 6. The British public library today - 7. The library for education and information - 8. The library for recreation ... 11. Public lending right - 12. The significance and limitations of the public library. Indexed.
Class No: 027.5

Databases

[1189]

The UK public libraries guide. Harden, S. *and* Harden, R., *comps.* World Wide Web resource

URL: http://dspace.dial.pipex.com/town/square/ac940/weblibs.html. Date reviewed 5th March 1998.

'The aim of these pages is to present the most complete and up to date picture of public library Internet activity in the

.... *(contd.)*
United Kingdom' (*Welcome page*). Includes 'UK public libraries on the Web', A-Z arranged links to the home pages of *c.*100 UK public library authorities.

The same compilers are also responsible for *Public libraries in Europe* (http://dspace.dial.pipex.com/town/square/ac940/eurolib.html) a less extensive site offering links to the home pages of selected European libraries.
Class No: 027.5(003.4)

Tables & Data Books

[1190]
CHARTERED INSTITUTE OF PUBLIC FINANCE AND ACCOUNTANCY. Statistical Information Service. **Public library statistics.** Actuals. 1962/63-. London, CIPFA, 1963-. Annual. £80. ISSN: 02604078.

Provides data on population served, items loaned, opening hours, stock, acquisitions, expenditure, income, etc. 1995/96 ed. (100p.) contains data for 159 UK public library authorities (95.2% of total), plus 31 from Ireland. Summary information precedes main tables.

CIPFA also issue *Public library statistics. Estimates* (Annual. ISSN: 03070552) giving projected expenditure, etc. for the forthcoming year. *Class No:* 027.5(083)

[1191]
Public library materials fund and budget survey. 1991/93-. Loughborough, Library and Information Statistics Unit, Department of Information and Library Studies, Loughborough University, 1992-. Annual. £22.50 ISSN: 09674888.

Continues *Public library bookfund estimates*, 1982-91.

'The aim of the survey is to enable public librarians to compare their own spending expectations with other authorities, and with recent history ... the main objective is to calculate percentage change from year to year' (*Introduction*) 1996/98 issue (1997. ii,245p.) has 1996/97 actual and 1997/98 estimated figures for total expenditure, total material expenditure, expenditure on books, expenditure on audio-visual materials, total staff, professional staff, number of service points and hours open.
Class No: 027.5(083)

Standards

[1192]
INTERNATIONAL FEDERATION OF LIBRARY ASSOCIATIONS AND INSTITUTIONS. Section for Public Libraries. **Guidelines for public libraries.** 3rd ed. München, Saur, 1986. 92p. (*IFLA publications, no.36.*) ISBN: 3598217668.

First published by IFLA as *Standards for public libraries*, 1973.

Offers guidelines on recommended provision for stock, staffing, service points, etc. Appendices (1/3 of book) present illustrative statistics from selected library systems. Of value, particularly for developing countries, but marred by 'an index of quite remarkable incompetence' (*British book news*, December 1986, p.686).
Class No: 027.5(083.74)

Histories

[1193]
KELLY, T. A History of public libraries in Great Britain, 1845-1975. 2nd ed. London, Library Association, 1977. xiii,582p. illus., plates, plans, map, ports. £55. ISBN: 0853652392.

1st ed. as *A History ... 1845-1965.* 1973.

16 chapters in 4 parts: The first phase, 1845-1886; From the Jubilee to the First World War, 1887-1918; Between the wars; The Second World War and after, 1939-1975. 13 appendices (3-4: Public library authorities, 1847-1972: dates of adoption and opening). Bibliography. Index. 'Readable, exhaustive and scholarly' (*British book news,* February 1974, p.92, on 1st ed.). The 2nd ed. has one additional chapter, minor amendments and an additional appendix on library authorities as at 1975. The definitive account.
Class No: 027.5(091)

Government Libraries

[1194]
World directory of national parliamentary libraries: including multi-national parliamentary libraries. Bonn, Deutscher Bundestag, 1985-. Biennial. ISSN: 10127690.

First published as *World directory of parliamentary libraries* 1983.

6th ed. (Kohl, E. *comp.* 1996. 2v.) contains information on 181 libraries arranged A-Z by country. Detailed data includes information on holdings, staffing and access arrangements. Many entries also provide a bibliography of publications by and about the library. Indexed.
Class No: 027.54

[1195]
—World directory of parliamentary libraries of federated states and autonomous territories. 1992/93-. Bonn, Deutscher Bundestag, 1993-. Quinquennial. ISSN: 09430113.

Initial issue: Kohl, E. *comp. & ed.* 2v. ISBN: 3893720111.

Covers libraries of sub-national legislative bodies (*e.g.* Canadian provinces, Australian states). Far from comprehensive, but detailed entries for libraries included.
Class No: 027.54

Children's Libraries

[1196]
ASSOCIATION FOR LIBRARY SERVICES TO CHILDREN. Special collections in children's literature: an international directory. Jones, D.J., *ed. & comp.* [3rd ed.]. Chicago, American Library Association, 1995. xiii,235p. illus. $40. ISBN: 0838934544.

First published as *Subject collections in children's literature* (1969); further ed. under present title 1982.

Covers over 300 US collections (by state) and 119 from 40 other countries. Entries give address and contact detail followed by descriptions of 25-200 words. Private collections excluded. Separate 'Subject listing' (p.99-189) for US collections has entries for author, illustrator and publisher names, as well as genres and subjects; no subject listing for other countries. General index (p.221-35). Patchy international coverage (*c.*30 entries for UK), but in the absence of any other source 'the definitive directory of special collections relating to children's literature' (*American reference books annual*, v.27, 1996, p.266).
Class No: 027.6-053

Bibliographies

[1197]
Children's services in the American public library: a selected bibliography. Thomas, F.H., *comp*. New York, Greenwood, 1990. xii,151p. £40.50;$49.95. (*Bibliographies and indexes in library and information science, no. 4.*) ISBN: 0313247218.

Contains entries for *c.*600 items, mainly periodical articles from titles such as *Library journal* or *Wilson library bulletin*, published before 1976. Arranged in 10 sections: 1. Historical focus; 2. Professional staff ... 6. Collection development; 7. Readers' services ... 10. Multi media. Author and subject indexes. Disappointing early cut off date, lacks statement of selection criteria and riddled with errors. 'Overall, there is a valuable idea behind this title, but it is poorly executed' (*American reference books annual*, v.22, 1991, p.258). *Class No:* 027.6-053(01)

[1198]
—VAN ORDEN, P. Library services to children: a guide to the research, planning and policy literature. Chicago, American Library Association, 1992 xiv,141p. ISBN: 0838905846.

Well produced bibliography of 'policy literature, historical works, research studies, reports and conference proceedings relating to public library services to children and children's librarianship' (p.vii). 298 annotated entries by title A-Z. Indexed by author and subject. *Class No:* 027.6-053(01)

Hospital Libraries

[1199]
Directory of domiciliary and hospital patients' library services in the United Kingdom. Collison, J.R., *comp.* London, Library Association Medical, Health and Welfare Libraries Group/Department of Library and Information Studies, Manchester Polytechnic, 1984. viii,854p. ISBN: 0950989703.

Questionnaire based data in two sections, Domiciliary library services (arranged alphabetically by library authority giving contact name, eligibility criteria, service description, material provided, deposit collections in homes, etc.) and Hospital patients' library services (arranged alphabetically by regional health authority, then district (private hospitals excluded)). Index of hospitals, district health authorities and place-names. Index of contacts (personal names). *Class No:* 027.6-056

[1200]
—Directory of domicilary library services: provided by English public library authorities. Donegani, K. *and* Lee, G., *comps.* Loughborough, Instant Library, 1991. [3],89p. £15. (*Instant Library guide, 1.*) ISBN: 1873511027.

Basic details only presented by library authority. Information gathered in connection with British Library Research & Development report 6045 *Library provision for the elderly and people with physical disabilities* (1991). *Class No:* 027.6-056

[1201]
Directory of medical and health care libraries in the United Kingdom and Republic of Ireland 1997-8. Forrester, W.H., *comp.* 10th ed. London, Library Association Publishing, 1997. xiv,273p. £35. ISBN: 1856042197.

First published 1957; 9th ed. 1994. Now appears every 2-3 years. Eds. 1-4 entitled *Directory of medical libraries in the British Isles.*

851 numbered entries arranged A-Z by name of library/organization. Also covers veterinary, pharmaceutical and occupational medicine libraries and information services run by medical charities. Standard data including detail on computerized facilities, publications and membership of library networks. Indexes of towns, personal names and hospitals. A useful source which could be enhanced by extending coverage to other medical collections, especially those in academic libraries. *Class No:* 027.6-056

[1202]
Guide to libraries and information sources in medicine and health care. Dale, P., *comp.* London, British Library Science Reference and Information Service, 1995. ii,162p. £39. (*Key resource series.*) ISBN: 0712308237.

'(A)ims to cover those libraries which are prepared to accept serious enquiries from outside' (*Preface*). 660 entries Abortion Law Reform Association ... York Health Library and Information Service, information including objectives and purpose (20-50 words), stock and coverage, hours and publications. Organization acronym, organization and subject indexes. Compared to *Directory of medical and health care libraries* (above) 'has a better coverage of medical charities, while the *Directory* has a better coverage of general hospitals' (*Reference reviews*, v.9(8), 1995, p.5). *Class No:* 027.6-056

[1203]
Health care librarianship and information work. Carmel, M., *ed.* 2nd ed. London, Library Association Publishing, 1995. xx,312p. £45. ISBN: 185604145x.

Previous ed. published 1981 as *Medical librarianship.*

22 chaps. (*e.g.* 3. Nursing, midwifery and health ... 14. Managing document delivery services ... 20. Professional associations for librarians in the health sector) each extensively referenced. List of acronyms and abbreviations (p.xv-xx); index. '(A)n invaluable resource for health service librarians' (*Journal of documentation*, v.52(4), December 1996, p.476). *Class No:* 027.6-056

[1204]
Hospital libraries and community care. Clarke, J.M. *and* Going, M.E., *eds.* 4th ed. London, Library Association, 1990. viii,274p. £35. ISBN: 0853655189.

1st ed. 1963 under title *Hospital libraries and work with the disabled;* 3rd ed. 1982 as *Hospital libraries and work with the disabled in the community.*

14 chapters: 2: Hospital libraries in the United Kingdom: recent developments (p.18-51) - 3: The organization and work of libraries in hospitals (p.52-85) ... 7: British official health publications ... 12: Library services to elderly people and people with disabilities. Further reading (p.257-60). Index. Changed emphasis in this ed. to reflect growing importance of care in the community. *Class No:* 027.6-056

Bibliographies

[1205]
Hospital and welfare library services: an international bibliography. Cumming, E.E., *comp.* London, Library Association, 1977. ix,174p. ISBN: 0853651396.

2,164 entries, chronologically arranged with occasional brief notes. Good coverage of foreign language material, introduction also in French and German. Let down by poor indexing: author index, country index (hundreds of entries under UK and US) and useless subject index with only 29 undivided headings. *Class No:* 027.6-056(01)

Prison Libraries

[1206]

MILTON, A. Directory of librarians in penal establishments. 2nd ed. [London], Library Association Prison Libraries Group, 1990. 31p.

At head of title page 'Library Association Prison Libraries Group'. First published 1989.

Lists librarians by name (p.7-20) with work address and posistion held. Further list of library authorities gives name of person responsible for prison library service.
Class No: 027.6-057

[1207]

VOGEL, B. Down for the count: a prison library handbook. Metuchen, N.J., Scarecrow Press, 1995 xi,193p. £29.50;$29.50. ISBN: 0810829274.

Strictly practical guide based on US experience. 15 chaps. covering all main aspects including collection management, space and equipment and staffing. Recommended reading (p.134-40), 9 appendices and index. *Class No:* 027.6-057

Bibliographies

[1208]

Prison librarianship: a selective, annotated, classified bibliography, 1945-1985. Hartz, F.R., *and others comps.* Jefferson, N.C., McFarland, 1987. ix,115p. £19.95;$19.95. ISBN: 089950258x.

185 substantially annotated entries arranged in 19 subject groups. Many of the entries are drawn from non-librarianship literature. Coverage mainly reflects US experience, although some items from or pertaining to other countries are included. Author and subject index.
Class No: 027.6-057(01)

[1209]

Prison libraries: a selective bibliography. Berry, J. *and* Fieldgate, J., *comps and* Morris, J., *rev. & ed.*. Prison Libraries Group of the Library Association, 1991. iv,32p. £5. ISBN: 1873710003.

Emphasises British material published 1960-90. *c.*225 briefly annotated entries in 11 sections (Policy documents... Prison library surveys... Education in penal establishments); author index. '(W)ell-produced and invaluable... should not be missed by anyone interested in the field' (*Library Association record*, v.93(9), September 1991, p.602).
Class No: 027.6-057(01)

Academic Libraries

[1210]

Academic libraries in the United Kingdom and Republic of Ireland. Harrold, A., *ed.* 3rd ed. London, Library Association Publishing, 1994. vii,148p. £30. ISBN: 185604114x.

1st ed. 1987 as *Libraries in colleges of further and higher education*; 2nd ed. 1992 under present title.

Questionnaire based, scope now extended to all higher and further education institutions. Full entries give controlling authority, chief librarian, hours, size of stock, institutional relationship, special collections, links with other institutions and brief history. Arranged A-Z by name of institution: library name, subject, special collections and geographic indexes. '(M)uch better than its predecessor ... (but) neither complete nor completely accurate' (*Reference reviews*, v.8(8), 1994, p.7). *Class No:* 027.7

[1211]

UK higher education and research libraries. Tilsed, I., *comp.* World Wide Web resource.

URL: http://www.ex.ac.uk/jtilsed/lib/uklibs.html. Date reviewed 7th March 1998. Part of Tilsed's *Library & related resources* site.

Provides links to the home pages of 140 UK academic libraries, including a few in the further education sector.
Class No: 027.7

Bibliographies

[1212]

KARP, R.S. The Academic library of the 90s: an annotated bibliography. Westport, Conn., Greenwood Press, 1994. viii,337p. £62.50;$69.50. (*Bibliographies and indexes in library and information science, 9.*.) ISBN: 0313293015.

Covers material published 1990-93. 1,662 entries with 50-100 word annotations in 6 broad categories. Does not provide the comprehensive coverage of the literature claimed, contains a number of typographical errors and is inadequately indexed. *Class No:* 027.7(01)

[1213]

LATHAM, S., ***and others.*** **Library services for off-campus and distance education:** an annotated bibliography Toronto, Canadian Library Association, 1991. xxii,249p. £31. ISBN: 0888022573, Canada; 1856040240, UK.

Co-published by the Library Association and the American Library Association.

'(C)oncerned with library support for post-secondary students and faculty'. 535 annotated entries for items, including theses and reports, published 1930 to early 1990. Continued by:- *Class No:* 027.7(01)

[1214]

—SLADE, A.L. *and* KASCUS, M.A. Library services for off-campus and distance education: the second annotated bibliography. Englewood, Colo., Libraries Unlimited, 1996. xxix,239p. £62.50;$65. ISBN: 1563084651.

518 further entries in 15 topical sections with author, geographic, institution and subject indexes. Aims at comprehensive coverage of the literature.
Class No: 027.7(01)

[1215]

NISONGER, T.E. Collection evaluation in academic libraries: a literature guide and annotated bibliography. Englewood, Colo., Libraries Unlimited, 1992. xix,271p. £32.95;$45. ISBN: 0872879259.

Selective listing of 617 items published since 1980. Takes a broad perspective, does not deal with issues such as routine selection or weeding. Topical arrangement in 12 chapters (*e.g.* Application of automation to collection evaluation'). Author/title and subject indexes; 5 p. glossary.
Class No: 027.7(01)

Periodicals

[1216]

Journal of academic librarianship. Greenwich, Conn., JAI Press, 1975-. Bi-monthly. $175. ISSN: 00991333.

One of the major periodicals in the field of academic librarianship, but as a reference source mainly valuable for the section 'The JAL guide to the professional literature'. This contains abstracts, annotations of new titles and summaries of reviews appearing in selected library, higher education and information technology journals. Emphasis is

.... *(contd.)*
on 'issues of immediate importance to academic libraries and higher education'. Author index. JAL also carries *c.*10 full length reviews in each issue. *Class No:* 027.7(051)

Tables & Data Books

[1217]
ASSOCIATION OF RESEARCH LIBRARIES. ARL statistics: a compilation of statistics from the one hundred and twenty members of the Association of Research Libraries. Washington, D.C., Association of Research Libraries, 1964-. Annual. $65. ISSN: 01472135.

Provides data for the major US academic libraries. 1995/96 v. (1997. 118p.) has detailed statistics for individual libraries on collections, personnel, services, etc., followed by rank order tables.

Current and back issues also Internet accessible at http://www.lib.virginia.edu/socsci/newarl. Features available include maps and graphics, customized queries and production of regionalized data.

A further source is *ACRL university library statistics ... a compilation of statistics from ... non-ARL university libraries* (Chicago, Association of College and Research Libraries, 1980-. Biennial). *Class No:* 027.7(083)

[1218]
—MOLYNEUX, R.E. The Gerould statistics, 1907/08-1961/62. Washington, D.C., Association of Research Libraries, 1986. viii,268p. $25. ISBN: 0918006112.

Extends the coverage of *ARL statistics.* 60 libraries covered, but not consistently.

Research library statistics 1907-8 through 1987-88 (Washington, D.C., Association of Research Libraries, 1990. 6 diskettes & documentation) is a database version incorporating additional ARL annual statistics to 1988. The data is also Internet accessible at gopher://arl.cni.org:70/11/stat/machine/. *Class No:* 027.7(083)

[1219]
STANDING CONFERENCE OF NATIONAL AND UNIVERSITY LIBRARIES. Annual library statistics. London, Standing Conference of National and University Libraries, 1981-. Annual. £35. ISSN: 13521020.

Title and format varies. Previously *University library expenditure statistics* (ISSN: 02683539).

The 1995/96 v. (1997. x, 106p.) contains data for 109 institutions. Coverage includes shelving, stock, clientele, loans, staff, expenditure and seating. Indexed. A disc version is also available. *Class No:* 027.7(083)

School Libraries

[1220]
HEEKS, P. Information providers in the school library field: a survey and directory. London, British Library, 1988. vi,80p. £7.50. (*British National Bibliography Research Fund report, v.34.*) ISBN: 0712331646.

Survey complemented by a list of 40 organizations A-Z including library schools, government departments and bodies such as the Book Trust, Educational Publishers' Association and Youth Libraries Group. *Class No:* 027.8

[1221]
LIBRARY ASSOCIATION. School Libraries Group. **The SLG directory to children's and school library services** in the British Isles. 2nd ed. Library Association, School Libraries Group, 1988. 45p. £2.50. ISBN: 0948933100.

Less informative than the title suggests, listing only the senior children's or school library service librarian of each education authority. Geographically arranged in the same order as *Libraries in the United Kingdom and the Republic of Ireland* (*q.v.*). Also includes personnel of library schools offering courses in library provision for young people and schools. *Class No:* 027.8

[1222]
RUDIN, C. The School librarian's sourcebook. New York, Bowker, 1990. xiii,504p. £34;$38. ISBN: 0835227111.

Critically annotated bibliography of 270, mostly recent, items relating to school librarianship in the US. Organized in 5 main sections covering administration, collections, services, user education and technology. Author, title and subject indexes. *Class No:* 027.8

[1223]
A Survey of library services to schools and children in the UK. Loughborough, Library and Information Statistics Unit, Department of Library and Information Studies, Loughborough University, 1991-. Annual. £22.50. ISSN: 13533118.

First published for 1990/91 as *A Survey of public library services to schools and children in England and Wales* (ISSN: 09674896).

The 1994/95 issue (Creaser, C. *comp.* 1995. vi,181p.) presents data at local authority level in main sections: Staffing; Public library services to children; School library services. Summary tables and commentary precedes. *Class No:* 027.8

028 Reading

Reading

[1224]
Best books: experts choose their favourites. Murray, C., *ed.* Oxford, Helicon, 1996. xiii,269p. £16.99. ISBN: 1859861342.

'New ed.' 1997 (£9.99. ISBN: 1859861954).

Topically arranged listing under 5 main sections: Aspects of society; Language and literature; The Arts; Science and technology; History. 6-12 books for each topic each selected and described by contributors. These include numerous famous names such as Brian Aldiss on science fiction, Malcolm Bradbury on the American novel and Anthony Clare on psychiatry. Introductions to each topic area. Lacks statement of selection criteria and other prefatory matter other than brief introduction by Doris Lessing. Nonetheless, a well-executed work, one of the few recent guides to general reading from a largely British perspective. *Class No:* 028

[1225]
—BRATMAN, F. *and* LEWIS, S. The Reader's companion: a book lover's guide to the most important books in every field of knowledge as chosen by experts. New York, Hyperion, 1994. 276p. $17.95. ISBN: 078686009x.

Pbk ed. also available ($9.95. ISBN: 0786880953).

Arranged in 9 broad topical sections. Contributions from over 200 'experts' including many famous names (*e.g.* J.K. Galbraith on economics). *Class No:* 028

[1226]
Books for college libraries: a core collection of 50,000 titles. 3rd ed. Chicago, American Library Association, 1988. 6v. ISBN: 083893353x.

V.1 Humanities (315p., 6,746 entries). V.2 Language and literature (607p., 14,102 entries). V.3 History (451p., 9,314 entries). V.4 Social sciences (541p., 11,016 entries). V.5 Psychology, science, technology, bibliography (450p., 8,482 entries). V.6 Index. First published 1967 (1056p.). 2nd ed. in 6v. 1975. Preceded by the A.L.A.'s *A List of books for college libraries* (1931-40).

Recommended core collection of monographs for undergraduate libraries, intended primarily as a selection tool. Confined to English-language material except for dictionaries and items which support language studies. Classroom texts excluded. Much expanded coverage of science and technology in this ed. Entries, unannotated, arranged by Library of Congress classification with subject data. Author and title index keyed to entry no.; subject index refers to class no. Also available on magnetic tape. *Class No:* 028

[1227]
An English library. Farrow, N., *and others eds.* 6th ed. Aldershot, Gower in association with the Book Trust, 1990. ix,385p. £19.95;$29.95. ISBN: 0566058189.

1st ed. 1943; 5th ed. 1963.

Compiled 'with one objective: to identify the books from the classical and modern heritage that will extend our enjoyment of reading' (Introduction p.vi). Over 2,500 titles, selected by 20 contributors. Briefly annotated entries in 15 categories (*e.g.* World literature in English, Children's literature, Drama, Biography, Travel, History, The Bible, Fine arts, Reference), each with an introductory section discussing the selection. Author and title index. Many entries omit publisher's name; prices not given. *Refer* (v.6(3), Autumn 1990, p.21-22) notes outdated editions in the reference books section. *Class No:* 028

[1228]
The Good book guide. London, The Good Book Guide, 1977-. Monthly. £24.

Frequency varies.

Intended as a guide for the general reader. Brief evaluative summaries for *c.*250 books published in Great Britain in each issue, many written by specialists. Linked to a book ordering service, but all titles selected and reviewed on merit. *Class No:* 028

[1229]
Good reading: a guide for serious readers. Weber, J.S., *ed.* 23rd ed. New York, Bowker, 1989. xxx,465p. £40;$44. ISBN: 0835227073.

First published as a pamphlet 1932. 22nd ed. 1985.

Lists and annotates *c.*2,500 titles in 7 subdivided topical sections, each with an introductory essay. A less comprehensive, but much cheaper, alternative to the same publisher's *Reader's adviser* (*q.v.*). *Class No:* 028

[1230]
Public library catalog: a guide to reference books and adult non-fiction. Yaakov, J., *ed.* 10th ed. New York, Wilson, 1994. vii,1325p. $230. (*Standard catalog series.*) ISBN: 0824208595.

First published 1934 as *Standard catalog for public libraries.* Now issued quinquennially, each ed. updated by annual supplements.

Selection of in print, non-fiction English language titles by a panel of public librarians. 7,735 entries by abridged Dewey classification giving basic bibliographical detail, price, annotation and for many items an evaluation from an identified source. Author, title and subject indexes, the latter containing analytical references to topics which appear in sections of composite works. Directory of publishers and distributors. Paperbound annual supplements each list about 1,000 further titles. *Class No:* 028

[1231]

—Best books for public libraries: the 10,000 top fiction and non-fiction titles. Arozena, S., *ed.* New Providence, N.J., Bowker, 1992. x,840p. £65;$75. ISBN: 0835230732.

10,293 actual entries for critically acclaimed titles published since 1965. Fiction arranged by genre, non-fiction (6,169 entries) classified by Dewey. Author, title and subject indexes. Fewer entries than *The Reader's catalog* (below) with many subjects under-represented. '(W)ill not compete with such standard tools for collection development as the *Public library catalog* and the *Fiction catalog*' (*Reference books bulletin 1992-93*, 1994, p.31). *Class No:* 028

[1232]

RAPHAEL, F. *and* **McLEISH, K. The List of books.** London, Mitchell Beazley, 1981. 160p. ISBN: 0855332239.

Select guide to 3,000 titles aimed at the 'reasonably literate person' (Introduction p.4). Briefly annotated entries in 36 subject sections A-Z (*e.g.* Anthropology ... Children's books ... Food and drink ... Travel and exploration). 4 preliminary lists including 'Books of the decade 1970-80'. Author index. Received a mixed critical response, largely owing to its attempt to evaluate and categorize each book under terms such as 'Seminal', 'Major masterpiece', 'Infuriating', etc. *Class No:* 028

[1233]

The Reader's adviser: a layman's guide to the literature. Sader, M., *ed.* 14th ed. New York, Bowker, 1994. 6v. £400;$500 (set price, v. also available individually). ISBN: 0835233200.

V.1 *The Best in reference works, British literature and American literature*; v.2 *The Best in world literature*; v.3 *The Best in social sciences, history and the arts*; v.4 *The Best in philosophy and religion*; v.5 *The Best in science, technology and medicine*; v.6 *Indexes*.

First published 1921. Early eds. with title *Bookman's manual.* 13th ed. 1986-88.

Volumes divided into 110 chapters contributed by 120 academics, librarians, etc. Each has a brief introduction followed by listings, beginning with general and reference works, then more specific titles by author, genre or topic. Many entries give brief annotations in addition to bibliographic citation, price and ISBN. Some out of print titles included. Individual volume indexes by subject, author and title in addition to the collective indexes in v.6. Fewer changes to this ed. than the 13th which expanded the number of volumes from 3 to 6. In the US can be 'heartily recommended for all but the smallest public library' (*Reference books bulletin* in *Booklist*, v.90(22), August 1994, p.2073). Elsewhere the American imprints may be an obstacle, but the work is an undoubted reference classic, the most comprehensive listing of general English language reading available.

CD-ROM version launched 1996 (Annual updating. $300 (single user). ISBN: 0835238490). Windows and Mac platforms with FolioViews software. Features include 3 search modes (browsing, author/title, query template using keywords and Boolean operators), hypertext links within entries and a 'Booklist' function enabling creation of customised bibliographies. *Class No:* 028

[1234]

The Reader's catalog: an annotated selection of more than 40,000 of the best books in print in over 300 categories. O'Brien, G.O., *and others eds.* 2nd ed. New York, Reader's Catalog, 1996. v,1969p. illus. $34.75. ISBN: 0924322012.

First published 1989.

Aimed at the general reader. Entries give basic bibliographical detail and in most cases a short annotation. Author and title indexes. 50% new material in this ed. The entire catalogue is to be made available for searching through the WWW offering enhanced cross-referencing and full Boolean searching, plus an additional database of over 300,000 titles. Further information at http://www.primarygroup.com/works/readcat.html. *Class No:* 028

[1235]

SONNENSCHEIN, W.S. The Best books: a reader's guide and literary reference, being a contribution towards systematic bibliography. 3rd ed. (entirely re-written). London, Routledge, 1910-35. 6v.

Reprinted Detroit, Gale, 1969. ISBN: 0810333627. First published 1887.

Pt.1: A. Theology; B. Mythology; C. Philosophy. (1910). Pt.2: D. Society; E. Geography. (1912). Pt.3: F. History and historical geography; G. Archaeology and historical collaterals. (1923). Pt.4: H. Natural science; H*. medicine and surgery; I. Arts and trades. (1926). Pt.5: K. Literature and philology. (1931). Pt.6: Authors, titles and subjects index. (1935).

'Records some 150,000 works, with dates of the first and last editions, and price, size and publishers' names, English and American' (Note to v.1). Brief annotations are given for some items. Now outdated, but still of some value for less recent books and as a comprehensive, systematic survey. Pt.6 includes a synopsis of the detailed classification scheme. *Class No:* 028

Children's Reading - Study & Criticism

CD-ROM

[1236]

Children's reference Plus: complete bibliographic, review and qualitative information books, reference books, serials, cassettes, software and videos for children and young adults. New Providence, N.J., Bowker, 1992-. CD-ROM database, updated annually. £520;$595.

Combines citations to children's material in sources such as *Books in print, Ulrich's international periodicals directory* and *Words on cassette*, with book summaries from Bowker titles (*e.g. Best books for children*), and the full text of reviews extracted from *Booklist, Kirkus reviews, Library journal, School library journal*, etc. Uses standard Bowker Plus software with DOS interface, up to 26 search criteria available. Not listed on Bowker WWW site 1998, current publication status uncertain. *Class No:* 028:087.5(003.40)

Internet

[1237]

The Children's literature Web guide: Internet resources related to books for children and young adults. Brown, D.K., *comp.* Calgary, Doucette Library of Teaching Resouces, Univ. of Calgary, 1994-. World Wide Web resource.

URL: http://www.acs.ucalcary.ca/kbrown/. Date reviewed 23rd July 1998.

.... *(contd.)*

Regularly updated and well maintained site offering links to hundreds of WWW resources on all aspects of children's literature. Links backed by brief descriptions, categories include book awards, best book listings, author sites, resources for teachers, Internet discussion groups and children's publishers and booksellers. Site search facility also provided. *Class No:* 028:087.5(003.41)

Bibliographies

[1238]

Children's literature: a guide to reference sources. Haviland, V., *comp.* Washington D.C., Library of Congress, 1966. x,341p., illus. ISBN: 0686979362.

First supplement. 1972. (vii,316p.); Second supplement. 1977. (x,413p. ISBN: 084440215x).

The main v. has 809 entries under broad topics such as Authorship, Illustration, Bibliography, plus 183 entries on International studies and National studies. Includes periodical articles, unpublished theses, records and tapes, as well as books and pamphlets. Index of authors, titles and subjects. The two supplements chiefly cover new material 1966-74, the latter having 929 entries in the same basic format as the parent volume. *Class No:* 028:087.5(01)

[1239]

Choosing books for young people: a guide to criticism and bibliography, 1945-1975. Ettlinger, J.R.T. *and* Spirt, D.L., *comps.* Chicago, American Library Association, 1982. 219p. ISBN: 0838903665.

Deals with any work of 16p. or longer which selects, criticizes or lists children's books. 600 titles arranged A-Z by author with subject index and added entry index of joint authors, titles, organizations and series. Much of the material is also to be found in Haviland (*q.v.*), but a valuable source, especially for its 'clear and complete annotations' (*RQ*, v.22 (3), Spring 1983, p.302).

Continued by *Choosing books for young people vol. 2: a guide to criticism and bibliography 1976-1984 (Ettinger, J.R.T. & Spirt, D.L. comps.* Oryx Press, 1987. 152p. ISBN: 0897742478), containing a further 415 entries.
Class No: 028:087.5(01)

[1240]

DENMAN-WEST, M.W. Children's literature: a guide to information sources. Englewood, Colo., Libraries Unlimited, 1998. xiv,187p. £36.95;$38.50. (*Reference sources in the humanities.*) ISBN: 1563084481.

Bibliography of bibliographies and other information sources. 478 annotated entries in 11 sections: Guides to award-winning books - Recommended reading - Multicultural literature - Subject bibliographies - Reference books - Biographies - Core periodicals/multimedia reviews - Nonprint media - Special collections of children's literature - Professional associations - The information superhighway via the Internet. Copyright date for nearly all printed material included after 1985. Author/title and subject indexes. Rather brief and some omissions, but the most up to date reference guide to children's literature available.
Class No: 028:087.5(01)

[1241]

HENDRICKSON, L. Children's literature: a guide to the criticism. Boston, Mass., G.K. Hall, 1987. xxvi,664p. $45. (*A reference publication in literature.*) ISBN: 0816186707.

Intended 'to draw together, for scholars and generalists, significant articles, books and dissertations relating to children's literature criticism that have originated in disparate disciplines and have been published in widely scattered popular and scholarly sources' (Preface). Covers fiction, drama, poetry and some non-fiction titles. Most items included published in the 1970s or 1980s. In 2 sections: A. Authors and their works (p.1-298); B. Subjects, themes and genres. Entries include descriptive annotations. Indexed by author, title, subject and critics. Appended lists of reference works and journals in children's literature.
Class No: 028:087.5(01)

[1242]

LEIF, I.P. Children's literature: a historical and contemporary bibliography. Troy, N.Y., Whitson, 1977. (4),xix,338p. ISBN: 0685880214.

An unannotated list of 2,473 items in sections: Children's literature today (by country etc.); Children's literature yesterday (histories by country, early publishers, bibliographical aids); School-books and religious tracts; Authors of children's books (A-Z p.137-248); Children's book illustrators (by artist p.249-98); Writing, publishing and reviewing. Author index. Aims to include 'virtually all the literature about children's literature'.
Class No: 028:087.5(01)

[1243]

LENZ, M.. *and* MEACHAM, M. Young adult literature and nonprint materials: resources for selection. Metuchen, N.J., Scarecrow Press, 1994. x,336p. £33.75;$37.50. ISBN: 0810829061.

Sections: I. Professional resources - II. Periodicals - III. Resources for research - IV. Specific genre and categorized selection tools - V. Subject-specialized bibliographies - VI. Using books with young adults - VII. Tools for selection of audiovisual materials. 694 entries with substantial and evaluative annotations. Emphasis is on works published 1988-1993. Includes a limited number of UK titles. Title and author/editor/illustrator indexes; list of publishers.
Class No: 028:087.5(01)

[1244]

Once upon ... a time for young people and their books: an annotated resource guide. Kohn, R., *comp.* Metuchen, N.J., and London, Scarecrow Press, 1986. v,211p. £20.25;$22.50. ISBN: 0810819228.

Briefly annotated guide to 829 bibliographies and other reference tools. Arranged by author with title and 220 heading subject index. Primarily American material, but a fair selection of British titles included.
Class No: 028:087.5(01)

[1245]

PELLOWSKI, A. The World of children's literature. New York and London, Bowker, 1968. x,538p., illus. ISBN: 0835201066.

Annotated bibliography of 4,496 numbered items including history and development of children's literature and libraries. International in scope, entries from 106 countries; includes monographs, histories, critical studies, anthologies, book lists and selection aids. Index has 15,000 entries.
Class No: 028:087.5(01)

[1246]

RAHN, S. Children's literature: an annotated bibliography of the history and criticism. New York, Garland, 1981. xxviii,451p. (*Garland reference library of the humanities, v.263.*) ISBN: 0824093577.

1,328 entries in 4 main sections: I. Aims and definitions - II. Historical studies: A. General; B. Specialized - III. Studies of genres - IV. Studies of authors (p.139-411): A. Individual; B. Group. Most entries for material published in the 1960's or 1970's, but coverage extends back to the nineteenth century. Includes periodical articles. Index (p.415-51). British material appears well-represented.
Class No: 028:087.5(01)

Encyclopaedias & Dictionaries

[1247]

CARPENTER, H. *and* **PRICHARD, M. The Oxford companion to children's literature.** Oxford, Oxford Univ. Press, 1984. x,587p., illus. £27.50;$55. ISBN: 0192115820.

More than 900 biographical entries for authors, illustrators, printers, publishers and educationalists. A further *c.*2,000 entries for major works of fiction, characters from books, genres, organizations, children's literature of specific countries and children's play and learning. Equal attention given to British, American and Commonwealth works. Well-written entries; comprehensively cross-referenced. Short on bibliographical guidance for further reading. A major contribution containing an enormous amount of information not readily obtainable from any other source. *Class No:* 028:087.5(03)

[1248]

CARRUTH, G. The Young reader's companion. New Providence, N.J., Bowker, 1993. xv,681p. illus. £33;$49.50. ISBN: 0835227650.

A-Z short entry encyclopedia . The *c.*2,000 entries include 750 for authors, 280 for historical persons and 200 for mythological or legendary figures. Remainder mostly for classic titles or plots. Good 20p. subject index. Informal presentation pitched directly at young people. 'Comprehensive and impressive' (*Choice*, v.31(4), December 1993, p.581). *Class No:* 028:087.5(03)

[1249]

FISHER, M. Who's who in children's books: a treasury of the familiar characters of childhood. London, Weidenfeld & Nicolson, 1975. 399p., illus. ISBN: 0297770373.

Incorporates certain entries from the same author's *Who's who of boys writers and illustrators* (London, The Author, 1964. 99p.).

Describes in detail *c.*1,000 characters from children's literature adding critical comment. 'Doctor Doolittle': 4 columns, 2 illus.; 'Paddington': 1 column, 3 illus. Titles of books concerned are appended. Cross-references. Attractively produced, over 400 illus. with 16 colour plates.
Class No: 028:087.5(03)

[1250]

—MORTIMORE, A.D. Index to characters in children's literature. Bristol, Mortimore, 1977. 191p. ISBN: 0950566500.

Brief index relating character to work and author. Mortimore later produced *Children's literary characters index 1981: the first supplement to 'Index to characters in children's literature'* (Bristol, Mortimore, 1981. 78p. ISBN: 0950566519). *Class No:* 028:087.5(03)

[1251]

HELBIG, A.K. *and* **PERKINS, A.G. Dictionary of American children's fiction.** Westport, Conn., Greenwood Press, 1985-86. 2v.

1859-1959 (1985. xv,666p. £62.95;$79.50. ISBN: 0313225907); *1960-1984* (1986. £67.50;$79.50. xvi,914p. ISBN: 0313252335).

The 1960-1984 v. has 1,550 entries based on 489 books, the 1859-1959 v. 1,226 entries based on 420 books. Selection of titles based on finalists for literary awards and established listings of recommended reading. Entries, in one A-Z sequence for authors, titles, major characters, settings, plots and other significant elements, vary in length from 4-5 lines to 1½ pages. Indexes (p.593-666, 1859-1959; p.753-914, 1960-1984) include pseudonyms, illustrators, genres, settings etc., not entered directly. 'Indispensable' (*Bulletin of bibliography*, v.55(2), June 1988, p.159).

Continued by *Dictionary of American children's fiction, 1985-1989* (Greenwood Press, 1993. x,368p. £49.50;$59.95 ISBN: 0313277192) containing over 400 entries based on 134 books and *Dictionary of American children's fiction, 1990-1994* (Greenwood Press, 1996. xiv,473p. £63.95;$79.50. ISBN: 0313287635) with 567 entries based on 189 books. *Class No:* 028:087.5(03)

[1252]

—HELBIG, A.K. *and* PERKINS, A.G. Dictionary of British children's fiction: books of recognized merit. Westport, Greenwood, 1989. 2v.(xx,1632p.). £135;$150. ISBN: 0313225915.

Similar to the American set (above). 1,626 entries based on 387 books published 1687-1985, chosen for inclusion from 21 award and citation lists. Author, title, character etc., entries as before; comprehensively indexed.
Class No: 028:087.5(03)

[1253]

—HELBIG, A.K. *and* PERKINS, A.G. Dictionary of children's fiction from Australia, Canada, India, New Zealand and selected African countries: books of recognized merit. Westport, Conn., Greenwood, 1992. xv,583p. £76.50;$89.50. ISBN: 0313261261.

Same pattern as the American and British titles, containing 726 entries based on 263 books by 166 authors. Books from Australia and Canada predominate.
Class No: 028:087.5(03)

[1254]

International companion encyclopedia of children's literature. Hunt, P., *ed.* London, Routledge, 1996. xv,923p. £85;$130. ISBN: 0415088569.

5 sections: I. Theory and critical approaches - II. Types and genres - III. The Context of children's literature - IV. Applications of children's literature - V. The World of children's literature. 86 entries or essays across the sections (*e.g.* Ideology (I); Animal stories (II); Libraries and research collections (III); Teaching fiction and poetry (IV)), the last containing 31 mainly geographically based accounts. Essays, many by distinguished contributors, average 5,000 words and conclude with appended references and further reading. Index (p.893-923). '(C)ommendable for its format and range of topics' (*Choice*, v.34(6), February 1997, p.944), although some essays omit discussion of recent issues and others reflect the writer's literary or political bent.
Class No: 028:087.5(03)

[1255]
JONES, R.E. Characters in children's literature. Detroit, Gale, 1997. xvi,529p. illus. £46;$60. ISBN: 0787604003.

Deals with more than 1,700 characters from 230 books by 152 writers. Entries, by author A-Z, give basic biographical detail with list of works, followed by analysis of plots and themes and detailed treatment of characters. Titles generally covered in 1-4 pages, entries include list of critical material and further reading. Character/title index. More characters than Fisher or Mortimore (*qq.v*), but selection of works has greater US bias. *Class No:* 028:087.5(03)

[1256]
—GILLESPIE, J.T. *and* NADEN, C.J. Characters in young adult literature. Detroit, Gale, 1997. xiv,535p. illus. £46;$60. ISBN: 0787604011.

Same format as Jones (above) dealing with more than 2,000 characters from 232 works by 148 authors.
Class No: 028:087.5(03)

[1257]
LEES, S. *and* MACINTYRE, P. The Oxford companion to Australian children's literature. Melbourne, Oxford Univ. Press in assoc. with ALIA Press, 1993. vii,485p. illus. £25;Aus$49.95. ISBN: 0195532848.

Contains about 1,600 entries for authors, illustrators, individual titles, subjects (Animal stories... Death...), and institutions (*e.g.* The Children's Library Guild of Australia). Bibliography (p.462-70); appendix listing book award winners. *Class No:* 028:087.5(03)

[1258]
—PRENTICE, J. *and* BENNETT, B. A Guide to Australian children's literature. Port Melbourne, D.W. Thorpe, 1992. viii,323p. £21.50;Aus$39.50. ISBN: 1875589112.

11 section reference guide. Includes a chronology, detail on special collections and awards, a bibliography of foreign language editions, a list of journals and magazines and an annotated listing of books, articles and videos concerning Australian children's literature. Indexed.
Class No: 028:087.5(03)

[1259]
Lexikon der Kinder- und Jugendliteratur: Personen-, Länder- und Sachartikel zu Geschichte und Gegenwart der Kinder- und Jugendliteratur. Doderer, K., *hrsg.* Weinheim, Beltz Verlag, 1974-81. 4v., illus. ISBN: 3407565119, Bd.1.

An important German language encyclopedia of children's literature, international in scope. Signed articles, most with bibliographical references. Reasonable coverage of English language subjects *e.g.* 'Blyton, Enid Mary', *c.*800 words, list of works, list of secondary literature (mainly German). V.4 contains supplementary articles and an index.
Class No: 028:087.5(03)

[1260]
—Kinder- und Jugendliteratur: ein Lexikon: Autoren, Illustratoren, Verlage, Begriffe. Baumgärtner, A.C. *and* Pleticha, H., *hrsg.* Meitlingen, Corian, 1995-. Looseleaf. ISBN: 3890481507.

To be issued in instalments. In 6 sections: T.1 *Autoren*; T.2 *Illustratoen*; T.3 *Verlage*; T.4 *Institutionen*; T.5 *Literarische*; T.6 *Themen/Aspekte*.

Intended as an update and replacement for Doderer (above). *Class No:* 028:087.5(03)

Reviews & Abstracts

[1261]
Children's literature abstracts. Austin, Tex., IFLA Children's Libraries Section/Round Table of Children's Literature Documentation Centres, 1973-. Quarterly. $32. ISSN: 03062015.

350-400 indicative abstracts per issue, drawing on *c.*70 perioidicals, including a few non-English titles. Abstracts signed, but short, rarely exceeding 100 words. Topical arrangement (*e.g.* Authors and illustrators ... Fantasy and science fiction ... National and minority literatures ... Young adult literarture). Separate index issued annually containing author/illustrator/subject/title and critic/editor/reviewer sequences. A supplementary series *Children's literature abstracts: books and pamphlets* is published semi-annually giving similar treatment to monograph material.
Class No: 028:087.5(048)

[1262]
Children's literature review: excerpts from reviews, criticism and commentary on books for children and young people. Detroit, Gale, 1976-. Irregular (approx 2-3 issues pa.). $110. ISSN: 03624145.

'Designed to provide a permanent, accessible record of ongoing scholarship'. Each v. deals with the work of a limited number of authors and illustrators. V.31 (Senick, G.J. *ed.* 1994. xv,269p.) treats 10 authors giving biographical detail, personal statements, critical writings and extracts from reviews of individual titles. International in scope, *c.*110 British authors covered in v.1-31. Cumulative index to authors, nationalities and titles in each v.
Class No: 028:087.5(048)

Indexes

[1263]
Children's book review index. Detroit, Gale, 1975-. Annual. $103. ISSN: 01475681.

Cites all reviews of children's books up to age 10 (grades K-5) that appear in any of the indexed sources for *Book review index* (*q.v.*). Entries arranged by author with title and, since 1986, illustrator indexes.
Class No: 028:087.5(048)(014)

[1264]
—Children's book review index: a master cumulation 1965-84. A cumulated index to more than 200,000 reviews of approximately 55,000 titles. Tarbert, G.C. *and* Beach, B., *eds.* Detroit, Gale, 1985. 5v. £325;$385. ISBN: 0810320460.

V.1-v.4 A-Z; v.5 Title index. Earlier cumulation covers 1969-81 (1982. 4v.).

Extends coverage of children's books back to the beginning of *Book review index*.
Class No: 028:087.5(048)(014)

Yearbooks & Directories

[1265]
Children's literature: annual of The Modern Language Association of America, Division on Children's Literature and The Children's Literature Association. New Haven, Conn., Yale Univ. Press, 1972-. Annual. ISSN: 00928208.

V.1-8 published by the Children's Literature Association.

Some issues devoted to a theme, *e.g.* v.20 discusses the work of Kipling. V.25 (1997. xvii,289p. illus.) has 11 articles of 10-30 pages and 7 reviews. Also contains 'Dissertations of note', an annotated listing (p.279-86) of *c.*50 titles. *Class No:* 028:087.5(058)

[1266]

Guide Européen du livre de jeunesse. Zoughabi, H., *éd.* Paris, Éditions du Cercle de la Librarie, 1994. 484p. FFr240. ISBN: 2765405506.

At head of title: Centre de promotion du livre de jeunesse Seine-Saint-Denis.

Directory of childen's book information. Country sections contain briefly annotated entries for publishers, authors, illustators, bookshops, libraries, specialist magazines, organizations, etc. Extended treatment for France (p.11-186); other detail includes list of children's literature reference works (p.449-457). *Class No:* 028:087.5(058)

[1267]

International directory of children's literature. Dunhouse, M.B., *comp.* New York, Oxford, Facts on File, 1986. 129p. ISBN: 0816014116.

Data from 84 countries. Chapters: 1) Children's literature publishers (over 50% of book) - 2) Children's magazines - 3) Children's literature magazines - 4) Children's literature organizations - 5) Children's literature fairs, seminars, conferences - 6) Children's literature prizes - 7) Major children's libraries and special collections - 8) Statistics on children's books. *Class No:* 028:087.5(058)

[1268]

International directory of children's literature specialists. Maissen, L., *ed.* München, Saur, 1986. 263p. ISBN: 3598106238.

Compiled under the auspices of the International Board on Books for Young People for UNESCO.

Alphabetical listing of 405 children's literature specialists from 32 countries in fields such as writing, illustration, publishing, bookselling, libraries, schools, reviewing, research and teaching. Subject index by 13 categories of specialism. *Class No:* 028:087.5(058)

Teaching Materials

[1269]

LUNDIN, A.H. *and* **CUBBERLEY, C.W. Teaching children's literature: a resource guide,** with a directory of courses. Jefferson, N.C., McFarland, 1995. vii,355p. £38.25;$42.50. ISBN: 0899509908.

In 3pts. Pt. I has 272 annotated entries for books, journal articles, etc. on the teaching of children's literature and the use of children's books. Pt. II contains 8 representative syllabi (*e.g.* Literature for young children Illinois State University); Pt. III comprises a directory of children's literature courses in US four-year colleges. Author/title index to pt. I (p.343-55). 'The layout is excellent and the breadth of material is extremely good ... (but) heavy US bias' (*Reference reviews*, v.9(5), 1995, p.38). *Class No:* 028:087.5(072)

Chronologies

[1270]

BINGHAM, J. *and* **SCHOLT, G. Fifteen centuries of children's literature:** an annotated chronology of British and American works in historical context. Westport, Conn., Greenwood, 1980. 1,540p., illus., facsims. £49.50;$55. ISBN: 0313221642.

'The purpose of this work is to provide a single, annotated chronological listing of significant or representative books written or used with or appropriated by British and American children from the sixth century to 1945' (Preface). 6 sections (Anglo-Saxon, ca.523-1099; Middle England, 1100-1499; Renaissance to Restoration, 1500-1659; Restoration to independence, 1660-1799; Nineteenth century, 1800-1899; Twentieth century, 1900-1945), each with an essay on the historical background and an annotated chronology. Lengthy bibliography of secondary sources (p.407-18). Index of authors, illustrators, translators and early publishers; index of titles cited in the chronological sections. Appendices include list of facsimiles and reprints of titles cited in the chronology. *Class No:* 028:087.5(090)

Histories

[1271]

AVERY, G. Behold the child: American children and their books 1621-1922. London, Bodley Head, 1994. xiii,226p. illus. ISBN: 0370319524.

Published in the US by John Hopkins Univ. Press ($29.95. ISBN: 0801850665).

First comprehensive history of pre-twentieth century American childen's literature. Chronological treatment in 7 chaps. Small type in double column format, black and white illustrations in text. Select bibliography (p.215-18); index. '(W)ill set standards for years to come ... a monumental work' (*The Horn book*, v.72(4), July/August 1996, p.483). *Class No:* 028:087.5(091)

[1272]

Children's literature: an illustrated history. Hunt, P., *ed.* Oxford, Oxford Univ. Press, 1995. xiv,378p. illus. £22.50;$45. ISBN: 0192123203.

12 chaps. in broadly chronological arrangement *e.g.* Morality and levity (1780-1820); Children's literature in America from the Puritan beginnings to 1870; Internationalism, fantasy and realism (1945-1970). Illustrations black and white except for 36 in colour (full page). Chronology (p.352-59), further reading (p.360-66) and index. *Class No:* 028:087.5(091)

[1273]

DARTON, F.J.H. Children's books in England: five centuries of social life. Alderson, B., *rev. & ed.* 3rd ed. Cambridge, Cambridge University Press, 1982. xviii,398p., illus., facsims. ISBN: 0521240204.

First published 1932; 2nd ed. (ed. K. Lines) 1958.

A classic account in 15 broadly chronological chapters covering to the close of the 19th century. This ed. is carefully edited and corrected by Alderson, with the emphasis on rectifying factual inaccuracies, leaving the original text unchanged as much as possible. Substantive new material in appendices *e.g.* 'Some additional notes on Victorian and Edwardian times' (p.316-29). 'Editors notes' (p.349-61). Fully revised 'General book list' (p.362-71). Index. *Class No:* 028:087.5(091)

[1274]

HURLIMANN, B. Three centuries of children's books in Europe. Alderson, B., *trans. and ed.* London, Oxford Univ. Press, 1967. xviii,297p. illus.(inc.pl.).

First published 1959 as *Europäische Kinderbücher in drei Jahrhunderten*. 2nd ed. 1963 of which this is the translation.

18 chapters on such themes as 'Jabberwocky', 'Education through pictures', 'Politics in children's books' and 'Men of letters who wrote for children'. Bio-bibliography (books on Grimm, etc., p.272-84). Index. *Class No:* 028:087.5(091)

[1275]

JACKSON, M.V. Engines of instruction, mischief and magic: children's literature in England from its beginnings to 1839. Lincoln, Neb., Univ. of Nebraska Press, 1989. xiv,304p., illus. ISBN: 0803225725.

Pbck. version in print ($16.50. ISBN: 0805275708).

10 chapter work which adopts a generally chronological approach. Gives greater emphasis to socio-political factors shaping the context of children's books than either Darton or Thwaite (*qq.v*). Selected bibliography (primary sources, bibliographies, etc., criticism and background (p.267-82)); index. An 'exemplary study - scholarly, readable and significant' (*The Horn book magazine*, July/August 1991, p.484). *Class No:* 028:087.5(091)

[1276]

MEIGS, C., *and others*. A Critical history of children's literature: a survey of children's books in English. Rev. ed. New York, Macmillan; London, Collier-Macmillan, 1969. xxviii,708p. ISBN: 0025839004.

1st ed. 1953.

In 4 pts.: Roots in the past up to 1840; Widening horizons 1840-1890; A rightful heritage 1890-1920; Golden years and time of tumult 1920-1967. Each section comprises *c.*12 contributed essays. Short bibliographies at most chapter ends. Index (p.669-708). Remains one of the more complete accounts of the history of children's literature.
Class No: 028:087.5(091)

[1277]

SMITH, E.S. The History of children's literature: a syllabus with selected bibliographies. Rev. & enl. ed. Chicago, American Library Association, 1980. xiii,290p. $40. ISBN: 0838902863.

Revised by M. Hodges and S. Steinfirst. First published 1937.

In 17 broadly chronological sections including The feudal age; Instruction and amusement: the eighteenth century; Early Victorian literature. Each section has a brief introduction, an 'outline' or programme for study and a detailed annotated bibliography of supporting literature. Most items retained from the 1st ed. with new material up to 1977. Author and title index. *Class No:* 028:087.5(091)

[1278]

THWAITE, M. From primer to pleasure in reading: an introduction to the history of children's books in England from the invention of printing to 1914 with an outline of some developments in other countries. 2nd ed. London, Library Association, 1972. x,340p., illus. ISBN: 0853654654.

A scholarly, chronological survey. 4 sections devoted to England (1. Sources - 2. Foundations - 3. The dawn of imagination - 4. Flood tide; the Victorian age and Edwardian aftermath, p.93-224), 1 section to children's books abroad (North America, Western Europe, Australia). Appendices: 1. Chronological table - 2. Bibliography: (p.283-313 by chapters and sections, 342 items, general sources annotated). Index (p.314-40). *Class No:* 028:087.5(091)

[1279]

TOWNSEND, J.R. Written for children: an outline of English-language children's literature. 6th ed. London, Bodley Head, 1995. xii,388p., illus. £9.99. ISBN: 0370315200.

Published in the US by Scarecrow Press ($37.50. ISBN: 0810831171). First published 1965.

Critical account of the development of children's literature with the emphasis on books of literary merit rather than

....(contd.)

reading matter generally. Chronological presentation, includes poetry and picture books. Geographic coverage extends to US and Commonwealth countries. A useful general history. *Class No:* 028:087.5(091)

Biographies

[1280]

American writers for children. Detroit, Gale, 1983-87. 4v., illus., ports, facsims. £107;$140 per v. (*Dictionary of literary biography 22,42,52,61.*)

The 4v. comprise: *American writers for children before 1900* (Estes, G. *ed.* xiii,441p. DLB.v.42. ISBN: 0810317206); *American writers for children, 1900-1960* (Cech, J. *ed.* xiv,412p. DLB,v.22. ISBN: 810311461); *American writers for children since 1960: fiction* (Estes, G. *ed.* xiii,488p. DLB,v.52. ISBN: 0810317303); *American writers for children since 1960; poets, illustrators and non-fiction authors* (Estes, G. *ed.* xiii,430p. DLB,v.61. ISBN: 0810317397).

171 essays across the four volumes, varying in length from 4-15 pages. Standard *Dictionary of literary biography* format including principal and secondary works, periodical publications, critical references and location of papers. Well illustrated with portraits and facsimiles.
Class No: 028:087.5(092)

[1281]

—British children's writers. Detroit, Gale, 1994-96. 4v. illus., ports., facsims. £107;$140 per v. (*Dictionary of literary biography, v.141,160,161,163.*)

The 4v. comprise: *British children's writers 1800-1880* (Khorana, M. *ed.* xvii,394p. DLB,163. ISBN: 0810393581); *British children's writers 1880-1914* (Zaidman, L.M. *ed.* xvii,390p. DLB,141. ISBN: 0810355558); *British children's writers 1914-1960* (Hettinga D.R. & Schmidt, G.D. *eds.* xv,422p. DLB,160. ISBN: 0810395557); *British children's writers since 1960* (Hunt, C.C. *ed.* xvii,394p. DLB,161. ISBN: 0810393565).

1880-1914 v. covers 24 writers including Belloc, Greenaway, Kipling, Potter and Stevenson. Separate chapter 'Minor illustrators' (p.312-21). *Class No:* 028:087.5(092)

[1282]

DOYLE, B. The Who's who of children's literature. London, Evelyn, 1968. xi,380p., illus. ISBN: 0238788121.

Bio-bibliographical entries for over 400 British, American and European writers and illustrators since 1800. In two A-Z sequences: writers, illustrators. 104 illus. 17p. bibliography. Very readable, with 'hearty prejudices' (*Times literary supplement*, no.3484, 5th December 1968, p.1370).
Class No: 028:087.5(092)

[1283]

KUNITZ, S.J. *and* HAYCRAFT, H. The Junior book of authors. 2nd ed. New York, Wilson, 1951. viii,309p., ports. $40.

First published 1934.

Biographical dictionary written for young readers. Entries, many of them autobiographical, arranged A-Z by surnames. 289 sketches, 129 new to this ed. The old ed. remains useful for the 108 sketches omitted. Continued by:-

More junior authors, (Fuller, M. *ed.* 1963. 235p. $35. ISBN: 0824200365), adding 268 sketches.

Third book of junior authors, (de Montreville, D. & Hills, D. *eds.* 1972. 320p. $40. ISBN: 08242048512).

Fourth book of junior authors and illustrators, (de Montreville, D. & Crawford, E.D. *eds.* 1978. 370p. $45.

.... *(contd.)*
ISBN: 0824205685).

Fifth book of junior authors and illustrators, (Holtze, S.H. *ed.* 1983. 357p. $48. ISBN: 0824206940).

Sixth book of junior authors and illustrators (Holtze, S.H. *ed.* 1989. 345p. $48. ISBN: 0824207777).

The *Seventh book of junior authors and illustrators* (Holtze, S.H. *ed.* 1996. vi,371p. ISBN: 0824208730) has 235 biographical sketches, each concluding with a selected bibliogaphy of works and references to additional sources. Also contains a cumulative index to the entire series.
Class No: 028:087.5(092)

[1284]
MUNROE, M.H. *and* **BANJA, J.R. The Birthday book:** birthdates, birthplaces and biographical sources for American authors and illustrators of children's books. New York, Neal-Schuman, 1991. xi,499p. £45;$49.95. ISBN: 1555700519.

Covers more than 7,000 individuals. Sources include *Authors of books for young people* and *Junior book of authors*. Indexed by birth month, year and place.
Class No: 028:087.5(092)

[1285]
Something about the author: facts and pictures about authors and illustrators of books for young people. Detroit, Gale, 1971-. approx. 5 issues pa. $96. ISSN: 0276816x.

A continuing series of compendia of biographical and bibliographical information, with illustrations, on selected children's authors and illustrators. Focusses on contemporary figures, but includes major authors and illustrators of the past (separate series *Yesterday's authors of books for children*, discontinued). Cumulated illustrator and author indexes in odd numbered vols. (v.57 onwards). V.89 (1997. xvi,328p.) profiles *c.*115 individuals.
Class No: 028:087.5(092)

[1286]
—Authors and artists for young adults. Detroit, Gale, 1989-. Semi-annual. $75. ISSN: 10405682.

A separate series aimed at adolescents. Considerable overlap with *Contemporary authors* (*q.v.*). V.21 issued 1997. 'One questions the need for another reworking of material already available ... the latest in Gale's efforts to fill library shelves and corner their budgets' (*American reference books annual*, v.23, 1992, p.454).
Class No: 028:087.5(092)

[1287]
—Junior DIScovering authors. Detroit, Gale, 1994. CD-ROM database. $250. ISBN: 0810358964.

Provides biographical detail, essays and bibliographies for 300 of the most studied authors of children's and young adult literature. Based on *Something about the author* and *Major authors and illustrators for young adults*.
Class No: 028:087.5(092)

[1288]
—Major authors and illustrators for children and young adults: a selection of sketches from *Something about the author*. Collier, L. *and* Nakamura, J., *eds.* Detroit, Gale, 1992. 6v. illus. $299. ISBN: 0810377020.

A cheaper alternative to the main series, containing updated and revised profiles for 800 of the most widely read authors and illustrators. *Class No:* 028:087.5(092)

[1289]
—Something about the author: autobiography series. Detroit, Gale, 1986-. Semi-annual. $96. ISSN: 08856842.

Each v. contains about 20 autobiographical essays. Additional information includes a bibliography of the author's book length work. V.25 issued late 1997. Cumulative indexes, as with the main *Something about the author*. *Class No:* 028:087.5(092)

[1290]
Twentieth-century children's writers. Berger, L.S., *ed.* 4th ed. Detroit, St. James Press, 1995. xxxi,1272p. £107:$140. (*Twentieth-century writers series.*) ISBN: 1558621776.

First published 1978; 3rd ed. 1989. Preface by N. Lewis (p.vii-xii).

Covers 'English language authors of fiction, poetry and drama' (p.xvii). More than 400 entries, arranged A-Z, providing biography, a complete list of all separately published books by category (including works for adults), critical assessments by contributors and, in the case of some living entrants, comments by the authors themselves. Appendix (p.1068-1104) of some important representative writers of the 19th century. 'Foreign language writers' with selected books in English translation (p.1107-11). Title index. 'For a one-volume quick source of information about children's authors this is the best source' (*American reference books annual*, v.27, 1996, p.492). Complemented by: *Class No:* 028:087.5(092)

[1291]
—Twentieth-century young adult writers. Berger, L.S., *ed.* Detroit, St. James Press, 1994. xxiii,830p. £107;$140. (*Twentieth-century writers series.*) ISBN: 1558622020.

406 entries for writers whose works appeal to readers ages 11-19. *Class No:* 028:087.5(092)

[1292]
WARD, M.E., *and others*. **Authors of books for young people.** 3rd ed. Metuchen, N.J., Scarecrow Press, 1990. iv,780p. £53.65;$65. ISBN: 0810822938.

First published 1964; 2nd ed. 1971, with supplement 1979.

Brief biographical detail for 4,000 authors A-Z based on a file maintained by Quincy Public Library, Illinois. Concentrates on contemporary authors 'whose biographies are difficult to locate'. Variable detail with highly selective bibliographies, but more entries than *Twentieth-century children's writers* so 'can serve as a quick identification tool for a large number of children's authors' (*Reference books bulletin* in *Booklist*, v.87(17), 1 May 1991, p.1728).
Class No: 028:087.5(092)

[1293]
Writers for children: critical studies of major authors since the seventeenth century. Bingham, J., *ed.* New York, Scribner, 1988. xiv,661p. ISBN: 0684181657.

Contributed essays averaging 6-8p. in length on 84 deceased writers Louisa May Alcott ... Charlotte Mary Yonge. Selected bibliography and list of critical biographical studies follows each essay. Indexed. Complemented by:-
Class No: 028:087.5(092)

[1294]
—Writers for young adults. Hipple, T.W., *ed.* New York, Scribner, 1997. 3v. $80. ISBN: 0684804743.

V.1 Aiken - Frank; v.2 Freedman - Paulsen; v.3 Peck - Zindel. Index.

Essays on 129 authors, average length 2,500 words. Aimed at 'rather bright seventh, eighth or nineth grades'.
Class No: 028:087.5(092)

Indexes

[1295]

Children's authors and illustrators: an index to biographical dictionaries. Nakamura, J., *ed.* 5th ed. Detroit, Gale, 1995. xcii,811p. £120;$156. (*Gale biographical index series, no.2.*) ISBN: 0810328992.

First published 1976; 4th ed. 1987.

Cites over 200,000 biographies of approximately 30,000 persons found in 650 reference books. Aims to cover "all known writers and illustrators of children's books whose work is accessible in the English language" (Introduction p.vii). Includes writers of adult fiction whose works have been adopted by children. Comprehensive, *c.*70 sources for A.A. Milne, *c.*66 for C.S. Lewis. 'This is the type of solid reference work that libraries and research collections eagerly await' (*American reference books annual*, v.27, 1996, p.494). *Class No:* 028:087.5(092)(014)

[1296]

Writers for young adults: biographies master index: an index to sources of biographical information about novelists, poets ... Nakamura, J., *ed.* 3rd ed. Detroit, Gale, 1989. lxix,183p. $92. ISBN: 0810318334.

1st ed. 1979; 2nd ed. 1984. New ed. due 1996.

Index to 145,000 articles, entries and essays on nearly 16,000 authors in 600 biographical dictionaries and similar sources. Includes articles etc., on writers of adult fiction whose work is suitable for young adults. Main sequence of citations arranged by author A-Z; bibliographic key to books indexed precedes. Complements *Children's authors and illustrators: an index to biographical dictionaries* (*q.v.*). *Class No:* 028:087.5(092)(014)

France

[1297]

DIAMENT, N. Dictionnaire des écrivains français pour la jeunesse 1914-1991. Paris, L'école des loisirs, 1993. 783p. illus. FFr780. ISBN: 2211071252.

A-Z listing of 300 authors with personal and professional details, discussion of work and list of books. Book title (p.703-650) and illustrator indexes.
Class No: 028:087.5(092)(44)

Canada

[1298]

STOTT, J.C. *and* **JONES, R.E. Canadian books for children: a guide to authors and illustrators.** Toronto, Harcourt Brace Jovanovich, 1988. viii,246p., illus. ISBN: 0774730811.

Critically assesses the work of 105 Canadian authors and illustrators of children's books. Also includes a list of Canadian English language children's book awards and winners. According to *Choice* (v.26(8), April 1989, p.1314) only about a third of the authors are in the Gale series *Something about the author* (*q.v.*).
Class No: 028:087.5(092)(71)

Australia

[1299]

Authors and illustrators of Australian children's books. McVitty, W., *ed.* New ed. Sydney, Hodder & Stoughton, 1990. 262p. illus. ISBN: 0340541695.

First published 1989.

Biographical summaries for writers and illustrators of children's books from early settlement to the present.

....(*contd.*)

Entries, A-Z, include a list of published works and references to critical material. Short bibliography; title index. *Class No:* 028:087.5(092)(94)

Black Races

[1300]

ROLLOCK, B.T. Black authors & illustrators of children's books: a biographical dictionary. 2nd ed. New York, Garland, 1992. xviii,234p. ports. $35. (*Garland reference library of the humanities, v.1316.*) ISBN: 082407078x.

1st ed. 1988.

Profiles over 150 black children's authors and illustrators (115 1st ed.) including a few from the Caribbean, Africa and the UK. Considerable overlap with other sources; 'article length does not appear proportional to the importance of the author or illustrator' (*American reference books annual*, v.24, 1993, p.484). *Class No:* 028:087.5(092)(=96)

Research Methods

[1301]

CHESTER, T.R. Children's books research: a practical guide to techniques and sources. Stroud, Thimble Press in association with Westminster College, Oxford, 1989. 76p. £3.50. ISBN: 0903355329.

Emphasis is on research methods, sections including 'Choosing your project', 'Writing the research proposal' and 'Using the library'. Brief discussion of the more important sources in the text. Books mentioned (p.57-60); Current periodicals (p.61-63); Booklist (p.67-74), drawing on Salway's *Reading about children's books* and *The Signal review*. A compact, well-written guide for those embarking on children's literature research. Complemented by:-
Class No: 028:087.5:001.891

[1302]

—Sources of information about children's books. Chester, T.R., *comp.* Stroud, Thimble Press in association with Westminster College, Oxford, 1989. 78p. ISBN: 0903355337.

Intended as a supplement to *Children's books research*. Main section comprises a list of 157 British collections specializing in children's literature and related materials (p.2-35). Entries include succinct descriptions; indexed. Further sections on 'Organizations and societies' and 'Printed sources' (p.53-78), a classified, annotated listing of mainly British publications. *Class No:* 028:087.5:001.891

[1303]

Research & professional resources in children's literature: piecing a patchwork quilt. Short, K.G., *ed.* Newark, Del., International Reading Association, 1995. ix,272p. table. $20.95. ISBN: 087207126x.

'(A)imed at elementary and middle school contexts, specifically preschool through grade 8 (age 14)' (*Introduction*, p.4). Annotated entries in 3 sections: I. Research on children's literature (subdivided, *e.g.*, Author and illustrator studies); II. Professional journals; III. Professional books on children's literature (divided by topic). Items included published 1985-1993, heavy US bias in selection. Author and subject indexes.
Class No: 028:087.5:001.891

Institutions & Associations

[1304]

Directory of institutions and organizations specialising in children's literature. International Board on Books for Young People. Paris, UNESCO, 1985. 213p. (*Studies on books and reading, no.23.*)

In two parts: Pt.1 Argentina-Israel. Pt.2 Japan-Yugoslavia. Compiled from information supplied by the national sections of the International Board. 228 entries from 49 countries. Includes children's information centres and libraries, associations of writers, research centres, publishers and publishers' associations. 15 topic subject index in each part. Similar to Dunhouse (*q.v.*), but the geographic coverage is not as wide and publishers have less prominence. The only British entry is the National Book League Centre for Children's Books.
Class No: 028:087.5:061:061.2

Children's Reading - Books

Bibliographies

[1305]

A Catalogue of the Spencer Collection of early children's books and chapbooks. Good, D., *comp.* Preston, Harris Public Library, 1967. xi,[l],307p.

Lists *c.*2,000 items with very brief bibliographical notes. 22 chapters; author and title indexes. *Class No:* 028-053(01)

[1306]

Kataloge der Internationalen Jugendbibliothek, Munich. Boston, Mass., G.K. Hall, 1968. 18v.

Alphabetischer Katalog 5v. (55,300 cards. ISBN: 00816107159); *Länderkatalog*. 4v. (52,300 cards. ISBN: 08161010186); *Systematischer Katalog* 2v. (23,900 cards. ISBN: 0816101086); *Titelkatalog* 4v. (47,700 cards. ISBN: 0816101116); *Illustratorenkatalog* 3v. (31,200 cards. ISBN: 0816101096).

Catalogues of a library with over 100,000 v., the largest special collection of its kind in the world. It covers picture books and books for children and young people, in all languages, plus pertinent theoretical and critical literature.
Class No: 028-053(01)

[1307]

LIBRARY OF CONGRESS. Rare Book Division. **Children's books in the Rare Book Division of the Library of Congress.** Totowa, N.J., Rowman and Littlefield, 1975. 2v. ISBN: 0874715792.

V.1. Author; v.2. Chronological.

Reproduces catalogue records for 15,000 items. Entries include many temporary cards not in the *National union catalog* (*q.v.*). *Class No:* 028-053(01)

[1308]

MANCHESTER POLYTECHNIC. Library. **Morality to adventure: Manchester Polytechnic's collection of children's books** 1840-1939. Shercliffe, W.H., *comp.* Manchester, Manchester Polytechnic Library in association with Bracken Books and Studio Editions, 1988. 203p., illus., plates. ISBN: 0901276189.

Catalogue of 2,649 numbered entries. Main strength of collection is in mid and late 19th century authors. Includes many titles not in the Osborne or Spencer collections. Subject arrangement in 21 sections, entries descriptively annotated. Indexed by author, title, editor, series, illustrator and local printers and publishers. *Class No:* 028-053(01)

[1309]

TORONTO PUBLIC LIBRARIES. The Osborne collection of early children's books, 1566-1910: a catalogue. St. John, J., *comp.* Toronto, Toronto Public Library, 1975-76. 2v. ISBN: 0919486541, v.1.

V.1 originally published 1958, reprinted with minor corrections 1966 and 1975. V.2 has title *The Osborne collection of children's books, 1476-1910.*

About 5,600 titles in author order. Appendices: Chronological list of editions; List of illustrators and engravers; List of publishers, booksellers and printers.
Class No: 028-053(01)

[1310]

UNIVERSITY OF READING. Library. **Catalogue of the collection of children's books 1617-1939** in the Library of the University of Reading. Cairns, E.M., *comp.* Reading, The Library, University of Reading, 1988. xi,265p., illus. (*Reading University Library publications, 5.*) ISBN: 0704909340.

Includes later reprints of pre-1940 imprints for which earlier copies not held. 3,364 entries in 24 section arrangement following that of the Osborne Collection. Index of authors, editors, translators, illustrators and engravers and titles. *Class No:* 028-053(01)

Ireland

[1311]

The Big guide to Irish children's books. [Morthreorai do leabehair Eireannacha don oige.] Coghlan, V. *and* Keenan, C., *eds.* Dublin, Irish Children's Book Trust, 1996. 159p. illus. £5.99. ISBN: 1872917011.

Chapters on different types of children's books, *e.g.* picture books, poetry, fantasy, backed by information children's book organizations, awards and publishers. '(E)xcellent, well-produced and value-for-money guide' (*Library Association record*, v.99(3), March 1997, p.164).
Class No: 028-053(01)(415)

Wales

[1312]

PHILLIPS, M. Llyfrau plant. [Children's books in Welsh.] Aberystwyth, Llyfrgell Genedlaethol Cymru, 1997. xii,302p. £30. ISBN: 090715882x.

5,441 entries for books published 1900-91 arranged chronologically. Based on the collection of the National Centre for Children's Literature. Includes books adopted/translated from other languages. Author/editor/translator, illustrator and title indexes. A further vol. for books published 1820-1900 is in preparation. *Class No:* 028-053(01)(429)

India

[1313]

Bibliography of children's books published in India. New Delhi, Children's Book Trust, 1983. vi,676p. £24.95. ISBN: 8170111587.

Aims to cover as many titles as possible. *c.*6,500 entries by language (about 20% English), then age range, most with one line annotations. List of publishers, but no indexes.
Class No: 028-053(01)(540)

Canada

[1314]

AMTMANN, B. Early Canadian children's books 1763-1840: a bibliographical investigation into the nature and extent of early Canadian children's books and books for young people. [Livres de l'enfance et livres de la jeunesse au Canada 1763-1840: étude bibliographique.] Montreal, The Author, 1976. xv,150p., plates.

593 numbered entries. Includes titles by non-Canadians relating to Canada. Gives references to bibliographic authorities *e.g.* Tremaine, Osborne collection (*qq.v.*). Followed by:- *Class No:* 028-053(01)(71)

[1315]

—AMTMANN, B. A Bibliography of Canadian children's books and books for young people 1841-1867. Montreal, The Author, 1977. 124p.

Unannotated author and title checklist. *Class No:* 028-053(01)(71)

USA

[1316]

Fiction, folklore, fantasy and poetry for children, 1876-1985: author index, illustrator index, title index, awards index. New York, Bowker, 1986. 2v.(xvii,2563p.). ISBN: 0835218317.

V.1. Authors, illustators; v.2. Titles, awards.

A retrospective bibliography of children's literature published in the US, compiled from sources such as *American book publishing record*, *Books in print* and *Publishers trade list annual* (*qq.v.*). *c.*133,000 titles included, age ranges 3-13, arranged in 4 sequences as in the subtitle. *Books in print* type format, some entries indicating grade levels and awards received. A 'monumental work' (*Reference and research book news*, v.2, Spring 1987, p.36) offering convenient access to basic bibliographical detail, although the information is available elsewhere for those prepared to seek it out. *Class No:* 028-053(01)(73)

[1317]

WELCH, D.A. A Bibliography of American children's books: printed prior to 1821. American Antiquarian Society and Barre Publishers, 1972. lxvi,516p. $60. ISBN: 0827171331.

Originally in 6 pts. in the *Proceedings of the American Antiquarian Society* 1963-67.

Author list 'primarily concerned with narrative books written in English designed for children under fifteen years of age' (p.liii). Index of printers, publishers and imprints. Locates copies in US libraries and the British Museum (Library). *Class No:* 028-053(01)(73)

Australia

[1318]

MUIR, M. *and* **WHITE, K. Australian children's books:** a bibliography. Carlton South, Vic., Melbourne Univ. P., 1992. 2v. Aus$150. (*Miegunyah Press series, no.7.*.) ISBN: 0522844561.

V.1, by Muir, covers 1774-1972; v.2, by White, covers 1973-1988. V.1 originally published in 2v. as *A Bibliography of Australian children's books* (London, Deutsch, 1970-76).

Provides thorough coverage. V.2, which identifies *c.*10,000 items, extends Muir's earlier landmark work. *Class No:* 028-053(01)(94)

[1319]

—O'NEILL, T. *and* O'NEILL, F. Australian children's books to 1980: a select bibliography of the collection held in the National Library of Australia. Canberra, National Library of Australia, 1989. xviii,260p. Aus$22.95. ISBN: 0642104646.

Records 1,972 titles. Detailed entries with short annotations and references to Muir (v.1 above). Arranged in chronological sections: author, illustrator and subject indexes. *Class No:* 028-053(01)(94)

Contemporary

[1320]

100 best books: the big stories for children. London, Young Book Trust, 1995-. Annual. £1.

'Young Book Trust paperback selection for children aged between 0 and 12+ years'. Continues the more substantial *Children's books of the year* published from 1970.

1995 ed. (32p. illus. ISBN: 0853534551) has briefly annotated entries with bibliographical detail, price and an indication of interest level and reading age. *Class No:* 028-053(01)"312"

[1321]

Best books for children: preschool through grade 6. Gillespie, J.T. *and* Naden, C.J., *eds.* 5th ed. New Providence, N.J., Bowker, 1994. xviii,1411p. $65. ISBN: 083523455x.

First published 1959. 1st ed. in revised format 1978; 4th ed. 1990.

A substantial and valuable classified listing. 15,647 entries (more than ½ new in this ed.), plus a further 1,493 citations in notes. Excludes out-of-print titles. Annotated entries note grade levels and price. Indexed by author, illustrator, title, subject and grade level. A 6th ed. is scheduled for publication late 1998 (ISBN: 0835240991). *Class No:* 028-053(01)"312"

[1322]

The Best in children's books: the University of Chicago guide to children's literature 1985-1990. Sutherland, Z., *and others eds.* Chicago, Univ. of Chicago Press, 1991. x,492p. £35.95;$45. ISBN: 0226780643.

Original vol. 1973, as *The Best in children's literature* (xii,484p. £23.95;$30. ISBN: 0226780570), replaces *Good books for children: a selection of outstanding children's books published 1950-1965.* Continued by vols. for 1973-78 (1980. xii,547p. £23.95;$30. ISBN: 0226780597) and 1979-84 (1986. x,511p. £35.95;$45. ISBN: 0226780600).

1,146 reviews for fiction and non-fiction titles. Arranged A-Z by author, reviews average 750 words. Also indicates age and grade range; books of special distinction asterisked. 6 indexes: title; developmental values; curricular use; reading level; subject; type of literature. '(C)ontinues to be a reliable, well-organized reference book for librarians, teachers, parents and students of children's literature' (*Reference books bulletin* in *Booklist*, v.88(9), 1 January 1992, p.846). *Class No:* 028-053(01)"312"

[1323]

Children's books in print: an author, title and illustrator index to books for children and young adults. New York, Bowker, 1969-. Annual. $159. ISSN: 00693480.

Subtitle varies.

Lists US published titles for children aged 3-18, basing entries on those in **Books in print** (*q.v.*). 115,430 titles listed 1997 in separate author/illustrator and title volumes. A CD-ROM version is available as *Children's books in print on disc* (ISSN: 10971459).

....(contd.)

Subject access is provided by the separately published *Subject guide to children's books in print* (1970-. Annual. ISSN: 00000167). *Class No:* 028-053(01)"312"

[1324]

Children's catalog. Price, A. *and* Yaakov, J., *eds.* 17th ed. New York, H.W. Wilson, 1996. xii,1373p. (*Standard catalog series.*) ISBN: 0824208056.

First published 1909; 16th ed. 1991. Now published quinquennially.

A catalogue of books suitable for pre-school to sixth-grade. Main sequence has 6,372 evaluatively annotated entries (60% non-fiction), classified by Dewey with an indication of age range. Extensive author, title and subject analytical indexing. Select list of recommended CD-ROM reference works (new to this ed.) and directory of publishers and distributors. Updated by annual supplements, that for 1997 (158p.) adding 703 titles. The longest established and probably best known annotated listing of children's books. *Class No:* 028-053(01)"312"

[1325]

DELONG, J.A. *and* **SCHWEDT, R.E. Core collection for small libraries:** an annotated bibliography of books for children and young adults. Lanham, Md., Scarecrow Press, 1997. vi,229p. £28.05;$29.50. ISBN: 0810832526.

Lists and briefly annotates 494 titles in sections: Picture books - Traditional literature - Modern fantasy - Multicultural books - Historical fiction - Contemporary fiction - Nonfiction - Poetry. Subject and author/title indexes. '(W)ould benefit from more balance between modern and older titles. Not an essential purchase' (*Reference books bulletin* in *Booklist*, v.94(3), 1st October 1997, p.352). *Class No:* 028-053(01)"312"

[1326]

The Elementary school library collection: a guide to books and other media phases 1-2-3. Williamsport, Pa., Bro-dart, 1965-. Biennial. $139.95.

Published annually 1965-77.

'Other media' includes filmstrips, video cassettes, sound recordings, computer software and CD-ROMs. Entries (more than 10,000 in 20th ed. 1996 (liv,1157p. ISBN: 0872721051)) organized by abridged Dewey classification with author, title, and subject indexes. Also available in CD-ROM format from 19th ed. (1994). '(W)ithout peer as a general selection tool for elementary schools' (*American reference books annual*, v.24, 1993, p.279). *Class No:* 028-053(01)"312"

[1327]

KONING, C. Good reading guide to children's books: inspire your child with a lifelong love of books. London, Bloomsbury, 1997. xiii,274p. £7.99. ISBN: 0747531986.

Lists more than 1,000 titles in sections: First books, first words and preschool - Primary school - Junior school - Secondary school - Information books. Entries give bibliographical detail and short annotation, but lack price or ISBN. Further sections for CD-ROMs (p.234-39) and major authors with brief biographical summaries (p.240-51). Indexed by subject, category, author and title. Has a number of shortcomings in selection and presentation, but one of the few recent British published guides to children's books. *Class No:* 028-053(01)"312"

[1328]

The School library selection of recommended titles. Barker, K., *ed.* Folkestone, Bailey Bros. and Swinfen on behalf of Bethany School, 1989. 44p. £5.95. ISBN: 0561003378.

Lists around 500 titles in separate sections for fiction and non-fiction, with a short list of journals. Unannotated entries giving author, title, publisher and ISBN only. Selection generally balanced and up-to-date, 'a welcome relief to the teacher-librarian trying to make sense of the wealth of books currently available' (*School librarian*, v.37(3), August 1989, p.124). *Class No:* 028-053(01)"312"

Adolescents

[1329]

Best books for young adult readers: grades 7-12. Calvert, S., *ed.* New Providence, N.J., Bowker, 1997. xx,747p. £50;$59.95. ISBN: 0835238326.

Combines and continues *Best books for junior high readers* (ISBN: 0835230201) and *Best books for senior high readers* (ISBN: 083523021X) both published 1991. Companion vol. to *Best books for children* (*q.v.*).

6,586 very briefly annotated entries (4,421 nonfiction titles) for books published 1990 to early 1996 suitable for readers aged 12-18. Detail includes review citations. Arranged by literary form and subject categories: author, title and subject/grade level indexes. Main rival to Wilson's *Middle and junior high school library catalog* and *Senior high school library catalog* (below). *Class No:* 028-053(01)-0053.7

[1330]

Books for teenagers: a recommended list for 13 years and upwards. Dublin, Dublin Corporation Public Libraries, Children's and Schools' Library Service, 1993. i,83p. ISBN: 0946841454.

Based on the stock of Dublin Public Libraries. *c.*1,250 unannotated entries under *c.*60 topical headings, *e.g.* Fantasy 13-15 years, Humour 15+ years. Author index. *Class No:* 028-053(01)-0053.7

[1331]

COOLING, W. Books to enjoy 12-16. Swindon, School Library Association, 1996. 32p. ISBN: 0900641770.

Annotated list of *c.*180 titles under theme and genre headings. Title and author/editor indexes. *Class No:* 028-053(01)-0053.7

[1332]

NAKAMURA, J., ***ed.*** **High-interest books for teens:** a guide to book reviews and biographical sources. 2nd ed. Detroit, Gale, 1988. xxxvi,539p. £85;$99. ISBN: 081031830x.

1st ed. 1981.

Aimed at the slow to average reader. Lists 3,500 titles by author. Gives review citations and at least one source of biographical information. Many titles included out of print, selection criteria not clearly defined, 'the editor is out of touch with the reading interests of today's young adults' (*Reference books bulletin* in *Booklist* v.84(22), August 1988, p.1903). A 3rd ed. is scheduled for 1999 (ISBN: 0810369257). *Class No:* 028-053(01)-0053.7

[1333]

Senior high school library catalog. Yaakov, J., *ed.* 15th ed. New York, H.W. Wilson, 1997. xi,1312p. (*Standard catalog series.*) ISBN: 0824209214.

First published 1926; now published quinquennially. Earlier eds. as *Standard catalog for high school libraries.*

Annotated list of 5,500 fiction and non-fiction titles for students grades 9-12. Arranged by Dewey classification with a separate listing for fiction. Extensive author, title and subject analytical indexing. Updated by annual supplements. *Class No:* 028-053(01)-0053.7

[1334]

—Middle and junior high school library catalog. Price, A. *and* Yaakov, J., *eds.* 7th ed. New York, H.W. Wilson, 1995. xiii,988p. (*Standard catalog series.*) ISBN: 0824208803.

First published 1965, issued quinquennially. Earlier eds. as *Junior high school library catalog.*

4,224 entries, classification and annual supplements as in *Senior high school library catalog.* *Class No:* 028-053(01)-0053.7

[1335]

The Young adult reader's adviser. Immell, M., *and others eds.* New Providence, Bowker, 1992. 2v. illus. £65;$79.95. ISBN: 0835230686.

V.1 *The Best in literature and language, arts, mathematics and computer science*; v.2 *The Best in social sciences and history, science and health.*

Aimed at young adults 12-18, based on *The Reader's adviser* (*q.v.*) and following much the same plan. About 17,000 titles included with brief annotations. Indexes in each vol. Surpasses rival works in number of entries and 'more than a bibliography - it is intended to be used by teens themselves' (*Reference books bulletin* in *Booklist*, v.88(19), 1 June 1992, p.1780). *Class No:* 028-053(01)-0053.7

Reviews & Abstracts

[1336]

Books for keeps: the children's book magazine. London, School Bookshops Association, 1980-. 6pa. £17.40. ISSN: 0143909x.

Incorporates *British book news: children's book review* (1983-88. ISSN: 02645637).

50-80 short (250 words or less), but signed, reviews in each issue. Also carries general articles on children's writers and book publishing, plus extensive advertising. *Class No:* 028-053(048)

[1337]

The Horn Book guide to children's and young adult books. Boston, Mass., The Horn Book, 1990-. Semi-annual. $35. ISSN: 1044405x.

Reviews virtually all hardback children's books published in the US. Fiction titles arranged by grade level and genre, non-fiction classified by Dewey. Indexed by author/illustrator, title, subject and series.

The *Horn book magazine* (1924-. Bi-monthly. $38. ISSN: 00185078), carries *c.*70 full length reviews of new children's books in each issue, plus annotated listings of new editions and reprints.

The Horn book index 1924-1989 (S.F. Day *comp.* Phoenix, Oryx Press, 1990. xiv,534p. £58.50;$65. ISBN: 0897741560) has an author/title sequence of *c.*80,000 entries and a 20p. subject index covering longer articles only. *Class No:* 028-053(048)

[1338]

—School library journal: the magazine of children's, young adult & school librarians. New York, School Library Journal, 1954-. Monthly. $79.50. ISSN: 03628930.

Another important source for reviews of new children's books published in the US. About ½ of each issue is devoted to short reviews. Also covers audiovisual materials and computer software and CD-ROMs. *Class No:* 028-053(048)

[1339]

The Junior bookshelf: a review of children's books. Huddersfield, 1936-96. 6pa. ISSN: 00226505.

Ceased publication December 1996. Almost exclusively devoted to reviews of new children's books with about 150 titles in each issue. Entries noted price and ISBN; annual index. *Class No:* 028-053(048)

[1340]

The School librarian. Swindon, School Library Association, 1937-. Quarterly. £45. ISSN: 00366595.

About 250 short reviews quarterly, occupying around 2/3 of each issue. Arranged in broad groups, mainly by age ranges (*e.g.* under eight; twelve to sixteen), with an author index. One of the major UK sources for reviews of children's books. *Class No:* 028-053(048)

Indexes

[1341]

PETTUS, E.S. *and* **PETTUS, D.D. Master index to summaries of children's books.** Metuchen, N.J., Scarecrow Press; London, Bailey Bros. and Swinfen, 1986. 2v. £80.55;$89.50. ISBN: 0810817950.

Index to *c.*18,000 summaries found in 86 bibliographies, children's literature textbooks and books of activities based on children's books published 1974-80. V.1 (xviii,1036p.) comprises 'Master index' of main entries under author/editor with bibliographical data, grade level and citation to summary. V.2 (352p.) is a title and subject index. Age range covered pre-school to primary (US grade 6). Selection aids not indexed. Based on American sources, 'in Britain its limitations are more evident than its usefulness' (*School librarian*, v.34(4), December 1986, p.393).

Listed as forthcoming 1998 Pettus, E.S. & Pettus, D.D. *Master index to more summaries of children's books, 1980-1990* (2v. ISBN: 0810832690). *Class No:* 028-053(048)(014)

Teaching Materials

[1342]

El-Hi textbooks and serials in print: including related teaching materials K-12. New York, Bowker, 1970-. Annual. $149. ISSN: 00000825.

Title varies: continues *American educational catalog* (1927-55) and *Textbooks in print* (1956-69).

Based on the catalogues of educational publishers. The 1997 v. (xxxviii,2056p.) lists 90,120 elementary, junior and senior high school and pedagogical titles. Arranged by subject under 21 broad and 321 specific categories; author, title, series, serials subject and serials title indexes. *Class No:* 028-053(072)

Awards & Prizes

[1343]

Children's books: awards and prizes: includes prizes and awards for young adult books. Children's Books Council, *comp. & ed.* New York, The Children's Books Council, 1969-. Irregular. $75. ISSN: 00693472.

Issued biennially until 1981; 8th ed. 1985, 10th ed. 1996.

Latest ed. (497p.) in 4 pts: US awards selected by adults; US awards selected by young readers; Australian, Canadian, New Zealand and UK awards; international and multinational awards. 213 awards and prizes covered, winners listed in chronological order. Title and author/illustrator index. Not the most comprehensive source, but 'a handy one-volume guide (which) provides quick and easy reference' (*American reference books annual*, v.28, (1997), p.426). *Class No:* 028-053(079.2)

[1344]

Children's literature awards and winners: a directory of prizes, authors and illustrators. Jones, D.B., *ed.* 3rd ed. Detroit, Gale, 1994. 688p. £72;$94. ISBN: 0810369001.

First published 1983; 2nd ed. 1988.

Contains information on 300 awards, including those discontinued, given in the US, other English speaking countries and internationally. Main section arranged A-Z by award giving name, granting organization, address, criteria and rules, purpose, history and winners (year, title, publisher, etc.). Author/illustrator, title, award, subject indexes. *Class No:* 028-053(079.2)

[1345]

Commended books for under-twelves: an annotated selection of children's books commended or shortlisted for the Carnegie Medal and other British awards 1954-1992. Campbell, A., *comp.* Swansea, Librarians of Institutes and Schools of Education, 1994. 27p. £5. ISBN: 0901922277.

100 entries in sections for single stories, short stories by one or more authors, and poetry and verse. Subject and title indexes.

Complemented by *Commended books for over-teens: an annotated selection of children's books commended or shortlisted for the Carnegie Medal and other British book awards 1955-1993* (Campbell, A. *comp.* Librarians of Institutes and Schools of Education, 1995. 32p. £5. ISBN: 0901922285). *Class No:* 028-053(079.2)

[1346]

Outstanding children's books: a list of 554 books which have won awards or official commendations during the period from 1930 to 1988, with an introduction and indexes. Campbell, A., *comp.* Swansea, Librarians of Institutes and Schools of Education, 1990. 50p. £4. ISBN: 090192220x.

Winners of 21 awards listed, including those not usually found elsewhere (*e.g.* Smarties Prize for Children's Books). Brief list of notable non-winners. Indexes of titles and authors/illustrators. Bibliography (p.47-48). Appendix on excluded awards. *Class No:* 028-053(079.2)

[1347]

SMITH, L.J. Children's book awards international: a directory of awards and winners from inception through 1990. Jefferson, N.C., McFarland, 1992. xxii,649p. £73.80;$82. ISBN: 0899506860.

Lists 425 current and discontinued awards made to authors and illustartors in 47 countries (Argentina ... Yugoslavia). Detail includes formal name, sponsoring organization, address, date established, format/amount, brief description and winners since inception (author, title, publisher and date only). Indexed by author, award and sponsor, illustrator and

....*(contd.)*

title. 24 British awards included. "(T)he most extensive directory available of award-winning titles for children" (*Choice*, v.30(9), May 1993, p.1449). *Class No:* 028-053(079.2)

Published Series

[1348]

ANDERSON, V. Fiction sequels for readers 10 to 16: an annotated bibliography of books in succession. 2nd ed. Jefferson, N.C., McFarland, 1998. v,176p. £26.95;$29.95. ISBN: 0786401850.

First published 1990.

1st ed. includes over 1,500 titles by 350 authors, mostly published since 1960 and still in print. Entries by author A-Z; title index only.

Forthcoming 1998 by Anderson *Sequels in children's literature: an annotated bibliography of books in succession or with shared themes and characters, K-6* (McFarland, 192p. £31.50;$35. ISBN: 0786402857). *Class No:* 028-053(082.1)

[1349]

ROMAN, S. Sequences: an annotated guide to children's fiction in series. Chicago, American Library Association, 1985. viii,134p. ISBN: 0838904289.

Selected fiction in series or sequence suitable for ages Grade 3 to young adult. Alphabetical author arrangement. Introductory notes critically outline each series, annotated entries for each book follow in suggested reading order. Title, main character and series indexes. *Class No:* 028-053(082.1)

[1350]

ROSENBERG, J.K. *and* **ROSENBERG, K.C. Young people's literature in series:** fiction. An annotated bibliographical guide. Littleton, Col., Libraries Unlimited, 1972. 176p. ISBN: 087287060x.

Companion v. by the same authors *Young people's literature in series: publishers' and non-fiction series. An annotated bibliographical guide* (Libraries Unlimited, 1973. 234p. ISBN: 0872870588).

Supplement to both v. *Young people's literature in series; fiction, non-fiction and publishers' series, 1973-1975* (1977. ISBN: 0872871401).

The original two volumes contain 7,451 entries (1,428 in the fiction volume, 6,023 in the non-fiction). Arranged A-Z by series title (or by author for untitled series). Annotations concern series not individual titles. *Class No:* 028-053(082.1)

[1351]

—ROSENBERG, J.K. *and* NICHOLS, C.A. Young people's books in series: fiction and non-fiction, 1975-1991. Englewood, Colo., Libraries Unlimited, 1992. x,424p. £26.75. ISBN: 0872878821.

Continues the three titles above. Fiction and non-fiction in separate sections, the latter restricted to titles currently available. Titles included in earlier works indicated; annotations as before. Indexed. More comprehensive and current than *Sequences* (above) and a rival to *Fiction index for readers 10 to 16* (*q.v.*). *Class No:* 028-053(082.1)

[1352]

Sequels, volume II. Children's books. Fraser, D., *comp.* 8th ed. Newcastle-under-Lyme, Association of Assistant Librarians, 1988. 145p. ISBN: 0900092718.

Companion v. to *Sequels. Volume I. Adult books*.

Lists children's books in series or sequence by author A-Z. The most comprehensive and up-to-date source for British published titles. Title/character index (p.135-45).
Class No: 028-053(082.1)

[1353]

YOUNG, P.H. Children's fiction series: a bibliography 1850-1950. Jefferson, N.C., McFarland, 1997. vii,307p. £49.50;$55. ISBN: 0786403217.

Entries for 1,243 series A-Z (p.11-204) giving author(s), illustrator(s) and publisher and listing known titles in chronological order. Author, illustrator and book title indexing. '(C)overage of British children's fiction series is decidedly eclectic and rather minimal' (*Reference reviews*, v.11(7), 1997, p.19). *Class No:* 028-053(082.1)

Illustrations

[1354]

CIANCIOLO, P.J. Picture books for children. 4th ed. Chicago, American Library Association, 1997. ix,213p. illus. £30.50;$38. ISBN: 0838907016.

First published 1973; 3rd ed. 1990.

A-Z entries by author giving bibliographical citation, content summary and recommended age range in 4 thematic sections. Also provides (new to this ed.) list of recommended resource books on visual art and book illustration. '(W)ide ranging topical listing, above all of US talent and book production, with many items of value - well worth getting by schools and libraries' (*Reference reviews*, v.11(8), 1997, p.6). *Class No:* 028-053(084.1)

[1355]

HARMS, J.M. *and* **LETTOW, L.J. Picture books to enhance the curriculum.** New York, H.W. Wilson, 1996. x,521p. $38. ISBN: 0824208676.

An index to more than 1,500 picture books. Main listing A-Z by author with very brief annotations. Books grouped by theme in separate section; title index. '(C)ommendable ... (but) physical arrangement and lack of detailed annotations detract from its usefulness' (*Reference books bulletin* in *Booklist*, v.93(22), August 1997, p.1930). *Class No:* 028-053(084.1)

[1356]

LIMA, C.W. *and* **LIMA, J.A. A to Zoo: subject access to children's picture books.** 5th ed. New Providence, N.J., Bowker, 1998. xxvii,1158p. $65. ISBN: 0835239160.

First published 1982; 4th ed. 1993.

Lists more than 14,000 fiction and non-fiction picture books for ages 3-7 under 800 subject headings. Separate listing by author giving full bibliographical detail; title and illustrator indexes. *Class No:* 028-053(084.1)

[1357]

Picture book index. Hobson, M. *and* Madden, J., *comps.* 3rd ed. Halifax, AAL Publishing, 1996. xi,70p. illus. £17.50. ISBN: 0900092955.

First published 1987; 2nd ed. 1991.

Companion to *Children's fiction index* (below). Groups recent in-print picture books under subject headings, such as 'Animal noises', 'Christmas', 'Ghosts' and 'Moon'. 2,484 entries each showing author, title, publisher, date and binding; illustrator's name not given. Highly selective and as the 'entries have no annotations ... prior knowledge (or trial

.... *(contd.)*

and error) is needed to know the age level for which a particular title is relevant' (*Reference reviews*, v.11(5), 1997 p.5). *Class No:* 028-053(084.1)

Fiction

[1358]

Children's fiction index. Madden, J. *and* Hobson, M., *comps.* 7th ed. Newcastle-Under-Lyme, Association of Assistant Librarians, 1993. [ii],61p. £20. ISBN: 0900092858.

First published 1964, earlier eds. as *Junior fiction index*. 6th ed., under current title, 1988.

Intended as an aid to the location of children's fiction on specific topics. Entries, for post 1980 mainly in print titles, arranged under *c.*450 headings such as 'Ashanti folk tales', 'Conkers' and 'Homelessness'. Picture books largely excluded, covered in **Picture book index** (above). This ed. an improvement on earlier efforts, but indexing still confined to a narrow range of titles. '(I)n danger of becoming an anachronism' (*Reference reviews*, v.8(7), 1994, p.36).
Class No: 028-053-3

[1359]

HOBSON, M. *and* **MADDEN, J. Children's fiction source book:** a survey of children's books for 6-13 year olds. 2nd ed. Aldershot, Scolar Press, 1996. ix,332p. £30.50;$64.95. ISBN: 1857420225.

First published 1992.

'(C)overs the best and most popular children's authors giving a biographical note, address and/or agent, awards and prizes, age-range and versions of their works with essential bibliographical details' (Preface, p.vii). About 150 authors covered, with *c.*50 word evaluative annotations for books. Various appendices including 'List of awards and prize winners'. Author, title and genre index. *Class No:* 028-053-3

[1360]

SPENCER, P. What do children read next? A reader's guide to fiction for children. Detroit, Gale, 1997. xvii,929p. £46;$55. ISBN: 0810364492.

'Vol. 2'. Earlier version with same title published 1994.

List of nearly 1,700 titles with grade level recommendations, brief descriptions and review citations. Comprehensively indexed.

Companion work *What do young adults read next? A reader's guide to fiction for young adults* (Spenser, P. Gale, 1997. xvi,692p. £46;$55. ISBN: 0810364492).
Class No: 028-053-3

Adolescents

[1361]

ANDERSON, V. Fiction index for readers 10 to 16: subject access to over 8200 books (1960-1990). Jefferson, N.C., McFarland, 1992. ix,477p. £35;$38.50. ISBN: 0899507034.

'Subject index' (p.1-123) lists books (author/title only) under more than 200 headings (Acting ... Writing). 'Annotated bibliography' (p.129-408) lists indexed books A-Z by author giving title, publisher, date and a 10-25 word description. Title index. 'In the absence of a British subject index to teenage fiction, this publication will help fill the gap' (*Library Association record*, v.95(4), April 1993, p.237). *Class No:* 028-053-3-0053.7

[1362]
Fiction for youth: a guide to recommended books. Shapiro, L.L. *and* Stein, B., *eds*. 3rd ed. New York, Neal-Schuman, 1992. xx,263p. ISBN: 1555701132.

First published 1980; 2nd ed. 1986.

Annotated list, mainly of adult titles, suitable for young people 13 to 18. Author arrangement; title and subject indexes. Offers a good selection, but 'weighted to providing books for the most able and the more mature' (*International review of children's literature and librarianship*, v.8(3), 1993, p.206). *Class No:* 028-053-3-0053.7

Fantasy Fiction

[1363]
COOK, E. The Ordinary and the fabulous: an introduction to myths, legends and fairy tales. 2nd ed. Cambridge, Cambridge Univ. Press, 1976. xx,182p. ISBN: 0521073464.

First published 1969.

A classic work on myths in children's literature. Includes a 'Short list of books' (p.123-77) comprising 370 briefly annotated entries. Index. *Class No:* 028-053-34

[1364]
LYNN, R.N. Fantasy literature for children and young adults: an annotated bibliography. 4th ed. New Providence, N.J., Bowker, 1995. lxxix,1092p. $55. ISBN: 0835234568.

1st ed. 1979; 2nd ed. 1983. Both published under the title *Fantasy for children: an annotated checklist and reference guide*. 3rd ed 1989.

Main section has 3,148 citations listing and describing over 4,800 novels and collections. Entries, in 13 subject groups (*e.g.* Animals, Time travel and fantasy), include citations to reviews. Further section has entries for 10,400 books, periodical articles, dissertations, etc. relating to fantasy literature for children. Author/illustrator, title and subject indexes. A 'monumental achievement' (*American reference books annual*, v.27, 1997, p.489). *Class No:* 028-053-34

[1365]
PFLIEGER, P. A Reference guide to modern fantasy for children. Westport, Conn., Greenwood Press, 1984. xvii,690p. £71.55;$79.50. ISBN: 0313228868.

A selective guide to approximately 100 books by 36 19th and 20th century authors (*e.g.* Charles Kingsley, Rudyard Kipling, C.S. Lewis, Walter de la Mare). Entries in dictionary format for authors, book titles, characters, places and magical objects. Author entries include lists of primary works and secondary material. *Class No:* 028-053-34

[1366]
The Storyteller's sourcebook: a subject, title and motif index to folklore collections for children. MacDonald, M.R., *ed.* Detroit, Gale, 1982. xviii,818p. $99. ISBN: 0810304716.

An index to folktales in 556 collections and 389 picture books published during the previous 20 years. In 4 parts: Motif index; Tale-title index; Subject index; Ethnic and geographic index, arranged by geographical area, subdivided and followed by an ethnic group index. *Class No:* 028-053-34

Historical Fiction

[1367]
ADAMSON, L.G. Recreating the past: a guide to American and world historical fiction for children and young adults. Westport, Conn., Greenwood Press, 1994. xxii,494p. £49.50;$59.95. ISBN: 0313290083.

Annotated list of 970 titles under 29 mainly geographic headings (*e.g.* The British Isles (p.49-110), United States (p.127-270)). Entries include plot synopsis, awards received and reading level. Seven useful appendices: 'Readability level' ... 'Works with protagonists or plots concerning minority groups' ... 'Country and dates of setting in Europe and the British Isles'. Index of authors, titles and illustrators (p.469-94). *Class No:* 028-053-38

[1368]
ADAMSON, L.G. A Reference guide to historical fiction for children and young adults. New York, Greenwood Press, 1987. xix,401p. £58.59;$69.50. ISBN: 0313250022.

The first such guide to children's historical fiction. Based on the work of 80 award winning authors writing post-1940. Entries in one dictionary sequence, for authors, titles, protagonists, historical persons, places and terms. *Class No:* 028-053-38

[1369]
Index to historical fiction for children and young people. Fisher, J., *comp.* Aldershot, Scolar Press, 1994. xvi,192p. illus. £30;$44.95. ISBN: 1859280781.

Entries for 461 titles by author A-Z each giving bibliographical detail, summary of about 100 words and age level. Title and subject indexes. All the books selected have been published in the UK, most within the previous 25 years. *Class No:* 028-053-38

Humour

[1370]
FAKIH, K.O. The Literature of delight: a critical guide to humorous books for children. New Providence, N.J., Bowker, 1993. ix,269p. $40. ISBN: 0835230279.

Contains 784 entries in 17 categories, mostly for titles published since 1980. In addition to bibliographical detail gives price, format (short story, poetry, etc.), grade level and 50-75 word annotation. Indexed by author, illustrator, title, subject and main character. *Class No:* 028-053-7

03 Reference Books

Reference Books

Bibliographies

English

[1371]

The American Library Association guide to information access: a complete research handbook and directory. Whiteley, S., *ed.* New York, Random House, 1994. xxv,533p. $19. ISBN: 0679750754.

Aimed at the general public. 4 main sections with 53 chapters: 2. Style manuals .... 5. Online public access catalogues ... 12. The Internet ... 15. Newspapers ... 19. Agriculture ... 31. The Home ... 46. Sports. Each chapter has a brief introduction followed by individual works with bibliographical citation and brief annotation. Topic index p.523-33). *Class No:* 03(01)=20

[1372]

AMERICAN LIBRARY ASSOCIATION. Social Responsibilities Round Table. Task Force on Alternatives in Print. **Alternative publications:** a guide to directories, indexes, bibliographies and other sources. Whitaker, C.S., *ed.* Jefferson, N.C., McFarland, 1990. v,90p. ISBN: 0899504841.

A guide to reference sources on alternative publications. 160 annotated entries in 4 main sections: Indexes and abstracts; Review sources; Subject and trade bibliographies (98 entries); Alternative mail order outlets. Indexed. Geographic coverage confined to the US. Replaces the much more extensive *Alternatives in print* (last published 1980) and *Field guide to alternative media* (1984).
Class No: 03(01)=20

[1373]

Encyclopedias, atlases & dictionaries. Sader, M. *and* Lewis, A., *eds.* New Providence, N.J., Bowker, 1995. xvi,495p. illus., maps. £70;$85. ISBN: 0835236692.

Replaces *General reference books for adults* (1988) and *Reference books for young readers* (1988).

Evaluates *c.*200 titles (*e.g.* 'Columbia encyclopedia', p.100-104) for authority, scope, accuracy, clarity, objectivity, accessibility, special features and format. Includes facsimile pages and comparative charts. Separate treatment of electronic sources and large print titles. Index (p.489-95). Thorough treatment for the limited range of titles covered. *Class No:* 03(01)=20

[1374]

—Topical reference books: authoritative evaluations of recommended resources in specialized areas. Sader, M., *ed.* New York, Bowker, 1991. xvii,892p. $109. (*Bowker buying guide series.*) ISBN: 0835230872.

Published in the same series as *General reference books for adults* (1988) now replaced by *Encyclopedias, atlases and dictionaries* (above).

Annotated entries for 1,200 in print titles under 91 subject

.... (*contd.*)
headings Advertising ... Zoology. Supplementary and new titles noted. Indexed by author, title, subject and LC and Dewey class nos. *Class No:* 03(01)=20

[1375]

Guide to reference books. Balay, R., *ed.* 11th ed. Chicago, American Library Association, 1996. xxvii,2020p. $275. ISBN: 0838906699.

Originated in A.C. Kroeger's *Guide to the study and use of reference books* (1902). 3rd-6th eds., (1917-36) by I.G. Mudge; 7th-8th eds. by C.M. Winchell (1951-67); 9th-10th eds. by E.P. Sheehy (1976-86). 10th ed. updated by supplement 1992 (x,613p. ISBN: 0838905889).

A further thorough revision of the standard US guide to reference books. 15,875 main entries (similar number to 10th ed.) amended up to the end of 1993, with some later titles. Selection based on works 'needed to support reference services in the general reference department of a large university library' (*Foreword*, p.xxii). 5 main sections (A. General reference works (including language dictionaries, biography, genealogy) - B. The humanities - C. Social and behavioral sciences - D. History and area studies - E. Science, technology and medicine), with 48 subsidiary subject divisions. Well set-out in 2 col. format with clear type; most subject divisions including introductory notes. Index (p.1597-2020) entries for authors, editors, compilers, sponsoring bodies, titles and subjects.

While the work has an understandable US slant, scope is international, with a fair proportion of foreign language titles. This ed. provides many improvements including a far higher proportion of science and technology works and greater emphasis on material relating to women and non-Western cultures. However, a large number of older entries appear to have been retained without amendment or pruning and there is still a failure to deal fully with electronic information sources. There is also a degree of uneveness between sections, perhaps resulting from the greater number of compilers involved with this edition.

Annotated listings acting as a partial update to *Guide to reference books* appear in the journal *College and research libraries* on a roughly semi-annual basis. 'Selected reference books' in V.58(5), September 1997, (p.465-80) notes 20 new titles and provides details on a similar number of revisions.
Class No: 03(01)=20

[1376]

HILLARD, J.M. Where to find what: a handbook to reference service. 3rd ed. Metuchen, N.J., Scarecrow Press, 1991. xviii,333p. ISBN: 0810816458.

First published 1975; 2nd ed. 1981.

'(A)imed more directly at the kind of questions received at the reference desk of public, school or smaller college libraries' (p.v). Descriptively annotated entries for English language titles, US published material predominating, under 607 subject headings 'Abbreviations and acronyms' ... 'Zoos'. 'Unfortunately, the editions of books listed are not always the most current ones' (*Reference books bulletin* in *Booklist*, v.88(1), 1 Sept. 1991, p.92).
Class No: 03(01)=20

[1377]

KATZ, W.A. Introduction to reference work. 7th ed. New York, McGraw-Hill, 1997. 2v.

V.1 *Basic information sources* (£32.99;$30.25. ISBN: 0070342776); v.2 *Reference services and reference processes* (£29.99;$27.50. ISBN: 0070342784). First published 1969; 6th ed. 1992.

V.1 has 3 parts: Introduction; Information control and access; Sources of information. The latter has 6 chapters covering encyclopedias, ready reference sources, biographical sources, dictionaries, geographical sources and government documents. Each chapter groups similar titles, provides evaluative and comparative commentaries and closes with a brief annotated list of 'Suggested reading'. North American bias, but some British titles included. From this ed. the focus is on online and CD-ROM sources, printed works generally given secondary treatment. V.2 is an overview of the principles and procedures of reference work. Vols. separately indexed. *Class No:* 03(01)=20

[1378]

Recommended reference books in paperback. March, A.L., *ed.* 2nd ed. Englewood, Co., Libraries Unlimited, 1992. xi,263p. £36.50;$47.50. ISBN: 1563080672.

1st ed. 1981. Earlier versions as *Reference books in paperback* (1972 and 1976).

Annotated listing of 993 titles selected for 'quality, availability and economy' (Preface). Similar structure to *American reference books annual* (*q.v.*). '(M)any (of the titles) are of American provenance and not really suitable for British libraries' (*Refer*, v.9(3), Autumn 1993, p.23).
Class No: 03(01)=20

[1379]

Reference and information services: an introduction. Bopp, R.E. *and* Smith, L., *eds.* 2nd ed. Englewood, Colo, Libraries Unlimited, 1995. xxiv,626p. £51.50;$47.50. (*Library science text series.*) ISBN: 156308130x.

Also available in pbck. (£37.95;$35. ISBN: 1563081296). First published 1991.

Mainly intended for library and information science students. In 2 pts: I. Concepts and processes (11 chaps., *e.g.* The Reference interview, Introduction to electronic reference sources); II. Information sources and their use (10 chaps., *e.g.* Directories, Biographical sources, Encyclopedias). Each chap. well structured with references and additional reading. Author/title and subject indexes. A rival to Katz's *Introduction to reference work* (above).
Class No: 03(01)=20

[1380]

Reference sources for small and medium-sized libraries. American Library Association. Reference and Adult Services Division. Reference Sources Committee, *comp and* Lang, J.P., *ed.*. 5th ed. Chicago, American Library Association, 1992. xvi,317p. $40. ISBN: 0838932932.

First published 1969; 4th ed. 1984. Eds. 1-3 as *Reference books for small and medium sized libraries.*

Aimed at college and school, as well as public libraries. 1,974 numbered entries in 22 subject sections based on Dewey classes. Brief annotations (signed), most titles in print. Includes microforms and CD-ROMs. Index of authors and titles. No subject index, but plentiful cross-references and a detailed contents list. *Class No:* 03(01)=20

[1381]

—DORITY, G.K. A Guide to reference books for small and medium-sized libraries 1984-1994. Englewood, Colo., Libraries Unlimited, 1995. xviii,372p. £59.50;$49. ISBN: 1563081032.

Earlier version, also by Dority, as *A Guide to reference books for small and medium-sized libraries, 1970-1982* (1984. xx,410p. ISBN: 0872874036).

975 main entries in 35 subject sections with a further 400 secondary citations. Notes availability of items in other formats such as CD-ROM. Based on reviews appearing in *American reference books annual* (*q.v.*). Further coverage in the annual *Recommended reference books for small and medium-sized libraries* (*q.v.*). *Class No:* 03(01)=20

[1382]

The Reference sources handbook. Lea, P.W. *and* Day, A., *eds.* 4th ed. London, Library Association, 1996. xvii,446p. £28.50. ISBN: 1856041778.

First published 1980; 3rd ed. 1990. Title of earlier eds. varies slightly; 3rd ed. as *Printed reference material.*

21 contributors, 16 chapters: 1. Reference publishing - 2. Bibliographies - 3. Dictionaries - 4. Encyclopedias - 5. Biographical sources - 6. Geographical sources - 7. Local history - 8. Community information - 9. Business and company information - 10. News and current affairs - 11. Periodicals - 12. Government publications - 13. Official publications of international organizations - 14. Statistical sources - 15. Grey literature, standards and patents - 16. Audiovisual materials. Each chapter usually gives a short general/historical introduction followed by brief descriptive and comparative annotations of individual items. References and suggestions for further reading at most chapter ends. Index of authors, titles and subjects (p.407-46). Despite some unevenness 'does a good job and remains a basic text for British libraries' (*Refer*, v.13(1), Winter 1997, p.10).
Class No: 03(01)=20

[1383]

SABLE, M.H. Research guides to the humanities, social sciences and technology: an annotated bibliography of guides to library resources and usage, arranged by subject or discipline of coverage. Ann Arbor, Pierian Press, 1986. xvi,181p. $35. (*Basic reference guides series, no.1.*) ISBN: 0876502141.

The 'guides listed are concerned primarily with the description of reference books in the field'. In depth coverage of 161 works, with the emphasis on English language titles published after 1970. Author and title indexes. *Class No:* 03(01)=20

[1384]

SHEARER, B.F. *and* **SHEARER, B.S.,** *comps.* **Finding the source:** a thesaurus index to the reference collection. London, Aldwych, 1981. xviii,545p. (*Studies in library science, no.5.*) ISBN: 0861720245.

'*Finding the source* consists of two sections: bibliographic citations to 2,000 reference books and a thesaurus index to the contents of the books cited' (p.xiv). Thesaurus index occupies p.179-545. Useful for pinpointing reference works on specific subjects, but the range of titles indexed is limited and now largely dated. *Class No:* 03(01)=20

[1385]

SWIDAN, E.A. Reference sources: a brief guide. Baltimore, Enoch Pratt Free Library, 1988. viii,175p. $7.95. ISBN: 0910556261.

First published 1947; 8th ed. 1978. Earlier eds. under title *Reference books: a brief guide.*

A standard US guide providing succinct comparative annotations for around 800 items. All subject areas covered except medicine, law and genealogy. Databases included for the first time in this ed., hence revised title.
Class No: 03(01)=20

Indexes

[1386]

Proper names master index: a comprehensive index of more than 200,000 proper names that appear as entries in standard reference works. Abate, F.R., *ed.* Detroit, Omnigraphics, 1994. 2v. $125. ISBN: 1558888373.

Indexes proper names, other than personal names, appearing in 68 works (*e.g. Benet's reader's encyclopedia, Halliwell's film guide*), including 12 Oxford companions. Limited overlap with Ryan's *First stop* (*q.v.*). 'In a suprising number of instances, the editor has not indexed the most recent edition of a source' (*Reference books bulletin* in *Booklist*, v.91(7), December 1 1994, p.709).
Class No: 03(01)=20(014)

Great Britain

[1387]

BRITISH COUNCIL. Reference works. 2nd ed. Manchester, The British Council, 1993. i,72p. £30. (*Core lists of library material.*) ISBN: 0863551548.

First published 1990.

Lists 706 basic reference items, nearly all published in the UK, giving bibliographical detail, Dewey class. no., 20-50 word descriptive annotation, ISBN, price and 4 level priority indicator (essential ... minority interest). Includes CD-ROMs. Entries arranged under subject headings Abbreviations ... Visual arts; author/title and class. no. index. '(B)iased towards British Council target users and therefore all subject areas are not covered to the same depth' (p.i). Nonetheless, a useful guide, especially valuable as a checklist for small to medium-sized libraries.
Class No: 03(01)=20(410)

India

[1388]

SHARMA, H.D. Indian reference sources: an annotated guide to Indian reference material. 2nd ed. Varanasi, Indian Bibliographic Centre, 1988. 2v. Rs400. ISBN: 8185131023.

V.1. Generalia and humanities; v.2. Social sciences, pure and applied sciences. First published 1972.

Selective guide to reference material published in India, or relating to India published elsewhere. Concentrates on those sources which are in print or readily available. Includes a proportion of works in Indian languages. About 5,500 entries in subject sections, with short descriptive annotations. Index in each volume. *Class No:* 03(01)=20(540)

South Africa

[1389]

MUSIKER, R. *and* **MUSIKER, N. Guide to South African reference books.** 6th ed. London, Mansell, 1997. vii,240p. £50;$80. ISBN: 0720122244.

First published 1955; 5th ed. 1971, with suppl. for 1971-76. This ed. also published as *South Africa* in Clio's *World bibliographical series.*

Aims 'to list reference works which provide information and facts on any South African subject' (*Introduction*, p.1). Bibliographies, except for 'a few basic cardinal subject bibliographies' excluded, covered in *South African bibliography* (*q.v.*). 1,139 entries in broad Dewey based subject groups with brief descriptive annotations. Author/title and subject indexes. *Class No:* 03(01)=20(680)

Canada

[1390]

Canadian reference sources: an annotated bibliography; general reference works, history, humanities. [Ouvrages de référence canadiens: une bibliographie annotée: ouvrages de référence généraux, histoire, sciences humaines.] Bond, M.E., *comp.* & *ed and* Caron, M.M., *comp.*. Vancouver, Univ. of British Columbia Press, 1996. xvi,1076p. Can$225. ISBN: 077480565x.

Intended to replace Ryder's *Canadian reference sources* (2nd ed. 1981).

'Includes reference sources of all types, in various formats, about Canada. Canadian and foreign publications which describe Canadian people, institutions, organizations, publications, art, literature, languages, history, etc. are cited and annotated' (p.xiii). 4,194 numbered entries in subject arrangement, annotations of 50-200 words. Name, title and English and French subject indexes. 'One of the most important Canadian reference works ever published' (*Choice*, v.34(4), December 1996, p.586).
Class No: 03(01)=20(71)

[1391]

Guide to reference materials for Canadian libraries. Nilsen, K., *ed.* 8th ed. Toronto, Univ. of Toronto Press for the Faculty of Library and Information Science, Univ. of Toronto, 1992. xv,596p. £32;Can$50. ISBN: 0802060048.

First published 1968; 7th ed. 1984. Earlier eds. as *Guide to basic reference materials for Canadian libraries.*

This ed. extensively revised and expanded. 4,668 entries, most briefly annotated for titles published to end of 1990. Classified arrangement with author, title and subject indexes. Now covering many general reference sources, in addition to those relating to Canada, this must be regarded as one of the more important English language guides.
Class No: 03(01)=20(71)

Australia

[1392]

MILLS, J.J. Information resources and services in Australia. Wagga Wagga, Centre for Information Studies, Charles Sturt Univ., 1990. 388p. (*Topics in Australasian library and information studies, no. 2.*) ISBN: 0949060089.

General guide with chapters on the reference interview, bibliographical control, ready reference sources, indexing and abstracting services, government publications, subject specific works, etc. Author, title, subject and database indexes. A 'good introduction to the type and scope of Australian reference sources' (*American reference books annual*, v.23, 1992, p.229). *Class No:* 03(01)=20(94)

German

[1393]

ALLISCHEWSKI, H. Bibliographienkunde: ein Lehrbuch mit Beschreibungen von mehr als 300 Druckschriftenverzeichnissen und allgemeinen Nachschlagewerken. 2. Aufl. neubearb. und erw. Wiesbaden, Reichert, 1986. xviii,380p. DM88. ISBN: 3882262532.

First published 1978.

A guide to bibliographies, library catalogues, biographical dictionaries and encyclopedias. Emphasis on German material, but scope is international, including a representative sample of British titles. *Class No:* 03(01)=30

[1394]

Ausgewählte Bibliographien und andere Nachschlagewerke: Generalregister zur gleichnamigen Rubrik in der *Zeitschriften für Bibliothekswesen und Bibliographie* 1974-1993. Krauch, S. *and* Schreiber, K., *bearbs*. Frankfurt am Main, Klostermann, 1995. 344p. DM128. (*Zeitschrift für Bibliothekswesen und Bibliographie: Sonderheft 61.*) ISBN: 3465026586.

Succeeds earlier index covering 1974-89.

Author/title and subject index to reviews of 1,422 new bibliographies and reference works which appeared in the bimonthly *Zeitschrift für Bibliothekswesen und Bibliographie* during the period. *Class No:* 03(01)=30

[1395]

TOTOK, W. *and* **WEITZEL, R. Handbuch der bibliographischen Nachschlagewerke.** Kernchen, H-J. *and* Kernchen, D., *hrsg*. 6., völlig neu bearb. Aufl. Frankfurt am Main, Klostermann, 1984-85. 2v. DM156, v.1; DM224, v.2. ISBN: 3465015924, v.1; 3465015940, v.2.

V.1 *Allgemeinbibliographien und allgemeine Nachschlagewerke* (xvi,472p.); v.2 *Fachbibliographien und fachbezogene Nachschlagewerke* (xviii,684p.). First published 1954; 5th ed. 1977.

About 6,000 entries, including subsumed references, mostly briefly annotated. V.1, in 17 main sections, covers general sources such as bibliographies of bibliographies, library catalogues, national bibliographies, theses, official publications, incunabula, encyclopedias, and biographical dictionaries. V.2 has 22 main subject sections each further subdivided. Author, title and subject index in each volume. Primarily German-language material, but English and other European languages are also fairly well represented. Strong on the general works covered in v.1, especially for European sources, but weaker in some subject areas, notably science and technology, where the sub-section for chemistry has only 34 entries. *Class No:* 03(01)=30

French

[1396]

BEAUDIQUEZ, M. *and* **BÉTHERY, A. Ouvrages de référence pour les bibliothèques:** répertoire bibliographique. 4. éd. Paris, Éditions du cercle de la librairie, 1995. 478p. FFr270. (*Collection bibliothèques.*) ISBN: 2765405913.

3rd ed. 1986 as *Ouvrages de référence pour les bibliothèques publiques*.

Expanded ed. of 1,304 entries (970 3rd ed.), now including items suitable for all types of libraries. Dewey based subject arrangement with fairly full analytical annotations. Includes some non-French works (*e.g.* nos.14-19 foreign language encyclopedias). Author/editor, title and subject index (p.445-78). *Class No:* 03(01)=40

[1397]

MALCLÈS, L-N. Les Sources du travail bibliographique. Genève, Droz, 1950-58. 3v. in 4.

1. *Bibliographies générales;* 2. *Bibliographies spécialisées: Sciences humaines* 2 pts.; 3. *Bibliographies spécialisées: Sciences exactes et techniques.*

Reprinted New York, French and European Publications, 1965: (v.1 ISBN: 0685359778; v.2 ISBN: 068535786; v.3 ISBN: 0685359794).

Guide to *c.*20,000 bibliographies and reference items, including major periodicals, important texts and other source material. In chapter form, beginning with a survey and then listing items in sections, each with an introduction. Many entries include an analysis of contents or annotation (*e.g. Index catalogue of The Library of the Surgeon-General's Office* US Army: nearly 1p.). Each volume has an author, anonymous title and subject index. A valuable French slanted source, which remains useful for older material. *Class No:* 03(01)=40

[1398]

PRÉVOTEAU, M-H. *and* **UTARD, J-C. Manuel de bibliographie générale.** Nouv. éd. Paris, Éditions du cercle de la librarie, 1996. 364p. FFr270. (*Collection bibliothèques.*) ISBN: 2765406332.

First published 1995.

Guide to bibliographical research. 10 chaps. of descriptive text, coverage including general dictionaries and encyclopedias, specialised dictionaries, statistical sources, etc. French sources emphasised, some treatment of CD-ROM, online and Internet databases. Author/title index. *Class No:* 03(01)=40

Italian

[1399]

MARTINUCCI, A. Guida alla bibliografia internazionale. Milano, Editrice Bibliografica, 1994. 288p. L60,000. (*Bibliografia e biblioteconomia. Fuori collana.*) ISBN: 8870753808.

Guide to bibliographies and related material. 958 entries (p.3-251) in 13 chapters for international bibliographies, library catalogues, national bibliographies, incunabula, periodicals, etc. Some entries include brief annotations. Author/title index. Reasonably strong on older material; weak on newer publications and no coverage of electronic information sources. *Class No:* 03(01)=50

Spanish

[1400]

Spanish-language reference books: an annotated bibliography. Bibliotecas para la Gente, Reference Committee, *comp*. Berkeley, Chicano Studies Library Publications Unit, Univ. Of California, 1989. viii,45p. (*Chicano Studies Library publications series, no.15.*) ISBN: 0918520150.

Brief guide with the emphasis on sources useful to Hispanic Americans. *Class No:* 03(01)=60

Russian

[1401]

MAICHEL, K. Guide to Russian reference books. Simmons, J.S.G., *ed.* Stanford, Ca., Hoover Institution on War, Revolution and Peace, Stanford University, 1962-67. 3v. (*Hoover Institution bibliographical series, nos. X, XVIII, XXXII.*)

.... *(contd.)*

V.I. *General bibliographies and reference books* (1962. 92p.); V.II. *History, auxillary historical sciences, ethnography and geography* (1964. 297p.); v.V. *Science, technology and medicine* (1967. 384p.). Originally projected for 5v. with a supplement and cumulated index.

Classified arrangement; each v. has an index. V.I-II remain valuable, the former having 379 well-annotated entries. *Class No:* 03(01)=82

[1402]

ZALEWSKI, W. Fundamentals of Russian reference work in the humanities and social sciences. New York, Russica, 1985. 170p. $16. (*Russica bibliography series, no.5.*) ISBN: 0898300975.

Aims to introduce 'the network of bibliographies and reference sources for Russian studies' (Introduction). In 2 pts: General, 5 chapters on publishing, bibliography, libraries, general bibliographies, non-bibliographic reference sources; Subject bibliographies, 6 chapters on Soviet bibliographic institutions, history, literature, linguistics and language studies, social sciences, humanities. Most entries unannotated, but commentary precedes each section. Unattractive typographical layout and inconsistent citation style, but useful as an update to Maichel (above). *Class No:* 03(01)=82

Chinese

[1403]

TÊNG, Saŭ-yü *and* **BIGGERSTAFF, K. An Annotated bibliography of selected Chinese reference works.** 3rd ed. Cambridge, Mass., Harvard Univ. Press, 1971. xi,250p. £9.50;$14. (*Harvard Yenching Institute studies, v.2.*) ISBN: 0674038517.

First published 1936; 2nd ed. 1950.

The 3rd ed. is 'so extensively revised that it may be considered practically a new work by the same compilers' (Foreword). Sections (each with introduction): 1. Bibliographies - 2. Encyclopedias - 3. Dictionaries - 4. Geographical works - 5. Biographical works - 6. Tables - 7. Yearbooks - 8. Sinological indexes. Combined index and glossary. Lengthy and valuable annotations in English. *Class No:* 03(01)=951

Japanese

[1404]

A Guide to reference books for Japanese studies. Rev. ed. Tokyo, International House of Japan Library, 1997. xiv,447p. ISBN: 4990002237.

Concentrates on humanities and social science resources. In 2 main sections: English-language materials (716 entries); Japanese-language materials (1,985 entries). Both sections arranged by subjects with brief annotations. Further listings of electronic resources and major Japanese libraries. Comprehensive, a more recent alternative to the American Library Association's *Guide to Japanese reference books* (1966) and supplement (1979). *Class No:* 03(01)=956

Handbooks & Manuals

[1405]

HEDE, A.A. Reference readiness: a manual for librarians, researchers and students. 4th ed. rev. & updated. Hamden, Conn., Library Professional Publications, 1990. xv,206p. £29.50;$33.50. ISBN: 0208022287.

1st ed. by S. Ziskind 1971; 3rd ed. 1984.

.... *(contd.)*

10 chapter annotated listing of printed and microform reference sources. '(N)ot intended as a text for reading *about* reference books, but rather to be used in conjunction with the examination of the works described to learn what they contain and when and how to use them' (Introduction p.xiii). Primarily for library school students. *Class No:* 03(035)

[1406]

TAYLOR, M. *and* **POWELL, R.R. Basic reference sources:** a self-study manual. 4th ed. Metuchen, N.J., Scarecrow, 1990. xvi,319p. £24.75;$32.50. ISBN: 081082244x.

First published 1973; 3rd ed. 1985.

Comprises a series of questions relating to the examination, use and comparison of major reference sources. Intended for the student, but also of wider application, highlighting some of the salient features of the 169 items analysed. *Class No:* 03(035)

Reviews & Abstracts

[1407]

American reference books annual. Englewood, Colo., Libraries Unlimited, 1970-. Annual. $95. ISSN: 00659959.

Aims to 'provide comprehensive coverage of English language reference books published in the United States and Canada'. Also covers a very limited number of British and Australian titles. Reviewing of new US books almost complete; serial publications reviewed at 4-5 year intervals. From 1993 includes reviews of CD-ROM reference products. Highly selective treatment of government publications (covered in *Government reference books* (*q.v.*)) and reprints. Publications of less than 48 pages and highly specialized material excluded. The 1997 ed. (v.28. xxvi,735p.) has 1,449 signed, critical reviews (considerably fewer than recent years due to 'production difficulties') in 37 main subject sections, with references to previous reviews and reviews in other periodicals. Indexed by author/title and subject; quinquennial cumulated indexes 1970/74-1990/94. Widest coverage of the US reference reviewing sources and a valuable selection tool for English-language materials, especially specialized titles. *Class No:* 03(048)

[1408]

—Best reference books, 1986-1990: titles of lasting value selected from *American reference books annual.* Wynar, B.S., *ed and* Dority, G.K., *comp.*. Englewood, Colo., 1992. xii,544p. £49.95;$75. ISBN: 0872879364.

1,211 reviews, selected from the 10,692 which appeared in the five years of *American reference books annual.* Some minor modifications to reflect new editions and other changes, but reviews otherwise unaltered.

Preceded by *Best reference books 1981-1985* (Wynar, B.S. *ed.* 1986. 504p. ISBN: 0872875547) and *Best reference books, 1970-1980* (Holte, S. and Wynar, B.S. *eds.* 1981. 408p. ISBN: 087287556). *Class No:* 03(048)

[1409]

—Recommended reference books for small and medium-sized libraries and media centers. Englewood, Colo., Libraries Unlimited, 1981-. Annual. £43.50;$45. ISSN: 02775948.

The 1995 ed., Wynar, B.S. *ed.* (xix,280p.) contains 525 original and unabridged reviews from *American reference books annual,* with the addition of codes to indicate suitability for particular types of library (*e.g.* S = School libraries). Same arrangement and indexing as the parent work. Complements *Reference sources for small and medium-sized libraries* (*q.v.*). *Class No:* 03(048)

[1410]

Reference and research book news: annotations and reviews of new books. Portland, Or., Book News, 1986-. Bimonthly. $100. ISSN: 08873763.

Issued quarterly until April 1989.

Provides short reviews of new books suitable for academic libraries. Includes a high proportion of reference works. A useful acquisition tool, but does not rival *Choice* (*q.v.*) in comprehensiveness or quality and length of reviews.
Class No: 03(048)

[1411]

Reference books bulletin: a compilation of evaluations... . Chicago, American Library Association, 1970-. Annual. ISSN: 87550962.

Issued under the auspices of the Reference Books Bulletin Board of the ALA.

Present title from 1983/84; previously *Reference and subscription book reviews.* Continues *Subscription books bulletin reviews,* published in 5v. for 1956/60-1966/68, (1961-68).

Extracted from the *Reference books bulletin* section of the semi-monthly *Booklist* (*q.v.*). Each v. reproduces *c.*500 reviews from the September to August issues of the previous year in Dewey based subject groups. Also includes several review articles and the annual general and electronic encyclopedia updates. Subject, type of material and title indexes. Not as comprehensive as *American reference books annual* (above), but the reviews are generally longer, better written and more considered. *Class No:* 03(048)

[1412]

Reference reviews: reviews of new reference materials prepared by librarians for librarians. Bradford, MCB University Press, 1987-. 8 pa. £1999;$2999. ISSN: 09504125.

Publisher varies. Subscribers have access to Internet based archive of issues from 1989.

Contains signed reviews of *c.*400-500 words in broad subject sections (*e.g.* General works, Sociology, Science, Literature, Area studies), with author and title indexes in each issue. Includes reference works for children and CD-ROMs. Number of reviews gradually increased in recent years; 517 titles covered 1996. The only British published periodical of its kind. *Class No:* 03(048)

[1413]

Reference reviews Europe annual. Firenze, Casalini Libri, 1995-. Annual. L24000. ISSN: 11246332.

Provides English-language summaries of reviews of reference material appearing in the German-language periodical *Informationsmittel für Bibliotheken.* 618 titles included in 1995 v. (1996. 205p.). Strong on German titles with a good election from other European countries, especially France, Italy and Scandinavia.

Reference reviews Europe developed from an Internet site of the same name. This continues to operate, providing summary translation of reviews from *Informationsmittel für Bibliotheken* on a quarterly basis. Site provided by Casalini from 1997 at http://rre.casalini.com. *Class No:* 03(048)

[1414]

Rettig on reference. Rettig, J., *comp.* Detroit, Gale, 1997-. World Wide Web resource.

URL: http://www.gale.com/rettig/rettig.html. Date reviewed 4th August 1998. Service hosted by H.W. Wilson before 1997.

Provides evaluative reviews of 200-300 words, all by

....(contd.)

Rettig, for new books and other sources including CD-ROMs and WWW sites. About 25 reviews each month, archived from 1997. *Class No:* 03(048)

[1415]

The Year in reference. 1993-94. Toase, C.A., *ed.* Andover, Gale Research International, 1994-95. 2v.

Ceased publication.

1993 v. (xliv,441p. ISBN: 1873471155) carried 275 reviews of new reference items published September 1992-August 1993. Reviews signed, mainly contributed by librarians and information specialists, generally 500-750 words in length. Author and title index. *Class No:* 03(048)

Indexes

[1416]

Book review index: reference books 1965-1984: a cumulated index to more than 87,000 reviews of approximately 40,000 reference titles that have been cited in *Book review index.* Beach, B., *ed.* Detroit, Gale, 1986. 700p. $130. ISBN: 0810321955.

Selected from *Book review index: a master cumulation 1965-1984* (*q.v.*). 470 sources indexed as listed on endpapers. Reference works broadly defined, including travel guides, repair manuals and non-reference items where the reviewer has commented on the work's reference value. Entries omit edition statement. Author arrangement A-Z, with title index, (p.511-700). *Class No:* 03(048)(014)

Periodicals

[1417]

Refer. London, Information Services Group of the Library Association, 1980-. 3pa. £15. ISSN: 01442384.

Journal of the Information Services Group of the Library Association.

Primarily a forum for news, views, comment and occasional reviews of interest to members of the ISG. Each issue also includes an invaluable section, 'Reference books you may have missed' by C.A. Toase, providing commentary on easily overlooked reference items, especially those recently published. *Class No:* 03(051)

[1418]

RQ. Chicago, American Library Association, 1960-. Quarterly. ISSN: 00337072.

Official publication of the Reference and User Services Association division of the American Library Association.

In addition to articles and news each issue carries good length signed reviews of new reference sources. V.36(4), Summer 1997, evaluates 3 databases, 25 reference books and 10 'professional materials'. *Class No:* 03(051)

[1419]

RSR/Reference services review. Ann Arbor, Pierian Press, 1973-. Quarterly. $79. ISSN: 00907324.

Originally carried reviews of new reference material, but now largely devoted to articles on a wide range of reference related topics. A particularly useful feature is the frequent appearance of bibliographical essays on often obscure topics. An example from v.25(1) is 'Coping with workplace change: an annotated bibliography of reources'. *Class No:* 03(051)

Histories

[1420]

Distinguished classics of reference publishing. Rettig, J., *ed.* Phoenix, Oryx. 1992. xv,356p. $55. ISBN: 0897746406.

Contains 31 chapters each providing 6-10 page accounts on the history and development of major English language reference works. Titles covered include *Bartlett's familiar quotations, Dictionary of national biography, Encyclopaedia Britannica, Guinness book of records, National union catalog, New York times index, Oxford English dictionary* and *Science citation index*. Accounts conclude with 20-30 item bibliographies. Index (p.339-56). A 'detailed and exceptionally well done piece of history, unique in its coverage ... (although) usefulness as a reference volume itself is limited' (*Library journal*, v.117(10), June 1 1992, p.110). *Class No:* 03(091)

Children

[1421]

BUCKINGHAMSHIRE COUNTY LIBRARY. Library and Information Service for Secondary Schools. **Reference material for the secondary school library.**
Hyland, S., *comp.* New ed. [Aylesbury], Buckinghamshire County Council, County Library, Library and Information Service for Secondary Schools, 1996. 35p. £4.99. (*Enquire within.*) ISBN: 0860595692.

First published as *Guide to reference books for schools*, 1986; ed. with current title 1991.

A slim guide, but useful as one of the only UK published titles to current children's reference material available. *Class No:* 03-0053

[1422]

Information books for children. Barker, K., *ed.* 2nd ed. Aldershot, Scolar Press, 1995. xiii,269p. £39.50;$64.95. ISBN: 1859280722.

First published 1992.

This ed. greatly expanded. Now contains *c.*1,500 critically annotated entries for non-fiction titles, including a number with reference value. Dewey classified arrangement; author, title and subject indexes. Titles evaluated suitable for children to age 16. Some uneven treatment, but of considerable value because of the lack of other British published works of this type.

Forthcoming from Scolar Press 1998: *Guide to children's reference books and multimedia material* (£35. ISBN: 1859282653). *Class No:* 03-0053

[1423]

NICHOLS, M.I. Guide to reference books for school media centers. 4th ed. Englewood, Colo., Libraries Unlimited, 1992. xiv,463p. £36.95;$40. ISBN: 0872878333.

First published 1973; 3rd ed. 1986.

Contains 2,200 critically annotated entries in 54 subject sections. Author/title and subject indexes. An established US source which shows some overlap with other Libraries Unlimited guides, especially *Recommended reference books for small and medium-sized libraries and media centers* (*q.v.*). *Class No:* 03-0053

[1424]

PETERSON, C.S. *and* FENTON, A.D. Reference books for children. 4th ed. Metuchen, N.J., Scarecrow Press, 1992. xiv,399p. £35.55;$45. ISBN: 0810825430.

First published as *Reference books for elementary and junior high school libraries* 1970; 3rd ed. under present title 1981.

Briefly annotated guide to 1,037 books published before

....(contd.)

June 1990, serially published titles included. Arranged under 120 subject headings within broad sections 'General reference', 'Humanities', 'Recreation', 'Science' and 'Social sciences'. Author/title and subject indexes. *Class No:* 03-0053

030 Encyclopaedias

Encyclopaedias

Bibliographies

[1425]

COLLISON, R.L. Encyclopaedias; their history throughout the ages; a bibliographical guide with extensive historical notes to the general encyclopaedias issued throughout the world from 350 B.C. to the present day. 2nd ed. New York and London, Hafner, 1966. xvi,334p. ISBN: 0028431006.

First published 1964.

8 chapters each with a short bibliography appended. Welcome concentration on older encyclopedias. Some lack of balance in treatment (*e.g. Encyclopaedia Britannica* receives a whole chapter (p.138-55); *Enciclopedia italiana* and the *Bol'shaia* - 1 page each only). Lengthy appendices on *The encyclopaedia metropolitana* and S.T. Coleridge (p.229-92). Appendix 4: 'List of encyclopaedias not mentioned in the text' (p.298-313). The detailed index lacks subject entries. *Class No:* 030(01)

[1426]

Dictionaries, encyclopedias and other word-related books. Brewer, A.M., *ed.* 4th ed. Detroit, Gale, 1988. 2v. £399;$520. ISBN: 0810304406.

Subtitle: *A Classed guide to dictionaries, encyclopedias, and similar works, based on Library of Congress MARC records and arranged according to the Library of Congress Classification System. Including compilations of acronyms, Americanisms, colloquialisms, etymologies, glossaries, idioms and expressions, orthography, provincialisms, slang, terms and phrases and vocabularies in English and all other languages.*

First published 1975; 3rd ed. 1982.

About 35,000 entries (3rd ed. 28,000) each with full Library of Congress cataloguing and subject headings. Subject and title indexes in v.2, rather than a keyword index as in previous eds. Minimal introductory information. Works relating to the English language occupy nearly 100 pages. *Class No:* 030(01)

[1427]

WALSH, S.P. Anglo-American general encyclopedias: a historical bibliography, 1703-1967. New York, Bowker, 1968. xix,270p. ISBN: 0835200264.

Guide to *c.*419 English-language encyclopedias, arranged A-Z (why not chronologically?), with critical annotations and bibliographical references. Appended chronology, general bibliography and indexes. *Class No:* 030(01)

Indexes

[1428]

First stop: the master index to subject encyclopedias. Ryan, J., *ed.* Phoenix, Oryx Press, 1989. xvii,1582p. £175.50;$215. ISBN: 0897743970.

Subject and keyword index to 40,000 topics treated in 430 English language subject encyclopedias. All titles indexed

.... *(contd.)*

are in print in the US and have analytical articles in excess of 250 words. 'Source list' p.1-12. Considered an 'excellent starting point' for background information by *Choice* (v.26(10), June 1989, p.1660). However, many indexing peculiarities are apparant (*e.g.* middle names indexed for biographical entries), and 'this otherwise useful work falls down because the editor has been content to let the computer find the keywords' (*Refer*, v.5(4), Autumn 1989, p.11).
Class No: 030(014)

[1429]

Subject index to feature articles and special reports in encyclopedia yearbooks, 1975-1991. Dilbert, S., *ed.* Hewlett, N.Y., Infodatafacts, 1992. 83p. $15. ISBN: 0962573906.

Covers yearbooks of the *Americana, Britannica, Collier's, Compton's* and *World book*, plus some medical and science annuals such as those of *Britannica*. Subject headings used based on *Sears*. '(P)robably safe to assume that there is little need for such a book' (*American reference books annual*, v.25, 1994, p.16). *Class No:* 030(014)

Handbooks & Manuals

[1430]

AMERICAN LIBRARY ASSOCIATION. Reference Books Bulletin Editorial Board. **Purchasing an encyclopedia:** 12 points to consider. Whiteley, S., *ed.* 5th ed. Chicago, Booklist, American Library Association, 1996. 43p. £6.50;$7.95. ISBN: 0838978231.

First published 1979; 4th ed. 1992.

Designed to assist in the evaluation of the major English language adult and children's sets, including online/CD-ROM versions. Based on reprints of reviews appearing in the *Reference books bulletin* section of *Booklist* (*q.v.*).
Class No: 030(035)

[1431]

AWE, S. ARBA guide to subject encyclopedias and dictionaries. 2nd ed. Englewood Colo., Libraries Unlimited, 1997. xxvi,482p. ISBN: 1563084678.

First published 1986.

Evaluates 1,086 mostly in print works (only 148 titles retained from previous ed.) in 36 subject sections. Reviews, partially rewritten, selected from *American reference books annual* (*q.v.*). Author/title and subject indexes. A valuable source which 'nicely complements *Guide to reference books* 11th edition, as only 473 entries appear in both sources' (*Choice*, v.35(3), November 1997, p.449).
Class No: 030(035)

[1432]

KISTER, K.F. Kister's best encyclopedias: a comparative guide to general and specialized encyclopedias. Phoenix, Oryx Press, 1994. xiv,506p. tables. £43.95;$42.50. ISBN: 0897747445.

1st ed. as *Best encyclopedias*, 1986, replacing Kister's *Encyclopedia buying guide: a consumer guide to general encyclopedias in print* (3rd ed. Bowker, 1981. First published 1976). This title succeeded S.P. Walsh's *General*

.... (contd.)
encyclopedias in print (9th ed. Bowker, 1973. First published 1963).

Main section offers in depth reviews of 58 general English language encyclopedias including single volume titles and those aimed at children and young adults. Each review divided into two sections: Facts (publishing history, no. of pages, articles, etc., price) and Evaluation (lengthy critical and comparative analysis followed by summary and review citations). Includes sections on encyclopedias available in electronic formats (p.255-98) and out-of-print (p.299-320). Further section 'Subject and foreign encyclopedias' gives briefer treatment to 800 specialized and 44 non-English general encyclopedias. Appended 'Encyclopedia resources' (annotated list of books and periodical articles about encyclopedias) and 'Directory of encyclopedia publishers and distributors'. Index. Especially thorough on the general English language sets, but well done throughout and unrivalled as the major current guide to encyclopedias.
Class No: 030(035)

English

Multi-Volume Works

[1433]

Chambers encyclopaedia. New rev. ed. London, International Learning Systems Corp. Ltd., [1973]. 15v. illus., maps.

Reprinted Pergamon Press, 1982.

First published 1859-1868, by William and Robert Chambers. (No connection with Ephraim Chambers *Cyclopaedia* (1725), the French translation of which (1745) gave inspiration to Diderot's *Encyclopédie*). Completely revised 1950; 4th new rev. ed. Oxford, Pergamon Press, 1967. 15v.

Over 23,000 articles, 4,000 contributors (listed per volume), 15 million words. Signed entries with short bibliographies (*e.g.* 'Archaeology', v.1, p.535-43, 13 lines of bibliography; 'Architecture', v.1, p.550-83, 2 columns of bibliography, 19p. of plates). V.15 *Indexes and maps* (xii,824p.) has a 44p. Bartholomew atlas and gazetteer, general index of 200,000 entries and references and a classified list of articles. At one time the major British alternative to the multi-volume encyclopedias published in the US, but now seriously out of date and useful only for historical and similar material. *Class No:* 030=20(003.8)

[1434]

Collier's encyclopedia: with bibliography and index. New York, P.F. Collier. Annual revision. 24v. illus., maps, tables. $850.

First published 1949-51 in 20 v. Issued as a 24 v. set since 1962. Published by Macmillan until 1993.

'Designed and built to fill the needs of the most exacting school and home users'. Broad entry approach with 23,000 articles, nearly all signed. The *c.*5,000 editors, advisors and contributors are mostly academics and include distinguished names such as Isaac Asimov, Margaret Mead and Reinhold Niebuhr. Many lengthy articles (*e.g.* 'Libraries', (v.14) p.559-99, *c.*40 illus., 1 chart). Biographical and geographical articles tend to be especially thorough and well-shaped (*e.g.* 'Ecuador', (v.8) p.542-49, 7 illus., 1 map). Currency is generally good, the 1997 revision having 57 new articles. A less satisfactory feature are the illustrations. About 50% remain black and white despite a programme of gradual replacement. While there are adequate cross-references (*c.*12,500), the set depends on the index in v. 24. At over 450,000 clearly displayed entries, including

.... (contd.)
illustrations and bibliography items, this is one of the most extensive of any English language encyclopedia. Also in this v. is *Collier's* other distinctive feature, a 11,500 item bibliography (p.1-200). Impressively up-to-date, this is in classified arrangement with one sentence annotations. While the whole set has an appreciable US slant, *Collier's* is a valuable second-string encyclopedia for the UK and elsewhere. An alternative to the *Britannica* and *Americana* for smaller public libraries and home use.

Collier's international yearbook is primarily concerned with the events of the previous year. Arrangement is A-Z with articles for countries, US states, major subjects and topical concerns. Includes 'Obituaries' and 'World facts and statistics' sections. A number of feature articles are also provided. One of the best encyclopedia yearbooks.

Collier's multimedia encyclopedia, a 3 disc CD-ROM, is the currently available electronic version (£75). The much improved 1998 release includes 17,000 articles from the print set, 8,000 photographs (nearly all new to the CD-ROM), 732 audio clips, 106 videos and a world atlas of 358 maps. Internet links, provided by Northern Light, are also available. *Class No:* 030=20(003.8)

[1435]

The Encyclopedia Americana. International ed. Danbury, Conn., Grolier. Annual revision. 30v. illus., ports., tables, maps.

First published 1829-33. The earliest US encyclopedia and largely based on *Brockhaus Konversations - Lexikon* (7th ed. 1827-29).

Over 6,000 contributors, c.52,000 articles (40% biographies), *c.*900p. per volume. Articles are signed and briefly state qualifications of contributor. Bibliographies appended for major topics. Stronger emphasis on North America than in comparable multi-volume sets, especially history, places and people. Also strong on science and technology (e.g. 'Aluminium': 5p., 8 illus., 2 diags., 6 references). Nearly 23,000 illus., judiciously placed, but of variable quality and with sparing use of colour (85% black & white). The index (v.30) is comprehensive with 353,000 entries, compensating for the limited number of cross-references in the text. 30 new articles added 1997 and 45 extensively altered. However, annual revision is not always as rapid or far-reaching as in competing encyclopedias. Outdated statistical data and bibliographies with no items published in the last 10-15 years are all too frequently encountered. This deficiency and an unattractive, old-fashioned appearance, largely resulting from the illustrations, are the *Americana's* major drawbacks. These must be balanced against scholarly and authoritative treatment of most topics and a level of comprehensiveness which makes it second only to the *Britannica* in the league table of English language encyclopedias.

The Americana annual (1923-) is divided into 4 major sections: Year in review; Feature articles; Alphabetical section; Statistical and tabular data.

The Encyclopedia Americana is also available on CD-ROM (launched 1995) and from 1997 through the Internet. The CD-ROM version contains the text of the printed volumes, 2,000 illustrations, WWW links and three additional reference titles, the *Merriman-Webster collegiate dictionary*, Helicon's *Chronology of world history* and Academic Press' *Dictionary of science and technology*. The Internet version is similar, but includes a greater number of WWW links. *Class No:* 030=20(003.8)

[1436]

Everyman's encyclopaedia. Girling, D.A., *ed.* 6th ed. London, Dent, 1978. 12v. (8,896p.), illus., diags., maps. £25 per v. ISBN: 0460040987.

First published 1913-14; 5th ed. 1967.

Around 50,000 articles from *c.*350 contributors, the vast majority British academics. Very lengthy articles are avoided. The longest, on USA (v.12, p.177-220) is sectionalised. British slant: London, Oxford and Cambridge institutes and colleges have separate entries; 'Cricket': 5p., 'Baseball': 1p. 13,500 biographies (Napoleon: 5 cols; Wellington: 1 col; Talleyrand: ½ col). Bibliographies are provided for longer articles. 5,600 black and white illus; coloured atlas appended to v.10. No index. Despite not having been updated for 20 years, remains of some value in the UK as one of the few multi-volume encyclopedias produced with a British readership primarily in mind. *Class No:* 030=20(003.8)

[1437]

The Hutchinson unabridged encyclopedia. Oxford, Helicon, 1996. 8v. ISBN: 1859860273.

The first British published adult multi-volume encyclopedia since *Everyman's* (above). Essentially an expansion of the single-volume *Hutchinson encyclopedia* (*q.v.*) based on Helicon's reference database. 3,500,000 words, 35,000 entries, over 3,000 illustrations (nearly all colour) and 250 tables and charts. Set out in 2 col. arrangement, articles are generally short as in the single vol. (*e.g.* Bern, 60 words; Baldwin, Stanley, 200 words) with longer entries for countries (*e.g.* Bolivia, 1¼cols., boxed data and short chronology) and major topics. Excellent system of cross-references (*c.*38,000); subject (grouped headings), people and general (45,000 entries) indexes in the final vol. *Class No:* 030=20(003.8)

[1438]

The Macmillan family encyclopedia. London, Macmillan. Regular revision. 21v. illus., ports., diags., tables, maps.

First published 1980. Published in the US with annual revision as *Academic American encyclopedia*. Also sold under various other titles including *Grolier academic encyclopedia* and *Lexicon universal encyclopedia*.

The most recently established of the English language multi-volume general encyclopedias. '(C)reated for students at the upper elementary level and in junior high school, high school or college and for the inquisitive adult' (Preface). More than 2,500 contributors, 30,000 articles, 18,000 illus. (predominantly col. and of a high standard) and 1,100 maps. Articles are brief to medium in length, mostly signed, over ½ with short appended bibliographies. Cross-references widely used in the text; v.21 *Index* has 200,000 entries, one of the fullest of its kind. A particular feature worthy of note is an attention to objectivity in dealing with controversial topics and a relative freedom from US bias. Currency is also good, the 1997 revision having 2,700 amended, plus 129 new articles. Negative features are closely spaced text and some lack of depth in the treatment of more complex subjects, especially those of a technical nature. Also available electronically as *The Grolier multimedia encyclopedia* (below). *Class No:* 030=20(003.8)

[1439]

—The Grolier multimedia encyclopedia. Grolier Electronic Publishing. Computer database.

Available either on CD-ROM (annual updating £75), from online hosts such a CARL or through the Internet on a subscription basis at http://gme.grolier.com/.

The first major encyclopedia to experiment with CD-ROM availability. The current disc is based on the text of the printed edition, but adds 5,000 further articles and includes 8,000 still pictures, 850 maps, plus video and sound clips and animations. Search software based on three modes, 'Article title list', 'Word search' and 'Knowledge tree' (hierarchical categories). Not as polished as some multimedia encyclopedias such as *Encarta*, but still one of the better products available. *Class No:* 030=20(003.8)

[1440]

The New Encyclopaedia Britannica. 15th ed. Chicago and London, Encyclopaedia Britannica. Annual revision. 32v. illus., ports., tables, maps.

From the 1985 printing comprises: Micropaedia (v.1-12); Macropaedia (v.13-29); Propaedia (1v.); Index (2v.).

The 15th ed. of the *Britannica* was first published in 1974 in 30v. comprising Micropaedia (10v.), Macropaedia (19v.) and Propaedia (1v.). The Micropaedia containing 100,000 brief entries, none longer than 750 words, was intended for ready reference, the bulk of the set being formed by the 4,200 lengthy articles of the Macropaedia. As then constituted the *Britannica* had no index, this function being performed by the Micropaedia. With the 1985 printing the *Britannica* was restructured, the main changes being a drastic reduction in the number of Macropaedia articles, the addition of two further Micropaedia volumes and most importantly, the provision of an index.

The largest, the longest established and the best known general encyclopedia in the English language, the *Britannica* contains *c.*44,000,000 words of text and 25,000 predominantly black and white illustrations and maps. The *c.*5,000 contributors, about ½ from the US, somewhat less than a ¼ from the UK, are listed in the Propaedia. Intended as 'a kind of preamble or antechamber to the world of learning that the rest of the encyclopedia aims to encompass' (Preface, p.v.), the Propaedia has references to the Macropaedia and Micropedia (*e.g.* 'The aims and organization of education' (p.215-16) has references to Macropaedia articles 'Philosophies of the branches of knowledge' and 'Teaching').

The 17v. Macropaedia 'Knowledge in depth' has 673 lengthy, scholarly articles covering 30p., with some much longer (*e.g.* 'Literature, the art of', 143p.). Generally confined to broad subjects (*e.g.* 'Christianity'; 'Reproduction and reproductive systems'), the Macropaedia also has articles for countries and regions (*e.g.* 'Norway', 15p. (subdivided) full page col. map, 2 illus., 1 further map, 1¼ columns of bibliography) and *c.*100 biographies (*e.g.* Darwin, Freud, Johnson, Lincoln, Rembrandt). Many of the articles, especially those on technical or complex subjects, are written at a level which put them beyond the understanding of the layperson. Lengthy bibliographies are appended (*e.g.* the article 'Chemical compounds' has 3p. of references).

The Micropaedia has *c.*64,500 entries averaging 275-300 words in length. Many biographical articles are included (*c.*33% of total), the more substantial of which have bibliographies (*e.g.* 'Nkrumah, Kwame', 1p., port., 8 references; 'Stresemann, Gustav', 1½p., 1 port., 9 references). Subjects treated in the Macropaedia also have entries, a policy which allows the Micropaedia to stand

....(contd.)
alone, but results in much unnecessary duplication. The final part of the *Britannica*, the 2v. index, has *c*.500,000 references and cross-references. Given the Macropaedia/Micropaedia division and the lengthy articles of the former, the index is a vital component of the set and should be the user's first port of call.

Revised on an annual basis, the 1995 printing having one new, 45 rewritten and 199 revised Macropaedia articles, the *Britannica* is kept impressively up-to-date. Illustrations may be sparse, paper quality relatively poor and the price well in excess of rivals, but when it comes to major considerations such as comprehensiveness and authority the *Britannica* is unbeatable. *Class No:* 030=20(003.8)

[1441]

—Britannica book of the year. Chicago and London, Encyclopaedia Britannica, 1938-. Annual. Illus., ports., tables., maps. ISSN: 00681156.

Spine title *Britannica world data*.

Content varies slightly, but usually contains a number of feature articles and a chronology of the past year. The main section, 'The year in review' is divided topically (*e.g.* Architecture; Disasters; Literature; Motion pictures; Sports and games) with various 'special reports' and biographies and obituaries following. 'Britannica update' reproduces selected Macropaedia articles or parts of articles which have been revised or re-written. The final section, 'World data' (grey edged paper), provides demographic, economic, transport, education, military, etc., statistics by country and comparative national statistics. Cumulative index covering the last 10 years. One of the best encyclopedia yearbooks, and an important reference source in its own right, especially for the statistical information collected under 'World data'.
Class No: 030=20(003.8)

[1442]

—Britannica CD. Chicago and London, Encyclopaedia Britannica, 1994-. CD-ROM database. £125.

1998 release is a 2 disc product: Disc 1 contains the 44 million words of the main set; Disc 2 provides multimedia features and the option to link to Internet sites.

Has most of the features of *Britannica online* (below) including the WWW based interface. An 'encyclopedia "first", not an encyclopedia pretending to be a television program or a box office hit' (*Database* v.19(1), February/March 1996, p.72) on the 1996 release.
Class No: 030=20(003.8)

[1443]

—Britannica online. Chicago and London, Encyclopaedia Britannica, 1994-. World Wide Web resource.

Accessible through subscription at http://www.eb.com. Updated on a continuous basis.

First multi-volume encyclopedia to be Internet accessible. The product has been developed and enhanced and now contains a wide range of features. These include (1998) 72,000 articles (3,000 of which not in the printed set), 12,000 illustrations, links to nearly 20,000 WWW sites selected by Britannica editors, a nations of the world section including maps and flags and special 'spotlight' features on current topics. Searching based on natural language, A-Z browsing and site map also available. Internet links can be opened directly from a hit list as well as articles. 'No other online encyclopedia currently offers the same combination of currency, visual appeal, textual breadth and depth and sophisticated search options' (*Reference books bulletin* in *Booklist*, v.94(5), November 1 1997 p.500).
Class No: 030=20(003.8)

[1444]

—Encyclopaedia Britannica. 1st-14th eds.

First published in Edinburgh 1768-71 (facsimile reprint, Routledge/Thoemmess Press, 1997. 3v. £499. ISBN: 0415149568). All the early editions are valuable from an historical point of view. The specifically Scottish bias should be noted, particularly the religious climate of Edinburgh.

Of the later editions those which retain most value now are the 9th and 11th and their supplements. The 9th ed. (24v. 1875-79), sometimes called 'the scholars' edition', was a great work of 19th century scholarship and many of its articles have hardly been bettered (*e.g.* that on the Renaissance). The 10th ed. (1902) consisted of 10 supplementary v. and an atlas, to be used together with the 9th ed. The 11th ed. (26v. 1910-11) was in many ways the best ever produced. Although there was a tendency to a greater number of shorter articles on specific topics, the set remained scholarly, carried a thorough index ('containing considerably more than 500,000 headings') and was well-illustrated for its time.

The next full scale ed. was the 14th (24v. 1929), basically a revision of the 11th, but with the text cut and the trend to shorter articles continued (eds. designated 12th and 13th formed supplements to the 11th, the former dealing with the First World War). The work, which had previously passed into American ownership, now had half American editors and contributors and was designed for a wider American as well as British public. In the years before the Second World War many of the features of the present encyclopedia were introduced. The words 'Fourteenth edition' disappeared from the title page about 1936, continuous revision was gradually adopted, although partially interrupted by the War, and the *Britannica book of the year* (1938-) established. The 14th ed. continued to provide the basic structure of the work until 1974 when the remodelled 15th ed. *The New encyclopaedia Britannica* (as described above) was first published.
Class No: 030=20(003.8)

[1445]

—The Treasury of the Encyclopaedia Britannica: more than two centuries of facts, curiosities and discoveries from the most distinguished reference work of all time. Fadiman, C., *ed.* New York, Viking, 1992. xxix,704p. illus. ISBN: 0670835684.

Reprints, usually in the form of extracts, material on specific topics and events or by renowned contributors (*e.g.* Trotsky on Lenin). '(P)rovides a glimpse of the history of this esteemed reference source' (*Reference books bulletin* in *Booklist*, v.89(6), November 15 1992, p.628).
Class No: 030=20(003.8)

Single-Volume works

[1446]

The Cambridge encyclopedia. Crystal, D., *ed.* 3rd ed. Cambridge, Cambridge Univ. Press, 1997. vi,1303,[128]p., illus., tables, maps. £35;$54.95. ISBN: 0521584590.

First published 1990; 2nd ed. 1994.

More entries (36,000 claimed) than the other British published one volume encyclopedias, achieved at the expense of text illustrations (1,000 diagrams and maps). Concise, well-written articles (*e.g.* 'Jupiter', *c*.360 words; 'Venezuela', *c*.350 words, 1 map; 'Royal Opera House', 35 words), including 6,000 biographies and 4,000 geographical entries. Aims to give special emphasis to technology, computer science, the environment, medicine and leisure interests. A unique and valuable feature is the 128p. 'Ready reference' section containing largely tabulated data in 11

....(*contd.*)
groupings. Individual tables include 'Saint's days', 'Airline designators', 'Counties of England' (area, population, administrative centre), 'Political leaders, 1900-1997' (by country), 'Competitive sports and games' (winners by sport) and 'Common abbreviations'. Extensive and effective use of cross-references (*c.*85,000) including references to 'Ready reference' data. The best of the British published single v. encyclopedias and 'must now be established as one of the most significant reference works of recent times' (*Reference reviews*, v.11(8), 1997, p.3). *Class No:* 030=20(003.9)

[1447]

—The Cambridge concise encyclopedia. Crystal, D., *ed.* 2nd ed. Cambridge, Cambridge Univ. Press, 1995. viii,1088p. illus., tables, maps. £17.95. ISBN: 0521550491.

First published 1992. A paperback version is available as *The Cambridge paperback encyclopedia* (2nd ed. 1995. £9.95. ISBN: 0521559685).

Abridgement of the main v. Nearly 20,000 entries, 570 maps and diagrams and 'Ready reference' section of 100p. *Class No:* 030=20(003.9)

[1448]

The Columbia encyclopedia. Chernow, B.A. *and* Vallasi, G.A., *eds.* 5th ed. New York, Columbia Univ. Press, 1993. xviii,3048p. illus., maps, tables. £49.99;$59.95. ISBN: 039562438x.

First published 1935; 4th ed. 1975 as *The New Columbia encyclopedia.*

6½ million words (*Everyman's encyclopaedia* 12 v. 8 million words) in over 50,000 unsigned articles. 'Germany': 12 columns, 1 map, bibliography of 20 items; 'Marxism': 1½ columns, 9 references; 'Rodin, Auguste': ½ column, 4 references; 'Wallasey': 30 words. Mostly solid text, with only slight concessions to illustrations. Good use of tables, *e.g.* for Nobel Prize winners, US national parks and monuments. US slant *e.g.* 'Cricket', 2/3 column; 'Baseball', 2¼ columns. No index but over 65,000 cross-references. By far the most comprehensive one volume general encyclopedia in the English language, which 'contains entries not found in even the largest sets' (*Reference books bulletin* in *Booklist*, v.90(2), September 15 1992, p.184).

A CD-ROM version was launched in 1996, based on the 1993 ed., but with 900 new and 3,000 revised entries. Also includes 260 maps. '(E)asy to use but lacks *Encarta's* state-of-the-art interface and has no graphics' (*Reference books bulletin* in *Booklist*, v.93(19/20), June 1997, p.1754). *Class No:* 030=20(003.9)

[1449]

—The Concise Columbia encyclopedia. Lagassé, P.G., *ed.* 3rd ed. New York, Columbia Univ. Press, 1994. [x],973p. illus., maps, charts, tables. £25;$49.95. ISBN: 0395624398.

First published 1983; 2nd ed. 1989. 2nd ed. forms the basis of the British published *Longman encyclopedia* (*q.v.*).

*c.*17,000 mainly short entries, as in the main set (*e.g.* 'Belloc, Hilaire', *c.*30 words; 'Chemical warfare', *c.*120 words; 'Down's syndrome', *c.*50 words), 2,000 new to this ed. Black and white illus., 100 tables and charts. 210 maps accompany country articles; full col. maps in centre pages as in previous eds. dropped. '(A)dmirably up-to-date' (*Reference books bulletin* in *Booklist*, v.91(4), 15 October 1994, p.450). Electronic versions also available online (FirstSearch), on CD-ROM, including as part of *Microsoft bookshelf*, and through several Internet providers such as America Online. *Class No:* 030=20(003.9)

[1450]

The Fontana dictionary of modern thought. Bullock, A. *and* Trombley, S., *eds.* New rev. ed. London, Fontana, 1988. xxvi,917p. £14.99. ISBN: 0006861296.

Published in the US as *The Harper dictionary of modern thought* (ISBN: 0060158697). First published 1977.

Takes 'key terms from across the whole range of modern thought, sets them within their context and offers short explanatory accounts (anything from ten to a thousand words) written by experts but in language as simple as can be used without over-simplification or distortion' (Preface p.vii). Scope extends beyond thought in the philosophical sense. Entries include: 'Corporatism', *c.*325 words 2 references; 'Laser surgery', *c.*360 words; 'My Lai', *c.*120 words. 'Modern' as in the title generally implies 20th century. 1,000 new entries in this ed. bringing total to 5,000. Biographical information now available in companion volume *Fontana dictionary of modern thinkers* (1989. ISBN: 0006369650). *Class No:* 030=20(003.9)

[1451]

The Guinness book of answers. 10th ed. Enfield, Guinness Publishing, 1995. 832p. illus., charts, tables. ISBN: 0851126596.

First published 1976; 9th ed. 1993.

Mainly comprises brief encyclopedia-type entries set out in broad subject sections (*e.g.* The Animal world, Architecture, Religion). Emphasis is on factual matter, especially statistical data. Heavy use of tables (*e.g.* Distance in kilometres between airports) and numerous listings (*e.g.* Famous writers). Countries of the world treated individually (p.568-712); separate section for the United Kingdom (p.713-93). Effective use dependant on the detailed analytical index (p.794-832). *Class No:* 030=20(003.9)

[1452]

The Guinness book of records. Enfield, Guinness Publishing, 1955-. Annual. £17.

Records must be 'measurable and comparable' and of widespread, preferably international, interest. Unique occurences, peculiarities or 'firsts' do not necessarily qualify for inclusion. 1998 ed. (352p. ISBN: 085112044X) in 14 sections: Human body - Human achievements - Size - Hobbies and pastimes - Taking it to the limit - Society - Money - Media - The Arts - Architecture and design - Science and technology - Earth - The Living world - Sport (longest section, p.268-335). Most data in short paragraphs *e.g.* 'Largest rodent' 20 words. Analytical index and a final page 'Getting into the book' providing information on the criteria for record inclusion. The standard guide and one of the most familiar general reference tools. A multimedia CD-ROM version has also been produced.
Class No: 030=20(003.9)

[1453]

The Guinness encyclopedia. Crofton, I., *ed.* 2nd ed. Enfield, Guinness Publishing, 1995. 784p. illus., diags., tables, maps. £35. ISBN: 0851126634.

First published 1990.

Differs from most other one volume encyclopedias (*e.g.* *Cambridge, Hutchinson*) in adopting a thematic approach. 12 sections: 1. The nature of the universe - 2. The restless earth (geology, climate, etc.) - 3. The living planet - 4. The human organism - 5. The world today - 6. Technology and industry - 7. A history of the world - 8. Religion and philosophy - 9. The visual arts - 10. Music and dance - 11. Language and literature - 12. The countries of the world. Each section divided into a series of double page spreads, *c.*320 in all, on individual topics (*e.g.* 'Coasts', 'Islamic art', 'Ancient

.... *(contd.)*
Egypt'). Index (p.744-84) acts as a specific subject key. Heavily illustrated in colour throughout (*c*.50% of entire work). Similar to the *Larousse desk encyclopedia* (below) but with more text, less use of tabulated data and poorer maps. An inadequate CD-ROM version has also been produced; 'has a half-baked and harried feel' (*Database*, v.19(1), February/March 1996, p.104).
Class No: 030=20(003.9)

[1454]

The Hutchinson encyclopedia. 11th ed. Oxford, Helicon, 1997. [vi],1199p. illus., maps, ports, tables. £40. ISBN: 1859862020.

First published 1948. Title varies, as *The Hutchinson 20th century encyclopedia* until 1981. 10th ed. 1992. Updating and minor amendment on an annual basis.

The longest established British one volume encyclopedia. Contains more than 26,000 short entries (*e.g.* 'Caxton, William', *c*.150 words; 'Italy', 3 cols., basic statistical tables and chronology; 'Clinton, Bill' *c*.300 words), with 2,600 supporting colour illustrations. and 600 maps. Provision of 1,250 quotations scattered in page margins adds little to reference value. Lacks a separate index but extensively cross-referenced. This ed. adds 20 longer articles or 'Focus features' (*e.g.* Ireland and the home rule campaign, The search for human origins) aimed at the National Curriculum and a 20p 'Factfile' containing tabulated data (*e.g.* Olympic games venues, Beaufort scale). Rivalled only by the *Cambridge* as the most comprehensive and effective of the British published single volume encyclopedias.

The Hutchinson encyclopedia is compiled from Helicon's reference database. This also forms the basis of the multimedia version (below) and *The Hutchinson unabridged encyclopedia* (*q.v.*). *Class No:* 030=20(003.9)

[1455]

—The Hutchinson multimedia encyclopedia. Oxford, Helicon, 199?-. CD-ROM database. £39.99.

Derived from the Helicon reference database and based on the single volume print ed. 1998 (ISBN: 1859862039) version contains 42,000 articles, 4,500 images, 439 audio clips, 52 video clips and 27 animations. Also features a 13,000 item timeline, an English dictionary and a dictionary of quotations. The only British produced multimedia encyclopedia and a real alternative to *Encarta* for UK users.

Several online versions of the *Hutchinson* have been made available. From 1998 Internet access is to be provided on a subscription basis in collaboration with British Telecom.
Class No: 030=20(003.9)

[1456]

Larousse desk encyclopedia. Hughes, J., *ed.* London, Larousse, 1995. 800p. illus., charts, maps. £30. ISBN: 075230013x.

Published as *The Larousse desk reference* in the US ($39.95. ISBN: 0752350064).

Topically arranged encyclopedia of 7 main sections: 1. Earth and universe - 2. Life on earth - 3. People - 4. History - 5. Science and technology - 6. Arts and culture - 7. International world. Each section subdivided (*e.g.* Arts and culture: Literature and drama, Theatre, film and television), with detailed contents page and icon based cross-reference system. Much use of tabulated and boxed data and over 2,000 colour illustrations. Colour country maps in International world section with map index. General index (p.763-800). 'Visual impact is the key to this volume' (*Choice*, v.33(6), February 1996, p.928).
Class No: 030=20(003.9)

[1457]

The Longman encyclopedia. Briggs, A., *ed.* Harlow, Longman, 1989. x,1178p. illus., diags., tables, maps. ISBN: 0582916208.

Based on the *Concise Columbia encyclopedia* 2nd ed. with extensive revisions to give a greater British orientation. *c*.17,000 undocumented entries from 120 contributors, all approved by a distinguished editorial board including Sir Herman Bondi, Stuart Hall and Mary Warnock. Average article length only 86 words, but countries and major topics given extended treatment (*e.g.* 'New Zealand' *c*.500 words, 1 map., list of post-war prime ministers; 'Magnetism', *c*.550 words). Closely spaced text in two column format supported by 500 illus., 250 diagrs., 36 tables and 150 text maps, all black and white. Separate 16p. col. atlas section. Fewer entries than some of the other one volume encyclopedias and visually not one of the most appealing, the *Longman's* main strength lies in the eminence and authority of the editors.
Class No: 030=20(003.9)

[1458]

The Macmillan encyclopedia. London, Macmillan, 1998. 1336p., illus., maps, diags. £29.99. ISBN: 0333696344.

Revised printings, incorporating updates and amendments, appear on an approximately annual basis. First published 1981.

Contains about the same number of entries (25,500) as *The Hutchinson encyclopedia* (*q.v.*). Mainly short entries (*e.g.* 'Lewes', *c*.35 words, 'Siena', *c*.90 words), but with a few longer articles (*e.g.* 'Mozart, Wolfgang Amadeus', *c*.300 words). Stronger coverage of the natural world, technology and commerce than some comparable encyclopedias. Illustrations (*c*.1,200) are relatively sparse and nearly all black and white. Also includes 19 grouped col. plates and maps. Regular updating permits the inclusion of a good number of entries for current topics (*e.g.* 'Dunblane gun laws', 'Taleban militia'). *Class No:* 030=20(003.9)

[1459]

Microsoft Encarta encyclopedia. [Redmond, Wa.], Microsoft, 1993-. CD-ROM database, updated annually.

Available in standard ($54.95) and deluxe ($79.95) editions. Comprises 2 CD-ROM discs. Also Internet accessible on a fee basis from http://encarta.msn.com.

Specially developed multimedia encyclopedia that takes the concept further than most of its rivals, the 1998 version offering 14,000 photographs and illustrations, 1,500 video clips, 2,300 sound clips and 10,000 WWW links. The accompanying text of 30,000 articles was originally based on the 29 v. *Funk & Wagnall's new encyclopedia*, but has now been greatly augmented. Other features include 'virtual tours' of famous buildings, etc., sidebar articles, a full dictionary and Internet links and updating options. Various language and national versions are available, that marketed in the UK containing material specific to a British audience (Deluxe ed. £79.99). Probably the best of the multimedia encyclopedias and certainly the best known. Although the text is less substantive and authoritative than some of its rivals, the range of multimedia features and ease of use make this an outstanding resource for school children and the general public. *Class No:* 030=20(003.9)

[1460]

The Random House encyclopedia. 3rd ed. New York, Random House, 1990. 2781p. illus., maps, charts. ISBN: 0394584503.

First published 1977; 2nd ed. 1983.

In 2 main sections, 'Colorpedia' and 'Alphapedia'. The 'Colorpedia', comprising over ½ of the entire volume is in 7 thematic sections (*e.g.* Life on earth; History and culture; Man and machines), each containing double page, heavily illustrated, articles on specific topics. The 'Alphapedia' has *c.*25,000 brief entries with cross-references to the 'Colorpedia'. Further 70p. atlas, bibliography and 'Time-chart' sections. Due to the work's structure '(l)ocating information on a specific topic can be frustrating' ... but those 'who want a one volume encyclopedia that encourages browsing and exploring will find this work highly suited to their needs' (*Reference books bulletin* in *Booklist*, v.87(9), 1 January 1991, p.946).

Abridged ed. published 1996 as *Random House concise encyclopedia* (727p. illus., maps. charts. $18. ISBN: 0679764542). Electronic versions of the main v. have also been produced. *Class No:* 030=20(003.9)

[1461]

ROBERTSON, P. The New Shell book of firsts. 3rd ed. London, Headline, 1994. xi,675p. illus. £10.99. ISBN: 0747210101.

First published 1974; 2nd ed. 1983.

Records firsts 'that have contributed to life as it is lived today, particularly those that have served to alter society' (Introduction, p.vii). Over 5,000 entries (1,000 new in this ed.): 'The First abortion, country to legalise' ... 'The First zip fastener'. Entries, 50-400 words in length, usually include a note on British firsts. Chronology (p.485-623); place and subject indexes. *Class No:* 030=20(003.9)

Children

[1462]

Children's Britannica. Sutton, M., *ed.* 4th ed. London, Encyclopaedia Britannica, 1988. 20v. illus., diags., maps. £199. ISBN: 085229218x.

First published 1960; 3rd ed. 1973. Extensively revised and reset for this ed. Minor updating and revision on an irregular basis.

About 3 million words in 4,230 articles. Generously, but not particularly attractively, illustrated with *c.*5,000 photographs (less than ½ in colour) and *c.*1,500 diagrams. Articles are lengthy where necessary (*e.g.* 'Aircraft', 8p., 2p. of diags., 6 illus.), but typically less than 1p. No bibliographies. V.19 contains an atlas section and gazetteer. V.20 comprises a *Reference index* of 30,000 dictionary entries, both for topics treated in the text (*e.g.* 'Matterhorn' *c.*25 words) and those not covered (*e.g.* 'Homs' (Syria) *c.*30 words). Intended for a younger age group than most other major children's encyclopedias and not a junior/adult set in the manner of *The World book*. In the US provides the main competition for the *New book of knowledge* (*q.v.*). In the UK has the advantage of relative freedom from American bias, the set being edited from London with many British contributors. One of the most widely sold sets for home use, also found in school and children's libraries.
Class No: 030=20-0053

[1463]

Compton's encyclopedia & fact-index. Chicago, Compton's Learning Company. Annual revision. 26v. illus., (incl. col.), diags., charts, maps. $415.

First published 1922. Present publisher from 1993, previously Encyclopaedia Britannica.

Intended for US junior and senior high school and middle elementary school students. Articles are generally curriculum orientated, and although often lengthy, written in a controlled vocabulary appropriate to the audience level. The 1997 revision contains 5,286 text articles v.1-25, supported by 22,000 illus. and 2,000 maps. About 500 articles are documented, around 1,000 signed. A feature of *Compton's* is the 30,000 entry 'Fact-index' used to provide information on topics considered too minor to warrant a full article. With good annual revision (211 updated articles and 434 new 'Fact-index' entries 1997) *Compton's* is second only to *The World book encyclopedia* (*q.v.*) as a leading set for the 9-18 age group and beyond.

Compton's was one of the first encyclopedias to experiment with electronic versions launching *Compton's multi-media encyclopedia* on CD-ROM in 1989. The current CD-ROM, *Compton's interactive encyclopedia*, is available in standard (single disc, $69.95) or deluxe (two discs, $89.95) eds. Each contains the full text of the printed set and a dictionary and thesaurus. The standard ed. adds *c.*8,000 illustrations, 100 videos and 6 hours of sound, while the deluxe has *c.*15,000 illustrations, 150 videos and 20 hours of sound. Both eds. allow monthly updating from the Internet, and have a range of special features such as timelines. *Compton's* is also available on America Online and Prodigy to subscribers. *Class No:* 030=20-0053

[1464]

Merit students encyclopedia. New York, Macmillan Educational Corp., 1991. 20v. Illus., diags., tables, maps.

First published 1967, then issued annually with revisions. Last updated 1991.

About 21,000 signed articles, ranging in length from one paragraph to over 60 pages. 20,000 illus. (only 25% in col.) and 1,350 maps. Phonetic pronunciation given for most entries. Lengthier articles have appended 'Books for further reading'. V.20 includes a good *c.*140,000 term subject index. Intended for children aged 10 and upwards. Was a major contender in the junior encyclopedia market, despite some problems with updating (especially bibliographies) and a less attractive appearance than some of its competitors.
Class No: 030=20-0053

[1465]

New book of knowledge. New York, Grolier Educational Corp. Annual revision. 21v. illus., diags., maps. $659.

First published 1912 as *The Book of knowledge*; present title from 1966.

Aimed primarily at the 7-14 age group. About 9,000 full articles A-Z, mostly signed, many by distinguished contributors. Careful use of language ensures material is presented in a clear, readable style. Text backed by *c.* 10,500 excellent illustrations, nearly all colour, which occupy about 1/3 of the total set. Each v. contains individual indexing (the only major encyclopedia to persist with this arrangement) cumulated in a 85,000 term general index in v.21. Major revision programme announced 1992, still in progress 1997, has updated many articles and revised layout of most volumes. Separately available *Home and school reading and study guides* (2pts.), includes a selected list of

....*(contd.)*
books and a guide for parents. The publishers also produce the *New book of knowledge annual*, first issued 1940.
Class No: 030=20-0053

[1466]

New standard encyclopedia. Chicago, Ferguson. Annual revision. 20v. illus., diags., maps.

First published 1910 as *Aiton's encyclopedia*; present title from 1930. Issued as 20 v. set from 1989.

Lesser known US orientated general encyclopedia, especially suitable for young adults. About 17,500 articles, mostly short, written in house, but authenticated by outside experts. Many illustrations added in recent updates, but majority still black and white. Well cross-referenced; v.20 comprises index of over 100,000 terms. *Class No:* 030=20-0053

[1467]

Oxford children's encyclopedia. Oxford, Oxford Univ. Press, 1996. 9v. Illus., diags., maps. £99. ISBN: 0199101736.

First published 1991 in 7v. Issued in the US as *Oxford American children's encyclopedia.*

An encyclopedia for younger children ages 7-13. Vols. 1-7, each of 192p., contain 1,528 articles, 400 of which relate directly to the school curriculum. V.8 is a separate biography v. with 555 brief articles. V.9 *Index* (112p.) has *c.*15,000 entries. The entire set is extremely well laid out with nearly 1,000 full colour illustrations and 250 maps. Revised set due for publication 1998 (£125. ISBN: 0199105065). A CD-ROM version with video, animations and sound clips is also available (£49.99. ISBN: 0192683403). *Class No:* 030=20-0053

[1468]

Oxford illustrated encyclopedia. Judge, H., *general ed.* Oxford, Oxford Univ. Press, 1985-93. 9v. illus., maps, charts, ports. £200;$265.

Thematically arranged: v.1 *The Physical world* (374p. ISBN: 0198691297); v.2 *The Natural world* (375p. ISBN: 0198691343); v.3 *World history from earliest times to 1800* (400p. ISBN: 0198691351); v.4 *World history from 1800 to the present day* (391p. ISBN: 019869136X); v.5 *The Arts* (502p. ISBN: 0198691378); v.6 *Invention and technology* (391p. ISBN: 0198691386); v.7 *The Universe* (199p. ISBN: 0198691408); v.8 *Peoples and cultures* (391p. ISBN: 0198691394). Completed by *Index and ready reference* (258p. ISBN: 0198691742).

Primarily for children aged 12 years and upwards. Distinguished volume editors include Sir Vivian Fuchs (v.1), John Julius Norwich (v.5) and Richard Hoggart (v.8). A-Z arrangement within volumes. Generally short entries (*e.g.* 'Glaciation', *c.*220 words 2 diags. (v.1); 'Mboya, Tom', *c.*80 words (v.4); 'Koran', *c.*125 words (v.8)). Attractively produced, about ½ the illustrations in colour. In addition to indexing (p.78-258) the final v. contains 200 quick reference tables (*e.g.* 'Chemical elements'; 'Rulers of England and the United Kingdom') and a separate section 'Figure in religion and myth' (p.1-44). *Class No:* 030=20-0053

[1469]

The World book encyclopedia. Chicago & London, World Book Inc. Annual revision. 22v. illus., diags., tables, maps. $644.

First published 1917.

V.1-21 A-Z; v.22 *Research guide and index.*

17,500 articles; 3,700 contributors and consultants; 28,000 illus. (22,000 in col.); 2,300 maps. Mostly short, carefully structured, signed articles written at the most appropriate vocabulary level for the anticipated readership. Thus 'Mouse' is written with the younger reader in mind, while 'Cell' is aimed at the older reader. Text backed by 1,700 bibliographies, mostly appended to longer articles, plentiful cross-references (*c.*100,000), and more illustrations (occupying 33% of the text) than any other English language encyclopedia. In addition to a detailed analytical index of over 150,000 entries, v.22 contains 200 reading and study guides on major topics. In 1992 World Book Inc. published a special edition for English-speaking readers outside North America. The same overall length and format as the main set, this contains articles especially lengthened or added for a wider readership (*e.g.* 'Australia, history of' 43p; 'Merseyside' 3p.; 'Drury Lane' 200 words). Extensively revised annually, *World book* is indisputably the leading all-purpose encyclopedia for those aged 10-18. It is also suitable for wider use and must be considered one of the pre-eminent sets in the English language.

The *World book year book* (first published 1922) is primarily an account of the events of the past year under the heading 'The world on file'. Also contains 'World book supplement', reprinting revised articles from the latest ed.

World Book Inc. have also produced various multimedia CD-ROM versions. Two main editions currently marketed, Standard and De Luxe, the latter now available in a version with IBM speech recognition technology. CD-ROM editions include 225,000 entries from the *World book dictionary*. An adapted Standard edition for the UK market (3 disc product) issued 1997 including animations, special project videos and Internet connection and online updating capability. *World Book* is also available online through FirstSearch.
Class No: 030=20-0053

German

[1470]

Allgemeine Encyklopädie der Wissenschaften und Künste... Ersch, J.S. *and* Gruber, J.G., *hrsg.* Leipzig, Brockhaus, 1818-89. 167v.

In sections: A-G (99v.); H-Lig (43v.); O-Phyxius (25v.).

Reprinted Graz, Akademische Druck- und Verlagsanstalt.

The most copious German encyclopedia, but incomplete. Scholarly, signed articles, particularly on languages, literature, biography and geography. Contains the longest article in any Western encyclopedia: 'Griechenland', v.80-87. 'Grossbritannien', 700p. Well-documented.
Class No: 030=30

[1471]

—Grosse vohlständiges Universal-Lexikon aller Wissenschaften und Künste... Halle, J.H. Zedler, 1732-50. 64v. ports. *Nöthige Supplement,* v.1-4 A-CAQ (1751-54).

Reprinted Graz, *Akademische Druck- und Verlagsanstalt,* 1962-63.

A detailed compendium of the sciences and arts, as known in the earlier 18th century. From v.18 (1738), includes biographies of eminent persons living at the time. Carefully compiled, a trustworthy source for historical information.
Class No: 030=30

[1472]

Brockhaus Enzyklopädie in vierundzwanzig Bänden. 19., völlig neubearb. Aufl. Mannheim, Brockhaus, 1986-96. 24v. & 6 v. suppls. Illus., tables, diags., maps. DM3996. ISBN: 3765311006.

Supplements comprise: Bd.25 *Personenregister*; Bd.26-28 *Deutsches Wörterbuch*; Bd. 29 *Wörterbuch Englisch*; Bd.30 *Ergänzungen A-Z*. Complemented by a *Weltatlas* (1993. 538p. ISBN: 3765311324). Updated by *Brockhaus Enzyklopädie. Jahrbuch* (1993-).

First published 1796-1808, as *Brockhaus' Konversations-Lexikon*. First post-war ed. (16th) as *Der Grosse Brockhaus*, 1952-63. 18th ed. issued in 15 v. 1977-82, being a condensed version of the 25 v. 17th ed. published 1966-81.

Continues the *Brockhaus* tradition of short articles (260,000) and plentiful, but small, illustrations (33,000). Longer articles are reserved for countries (*e.g.* 'Ägypten' (Egypt), 17 cols., 2 maps, 3 illus., 3 tables, *c.*25 item bibliography) and major topics. Especially well documented (*e.g.* short article 'Knossos' (2 cols.) has 5 references), all bibliographies revised.

A new ed., *Brockhaus: Die Enzyklopädie in 24 Bänden* (20. Aufl. DM4656. ISBN: 3765331007), began publication 1996 reaching Bd.13 Lah-Maf late 1997.

A number of smaller sets are derived from this most highly regarded of German language encyclopedias. Recent examples include *Der Brockhaus: in drei Banden* (1995. 3v. DM249. ISBN: 3765328014), *Der Brockhaus in 15 Bänden* which began publication 1997 and is to contain 140,000 entries (DM720. ISBN: 3765328014) and *Der Brockhaus in einem Banden* (below). *Class No:* 030=30

[1473]

—Der Brockhaus in einem Band. 7. voll. uberarb. und. aktualis. Aufl. Mannheim, Brockhaus, 1996. 1128p., illus., maps. DM49.90. ISBN: 3765316768.

Compact one volume ed. of *Brockhaus* containing *c.*55,000 entries and 4,500 mostly marginal illus. Short entries, rarely exceeding 200 words, but comprehensive international treatment. Updating eds. appear on a regular basis. *Class No:* 030=30

[1474]

Die Grosse Bertelsmann Lexikothek. Lexikon Inst. Bertlesmann, *hrsg.* Gutersloh, Bertlesmann Lexikon-Verlag, 1984-85. 30v. illus., tables, maps. ISBN: 3570089037.

Comprises *Bertlesmann Lexikothek Themenbände* of 15 v. (ISBN: 3570089037), complemented by *Der Bertlesmann Lexikon* (ISBN: 3570088995). Thematically arranged vols. contain lengthy articles with separate atlas; approx. Well illustrated, mostly in colour. *Class No:* 030=30

[1475]

—Bertelsmann discovery: das grosse Universallexikon auf CD-ROM. München, Bertelsmann, 1996-. CD-ROM database, annual updating. DM198. ISBN: 3577111429, (1997 release).

Developed from Bertelsmann's 20 v. *Universallexikon*. Over 100,000 short entries with 2,400 illustrations, 2,000 maps and interactive graphics, 60 minutes of sound and 30 minutes of video sequences. An alternative multimedia encyclopedia is the German version of *Microsoft Encarta* which contains fewer, but much longer entries, and is generally better produced. *Class No:* 030=30

[1476]

Meyers enzyklopädisches Lexikon in 25 Bänden. 9., völlig neubearb. Aufl. Mannheim, Bibliographisches Institut, 1972-84. 32v. DM4200. ISBN: 3411012501.

Bd.1-25, A-Z; Bd.26, *Nachträge* (2. Aufl. 1984); Bd.27, *Weltatlas;* Bd.28, *Personenregister;* Bd.29, *Bildwörterbuch, Deutsch-Englisch-Französich;* Bd.30, *Deutsches Wörterbuch.*

First published 1839-52; 8th ed. 1936-42 (v.1-9, 12) as *Meyers Konversations Lexikon.* The firm of Meyer, which openly hailed the coming of National Socialism in 1933, was liquidated in 1946. From then until re-unification two versions of *Meyers* appeared, the 25v. set published from Mannheim and an East German rival, *Meyers neues Lexikon* (see note under next entry), published from Leipzig.

The most comprehensive of the German 20th century encyclopedias. Each volume has 800-900p., with many brief entries, as well as lengthy signed articles (*e.g.* in v.1 'Africa on the road to self-determination'). Biographies include living persons. Well documented. Many small illus., maps and plans and 2 column format, with closely spaced text, give a somewhat cluttered appearance. Kept up to date by *Meyers enzyklopädisches Lexikon. Jahrbuch,* 1973-. (1974-). *Class No:* 030=30

[1477]

Meyers neues Lexikon. Meyers Lexikonredaktion, *hrsg. u. bearb.* Mannheim, Meyers Lexikonverlag, 1993. 10v. illus., diags., maps. DM980. ISBN: 3411075112.

Earlier version published in 8v. 1978-81.

Approx. 5280p. of mainly brief entries (*e.g.* 'Mikroprozessor' *c.*125 words) in 2 col. format. Occasional longer entries (*e.g.* 'Ungarn' (Hungary) 3½p., 1 map.), all undocumented. Abundant illus., (*c.*16,500) many in col.

An 18v. set under the same title was published in the former East Germany by VEB Bibliographisches Institut, 1972-78 (2. Aufl., first issued in 8v. 1962-64). Containing *c.*120,000 entries this retains some value, despite a pronounced Marxist-Leninist slant to many articles. *Class No:* 030=30

Dutch

[1478]

Grote Nederlandse Larousse encyclopedie: in vizfentwintig delen. s'Gravenhage, Scheltens & Giltay, 1971-83. 25v. illus., maps. Atlas 1980. 4v. Decenium serie 1982-83.

Modelled on the *Grande Larousse encyclopédie* (1960-64. 10v.). Each volume has *c.*700p. with an appended grouped bibliography (*e.g.* v.1: p.663-70). Illus. are mostly black-and-white, marginal. The *Atlas,* 296p. has an index-gazetteer with *c.*30,000 entries. The *Decenium serie* covers the 1940's to 1970's in 4 separate volumes. Each has a chronology, analysis of major trends under 6 major subject groupings, country by country accounts and an index. Cumulative index to personal names in the *Decenium serie* with notes (56p.). *Class No:* 030=393

[1479]

Grote Winkler Prins encyclopedie: in 26 delen. 9 geheel nieuwe druk. Amsterdam, Elsevier, 1990-1993. 26v. illus. (incl.col.), diagrs.,tables,maps. ISBN: 9010090019.

First published 1870-82 with title *Winkler Prins' Algemeene encyclopaedie.* 8th ed. 1979-84 (24v.).

The major Dutch encyclopedia and a set of international standing. Originally based on *Brockhaus*, each v. contains *c.* 600 pages of well-written articles, many of considerable length (*e.g.* 'Denmarken': 10½p., 6 illus., map, subdivisions

....(*contd.*)
for economy, history, literature, etc. Good international coverage *e.g.* 'Kingston-upon-Hull': *c.*150 words. Impressive bibliographies appended to many articles, *e.g.* 'Pompidou, Georges': *c.*200 words, 7 refs. Frequent use of boxed data and reasonable number of illus., about 50% in colour. *Supplement 1994* (612p. illus., maps) contains new and revised articles. Annual *Jaarboek* provides additional updating. *Class No:* 030=393

Norwegian

[1480]

Aschehoug og Gyldendals store norske leksikon. Oslo, Kunnskapsforlaget, 1978-81. 12v. illus. (incl.col.), maps. ISBN: 8257300373.

A well-planned, comprehensive encyclopedia, international in scope, each volume averaging 775p. Articles are generally short, (*e.g.* 'Goya' nearly 1 column, 3 col.illus., 4 references or 'Humberside' 8 lines), but longer for major topics or countries (*e.g.* 'Japan' 17 pages, 2 maps, sectional arrangement, references for each section). Many small illus. boxed data in colour. Each volume has an index. Supplement covering period to 1983 issued 1984 as v.13 (518p. ISBN: 8256302163). Further supplement for 1984-89 published 1989 as v.14 (484p. ISBN: 8257303204), with updating in *Supplement 1992* (611p. ISBN:8257304875).

Aschehoug og Gyldendals store norske leksikon 3. utg. began publication 1995 (Kunnskapsforlaget. ISBN: 8257306762). *Class No:* 030=396

[1481]

Aschehougs Konversasjonslexikon. Holmesland, A., *Red. (etc.).* 5 utg. Oslo, Aschehougs, 1968-73. 19v. & Registerverband. illus.,ports.,maps.

First published 1907-13. 4th ed. 1954-61.

Articles range in length from a few lines to many pages (*e.g.* 'Danmark': v.4, cols: 468-541; 'England': v.5, cols. 658-701). Pronunciation given. Strong on Norwegian biography, places and institutions. Bibliographies are rather scanty; many small illus., including portraits. V.20, the index, has *c.*300,000 entries. *Class No:* 030=396

[1482]

Norsk Allunnebok... Sudmann, A., *Red.* Oslo, Fonna, 1948-66. 10v. illus.,plates,maps.

First encyclopedia entirely in the *nynorsk* (landsmal) language. 235 contributors. Excellent for Norwegian matter including virtually every named place and geographical feature in the country. Also emphasises Norwegian legends and traditions, history and social conditions, language and literature. Illus. rather small; some full plates; a few colour plates. All maps are in the atlas volume which has a gazetteer of the place-names mentioned in the encyclopedia. *Class No:* 030=396

Swedish

[1483]

Nationalencyklopedin. Ett uppslagsverk på vetenskaplig grund utarbetat på initiativ av Statens Kulturråd. Höganäs, Bokförlaget Bra Böcker, 1989-96. 20v. illus., ports., diags., maps. ISBN: 917024619x.

A new Swedish language encyclopedia on a grand scale. Articles tend to be short (*e.g.* 'Kampala', *c.*100 words; 'Kerouac, Jack', *c.* 150 words), but with longer entries for countries (*e.g.* 'Japan', 18p. (subdivided), 4 maps, 4 charts, brief historical chronology, list of prime ministers). Technical and related subjects treated in some depth (*e.g.* 'Algebra', 3p. numerous tables; 'Plattektonik', 6 cols., map, diag., 5 refs.). Longer articles signed; short bibliographies for major topics. Complemented by 3 vol. *Ordbok* (1996. ISBN: 9171199705). The most up-to-date and comprehensive Swedish language encyclopedia available. *Class No:* 030=397

[1484]

—Bra Böckers Lexikon. 4., omarb., aktualiserade och utokade uppl. Höganäs, Bokförlaget Bra Böcker, 1991-. Illus., tables, maps. ISBN: 9171330828, (v.1).

Latest ed. of the other major contemporary Swedish general encyclopedia, produced by the publisher of *Nationalencyklopedin* to the same high standard. *Class No:* 030=397

[1485]

Nordisk familjebok: Konversationslexikon och realencyklopedi. Meijer, B., . Ny. [2] reviderad och rikt illustrerad uppl. Stockholm, Nordisk Familjebokens Förlag, 1904-26. 38v. illus.

Two further eds. published: - encyklopedi och konversationslexikon. 3., väsentligt omarbetade och koncentrerade uppl. Huvudredaktör, E. Thyselius. (Stockholm, Familjebokens Förlag, 1923-27. 23v. illus.)

- 4. Väsentligt omarbetade och koncenterade uppl. Under redaktion av S.-E.S. Bergelin. Redaktionskretaer, G. Åkerholm. (Malmö, Förlagshuser Norden, 1951-56. 22v. illus.).

The 3rd ed. is basically a revision and reduction of the 2nd. Both remain valuable for historical, biographical and literary subjects. Brief bibliographies for longer articles; many illus., those in the text being smallish and unclear.

The 4th ed. is largely a reduction of the 3rd., but revised and brought up to date. Numerous articles, short, unsigned and without bibliographies. Illus. are good being based on those in *Svensk uppslagsbok* (below), but smaller and fewer. *Class No:* 030=397

[1486]

Svensk uppslagsbok. 2. omarb. och utvidgade uppl. Malmö, Förlagshuset Norden, 1947-55. 32v. illus., ports., maps, plans.

Revision and expansion (larger format) of 1st ed. (1929-37. 30v. & suppt.).

Articles vary in length from short definitions to full-length treatment (*e.g. c.*19p. on Africa). Pronunciations given; also derivations of terms, especially those not of Scandinavian origin. Many biographies especially of living people. Longer articles have lengthy bibliographies (*e.g.* 3 cols. for US). Illus. are excellent, with some coloured plates, especially for art and natural history. Maps in black-and-white; important ones coloured. Plans for world's major cities and many Swedish towns. The major Swedish encyclopedia of its day and still valuable, especially as a source of information on Sweden and Scandinavia. *Class No:* 030=397

Danish

[1487]

Gyldendals leksikon 1-10. København, Gyldendalske Bokhandel, 1977-78. 10v. illus., ports., maps. Supplement 1984.

About 75,000 entries mostly short. 'Australia': *c.*9 columns of text; 2½p. of maps; no bibliography. Each volume has *c.*450p. 15,000 illus; marginal portraits; location maps. 43p. of two-colour maps. V.10 has an index of

....(*contd.*)

*c.*15,000 literary titles, musical compositions and works of art. The supplement (494p.) updates existing material and adds further entries. *Class No:* 030=398

[1488]

Salmonsens Konversationsleksikon. 2.udg. København, Schultz, 1915-30. 26v. illus., maps, plans.

First published as *Salmonsens Store illustrerede konversationsleksikon* (1893-1911. 19v.).

Stronger on arts, literature and history than science and technology. Nearly all articles are signed, the longer of them carrying lengthy bibliographies. Many illus., maps and detailed town plans. Bears comparison, in reputation, with the *Encyclopaedia Britannica,* 11th ed.

Supplemented by the monthly *Salmonsen Leksikon tidskrift* (København, Schultz, 1941-57, Aarg. 1-15; biennial indexes). *Class No:* 030=398

[1489]

Den Store danske encyklopaedi. København, Danmarks Nationalleksikon, 1994-. Illus., diags., maps. DKr16,000. ISBN: 8777890450.

Encyclopedic dictionary containing numerous short entries in 3 col. format. Good international coverage (*e.g.* 'Indepenedent' (British newspaper) *c.*75 words) with longer entries for countries and major topics (*e.g.* 'Indien' (India) 21 pages, including maps and tables). Some articles signed, but bibliographies not appended. Well illustrated throughout, mostly in colour. Scheduled for completion in 20 vols., v.9 *Hostie - Janteloven* issued 1997. *Class No:* 030=398

French

[1490]

DIDEROT, D. Encyclopédie, ou Dictionnaire raisonné des sciences, des arts et des métiers par une société des gens de lettres. Paris, Briasson, 1751-80. 35v. illus.

Mis en ordre et publié par D. Diderot, et quant à la partie mathématique, par J. d'Alembert. Widely known as Diderot. Various editions.

'One of the greatest and most remarkable literary enterprises of the 18th century ... No encyclopaedia perhaps has been of such political importance, or has occupied as conspicuous a place in the civil and literary history of its century. It sought not only to give information, but to guide opinion', being theistic and heretical (*Encyclopaedia Britannica* 11th ed. 1910, v.9, p.375-76). Gives prominence to technologies and trades, dealing only incidentally with history and biography. *Class No:* 030=40

[1491]

Encyclopaedia universalis. [4. éd.]. Paris, Encyclopaedia Universalis, 1996. 27v. illus. (incl. col.), facsims, ports., maps, tables. ISBN: 2852292874.

V.1-23 *Corpus*; 4v. *Thesaurus-Index*. First published in 20v. 1968-75; 3rd ed. 1990.

Invites comparison with Britannica 3 (1974), in that v.1-23 function as a Macropaedia and the *Thesaurus index* as a Micropaedia. The Corpus has over 10,000 lengthy articles, with many illustrations, tables and plans. Articles are well sectionalized, signed and have appended bibliographies. The Thesaurus contains *c.*52,000 capsule entries and makes reference to longer Corpus articles. Conceived on a grand scale and executed to the highest standards; the most comprehensive current French language general encyclopedia.

Supplements to the 1st ed. were published 1980 and 1984. Further suppl., designed primarily to update the 2nd ed., but

....(*contd.*)

also functioning as third supplement to the original set, issued 1990. A CD-ROM version of the encyclopedia is also available. The annual *Universalis*, first published 1973, provides additional updating. 1997 ed. (573p. ISBN: 2852293242), subtitled *La Politique, les connaissances, le culture en 1983* contains lengthy essays on topical subjects, a chronology, biographical portraits and a cumulated index 1993-97. *Class No:* 030=40

[1492]

Encyclopédie Bordas. Thomas, J., *dir.* Paris, Bordas, 1994. 10v. illus., plates, diagrs., maps. FFr6400. ISBN: 2907092316, (v.1).

Earlier *Bordas encyclopédie,* 23v. (1968-75) and *Nouvelle encyclopédie Bordas*, 10v. (1985-86).

Aimed at senior school students and the general public. 5,744 pages, well illustrated mostly in colour. A CD-ROM version is available as *Encyclopédie Bordas multimédia.* The print set can also be purchased with a French language dictionary and a separate electronic index. *Class No:* 030=40

[1493]

Grand Larousse universal. Rev. et corr. éd. Paris, Larousse, 1994. 15v. illus., maps, charts. FFr7980. ISBN: 2031023306.

First published as *Grand dictionnaire encyclopédie Larousse* (below). Initial ed. under preent title 1989.

An encyclopedic dictionary of short entries, generally less than 300 words in length. More substantial entries for countries, French cities and some major topics. Bibliographies for lengthier articles placed at end of sequence, nearly all references French language. Nearly 200,000 entries across the 15 v. A CD-ROM version with 72,000 entries, 3,500 illustrations, video clips, etc. is available as *Larousse multimédia encyclopédie* (Liris Interactive, 1996. FFr499). Internet access is also available through CompuServe. *Class No:* 030=40

[1494]

—Grand dictionnaire encyclopédique Larousse. Paris, Larousse, 1982-85. 10v. illus., maps., charts. ISBN: 2031023004.

Derives many of its encyclopedic entries from *La Grande encyclopedie* (below). *c.*190,000 mainly short articles with liberal use of illustration (23,000, plus *c.*1,300 maps). Bibliographies provided for major articles, but filed at the end of each letter.

The earlier *Grand Larousse encyclopédique en dix volumes* (Paris, Larousse, 1960-64. 10v. Supplements 1968 and 1975), is on much the same plan. The progenitor *Grand dictionnaire universel du XIXe siècle* (Larousse, 1865-85. 17v. Facsimilie reprint Lacour, 1990-92. FFr8400. ISBN: 286971193X) is an outstanding example of the encyclopedia dictionary, still having some value as a source of biographical and historical data. *Class No:* 030=40

[1495]

La Grande encyclopédie. Paris, Larousse, 1971-78. 20v. & index, illus., charts, diags., tables, maps.

Many short entries, plus *c.*8,000 longer signed articles ('Monteverdi': nearly 3p., with 1 col. portrait, music examples, a boxed list of chief compositions and 14 lines of bibliography). Emphasises 20th century achievements, thus supplementing the earlier *La Grande encyclopédie* (below), but dispenses with the language dictionary function. French slant ('Rouen': 6p., 2 maps, 1 illus., 1 diag.; 'Brisbane': ½p.). 14,000 illus. the majority in good colour. The index

....*(contd.)*
([viii], 649p.) is claimed to have **400,000** entries.

Updated by supplements (1981, 1985 and 1990). *Atlas général Larousse* (1976. [vii], 184 & 128p., first published 1973), is a separate atlas volume with a gazetteer of 54,000 entries. *Class No:* 030=40

[1496]

La Grande encyclopédie: inventaire raisonné des sciences, des lettres et des arts, par une société de savants et de gens des lettres. Paris, Lamirault, 1886-1902. 31v. illus., maps.

Has been compared to the 9th ed. of the *Encyclopaedia Britannica* (1875-89) for its scholarly, signed articles and its valuable bibliographies. Apart from lengthier contributions (*e.g.* on Voltaire, by G. Lanson: v.31, p.1117-29, with 1½ columns of bibliography), it has many brief entries (*e.g.* definitions of technical terms). Excellent on historical aspects of subjects, for biographies, and as a gazetteer of France. *Class No:* 030=40

[1497]

Quid. Frémy, D. *and* Frémy, M., *eds.* Paris, Laffont, 1963-. Annual.

A systematically arranged 1 v. encyclopedia that spans the sciences, arts and social sciences. 1995 v. (1994. 2078p. illus., ports., tables, maps, plans) continues the format established in previous editions. Includes a lengthy section on countries A-Z (p.934-1261). France separately treated under headings such as History, Institutions, Regions (p.632-900). 3 column format throughout, limited illus., but much use of boxed data. Thorough index (p.1974-2078). A mine of information widely used in France by students and public at large. *Class No:* 030=40

[1498]

Théma encyclopédie Larousse. Paris, Larousse, 1993-94. 6v. illus., maps., tables. ISBN: 2031522701.

V.1 *Les Hommes et leur histoire* (575p.); v.2 *Le Monde d'aujourd'hui* (575p.); v.3 *Sciences et techniques* (551p.); v.4 *Arts et culture* (559p.); v.5 *Sciences de la vie* (560p.); v.6 *Index générale.* First published 1990-91.

Thematically arranged encyclopedia intended for older students and the general public. Heavily and effectively illustrated. *Class No:* 030=40

Catalan

[1499]

Gran enciclopedia catalana. Barcelona, Fundació Enciclopedia Catalana, 1970-1980. 15v. illus. (incl. col.), facsims., ports., tables, maps. ISBN: 8430055118.

International in scope; signed articles. Each volume has *c.*850p. No bibliographies. Many coloured illus. Well produced.

Updated by supplementary vols. (v.16. 1983. 827p; v.17. 1989. 800p; v.18. 1993. 576p.) maintaining the structure and standards of the original set. *Class No:* 030=499

Italian

[1500]

Dizionario enciclopedico italiano. Roma, Istituto della Enciclopedia Italiana, fondata da G. Treccani, 1955-61. 12v. illus., maps.

Appendice 1963 (217p.); *Atlante e repertorio geografico* 1973; *Appendice* 1974 (972p.); *Secondo Supplemento* 1984 (1016p.).

An encyclopedic dictionary in the *Brockhaus* manner (*i.e.,* many shorter entries for biographical and gazetteer data, definitions, etc.). Lengthier articles on countries and the likes with emphasis on things Italian (*e.g.* 'Italia': 72p.; 'Inghilterra' 8p., plus 2p. of plates). The article 'Suora', on nuns, occupies 13½ columns and provides a directory of religious congregations in Italy. No bibliographies or signed articles. Attractive layout, despite the 3-column page: good typography; well illustrated. The excellent maps (some folding) are by Vallardi and Touring Club Italiano. *Atlante e repertorio geografico* includes a 119p. atlas and gazetteer with *c.*60,000 entries. The 1984 supplement provides new and updated articles with a greater emphasis on technical subjects than in the original set. Includes 'Italia' (16p.) and 'Inghilterra' (2p.). Errata to original volumes (p.1011-16). *Class No:* 030=50

[1501]

Enciclopedia. Torino, Einaudi, 1977-84. 16v. illus. (some col.), plans, charts. L160,000 per v.

An encyclopedia of *c.*500 entries on broad topics. Articles are lengthy, signed and well documented with notes and references to related entries (*e.g.* 'Armonia': v.1. p.841-67, bibliography of 43 items and a note on vocabulary). Plates are grouped, but graphs, plans and charts are in the text. V.15 is devoted to 43 subject-themes (*e.g.* 'Violenza' 28 pages, 16 references and a glossary). V.16 comprises an alphabetical index together with extensive charts representing the interrelationships of subjects. *Class No:* 030=50

[1502]

Enciclopedia europea. Milano, Garzanti, 1976-84. 12v. illus., ports., tables, maps, plans.

A global encyclopedia, mainly of brief articles, but with some longer entries. Each volume has *c.*1100p. Much use of small black-and-white marginal illus. and maps, the latter of inferior quality. 'Atene': v.1, p.772-81, 22 illus., 1 map, 3 plans; 'Agopuntura': 2½p., 7 illus.; 'Ariosto': 7 columns, 9 illus. No appended bibliographies but liberal use of bibliographical references in the text. The final volume comprises an index, a 24 section classified bibliography in discursive format and statistical tables. *Class No:* 030=50

[1503]

Enciclopedia italiana di scienze, lettere ed arti. Roma, Istituto della Enciclopedia Italiana, fondata da G. Treccani, 1929-39. 36v. illus., maps. L13,000,000.

Appendice I. 1938; *Appendice II.* 1938-48 (1948-49). 2v.; *Appendice III.* 1949-60 (1961). 2v.; *Appendice IV.* 1961-78. (1978-81). 3v. *Appendice V.* 1979-92 (1991-).

A massive and prestigious work. All articles are signed (*e.g.* 'Inghilterra'. 67p. subdivided History; Language; Ethnology and folklore; Art; Music; Literature: 10 double-pages of photogravure illus.; maps and illus. in text). Bibliographies are ample and include periodical articles. The article 'Fascismo' (v.14) has a section 'Dottrina', by Mussolini (p.847-51). The index (v.36) contains *c.*400,000 entries. Generous page size, fine quality plates, text illus., and maps by Touring Club Italiano.

Appendice I carries errata and corrigenda for v.1-35, but has no index, *Appendice II* providing a combined index. *Appendice V*, covering 1979-92, began publication 1991 (v.4 *P-Sn.* 1994. 827p.). Contains a mixture of new and updating articles (*e.g.*. 'Psichiatria' 4p., plus 1 col. of refs.). Same format and lavish col. plates as the main set. These appendices are true supplements, unlike the yearbooks put out by many other encyclopedias.

Enciclopedia del novecento (Roma, Istituto della

....(contd.)
Enciclopedia Italiana, 1978-89. 8v.) focuses on the 20th century, but is otherwise similar in style. V.8 has subtitle *Supplemento.* *Class No:* 030=50

[1504]
Grande dizionario enciclopedico UTET. Fondato da P. Fedele. 4 ed. Torino, Unione Tipografico-Editrice, 1984-93. 25v. illus., plates, diags., maps. L180,000 per v. ISBN: 8802039216, v.1.

First published 1933-40. 3rd ed. 1966-75 in 20v.

Bears some resemblance to the 36v. *Encicplopedia italiana di scienze, lettre ed arti* (1929-39) in format and of similar standing as one of the major established and authoritative Italian encyclopedias. V.1-20 contain mainly short articles, but with some longer for major subjects or countries (*e.g.* 'Nuova Zelanda' (New Zealand) 5½p., boxed statistical data, 5 refs). Longer articles are signed and have appended bibliographies. Impressive international coverage (*e.g.* 'Hamilton, Lady Emma' *c.*220 words, 4 refs.; 'Amundsen, Roald Engelbert' *c.*400 words, 3 refs., port). Well cross-referenced between articles. V.21, *Grande atlante geografico e storico,* is beautifully produced containing 357p. of general and 173p. of historical maps. Further 3v. as *Dizionario dei capola vori* emphasising Italian works. The set is completed by a 785p. index.

Appendice 1997 (viii,915p. illus., maps. ISBN: 8802051852) comprises updating articles (p.3-572) including many biographies, and 'I pasei del mondo' (p.573-873). Indexed. *Class No:* 030=50

Rumanian

[1505]
Dicţionar enciclopedic. Popa, M.D. Bucureşti, Editura Enciclopedică, 1993-. ISBN: 9734500465.

V.1 A-C (xvi,506p.) is in 3 col. format with dense text on poor quality paper. Articles are, however, well written and international in scope (*e.g.* 'Basildon') and backed by good illustrations and 14 pages of grouped colour plates. V.2 D-G (1996. xv,529p.) is similar, but is printed on better quality paper. When complete will replace the communist era *Dicţionar enciclopedic Român* (1962-66. 4v.).
Class No: 030=590

Spanish

[1506]
Diccionario enciclopédico España. 10. ed. Madrid, Espasa-Calpe, 1987-88. 24v. illus., tables, maps.

Regularly updated encyclopedic dictionary of 250,000 entries, a large proportion of which are biographical. Also strong on geographical topics with a pronounced bias towards Spain and Hispanic America. Dictionary definitions, with French, English, Italian and German equivalents, plus etymology. No bibliographies. Very well illustrated in colour. Several abridged versions (*e.g.* *Diccionario enciclopédico Espasa 5.* Madrid, 1993. ISBN: 8423962008), including an annually updated single volume (*Diccionario enciclopédico Espasa 1*), also available. *Class No:* 030=60

[1507]
Enciclopedia universal ilustrada europeo-americana. Barcelona, Espasa, 1905-33. 80v. in 81, illus., maps *Suplemento anual,* 1934-. ISBN: 8423945006.

A-Z v.1-70 in 71v. *Apéndice,* v.1-10.

1,000,000 unsigned articles. Excels in short articles and as a gazetteer *cum* biographical dictionary. As a language dictionary, gives etymology and translates many terms into French, Italian, English, German, Portuguese, Catalan and Esperanto. Major subjects (*e.g.* countries) are treated at length and well documented (*e.g.* Abyssinia: 3 columns of bibliography). Outstandingly strong on the Iberian Peninsula and Latin America. Includes town plans not merely of towns in Spain and Hispanic America but such places as Weston-super-Mare and Yaroslavl. Illus. are, however, not of a high quality.

Apéndice A-Z (Madrid, Espasa-Calpe, 1996. xv,1495p. illus., tables, maps. ISBN: 8423975916) is a new updating supplement of generally short articles with black and white illustrations in the manner of the main set. The *Suplemento anual* has appeared biennially since 1953-54 (previously irregular). The 1995/96 ed. (Madrid, Espasa-Calpe, 1995. 1468p. ISBN:8423943666) is in topical sections *e.g.* 'Ecologia'; 'Matemátics'. Also includes 'Biografia y necrologia', 'Cronologia' and 'Geografia e historia' (by countries A-Z, p.471-984). Each supplement contains an index; a cumulation covering 1934-80 has also been published. *Class No:* 030=60

[1508]
Gran enciclopedia Rialp. 7. ed. Madrid, Ediciones Rialp, 1992. 24v.

Rev. eds. issued at regular intervals. Updated by *Suplemento* issued as v.25.

Features lengthy signed articles, most with bibliographies. The original ed. contained over 15,000 entries and 20,000 illus. The revised eds. contain relatively minor amendments and do not significantly modify the structure of the original. Ranks only behind *Enciclopedia universal ilustrada europeo-americana* (above) in the league table of Spanish encyclopedias. *Class No:* 030=60

[1509]
Salvat universal diccionario enciclopédico. Barcelona, Salvat, 1993. 20v. illus., charts, maps. ISBN: 8434547031.

Regularly updated. First published as *Diccionario Salvat* in 9v. with an appendix, 1907-13. Then issued under title *Diccionario enciclopédico Salvat universal.*

A popular-type encyclopedia-dictionary, including many short entries and definitions as well as longer articles. 800,000 definitions, 200,000 entries, 100,000 longer articles, 22,000 illus. and 1,500 maps in the current ed. Several further print versions (*e.g.* *Diccionario enciclop^edico Salvat* 1995. 13v. ISBN: 8434593416) and a CD-ROM (*Enciclopedia multimedia Salvat en CD-ROM* ISBN: 8434594871) also available. *Class No:* 030=60

Portuguese

[1510]
Grande enciclopédia portuguesa e brasileira. Lisboa, Editorial Enciclopédia, 1935-57. 37v.

A dictionary encyclopedia on a grand scale, primarily concerned with Portugal and the Portuguese language, but including some international coverage (*e.g.* 'Londres' and 'Madrid' 2 cols. each, but 'Macau' 12p.). Small print and unattractive layout with plentiful, but poor quality, black and white illustrations.

.... (contd.)

A 3v. appendix published as v.38-40 (1958-60) updates the main set; v.40 includes a comprehensive list of Portuguese abbreviations.

A further supplement *Actualiação* published in 10v. 1981-87. Articles are lengthier and less biased towards Portugal than in the original set (*e.g.* 'Afghanistan' 8½ cols., 5 col. illus., 1 map; 'Schweitzer, Albert' c.400 words). Presentation is also much improved. Additional updating is available in the annual *Livro do ano*. *Class No:* 030=690

[1511]

Verbo: Enciclopédia luso-brasileira da cultura. Lisboa, Editorial Verbo, 1963-91. 22v. illus. (incl.col.), maps.

Signed and documented articles, mainly concerning Portugal and Brazil, but not neglecting other parts of the world. Extensive use of coloured illustrations. Main set complete in 18 vols., v.19-22 are updating supplements. *Class No:* 030=690

Greek

[1512]

Papyros-Larousse genikē pankosmios enkylopaideia. Athens, (Scientific Society of Greek letters, 'Papyros'), 1963. 12v. illus., (incl.col.), maps.

Based on the *Grand Larousse encyclopédique* (1960-64. 10v.), but incorporating a full dictionary of the Greek language, plus a Greek slant in the encyclopedic articles.

A more recent Greek encyclopedia is the thematically arranged *Epaidentiké Hellēnike enkyklopaideia: thematike kav alphavētikē enkyklopaideia* (Athens, Ekdotike Athēnon, 1983-) scheduled for completion in 35 v. *Class No:* 030=77

Russian

[1513]

Bol'shaia sovetskaia entsiklopediia. Prokhorov, A.M., *ed.* 3. izd. Moskva, 'Sovetskaia Entsiklopediia', 1969-83. 30v. & index.

About 100,000 entries. More factual in approach than the earlier eds. (below), but the communist viewpoint is maintained. Thus the US declaration of independence is briefly dismissed as the product of a bourgeois revolution, while the entry for Glasgow concentrates on the strikes that occurred there. Emphasis on the Soviet Union is also marked. The entry for Azerbaijan (v.1) covers 70p. divided into over 20 sections, with 5 illus., 8 tables, 3 maps and ½ column of bibliography. White paper and cleaner type than in the previous ed., but the illus. remain of poor quality.

The earlier eds. remain important, both because of their sheer size and the way in which they reflect the changes in Soviet ideological outlook. *Class No:* 030=82

[1514]

—Bol'shaia sovetskaia entsiklopediia. 2. izd. Moskva, 'Sovetskaia Entsiklopediia', 1949-58. 51v. & index.

In comparison with the 1st ed. stresses economic, industrial and technical aspects. Stated to be 'purged of the gross theoretical and political errors of the earlier edition', reflecting official Soviet thinking (*e.g.* excision of article on Beria and delay in publishing until 1957 of v.40, which carries the article on Stalin). V.51 is a supplement to the main sequence with many biographical articles, some new, others for persons with rehabilitated reputations. The index (1960. 2v. 1575p.) covers 200,000 terms.
Class No: 030=82

[1515]

—Bol'shaia sovetskaia entsiklopediia. Bukharina, N.I. *and* Kuibysheva, V.V., *reds.* Moskva, 'Sovetskaia Entsiklopediia', 1926-47. 65v.

A comprehensive encyclopedia, on a generous scale. Signed articles, most with bibliographies. Articles tend to be longer than in the 2nd ed. *Class No:* 030=82

[1516]

Bol'shoi entsiklopedicheskii slovar'. Prokhorov, A.M., *red.* Izd. 2., perer. dop. Moskva, Bol'shaia Rossiiskaia entsiklopediiā, 1997. 1434p. illus., maps., tables. ISBN: 5852701602.

First published in 2 v. 1991, 1 v. version 1994. Continues *Sovetskii entsiklopedicheskii slovar'* published in four editions 1979-89.

Dictionary encyclopedia, Spartan in appearance with condensed text and sparse, poor quality black and white illus. Content is, however, thorough with better international coverage than similar Russian works (*e.g.* 'Coventry', 25 words; 'Trinidad and Tobago', 100 words, small map).
Class No: 030=82

[1517]

Great Soviet encyclopedia. New York, Macmillan; London, Collier Macmillan, 1973-83. 31v. $1,700.

A translation of the 3rd ed. of the *Bol'shaia sovetskaia entsiklopediia.*

'This English edition of the Great Soviet Encyclopedia is a faithful translation ... unannotated and as true as possible in content and meaning intended by the editors of the original edition in Russian' (Publisher's foreword v.1,p.v.). Only 1% of the text is apparantly omitted, largely dictionary and gazetteer entries. All bibliographies appended to articles in the original ed. are listed in translation, but maps and illustrations are not reproduced. Because entries per volume are taken from the Russian, the English translation of headwords and therefore articles, sets up a different A-Z order. Thus while two-thirds of v.1 contains articles under the letter 'A', it also carries the articles 'English Civil War', 'Forklift' and 'Zulu War'. This problem is to a large extent overcome by the use of the index volume, which contains entries for every article title, as well as all significant references within articles. V.31, the final volume, is a translation of v.24 of the Russian ed. devoted to the Soviet Union. This, and indeed the entire set, forms a major resource for the study of the former Soviet Union, offering the English speaker an accessible statement of the pre-Gorbachev view. *Class No:* 030=82

Byelorussian

[1518]

Belaruskaia entsyklapediya. Pashkou, H.P. Minsk, Belaruskaia Entsyklapediya, 1996-. ISBN: 9851100358.

New good quality encyclopedia mainly of short entries (*e.g.* Alabama 40 words; Antwerp, 100 words). Some longer articles most of which are signed and have appended bibliographies. Well endowed with illustrations, about 50% in colour. 5 vols. published to end of 1997.
Class No: 030=826

Ukranian

[1519]

Ukrains'kyi radians'kyi entsyklopedychnyi slonyk .... Babychev, F.S., *red.* Vyd. 2. Kyiv, Holovna redaktsiia Ukrains'koi Radianskoi Entsyklopedii, 1986-87. 3v. illus.

Encyclopedic dictionary. Features many small black and white illus. Longer entries for countries and major topics, *e.g.* Iraq 5 cols., with 3 illus., map and 6 item bibliography. *Class No:* 030=83

Polish

[1520]

Nowa encyklopedia powszechna PWN. Warszawa, Pánstwowe Wydawnictwo Naukowe, 1973-76. 4v. illus. (incl.col.), maps., tables. ISBN: 8301110961.

Replaces *Encyklopedia powszechna PWN* issued in 4 v. 1973-76.

An encyclopedia in the *Brockhaus* style with mostly short entries in 3 col. arrangement. Longer articles for countries (*e.g.* 'Bolivar' (Bolivia), 1½p., 2 illus., 1 map, 1 table). and major subjects, often with appended bibliographies. Coverage impressively international (*e.g.* 'Bellingham' (England), 20 lines); plentiful illustrations, mainly in colour. Scheduled for completion in 6 v. *Class No:* 030=84

[1521]

—Encyklopedia popularna PWN. Wyd. 27, zm. i uzup. Warszawa, Wydawnictwo Naukowe PWN, 1997. 1023p. illus., maps. ISBN: 830112301x.

Latest ed. of annually revised 1 v. encyclopedia. Very short entries in condensed format. Occasional expanded coverage for countries *e.g.* 'Meksyk' (Mexico) *c.*300 words, 2 illus., 2 maps. *Class No:* 030=84

[1522]

Wielka encyklopedia powszechna PWN. Warszawa, Pánstwowe Wydawnictwo Naukowe, 1962-70. 12v. & supplement, illus.,maps.

'Large general encyclopedia'. About 82,000 entries, longer articles being signed, with short bibliographies. 12,000 illus., many of them small; plans of Polish towns; 120 maps in colour; music examples. The article 'Polska' (v.9, p.5-229) is in 23 sections with a sub-section bibliographies, 5 double-sided map plates, plus 18 other coloured maps. The article 'Chopin' is relatively short at 2½ columns, 1 port. and 12 references up to 1960. 'Politically, the work is only just detectable as coming from a communist country' (*Times literary supplement,* no.3213, 27 September 1963, p.771).

The Supplement has *c.*1,500 new entries, various appendices and also corrigenda.

Older Polish encyclopedias are the elaborate *Encyklopedyja powszechna* (Warszawa, 1859-68. 28v.) and S. Orgelbranda *Encyklopedja powszechna z illustracjami i mapami* (Warszawa, Orgelbrand, 1898-1904. 16v.). *Class No:* 030=84

Czech

[1523]

Ilustrovaná encyklopedie. Praha, Encyklopedický, 1995. 3v. illus., maps. ISBN: 8090164730.

45,000 very short entries in 3 col. arrangement (*e.g* 'Shaw, George Bernard', 20 words; 'rýže' (rice), 40 words). Some longer entries for countries and major topics (*e.g* 'Francie' (France), 2p. with good map and chronological table). Many small illustrations, mainly in colour. Not as comprehensive as *Mala Československá encyklopedie* (below), but free of its Marxist-Leninist perspective. *Class No:* 030=850

[1524]

Malá Československá encyklopedie. Praha, Československá Akademie Věd Encyklopedický Institut, 1984-87. 6v. illus.,tables,plates,maps.

Over 100,000 unsigned, short articles without bibliographies in volumes averaging 900p. 3 column format, many black and white illustrations with grouped coloured plates. Comprehensive international coverage. 'Towton, (Battle of)': 8 lines; 'Trinidad and Tobago': 1 column, map and chronological table. V.1 contains an extensive article on Czechoslovakia (p.809-27). Succeeds the earlier Czechoslovakian communist encyclopedia *Prirucni slovnik naučný,* 1963-67, 4v. *Class No:* 030=850

[1525]

Ottův slovník naučný. Illustrovaná encyklopie obecných vědomosti. Praze, Otto, 1888-1909. 27v. & suppt. illus.,maps.

Still a valuable encyclopedia. Particularly important 'for its information about the Czech Estates and their family history. It contains many outstanding entries including the articles on Wallenstein by the great Czech historian Pekař (*Times literary supplement,* no.3458, 6 June 1968 p.605). *Ottův slovník nove doby* (Praze, Otto, 1930-43. v.1-6, pt.2 (A-UZOK) illus., maps) is an updating supplement that was never completed because of the Nazi occupation. *Class No:* 030=850

Slovak

[1526]

Malá slovenská encyklopédia. Bratislava, Encyklopedicky ustav Slovenskej akadémie vied: Goldpress, 1993. 822p. tables. ISBN: 8085584123.

Cover title 'Beliana'.

Dictionary encyclopedia of 40,000 entries, *e.g* 'Innsbruck' 25 words, 'Danska' (Denmark) 350 words. Condensed two col. format, no illustrations. *Class No:* 030=854

Bulgarian

[1527]

Kratka bŭlgarska entsiklopediia. Sofia, Izdat na Bulgarskata Akademiia na Naukite, 1963-69. 5v. illus., maps.

'Short Bulgarian encyclopedia'.

V.4: 660p. Many portraits. Longer articles (unsigned) carry bibliographies (*e.g.* 'Paris': 3½ cols; 7 lines of bibliography; 'Sofia': 5½ cols. plus 2p. of plates; 7 lines of bibliography; 2 plans; 4 illus.). Some folding maps, well coloured. Good col. illus.; black-and-white illus. (1-2 per page) less good. The entry 'Bulgariya' (p.321-405) has 24 sections each with short bibliography. *Class No:* 030=867

[1528]

Suvremenna bŭlgarska entsiklopediia. Veliko Turnovo, Izd-vo 'Elpis'; Izd-vo 'Feniks', 1993-.

New Bulgarian language encyclopedia. V.IVa *Oshov-Tants* (1994. 608p. ISBN: 954557003X) contains variable length entries in 2 col. format with plentiful black and white illustrations. *Class No:* 030=867

Lithuanian

[1529]

Lietuviškoji tarybinė enciklopedija. Vilnius, Liedykla 'Mokslas', 1976-84. 12v. illus. (incl. col.), ports., diagrs., maps.

A medium-sized encyclopedia. 'Automobiles': 4p. with 7 photographs and 25 line drawings (7 with keyed parts). 'Algeria': 4½p., sectionalized, 6 illus. (1 col.), 2 ports., 2 maps. Bibliographies appended to major articles, many citations to Russian language works. Includes town plans, *e.g.* of Peking. Col. illus. lack sharpness. A supplement (1985. 640p.) carries new and updated articles.

The older *Lietuviu enciklopedija* ([Boston, Mass.], Lietuviu Enciklopedijos Leidykla, [1953-69]. 36v. illus.) has marked emphasis on Lithuania and Lithuanians.
Class No: 030=882

Latvian

[1530]

Latvijas padomju enciklopēdija. Riga, Galvenā enciklopēdiju redakeija, 1981-1987. 10v. illus. (incl. col.), maps.

Each volume has *c.*750 pages with many illustrations and good quality maps. Mainly short entries, similar in style to *Eesti nõukogude entsiiklopeedia* (*q.v.*), but better produced.
Class No: 030=883

[1531]

—Enciklopēdiska vārdnīca. 2. sēj. Riga, Latvijas enciklopēdiju redakcija, 1991. 2v. maps. ISBN: 5899600225.

Dictionary encyclopedia, few entries exceed 100 words.
Class No: 030=883

Hindi

[1532]

Hindi Viśvakośa. Varma, D., *and others eds.* Benares Nagaripracarini Sabha, 1960-70. 12v. illus. (incl.col.),maps.

'Hindi encyclopedia'. International in scope. Some articles carry bibliographies. Index for set in v.12. A 'solid, useful reference tool' (Scholberg, H. *The Encyclopedias of India* (p.35)). *Class No:* 030=914.3

Hebrew

[1533]

ha-Enziklopedyah ha-Ivrit. Tel Aviv, Encyclopaedia Publishing Co., 1949-83. 32v. illus., ports.

Protracted publication necessitated the issue of an interim supplement to v.1-16 in 1966. A further supplement appeared in 1983.

Also refered to as 'Encyclopaedia Hebraica'. A scholarly work, in Hebrew, with signed and documented articles. Only occasional plates. International in scope. 'The most ambitious Jewish encyclopedia ever attempted ...; a general Jewish and Israel reference work' (*Encyclopaedia Judaica,* v.6, col.733). *Class No:* 030=924

[1534]

—ha-Entsiklopedyah ha-Yiṙe'elit ha-kelalit: hadashah makifah. Jerusalem, Keter, 1987-89. 4v. illus. ISBN: 9650700102.

A newer general encyclopedia. Short entries, well illustrated. *Class No:* 030=924

Turkish

[1535]

Türk ansiklopedisi. Ankara, Milli Eğitim Basimevi, 1946-84. 33v.

V.1-4 published under the title *Inönü ansiklopedisi.*

Comprehensive international coverage in volumes averaging 500p. The mainly short articles are signed in later volumes. Black and white illustrations and a few poor quality maps. Protracted publication has made the earlier volumes seriously dated. A more up-to-date, but shorter, Turkish general encyclopedia is the well illustrated *Yeni Türk ansiklopedisi* (Istanbul, Otüken, 1985. 12v.).
Class No: 030=943.5

Hungarian

[1536]

Magyar nagylexikon. Budapest, Akadémiai Kiadó, 1993-. Illus., diags., maps. ISBN: 9630566117.

V.1 (xxxi,832p.) contains mainly short entries in 2 col. format. Impressive international coverage (*e.g.* 'Alcott, Louisa May', *c.*50 words, list of works). Longer entries for major countries (*e.g.* 'Amerikai', *c.*35p.) Scientific and technical subjects given thorough treatment. Extensive use of cross-references.

Other recent Hungarian language encyclopedias from Akadémiai Kiadó include the 3 v. *Magyar Larousse* (1991-94. ISBN: 9630558564) and 2 v. *Akadémiai kislexikon* (1989-90. ISBN: 9630552795). *Class No:* 030=945

[1537]

Révai nagy lexikona: az ismeretek enciklopéd. Budapest, Révai Testverek, 1911-35. 21v. illus.

V.20-21 (1927; 1935) are supplements.

Articles are unsigned, but the more important have bibliographies appended (*e.g.* the 100p. entry on Hungary in v.13 has 6 columns of bibliography). Good illus.
Class No: 030=945

[1538]

Uj magyar lexikon. Budapest, Akadémiai Kiadó, 1959-62. 6v. & supplement, illus.,maps.

'New Hungarian encyclopedia', edited by the Hungarian Academy of Sciences. Each volume has *c.*800p. and 10 plates. Mainly short articles, no bibliographies. Marxist-Leninist viewpoint. Updating supplements 1972 and 1981. Now superseded by the ongoing *Magyar nagylexikon* (above). *Class No:* 030=945

Finnish

[1539]

Otavan suuri ensyklopedia. Helsinki, Otava, 1976-82. 12v. illus., maps, tables.

Based on the French *La Grande encyclopédie* (*q.v.*).

About 5,000 signed articles with short bibliographies. Well illustrated. The emphasis is on humanities subjects.
Class No: 030=945.41

[1540]

Uusi tietosanakirja. Helsinki, Tietosanakirja Oy, 1960-66. 24v. illus., plates, maps.

First published 1931-39.

'New encyclopedia'. Based largely on the Swedish *Nordisk familiebok* and *Brockhaus,* but much expanded with original articles by Finnish contributors, especially on Finland and its people. The largest Finnish encyclopedia ever published, with over 125,000 unsigned entries,

.... *(contd.)*
(*c.*24,000 text columns), over 22,000 black-and-white illus., 1,200 col. plates and 400 maps. V.24 is an index. Handy volume size and good paper. *Class No:* 030=945.41

Estonian

[1541]
Eesti nõukogude entsiiklopeedia. Tallinn, [Valgus], 1968-78. 9v. illus. (incl. col.), maps.

Short entries, v.9 including the index (p.237-784). Marginal illus., those in black-and-white being rather poor. Coloured maps. *Class No:* 030=945.45

Japanese

[1542]
Nihon daihyakka zensho. [Encyclopedia Nipponica.] Tokyo, Shōgakukan, 1984-89. 25v. illus. (incl. col.).

Earlier version in 23 v. 1972-73.

130,000 articles, many with bibliographies. 50,000 colour illustrations. Updating supplement with cross-references to main set issued 1994. *Class No:* 030=956

[1543]
Sekai daihyakka jiten. Tokyo, Heibonsha, 1988. 34v. illus., maps. ISBN: 4582022006.

First published 1955-63.

About 90,000, mainly brief, entries from 7,000 contributors. 20,000 illustrations nearly half in colour. Well cross-referenced; 400,000 term index. Final two vols. comprise atlases of Japan and the globe. Updating in the annual *Heibonsha hyakka nenkan*. *Class No:* 030=956

Indonesian

[1544]
Ensiklopedi nasional Indonesia. Jakarta, PT Cipta Adi Pustaka, 1988-91. 18v. illus., charts, maps. ISBN: 9798265114.

International in scope but with emphasis on Indonesia. Variable length entries (*e.g.* 'London' 30 lines; 'Korea', including separate sections for North and South, 11 pages) in two column format with mainly black and white illustrations. Comprehensive index in final v. *Class No:* 030=992

04 Essays, Reprints, Theses, Reviews

Essays & Festschriften

Bibliographies

[1545]
Essay and general literature index. 1900/1933-. New York, Wilson, 1934-. Semi-annual, with cumulations. $125. ISSN: 0014083x.

Continues *A.L.A. index to general literature* (2nd ed. 1901-14), covering (with a supplement) up to 1910.

Basic publication on a semi-annual basis with issue in June, followed by annual cumulation. Permanent cumulation published every 5 years, first issued 1955/59. Earlier cumulations 1900/33, 1934/40, 1941/47 and 1948/54.

Author and subject index in one sequence to essays published in collections, with particular emphasis on the humanities and, since 1970, the social sciences. 1996 cumulation indexes 4,238 essays and articles in 312 collections. The 1990/94 cumulation (Greenfieldt, J. *ed.* 1995. 2042p. $245. ISBN: 0685458369), indexes 18,959 essays, bringing the total number covered to nearly 300,000. Database access to records 1985 onwards through Wilsonline, UMI ProQuest and SilverPlatter. Annually updated CD-ROM from Wilson ($695) or SilverPlatter (£580). 'As a means to buried articles and essays on a wide range of disciplines - as well as on the lives and works of scholars and other figures throughout world history - *EGLI* remains without peer' (*American reference books annual*, v.27, 1996, p.30). *Class No:* 04.0(01)

[1546]
—Essay and general literature index: works indexed 1900-1969. New York, Wilson, 1972. 437p. $43. ISBN: 0824205030.

Lists, under authors, the 9,917 collections indexed. Cross-references from titles, pseudonyms, translators, joint authors and editors. *Class No:* 04.0(01)

[1547]
LEISTNER, O. Internationale Bibliographie der Festschriften von der Anfängen bis 1979 mit Sachregister. [International bibliography of Festschriften from the beginnings until 1979 with subject index.] 2nd ed. Osnabrück, Biblio Verlag, 1984-89. 3v. DM850. ISBN: 3764812753.

1st ed. 1976 (1v.) gave coverage to 1974.

Considerably expands the coverage given by the 1st ed., listing over 30,000 Festschriften. The main body of the work comprises entries under persons honoured, giving basic bibliographical detail and birth and death dates, but with no attempt to list contents or contributors. Includes Festschriften dedicated to corporate bodies or published as issues of periodicals. V.3 includes a subject index, German language headings only, and supplementary entries to v.1-v.2.
Class No: 04.0(01)

[1548]
—Internationale Jahresbibliographie der Festschriften. 1980-. [International annual bibliography of Festschriften. 1980-.] Zeller, O. *and* Zeller, W., *hrsg.* Osnabrück, Dietrich, 1982-. Annual. DM1,400. ISSN: 07242298.

Continues Leistner's 2nd ed. (above), but provides more detail and greater depth of indexing. Now arranged in 5 sections published in 4 volumes: A. Festschriften in the alphabet of the honoured (including full list of contents with name of contributor) - B. Festschriften by fields of knowledge (classified) - C. Contributions by keywords (in German with English and French references) - D. Keyword index of contributions (refering to C) - E. Author index of contributors. Over 500 Festschriften indexed annually. *Alphabetisches Register* to the first 10v. published 1992 (2v. ISBN: 3891860129). *Class No:* 04.0(01)

[1549]
NEW YORK PUBLIC LIBRARY. Research Libraries. **Guide to Festschriften.** Boston, Mass., G.K. Hall, 1977. 2v. ISBN: 0816100691.

V.1 *The Retrospective Festschriften collection of the New York Public Library: materials catalogued through 1971* (iii,597p.).

V.2 *A Dictionary catalog of Festschriften in the New York Public Library (1972-1976) and the Library of Congress (1968-1976)* (ii,467p.).

V.1 reproduces catalogue cards, 10 to the page, in main entry order only. About 6,000 entries, some listing contents. Lacks an index. V.2 is computer produced, in dictionary catalogue format, with multiple entry points including subject headings. Contents frequently listed. *Class No:* 04.0(01)

Reprints

Bibliographies

[1550]
BookVault: the UMI Books on Demand database. Ann Arbor, UMI, 1995-. CD-ROM database, updated annually. $99.

Title from title screen.

Provides basic bibliographical information on 134,000 titles available as reprints through the Books on Demand service. Windows and DOS versions, same software as Bowker's *Books in print* database. Search options include author, title, publisher, publication date and ISBN.
Class No: 04.04(01)

[1551]
Catalog of reprints in series. Orton, R.M., *ed.* 21st ed. Metuchen, N.J. Scarecrow Press, 1972. 929p. ISBN: 0810804387.

First published 1940. 20th ed. 1965; suppt. 1967. No further eds. published.

Pt.1: Author and title list (references from titles to authors). Pt.2: Publishers and series. Includes 'not only

....*(contd.)*
reprints from original plates, but also volumes with text unchanged but newly reset and also collections from many sources' (*Preface*). *Class No:* 04.04(01)

[1552]

Guide to reprints: an international bibliography of scholarly reprints. Kent, Conn., Guide to Reprints Inc., 1967-. Annual. $170. ISSN: 00728667.

A cumulating bibliography of currently available photo-offset reprints from around 400 publishing firms worldwide. To be included reprints must be full or not less than 75% of original size and published in an edition of 200 or more copies. Serials, government publications and collections covered as well as monographs. Information, as supplied by publisher, includes author, title, no. of vols., original publication date, ISBN, publisher and price. Date of reprint not given. Entries in author arrangement A-Z; no indexes. *Class No:* 04.04(01)

[1553]

Internationale Bibliographie der Reprints. [International bibliography of reprints.] München, Verlag Dokumentation (v.1), Saur (v.2), 1976-80. 2v. in 4. ISBN: 3794034333, v.1; 3598034342, v.2.

V.1: *Books and serials*. Gnirss, C. *ed.* (Pt.1 A-K; Pt.2 L-Z; Pt.3 Index). V.2: *Periodicals, newspapers, annuals, conference reports etc*. Dettweiler, H. *ed.*

V.1 lists 52,000 titles reprinted up to the end of 1973. The 'term 'reprint' is here used to describe all reprinted works reproduced by photochemical means in so far as the publisher is not identical with the publisher of the original work' (Foreword p.ix). Entries based on publishers' catalogues, lists etc. V.2 lists approx. 6,000 reprints from 260 publishers to Summer 1979. Same inclusion criteria and compilation methods as v.1, except new impressions by the original publisher are included. *Class No:* 04.04(01)

Pamphlets

Bibliographies

[1554]

Vertical file index: guide to pamphlets and references to current topics. 1932/34-. New York, Wilson, 1935-. Monthly (except August). $50. ISSN: 00424439.

As *Vertical file service catalog*, 1932-54.

Covers pamphlet and other minor paperbound material published in the English language in US and Canada. Entries in subject order A-Z, give full bibliographical detail and very brief abstracts. Title index in each issue; subject indexes in quarterly and semi-annual nos. Handy for the selection of free and inexpensive publications and tracing propaganda and similar material. Each issue also carries 'References to current topics', an index to articles of topical interest in US magazines. *Class No:* 041(01)

Theses & Dissertations

[1555]

Guide to the availability of theses. Borchardt, D.H. *and* Thawley, J.D., *comps*. München, Saur, 1981. 443p. (*IFLA publications, no. 17.*) ISBN: 3598203942.

Compiled for the Section of University Libraries and other General Research Libraries.

Based on a questionnaire to which 698 institutions from 85 countries responded. Information given: name, address, library name, type of theses deposited, copyright, bibliographic control, consultation restrictions, borrowing, copying, inter-library loan, abstracts, other libraries or institutions receiving copies, publications listing theses. Geographic arrangement; index of institutions. 48 entries for Great Britain, 180 for US. *Class No:* 043

[1556]

—Guide to the availability of theses. II. Non-university institutions. Allen, G.G. *and* Deubert, K., *comps*. München, Saur, 1984. 124p. (*IFLA publications, no.29.*) ISBN: 3598203942.

Covers a further 199 institutions in 24 countries. Includes data for some university institutions omitted from the parent volume. *Class No:* 043

Bibliographies of Bibliographies

[1557]

A Guide to theses and dissertations: an international bibliography of bibliographies. Reynolds, M.M., *ed.* 2nd ed. Phoenix, Oryx, 1985. vii,263p. ISBN: 0897741498.

1st ed., Detroit, Gale, 1975.

Identifies and annotates nearly 3,000 bibliographies (some hidden in journals) of US and foreign theses and dissertations. Arranged in 17 subject groups with subdivisions. Universal and national lists precede (p.1-19), of 34 and 165 entries respectively. Indexes of institutions, names and journal titles and subjects. Excludes general bibliographies of a single university, although institution specific subject bibliographies are covered.
Class No: 043(009)

Handbooks & Manuals

[1558]

ALLISON, B. The student's guide to preparing dissertations and theses. London, Kogan Page, 1997. ix,86p. £8.99. ISBN: 0749421932.

Basic guide designed for both undergraduate and postgraduate research. 24 sections in 2 main chaps., 'Contents' and 'Presentation and style'. Index. An alternative to the numerous guides based on US requirements and practice. *Class No:* 043(035)

[1559]

BALIAN, E.S. The Graduate research guidebook: a practical approach to doctoral/masters research. 3rd ed. Lanham, Md., Univ. Press of America, 1994. 289p. illus., tables. £62.50;$74.50. ISBN: 0819194700.

Rev. ed of *How to design, analyse and write doctoral or masters research*, first published 1983, 2nd ed. 1988.

1st ed. (xviii,249p.) in 10 sections: 1. Developing research ideas - 2. Literature reviews ... 5. Instrumentation and testing ... 7. Statistical analysis ... 10. The Final report

.... *(contd.)*
presentation. Includes worksheets and numbered checklists. References and selected reading at chapter ends. Indexed. *Class No:* 043(035)

[1560]

MADSEN, D. Successful dissertations and theses: a guide to graduate student research from proposal to completion. San Francisco, Jossey-Bass, 1992. xix,216p. facsims. $22. ISBN: 1555423892.

Another example of the many US published guides to theses and dissertation research and presentation. Step-by-step approach in 9 chapters (*e.g.* 'Selecting and shaping the topic'; 'Employing basic research sources and techniques'; 'Using the library and locating essential resources'). References (p.193-207). Indexed. *Class No:* 043(035)

[1561]

TURABIAN, K.L. A Manual for writers of term papers, theses and dissertations. 6th ed. Chicago, Univ. of Chicago Press, 1996. ix,308p. tables, diags. £10.25;$12.95. (*Chicago guides to writing, editing and publishing.*) ISBN: 0226816273.

Revised and expanded by J. Grossmann and A. Bennett. First published 1937; 5th ed. 1987. Title varies slightly.

The standard guide to style in the presentation of theses and dissertations. Based on the 14th ed. of *The Chicago manual of style.* 14 chapters including spelling and punctuation, capitalization, quotations, tables, illustrations, documentation (chaps. 8-12), preparing the manuscript and formats and layout. Each chap. carefully structured with numerous examples; further section of 'Sample pages' (p.256-81). Selected bibliography; indexed. *Class No:* 043(035)

[1562]

—TURABIAN, K.L. A Manual for writers of research papers, theses and dissertations. First British ed. London, Heinemann, 1982. viii,228p. ISBN: 043479970x.

Prepared by J.E. Spink.

Based on the 4th ed. (1973). 'Only the section on the treatment of legal documents has required substantial revision' (Preface p.vii). Otherwise, with the exception of some rearrangement and alteration to comply with British methods, the text is largely unchanged. *Class No:* 043(035)

Standards

[1563]

BRITISH STANDARDS INSTITUTION. Presentation of theses and dissertations. 2nd ed. London, British Standards Institution, 1990. 27p. £50. (*BS 4821.*) ISBN: 0580178137.

First published 1972.

Includes advice on paper quality, design, sequence of material, methods of producing text, quality of typeface, tables, illustrations, footnotes and endnotes and bibliographical references. *Class No:* 043(083.74)

Worldwide

[1564]

Comprehensive dissertation index, 1861-1972. Ann Arbor, Xerox University Microfilms, 1973. 37v. ISBN: 0835700801.

Contents: v.1-4: Chemistry; v.5: Mathematics and statistics; v.6: Astronomy and physics; v.7: Physics; v.8-10: Engineering; v.11-13: Biological sciences; v.14: Health and environmental sciences; v.15: Agriculture; v.16: Geography and geology; v.17: Social sciences; v.18-19: Psychology; v.20-24: Education; v.25-26: Business and economics; v.27: Law and political science; v.28: History; v.29-30: Language and literature; v.31: Communication and the arts; v.32: Philosophy and religion; v.33-37: Author index.

Entries for more than 417,000 dissertations. Based on *Dissertations abstracts, Doctoral dissertations accepted by American universities, List of American doctoral dissertations* and various lists, often unpublished, of individual universities. Aims at full coverage for the US, with some Canadian and foreign dissertations included. Within each subject volume the listing is A-Z by keyword, entries giving citation to *Dissertation abstracts* and other sources.

Continued by *Comprehensive dissertation index: supplement* (1973-. Annual). 1996, issued as a 5 v. set (v.1-2 Sciences; v.3-4 Social sciences and humanities; v.5 Author index), lists 55,467 dissertations. Cumulations provided as *Comprehensive dissertation index: ten year cumulation, 1973-1982* (1984. 38v. ISBN: 0835706397), superseding earlier cumulation 1973-1977) and *Comprehensive dissertation index: five year cumulation, 1983-1987* (1989. 22v. ISBN: 0835708322). Both arranged by subject in similar sequence to the 1861-1972 cumulation, with author indexes. *Class No:* 043(100)

[1565]

Dissertation abstracts international. Ann Arbor, University Microfilms International, 1938-. Monthly.

Title varies: *Microfilm abstracts,* 1938-51; *Dissertation abstracts,* 1952-1969.

Published in 3 sections: A: *The Humanities and social sciences* (Monthly. ISSN: 04194209); B: *The Sciences and engineering* (Monthly. ISSN: 04194217); C: *Worldwide* (Quarterly. ISSN: 10427279, until 1989 as *European abstracts* (ISSN: 03076075)). A and B as separate sections from 1966; C published from 1977. Most dissertations abstracted in series A & B are microfilmed and available for purchase from University Microfilms International. Series A & B are also issued as a monthly microfiche service.

Includes *c.*45,000 dissertations annually from more than 1,000 institutions. Abstracts, up to 350 words, in classified arrangement with title, author's name, degree, awarding institution, year, pagination, adviser and UMI order no. British doctoral dissertations from most major universities now included, but the vast majority of dissertations remain of North American origin. Title keyword and author indexes in each monthly issue. Section C covers dissertations in all subject areas. Coverage extended 1989, although the total number of participating institutions remains small in comparison with A and B and is still predominantly European.

Dissertation abstracts is searchable online various services including DataStar, Dialog (file 35), OCLC, SilverPlatter and STN International. Abstracts available for dissertations from July 1980, citations only prior to this date. Since 1988 has also included masters theses from *Masters abstracts international* (*q.v.*). CD-ROM versions are available from SilverPlatter and UMI (quarterly updating) with various subscription and backfile options. Records for dissertations 1997 to date currently (July 1998) also searchable through the Internet without charge at http://www.umi.com/dissertations/. *Class No:* 043(100)

Great Britain

[1566]
The Brits index: an index to the British theses collections (1971-1987) held at the British Library Document Supply Centre and London University. Godstone, British Theses Service, 1989. 3v. ISBN: 0576400181.

V.1 Author; v.2 Subject; v.3 Title. The British Theses Service was established in 1984 by the British Library Document Supply Centre (BLDSC) and Information Publications International, with the objective of improving access to British doctoral dissertations.

Based on the BLDSC microfilming programme begun in 1971 and London University's independent service begun in 1981. 68,000 entries: minimal bibliographical detail of author, title, university, no. of pages, date and order no. Subject volume organized by 3 major and 643 subsidiary groups. Includes only theses from the date of an institution's participation in the BLDSC programme (*e.g.* Manchester Univ. 1984; Bristol University 1985). Updated by supplements for 1988 and 1989, the latter (1990. [xiv],343p. ISBN: 0576400254) listing *c.*7,000 theses.
Class No: 043(410)

[1567]
Index to theses: with abstracts accepted for higher degrees by the universities of Great Britain and Ireland. 1950/51-. London, Aslib, 1953-. 4-5 issues annually. £165. ISSN: 00736066.

Frequency varies: annual to 1975, then semi-annual; current frequency from 1986.

From v.35 (1986) includes abstracts of up to 300 words and a greatly enhanced subject index. Previous volumes gave bibliographical citation only, with *Abstracts to theses* available as a separate microfiche service from v.26. Excludes degrees awarded solely for published work and those dissertations submitted in partial fulfilment of the requirements of a higher degree in conjunction with another examination (no abstracts for non-doctoral dissertations). Classified arrangement in 11 major classes Arts and humanities ... Civil and chemical engineering, with 70 subclasses and 325 subdivisions. British Library Document Supply Centre shelfmarks appended where available. Author and subject indexes. 14,848 numbered entries in issues for 1997. Records 1970 to date also available to subscribers at no extra cost through the Internet at http://www.theses.com. This is an invaluable service, especially as retrospective searching of the printed issues is extremely time consuming due to the lack of consolidated indexing.
Class No: 043(410)

[1568]
—UNIVERSITY OF CAMBRIDGE. Board of Graduate Studies. Titles of dissertations approved for the Ph.D., M.Sc. and M.Litt degrees in the University of Cambridge during the academic year... . 1957/58-. Cambridge, Cambridge University Board of Graduate Studies, 1959-. Annual.

Preceded by *Abstracts of dissertations approved for the Ph.D., M.Sc and M.Litt degrees* covering 1925/26-1956/57 (1927-59).

Arranged by faculties A-Z, then departments; name index. Recent issues appear restricted to doctoral dissertations.
Class No: 043(410)

[1569]
—UNIVERSITY OF OXFORD. Successful candidates for the degrees of D.Phil., M.Litt., M.Sc. and Diploma in Law with titles of their theses. Oxford, 1950-. Annual.

Title varies. Preceded by *Abstracts of dissertations for the degree of Doctor of Philosophy,* 1925-40 (1928-47 12v.). Included B.Litt and B.Sc. theses 1926-39 in two special lists in v. 10 and 12.

Arranges theses by faculty, then term, within D.Phil, M.Litt, M.Sc., etc. sequences. Gives title, author and college only; author index. *Class No:* 043(410)

[1570]
Retrospective index to theses of Great Britain and Ireland, 1716-1950. Bilboul, R.R. *and* Kent, F.L., *eds.* Santa Barbara, Ca. and Oxford, ABC-Clio , 1975-77. 5v. & addendum. ISBN: 090345002x.

V.1 *Social sciences and humanities* (1975. (7),x,393p. £78); v.2 *Applied sciences and technology* (1976. (7),xii,159p. £37.50); v.3 *Life sciences* (1977. (7),xii,327p. £66); v.4 *Physical sciences* (1976. (7),xii,99p. £31.50); v.5 *Chemical sciences* (1976. (7),xii,251p. £52); *Addendum* (1977. 26p.).

Designed to precede *Index to theses* (above). Includes *c.*50,000 theses in all; *c.*13,000 in v.1. Each v. has subject and author indexes. *Class No:* 043(410)

Germany

[1571]
Bibliographie der geheimen DDR-Dissertationen. [Bibliography of secret dissertations in the German Democratic Republic.] München, K.G. Saur, 1994. 2v. DM398. ISBN: 3598112092.

V.1 Bibliography; v.2 Index.

Covers restricted access dissertations not included in *Deutsche Nationalbibliographie. Reihe C: Dissertation und Habiilitationen* and *Jahresverzeichnis der Hochschulschriften* (below). 9,805 items recorded; geographic, personal name, subject and author indexing. *Class No:* 043(430)

[1572]
Deutsche Nationalbibliographie: und Bibliographie der im Ausland erschienenen deustchsprachigen Veröffentlichungen. Reihe H. Hochschulschriften. Frankfurt am Main, Buchhändler-Vereinigung, 1991-. Monthly. ISSN: 09390588.

A subseries of the German national bibliography. Continues *Deutsche Bibliographie: Hochschulschriften-Verzeichnis*, published from 1972 (ISSN: 03014665) and incorporates *Reihe C, Dissertationen und Habilitationsschriften*, a subseries of the former East German national bibliography.

Classified list of new German-language theses (Austrian and Swiss titles from 1993). Author, title and subject keyword indexes. A CD-ROM version, *Hochschulschriften*, containing records from 1945 and using the same software as *DNB-Aktuell*, is also available. *Class No:* 043(430)

[1573]
Gesamtverzeichnis deutschsprachiger Hochschulschriften (GVH) 1966-1980. Gorzny, W., *hrsg.* München, Saur, 1983-89. 40v. DM12800. ISBN: 3598306008.

Lists 300,000 dissertations and similar material from West and East German, Swiss and Austrian universities. Largely based on published bibliographies such as *Deutsche Bibliographie. Hochschulschriften-Verzeichnis.* Includes 16

....*(contd.)*
index volumes. Companion series to *Gesamtverzeichnis des deutschprachigen Schrifttums ausserhalb des Büchhandels 1966-1980* (*q.v.*). *Class No:* 043(430)

[1574]

Jahresverzeichnis der Hochschulschriften. 1885/86-1987. Leipzig, VEB Bibliographisches Institut, 1887-1990. Annual. ISSN: 0323455x.

Title varies; 1935-69 as *Jahresverzeichnis der deutschen Hochschulschriften.* Publisher also varies. Ceased publication on re-unification.

The original German list. Continued to cover all of Germany after 1945, despite publication from Leipzig. Dissertations of the Technische Hochschulen included from 1913 and the Hochschulen der Länder from 1924. Jahr. 100 for 1984 (1987) had 10,377 entries, separate sections for East and West Germany. Arranged by place then university; author and subject indexes. *Class No:* 043(430)

[1575]

KÖSSLER, F. Verzeichnis von Programm-Abhandlungen deutscher, österreichischer und schweizerischer Schulen der Jahre 1825-1918: alphabetisch geordnet nach Verfassern. München, Saur, 1987-91. 5v. DM980 per v., (except v.5 DM248). ISBN: 3598106653.

V.1-v.4 A-Z with *Orts- und Schulregister* in v.4; v.5 *Ergänzungsband.*

Lists 55,000 scholarly pamphlets form German, Austrian and Swiss academic institutions. Author arrangement; institution, but no subject index. *Class No:* 043(430)

[1576]

MUNDT, H. Bio-bibliographisches Verzeichnis von Universitäts- und Hochschuldrucken (Dissertationen) vom Ausgang des 16. bis Ende des 19. Jahrhunderts. Leipzig, Carlsohn (Bd.1-2), München, Verlag Dokumentation (Bd.3), Munich, Saur (Bd.4), 1936-1980. 4v. ISBN: 3598028156.

Bd.1 Lfg. 1-9 A-Kühn (1934-36). Bd.2 Lfg. 10-13 Kühn-Ritter (1937-42). Completed by Bd.3 Ritter-Z (1977) and Bd.4 Personenregister (1980), both edited by K. Wickert. Bd.1-2 reprinted New York, Johnson, 1965.

Arranged alphabetically by name of respondent, with brief biographical data on the persons concerned with the dissertations. Includes some Swedish and Dutch dissertations. *Class No:* 043(430)

Austria

[1577]

Gesamtverzeichnis österreichischer Dissertationen. 1966-84. Wien, Verband der wissenschaftlichen Gesellschaften Österreichs Verlag, 1967-89. Annual. ISSN: 00724165.

Arranged by university with author, subject, name and place indexes. Each new annual made additions/corrections to previous volumes.

A cumulated index, *Gesamtverzeichnis österreichischer Dissertationen. Systematisches Register. 1966/1975* (656p.), containing 37,000 entries for 11,849 dissertations was published 1986. *Class No:* 043(436)

[1578]

Österreichische Bibliographie. Reihe B: Verzeichnis der Österreichischen Hochschulschriften. Wien, Österreichische Nationalbibliothek, 1987-. Quarterly, with annual index. ISSN: 10231897.

The current list issued as a sub-series of the national bibliography. About 3,000 entries in each issue; classified arrangement, author and title keyword indexes.
Class No: 043(436)

Hungary

[1579]

KÁLLAY, J. Kandidátusi és doktori disszertációk (1953-1975, január 31). Budapest, Magyar Tudományos Akadémia Könyvtára, 1978. 358p. (*A Magyar Tudományos Akadémia Könyvtára Kézirattárának katalógusai, 10.*) ISBN: 9637301267.

Cumulates issues of the irregularly published *Kandidátusi és doktori disszertációk katalógusa.*

Lists theses acquired by the library of the Hungarian Academy of Sciences. Around 6,000 entries in 24 subject classes.

Continued by supplements for February 1975-1980 (Abaffy, C.M. 1981. 150p. ISBN: 9637301387) and 1980-1984 (Horanyi, K. 1988. 196p. ISBN: 9637302417).
Class No: 043(439)

France

[1580]

ATELIER NATIONAL DE REPRODUCTION DES THÈSES DE LILLE. Catalogue des thèses reproduites. 1988-. Lille, Atelier national de reproduction des thèses de Lille, 1990-. 3 issues pa. ISSN: 02941767.

Based on data from units at Lille and Grenoble universities entrusted with reproducing theses submitted to French universities. Science and technology theses excluded. Entries, in classified order, give author, title, type of degree and university (coded). Author index. *Class No:* 043(44)

[1581]

Inventaire des thèses de doctorat soutenues devant les universités françaises. 1981-. Paris, Centre national du Catalogue collectif national, 1982-. Annual.

Continues *Catalogue des thèses de doctorat soutenues devant les universités françaises* (below).

Published in 3 series: *Droit, sciences économiques, sciences de gestion, lettres, sciences humaines, théologies* (ISSN: 0290439X); *Sciences*; *Médicine, pharmacie, chirurgie, dentaire, odontologie, médicine vétérinaire* (ISSN: 07667094). Basic details (author, title, university, date of submission, etc.) in classified order with author and university indexes. Last print issues 1995. Updated data searchable through the Internet as *Téléthèses* (Telnet connection from http://www.abes.fr/teleth.htm). File contains records for 320,830 theses 1997 with coverage back to 1973 (except medicine). A CD-ROM version, *DocThèses*, is also available from Chadwyck-Healey (semi-annual updating, £675). *Class No:* 043(44)

[1582]

—Catalogue des thèses de doctorat soutenues devant les universités françaises. 1884/85-1977/80. Paris, Cercle de la Librairie, 1885-1984. Annual.

Title varies: as *Catalogue des thèses et écrits académiques* 1884-1959. Publisher also varies. Ceased with combined volume for 1977/80.

Arranged under university A-Z 1884-1913; from 1914 to 1972 under faculties subdivided by university; author index introduced 1957. From 1973 changed format completely to a classified listing with author and subject indexes. The annual Supplément D of *Bibliographie de la France* also listed theses received on legal deposit 1931-70. Two 19th century lists provide earlier coverage:- *Class No:* 043(44)

[1583]
—MOURIER, A. *and* DELTOUR, F. Notice sur le doctorat ès lettres, suivie du Catalogue et d'analyse des thèses françaises et latines admises par les facultés des lettres depuis 1810. 4. éd. Paris, Delalain, 1880. 442p.

Annual supplements continue coverage to 1901/2.

Arranged chronologically and by university faculties. Includes summaries of theses contents. Subject and author indexes.

The second list, A. Maire's *Répertoire alphabétique des thèses de doctorat ès lettres des universités françaises, 1810-1910* (Paris, Picard, 1903. vi,227p.), is largely complementary, but is arranged alphabetically by author with a subject index and chronological list by universities.
Class No: 043(44)

Italy

[1584]
Bibliografia nazionale italiana: nuova serie del *Bollettino delle pubblicazioni italiane ricevuto per diritto di stampa.* Tesi di dottorato. Roma, Istituto centrale per il catalogo unico delle biblioteche italiane e per le informazioni bibliografiche, 1995-. Semi-annual. ISSN: 11250895.

New series of the Italian national bibliography. Issued with floppy disc. A retrospective vol., *Tesi di dottorato 1987-1993* (1996 909p. ISBN: 8871070674), is also available.
Class No: 043(450)

RSFSR

[1585]
Katalog doktorskikh i kandidatskikh dissertatsiĭ, postupivshikh v Rossiĭsktuiu gosudarstvennuiū biblioteku. Moskva, Biblioteka, 1958-. 25 pa.

Catalogue of doctoral and masters dissertations received by the Russian State Library. Content, frequency and title varies: as *Katalog kandidatskikh i doktorskikh dissertatsii...* 1974-89, current title from 1992. *Class No:* 043(470)

[1586]
Letopis' avtoreferatov dissertatsiĭ. Moskva, Izd-vo 'Knizhnaia palata', 1993-. Monthly. ISSN: 08695954.

Continues *Knizhnaia letopis'. Dopolnitel'nyi vypusk. Avoreferaty dissertatsii* issued 1981-92 (ISSN: 02071126).

Classified arrangement with abstracts. Includes some dissertations written outside Russia relating to the country.
Class No: 043(470)

Finland

[1587]
MÄKELÄ-HENRIKSSON, E. *and* PUUPPONEN, T. **Helsingin yliopiston väitöskirjat** 1828-1977. [Dissertations at the University of Helsinki 1828-1977.] Helsinki, Helsingin yliopiston kirjasto, 1978. xiv,222p. (*Helsingin yliopiston kirjaston julkaisuja, 41.*) ISBN: 9514515021.

Title also in Swedish.

Author list of 4,730 dissertations giving title, date defended, type of thesis and series (if applicable). No subject index, but index to faculties and divisions (p.183-222).
Class No: 043(480)

Norway

[1588]
ANDRESEN, G.W. Doctores kreert ved Universitetet i Oslo, 1817-1961: en bibliografi... Oslo, Universitets Forlaget, 1962. 100p.

University of Oslo doctoral dissertations, arranged chronologically under faculty. Author index.

Continued by the same author's *Doctores kreert ved Universitetet i Oslo, 1961-1972: bibliografi* (Oslo, Universitetsbiblioteket i Oslo, 1974. 71p.) listing a further 511 dissertations. Current Norwegian dissertations are recorded in the national bibliography *Norsk bokfortegnelse* (*q.v.*) and associated databases. *Class No:* 043(481)

Sweden

[1589]
Doktorsavhandlingar vid svenska universitet och högskolor. 1986/87-. Henån, Slussens Bokförlag, 198?-. Annual. ISSN: 0284785x.

English title: *Doctoral dissertations at Swedish universities.*

The 1992/93 vol. (1995. iv,90p.) is a classified listing of 1,266 dissertations submitted to 14 institutions. Author index. Most dissertations listed have English-language titles. Doctoral dissertations are also included in the national bibliography *Svensk bokförteckning* (*q.v.*).
Class No: 043(485)

[1590]
TUNELD, J. Akademiska avhandlingar vid Sveriges universitet och högskolor läsåren, 1910/11-1939/40: bibliografi. Lund, [Ohlsson], 1945. 336p.

Author list, with classified index.

Preceding lists stretch back to the 18th century: Liden, J.H. *Catalogus disputationum* (Uppsala, 1778-80; supplement, 1820); Marklin, G. *Catalogus disputationum* (Uppsala, 1820; 1856); Josephson, A.G.S. *Avhandlingar ock program utgivna vid svenska ock finska akademier ock skolor, 1855-1890: bibliografi* (Uppsala, 1891-7. 2v.); Nelson, A.H. *Akademiska afhandlingar vid Sveriges universitet och högskolor läsåren 1890/91-1909/10* (Uppsala, 1911). *Class No:* 043(485)

Denmark

[1591]
COPENHAGEN. Universitet. Bibliotek. **Danish theses for the doctorate** and commemorative publications of the University of Copenhagen, 1836-1926: a biobibliography. København, Levin and Munksgaard, 1929. xvi,395p.

Two sequences, the first classified, the second author, with biographical data. Subject index.

Continued by *Danish theses for the doctorate, 1927-1958: a bibliography* (København, Univ. Library, 1962. xiv,249p.) containing 1,389 entries with a subject index.
Class No: 043(489)

Netherlands

[1592]
Bibliografie van Nederlandse Proefschriften. 1977-86. [Dutch theses.] Utrecht, Bibliotheek der Rijksuniversitet te Utrecht, 1980-90. Annual. ISSN: 01669966.

Arranged by broad subject group, then author. Most entries with an English translation of title. Author, but no detailed subject index. Issue 10 for 1986 (1990. xi,177p.)

....*(contd.)*
had 1,180 entries. Bibliographical detail of current Dutch dissertations can be found in *Brinkman's cumulatieve catalogus van boeken* (*q.v.*). *Class No:* 043(492)

[1593]
Catalogus van academische geschriften in Nederland verschenen. 1924-76. Utrecht, Nederlandsche Vereeniging van Bibliothecarissen, 1925-79. Annual.

Title and publisher vary. Cumulations for 1941-45 (1949) and 1946-49 (1952). Re-numbered 'Nieuwe reeks' from 1962.

Arranged under universities and faculties, with author index. Up to and including 1945 covered the Netherlands Indies. *Class No:* 043(492)

Belgium

[1594]
BELGIUM. Ministère des Affaires Etrangères. **Répertoire des thèses de doctorat.** 1971/72-1983/84. [Repertorium van doctorale proefschriften.] Bruxelles, Ministère des Affaires Etrangères, 1973-1985. Annual. ISSN: 03043533.

The final issue (266p.) listed 675 dissertations A-Z by author with an extensive KWIC subject index. Belgian theses are listed in the national bibliography *Bibliographie de Belgique* (q.v.). *Class No:* 043(493)

Switzerland

[1595]
Jahresverzeichnis der schweizerischen Hochschulschriften. 1897-1991. [Catalogue des écrits académiques suisses.] Basel, Verlag der Universitätsbibliothek, 1898-1994. Annual.

Publisher varies.

Cumulated index *Verfasser-Register zu den Jahrgängen 1897/98-1922/23* (Basel, Univ. Bibliothek, 1927).

Arranged by university then faculty. The final issue (94 Jahr. 1994. 288p.) had 2,253 entries from 11 institutions. Author index. More recent Swiss dissertations are searchable as part of *Helveticat*, the Schweizerische Landesbibliothek catalogue, at http://www.snl.ch. *Class No:* 043(494)

Hong Kong

[1596]
UNIVERSITY OF HONG KONG. University of Hong Kong theses and dissertations, 1941-1985. Hong Kong, University Libraries, University of Hong Kong, 1986. 323p. ISBN: 9627202010.

1,607 entries mostly for English language theses and dissertations, arranged by department then chronologically. Author, subject and Chinese author index.
Class No: 043(512.317)

India

[1597]
A Bibliography of doctoral dissertations accepted by Indian universities 1857-1970. New Delhi, Inter-University Board of India, 1974-75. 4v.

Supersedes the irregular *Bibliography of doctorate theses in science and arts accepted by Indian universities,* also published by the Board.

Lists 19,593 dissertations written in all Indian languages in volumes for biology, physical sciences, social sciences and humanities. Dewey based classified arrangement. Author and subject index in each volume. 505.00/00$aContinued by *Bibliography of doctoral dissertations 1970-1975* (New Delhi, Association of Indian Universities, 1979-80. 3v.). Current dissertations are listed in:- *Class No:* 043(540)

[1598]
—Bibliography of doctoral dissertations. 1976/77-. New Delhi, Association of Indian Universities, 1979-. Annual.

Issued in 2 pts. *Natural and applied sciences* and *Social sciences and humanities.*

Continues the format of the earlier cumulations. Comprehensive and reasonably up-to-date, the 1992 social sciences and humanities v. (1995) has 4,362 entries with a keyword and author index. *Class No:* 043(540)

Israel

[1599]
Bibliyografyah shel 'avodat doktor be-mada'e ha-ruah veha-hevrah she-nikhtevu be-universita'ot Yiśr'el. Yerashalayim, Bet ha-sefarim ha-le'umi veha-universita'i, 1992. 284p. (*Pirsume Bet ha-sefarim mis 8.*) ISBN: 9652222682.

Added title page *Bibiliography* (sic) *of doctoral dissertations in the humanities and the social sciences submitted to Israeli universities.*

1,976 entries for dissertations completed since 1936.
Class No: 043(569.4)

Nigeria

[1600]
Nigerian theses: a list of theses on Nigerian subjects and of theses by Nigerians. Toye, B.O., *comp.* 2nd ed. Ibadan, Univ. Press, 1992. x,257p. ISBN: 9781212160.

First published 1965.

3,357 entries for theses written 1965-78.
Class No: 043(669)

[1601]
OFORI, P.E. *and* **AMUNE, S.A. Retrospective index to Nigerian doctoral dissertations** and masters theses, 1895-1980. V.1. Science and technology. Zaria, Gaskiya Corp., 1984. xix,228p. ISBN: 9781940004.

2,122 entries by broad subject. Includes theses submitted to British and US universities. V.2 to cover humanities and social sciences. *Class No:* 043(669)

South Africa

[1602]
Gesamentlike katalogus van proefskrifte en verhandelinge van die Suid-Afrikaanse universiteite 1918-1984. [Union catalogue of theses and dissertations of South African universities 1918-1984.] Potchesfstroom, Ferdinand Postma-Biblioteek, 1984. Microfiche.

35 microfiche. Earlier microfiche cumulation covering 1918-77 (1978), with updating supplement 1978-83.

Incorporates A.M.L. Robinson's *Catalogue of theses and dissertations accepted for degrees by South African universities, 1918-1941* (1943) and S.L. Malan's *Union catalogue of theses and dissertations of South African universities, 1942-1958* (1959), plus supplements.

The main sequence lists 30,466 theses. Includes subject and keyword in context indexes.

South African theses are also recorded in *South African studies CD-ROM* available from NISC (quarterly updating, £500. ISSN: 10254015). *Class No:* 043(680)

Canada

[1603]

Canadian theses, 1960/61-. [Thèses canadiennes. 1960/61-.] Ottawa, National Library of Canada, 1962-. Semi-annual. ISSN: 00689874.

Published on a mainly annual basis until 1976/77-1979/80 (2v. A-Lit; Math-Z). From 1980/81- (1984-) issued semi-annually in microfiche format only.

Includes theses published outside Canada that have a Canadian author or association. Microfiche comprises 2 registers and 4 indexes (author/title, keyword, Dewey classification, ISBN). 5 year cumulations available from 1980/81. Records also searchable online. *Class No:* 043(71)

[1604]

—CANADIAN BIBLIOGRAPHIC CENTRE. Canadian graduate theses in the humanities and the social sciences 1921-1946. Ottawa, Printer to the King, 1951. 194p.

3,043 theses in subject arrangement. *Class No:* 043(71)

[1605]

—Canadian theses, 1947/1960. [Thèses canadiennes, 1947-1960.] Ottawa, National Library of Canada, 1973. 2v.

Arranged by subjects, sub-divided by institution. Author index. *Class No:* 043(71)

[1606]

ROBITAILLE, D. *and* **WAISER, J. Theses in Canada:** a bibliographic guide. [Thèses au Canada: guide bibliographique.] Ottawa, National Library of Canada, 1986. xi,72p. ISBN: 066053228x.

1st ed. 1978 as *Theses in Canada: a guide to sources of information about theses completed or in preparation.*

Covers monograph and serial sources. 331 numbered entries in 3 sections: General bibliographies (13 entries) - Theses lists by university - Specialized bibliographies. Author and subject indexes. *Class No:* 043(71)

USA

[1607]

American doctoral dissertations. 1955/56-. Ann Arbor, University Microfilms International, 1957-. Annual. ISSN: 0065809x.

Compiled for the Association of Research Libraries.

Preceded by Library of Congress. Catalog Division. *List of American doctoral dissertations printed in 1912-38* (Washington, D.C., Government Printing Office, 1913-39. 27v.) and *Doctoral dissertations accepted by American universities* 1933/34-1954/55 (New York, Wilson, 1934-56. Annual).

Compiled from *Dissertation abstracts international* (*q.v.*) and information gathered directly from universities. Classified arrangement under *c.* 75 main headings with author index. Entries give author, title, degree, date, and UMI order number. 1995/96 annual (1997. xii,876p.) has 41,565 citations, Canadian dissertations included. *Class No:* 043(73)

[1608]

Guide to lists of masters' theses. Black, D.M., *comp.* Chicago, American Library Association, 1965. 144p.

A briefly annotated guide to the identification of unpublished masters' theses. It 'includes all lists of masters' theses written in colleges and universities of the United States and Canada, through the year 1964' (*Preface*). Parts: 1. Sources of lists - 2. General lists - 3. Lists ... in special fields (by subjects, A-Z) - 4. Lists ... of specific institutions. About 700 lists are recorded. Deals only with printed sources. *Class No:* 043(73)

[1609]

Masters abstracts international: the humanities and social sciences; the sciences and engineering. Ann Arbor, University Microfilms International, 1962-. Bi-monthly. $320. ISSN: 08989095.

Title previously *Masters abstracts: a catalog of selected masters theses on microfilm* (ISSN: 00255106).

Despite revised title, coverage is confined to a limited number of participating institutions, nearly all US or Canadian. Abstracts Spring 1988 onwards also available in full as part of the *Dissertation abstracts* (*q.v.*) online and CD-ROM database. *Class No:* 043(73)

[1610]

Master's theses directories. Ceader Falls, Ia., H.M. Silvey, 1993-. Annual. $87.95. ISSN: 10725903.

'Education, arts and social sciences, natural and technical sciences in the United States and Canada'. Combines *Master's theses directories. Arts and social sciences* issued from 1976 (ISSN: 10669795), *Master's theses directories. Education* (ISSN: 10725911) and *Master's theses directories. Natural and technical sciences* issued from 1957 (ISSN: 10698973). Also available on CD-ROM (ISSN: 10800921). *Class No:* 043(73)

Philippines

[1611]

Philippine national bibliography. Part 2. Theses and dissertations. Manila, National Library of the Philippines, 1985-. Annual. ISSN: 01162705.

Retrospective coverage in Nemenzo, C.A. *comp. Graduate theses in Philippine universities and colleges 1908-1969: an annotated bibliography* (Manila, Phillipine Center for Advanced Studies, 1974. x,1718p.) and *Annotated bibliography of theses and dissertations written during the ten-year period May 1973 to April 1984* (Manila, Philippine Association for Graduate Education, 1984. 398p.). *Class No:* 043(914)

New Zealand

[1612]

JENKINS, D.L. Union list of the theses of the University of New Zealand, 1910-1954. Wellington, New Zealand Library Association, 1956. 272p.

Includes overseas theses of New Zealand interest, and theses presented by New Zealanders while overseas. Doctorate, medical and dental theses arranged chronologically; masters' theses in A-Z order of subject. Author index. Gives locations where known. *Class No:* 043(931)

[1613]

—JAMIESON, D.G. Union list of theses of the universities of New Zealand: supplement 1955-1962... Wellington, New Zealand Library Association, 1963. 86p.

Includes additions and corrections to the 1910-54 list.

Another supplement for 1963-67 published under this title 1968. Further supplements as *Union list of higher degree theses in New Zealand libraries* cover 1968-70 (1972); 1971-75 (1976); 1976-78 (1980); 1979-82 (1984). Recent New Zealand theses are included in *Index New Zealand* (*q.v.*). *Class No:* 043(931)

Australia

[1614]

Union list of higher degree theses in Australian university libraries. Cumulative ed. to 1965. Wylie, E., *ed.* Hobart, Univ. of Tasmania Library, 1967. xii,568p.

First published 1959 (edited by M.J. Marshall): supplements 1-3, 1961-63.

6,500 numbered items - theses submitted 'for a Master's degree or a Doctorate at an Australian University for which a copy is held in an Australian University library' (Explanatory notes). Arranged under grouped subjects (Religion - Agriculture). 14 library locations. Author index; index to subject headings.

Continued by supplements for 1966/68, 1969/71, 1972/73 and 1974, published 1971-76 by the University of Tasmania. *Class No:* 043(94)

Reports

[1615]

AUGER, C.P. Information sources in grey literature. 4th ed. London, Bowker Saur, 1998. ix,177p.illus., facsims. £58. (*Guides to information sources.*) ISBN: 1857391942.

1st ed. 1975 as *Uses of reports literature*; 3rd ed. 1994.

12 chapters: 5 general (1. The nature and development of grey literature ... 3. Bibliographical control, cataloguing and indexing - 4. Specialist means of distribution, microforms and the Internet - 5. Theses, translations and meetings papers); 7 specialised (aerospace, life sciences, business and economics, European Community, education, energy, science and technology). Appendices on keys to report series codes, trade literature and points of contact. Indexed. Now updated every 4-5 years, but amount of revision is small, only substantial changes in this ed. being chapter on European Community and limited information on Internet sources. *Class No:* 047

[1616]

British national bibliography for report literature. Boston Spa, British Library, 1981-. Monthly. £98. ISSN: 14600390.

Supersedes *BLLD announcement bulletin.* Current title from January 1998, previously issued as *British reports, translations and theses* (ISSN: 09594922).

Lists 'reports and other material published in the United Kingdom by non-trade publishers such as research organisations, universities, charities and pressure groups, which have been acquired by the British Library. UK doctoral theses are also included' (*Preface*, January 1998). Entries, in classified arrangement include BLDSC stock no. Subject keyword index in each issue (cumulating quarterly microfiche indexes by author, report no., and keyterm provided to 1997 apparently discontinued). The major source for British 'grey literature'. Material included also appears in the *SIGLE* database (below). *Class No:* 047

[1617]

Report series codes dictionary: a guide to more than 20,000 alphanumeric codes used to identify technical reports. Aronson, E.J., *ed.* 3rd ed. Detroit, Gale, 1986. x,647p. £155;$180. ISBN: 0810321475.

Rev. ed. of *Dictionary of report series codes* (2nd ed. Special Libraries Association, 1973; first published 1962).

Key to codes used by 10,000, mainly US, corporate authors. Covers predominantly science and technology, but

.... *(contd.)*

reports series in some other subject areas also included. 2 major sections: report series codes, A-Z; corporate author or issuing agencies, A-Z. *Class No:* 047

[1618]

Reports index. Leatherhead, Langley Associates, 19??-. 3pa. £295 (full service).

Print (3v.), diskette or CD-ROM versions available.

Covers reports and surveys from more than 1,500 commercial publishers, government departments, consultancies, academic institutions, research centres and think tanks and supranational organizations such as UN, OECD and EC. Subject scope includes market research, intelligence and statistics, business and management and social policy, education, health and environment issues. Records provide title, classification/subject, author, publisher/vendor, contact details, and in most cases, price, pages and abstract. *Class No:* 047

[1619]

SIGLE: system for information on grey literature in Europe. The Hague, European Association for Grey Literature Exploitation, 1984-. Computer database.

Available online through BLAISE, SUNIST and STN (updated monthly) and on CD-ROM from SilverPlatter (updated semi-annually, £688 p.a.). Produced by a consortium of European documentation centres, UK records input by the British Library Document Supply Centre.

Covers 'grey' or 'non-conventional' literature *e.g.* research reports, theses, proceedings, translations, official documents, internal communications, etc. Confined to documents made publicly available since 1981. Emphasis on technical subjects, large percentage of material in English. *c.*500,000 records 1998 from 9 European countries. UK entries also appear in *British national bibliography for report literature* (above). *Class No:* 047

Abstracts

[1620]

The Index and abstract directory: an international guide to services and serials coverage. 3rd ed. Birmingham, Ala., EBSCO Publishing, 1994. 2v. (xliii,3561p.). ISBN: 0913956740.

First published 1989; 2nd ed. 1990. Partially based on EBSCO's *Serials directory* (*q.v.*).

V.1 lists 56,000 current serials (35,000 2nd ed.) A-Z giving full bibliographical detail and description of content, followed by titles of publications where the serial is indexed/ abstracted. Wherever possible information is also given on dates covered, whether indexing/abstracting is full or selective and online/CD-ROM availabilty. V.2 contains 'Index/abstract title listings' (p.1665-3554) providing bibliographical information and descriptions for 950 active services (up 200 from 2nd ed.), with lists of titles indexed/ abstracted. Includes indexing/abstracting services available as online or CD-ROM databases. Separate 'Index/abstract services subject index'. Mainly valuable as a directory of abstracting and indexing services, but with v.1 listing so many titles, can also function as a general serials guide. *Class No:* 048.3

[1621]

STEPHENS, J. Inventory of abstracting and indexing services produced in the UK. 3rd ed. London, British Library, 1986. viii,238p. £29. (*British Library information guide, 2.*) ISBN: 0712330801.

1st ed. 1978 by G. Burgess and others (*BL Research and development report, no.5420*); 2nd ed. 1983 by G. Stephens (*BL Library and information research report, no.21*).

Lists 430 services A-Z. Includes all types of secondary services from card files to computer databases. Entries give producer, contact, subject scope, subject classification, sources (type of material covered), languages, geographic area, cost, start date, frequency/size of updates, online access, availability and additional notes. Broad and specific subject heading indexes. Further indexes of responsible authorities and database hosts. *Class No:* 048.3

Handbooks & Manuals

[1622]

CREMMINS, E.T. The Art of abstracting. Arlington, Va., Information Resources Press, 1996. xvii,230p. diags. $34.95. ISBN: 0878150668.

First published 1982.

21 chaps. in 6 main sections, *e.g.* Analytical reading; Editing or revising 'author' abstracts; Abstracting as a profession. 7 appendices including 'Abstract of the American National Standards for Abstracting' and 'Selected annotated bibliography on abstacting' (*c.*40 items). Glossary and index. The standard source, 'analysis ... is perceptive (the) prose lucid and there are copious worked examples' (*Library Association record*, v.98(8), August 1996, p.427). *Class No:* 048.3(035)

Histories

[1623]

MANZER, B.M. The Abstract journal 1790-1920: origin, development and diffusion. Metuchen, N.J., Scarecrow Press, 1977. ix,312p. £24.75. ISBN: 0810810476.

Two main chapters: IV. Chronicle of the abstract journal (p.66-107); V. Analysis and interpretation (p.108-197), including sponsorship, subject diffusion, geographic diffusion, duration, arrangement, frequency, etc. 6 valuable appendices: 1. Abstract journals 1790-1920 (A-Z international list); 2. Chronology of abstract journals; 3. Subject list of abstract journals 1790-1920; 4. Indexing publications appearing independently of journal publication; 5. Journals which contain bibliographic sections noting contents of the other journals; 6. Major review journals. List of references (p.277-86). Name, title and subject indexes. *Class No:* 048.3(091)

Book Reviews

[1624]

Booklist. Chicago, American Library Association, 1905-. Semi-monthly, (monthly July and August). $69.50. ISSN: 00067385.

Incorporates *Subscription books bulletin* from September 1956; issued under the title *The Booklist and subscription books bulletin* until 1969.

'The purpose of *Booklist* is to provide a guide to current print and audiovisual materials worthy of consideration for purchase by small and medium-sized public libraries and

....*(contd.)*

school library media centers. A review in *Booklist* constitutes a recommendation for library purchase'. Signed, measured reviews of 100-200 words in sections for fiction and non-fiction. Extensive coverage of children's books (Books for older readers; Books for middle readers; Books for the young; Series roundup). Reviews of audio-visual material included since 1969. Index in each issue, cumulated semi-annually.

Each issue also contains *Reference books bulletin,* providing longer in depth reviews of new reference material, overseen by the ALA's Reference Books Bulletin Editorial Board. Cumulations of this section, which continues *Subscription books bulletin,* are published annually, also under the title ***Reference books bulletin*** (*q.v.*).

Since 1993 ***Booklist*** has also been available as a CD-ROM database from SilverPlatter (quarterly updating; £478), containing reviews from 1990 onwards. *Class No:* 048.83

[1625]

Choice: current reviews for academic libraries. Middletown, Conn., Association of College and Research Libraries, 1964-. Monthly, (except July/August). $185. ISSN: 00094978.

Each issue covers *c.*600 books, CD-ROMs and other items with carefully, concisely written 175-200 word critical and comparative reviews, signed since 1984. Subject arrangement in main sections: Reference; General; Humanities; Science and technology; Social and behavioral sciences. Author and title indexes, cumulated annually. Issues also normally contain a feature article and a bibliographic essay (*e.g.* 'The Roots of evolutionary ideas' in v.35(6), February 1998). Quarterly updated CD-ROM (£634) and Internet (£793) database versions available from Silver Platter, containing reviews from 1987. Records are also searchable online through the CARL Systems Network, updated monthly. The best general selection tool for university and college libraries. *Class No:* 048.83

[1626]

London review of books. London, London Review of Books, 1979-. Semi-monthly. £59.95. ISSN: 02609592.

Covers fewer books than the ***TLS*** (*c.*30 per issue), but reviews are often longer and of a similar overall standing. As with the ***TLS*** concentrates on literary, historical and philosophical works and often groups reviews. Also available in microform from UMI. *Class No:* 048.83

[1627]

New York Times book review. New York, New York Times, 1896-. Weekly. $52. ISSN: 00287806.

Resembles the ***TLS***, but contains a greater number of short reviews and has a heavier advertising content. Includes regular feature articles (*e.g.* crime). Also available in microform from UMI and as part of the New York Times WWW site at http://www.nytimes.com. *Class No:* 048.83

[1628]

—The New York review of books. New York, New York Review of Books, 1963-. Semi-monthly, (except monthly January, July, August and September). $55. ISSN: 00287504.

About 20-35 full-length, well-written reviews per issue. *Class No:* 048.83

[1629]

TLS. The Times literary supplement. London, Times Supplements, 1902-. Weekly. ISSN: 0307661x.

About 2,500 reviews pa., often a model of their kind, 'detached, measured and intelligent'. Emphasis on the humanities; subjects normally covered: art, bibliography, biography and memoirs, education, fiction, history, literature, natural history, poetry, politics, religion and travel. Reviews (now signed) do not invariably appear promptly and two or three books on the same subject may well and effectively be dealt with together. Each issue also contains a 'Listings' section, giving bibliographical detail of *c.*100 new works in subject groupings.

Also available on CD-ROM from Chadwyck-Healey (£295). First disc, published 1997, contains text from October 1994 to December 1996; further updating to be on an annual basis. Since 1973 the *TLS* has been indexed in *The Times index* (*q.v.*). Indexing from inception is provided by *The Times literary supplement index* (*q.v.*).

Class No: 048.83

Handbooks & Manuals

[1630]

Reviews and reviewing: a guide. Walford, A.J., *ed.* London, Mansell, 1986. vii,248p. £55. ISBN: 0720118239.

Collection of 14 essays, 6 by Walford, which aim 'to provide guide-lines for the reviewing of books and audio-visual materials in a variety of disciplines. In addition there are lists of reviewing journals, which are extensively annotated ...'. 2 general essays on reviewing followed by 12 relating to specific materials or disciplines (*e.g.* Reference books; Social sciences; Medicine; Music; Children's books). Appendices: A. Select list of indexes to reviews; B. Select and annotated bibliography (*c.*55 items). Index. Succeeds admirably in its intentions; also useful for tracing sources of reviews. *Class No:* 048.83(035)

Great Britain

[1631]

British book news: the British Council's monthly survey for book buyers throughout the world. London, British Council, 1940-93. Monthly. ISSN: 00070343.

Published as *Selection of books* 1940. Subtitle varies. The monthly parts cumulated annually until 1950. Ceased publication with the December 1993 issue.

Until April 1987 provided signed critical reviews. After this date merely listed new titles (*c.*700 per issue) in 8 subject sections, with bibliographical detail and brief descriptive annotations. Also carried articles of interest to librarians and those involved in the book trade.

Class No: 048.83(410)

France

[1632]

Bulletin critique du livre français. Paris, Association des amis du Bulletin critique du livre français, 1945-. 11 p.a. FFr1450. ISSN: 00074209.

Publication suspended December 1992, resumed October 1995.

Contains short, signed reviews for new French books in all subject areas. Information includes price, ISBN and note indicating audience level. Indexed by author, title, publisher, etc., cumulated annually. *Class No:* 048.83(44)

Italy

[1633]

Libri e riviste d'Italia: rassegna di informazione culturale e bibliografica. Roma, Ministero per i Beni Culturali e Ambientali, 1958-. Quarterly. L22000. ISSN: 00242683.

Title and frequency varies. As *Libri e riviste* 1950-57.

Each issue contains *c.*75 lengthy reviews of important new Italian books in 9 classified sections. Also includes a section providing annotated summaries of the contents of major periodicals. Index in each issue, cumulated in final issue of each year. An English language edition, *Italian books and periodicals* (ISSN: 00212881), is published semi-annually. French, German, and Spanish versions also issued.

Class No: 048.83(450)

Canada

[1634]

Canadian book review annual. 1975-. Toronto, Canadian Book Review Annual, 1976-. Annual. Can$110. ISSN: 0383770x.

Published by Simon & Pierre to 1991.

Contains signed reviews (200-400 words), by subject specialists, of English language trade books with a Canadian imprint. The 1996 v. (1997. 617p.) reviews *c.*2,000 titles, reprints and selected federal government publications included. Arranged in 6 subject sections with 56 subdivisions; author/title/subject index.

Class No: 048.83(71)

Australia

[1635]

GNAB: guide to new Australian books. Melbourne, D.W. Thorpe in assoc. with the National Centre for Australian Studies, 1990-. 3 pa. Aus$57. ISSN: 10355391.

Contains summary reviews (30-50 words) for nearly all newly published Australian books or books with an Australian content. Title arrangement with author/editor/illustrator and subject indexing. Also includes more in-depth reviews of notable books (4-6 per issue) and a subject listing of forthcoming titles. *Class No:* 048.83(94)

Indexes

[1636]

Book review digest. New York, Wilson, 1905-. Monthly (except February and July), annual cumulation. ISSN: 00067326.

A digest and index of book reviews in *c.*90 US and British periodicals (including *English historical review, The Economist, London review of books, New statesman and society, Times literary supplement*). To be eligible for inclusion a work must be published in the US and Canada and have been reviewed by at least two of the periodicals indexed if a non-fiction title, or three if a work of fiction. Includes reviews of children's books; government publications, textbooks and technical works in science and law excluded. Reviews arranged by author A-Z; subject and title indexes in each issue. About 8,000 books covered annually. Records 1983 to date also available as an online/WWW database (Wilsonline, Dialog, OCLC, SilverPlatter, UMI ProQuest, quarterly updating) and on CD-ROM (Wilson or SilverPlatter, quartely updating, ISSN: 10767045). Mainly useful for the digests, as the range of periodicals indexed is restricted compared with *Book review index* (below). *Class No:* 048.83:014.3

[1637]

—Book review digest: author/title index, 1905-1974. Dunmore-Leiber, L., *ed.* New York, Wilson, 1976. 4v. ISBN: 0824205898.

Author/title index in one sequence with cross-references from joint authors, pseudonyms etc. About 300,000 books covered.

Two further cumulations, *Book review digest: author/title index 1975-1984* (1986. 1488p. $65. ISBN: 0824207297) and *Book review digest: author/title index 1985-1994* (1996. 1261p. ISBN: 0824209079), cover 60,000 and 62,000 titles respectively. *Class No:* 048.83:014.3

[1638]

Book review index. Detroit, Gale, 1965-. 3 issues pa., with annual cumulation. $240. ISSN: 05240581.

Frequency varies. Monthly, with quarterly and annual cumulations 1965-69, then suspended. Resumed with 6 issues pa. and annual cumulation 1972, 1970-71 cumulations published retrospectively. Reduced number of issues since 1993.

Indexes reviews of books and periodicals in more than 600 publications ranging from scholarly journals to general interest magazines such as *Newsweek.* Includes a number of titles published in the UK (*e.g. Critical quarterly, Library Association record, Times literary supplement*). Reviews broadly defined to encompass all critical statements, even if in the form of brief annotations or listings. Entries, by author A-Z, omit reviewer's name. Reviews of children's literature extracted for inclusion in *Children's book review index* (*q.v.*). As from the first issue of 1998 provides citations to online book reviews. Available online through Dialog (File 137) for citations 1969 onwards, 3 updates annually. Gale also produce a CD-ROM version (£1025;$1,295).
Class No: 048.83:014.3

[1639]

—Book review index: a master cumulation 1965-1984: a cumulated index to more than 1,605,000 reviews of approximately 740,500 titles. Tarbert, G.C. *and* Beach, B., *ed.* Detroit, Gale, 1985. 10v. £1130;$1,315. ISBN: 0810305771.

Supersedes *Book review index: a master cumulation 1969-1979* (1980. 7v.).

Cumulative indexes for periodicals and reference books also published as *Book review index: periodical reviews 1976-1984* and *Book review index: reference books 1965-1984.*

Further cumulation, *Book review index: a master cumulation 1985-1992: a cumulated index to more than 1,000,000 reviews of approximately 500,000 titles* (Walker, N.E. & Baer, B. *eds.* 1994. 6v. £720;$1315. ISBN: 0810396262), extends coverage. *Class No:* 048.83:014.3

[1640]

Combined retrospective index to book reviews in scholarly journals, 1886-1974. Farber, E.I., *ed.* Arlington, Va., Carrollton Press, 1979-82. 15v. ISBN: 0840801572, v.1.

V.1-12 Authors; v.13-15 Titles.

Offers access to more than 1,000,000 book reviews which appeared in 459 journals, mainly in the subject areas of history, politics and sociology. Most reviews not previously indexed. Includes many journals published outside the US, British titles well-represented (*e.g. British journal of sociology, English historical review, Political studies*). Entries in author volumes give title and abbreviated citation to journal with volume, date and initial page of review.

....*(contd.)*

Entries in title volumes refer to author entries. A valuable source, compensating for the restricted coverage of scholarly journals in *Book review digest. Class No:* 048.83:014.3

[1641]

—Combined retrospective index to book reviews in humanities journals, 1802-1974. Farber, E.I., *ed.* Woodbridge, Conn., Research Publications, 1982-84. 10v.

V.1-9 Authors; v.10 Titles.

Companion set, giving access to a further 500,000 reviews with the emphasis on literary, philosophy and music journals. Same format, with the exception that reviewers' names are added to entries whenever they have been identified. *Class No:* 048.83:014.3

[1642]

FORSTER, A. Index to book reviews in England 1749-1774. Carbondale, Ill., Southern Illinois Univ. Press, 1990. xi,301p. $44.95. ISBN: 0809314061.

Cites review sources for 3,023 fictional, poetical and dramatic titles. Journals indexed include *The Monthly review, Critical review* and *The Gentleman's magazine.* Continued by:- *Class No:* 048.83:014.3

[1643]

—FORSTER, A. Index to book reviews in England 1775-1800. London, British Library, 1997. lii,490p. £85. ISBN: 0712304185.

Review sources for a further 4,984 works in 14 major and 13 minor titles, including several Scottish and Irish magazines. The 'indispensable source for studying the reception of *belles lettres* during the last half of the eighteenth century' (*Reference reviews* v.11(7), 1997, p.5).
Class No: 048.83:014.3

[1644]

A Guide to book review citations: a bibliography of sources. Gray, R.A., *comp.* Columbus, Ohio State Univ. Press, 1968. xvi,223p. (*The Ohio State University Libraries publications, no.2.*)

A guide 'to those indexes and bibliographies which are likely to yield the largest number of review references for any given book irrespective of its date, its subject or the language in which it is written' (Introduction p.1). 512 entries arranged in 8 broad classes; annotations on scope and organization. Subject, personal name, title, chronological and country of origin indexes. *Class No:* 048.83:014.3

[1645]

An Index to book reviews in the humanities. Williamstown, Mich., Philip Thomson, 1960-91. Annual. ISSN: 00735892.

Published quarterly 1960-62, 1961-62 cumulated annually. Cumulation for 1960 not issued until 1978. Ceased publication with issue for 1990.

Indexed book reviews appearing in *c.*475 periodicals. 'Humanities' regarded as art, biography, drama and dance, folklore, language, literature, music, philosophy, travel and adventure. From 1971 indexed all reviews (formerly selective) in periodicals covered, except those for children's books. *Class No:* 048.83:014.3

[1646]

Internationale Bibliographie der Rezensionen Wissenschaftlicher Literatur. [International bibliography of book reviews of scholarly literature.] Zeller, O. *and* Zeller, W., *hrsg.* Osnabrück, Dietrich, 1971-. Semi-annual. DM2900. ISSN: 0020918x.

Each semi-annual issue in 3v. A companion publication to *Internationale Bibliographie der Zeitschriftenliteratur* (*q.v.*). Revives *Bibliographie der Rezensionen und Referate*

....(contd.)
(below).

Main section of each issue (pt. A) arranges reviewed works under German keywords (English and French references), with bibliographical detail and review citation (title coded). Other sections comprise keyword index (keywords divided into 18 fields of knowledge), index of reviewed works by author, reviewer index (a feature not found in most other book review indexes) and list of periodicals to which the coded citations in pt. A refer. Cumbersome to use, but offers good international coverage and is especially useful for tracing reviews of non-English language titles. A CD-ROM version is also available. (DM2900). *Class No:* 048.83:014.3

[1647]

—Bibliographie der Rezensionen und Referate. 1900-43. Leipzig, Dietrich, 1901-44. (*Internationale Bibliographie der Zeitschriftenliteratur, Abt. C.*)

Indexed reviews of worthwhile German and (1925-43) non-German books. The 1900-11v. indexed only German reviews; the 1912-43v. appeared in two series, numbered alternately, one indexing book reviews in German periodicals and the other in non-German journals. The journals cited are those indexed Abt.A and B of the *Internationale Bibliographie der Zeitschriftenliteratur* (*q.v.*), providing an immense range of 6,000 titles. No indexes. *Class No:* 048.83:014.3

[1648]

The New York Times book review index, 1896-1970. New York, Arno Press, 1973. 5v. $600. ISBN: 0405124945.

V.1 Author index; v.2 Title index; v.3. Byline index; v.4. Subject index; v.5 Category index.

About 800,000 entries. The 'Byline index' lists reviewers and authors of essays, articles, columns, letters etc. The 'Category index' is by genres *e.g.* anthologies, children's fiction, poetry, reference works. *Class No:* 048.83:014.3

[1649]

The Times literary supplement index: 1940-1980. Reading, Research Publications, 1982. 3v. £695. ISBN: 0903712942.

Contains references to reviews, leading articles, letters and poems. About 500,000 entries for personal names, titles and subjects in separate sequences within one A-Z order. Of questionable value in view of the coverage provided in other indexing services such as *British humanities index* and *Book review digest* (*qq.v.*).

Earlier coverage is provided by *The Times literary supplement index: 1902-1939* (1978. 2v. £335). A further cumulation is available covering 1981-85 (1986. viii,407p. £335. ISBN: 090751474X). Primary Source Media (successor of Research Publications) also produce an annual index in tabloid format (£70). Electronic indexing of current issues is provided on the same publisher's CD-ROM *BNI: British newspaper index* (*q.v.*). *Class No:* 048.83:014.3

Latin America

[1650]

Guía a las reseñas de libros de y sobre Hispanoamérica 1960/64-. [A Guide to reviews of books from and about Hispanic America. 1960/64-.] Ponce, Puerto Rico, Ediciones AMM, 1965-. Annual (irregular) $115.

Chequered publication history. Initial vol. for 1960/64 published in Puerto Rico, with further vol. for 1965 (1973). Then issued from US beginning with 1972/73 (1976), mostly on an annual basis, later vols. published by Garland. Publication now returned to Puerto Rico, current status

....(contd.)
uncertain.

Indexes and summarises (in language of review) reviews of books from all subject areas. Scope extends to Brazil, the English, French and Dutch speaking Caribbean and Hispanics in the US. The 1985 issue (1989. xlv,1940p.), which appears to be the last published, summarises 3,303 reviews (mostly Spanish language) from 400 periodicals. *Class No:* 048.83:014.3(729.99)

05 Periodicals

Periodicals

Abbreviations & Symbols

[1651]

BRITISH STANDARDS INSTITUTION. Abbreviation of title words and titles of periodicals. London, British Standards Institution, 1985. 6p. (BS 4148). £20. ISBN: 0580145697.

First published 1967; revised 1970. Confirmed 1990.

Identical with International Organization for Standardization *Documents: rules for the abbreviation of title words and titles of publications* (ISO 4 1984). Main sections: Scope - Definitions - Rules for word abbreviations - Rules for title abbreviations. To be used in conjunction with *List of serial title word abbreviations* (below). *Class No:* 050(003)

[1652]

INTERNATIONAL SERIALS DATA SYSTEM *and* INTERNATIONAL ORGANIZATION FOR STANDARDIZATION. List of serial title word abbreviations. Paris, ISDS; Geneva, ISO, 1985. 215p. ISBN: 2904938028.

First published 1974 under title *Documentation: international list of periodical title word abbreviations* (ISO 833). Updated by semi-annual supplements to 1984.

28,000 words/roots from 45 languages in alphabetical order regardless of accents or diacritics, followed by standardized abbreviation. Conforms to ISO 4 (above as BS 4148), and intended for use with this publication. Continued by *List of serial title word abbreviations. Supplement* (Paris, ISDS, etc., 1986-. ISSN: 02590018). Also available as part of the *ISSN compact* CD-ROM database (*q.v.*).
Class No: 050(003)

[1653]

LEISTNER, O. *and* BECKER, H. ITA. Internationale titelabkürzungen von Zeitschriften, Zeitungen, wichtigen Handbüchern, Wörterbüchern, Gesetzen, Institutionen usw. [ITA. International title abbreviations of periodicals, newspapers, important handbooks, dictionaries, laws, institutions etc.] 6 erw. Aufl. Onsabrück, Dietrich, 1995. 2v. DM890. ISBN: 3891860161.

1st ed. 1967; 5th ed. 1993.

Contains *c.*73,000 abbreviations A—Z with expansion, place of publication and dates of issue. Generally inferior to the Gale title (below), but good on non-english language periodicals. V.2 also contains several 'special lists' (*e.g.* Abbreviations used for the Roman Catholic orders).
Class No: 050(003)

[1654]

Periodical title abbreviations. Alkire, L.G., *comp. and ed.* Detroit, Gale, 1969-. Irregular. £172;$215 per vol. ISSN: 07377843.

Subtitled: *Covering: periodical title abbreviations and selected monograph abbreviations in science, the social sciences, the humanities, law, medicine, religion, library science, engineering, education, business, art and many*

....*(contd.)*
other fields.

Published in 2 main v.: v.1 *Periodical title abbreviations: by abbreviation*; v.2 *Periodical title abbreviations: by title.* Inter-edition supplement as v.3.

Abbreviations taken from *c.*125 sources. Descriptive rather than prescriptive, intended 'merely as a record of myriad ways in which commonly used indexing and abstracting services abbreviate periodical titles'. About 159,000 entries in 10th ed. (1995). *Class No:* 050(003)

CD-ROM

[1655]

ENSOR, P. *and* HARDIN, S. CD-ROM periodical index: a guide to abstracted, indexed and fulltext periodicals on CD-ROM. Westport, Conn., Meckler, 1992. vii,420p. (*Supplement to computers in libraries, 48.*) ISBN: 0887368034.

List of 77 databases (ABI/Inform ... Wilson business abstracts) indicating titles indexed or provided in fulltext, followed by index of *c.*30,000 periodicals citing CD-ROM service which provides coverage. Some inconsistencies (*e.g.* dates of periodical coverage not always given) and errors, but a useful first effort. *Class No:* 050(003.40)

Internet

[1656]

Directory of electronic journals, newsletters and academic discussion lists. Washington, D.C., Association of Research Libraries, 1991-. Annual. ISSN: 10571337.

7th ed. (1998. 950p.) has over 7,000 listings including 'zines' and professional electronic conferences. Entries include brief description, URL/subscription information, ISSN, first issue date, frequency and contact detail. Indexed by keyword, publisher/distributor and title. Now established as the standard source. Internet version also available on subscription basis through http://arl.cni.org.
Class No: 050(003.41)

[1657]

e.journal. World Wide Web resource.

URL: http://www.edoc.com/ejournal. Date reviwed 18th July 1998.

'A service provided by e.doc'. Part of the WWW Virtual Library.

Provides links to *c.*2,000 electronic journals. Main listing by category (*e.g.* Academic and reviewed journals; Email newsletters; Political), most entries with brief descriptive detail. *Class No:* 050(003.41)

[1658]

Ejournal site guide: a metasource. Jones, J., *comp.* Univ. of British Columbia. World Wide web resource.

URL: http://www.library.ubc.ca/ejour/. Date reviewed 18th July 1998.

'Provided here is a selected and annotated set of links to *sites* for ejournals, which in turn provide links to individual titles and/or to other collections of links' (*Home page*). 35 sites listed by name and subject. *Class No:* 050(003.41)

[1659]

Net.journal directory: the catalog of full text periodicals archived on the World Wide Web. Hillsdale, N.J., Hermograph Press, 1997-. Semi-annual.

First issue (270p. ISBN: 0965677591) covers nearly 7,000 periodicals 'whose full text may be read online or immediately downloaded'. Titles listed A-Z, detail includes fees, formats and issues available. Newspapers excluded. *Class No:* 050(003.41)

Micromaterials

[1660]

Serials in microform. Ann Arbor, University Microfilms International, 1972-. Annual. $15. ISSN: 03612740.

Absorbed *Newspapers in microform* from 1992.

The 1997 international ed. (1313p.) lists over 19,000 serials, 10,000 of which are current. Title arrangement with basic details including microformat and price; subject listing (p.1175-313). Also Internet accessible (http://www.umi.com) with ISSN, keyword, etc. searching. All titles listed are available for purchase from UMI. *Class No:* 050(003.5)

Bibliographies of Bibliographies

[1661]

BESTERMAN, T. Periodical publications: a bibliography of bibliographies. Totowa, N.J., Rowmann & Littlefield, 1971. 2v. (*The Besterman world bibliographies.*) ISBN: 087471043x.

Extracted from Besterman's *A World bibliography of bibliographies* 4th ed. (*q.v.*).

5 main sections: Union catalogues - General - Subjects - Countries - Indexes to periodicals. Excludes almanacs and directories. *Class No:* 050(009)

[1662]

Periodical directories and bibliographies: an annotated guide to approximately 350 directories, bibliographies and other sources of information about English-language periodicals from 1850 to the present including newspapers, journals, magazines, newsletters and other serial publications. Tarbert, G.C., *ed.* Detroit, Gale, 1987. 195p. $60. ISBN: 0810314746.

347 numbered entries alphabetical by title with subject index. Information includes publisher, scope, description of contents, arrangement, indexes, price and date/frequency. Many entries incomplete, some providing title and date only. Criticised *RQ* (v.26(4), Summer 1987, p.518-20) for many omissions and poor subject indexing. *Class No:* 050(009)

[1663]

VESENYI, P.E. An Introduction to periodical bibliography. Ann Arbor, Pierian Press, 1974. ix,382p. ISBN: 0876500459.

In 2 pts. Pt. I is a chronological survey of the development of periodical bibliographies (including indexes, abstracting journals, union lists, directories) in 8 chapters. Pt. II 'Bibliography section' (p.133-348) is an annotated list of

....(*contd.*)

more than 400 indexing and abstracting services A-Z by title. Index to pt. I; subject guide to pt. II.
Class No: 050(009)

Bibliographies

[1664]

BARLOW, R.G. The Fifth directory of periodicals: publishing articles on American and English language and literature, criticism and theory, film, American studies, poetry and fiction. Athens, Ohio, Swallow P./Ohio Univ. Press., 1992. xxxiii,349p. $49.95. ISBN: 0804009589.

Also available in pbck. ($24.95. ISBN: 0804009627). First published 1959; previous ed.1974

Intended 'as a reference guide to a number of scholarly journals to which they (scholars) may submit manuscripts for publication' (*Introduction*). *c.*600 titles in six categories detail including subscription rates, fields of interest and manuscript requirements. Indexed. US titles predominate.
Class No: 050(01)

[1665]

BIBLIOTECA NACIONAL. (SPAIN). Catálogo de publicaciones periódicas. Madrid, Chadwyck-Healey, 1990. Microfiche. £460.

133 microfiche.

Catalogue of the largest collection of Spanish-language periodicals in existence. 35,000 entries for scholarly and technical journals, newspapers, annuals, etc., received to June 1990. *Class No:* 050(01)

[1666]

BIBLIOTHÈQUE NATIONALE. (FRANCE). Département des Périodiques. **Catalogue collectif des périodiques du début du XVIIe siècle à 1939** conservés dans les bibliothèques de Paris et dans le bibliothèques universitaires des départements. Paris, Bibliothèque Nationale, 1967-82. 5v. ISBN: 2717716165.

V.1-v.4 A-Z; v.5 *Additions et corrections. Tables des collectivités citées.*

Lists *c.*75,000 titles held by 73 co-operating libraries with the emphasis on French titles. Excludes newspapers after 1849, certain other categories, as well as Slavic periodicals in Cyrillic (covered in *Catalogue collectif ... Périodiques slaves et caractères cyrilliques* (*q.v.*)). *Class No:* 050(01)

[1667]

—Inventaire des périodiques étrangers et des publications en série étrangères reçus en France par les bibliothèques et les organismes de documentation en 1965. 4. éd. Paris, Bibliothèque Nationale, 1969. 1207p.

First published 1956.

Lists *c.*43,000 titles held by 2,300 co-operating libraries. Updated by a listing of new and revised titles 1965-82 (1983. 2v. ISBN: 2717716688). *Class No:* 050(01)

[1668]

BIBLIOTHÈQUE NATIONALE. (FRANCE). Département des Périodiques. **Catalogue général des périodiques de la Bibliothèque Nationale** des origines à 1959. Paris, Chadwyck-Healey, 1987. Microfiche. £3,840. ISBN: 2869760108.

Comprises 1,344 microfiche, including an *Annexe: addenda et errata* of 48 microfiche. Accompanied by a printed *Guide de l'utilisateur du 'Catalogue général des périodiques de la Bibliothèque nationale'* by E. Delaunay (1988).

A complete inventory of the periodical holdings of the Bibliothèque Nationale to 1959. Incorporates the

....(*contd.*)
Bibliothèque Nationale holdings from the *Catalogue collectif ... à 1939* and consolidates various other listings including *Catalogue collectif ... Périodiques slaves en caractères cyrilliques* and *Bibliographie de la presse française politique et d'information général* (*qq.v.*). Over 300,000 entries A-Z by title. Contains many titles not listed in other general periodicals catalogues. *Class No:* 050(01)

[1669]
BRITISH MUSEUM. Department of Printed Books. **Catalogue of the printed books in the library of the British Museum: periodical publications.** Rev. ed. London, British Museum, 1899-1900. 6 pts. and index.

Arranged by place of publication, A-Z with an index of titles. Excludes newspapers after 1800, and publications of societies and institutions; includes annuals but not directories or almanacs. *c.*25,000 titles listed. *Class No:* 050(01)

[1670]
British union-catalogue of periodicals: a record of periodicals of the world, from the seventeenth century to the present day, in British libraries. Stewart, J.D., *and others eds.* London, Butterworths, 1955-58. 4v .

Edited for the Council of the British Union-Catalogue of Periodicals. Supersedes *Union catalogue of the periodical publications in the university libraries of the British Isles ...* (London, Joint Standing Committee on Library Co-operation, 1937. xii,712p.).

Lists more than 140,000 titles permanently filed in 441 libraries in the UK. Includes annuals, but excludes newspapers after 1799, directories and time-tables, and some ephemera. Arrangement is by earliest title (or by earliest form of society), with liberal references. Gives changes of title, volume numbering and dates, and notes existence (but not locations) of cumulated indexes. V.4 includes a separate list of numerical titles (*e.g.* 24th Battalion).

A *Supplement to 1960,* Stewart, J.D. ed. (1962. 991p.), includes new periodicals, amended entries and titles not reported in the earlier volumes. Continued by:-
Class No: 050(01)

[1671]
—British union-catalogue of periodicals, incorporating 'World list of scientific periodicals'. New periodical titles. 1960/68-80. London, Butterworths, 1964-81. Quarterly, with annual cumulations.

A cumulative issue for 1960-68 was published 1970 (ISBN 0408700300). Ceased publication 1980; continued in part by *Serials in the British Library* (*q.v.*).

The incorporated *World list of scientific periodicals* was published by Butterworths in 4 eds. 1925/27-1963/65.
Class No: 050(01)

[1672]
CAMBRIDGE UNIVERSITY. Library. **Cambridge union list of serials.** Cambridge, Cambridge University Library, 1985-. Microfiche. Cumulations issued semi-annually. ISSN: 02690330.

Title varies, initially as *List of serials available in Cambridge University Library and other libraries connected with the University.* Merges two paper publications *Current serials available in the University Library* ... published in various eds. from 1955 and *Non-current serials* last published 1978, with a supplement 1980.

Lists more than 100,000 current and non-current serials held by the University and departmental libraries. The list is also searchable by title and title keyword through the Internet

....(*contd.*)
as part of Cambridge University Library's OPAC at http://www.lib.cam.ac.uk/Catalogues/OPAC/serials.htm.
Class No: 050(01)

[1673]
The **International directory of little magazines and small presses.** Fulton, L., *ed.* Paradise, Ca., Dustbooks, 1965-. Annual. $47.95.

Early issues under title *Directory of little magazines.*

Lists magazines and small presses in one A-Z sequence. For magazines information includes name of press, editor, address, foundation date, type of material published, circulation, frequency, subscription price, average size, whether reviews included, etc. Regional (US state and country) and broad subject heading ('Crime', 'Music' 'Occult') indexes. Coverage predominantly of US and Canadian titles, but a reasonable number of British magazines and presses also included. *Class No:* 050(01)

[1674]
ISSN compact. Paris, International Serials Data System International Centre, 1992-. CD-ROM database, updated quarterly. ISSN: 10184783.

Distributed by Chadwyck-Healey.

Database of the international organization responsible for assigning ISSNs. Contains over 850,000 records 1997, 40,000 new entries and 60,000 updates annually. Standard bibliographical data for most titles including place of publication, publisher, start date, frequency, language, CODEN, DDC no. and related titles. Software (Online Computer Systems) provides search and browse modes, based on 25 indexes. Database also incorporates the *List of serial title word abbreviations* (*q.v.*). More records than most other bibliographies of serials, but as amendments are made only when a new ISSN is assigned, does not always offer up-to-date information on changed titles or cessations in the manner of sources such as *Ulrich's* (*q.v.*).
Class No: 050(01)

[1675]
KATZ, B. *and* **KATZ, L. Magazines for libraries:** for the general reader and school, junior college, college, university and public libraries. 9th ed. New Providence, N.J., Bowker, 1997. xxiii,1402p. $170. ISBN: 0835239071.

First published 1969; 8th ed. 1995.

More than 7,800 entries in the 8th ed., 1,300 new, most entries revised. Arranged in 145 subject sections (Abstracts and indexes - Women: feminist and special interest). In addition to standard bibliographical detail, entries include price, circulation, audience level, availability in other formats and where indexed. Annotations of 75-125 words occasionally fail to note recent developments. Title and subject indexes. 'The enjoyable writing style and the logical overall organization will satisfy all levels of library users who are seeking advice on which periodical to read, research or purchase' (*American reference books annual*, v.27, 1996, p.32). Also available as part of *Ulrich's on disc*, the CD-ROM version of *Ulrich's international periodicals directory* (below). *Class No:* 050(01)

[1676]
Keyword index to serial titles. Boston Spa, British Library Document Supply Centre, 1980-. Microfiche. Quarterly. £330pa. (annual issue £125). ISSN: 01439553.

Often referred to as *KIST*. Also available as a BLAISE database, updated quarterly.

Keyword-out-of-context listing, based on the Document Supply Centre's (DSC) master file, non-current titles

....(contd.)

included unlike in *Current serials received* (below). Also covers titles held by the British Library Science Reference and Information Service, British Library Humanities and Social Sciences, Science Museum Library, the library of Imperial College and Cambridge University Library. Over 500,000 records 1997, unnumbered serials and finite series excluded. Many entries provide notes on changed titles, cessation dates, etc. Useful both as a unified key to the vast serial holdings of the British Library and as a source of basic bibliographical data. *Class No:* 050(01)

[1677]

—Boston Spa serials. Boston Spa, British Library Document Supply Centre, 1989-. CD-ROM database. Updated discs issued semi-annually. £325.

Based on the DSC serials holdings file, including, as with *Keyword index to serial titles,* records for the Science Reference and Information Service, Humanities and Social Sciences (BL) Science Museum and Cambridge University. Uses the same software as other British Library CD-ROMs with search and browse options. Indexes include keyword, title, ISSN and DSC shelfmark. *Class No:* 050(01)

[1678]

—Current serials received. Boston Spa, British Library Document Supply Centre/Science Reference and Information Service, 1965-. Annual. ISSN: 03090655.

First published as *Current serials received by the N.L.L.* Issued annually from 1978.

The 1998 ed. (552p.) lists over 60,000 titles in all subject areas currently received by the Document Supply Centre and Science Reference and Information Service. In 3 pts: Current serial titles except for Cyrillic - Cyrillic titles (transliterated) - Cover-to-cover translations of Cyrillic titles. Entry consists simply of title and DSC shelf-mark. Primarily for inter-library loan use, but also functions as a handy checklist. Also freely searchable through the Internet with title browse and keyword search options at http://www.bl.uk/serials/. *Class No:* 050(01)

[1679]

London union list of periodicals: central area 1995. Stallion, M., *comp.* [3rd ed.]. [Leigh-on-Sea], M. Stallion on behalf of the London Reference Group, 1995. Unpaged. ISBN: 0951818414.

Looseleaf in a ring binder. First published 1969; 2nd ed. 1991.

Covers the Corporation of London, City Business Library and the boroughs of Camden, Hackney, Islington, Kensington & Chelsea, Tower Hamlets and Westminster. A-Z title listing, no holdings data. *Class No:* 050(01)

[1680]

Myriade: le catalogue collectif national des publications en série sur CD-ROM. Paris, Centre National du CCN/ Ministère de l'Education Nationale ..., 1991-. Computer database; updated semi-annually. £675.

Distributed by Chadwyck-Healey.

Union catalogue of more than 250,000 serial titles in nearly 3,000 French libraries of all types. Full bibliographical data (title, previous title(s), publisher, etc.), with publication history, current status and holding libraries (includes address, access rules, hours, etc.). Also available online through SUNIST as *Catalogue collectif national. Myriade Plus* is a more sophisticated CD-ROM version aimed at professional users. *Class No:* 050(01)

[1681]

New serial titles: a union list of serials held by libraries in the United States and Canada. Washington, D.C., Library of Congress, Cataloging Distribution Service, 1953-. Monthly. $530. ISSN: 00286680.

Current subscription includes 8 monthly and 3 quarterly issues with an annual cumulation. Prepared by the Serial Record Division of the Library of Congress, from records created and maintained as part of the CONSER programme.

Lists periodicals received by the Library of Congress and 650 other libraries. Titles covered are those which meet the AACR2 definition of a serial. Newspapers excluded. Each issue arranged A-Z by title, with entries in the form of catalogue records, including ISSN and subject tracings. ISSN index in each issue, cumulated annually. Until 1981 covered only records for periodicals that began publication after 1950, but now includes all serials regardless of date of initial issue. A major tool for the bibliographic control of serials.

Quinquennial cumulations published for 1971/75 (2v. $170), 1975/80 (2v. $225) and 1981/85 (6v. $350). Further cumulation 1986/89 (6v. $450). Earlier cumulation for 1950/70 (below).

CONSER records are also available on fiche as *CONSER microfiche* (Ottawa, National Library of Canada/ Washington, D.C., 1975/78-. ISSN: 07073747) and online and through the Internet (http://www.loc.gov) as part of the Library of Congress catalogues. *Class No:* 050(01)

[1682]

—New serial titles: a union list of serials commencing publication after December 31, 1949; 1950-1970 cumulative. Washington, D.C., Library of Congress, New York, Bowker, 1973. 4v. ISBN: 0835205568.

More than 250,000 entries with an average of 6 locations for each title. Incorporates 13,000 revisions and numerous new locations, plus ISSN's and country codes. V.4 concludes with a 'Changes in serials' section. 505.00/00$aComplemented by *New serial titles, 1950-1970: a subject guide (Koltay, E.I. ed.* New York, Bowker, 1975. 2v. ISBN: 0835208206). *Class No:* 050(01)

[1683]

—Union list of serials in libraries of the United States and Canada. Titus, E.B., *ed.* 3rd ed. New York, Wilson, 1965. 5v.

Prepared under the sponsorship of the Joint Committee on the Union List of Serials with the cooperation of the Library of Congress.

First published 1927, (supplements, 1925-32. 2v.); 2nd ed. 1943, (supplements, 1941-49. 2v.).

Lists 156,449 serials held by 956 libraries which began publication before 1950. Excludes most government publications, US and most foreign newspapers, house organs and periodicals of an ephemeral nature. Continued by *New serial titles* (above). *Class No:* 050(01)

[1684]

Nordisk samtkatalog över periodika. [Nordic union catalogue of periodicals.] Oslo, Universitetsbiblioteket Oslo. Computer database.

Known as *NOSP*. Available online through the TRIP system or the Internet (subscription basis). CD-ROM and microfiche versions also available.

Online file contains records for 142,000 periodicals in more than 600 Scandinavian libraries with an ISSN. CD-ROM adds titles without an ISSN. *Class No:* 050(01)

[1685]

NUCOS: national union catalogue of serials held in Australian libraries. Canberra, National Library of Australia, 1984-. Microfiche. ISSN: 08129258.

Cumulating microfiche, semi-annual updating.

Lists and locates over 300,000 serial titles in more than 600 Australian libraries. A CD-ROM version, *Serials in Australian libraries: NUCOS on disc*, is also available (Melbourne, Informit. 3 updates annually, £740).

Class No: 050(01)

[1686]

SALSER: Scottish academic libraries SERials. Edinburgh, EDINA. World Wide Web resource.

URL: http://edina.ed.ac.uk/salser. Date reviewed 4th August 1998.

WWW based catalogue of the serial holdings of 13 Scottish university libraries, the public libraries of Glasgow and Edinburgh, the National Library of Scotland and a number of smaller research libraries. *Class No:* 050(01)

[1687]

The Serials directory: an international reference book. Birmingham, Ala., EBSCO Publishing, 1986-. Annual. $339. ISSN: 08664179.

12th ed. (1998) issued in 5 vols: v.1-3 Serials listing; v.4 Newspapers. Alphabetical title index; v.5 Indexes.

Major international current serials directory, including 10,000 newspapers, based on EBSCO's (subscription agents) internal database, CONSER and ISSN Register records and questionnaire returns. Over 150,000 entries under *c.*150 main and *c.*350 subsidiary headings. Standard data, including Library of Congress, Dewey, UDC and NLM class nos., ISSN, CODEN, country of publication, title, variant title, dates of publication, frequency, price, publisher, index availability, advertising data, circulation, description (50 words) and where indexed/abstracted. Two cumulative updating supplements issued between eds. Also available online (EBSCOhost) and as a CD-ROM database (updated quarterly) with additional titles and full CONSER MARC records for each citation. The inevitable comparison is with *Ulrich's international periodicals directory* (*below*). *The Serials directory* includes a similar number of titles and has slightly fuller information for most entries. On the negative side it is less well laid out and, despite improvements, is not as fully or accurately indexed. Overall *Ulrich's* probably remains the better source and certainly continues to be preferred by most UK libraries.

Class No: 050(01)

[1688]

Serials in the British Library. Boston Spa, British Library, National Bibliographic Service 1981-. Quarterly, 4th issue annual cumulation. £175. ISSN: 02600005.

Continues in part *British union-catalogue of periodicals: incorporating 'World list of scientific periodicals'. New periodical titles* (*q.v.*). Until the end of 1986 annual cumulation issued separately on microfiche.

A 'catalogue of new and retitled UK and overseas serial publications received by the British Library ... It does not include all the serials acquired by the British Library primarily for loan and document supply' (Preface). 10,000-12,000 titles listed annually, including newspapers, annuals, proceedings, translations and monographic series. Entries arranged alphabetically by catalogue headings according to BLAISE filing rules. Computer-produced keyword index in each issue, includes many insignificant access points.

....*(contd.)*

A microfiche cumulation, *Serials in the British Library 1976-1986* (57 microfiche), lists 57,000 titles.

Class No: 050(01)

[1689]

SMITH, A.M. Free magazines for libraries. Langston, D.J. 4th ed. Jefferson, N.C., McFarland, 1994. ix,293p. £25.65;$28.50. ISBN: 0899509479.

First published 1980; 3rd ed. 1989.

Annotated guide to house magazines, mainly from US corporate organizations, available on free subscription. Approximately 700 entries in *c.*70 subject categories Abstracts and indexes - Women's interests. Data includes date founded, frequency, editor, publisher, illustrations, circulation, samples, where indexed, and suggested audience. Indexed. *Class No:* 050(01)

[1690]

Ulrich's international periodicals directory: including Irregular serials and annuals. New York, Bowker, 1932-. Annual. £385;$459.95. ISSN: 00000175.

Title varies: *Periodicals directory,* 1932-38; *Ulrich's periodicals directory,* 1943-63. Frequency also varies; irregular until 1969, then biennial. From the 27th ed. 1988/89 merged with *Irregular serials and annuals* (first published 1967) and issued annually. Now published as a 5 v. set.

The most widely used directory of current serials based on Bowker's international serials database. Includes 'all publications that meet the definition of a serial except administrative publications of major government agencies below state level that can easily be found elsewhere, membership directories, comic books and puzzle and game books' (Preface p.viii, 1998). Includes annuals and other less frequently published titles since the incorporation of *Irregular serials and annuals.* V.1-3 comprise a 'classified list' (A-Z by title under 869 subject headings), entries including Dewey class no./LC class no., ISSN, CODEN, language, frequency, date first published, publisher, price, contact detail with email and URL addresses, editor, where indexed, online/CDROM availability, title changes, whether refereed, document suppliers (BLDSC nos. where applicable) and, for many titles, a 10-50 word descriptive annotation. V.4 has sections: Cross-index to subjects; Cessations (A-Z title list of serials reported ceased in the last 3 years); ISSN index; Title index; Title change index. V.5 *Newspapers*, introduced from 1993/94 ed., has entries for 7,000 daily and weekly US newspapers with a separate title index. Also contains indexes of serials available online or on CD-ROM and an index of publications of international organizations. 36th ed. 1998 lists more than 156,000 current titles (7,000 new entries). Kept up to date by the semi-annual *Ulrich's update*, issued from the 17th ed. Searchable online (monthly updating) through Dialog (file 480), LEXIS-NEXIS, Ovid (ULRI) and Silver-Platter. CD-ROM version, *Ulrich's on discs* (updated quarterly, £450. ISSN: 00001724), uses standard Bowker software and offers 24 search criteria. Online versions include information on discontinued titles and the CD-ROM incorporates full text reviews from *Magazines for libraries* (above). Well-organized and accurate, with wide internationa

Class No: 050(01)

[1691]

Union list of serials in the social sciences and humanities held by Canadian libraries. [Liste collective des publications en séries dans le domaine des sciences sociales et humaines dans les bibliothèques canadiennes.] Ottawa, National Library of Canada, 1981- Semi-annual. ISSN: 02273187.

Microfiche. Companion series *Union list of scientific serials in Canadian libraries.*

Cites *c.*200,000 titles. Includes some general interest science and technology serials. Newspapers and house organs excluded. Also available online as *CANUCS* and on CD-ROM as part of the *Romulus* database (Ottawa, National Library of Canada, 1992-. Semi-annual updating. ISSN: 11888741). *Class No:* 050(01)

[1692]

Willing's press guide: a guide to the press of the United Kingdom and to the principal publications of Europe, the Americas, Australasia, Asia, Africa and the Middle East. Teddington, Hollis Directories, 1874-. Annual. £189. ISSN: 00000213.

Publisher varies. 1998 ed. in 2v: v.1 *United Kingdom* (1432p.); v.2 *International* (1341p.).

'Press' includes 'newspapers, free sheets, magazines, journals, newsletters and any other publication appearing on a regular basis'. The UK v. has over 15,000 entries A-Z by title, information given including ISSN, publisher, foundation date, frequency, price, circulation, senior personnel, summary of contents (10-50 words), readership/target audience and advertising data. Separate lists of new and recently ceased titles (publisher and title sequences) and publishers and their titles. Classified index to periodicals and newspaper index precedes main listing. The *International* v. is arranged by country in regional sections (*e.g.* Europe, The Americas) with a publisher listing, a classified index and index to newspapers by country. Invaluable for library and desk use. Especially strong on British newspapers and general interest magazines. *Class No:* 050(01)

[1693]

Zeitschriften-Datenbank. (ZDB). Berlin, Deutsches Bibliotheksinstitut. Computer database and microfiche service. DM490 (microfiche). ISSN: 01718932.

Searchable online through STN International and the Deutsches Bibliotheksinstitut's Internet service DBI-LINK (http://www.dbilink.de). CD-ROM also available (DM1600). Microfiche cumulations issued semi-annually. 36th ed. April 1997 (533 microfiche).

Union catalogue of the serials holdings of major German academic and research libraries. Contains details of *c.*950,000 titles 1997 with over 4.3 million locations. *Class No:* 050(01)

Children

[1694]

Children's periodicals of the United States. Kelly, R.G., *ed.* Westport, Conn. and London, Greenwood, 1984. xxix,591p. £67.50;$79.50. (*Historical guides to the world's periodicals and newspapers.*) ISBN: 0313221170.

Intended to 'provide brief authoritative descriptions of a broad sample of American periodicals for children' (Preface). The earliest title included is *Children's magazine* established 1789, the latest *Cobblestone* established 1980. Entries, average length 5 pages, give a full description of the title and its contents. Details of bibliographic sources and locations are presented under the heading 'Information

....*(contd.)*

sources', notes on title changes, publishers, editors etc. under the heading 'Publication history'. Selected bibliography (p.543-52). Chronological and geographical lists of titles. An 'impressive volume' (*Library Quarterly*, v.55(4), October 1985, p.475), despite a degree of unevenness in entry detail. *Class No:* 050(01)-0053

[1695]

Magazines for kids and teens. Rev. ed. Glassboro, N.J., Educational Press Association of America/Newark, N.J, International Reading Association, 1997. x,118p. $15.95 ISBN: 0872072436.

First published 1994.

1st ed. (101p.) lists and briefly describes 249 magazines suitable for children aged 2-17 years. A-Z title arrangement; indexed by age/grade level and subject. *Class No:* 050(01)-0053

[1696]

Magazines for young people. Katz, B. *and* Katz, L., *eds.* 2nd ed. New Providence, N.J., Bowker, 1991. xxv,361p. $38. ISBN: 0835230090.

'A Children's magazine guide companion volume' (cover). First published as *Magazines for school libraries*, 1987.

Modelled on *Magazines for libraries* (*q.v.*). Entries for over 1,000 titles in 3 sections: Children's magazines (*c.*100 titles); Young adult magazines (ages 14-18); Professional education and library journals (*c.*175 titles). Detail includes intended audience, where indexed and evaluative annotation. Title/subject and titles by age group indexes. An 'excellent work of reference, which is to be thoroughly recommended wherever and whenever the American emphasis poses no difficulty' (*Reference reviews*, v.6(6), 1992, p.4). *Class No:* 050(01)-0053

Women

[1697]

HUMPHREYS, N.K. American women's magazines: an annotated historical guide. New York, Garland, 1989. xiii,303p. (*Garland reference library of the humanities, v.789.*) ISBN: 0824075439.

A bibliography of writings about American women's magazines from the late 19th century to 1987. 888 entries, arranged by author in 6 sections. 1. Early women's rights periodicals - 2. Feminist periodicals - 3. Early women's magazines - 4. Twentieth century women's magazines - 5. Women's pages in newspapers - 6. Confession/romance magazines. Subject index. *Class No:* 050(01)-0055.2

[1698]

Sources on the history of women's magazines, 1792-1960: an annotated bibliography. Zuckerman, M.E., *comp.* New York, Greenwood, 1991. xxiii,297p. $59.55. (*Bibliographies and indexes in women's studies, no. 12.*) ISBN: 0313263787.

Annotated entries of up to 100 words for material relating to women's magazines which began publication before 1960. Topical arrangement in 10 chapters. Final chap. lists 62 'Selected archives, special sources and manuscript collections'. Author and subject indexes. More extensive than Humphreys (above), but excludes underground sources concentrating on popular titles. 'In addition to general sources ... includes useful material on images of women in other media, sources on advertising and market research, and biographical resources on the magazines' publishers' (*Choice*, V.29(7), March 1992, p.1058). *Class No:* 050(01)-0055.2

[1699]
WHITE, C.L. Women's magazines, 1693-1968. London, Michael Joseph, 1970. 348p. tables. ISBN: 0718106873.

A sociological study of women's magazines in Britain, which includes a useful chronological listing of titles (p.305-17) with British Library locations, statistical tables on circulation and a bibliography of secondary sources.

Class No: 050(01)-0055.2

[1700]
Women's periodicals and newspapers from the 18th century to 1981: a union list of holdings of Madison, Wisconsin libraries. Danky, J.P., *ed and* Hady, M.E., *and others comps.*. Boston, Mass., G.K. Hall, 1982. xxiv,376p. (*A reference publication in women's studies.*) ISBN: 0816181071.

Primarily based on the holdings of the Wisconsin State Historical Society, believed to be one of the strongest collections of women's periodicals and newspapers in North America. 1,461 entries, predominantly for titles published in the US. Broad scope including literary, political and historical journals as well as general newspapers and magazines. Arranged by title A-Z, with geographic, editor, publisher, subject, foreign language, catchword/subtitle and chronological indexes, the latter in graphic format.

Class No: 050(01)-0055.2

[1701]
Women's periodicals in the United States: social and political issues. Endres, K.L. *and* Lueck, T.L., *eds.* Westport, Conn., Greenwood Press, 1996. xxv,525p. £87.95;$110. (*Historical guides to the world's periodicals and newspapers.*) ISBN: 0313286329.

Contains historical essays on 76 titles with chronology, general bibliography and index.

Complemented by the same editors' *Women's periodicals in the United States: consumer magazines* (Greenwood Press, 1995. xvii,501p. £89.50;$99.50. ISBN: 0313286310) profiling 75 titles. Together these works help to make up for the relative neglect of women's magazines by Mott (*q.v.*).

Class No: 050(01)-0055.2

Handbooks & Manuals

[1702]
Guide to special issues and indexes of periodicals. Uhlan, M. *and* Katz, D.B., *eds.* 4th ed. New York, Special Libraries Association, 1994. 223p. $56. ISBN: 0871112639.

First published 1962; 2nd ed. 1976.

Lists special issues, (directories, buyers' guides, conference issues, reviews etc.), produced on a regular basis by 1,748 US and Canadian periodicals. Data includes price, month of publication and date first produced. Arranged under periodical title A-Z with classified listing and subject index. *Class No:* 050(035)

Reviews & Abstracts

[1703]
Book review index: periodical reviews 1976-1984: a cumulated index to more than 15,000 reviews of approximately 5,300 periodicals that have been cited in *Book review index*. Beach, B., *ed.* Detroit, Gale, 1987. 295p. $80. ISBN: 0810343649.

Indexes reviews in 273 publications. Periodicals defined as 'non-book publications with a continuing, specific title that are published at stated intervals, usually more often than once a year' (Introduction p.7). Includes reviews of children's magazines and newspapers. *Class No:* 050(048)

[1704]
Serials review. Greenwich, Conn., JAI Press, 1975-. Quarterly. $175. ISSN: 00987913.

Previously published by Pierian Press.

Originally concentrated on reviewing new or established periodicals, but issues are now predominantly devoted to short articles on a wide range of topics relating to serials librarianship and publishing. Examples from v.22(4) 1996 include 'Serials information in the OPAC' and 'A Critical look at the availability of gay and lesbian periodical literature in libraries and standard indexing services'. A particularly valuable reference feature is the section 'Serials review index' which appears in every other issue. That in v.22(4) lists reviews of *c.*475 serials in 175 periodicals.

Class No: 050(048)

Great Britain

[1705]
TIMES, The. Tercentenary handlist of English and Welsh newspapers, magazines and reviews.
Muddiman, J.G., *comp.* London, The Times, 1920. 324,[1],xxxvp.

Reprinted London, Dawsons, 1966.

Section 1: The London and suburban press (1620-1919); section 2: The provincial press (1701-1919). Both sections arranged chronologically with title indexes. About 20,000 items listed, but limited by its reliance on the collections of the British Museum (Library) and a few other libraries (notably the Bodleian). Sometimes referred to as J.G. Muddiman's handlist.

Addenda were published in *Notes and queries* v.8 (1921) and v.10 (1922). *Class No:* 050(410)

17th & 18th Centuries

[1706]
BODLEIAN LIBRARY. A Catalogue of English newspapers and periodicals in the Bodleian Library, 1622-1800. Milford, R.T. *and* Sutherland, D.M., *comps.* Oxford, Oxford Bibliographical Society, 1936. 184p.

Also in the Oxford Bibliographical Society's *Proceedings and papers,* v.4(2), 1936, p.163-346.

Arranged alphabetically by titles, with index of editors, authors and contributors. In spite of title, covers Great Britain and Ireland. *Class No:* 050(410)"16/17"

[1707]
CRANE, R.S. *and* **KAYE, F.B. A Census of British newspapers and periodicals, 1620-1800.** Chapel Hill, Univ. of North Carolina Press, 1927. 205p.

Reprinted London, Holland Press, 1966.

Gives complete holdings of 38 American libraries and partial holdings of 24; lists 984 items found in American libraries, with locations, and 1,445 not found. Alphabetical arrangement with chronological and geographic (places other than London) indexes. *Class No:* 050(410)"16/17"

17th Century

[1708]
British newspapers and periodicals 1641-1700: a short-title catalogue of serials printed in England, Scotland, Ireland and British America. Nelson, C. *and* Seccombe, M., *comps.* New York, The Modern Language Association of America, 1987. xx,724p. $300. ISBN: 0873521749.

The first work to comprehensively cover the period, as Wing (*q.v.*) excludes serials other than annuals. 711

.... *(contd.)*

newspapers and periodicals listed, A-Z by earliest title, giving dates, periodicity, editor, citations to bibliographical authorities, etc. Includes newsheets, literary and leisure miscellanies, trade bulletins and official journals. Separate entry for every issue of each title identifying number, date and imprint and listing holding libraries (*c.*150 predominantly UK and US). 6 indexes: chronological, publisher/printer, editor/author, subject, geographical, foreign language. Appendix: 'Checklist of serials printed 1701-2' giving coverage to start of McLeod and McLeod (below). *Class No:* 050(410)"16"

[1709]

DAHL, F. A Bibliography of English corantos and periodical newsbooks, 1620-1642. London, Bibliographical Society, 1952. [ii],282p. facsims.

Available from Oxford Univ. Press (£15. ISBN: 0197217176).

404 items. Gives locations; bibliography of sources. *Class No:* 050(410)"16"

18th & 19th Centuries

[1710]

WARD, W.S. Index and finding list of serials published in the British Isles, 1789-1832. Lexington, Univ. of Kentucky Press, 1953. xiv,180p.

Paperback reprint available from Books on Demand ($59. ISBN: 0317103954).

5,250 items with locations in 359 British, American and Canadian libraries and newspaper offices. Gives place of publication, volume numbering, dates and frequency; bibliography.

A further 200 items (locations not indicated) are added by Ward's article, *Index and finding list of serials published in the British Isles 1789-1832: a supplementary list* in the *Bulletin of the New York Public Library,* v.77(3), Spring 1974, p.291-97. *Class No:* 050(410)"17/18"

[1711]

—WARD, W.S. British periodicals and newspapers, 1789-1832: a bibliography of secondary sources. Lexington, Univ. Press of Kentucky, 1972. 400p. ISBN: 0813112710.

A companion v. to the above. Subject arrangement with author index. *Class No:* 050(410)"17/18"

18th Century

[1712]

CRANFIELD, G.A. A Handlist of English provincial newspapers and periodicals, 1700-1760. [Rev. ed]. Cambridge, Cambridge Univ. Press, 1961. viii,30[13]p.

First published 1952. The additional 13p. comprise additions and corrections to the 1952 ed. extracted from the *Transactions of the Cambridge Bibliographical Society* v.2, 1954-58, p.269-74 and p.385-89.

Arranged by place of publication; names printers; gives locations in libraries, newspaper offices and private collections. Indexes of printers and changed titles. *Class No:* 050(410)"17"

[1713]

McLEOD, W.R. *and* McLEOD, N.B. A Graphical directory of English newspapers and periodicals, 1702-1714. Morgantown, W. Va., School of Journalism, University of West Virginia, 1982. Various pagings. ISBN: 0930362055. Spiral bound.

Intended to provide complete coverage for the reign of Queen Anne. Data on each title displayed in graphical form showing individual issues and dates covered. Separate section of written descriptions. Index of printers, publishers and booksellers. Chronological index. Continues the comprehensive coverage of Nelson and Seccombe (above). *Class No:* 050(410)"17"

19th & 20th Centuries

[1714]

REED, D. The Popular magazine in Britain and the United States, 1880-1960. London, British Library, 1997. viii,287p. illus., facsims., plates. £45. ISBN: 0712304177.

'This is a mapping exercise. Its object is to describe directly and by comparison; to refine terms of discussion; to outline some generic aspects of the modern magazine and establish a perspective on the changes wrought on those elements' (*Introduction*, p.1). Mainly chronological approach in 7 chaps., each extensively documented. 49 plates, including 11 in colour. Appendices analysing the contents of 28 titles (p.235-62), bibliography (p.263-77) and index. '(S)crupulous and penetrating research' (*Reference reviews*, v.12(1), 1997, p.19). *Class No:* 050(410)"18/19"

Victorian Age

[1715]

Union list of Victorian serials: a union list of selected nineteenth-century British serials available in United States and Canadian libraries. Fulton, R.D. *and* Colee, C.M., *eds.* New York, Garland, 1985. xxvii,732p. (*Garland reference library of the humanities, v.530.*) ISBN: 0824088468.

A selective finding list, titles included being based on those listed in the *New Cambridge bibliography of English literature* (*q.v.*) with the addition of some scientific serials. 1,179 entries each with column number in the above work and item number in *The Waterloo directory of Victorian periodicals* (below). Locations for *c.*350 libraries (19 Canadian). List of libraries. *Class No:* 050(410)"1837-1901"

[1716]

Victorian periodicals: a guide to research. Vann, J.D. *and* VanArsdel, R.T., *eds.* New York, Modern Language Association of America, 1978. xi,188p. $37.50. (*Reviews of research, 4.*) ISBN: 0873522567.

8 contributed chapters including: II. The bibliographic control of Victorian periodicals; III. Finding lists for Victorian periodicals; IV. Biographical sources. Indexed. *Class No:* 050(410)"1837-1901"

[1717]

—Victorian periodicals: a guide to research. Volume 2. Vann, J.D. *and* VanArsdel, R.T., *eds.* New York, Modern Language Association of America, 1989. viii,177p. $37.50. (*Reviews of research, 7.*) ISBN: 0873522648.

12 further contributions including 'British women's serials', 'Magazines for children' and 'The Welsh periodical press'. Various appendices update chapters in the previous volume. Indexed. *Class No:* 050(410)"1837-1901"

[1718]
Victorian periodicals and Victorian society. Vann, J.D. *and* VanArsdel, R.T., *eds.* Aldershot, Scolar Press, 1994. xiii,370p. £65;$125. ISBN: 0859679446.

Collection of 18 bibliographical essays on a wide range of topics (Law ... Science ... Theatre ... Advertising ... Temperance ... Student's journals). Indexed (p.339-70). '(T)houghtful introduction to a broad topic' (*Reference reviews*, v.8(7), 1994, p.9). *Class No:* 050(410)"1837-1901"

[1719]
—Periodicals of Queen Victoria's empire: an exploration. Vann, J.D. *and* VanArsdel, R.T., *eds.* London, Mansell, 1996. x,371p. tables, maps. £55;$80. ISBN: 072012333x.

First published in Canada by Univ. of Toronto Press.

Further bibliographical essays covering Australia, Canada, India, New Zealand, Southern Africa and 'Outposts of Empire'. Longest chap. for Canada (p.60-174) includes a lengthy annotated bibliography. Index (p.337-71). *Class No:* 050(410)"1837-1901"

[1720]
The Waterloo directory of Victorian periodicals 1824-1900. Phase I. Wolff, M., *and others eds.* Waterloo, Ont., Wilfrid Laurier Univ. Press for the Univ. of Waterloo, 1976. xxvii,1187p. ISBN: 0889200262.

Sponsored by the Research Society for Victorian Periodicals and Waterloo Computing in the Humanities. Available as a Pergamon Reprint ($529. ISBN: 0080260799).

Checklist of 28,995 entries, including about 4,000 cross-references. 'The conditions for inclusion are only that a periodical be published in Great Britain ... or be related to one that was. The definition of a periodical ... is a publication intended to be produced at regular intervals, for an indefinite period of time. So newspapers, magazines, reports of societies, monthly bulletins, annuals and almanaks are included' (p.xvi). Entries arranged by title A-Z: variable descriptive data from subtitle, numbering, dates, editor(s), place of publication, publisher, printer, price, size, frequency, illustrations, circulation, issuing body, indexing, notes, mergers and subsidiary and alternate titles. The most comprehensive source, more than doubling the *c.*11,000 entries for Victorian periodicals in the *Tercentenary handlist of English and Welsh magazines and newspapers (1920).* Forms the basis for the more extensive Phase II, two volumes of which, *The Waterloo directory of Irish newspapers and periodicals* (1987) and *The Waterloo directory of Scottish newspapers and periodicals* (1989), have so far been published. *Class No:* 050(410)"1837-1901"

Contemporary

[1721]
Current British journals 1992: a bibliographical guide. Toase, M., *ed.* 6th ed. Boston Spa, British Library Document Supply Centre, 1992. [vi],783p. ISBN: 0712320881.

First published 1962 as *Guide to current British periodicals*; 5th ed. 1989. No further eds. planned.

Contains information on 8,362 titles (8,160 5th ed.). Excludes newspapers, house journals, local magazines below county level, members' bulletins, etc. Entries, classified by UDC, give title, year of first issue, previous title, price, frequency, no. of pages per issue, policy on advertising, whether book reviews included, availability of indexes, sponsor, ISSN, additional formats, where indexed/abstracted, publisher name and address, and brief subject description. Indexed by title, subject, sponsoring body and ceased title (since 5th ed.). *Class No:* 050(410)"312"

[1722]
GÖRTSCHACHER, W. Little magazine profiles: the little magazines in Great Britain, 1939-1993. Salzburg, Univ. of Salzburg, 1993. ii,751p. (*Salzburg studies in English literature, poetic drama & poetic theory.*) ISBN: 3705206087.

Includes the 'History of little magazines 1939-1993' (p.88-254) and full profiles of 18 titles (*e.g. Stand, Orbis, PN review*, p.505-690). Bibliography (p.693-716); index. *Class No:* 050(410)"312"

[1723]
ISSN UK Centre for Serials. London, British Library, 1989-. Computer database.

Available through BLAISE-Line, updated monthly. Previously as *National Serials Data Centre file.*

Database of Centre, established by the British Library in 1974, responsible for assigning ISSNs to serials with a British imprint. Coverage ranges from scientific journals, yearbooks and business publications to magazines, comics and local society publications. At March 1997 the database contained 51,968 records, approximately 4,000 additions annually. *Class No:* 050(410)"312"

[1724]
NOYCE, J.L. The Directory of British alternative periodicals, 1965-1974. Hassocks, Harvester Press; Atlantic Highlands, Humanities Press, 1979. xiii,359p. ISBN: 0855271043.

Covers 1,256 titles A-Z, including some from 1975. Publications devoted to poetry and traditional politics largely excluded. Very full data for most entries, including description (history, aims, assessment of influence, variant titles, irregularities in numbering etc.), indexes, library holdings and references. Index of personal names, place-names, organizations and subjects. A 'superb job' (*Choice*, v.16(9), November 1979, p.1154). *Class No:* 050(410)"312"

[1725]
Small press guide: a detailed guide to poetry and small press magazines. London, Writer's Bookshop, 1996-. Annual. £9.99.

The 1997 issue (2nd ed. 373p. ISBN: 0952911905) lists over 500 magazines A-Z by title. Entry detail includes frequency, subscription, type of writing, contact information, etc. and a brief general description. Further list of titles for which full information unavailable (p.315-71). *Class No:* 050(410)"312"

[1726]
—Small presses & little magazines of the UK and Ireland: an address list. Finch, P., *comp.* Cardiff, HMSO Oriel Bookshop, 198?-. Irregular.

Published in conjunction with the Association of Little Presses.

The 12th ed. (1996. 74p. ISBN: 0946329230) has about 350 entries for magazines (p.7-37). *Class No:* 050(410)"312"

[1727]

Walford's guide to current British periodicals in the humanities and social sciences. Walford, A.J., *ed.* London, Library Association, 1985. vi,473p. ISBN: 0853656762.

Selective coverage of over 3,000 titles classed by UDC. The well annotated entries include foundation date, frequency, publisher, price, ISSN, and whether indexed by *British humanities index* (*q.v.*). Excludes house journals, annuals (except bibliographies), college and school magazines, local/diocesan publications and newspapers. Title, subject and sponsoring body index. '(T)horough and meticulous' (*Library review*, v.35, Autumn 1986, p.212). *Class No:* 050(410)"312"

Scotland

[1728]

COUPER, W.J. The Edinburgh periodical press; being a bibliographical account of the newspapers, journals and magazines issued in Edinburgh from the earliest times to 1800. Stirling, Mackay, 1908. 2v. facsims.

V.1 1642-1711; v.2. 1711-1800. Supplements appeared in *Scottish notes and queries,* 3rd series, v.8-13 (1930-35). *Class No:* 050(411)

[1729]

The Waterloo directory of Scottish newspapers and periodicals: 1800-1900. North, J.S., *ed.* Waterloo, Ont., North Waterloo Academic Press, 1989. 2v., facsims. ISBN: 0921075057.

Published as the second part of Phase II of the Waterloo periodical directory series.

More thorough than the Irish companion v. (below), based on research in 80 Scottish libraries. 7,300 entries arranged by earliest title, with cross-references to changed titles, subtitles and issuing bodies. In addition to full bibliographical detail, entries give circulation figures, indexing sources (including *Wellesley index to Victorian periodicals,* (*q.v.*)), general comments, subjects and locations in Scottish and a few other British libraries. Around 2,400 entries also include photofacsimile title pages. Subject, place and personal name indexes. *Class No:* 050(411)

Ireland

[1730]

Irish periodicals: first published before 1901: a union list of Northern Ireland library holdings. McAllister, K., *ed.* Omagh, Library Local Studies Panel, 1995. 95p. £5. ISBN: 0951651013.

Covers 16 libraries including the Linen Hall Library and Queen's University. Entries, arranged A-Z by title, give full holdings details, notes on title changes and ref. no. in *The Waterloo directory of Irish newspapers and periodicals* (below). *Class No:* 050(415)

[1731]

The Waterloo directory of Irish newspapers and periodicals, 1800-1900. North, J.S., *ed.* Waterloo, Ont., North Waterloo Academic Press, 1986. 838p. $300. ISBN: 0921075006.

Published as the first part of Phase II of the Waterloo periodical directory series.

Increases almost fourfold the number of Irish titles listed in *The Waterloo directory of Victorian periodicals 1824-1900* (*q.v.*). 3,932 numbered entries including annual reports, almanacs and directories. Arranged by earliest title, cross-referenced from changed titles, subtitles and issuing bodies.

....*(contd.)*

Full bibliographical information and publishing history with at least one location, mostly in Irish libraries. Subject, place and personal name indexes (p.521-838). *Class No:* 050(415)

Wales

[1732]

WALTERS, H. Llfryddiaeth cylchgronau Cymreig 1735-1850. [A Bibliography of Welsh periodicals 1735-1850.] Aberystwyth, Llyfrgell Genedlaethol Cymru/National Library of Wales, 1993. lviii,109p. facsims. £22. ISBN: 0907158706.

Parallel Welsh text and English translation.

Covers titles published in Wales, including those in English, and of Welsh association issued overseas. 195 entries with full detail of title changes, editors, frequency, sources, etc. Thoroughly indexed; extensive 'Select bibliography' (p.xlvii-lviii). '(S)cholarly' (*Library Association record*, v.96(8), August 1994, p.453). *Class No:* 050(429)

Germany

[1733]

BÖNING, H. Deutsche Presse: Biobibliographische Handbücher zur Geschichte deutschsprachigen periodischen Presse von den Aufängen bis 1815. Stuttgart-Bad Cannstatt, Frommann-Holzboog, 1996-. ISBN: 3772815898.

Scheduled for 40 v. Bd.1 *Hamburg. Kommentierte Bibliographie der Zeitungen, Zeitschriften, Intelligenzblätter, Kalender und Almanache sowie biographische Hinweise zu Herausgebern, Verlegern und Druckern periodischer Schriften* issued in 3 pts., DM510 each.

To cover all Germany, Austria and German-speaking Switzerland. Full bibliographical detail and substantive annotations for each entry. Chronological arrangement; person, institution, subject, place and title indexing. 1,018 titles in Bd.1, far more comprehnsive than Kirchner (below) for the same region. '(Y)et another huge and extremely useful German bibliographical project' (*The Library*, v.19(3), September 1997, p.267).

The recently begun microfiche project *Deutsche Zeitschriften des 18. und 19. Jahrhünderts: Microfiche-Volltext* (Hildesheim, Olms, 1995-) is to include a CD-ROM index. *Class No:* 050(430)

[1734]

Deutsche Bibliographie. Zeitschriften-Verzeichnis: Neuerscheinungen, Änderungen und Abschlüsse: Verzeichnis aller im Wöchentlichen Verzeichnis angezeigten deutschen und im Ausland erscheinenden deutschsprachigen Zeitschriften und zeitschriftenartigen Reihen. 1945/52-. Deutschen Bibliothek, *bearb.* Frankfurt am Main, Buchhändler-Vereinigung, 1954-89. Irregular. ISSN: 01701002.

Subtitle varies. Initial v. for 1945-52; further coverage for 1953-57, 1958-70, 1971-76, 1977-80 and 1981-85, each published in parts. Periodicals now included in the quinquennial cumulations of the full German national bibliography *Deutsche Nationalbibliographie ... Monographien und Periodika - Fünfjahrverzeichnis* (*q.v.*).

Included serials published in East Germany, Austria, Switzerland and the German language elsewhere. Each set in 2 pts: classified section giving bibliographical detail with notes on title changes, irregular publication patterns, etc; index section providing access by title, editor/publisher/responsible body and subject. *Class No:* 050(430)

[1735]

Deutschsprachige Zeitschriften: Deutschland - Österreich - Schweiz: und ausgewählte internationale wissenschaftliche Zeitschriften, Loseblatt-Werke, Jahrbücher, Periodika auf CD-ROM und Online. Köln, Verlag der Schillerbuchhandlung Hans Banger, 1956-. Annual. DM146. ISSN: 04190054.

Until 1967 published as *Anschriften deutschsprachigen Zeitschriften.* Subtitle also varies.

Jahr. 41 (1997. 1604p.) lists *c.*17,800 periodicals published in Germany, Austria and Switzerland. Brief information for each entry includes publisher, frequency, price and ISSN. Plentiful cross-references from alternate and abbreviated titles. Further listings by ISSN and broad subject group (p.997-1217). Separate sequences for looseleaf, yearbook and CD-ROM and online titles (p.1221-581). Also available on CD-ROM as *Der 'Banger' auf CD-ROM* (DM249. ISSN: 0949863X). The main alternative to *Stamm: Leitfaden für Presse und Werbung (q.v.).*
Class No: 050(430)

[1736]

KIRCHNER, J. Bibliographie der Zeitschriften des deutschen Sprachgebietes bis 1900. Stuttgart, Hiersemann, 1969-89. 4v. ISBN: 3777266175.

Bd.1. *Von den Anfängen bis 1830* (1969. xv,489p. DM460); Bd.2. *1831-1870* (1977. xi,400p. DM460); Bd.3. *1871-1900* (1977. xi,730p. DM490); Bd.4. *Register zur bibliographie... . Teil 1. Alphabetisches Titelregister* (1989. x,551p. DM490).

A bibliography and union list. Arranged by subject, then chronologically. Notes title changes and editors. Locations in more than 100 libraries. Each v. has its own index. V.4 pt.1 cumulated title index; the projected v.4 pt.2 is to index publishers, places of publication and editors.
Class No: 050(430)

Refugees

[1737]

MAAS, L. Handbuch der deutschen Exilpresse 1933-1945. München, C. Hanser, 1976-90. 4v. (*Sonderveröffentlichungen der Deutschen Bibliotek, 2... etc.*.) ISBN: 3446120592, v.1.

V.1-v.2 comprise a title list of 436 newspapers, magazines, information sheets, bulletins and circulars produced or decisively influenced by German exiles. A major feature is the full listing of contributing authors provided for each title. Locations given for 31 libraries including Library of Congress and New York Public Library. V.3 contains name and pseudonym, organization, country and place indexes. V.4 *Die Zeitungen des deutschen Exils in Europe von 1933 bis 1939 in Einzeldarstellungen* contains 2-3 page accounts by broad subject groups.
Class No: 050(430)-0054.7

Czech

[1738]

HNIKOVA, D. Přeheld periodického tisku v České Republice roce 1990. Praha, Narodni knihovna v Praze, 1991. 3v. ISBN: 807050112x.

V.1-v.2 have records for 4,046 current titles in 16 broad subject sections. V.3 contains title, publisher and place of publication indexes. *Class No:* 050(437.1)

Poland

[1739]

Bibliografia wydawnichw ciągłych 1981-. Warszawa, Biblioteka Narodowa, 1984-. Irregular. Z300,000. ISSN: 02394421.

Title varies. Replaces *Bibliografia czasopism i wydawnichw zbiorowych,* issued as an annual for 1958-60 and again for 1971 and 1972/74 (1960-78).

The current listing based on a looseleaf quarterly insert in the main national bibliography, *Przewodnik bibliogaficzny (q.v.).* Cumulation 1996 under title *Bibliografia wydawnichw ciągłych nowych, zawieszonych i zmieniajacych tytul, 1985-1994.* (263p. ISBN: 837009822). *Class No:* 050(438)

[1740]

KOWALIK, J. Bibliografia czasopism polskich wydanych poza granicami Kraju od września 1939 roku. [World index of Polish periodicals published outside of Poland since September 1939.] Lublin, Katolicki Universytet Lubelski, 1976. 4v.

Supersedes *Catalogue of periodicals in Polish or relating to Poland and other Slavonic countries published outside Poland since September 1st 1939*; comp. by M. Danilewicz and G. Sadowska. 2nd ed. (London, Polish Library, 1971. 126p. 0902763032. First published 1964).
Class No: 050(438)

[1741]

—KOWALIK, J. World index of Polish periodicals published outside of Poland since September 1939: volume 5: a tentative bibliography. San Jose, American Polish Documentation Studio, 1984. 2pts. illus.

Pt.1 registers 361 titles in Polish or related to Poland published 1973-84. Pt.2 has 261 supplementary and 93 revised entries for 1939-72. *Class No:* 050(438)

[1742]

UNIWERSYTET JAGIELLOŃSKI. Katalog czasopism polskich Biblioteki Jagiellońskiej. Wyd. 2. Kraków, Uniwersytet Jagiellońskiego, 1974-86. 9v. in 10. (*Varia zesz, 94... etc.*.) ISBN: 8323300887, v.9.

A catalogue of Polish periodicals held by the University Library. Forms the most comprehensive retrospective bibliography available. *Class No:* 050(438)

Hungary

[1743]

Magyar nemzeti bibliográfia. Új periodikumok. Budapest, Országos Széchényi Könyvtár, 1996-. Monthly. ISSN: 12196835.

Issued as a section of *Magyar nemzeti bibliográfia. Könyvek bibliográfiája* 1991-95.

Lists new and changed serials. Excludes directories, reports, specialist abstract and indexing services, newsletters, etc. A-Z title arrangement with issuing body, geographical and ISSN index. 1,030 entries in issues for 1997. A CD-ROM version is also available (ISSN: 14165414). Preceded by:- *Class No:* 050(439)

[1744]

—Magyar nemzeti bibliográfia. Idöszaki kiadványok bibliográfiája. 1981-90. Budapest, Országos Széchényi Könyvtär, 1983-94. Annual. ISSN: 02314592.

Continues Kurrens idöszaki kiadványok: a magyar országon megjelenó idöszaki kiadványok bibliográfiája, 1976-82 (ISSN: 01340247).

Title listing with indexes. A cumulated index is available for 1981-85 (1988. 2v.). *Class No:* 050(439)

France

[1745]

BÉTHERY, A. Revues et magazines d'aujourd'hui: guide des périodiques à l'intention des bibliothèques publiques. 3e. éd. rev. & augm. Paris, Éditions du Cercle de la Librairie, 1990. 396p. FFr240. (*Collections bibliothèques.*) ISBN: 2765404380.

Earlier eds. 1978 and 1985 as *Les Périodiques: guide à l'intention des bibliothèques publiques.*

A useful selective guide to French periodicals suitable for public libraries, similar in concept to *Magazines for libraries* (*q.v.*). 763 critically annotated entries (638 previous ed.) in Dewey based subject groups. Indexed. *Class No:* 050(44)

[1746]

Bibliographie nationale française. Publications en série. Paris, Bibliothèque nationale, 1977-. Monthly, with annual index. FFr1630. ISSN: 11423269.

Title and publisher varies. As *Bibliographie de la France. Supplément I. Publications en série* (ISSN: 01501399), until 1989.

UDC classified list of new or revised serial titles. Entries giving full bibliographical citation including frequency statement and ISSN. Title, collective author and subject indexes, cumulated annually. The issues for 1997 record 7,207 titles. *Class No:* 050(44)

[1747]

BIBLIOTHÈQUE NATIONALE. (FRANCE). Bibliographie de la presse française politique et d'information générale, des origines à 1944. Paris, Bibliothèque Nationale, 1964-. ISBN: 2717700048.

Originally intended as a continuation of Hatin (below). Title and coverage changed after 1980, previously as *Bibliographie ... générale, 1865-1944.* To be issued in 89 fasc., one for each *département.* Fasc. published as completed, numbered alphabetically by name of *département.*

Fasc. arranged A-Z by title with chronological indexes: *e.g.* Pas-de-Calais (Fasc. 62. 1968. 116p.) lists *c.*725 titles with full bibliographical details (p.13-88); chronological index (p.90-116). Latest published *Tarn* (Facs. 81. 1996. 85p. FFr138. ISBN: 2717719814).

Titles 1945-58 omitted from fasc. published before 1980 are recorded in Guillauma, Y. *La Presse politique et d'information générale de 1944-1958: inventaire des titres* (Paris, Guillauma, 1995. 620p. FFr1300. ISBN: 2950931502). *Class No:* 050(44)

[1748]

BIBLIOTHÈQUE NATIONALE. (FRANCE). Catalogue des périodiques clandestins diffusés en France de 1939 à 1945, suivi d'un catalogue des périodiques clandestins diffusés à l'étranger. Roux-Fouillet, R., *comp.* Paris, Bibliothèque Nationale, 1954. xxiii,282p. FFr75.

1,106 numbered entries: 1. Périodiques diffusés en France (1-1,015) - 2. Périodiques diffusés à l'étranger (1,016-1,106). Bibliothèque Nationale press-marks are given. Index of names, places and titles. *Class No:* 050(44)

[1749]

BIBLIOTHÈQUE NATIONALE. (FRANCE). Répertoire de la presse et des publications périodiques françaises. 1977/1978. 6. éd. Paris, Bibliothèque Nationale, 1981. 2v. (xxiv,962p.; 963-1599[1]p). ISBN: 2717716009.

V.1 *Répertoire systématique des périodiques vivants;* v.2 *Index alphabétique des titres. Index alphabétique collectivités. Liste des périodiques disparus entre le 1er octobre 1968 et le 31 décembre 1976.*

....(*contd.*)

Earlier eds. cover 1956/57 (1958); 1957/60 (1961); 1960/63 (1964); 1963/66 (1968); 1966/71 (1973).

V.1 lists 20,399 titles current January 1977-March 1978 in modified UDC order with Bibliothèque Nationale press-marks and ISSN. *Class No:* 050(44)

[1750]

HATIN, E. Bibliographie historique et critique de la presse périodique française, ou Catalogue systématique et raisonné de tous les écrits périodiques de quelque valeur publiés ou ayant circulé en France depuis l'origine du journal jusqu'á nos jours. Paris, Firmin-Didot, 1866. cxxviii,660p.

Reprinted Paris, Ed. Anthropos, 1965.

Chronologically arranged, 1631-1865. Historical, descriptive and critical notes on *c.*5,000 journals. Title index. Partially replaced by Sgard (below).
Class No: 050(44)

[1751]

SGARD, J. Dictionnaire des journaux: 1600-1789. Paris, Universitas/Oxford, Voltaire Foundation, 1991. 2v. FFr1,500. ISBN: 2740000049.

Prelim. ed. *Bibliographique de la presse classique (1600-1789),* 1984.

Attempts coverage of all French language titles of the period. Periodical defined as publication with stable format and title, issued regularly and containing recent information. 1,267 entries (many more than Hatin (above) for the same period) alphabetically arranged by title. Very full detail including title changes, dates of publication, physical description, general contents analysis, name of founder, refrences in contemporary literature, citations to recent books/articles and locations (including British Library). V.2 provides indexing by collaborator, place of publication, printer/publisher, cited author, editor and contributor and date. *Class No:* 050(44)

Italy

[1752]

Bibliografia dei periodici del periodo fascista, 1922-1945: posseduti dalla biblioteca della Camera dei deputati. Gulli Pecenko, D. *and* Nasi Zitelli, L., *comps.* Roma, Camera dei deputati, 1983. 269p. L19,000.

Catalogue of 955 titles in all subjects held by the library of the Chamber of Deputies. Full entries, including bibliographical notes. Bibliography (p.211-25). Title arrangement with subject, personal name and organization indexes. *Class No:* 050(450)

[1753]

Bibliografia nazionale italiana: nuova serie del *Bollettino delle pubblicazioni italiane ricevute per diritto di stampa.* Periodici. Roma, Istituto centrale per il catalogo unico delle biblioteche italiane e per le informazioni bibliografiche, 1995-. Semi-annual. ISSN: 11250887.

New series of the Italian national bibliogaphy. DDC classified listing with responsible body/title and subject indexes. 798 serials recorded 1997. *Class No:* 050(450)

[1754]

Catálogo dei periodici italiani. Maini, R., *ed.* Milano, Editrice Bibliografica, 1981-. Irregular. L270,000

Succeeds *Elenco dei quotidiani e periodici italiani* (1974).

The 6. ed. (1996. xxii,1019p. ISBN: 8870754456) lists 13,566 titles A-Z current at 31 December 1995, with information on foundation date, frequency, circulation, editor, publisher, address, ISSN, price, etc. House organs, limited circulation titles, journals of educational institutions

.... *(contd.)*
and official bulletins excluded. Separate list by detailed subject headings (p.551-810). Indexed by place of publication, publisher, ISSN and titles ceased since previous ed. *Class No:* 050(450)

[1755]
ISTITUTO CENTRALE PER IL CATALOGO UNICO DELLE BIBLIOTECHE ITALIANE E PER LE INFORMAZIONI BIBLIOGRAFICHE. Periodici italiani 1968-1981. Roma, ICCU, 1983. 612p.

Based on titles received under legal deposit at the National Library, Florence. 10,872 numbered entries arranged alphabetically by title. Indexes of title changes, supplements, editors and organizations. *Class No:* 050(450)

[1756]
—CENTRO NAZIONALE PER IL CATALOGO UNICO DELLE BIBLIOTECHE ITALIANE E PER LE INFORMAZIONI BIBLIOGRAFICHE. Bibliografia nazionale italiana: periodici 1958-1967. Roma, ICCU, 1972. 229p. L.26,000.

Title and responsible body listing in one sequence.
Class No: 050(450)

[1757]
—ISTITUTO CENTRALE PER IL CATALOGO UNICO DELLE BIBLIOTECHE ITALIANE E PER LE INFORMAZIONI BIBLIOGRAFICHE. Periodici italiani 1886-1957. Roma, ICCU, 1980. 940p. L.72,800.

Reproduced from the *Catalogo cumulativo 1886-1957 del Bollettino delle pubblicazioni italiane ... (q.v.).*
Class No: 050(450)

Malta

[1758]
SAPIENZA, A.F. A Checklist of Maltese periodicals and newspapers in the National Library of Malta (formerly Royal Malta Library) and the University of Malta Library. Msida, Malta Univ. Press, 1977. *c.*350p.

Dates back to 1798 (*Le Journal de Malta*). Cut-off date end of 1973. 1,200 entries arranged A-Z by title giving frequency, date first published, place of publication, and last issue (if ceased). Some entries annotated. No indexes.
Class No: 050(458.2)

Spain

[1759]
Bibliografía española: publicaciones periódicas. Madrid, Biblioteca Nacional, 1979-. Frequency varies, now annual. Ptas2,000. ISSN: 11346620.

Part of the Spanish national bibliography. Current title from 1993, previously *Bibliografía española: suplemento de publicaciones periódicas* (ISSN: 02108372).

1995 issue (1996. viii,235p.) lists 3,444 new, changed or ceased titles by major UDC classes. Indexed by responsible body/personal author, title and ISSN. *Class No:* 050(460)

[1760]
CENTRE D'ESTUDIS HISTÒRIES INTERNACIONALS. Premsa clandestina i de l'exili (1939-1976): inventori de la col-lecció del C.E.H.I. Barcelona, C.E.H.I., 1977. 87p. ISBN: 8460009203.

Title list of 742 numbered entries. Index to publishing organizations p.81-87. *Class No:* 050(460)

[1761]
CENTRO DE INFORMACIÓN Y DOCUMENTACIÓN CIENTIFICA. Directorio de revistas españolas de ciencias sociales y humanas. 2. ed. Madrid, CINDOC, 1994. 284p. ISBN: 8400073932.

First published 1987.

Entries for 1,462 current periodicals A-Z by title with basic publication details only. Various indexes including broad subject, ISSN and publisher. *Class No:* 050(460)

[1762]
Periodicos y revistas españolas e hispanoamericanos. Barcelona, Centro de Investigaciones Literarias Españolas e Hispanoamericanos, 1989. 2v. ISBN: 8487411010.

Intended for biennial publication.

V.1 comprises an A-Z list of Spanish language serials, regardless of place of publication. Entry detail includes frequency, start date, price, contents, publisher/distributor, subjects and editorial personnel. V.2 provides a subject index, additional sections on Catalan, Basque and Galician titles and a listing of reference serials, directories etc.
Class No: 050(460)

[1763]
RUIZ DE GAUNA, A. Catálogo de publicaciones periódicas vascas de los siglos XIX y XX. San Sebastian, Eusko IkasKuntza, 1991. 710p., tables, maps. ISBN: 8487471277.

Lists 2,199 titles published in the Basque region, including those in Spanish. Title arrangement; chronological, place of publication, subject and responsible body indexing. Bibliography of sources (p.681-710). *Class No:* 050(460)

Portugal

[1764]
UNIVERSIDADE DE COIMBRA. Biblioteca Geral. **Publicações periódicas portuguesas** existentes na Biblioteca Geral da Universidade de Coimbra (1641-1910). Coimbra, Biblioteca Geral de Universidade, 1983. 318p. Esc.1,600. (*Catálogas e bibliografias, 1.*) ISBN: 9726161061.

Catalogue of 2,295 periodicals arranged alphabetically by title. Bibliographical citation only. Place and editor/ publisher/institutional body indexes.

Continued by *Publicações periódicas portuguesas existentes na Biblioteca Geral da Universidade de Coimbra (1911-1926).* (Biblioteca Geral..., 1991. 271p. (Catálogas e bibliografias, 7). ISBN: 972616009X). *Class No:* 050(469)

RSFSR

[1765]
ANDREEVA, W.F. *and* **MASKOVA, M.V. Russkaya periodicheskaya pechat'** ... Annotiravannyi ukazatel. Moskva, Kniga, 1977. 184p.

Supplements but does not replace *Obshchie bibliografii russkikh periodicheskikh izdanii, 1703-1954 ...*, (1956).

'The Russian periodical press (general and subject bibliographies 1703-1975). An annotated bibliography'. 318 entries. *Class No:* 050(470)

[1766]
BIBLIOTHÈQUE NATIONALE. (FRANCE). Département des Périodiques. **Catalogue collectif des périodiques conservés dans les bibliothèques de Paris** et dans les bibliothèques universitaires de France. Périodiques slaves en caractères cyrilliques. État des collections en 1950. Paris, Bibliothèque Nationale, 1956. 2v. FFr100.

.... *(contd.)*
A union list of 7,000 titles in 46 libraries.
- *Addenda et errata. État général des collections en 1960.* (Paris, 1965. 222p). *Class No:* 050(470)

[1767]
—BIBLIOTHÈQUE NATIONALE. (FRANCE). Catalogue des périodiques russes: des origines à 1970 conservés à la Bibliothèque Nationale. Paris, Bibliothèque Nationale, 1978. xii,550p. FFr50. ISBN: 2717713921.
2,300 entries. *Class No:* 050(470)

[1768]
Gazety SSSR 1917-1960: bibliograficheskii spravochnik. Moskva, Izdatel'stvo 'Kniga', 1970-84. 5v.
V.1 has entries for the periodical publications of Moscow, Leningrad and the capitals of Soviet republics. V.2-v.4 cover remaining Soviet cities in one A-Z title sequence. 12,875 numbered entries across the 4 volumes. V.5 provides place, subject and abbreviation indexes to v.2-v.4. V.1 has separate title, subject and abbreviation indexes. *Class No:* 050(470)

[1769]
Letopis' periodicheskikh i prodolzhainschihikhsia izdanii. 1971-. Moskva, Kniga, 1977-. Irregular, cumulations on a quinquennial basis. ISSN: 02016265.
'Record of periodical and serial publications'. Supersedes the annual *Letopis' periodicheskikh izdanii SSSR,* 1933-70, publication suspended 1940-45. Now issued in separate volumes for journals (*Zhurnaly* ISSN: 0206257), newspapers (*Gazety* ISSN: 0206389), collections (*Sborniki* ISSN as *Gazety*) and bulletins (*Biūlleteni* ISSN: 02016837).
The current listing. Full information for each title.
Class No: 050(470)

[1770]
LIBRARY OF CONGRESS. Half a century of Soviet serials, 1917-1968: a bibliography and union list of serials published in the U.S.S.R. Smits, R., *comp.* Washington, D.C., Library of Congress, 1968. 2v. (xv,860p.; xiii,861-1661p.).
Earlier ed., *Serial publications of the Soviet Union 1939-1957* (1958), included an English-language subject index.
29,761 entries (27,099 numbered items, plus interpolations), with over 28,000 cross-references. Locations in *c.*500 US and Canadian libraries. 'Included are all known serial publications appearing in the Soviet Union at regular or irregular intervals since 1917, in all except Oriental languages, such as Armenian, Georgian, Kirghiz, etc. These are included only if they have a Russian language title page and some contributions in Russian' (*Preface*).
Class No: 050(470)

[1771]
LISOVSKII, N.M. Bibliografiīā russkoi periodicheskoi pechati, 1703-1900 gg. (Materialy dlia istorii russkoi zhurnalistiki). Petrograd, 1915. xvi,1067p.
Also published 1915 as *Russkaia periodicheskaia pechat', 1703-1900 gg.,* plus tables. This ed. reprinted Bell & Howell, 1967.
'Bibliography of the Russian periodical press, 1703-1900: materials for the history of Russian journalism'. Lists 2,900 titles by date of foundation; indexed by subject (in 3 pts: St. Petersburg, Moscow and provincial periodicals) publishers and editors. *Class No:* 050(470)

[1772]
—Bibliografiīā periodicheskikh izdanni Rossii, 1901-1916. Barashenkova, V.M., *red.* Leningrad, Publichnaia Biblioteka, 1958-61. 3v. & index.
Lists 9,713 periodicals and newspapers with full bibliographical detail. *Class No:* 050(470)

[1773]
Periodicheskaia pechat' SSSR, 1917-1949: bibliograficheskii ukazatel'. Moskva, Vsesoiuznaia Knizhnaia Palata, 1955-63. 9v. in 10, & index.
A detailed and exhaustive bibliography, continuing Barashenkova (above), but excluding newspapers. Each v. is devoted to a specific subject field (*e.g.* v.1 (2pts): social sciences and history; v.2: natural sciences and mathematics; ... v.8: language, literature and art; v.9: publishing, library science and bibliography) and has its own title, languages (other than Russian), place of publication and publishing body indexes, cumulated in the final v. master index. Continued by the quinquennial cumulations of *Letopis' periodicheskikh izdanii SSSR* and its successors.
Class No: 050(470)

[1774]
Svodnyi katalog serialnykh izdanni Rossii, 1801-1825. Rebrieva, T.B. Sankt-Peterburg, Izd-vo Rossiiskoi natsionalnaīā biblioteki, 1997-. ISBN: 571960975x.
'Union catalogue of serials published in Russia 1801-1825'. V.1 *Zhurnaly A-V* (xii,844p.). *Class No:* 050(470)

Refugees

[1775]
OSSORGUINE-BAKOUNINE, T. L'Emigration russe en Europe: catalogue collectif des périodiques en langue russe. 2 éd. rev. et comp. Paris, Institut d'études slaves, 1981-90. 2v. (*Bibliothèque russe de l'Institut d'études slaves, v.50.*)
V.1: 1855-1940 (355p. ISBN: 2720402486); v.2: 1940-1970 (147p. ISBN: 2720401668). First published 1976-77, also in 2v., the latter covering to 1970 rather than 1979.
1,926 numbered entries. Bibliographical citations in Russian, notes, etc. in French.
Indexing for 45 titles is available in *L'Emigration russe: revues et recueils, 1920-1980: index général des articles (Gladkova, T. & Ossorguine-Bakounine, T. eds.* Paris, Institut d'études slaves, 1988. (Bibliothèque russe de Institut d'études slaves, v.81). 661p.). *Class No:* 050(470)-0054.7

Latvia

[1776]
EGLE, K., ***and others.*** **Latviešu periodika 1768-1940.** Riga, Zinātne, 1976-89. 3v. in 4. ISBN: 5796601288.
V.1 1768-1919; v.2-3 1920-40.
Title listing of 1,408 Latvian periodicals. V.2 contains revolutionary and Soviet titles, v.3(1) other titles (v.3(2) is an index). Further v. for 1940-45, issued 1995 (416p. ISBN: 9984538036), includes a supplement to v.1-3.
Class No: 050(474.3)

Lithuania

[1777]
Bibliografijos žinios: serialiniai leidiniai. Lietuvos valstybinés bibliogafijos rodyklé. [Bibliographical news: serials. Lithuanian national bibliographical index.] Vilnius, Lietuvos Nacionaliné Martyna Mažvyda Biblioteka, 1995-. Annual. ISSN: 13921754.

....*(contd.)*

Covers magazines, newspapers, research serials, collections and bulletins. 1996 issue (1997. 53p.) lists 858 titles *Class No:* 050(474.5)

[1778]

Lithuanian periodicals in American libraries: a union list. Balys, J., *comp.* Washington, D.C., Library of Congress, 1982. xi,125p. ISBN: 0844404012.

Includes titles in Lithuanian published outside Lithuania. 888 entries by title; place of publication index and subject guide. *Class No:* 050(474.5)

Finland

[1779]

KURIKKA, J. *and* **TAKKALA, M. Suomen aikakauslehdistön bibliografia 1782-1955.** [Bibliography of Finnish periodicals 1782-1955.] Helsinki, Helsingin yliopiston kirjastal, 1983. vii,463p. (*Helsingin yliopiston kirjaston julkaisuja, 47.*)

Introduction in Finnish, Swedish and English. Russian titles are separately listed. Excludes annuals, ephemera, mimeographed titles, foreign titles printed in Finland and Finnish language titles printed outside Finland. Arranged by latest title, giving previous title, publisher's name, date of first issue, frequency, whether indexed, special issues and supplements and editors' names. 4,156 numbered entries and 38 Russian titles. Indexes of publishers, editors.
Class No: 050(480)

[1780]

—TAKKALA, M., *and others.* Suomen aikakauslehdistön bibliografia 1956-1977. [Bibliography of Finnish periodicals 1956-1977.] Helsinki, Helsingin yliopiston kirjastol, 1986. v,632p. (*Helsingin yliopiston kirjaston julkaisuja, 48.*)

7,260 entries. Same scope and format as original v. (above). *Class No:* 050(480)

[1781]

KYTÖMÄKI, P., *and others.* **Suomalaiset ja yhteisophjoismaiset tieteelliset** kausijulkaisnt kansainvälisissä bibliografioissa ja viitetietokannoissa. [Finnish and internordic periodicals in international bibliographies and databases.] Oulu, Oulun Ylipisto, 1990. 118p. (*Oulun Ylipiston kirjaston julkaisnja, 21.*) ISBN: 9514228545.

Useful checklist indicating indexing sources for 468 Finnish and 79 internordic titles. *Class No:* 050(480)

Norway

[1782]

Norsk periodikafortegnelse. 1993-. [Norwegian list of serials.] Oslo, Universitetsbiblioteket i Oslo, 1995-. Annual. ISSN: 08053340.

Records new, ceased or changed titles. Data is available online in the *NORPER* database through the TRIP service, 15,000 records June 1997. The CD-ROM *Nasjonalbibliografiske data* also covers serial publications.

An additional printed source is *Norske tidsskrifter 1971/1983* [*Norwegian periodicals 1971-1983*] (Oslo, Universitetsbiblioteket i Oslo, 1994. vii,554p. ISBN: 8270002321). *Class No:* 050(481)

[1783]

Norske tidsskrifter: bibliografi over periodiski skrifter i Norge inntil 1920: kronologisk utgave. Oslo, Universitsbibliteket, 1984. xv,188p. facsims. ISBN: 82700001252.

Earlier ed., arranged by title, published 1940.

Chronological listing by year first published to 1920. Details include publication dates, notes on title changes, frequency and editors. 2,252 entries, 1,135 for the nineteenth century or earlier. Geographic and institution indexes. *Class No:* 050(481)

Sweden

[1784]

LUNDSTEDT, B.W. Sveriges periodiska litteratur. Bibliografi. Stockholm, Iduns Tryckeri, 1895-1902. 3v.

1. *Stockholm och landsorten, 1645-1812* (1895); 2. *Stockholm, 1813-1894* (1896); 3. *Landsorten, 1813-1899* (1902). Reprinted Stockholm, Redivina, 1969.

Includes newspapers. The final volume includes title, institution, pseudonym and subject indexes.
Class No: 050(485)

[1785]

Svensk periodicaförteckning: tidskrifter, årsböcker, dagstidningar och rapportserier. [Current Swedish periodicals.] Bibliografiska avdelningen vid Kungl. biblioteket. Stockholm, Tidningsaktiebolaget Svensk Bokhandl, 1968-. Triennial. Kr860. ISSN: 11041102.

Current title from 1994, previously *Svensk tidskriftsförteckning* (ISSN: 05860431).

From title change covers periodicals, newspapers, research reports and annuals. Excludes serials of a local or private nature. Arranged by title A-Z, with classified index.
Class No: 050(485)

Denmark

[1786]

Dansk periodicafortegnelse. 1976-85. [The Danish national bibliography: serials.] Ballerup, Bibliotekscentralens, 1990. cxxii,769p. ISBN: 8755218008.

Compiled by the Royal Library in conjunction with Bibliotekscentralens, the Danish Library Bureau. Vol. with same title covers 1970-75 (1977. 308p. ISBN: 8755204325). Earlier coverage in *Dansk tidsskriftfortegnelse* (below).

Includes newspapers, serial titles in book form and annuals. Entries in A-Z title arrangement, followed by UDC classed listing. Titles published in Danish outside Denmark also covered; separate listing of Greenlandic and Faroese serials. Records are also available as part of the Royal Library's *REX* database (Internet http://kb.dk.natbib/) and on CD-ROM. *Class No:* 050(489)

[1787]

Dansk tidsskriftfortegnelse. 1960-69. [The Danish national bibliography: periodicals. 1960-69.] København, Bibliotekscentralen, 1971. xvi,148p. ISBN: 8755200559.

About 4,000 entries in classified arrangement. Earlier eds. cover 1950-53 (1955) and 1954-59 (1962).
Class No: 050(489)

Iceland

[1788]

Íslensk tímarit í 200 ór: íslensk blöð og tímarit frá upphafi til 1973. [200 years of Icelandic periodicals: a bibliography of Icelandic newspapers and other serial publications 1773-1973.] Kvaran, B. *and* Sigurðosson, E., *comps*. Reykjavik, 1991 xx,205p. ISBN: 9979906758.

Earlier mimeographed ed. covering to 1966 published 1970.

Title listing with brief bibliographical details. Indexed by place of publication (p.163-205).

Supplemented by Baldursdottir, H. *Íslensk blöð og tímarit 1974-1993: skra um íslensk blöð og tímarit 1974-1993* (Reykjavik, Landsbókasafn Íslands, 1994. xii,502p. ISBN: 997980016X). *Class No:* 050(491.1)

Belgium

[1789]

Catalogus van Belgische en Luxemburgse periodiken. 6. uitg. Brussel, Nederlandse Kamer van Koophandel voor België en Luxemburg, 1988. 187p.

First published 1962.

Main listing A-Z by title; classified sequence under 114 headings. *Class No:* 050(493)

Switzerland

[1790]

BLASER, F. Bibliographie der schweizer Presse mit Einschluss des Fürstentums Liechtenstein. [Bibliographie de la presse suisse.] Basel, Birkhäuser Verlag, 1956-58. 2v. (*Quellen zur Schweizer Geschichte. N.F. Abt. 4: Handbücher, Bd. 7.1, 2.*)

A carefully compiled title-list of *c.*10,000 Swiss and Liechtenstein periodicals. Omits scientific and literary periodicals. Historical and bibliographical notes; locations in Swiss libraries. Chronological index; list of places of printing and of printing presses. *Class No:* 050(494)

[1791]

Schweizerische Zeitschriftenverzeichnis. 1951/55-. [Répertoire des périodiques suisses. 1951/55-.] Zurich, Des Schweizerischen Buchhändler- und Verleger- Verbandes, 1956-. Quinquennial. ISSN: 10128387.

Forms part of the Swiss national bibliography.

Lists all periodicals (but not newspapers) published during the five-year period; includes directories, annuals and more important federal, cantonal and municipal periodicals. Full information for each title including frequency, year of foundation, editor, format, price, ISSN and title changes. The 1991-95 v. (1996. ix,486p.), has 8,194 numbered entries in 24 major subject groups with title (p.429-486) and title keyword (5 microfiche) indexes. *Class No:* 050(494)

Yugoslavia

[1792]

Bibliografija Jugoslavije. Serijske publikacije. Beograd, Jugoslovenski Bibliografski Institut, 1956-. Annual. ISSN: 03500349.

Published as *Bibliografija Jugoslovenske periodike* 1956-74.

Series of the Yugloslav national bibliography. Lists current periodicals and newspapers. UDC classified arrangement. *Class No:* 050(497.1)

Bulgaria

[1793]

Bŭlgarski periodichen pechat: vestnitsī, spisaniīa biuletini i periodichni sbornitsī. Sofiīa, Narodna Biblioteka Kiril i Metodiĭ, 1965-. Annual. US$60. ISSN: 03239764.

'Bulgarian periodicals, newspapers, journals, bulletins and periodical collections'. Published as series 4 of the Bulgarian national bibliography.

The current list, giving data on number of issues published and new titles. *Class No:* 050(497.2)

[1794]

SPASOVA, M.V. Bŭlgarski periodichen pechat 1944-1969: bibliografski ukazatel. Sofiīa, Narodna Biblioteka Kiril i Metodiĭ, 1975. 3v.

Title list of 3,632 Bulgarian language and 225 foreign language periodicals published in Bulgaria during the period. Full information for each title, including exhaustive records of parts issued. V.3 contains an index and tables indicating years each title was published. *Class No:* 050(497.2)

[1795]

—Bŭlgarski periodichen pechat 1844-1944: anotiran bibliografski ukazatel. Ivanchev, D.P., *comp.* Sofiīa, Nauka ilzkustvo, 1962-69. 3v.

Companion volume to the above. Similar format, v.3 includes foreign language titles published in Bulgaria and an index. *Class No:* 050(497.2)

Rumania

[1796]

Publicaţiile periodice româneşti: ziare, gazete, reviste. Bucureşti, Editura Academiei Republicii Socialiste Româna, (previously Socec), 1913-.

3 volumes published to date. V.1 Catalog alfabetic, 1820-1906. (1913). V.2 Catalog alfabetic, 1907-1918. Supplement 1790-1906. (1969). 1919-1924 (1987).

The latest volume has 3,398 entries in title order for all periodicals published during the period. Very full information including notes on supplements, title changes etc. *Class No:* 050(498)

[1797]

RĂDUICĂ, G. *and* **RĂDUICĂ, N. Dicţionarul presei românesti:** 1731-1918. Bucureşti, Editura Stiintifica 1995. 552p. illus., plates. ISBN: 9734401238.

More titles than *Publicaţiile perodice româneşti* (above), but generally less full descriptions. Entries in A-Z title arrangement with name, place and year of publication indexes. English summary of contents; printed on poor quality paper. *Class No:* 050(498)

Asia—Far East

[1798]

BRITISH LIBRARY. Document Supply Centre. **Current Oriental serials.** Boston Spa, British Library Document Supply Centre, 1995. vp. ISBN: 071232139x.

Lists 3,392 titles published in Japan, China, Hong Kong, Korea and Taiwan. Includes serials published in English. The Document Supply Centre's files of current Chinese and Japanese serials are also available in PDF format from the British Library through http://portico.bl.uk/. A further printed listing of Japanese titles, *Current Japanese serials* (*q.v.*), issued 1997. *Class No:* 050(51/52+57)

China

[1799]

CHINA LIBRARY GROUP. Chinese union list of serials. [London], British Library Oriental Collections, 1992. Unpaged.

No frills computer produced list of titles held by UK libraries. Entries, under transliterated title, include reasonably full holdings data. *Class No:* 050(510)

[1800]

China press and publicity directory 1985. Guo-Gan, G., *and others eds*. Beijing, Modern Press; London, Longman, 1985. (Distr. by Gale in North America). xxxix,360p. ISBN: 058297819x.

Lists 1,682 periodicals and newspapers under 21 subject headings. Gives title in English and Chinese (transliterated and phonetic alphabet), frequency, year founded, names of editorial board, publisher's address, overseas distributor, 1983 circulation and brief description. Further sections on 'Publishers', 296 entries regionally arranged and 'Booksellers', 375 entries, including foreign language bookstores. Each section separately indexed.
Class No: 050(510)

[1801]

Chinese periodicals in the Library of Congress. Huang, H.C., *comp*. Washington D.C., Library of Congress, 1978. 521p. $39. ISBN: 0844402222.

Romanized title (modified Wade-Giles) listing of 6,400 titles, in all subjects, issued during the period 1868-1975 held by the Orientalia Division. Gives Chinese title, place of publication, issuing body, frequency and Library of Congress holdings. *Class No:* 050(510)

[1802]

CONTEMPORARY CHINA INSTITUTE. A Bibliography of Chinese newspapers and periodicals in European libraries. London, Cambridge University Press, 1975. viii,1025p. (*Contemporary China Institute publications.*) ISBN: 0521209501.

Covers over 100 libraries including those in the former Soviet Union and Eastern Europe. UK libraries include the British Museum (British Library), the university libraries of Cambridge, Durham, Edinburgh and Leeds, and SOAS. Arranged alphabetically by romanized title. Entries give title in Chinese characters, place of publication, editor, publisher, dates, frequency and notes. Cut off date 1972.
Class No: 050(510)

[1803]

TUNG, J. Bibliography of Chinese academic serials, pre-1949: material in the Hoover Institution on War, Revolution and Peace. Stanford, Ca., Hoover Institution, 1982. v,107p. ISBN: 0871926624.

Lists holdings of the Hoover Institution's East Asian Collection. Romanized Wades-Giles alphabetical arrangement, bibliographical data in Chinese characters. Includes many titles unique outside China. Tung has also produced *Bibliography of Chinese government serials, 1800-1949* (Hoover Inst., 1979. 136p. ISBN: 0817942424).
Class No: 050(510)

Hong Kong

[1804]

KAN, L-B. *and* **CHU, G.H.L. Serials of Hong Kong 1845-1979.** Hong Kong, Chinese University of Hong Kong, 1981. x,186p. (*University library bibliographical series, no.4.*)

1,966 numbered entries, (55% Chinese language publications, titles transliterated), giving frequency, Chinese

.... (contd.)

title, publisher, dates and brief notes. Broad heading subject index and Chinese title index. Newspapers excluded, covered in *Newspapers of Hong Kong* (*q.v.*). For official serials see *An Annotated guide to serial publications of the Hong Kong government* (*q.v.*). *Class No:* 050(512.317)

Korea

[1805]

Standortkatalog koreanischer Zeitschriften in Europa. Adami, N.R., *ed.* Berlin, Staatsbibliothek Prussischer Kulturbesitz, 1981-87. 2v. ISBN: 3880530327.

Ed. by N.R. Adami for the Association of Korean Studies in Europe. Lfg.1 1981; Lfg.2-3 1987.

A union catalogue of Korean periodicals in European libraries. Arranged A-Z by transliterated title. German introduction. British libraries represented include the British Library, School of Oriental and African studies, Cambridge University, Oriental Institute Oxford and Durham University. *Class No:* 050(519)

[1806]

Union list of Korean serials in East Asian libraries in the United States. Choo, Y.K., *comp*. Ann Arbor, Association for Asian Studies, 1994. 263p. $20. ISBN: 0924304219.

Covers 10 major collections including the Library of Congress and Harvard Yenching Library. Entries, with Korean and transliterated title, include holdings data. Newspapers and some recent titles omitted.
Class No: 050(519)

Japan

[1807]

BRITISH LIBRARY. Document Supply Centre. **Current Japanese serials.** Bangerter, N. *and* Brittain, H., *comps. & eds*. Boston Spa, British Library Document Supply Centre, 1997. vp.

Lists more than 2,400 serials received at 30th June 1997. Also Internet accessible as a PDF file through the British Library WWW pages at http://portico.bl.uk/.
Class No: 050(52)

[1808]

CARNELL, P.W. Check-list of Japanese periodicals held in British university and research libraries. 2nd ed. Sheffield, Sheffield University Library, 1976-77. 2v. ISBN: 090328412x.

Pt.1: *Japanese titles.* (1976 (2), v,305p.). Pt.2: *Index of Western-language sub-titles and subject index.* (1977 (2), i,60,i,61p.).

Supplement No. 1 (1978 i,81,(25)p.).

1st ed. (1v.) 1971, by S.M. Mandahl and P.W. Carnell.

Pt.1 arranged A-Z by transliterated title.
Class No: 050(52)

[1809]

Japanese periodicals and newspapers in Western languages: an international union list. London, Mansell, 1979. xxviii,235p. ISBN: 0720109345.

Holdings of *c.*800 US, British, Canadian and Japanese libraries. 3,500 titles. Compiled from other lists *e.g. New serial titles; British union catalogue of periodicals.* About 220 British libraries covered. *Class No:* 050(52)

[1810]
National union list of current Japanese serials in East Asian libraries of North America. Makino, Y. *and* Miki, M., *comps*. Association for Asian Studies Committee on East Asian Libraries Subcommittee on Japanese Materials, 1992. 485p.

Basic holdings list for 32 US and Canadian libraries arranged by transliterated title. Entries include foundation date, frequency and English translation of title. No indexes. An earlier list, *Current Japanese serials in the humanities and social sciences received in American libraries* (Bloomington, Indiana Univ. Library, 1980) covered 58 libraries. *Class No:* 050(52)

[1811]
Zasshi shinbun sōkatarogu. [Periodicals in print.] Tokyo, Media Research Center, 1979-. Annual.

The standard directory of current Japanese periodicals. The 1996 ed. lists 20,142 titles, including newspapers, under *c.*275 subject categories. Publisher and title indexes. Also available on CD-ROM. *Class No:* 050(52)

Asia—Middle & Near East

[1812]
AHMED-BIOUD, A. 3200 revues et journaux arabes de 1800 à 1965: titres arabes et titres translittéres. Paris, Bibliothèque Nationale, 1969. 252p.

Published with the assistance of the French National Commission of UNESCO.

Entry is under the Arabic title followed by romanized form. Data: first year and place of publication; type of information supplied (*e.g.* social or political questions; general subjects; medical review). *Class No:* 050(53+56)

[1813]
AMAN, M.M. Arab periodicals and serials: a subject bibliography. Garland, New York and London, 1979. x,252p. ISBN: 0824098161.

A guide to current and ceased titles published in Arabic, English, French and other European languages in Arab countries and the Western hemisphere. 2,711 unannotated, numbered entries arranged in 52 subject categories. All entries in roman script (Arabic titles transliterated). No title or geographic index. *Class No:* 050(53+56)

[1814]
ATABAKI, T. *and* **RUSTAMOVA-TOWHIDI, S. Baku documents:** union catalogue of Persian, Azerbaijani, Ottoman Turkish and Arabic serials and newspapers in the libraries of the Republic of Azerbaijan. London, Tauris Academic Studies, 1995. xiv,332p. £50;$75. ISBN: 1850438366.

Data on 1,040 serials in 16 languages. Title arrangement with language, place of publication and 'specialization' (broad topic) indexing. *Class No:* 050(53+56)

[1815]
Guide to current Gulf periodicals: newspapers, magazines, bulletins in the Arab Gulf states. Arab Gulf States Information Documentation Center, *and others comps*. Baghdad, Arab Gulf States Information Documentation Center, etc., 1988. vp.

Title also in Arabic; text in Arabic. Updates a number of earlier publications.

771 entries for periodicals published in Bahrain, Kuwait, Iraq, Oman, Qatar, Saudi Arabia and United Arab Emirates. *Class No:* 050(53+56)

[1816]
Union catalogue of Arabic serials and newspapers in British libraries. Auchterlonie, P. *and* Safadi, Y., *eds*. London, Mansell, 1977. xvi,146,(2)p. ISBN: 0720106362.

Sponsored by the Middle East Libraries Committee.

About 1,000 entries A-Z by Arabic title (word by word in Library of Congress transliteration scheme), and by translated title. Entries give place of publication, frequency, first and last dates of issue, languages, locations and holdings and variant titles. Indexes in transliteration and Arabic script. *Class No:* 050(53+56)

Asia—South & South East

[1817]
The Bibliography of South Asian periodicals: a union-list of periodicals in South Asian languages. Shaw, G.W. *and* Quaraishi, S., *comps*. Brighton, Harvester Press, 1982. xii,135p. ISBN: 0710804709.

Union list of serials, in or partially in, South Asian languages held by the British Library, Bodleian, Cambridge University, Durham University, India Office and the School of African and Asian Studies. Geographic coverage is for India, Pakistan, Bangladesh, Nepal, Bhutan, Sikkim and Afghanistan. A few titles published outside these states, (*e.g.* Urdu newspapers published in Great Britain), are also included. Arranged in 32 language sections, all entries in roman script. Lacks title or other indexes.
Class No: 050(54+59)

India

[1818]
Directory of periodicals published in India. 1991. Kaur, S. *and* Sapra, P., *comps*. 2nd ed. New Delhi, Sapra and Sapra, 1991. xxvii,515p.

1st ed. 1988.

Lists *c.*7,200 current titles (2,000 new in this ed.), excluding irregularly published items, newspapers, house organs and annual reports. Includes titles in Indian languages other than English (*c.*40% of total). Classified arrangement, entries give ISSN, publisher and address, frequency, foundation date, previous titles and subject annotation. Separate listing 'Status of unknown/unconfirmed titles'. Title index. *Class No:* 050(540)

[1819]
KUMAR, R.P. Research periodicals of colonial India 1780-1947. Delhi, Academic Publications, 1985. viii,230p. (*Academic series in library and information science, v.2.*)

'Bibliographical census' of titles published during the period with dates (p.30-136). Followed by discussion of contents, publishing history and scholarly significance of titles in chapters: religion and philosophy, sciences, social sciences, Indology and Orientalia. Coverage mostly of English language publications. Bibliography (p.219-24); inadequate index (p.225-30). *Class No:* 050(540)

[1820]
TULIP: the universal/union list of Indian periodicals. Nagar, M.L. *and* Nagar, S.D., *project directors*. Columbia, Mo., International Library Center, 1986-91. ISBN: 0943913039.

V.1-8 titles; v.9-10 subject index.

Catalogue of titles published to 1980 based on the holdings of Indian, US and British research libraries. Computer produced, full information for each entry, about 10,000 titles recorded. Subject indexing under detailed headings. '(A)

.... *(contd.)*
remarkable bibliographic effort and an indispensable tool for serious scholars of India' (*American reference books annual*, v.20, 1989, p.30-31). *Class No:* 050(540)

Pakistan

[1821]
HASSAN, M. Pakistani serials: a bibliographic control list. [Islamabad], M. Hassan; Rawalpindi, Federal Book Corp., 1990. xvi,290p.

Comprehensive guide to Pakistani serials. Indexed. *Class No:* 050(549)

Iran

[1822]
Rāhnamā-yi Majalbh-hāyi Irān. [Directory of Iranian periodicals.] Tehran, National Library of the Islamic Republic of Iran, 1969-. Irregular. ISSN: 00849960.

Title varies.

Includes a limited number of English and other foreign language titles in a separate section. *Class No:* 050(55)

[1823]
Union catalogue of Persian serials and newspapers in British libraries. Sims-Williams, U., *ed.* London, Ithaca Press, 1985. xv,149p. ISBN: 0863720390.

At head of title: Middle East Libraries Committee.

Locates titles, including those only partially in Persian, or in Dari or Tajik, in British libraries. 640 numbered entries arranged alphabetically by title. Holdings data for 16 libraries with basic bibliographical detail including changed and variant titles, notes on supplements and indexes. Bibliography (p.141-2). Chronological and responsible institution indexes. *Class No:* 050(55)

Turkey

[1824]
Periodicals in Turkish and Turkic languages: a union list of holdings in UK libraries. Waley, M.S., *ed.* Oxford, Middle East Libraries Committee, 1993. 95p. £20. ISBN: 0948889063.

Covers 'periodicals and newspapers wholly or partly in modern and Ottoman Turkish and in other languages of the Turkic group regardless of country or date'. *c.*1,200 records based on 11 collections. Title arrangement; no indexes. *Class No:* 050(560)

Israel

[1825]
TRONIK, R. Israeli periodicals and serials in English and other European languages: a classified bibliography. Metuchen, N.J., Scarecrow Press, 1974. xiii,193p. ISBN: 0810806827.

Entries for 1,100 titles published since the establishment of Israel as a state. Includes periodicals published in French, German, Spanish, Italian and Portuguese as well as English. Title index.

A supplement was published in *Serials librarian*, v.4(4), Summer 1980, p.427-62. Further updating also provided by Brown, M. *Directory of Israeli English-language periodicals* (Kiryat Shmonah, Israel Book Bulletin Publications, 1986. 42p.) which lists 172 predominantly science and technology titles. *Class No:* 050(569.4)

Jordan

[1826]
Directory of Jordanian periodicals. Elayyan, R. *and* Ajamieh, Y.A., *comps.* Amman, Jordan Library Association, 1982. v.p. (*JLA publications, 7.*)

Separate lists of 304 Arabic and 38 English titles each with a subject index. *Class No:* 050(569.5)

Asia—South East

[1827]
Southeast Asian periodicals: an international union list. Nunn, G.R., *comp.* London, Mansell, 1977. xxiii,456p. ISBN: 0720107253.

Lists 26,000 periodicals published 1800-1975. Excludes newspapers, but includes government serials. Arranged A-Z by title within country of publication sections. Locations for South East Asian, European and North American libraries. *Class No:* 050(59)

[1828]
—MOON, B.E. Periodicals for South-East Asian studies: a union catalogue of holdings in British and selected European libraries. London, Mansell, 1979. xix,610p. £80;$140. ISBN: 072010730x.

Includes many titles published in South East Asia. Gives more British locations than Nunn (above). Entries in title order A-Z with basic bibliographical detail. Lacks indication of publication frequency or a subject index. *Class No:* 050(59)

Malaysia

[1829]
ROFF, W.R. Bibliography of Malay and Arabic periodicals published in the Straits Settlements and Peninsular Malay States, 1876-1941: with an annotated list of holdings in Malaysia, Singapore and the United Kingdom. London, Oxford University Press, 1972. [vii],74p. £10. (*London oriental bibliographies, v.3.*) ISBN: 0197135722.

Rev. ed. of the same author's *Guide to Malaysian periodicals, 1876-1941* (Singapore, 1961).

Chronologically arranged with title and name indexes. Includes microfilm holdings. Bibliography (p.65-66). *Class No:* 050(595)

Singapore

[1830]
A List of Singapore periodicals in Chinese held by the Department of Oriental Manuscripts and Printed Books the British Library. Chng, D.Y.K., *comp.* New ed. Singapore, National Library, 1987. 60p.

Bibliographical data in English. Includes holdings details. *Class No:* 050(595.13)

Africa

[1831]
The African book world and press directory. [Répertoire du livre et de la presse en Afrique.] Zell, H.M., *ed.* 4th ed. London, Zell, 1989. xxi,306p. £75;$135. ISBN: 0905450507.

1st ed. 1977; 3rd ed. 1983.

Deals with 51 African states. Information presented by country A-Z in 11 sections including, 'Periodicals and

.... *(contd.)*
magazines' and 'Major newspapers'. Appendix: 'African news agencies'. Subject index to periodicals and magazines. *Class No:* 050(6)

[1832]

Periodicals from Africa: a bibliography and union list of periodicals published in Africa. Travis, C. *and* Alman, M., *comps.* Boston, Mass., G.K. Hall, 1977. xvii,619p. £62.50. *(Bibliographies and guides in African studies.)* ISBN: 0816179468.

At head of title: Standing Conference on Library Materials on Africa.

Aims to provide 'as comprehensive list as possible of periodical titles published in Africa ... and give locations for those titles held in libraries in the United Kingdom' (p.ix). 17,000 entries; 60 UK locations. Wide definition of periodicals including bulletins, annuals, non-commercial newspapers, transactions and proceedings. Excludes daily newspapers, government departmental reports and publishers' series. Entries in country sections A-Z, Egypt excluded. Coverage for South Africa partial in that only periodicals held in UK libraries included. Entries corrected up to October 1975. Title index, but no index of languages or subjects. The most extensive bibliography of African periodicals published.

A *First supplement* (Blake, D. & Travis, C. *comps.* 1984. xvii,217p. ISBN: 0816185255) adds a further 7,000 entries for omissions and new titles to 1979. *Class No:* 050(6)

[1833]

THOMASSERY, M. Catalogue des périodiques d'Afrique noire francophone (1858-1962) conserveés à l'IFAN. Dakar, IFAN, 1965. 117p. *(Institut Français d'Afrique Noire. Catalogues et documents, 19.)*

884 titles, A-Z. Details of issuing body, frequency, size, form of publication and IFAN holdings. Indexes of location and subject, publishing bodies, editors, etc. as well as a chronological index. *Class No:* 050(6)

Tunisia

[1834]

HAMDANE, M. Guide des périodiques parus en Tunisie: de 1838 au 20 mars 1956. Tunis, Fondation Nationale pour la Traduction l'Etablissement des textes et les Etudes, 1989. 2v. ISBN: 9973911318.

Title also in Arabic. V.1 covers Arabic titles, v.2 those published in European languages. Periodicals issued after independence are listed in the same author's *Guide des périodiques parus en Tunisie de l'indépendance à 1993* (Tunis, Centre du Documentation Nationale, 1994. 2v. ISBN: 9973915550). *Class No:* 050(611)

Senegal

[1835]

BOUSCARLE, M-E. Les Publications en série éditées au Sénégal 1856-1982: liste provisoire. Paris, Bibliothèque Nationale, 1987. viii,107p. *(Etudes, guides et inventaires, no.7.)* ISBN: 2717717587.

692 entries for titles held by the Bibliothèque Nationale (Paris). *Class No:* 050(663)

Nigeria

[1836]

IBADAN UNIVERSITY. Library. **Nigerian periodicals and newspapers 1950-1970:** a list of those received by Ibadan University under the country's various deposit legislations from April 1950 to June 1970. Ibadan, Ibadan University Press, 1971. v,122p.

Supplement 1971-74 (1975). *Class No:* 050(669)

Africa—East & Equatorial

[1837]

LIBRARY OF CONGRESS. Library of Congress Office, Nairobi. **Accessions list Eastern and Southern Africa: serials supplement.** Nairobi, Library of Congress Office, 1968-. Biennial. ISSN: 10743820.

Annual until 1995/96. Present title from 1993, previously *Accession list Eastern Africa...* . Supplement to *Accessions list Eastern and Southern Africa (q.v.).*

Provides full Library of Congress records for titles currently received by the Nairobi Office. *Class No:* 050(67)

Kenya

[1838]

Kenyan periodicals directory. Nairobi, Kenya National Library Service, National Reference and Bibliographic Department, 1984-. Biennial (irregular).

Intended for biennial publication, but 1984 (ix,55p.) appears to be only volume issued.

Lists *c.*420 titles including newspapers and foreign serials relating to Kenya. A further source is *Union list of periodicals in Kenyan libraries* ([Nairobi], Univ. of Nairobi Library, 1993. vi,389p.). *Class No:* 050(676.2)

Mozambique

[1839]

ROCHA, I. Catálogo dos periódicos e principais seriados de Moçambique: da introdução de tipografia à independência (1854-1975). Lisboa, Edições 70, 1985. 175p., plates.

Entries for 1,000 titles. Subject, name, place and language, (other than Portuguese), indexes.
Class No: 050(679)

South Africa

[1840]

South African periodical publications, 1800-1875: a bibliography. Saul, C.D., *comp.* Cape Town, Univ. School of Librarianship, 1949. 45p.

Excludes newspapers, government publications and certain annuals. Locates copies in South African libraries.
Class No: 050(680)

[1841]

SWITZER, L. *and* SWITZER, D. The Black press in South Africa and Lesotho: a descriptive bibliographic guide to African, coloured and Indian newspapers, newsletters and magazines, 1836-1976. Boston, G.K. Hall, 1979. xix,307p. *(Bibliographies and guides in African studies.)* ISBN: 0816181748.

Covers serial publications 'directed at or intended for' (*Introduction* p.vii) a non-white audience. 712 numbered entries giving title with English translation, dates, frequency, brief description and history and locations in South African libraries. Comprehensive, including official and semi-

.... *(contd.)*
official, political, religious, student, teacher, special and general interest publications. *c.*175 item bibliography of secondary sources (p.279-90). *Class No:* 050(680)

Zimbabwe

[1842]
BARRY, P. Zimbabwe periodicals: a bibliography. Harare, National Archives, 1988. 56p. (*National Archives bibliographies series, no. 4.*)
Classified list of 571 titles including official serial publications. *Class No:* 050(689.1)

Canada

[1843]
Canadian serials directory. [Répertoire des publications sériés canadiennes.] Ripley, G., *ed.* 3rd ed. Toronto, Reference Press, 1987. 396p. ISBN: 0919981100.
First published 1972; 2nd ed. 1977.
Lists about 4,000 current Canadian periodicals, magazines, newsletters, daily newspapers, annuals, proceedings, etc. Full detail given, including editor, publisher, address, former title(s), type of publication, format, pagination, date of first issue, where indexed, whether advertising accepted, circulation, ISSN and price. French language titles described in French. Separate list of titles by subject headings (p.265-318); publisher and sponsor index. A 4th ed. is scheduled for publication November 1998 (Can$55. ISBN: 091998133X). *Class No:* 050(71)

[1844]
Checklist of Canadian ethnic serials. Bogusis, R., *comp.* Ottawa, National Library of Canada, Newspaper Division, Public Services Branch, 1981. viii,381p. Can$50.
3,000 entries for newspapers, periodicals, church bulletins, directories, almanacs, yearbooks and conference proceedings. Arranged by ethnic group with title index. Locates titles in Canadian and foreign libraries.
Class No: 050(71)

Quebec

[1845]
BEAULIEU, A., ***and others*****. La Presse québécoise des origines à nos jours.** 2. ed. Québec, Presse de l'Université Laval, 1973-90. 10v. ISBN: 0774666587.
V.1 1764-1859; v.2 1860-1879; v.3 1880-1895; v.4 1896-1910; v.5 1911-1919; v.6 1920-1934; v.7 1935-1944; v.8 1945-1954; v.9 1955-1963; v.10 1964-1975.
1st ed. as *Les Journaux de Québec de 1764 à 1964.* (Québec, Presse de l'Université Laval, 1965. 329p.).
A comprehensive survey of 6,200 periodicals published in Quebec, including English language titles, arranged chronologically. Details for each title include dates and place of publication, circulation, proprietor and extensive publishing history. Locations for Quebec and Ontario libraries. Indexes, including title, in each volume; cumulative index to v.1-7 1987. *Class No:* 050(714)

Mexico

[1846]
Catálogo general de publicaciones periódicas mexicanas. Mexico, DIRSA, 1984-. Annual (irregular). ISSN: 01855573.
Directory of current Mexican periodicals including yearbooks and CD-ROMs. 1993 issue (250p.) lists *c.*3,900 titles in classified order, entries with price and ISSN. Title and geographic indexes. *Class No:* 050(72)

Caribbean

[1847]
Current Caribbean periodicals and newspapers: a guide for the English-speaking region. Evelyn, S., *comp.* St. Augustine, Trinidad, Assoc. of Caribbean Univ. Research and Institutional Libraries, 1988. xi,88p.
Developed as a source tool for *CARINDEX* (*q.v.*). 1,048 entries, including discontinued titles that began publication after 1962. UDC classed arrangement with title, subject and country indexes. *Class No:* 050(729)

Cuba

[1848]
BIBLIOTECA NACIONAL JOSE MARTI. Catálogo de publicaciones periódicas cubanas de los siglos XVIII y XIX. La Habana, Departamento Coleccion Cubana Biblioteca Nacional Jose Marti, 1965. 246p.
716 entries; chronological, place and subject indexes.
Class No: 050(729.1)

[1849]
A Survey of Cuban revistas, 1902-1958. Esquenazi-Mayo, R., *comp.* Washington, D.C., Library of Congress, 1993. xxii,112p. ISBN: 0844407585.
Lists 558 titles, with 122 held by the Library of Congress given detailed treatment. Bibliography of 102 items; indexed. *Class No:* 050(729.1)

Latin America

[1850]
COVINGTON, P.H. Indexed journals: a guide to Latin American serials. Madison, Wi., Seminar on the Acquisition of Latin American Library Materials, 1983. iv,458p. (*SALALM bibliography series, no.8.*)
'This guide consists of (1) a description and evaluation by discipline of the principal indexes and abstracts which cover journals published in or relating to Latin America and (2) a list of these journals with an indication of those indexes and abstracts in which each is covered' (Preface p.iii). Covers *c.*100 indexes and abstracts and *c.*1,500 journal titles. Also contains a subject classification of journals by 23 subject headings. *Class No:* 050(729.99)

[1851]
LA PLATA. UNIVERSIDAD NACIONAL. Biblioteca. **Catálogo de periódicos sudamericanos** existentes en la Biblioteca Pública de la Universidad, 1791-1861. La Plata, 1934. xi,231p.
An annotated, A-Z title list of 522 periodicals published in Argentina, Bolivia, Brazil, Chile, Colombia, Ecuador, Paraguay, Peru and Uruguay. Chronological list follows, with geographical index and index of editors etc.
Class No: 050(729.99)

[1852]

Periodicos y revistas españolas e hispanoamericanos. Barcelona, Centro de Investigaciones Literarias Españolas e Hispanoamericanos, 1989. 2v. ISBN: 8487411010.

V.1 comprises an A-Z list of Spanish language serials, regardless of place of publication. Entry detail includes frequency, start date, price, contents, publisher/distributor, subjects and editorial personnel. V.2 includes a subject index and a listing of reference serials, etc. A welcome addition to the ranks of periodical directories, especially valuable for its coverage of Latin American titles. *Class No:* 050(729.99)

[1853]

Serial publications available by exchange: Spanish South America. Sonntag, G., *comp. & ed.* Albuquerque, N.M., SALALM Secretariat, General Library, Univ. of New Mexico, 1995. vii,182p. $22.00. (*SALALM bibliography and reference series, 37.*) ISBN: 0917617460.

Companion titles are: *Latin American serial publications available by exchange: Mexico, Central America and Panama* (Miller, S. *comp.* SALALM Secretariat, 1992. 86p. ISBN: 091761290) and *Serial publications available by exchange: Caribbean area* (Miller, S. & Sonntag-Grigera, G. *comps. & eds.* SALALM Secretariat, 1994. vii,48p. $19.50. ISBN: 0917617452). *Class No:* 050(729.99)

USA

[1854]

Association periodicals: a directory of publications issued on a continuing basis by all types of national nonprofit membership organizations of the United States. Allard, D.M. *and* Thomas, R.C., *eds.* Detroit, Gale, 1988. 3v. ISBN: 0810320827.

V.1 *Business, finance, industry and trade;* v.2 *Science, medicine and technology;* v.3 *Social sciences, education and humanities.* Published as a supplement to the *Encyclopedia of associations* (*q.v.*).

Lists 10,811 titles in subject sections. Periodicals broadly defined. Indexes in each v., cumulated in v.3.
Class No: 050(73)

[1855]

—Corporate magazines of the United States. Riley, S.G., *ed.* Westport, Conn., Greenwood Press, 1992. xiii,281p. £71.55;$79.50. (*Historical guides to the world's periodicals and newspapers.*) ISBN: 0313275696.

Detailed entries for 51 titles A-Z giving history, locations, etc. Appended list of other magazines not profiled.
Class No: 050(73)

[1856]

—Trade, industrial and professional periodicals of the United States. Endres, K.L., *ed.* Westport, Conn., Greenwood Press, 1994. ix,467p. £89.50;$105. (*Historical guides to the world's periodicals and newspapers.*) ISBN: 0313280428.

3-15p. profiles of 66 titles chosen for their 'historical importance, dominance in the field and editorial excellence'. '(C)ontains such a motley assortment of titles ... difficult to think of uses for it in most reference collections' (*Choice*, v.32(3), November 1994, p.438). *Class No:* 050(73)

[1857]

EDGAR, N.L. A History and bibliography of American magazines 1810-1820. Metuchen, N.J., Scarecrow, 1975. v,379p. ISBN: 0810808218.

The history section of 4 chapters is followed by a detailed bibliography (p.85-258) listing 223 titles A-Z with full bibliographical detail and annotations. Chronological listing (p.294-308); register of printers, publishers, editors and engravers. Select bibliography (p.355-69). Index.
Class No: 050(73)

[1858]

Encyclopedic directory of ethnic newspapers and periodicals in the United States. Wynar, L.R. *and* Wynar, A.T., *eds.* 2nd ed. Littleton. Co., Libraries Unlimited, 1976. 256p. ISBN: 0872871541.

1st ed. 1972.

Survey based directory of 977 publications from 63 ethnic groups, arranged in 51 sections. Each section sub-divided into native language (and bi-lingual) and English language listings. Full bibliographical data for each entry with English translation of title and note on objective and scope. Statistical appendix; title index. Partially updated by:-
Class No: 050(73)

[1859]

—Ethnic periodicals in contemporary America: an annotated guide. Ireland, S.L.J., *comp.* Westport, Conn., Greenwood Press, 1990. xvi,222p. £40.50;$49.50. (*Bibliographies and indexes in ethnic studies, no.3.*) ISBN: 0313268177.

Questionnaire based guide to 290 magazines and newspapers. Arranged by ethnic group giving basic directory details and a short description. Because of the limited number of entries, must be seen as a supplement rather than a replacement for Wynar (above).
Class No: 050(73)

[1860]

HOORNSTRA, J. *and* **HEATH, T. American periodicals 1741-1900:** an index to the microfilm collections: *American periodicals, 18th century; American periodicals, 1800-1850; American periodicals, 1850-1900, Civil War and Reconstruction.* Ann Arbor, University Microfilms International, 1979. xv,341p. $75. ISBN: 0835603746.

Cumulative index to respectively 88, 923 and 117 titles in the three collections. Main index by title (p.1-230) including full bibliographical information; briefer indexes by subject, editor and reel no. *Class No:* 050(73)

[1861]

Index to city and regional magazines of the United States. Riley, S.G. *and* Selnow, G.W., *comps.* Westport, Conn., Greenwood Press, 1989. [ix],130p. tables. £38.75;$42.95. (*Historical guides to the world's periodicals and newspapers.*) ISBN: 0313268401.

Lists nearly 1,000 general interest titles published during the period 1950-88. Main sequence A—Z by title gives dates, magazine type, frequency, etc. and OCLC derived holdings data. Separate chronological and geographic (state) listings. Appendix of *c.*500 titles published before 1950.

Companion v. by the same compilers *Regional interest magazines of the United States* (Greenwood Press, 1991. xiii,418p. £85.50;$99.50. ISBN: 0313268401) contains detailed profiles of 86 titles. *Class No:* 050(73)

[1862]

MOTT, F.L. A History of American magazines. Cambridge, Mass., Belknap Press of Harvard Univ. Press, 1930-68. 5v. illus., ports., facsims. ISBN: 0674395506, v.1.

Available from Books on Demand, approx. $180 per v.

V.1: 1741-1850; v.2: 1850-1865; v.3: 1865-1885; v.4: 1885-1905; v.5: 1905-1930.

A full, well-documented survey, the 5v. containing sketches of 229 important magazines. V.5, which deals with 21 magazines A-Z, beginning with *The American mercury* and ending with *The Yale review*, includes a cumulative index to all 5v. (p.353-595). *Class No:* 050(73)

[1863]

—American mass-market magazines. Nourie, A. *and* Nourie, B., *eds*. Westport, Conn., Greenwood Press, 1990. x,611p. £85.50;$99.50. (*Historical guides to the world's periodicals and newspapers*.) ISBN: 0313252548.

Profiles of 2-6p. for 106 titles published from the 18th century to the present. Wide range of titles covered *e.g. Harpers, Mother earth news, National enquirer, Rolling stone, Sports illustrated*. '(M)any more recent titles than Mott, and a more general scope than other titles, this work will be of value to most larger libraries' (*RQ*, v.30(3), Spring 1991, p.411). *Class No:* 050(73)

[1864]

—TEBBEL, J. *and* ZUCKERMAN, M.E. The Magazine in America 1741-1990. New York, Oxford Univ. P., 1991. viii,433p. £30;$35. ISBN: 0195051270.

27 chapter thematic history (*e.g.* Magazines as political weapons in the class struggle; Changing concepts in women's magazines; Pulps and science fiction) which concentrates on the period since 1918. Full bibliography (p.383-97); index. Complements and continues Mott. '(R)ecommended for the reference shelf' (*Choice*, v.29(5), January 1992, p.748). *Class No:* 050(73)

[1865]

The National directory of magazines: the most comprehensive guide to US & Canadian magazines. New York, Oxbridge Communications, 1988-. Annual. $495. ISSN: 08954321.

Current information on *c.*20,000 titles under 175 subject headings Accountancy...Zoology. Excludes scholarly journals, newspapers, newsletters and house organs. Aimed largely at media buyers, entries containing detailed circulation and advertising data. Useful for tracing obscure titles and local and regional publications, but 'no substitute for the major bibliographical directories' (*Library acquisitions: practice and theory*, v.17(3), Fall 1993, p.394). Also available on CD-ROM and through the Internet as part of Oxbridge Communications freely accessible *Mediafinder* site (http://www.mediafinder.com/). *Class No:* 050(73)

[1866]

The Standard periodical directory. New York, Oxbridge Communications, 1964-. Annual. $695. ISSN: 00856630.

Published annually from 1987, previously irregular.

The 21st ed. (1998) has entries for more than 90,000 periodicals mostly published in the US and Canada. Periodical defined as any publication having a frequency of issue at least once every two years. Includes consumer magazines, directories, government publications, house organs, newsletters, newspapers, trade journals, transactions and proceedings of scientific societies, yearbooks, etc. Data for each title includes publisher, editor and other senior personnel, target audience, frequency, year established, where indexed/abstracted, online availability, subscription

.... *(contd.)*

rates, circulation, advertising rates, physical characteristics, availability in other media and ISSN. Entries in 261 subject sections; online and title/ISSN indexes, with cross-index to subjects preceeding main listing. Geared to the general public, but gives wider coveage of North American titles than either *Ulrich's periodical directory* or *The Serials directory* (*qq.v.*). Also available on CD-ROM (quarterly updating) and through the Internet as part of Oxbridge Communications freely accessible *Mediafinder* site (http://www.mediafinder.com/). *Class No:* 050(73)

Black Races

[1867]

DANIEL, W.C. Black journals of the United States. Westport, Conn., and London, Greenwood, 1982. x,429p. £67.50;$79.50. (*Historical guides to the world's periodicals and newspapers*.) ISBN: 0313207046.

Detailed treatment, including historical essays and bibliographical data, for *c.*175 titles published 1827 to date. Excludes newspapers. *Class No:* 050(73)(=96)

[1868]

POTTER, V.R. A Reference guide to Afro-American publications and editors, 1827-1946. Ames, Iowa State Univ. Press, 1993. xii,104p. £19.95;$26.95. ISBN: 0813806771.

Based on W.H. Brown's *Checklist of negro newspapers in the United States (1827-1946)* (1946).

Reprints Brown's checklist of 467 titles with corrections, additions and indexing. *Class No:* 050(73)(=96)

[1869]

UNIVERSITY OF WISCONSIN-MADISON *and* STATE HISTORICAL SOCIETY OF WISCONSIN. Black periodicals and newspapers: a union list of holdings in libraries of the University of Wisconsin and the Library of the State Historical Society of Wisconsin. Strache, N.E., *and others*. 2nd rev. ed. Madison, The Society, 1979. xiii,83p. ISBN: 0870201786.

Lists over 600 periodicals A-Z by title, with geographic and subject indexes. The holdings of the two libraries are believed to constitute 'one of the strongest collections in the field' (Introduction). *Class No:* 050(73)(=96)

Amerindians, North

[1870]

Native American periodicals and newspapers 1828-1982: bibliography, publishing record and holdings. Danky, J.P., *ed and* Hady, M.E., *comp.*. Westport, Conn., Greenwood Press, 1984. xxxii,532p. £67.50;$79.50. ISBN: 0313237735.

Selective coverage of 1,164 titles, including political and literary journals, published in the United States or Canada by or about Native Americans. 71% of the titles included are held in the specialist collection developed by the State Historical Society of Wisconsin. *Class No:* 050(73)(=97)

[1871]

—American Indian and Alaska native newspapers and periodicals. Littlefield, D.F. *and* Parins, J.W., *comps.* Westport, Conn., Greenwood Press, 1984-86. 3v. $105 per v. (*Historical guides to the world's periodicals and newspapers.*)

1826-1924 (ISBN: 0313232645); 1925-1970 (ISBN: 0313234272); 1971-1985 (ISBN: 031324846).

....*(contd.)*

Fewer titles than Danky & Hady, but in depth profiles of those included. Appendices list titles by date of first issue, location and tribal affiliation. *Class No:* 050(73)(=97)

Brazil

[1872]

Guia de publicações seriadas brasileiras. Brasília, Instituto Brasileira de Informaçao em Ciência e Tecnologia, 1987. 671p. ISBN: 8570130104.

Rev ed. of *ISSN: publicações periódicas brasileiras* (1983).

Broad subject listing of c.1,700 titles. Includes title and ISSN indexes. *Class No:* 050(81)

[1873]

LIBRARY OF CONGRESS. Library of Congress Office, Brazil. **Accessions list Brazil and Uruguay: annual list of serials.** 1975-91. Rio de Janeiro, Library of Congress Office, 1976-92. Irregular. ISSN: 01461060.

As *Accessions list Brazil: annual list...* until 1989. Supplement to *Accessions list: Brazil and Uruguay* (*q.v.*). *Cumulative list of serials 1975-1980* issued 1982 (759p.); subsequent publication biennial and annual.

The 1975-80 cumulation has approx. 6,500 entries. A further source of information on current Brazilian periodicals is *Anuário brasileiro de mídia* (*q.v.*). *Class No:* 050(81)

Argentina

[1874]

Catálogo de publicaciones en serie argentinas con registro de ISSN. Buenos Aires, Centro Argentino de Información Cientifica y Technológia, 1993. viii,339p. ISBN: 9506920206.

Rev ed. of *Publicaciones periodicas argentinas 1981*. Includes supplements 1983 and 1989 and new material. A further title is *Catálogo de publicaciones seriadas argentinas* (Buenos Aires, Instituto Nacional de Estadistica y Censos, 1988. viii,172p.). *Class No:* 050(82)

Chile

[1875]

La Revista chilena en venta. Santiago de Chile, Servicio de extension de cultura chilena, 1975-. Irregular.

Latest 1981-84 (1986. v,63p.) and 1985-94 (1995. xii,247p.).

Each v. lists Chilean periodicals current during the period. Broad subject arrangement with title index.
Class No: 050(83)

Bolivia

[1876]

TICHAUER, W.G. *and* **ARZE RAMIREZ, M.R. Bibliografía de revistas bolivianas 1962-1991:** con indices de materias, editoriales y lugares de edición. Cochabamba/ La Paz, Editorial 'Los Amigos del Libro', 1992. 103p.

Provides brief bibliographical detail for 449 titles. Subject, publisher and place of publication indexes.
Class No: 050(84)

Colombia

[1877]

Colombian serial titles in the University of Illinois Library at Urbana-Champaign. Mundo Lo, S. de, *comp.* Austin, SALALM, 1978. 130p. (*Seminar on the Acquisition of Latin American Library Materials, bibliography, no.4.*)

A list of more than 500 current and ceased periodicals arranged alphabetically by title. Appendix on the history of Colombian serial bibliographies (p.117-22).
Class No: 050(86)

Australasia & Oceania

[1878]

Periodicals in print: Australia, New Zealand and the South Pacific. Toowong, ISA Ausralia, 1981-. Annual. £50;Aus$85. ISSN: 13328395.

Title varies. Initially as *Australian serials in print*, replacing the National Library's *Current Australian serials* (1963-75). Later issues as *Australian periodicals in print*, then *Periodicals in print: Australia, New Zealand and Papua New Guinea*, publisher D.W. Thorpe, ISSN: 10302476.

The 14th ed. (1997. xvi,844p.) has 14,630 entries, 11,498 of which are for Australian titles. Includes periodicals published elsewhere about the region; excludes annual reports, free newspapers, comics, school magazines, etc., except those from Papua New Guinea and the South Pacific. Main section lists titles A-Z with a brief description and standard data such as frequency, publisher, editor, advertising and circulation. Lists of ceased titles and publishers with addresses. Classified (subject) list and ISSN index. *Class No:* 050(9)

Indonesia

[1879]

A Checklist of Indonesian serials in the Cornell University Library (1945-1970). Thung, Y. *and* Echols, J.M., *comps.* Ithaca, N.Y., Cornell University, Department of Asian Studies, 1973. 225p. (*Cornell University Southeast Asia program data papers, no.89.*)

Reprint available from Books on Demand ($65.90. ISBN: 0835736784). An earlier ed. by the same authors covered 1945-1965.

Lists 2,269 serials by title including government publications, annual reports and publications of commercial organizations. *Class No:* 050(910)

[1880]

PERPUSTAKAAN NASIONAL (Indonesia). **Katalog majalah terbitan Indonesia:** kumulasi 1779-1980 (A-Z). [Catalogue of Indonesian serials.] [Jakarta], Perpustakaan Nasional, Departemen Pendidikan dan Kebudayaan, [1985]. viii,412p.

Replaces 3v. listing (1779-1927, 1928-41 and 1942-80) published 1981-83.

A-Z list of *c.*7,500 titles published in Indonesia based on the holdings of Perpustakaan Nasional (National Library). Lacks indexes. *Class No:* 050(910)

Philippines

[1881]

GOLAY, F.H. *and* **HAUSWEDELL, M.H. An Annotated guide to Philippine serials.** Ithaca, Cornell University, Department of Asian Studies, 1976. viii,131p. $39.80. ISBN: 0877271011.

Reprint available from Books on Demand ($43.70. ISBN:

....*(contd.)*
0835736806).

Based on the holdings of the Southeast Asia collection of Cornell University Library. Full bibliographical details with brief annotations in non-governmental and government sections. Indexed by issuing body. *Class No:* 050(914)

New Zealand

[1882]
New Zealand serials. Wellington, National Library of New Zealand, 1992. Microfiche. NZ$170.

In 4 sections: Register of full records, Author/title index, Subject index, Publishers' address list.

14 microfiche set listing all the serials contained in the *New Zealand national bibliography* (*q.v.*) from 1982 to February 1992. *Class No:* 050(931)

Australia

[1883]
Checklist of nineteenth century Australian periodicals. Pong, A., *comp.* Bundoora, The Borchardt Library, La Trobe University, 1985. 49p. Aus$10. (*La Trobe University Library publication, no.29.*) ISBN: 085816602x.

A preliminary to the projected compilation of an index of major Australian periodicals of the pre-1945 period. Short-title entries arranged alphabetically: basic bibliographical data; cross-references between title changes; some annotations. Excludes annuals, government gazettes and titles included in *Newspapers in Australian libraries ... Part 2. Australian newspapers* (*q.v.*). *Class No:* 050(94)

[1884]
STUART, L. Nineteenth century Australian periodicals: an annotated bibliography. Sydney, Hale and Iremonger, 1979. viii,200p. illus. ISBN: 0908094531.

A-Z list of 449 titles which contain 'literary features' (Introduction). Includes holdings data for major Australian libraries. Bibliography (p.176-182). Index of printers, publishers, proprietors, noted contributors and artists (p.183-199). *Class No:* 050(94)

Papua—New Guinea

[1885]
Checklist of current Papua New Guinea periodicals. Lea, M.A. *and* Rannells, E., *comps.* Lae, Matheson Library, Papua New Guinea University of Technology, 1985. 60p. (*Matheson Library occasional bibliography, no.1.*)

Comprehensive list of over 400 titles based on the collections of the Matheson Library and the National Library of Papua New Guinea. *Class No:* 050(954)

Jews

[1886]
Directory of world Jewish press and publishing. Jerusalem, The Directory, 1984. 134p.

Earlier coverage provided by *The Jewish press of the world,* J. Fraenkel ed., published irregularly 1953-1972.

Worldwide list of current titles. 866 entries arranged geographically with data for address, editor, foundation date, publisher, language, frequency, circulation, affiliation, etc. Includes bulletins, magazines, newsletters and a few irregular publications in a separate section. 42 entries under the heading England. Title index. *Class No:* 050(=924)

[1887]
Jewish serials of the world: a research bibliography of secondary sources. Singerman, R., *comp.* Westport, Conn. and London, Greenwood Press, 1986. xxii,377p. £58.50; $65. ISBN: 0313244936.

Based largely on the collection of the Price Library of Judaica, University of Florida. 3,035 numbered entries for books and articles in country sections (105 Great Britain, 769 US). Also has sections on multinational, Hebrew, Judezmo and Yiddish serials. Cross-referenced; author and subject indexes. 'A splendid job' (*Library quarterly,* v.57(2), April 1987, p.241). *Class No:* 050(=924)

Indexes

Bibliographies

[1888]
The Index and abstract directory: an international guide to services and serials coverage. 3rd ed. Birmingham, Ala., EBSCO Publishing, 1994. 2v. (xliii,3561p.). ISBN: 0913956740.

First published 1989; 2nd ed. 1990. Partially based on EBSCO's *Serials directory* (*q.v.*).

V.1 lists 56,000 current serials (35,000 2nd ed.) A-Z giving full bibliographical detail and description of content, followed by titles of publications where the serial is indexed/abstracted. Wherever possible information is also given on dates covered, whether indexing/abstracting is full or selective and online/CD-ROM availability. V.2 contains 'Index/abstract title listings' (p.1665-3554) providing bibliographical information and descriptions for 950 active indexing/abstracting services (up 200 from 2nd ed.). Separate 'Index/abstract services subject index'. The most up-to-date and comprehensive guide available.
Class No: 050:014.3(01)

[1889]
Indexes, abstracts and digests: a classified bibliography reproduced from Library of Congress cards arranged according to the Library of Congress classification system. Brewer, A.M., *ed.* Detroit, Gale, 1982. xviii,801p. $220. ISBN: 0810316862.

Reproduces Library of Congress cards which include the words index(es), abstract(s) or digest(s) in the title or subject tracings. About 6,000 entries. Includes some foreign language items. Appended section of LC cards without class nos. (p.696-801). Keyword index to the classification (p.xiii-xviii). Reproductions of good quality.
Class No: 050:014.3(01)

[1890]
MARCONI, J.V. Indexed periodicals: a guide to 170 years of coverage in 33 indexing services. Ann Arbor, Pierian Press, 1976. xxvi,416p. ISBN: 087650005x.

A-Z listing of 11,000 periodicals 1802 to mid-1973, identified as being indexed in 33 US, British and Canadian periodical indexes. Includes all the H.W. Wilson indexes (with the exception of *Bibliographic index), British humanities index, British technology index, Canadian index to periodicals* and *Index to legal periodicals.* Information for each indexed title includes volumes and dates covered and full detail of title changes, suspensions and mergers.
Class No: 050:014.3(01)

[1891]

NEW YORK PUBLIC LIBRARY. A Check list of cumulative indexes to individual periodicals in the New York Public Library. Haskell, D.C., *comp.* New York, New York Public Library, 1942. [iii],370p.

Reprinted Detroit, Gale 1969.

About 6,000 entries, arranged A-Z by titles of periodicals indexed. Defines a cumulative index as 'one which indexes at least three volumes of a file, and makes at least a slight attempt at the classification of the periodical's contents, either an arrangement by authors or by subjects' (Preface). *Class No:* 050:014.3(01)

Developing Countries

[1892]

GORMAN, G.E. *and* **MILLS, J.J. Guide to current indexing and abstracting services in the Third World.** London, Zell, 1992. xvii,260p. £45;$85. ISBN: 090545085x.

Analytical entries for *c.*125 abstracting and indexing titles produced in Third World countries, including those relating to specific subjects (*e.g. Irrigation and power abstracts; Educational abstracts for Tanzania*). A-Z title order; bibliographical citation plus full detail under headings scope, arrangement, main content, assessment of content. Subject and geographic index. Appendix of additional titles not available for analysis. *Class No:* 050:014.3(01)(4/9-77)

Worldwide

[1893]

Internationale Bibliographie der Zeitschriftenliteratur aus allen Gebieten des Wissens. 1963/64-. [International bibliography of periodical literature covering all fields of knowledge. 1963/64-.] Zeller, O. *and* Zeller, W., *hrsg.* Osnabrück, Dietrich, 1965-. Semi-annual. DM4900. ISSN: 00209201.

Also known as 'IBZ'. Three sister publications, *Internationale Bibliographie der Rezensionen, Internationale Jahresbibliographie der Festschriften* and *Internationale Jahresbibliographie der Kongressberichte*, cover book reviews, Festschriften and conference proceedings respectively.

Continues *Bibliographie der fremdsprachigen Zeitschriftenliteratur* (1911-64) and *Bibliographie der deutschen Zeitschriftenliteratur* (1896-1964).

Indexes *c.*250,000 articles in about 9,000 periodicals. Revised format from v.19(2) 1983. Each semi-annual issue in 6v.: v.1-5 Index rerum; v.6 Autores. Periodica (Index Systematicus (keywords organinized by fields of knowledge) dropped from second issue of 1995). Index rerum (subject index) comprises German language keyword index (English and French keywords refer to German entries), giving coded references to periodical titles and article citations. The Autores section provides an author index, while the Periodica section lists periodicals indexed by the code number quoted in the Index rerum entries. A CD-ROM version is also available containing records from 1989. The only general periodical index providing international coverage on such a scale. Remains of some value in larger academic libraries, especially for German language material. *Class No:* 050:014.3(100)

[1894]

—Bibliographie der fremdsprachigen Zeitschriftenliteratur. [International index to periodicals.] Leipzig, Dietrich, 1911-64.

Published as Abt.B of the earlier *Internationale Bibliographie der Zeitschriftenliteratur*. Issued in 2 series, 1911-19 and 1925-64; 1943/44-1948 not published.

Indexed nearly 1,500 non-German language periodicals. Similar arrangement to *Bibliographie der deutschen Zeitschriftenliteratur* (*q.v.*). *Class No:* 050:014.3(100)

[1895]

—Internationale Bibliographie der Zeitschriftenliteratur. Register der Schlagwörter 1896-1974. Zeller, O., *hrsg.* Osnabrück, Dietrich, 1975. 2v.

Index of keywords used since the inception of *Internationale Bibliographie der Zeitschriftenliteratur*. *Class No:* 050:014.3(100)

English

[1896]

Academic index. Foster City, Ca., Information Access Co., 1987-. Computer database.

Accessible online through CARL, Dialog (file 88), Data-Star and the Internet (SilverPlatter), updated monthly. Various CD-ROM versions also available (see below).

Indexes approx. 1,600 commonly held English-language scholarly and general interest periodicals. Core titles covered back to 1976, recent articles with abstracts. Selected full text for many titles. Full indexing of each journal covered, extending to news reports, editorials, reviews, etc.

Three main CD-ROM versions of *Academic index* are currently available: *Academic ASAP*, indexing 500 titles with full text coverage for 250; *Expanded academic index*, corresponding to the online version, indexing 1,580 titles with full text for 750; *General periodicals index*, indexing 1,000 titles with full text for 700. Each disc contains indexing for current and 3 previous years; full text coverage is for current and previous 2 years.

General academic index (monthly updating, £1,495) is a further product designed especially for the UK and Europe. In addition to coverage of 350 periodicals, many with a British imprint, it includes indexing for the *Guardian, Independent* and *Times*. Most titles indexed from 1992, some covered back to 1989. Brief abstracts provided for the majority of citations.

The Info Access family of CD-ROMs use the InfoTrac software system supporting advanced and novice search modes. Libraries may add customized holdings data. Information Access Company have also recently launched an Internet service *InfoTrac SearchBank custom* allowing libraries to create their own database of indexed and full text titles. *Class No:* 050:014.3(100)=20

[1897]

Academic search. Peabody, Mass., EBSCO, 1993-. Computer database. ISSN: 10712720.

Available in a range of online, Internet subscription (EBSCOhost) and CD-ROM options.

Provides indexing and abstracting of titles selected for their relevance to academic libraries. American published periodicals predominate, but a good range of British and other non-US English language titles included. Indexing under Library of Congress subject headings, *c.*50 word summaries added to entries. Coverage for most titles back to 1990.

The main database *Academic search fulltext* (EBSCOhost)

.... *(contd.)*
indexes and abstracts 3,500 titles with full text coverage for 1,000. Also covers the *New York times, Wall Street journal* and *Christian Science monitor*. *Elite* and *Premier* subsets available including 2,100 and 550 titles respectively, both also issued on CD-ROM. Versions without full text are available as *Academic abstracts*. EBSCO also provide the *Magazine article summaries* series of databases (*q.v.*) intended mainly for public libraries.
Class No: 050:014.3(100)=20

[1898]

Alternative press index: an index to alternative and radical publications. Baltimore, Md., Alternative Press Center, 1969-. Quarterly, final issue annual cumulation. ISSN: 0002662x.

Subject index to around 225 left-wing, feminist, black and minority group, environmental and similar periodicals and newspapers. Wide ranging coverage including a number of scholarly journals *e.g. Black scholar, Science and society, Women's studies quarterly*. Geographic coverage largely restricted to North America, but a few British published titles, *e.g. Economy and society* and *New left review*, also included. A 'mainstay of reference indexes, due to its unique scope and its breadth of treatment' (*American reference books annual*, v.28, 1997, p.31). Also available as a quarterly updated CD-ROM from NISC.
Class No: 050:014.3(100)=20

[1899]

—The Left index: a quarterly index to periodicals on the left. Santa Cruz, Ca., Reference and Research Services, 1982-. Quarterly. ISSN: 07332998.

'Journals selected for inclusion ... have a Marxist, radical, or left perspective and contain lengthy, critical, analytical material. Newsletters and newspapers are not included'. Fewer titles than *Alternative press index*, averaging around 95 in each issue, including a few published in the UK. Main entry by author name with separate 'Book review index' and subject index, the latter cumulated in final issue for each year. *Class No:* 050:014.3(100)=20

[1900]

Annual magazine subject index: a subject index to a selected list of American and English periodicals and society publications. 1907-1949. Boston, Mass., Faxon, 1908-52. 43 annual v.

Generally aimed to cover only periodicals not indexed elsewhere, a policy which led to variations in coverage from year to year as other indexes added or dropped titles. Early volumes show some continuation in the titles previously indexed in Poole (*q.v.*). The initial volume, published as *Magazine subject index* included retrospective indexing of 44 titles from their inception. Although the titles indexed were predominantly of general interest, there was a marked bias towards history, especially US state and local history (periodicals in this subject area excluded from the policy of not indexing titles covered elsewhere). Also strong on art, architecture, outdoor life, education and political science.
Class No: 050:014.3(100)=20

[1901]

—Cumulated magazine subject index, 1907-1949. Boston, Mass., G.K. Hall, 1964. 2v. ISBN: 0816104018.

Cumulates the 43 annual volumes in one A/Z sequence. 253,000 entries, indexing 356 magazines.
Class No: 050:014.3(100)=20

[1902]

ArticleFirst. Dublin, Ohio, OCLC, Online Computer Library Center. Computer database.

Available on FirstSearch, file updated daily.

Provides indexing for about 12,500 core English-language periodicals in all subject areas from 1990 or later. Selection aimed at academic libraries. A complementary database *ContentsFirst*, allowing browsing and searching of the periodicals indexed in *ArticleFirst*, is also available.
Class No: 050:014.3(100)=20

[1903]

Comprehensive index to English-language little magazines 1890-1970. Series one. Sader, M., *ed.* Millwood, N.Y., Kraus-Thomson, 1976. 8v. ISBN: 0527003700.

Personal name index to 100 little magazines of which 59 are American. British titles covered include *Life and letters, Poetry quarterly* and *Stand.* About 200,000 entries in sequences for 'Works by' and/or 'Works about' under each name heading. Each entry includes a note on the form of contribution (poem, play, photograph etc.).
Class No: 050:014.3(100)=20

[1904]

Faxon finder. Cambridge, Mass., Faxon Research Services, 1993-. Computer database

Available online through Faxon or as a monthly updated CD-ROM.

Contents listing based index to 12,000 periodicals in all subject areas covering January 1990 onwards. Over 7,000,000 citations 1997, including book reviews, proceedings and editorials. Unlike some similar services coverage extends to a limited number of foreign language titles. *Class No:* 050:014.3(100)=20

[1905]

Humanities index. New York, Wilson, 1974-. Quarterly, with annual cumulation. ISSN: 00955981.

Continues in part *Social sciences and humanities index* (below).

Cover to cover indexing of 400 English language periodicals in the fields of archaeology and classical studies, area studies, folklore, history, language and literature, performing arts, philosophy, religion and theology. Includes numerous British titles *e.g. Antiquity, British journal of aesthetics, History, Mind, Past and present*. Arranged in standard Wilson format, subject and author entries in one A-Z sequence. Separate list of book reviews. Records 1984 to date searchable online through Ovid and WilsonLine. Quarterly updated CD-ROM version, also with data from 1984, available from Wilson and SilverPlatter. Enhanced database version as *Humanities abstracts* (below).
Class No: 050:014.3(100)=20

[1906]

—Humanities abstracts. New York, Wilson, 1996-. Computer database.

Searchable online through several hosts including Dialog, OCLC and WilsonLine. Also available on CD-ROM updated monthly, quarterly or 9 times per annum and through WilsonWeb and other Internet based subscription services.

Indexing for titles covered by *Humanities index* back to 1984 with abstracting from March 1994. A further version, *Humanities abstracts full text*, indexes and abstracts the same periodicals but with the addition of full text for 96 titles from January 1995. *Class No:* 050:014.3(100)=20

[1907]

—Social sciences and humanities index: formerly *International index*. 1907/15-64. New York, Wilson, 1916-74. Quarterly, with cumulations.

As *Readers' guide to periodical literature supplement*, (covering 1907-19), 1916-20; as *International index to periodicals* 1916-65.

Up to 1928 *International index* covered education periodicals, now indexed in *Education index* (1929-), and up to 1945 also covered a number of foreign-language periodicals. As *Social sciences and humanities index* covered about 200 titles of which around 30 were British. From 1974 divides into *Humanities index* (above) and *Social sciences index*. *Class No:* 050:014.3(100)=20

[1908]

Inside social sciences and humanities. Boston Spa, British Library Document Supply Centre, 1996-. CD-ROM database. £500.

Each disc contains 6 months' data (current month plus previous 5 months). Companion disc *Inside science* (£600). Partially continues *Inside information* begun in 1993.

The British Library Document Supply Centre also provide the Internet accessible *Inside web* service. This allows searching of the 20,000 current journals covered by *Inside social sciences and humanities* and *Inside science*, access to 16,000 conference proceedings (*Inside conferences* (*q.v.*)) as well as making available title level information on 250,000 other journals held by the British Library.

Primarily a current awareness service, containing the contents pages of the 7,000 most frequently requested humanities and social science periodicals held by the Document Supply Centre. Uses same software as other British Library CD-ROMs with search and browse options. Additional features include facility to indicate local holdings and hypertext searching by selecting words from a full display. *Class No:* 050:014.3(100)=20

[1909]

Periodical abstracts. Ann Arbor, University Microfilms International, 1989-. Computer database.

Available online through a number of vendors including OCLC and Dialog (*Newspaper and periodical abstracts*, file 484). A number of CD-ROM versions are currently marketed. These include: *Periodical abstracts library edition*, 572 titles; *Periodicals abtracts research I*, 1,065 titles; *Periodical abstracts research II*, 1,691 titles. In addition versions with some full text are available (*Periodical abstracts plus text*). *General periodicals on disc* and derivatives are similar but the full text provided is in the form of exact copies of the articles as they appeared in the original journals. All databases use UMI's Proquest software.

Stands with Information Access Company's *Academic index* and EBSCO's *Academic search* as one of the major online/CD-ROM general periodical indexes. Coverage for many titles is from 1986 (longer than some other services) and although the periodicals included are predominantly North American a reasonable number from elsewhere are available. Further CD-ROMs based on *Periodicals abstracts* include the *Resource/One ondisc* series (standard, *Select* and *Fulltext*), covering general interest titles and intended mainly for public and secondary school libraries.
Class No: 050:014.3(100)=20

[1910]

Periodicals contents index. Cambridge, Chadwyck-Healey, 1993-. Computer database.

Available on CD-ROM and through the WWW on a subscription basis. UK academic libraries also have the option of WWW and Telnet access through the Edina service. The database is still in the process of compilation with new segments added every 2 months. A subset is available as *Periodicals contents index literature*.

A major retrospective index to periodicals in the humanities and social sciences based on the holdings of Harvard University. Most titles covered are English-language, but a number in other European languages are also included. Well over 2,000 titles indexed 1998, providing access to over 8 million articles. Indexing is from title inception to 1990, with searching on a full range of fields including article title, keyword and author. Table of contents browsing also available. Periodicals assigned to 37 broad subject categories enabling a degree of subject searching. When complete will encompass 3,500 journals and 15 million articles and will form one of the most important periodical indexes ever produced.
Class No: 050:014.3(100)=20

[1911]

Poole's index to periodical literature. 1802-1906. Boston, Mass., Osgood; London, Turner, 1882-1908. 6v.

V.1 1802-81; 1st Suppl. 1882-86; 2nd Suppl. 1887-92; 3rd Suppl. 1892-96; 4th Suppl. 1897-1901; 5th Suppl. 1902-6.

Original v. and suppls. reprinted (Peter Smith. ISBN: 084465695x).

The only general periodical index covering so long a period. Confined to American and English titles. Indexes nearly 600,000 articles in 479 periodicals. Invaluable within its limits as a key to 19th century magazine literature. A subject index only with title entries for works of fiction etc. No author entries, except for biographical or critical works, although the author's name does appear in parentheses in each subject entry. Entries do not give full pagination or date of articles. This deficiency is met by *Poole's index: date and volume key*. M.V. Bell and J.C. Bacon (Chicago, Association of College and Research Libraries, 1957. 61p. (ACRL monograph, 19)). *Class No:* 050:014.3(100)=20

[1912]

—Cumulative author index for *Poole's index to periodical literature* 1802-1906. Wall, C.E., *and others comps. & eds.* Ann Arbor, Pierian Press, 1971. ix,488p. ISBN: 0876500068.

Displays in one A-Z sequence all author names which appear in parentheses in entries in Poole. 300,000 citations. Computer produced and visually unattractive.
Class No: 050:014.3(100)=20

[1913]

UnCover. Denver, Colo., UnCover Co., 1993-. Computer database, updated daily.

Originally available on a fee basis by CARL, now accessible free of charge through the Internet at several URLs including http://www.carl.org/uncover.

Mainly intended as a document delivery service, but also available for searching only without charge or prior registration. Database contains table of contents information for over 17,000 English language periodicals from October 1988. Search paths include author and keyword; title file browsable. Contents pages can be recreated online. About 5,000,000 articles in total, updated daily. Valuable, especially where other online or CD-ROM general periodical indexes are not accessible, but the 'absence of subject

....*(contd.)*
indexing and a controlled vocabulary (are) a major limitation for comprehensive subject searching' (*Database*, v.19(4), August/September 1996, p.94).
Class No: 050:014.3(100)=20

Great Britain

[1914]
BLOOMFIELD, B.C. An Author index to selected British 'Little magazines' 1930-1939. London, Mansell, 1976. xiii,153p. ISBN: 0720105420.

11,000 entries for 73 titles most of which are not indexed in *Comprehensive index to English-language little magazines* (*q.v.*). Most magazines indexed in full. Lists reviews and reviewers. *Class No:* 050:014.3(410)

[1915]
British humanities index. 1962-. East Grinstead, Bowker-Saur, 1963-. Quarterly, with separate annual cumulation. £480. ISSN: 00070815.

Published by Library Association Publishing until January/March 1990. Issued in 3 quarters with an annual cumulation until 1968. Continues in part *Subject index to periodicals* (below).

Indexes *c.*300 British periodicals and newspapers. Humanities interpreted broadly to include the arts, music, philosophy, religion, literature, economics, politics, history and society. Also indexes selected non-specialist articles of popular interest in science and technology. Newspaper coverage restricted to articles of comment and analysis of at least 30 column inches in the *Times, Guardian, Independent*, etc. Revised format from 1993. Main listing, 'Abstracts sequence', arranges entries by subject heading with brief *c.*50 word abstract. Separate subject (other elements in heading), author and source (titles included) indexes. A very valuable source for a wide range of British periodical literature, 20,312 entries in the 1997 annual cumulation.

A quarterly updated CD-ROM version is available under the title *BHI Plus* (£850. ISSN: 09668772) covering records 1985 to date. DOS and Windows interface with 12 search paths, browse indexes and 5 display and output formats. *BHI* is also available as an online database though DataStar.
Class No: 050:014.3(410)

[1916]
—Subject index to periodicals. 1915-61. London, Library Association, 1919-62. Annual, (quarterly issues 1954-61).

As the *Athenaeum subject index to periodicals* 1915-16. Frequency varies: annual 1915-22, 1926-53; quarterly with annual cumulations, 1954-61. 1923-25 partly compiled, but never published.

Issued as class lists with author indexes 1915-22, those for 1915-16 cumulated and published in 1v. 1919. Published as a subject index from 1926. From 1947 confined almost entirely to British periodicals (foreign titles dropped during World War II, except for some US titles discontinued 1947). During the 1950's indexed about 325 periodicals annually. With cessation of publication in 1961 continued by *British humanities index* (above) and *British technology index*, later *Current technology index*. *Class No:* 050:014.3(410)

[1917]
Clover information index. Woodrow, M., *ed.* Biggleswade, Clover Publications, 1975-. Quarterly, (final issue annual cumulation). £52. ISSN: 01401939.

Companion publication *Clover newspaper index* (*q.v.*).

Indexes *c.*110 popular interest magazines *e.g. Amateur gardening, Good housekeeping, History today, New scientist, Sky & telescope, Which*. Entries under specific headings A-Z, indexing based on 'modified free language'. Where title unclear entries include brief explanatory note on article content. Some 3 year cumulations, *e.g.* 1985/87. Also issued on CD-ROM, the current file covering from 1990 (quarterly updating, £119), the retrospective file 1982-90 (£99). An online service to UK libraries through CHEST is anticipated. Mainly a source for public libraries, but for some titles provides the only indexing available.
Class No: 050:014.3(410)

[1918]
Wellesley index to Victorian periodicals, 1824-1900: tables of contents and identification of contributors with bibliographies of their articles and stories and an index of initials and pseudonyms. Houghton, W.E., *ed.* Toronto, Univ. of Toronto Press; London, Routledge & Kegan Paul, 1966-89. 5v. £500 (set) ISBN: 0802027199, set.

Identifies nearly 12,000 authors as the anonymous or pseudonymous contributors to 43 major British monthlies and quarterlies. Titles indexed include: *The contemporary review, The Edinburgh review* (from 1802), *The quarterly review* (v.I); *The fortnightly review, The London review* (v.II); *Westminster review* (v.III); *British quarterly review, London quarterly review* (v.IV). V.I-v.IV each in 3 pts: A. 'Table of contents and identification of contributors (introductory essay for each title followed by table of contents for every issue, including the authorial signature, the *Index* attribution and evidence for that attribution); B. Bibliography of contributors (bibliographies of the identified contributors, together with biographical data and source of that data); C. Index of pseudonyms and initials (alphabetical table of identified and unidentified pseudonyms and initials). V.V *Epitome and index* consolidates the entries from part B of v.I-v.IV in one A-Z sequence. Also includes appendices: I. Items in part A of volumes I-IV altered in their appendices; II. Corrections and additions to volumes I-IV.

A CD-ROM version, to include a few additional periodicals and material from *Victorian periodicals review*, announced for December 1998 (Routledge. £1,795. ISBN: 0415193451). *Class No:* 050:014.3(410)

[1919]
—BOYLE, A. An Index to the annuals. V.1: The authors (1820-1850). Worcester, A. Boyle, 1967. xii,344,3p.

A-Z list of writers with their contributions to each annual, plus an A-Z list of titles. The annuals range from such ephemera as *Drawing-room scrap book* to the more memorable *Janus* (1826). Three indexes: authors (named or identified); contributions 'by the author(s) of'; anonyma. No list of annuals indexed. *Class No:* 050:014.3(410)

Scotland

[1920]
CAMERON, S.H.M. Index to Scottish Gaelic periodicals 1871-1975. Willingham, S.H.M. Cameron, 1996. Unpaged. ISBN: 0952769107.

Indexes selected articles in Gaelic, or articles about the Gaelic language, in 29 periodicals. 1,535 numbered entries

.... *(contd.)*
arranged topographically by Scottish regions with place and personal name indexes. Covers to inception of *Bibliography of Scotland* (*q.v.*). *Class No:* 050:014.3(411)

Commonwealth

[1921]

Index to Commonwealth little magazines. 1964/65-1990/92. Troy, N.Y., Whitson, 1966-93. 11v.

Published in biennial or triennial vols. Final vol. to appear that for 1990/92. Most vols. in print, price varies.

Author and subject index in one alphabetical sequence. Book reviews, editorial notes and news items included if more than 500 words. Titles indexed are those 'which are not generally covered by other indexing services'. 1990/92 vol. indexes only 15 titles (10 from UK), a marked reduction on earlier efforts, 1976/79 indexing 36.
Class No: 050:014.3(41-44)

Wales

[1922]

Subject index to Welsh periodicals. 1931-80. Aberystwyth, National Library of Wales, 1934-86. Irregular. ISSN: 0140265x.

Published by the Library Association, Wales and Monmouthshire Branch 1934-64 in 7v., covering 1931-55. Later volumes, 1968-70 (1978. xi,136p.), 1971-76 (1983. 304p.) and 1977-80 (1986. 200p.), published by the National Library of Wales. Partially continued by *Llfryddiaeth Cymru* (*q.v.*).

Indexed both periodicals published in Wales and periodicals published elsewhere of Welsh interest. Periodicals included concerned principally with Welsh literature and history. 87 titles published in Wales indexed 1977-80, English language subject headings used throughout. *Class No:* 050:014.3(429)

Germany

[1923]

Bibliographie der deutschen Zeitschriftenliteratur, mit Einschluss von Sammelwerken. 1896-64. Leipzig, Dietrich, 1897-1964. Semi-annual.

Published as Abt.A of the old *Internationale Bibliographie der Zeitschriftenliteratur.* Merged with *Bibliographie der fremdsprachigen Zeitschriftenliteratur* 1964 to form the current *Internationale Bibliographie der Zeitschriftenliteratur* (q.v.).

Over 4,000 titles indexed in later volumes giving very comprehensive coverage of scholarly German periodical literature. Most volumes published as an A-Z subject index, with coded references to periodicals and a subsidiary author index.

A 20v. *Ergänzungsband,* published 1908-42, provides retrospective coverage to 1861. *Class No:* 050:014.3(430)

[1924]

Index deutschsprachiger Zeitschriften 1750-1815. Hildesheim, Olms Neue Medien, 1990. Microfiche.

At head of fiche *Zeitschriften-Index 1750-1815.* Comprises 28 microfiche, printed guide and list of titles indexed.

Indexes approx. 200 titles in separate author, subject keyword, name, geographical, illustration and book review sequences. *Class No:* 050:014.3(430)

[1925]

Zeitschriftendienst ZD: nachweis von Aufsätzen aus rund 195 deutschsprachigen Zeitschriften. Berlin, Deutsches Bibliotheksinstitut, 1965-. Monthly, with 3 cumulations pa. ISSN: 09341897.

Format and frequency varies: bimonthly until 1988, then monthly microfiche service.

Subject index to articles in 195 general interest German language periodicals. Cumulations available for 1984-89, 1990-92, and 1993-95. Indexing 1987 to date also available on diskette and CD-ROM, with recent issues Internet accessible at http://www.dblink.de. Mainly intended for larger public collections, more comprehensive coverage of German scholarly periodicals is available in *Internationale Bibliographie der Zeitschriftenliteratur* (*q.v.*).
Class No: 050:014.3(430)

Czech

[1926]

Česká národní bibliografie: Články v českých časopisech. 1953-. Praha, Národní knihovna České republiky, 1954-. Computer database. ISSN: 12108952.

'Articles in Czech periodicals'. Part of the Czech national bibliography. The printed *Články v českých časopisech* ceased publication 1990. Now available only on diskette, CD-ROM and through the Internet.
Class No: 050:014.3(437.1)

Poland

[1927]

Bibliografia Zawartości Czasopism. Warszawa, Biblioteka Narodowa, Instytut Bibliograficzny, 1947-. Monthly. ISSN: 00061093.

Index to Polish periodicals in all subject fields. Over 40,000 entries annually in classified arrangement; author and subject indexes in each issue. *Class No:* 050:014.3(438)

Hungary

[1928]

Magyar nemzeti bibliográfia. Időszaki kiadványok repertóriuma. Budapest, Országos Széchényi Könyvtár, 1977-. Monthly. Ft2400. ISSN: 01336894.

Published as a supplement to the Hungarian national bibliography. Continues the semi-monthly *Magyar folyóiratok repertóriuma* 1946-77 and assumes its numbering.

Promptly produced classified index, 1995 issues containing 13,741 entries. Author and subject indexes in each issue. *Class No:* 050:014.3(439)

France

[1929]

French periodical index. 1973/74-96. Ponchie, J-P., *comp.* Morgantown, Ponchie, 1976-97. Annual. ISSN: 03625044.

Initial issues published by Faxon. Listed as ceased publication by *Ulrich's international periodical directory* 1997/98.

Subject index to articles in general interest French-language periodicals. Number of titles indexed in each issue has varied. Some French periodicals are also indexed in the Quebec published *Repère* (*q.v.*). *Class No:* 050:014.3(44)

Portugal

[1930]

Sumários das publicações periódicas portuguesas: ciências humanas, socias, puras e aplicadas. Coimbra, Biblioteca Geral da Universidade de Coimbra, 1979-. 10 pa., issues consolidated. ISSN: 08700257.

Numbered on the basis of 10 pts. per v., but issues are combined and appear less frequently (*e.g.* v.XVII no.1/10 for 1995 (1996. 421p.)).

Reproduces the contents pages of Portuguese periodicals. Broad subject arrangement based on Dewey classification, with author article and periodical title indexes.

Class No: 050:014.3(469)

RSFSR

[1931]

Letopis' zhurnal'nykh statei. Moskva, Izd-vo Kniznaiā palata, 1926-. Weekly (since 1944). US$175. ISSN: 00241202.

As *Zhurnal'naya letopis,* 1926-37.

'Record of periodical articles'. Indexes journals and other serial publications in all subject areas. 73,646 articles indexed 1996. Excludes popular and children's magazines and government publications. Now arranged in UDC classified order (previously 50 subject classes of the Soviet classification scheme) with personal and geographical name indexes in each issue. *Class No:* 050:014.3(470)

[1932]

MASANOV, I.I., ***and others*. Ukazateli soderzaniia russkikh zurnalov i prodolzajuscihija izdanij 1755-1970gg.** [Indexes of the contents of Russian journals and serial publications, 1755-1970.] Moskva, Kniga, 1975. 438p.

Annotated bibliography of general and specialized indexes published in Russian and in Russia, both those of several periodicals and those of individual titles. Reprinted, with a new English introduction and 133 further items, by Oriental Research Partners, Newtonville, Mass., 1979.

Class No: 050:014.3(470)

Finland

[1933]

Suomalaisia aikakauslehtiartikkeleita: uutuusindeksi. Helsinki, Kirjastopalveln, 1982-. Quarterly. ISSN: 03594459.

Preceded by the annual *Suomen aikakauslehti-indeksi* (ISSN: 00819395) giving coverage from 1959. Earlier retrospective coverage provided by *Suomen aikakauslehti-indeksi, 1803-1963* (M. Palperi *ed.* Turku, Turun Yliopiston Kirjasto, 1974. vii,211p.).

UDC classified index. Also available online and on CD-ROM as *Aleksi*. *Class No:* 050:014.3(480)

Norway

[1934]

Norske tidsskriftartikler: NOTA. 1980-. Oslo, Universitetsbiblioteket i Oslo, 1981-. Annual. ISSN: 0332978x.

Issued quarterly with annual cumulation to 1993.

'The Norwegian index to periodical articles'. Includes book reviews. Entries in Dewey classified order with name/institution, place and subject indexes. 1993 cumulation (1994. 692p.) indexes 14,121 items. Cumulated microfiche ed. for 1980-89. Also available online as *NORART* (*c.*125,000 citations), incorporating records from the health and social affairs index *HelseNOTA*, and on CD-ROM as part of the quarterly updated *Nasjonalbibliografiske data*.

Class No: 050:014.3(481)

[1935]

—Norsk tidsskriftindex 1918-65. Oslo, Steenske Forlag, 1919-71. Annual.

Publisher varied.

Classified index to *c.*300 Norwegian periodicals as well as leading daily newspapers (from 1933). Separate subject indexes on a roughly quinquennial basis 1918-50. Biographical articles separately indexed from 1931 in *Biografske artikler i norske tidsskrifter*.

Class No: 050:014.3(481)

Sweden

[1936]

Svenska tidskriftsartiklar: ett register över innehållet i cirka 450 tidskrifter. Lund, Bibliotekstjänst, 1952-. Monthly, with annual cumulation. Kr4100. ISSN: 00396915.

As *Svenska tidskriftsindex* to 1960. Limited earlier coverage in Lange, A. *Svenska tidskritsartiklar 1940-1945: ett urval* (Boras, Hogskolon i Boras, 1985. vi, 527p.).

Classified index to Swedish periodical literature. Annual cumulation 1995 (1996. ix,552p.) has 17,495 entries with name and subject index and list of periodicals covered. Entries 1979- also available online as part of the *Artikel-sök* database of Bibliotekstjänst and on CD-ROM as *CD:ArtikelSök*. *Class No:* 050:014.3(485)

Denmark

[1937]

Artikelbasen. 1981-. Ballerup, BiblioteksCenter, 1994-. Computer database. Kr8570. ISSN: 13956345.

Available online and on CD-ROM (quarterly updating). Incorporates records from the the printed *Dansk artikelindeks* (ISSN: 0106147X) published bi-monthly with annual cumulation 1981-93. *Dansk artikelindeks* formed from the merger of *Dansk tidsskrift-index* (below), and *Avis-kronik-index* (*q.v.*).

Indexes articles from 800 current Danish periodicals and annuals and 8 newspapers 'of more than 6,000 typographical units'. Includes interviews; excludes editorials and articles detailing internal affairs of associations, etc. 500,000 references 1996 with 30,000 additions annually. Earlier indexing of Danish periodical literature in:-

Class No: 050:014.3(489)

[1938]

—Dansk tidsskrift-index 1915-78. København, Hagerup (then Bibliotekscentralens), 1916-80. Annual. ISSN: 00116521.

Later volumes indexed *c.*400 titles from all subject areas in Dewey classified arrangement. Author and subject indexes. *Stedregister til Dansk tidsskrift-index 1915-1970* by T. Sørensen and H. Michelson (1970), cumulates entries of interest for the study of Danish local history.

Class No: 050:014.3(489)

[1939]

—Danske blandede tidsskrifter, 1815-1922. Inholdsoversigt til 27 danske tidsskrifter. Thomsen, S., *red.* København, Bianco Lunos, 1928-29. 2v.

Issued by the Københavns Kommunebiblioteker.

Indexes articles from 27 general or miscellaneous periodicals, 5 of which were covered thereafter by *Dansk tidsskrift-index.* V.1: Faglitteratur (scientific); v.2: Skøonlitteratur (belleslettres) etc., including music.
Class No: 050:014.3(489)

Netherlands

[1940]

Nijhoffs index op de Nederlandse periodieken van algemene inhoud. The Hague, Nijhoff, 1910-1973. Monthly.

Title varied. Ceased publication with v.60 for 1970, published 1973.

An author and subject index to general periodicals covering about 50 titles in the later years of publication. Annual author and keyword subject index from 1925.
Class No: 050:014.3(492)

Yugoslavia

[1941]

Bibliografija Jugoslavije: članci i prilozi u serijskim publikacijama. Beograd, Bibliografski Inst. FNRJ, 1950-. Monthly.

Part of the Yugoslav national bibliography. Frequency varies.

'Articles and book reviews in journals'. Published in 3 series: A *Drustvene nauke* (ISSN: 03525899); B *Pirodne primenjene, medicinske i tehnicke nauke* (ISSN: 03525945); C *Umetnost, sport, filologija, knjizennost* (ISSN: 03525996).
Class No: 050:014.3(497.1)

Bulgaria

[1942]

Letopis na statiite ot bŭlgarskite spisannia i sbornitsi. Sofia, Narodna Biblioteka Kiril i Metodii, 1952-. Semi-monthly. US$58. ISSN: 03240398.

Series 5 of the Bulgarian national bibliography. Published monthly 1952-71 as *Letopis na periodichniia pechat.*

'Articles from Bulgarian journals and collections'. UDC classified arrangement; annual index. Newspaper articles, included until 1971 title change, are separately indexed in the monthly *Letopis na statiite ot bŭlgarskite vestnistsi* (ISSN: 03240347). *Class No:* 050:014.3(497.2)

Rumania

[1943]

Bibliografia natională română. Publicaţii seriale. Bucureşti, Biblioteca Natională a Romanie, 1953-. Semi-annual. ISSN: 1221180x.

Sub-series of the Rumanian national bibliography. Title and frequency varies: current title from 1992, previously *Bibliografia Republicii Socialiste România. Articole din publicaţii periodice si seriale* issued semi-monthly.
Class No: 050:014.3(498)

[1944]

—ACADEMIA REPUBLICII SOCIALISTE ROMÂNIA. Bibliografia analitica a periodicelor Româneşti. Bucureşti, Editura Academiei Republicii Socialiste România, 1966-.

V.1 1790-1850, pts. 1-3 (1966-67); v.2 1851-58, pts. 1-3 (1970-72).

Retrospective coverage of Rumanian periodicals, also classified by UDC. Concentrates on articles of a political, economic or cultural nature. V.1 has 24,105 entries, v.2 24,123. *Class No:* 050:014.3(498)

China

[1945]

Chung-kuo hsüeh shu chih mu tz'u so yin. [Index to contents of Chinese academic journals.] Seoul, Korea, Center for Materials on Chinese Studies, 1994-. Quarterly.

All contents and indexing in Chinese. 200 journals covered, including those from Taiwan, Hong Kong, Japan and Korea relating to China. Each issue in 2pts: list of journals with contents; author and word index.
Class No: 050:014.3(510)

Japan

[1946]

Current contents of academic journals in Japan: the humanities and social sciences. 1970-. Tokyo, Center for Academic Publications Japan, 1971-. Annual. $85. ISSN: 03867293.

The 23rd volume (1996. 447p.) has entries for 5,296 articles from 298 journals. Dewey based arrangement under 39 subject groups. List of journals indexed precedes; author index. *Class No:* 050:014.3(52)

[1947]

Zasshi kiji sakuin: Jinbun shakai-hen. Tokyo, Kokuritsu Kokkai Toshokan, 1948-. Quarterly. ISSN: 00215341.

Printed issues ceased 1996. Continues as a quarterly updated CD-ROM, current disc including data from 1990.

'Japanese periodical index: humanities and social sciences'. Based on the acquisitions of the National Diet Library. Printed issues in classified arrangement with author index. Various subject based cumulative eds. also published. An online version is available through the National Diet Library. *Class No:* 050:014.3(52)

Asia—Middle & Near East

[1948]

Al-Fihrist. Bayrut, 1981-. Quarterly (parts often combined). US$200. ISSN: 0257439x.

English subtitle *Index to Arabic periodical literature.*

Index to over 200 periodicals published in the Arab world and in Arabic elsewhere. Includes a few articles in Western languages. Subject arrangement under detailed headings; well cross-referenced. Author index.
Class No: 050:014.3(53+56)

India

[1949]

Guide to Indian periodical literature (social sciences and humanities). Gurgaon, Indian Documentation Service, 1964-. Quarterly, with annual cumulation. Rs3,000;$250. ISSN: 00175285.

Published monthly for 8 issues in 1964 then suspended. Resumed publication in 1967 on a quarterly basis. Annual

....(contd.)
cumulations subsequently published to cover 1964-66, plus retrospective v. for 1963. Last annual cumulation currently available 1993 (1997).

An A-Z author and subject index in one sequence following the style of the H.W. Wilson publications. Coverage gradually increased, now indexing around 500 titles pa. Includes essays and book reviews.
Class No: 050:014.3(540)

[1950]

—Index India. Jaipur, Rajasthan Univ., Library, 1967-. Quarterly. Rs1200. ISSN: 00193844.

Issues often combined *e.g.* v.26/27 for 1992/93 (1996. xxiii,444p.).

An alternative source to *Guide to Indian periodical literature*, but not as prompt in appearance and generally less comprehensive in coverage. *Class No:* 050:014.3(540)

Turkey

[1951]

Türkiye makaleler bibliyoğrafyasi. Ankara, Millî Kütüphane Başimevi, 1952-. Monthly. US$48. ISSN: 00414344.

Publisher and frequency varies. English subtitle *Bibliography of articles in Turkish periodicals.*

Based on material received by the National Library. Includes conference and seminar papers. Dewey classified arrangement, with author index in each issue. 15,000-20,000 items indexed annually. *Class No:* 050:014.3(560)

Malaysia

[1952]

Indeks Majalah Malaysia. [Malaysian periodicals index.] Kuala Lumpur, Perpustakaan Negara Malaysia, 1974-. Semi-annual. US$35. ISSN: 01265040.

Companion index to *Indeks suratkhabar Malaysia* (newspapers *(q.v.)) and Indeks persidangan Malaysia* (conference proceedings). Earlier coverage provided by *Index to current Malaysian, Singapore and Brunei periodicals* published 1969-71 for 1967-68.

Indexes *c.*105 Bahasa Malay, English, Chinese and Tamil periodicals by subject and author/title in separate Roman and non-Roman script sections. Some publication delay, second issue for 1991 not published until 1996.
Class No: 050:014.3(595)

Singapore

[1953]

Singapore periodicals index 1969/70-. Singapore, National Library, 1974-. Annual. ISSN: 0218902x.

Continues in part *Index to current Malaysian, Singapore and Brunei periodicals* published 1969-71 for 1967-68. Printed index (ISSN: 03777928) ceased with issue for 1993. Now continues on CD-ROM, discs containing records from 1981.

The 1993 print issue (1994. vp.) indexes 5,369 articles from 156 periodicals published in Singapore. Most articles of less than 750 words omitted. Separate English/Malay (vast majority of entries) and Chinese sections, both arranged by Library of Congress subject headings with author indexes. *Class No:* 050:014.3(595.13)

Africa

[1954]

Africa index to continental periodical literature. Oxford, Zell, 1976-89 Annual. ISSN: 03784797.

Indexed 'selected scholarly and semi-scholarly journals published ... within the African continent excluding South Africa'. Also covered reports literature, conference proceedings and papers presented at seminars held in African countries. Broad subject arrangement with author and subject indexes. *Class No:* 050:014.3(6)

[1955]

Quarterly index to periodical literature, Eastern and Southern Africa. Nairobi, Library of Congress Office Nairobi, 1991-. Quarterly. ISSN: 10181555.

Index to around 300 predominantly English language titles. Citations arranged by registry no. within broad subject groupings. Author, geographical, detailed subject, article title and journal title indexes in each issue cumulated annually. Last issue for 1996 brings total no. of entries since inception to 17,564. A partial replacement for the defunct *Africa index to continental periodical literature* (above).
Class No: 050:014.3(6)

South Africa

[1956]

Index to South African periodicals. [Repertorium van Suid Afrikaanse tydskrifartikels. 1940-.] Pretoria, State Library, 1941-. Semi-annual (CD-ROM database). R2,400. ISSN: 10217509.

Publisher, frequency and format varies. Printed index (ISSN: 03790584) to 1980 with cumulations 1940-49 (4v.) and 1950-59 (3v.). Then issued on microfiche to 1986 (microfiche cumulations for 1960-69 and 1970-79). Indexing for 1987 onwards on CD-ROM disc, *Index to South African periodicals 1987+, theses and dissertations 1918+*, incorporating records from *Gesamentlike katalogus van proefskrifte* (*q.v.*).

Author and subject index to about 450 periodicals published in South Africa. Scholarly journals indexed in full, other titles selectively. Also available for online searching through SABINET.

Records from *Index to South African periodicals* are a major component of the *South African studies CD-ROM* available from NISC (Quarterly updating. £500. ISSN: 10254015). *Class No:* 050:014.3(680)

Canada

[1957]

Canadian index. Toronto, Micromedia, 1985-. Monthly, with semi-annual cumulations. Can$130. ISSN: 11924160.

Formed from the merger of *Canadian magazine index* (1985-92. ISSN: 08298777), *Canadian news index* (1977-92. ISSN: 02257459) (*q.v.*) and *Canadian business index* (ISSN: 02278669).

Now the largest Canadian periodical index covering 550 titles including 350 academic and popular periodicals, 200 trade and business publications, 55 French-language titles and 8 daily newspapers. Main listing by subject with corporate and personal name indexes. Also available in microform. Online versions are available from various vendors including Dialog as part of *Canadian business and current affairs* (file 262). Several CD-ROM versions are also produced including *Canadian business and current affairs fulltext* from SilverPlatter (records 1993-, monthly updating, 130 fulltext titles). *Class No:* 050:014.3(71)

[1958]

Canadian periodical index. [Index périodiques canadiens.] Scarborough, Ont., Gale Canada, 1949-. Monthly, with annual cumulation. ISSN: 00084719.

Published by the Canadian Library Association until 1986, Info Globe until 1994. As *Canadian index to periodicals and documentary films* 1949-63; cumulation 1948-59 (1962. 1180p.).

Covers over 400 Canadian periodicals, plus 25 major US titles dealing with North American and international affairs. Author, corporate name and subject entries in a single alphabetical sequence. Book and other reviews listed under form heading by title. About 15% of entries are for French language articles. Records 1988 onwards searchable through GaleNet as *CPI.Q*, fulltext provided for 150 titles from 1995. A bi-monthly updated CD-ROM version is also available. *Class No:* 050:014.3(71)

[1959]

—Canadian periodical index 1920-1937: an author and subject index. Heggie, G., *and others comps.* Ottawa, Canadian Library Association, 1988. viii,567p. ISBN: 0888021879.

Indexes 20 English language titles. The period 1938-47 is covered by 10 annual indexes published by the Ontario Department of Education (Public Libraries Branch) under the title *Canadian periodical index*. The forerunner of the current index, these cumulate quarterly indexes originally appearing in the *Ontario review*. *Class No:* 050:014.3(71)

Quebec

[1960]

Repère: index analytique d'articles de périodiques de langue française. Montreal, Bibliothèque nationale du Quebec/ Services documentaires multimedia, 1984-. Bimonthly, with annual cumulation. Can$205. ISSN: 08228833.

Formed from the merger of *RADAR: répertoire analytique d'articles de revues du Québec* (1972-83) and *Periodex* (1972-83), which covered French language titles published elsewhere. Present title from 1995, formerly *Point de repère*.

Author and subject index to nearly 300 scholarly and general interest French language periodicals in all subject areas. Quebec published titles predominate, but periodicals published in France, Belgium and Switzerland included. Also available in microfiche and as an online and CD-ROM database (SilverPlatter). Electronic versions now include some fulltext articles. *Class No:* 050:014.3(714)

Caribbean

[1961]

CARINDEX: social sciences and humanities. 1982-. St. Augustine, Trinidad, Main Library, Univ. of the West Indies, 1985-. Semi-annual. TT$45. ISSN: 02507617.

Companion to *CARINDEX: science and technology* and *CARINDEX: abstracts of the agricultural literature of the Caribbean*.

Index to periodical articles, conference proceedings, reports and theses issued in the English-speaking Caribbean. Entries, by LC based subject groups, include good length abstracts; author and specific subject indexes. Separate listings of poems, short stories and book reviews. V.6(1) for 1990 (not issued until 1997) brings the total no. of entries to 3,111. *Class No:* 050:014.3(729)

Latin America

[1962]

Citas Latinoamericanas en ciencias sociales y humanidades: CLASE. 1976-. México, Centro de Información Científica y Humanística, Universidad Nacional Autónoma de México, 1978-. Quarterly. US$190. ISSN: 01850903.

Title varies slightly.

Broad entry subject index to 800 social science and humanities periodicals published in Latin America. Author and subject keyword indexes. Also available online and on CD-ROM as part of *BIBLAT: bibliografía sobre America Latina e información*. *Class No:* 050:014.3(729.99)

[1963]

HAPI: Hispanic American periodicals index, 1970/74-. Los Angeles, University of California, Los Angeles, Latin American Center, 1977-. Annual. $400. ISSN: 02708558.

Retrospective volume for 1970/74 published in 3 v. 1980 (v.1-2 Subjects; v.3 Authors. ISBN: 08790340922). With *Index to Latin American periodical literature* (below), provides unbroken coverage from 1929.

Indexes 'by subject and author articles, documents, reviews, bibliographies, original literary works and other items appearing in nearly two hundred fifty journals published throughout the world which regularly contain information on Latin America. Also indexed are leading journals treating the United States-Mexico border region and Hispanics in the United States'. Scientific and technological journals excluded. Book reviews in separate sequence. Consistently high standard of indexing and production. Database version, *HAPI online* searchable through CitaDel and UCLA, contains 210,000 records. *HAPI* records 1970 onwards are also available as part of NISC's semi-annually updated CD-ROM *Latin American studies - volume 1* ($1,095). *Class No:* 050:014.3(729.99)

[1964]

—PAN AMERICAN UNION. Columbus Memorial Library. Indice general de publicaciones periódicas latino-americanas: humanidades y ciencias sociales. [Index to Latin American periodicals: humanities and social sciences.] Boston, Mass., G.K. Hall, 1961-70. Quarterly, with annual cumulation.

Ceased with v.10 no.2: last cumulation for v.9.

Alphabetical subject listing under Spanish form of heading from v.3. Annual cumulations do not interfile entries, but reproduce the quarterly issues with the addition of an integrated author index. *Class No:* 050:014.3(729.99)

[1965]

—PAN AMERICAN UNION. Columbus Memorial Library. Index to Latin American periodical literature, 1929-1960. Boston, Mass., G.K. Hall, 1962. 8v.

Continued in 2 supplements: 1961-65 (2v. 1968) and 1966-70 (2v. 1980). The 1961-65 volumes exclude material indexed in *Indice general de publicaciones periódicas latino-americanas* (above).

The original set photolithographically reproduces 250,000 catalogue cards on *c.*6,000p. The *c.*3,000 periodicals are generally of Latin American origin, but many others, containing articles on Latin America or by Latin American authors are included. Until 1951, except for well-known authors and authors of articles having literary value, entries are for subjects only. The 2nd supplement has *c.*50,000 entries. *Class No:* 050:014.3(729.99)

[1966]

LEAVITT, S.E., ***with others.*** **Revistas hispanoamericanas:** indice bibliográfico, 1843-1935. Santiago de Chile, Fondo Histórico y Bibliográfico José Toribio Medina, 1960. xxiii,589p.

An index to 30,107 articles in 56 periodicals. Three main sections: Materias (13 subject classes: Bibliografía - Biografía y autobiografía - Revistas de libros - Teatro ... Poemas en prosa - Viajes) - Miscelanea (Anécdotas, etc.) - Traducciones (sub-divided by languages, A-Z). Name index (detailed, non-analytical). Appendix listing US libraries holding periodicals indexed. *Class No:* 050:014.3(729.99)

USA

[1967]

Access: the supplementary index to periodicals. Birmingham, Ala., John Gordon Burke, 1975-. 3 pa., final issue annual cumulation. $167.50. ISSN: 00955698.

Initially as *Access: the index to little magazines*.

Concentrates on new and fringe titles, especially those not indexed by *Readers' guide* (*q.v.*). Author and subject sequences, the latter under specific headings. Includes reviews. 108 titles currently covered. '(M)ay have limited value for large academic libraries where the collection encompasses a large number of subject indexes and online indexing systems' (*American reference books annual*, v.27, 1996, p.29). Records from 1988 also available as a SilverPlatter CD-ROM database, updated semi-annually. *Class No:* 050:014.3(73)

[1968]

Index to little magazines. 1940-1966/67. Denver, Swallow, 1948-70. Irregular.

Commenced publication as an annual with the issue for 1948 (1949), continuing on this basis until 1952. Then issued biennially until 1966/67 (1970), with the exception of 1953/55 (1957).

Retrospective volumes, compiled by S.H. Goode, also published for 1940/42 (Johnson Reprint Corp., 1967. 234p.) and 1943/47 (Swallow, 1965. iii,287p.).

The 1943/47 v. indexes 43 US titles not indexed elsewhere. Author/subject indexing with subject headings kept to a minimum. Editorials, graphic art and book reviews omitted. Coverage further extended retrospectively by:- *Class No:* 050:014.3(73)

[1969]

—Index to American little magazines, 1920-1939. Goode, S.H., *comp.* Troy, N.Y., Whitson, 1969-74. 2v.

Indexes 33 titles. *Class No:* 050:014.3(73)

[1970]

—Index to American little magazines, 1900-1919: to which is added a selected list of British and continental titles for the years, 1900-1950, together with addenda and corrigenda to previous indexes. Goode, S.H., *comp.* Troy, N.Y., Whitson, 1974. 3v. ISBN: 0878750266.

Indexes a wider range of magazines than the volumes covering 1920-1966/67. Otherwise maintains the same style of indexing, including the minimal use of subject headings. 102 titles covered. *Class No:* 050:014.3(73)

[1971]

Magazine article summaries. Birmingham, Al., EBSCO. Computer database, etc.

Originally a weekly print service (ISSN: 08953376) developed from *Popular magazine review* (ISSN: 07403763).

An index to more than 400 general interest magazines and business periodicals published in the US. Also includes the *New York times* and *Magill book reviews*. Now available under the title *MAS full text* on CD-ROM and online (EBSCOhost) in several versions. The full service, *Ultra* (EBSCOhost only), provides the full text of 400 titles with indexing and abstracting for an additional 590. Other services *Premier*, *Select* and *Elite*, offer access to a reduced number of titles. Many of the magazines are also indexed in the further EBSCO database *MasterFile*, covering general interest periodicals. EBSCO also produce *Academic search*, a series of complementary databases aimed at the academic sector. *Class No:* 050:014.3(73)

[1972]

Magazine index. Foster City, Ca., Information Access Corp. Computer database.

Developed from a microfiche sevice begun in 1977.

Indexes 500 popular magazines published in the US and Canada, including sports, consumer and children's titles and the *New York times* and *Wall Street journal*. Complete indexing of the magazines covered, *e.g.* reviews, editorials, product evaluations.

Magazine index is searchable online through a variety of online hosts including Data-Star and Dialog (file 47). The CD-ROM version, *Magazine index ASAP* available from Information Access and SilverPlatter, includes the full text of 300 titles. Records from *Magazine index* are also a component of other Information Access database products including *General periodicals index* and *General reference center*. *Class No:* 050:014.3(73)

[1973]

Nineteenth century readers' guide to periodical literature, 1890-1899, with supplementary indexing, 1900-1922. Cushing, H.G. *and* Morris, A.V., *eds.* New York, Wilson, 1944. 2v.

Originally intended as part of an index to cover the entire nineteenth century, no further volumes have been published.

Indexes 51 titles, 14 of them beyond 1899 to the date of their inclusion in other Wilson indexes. Some of the titles indexed are also covered in Poole (*q.v.*), but the indexing here is more thorough, offering access by author (articles published anonymously identified where possible), illustrator and subject. *Class No:* 050:014.3(73)

[1974]

Readers' guide to periodical literature (Unabridged): an author subject index to selected general interest periodicals of reference value in libraries. 1900-. New York, Wilson, 1905-. Monthly (except March, April, September, October, December semi-monthly), with quarterly and annual cumulations. $200. ISSN: 00340464.

Annual cumulations began 1965, earlier cumulations cover longer periods; v.1 covers 1901-04.

The longest established of the general US periodical indexes now covering 240 titles. Also includes the *New York times* from late 1993. In one A-Z sequence of authors and subjects, except for book review citations. Valuable for its coverage of popular periodicals, sound indexing and frequency. The longest established and best known of the US published general indexes to periodicals. Records 1983 to

....(contd.)
date also available online through Wilsonline updated weekly and on CD-ROM (SilverPlatter and Wilson).
Class No: 050:014.3(73)

[1975]
—Abridged readers' guide to periodical literature: author and subject index to a selected list of periodicals. New York, Wilson, 1936-. Monthly (except June to August), with annual cumulation. $100. ISSN: 0001334x.

Indexes *c.*82 of the titles covered in the main *Readers' guide*. Intended for school and smaller public libraries.
Class No: 050:014.3(73)

[1976]
—Readers' guide abstracts. New York, Wilson, 1984-. Computer database.

Searchable through a number of online systems including FirstSearch and Ovid, as well as Wisonline (updated twice weekly). Also available on CD-ROM updated monthly or quarterly.

Covers the same titles as the main *Readers' guide* with the addition of *c.*125 word abstracts. About 75,000 articles abstracted annually.

Readers' guide abstracts select edition is a further version covering selected articles only and aimed at smaller libraries. *Readers' guide abstracts full text* is a recently launched online (Dialog and Wilson) and CD-ROM service (CD-ROM updated monthly or quarterly). Abstracting is of the same titles as *Readers' guide abstracts* but with the addition of either 120 (Mega ed.) or 60 (Mini ed.) titles in full text.
Class No: 050:014.3(73)

Indonesia

[1977]
Indeks majalah ilmiah Indonesia. [Index of Indonesian learned periodicals.] Jakarta, Pusat Dokumentasi dan Informasi Ilmiah, 1960-. Semi-annual. US$40. ISSN: 02166216.

Title varies; present form from 1980.

The first issue for 1996 (1996. viii,236p.) indexes 1,499 articles from 104 periodicals. Dewey classified arrangement with author, keyword and geographical indexes. All entries include English translation of title.
Class No: 050:014.3(910)

Philippines

[1978]
Index to Philippine periodicals. 1955-. Quezon City, University of the Philippines, 1956-. Quarterly (some issues semi-annual). US$60. ISSN: 0073599x.

Began publication as a quarterly, then issued semi-annually with increasingly poor currency, 1980-84 not published. Re-launched on a quarterly basis 1988.

Indexes about 140 titles, entries in dictionary format. Includes book reviews. *Class No:* 050:014.3(914)

New Zealand

[1979]
Index New Zealand. Wellington, National Library of New Zealand, 1988-. Quarterly. NZ$225 (higher rate overseas). ISSN: 01136526.

Replaces *Index to New Zealand periodicals* (below). Quarterly cumulating microfiche in 3pts: General, Research, Book review. Five year cumulation 1987-91. Also available as a quarterly updated CD-ROM (NZ$1,440. ISSN: 11731869) and as an online database (KiwiNet).

Subject index to periodical articles, books, theses, reports, etc., published in New Zealand and the South Pacific or relating to the area. Electronic versions give access to well over 100,000 records. *Class No:* 050:014.3(931)

[1980]
Index to New Zealand periodicals. Wellington, New Zealand Library Association, 1940-87. ISSN: 00735957.

Frequency varies. From 1950-65 included the *Current national bibliography of New Zealand books and pamphlets* (*q.v.*). Annual 1957-78. From 1979 3 issues pa. with annual cumulation.

Later issues indexed *c.*200 New Zealand periodicals in one author and subject sequence. Also covered articles dealing with New Zealand in overseas periodicals. Ceased publication with cumulation for 1986. Replaced by *Index New Zealand* (above). *Class No:* 050:014.3(931)

Australia

[1981]
Australian periodical index 1944/49-1960/63. Sydney, New South Wales Public Library, 1950-64. Irregular.

As *Index to periodicals* to 1956, published in 3v., covering 1944-June 1949, July 1949-51, 1952-55. From 1956 published as a supplement to the Library's monthly catalogue.

Covered Australia, New Zealand, S.W. Pacific, Antarctic; limited to periodicals not covered by other indexes.
Class No: 050:014.3(94)

[1982]
AUSTROM: Australian social science, law and education databases. Melbourne, Royal Melbourne Institute of Technology, 1990-. CD-ROM database, updated quarterly or semi-annually. Aus$1,495. ISSN: 10352171.

Also available from SilverPlatter.

Combines a number of Australian indexes and databases including *AEI: Australian education index, ALISA: Australian library & information science abstracts* (*q.v.*), *APAIS: Australian Public Affairs Information Service, AUSPORT* and *Australian family & society abstracts*.
Class No: 050:014.3(94)

Jews

[1983]
Index to Jewish periodicals: an author and subject index to selected English language journals of general and scholarly interest. Koppel, L.P., *ed.* Cleveland Heights, Oh., Index to Jewish Periodicals, 1963-. Annual. $100. ISSN: 00194050.

Issued semi-annually to 1986 (numbered as a quarterly).

Indexes *c.*70 titles published for a Jewish audience or devoted to the study of Jews or Judaism. US issued journals predominate, but a few from the UK (*e.g. L'Eylah, Manna*), Israel and elsewhere are also covered. Includes book reviews. Also available as a CD-ROM database ($285).
Class No: 050:014.3(=924)

Children

[1984]
Children's magazine guide: subject index to children's magazines. New Providence, N.J., Bowker, 1948-. 9pa., with annual cumulation. $55. ISSN: 07439873.

As *Subject index to children's magazines* (ISSN: 00394351) until 1981. Publication by Bowker from 1993.

....*(contd.)*

Aimed at children through to about age 14. Now indexes 51 titles, including 14 'professional' journals intended for teachers or school librarians. The longest established and for many years the only major index to periodical literature for children. *Class No:* 050:014.3-0053

[1985]

Primary search. Peabody, Ma., EBSCO, 1994-. CD-ROM database, updated 3 times pa. $549.

Indexes over 100 US published children's interest periodicals, including nearly all those covered by *Children's magazine guide* (above). Full text provided for 33 titles, also includes material of interest to teachers and librarians. Search structure designed for direct use by children. *Middle search*, an associated product intended for older children (3 updates annually, ISSN: 10712755), covers 170 titles including 52 full text. *Class No:* 050:014.3-0053

[1986]

Readers' guide for young people. New York, Wilson, 1996-. Computer database. ISSN: 10937838.

CD-ROM (monthly, 9pa. or quarterly updates) or WWW (WilsonWeb, twice weekly updates) access.

Provides abstracts and indexing for 64 periodicals including 9 'professional' publications. 21 of the titles also available in full text. *Class No:* 050:014.3-0053

Information Management

[1987]

GRAHAM, M. *and* **BUETTEL, F. Serials management:** a practical handbook. London, Aslib, 1990. ix,179p. £28. ISBN: 085142239x.

A basic reference handbook for both practitioners and library school students. 9 contributed chapters in 4 main sections: Collection development; Collection management; Automation; Standards. Appendices: Training organizations for serials management; Serials subscription agents; Binders (6 entries only); Equipment suppliers for serials management. Index. *Class No:* 050:025.4

[1988]

International directory of serial specialists. Whiffin, J.I., *ed.* Binghamton, N.Y., Haworth Press,, 1995. xii,156p. $24.95. ISBN: 1560249439.

Detailed entries for 146 experts from 44 countries 'who can supply specialized information on the serials literature of the national imprint, and/or serials bibliographic control, management and conservation in their respective territories' (p.ix). Based on 1986 survey, some data apparently not updated. Name and area of expertise indexes. '(C)ompetent (but) does seem a somewhat incestuous sort of publication of very limited interest even to serials librarians' (*Reference reviews*, v.9(8), 1995, p.6). *Class No:* 050:025.4

[1989]

International subscription agents. Wilkas, L.R., *comp.* 6th ed. Chicago, American Library Association, 1994. xxii,410p. £31.50;$35. ISBN: 0838906222.

First published 1963; 5th ed. 1986.

Directory of 250 subscription agents. Entries, A-Z by country, provide detailed information on materials handled, services offered, computerized services, catalogues, charging policies, etc. *Class No:* 050:025.4

[1990]

—ALFRED M. GOODLOE ASSOCIATES. Guide to international subscription agencies: a research report. 2nd ed. New York, Direct International, 1996. 220p. $145. ISBN: 0961640987.

Looseleaf. First published 1990.

Questionnaire based; entries for 358 companies. "(F)ails to distinguish between booksellers and subscription agents, and applies no quality control to the questions it asks". (*Serials*, v.9(3), November 1996, p.359). *Class No:* 050:025.4

[1991]

LEONG, C.H. Serials cataloging handbook: an illustrative guide to the use of AACR2 and LC rule interpretations. Chicago, American Library Association, 1989. xiii,313p. $55. ISBN: 0838905013.

'The objective of this handbook is to aid the cataloger in applying general rules or procedures in the context of a specific problem situation in the cataloging of serials' (Introduction p.xi). 200 entries with 178 cataloguing examples in 17 sections. *Class No:* 050:025.4

[1992]

TUTTLE, M. Managing serials. Greenwich, Conn., JAI Press, 1996. xix,347p. tables. £49.95;$73.25. (*Foundations in library and information science, v.35.*.) ISBN: 0762301007.

Based on *Introduction to serials management* (JAI Press, 1983).

14 chaps: 1. The Nature of serials - 2. Serials publishing trends ... 6. Subscription agents and other serials suppliers ... 10. Cataloging serials ... 12. Preserving library serials ... 14. Access to serials: serials outside the library. Index. Emphasises serials work in academic libraries. '(C)omprehensive, informative, insightful survey' (*Journal of academic librarianship*, v.23(3), May 1997, p.245). *Class No:* 050:025.4

Gentleman's magazine

[1993]

The Gentleman's magazine, or, Monthly intelligencer. v.1-v.303, no.3, January 1731-September 1907.

Volume numbering is irregular: v.53-103 each in two parts, counted but not issued as 53-154; 'new series, v.1-45' counted but not issued as 155-99; v.200 omitted in numbering; v.201-19 also as 'new series, v.1-19'; v.220-24 also issued as 'new series, v.1-5'; v.225-41 issued as 'entirely new series v.1-17'; v.242-48 issued as 'v.240-46'. Continued as a four page leaflet to reserve copyright until September 1922.

Usual contents: summaries of news and essays from other periodicals; lists of births, deaths, marriages and appointments; commodity prices, daily weather, stocks and shares; new books; poetry; literary, historical and biographical articles. Changed in character in June 1868 by dropping the reference material in favour of fiction and other ephemera. Selected articles are collected as *The Gentlemen's magazine library*, 29v. in 30, 1883-1905.

Indexes: Ayscough, S. *A General index to the first fifty-six volumes* ... [1731-86] (London, Henry, 1789. 2v.); Nichols, J. *A General index to the 'Gentleman's magazine' from the year 1787 to 1818* ... (London, Nichols, 1821. 2v.); these two indexes do not distinguish between persons of the same surname.

Other indexes include: Farrar, R.H. *An Index to the biographical and obituary notices ... 1731-1780* (London,

.... *(contd.)*
British Record Society, 1891. vii,677p.); St. Barbe, C. *A Complete list of the plates and wood-cuts ... 1731-1818 ...* (London, Nichols, 1821. viii,225p. ports).

As with *Notes and queries* (below) the full text of *The Gentleman's magazine* is to be made Internet accessible as part of the Internet Library of Early Journals project (http://www.bodley.ox.ac.uk/ilej). *Class No:* 050GEN

Notes and queries

[1994]

Notes and queries: for readers and writers, collectors and librarians. Oxford, Oxford Univ. Press, 1849-. Quarterly. £70;$130. ISSN: 00293970.

Publisher, subtitle and frequency vary. Semi-monthly until 1953; monthly 1953-76; bi-monthly 1977-83; quarterly 1984-. Until 1933 was numbered in 13 series of 12 volumes each; now numbered in one sequence as though starting in 1849. Cumulated indexes published to correspond with the 13 series; annual indexes for recent volumes. The subject headings used in the earlier indexes are selective and somewhat unreliable.

The longest established periodical of its kind, for many years primarily concerned with answering queries posed by readers. Current issues continue to feature a small number of readers' queries and replies, but each issue is now largely made up of short notes and reviews, with a few longer articles. Subject coverage remains 'devoted principally to English language and literature, lexiography, history and scholarly antiquarianism. Emphasis is on the factual rather than the speculative'. The older volumes are valuable as a source of quotations, for bibliographies on minor subjects and for the factual and other information presented in response to reader enquiries. The full text of issues 1849-69 have been made available through the Internet as part of the Internet Library of Early Periodicals project (http://www.bodley.ox.ac.uk/ilej/); further issues to follow. *Class No:* 050NOT

Directories

[1995]

BRITISH LIBRARY. Science Reference and Information Service. **Guide to directories at the Science Reference and Information Service.** Gilbert, J., *comp.* 3rd ed. London, British Library, 1992. v,137p. ISBN: 071230777x.

Previous eds., both published 1986, as *Directories held by the Science Reference and Information Service*.

Lists more than 2,500 directories held at SRIS. Includes professional directories, directories of learned bodies and associations in science and technology and a wide selection of trade and business directories. Brief bibliographical details only in SRIS shelfmark order; title and subject indexes. '(D)esigned for librarians by librarians, and is off-putting to the casual user' (*Aslib information*, v.21(3), March 1993, p.127). *Class No:* 058

[1996]

The Dawson top 4,000 directories and annuals. Wellingborough, Dawson Book Division, 1980-. Irregular. £65. ISSN: 02689928.

Published by Alan Armstrong on an annual basis 1980-87 under the title *The Top 1,000 directories and annuals.* Later eds. issued irregularly as *The Top 3,000 directories and annuals*.

The 12th ed. (1995. vii,454p.) has 4,045 actual entries by title A-Z (p.1-294). Gives title, publisher, editor, date of recent eds., ISBN, price and a brief description rarely exceeding 50 words. Includes a number of bibliographical annuals (*e.g.* *Books in print*). Supplementary listings: Alternative media (titles available on CD-ROM, online, etc.); Directories by month and year of issue (a useful feature not found in most other guides); Directories by publisher; Subject index (broad categories, *e.g.* 300 entries under 'Business UK and international'); Publisher index. Better international coverage and slightly more up to date than the main UK published rival *Current British directories* (*q.v.*). *Class No:* 058

[1997]

Directories in print: a descriptive guide to print and non-print directories, buyer's guides, rosters and other address lists of all kinds. Detroit, Gale, 1980-. Annual. ISSN: 0899353x.

Published as *Directory of directories* until 1987; subtitle varies.

15,092 entries in the 14th ed. (1997. 2v.), the majority for titles published in the US. Arranged under 26 subject groupings (General business ... Library and information science ... Medicine ... Education ... Hobbies and leisure activities). Up to 28 data elements for each entry including title, publisher, email address and URL (new in this ed.), coverage, entries, language, indexes, pages, frequency, former title(s), price, and online availability/alternative formats. V.2 contains an 'Alternative format index' (directories available electronically), subject index (*c.*4,700 LC based subject headings) and title and keyword index. Kept up-to-date by an inter-edition supplement. Available online as part of the *Gale database of publications and broadcast media* (Dialog File 469; GaleNet) and on CD-ROM as a component of *Gale's ready reference shelf.* Unrivalled coverage, the essential key to directories and a useful pointer to sources for many reference enquiries. *Class No:* 058

[1998]

International bibliography of special directories. [Internationale Bibliographie der Fachaddressbücher.] Lengenfelder, H., *ed.* 7th ed. München, Saur, 1983. xx,474p. (*Handbook of international documentation and information, v.5.*) ISBN: 3598205201.

First published 1962, 6th ed. 1978, all with title *International bibliography of directories.*

5,630 entries for directories published in over 50 countries. Arranged in 7 main sections divided into 72 subject groups. Entries give bibliographical detail and in some cases the number of items listed. Lacks subject or any other indexes. No longer useful as a current source, but retains some historical value. *Class No:* 058

Europe

[1999]

Current European directories. O'Connor, T., *comp. & ed.* 3rd ed. Beckenham, CBD Research, 1994. xx,488p. £140. ISBN: 0900246642.

First published 1969; 2nd ed. 1981.

Similar scope and detail to *Current British directories* (below), but UK titles excluded. *c.*4,000 entries (over double previous ed.), with some coverage of Eastern Europe including the former Soviet Union. Main listing by country A-Z, preceeded by section for European wide directories (p.1-90). Publisher, subject (with English, French and German headings) and title indexes. 'Clearly presented and thoroughly indexed' (*Reference reviews*, v.9(5), 1995, p.6). *Class No:* 058(4)

[2000]

Directories in Europe. Bruxelles, European Association of Directory Publishers, 199?-. Biennial (irregular).

Title also in French and German. Initial issues as *Directories: successful advertising media.*

The 1996/97 issue (392p. tables) has brief details of directories from 172 members of the European Association of Directory Publishers. Also available on CD-ROM. '(V)ery much more of a trade catalogue than a directory' (*Managing information*, v.4(4), May 1997, p.48). *Class No:* 058(4)

[2001]

SHAW, G. *and* **COLES, T. A Guide to European town directories.** V.1. Germany, Austria, Switzerland and Scandinavia. Aldershot, Ashgate, 1997. xiv,327p. illus., tables, maps. £55;$93.95. ISBN: 1859280242.

Intended as 'a detailed source guide to directories, especially their contents and, most important, their reliability'. Limited to titles published before 1950. Arranged in country sections, each beginning with a narrative account of directory publishing followed by bibliographical listings arranged under place and title. Full information including library location; place index for each country and general index (p.323-27). A second vol. is to cover France and southern Europe. *Class No:* 058(4)

Great Britain

[2002]

Current British directories: a guide to directories published in the British Isles. Murphy, S. *and* Henderson, C.A.P., *comps.* 12th ed. Beckenham, CBD Research, 1993. xii,470p. £140;$235. ISBN: 090024660x.

First published 1953; 11th ed. 1988.

Directories defined as 'any works which enable a searcher to locate, identify or obtain further information about a person, organization or other unit; or which provide the searcher with a list of persons, organizations or other units in a particular industry, trade or group, or in a specific area' (p.vii). Includes directories published in Ireland. 4,127 entries (1,200 new to this ed.) in one A-Z sequence. Data includes publisher, date first issued, frequency, no. of pages, price, ISSN, description of content (10-100 words), geographic area of coverage and former title(s). Publisher index; subject index (p.397-470) under detailed headings. Fuller data than *The Dawson top 4,000 directories and annuals* (*q.v.*). *Class No:* 058(410)

[2003]

Directory of UK directories. Fairford, Marketing Data, 1992. 89p.

Title keyword entries (*e.g.* 'Architecture and planning, Directory of official') for about 900 directories. Contains many helpful cross-references (*e.g.* 'Garden equipment see Horticultural Trade Association year book'). Limited number of titles covered. Information for those included confined to publisher and address, date of latest ed., price and 1-2 line description. *Class No:* 058(410)

[2004]

DIRECTORY PUBLISHERS ASSOCIATION. Membership book. London, AP Information Services on behalf of the Directory Publishers Association, 1983-. Annual. ISBN: 1854382357.

The 1997 ed. (224p. ISBN: 0906247799) lists over 80 members of the DPA. For each gives address and contact detail, and a full list of published titles with price and 10-30 word descriptive annotation. Subject, directory title and personal name indexes (p.172-224). *Class No:* 058(410)

[2005]

SHAW, G. *and* **TIPPER, A. British directories: a bibliography** and guide to directories published in England and Wales (1850-1950) and Scotland (1773-1950). 2nd ed. London, Mansell, 1997. xi,459p. illus., tables. £75;$150. ISBN: 0720123291.

First published by Leicester Univ. Press, 1988; pbck. ed. 1992.

Extends and complements the work of J.E. Norton, *Guide to the national and provincial directories of England and Wales, excluding London published before 1856* (1950) and C.W.F. Goss, *The London directories 1677-1855* (1932).

Lists 2,200 titles in nearly 18,000 vols. 3 main sections: Introduction and guide (previous works and guides, trends in directory publication, use in historical studies); Bibliography (p.63-418); Library holdings and index. Mainly covers local directories, entries arranged geographically by pre-1974 county boundaries. Commercial, industrial and trade directories in a separate section (p.379-418). Indexed by publisher, place and subject. *Class No:* 058(410)

[2006]

—ATKINS, P.J. The Directories of London 1677-1977. London, Mansell, 1990. [vi],732p. plates. £90;$150. ISBN: 0720120632.

Succeeds C.W.F. Goss's *The London directories 1677-1855,* (1932).

Adds greater depth to Shaw and Tipper (above), giving specialized treatment to London directories. Arranged A-Z by title in sections for general directories, specialist directories and suburban and local directories. Indexed by title, publisher and place (local and suburban directories). 5,827 entries. Although title limits coverage to 1977, listing of editions continues to 1989. '(R)emarkably few errors ... this book will be invaluable not only for local studies but also for many geographical and historical purposes' (*Refer,* v.6(3), Autumn 1990, p.22-23). *Class No:* 058(410)

Canada

[2007]

NATIONAL LIBRARY OF CANADA. Canadian directories 1790-1987: a bibliography and place-name index. [Annuaires canadiens: une bibliographique et un index des noms de lieux.] Bond, M.E., *comp.* Ottawa, National Library of Canada, 1989. 3v. ISBN: 0660547864.

Partially updates Ryder (below) listing the holdings of the

.... *(contd.)*
National Library and National Archives. *c.*1,200 entries in v.1 for directories of provinces, cities, towns, etc., other directories (*e.g.* professions, ethnic groups) excluded. Place-name index (21,500 entries by province) in v.2-3.
Class No: 058(71)

[2008]
—RYDER, D.E. Checklist of Canadian directories, 1790-1950. [Répertoire des annuaires canadiens, 1790-1850.] Ottawa, National Library of Canada, 1979. xvii,288p. Can$10.95. ISBN: 066050409x.

Covers to the commencement of *Canadiana,* (*q.v.*) the national bibliography. Concentrates on town directories. Entries arranged geographically by province then town. Locates copies in the National Library, the Public Archives and provincial archives and public libraries within the geographical area covered by the directory.
Class No: 058(71)

USA

[2009]
Guide to American directories. Klein, B., *ed.* Coral Springs, Fla., B. Klein Publications, 1954-. Irregular. $95. ISSN: 05335248.

Publisher varies.

The 13th ed. (1994. x,505p. ISBN: 0873400135) lists *c.*10,000 directories under 180 subject categories (Accounting and accountants ... Zoology and animal sciences). Entries give title, brief description, frequency, publisher and cost. Subject and alphabetical indexes. Includes about 1,000 titles published outside the US. Cheaper, and some unique entries, but in all other respects an inferior product to Gale's *Directories in print* (*q.v.*).
Class No: 058(73)

[2010]
SPEAR, D.N. Bibliography of American directories through 1860. Worcester, Mass., American Antiquarian Society, 1961. 389p.

Reprinted 1978 (Westport, Conn., Greenwood Press. £53.95;$65. ISBN: 0313202516).

1,647 entries, arranged A-Z by place, with locations for national collections (especially American Antiquarian Society which holds 1,100 of the titles). Plentiful cross-references for places covered, but no indexes (*e.g.* for compilers).
Class No: 058(73)

Australia

[2011]
Directory of Australian directories. Reid, R.S., *comp. & ed.* 2nd ed. Port Melbourne, D.W. Thorpe, 1991. 255p. ISBN: 090053280x.

1st ed., published by Library Assoc. of Australia, 1987.

895 entries arranged under 32 categories (*e.g.* Business, trade, commerce; Library and information sciences; Women's organizations and services). Standard data for each title including scope, arrangement, indexes, frequency, former title(s) and price. Subject, place (by state), title and author/editor indexes. An 'exemplary, highly professional reference work' (*Reference reviews*, V.6(1), 1992, p.6).
Class No: 058(94)

06 Organizations & Associations

Organizations & Associations

Worldwide

[2012]

International organizations: a guide to ... international nonprofit membership organizations including multinational and binational groups, and national organizations based outside the United States, concerned with all subjects or areas of activity. Detroit, Gale. Annual. $530. ISSN: 10410023.

Published as v.4 of the *Encyclopedia of associations* (*q.v.*). Recent issues in 2v., main listings and separate indexes. Updated by inter-edition supplement.

The 31st ed. (1997) has entries for 6,500 multinational and binational organizations and 12,900 national organizations in more than 200 countries. Arranged in 15 broad subject sections: information given similar to the *Encyclopedia of associations*, including date founded, executives, budget, brief description, services, affiliates, publications and conferences. V.2 comprises geographic (country, then city), executive and name and keyword indexes. Searchable online through Dialog (file 114), LEXIS-NEXIS and GaleNet as component of *Encyclopedia of associations*. Available on CD-ROM as part of *Associations unlimited* and *Gale's ready reference shelf*. *Class No:* 061(100)

[2013]

OWEN, R. The Times guide to world organizations: their role & reach in the new world order. London, Times Books, 1996. 254p. ISBN: 0723007896.

'(A)ims to include most significant UN bodies and non-governmental agencies (NGOs) with a global reach, a substantial budget and an international mandate' (*Preface*, p.7). *c.*160 main entries in topical sections: 1. Regional ... 5. Military and security ... 10. Aid ... 16. Medical and health ... 23. Transport and travel. Detail, includes contact information, objectives, main activities, leadership, budget and affiliations. Further section 'Other organizations' contains abbreviated information on 55 additional bodies. Organization and personal name index (p.249-54). Handy and compact, but does not rival Schiavone (below). *Class No:* 061(100)

[2014]

SCHIAVONE, G. International organizations: a dictionary. 4th ed. London, Macmillan, 1997. 334p. tables. £69. ISBN: 1561591955.

1st ed. 1983; 3rd ed. 1992.

Main body of work consists of descriptive and historical entries for approx 170 organizations, (*e.g.* International Monetary Fund (p.168-74), Organization of American States (p.220-25), Universal Postal Union (p.286-88)), A-Z by name. Longer entries include list of publications and references. Further tables show country membership of UN and specialized agencies and membership of regional organizations. Foundation date, classified, acronym and name (organization) indexes. 'In many libraries ...

.... *(contd.)*

particularly those which are not research orientated and have limited budgets, Schiavone's work will be the reference source of choice on international organizations' (*Reference reviews*, v.11(6), 1997, p.5). *Class No:* 061(100)

[2015]

SCHRAEPLER, H-A. Directory of international organizations. Washington, D.C., Georgetown Univ. Press, 1996. xxx,424p. £50.75;$65. ISBN: 0878406077.

Pbck. ed. also available (£19.50;$24.95).

Basic directory offering 3-10 page profiles of international organizations. Arranged in 6 sections: I. United Nations - II. North Atlantic Treaty Organization - III. Regional organizations of worldwide importance - IV. Economic organizations of worldwide importance - V. The Commonwealth and Commonwealth of Independent States - VI. Other organizations of worldwide relevance. Fewer entries than Schiavone (above) and less factual detail, but still 'a convenient, one-volume overview of major international organizations' (*American reference books annual*, v.28, 1997, p.278). *Class No:* 061(100)

[2016]

UNION OF INTERNATIONAL ASSOCIATIONS. The 1978 international organizations founded since the Congress of Vienna: chronological list. Brussels, Union of International Associations, 1957. xxviii,204p. (*Documents, no.7.*)

Chronological list 1815-1956 with two earlier entries. Details: date; place; name (and later name(s)); UDC number. English and French subject index. 585 of the organizations had ceased operation at the time of compilation. *Class No:* 061(100)

[2017]

Yearbook of international organizations. Union of International Associations, *ed.* München, Saur, 1948-. Annual. £845;$1155. ISSN: 00843814.

Published annually since 1983 (previously approximately biennial), now in 4 volumes: 1. *Organization descriptions*; 2. *Country directory of secretariats and membership*; 3. *Subject directory and index*; 4. *International organization bibliography and resources*.

The 34th ed. for 1997/98 has information on 24,248 organizations in v.1 A-Z by title. Entries, based largely on information supplied by organizations, vary in length from a few lines to five or more pages. Detail normally includes history, structure, membership, description of activities and publications, with standard additional data such as address of main office, names of executive officers and foundation date. V.2 is a geographical index of organizations in two sections, the first listing principal and secondary secretariats located in the country, the second organizations of which the country is a member. V.3 classifies organizations under 2,000 categories and provides an A-Z keyword index. V.4, introduced from 1996/97, includes major periodical publications of international organizations together with bibliographic information on reseach into non-governmental organizations taken from *Encyclopedia of world problems and human potential*. Also available on CD-ROM as

....(contd.)

Yearbook Plus: international organizations and biographies (annual updating, £995) containing additional data from *Who's who in international organizations* (below). The major source, more comprehensive and detailed than Gale's *International organizations* (above). *Class No:* 061(100)

Abbreviations & Symbols

[2018]

Internationale Organisationen: Bezeichnungen, Abkürzungen, Akronyme. [International organizations: designations, abbreviations, acronyms.] Berlin, Walter de Gruyter, 1985. xi,640p. £51.85;DM128. (*Terminologische Schriftenreihe, Bd. 2.*) ISBN: 3110100428.

Published under the auspices of the Foreign Office Language Services Division of the German Federal Republic.

Contains in up to 7 languages (German (base language), plus English, French, Spanish, Dutch, Italian and Russian), the designations of bilateral or multilateral organizations, conferences, programmes, institutes, etc., together with their respective abbreviations. Includes references to higher ranking organizations, explanations (in German) and cross-references to alternative designations. Alphabetical, keyword, abbreviation and hierarchical index.
Class No: 061(100)(003)

Bibliographies

[2019]

ATHERTON, A.L. International organizations: a guide to information sources. Detroit, Gale, 1976. xxviii,350p. $68. (*International relations informations guide series, 1.*) ISBN: 0810313243.

1,532 annotated entries for English language sources. Topical arrangement with author, title and subject indexes. *Class No:* 061(100)(01)

[2020]

BAER, G.W. International organizations, 1918-1945: a guide to research and research materials. Rev. ed. Wilmington, Del., Scholarly Resources, 1991. xix,212p. £35.95;$65. ISBN: 0842023097.

First published 1981.

General treatment of materials such as archives followed by chapters on specific topics and bodies (*e.g.* League of Nations). Author index. *Class No:* 061(100)(01)

Indexes

[2021]

Organizations master index. Allard, D.M., *ed.* Detroit, Gale, 1987. 1120p. £110;$125. ISBN: 0810320797.

Subtitle: *A Consolidated index to approximately 50 directories, handbooks, yearbooks, encyclopedias and guides providing information on approximately 150,000 national and international associations, government agencies and advisory organizations, foundations, research centers, museums, religious groups, political organizations, labor unions and other organizations, institutions and programmes of all kinds in the United States, Canada and world wide.*

Intended to facilitate the search for information on national and international organizations. Sources include *American art directory*, *Encyclopedia of assocations (q.v.)*, *Foundation directory (q.v.)*, *Literary market place* and *World nuclear directory*. Each entry gives organization name, sponsor or

....(contd.)

parent organization, location (city, state, country) and a code identifying the source where information about the organization can be found. *Class No:* 061(100)(014)

Biographies

[2022]

Who's who in international organizations: a biographical encyclopedia of more than 13,000 leading personalities. Jenkins, J.C., *ed.* 2nd ed. München, Saur, 1996. 3v. £325;$385. ISBN: 3598112394.

At head of title: Union of International Organizations.

Biographies (v.1-2) for personalities from 11,339 organizations. All entries give name, current position and mailing address, with additional detail such as date of birth, awards interests, posts held and publications as available. V.3 comprises name by organization, name by area of concern (*e.g.* Biosciences/Growth; International relations) and name by country of citizenship indexes.
Class No: 061(100)(092)

Europe

[2023]

COMMISSION OF THE EUROPEAN COMMUNITIES. Répertoire des organisations professionelles de la Communauté européenne. [Directory of European Community trade and professional associations.] 5th ed. Luxembourg, Office des Publications Officielles des Communantés Européennes; Bruxelles, Editions Delta, 1992. 516p. ECU79. (*Information management series.*) ISBN: 9282641627.

Previous ed. 1990.

568 entries in sections Chambers of commerce - Industry - Crafts - Small and medium sized enterprises - Trade - Transport - Professions - Other activities - Unions - Consumer and other organizations - Miscellaneous. Associations must have a permanent secretariat or other organizational structure at European level, or have a membership predominantely drawn from EC countries. Data includes name, year founded, names of senior officials, address and list of national member associations. Acronym/abbreviation, subject and name indexes. '(U)p to date and reasonably priced' (but) 'a useful rather than essential purchase for a general reference library' (*The Year in reference*, 1993, p.9). *Class No:* 061(4)

[2024]

The Directory of EU trade and professional associations and their information. [Annuaire des associations professionelles communautaires et leurs information.] 2nd rev. ed. Genval, Bel., Euroconfidential, 1996. 335p. £110. ISBN: 2930066261.

'(S)eeks to identify the different sources of information offerred by EU trade and professional associations and provide comprehensive details about each association's membership' (Introduction). Approx. 650 associations A-Z by acronym. Variable data in condensed four column layout. Association name and keyword indexes. *Class No:* 061(4)

[2025]

Pan-European associations: a directory of multi-national organisations in Europe. Henderson, C.A.P., *ed.* 3rd ed. Beckenham, CBD Research, 1996. iv,306p. £94. ISBN: 0900246731.

First published 1983; 2nd ed. 1991.

Covers European voluntary organizations which represent membership, either throughout Europe, or in a significant number of countries. Also includes international voluntary organizations whose membership is almost exclusively European. About 2,300 entries (p.1-251) Academica Europaea ... Zinc Oxide Producers' Association, with numerous cross-references mainly to names in other languages. About 50% of associations included are from professional fields, the majority of the remainder are trade organizations. Data includes full contact information with email and URL, activities, country memberships, affiliations and publications. Separate list of 'Unverified and lost associations' (p.253-59). Abbreviations index (p.261-75); subject index (p.277-306). Includes some bodies not in the *Yearbook of international organizations* (above). *Class No:* 061(4)

[2026]

—Directory of pan-European organisations. London, Euromonitor, 1992. vii,258p. £160;$335. ISBN: 0863384056.

Includes pan-European official, semi-official and voluntary organizations, plus international organizations whose membership and sphere of activity is largely confined to Europe. Entires A-Z by English title with variable data on objectives, structure, membership, activities, regular publications, etc. Separate subject listing of statistical sources. Indexed by acronym and subject (190 headings). Less comprehensive than its CBD rival (above), trade organizations predomintating. *Class No:* 061(4)

[2027]

SCHRAEPLER, H-A. European handbook of organisations. London, Whurr Publishers, 1993. xii,177p. tables. £40. ISBN: 1870332296.

Also available in pbck. (£17.50. ISBN: 1870332342).

Guide, for a general audience, 'to the purposes, structures and activities of those European and international organisations that influence European affairs' (p.v.). Contents: I. The Conference on Security and Cooperation in Europe; II. European Union; III. European organisations (22 entries, *e.g.* European Space Agency, Danube Commission); IV. Military alliances; V. Other organisations with economic and political relevance for Europe (*e.g.* OPEC). Tables indicating memberships by country (p.149-64). Abbreviations, bibliography and index. *Class No:* 061(4)

[2028]

URWIN, D.W. Historical dictionary of European organizations. Metuchen, N.J., Scarecrow Press, 1994. xxx,389p. £44.55;$49.50. (*International organizations series, 4.*) ISBN: 0810828383.

Dictionary (p.7-310) has *c.600 variable length entries for organizations, agreements, individuals, etc. (e.g.* Council for Mutual Economic Assistance' 3p., 'Jenkins, Roy' 1p.). Complemented by bibliography (p.315-89) in 18 topical sections. '(D)oes not define its subject matter in a clear manner, covers more or less post-war European history in general and duplicates to a considerable extent the volume that launched this series of historical dictionaries, Desmond Dinan's *Historical dictionary of the European Community* (*Reference reviews*, v.9(5), 1995, p.10). *Class No:* 061(4)

Great Britain

[2029]

Associations and professional bodies of the United Kingdom: an alphabetical and subject-classified guide to over 3,700 organisations. Ramscar, J., *ed.* 14th ed. London, Gale, 1995. vi,863p. £115. ISBN: 0787607355.

First published 1962; 13th ed. 1994. Title and publisher varies: previously as *Trade associations and professional bodies of the United Kingdom.*

Also includes trade unions, livery companies and charities. Main section (p.1-758) lists organizations A-Z giving name, address, contact name, date founded, no. of members, no. of staff, affiliated organizations, member profile (*c.*15-20 words) and objectives (*c.*20-50 words). Separate lists of 'Chambers of commerce, trade, industry and shipping' (p.759-67) and 'United Kingdom offices of overseas chambers of commerce'; appended 'List of organisations with unknown addresses'. Subject (broad term) and geographic indexes. *Class No:* 061(410)

[2030]

Councils, committees & boards: including government agencies & authorities: a handbook of advisory, consultative, executive, regulatory & similar bodies in British public life. Henderson, C.A.P., *ed.* 10th ed. Beckenham, CBD Research, 1998. viii,439p. ISBN: 0900246790.

First published 1970; 9th ed. 1995. A companion volume to *Directory of British associations* (below).

Arranged A-Z by names of bodies. Wide ranging coverage, c.1,600 entries (*e.g.* Jewish Marriage Council; Sugar Beet Research and Education Committee) including the National Health Service, tourist boards, consumer councils and passenger transport authorities and executives. Excludes purely local bodies, sub-committees or working parties responsible to a superior committee and government committees composed solely of officials of a government department. Data for each body includes postal address, email and URL, establishment date, previous name(s), membership, terms of reference, objects/duties and or mission statement, activities and publications. Abbreviation, chairmen and other senior personnel and subject indexes. *Class No:* 061(410)

[2031]

Directory of British associations: & associations in Ireland. Henderson, S.P.A. *and* Henderson, A.J.W., *eds.* 13th ed. Beckenham, CBD Research, 1996. xvi,626p. £142.50. ISBN: 0900246766.

First published 1965; 12th ed. 1994. Editions now appear biennially.

The major British directory of associations covering 'national associations, societies, institutions and similar organisations in all fields of activity which have a voluntary membership. Regional and local organisations concerned with important industries and trade ... are included, as are local chambers of commerce and county agricultural, archaeological, historical, natural history and similar organizations' (Introduction p.ix). Questionnaire based, about 7,000 organizations included. Heavy use of coded data. Entries, A-Z by name, give date founded, address etc. (including email), name of secretary or other senior officer, type of constitution, branches, organization type, activities, affiliations, membership, publications and former names. Separate list of 'Unverified and lost associations' (blue pages). Abbreviations index. Subject index under detailed headings (p.535-626); ample cross-references. Also available on CD-ROM (£200). *Class No:* 061(410)

[2032]

Key organisations: the address list of the year. Carlisle, Carel Press, 1995-. Annual. £12.50.

1997 issue (41p. ISBN: 187236537X) gives postal address, tel. no., fax. no., email, URL, and one line description for *c.*1,500 UK organizations. Thematic guide under headings such as animals, family and sport and leisure precedes main listing. Aimed primarily at schools, '(m)ost general libraries will prefer the *Directory of British associations*' (*Refer*, v.12(2), Spring 1996, p.22).
Class No: 061(410)

[2033]

The Voluntary agencies directory. London, NCVO Publications, 1928-. Biennial. £20.

Title and frequency varies. First published as *Voluntary social services: handbook and directory*, 1928, revised six times 1948-70, with 2nd ed. 1973 and 3rd ed. 1978. 4th ed. (1980) and subsequent eds. as *Voluntary organizations: an NCVO directory*. Present title from 9th ed. (1987); published annually since 1995.

The 17th ed. (1998. xi,448p. ISBN: 0719915120) has entries for over 2,500 organizations A-Z. 'Voluntary agency is interpreted broadly as a self-governing body of people who have joined together voluntarily to take action for the betterment (as they perceive it) of the community and are established otherwise than for financial gain. Organisations affiliated to any political party are not eligible for inclusion' (p.xi). Not restricted to the social service sector, including a wide range of organizations (*e.g.* British Tarantula Society; Farming and Wildlife Advisory Group; Plain English Campaign; Third World First). Typical entry gives address, director (or equivalent), contact and date founded, with brief descriptive paragraphs on objects and activities and coded data for membership, publication production, income and expenditure, etc. Useful addresses, (p.346-58); abbreviations and acronyms, (p.362-75); classified index, (p.378-445). A less wide ranging, but cheaper, alternative to sources such as the *Directory of British associations* (above).
Class No: 061(410)

Scotland

[2034]

BRANDER, M. The World directory of Scottish associations. [2nd ed.]. Glasgow, Neil Wilson Publishing, 1996. [xv],281p. £14.95;$22.95. ISBN: 1897784279.

First published 1979.

Covers 'societies, clubs and associations throughout the world, as well as in Scotland itself, connected with Scottish heritage in one way or another' (*Preface*). Includes clan societies, Burns clubs, dance groups, Highland Games societies and pipe bands. *c.*2,000 entries in 50 country sections many with brief descriptions of aims and activities. Indexed (p.256-81). *Class No:* 061(411)

[2035]

MacDONALD, F. The Scottish companion. 1989/90. 3rd ed. Ayr, Carrick Publishing, 1989. 176p. £20. ISBN: 0946724210.

First published 1985; 2nd ed. 1987.

A directory of 1,100 Scottish institutions, societies and associations. Local branches of national bodies generally excluded. Arranged A-Z by title giving address, foundation date, principal officers and a 25-50 word description. Separate lists of Scottish secondary schools and MPs. Subject index under 35 headings (p.166-76).
Class No: 061(411)

Commonwealth

[2036]

Directory of Commonwealth organizations: official and unofficial organizations of the Commonwealth. 4th ed. London, Commonwealth Secretariat, 1991. 166p. £5. ISBN: 0850923654.

First published 1977; 3rd ed. 1985 under title *Commonwealth organizations: a directory of official and unofficial organizations active in the Commonwealth.*

In 2pts., the first describing the Commonwealth Secretariat and related bodies, the second general government and non-government organizations. *Class No:* 061(41-44)

Wales

[2037]

WALES COUNCIL FOR VOLUNTARY ACTION. Directory of voluntary organisations in Wales: national contacts 1997. [Cyfeiriadur mudiadau gwirfoddal yng Nghymru: cysylltiadu cenedlaethol.] 4th ed. Caerphilly, Welsh Council for Voluntary Service, 1996. 82p. ISBN: 1871094526.

First published 1988; 3rd ed. 1994.

Questionnaire based directory of nearly 400 entries. Covers both Welsh national organizations and UK national organizations able to provide regional contacts in Wales. Entry detail, in English and Welsh, includes contact detail, objectives, actvities and publications. Broad term subject index (p.11-19). *Class No:* 061(429)

Poland

[2038]

Informator nauki polskiej. Warszawa, Ośrodek Przetwarzania Informacji, 1958-. Annual (irregular). ISSN: 0537667x.

Ed. 26 1995/96 (5v. in 6) covers a wide range of organizations including learned societies, universities and other advanced educational institutions. Main listings in v.2 *Instytucje naukowe*; v.4 *Ludzie nauki* has biographical information. *Class No:* 061(438)

France

[2039]

GAFA: guide annuaire des fondations et des associations. Paris, Éditions SA2, 198?-. Irregular. FFr620. ISSN: 11641975.

Lists French foundations and associations by fields of activity. Acronym, name and subject indexes. 5. éd. now available (1997. xxvi,483p.). *Class No:* 061(44)

Norway

[2040]

Norske organisasjoner. Oslo, Fabritius, 1966-. Irregular. NKr389.

First published as *Oppslagsboken Norske organisasjoner*.

Directory of Norwegian trade associations, research institutions, political parties, pressure groups and professional bodies. Latest ed. 1993 (Hallenstvedt, A. & Trollvik, J. *red.* xvi,704p. ISBN: 8207009691).
Class No: 061(481)

Japan

[2041]

Japan directory of professional associations. 3rd ed. Tokyo, Intercontinental Marketing, 1994. 420p. £125;$300. ISBN: 4900178098.

First published 1984; 2nd ed. 1988.

Covers approx. 8,600 academic, commercial, cultural, industrial, professional, research and technical associations. Arranged in alphabetical order by English name with Japanese name (romanized) and address. More complete entries also give senior personnel, EMail/Internet address, no. of staff, purpose/activity and whether a library is maintained. Indexed by Japanese name and subject. Also available on diskette. 4th ed. scheduled for 1998.
Class No: 061(52)

Asia—South & South East

[2042]

An Alternative directory of nongovernmental organizations in South Asia. Nachowitz, T., *ed.* Rev. ed. Syracuse, N.Y., Maxwell School of Citizenship and Public Affairs, Syracuse Univ., 1990. xii,82p. $15. (*Foreign and comparative studies South Asian series, 14.*) ISBN: 0915984415.

First published 1989.

Lists organizations in India, Pakistan, Bangladesh, Sri Lanka and Nepal under 24 headings (Alternative travel and tourism ... Environment ... Human rights ... Women). Most entries include 50-200 word descriptions. Indexed. '(N)ot comprehensive, but is a good addition to the literature' (*Choice*, v.28(8), April 1991, p.1283).
Class No: 061(54+59)

Africa

[2043]

DELANCEY, M.W. *and* **MAYS, T.M. Historical dictionary of international organizations in sub-Saharan Africa.** Metuchen, N.J., Scarecrow Press, 1994. lviii,517p. maps. £60.75;$69.50. (*International organizations series, 3.*) ISBN: 0810827514.

'The Dictionary' (p.27-284) has 50-200 word entries for *c.*250 organizations. 'The Bibliography' (p.285-483) is an unannotated listing of *c.*1,500 items. Acronym key and chronology precede; appendices include classification of organizations by field of activity. 'There is no comparable work' (*Choice*, v.32(8), April 1995, p.1282).
Class No: 061(6)

[2044]

FREDLAND, R. A Guide to African international organizations. London, Zell, 1990. vii,315p. tables, maps. $85. ISBN: 0905450906.

'This volume serves two purposes. First, it is a compilation of about 400 *intergovernmental* organizations which have existed and still do exist in Africa. Second, it offers a commentary about the institution of African international organizations ...' (Foreword p.vii). Main section (p.49-157) gives name, acronym, when founded, headquarters and brief description of objectives; section (p.15-47), on the main international organizations (OAU, EAC, OCAM, ECOWAS, SADCC, UDEAC, PAC, ADB), precedes. Supported by 'Individuals in the leadership of African international organizations' (p.159-75) giving biographical data on 120 persons, and a chronology (p.177-79). 6 appendices including a listing of acronyms and

.... *(contd.)*

individual country memberships. 10 maps; bibliography (p.291-305). Somewhat meagre index, but otherwise superbly done. *Class No:* 061(6)

[2045]

SÖDERBAUM, F. Handbook of regional organizations in Africa. Uppsala, Nordiska Afrikansinstitutet, 1996. 161p. chart. SKr150. ISBN: 9171064001.

In 2pts. I. 'Main regional organizations in Africa' has detailed entries for 15 organizations including the African Development Bank, OAU and South African Customs Union. Pt. II. 'Other regional organizations in Africa' has shorter entries, *e.g.* 'Club of the Sahel' ½p., 'Lake Victoria Fisheries Commission' 9 lines. List of acronyms and A-Z list of organizations as appendices. *Class No:* 061(6)

South Africa

[2046]

Bridge: a directory of organisations at work in South Africa. Johannesburg, Human Awareness Programme Organisational Development Services, 1980-. Irregular.

Title varies slightly.

The 1995 ed. (241p.) is a directory of South African organisations with the emphasis on those concerned with education, health welfare, religious and social matters. Further listings of conference centres and university libraries. *Class No:* 061(680)

[2047]

Directory of South African associations. [Gids van Suid-Afrikaanse verenigings.] Pretoria, Council for Scientific and Industrial Research, Division of Information Services, 1990-. Irregular.

1992/93 ed. (1993. 488p.) is an A-Z listing. Excludes political parties and religious denominations. Subject keyword index and list of acronyms. *Class No:* 061(680)

Canada

[2048]

Associations Canada: the directory of associations in Canada. Toronto, Canadian Almanac & Directory Publishing, 1991-. Annual. Can$289. ISSN: 11869798.

The 1998/99 ed. lists more than 21,000 Canadian industrial, commercial, professional, charitable and special interest associations and international organizations active in Canada. Comprehensively indexed by subject, place, acronym, Internet and email address, budget, etc. Also available on CD-ROM (Can$389. ISSN: 12093726). Slightly more entries than *Directory of associations in Canada* (below). *Class No:* 061(71)

[2049]

Directory of associations in Canada. [Répertoire des associations du Canada.] Toronto, Micromedia, 1973-. Annual. ISSN: 03160734.

Biennial 1973-82. Publisher varies, formerly Univ. of Toronto Press.

Covers non-profit and non-governmental associations including foundations and research institutions, international and foreign associations with offices or affiliates in Canada and local branches of national associations. Brief data such as name of chief executive or equivalent, no. of staff, no. of members, titles of publications, conference dates and descriptive note. Main (keyword) index; further indexes

....(contd.)
including acronym, personal name and budget. The 18th ed. (1997. xvi,1307p.) lists *c.*17,000 associations and is the first to include URLs. *Class No:* 061(71)

USA

[2050]

Encyclopedia of associations. Detroit, Gale, 1956-. Annual. $570. ISSN: 00710202.

Title varies: early editions as *Encyclopedia of American associations*. Now published in 3 volumes: v.1 *National organisations of the US*; v.2 *Geographic and executive indexes*; v.3 *Supplement*.

Subtitle of 33rd ed. (1998) *A Guide to over 23,000 national and international organizations, including: trade, business and commercial; environmental and agricultural; legal, governmental, public administration and military; engineering, technological and natural and social sciences; educational, cultural and social welfare; health and medical; public affairs; fraternal, nationality and ethnic; religious; veterans, hereditary and patriotic; hobby and avocational; athletic and sports; labor unions, associations and federations; chambers of commerce and trade and tourism; Greek letter and related organizations, and fan clubs*.

V.1 *National organizations of the US* in 3 pts. Pts.1-2 contain entries for 22,761 non-profit American membership organizations of national scope arranged according to 18 subject groups. Up to 33 categories of information given for each entry, including address, chief official and title, founding date, no. of members, staff, budget, regional state and local groups, description (50-200 words), computer services, affiliations, publications and conventions/meetings. Name and keyword index issued as pt.3 of v.1 includes references to organizations listed in *International organizations* (*q.v.*). V.2 of the set offers further indexing by state/city and executive name. V.3 is an inter-edition supplement containing new and updated entries.

The entire set, together with the associated publications *International organizations* and *Regional, state and local organizations* (below), is searchable online through Dialog (file 114) and GaleNet. Also available on CD-ROM (semi-annual updating, £1,070) as *Associations unlimited*. Electronic versions contain additional data on government nonprofit organizations and the full text of printed materials for about 2,000 major associations. *Class No:* 061(73)

[2051]

—Gale encyclopedia of business and professional associations: a guide to more than 8,000 business, professional, trade and related organizations. Huellmantel, M.B., *and others eds.* Detroit, Gale, 1995. xxvii,1184p. $75. ISBN: 0787602949.

Offshoot of *Encyclopedia of associations*, intended as a rival to *National trade and professional associations of the United States* (below). 8,161 entries. *Class No:* 061(73)

[2052]

—Regional, state and local organizations: a guide to ... United States nonprofit membership organizations with interstate, state, intrastate, city or local scope, membership and interest concerned with all areas of activity. Detroit, Gale, 1987-. Irregular (now appearing annually). $510 (individual vols. $130). ISSN: 08942846.

Issued in 5v. V.1 *Great Lakes states*; v.2 *Northeastern states*; v.3 *Southern and Middle Atlantic states*; v.4 *South Central and Great Plains states*; v.5 *Western states*.

Includes local affiliates, chapters, branches, etc. of national associations. State then city arrangement. Briefer

....(contd.)
entries, but otherwise similar format and style to the *Encyclopedia of associations*. Name and keyword index in each v. Over 100,000 entries in 6th ed. (1997). Records are also available as part of the *Associations unlimited* database (above). *Class No:* 061(73)

[2053]

National directory of nonprofit organizations. Detroit, Taft Group/Gale, 1989-. Annual. ISSN: 10488154.

Issued in 3v. Originally published as the *Taft directory of nonprofit organizations*.

1995 ed. has basic detail on 185,000 organizations with annual revenue in excess of $100,000. *Class No:* 061(73)

[2054]

National trade and professional associations of the United States. Washington, D.C., Columbia Books, 1966-. Annual. $85. ISSN: 0734354x.

Title varies; previously *Directory of national trade and professional associations of the United States*.

The 32nd ed. (1997. 694p.) lists about 7,625 trade associations, labour unions, professional, scientific and other 'national groups composed of combinations united for a common purpose'. Excludes fraternal, sporting, patriotic and hobby associations. Brief data only including membership, budget, publications and annual meetings. Subject, geographic, budget size, executive and acronym indexing. A cheaper and generally accurate alternative to the *Encyclopedia of associations* (above), but far fewer entries and less information. A companion v., *State and regional associations of the United States* (9th ed. 1997. ISBN: 1880873230), is also available. *Class No:* 061(73)

Australia

[2055]

Directory of Australian associations. Melbourne, Vic., Information Australia, 1978-. Irregular (currently revised and updated every 4 months). ISSN: 0110666x.

Ed.30, November 1997-March 1998 (1997. vi,[56],864p.), has 5,017 entries, including international and foreign associations with branches/offices in Australia, state wide associations and associations in the major metropolitan areas. Student organizations, local community associations, etc. excluded. Full detail (*e.g.* address including email and URL, senior personnel, membership, frequency of meetings, publications) with summary description of objectives/activities. Arranged by broad headings; alphabetical, subject and acronym indexes. *Class No:* 061(94)

Non-Government Organizations

Learned Societies

[2056]

International encyclopedia of learned societies and academies. Kiger, J.C., *ed.* Westport, Conn., Greenwood Press, 1993. xiii,377p. £85.50;$99.50. ISBN: 0313276463.

Companion v. to the same author's *Research institutions and learned societies* (*q.v.*). Provides 2-6p. profiles of 103 societies and academies from 50 countries. Draws heavily on official histories, with limited current information. UK bodies include British Academy, Royal Academy of Arts and Royal Society. Appendices list institutions by foundation date, outline name changes and group by subject. Index (p.353-71). *Class No:* 061.22

[2057]

World guide to scientific associations and learned societies. Zils, M., *ed.* 7th ed. München, Saur, 1998. xiv,529p. £215;$300. (*Handbook of international documentation and information, v.13.*) ISBN: 3598205813.

First published 1974 as *World guide to scientific organizations*; 6th ed. 1994.

6th ed. (xiv,524p.) has 17,190 entries in country sections for associations and societies 'from the fields of science, culture and technology'. Wider scope than the title suggests, UK associations/societies including The Museums Association, Royal Institute of International Affairs and Society of Indexers. Information includes name, address, year of foundation, no. of members, chief officers, area of activity, and periodical publications. Condensed text in 4 col. format, many entries lack full detail. Association name, subject and publications index. Some overlap with other sources such as *World of learning*. *Class No:* 061.22

[2058]

World of learning. London, Europa, 1947-. Annual. £225. ISSN: 00842117.

Entries for major countries include sections 'Learned societies' and 'Research institutions'. 'Sweden' (p.1397-416, 48th ed. 1998) has brief details for 50 and 34 bodies respectively. *Class No:* 061.22

Internet

[2059]

Scholarly societies project. Parrot, J., *ed.* Waterloo, Ont., Univ. of Waterloo, 1995-. World Wide Web resource.

URL: http://www.lib.uwaterloo.ca/society/overview.html. Date reviewed 22nd July 1998. Part of the University of Waterloo electronic library.

Main links are to WWW sites of 1,250 scholarly societies world wide through subject, society name and founding date listings. Also provides links to international unions, meeting/conference announcement lists, full text serials and Internet based essays and other commentaries concening scholarly societies. Fielded searching of society data also available. A well maintained and regularly updated site.
Class No: 061.22(003.41)

Europe

[2060]

Directory of European professional & learned societies. Greenslade, S., *ed.* 5th ed. Beckenham, CBD Research, 1995. xvi,412p. £125;$262.50. ISBN: 0900246707.

Distributed in the US by Gale. Title, introductory matter and subject indexes also in French and German. Replaces *Directory of European associations. Part 2. National learned, scientific and technical societies*, first published 1975. Current title and format from 4th ed. 1989. Companion to *Directory of European industrial and trade associations* and *Directory of European medical organizations.*

Excludes British, pan-European or international associations. About 3,000 entries A-Z by society name. A full entry provides name, acronym, foundation date, address, objectives, affiliations, official languages, membership of international organizations, publications, former names and notes. Separate list of unverified societies; abbreviation and subject indexes. *Class No:* 061.22(4)

Great Britain

[2061]

FOUNDATION FOR SCIENCE AND TECHNOLOGY. The Register of learned and professional societies. London, Foundation for Science and Technology, 1986-. Irregular.

The 1994/95 ed. [4th] (1994. xi,255p. ISBN: 1872387063) has entries for over 400 societies A-Z. Information for each includes address, senior employee, contact name, statement of aims (one sentence), no. of members, qualifications awarded, principal publications, short list of activities and a description of facilities. Wide range of bodies covered *e.g.* General Council and Register of Naturopaths, Institute of Chartered Accountants in England and Wales, Royal College of Art, Society for Libyan Studies. List of 'Societies for which no details are held' with addresses (p.217-43); very basic subject index (p.245-85). Not a substitute for the CBD family of directories. *Class No:* 061.22(410)

Germany

[2062]

Vademecum deutscher Lehr- und Forschungsstätten: Stätten der Forschung. Bonn, Raabe, 1955-. Irregular. DM590. ISSN: 00835080.

First published as *Vademecum deutscher Forschungsstätten*; present title from 4th ed. 1964. 9th ed. 1989.

A well-established directory of research institutions and learned societies, including industrial and public institutions and institutes of universities. 11.Aufl. (1994. 2.v.) has over 12,500 entries in 5 main sections: A. Geisteswissenschaften - B. Naturwissenschaften - C. Biowissenschaften - D. Ingenieurwissenschaften - E. Bibliotheken, Archive, Dokumentationsstellen, Museen, etc. Entries include address, parent organization, management, key staff, subject area and research projects. Place, name and subject indexes in v.2 (p.1587-2051). Also available online through STN International and on CD-ROM (annual updating, DM1610). A looseleaf version under title *Vademecum, Stätten der Forschung* began publication 1996. *Class No:* 061.22(430)

Italy

[2063]

ISTITUTO NAZIONALE DELL'INFORMAZIONE. Doc Italia: annuario degli enti di studio, cultura, ricerca e informazione. Roma, Editoriale Italiana, 1972-. Irregular. L250,000. ISSN: 03915018.

Continues *Doc; documentazione*.

A-Z list of Italian learned societies, scholarly institutions etc., with the emphasis on research organizations. Gives address, foundation date, constitution, senior personnel, notes on scope and activities and periodical publications. Subject and acronym indexes. Over 7,000 listings in 6th ed. for 1992/93 (1992. 1631p.). *Class No:* 061.22(450)

RSFSR

[2064]

A Scholars' guide to humanities and social sciences in the Soviet successor states: the Academies of Sciences of Russia, Armenia, Azerbaidzhan, Belarus, Estonia, Georgia, Kazakhstan, Kirghizstan, Latvia, Lithuania, Moldova, Tadzhikistan, Turkmenistan, Ukraine and Uzbekistan. [2nd ed.]. Armonk, N.Y., M.E. Sharpe, 1993. xv,228p. £175.50;$215. ISBN: 0873328310.

Joint project of the Institute of Scientific Information in the

....*(contd.)*
Social Sciences (INION), Russian Academy of Sciences and the Kennan Institute for Advanced Russian Studies, Woodrow Wilson International Center for Scholars. 1st ed. as *A Scholars' guide to humanities and social sciences in the Soviet Union* (1985).

In 2pts. The first deals with the Russian Academy of Sciences (p.13-106) including information on 70 constituent divisions, the second (p.109-94) gives similar treatment to the Academies of Sciences of the other states (*e.g.* Institute of Psychology Georgian Academy of Sciences; Institute of History of Moldova Academy of Sciences). Impressively detailed entries, entirely in English, cover history, structure, staff, research areas, serial publications, library and archive collections, etc. Subject and supervisor indexes.
Class No: 061.22(470)

China

[2065]
Directory of Chinese learned organizations. Beijing, World Publishing Corporation, 1990. iv,775p. £85.50;$159. ISBN: 0387530134.

Distr. worldwide by Springer-Verlag, Berlin.

More wide-ranging than the title suggests. 5 sections: Research institutions (2,391 entries); Universities and colleges (590 entries); Societies and associations (404 entries); Public and special libraries (129 entries); Museums (89 entries). Variable data for each organization, but a good number have descriptions and all are coded to indicate subject scope and geographic location. Category (subject), geographic and Chinese phonetic indexes.
Class No: 061.22(510)

Social, Sports & Literary Clubs & Associations

[2066]
The 1990 British club year book and directory. 7th ed. London, Eagle Commercial Publications, 1990. vii,612p. ISBN: 0951558307.

First published 1961, 6th ed. 1982.

Coverage includes sports clubs (*e.g.* bowls, golf, rugby) leisure interest clubs (*e.g.* antiques, camera, horticulture), social clubs, political clubs and various other general clubs and similar organizations. Brief entries, arranged in 120 categories Alcuin ... YWCA, giving address, tel. no. and contact (secretary etc.) only. Includes full listings of branches of nationally organized clubs (*e.g.* English Golf Union). Listing of working men's clubs (p.128-73). A useful source, worthy of more regular updating.
Class No: 061.237

Foundations & Endowments

[2067]
International encyclopedia of foundations. Kiger, J.C., *ed.* Westport, Conn., Greenwood, 1990. xxi,335p. £76.50$89.50. ISBN: 0313259836.

Information on the history and operations of 145 foundations in 31 countries, US excluded. All entries include references to further information sources. '(P)rovides more depth than *The International foundation directory*' (*Choice*, v.28(2), October 1990, p.284), but much narrower coverage and no substitute for this work as a source of current information. *Class No:* 061.27

[2068]
The International foundation directory 1996. 7th ed. London, Europa Publications, 1996. xiii,817p. £95;$190. ISBN: 1857430174.

First published 1974; 6th ed. 1994.

To be included foundations must be independent, recognised as charitable, permanently established, allocate funds on a discretionary basis and operate or have an impact across national boundaries. *c.*1,500 entries (300 more than the 6th ed.) arranged by 100 host countries Albania-Zambia. Each entry gives title, brief history and objectives, activities, publications, financial detail, senior personnel and address. UK foundations p.447-556, US p.557-693. Masterful introduction by H.V. Hodson (p.1-17) provides historical perspective. Brief select bibliography. Index of foundation names; index of main activities (11 broad headings only).
Class No: 061.27

Europe

[2069]
Selected bibliography on foundations and corporate funders in Europe: an annotated bibliography of regional, national and European-level funding directories, legal, fiscal and management titles and publications of members of the European Foundation Centre. Garonzik, E. *and* Hadju, A., *comps*. Brussels, European Foundation Centre, 1994. viii,69p. ISBN: 2930107006.

260 entries mostly for reports, newsletters, brochures, etc.
Class No: 061.27(4)

Germany

[2070]
Verzeichnis der deutschen Stiftungen. Bundesverband Deutscher Stiftungen e.V., *hrsg*. [2. Aufl.]. Darmstadt, Hoppenstedt, 1994. xix,1061p. DM245. ISBN: 3820303219.

First published 1991.

Lists 6,812 German foundations, charitable trusts, etc. A-Z (p.1-891) giving basic information only. Indexed by area of interest (13 broad categories) and location.
Class No: 061.27(430)

Spain

[2071]
Directorio de las fundaciones españolas. Madrid, Centro de Fundaciones, 1994. 539p. Ptas. 7200. ISBN: 8481980242.

Geographically arranged directory of 2,716 Spanish foundations, many government related.
Class No: 061.27(460)

USA

[2072]
The Foundation directory. New York, The Foundation Center, 1960-. Annual. $190. ISSN: 00718092.

Frequency varies: originally irregular, then biennial.

Foundation defined as a 'nongovernmental, nonprofit organization with its own funds (usually from a single source, either an individual family or corporation) and program managed by its own trustees and directors, which was established to maintain or aid educational, social, charitable, religious or other activities serving the common welfare, primarily by making grants to nonprofit organizations'. To be included a foundation must have assets of at least $2,000,000 or give in excess of $200,000 annually (foundations not meeting these criteria separately treated in

....(contd.)
The Foundation directory part 2 (below)). Coverage confined to the US. Arranged geographically by state; various indexes including donors/officers/trustees, geographic, type of support, subject and foundation name. 7,961 entries in the 19th ed. (1997. xxxviii,2172p.). Also available online through Dialog (File 26), updated annually, and on CD-ROM as *FC search the Foundation Center database on CD-ROM*, updated semi-monthly ($1,195). *Class No:* 061.27(73)

[2073]

—The Foundation directory part 2. New York, The Foundation Center, 1990-. Annual. $185. ISSN: 10586210.

Covers foundations with assets of $1,000,000-$2,000,000 or annual grantmaking programmes of $50,000-$200,000. *Class No:* 061.27(73)

Conferences

Abbreviations & Symbols

[2074]

Directory of acronyms and abbreviations: derived from the British Library's catalogue of conference proceedings. 1993-. Boston Spa, British Library Document Supply Centre, 1993-. Biennial (approx.) £27. ISSN: 13586955.

3rd ed. (1998. 192p.) expands more than 9,000 acronyms present in the *Index to conference proceedings* (*q.v.*) database. In addition to conference titles, acronyms may relate to organizations, societies, etc., or scientific and medical terms. *Class No:* 061.3(003)

Internet

[2075]

The Directory of scholarly and professional E-conferences. Kovacs, D., *comp*. World Wide Web resource.

URL: http://n2h2.com/KOVACS/. Date reviewed 22nd July 1998.

Previously titled *Directory of scholarly electronic conferences*. An annual print version is also issued by the Association of Research Libraries (as component of *Directory of electronic journals ...* (*q.v.*)).

Lists, organizes and evaluates discussion lists, newsgroups, mailing lists, etc. of 'interest to scholars and professionals in their scholarly, pedagogical and professional activities'. Records include name, subscription and other addresses, whether moderated, archive availabilty and keywords. Records accessed either from fielded search option or subject category and alphabetical browse lists. Established as the major information source on 'worthwhile' electronic conferences and similar Internet based communication. *Class No:* 061.3(003.41)

Dictionaries

[2076]

COMMISSION OF THE EUROPEAN COMMUNITIES *and* INTERNATIONAL ASSOCIATION OF PROFESSIONAL CONGRESS ORGANISERS. Congress terminology. Luxembourg, Office for Official Publications of the European Community, 1987. 172p. ECU35. ISBN: 9282566102.

A tool for those who operate in a professional capacity in the congress sector. It's 'fundamental aim is to standardize congress terminology' (p.5). 335 terms arranged A-Z in

....(contd.)
English with equivalents in French, German, Spanish and Italian. Brief definitions in English only. 5 language index section (p.123-72). *Class No:* 061.3(038)

[2077]

Conference terminology: a manual for conference-members and interpreters in English, French, Spanish, Russian, Italian, German, Hungarian. Herbert, J., *ed.* 2nd rev. & augm. ed. Amsterdam, Elsevier, 1976. [16],207p. £68.65;$130.25. (*Glossaria interpretum.*) ISBN: 0444413545.

First published 1957. Hungarian has been added to this 2nd ed.

756 numbered English entries, with equivalents in the other six languages. Six sections (subdivided): A. Types of meetings - B. Preparation of the meeting - C. Documents - D. Composition of a conference - E. Votes and elections - F. Debates. Many compounded expressions (*e.g.* 'draft resolutions', 'confidential documents'). Seven language indexes. *Class No:* 061.3(038)

Worldwide

[2078]

EventLine. Amsterdam, Elsevier, 1990-. Computer database.

Available online, vendors include Datastar (EVNT), Dialog (File 165), OCLC, Questel Orbit and STN International. Updated monthly.

Database directory of past and forthcoming conferences, symposia, seminars, workshops, trade fairs, exhibitions and major sporting events. Information on 40,000 events added annually, database now comprises over 400,000 records. Each event coded from 700 subject classifications, data includes event title, subject, type, date, venue and contacts (including email and URL addresses). Also available as a quarterly updated CD-ROM (£480). *Class No:* 061.3(100)

[2079]

International congress calendar. Union of International Associations, *ed.* Brussels, Union of International Associations, 1961-. Quarterly. $395. ISSN: 05386349.

Issued in 4 editions annually, each of which supersedes the last.

Covers conferences of international organizations and important national bodies. Geographical and chronological sections, each giving date and place of conference and, as available, address of organizing body, estimated number of participants, number of countries represented, concurrent exhibitions and references to organization entries in the *Yearbook of international organizations* (*q.v.*). About 10,000 announcements annually, many for conferences several years ahead. Subject/organization index based on significant keywords in the organization name or name of principal conference theme. *Class No:* 061.3(100)

[2080]

World meetings: social & behavioral sciences, human services & management. New York, World Meetings Publications, Macmillan Library Reference, 1971-. Quarterly. $180. ISSN: 01946161.

A 2 year registry of future meetings, seminars, conferences, exhibitions and other events. Main entry section lists meetings in 8 sub-sections, one for each quarter of the 2 year period. Each entry gives meeting title, location, date, sponsor, contact, brief description of planned content, estimated attendance, papers deadline, availability of papers, abstracts, etc. and no. of exhibitors. Quarterly issues completely revised and updated, new/revised entries

....(contd.)
indicated. Main section preceeded by 6 indexes: subject (27 categories); date; location; publisher; deadline (submission of papers); sponsor. *Class No:* 061.3(100)

Histories

[2081]
UNION OF INTERNATIONAL ASSOCIATIONS. Les Congrès internationaux de 1681 à 1899: liste complète. [International congresses, 1681 to 1899, full list.] Bruxelles, Union of International Associations, 1960. 76p. (*Documents, no.8; Publication no.164.*)

Nearly 1,500 international congresses are listed chronologically, with places of meeting and dates. Keyword indexes in French and English. *Class No:* 061.3(100)(091)

[2082]
—UNION OF INTERNATIONAL ASSOCIATIONS. Les Congrès internationaux de 1900 à 1919: liste complète. [International congresses, 1900 to 1919, full list.] Bruxelles, Union of International Associations, 1964. 143p. (*Documents, no.14; Publication no.188.*)

Lists 2,528 international congresses. Includes a cumulative subject index to both volumes (1681-1919).
Class No: 061.3(100)(091)

USA

[2083]
World meetings: United States & Canada. New York, World Meetings Publications, Macmillan Library Reference, 1963-. Quarterly. $195. ISSN: 00438693.

Covers medical, scientific and technical meetings. Same format as *World meetings: social & behavioral sciences... (q.v.)*.

A further companion title, published from 1968, is *World meetings: outside United States & Canada* (Quarterly. $195. ISSN: 00438677). *Class No:* 061.3(73)

Conference Proceedings

[2084]
Bibliographic guide to conference publications. 1975-. Boston, Mass., G.K. Hall, 1976-. Annual. $365. ISSN: 03602729.

Dictionary catalogue of proceedings, reports and summaries of conferences, meetings and symposia. Based on material catalogued by the New York Public Library Research Libraries and Library of Congress. International in scope, but with a bias towards English language and US material. *Class No:* 061.30

[2085]
The Directory of published proceedings. Harrison, N.Y., InterDok Corp., 1966-.

Known as 'InterDok'. Published in 3 series:-

Series SEMT: Science/engineering/medicine/technology. 1966-. 10pa., cumulated into annual v. Cumulated index supplement published 3 times pa., cumulated indexes for annual v. every 2-5 years ($575. ISSN: 00123293.

Series SSH: Social sciences/humanities. 1968-. Quarterly, final issue with cumulative index; cumulative v. published at 4 yearly intervals ($375. ISSN: 00123307).

Series PCE: Pollution control/ecology. 1974-. Annual ($150. ISSN: 00935816).

Cites 'preprints and published proceedings of congresses, conferences, symposia, meetings and seminars that have all taken place worldwide'. Primary arrangement chronological

....(contd.)
by year, then month. Entries include conference details (date, location, acronym, theme, sponsoring organization), title of published proceedings, series information, editor, publisher, acquisition detail and subject descriptors. Editor and subject/sponsor indexes. Series SSH carries about 700 entries in each issue. Entries in Series PCE abstracted from SEMT and SSH. Withdrawn as a Data-Star database December 1997. *Class No:* 061.30

[2086]
Index to conference proceedings. Boston Spa, British Library BSDS Publications, 1964-. Monthly, with annual cumulation. £104. ISSN: 09594906.

Title varies slightly: as *Index of conference proceedings received* until the end of 1987.

Based on the conference proceedings acquisition programme of the Document Supply Centre. The Centre 'endeavours to obtain all "worthwhile" conference publications regardless of subject or language and covers all types of publication format with the exception of audiovisual material'. Indexing by subject, key term derived from conference title or organizing/sponsoring body. Entry detail includes date and venue, conference title, publisher/ sponsoring body, document description, ISSN and DSC stock no. About 16,000 proceedings indexed annually.

Index to conference proceedings is also searchable online through BLAISE, updated monthly, and OCLC (*ProceedingsFirst*). The CD-ROM equivalent is *Boston Spa conferences on CD-ROM* (quarterly updates, £350), offering search and browse options on up to 13 different indexes.
Class No: 061.30

[2087]
—Index of conference proceedings received, 1964-1988. London, Saur, 1989. 26v. £3,562. ISBN: 0862918987.

Also available in microfiche.

Indexes more than 270,000 proceedings under 750,000 subject key terms. 'Although now the largest bibliography in its field, this remains essentially a finding list to such material held by the Document Supply Centre, and must be accepted as such' (*Reference reviews* v.3(4), December 1989, p.153). Major limitations include identification of books and serials containing proceedings by DSC stock no., rather than title, and key terms based strictly on title and organizing/sponsoring body. *Class No:* 061.30

[2088]
—Inside conferences on CD-ROM. Boston Spa, British Library Document Supply Centre, 1993-. CD-ROM database. £500.

Issued quarterly, discs cumulate annually. Annual backfiles from 1993 also available.

Contains bibliographical details of the individual papers that make up the proceedings indexed in *Index to conference proceedings* (above). Windows and DOS interfaces with similar search software to other British Library Document Supply Centre CD-ROMs. Search options include keyword, paper author(s), keyword in paper title, conference venue and publisher. A major tool for tracing conference literature, which has no printed equivalent. The British Library WWW database *Inside Web* (*q.v.*) also contains paper level records for conference proceedings. Online versions are available through Dialog (File 65, updated weekly) and OCLC (*PapersFirst*, Epic and FirstSearch, 24 updates annually).
Class No: 061.30

[2089]

Index to social sciences & humanities proceedings. Philadelphia, Institute for Scientific Information, 1979-. Quarterly, final issue annual cumulation. $1,025. ISSN: 01910574.

Indexes published proceedings of conferences, seminars, symposia, colloquia, conventions, etc. International in scope, including some non-English language material. Excludes proceedings in which the majority of the material is not printed for the first time, or is in the form of abstracts. Main listing by proceedings number gives location and date, bibliographical detail of proceedings, title of papers and authors (address given for first author). 6 indexes: category (69 broad categories); permuterm subject; sponsor; author/editor; meeting location; corporate (geographic and organization sections). 3,560 proceedings indexed 1996. Available as a CD-ROM database from 1994 (quarterly updating) containing data from 1990. Entire index also accessible online through DIMDI; updated weekly, records 1997 forward with searchable abstracts. *Class No:* 061.30

[2090]

International congresses and conferences, 1840-1937: a union list of their publications available in libraries of the United States and Canada. Gregory, W., *ed.* New York, Wilson, 1938. 229p.

Reprinted Millwood, N.Y., Kraus, 1980. ISBN: 0527445002.

A-Z arrangement, with subject index. Includes unofficial reports; excludes diplomatic conferences and League of Nations. *Class No:* 061.30

[2091]

Internationale Jahresbibliographie der Kongressberichte. 1984-. [International annual bibliography of congress proceedings.] Osnabrück, Dietrich, 1987-. Annual. DM1200. ISSN: 09331905.

Issued in 3v. Proceedings indexed in main sequence, 'Alphabetical list of congresses', by German language thematic heading (English and French cross-references). Entry includes brief detail of conference and publication and full list of papers presented. 2 further sections: B. Congresses by fields of knowledge (themes listed under 15 basic subject headings); C. Author index of contributions. International coverage, good for European conferences, but British and US libraries will generally prefer *Index to conference proceedings* and *Proceedings in print* (*qq.v.*). *Class No:* 061.30

[2092]

Proceedings in print. Halifax, Mass., Proceedings in Print, 1964-. Bimonthly. $680. ISSN: 00329568.

Initially confined to science and technology proceedings, but since 1967 has covered all subject areas and all languages. Now indexes about 3,500 proceedings annually. Conference proceedings defined to include symposia, lecture series, hearings, seminars, courses, colloquia and meetings. Entries, under conference title, give place, date, sponsoring agency, details of proceedings and where published. Order information and price added where possible. Index of corporate authors, sponsoring agencies, editors and subject headings in each issue. Cumulated annual index available as separate subscription. *Class No:* 061.30

[2093]

STAATSBIBLIOTHEK DER STIFTUNG PREUSSISCHER KULTURBESITZ. Gesamtverzeichnis der Kongress-Schriften in Bibliotheken der Bundesrepublik Deutschland einschliesslich Berlin (West). Schriften von und zu Kongressen, Konferenzen, Kolloquien, Symposien, Tagungen, Versammlungen und dergleichen vor 1971 mit Besitznachweisen Stand 1976. [Union list of conference proceedings in libraries of the Federal Republic of Germany including Berlin (West).] München, Verlag Dokumentation, 1976. 2v. ISBN: 3794030001.

Lists publications from and for congresses, colloquia, symposia, meetings etc., held before 1971 with libraries' holdings as of 1976. Excludes proceedings of conferences held in Germany. Main listing in v.1 by conference name or organizing body; v.2 is a keyword name and title index.

Initial supplement 1978 (viii,498p.). Further supplements, 1980 (viii,834p. ISBN: 3794030060) and 1982 (xii,602p. ISBN: 3598104340), include proceedings of conferences held in Germany. Continued updating by an annual microfiche listing produced by the Deutsches Bibliotheksinstitut (ISSN: 01729810. 11 Ausg. 1996. 48 microfiche. DM48. ISBN: 3870680113). An online database version is also available. *Class No:* 061.30

Exhibitions & Fairs

[2094]

Exhibition bulletin. London, Exhibition Bulletin, 1948-. Monthly. £50. ISSN: 00144649.

Lists exhibitions and trade fairs up to three years ahead. Arranged in 5 sections: UK exhibitions - London, then alphabetical by town; UK exhibitions - classified index in alphabetical order; European exhibitions - by country and town; Worldwide exhibitions (excluding UK and Europe); Classified index (excluding UK and Europe). Basic detail for each exhibition only. *Class No:* 061.4

[2095]

MessePlanner: Messen und Ausstellungen international. [Schedule of fairs and exhibitions worldwide.] Frankfurt am Main, Verlag für Messen, Ausstellungen und Kongresse, 1919-. Semi-annual (June & December).

The longest established, and probably the fullest, listing of international fairs and exhibitions. Data for up to 3 years ahead in sections for Germany and Europe and the rest of the world. Entries (headings and data in German) give information as supplied by organizers including date, title, registration deadline, frequency, main product/group sectors, whether event open to the general public, net exhibit space, profile of exhibitors and profile of attendees. Further lists of exhibitions in chronological order, fairs and exhibitions by branch of business, conference halls and fairs and exhibitions services (yellow pages).

The same publisher also produces an English-language version under the title *International tradeshows directory*. The Internet site http://www.expobase.com contains data from MessePlanner and related listings. *Class No:* 061.4

[2096]

The World directory of exhibitions and trade fairs. London, Euromonitor, 1995-. Annual (irregular).

Initial issue (vii,396p. ISBN: 0863384536) is 'a guide to the major international events in more than 90 countries worldwide, covering both industrial and consumer sectors. Coverage is focussed on events which run on a regular,

....*(contd.)*
periodic basis'. Two main sections listing exhibition/trade fairs by name and organizers by continent/country; sector, classified and organizer indexes. *Class No:* 061.4

Histories

[2097]
Historical dictionary of world's fairs and expositions 1851-1988. Findling, J.E. *and* Pelle, K.D., *eds.* New York, Greenwood, 1990. xix,443p. illus., tables. £71.55;$79.50. ISBN: 0313260230.

Provides 2-8p. historical and cultural reviews of 96 fairs and exhibitions beginning with the Crystal Palace Exhibition of 1851 and concluding with the Glasgow Garden Festival (1988). Each entry includes a brief bibliographic essay. Some unevenness in the description, some similar fairs excluded (*e.g.* Liverpool and Stoke-on-Trent garden festivals). 6 appendices: A. Bureau of International Exhibitions; B. Fair statistics (attendance, profit/loss, etc.); C. Fair officials; D. Fairs not included; E. Fairs that never were; F. Fairs yet to come (6 entries only). Bibliography, (p.411-17); index. *Class No:* 061.4(091)

Bibliographies

[2098]
SMITHSONIAN INSTITUTION. Libraries. **The Book of fairs:** materials about world's fairs, 1834-1916, in the Smithsonian Institution Libraries. Chicago, American Library Association, 1992. xx,268p. illus. £90;$99. (*Smithsonian Institution research guide, no. 6.*) ISBN: 0838905560.

Annotated list of 1,679 items, mostly catalogues, brochures, guides, etc., relating to 185 fairs. Secondary materials such as historical studies generally excluded. Lengthy introductory essay 'The Literature of international expositions' (p.1-62). Chronological listing of fairs as appendix; general and title indexes.
Class No: 061.4(091)(01)

Research Establishments

Worldwide

[2099]
Current research worldwide. London, Cartermill International, 1991-. CD-ROM database, updated semi-annually. £850.

Previous title *World research database*. Incorporates data from a variety of other sources such as *Current research in Europe* and *Industrial research in the United Kingdom*.

The 1997 release includes information on 29,000 research establishments in more than 150 countries.
Class No: 061.62(100)

[2100]
DAY, A. Think tanks: an international directory. Harlow, Longman Current Affairs, 1993. viii,616p. £135. ISBN: 0582209056.

'Broadly speaking, government bodies and university departments have been excluded in the case of the United States, Britain and more developed countries... . In the case of other countries, self-definition as a think tank has been more readily accepted' (*Introduction*, p.vii). 783 variable length entries by country Argentina ... Zaire. Information usually includes address, foundation date, staff, membership,

....*(contd.)*
historical highlights, current research and periodical publications. Classification by orientation or main policy sphere; index. *Class No:* 061.62(100)

[2101]
—NATIONAL INSTITUTE FOR RESEARCH ADVANCEMENT (Japan). NIRA's world directory of think tanks. 2nd ed. Tokyo, National Institute for Research Advancement, 1996. xviii,642p. ISBN: 4795560099.

First published 1993.

Emphasis is on 'public policy research organizations that focus on the social issues facing today's society'. *c.*220 entries for think tanks in 68 countries (13 UK, including Adam Smith Institute and Royal Institute of International Affairs). Government organizations excluded. Indexed.
Class No: 061.62(100)

[2102]
International research centers directory. Detroit, Gale, 1982-. Annual (irregular) £341;$449. ISSN: 02782731.

Now appears to be issued on an annual basis. 10th ed. (Wood, D. *ed.* 1997. xiv,1275p.) has subtitle: *A World guide to government, university, independent non-profit and commercial research and development centers, institutes, laboratories, bureaus, test facilities, experimental stations, research parks and data collection and analysis centers, as well as foundations, councils and other organizations which support research.*

8,163 entries for research centres in more than 150 countries (*c.*380 for UK). Excludes US and Canada, covered in *Research centers directory* (below). Entries include name (English and indigenous), contact detail including email and URL, date founded, short desciption, no. of staff by category, memberships, research activities, resources, publications, meetings, awards, services and library holdings. Country, subject and master indexes. Also searchable online as part of the *Research centers and services directory* database on Dialog (file 115) and GaleNet.
Class No: 061.62(100)

Pacific Ocean

[2103]
Pacific research centres; a directory of scientific, industrial, agricultural and biomedical laboratories. Harlow, Longman, 1993-. Irregular. £250. (*Reference on research.*)

Companion v. to *European research centres* (below). 3,500 entries in 4th ed. (1993. vii,392p. ISBN: 0582216699) for centres in Australia, China, Hong Kong, Indonesia, Japan, Korea, Malaysia, New Zealand, Philippines, Singapore, Thailand, Vietnam and other Pacific region states. Separate lists of trade associations and societies (p.275-98). Establishment title and subject indexes.
Class No: 061.62(265)

Europe

[2104]
Directory of European research and development. East Grinstead, Bowker Saur, 1995-. Annual (irregular).

1995 v. (2v. $450. ISBN: 185739092X) has entries for 20,272 organizations (3,390 UK) with country and field of research indexes (v.2). Complemented by *Who's who in European research and development* (Bowker Saur, 1995. xxii,800p. $400. ISBN: 1857390970) containing over 10,000 biographical profiles. Extended version also available online

....(*contd.*)
(DataStar) and on CD-ROM as *European research and development database* (CD-ROM annual updating, £995). *Class No:* 061.62(4)

[2105]

European research centres: a directory of scientific, technological, agricultural and biomedical laboratories. 10th ed. Harlow, Longman, 1995. 2v. £365. (*Reference on research.*) ISBN: 0582256925.

9th ed. 1993.

9th ed. covers research centres, research funding organizations and universities. 12,000 entries, arranged by country (UK 3,076), former Soviet Union excluded. Variable amounts of data for each centre, but research activities often described at length. Also typically notes parent body, key personnel, annual expenditure, publications and clients. Establishment title and subject indexes in v.2. Provides better coverage of European research institutes than Gale's *International research centers directory* (above). *Class No:* 061.62(4)

Great Britain

[2106]

Centres, bureaux & research institutes: the directory of UK concentrations of effort, information and expertise. Riley, S., *ed.* 3rd ed. Beckenham, CBD Research, 1996. ix,402p. £115. ISBN: 0900246723.

First published 1987, 2nd ed. 1993; both under title *Centres and bureaux.*

Covers 'organizations which are concentrations of some kind of effort and expertise, or which provide information to the general public. Many of those listed sell their services to specialised (usually institutional) customers' (Introduction). With a few exceptions most organizations included have 'centre', 'bureau' or 'institute' as part of their title (*e.g.* Cognac Information Centre; National Children's Bureau; Institute of Polarology). Approximately 2,000 entries arranged alphabetically by title giving year established, address, branches, membership, finance, sponsors, objects, previous names and notes. Some composite entries *e.g.* Citizen's Advice Bureaux. Indexed by abbreviation, sponsor (universities) and subject. 7 p. list of 'Unverified and lost entries'; lacks a geographic index. A useful addition to the CBD family of directories, including organizations not readily found elsewhere. *Class No:* 061.62(410)

India

[2107]

Handbook of research institutions in India. Indian Bibliographic Centre, *ed.* Varanasi, Indian Bibliographic Centre, 1995. 280p. Rs600. ISBN: 8185131112.

Lists over 500 institutions A-Z in separate social sciences and humanities and pure and applied sciences sections. Basic data for each institution outlining scope of research, but with the emphasis on library facilities and publications. 'Index of institutional heads' (p.268-80). *Class No:* 061.62(540)

USA

[2108]

Research centers directory. Detroit, Gale, 1960-. Annual (formerly irregular). £365;$470. ISSN: 00801518.

1st ed. 1960 as *Directory of university research bureaux and institutes*. Now published annually. 23rd ed. (Wood, D. *ed.* 1998. 2v.) has subtitle *A Guide to over 14,100 university-related and other nonprofit research organizations established on a permanent basis and carrying on continuing research programs in agriculture, astronomy and space sciences, behavioral and social sciences, biological sciences and ecology, business and economics, computers and mathematics, education, engineering and technology, government and public affairs, humanities and religion, labor and industrial relations, law, medical sciences, physical and earth sciences and regional and area studies.*

US companion v. to *International research centers directory* (above). Includes Canada. US government research centres separately covered in *Government research directory* (below). Entries in 17 subject sections v.1; subject, geographic, personal name and master indexes v.2. Updated by inter-edition supplement *New research centers.* Also searchable online as part of the *Research centers and services directory* database on Dialog (file 115) and GaleNet. *Class No:* 061.62(73)

[2109]

—Government research directory. Detroit, Gale, 1980-. Irregular (now approx. annual). £357$465. ISSN: 08823766.

9th ed. (Barrett, J.K. & Hubbard, M.M. *eds.* 1996. xiii,1037p.) has subtitle: *A Descriptive guide to more than 4,200 US government research and development centers, institutes, laboratories, bureaus, test facilities, experiment stations, data collection and analysis centers and grants management and research coordinating offices in agriculture, commerce, education, energy, engineering, environment, the humanities, medicine, military science and basic and applied sciences.*

4,231 actual entries (134 for Canada) arranged under departmental and other government headings. Entries typically give name of research unit, contact details, organizational notes, statement of research activities and fields, special resources and publications and services. Subject, geographic and master indexes. Available online as part of *Research centers and services directory* through Dialog (file 115) and GaleNet. *Class No:* 061.62(73)

[2110]

—Research services directory: a one-stop guide to commercial research activity. Detroit, Gale, 1981-. Irregular. £261;$340. ISSN: 02781743.

Covers independent commercial laboratories, contract engineers, market and survey research organizations, medical diagnostic facilities, product research and development firms, defence contractors, management consultants, information brokers, etc. Over 4,700 entries in the 6th ed. (1995. xiv,931p.). Includes firms conducting in-house research. Alphabetical, geographic, personal name and subject indexes. *Class No:* 061.62(73)

[2111]

Research institutions and learned societies. Kiger, J.C., *ed.* Westport, Conn., Greenwood Press, 1982. xxv,551p. £49.50;$55. (*Greenwood encyclopedia of American institutions, no.5.*) ISBN: 0313220611.

Provides 5-7p. historical sketches of 164 US 'non-governmental, not-for-profit organizations aiding the promotion or performance of basic research and the advancement of knowledge' (Preface p.xxi). Each sketch concludes with references to further sources of information. Various appendices (p.495-525) including a chronology and a listing by areas of subject activity. *Class No:* 061.62(73)

Australia

[2112]

The Australian directory of academic and research associations. Kenmore, Qld., Academic Information Services, 1992-. Annual (irregular). ISSN: 10386459.

4th ed. (Edwards, G. & Sullivan, T. *comps. & eds.* xvi,234p.) contains information on over 900 research associations A-Z by name. Broad heading subject index (p.203-11); annotated list of Australian research journals (p.215-34). *Class No:* 061.62(94)

Festivals

[2113]

SHEMANSKI, F. A Guide to world fairs and festivals. Westport, Conn., Greenwood Press, 1985. viii,309p. £38.75;$42.95. ISBN: 0313207860.

Descriptive entries for fairs and festivals of all types including religious events, arts and literary festivals, agricultural and flower shows, historic commemorations, New Years celebrations and patriotic observances. 75 countries covered Antigua ... Zambia, (US excluded). 19 UK entries ranging from local events such as the Broadstairs Dickens Festival to Crufts Dog Show and the Edinburgh Festival. Calendar of fairs and festivals (by country then date p.189-246); appendix by type of event (p.247-99). Index.
Class No: 061.7

[2114]

—SHEMANSKI, F. A Guide to fairs and festivals in the United States. Westport, Conn., Greenwood Press, 1984. viii,339p. £43.95;$47.95. ISBN: 0313214379.

Companion v. to *A Guide to world fairs and festivals.* Several hundred events described. Arranged by state, then city or town. Appendix by type of event and a calendar of events by state and month. *Class No:* 061.7

Museums

Internet

[2115]

World Wide Web virtual library: museums: a comprehensive directory of online museums and museum-related resources. Brown, J., *comp.* Paris, International Council of Museums, 1994-. World Wide Web resource.

URL: http://www.icom.org/vlmp. Date reviewed 13th July 1998. Various mirror sites available, UK http://cs.rdg.ac.uk/vlmp.

The most well-known and probably the largest Internet site offering links to musuem and exhibition WWW resources. Well structured, indexed and maintained, museums links in country sections, over 200 for UK. *Class No:* 069(003.41)

Bibliographies

[2116]

Bibliographie muséologique internationale. 1967-85. [International museological bibliography.] Paris, Unesco/ICOM Documentation Centre, 1969-88. Annual.

1967-71 appeared as a supplement to *ICOM news*; some issues combined. Publisher varied.

Later issues based on material received at the Unesco/ICOM Documentation Centre. Entries in masterfile number order (previously classified); extensive indexes.
Class No: 069(01)

[2117]

A Bibliography of museum studies. Knell, S.J., *comp. & ed.* 11th ed. Aldershot, Scolar Press, 1994. viii,248p. £45;$69.95. ISBN: 1859280617.

Previously published by the Dept. of Museum Studies, Univ. of Leicester as the *Bibliography of museum studies training.* 10th ed. 1991 entitled *Museum studies bibliography.*

This greatly expanded ed. has a wider orientation than previous efforts. Unannotated entries for books, periodical articles, etc. in 12 sections (*e.g.* Collection studies and museum history; Museum management), each subdivided. New material especially well represented. Author but no subject index.

G. Kavanagh's *A Bibliography for history, history curatorship and museums* (Scolar Press, 1996. viii,221p. £30;$54.95. ISBN: 1859282032), containing *c.*2,500 citations in 25 topical sections, appears to be a companion work. *Class No:* 069(01)

[2118]

BORHEGYI, S.F. de *and* **DODSON, E.A. A Bibliography of museums and museum work** 1900-1960. Milwaukee, Milwaukee Public Museum, 1960. 72p. (*Milwaukee Public Museum. Publications in museology, 1.*)

Lists *c.*1,000 publications in 16 topical sections. Author index. US material predominates. A supplementary volume by the same authors, listing a further *c.*1,200 items, was published in 1961. *Class No:* 069(01)

[2119]

The Museum: a reference guide. Shapiro, M.S. *and* Kemp, L.W., *eds.* Westport, Conn., Greenwood, 1990. xiv,385p. £62.95;$75. ISBN: 0313236860.

Comprises 11 essays, either on information sources in relation to particular types of museum (*e.g.* natural history, folk), or aspects of museology (*e.g.* museum education). Each essay in standard format giving a historical outline, survey of the sources and bibliography. 3 appendices: Museum directories (annotated list); Archives and special collections; Museum-related periodicals. 'Chapter bibliographies are current and full, but the appendices do not always cite the most current editions and some valuable publications of the last five years are inexplicably omitted' (*Choice*, v.28(4), December 1990, p.612).
Class No: 069(01)

[2120]

Museum abstracts: a monthly information service. Edinburgh, Scottish Museums Council, 1985-. Monthly, (first v. quarterly). £50. ISSN: 02678594.

Current publication status uncertain. Incorporated *Museum abstracts international* (ISSN: 09600183) 1993.

Based on periodicals received at the Scottish Museums Council's Information Centre. About 150 short abstracts (100-150 words) in each issue arranged in subject sections (*e.g.* Administration and finance; Legislation and policy; Training and professional development). *Class No:* 069(01)

[2121]

WOODHEAD, P. *and* **STANSFIELD, G. Keyguide to information sources in museum studies.** London, Mansell, 1994. xiv,224p. £60;$65. ISBN: 0720121515.

'(A)ims to provide an integrated guide to the documentation, reference aids and key organizational sources of information about museums and museum studies worldwide' (Introduction p.xi). In 3 pts: I. Overview of museum studies and its literature (8 discursive chapters, each with references) - II. Bibliographical listing of sources of

....(contd.)
information (446 annotated entries, a high proportion for works discussed in pt.I) - III. Listing of selected organizations (100 entries, also annotated). Pt.II, subdivided by form of material, includes entries for 71 museum directories. Entries in III note publications. Indexed. '(An) indispensable work of reference for any museum or heritage studies collection, and probably helpful in any college or public reference collection' (*Managing information*, v.2(3), March 1995, p.48). *Class No:* 069(01)

Handbooks & Manuals

[2122]
EDSON, G. *and* **DEAN, D. The Handbook of museums.** London, Routledge, 1994. xv,302p. diags. £40;$45. (*The Heritage*.) ISBN: 0415099528.

'(O)ffers a broad base of information designed to present both the theory and practice of the museum profession' (Preface p.xiii). Prescriptive approach in 5 main sections: I. Museum role and responsibility - II. Museum collection management and care - III. Interpretation and communication - IV. Professionalism and ethics - V. Support material (includes glossary (p.289-95) and bibliography (p.296-99)). Indexed. *Class No:* 069(035)

[2123]
LORD, B. *and* **LORD, G.D. The Manual of museum management.** London, The Stationery Office, 1997. xiii,261p. illus., tables. £25;$49. ISBN: 0112905188.

3 main sections: 1. The Objective of museum management - 2. Who: the structure of museum organisation (mode of governance, the board, staff, role of volunteers) - 3. How: methods of museum management (executive role, collection management, finance). Various contributed case studies interspersed in text (*e.g.* Exhibition teams at the Field Musuem of Natural History, Chicago); glossary (p.227-51) and index. *Class No:* 069(035)

[2124]
Manual of curatorship: a guide to museum practice. Thompson, J.M.A., *and others, eds.* 2nd ed. London, Butterworth-Heinemann, 1992. xvii,756p. illus., charts. £75;$139.95. ISBN: 0750603518.

First published 1984.

A comprehensive reference book of museum work based on British experience and practice. 71 chapters in 5 sections: The Museum context - Management and administration - Conservation - Collection research - User services. Bibliographies follow most chapters, often lengthy. Appended 'Code of conduct for museum professionals'; subject index (p.725-56). *Class No:* 069(035)

[2125]
The Manual of museum planning. Lord, G.D. *and* Lord, B., *eds.* London, HMSO, 1991. xvi,361p. diags.,charts. £37.50. ISBN: 0112904831.

Aims to provide practical advice on the planning process for any museum capital project. 21 contributed chaps. (*e.g.* Planning for safety and security; Preparing the brief; Cost control); glossary and 6½p. bibliography.
Class No: 069(035)

Dictionaries

[2126]
Dictionarium museologicum. Éri, I. *and* Bèla, V., *eds.* Budapest, Hungarian Esparanto Association, 1986. lv,774p. ISBN: 9635711743.

Published for the International Council of Museums. International Committee for Documentation. Working Group on Terminology.

Not a museological dictionary, but a two part multilingual vocabulary of technical terms of importance in museum work. 1,632 terms in 19 European languages and Esparanto are set out under English lead term, followed by alphabetical word indexes for each language. Appendices of German, Czech and Dutch terms with English definitions. The first 'comprehensive terminology of museum theory and practice' (*Museum news*, v.66(6), July/August 1988, p.71).
Class No: 069(038)

Worldwide

[2127]
HUDSON, K. *and* **NICHOLLS, A. The Directory of museums and living displays.** 3rd ed. Macmillan, Basingstoke; Stockton Press, New York, 1985. xvii,1047p. ISBN: 0333362659, UK; 0943818176, US.

1st ed. 1975 and 2nd ed. 1981 as *The Directory of world museums.*

Claims to list 35,000 museums with 'living displays', defined as 'zoos, aquaria, botanical gardens and living history farms', included for the first time in this edition. Listing by country in three-column A4 format. General note on each country, museums listed under town, then A-Z. Entries give only address and brief uncritical note on museum holdings. No subject index. Needs updating.
Class No: 069(100)

[2128]
Museums of the world. Bartz, B., *ed.* 6th rev. & enl. ed. München, Saur, 1997. viii,673p. illus. £350;$425. (*Handbook of international documentation and information, v.16.*) ISBN: 3598206054.

First published 1973; 5th ed. 1995.

Lists 27,380 museums of all kinds. Typical entry comprises name of museum (English translation where necessary), address and contact detail including email and WWW, museum type, foundation date, director, brief description of collection (10-50 words) and facilities. Arranged A-Z by country, then town. Museum name, person (subject of collection) and comprehensive general subject (*c.*220 headings) indexes. Apart from the subject index, which is especially useful, best regarded as a glorified address list as the descriptive detail is too short for most purposes. *Class No:* 069(100)

Bibliographies

[2129]
World museum publications 1982: a directory of art and cultural museums, their publications and audiovisual materials. New York, Bowker, 1982. 711p. ISBN: 0835214443.

Evolved from *Art books 1950-1979* (1979) and *1876-1949* (1981).

Guide to 21,877 museum publications, 8,675 audiovisual items and 10,040 museums. Arranged by country; indexes of publication titles and museums. *Class No:* 069(100)(01)

Children

[2130]

ZUCKER, B.F. Children's museums, zoos and discovery rooms: an international reference guide. New York and London, Greenwood Press, 1987. viii,269p. £53.95;$59.95. ISBN: 031324538x.

Very selective coverage of 235 children's museums, or museums with special children's areas, in 19 countries Australia-Zimbabwe. Entries lack directory information, but provide detailed descriptions of the museum's contents and history and include bibliographic references. US emphasis, 155 of 210 pages of text devoted to US. Useful bibliography (p.241-60); indexes.

Listed as forthcoming by Greenwood Press early 1998: *Children's museums: an American guidebook* (ISBN: 0786404434). *Class No:* 069(100)-0053

Europe

[2131]

European museum guide. Museum Media Publications. World Wide Web resource.

URL: http://www.museumguide.com. Date reviewed 10th July 1998.

Provides information and links for museums in 12 countries. Also includes links and data for major exhibitions. *Class No:* 069(4)

[2132]

HUDSON, K. *and* **NICHOLLS, A. The Cambridge guide to the museums of Europe.** Cambridge, Cambridge Univ. Press, 1991. xxvi,509p. illus., maps. ISBN: 0521371759.

Contains *c.*2,000 entries. Intended primarily for 'more active and independent tourists' (p.vii), aiming to cover all the major national and regional museums with a selection of special interest collections. Most local museums of a general nature excluded. Confined to Western Europe; 380 UK museums included. Arranged by country then town, entries give address, hours, admission details, facilities etc., and a descriptive note of 50-300 words. 500 illus.; 12 locational maps. Indexes of subjects, museum names and museums associated with individuals. The first guide to European museums and 'outstanding for its range, balance and quality of entries' (*Reference reviews,* v.5(3), 1991, p.8). *Class No:* 069(4)

[2133]

New museums in Europe 1977-1993. Negri, M., *ed.* Milan, Mazzotta, 1994. 348p. illus. ISBN: 8820210924.

Text by K. Hudson.

Contains brief descriptions of *c.*600 museums which have been candidates for the European Museum of the Year Award. Arranged by year of candidature; index of museums by country and town. *Class No:* 069(4)

Great Britain

[2134]

Exploring museums. Matyjaszkiewicz, K., *series ed.* London, HMSO, 1989-93. 10v. £3.95 per v.

At head of title 'A Museums Association' guide.

Published 1989: *London* (xii,110p. ISBN: 0112904653); *North east England* (xiv,160p. ISBN: 011290470x); *North west England and the Isle of Man* (xiv,114p. ISBN: 0112904734); *South west England* (xiv,114p. ISBN: 0112904696). Published 1990: *The Home counties* (xiv,122p. ISBN: 0112904718); *Ireland* (xiv,85p. ISBN: 0112904750); *Scotland* (xiv,122p. ISBN: 0112904742); *Wales* (xiv,114p. ISBN: 011290467x). Published 1992: *Southern England and the Channel Islands* (xiv,114p. ISBN: 0112904688). Published 1993: *East Anglia* (xii,108p. ISBN: 0112904726). No coverage for the Midlands.

Regional guides to major museums in which the editors of each volume 'have tried to put themselves in the shoes of the general museum visitor and present a personal rather than official view'. Lengthy descriptive entries, heavily illustrated. Arrangement A-Z by town; each v. has museum name and subject indexes. *Class No:* 069(410)

[2135]

HUDSON, K. *and* **NICHOLLS, A. The Cambridge guide to the museums of Britain and Ireland.** Rev. paperback ed. Cambridge, Cambridge Univ. Press, 1989. x,[16],452p. illus., maps. ISBN: 0521322723.

Hardback ed. 1987.

Aimed at 'absolute completeness' of coverage (Introduction p.ix). Entries for over 2,000 museums, art galleries and historic houses arranged under towns A-Z. Gives address, opening hours, name of curator, symbols to indicate visitor facilities and brief description of museum contents. Over 400 illustrations, some in colour; 16p. map section locates towns with museums. Indexes of museum names, subjects and museums associated with individuals. *Class No:* 069(410)

[2136]

Museum and special collections in the United Kingdom. Dale, P., *ed.* 2nd ed. London, Aslib, The Association for Information Management, 1996. vi,454p. £98. ISBN: 0851423485.

On title page: Museums Association. First published 1993.

Covers 2,134 museums and other institutions (1,225 1st ed.), such as libraries and historic houses, holding 'collections of artefacts which are unusual, important or especially noteworthy' (Introduction, p.v). Entries provide fairly brief detail under headings Main collections, Special collections and Catalogues. Omits some important museums (data questionnaire based) and lacks in-depth information on collection contents. Mainly valuable for the very full subject index (p.377-454). *Class No:* 069(410)

[2137]

Museums and galleries. Hobsons, Cambridge, 1955-. Annual. £8.95.

Title and publisher varies. Before 1997 issued under title *Museums and galleries in Great Britain and Ireland* (ISSN: 01416723).

The 1996 ed. (xxiv,221p. illus.) has information on over 1,400 museums and galleries arranged by county then town. Entries include descriptive detail (usually less than 100 words), opening hours, admission prices and location (railway station/roads). Separate list of services (military) museums (p.178-83). Subject, location and museum/gallery name indexes and directory of suppliers of products and services. Numerous advertisments in the text and mainly intended for the tourist, but a handy, up-to-date source which gives surprisingly comprehensive coverage. *Class No:* 069(410)

[2138]

Museums yearbook: including a directory of museums and galleries of the British Isles. London, Museums Association, 1955-. Annual. £85. ISSN: 03077675.

Title varies, previously *Museum calendar.*

Bulk of each yearbook comprises a directory (p.17-318 1997/98 ed.) listing museums by place A-Z. Information given includes contact detail with email and WWW addreses,

.... *(contd.)*
brief description of collections, scope, opening hours, admission charges, facilities, services (*e.g.* tours), attendance figures, name of governing body and senior staff (full list with post held and qualifications). Some extensive entries *e.g.* Victoria and Albert Museum 6 cols., but descriptions of actual collections limited. Other sections include 'Museum and gallery organisations' and 'Buyer's guide to suppliers and services'. Also lists professional (individual) and other members of the Museums Association. Indexed by museum name and county. *Class No:* 069(410)

[2139]

The Times museums & galleries: passport guide. Tait, S., *ed.* 2nd ed. London, Spero Communications, 1990. 456p. illus., maps. £7.95. ISBN: 1872765009.

First published 1989. Issued in conjunction with the 'Passport to museums' concession scheme.

Popular guide in 11 regional sections. About 1,400 entries including 3-4 line descriptions of museums. Subject (p.24-36) and museum name (p.425-52) indexes; 11 maps.
Class No: 069(410)

Bibliographies

[2140]

Bibliography of museum and art gallery publications and audiovisual aids in Great Britain and Ireland. Cambridge, Chadwyck-Healey, 1978-80. 2v.

1st ed. 1977 ed. by J. Lambert (1978. 372p.); 2nd ed. 1979/80 ed. by M. Roulstone (1980. 450p.). No more published.

The 2nd ed. listed publications of 955 institutions (1st ed. 922), including stately homes, the National Trust, Dept. of the Environment and Arts Council. 'Audiovisual aids' range from slides and films to records and sound recordings and photographs and postcards. Arranged alphabetically by institution; geographic, author and subject indexes.
Class No: 069(410)(01)

Scotland

[2141]

Scottish museums and galleries: the guide. Aberdeen, Aberdeen University Press and Scottish Museums Council in association with The Sunday Mail, 1990. xiii,110p. illus., plates, maps. £4.99. ISBN: 0080379745.

Earlier coverage in *Scottish museums and galleries guide* (Edinburgh, Polygon, 1986).

Regionally arranged directory of *c.*400 museums. Brief entries only, giving address, governing body/owner, hours, facilities and a short description. Indexed by museum name.
Class No: 069(411)

Ireland

[2142]

ORAM, H. Irish museums and heritage centres. Belfast, Appletree Press, 1996. 96p. illus., maps. £3.99. ISBN: 0862815487.

Pocket-sized guide aimed at the tourist. A-Z town arangement, with the emphasis on practical matters such as opening hours. *Class No:* 069(415)

Germany

[2143]

Der Deutsche Museumsführer in Farbe: Museen und Sammlungen in der Bundesrepublik Deutschland und West-Berlin. Mörmann, K., *hrsg.* 3.Aufl. Frankfurt-am-Main, Krüger-Verlag, 1986. 1056p. illus. ISBN: 3810512117.

1st ed. 1979. 2nd ed. 1983.

Museum guide for the former West Germany. Entries are under town Aachen-Zwiesel. Basic information for each museum including a short description of the contents and any special features. Attractively produced, many colour illustrations. Museum name index, but no subject index in this ed. *Class No:* 069(430)

[2144]

Museums-Fahrplan: ein Streifzug durch die Deutsche Museumslandschaft. Troisdorf, CED CD-ROM Verlag, 1996. CD-ROM database. (*DM98.*.) ISBN: 3932045009.

Contains questionnaire derived information on 4,200 German museums of all types. Some entries contain only an address, others lengthy descriptions backed by illustrations and video clips. More entries than in the Germany section of *Museums of the world* (*q.v.*). *Class No:* 069(430)

Austria

[2145]

DAWID, M. *and* **EGG, E. Der Österreichische Museumsführer in Farbe:** Museen und Sammlungen in Österreich. 4 neu. und erw. Aufl. Innsbruck, Pinguin-Verlag, 1991. 495p. illus.

Guide to 900 Austrian museums and collections. Brief descriptions with attractive colour illustrations. Name and subject indexes. *Class No:* 069(436)

Poland

[2146]

WAISNER-NIEDUSZYNSKA, J. *and* **DARNENTKA, E. Wykaz muzeów w Polsce,** sierpien 1993. Warszawa, Ośrodek Dokumentacji Zabytkó, Ozral Musealnictwa, 1993. 65p.

Lists Polish museums by town giving contact information and name of curator only. Subejct index (p.37-65).
Class No: 069(438)

France

[2147]

CABANNE, P. Le Nouveau guide des musées de France. Paris, Larousse, 1997. 997p. maps. FFr195. ISBN: 2035114012.

Earlier eds. 1984-90 under title *Guide des musées de France*.

Covers over 2,000 museums including 5 in Monaco and 14 in French territories overseas. Arranged by *département,* then town, in 24 regional sections. Entries give address, opening hours and detailed description of museum contents. Town, museum name, artists and persons as subjects of collections and general indexes (p.914-97).
Class No: 069(44)

[2148]

—MORLEY-SCHAEFFER, A. *and* LE VAVASSEUR, G. Le Guide Seat des musées: 7,000 musées & collections en France. Paris, Le Cherche Midi, 1992. 524p. FFr120. (*Collection 'Guides'*.) ISBN: 2862742481.

Basic guide mainly useful for the large number of collections covered. Short entries concentrate on practical matters such as opening hours, location, etc.
Class No: 069(44)

Italy

[2149]

Musei d'Italia. [Milano], G. Mondadori, 1997. 323p. illus. (*Bell'Italia grandi guide, 3.*) ISBN: 8837415575.

Regionally arranged directory of about 2,700 entries. Brief detail for most museums with little information on contents. Includes 500 coloured illustrations of museum artefacts. Location index.

An older guide is *Tutti i musei d'Italia* (Editoriale Domus, 1984. 854p. ISBN: 8872120101). This provides lengthy collection descriptions for many of the *c.*1,500 museums covered as well as a bibliography of Italian museum guides
Class No: 069(450)

Spain

[2150]

AVELLANOSA, T. *and* FRANCISCO, C. de. Guía de los museos de España. Madrid, Espasa Calpe, 1995. xv,659p. illus. (*Guías Espasa, 6.*) ISBN: 8423980375.

Arranged in sections for major towns. *c.*1,300 entries each giving basic details of facilities, etc., followed by descriptions of important collections. Museum name, subject and artist and other named person indexes.

The Ministeio de Cultura España also maintains *Censo de museos de España*, an online database of Spanish museums and collections. This is based on the printed directory *Museos y colecciones de España* published in a 5th ed. 1990, first issued 1969. *Class No:* 069(460)

RSFSR

[2151]

BAIKOVA, I. Museums in and around Moscow: a guide. Moskva, Radguga Publishers, 1983. 197p. plates, map. ISBN: 0828529205.

Lengthy descriptions of 73 museums in 5 chapters. Two further English language guides are *The Museums of Leningrad* (Moskva, Progress Publishers, 1982) and *Museums of Kiev* (Radguga Publishers, 1984).
Class No: 069(470)

[2152]

Muzei Rossii: spravochnik. Gavrilov, I.A., *red.* Moskva, M-vo kul'tury Rossii, Glavnyi informatsionno-vychislitel'nyi tsentr, 1993. 4v. ISBN: 5900104095.

Published by the Ministry of Culture. Replaces *Muzei SSSR* (1990).

Subject based directory. Includes detail on individual collections. *Class No:* 069(470)

Finland

[2153]

Suomen museot. [Finnish museums.] Hallstrom, J., *ed.* Helsinki, Suomen museoliitto, 1997. 153p. illus. (*Suomen museoliiton julkaisuja, 43.*) ISBN: 9519426191.

Earlier eds. 1979, 1986 and 1990.

Comprehensive guide by town. Includes brief English language descriptions of museum contents. Finnish and English indexes. *Class No:* 069(480)

Sweden

[2154]

Museer i Sverige. Stockholm, Svenska turistföreningen, 1996. 240p. illus. maps. ISBN: 9171561447.

Earlier ed. under same title 1990.

Guide to more than 475 Swedish museums arranged A-Z by town. Entries include practical matters and short museum descriptions summarised in English. Museum name and category indexes. *Class No:* 069(485)

Denmark

[2155]

SVENDSEN, P. Museer og seværdigheder i Danmark. [Frederiksberg], Branner og Korch, 1989-90. 2v. illus., maps. ISBN: 8741155874.

V.1. *Sjælland, Lolland, Falster, Møn og Bornholm.* V.2. *Jylland, Fyn og omliggende øer*

Comprehensive guide to Danish museums, historic sites, zoos, etc. Entries provide basic detail such as hours, admission price, facilities, plus a good description of the collection and its development. Tabulated museum name/subject index in each vol. *Class No:* 069(489)

Netherlands

[2156]

Nederland museumland: gids langs meer dan 900 Nederlandse musea. Nieuw ed. Leiden, Sticting Museumjaarkaart, 1992. 311p. illus., maps. ISBN: 9066113723.

Earlier ed. 1988.

Entries, in regional sections, briefly describe collections and give basic details such as hours, facilities, etc. Place name index. *Class No:* 069(492)

Switzerland

[2157]

Schweizer Musueumsführer: mit Einschluss Fürstentums Liechtenstein. [Guide des musées Suisses.] Verband der Museen der Schweiz, *hrsg.* 7.Aufl. Basel, Friedich Reinhardt, 1996. 500p. SFr34. ISBN: 3724509065.

First published 1965 as *Museen und Sammlungen der Schweiz*; 6th ed. 1993.

Regularly updated guide to Swiss museums. Entries, arranged by town, in German, French or Italian according to museum location. Detail includes practical matters and brief descriptions of collections. Indexed. *Class No:* 069(494)

Japan

[2158]

ROBERTS, L.P. Roberts' guide to Japanese museums of art and archaeology Rev. & updated ed. Tokyo, Simul Press, 1987. iv,383p. illus. Y3,500 ISBN: 4377507370.

First published as *The Connoisseur's guide to Japanese museums*; 2nd ed. under present title 1978.

The more widely available 2nd ed. (Tokyo, Kodansha International. ISBN: 0870113062) has 355 descriptive entries A-Z. *Class No:* 069(52)

India

[2159]

PUNJA, S. Museums of India. Hong Kong, Odyssey Guides, 1991. 307p. illus., maps. £9.95. ISBN: 9622171958.

Attractively illustrated guide aimed at the tourist. Good descriptions of major collections by city, followed by 'Reference section' containing a list of museums by state, glossary and 'Chronology, historical sites and related museums'. Indexed. *Class No:* 069(540)

Israel

[2160]

ROSOVSKY, N. *and* **UNGERLEIDER-MAYERSON, J. The Museums of Israel.** New York, Harry N. Abrams, 1989. 256p. illus., maps. ISBN: 0810924226.

8 section guide (Jerusalem - Tel Aviv ... Southern Coast and Negev) to 120 museums. Many collections described at length *e.g.* Tel Aviv Museum of Art (p.103-9). Attractively illustrated. Subject, museum name and location index. *Class No:* 069(569.4)

Africa

[2161]

The Directory of museums in Africa. [Répertoire des musées en Afrique.] Unesco/ICOM Documentation Centre, *comps and* Peters, S., *ed.*. London, Kegan Paul, 1989. 211p. illus. £45. ISBN: 0710303785.

Text in English or French. Updates *Directory of African museums* (1981).

Details for 503 museums in 48 countries, South Africa excluded. Also includes zoos, botanical gardens etc. Full entries give address, chief officer, status, hours, charges, collections (list of subjects), services, history and publications. Information for many museums incomplete. *Class No:* 069(6)

Canada

[2162]

The Official directory of Canadian museums and related institutions. [Répertoire officiel des musées canadiens et des institutions connexes.] Ottawa, Canadian Museums Association, 1968-. Irregular. ISSN: 08290474.

Title varies slightly; initially as *Directory of Canadian museums and related institutions.*

'Related institutions' include art galleries, archives, historic sites, zoos, nature parks, etc. 1993/94 ed. (1992. xxx,411p.) has more than 2,000 entries. Information, presented in provincial sections then by town, gives address, director, senior staff, *c.*50 word description of collection, activities, publications, admission details and governing authority. Various indexes, including museums by 23 subject categories. *Class No:* 069(71)

USA

[2163]

The Official museum directory. New Providence, N.J., National Register Publishing, 1961-. Annual. $210. ISSN: 00906700.

As *Museum directory of the United States and Canada* 1961-65. Annual since 1980; until recent issues published by the American Association of Museums.

The 28th ed. (1997) is in 2 vols. V.1 has entries for more than 7,700 US museums (coverage of Canadian museums discontinued from 1984). Fairly brief information on personnel, governing authority, type of museum, collections, facilities, activities, publications, hours, admission prices and attendance. Lacks detailed descriptions of museum contents. Arranged by state, then city, with museum name, personnel, museum category and collection indexes. Appended 'Museums on the World Wide Web'; introductory information on the American Museums Association. V.2 is *Products and services* directory.

Guides to state and city museums are also useful, especially as they often contain more expansive information on collections. Recent examples include *New York city museum guide* (Ward, C. *ed.*. Dover Publications, 1995. 122p. ISBN: 0486286398) and *Museums of the San Francisco Bay Area* (Danto, E. 2nd ed. Eldan Press, 1998. 119p. ISBN: 0961512881). *Class No:* 069(73)

Jews

[2164]

The World directory of Jewish museums. Jerusalem, The Center for Jewish Art, The Hebrew University and Eliezer Fisher, 1994. 171p. ISBN: 9653950051.

Pocket-sized guide to 150 museums. Continent/country arrangment, only one UK collection (Jewish Museum, Manchester), many museums included located in Poland and the former Soviet Union. Variable length entries, usually with brief description and notes on publications; index of cities. *Class No:* 069(=924)

Information Management

[2165]

BIERBAUM, E.G. Museum librarianship: a guide to the provision and management of information services Jefferson, N.C., McFarland, 1994. ix,179p. illus., diags. £40.50;$45. ISBN: 0899509711.

Brief 7 chap. guide covering collections and bibliographic processes, space and equipment, administration and technology. 7 appendices including 'Sample collection development policy' and 'Related associations and organizations'. Good topically arranged bibliography of 300 entries; index. '(A)ddressed to museum staff and is intended to serve as a supplement to developmental consultation with special librarians' (*Libraries and culture*, v.32(2), Spring 1997, p.276).

Listed as forthcoming by Gower late 1997: *Information management in museums* (*c.*£39. ISBN: 0566077760). *Class No:* 069:025.4

Classification Systems

[2166]

BLACKABY, J.R. The Revised nomenclature for museum cataloging: a revised and expanded version of Robert G. Chenhall's system for classifying man-made objects. Nashville, American Association for State and Local History, 1988. 513p. ISBN: 0910050937.

.... *(contd.)*

Reprinted 1995 (Alta Mira Press. $65. ISBN: 0761991476). Previous ed. by Chenhall as *Nomenclature for museum cataloging* (1978).

2 main sections: 'Hierarchical list of preferred terms'; 'Alphabetical list of preferred terms'. Preceded by introductory matter. Based on major artefact categories; includes a partial lexicon expandable by the user.
Class No: 069:025.44

[2167]

SHIC WORKING PARTY. Social history and industrial classification (SHIC): a subject classification for museum collections. 2nd ed. Cambridge, Museums Documentation Association for the SHIC Working Party, 1993. Looseleaf. ISBN: 0905963911.

First published 1983.

Classification system for materials relating to human history. Complemented by *Simple subject headings based on the Social History and Industrial Classification* (Cambridge, Museum Documentation Assoc., 1996. vi,72p. ISBN:190064200X). *Class No:* 069:025.44

Education Courses

[2168]

DANILOV, V.J. Museum careers and training: a professional guide. Westport, Conn., Greenwood Press, 1994. xi,546p. £71.50;$85. ISBN: 031328105x.

In 2pts. 'History and types of museum careers and training' discusses development and current state of museum profession and training in 11 chaps. (*e.g.* Museum salaries and benefits; Graduate programs). 'Directory of museum training programs' (p.176-508) has more than 700 entries, mostly for the US but with a few for other countries. Selected bibliography; index. *Class No:* 069:377.3

[2169]

EDSON, G. International directory of museum training. London, Routledge, 1995. xiv,411p. £55;$49.95. (*Heritage con-preservation management.*) ISBN: 0415122570.

Training programs directory (p.65-348) has 235 entries A-Z by country. Questionnaire based data with supplementary descriptive detail. Heavy US bias (p.166-347), only 3 entries for Germany and 2 for France (UK p.152-65). Glossary of museum training terms (p.367-75) and select bibliography (p.379-91). Indexed by training level, discipline, financial aid and training agency. *Class No:* 069:377.3

07 Journalism & Newspapers

Journalism & Newspapers

Mass Media

Bibliographies

[2170]

BLOCK, E.S. *and* **BRACKEN, J.K. Communication and mass media:** a guide to the reference literature. Englewood, Colo., Libraries Unlimited, 1991. xii,198p. (*Reference sources in the humanities.*) ISBN: 0872878100.

Annotated listing of 483 English language sources nearly all published since 1970. Coverage includes a few online and CD-ROM databases and core peridoicals. Entries arranged according to material type (*e.g.* Bibliographies); subject and author/title indexes. 'Institutions with strong programs in communication will want this title. Others can get by with Cates and Blum/Wilhoit' (*Choice*, v.29(6), February 1992, p.870). *Class No:* 070.0(01)

[2171]

BLUM, E. *and* **WILHOIT, F.G. Mass media bibliography:** an annotated guide to books and journals for research and reference. 3rd ed. Urbana, Univ. of Illinois Press, 1990. viii,344p. $49.95 ISBN: 0252017064.

1st ed. 1972 (itself a reworking of Blum's *Reference books in the mass media,* 1962) and 2nd ed. 1980 as *Basic books in the mass media.*

'All titles give information about some aspect of mass communication - theory, structure, economics, function, research, content, effects. Many are reference works. ... All entries have one common factor: they treat the subject in broad general terms' (Preface p.vii). Expanded from 1,179 to 1,947 entries in this ed. 9 main sections: General communications - Broadcasting media - Print media - Film - Advertising and public relations - Bibliographies - Directories and handbooks - Journals - Indexes to the mass communication literature. Well-written *c.*150 word evaluative annotations. Author, title and subject indexes. US bias and confined to English language material, but an excellent, established source. *Class No:* 070.0(01)

[2172]

Communication abstracts: an international information service. Thousand Oaks, Ca., Sage, Periodicals Press in cooperation with the School of Communication and Theater, Temple University, 1978-. Bi-monthly. $498. ISSN: 01622811.

Abstracts about 1,500 items annually on a range of mass media fields, including mass communication, advertising and marketing, broadcasting, journalism, public relations, radio and television and communication theory. Covers books and reports as well as periodical articles. Arranged in 16 topical groups, with further section of briefly noted items. Subject and author indexes in each issue, author index cumulated in the final issue of year. *Class No:* 070.0(01)

[2173]

—Index to journals in communication studies through 1990. Matlon, R.J. *and* Oritz, S.P., *eds.* 4th ed. Annandale, Va., Speech Communication Association, 1992. 2v. ISBN: 0944811086.

First published 1974.

V.1 contains tables of contents for 19 titles from their inception to 1990. V.2 comprises contributor, classified and keyword indexes. Considerable overlap with *Communication abstracts*, but more convenient for retrospective searching and 'a valuable source for academic libraries that support programs in speech communication, journalism or mass media' (*American reference books annual*, v.24, 1993, p.403). *Class No:* 070.0(01)

[2174]

Information sources for the press and broadcast media. Eagle, S., *ed.* London, Bowker-Saur, 1991. xiii,219p., diags. £41;$70. (*Guides to information sources.*) ISBN: 0862919002.

14 contributed essays (2. Information resources and the television programme maker. ... 5. Use of information in the US media. ... 7. The newspaper library in the information age. ... 13. Film and videotape sources in the UK.) identifying sources and discussing their access and use. Appendix of online databases mentioned in the text. Index. Commendable emphasis on electronic sources, but some essays lean heavily on personal experience and do not give a complete perspective.

2nd ed. scheduled for August 1999 (*c.*£45. ISBN: 1857392612). *Class No:* 070.0(01)

[2175]

LENT, J.A. Global guide to media & communication. München, George Kurian Reference Books, 1987. xii,145p. $70. ISBN: 3598107463.

Bibliography of 'key items in understanding the mass communication of a country or region' (Preface). Includes periodical articles and dissertations. About 4,000 entries, some briefly annotated, in geographic sections. US excluded. Lack of any indexing and unevenness of coverage between the geographic sections devalues this otherwise unique source. *Class No:* 070.0(01)

Scandinavia

[2176]

NORDICOM: bibliography of Nordic mass communication literature. Århus, Nordic Documentation Center for Mass Communication Research, 1975-. Annual. ISSN: 0909914x.

Danish title: *NORDICOM: bibliografi over nordisk massenkommunikationslitteratur*. From 1994 merges *NORDICOM index* (ISSN: 09092773) and *NORDICOM document list* (ISSN: 01051385).

Comprehensive bibliography of mass media literature published in Scandinavia, coverage including chapters in books, periodical articles, dissertations and reports. Entries provide full bibliographical detail, abstract and keywords.

.... *(contd.)*

Also available online (*NCOM*) and on CD-ROM, database versions containing 25,000 records 1997.
Class No: 070.0(01)(48)

Africa

[2177]

WALSH, G. The Media in Africa and Africa in the media: an annotated bibliography. London, Zell, 1996. xvii,291p. $100. ISBN: 1873836813.

1,755 entries in press, broadcasting, film and general (works dealing with more than one medium as well as works on mass communication and theoretical issues) sections. Annotations of 1-5 lines. Author and subject/geographical indexes. *Class No:* 070.0(01)(6)

Caribbean

[2178]

Bibliographic guide to Caribbean mass communication. Lent, J.A., *comp.* Westport, Conn., Greenwood Press, 1992. xi,301p. £58.50;$65. (*Bibliographies and indexes in mass media and communications, no. 5.*) ISBN: 0313282102.

Replaces Lent's *Caribbean mass communications: a comprehensive bibliography* (Los Angeles, Crossroads Press, 1981).

3,695 entries for material of all types. Companion v. in same series (no. 6), *Bibliography of Cuban mass communication* (1992. xi,357p. £62.55;$69.50. ISBN: 0313284555), contains entries for 4,315, mainly Spanish language, items. Both volumes marked by 'little selectivity and no annotations' (*Choice*, v.30(10), June 1993, p.1607).
Class No: 070.0(01)(729)

Women

[2179]

Women and mass communications: an international annotated bibliography. Lent, J.A., *comp.* New York, Greenwood Press, 1991. xvii,481p. £76.50;$89.50. (*Bibliographies and indexes in women's studies.*) ISBN: 0313265798.

3,235 numbered entries for items on images of women in the mass media, women as an audience, women practitioners, women's media, etc. Broad geographic arrangement by continent; author and subject indexes. Appendix: 'Organizations, periodicals and other resources'. Impressive coverage of reports, papers and non-UMI dissertations, but marked American bias (material relating to US 210p.). '(T)he only large-scale bibliography of its kind' (*Choice*, v.28(11/12), July/August 1991, p.1761).
Class No: 070.0(01)-0055.2

Encyclopaedias & Dictionaries

[2180]

ELLMORE, R.T. NTC's mass media dictionary. Lincolnwood, Ill., National Textbook Co., 1991. xi,668p. £23.95;$39.95. ISBN: 0844231851.

Offers more than 20,000 short definitions. Extensive cross-referencing. Coverage extends to related fields such as acting, graphic arts, public relations and print technologies. As a result 'sometimes the definitions are a bit skimpy' (*Choice*, v.29(2), October 1991, p.256).
Class No: 070.0(03)

[2181]

WATSON, J. *and* HILL, A. A Dictionary of communication and media studies. 4th ed. London, Arnold, 1997. xii,251p. illus., tables. £12.99;$18.95. ISBN: 0340676353.

First published 1984, 3rd ed. 1993.

Broad scope dictionary of around 1,600 terms, many with lengthy definitions *e.g.* 'Commercial radio' *c.*900 words; 'Maslow's hierarchy of needs' *c.* 500 words; 'Reithian' *c.*250 words. Extensively cross-referenced; entries include source references and occasional further reading. Useful abbreviations (p.vii-xii). '(S)pecialized no-frills dictionary designed for the academic study of communications and media' (*Reference books bulletin* in *Booklist*, v.93(19/20), June 1997, p.1754). *Class No:* 070.0(03)

[2182]

—PRICE, S. The Complete A-Z media and communication handbook. London, Hodder & Stoughton, 1997. 258p. illus. £8.99. ISBN: 034069131x.

Similar in scope and objective to Watson & Hill (above). *c.*2,500 entries (*e.g.* 'News international' *c.*200 words; 'Regional press' *c.*25 words), with bibliography (p.254-58).
Class No: 070.0(03)

[2183]

WEINER, R. Webster's New World dictionary of media and communications. New York, Macmillan, 1996. iv,676p. $39.95. ISBN: 0028614747.

Rev. & updated ed.

Also available in pbck. ($27.95. ISBN: 002860116). First published 1990.

35,000 definitions of 10-200 words. Coverage includes advertising, book production, broadcasting, computers, fashion, marketing, publishing, radio, television, typography, etc. Includes some entries for associations, companies, individuals and publications. American bias, but a few entries relating to the UK (*e.g.* 'Granada Group', 14 words). 'By far the largest and most current work of its kind ... (a) work of impressive quality' (*Library journal*, v.122(7), April 15th 1997, p.74). *Class No:* 070.0(03)

USA

[2184]

HOLLIS, D.W. The ABC-Clio companion to the media in America. Santa Barbara, ABC-Clio, 1995. xiii,352p. illus. $55. (*ABC-Clio companions to key issues in American history and life.*) ISBN: 087436776x.

Encyclopedic guide 'focussed upon (1) notable "firsts" in the history of the media in America, and (2) organs and personalities of influence' (*Preface*, p.ix). 200 entries of 800-1500 words *e.g.* 'Hearst, William Randolph' 2p., photo., 1 ref; 'National News Council' 1p., 1 ref; 'Raleigh News and Observer' 1½p. 1 ref. Short chronology, bibliography and index. '(N)ot as thorough as Donald Paneth's *The Encylopedia of journalism*' (*q.v.*) (*Choice*, v.33(5), January 1996, p.756). *Class No:* 070.0(03)(73)

[2185]

HUDSON, R.V. Mass media: a chronological encyclopedia of television, radio, motion pictures, magazines, newspapers and books in the United States. New York, Garland, 1987. xxxviii,435p. (*Garland reference library of social science, v.310.*) ISBN: 0824086953.

Intended to provide 'one handy comprehensive reference for historical facts about the mass media in the United States' (p.xix). Arranged in chronological sections 'Founding period 1638-1764' ... 'Economic and legal challenges 1973-1985'. Concentrates on brief factual information such as foundation

....(contd.)
dates of newspapers. Index (p.361-435). Main section preceded by 'Selected firsts in the mass media'. Of some reference value but poorly organized and indexed.
Class No: 070.0(03)(73)

Handbooks & Manuals

Worldwide

[2186]

The World's news media: a comprehensive reference guide. Dorst, H., *ed.* Harlow, Longman Current Affairs, 1991. xi,604p. £124;$198. ISBN: 0582085543.

Distributed in the US by Gale.

Provides information on news media in 118 countries A-Z. About half of each country entry comprises background information such as recent history and statistical data (boxed). Directory section then lists national and regional newspapers, news magazines, broadcasting organizations, news agencies, media pressure groups, professional associations, publishing and broadcasting groups, etc. Variable data for each including contact details, circulation figures, political orientation and history. Separate sections: 'Regional media' (by continent); 'World media'. Appendices list primary sources of official information and newspaper publishing and journalists' associations. A mine of information which could have been improved by more detailed treatment of major countries and the provision of indexes. *Class No:* 070.0(035)(100)

[2187]

World media handbook. United Nations. Department of Public Information. Programme Evaluation and Communication Research Unit, *comp.*. New York, United Nations, 1990-. Irregular. $65.

First published 1990; further eds. 1992 and 1995.

Provides summary information on the mass media in individual countries. 1995 ed. (viii,308p. ISBN: 9211005744) lists newspapers (max. 25) and periodicals (max. 30) by country, with further brief information on broadcast and television stations, news agencies, media related associations and communication educational institutions. No indexes, restricted coverage and some errors, but '(e)specially as a source of communication statistics on less developed countries, this handbook is a unique addition to reference collections' (*Journal of government information*, v.24(1) Jan/Feb 1997, p.70).
Class No: 070.0(035)(100)

Asia—Middle & Near East

[2188]

KAMALIPOUR,, Y.R. *and* **MOWLANA, H. Mass media in the Middle East:** a comprehensive handbook. Westport, Conn., Greenwood Press, 1994. xvii,333p. tables. £62.50;$69.50. ISBN: 0313285357.

Covers 21 states including Arab countries in North Africa, Cyprus, Israel and Turkey. For each provides general survey of media with sections on newspapers, radio, television, cinema, news agencies, etc. References at chap. ends. 40 tables, glossary, bibliographical essay and index.
Class No: 070.0(035)(53+56)

USA

[2189]

Handbook on mass media in the United States: the industry and its audiences. Thomas, E.K. *and* Carpenter, B.H., *eds.* Westport, Conn., Greenwood Press, 1994. xv,325p. tables, diags. £67.50;$79.50. ISBN: 0313278113.

Aimed at students and the general reader offering 'succinct surveys of the history, organization, role, current issues and outlook for the future of different segments of the industry' (*Preface*, p.ix). 16 chaps: 1. Advertising ... 4. Films ... 6. Newspapers ... 9. Recordings ... 11. Minorities ... 14. Disabled audiences ... 16. Sports audiences. Bibliographies and lists of periodicals and organizations at chap. ends; brief index. '(H)andy, but pricey' (*RQ*, v.34(4), Summer 1995, p.520). *Class No:* 070.0(035)(73)

Glossaries

[2190]

CLARKE, P., *and others.* **French glossary of media terms:** French-English/English-French. London, Impact Books, 1994. 184p. illus. £6.95. ISBN: 1874687447.

Translations for over 4,000 terms.
Class No: 070.0(038.1)

[2191]

European media terms glossary. London, Maclean Hunter, 1994-. Irregular. ISSN: 1357096x.

Alternate title *BRAD European media terms glossary*.

English, French, German, Italian and Spanish listings, about 1,200 terms covered. *Class No:* 070.0(038.1)

Yearbooks & Directories

Worldwide

[2192]

Benn's media: the guide to newspapers, periodicals, television, radio and other media. Tonbridge, Miller Freeman, 1846-. Annual. £99 per v. ISSN: 09684557.

Title and publisher varies: as *Newspaper press directory* until 1977; publisher Mitchell until 1948.

Format also varies. 1997 ed. issued in 3 vols: 1. *United Kingdom* (viii,946p.); 2. *Europe* (viii,511p.); 3. *World* (viii,734p.).

The UK v. has sections for publishing houses, national newspapers, regional newspapers (by county and town, A-Z list of towns precedes), consumer periodicals, business and professional periodicals (by subject groups, p.395-749), reference publications, broadcasting, other media (cinema, outdoor advertising, etc.), media organizations and media services. The European and world vols. are arranged in country sections, but otherwise offer similar, if less complete, data. Master index in each v. Fuller information than in its closest rival *Willing's press guide* (*q.v.*). The most widely available UK published media directory, greatly enhanced in recent years by expanded overseas coverage.
Class No: 070.0(058)(100)

Europe

[2193]

European media directory: the classified guide to European media and editorial contacts. London, Two-Ten Communications, 1989-. Semi-annual.

Issued in 2v.: v.1 *Trade and technical* (ISSN: 09551581); v.2 *News and consumer* (ISSN: 09682694). Two-Ten Communications also produce the bimonthly *UK media*

....(contd.)
directory.

July 1997 issue has more than 22,000 entries with 32,000 named editorial contacts. Data for most titles restricted to publisher address, frequency, circulation and contact name(s). V.2 includes some TV and radio stations. Subject, then country, arrangement (except newspapers); subject and title indexes in each v. *Class No:* 070.0(058)(4)

[2194]

Mercator media guide. Cardiff, Mercator Media Project, University of Wales Press, 1993-. ISBN: 0708312047.

V.1 1993 (Davies, J. *ed.* x,224p. £9.95. ISBN: 0708312407) and v.2 1996 (Jones, E.H.G. *ed.* xii,273p. £12.95. ISBN: 0708313817); third vol. anticipated.

Guide to newspapers, magazines and radio and television stations in European Community minority languages and regions. 9 languages in v.1 (*e.g.* Basque, Cornish, Scottish Gaelic, Welsh), 10 languages or regions in v.2 (*e.g.* Corsican, the South Tyrol, Galician, Sorbian). Descriptive entries of up to 1p. No indexes. *Class No:* 070.0(058)(4)

Great Britain

[2195]

BRAD. Barnet, EMAP Business Communications, 1954-. Monthly. £200. ISSN: 09547746.

Title, publisher and format varies; previously subtitled *British rate and data.*

Sections (August 1997, 757p.): Consumer press (p.49-256), *c.*3,250 titles in sections Almanacs...Woodworking; Electronic & outdoor media (p.257-316) including television, video, radio, outdoor and poster advertising and Internet and CD-ROM; Business press (p.317-756), 8,000 titles in classified arrangement. Newspapers previously included now separately covered in *BRAD newspapers* (*q.v.*). Alphabetical title index (yellow pages) precedes main listings. Online version available as *BRADbase media selector*. Mainly for the advertising trade, but full detail provided (publisher, frequency, price, descriptive profile, etc.) and frequency of appearance make this a useful tool for tracking changes in British periodical publishing. *Class No:* 070.0(058)(410)

[2196]

Editors media directories. London, Media Information, 1981-. Monthly, etc. £450.

Issued in 6 vols: 1. *National media* (Monthly. ISSN: 02687542); 2. *Business and professional* (Quarterly. ISSN: 02687550); 3. *Provincial newspapers and town guide* (3 pa. ISSN: 02687569); 4. *Consumer and leisure magazines* (Quarterly. ISSN: 02687577); 5. *Radio and TV programmes* (Semi-annual. ISSN: 02687585); 6. *Freelancers, writer's guilds and London correspondents of the foreign press* (Annual. ISSN: 02687631). *Class No:* 070.0(058)(410)

[2197]

The Media guide. London, Fourth Estate, 1992-. Annual. £12

Intended mainly as a 'handbook for those working in the media, those who want to work in it and those who work with journalists and broadcasters'. 1998 ed. (Fisher, P. & Peak, S. *eds.* 409p. ISBN: 1857022639X) has sections: 'Press', listing national and regional daily and most weekly local newspapers, plus some news magazines, book publishers and press agencies; 'Broadcasting', BBC, independent TV, satellite/cable, radio, film libraries; 'Cross media', *e.g.* law and media, advertising and PR, annual media events; 'Contacts', phone nos. etc. under headings such as The State, Disasters and emergencies and Pressure groups. Index. Cheap and basic, but valuable as a quick reference source for a wide range of information relating to the British media. *Class No:* 070.0(058)(410)

[2198]

The Media UK Internet directory. London, Media UK. World Wide Web resource.

URL: http://www.mediauk.com/. Date reviewed 4th July 1998.

Main coverage for television, radio, newspapers and magazines and press agencies. Entries, arranged under categories (*e.g.* daily newspapers), include basic details with links to Internet site and email addresses. Also features a search facility, a point and click map for links to UK local newspapers and a student media directory.
Class No: 070.0(058)(410)

[2199]

Pims United Kingdom media directory. London, Pims, 1981-. Monthly. £344. ISSN: 02615169.

Lists contacts by specialism for newspapers (national and regional), news agencies, trade and technical publications, consumer magazines, radio and television, etc. Index in each issue. Also available as an online database and on CD-ROM.

Other titles from Pims, all published semi-annually: *Pims European consumer directory* (ISSN: 09576916); *Pims European national newspapers directory* (ISSN: 13584472); *Pims USA consumer directory* (ISSN: 09576908); *Pims USA newspapers directory* (ISSN: 09558675).
Class No: 070.0(058)(410)

Germany

[2200]

Stamm: Leitfaden für Presse und Werbung: Nachweis und Beschreibung periodischer Druckschriften sowie aller Werbemöglichkeiten in Deutschland und der wichtigsten im Ausland. Stamm, W. Essen, Stamm, 1947-. Annual. DM194. ISSN: 09423869.

English title: *Annual directory through press and advertising: bibliography and description of newspapers and periodicals and of all advertising possibilities in Germany as well as of the most important abroad.*

Sections: 1. Newspapers - 2. Free-distribution newspapers - 3. Magazines and annual publications - 4. Press and information services, other publications - 5. Foreign countries - 6. Broadcasting and cinema - 7. Outdoor advertising - 8. Other possibilities of advertising - 9. Other addresses and advertising. Thumb index. Includes data for *c.*20,000 newspapers and serials published in Germany, plus many others issued elsewhere.

Separate directories now also available for Austria and Switzerland as *Stamm Österreich* (1994-. ISSN: 09465014) and *Stamm Schweiz* (1995-. ISSN: 09488669).
Class No: 070.0(058)(430)

France

[2201]

Annuaire de la presse et de la publicité: et de la communication. Paris, Écran Publicité, 1878-. Annual. ISSN: 00662585.

Title and publisher varies.

The 110th ed. (1997. 701p.) has 4 main sections: Organismes professionnels - Presse - Agences - Publicité. Press section (p.17-510) divided into various listings for national and regional newspapers, titles for the general public (by topic), professional and commercial titles,

....(contd.)
newsletters and scientific publications. Brief entries give basic information such as contact detail, foundation date, frequency and price only. Index (p.637-701) of titles, societies and organizations. *Class No:* 070.0(058)(44)

Italy

[2202]
Guida della stampa periodica italiana. 10. ed. Roma, Unione Stampa Periodica Italiana, 1995. 1011p. L100,000. ISBN: 8876217347.

1st ed. 1969; 9th ed. 1991.

Sections for daily newspapers, picture magazines, local and political newspapers (subdivided by region), periodicals by subject (p.101-453), society and association periodicals, information agencies, Italian language newspapers overseas and radio and television stations. Basic details for each entry only. Full treatment of legislation relating to the media and statistical tables (p.533-918); index and contents summary. *Class No:* 070.0(058)(450)

RSFSR

[2203]
The media guide CMN: to the former Soviet Union & the Baltic states. London & Moscow, CIS Information Publishing, 1996-. Annual. ISSN: 13636502.

First issue (xi,521p.) divided into English and Russian sections. Former (p.1-240) provides editorial and statistical overviews followed by a directory section listing newspapers, magazines and periodicals, radio and TV stations, etc., by media type and country. Comprehensively indexed. *Class No:* 070.0(058)(470)

Scandinavia

[2204]
Media Scandinavia. København, Danske Reklamebureauers Brancheforening, 1952-. Annual. DK Kr735. ISSN: 00765821.

Title varies: originally *Eberlins Bladliste,* then *Media.*

Contains information on advertising media in Denmark, Greenland, The Faroe Islands, Norway, Sweden, Finland and Iceland. Entry detail in Danish, with English headings, table of contents and introductory matter. A useful source of information on current newspapers and magazines, trade and technical journals, yearbooks and directories. Also has sections on television and radio stations, outdoor advertising, fairs and exhibitions and advertising agencies. Data is most comprehensive for Denmark. *Class No:* 070.0(058)(48)

Africa

[2205]
Directory of African media. Maja-Pearce, A., *ed.* Bruxelles, International Federation of Journalists, 1996. 384p.

Also published in French as *Annuaire de la presse africaine.*

Lists newspapers and magazines by country A-Z. Full entries give contact information, publisher, editorial staff, date founded, frequency, circulation, etc. For many countries covers only a handful of titles. Various appendices including 'National journalists' organizations' and 'List of African periodicals in Europe and North America'. *Class No:* 070.0(058)(6)

USA

[2206]
Gale directory of publications and broadcast media: an annual guide to publications and broadcasting stations, including newspapers, magazines, journals, radio stations, television stations and cable systems. Detroit, Gale, 1987-. Annual. $425. ISSN: 10487972.

Issued in 3v. Continues the long established *Ayer directory of publications,* first published 1880 (as *IMS/Ayer directory of publications,* 1983-86).

Radio and television stations and cable systems included since 1990. Geographic coverage confined to North America. 34,628 entries in v.1-2 of 131st. ed. (1998), arranged by state and town. Print entries include publisher, address, description (1-2 lines), date founded, frequency, size, editorial personnel, ISSN, subscription rates, online availability, alternate formats and variant names. Excludes newsletters and directories. V.3 contains maps, statistical tables and publisher, subject, editorial name, and master name/keyword indexes. An inter-edition supplement *Gale directory of publications update* reports changes and adds new entries. The directory is searchable online as part of the *Gale database of publications and broadcast media* (Dialog (file 469) and GaleNet). Also available on CD-ROM both as a separate disc and as component of *Gale's ready reference shelf.* *Class No:* 070.0(058)(73)

[2207]
Gebbie Press: all-in-one directory. New Paltz, N.Y., Gebbie Press, 1972-. Annual. $95. ISSN: 00978175.

Lists business, trade and consumer periodicals and magazines (white pages), news syndicates, daily, weekly, Black and Hispanic newspapers (yellow pages) and cable networks, TV stations and radio stations (grey pages). Minimal data compared with sources such as the *Gale directory* (above), but adequate for basic details such as publisher address or publication frequency.
Class No: 070.0(058)(73)

[2208]
The Working press of the nation. New Providence, N.J., Bowker, 1945-. Annual (since 1959). $399. ISSN: 00841323.

Published by Bowker from 47th ed. (1997), previously National Research Bureau (Chicago). Now issued in 3v.: 1. *Newspaper directory*; 2. *Magazines and internal publications directory*; 3. *TV & radio directory*.

Aimed at journalists and those working in the media and related fields. V.1 includes weekly and local newspapers. V.2 lists over 5,500 magazines (by subject), the internal publications of 1,500 companies and 1,500 newsletters. V.3 has over 15,000 listings for TV and radio stations.
Class No: 070.0(058)(73)

Biographies

[2209]
Who's who in mass communication. Dziki, S., *and others eds.* 2nd rev. ed. München, Saur, 1990. xi,191p. $135. ISBN: 3598108842.

At head of title: The Press Research Centre, Cracow on behalf of the International Association for Mass Communication Research. Rev. ed. of *World directory of mass communication researcher's* (Krakow, Press Research, 1984.)

Contains 1,124 entries A-Z for researchers in the field of mass communication. Variable data on educational qualifications, career, memberships and publications. '(T)his

....*(contd.)*
work is scanty ... . In addition, it is disturbing to find someone listed who died in the mid-1980s'. (*American reference books annual*, v.22, 1991, p.376).
Class No: 070.0(092)

The Press

Bibliographies

[2210]
HAGELWEIDE, G. Literatur zur deutschsprachigen Presse: eine Bibliographie von den Aufängen bis 1970. München, Saur, 1985-. DM360 per v. (*Dortmunder Beiträge zur Zeitungsforschung, Bd.35.*) ISBN: 3598212844.

Bibliography of German language literature on all aspects of the press, international in scope. Unannotated entries in classified arrangement. Publication of Bd. 8 (1997) brings total no. of items to 89,198. Now scheduled for 14 v. (originally 9), subject index to complete set.
Class No: 070.1(01)

[2211]
McCOY, R.E. Freedom of the press: an annotated bibliography. Carbondale, Ill., Southern Illinois Univ. Press, 1968. v.p. $44.95. ISBN: 0809303353.

About 8,000 entries for books, pamphlets, articles, dissertations, films and other materials relating to the freedom of the press in the English-speaking world.

Continued by the same author's *Freedom of the press: a bibliocyclopedia: ten year supplement (1967-1977)* (Southern Illinois Univ. Press, 1979. 557p. $44.95. ISBN: 0809308444) and *Freedom of the press: an annotated bibliography: second supplement, 1978-1992* (Southern Illinois Univ. Press, 1993. xiv,441p. $100. ISBN: 0809315831). '(T)hese volumes are the major reference sources on this topic' (*Choice*, v.31(10), June 1994, p.1558).
Class No: 070.1(01)

[2212]
PAINE, F.K. *and* **PAINE, N.E. Magazines: a bibliography for their analysis** with annotations and a study guide. Metuchen, N.J., Scarecrow Press, 1987. vii,690p. £56.25;$62.50. ISBN: 0810819759.

Gives selective coverage of books, journal articles and dissertations written about magazines. 2,200 annotated entries, mostly for items published since 1978, although a few important earlier works are also included. Separate 'Study guide' section listing journals, newspapers, reference sources and indexes relevant to the study of magazines. US emphasis, although some British items included. Subject index, lacking in specificity; no author or title index.
Class No: 070.1(01)

Encyclopaedias & Dictionaries

[2213]
World press encyclopedia. Kurian, G.T., *ed.* London, Mansell, 1982. 2v. (xix,1202p.). ISBN: 0720116465.

Published in the US by Facts on File (ISBN: 0871966212). Reprint avaialable from Books on Demand ($180. ISBN: 078371579x).

Intended as a 'definitive survey of the press in 180 countries' (Preface v.1 p.xiii). 4 sections. 'The international press', comprises 6 essays (*e.g.* Comparative press laws). The main section, 'The world's developed press', covers 83 countries Albania-Zimbabwe. Each country arranged under headings (*e.g.* Censorship) with summary, chronology and bibliography. Remaining sections, 'Smaller and developing

....*(contd.)*
press systems' (33 countries) and 'Minimal and underdeveloped press systems' (65 countries) with briefer information. 4 appendices including 'News agencies of the world'. Detailed index (p.1171-202). A major compilation which retains some value, despite the appearance of more up-to-date alternatives such as *The World's news media* (*q.v.*). *Class No:* 070.1(03)

Great Britain

Bibliographies

[2214]
The Newspaper press in Britain: an annotated bibliography. Linton, D. *and* Boston, R., *eds.* London, Mansell, 1987. xvii,361p. ISBN: 0720117925.

The first significant bibliography of the British newspaper press. 2,909 critically annotated entries for books, articles and theses on 'printed news journalism' from the earliest times to the present. Coverage includes photojournalism, cartoon illustration and news agencies. Arranged A-Z by author with an index of subjects, newspaper titles and persons. Appendices on the chronology of British newspaper history 1476-1986 and archival sources for *c.*155 individual newspapers and authors. *Class No:* 070.1(410)(01)

[2215]
—LINTON, D. The Twentieth-century newspaper press in Britain: an annotated bibliography. London, Mansell, 1994. xxi,386p. £70;$120. ISBN: 0720121590.

Based on the 1987 v., but with wider selection criteria (essayists, dramatists, critics, sports reporters etc., as well as news journalists) and excluding material not relating to the present century. 3,779 entries A-Z by author with a preliminary listing of 97 'Reference works'. Annotations rarely exceed 50 words. 'Chronology of the British newspaper press 1900-1994' (p.358-65). Index. '(A) useful and comprehensively analytical work with subject matter ranging from free newspapers to D notices, cartoons and crossword puzzles' (*Refer*, v.11(2), Spring 1995, p.19).
Class No: 070.1(410)(01)

[2216]
The Nineteenth-century periodical press in Britain: a bibliography of modern studies 1901-1971. Madden, L. *and* Dixon, D., *comps.* New York, London, Garland, 1976. xiv,280p. (*Garland reference library of the humanities, v.53.*) ISBN: 0824099451.

2,632 entries including books, theses and articles from over 100 journals. In 4 sections: A. Bibliographies, finding lists and reports on bibliographical projects; B. General history of periodicals and newspapers; C. Studies of individual periodicals and newspapers (A-Z by title); D. Studies and memoirs of proprietors, journalists and contributors. Some entries annotated, some references to *Dictionary of national biography* and Boase *Modern English biography*. Author index.

Updated by Uffelman, L.K. *and others*, *The Nineteenth-century periodical press in Britain: a bibliography of modern studies, 1972-1987* (Victorian Periodicals Press. 132p. $19.95. ISBN: 00963462601). *Class No:* 070.1(410)(01)

[2217]
WEED, K.K. *and* **BOND, R.P. Studies of British newspapers and periodicals** from their beginning to 1800: a bibliography. Chapel Hill, Univ. of North Carolina Press, 1946. London, Oxford Univ. Press, 1947. vi,233p. (*Studies in philology, extra series, no.2.*)

Bibliography of books and periodical articles in subject sections. About 2,100 entries. Includes materials on individual newspapers and periodicals and also general subjects such as freedom of the press and stamp duty.
Class No: 070.1(410)(01)

Encyclopaedias & Dictionaries

[2218]
Encyclopedia of the British press 1422-1992. Griffiths, D., *ed.* Basingstoke, Macmillan, 1992. x,694p. ISBN: 0333529847.

Published in the US by St. Martins Press ($79.95. ISBN: 0312086334).

Contains *c.*3,000 articles on 'newspapers, journalists and personalities, national and provincial newspapers, and terms, ideas, places and events' (Foreword p.vii). Most entries for journalists (*e.g.* 'Stead, William Thomas' *c.*900 words) or newspapers (*e.g.* 'Yorkshire Post' *c.*700 words plus list of editors). Bibliographical citations to items by or about individuals with entry; 'Thematic bibliography' (p.691-94). Main section preceded by 6 essays outlining broad history of the press (p.1-64). Various appendices inluding brief chronology, 1991 circulation figures, list of editors and information on organizations such as BL Newspaper Library, National Union of Journalists and Reuters. Impressively comprehensive this momentous publication, which was 5 years in the making, is the only work of its kind on the British press. *Class No:* 070.1(410)(03)

Histories

[2219]
BLACK, J. The English press in the eighteenth century. London, Croom Helm, 1987. xv,321p. ISBN: 0709939248.

Available from Ashgate (£40. ISBN: 0751200077). Earlier coverage of the 18th century provincial press provided by G.A. Cranfield's *The Development of the provincial newspaper, 1700-1760* (1962).

General introduction to the London and provincial press. Thematic chapters (*e.g.* 5. The press and the constitution; 6. Controlling the press: censorship and subsidies). References at chapter ends; bibliography (p.317-21). Index of titles (newspapers). Contains a great deal of information, but as a historical work 'short on conclusions and summaries' (*The Library. Sixth series.* v.10(2), June 1988, p.172).
Class No: 070.1(410)(091)

[2220]
Newspaper history from the seventeenth century to the present day. Boyce, G., *and others eds.* London, Constable for the Press Group of the Acton Society, 1978. 423p. illus., ports. (*Communication and society.*) ISBN: 0094623007.

A collection of essays, concentrating on the 19th-20th centuries. In 4 parts: 1. Historical perspectives; 2. The structure, ownership and control of the press; 3. The organization and occupation of journalism; 4. Press, politics and society. Appended: A national press archive; Select bibliography; Newspaper chronology, 1621-1977. Index. Despite 'rather incoherent organization, an extremely

....*(contd.)*
inportant and worthwhile' history of the British press (*Library review*, v.29(2), Summer 1979, p.113-4).
Class No: 070.1(410)(091)

[2221]
TIMES, The. **The History of 'The Times'.** London, 'The Times', 1935-93. 6v. in 7, illus., ports.

V.1 1785-1841. (1935). V.2 1841-84. (1939). V.3 1884-1912. (1947). V.4 1912-48. (1952). V.5 1939-66. (1984. ISBN: 0723002622). V.6 1966-81. (1993. ISBN: 0723006105).

The most comprehensive history available. V.4 (in 2 pts., 1912-20 and 1921-48), includes an appendix (p.1130-36) showing proprietors, editors, policy and price of London daily newspapers contemporary with *The Times.* V.5 by I. McDonald, published to mark the newspaper's 200th anniversary, goes back over ground transversed in v.4, which gave coverage only of an 'abbreviated nature' to the period 1939-48. The latest v., *The Thomson years* by J. Grigg, covers to the Murdoch takeover. Includes an appended list of editorial and senior management personnel and a chronology. *Class No:* 070.1(410)(091)

Germany

[2222]
Geschichte der deutschen Presse. Berlin, Colloquium Verlag, 1966-1986. 4v. (*Abhandlungen und Materialen zur Publizistik, Bd.5, etc.*.)

History of the German press. V.1 *Deutsche Presse bis 1815* (1969, reprinted with supplementary material 1986. 360p. DM88. ISBN: 389166818X); v.2 *Deutsche Presse im 19. Jahrhundert* (1966. 392p. DM98. ISBN: 3891668031); v.3 *Deutsche Presse 1914-1945* (1972. 592p. DM118. ISBN: 389166804x); v.4 *Pressepolitik für Deutsche 1945-1969* (1986. 524p. DM108. ISBN: 3891668058). Each v. individually indexed with a bibliography.
Class No: 070.1(430)

France

[2223]
Histoire générale de la presse française. Bellanger, C., *and others eds.* Paris, Presses Universitaires de France, 1969-76. 5v. illus.

V.1: *Des origines à 1814.* (1969. 652p. ISBN: 213030284x); v.2: *De 1815 à 1871.* (1969. 472p. ISBN: 2130302580); v.3: *De 1871 à 1940.* (1972. 688p. ISBN: 2130321496); v.4: *De 1940 à 1958.* (1975. 488p. ISBN: 2130335411); v.5: *De 1958 à nos jours.* (1976. 576p. ISBN: 2130336132).

A full history of the French press, wide in scope, including regional and local newspapers and special interest publications. Detailed indexes of personal names and newspaper titles in each volume. Extensive bibliographies in v.1-3 and v.5, (bibliography for 1940-1958 in v.5); v.5 also includes a supplementary bibliography for v.1-3.
Class No: 070.1(44)

Italy

[2224]
Storia della stampa italiana. Castronovo, V. *and* Tranfaglia, N., *eds.* Rome, Laterza, 1976-94. 7v.

V.1 *La Stampa italiana del Cinquecento all'Ottocento.* (1976. 566p.); v.2 *La Stampa italiana del Risorgimento.* (1979. 601p.); v.3 *La Stampa italiana nell'età liberale.*

.... *(contd.)*
(1979. 429p.); v.4 *La Stampa italiana nell'età fascista.* (1980. 385p.); v.5 *La Stampa italiana dalla Resistenza agli anni Sessanta.* (1980. 330p.); v.6 *La Stampa italiana del neocapitalismo.* (1976. 608p.); v.7 *La Stampa italiana nell'età della Tv 1975-1994.* (1994. 646p. ISBN: 8842045098).

Each volume separately indexed. Various appendices present factual data *e.g.* 'La proprieta dei giornali dal 1861 al 1975', v.6, (p.514-82). A revised ed. of v.4 was issued under the title *La Stampa del regime fascista,* in 1986. *Class No:* 070.1(450)

Sweden

[2225]

RYDÉN, P. Anteckningar till en svensk presshistorisk bibliografi. Lund, Lunds Universitet, 1971. v,324p.

All Swedish language items. Section on individual publications (p.119-218); section on journalists (p.219-92). Name and subject index. *Class No:* 070.1(485)

Denmark

[2226]

ELVIUS, B. *and* **FALD, K. Litteratur om dansk presse** 1951-1969: en bibliografi. Århus, Institut for Presseforskning, 1973. 425p.

Bibliography of publications, including periodical articles and parts of composite works, on the Danish press. Classified arrangement with author, subject, newspaper, other serials and person as subject indexes. *Class No:* 070.1(489)

Belgium

[2227]

LEENAERTS, R.J. De Periodieke drukpers in Belgie: de geschiedenis van de periodieke drukpers in Belgie van 1605 tot op heden. [La Presse périodique en Belgique: sources pour l'histoire de la presse périodique en Belgique depuis 1605 à nos jours.] Torhout, Flandria Nostra, 1987. 3v.

Contains briefly annotated entries for 7,877 items relating to the history of the periodical press in Belgium; index in v.3. *Class No:* 070.1(493)

Nigeria

[2228]

Press in Nigeria: an annotated bibliography. Ogbondah, C., *comp.* Westport, Conn., Greenwood Press, 1990. xv,127p. $38.75;$42.95. *(African special bibliographic series, no.12.)* ISBN: 0313265216.

'(S)teers a pioneering academic exercise in bibliographical compilation on Nigerian mass communication' (p.xiii). 501 numbered entries A-Z by author; annotations average 100 words. Index (p.113-27). *Class No:* 070.1(669)

Canada

[2229]

An Annotated bibliography of works on daily newspapers in Canada 1914-1983. [Une Bibliographie annotée des ouvrages portant sur les quotidiens canadiens.] Sotiron, M., *ed.* Montreal, Inkstain Publications, 1987. 288p. ISBN: 096931020x.

Coverage includes freedom of the press, news ownership, advertising and ethics, and history of newspapers.

.... *(contd.)*
Approximately 3,750 entries arranged geographically. French language entries (*c.*500) grouped under Quebec. Subject and author indexes. *Class No:* 070.1(71)

USA

[2230]

The Ethnic press in the United States: a historical analysis and handbook. Miller, S.M., *ed.* New York, Greenwood Press, 1987. xxii,437p. £76.50;$89.50. ISBN: 0313238790.

The 'press is basically defined as newspapers of general circulation rather than special interest publications' (Introduction p.xii). Covers 27 ethnic groups in separate chapters: The Arabic language press ... The Ukranian press. In depth historical treatment. The 'chapter bibliographies are richly detailed and together form one of the fullest bibliographies to date compiled' (*Journalism history,* v.14(4), Winter 1987, p.131-32). *Class No:* 070.1(73)

[2231]

SCHWARZLOSE, R.A. Newspapers: a reference guide. New York and London, Greenwood, 1987. xxxvii,417p. £76.50; $89.50. *(American popular culture.)* ISBN: 0313236135.

Selective guide to the literature on US newspapers from the beginning to the mid 1980s. Presentation as narrative essays, each with attached bibliography: 'Providing newspapers' - 'Newspapers and society' - 'Newspapers and the law' etc. Approximately half the coverage is for newspaper history. Includes appendix on major research collections. Well indexed (p.337-417). Warmly received, 'no comparable book about the press' (*Choice,* v.25(10), June 1988, p.1546). *Class No:* 070.1(73)

Newspapers

Databases

[2232]

News information online, CD-ROM and Internet sources. Spencer, N., *comp.* London, British Library Science Reference and Information Service, 1997. vi,64p. ISBN: 0712308334.

'The focus of the guide is on commercial economic and political news as well as current affairs and will be of particular, though not exclusive, value to the commercial researcher' (Preface). 5 sections: 1. News databases available via commercial online services - 2. News CD-ROM databases - 3. Online databases and CD-ROM product files (brief detail including 5-20 word descriptions) - 4. Online services and CD-ROM publishers/vendors - 5. News on the World Wide Web. *Class No:* 070.2(003.4)

[2233]

Newspapers online: a guide to searching daily newspapers whose articles are online in full text, including geographic indexes. Bjørner, S.N., *comp. & ed.* 3rd ed. Needham Heights, Mass., BiblioData, 1995. Looseleaf. $99. ISBN: 1879258129.

First published 1992; no further eds. are planned.

Covers more than 200 newspapers A-Z by title. Entries include online vendors, CD-ROM availability and searching advice. Comprehensively indexed. *Class No:* 070.2(003.4)

Internet

[2234]

Ecola newstand: a guide to English language media online. Ecola Design, 1995-. World Wide Web resource.

URL: http://www.ecola.com/news. Date reviewed 30th June 1998.

Provides links to 6,400 newspapers and magazines with an Internet presence. Sites included are actively updated and offer unrestricted access. Geographic arrangement with publication name search facility. *Class No:* 070.2(003.41)

Micromaterials

[2235]

LIBRARY OF CONGRESS. Catalog Management and Publications Division. **Newspapers in microform.** United States and foreign countries 1948-1983. Washington DC., Library of Congress, 1984. 3v. ISSN: 00979627.

V.1 US A-O. V.2 US P-Z. Title index. V.3 Foreign countries.

Cumulates: *Newspapers in microform: United States, 1948-1972,* (1973); *Newspapers in microform: foreign countries, 1948-1972,* (1973); the respective quinquennial supplements covering 1973-77 (1978); the 1978-82 issues of the now ceased annual *Newspapers in microform,* (US and foreign titles in separate sequences with combined indexes), plus new reports received in 1983.

Serves as an international union catalogue of microformed newspapers reported to the Library of Congress. Geographically arranged entries under newspaper title giving publication dates, frequency and microform holdings of reporting institution. Includes details of holdings of *c.*75 British institutions. Wide international coverage; there 'is no substitute for this work' (*Microform review,* Summer 1986, p.193). *Class No:* 070.2(003.5)

Bibliographies

[2236]

BRITISH LIBRARY. Newspaper Library. **Catalogue of the Newspaper Library, Colindale.** London, British Museum Publications for the British Library, 1975. 8v. ISBN: 0714103527.

V.1: London. (654p.); v.2: England and Wales, Scotland, Ireland. (672p.); v.3: Aden-New Guinea. (416p.); v.4: New Zealand-Zanzibar. (320p.); v.5: Titles, A-E. (600p.); v.6: Titles, F-L. (604p.); v.7: Titles, M-R. (604p.); v.8: Titles, S-Z. (604p.). Supersedes *Catalogue of printed books. Supplement: Newspapers published in Great Britain and Ireland, 1800-1901.* (London, British Museum, 1908. 532 cols.).

Compiled from the working catalogue of the Colindale collection. UK titles and amendments included up to the end of 1970, overseas titles and amendments up to the end of 1971. Covers 'London newspapers and journals from 1801 onward, English provincial, Scottish and Irish newspapers from about 1700 onward and large collections of Commonwealth and foreign newspapers' (Introduction). Excludes London newspapers published before 1801 (in separate BL Burney Collection) and newspapers in oriental languages. V.1 includes national newspapers published in London. Entries give title, dates, notes on changed titles, etc. and extent of the Library's holdings.
Class No: 070.2(01)

[2237]

CENTER FOR RESEARCH LIBRARIES. Foreign newspapers held by the Center for Research Libraries. Smets, K. *and* Pilecky-Dekajlo A., *comps.* Chicago, Center for Research Libraries, 1992. 2v.

Lists 5,562 titles from 156 countries of which 328 currently received. Separate title and geographical sequences, entries include bibliographical detail and summary holdings data. *Class No:* 070.2(01)

[2238]

Hosnill: a handlist of selected newspaper holdings, national, regional and foreign in London public libraries. Croydon Libraries. Museum and Arts, Reference and Information Service, *comp.* Croydon, Croydon Libraries, Museum and Arts, Reference and Information Service, 1973-. Irregular.

No. XV issued 1997 (iv,33p. ISBN: 0903712407), new eds. now appearing on approx. annual basis.
Class No: 070.2(01)

[2239]

Internationale Zeitungsbestände in Deutschen Bibliotheken: ein Verzeichnis von 18000 Zeitungen, Amtsblättern und zeitungsähnlichen Periodika mit Besitznachweisen und geographischern register. Walravens, H., *hrsg.* 2 Aufl. München, Saur, 1993. xxi,801p. DM498. ISBN: 3598111541.

First published as *Standortverzeichnis ausländischer Zeitungen und Illustrierten in Bibliotheken und Institutionen der Bundesrepublik Deutschland einschliesslich Berlin (West)* (Pullach, Verlag Dokumentation, 1973. 334p.).

Union catalogue of international newspapers in German libraries. 18,000 entries including news magazines, official gazettes and similar publications. Geographical index.
Class No: 070.2(01)

[2240]

LIBRARY OF CONGRESS. Serial and Government Publications Division. **Newspapers currently received in the Library of Congress.** Washington, D.C., Library of Congress, 1968-. Biennial (irregular). ISSN: 00936464.

Title varies slightly: early eds. as *Newspapers currently received and permanently retained in the Library of Congress.*

The 12th ed. (1990. vii,47p.), lists 359 US and 1,134 foreign newspapers received and retained on a permanent basis. Arranged geographically. *Class No:* 070.2(01)

[2241]

—LIBRARY OF CONGRESS. An Annotated list of selected newspaper reference works located at the Library of Congress. Connell, J.J., *comp.* Washington, D.C., United States Newspaper Program, 1992. ii,132p.
Class No: 070.2(01)

[2242]

World list of national newspapers: a union list of national newspapers in libraries in the British Isles. Weber, R., *comp.* London, Butterworths, 1976. 95p. ISBN: 0408708174.

Published under the auspices of the Standing Conference of National and University Libraries in contract with the Social Science Research Council.

Reports holdings for over 1,500 newspapers in major British libraries with the exception of the British Library Newspaper Library (Colindale). Includes British and Irish national newspapers and regional newspapers which carry a significant amount of national news. Excludes emigré, political, religious, military and cultural titles, unless of national significance. In A-Z title order, with index of

....*(contd.)*
newspaper titles by country (p.75-88). Updated by *World list of national newspapers: revised entries: March 1984,* published as *British Library Newspaper Library newsletter. Supplement no.1* (1984. 7p.). *Class No:* 070.2(01)

Europe—Eastern

[2243]
Union list of Slavonic and East European newspapers in British libraries. Szkuta, M., *comp.* London, British Library Slavonic and East European Collection, 1992. Unpaged.

Covers 22 libraries. Entries, A-Z by country then title, give date publication began, frequency and holdings statement with indication of format *e.g.* microfilm. Includes the Asian republics of the former USSR.
Class No: 070.2(401)

Great Britain

[2244]
Bibliography of British newspapers. Toase, C.A., *gen. ed.* London, British Library, 1975-.

V.1 *Wiltshire* (Bluhm, R.K. *ed.* 1975. 28p. ISBN: 0853650381); v.2 *Kent* (Bergess, W.F. *and others eds.* 1982. xviii,139p. £15. ISBN: 0712300074); v.3 *Durham and Northumberland* (Manders, F.W.D. *ed.* 1982. xvi,65p. ISBN: 0712301240); v.4 *Derbyshire* (Mellors, A. & Radford, J. *eds.* 1987. xv,74p. £15. ISBN: 0712301240); v.5 *Nottinghamshire* (Brook, M. *ed.* 1987. xvii,62p. £15. ISBN: 0712300619); v.6 *Cornwall: Devon* (Rowles, J. & Maxted, I. *eds.* 1991. xiv,123p. ISBN: 0712302239). V.1 published as a pamphlet by the Library Association Reference, Special and Information Section.

Eventual objective is to cover the entire British Isles based on pre-1974 county boundaries. Confined to newspapers providing general news. Format of volumes varies. Latest has main section listing newspapers A-Z by title. Separate section by town A-Z locates files in libraries, publisher's offices, record offices and other collections. Further 'Chronologies' section listing newspapers by town and date. Historical accounts and indexes also noted.
Class No: 070.2(410)

[2245]
BRAD newspapers. London, EMAP Business Communications, 1994-. Monthly.

An offshoot of the main *BRAD* (*q.v.*). Separate sections for national and regional titles (by county); title index (yellow pages). Concentrates on advertising rates and data, but includes publisher, frequency, price, etc. More comprehensive and up-to-date than *Willing's press guide* (*q.v.*). *Class No:* 070.2(410)

[2246]
Local newspapers and periodicals of the nineteenth century: a checklist of holdings in provincial libraries. Dixon, D., *comp.* Leicester, University of Leicester, Victorian Studies Centre, 1973. 2v.

V.1: *Aylesbury-Hereford.* [2],30 leaves; v.2: *Hereford-York.* [1],31-62.

The 'information is based largely upon examination of the catalogues of local history collections in the libraries'. Arranged by place A-Z; entries give title and dates held only. *Class No:* 070.2(410)

[2247]
Newsplan. London, British Library, 1986-96. 10v. £30 (per v., most in print).

Initial vol. *Report of the pilot project in the South West* (1986. ISBN: 0712330577). Further vols., with title *Report of the Newsplan project in...*, for the East Midlands (1989. ISBN: 0712301860), Northern region (1989. ISBN: 0712301836), North Western region (1990. ISBN: 0712302212), Yorkshire and Humberside (1990. ISBN: 0712302182), West Midlands (1990. ISBN: 0712302360), Ireland (1992. ISBN: 0712302824), Wales (1994. ISBN: 0712303154), Scotland (1994. ISBN: 071230360X) and London and South Eastern region (1996. ISBN: 0712304878). Various updates also issued, *e.g. Newsplan in Yorkshire and Humberside: cumulative update of local newspaper holdings 1990-1995.*

'Newsplan' is a BL Newspaper Library project intended to locate surviving files of newspapers in the regions in order that the contents might be preserved in microfilm. Each v. contains a listing, either by title or locality, giving brief bibliographical details and holding libraries with notes on condition, etc. *Class No:* 070.2(410)

Scotland

[2248]
Directory of Scottish newspapers. Ferguson, J.P.S., *comp.* Edinburgh, National Library of Scotland, 1984. xviii,155p. 1 facsim. £10. ISBN: 0902220403.

Succeeds Ferguson's *Scottish newspapers held in Scottish libraries,* 1956.

Details, as at December 1979, of the newspaper holdings of 57 Scottish libraries and many Scottish newspaper publishers. Also includes 80% of the Scottish newspaper holdings of the British Library extracted from the general catalogue to 1975. 1,178 entries arranged by title giving publication dates and cross-references to earlier titles. Includes newspapers of a political or religious character, but not house or trade journals. Indexed by town with lists of titles published. *Class No:* 070.2(411)

Ireland

[2249]
MUNTER, R.L. A Handlist of Irish newspapers, 1685-1750. Cambridge, Bowes & Bowes, 1961. xiii,36p. (*Cambridge Bibliographical Society. Monograph no.4.*)

Geographically arranged list with locations in Irish and British libraries. Munter later published a historical account for much the same period, *The History of the Irish newspaper, 1685-1760.* (London, Cambridge University Press, 1967. xiii,217p.), which includes a useful bibliography (p.192-207). *Class No:* 070.2(415)

Northern Ireland

[2250]
Northern Ireland newspapers, 1737-1987: a checklist with locations. 2nd rev. ed. Belfast, Library Association, Northern Ireland Branch, 1987. vi,63p. ISBN: 0906066034.

First published 1979.

Alphabetical title list of more than 250 entries. Holdings detail for 23 libraries in Northern Ireland, plus the British Library, Cambridge University and the National Library of Ireland. *Class No:* 070.2(416)

England

[2251]

Early English newspapers: bibliography and guide to the microfilm collection. Cox, S.M. *and* Budeit, J.L., *comps.* Woodbridge Ct. and Reading, Research Publications, 1983. vi,80p. $95. ISBN: 0892350768.

Title list of British Library Burney Collection and Bodleian Library newspapers microfilmed by Research Publications as *Early English newspapers.* Gives publication dates and reel location only. *Class No:* 070.2(420)

[2252]

GIBSON, J.S.W. Local newspapers 1750-1920: England and Wales, Channel Islands, Isle of Man: a select location list. Birmingham, Federation of Family History Societies, 1987. 64p. £2. ISBN: 0907099467.

Indicates which newspapers have been published in specific places and libraries/record offices, (including Colindale), where they can be consulted. Based on the British Library's *Catalogue of the newspaper Library, Colindale* (*q.v.*), arrangement by county then town. Titles published for less than four years or in Welsh excluded. Complements Dixon (*q.v.*). *Class No:* 070.2(420)

Germany

[2253]

HAGELWEIDE, G. Deutsche Zeitungsbestände in Bibliotheken und Archiven. Düsseldorf, Droste Verlag, 1974. 372p. (*Bibliographien zur Geschichte des Parlamentarismus und der politischen Partein. Heft 6.*)

A union list of German newspapers published 1700-1969 held in 530 German and 49 foreign collections. 2,018 entries for an overall number of 4,411 titles. Geographically arranged by 222 places of publication within the German frontiers of 1937. Register of places of publication precedes the main catalogue. Title index (p.309-47). English language introduction (p.18-26). *Class No:* 070.2(430)

Austria

[2254]

Verzeichnis Österreichischer Zeitungen 1800-1945: vermehrt durch Bestände ausländischer Zeitungen in Österreichischen Zeitschriftendatenbank an der Österreichischen Nationalbibliothek. Sagl, H., *hrsg.* Wien, Österreichische Nationalbibliotek, 1993. 578p.

Compiled from the database of Austrian periodicals maintained by the Österreichische Nationalbibliotek. Includes supplementary information on foreign newspapers held by Austrian libraries. *Class No:* 070.2(436)

France

[2255]

BIBLIOTHÈQUE NATIONALE. (FRANCE). Répertoire collectif des quotidiens et hebdomadaires publiés dans les départements de la France métropolitaine de 1944 à 1956 et conservés dans les archives et bibliothèques de France. Paris, Institut Français de Presse (Université de Paris), 1958. v,153p.

A-Z title list, gives title, location, place of publication, date of first issue and whether file is complete (details of files are not given). Continued by: *Class No:* 070.2(44)

[2256]

—BIBLIOTHÈQUE NATIONALE. (FRANCE). Catalogue collectif des journaux quotidiens d'information générale publiés en France métropolitaine de 1957 à 1961. Paris, Bibliothèque Nationale, 1962. 129p. *Class No:* 070.2(44)

RSFSR

[2257]

AKADEMIYA NAUK SSSR. Biblioteka. **Russkie dorevoliutsionnye gazety** v fondakh Biblioteka Akademiya Nauk SSSR, 1703-1916. Leningrad, Biblioteka Akademiya Nauk SSSR, 1984. 2v.

4,480 entries giving basic bibliographical detail only. Geographic index. *Class No:* 070.2(470)

[2258]

KUZNESTOV, I.V. *and* **FINGERIT, E.M. Gazetnyi mir Sovetskogo Soyuza 1917-1970.** Moskva, Izd-vo Mosk, 1972-76. 2v. facsims.

V.1 lists titles in 8 chronological sections with the focus on the immediate post-revolutionary period. V.2 has sections for 15 Soviet republics. Each volume separately indexed. *Class No:* 070.2(470)

[2259]

LIBRARY OF CONGRESS. Slavic and Central European Division. **Russian, Ukrainian and Belorussian newspapers, 1917-1953:** a union list. Horecky, P.L., *comp.* Washington D.C., Library of Congress, 1953. xi,218p.

Arranged by place of publication, with title index. Lists 859 newspapers in 39 US libraries. *Class No:* 070.2(470)

Finland

[2260]

KAARNA, V. *and* **WINTER, K. Suomen sanomalehdistön bibliografia,** 1771-1963. [Bibliography of the Finnish newspapers, 1771-1963.] Helsinki, Yliopisto Kirjasto, 1965. 130p. (*Helsingin Yliopiston Kirjaston julkaisuja, 31.*)

Title also in Swedish.

A-Z title list of nearly 1,250 Finnish newspapers. Details on political affiliation, title changes, place of printing and publication etc. Locality and chronological sequences follow. *Class No:* 070.2(480)

Norway

[2261]

Norsk aviser 1763-1969: en bibliografi. Oslo, Universitetsbiblioteket, 1973-74. 2v.

V.1 *Alfabetisk fortegnelse.* (594p.); v.2 *Registerband* (285p.).

Bibliography of Norwegian newspapers. Full entries, giving place of publication, dates, changes of title, editors, etc. Index vol. has name and place sequences. *Class No:* 070.2(481)

Sweden

[2262]

TOLLIN, S. Svensk dagspress 1900-1967: en systematisk och kommenterad kartläggning. Stockholm, TUs Förlags, 1969. 169p.

Title list of newspapers published during the period noting political affiliation and circulation figures. Geographic index (p.148-66). *Class No:* 070.2(485)

Denmark

[2263]

Topografisk, kronolisk fortegnelse over danske, faeroske og gronlanske aviser 1648-1975. København, Minerva Mikrofilm Aps, 1977. 47p.

List of Danish etc. newspapers arranged by region, then town, then in order of foundation. Changed titles and dates of issue given. Copenhagen (p.27-35). Appended list of microfilmed newspapers. *Class No:* 070.2(489)

China

[2264]

Chinese newspapers in the Library of Congress: a bibliography. Huang, H.C. *and* Jen, H.C., *comps*. Washington D.C., Library of Congress, 1985. 206p. ISBN: 0844404810.

List of 1,200 titles published 1870 to the present held by the Chinese and Korean section. Romanised title entries, (modified Wade-Giles), giving title in Chinese characters, place of publication and date of holdings. Place index. The most comprehensive Western language list available.
Class No: 070.2(510)

[2265]

GOODMAN, D.S.G. Research guide to Chinese provincial and regional newspapers. London, Contemporary China Institute, School of Oriental and African Studies, 1976. v,140p. £1. (*Research notes and studies, no.2.*) ISBN: 0728600366.

Indicates availability of 39 titles published since 1939 in the Library of Congress, China Research Institute (Hong Kong) and the East Asian Library of the Hoover Institution. Tabulated format with appended notes.

Goodman, D.S.G. *and* Saich, T. *Chinese local newspapers at SOAS* (Contemporary China Institute, 1978. iii,83p. (*Research notes and studies, no.4*) £1. ISBN: 0728600625) has information for about 50 titles.
Class No: 070.2(510)

Asia—Middle & Near East

[2266]

LIBRARY OF CONGRESS. African and Middle Eastern Division. **Arab-world newspapers in the Library of Congress.** Selim, G.D., *comp*. Washington D.C., Library of Congress, 1980. v,85p. (*Near East series, no.1.*)

Lists newspapers held by the Library of Congress published in Arab countries in Arabic or Latin scripts, together with Arabic titles published elsewhere. 575 entries arranged by language, including 90 French and 57 English titles. Arabic and Western language title indexes. Index of place-names. *Class No:* 070.2(53+56)

India

[2267]

Press in India: annual report of the Registrar of Newspapers for India under the Press & Registration of Books Act, 1867. New Delhi, Ministry of Information and Broadcasting, 1957-. Annual.

Subtitle and publisher varies.

1995 report (x,437p.) provides statistical and other data on Indian newspapers and periodicals, regional titles included. Does not provide full bibliographical or contact information.
Class No: 070.2(540)

Iran

[2268]

LIBRARY OF CONGRESS. African and Middle Eastern Division. **Persian and Afghan newspapers in the Library of Congress** 1871-1978. Pourhadi, I.V., *comp*. Washington D.C., Library of Congress, 1979. xiv,101p. ISBN: 0844402834.

Annotated list of 326 Persian and 23 Afghan newspapers. Title order with chronological, place of publication and name (publisher/editor/owner) indexes. All entries include English translation of title. *Class No:* 070.2(55)

Asia—South East

[2269]

Burmese and Thai newspapers: an international union list. Nunn, G.R., *comp*. Tapei, Chinese Materials and Research Aids Service Center, 1972. xii,44p. (*Chinese Materials and Research Aids Service Center occasional series, no.13.*)

Covers 250 Thai and 30 Burmese newspapers. A further 76 Burmese newspapers are listed without holdings information. *Class No:* 070.2(59)

[2270]

Singapore, Malaysian and Brunei newspapers: an international union list. Lim, P.P.H:, *comp*. Rev. & enl. ed. Singapore, Institute of Southeast Asian Studies, 1992. xxiii,168p. S$38. (*Institute of Southeast Asian studies library series, no. 19.*) ISBN: 9813016353.

First published 1970 as *Newspapers published in the Malaysian area.*

Aims to list and locate all newspapers known to have been published. Locations, which include the British Library, Library of Congress and National Library of Australia, include holdings detail. *Class No:* 070.2(59)

[2271]

Vietnamese, Cambodian and Laotian newspapers: an international union list. Nunn, G.R., *comp*. Taipei, Chinese Materials and Research Aids Service Center, 1972. xiii,104p. (*Chinese Materials and Research Aid Service Center occasional series, no.12.*)

Lists 764 newspapers published in Vietnam, 142 in Cambodia and 41 in Laos. Locations include the Bibliothèque Nationale, Paris and US collections.
Class No: 070.2(59)

Africa

[2272]

African newspapers in the Library of Congress. Pluge, J., *comp*. 2nd ed. Washington D.C., Library of Congress, 1984. ix,144p. ISBN: 0844404578.

1st ed. 1977.

931 titles, an increase of 322 on the 1st ed., arranged in 52 country sections. Frequency and establishment date given where known. Includes ceased titles. *Class No:* 070.2(6)

[2273]

STANDING CONFERENCE ON LIBRARY MATERIALS ON AFRICA. African newspapers on microfilm. McKee, M.D., *comp*. [London], SCOLMA, 1973. 58p. £0.50. Mimeographed. ISBN: 0901877883.

About 600 titles, A-Z with details of holdings. 14 locations (3 in South Africa, 4 in UK, 5 in US, 1 each in France and Switzerland). *Class No:* 070.2(6)

South Africa

[2274]

South African newspapers on microfilm. Coetzee, J.C., *comp and* Van der Walt, H., *ed.*. 2nd ed. Pretoria, State Library, 1991. x,93p. R35.20. (*Contributions to library science, no. 35.*) ISBN: 0798913711.

1st ed. 1975.

Information on microfilm availability of 376 titles. Entries include dates held and notes; geographic and title indexes. *Class No:* 070.2(680)

[2275]

STATE LIBRARY. (South Africa). **A List of South African newspapers,** 1800-1982. Pretoria, State Library, 1983. xv,253p. ISBN: 0798901292.

Replaces *Union list of South African newspapers, 1800-1949,* South African Public Library, 1950.

2,280 entries arranged alphabetically by title giving dates of publication, frequency and holdings data for South African and selected overseas libraries including the British Library and Library of Congress. Separate geographic listing by towns (p.181-253). *Class No:* 070.2(680)

Canada

[2276]

NATIONAL LIBRARY OF CANADA. Union list of Canadian newspapers. [Liste collective des journaux canadiens.] Ottawa, Minister of Supply and Services, 1988-. Annual (irregular). ISSN: 08405832.

Issued in microfiche. Preceded by a paper ed. (1977. xxix,483p. ISBN: 0662005162).

Amalgamation of the 1977 list, subsequent acquisitions recorded by the National Library, entries from a *Checklist of Canadian ethnic serials* (*q.v.*) and input from provincial inventories. Initial issue (33 microfiche) has about 18,000 records, representing the newspaper holdings of more than 750 Canadian libraries.

The National Library of Canada's WWW home page (http://www.nlc.-bnc.ca) includes *Canadian newspapers on microform held by the National Library of Canada.* *Class No:* 070.2(71)

Caribbean

[2277]

Colonial British Caribbean newspapers: a bibliography and directory. Pactor, H.S., *comp.* Westport, Conn., Greenwood Press, 1990. xiii,144p. £53.95;$65. (*Bibliographies & indexes in world history, v.19.*) ISBN: 0313272328.

677 titles arranged alphabetically by colony. Brief entries giving dates of publication and locations, with further limited information on editor, publisher, circulation and title changes as available. Selected sources (p.124-27). Newspaper and editor indexes. *Class No:* 070.2(729)

Latin America

[2278]

CHARNO, S.M. Latin American newspapers in United States libraries: a union list. Austin, University of Texas Press for the Conference on Latin American History, 1969. xv,619p. (*Conference on Latin American history, publication no.2.*) ISBN: 0292784031.

Compiled in the Serial Division, Library of Congress.

About 5,500 titles, locations in 70 libraries.
Class No: 070.2(729.99)

USA

[2279]

ADAMS, D.K. American newspaper holdings in British and Irish libraries. Produced for the British Association for American Studies by the David Bruce Centre for American Studies, University of Keele. Keele, 1974. [iii],94p.

A revised and modified version of *List of American newspapers up to 1940, held by libraries in Great Britain and Ireland,* by B.R. Crick and A. Daltrop (Edinburgh, British Association for American Studies, 1958).

Index 1: An alphabetical list of titles held (*c.*700 titles). Index 2: A list of titles held, under place of publication. Appended list of underground newspapers (on microfilm) held by the Univ. of Exeter Library. *Class No:* 070.2(73)

[2280]

—KEMBLE, J. *and* DAS, P. United States and Canadian holdings in the British Library Newspaper Library. London, Eccles Centre for American Studies, The British Library, 1996. 92p. ISBN: 0712344071.

'One of the main aims of the guide is to provide direct access to holdings pertinent to individual states and provinces as the Newspaper Library's catalogue arrangement is by title and town only' (Introduction, p.1). 1,384 US and 526 Canadian entries, each with detailed holdings data and shelfmark. *Class No:* 070.2(73)

[2281]

American newspapers, 1821-1936: a union list of files available in the United States and Canada. Gregory, W., *ed.* New York, Wilson, 1937. 791p.

Published under the auspices of the Bibliographical Society of America. Reprinted New York, Kraus, 1967 ($200. ISBN: 0527022500).

Lists 37,000 items in libraries, newspaper offices, private collections, etc. Organized by states, then A-Z by towns. Appended bibliography of union lists of newspapers (p.787-89). *Class No:* 070.2(73)

[2282]

BRIGHAM, C.S. History and bibliography of American newspapers, 1690-1820. Worcester, Mass., American Antiquarian Society, 1947. 2v.

Reprinted 1976 (Greenwood. $165. ISBN: 0837186773).

Lists 2,120 newspapers: arrangement is by states A-Z, then by towns A-Z. Notes changes of titles, editors etc. Locations of files in the US are given.

Updated by Brigham in 'Additions and corrections ...', (1962. 50p.), reproduced from the *Proceedings of the American Antiquarian Society* April 1961.
Class No: 070.2(73)

[2283]

—LATHEM, E.C. Chronological tables of American newspapers, 1690-1820: being a tabular guide to holdings of newspapers published in America through the year 1820. [Worcester, Mass.], American Antiquarian Society, 1972. 131p. $40. ISBN: 0827172044. *Class No:* 070.2(73)

[2284]

United States Newspaper Program national union list October 1993. 4th ed. Dublin, Ohio, OCLC, 1993. 70 microfiche, plus 1 pamphlet.

First published 1985; 3rd ed. 1989.

Based on data entered into the OCLC system by participants in the US Newspaper Program. Over 100,000 entries, A-Z by title, with full bibliographical detail. Date of publication, topic, place of publication and place name indexes. Also available online through OCLC.
Class No: 070.2(73)

Black Races

[2285]

HENRITZE, B.K. Bibliographical checklist of African American newspapers. Baltimore, Md., Genealogical Publishing, 1995. xxvii,206p. ISBN: 0806314575.

Entries for 5,539 titles 'that have served Americans of African descent'. Arranged by state, then city with frequency, dates published and sources in which title identified. Newspapers defined to include many topical and religious publications. Bibliography (p.155-70); index. 'The principal value of the checklist is that it combines entries from numerous sources into one volume' (*American reference books annual*, v.27, 1996, p.399).
Class No: 070.2(73)(=96)

Indonesia

[2286]

NUNN, G.R. Indonesian newpapers: an international union list. Taipei, Chinese Materials and Research Aids Service Center, 1971. xv,131p. (*Chinese Materials and Research Aids Service Center occasional series, no.14.*)

Holdings of *c.*1,000 newspapers published in Indonesia, with locations in Djakarta, The Hague and Amsterdam and in major libraries in the US. Title-index.
Class No: 070.2(910)

[2287]

PERPUSTAKAAN NASIONAL (Indonesia). **Katalog surat kabar:** koleksi Perpustakaan Nasional, 1810-1984. [Catalogue of newspapers.] Santoso, W., *ed.* Jakarta, Perpustakaan Nasional, Departemen Pendidikan dan Kebudayaan, [1984]. xxiii,246p.

Replaces *Katalogus suratkabar-, koleksi Perpustakaan Museum Pusat 1810-1973* (1973).

Lists about 1,400 newspapers held by Perpustakaan Nasional (National Library), the vast majority Indonesian. Title arrangement with place of publication indexes.
Class No: 070.2(910)

Philippines

[2288]

Philippine newspapers: an international union list. Saito, S. *and* Mak, A.W., *comps.* Honolulu, Philippine Studies Program, Center for Asian and Pacific Studies, University of Hawaii, 1984. xv,273p. (*Philippine studies occasional paper no.7.*)

Preceded by ***Philippine newspapers in selected American libraries: a union list,*** S. Saito (1966).

Two part list by place of publication and repository of 432 titles held at 35 locations in the Philippines, United States, Canada, Australia and Great Britain (British Library, SOAS, University of Hull). Title index. *Class No:* 070.2(914)

New Zealand

[2289]

HARVEY, D.R. Union list of newspapers preserved in libraries, newspaper offices, local authority offices and museums in New Zealand. Wellington, National Library of New Zealand, 1987. 326p. NZ$22.05. ISBN: 0477074049.

Also available on microfiche (ISBN: 0477074057). Revised ed. of *Union list of New Zealand newspapers before 1840: preserved in libraries, newspaper offices, local authority offices and museums in New Zealand* (1985).

.... *(contd.)*

Includes all newspapers published in New Zealand from 1840 to the end of 1986 and holdings of overseas newspapers published after 1800. *Class No:* 070.2(931)

Australia

[2290]

NATIONAL LIBRARY OF AUSTRALIA. Newspapers in Australian libraries: a union list. 4th ed. Canberra, National Library of Australia, 1984-85. 2v.

Pt.1. *Overseas newspapers* (xvii, 190p. ISBN: 0642992983); pt.2. *Australian newspapers* (v.p. ISBN: 0642993270). First published 1959-60; 3rd ed. 1974-75.

Pt.2. of 3rd ed. lists 4,006 titles in more than 450 locations. Arranged by state or territory, then town. Entries include a brief note on publication history. Further sections 'Ships and miscellaneous newspapers' and 'Papua New Guinea'. Title index. *Class No:* 070.2(94)

Indexes

Internet

[2291]

News index. News index, 1996. World Wide Web resource.

URL: http://www.newsindex.com. Date reviewed 29th June 1998.

Provides keyword indexing for articles appearing in Internet versions of over 300 newspapers and news sources. Restricted to recent issues, archive sevice not provided. UK titles covered include *Electronic telegraph, Independent* and *Times*. *Class No:* 070.2:014.3(003.41)

Bibliographies

[2292]

BUDER, J. Die Inhaltserschliessung von Zeitungen: eine internationale Übersicht über Zeitungsindices und Zeitungsinhaltsbibliographien. Berlin, Deutscher Bibliotheksverband, Arbeittselle für das Bibliothekswesen, 1978. 119p. (*Bibliothesdienst. Beiheft 133.*) ISBN: 3870651330.

An international bibliography of newspaper indexes. 240 entries arranged alphabetically by country. Includes a general introduction and notes on the development of newspaper indexing in individual countries. Title index.
Class No: 070.2:014.3(01)

Great Britain

[2293]

BNI: British newspaper index. Reading, Primary Source Media, 1991-. Computer database.

Current CD-ROM (quarterly updating) from 1995 (start up subscription £1,695, continuing subscription £1,095); backfile 1990-94 (£3,025). Internet access scheduled for 1998.

Covers *The Times, Sunday times, Times educational supplement, Times higher education supplement, Times literary supplement, Financial times* 1990 onwards, *Independent* and *Independent on Sunday* 1991 onwards, *Guardian* and *Observer* 1995 onwards and the *Daily Telegraph* and *Sunday Telegraph* 1997 onwards. Features browsable index plus searching by a variety of variables including newspaper name, publication date, headline, keywords and journalist. Expensive, especially in comparison with *Clover newspaper index* (below), but 'any

....(contd.)
library looking for a CD-ROM product which can be used effectively by most, without intensive training, would do well to look at BNI' (*Reference reviews*, v.8(3), 1994, p.8).
Class No: 070.2:014.3(410)

[2294]

Clover newspaper index. Biggleswade, Clover Publications, 1986-. Weekly, (46 issues pa.), with half-yearly cumulated indexes. £215.

Covers the *Daily telegraph*, *Economist* (from 1992), *European* (also from 1992), *Financial times*, *Guardian* (including *Guardian weekend*), *Independent*, *Observer* and *Times* (including the *TES*, *THES* and *TLS*). Indexing of *The Scotsman* is planned. Coverage comprehensive for all major articles; most shorter items down to 3½ col. inches also indexed. Entries under detailed subject headings with reference to article title, newspaper, date, page and column. Reviews entered under headings Book reviews, Film reviews, etc. Very promptly produced, normally available within two weeks of the issue indexed. A CD-ROM version covering 1992 to date, with a separate retrospective file 1986-92, is also available (current £499 or £795 (quarterly or 10 annual updates); backfile £199). Print subscribers have access to the latest data on a weekly basis through Clover Publication's World Wide Web site. An online service to UK libraries through CHEST is anticipated (weekly updating, £335). *Class No:* 070.2:014.3(410)

[2295]

The Guardian index. 1986-. Ann Arbor, University Microfilms International, 1987-. Monthly (8 monthly issues; 4 quarterly cumulations; annual cumulation). ISSN: 08864667.

Covers *The Guardian* and *Guardian weekly*. Indexes news items, feature articles, editorials, editorial cartoons, important letters, commentaries, sports articles, business and financial reports and reviews. Indexing based on 8,000 term controlled vocabulary. Entries include 20-30 word abstracts. Book reviews grouped under heading 'Books', then subdivided by author. Similar treatment for films, etc. *The Guardian* 1990 onwards is also available as a full text CD-ROM database from Chadwyck-Healey.
Class No: 070.2:014.3(410)

[2296]

Palmer's index to The Times newspaper, October 1790-June 1941. London, Palmer, 1868-1943. Quarterly.

Began publication with October-December 1867, then issued quarterly. Indexing of 1790-September 1867 begun 1875 with publication of July-September 1867. Further publication then in reverse order over a long period to 1925.

Briefer entries and less accurate indexing than *Index to The Times* (below), but valuable because it goes back almost to the beginning of *The Times*. Deaths are grouped under that heading, with no references in the body of the index.
Class No: 070.2:014.3(410)

[2297]

—Palmer's index to The Times 1790-1905. Cambridge, Chadwyck-Healey, 1993-95. Computer database.

Issued on one CD-ROM disc with DOS interface (£4,800). Includes user manual and single-sheet quick reference guide. Subscription based World Wide Web access launched 1998 (£500 initial annual fee).

Cumulates more than 450 printed issues. Data entered with minimal editorial intervention, so many of the quirks of the printed vols. persist. Searches can be restricted to any period and combined using Boolean operators. Main

....(contd.)
headings and keywords also browsable. 'Very "user friendly" ... has enormous potential' (*Reference reviews*, v.8(3), 1994, p.9). *Class No:* 070.2:014.3(410)

[2298]

—The Times index. 1785-1790. Reading, Newspaper Archive Developments, 1978-83. 5v. ISBN: 0903713853, v.1.

Gives coverage of the first half-dozen years of *The Times*, or *The Daily universal register* as it was until 1787. Wherever possible employs the headings used in the modern index. A few issues which were unobtainable not indexed.
Class No: 070.2:014.3(410)

[2299]

The Times index. Reading, Primary Source Media, 1973-. Monthly, with annual cumulation. £610. ISSN: 02600668.

Quarterly 1973-76; annual cumulation from 1977.

Compiled from the final edition of each day. Also covers *The Sunday Times*, *The Times literary supplement*, *The Times educational supplement*, *The Times Scottish educational supplement* and *The Times higher educational supplement*. Detailed indexing; many major headings (*e.g.* Athletics; Law; Science and technology) extensively subdivided. Reviews grouped (*e.g.* Books (titles and reviews), Theatrical productions). References to date, page and column. Several months' time lag in appearance. *The Times* 1990 onwards is also available as a full text CD-ROM database from Chadwyck-Healey. During the suspension of publication of Times newspapers from 1st December 1978-12th November 1979 indexing was for the *Daily telegraph* and *Sunday telegraph*. Earlier coverage available in:-
Class No: 070.2:014.3(410)

[2300]

—The Index to The Times, 1906-1980. Cambridge, Chadwyck-Healey, 1998-. Computer database.

Available on CD-ROM (£20,000) or through the World Wide Web (£1,950 annual subscription). Data made available in installments, schedule 1 covering 1970-80 released April 1998, completion expected December 1999.

Converts the many printed indexes into a single file. Completed database to contain in excess of 12,000,000 records. *Class No:* 070.2:014.3(410)

[2301]

—THE TIMES. Index to The Times. London, The Times, 1906-72. Frequency varies.

Title varies: *The Annual index to The Times,* 1906-13; *The Official index to The Times,* 1914-January/February 1957. Frequency: monthly, with annual cumulations 1906-13: quarterly July 1914-56; bi-monthly, 1957-72.

Much the same format as the current index. Covered *The Times literary supplement,* 1906-21.
Class No: 070.2:014.3(410)

Germany

[2302]

Zeitungsindex: Verzeichnis wichtiger Aufsätze aus deutschsprachigen Zeitungen. Gorzny, W., *hrsg*. Pullach bei München, W. Gorzny, 1974-. Monthly, with annual cumulation. ISSN: 03400107.

Frequency varies: issued quarterly until 1993. Publisher also varies: Verlag Dokumentation, 1974-79, then Saur.

Subject index to articles in major German language newspapers *e.g. Frankfurter Allgemeine Zeitung, Der Spiegel, Die Welt.* Includes one Austrian and two Swiss titles. Main sequence of entries under keywords with further

....(*contd.*)
sections for literary, film and theatrical reviews. A CD-ROM version covering 1982-89 has also been issued by K.G.Saur. *Class No:* 070.2:014.3(430)

France

[2303]

Index Le Monde. Reading, Primary Source Media, 1987-. Monthly, with annual cumulation. £410. ISSN: 09537171.

Similar in layout to *The Times index* (*q.v.*). Subject terms in French. Includes the various supplements.

In addition to the current index retrospective vols. are available for 1944-51 and 1965-68. Primary Source Media (previously Research publications) have embarked on a programme to close the gap from 1969 by publishing a series of retrospective annual indexes, coverage extending back 1982 in 1996. An *Index Le Monde sur CD-ROM* is available containing records from 1990 (updated monthly, £410 for annual subscription, £1,140 for backfile). A full text CD-ROM version of the newspaper is also produced. *Class No:* 070.2:014.3(44)

RSFSR

[2304]

KUZMIN, S.A. Ukazateli soderzhaniia russkikh dorevoliutsionnykh gazet. Leningrad, Biblioteka Akademii nauk SSSR, 1986. 126p.

List of indexes to newspapers of the pre-revolutionary period. *Class No:* 070.2:014.3(470)

[2305]

Letopis' gazetnykh statei. Moskva, Izd-vo Kniznaīā palata, 1936-. Weekly. US$414. ISSN: 00241172.

Frequency varies: originally weekly, then monthly to 1974; bi-monthly 1975-76; weekly 1977-.

'Record of newspaper articles'. Now arranged by UDC (previously 50 subject classes of the Soviet system), with personal and geographical name indexes. Gives good coverage of the Russian press with about 45,000 entries annually. *Class No:* 070.2:014.3(470)

Sweden

[2306]

LITERATURVETENSKAPLIGA INSTITUTIONEN I LUND. Svenskt pressregister. Lund, Bibliotekstjänst, 1967-. ISSN: 0282731x.

V.1: 1880-85 (1967); v.2: 1886-90 (1969); v.3: 1891-94 (1973); v.4: 1895-97 (1985); v.5: 1898-1900 (1989).

Classified index to reviews of literature, music, theatrical performances, art exhibitions and cultural events which appeared in Swedish newspapers during the years covered. Includes reviews of non-Swedish literature, etc. *Class No:* 070.2:014.3(485)

[2307]

Svenska tidningsartiklar: register över tidningsartiklar och recensioner. Lund, Bibliotekstjänst, 1953-. Monthly, with annual cumulation. Kr3800. ISSN: 00396907.

Current title from 1961. Formerly *Svensk tidningsindex.*

Indexes articles and reviews in 32 newspapers. Classified arrangement with name index. Book, film, theatrical, musical and art reviews in separate section. About 12,500 entries annually. Also available in microfiche, online as part of the *ArtikelSök* database (records 1979 to date) and on CD-ROM as a component of *CD:ArtikelSök*. *Class No:* 070.2:014.3(485)

Denmark

[2308]

Avis-kronik-index. København, Bibliotekscentralens, 1940-78. Monthly with annual indexes.

Merged with *Dansk tidsskrift-index* (*q.v.*) in 1979 to form *Dansk artikelindeks*, which is now incorporated into the computer database *Artikelbasen* (*q.v.*).

Classified index to Danish newspapers. Included reviews. *Class No:* 070.2:014.3(489)

India

[2309]

Indian press index. Delhi, Delhi Library Association, 1968-. Monthly (many issues combined). Rs.300. ISSN: 00196177.

Covers 17 English language Indian newspapers, including the *Hindustan times* and the *Times of India*. Main 'Alphabetical index' of subjects with author and geographical indexes. Book reviews dealt with in separately published quarterly supplement. *Class No:* 070.2:014.3(540)

Malaysia

[2310]

Indeks suratkhabar Malaysia. [Malaysian newspaper index.] Kuala Lumpur, Perpustakaan Negara Malaysia, 1979-. Quarterly (semi-annual 1979-1982). ISSN: 01269062, (Malay); 01277448, (English).

Published in two sub-series, one covering Malay language newspapers the other English language titles (*New Straits times* and *The Star*). Serious publication delays, issues seem to take about six years to appear. *Class No:* 070.2:014.3(595)

Canada

[2311]

BURROWS, S. *and* **GAUDET, F. Checklist of indexes to Canadian newspapers.** Ottawa, National Library of Canada, 1987. 148p. Can$16.95. ISBN: 0660537354.

Text in English and French with French text on inverted pages.

Based on a survey of Canadian libraries, archives, newspaper offices and genealogical and historical societies. Access to 324 indexes or clipping files for around 750 titles in 260 locations. Arranged by indexing institution indicating titles indexed, type of entry, access conditions, etc. Newspaper title and geographic indexes. *Class No:* 070.2:014.3(71)

[2312]

Canadian news index. Toronto, Micromedia, 1977-92. Monthly, with annual cumulation. ISSN: 02257459.

As *Canadian newspaper index* 1977-79. From 1993 continues as part of *Canadian index* (*q.v.*).

7 newspapers covered: *Calgary herald, Globe & mail* (Toronto), *Halifax chronicle herald, Montreal gazette, Toronto star, Vancouver sun,* and *Winnipeg free press.* Detailed subject and personal name indexing (in separate sequences), including editorials, some letters and reviews. *Class No:* 070.2:014.3(71)

USA

[2313]

MILNER, A.C. Newspaper indexes: a location and subject guide for researchers. Metuchen, N.J., Scarecrow Press, 1977-82. 3v.

V.1 1977 (xii,210p. $25. ISBN: 0810810662); v.2 1979 (ix,203p. $25. ISBN: 0810812444); v.3 1982 (x,181p. $22.50. ISBN: 0810814935).

Concentrates on unpublished indexes maintained by libraries, newspaper publishers, historical societies etc. Compiled from questionnaire returns. Aimed at genealogists and local historians. *Class No:* 070.2:014.3(73)

[2314]

National newspaper index. Foster City, Ca., Information Access Corporation, 1979-. Computer database.

Available as an online database through a variety of hosts including CARL, Dialog (file 111) and LEXIS-NEXIS. On Dialog updated monthly with data added daily to *Newsearch* (file 211). CD-ROM version issued by publisher (monthly updating, £1000) covering current and 3 previous years. Also available from SilverPlatter as an Internet accessible database (rolling 4 years data) and as a component of Information Access Company's *InfoTrac* system.

Indexes the *Christian science monitor, New York times* (including *New York times book review* and *New York times magazine*), *Wall Street journal* and from 1982 the *Los Angeles times* and *Washington post.* Full indexing for each title, only weather charts, horoscopes, editorial cartoons, etc. excluded. 4,300,000 records in full file 1998.
Class No: 070.2:014.3(73)

[2315]

New York Times index. New York, New York Times, 1913-. Semi-monthly; quarterly interim and annual cumulated indexes. ISSN: 0147538x.

Frequency varies: originally quarterly, monthly until 1947, then weekly for a long period. Annual cumulations from 1931, quarterly interim cumulations from 1978.

Subject, geographic, organization and personal name headings in one A-Z sequence. More detailed than *The Times index* (London), in that entries for significant news articles, editorial matter and special features include short abstracts, which are often sufficiently detailed to answer a query without reference to the paper itself. Various online and CD-ROM indexes also provide coverage including *Newspaper abstracts* and *National newspaper index* (*qq.v.*). The *New York times* Internet site (http://www.nytimes.com) includes an archive feature allowing registered users access to 365 days back copies.

Indexing for the years 1851-1912 is available in *New York Times index. Prior series* (New York, Bowker, 1966-76. 15v.). Volumes cover varying periods, (*e.g.* v.1 1851-62), some representing new indexing, others being reproductions of indexes previously compiled for internal use. A cumulated index to personal names is also available:-
Class No: 070.2:014.3(73)

[2316]

—FALK, B.A. *and* FALK, V.R. Personal name index to 'The New York times index' 1851-1974. Succasunna, N.J., Roxbury Data Interface, 1976-83. 22v. $1025. ISBN: 089902100x.

About 3,000,000 entries. Includes obituary listings. Continued by ***Personal name index to The New York times index, 1975-1996 supplement*** (Sparks, Nev., Roxbury Data Interface, 1998-. ISBN: 0899020968. (Replaces earlier supplements including a 6 v. set for 1975-93)).
Class No: 070.2:014.3(73)

[2317]

Newspaper abstracts. Ann Arbor, University Microfilms International. Computer database.

Available online for records 1989 onwards through several vendors including Dialog (as part of *Newspaper and periodical abstracts* (*q.v.*), file 484), OCLC, Ovid and SilverPlatter. Weekly or monthly updating. 1984-88 in separate Dialog database *Newspaper abstracts* (file 603). CD-ROM versions from publisher in two subscription options: 'National edition' (*New York times, Wall Street journal, Christian science monitor, Washington post* and *Los Angles times*); 'Complete edition' (above titles plus *Atlanta constitution, Boston globe, Chicago tribune* and *USA today*). The 'National edition' is a 2 disc service with 1985-87 as a backfile; the 'Complete edition' is available as a 3 disc set (1985-86 & 1987-88 backfiles). Both versions updated monthly. The database is also available as a component of UMI's *ProQuest* service.

Indexes news articles, reviews, editorials, commentaries, etc. 15-40 word abstracts added to entries. Additional titles indexed in some database versions. The main rival to *National newspaper index* (above).
Class No: 070.2:014.3(73)

[2318]

Newspaper source. Ipswich, Mass., Ebsco, 1996-. Computer database. ISSN: 10912614.

Available on CD-ROM or online through EbscoHost.

Includes the full text of the *Christain science monitor* and indexing and abstracting for the *New York times, Wall Street journal* and *USA today* from January 1995.
Class No: 070.2:014.3(73)

Libraries

[2319]

News media libraries: a management handbook. Semonche, B.P., *ed.* Westport, Conn., Greenwood Press, 1993. xx,656p. illus., diags. £67.95;$79.50. (*The Greenwood library management collection.*) ISBN: 0313279462.

Aimed mainly at practising news librarians. 30 contributed chapters: 1. News library history ... 8. The Clipping collection ... 11. The Electronic news library ... 19. Newspaper indexing policies and procedures ... 26. Television news libraries ... 30. The Newspaper Association of America Library. Some chapters documented, others with appended listings, chronologies, etc. Brief directory of news media organizations, glossary and 'News libraries: a selective bibliography' (p.595-613). Name and subject indexes. Based on US practice and sources, but thorough and well structured treatment will have relevance elsewhere.
Class No: 070.2:061:026/027

[2320]

Newspaper libraries: a bibliography, 1933-1985. Wall, C.J., *comp.* Washington, D.C., Special Libraries Association, 1986. 126p. ISBN: 0871113198.

Reprint available from Book on Demand ($32.80. ISBN: 0608007617).

Aims at comprehensive coverage of English language material, including chapters in books, journal articles, pamphlets and unpublished reports. Unannotated entries arranged alphabetically in chapters such as history, organization and administration, newspaper indexing and automation. *Class No:* 070.2:061:026/027

Newsletters

[2321]

Hudson's subscription newsletter directory. Rhinebeck, N.Y., Hudson's Subscription Newsletter Directory, 1977-. Annual (irregular). $185. ISSN: 10468110.

The smallest directory of newsletters in terms of number of entries, but international in scope unlike its competitors *Newsletters in print* and *Oxbridge directory of newsletters* (below). The 1996 issue (13th ed. x,450p.) lists over 4,800 titles under 169 subject headings, entries including editor, publisher, subscription detail/price, frequency, year founded and brief (10-20 word) description of contents. Multiple publisher, geographic, alphabetical (major publisher and newsletter title), editorial and publishing personnel indexes. *Class No:* 070.20

[2322]

Newsletters in print. Detroit, Gale, 1966-. Annual (approx). $281.75 ISSN: 08990425.

Subtitle: *A Descriptive guide to subscription, membership and free newsletters, bulletins, digests, updates and similar serial publications issued in the United States and Canada and available in print and online.*

First published 1966 as *National directory of newsletters and reporting services*; 2nd ed. issued in 8 pts., 1978-84. 3rd ed. as *Newsletters directory*, 1987. Current title from 4th ed. 1988.

To be included newsletters must be serial in nature, of national or broad regional interest and treat specialized interests or topics. The 10th ed. (1997. xviii,1600p.) has more than 11,500 entries in 33 subject sections, information including editor, 10-50 word description, intended audience, foundation date, frequency, circulation, ISSN and online availability. 6 indexes including title and keyword, publisher, subject and online availability. Also a component of *Gale database of publications and broadcast media* available online through Dialog (File 469) and GaleNet or on CD-ROM. *Class No:* 070.20

[2323]

Oxbridge directory of newsletters: the most comprehensive guide to US and Canadian newsletters. New York, Oxbridge Communications, 1979-. Annual (Irregular). $495. ISSN: 01637010.

Produced by the publisher of the *Standard periodical directory* (*q.v.*). The 1994 issue (12th ed. 1434p.) lists over 20,000 publications under *c.*250 subject categories. Entries lack the descriptive detail of those in *Newsletters in print.* Publisher, publisher by state, title and title change indexes. Also available on CD-ROM (quarterly updating) and through the Internet as part of Oxbridge's freely accessible *Mediafinder* site (http://www.mediafinder.com/). *Class No:* 070.20

Journalism

Bibliographies

[2324]

CATES, J.A. Journalism: a guide to the reference literature. 2nd ed. Englewood, Colo., Libraries Unlimited, 1997. xv,317p. £43.50;$45. (*Reference sources in the humanities.*) ISBN: 1563083744.

First published 1990.

Selective guide to the English language reference literature on print and broadcast journalism. Includes bibliographies, encyclopedias, dictionaries, indexes and abstracts, biographical sources, directories, handbooks and manuals, style books, etc. 789 numbered entries (503 1st ed.) with well-written evaluative annotations; a further 192 entries for core periodicals, societies, institutions, research centers, archives and media institutes. Appendix: Database service suppliers and vendors. Author/title and subject indexes. Much more detailed and up-to-date than *The Journalist's bookshelf,* (*q.v.*); this ed. has 'solidified its reign as the benchmark for guides to journalism literature' (*Choice*, v.35(3), November 1997, p.452). *Class No:* 070.4(01)

[2325]

GREENBERG, G.S. Tabloid journalism: an annotated bibliography of English-language sources. Westport, Conn., Greenwood Press, 1996. xi,187p. £57.95;$65. (*Bibliographies and indexes in mass media and communications, 10.*) ISBN: 0313295441.

819 annotated entries in 5 chapters: 1. Primary sources - 2. U.S. print journalism - 3. U.S. television - 4. Legal implications - 5. International perspectives (15 country sections, 'England' 94 entries). Author and subject indexes. '(C)annot be relied on for comprehensiveness' (*American reference books annual*, v.28, 1997, p.345), but a better starting point for material on tabloid journalism than more general sources. *Class No:* 070.4(01)

[2326]

PRICE, W.C. The Literature of journalism: an annotated bibliography. Minneapolis, Univ. of Minnesota Press, 1959. xviii,489p.

Available from Books on Demand ($144.50. ISBN: 01317104349).

Some 3,150 annotated entries for books in English on journalism and related subjects (*e.g.* radio, advertising, public opinion) in classified order. Lists histories of individual newspapers and biographies of journalists. 'The base of the book is frankly historical and biographical with more than two fifths of all the titles in these two categories' (*Foreword*). Author and subject index.

Supplemented by W.C. Price and C.M. Pickett's *An Annotated journalism bibliography, 1958-1968* (Minneapolis, Univ. of Minnesota Press, 1970. 285p.). This has nearly 2,200 items in author sequence, with a detailed subject index and liberal cross-references. *Class No:* 070.4(01)

Handbooks & Manuals

[2327]

MACDOWALL, I. The Reuters handbook for journalists. London, Butterworth-Heinemann, 1992. x,183p. £16.99. ISBN: 0705065510.

Main text (p.1-165) comprises *c.*1,250 short entries for organizations, countries, subjects, etc. Some longer grouped entries *e.g.* 'Oil terms and definitions'. Also covers practical matters, *e.g.* 'Punctuation'. Appended: 'Technical glossary' of computer and data transmission terms commonly used by journalists; 'Business abbreviations'. *Class No:* 070.4(035)

[2328]

SPARK, D. A Journalist's guide to sources. Oxford, Focal Press, 1996. vi,398p. £16.99;$28.95. (*Journalism media manual.*) ISBN: 024051470x.

Mainly a listing of contact addresses with telephone nos. (no email or URLs). Broad topic then subject arrangement *e.g.* 'Aluminium', 5 associations and companies; 'Landmines', 2 organizations. Indexed (p.379-97). *Class No:* 070.4(035)

Dictionaries

[2329]

ROTH, M.P. Historical dictionary of war journalism. Westport, Conn., Greenwood Press, 1997. xi,482p. £51.95;$85. ISBN: 0313291713.

Most entries for war journalists, photograhers and artists. Also includes entries for individual wars and terms relevant to the history of war reporting, *e.g.* 'Newsreel companies'. Entries vary in length, .*e.g.* 'Hare, James H.', 2p., 3 refs; 'Kingsley, Mary', 8 lines, 1 ref. Concentrates on US personalities and wars in which US involved. 17 appendices (p.361-462), *e.g.* 'American Civil War correspondents', 'Pulitzer prizes for war reporting'. Selected bibliography; index. '(B)est used as an introduction to the scattered literature of war and its writers, many of whom are not household names' (*Choice*, v.35(3), November 1997, p.462). *Class No:* 070.4(038)

Theses

[2330]

Journalism and mass communication abstracts. Columbia S.C., Association for Education in Journalism and Mass Communication, 1963-. Annual. ISSN: 1077694x.

Issued under title *Journalism abstracts* (ISSN: 00754412) until v.32 (1994).

Provides lengthy abstracts of doctoral and masters theses in journalism and related areas submitted to US and Canadian universities. About 250-300 abstracts annually arranged A-Z by author name with subject and institution indexing. *Class No:* 070.4(043)

Yearbooks & Directories

[2331]

NATIONAL UNION OF JOURNALISTS. Freelance directory. London, National Union of Journalists, 1971-. Irregular.

10th ed. (1995. x,382p. ISBN: 0951457829) lists names, addresses and specialist skills of almost 1,500 freelance members of the NUJ. Skills and geographical index. *Class No:* 070.4(058)

Biographies

[2332]

Journalist biographies master index: a guide to 90,000 references to historical and contemporary journalists in 200 biographical directories and other sources. Abrams, A.E., *ed.* Detroit, Gale, 1979. xxvi,380p. $90. (*Gale biographical index series, no.4.*) ISBN: 0810310864.

'Journalists' are defined as 'persons who have devoted a significant part of their careers to newspapers, magazines or the broadcast media'. Sources indexed include *Dictionary of American biography, Contemporary authors* and *Who's who in America.* A few sources relating to Britain also covered *e.g. British authors of the nineteenth century, Who's who.* *Class No:* 070.4(092)

Laws

[2333]

McNae's essential law for journalists. Welsh, T. *and* Greenwood, W., *eds.* 14th ed. London, Butterworth, 1997. xiii,335p. ISBN: 0406895449.

First published 1954; new eds. now appear every 2-3 years.

Updated to 1st May 1997. Standard legal guide, useful for

....(*contd.*)

both practising journalists and students. Topical arrangement in 33 sections *e.g.* Divorce, Contempt of court, Criminal libel, slander and malicious falsehoods. Glossary, booklist and comprehensive index. *Class No:* 070.4(094.1)

USA

Bibliographies

[2334]

WOLSELEY, R.E. *and* **WOLSELEY, I. The Journalist's bookshelf:** an annotated and selected bibliography of the United States print journalism. 8th ed. Indianapolis, Berg, 1986. xiii,400p. $38.50. ISBN: 0897301390.

First published 1939; previous ed. 1961.

2,427 entries for books on US print journalism. Heavy emphasis on biographical works. Retains many items from earlier eds. Arranged in subject categories; author and title indexes. Useful historically, but 'retention of the old, particularly in the skills area, drains value from the book as a tool for contemporary teachers, students and professionals'. (*Journalism history,* v.13(2), Summer 1986, p.72-3). *Class No:* 070.4(73)(01)

Encyclopaedias

[2335]

PANETH, D. The Encyclopedia of American journalism. New York, Facts on File, 1983. ix,548p.illus. ISBN: 0871964279.

Covers newspapers, magazines, media personalities, technology, politics of the media etc. Although the focus is on the US 'contains various references to certain origins, earlier and foreign' (Introduction p.vii). About 2,500 entries A-Z of varying length (*e.g.* 'Freedom of Information' 2 cols; 'McLuhan, Marshall *c.*225 words; 'Copycutter' 3 lines). Major entries include bibliographical references. Subject index. *Class No:* 070.4(73)(031)

Histories

[2336]

American journalism history: an annotated bibliography. Sloan, W.D., *comp.* Westport, Conn., Greenwood, 1989. xv,344p. £67.50;$79.50. (*Bibliographies and indexes in the mass media and communication, no.1.*) ISBN: 0313263507.

Covers 2,657 books, articles and dissertations published 1810-1988. Broadly chronological arrangement in 16 chapters including 'Broadcasting 1920-present' and 'Research guides and information works'. Entries carefully annotated, often at considerable length. Subject index. Some errors and omissions, but 'destined to be a seminal reference source in history, journalism and mass communication' (*Choice,* v.27(2), October 1989, p.293). *Class No:* 070.4(73)(091)

[2337]

Guide to sources in American journalism history. Caswell, L.S., *ed. & comp.* New York, Greenwood, 1988. vii,319p. £58.50;$65. (*Bibliographies and indexes in mass media and communication, no.2.*) ISBN: 0313261784.

Prepared under the auspices of the American Journalism Historians' Association.

Primarily a directory of archival and manuscript collections (p.99-276), arranged by repository in state sections. Entries include personal dates, type of collection, inclusion dates, access conditions etc. Preceded by 7 essays,

.... *(contd.)*
including 'Bibliographies for journalism history' and 'The United States newspaper program'. Comprehensively indexed (p.277-319). *Class No:* 070.4(73)(091)

Biographies

[2338]
American newspaper journalists. Ashley, P.J., *ed.* Detroit, Gale, 1983-85. 4v. illus.,plates,facsims. $140 per v. (*Dictionary of literary biography, v.23, 25, 29, 43.*)

In 4v.: *1690-1872* (1985. xiv,527p. ISBN: 0810317214); *1873-1900* (1983. xiv,392p. ISBN: 0810311453); *1901-1925* (1984. xiv,385p. ISBN: 0810317044); *1926-1950* (1984. xiv,410p. ISBN: 0810317079).

Collectively the 4v. contain 199 biographical sketches including Benjamin Franklin, William Lloyd Garrison, Tom Paine, A. Bierce, W.R. Hearst, R. Lardner, Walter Lippman and Josey Patterson. Contributed essays give career details, birth and death dates, positions held, list of major publications, secondary sources, and manuscript locations. A 'trustworthy source of evaluative biographies' (*Wilson library bulletin,* v.59(4), December 1984, p.289, on the 1926-1950 v.). *Class No:* 070.4(73)(092)

[2339]
—American magazine journalists. Riley, S.G., *ed.* Detroit, Gale, 1988-94. 4v. illus., plates, facsims. $140 per v. (*Dictionary of literary biography, v.73, 79, 91, 137.*)

In 4v.: *1741-1850* (1988. xv,430p. ISBN: 081034551x); *1850-1900* (1989. xvii,387p. ISBN: 0810345579); *1900-1960* (1990. xv,401p. ISBN: 0810345714); *1900-1960: second series* (1994. xi,411p. ISBN: 0810353962).

High degree of duplication in coverage with other *DLB* volumes, including *American newspaper journalists,* but entries slanted towards the individual's contribution to magazine journalism. A further *DLB* v., also by Riley, is *American newspaper publishers, 1950-1990* (1993. ISBN: 0810353865). *Class No:* 070.4(73)(092)

[2340]
APPLEGATE, E. Journalistic advocates and muckrakers: three centuries of crusading writers. Jefferson, N.C., McFarland, 1997. viii,219p. £35.95. ISBN: 0786403659.

101 biographical sketches for mostly US writers who posed 'why not' questions. Most entries conclude with brief list of representative works; index of people and publications. '(U)nclear focus, limited scholarship, and lack of uniqueness' (*Reference books bulletin* in *Booklist*, v.94(5), November 1 1997, p.515). *Class No:* 070.4(73)(092)

[2341]
Biographical dictionary of American journalism. McKerns, J.P., *ed.* New York, Greenwood, 1989. xiv,820p. $59.95. ISBN: 0313238189.

Contains nearly 500 sketches of persons who contributed to American journalism 1690 to the present. Includes reporters, editors, publishers, columnists, cartoonists, photographers etc. Sketches follow format of *Dictionary of American biography,* each concluding with a two part bibliography listing significant works by the subject and books, articles etc. about the subject, including citations to other biographical dictionaries. List of journalists by specialism *e.g.* Columnists, Sports journalism (p.771-85). Index. Remains the best source available, covering more journalists than the Gale set and giving greater detail than Downs, Paneth or Taft (*qq.v*). *Class No:* 070.4(73)(092)

[2342]
DOWNS, R.B. *and* **DOWNS, J.B. Journalists of the United States:** biographical sketches of print and broadcast news shapers from the late 17th century to the present. Jefferson, N.C., McFarland, 1991. vii,391p. £44.95;$39.95. ISBN: 089950549x.

Offers *c.*500 well written sketches mostly less than a page in length. A-Z arrangement with good index of personal names, newspaper titles, organizations and topics. Brief bibliography. '(R)ich in 18th and 19th century biography, but alas journalists of the 'present' are only the most high profile names' (*Library journal,* v.117(1), January 1992, p.106). *Class No:* 070.4(73)(092)

[2343]
RILEY, S.G. Biographical dictionary of American newspaper columnists. Westport, Conn., Greenwood Press, 1995. xii,411p. £71.50;$79.50. ISBN: 0313291926.

About 600 entries, average length 250 words, for columnists of 'relatively general interest'. Detail includes citations to all known works by or about columnist. Some overlap with other sources especially *American newspaper journalists* and *Biographical dictionary of American journalism* (above), but 'enriches journalism reference' (*Rettig on reference,* January 1996, http://www.hwilson.com/retjan.html). *Class No:* 070.4(73)(092)

[2344]
—APPLEGATE, E. Literary journalism: a biographical dictionary of writers and editors. Westport, Conn., Greenwood Press, 1996. xxi,386p. £67.95;$85. ISBN: 0313299498.

Covers about 150 writers and editors 1700 to present, US figures predominating. 1-2p. entries include occasional quotations from works. '(T)he entries are much shorter than the lengthy articles appearing in *American magazine journalist(s)*' (above) (*Reference books bulletin* in *Booklist*, v.93(9-10), January 1-15 1997, p.898).
Class No: 070.4(73)(092)

[2345]
TAFT, W.H. Encyclopedia of twentieth-century journalists. New York and London, Garland, 1986. xv,408p. $41.95. (*Garland reference library of the humanities, v.493.*) ISBN: 0824089618.

Contains brief biographical sketches of *c.*1,000 personalities including editors, publishers, columnists, photographers and cartoonists. Better biographical coverage for the period than Paneth (*q.v.*), but the 'technical flaws', as detected by *Choice* (v.24(1), September 1986, p.94), call into question its value as an authoritative source.
Class No: 070.4(73)(092)

News Digests

Worldwide

[2346]
Archiv der Gegenwart: die Weltweite Dokumentation für Politik und Wirtschaft. Bonn, Siegler, 1931-. Semi-monthly. DM460. ISSN: 00038865.

Publication suspended 1945-49. Publisher varies, Siegler since 1961.

Resembles *Keesing's* (*q.v.*), based on press reports, news broadcasts, etc. International coverage, but with a slant to German affairs or issues of German interest. Also available on microfiche and CD-ROM. *Class No:* 070.40(100)

[2347]

Facts on file: world news digest with index. New York, Facts on File, 1940-. Weekly. $725. ISSN: 00146641.

Weekly looseleaf issues for insertion in binder. Twice monthly cumulating indexes (blue pages), consolidated quarterly (yellow pages). Full colour Rand McNally quick reference atlas issued annually. Bound annual volumes issued as *Facts on file yearbook* available for separate purchase (ISSN: 01960040. $100). Five yearly indexes published from 1946/50 onwards.

Based on the contents of more than 70 US and foreign newspapers and magazines including *The Times, Guardian* and *Economist.* Wide-ranging coverage, extending to economics and business, science and technology and social developments, as well as general news stories. Less detailed treatment of diplomatic topics and more popular in style than *Keesing's.* In many issues nearly half the content relates to the US. Searchable online through CARL and NEXIS. Records 1980 onwards also available as *Facts on File news digest CD-ROM*, either from the publisher (annual updating, $695) or EBSCO (quarterly updating, $795). CD-ROM with menu driven or command level searching 'provides a powerful tool that is ... exceptionally easy to use' (*Choice*, v.32(8), April 1995, p.1283-84). *Class No:* 070.40(100)

[2348]

—Editorials on file: newspaper editorial reference service with index. New York, Facts on File, 1970-. Semi-monthly. $450. ISSN: 00130966.

Looseleaf. Also available in microfiche.

Comprises reprints from major US and Canadian newspapers. About 200 full text editorials in each issue covering an average of 10 topics. Indexes cumulate quarterly. *Class No:* 070.40(100)

[2349]

Keesing's record of world events. London, Keesing's Worldwide, 1931-. Monthly. £160. ISSN: 09506128.

Looseleaf with annual binder. Frequency weekly 1931-72. Published as *Keesing's contemporary archives* 1931-86.

Records national and international affairs, 'based on constant monitoring of the world's press and information sources by experienced research editors'. Format has varied. Each issue now contains news stories from the previous month arranged in sections Africa - Americas - Asia-Pacific - Europe - Middle East - International. Sections headed by major articles giving extended coverage, followed by concise, factual entries. Extensive cross-referencing, including citation to last article on topic. 'Annual reference supplement' (79p. 1996) contains up-to-date background briefing documents and basic political and economic data for every country. 'Outline' index in each issue; twice yearly cumulative subject (yellow pages) and name (pink pages) indexes. Stronger on international affairs than its main rival *Facts on file* (above), but economics and business are comparatively neglected. Also available in microfiche and as a quarterly updated CD-ROM. Latter now marketed by Chadwyck-Healey covering records 1960 to date and using FolioViews software (£650 annual licence).
Class No: 070.40(100)

[2350]

Summary of world broadcasts. Caversham Park, Reading, BBC, 1939-. Daily (6 days a week) and weekly. Various subscription rates, approx £470 per series.

As *Daily digest of world broadcasting*, 1939-47.

Format varies. From 1993 main series issued daily in 5 parts: 1. *Former USSR* (ISSN: 13508148); 2. *Central Europe and the Balkans* (ISSN: 13521365); 3. *Asia-Pacific* (ISSN:

.... (contd.)

13521403); 4. *Middle East* (ISSN: 13508199); 5. *Africa, Latin America and the Caribbean* (ISSN: 13508245). Each part complemented by a *Weekly economic report* containing economic, scientific and technical information (approx. £335 per series).

Summaries of transmissions from foreign broadcasting services. 'All items or passages described as Text or Excerpt(s), or words given in quotation marks, are a verbatim translation of the original, or are the actual words where these were given in English'. Authoritative and prompt in appearance. Searchable online through LEXIS, FT Profile and DataStar. An Internet version, delivered by ftp, is also available (sample pages at http://www.monitor.bbc.co.uk) at £550 per main series.
Class No: 070.40(100)

Great Britain

[2351]

Keesing's UK record. Cambridge, Cambridge International Reference on Current Affairs, 1988-. Quarterly. ISSN: 0952195x.

Looseleaf with annual binder; issued bi-monthly until 1996.

Gives more extensive coverage of the UK than *Keesing's record of world events* (above). Apr/June 1997 issue in main sections: Events of the month (calendar of principal occurrences); Government and politics; Defence and internal security; Local government and regional affairs; Social affairs; Legislative summary; Obituaries. Special *General election results supplement* gives coverage at constituency level. Index in each issue, cumulated annually.
Class No: 070.40(410)

RSFSR

[2352]

Current digest of the post-Soviet press. Columbus, Ohio, Current Digest of the Post-Soviet Press, 1949-. Weekly. $935. ISSN: 10677542.

Established by the American Council of Learned Societies and the Social Science Research Council (US). Later issued by the American Association for the Advancement of Slavic Studies. Now published independently. Present title from 1992; previously *Current digest of the Soviet press* (ISSN: 00113425).

Provides English translations or abstracts of articles appearing in about 50 newspapers and magazines published in the states of the former Soviet Union. Quarterly and annual (from 1976) indexes issued on separate subscription. Searchable online through NEXIS; a CD-ROM version for records from 1982 is also available using FolioViews software. *Class No:* 070.40(470)

Asia

[2353]

Asian recorder: weekly digest of Asian events with index. New Delhi, Ashish Publications, 1955-. Weekly. $185. ISSN: 00044644.

Looseleaf with ringbinder.

Reports on events by country A-Z, as well as Asian events generally. Nearly all reports based on extracts from the Indian press; source of entries acknowledged. Quarterly and annual indexes. *Class No:* 070.40(5)

Canada

[2354]

Canadian news facts: the indexed digest of Canadian current events. Toronto, Marpep Publishing, 1967-. Semi-monthly. Can$289. ISSN: 00084565.

Publisher varies.

Comprehensive news reference system providing reports of current events as gleaned from 20 Canadian newspapers, the *New York Times*, government publications, private reports and the Canadian Press Service. Continuous pagination; semi-annual and annual subject/name indexes. *Class No:* 070.40(71)

USA

[2355]

Broadcast news. Woodbridge Conn., Primary Source Media, 1993-. CD-ROM database, updated monthly. £995.

Provides full text transcripts for news and current affairs programmes broadcast on CNN, NPR (National Public Radio), ABC News and PBS television and radio networks. About 30,000 records per year on annual cumulating disc. Features include timeline of key events, images and bibliography for further reference. *Class No:* 070.40(73)

08 Polygraphies

Publishers' Series

[2356]

Books in series: original, reprinted, in-print, and out-of-print books, published or distributed in the US in popular, scholarly and professional series. 4th ed. New York, Bowker, 1985. 6v. £378. ISBN: 0835219380.

Contents: v.1 *Series heading index. Subject index to series. Series index AAAS - Introductory handbook to art & design;* v.2 *Introductory mathematics for scientists and engineers - Zurich. Jung Institut Studies;* v.3 *Authors index. AB - Konig, H.W.;* v.4 *Authors index. Koo, Robert - Zzizinga, A.;* v.5 *Titles index. A.A. Milne - Mechanics of materials;* v.6 *Titles index. Mechanics of particular materials - ZZ.* Directory of publishers and distributors in v.4. First published 1976; 3rd ed. 1980.

286,754 titles in 26,642 series. Definition of series based on the Anglo-American cataloguing rules, entries mainly derived from Bowker's *American book publishing record* and *Books in print* databases. Excludes series for children, school textbooks in series, US government documents in series and series included in *Books in series 1876-1949* (below).

Continued by *Books in series, 1985-1989* (New York, Bowker, 1989. 2v. $199.95. ISBN: 0835226794). As 'information comes directly from publishers or their catalogs, variant forms may disrupt strict alphabetical listings' (*American reference books annual*, v.21, 1990, p.7). *Class No:* 082.1

[2357]

—Books in series, 1876-1949: original, reprinted, in-print and out-of-print books, published or distributed in the US in popular, scholarly and professional series. New York, Bowker, 1982. 3v. £175. ISBN: 0835214435.

Similar format to the main *Books in series:* v.1 *Series heading index. Subject index to series. Series;* v.2 *Authors;* v.3 *Titles.*

Cites *c.*67,000 titles in 9,300 series. *Class No:* 082.1

[2358]

Titles in series: a handbook for librarians and students. Baer, E.A., *comp.* 3rd ed. Metuchen, N.J., Scarecrow Press, 1978. 4v. ISBN: 0810810433.

V.1 *Titles in series A-I;* v.2 *Titles in series J-Z;* v.3 *Author/title index A-L;* v.4 *Author/title index M-Z. Series title index. Directory of publishers.*

First published 1953-61 (3v.). 2nd ed. 1964 (2v. plus Supplements 1-3. 1967-74).

Includes '69,657 book titles published in America and foreign countries prior to January 1975' (Preface p.v.). Within series titles listed in numerical order when allocated, otherwise chronological (*e.g.* lecture series) or A-Z. 'Well-researched, easy to use' (*Library review,* v.29(1), Spring 1980, p.50). *Class No:* 082.1

Audio-Visual Materials

Databases

[2359]

AVMARC. London, British Library, 1981-. Computer database.

'Audiovisual machine readable catalogue' searchable through BLAISE-Line and BLAISE-Web. Includes material recorded in the printed *British catalogue of audio-visual materials* (below). 22,653 records January 1995, file not updated. *Class No:* 084/086(003.4)

Bibliographies

[2360]

British catalogue of audio-visual materials: a subject catalogue of audio-visual materials processed by the British Library/Inner London Education Authority Learning Materials Recording Study. London, British Library, Bibliographic Services Division, 1979. 487p. £15. ISBN: 0900220775.

Designated '1st experimental ed.'. Supplements 1980 (220p. £12.50. ISBN: 0900220856) and 1983 (147p. £12.50. ISBN: 0712310096).

Includes slides, filmstrips, spoken word sound recordings, tape slides, overhead projections and educational kits, as well as some print materials such as wall charts. Major exclusions are 16mm films (apart from those provided by the British Universities Film Council), videorecordings and musical sound recordings. About 5,300 entries in Dewey classified arrangement; author/title/series and subject indexes.

The two supplements, similarly arranged, add 2,300 and 1,200 items respectively. Records are largely derived direct from publishers, rather than from the ILEA as previously. *Class No:* 084/086(01)

[2361]

LIBRARY OF CONGRESS. National union catalog. Audiovisual materials. Washington, D.C., Library of Congress, 1983-. Quarterly. $115. ISSN: 07347669.

Microfiche. Continues the paper *Audiovisual materials* issued quarterly, final issue annual cumulation, 1979-82.

Covers films, filmstrips, sets of transparencies, slide sets, videorecordings and kits catalogued by the Library of Congress. Entries in register format, with name, title, series and subject indexes. Nearly 300,000 items included. Also Internet accessible as part of *The Library of Congress catalogs (q.v.)* WWW site at http://lcweb.loc.gov/catalog. *Class No:* 084/086(01)

Reviews & Abstracts

[2362]

Media review digest: the only complete guide to reviews of non-book media. Ann Arbor, Pierian Press, 1970-. Annual with semi-annual supplement. $245. ISSN: 03637778.

As *Multi media review index* 1970-72.

Largely limited to film and video, but also covers records, tapes, slides, transparencies, illustrations, charts, media kits and, from 1995, CD-ROMs. 1996 v. contains about 42,000 citations with brief descriptive notes and general, A-Z subject, reviewer and other indexes. '(A)n enormous and useful compilation' (*American reference books annual*, v.28, 1997, p.7). *Class No:* 084/086(048)

Yearbooks & Directories

[2363]

AV market place: the complete business directory of products & services for the audio video industry including: audio visual, computer systems, film, video, programming, with industry yellow pages. New Providence, N.J., Bowker, 1969-. Annual. £130;$159.95. ISSN: 10440445.

Title varies: as *Audiovisual market place* (ISSN: 00670553) 1969-83.

Primarily a directory of products, services and suppliers. Geographic coverage confined to US and Canada. 1997 ed. (xii,1519p.) has entries for more than 7,000 companies under *c.*1,250 classifications (p.21-877). Company directory (p.881-1146). Also lists associations, film and television commissions, awards and festivals, conferences, periodicals and reference books. 'Industry yellow pages' (p.1245-1519) provides an index of organizations and personal names. *Class No:* 084/086(058)

Archives

[2364]

CORNISH, G.P. Archival collections of non-book materials: a listing and brief description of major national collections. Boston Spa, British Library, 1986. vii,41p. (*British Library information guide, 3.*) ISBN: 071233081x.

Updates J. Line's *Archival collections of non-book materials: a preliminary list indicating policies for preservation and access* (1977. BL R & D Report 5330).

Briefly describes 22 major national archives of non-book materials including sound recordings, visual recordings (film, video, photographs and slides) mixed media and graphics. Excludes collections which are specialized both by subject or format. *Class No:* 084/086(093.20)

[2365]

Directory of audiovisual resources in the East Midlands. Cornish, G.P., *comp.* Boston Spa, British Library Document Supply Centre, 1988. Unpaged. ISBN: 0712320482.

Entries for 131 collections, arranged by county, giving contact name, restrictions, loan availability, broad and special subject areas and collection size. Subject index.

Cornish has also compiled the similar *Directory of audiovisual resources in Yorkshire and Humberside* 2nd ed. (Boston Spa, British Library Document Supply Centre, 1988. [24]p. ISBN: 0712320526). Another regional guide is *NEMROC directory of audiovisual resources,* Hetherington, J. and Wilkinson, F. *comps.* (Sunderland, North East Media Resources Organizing Committee, 1988. [12]p. ISBN: 0712320512). *Class No:* 084/086(093.20)

[2366]

INTERNATIONAL ASSOCIATION OF SOUND AND AUDIOVISUAL ARCHIVES. IASA directory. London, International Association of Sound and Audiovisual Archives, 1997-. Biennial.

Replaces *IASA membership list* published 1989.

1997 issue (43p.) is a basic membership listing in separate sequences for institutional and individual members. Country index. *Class No:* 084/086(093.20)

[2367]

ROWAN, B.G. *and* **WOOD, C.J. Scholars' guide to Washington, D.C. media collections.** Washington, D.C., Woodrow Wilson Center Press/Baltimore, John Hopkins Univ. Press, 1994. xxvii,189p. $45; paper ed. $19.95. ISBN: 0943875544.

Updates *Scholars' guide to Washington, D.C. film and video collections* (1980) and *Pictorial resources in the Washington, D.C. area* (1976).

Briefly describes the collections of 131 institutions. Detailed treatment of sound recordings is available in *Scholars' guide to Washington, D.C. for audio resources* (*q.v.*). *Class No:* 084/086(093.20)

Information Management

[2368]

FOTHERGILL, R. *and* **BUTCHART, I. Non-book materials in libraries:** a practical guide. 3rd ed. London, Bingley, 1990. vi,319p. £30. ISBN: 085157436x.

Previous eds. 1980 and 1984.

Includes treatment of optical storage systems (videodiscs, CD-ROMs), databases and interactive video, as well as more traditional non-book materials. Bibliography (p.304-8); index. *Class No:* 084/086:025.4

[2369]

FROST, C.O. Media access and organization: a cataloging and reference sources guide for nonbook materials. Englewood, Colo., Libraries Unlimited, 1989. xxi,265p. £30.50;$31.50. ISBN: 0872875830.

Separate sections for cartographic materials, sound recordings, films and videorecordings, graphic materials, computer files, three dimensional artefacts and realia and microforms. Each offers commentary and guidance on cataloguing, with examples, followed by an annotated listing of important reference sources. Brief index (p.259-65). *Class No:* 084/086:025.4

[2370]

OLSON, N.B. Cataloging of audiovisual materials: a manual based on AACR2. 3rd ed. DeKalb, Ill., Minnesota Scholarly Press, 1992. xii,335p., illus. $65. ISBN: 0933474482.

First published 1981; 2nd ed. 1985.

Coverage includes cartographic materials, computer files and microforms. Refers to relevant AACR2 rules and makes frequent use of illustrative examples. Indexed. *Class No:* 084/086:025.4

Bibliographies

[2371]

Audiovisual librarianship: a select bibliography, 1965-1983. Liebscher, P., *comp.* London, Aslib and Library Association Audiovisual Groups, 1984. iv,177p. ISBN: 0950977209.

Partially based on references published in the

....*(contd.)*
'Bibliographic update' column of *Audiovisual librarian.* (below). 1,703 entries, some annotated, in subject arrangement. *Class No:* 084/086:025.4(01)

Periodicals

[2372]
Audiovisual librarian: multimedia information. Aberystwyth, Audiovisual Librarian, 1973-. Quarterly. £55. ISSN: 03023451.

Official journal of the Multimedia Groups of Aslib and the Library Association.

In addition to a number of articles each issue usually contains: 'Seen and heard' giving news, forthcoming events and information on equipment/services; 'Bibliographic update' providing citations to *c.* 50 recently published articles relating to audiovisual librarianship; 'Reviews' covering books, videos, hardware, etc; 'Publications' detailing new audiovisual and print titles.
Class No: 084/086:025.4(051)

Illustrations

[2373]
APPEL, M.C. Illustration index VII: 1987-1991. Metuchen, N.J., Scarecrow Press, 1993. ix,492p. £53.55;$59.50. ISBN: 0810826593.

First published 1957 covering 1950-June 1956: supplement extending coverage to 1959 (1961). New '2nd ed.' combining the earlier issues, adding new material and extending coverage to June 1963 (1966). Subsequent issues supplement this volume as follows: July 1963-1971 (1973); 1972-1976 (1980. $39.50. ISBN: 0810812738); 1977-1981 (1984. $39.50. ISBN: 0810816563); 1982-1986 (1988. £38.25;$49.50. ISBN: 080821468).

Indexes 10 periodicals *American heritage, Gourmet, Life, National geographic, National wildlife, Natural history, Smithsonian, Sports illustrated, Travel and leisure, Travel/Holiday.* Each illustration treated separately: 19,000 individual subject headings encompassing 28,000 entries. Alphabetical arrangement; well cross-referenced. Entry includes indication of type of illustration if not a photograph, whether colour or black and white and code indicating size.
Class No: 084

[2374]
BRITISH ASSOCIATION OF PICTURE LIBRARIES AND AGENCIES. BAPLA directory. London, BAPLA, 1981-?. Irregular. ISSN: 02692023.

1997 v. (128p.) lists 335 member libraries A-Z with 50-75 word descriptions and detail such as search fee, hours and email/WWW address. Broad heading 'Subject list' precedes. Separate section for associate members. Updated information available from BAPLA WWW site at http://www.bapla.org.uk. *Class No:* 084

[2375]
ELLIS, J.C. Index to illustrations. Boston, Mass., Faxon, 1966. xi,682p. (*Useful reference series, no. 95.*) ISBN: 0873050959.

Contains *c.*30,000 references in all fields, but excludes nature illustrations, (separately covered in *Nature and its applications* (Faxon, 1949.)). List of books and 8 periodicals cited, p.xi. Remains a valuable tool. *Class No:* 084

[2376]
EVANS, H. *and* **EVANS, M. Picture researcher's handbook:** an international guide to picture sources and how to use them. 6th ed. London, Routledge, 1996. xx,649p. £50. (*A Blueprint book.*) ISBN: 0415151260.

1st ed. 1975; 5th ed. (Blueprint) 1992.

Sources include picture libraries, general libraries, commercial picture and press agencies, museums, art galleries, archives and historical societies. In 4 sections: General 390 entries; Regional (material covering several countries) 116 entries; National (material relating to a particular country) 256 entries; Specialist (subdivided in 11 subject categories 'Art, architecture and archaeology ... Natural history ... Various') 630 entries. Information includes address, brief description of material held, stock size, research facilities, hours, loan procedures/fees and catalogues/literature. Subject, place (geographic) and source indexes. The established and pre-eminent reference for information on picture collections. *Class No:* 084

[2377]
EVANS, H. *and* **EVANS, M. Sources of illustrations, 1500-1900.** Bath, Adams & Dart, 1971. [6], 162p. illus.,facsims.,ports. ISBN: 0239000951.

Indicates the scope and range of illustrative material available before photography came into general use (*e.g.* wood engraving, line engraving on metal, lithograph etc.). 192 representative illustrations reproduced in approximate chronological order (p.24-153) with short annotations. Brief list of sources (p.156-61), including public collections and commercial picture libraries (each listing divided by country). Some useful books (p.162). *Class No:* 084

[2378]
McKEOWN, R. National directory of slide collections. London, British Library, 1990. viii,310p. £20. (*British Library information guide, 12.*) ISBN: 0712332081.

Compiled from data collected for the *National survey of slide collections* (1989. British Library research paper, 67).

A first attempt at establishing a complete listing of UK slide collections. Coverage mainly of non-commercial collections in academic and public libraries, museums and galleries, research units, professional associations, teaching hospitals etc. About 950 entries in A-Z order of holding institution, giving data on collection size, subject coverage, opening hours, access conditions and contact person. Subject and geographical indexes. *Class No:* 084

[2379]
Picture sources UK. Eakins, R., *ed.* London, Macdonald, 1985. 474p. ISBN: 0356100782.

Replaces Nunn, G.W.A. ed. *British sources of photographs and pictures,* 1952.

Information on 1,141 collections of photographs, prints and other visual material presented in 14 subject chapters. For each collection gives address, approximate no. of items held, dates of subject matter, detailed listing of subjects covered and access conditions. Collection and subject indexes. Needs updating, now largely superseded by the *Picture researcher's handbook* (above). *Class No:* 084

[2380]
ROBL, E.H. Picture sources 4. New York, Special Libraries Association, 1983. xi,180p. illus., plates. $10. ISBN: 0871112744.

First published 1959; 3rd ed. 1975.

Information on nearly 1,000 picture sources in the US and Canada. For each collection gives address, contact name,

....*(contd.)*
number and type of items held, subject and chronological coverage and access conditions. Detailed subject index; collection and geographic indexes. *Class No:* 084

[2381]
UNITED STATES. National Archives and Records Administration. Still Picture Branch. **Guide to the holdings of the Still Picture Branch of the National Archives.** Washington, D.C., National Archives and Records Administration, 1990. x,166p. $25. ISBN: 0911333835.

Describes material from 170 US government departments and agencies including photographic prints, negatives, posters and transparencies. Excludes visual material from textual records housed in other branches of the National Archives. *Class No:* 084

Research Methods

[2382]
EVANS, H. Practical picture research: a guide to current practice, procedure, techniques and resources. London, Blueprint, 1992. xi,265p. illus. £45. ISBN: 0948905786.

Rev. ed. of *The Art of picture research* (Newton Abbot, David & Charles, 1979).

Largely intended for the professional picture researcher. 6 sections: 1. The Picture researcher (qualifications, career opportunities, etc.) - 2. Picture sources (private, commercial, etc.) - 3. Procedure (access, fees, copyright, etc.) - 4. Picture selection - 5. The Assignment - 6. Reference (annotated lists of associations and other organizations, libraries, services, reference books; also glossary). 'An essential guide ... if you only have room for one book on the subject this is it' (*The Year in reference*, 1993, p.30).
Class No: 084:001.891

[2383]
SCHULTZ, J. *and* **SCHULTZ, B. Picture research:** a practical guide. New York, Van Nostrand Reinhold, 1991. ix,326p. illus. $42.95. ISBN: 0442318405.

8 chapters include information on production and reproduction of photographs, researchers and buyers, museums and archives, commercial picture agencies, legal matters, and electronic picture transmission and research. Good glossary (p.291-98) and well annotated bibliography of *c.*100 items. Indexed. *Class No:* 084:001.891

Information Management

[2384]
Picture librarianship. Harrison, H.P., *ed.* London, Library Association, 1981. xii,542p. (*Handbooks on library practice.*) ISBN: 0853659125.

Reprint available from Books on Demand ($157.90. ISBN: 0783753225).

In 2 pts: 1. Techniques and organization (13 sections; including selection, presentation and storage, microforms, copyright, education and training); 2. Case studies and surveys of picture libraries (26 sections; including the National Film Archive, art galleries and museums, public libraries, commercial libraries). Extensive bibliography (p.495-517); comprehensively indexed. A substantial work, still unrivalled in the field. *Class No:* 084:025.4

[2385]
SUTCLIFFE, G. Slide collection management in libraries and information units. Aldershot, Gower, 1995. xii,219p. illus., tables. £45. ISBN: 0566075806.

8 chapters including the literature of slide collection management (discursive treatment), slide management and retrieval packages, medical slide collections and optical systems and the slide. Useful bibliography (p.157-78). 6 appendices including glossary and 'Professional associations and other relevant bodies'. Index. '(V)ery much a first-hand account of someone who has experience of working with slides' (*Managing information*, v.2(5), May 1995, p.57).
Class No: 084:025.4

Microfilms

Bibliographies

[2386]
Bibliographic guide to microform publications. Boston, Mass., G.K. Hall, 1987-94. Annual. ISSN: 08913749.

Listed non-serial microforms catalogued by the New York Public Library and the Library of Congress. Included original publications filmed for archival purposes, as well as commercially available microforms. In dictionary format.
Class No: 084.0(01)

[2387]
BODLEIAN LIBRARY. A Guide to microform holdings in the Bodleian Library. 4th ed. Oxford, Bodleian Library, 1995. [iv],48p.

Previous ed. 1993

Useful list of 524 microforms with full bibliographical detail and locations. Main headings: Catalogues and bibliographies - Official publications, statistics and state papers - Collections - Newspapers. Index (p.39-48).
Class No: 084.0(01)

[2388]
BRITISH LIBRARY. Microform research collections at the British Library. Carpenter, R., *ed.* London, British Library, 1989. 46p.

Replaces earlier partial listings especially *Microform research collections at the British Library Lending Division* (2nd ed. 1985, first published 1983).

The first consolidated listing for the British Library, covering 346 collections, including those held at the Document Supply Centre, as well as the major London collections. Confined to commercially produced microform sets of previously published or unpublished documents, microforms which comprise a single item excluded. In A-Z title order, entries include BL locations but not pressmarks. Index of titles, persons and bodies and broad subjects.
Class No: 084.0(01)

[2389]
Guide to microforms in print: incorporating International microforms in print. Author/title. München, Saur, 1961-. Annual. DM596;$285. ISSN: 01640747.

Title varies slightly; as *International microforms in print* 1974/75. Published by Meckler until 1990. 1997 issued in 2v.

Covers microfilmed books, journals, newspapers, government publications, archival material, collections, etc., available from publishers worldwide. Excludes theses and dissertations. Entries, arranged by title with cross-references from authors/editors, give basic bibliographical detail, type of microform (coded), price and ISBN. List of publishers and distributors. *Class No:* 084.0(01)

[2390]

—Guide to microforms in print: incorporating International microforms in print. Subject. München, Saur, 1962-. Annual. DM596;$285. ISSN: 01638386.

Companion volume to the above, listing microfilms by modified Dewey classification. Index to persons as subjects.

Guide to microforms in print. Supplement (1979-. ISSN: 01640739) appears approximately 6 months after the annual v., listing newly available microforms in author/title and subject sequences. *Class No:* 084.0(01)

[2391]

International guide to microform masters. München, Saur, 1995-. CD-ROM database. £1,625.

Annually updated, Windows based, two disc product with German and English interface. Disc 1 enables complete searching of database and viewing of brief citation. Disc 2 displays full citation.

Records the collections of over 200 libraries and research institutes in North America and Europe in well over 1,400,000 entries. Full bibliographical data and technical information on the type of film used. More than 30 search options including publisher of original work and year filmed. *Class No:* 084.0(01)

[2392]

LIBRARY OF CONGRESS. Humanities and Social Sciences Division. **A Guide to the microform collections in the Humanities and Social Sciences Division of the Library of Congress.** Frazier, P., *ed.* Washington, D.C., Library of Congress, Humanities and Social Sciences Division, 1996. v,341p. ISBN: 0844409316.

Replaces *Microform collections and selected titles in microform in the Microform Reading Room* (1987) and *First supplement* (1991).

Entries A-Z by main entry with short description, Library of Congress subject headings and notes on finding aids, guides, etc. Indexed by format and subject.

Also Internet accessible at gopher://marvel.loc.gov:70/00/research/collections.catalogs/collections/micro/intro.mrv. *Class No:* 084.0(01)

[2393]

Microform research collections: a guide. Dodson, S.C., *ed.* 2nd ed. Westport, Conn. and London, Meckler, 1984. xxxv,670p. £72. (*Meckler publishing series in library micrographics management, 9.*) ISBN: 0930466667.

1st ed. 1978.

A detailed, well-written guide to 374 major research collections (nearly twice as many as the 1st ed.) from 59 publishers. Arranged alphabetically by collection title, entries give publisher, format, price, review citation, arrangement and bibliographical control, bibliographies and indexes covering the collection and scope and content. Author, editor, compiler, title and subject index to the collections (p.619-70); also indexes the bibliographies, guides etc. upon which the collections are based. *Class No:* 084.0(01)

[2394]

Micropublishers' trade list annual. Alexander, Va., Chadwyck-Healey, 1978-1995. Irregular (Microfiche). ISSN: 03612635.

Cover title *MTLA the micropublishers' trade list annual.* Ceased publication with 1994/95.

Reproduced the catalogues and brochures of micropublishers worldwide. Issued as a set of microfiche in a ring binder (174 fiche 1994/95), with a paper index to publishers. *Class No:* 084.0(01)

[2395]

Mikfroform-Sammlungen in wissenschaftlichen Bibliotheken der Bundesrepublik Deutschland einschliesslich Berlin (West): ein Verzeichnis umfangreicher Erwerbungen. Hohoff, U., *bearb.* Berlin, Deutsches Bibliotheksinstitut, 1990. 141p. DM28. ISBN: 3870683791.

Preliminary listing of microfilm collections in German research libraries. Over 400 collections briefly described. *Class No:* 084.0(01)

[2396]

NATIONAL LIBRARY OF SCOTLAND. Microform research collections in major Scottish libraries. [2nd ed.]. Edinburgh, National Library of Scotland, 1993. vi,92p. ISBN: 1872116159.

First published 1987.

Covers the National Library of Scotland, the 8 older university libraries, the Mitchell Library Glasgow, Edinburgh Central Library and National Museums of Scotland. Concentrates on commercially available collections, in house microforms and microforms of individual newspapers excluded. Subject arrangement in 26 sections; keyword index. *Class No:* 084.0(01)

[2397]

National register of microform masters. 1965-1983. Washington D.C., Library of Congress, 1965-84. Annual. ISSN: 00903299.

Frequency varies; initially irregular, then annual.

Covered both commercial and non-profit microform producers. Only technical reports, typescript translations, manuscripts and US doctoral dissertations and masters theses excluded. From 1970 arranged by main entry, prior to this date by LC card no. A 6v. cumulation (*National register of microform masters: 1965-75*) published 1976, presents all entries, including those dating from before 1970, in a single main entry sequence. *Class No:* 084.0(01)

[2398]

PHILADELPHIA BIBLIOGRAPHICAL CENTER AND UNION LIBRARY CATALOGUE. Union list of microfilms. Rev., enl. and cumulated ed. Ann Arbor, Mich., Edwards, 1951. xvip,1961cols.

First published 1942, updated by 5 supplements. Supplement to this ed. covering 1949-59 issued in 2v., 1961.

The 1951 cumulated ed. lists *c.*25,000 titles held by 197 libraries. The 1949-59 supplement has *c.*52,000 entries for microfilms in 215 libraries. Newspapers are included in the 1951 ed., but not in the supplement since they are recorded in *Newspapers in microfilm* (*q.v.*). *Class No:* 084.0(01)

[2399]

Register of preservation microforms. London, British Library. Computer database.

Available through BLAISE-Line and BLAISE-Web, updated monthly.

Records microforms created by the National Preservation Office of the British Library for books and serials in danger of deterioration. Also covers microforms produced as part of *The Nineteenth century* British Library/Chadwyck-Healey joint project. Detail includes brief description of original, location of copies and locations of microforms produced. At the beginning of 1995 the file contained 105,315 records. *Class No:* 084.0(01)

Indexes

[2400]
Index to microform collections. Niles, A., *comp*. Westport, Conn., Meckler, 1985-88. 2v. £20(v.1);£105(v.2). (*Meckler series in library micrographics management, 11,13.*) ISBN: 0930466756, v.1; 0887360610, v.2.

Provides author and title access to over 20,000 individual monographs contained in large microform sets. 26 collections indexed in v.1, including *British trade union history* (World Microfilm Publications), *Early English courtesy books* (Bell and Howell) and *Source materials in the field of theatre* (University Microfilms International). 44 collections in v.2, *Archives de la linguistique française ... The works and sources of David Ricardo*. Both volumes include complete contents lists for each set.
Class No: 084.0(014)

Reviews & Abstracts

[2401]
Microform & imaging review. München, K.G. Saur, 1972-. Quarterly. DM268;$150. ISSN: 09495770.

Current title from 1996, previously *Microform review* (ISSN: 00026530). Published by Meckler until 1991.

In addition to articles on microform and imaging publishing and technology, each issue carries 3-4 reviews and a 'Comment and news' section. Index to reviews in each issue; ten year index, *Microform review cumulative index volumes 1-10, 1972-1981*, J. Wellington *ed.* (1982. ISBN: 0930466578). Further cumulative index for 1985-88 in v.26(3), Summer 1997, p.121-27; index from 1989 anticipated. *Class No:* 084.0(048)

[2402]
—Cumulative microform reviews, 1977-1984. Westport, Conn., Meckler, 1986. 1047p. ISBN: 0887360181.

Reproduces over 500 reviews from *Microform review*. Subject arrangement with title index. Earlier v. *Cumulative microform reviews, 1972-1976* (Meckler, 1978. 619p. 0913672270). *Class No:* 084.0(048)

Yearbooks & Directories

[2403]
Microform market place: an international directory of micropublishing. München, Saur, 1974-. Biennial/triennial. DM120;$75. ISSN: 03620999.

Previously published by Meckler.

The only directory devoted entirely to micropublishers. Gives address, key personnel, details of publishing programme and order information. Around 475 entries in the 1995/97 ed. (1997. viii,223p.), UK micropublishers well-represented. Geographic and broad term subject indexes. Lists of discontinuations, acquisitions and name changes; list of organizations. Also contains section 'Information sources', an annotated listing of 70 titles useful to the microform user 'faced with making decisions about microforms or microform equipment'. *Class No:* 084.0(058)

Information Management

[2404]
Preservation microfilming: a guide for librarians and archivists. Fox, L.L., *ed.* 2nd ed. Chicago, American Library Association, 1996. xxx,394p. illus. $70. ISBN: 0838906532.

Edited for the Association of Research Libraries. First published 1987.

....(contd.)

6 main chaps. each extensively divided by topic, covering selection of materials, production and preparation, standards and practices, bibliographic control and costs. 6 appendices including 'Resources for preservation microfilming' comprising list of institutions with brief details. Glossary (p.355-75); index. *Class No:* 084.0:025.4

[2405]
TEAGUE, S.J. Microform, video and electronic media librarianship. London, Butterworths, 1985. viii,150p. illus. £20. ISBN: 0408014016.

First published under title *Microform librarianship*, 1977. 2nd ed. 1979.

Despite the revised title of this ed., still largely concerned with microforms. 11 chapters, covering microforms in libraries, micropublishing, library catalogues, data services copying from non-book media and information technology. Includes a useful survey of the major micropublishers and their products. Index (p.146-50). *Class No:* 084.0:025.4

Sound Recordings

[2406]
Directory of recorded sound resources in the United Kingdom. Weerasinghe, L., *comp* *and* Silver, J., *researcher*. London, British Library, 1989. xxii,173p. £30. ISBN: 0712305025.

Based on the *National register for collections of recorded sound* database maintained by the British Library. Covers 489 collections of music, spoken literature and history, speeches, dialects, recordings for the blind, and transport, machinery and wildlife noises. Standard information for each collection including details of available written transcripts, finding aids, publications and complimentary non-sound resources. Repository organizations include libraries, museums, archives, learned societies and radio stations. Indexed (p.143-73) by topics, genres, events, geographic regions and corporate and individual names. A valuable and much-needed tool, although far from comprehensive in coverage. *Class No:* 086.7

[2407]
HEINTZE, J.R., *and others*. **Scholars' guide to Washington, D.C. for audio resources:** sound recordings in the arts, humanities, social, physical and life sciences. Washington, D.C., Smithsonian Institution Press, 1985. xiv,395p. £25;$29.95. (*Scholars' guide to Washington, D.C. no. 11.*) ISBN: 0874745160.

Published for the Woodrow Wilson International Center for Scholars. Also available in pbk. (£12.50;$15. ISBN: 0874745179).

Surveys over 400 collections, including those in libraries, archives, museums, embassies, government agencies etc. Arranged alphabetically by name of collection within classified sections; indexed by personal name, subject, organization/institution. Bibliography (p.361-63).
Class No: 086.7

Bibliographies

[2408]
British words on cassette 1992: a directory of spoken word cassettes produced in the UK. London, Bowker-Saur, 1992. vii,173p. £25;$40. ISBN: 1857390857.

Revised and expanded ed. of *British words on tape* (Meckler, 1990. x,161p. ISBN: 0887366198).

UK counterpart of *Words on cassette* (below) listing 6,200 titles. Covers 'popular fiction, classic literature, drama,

.... *(contd.)*

poetry, children's books, educational materials and recordings of sounds' (p.vii). Full entries by title (p.1-91) include author, reader, no. of cassettes, length of play, order no., price, rental charge, publisher and notes. Separate author, reader and subject (225 categories) indexes. List of publishers and distributors. *Class No:* 086.7(01)

[2409]

POSTGATE, M. A Few well-chosen words: recommended spoken word recordings. Harrow, Gramophone Publications, 1995. 256p. £6.95. ISBN: 0902470531.

Provides 100-400 word evaluative reviews in sections: Full-length books - Abridged novels, non-fiction and short stories - Poetry - Drama - Humour - Documentaries, memoirs and diaries - Recordings for children. Entries include detail of reader, producer, running time, etc. Indexed by author, title and reader. *Class No:* 086.7(01)

[2410]

Words on cassette: combining Meckler's *Words on tape* with Bowker's *On cassette*. New York, Bowker, 1992-. Annual. $149.95.

Merges *Words on tape* (1984/85-91. ISSN: 87553579) and *On cassette* (1989-91).

The equivalent of *Books in print* for spoken word audio cassettes. The 1997 ed. (2v. ISBN: 0835239144) lists 57,400 recordings of literary, business, historical, political, biographical and humorous works, available in the US from 2,000 producers. Full entries by title in v.1 give author, reader/performer, no. of cassettes, running time, publication date, price/rental cost and producer/distributor. Many entries also have a brief descriptive annotation. Author, reader/performer, subject and distributor/producer indexes in v.2. *Class No:* 086.7(01)

[2411]

—WYNNE, J. Listener's guide to audio books: reviews, recommendations and listings for more than 2,000 titles. New York, Simon & Schuster, 1995. 447p. $14. ISBN: 0684802392.

'A Fireside book'.

Arranged by category with an author/title index. Information includes author, reader/performer, summary, length and publisher. '(N)o challenge at all to the excellent annual *Words on cassette*' (*Choice*, v.33(6), February 1996, p.936). *Class No:* 086.7(01)

Information Management

[2412]

WARD, A. A Manual of sound archive administration. Aldershot, Gower, 1990. xi,299p. illus., diags. $59.95. ISBN: 0566055716.

6 main chaps: What are sound archives? - Acquiring sound archives - Copyright and public access - Documentation - Accommodation, equipment, facilities - Conservation of sound archives. Further reading (p.195-99); various appendices including a good glossary (p.229-73). Indexed. *Class No:* 086.7:025.4

087 Government Publications

Government Publications

Bibliographies

[2413]
AMERICAN LIBRARY ASSOCIATION. Government Documents Round Table. **Guide to official publications of foreign countries.** Westfall, G., *ed.* 2nd ed. [Bethesda, Md.], Congressional Information Service, 1997. xxii,494p.

First published 1990.

Contains annotated entries for the major official publications of 178 states, with the emphasis on current materials, serials strongly represented. Up to 19 categories of publication for each country including general guides, bibliographies and catalogues, government directories, statistical yearbooks, legislative proceedings, census reports and publications on health, labour, education, etc. This ed. includes publications available in electronic form. About 4,500 entries overall detail for each including title with English translation, date(s), name of responsible agency, frequency of issue, availability and annotation of 50-200 words. No indexes, but an immensely valuable compilation, generally more thorough and current than *Information sources in official publications* (below). *Class No:* 087.7(01)

[2414]
A Guide to official gazettes and their contents. Roberts, J.E., *comp.* Washington, D.C., Library of Congress Law Library, 1985. Unpaged.

Based on the holdings of the Library of Congress. Includes entries for all sovereign states as well as some 'semi-dependent entities' (*e.g.* Northern Ireland, Falkland Islands). In A-Z order of country, giving gazette title, commonly used abbreviation, frequency of publication, language(s) of publication and list of contents, including separately published parts and supplements and indexes. Lacks detail of title changes. This and other additional information available in the earlier *Government gazettes: an annotated list of gazettes held in the Dag Hammarskjold Library* (United Nations, 1964). *Class No:* 087.7(01)

[2415]
Information sources in official publications. Nurcombe, V.J., *ed.* London, Bowker Saur, 1997. xxvii,564p. £65;$95. (*Guides to information sources..*) ISBN: 1857391519.

Country-by-country coverage in 11 sections *e.g.* North America ... Australasia ... Former Soviet Union ... Western Europe. Initial section on United Nations and other international organizations (EU under Western Europe). All major states covered. For most includes information on government structure, publishing activities and bodies, bibliographic control and access to collections. Detail on specific publications given in form of italicised title and brief description in text. Index (p.529-64) includes names of governing bodies and their official gazettes, national bibliographies, etc., although 'titles of publications not generally indexed'. Some sections a little sketchy (*e.g.* Asia)

....(contd.)
and others not completely up to date, but overall 'impressively researched, massively detailed and well organised ... a must for any half-decent reference collection' (*Reference reviews*, v.12(1), 1998, p.6).
Class No: 087.7(01)

[2416]
List of the serial publications of foreign governments, 1815-1931. Gregory, W., *ed.* New York, Wilson, 1932. x,720p.

Reprinted Kraus, 1966. ISBN: 0527574007.

Union list of about 30,000 non-American government serials, with holdings in some 85 US libraries. Entry is under country, subdivided by departments, ministries etc.
Class No: 087.7(01)

[2417]
NEW YORK PUBLIC LIBRARY. Research Libraries. **Catalog of government publications in the Research Libraries.** Boston, Mass., G.K. Hall, 1972. 40v. ISBN: 0816107815.

Updated by *Dictionary catalog of government publications: supplement 1974* (Boston, G.K. Hall, 1976. 2v. $240. ISBN: 0816100608).

The main catalog comprises 561,000 photolithographed catalogue cards for the 'fundamental documents of all national and colonial governments so far as they have been published or obtainable'. Holdings are strongest for the US, Great Britain, Western Europe and Scandinavia. Entry is under political units subdivided by department etc. Within headings serials are arranged alphabetically, monographs chronologically. Continued by two annual publications *Bibliographic guide to government publications - foreign* (below) and *Bibliographic guide to government publications - US* (*q.v.*). *Class No:* 087.7(01)

[2418]
—Bibliographic guide to government publications - foreign. 1975-. Boston, Mass., G.K. Hall, 1976-. Annual. $720. ISSN: 0360280x.

Based on material catalogued by the Library of Congress. Includes official gazettes, parliamentary debates and papers, session law, treaties, departmental reports, censuses and statistical annuals. Publications of international and regional agencies, state and provincial governments and major cities also covered. In dictionary catalogue format with bold-face upper case subject entries under Library of Congress headings. 2 v. for 1995 list items catalogued September 1994-December 1995. *Class No:* 087.7(01)

Periodicals

[2419]
Journal of government information: an international journal of issues and information resources. Tarrytown, N.Y., Pergamon Press, 1973-. Bi-monthly. $472. ISSN: 13520237.

Title and frequency varies. Current title from v.21 1994; previously *Government publications review* (ISSN: 02779390). Published quarterly 1973-81.

Most issues have 4-5 articles on document production, distribution, library handling and use, with a similar number

....(contd.)

of reviews of new publications. From 1982 the last issue of each year has been devoted to an annotated listing of notable new government publications worldwide (formerly covered in the separately published part B). V.22(6), 1995, has 536 entries, 278 of which are for US federal, state or local publications. A further regular feature is the unnanotated listing 'Recent literature on government information'. V.23(2), 1996, cites *c.*450 items under this heading, including reports and book chapters. *Class No:* 087.7(051)

Europe—Western

[2420]

Official publications of Western Europe. Johansson, E., *ed.* London, Mansell, 1984-88. 2v. $120 per. v. ISBN: 0720116236, v.1; 0720116627, v.2.

V.1 *Denmark, Finland, France, Ireland, Italy, Luxembourg, Netherlands, Spain and Turkey.* (xvi,313p.). V.2 *Austria, Belgium, Federal Republic of Germany, Greece, Norway, Portugal, Sweden, Switzerland and United Kingdom.* (x,278p.).

Intended 'to present a state-of-the-art record of government publishing in the late twentieth century and to provide a practical reference work of lasting value' (Preface v.2 p.x). Separate chapters for each country, contributed by specialists, in standard format with slight variations: 1. Introduction - 2. Principal government publications (central government) - 3. Manner of publication - 4. Bibliographic control - 5. Local government publications - 6. Library collections and availability - 7. Bibliography. V.1 includes chapter 'The art and acquisition of foreign official publications'. Both volumes indexed by organization/title and subject. Shows 'little overlap with other works in English' (*Choice*, v.26(4), December 1988, p.631).
Class No: 087.7(400)

Europe—Eastern

[2421]

Official publications of the Soviet Union and Eastern Europe, 1945-1980: a select annotated bibliography. Walker, G., *ed.* London, Mansell, 1982. xxviii,624p. £85;$130. ISBN: 0720116414.

Selective coverage in separate chapters for Albania, Bulgaria, Czechoslovakia, German Democratic Republic, Hungary, Yugoslavia, Poland, Rumania and the USSR. Official publications widely interpreted. Categories include constitutional documents; law codes; Party documents; statistics; economic, military, social and cultural affairs; leaders' works. Does not attempt documentation below the national level. Soviet Union afforded most detailed treatment. Title name/index of entries. *Class No:* 087.7(401)

Great Britain

[2422]

BUTCHER, D. Official publications in Britain. 2nd ed. London, Library Association, 1991. xiii,192p. £35. ISBN: 085157422x.

1st ed. 1982.

'(E)xamines the nature and organization of official publishing in Britain at national, regional and local levels, the extent and adequacy of bibliographic control and the ways in which these publications may be selected and acquired' (*Preface* p.ix). 7 documented chapters: 1. The scope and structure of official publishing in Britain - 2. Parliamentary publications - 3. Government department

....(contd.)

publishing - 4. National and regional public bodies - 5. Bibliographic control and selection sources (p.125-49) - 6. The availability of official publications - 7. Local government publishing. Index (p.185-92). Includes coverage of online and CD-ROM sources. Concise and up-to-date, 'anyone new to the subject would be hard-pressed to find a better introduction' (*Government libraries journal*, v.2(1), 1992, p.8). *Class No:* 087.7(410)

[2423]

Directory of British official publications: a guide to sources. Richard, S., *comp.* 2nd ed. London, Mansell, 1984. xxxvi,431p. $120. ISBN: 0720117062.

1st ed. 1981.

A directory of 1,283 official publishing bodies. Wide ranging coverage including organizations as diverse as the Arts Council, Commonwealth Secretariat, National Gas Consumers' Council and the Weed Research Organization. 15 sections: I/VI UK, Great Britain, England and Wales - VII/IX Northern Ireland - X/XIII Scotland - XIV Wales - XV Isle of Man and Channel Islands. Entries for each body provide a general overview of publishing activity, with the emphasis on publication lists and serial titles. Now overtaken by changes in government structure, but still of occasional value for identifying older material. *Class No:* 087.7(410)

[2424]

PEMBERTON, J.E. British official publications. 2nd rev. ed. Oxford, Pergamon, 1973. xiv,328p. facsims, tables. $137. ISBN: 0080177972.

First published 1971.

17 chapters: 1. British Parliamentary government - 2. Official publications: classification and indexes ... 5. Command Papers ... 8. Parliamentary debates ... 12. Non-parliamentary publications - 13. Reference books (arranged by titles) - 14. Statistics (subjects A-Z) ... 17. Non-HMSO official publications (departments A-Z). Sound index of subjects and titles. Now very dated, but because of the limited number of alternative guides to British government publications, remains of some value. *Class No:* 087.7(410)

[2425]

RODGERS, F. A Guide to British government publications. New York, H.W. Wilson; London, Mansell, 1980. xviii,750p. ISBN: 0824206177.

3 parts (29 chapters): I. General (*e.g.* The evolution of official printing and publishing; General catalogues and indexes) - II. Parliamentary (*e.g.* Reports of debates) - III. Executive agencies (*e.g.* Central control (including the Cabinet Office, Civil Service Department); Financial control; Industrial resources (including British Aerospace, Post Office); Education and libraries; Scotland; Wales and Northern Ireland; Miscellaneous agencies (*e.g.* HMSO)). Glossary (p.687-90). Detailed analytical index (p.691-750). Brief historical notes precede discussion of the most important publications of each department/agency. Despite its age, remains one of the most useful and extensive surveys of British official publishing. *Class No:* 087.7(410)

Databases

[2426]

UKOP: catalogue of United Kingdom official publications. Cambridge, Chadwyck-Healey; London, HMSO, 1989-. Computer database. £925. ISSN: 09620737.

Available either on CD-ROM (bimonthly updating, £990) or through the World Wide Web (monthly updating). Direct access to full text of selected publications to be introduced

....*(contd.)*
from early 1998.

Amalgamates The Stationery Office's catalogues with Chadwyck-Healey's *Catalogue of British official publications not published by The Stationery Office* (*qq.v.*). 360,000 records for publications from 1980, 2,000 entries added monthly. Searchable fields include corporate author, personal author or chairperson, title, series title, subject or keyword, year of publication, publisher, ISBN/ISSN and price. Searches can be limited (*e.g.* in-print or out-of-print; Stationery Office publications or non-Stationery Office publications). Occasional indexing peculiarities and not as frequently updated as the printed indexes on which it is based. Otherwise of immense value, eliminating the need to distinguish between Stationery Office and non-Stationery Office published material when attempting to trace official publications. *Class No:* 087.7(410)(003.4)

Internet

[2427]

BOPCAS: British official publications current awareness service. Southampton, Univ. of Southampton, 1995-. World Wide Web resource.

URL: http://www.soton.ac.uk/opcas. Date reviewed 9th June 1998. Initially title *NUKOP: new United Kingdom official publications.*

Based on accessions to the Ford Collection of British official publications at Southampton University. Data for publications from 1995, file updated at least weekly. Approx. 9,500 items recorded June 1998, entries including full bibliographical detail, ISBN, price and subject keywords. Database specifically designed to provide email current awareness service, but search and browse options also supported. *Class No:* 087.7(410)(003.41)

[2428]

Her Majesty's Stationery Office (World Wide Web site). London, HMSO. World Wide Web resource.

URL: http://www.hmso.gov.uk/. Date reviewed 9th June 1998.

WWW site of the surviving post-privatisation HMSO, as distinct from The Stationery Office publisher of *The Stationery Office annual catalogue* (*q.v.*). Main reference value of site is the full text access provided to recent official publications backed by a Muscat search engine. This enables rapid retrieval of recent publications based on keywords, etc. At June 1998 full text was available for Acts of Parliament from January 1996 and Statutory Instruments and Measures of the General Synod of the Church of England from January 1997. *Class No:* 087.7(410)(003.41)

Bibliographies

[2429]

British government publications: an index to chairmen and authors. Richard, S., *comp.* London, Library Association, 1974-84. 4v. £55 per v.

V.I 1800-1899 (1982. ix,196p. ISBN: 0853657432); v.II. 1900-1940 (1974, reissued 1982. iii,174p. ISBN: 0853654271); v.III 1941-1978 (1982. vii,152p. ISBN: 085365753x); v.IV 1979-1982 (1984. vii,95p. ISBN: 0853657564).

Compiled for the Reference, Special and Information Section of the Library Association. V.I has variant subtitle *An Index to chairmen of committees and commissions of inquiry.* V.III cumulates earlier indexes for 1941-66 (2nd ed. 1973) and 1967-71 (1976) compiled by A.M. Morgan and

....*(contd.)*
L.R. Stephen.

Identifies government reports which are often known only by chairman's or author's name. Excludes annual and other periodic reports, accident inquiry reports and reports prepared by government officials in the course of their duties. Coverage in v.4 extended to non-HMSO publications. Arrangement is A-Z by latest form of chairman's name with chronological suborder. Cross-references from earlier forms of name. Entries give report title, date, responsible department and, if a Parliamentary paper, the Parliamentary reference. No subject or other indexes.
Class No: 087.7(410)(01)

[2430]

—Index to chairmen: reports of official committees. London, The Stationery Office, 1982-. Quarterly, with annual cumulation. £8.50. ISSN: 14628104.

Current title from 1997: previously *Committee reports published by HMSO: indexed by chairmen* (ISSN: 02672146).

Change of scope from title change, no longer indexing chairmen of Parliamentary select or standing committees. Entries A-Z by surname (or title in case of nobility), with full bibliographical detail, price and ISBN.
Class No: 087.7(410)(01)

[2431]

Catalogue of British official publications not published by The Stationery Office. Cambridge, Chadwyck-Healey, 1980-. Bi-monthly, with annual cumulation. £295. ISSN: 02605619.

Current title from 1996, previously *Catalogue of British official publications not published by HMSO.*

Covers publications of 'over 500 organisations financed or controlled completely or partially by the British government, which are not published by The Stationery Office. These organisations divide broadly into government departments, nationalized industries, research institutes, quangos and other official bodies'. Material covered includes periodicals and other serials, single sheet updates and appendices, leaflets and publicity material (if of value), maps, posters and audio-visual aids. Ephemeral material, circulars, internal memoranda and reports and material well catalogued elsewhere (*e.g.* Ordnance Survey maps, patents) excluded. Arranged A-Z by publishing body with a separate sequence for periodicals, entries give full bibliographical information, purchase detail and price. Indexed by personal name, corporate author and subjects in one sequence. Further microfiche identification number and source of publication indexes. 1996 cumulation (539p.) contains 10,662 entries. Records 1980 to date are also available as part of the database *UKOP: catalogue of United Kingdom official publications* (*q.v.*).

Various government departments publish their own list of publications on a regular basis. Examples include Department of the Environment, Transport and the Regions *Publications - monthly list* (ISSN: 1359885) and Department of Trade and Industry *DTI publications in print.*
Class No: 087.7(410)(01)

[2432]

—Keyword index to British official publications not published by HMSO. Cambridge, Chadwyck-Healey, 1983-. Bi-monthly.

Bi-monthly cumulating issues with final annual cumulations.

Indexes significant words from the titles of publications in the main *Catalogue* (above). *Class No:* 087.7(410)(01)

[2433]

A Numerical finding list of British Command Papers published 1833-1961/62. Di Roma, E. *and* Rosenthal, J.A., *comps.* New York, New York Public Library and Arno Press, 1967. 148p. ISBN: 0871045052.

Reprinted 1971.

Eliminates the need to consult annual numerical lists in order to trace a particular Command Paper.

1962/63-1976/77 covered by *British Command Papers: a numerical finding list,* McBride, E.A. comp. (Atlanta, Ga., Emroy General Libraries, 1982. 35p.). Both lists incorporate a few corrections, but make no systematic attempt to check for errors. *Class No:* 087.7(410)(01)

[2434]

STATIONERY OFFICE. (Great Britain). **The Stationery Office annual catalogue.** 1922-. London, The Stationery Office, 1923-. Annual. ISSN: 09518584.

Cumulates the *Daily list* and *The Stationery Office monthly catalogue* (below). Published as *Government publications* 1972-84 and *HMSO annual catalogue* 1985-95. Earlier titles: *Consolidated list of government publications* (1922-53); *Government publications catalogue* (1954-55); *Catalogue of government publications* (1956-71). Preceded by a *Quarterly list* 1897-1921.

Lists all of the 8-9,000 items published by The Stationery Office annually, except statutory instruments and statutory rules of Northern Ireland (separately covered, see below). In 3 main sections: Parliamentary publications, listed numerically by type of publication (House of Lords papers; House of Lords bills; House of Lords debates; House of Lords journals; House of Commons papers; House of Commons debates; House of Commons bulletins, etc.; House of Commons bills; Command Papers; Public General acts; Local acts; Measures of the General Synod); Classified section, including all non-Parliamentary publications and Parliamentary publications (excluding bills, acts, debates and measures), listed under the responsible department or body; Northern Ireland publications. Alphabetical (subject terms, authors, chairmen, editor) index; ISBN index. Preliminary section 'Where to consult Stationery Office publications', lists UK libraries receiving the full selected subscription service. Also available online for records 1976 to date through BLAISE, updated monthly. Records 1980 to date are searchable as part of the database *UKOP: catalogue of United Kingdom official publications* (*q.v.*).

The Stationery Office monthly catalogue (£19. ISSN: 02637197) is in much the same format as the annual. *Daily list* (£87 daily. ISSN 9051843x) forms the basis of the later cumulations. Recent issues are now Internet accessible at http://www.national-publishing.co.uk/d-listfr.html. Statutory instruments included in the daily list are cumulated in *List of statutory instruments together with the list of statutory rules of Northern Ireland for the month of ...* (£33. ISSN: 02672979), with annual cumulation. The full text of statutory instruments from 1980 or 1987 are also available online and on the CD-ROM *SI CD: statutory instruments database* (London, Context and The Stationery Office, 1995-. Quarterly. ISSN: 13511084).

Other supporting publications to the *Annual catalogue* include *The Stationery Office in print on microfiche* (Bi-monthly. £100. ISSN: 02671727) and *The Stationery Office agency catalogue* (Annual, formerly *International organizations catalogue*. £8.00. ISSN: 09557601) listing publications of European and international organizations for which The Stationery Office is the UK agent.
Class No: 087.7(410)(01)

[2435]

—Catalogues and indexes of British government publications, 1920-1970. Bishops Stortford, Chadwyck-Healey, 1974. 5v.

V.1 *Consolidated indexes to British government publications 1936-1970* (*c.*257p. ISBN: 085964006x); v.2 *Annual catalogues of British government publications 1920-1935* (*c.*900p. ISBN: 0859640078); v.3 *Annual catalogues of British government publications 1936-1950* (*c.*530p. ISBN: 0859640086); v.4 *Annual catalogues of British government publications 1951-1960* (*c.*570p. ISBN: 0859640094); v.5 *Annual catalogues of British government publications 1961-1970* (*c.*900p. ISBN: 0859640108).

A reduced size reprint of the annual catalogues (v.2-5) and the consolidated indexes (v.1). The reduction of 4p. of originals into 1p. necessitates use of a magnifying lens for reading purposes.

Catalogues for the period 1894-1919 are available as microfiche sets, publisher also Chadwyck-Healey: *Annual catalogues of British official and Parliamentary publications 1894-1910* (12 fiche. ISBN: 0859640167); *Annual catalogues of British official and Parliamentary publications 1911-1919* (8 fiche. ISBN: 0859640175).
Class No: 087.7(410)(01)

[2436]

—Cumulative index to the annual catalogues of Her Majesty's Stationery Office publications 1922-1972. Blackmore, R.M., *and others comps.* Washington, D.C. and Inverness, Carrollton Press, 1976. 2v. ISBN: 0840801408.

Merges 23 annual and quinquennial indexes into one A-Z author and subject sequence. Each entry has a unique numerical address, representing the year and page number in the annual catalogues. Has 'all the deficiencies of the original indexes and it lacks adequate cross-references' (*College and research libraries,* v.38(4), July 1977, p.323).

The *Cumulative index* is a companion to the microfilm ed. of HMSO publications of the same period: *The Controller's Library Collection of HMSO publications, 1922-1972* (Arlington, Va., United States Historical Documents Institute, 1976-78). *Class No:* 087.7(410)(01)

[2437]

—GREAT BRITAIN. Her Majesty's Stationery Office. Consolidated index to government publications. 1936/40-1976/80. London, HMSO, 1952-82. Quinquennial.

Largely superseded by the Carrollton Press cumulated index (above). *Class No:* 087.7(410)(01)

[2438]

—GREAT BRITAIN. Her Majesty's Stationery Office. The Sales catalogues of British government publications, 1836-1921. Dobbs Ferry, N.Y., Oceana, 1977. 4v. ISBN: 0379005506.

V.1 1836-1889; v.2 1890-1900; v.3 1901-1911; v.4 1912-1921.

Slightly reduced photographic reprint of the surviving lists. Includes a historical introduction.
Class No: 087.7(410)(01)

Periodicals

[2439]

BRITISH LIBRARY. Checklist of British official serial publications 1987. Finnie, H., *comp.* 12th ed. London, British Library, 1987. viii,74p. £10. ISBN: 0712300171.

1st ed. 1967, then approx. annual to 11th ed. 1980.

Lists A-Z by title 'serials issued by the United Kingdom central government departments and other agencies, and by

.... (contd.)
bodies established, controlled or financed by the UK government' (Introduction). Exclusions: Parliamentary papers; publications of nationalised industries, public corporations, bodies with regional responsibilities only, tourist boards and museums and galleries; local interest publications; offprints, forms and examination questions. Brief entries giving issuing body, frequency and availability data only. Index of issuing bodies.
Class No: 087.7(410)(051)

Ireland

[2440]
EIRE. Stationery Office. **Catalogue government publications.** [Foilseachain rialtais] Dublin, Stationery Office, 1922-. Quarterly.

Published annually until 1941. Consolidated listings issued on a 3,4 or 5 yearly basis until 1956-60.

Cumulated from listings in the weekly *Update of government publications*. Separate sections for acts, bills, parliamentary publications, departmental publications, statutory instruments, etc. Also lists EU, UN and other international body publications available through the Stationery Office. *Class No:* 087.7(415)

[2441]
MALTBY, A. *and* **MALTBY, J. Ireland in the nineteenth century:** a breviate of official publications. Oxford, Pergamon Press, 1979. xxix,269p. facsims. (*Guide to official publications, v.4.*) ISBN: 008023688x.

Lists more than 300 publications, with summaries of contents. 'Essentially a bibliographical tool for specialists ... Its authors have shown considerable skill and thoroughness' (*British book news,* April 1980, p.211).
Class No: 087.7(415)

[2442]
MALTBY, A. *and* **McKENNA, B. Irish official publications:** a guide to Republic of Ireland papers with a breviate of reports 1922-1972. Oxford, Pergamon Press, 1980. xi,377p., illus., facsims. $170. (*Guide to official publications, v.7.*) ISBN: 0080237037.

Guide (p.1-22). Breviate classes: 1. Government - 2. Economics, finance, labour - 3. Industry and technology - 4. Agriculture - 5. Energy resources - 6. Legal matters, police - 7. Transport and communications - 8. Education and culture - 9. Welfare, health and safety - 10. Housing and town planning. Includes appendix selectively listing annual and other reports to 1979. Name index; analytical subject index.
Class No: 087.7(415)

[2443]
—FINEGAN, R.B. *and* WILES, J.L. Irish government publications: a select list, 1972-1992. Blackrock, Irish Academic Press, 1995. 58p. Ir£17.50. ISBN: 0716525240.

Intended to continue Maltby and McKenna (above) and P. & G. Ford's *Select list of reports and inquiries of the Irish Dail and Senate 1927-1972* (1974).

Selective list by topic, *e.g.* Economic policy: development and trade. Confined to Stationery Office publications. Supplementary listing, 'Publications of the National Economic and Social Council'. Index. *Class No:* 087.7(415)

Northern Ireland

[2444]
Annual list of publications. Belfast, HMSO, 1948-87. Annual.

Preceded by *Consolidated list of the publications of the government of Northern Ireland, 1921-1937* (1938) and *Consolidated list of publications, 1938-1947* (1949).

Last published as an annual for 1986; monthly issues for 1987. The *Stationery Office annual catalogue* (*q.v.*) has a section 'Northern Ireland publications'.
Class No: 087.7(416)

Germany

[2445]
CHILDS, J.B. German Federal Republic official publications, 1949 to 1957, with inclusion of preceding zonal official publications: a survey. Washington D.C., Library of Congress, 1958. 2v. in 1.

Lists 7,500 publications under issuing body, with zonal publications in final section. Indicates Library of Congress holdings. No indexes.

Childs is also responsible for a similar list for East Germany, *German Democratic Republic official publications with those of the preceding zonal period, 1945-1958* (Washington D.C., Library of Congress, 1960-61. 4v.).
Class No: 087.7(430)

[2446]
Deutsche Bibliographie. Verzeichnis amtlicher Druckschriften: Veröffentlichungen der Behörden, Körperschaften, Anstalten und Stiftungen des öffentlichen Rechts sowie der wichtigsten halbamtlichen Institutionen in der Bundesrepublik Deutschland und West-Berlin. 1957/58-1981/82. Frankfurt am Main, Buchhändler-Vereinigung, 1963-84. Biennial. ISSN: 01701258.

In 4 main sections: federal publications; state (Länder) publications; cities (over 100,000 population); church bodies. Included publications of many semi-official bodies. Agency, place, title and catchword and personal name indexes. Final issue 1981/82 published in 3 pts: (Lfg.1. Bund, Baden-Württemberg-Bayern; Lfg.2. Berlin-Schleswig-Holstein, Kommunen, Kirchen; Lfg.3. Register).
Class No: 087.7(430)

[2447]
Monatliches Verzeichnis der reichsdeutschen amtlichen Druckschriften... Berlin, Reichs- und Staatsverlag GmbH., 1928-44. 17v.

The pre-war list of German official publications.
Class No: 087.7(430)

France

[2448]
Bibliographie nationale française. Publications officielles. Paris, Bibliothèque Nationale, 1975-. Bimonthly. FFr1170. ISSN: 11423277.

Continues *Bibliographie de la France. Supplément F: Publications officielles,* 1950-74. Title varies slightly; previously *Bibliographie de la France. Supplément II. Publications officielles.*

Lists about 2,750 publications annually. In 7 sections: Budgets, lois et traités - Assemblées constitutionnelles - Cours et jurisdictions - Administration centrale - Administration locale - Établissements publics et enterprises nationalisées - Organizations intergovernmentales. Entries

....(*contd.*)

include subject data. Title, collective author, personal name and subject index in each issue, cumulated annually.
Class No: 087.7(44)

[2449]

WESTFALL, G. French official publications. Oxford, Pergamon Press, 1980. xv,209p. facsims. (*Guide to official publications, v.6.*) ISBN: 0080218385.

13 sections: 1. Introduction - 2. Official publishing: policy and programs - 3. Bibliographical control ... 5. The *Journal officiel* ... 8. The President and the government - 9. Economic affairs: the economy and public finance ... 13. The judiciary. Subject and corporate author index; personal author index. Acronyms. Selected title/series titles index. Still the only substantial English-language guide.
Class No: 087.7(44)

Italy

[2450]

ALBERANI, V. Pubblicazioni ufficiali italiane. Roma, Associazione italiana biblioteche, 1995. 91p. L12,000. (*ET enciclopedia tascabile 7.*) ISBN: 8878120294.

Brief discursive guide to Italian official publishing. Arranged by publication type, *e.g.* Pubblicazioni legali delle regioni; useful bibliography (p.79-91).
Class No: 087.7(450)

[2451]

Pubblicazioni edite dallo Stato o col suo concorso... Roma, Libreria dallo Stato, 1924-74. Irregular.

Original v. covers 1861-1923 (668 cols.). Supplements: 1924-30 (1931); 1931-35 (1937); 1936-40 (1942); 1941-44 (1969); 1945-60 (1974).

'Publications edited by the state or with state support'. From 1941 publications listed under ministry then department or other body. *Class No:* 087.7(450)

Spain

[2452]

Publicaciones oficiales. Boletin de novedades. Madrid, Ministerio de la Presidencia Servica Central de Publicaciones, 1986-. 3 issues annually. ISSN: 02135760.

Lists new government publications by issuing agency, giving full bibliographical detail, price and ISBN. Title/personal author indexes in each issue. Cumulated vols. published at intervals *e.g. Catalogo general publicaciones oficiales 1992-1994* (Madrid, 1995. 376p. ISBN: 8474711142). *Class No:* 087.7(460)

[2453]

SPAIN. Ministerio de Información y Turismo, Secretariá General de Tecnica Servico de Documentacion. **Censo de las publicaciones oficiales españoles, 1939-1964.** Madrid, Ministerio de Información y Turismo, Secretariá General de Tecnica Servico de Documentacion, 1966. 4v. in 6.

V.1 *Ministerios de trabajo, información y turismo, vivienda*; v.2 *Ministerios de ejécrito, marina, aire*; v.3 *Ministerios de agricultura, comercio, hacienda, industria, obras públicas*; v.4 *Ministerios de educación nacional.*

Gives basic bibliographical detail only. Indexed by author, title and publishing body in each volume.
Class No: 087.7(460)

Finland

[2454]

Valtion virallisjulkaisut. [Government publications in Finland.] Helsinki, Eduskunnan kirjasto, 1961-. Annual. ISSN: 04305094.

Title also in Swedish *Statens officiella publikationer.*

Issued by the Parliamentary Library. Excludes maps and publications of state controlled companies, state supported organizations and educational institutions. 2,986 entries in the 1995 annual (1997. xiv,284p.). Arranged by issuing body A-Z with name, series and subject indexes.
Class No: 087.7(480)

Norway

[2455]

Bibliografi over Norges offentlige publikasjoner, 1956-90. Oslo, Universitetsbiblioteket i Oslo, 1957-91. Annual. ISSN: 04748050.

Based on legal deposit. From Årg.20 1975 in 2 pts., Del.1 covering books, serials, reports etc., Del.2 covering other material such as circulars and memoranda. Some government publications are recorded in the national bibliography *Norsk bogfortegnelse* (*q.v.*).
Class No: 087.7(481)

Sweden

[2456]

Statliga publikationer årsbibliografi. 1931/33-94. [Swedish government publications annual bibliography. 1931/33-95.] Stockholm, Riksdagsbiblioteket, 1934-. Annual. ISSN: 02838826.

Title varies: as ***Årsbibliografi över Sveriges offentliga publikationer*** until 1976, then as *Sveriges statliga publikationer* to 1985. Ceased publication with volume for 1994.

Based on accessions to the Parliament Library (Riksdagsbiblioteket). Arranged by issuing body A-Z; subject and personal name indexes. The 1994 v. (xxiv,313p.) contained 5,376 entries. Records from 1995 onwards available from the *Rixlex* database (http://www.riksdagen.se). *Class No:* 087.7(485)

Denmark

[2457]

Bibliografi over Danmarks Offentlige Publikationer, 1948-. København, Danmarks Institut for International Udveksling af Publikationer, 1949-. Annual. Kr325. ISSN: 00676543.

At head of title Impressa publica Regni Danici. Title varies; 1948-59 as ***Bibliografisk, Fortegnelse over statens Tryksager og statsunderstøttede Publikationer.***

Section for Folketinget (Parliament) then ministries A-Z. Serial and monograph publications listed separately within sections. Indexes of institutions and periodicals, subjects and authors. Prefatory matter in English. V.49 for 1996 records 3,537 publications. Also available as part of the Royal Library's *REX* database Internet accessible at http://www.kb.dk.natbib/. *Class No:* 087.7(489)

Netherlands

[2458]

Bibliografie van in Nederland verschenen officiële uitgaven bij rijksoverheid en provinciale besturen. s'Gravenhage, Koninklijke Bibliotek, 1929-88. Annual. ISSN: 01652958; 01652958.

Title varied. Main title *Nederlandsche overheidsuitgaven* with variant subtitles, 1929-52. As *Bibliografie van in Nederland verschenen officiële en semi-officiële uitgaven* 1953-76.

Included publications of government sponsored research agencies, educational institutions etc., as well as publications of provincial authorities.

Current Netherlands official publications are listed in *Nederlandse bibliografie B lijst* and subsequently in *Brinkman's cumulative catalogus* (*q.v.*).
Class No: 087.7(492)

Belgium

[2459]

WEERDT, D., *and others*. **Bibliographie rétrospective des publications officielles de la Belgique, 1794-1914.** Louvain, Nauwelaerts, 1963. 427p. (*Cahiers de la Centre Interuniversitaire d'Histoire Contemporaine, no.30.*)

3,471 numbered, unannotated entries, in three main periods (Période français - Période hollandaise - Période 1830-1914), with A-Z title sub-division. Bibliothèque Royale call numbers. Bibliography (p.424-6). Indexes: authors; places and subjects. *Class No:* 087.7(493)

Switzerland

[2460]

SCHWEIZERISCHEN LANDESBIBLIOTHEK. **Bibliographie der schweizerischen Amtsdruckschriften.** 1946-. [Bibliographie des publications officielles Suisses. 1946-.] Bern, Schweizerischen Landesbibliothek, 1947-. Biennial. ISSN: 05230330.

Based on Schweizerischen Landesbibliothek accessions. Covers federal, cantonal and major municipal monograph publications in separate sections, departmentally and geographically subdivided. Index. *Class No:* 087.7(494)

Hong Kong

[2461]

CHU, G.H.L. *and* KAN, L-B. **An Annotated guide to serial publications of the Hong Kong government.** Hong Kong, Chinese University of Hong Kong, 1979. viii,142p. (*University library bibliographical series, no.3.*)

Main entry listing of 302 titles issued during the period 1841-1978. Extensively cross-referenced; subject index.
Class No: 087.7(512.317)

Japan

[2462]

A Checklist of Japanese government publications. Oikawa, A., *and others eds.* Tokyo, Tsukuba Shuppankai, 1987. 2v. (*East Asia library series, 6.*.) ISBN: 4924753025.

Records the holdings of the East Asiatic Library, Univ. of California, Berkeley and the East Asian Collection, Hoover Institution, Stanford Univ. 8,908 entries; name, series, author and title keyword indexing in v.2.
Class No: 087.7(52)

[2463]

KUROKI, T. **An Introduction to Japanese government publications.** Oxford, Pergamon Press, 1981. x,204p. table. (*Guide to official publications, v.10.*) ISBN: 0080246796.

First published 1972 by Gyostel Ltd., in Japanese. Translated by M. Kishi, with an annotated bibliography by C. Hayeshi.

4 parts: 1. Structure of government publications - 2. Publication and distribution of government publications - 3. Retrieval - 4. Annotations of government publications (*e.g.* periodicals; White Papers; investigations, statistics, reports). 4 appendices; analytical index (p.201-4). Now very out of date, but remains the only substantial English-language guide available. *Class No:* 087.7(52)

[2464]

LIBRARY OF CONGRESS. **Japanese national government publications** in the Library of Congress: a bibliography. Ohta, T.Y., *comp.* Washington D.C., Government Printing Office, 1980. v,402p. ISBN: 0844403261.

3,376 entries mainly for material acquired since 1956. In 4 sections: 1. Legislative branch - 2. Executive branch - 3. Judicial branch - 4. Public corporations and research institutions. Romanized Japanese and English title indexes. Includes a large number of serial publications.
Class No: 087.7(52)

India

[2465]

Catalogue Government of India publications & periodicals. New Delhi, Department of Publication, 1959-. Irregular.

Title varies; issued on an irregular basis with various supplements.

Lists 'important' titles available for sale. 7,813 entries in 1993 issue. A typescript monthly, *List of Government of India publications and periodicals* (title varies), provides further coverage. *Class No:* 087.7(540)

[2466]

DATTA, R. **Union catalogue of the Central government of India publications** held by libraries in London, Oxford, and Cambridge. London, Mansell, for the University of Cambridge, Centre for South Asian Studies, 1970. [6]p.471 cols. ISBN: 0720101433.

Covers English language publications, mainly in the social sciences, published between independence and 1968. Holding libraries: British Library; Foreign and Commonwealth Office; Institute of Commonwealth Studies; India House; Indian Institute, Oxford; Royal Institute of International Affairs; India Office; British Library of Political and Economic Science; Royal Commonwealth Society; Centre for South Asian Studies, Cambridge University; School of Oriental and African Studies.
Class No: 087.7(540)

[2467]

Government books in print 1994. Khurana, J.S. *and* Khurana, M.S., *comps.* 2nd ed. Delhi, Bookwell Publications, 1994. lxxii,214p. Rs250 ISBN: 8185040044.

1st ed., *Government books in print 1986*, published 1987.

List of available publications issued 1980 to 31st January 1994. Arranged by 27 ministries, some divided by directorate, topic, etc. Entries give title, date, pagination and price only. Title index (p.i-lxxii). *Class No:* 087.7(540)

[2468]

MacDONALD, T. Union catalogue of the serial publications of the Indian government, 1858-1947, held by British libraries. Cambridge, Mansell, for the University of Cambridge, Centre for South Asian Studies, 1973. 154p. ISBN: 0720103630.

Limited to English language titles published by the Central or Provincial Governments and the Governments of the major Princely states. *Class No:* 087.7(540)

[2469]

SINGH, M. Government of India publications. New Delhi, Budda's Press, 1982. 176p.

Replaces the same author's *Government publications of India: a survey of their nature bibliographical control and distribution systems* (1967).

In 2pts: Pt.1 discusses the nature and scope of government publishing in India in 5 chapters; pt.2 is a 'Select bibliography' of 789 government publications arranged A-Z by issuing body. Name and subject index to the bibliography. *Class No:* 087.7(540)

[2470]

—SINGH, M. State government publications in India. Delhi, Academic Publications, 1985. 2v.(659p.). (*Academic series in library and information science, no.3.*)

Intended as a companion to *Government of India publications* (above). Brief introductory chapters followed by a 'Bibliography of State government publications' (p.43-648). Includes publications of the Union territories. Entries under state, A-Z. Personal name but no subject index. *Class No:* 087.7(540)

Sri Lanka

[2471]

MacDONALD, T. Union catalogue of government of Ceylon publications held by libraries in London, Oxford and Cambridge. London, Mansell, for the University of Cambridge, Centre for South Asian Studies, 1970. [6]p. 75 cols. ISBN: 0720101425.

Government of Ceylon publications since independence, as held in 18 libraries. *Class No:* 087.7(548.7)

Pakistan

[2472]

MORELAND, G.B. *and* **SIDDIQUI, A.H. Publications of the government of Pakistan 1947-1957.** Karachi, Institute of Public and Business Administration, University of Karachi, 1958. iv,187p.

Lists 1,578 publications by department. Subject index. Continued by:- *Class No:* 087.7(549)

[2473]

—SIDDIQUI, A.H. A Guide to Pakistan government publications 1958-1970. Karachi, National Book Centre of Pakistan, 1973. 276p.

Additional coverage to 1976 given in Siddiqui's *A guide to Pakistan government publications 1971-1976* (Karachi, National Book Council of Pakistan, 1978. 132p.).

3,331 publications listed for 1958-70, 1,730 for 1971-76. *Class No:* 087.7(549)

[2474]

SIDDIQUI, A.H. Pakistan government publications: their nature, content, production and distribution. Lahore, Vanguard Books, 1981. 97p.

Provides a general overview of Pakistan government publishing. Includes descriptions of the functions of various ministries and government departments. *Class No:* 087.7(549)

[2475]

Union catalogue of the government of Pakistan publications held by libraries in London, Oxford and Cambridge. Datta, R., *ed.* London, Mansell, 1967. (v),116 cols.

About 1,000 publications of the Pakistan government, 1947-66. Includes serials. 11 locations. *Class No:* 087.7(549)

Israel

[2476]

Israel government publications. Jerusalem, State Archives, 1956-. Annual.

Title also in Hebrew. Frequency varies, previously monthly. Preceded by *List of government publications* 1952-56. Cumulation, *Israel government publications 1948-64* (Jerusalem, Government Printer, 1972).

Separate lists of English and Hebrew publications, both arranged under issuing body with title and general indexes. Hebrew section, by far the longest, also includes a few Arabic language items. Additional coverage of publications of local authorites, state corporations and the Army on a selective basis. *Class No:* 087.7(569.4)

Africa

[2477]

BOSTON UNIVERSITY. Libraries. **Catalog of African government documents.** 3rd ed. Boston, Mass., G.K. Hall, 1976. vi,679p. ISBN: 0816100365.

1st and 2nd eds. as *Catalog of African government documents and African area index,* 1960 and 1964.

Reproduces catalog cards for over 13,000 monograph and serial titles held by one of the strongest US collections of African government publications. Arranged by modified Library of Congress classification with alphabetical country index. *Class No:* 087.7(6)

[2478]

LIBRARY OF CONGRESS. General Reference and Bibliography Division. Reference Department. **Portuguese Africa: a guide to official publications.**
Gibson, M.J., *comp.* Washington D.C., Library of Congress, 1967. xv,217p.

2,831 numbered items covering Angola, Cape Verde Islands, Mozambique, Portuguese Guinea, São Tomé e Principe and Portuguese publications relating to the colonies. 33 library locations. Index. *Class No:* 087.7(6)

[2479]

—LIBRARY OF CONGRESS. General Reference and Bibliography Division. Reference Department. Spanish-speaking Africa: a guide to official publications.
Rishworth, S.K., *comp.* Washington D.C., Library of Congress, 1973. xiii,66p.

640 entries. Indexed. *Class No:* 087.7(6)

[2480]

WESTFALL, G. French colonial Africa: a guide to official publications. London, Zell, 1992. x,226p. £40;$85. ISBN: 1873836600.

In 5 sections: I. Guides and bibliographies - II. French colonial archives - III. Publications of the central administration - IV. Semi-official publications - V. Publications of colonial governments (including bibliography of major publications by colony p.113-98). Indexed.

Consolidates, but does not entirely replace, two Library of Congress guides to the government publications of the former French Africa: *French-speaking west Africa: a guide to official publications*, Witherell, J.W. *comp.* (Washington, D.C., 1967. xii,201p.); *French-speaking central Africa: a guide to official publications*, Witherell, J.W. *comp.* (Washington, D.C., 1973. xiv,314p. ISBN: 0844400335).
Class No: 087.7(6)

Sierra Leone

[2481]

LIBRARY OF CONGRESS. General Reference and Bibliography Division. Reference Department. **Official publications of Sierra Leone and Gambia.**
Walker, A.A., *comp.* Washington D.C., Library of Congress, 1963. xii,92p.

Principal contents: Publications of the Sierra Leone Company - Publications of Sierra Leone (p.3-49) - British publications on Sierra Leone - Publications of the Gambia (p.62-79) - British publications on the Gambia. 720 numbered items. Author and subject index. Locations in the Library of Congress and 19 other US libraries.
Class No: 087.7(664)

Ghana

[2482]

LIBRARY OF CONGRESS. General Reference and Bibliography Division. Reference Department. **Ghana: a guide to official publications, 1872-1968.** Witherell, J.W. *and* Lockwood, S.B., *comps.* Washington D.C., Library of Congress, 1969. xi,110p.

1,283 entries covering documents issued by the Gold Coast (1872-1957) and Ghana (1957-68), British official publications relating to the Gold Coast, and British, League of Nations and United Nations materials on British Togoland. Author and subject index. *Class No:* 087.7(667)

Nigeria

[2483]

LIBRARY OF CONGRESS. General Reference and Bibliography Division. Reference Department. **Nigeria: a guide to official publications.** Lockwood, S.B., *comp.* Washington D.C., Library of Congress, 1966. xii,166p.

Revision of *Nigerian official publications 1869-1959: a guide,* comp. by H.F. Conover, 1959.

4 main sections: Nigeria, 1861-1914; Nigeria, 1914-1965, (subdivided: Federal government; Eastern Nigeria; Mid-West Nigeria; Northern Nigeria; Western Nigeria; Southern Cameroons); British publications relating to Nigeria and the British Cameroons; League of Nations and United Nations publications relating to the British Cameroons. 2,451 numbered entries, primarily for post-1959 publications. Locations in 34 US libraries. Index (p.151-66). Continued by:- *Class No:* 087.7(669)

[2484]

—Nigerian government publications, 1966-1973: a bibliography. Stanley, J., *comp.* Ile-Ife, Univ. of Ife Press, 1975. x,193p.

2,660 numbered items in sections for Nigeria (nos.1-1100) and the 14 states. Name and subject indexes.

Further limited coverage provided by F. Songonuga *comp. A Selective bibliography of Nigerian government publications, 1973-1977* (in *A Current bibliography on African affairs,* v.11(4), 1978-79, p.361-77), listing 256 items. *Class No:* 087.7(669)

Africa—East & Equatorial

[2485]

LIBRARY OF CONGRESS. General Reference and Bibliography Division. Reader Services Department. **East African community: subject guide to official publications.**
Howell, J.B., *comp.* Washington, D.C., Library of Congress, 1976. xvi,272p. ISBN: 0844402087.

Covers 'official publications of the East African Community and its predecessors for the period 1926 to 1974, and of the East African region (including Kenya, Tanzania and Uganda) for the period 1859 to 1974 issued by Great Britain or one of the three partner states' (Preface). 1,812 entries annotated where necessary. Sources include not only major US libraries but also the Foreign and Commonwealth Office Library and the Royal Commonwealth Society Library. Arranged in 23 subject sections; index (p.219-72). *Class No:* 087.7(67)

[2486]

LIBRARY OF CONGRESS. General Reference and Bibliography Division. Reference Department. **Official publications of British East Africa.** Connover, H.F. *and* Walker, A.A., *comps.* Washington D.C., Library of Congress, 1960-63. 4v.

Pt.1 *The East African High Commission and other regional documents;* pt.2 *Tanganyika*; pt.3 *Kenya and Zanzibar;* pt.4 *Uganda.*

3,063 numbered items in all. Name and subject indexes. Partly superseded by later publications, *e.g., Uganda: a subject guide to official publications* (1977) (below).
Class No: 087.7(67)

Uganda

[2487]

LIBRARY OF CONGRESS. General Reference and Bibliography Division. Reader Services Department.
Uganda: subject guide to official publications.
Gray, B.A., *comp.* Washington, D.C., Library of Congress, 1977. xvi,271p. ISBN: 0844402451.

Updates *Official publications of British East Africa. Pt.4 Uganda* (above).

Lists 2,442 items published 1893-1974. 'Every attempt has been made to include documents issued by Uganda, Great Britain and the East African Common Services Organization and its predecessors before October 1962, and by Uganda, the East African Common Services Organization and the East African Community after independence' (Preface p.vii). Comprehensively indexed (p.225-70).
Class No: 087.7(676.1)

Kenya

[2488]

KENYA. National Archives. **A Guide to government monographs, reports and research works.** Nairobi, National Archives, 1984. i,157p.

In addition to central government publications includes some items issued by provincial and district authorities. Also covers theses and dissertations. *Class No:* 087.7(676.2)

[2489]

LIBRARY OF CONGRESS. General Reference and Bibliography Division. Reader Services Department. **Kenya: subject guide to official publications.** Howell, J.B., *comp.* Washington D.C., Library of Congress, 1978. xix,423p. ISBN: 0844402621.

Updates *Official publications of British East Africa. Pt.3 Kenya and Zanzibar* (above).

3,048 entries for publications issued 1886-1975. Covers Republic of Kenya, Kenya Colony and Protectorate, British publications dealing with Kenya and East African Community etc. as in *Uganda: subject guide to official publications* (above). Indexed. *Class No:* 087.7(676.2)

Africa—Southern

[2490]

LIBRARY OF CONGRESS. General Reference and Bibliography Division. Reference Department. **Botswana, Lesotho and Swaziland: a guide to official publications** 1868-1968. Balima, M.G., *comps.* Washington D.C., Library of Congress, 1971. xvi,84p. ISBN: 0844400033.

791 entries, some briefly annotated. Sections: Basutoland, Lesotho; Bechuanaland, Botswana; Swaziland; High Commission Territories; Cape of Good Hope; Great Britain; Republic of South Africa and Transvaal Colony. Explanatory notes precede some sections. Indexed. *Class No:* 087.7(68)

South Africa

[2491]

KOTZÉ, D.A. Bibliography of official publications of the black South African homelands. 2nd rev. ed. Pretoria, University of South Africa, 1983. xxvi,119p. map. ISBN: 0869812866.

1st ed. 1979.

'This bibliography embraces official publications of self-governing Black homelands in South Africa and of territorial assemblies prior to their attainment of self-government' (Introduction p.xi). Gives coverage to the end of 1981. In 10 sections Bophuthatswana-Venda. All entries in English irrespective of language of publication. Notes University of South Africa holdings. *Class No:* 087.7(680)

Swaziland

[2492]

STATE LIBRARY. (South Africa). **Swaziland official publications** 1880-1972: a bibliography of the original and microfiche edition. Pretoria, State Library, 1975. xi,190p. map. ISBN: 0798900318.

A classed bibliography of 824 entries. Includes British official publications dealing with Swaziland, publications of the High Commissioner for Basutoland, the Bechuanaland Protectorate and Swaziland containing material on Swaziland and some semi-official publications. Indexed.
Class No: 087.7(683.4)

Zimbabwe

[2493]

LIBRARY OF CONGRESS. General Reference and Bibliography Division. Reference Department. **The Rhodesias and Nyasaland: a guide to official publications.** Walker, A.A., *comp.* Washington D.C., Library of Congress, 1965. xv,285p.

Contents: Publications of the Central African interterritorial agencies prior to federation - Publications of the Federation of Rhodesia and Nyasaland - Publications of Northern Rhodesia - Publications of Southern Rhodesia - Publications of Nyasaland - British publications relating to the central African territories - Publications of the British South Africa Company. 1,889 numbered items. Index (p.259-85). *Class No:* 087.7(689.1)

Madagascar

[2494]

LIBRARY OF CONGRESS. General Reference and Bibliography Division. Reference Department. **Madagascar and adjacent islands: a guide to official publications.** Witherell, J.W., *comp.* Washington, D.C., Library of Congress, 1965. xiii,58p.

927 numbered items. Covers Madagascar, Comoro Islands, Réunion, Mauritius, Seychelles. Author and subject index. *Class No:* 087.7(691)

Canada

[2495]

BISHOP, O.B. Canadian official publications. Oxford, Pergamon Press, 1981. x,297p. (*Guides to official publications, v.9.*) ISBN: 0080246974.

18 chapters: 1. Canadian parliamentary government. ... 3. Official publications: classification and indexes. ... 5. House of Commons and Senate papers. ... 8. Acts. ... 12. Departmental commissions and committees. ... 15. Reference books (p.201-16; titles, A-Z). ... 18. Obtaining Canadian government publications. Extensive index (p.265-97). Dated, but remains a standard source.
Class No: 087.7(71)

[2496]

Government of Canada publications: quarterly catalogue. [Publications du government du Canada: catalogue trimestriel.] Ottawa, Canada Communications Group Publishing, 1953-. Quarterly. Can$76. ISSN: 07090412.

Title and publisher vary. As *Canadian government publications catalogue* 1953-69. Current title and publisher from 1979. Coverage of Canadian official publications prior to 1953 provided by *Catalogue of official publications of the Parliament and government of Canada,* 1928-48.

Contains publications listed in *Weekly checklist of Canadian government publications* (1978-. ISSN: 07064659. Recent issues Internet accessible at http://dsp-psd.pwgsc.gc.ca/dsp-psd/Checklist/lists-e.html). Separate English and French sections in 2 pts: 1. Parliamentary publications (subdivided Statutes - Senate - House of Commons, etc.); 2. Departmental publications (A-Z by department). Bilingual author, title and subject index cumulated annually. Also available in microfiche from Micromedia. *Class No:* 087.7(71)

[2497]

Microlog: Canadian research index. Toronto, IHS/ Micromedia, 1979-. Monthly, with annual cumulation. ISSN: 1196099x.

Title format varies. Supersedes *Publicat, Pro File* and *Urban Canada.*

Index to Canadian government and research literature produced by federal, provincial and municipal bodies, and institutions receiving research grants. About 8,000 items included annually. From 1998 printed monthly has main listing by title giving full bibliographical detail. Abstracts, previously provided, now only available with electronic versions. Corporate name, personal name, subject and series indexes. Online versions from CAN/OLE and Info Globe. Also available on CD-ROM and as an ERL compliant database using SilverPlatter (SPIRS) software (records 1982 to date, file updated monthly or quarterly).
Class No: 087.7(71)

[2498]

PROSS, C.A. A Guide to the identification and acquisition of Canadian government publications: provinces and territories. 2nd ed. Halifax, Nova Scotia, Dalhousie University, 1983. 103p. £10;Can$11.50. (*Dalhousie University Libraries/Dalhousie University School of Library Service, occasional paper, 16.*) ISBN: 0770301657.

1st ed. 1977.

Discusses the major catalogues, bibliographies, guides etc. in 6 chapters. Bibliographical references in text; chapter 6 comprises series of tables indicating holdings of major provincial publications in selected Canadian libraries.
Class No: 087.7(71)

Mexico

[2499]

KER, A.M. Mexican government publications: a guide to the more important publications of the national government of Mexico, 1821-1936. Washington D.C., US Government Printing Office, 1940. xxi,333p.

Reprinted Gordon Press, 1976. ($59.95. ISBN: 0849006155).

Based on the collections of the Library of Congress. Arranged by issuing body; title and general index. Continued by:- *Class No:* 087.7(72)

[2500]

—FERNÁNDEZ DE ZAMORA, R.M. Las Publicaciones oficiales de México: guia de publicaciones periódicas y seriadas, 1937-1970. México, Universidad Nacional Autónoma de México, Instituto de Investigaciones Sociales, 1977. 238p. (*Universidad Nacional Autónoma de México. Instituto de Investigaciones Bibliográficas. Ser. guias, 5.*)

First published 1967 covering 1937-67, author as R.M. Fernández Esquivel.

Introductory chapters followed by full listings of serial publications under issuing bodies. Title and subject index.
Class No: 087.7(72)

Latin America

[2501]

Guide to the official publications of the other American republics. Childs, J.B., *ed.* Washington D.C., Library of Congress, 1945-49. 19v.

Reprinted New York, Johnson Reprint Corp., 1965 in 2v. (v.1: Argentina-Ecuador; v.2: El Salvador-Venezuela).

....(contd.)

Bibliographical guide with extensive notes on the development of government publishing. Each country volume separately indexed. *Class No:* 087.7(729.99)

[2502]

Latin American serial documents: a holdings list. Mesa, R.Q., *comp.* Ann Arbor, University Microfilms International, 1968-77. 12v.

V.1, Colombia; v.2, Brazil; v.3, Cuba; v.4, Mexico; v.5, Argentina; v.6, Bolivia; v.7, Chile; v.8, Ecuador; v.9, Paraguay; v.10, Peru; v.11, Uruguay; v.12, Venezuela. V.5-6 originally published by Bowker; all volumes currently available from UMI, separately priced.

Each volume indicates holdings in US and Canadian libraries for as many serial documents as could be identified from the time of the country's formation or independence. Coverage is most detailed for Argentina, Mexico and Chile. Brazil is comparatively neglected, but complementary coverage is provided in Lombardi (*q.v.*).
Class No: 087.7(729.99)

USA

[2503]

Informing the nation: a handbook of government information for librarians. O'Hara, F. J., *ed.* New York, Greenwood, 1990. xvii,560p. facsims. £58.50;$69.50. ISBN: 0313272670.

Reprints selected official manuals, guides, etc. to organizations that produce government information (*e.g. Information about the National Archives for prospective researchers*). In 5 sections (II. Depository libraries and the Superintendent of Documents Classification Scheme - III. Congress, Laws and Regulations ... V. United Nations), each with introductory matter and a list of further reading. Indexed. *Class No:* 087.7(73)

[2504]

LIBRARY OF CONGRESS. Serial and Government Publications Division. **Popular names of US government reports:** a catalog. Bernier, B.A. *and* Wood, K.A., *comps.* 4th ed. Washington D.C., Library of Congress, 1984. x,272p. ISBN: 0844401749.

1st ed. 1966; 3rd ed. 1976.

Lists 1,555 US government reports under popular name as referred to in the media etc. Full Library of Congress cataloguing record reproduced for each report. Separate list of 100 unidentified reports (p.245-49). Corporate author and subject indexes. *Class No:* 087.7(73)

[2505]

MOREHEAD, J. Introduction to United States government information sources. 5th ed. Englewood, Co., Libraries Unlimited, 1996. xxi,333p. illus. tables. £52.95;$40. (*Library science text series.*) ISBN: 1563084856.

First published 1975; 4th ed. 1992. Eds. 1-3 as *Introduction to United States public documents.*

Narrative 'account of the general and specialized sources, in print and nonprint formats, that comprise the bibliographic and textual structure of federal government information' (Preface p.xix). 11 chaps. (1. Public access in the electronic age ... 4. General catalogs, indexes, bibliographies, and selected reference sources ... 6. The Presidency ... 9. Statistical sources ... 11. Geographic information sources), each subdivided by topic, department, etc. Personal name, title/series and subject indexes. '(P)rovides a useful first

....*(contd.)*
source for descriptions of data sources to try' (*Journal of government information*, v.24(2), May/June 1997, p.224).
Class No: 087.7(73)

[2506]
ROSS, J.M. How to use the major indexes to US government publications. Chicago, American Library Association, 1989. iii,37p. illus. $5. ISBN: 0838905099.

Deals with subject searching of *American statistics index,* the 3v. CIS annuals, *Index to US government periodicals* (*q.v.,*) *Congressional record* and *Monthly catalogue* (*q.v.*). Includes model searches and sample pages. Can be 'easily understood by a person with no US government documents experience' (*Reference books bulletin* in *Booklist,* v.86(8), 15 December 1989, p.856). *Class No:* 087.7(73)

[2507]
SEARS, J.L. *and* **MOODY, M.K. Using government information sources:** print and electronic. Phoenix, Oryx Press, 1994. 539p. illus., maps. £124;$115. ISBN: 0897746708.

First published in 2 v. 1985-86 as *Using government publications* (v.1 *Searching by subject and agencies* (viii,216p.); v.2 *Finding statistics and using special techniques* (viii,231p.)).

A guide to tracing information on a wide range of topics. V.1 of the first ed. contains 20 chapters on subject based searches (*e.g.* foreign policy, tax information), with 4 further chapters on agency searching (*e.g.* administrative decisions). V.2 has 14 chapters on statistical searching (*e.g.* economic indicators, employment) and 9 on special techniques (*e.g.* National Archives, treaties). Each chapter designed to be self-sufficient following a set format of suggested search strategy, checklist of sources and narrative description. '(O)ne of the best of the several guides that have been published in recent years' (*American reference books annual,* v.26, 1995, p.43). *Class No:* 087.7(73)

Databases

[2508]
The Federal data base finder: a directory of free & fee-based databases & files available from the federal government. Lesko, M. *and* Murray, T., *eds.* 4th ed. Kensington, Md., Information USA, 1995. vi,1253p. £96;$125. ISBN: 0787603619.

First published 1984; 3rd ed. 1990.

Covers databases available online, on CD-ROM, diskette, tape, etc. Arranged by department or agency, entries with descriptive annotations of 50-250 words. Indexed.
Class No: 087.7(73)(003.4)

CD-ROM

[2509]
Government CD-ROMs: a practical guide to searching electronic databases. Maxymuk, J., *ed.* Westport, Conn., Mecklermedia, 11994. xix,324p. illus., diags., tables. £31.50. (*Supplement to computers in libraries, 71.*) ISBN: 0887368875.

Attempts to classify and describe government CD-ROMs with the emphasis on practical matters such as installation, search procedures, etc. 12 chapters, most devoted to specific titles *e.g.* 5. The 1987 economic census on CD-ROM. Useful apppendix 'An Annotated list of GPO CD-ROMs' (p.279-314). Index. *Class No:* 087.7(73)(003.40)

Internet

[2510]
NOTESS, G.R. Government information on the Internet. Lanham, Md., Bernan Press, 1997. xxv,778p. illus. $45. ISBN: 0890590818.

Also available in pbck. ($24. ISBN: 0890590419).

Probably the best of a number of recent guides to US government information available through the Internet. Over 1,200 distinct resources recorded, each entry including URL, sponsoring agency, descriptive summary and subject headings. Indexed. *Class No:* 087.7(73)(003.41)

Bibliographies of Bibliographies

[2511]
Cumulative subject guide to US government bibliographies, 1924-1973. Kanely, E.A., *comp.* Washington D.C., Carrollton Press, 1976. 7v. ISBN: 0840801505, v.1.

Over 40,000 entries by subject A-Z, taken from 50 years of the *Monthly catalog* (*q.v.*). Includes bibliographies appended to other publications. Entries keyed to the same publisher's microfiche full-text collection *US government bibliography masterfile.* The final v. is an index listing all entries in Superintendent of Documents classified order.
Class No: 087.7(73)(009)

[2512]
DOW, S.L. State document checklists: a historical bibliography. Buffalo, N.Y., William S. Hein, 1990. 224p. $40. ISBN: 0899417396.

Lists bibliographies, checklists, etc. by state. Includes both regularly published and single issue titles; checklists published by individual agencies excluded. Lengthy introductory survey (p.11-50); 'Sources consulted' (p.201-10). Title index. *Class No:* 087.7(73)(009)

[2513]
ZINK, S.D. United States government publications catalogs. 2nd ed. Washington D.C., Special Libraries Association, 1988. 292p. ISBN: 087111335x.

Available from Books On Demand ($89. ISBN: 0783786794). First published 1982.

Bibliography of catalogues, bibliographies and publication lists produced by US government agencies. 372 numbered and annotated entries in SuDoc classified order. Title and subject indexes. Catalogues of retrospective materials excluded. *Class No:* 087.7(73)(009)

Bibliographies

[2514]
Bibliographic guide to government publications - US. 1975-. New York, G.K. Hall, 1976-. Annual. $620. ISSN: 03602796.

Issued in 2 v. Continues in part the New York Public Library's *Catalog of government publications* and forms a companion volume to *Bibliographic guide to government publications - foreign* (*qq.v.*).

Lists publications catalogued during the past year by the Library of Congress. In addition to Federal government material includes state, municipal and local publications. Full bibliographical records in dictionary format with Library of Congress subject headings. *Class No:* 087.7(73)(01)

[2515]

Government reference books: a biennial guide to US government publications. 1968/69-. Englewood, Co., Libraries Unlimited, 1970-. Biennial. $67.50. ISSN: 00725188.

An 'annotated guide to atlases, bibliographies, catalogs, compendia, dictionaries, directories, guides, handbooks, indexes and other reference monographs issued by agencies of the United States government during the most recent two year period' (Introduction 12th ed. p.xi). In 4 main sections: 1. General library reference; 2. Social sciences; 3. Science and technology; 4. Arts and humanities. Personal author, title and subject index. Most serial titles excluded from 9th ed., covered in *Government reference serials* (*q.v.*). Recent publication on triennial basis, 1994/96 (ISBN: 1563084333) announced late 1997. *Class No:* 087.7(73)(01)

[2516]

—HARDY, G.J *and* ROBINSON, J.S. Subject guide to U.S. government reference sources. 2nd ed. Englewood, Co., Libraries Unlimited, 1996. xxi,358p. £43.50;$45. ISBN: 156308189x.

First published under current title 1985. Earlier ed. by S. Wynkoop 1972 as *Subject guide to government reference books*.

1,302 numbered entries (894 new to this ed.) in 4 main sections (each subdivided): General reference sources - Social sciences - Science and technology - Humanities. 'Emphasis is on depository titles at least 80 pages long' (*Introduction*, p.xv), CD-ROMs and Internet sites also covered. Annotated entries include SuDoc, LC card and OCLC numbers. Index (p.301-358).
Class No: 087.7(73)(01)

[2517]

—State blue books, legislative manuals and reference publications: a selective bibliography. Hellebust, L., *ed.* Topeka, Ka., Government Research Service, 1990. ii,142p. ISBN: 0961522771.

Annotated entries for currently published titles. State-by-state arrangement. Continued on an annual basis by *State reference publications: a bibliographic guide to state blue books, legislative manuals and other general reference sources* (Government Research Service, 1991-. ISSN: 10570586). *Class No:* 087.7(73)(01)

[2518]

Guide to U.S. government publications. Andriot, D., *ed.* Manassas, Va., Documents Index, 1973-. Annual (previously irregular). $325. ISSN: 00923168.

Format varies: 1973-76 looseleaf with updates; 1976-80 hardback in 4v., revised every 6 months; 1980-85 in 2v., 1 covering existing agencies (annual), the other abolished agencies (irregular). From 1986 published in 1v.

Intended as 'a comprehensive, yet concise annotated guide to important series, periodicals, and reference tools published by U.S. government agencies'. 1997 ed. (xxix,1670p.) has main listing by SuDoc classification (p.1-893), some entries with brief annotations. Further sections: Agency class chronology (p.897-977), giving complete history of current class. no. assignments; Agency index (p.979-1018); Title index (p.1019-170); Keyword in title index (p.1173-670). '(H)ard to imagine anyone working in government documents without this guide' (*American reference books annual*, v.25, 1994, p.23).
Class No: 087.7(73)(01)

[2519]

HOFFMANN, F.W. *and* **WOOD, R.J. Guide to popular US government publications.** 4th ed. Englewood, Co., Libraries Unlimited, 1997. xxx,285p. £33.50;$39.95. ISBN: 1563084627.

Previous eds. under this title 1986, 1990 and 1993. Earlier coverage in W.L. Newsome's *New guide to popular government publications* ... (1978) and L.C. Pohle's *Guide to popular government publications* ... (1972).

Mainly intended for the general public and students. This ed. focusses on publications issued 1992 to 1996, but includes others which remain topical or are part of a long-standing series. 1,400 entries with short annotations under *c.*50 subject headings. Title and subject indexes.
Class No: 087.7(73)(01)

[2520]

Monthly catalog of United States government publications. Washington, D.C., U.S. Government Printing Office, 1895-. Monthly. ISSN: 03626830.

Title varies: originally *Catalogue of United States public documents*, then *Monthly catalog; United States public documents* and *United States government publications: monthly catalog;* current title since 1950.

Arranged by Superintendent of Documents classification (department or bureau before 1976). Until 1996 printed issues contained full Anglo-American cataloguing for each entry with comprehensive indexing by author, title, subject (Library of Congress headings), series/report no., contract no., stock no. and title keyword. From 1996 only short entries and a title keyword index are provided. Electronic versions continue to offer full data.

Records 1976 to date are searchable through a variety of online vendors including Dialog (File 166) and OCLC. A number of CD-ROM products covering the same time span are also available (*e.g., Government publications index* (Information Access. £1,000); *GPO* (SilverPlatter. £502)). Records 1994 to date are freely accessible through the Internet at http://www.access.gpo.gov/su-docs/dpos/adpos400.html. The daily updated file provides access to the most recent publications, but effective retrieval is inhibited by limited search facilities.

Various complementary publications are issued notably *Monthly catalog of United States government publications. Periodicals supplement* (Annual. $29. ISSN: 8755528x).

A number of cumulated indexes have been published on a commercial basis (*e.g. Monthly catalog of United States government publications. Cumulative index* (Phoenix, Oryx Press. 1976-80 6v. 1981-85 7v. ISBN: 0897743806)).
Class No: 087.7(73)(01)

[2521]

—Cumulative subject index to the 'Monthly catalog of United States government publications': 1900-1971. Buchanan, W.W. *and* Kanely, E.M., *comps.* Washington, D.C., Carrollton Press, 1973-75. 15v. ISBN: 0840800010, v.1.

Provides cumulative subject indexing to over 800,000 publications. Coverage extended back to 1895 by *Cumulative subject index to the Monthly catalog of United States government publications, 1895-1899* (Washington, Carrollton Press, 1977. 2v.). *Class No:* 087.7(73)(01)

[2522]

—GPO sales publications reference file. Washington, D.C., U.S. Government Printing Office, 1978-. Microfiche. Bimonthly, with updates in alternate months. $145.

Catalogue of all publications and subscription services currently available. Also freely available through the Internet (http://www.access.gpo.gov./su-docs/sale/prf/prf.html) as *GPO sales product catalog*. Discontinuation of the microfiche service is planned. *Class No:* 087.7(73)(01)

[2523]

—HICKCOX, J.H. United States government publications: a monthly catalogue 1885-1894... Arlington, Va., Carrollton Press, 1978. 10v. in 6.

Reprint of the 10v. catalogue originally privately compiled by Hickcox. Superintendent of Documents classification numbers added. *Class No:* 087.7(73)(01)

[2524]

Monthly checklist of state publications. Washington, D.C., Library of Congress, 1910-. Monthly. $32. ISSN: 00270288.

Record of state documents received by the Library of Congress. Arranged A-Z by state with sub-arrangement of issuing agencies. Subject index in each issue. Excludes ephemeral items. *Class No:* 087.7(73)(01)

[2525]

PEARSON, J.A. *and* **TULL, P. U.S. government directories,** 1982-1995. Englewood, Co., Libraries Unlimited, 1998. xvii,159p. £43.50;$45. ISBN: 156308290x.

Covers directories (and directory type publications) of areas and places, organizations, businesses, individuals, laws, activities, etc. Includes directories in electronic formats. Preceded by:-

Gray, C.S. *U.S. government directories 1970-1981* (Libraries Unlimited, 1984. xi,260p. ISBN: 0872874141). A similar source is Larson, D.R. *Guide to U.S. government directories, 1970-1980* (Phoenix, Oryx Press, 1981. xvi,191p. ISBN: 0912700637), with supplementary *Guide to U.S. government directories volume 2* (1985. 214p. ISBN: 0897741625). *Class No:* 087.7(73)(01)

[2526]

United States government publications: an author index representing pre-1956 holdings of American libraries reported to the 'National Union Catalog' of the Library of Congress. London, Mansell, 1980. 16v. ISBN: 0720115094.

A reprint of v.609-24 of the *National union catalog pre-1956 imprints* (*q.v.*), containing the author heading 'United States' and its subdivisions. *Class No:* 087.7(73)(01)

[2527]

UNITED STATES. Superintendent of Documents. **Catalog of the public documents of Congress** and of all departments of the government of the United States for the period March 4, 1893 - December 31, 1940. Washington D.C., Government Printing Office, 1896-1945. 25v.

Known as the 'Document catalog'. Dictionary arrangement. *Class No:* 087.7(73)(01)

[2528]

UNITED STATES. Superintendent of Documents. **Checklist of United States public documents, 1789-1909.** 3rd ed. Washington D.C., Government Printing Office, 1911. 1709p.

Reprinted New York, Kraus Reprint, 1962.
Class No: 087.7(73)(01)

[2529]

WILLIAMS, W.J. Subject guide to major United States government publications. 2nd ed. Chicago, American Library Association, 1987. xi,257p. ISBN: 0838904750.

1st ed. by E. Jackson, 1968. Earlier work with same title by Melinat & Hirsberg, 1947.

Covers from the inception of federal government to 1986. 60% new material in this ed., titles selected 'with an eye to their enduring significance' (p.ix). Briefly annotated entries arranged by modified Library of Congress subject headings. 2 valuable appendices: I. Guides, catalogs and indexes and directories; II. Subject bibliographies. Title index. '(S)election of titles is excellent' (*American reference books annual*, 1988, p.32). *Class No:* 087.7(73)(01)

Periodicals

[2530]

Government reference serials. Schwarzkopf, L.C., *comp.* Englewood, Co., Libraries Unlimited, 1988. 344p. £46.50;$48. ISBN: 0872874516.

Covers titles distributed through GPO's depository library programme issued biennially or more frequently. 583 annotated entries following organizational pattern of *Government reference books* (*q.v.*). Annotations include full publishing history of title. *Class No:* 087.7(73)(051)

[2531]

U.S. government periodicals index. 1993-. Bethesda, Md., Congressional Information Service, 1994-. Quarterly, with annual cumulation $795. ISSN: 10763163.

Revives *Index to U.S. government periodicals* (below).

Subject and name index to around 180 titles, most not indexed elsewhere. '(A)imed at the taxpaying citizen who might have a nonprofessional's interest in, for example, the space program or the activities of the State Department' (*Journal of government information*, v.22(2), March/April 1995, p.181). 2,500 entries quarterly, in-house newsletters and serial monographs excluded. Retrospective coverage to bridge the 1988-92 gap in progress. Also available as a quarterly updated CD-ROM database.
Class No: 087.7(73)(051)

[2532]

—Index to U.S. government periodicals. Chicago, Infordata International, 1974-87. Quarterly, 4th issue annual cumulation. ISSN: 00984604.

Covered a similar number of titles to *U.S. government periodicals index* (above). Author and subject entries in one A-Z sequence. Also issued in microfiche.
Class No: 087.7(73)(051)

Brazil

[2533]

LOMBARDI, M. Brazilian serial documents: a selective and annotated guide. Bloomington, Indiana University Press, 1974. xxviii,445p. ISBN: 0253312620.

Reprint available from Books on demand ($138.50. ISBN: 0835773876.

1,367 annotated entries in 4 parts (divided into 23 chapters): Federal Republic; Legislature; Executive; Judiciary. Notes on origins and resources of each agency. Serials which ceased publication before 1961 not treated in full. Detailed index (p.367-441). *Class No:* 087.7(81)

Chile

[2534]

Publicaciones oficiales de Chile, 1973-1983. Sanz, M.T., *dir.* Santiago, Instituto Profesional de Santiago, Escuela Bibliotecología y Documentación, 1985. 196p.

Comprehensive listing of 4,416 items by issuing agency. Agency (subsidiary) and personal name indexes. *Class No:* 087.7(83)

Venezuela

[2535]

Catálogo de publicaciones oficiales 1840-1977. Martínez de Cartay, B., *comp.* Merida, Imprenta Oficial del Estado Merida, 1978. 445p.

At head of title page Republica de Venezuela. Instituto Autonomo Biblioteca Nacional. Seccion de Publicaciones Oficiales.

Lists 3,865 national government publications in A-Z responsible body order. *Class No:* 087.7(87)

Philippines

[2536]

Checklist of Philippine government documents 1917-1949. Rebadavia, C.B., *comp and* Verzosa, M.P., *ed.*. Quezon City, University of the Philippines Library, 1960. xv,817p.

The main retrospective listing containing 6,469 annotated entries. Earlier coverage provided by E.O. Elmer's *Checklist of publications of the government of the Philippine Islands, September 1 1900 to December 31 1917* (1918). Period to 1958 covered by A.C. Ponce & J.C. Yacto's *List of Philippine government publications, 1945-1958* (2v. 1959-60). *Class No:* 087.7(914)

[2537]

—Checklist of Philippine government publications. Manila, National Library, 1958-73. Annual.

Ceased publication. *Bibliographic services throughout the world. Supplement 1983-84,* p.202, also lists Austria, C.S. *Checklist of Philippine government documents 1963-1973* (Quezon City, University of the Philippines, 1985). *Class No:* 087.7(914)

Australia

[2538]

Australian government publications. 1961-. Canberra, National Library of Australia, 1962-. Microfiche, updated quarterly. Aus$70. ISSN: 00671878.

Annual 1961-70; quarterly 1972-87, with 4th issue annual cumulation (1971 quarterly with separate annual cumulation). From 1988 available only on microfiche, each quarterly issue cumulative. Earlier coverage provided by *Monthly list of Australian government publications* (1952-60), cumulated as *Annual catalogue of Australian government publications.*

Lists material issued by the agencies of the Commonwealth of Australia and its territories, the States of Australia and the Northern Territory and local government authorities. Includes pamphlets, leaflets, posters, serials, individual Acts, Bills and Ordinances, projected media, sound recordings and maps. Microfiche in separate author/title and subject sequences, the former including personal and series names, the latter under Library of Congress headings. Records 1983-1987 also available as a closed file on OZLINE.

State government publications are also separately recorded

....*(contd.)*
in lists compiled by State libraries, *e.g. Victorian government publications* (Melbourne, State Library of Victoria, 1976-. Monthly, with annual cumulation. ISSN: 03132463). *Class No:* 087.7(94)

[2539]

BORCHARDT, D.H. Australian official publications. Melbourne, Longman Cheshire, 1979. xii,365p. tables. ISBN: 0582714613.

9 essays by specialists on government in Australia and its written records (1. Federal and state government ... 3. Federal and state government publications - 4. Parliamentary publications ... 6. Publications issued by government departments, statutory authorities and local government authorities ... 8. Bibliographic control - 9. Access to Australian official publications. Index. Now largely superseded by Harrington (*q.v.*). *Class No:* 087.7(94)

[2540]

COXON, H. Australian official publications. Oxford, Pergamon Press, 1980. xvi,211p. facsims. (*Guide to official publications, v.5.*) ISBN: 0080231314.

'Aimed at a general readership' (Preface). Contents: 1. The Commonwealth Parliament - 2. Commonwealth Departments and statutory authorities - 3. Distribution and availability - 4. The states of Australia - 5. The internal Territories - 6. The bibliography of Australian official publications (p.187-99). Appendices (*e.g.* 'Dates of sessions of the Commonwealth Parliament, 1901-1978'). 43 facsims; footnotes. Analytical index. *Class No:* 087.7(94)

[2541]

HARRINGTON, M. The Guide to government publications in Australia. Canberra, Australian Government Publishing Service, 1990. viii,164p. facsims. Aus$11.95. ISBN: 0644114401.

Main contents: 1. Government in Australia - 2. Government printing and publishing in Australia - 3. Parliamentary publications: non-legislative material - 4. Parliamentary publications: law - 5. Executive publications; law and official gazettes - 6. Executive publications: publications of government agencies - 7. Judicial publications and decisions - 8. Publications of intergovernmental organisations - 9. Access to government publications: list of publications - 10. Access to government publications. Bibliography; index. Includes some consideration of state and other non-Commonwealth publications. Chap. 10 reproduces sample pages. The current standard guide, 'compiled with great care and written in a style that rises above the factual to touch at times on elegance' (*American reference books annual,* v.23, 1992, p.21). *Class No:* 087.7(94)

Information Management

[2542]

The Bibliographic control of official publications. Pemberton, J.E., *ed.* Oxford, Pergamon Press, 1982. 172p. illus. £24. (*Guides to official publications, v.11.*) ISBN: 0080274196.

Published 'with the object of stimulating progress towards the establishment of a comprehensive system for the bibliographic control of official publications' (Preface p.7). 11 contributed chapters outlining systems of bibliographic control used in individual libraries (*e.g.* 3. Treatment of official publications in the Library of Parliament, Ottawa ... 9. The University of Virginia Documents Classification System). *Class No:* 087.7:025.4

[2543]

Directory of specialists in official publications. Nurcombe, V.J., *comp.* 3rd ed. [Winsford], Library Association Information Services Group, Standing Committee on Official Publications, 1992. 38p. £7. ISBN: 095120114x.

First published 1985; 2nd ed. 1988.

Questionnaire based. Entries give name, job title, address and tel. no. only. Geographic arrangement: English counties; Scottish regions etc. Name and expertise indexes. Fewer entries than previous eds., but 'cheap and convenient ... for anyone needing to inquire about official publications and wondering whom to ask for' (*The Year in reference*, 1993, p.14). *Class No:* 087.7:025.4

[2544]

GARNER, D.L. *and* **SMITH, D.H. The Complete guide to citing government information resources:** a manual for writers and librarians. Rev. ed. Bethesda, Md., Congressional Information Service, 1993. xvii,222p. ISBN: 0886922542.

Rev. ed. of *The Complete guide to citing government documents* (1984).

Designed to supplement standard citation manuals. 5 main chaps: United States government (p.15-66) - State, local and regional government - International/IGO (UN, EC, OAS) - Foreign government - Electronic formats. Sub-arrangement under specific headings (*e.g.* 'Budget of the United States', 'Clearinghouse documents'). Glossary (p.199-206); index. *Class No:* 087.7:025.4

Bibliographies

[2545]

Government documents in the library literature, 1909-1974. Schorr, A.E., *comp.* Ann Arbor, Pierian Press, 1976. vii,110p. ISBN: 0876500718.

The 'purpose of this volume is to provide librarians with a comprehensive bibliographic guide to the literature on United States Federal, state and municipal documents and United Nations and League of Nations documents' (Introduction p.v). 1,206 numbered, unannotated entries in 5 sections. Indexed by state and personal name. *Class No:* 087.7:025.4(01)

[2546]

SCHORR, A.E. Federal documents librarianship, 1879-1987. Juneau, Denali Press, 1988. 215p. $25. ISBN: 0938737147.

Bibliographical guide to the literature on United States government information policy. 2,153 unannotated entries including periodical articles, chapters, conference proceedings and theses. Classified arrangement in 10 sections; author index, 'a detailed subject index would increase this guide's usefulness' (*American reference books annual,* v.20, 1989, p.25). *Class No:* 087.7:025.4(01)

Libraries

[2547]

AMERICAN LIBRARY ASSOCIATION. Government Documents Round Table. **Directory of government documents collections & libraries.** Kapfer, M.A., *ed.* 7th ed. Bethesda, Md., Congressional Information Service, 1997. xv,624p. ISBN: 0912380152.

1st ed. 1974; 6th ed. 1991.

Main section 'Guide to libraries, collections and staff' (p.1-240) covers more than 2,000 collections, including all depository libraries. Indexed by library, documents

....(*contd.*)

collections (state, local, international, foreign), special collections and personal names. Various other listings such as 'State document authorities' and 'Association and government offices'. *Class No:* 087.7:061:026/027

[2548]

—Directory of foreign document collections. Turner, C.A., *comp.* New York, UNIPUB for the Government Documents Round Table, American Library Association, 1985. vii,148p. ISBN: 0890590451.

Identifies *c.*145 US and Canadian libraries which collect government publications of other countries. Main sequence by library with separate country listing. Excludes highly specialized collections. *Class No:* 087.7:061:026/027

[2549]

Directory of official publications in Scotland. Anderson, G., *comp.* Edinburgh, Scottish Working Group on Official Publications, 1991. vi,110p. £10. ISBN: 1873642008.

Guide to main collections of official publications in Scotland. Covers National Library of Scotland, 8 university libraries, the public reference libraries of Glasgow and Edinburgh, the Advocates Library, Scottish Office Library and Scottish Educational Trust for United Nations and International Affairs. Arranged by institution. Strengths of collections in specific areas indicated by 3 gradings 'basic', 'intermediate' and 'extensive'; only occasional detail of actual holdings. Index of countries, international bodies, etc. (p.96-110). *Class No:* 087.7:061:026/027

09 Rare Books & Manuscripts

Rare Books

[2550]

BRUNET, J.C. Manuel du libraire et de l'amateur de livres ... 5.éd. Paris, Didot, 1860-80. 6v.; Supplément 2v.

First published 1810. Reprinted Paris, Maisonneuve et Larose, 1965-66. 7v. Available from French & European Publications, $1,200 (ISBN: 0785952187).

V.1-5 form an A-Z author list of 47,500 rare, valuable, noteworthy and otherwise remarkable books, irrespective of language (but particularly strong for French titles), published up to *c.*1850. Gives details of various editions, forgeries; gives full collation for early books; appended notes on sale prices fetched in France and England over a hundred year period. V.6 is a classified list based on the Brunet scheme (5 main classes: Theology; Jurisprudence; Sciences and Arts; Belles-lettres; History), plus some additional titles. The *Supplément*, similarly arranged, adds *c.*12,500 entries.

Dictionnaire de géographie ancien et moderne à l'usage du libraire et de l'amateur de livres, by P. Deschamps (Paris, Didot, 1870. 1591 cols; reprinted Paris, Maisonneuve et Larose, 1964) as a further supplement lists ancient Greek and Latin place-names, with modern equivalents and printing press details. H. Cotton's *The Typographical gazetteer* (Oxford, Clarendon Press, 1825) a guide to places where rare books were printed, was reprinted in 1975 (Detroit, Gale. xvi,219p. ISBN: 0686568141). *Class No:* 090.0

[2551]

—GRAESSE, J.G.T. Trésor de livres rares et précieux ... Dresden, Kuntze, 1859-96. 7v.

Various reprints include Altmann (Berlin, 1922), AMS Press, (1972) and Malavasi (Milano, 1993).

Claims 100,000 entries and is particularly strong for German titles, thus supplementing Brunet. Authors A-Z (v.1-6); supplement (v.7). Like Brunet, gives sale prices and other bibliographical notes. No classified or A-Z subject index.

Brunet and Graesse between them constitute the main key to noteworthy books published during the first four centuries of European printing. *Class No:* 090.0

[2552]

ILLINOIS UNIVERSITY Library. **Catalog of the Rare Book Room, University Library, University of Illinois,** Urbana-Champaign. Boston, G.K. Hall, 1972. 11v. $1,450. ISBN: 0816109389.

V.1-9 A-Z: v.10 *Baskette shelflist; Churchill catalog and supplement; Hollander catalog and supplement; Meine shelflist*: v.11 *Catalog of the Wells collection*.

About 213,000 entries representing a collection of nearly 100,000 volumes. The main strength of the Rare Book Room is the great Milton Collection listing 100 editions and 3,000 works about him. The H.G. Wells and Churchill collections are also notable, the latter comprising 1,800 items. A *First supplement* (1978. ISBN: 0816100985) records a further

.... *(contd.)*

11,000 items added to the collection 1972-77. For incunabula see *Incunabula in the University of Illinois Library (q.v.)*. *Class No:* 090.0

[2553]

NEW YORK PUBLIC LIBRARY. Research Libraries. Rare Book Division. **Dictionary catalog of the Rare Book Division.** Boston, Mass., G.K. Hall, 1971. 21v. $2,280. ISBN: 0816107823.

V.21 *Appendix. Broadsides*. A *First supplement* was published 1973 (745p.).

About 375,000 photolithographed catalogue cards, representing *c.*90,000 books and pamphlets from the 15th century to recent private and special press books. The major strength of the collection lies in its historical Americana. *Class No:* 090.0

[2554]

—NEW YORK PUBLIC LIBRARY. Research Libraries. Rare Book Division. The Imprint catalog of the Rare Book Division. Boston, Mass., G.K. Hall, 1979. 21v. $2,430. ISBN: 0816100926.

Entries arranged alphabetically according to anglicized form of name of cities, towns and ships. About 320,000 reproduced cards for 12,000 places. Includes some entries for important books in other collections (*e.g.* Spencer Collection), and a few for books not held by the NYPL. 'No other reference source brings together as many items according to their geographical place of publication' (Introduction v.1 p.iii). *Class No:* 090.0

Canada

[2555]

GAUVIN, D. Guide canadien du livre rare. [Canadian guide to rare books.] Montreal, D. Gauvin, 1989. x,217p. ISBN: 298015010x.

In 2 pts: 'Bibliophilism' contains basic information on collecting with bibliography of books, directories, periodicals, etc; 'Directory of useful addresses' has detail of Canadian, US and European antiquarian booksellers, Canadian collectors, book collecting associations, etc. Misleadingly entitled with 'odd and uneven coverage' (*Canadian library journal*, v.47(3), June 1990, p.209). *Class No:* 090.0(71)

Australia

[2556]

WANTRUP, J. Australian rare books 1788-1900. Sydney, Hordern House, 1987. x,468p. facsims. Aus $135. ISBN: 0958847827.

Discusses 265 books published in Australia, or about the discovery and exploration of Australia, in 5 chronological chapters. 3 further chapters on bookplates and book collecting. Includes recent sale price data. Primarily for the book collector, but considered (*Times literary supplement*, no.4394, 19th June 1989, p.670), to contribute 'more

....*(contd.)*
genuinely useful additions to bibliographical knowledge than the officially sponsored addenda' (Ferguson *Bibliography of Australia: addenda 1986* (q.v.)). *Class No:* 090.0(94)

Book Collecting

[2557]
AHEARN, A. Collected books: the guide to values. 1998 ed. New York, Putnam's, 1997. viii,769p. $75. ISBN: 0399142797.

First published 1991.

Aims to provide a basis for identifying and pricing mostly literary first editions. A-Z arrangement by author giving basic bibliographical details, occasional notes and estimated price. Bibliographical references (p.729-69).
Class No: 090.1

[2558]
—AHEARN, A. *and* AHEARN, P. Book collecting: a comprehensive guide. 1995 ed. New York, Putnam's, 1995. xiv,480p. illus. $35. ISBN: 0399140492.

First published 1989; designed to succeed V.A. Bradley's *Book collector's hand book of values,* also published by Putnam's.

Not as comprehensive as the title suggests, p.129-428 offering a listing of first editions/first printings with retail price estimates for 1978, 1986 and 1995. Preceeding pages offer general guidance; various appendices. Also available on CD-ROM. *Class No:* 090.1

[2559]
Book collecting: a modern guide. Peters, J., *ed.* New York, Bowker, 1977. xix,288p. illus. £35;$39.95. ISBN: 0835209857.

A well balanced guide of 12 contributed chapters covering all aspects of book collecting including buying from dealers, buying at auction, descriptive bibliography, fakes, forgeries and facsimilies, physical care and organizing a collection. The final chapter 'The Literature of book collecting' by G.T. Tanselle (p.209-71) is particularly valuable.

Peters also edited *Collectible books: some new paths* (New York, Bowker, 1979. xxxii,294p. illus. ISBN: 0835211541) and *The Bookman's glossary* 6th ed. (New York, Bowker, 1983. ix,223p. £35;$39.95. ISBN: 0855216861), the latter defining *c.*2,000 terms, including those used in the antiquarian book trade. *Class No:* 090.1

[2560]
Collecting children's books. Jackson, C., *ed and* Book and Magazine Collector, *comp.*. London, Diamond, 1995. 303p. illus. £19.95. ISBN: 0951555375.

Comprises listing (p.20-303) of 266 authors/illustrators/ series A-Z with bibliographical detail and current value of first editions. Over 9,000 titles covered; brief biographical notes for many individuals. *Class No:* 090.1

[2561]
ELLIS, I.C. Book finds: how to find, buy and sell used and rare books. New York, Berkley, 1996. xii,271p. $13. ISBN: 0399519785.

New guide aimed at the general collector. 12 chaps. *e.g.* 3. Edition, condition and scarcity; 9. Book repair, restoration, cleaning and care. Final chap. (p.225-248) comprises list of 1,001 collectible books. Appendix, glossary and index. *Class No:* 090.1

[2562]
MILLER, S. Book collecting: a guide to antiquarian and second hand books. Royston, Provincial Booksellers Fairs Association, 1994. ix,190p. illus., facsims. £12.95. ISBN: 0952412217.

Basic guide under headings such as 'Signatures' (4p.), 'Binding the book' (6p.), 'The Dust jacket' (3p.) and 'Auctions' (3p.). Indexed. *Class No:* 090.1

[2563]
RICCI, S. de. The Book collector's guide: a practical handbook of British and American bibliography. Philadelphia & New York, Rosenbach, 1921. xviii,649p.

Reprinted New York, Franklin, 1970. (ISBN: 0833729802).

Lists by authors (or anonymous titles), A-Z 'the two or three thousand British and American books which fashion has decided are the most desirable for the up-to-date collector' (Preface). Covers the period from Chaucer to Swinburne, reinforcing Lowndes' *Bibliographer's manual of English literature* (*q.v.*). Includes bibliographical descriptions. Bibliography p.xv-xviii. *Class No:* 090.1

[2564]
UDEN, G. Understanding book-collecting. Woodbridge, Antique Collectors' Club, 1982. 279p. illus. £14.95;$29.50. ISBN: 0907462138.

Reprinted 1983. Paperback ed. 1986 (ISBN: 1851490280).

Wide-ranging study. Begins with chapters on the language of book collecting followed by treatment by type of book collected (*e.g.* illustrated books, private press books etc.). Also covers book care and conservation. Glossary (p.241-57); index. One of the more valuable overviews of book collecting. *Class No:* 090.1

Encyclopaedias & Dictionaries

[2565]
BERNARD, P. Antiquarian books: a companion for booksellers, librarians and collectors. Aldershot, Scolar Press, 1994. xiv,461p. illus. £55;$84.95. ISBN: 0859679306.

Published in the US by Univ. of Pennsylvannia Press (ISBN: 0812232682).

Contains about 400 short entries for terms, persons, etc. relating to the antiquarian book trade interspersed with longer articles. Latter include 'Colour book plates' (6p.) and 'Incunabula' (6½p.). Short entries usually less than 200 words, *e.g.* 'False imprint' *c.*75 words. Many black and white illus., some entries with bibliographical citations. A valuable new work, useful in a wide variety of situations.
Class No: 090.1(03)

[2566]
CARTER, J. ABC for book collectors. 7th ed. London, Werner Shaw, 1994. 224p. $25. ISBN: 0907961061.

Published in US by Oak Knoll Books (ISBN: 1884718051). First published 1952; 5th ed. 1972. 6th ed. 1980 prepared from Carter's annotated copy by N. Barker. This ed., with further corrections and additions, also prepared by Barker.

Intended for the amateur collector. Over 450 entries, some of them brief definitions (*e.g.* 'Tail': 15 words) and others lengthy discussions (*e.g.* 'Errata': 1½p.). Includes a few entries for bibliographers (*e.g.* Hain, Proctor, Wing). Entries for printers, presses, publishers etc. kept to a minimum. Confined to British and American terminology. '(M)ore than a reference manual. It is the learned advice of an experienced collector, and a worthy companion for

....*(contd.)*
beginning bibliophiles and rare book librarians' (*Rare books and manuscript librarianship*, v.10(2), 1995, p.104).
Class No: 090.1(03)

Yearbooks & Directories

[2567]
International directory of book collectors 1993-95: a directory of book collectors in the United Kingdom, Ireland, America, Canada and the rest of the world. Sheppard, R., *comp.* 5th ed. Beckenham, Trigon Press, 1992. xvi, 260p. £28. ISBN: 0904929310.

First published 1976; 4th ed. 1985.

Questionnaire based giving address, main and subsidiary subjects/authors collected, membership of bookman's club or society, etc. 2,000 entries A-Z by name in sections for UK and Ireland, US and Canada and rest of the world. Indexed by subject speciality and collected authors and illustrators. 'Books for bookmen' (p.viii-xvi) offers brief notes on 16 recent books on book collecting. *Class No:* 090.1(058)

Biographies

[2568]
American book-collectors and bibliographers. Rosenblum, J., *ed.* Detroit, Gale, 1994-97. 2v. illus., plates, facsims. $140. (*Dictionary of literary biography, v.140, 187..*)

First series (1994. xviii,408p. ISBN: 0810353997); *Second series* (1997. xix,431p. ISBN: 078761842X).

The *First series* has 43 entries, *e.g.* 'Hubert Howe Bancroft', 'Henry E. Huntington', 'Gordon Norton Ray', 'John Pierpont Morgan', in standard DLB style. Checklist of further readings (p.343-45).

Forthcoming 1998 *Nineteenth-century British book collectors and bibliographers* (DLB v.184. ISBN: 0787610739). *Class No:* 090.1(092)

[2569]
Contributions towards a dictionary of English book-collectors: as also of some foreign collectors whose libraries were incorporated in English collections, or whose books are chiefly met with in England. Quaritch, B., *ed.* London, Quaritch, 1892-1921. 14 pts.

Reprinted Nieuwkoop, De Graaf, 1969. (350p. ISBN: 9060041356).

78 extensive articles on famous book-collectors, A-Z. An important source for establishing provenances, since it notes the more important items collected and the dispersal of collections. *Class No:* 090.1(092)

[2570]
DICKINSON, D.C. Dictionary of American book collectors. Westport, Conn., Greenwood, 1986. xvi,383p. £58.50;$69.50. ISBN: 0313225443.

Covers 359 major collectors who died before 1985. Entries include biographical details, narrative discussion of collectors' interests and collections and selective bibliography of primary and secondary sources. Subject and general index; chronological list of major book auctions 1860-1984. Carefully researched and well presented, 'fills a real need' (*Library quarterly*, v.57(1), January 1987, p.125).
Class No: 090.1(092)

Manuscripts

[2571]
ALEXANDER TURNBULL LIBRARY *and* NATIONAL ARCHIVES OF NEW ZEALAND. The National register of archives and manuscripts in New Zealand. Wellington, National Library of New Zealand, 1979-. Irregular. ISSN: 01107178.

Replaces *Union catalogue of New Zealand and Pacific manuscripts in New Zealand libraries.* (Wellington, Alexander Turnbull Library, 1968-69. 2v.).

Issued in instalments of 250 entries, four instalments making up one volume (A 1979-82; B 1983-90; C 1991-). Covers libraries, museums, historical societies, organizations, National Archives and private individuals. Entries, in standard format, include full descriptions. Cumulative name, geographic and subject indexes to completed volumes. Also available on microfiche.
Class No: 091

[2572]
BIBLIOTECA NACIONAL. (SPAIN). Inventario de manuscritos de la Biblioteca Nacional. Madrid, Ministerio de Cultura, Dirección del Libro y Bibliotecas, 1953-.

13 v. published to 1995 (MSS. 1-9500). Name index and tables in each v. *Class No:* 091

[2573]
BIBLIOTHÈQUE NATIONALE. (FRANCE). Département des Manuscrits. **Bibliothèque Nationale, Département des Manuscrits: inventaire des instruments de recherche:** manuscrits occidentaux. Paris, Chadwyck-Healey, 1989. 2,620 microfiche & 27p. printed index.

Reproduces 200 catalogues of Western manuscripts in the Bibliothèque Nationale, most long out-of-print, many never before published. Examples include *Inventaire sommaire des manuscrits grecs* (1886-1898), *Catalogue général des manuscrits français. Nouvelles acquisitions...* (1899-1918) and *La Librairie de Charles V* (1968). Catalogues arranged in broad groupings (*e.g.* Greek manuscripts; Special collections; Iconography); printed index with title *Les Catalogues des manuscrits occidentaux de la Bibliothèque Nationale...* . *Class No:* 091

[2574]
BODLEIAN LIBRARY. A Summary catalogue of Western manuscripts in the Bodleian Library, Oxford. Madan, F., *and others.* Oxford, Clarendon Press, 1895-1953. 6v. in 7 & index.

V.I. *Historical introduction and conspectus of shelfmarks* (1953). V.II. Pt.I. *Collections received before 1660 and miscellaneous MSS. acquired during the first half of the 17th century* (1922). V.II. Pt.II. *Collections of miscellaneous MSS. acquired during the second half of the 17th century* (1937). V.III. *Collections received during the 18th century* (1895). V.IV. *Collections received during the first half of the 19th century* (1897). V.V. *Collections received during the second half of the 19th century and miscellaneous manuscripts acquired between 1695 and 1890* (1905). V.VI. *Accessions, 1890-1915* (1924). V.VII. *Index* (1953).

Reprinted with new introductory matter and corrections, München, Kraus Reprint, 1980. *Class No:* 091

[2575]
—CLAPINSON, M. *and* ROGERS, T.D. Summary catalogue of post-medieval Western manuscripts in the Bodleian Library, Oxford. Acquisitions 1916-1975 (SC 37300-55936). Oxford, Clarendon P., 1991. 3v. £325;$700. ISBN: 0199521093.

Excludes manuscripts on deposit, some collections of recent political papers (listed in appendix), manuscripts relating to Oxford, Oxfordshire and the University, deeds and charters, music, microfilms and facsimilies. Shelfmark arrangement; general index in final v. offering access by persons, places and, to a limited extent, subjects.
Class No: 091

[2576]
—Select index of manuscript collections in Oxford libraries outside the Bodleian. Morgan, P., *comp.* Oxford, Bodleian Library, 1991. 50p. £5. ISBN: 1851240241.

Expanded and corrected version of list published as Appendix II of the author's *Oxford libraries outside the Bodleian* 2nd ed. (1980).

'(A)ims to provide a rough summary guide to the (chiefly modern) non-archival material scattered around the numerous libraries in Oxford that do not appear in H.O. Coxe *Catalogus codicum MSS. qui in collegiis aulisque Oxoniensibus hodie adservantur,* (1852)' (*Preface*).
Class No: 091

[2577]
—WATSON, A.G. Catalogue of dated and datable manuscripts in Oxford libraries. Oxford, Clarendon Press, 1984. 2v. V.I *The Text.* (176p.); v.II *The Plates.* (818l.). ISBN: 0198181973.

Second British catalogue in the series on dated and datable manuscripts initiated by the Comité International de Paléographie. Reprinted K.G. Saur 1996 (DM698. ISBN: 3598113157).

Physical description, evidence of date, summary history and bibliography for 882 manuscripts written up to 1550 in the Department of Western Manuscripts of the Bodleian Library (711 entries) and the libraries of Oxford colleges. Date and name indexes. *Class No:* 091

[2578]
BRITISH LIBRARY. Department of Manuscripts. **Index of manuscripts in the British Library.** Cambridge, Chadwyck-Healey, 1984-86. 10v. £1750;$3,450. ISBN: 0859641406.

The product of over twenty years' editorial work consolidating the indexes to over 30, mostly published, catalogues including the 'Additional' series to 1950, *Index to charters and rolls in the Department of Manuscripts* ... (1912), *Catalogue of manuscripts in the Cotton Library* ... (1812), *Catalogue of the Stowe manuscripts* (1895) and *Index to the Sloane manuscripts* ... (1904). Personal and place-name index only, all subject entries removed unless they could be relocated under the name of a place. Form of entry for personal names based on the *Dictionary of national biography.* Entries give name of manuscript, name of collection in abbreviated form, number within collection and folio number. 4 column format, index slips photographically reproduced. Well over 1,000,000 entries. A 'marvellous key with which to unlock the British Library's great manuscript collections ... it will be used by some as a substitute for, rather than a key to, the catalogues' (*Times literary supplement,* no.4269, January 25th 1985, p.103).
Class No: 091

[2579]
—ALSTON, R.C. Books with manuscripts: a short title catalogue of books with manuscript notes in the British Library, including books with manuscript additions, proofsheets, illustrations, corrections. London, British Library, 1993. xiii,663p. £60;$120. ISBN: 0712303294.

Limited to items listed in *The British Library general catalogue.* About 25,000 entries, mostly unascribed. Owner and author indexes. *Class No:* 091

[2580]
—ALSTON, R.C. Handlist of library catalogues and lists of books and manuscripts in the British Library Department of Manuscripts. London, Bibliographical Society, 1991. iv,87p. (*Occasional papers of the Bibliographical Society, no. 6.*)

Lists catalogues, etc. produced by BL's Dept. of Manuscripts and its predecessors from the late 17th century onwards. Excludes material in *Handlist of unpublished finding aids to the London collections* (*q.v.*). Brief entries only; subject, collection and compiler indexes (p.67-87). Mainly of historical interest. *Class No:* 091

[2581]
BRITISH MUSEUM. Catalogue of additions to the manuscripts in the British Museum. London, British Museum, 1843-1982.

Preceded by Ayscough, S. *A Catalogue of the manuscripts preserved in the British Museum hitherto undescribed* ... (London, 1782. 2v.) and *Index to the additional manuscripts with those of the Egerton Collection preserved in the British Museum and acquired in the years 1783-1835* (London, 1849). A new catalogue of the manuscripts described in Ayscough has been published as *Catalogue of additions to the manuscripts 1756-1782* (London, British Library, 1977. ISBN: 0714104906).

Catalogue of additions series published as follows: 1836-40 (1843); 1841-45 (1850); 1846-47 (1864); 1848-53 (1866); 1854-75 (1877-80); 1876-81 (1882); 1882-87 (1889); 1888-93 (1894); 1894-99 (1903); 1900-5 (1907); then on a quinquennial basis with the exception of 1935-45 (1970) to 1951-55 (1982). All vols. available from the British Library, price varies. Continued by the *New series* (below).

The 'Additional' series is by far the largest collection of manuscripts and comprises all acquisitions since 1756 with the exception of those which form closed collections. Numbers begin at 4101, following the Sloane MSS 1-4100. The last v. published *Catalogue of the additions to the manuscripts 1951-1955* (2v. (Pt.1 Descriptions. Pt.2 Index) £90. ISBN: 0904654699) did not appear until 1982. The new series (below) aims to provide less protracted coverage and fill the gap back to 1956. In the meantime the *Rough register of acquisitions of the Department of Manuscripts, British Library,* prepared by the List and Index Society and published in a number of vols. from 1974, remains a helpful interim source.

Catalogues of special collections of manuscripts include *Index to the Sloane manuscripts in the British Museum* (1904), *Catalogue of the Stowe manuscripts in the British Museum* (2v. 1895-96) and *Catalogue of the Western manuscripts in the Old Royal and King's collections* (4v. 1921). Recent 'additions' catalogues of this type include *Catalogue of additions to the manuscripts: the Blenheim Papers* (British Library, 1985. 3v. £115. ISBN: 0712300198), *Catalogue of additions to the manuscripts: the Cecil Chelwood papers.* (British Library, 1991. x[ix],171p.]. £30. ISBN: 0712301526) and *Catalogue of additions to the manuscripts: the Yelverton manuscripts* (British Library, 1994. 2v. £85. ISBN: 0712303553). *Class No:* 091

[2582]

—BRITISH LIBRARY. Department of Manuscripts. Catalogue of additions to the manuscripts. New series. London, British Library, 1993-. Quinquennial.

Intended both as an ongoing listing and to provide coverage back to the 1951-55 v. of the original *Catalogue and additions* series (above). Began publication with 1986-90 issued in 3 v. (I. *Descriptions 1986-1988*; II. *Descriptions 1989-1990*; III. *Index* (£125. ISBN: 0712303057)). Retrospective set for 1981-85 issued 1994 (2v. £85. ISBN: 0712303413) followed by 1976-80 in 1995 (2 v. £85. ISBN: 0712304290). 1966-70 (ISBN: 0712345701) and 1956-65 (ISBN: 0712345671) listed for publication as 3 v. sets 1998.

More summary treatment of larger collections than previously. 1986-90 set covers additional manuscripts 63650-70637, Egerton manuscripts 3813-3867, Additional charters and rolls 76609-76772 and 76792-76836, and Egerton charters and rolls 8853-8858. Index of personal names only. *Class No:* 091

[2583]

—WATSON, A.G. Catalogue of dated and datable manuscripts *c.*700-1600: in the Department of Manuscripts, the British Library. London, British Library, 1979. 2v. ISBN: 0714104876.

First British catalogue in the series on dated and datable manuscripts initiated by the Comité International de Paléographie. Reprinted K.G. Saur 1997 (ISBN: 3598113137).

V.1 describes 953 manuscripts. Entries include evidence of date and origin and bibliographical references. Name index. V.2 comprises 915 black and white plates. *Class No:* 091

[2584]

CAMBRIDGE UNIVERSITY. Library. **A Catalogue of the manuscripts preserved in the library of the University of Cambridge.** Luard, H.P. Cambridge, Cambridge Univ. Press, 1856-67. 5v. + Catalogue of Adversaria and index.

Reprinted Olms (DM980. ISBN: 3487069873).

Excludes Orientalia. *Class No:* 091

[2585]

—CAMBRIDGE UNIVERSITY. Library. Summary guide to accessions of Western manuscripts (other than medieval) since 1867. Owen, A.E.B. Cambridge, Univ. Library, 1966. 48p. *Class No:* 091

[2586]

—ROBINSON, P.R. Catalogue of dated and datable manuscripts *c.*737-1600 in Cambridge libraries. Cambridge, D.S. Brewer, 1988. 2v. V.I *The Text.* (130p.); v.II *The Plates.* (390l.). £250;$450. ISBN: 0859912493.

Third British catalogue in the series on dated and datable manuscripts initiated by the Comité International de Paléographie.

Describes 394 manuscripts, 117 in the University Library, the remainder in college libraries and the Fitzwilliam Museum. Similar format to the Oxford companion volume (Watson (*q.v.*)), but with more extensive indexing. *Class No:* 091

[2587]

CANADA. Public Archives *and* **CANADA.** Humanities Research Council. **Union list of manuscripts in Canadian repositories.** [Catalogue collectif des manuscrits des archives canadiennes.] Maurice, E.G., *ed.* Rev. ed. Ottawa, Public Archives Canada, 1975. 2v.

Earlier ed. 1968. Updated by supplements for 1976, 1977-78, 1979-80 and 1981-82.

.... *(contd.)*

The original set describes approximately 27,000 manuscript collections in 215 repositories under names of individuals, corporate bodies etc., which created or received the papers. Index of collections by repository; general index. *Class No:* 091

[2588]

Catalogue général des manuscrits des bibliothèques publiques de France. Paris, Various publishers, (originally Imprimerie Imperiale now Centre National de la Recherche Scientifique), 1848-.

Title varies. First series published 1848-1885 in 7v. (reprinted Farnborough, Gregg, 1969). New series commenced 1886 reaching v.48 in 1933 when publication was suspended. Resumed 1951; recent years have seen the production of further volumes *e.g.* v.64 *Versailles* (1990. 478p. ISBN: 222204362X). *Class No:* 091

[2589]

—POPOFF, M. Index général des manuscrits: decrits dans le *Catalogue général des manuscrits des bibliothèques publiques de France*. Paris, Références, 1993. 3v. ISBN: 2908302306.

184,000 entry personal name, place, etc. index complete to v.63. An impressive and painstaking compilation, essential for the effective exploitation of the rich collections catalogued in the main volumes. *Class No:* 091

[2590]

EDINBURGH UNIVERSITY. Library. **Index to manuscripts.** Boston, Mass., G.K. Hall, 1965. 2v. $220. ISBN: 0816113564.

30,000 cards photolithographically reproduced, covering more than 8,000v. and 28,000 other separate pieces of post-medieval Western MS. materials. A *First supplement* (Boston, Mass., G.K. Hall, 1981, iii,609p. $175. ISBN: 0816103194) reproduces a further 12,750 cards for material acquired up to 1979. *Class No:* 091

[2591]

A Guide to modern manuscripts in the Princeton University Library. Delaney, J.M., *ed.* Boston, Mass., G.K. Hall, 1989. 2v. $275. ISBN: 0816104697.

V.1: *Collection descriptions and related indexes.* (xxxii,1035p.). V.2: *Summaries of holdings by author.* (xiii,809p.).

Describes 646 collections in 5 divisions of the library's Department of Rare Books and Special Collections (Manuscripts Division; Seeley G. Mudd Manuscript Library; the William Seymour Theatre Collection; Western Americana and Historic Maps; Robert H. Taylor Library). Modern interpreted as post-1500. *Class No:* 091

[2592]

HOUGHTON LIBRARY. Catalogue of manuscripts in the Houghton Library, Harvard University. Alexander, Va., Chadwyck-Healey, 1986. 8v. £1,250;$2,649. ISBN: 0898870402.

Reproduces 136,000 cards from the main manuscript catalogue as at April 1985. Entries for all principal authors, correspondents and addresses. Also includes numerous genre headings such as 'Sermons' and 'Diaries'. 3 column format, filing A-Z by main heading. Some entries include brief descriptions. A major catalogue of a rich general collection, especially strong in American and European literary manuscripts. Medieval and Renaissance manuscripts are fully described in *Catalogue of medieval and Renaissance manuscripts in the Houghton Library*... (*q.v.*). *Class No:* 091

[2593]

JAMES, M.R. *and* **JENKINS, C. A Descriptive catalogue of the manuscripts in the Library of Lambeth Palace.** Cambridge, Cambridge Univ. Press, 1930-32. 871p,. £70. ISBN: 0950243221.

Published in 5 parts.

Mainly medieval manuscripts. Recatalogues much of the material described in the first printed catalogue by H.I. Todd *Catalogue of the archiepiscopal manuscripts in the Library at Lambeth Palace* (1812, reprinted Gregg, 1965. £55. ISBN: 0576700460x). Continued by:- *Class No:* 091

[2594]

—BILL, E.G.W. A Catalogue of manuscripts in Lambeth Palace Library. Oxford, Clarendon Press, 1972-83. 3v.

MSS. 1222-1860 (1972. viii,442p.); *MSS. 1907-2340* (1976. xi,379p. ISBN: 0199200793); *MSS. 2341-3119 (excluding 2690-1750)* (1983. viii,397p. ISBN: 0199201358).

Continues the numerical sequence originally established by Todd. The excluded manuscripts are separately described by Bill in *Catalogue of the papers of Roundell Palmer (1812-1895) first Earl of Selborne* (1967) (MSS. 1861-1906) and *The Queen Anne churches* (1979) (MSS. 2690-2750). *Class No:* 091

[2595]

LIBRARY OF CONGRESS. Special Materials Cataloging Division. **National union catalog of manuscript collections.** 1959/61-93. Washington D.C., Library of Congress, Cataloging Distribution Service, 1962-94. Frequency varies, mostly annual. ISSN: 00900044.

Based on holdings reported to the Library of Congress by repositories throughout the United States. Manuscripts reported largely personal papers, manuscripts or typescripts, originals or copies, of letters, memoranda, diaries, log books, drafts and the like. From 1970 also included oral history transcripts and collections containing sound recordings. The final v. (1994. lxxiii,268p.), the 29th in series, reported 1,758 collections held by 52 repositories, 24 reporting for the first time. This brought the total to 72,300 collections located in 1,406 different repositories. Subject, personal, family and corporate name and place indexes for 1959/62, 1963/66 (bound with 1966 catalogue), 1967/69 (bound with 1969 catalogue), 1970/74 (bound with 1973/74 catalogue), 1975/79, 1980/84, 1986/90 and 1991/93. These indexes partially replaced by cumulations from Chadwyck-Healey (below).

Since the cessation of the printed vols. the Library of Congress has continued to produce cataloguing in the RLIN database for libraries unable to produce their own manuscript cataloguing in RLIN or OCLC. Detail and data Internet accessible through http://lcweb.loc.gov/coll/nucmc/nucmc.html. Chadwyck-Healey's database *Archives USA*, available either on CD-ROM (annual updating) or through the Internet on a subscription basis (http:archives.chadwyck.com/infopage.ausa.abt.htm), also contains *NUCMC* records from 1959. *Class No:* 091

[2596]

—LIBRARY OF CONGRESS. Index to personal names in the National union catalog of manuscript collections 1959-1984. Alexandria, Va., Chadwyck Healey, 1988. 2v. £280;$589. ISBN: 0898870372.

'(B)rings together for the first time in one alphabetical sequence all the personal and family names appearing in the descriptions of manuscript collections catalogued from 1959 to 1984' (Introduction p.vii). Around 200,000 entries; includes many corrections and revisions. *Class No:* 091

[2597]

—LIBRARY OF CONGRESS. Index to subjects and corporate names in the National union catalog of manuscript collections 1959-1984. Alexandria, Va., Chadwyck-Healey, 1994. 3v. $825. ISBN: 0898871077.

Companion set to the above. 300,000 entries.
Class No: 091

[2598]

MAZZATINTI, G., ***and others*. Inventari dei manoscritti delle biblioteche d'Italia.** Florence. R. Olschki, 1890-.

First 75 volumes reprinted 1955-69. All vols. in print, L110,000 each.

Arranged under towns. V.107 *Camerino, Biblioteca Comunale Valentiniana* (243p. ISBN: 8822241371) published 1993. *Class No:* 091

[2599]

NATIONAL LIBRARY OF SCOTLAND. Catalogue of manuscripts acquired since 1925. Edinburgh, HMSO, 1938-.

V.1: *Manuscripts 1-1800. Charters 1-900.* (1938. xvi,551p.). V.2: *Manuscripts 1801-4000. Charters and formal documents 901-2634.* (1966. vii,904p.). V.3: *Manuscripts 4001-4940. Blackwood papers 1805-1900.* (1968. vii,331p. ISBN: 01149006x). V.4: *Manuscripts 4941-6405. Charters and other formal documents 2635-6000.* (1982. vii,579p. £35. ISBN: 0114920052). V.5: *Manuscripts 6406-7529. Charters and other formal documents 6001-7636.* (1986. vi,421p. £60. ISBN: 0114931194). V.6: *Manuscripts 7530-8022. Scottish foreign mission records 1827-1929.* (1984. vii,789p. ISBN: 0114903123). V.7: *Manuscripts 8023-9500. Charters and other formal documents 7637-8500.* (1989. vii,467p. ISBN: 0114934509). V.8: *Manuscripts 9501-11000. Charters and other formal documents 8501-8970.* (1992. vii,773p. ISBN: 0114941505).

Manuscripts listed in v.1 described in v.2. Each volume extensively indexed. V.6 published out of sequence.
Class No: 091

[2600]

—NATIONAL LIBRARY OF SCOTLAND. Summary catalogue of the Advocates' manuscripts. Edinburgh, HMSO, 1971. viii,165p. ISBN: 0114903123. *Class No:* 091

[2601]

NEW YORK PUBLIC LIBRARY. Dictionary catalog of the Manuscript Division. Boston, Mass., G.K. Hall, 1967. 2v. (1,155p.). $180. ISBN: 0816107505.

24,000 catalogue cards, photolithographically reproduced. Entries embrace names, subjects, geographical areas and types of manuscripts (*e.g.* account-books, diaries, log-books, maps, literary typescripts). *Class No:* 091

Handbooks & Manuals

[2602]

BRASWELL, L.N. Western manuscripts from classical antiquity to the Renaissance: a handbook. New York, Garland, 1981. xxi,382p. (*Garland reference library of the humanities, v.139.*) ISBN: 0824095413.

A bibliographical guide of 2,074 briefly annotated entries. Arrangement reflects the order in which a researcher would examine a manuscript *i.e.*, from identification to transcript to edition. 15 chapters: I. Bibliographical materials - II. Libraries - III. Microforms - IV. Incipits - V. Special subjects: indexes, lists, catalogues and repertoria - VI. Paleography, writing and scripts - VII. Diplomatics and archives - VIII. Fragments, booklets and related problems - IX. Decoration and illumination - X. Music - XI.

....*(contd.)*
Codicology: the manuscript book - XII. Reference works - XIII. Manuscripts and their contexts - XIV. Journals - XV. Textual criticism. Each chapter preceded by a contents listing and subject guidance. Extensively cross-referenced. Index (p.359-82). *Class No:* 091(035)

Dictionaries

[2603]
MUZERELLE, D. Vocabulaire codicologique: répertoire méthodique des termes français relatifs aux manuscrits. Paris, Editions CEMI, 1985. 265p. plates. ISBN: 2903680043.

Terms in classified order in 7 sections: 1. Les Supports de l'ecriture - 2. Le Copiste et son materiel - 3. La Fabrication du livre - 4. La Copie et le texte - 5. La Decoration - 6. La Reliure - 7. Transmission et conservation. Bibliography (p.19-28); index (p.235-63). A well-structured valuable work, 'essential equipment in the manuscript departments of this country's libraries' (*Book collector,* v.37(2), Summer 1988, p.279). *Class No:* 091(038)

Periodicals

[2604]
Scriptorium. Revue internationale des études relatives aux manuscrits. 1946/47-. Bruxelles, Centre d'Étude des Manuscrits, 1947-. 2pa. BFr3800. ISSN: 00369772.

English sub-title 'International review of manuscript studies'. Contributions predominantly in French, some articles in English and other European languages.

An important scholarly journal, including well-documented articles and various notes, but most valuable for 'Bulletin codicologique', a comprehensive bibliography of recent contributions to manuscript studies. Produced by the Centre International de Codicologie, 'Bulletin codicologique' carries signed and annotated entries (750 v.49, 1995) in author/ anonymous title order for books, periodical articles, catalogues etc.

Cumulated indexes to *Scriptorium,* including 'Bulletin codicologique' entries, published as follows: v.1-30 (1947-76) (1984); v.31-40 (1977-86) (1987); supplementary index v.1-30, alleviating deficiencies in the earlier cumulation, (1988): all ed. by E. Manning. *Class No:* 091(051)

Anglo-Saxon

[2605]
KER, N.R. Catalogue of manuscripts containing Anglo-Saxon. Oxford, Clarendon, 1990. lxiii,579p. facsims. £77.50. ISBN: 0198112513.

Originally published 1957. This version unchanged except for addition of *A Supplement to 'Catalogue of manuscripts containing Anglo-Saxon'* reprinted from *Anglo-Saxon England*, 5, (1977), p.121-31.

Catalogue (p.1-474), arranged by location or owner, A-Z (*e.g.* Oxford. Bodleian, Ashmolean etc., p.349-437). Introduction includes valuable notes on the palaeography and history of the principal MSS. Appendix of manuscripts containing Anglo-Saxon written by foreign scribes (p.475-86). Bibliography (p.485-510). Index of the contents of the manuscripts (p.517-50). Palaeographical and historical index (p.551-58). Index of owners (p.559-67). 8 facsims.
Class No: 091=20.0

French

[2606]
BIBLIOTHÈQUE NATIONALE. (FRANCE). Département des Manuscrits. **Catalogue général des manuscrits français.** Paris, Bibliothèque nationale, 1868-.

Published in various series beginning with *Ancien fonds français*. Additions series, *Nouvelles acquisitions françaises*, began 1899, reaching No.22811 in 4 v. by 1917. *Table générale alphabétique* in 6 v. 1931-48. Further v. covering new acquisitions, including *Catalogue des nouvelles acquisitions françaises, 1958-1971* (1981).
Class No: 091=40

Spanish

[2607]
BRITISH MUSEUM. Catalogue of the manuscripts in the Spanish language in the British Museum. Gayangos, D.P. de, *comp*. London, Trustees of the British Museum, 1875-93. 4v.

Reprinted British Library, 1977 (£95. ISBN: 0714104914).

Descriptions of manuscripts, letters and state papers in the Spanish language acquired up to 1867 with an appendix of later additions in v.4. In 5 classes: I. Theology - II. Belles-lettres and science - III. History and political - IV. Works and tracts relating to Asia, Africa and America - V. Spanish settlements in America. *Class No:* 091=60

[2608]
MARTÍN ABAD, J. Manuscritos de España: guia de catálogos impresos. Madrid, Arco, 1989. 326p. ISBN: 8476350600.

Contents: Catálogo des catálogos de bibliotecas españoles (p.25-248); Catálogo de catálogos de bibliotecas extranjeras; Catálogo de bibliotecas dispersas. 941 fully annotated entries; name, subject, place, archive and library and collection indexes. *Suplemento* 1994 (Ptas1100. ISBN: 847635150X). *Class No:* 091=60

Portuguese

[2609]
The Portuguese manuscript collection of the Library of Congress: a guide. Lund, C.C. *and* Kahler, M.E., *comps*. Washington D.C., Library of Congress, 1980. xi,187p. ISBN: 0844403296.

Annotated list of 537 manuscripts. Index to personal names, places and some titles, (p.159-87).
Class No: 091=690

Latin

[2610]
BIBLIOTHÈQUE NATIONALE. (FRANCE). Département des Manuscrits. **Catalogue général des manuscrits latins.** Paris, Bibliothèque nationale, 1939-.

V.I 1-1438 (1939); v.II 1439-2692 (1940); v.III 2693-3013A (1952); v.IV 3014-3277 (1958); v.V 3278-3535 (1966); v.VI 3536-3775B (1975); v.VII 3776-3835 (1988). Separate index vols. published as follows: 1-2692 (1968); 2693-3775B plus Incipit A-Z (3v. 1981-83); 3776-3835 (1991). *Class No:* 091=71

[2611]

Catalogue des manuscrits en écriture latine: portant des indications de date, de lieu ou de copiste. Samaran, C. *and* Marichal, R., *eds.* Paris, Centre National de la Recherche Scientifique, 1959-84. 7v.

French contribution to the international series of catalogues of datable manuscripts promoted by the Comité International de Paléographie.

V.1 covers the Musée Conde and small Parisian collections, v.2-v.4 the Bibliothèque Nationale, v.5-v.7 French regional collections (*e.g.* v.7 *Ouest de la France et pays de Loire.* 1984. 653p. ISBN: 222203437x). Each volume separately indexed. *Class No:* 091=71

[2612]

—Datierte Handschriften in Bibliotheken der Bundesrepublik Deutschland. Stuttgart, Hiersmann, 1984-.

The German contribution to the Comité International de Paléographie series. Bd.1 *Die datierten Handschriften der Stadt und Universitätsbibliothek Frankfurt am Mainz* (Powitz, G. viii,362p. DM 590. ISBN: 3777284270), includes 337 plates. Latest v., Bd. 4 *Die Datierten Handschriften der Bayerischen Staatsbibliothek München. Teil 1. Die deutschen Handschriften bis 1450.* (Schneider, K. xxxviii,390p. DM540. ISBN: 3777294160), published 1994.

Other countries which have produced catalogues as part of the project include Austria, Belgium, France (as above), Holland, Italy, Sweden and Switzerland. The 3 British contributions to date, covering the British Library, Oxford libraries and Cambridge libraries, are separately entered. *Class No:* 091=71

[2613]

Codices latini antiquiores: a palaeographical guide to Latin manuscripts prior to the ninth century. Lowe, E.A., *ed.* Oxford, Clarendon Press, 1934-66. 11pts. and supplement. Facsims.

Edited under the auspices of the Union Académique Internationale for the American Council of Learned Societies and the Carnegie Institution of Washington.

Pt.I. *Vatican City;* pt.II. *Great Britain and Ireland;* pt.III. *Italy: Ancona-Novara;* pt.IV. *Italy: Perugia-Verona;* pt.V. *Paris;* pt.VI. *France;* pt.VII. *Switzerland;* pt.VIII. *Germany: Altenburg-Leipzig;* pt.IX. *Germany: Maria Laach-Würzburg;* pt.X. *Austria, Belgium, Czechoslovakia, Denmark, Egypt, Holland;* pt.XI. *Hungary, Luxembourg, Poland, Russia, Spain, Sweden, the United States and Yugoslavia.*

'(T)he interest of the work is almost wholly palaeographical. Its aim is to place before scholars succint descriptions, based upon examination of the originals, of all known Latin manuscripts on papyrus, parchment, or vellum which may be regarded as older than the ninth century, accompanied by a specimen, unreduced, of the script and supplemented by a select bibliography' (Introduction v.1 p.vii). The supplement (1971) brings the total no. of manuscripts covered to 1,811 and contains an author index to the preceding 11pts.

Pt.II. *Great Britain and Ireland* issued in a 2nd ed. 1972, correcting errors and incorporating the results of later scholarship. *Class No:* 091=71

[2614]

JEUDY, C. *and* **RIOU, Y-F. Les Manuscrits classiques latins des bibliothèques publiques de France.** Paris, Centre National de la Recherche Scientifique, 1989-.

V.1 Agen-Évereux (xxviii,780p. 25 plates. FFr990. ISBN: 2222040892).

V.1 describes 314 manuscripts of the 8th to 15th centuries held by 36 libraries. *Class No:* 091=71

[2615]

KRISTELLER, P.O. Latin manuscript books before 1600: a list of the printed catalogues and unpublished inventories of extant collections. Krämer, S., *ed.* 4th ed. rev. & enl. ed. München, Monumento Germaniae Historica, 1993. xxxvi,941p. (*Monumenta Germaniae Historica, 13.*) ISBN: 3886121135.

First published in 2 separate parts in *Traditio* (v.6, 1948, p.227-317; v.9, 1953, p.393-418) on printed catalogues and unpublished inventories respectively. 2nd ed. 1960, reprinted as the 3rd ed. 1965 (New York, Fordham Univ. P. ISBN: 0823203808) with the addition of supplementary material.

This ed. greatly enlarged giving coverage to mid 1992. Concentrates on material in public collections. Sections: A. Bibliography and statistics of libraries and their manuscripts (p.1-20) - B. Works describing manuscripts of more than one city (p.21-234) - C. Printed catalogues and handwritten inventories of individual libraries by cities (p.235-936) - D. Directories and guides to libraries and archives (p.937-941, new to this ed.). Impressively comprehensive, a major source of reference in manuscript studies. *Class No:* 091=71

[2616]

—CRANZ, F.E. A Microfilm corpus of the indexes to printed catalogues of Latin manuscripts before 1600. New London, Conn., Connecticut College, 1982. Microfilm.

In 2 pts: 1. 'Text' (ix,609p.); 2. Microfilm (39 35mm reels).

Reproduces the indexes to the published titles listed in Kristeller's 3rd ed. (1965). *Class No:* 091=71

Greek

[2617]

OLIVER, J-M. Répertoire des bibliothèques et des catalogues de manuscrits grecs: de Marcel Richard. 3.éd. Turnhout, Brepols, 1995. xvi,952p.

First published 1948; 2nd ed. 1958, with updating suppl. 1964.

2,507 numbered entries in sections: I. Bibliographie - II. Recueils de travaux - III. Catalogues spécialisés - IV. Catalogues régionaux et répartition par pays... . - V. Villes et autres lieux. Bibliographical notes on some items; extensive cross-referencing. Two appendices providing concordance with 2nd ed. and list of citations. Index (p.899-952). *Class No:* 091=77

[2618]

TURYN, A. Dated Greek manuscripts of the thirteenth and fourteenth centuries in the libraries of Great Britain. Dumbarton Oaks, Center for Byzantine Studies, 1980. 198p. $65. (*Dumbarton Oaks studies, no.17.*) ISBN: 0884020770.

The same author has also published *Dated Greek manuscripts of the thirteenth and fourteenth centuries in the libraries of Italy* Champaign, Univ. of Illinois Press, 1972. 2v. ISBN: 0252000838.

Describes and analyses all extant Greek manuscripts of the period in British libraries. 68mss. from 11 libraries, illustrated with 126 plates. Full discussion of each ms. including bibliographical citations. *Class No:* 091=77

Slavonic

[2619]
A Union catalogue of Cyrillic manuscripts in British and Irish collections. Cleminson, R., *comp.* London, School of Slavonic and East European Studies, Univ. of London, 1988. xii,352p., plates. ISBN: 0903425149.

At head of title 'The Anne Pennington Catalogue'.

Contains descriptions of 204 manuscripts comprising all Cyrillic codices located in British and Irish collections (159 in number), plus fragments of such codices and inscriptions and additions in Cyrillic in codices in other scripts. Charters, letters and similar documents excluded, covered in J.M. Hartley's *Guide to documents and manuscripts in the United Kingdom relating to Russia and the Soviet Union* (1987). Arranged by place A-Z, then institution. Entries 49-119 British Library, 142-198 Bodleian Library. References (p.317-21). Chronological, linguistic, personal name, place, work and incipit indexes. *Class No:* 091=81

Indic

[2620]
SOMADASA, K.D. Catalogue of the Hugh Nevill collection of Sinhalese manuscripts in the British Library. London, British Library, with the Pali Text Society, 1987-95. 7v. £50-75 per v. ISBN: 0712301399, (v.1).

Documents a collection of over 2,000 texts, the largest outside Sri Lanka. Final v. provides indexes.
Class No: 091=911

[2621]
—INDIA OFFICE LIBRARY AND RECORDS. Catalogue of the Sinhalese manuscripts in the India Office Library. Wijayaratne, D.J., *comp and* Reynolds, C.H.B., *ed.*. London, India Office Library and Records, 1981. viii,73p. ISBN: 0903359332. *Class No:* 091=911

Iranian Languages

[2622]
BLUMHARDT, J.F. *and* **MacKENZIE, D.N. Catalogue of the Pashto manuscripts in the libraries of the British Isles.** London, Trustees of the British Museum and Commonwealth Relations Office, 1965. xii,147p.

Reprint, State Mutal Book and Periodical Service ($210. ISBN: 068505733x).

First union catalogue of manuscripts in a single Asian language in British libraries. Describes 170 manuscripts, 69 in the British Museum (Library), 60 in the India Office Library. Title and person indexes. *Class No:* 091=915

Persian (Farsi)

[2623]
ETHÉ, H. Catalogue of Persian manuscripts in the India Office Library. Oxford, For the India Office, 1903-37. 2v.

Facsim ed. in 1v. published by the India Office Library and Records 1980 (ISBN: 0903359251).
Class No: 091=915.5

[2624]
RIEU, C. Catalogue of Persian manuscripts in the British Museum. London, British Museum, 1879-83. 3v.

Reprinted 1966 (£60. ISBN: 0714106445). *Supplement* 1895, reprinted 1977 (£20. ISBN: 0714106623).

The original set describes 2,536 manuscripts, 429 entries in v.3 belonging to the Elliot Collection relating almost exclusively to Indian history. The supplement describes a further 425 items. Updated by: *Class No:* 091=915.5

[2625]
—MEREDITH-OWENS, G.M. Handlist of Persian manuscripts 1895-1966. London, British Museum, 1967. x,126p. £10. ISBN: 0714106305.

Minimal information on 972 manuscripts.
Class No: 091=915.5

Celtic Languages

[2626]
BRITISH LIBRARY. Department of Manuscripts. **Catalogue of Irish manuscripts in the British Library:** [formerly British Museum]. Dublin, School of Celtic Studies, Dublin Institute for Advanced Studies, 1992. 2v. £35. ISBN: 1855001527.

Second v. contains lengthy introduction, general index and index of initia. Originally published in 3 v. as *Catalogue of Irish manuscripts in the British Museum* (1926-53).

Lists of Irish manuscripts are recorded in A.R. Eager's *A guide to Irish bibliographical material* (*q.v.*).
Class No: 091=916

[2627]
Catalogue of Gaelic manuscripts in selected libraries in Great Britain and Ireland. Mackenhnie, J., *comp.* Boston, Mass., G.K. Hall, 1973. 2v.(1456p.). $265. ISBN: 0816108323.

72,800 entries for Irish, Welsh, Scottish and English Gaelic manuscripts in the National Library of Scotland, the university libraries of Edinburgh, Glasgow and Aberdeen, the Royal Irish Academy, Dublin and the British Museum (Library). *Class No:* 091=916

[2628]
NATIONAL LIBRARY OF IRELAND. Catalogue of Irish manuscripts in the National Library of Ireland. Dublin, Institute for Advanced Studies, 1961-. Irregular. ISSN: 07911890.

Began publication with Fasc.II MSS. G15-G69. Fasc.I published 1968, Fasc.III 1976. Latest to appear Fasc.XIII MSS. G700-G773 (1996. 130p. ISBN: 1855001772).
Class No: 091=916

Semitic Languages

[2629]
DESREUMAUX, A. Répertoire des bibliothèques et des catalogues de manuscrits syriaques. Paris, Éditions du Centre National de la Recherche Scientifique, 1991. 285p. FFr200. ISBN: 2222045487.

List of libraries by country (p.25-47); bibliography of 858 catalogues and other works relating to Syriac manuscripts (p.49-266). Name index. *Class No:* 091=92

[2630]
SHUNNAR, Z. Katalog Samaritanischer Handschriften I. Berlin, Seitz, 1974. 257p. illus.

Covers the British Museum (Gaster Collection), thereby complementing the Margoliouth catalogue (below). Other collections include those in the Library of Congress, New York Public Library and Yale University.
Class No: 091=92

Hebrew

[2631]
Catalogue of the Hebrew manuscripts in the Bodleian Library and in the college libraries of Oxford: including MSS. in other languages which are written with Hebrew characters or relating to the Hebrew language or literature; and a few Samaritan MSS. Neubauer, A., *comp.* Oxford, Clarendon Press, 1994. xxxii,1167p. £80;$145. ISBN: 0199513570.

Reprint: first published by Clarendon Press 1886.

2,451 entries; indexed. Reprint accompanied by *Catalogue of the Hebrew manuscripts in the Bodleian Library: supplement of addenda and corrigenda to vol. 1 (A. Neubauer's catalogue)* (Beit-Arie, M. *comp.* & May, R.A. *ed.* Oxford, Clarendon Press, 1994. xxxi,595p. plates. £60;$98. ISBN: 0198173865). *Class No:* 091=924

[2632]
The Collective catalogue of Hebrew manuscripts: the Institute of Microfilmed Hebrew Manuscripts, the Department of Manuscripts, the Jewish National and University Library. Paris, Chadwyck-Healey, 1989. Microfiche. £3,850.

862 microfiche and *User's guide* (ISBN: 2869760213).

Reproduces records from the catalogues of both institutions, the former holdings details of around 50,000 codices and 200,000 fragments found in 700 collections in 30 countries. Information presented in 12 sequences, including author and name file (196 fiche), subject file (240 fiche), geographic index file, title file and library catalogue file. *Class No:* 091=924

[2633]
MARGOLIOUTH, G. Catalogue of the Hebrew and Samaritan manuscripts in the British Museum. London, British Museum, 1899-1935. 4v.

Pts.1-3, by G. Margoliouth published 1899-1915. (Reprinted 1964 omitting plates. £10 per v. ISBN: 0714106194). Pt.4, *Introduction, indexes, brief descriptions of accessions and addenda and corrigenda* by J. Leveen published 1935. (Reprinted 1978. £15. ISBN: 07141066194).

Supplemented by *Catalogue of Hebrew manuscripts in the Gaster Collection, The British Library* (London, Hebrew Section, Oriental and India Office Collections, 1996). Forthcoming 1998: *Catalogue of Samaritan manuscripts now in the British Library* (ISBN: 0712345744). *Class No:* 091=924

[2634]
REIF, S.C. Hebrew manuscripts at Cambridge University Library: a description and introduction. Cambridge, Cambridge Univ. Press, 1997. xx,626p. plates. £75:$125. (*Univ. of Cambridge Oriental publications, 52.*) ISBN: 052158339x.

Arranged in 23 categories, Bible texts ... Liturgy ... Philosophy ... Other material relating to Hebraica and Judaica. Taylor-Schechter Collection excluded. Entries include classmark, full physical description, published references and provenance. 12 indexes (*e.g.* titles, sources, names and scribes); historical introduction (p.1-35). *Class No:* 091=924

Arabic

[2635]
BIBLIOTHÈQUE NATIONALE. (FRANCE). Catalogue des manuscrits arabes. Paris, Bibliothèque Nationale, 1972-95. ISBN: 2717713956.

Première partie: manuscrits chrétiens. V.I. Nos.1-323 (1972. 279p.). V.II. Manuscrits dispersés entre les nos. 780 et 6933 (1974. 194p.).

Deuxième partie: manuscrits musulmans. V.I. Fasc.1. Les manuscrits du Coran: aux origines de la calligraphie Coranique (1983. 180p.); V.I. Fasc.2. Les manuscrits du Coran: du Maghreb à l'Insulinde (1985. 170p.) (v.I describes manuscripts nos. 324-589). V.II. Nos. 590-1120 (1978. 370p.). V.III. Nos. 1121-1464 (1985. 328p.). V.IV. Index de tomes II et III nos. 590-1464 (1985. 231p.). V.V Nos. 1465-1685 (1995. 333p.).

Catalogue of the richest collection in the Western world. Adds to and revises W. de Slane's *Catalogue des manuscrits arabes* (1883-95) and E. Blochet's *Catalogue des manuscrits arabes des nouvelles acquisitions 1884-1924* (1925). *Class No:* 091=927

[2636]
BRITISH LIBRARY. Oriental and India Office Collections. **A Classified handlist of Arabic manuscripts acquired since 1912.** Vassie, R., *ed.* London, British Library, 1995. 2v. £25 per v.

V.1 *Islamic law* (ISBN: 0712303464); v.2 *Qur'ānic science and health.* Continues *A Descriptive list of manuscripts acquired by the Trustees of the British Museum since 1894* (1912) which follows Rieu's *Supplement to the Catalogue of Arabic manuscripts in the British Museum* (1894).

First of a projected series of vols. to list the British Library's Arabic manuscripts. V.1 contains 481 entries, v.2 515. Indexes in each v. *Class No:* 091=927

[2637]
HUISMAN, A.J.W. Les Manuscrits arabes dans le monde: une bibliographie des catalogues. Leiden, E.J. Brill, 1967. 99p. FFr48. ISBN: 9004009752.

Revises and updates M.J. Vajda's *Répertoire des catalogues et inventaires de manuscrits arabes* (1949).

Arranged A-Z by country. Includes catalogues of collections in Arab countries as well as the Western world. *Class No:* 091=927

[2638]
PRINCETON UNIVERSITY. Library. **Catalogue of Arabic manuscripts (Yahuda section) in the Garrett Collection** Princeton University Library. Mach, R. Princeton, Princeton Univ. Press, 1977. viii,515p. £170;$250. ISBN: 0691039089.

Collection acquired 1942. 5,275 entries, classified arrangement. Somewhat meagre information given. Index of authors and titles. Supplemented by:- *Class No:* 091=927

[2639]
—PRINCETON UNIVERSITY. Library. Handlist of Arabic manuscripts (New series) in the Princeton University Library. Mach, R. *and* Ormsby, E.L. Princeton, Princeton Univ. Press, 1985. xiv,393p. £80;$99.50. (*Princeton studies in the Near East.*) ISBN: 0691054290.

Concise descriptions of 1,626 manuscripts collected 1955-1982, predominantly Shihite works from the early period to the present century. Probably the richest collection in this area in the Western world. *Class No:* 091=927

[2640]

WITKAM, J.J. Catalogue of Arabic manuscripts in the Library of the University of Leiden and other collections in the Netherlands. Leiden, Leiden Univ. Press/Brill, 1983-. Fasc.1-. ISBN: 9004079378.

Fasc. 5 issued 1989. To replace *Handlist of Arabic manuscripts in the Library of the University of Leiden and other collections in the Netherlands* (Voorhoeve, P. *comp.* 2nd ed. 1980. ISBN: 9060214714).

To cover the 4,000 Arabic manuscripts held by the university. The early fascicules catalogue those parts of the collection not listed by Voorhoeve. *Class No:* 091=927

[2641]

World survey of Islamic manuscripts. Roper, G., *ed.* London, Al-Furqan Islamic Heritage Foundation, 1991-94. 5v. £96.50 per v. ISBN: 1873992025.

Inaugural volume (1991); v.1-3 (1992-94); v.4 *Supplement, including indexes of languages, names and titles...* . (1994). An Arabic translation began publication 1997 (ISBN: 1873992041).

'"Islamic" for our purposes means written in the Arabic script, in any of the languages that have used this script, regardless of the subject matter or content of the texts. Not only Muslim, but also most Christian Arabic manuscripts are therefore included; but Arabic, Persian and Turkish manuscripts written in other scripts ... are generally excluded' (p.xv, v.1). Collections of archives, documents, letters, etc., mostly omitted. Arranged in country sections Afghanistan ... Yugoslavia. Format varies slightly, country entries generally list union catalogues and surveys followed by details of individual collections (brief notes including holdings summary) and a bibliographical appendix. *Class No:* 091=927

Hamitic Languages

[2642]

BAYLOT, R. *and* **RODINSON, M. Répertoire des bibliothèques et des catalogues de manuscrits éthiopiens.** Paris, Centre national de la recherche scientifique/Turnhout, Brepols, 1995. 118p. FFr355. (*Documents, études et répertoires.*) ISBN: 2271052157.

Similar in function and plan to Coulie (below). *Class No:* 091=93

[2643]

STRELCYN, S., *comp.* **Catalogue of Ethiopian manuscripts in the British Library** acquired since the year 1877. London, British Museum Publications, 1978. xvi,184p. 16p. plates. £35. ISBN: 0714106496.

Describes 108 manuscripts. Continues Wright, W. *Catalogue of the Ethiopic manuscripts in the British Museum acquired since the year 1847* (London, Trustees of the British Museum, 1877. 366p. 12p. plates). *Class No:* 091=93

Caucasian Languages

[2644]

COULIE, B. Répertoire des bibliothèques et des catalogues de manuscrits arméniens. Turnhout, Brepols, 1992. xiii,265p. ISBN: 2503502539.

Main section (p.13-229) is an international listing of libraries by city A-Z outlining collections, indicating notable manuscripts and citing relevant catalogues, etc. List of works cataloguing Armenian manuscripts precedes. Index of manuscripts. *Class No:* 091=946

Oriental

[2645]

Oriental manuscripts in Europe and North America: a survey. Pearson, J.D., *comp.* Zug, Inter Documentation, 1971. lxxx,515p. ISBN: 385750000x.

Published with the assistance of UNESCO. A development and extension of Pearson's *Oriental manuscript collections in Great Britain and Ireland* (London, Royal Asiatic Society, 1954).

An attempt to identify collections of manuscripts in Oriental and Asiatic languages. Arranged in language sections, collections discussed geographically by European or North American country. Includes notes on collection size, development and catalogues. Indexes of former owners of manuscripts and libraries and other collections. *Class No:* 091=95

Indonesian

[2646]

PIGEAUD, T.G.T. Literature of Java: catalogue raisonné of Javanese manuscripts in the Library of the University of Leiden and other public collections in the Netherlands. The Hague, Nijhoff, 1967-80. 4v. illus., facsims., maps.

V.1: *Synopsis of Javanese literature, 900-1900 A.D.* (1967. xx,325p.). V.2: *Descriptive lists of Javanese manuscripts* (1968. xv,972p.). V.3: *Illustrations and facsimilies of manuscripts, maps; addenda and a general index of names and subjects* (1970. xvii,441p.). V.4: *Supplement.* (1980. xxiii,390p. Published by Leiden University Press. ISBN: 9060214536). *Class No:* 091=992

[2647]

RICKLEFS, M.C. *and* **VOORHOEVE, P. Indonesian manuscripts in Great Britain:** a catalogue of manuscripts in Indonesian languages in British public collections. Oxford, Oxford Univ. Press, 1977. xxix,237p. £25. (*London Oriental bibliographies, v.5.*) ISBN: 0197135927.

Lists 1,200 manuscripts. Bibliography (p.188-202). *Class No:* 091=992

Middle Ages

[2648]

BANKS, D.H. Medieval manuscript bookmaking: a bibliographic guide. Metuchen, N.J. and London, Scarecrow Press, 1989. viii,282p. £26.25;$32.50. ISBN: 0810822741.

7 chapters: I. Introduction - II. Books in the middle ages - III. Medieval libraries - IV. The manuscript book and the Church - V. Universities and books - VI. Economic and social conditions and their impact on books - VII. Science and technology. Bibliography (p.139-273) listing the 1,044 items discussed in the text. Excludes some 'specialized subjects, for instance music and paleography...' (Preface p.vii). Index (p.275-82). *Class No:* 091"01/14"

[2649]

BEINÉCKE RARE BOOK AND MANUSCRIPT LIBRARY. Catalogue of medieval and Renaissance manuscripts in the Beinécke Rare Book and Manuscript Library, Yale University. Binghamton, N.Y., Centre for Medieval and Early Renaissance Studies, 1984-.

V.1 *MSS. 1-250* (1984. xxii,420p. 32 plates. $55). V.2 *MSS. 250-500* (1987. xiv,574p. 64 plates. $55). V.3 *Marston manuscripts* (1992. xxxii,648p. 64 plates. $60).

Entry format similar to Ker (*q.v.*), heading, contents, physical descriptions, provenance and bibliography. Each volume extensively indexed; black and white plates. A

....*(contd.)*
significant work, 'its breadth and generous indexing make it a valuable reference tool even for medieval and Renaissance scholars who have little interest in the particular manuscripts in the Beinécke' (*American reference books annual*, v.25, 1994, p.14). *Class No:* 091"01/14"

[2650]
—HOUGHTON LIBRARY. Catalogue of medieval and Renaissance manuscripts in the Houghton Library, Harvard University. Binghamton, N.Y., Medieval and Renaissance Texts and Studies, 1995-.

V.1 *MSS Lat 3-179* (xxxv,347p. 67 plates. $40. ISBN: 0866981853).

Similar to the Yale set (above). Four further volumes are projected. *Class No:* 091"01/14"

[2651]
GENEVAIS, A-M. Bibliothèques de manuscrits médiévaux en France: relevé des inventaires du VIIIe au XVIIIe siècle. Paris, Éditions du Centre National de la Recherche Scientifique, 1987. xix,388p. FFr285. ISBN: 2222041015.

Similar to Ker (*q.v.*) in concept, listing catalogues, etc. relating to medieval manuscripts held by French libraries. 1,938 entries arranged by author/institution; indexed. *Class No:* 091"01/14"

[2652]
Gesamtindex mittelalterlicher Handschriftenkataloge: Kumulation der Register der seit 1945 in der Bundesrepublik Deutschland erschienenen Handschriftenkataloge. Staatsbibliothek zu Berlin. Preussischer Kulturbesitz, *hrsg.* Wiesbaden, Harrassowitz, 1995. Microfiche. DM198. ISBN: 3447037466.

Comprises *Kreuzregister* (14 microfiche), *Initienregister* (10 microfiche) and explanatory booklet (22p.).

Union index to German catalogues of medieval manuscripts. 130 works produced since 1945 included. A database version is also freely available through Deutsches Bibliotheksinstitut's DBI-Link Internet service at http://dbix01.dbi-berlin.de:6100/DBI/logon.html. *Class No:* 091"01/14"

[2653]
HUNTINGTON LIBRARY. Guide to medieval and Renaissance manuscripts in the Huntington Library. Dutschke, C.W., *and others, comps.* San Marino, Ca., Huntington Library Publications, 1989. 2v. $95. ISBN: 0873280822.

The most detailed of a series of descriptive guides to the collections of the Huntington Library. Includes 320 manuscripts in Latin script and 2 in Greek. Indexes of dated manuscripts, manuscripts cited, scribes and artists. A 'fine example of modern cataloguing practice' (*Times literary supplement,* no.4521, November 24th 1989, p.1307). *Class No:* 091"01/14"

[2654]
KER, N.R. Medieval manuscripts in British libraries. Oxford, Clarendon Press, 1969-. Facsims.

V.I. *London.* (1969. xxxviii,437p. ISBN: 0198182198); v.II. *Abbotsford-Keele.* (1977. xliii,999p. ISBN: 0198181620); v.III. *Lampeter-Oxford.* (1983. xxxvi,735p. ISBN: 0198181957); v.IV. *Paisley-York.* (1992. xl,826p. £95. ISBN: 0198181965).

'The British Museum ... the National Libraries of Scotland and Wales, the Bodleian Library and Cambridge University Library are beyond my scope. They figure only as headings in which reference are made to printed or unprinted catalogues. For other libraries *Medieval manuscripts in British libraries* is intended to provide information about manuscripts, other than muniments and binding fragments, written before 1500, in Latin or a Western European language, either by reference to an existing catalogue or by my own descriptions'. (Preface v.I p.v-vi). Full descriptions for previously uncatalogued items including text, make up, decoration, etc. A final v. to contain addenda and indexes is projected. *Class No:* 091"01/14"

[2655]
LIBRARY OF CONGRESS. Medieval and Renaissance manuscript books in the Library of Congress: a descriptive catalog. Schutzner, S., *comp.* Washington D.C., Library of Congress, 1989-. $62. ISBN: 0844405167, v.1.

Projected for 3v. V.1: *Bibles, liturgy, books of hours* (xi,421p. col.plates).

V.1 describes 64 Bibles and liturgical and paraliturgical texts. 26 col.plates. Index. Two further volumes projected, to cover canon law and theology and secular manuscripts, yet to appear early 1998. *Class No:* 091"01/14"

[2656]
RICCI, S. de *and* WILSON, W.J. Census of medieval and Renaissance manuscripts in the United States and Canada. New York, Wilson, 1935-40. 3v.

Published under the auspices of the American Council of Learned Societies. (Reprinted New York, Kraus, 1961).

Covers the period to 1600. Arranged by states, cities and libraries (v.1: Alabama-Massachusetts; v.2: Michigan-Wisconsin, Hawaii, Canada; errata and addenda; v.3: Indices, 6 in all - General index of names, titles and headings; Scribes, illuminators, cartographers; Incipits; Gregory numbers for Greek New Testament manuscripts; Present owners; Previous owners). About 10,000 items are briefly described. *Class No:* 091"01/14"

[2657]
—RICCI, S. de. Supplement to the Census ... Originated by C.U. Faye; continued and edited by W.H. Bond. New York, Bibliographical Society of America, 1962. xvii,626p.

Similar in pattern, with cross-references to the main work. *Class No:* 091"01/14"

[2658]
SINCLAIR, K.V. Descriptive catalogue of mediaeval and Renaissance Western manuscripts in Australia. Sydney, Sydney Univ. Press, 1969. xvi,504p. illus. ISBN: 0424057603.

Identifies and meticulously records the codicological and textual elements of 264 manuscripts in public and private collections. *Class No:* 091"01/14"

[2659]
—MANION, M., *and others*. Medieval and Renaissance manuscripts in New Zealand collections. Melbourne and London, Thames & Hudson, 1989. 200p. plates (some col.). £34. ISBN: 0500235449.

Detailed descriptions of 181 manuscripts in public and private collections, with the emphasis on illuminated manuscripts. Indexed. *Class No:* 091"01/14"

Renaissance

[2660]
Iter italicum: a finding list of uncatalogued or incompletely catalogued humanistic manuscripts of the Renaissance in Italian and other libraries. Kristeller, P.O., *comp.* London, The Warburg Institute; Leiden, E.J. Brill, 1963-97.

V.I. *Italy. Agrigento to Novara.* (1963. xxviii,533p.

....(contd.)

£106). V.II. *Italy. Orvieto to Volterra. Vatican City*. (1967. xv,736p. £129.50). V.III. *Alia itinera I. Australia to Germany*. (1983. xxxviii,747p. £128.75). V.IV. *Alia itinera II. Great Britain to Spain*. (1989. xxii,812p. £152). V.V. *Alia itinera III and Italy III. Sweden to Yugoslavia, supplement to Italy A-F*. (1990. xxii,642p. £173.50). V.VI. *Italy III and alia itinera IV. Supplement to Italy G-V, supplement to Vatican and Austria to Spain*. (1992. xxiv,595p. £173.50).

V.I-II and IV have their own indexes. Separate index to v.III (1987. £17.75); indexes and addenda to v.V (1993. £26.50) and v.VI (1996. £24). The newly issued *A Cumulative index to volumes I-VI ....* (1997. vi,581p. ISBN: 9004105921) attempts to 'collect all mentions of the same person under a single entry' (*Preface*).

Intended as a finding list, the 'main emphasis is on the textual content of the manuscript listed, as against their script and decoration, external appearance, provenance and history' (Preface p.xiii). Originally confined to Italian libraries, coverage has been extended worldwide. The section for Great Britain includes *c*.135 holding institutions arranged by town. Supplementary material in v.V-VI based on recently published material and new contributions from scholars and librarians. A CD-ROM version with Windows and DOS interface and issued 1995 (1 CD-ROM and Manual (39p.). $1,303.50. ISBN: 9004101225)
Class No: 091"1095-1300"

Illuminated Manuscripts

[2661]

Corpus de manuscrits enluminés des collections publiques des départements. Paris, Éditions du centre national de la recherche scientifique, 1991-.

V.1 *Manuscrits enluminés de Dijon* (387p. FFr550. ISBN: 2222043557) describes 350 manuscripts with 148 plates, mainly black and white. Indexed. Further v. yet to appear 1997. *Class No:* 091.3

[2662]

MANION, M. *and* **VINES, V.F. Medieval and Renaissance illuminated manuscripts in Australian collections.** Melbourne and London, Thames and Hudson, 1984. 240p. plates. £28;Aus$85. ISBN: 0500233810.

Lengthy descriptions under headings: ownership; text; decoration; programme of decoration; commentary; bibliography. 302 illustrations, 48 in colour. Index (p.235-40). Supplements Sinclair (*q.v.*). *Class No:* 091.3

[2663]

PÄCHT, O. Book illumination in the middle ages: an introduction. London, Harvey Miller Publishers; Oxford, Oxford Univ. Press, 1986. 223p. illus., plates. £36. ISBN: 0199210608.

Paperback ed. 1994 (£19.95. ISBN: 1872501761).

Thematic, rather than chronological, analysis from the point of view of format and style. Includes chapters on the initial letter, Bible illustration, didactic miniatures, illustration of the apocalypse and illustration of the psalter. Careful use of examples; 32 full colour plates, 210 illustrations. Select bibliography, bibliography of the works of Pächt. Well received, 'by far the best introduction for the student and teacher' (*Manuscripta*, v.32(1), March 1988, p.50-51). *Class No:* 091.3

[2664]

PÄCHT, O. *and* **ALEXANDER, J.J.G. Illuminated manuscripts in the Bodleian Library,** Oxford. Oxford, Clarendon Press, 1966-73. 3v. facsims.

V.1: *German, Dutch, Flemish, French and Spanish schools*. (1966. xii,108p. 66 plates); v.2: *Italian school*. (1970. xii,161p. 88 plates. ISBN: 0198171692); v.3: *British, Irish and Icelandic schools: with addenda to volumes 1 and 2*. (1973. xiii,167p. 120 plates. ISBN: 0198171854).

An invaluable survey of the Bodleian's collections. Excludes manuscripts after 1800 and most post-medieval manuscripts containing topographical or heraldic drawings. Over 3,000 manuscripts briefly described across the 3v.; black and white plates. Each volume includes indexes of texts and authors, illuminators and scribes, persons (mainly owners) and places. *Class No:* 091.3

[2665]

—ALEXANDER, J.J.G. *and* TEMPLE, E. Illuminated manuscripts in Oxford college libraries, the university archives and the Taylor Institution. Oxford, Clarendon Press, 1985. 142p. (71 leaves). £50. ISBN: 0198173814.

Compiled to complement the 3v. survey of the Bodleian (above). 1,012 entries. *Class No:* 091.3

[2666]

—Illuminated manuscripts: an index to selected Bodleian Library colour reproductions. Ohlgren, T.H., *ed.* New York, Garland, 1977. xxiv,646p. (*Garland reference library of the humanities, v.89.*) ISBN: 0824098846.

An index to those manuscripts reproduced on 35mm colour microfilm. Further coverage provided by Ohlgren, T.H. *ed. Illuminated manuscripts and books in the Bodleian Library: a supplement index*. (New York, Garland, 1978. xxxii,583p. Garland reference library of the humanities v.123. ISBN: 082409820x). *Class No:* 091.3

[2667]

A Survey of manuscripts illuminated in the British Isles. Alexander, J.J.G., *general ed.* Oxford, Harvey Miller in conjunction with Oxford Univ. Press, 1975-96. Facsims.

V.1. *Insular manuscripts from the 6th to the 9th century* (Alexander, J.J.G. 1978. 219p. £82. ISBN: 0905203011). V.2. *Anglo-Saxon manuscripts, 900-1066* (Temple, E. 1976. 243p. £44. ISBN: 0856020168). V.3. *Romanesque manuscripts, 1066-1190* (Kaufman, C.M. 1978. 235p. ISBN: 0856020176). V.4. *Early Gothic manuscripts* (Morgan, N.J. In 2 pts: I. *1190-1250* (1982. 276p. £65. ISBN: 0199210268); II. *1250-1285* (1988. (374p. £78. ISBN: 0905203534)). V.5. *Gothic manuscripts, 1285-1385* (Sandler, L.F. In 2 pts: I. *Text and illustration* (1986. 70p. 419 plates £80. ISBN: 0199210373); II. *Catalogue* (1986. 231p. £80. ISBN: 0199210373)). V.6. *Later Gothic manuscripts, 1390-1490* (Scott, K.L. 1996. £140. ISBN: 0905203046. In 2 pts: I. *Text and illustrations*; II. *Catalogues and indexes*).

Provides an illustrated corpus of all the most important manuscripts illuminated in Britain. Detailed treatment of each manuscript, including full description and notes on provenance, published literature and exhibitions. Indexes in each volume. *Class No:* 091.3

[2668]

—Insular and Anglo-Saxon illuminated manuscripts: an iconographic catalogue *c.*AD625 to 1100. Ohlgren, T.H., *comp. and ed.* New York, Garland, 1986. xxvii,400p. 50 plates. ISBN: 0824086511.

Designed to supplement the appropriate volumes of *A survey of manuscripts illuminated in the British Isles.* 222 main entries; comprehensively indexed. *Class No:* 091.3

[2669]

—A Survey of manuscripts illuminated in France. Avril, F. *and* Alexander, J.J.G., *eds.* London, Harvey Miller, 1996-.

V.1 *Romanesque manuscripts: the twelfth century* (Cahn, W. 2v. (I. *Text and illustrations* 48p. 374plates; II. *Catalogue* (217p.). £125;$220. ISBN; 1872501605(set)).

Largely modelled on *A Survey of manuscripts illuminated in the British Isles* (above). Further volumes in preparation for Frankish, Gothic and Renaissance manuscripts.
Class No: 091.3

[2670]

WORMALD, F. *and* GILES, P.M. A Descriptive catalogue of the additional illuminated manuscripts in the Fitzwilliam Museum. Cambridge, Cambridge Univ. Press, 1982. 2v. (xiv,402p. £130. ISBN: 0521245818; 403-808p. £140. ISBN: 0521245826).

500 additional manuscripts acquired since M.R. James's *A Descriptive catalogue of the manuscripts in the Fitzwilliam Museum* (1895). Excludes the McClean bequest covered by M.R. James's *A descriptive catalogue of the McClean collection of manuscripts in the Fitzwilliam Museum* (1912). Includes an iconographic and general index to authors, artists, scribes, previous owners and places.
Class No: 091.3

Glossaries

[2671]

BROWN, M.P. Understanding illuminated manuscripts: a guide to technical terms. J. Paul Getty Museum in assoc. with the British Library, 1994. 127p. illus., plates. £9.95;$13.95. ISBN: 0712303405.

Offers readable explanations of *c.*500 terms frequently encountered in the study of Western manuscripts. Most entries fairly brief (*e.g.* 'Headpiece', 40 words; 'Obit', 20 words). Occasional illustrative col. plates. Mainly for the general public and students, but not without value to the professional. *Class No:* 091.3(038.1)

[2672]

VALENTINE, L.N. Ornament in medieval manuscripts: a glossary. London, Faber and Faber, 1965. 108p. illus.

Contents: 1. Elements of pattern - 2. Ornament in its simplest form - 3. Developed ornament - 4. Colours - 5. The page - 6. Lettering terms - 7. Initials - 8. Useful descriptive terms and definitions. Appendix (p.81-95): Leaves, fruit, flowers as sources of ornament; supernatural, mythical creatures (medieval, classical); crosses; flags; haloes. 'Books of reference' (p.96); index (p.97-108). Numerous small black and white drawings. *Class No:* 091.3(038.1)

Histories

[2673]

DE HAMEL, C. A History of illuminated manuscripts. 2nd ed., rev. & enl. London, Phaidon, 1994. 272p. plates. £34.99;$55. ISBN: 0714829498.

Pbk. ed. also available (1997. £22;$35. ISBN: 0714834521).

.... *(contd.)*

Provides a more general approach than Pächt (*q.v.*), having 8 broadly chronological chapters each focussing on groups who made and used illuminated manuscripts (*e.g.* 'Books for monks' (12th century); 'Books for aristocrats' (14th century). 240 plates, mostly col., each with a descriptive annotation. Bibliography (p.258-63); index of manuscripts and a general index. '(A) real tour-de-force' (*Rare books newsletter*, no.50, July 1995 p.68).
Class No: 091.3(091)

Hebrew

[2674]

NARKISS, B. Hebrew illuminated manuscripts in the British Isles: a catalogue raisonné. Oxford, Oxford Univ. Press, 1982. 2v. £70;$90. ISBN: 0197259774.

61 Spanish and Portuguese manuscripts in ample detail, with full indexes and glossary. Separate vol. of 171 plates. Guide to Sephardic schools of illumination.
Class No: 091.3=924

Autographs

[2675]

Autographs and manuscripts: a collector's manual. Berkeley, E., *ed.* New York, Scribners, 1978. xviii,565p. illus. ISBN: 0684156229.

Sponsored by the Manuscripts Society. Contains 40 articles *e.g.* collecting fundamentals; language and procedures; areas of specialization. Full bibliography and glossary. Many illustrations, detailed index.
Class No: 091.5

[2676]

BENJAMIN, M.A. Autographs: a key to collecting. New York, Walter R. Benjamin Autographs, 1963. xxii,313p. plates., tables.

Corrected and revised version of ed. first published 1946. Includes new preface and selected list of reference works. Reprint available from Dover Publications (1986. $10.95. ISBN: 0486250350).

Pt.1 discusses autographs and collecting under 12 headings, *e.g.* 'What to collect'; 'Facsimilies, reproductions and manuscript copies'. Pt.2 deals with care and preservation and arrangement of collections. List of reference works (p.283-89); index. *Class No:* 091.5

[2677]

RAWLINS, R. Four hundred years of British autographs: a collector's guide. London, Dent, 1970. 188p. facsims. ISBN: 0460039679.

Autographs are grouped by categories, p.51-174 (sovereigns; royalty; politicians; men of the church; men of law; men of action; pioneers and benefactors; scientists and scholars; literary figures; artists; musicians; personalities of the theatre; Empire and Commonwealth personalities; magnates of commerce and industry; sportsmen). About 8 autographs per page. Unannotated bibliography of works on autograph collecting (p.175-7). Index. *Class No:* 091.5

[2678]

RAWLINS, R. The Guinness book of autographs. Enfield, Guinness Superlatives, 1977. [viii],244p. illus., facsims. ISBN: 0900424737.

International in scope, reproducing autographs of around 1,600 individuals from all walks of life, from the 8th century to the present. Arranged A-Z by name, brief biographical details in right hand column, autograph, occasionally with

.... (contd.)
variant forms, in left hand column. A few grouped entries; *e.g.* 'British prime ministers', 'The presidents of the United States'. Some overlap with *Four hundred years of British autographs* (above). *Class No:* 091.5

[2679]
SANDERS, G., *and others*. Collector's guide to autographs. Radnor, Pa., Wallace-Homestead, 1990. xiv,225p. illus., facsims. (*Wallace-Homestead collector's guides series.*) ISBN: 0870695568.

15 chap. guide covering topics such as forgery, obtaining autographs, care and preservation, computerization of collection, etc. Brief list of autograph dealers, galleries and publications; short annotated bibliography.

Sanders is also responsible for *The Sanders price guide to autographs: the world's leading autograph pricing authority* (4th ed. Alexander, N.C., Alexander Books, 1997. xii,608p. $24.95. ISBN: 1570900329) listing more than 50,000 current prices. *Class No:* 091.5

Incunabula

Databases

[2680]
Incunabula short title catalogue. London, British Library, 1984-. Computer database.

Online access via BLAISE-LINE. File updated monthly.

An ongoing project to record in short-title form all books and other material printed with movable type before 1501. Developed from two major national union catalogues of incunabula, Goff's *Third census* and the *Indice generale degli incunaboli delle biblioteche d'Italia* (*qq.v.*). These sources supplemented by data for incunabula held by the British Library and other libraries in the UK and abroad. Records include bibliographical references and locations with notes on textual and printing history, etc., if BL holds a copy. Now contains more than 28,000 records, over 85% of known incunabula. *Class No:* 093(003.4)

[2681]
—The Illustrated ISTC on CD-ROM. Reading, Primary Source Media in assoc. with the British Library, 1996-. CD-ROM database. £1,995.

Issued on two CD-ROM disc with user manual (73p.). MS-Windows software. Annual cumulative updates envisaged over ten year period.

Contains the complete textual database of the online *ISTC* and 10,000 key images of original incunabula editions. Each annual update to add approx. 10,000 additional images. A major reference source combining bibliographical data and images of incunabula on an unprecedented scale. 'It is hard to see how any library supporting research can fail to acquire this indispensable tool' (*The Library*, v.19(3), September 1997, p.265). *Class No:* 093(003.4)

Bibliographies of Bibliographies

[2682]
BESTERMAN, T. Early printed books to the end of the sixteenth century: a bibliography of bibliographies. 2nd ed. rev. and much enl. Geneva, Societas Bibliographica, 1961. 344p.

Reprinted New York, Rowman & Littlefield, 1969 (0874710472). First published 1940.

.... (contd.)
2,389 numbered entries giving full pagination and stating number of items listed. Divided into 'Block books' (p.13-14) and 'Books printed from type', subdivided Bibliographies of bibliographies; Bibliographies (general; select; special: subjects; special: countries); Library catalogues. Indexed (p.309-64) by author, subject, printer and bookseller, printing-place, libraries (public and private).
Class No: 093(009)

[2683]
Der Buchdruck im 15 Jahrhundert: eine bibliographie. Corsten, S. *and* Fuchs, R.W., *hrsg.* Stuttgart, Hiersmann, 1988-93. 2v. DM1300 (Bd.1); DM260 (Bd.2). (*Hiersemanns bibliographische Handbücher, Bd. 7.*) ISBN: 3777288128.

A bibliography on all aspects of the fifteenth century printed book. International in scope, over 15,000 entries for books, book chapters, articles, etc. Main listing in v.1 (xviii,699p.). Contents: I. Allgemeiner Teil (p.3-280) 1. Buchdruck und Buchhandel des 15 Jahrhunderts; 2. Das Buch des 15 Jahrhunderts; 3. Wiegendruckforschung - II. Regionaler Teil A: Länder (p.281-415) - III. Regionaler Teil B: Orte (p.415-699), divided by place and printer. Includes valuable lists of general catalogues of incunabula by country (p.186-96) and incunabula catalogues of libraries (p.199-272). V.2 *Nachträge Ergänzungen. Die Register* (vii,164p. ISBN: 3777293229) contains additional items and indexes. The most complete bibliography for the study of incunabula yet compiled, 'indispensable not only to incunabulists ... but to the far greater number of researchers and scholars concerned with other aspects of the fifteenth century' (*The Library. Sixth series*, v.XI(3), September 1989, p.277).
Class No: 093(009)

[2684]
Catalogues of incunabula (in *The Library*, Sixth series, v.XIII(3), Sept. 1991, p.267-84).

Survey article which discusses 7 of the more important recently published or ongoing catalogues of incunabula. Compiled by members of the British Library's *ISTC* team. Includes a useful account of the *Gesamtkatalog* (*q.v.*).
Class No: 093(009)

[2685]
STILLWELL, M.B. Incunabula and Americana 1450-1800: a key to bibliographical study. New York, Columbia Univ. Press, 1931. xviii,483p. facsims.

Reprinted New York, Cooper Square Publishers, 1961.

In 3 main pts: I. Incunabula; II. Americana; III. Reference sections. Pts. I and II comprise 8 discursive chapters. Pt. III (p.175-448) in 8 sections: 1. Notes and definitions - 2. Foreign bibliographical terms - 3. Latin contractions and abbreviations - 4. Place-names of fifteenth century printing towns - 5. Incunabula: selected bibliographies and monographs (600 annotated entries) - 6. Fifteenth century woodcuts, etc: selected monographs - 7. Americana: selected bibliographies and monographs (627 annotated entries) - 8. Miscellanea: selected monographs. Index. Remains a valuable guide, especially for the annotated bibliographies.
Class No: 093(009)

Bibliographies

[2686]
BADALIC, J. Inkunabule u Narodnoj Republici Hrvatskoj. Zagreb, 1952. x,[2],258,[1]p. facsims., map.

At head of title page: 'Djela Jugoslavenske Akademije Znanosti i Umjetnosti'.

Catalogue of incunabula in Croatian libraries. 1,124

.... *(contd.)*

numbered entries. Index of places of printing and publishers; concordances. A second catalogue of incunabula in the libraries of the former Yugoslavia is:- *Class No:* 093(01)

[2687]

—GSPAN, A. *and* BADALIC, J. Inkunabule v Sloveniji. [Incunabula quae in Slovenia asservantur.] Ljubljana, 1957. 493,[2]p, facsims., maps.

At head of title page: 'Slovenska Akademija Znanosti in Umetnosti Academia Scientiarum et Artium Slovenica'.

Incunabula catalogue for Slovenia. 847 brief entries, plus references to sources. Indexes of names, locations, library location numbers, concordances and places of printing, etc. *Class No:* 093(01)

[2688]

BAYERISCHE STAATSBIBLIOTHEK. Inkunabelkatalog. Wiesbaden, Ludwig Reichert Verlag, 1988-. DM390 (Bd.1-2); DM490 (Bd.3). ISBN: 3882264500.

Catalogue of the foremost German incunabula collection. Bd.1 *A-Brev* (596p.) deals with 1,883 editions. Generous 2 column format with full detail of individual copies including provenance. References to other catalogues; concordances with the *Gesamtkatalog* and Hain. Bd.3 *Gras-Mans* (612p.) published 1993. *Class No:* 093(01)

[2689]

BIBLIOTECA NACIONAL. (PORTUGAL). Catálogo de incunábulos. Introdução, organização e indices por M. Valentino C.A. sul Mendes. Lisboa, Biblioteca Nacional, 1988. 442p. plates.

Well-produced catalogue of 1,359 entries arranged by author. Concordances with the *Gesamtkatalog*, Hain, Copinger, Haebler, *Bibliografia geral portuguesa* and Anselmo, A. *Origens da imprensa em Portugal* (1981). 16 plates. Indexed by secondary author (collaborators, illustrators, etc.), place of printing and printer. *Class No:* 093(01)

[2690]

BIBLIOTECA NACIONAL. (SPAIN). Catálogo general de incunables en bibliotecas españolas. Madrid, Ministerio de Cultura, Direccion General del Libro y Bibliotecas, 1989-90. 2v. plates. ISBN: 8474834619.

Brief entry catalogue locating 6,295 editions in *c.*200 Spanish libraries. Good introduction and bibliography v.1. Extensive indexing (p.423-773) and concordances v.2. Further *Addenda y correcciones* published 1994. (89p. ISBN: 84748183X). *Class No:* 093(01)

[2691]

BIBLIOTHÈQUE NATIONALE. (FRANCE). Catalogue des incunables. Paris, Bibliothèque Nationale, 1982-. ISBN: 2717716092.

V.2, *H-Z et Hebraica* ([16],xvii,783p.), published in 4 fascs. (H-L, M-O, P-R, S-Z) 1982-85 (all in print, price varies). Publication of V.1 now in process: Fasc. 1. *Xylographes et A* (1992. xxvi,[31],203p. FFr330); Fasc. 2. *B* (1996. 446p. FFr440). Final index v. to complete set.

V.2 intended as a partial update to Pellechet (below), but covering only the holdings of the Bibliothèque Nationale. *c.*4,350 items, full bibliographical detail provided for titles not catalogued elsewhere. 16p. supplement of additions and corrections. Departs from practices of most other incunabula catalogues; long review in *The papers of the Bibliographical Society of America* (v.80(3), 1986, p.381-86). V.1. Fasc. 1, which contains 818 entries and 108 black and white plates, drops many of the policies of v.2. Xylographies dealt with in preliminary pages. *Class No:* 093(01)

[2692]

—FRANCE. Direction du livre et de la lecture. Catalogues régionaux des incunables des bibliothèques publiques de France. Paris, Klincsieck/Aux Amateurs de Livres, 1979-.

Planned for 21v. Publisher varies.

V.I *Bibliothèques de la région Champagne-Ardenne* J-M. Arnoult (xi,457p.) covers 17 libraries. Author/anonymous title order with place of printing, printer/bookseller and provenance indexes. Concordances with the major bibliographies and catalogues of incunabula. Includes notes on the development of the collections covered. Publication proceeding, V.XIV *Région Poitou-Charente - Région Limousin* H. Richard (341p. FFr350. ISBN: 2252030356) appearing 1996. *Class No:* 093(01)

[2693]

—PELLECHET, M.L.C. Catalogue général des incunables des bibliothèques publiques de France. Paris, Picard, 1897-1909. 3v.

1: *Abanco-Biblia.* (1897); 2: *Biblia pauperum-Commandements.* (1905); 3: *Compagnies-Gregorius Magna.* (1909). V. 2-3 edited from Pellechet's manuscripts by L. Polain; no further parts published. Reprinted (Nendeln, Kraus Thomson, 1970) in 26v., v.4-26 comprising photo-reproductions of the manuscripts of volumes not originally published.

5,394 items, with full bibliographical descriptions. *Class No:* 093(01)

[2694]

BRITISH MUSEUM. Department of Printed Books. **Catalogue of books printed in the XVth century** now in the British Museum. London, 1908-85. 12v.

Pt.1. *Xylographica and books printed with types at Mainz, Strassburg, Bamberg and Cologne.* (1908. xxviii,312p.); pt.2. *Germany: Eltvil-Trier.* (1912. xvii,313-620p.); pt.3. *Germany: Leipzig-Pforzheim; German-speaking Switzerland and Austria-Hungary.* (1913. xl,621-864p.); pt.4. *Italy: Subiaco and Rome.* (1916. xvi,145p.); pt.5. *Venice* (1924. [lv],147-598p.); pt.6. *Italy: Foligno, Ferrara, Florence, Milan, Bologna, Naples, Perugia and Treviso.* (1930. l,599-899p.); pt.7. *Italy: Genoa-Unassigned Addenda.* (1935. lxxxviii,901-1213p.); pt.8. *France: French-speaking Switzerland.* (1949. lxxxvii,441,21p.); pt.9. *Holland and Belgium.* (1962. lxi,222p.); pt.10. *Spain, Portugal.* (1971. lxxv,92[2]p.); pt.12. *Italy (Supplement)* (1985. x,93p.).

A photolithographic reprint of pts.I-VIII, (London, British Museum, 1963) reproduces the Museum's working copy which contains numerous manuscript additions and corrections. Pt.9 separately reprinted 1967.

Gives full bibliographical descriptions, each volume including excellently reproduced facsimiles of a sampling of the characteristic types in use. Arranged by 'Proctor order' *i.e.* by countries, towns and presses chronologically. Pt.3 has an introduction to the whole of the German section with a typographical map and indexes to Hain's and Proctor's numbers. Pt.7 has an introduction to the whole of the Italian section with similar indexes. The 1985 supplement to the Italian section corrects some entries and adds 216 editions acquired 1935-84.

Proctor's *An index to the early printed books...*, pt.1 (below) provides the basis for this much fuller catalogue. *Class No:* 093(01)

[2695]

—PROCTOR, R. An Index to the early printed books in the British Museum with notes on those in the Bodleian Library. London, Kegan Paul, 1898-1938. 4v.

Supplements 1898-1902 (London, 1900-03. 5pts.). Reprinted Philadelphia, Saifer, 1960.

In 2pts: 1. *To 1500*. v.1 (1: Germany. 2: Italy) 1898 (3: Switzerland to Montenegro, including France, Netherlands, Austria-Hungary, Spain, England, Scandinavia, Portugal. 4: Registers) 1899. 2. *1501-1520* (1: Germany) 1903. (2: Italy. 3: Switzerland and Eastern Europe. by F. Isaac, Quaritch, 1938).

Arranged by countries, towns and presses chronologically; 1 or 2 line entries only, but giving Hain references and type numbers. *Class No:* 093(01)

[2696]

CAMBRIDGE UNIVERSITY. Library. **A Catalogue of the fifteenth-century printed books in the University Library, Cambridge.** Oates, J.C.T., *comp*. London, Cambridge Univ. Press, 1954. xiii,898p. illus., facsims.

'The purpose of this volume is to list all the fifteenth-century books in the Cambridge University Library, to direct the reader to the best-published description of certain books, to supplement published descriptions when they appear inadequate or inaccurate, and to describe the peculiarities and the provenance of the Cambridge copy' (Preface). 4,249 (22 of them lost incunabula) items are described, arrangement being based on Proctor-order. Indexes: authors and anonymous titles; printers and places; provenances; Hain/Cambridge University Library numbers. Particularly rich in holdings of Low Countries' imprints. A brief history of the Collection (p.1-51); references (p.52-57). *Class No:* 093(01)

[2697]

Catalogus incunabulorum quae in bibliothecis publicis Hungariae asservantur. Sajó, G. *and* Soltész, E., *comps*. Budapest, Aedibus Academiae Scientiarum Hungaricae, 1970. 2v. (1,444p.), plates.

A comprehensive, well-produced union catalogue of incunabula in 56 Hungarian libraries. Around 50% of the 7,107 copies are held by the National Széchényi Library, the Library of the Hungarian Academy of Sciences and the University Library, Budapest. Lengthy introduction and notes in English. Thoroughly indexed; 78 plates in v.2. *Class No:* 093(01)

[2698]

Gesamtkatalog der Wiegendrucke. Kommission für der Gesamtkatalog der Wiegendrucke, *hrsg*. Leipzig, then Stuttgart, Hiersemann, 1925-. DM460 per v. ISBN: 3777268143.

7 complete volumes and Bd.8 Lfg.1 covering A-Federicis issued to 1940. Publication then interrupted by World War II. A new ed., compiled at the Deutschen Staatsbibliothek, Berlin and published from Stuttgart by Hiersemann, commenced 1972 with a revised Bd.8 Lfg.1. Bd.8 completed 1978. Bd.9, also issued in parts, completed 1991 covering Fogeda-Grassus. Bd.1-7 reprinted without revisions, Kraus 1968-81.

Intended to be an author union catalogue of all known incunabula estimated at some 40,000. When complete will effectively replace Hain's *Repertorium bibliographicum* and its supplements. Entries slightly fuller than in the British Museum *Catalogue of books printed in the XVth century* (*q.v*). References given to Hain, Copinger, Reichling, Proctor, British Museum catalogue and national catalogues of incunabula. From Bd.8 attempts to locate all recorded

....(contd.)

copies, locations previously being selective for items available in multiple copies. Bd.10 Lfg.2 published 1994 brings the total no. of entries to 11,786. *Class No:* 093(01)

[2699]

GOFF, F.R. Incunabula in American libraries: a third census of fifteenth century books recorded in North American collections. New York, Bibliographical Society of America, 1964. lxiii,798p.

Supersedes the *First census* of 1919 and M.B. Stillwell's *Second census*, 1940.

An author list, recording 47,188 copies of 12,599 titles, held by 464 institutions and 296 private collections. Abbreviated entries give short title, place, printer, date, physical description, references to printed catalogues and locations. Register of owners (p.xxiii-li); list of sources (p.liii-lxiii). Appended: tables of variant author forms and entries; index of printers and publishers; concordances to the *Gesamtkatalog*, Hain, Proctor and Stillwell's *Second census*; list of deletions from the *Second Census*; addenda.

A Supplement, (New York, Bibliographical Society of America, 1972. xii, 104p. $20. ISBN: 0914930028), adds 324 titles in 3,560 copies.

A reprint of the 1964 ed., (Millwood, N.Y., Kraus Reprint, 1973. ISBN: 0527342009), is reproduced from a copy annotated by Goff, and includes handwritten corrections and notes on dealers' and auction house prices. *Class No:* 093(01)

[2700]

GUARNASCHELLI, T.M. *and* **VALENZIANI, I. Indice generale degli incunaboli delle biblioteche d'Italia,** a cura del Centro Nazionale d'Informazioni Bibliografiche. Roma, Libreria dello Stato, 1943-81. 6v.

Issued under the auspices of the Ministero dell' Educazione Nazionale.

Serves as a national census. 10,446 editions A-Z by author in the first 5v. (v.5 in print L100,000). Gives locations not only in state libraries but also in libraries of local cultural institutions and of religious orders (list in v.1. p.xiii-xix). List of sources appears in each volume.

V.6 *Aggiunte, correzione, indici* (L110,000) comprises corrections in 250p. related to the original serial no.; list of 88 Hebrew incunabula; indexes of secondary authors, commentators, translators, printers and publishers and places; list of plates; concordances to Hain and the *Gesamtkatalog*. *Class No:* 093(01)

[2701]

HAIN, L.F.T. Repertorium bibliographicum ad annum MD. Stuttgart, Cotta, 1826-38. 2v. in 4.

Reprinted Milan, Görlich, 1966.

An author list, with items numbered 1-16299. Bibliographical descriptions are of medium length. Index of towns and printers. Items personally examined by Hain are asterisked. Frequently cited in subsequent catalogues of incunabula.

An index of printers is provided by K. Burger's *Ludwig Hain's Repertorium bibliographicum. Register* (Leipzig, Harrassowitz, 1891. Reprinted Nendeln, Kraus, 1968). Supplements to Hain:- *Class No:* 093(01)

[2702]

—BURGER, K. Supplement zu Hain und Panzer ... Leipzig, Hiersemann, 1908. 440p.

The work by Panzer is the *Annales typographici ... ad annum 1536* by G.W. Panzer (Nuremburg, 1793-1803, 11v.), arranged A-Z by the Latin names of towns, with chronological sub-division. V.1-v.5 cover to 1500, v.6-v.11 to 1536. *Class No:* 093(01)

[2703]

—COPINGER, W.A. Supplement to Hain's Repertorium bibliographicum; or, Collections towards a new edition of that work. London, Sotheran, 1895-1902. 2v. in 3.

Reprinted, Leipzig, Lorentz, 1926.

Includes 6,000 additions and 7,000 corrections.

Class No: 093(01)

[2704]

—REICHLING, D. Appendices ad Hainii-Copingeri Repertorium bibliographicum: additiones et emendationes. Monaco, Rosenthal, 1905-11. 7v. in 8; Supplementum. 1914.

Reprinted, Milan, Görlich, 1953. *Class No:* 093(01)

[2705]

HARVARD UNIVERSITY. Library. **A Catalogue of the fifteenth-century printed books in the Harvard University Library.** Walsh, J.E., *comp.* Binghamton, N.Y., Medieval & Renaissance Texts and Studies, 1991-97. 5v. (*Medieval & Renaissance texts and studies, 84, 97, 119, 150, 171.*.) ISBN: 0866980962.

V.I. *Books printed in Germany, German-speaking Switzerland and Austria-Hungary* (1991. xxv,617[21]p., plates. $45). V.II. *Books printed in Rome and Venice* (1993. xii,672[18]p., plates. $50). V.III. *Books printed in Italy with the exception of Rome and Venice* (1994. xii, 397p. plates. $50). V.IV *Books printed in France, The Netherlands, the Iberian Peninsula, England and Montenegro. Hebraica and supplementary entries* (1996. xvii,330p. plates. $45). V.V *A Brief history of the collection. Cumulative indexes.* (1997. ix,478p. plates. $45).

Contains records for 3,517 editions (4,187 copies) in all libraries of the Harvard system. Full detail with descriptive notes and references to appropriate authorities. Comprehensively indexed including author/title, editors and translators, printers and places and provenance. Concordances with Hain, Proctor, the *Gesamtkatalog* and Goff. *Class No:* 093(01)

[2706]

ILLINOIS UNIVERSITY Library. **Incunabula in the University of Illinois Library** at Urbana-Champaign. Harman, M., *comp.* Urbana, Univ. of Illinois Press, 1979. v,251p. (*Robert B. Downs publication fund, no.5.*) ISBN: 0252007891.

Catalogue of one of the larger US collections of incunabula. Describes 1,083 copies, 103 otherwise unrepresented in US collections. Entries in alphabetical author order, with title, country, city and printer and chronological indexes. Concordances with Goff, the *Gesamtkatalog, Hain, Proctor, Copinger and Reichling.* *Class No:* 093(01)

[2707]

Incunabula in Dutch libraries: a census of fifteenth-century printed books in Dutch public collections. Van Thienen, G., *ed.* Nieuwkoop, B. De Graff, 1983. 2v. DFl350. (*Bibliotheca bibliographica Neerlandica, 17.*) ISBN: 9060043758, v.1; 906004374x, v.2.

Modelled on Goff (*q.v.*). V.1 contains entries for 4,759 editions representing 7,940 copies in 85 libraries. Includes 1,200 imprints from the Low Countries. V.2 comprises place, printer and general indexes and concordances to the Gesamtkatalog, Hain, Copinger, Reichling, Campbell and Goff. Well planned and presented, an 'admirable addition to the shelf of essential catalogues of incunables' (*Book Collector*, v.32(1), Spring 1985, p.115). *Class No:* 093(01)

[2708]

Inkunabelkatalog der Stadt- und Universitätsbibliothek und anderer öffentlicher Sammlungen in Frankfurt am Main. Ohly, K. *and* Sack, V. Frankfurt am Main, Klostermann, 1967. xlv,727p. DM485. (*Kataloge der Stadt-und Universitätsbiblothek, Frankfurt am Main, Bd.1.*) ISBN: 3465007344.

Issued in 5 Lfg.

3,076 numbered items. 'Proctor' index of places of printing, printers and their products. Concordances to the *Gesamtkatalog* and Hain. Name and subject list. List of sources pxxix-xliii. Well-produced. *Class No:* 093(01)

[2709]

Inkunabeln in Baden-Württemberg: Bestandskataloge. Universitätsbibliothek Tübingen, *hrsg.* Wiesbaden, Harrassowitz, 1993-.

One of a several important new German incunabula catalogues. V.1 *Katalog der Inkunabeln in Bibliotheken der Diözese Rottenburg-Stuttgart* (341p. plates. DM98. ISBN: 3447034025) has 641 full entries with notes. Main, printer/publisher, etc. indexes; concordances. *Class No:* 093(01)

[2710]

Inkunabuły w bibliotekach Polskich: centralny katalog. [Incunabula quae in bibliothecis Poloniae asservantur.] Wrocław, Zakład Narodowy Imienia Ossolińskich, 1970. 2v.

Catalogue of 5,768 incunabula (19,207 copies) in 108 Polish public and private collections. Place and printer indexes; concordances with the *Gesamtkatalog*, Hain, etc. *Class No:* 093(01)

[2711]

KOTVAN, I. Inkunábuly na slovensku. [Incunabula quae in biblothecis Slovaciae asservantur.] Martin, Matica Slovenská, 1979. 560p. plates.

Describes 1,523 copies of 1,236 titles (2/3 German) in 50 Slovakian libraries. Set in *Gesamtkatalog* style. English summary to introduction. Provenance, library and chronological indexes. With E. Frimmova, Kotvan has also produced *Inkunábly Slovenskej národnej knižnice Matice Slovenskej v Martin* (Martin, Matica Slovenská 1988. 262p. plates). *Class No:* 093(01)

[2712]

—RIEDL, M. Katalog prvotisku jiholčeských knihoven. Praha, Státní Pedagogické Nakladatelstvi, 1974. 478p.

Catalogue of 1,026 incunabula in the libraries of southern Bohemia. Brief introduction in English. *Class No:* 093(01)

[2713]
MADSEN, V. Katalog over det Kongelige Biblioteks inkunabler. København, Levine & Munksgaard, 1931-38. 2v. in 6 pts.

4,265 entries covering the holdings of the Royal Library. A further supplementary volume, *Accessions 1938-1962 inkunabler l andre biblioteker registre* (København, Det Kongelige Bibliotek, 1963. 104p.), lists new accessions (items 4266-4395) and the holdings of other Danish libaries (items 1-87). *Class No:* 093(01)

[2714]
POLAIN, L. Catalogue des livres imprimés au quinzième siècle des bibliothèques de Belgique. Bruxelles, Société des Bibliophiles, 1932. 4v. Facsims.

4,109 items with full bibliographical descriptions. V.4 includes a list of facsimiles (which are always appropriately placed in the text), a concordance of *Gesamtkatalog*, Hain etc., numbers, lists of printers and engravings and a general index. Locations in Belgian libraries are given.

Supplement (Bruxelles, Tulkens, 1978. xv,622p.) corrects the earlier volumes and adds 695 new entries.
Class No: 093(01)

[2715]
RHODES, D.E. A Catalogue of incunabula in all the libraries of Oxford University outside the Bodleian. Oxford, Clarendon Press, 1982. xli,444p. 8p. plates, facsims. £98. ISBN: 0198181752.

Lists, A-Z by author, 1,847 titles in 2,585 copies. Strongest collections held by All Souls, New College, Queens and Corpus Christi. Entries include references to standard works, locations with pressmarks and notes on provenance, imperfections and bindings. Concordances with Goff, the *Gesamtkatalog* and Duff. Indexes of libraries, towns, printers and provenances, the latter 'notable among an admirable series of indexes' (*Book collector*, v.32(3), Autumn 1983, p.360-63). *Class No:* 093(01)

[2716]
SACK, V. Die Inkunabeln der Universitätsbibliothek und anderer öffentlicher Sammlungen in Freiburg im Breisgan und Umgebung. Wiesbaden, Harrasowitz, 1985. 3v. DM614. (*Kataloge der Universitätsbibliothek Freiburg im Breisgan Bd.2 Teile1-3.*) ISBN: 3447023198.

Based on the rich holdings of Freiburg University, describing 3,775 incunabula, 274 of which are duplicates. Bd.3 comprises full indexes and concordances to the *Gesamtkatalog*, Hain Copinger and Reichling. A 'point of reference for any studies dealing with 15th century imprints' (*American notes and queries*, v.24(9/10), May/June 1986, p.158). *Class No:* 093(01)

[2717]
Uchetnyi spiosk sobraniia inkunabulov. Gorfunkel, A.M., *red.* Sankt-Peterburg, Gos. Publichnaia Biblioteka im. M.E. Saltykova-Shchedrina, 1981-.

Register of the largest Russian incunabula collection held at the Saltykova-Shchedrina State Public (now Russian National) Library. V.4 Horius-L published 1992.
Class No: 093(01)

Hebrew

[2718]
GOLDSTEIN, D. Hebrew incunables in the British Isles: a preliminary census. London, British Library, 1985. xi,42p. plates. £9.50. ISBN: 0712300473.

106 editions represented by 398 copies in 12 libraries. Also indicates if copies exist in private hands. 'Proctor order' arrangement town by town then printer. 'Admirably concise' (*Times literary supplement*, no.4326, 28 February 1986, p.229). *Class No:* 093=924

[2719]
Hebrew incunabula in public collections: a first international census. Offenberg, A.K., *comp.* Nieuwkoop, De Graaf, 1990. lxxiv,214p. DFl90; $77.50. (*Bibliotheca humanistica & reformatorica, xlvii.*) ISBN: 9060044045.

Lists 139 editions by main entry with locations and citations to relevant literature. Concordances; place and printer, Hebrew title and general name indexes. Further 'List of copies printed on parchment'. *Class No:* 093=924

Private & Small Presses

[2720]
CAVE, R. The Private press. 2nd ed. rev. & enl. New York, Bowker, 1983. xvi,389p., illus. £70;$64.95. ISBN: 0835216950.

1st ed. 1971.

Surveys the history and publishing of selected presses in 27 broadly chronological chapters. Concentrates on the English-speaking world, including Canada, Australia and New Zealand. Extensive bibliography (p.349-62). Index.
Class No: 094.1

[2721]
FRANKLIN, C. The Private presses. 2nd ed. Aldershot, Scolar Press, 1991. 378p., illus. £39.50;$63.95. ISBN: 0859678350.

1st ed. Studio Vista, 1969.

8 chapters dealing with 11 presses (The Daniel Press and nineteenth century Oxford ... Golden Cockerel and Shakespeare Head (p.19-151)),plus 'Et Cetera' and 'Collecting'. Select bibliography of the presses (p.183-360) including short physical descriptions of books, references to published bibliographies (especially Tomkinson (*q.v.*)) and auction prices. Author and title indexes. *Class No:* 094.1

[2722]
GLAZIER, L.P. Small press: an annotated guide. Westport, Conn., Greenwood Press, 1992. xiv,123p. £44.95;$55. ISBN: 0313283109.

Covers sources for the study of literary small presses, focussing on the contemporary US. 174 entries for books, periodical articles, chapters, etc., published since 1960. Includes press directories, bibliographies and catalogues; items devoted exclusively to a single author omitted. Indexed. An 'invaluable resource ... that contains informed and insightful annotations on well-chosen materials' (*Library journal*, v.117(20), December 1992, p.124).
Class No: 094.1

[2723]
RANSOM, W. Private presses and their books. New York, Bowker, 1929. 493p.

Reprinted 1963 (Duschnes), 1976 (AMS Press. ISBN: 0404147321) and 1992 (Cummins $75. ISBN: 1882860055).

Narrative account of the private press with a checklist of presses (p.189-451). Checklist in A-Z order of press, giving brief historical notes and a list of titles. Index. Ransom also produced *Selective checklists of press books* (*q.v.*).
Class No: 094.1

[2724]

Seventh international directory of private presses: letterpress. Westreich, A. *and* Westreich, B., *eds.* Sacremento, Ca., ERS, 1995. 173p.

6th ed. 1993.

North American presses predominate, despite title.

Class No: 094.1

[2725]

—The First check-log of private press names. Lieberman, E.K. 3rd. ed. White Plains, N.Y., Herity Press, 1962. 24p.

First published 1960.

List of *c.*1,250 names of presses 1475 to 1960.

Class No: 094.1

[2726]

Small press yearbook. Small Press Group of Great Britain, *comp.* London, The Group, 1989-94. Annual. ISSN: 00959847.

Ceased publication with 1994.

Final ed. (238p.) mainly comprised A-Z listing of UK small presses, some with details of publishing activity and major titles. *Class No:* 094.1

[2727]

Small presses & little magazines of the UK and Ireland: an address list. Finch, P., *comp.* Cardiff, HMSO Oriel Bookshop, 198?-. Irregular.

Published in conjuction with the Association of Little Presses.

The 12th ed. (1996. 74p. ISBN: 0946329230) lists about 475 small presses giving address and one line description. Also has basic detail on *c.*350 magazines. *Class No:* 094.1

Bibliographies

[2728]

BROWN, P.A.H. Modern British and American private presses, (1850-1965): holdings of the British Library. London, British Museum Publications for the British Library, 1976. [3],211p. £20. ISBN: 0714103675.

Reproduces entries from the British Library (British Museum) *General catalogue of printed books*. Arranged A-Z under press, then by year and author. Index of authors and anonymous titles. Some works in English published by presses in non-English speaking countries included. Coverage less full for US presses. *Class No:* 094.1(01)

[2729]

DOBELL, B. Catalogue of books printed for private circulation. London, the Author, 1906. 238p.

Reprinted 1966 (Gale. ISBN: 0810333031).

Lists *c.*2,500 items by authors or anonymous titles, A-Z, in two sequences. Gives 'not only the titles of the books, but also some notice of their contents and character' (Introductory note), with anecdotes and quotations interspersed. *Class No:* 094.1(01)

[2730]

Little press books in print. Oxford, Association of Little Presses, 1984-. Annual. £3.00.

Issue no.14 for 1997 in two main parts: 'Presses advertise their own publications etc' reproduces catalogues and publicity material of presses; 'Author index of books in print' lists about 1,350 titles. *Class No:* 094.1(01)

[2731]

MARTIN, R.J. Bibliographical catalogue of privately printed books. 2nd ed. London, 1854. xxv,593p.

First published 1834 as *Bibliographical catalogue of books privately printed, including those of the Bannatyne, Maitland and Roxburghe clubs, and of private presses at Darlington. Auchinleck, Lee Priory, Newcastle, Middle Hill and Strawberry Hill.* Reprinted 1970 (New York, Franklin).

2nd ed. revises and expands the chronological list of books 1672-1833, in 1st ed., and extends it to 1853 (1,750 items), but omits the second section (A-Z list of private press publications). Index of authors and titles.

Class No: 094.1(01)

[2732]

Private press books 1959-. Pinner, Private Libraries Association, 1960-. Annual (irregular). ISSN: 00795402.

Some v. combined *e.g.* 1981/84 (1987); last v. currently available 1991.

Checklist of books issued by private presses during the year. International in scope, but usually confined to English language texts. Arranged by press, entries (174 in v. for 1991 (1993. 80p. ISBN: 0900006263)) give full bibliographical detail, physical description and price. Each issue also contains a very useful feature, 'The literature of private printing', a listing of books and journal articles relating to private presses (124 entries in v. for 1991). Reviews of individual titles excluded. *Class No:* 094.1(01)

[2733]

RANSOM, W. Selective checklists of press books: a compilation of all important & significant private presses or press books which are collected. New York, Duschnes, 1963. iii,420p.

First published 1945-50, in 12 pts. Reprinted 1992 (Cummins. $75. ISBN: 1882860039).

About 3,000 items, covering the products of 56 presses. Index of presses precedes. *Class No:* 094.1(01)

[2734]

RIDLER, W. British modern press books: a descriptive check list of unrecorded items. New enl. ed. Folkestone, Dawson, 1975. xvi,331p. ISBN: 0712906835.

A reprint with addenda and index; first published 1971.

Unrecorded items are those which do not appear in individual press bibliographies or Tomkinson or Ransom (*qq.v.*). Lists *c.*2,000 items from 96 presses (Alcuin Press ... Yellowsands Press). Brief bibliographical descriptions and cross-references between presses. *Class No:* 094.1(01)

[2735]

Small press record of books in print. Fulton, L., *ed.* Paradise Ca., Dustbooks, 1966-. Annual. $55. ISSN: 01489720.

1st issue 1966-68, 2nd issue 1969-72; then annual. Now appears to be available only on CD-ROM. The same publisher also issues *International directory of little magazines and small presses* (*q.v.*). and *The Directory of small press/magazine editors and publishers.*

Recent eds. have entries for about 35,000 books, pamphlets, broadsides, posters and poem cards listed as available in the catalogues of 5,000 small publishers worldwide. Main sequence A-Z by author, many entries with brief annotations. Title, publisher (with addresses) and subject indexes, the latter under broad headings.

Class No: 094.1(01)

[2736]
—Small press review. Fulton, L., *ed.* Paradise, Ca., Dustbooks, 1967-. Bi-monthly. $31. ISSN: 00377228.

Each issue has 10-12 lengthy reviews of new publications, news articles and notes. *Class No:* 094.1(01)

[2737]
TOMKINSON G.S.A., Sir. A Select bibliography of the principal modern presses, public and private, in Great Britain and Ireland. London, First Edition Club, 1928. xxiv, 238p. illus.

Reprinted 1975 (Dawson. ISBN: 0721906495).

Lists *c.*1,500 titles from nearly 100 presses A-Z. Entries give full bibliographical detail and physical description. Brief notes on the history of each press. *Class No:* 094.1(01)

[2738]
TRATT, G. Check list of Canadian small presses: English language. Halifax, N.S., Dalhousie University, School of Library Science, 1974. 153p. (*Dalhousie University Library. Occasional paper series, no.6.*)

Gives the history of each press and lists books published. Continued by:- *Class No:* 094.1(01)

[2739]
—Literary presses in Canada, 1975-1985: a check list and bibliography. Melanson, H., *comp.* Halifax, N.S., Dalhousie University, School of Library and Information Studies; London, Vine Press, 1988. iii,187p. Can$16.50. (*Dalhousie University. School of Library and Information Studies. Occasional papers series, no.43.*) ISBN: 0770397174.

About 4,300 books, pamphlets and broadsides listed by press. Includes bibliographies of articles about presses. No title index. *Class No:* 094.1(01)

First Editions

[2740]
Breese's guide to modern first editions. Breese, M., *comp.* London, Breese Books, 1993. 228p. plates. £37.50. ISBN: 0947533362.

Practical guide with prices to the first editions of 29 'most collectible' authors Kingsley Amis ... Virginia Woolf. Further listings: 'Ultra modern', 'The Angry young men', 'Some miscellaneous writers'. 1p. author index.
Class No: 094.4

[2741]
BRUSSEL, I.R. Anglo-American first editions... London, Constable; New York, Bowker, 1935-36. 2v. facsims.

Pt.1 *East to West, 1826-1900*, describes first editions of *c.*250 works by English authors, published in America before their publication in England (26 authors, A-Z, including Wilkie Collins, Dickens, Thackeray and Trollope); index. Pt.2 *West to East, 1786-1930*, describes first editions of *c.*300 works by US authors, whose books were published in England before their publication in America (22 authors, A-Z, including Henry James, Mark Twain and Fenimore Cooper). Index. *Class No:* 094.4

[2742]
CONNOLLY, J. Modern first editions: their value to collectors. 4th ed. London, Little, Brown and Co., 1993. 343p. plates. ISBN: 0316903639.

First published as *Collecting modern first editions* 1977; 3rd ed. 1987.

Selective guide to values for British and US authors on a 26 point scale ranging from £5 to £12,000 and over. Entries for each author include brief biographical notes. Rambling introduction dispenses advice on collecting. No indexes. Mixed critical reception for this and earlier eds. '(D)oes provide useful information (but) valuations must be treated with a dose of scepticism' (*Library review*, v.43(3), 1994, p.71). *Class No:* 094.4

[2743]
First editions: a guide to identification. Statements of selected North American, British Commonwealth and Irish publishers on their methods of designating first editions. Zempel, E.N. *and* Verkler, L.A., *eds.* 3rd ed. Peoria Ill., Spoon River Press, 1995. viii,515p. $35. ISBN: 0930358139.

First published 1984; 2nd ed. 1989.

Based on eds. 1-3 of H.S. Boutell's *First editions of today and how to tell them* (1928-49) and Zempel and Verkler's *A First edition* (1977).

About 2,900 statements (1,200 more than 2nd ed.) arranged by publisher A-Z. Statements generally reproduced verbatim, small publishers well represented. '(U)nique and useful' (*Choice*, v.33(7), March 1996, p.1094).
Class No: 094.4

[2744]
TANNEN, J. How to identify and collect American first editions: a guide book. 2nd ed. rev. & enl. New York, Arco, 1985. xvi,142p. ISBN: 0668065265.

1st ed. 1976.

In 2 pts: a list of 392 American publishers with information on how to identify and collect their first editions; 8 chapter guide to collectible areas such as Americana, children's books and science fiction. Bibliography p.127-33. Index. Less comprehensive than Zempel and Verker.
Class No: 094.4

[2745]
WARD, K.A. First editions: a field guide for collectors of English and American literature. Aldershot, Scolar Press, 1994. xxiv,391p. ISBN: 0859679802.

Paperback ed. in print £12.95;$29.95 ISBN: 1859281281.

Entries, A-Z by name for 'the most important works of the major figures of literature', include notes and estimated price. Some bias against living authors. No indexes. '(H)as the appearance of a bookseller's private notebook ... as a guide for a general audience of collectors, it is difficult to see the book's purpose and too easy to discover its shortcomings' (*Papers of the Bibliographical Society of America*, v.89(2), June 1995, p.209). *Class No:* 094.4

Bookbindings

[2746]
BRESLAUER, B.H. The Uses of bookbinding literature. New York, Book Arts Press, School of Library Service, Columbia Univ., 1986. 44p. (*Book Art Press occasional publications, no.1.*)

Concentrates on works that describe the history and design

....*(contd.)*
of bindings. Narrative format, with a 'List of books and articles mentioned in the text' (p.33-44). A 'welcome reference work for historians of the book' (*Bulletin of bibliography*, v.45(1), March 1988, p.66). *Class No:* 095

[2747]
FOOT, M.M. The Henry Davis gift: a collection of bookbindings. London, British Library, 1978-83. 2v.

V.1 *Studies in the history of bookbinding* (352p. ISBN: 0714103918). V.2 *A Catalogue of North European bindings* (446p. £90. ISBN: 0904654737).

The collection, probably the foremost amassed this century, came to the Library in 1968. V.1 comprises a series of studies built around one or two bindings, concentrating on those not previously the object of detailed study. V.2 is a catalogue of 368 bindings arranged by country of origin, then chronologically. Entries include brief description, provenance, and where available, references, comparative material, literature and notes. Both volumes have binder and owner indexes. *Class No:* 095

[2748]
NEEDHAM, P. Twelve centuries of bookbindings 400-1600. New York, The Pierpont Morgan Library; London, Oxford Univ. Press, 1979. xxvii,338p. illus., col. plates. ISBN: 0192115804.

Traces the history of bookbinding to the end of the sixteenth century through consideration of 100 examples in The Pierpont Morgan Library, probably the finest collection in the US. Detailed, well-referenced descriptions. Works cited (p.311-23). Indexes. *Class No:* 095

[2749]
NIXON, H.M. History of decorated bookbinding in England. Foot, M.M., *ed.* Oxford, Clarendon, 1992. xviii,124p. plates. £42.50. (*Lyell lectures in bibliography*.) ISBN: 0198181825.

Continued by Foot after Nixon's death.

Six chapter survey of bindings with the emphasis on the period before 1800. 12 colour and 128 black and white plates. Index. A 'potted history at best (but)... to be welcomed as the only introduction to the subject available' (*The New bookbinder*, v.12, 1992, p.97). *Class No:* 095

[2750]
—NIXON, H.M. Five centuries of English bookbinding. London, Scolar Press, 1978. 241p. plates. ISBN: 0859674118.

Reproduces Nixon's descriptions of bindings published in the *Book collector* over 25 years (1952-77). 100 bindings covered. Bibliography (p.225-31); index. *Class No:* 095

[2751]
WARD, P. Contemporary designer bookbinders: an illustrated directory. [Relieurs d'art contemporains: un répertoire illustré.] Cambridge, Oleander Press, 1995. 218p. illus. £30;$45. ISBN: 0906672368.

Two pages for each artist, one with curriculum vitae, 'aesthetic statement' and portrait, other with reproduction of representative bindings (black and white). International in scope; some entries in French. A further v. is anticipated. *Class No:* 095

Illustrated Books

Bibliographies

[2752]
Book illustration and decoration: a guide to research. Brenni, V.J., *comp.* Westport, Conn., Greenwood Press, 1980. viii,191p. £58.50;$69.50. (*Art reference collection, no.1.*) ISBN: 0313223408.

A bibliography 'concerned primarily with illustration and decoration inside the book ... rather than the cover' (Preface p.vii). Covers all periods and countries. Exhibition and sale catalogues included if they contain essays and/or illustrations. 2,114 unannotated entries in 11 chapters: 1. Reference works - 2. Book decoration - 3. Manuals of illustration and other writing techniques - 4. History of methods of illustration - 5. History of book illustration from ancient times to the present day - 6. History of book illustration and decoration in the countries of the world - 7. Illustration and decoration in children's books - 8. Science and technology - 9. Medicine - 10. Music - 11. Geography and history. Includes non-English language material. Author and subject indexes. *Class No:* 096(01)

Histories

[2753]
BLAND, D. A History of book illustration: the illuminated manuscript and the printed book. 2nd ed. London, Faber & Faber, 1969. 459p. illus., plates. ISBN: 0571046878.

First published 1958.

Remains the most comprehensive and authoritative history of book illustration. International in scope, including the Far East, Near East and the Americas. 8 chronological chapters, mainly subdivided geographically. 404 facsimiles, some in colour, giving size of originals, date, artist, etc. Index gives MS. references to British Museum (Library) and Bibliothèque Nationale. Short chapter bibliographies (p.437-41). *Class No:* 096(091)

[2754]
HARTHAN, J. The History of the illustrated book: the Western tradition. London, Thames & Hudson, 1981. 288p. illus., plates. £35. ISBN: 0500233160.

Pbck. reprint 1997 (£24.95;$39.95. ISBN: 0500279462).

An attempt at a full history from ancient times to date by a former keeper of the National Art Library. 7 chronological chapters: 1. Manuscripts - 2. The birth of printing - 3. The Renaissance - 4. The Baroque - 5. The Rococo - 6. Romanticism and the mass market (1800-80) - 7. The book beautiful and after (1880-1980). Each chapter thematically and geographically subdivided (*e.g.* chap. 7 'The private press movement', 'American illustration', 'Surrealism and art deco'). 465 illustrations including 33 col. plates. Limited bibliography (p.283-84); index. An ambitious, well-produced survey; the emphasis is on illustration as an art form and the historical and cultural context rather than techniques.
Class No: 096(091)

Biographies

[2755]
OSTERWALDER, M. Dictionnaire des illustrateurs. Neuchâtel, Ides et Clendes, 1989-.

V.1 *1800-1914, illustrateurs, caricaturistes et affichistes* (Nouv. ed. 1989. 1223p. FFr780. ISBN: 2825800309); v.2

.... *(contd.)*
1890-1945, XXe siècle, première génération, illustrateurs du monde entier nés avant 1885... (1992. 1384p. FFr780. ISBN: 2825800392). V.1 first published Paris, Hubschmid & Bouret, 1983.

International coverage, entries gives brief biographical detail and list works illustrated. Further vols. for 1500-1800 and the 20th century were intended. *Class No:* 096(092)

Great Britain

[2756]
HAMMELMANN, H. Book illustrators in eighteenth-century England. Edited and completed by T.S.R. Boase. New Haven, Conn., Yale Univ. Press for the Paul Mellon Centre for Studies in British Art, 1975. xiv,120p., 40p. of plates. (*Studies in British art.*) ISBN: 0300018959.

Biography and artistic history for 263 illustrators. Entries include list of works illustrated and bibliographical references. Essay 'Book illustration in the eighteenth century' (p.1-10). 45 well-chosen plates. Author and anonymous title and general indexes. 'Indispensable for libraries collecting in English art and literature' (*Library journal*, v.101(6), 15th March 1976, p.801).
Class No: 096(410)

[2757]
HODNETT, E. Five centuries of English book illustration. Aldershot, Scolar Press, 1988. 364p. illus., plates. £75;$124.95. ISBN: 0859676978.

Aims to 'present the first one-volume, selective, comprehensive and critical record of literary illustration in England' (Introduction). In 2 parts: Pt.1 a critical account in 11 chronological sections; Pt.2 a selective catalogue of 250 illustrators and 2,700 books. Limited to artists resident in England or books printed in England. Children's books excluded. Index of illustrators. 'Large impressive and expensive' with 'highly subjective judgements on the merits of individual authors' (*Library Association Record*, v.90(10), October 1988, p.598); 'rich but fragmented treatment of periods' (*Times Literary Supplement*, no.4467, 11-17 November 1988, p.1261). *Class No:* 096(410)

[2758]
HORNE, A. Dictionary of twentieth century British book illustrators. Woodbridge, Antique Collectors' Club, 1994. 456p. illus. £39.50;$79.50. ISBN: 1851491082.

Intended as a continuation of Houfe (below). Biographical profiles for about 1,000 individuals with notes on books and magazines illustrated, exhibitions, etc. 5 brief introductory essays including 'Some notes on children's book illustration 1915-1985' by B. Alderson (p.45-63). 300 black and white and 150 colour illustrations. Short bibliography. Some omissions, but 'a delightful and informative work of reference, certainly the most up-to-date and probably the best available work on the subject' (*Library Association record*, v.97(4), April 1995, p.231). *Class No:* 096(410)

[2759]
HOUFE, S. The Dictionary of 19th century British illustrators and caricaturists. [Rev. ed.]. Woodbridge, Antique Collectors' Club, 1996. 367p. plates., ports. £39.50;$79.50. ISBN: 1851491937.

First published 1978. Further ed. 1981 as *The Dictionary of British book illustrators and caricaturists 1880-1914.* Included 11 chaps. of introductory material most of which is omitted from this ed.

Mainly short entries giving basic biographical detail, summaries of work, notes on material illustrated (including

.... *(contd.)*
magazines), exhibitions, collections holding examples of work and bibliography. Some longer entries for major illustrators (*e.g.* Bateman 1½ col.). Includes over 300 predominantly black and white illustrations. Introduction (p.8-40) and bibliography (p.366-68); no indexes. 'The strength of the *Dictionary* is its bibliographical and visual data ... (it) falls short of a scholarly biography or sustained piece of academic criticism' (*The Library*, v.18(2), June 1996, p.167). *Class No:* 096(410)

[2760]
PEPPIN, B. *and* **MICKLETHWAIT, L. Dictionary of British book illustrators:** the twentieth century. London, Murray, 1983. 336p. ISBN: 0719539854.

Published in the US as *Book illustrators of the twentieth century* (Arco. ISBN: 0668056703).

Comprehensive coverage 'primarily of fiction and poetry illustrators, whose work was first published in Britain between 1900 and 1975' (Foreword). Over 800 entries, *c.*350 accompanied by an example of the illustrator's work. Information given includes basic biographical detail, discussion of subjects and style, list of books illustrated, list of periodicals to which the artist contributed and reference bibliography. Book lists based on the British Library catalogue supplemented by information gleaned elsewhere.
Class No: 096(410)

[2761]
RAY, G.N. The Illustrator and the book in England from 1790-1914. Oxford, Oxford Univ. Press; New York, Pierpont Morgan Library, 1976. xxxiii,336p. plates. ISBN: 0195198832, O.U.P.

Based on an exhibition of Ray's collection at the Pierpont Morgan Library.

In print as an unabridged slightly altered paperback ed. New York, Dover Publications, 1991. (£29.95;$24.95. ISBN: 0486269558).

Catalogue in sections: The forerunners; William Blake ... Arthur Rackham; Other illustrators who drew for the 3 colour process. Describes 333 volumes. Plates (p.213-312); index (includes illustrations). *Class No:* 096(410)

[2762]
TOOLEY, R.V. English books with coloured plates 1790 to 1860: a bibliographical account of the most important books illustrated by English artists in colour aquatint and colour lithography. Rev. ed. Folkestone, Dawson, 1979. x,452p. ISBN: 0712909052.

First published 1935 (Ingpen & Grant) as *Some English books with coloured plates*. 2nd ed. 1954 (Batsford) as *English books with coloured plates*. This ed. reprinted 1973 (Dawson ISBN: 0712905839) and 1987 (Batsford ISBN: 0713457856).

A checklist of over 500 items, illustrations being recorded in detail. This (1979) ed., is a reprint of the 2nd ed., with some additional information supplemented to the main body of the text, and an appendix of 41 additional entries (p.425-52). 'Its principal virtues are thoroughgoing collations and the occasional notes that mark discrepancies between editions' (*Library quarterly*, v.51(1), January 1981, p.142).
Class No: 096(410)

Germany

[2763]

KUNZE, H. Geschichte der Buchillustration in Deutschland: das 16. und 17. Jahrhundert. Frankfurt am Main, Insel, 1993. 2v. illus., plates. DM980. ISBN: 345816183x.

Follows previous v. on 15th century published 1975.

V.1 contains text (completed 1985 with more recent scholarship cited) giving chronological then topical treatment. V.2 presents 540 black and white plates (small illus. also in v.1). '(S)erious and wide-ranging' (*Book collector*, v.44(4), Winter 1995, p.589). *Class No:* 096(430)

USA

[2764]

American book and magazine illustrators to 1920. Smith, S.E., *and others eds.* Detroit, Gale, 1998. xviii,450p., illus. (*Dictionary of literary biography, v.188.*) ISBN: 0787618438.

Covers through to the so-called 'Golden Age' of American book illustration. 42 entries including 'several now lesser-known illustrators as well as individuals who are better known today as "fine artists"' (*Introduction*, p.xiii). *Class No:* 096(73)

[2765]

BEST, J.J. American popular illustration: a reference guide. Westport Ct., Greenwood Press, 1984. x,171p. £45;$52.95. (*American popular culture.*) ISBN: 0313233896.

Discusses sources relating to book and magazine illustration in 6 chapters: 1. A historical overview - 2. History and aesthetics of American illustration - 3. Major illustrated works: bibliographies and books - 4. The major illustrators - 5. The social and artistic context of illustration - 6. Illustration media. Bibliographical citations at chapter ends. Brief bibliography of illustrated books (p.157-62). Index. *Class No:* 096(73)

Children

[2766]

Illustrators of children's books 1744-1945. Mahony, B.E., *comp.* Boston, Mass., Horn Book, 1947. xvi,527p. illus. ISBN: 0876750153.

In 3 pts. I. History and development; II. Biographies (p.265-376), covering about 400 artists; III. Bibliographies (p.379-519), subdivided 'A bibliography of illustrators and their works' (p.383-448) and 'A bibliography of authorship' (p.449-519).

Supplements published as follows:- Mahoney, B.E. *Illustrators of children's books 1946-1956* (Horn Book, 1958. xvii,299p. ISBN: 0876750161); Kingman, L. and others *Illustrators of children's books 1957-1966* (Horn Book, 1968. xvii,295p. ISBN: 087675017x); Kingman, L. and others *Illustrators of children's books 1967-1976* (Horn Book, 1978. xiv,290p. £35;$35.95. ISBN: 0876750188).

The 1967-76 supplement is in 4 pts: I. A decade of illustration in children's books (4 essays); II. Biographies (illustrators active 1967-76); III. Bibliographies (illustrators and authors); IV. Appendix (including cumulative index to biographies and bibliographies in the original work and the 3 supplements). *Class No:* 096-0053

[2767]

MARANTZ, S.S. *and* **MARANTZ, K.A. The Art of children's picture books:** a selective reference guide. 2nd ed. New York, Garland, 1995. xx,293p. £25.20;$43. (*Garland reference library of the humanities, v.1636.*) ISBN: 0815309376.

First published 1988.

Contents: I. History of children's picture books - II. How a picture book is made - III. Criticism of children's picture books - IV. Artists anthologized - V. Books, articles and audiovisual materials on individual picture book artists - VI. Guides and aids to futher research - VII. Some collections and/or repositories of materials on picture books and their creation (*c.*25 collections only). 844 bibliographical entries with annotations of 50-60 words across the sections (451 1st ed.). US materials predominate although some British and foreign language material included. Artist/author/editor/compiler and title indexes. No subject index. *Class No:* 096-0053

[2768]

WHALLEY, J.I. *and* **CHESTER, T.R. A History of children's book illustration.** London, John Murray with the Victoria and Albert Museum, 1988. 268p., illus., plates. ISBN: 0719545846.

US ed. as *The Bright stream: a history of children's book illustration* (Boston, Mass., Godine, 1994. ISBN: 0879237961).

The first general survey of children's book illustration, based largely on British books. Coverage includes chapbooks, picture sheet books, comics and books of instruction. 12 chronological chapters, 172 illustrations, 37 colour plates. Bibliography, *c.*140 items (p.249-52). Bibliographical notes to the illustrations. 'Designed to become the standard work for librarians and collectors' (*Bookseller*, 14th October 1988, p.1539). *Class No:* 096-0053

Bookplates

[2769]

Bookplates in the news 1970-1985: a collection of sixty issues of the Newsletter of the American Society of Bookplate Collectors and Designers, including a general index and an illustration index to bookplates, artists and owners. Arellanes, A.S., *ed.* Detroit, Gale, 1986. xii,640p. illus. $74. ISBN: 0810342928.

Includes over 250 illustrations. A 'fine and substantial book ... a very rich source of information' (*Bookplate journal*, v.5(1), March 1987, p.47). *Class No:* 097

[2770]

BUTLER, W.E. *and* **BUTLER, D.J. The Golden era of American bookplate design** 1890-1940. London, Bookplate Society & Forlaget Exlibristen, 1986. 165p. plates. ISBN: 8773171255.

The first substantial reference aid to modern American bookplate design. Discusses the work of *c.*100 designers in sections: The acknowledged masters; The unacknowledged masters; Other bookplate designers of note. Index (p.149-65). *Class No:* 097

[2771]

BUTLER, W.E. *and* **BUTLER, D.J. Modern British bookplates.** Cambridge, Silent Books, 1990. 60p. illus. £6.95. ISBN: 1851830235.

Brief account which includes an A-Z directory of designers (p.25-49). *Class No:* 097

[2772]

JOHNSON, F. A Treasury of bookplates: from the Renaissance to the present. New York, Dover Publications, 1977. vii,151p. illus. £8.95; $6.95. ISBN: 0486234851.

Collection of 761 outstanding bookplate designs from 1450 to the 20th century. Lacks information on the medium, original size or exact date, captions indicating artist and original owner only. Index of artists. *Class No:* 097

[2773]

LEE, B.N. Early printed book labels: a catalogue of dated personal labels and gift labels printed in Britain to the year 1760. Pinner, Private Libraries Association and the Bookplate Society, 1976. xxii,185p. illus. £14;$28. ISBN: 0900002727.

Limited ed.

Detailed descriptions of 506 book labels arranged chronologically. Selected illustrations only. Introductory essay (p.ix-xx). Appendices: Early American labels; Printers gifts; Book stamps. Indexes of names and college and university gift labels. *Class No:* 097

[2774]

—LEE, B.N. British Royal bookplates: and ex-libris of related families. Aldershot, Scolar P., 1992. vii,260p. illus. £65; $120. ISBN: 0859678830.

Illustrates and describes 172 bookplates with a further 37 as addenda. Select bibliography; index. '(C)omprehensive and beautifully illustrated' (*Manuscripta*, v.36(3), November 1992, p.252).

Lee has also produced a useful general history *British bookplates: a pictorial history* (Newton Abbot, David & Charles, 1979. 160p. illus. ISBN: 071537785x).
Class No: 097

Bibliographies

[2775]

ARELLANES, A.S. Bookplates: a selective annotated bibliography of the periodical literature. Detroit, Gale, 1971. xxxviii,474p. plates. $40. ISBN: 081030340x.

5,445 periodical articles are listed under nearly 600 journals, chronologically. Entries briefly annotated. 81 colour plates. Good author and subject indexes.
Class No: 097(01)

[2776]

A Bibliography of bookplate literature. Grimm, V.B., *comp and* Fuller, G.W., *ed.*. Spokane, Spokane Public Library, 1926. 151p.

Originally published as a limited ed. of 500 copies. Reprinted 1973 (Detroit, Gale. ISBN: 081033190x), currently available from Omnigraphics ($48. ISBN: 1558889337).

Unannotated bibliography of *c.*1,250 books, brochures and periodical sets. *Class No:* 097(01)

Periodicals

[2777]

The Bookplate journal. London, The Bookplate Society, 1983-. Semi-annual. £30. ISSN: 02643693.

Issues normally contain several articles, a portrait of a particular bookplate with notes, a profile of an artist and a book review. *Class No:* 097(051)

Prohibited Books

[2778]

FOERSTEL, H.N. Banned in the USA: a reference guide to book censorship in schools and public libraries. Westport, Conn., Greenwood Press, 1994. xxii,231p. £40.50;$45. ISBN: 0313285179.

Deals with contemporary book censorship. Most valuable section (p.135-215) identifies the 50 most censored titles. Further section describes 8 major banning incidents 1976-92. Short on other reference information. Select bibliography and index. *Class No:* 098.1

[2779]

HAIGHT, A.L. Banned books: 387 B.C. to 1978 A.D. New York, Bowker, 1978. xxv,196p. ISBN: 0835210782.

Updated and enl. by C.B. Grannis. First published 1935 as *Banned books: informal notes ...*; 3rd ed. 1970.

Presents examples of actual or attempted book bannings worldwide, but with the emphasis on recent US episodes. Chronological arrangement; 60 new entries in this ed. 5 appendices relating to US censorship, court decisions etc. Select bibliography (p.179-82). Index. *Class No:* 098.1

Other Printed Works

Erotic Books

[2780]

CEREZO, J.A. Bibliotheca erotica: sive apparatus a catalogum librorum eroticum (ad usum privatum). Madrid, Ediciones El Museo Universal, 1993. xiii,338p. ISBN: 8488427077.

Author A-Z listing of 684 bibliographies, catalogues, dictionaries, anthologies, etc., concerning erotica. Original works of literature and art excluded. Entries include library locations and occasional notes. Frequent errors and omissions; inferior to *Selten und gesucht* (below).
Class No: 099.0

[2781]

McCORMICK, D. Erotic literature: a connoisseur's guide. New York, Continuum, 1992. 263p. £21.95. ISBN: 0826405746.

Main section (p.86-226) profiles *c.*200 writers Abélard-Zola whose works are considered erotic in whole or in part. Entries, ranging from a few lines to several pages, include quotations of characteristic passages. Glossary (p.237-49); select bibliography and index. *Class No:* 099.0

[2782]
MENDES, P. Clandestine erotic fiction in English 1800-1930: a bibliographic study. Aldershot, Scolar Press, 1993. xviii,479p. facsims. £85;$124.95. ISBN: 0859679195.

Main section (p.127-407) comprises chronological listing of *c.*280 books published 1885-1930 with full bibliographical detail and notes. Supporting sections include checklists of clandestine catalogues and pamphlets. Earlier titles briefly listed in 'A Supplementary short-title checklist of erotic fiction in English 1800-1884' (p.425-33). Various appendices; indexed by theme, title and publisher/printer/author. '(E)xcellently produced ... should certainly not be overlooked by the social historian' (*The Library. Sixth series*, v.XVII(3), September 1995, p.18-19).
Class No: 099.0

[2783]
PIA, P. Les Livres de l'Enfer: bibliographie des ouvrages érotiques dans leurs différentes éditions du XVIe siècle à nos jours. Paris, C. Coulet et A. Faure, 1978. 2v. ISBN: 290268701x.

Catalogues and describes 1,730 items held by the Bibliothèque Nationale. Entries, arranged by title, provides detailed notes on contents, publishing history, physical appearance, etc. Classified list; name index. Preceded by Guillaume Apollinaire and other's *L'Enfer de la Bibliothèque Nationale: catalogue critique des collections* ... Nouv. ed. 1919. (Reprinted Geneva, Slatkine, 1970). *Class No:* 099.0

[2784]
The Private case: an annotated bibliography of the private case erotica collection in the British (Museum) Library. Kearney, P.J., *comp.* London, Jay Landesmann, 1981. 354p. £45. ISBN: 0905150224.

Limited ed. Includes an introduction by G. Legman.

1,920 entries for items mainly gained through donation. Arranged by author where known, otherwise pseudonym or title. Index of anonymous or pseudonymous works to which authors have been ascribed. Lacks other indexes, a deficiency remedied by Libenzell (below). *Class No:* 099.0

[2785]
—LIBENZELL, T. Smut in the British Library: register zu Kearney's Private Case. Hamburg, Bell, 1986. 88p. (*Arcana bibliographica, 8.*) ISBN: 3923308531.

Provides personal name, title, language (other than English and French) and publisher indexes to *The Private case*. German language introduction. *Class No:* 099.0

[2786]
Selten und gesucht: bibliographien und ausgewählte Nachschlagewerke zur erotischen Literatur. Bayer, F. *and* Leonhardt, K.L., *bearbs.* Stuttgart, Hiersemann, 1993. xi,416p., illus. DM560. (*Hiersemann bibliographische handbücher, 10.*.) ISBN: 3777293016.

Provides annotated entries for 582 bibliographies and other reference works relating to erotic literature. Arranged by category with extensive contents listing and cross-references; name, title, publisher and subject indexes. Detailed and scholarly, identifying and describing far more material than Deakin (below). *Class No:* 099.0

[2787]
—Catalogi librorum eroticorum: a criticial bibliography of erotic bibliographies and book catalogues. Deakin, T.J., *comp.* London, Cecil & Amelia Woolf, 1964. xii,28p. £9.95. ISBN: 090082106x.

Brief pamphlet containing approximately 80 critically annotated entries. Confined to the erotica of Western Europe. Indicates holdings for the British Museum (Library),

....*(contd.)*
Bibliothèque Nationale (Paris), Bodleian Library, Cambridge University Library and the Institute of Sex Research, Bloomington, Indiana. Author arrangement; title and name indexes. *Class No:* 099.0

Miniature Books

[2788]
A Bibliography of miniature books (1470-1965). Welsh, D.V., *comp and* Weber, F.J., *ed.*. Cobleskill, N.Y., K.I. Rickard, 1989. viii,250p.

Contains 7,271 entries for miniature books published up to 1965. Author arrangement with brief bibliographical detail; no information on bindings or annotations. Indexed by short title only. Some inconsistencies and duplicate entries, but there 'is no bibliography of miniature books comparable to this volume, and those interested in these books will cite the Welsh number in their articles and catalogs for years to come' (*American reference books annual*, v.22, 1991, p.6).
Class No: 099.1

[2789]
BONDY, L.W. Miniature books: their history from the beginnings to the present day. London, Sheppard Press, 1981. x,221p. illus. (some col.), 1 port. ISBN: 0900661232.

Reprinted Farnham, Richard Joseph, 1994. (£24. ISBN: 1872699162).

Narrative account in 23 chapters, each focussing on a specific topic (*e.g.* 5. Thumb bibles ... 9. English children's books after 1800... 13. David Bryce and Sons of Glasgow). Bibliography (p.203-7); indexes of authors/titles and publishers/printers. *Class No:* 099.1

[2790]
WEBER, F.J. A Select guide to sources for miniature books, 1879-1992. Fullerton, Ca., Lorson's Books and Prints, 1992. ix,82p.

Printed in limited press run of 300 copies.

Lists 254 items including 55 books and 57 periodical articles. *Class No:* 099.1

7 The Arts

The Arts

Bibliographies

[2791]

ADAM project: an art, design, architecture and media information gateway. Farnham, Surrey, Surrey Institute of Art & Design, 1996-.

Part of the UK Electronic Libraries Programme (e-Lib); project director e-mail: <mwilks@surrart.ac.uk>

UK-based information gateway project, scheduled to be completed at the end of 1998. Intended to give access to Internet resources and links to other online services; selection criteria, interface, linkages are the subject of discussion with the art community. Major participant with Surrey Institute is the University of Northumbria at Newcastle, which will host the server; other participants include the National Art Library and Tate Gallery.
Class No: 7.0(01)

[2792]

ARNTZEN, E.M. *and* **RAINWATER, R. Guide to the literature of art history.** Chicago, American Library Association; London, Art Book Co., 1980. 616p. ISBN: 0905309057.

A major guide, containing over 4,000 entries with descriptive critical annotations. Intended for scholarly researchers, but including all basic materials. Main subject areas: painting, sculpture, architecture, prints, drawings, photographs, decorative arts. Organized into four categories: general reference sources, general primary and secondary sources, the particular arts, and serials. Author/title index and detailed subject index. The cut-off date was 1977, but retrospective value is good. *Class No:* 7.0(01)

[2793]

Art book review quarterly: an international review of art literature. London, Art Book Review, 1982-. £22pa. ISSN: 0263709x.

Paper version published quarterly; Internet version at Website <http://www.atrium.co.uk>.

Lengthy reviews, short notices; provides a useful current commentary. Website lists over 3000 current art titles.
Class No: 7.0(01)

[2794]

Art index: an author and subject index to domestic and foreign art periodicals and museum bulletins covering archaeology, architecture, art history, arts and crafts, city planning, fine arts, graphic arts, industrial design etc. New York, H.W. Wilson, 1929-. $185pa.; CD-ROM $1495.00 (covers 1984 to date; new disc each quarter.) ISSN: 00043222.

Quarterly with annual cumulations; 3-year cumulations 1929-1953; 2-year cumulations 1953-1967, then annual. Available online and on CD-ROM from 1984. *See also Wilson Art Abstracts.*

Wide international coverage, and comprehensive in all aspects of visual arts. Covers 250 serials, bulletins, exhibitions. Subjects include archaeology, architecture, art history, film, industrial and interior design, landscape and town planning, photography, television etc. Single alphabetical sequence; separate index of book reviews.
Class No: 7.0(01)

[2795]

Art/Kunst: International bibliography of art books, 1972-. Basel, Jaeggi AG, 1988-.

Annual. Published 1973-1987 by Helbing & Lichtenhahn, Basle.

Classified bibliography of art books published worldwide. Index of authors, editors, artists. Includes museum guides, exhibition catalogues. Text in English, French and German.
Class No: 7.0(01)

[2796]

Art on screen on CD-ROM. Boston, G.K. Hall, 1996. CD-ROM. £410.00; annual update £205.00. ISBN: 0783821530.

Database of the Program for Art on Film; printed vols. issued as *Art on screen* (1992) and *Architecture on screen* (1994).

Filmographies for the visual arts, covering over 22,000 films and videos from 70 countries; mainly 1970 to the present, but some limited coverage 1915-1969. Includes fine arts, architecture, photography, decorative arts, design, folk art etc. Entries give title of film, synopsis of content, language, production date, format, distribution sources.
Class No: 7.0(01)

[2797]

ARTbibliographies MODERN: abstracts of the current literature of modern art, photography and design. Oxford, Clio Press, 1973-. $1350.00 CD-ROM for print subscribers; $1800.00 for non-print subscribers; network prices extra. ISSN: 0300466x.

Regarded as the successor to the defunct *Literature of Modern Art (LOMA)* 1971-1973 which covered 1969-1971. This present work therefore begins at volume 4 in 1973. Online service began from volume 5. Now annual CD-ROM service covering 1984 onwards; 'expanded' version covers 1974 onwards.

Abstracts about 12,000 items each year in a single A/Z sequence of subjects, artists, groups, collectors, critics, etc. culled from 500 art journals, museum bulletins, exhibition catalogues, and monographs covering all aspects of 19th and 20th century art. Author and museum/gallery indexes. The CD-ROM is easy to install and has well-written documentation. 'The principal goal seems to be to amass a preset number of about 12,000 abstracts per annum from worldwide sources. This assures quantity but not necessarily reliability.' (*Choice,* 31(10) June 1994. p1564-5.)
Class No: 7.0(01)

[2798]
Arts and humanities citation index. Philadelphia, PA, ISI, 1978-. $5,000 for 3 years service.

2 interim issues pa., and annual cumulation. Available online and on CD-ROM.

Indexes over 6,000 key journals from all countries in archaeology, architecture, art, Asian studies, classics, dance, film TV and radio, folklore, history, music, philosophy, theatre etc. Every substantive item is indexed in 1400 journals, and selective coverage of a further 4700. Book reviews included. 'An intricate but rewarding database that responds well to creative searching' (*Choice,* 24,9. May 1987, p.1384). *Class No:* 7.0(01)

[2799]
Bibliographic guide to art and architecture. Boston, G.K. Hall, 1975-. c950p. £280.00 per vol. ISSN: 03602699.

Published annually. Serves as the annual supplement to the NYPL Dictionary Catalog of the Art & Architecture Division (G.K. Hall, 1975).

Lists publications catalogued by the New York Public Library and the Library of Congress. *Class No:* 7.0(01)

[2800]
Bibliography of the history of art. Bibliographie d'histoire de l'art. Los Angeles/London/Vandoeuvre-les-Nancy, Getty Trust Publications/INIST Diffusion, 1990-. $425.00pa. CD-ROM $700.00.

Replaces *Répertoire d'art et d'archéolgie* and *Répertoire international de le litterature de l'art* (RILA). Issued quarterly, with annual cumulative index. Online access available. Various CD-ROM versions 1996 onwards, in French and English.

Over 400,000 records, with 24,000 citations added per year; abstracts presented in French or English. Covers Western art from late antiquity to the present. Joint venture of INIST (CNRS Institut de l'Information Scientifique et Technique) and AHIP (The Getty Art History Program). Abstracts books (including catalogues), all periodical content (interviews, obituaries, reviews, letters etc.), proceedings, Festschriften, essays, dissertations; but not annual reports, auction catalogues, films or newspapers. 'Handsomely produced, well-organized and economically priced, and it has successfully solved the problem of its use of both English and French. It provides greater and wider coverage than both of its predecessors put together.' (*Art Libraries Journal,* 16(4) 1991. p.20-30.) *Class No:* 7.0(01)

[2801]
CENTRAL INSTITUTE FOR ART HISTORY, Munich. **Catalogs of the library of the Central Institute for Art History, Munich.** Munich, K.G. Saur. 649 microfiche, and printed guide. $5,000 (available separately).

Part one covers book and serial holdings until 1982 (272,000 cards, 199 fiche); part two covers articles and essays, reviews in periodicals, Festschriften etc. from 1950; part three is the subject catalog (500,000 cards on 270 fiche). Major collection particularly strong in aesthetics, iconography, and French art. *Class No:* 7.0(01)

[2802]
CHAMBERLIN, M.W. Guide to art reference books. Chicago, American Library Association, 1959. xiv,416p.

2,565 systematically annotated entries. 19 chapters: Bibliography-Indexes-Directories - Sales records - Reproductions - Dictionaries and encyclopedias - Biography - Iconography - methodology - Histories and handbooks of art: Architecture, Sculpture - Drawings - Painting - Prints and engravings - Applied arts - Documents and sources - Periodicals (items 2121-3270, indicating which periodicals are covered by particular indexing series) - Serials. Appendix: Special collections and resources (items 2490-2565); covering US and W. Europe. Includes costume, but excludes advertising art, arms and armour, book arts, calligraphy, caricature, city planning, the dance and heraldry, 'how-to-do-it' books, interior decoration (except furniture and textiles), landscape gardening, numismatics, photography, music, sports and pastimes, and theatre. Standard books are indicated. Authoritative, if dated.
Class No: 7.0(01)

[2803]
EHRESMANN, D.L. Fine arts: a bibliographic guide to basic reference works. 3rd ed. Littleton,CO, Libraries Unlimited, 1992. 373p. £50.00. ISBN: 0872876403.

First published 1976.

Numbered and briefly annotated entries, with interpolations for books and articles. *Part 1:* Reference works (Bibliographies; Library catalogs; Indexes; Directories; Dictionaries; and encyclopedias; Iconography) *Part 2:* Histories and handbooks (Prehistoric and primitive art; Periods of Western art history; National histories and handbooks of European art; Oriental art; New World art; Art of Africa and Oceania (including Australia), Cross-references. Coverage of pt.2 is restricted to books in Western European languages. Detailed analytical index. Annotations stress special features *e.g.* glossaries, chronological charts, specially good illus., and bibliographies. Updates but does not supersede Chamberlin.
Class No: 7.0(01)

[2804]
FREER GALLERY OF ART. Dictionary catalog of the library of the Freer Gallery of Art. Boston, G.K. Hall, 1967. 6v.

Access by author, subject and title to western language (vols. 1-4) and oriental language (vols. 5-6) monographs and serials; includes analytics for major serials.
Class No: 7.0(01)

[2805]
FREITAG, W.M. Art books: a basic bibliography of monographs on artists. 2nd.ed. New York, Garland, 1997. xxvi,542p. £72.00. ISBN: 0824033264.

All countries and periods, artists and architects, and specializing in monographs not cited in other standard sources. 'An extremely useful work that will easily assume a place next to Arntzen, Ehresmann, and Chamberlin on any art librarians shelf'. (*Art Libraries Journal* 11(3)1986. p.35-37, commenting on the first ed.). *Class No:* 7.0(01)

[2806]
GERMAN ARCHAEOLOGICAL INSTITUTE. Rome. **Index der antiken Kunst und Architektur,** Index of ancient art and architecture. London, Saur, 1987-1991. *c.*4000 microfiche. £5,200. ISBN: 3598320701.

Microfiche series based on the Institute's collection of 300,000 photographs; covers architecture, sculpture, sarcophagi, reliefs, vases, inscriptions, mosaics, and small art objects. *c.*3,250 fiche comprise the photographic inventory, the remainder form the catalogue.
Class No: 7.0(01)

[2807]

HARVARD UNIVERSITY. Fogg Art Museum. **Catalogue of the Harvard University Fine Arts Library.** Boston, G.K. Hall, 1973. 15v. + 3v. supplement.

412,000 + 58,500 photolithographed catalogue cards, reproduced 33 to the page. A dictionary catalogue that reflects the combined strengths of the Fogg Museum and the Widener Library. It covers the history of arts in all periods, with emphasis on the Western tradition. V.15 (681p.), 'Catalogue of auction sales catalogues' has 22,400 main-entry cards. *Class No:* 7.0(01)

[2808]

METROPOLITAN MUSEUM OF ART. New York. **Library catalogue of the Metropolitan Museum of Art.** 2nd rev. ed. Boston, G.K. Hall, 1986. 2500p. (4v.). £489. ISBN: 0816104069.

First edition 1960, with 8 supplements 1962-80; second edition 1980 (48v.) with supplements 1982 and 1986 (4v.).

Dictionary catalogue including coverage of sales catalogues indexed by subject & auction house. New headings in the second edition reflect trends and new movements; cross-references. Revised second edition abandons the technique of reproducing the catalogue cards. *Class No:* 7.0(01)

[2809]

NEW YORK PUBLIC LIBRARY. Dictionary catalog of the Art and Architecture division. Boston, G.K. Hall, 1975. 30v.

Supplement 1974 (566p.; published 1975). Thereafter supplemented by the *Bibliographic guide to art and architecture. (q.v.).*

Almost 500,000 catalogue cards reproduced, representing over 100,000 volumes on painting, drawing, sculpture, and the history and design aspects of architecture and the applied arts - one of the largest research collections of its kind. *Class No:* 7.0(01)

[2810]

Répertoire d'art et d'archéologie. Paris, Morance, 1910-.

From 1990 replaced by *Bibliography of the history of art (q..v.).*

Annual bibliography, arranged by broad categories of countries and periods. Indexes by artist, author, and subject. *Class No:* 7.0(01)

[2811]

Répertoire international de la littérature de l'art. Williamstown, Mass., College Art Association of America, 1975-. $150.00. ISSN: 01455982.

From 1990 replaced by *Bibliography of the history of art (q.v.).* Cumulative indexes issued for 1975-79, and 1980-84. Online access; CD-ROM backfile issued 1996 by Getty Trust Publications. Also Internet access at Website <http://www.ahip.getty.edu/ahip/home.html> *Class No:* 7.0(01)

[2812]

ROBINSON, D. Fine art periodicals: an international directory of the visual arts. Voorheesville,NY, Peri, 1991. 570p. ISBN: 1879796031.

2790 titles under broad subject arrangement; some more titles and more information than Ulrich. *Class No:* 7.0(01)

[2813]

VARLEY, G. Art and design documentation in the UK and Ireland: a directory of resources. West Bromwich, ARLIS, 1993. 241p. £50.00. ISBN: 0951967428.

400 entries - name, address, contact, stock and subject, hours, access, services, publications. Regional index; subject index. *Class No:* 7.0(01)

[2814]

VICTORIA AND ALBERT MUSEUM. London. Library. **Complete author catalogue.** Brighton, Harvester Press Microform Publications, 1987. $3950.

Holdings up to the end of 1986. 400,000 entries on microfiche; includes books, serials, periodicals and annuals. *Class No:* 7.0(01)

[2815]

Wilson art abstracts. New York, H.W. Wilson, 1995-. CD-ROM. $2870.00 full annual subscription (12 discs); various reductions for reduced frequency.

Standard service consists of a monthly disc; Internet access to be made available - check Website at <http://wilsonweb.hwwilson.com>

Cover-to-cover abstracting of 260 publications worldwide; wide range of subject coverage: antiques, architecture, art history, crafts, decorative arts, folk art, graphic arts, interior design, landscape architecture, motion pictures, painting, photography, pottery, sculpture, television, textiles. Access by keyword, artist name, subject terms, words in the abstracts. Abstracts of 50-150 words, noting illustrations, maps, portraits, etc. Full abstracting service began in 1995, and 2000 items are added each month; discs also contain index entries back to 1984, taken from *Art index* records. Brief technical review in *Information world review*, July/August, 1998, p.27. *Class No:* 7.0(01)

Women

[2816]

ANDERSON, J.A. Women in the fine arts: a bibliography and illustration guide. Jefferson,NC, McFarland, 1991. 362p. $49.95. ISBN: 0899505414.

Covers the Renaissance to the present day; material is categorized into general reference, periodicals, exhibition catalogues, and newspapers. The primary arrangement is by author, with an artist index. References to any one artist could appear in any of the categories, and thus four access points could be indicated. Coverage of exhibition catalogues is good; there is a US emphasis, although the work is international. Illustrations in the sources are noted. *Class No:* 7.0(01)-0055.2

[2817]

PILAND, S., *ed.* Women artists: an historical, contemporary and feminist bibliography. 2nd.ed. Metuchen, NJ, Scarecrow Press, 1994. 454p. £50.50. ISBN: 0810825597.

First ed. published 1978.

185 artists are represented, from the 10th century to 1930. Some problems are noted (*American reference books annual*, 1996, p423) including inconsistencies in format, omissions of key sources, incomplete citations, superficial biographical information. Heavy US bias. *Class No:* 7.0(01)-0055.2

Encyclopaedias & Dictionaries

[2818]

The Book of art: a pictorial encyclopedia of painting, drawing, and sculpture. Read, H., *ed.* Rev.ed. Danbury, Conn., Grolier, 1994. 10v., illus. $339.00. ISBN: 0717273563.

Scholarly survey of the history of art, national schools, individual artists; despite the title, architecture and the decorative arts are also included. 8 vols. concentrate on Western art; one vol. covers Chinese and Japanese art; final vol. outlines the basis of art criticism - styles, genres, etc.,

....(contd.)
and contains a glossary and index. Some 630 artists are discussed; 5000 plates and other illustrations captioned with artists, date, media, size, location. *Class No:* 7.0(03)

[2819]
CHILVERS, I., ***ed.*** **The Concise Oxford dictionary of art and artists.** 2nd.ed. Oxford, OUP, 1996. 584p. £6.99. ISBN: 0192800485.

Previous ed. 1990.

Alphabetical arrangement of names and terms; covers Western painting, sculpture, and graphic art. Artist biographies, groups, styles, movements, critics, patrons, dealers and collectors, museums and galleries; scope: fifth century BC to present. *Class No:* 7.0(03)

[2820]
CHILVERS, I. ***and*** **OSBORNE, H.** ***and*** **FARR, D.,** ***eds.*** **The Oxford dictionary of art.** Rev.ed. Oxford, OUP, 1997. 1008p. £25.00. ISBN: 0198600844.

Based on Oxford Companions to *Art, Twentieth-Century Art*, and *Decorative Arts*.

Entries cover major names in Western art including historians, artists, collectors, dealers, and terms, schools, techniques, styles and genres. Covers fifth century BC to present day, Western culture only. 3,000 entries in alphabetical arrangement include no artists born after 1945; this ed. is extensively re-written and has 300 completely new entries. Architecture is excluded. 2 column layout is close but clear; abundant cross-references indicated by asterisk; no illus. *Class No:* 7.0(03)

[2821]
Dictionary of art. Turner, J., *ed.* London, Macmillan, 1996. 30,200p.(34v.), illus. £5750.00. ISBN: 1884446000.

An online version is expected at the end of 1998.

45,000 articles and over 15,000 illustrations; the work of 6700 contributors from 120 countries. The largest and most comprehensive encyclopedia of the visual arts ever attempted, which must become the definitive source for many decades. Coverage is international, and ranges from prehistory to the present day; painting, sculpture, decorative arts, architecture, restoration, conservation, furniture, design, jewellery, graphic arts, photography, patrons, teachers, collectors are included. Equal emphasis is given to Western and Non-Western cultures; entry for *Africa* (v.1) extends to 200p., with 163 illus. and maps.

About half of all entries are biographies: typical example (such as *Michelangelo*, 30 pages) begins with a table of contents, life and work, working techniques and methods, character and personality, critical reception, bibliography - general, monographs, exhibition catalogues and congresses, specialist studies. There are 500 entries for styles, schools, groups; 800 on forms, themes, subjects.

Entry *Bibliography of art* (v.4, p20-28; by Lee Sorensen) offers introduction, history, catalogues and classification schemes, bibliographies, reference works, histories, databases, specialist formats, exhibition catalogues, image collections. Many citations are out-dated - possibly as the work has been in progress for 14 years; reference to *Walford* is to 1980 ed. Entry for *Encyclopedias and dictionaries* (v.10, p203-214) divides into 6 time periods and gives lengthy bibliography after each; similar problem of old eds. of standard works. Entry *Periodical* (v.24, p420-453) is very thorough, listing journals by styles and periods, including futurism, expressionism, cubism, vorticism, dada etc; regional and national surveys by continent (Europe A/Z by country, each categorised and giving bibliography.)

Illus. mainly monochrome but with small sections of

....(contd.)
plates, and 1000 commissioned line drawings. Appendices (v.33) give locations of galleries etc., periodical titles, reference works, non-Western dynasties and peoples. Index (v.34) contains over 700,000 entries.

Generally received with critical acclaim; *Choice* (34(5); January 1997; p761-2) describes it as an 'extraordinary achievement'; *Reference books bulletin* (93(8); 1996; p742-3) judges that its 'interdisciplinary, context-based approach also makes it one of the most important publishing efforts for related disciplines such as anthropology, archaeology, ethnology, theater, and the history of culture.'
Class No: 7.0(03)

[2822]
Encyclopedia of world art. New York, J. Heraty Associates, 1959-68. 15v. illus., plates, maps. $1495. ISBN: 007019467x.

Supplementary volumes issued 1983 (vol.16) and 1987 (vol.17).

About 1,000 entries in main work; monographic treatment (*e.g. Baroque Art,* v.2, cols. 255-361; 89 illustrations; 8½ cols. of bibliography). Contributors are international scholars and specialists; coverage centres on historical, conceptual and systematic, and geographical viewpoints. Vol.15 is a comprehensive index with 20,000 entries. Wide coverage, but not photography, nor theatre.
Class No: 7.0(03)

[2823]
Hutchinson dictionary of the arts. Oxford, Helicon Publishing, 1994. 564p. £20.00. ISBN: 009177652x.

6000 entries - definitions, terms, individual movements, styles etc. covering architecture, artistic theory, cinema, craft and design, dance, music, mythology, painting, photography, sculpture, theatre. 'The best buy presently available in a one-volume work that covers all the major arts.' 'Highly accessible...and an indispensable permanent source of reference.' (*Reference reviews,* 8(7) 1994. p.29.)
Class No: 7.0(03)

[2824]
MURRAY, P. ***and*** **MURRAY, L. The Penguin dictionary of art and artists.** 7th ed. London, Penguin, 1997. xiv,580p. £6.99. ISBN: 0140513000.

First published 1959.

A/Z by topic (outlined pviii-xiii) and 1200 biographical entries, covering all major artists 1300 to the present; this ed. provides several new entries for modern American artists. Includes terms, processes, movements, styles, techniques; cross-references. *Class No:* 7.0(03)

[2825]
The Oxford companion to art. Osborne, H., *ed.* Oxford, Clarendon Press, 1970. xii, 1277p., illus. £32.50. ISBN: 019866107x.

Latest reprint 1997.

76 contributors; about 3,000 entries ranging in length from 10 lines to 10p. (*e.g.* 'Roman art'), 'Pop art': 1 column. Coverage allows comparatively more space to contemporary art movements; includes architecture and ceramics but not practical or performing arts. Admirable bibliography of 2,969 references from the text is appended in 5 sections. Numerous smallish black-and-white illustrations. Designed as a non-specialist introduction to the fine arts. Still a highly-regarded source despite its age. *Class No:* 7.0(03)

[2826]
The Oxford illustrated encyclopaedia of the arts. Norwich, J.J., *ed.* Oxford, OUP, 1990. 512p. illus. £25. ISBN: 0198691378.

Volume 5 of the *Oxford Illustrated Encyclopedia*.

Over 3000 A/Z entries on art, architecture, dance, sculpture, music, theatre, cinema, photography, literature and the decorative arts, from pre-history to the present. Entries vary in length from 50-1000 words; 350 illustrations, 175 in colour. 120 contributors. An excellently-produced and authoritative single-volume source. *Class No:* 7.0(03)

Handbooks & Manuals

[2827]
MAYER, R. Artist's handbook of materials and techniques. 5th ed. London, Faber, 1991. xv,761p. ISBN: 0571143318, pbk; 0571150675.

A thorough treatment; coverage includes pigments, oils, acrylics, tempera, grounds, watercolour, gouache, pastel, encaustic, mural, solvents and thinners, glues, wax, chemistry, conservation, inks, brushes etc. Numerous appendices and tables. Bibliography in category order (pp.675-711) and a good index (pp.713-761).
Class No: 7.0(035)

[2828]
SMITH, S. The Artist's manual. 2nd ed. London, Macdonald, 1990. 320p. illus. £11.95. ISBN: 0356196062.

Originally hardback edition 1980.

Practical guide to artistic media: painting, drawing, designing, sculpting. Step-by-step instruction, based on small illustrations and descriptive text. Analytical index.
Class No: 7.0(035)

Dictionaries

[2829]
ATKINS, R. Artspeak: a guide to contemporary ideas, movements, and buzzwords, 1945 to the present. 2nd.ed. New York, Abbeville, 1997. 208p., illus. £19.00. ISBN: 0789204150.

This ed. includes 120 entries relating to art movements in America and Europe from 1945. Plenty of nebulous jargon is explained. *Class No:* 7.0(038)

[2830]
Dictionary of the arts. New York, Facts on File, 1994. 564p. $29.95. ISBN: 081603205x.

Concise general resource of terms and personal names; 6000 entries of all periods of Western art. Clear layout and comprehensive scope, but only suitable at an introductory level. *Class No:* 7.0(038)

[2831]
DURO, P. *and* **GREENHALGH, M. Essential art history.** London, Bloomsbury, 1994. 311p. £12.50. ISBN: 074751402x.

Dictionary of 700 art history terms; Western emphasis. Architecture is not included, and there are no illustrations. Bibliographic references follow about half the entries. Good on recent material, but the *Oxford dictionary of art* is fuller, and Lucie-Smith (below) has the advantage of good illustrations. *Class No:* 7.0(038)

[2832]
EHRESMANN, J.M., ***ed.*** **Pocket dictionary of art terms.** 3rd ed. New York, Bulfinch, 1992. 160p. £5.99. ISBN: 0821219057.

Coverage: styles, schools and movements, techniques and physical properties of painting, sculpture, applied and decorative arts, architecture and philosophy. Bibliography.
Class No: 7.0(038)

[2833]
FERMENT, C. Dictionnaire des termes de l'art: Anglais-Francais, Francais-Anglais. Paris, Maison du Dictionnaire, 1994. 490p. 350FF. ISBN: 2856080596.

8000 entries, with some brief explanations, covering painting, sculpture, architecture, decorative arts, furniture, numismatics. Very thorough and reliable.
Class No: 7.0(038)

[2834]
Glossarium artis: systematic glossary of art terms. Tübingen, Niemayer, 1971-. 9v., illus.

Terms in English, French, German; illustrated with line drawings, bibliographies, Latin terms where necessary.

Volumes are as follows:

V.1 *Castles.* 2nd ed., 1977. 280p.
V.2 *Liturgical objects.* 2nd ed., 1982. 150p.
V.3 *Arches and arcades.* 2nd ed., 1982. 160p.
V.4 *Ornaments and liturgical books.* 2nd ed., 1982. 202p.
V.5 *Staircases.* 2nd rev.. ed., 1985. 278p.
V.6 *Vaults.* 3rd rev. ed., 1988. 300p.
V.7 *Fortifications.* New ed. in preparation.
V.8 *The historic monument.* 1981. 320p.
V.9 *Towns.* 1987. 408p. *Class No:* 7.0(038)

[2835]
IFLA SECTION OF ART LIBRARIES. Multilingual glossary for art librarians. 2nd.ed. Munich, K.G. Saur, 1996. 181p. £46.50. ISBN: 3598218028.

First published 1984 as *Art librarians' glossary*.

600 (English) terms are briefly defined with equivalent terms in Dutch, French, German, Italian, Spanish, Swedish, and variant US spellings. Indexes (p135-180) in each of these languages. *Class No:* 7.0(038)

[2836]
LUCIE-SMITH, E., ***ed.*** **Dictionary of art terms.** London, Thames & Hudson, 1984. 208p. illus. £10.50. ISBN: 0500233896.

Over 2,000 entries, including the vocabulary of the arts of India, China, Japan, Malaysia, Oceania, Africa, pre-Columbian America, as well as Western art. 'Almost everyone concerned with the history of art will find invaluable the clear, brief definitions' (*TLS* April 8, 1988,p.397). *Class No:* 7.0(038)

[2837]
RÉAU, L. Dictionnaire polyglotte des termes d'art et d'archéologie. Paris, Presses Universitaires de France, 1977. viii,247p. £60.

At head of title-page. Comité International d'Histoire de'Art. Published with Unesco support.

About 8,500 French-base terms covering art and archaeology, with equivalents in other European languages, particularly Italian, Spanish, English, German and Russian (transliterated). Other languages less regularly covered: Greek, Latin, Portuguese, Dutch, Danish, Swedish, Czech and Polish. 1977 ed. adds German, English and Italian reverse indexes. *Class No:* 7.0(038)

[2838]

WALKER, J.A. Glossary of art, architecture and design since 1945; terms describing movements, styles, groups and organizations derived from the vocabularies of artists, critics, and curators. 3rd ed. London, Library Association Publishing, 1992. 402p., illus. £49.50. ISBN: 0851576398.

700 definitions of groups, styles etc. that have evolved since 1945; international in scope, and based on published literature. Concepts and theoretical ideas are a valuable feature; cross-references, indexes of artists, art groups, and art concepts. Bibliographies follow many entries.
Class No: 7.0(038)

Reviews & Abstracts

[2839]

Art and archaeology technical abstracts. New York, Institute of Fine Arts, New York University for the International Institute for the Conservation of Historic and Artistic Works (London) and the Getty Conservation Institute (Malibu) 1966-. $60. ISSN: 00042994.

Semi-annual. Formerly *I.I.C. abstracts* (London, International Institute for Conservation of Museum Objects, 1955-. v.1-5 2pa). 2v. cumulative author/subject index covering 1974-1988 issued 1997 by Getty Trust Publications.

Signed, indicative and informative abstracts. 11 sections: A. General methods and applications - B. Papers - C. Wood - D. Fibres and textiles - E. Paint and paintings - F. Glass and ceramics - G. Stone and masonry - H. Metals - I. Photographs and other audio visual materials - J. Other natural and synthetic organic materials - K. Information sources (including motion pictures and slides). Appended lists of contributors and authors in each issue. Annual subject index. *Class No:* 7.0(048)

Periodicals & Progress Reports

[2840]

FRICK ART REFERENCE LIBRARY. Original index to art periodicals. Boston, G.K. Hall, 1983. 12v.

Detailed analytical entries compiled by the Frick Library 1923-1969, but covering many 19th century journals. French and Italian material strong; entries include galleries, exhibitions, artists, portraits etc. A Supplement covers 1961-1974. *Class No:* 7.0(05)

[2841]

ROBINSON, D. Fine art periodicals: an international directory of the visual arts. Voorheesville,NY, Peri, 1991. 570p. ISBN: 1879796031.

2790 titles in broad subject arrangement; some more titles and more information than Ulrich. *Class No:* 7.0(05)

[2842]

Zeitschrift für Kunstgeschichte. Munich, Deutsche Kunstverlag, 1932-. DM150. ISSN: 00442992.

Issued quarterly.

Publisher and frequency vary. Preceded by *Repertorium für Kunstwissenshaft* (1876-1931).

Carries an annual bibliography 'Bibliographischer Teil' as the November/December issue of each year. About 3,000 unannotated entries, systematically arranged (Allegemeines - Ikonographie - Kunst nach Ländern - Baukunst - Ornamentik - Bauplastik - Dekoration - Gardenkunst - Plastik - Malerei und Graphik - Glasmalerei ... Bucheinbände). Author index. International and wide-ranging 'Unique and indispensable for

.... (contd.)

the art historian' (Arntzen, E., and Rainwater, R. *Guide to the literature of art history* (1980), entry A18.
Class No: 7.0(05)

Periodicals

[2843]

Apollo: the international magazine of the arts. London, Apollo Magazine, 1925-. £70pa. ISSN: 00036536.

Monthly. Also available on microfilm.

Covers art history, antiques, and auctions; valuable for scholars, dealers, and collectors. Illustrated advertisements. Gallery news, letters, book reviews. *Class No:* 7.0(051)

[2844]

Art documentation: the bulletin of the Art Libraries Society of North America. Tucson, Az, ARLIS/NA, 1982-. $75pa. ISSN: 07307187.

Issued quarterly, formerly *ARLIS/NA Newsletter* (1972-81).

Excellent journal source for articles on art librarianship, slide and photography curatorship, art history, book publishing, art bibliography. Regular sections of book reviews and publications received. *Class No:* 7.0(051)

[2845]

Art history. Oxford, Blackwell, 1978-. £44pa. (£73 to institutions.) ISSN: 01416790.

Issued quarterly.

Authoritative, scholarly book reviews are a regular feature; typically about 10-12 of 500 words or more.
Class No: 7.0(051)

[2846]

Art libraries journal. London, ARLIS, 1976-. £29pa. ISSN: 03074722.

Issued quarterly.

Good selection of articles on art librarianship, book reviews, bibliographies. 'Truly international rather than UK-oriented'. (*Art Documentation* 6,2. Spring 1987, p.42).
Class No: 7.0(051)

[2847]

Arts Review. London, Arts Review, 1949-. £24pa; (£44 to institutions). ISSN: 00041140.

25 issues per year.

Each issue contains arts news, features, saleroom news, articles, London and regional reviews (galleries, exhibitions, and events). Pull-out exhibition guide. *Class No:* 7.0(051)

[2848]

The Burlington magazine. London, Burlington Magazine Publications, 1903-. £132pa.

Monthly.

Academic international arts periodical covering all periods. Illustrated; book reviews. Annual index; Cumulative index 1962-72, and 1972-82. *Class No:* 7.0(051)

[2849]

Gazette des beaux-arts. Paris, Presses Universitaires de France, 1859-. £90pa. ISSN: 00165530.

10 issues pa.

Scholarly art history journal with material in French & English. 'One of the oldest and most respected art journals' (Arntzen & Rainwater, 1980). *Class No:* 7.0(051)

Yearbooks & Directories

[2850]

Art world directory: 1998/99 incorporating *Arts Review* yearbook. 25th.ed. London, Arts Review in association with Nautilus, 1998. 356p., illus. £12.95. ISBN: 090483123x.

Entries cover galleries (public and commercial), museums, sculpture parks, auction houses, publishers, art bookshops, courses, schools and colleges, art societies and organisations, regional arts boards, consultants, materials; diary of exhibitions and competitions; space for hire, index of artists and general index. *Class No:* 7.0(058)

[2851]

Artyear 1998: international exhibition guide. Merz, B. *and* Blanchard, P., *eds*. Bologna, Hopefulmonster, 1997. 400p., illus. £7.95. ISBN: 8877570768.

Guide to exhibitions of art and architecture in museums worldwide; also information on permanent collections, opening hours, prices etc. *Class No:* 7.0(058)

[2852]

International directory of arts: 1997/98. 23rd ed. Munich, K.G.Saur, 1997. 695, 772, 658p. (3v). £245.00. ISBN: 3598230753.

Volume 1: museums and public galleries, universities, art schools, associations; v.2: dealers, commercial galleries, auctioneers, restorers, publishers, periodicals, booksellers. 150,000 entries from 140 countries. Arranged throughout by country. V.3 is Index of persons (directors, curators, presidents, scientific staff of museums etc.) and index of institutions and companies. *Class No:* 7.0(058)

[2853]

Writers' and artists' yearbook. London, A. & C. Black. c700p. £11.99.

Annual.

Sections relevant to performing arts and broadcasting (script markets for theatre, radio, television, and films; list of specialist agents); illustration & design, including art agents, & firms requiring drawings & designs; photography; picture research; music, including list of UK and US publishers. General information on finance, law and regulations, publishing practice, preparation of materials. List of societies & prizes. *Class No:* 7.0(058)

Quotations

[2854]

CROFTON, I., *comp*. A Dictionary of art quotations. London, Routledge, 1988. 223p. £12.95. ISBN: 0415003229.

Quotations from artists, and reactions to their work. Emphasis on Western fine arts, arranged in one alphabetical sequence of 371 topics. Minimal citation details; author and subject indexes. *Class No:* 7.0(082.2)

[2855]

LA COUR, D.W., *comp*. Artists in quotation: a dictionary of the creative thoughts of painters, sculptors, designers, writers, educators, and others. Jefferson, NC., McFarland, 1989. 208p. $29.95. ISBN: 0899503799.

About 2,000 entries, arranged under 160 topics A/Z; chronological sub-arrangement, with detailed subject index. *Class No:* 7.0(082.2)

Histories

[2856]

GOMBRICH, E.H. The Story of art. 16th ed. London, Phaidon, 1995. 688p., illus. £29.99. (Pbk £19.99.) ISBN: 071483355x.

First published 1950.

One of the most successful general histories; begins with prehistoric art and ancient America and has some material on Islam and China but otherwise concentrates on mainstream Western art. This ed. has been re-designed; text and bibliographies have been revised, and new artists have been included. Almost all illus. are in colour. Excellent coverage in a clear style. *Class No:* 7.0(091)

[2857]

HONOUR, H. *and* FLEMING, J. A World history of art. 3rd ed. London, Lawrence King, 1991. 766p. illus. £19.95. ISBN: 1856690008; 1856690059, Pbk.

Published in the US by Prentice-Hall as *The visual arts: a history*.

Concise and well organized, and covering art of all countries and periods. An excellent single-volume source, with over 1100 illustrations. Detailed index to text and illustrations. *Class No:* 7.0(091)

[2858]

HOOKER, D., *ed*. Art of the Western World. London, Boxtree, 1991. 464p. illus. ISBN: 1852831626, pbk.

First published in hardback 1989.

Intended as a companion to the television series *Art of the Western World* produced by TVS for Channel 4 UK. 18 chronological chapters by well-known specialist contributors cover the major periods from Greek and Roman art to post-modernism. Excellent illustrations; each chapter also contains two double-page features examining in detail a crucial work of the period, in addition to its inclusion in the main text. Three 3-hour videotapes are available to accompany the book. *Class No:* 7.0(091)

[2859]

JANSON, H.W. History of art: a survey of the major visual arts from the dawn of history to the present day. 5th ed. London, Thames & Hudson, 1994. 960p., illus. £48.00. ISBN: 0500237514.

A comprehensive and reliable basic history, well indexed and with a good bibliography. Over 1200 illustrations, half in colour. *Class No:* 7.0(091)

[2860]

Oxford history of art. Oxford, Oxford University Press, 1997-.

A new series to rival the two collections below; publication began in 1997 and some 45 titles are currently available with many others announced for 1999. Prices are generally £30.00 in hardback and £8.99 in paperback, although some more extensive survey volumes are issued in a higher-price paperback only.

Four sub-series are intended: Western art; Western architecture; world art; themed volumes (*eg: Art and film; Women in art*). All types and media of art are included within each sub-series; layout is clear, and highlights key items in box features. Standards of illustration are excellent (c.150 in each vol., about half in colour). Authors are generally younger academics. Notes on sources and brief bibliographies are included. *Class No:* 7.0(091)

[2861]

Pelican history of art. London, Yale University Press, 1992-. 40v. £16.95 - £50.00.

Formerly published by Penguin Books from 1953. Some older vols are still in print, but new editions are being prepared for many of the titles, and these are gradually appearing in a slightly larger format than the original Penguin versions. The illustrations are greatly enhanced.

An enormously influential, scholarly series. Titles range from prehistoric art to the twentieth century, and from Europe to the Far East. Begun by Nicholaus Pevsner in the 1940s, it has been described as 'the most important series of art books published in the English-speaking world since 1945.'(James Hall; *Guardian,* June 6, 1992, p.27.) Many titles have become established classics. *Class No:* 7.0(091)

[2862]

World of art. London, Thames & Hudson. 140 vols.

Established as a major series of paperbacks - almost all at the bargain price of £6.95 - *World of art* combines specialist contributions in a compact format with very high quality illustrations. New titles are issued regularly and revisions of existing titles appear frequently. The titles are grouped into categories: reference works, ancient and classical, world art, painters and sculptors, Western art, British art and architecture, 20th century, architecture and architects, decorative arts, design and graphic arts, performing arts, and music. Special fields have also been covered (for example posters, photomontage, furniture). Wide coverage, reliable texts, and excellent value. Some of the series have become classics in art publishing, and many of the most respected names in their fields have contributed. At present (1998) 40 new titles are reported to be in preparation.
Class No: 7.0(091)

Bibliographies

[2863]

LINCOLN, B.W. Festschriften in art history, 1960-1975; bibliography and index. London, Garland, 1988. 220p. $40. ISBN: 0824084977.

International coverage, over 5000 entries including all European languages. Indexes by subject, authors, dedications. 'Completes the indexing in art history ... detailed and meticulous' (*Choice* 25(10) June 1988, p.1538). *Class No:* 7.0(091)(01)

Maps & Atlases

[2864]

STEER, J. ***and*** **WHITE, A. Atlas of Western art history:** artists, sites and movements from Ancient Greece to the modern age. New York, Facts on File, 1994. 335p., illus. £39.95. ISBN: 081602457x.

Places developments in Western art in a geographical and historical context. Chronological arrangement under five main divisions - ancient world, medieval world, renaissance, baroque and rococo, modern world. 140 broad themes are identified and explored. Maps on each right-hand page expand on the text; somewhat over-eager in places, but a fascinating new resource. 300 colour illustrations.
Class No: 7.0(091)(084.3)

Biographies

[2865]

BÉNÉZIT, E. Dictionnaire critique et documentaire des peintres, sculpteurs, dessinateurs, et graveurs de tous les pays. Paris, Grund, 1976. 10v. $695.00. ISBN: 0865359212.

First published in three volumes 1911-1923; previous edition 1948-1955 in eight volumes.

Coverage of all countries and all periods. Probably one of the most important biographical sources in the art world, including almost 300,000 biographies of artists. Length of entries varies from a few lines to lengthy signed articles. Entries carry details of prizes, holding museums and collections, sale prices, and bibliographies. 'After Thieme-Becker the most useful universal dictionary of artists' (Arntzen & Rainwater (1980) p.44). *Class No:* 7.0(092)

[2866]

BUSSE, J. Internationales Handbuch aller Maler und Bildhauer des 19. Jahrhunderts. Wiesbaden, Busse Kunst Dokumentation/London, G. Prior, 1977. 1403p.

Data on over 70,000 painters, sculptors and graphic artists of the Western World who were still living after 1806 and/or were born before 1880, - their dates, nationality, major residences, special media and subjects, plus references to the literature (13 sources *e.g.* Thieme-Becker). Especially complete on German-speaking countries. *Class No:* 7.0(092)

[2867]

CAPLAN, H.H. The Classified directory of artists' signatures, symbols and monograms. 2nd ed. London, Grahame, 1982. 873p. $125.00. ISBN: 0860436586.

Several thousand artists are included; the first section presents signatures arranged alphabetically, the second monograms under first letter, the third illegible signatures under the first recognisable letter, and the fourth symbols arranged by general shape. *Class No:* 7.0(092)

[2868]

—CAPLAN, H.H. The Classified directory of artists' signatures, symbols and monograms: American artists with new UK additions. London, Grahame, 1987. 564p. ISBN: 0950889318.

Separate sections cover signatures, symbols, illegible and misleading signatures etc. Cross references, and formatted data pages. Includes 18th, 19th, and 20th century artists.
Class No: 7.0(092)

[2869]

CASTAGNO, J. Artists as illustrators: an international directory with signatures and monograms, 1800-Present. Metuchen, NJ, Scarecrow, 1989. 645p. $127.50. ISBN: 0810821680.

Alphabetical listing of nineteenth and twentieth century European and North American illustrators of books, magazines, covers, and posters. Biographical data, and bibliographical sources. Some one third of the 14,000 entries have a facsimile signature. *Class No:* 7.0(092)

[2870]

CASTAGNO, J. Artists' monograms and indiscernable signatures: an international directory, 1800-1991. Metuchen,NJ, Scarecrow Press, 1991. 538p. ISBN: 0810824159.

5200 signatures representing 3700 artists; monograms are grouped in six categories. Basic data is given and a key to sources for further information. *Class No:* 7.0(092)

[2871]
CASTAGNO, J. Old masters signatures and monograms, 1400-born1800. Metuchen, NJ, Scarecrow Press, 1996. 396p. £104.50. ISBN: 0810830825.

Continues the pattern of the item above.
Class No: 7.0(092)

[2872]
Dizionario enciclopedico bolaffi dei pittori e degli incisori italiana. Torino, Bolaffi, 1972-1976. 11v.

Highly detailed, illustrated, dictionary of Italian printers and engravers from the eleventh to twentieth centuries. Covers 12,000 artists, including many obscure and lesser names. *Class No:* 7.0(092)

[2873]
GOWING, L., *ed.* A Biographical dictionary of artists. Rev.ed. London, Macmillan /New York, Facts on File, 1995. xvi,784p., illus. $50.00/£35.00. ISBN: 0816032521.

90 contributors; 1,340 main entries for printers, sculptors, painters, architects worldwide. Chronology; glossary. Index includes 1,000 additional names with very brief details. 800 illustrations. Brief bibliography after many entries.
Class No: 7.0(092)

[2874]
Internationale Künstlerdatenbank. [World biographical dictionary of artists.] Munich, K.G.Saur, 1996. CD-ROM. DM2400.

Assembled by the team responsible for AKL. (*See* Meissner, below.)

IKD contains biographical information derived from the 148,000 articles in *Thieme-Becker,* together with 19,000 artists mentioned in the text of that work but who have no discrete entries, 18,000 cross-references, and 10,000 other artists mentioned only in family groupings; to these are added the entries from the first 12 vols. of AKL. Searchable by 26 fields, including name, date, place, etc.
Class No: 7.0(092)

[2875]
MAILLARD, R., *ed.* Dictionnaire universal de la peinture, des origines à nos jours. Paris, Le Robert, 1977. 6v., illus. £215.

3,500 entries, A-Z, with numerous cross-references. Includes design, engraving, tapestry, mosaic, glass and other related fields. Strong on movements and contemporary artists, with evaluative comments. Appended vocabulary of technical and aesthetic terms, and a directory of 500 museums and galleries. 2,700 coloured illus. in all.
Class No: 7.0(092)

[2876]
MEISSNER, G., *ed.* Allgemeines Künstlerlexicon. Die bildenden Künstler aller Zeiten und Volker. Munich, K.G.Saur, 1983-. c750p. per vol. DM398 per vol. ISBN: 359822740x.

In progress; 78 vols. are envisaged; 16 vols. and 2 index vols. so far issued.

Includes traditional fine arts, applied & decorative arts. Data comprises biographical outline & career summary, works & locations, writings, exhibitions, bibliography, references to unpublished sources. AKL should eventually outstrip *Thieme-Becker* for currency and comprehensiveness, and will carry details of over 500,000 names. CD-ROM version incorporated in *Internationale Künstlerdatenbank* above. *Class No:* 7.0(092)

[2877]
NAYLOR, C., *ed.* Contemporary artists. New ed. London, St. James Press, 1996. 1340p. £120.00. ISBN: 1558621830.

900 entries, both established figures and newcomers who have attracted critical acclaim. No figure deceased prior to 1965 is included. US bias, as the new nationality index reveals. Critical essay with personal data, and details of awards, exhibitions, etc. 600 photographs. Retention of earlier editions recommended. *Class No:* 7.0(092)

[2878]
NEW YORK PUBLIC LIBRARY. Artists file. Cambridge, Chadwyck-Healey, 1987-. 11000 microfiche. $20,000.

Extensive biographical source covering over 90,000 artists, sculptors, architects, jewellers, designers etc; reproduces files held by NYPL containing exhibition information, clippings, obituaries, reviews, photographic reproductions. Earliest item 1895, but most dated 1930-1979. Methodically assessed in *Art Documentation* 8(3) Fall 1989, p.149-50. *Class No:* 7.0(092)

[2879]
THIEME, U. *and* BECKER, F. Allgemeines Lexikon der bildenden Künstler von der Antike bis zur Gegenwart. Leipzig, Seemann, 1907-50. 37v.

Reprinted Seemann, 1965. Also Somerset House (Teaneck, NJ). CD-ROM version incorporated in *Internationale Kunstlerdatenbank* above.

About 400 contributors; *c.*40-50,000 entries for painters and engravers, plus some architects and sculptors. V.37 covers anonymous artists and monogrammists. Longer articles are signed and well documented (*e.g.* 'Sir Joshua Reynolds': 3 columns, - 1 col. of biographical data, listing and locating paintings; 2 cols. of bibliography: works by Reynolds, then material on him, - monographs, catalogues, periodical articles, etc.). That on Poussin, by Walter Friedlander, v.27, p.321-7, has sections on biography, artistic development, paintings (6½ cols.) and bibliography (1. col).

The most extensive dictionary of its kind (each v. has *c.*600p., double column). Includes living artists, but in this respect is supplemented by: Vollmer, H. *Allgemeines Lexikon des bildenden Künstler des XX. Jahrhunderts.* Leipzig, Seemann, 1953-62. 6v. This is arranged on the same detailed pattern as Thieme and Becker.
Class No: 7.0(092)

[2880]
Union list of artist names. New York, G.K.Hall, 1994. 2912p.(4v.)/6 diskettes. $495.00. ISBN: 0816107254.

Available in a printed form, and on diskette.

ULAN is a comprehensive database of artists' and architects' names, including bibliographical data; developed by the Getty Art History Information Programme (AHIP), it includes over 200,000 names representing over 100,000 people. There are 190,000 citations to sources, and a bibliography of major source materials. Variations in spelling are recorded, and life dates. All periods, but mainly post-mediaeval; international, but with a Western emphasis. Created by the merged authority files of 7 AHIP projects and two other Getty programmes. *Class No:* 7.0(092)

[2881]

Who's who in art: biographies of leading men and women in the world of art today - artists, designers, craftsmen, critics, writers, teachers, curators. 26th ed. London, Art Trade Press, 1994. xxiv, 622p. £30. ISBN: 0900083131.

Covers some 3,000 names, mainly British but with a good international spread. Details of schools and academies; entries include awards, publications, agent addresses. Appendix of signatures and monograms. *Class No:* 7.0(092)

Women

[2882]

DUNFORD, P. A Biographical dictionary of women artists in Europe and America since 1850. New York, Harvester Wheatsheaf, 1990. 340p. illus. £60. ISBN: 0710811446.

Entries arranged alphabetically, and give dates, nature of work, professional biography, location of major items, and bibliographies. *Class No:* 7.0(092)-0055.2

[2883]

GAZE, D., *ed*. Dictionary of women artists. London, Fitzroy Dearborn, 1997. xlviii,1400p.,(2v.) illus. £175.00. ISBN: 1884964214.

The work of 23 advisers and 330 collaborators; includes painters, sculptors, ceramicists, textile artists, photographers etc. Anglo-American bias, but coverage is reckoned very good; preponderance of emphasis towards the modern era. Introductory surveys cover topics such as convents, guilds, court artists, academies, copyists, training and professionalism, feminism. Entries give brief biography, principal exhibitions, writings, bibliography, then lengthy commentary. Generally well-reviewed, but some omissions are noted. Good reproduction of the artist's work appears in each entry. General bibliography p.xxxi-xlviii.
Class No: 7.0(092)-0055.2

[2884]

PETTEYS, C., *ed*. Dictionary of women artists: an international dictionary of women artists born before 1900. Boston, G.K. Hall, 1985. 851p. £45. ISBN: 0816184569.

Over 21,000 entries for painters, sculptors, print-makers, illustrators. Good general bibliography of 1500 major items. 'Primary reference tool for years to come' (*Art Documentation* 4(3) Fall 1985 p.127). *Class No:* 7.0(092)-0055.2

Persia, Ancient

[2885]

POPE, A.U. *and* **ACKERMAN, P., *eds*. A Survey of Persian art** from prehistoric times to the present. Ashiya, Japan, SOPA, 1981. 3,816p. (16v. in 18); 3737 plates. £875. ISBN: 4893600117.

First published Oxford, OUP, 1938-58 in 7 vols. Reissued 1964 in 13 vols. 1981 version adds three further volumes.

Volumes cover Pre-Islamic art (v.1,2,7); architecture (vols. 3,8); pottery and faience (vols. 4,9); arts of the book (vol. 5a,10); textiles (vol.5b,11); carpets (vol.6a,12); metalwork and minor arts (vol.6b,13); new studies (v.14); bibliography and indexes, updates etc. (v.15); further bibliography etc. (v.16). Although dated in places these volumes are 'without doubt the single most essential source on the subject of Persian art' (*Hali* 28,Oct-Dec 1985, p.73/5). *Class No:* 7.0(355)

Great Britain

Encyclopaedias

[2886]

BINDMAN, D., *ed*. Thames and Hudson encyclopaedia of British art. London, Thames & Hudson, 1985. 320p. illus. £10.50. ISBN: 0500234205.

Paperback edition 1988 (050020229x, £6.95.)

Covers painting, sculpture, printmaking from Anglo-Saxon periods to the present day. Alphabetical arrangement for artists, styles, schools and groups, types of production, individual works and groups of works, techniques, galleries, societies, art schools, periodicals, patronage. Subject index; bibliography. World gazetteer of museums and galleries containing British art. 316 monochrome illustrations.
Class No: 7.0(410)(031)

Yearbooks & Directories

[2887]

Art world directory: 1998/99 incorporating *Arts Review* yearbook. 25th.ed. London, Arts Review in association with Nautilus, 1998. 356p., illus. £12.95. ISBN: 090483123x.

Entries cover galleries (public and commercial), museums, sculpture parks, auction houses, publishers, art bookshops, courses, schools and colleges, art societies and organisations, consultants, materials; diary of exhibitions and competitions; space for hire, index by artist and general index. *Class No:* 7.0(410)(058)

[2888]

British art and antiques yearbook. London, Antique Collector Magazine, 1978-. £7.50. ISSN: 01408763.

Directory and guide to over 5,000 antique and fine art dealers, auctioneers, and restorers. Indexes by place, speciality, business name. *Class No:* 7.0(410)(058)

[2889]

The Lund Humphries calendar of art exhibitions in UK public galleries and museums, 1998-9. London, Lund Humphries, 1998. 96p., maps. £6.99. ISBN: 0853317097.

Information on about 1000 exhibitions over 18 months; arranged alphabetically by city, then venue. Symbols indicate if a catalogue is available; venues of touring exhibitions are cross-referenced. 10 city-centre maps.
Class No: 7.0(410)(058)

[2890]

ROSS, J., *ed*. Directory of exhibition spaces. 4th.ed. Sunderland, AN Publications, 1995. 287p. ISBN: 0907730272.

Lists public and private spaces, specialist galleries, museums, art centres, venues in libraries, educational establishments, hospitals, heritage and community centres, pubs, cafes, theatres, etc. A total of 1665 spaces are listed in all parts of the UK, with full address, contact data, space details, services, costs. All fields are included from fine arts and crafts to live art. *Class No:* 7.0(410)(058)

[2891]

WADDELL, H. London art and artists guide. 7th ed. London, London Art & Artists Guide, 1997. 233p., illus., maps. £9.95. ISBN: 0952000415.

1st.ed. published 1979.

Information on galleries and museums in London (over 600 entries), bookshops, workshops, art schools, studios, commerical galleries, art competitions, parks, markets. Overview sections such as *Hidden backstreets; Riverside London*. *Class No:* 7.0(410)(058)

Gazetteers

[2892]
ARNOLD, A., *comp*. The Art atlas of Britain and Ireland. London, Viking Penguin in association with the National Trust, 1991. 489p., illus., maps. £25.00. ISBN: 0670819255.

Regional arrangement with discursive treatment and highlighting of key works with illustrations; this is followed by a gazetteer (pp. 325-447) arranged A/Z by county with brief entries for collections giving address and telephone numbers, opening hours, location, summary of holdings. Good index of artists, places, picture titles.
Class No: 7.0(410)(083.86)

Histories

[2893]
The Cambridge guide to the arts in Britain. Ford, B., *ed*. Cambridge, CUP, 1988-. 9v., illus. £37.50. per vol.

Volume 1: Prehistoric, Roman & early Mediaeval (1988; 318p.; 0521309719) Volume 2: Middle Ages (1988; 312p.; 0521309751) Volume 3: Renaissance & Reformation (1989; 356p.; 052130976x) Volume 4: Seventeenth century (1990; 360p.; 0521309778) Volume 5: Augustan Age (1990) Volume 6: Romantics to early Victorians (1990; 352p.; 0521309794) Volume 7: Later Victorian age (1990; 363p.; 0521309808) Volume 8: Edwardian Age and the Inter-war years (1989; 367p.; 0521309816) Volume 9: Since the second world war (1988; 380p.; 0521327652). Chronological, cross-disciplinary account; separate chapters devoted to major branches of the arts: literature, music, drama, visual arts, crafts, architecture. Introductory chapter; detailed appendices with bibliographies, further reading, and brief biographies. *Times Literary Supplement* review (Feb.3 1989. p.116) calls it an 'ambitious venture', but comments on uneven treatment. *Class No:* 7.0(410)(091)

[2894]
GRAHAM-DIXON, A. A History of British art. London, BBC Publications, 1996. 256p., illus. £25.00. ISBN: 0563370440.

Written in parallel with a BBC television series; offers an idiosyncratic but exciting approach to British art, with an emphasis on the social and political backgrounds. Points out relationships between various phases of art, and between traditions of other countries. *Class No:* 7.0(410)(091)

Scotland

[2895]
McEWAN, P.J.M. Dictionary of Scottish art and architecture. Woodbridge, Suffolk, Antique Collectors' Club, 1995. 626p., illus. £50.00. ISBN: 1851491341.

Includes artists Scottish by birth, ancestry or marriage, or associated with Scottish art, who have exhibited at least one work in a major exhibition. 11,000 entries cover painters, engravers, etchers, architects, carvers, textile artists, illustrators, jewellers, masons, photographers etc. Entries range from a single line to several paragraphs; locations of works and bibliographies are provided where possible.
Class No: 7.0(411)

Ireland

[2896]
BREFFNY, B., *ed*. Ireland: a cultural encyclopedia. London, Thames & Hudson, 1983. 256p., illus. £14.95. ISBN: 0500013047.

Broad coverage includes costume, furniture, crafts, ceramics, architecture, painting, sculpture etc. Subject and biographical entries, by 45 specialist contributors. Lists museums, galleries, houses, gardens. *Class No:* 7.0(415)

Biographies

[2897]
STRICKLAND, W.S. A Dictionary of Irish artists. Rev. ed. Dublin, Irish Univ. Press, 1969. 598,728p., (2v.). ISBN: 0716506025.

Originally published Dublin: Maunsel, 1913.

Includes 'not only every artist of any note who has worked in Ireland but those of Irish birth ... who have followed this profession in England and elsewhere' (*Preface*). Excludes architects. Entries carry detailed lists of works. V.2 has detailed index (p.665-728) of names and subjects of pictures, sculpture, etc. names of owners and places where pictures are; also an appendix; 'Art institutions in Ireland'. 150 portraits. *Class No:* 7.0(415)(092)

Women

[2898]
RYAN-SMOLIN, W., *and others*. Irish women artists: from the eighteenth century to the present day. Dublin, National Gallery of Ireland/Douglas Hyde Gallery, 1987. xxxxviii,208p. illus. £18. ISBN: 0903162407.

Exhibition catalogue.

Covers chiefly painting and sculpture with some stained glass and prints. 13 essays on various aspects; catalogue p.81-146. Dictionary of Irish women artists (including those not represented in the exhibition) p.147-195. Bibliography; various indexes. Intended to be comprehensive pre-1943.
Class No: 7.0(415)(092)-0055.2

England

Histories

[2899]
DODWELL, C.R. Anglo-Saxon art: a new perspective. Manchester, University Press, 1982. x,353p., illus.

8 chapters: 1. Art survivals and written sources - 2. Anglo-Saxon art - 3. Artists and craftsmen in Anglo-Saxon England - 4. Painting and carving - 5. Textiles - 6. Costume and vestments - 7. Jewellery, silver and gold - 8. Anglo-Saxon art and the Norman Conquest. Abbreviations for sources most frequently cited, p.235-331. Analytical index. p.333-53. 63 plates (8 in colour). Emphasises the Anglo-Saxons' leading arts; goldwork and embroidery. 'This is an important book for art historians, but is so lucidly written that it will also provide stimulating access to the subject for the student and general historian' (*British book news*, March 1983, p.179). *Class No:* 7.0(420)(091)

[2900]
The Oxford history of English art. Boase, T.S.R., *ed.* Oxford, Clarendon Press, 1949-. 11v., illus.

1: *English art to A.D. 871.*
2: *English art, 871-1100*, by V. Talbot-Rice. 1952.
3: *English art, 1100-1216*, by T.S.R. Boase. 1951.
4: *English art, 1216-1307*, by P. Brieger. 1957.
5: *English art, 1307-1461*, by Joan Evans. 1949.
6: *English art, 1461-1553.*
7: *English art, 1553-1625*, by E.B. Mercer. 1962.
8: *English art, 1625-1714*, by M. Whinney and O. Millar. 1957.
9: *English art, 1714-1800*, by J.T.A. Burke.
10: *English art, 1800-1870*, by T.S.R. Boase.
11: *English art, 1870-1940*, by D. Farr. 1978.

Aims 'to set out chronologically the development of the visual arts as part of the general history of England' (*Preface*), and treatment of subjects resembles that given in the *Oxford history of England*. V.11 (xxxi, [1], 405, 120p.) covers painting, sculpture, architecture and the decorative arts in 6 parts (12 chapters). Footnotes, Bibliography, grouped, p.367-78. 120 pages of plates. Now seems very dated in some aspects, but a respected source.
Class No: 7.0(420)(091)

Biographies

[2901]
HALL, M., *ed*. Artists of Cumbria: an illustrated dictionary of Cumberland, Westmorland. South Lancashire and North West Yorkshire painters, sculptors, draughtsmen and engravers born 1615-1900. Newcastle-upon-Tyne, M. Hall, 1979. 112p.,illus. £9.50. ISBN: 0903858010.
Includes 110 illustrations. *Class No:* 7.0(420)(092)

[2902]
HALL, M., *ed*. Artists of Northumbria: an illustrated dictionary of Northumberland, Durham, and North Yorkshire painters, sculptors, draughtsmen and engravers born between 1625 and 1900. 2nd ed. Newcastle-upon-Tyne, M. Hall, 1982. 208p.,illus. £17.50. ISBN: 0903858029.
First published 1973.
Second edition contains 199 illustrations.
Class No: 7.0(420)(092)

[2903]
TURNBULL, H. Artists of Yorkshire: a short dictionary (artists born before 1921). Snape, Dedale, Thornton Gallery, 1976. xiv,68p.,illus. £3.75. ISBN: 0950534102.
Notes on 'the recorded painters, engravers and sculptors who have lived or worked in Yorkshire' (*e.g.* Henry Moore: 1 column; Sir William Rotherstein: ½ col.). Preliminaries list principal societies, academies and exhibition galleries; Principal public art galleries in Yorkshire; abbreviations. Appended: 'Principal sources and bibliography', p.67-68.
Class No: 7.0(420)(092)

Wales

Histories

[2904]
ROWAN, E. Art in Wales 1850-1980: an illustrated history. Cardiff, University of Wales Press, 1985. 188p.,illus. £35. ISBN: 0708308546.
Useful summary; 44 of the 178 illustrations are in colour.
Class No: 7.0(429)(091)

[2905]
ROWAN, E. Art in Wales 2000 BC-AD 1850: an illustrated history. Cardiff, Welsh Arts Council/University of Wales Press, 1978. 127p.,illus. £6.95. ISBN: 0708306748.
Includes bibliographies for each chapter. 136 illustrations.
Class No: 7.0(429)(091)

Biographies

[2906]
REES, T.M. Welsh painters, engravers, sculptors (1527-1911). Caernarvon, Welsh Publishing Co., 1912. 188p.,illus.
150 biographies including lists of works, often with a description and location. 30 portraits.
Class No: 7.0(429)(092)

France

[2907]
Art and architecture in France: the French photographic archives. London, Mindata, 1983,. 1021 microfiche. £2,025.
Available separately by sections.
First series deals with *Fine and decorative arts in France*, presenting 70,000 images; nine sections cover paintings in the Louvre, paintings in provincial museums, drawings in the Louvre, drawings in provincial museums, sculpture, decorative art, antiquities, manuscripts, indexes. Second series *Architecture and early photography in France* offers 28,000 images in two sections: architecture and monuments; Paris views and early photographs. *Class No:* 7.0(44)

Italy

[2908]
KUNSTHISTORISCHES INSTITUT. Florence. **Katalog des Kunsthistorisches Instituts in Florenz.** Boston, G.K. Hall, 1964. 5159p. (9v.).
Supplements 1-3 (1968-78) cover 4,346p. (6v.).
94,900 photolithographically reproduced catalogue cards, in all. The collection (over 60,000v.) specialises in the history of Italian art from early Christian times to the present. An author catalogue; museum catalogues appear under name of town. *Class No:* 7.0(450)

Spain

Biographies

[2909]
RAFOLS, J.F. Dicionario biografico de artistas de Cataluna desde la epoca romona hastra nuestras dias. Barcelona, Milla, 1951-54. 3v. illus.
About 20,000 short biographical notes on Catalan artists, including musical-instrument makers and naval engineers, A-Z. V.3 includes sections on the various arts practised in Catalonia and a list of artists, by centuries. Each volume has a name index. No bibliographies. *Class No:* 7.0(460)(092)

Portugal

Biographies

[2910]
PAMPLONA, F. Dicionário de pintores e escultores portugueses on que trabalharam em Portugal. Santo Silva, R., *ed.* [Lisbon] 1954-59. 4v., illus.
About 2,000 entries for Portuguese painters and sculptors,

.... (contd.)
including foreign-born artists who worked in Portugal. Many articles carry bibliographies; facsimile signatures in some cases. *Class No:* 7.0(469)(092)

USSR

[2911]
AKADEMIYA NAUK SSSR. Istoriya russkogo iskusstvo. Grabaria, I.E., *ed.* Moscow, Akademiya Nauk, 1953-68. 13v. in 16., illus.

'A history of Russian art'. V.1-5 cover the period up to *c.*1750; V.11-12 deal with 1917-41; v.13 is a supplement, the work of 10 contributors (with sections on graphic and decorative arts). Well documented: many footnote references; appended bibliography per volume (*e.g.* v.5; p.527-37). Illus. (v.13: over 200 black-and-white and coloured illus.) are mediocre. 'These volumes vary in quality a great deal. Those concerned with the period 1907-17 (v.10, bk. 2) & 1917-21 (v.11) are not detailed and at times are factually inaccurate' (Auty, R., and Obolensky, D., eds. *Companion to Russian studies,* v.3, p.173). *Class No:* 7.0(47)

[2912]
AUTY, R. *and* **OBOLENSKY, D.,** *eds.* **Companion to Russian studies, vol 3:** an introduction to Russian art and architecture. Cambridge, CUP, 1980. xiii,194p., illus. £15. ISBN: 0521838411.

4 parts: 1. Art and architecture of Old Russia, 988-1700, and 2. Art and architecture in the Petersburg age, 1700-1860 (both by R. Miller-Gulland); 3. Art and architecture in the age of revolution, 1860-1917, and Art and architecture in Soviet Russia, 1917-1972 (both by John Bowlt). 'Guide to further reading' (with brief critical comments), grouped, p.173-81. Analytical index, p.183-94. A scholarly introduction. *Class No:* 7.0(47)

[2913]
WARD, C.A. Moscow and Leningrad: a topographical guide to Russian cultural history. Volume 2: writers, painters, musicians and their gathering places. Munich, K.G. Saur, 1990. 350p. £39. ISBN: 3598108346.

Guide to the houses, studios, cafés etc. of Russian musical, literary, artistic and cultural life, 1700-1925. Index of all names, listing of museums. Pre- and post-revolutionary street names. *Class No:* 7.0(47)

Biographies

[2914]
MILNER, J. Dictionary of Russian and Soviet artists, 1420-1970. Woodbridge, Suffolk, Antique Collectors' Club, 1993. 483p. £70.00. ISBN: 1851491821.

2200 entries; good range of data. Generous bibliographies; transliteration guide. Nearly 400 excellent illustrations, each having complete description, location and commentary. *Class No:* 7.0(47)(092)

Norway

Biographies

[2915]
Norsk kunstnerleksikon: bildende kunstnere - arkitekter - kunsthåndverkere. Oslo, Universitetsforlagt, 1981-85. 3v. £135. ISBN: 8200056899.

Alphabetical dictionary of Norwegian artists, written in Norwegian, under the direction of the Norwegian National

.... (contd.)
Gallery. Covers the Reformation to the present day, but very selective post-1940. Mainly painters, sculptors and printmakers, but some textile artists, architects, craftsmen and designers. Detailed biography & thorough bibliographies. Unillustrated. 'A tremendous effort' (*Art Libraries Journal* 9(2) 1984. p.83). *Class No:* 7.0(481)(092)

Sweden

Biographies

[2916]
Svenskt konstnärslexikon... Malmö, Allhens Verlag, 1952-67. 5v.,illus.

'Dictionary of Swedish artists'.

Entries, mostly signed and of good length, on *c.*12,500 artists. Some articles carry bibliographies, although references are less precise than those in Weilbach's dictionary of Danish artists (*q.v.*). Lavishly illustrated with small portraits, etc. (*c.*2 per page) and many good full-page half-tone reproductions of works, several in colour. Includes living artists. *Class No:* 7.0(485)(092)

Denmark

[2917]
WEILBACH, P. Kunstnerlexikon. Copenhagen, Aschenhoug Dansk Forlag, 1947-52. 3v.,illus.

First published 1877-78 as *Dansk Kunstnerlexikon.*

Dictionary of Danish artists and also foreign artists who worked in Denmark and influenced Danish art: Signed articles of good length, with excellent detailed references in bibliographies appended. V.1 (A-H) includes list of medals and awards, scholarships and bursaries, plus chronological lists of Danish art exhibitions, at home and abroad. Supplement in v.3 contains additions and corrections, with a topographical index to architectural works mentioned in the text. The standard work of its kind. *Class No:* 7.0(489)

Balkan States

[2918]
CURČIČ, S. Art and architecture in the Balkans: an annotated bibliography. Boston, G.K. Hall, 1984. xxv,427p. £65. ISBN: 0816183260.

Covers mediaeval art and architecture in four main sections: Balkans, Albania, Bulgaria, Yugoslavia, each subdivided by architecture, painting, sculpture, minor arts, iconography etc. Lists of principal bibliographical sources and periodicals. Author and general index. *Class No:* 7.0(497)

Asia

[2919]
YAMAMOTO, C. Introduction to Buddhist art. New Delhi, Adity Prakashan, 1990. xxiv,360p., illus. Rs.750. ISBN: 8185179441.

Survey of the history of Buddhist art from Indian origins to its final developments in Japan. It gives the main outlines of its evolution in India, Srilanka, Indonesia, Kambuja, Vietnam, Thailand, Burma, Afghanistan, Chinese Turkistan, China, Korea and Japan. *Class No:* 7.0(5)

China

[2920]

Chinese art. 2nd English ed. London, Phaidon, 1980. 263,277,243p. (3v.), illus. ISBN: 0714821349, v.1; 0714821357, v.2; 0714821365, v.3.

Translated from the French *Arts de la Chine* (Switzerland, Office du Livre, 1961). First English ed. Oldbourne Press 1963-66.

Volume 1:- Bronzes, jade, sculpture, ceramics. Chronology of Chinese dynasties, bibliography. Written by D. Lion-Goldschmitt & J-C. Moreau-Gobard; tran. D. Imber. Volume 2:- Gold, silver, later bronzes, enamel, laqueur, wood. Authors: R. S. Jenyns & W. Watson. Volume 3:- Textiles, glass, carvings, bottles, etc. Same author as vol.2. The three volumes are extensively illustrated, and chart the major stages of Chinese art over 4,000 years. *Class No:* 7.0(510)

[2921]

MUNSTERBERG, H. Dictionary of Chinese and Japanese art. New York, Hacker, 1981. 354p. £35. ISBN: 0878172483.

2,500 brief entries cover artists, periods, schools, motifs, locations and buildings, techniques, concepts. Brief definitions and explanations. Bibliography p.353-4.
Class No: 7.0(510)

[2922]

SEYMOUR, N.N. An Index-Dictionary of Chinese artists, collectors, and connoisseurs with character identification by modified stroke count. Metuchen, NJ, Scarecrow, 1988. 1004p. $82.50. ISBN: 0810820919.

Contains brief information on over 5,000 Chinese names from T'ang Dynasty to present day, with references to other sources. *Class No:* 7.0(510)

Bibliographies

[2923]

VANDERSTAPPEN, H.A., *ed*. The T.L. Yüan bibliography of Western writings on Chinese art, 1920-1965. London, Mansell, 1975. xlvii,606p.

A classified bibliography of 8,954 numbered entries on Chinese art and archaeology. 2 sections: the first lists books and exhibition catalogues; the second, periodical articles and special studies. Both sections have divisions: 1. General - 2. Archaeology - 3. Architecture - 4. Calligraphy - 5. Paintings - 6. Graphics - 7. Sculpture - 8. Bronze - 9. Ceramics - 10. Decorative arts and handicrafts. List of sources, p.xi-xxxv. Author index; index to collectors and collections. No subject index. *Class No:* 7.0(510)(01)

Japan

[2924]

MASON, P. History of Japanese art. New York, Abrams, 1993. 431p. $60.00. ISBN: 0810910853.

Major overview of all the visual arts; thorough and extensive including coverage of the first half of the twentieth century. Good quality illustrations. Scholarly, but not pedantic. (*Choice,* 30(10) June 1993. p1617.)
Class No: 7.0(52)

Biographies

[2925]

ROBERTS, L.P. A Dictionary of Japanese artists: painting, sculpture, ceramics, prints, lacquer. New York, Weatherhill, 1977. 312p. £22.50. ISBN: 0834801132.

Reissued Apollo Books, NY, 1989 (0317549413).

Information on 3000 figures from earliest times to 1972; alphabetical arrangement with personal and career details, character index by radical number and stroke order.
Class No: 7.0(52)(092)

[2926]

SELF, J. *and* HIROSE, N. Japanese art signatures: a handbook and practical guide. London, Bamboo Publishing, 1987. 399p. illus., facsims, tables. £19.50. ISBN: 1870076044.

Illustrates 1600 characters, their groupings and classifications, over 11,000 names of artists and craftsmen, and debased and variant characters. Guides to reading names of provinces and towns, dates, proper names. 300 facsimile woodblock print signatures. Radical & stroke-count indexes. Bibliography p.367-375. *Class No:* 7.0(52)(092)

[2927]

TAZAWA, Y., *ed*. Biographical dictionary of Japanese art. Tokyo, New York, Kodansha International, 1981. 825p. illus. £35.75. ISBN: 0870114883.

Covers 863 artists in 14 categories of fine arts, architecture and crafts, 250AD to the present. Arrangement by medium with A/Z entries for significant figures. Names given in Roman and Japanese characters; dates, narrative biographical and artistic data; significant works and locations. Appendices include lineage of 67 schools of artists; 64-page bibliography; glossary. Up to four illustrations per page. *Class No:* 7.0(52)(092)

Women

[2928]

FISTER, P. *and* YAMAMOTO, F.Y. Japanese women artists 1600-1900. Lawrence, Kansas, Spencer Museum of Art, 1988. 197p. illus. ISBN: 0913689254.

Exhibition catalogue; reissued London: Harper and Row, 1989 (£11.50. 0064301818).

Covers 27 painters, print-makers, & potters. Chronological arrangement; substantial biographies & detailed description of exhibited works. Bibliography; index.
Class No: 7.0(52)(092)-0055.2

India

[2929]

BHATTACHARYYA, T. The Canons of Indian art: a study of Vãstuvidyã. 2nd ed. Calcutta, Firma K.L. Mukhopadhyay, 1967. xvi, 506p., illus.

First published 1963.

Includes ancient Indian texts on the theory and technique of sculpture, painting, iconography and some minor arts and crafts. Contains 30 chapters, 8 appendices, 12 tables, bibliography and index. *Class No:* 7.0(540)

[2930]

HAVELL, E.B. A Handbook of Indian art. Varanasi, Indic Academy, 1972. xvi,222p., illus.

First published 1920.

15 chapters grouped into three sections, one each on architecture, sculpture and paintings. It attempts to explain the ideals and modes of expression in Indian arts of Ancient

....(*contd.*)
and Moughal periods. Provides a concise survey of the whole subject in a lucid language and tries to tackle some problems of religious themes. *Class No:* 7.0(540)

[2931]
MICHELL, G. Architecture and art of Southern India: Vijayanagara and the successor states. Cambridge/New York, Cambridge University Press, 1995. xxii,302p., illus., maps. £50.00. ISBN: 0521441102.

Major scholarly survey, forming part of the authoritative *New Cambridge History of India*. *Class No:* 7.0(540)

[2932]
ROWLAND, B. The Art and architecture of India: Buddhist, Hindu, Jain. 3rd ed. Harmondsworth, Penguin Books, 1971. xxi,314p., illus. ISBN: 0140561021.

Six sections further split into 24 chapters describe the subject from ancient Gupta period to the 13th century. The sixth Section describes the Indian art in Sri Lanka and South East Asia up to 18th century. Notes, glossary and a broadly classified bibliography are given at the end.
Class No: 7.0(540)

[2933]
SIVARAMAMURTY, C. The Art of India. New York, Abrams, 1977. 603p., illus. ISBN: 0810906309.

Divided into 14 chapters, this volume contains a critical evaluation and description of Indian art history from the ancient to the Moughal periods. Each chapter is a self-contained essay on a particular aspect. Integrates art with culture, mythology and religion. Chronology, glossary and 'Symbolism in art' are useful appendices. Profusely illustrated with 1175 illustrations of which 1000 are photographic plates. *Class No:* 7.0(540)

Bibliographies

[2934]
CHANDRA, J., *comp*. Bibliography of Indian art, history and archaeology: Volume 1, Indian art. New Delhi, Delhi Printers Parakashan, 1978. lxiii,316p.

Lists 8,329 entries in six parts. Pt.I Indian art - Pt.II Indian architecture - Pt.III Indian sculpture - Pt.IV Indian painting - Pt. V Handicrafts - Pt. VI Greater India. Each part is further divided minutely into unnumbered chapters, in which references are arranged by author and provide full bibliographic details. Book entries are analytical referring to the specific pages of the relevant text. References in Roman script have been taken from literature in English, Hindi and also from some European languages.
Class No: 7.0(540)(01)

Encyclopaedias & Dictionaries

[2935]
Indian art collection. New Delhi, Cosmo Publications, 1990. 3,500p.(22v.), illus. Rs16,500.

Reprint collection based on a number of older monographs.

Encyclopaedic survey of Indian architecture, sculpture, mural paintings, artifacts etc. *Class No:* 7.0(540)(03)

Dictionaries

[2936]
SHUKLA, L.K. A Study of Hindu art and architecture, with special reference to terminology. Varanasi, Chowkhamba Sanskrit Series, 1972. vii,297p., illus.

Authoritative and encyclopaedic summary and glossary of Hindu art - the *Vastu Sastra*. Covers all aspects of art, architecture and town planning, temple art, sculpture, iconography and Hindu paintings. Investigates the relation of 64 arts with those treated in classical Indian texts. Descriptive terminology covers all the Indian arts and architecture. Closes with a bibliography of 65 references and an index. *Class No:* 7.0(540)(038)

Histories

[2937]
SWARUP, S. 5000 years of arts and crafts in India and Pakistan: a survey of sculpture, architecture, painting, dance, music, handicrafts and ritual decorations from the earliest times to the present day. Bombay, D.B. Taraporevala, 1968. 256p., illus.

Short and simple outline, but comprehensive history of various Indian arts of the last 5,000 years. Chap. 1. Introduction - Chap. 2. Sculpture - Chap. 3. Architecture - Chap. 4. Paintings - Chap. 5. Dance - Chap. 6. Music - Chap. 7. - Handicrafts - Chap. 8. Handicrafts. Each chapter further subdivided into sub-headings. Closes with a glossary (250 terms) and a bibliography of 200 references.
Class No: 7.0(540)(091)

Islamic World

Bibliographies

[2938]
CRESWELL, K.A.C. A Bibliography of the architecture, art, and crafts of Islam to 1960. Cairo, American University at Cairo Press, 1961. 1330p.

Supplement 1960-1972 (366p) issued 1973.

Part 1 (architecture) divided by country (p.1-478). Part 2 (arts & crafts) divided by craft, material and country (p.479-1330). Author index. *Class No:* 7.0(5.297)(01)

Africa

Periodicals & Progress Reports

[2939]
BURT, E.C., *comp*. Serials guide to ethnoart: a guide to serial publications on visual arts of Africa, Oceania and the Americas. Westport, CT, Greenwood Press, 1990. 368p. $65. ISBN: 0313273324.

Extracted from *EthnoArts Index* database (1987-.); formerly *Tribal Arts Review* (1984-6).

Notes editorial policy, specialities, subscription data, book and exhibition reviews, indexing arrangements. Appendices by geographical area. *Class No:* 7.0(6)(05)

Nigeria

[2940]
DARK, P.J.C., *comp*. An Illustrated catalogue of Benin art. Boston, G.K. Hall, 1982. 332p., illus. $75. ISBN: 0816103828.

A subject catalogue listing over 600 works of art created in Benin (Nigeria) from *c.*1000 A.D. to the 20th century, -

.... *(contd.)*
ironwork, ivory carvings and especially bronze sculptures. Separate lists of collections and published photographs of particular objects. 85 illus. *Class No:* 7.0(669)

[2941]
Nigerian artists: a who's who and bibliography. London, Zell/Bowker Saur, 1990. 700p. £60. ISBN: 0905450826.

Biographical dictionary of over 400 artists, followed by a comprehensive bibliography on modern Nigerian art. *Class No:* 7.0(669)

Africa—East & Equatorial

[2942]
BIEBUYCK, D.P. The Arts of Central Africa: an annotated bibliography. Boston, G.K. Hall, 1987. 300p. $49. ISBN: 0816186014.

1,920 citations covering general studies on African art, ethnographies, travelogues, bibliographies. Geographic regions subdivided by ethnic group. Mainly English-language sources, but some French, German etc. Detailed index. 'Excellent index ... misleading title - the book concentrates on the arts of Zaire'. (*Choice* 24,11/12, July/Aug.1987. p.1672). *Class No:* 7.0(67)

South Africa

Biographies

[2943]
BERMAN, E. Art and artists of South Africa: an illustrated biographical dictionary and historical survey of painters, sculptors and graphic artists since 1875. Rev. ed. Cape Town/Rotterdam, A.A. Balkema, 1983. 564p. 48 plates. ISBN: 0869611445.

Over 400 entries with lists of exhibitions, works in public collections, bibliographic references. Historical survey, list of participants in major exhibitions 1902-1979. Bibliography. *Class No:* 7.0(680)(092)

[2944]
OGILVIE, G., ***comp*****. The Dictionary of South African painters and sculptors.** Johannesburg, Everard Read, 1988. 799p. ISBN: 0620126639.

Over 1800 exponents of Western art listed A/Z; criteria for inclusion are to have lived or worked in South Africa/Namibia. Features Dutch, English and French settlers, artists trained overseas, current generation. Standard data includes personal profile, exhibitions, galleries where represented, public commissions, literature references. 80 full-page colour illustrations. Bibliography p773-81; directory of useful addresses p783-93. *Class No:* 7.0(680)(092)

Canada

[2945]
Art and architecture in Canada: a bibliography/Bibliographie sur l'art et l'architecture au Canada. Singer, L. *and* Williamson, M., *eds*. Montreal, Concordia University, 1985-.

Aims to list over 9,000 books, articles, exhibition catalogues, and theses, published 1820-1981, covering Canadian, Indian, and Inuit art, folk arts, decorative arts, photography, museums, government & the arts, art education. Classified arrangement. *Class No:* 7.0(71)

Biographies

[2946]
Artists in Canada: a union list of files. Ottawa, National Gallery Association, 1982. vi,358p. ISBN: 0888844840.

Lists and describes files held in 20 Canadian libraries on Canadian artists, artists of other nationalities active in Canada, Canadian-born artists active elsewhere (thus covering British military topographical artists of the colonial period), nineteenth century illustrators and engravers, and American artists of all periods. 21,000 entries, listing dates, media, locations. 'Exhaustive coverage' (*Art Documentation* 2,2. May 1983. p.80). *Class No:* 7.0(71)(092)

Latin America

[2947]
BAILEY, J.W., ***ed*****. Handbook of Latin American art ...:** a bibliographical compilation. Oxford, ABC-Clio, 1984-. 579,614,540p. (3v.). £60. per volume. ISBN: 0874363845, 1(i); 0874363896, 1(ii); 0874363853, 2.

Volume 1 (parts 1 & 2) cover art of the nineteenth and twentieth century in North America (part 1) and South America (part 2); volume 2 covers art of the colonial period. A further part (volume 3) is planned to cover art of the ancient period. Some 16,000 items are mentioned: books, articles, anthologies, catalogues, reports, extracted from *Handbook of Latin American Studies* 1936-1984, Library of Congress shelflist, etc. Divided by region, country, topic. Indexes. *Class No:* 7.0(729.99)

[2948]
FINDLAY, J.A. Modern Latin American art: a bibliography. London, Greenwood Press, 1983. 301p. £40.50. ISBN: 0313237573.

Covers books, exhibition catalogues, and journal titles (not articles) arranged by subject with geographical divisions. Omits work on individual artists. Includes Central America & the Caribbean. Reflects the holdings of the Museum of Modern Art Library, New York. *Class No:* 7.0(729.99)

USA

[2949]
KARPEL, B., ***ed*****. Arts in America.** Washington, DC, Smithsonian Institution Press, 1979. 4v.

25,000 entries in 21 subject areas covering architecture, decorative arts, design, sculpture, painting, graphic arts, photographs, film, theatre, dance, music, art of Native Americans, art of the West, serials, periodicals, dissertations, theses, visual resources. Includes books, exhibition catalogues, bibliographies. Vol.4 contains indexes by authors, artists, subjects, selected titles. *Class No:* 7.0(73)

Bibliographies

[2950]
ARCHIVES OF AMERICAN ART. Card catalog of the manuscript collections of the Archives of American Art. Wilmington, Del, Scholarly Resources; 1981-1985. 5,500p. (10v. and supplement). $750.00. ISBN: 0842022414.

Main volumes published 1981, with a supplement to 1984(1985). Covers six million items in 5,000 collections now held at the Smithsonian Institution. Biographical approach by artist name; all items are available on microfilm for loan. *Class No:* 7.0(73)(01)

Yearbooks & Directories

[2951]

American art directory 1997/98. 56th.ed. New Providence, NJ, R.R.Bowker, 1997. 906p. ISBN: 0835238199. ISSN: 00656968.

Lists over 2000 art institutions in the United States and Canada, including museums, art galleries, libraries, art schools, state art councils, exhibition booking agencies, scholarships etc. Indexes by subject, people, organisations. Contact data and basic information; no email addresses or Websites given. *Class No:* 7.0(73)(058)

Biographies

[2952]

CASTAGNO, J. American artists: signatures and monograms, 1800-1989. Metuchen, N.J., Scarecrow Press, 1990. 826p., illus. $145. ISBN: 0810822490.

Alphabetical arrangement of facsimile signatures and monograms of over 5,000 US, Canadian and Latin American artists. Data includes nationality, dates, references to standard source and catalogues. Supplementary sections cover alternative names, indecipherable marks, initials. A later volume covering Latin America alone is now available; *see entry at* 7.0(8)(092). *Class No:* 7.0(73)(092)

[2953]

CUMMINGS, P., *comp.* **Dictionary of contemporary American artists.** 6th ed. New York, St. Martins Press, 1994. 786p. $85.00. ISBN: 0312084404.

Includes 900 painters, sculptors, printmakers; illustrated, and with good bibliographies. Also details of schools, awards, teachers, dealers, exhibitions. 150 monochrome illus. This ed. appears to be a more significant revision than previous re-issues. General bibliography at end covers 55p. *Class No:* 7.0(73)(092)

[2954]

FALK, P.H. Dictionary of signatures and monograms of American artists: from the colonial period to the mid-twentieth century. Land O'Lakes, FL, Sound View Press, 1989. 556p. $115.00. ISBN: 0932087043.

8,000 facsimile signatures used by 3,000 painters, sculptors, illustrators, cartoonists and printmakers. *Class No:* 7.0(73)(092)

[2955]

FALK, P.H. Who was who in American art: compiled from the original 34 volumes of American Art Annual ... Madison, CT, Sound View Press, 1985. 707p. £85. ISBN: 0932087000.

Alphabetical listing of artists, craftspeople, photographers, cartoonists, critics and historians taken from *AAA* 1898-1933 and *Who's Who in American Art* 1935-1947. 25,000 entries with wide range of data; 'an invaluable source' (*Choice* 23(6) Feb. 1986. p.855). *Class No:* 7.0(73)(092)

[2956]

HUGHES, E.M. Artists in California 1786-1940. 2nd ed. San Francisco, Hughes, 1989. 637p. $60. ISBN: 0961611219.

Index of over 14,000 artists: painters, sculptors, printmakers, etchers, muralists, pastellists, illustrators, teachers, commercial artists, engravers, woodcarvers, lithographers. Excluding photographers, craftsmen, architects. Bibliography p.631-7. *Class No:* 7.0(73)(092)

[2957]

OPITZ, G.B., *ed.* **Mantle Fielding's dictionary of American painters, sculptors and engravers.** 2nd ed. New York, Apollo Books, 1986. 1,081p. $85.00. ISBN: 0938290045.

First revision by Opitz 1983; originally published 1926.

Concise with good coverage of minor figures; over 13,000 names included. *Class No:* 7.0(73)(092)

[2958]

SAMUELS, P. *and* **SAMUELS, H. The Illustrated biographical encyclopedia of artists of the American West.** New York, Doubleday, 1976. xxvi,549p., illus. ISBN: 0385017308.

A/Z (Abdy-Zorach) of 1700 painters, printmakers, illustrators, sculptors from the European artist-explorers to the 1950's. Data includes full name, dates, specialities, collections, awards, signature, references. *Class No:* 7.0(73)(092)

[2959]

Who's who in American art 1995-1996. 21st.ed. Providence NJ, R.R. Bowker, 1995. 1521p. £150.00. ISBN: 0835235718. ISSN: 00000191.

Revised every 2 or 3 years.

Biographical details of over 11,800 artists, administrators, historians, educators, collectors, critics, curators, dealers in the US, Canada & Mexico. 600 new entries in this ed. Geographic index; professional classification index. Obituaries section, cumulative from 1953. *Class No:* 7.0(73)(092)

Women

[2960]

CHIARMONTE, P. Women artists in the United States: a selective bibliography and resource guide on the fine and decorative arts, 1750-1986. Boston, G.K. Hall, 1990. 1024p. $65.00. ISBN: 081618917x.

3,000 artists represented in entries covering almost 4,000 published items. Brief summaries of each publication. Part one - critics, organizations and resources, includes repositories and collections, biographical tools; part two examines the literature on women's art (painting, sculpture, photographs, performance, ceramics, crafts etc.) and lists documents on artists A/Z. Indexes by author/title, and artist name. *Class No:* 7.0(73)(092)-0055.2

[2961]

HELLER, J. *and* **HELLER, N.G.,** *eds.* **North American women artists of the twentieth century:** a biographical dictionary. New York, Garland, 1995. 612p., illus. $125.00. ISBN: 0824060490.

1500 women artists from the US, Canada and Mexico; concise biography, exhibition information, and brief bibliography. Criteria for inclusion are residence or work in the relevant countries, date-of-birth before 1960, and proven status by exhibition participation and literature. Covers painting, performance art, sculpture, printmaking, ceramics, textiles, metal arts, photography. 100 monochrome illustrations. Unevenness of coverage is noted, and some lack of currency, but 'even an imperfect source on women artists is welcome if it is as comprehensive as this one' (*Reference books bulletin*, 15/10/1995; p429.) 'An excellent and timely reference work' (*American reference books annual*, 1996; p425.) *Class No:* 7.0(73)(092)-0055.2

[2962]

TUFTS, E. American women artists, past and present: a selected bibliographical guide. New York, Garland, 1984, 1989. 450,491p. (2v.) illus. $47; $57. ISBN: 0824090705, v.1; 0824015118, v.2.

Volume one (1984) is updated and supplemented, but not replaced. The second volume includes 1,250 names (volume one, 519 artists) 1670-1960. All types of media, but not architects. No annotations, simply listings of English-language sources. Illustrations of limited value. 'Useful for finding information on lesser-known women artists' (*Choice* 27(6) February 1990, p.938). *Class No:* 7.0(73)(092)-0055.2

Black Races

Bibliographies

[2963]

IGOE, L.M. 250 years of Afro-American art: an annotated bibliography. London, Bowker, 1981. 1266p. ISBN: 0835213765.

Covers books, exhibition catalogues, periodicals, newspapers, announcements, flyers, theses, correspondence. 25,000 citations on 3,900 artists. Drawing, painting, sculpture, prints, crafts, photography, architecture are included. List of examples in published sources. 'Will undoubtedly become the authoritative bibliography in the field'. (*Art Documentation* 1(2) May 1982, p.84-85).
Class No: 7.0(73)(=96)(01)

America—South

Biographies

[2964]

CASTAGNO, J. Latin American artists' signatures and monograms: colonial era to 1996. Metuchen, NJ, Scarecrow Press, 1997. 600p. £137.50. ISBN: 0810832933.

Similar format to other compilations by this author; efficient arrangement. *Class No:* 7.0(8)(092)

Peru

Bibliographies

[2965]

SILVERMAN, H. Ancient Peruvian art: an annotated bibliography. Boston, G.K. Hall, 1996. 252p. $100.00. ISBN: 0816190607.

Covers books, journal articles, exhibition catalogues; international scope. Includes various media - pottery, murals, monuments, textiles, shells, land sculpture, metal arts, woodcarving. Some 1500 citations with good annotations. *Class No:* 7.0(85)(01)

Australasia & Oceania

Periodicals & Progress Reports

[2966]

BURT, E.C., ***comp.*** **Serials guide to ethnoart:** a guide to serial publications on visual arts of Africa, Oceania and the Americas. Westport, CT, Greenwood Press, 1990. 368p. $65. ISBN: 0313273324.

Extracted from *EthnoArts Index* database (1987-.); formerly *Tribal Arts Review* (1984-6).

....(contd.)

Notes editorial policy, specialities, subscription data, book and exhibition reviews, indexing arrangements. Appendices by geographical area. *Class No:* 7.0(9)(05)

Australia

[2967]

McCULLOCH, A. ***and*** **McCULLOCH, S. Encyclopaedia of Australian art.** 3rd.ed. London, Herbert Press /Honolulu, University of Hawaii Press, 1994. 878p., illus. £35.00. ISBN: 1871569737.

First published 1968; rev. ed. 1981; 2nd. ed. 1984.

3000 entries cover all aspects of Australian art - painting, sculpture, prints, art critics, photography - from 1770 to the present. This revision incorporates about one third new material. Artist entries give brief biographical and professional data, awards, exhibitions, galleries where works are located - over half the entries are for living artists. Illustrations are mainly small and monochrome but there are 7 sections of colour plates. Appendices list galleries, exhibitions, prizes, art periodicals etc. Index by artist names.
Class No: 7.0(94)

Bibliographies

[2968]

Australian art index. Canberra, Australian National Gallery, 1984-.

Available online through AUSINET, or on microfiche.

A group of databases consisting of Australian Art Index (AARTI), ARTSDOC, ARCH (Architecture) and the Crafts Council of Australia's *Index to crafts journals*.
Class No: 7.0(94)(01)

Biographies

[2969]

Australian artists' index: a biographical index of Australian artists, craft workers, photographers and architects. Sydney, ARLIS/ANZ, 1986. 432p. A$25. ISBN: 0947101004.

Alphabetical listing of over 10,000 Australian artists and craftsmen since 1788. Each entry lists general sources which provide biographical information - 416 such works being indexed. 'Good value for money and will save much time and effort in research' (*Art Libraries Journal* 13(4) 1988, p.35). *Class No:* 7.0(94)(092)

Jews

[2970]

Index of Jewish art: iconographical index of Hebrew illuminated manuscripts. Munich, K.G. Saur for the Israel Academy of Sciences and Humanities, 1981-89. 3v. ISBN: 9652080527.

Index cards with introductory notes; each volume folder contains also numerous illustrations. The third volume is the *Rothschild Miscellany*. *Class No:* 7.0(=924)

[2971]

KANIEL, M. Guide to Jewish art. New York, Philosophical Library, 1988. 192p. illus. £35.50. ISBN: 0802225535.

Straightforward & comprehensive guide; well illustrated.
Class No: 7.0(=924)

Bibliographies

[2972]

MAYER, L.A. Bibliography of Jewish art. Kurz, O., *ed.* Jerusalem, Magnes Press, Hebrew University, 1967. 374p.

3,016 numbered entries, with interpolations; occasional brief bibliographical notes; references to reviews. Titles in Hebrew are not transliterated. Coverage; the period A.D.70 (destruction of the Temple) to 1830. Excludes all works by Christian artists dealing with Biblical subjects or symbols of Judaism, and also historical documents (unless of clearly artistic value), newspaper articles, and preliminary archaeological reports (if later finalised). 28 sources listed, p.17-18. Analytical index. 'The most authoritative work in the field' (Arntzen, E., & Rainwater, R. *Guide to the literature of art history* (1980), entry A 192).
Class No: 7.0(=924)(01)

Islamic Peoples

[2973]

PAPADOPOULO, A. Islam and Muslim art. London, Thames & Hudson, 1980. 631p. illus. £55. ISBN: 0500233071.

Original French edition, Paris, Mazenod, 1976.

7 parts: 1. Islam and Muslim civilization - 2. The Muslim arts (*e.g.* 'The miniature', p.89-122) - 3. Architecture (*e.g.* 'The origins of the mosque'; 'Civil architecture in Islam', p.293-380) - 4. The image as document - 5. The principal sites of Muslim art (p.477-560) - 6. Prayer halls and other interiors - 7. A lexicon (political figures and holy men; theologians and mystics, philosophers and scientists; historians and geographers; poets and prose writers; painters; calligraphers; architects). Glossary; Notes. Bibliography (grouped) p.615-9. Analytical index. 1,100 fine illustrations. *Class No:* 7.0(=95.297)

Thesauri

[2974]

Art and architecture thesaurus. 2nd.ed. Oxford, OUP, 1994. 2186p. (5v.). £200. ISBN: 0195088840.

Also published in electronic edition; manual and diskettes (Oxford, Oxford Electronic Publishing, 1990; 0195066367). Annual supplements for both formats. Separate *Guide to indexing and cataloguing with the Art and Architecture Thesaurus* available. (ISBN: 0195088808; $35.00.)

Also available online through Research Libraries Information Network (RLIN).

Expanded vocabulary for the description of art, architecture, decorative arts, material culture, and archival materials. *Class No:* 7.0:025.43

Libraries

[2975]

Picture librarianship. Harrison, H.P., *ed.* London, Library Association Publishing, 1981. xii,542p. £40.00. ISBN: 0853659125.

Section 1: techniques and organizations (photographic sources p.35-54) selection, presentation & storage, arrangement & indexing, microforms, education & training. Section 2: case studies and surveys of picture libraries (26 divisions including the National Film Archive, art galleries and museums, public libraries, commercial libraries.) Bibliography p.495-517; out-of-date in some aspects, but still a standard source. *Class No:* 7.0:061:026/027

Handbooks & Manuals

[2976]

PACEY, P., *ed.* Art library manual: a guide to resources and practice. London, Bowker in association with ARLIS, 1977. xviii,423p.

21 contributors (20 of them British). 24 sections: 1. General art bibliographies - 2. Quick reference material - 3. The art book - 4. Museum and gallery publications - 5. Exhibition catalogues - 6. Sales catalogues and the art market - 7. Standards and patents - 8. Trade literature - 9. Periodicals and serials - 10. Abstracts and indexes - 11. Theses - 12. Primary sources - 13. Out of print materials - 14. Reprints - 15. Microforms - 16. - Sound recordings, video and films - 17. Slides and filmstrips - 18. Photographs and reproductions of works of art - 19. Photographs as works of art - 20. Printed ephemera - 21. Book design and illustration (p.337-54; 4p. of bibliography) - 22 Artists' books and book art - 23. Loan collections of original works of art - 24. Illustrations. Appendix 1: Other libraries and organizations as sources of information; 2. Conservation. Chapter references; appended bibliographies. Analytical index, p.404-23.

A most respected and valuable source; now in need of revision in many areas. Pacey's *Reader in art librarianship* (Munich, K.G.Saur, 1985; ISBN: 3598203985) augments the manual to some extent, but never achieved the same status.
Class No: 7.0:061:026/027(035)

Yearbooks & Directories

[2977]

VIAUX, J., *comp.* IFLA directory of art libraries. New York, Garland, 1985. xxi, 480p. $88.00. ISBN: 0824089138.

Lists libraries in over fifty countries, excluding US and Canada. Standardised data; subject index. Detailed review in *Art Libraries Journal* (v.11(1) 1986, p.36-38) commends the work but points out several faults and omissions.
Class No: 7.0:061:026/027(058)

Great Britain

Yearbooks & Directories

[2978]

McKEOWN, R. National directory of slide collections. London, British Library, 1990. viii,310p. (*British Library Information Guide, 12.*) ISBN: 0712332081. ISSN: 02691809.

Compiled from data collected in the *National Survey of Slide Collections* (BL Research Paper 67), and containing mainly non-commercial collections. Arranged in alphabetical name order, with subject and geographical indexes. Contains data on about 950 collections, giving size, coverage, access, facilities, charges, & contact name.
Class No: 7.0:061:026/027(410)(058)

Museums

Yearbooks & Directories

[2979]

JACKSON, V., *ed.* Art museums of the world. London, Greenwood Press, 1987. xiv,1681p. (2v.). £136.50. ISBN: 0313213224.

Articles on the history and collections of over 200 major institutions. Administrative details and selective analysis of

....*(contd.)*
the collections. Lists library facilities. Extensive bibliographies; 11-page glossary; copious index.
Class No: 7.0:061:069(058)

Aesthetics

[2980]
BEARDSLEY, M.C. Aesthetics: from classical Greece to the present. Tuscaloosa, University of Alabama Press, 1976. 414p. £9.95. ISBN: 0817366237.
Originally published London (Collier Macmillan, 1966).
12 sections, each with appended bibliography: 1. First thoughts - 2. Plato - 3. Aristotle - 4. The later Classical philosophers - 5. The Middle Ages - 6. The Renaissance - 7. The Enlightenment: Cartesian rationalism - 8. The Enlightenment: Empiricism - 9. German idealism - 10. Romanticism - 11. The artist and society - 12. Contemporary development (Croce and the Metaphysicians; Santayana and Dewey; Semiotic approaches; Marxism-Leninism; Phenomenology and Existentialism; Empiricism). Bibliography p.289-98. General bibliography, p.17-18. Non-analytical index, p.399-414. Standard text. *Class No:* 7.01

Periodicals

[2981]
British journal of aesthetics. London, OUP for the British Society of Aesthetics, 1960-. £33pa. ISSN: 00070964.
Quarterly.
Extensive book review section. *Class No:* 7.01(051)

[2982]
Journal of aesthetics and art criticism. Alberta, Canada, University of Alberta/American Society of Aesthetics. 1941-. $30. ISSN: 00218529.
Quarterly.
Interdisciplinary scholarly journal relating to the visual arts, theatre, music and literature. Includes bibliographies.
Class No: 7.01(051)

Design

Bibliographies

[2983]
Design and applied arts index. Mayfield, East Sussex, Design Documentation, 1988-. £175pa. ISSN: 09530681.
Two issues pa in printed format; four issues pa for CD-ROM.
International index to 300 current design and design-related journals, and exhibition catalogues, theses, film and video material. Includes industrial and vehicle design, architecture, interior design, environmental, computer-aided and furniture design, ceramics, glass, jewellery, fashion, typography, book design, advertising, retail design, theatre, ergonomics, disabled. Single alphabetical sequence of subjects, authors, designers; brief annotations. 'Valuable key to ... data never systematically indexed before nor easily accessible anywhere else' (*Art Libraries Journal* 13(4). 1988. p.32-33). Database now has over 100,000 references, including 35,000 individual names. Journals indexed are listed at start of each issue, and on CD-ROM.
Class No: 7.011(01)

[2984]
GODFREY, J. *and* **McKEOWN, R.,** *eds.* **Visual resources for design.** Wolverhampton, ARLIS/UK & Ireland Visual Resources Committee, 1995. £20.00. ISBN: 0951967444.
Lists image sources and suppliers of audio-visual materials to support design history and practice; gives full contact details, availability of catalogues etc. Detailed indexes by format and by subject. *Class No:* 7.011(01)

Encyclopaedias & Dictionaries

[2985]
BYARS, M., *ed.* **The Design encyclopedia.** London, Laurence King, 1994. 672p., illus. £29.50. ISBN: 1856690474.
4000 entries compiled by an international team; covers Europe, America, Australasia, Japan. Designer entries give full biography, details of education, major works, exhibitions and awards. Includes furniture, textiles, glass, metalwork, wallpaper, interiors, ceramics, industrial designers; no coverage of fine arts, photography, architecture, fashion, or vehicle design. Other entries discuss companies, materials, groups, movements. 120 monochrome illustrations; bibliography. *Class No:* 7.011(03)

[2986]
DALLEY, T., *ed.* **The Complete guide to illustration and design:** techniques and materials. New ed. Oxford, Phaidon, 1984. 224p.,illus.,tables. £14.95. ISBN: 0714823473.
2 parts: Illustration (Introduction. 1. Pencils and other point media; 2. Pen and ink; 3. Oils and other paint media; 4. Printmaking; 5. Technical illustration) - Graphic design (Introduction. 6. Design equipment; 7. Copying and photoprinting; 8. Design and typography; 9. Design procedures; 10. Design and photography; 11. Reproduction and printing). Glossary, p.208-213. Paper and sizes. Manufacturers and suppliers. Index, p.218-24. Step-by-step instruction, profusely illustrated (550 illus., 250 in colour), with descriptive captions. *Class No:* 7.011(03)

[2987]
JULIER, G. Thames and Hudson encyclopedia of twentieth century design and designers. London, Thames and Hudson, 1993. 216p.,illus. £6.95. ISBN: 0500202699.
Over 500 entries cover movements and -isms of the twentieth century, theory, management, promotion, critics, teachers, company histories, graphics, products, interiors, furniture, industrial and architectural design. Good subject index; bibliography. *Class No:* 7.011(03)

[2988]
QUINN, G., *ed.* **Encyclopedia of illustration:** compilation of more than 5,000 illustrations and designs. London, Studio Editions, 1990. 384p.(mainly illus.). £55. ISBN: 0851703608.
16 chapters range over people, occupations, transport, leisure & sport, music, costume, heraldry & armour, ornament & alphabets, architecture, anatomy & medicine, flowers, animals, insects, birds, fish. Examples of how artists have drawn various themes; all periods and countries.
Class No: 7.011(03)

Yearbooks & Directories

[2989]
International design yearbook. London, Laurence King. c250p., illus. £42.00. ISSN: 02692007.

Annual; first published 1985.

Covers furniture, lighting, tableware, textiles and other products by new and established designers; international; high standard of illustration, and technical data for each object. Reference section gives biographies, list of suppliers and addresses, update of design acquisitions at major museums. *Class No:* 7.011(058)

Standards

[2990]
CHIARA, J., *et al.* Time-saver standards for interior design and space planning. New York, McGraw-Hill, 1991. 1162p. ISBN: 0070162999.

Standard dimensions and sizes of details are given on clearly drawn graphic illustrations. 5 sections: houses, offices, commercial spaces; construction details; woodwork; specialities; general reference data. Extensive subject index. *Class No:* 7.011(083.74)

Histories

[2991]
CONWAY, H., *ed.* Design history: a students handbook. New ed. London, Routledge, 1992. 224p. £10.99. ISBN: 0415084733.

Bibliographic guide to the design history of ceramics, graphic design, furniture, fashion design, interior design, presented by an authority in each field. Annotations; bibliography; index. *Class No:* 7.011(091)

[2992]
SPARKE, P. A Century of design. London, Mitchell Beazley, 1998. 272p., illus. £35.00. ISBN: 1840000007.

Overview of 20th.century design - glass, furniture, ceramics, industrial products, cars, graphics. Chapters cover Conservative Modernism, Progressive Modernism, New Modernism etc. Over 250 colour illustrations; directory of manufacturers and design collections; glossary; bibliography. *Class No:* 7.011(091)

Biographies

[2993]
DORMER, P., *ed.* The Illustrated dictionary of twentieth century designers. London, Quarto, 1991. 256p., illus. £19.95. ISBN: 0747202680.

First published by Headline, 1990.

400 brief biographies and examples of work covering architecture, industrial design, interior decoration, fashion, graphics, textiles, and applied art in general. 350 colour photographs. *Class No:* 7.011(092)

[2994]
MORGAN, A.L. *and* NAYLOR, C., *eds.* Contemporary designers. 3rd ed. London, St. James Press, 1994. 1000p., illus. £98. ISBN: 1558621849.

800 entries on graphic, industrial/product, fashion, textile, interior, film, stage, set, and costume designers worldwide. Alphabetically by name, with biographical details, statement by contributor and designer, list of references. Over 500 illustrations. *Class No:* 7.011(092)

Great Britain

Bibliographies

[2995]
COULSON, A.J. A Bibliography of design in Britain, 1851-1970. London, Design Council, 1979. 308p.

3 main sections: fostering design, design and designers, areas of design activity. Wide range of books and articles; broad subject guide but no detailed indexes. *Class No:* 7.011(410)(01)

20th Century

[2996]
PILE, J. Dictionary of twentieth century design. Oxford, Facts on File, 1994. 312p., illus. £22.95. ISBN: 0816018111.

Alphabetical arrangement covering all areas of design, interior furnishing, tableware, glassware, silverware, graphic design; includes styles, periods, designers, manufacturers, technical terms. *Class No:* 7.011"19"

Colour

[2997]
KORNERUP, A. The Methuen handbook of colour. New ed. London, Methuen, 1989. £30.

First published in UK 1963.

Universal ready-reference guide for technicians, designers etc. Plates of 1266 coded colour samples with fully cross-referenced descriptive glossary of colour names. Chart of names used by British paint manufacturers. British Standard colour ranges. *Class No:* 7.017

Art Techniques

Handbooks & Manuals

[2998]
HEBBLEWHITE, I. Artists' materials: an international comparative directory. London, Phaidon, 1986. 288p. illus., tables, charts. ISBN: 0714824321.

Five main sections list and evaluate, mainly in chart form: supports, including canvas, paper & board; studio furniture & equipment, drawing & calligraphy instruments; brushes and knives; colour and paints, inks, etc. Technical specifications are noted, and manufacturers and suppliers listed. *Class No:* 7.02(035)

[2999]
MAYER, R. The Artist's handbook of materials and techniques. 5th ed. London, Faber, 1991. 800p. £30.00. ISBN: 0571150675.

First published 1940.

Good coverage of pigments, colours, solvents, new materials, conservation methods etc. Bibliographies to many entries. *Class No:* 7.02(035)

Dictionaries

[3000]
MAYER, R. HarperCollins dictionary of art terms and techniques. Sheehan, S., *ed.* 2nd ed. New York, Harper Perennial, 1991. 474p. $25.00. ISBN: 0062715186.

First edition as *Dictionary of art terms and techniques,* 1969, reprinted 1981.

Over 3,000 authoritative entries - schools, periods, styles, technical terms - thoroughly updated for the new edition.

....(*contd.*)

Line drawings, but photographs are no longer included; layout much condensed. Excellent basic bibliography at end. *Class No:* 7.02(038)

Repair & Restoration

[3001]

GUILD OF MASTER CRAFTSMEN. Care and repair. Lewes, East Sussex, Guild of Master Craftsmen Publications, 1989. 159p.,illus. £12.50. ISBN: 0946819157.

Formerly *Guide to restoration experts.*

Lists craftsmen whether members of the Guild or not. Sections cover antique restorers (by speciality), building restorers (by speciality), suppliers of materials (30 sub-headings). Lists of advisers, courses, organizations, publications, specialist bookshops. *Class No:* 7.025.4

Periods & Styles

Primitive & Prehistoric

[3002]

BAHN, P.G. The Cambridge illustrated history of prehistoric art. Cambridge, Cambridge University Press, 1997. 352p., illus. £24.95. ISBN: 0521454735.

A curiously empty area of publishing is now filled with an outstanding new title; fully international in scope with historical notes on the discovery and appreciation of prehistoric art. 165 colour plates show the art itself - including the most recent finds - and drawings by explorers from the 1600s onwards. *Class No:* 7.031

[3003]

SANDARS, N.K. Prehistoric art in Europe. 2nd ed. Harmondsworth, Middx., Penguin, 1985. 512p. illus. £16.95. (*Pelican History of Art.*) ISBN: 0140561307.

First edition 1968.

Coverage includes: 1. The beginnings (30,000-15,000 B.C.) - 2. Upper Palaeolithic art, 15,000-8,000 B.C. - 3. Mesolithic art, 8,000-2,000 B.C. - 4. Neolithic art in Southern Europe, 5,000-2,000 B.C. - 5. From the Mediterranean to the Baltic, 4,000-2,000 B.C. - 6. Bronze age art, 2,000-1,200 B.C. - 7. Ferment and new beginnings, 1,200-500 B.C. - 8. Continental art in the last centuries B.C. - 9. Insular la Tène and the problem of La Tène art - 10. Postscript. Bibliography (by chapters). 104 line-drawings; 192 appended pages of plates. Analytical index. *Class No:* 7.031

Ancient Egypt

[3004]

GAY, R. The Art of ancient Egypt. London, British Museum Press, 1997. 288p., illus. £28.50. ISBN: 0714109886.

History of Egyptian art from the earliest dynasties to the Ptolemaic period; chapters include plenty of background and explanation. The excellent illustrations (over 300, half in colour) depict major objects from the British Museum and other European, Egyptian and US collections to support the text. Chronology and bibliography. *Class No:* 7.031(32)

Ancient World

[3005]

AMIET, P., *and others*. Art in the ancient world: a handbook of styles and forms. London, Faber, 1981. 567p. illus., maps. ISBN: 0571117430.

Covers Iran, Mesopotamia, the Levant, Egypt, Greece, Etruria, Rome. Lists major museums, includes bibliographies and glossary. Discusses and illustrates forms in architecture, decoration, reliefs, sculpture, ceramics, metalwork etc. *Class No:* 7.032

Ancient Greece

[3006]

BOARDMAN, J., *ed.* The Oxford illustrated history of classical art. Oxford, Oxford University Press, 1993. 544p. £35.00. ISBN: 0198143869.

Account of the arts of Greece and Rome from the 10th century BC to the 4th century AD. Origins, development, diffusion, patronage are explored through well chosen examples; 500 monochrome illustrations and 50 colour plates. Bibliography and index. *Class No:* 7.032(37)

[3007]

PEDLEY, J.G. Greek art and archaeology. 2nd.ed. London, Calmann & King, 1997. 384p., illus. £14.95. ISBN: 1856691098.

First ed. published 1992.

Chronological account of the development of Greek art and civilisation from the earliest island cultures through to the Hellenistic period. Latest archaeological finds are incorporated. High standard of illustrations (460 total, 40 in colour), and clear diagrams. *Class No:* 7.032(37)

[3008]

RICHTER, G.M.A. A Handbook of Greek art: architecture, sculpture, genre, coins, jewellery, metalwork, pottery and vase painting, glass, furniture, textiles, paintings and mosaic: a survey. Rev. ed. London, Phaidon, 1989. 431p. illus. £9.95. ISBN: 0714824968.

First published 1959; 7th ed. 1983.

16 chapters, with notes and chapter bibliographies, p.388-98. Tentative chronology of Greek sculptural works, *c.*850-100 BC. Short glossary. General bibliography, p.399-410. Index of names. 520 half-tone illus. A standard work intended for the student and intelligent amateur. *Class No:* 7.032(37)

[3009]

ROBERTSON, M. A History of Greek art. Cambridge, CUP, 1975. v,835p. (2v.) illus.,maps. £85. ISBN: 0521202779.

V.1 (xviii,611p.) has contents: Prologue: art in Greece before the Iron Age - 9 chapters: 1. The seeds of Greek art. 2. The beginnings of monumental Greek art - 3. Ripe archaic art - 4. The great change: late Archaic and early Classical - 5. The Classical moment - 6. Development into the fourth century - 7. The second change: Classical to Hellenistic - 8. Hellenistic art. Epilogue: Greek art and Roman. V.2 (v, 613-835p) has voluminous notes on v.1 (p.613-39); 'Abbreviations and bibliography' p.740-59 (authors, A/Z) and 178p. of plates. General index; index of museums and collections (p.817-35). A scholarly survey covering *c.*1000B.C. to the first century B.C. V.1 concentrates on Greek sculpture and painting, dealing only marginally with architecture. Well produced, although *TLS* no.3883, 13 August 1976, p.1011-2 criticises choice and quality of illus. 'A considerable intellectual achievement' (*British Book news*, June 1976, p.448). *Class No:* 7.032(37)

Ancient Rome

[3010]

BOARDMAN, J., *ed.* The Oxford illustrated history of classical art. Oxford, Oxford University Press, 1993. 544p. £35.00. ISBN: 0198143869.

See entry at 7.032(37). *Class No:* 7.032(38)

[3011]

GRANT, M. Art in the Roman Empire. London, Routledge, 1995. xxii,146p., illus., maps. £25.00. ISBN: 0415120314.

Major, scholarly work; extensive bibliography p134-141. *Class No:* 7.032(38)

[3012]

HENIG, M., *ed.* A Handbook of Roman art: a survey of the visual arts of the Roman world. London, Phaidon, 1983. 320p.,illus.,maps,plans. £15. ISBN: 0714823015.

The work of 11 specialists, covers a variety of arts, from Early Rome to Late Antiquity. Covers not only Rome and Italy but also the provinces of the Empire, - a neglected area. It forms a companion to G.M.A. Richter's *A handbook of Greek art (q.v.).* *Class No:* 7.032(38)

[3013]

RAMAGE, N.H. *and* RAMAGE, A. Roman art. 2nd.ed. London, Calmann & King, 1996. 320p., illus. £14.95. ISBN: 1856690784.

First ed. published 1991.

Very clear and well-presented guide to the painting, sculpture, mosaics, architecture of ancient Rome. Arranged by historical period, with discussion of background myths, literature etc. Over 400 illustrations, 36 in colour. *Class No:* 7.032(38)

China

[3014]

RAWSON, J. Ancient China: art and archaeology. London, British Museum, 1980. 240p., illus. £8.95. ISBN: 0714114154.

5 chapters, spanning *c.*5000B.C. to A.D.220: 1. The Neolithic - 2. The Shan dynasty - 3. The Western Zhou - 4. The Eastern Zhou - 5. The Han dynasty. Bibliography (grouped), p.221-8. General index. Index of characters: Chinese characters with pinyin and Wade-Giles transliteration. Index of objects by reference number. 192 illus., with descriptive captions. Well produced. *Class No:* 7.032(510)

Egypt

[3015]

SALEH, M. *and* SOUROUZIAN, H. The Egyptian Museum, Cairo. Munich, Prestel Verlag, 1987. 268p. illus. £27.50. ISBN: 3791307975.

The official catalogue and standard work on the collection. 'Beautifully illustrated and highly informative ... complete with a helpful glossary of terms and an extensive bibliography' (*Apollo* August 1989, p.140). *Class No:* 7.032(620)

Mediaeval & Byzantine

[3016]

ERLANDE-BRANDENBURG, A. Gothic art. New York, Abrams, 1989. 630p. illus. $135. ISBN: 0810906317.

122-page introductory essay; four main sections on stylistic periods, each subdivided by subjects: architecture, sculpture, painting, metalwork etc., then further divided by

....(contd.)

country or region. Appendix shows monuments with descriptions, plans etc. 935 illustrations, 170 in colour. Glossary, bibliography, index. 'Comprehensive survey' (*Choice* 27(8) April 1990, p.1309). *Class No:* 7.033

[3017]

RODLEY, L. Byzantine art and architecture: an introduction. Cambridge, Cambridge University Press, 1994. xiv,380p., illus. ISBN: 0521354404.

Divided into conventional periods of Byzantine history (Early Christian, 6th century, Dark Age and Iconoclasm, Macedonian Dynasty, Comnene Dynasty, Latin Occupation, Palaiologan Period). Each chapter treats architecture, sculpture, monumental art, minor arts, illuminated manuscripts and general synopsis. Appendices cover Armenian art and architecture, the Copts, Byzantine ceramics, coins and seals, list of emperors. Glossary; bibliography. Well illustrated with monochrome photographs, plans and maps (over 300 in total). *Class No:* 7.033

Bibliographies

[3018]

Dumbarton Oaks bibliographies based on *Byzantinische Zeitschrift.* Allen, J.S. London, Mansell, 1973-81. 1095,586,408p. (3v.). £180. ISBN: 0720102170, v.1; 0720102189, v.2; 0720115868, series 2, v.1.

Series one *Literature on Byzantine Art,* 1892-1967 is divided by location (vol.1, issued in 2 parts) and by category (vol.2). Series two *Literature in various Byzantine desciplines* 1892-1977 covers *Epigraphy* in its first volume (1981). The volumes form the cumulative index to the annotated bibliographies of *BZ.* *Class No:* 7.033(01)

Great Britain

[3019]

LEHMANN-BROCKHAUS, O., *ed.* Lateinische Schriftquellen zur Kunst in England, Wales und Schottland vom Jahre 901 bis zum Jahre 1307. Munich, Prestelverlag, 1958-60. 5v.

Extracts from Latin source material on medieval British art. V.1-3 have entries for 6,773 items, with citations from the Latin texts. Main sources: the Rolls Series, Camden Society, Caxton Society, Surtees Society and Oxfordshire Record Society publications, Monumenta Germaniae Acta Sanctorum, and Migne's *Patrologiae cursus completus.* V.1-2 are in topographical order. The valuable indexes constituting v.4-5 are the outstanding features of the work. Thus, v.5 has 542p. of subject index and indexes of iconography and hagiography (*e.g.* 'Maria (N.T.)': p.513-519, set solid. 'An indispensable tool in English Medieval art studies' (*Burlington magazine,* v.103, no.700, July 1961, p.325). *Class No:* 7.033(410)

Renaissance

[3020]

BOBER, P.P. *and* RUBINSTEIN, R.O. Renaissance artists and antique sculpture: a handbook of sources. London, Harvey Miller/OUP, 1986. 522p. illus. £45. ISBN: 0199210292.

Divided into two parts: Greek and Roman gods and myths, and Roma triumphans - Roman history and life, the volume catalogues 203 sculptures known to Renaissance artists with

.... *(contd.)*
the works inspired by them. Full description including present location; extensive bibliography, indexes of artists, collections, and an analytical index. *Class No:* 7.034

Italy

[3021]
HALE, J.R. A Concise encyclopaedia of the Italian Renaissance. London, Thames & Hudson, 1983. 360p., illus., maps. £5.95. ISBN: 0500201919.

Latest reprint 1989.

32 contributors. About 750 entries ('Titian': 2½ columns; 1 illus. 3 references; 'Lorenzo de Medici': 21/3 cols; 4 references). Appendices include a glossary of Italian terms; bibliographical note on the chief relevant works. 237 black-and-white illus., 11 genealogical and 1 chronological table. Subject index precedes. 'Well organized' (*Art documentation,* v.1 no.5, Summer 1982, p.135).
Class No: 7.034(450)

[3022]
HARTT, F. A History of Italian Renaissance art: painting, sculpture, architecture. 4th ed. London, Thames & Hudson, 1994. 704p., illus. £38. ISBN: 0500236771.

First published 1970.

3 parts: 1. The late Middle Ages; 2. The Quattrocento; 3. The Cinquecento. Subdivision by place or form of art, much of the text being devoted to individual works. Includes glossary, further reading, analytical index. Over 100 colour plates and numerous black-and-white illus.; captions state medium, size and location. A standard one-volume history of the period. *Class No:* 7.034(450)

[3023]
VASARI, G. Le Vite de'piu eccelenti pittori, scultori, e architectori.... Milanesi, G., *ed.* Florence, Sansoni, 1900. 9v.

Reprinted 1906, 1973. Also available in the Dent Everyman Library in 4 vols, edited by William Gaunt.

First published 1550. The most reliable English translation is that by Gaston du C. De Vere, - *Lives of the most eminent painters, sculptors and architects* (London, Macmillan, 1912-15; reprinted AMS Press, 1976). 10v. 500 illus).

The classic biographical source on the Renaissance Italian artists. 'Important for the critical apparatus based on research with documents' (Arntzen, E., and Rainwater, R. *Guide to the literature of art history (1980), entry H48, 48A).* *Class No:* 7.034(450)

Classicism

[3024]
ACKERMANN, H.C. *and* **GISLER, J.R.,** ***eds.*** **Lexicon iconographicum mythologiae classicae.** Zurich, Artemis, 1981-. 2v., in 4., illus.

Intended to be a 7 vol. set, each in two parts (texts & plates).

Dictionary of iconography of Greek, Etruscan and Roman mythology. Ranges from early Greek (Mycenean) period to early Christian period. Signed articles (in English, German, French or Italian) with bibliographies. Cross references. The final volume of LIMC will be an index. *Class No:* 7.035

[3025]
PRESTON, P. Dictionary of pictorial subjects from classical literature: a guide to their identification in works of art. New York, Scribners, 1983. xxii,311p.illus. £39.95. ISBN: 068417913x.

Alphabetical arrangement of visual representations of topics from classical literature, identified by objects or activities rather than the characters. Explanations and citations. Line drawings; cross-references. List of Greek names with Roman equivalents; works cited; bibliography.
Class No: 7.035

[3026]
REID, J.D. The Oxford guide to classical mythology in the arts, 1300-1990s. Oxford, Oxford University Press, 1993. 1310p.(2v.) £140.00. ISBN: 0195049985.

References to the treatment of classical Greek and Roman mythological figures and stories in most media. 30,000 works of art are cited in 205 sub-divisions. Thematic categories for complex entries. References in every case to catalogues or learned publications. (Review in *Choice,* 31(4) December 1993, p589/90.) *Class No:* 7.035

Modern Art

[3027]
ARNASON, H.H. A History of modern art: painting, sculpture, architecture. Wheeler, D., *ed.* 4th ed. London, Thames & Hudson, 1989. 744p. illus. £29.95. ISBN: 0500235414.

First published 1969.

24 parts (1. Painting in the nineteenth century ... 7. Expressionism in Germany ... 15. Dada ... 20. Painting and sculpture in the United States, to 1950 ... 24. New dimensions in the 1960s and 1970s.) Bibliography. Index.
Class No: 7.036

Bibliographies

[3028]
MUSEUM OF MODERN ART. New York. **Annual bibliography of modern art.** Boston, G.K. Hall. c650p. ISBN: 0783820313, 1996 ed.

Annual series.

Wide coverage; includes all types of material. Data comprises author, title, place and date of publication, publisher, collation, ISBN, LC number, subject headings.
Class No: 7.036(01)

[3029]
MUSEUM OF MODERN ART. New York. **Catalog of the library.** Boston, G.K. Hall, 1976. 14v.

Photographic reproduction of the dictionary catalogue; includes citations to periodical articles not covered by *Art Index* or *RILA*. *Class No:* 7.036(01)

Encyclopaedias & Dictionaries

[3030]
Multimedia dictionary of 20th century art. London, Thames & Hudson, 1996. CD-ROM. £69.95. ISBN: 0500100152.

Windows and Macintosh versions available.

Entries for 2500 artists, groups, movements, galleries; over 3500 reproductions. Audio and video clips to support entries. Generally enthusiastically received by the art press, and judged to be sophisticated technically but remaining easy to use. *Class No:* 7.036(03)

[3031]

The Oxford companion to twentieth century art. Osborne, H., *ed.* Oxford, OUP, 1981. 672p. illus. £12.95 (pbk). ISBN: 0192820761.

Scheduled revision has resulted in a totally new work - see *Oxford Dictionary of twentieth century art* below; this volume retains some value.

A/Z entries cover biographies, accounts of movements & associations, elucidation of terms, historical perspectives. 300 reproductions in 8 plate sections (Expressionism; Cubism; Surrealism; Constructivism; American art to 1960; abstract art after 1960; Pop art; artists & countries outside major movements). *Class No:* 7.036(03)

[3032]

The Oxford dictionary of twentieth century art. Chilvers, I., *ed.* Oxford, Oxford University Press, 1998. 670p. £25.00. ISBN: 0192116452.

Originally planned as an update of the entry above, but extensive retreatment led to a new title.

Covers 1000 artists; also movements and styles; techniques and terms; schools and galleries; writers and critics. 2-column layout is easy to scan, but there are no illustrations. Established names and new figures are represented - *Futurism* 4 columns; *Picasso* 5 columns; *Rachel Whiteread* 1 column; *Damien Hirst* 1 column.
Class No: 7.036(03)

Quotations

[3033]

ROBERTSON, J. Twentieth century artists on art: an index to artists' writings, statements, and interviews. Boston, G.K. Hall, 1986. £22.50. ISBN: 0816187142.

Over 5000 artists of 60 nationalities in some 1400 citations from 495 sources including anthologies, books of essays, periodicals, exhibition catalogues. Wide range of subjects covered. 'Valuable addition to the reference collection' (*Art Documentation* 5(3) Fall 1986, p.139); 'Highly recommended' (*Choice* 23(9) May 1986, p.1374).
Class No: 7.036(082.2)

Portugal

[3034]

TANNOCK, M. Portuguese twentieth century artists: a biographical dictionary. Chichester, Phillimore, 1978. 192p. illus. £25. ISBN: 0850333121.

Covers 2150 artists active 1900-1974. Brief data, exhibitions, prizes, awards. List of museums. 94 colour plates and 287 monochrome illustrations.
Class No: 7.036(469)

India

[3035]

GHOSE, D.C. Bibliography of modern Indian art.
Kaul, K.L., *ed.* New Delhi, Lalit Kala Academy, 1980. 249p.

Bibliography of contemporary Indian art covering the period 1900 to 1976. List of journals and periodicals. Lists documents mainly in the English language: 2,550 periodical articles and exhibition catalogues. Several appendices.
Class No: 7.036(540)

Art Deco

[3036]

ARWAS, V. Art Deco. Rev ed. New York, Abrams, 1992. 316p. $75.00. ISBN: 0810919265.

Originally published 1980.

Covers furniture, jewellery, sculpture, painting, graphic arts, bookbinding, glass, ceramics; includes biographies of artists. 436 illustrations. 'Expert survey of the masterpieces of the art deco aesthetic has been *the* key volume on the subject.' (*Reference books bulletin*, 1/10/92. p226.)
Class No: 7.036ART

[3037]

BAYER, P. Art Deco architecture: design, decoration and detail from the Twenties and Thirties. New York, Abrams, 1992. 224p. $49.50. ISBN: 0810919230.

Thorough study with 370 illustrations of key buildings - exhibition pavilions, houses and hotels, offices, cinemas, monuments, stores, restaurants, factories, civic buildings. Commentary is 'rich in history and description...artistic and social context.' (*Reference books bulletin*, 1/11/92. p478.)
Class No: 7.036ART

[3038]

DUNCAN, A., *ed.* The Encyclopedia of art deco. New York, Dutton, 1988. 192p. $29.95. ISBN: 0525246134.

Background and biography by expert hands. Well illustrated. *Class No:* 7.036ART

Dada

[3039]

DACHY, M. The Dada movement, 1915-1923. New York, Skira/Rizzoli, 1990. 230p., illus. £55. ISBN: 0847811107.

Three basic periods of Dada explored, with excellent illustrations. Many minor figures are discussed, as well as the key names. 'Indispensable survey' (*Choice*, October 1990, p.293). *Class No:* 7.036DAD

Earth scale art

[3040]

HAVLICE, P.P. Earth scale art: a bibliography, directory of artists and index of reproductions. London, McFarland, 1984. 138p. $35. ISBN: 0899500722.

Four main sections: bibliography of general articles (mainly 1970s); individual artists (A/Z of 32 names with details); author index; index to works by titles (approx 500 cited). *Class No:* 7.036EAR

Fauvism

[3041]

CLEMENT, R. Les Fauves: a sourcebook. Westport,CT, Greenwood Press, 1994. 683p. $115.00. ISBN: 0313283338.

A well researched title, being mainly an annotated bibliography. Section on each artist gives a biography, chronology, and primary and secondary bibliography.
Class No: 7.036FAU

Folk art

[3042]

MEYER, G.H., *ed.* Folk artists biographical index. Detroit, Gale Research, 1987. 496p. $40. ISBN: 0810321459.

Published in association with the Museum of American Folk Art; identifies 206 sources on some 9,000 American folk artists. Standard data on personal details, career,

.... (contd.)
locations of work. Indexes by museums, ethnic group, geographic location, media, type of work. Wide interpretation of folk art, covering seventeenth century to the present. Useful but imperfect (*Art Libraries Journal* 13(1) 1988 p.28-33). *Class No:* 7.036FOL

[3043]
MUSEUM OF AMERICAN FOLK ART. Encyclopedia of twentieth century American folk art and artists. Abbeville, C. & J. Rosenak, 1990. 416p. $75.00. ISBN: 1558590412.
255 illustrated biographical accounts, with interviews and photographs. List of exhibitions 1924-1990. Extensive bibliography and thorough index. 'Authoritative and handsome.' (*Reference books bulletin,* July 1991. p2069/70.) *Class No:* 7.036FOL

[3044]
SELLEN, B.C. Twentieth century American folk, self-taught, and outside art. New York, Neal-Schuman, 1993. 462p. $90.00. ISBN: 1555701426.
Classified directory and bibliography of information sources - commercial galleries, centres and museums, exhibitions, organizations and associations, courses and programmes; newsletters, journals, books, catalogues, articles in journals and newspapers, audio-visual materials. *Class No:* 7.036FOL

Naive art

[3045]
MERIN, O.B. *and* **TOMASEVIC, N.B.,** ***eds*****. World encyclopedia of naive art.** New ed. London, Bracken Books, 1987. 735p. illus. £21.95. ISBN: 0851701273.
Main part consists of biographical dictionary featuring 800 artists; also historical surveys of naive art in individual countries, lists of exhibitions, museums, galleries. Bibliography; good illustrations, many in colour. *Class No:* 7.036NAI

Pop art

[3046]
LIVINGSTONE, M. Pop art: a continuing history. New York, Abrams, 1990. 366p., illus. $49.50. ISBN: 0810937077.
An authoritative survey of 30 years of Pop Art. Discusses the work of 130 artists in comic strips, commercials, consumer products. 300 colour plates. *Class No:* 7.036POP

Ornamentation

[3047]
JONES, O. The Grammar of ornament, illustrated by examples from various styles of ornament. London, Quaritch, 1910. 157p., illus.
First published 1856. Reprinted Van Nostrand Reinhold, 1974.
Chapters 1-20 (1. Ornament of savage tribes; 2. Egyptian ornament ... 20. Leaves and flowers from nature): the various classes and types of decorative art of the past, from primitive times to the 17th century, with a list of 'general principles'. Chapter references. Also essays on the ornament of the Renaissance and Italian periods, by M. Digby Wyatt. 112 col. plates. 'A splendid corpus of historic ornament from all over the world; first produced during the Arts and Crafts movement in England' (Arntzen, E., and Rainwater, R. *Guide to the literature of art history* (1980), entry P.72. *Class No:* 7.04

Dictionaries

[3048]
LEWIS, P. *and* **DARLEY, G. Dictionary of ornament.** London, Pantheon, 1986. 319p. £22.00. ISBN: 0394509315.
European and North American material; covers styles, patterns, motifs, techniques, and individuals. Over 1,000 entries, and valuable visual key. Photographic surveys of significant motifs and techniques under such headings as 'animal forms', 'linear decoration'. Ranges from Renaissance to present day with emphasis on use of treatises, pattern and design books. *Class No:* 7.04(038)

Islamic World

[3049]
HUMBERT, C. Islamic ornamental design: 1001 ornamental motifs. London, Faber, 1980. 236p. illus. ISBN: 057111587x.
Information followed by illustrated catalogue of examples under headings: script, calligraphy, epigraphy, geometric, plants, floral, etc. Locations noted; index by country and date. *Class No:* 7.04(5.297)

Jews

[3050]
KEEN, M. Judaica: Jewish ritual objects in the Victoria and Albert Museum. London, HMSO, 1990. 120p. illus. £20. ISBN: 0112904491.
Catalogue of Jewish artefacts in the Museum, ranging from everyday items to ceremonial pieces. Full description and explanation, with good illustration. *Class No:* 7.04(=924)

Symbols & Allegories

[3051]
BIEDERMANN, H. Dictionary of symbolism. New York, Facts on File, 1992. 465p. $45.00. ISBN: 0816025932.
600 entries for 2000 symbols, mainly based on European heritage. Limited coverage of Asian, African and New World symbols; references to literature, myth, associations, historical use. *Class No:* 7.045

[3052]
CARR-GOMM, S. The Dictionary of symbols in Western art. New York, Facts on File/Oxford, Helicon, 1995. 240p., illus. £9.99. ISBN: 185986175x, UK; 0816033013, US.
A/Z listing of individuals (religious, mythological, historical), fictitious characters, themes, symbols, emblems, attributes, abstract ideas, used in Western art from the Renaissance to the present. *Class No:* 7.045

[3053]
CHEVALIER, J. *and* **GHEERBRANT, A.,** ***eds*****. A Dictionary of symbols.** Oxford, Blackwell Reference, 1994. 1174p. ISBN: 0631192654.
Translated from French original.
15 contributors from varied backgrounds - anthropology, ethnology, psychotherapy, art history - give this work an edge in exploring meanings that are elusive from a

....(contd.)
conventional approach. Examines folklore, literary and artistic sources. Regarded as a standard work in France. Bibliography p1150-74. *Class No:* 7.045

[3054]
DREYFUSS, H. Symbol source book: an authoritative guide to international graphic symbols. New York, Van Nostrand Reinhold. 1984. 292p., illus. £18.95. ISBN: 0442218060.

Hardback edition McGraw Hill, 1972.

Mainly diagrams laid out in subject groups (medicine, geography, music etc.) with explanation. Multi-language introductory contents section. Bibliography p.252-267; index p.268-292. *Class No:* 7.045

[3055]
HALL, J., ***ed*****. Illustrated dictionary of symbols in Eastern and Western art.** New York/London, Icon Editions/ HarperCollins, 1994. 244p. illus. $30.00. ISBN: 0064333140.

Wide scope; six thematic parts - abstract signs, animals, artifacts, earth and sky, human body and dress, plants. Small illus. for each entry; references to literature. Geographic index, chronological tables, general index. *Class No:* 7.045

[3056]
LIUNGMAN, C.G. Dictionary of symbols. Oxford, ABC-Clio, 1991. 596p. ISBN: 0874366100.

Originally published in Sweden; in 1974.

Covers Western cultural history from the earliest times to the present, old ideograms, modern signs and symbols, instrument panels. 1500 symbols in 54 main groups determined by shape; simple line drawings with annotations. Word index; graphic index (in group order); graphic search index (explanatory aid). *Class No:* 7.045

[3057]
ROBERTS, H.E., ***ed*****. Encyclopedia of comparative iconography:** themes depicted in works of art. London, Fitzroy Dearborn, 1998. 1400p.,(2v.) illus. £175.00. ISBN: 1579580092.

Compares the use of iconographic themes from mythology, the Bible and other sacred texts, literature, popular culture as seen in works of art in various periods and cultures. *Class No:* 7.045

Bibliographies

[3058]
LURKER, M., ***and others*****. Bibliographie zur Symbolkunde.** Baden-Baden, Verlag Heitz. 1964-68. 3v.

1. *Kunstgeschichte-Archäologie-Prähistorie.*
2. *Symbolerscheinungen.*
3. *Autorenregister. Sachregister. Nachträge.*

An extensive, systematically arranged bibliography. V.1 (viii, 215p.) has 4,521 numbered entries in 14 sections (Bibliographien - Periodica - Lexica ... Auswahl aus der Literatur des 16-18. Jahrhunderts ... Volkshunde und Kulturgeschcichte - Kultsymbolik ... Literature ... Psycholtherapie). V.2 deals with types of symbols (*e.g.* plants, animals); v.3, - author and subject indexes, plus a supplement to v.1-2. *Class No:* 7.045(01)

England

[3059]
DIEHL, H. Index of icons in English emblem books, 1500-1700. London, University of Oklahoma Press, 1986. xiii,258p. illus. £29.25. ISBN: 0806119896.

Alphabetical listing, p.9-225, of 'every icon in every English emblem book ... printed in the 16th. and 17th. centuries' (Preface). Entries give motto, description, epigram or interpretation. Cross-references. Illustrations p.228-252. Bibliography p.253-4. Index. *Class No:* 7.045(420)

Christian Iconography

[3060]
APOSTOLOS-CAPPADONA, D. Dictionary of Christian art. New York, Continuum Publishing, 1994. 376p., illus. $39.50. ISBN: 082640779x.

Over 1000 entries explain the signs, symbols, figures, animals, topics, colours, fauna, architectural elements, etc. that have appeared in Christian art. Entries range from 50 words to several hundred; cross-references indicated by asterisks. About 150 illustrations. Bibliography of 70 items. *Class No:* 7.046

[3061]
CHRISTE, Y., ***and others*****. Art in the Christian world 300-1500:** a handbook of styles and forms. London, Faber, 1982. 504p. ISBN: 0571119417.

Originally published 1982, Office du livre S.A. Fribourg.

Divided into principal periods, with useful line drawings and maps. Glossary, and lists of major museums. Concise bibliography follows the introduction to each division. No index. *Class No:* 7.046

[3062]
MURRAY, P. ***and*** **MURRAY, L. The Oxford companion to Christian art and architecture.** Oxford, Oxford University Press, 1996. xi,596p, illus. £30.00. ISBN: 0198661657.

General essays on periods and styles (Early Christian, Byzantine, Carolingian, Ottonian, Romanesque, Anglo-Saxon, Irish, Gothic, Renaissance, Baroque) with shorter entries describing specific works, artists, themes, images. Discussion of major traditions and beliefs that appear in art works; saints, popes, rulers; significant places and buildings. Glossary and bibliography. *Class No:* 7.046

[3063]
SCHILLER, G. Iconographie der christlicher Kunst. 2nd ed. Gütersloh, Gütersloher Verlagshaus Gerd Mohn, 1969-80. 473,692,604,341,472, (4v. in 5), illus.

Supplement including name and place indexes issued by same publisher, 1980. Vols. 1 & 2 issued in English translation by Janet Seligman as *Iconography of Christian Art* (Lund Humphries).

Volumes cover various aspects of Christian art, Incarnation, Passion, Ascension, Virgin Mary, apocalypse, etc. in narrative format. Each volume has a bibliography, indexes to texts and subjects, monochrome illustrations. Corrected impression now in progress. Vol. one issued 1981, two 1983, three 1986, four (part one) 1987, four (part two) 1980, five (now split into two parts) 1990 and 1991. *Class No:* 7.046

Industrial Design

Yearbooks & Directories

[3064]

British design and art direction annual 1997. London, Laurence King, 1997. 580p., illus. £60.00. ISBN: 1856691144.

Annual; four-disc CD-ROM published in conjunction, presenting each image, commercial, video, radio advert etc in its original media. (ISBN: 1856691233; £150.00.)

Published on behalf of the Designers and Art Directors Association of the UK; profiles the best of British and international design in advertising, editorial and graphic products (posters, books, typography, illustration), radio, television, cinema commercials, multi-media products. Lists awards; member list appended. Mainly consists of 200 illustrations and captions. *Class No:* 7.05(058)

Collectors & Collecting

[3065]

Akoun: international auction art 1998. Paris, Amateur, 1998. 1800p. £28.00. ISBN: 2859172505.

Guide to the auction prices of paintings, watercolours, gouaches, drawings, prints, posters, photographs, miniatures, sculptures, bronzes etc. Total of about 60,000 artists represented; international coverage of sales. French text, but key words are translated into several languages. *Class No:* 7.074

[3066]

Annuel des arts 1997. Wilder, F. Paris, EVW Saint-Ouen, 1997. 1447p. £70.00. ISBN: 2852990296.

Annual.

Records sales of artists work throughout the world during 1996. Arranged by title, with note of technique, size, signature, date, auction details, prices in francs, dollars and currency of sale. Text in French. *Class No:* 7.074

[3067]

Art at auction in America. Silver Spring, MD, Krexpress, 1993. $35.00. ISBN: 0962492639. ISSN: 10464999.

Prices of artworks, from all parts of the world, sold at US auction houses; some 20,000 items at 16 houses included. Arranged alphabetically by artist; convenient format and low price, but small type and abundant abbreviations. *Class No:* 7.074

[3068]

Art price index international. Falk, P.H., *et al.* Madison,CT, Sound View Press. c3000p.(2v.)

Annual.

Claims to be the most comprehensive and lowest priced compilation of auction records. Includes 160,000 results from 400 auction houses in 27 countries. Covers paintings, works on paper, sculpture, prints; arranged alphabetically by artist (over 51,000), and gives name, nationality, dates, medium, sale date, size, house, lot number, price in sterling and local currency. Reckoned comprehensive and easy to consult. (*Choice,* 31(10) June 1994. p.1547.) *Class No:* 7.074

[3069]

The Art price indicator 1998. Paris, ADEC, 1998. 1792p. £9.95. ISBN: 2907129112.

Provides representative prices as a guideline to sellers; contains entries for 50,000 artists working in media of painting, drawing, printing, sculpture and photography. *Class No:* 7.074

[3070]

Art sales index. Hislop, R., *ed.* Weybridge, Art Sales Index. c3500p (2v) per annum. ISSN: 01430688.

Also available on microfiche (6pa.) and online as *Art Quest,* continuously updated.

Printed volumes comprise:- vol.1: A-K by artist to oil paintings, works on paper; also miniatures, photographs and prints. Vol.2: L-Z by artist to oil paintings, works on paper; also sculpture, bronzes, and three-dimensional works. Entries give full name, dates, nationality, prices in sterling and US dollars, date and place of sale etc. Includes details of over 100,000 sale results from 2300 sales at 390 auction houses each year. 38,000 artists represented. *Class No:* 7.074

[3071]

CARNEVALLE, D. *and* **JONES, S.K. Collectibles market guide and price index:** to limited edition plates, figurines, bells, graphics, ornaments and dolls. 7th ed. Grand Rapids, MI, Collectors' Information Bureau, 1990. 288p. illus. $16.95. ISBN: 0930785053.

Discusses trends in an expanding market for limited edition commemorative artefacts. Chapters on manufacturers and artists; directory of museums, organizations; glossary of terms. Discussion of major series or collections; price guide at end covers about 20,000 distinct items. *Class No:* 7.074

[3072]

CURTIS, T. The Lyle price guide: printed collectibles. Galashiels, Lyle Publishers, 1994. 448p. £14.95. ISBN: 0862481562.

Prices paid at auction for books, advertisements, bags, wrappers, cigarette packets, railway tickets, etc. Photographs of 3000 items. *Class No:* 7.074

[3073]

Getty provenance index. Los Angeles, Getty Trust Publications, 1996. CD-ROM. $900.00. ISBN: 0892364181.

Also available on a trial basis on the Internet at Website <http://www.ahip.getty.edu/ahip/home.html>

The index is the work of 12 international institutions; a series of databases assist in the tracing of the origins of works of art by providing information on earlier collections. Databases comprise inventories of notable 17th. and 18th.century collections in Italy, Spain, the Netherlands, etc. and records of painting auctions in the UK, France and the Netherlands in the 19th.century. *Class No:* 7.074

[3074]

GRAVES, A. Art sales from early in the eighteenth century to early in the twentieth century. Weston-super-Mare, Kingsmead Reprints, 1973. 1138p. (3v.). £50. ISBN: 0901571636.

Originally published London: Graves, 1918-21.

Alphabetical arrangement, with notes on prices and original owners. *Class No:* 7.074

[3075]

International auction records. Zurich, Editions Acatos. c2200p. illus. £109.00.

Annual; this series began 1961/62 as *Annuaire international des ventes,* continued under present title from 1967/68, originally by Editions Publisol (New York, & Paris), and various other imprints.

60,000 prices from over 2,000 sales; sections on prints, drawings, watercolours, gouaches, pastels etc., each A/Z by artist; chronological order of works; catalogue numbers. Monochrome and colour illustrations. *Class No:* 7.074

[3076]

LANCOUR, H. American art auction catalogues, 1785-1942: a union list. New York, NYPL, 1944. 377p.

Originally published 1943/1944 in *Bulletin of the New York Public Library*.

Checklist of over 7,000 auction sale catalogues; a classic work. *Class No:* 7.074

[3077]

LUGT, F. Répertoire des catalogues de ventes publiques intéressant l'art ou la curiosité. The Hague, Nijhoff, 1938-1953. 3v.

A chronological list of over 58,000 catalogues of European sales held between 1600 and 1900.
Class No: 7.074

[3078]

MARSH, M., *ed.* Miller's picture price guide. London, Miller. c640p. £25.00.

Annual.

Aimed at the professional dealer or the private collector, this volume is especially to be recommended for the wealth of illustrations - 200 colour and 4000 monochrome. Glossary and index. *Class No:* 7.074

[3079]

Mayer international auction records on CD-ROM. London, Digital Media Resources Ltd, 1997. CD-ROM.

Also available on the Internet at Website: <http://www.artlibrary.com/mayer>

1997 CD-ROM covers 1987-1996; six-monthly updates.

Printed vols still available from Editions Acatos in Lausanne: titled 'Le Guide Mayer', the 1997 set - '35th year of publication' - (5110p; 2v. ISBN: 2940033234)) gives 120,000 prices from 2800 sales.

Covers prints, drawings, watercolours, paintings, sculpture. 1997 CD-ROM holds 750,000 records from 800 auction houses in 45 countries. Database can be searched by artist name, school, medium, title, seller, city or date of sale etc. Records can be retrieved in English or French.
Class No: 7.074

[3080]

Miller's price guide series. London, Reed International Books.

Illustrated series of guides for collectors; subjects covered include:- Collectables; Art Nouveau & Art Deco; Pine & Country Furniture; Antiques; Furniture; Pottery & Porcelain; Victoriana; Prints & Posters; and many others.
Class No: 7.074

[3081]

Price guide series. Woodbridge, Suffolk, Antique Collectors Club, 1970-.

A series of volumes providing authoritative valuations and identification hints. All are extensively illustrated. Titles in the series include:- Automobilia; Antique edged weapons; Antique furniture; Antique silver; Baxter prints; Black & white pot-lids; Bronze sculptures; Clocks 1840-1940; Collectible antiques; Dolls; Eighteenth century English porcelain; Eighteenth century English pottery; Jewellery; Metal toys; Models of W.H. Goss; Nineteenth & twentieth century British porcelain; Nineteenth & twentieth century British pottery; Nineteenth century European furniture; Old Sheffield plate; Victorian and Edwardian furniture; Victorian silver. *Class No:* 7.074

[3082]

REITLINGER, G. The Economics of taste. New York, Hacker, 1983. xl,1921p. illus. £100. ISBN: 0878172882.

Originally published London, Barrie & Rockliff, 1961-70 in 3 volumes.

1. *The rise and fall of picture prices, 1760-1960.* 2. *The rise and fall of objets d'art prices since 1950.* 3. *The art market of the 1960s.* V.1 is an historical survey of the period, plus 'Sales and analysis of the most popular painters, 1760-1960' (A/Z) and bibliography. Index of artists; index of collectors, dealers and others. V.2 takes selected types of objets d'art (Arms and armour ... Tapestry). Bibliography. Index. V.3 has parts: 1. Paintings and drawings (under artists, A/Z and under schools); 2. Sales analysis of sculpture; 3. Objets d'art. No bibliography or index. Valuable 'Explanatory note', and 'Introduction: Art and inflation'. *Class No:* 7.074

[3083]

SCIPIO: Sales catalog index project input online.

About 100,000 records accessible via the Research Libraries Information Network (RLIN). As part of the Getty Provenance Index (*qv.*) records are available on a trial basis on the Internet at Website <http://www.ahip.getty.edu/ahip/home.html>

Database of catalogues from 3,000 auction houses of all sizes worldwide, held by the libraries of the Art Institute of Chicago, Cleveland Museum of Art, Metropolitan Museum of Art, National Gallery of Art etc. Coverage from 1599 to the present. *Class No:* 7.074

[3084]

Sotheby's Art at auction: the year in review. London, Conran Octopus, 1967-. c350p., illus. £50.00. ISSN: 00846783.

An excellent annual record; lavishly produced and illustrated, with review features as well as sale details.
Class No: 7.074

[3085]

World collectors annuary. Kinderhook,NY, ibd for World Collectors Publications, 1946-. 735p.(Vol. 42, 1991/2.) $175.00.

Published annually; cumulative index to volumes 1-24 (Voorburg, World Collectors, 1976). Various other imprints at earlier stages.

Covers graphic art sales in Europe and the USA; an important source with excellent detail. *Class No:* 7.074

Glossaries

[3086]

BERNASCONI, J.R. Wordsworth guide to antiques and fine arts. Ware, Wordsworth Reference, 1995. xviii,595p.,illus. ISBN: 1853263435.

Originally published as *Collectors' glossary of antiques and fine arts* (London: Estates Gazette, 1971)

Wide ranging list of terms, with adequate illustrations.
Class No: 7.074(038.1)

Antiques

[3087]

CURTIS, T. Popular antiques and their values, 1800-1875. Galashiels, Lyle, 1990. 255p. illus. £7.95. ISBN: 0862481201.

Small monochrome illustrations grouped by subject, with brief description and estimate of price. Index.
Class No: 7.074.0

[3088]
CURTIS, T. Popular antiques and their values, 1875-1950. Galashiels, Lyle, 1990. 255p. illus. £7.95. ISBN: 086248121x.
Small monochrome illustrations grouped by subject. China: 76 subheadings. Brief description and price guide. Index. *Class No:* 7.074.0

[3089]
The Lyle official antiques review price guide. Curtis, T., *ed.* Galashiels, Lyle Publications. c850p.,illus. £19.95.
Annual.
Illustrates and describes some 9,000 items under 375 broad subject categories, including a price guide. Photographs are mainly monochrome, but some colour. Much useful information is included at the beginning - silver marks, glossary of terms, details of feet, handles, legs, pediments, etc. Glossary and index. *Class No:* 7.074.0

[3090]
MILLER, J. *and* **MILLER, M. Miller's antiques price guide.** London, Mitchell Beazley. c800p., illus. £22.50.
Annual.
Illustrates & describes over 10,000 items grouped under 70 subject headings, with price guide. Comprehensive coverage - furniture, carpets, pottery, porcelain, glass, silver, dolls, etc. etc. Directories of auctioneers, specialists; index to advertisers. *Class No:* 7.074.0

[3091]
MILLER, J. *and* **MILLER, M.,** ***comps*. Miller's collectables price guide.** Tenterden, Miller's. c500p. illus. £17.99.
Annual.
Alphabetical arrangement (Aeronautica - Vesta cases) Photographic illustrations grouped by subjects, with descriptions and valuations. Directory of specialist dealers. Calendar of fairs, directory of markets and centres (both by county). Index. *Class No:* 7.074.0

[3092]
RINKER, H.L., ***ed*. Warman's antiques and their prices.** 25th ed. Radnor, PA, Wallace-Homestead/Chilton Book Co., 1991. 700p. £11.50. ISBN: 0870695924.
Valuable especially to the North American collector; a special strength lies in its coverage of American glass. Good illustrations. *Class No:* 7.074.0

Bibliographies

[3093]
FRANKLIN, L.C. Antiques and collectibles: a bibliography of works in English, 16th century to 1976. Metuchen, NJ, Scarecrow, 1978. xxiii,1091p. ISBN: 0810810921.
Almost 11,000 items covering all types of printed materials including trade and exhibition catalogues. Subject groups range over furniture, ceramics, glass, metalwork, wood, ivory, costume, ecclesiastical antiques; folk art, paper, toys, firearms, domestic appliances etc. etc., totalling 33 sections each further subdivided. Glossary; author and subject indexes. *Class No:* 7.074.0(01)

Great Britain

Yearbooks & Directories

[3094]
ADAMS, C., ***comp*. Guide to the antique shops of Britain.** Woodbridge, Suffolk, Antique Collectors' Club. c850p. illus., maps. £14.95.
First published 1972, issued annually.

....*(contd.)*
7,000 dealers listed, with name, address, telephone number, hours of opening, size of showroom. Type of stock, price range, attendance at fairs, services offered, etc. Geographic arrangement. Index of packers, exporters, auctioneers. List of fairs; index of names, subjects. Many advertisements. *Class No:* 7.074.0(410)(058)

[3095]
BRITISH ANTIQUE DEALERS' ASSOCIATION. Handbook. London, BADA, 1986-. £7.50.
Annual.
Illustrated guide to members' shops; indexes; classified by specialist areas and geographically.
Class No: 7.074.0(410)(058)

[3096]
British art and antiques yearbook. London, Antique Collector Magazine, 1978-. £7.50. ISSN: 01408763.
Directory and guide to over 5,000 antique and fine art dealers, auctioneers, and restorers. Indexes by place, speciality, business name. *Class No:* 7.074.0(410)(058)

[3097]
HORNSBY, P. Guide to British antiques fairs. Witney, P&J Hornsby. c190p. £4.95.
Annual.
Over 100 fairs are described, and a further 100 mentioned. Full entries give dates, name, addresses, location, visitor facilities, specialities, catalogues, entry cost, vetting services. Geographical index; list of organisers.
Class No: 7.074.0(410)(058)

Matchbox Labels

[3098]
GLADWISH, V.E.R. The Gladwish encyclopedia of matchbox labels. 3rd. ed. Taunton, Universal Phillumenists Exchange Club, 1979-84.
The basic work in its field. *Class No:* 7.074.2

[3099]
LUKER, J.H. Matchbox label collectors' catalogue encyclopedia. Camberley, J.H. Luker, 1979-. 12v.
One of several similar works by the same author/ publisher; these include *Encyclopedia phillumenica* (the Matchbox Label Collectors' Encyclopedia, 2v. 1975; 0905040007) and the *Matchbox label collectors' catalogue* (several volumes, 1976-). A detailed list is given in the *British Library Catalogue 1976-1982 supplement,* vol.28., p.245-6. *Class No:* 7.074.2

Cigarette Cards

[3100]
LAKER, I. Catalogue of British and foreign cigarette cards 1988-1989. Somerset, London Cigarette Card Co. 1988. 132p. illus. £6.50. ISBN: 0903790513.
Issued annually.
Comprehensive guide, with 340 illustrations.
Class No: 7.074.4

[3101]
LONDON CIGARETTE CARD CO. Complete catalogue of British cigarette cards. 2nd ed. Exeter, Webb & Bower, 1982. 256p. illus. ISBN: 090667285x.
Three main sections: history, collecting; illustrations divided by subjects; catalogue A/Z by publishers. Full details; bibliography. Catalogues over 4500 sets, with 800 colour illustrations. *Class No:* 7.074.4

[3102]

LONDON CIGARETTE CARD CO. The Illustrated catalogue of British and international cigarette cards. Camberley, Webb & Bower. 1990. 320p., illus. £12.95. ISBN: 0863504094.

Includes UK sets, and those issued in the US, Australia, NZ, South Africa, Canada, Japan, Korea, India, West Indies, Denmark, Switzerland, Malta etc. Colour illustrations of examples. *Class No:* 7.074.4

Paper Money

[3103]

PICK, A. Standard catalog of world paper money. Bruce, C. *and* Shafer, N., *eds*. 7th ed. Iola, Wisc, Krause, 1994-96. 928,1087, 720p. (3v.), illus., maps. $60.00. per vol. ISBN: 0873412087, v.1; 0873412079, v.2; 087341425x, v.3.

Volume one (1995) covers *specialized issues* (early US provincial and state notes, regional, military issues etc.); volume two (1994) *general issues.* (legal tender paper money currency issues from 300 past & current governments late 1600s to 1990s.). Volume 3 (1996) *modern issues 1961-1996* (250 issuing authorities.) Each vol. arranged A/Z by country, then chronological. Each note illustrated & valued. Glossary; bibliography. *Class No:* 7.074.6

Bibliographies

[3104]

McKERCHER, M., *ed*. Paper money: a bibliography. London, Spink, 1979. 72p. £6. ISBN: 0900696923.

Simple listing of monographs, articles etc.
Class No: 7.074.6(01)

Histories

[3105]

HEWITT, V., *ed*. The Banker's art: studies in paper money. London, British Museum, 1995. 168p., illus. £30.00. ISBN: 0714108790.

Interesting, authoritative review; useful for amateurs.
Class No: 7.074.6(091)

Postcards

[3106]

BONYNGE, R. Theatrical postcards: a collector's guide. London, Batsford, 1988. 128p. £12.95. ISBN: 0713457872.

Guide to collecting and categorising, with sources, prices and a commentary on some 200 illustrated examples.
Class No: 7.074.8

[3107]

COYSH, A.W. Dictionary of picture postcards in Britain, 1894-1939. Woodbridge, Suffolk, Antique Collectors' Club, 1984. 310p. illus. £19.50. ISBN: 1851490159.

Also paperback edition, 1986.

Alphabetical arrangement by subject, artist, photographers, advertisers, publishers. Index of place names. Bibliography. 546 illustrations, 77 in colour.
Class No: 7.074.8

[3108]

Stanley Gibbons postcard catalogue. Holman, J.R., *ed.* 5th ed. London, Stanley Gibbons, 1986. 336p., illus. £5.95. ISBN: 085259142x.

Subjects: Accessories - Advertising - Animals/Birds/Fish/ Insects ... Social history/Topographical - Theatre/Wireless/ War. Data: artist's name; publisher; thematic price. Classified index precedes. *Class No:* 7.074.8

[3109]

VENMAN, J. *and* MEAD, R. The RF postcard price guide. Ochiltree, Ayrshire, Richard Stenlake, 1995. 132p., illus. £6.99. ISBN: 1872074553.

Arranged under broad headings A/Z (advertising - topographical) with over 200 illustrations. Clear layout; efficient general index and index of artists. A useful addition. *Class No:* 7.074.8

71 Town & Country Planning. Landscapes

Town & Country Planning

Bibliographies

[3110]

GRETES, F.C. Directory of international periodicals and newsletters on the built environment. 2nd ed. New York, Van Nostrand Reinhold, 1992. 442p. $79.95. ISBN: 0442007922.

Fourteen sections cover architecture, preservation, interior design, landscape etc. 1600 periodicals are noted from professional, private and commercial sources in 57 countries. (English language or English summary only.) Full data and annotation. Lists indexes and abstracts; title and geographic indexes. *Class No:* 711(01)

[3111]

Planning and development digest. Glasgow, Planning Exchange, 1985-. £69. ISSN: 02677385.

Monthly; previously *Planning Information Digest.* Annual cumulations.

Abstracting service covering books, reports, & 300 current journals. Subject arrangement under main headings, with author & subject indexes. *Class No:* 711(01)

[3112]

SUTCLIFFE, A. The History of urban and regional planning: an annotated bibliography. London, Mansell, 1981. 284p. £30. ISBN: 0720109019.

1400 entries mainly after 1945; eight major categories - planning histories; definitions, methods; encyclopedias, guides and bibliographies; planning, international; planning by country; towns and cities; individual planners: antecedents. Name and author index. *Class No:* 711(01)

Dictionaries

[3113]

LOGIE, G., *comp*. Elsevier's dictionary of physical planning in six languages. Amsterdam, Elsevier, 1989. 468p. £95. ISBN: 0444705090.

Alphabetically in English with other language equivalents - French, Italian , Dutch, German, Swedish. Indexes in these languages to the English term. Bibliography.
Class No: 711(038)

[3114]

LOGIE, G., *ed*. International planning glossaries. Amsterdam, Elsevier, 1978-1986. 266,296,290,304,254p. (5v.). £50 per vol. ISBN: 0444417303, v.1; 0444418881, v.2; 0444420649, v.3; 0444422811, v.4; 0444426086, v.5.

Previous series published by the author 1975-81.

Volumes cover population (1978), transport (1980), employment and industry (1982), land resources (1984), planning and development (1986). Entries arranged under broad subject headings (*e.g.* vol.3 employment, minerals, extraction, energy etc.) subdivided as necessary. Short introduction to each section. *Class No:* 711(038)

Periodicals & Progress Reports

[3115]

Planning perspectives: an international journal of history, planning and the environment. London, Spon, 1986-. £145pa. ISSN: 02665433.

Issued three times pa.

Scholarly papers on the history of town and environmental planning. Book reviews are a major feature (*e.g.* vol.5 no.1. January 1990. p.95-124). *Class No:* 711(05)

[3116]

Planning week: journal of the Royal Town Planning Institute. London, RTPI, 1973-. ISSN: 13528424.

Previously *Royal Town Planning Institute Journal, The Planner.*

Professional journal featuring news, events, legal notes etc. *Class No:* 711(05)

[3117]

Town and country planning. London, Town & Country Planning Association, 1904-. £52pa. ISSN: 00409960.

Issued monthly.

Articles on current issues; reports, book reviews.
Class No: 711(05)

[3118]

Town planning review. Liverpool, University of Liverpool, 1910-. £30pa. (£60 institutional.) ISSN: 00410020.

Issued quarterly.

Scholarly, with British emphasis; usually 10-15 book reviews (700-1,000 words each) per issue.
Class No: 711(05)

Great Britain

[3119]

CULLINGWORTH, J.B. Town and country planning in Britain. 12th rev. ed. London, Routledge, 1997. 416p. £50.00. ISBN: 0415139120.

First published 1964.

Highly regarded standard textbook on environmental planning, planning controls and legislation. References & further readings; index. *Class No:* 711(410)

[3120]

MORGAN, P.H. *and* NOTT, S. Development control: law, policy and practice. 2nd.ed. London, Butterworth, 1995. xx,395p. ISBN: 0406050031.

Previous edition 1988.

Covers regional planning, city planning and redevelopment law in England and Wales; basic law expanded with examples of policy in action.
Class No: 711(410)

Yearbooks & Directories

[3121]

Directory of official architecture and planning, 1996. London, Pitman Publishing, 1995. 359p. ISBN: 027361682x.

Covers UK legislation, Parliamentary committees,

.... *(contd.)*
university departments, development and planning bodies, public services, statutory authorities, parks and tourist boards; directory of organisations. *Class No:* 711(410)(058)

Land Use

[3122]

GODFREE, S., ***comp.*** **Land use gazetteer:** the comprehensive guide to land uses and their use classes. Deal, Kent, Leaf Coppin Publishing, 1988. 224p. £18.50. ISBN: 0951342606.

Covers over 10,000 separate uses; four main sections - land use (A/Z); new classes related to old; old classes related to new; permitted development (A/Z). Appendix of statutory instruments and circulars. *Class No:* 711.14

Town Planning

Bibliographies

[3123]

DUENSING, E.E. Information sources in urban and regional planning: a directory and guide to reference materials. New Brunswick,NJ, Center for Urban Policy Research, 1994. 178p. $24.95. ISBN: 0882851462.

6 sections: dictionaries and glossaries, indexes and abstracts, directory of directories, classified directory of planning and planning-related organizations (pp.59-128), appendices (earlier bibliographic guides, online database vendors, directories of state data centers, graduate education programs), indexes by author, organization and title. *Class No:* 711.4(01)

[3124]

RUSSELL, T. The Built environment: a subject index 1800-1960. Godstone, Surrey, Gregg Publishing, 1989. 1076,1042,1114,1184p. (4v.). ISBN: 0576400068.

Volume 1: Town planning & urbanism, architecture, gardens & landscape design.

Volume 2: Environmental technology, constructional engineering, building & materials.

Volume 3: Decorative art & industrial design, international exhibitions & collections, recreation & performing arts.

Volume 4: Public health, municipal services, community welfare.

Arranged by subject categories within each volume, entries are extremely brief, often lacking full bibliographic detail. *Class No:* 711.4(01)

Handbooks & Manuals

[3125]

MILLS, E.D., ***ed.*** **Planning:** the architects' handbook. 10th ed. London, Butterworths, 1985. 658p.,illus., diagrs., tables. £69.50. ISBN: 0408012137.

First published 1936; 9th ed. 1972.

Part 1: technical data; part 2: building types; part 3: reference data including bibliography, planning data, planners, engineers, surveyors. Subject index. *Class No:* 711.4(035)

[3126]

MORRIS, E. British town planning and urban design: principles and policies. Harlow, Longman, 1997. 296p.,illus. £20.99. ISBN: 0582234964.

History and discursive treatment of how planning regulations have been applied in Great Britain. *Class No:* 711.4(035)

Histories

[3127]

GUTKIND, E.A., ***and others.*** **International history of city development.** London, Collier Macmillan. 1964-72. 8v. illus., maps.

1. *Urban development in Central Europe.* 1964. 2. *Urban development in the Alpine and Scandinavian countries.* 1965. 3/4. *Urban development in Southern Europe* (Spain and Portugal; Italy and Greece). 1967-69. 5/6. *Urban development in Western Europe* (France and Belgium; Netherlands and Great Britain). 1970-71. 7. *Urban development in East-Central Europe: Poland, Czechoslovakia and Hungary.* 1972. 8. *Urban development in Eastern Europe: Bulgaria, Romania and USSR.* 1972. V.6 (xv, 512p.) devotes chapters 5-10 to Great Britain (5. Origin and spread of settlement - 6. The Roman interlude - 7. Invasion and settlement - 8. The Middle Ages - 9. Utopia. Reality. Subtopia - 10. City survey (24 cities).). 294 captioned illus. in all. Bibliography, p.487-504 (Great Britain: 492-504). Detailed index. *Class No:* 711.4(091)

Landscape Planning

[3128]

LISNEY, A. ***and*** **FIELDHOUSE, K.** ***and*** **DODD, J.,** ***eds.*** **Landscape design guide.** Vol 1: soft landscape; Vol.2: hard landscape. Aldershot, Gower, 1990. 224,215p. (2v.). £70. ISBN: 0566090171, v.1; 0566090198, v.2.

Volume one covers planting design including selection and techniques; second volume examines paving, enclosure methods, fittings. *Class No:* 712.2

Bibliographies

[3129]

Landscape architecture sourcebook: a guide to resources on the history and practice of landscape architecture in the United States. Vogelsong, D., *ed.* Detroit, Omnigraphics, Inc., 1996. 375p. $45.00. ISBN: 0780801962.

Annotated listings of a wide range of recently published English-language publications, institutional resources, and other information sources; despite the title, there is some international coverage. Electronic formats are included - databases, network resources and discussion lists, Web sites. 10 major sections: reference works, general texts and histories, architects and firms, handbooks, plant and materials, core works on places and projects, environmental concerns, periodicals, institutional resources, computer and media resources. Chapter on 'Core works' is divided: gardens, parks and public lands, city planning/urban landscape design, landscape preservation and restoration, special projects and sites. Full bibliographic data is included, and a single paragraph annotation. Institutional resources have address, contact information and Web sites. *Class No:* 712.2(01)

[3130]

POWELL, A. Bibliography of landscape architecture, environmental design and planning. London, Mansell, 1987. 312p. £45. ISBN: 0897742508.

Very comprehensive bibliography of some 8,500 citations under one hundred subject headings. Reckoned complete 1950-1985. 'An essential reference tool' (*Choice*, March 1988). *Class No:* 712.2(01)

Handbooks & Manuals

[3131]

NELISCHER, M., ***ed.*** **Handbook of landscape architectural construction.** Volume 1: Construction. 2nd ed. Washington, Landscape Architecture Foundation, 1985. 385p., illus., diagrs., tables. $45. ISBN: 0941236099.

First published 1976; volume one of a projected 4-volume series.

12 sections provide data for the preparation & layout of construction plans. 16 named contributors. Based on US practice. Volume 2 (1988) covers Site Works; vols. 3 & 4 will deal with services & materials. *Class No:* 712.2(035)

[3132]

RUBENSTEIN, H.M. A Guide to site planning and landscape construction. 4th.ed. New York/Chichester, Wiley, 1996. x,412p.,illus.,maps. £55.00. ISBN: 0471129321.

Previous edition 1987 as 'A Guide to site and environmental planning'.

Covers landscape architecture and the planning of building areas. *Class No:* 712.2(035)

[3133]

Spon's landscape and external works price book 1998. London, Spon, 1997. 288p. £62.50. ISSN: 02674181.

Intended to assist the landscape designer or contractor; covers recent legislation, fees & preliminaries, cost information, British Standards, estimating. List of manufacturers & suppliers. Index. Quarterly *Price Book Update* available. *Class No:* 712.2(035)

Standards

[3134]

HARRIS, C. ***and*** **DINES, D.T. Time-saver standards for landscape architecture.** 2nd.ed. New York/London, McGraw-Hill, 1997. 960p. illus. £86.99. ISBN: 0070267251.

Previous edition 1988.

Covers over 50 technical topics related to landscape operations; standards, procedures, devices. 1500 illustrations. *Class No:* 712.2(083.74)

Histories

[3135]

GILG, A.W. Countryside planning: the first half century. 2nd.ed. New York/London, Routledge, 1996. xiv,291p.,illus.,maps. ISBN: 0415054893.

Previous edition 1978 (Newton Abbot: David & Charles.)

History of regional planning, rural land use, environmental policy in Great Britain. Useful maps etc. *Class No:* 712.2(091)

Recreational Planning

Dictionaries

[3136]

SMITH, S.L.J. Dictionary of concepts in recreation and leisure studies. Westport, CT, Greenwood Press, 1990. 372p. $56. ISBN: 0313252629.

Definition of terms such as 'national park', 'environment', 'holiday', 'wilderness'; entries discuss historical development of the term, different current opinions, suggested standard definition, and a bibliography usually of 10-30 scholarly sources. Cross-references; index. *Class No:* 712.25(038)

Gardens & Parks

[3137]

CROWE, S. Garden design. Woodbridge, Suffolk, Antique Collectors' Club, 1994. 296p., illus. £30.00. ISBN: 1870673085.

Thorough history, with discussion of principles and their applicability in contemporary landscape. 300 illustrations, half in colour, and additional drawings. *Class No:* 712.26

[3138]

PAUL, A. ***and*** **REES, Y. The Garden design book.** London, HarperCollins, 1992. 256p. £15.00. ISBN: 0004125932.

Suggested designs by 15 professional designers - city, country, water, entrances, paths, walls, pergolas, sculpture, awnings, trees, shrubs, grasses, ferns, bulbs, trellises, containers. 350 colour plates. *Class No:* 712.26

[3139]

VERNEY, P. ***and*** **DUNNE, M. The Genius of the garden.** London, Webb & Bower, 1989. 120p., illus. £20. ISBN: 0863502075.

Basically a discussion of garden design, looking at first principles, practical devices, ornament, planning etc. Illustration from all types of terrain and scale. *Class No:* 712.26

Bibliographies

[3140]

DESMOND, R. A Bibliography of garden history. London, Garden History Society, 1990. xvp.

Published as an appendix to *Garden History: the journal of the Garden History Society* vol.18, no.1, Spring 1990.

183 items arranged by subject, with a list of relevant libraries & record offices. *Class No:* 712.26(01)

[3141]

Garden literature: an index to periodical articles and book reviews. Boston,MA, Garden Literature Press, 1992-. 220p.(Vol.1, no.1.) $75.00. ISSN: 10613722.

Quarterly, with expected annual cumulation.

Covers specialist titles and general literature, suitable for professionals and amateurs. 'Broad range of periodicals from *Architectural digest* to the *New Yorker,* including along the way many titles devoted to environmental issues and alternative farming.' (*Choice,* 30(6) February 1993. p.939.) *Class No:* 712.26(01)

Encyclopaedias & Dictionaries

[3142]

GOODE, P. ***and*** **LANCASTER, M.,** ***eds.*** **The Oxford companion to gardens.** Oxford, OUP, 1986. 635p. illus. £32.50. ISBN: 0198661231.

Paperback edition with revisions, 1991. (0192861387; £15.00.)

Alphabetical arrangement covering garden history, garden and landscape design and designers, concepts and technical terms. Over 1500 entries, more than 700 being for individual gardens. Entries for countries outline historical development.

.... *(contd.)*
Cross-references; bibliography. 'The value of having access to information ... from all parts of the world capsulized in one volume cannot be overestimated' (*Art Libraries Journal* 12(3), 1987. p.50-52). *Class No:* 712.26(03)

Periodicals

[3143]
Journal of garden history: an international quarterly. Basingstoke, Hants, Taylor & Frances, 1981-. £114pa. ISSN: 01445170.

Documentation of individual gardens, conservation & restoration of historic gardens, aesthetics. Book reviews. *Class No:* 712.26(051)

Histories

[3144]
SYMES, M. A Glossary of garden history. Princes Risborough, Shire, 1993. 144p., illus. £6.99. ISBN: 0747802238.

Informative definitions of terms, concentrating on British gardens, and providing photographs and illustrations where neeeded. *Class No:* 712.26(091)

[3145]
THACKER, C. The History of gardens. New ed. London, Croom Helm, 1985. 288p., illus. £13.95. ISBN: 0709943156.

Traces developments from ancient ideas of 'paradise' to present day; individual gardens are identified and discussed to illustrate points. Worldwide coverage including Chinese, Japanese, Islamic, and European ideas.
Class No: 712.26(091)

[3146]
VERCELLONI, V. European gardens: an historical atlas. [Atlante storico dell'idea di giardino europeo] New York, Rizzoli, 1990. 207p., illus. ISBN: 0847812944.

Historical survey from Egyptian and Hellenistic times to the Garden City movement of the early 20th century. 200 illustrations (105 in colour) cover a wide range of periods and countries. Concepts of the garden are discussed, and the evolution of styles. Bibliography p.201-2.
Class No: 712.26(091)

Great Britain

[3147]
HADFIELD, M. A History of British gardening. 3rd ed. London, Murray, 1979. 509p. illus., plans. £15. ISBN: 0719536448.

Paperback issue 1985. First published 1960 as *Gardening in Britain.*

8 chapters: 1. From Eden to Utopia, to 1529 - 2. From Utopia to Paradise, 1530/1629 - 3. From the knot to the parterre, 1630/1659 - 4. France triumphant, 1660/1719 - 5. The landskip, 1720/1780 - 6. From picturesque to gardenesque, 1781/1840 - 7. The glorious Victorians, 1814/1882 - 8. Nature returns as science advances, 1883-1939. Footnotes. Appendix: 1939/1978 (p.431-54). Bibliographical notes (by chapters), p.455-74. Detailed index (*c.*4,000 entries), p.475-507; index to Appendix, p.508-9. 'Will for long be the standard work on gardening in England' (*Journal of the Royal Horticultural Society,* on the 1st ed.). *Class No:* 712.26(410)

[3148]
TURNER, T. English garden design: history and styles since 1650. Woodbridge, Suffolk, Antique Collectors' Club, 1986. 240p., illus. £29.95. ISBN: 0907462251.

Standard text with descriptions of gardens through the ages; theories, evolution, conflicts, major personalities. 300 illustrations, 70 in colour. *Class No:* 712.26(410)

Bibliographies

[3149]
DESMOND, R. Bibliography of British gardens. Winchester, St. Paul's Bibliographies, 1984. viii,318p. illus. £37.75. ISBN: 090679515x.

Select bibliography incorporating references from horticultural literature; 450 sources include journals, topographies, county histories. 5,500 sites included, in chronological order, ranging from botanic gardens, cemeteries, municipal parks, to private houses, stately homes. Bibliography; county index. 'Invaluable as a research tool ... most comprehensive available' (*Garden History* 13(1) Spring 1985. p.75,81).
Class No: 712.26(410)(01)

Yearbooks & Directories

[3150]
ROSE, G. *and* **KING, P.,** *eds.* **The Good gardens guide 1999:** over 1000 of the best gardens in the British Isles and Europe. London, Ebury Press, 1998. 624p., maps. £14.99. ISBN: 0091863538.

Covers gardens in the UK & Ireland, and selectively in Europe, with information on location, admission, facilities, description, seasonal features, grading. Arranged by county for UK. *Class No:* 712.26(410)(058)

[3151]
ROYAL HORTICULTURAL SOCIETY. RHS gardener's yearbook. London, Dorling Kindersley, 1997. 320p. £9.99. ISBN: 075130560x.

Issued annually; first ed. 1994.

Essential information for gardeners, including events, news, reviews, plants, products, and details of 500 gardens recommended for visiting. *Class No:* 712.26(410)(058)

Biographies

[3152]
HADFIELD, M., ***and others.*** **British gardeners:** a biographical dictionary. London, Zwemmer with Condé Nast, 1980. 320p. illus., plans. £12.50. ISBN: 0302005412.

Some 500 entries and 1,000 illustrations; good coverage of famous figures with lists of work and plans. No bibliographies; good index of names and places. Handsomely produced. *Class No:* 712.26(410)(092)

Scotland

[3153]
Gardens of Scotland. Kirkcaldy, Scotland's Garden Scheme, 1997. 164p. £3.00. ISBN: 0901549126. ISSN: 0967831x.

A guide to 350 Scottish gardens open for charity on an occasional basis. *Class No:* 712.26(411)

[3154]

LAND USE CONSULTANTS. An Inventory of gardens and designed landscapes in Scotland. Glasgow, Land Use Consultants, 1987. 35,390,329,432,434p. (5v.), illus., maps, plans. £70. ISBN: 0902226916, v.1; 0902226924, v.2; 0902226932, v.3; 0902226940, v.4; 0902226959, v.5.

Report to the Countryside Commission for Scotland, and Historic Buildings and Monuments Directorate, Scottish Development Dept. Volume one contains a summary, with bibliography. Volumes 2-5 cover: Dumfries, Galloway & Strathclyde; Highland, Orkney, & Grampian; Tayside, Central & Fife; Lothian & Borders. Within each volume, arrangement is alphabetical by garden or site. Standard entries discuss extent, historical influences, components including architectural features, woodland, walls, water etc. access, condition & potential, assessment of significance.
Class No: 712.26(411)

England & Wales

[3155]

Gardens of England and Wales open for charity 1998: a guide to 3500 gardens not normally open to the public. Guildford, National Gardens Scheme, 1998. 448p. illus., maps. £4.50. ISSN: 13650572.

Issued annually.

List of gardens occasionally open as part of the National Gardens Scheme; arranged by county, then chronological list, and alphabetical list of gardens with brief description, access & facilities. *Class No:* 712.26(42)

[3156]

HOLLIS, S. *and* **MOORE, D. The Shell guide to the gardens of England and Wales.** London, Deutsch, 1989. 400p., illus, maps. £17.95. ISBN: 0233983910.

Discusses 350 gardens of all sizes and in all types of country. Clear indication of location, opening arrangements, key features. Excellent illustrations; gazetteer.
Class No: 712.26(42)

[3157]

National Trust gardens handbook. Bromley, Kent, National Trust, 1993. 176p., illus. £4.50. ISBN: 0707802008.

Directions, maps and general information on the NT's 126 gardens. *Class No:* 712.26(42)

Environmental Protection

Yearbooks & Directories

[3158]

The Environment encyclopedia and directory: a world survey. 2nd.ed. London, Europa Publications, 1997. 500p. £210.00. ISBN: 185743028x.

International directory of 3000 governmental and non-governmental organisations with contact details, Web sites etc, brief outline of aims; A/Z by country with subject index. Who's Who with biographical details of 700 active personalities; glossary (1000 definitions); detailed maps; bibliography of over 1000 relevant journals.
Class No: 719(058)

Great Britain

Yearbooks & Directories

[3159]

Conservation sourcebook. New ed. London, HMSO for Museums & Galleries Commission, 1991. 160p. £13.95. ISBN: 0112904939.

Originally published by the Crafts Commission.

Details of UK national and regional organizations involved in the conservation of buildings and objects, including research bodies, societies, collectors' associations, quangos. Data include name, address, aims, history, publication, services, awards available. *Class No:* 719(410)(058)

[3160]

COUNTRYSIDE COMMISSION. Directory of areas of outstanding natural beauty. Cheltenham, Countryside Commission, 1989. 163p., maps (loose-leaf binder). £10.

Official listing by the CC National Parks & Planning Branch of 38 AONBs. Description, pressures, policies, documentation, management mechanisms, staffing. Conservation organizations, contacts, maps.
Class No: 719(410)(058)

[3161]

Who's who in the environment: England. Cowell, S., *ed.* London, Environment Council, 1990. 337p. ISBN: 0903158353.

Similar publication for Scotland (1989; 2nd ed.). Wales and Northern Ireland expected.

Lists organizations alphabetically (p.1-323) covering about 1,000 regional and national bodies. Contact name, address, details of publications, membership total etc.
Class No: 719(410)(058)

National Trust

[3162]

GREEVES, L. *and* **TRINICK, M. The National Trust guide.** New ed. London, National Trust. 1997. 426p. illus., maps. £24.99. ISBN: 070780261x.

Covers all NT properties in England, Wales and Northern Ireland, with full description, history, and outline of special features. *Class No:* 719:061:061.2

[3163]

NATIONAL TRUST. The National Trust handbook for members and visitors 1998. Bromley, National Trust, 1998. 320p., illus., maps. ISBN: 0707801605.

Annual.

Directory of properties, arranged by region in England (South West, South & South East, London, East, Central, North West, North East), Wales & Northern Ireland. Index by property name, and by county. Area maps at front. Brief descriptions, location, opening times, facilities.
Class No: 719:061:061.2

72 Architecture

Architecture

Bibliographies

[3164]

Architectural publications index. London, Royal Institute of British Architects, 1995-. ISSN: 13570536.

Based on the earlier *Architectural periodicals index*, issued from 1972; prior to that *RIBA library bulletin,* from 1946.

CD-ROM subject index to some 400 periodical titles from 45 countries held in the British Architectural Library. British and foreign material, covering architecture and allied arts, constructional technology, design and environmental studies, landscape, planning, and research. Some coverage of interiors, decoration, painting, sculpture, furniture etc. where relevant to architecture. 150,000 records from 1978 onwards are included on the CD-ROM, which is updated and issued quarterly. In addition, 18,000 records cover books, exhibition catalogues, technical reports, and audio-visual materials held in the BAL. *Class No:* 72.0(01)

[3165]

Avery Index to architectural periodicals. Avery Architectural Library, Columbia University. Boston, G.K. Hall, 1994-. CD-ROM. $995.00 pa. ISBN: 0783820291.

Internet access at Website <http://www.ahip.getty.edu/ahip/home.html>

Also available online on RLIN (Research LIbraries Information Network). Printed annual supplement still available (18th.ed. 1996; 4v.)

CD-ROM, updated and issued annually, contains some 150,000 records from 1977 to date. Over 700 periodicals are indexed from the US and abroad; coverage includes art history, archaeology, landscape architecture, decorative arts, interior decoration, urban planning and housing, conservation. *Class No:* 72.0(01)

[3166]

Bibliographic guide to art and architecture. Boston, G.K. Hall, 1975-. c950p. £280.00 per vol. ISSN: 03602699.

Published annually. Serves as the annual supplement to the NYPL Dictionary Catalog of the Art & Architecture Division (G.K. Hall, 1975).

Lists publications catalogued by the New York Public Library and the Library of Congress. *Class No:* 72.0(01)

[3167]

EHRESMANN, D.L. Architecture: a bibliographic guide to basic reference works, histories, and handbooks. Littleton, Col., Libraries Unlimited, 1984. 354p. £68.75. ISBN: 0872873943.

An annotated bibliography mainly of English language material; US emphasis. Covers books published 1875-1980; two sections deal with reference works and general histories and handbooks. Eight further sections offer a chronological arrangement, and the final four sections are divided geographically. Author/title and subject indexes.
Class No: 72.0(01)

[3168]

GERMAN ARCHAEOLOGICAL INSTITUTE. Rome. **Index der antiken Kunst und Architektur,** Index of ancient art and architecture. London, Saur, 1987-1991. *c.*4000 microfiche. £5,200. ISBN: 3598320701.

Microfiche series based on the Institute's collection of 300,000 photographs; covers architecture, sculpture, sarcophagi, reliefs, vases, inscriptions, mosaics, and small art objects. *c.*3,250 fiche comprise the photographic inventory, the remainder form the catalogue.
Class No: 72.0(01)

[3169]

HALL, R. de Z. A Bibliography on vernacular architecture. Newton Abbot, David & Charles, 1972. 191p.

Compiled on behalf of the Vernacular Architecture Group (currently based in Aberystwyth), which issues an irregular supplement: latest (described as Vol. 3) covers 1977-1989 and was issued in 1992. (144p.; ISBN: 0906259010)

Classified bibliography to the end of 1970 on UK domestic buildings; mainly local & regional publications. About 2,000 entries classified to cover general, regional and local studies; rural and urban buildings; construction techniques and building materials; economic & social background. Author index. *Class No:* 72.0(01)

[3170]

MACE, A. The Royal Institute of British Architects: a guide to the manuscript collection. London, Mansell, 1997. 448p., illus. £80.00. ISBN: 0720121957.

Guide to an important and fascinating collection; thorough indexing. *Class No:* 72.0(01)

[3171]

NEW YORK PUBLIC LIBRARY. Dictionary catalog of the Art and Architecture division. Boston, G.K. Hall, 1975. 30v.

Supplement 1974 (566p.; published 1975). Thereafter supplemented by the *Bibliographic guide to art and architecture.* (*q.v.*).

Almost 500,000 catalogue cards reproduced, representing over 100,000 volumes on painting, drawing, sculpture, and the history and design aspects of architecture and the applied arts - one of the largest research collections of its kind.
Class No: 72.0(01)

[3172]

NURCOMBE, V.J., *ed.* Information sources in architecture and construction. 2nd.ed. East Grinstead, Bowker Saur, 1996. 489p. £60.00. ISBN: 1857390946.

Early chapters cover information retrieval, libraries, periodicals, databases, and specialised information management. Subject chapters examine standards, geographical information systems, CAD, costings, quality assurance, contracts. Detailed bibliographical source lists.
Class No: 72.0(01)

[3173]

RIBA list of recommended books. London, RIBA Publications for the British Architectural Library, 1969-. c.50p. Gratis.

Issued annually; 1998 list is the 27th.ed.

Important summary of new literature, compiled and revised by the Professional Literature Committee, a subcommittee of the Library Board of the Royal Institute of British Architects. Over 900 entries arranged in subject categories, with A/Z index of subjects. *Class No:* 72.0(01)

[3174]

SAVAGE, N., ***and others, eds*****. Early printed books 1478-1840:** catalogue of the British Architectural Library Early Imprints Collection. East Grinstead, Bowker-Saur, 1994-. 5v. £200.00 per vol. ISBN: 1857390083, v.1.

Planned as a four-vol. set and an index vol. Vol. 1(1994), v.2(1995) and v.3(1996) available; v.4 expected 1998; index vol. expected 1999.

Catalogue of a magnificent and important collection. Complete work will include some 4000 items with full bibliographic description, especially noting illustrations. In addition to architecture, much material on related topics - heraldry, ornament, statuary etc, *Class No:* 72.0(01)

[3175]

WAYNE, K.M., ***ed*****. Architecture sourcebook:** a guide to resources on the practice of architecture. Detroit, Omnigraphics, Inc., 1997. 417p. $45.00. ISBN: 0780800249.

Part one: building types - 14 chapters covering offices, health care, cultural, government and public, housing, industrial, libraries, sport etc., giving reference sources, associations, bibliographies, periodicals; annotated listings throughout. Part two: 4 chapters on dictionaries and encyclopedias, indexes, handbooks and manuals, and periodicals for a core collection. Appendices identify architectural collections in the US, and publication sources. Author/title, and subject indexes. *Class No:* 72.0(01)

[3176]

WODEHOUSE, L. Indigenous architecture worldwide: a guide to information sources. Detroit, Gale Research, 1980. x, 392p.

About 2,000 annotated entries. Part 1: 'Indigenous architecture worldwide', p.23-230, with chapters on Africa, the Americas, Asia, Australia, and Europe, subdivided into countries. Part 2: 'The vernacular as a nineteenth century revival style and an influence in twentieth-century architecture' (4 sections: Selections of general reference works - British architects - European architects - American architects). Author, title, geographic and building location, and subject indexes. *Class No:* 72.0(01)

Encyclopaedias

[3177]

CALLOWAY, S., ***ed*****. The Elements of style:** an encyclopedia of domestic architectural detail. Rev.ed. London, Mitchell Beazley, 1996. 568p., illus. £45.00. ISBN: 1857328345.

Previous ed. 1991.

Respected guide to architectural decoration; fine illustrations; bibliography p.557-9. *Class No:* 72.0(031)

[3178]

Encyclopedia of architecture: design, engineering and construction. Wilkes, J.A., *ed*. New York, Wiley, 1988-1990. 4,000p. (5v). £779.00. ISBN: 0471633518.

Sponsored by the American Institute of Architects, this set has become a standard source. Emphasizes processes and technology, but also covers history, aesthetics and biography. Specialist contributors, numerous bibliographies, illustrations and tables. Volume 5 (pp.442-659) contains an updating supplement and general index to the set. 'The range of subjects it attempts to cover is both disparate and questionable'. (*Architectural Review*, CLXXXIV, no.1102, Dec. 1988, p.10). *Class No:* 72.0(031)

[3179]

FLEMING, J., ***ed*****. The Penguin dictionary of architecture.** 4th ed. Harmondsworth, Middx, Penguin, 1991. 512p. illus., plans. £6.99. ISBN: 0140512411.

First published 1966.

Entries for terms, countries, styles, movements, biographies, etc. and cross-references. Small but clear line-drawings. No bibliographies. A bargain.
Class No: 72.0(031)

[3180]

OLIVER, P., ***ed*****. Encyclopedia of vernacular architecture of the world.** Cambridge, Cambridge University Press, 1997. 2500p.(3v.), illus. £695.00. ISBN: 0521564220.

The work of over 750 contributors from 80 countries. V.1: approaches and concepts; cultural traits and attributes; environment; materials and resources; production and components; service systems; symbolism and decoration, typologies; uses and functions. V.2: Asia; Australia and Oceania; Europe and Eurasia; Mediterranean & S.W. Asia. V.3: Latin America; North America; Sub-Saharan Africa. Lexicon of 500 terms used in vernacular architecture; glossary of 1200 specialist terms; bibliography of over 9000 items. Almost 3000 illustrations, including 1000 diagrams.
Class No: 72.0(031)

[3181]

SHARP, D., ***ed*****. The Illustrated dictionary of architects and architecture.** London, Headline, 1991. 256p. £19.95. ISBN: 0747202710.

Two-thirds of the book form a biographical dictionary, well-stocked with detail on post-1550 practitioners; the final third is a sound general history of architecture, superbly illustrated. Useful cross-references from biographies to history. *Class No:* 72.0(031)

[3182]

VYNCKT, R.J.V. International dictionary of architects and architecture. London, St.James Press/Detroit, Gale Research, 1993. 1115,1046p.(2v.). £175.00. ISBN: 1558620893.

Volume 1: 523 biographies, with chronology, bibliography, signed critical essay. Volume 2: 467 individual buildings discussed, in chronological arrangement. 1000 photographs (of disappointing quality) and plans. No cross-references between volumes; citation methods poor. 'Most essays are excellent, with pithy summaries.' (*Choice*, 31(6) February 1994. p916.) *Class No:* 72.0(031)

[3183]

YARWOOD, D., ***ed*****. Encyclopedia of architecture.** New ed. London, Batsford, 1993. 448p. £19.99. ISBN: 0713473762.

A reasonable treatment, with British emphasis. Over 1,200 entries, A-Z. Longer articles (*e.g.* Country houses) include a glossary. Cross references; over 200 photographs and 800 line drawings. 4,000 index entries. *Class No:* 72.0(031)

Handbooks & Manuals

[3184]
BRERETON, C. The Repair of historic buildings: advice on principles and methods. 2nd.ed. London, English Heritage, 1995. 67p., illus. ISBN: 1850745277.

Previous ed. 1991.

Good basic guide to the conservation and restoration of buildings. Bibliography p64-67. *Class No:* 72.0(035)

[3185]
SALISBURY, F. The Architect's handbook for client briefing. London, Butterworth, 1990. 212p. illus. £27.50. ISBN: 0408500204.

Detailed guidance on the architect-client relationship, setting out essential activities, liaison between design team and client organization. *Class No:* 72.0(035)

Dictionaries

[3186]
BUCHER, W., *ed*. Dictionary of building preservation. New York/Chichester, Wiley, 1996. 560p., illus. £30.00. ISBN: 0471144134.

Extensive list of terms relating to all aspects of preservation; bibliography p.555-560. *Class No:* 72.0(038)

[3187]
CHING, F.D.K. A Visual dictionary of architecture. New York, Van Nostrand, 1995. 320p., illus. £26.00. ISBN: 0442009046.

Terms grouped into large sectors: design, hardware, history, ornament etc; definitions are thus provided in a context of related terms. Each definition is accompanied by a line drawing. *Class No:* 72.0(038)

[3188]
CURL, J.S. Encyclopaedia of architectural terms. Donhead St. Mary, Donhead, 1993. 364p., illus. £47.50. ISBN: 1873394047.

Reprinted in paperback 1997; same ISBN.

Definitions ranging from two words to four pages in length, with line drawings or photographs on almost every page. All example are British. Cross-references are frequent, and can be difficult to follow as arrows are used to signal them; locations of illustrations are not always easy to trace - they are sometimes grouped away from the individual entries. Four-page select bibliography follows the main text. *Class No:* 72.0(038)

[3189]
FORBES, J.R. Dictionary of architecture and construction: French/English and English/French. 2nd ed. Paris, Technique & Documentation (Lavoisier), 1988. 416p. $175. ISBN: 2852064448.

23,000 entries covering a wide range of topics including historic architecture, traditional techniques, tools, machinery, conservation, civil engineering, town planning, quantity control, soil mechanics etc. Alphabetical listing of keywords and compounds with related terms. Appendices cover standards, timbers, bricks. *Class No:* 72.0(038)

[3190]
GELBRICH, U. Dictionary of architecture and building: English-German. Amsterdam, Elsevier, 1989. 418p. £94. ISBN: 0444988645.

30,000 terms and compound words relating to architecture, building, carpentry, joinery, heating, plumbing, lighting, materials etc. List of abbreviations. *Class No:* 72.0(038)

[3191]
GRECH, C., *ed*. Multilingual dictionary of architecture and building terms. London, E.& F.N.Spon, 1996. 384p. £40.00. ISBN: 0419199209.

Efficient and comprehensive; clear layout. *Class No:* 72.0(038)

[3192]
HARRIS, C.M., *ed*. Dictionary of architecture and construction. 2nd ed. New York, McGraw-Hill, 1993. 924p., illus. £40.00. ISBN: 0070268886.

The work of 52 expert contributors; 20,000 entries illustrated by 2,000 line drawings. Covers design, appearance, installation, ceramic surfaces, landscape architecture, ancient and classical styles, mediaeval, renaissance, and modern periods. *Class No:* 72.0(038)

[3193]
LEVER, J. *and* HARRIS, J. Illustrated dictionary of architecture 800-1914. 2nd.ed. London, Faber, 1993. 218p. illus. £40.00. ISBN: 0571137652.

First ed. 1966 as *Illustrated glossary of architecture 850-1830.*

Alphabetically listed terms p.1-44; each is explained by the use of illustrations of UK buildings (plates p.47-218). This ed. has been reset; contains about 1000 terms, with extended coverage on the period 1830-1914; excellent photographs and drawings. *Class No:* 72.0(038)

[3194]
VANDENBERGHE, J.P., *comp*. Elsevier's dictionary of architecture in five languages. Amsterdam, Elsevier, 1988. 519p. illus. £90. ISBN: 0444429328.

English base, listing other language equivalents - French, Spanish, German and Dutch. Indexes of terms in these languages cross-referenced to the English. Covers architects office practice, planning, techniques, elements of building, ornamentation. Bibliography. *Class No:* 72.0(038)

Periodicals & Progress Reports

[3195]
Architect's journal. London, Architectural Press Ltd., 1895-. £90pa. ISSN: 00038466.

Issued weekly.

Although primarily a news and features magazine, a small number of signed book reviews is usually included. *Class No:* 72.0(05)

[3196]
Architectural review. London, Architectural Press, 1897-. £55pa. ISSN: 0003861x.

Issued monthly.

Usually includes 5 or 6 substantial book reviews (1,500 words) in addition to new product reviews, and major theme-related features. *Class No:* 72.0(05)

Yearbooks & Directories

[3197]
International architecture yearbook. Mulgrave, Vic, Australia, Images Publishing Group, 1997. 416p., illus. ISBN: 1875498877.

1997 ed. is described as 'no.4.'

International review of the leading architectural projects of the year; over 600 photographs, drawings etc. Critical appraisal is included; over 100 architects are featured in this ed. *Class No:* 72.0(058)

[3198]

ROYAL INSTITUTE OF BRITISH ARCHITECTS. International directory of practices. London, RIBA. ISSN: 02690837.

Revised regularly.

Classified chart of practices by expertise or specialization. Alphabetical list of practices. Geographical listing (by country); name & basic contact data. *Class No:* 72.0(058)

Drawings

[3199]

ROYAL INSTITUTE OF BRITISH ARCHITECTS. Catalogues of the drawings collection of the Royal Institute of British Architects. Aldershot, Gregg, 1969-89. 20v.

Catalogues of the general collection were issued in 8 volumes 1969-84, each priced at £95.00 and containing illustrations. A further 11 volumes cover the special collections (*e.g.* Edwin Lutyens, 1973; Inigo Jones & John Webb, 1973). A cumulated index was issued in 1989 (£225.00; ISBN: 0576400041; 602p.).
Class No: 72.0(084.11)

[3200]

TEAGUE, E.H., *comp*. World architecture index: a guide to illustrations. Westport,CT, Greenwood Press, 1991. 447p. ISBN: 0313225524.

7000 illustrations indexed from 108 standard English-language architectural books published from the late 1950s onwards. All styles and eras, but mainly Western. Indexes by site, architect, building type, specific structures.
Class No: 72.0(084.11)

Chronologies

[3201]

YARWOOD, D. A Chronology of western architecture. New York, Facts on File, 1988. 224p. $29.95. ISBN: 0816018618.

Unique format describes architectural developments with facing page showing political, scientific and cultural events. Sketches and plans; useful if sometimes idiosyncratic.
Class No: 72.0(090)

Histories

[3202]

FLETCHER, B. A History of architecture.
Cruickhank, D., *ed.* 20th.ed. Oxford, Architectural Press, 1996. xxxviii,1794p., illus. £75.00. ISBN: 0750622679.

First published 1896.

Sir Bannister Fletcher's work has long been regarded as the standard historical source; over one third of this edition is new. Part 1 - Egypt, Near East, Asia, Greece, Hellenistic kingdoms; part 2 - Europe and Mediterranean to Renaissance (including prehistoric, Rome, Russia); part 3 - Islam; part 4 - pre-colonial cultures outside Europe; part 5 - Renaissance and after in Europe and Russia; part 6 - colonial and post-colonial periods outside Europe (Africa, Americas, China, Japan/Korea, S.E.Asia, India/Pakistan, Australasia); part 7 - 20th century (international, extending in total to 350p.) Glossary; bibliography p.1671-1712 arranged by the 58 chapters; detailed index p.1731-1794 (close printed, 3 column.). 18 colour plates and 850 pages of photographs, drawings, maps etc. Chronological tables.
Class No: 72.0(091)

[3203]

HARPER, R.H. Victorian architectural competitions: an index to British and Irish architectural competitions in *The Builder* 1843-1900. London, Mansell, 1983. xxxviii,416p. £35. ISBN: 0720116856.

Substantial introduction giving background data, followed by the index: part 1- geographical; part 2- architects & assessors; part 3- building types. Bibliography; chronology.
Class No: 72.0(091)

[3204]

JONG, C. *and* MATTIE, E. Architectural competitions. Cologne, Taschen, 1994. 740p.(2v.) £50.00. ISBN: 3822889296.

Volume 1: 1792-1947; volume 2: 1947-1993. Chronological arrangement, international scope. Over 1500 illustrations and plans. Bibliography and index.
Class No: 72.0(091)

[3205]

NUTTGENS, P. The Story of architecture. 2nd.ed. London, Phaidon, 1997. 352p., illus. £25.00. ISBN: 071483615x.

Revised and expanded, new maps, time charts, and biographies; layout has been redesigned with many new illustrations. Nuttgens' style is clear and very readable, and concentrates on the human element in architecture. Coverage is international, of all periods; generally impressive. Over 400 illustrations; good bibliography. *Class No:* 72.0(091)

[3206]

Pelican history of art. Harmondsworth, Penguin Books, 1953-.

From 1992 taken over by Yale University Press. *See* entry at 7.0(091) for fuller details.

Many volumes in this extraordinarily important series are concerned in whole or part with the history of architecture.
Class No: 72.0(091)

[3207]

PEVSNER, N. A History of building types. London, Thames & Hudson, 1997. 352p., illus. £29.95. ISBN: 0500271747.

Re-issue of the 1976 original.

Covers national monuments, government buildings (by period), theatres, libraries, museums, hospitals, prisons, hotels, exchanges/banks, warehouses, railway stations, market halls, exhibition buildings, shops and stores, factories. Idiosyncratic, but perceptive commentary; bibliography; abundance of monochrome illustration.
Class No: 72.0(091)

[3208]

PEVSNER, N. An Outline of European architecture. New ed. London, Penguin, 1990. 496p. illus. ISBN: 0140135243.

First published 1943. 7th ed. published 1963.

Chronological arrangement of chapters covering fourth century AD to the 1950s. A standard, authoritative work in a convenient, single-volume format. Excellent narrative text, but illustrations (monochrome) although adequate are poor by current standards. Glossary, with line drawings, p.473-5; bibliography p.457-470, arranged by period and country.
Class No: 72.0(091)

[3209]

PORTOGHESI, P., *ed*. Dizionario enciclopedico di architectura e ubanistica. Rome, Instituto Editoriale Romano, 1968-9. 6v., illus., plates, plans, diagrams.

Scholarly approach to historical architecture; signed articles by 114 contributors. Entries include over 8000 biographies, also building types, terms, concepts, styles, principal cities (500 entries), geographical areas, ethnic

....*(contd.)*
groups. 'Indispensable as a reference tool for architectural historians' (Arntzen & Rainwater *Guide to the literature of art history* (1980) J29). *Class No:* 72.0(091)

[3210]
WATKIN, D. A History of Western architecture. 2nd.ed. London, Calmann & King, 1996. 608p., illus. £19.95. ISBN: 1856690822.

First ed. published 1986.

Takes a Marxist view of architecture as a living continuity, not a museum of styles and revivals. Chapters are arranged in a broad chronology, with almost half the book concentrating on the 19th.century onwards. This ed. contains chapters on Modernism after 1945, post-Modernism, architecture for the millennium; Nearly 800 excellent illustrations, some 50 in colour. Glossary; bibliography.
Class No: 72.0(091)

[3211]
World atlas of architecture. London, Mitchell Beazley, 1984. 408p. illus., maps, charts, diagrams. £29.95. ISBN: 0855335408.

First published 1981 as *Le Grand Atlas de l'Architecture Mondiale* (Paris) which was partly based on Mitchell Beazley's *Great Architecture of the world* (1975).

Six main sections: non-European civilizations, ancient world, late antiquity & early mediaeval, mediaeval, age of classicism, modern era. 725 photographs, 111 reproductions, 36 maps, 20 charts, 174 architectural plans. Glossary; index; chronological tables; subject index.
Class No: 72.0(091)

Bibliographies

[3212]
WHITTINGTON, C. Architectural history: a core collection. *Reference Services Review* 15(2) 1987. p.37-45.

Introductory section leads to an annotated list featuring several encyclopedias and dictionaries, biographies, guides and handbooks, bibliographies, and published indexes.
Class No: 72.0(091)(01)

Biographies

[3213]
Avery obituary index of architects. Avery Architectural Library, Columbia University. 2nd ed. Boston, G.K. Hall, 1980. 530p. ISBN: 0816110689.

Now incorporated into *Avery Index of Architectural Periodicals.*

Over 17,000 entries; worldwide coverage, and including significant art historians, archaeologists, city planners.
Class No: 72.0(092)

[3214]
EMANUEL, M., *ed.* Contemporary architects. 3rd ed. New York/London, St. James' Press, 1994. 1125p., illus. £100.00. ISBN: 1558621822.

First edition 1980.

585 entries; 70 are new to this ed. and existing entries have been updated. Includes living architects and influential names from the past. Substantial entries are written by authoritative contributors and include biographical data, awards received, list of works and projects, major exhibitions, publications by and about the architect, critical appraisal, and photograph of at least one representative work. Now includes engineers, theorists, and landscape

....*(contd.)*
architects; cross references to names in earlier eds. Index of major buildings arranged geographically by country.
Class No: 72.0(092)

[3215]
FELSTEAD, A. *and* **FRANKLIN, J.** *and* **PINFIELD, L.,** *comps.* **Directory of British architects, 1834-1900.** London, RIBA/Mansell, 1993. 1035p. £165.00. ISBN: 0720121582.

7000 names are included, with details of dates, addresses, professional achievements, bibliographic references. Excellent for minor architects. *Class No:* 72.0(092)

[3216]
PLACZEK, A.K., *ed.* **The Macmillan encyclopedia of architects.** London, Macmillan, 1982. 2,400p. (4v). £312.00. ISBN: 0029250005.

A source for all areas and periods; distinguished panel of advisors. All aspects of work are covered, including engineers, planners. Over 2,450 biographies; signed entries by over 600 contributors, with list of main works. Glossary: 1,000 illustrations; indexes contain over 20,000 entries. Marred by some poor editing, especially in the index.
Class No: 72.0(092)

[3217]
VYNCKT, R.J.V. International dictionary of architects and architecture. London, St.James Press/Detroit, Gale Research, 1993. 1115,1046p.(2v.) £175.00. ISBN: 1558620893.

Substantial biographical element; *see* fuller entry at 72.0(031). *Class No:* 72.0(092)

Laws

[3218]
GREENSTREET, R. *and* **CHAPPELL, D.,** *eds.* **Legal and contractual procedures for architects.** 3rd ed. London, Butterworth, 1990. 112p. illus. £16.95. ISBN: 0408040777.

A sourcebook of practical information featuring various checklists, diagrams, forms, case studies.
Class No: 72.0(094.1)

Europe

[3219]
SACHAR, B. Atlas of European architecture. New York, Van Nostrand Reinhold, 1984. xi, 369p. $37.95. ISBN: 0442281498.

Arranged by country, then city, with chronological listings of buildings giving copious detail and photograph. Well indexed, including architect and artist index.
Class No: 72.0(4)

[3220]
YARWOOD, D. The Architecture of Europe: the nineteenth and twentieth centuries. London, Batsford, 1991. 192p., illus. £19.95. ISBN: 0713466057.

Narrative survey noting how the technical advances and possibilities of the period are reflected in architecture.
Class No: 72.0(4)

Bibliographies

[3221]
SAGVARI, A., *ed*. The Capitals of Europe: a guide to the sources for the history of their architecture and construction. Munich, K.G. Saur, 1980. 359p., illus.

Sponsored by the International Council on Archives.

Covers 28 cities: Amsterdam, Ankara, Athens, Belgrade, Berlin, Bern, Bonn, Brussels, Bucharest, Budapest, Copenhagen, Dublin, Helsinki, Lisbon, London, Madrid, Moscow, Nicosia, Oslo, Paris, Prague, Reykjavik, Rome, Sofia, Stockholm, Valetta, Vienna, Warsaw. Section bibliographies plus notes on documentary sources. 14 statistical tables. 104 plates. *Class No:* 72.0(4)(01)

Great Britain

[3222]
COLVIN, H.M., *ed*. The History of the King's Works. London, HMSO.1963-82. 6v., illus., plans.

1-2: *The Middle Ages*, 1963. xxv, xiv, 1139p.

3-4: *1485-1660*. 1975-82. xxv. 469p. + xxviii, 826p.

5: *1660-1782*. 1976. xxiv, 535p.

6: *The period of reform and experiment, 1782-1851*. 1973. xxvii, 744, [66]p.

An exhaustive, lavishly illustrated history of all public buildings for government, defence, royal pleasure and worship in England (and Wales) from before the Norman Conquest up to the mid-19th century. V.1-2 carry a separate portfolio of folding plans on Dover Castle, Tower of London, Westminster Palace and Windsor Castle. V.1 has a chapter, 'The King's Works in Wales, 1277-1330', also available separately. V.3 includes a pt.4, 'The King's Works in France'. Seven large-scale plans accompany the series.

'An unrivalled & authoritative source book and reference work for historians of politics and of the building professions' (*British book news*, June 1983, p.378).
Class No: 72.0(410)

[3223]
Historic buildings in Britain: Royal Commissions on ancient and historic monuments and constructions England/Scotland/ Wales. Cambridge, Chadwyck-Healey, 1985. 333 microfiche. £1,180.

7,500 photographs with text from the inventories of the Commissions 1910-1979, describing remains pre-1714 arranged by parish. Includes 70 published volumes containing maps, plans and photographs.
Class No: 72.0(410)

Bibliographies

[3224]
HARRIS, E. *and* SAVAGE, N., *ed*. British architectural books and writers 1556-1785. Cambridge, CUP, 1990. 528p. illus. £75. ISBN: 0521385512.

Comprehensive and scholarly survey of a complex and uncharted wealth of material. Essential for historians, collectors. Substantial general introduction on bibliographical history; entries for 220 authors with biographical essay (lengths vary from 100-6,000 words) and list of publications in all known editions - about 1,000 books in total from 400 titles. Locations in UK & US libraries noted. Chronological list of titles; extensive name, place & subject index.
Class No: 72.0(410)(01)

[3225]
KAMEN, R.H. British and Irish architectural history: a bibliography and guide to sources of information. London, Architectural Press, 1981. 249p. £30. ISBN: 0851390773.

Selective, annotated bibliography containing 870 entries systematically arranged, cross-referenced, and indexed. Covers published and unpublished sources, periodicals. Lists of photographic collections, archives, slide libraries. 'A major sourcebook for the architectural historian' (*Garden History* 11(1) Spring 1983, p.88). *Class No:* 72.0(410)(01)

Biographies

[3226]
COLVIN, H.M. A Biographical dictionary of British architects 1600-1840. 3rd. ed. New Haven/London, Yale University Press for the Paul Mellon Centre for Studies in British Art, 1995. 1248p. £60.00. ISBN: 0300060912.

First published 1954 as *A Biographical Dictionary of English Architecture 1660-1840*.

Fully revised with over 150 new entries; now covers 2000 architects who practiced in England, Scotland and Wales. Introductory historical essay, then alphabetical listing with personal and professional data, including important buildings, brief assessment, references to illustrations and published descriptions, and bibliographies. Useful appendices; indexes of persons, buildings, and places.
Class No: 72.0(410)(092)

[3227]
ROYAL INSTITUTE OF BRITISH ARCHITECTS. British architectural biography 1834-1914. London, RIBA, 1988-.

A project to create an on-line database of RIBA nomination papers filled in by architects 1834 onwards. Gives names, addresses, date of election. From 1870 includes description of professional education, and a list of buildings designed. *Class No:* 72.0(410)(092)

Scotland

[3228]
FAWCETT, R. The Architectural history of Scotland. Edinburgh, Edinburgh University Press, 1994. 350p. £35.00. ISBN: 0748604650.

First of a proposed series of 7 volumes.

Comprehensive survey of the late 14th - 16th centuries, looking in detail at specific building types - cathedrals, churches, castles and palaces - and relating these to changing social patterns and outside architectural influences. 200 illustrations and plans. *Class No:* 72.0(411)

[3229]
McKEAN, C., *ed*. Illustrated architectural guides. Edinburgh, Rutland Press, 1986-. ISBN: 1873190255, (West Lothian vol.).

'Landmark Trust Series' issued with the collaboration of RIAS (Royal Incorporation of Architects in Scotland) and with various other editors in addition to McKean. 28 vols. cover the whole of Scotland, and some have in appeared in 2nd.eds.

Selective guides in a pocket-sized format; valuable for their high standard of work and reliable information.
Class No: 72.0(411)

[3230]

PEVSNER, N., ***ed.*** **The Buildings of Scotland.** Harmondsworth, Penguin, 1978-. £30.00 per vol.

An 11 volume series. General chapters on types of building in the area are followed by a descriptive gazetteer of buildings, towns and villages, churches, public buildings, villas, farms. Glossary; index of plates; index of artists; index of places. Pocket-sized. Volumes so far published are *Lothian* (1978), *Edinburgh* (1984), *Fife* (1988), *Glasgow* (1990), *Highlands and Islands* (1992); remaining volumes will cover *Borders; Grampian; Strathclyde North and Central; Strathclyde South; Tayside; Dumfries and Galloway*. *Class No:* 72.0(411)

Ireland

[3231]

CRAIG, M. The Architecture of Ireland, from the earliest times to 1880. 2nd ed. London, Batsford/Dublin, Eason, 1989. 358p., illus. £17.95. ISBN: 0713425873.

Chapters cover chronological periods and building types; bibliography and index. *Class No:* 72.0(415)

[3232]

PEVSNER, N., ***ed.*** **The Buildings of Ireland.** Harmondsworth, Penguin. 1979-. £30.00 per vol.

Series of 9 volumes devoted to a comprehensive survey of Ireland's buildings. Each of the country's 32 counties will be dealt with, allowing 1v. to Dublin, city and county, and 2v. each to Ulster, Munster, Leinster and Connaught.

Volumes so far published are *North-West Ulster* (1979), and *North Leinster* (1993). *Class No:* 72.0(415)

Biographies

[3233]

LOEBER, R. A Biographical dictionary of architects in Ireland 1600-1720. London, John Murray, 1981. 127p. ISBN: 0719538327.

Alphabetical by name, giving personal and professional data and listing all significant buildings. Bibliographic references; index of person & places.
Class No: 72.0(415)(092)

England

[3234]

PEVSNER, N., ***ed.*** **The Buildings of England.** Harmondsworth, Penguin, 1966-1996. 33v., illus. £35.00 per vol.

Comprehensive and respected pocket-sized county series, each arranged A/Z by place with descriptions of buildings. Glossary; indexes to plates, persons, and places.

The original series is gradually being revised and republished in a taller format, with improvements to the illustrations; although the series is now apparently complete, new eds. will continue to appear.

A CD-ROM index is available to the series; this allows access by category of building, place names, period, artist, specific features etc. and is sold by the compiler (M. Good, 11 Australia Court, Oxford Road, Cambridge CB3 0JA, UK; £100.00.) *Class No:* 72.0(420)

Glossaries

[3235]

CURL, J.S. English architecture: an illustrated glossary. 2nd ed. Newton Abbot, David & Charles, 1986. 192p. illus., plans. £10.95. ISBN: 0715388878.

Concise alphabetical listing, illustrated with photographs, drawings and diagrams. Includes many Scottish terms. Five-column entry for *symbol* lists motifs, and their meaning or referents. *Class No:* 72.0(420)(038.1)

Histories

[3236]

TAYLOR, H.M. *and* **TAYLOR, J. Anglo-Saxon architecture.** Cambridge, University Press, 1965-78. 1118p.(3v.), illus., maps. £110 (vol. 1 & 2); £75 (vol. 3). ISBN: 0521066115, v. 1 & 2; 0521216923, v.3.

Paperback edition of vols. 1 & 2 issued 1981; new paperback edition 1984.

An inventory, concerned with the architecture of churches, with a few brief references to monastic sites where excavation has given reliable evidence about domestic buildings. Thus v.3 (xx, 735-1116p.) has 19 chapters (1-4, introductory; 5. Major arches - 6. Doorways - 7. Windows ... 9. Towers ... 15. Anglo-Saxon church plans ... 17. Decoration ... 19. Dating sequences and date ranges) and concentrates on principal architectural features and ornament of 267 Anglo-Saxon churches. Appendices: addenda & corrigenda to v.1-2, bibliography, p.1087-92, and analytical index to all 3 v. 112pl., 178 tables.

V.1-2 available in reduced-format paperback and covering 415 Anglo-Saxon buildings, are intended as a field guide. The whole is the definitive work on the subject.
Class No: 72.0(420)(091)

Wales

[3237]

PEVSNER, N., ***ed.*** **The Buildings of Wales.** Harmondsworth, Penguin, 1979-. £30.00.per vol.

A series to be completed in 6 volumes. Volumes for *Clwyd, Glamorgan* and *Powys* are available; forthcoming volumes will cover *Dyfed; Gwent; Gwynnedd.*

Volumes in the series examine prehistoric and Roman remains, and all surviving buildings of importance from all periods. Gazetteer; architectural glossary; language glossary. Indexes of plates; architects, etc. *Class No:* 72.0(429)

USSR

[3238]

BRUMFIELD, W.C. A History of Russian architecture. Cambridge, Cambridge University Press, 1993. 644p. £65.00. ISBN: 0521403332.

Some of the text originally issued as *Gold in azure,* 1984.

Excellent photographs, plans etc. Meticulous documentation. 'Encyclopedic in length and exhaustive in its treatment.' (*Choice,* 31(10) June 1994. p1568.)
Class No: 72.0(47)

[3239]

FAENSEN, H. *and* **IVANOV, V. Early Russian architecture.** London, Elek, 1975. 536p., illus. £25. ISBN: 0236176307.

A definitive guide to the period 1,000-1,700 when most work depended on the church. Part one explains design and decoration of churches, influence of the liturgy, development of arts from Byzantine origins to native forms. Part two lists

.... (contd.)

and describes every major building or monument, with background and plans. 420 plates, over 80 in colour. Bibliography p.516-527. *Class No:* 72.0(47)

[3240]

HAMILTON, G.A. The Art and architecture of Russia. 3rd ed. Harmondsworth, Penguin, 1983. 488p.,illus. £16.95. (*Pelican History of Art.*) ISBN: 0140561064.

First published 1954.

5 parts: 1. Kievan Russian - 2. Icon-painting - 3. The art of Muscovy - 4. St. Petersburg - 5. Modern Russian art, 1814-1971. Chapter notes, general bibliography (with brief annotations), analytical index. *Class No:* 72.0(47)

Balkan States

[3241]

CURČIĆ, S. Art and architecture in the Balkans: an annotated bibliography. Boston, G.K. Hall, 1984. xxv,427p. £65. ISBN: 0816183260.

Covers mediaeval art and architecture in four main sections: Balkans, Albania, Bulgaria, Yugoslavia, each subdivided by architecture, painting, sculpture, minor arts, iconography etc. Lists of principal bibliographical sources and periodicals. Author and general index.
Class No: 72.0(497)

India

[3242]

ACHARYA, P.K. An Encyclopedia of Hindu architecture. Bhopal, J.K. Publishing House, 1978. xxiv,684p.

First published in 1927 under the title; *Indian architecture according to Manasara-Silpa-Sastra and a dictionary of Hindu architecture*. (Bombay, OUP).

Based on a text and rendering of the classical Indian architect Mansara (Ca 500-700 AD). It is a monumental work with 3,000 terms relating to architecture, sculpture and cognate arts found in Mansara. About 25% of them are architectural terms of importance. Each entry is illustrated with copious quotations from the ancient literature of India; sources are both literary and archaeological.
Class No: 72.0(540)

[3243]

The Penguin guide to the monuments of India. Michell, G. *and* Davies, P., *eds*. New ed. Harmondsworth, Penguin, 1990. 520,606p. (2v.), illus. £30 per vol. ISBN: 067080696x, v.1; 0670808474, v.2.

Volume one deals with Buddhist, Hindu and Jain cultures (G. Michell); volume two covers Islamic, Rajput and European (P. Davies). *Class No:* 72.0(540)

Dictionaries

[3244]

NATH, R. Jharokha: an illustrated glossary of Indo-Muslim architecture. Jaipur, Historical Research Documentation Programme, 1985. 128p., illlus.

Lists 1386 Arabic, Persian, Sanskrit, Hindi and English terms. Several illustrations; detailed index.
Class No: 72.0(540)(038)

Histories

[3245]

FERGUSON, J. History of Indian and Eastern architecture. Burgers, J. *and* Spiers, P., *eds*. New ed. New Delhi, Munshiram Manoharlal. 1976. 2v., illus.

First edition 1967.

Divided into 9 books. (Vol.1). Book I. Buddhist architecture - Book II. Architecture in the Himalayas - Book III. Dravidian Style - Book IV. Chalkyan Style. (Vol.2): Book V. Jaina architecture - Book VI - Northern or Indo-Aryan Style - Book VII. Indian Saracenic architecture. Book VIII. Further India - Book IX. China and Japan. Profusely illustrated with photographs, line drawings and sketches.
Class No: 72.0(540)(091)

[3246]

TADGELL, C. History of architecture in India. London, Phaidon, 1993. 408p. £19.95. ISBN: 0714829609.

Draws together the elements of Vedic and native traditions, Hindu, Buddhist, Islamic, and secular architecture, and the British Raj. Over 500 illustrations.
Class No: 72.0(540)(091)

Pakistan

[3247]

MUMTAZ, K.K. Architecture in Pakistan. Singapore, Concept Media Ltd., 1985. 206p., illus. ISBN: 997184141x.

Concisely presents the history of architecture in the area now in Pakistan from 2500 BC to contemporary period, through the Moughal (14th century) to the British India monuments and bringing it up to date to 1980s. Profusely illustrated with over 230 black and white architectural plans. Closes with a glossary of terms, a chronology and an index of places, people and building types. Provides a bibliography of 100 references. *Class No:* 72.0(549)

Islamic World

Bibliographies

[3248]

CRESWELL, K.A.C. A Bibliography of the architecture, art, and crafts of Islam to 1960. Cairo, American University at Cairo Press, 1961. 1330p.

Supplement 1960-1972 (366p) issued 1973.

Part 1 (architecture) divided by country (p.1-478). Part 2 (arts & crafts) divided by craft, material and country (p.479-1330). Author index. *Class No:* 72.0(5.297)(01)

Dictionaries

[3249]

PETERSEN, A. Dictionary of Islamic architecture. London, Routledge, 1996. 342p., illus. ISBN: 0415060842.

Covers all periods, and all locations from West Africa through the Middle East to Indonesia, and includes Islamic influence throughout the world. A/Z arrangement of 500 entries - artistic, technical, archaeological, cultural, biographical - fully cross-referenced and indexed. Definitions of building types, descriptions of specific monuments, summaries of regional styles; brief bibliography with each entry. Plans and sketch maps included. 'Indispensible reference tool for all academics, students and researchers involved in the study of Islamic architecture and archaeology.' (*Reference reviews*, 10(5), 1996; p28-9.)
Class No: 72.0(5.297)(038)

Canada

[3250]

Art and architecture in Canada: a bibliography/Bibliographie sur l'art et l'architecture au Canada. Singer, L. *and* Williamson, M., *eds.* Montreal, Concordia University, 1985-.

Aims to list over 9,000 books, articles, exhibition catalogues, and theses, published 1820-1981, covering Canadian, Indian, and Inuit art, folk arts, decorative arts, photography, museums, government & the arts, art education. Classified arrangement. *Class No:* 72.0(71)

USA

[3251]

America preserved: a checklist of historic buildings, structures, and sites. 2nd.ed. Washington, DC, Library of Congress, Cataloging Distribution Service, 1995. 1152p., illus. $79.00. ISBN: 0160452554.

First ed. as *Historic America*, 1983.

The *National Register of Historic Places (see* entry below) is the standard reference source; *America preserved*, which is more comprehensive, is an updated ed. of the Checklist that provides access to the *Historic American Buildings Survey (see* entry below) and the *Historic American Engineering Record*. This ed. adds 14,000 entries and gives more documentation for each site, but has fewer illustrations and lacks the essays on preservation which appeared in the 1983 ed. *Class No:* 72.0(73)

[3252]

Historic American buildings survey. Cambridge, Chadwyck Healey, 1984. 1567 microfiche. $6,500.

Certain sections (*e.g.* Victoria County, District of Columbia) available in print from University Press of Virginia.

45,000 photographs and 35,000 pages of text covering 20,000 sites and structures throughout the US. Compiled from Library of Congress Prints and Photographs Division Archives, and containing the entire *National Register of Historic Places.*(*See* entry below.) 'Will enrich the field for many years' (*Choice* 25(7) March 1988. p.1056).
Class No: 72.0(73)

[3253]

MULLINS, L.C. Architectural treasures of early America. New ed. Washington, DC, National Historical Society,1987. 4v. (240,236,248,248p.). ISBN: 1555620388, v.1; 1555620396, v.2; 155562040x, v.3; 1555620418, v.4.

Originally published 1914-1940 as White Pine Series of Architectural monographs.

A reorganization of the earlier publication, with good illustrations, and plenty of detail. Volume one deals with Early American design, two with Early Architecture of the South, three with New England by the Sea, and four with Colonial Architecture of the Mid-Atlantic.
Class No: 72.0(73)

[3254]

National register of historic places. Washington,DC, National Park Service/Preservation Press, 1976.

Supplement covering 1966-1994 issued 1994 (923p., ISBN: 0891332545.)

State by state list of the 62,000 buildings, structures, sites etc. on the Register to date. A small number of illustrations; maps. (*See also Historic American buildings survey* above.)
Class No: 72.0(73)

[3255]

PACKARD, R.T., ***ed.*** **Encyclopedia of American architecture.** 2nd.ed. New York, McGraw-Hill, 1995. 724p., illus. $89.50. ISBN: 0070480109.

First ed. by W.D. Hunt, 1980.

Fully updated, this edition contains much new material: factual, biographical, technical; articles on postmodernism, accessibility, environmental protection, computer applications, etc. have been added. More than 500 colour photographs have also been included, and these now dominate the book. Articles are a mix of biography, history, building types, materials etc, and are not analytical. 'However one may feel about the sometimes pedestrian text, the illustrations show the best contemporary American buildings to advantage.' (*American reference books annual*, 1996; p432.) *Class No:* 72.0(73)

[3256]

SMITH, G.E.K. The Architecture of the United States: an illustrated guide to notable buildings A.D.1115 to the present open to the public. New York, Anchor Press/Doubleday in association with the Museum of Modern Art, New York, 1981. 755,749,817p.(3v.) ISBN: 0385146736, v.1; 0385146752, v.2; 0385146779, v.3.

Condensed version issued 1996; *see Sourcebook of American architecture* below.

3 vols; v.1 - New England and the mid-Atlantic states; v.2 - South and the MidWest; v.3 - Plains states and the FarWest. Each vol. arranged A/Z by state, then A/Z by town/city. Monochrome illustration of almost all entries; full address, brief history and description. Each vol. has a glossary, and 20p. double-column index.
Class No: 72.0(73)

[3257]

SMITH, G.E.K. Source book of American architecture: 500 notable buildings from the 10th century to the present. Princeton, Princeton Architectural, 1996. 678p., illus. $50.00. ISBN: 1568980248.

Updated and condensed version of *The Architecture of the United States,* (3v.; 1981). (*See above.*)

Personal selection; every state is represented. Reduces previous ed. total of 1400 buildings to 500, of which half are 20th.century. Entries are full of detail and history, each has a monochrome photograph, and for post-1900 structures give bibliographic citations. Buildings chosen are all open to the public. Maps; glossary; index by architects/designers, building types; bibliographic review. *Class No:* 72.0(73)

Bibliographies

[3258]

MARKOVITZ, A.L., ***ed.*** **Historic preservation:** a guide to information sources. Detroit, Gale Research, 1980. xiv,279p.

827 entries (items 1-659 (*i.e.* sections 1-12) annotated. Sections: 1. General reference works - 2. Historical and current overviews - 3. Financial, legal and planning aspects ... 5. Guidebooks ... 8. Renovation, restoration, and re-use of existing buildings ... 11. Natural landscapes - 12 Losses - 13. Periodicals - 14. A checklist of historic American buildings. Appendix: 'Developing the historic preservation library'. 'Select list', p.201-3 (books, periodicals). Organization, title and subject indexes. US-slanted. 'Reasonably comprehensive and excellently organized' (*ARLIS/NA Newsletter*, v.9, no.2, February 1981, p.64).
Class No: 72.0(73)(01)

Biographies

[3259]
KRANTZ, L. American architects: a survey of award-winning contemporaries and their notable works. Oxford, Facts on File, 1989. 301p. illus. £35. ISBN: 0816014205.

Alphabetical list of 400 living architects, with detail on career and list of buildings. *Class No:* 72.0(73)(092)

Women

[3260]
DOUMATO, L. Architecture and women: a bibliography detailing women architects, landscape architects, designers, critics and writers, and women in related fields working in the United States. London, Garland, 1988. 269p. $40. ISBN: 0824041054.

General works listed by form, then bibliography of 128 individuals listing sources, exhibitions. Mainly nineteenth century to present day; sources include published interviews. *Class No:* 72.0(73)(092)-0055.2

Australia

Histories

[3261]
SAUNDERS, D., *ed.* **Manual of architectural history sources in Australia.** Adelaide, University of Adelaide Dept., of Architecture, 1981. 534,390,430p. (3v.).

Vol. one: New South Wales & South Australia; vol. two: Victoria & Western Australia; vol. three: Tasmania & Queensland, & index to vols. 1-3. Expands & updates the *Manual of architectural history research* (Sydney, 1977) & identifies and lists libraries, archives, government departments, etc. Data presented in a standardized format. *Class No:* 72.0(94)(091)

Thesauri

[3262]
Art and architecture thesaurus. 2nd.ed. Oxford, OUP, 1994. 2186p. (5v.). £200. ISBN: 0195088840.

Also published in electronic edition; manual and diskettes (Oxford, Oxford Electronic Publishing, 1990; 0195066367). Annual supplements for both formats. Separate *Guide to indexing and cataloguing with the Art and Architecture Thesaurus* available. (ISBN: 0195088808; $35.00.)

Also available online through Research Libraries Information Network (RLIN).

Expanded vocabulary for architecture and art resources generally. *Class No:* 72.0:025.43

[3263]
Thesaurus of monument types: a standard for use in archaeological and architectural records. Swindon, Royal Commission on the Historic Monuments of England/ English Heritage, 1995. xxviii,322p. (loose-leaf). ISBN: 1873592205.

Derives from *Revised thesaurus of architectural terms* (1989) and the *Thesaurus of archaeological site types* (1992).

Aims to aid consistency between national and local records to support efficient data transfer; 7000 terms in hierarchical order with scope notes. *Class No:* 72.0:025.43

Design & Specification

[3264]
EVANS, L. Illustration guide: for architects, designers, and students. New York, Van Nostrand Reinhold, 1982/1988. 304,288p. (2v.) chiefly illus. £22.50/£25. ISBN: 0442221991, v.1; 0442222912, v.2.

Each volume contains over 2,000 line drawings of foreground and background materials, trees, plants, people & vehicles. Standard scales. *Class No:* 72.01

[3265]
KENDALL, M.S. Site design graphics. New York, Van Nostrand Reinhold, 1989. 512p.,illus. £49. ISBN: 0442234309.

4000 computer generated illustrations of standard site elements at many scales and angles of view, for use in preparation of design drawings and construction documents. Aimed at architects, planners etc. Index. *Class No:* 72.01

[3266]
NEUFERT, E. Architects' data. 3rd ed. Oxford, Blackwell, 1987. 433p. illus., diagrams, tables. £21.50. ISBN: 0632023392.

First published in Germany 1936; first English edition 1970.

Provides data for the initial planning of an architectural project. Over 200 building types covered under broad headings - community, commerce, leisure etc. Bibliography (655 items). Index. *Class No:* 72.01

[3267]
RAMSEY, C.G. *and* **SLEEPER, H.R. Ramsey/Sleeper architectural graphic standards.** 9th ed. New York/ Chichester, Wiley in association with the American Institute of Architects, 1994. 928p. (chiefly illus., charts, tables). £150. ISBN: 0471533696.

First published 1932. Cumulative supplement issued annually - latest: 1997. (332p.; ISBN: 0471180130; £65.00.). Available on CD-ROM (ISBN: 0471076864; £200.00.).

19 sections (*e.g.* masonry, doors and windows, electrical) present construction and design data in graphic and tabular form with explanatory text. Some major revisions for this edition; 60% of the material is reckoned to be new. 10,500 illustrations. Over 200 contributors. Detailed index. *Class No:* 72.01

[3268]
STITT, A. Architect's detail library. New York, Van Nostrand Reinhold, 1989. 666p. $89.95. ISBN: 0442205295.

Line drawings of over 2,000 construction components, drawn to scale. Intended to be used to save time in drafting standard details. *Class No:* 72.01

[3269]
WATSON, D. *and* **CROSBIE, M.** *and* **CALLENDER, J.H. Time-saver standards for architectural design data.** 7th.ed. London, McGraw-Hill, 1997. 1024p., illus. £99.99. ISBN: 0070685061.

Previous ed. 1982.

Especially useful for modern styles; includes bibliographical references. *Class No:* 72.01

Handbooks & Manuals

[3270]

SMITH, R.J. Directory of specialist crafts for architects and builders. London, Hale, 1990. 448p. £18.95. ISBN: 0709038344.

Trade directory for specialist features.
Class No: 72.01(035)

[3271]

Spon's architects' and builders' price book 1998. 123rd. ed. London, Spon, 1998. 908p. £70.50. ISSN: 03063046.

Sections cover fees, wages, prices for measured work, estimating, tables and memoranda. Index. Useful addresses.
Class No: 72.01(035)

Periods & Styles

Ancient World

Asia—Near East

[3272]

LEICK, G. Dictionary of ancient Near-Eastern architecture. London, Routledge, 1988. xix,261p.,illus., maps. £40. ISBN: 0415002400.

Alphabetical sequence of architectural terms and techniques, ornament, sites, and regional entries. Cross-references; index. 175 photographs, line drawings and plans.
Class No: 72.032(56)

Mediaeval

England

Biographies

[3273]

HARVEY, J. English mediaeval architects: a biographical dictionary down to 1550, including master masons, carpenters, carvers, building contractors and others responsible for design. Rev. ed. Gloucester, Alan Sutton, 1984. lxiii,479p. £30. ISBN: 0862990343.

First published 1954. Brief supplement published by Pinhorns, 1987 (09012622422). Also available from St. Martins Press, New York (1987).

Alphabetical arrangement giving personal and professional information collected from a range of documentary sources. Cross-references; general index; county index; subject index of buildings; chronological table.
Class No: 72.033(420)(092)

Classicism

[3274]

ADAM, R. Classical architecture: a complete handbook. London, Viking, 1990. 320p. £30. ISBN: 0670826138.

Detailed examples of all aspects of classical design up to the present day. *Class No:* 72.035

[3275]

CHITHAM, R. The Classical orders of architecture. London, Butterworth Architecture, 1985. 160p., illus. £19.50. ISBN: 0851397794.

Covers elements, details, rules of composition, illustrated by 50 line drawings. Introduction gives history, details of the orders, use. Glossary p.145-59; brief bibliography p.160.
Class No: 72.035

Modern

[3276]

Introduction to twentieth century architecture. London, Apple Press, 1989. 128p.,illus. £8.95. ISBN: 1850761825.

Divided into 4 periods: 1900-1918, 1918-1945, 1945-1970, 1970-1990. A selective introduction covering domestic and commercial buildings, in urban and rural settings, copiously illustrated. Bibliography; index. *Class No:* 72.038

[3277]

LAMPUGNANI, V.M., *ed.* **Thames and Hudson encyclopedia of twentieth century architecture.** London, Thames & Hudson, 1988. 384p., illus. £6.95 (paper). ISBN: 0500202346.

Hardback edition 1986; German original (Stuttgart, 1983) based on the *Encyclopedia of Modern Architecture* (Munich, Zurich, 1963).

Distinguished contributors; includes biographies, surveys of styles, movements etc. About 500 monochrome illustrations. *Class No:* 72.038

[3278]

ROWLAND, A. Bauhaus source book. London, Phaidon, 1990. 180p. illus. £19.95. ISBN: 0714826251.

A reference guide to the Bauhaus style and its worldwide influence. Concepts and personalities are examined; abundantly illustrated. *Class No:* 72.038

Bibliographies

[3279]

SHARP, D. Sources of modern architecture: a critical bibliography. 2nd ed. London, Granada, 1981. 192p., illus.

First published 1967 (Lund Humphries) based on articles that appeared in *Architectural Association Journal.*

3 sections: Biographical bibliography, p.16-143 (Aalto, Alvar ... Yorke, F.R.S.); Subject bibliography, p.145-62; National bibliography, p.163-75 (Austria ... USSR). 'A select list of architectural periodicals', p.177-81. Index of architects (in bold) and authors, p.183-92. Reflects 'the vast increase over the past two decades in the literature on modern architecture, architectural theory, aesthetics, design, history, construction and planning' (***Introduction***). 'The standard biographical source' (*Choice*, v.19. nos.11/12, July/August 1982, p.1543). *Class No:* 72.038(01)

Great Britain

[3280]

GLANCEY, J. New British architecture. London, Thames & Hudson, 1989. 192p., illus. £20 (£14.95 Pbk.). ISBN: 0500341079; 0500276072, paper.

Considers domestic, industrial, commercial, public buildings of recent years; influences of conservation, social policy etc., noted. Useful synopsis. Bibliography.
Class No: 72.038(410)

Netherlands

[3281]

GROENENDIJK, P. *and* **VOLLAARD, P.,** *eds.* **Guide to modern architecture in the Netherlands.** Rotterdam, Uitgeverij Publishers, 1986. £21.

Covers 500 buildings arranged in 14 geographic areas, each with map. Buildings are listed 3 per page with recent photograph, date, details of architect, bibliographic references. Descriptions in Dutch and English. Indexes by

....(contd.)
architect, building type, chronology, names. 'Such thoroughness is welcome' (*Architectural Review* clxxxii, no.1087, Sept. 1987. p.12). *Class No:* 72.038(492)

Types of Buildings

Theatres & Cinemas

[3282]

STOTTARD, R. Theatre and cinema architecture: a guide to information sources. Detroit, Gale Research, 1978. ix,368p.

1,824 briefly annotated entries. 3 parts (21 chapters): 1. General references (1. Bibliographies; 2. Periodicals) - 2. Theatre architecture (general, then by periods and countries), p.11-307. - 3. Cinema architecture. 4 indexes: Authors; Architects, designers, consultants and decorators; Theatre and cinema; Subject. Covers theatres, cinemas, opera houses and dance halls; includes biographies of architects and histories of particular theatres. Priority is given to publications in English. *Class No:* 725.82

Religious Architecture

[3283]

DAVIES, J.G. Temples, churches and mosques: a guide to the appreciation of religious architecture. Oxford, Blackwell, 1982. x,262p., illus., maps.

10 chapters. 1. The temples of the Nile - 2. Aegean architecture - 3. The sanctuary of Classical Greece - 4. The Hellenistic and Roman periods - 5. Early Christian architecture and the Byzantine achievement - 6. Mosques and Madrasas - 7. Romanesque and Mannerism - 10. Baroque and Rococo. Appendix; 'Introducing the fundamentals of architectural appreciation': Further reading (by chapters and appendix), p.249-51. Index of places and buildings, p.252-5. Non-analytical general index, p.256-62. 98 plans; locating maps. *Class No:* 726.5

India

[3284]

MEISTER, M.W. Encyclopedia of Indian temple architecture. Dhaky, M.A., *ed.* New Delhi, OUP for American Institute of Indian Studies at Varanasi, 1986-.

Still in progress; each volume is to be in 4 or 5 parts, each divided into separate books of text and photographs, drawings etc.

Covers South India 200BC to 1324AD, featuring Colas, Pandyas, Multtaraiyars, Irrukuvels, Paluvettaraiyars and other dynasties of the lower South. Regional and chronological arrangement, with entries by name of site. 'An ambitious and exhaustive survey' (*Architectural Review* CLXXXV, no.1108, June 1989, p.12). Bibliographies are included. *Class No:* 726.5(540)

Churches

England & Wales

[3285]

BETJEMAN, J., *ed.* Sir John Betjeman's guide to English parish churches. Kerr, N., *ed.* Rev ed. London, HarperCollins, 1993. 764p. illus., maps. £25.00. ISBN: 0002177277.

First published 1958; 2v. ed. (1968) as *Collins' Pocket guide to English parish churches.* (*The South.* 447p.; *The North.* 384p.).

Selective and quirky, with too much Victoriana, but still a classic compilation. Gazetteer format, arranged by historic counties. Includes Wales, Channel Islands and Isle of Man; Church of England buildings only, and no cathedrals, abbeys, chapels. Brief glossary. Index of architects, artists, places. *Class No:* 726.54(42)

England

[3286]

HUMPHRY, S.C., *ed.* Churches and chapels of Northern England. London, A. & C. Black, 1991. 544p., illus., maps, plans. £14.95. ISBN: 0713631716.

Historical introduction (p.11-40), glossary; arranged by counties, Cheshire - Yorkshire, West Riding. Indexes of architects, artists, craftsmen. *Class No:* 726.54(420)

[3287]

HUMPHRY, S.C., *ed.* Churches and chapels of Southern England. London, A. & C. Black, 1991. 667p., illus., maps, plans. £14.95. ISBN: 0713630299.

Historical introduction (p.11-40), glossary; arranged by counties, Bedfordshire - Wiltshire. Indexes of architects, artists, craftsmen. *Class No:* 726.54(420)

Abbeys & Cathedrals

England & Wales

[3288]

HARVEY, J. Cathedrals of England and Wales. 2nd ed. London, Batsford, 1988. 192p.,illus., plans, maps. £13.95. ISBN: 0713458712.

First published 1950 as *The English Cathedrals.*

Includes historical and descriptive notes on each cathedral. Glossary; bibliography; index. *Class No:* 726.6/.7(42)

[3289]

NEW, A.S.B. A Guide to the abbeys of England and Wales. London, Constable, 1985. 480p. illus. £7.95. ISBN: 009463520x.

Pocket guide arranged alphabetically by place. Glossary. *Class No:* 726.6/.7(42)

[3290]

NEW, A.S.B. A Guide to the cathedrals of Britain. London, Constable, 1980. 462p. illus., maps, plans. £4.95.

A pocket guide to 106 cathedrals, - all the cathedrals of Britain, regardless of denomination, arranged under places, A-Z, p.16-444. Many small plans, indicating clerestory height, with a deeper shading for towers and domes. 'York Minster': p.433-41; 1 illus., 1 ground plan. Glossary, p.5-15. Appended lists: Some ex-cathedrals (27); Architects and designers; Embroiderers, tapestry-makers, illustrators; Furniture makers; Glass artists; Metalworkers; Mosaic and ceramic artists; Organ builders; Painters; Sculptors. Well-produced. *Class No:* 726.6/.7(42)

[3291]

THOROLD, H. Collins guide to cathedrals, abbeys and priories of England and Wales. London, Collins, 1986. 352p.,illus. £15. ISBN: 0002172410.

Covers all Anglican cathedrals and those abbey and priory churches still used for worship. Grouped by diocese; 300 illustrations. 'It is the priories and the parish church cathedrals that are best served by this book'. (*Royal Society of Arts Journal,* January 1987, p.166-7). *Class No:* 726.6/.7(42)

England

[3292]

PEVSNER, N. *and* **METCALF, P. The Cathedrals of England.** Harmondsworth, Viking, 1985. 381,399p. (2v.), illus., plans. ISBN: 0670801240, v.1; 0670801259, v.2.

Volume one covers Southern England; volume two Midlands, Eastern and Northern England. Describes 62 cathedrals from the Middle Ages to the 20th century. Metcalf has re-edited and updated descriptions from Pevsner's *Buildings of England* series. Entries include building chronology, detailed description, glass, sculpture, paintings etc. Glossary. Over 180 illustrations in each volume. *Class No:* 726.6/.7(420)

Domestic Architecture

[3293]

BRUNSKILL, R.W. Illustrated handbook of vernacular architecture. 3rd ed. London, Faber, 1987. 256p., illus., maps, plans. £7.50. ISBN: 0571139167.

First published 1971.

Systematically covers the design and architecture, materials, construction methods and ornamentation used in traditional domestic and small industrial buildings to the nineteenth century. 82 photographs, 790 line illustrations, glossary, bibliography, index. *Class No:* 728

Great Britain

Bibliographies

[3294]

ARCHER, J. The Literature of British domestic architecture 1715-1842. Cambridge, Mass., M.I.T. Press, 1985. 1078p. plates. £107.95. ISBN: 0262010763.

Good introductory chapters and an excellent annotated bibliography of eighteenth and nineteenth century British and Irish publications. Main section contains works with original designs for domestic structures, with some agricultural buildings and landscape design. 'A splendid addition to architectural scholarship'. (*Art Documentation* 4(4) Winter 1985. p.183). *Class No:* 728(410)(01)

Scotland

[3295]

MacGIBBON, D. *and* **ROSS, T. The Castellated and domestic architecture of Scotland,** from the twelfth to the eighteenth century. New ed. Edinburgh, Mercat Press, 1971. xl,3068p. (5v.), illus. £125. ISBN: 0901824186.

First published Edinburgh: Douglas, 1887-92.

Standard source, with descriptions of 1,000 keeps, houses, tolbooths, town halls, churches, & monuments. Index. *Class No:* 728(411)

Greece

[3296]

PHILIPPIDES, D., *ed.* **Greek traditional architecture.** Athens, Melissa, 1983. 6v.

8 volumes are projected. Vols. 1 & 2 are currently available in English. Self-contained chapters separately available.

Vol. one covers Eastern Aegean, Sporades, Ionian islands; vol. two Santorini. Historical introductions followed by detailed descriptions. Copious illustration of internal and external features in colour & monochrome. 'Architectural

....(contd.)

documentation of physical remains already in many places fast crumbling' (*Times Literary Supplement* 22/28 December 1989, p.1424). *Class No:* 728(495)

Houses

Great Britain

[3297]

HARRIS, J. A Country house index: an index of over 2,000 country houses illustrated in 107 books of country views published between 1715 and 1872, together with a list of British country-house guides and country-house art collections/catalogues for the period 1726-1880. 2nd ed. London, Pinhorns, 1979. iv,45p. £7. ISBN: 0901262218.

First published 1971.

Index of country houses, p.3-30, with key (*i.e.,* sources). Appended list of country-house guides. Author is Curator, Drawings Collection, Royal Institute of British Architects. *Class No:* 728.1(410)

[3298]

HOLMES, M. The Country house described: an index to the country houses of Great Britain and Ireland. Winchester, St. Paul's Bibliographies/V&A, 1986. 320p. illus., bibliog. £35. ISBN: 0906793397.

Entries for 4,000 houses based on the contents of 135 general architectural books, county histories, guides, sale catalogues, and some periodicals (all held in the National Art Library, Victoria & Albert Museum). Three main sequences cover England & Wales, Scotland, Ireland. 'Diligently researched' (*Antique Collector,* December 1986, p.87). *Class No:* 728.1(410)

Manor Houses & Stately Homes

Great Britain

Yearbooks & Directories

[3299]

Historic houses, castles and gardens open to the public 1998. Alcock, S., *ed.* 44th ed. London, Johansens, 1998. 288p. illus., maps. £6.95. ISBN: 1860175066.

Published annually since 1954.

Useful introductory sections preface the main directory of over 2000 properties, and gardens, arranged in order of counties (England, Wales, Irish Republic, Northern Ireland) and by region (Scotland). Selective coverage of similar sites in Belgium, France, Germany. Many entries feature colour photographs; standard data includes a brief description, access arrangements, charges, facilities, opening hours, telephone number. Index of properties, and maps. Numerous advertisements provide additional information. *Class No:* 728.8(410)(058)

[3300]

National Trust historic houses handbook. Bromley, Kent, National Trust, 1993. 256p., illus. £4.50. ISBN: 0707801613.

Concentrates on the architectural history of the NT's houses, and the treasures they contain. *Class No:* 728.8(410)(058)

[3301]

TYACK, G. *and* **BRINDLE, S. Blue guide to country houses of England.** London, A. & C. Black, 1994. 608p. £15.99. ISBN: 0713637803.

400 entries give main features and contents, opening times, location, refreshments, etc. Other sources may be more comprehensive, but this 'gives more information about what is worth seeing.' (*Reference reviews,* 8(5) 1994, p32.) *Class No:* 728.8(410)(058)

Scotland

[3302]

TRANTER, N. The Fortified house in Scotland. Edinburgh, Mercat Press, 1977. 5v. (each 200p.,illus). £7.95 per vol. ISBN: 0901824429, v.1; 0901824437, v.2; 0901824445, v.3; 0901824453, v.4; 0901824461, v.5.

First published by Oliver & Boyd, 1962-70.

Volumes are 1: South-East Scotland, 2: Central Scotland, 3: South-West Scotland, 4: Aberdeenshire, Angus, & Kincardinshire, 5: North-West Scotland.

Each volume is arranged by county and aims to describe the aspect, situation, special features, and history of each fortified house, with notes on builders and owners. Covers 500 houses in all. *Class No:* 728.8(411)

USA

Yearbooks & Directories

[3303]

VILA, B. Guide to historic homes of the Mid Atlantic. New York, Lintel/Morrow, 1993. 316p. $15.00. ISBN: 0688124941.

Companion volumes cover the South (1993), New England (1993), Midwest (1994), Great Plains and the West (1994).

Arranged by state, then city or town. Maps and directory with access details; entries explain historical significance, famous occupants, collections etc. Monochrome photographs. *Class No:* 728.8(73)(058)

Castles

Great Britain

Bibliographies

[3304]

KENYON, J.R., *ed.* **Castles, town defences and artillery fortifications in Britain and Ireland:** a bibliography. London, Council for British Archaeology, 1978-. 3v. £4.50; £4.95; £12. ISBN: 0900312610, v.1; 0906780314, v.2; 187241401x, v.3.

The first volume (1978) covers the years 1945-1974, and includes books, pamphlets, periodical articles and miscellaneous materials. Updated by two further volumes in 1983 and 1990. *Class No:* 728.81(410)(01)

73 Sculpture, Plastic & Metal Arts

Sculpture, Plastic & Metal Arts

Handbooks & Manuals

[3305]

MOULIN, R., ***ed.*** **A Handbook for plastic artists.** 2nd ed. Luxembourg, Office for Official Publications of the European Community/HMSO, 1988. 222p. £18.75. ISBN: 9282571076.

A directory and data handbook to inform plastic artists of the measures available to assist them. Arranged by EC country within which are the following sections: art in society (patronage & art market), artists' associations, legal aspects, economic aspects, display centres, addresses of associations and galleries. Periodicals list.
Class No: 73.0(035)

Biographies

[3306]

PYKE, E.J. A Biographical dictionary of wax modellers. Oxford, OUP, 1973. lxvi, 216p. illus., plates. £40. ISBN: 0198171943.

3 supplements have been issued by the author (1981, 1983, 1986).

Alphabetical list of modellers, with notes on techniques, extant works, references. Bibliography p.164-176. Detailed index including references to the plates.
Class No: 73.0(092)

Sculpture

Periodicals & Progress Reports

[3307]

The Sculpture journal. Trusted, M., *ed.* London, Public Monuments and Sculpture Association, 1997- . 88p., illus.(v.1). £25.00. ISSN: 13662724.

First issue 1997.

Periodical devoted to sculpture and public monuments; discussions, reviews, notes on recent work etc.
Class No: 730(05)

Europe

Dictionaries

[3308]

BASSETT, J. ***and*** **FOGELMAN, P. Looking at European sculpture:** a guide to technical terms. London, V & A Publications, 1997. 103p., illus. £8.95. ISBN: 089236291x.

Collaborative production with the J. Paul Getty Museum.

Concise and readily understandable dictionary of terms; 50 colour illustrations and others in monochrome; brief bibliography. *Class No:* 730(4)(038)

Histories

[3309]

POPE-HENNESSY, J., ***ed.*** **A History of Western sculpture.** London, Michael Joseph, 1967-1969. 352, 368, 352, 352p. (4v).

A monumental and excellent reference source: vol. 1 features classical sculpture (G.M.A. Hanfmann); vol. 2 mediaeval sculpture (R. Salvini); vol. 3 renaissance to rococo (H. Kentner); vol. 4 nineteenth and twentieth centuries (F. Licht). Historical and social background explored; excellent illustrations. *Class No:* 730(4)(091)

Great Britain

[3310]

GUNNIS, R. Dictionary of British sculpture 1660-1851. Rev. ed. London, Abbey Library, 1968. 514p. illus.

First published 1953.

Over 1,000 entries giving biographical information, titles and dates of important works, selected exhibitions, and bibliographical references. A recognized, indispensable source. *Class No:* 730(410)

[3311]

READ, B. Victorian sculpture. New Haven, Conn., Yale Univ. Press, 1982. x,414p.,illus. £55. ISBN: 0300025068.

Covers 'Sculpture in Britain between about 1830 and about 1914' (*Preface*), although largely 1830-70. 4 parts: 1. The position of Victorian sculpture - 2. The life and the works - 3. Classes apart (*e.g.* Architectural sculpture: Gothic; religious) - 4. The end of the century. References, p.87-96; bibliography, p.397-403. Analytical, small-type, index, p.404-14. 'Densely factual but considerable humour and a sharp eye for anecdotal detail' (*British book news,* November 1982, p.696). *Class No:* 730(410)

London

[3312]

BLACKWOOD, J. London's immortals: complete outdoor commemorative statues. London, Savoy Press, 1989. 390p., illus. £30. ISBN: 0951429604.

Comprehensive survey; over 300 illustrations, mainly monochrome. *Class No:* 730(421)

France

[3313]

SOUCHAL, F. French sculptors of the seventeenth and eighteenth centuries: the reign of Louis XIV; Catalogue raisonné. Oxford, Bruno Cassirer, 1977-87. 391,464,480p. (3v.), illus. £75 per vol. ISBN: 0851810624, v.1; 0851810438, v.2; 0851810535, v.3.

Concise catalogue entries; monochrome illustrations; analytical index. 'Vast assemblage of learning' (*Royal Society of Arts Journal* Feb. 1988. p.202).
Class No: 730(44)

Bibliographies

[3314]

LYMAN, T.W. *and* **SMARTT, D. French Romanesque sculpture:** an annotated bibliography. Boston, G.K. Hall, 1987. 463p. $49. ISBN: 0816183309.

Covers the period 1000-1200AD in publications (French & English) dating from 1670-1984. 2000 entries in three chronological divisions. Detailed indexes. Fully analysed in *Art Libraries Journal* 14(2) 1989, p.43-45.

Class No: 730(44)(01)

Biographies

[3315]

LAMI, S. Dictionnaire des sculpteurs de l'école française. Paris, Champion, 1898-1921. 8v.

Reprinted by Kraus (Liechstenstein, 1970).

1: *Du Moyen Age au règne de Louis XIV*. 1898. viii, 593p.

2: *Sous la règne de Louis XIV*. 1906. vi, 504p.

3/4: *Au dix-huitième siècle*. 1910-11. 2v.

5/8: *Au dix-neuvième siècle*. 1914-21. 4v.

Biographies, A-Z, include chronological list of works, their location and references to the literature (*e.g.* 'Rodin', v.8, p.161-78: career; works, p.165-74; bibliography, p.174-8). Includes foreign sculptors who came to and worked in France until their death. 'A fundamental reference and research tool' (Arntzen, E., and Rainwater, R. *Guide to the literature of art history* (1980), entry K115).

Class No: 730(44)(092)

Italy

[3316]

POPE-HENNESSY, J. *and* **LIGHTBROWN, R. Catalogue of Italian sculpture** in the Victoria and Albert Museum. London, HMSO, 1964. 3v., illus. £70. ISBN: 0112903673.

1. *Text: Eighth to fifteenth century*. xvi,395p.
2. *Text: Sixteenth to twentieth century*. v, [1], 399-767p.
3. *Plates*. [v], 426p.

A new catalogue, not a revision of the 1932 ed., covering the world's largest single collection. 745 items in all, descriptions in v.1-2 sometimes running to over 1 page. V.2 includes a bibliography (p.700-8) and indexes of artists, provenance, sculptors mentioned in the text, and numbers. V.3 contains 736 half-tone plates. *Class No:* 730(450)

[3317]

POPE-HENNESSY, J. Introduction to Italian sculpture. 4th ed. London, Phaidon, 1996. 288,444,560p. (3v.), illus. £65, £80, £95. ISBN: 0714830143, v.1; 0714830151, v.2; 071483016x, v.3.

Volumes first published 1955, 1958, 1963.

Coverage: Gothic sculpture; Renaissance sculpture; High Renaissance and Baroque. Each volume arranged in sections on major artists and areas of activity (Humanist tombs; portrait busts). Notes on sculptors and plates. Bibliographies; index of places, sculptors. Profusely illustrated.

Class No: 730(450)

Bibliographies

[3318]

GLASS, D. Italian Romanesque sculpture: an annotated bibliography. Boston, G.K. Hall, 1983. 302p. ISBN: 0816183317.

Subject arrangement; 17 sections, some with detailed subdivisions. Author index; analytical index to regions and sites. *Class No:* 730(450)(01)

[3319]

WILK, S.B., ***ed*****. Fifteenth century Italian sculpture:** an annotated bibliography. Boston, G.K. Hall, 1986. 474p. £52. ISBN: 0816185506.

Comprehensive, specialist volume.

Class No: 730(450)(01)

India

[3320]

PAL, P. Indian sculpture: a catalogue of the Los Angeles County Museum of Art Collection. Berkeley, University of California Press, 1990. 2v. ISBN: 0520064771.

Vol. one covers 500BC-700AD; vol. two 700-1800. Detailed descriptions and illustrations of an outstanding collection. Includes stone, metal, ivory, wood; arranged by region, and including Pakistan & Afghanistan. Author is the Museum's Senior Curator of Indian & S.E. Asian Art.

Class No: 730(540)

USA

[3321]

Gothic sculpture in America: Volume 1 - the New England museums. Gillerman, D., *ed*. London, Garland, 1989. 403p. $99. ISBN: 0824084624.

First volume of a series that will catalogue all monumental European Gothic stone or wood sculpture held in American public collections. 275 objects photographed, described, with bibliography. Index to sculptors, dealers, subjects & provenance. 'Important catalog ... essential for research libraries' (*Choice* 27/10 June 1990. p.1669).

Class No: 730(73)

Biographies

[3322]

OPITZ, G.B., ***ed*****. Dictionary of American sculptors,** eighteenth century to the present. New York, Apollo Books, 1984. 656p. illus. $75. ISBN: 0938290037.

Over 5000 alphabetical entries, mainly brief biography and major pieces. 200 photographs. '... tackling a difficult job and doing it so well' (*Sculpture Review* 33(4) Winter 1984/5 p.26-7). *Class No:* 730(73)(092)

Women

[3323]

JONES, V.W. Contemporary American women sculptors. Phoenix, Oryx, 1986. x, 665p. £92. ISBN: 0897741390.

Entries for over three hundred sculptors, with details of media, exhibitions, awards, bibliography, and photographs. Double page spread for each individual includes a personal statement, an illustration of a typical work, and specimen signature. *Class No:* 730(73)(092)-0055.2

Materials

[3324]

BECKWITH, J. Ivory carvings in early medieval England. New ed. Oxford, OUP, 1982. 168p., illus. £62. ISBN: 0199210071.

First published in 1972.

3 parts: 1. The heroic age of the 7th and 8th centuries - 2. The 10th-century monastic reform and its aftermath - 3. The English genius in the 12th century. Notes, p.111-6; catalogue; index. 270 illus. *Class No:* 730.023

Wood

[3325]

PINTO, E.H. Treen and other wooden bygones: an encyclopedia and social history. London, Bell, 1976. 458p. illus. ISBN: 0713515333.

Reprint of 1969 issue.

28 main headings (Apothecary - watch stands) each beginning with an historical introduction, then listing & describing objects in A/Z order. 3,300 objects illustrated in 460 plates. Bibliography, glossary, index. (The Pinto Collection is now housed in Birmingham City Museum & Art Gallery). *Class No:* 730.023.1

Stone

England & Wales

[3326]

DARKE, J. The Monument guide to England and Wales. London, Macdonald, 1991. 256p. illus. £19.95. ISBN: 0356176096.

Narrative survey of principal monuments, giving details of sculptor, locations, style, state of repair. Biographical background supplemented with anecdotes.
Class No: 730.023.2(42)

[3327]

LANG, J.T. The Corpus of Anglo-Saxon stone sculpture: vol.3 - York and Eastern Yorkshire. Oxford, OUP/British Academy, 1990. 480p. illus. £75. ISBN: 0197260799.

Earlier volumes cover *County Durham and Northumberland* (1984) and *Cumberland, Westmorland and Lancashire North-of-the-Sands* (1988).

A detailed and scholarly photographic record with descriptions and historical notes. Important introduction.
Class No: 730.023.2(42)

[3328]

—CRAMP, R., *ed.* General introduction to the Corpus of Anglo-Saxon stone sculpture. Oxford, OUP, 1990. 52p. £9.95. ISBN: 0197260985.

Companion volume to the series.

Discusses dating methods, epigraphs, carving technique, forms, shapes, decoration etc. *Class No:* 730.023.2(42)

Metal

[3329]

FORRER, L. Biographical dictionary of medallists, coin-, gem-, and seal engravers, mint-masters etc... London, Spink, 1904-30. *c.*8000p. (6v. and 2 supplement) illus., plates.

Reprinted by Franklin (NY) 1971, and Baldwin (London) 1980.

Alphabetical arrangement covering over 6,000 entries 500BC-1900AD. Details include references to major work and bibliography; entries vary from two lines to several pages. Principal sources of information listed in v.1 p.xxxix-xlviii; further bibliography; v.8 p.368, followed by index of illustrations p.369-461. *Class No:* 730.023.3

Seals

Great Britain

[3330]

PUBLIC RECORD OFFICE. London. **Catalogue of seals in the Public Record Office.** Personal seals, vols 1 & 2; Monastic seals. London, HMSO., 1978-86. 82,129,160p. (3v.), illus. £8; £15; £25. ISBN: 0114400849, v.1; 011440111x, v.2; 0114401934, v.3.

Vols. 1 & 2 *Personal seals* compiled by R.M. Ellis illustrate the seals with description, date, design, size, colour etc. List of owners. Vol.2 supplements & corrects vol.1. Vol.3 covers *Monastic seals. Class No:* 736.3(410)

Coins

[3331]

BRITISH MUSEUM. Department of Coins and Medals. **Catalogue of coins.** London, British Museum Press, 1873-. Several series, most multi-volume. All illus. with plates.

Although slow in publication, still in progress. Many volumes out-of-print.

Major series of titles, which include:-

A catalogue of Greek coins, by R.S. Poole [and others]. 1873-1927. 29v.

Principal coins of the Romans, by R.A.G. Carson. 1978-83. 3v.

A catalogue of coins of the Roman Republic, by H.A. Grueber. 1910. 3v.

A catalogue of coins of the Roman Empire, by M. Mattingly [and others]. 1923-64. 6v. (v.2, 5, 6. 2nd ed. 1976).

A catalogue of coins of the Vandals, Ostrogoths and Lombards, etc. by W. Wroth. 1961.

The Carolingian coins in the British Museum, by R.H.M. Dolley and K.F. Morrison. 1966.

A catalogue of Imperial Byzantine coins, by W.Wroth. 1908. 2v.

A catalogue of English coins: Anglo-Saxon series, by C.F. Keary and H.A. Grueber. 1887-93. 2v.

A catalogue of English coins: the Norman Kings, by G.C. Brooke. 1916. 2v.

English copper, tin and bronze coins in the British Museum, 1558-1958. by C.W. Peck. 1960.

Catalogue of the Oriental coins in the British Museum, by R.S. Poole. 1875-90. 10v.

Catalogue of the Indian coins in the British Museum, by E.J. Rapson. 1908.

Catalogue of the coins of ancient India, by J. Allan. 1936.

Catalogue of the coins of the Gupta Dynasties and of Sasanka, King of Gauda, by J. Allan. 1914.

British Iron Age coins in the British Museum, by R. Hobbs. 1996.

Catalogue of the Celtic coins in the British Museum, by D.F. Allen. 1990-95. 3v.

Catalogue of the Aksumite coins in the British Museum, by S.C. Munro-Hay. 1996.

Coin hoards from Roman Britain, by R. Bland & A. Burnett. 1980-1992. 9v. *Class No:* 737

[3332]

KRAUSE, C.L. *and* **MISHLER, C. Standard catalog of world coins 1998.** 25th. ed; editorial assistance from C.R. Bruce. Iola, Wis, Krause Publications, 1997. 1792p. illus., tables, maps. $47.95. ISBN: 0873414977.

This ed. introduces a major change in the pattern of publication; this main vol. covers only 1901 to the present. 3 other vols. are now published: 1801-1900 (1st.ed. 1996; ISBN: 0873414276); 1701-1800 (2nd.ed. 1997; ISBN: 0873415264); 1601-1700 (1st.ed. 1996; ISBN: 0873412710).

Each of the 4 vols. is arranged A/Z by country then chronologically by coin denominations. Over 59,000 full size photographs in the 20th.century vol., and c20,000 in each of the others. Full details, current values, monogram chart, identification key. Good introductory data on symbols, marks etc. Guide to Eastern mint names. In its new pattern, this must become the accepted international source.
Class No: 737

[3333]

KRAUSE, C.L. *and* **MISHLER, C. Standard catalog of world gold coins.** 3rd ed. Iola, Wisc, Krause Publications, 1992. 848p. $60.00. ISBN: 0873412133.

Well organized, well produced, and exhaustive.
Class No: 737

Bibliographies

[3334]

AMERICAN NUMISMATIC SOCIETY. Dictionary and auction catalogues of the library.... Boston, G.K. Hall, 1962. 5920p. (7v.).

Supplements issued 1967, 1973, and 1978 (2v.).

The main volumes reproduce 123,300 catalogue cards, including many entries for periodical articles. The 3 *Supplements* add 63,500 entries. The Society's Library is the most comprehensive of its kind in America, containing over 50,000 items covering every phase of numismatics.
Class No: 737(01)

[3335]

BROWN, I.D. *and* **DOLLEY, M. A Bibliography of coin hoards of Great Britain and Ireland,** 1500-1967. London, Royal Numismatic Society and Spink & Sons, 1971. 88p., tables.

Part 1: Great Britain (Hoards deposited in England & Wales, 1500-1697; Great Britain, 1697-1967, - Scotland from 1707; Scotland, 1500-1707; Uncertain; Coins in wrecks from the coasts of Great Britain and Ireland). Hoards deposited in Holland, Belgium and Luxembourg, France, Scandinavia, Asia, Africa, Northern America, Australia - Part 2: Hoards of Ireland, p.63-82. Data: item no.; nature; country and map reference; date of deposit/find; contents; references. Sources (articles), p.15-18; Selected lists of review articles, p.19. *Class No:* 737(01)

[3336]

—THOMPSON, J.D.A. Inventory of British coin hoards, AD 600-1500. London, Royal Numismatic Society, 1956. 216p., illus. £18. ISBN: 0901405108.

Covers the earlier period. *Class No:* 737(01)

[3337]

CLAIN-STEFANELLI, E.E. Numismatic bibliography. 2nd ed. New York, Saur, 1985. xxii, 1848p. $125. ISBN: 3598075073.

Covers 1700 to 1981; 18,000 citations, mainly monographs with some journal articles, major exhibitions, sales catalogues, conference proceedings. Additional 6,000 references to related areas, counterfeiting, paper money, tokens etc. Alphabetically by author within chronological periods and geographic divisions. Five indexes, cross-references. 'An impressive achievement' (*Choice* 23,9 May 1986, p.1369). *Class No:* 737(01)

[3338]

HARNSBERGER, R.S. Numismatics: a core collection. *Reference Services Review* 16(4) 1988. p.57-64.

Brief introduction, then listing of items with substantial annotations. Arranged under headings - general reference, Ancient Greece, Ancient Rome. Byzantine Empire, Mediaeval Europe, general worldwide, United States, commemorative medals. *Class No:* 737(01)

[3339]

Numismatic literature. New York, American Numismatic Society, 1947-.

2pa.; originally quarterly.

Classified abstracting service for books and periodicals; separate sections of reviews and obituaries. Author and subject indexes. Highly regarded for coverage and accuracy.
Class No: 737(01)

Encyclopaedias & Dictionaries

[3340]

CRIBB, J. *and* **COOK, B.** *and* **CARRADICE, I. The Coin atlas:** the world of coinage from its origins to the present day. London, Macdonald/Spink, 1990. 337p. illus., maps, tables. £19.95. ISBN: 0356174867.

Five main sections by continent, then country by country analysis over 2600 years. Over 100 maps, 1800 illustrations; glossary; bibliography; index. *Class No:* 737(03)

[3341]

JUNGE, E. World coin encyclopedia. London, Barrie & Jenkins, 1984. 297p. illus. ISBN: 0091551404.

Over 1,500 entries and 450 illustrations covering names of coins, terminology, persons and places, with emphasis on classical and European coinage. Bibliography of 500 items. 'Scholarly reference source' (*Choice* 22(10) June 1985. p.1474). *Class No:* 737(03)

Dictionaries

[3342]

DOTY, R.G. Encyclopedic dictionary of numismatics. London, Hale, 1982. xii,355p., illus. £25.

US title as *The Macmillan encyclopedia of numismatics*.

About 450 entries, A-Z, with numerous cross-references. 'Denier': 2 columns, 2 illus., 6 cross-references; 'Groat': nearly 2 columns, 2 illus., 6 cross-references. Includes related fields, *e.g.* medals, tokens, decorations and paper money. Over 650 illus. Sectional bibliography, p.349-55. 'Admirable successor to Albert Frey's *Dictionary of numismatic names* (originally published 1917) as the standard' (*Wilson library bulletin,* October 1982, p.174). Author is Associate Curator at the American Numismatic Society. *Class No:* 737(038)

[3343]

FREY, A.R. Dictionary of numismatic names with addenda. With glossary of numismatic terms in English, French, German, Italian, Swedish. London, Spink/ Organization of International Numismatics, 1973. 311p. 94p. tables.

Originally published by American Numismatic Society 1917, reissued Barnes & Noble 1947.

Incorporates some wholly new material from the American Numismatic Association's *Dictionary of Numismatic Terms,* otherwise preserves original entries. Includes slang & popular names; geographical index, paper money index. Glossary lists some 300 terms. *Class No:* 737(038)

Yearbooks & Directories

[3344]

Coin year book. 5th.ed. Honiton, Devon, Token Publishing Ltd, 1998. £9.95. ISBN: 1870192168.

Compiled by the staff of *Coin News.*

Contents include glossary, mintmarks, price guide (p109-246), banknote section, directory of museums, libraries, organisations. *Class No:* 737(058)

Great Britain

[3345]

BRITISH ACADEMY. London. **Sylloge of coins of the British Isles.** Oxford, OUP, 1958-.

Recent volumes have also been issued by other publishers (Spink, British Museum, etc.).

A series of inventories of British coins in major collections in the UK and elsewhere (*e.g.* State Museum, Berlin). Begins with *Fitzwilliam Museum, Cambridge, part 1: Ancient British & Anglo-Saxon Coins* (P. Grierson, 1958). A massive project likely to be in progress for many years; recent volumes include *J.J. North Collection: Edwardian silver coins 1279-1351* (0197260756; 1989; £35.00); *Norweb Collection: tokens 1575-1750 part 2: Dorset, Durham, Essex & Gloucestershire* (Spink, 1988; 0907605230; £20.00), and *John Morcum collection of western Greek bronze coins* (Oxford University Press & Spink, 1995; 0197261523; £30.00). *Class No:* 737(410)

[3346]

British coins market values 1998. Croydon, Link House, 1997. 130p., illus. £5.95. ISBN: 0862961459.

Published annually.

Brief, simple, inexpensive but reliable guide for collectors. Includes all English, Scottish and Irish coins.
Class No: 737(410)

[3347]

Coincraft's 1998 standard catalogue of English and UK coins, 1066 to date. London, Coincraft, 1998. 700p., illus. £19.95. ISBN: 0862961459.

Annual.

Contains 50,000 prices; coins are well illustrated. Other features include a glossary, history of British coinage, index of engravers and designers. *Class No:* 737(410)

[3348]

Coins of England and the UK, 1998. 33rd.ed. London, Spink, 1998. xix,411p., illus., maps. ISBN: 0907605907.

First published in 1929 with the title *A Catalogue of coins of Great Britain and Ireland.* Later became *Standard catalogue of British coins* (eds. B. Mitchell & B. Reeds), published by Seaby which company was absorbed by Batsford; in 1996 the title was transferred to Spink.

....*(contd.)*

Chronological arrangement, with excellent illustrations. Prices and several supporting features. Bibliography.
Class No: 737(410)

[3349]

MANVILLE, H.E. *and* **ROBERTSON, T.J. British numismatic auction catalogues** 1710-1984. London, A.H. Baldwin, 1986. 438p., illus. £40. ISBN: 0906919142.

Comprehensive survey & descriptions.
Class No: 737(410)

Scotland

[3350]

BATESON, J.D. Coinage in Scotland. London, Spink, 1997. 175p., illus. £19.99. ISBN: 0907605745.

Historical discussion and descriptions; good illustrations and maps of mint locations. Likely to become a standard source. *Class No:* 737(411)

Commonwealth

[3351]

Spink's catalogue of British colonial and Commonwealth coins: standard reference with valuations. Clermont, A.P., *ed.* London, Spink, 1986. 704p., illus. £22.50. ISBN: 0907605192.

Alphabetically arranged by country, then chronologically and by denomination. 7,700 illustrations with description and current valuation. *Class No:* 737(41-44)

USA

[3352]

ALEXANDER, D.T., *ed.* **The Coin World comprehensive catalog and encyclopedia of United States coins.** Pharos/ World Almanac, 1990. 456p., illus. $29.95. ISBN: 088687484x.

Well researched and comprehensively indexed; coin auction catalogues are included in the Bibliography. Includes colonial and early state coins and tokens. 800 coins are illustrated. *Class No:* 737(73)

[3353]

BARTIMORE, J., *ed.* **United States coin book:** definitive US coins. Hughes, R.P., *ed.* 11th ed. Ely, Cambs., F. Fell, 1990. x,181p., illus. £11.95. ISBN: 0811900371.

Good source for US coinage; 171 illustrations.
Class No: 737(73)

[3354]

BREEN, W. Complete encyclopaedia of US and Colonial coins. New York, Doubleday, 1987. 754p. $100.00. ISBN: 0385142072.

Comprehensive from 1616; 8,000 entries in eight sections, with chronological lists and good illustrations. Full details given, including some auction prices. Bibliography, abbreviations, glossary. *Class No:* 737(73)

[3355]

YEOMAN, R.S. *and* **BRESSETT, K.,** *eds.* **A Guide book of United States coins,** 1996. 49th.ed. Racine,Wis, Western Publishing, 1995. 311p., illus. $7.95. ISBN: 0307199029.

Published annually.

Standard guide for collectors and dealers; preliminaries give definitions of terminology and concise history. Chronological listing of colonial and US coins, tokens, medals and related materials. For each item there is an illustration, note on variations, history, and suggested market

.... (contd.)
value. Commemorative and private issues also included in section at the end. Clear layout with bold heads.
Class No: 737(73)

Ancient Times

[3356]
JONES, J.M., *ed.* **Dictionary of ancient Greek coins.** London, Seaby, 1986. 256p., illus., tables. £25. ISBN: 0900652810.
Includes 300 illustrations. 3 tables. A useful summary.
Class No: 737"-"

[3357]
JONES, J.M. Dictionary of ancient Roman coins. London, Seaby, 1990. 329p., illus. £30. ISBN: 185264026x.
Companion volume to the *Dictionary of Ancient Greek coins* (1986). *Class No:* 737"-"

Middle Ages

[3358]
GRIERSON, P. *and* **BLACKBURN, M. Medieval European coinage:** with a catalogue of the coins in the Fitzwilliam Museum. Volume one: early middle ages, fifth to tenth century. Cambridge, CUP, 1986. 674p. £60.00. ISBN: 0521260094.
The definitive, classic work; thirteen volumes are envisaged. 'Scholarly work of the highest order' (*American Reference Books Annual*, 1988). *Class No:* 737"01/14"

20th Century

[3359]
SCHÖN, G. World coin catalogue, twentieth century. 6th ed. London, Seaby, 1987. 1633p. illus. £12.50. ISBN: 185264012x.
Alphabetical by country or territory, then in chronological order of issue. Full description and estimated market value. Over 3,000 actual-size photographic illustrations.
Class No: 737"19"

Medals

Periodicals

[3360]
The Medal. London, British Art Medal Trust, 1982-. £20pa. ISSN: 02637707.
2 issues pa.
Includes regular book reviews. 'High standard of scholarship and production' (*RSA Journal,* Sept, 1986. p.693-4). *Class No:* 737.2(051)

Yearbooks & Directories

[3361]
Medals year book 1998. Brant, J.G., *ed.* 4th. annual ed. Honiton, Devon, Token Publishing, 1997. 336p.,illus. ISBN: 1870192141.
Editorial team includes staff of *Medals news.*
Market review; covers awards, orders, decorations, campaign medals, coronation and jubilee medals etc. Dealer directory. Military book stockists (p264-271). Directory of

.... (contd.)
societies, museums, collections, fairs, researchers, auctioneers. Abbreviations found on medals. Detailed index.
Class No: 737.2(058)

Great Britain

[3362]
ABBOTT, P.E. *and* **TAMPLIN, J.M.A. British gallantry awards.** 2nd ed. Colchester, J.B. Hayward, 1981. xx,316p. illus. £25. ISBN: 0903754258.
Covers period 1855-1979; 44 illustrated chapters each on a separate award. Standardized approach under headings: origin and development, description, verification and citations, numbers awarded, illustrative award. Ribbon chart and key. Index to recipients mentioned. Bibliography.
Class No: 737.2(410)

[3363]
BROWN, L.A. A Catalogue of British historical medals 1760-1960. London, Seaby, 1980-. 469,496,432p. (3v.), illus. £60. (v.1); £95 (v.2); £75 (v.3). ISBN: 090065256x, v.1; 0900652926, v.2; 0907605540, v.3.
One further volume was planned.
Volumes cover 1760-1837, 1837-1901, 1901-1960. Information given includes date of issue, subject, metal, size, artist/designer/publisher, description, bibliographic references, collections, historical or biographical notes. Inscriptions noted, and translated. Indexes. Extensively illustrated. *Class No:* 737.2(410)

[3364]
EIMER, C. British commemorative medals and their values. London, Seaby, 1987. 265p. illus. £35. ISBN: 0900652942.
Catalogues over 2000 medals with historical and biographical details. Price guide included. 'Essential reference work for collectors' (*Antique Collector,* October 1987, p.121). *Class No:* 737.2(410)

[3365]
FEARON, D. Spink's catalogue of British commemorative medals 1558 to the present day, with valuations. Exeter, Webb & Bower, 1984. 192p. illus. ISBN: 0863500293.
Introductory section on collecting then systematic chronological catalogue with detailed descriptions, followed by illustrations (p.98-189). Index of medallists; further reading. *Class No:* 737.2(410)

[3366]
JOSLIN, E.C., *and others.* **British battles and medals.** 6th ed. London, Spink, 1988. 299p. illus. £35. ISBN: 0907605257.
This edition revised by L.L. Gordon.
Catalogue of every campaign medal and bar awarded since the Armada. Details of military background. 'Drawing extensively on existing reference sources, the information has been updated and 'pruned'. and an extensive index included to make the book as accessible as possible' (*Antique Collector* November 1989, p.154). *Class No:* 737.2(410)

[3367]
LITHERLAND, A.R. *and* **SIMPKIN, B.T.,** *eds.* **Spink's catalogue of British and associated orders, decorations and medals.** 6th ed. London, Spink, 1990. 224p. illus. £25. ISBN: 090760532x.
Previous edition published as *Spink's Catalogue of British and associated orders, decorations and medals* (Exeter,

....(contd.)
Webb & Bower, 1983).
Well illustrated; bibliography and index.
Class No: 737.2(410)

Germany

[3368]
TRUSTED, M. German Renaissance medals. London, Victoria & Albert Museum, 1990. 192p. illus. £47.50. ISBN: 1851770135.
Catalogue of the Museum's collection, with background notes on purpose, context, identification.
Class No: 737.2(430)

Ceramics & Pottery

Bibliographies

[3369]
CAMPBELL, J.E., *ed.* Pottery and ceramics. a guide to information sources. Detroit, Gale Research, 1978. xii,241p. $68. ISBN: 0810312743.
Covers ancient as well as contemporary ceramics. Mostly limited to English-language material. Lists ceramic periodicals, ceramic organizations and museum collections in the US. Author, title and subject indexes. *Class No:* 738(01)

[3370]
SOLON, M.L., *ed.* Ceramic literature: an analytic index to the works published in all languages on the history and the technique of the ceramic art. New York, Saur, 1987. 660p. $115. ISBN: 3598072279.
First published 1910.
Valuable historical source. *Class No:* 738(01)

Encyclopaedias & Dictionaries

[3371]
CAMERON, E. Encyclopedia of pottery and porcelain: the 19th and 20th centuries. London, Faber, 1986. 366p., illus. £10. ISBN: 0571113974.
Supplements Honey's *European ceramic art* (1949-52) (*q.v.*).
Covers world ceramics 1800-1960; about 2500 cross-referenced entries for factories, techniques, styles, designers, potters and decorators. Selective bibliographies cover most entries. Over 550 illustrations, and 155 potter's marks. *Class No:* 738(03)

[3372]
COYSH, A.W. *and* HENRYWOOD, R.K. The Dictionary of blue and white printed pottery 1780-1880. Woodbridge, Suffolk, Antique Collectors Club, 1982-1989. 420,239p. (2v.), illus. £29.95; £25. ISBN: 0907462065, v.1; 1851490930, v.2.
Volume 1 is an alphabetical listing of 2300 entries for potteries, terms, pattern names, personal & place names, series. Appendices cover potters marks, source books, maps. Brief bibliography. Volume 2 contains 1000 additional entries and supplementary information. *Class No:* 738(03)

[3373]
FOURNIER, R. Illustrated dictionary of pottery decoration; techniques materials and history. New York, Prentice Hall, 1986. 264p. $29.95. ISBN: 0671613766.
Mainly concerned with handmade pottery; several hundred entries, with cross references. *Class No:* 738(03)

[3374]
HONEY, W.B. European ceramic art, from the end of the Middle Ages to about 1815. London, Faber, 1949-52. 53,788p. (2v.).
Volume 1 is mainly plates (192, 24 colour) with introduction (Reissued in a second edition, 1963). Volume 2 contains alphabetical entries on factories, types of ware, artists, techniques, collectors. Bibliography p.17-27; index to marks p.683-788. Cameron continues where this work finishes. *Class No:* 738(03)

[3375]
PENKALA, M. European pottery: a handbook for the collector. 3rd ed. Schiedam, Netherlands, Interbook International, 1980. 472p. illus. £51. ISBN: 9063970269.
Arranged by country, then town with entries for all factories. 5,816 marks on Maiolica, Faience & Stoneware illustrated. Bibliography p.459-462. Index to persons & factories. *Class No:* 738(03)

[3376]
SAVAGE, S. *and* NEWMAN, H. An Illustrated dictionary of ceramics. London, Thames & Hudson, 1985. 320p. illus. £16.95. ISBN: 0500273804.
Paperback reprint of the 1974 edition, but without the colour illustrations.
Subtitled 'defining 3,054 terms relating to wares, materials, processes, styles, patterns and shapes from antiquity to the present day'. Alphabetical entries with cross-references. Over 600 small monochrome illustrations.
Class No: 738(03)

Handbooks & Manuals

[3377]
BIRKS, T. The Complete potter's companion. New ed. London, Conran Octopus, 1997. 192p., illus. £14.99. ISBN: 185029917x.
Previous ed. 1993.
General introduction to the craft skills, with some fine photography. Bibliographical references.
Class No: 738(035)

[3378]
FRENCH, N. The Potter's directory of shape and form. London, A.& C. Black, 1998. 80p., illus. £14.99. ISBN: 0713648791.
Concise paperback guide to over 600 ceramic shapes and forms with silhouette illustrations. Discussion of problems, solutions, materials and techniques. *Class No:* 738(035)

[3379]
HAMER, F. *and* HAMER, J. The Potter's dictionary of materials and techniques. 3rd ed. London, A. & C. Black, 1991. 394p. illus. ISBN: 0713633379.
Standard reference book for craft potters; includes data on behaviour of clays and glazes, sources and character of materials, notes on historical development, and terminology. Numerous excellent diagrams, drawings and photographs. Bibliography; list of suppliers. *Class No:* 738(035)

[3380]

LEACH, B. A Potter's book with special reference to Chinese and Japanese pottery. 2nd ed. London, Faber, 1945. xxvii, 294p.

Eight chapters covering materials and products, the making of clays, shapes, decorations, pigments, glazes, kilns, and workshops. Glossary. *Class No:* 738(035)

[3381]

PETERSON, S. The Craft and art of clay: a complete potter's handbook. 2nd.ed. London, Overlook Press/ Calmann & King, 1996. 400p., illus. $65.00. ISBN: 0879516348.

Originally published as *The Complete pottery course.*

Step-by-step guides to hand, wheel, and plasterwork techniques; many examples of new pieces by international artists. Colour charts, glaze combinations, technical information. Brief history of ceramics links past and present techniques. Over 1200 illustrations, 300 in colour. *Class No:* 738(035)

[3382]

WARDELL, S. Slipcasting. London, A.& C.Black, 1997. 128p., illus. £10.99. ISBN: 0713640677.

Handbook to this technique; useful illustrations, some in colour. *Class No:* 738(035)

Great Britain

[3383]

GODDEN, G.A. The Concise guide to British pottery and porcelain. London, Barrie & Jenkins, 1990. 224p. illus. £8.99. ISBN: 0712636005.

Revised edition of *The Observer's book of pottery and porcelain* by Mary & Geoffrey Payton (Warne, 1973).

Alphabetical arrangement of entries covering styles, potteries, types of ware. Bibliography p.206-213. 8 pages of plates; index. *Class No:* 738(410)

[3384]

GODDEN, G.A. An Illustrated encyclopaedia of British pottery and porcelain. 2nd ed. London, Barrie & Jenkins, 1980. 390p., illus., plates. £30. ISBN: 0214206920.

Designed to be used in conjunction with books on pottery and porcelain marks. Historical summary, and glossary, followed by pictorial survey of over 2000 'documentary examples of English ceramic art', arranged alphabetically by manufacturer, 1650-1900. *Class No:* 738(410)

[3385]

HENRYWOOD, R.K. An Illustrated guide to British jugs: from medieval times to the twentieth century. Shrewsbury, Swan Hill, 1997. 256p., illus. £35.00. ISBN: 1853107476.

Authoritative guide; brief bibliography; 16pp of plates. *Class No:* 738(410)

Histories

[3386]

CLARK, G. The Potter's art: a complete history of pottery in Britain. London, Phaidon, 1995. 240p., illus. £39.99. ISBN: 0714832022.

Comprehensive: from the rudimentary pots of the Middle Ages to modern studio work. 4 sections: peasant, industrial, artist, studio potters. Developments in style and fashions; working conditions, status and lifestyle of workers. Chronology, glossary, bibliography; 200 colour illustrations and many others in monochrome. *Class No:* 738(410)(091)

Biographies

[3387]

CARTER, P. Dictionary of British studio potters. Aldershot, Scolar Press, 1990. 201p., illus. £30. ISBN: 0859678008.

Biographical guide to over 170 major twentieth-century potters. Full page for each potter giving details, example, marks. List of galleries, auctions, collections. Bibliography. *Class No:* 738(410)(092)

[3388]

COOPER, E. *and* **LEWENSTEIN, E.,** ***ed.*** **Potters:** an illustrated directory of the work of fellows and professional members of the Craftsmen Potters Association of Great Britain: a source for studying pottery in the United Kingdom. 10th ed. London, Ceramic Review Publishing for the Craftsmen Potters Association, 1994,. 276p. illus., maps. £7.95. ISBN: 0952357607.

One-page entries give biographical and professional data on potters; lists addresses, courses, events, exhibitions. *Class No:* 738(410)(092)

England

[3389]

LEWIS, G. Collector's history of English pottery. 4th ed. Woodbridge, Suffolk, Antique Collectors' Club, 1987. 360p. illus. £29.50. ISBN: 1851490566.

First published 1969.

26 sections each covering a different type or family of pottery (*e.g.* 2 slipware; 10 Pearl ware; 22 Decorative Victorian tiles) over 700 illustrations, 54 in colour. End of section bibliographies, and general bibliography p.351-5. Efficient index. *Class No:* 738(420)

Encyclopaedias

[3390]

HONEY, W.B. English pottery and porcelain. Charleston, R.J., *ed.* 6th ed. London, Black, 1969. xvi,287p., illus.

Reprinted New York: Alpine, 1981. First published 1933.

3 parts: 1. Earthenware and stoneware to the end of the 18th century - 2. English porcelain of the 18th century - 3. 19th-century pottery and porcelain. Section on collection, p.243-58. Bibliography, p.271-7. 24 plates. The reviser was the Deputy Keeper of the Department of Ceramics, Victoria and Albert Museum. A standard work. *Class No:* 738(420)(031)

China

[3391]

VAINKER, S.J. Chinese pottery and porcelain. London. British Museum Press, 1990. 240p., illus. £19.95. ISBN: 0714114480.

Covers neolithic period to the present, describing styles, function, physical composition. Appendices provide detailed technical data on clays, glazes, and kilns. *Class No:* 738(510)

Japan

[3392]

PENKALA, M. Survey of Japanese ceramics: a guide for the collector and dealer. Schiedam, Netherlands, Interbook International, 1981. 296p. illus. £51. ISBN: 9063970277.

Extensively illustrated; bibliography, index. *Class No:* 738(52)

USA

Bibliographies

[3393]

STRONG, S.R. History of American ceramics: an annotated bibliography. Metuchen, NJ, Scarecrow Press, 1983. xxii, 184p. £17.50. ISBN: 0810816369.

Includes books, pamphlets, exhibition & trade catalogues, theses & dissertations, from Colonial times to 1966. 22 sections - bibliographies, dictionaries & encyclopaedias, marks, general history, specific topics (*e.g.* folk pottery, dinnerware etc.), individual potters & potteries. Subject, author, & title indexes. *Class No:* 738(73)(01)

Histories

[3394]

CLARK, G. American ceramics 1876 to the present. New York, Abbeville, 1988. 351p. $62.50. ISBN: 0896597431.

Revision of *Century of ceramics in the United States*. 1979.

Historical account with good illustrations, and discussion of key figures. *Class No:* 738(73)(091)

[3395]

LEVIN, E. The History of American ceramics 1607 to the present: from pipkins and bean pots to contemporary forms. New York, Abrams, 1988. 352p., illus. £40.00. ISBN: 0810911728.

Reprinted 1997.

Complete historical survey from an authoritative author; covers early forms, through art potteries of the 1800s, Art Nouveau, Art Deco, commercial manufacture, and modern works. Over 350 illustrations, 100 in colour; bibliography. *Class No:* 738(73)(091)

Ancient Times

[3396]

Corpus vasorum antiquorum. Paris, Champion, and others, 1922-.

At head of title: 'Union Académique Internationale'.

Issued in portfolio fascicules, each with *c.*50-60p. of plates and devoted to the painted vases in a particular national museum (*e.g. New Zealand*, fasc.16: *The Los Angeles County Museum of Art*. pt.1. 64p., 60p. of plates, 12 drawings. California Univ. Press, 1977). Some fascs. have native imprints, the series being planned in *c.*200 fasc. *Konkordanz zum 'corpus vasorum antiquorum'*, by Jan W. Crous (Rome, Bretschneider, 1942. 244p.) covers the first 74 fascs., to 1940. *Class No:* 738"-"

[3397]

HAYES, J.W. Handbook of Mediterranean Roman pottery. London, British Museum, 1997. 108p., illus. £14.99. ISBN: 0714122165.

Describes processes of manufacture and decoration, trading patterns and use. Identification guide with drawings and photographs. Some bibliographic references. *Class No:* 738"-"

Ceramic Marks

[3398]

CHAFFERS, W. Collector's handbook of marks and monograms on pottery and porcelain. 4th ed. London, Wordsworth Editions, 1988. 272p., illus. £4.99. ISBN: 1853269158.

....*(contd.)*

This edition previously issued 1968 by Reeves (London). Lists about 5,000 marks; selected from Chaffer's *Marks and monograms*. *Class No:* 738.0

[3399]

CHAFFERS, W. Marks and monograms on European and Oriental pottery and porcelain. 15th rev. ed. London, Reeves, 1965. 635,443p. (2v.) illus. £40. ISBN: 0721100511.

First published 1863.

V.1: *Continental & Oriental pottery* - v.2: *British pottery*. (British pottery manufacturers in 1900, 1964, p.390-408. Selected bibliography (p.328-38) includes contents-listing of transactions. In the 15th ed. the accounts of Bow, Longton Hall and Lowestoft have been completely rewritten. The standard work on pottery marks. *Class No:* 738.0

[3400]

CUSHION, J.P. *and* **HONEY, W.B. Handbook of pottery and porcelain marks.** 5th ed. London, Faber, 1996. vii,304p.,illus.,maps. £35.00. ISBN: 0571179231.

First published 1956; 4th. ed. 1980.

Records over 4000 marks for 21 countries, Austria ... Switzerland. 'Great Britain & Ireland' has appendices including: 'Index of names and dates of manufacturers, retailers, wholesalers and others who registered designs from 1842 to 1883'. Detailed index, with *c.*7,500 entries. *Class No:* 738.0

[3401]

DANCKERT, L. Directory of European porcelain: marks, makers and factories. [Handbuch des europäischen Porzellands.] London, N.A.G., 1981. 688p., illus. £30.00. ISBN: 0719800137.

Reprinted 1995.

Standard and comprehensive handbook; bibliography pp684-688. *Class No:* 738.0

Great Britain

[3402]

COPELAND, R. Spode and Copeland marks. London, Studio Vista, 1993. 173p., illus. £35.00. ISBN: 0289800692.

Contains a chronology, brief catalogue of marks, full and illustrated list of marks, pattern numbers with period and dates; appendices show families, forms, sizes, rarities, popular patterns. Bibliography p.172-3. *Class No:* 738.0(410)

[3403]

CUSHION, J.P. Pocket book of British ceramic marks. New ed. London, Faber, 1983. 439p.,illus. £7.99. ISBN: 0571131085.

A very useful summary. 3,000 entries, with over 800 reproductions of marks under towns arranged alphabetically. Index of manufacturers, names, and initials. *Class No:* 738.0(410)

[3404]

GODDEN, G.A. Encyclopaedia of British pottery and porcelain marks. 2nd rev. ed. London, Jenkins, 1968. 766p., illus. £45. ISBN: 0257657827.

First published 1964.

Lists 4,400 British ceramic marks, under potters' names, A-Z. Appended: List of unidentified marks; Glossary. Indexes of monograms, sizes and devices. A comprehensive and accurate encyclopaedia. *Class No:* 738.0(410)

[3405]

—GODDEN, G.A. The Handbook of British pottery and porcelain marks. New ed. London, Jenkins, 1975. 288p., illus. £6.99. ISBN: 0214201929.

An abridgement of the *Encyclopaedia* in a more convenient format. *Class No:* 738.0(410)

China

[3406]

DAVISON, G. Guide to marks on Chinese porcelain. London, Bamboo Publications, 1987. 105p. illus. £10. ISBN: 1870076036.

Includes 450 diagrams. *Class No:* 738.0(510)

USA

[3407]

DEBOLT, C.G. The Dictionary of American pottery marks: whiteware and porcelain. New York, C.E. Tuttle, 1989. 153p. $27.95. ISBN: 0804870276.

199 manufacturers are listed, with reproductions of relevant marks. Well indexed. *Class No:* 738.0(73)

Porcelain

[3408]

BATTIE, D., ***ed.*** **Sotheby's concise encyclopedia of porcelain.** London, Sotheby Publications, 1990. New York, Little, Brown, 1990. 208p., illus. £30. ISBN: 1850292515.

Paperback version of this edition issued 1994. (1850296480; £14.99)

Concise historical narrative and excellent illustrations; includes fakes and forgeries. 'In the absence of comparable works, a useful overview of the subject'. (*Reference reviews*, 9(2), 1995. p31.) Glossary of terms; bibliography, lists of major factories, and of important names in the development of porcelain. *Class No:* 738.1

Europe

[3409]

GODDEN, G.A. The Concise guide to European porcelain. London, Barrie & Jenkins, 1996. 255p., illus. £14.99. ISBN: 0712645829.

Thoroughly reliable and authoritative work in a convenient format. Bibliography pp241-248. *Class No:* 738.1(4)

[3410]

PENKALA, M. European porcelain: a handbook for the collector. 3rd ed. Schiedam, Netherlands, Interbook International, 1980. 256p. illus. £45. ISBN: 9063970250.

Arranged by country then factory, with data on principal artists. 5,780 marks & signs of painters & modellers illustrated. Bibliography; index. *Class No:* 738.1(4)

Great Britain

[3411]

ATTERBURY, P. ***and*** **BATKIN, M. The Dictionary of Minton.** Rev.ed. Woodbridge, Antique Collectors' Club, 1996. 368p. illus. £35.00. ISBN: 1851492720.

A comprehensive history and survey of the Minton Pottery Company, works, designers, founders. Major personalities are discussed. Over 600 illustrations, 65 in colour. *Class No:* 738.1(410)

[3412]

CURTIS, T. The Lyle price guide: Doulton. Galashiels, Lyle Publishers, 1994. 448p. £14.95. ISBN: 086248152x.

4500 items listed - figures, toby jugs, animals, art pottery, bookends, stoneware, etc. 2500 photographs. *Class No:* 738.1(410)

[3413]

CUSHION, J.P. ***and*** **CUSHION, M. Collector's history of British porcelain.** Woodbridge, Suffolk, Antique Collectors' Club, 1992. 448p., illus. £45.00. ISBN: 1851491554.

Comprehensive overview of the manufacture of porcelain in Great Britain from the mid-eighteenth century to the present. Covers materials and techniques, individual factories, studio potters, decorators, designs and forms. *Class No:* 738.1(410)

[3414]

GODDEN, G.A. Encyclopaedia of British porcelain manufacturers. London, Barrie & Jenkins, 1988. 855p. £50. ISBN: 0712621008.

Introductory essays on types of body and makers' marks and pattern numbers. Checklist of manufacturers 1740-1840 by decade. Alphabetical listing of all manufacturers including studio potters. Concise histories, individual biographies, showing marks where known. 450 illustrations; bibliography; index. 'An absolutely indispensable reference work' (*Apollo,* October 1989. p.285). *Class No:* 738.1(410)

[3415]

HONEY, W.B. Old English porcelain: a handbook for collectors. Barrett, F.A., *ed.* 3rd ed. London, Faber, 1977. xxxiv,440p.,illus. £13.

First published 1928.

17 sections: 1. Introduction - 2. Chelsea - 3. Bow - 4. Derby - 5. Longton Hall - 6. Lowestoft - 7. Lund's Bristol and early Worcester - 8. Worcester (p.229-85; 25 illus.) - 9. Caughley - 10. Liverpool - 11. Pinkton - 12. Nantgarw and Swansea - 13. Coalport - 14. Plymouth and Bristol - 15. Staffordshire - 16. Swinton (Rockingham) - 17. Miscellaneous factories... Appendix A: Marks; B. English porcelain bodies. Locations of collections referred to in the text. Bibliography (by sections). p.414-23. Many footnotes. 136 illus. Analytical index, p.425-50. The standard general guide to English porcelain, 1745-1850. *Class No:* 738.1(410)

[3416]

MESSENGER, M. Coalport 1895-1926. Woodbridge, Suffolk, Antique Collectors' Club, 1995. 424p., illus. £45.00. ISBN: 1851491120.

Traces the development of the John Rose Company from the beginning to the demise of the Coalport factory. Much new information presented - unpublished patterns, profiles of wares, reviews of individual artists and independent decorators. Appendices include marks used; bibliography. 44 colour plates and some 400 other illustrations. The standard work on Coalport. *Class No:* 738.1(410)

[3417]

REILLY, R. Wedgwood: the new illustrated dictionary. Woodbridge, Suffolk, Antique Collectors' Club, 1994. 516p., illus. £45.00. ISBN: 1851492097.

Revised and enlarged version of *The Dictionary of Wedgwood*, 1980 by R. Reilly & G. Savage.

Covers all the ranges of wares, with details of the manufacturing processes, styles, subjects. Over 1200 illustrations, mainly monochrome. *Class No:* 738.1(410)

[3418]

REILLY, R. Wedgwood Jasper. London, Thames & Hudson, 1994. 416p., illus. £36.00. ISBN: 0500016240.

Narrative chronology of the firm and detailed account of principal products; dates, descriptions. Appendices of trademarks, cameos, intaglios, medals, medallions, plaques, busts and figures. Excellent illustrations. 'The definitive work on the subject for many years to come'.(*Reference reviews*, 9(2), 1995. p31.) *Class No:* 738.1(410)

[3419]

SANDON, J. *and* **SANDON, H. Dictionary of Worcester porcelain.** Woodbridge, Antique Collectors' Club, 1991. 402p. £45.00. ISBN: 1851491562.

This volume covers 1751-1851; a second volume is expected, and will cover the later period.

Well illustrated, and with good detail of pieces and designs. *Class No:* 738.1(410)

[3420]

WILLIAMS, P. Wedgwood: a collector's guide. London, Grange, 1997. 128p., illus. £7.99. ISBN: 1856278182.

Originally published: London, Apple, 1992.

Convenient, concise handbook for amateur collectors. *Class No:* 738.1(410)

China

[3421]

VAINKER, S.J. Chinese pottery and porcelain. London. British Museum Press, 1990. 240p., illus. £19.95. ISBN: 0714114480.

Covers neolithic period to the present, describing styles, function, physical composition. Appendices provide detailed technical data on clays, glazes, and kilns. *Class No:* 738.1(510)

Metal Arts

Goldsmiths & Silversmiths

Encyclopaedias & Dictionaries

[3422]

BRETT, V. Sotheby's directory of silver 1600-1940. London, Philip Watson for Sotheby's Publications, 1986. 432p. ISBN: 0856671932.

Directory is divided by country; useful introduction. Brief bibliography and indexes of objects, goldsmiths, assay masters, designers, engravers, heraldry and inscriptions. Concentrates on some 2,000 pieces sold at Sotheby's 1920-1985. *Class No:* 739.1(03)

[3423]

CLAYTON, M., *ed.* **The Collectors' dictionary of the silver and gold of Britain and North America.** 2nd ed. Woodbridge, Suffolk, Antique Collectors' Club, 1985. 480p., illus. £35. ISBN: 090746257x.

First published 1971.

Includes brief biographies as well as entries on silver & gold ware. Short bibliographies are appended to many entries. Cross-references; tables; general bibliography. 78 colour plates and over 700 monochrome illustrations. Tables of hallmarks. *Class No:* 739.1(03)

[3424]

NEWMAN, H. An Illustrated dictionary of silverware. London, Thames & Hudson, 1987. 367p. £22.50. ISBN: 0500234566.

Covers UK and North America, and includes wares, techniques, designers, and makers, 1500 to the present. Well illustrated and with plentiful bibliographic notes. 'Excellent, much-needed work' (*Choice*, March 1988). *Class No:* 739.1(03)

[3425]

TRUMAN, C., *ed.* **Sotheby's concise encyclopaedia of silver.** London, Conran Octopus, 1994. 208p., illus. £35.00. ISBN: 1850294224.

Essays by 13 specialists; glossary; brief biographies; hallmarks described. *Class No:* 739.1(03)

[3426]

WALDRON, P. Price guide to antique silver. 2nd. ed. Woodbridge, Suffolk, Antique Collectors' Club, 1992. 368p., illus. £35.00. ISBN: 1851491651.

Compiled by the head of Sotheby's silver dept., using the firm's photographic archives to illustrate styles, factors affecting value, potential for fakes etc. Almost 1200 illustrations. *Class No:* 739.1(03)

Biographies

Women

[3427]

GLANVILLE, P. *and* **GOLDSBOROUGH, J.F. Women silversmiths 1685-1845.** London, Thames & Hudson, 1990. 176p. illus. £28. ISBN: 0500235783.

Includes a scholarly discussion of forms, styles, techniques, decoration, and major individual works. *Class No:* 739.1(092)-0055.2

Great Britain

[3428]

HELLIWELL, S. Understanding antique silver plate. Woodbridge, Suffolk, Antiques Collectors' Club, 1996. 208p., illus. £25.00. ISBN: 185149247x.

Covers Old Sheffield Plate and Electroplate; arranged by areas of interest - candlesticks; cutlery; drinking vessels etc. Suggested valuations included. Over 300 illustrations, 45 in colour. *Class No:* 739.1(410)

[3429]

HUGHES, G.B. Antique Sheffield plate. London, Batsford, 1990. 304p. £50. ISBN: 0713465859.

Full explanation of process, techniques, developments, ranges of typical products. *Class No:* 739.1(410)

[3430]

POOLE, T.R. Identifying antique British silver. London, Bloomsbury, 1988. 327p. illus., charts. £25. ISBN: 0747500924.

Sections on hallmarks, punch shapes, date letters, styles, chronology. Alphabetical illustrated dictionary of artefacts (p.39-131), alphabetical and descriptive list of makers' marks (p.136-321). Bibliography; glossary. *Class No:* 739.1(410)

[3431]

WATSON, B.W., ***ed.*** **The Sheffield Assay Office register:** a copy of the register of the persons concerned in the manufacture of silver wares, and of the marks entered by them from 1773 to 1907. 2nd ed. Sheffield, Sheffield Assay Office, 1989. xvi,104p. £25. ISBN: 1872212018.

Previous edition Sheffield, Townsend, 1911.

Index of names connected with a major centre.

Class No: 739.1(410)

London

[3432]

CULME, J. The Directory of gold and silversmiths, jewellers and allied traders 1838-1914: from the London Assay Office registers. Woodbridge, Suffolk, Antique Collectors' Club, 1987. 546, 340p. (2v.). £145. ISBN: 0907462464.

Detailed biographies of individuals and companies in Volume 1; Volume 2 contains some 12,000 illustrations of all makers' marks registered at Goldsmiths Hall 1838-1914, arranged alphabetically and giving name and occupation.

Class No: 739.1(421)

[3433]

HEAL, A. The London goldsmiths, 1200-1800: a record of the names and addresses of the craftsmen, their shop signs and trade cards, compiled ... from the records of the Goldsmith's Company ... Newton Abbott, David & Charles, 1972. 279p. illus.

Originally published: Cambridge, CUP, 1935.

7,000 names are featured; illustrations of signs and cards.

Class No: 739.1(421)

Hallmarks

[3434]

BRADBURY, F. Book of hallmarks: a guide to marks of origin on British and Irish silver, gold and platinum, and on foreign imported silver and gold plate 1544-1980. Old Sheffield plate-makers marks, 1743-1860. Rev. ed. Sheffield, J.W. Northend, 1989. 112p.,illus. £9.50. ISBN: 0901100226.

Previous edition 1980.

Small format, comprehensive handbook.

Class No: 739.10

Great Britain

[3435]

CHAFFERS, W. Hallmarks on gold and silver plate, illustrated with revised tables of annual date letters employed in the Assay Offices of England, Scotland and Ireland. Markham, C.A., *ed.* 10th ed. London, Reeves, 1922. liv,395p., illus., tables.

First published 1865.

Includes historical data, tables of marks, notes on standards, assaying, etc., a chronological list of specimens of plate, and an extensive bibliography (p.374-83). General index. A standard work on the subject.

Class No: 739.10(410)

[3436]

—CHAFFERS, W. Handbook to hallmarks on gold and silver plate, Great Britain and Ireland, with tables of the annual date letters employed in the Assay Offices. Blunt, C.G.E., *ed.* 11th ed. London, Reeves, 1975. vii,135p.,illus. £12.50. ISBN: 0721103081.

First published 1897.

A reduced version of *Hallmarks.* *Class No:* 739.10(410)

[3437]

PICKFORD, I., ***ed.*** **Jackson's silver and gold marks of England, Scotland and Ireland:** a revised edition with 10,000 corrections of Sir Charles Jackson's classic work. Woodbridge,Suffolk, Antique Collectors' Club, 1990. 766p. £45. ISBN: 0907462634.

First published 1905; last revised 1921.

Arranged by region, using chronological charts, and photographs to illustrate the marks. Bibliography; indexes of initials, and symbols. *Class No:* 739.10(410)

[3438]

—PICKFORD, I., *ed.* Pocket edition Jackson's hallmarks of England, Scotland and Ireland. Woodbridge, Suffolk, Antique Collectors' Club, 1993. 172p., illus. £6.95. ISBN: 1851491287.

Abbreviated version of the main work, featuring 1000 of the most prominent and interesting makers and their marks.

Class No: 739.10(410)

England

[3439]

BLY, J. Discovering hallmarks on English silver. 8th.ed. Princes Risborough, Shire, 1997. 72p.,illus. £4.50. ISBN: 0747803498.

Concise and accessible guide for amateurs.

Class No: 739.10(420)

[3440]

JONES, K.C., ***ed.*** **The Silversmiths of Birmingham and their marks, 1750-1980.** London, NAG Press, 1981. 415p.,illus., tables, maps. £30. ISBN: 0719800021.

Five sections cover history; organization & management of labour; major silversmiths, bullion dealers and companies; makers' marks; glossary of decorative terms & techniques. Bibliography; index. 'The book's fundamental service is to record exactly the punchmarks of 2,400 silversmiths ...' (*RSA Journal* July 1983, p.486). *Class No:* 739.10(420)

London

[3441]

GRIMWADE, A.G. London goldsmiths 1697-1837: their marks and lives from the original registers of Goldsmiths' Hall and other sources. 3rd. rev. ed. London, Faber, 1990. 752p. illus. £60. ISBN: 0571152384.

Alphabetical list of all known makers' marks (3,914 illustrated) with substantial dictionary of the makers (almost 2,600). *Class No:* 739.10(421)

Jewellery

Encyclopaedias

[3442]

BAGLEY, P. Encyclopedia of jewellery techniques. New ed. London, Batsford, 1989. 192p. illus. £12.95. ISBN: 0713442565.

Alphabetical sequence covering materials, equipment,

....(*contd.*)
processes, tools, giving definitions and explanations. 344 photographs and line drawings, diagrams.
Class No: 739.2(031)

Dictionaries

[3443]
FORGET, C., ***comp*****. Elsevier's dictionary of jewellery and watchmaking** in five languages. Amsterdam, Elsevier, 1984. viii,508p. £103. ISBN: 044442279x.
Covers English, French, German, Italian and Spanish; English base p.3-344 with indexes from the other languages. Over 5,500 entries. *Class No:* 739.2(038)

Histories

[3444]
BURY, S. Jewellery 1789-1910. Woodbridge, Antique Collectors' Club, 1990. 750p. (2v.). £75. ISBN: 185149104x.
Detailed examination of fashions and styles through the 19th century, with commentary on developments based on new materials and techniques. *Class No:* 739.2(091)

[3445]
DUBIN, L.S. The History of beads from prehistory to the present. London, Thames & Hudson, 1987. 364p. illus. £36. ISBN: 0500235074.
Covers the uses and symbolism of beads in prehistoric, Roman, Islamic, Christian, Asian, African, and early American cultures. *Class No:* 739.2(091)

[3446]
MASCETTI, D. *and* **TRIOSSI, A. Earrings from antiquity to the present.** London, Thames & Hudson, 1990. 245p.,illus. £30. ISBN: 0500014930.
Introductory sections chart the history of earrings from the ancient world, classical times, Byzantium, to the 19th & 20th centuries. Key names are extensively discussed; excellent illustrations. Both authors are with Sotheby's.
Class No: 739.2(091)

[3447]
NEWMAN, H. *and* **ROBERTSON, R. An Illustrated history of jewellery.** Rev. ed. London, Thames & Hudson, 1987. 352p. illus. £12.95. ISBN: 0500274525.
2500 entries include definitions of terms relating to materials, processes, and types, descriptions of named items, biographical entries for designers and makers, and topographical entries. 16 colour plates, and 632 monochrome illustrations. Line drawings.
Class No: 739.2(091)

Biographies

[3448]
SNOWMAN, A.K., ***ed*****. The Master jewellers.** London, Thames & Hudson, 1990. 278p., illus. £28. ISBN: 0500235902.
15 chapters, written by acknowledged experts, cover many aspects of jewellery, including aesthetic, social, and business. From 1850 to the present. Good coverage of the work of major names (*e.g.* Fabergé, Cartier). Fine illustrations. *Class No:* 739.2(092)

Great Britain

Yearbooks & Directories

[3449]
British Jeweller yearbook. London, EMAP. c275p. £35.00. ISSN: 13570052.
Annual.
Data on hallmarking, gold prices, standards, ring sizes, punchmarks, trade names; directory of courses, trade fairs, members of organizations. *Class No:* 739.2(410)(058)

USA

Histories

[3450]
FALES, M.G. Jewelry in America: 1600-1900. Woodbridge, Suffolk, Antique Collectors' Club, 1995. 447p., illus. £35.00. ISBN: 1851492232.
Identifies jewellery worn in America, whether manufactured there or elsewhere; notes developments in forms, styles, materials and techniques. Over 500 illustrations, half in colour. *Class No:* 739.2(73)(091)

Copper, Bronze etc.

Brass

[3451]
SCHIFFER, P. *and* **SCHIFFER, N. The Brass book:** American, English and European, fifteenth century through 1850. Exton, Penn, Schiffer, 1978. xii,447p.,illus. £48. ISBN: 091683817x.
Re-issued 1987.
Historical introduction (p.15-32) followed by alphabetically arranged sections on brass objects (Andirons - warming pans). Large sections on andirons, candlesticks, fire-place accessories, kettles, tobacco boxes. Smaller sections include scientific instruments, lamps & lanterns, horse brasses, tableware etc. Dating charts; representative items described & illustrated. Catalogue of 18th century furniture brass reproduced p.413-43. Bibliography; index.
Class No: 739.5BRA

Great Britain

[3452]
BERTRAM, J., ***ed*****. Monumental brasses as art and history.** Stroud, Alan Sutton, 1996. xxi,218p., illus. £29.50. ISBN: 0750910518.
Co-published with the Monumental Brass Society.
Useful discussion and description; bibliography pp201-206. *Class No:* 739.5BRA(410)

[3453]
LACK, W., ***ed*****. Index to Monumental Brass Society transactions,** bulletins, and portfolios 1887-1986. London, W. Lack/Monumental Brass Society, 1987. 222p. £12. ISBN: 0951157108.
Comprehensive and efficient key.
Class No: 739.5BRA(410)

[3454]
LESTRANGE, R. British monumental brasses. London, Thames & Hudson, 1972. 150p., illus.
A catalogue of over 9,000 brasses under countries, counties and then churches, A-Z. Appendices on crosses, chalice brasses, etc. 'General books of reference', p.149-50.
Class No: 739.5BRA(410)

[3455]

STEPHENSON, M. A List of monumental brasses in the British Isles. London, Headley, 1926. xvi,718p.

Appendix (pp.719-849) issued 1938.

Arranged under English counties, then under Ireland, Scotland, Wales and Isle of Man. Also sections: 'Museums and associations'; 'Private possession'; 'Derelicts'. Detailed analytical index (p.593-716) of *c.*7,500 entries. Supersedes pt.2 of the old classic on the subject: Haines, H. *Manual of monumental brasses* (1861). *Class No:* 739.5BRA(410)

England

[3456]

COALES, J., *ed.* Earliest English brasses: patronage, style and workshops. 1270-1350. London, Monumental Brass Society. 1987. 234p., illus. £12.95. ISBN: 0950129852.

Survey of extant brasses; county summary list p.180-215. Bibliographic citations p.216-9. Index by place, and names. 219 illustrations. *Class No:* 739.5BRA(420)

[3457]

HESELTINE, P. Oxford brasses. London, Batsford, 1990. 96p. illus. £12.95. ISBN: 0713461241.

Illustrated guide to medieval and Tudor brasses in Oxford colleges and churches. *Class No:* 739.5BRA(420)

Bronze

[3458]

BERMAN, H. Encyclopedia of bronzes: sculptors and founders, 1800-1930. New York, Editions Publisol, 1988. 4v., illus. $265. ISBN: 0917350057.

Originally published Chicago; ABAGE Publishers, 1974-80 as *Bronzes.*

Brief catalogue entries (title; sculptor; date of cast; country of origin; patination; height; founder), with monograms. Chief feature: the 4877 brilliant photographs. V.1 (p.1-224) has foreword ('Criteria for evaluation of bronzes'); Part 1: Bronze sculptors; Photographic section, p.15-188; Part 2: General references (*i.e.,* appendices); *e.g.* Founders' seals; Care, cleansing and protecting of bronzes. How to photograph bronzes. Partly analytical index.
Class No: 739.5BRO

[3459]

MACKAY, J. The Dictionary of Western sculptors in bronze. Woodbridge, Suffolk, Antique Collectors' Club, 1977. 414p. £25. ISBN: 0902028553.

About 800 entries, A-Z, from the beginning of the 18th century to about 1960, and covering 'Western Europe and most westernised parts of the world, such as America and Australia'. Oriental sculpture is included, if in the western idiom. Lengthier entries have references (*e.g.* John Gibson: 1/3 column, 2 references). Family trees, p.407-12. Select bibliography (9 sections). p.413-4. 'The primary purpose ... is to enable the collector, dealer and student to identify bronzes that bear a signature' (*Author's preface*). No ports. or illus. *Class No:* 739.5BRO

[3460]

THOMAS, G. Bronze casting: a manual of techniques. Marlborough, Crowood Press, 1995. 128p.,illus. £17.99. ISBN: 1852239387.

Describes the techniques in detail, using the example of a modelled head. Also covers clay, wax and plaster processes. 100 monochrome illustrations. *Class No:* 739.5BRO

Pewter

[3461]

COTTERELL, H.H. Old pewter: its makers and marks in England, Scotland and Ireland. London, Batsford, 1929. xv,432p. plates, illus.

Introduction on history, marks and collecting. Alphabetical list of pewterers with illustration of their marks where known. Alphabetical list of initialled marks, obscure marks, devices, 'hall-marks'. Bibliography. 6 fold-out plates of London and Edinburgh Touchplates. *Class No:* 739.5PEW

[3462]

PEAL, C.A. More pewter marks. Norwich, Christopher Peal for the Pewter Society, 1976. 117p. illus. £25. ISBN: 0950528803.

Published as a supplement to H.H. Cotterell's *Old Pewter* (1929). An addendum was published in 1977 (33p. illus., £5.; 0950528811).

Six sections - named marks, initialled marks, obscure marks, hall marks, spoon marks, fakes. Alphabetical entries, well illustrated, but lacking index, poorly formatted.
Class No: 739.5PEW

[3463]

STARÁ, D. Pewter marks of the world. London, Hamlyn. 1977. 260p., illus.

Translation of original Czech edition, published in Prague.

Identifies 1,940 marks (plates, p.32-232); data include name of pewterer or factory, place, the date pewterer passed examination, etc.; year of pewterer's death, Pewter marks are arranged by designs (*e.g.* letters, nos.1-377; animals, 640-934; plants, 1102-1325. Introductory section on history of marks in individual states, Austria ... USA. Index of places; index of names. *Class No:* 739.5PEW

Arms & Armour

[3464]

CURTIS, T. The Lyle price guide to militaria, arms and armour. Galashiels, Lyle Publishing, 1993. 448p. £14.95. ISBN: 0862481481.

Price guide and 3000 illustrations of 200 categories and sub-divisions of weapons and equipment. 4 sections: edged weapons; flintlock and matchlock weapons; militaria; percussion weapons. High standard of production, background information, and excellent illustrations make this an essential reference tool. *Class No:* 739.7

[3465]

GYNGELL, D.S.H. Armourers' marks: being a compilation of the known marks of armourers, swordsmiths and gunsmiths. London, Thompson, 1959. xi,131p, illus.

Marks arranged under countries, A-Z. Enlarged reproductions, to facilitate easy recognition. Unidentified armourers, swordsmiths, etc., p.114-26. Bibliography, p.129. 'Sale catalogues in which marks are reproduced', p.131. Index of craftsmen, p.vi-ix. A-Z list of symbols and marks, p.x-xi. *Class No:* 739.7

Encyclopaedias & Dictionaries

[3466]

EVANGELISTA, N. The Encyclopedia of the sword. Westport,CT, Greenwood Press, 1995. xxiv,690p., illus. $79.50. ISBN: 0313278962.

Covers artistic, cultural, historical, literary, symbolic aspects of the sword in all periods, worldwide. Several hundred short entries concentrate on European classical fencing, with treatment of contemporary practice, history

.... *(contd.)*
and specialised terminology. But also good coverage of Japan and other non-European countries, swords in literature and cinema, etc. 250 types of sword are identified and described. Appendices list sword categories, fencing organisations. *Class No:* 739.7(03)

[3467]
TARASSUK, L. *and* **BLAIR, C.,** *ed.* **The Complete encyclopaedia of arms and weapons.** London, Batsford, 1982. 544p. illus. ISBN: 0713415959.
Alphabetical sequence covering weapons, styles of armour, component parts; all periods and places. Nine named contributors; numerous detailed & systematic illustrations and diagrams. 90 colour plates. Good coverage of obscure oriental & classical terms. Bibliography p.536-44. *Class No:* 739.7(03)

Glossaries

[3468]
STONE, G.C. A Glossary of the construction, decoration and use of arms and armour in all countries and in all times ... London, Arms & Armour Press, 1978. vi,694p., illus.
Reprint of the 1924 publication (Southwark Press).
About 15,000 entries, A-Z, illustrated, where possible. Essentially an historical approach (*e.g.* no entry for, or reference to, the rifle). Treatment is international. Thus, Japanese weapons receive considerable attention. 'Spear': p.572-7; 8 illus. of 86 specimens. Entries cite sources. Bibliography, p.687-94. 3,500 small half-tones.
Class No: 739.7(038.1)

Scotland

[3469]
WHITELAW, C.E. Scottish arms makers: a biographical dictionary of makers of firearms, edged weapons and armour working in Scotland from the 14th century to 1870. London, Arms & Armour Press, 1976. 339p. illus. £11.50. ISBN: 0853682011.
Dictionary of craftsmen under towns; glossary; detailed index p.320-339. *Class No:* 739.7(411)

Firearms & Pistols

[3470]
SCHWING, N. *and* **HOUZE, H. Standard catalog of firearms.** 5th.ed. Iola,Wis, Krause, 1995. 912p., illus. $27.95. ISBN: 0873413512.
10,000 models of guns and over 1,000 manufacturers are listed, with brief historical notes; many illustrations. Pricing information has been updated. *Class No:* 739.74

Great Britain

[3471]
NEAL, W.K. *and* **BACK, D.H.L. British gunmakers:** their trade cards, cases and equipment, 1760-1860. Warminster, Compton Press, 1980. 300p., illus. ISBN: 0900193581.
Scholarly detailed work in this specialized field.
Class No: 739.74(410)

[3472]
NEAL, W.K. *and* **BACK, D.H.L. Great British gunmakers, 1740-1790.** London, Sotheby Publications, 1975. 196p., illus. ISBN: 0856670154.
A companion volume covering 1540-1740 is expected. Historical commentary and full discussion and illustration of important pieces. *Class No:* 739.74(410)

London

[3473]
BLACKMORE, H.L. A Dictionary of London gunmakers 1350-1850. London, Phaidon, 1986. 222p., illus. £70. ISBN: 0714880213.
Historical overview precedes the 170p. dictionary of individual and company names. Each entry gives full name and variants, trade, dates, address, and brief information on significant designs, innovations, etc. 260 gunmakers' marks illustrated; 9 brief appendices. 'Uniquely valuable treasury' (*Antique Collector,* August 1986, p.63) 'of quite outstanding importance' (*British Book News* October 1986, p.596).
Class No: 739.74(421)

[3474]
BROWN, N. London gunmakers. London, Christies, 1998. 296p., illus. £65.00. ISBN: 0903432528.
Encyclopedic coverage from 14th century, but with fullest information on 19th and 20th century makers; claims to include all London makers, giving the history of 48 firms and 15 shooting schools, along with a quantity of miscellaneous facts and figures. Lists serial numbers and makers' records; brand names; trade patents; proof marks; date marks, etc. Names of presidents, secretaries, chairmen of various associations and clubs. Brief bibliography.
Class No: 739.74(421)

USA

[3475]
FLAYDERMAN, N. Guide to antique American firearms and their values. 6th ed. London, Arms & Armour Press, 1994. 624p. illus. £19.95. ISBN: 0873491629.
A comprehensive guide; over 900 illustrations.
Class No: 739.74(73)

74 Decorative Arts & Drawing

Decorative Arts & Drawing

Bibliographies

[3476]
AMES, K.L. *and* **WARD, G.W.R.,** *eds.* **Decorative arts and household furnishings in America, 1650-1920:** an annotated bibliography. Virginia University Press for Winterthur Museum, 1990. 392p. $60. ISBN: 0912724196.

Contains 21 individual bibliographies with introductions by expert hands. Covers domestic architecture, furniture, metals, glass, ceramics, textiles, clocks, Arts & crafts movement, etc. Good coverage of materials, well annotated. *Class No:* 740(01)

[3477]
DEWINTER, P.M. European decorative arts 1400-1600: an annotated bibliography. Boston, G.K. Hall, 1988. 343p. $75. ISBN: 081618612x.

Over 2,200 briefly annotated references to works on clerical and secular furnishings. 38 chapters, omits popular works. *Class No:* 740(01)

[3478]
EHRESMANN, D.L. Applied and decorative arts: a bibliographic guide. 2nd ed. Littleton,CO, Libraries Unlimited, 1993. 629p. £45.00. ISBN: 0872879062.

2482 entries, almost 1000 new to this edition. Covers ceramics, costume, furniture, glass, leather, metalwork, textiles; new features for this edition include wallpaper, regional arts, individual designers. Chapters discuss individual media, then use standard sub-divisions - reference works, chronologies, regions, factories, designers, individual pieces. Western language material - two-thirds English; annotations are descriptive, but include some evaluative comments. Author/title and subject indexes. 'Essential arts reference source.' (*Reference books bulletin,* 15/10/93. p465/6.) *Class No:* 740(01)

Encyclopaedias & Dictionaries

[3479]
DIAGRAM GROUP. Handbook of arts and crafts: the encyclopedia of the fine, decorative and applied arts. Lawther, G., *ed.* London, Harrap, 1981. 319p., illus.

'Examples from over 150 specialized fine and applied arts, involving the use of over 2000 tools. Each skill is illustrated by an example of the art form, or by a documentary illustration of the artists at work' (*Foreword*). Closely subdivided: Introduction - Writing on bone and stone ... Development of the pen ... Printing type ... Photography ... Oil painting ... Brass rubbing ... Pottery (p.86-109) ... Plaster ... Metal ... Wood sculpture ... Carving ... Glossary (p.180-201) ... Precious metals ... Beadmaking ... Weaving ... Crochet ... Millinery ... Leather decoration. Bibliography (general: 18 sections), p.310-1. Analytical index p.313-9. Over 4,000 illus., mainly two-colour. Well produced. *Class No:* 740(03)

[3480]
FLEMING, J. *and* **HONOUR, H. The Penguin dictionary of decorative arts.** Rev. ed. London, Viking, 1989. 935p. illus. £30. ISBN: 0670820474.

A concise guide to Western decorative arts from the Middle Ages to the present. Almost 5000 entries and over 1000 illustrations. Alphabetical arrangement of designers, craftsmen, movements, styles, techniques, materials, terms. Almost every entry has a bibliographic citation, and there are many cross-references. *Class No:* 740(03)

[3481]
The Oxford companion to the decorative arts. Osborne, H., *ed.* Oxford, OUP, 1985. xiv,880p. illus. £14.95. ISBN: 0192818635.

Paperback version of the 1975 edition.

About 1,000 entries A/Z including biographies. Bibliography of 940 numbered items with references from the text. *Class No:* 740(03)

[3482]
Phaidon encyclopedia of the decorative arts, 1890-1940. Garner, P., *ed.* New ed. London, Phaidon, 1988. 320p., illus. £14.95 (pbk). ISBN: 0714825344.

Hardback edition published 1978; US edition as *The Encyclopedia of decorative arts, 1890-1940* (Van Nostrand Reinhold, 1978).

11 contributors, 3 parts: 1. Styles and influences in the decorative arts, 1890-1940 - 2. Designs and designers, 1890-1940 (France, UK., Germany and Austria, etc.) - 3. The background (The great exhibitions. Photography and the cinema. Painting and the decorative arts. Literature and the decorative arts). Appended: 'Major craftsmen and designers, 1860-1940'. Bibliography, p.310-12. Glossary. Index. Nearly 500 illus. (150 in colour).

French translation and adaptation as *Encyclopédie visuelle des arts decoratifs, 1890-1940* (Paris, Bordas-Elsevier, 1981) and recommended for 'well-informed amateurs and specialists' (*Bulletin critique du livre français,* no.433, January 1982, entry 117703). *Class No:* 740(03)

Histories

[3483]
BRIDGEMAN, H. *and* **DRURY, E. The Encyclopedia of Victoriana.** London, Macmillan, 1975. 368p., illus.

29 specialist contributors; 19 chapters divided by type of material (glass, furniture, textiles, wallpaper, etc.) and examining UK and US developments. Describes artifacts, and gives details of designers and makers. Glossary, brief bibliography. Excellent illustrations. *Class No:* 740(091)

[3484]
GRUBER, A. The History of decorative arts. The Renaissance and mannerism in Europe. New York, Abbeville, 1994. 495p. $150.00. ISBN: 1558598219.

The first in a projected series of three vols.

Survey of the decorative arts from the Middle Ages to the 20th. century; essays on decorative elements - interlace, rinceaux, grotesque, Moorish tracery, strapwork and cartouches. Glossary, biographical notes, extensive

.... (contd.)
bibliography. 'Fills a great need for placing these neglected aspects of visual culture in the wider framework of art history.' (*Choice,* April 1995, p1288.) *Class No:* 740(091)

Biographies

Women

[3485]
PRATHER-MOSES, A.I. International dictionary of women workers in the decorative arts: a historical survey from the distant past to the early decades of the twentieth century. Metuchen, NJ, Scarecrow Press, 1981. xvii,200p. £17.50. ISBN: 0810814501.

A/Z arrangement of 900 entries with brief data. List of sources; subject index. *Class No:* 740(092)-0055.2

Marks & Monograms

[3486]
GOLDSTEIN, F. Monogramm Lexikon: internationales Verzeichnis der Monogramme bildender Künstler seit 1850. Berlin, de Gruyter, 1964. viii,931p., illus.

About 20,000 monograms worldwide, with small but clear reproductions (p.1-810). Supplementary lists of figures and signs, of anonymous artists, and of cyrillic characters. Name index, p.835-931. *Class No:* 740.0

[3487]
HASLAM, M. Marks and monograms: the decorative arts, 1880-1960. Rev.ed. London, Collins & Brown, 1995. 448p.illus. £35.00. ISBN: 1855850249.

Previous edition as *Marks and monograms of the modern movement* (Guildford: Lutterworth, 1977.)

Excellent coverage within its date period. *Class No:* 740.0

[3488]
NAGLER, G.K. Die Monogrammisten. Andersen, A.G. *and* Claus, C., *eds.* Nieuwkoop, DeGraaf, 1966. 5v., illus. $546.

Reprint of 1871-2 edition, and index (1920).

More than 30,000 monogram facsimiles. *Class No:* 740.0

[3489]
NAHUM, P. Monograms of Victorian and Edwardian artists. London, Victoria Square Press, 1976. 326p. ISBN: 0950529508.

Identifies 4000 monograms of artists, illustrators, architects and craftsmen working 1830-1930. Two main sections: monograms in alphabetical order with artist details (several entries if more than one interpretation is possible); alphabetical index of artists. Brief bibliography.
Class No: 740.0

[3490]
RIS-PAGUOT, O.T. Dictionnaire encyclopédie des marques et monogrammes ... Paris, Laurens, 1893. 2v., illus.

Reprinted New York, Franklin, 1964.

Over 12,000 marks, ciphers, and initialisms for painters, jewellers, ceramicists, sculptors, textile artists, engravers, designers, founders, etc., etc. *Class No:* 740.0

Drawing

[3491]
ASHMOLEAN MUSEUM. Oxford. **Catalogue of the collection of drawings.** Oxford, Clarendon Press, 1938-. v.1-, illus.

1. *Netherlandish, German, French and Spanish schools,* by K.T. Parker. 1939.
2. *Italian schools,* by K.T. Parker. 2v. (1: Text. xx,575p.; 2: Plates. (240 pl.). 1956.
3. *Supplement,* by H. Macandrew. 1980. xxi,368p. 10 pl.
4. *Earlier British drawings,* by D.B. Brown. 1982. 672p.

V.1 has descriptions of 1,625 drawings, with notes on collections, exhibitions and reproductions; index of artists; 104 plates. In v.2 primary arrangement is by century, with artists A-Z under each; prefixed by list of sources referred to. V.4 covers artists born before 1775; over 560 drawings reproduced in microfiche (slip-case inside back cover). V.2 is considered 'indispensable for study in the field' (Arntzen, E., and Rainwater, P., *Guide to the literature of art history,* item L55). *Class No:* 741

[3492]
BRITISH MUSEUM. Department of Prints and Drawings. **A Handbook to the drawings and watercolours in the Department of Prints and Drawings.** Popham, A.E. London, British Museum, 1939. 144p., illus.

General notes are followed by 10 country chapters. Very brief biographical references, with dates, to *c.*1,200 artists. Appendices: 1. The growth of the British Museum Collection; 2. Collectors of drawings; 3. Reproductions of drawings. Index of artists, p.135-44. 8 plates. The author was Deputy Keeper of Prints and Drawings. *Class No:* 741

Encyclopaedias & Dictionaries

[3493]
ASHWIN, C. Encyclopedia of drawing: materials, technique and style. London, Batsford, 1982. 264p., illus.

Entries: Abstraction ... Water colour. 'Caricature': p.42-47; 'Grip': p.110-3. Cross-references in bold. Index to artists, p.261-4. 258 illus. (incl. 19 in colour). The text is not confined to technical information in the narrow sense but approaches drawing also 'as a means of recording and communicating information, feelings and opinions' (*Preface*). *Class No:* 741(03)

Great Britain

[3494]
BRITISH MUSEUM. Department of Prints and Drawings. **Catalogue of British drawings,** supplemented by a list of foreign artists' drawings connected with Great Britain. London, BM, 1960-. v.1.-, illus.

Replaces L. Binyon's *Catalogue of drawings by British artists* (1898-1907. 4v.).

V.1 (2pts: Text; Plates): *XVI & XVII centuries,* by E. Croft-Murray and P. Hobson.

The text (xliii, 619p.) consists of a catalogue (artists, A-Z) in 2 main parts: 16th and early 17th century, p.1-86; 17th century, p.87-555, plus a handlist of drawings by foreign artists (p.556-8). For each work: inscription; engraving; bibliography; biographical note; description. Index of provenances, p.579-87; list of works referred to, p.588-97; index (11pts.) of subjects of drawings ('Ancient history,

.... (contd.)
allegory and mythology' ... 'Topography'). Plates in v.1 comprise 297 half-tones, plus 8 colour plates.
Class No: 741(410)

[3495]
HARRIS, J., ***comp.*** **A Catalogue of British drawings for architecture, decoration, sculpture and landscape gardening,** 1550-1900, in American collections. Boston, G.K. Hall, 1971. 355p. illus. $185. ISBN: 083980766x.
Lists 5,000 drawings, illustrating the impact of English architecture on America. *Class No:* 741(410)

Ireland

[3496]
NATIONAL GALLERY OF IRELAND. Summary catalogue of drawings, watercolours and miniatures. Le Harivel, A., *ed.* Dublin, National Gallery of Ireland, 1984. xxviii,846p. illus. £40. ISBN: 0903162105.
Over 5000 items illustrated and described; eleven appendices, of which the last is an index to artists.
Class No: 741(415)

France

[3497]
OSTERWALDER, M. Dictionnaire des illustrateurs, 1800-1914: illustrateurs, caricaturistes et affichistes. Paris, Hubschmid & Bouret, 1983. 1221p. illus. £35. ISBN: 2859720081.
Emphasis on French artists but covers a wide range of European and American figures. Over 1000 entries give concise biographical data, bibliography of writings, reproduction of a work. General bibliography and extensive indexes. 'Provide already accessible if somewhat dispersed information in a compact form' (*Print Quarterly* 2(4) December 1985 p.324-5). *Class No:* 741(44)

Italy

[3498]
BRITISH MUSEUM. Department of Prints and Drawings. **Italian drawings in the Department of Prints and Drawings.** London, BM, 1950-82. 5v. in 9.
1. *The fourteenth and fifteenth centuries*, by A.E. Popham and P. Pouncey. 1950. 2v. (Catalogue; Plates).
2. *Michelangelo and his studio*, by J. Wilde. 1953.
3. *Raphael and his circle*, by P. Pouncey and J.A. Gere. 1962. 2v. (Catalogue; Plates).
4. *Artists working in Parma in the sixteenth century*, by A.E. Popham. 1967. 2v. (Catalogue; Plates).
5. *Artists working in Rome, c.* 1550-*c.* 1640, by J.A. Gere and P. Pouncey. 1982. 2v. (Text; Plates).
The 1967v. covers the work of Corregio, Anselmi, Rondanti, Gatti, Gambara, Orsi, Parmigianino, Bedoli, Bertoja. Entries in v.1 give description, provenance and references. List of sources, p.xi-xiii. V.2 has 152 plates.
Class No: 741(450)

Netherlands

[3499]
BRITISH MUSEUM. Department of Prints and Drawings. **Catalogue of drawings by Dutch and Flemish artists preserved in the Department of Prints and Drawings.** Hind, M. London, BM, 1915-32. 5v., illus.
1. *Drawings by Rembrandt and his school.* 1915.

.... (contd.)
2. *Drawings by Rubens, Van Dyck and other artists of the Flemish School of the 17th century.* 1927.
3./4. *Dutch drawings of the 17th century.* 1926-31. 3v.
5. *Dutch and Flemish drawings of the 15th and 16th centuries*, by A.E. Popham. 1932. *Class No:* 741(492)

Technique

[3500]
DALLEY, T., ***ed.*** **The Complete guide to illustration and design:** techniques and materials. New ed. Oxford, Phaidon, 1984. 224p.,illus.,tables. £14.95. ISBN: 0714823473.
2 parts: Illustration (Introduction. 1. Pencils and other point media; 2. Pen and ink; 3. Oils and other paint media; 4. Printmaking; 5. Technical illustration) - Graphic design (Introduction. 6. Design equipment; 7. Copying and photoprinting; 8. Design and typography; 9. Design procedures; 10. Design and photography; 11. Reproduction and printing). Glossary, p.208-213. Paper and sizes. Manufacturers and suppliers. Index, p.218-24. Step-by-step instruction, profusely illustrated (550 illus., 250 in colour), with descriptive captions. *Class No:* 741.02

[3501]
HAYES, C., ***ed.*** **The Complete guide to painting and drawing techniques and materials.** New ed. Oxford, Phaidon, 1984. 224p.,illus. £11.95. ISBN: 0714823481.
A step-by-step guide in 17 chapters, including: 3. Oils; 4. Acrylics; 5. Tempera; 6. Fresco; 7. Exterior painting; 8. Water colour; 9. Gouache; 10. Pastels; 11. Charcoal; 12, Pen and Ink; 13. Pencil; 14. Airbrushing; 15. Drawing aids; 16. Printmaking; 17. Presentation and storage. Glossary. Manufacturers and suppliers. Analytical index, p. 216-22. Attractively produced (817 illus., of which 341 are in colour). *Class No:* 741.02

Dictionaries

[3502]
GOLDMAN, P. Looking at prints, drawings and watercolours; a guide to technical terms. London, British Museum Publications, 1989. 64p. £7.50. ISBN: 0892361484.
Readable and authoritative list of terms, processes, materials, tools. Cross references and bibliography.
Class No: 741.02(038)

Cartoons & Caricature

[3503]
GIFFORD, D. Encyclopedia of comic characters. Harlow, Longman, 1987. 256p. illus. ISBN: 0582892945.
Over 1200 entries covering 150 years of mainly British characters, but including well-known American and foreign names. Alphabetical arrangement, each entry with illustration. Details of illustrator, comic, dates, publisher etc. Index of comics and creators. *Class No:* 741.5

[3504]
HORN, M., ***ed.*** **The World encyclopedia of cartoons.** Detroit, Gale Research with Chelsea House Publishers, 1980. 787p.(6v.), illus. $125. ISBN: 0877543992.
22 contributors. 1,200 entries, A/Z giving biographies, data on characters, plots, etc., of cartoons, caricatures and animation (*e.g.* Fantasia, Donald Duck). Hundreds of black-and-white illus., plus colour section. Appended chronology,

....(*contd.*)

glossary, bibliography and indexes. 'Well planned and carefully edited' (*RQ*, v.20(2), Winter 1980, p.219-20).

Class No: 741.5

Bibliographies

[3505]

EUROPEAN CARTOON ARTS NETWORK. CartooNet. Brighton, Pavilion Internet, 1995.

Website at <http://www.pavilion.co.uk/cartoonet/>

Sponsored by Pavilion Internet plc and supported by the European Union, the network provides a communications link between cartoon artists throughout Europe, encourages federated working practices, agency and other trading arrangements. *Class No:* 741.5(01)

[3506]

GERBER, E. *and* **GERBER, M. The Photo Journal guide to comic books.** Gerber Publishing/Quality Books, 1990. 856p. (2v.). $145. ISBN: 096233281x.

Lists titles with predecessors, variants, changes, sets, series, etc. Colour reproduction of nearly all covers; period mainly 1933-65. Title, artists and character indexes.

Class No: 741.5(01)

[3507]

GIFFORD, D. American comic strip collections: the evolutionary phase, 1884-1939. Boston, G.K. Hall, 1990. 240p., illus. $50. ISBN: 0816172706.

Published in UK as *The American comic book catalogue: the evolutionary era, 1884-1939.* (Mansell, 1990.)

Covers books and strips: 'very complete chronological listing that will be an invaluable reference tool' (*Library Journal* Sept. 15. 1990; p.70). *Class No:* 741.5(01)

[3508]

LENT, J.A., ***comp*****. Animation, caricature, and gag and political cartoons** in the United States and Canada: an international bibliography. Westport, CT, Greenwood Press, 1994. xx,415p. $75.00. ISBN: 0313286817.

Focusses on those areas of comic art that do not include books and strips; one general chapter, one chapter devoted to Canada, but otherwise all US material. Author and subject indexes (creators, characters, titles, fanzines, companies etc.) *Class No:* 741.5(01)

[3509]

LENT, J.A., ***comp*****. Comic art of Europe:** an international, comprehensive bibliography. Westport,CT, Greenwood Press, 1994, 663p. $95.00. ISBN: 0313282129.

Companion volume *Comic art in Africa, Asia, Australia and Latin America: a comprehensive, international bibliography* published 1996; (518p; 0313293430.)

Arranged A/Z by 29 countries; wide coverage of various aspects of comic art. Hailed as 'indispensible' (*Choice*, January 1995; p752-754.) *Class No:* 741.5(01)

[3510]

LENT, J.A., ***comp*****. Comic books and comic strips in the United States:** an international bibliography. Westport, CT, Greenwood Press, 1994. 596p. $85.00. ISBN: 0313282110.

Three main sections: comic books and strips (subheadings for education and culture, ethnicity, minorities, racism, women); comic books (subheadings for historical aspects, makers and their works, legal aspects); comic strips (titles and characters, cartoonists.) Citations within sections further divided by artist, genre, subject etc. *Class No:* 741.5(01)

[3511]

SCOTT, R., ***comp*****. The Comic Art Collection catalog:** an author, artist, title and subject catalog of the Comic Art Collection Division, Michigan State University Libraries. Westport,CT, Greenwood Press, 1993. 1435p. $199.95. ISBN: 0313283257.

70,000 items - US comic books collected since 1970. 'Splendidly catalogued and indexed.' 'Remarkable bibliographic accomplishment.' (*Choice*, 31(5) January 1994. p756.) *Class No:* 741.5(01)

Encyclopaedias & Dictionaries

[3512]

Comic book price guide, 1993. London, Titan Books, 1993. n.p. £12.99.

Continues *The Official comic book price guide.*

Guide to an increasingly collectable area.

Class No: 741.5(03)

Histories

[3513]

KUNZLE, D. The History of the comic strip: the nineteenth century. Berkeley, University of California Press, 1990. 411p.,illus. $85. ISBN: 0520057759.

Earlier history was traced in a previous volume (*The Early Comic Strip*, 1974) by the same author, and this volume continues by covering the major period of cartoon & caricature. Discusses the magazines in which such work appeared. *Class No:* 741.5(091)

[3514]

SABIN, R. Comics, comix and graphic novels: a history of comic art. London, Phaidon, 1996. 240p., illus. £39.99. ISBN: 0714830089.

Comic traditions of the USA, UK, Europe and Japan; arranged thematically - humour, adventure etc., highlighting creators and characters. Over 600 illustrations, mainly in colour. Brief bibliography. *Class No:* 741.5(091)

Great Britain

[3515]

GIFFORD, D. The British comic catalogue 1825-1986. London, Mansell, 1988. 272p. £30.

Covers 3000 items from the first picture papers to recent underground publications. Lists and describes reprints of American and other foreign material. Indexed by artists.

Class No: 741.5(410)

Biographies

[3516]

BRYANT, M. *and* **HENEAGE, S.,** ***comps*****. Dictionary of British cartoonists and caricaturists,** 1730-1980. Aldershot, Scolar Press, 1994. 252p. £29.50. ISBN: 0859679764.

500 entries, giving dates, brief biographies, notable work, publications, exhibitions, location of collections, biographies or autobiographies. Some sample illustrations. Uneven coverage - Gillray and Hogarth both receive 1 column and full page example, Searle 2 columns and full page example, Scarfe 1 column but no example. Cross-references unreliable: 'Trog' *see* Fawkes is in, but no reference from 'Bristow' to Dickens. *Class No:* 741.5(410)(092)

[3517]
CLARK, A. Dictionary of British comic artists, writers and editors. London, British Library, 1997. 196p., illus. £40.00. ISBN: 0712345213.

Coverage is only of people who have worked on comic strips, books etc. (not political cartoonists or other independents.) Arranged A/Z; entries range from a single line, to full page and more with example drawing. Bibliography p195-6. *Class No:* 741.5(410)(092)

USA

[3518]
GOULART, R., ***ed.*** **Encyclopedia of American comics:** from 1897 to the present. Oxford, Facts on File, 1990. 408p., illus. £19.95. ISBN: 0816018529.

Covers adventure, humour, romance, superhero etc; entries for creators, strip titles - about 650 in all arranged A/Z. Entries about specific comics give history, content, syndication; especially useful for 1980's material.
Class No: 741.5(73)

Australia

[3519]
JENSEN, J. Australasian cartoonists in Britain 1889-1988. London, Menzies Centre for Australian Studies, 1989. 22p. illus. £1.50. ISBN: 0902499971.

Brief summary; 8 illustrations. *Class No:* 741.5(94)

Libraries

USA

[3520]
SCOTT, R.W. Comics librarianship: a handbook. Jefferson,NC, McFarland, 1990. 188p. $32.50. ISBN: 0899505279.

Fully describes the range of materials, history of US comic art; preservation, cataloguing; list of major collections. Author is comics librarian at Michigan State University Library, and responsible also for the *Comic art collection catalog*. *Class No:* 741.5:061:026/027(73)

Silhouettes

Great Britain

[3521]
McKECHNIE, S. British silhouette artists and their work, 1760-1860. London, Sotheby Parke Bernet, 1978. 799p. illus. ISBN: 0856670367.

Part 1 covers historical & technical background; part 2 discusses costume - a guide to the attribution & dating of silhouettes; part 3 lists artists, arranged alphabetically in 7 sections according to technique used. Technical glossary; bibliography; appendices include engravers & publishers, artists who worked in the US. *Class No:* 741.7(410)

Lettering & Signwriting

[3522]
CHILD, H., ***ed.*** **The Calligrapher's handbook.** London, A & C Black, for the Society of Scribes and Illuminators, 1985. 272p. illus. £14.99. ISBN: 071362695x.

First published 1957.

Coverage includes choice and preparation of writing surfaces, illumination & the use of gold leaf, writing implements, pigments and inks, scripts and handwriting, binding, reproduction. 'Standard work of reference on the craft' (*RSA Journal,* February 1987, p.249).
Class No: 744.9

[3523]
Contemporary calligraphy: modern scribes and lettering artists, 2. New York, Taplinger, 1986/London, Trefoil Books 1988. 168p. illus. £14.95. ISBN: 0862940729, UK.

Contemporary Calligraphy 1 appeared in 1980.

Produced in collaboration with the Society of Scribes and Illuminators in the UK. 280 examples (26 in colour) by 124 calligraphers from 14 countries. Updates activity since 1980.
Class No: 744.9

Bibliographies

[3524]
DAVIS, J.Y. ***and*** **RICHARDSON, J.V. Calligraphy:** a sourcebook. Littleton,CO, Libraries Unlimited, 1982. 222p. $35. ISBN: 0872872777.

Bibliography of English language books, articles and a/v materials covering all periods and places. Sections deal with general calligraphy; Latin alphabet; Mayan script; Greek letters; Egyptian letters; Near Eastern scripts; Arabic calligraphy; Hebrew letters; Indian calligraphy; Chinese; Japanese; Korean; Tibetan calligraphy. Appendices include list of major Western societies; index. *Class No:* 744.9(01)

Textile Arts

Bibliographies

[3525]
ARTHUR D. JENKINS LIBRARY. Rug and textile arts. a periodical index, 1890-1982. Boston, G.K. Hall, 1983. 472p.

Indexes 300 Journals; reproduces catalogue card entries with full bibliographical details. Two sequences - author, and subject index. *Class No:* 745.52(01)

Encyclopaedias & Dictionaries

[3526]
JERDE, J. Encyclopedia of textiles. New York, Facts on File, 1992. 260p. ISBN: 0816021058.

Aimed at a general readership; covers all types of textiles, history, manufacturing, statistics, production. Synthetic fibre guide. Alphabetical arrangement with many cross-references. Very good illustrations; bibliography includes many standard works and trade association publications.
Class No: 745.52(03)

Periodicals & Progress Reports

[3527]

Hali: the international magazine of antique carpet and textile art. London, Hali Publications, 1978-. £56.00. ISSN: 01420798.

Index 1978-1989 (1990) also published (76p.; 095161990). Book reviews are a regular feature. *Class No:* 745.52(05)

Histories

[3528]

GEIGER, A. A History of textile art. London, Pasold Research Fund in association with Sotheby Parke Bernet, 1979. 317p., illus. ISBN: 0856670533.

Originally 1972 as *Ur Textilkonstens Historia.*

Discusses materials, implements, fabrics, development, Asia, Europe, Scandinavia, dyeing, printing, trade, conservation. Bibliography p.290-305. Line drawings in text, and 95 monochrome plates at end.
Class No: 745.52(091)

[3529]

ROTHSTEIN, N. Silk designs of the eighteenth century in the collection of the Victoria and Albert Museum, London. London, Thames & Hudson, 1990. 352p. illus. £55. ISBN: 0500235899.

Catalogue of the designs in the world's most extensive collection; data on designers, weavers; journeymen, mercers, etc. Almost 500 illustrations.
Class No: 745.52(091)

Peru

[3530]

D'HARCOURT, R. Textiles of ancient Peru and their techniques. Seattle, University of Washington Press, 1987. 303p. illus. ISBN: 0295963314.

First published 1934; this version, translated from the French, is a reprint of the 1962 edition.

Three main sections: text, plates, and description of plates, cross-referenced. Chapters comprise a classification of fabric technique and structure, illustrated by 104 structural and schematic drawings, and 117 pages of monochrome photographs. 'Remains unchallenged more than fifty years after its first production ... a cornerstone of the work of several generations of textile scholars' (*Hali,* no.46. August 1989, p.51). *Class No:* 745.52(85)

Tapestries & Carpets

[3531]

BLACK, D., *ed.* World rugs and carpets. Feltham, Middx, Country Life Books, 1985. 256p., illus., maps. £12.95. ISBN: 0600358968.

Published in the US as the *Macmillan Atlas of Rugs and Carpets.*

Chapters describe weaving methods, history, work of individual countries. Main function is a gazetteer arranged by geographical region. Excellent illustrations.
Class No: 745.521

France

[3532]

Inventaire général des monuments et des richesses artistiques de la France. Tapisserie. Vialot, N. Paris, Imprimerie Nationale, 1971. xx,148p., illus. FF.75.

'The most useful, authoritative reference work on the techniques, terminology and methodology for the study of tapestries' (Arntzen, E. and Rainwater, R. *Guide to the literature of art history* (1980), item P639.)
Class No: 745.521(44)

Asia—Near East

[3533]

BENNETT, I., *ed.* Oriental rugs. Woodbridge, Suffolk, Antique Collectors' Club, 1981-96. 375,264,184,272,320p. (5v.), illus. £45.00. per vol. ISBN: 0902028588, v.1; 090746212x, v.2; 1851491449, v.3; 1851490914, v.4; 1851491368, v.5.

Volume 1 (1981) deals with Caucasian rugs; volume 2 (by Erich Aschenbrenner) covers Persian rugs. Volume 3 (3rd ed. 1990) by R.D. Parsons deals with carpets of Afghanistan; volume 4 (1989) by K. Zipper & C. Fritzche deals with Turkish rugs; volume 5 (1996) by U. Jourdan concentrates on the work of the Turkoman tribes (Turkmenistan, Uzbekistan, north-east Iran, northern Afghanistan). All volumes are illustrated to a very high standard, and have notes on the social background of the areas. *Class No:* 745.521(56)

[3534]

EILAND, M.L. Oriental rugs: a complete guide. Rev.ed. London, Calmann & King, 1998. 352p., illus.

First published 1973.

Recognised as an authoritative source; latest ed. updates the whole text with much new information on traditional areas, and new coverage of China, India, Tibet, Mongolia, North Africa, and the Balkans. Over 300 illustrations in colour - all new for this ed. -and 17 maps.
Class No: 745.521(56)

[3535]

FORD, P.R. Oriental carpet design: a guide to traditional motifs, patterns and symbols. 2nd ed. London, Thames & Hudson, 1989,. 352p., illus., maps. £38. ISBN: 0500233284.

Entries grouped according to basic characteristics of the patterns; bibliographies, indexes. Over 800 illustrations.
Class No: 745.521(56)

[3536]

NEFF, I.C. *and* MAGGS, C.V. Dictionary of oriental rugs, with a monograph on identification by weave. Johannesburg & London, Donker, 1977. 237p. illus. ISBN: 0949937355.

Monograph p.18-51; dictionary p.53-143. Bibliography p.148-51. 84 colour plates with descriptive captions giving dimensions and period. Fold out map showing major oriental rug weaving areas. *Class No:* 745.521(56)

Encyclopaedias & Dictionaries

[3537]

STONE, P. The Oriental rug lexicon. London, Thames & Hudson, 1997. 288p., illus. £19.95. ISBN: 0500279497.

Terminology explained with abundant illustration.
Class No: 745.521(56)(03)

Turkey

[3538]

BUTTERWECK, G. *and* **ORASCH, D. Handbook of Anatolian carpets.** Vienna, Butterweck, 1986. 255p., illus., maps. £53. ISBN: 3900548005.

3 volumes planned.

Reference and classification guide for collectors, dealers and buyers. 350 design types illustrated in 800 monochrome and 200 colour reproductions. Bibliographies, structural analysis of each type. *Class No:* 745.521(560)

Jews

[3539]

FELTON, A. Jewish rugs and carpets. Woodbridge, Suffolk, Antique Collectors' Club, 1997. 220p., illus. £35.00. ISBN: 1851492593.

First authoritative survey of an apparently undocumented topic; extensively illustrated - almost all in colour.
Class No: 745.521(=924)

Needlework & Handicrafts

Software

[3540]

LARSON, L. Software directory for fibre artists. 3rd.ed. Camrose,AB (Canada), Studio Word Processing Ltd, 1995. 246p. $35.00. ISBN: 0969551789.

Formerly *Software for weavers - a resource.*(1986; 2nd.ed 1988.)

Includes knitting, needlework, quilting, sewing, weaving, profiles of industrial and commercial artists using software programs, resource lists, sample printouts; 275 programs are discussed, noting hardware and system requirements, with contact data to confirm availability and price. Glossary; six-page bibliography. *Class No:* 746(003.42)

Bibliographies

[3541]

Index to craft journals. Surry Hill,NSW, Crafts Council of Australia, 1979-. $118.00.

Indexes the contents of 74 craft journals; author arrangement with indexes of craftspersons' names, subject fields, studio or workshop name. *Class No:* 746(01)

[3542]

MAKOWSKI, C.L. Quilting 1915-1983: an annotated bibliography. Metuchen, NJ, Scarecrow Press, 1986. 165p. £15. ISBN: 0810818132.

Useful work in an area of little scholarly attention.
Class No: 746(01)

Encyclopaedias & Dictionaries

[3543]

Anchor manual of needlework. 4th ed. London, Batsford, 1990. 499p., illus. £17.95. ISBN: 0713460873.

First edition 1958.

Covers sewing, embroidery of all types, lace, crochet. Very full and detailed explanation, with over 1200 diagrams and photographs. Extensive index to subjects and stitches.
Class No: 746(03)

[3544]

CAULFEILD, S.F.A. *and* **SAWARD, B.C. Dictionary of needlework.** New ed. London, Blaketon Hall, 1989. 536p., illus. £14.95. ISBN: 0907854109.

Originally published 1882; earlier reprint 1982 (Hamlyn).

Detailed coverage, with historical notes on development. Many cross-references; over 800 engravings.
Class No: 746(03)

[3545]

Complete guide to sewing. London, Hodder & Stoughton/ Reader's Digest 1978. 528p. illus., diagrams. £16.95. ISBN: 0276001826.

Latest reprint 1989.

Two main sections: sewing tools and techniques p.8-436; sewing projects p.439-516. 2000 illustrations and diagrams. Index. *Class No:* 746(03)

[3546]

DILLMONT, T. Encyclopaedia of needlework. Rev. ed. London, Bracken Books, 1988. 830p. illus. £6.95. ISBN: 1851700145.

Originally published 1886 and revised at intervals; available in several language versions.

20 sections cover plain sewing, embroidery, tapestry, knitting, crocheting, openwork etc., with instructions or tracing. Abundant illustrations. *Class No:* 746(03)

[3547]

Step-by-step needlecraft encyclopedia. Rev. ed, London, Dorling Kindersley, 1995. 512p., illus. £25.00. ISBN: 0751302945.

Previous ed. as *The Good Housekeeping step-by-step encyclopaedia of needlecraft.*

Good range of craft coverage; illustrations mainly monochrome, but clear. *Class No:* 746(03)

[3548]

TORBET, L., ***ed.*** **Encyclopedia of crafts.** New York, Scribner, 1980. 3v.

12,000 entries on craft terms; some entries are very extensive, and cross-references are included.
Class No: 746(03)

Dictionaries

[3549]

CLABBURN, P. The Needleworker's dictionary. London, Macmillan, 1976. 296p. illus. ISBN: 0333187563.

2,000 alphabetical entries; international & historical coverage; bibliography p.288-92. 350 photographs, 300 drawings, 56 colour plates. *Class No:* 746(038)

Yearbooks & Directories

[3550]

The Craftworker's yearbook 1998. Stoke-on-Trent, Write Angle Press, 1997. 216p. ISBN: 0952073765.

Annual.

Lists craft fairs with diary of shows, festivals p37-146; also advice on pricing, insurance, directories of organisers, guilds, associations. *Class No:* 746(058)

Weaving

Bibliographies

[3551]
BUSCHMAN, I. Handweaving: an annotated bibliography. Metuchen,NJ, Scarecrow Press, 1991. 250p. ISBN: 0810824035.
553 books, reference works and journals are discussed; covers processes, history, artistry - especially of Native Americans. Indexes by author, title, subject.
Class No: 746.1(01)

Lacemaking

Encyclopaedias & Dictionaries

[3552]
GWYNNE, J.L. The Illustrated dictionary of lace. London, Batsford, 1996. 224p., illus. £25.00. ISBN: 0713478217.
High standard of illustration makes this a valuable review. *Class No:* 746.2(03)

[3553]
REIGATE, E. An Illustrated guide to lace. Woodbridge, Suffolk, Antique Collectors' Club, 1986. 264p., illus. £25.00. ISBN: 1851490035.
Valuable especially for the quality and quantity of illustrations - 700 monochrome and a small number in colour. *Class No:* 746.2(03)

[3554]
STILLWELL, A. Cassell illustrated dictionary of lacemaking. London, Cassell, 1996. 253p., illus. £18.99. ISBN: 0304341452.
Useful general source - terms, materials, tools, techniques etc. *Class No:* 746.2(03)

[3555]
WHITING, G. Lace guide for makers and collectors; with bibliography and five-language nomenclature. New York, Dutton, 1920. 415p., illus.
A standard source, with terms listed in English, French, Spanish, Italian, & German. Instructions for making various types of lace; extensively illustrated. *Class No:* 746.2(03)

Embroidery

Bibliographies

[3556]
COPELAND, K. Embroidery and needlepoint: an information sourcebook. Phoenix, Oryx, 1989. 150p. $46.50. ISBN: 089774442x.
Covers 1950 onwards and scans 91 monographs and journals. Arranged by technique with annotations. Some foreign language material; pattern books included but not ephemeral pamphlets. *Class No:* 746.3(01)

Encyclopaedias & Dictionaries

[3557]
EATON, J., *ed.* Mary Thomas's Dictionary of embroidery stitches. Rev. ed. London, Hodder & Stoughton, 1989. 208p. illus. £12.95. ISBN: 0340510757.
First published 1934.
14 sections covering 400 different stitches (100 new to this edition) grouped by usage. 500 illustrations; index.
Class No: 746.3(03)

[3558]
SWIFT, G. The Batsford encyclopedia of embroidery techniques. London, Batsford, 1984. 240p., illus. £15.95. ISBN: 0713467819.
Covers styles, techniques, terms of hand and machine embroidery. 370 alphabetically arranged entries; 500 photographs and line-drawings. Good bibliography p.229-236; list of collections. *Class No:* 746.3(03)

Crochet & Knitting

[3559]
COMPTON, R. The Illustrated dictionary of knitting. London, Batsford, 1988. 272p. diagrs., charts. £17.95. ISBN: 0713448636.
Over 500 main entries arranged alphabetically; line illustrations and photographs. *Class No:* 746.4

Interior Decoration

[3560]
BANHAM, J., *ed.* Encyclopedia of interior design. London/ Chicago, Fitzroy Dearborn, 1997. 1450p.(2v.), illus. £175.00. ISBN: 1884964192.
Very wide coverage of topics, from the established and expected names and obvious subjects to detailing features (*chintz, linoleum*) and room types. Good illustrations; bibliographies follow many entries. 'Especially useful for its careful attention to every type of room including boudoirs, offices, billiard rooms, nurseries, and parlours. The bibliographies too are well done.' (*Refer*, 13(3) Autumn 1997; p7-8.) *Class No:* 747

[3561]
DIZIK, A.A. Concise encyclopaedia of interior design. 2nd ed. New York, Van Nostrand, 1988. 220p. $36.95. ISBN: 0442221096.
First published 1976 as *Encyclopaedia of Interior Design and Decoration.*
Covers styles, principles, and details. Illustrations not in colour. *Class No:* 747

[3562]
HOSKINS, L., *ed.* The Papered wall: history, pattern, technique. New York, Abrams/ London, Thames & Hudson, 1994. 256p., illus. £32.00. ISBN: 050023695x.
Mainly historical treatment by team of contributors based in European and US museums. Covers earliest European wall decorations to the present day; chapters on restoration and care. Readable and scholarly text; high standard of illustration, many in colour. Extensive bibliographies, glossary, list of important collections, suppliers of historic patterns, list of organisations involved in the subject.
Class No: 747

Yearbooks & Directories

[3563]
Design directory 97/98. 2nd.ed. Hove, East Sussex, Information Works Ltd, 1997. 212p. ISBN: 0952652617.
Biennial.
Publisher has announced a *European design directory*, scheduled for 1998.
Arranged A/Z by company p3-146, then expertise indexes - architecture, ergonomics, exhibitions, graphic, industrial, interior, landscape, product, etc. *Class No:* 747(058)

[3564]
Interior design handbook 1997. 15th ed. London, Interior Design Handbook 1997. 418p., illus. £57.00.

4500 listings by product type; includes building elements, services, lighting, communications, security, bathroom and sanitary fittings, kitchens, floor finishes, wall finishes, window treatments, materials (paint, stone, glass etc), furniture, garden fittings. Directory of exhibitions, showrooms, advisory services, associations, organisations. Brief list of publications p.387-8. Subject index; manufacturers' index. *Class No:* 747(058)

England

[3565]
GORE, A. The History of English interiors. London, Phaidon, 1990. 192p. illus. £29.99. ISBN: 0714826111.

Historical survey using newly commissioned photographs, and contemporary sources. Records all styles and periods from Norman times, through Gothic, Renaissance, Baroque, Rococo, Palladian etc. Influences of major figures explained. Over 200 illustrations. *Class No:* 747(420)

[3566]
MURRAY, E.C. Decorative painting in England 1537-1837. Feltham, Country Life, 1962-1970. 326p. 382p. illus. £20 (v.2). ISBN: 0600430871, v.2.

Volume 1 (1962) deals with the Early Tudors to Sir James Thornhill; volume 2 (1970) covers 18th and early 19th centuries. Details of the painting of ceilings, walls, and woodwork. Catalogue of artists, biographical notes, bibliography. *Class No:* 747(420)

Glass & Crystal Ware

Bibliographies

[3567]
BUSH, L.K. *and* **PERROT, P.N.,** *comps.* **The History and art of glass:** index of periodical articles, 1956-1979. Boston, G.K. Hall/Corning Museum of Glass, 1982. vii,876p. ISBN: 0816113033.

Also supplement (1984) covering 1980-82. (0816104271; $100.00.)

Indexes over 500 journals held in the Corning Museum, and conference proceedings, chapters in annuals etc. Three broad categories: general, technology (including conservation), and history (subdivided by period and country). Separate sections of modern glass, stained glass, beads. Indexes of authors, and of book reviews.
Class No: 748(01)

[3568]
CORNING MUSEUM OF GLASS. Trade catalogues from the Corning Museum of Glass. New York, Clearwater, 1987. 5090 microfiche, printed guide. $10,500 (Guide $95.). ISBN: 0883540762, guide.

Lists 2,360 catalogues, covering 500 years of glass production in US and Europe. Printed guide contains full bibliographic citations and geographical and chronological indexes. *Class No:* 748(01)

[3569]
DUNCAN, G.S., *comp.* **Bibliography of glass** (from the earliest records to 1940). Dimbleby, V., *ed.* London, Dawson for the Society of Glass Technology, 1960. viii, 544p.

15,752 numbered entries, under authors A/Z with supplement. Subject index. 'Rich in references to stained glass, to historical contributions, to records (including sales catalogues) of former collections of glass and glassware, as well as to the development of glass technology, and of the "aids" to the production and working of glass' (*Preface*).
Class No: 748(01)

[3570]
New glass review: annual compendium of contemporary glass made in the previous calendar year. Corning,NY, Corning Museum of Glass, 1976-. $6.00 pa. ISSN: 0275469x.

Annual; previously *Contemporary Glass* (1976-78).

Lists books & journals acquired during the year by the Museum, which aims to buy every relevant publication.
Class No: 748(01)

Encyclopaedias & Dictionaries

[3571]
BRAY, C. Dictionary of glass: materials and techniques. London, A&C Black/ Pennsylvania, University of Pennsylvania Press, 1995. 240p., illus. £35.00. ISBN: 0713640081.

Covers technical and artistic aspects, with some historical background. A/Z listing of words and phrases - technical terms, materials, equipment, processes, practices; entries range from simple definitions to longer articles. Good standard of illustrations - photographs and diagrams. Appendices list suppliers, academic courses, museums with fine collections, and a general bibliography.
Class No: 748(03)

[3572]
NEWMAN, H. An Illustrated dictionary of glass. London, Thames & Hudson, 1987. 308p. illus. £12.95 (pbk). ISBN: 0500274517.

First published 1977.

Alphabetical entries for types, techniques, decorative styles, makers & manufacturers, including histories of major factories. Subtitle adds: '2442 entries, including definition of wares, materials, processes, forms and decorative styles ... from antiquity to the present.' *Class No:* 748(03)

Periodicals & Progress Reports

[3573]
Journal of glass studies. Corning, NY, Corning Museum of Glass, 1959-. ISSN: 00754250.

Excellent, well illustrated, scholarly source. Regularly features a checklist of recently published articles, books, and papers. *Class No:* 748(05)

Histories

[3574]
LIEFKES, R., *ed.* **Glass.** London, V.&A. Museum Publications, 1997. 160p., illus. £25.00. ISBN: 1851771972.

9 contributors survey glass from the ancient and Islamic world, through mediaeval Europe, to 19th century manufacture, and 20th century studio work. Concise in format, but authoritative; 200 excellent illustrations mostly colour; glossary; brief bibliography. *Class No:* 748(091)

Great Britain

[3575]

HAJDAMACH, C.R. British glass 1800-1914. Woodbridge, Suffolk, Antique Collectors' Club, 1991. 466p., illus. £45.00. ISBN: 1851491414.

Established as the standard work on British 19th century glass; factual and authoritative. Some 480 illustrations, 50 in colour. *Class No:* 748(410)

Stained Glass

[3576]

Corpus vitrearum medii aevi. Publishers vary, 1956-. Oxford, OUP, 1979 - (UK vols.). 3v. (UK). illus., maps, plans. £90; £195; £29.50 (UK vols). ISBN: 0197259707, v.1; 0197259952, v.2; 0197259952, v.3.

Publisher varies with country of origin; 90 volumes are planned. Sponsored by various learned societies in Europe, and supported by Unesco.

An international inventory of stained glass still extant. Emphasis on history, biographies and iconography. UK volumes so far published cover (1) County of Oxford (1979), (2) Christ Church Cathedral, Canterbury (1981), and (3) York Minster, fascicle 1 (1987). *Class No:* 748.02

Bibliographies

[3577]

BRADY, D. *and* **SERBAN, W. Stained glass:** a guide to information sources. Detroit, Gale Reserch, 1980. xiii,572p. $68. ISBN: 0810314452.

1,722 numbered entries. 16 chapters: 1. Pathfinder (*e.g.* bibliographies, indexes, encyclopaedias) - 2. General reference sources - 3. Bibliography - 4. Dissertations and theses - 5. Periodicals - 6. Library collections - 7. Archives and manuscript collections - 8. Museums - 9. Organizations - 10. Schools and workshops - 11. Craft events; exhibitions and fairs - 12. Market place: shops and galleries - 13. Supplies sources - 14. Computerized information retrieval systems - 15. A selected guide to government resources (US government; state government; international (*i.e.* foreign) government) - 16. Science and technology sources. Author, title and subject (general; name; place) indexes, p.459-72. Books cited are largely US. *Class No:* 748.02(01)

[3578]

CAVINESS, H. Stained glass before 1540: an annotated bibliography. Boston, G.K. Hall, 1983. 304p. $54. (*Reference Publications in Art History*.) ISBN: 0816183325.

2,000 entries subdivided into broad subject areas, with a sequence on various countries. Chronological arrangement within each section; author index, index of glass painters, designers, and topographical index. 'A useful way into the material' (*Journal of Stained Glass* 18(1) 1983/4, p.107-9). *Class No:* 748.02(01)

[3579]

EVANS, D. A Bibliography of stained glass. London, Brewer, 1982. 201p. £40. ISBN: 0859910873.

Lists over 6,000 items of all types; international coverage, and all periods. Alphabetical arrangement by author, or location, or title; subject index under major sub-headings. *Class No:* 748.02(01)

Handbooks & Manuals

[3580]

MADDY, D.L., ***et al.*** **SGAA reference and technical manual:** a comprehensive guide to stained glass. 2nd ed. Stained Glass Association of America, 1992. 785p., illus. $225.00. ISBN: 0961964014.

Detailed text with illustrations; valuable source for artists, enthusiasts and specialists. (*Library Journal,* 1 April 1993. p.94.) *Class No:* 748.02(035)

Great Britain

[3581]

COWEN, P. A Guide to stained glass in Britain. London, Michael Joseph, 1985. 280p., illus., charts, maps. £14.95. ISBN: 0718125673.

First part contains an introduction on history and design (p.4-67); second part is county-by-county gazetteer. 600 main entries, & 1500 single-line entries. Glossary; thematic guide; bibliography; various indexes. 54 colour illustrations and numerous monochrome. *Class No:* 748.02(410)

Furniture

Encyclopaedias & Dictionaries

[3582]

ARONSON, J. The Encyclopedia of furniture. New ed. London, Batsford, 1989. 496p., illus. £15.95. ISBN: 071345881x.

First published 1938. Re-issued as *The new encyclopedia of furniture* (New York, Crown, [1967]. ix,484p.).

Substantial articles, also *c.*2,500 separate descriptive definitions. 'A glossary of designers and craftsmen'. The examples are largely of US origin or in US museums. A popular standard work; 2000 illustrations.
Class No: 749.1(03)

[3583]

BOYCE, C., *ed.* **Dictionary of furniture.** Oxford, Facts on File, 1985. 331p. illus. £21.95. ISBN: 0816010420.

Brief entries cover all countries and all periods, and extend well into the twentieth century. A useful adjunct to Aronson. Over 2,000 entries, and 400 line drawings, Ancient Egypt to post-modernism, Far East to the Americas. Abundant cross-references. 'Recommended for all subject collections' (*Library Journal* March 1986, p.60-61) 'Serious flaws in conception limit the usefulness' (*Choice* 23(9) May 1986, p.1519). *Class No:* 749.1(03)

[3584]

GLOAG, J. *and* **EDWARDS, C.,** ***eds*****. John Gloag's Dictionary of furniture.** Rev. ed. London, Unwin Hyman, 1990. 229p. illus. £20. ISBN: 0044407742.

2500 entries covering 1100 AD to the present day; history and design are included, with discussion of materials, craft skills. Tables of periods, forms etc. *Class No:* 749.1(03)

[3585]

HABEGGER, J. *and* **OSMAN, J.H. Sourcebook of modern furniture.** 2nd.ed. New York/London, W.W.Norton, 1997. 576p., illus. £50.00. ISBN: 0393730107.

First ed. 1989.

'Definitive visual and factual reference to the more influential furniture...designs in the twentieth century'

....(contd.)
(*Choice*, March 1989, commenting on the 1989 ed.). Substantial bibliography, designer index, manufacturers' addresses. *Class No:* 749.1(03)

[3586]
PAYNE, C. Miller's collecting furniture: the facts at your fingertips. 2nd.ed. London, Mitchell Beazley, 1998. 192p.illus. £12.99. ISBN: 1840000538.
Divided into types of furniture, with good illustrations. Bibliography and index. *Class No:* 749.1(03)

[3587]
PAYNE, C., ***ed*****. Sotheby's concise encyclopaedia of furniture.** London, Conran Octopus, 1989. 208p. illus. £25. ISBN: 1850291977.
Covers earliest times to 1988; chronological arrangement of chapters, discussing styles, countries etc. Select bibliography, glossary, drawings and 300 colour photographs. *Class No:* 749.1(03)

Great Britain

[3588]
ANDREWS, J. British antique furniture. Woodbridge, Suffolk, Antique Collectors' Club, 1989. 392p., illus. £35.00. ISBN: 1851490906.
Comprehensive and authoritative; introduction to the furniture, advice on identification, the market, fakes, forgeries, improvements, restoration; how to buy. 1300 excellent illustrations, 120 in colour. *Class No:* 749.1(410)

[3589]
Pictorial dictionary of British 19th century furniture design. Woodbridge, Antique Collectors' Club, 1977. xlvii,583p. illus. £27.50.
Sections: Bedroom furniture; Cabinets; Chairs; Chests; Couches; Desks; Hall stands; Mantelpieces; Mirrors; Screens; Shelves; Sideboards; Tables; Miscellaneous; General views (of interiors with furniture). Prelims. include: Key dates; Contemporary sources quoted; 'The designers and design books', p.xix-xliv. 'Planned to show the complete range of Victorian furniture in illustrations drawn from contemporary sources' (*Introduction*). *Class No:* 749.1(410)

[3590]
WHITE, L. Pictorial dictionary of British 18th century furniture design. Woodbridge, Suffolk, Antique Collector's Club, 1991. 520p., illus. £65. ISBN: 1851491058.
Includes designs from 120 sources, which are listed. Over 3,000 illustrations. *Class No:* 749.1(410)

Scotland

[3591]
BAMFORD, F. A Dictionary of Edinburgh wrights and furniture makers 1660-1840. London, Furniture History Society, 1983. 137p., illus. £12. ISBN: 0903335042.
Biographical details, place and type of work. Glossary; 92 monochrome plates. *Class No:* 749.1(411)

England

[3592]
BEARD, G. ***and*** **GILBERT, C.,** ***eds*****. Dictionary of English furniture makers 1660-1840.** London, Furniture History Society/W.S. Maney 1986. 1084p. £100.00. ISBN: 0901286184.
Index volume published 1993 (0903335077) includes 30,000 names.

....(contd.)
The definitive work; over four hundred specialist contributors. 50,000 entries give very basic details, but significant figures receive longer entries with details of commissions. Comprehensive coverage of all relevant trades; photographic key to maker identification. 'A serious attempt to create a firm basis of objective information'. (*Furniture History* 23, 1987. p.127-8).
Class No: 749.1(420)

[3593]
EDWARDS, R. Shorter dictionary of English furniture. New ed. London, Hamlyn, 1987. 688p., illus. £29.95. ISBN: 0600554015.
First published 1964.
Concentrates on domestic furniture. 'Standard reference work' (*Antique Collector* 1987, p.98). *Class No:* 749.1(420)

[3594]
MacQUOID, P. ***and*** **EDWARDS, R. The Dictionary of English furniture,** from the Middle Ages to the late Georgian period. 2nd ed. Woodbridge, Antique Collectors' Club, 1983-6. 3v., illus. £85. ISBN: 185149037x.
First published 1924-7; this paperback edition is a reprint of the 2nd ed. published by Country Life Books, 1954. Reprinted 1990.
Of particular value is the detailed attention paid, in text and illus., to different articles of furniture (*e.g.* the articles on various types of table ('Tables, Artists and Reading' ... 'Tables, Work') occupy p.185-325, with 423 illus. Includes biographies; articles are signed; many cross-references; literature references in the text. 43 col. plates, and over 2500 monochrome illustrations in total. A most important work, textually and pictorially. *Class No:* 749.1(420)

[3595]
MacQUOID, P. A History of English furniture. London, Lawrence, 1904-8. 1091p. (4v.).
Re-issued in 2 vols., Woodbridge: Antique Collectors' Club, 1987. (£70; 1851490523) *and* in 1 vol, London: Bracken Books, 1988. (£20; 1851700803).
1. *The age of oak.* 2. *The age of walnut.* 3. *The age of mahogany.* 4. *The age of satinwood.* 'A classic, dated account of the development of English furniture, 16th to 18th centuries, plus discussions of foreign influences, political and social climate, social history, and the contemporary architectural practice which all helped determine the evolution of style' (*TLS* no.3691, 1 December 1972, p.1457). Each volume has an index. 935 illus. in all.
Class No: 749.1(420)

[3596]
VICTORIA AND ALBERT MUSEUM. London. **Catalogue of English furniture and woodwork.** Smith, H.C., *and others*. London, HMSO, 1927-31. 4v., illus.
1. *Gothic and early Tudor*, by H.C. Smith. 1929.
2. *Late Tudor and early Stuart* (1558-1660). 1930.
3. *Late Stuart to Queen Anne*, by O. Brackett, 1927.
4. *Georgian*, by R. Edwards, 1931 (3rd ed. 1958).
Each volume includes many excellent illus. and a short but valuable bibliography. *Class No:* 749.1(420)

London

[3597]
HEAL, A. The London furniture makers, from the Restoration to the Victorian era, 1660-1840: a record of 2,500 cabinet makers, upholsterers, carvers and gilders ... London, Batsford, 1953. xx,276p. illus.
2 main parts: 1. Selected list of cabinet makers, etc.,

....(*contd.*)
illustrated with reproductions of trade cards (p.3-212) - 2. Old English furniture and its makers; the problem of identification, with examples of authenticated pieces. Bibliography and notes on illus. (which include 52 plates). 'Cabinet-makers not in 'Heal', or Eighteenth and nineteenth century trade cards of furniture in the John Johnson Collection of printed ephemera', by P. Agius, appeared in *Furniture history*, v.10, 1974, p.82-84.
Class No: 749.1(421)

France

[3598]

VIAUX, J. Bibliographie du meuble (Mobilier civil français). Paris, Société des Amis de la Bibliothèque Forney, 1966. v,587p. and supplement 624p. FFR.400 (both vols). ISBN: 2906869023, supplement.

Supplement covers 1965-85 (published by Agence Culturelle de Paris, 1988).

Total of 7,500 references, including theses. Division into period, region, and named designers. Grouped entries for museums, collections, techniques of manufacture. Wide coverage of related topics, and of source materials. Supplement lists major trade catalogues, and indexes to both volumes for makers, collectors, places, authors etc. 'Indefatigable documention of French furniture which is hard to overpraise' (*Art Libraries Journal* 14(3) 1989, p.25-27).
Class No: 749.1(44)

USA

[3599]

BATES, E.B. *and* **FAIRBANKS, J.L. American furniture, 1620 to the present.** New York, Marek/Putnam, 1981. 561p.

Comprehensive coverage by period, with useful illustrations. Extensive social and historical commentary. Glossary of cabinet makers' terms, and bibliography.
Class No: 749.1(73)

75 Painting

Painting

[3600]
HAVLICE, P.P. World painting index. Metuchen, NJ, Scarecrow, 1977-1996. 2136, 1233, 1879p.(3 x 2v). $149.50 (2nd. supplement.) ISBN: 0810810166, 2v; 0810815311, Supplement; 0810830205, Second supplement.

Issued as a two volume set in 1977; supplement 1973-1980, issued as two volumes 1982; supplement 1980-1989 issued as two volumes 1995.

Index to reproductions of paintings in art books and catalogues; covers European and American work in some 2,000 sources published from 1945. *Class No:* 75.0

[3601]
NATIONAL GALLERY. London. **Complete illustrated catalogue.** Baker, C. *and* Henry, T., *comp.* London, National Gallery, 1995. 810p., illus. Also CD-ROM ed. (2nd.ed.;1997). £45.00; (CD-ROM £55.00). ISBN: 1857090500, (Print); 1857091949, (CD-ROM).

Some 2200 works of art are included; each painting and sculpture in the Gallery is illustrated and briefly described; small photographs are reproduced three to a page, mostly in colour. Data gives attribution, date, dimensions, medium, provenance etc, and a 50- to 100-word annotation, with bibliographical references. Brief biography of each artist located with first work shown. Full bibliography at end of volume, and comprehensive analytical index.

Companion CD-ROM is Macintosh and Windows compatible; scrolling list of artists leads to biography and small illustrations. Clicking on any image produces larger image which can be viewed at large scale in sections, and several choices - bibliography, subject matter terms, literary sources etc. Full text of commentary is searchable by any word. Text can be printed out, but not images.
Class No: 75.0

[3602]
NATIONAL GALLERY OF CANADA. Catalogue of the National Gallery of Canada: European and American painting, sculpture, and decorative arts. Laskin, M. *and* Pantazzi, M., *eds.* Chicago, Chicago University Press/ National Gallery of Canada, 1987. 3v., illus. £77.95 (v.1). ISBN: 0226563367, v.1.

Volume 1: 1300-1800; volume 2: nineteenth century; volume 3: twentieth century. List of works, biographical data, condition, provenance, exhibition history, references. Each entry is illustrated; 8 indexes including subject, former owners, location of related works. *Class No:* 75.0

[3603]
TATE GALLERY. London. **[Catalogue of the Tate collection].** London, Hub Communications Company for the Tate Gallery.

Website at <http://www.tate.org.uk>

The site's key features include an online catalogue of the Tate collection, with a complete listing of its 25,000 works

.... *(contd.)*

with thousands of images. Also carries information on special exhibitions, events and services, and information on the Gallery sites in Liverpool and St.Ives. *Class No:* 75.0

[3604]
TATE GALLERY. London. **Illustrated catalogue of acquisitions.** London, Tate Gallery, 1990. 672p. illus. £25.00. ISBN: 1854371649.

Covers 1986-88. Earlier volumes cover 1980-82 (1984), 1982-84 (1986) and 1984-86 (1989).

Over 1000 entries, with 630 illustrations. For works in the modern collection, information is based on interviews with the artists. *Class No:* 75.0

[3605]
WRIGHT, C., *comp.* **The World's master paintings:** from the early Renaissance to the present day; a comprehensive listing of works by 1300 painters and a complete guide to their locations worldwide. New York, Routledge, 1992. 854,953p.(2v.) $350.00. ISBN: 0415022401.

Personal preferences, but a very interesting work. 4 parts: index of painters, list of paintings, list of locations, title index of paintings. Brief biographies are given, and valuable bibiographic references; each entry in list of locations gives a bibliography for the collection and key holdings, and list of painters represented. 'By compiling even a selective list of 1300 different artists and their paintings, and linking them to the collections that own them, he has filled one of the largest gaps in the bibliography of painting history...Thoughtful arrangement and high production standards.' (*Choice,* 30(3) November 1992. p451.) *Class No:* 75.0

Yearbooks & Directories

[3606]
CURTIS, T. The Lyle painting price guide. Galashiels, Lyle Publishing. c600p. £16.95.

Annual.

International coverage, arranged by artist, giving price and authenticity detail. Good introduction and summary of trends. 'This is probably the most comprehensive illustrated survey of paintings sold at auction and, as such, is an essential reference tool.' (*Reference reviews,* 8(2) 1994. p30.) *Class No:* 75.0(058)

Biographies

[3607]
Bryan's Dictionary of painters and engravers. Williamson, G.C., *ed.* Port Washington, NY, Kennicat Press, 1964. 363,291,393,308,425p. (5v.), illus.

First published in 2 vols., 1816; subsequent editions 1849, 1884-9, 1903-4 (fourth edition, reprinted here).

Brief, authoritative entries; titles & location of work. A respected historical source. Monochrome plates bound in each volume. *Class No:* 75.0(092)

[3608]

COURTAULD INSTITUTE OF ART. London. **A Checklist of painters.** *c.*1200-1994. 2nd.ed. London, Fitzroy Dearborn, 1995. xvi,557p. $95.00. ISBN: 1884964370.

A preliminary database *Checklist of British artists* developed from this publication and covering 1200-1900 is available from the Witt Library at the Courtauld Institute. In 1992 a printed version was issued. (ISBN: 095183270; £30.00.)

There are about 66,000 artists represented in the Witt Library and the number of reproductions is in excess of 1,700,000. Data on each artist (A-Z): name; nationality; dates. 'It will be invaluable to students and to anyone in search of information about painters of fame or promise in reproductions of their works' (*British book news*, February 1979, p.165, commenting on the 1st.ed).
Class No: 75.0(092)

[3609]

FREDERICKSEN, B.B., *ed.* **The Index of paintings sold in the British Isles during the nineteenth century;** the provenance index of the Getty Art History Information Program. Los Angeles/London, Getty Trust Publications, 1988-. 1047p(v.1); 689,716p (2v)(v.2); 704,748p(2v)(v.3); 583,653p(2v)(v.4) ISBN: 0874365260, v.1; 0892363967, v.4(2).

Originally issued in part by Clio Press, and by K.G.Saur.
See also entry at 7.074 for the *Getty provenance index.*

The beginning of an enormous project. First volume, 1988 covers 1801-1805; second volume, 1990 covers 1806-1810; volume three, 1992, covers 1811-1815; fourth volume, 1996, covers 1816-1820. Indexes 356 catalogues - 20% more than are in Lugt - and private contract sales. A/Z index of artists; list of owners. *Class No:* 75.0(092)

[3610]

Kindlers Malerei Lexikon. Munich, Deutscher Taschenbuch Verlag, 1976. 15v., illus.

Originally as *Kindlers Malerei Lexikon* (Zurich, Kindler, 1964-71. 6v.: 1-5: A-Z; v.6; *Begriffe und Register*).

Edited by international team of 15 specialists. V.1-12: Artists (Velasquez, v.12, p.142-52; 10 illus. (3 in colour); artist's signature; 28½ lines listing major paintings, with location and size; 4 references). V.13-14; subjects/concepts (*e.g.* 'Barock': v.13, p.102-16; 4 illus. (1 inc colour), 2 columns of bibliography). V.15: Index (234p.), in 3 sequences, - names; locations; authors. About 1,200 colour reproductions; 3,000 in black-and-white. 'A singularly useful and reliable reference work' (*American notes & queries*, September 1978, p.12). 'Britain is altogether well looked after. The Italian baroque is the one inadequately covered area' (*Times literary supplement*, no.3518, 31 July 1969, p.850). *Class No:* 75.0(092)

[3611]

TATE GALLERY. London. **Index to the Tate Gallery archive.** London, Ormonde Publishing. 122 microfiche. £130. ISBN: 0907716113.

12,000 images and brief introductory notes; covers over 26,000 index cards and related documentation on 20th century British artists, artists who have worked in Britain, and 20th century artists worldwide. Includes 2,500 photographs and posters. *Class No:* 75.0(092)

Great Britain

[3612]

PENDRED, G.L., *comp.* **An Inventory of British sporting art in United Kingdom public collections.** Woodbridge, Suffolk, Boydell & Brewer, 1987. v,266p. £29.50. ISBN: 0851154654.

Compiled on behalf of British Sporting Art Trust, lists sporting art from mid-17th century in 200 national and provincial galleries, museums, institutions and National Trust properties. Index of galleries; index of artists.
Class No: 75.0(410)

[3613]

WATERHOUSE, E.K. Painting in Britain, 1530-1790. 5th.ed. London, Yale University Press, 1994. 387p.,illus. £45.00; pbk £16.95. (*Pelican History of Art.*) ISBN: 0300058322.

First published 1953.

Comprehensive, and very carefully compiled; a classic in its field. Extensive notes and bibliography.
Class No: 75.0(410)

Biographies

[3614]

BRYANT, B. Dictionary of British Romantic painters, 1780-1840. Woodbridge, Suffolk, Antique Collector's Club, 1993. 569p., illus. £55.00. (*Dictionary of British art, volume 3.*) ISBN: 1851491333.

4000 artists are listed, from a period that has been neglected. 600 illustrations, about 60 in colour.
Class No: 75.0(410)(092)

[3615]

DOLMAN, B. Dictionary of contemporary British artists. Woodbridge, Suffolk, Antique Collectors' Club, 1981. 553p. £25.00. ISBN: 0902028995.

New edition based on the 2nd ed. 1929.

Alphabetically arranged biographies of leading artists, collectors, critics, and curators. Appendices include obituaries, associations and clubs, monograms and signatures. *Class No:* 75.0(410)(092)

[3616]

GRAVES, A. The British Institution 1806-1867; a complete dictionary of contributors and their work from the foundation of the Institution. Weston-Super-Mare, Kingsmead Press, 1969. 618p. £25. ISBN: 0901571113.

First published 1908.

28,000 works listed; arranged alphabetically by artist, and chronological list of works. Index of portraits, etc.
Class No: 75.0(410)(092)

[3617]

GRAVES, A., *comp.* **A Dictionary of artists who have exhibited works in the principal London exhibitions** from 1760-1893. 2nd ed. Weston-Super-Mare, Kingsmead Press, 1984. 314p. £30. ISBN: 090157113x.

First edition 1884; this edition first published 1895, reprinted 1901.

Over 22,000 names listed; tabular, alphabetical arrangement of artists giving name, town, years of activity, speciality etc. *Class No:* 75.0(410)(092)

[3618]
GRAVES, A. The Royal Academy of Arts: a complete dictionary of contributors and their work from its foundation in 1769 to 1904. Weston-Super-Mare, Kingsmead Press, 1989. *c.*3200p. (8v. in 4). £300. ISBN: 1850260125.

Reprint of original edition (Graves/Bell) 1905-6.

Chronological list of paintings with title, date, and catalogue number. *Class No:* 75.0(410)(092)

[3619]
GRAVES, A. The Society of Artists of Great Britain 1760-1791; the Free Society of Artists 1761-1783: a complete dictionary of contributors and their work from the foundation of the societies to 1791. Weston-Super-Mare, Kingsmead Press, 1969. 354p. illus. £25.

Reprint of original edition (Bell/Graves) 1907.

Lists over 13,000 works; arranged alphabetically by artist with chronological list. Index of portraits etc. Brief accounts of the societies. *Class No:* 75.0(410)(092)

[3620]
JOHNSON, J. *and* **GREUTZNER, A. The Dictionary of British artists 1880-1940;** an Antique Collectors' Club Research project listing 41,000 artists. Woodbridge,Suffolk, Antiques Collectors's Club, 1986. 567p. £45.00. (*Dictionary of British art, volume 5.*.) ISBN: 0902028367.

Reprint of 1976/77 issue. Continuation of Graves' *Dictionary of artists 1760-1893* (1901). (*See* entry above.)

Comprehensive coverage, brief but adequate biographical notes. Alphabetical arrangement, heavily abbreviated entries. London and regional coverage using exhibition catalogues and collections. *Class No:* 75.0(410)(092)

[3621]
PAVIÈRE, S.H. Dictionary of British sporting painters. Rev. ed. Leigh-on-Sea, F. Lewis, 1980. 93p. plates. ISBN: 0853179409.

First published 1965.

Brief biographical and professional details. 48 monochrome plates. *Class No:* 75.0(410)(092)

[3622]
ROYAL ACADEMY OF ARTS. London. **Royal Academy exhibitors 1905-1970;** a dictionary of artists and their work in the Summer Exhibitions. Wilts, Hilmarton Manor Press, 1986. 4v. £200. ISBN: 0904722090, v.1; 0904722104, v.2; 0904722112, v.3; 0904722120, v.4.

Originally published in 6 vols, 1973-82 (EP Publishing). Further volume covering 1971-89 issued by same publisher 1989 (558p.; £50.; 0904722198).

Continues Graves's *Complete Dictionary;* details of artists, address, titles, catalogue numbers etc.
Class No: 75.0(410)(092)

[3623]
ROYAL ACADEMY OF ARTS. London. **Royal Academy of Arts directory of membership:** from the foundation in 1768 to 1995, including honorary members. Popp, G. *and* Valentine, H., *comps*. London, Royal Academy of Arts Library, 1996. xi,163p. ISBN: 0900946482.

The official listing of all members.
Class No: 75.0(410)(092)

[3624]
WATERHOUSE, E.K. Dictionary of eighteenth century painters in oils and crayons. Woodbridge, Suffolk, Antique Collectors' Club, 1981. 442p. illus. £45.00. (*Dictionary of British art, volume 2.*) ISBN: 0902028936.

Alphabetical sequence giving biographical data, commentary on type of work. Illustrated throughout with small monochrome reproductions; 12 colour plates. Bibliography p.436-9. Chronology of dated works, 1700-1800. *Class No:* 75.0(410)(092)

[3625]
WATERHOUSE, E.K. Dictionary of sixteenth and seventeenth century British painters. Woodbridge, Suffolk, Antique Collectors' Club, 1988. 308p. illus. £45.00. (*Dictionary of British art, volume 1.*) ISBN: 1851490361.

500 entries; alphabetical listing giving brief biographical and professional data. Cross-references; bibliography. 290 illustrations (40 colour). *Class No:* 75.0(410)(092)

Women

[3626]
LAPERRIERE, C.B., *ed.* **The Society of Women Artists exhibitors 1855-1996.** Calne, Wilts, Hilmarton Manor Press, 1997. 1600p. (4v.) £200.00. ISBN: 0904722309.

Complete dictionary of all the artists who exhibited at the RSWA annual exhibitions, recording all their works of art; standard format of data presentation, giving only information known from the exhibition registers. Covers 76,000 works by 11,500 artists. *Class No:* 75.0(410)(092)-0055.2

Scotland

[3627]
RINDER, F. *and* **McKAY, W.D. The Royal Scottish Academy 1826-1916;** a complete list of the exhibited works... Weston-Super-Mare, Kingsmead Press, 1975. 505p. £25. ISBN: 0901571733.

Originally published Glasgow: James Maclehose. 1917.

Introduction to Academy, history, lists of officials, members. Catalogue arranged alphabetically by artist name with dates and titles of works exhibited etc. Indexes.
Class No: 75.0(411)

Biographies

[3628]
BILLCLIFFE, R., *comp.* **Royal Glasgow Institute of Fine Arts 1861-1989:** a dictionary of exhibitors at the annual exhibitions. Glasgow, Woodend, 1992. c1600p. (4v.) £50 per vol. ISBN: 0951594508, Vol. 1; 0951594516, Vol. 2; 0951594524, Vol. 3; 0951594532, Vol. 4.

Volumes are alphabetical: A-D, E-K, L-P, Q-Z.
Class No: 75.0(411)(092)

[3629]
HALSBY, J. *and* **HARRIS, P. Dictionary of Scottish painters.** 1600-1960. Edinburgh, Canongate, 1991. 236p.,illus. £30. ISBN: 0862413281.

Over 2,000 entries with brief biographical details. 300 colour illustrations. Career summaries include exhibitions, honours, institutional affiliations. *Class No:* 75.0(411)(092)

Ireland

[3630]

McCONKEY, K. Free spirit: Irish art 1860-1960. Woodbridge, Suffolk, Antique Collectors' Club, 1990. 228p., illus. £29.50. ISBN: 1851491279.

Covers the work of 52 major artists, and discusses the influences on Irish art from Europe and within Ireland. 175 illustrations, 60 in colour. *Class No:* 75.0(415)

[3631]

NATIONAL GALLERY OF IRELAND. Illustrated summary catalogue of paintings. Dublin, Gill & Macmillan, 1981. xxxxii,363p. illus. £35. ISBN: 071711144x.

2200 paintings illustrated and described. Various appendices. *Class No:* 75.0(415)

Biographies

[3632]

CROOKSHANK, A. *and* **FITZGERALD, D.J.V. The Painters of Ireland,** *c.*1660-1920. London, Barrie & Jenkins. 1978. 303p., illus.

15 chapters: 1. The seventeenth century - 2. Portrait painters, 1700-1950 ... 4. The Dublin Society School and the Pastelists ... 8. Landscapes - 9. Foreigners in Ireland and decorative painters ... 14. The influence of Antwerp, Paris, Brittany and London - 15. Nineteenth-century subject pictures and portraits. Notes, p.287-91. Bibliography (books and pamphlets; catalogues). Appendix 1: The Dublin Society's Drawing Academy; 2. The Metropolitan School of Art, Dublin. Non-analytical index (p.299-303), but including names of paintings. *Class No:* 75.0(415)(092)

[3633]

SNODDY, T. Dictionary of Irish artists: 20th century. Dublin, Wolfhound, 1996. 800p.,illus. £50.00. ISBN: 0863275621.

500 painters, sculptors, designers etc. Arranged A/Z; entries give biographies, careers, location of principal works, literature references. Bibliography p501-2. No illustrations. *Class No:* 75.0(415)(092)

Wales

Biographies

[3634]

DUNTHORNE, K.B., *ed.* **Artists exhibited in Wales,** 1945-74. Cardiff, Welsh Arts Council, 1978. vii,344p. £6.50. ISBN: 0950045586.

Entries arranged alphabetically. Adamson, H. Leslie ... Zobole, E. 'Richards, Ceri' (p.215-8) has data; biography; exhibitions; awards; prizes; commissions; books; films; articles, reviews; collections; other information.
Class No: 75.0(429)(092)

Spain

Histories

[3635]

POST, C.R. A History of Spanish painting. Cambridge, Mass., Harvard Univ. Press, 1930-70. 14v. in 19, illus.

Available from Kraus Reprint (0527720003; $1.000).

An exhaustive survey, going up to the mid-16th century, copiously and well illustrated. Each volume, devoted to a particular phase of Spanish painting, contains a bibliography, plus indexes of artists and places. V.11, *The Valencian School in the early Renaissance,* carries an additional bibliography for v.1-10. Footnote references on almost every page. V.14, *The later Renaissance in Castile,* includes Professor Post's personal biography and a bibliography of the author. 104 plates. *Class No:* 75.0(460)(091)

Biographies

[3636]

FRICK ART REFERENCE LIBRARY. Spanish artists from the fourth to the twentieth century: a critical dictionary. Boston, G.K.Hall, 1994-7. 2700p. (4v.) $420 per set. ISBN: 0816106142.

3 vols. and index vol.

Annotated checklist of 10,000 painters, sculptors, draftsmen, printmakers, architects and applied artists; users' guide explains entries which give dates, alternative name forms, field of work, bibliographic references. Extensive general bibliographies. 'The result of meticulous and thorough authority work, and it will prove essential for research.' (*Choice,* 32(1) September 1994, p78.)
Class No: 75.0(460)(092)

[3637]

PALOMINO, A. Lives of the eminent Spanish painters and sculptors. Ayala Malory, N., *trans.* Cambridge, CUP, 1987. xviii,405p. £27.50. ISBN: 0521334748.

First published 1724 and re-issued many times.

226 biographies ranging from short paragraphs to 20,000 word entries. Chronological order by date of death. This edition annotated with additional information. Table of names. Bibliography p.389-97. General index. 'Minor objections ... pale in front of the monumental work carried out by Prof. Ayala. Her translation ... will become an indispensable aid in research' (*Times Literary Supplement* 20/26 January 1989). *Class No:* 75.0(460)(092)

Belgium

Biographies

[3638]

BERKO, P. *and* **BERKO, V. Dictionary of Belgian painters born between 1750 and 1875.** Brussels, Editions Laconti, 1981. 922p. illus. £86. ISBN: 2870080131.

Translated from French original.

Provides 1150 illustrations, 250 in colour.
Class No: 75.0(493)(092)

China

[3639]

CAHILL, J. An Index of early Chinese painters and painting: T'ang, Sung, and Yuan. Berkeley, University of California Press, 1980. 391p. $47.50. ISBN: 0520035763.

Basic division into periods; *painters* are listed with brief biographical data, ownership of works, reproductions etc.; chapters covering *paintings* are arranged by subject.
Class No: 75.0(510)

[3640]

SUZUKI, K., ***ed.*** **Comprehensive illustrated catalog of Chinese paintings.** New York, Columbia Univ. Press, 1982. 5v., illus. $145 per vol. ISBN: 086008308x, v.1; 0860083098, v.2; 0860083101, v.3; 086008311x, v.4; 0860083128, v.5.

1. *United States and Canada*. 460p. (38 collections; 1,900 illus.).
2. *Southeast Asia and Europe*. 410p. (42 collections; 1,260 illus.).
3. *Japan*. Part 1: *Museums*. 440p. (30 collections; 1,920 ilus.).
4. *Part 2: Temples, shrines and individuals*. 440p. (290 collections. 2,000 illus.).
5. *Collector, subject and artist indexes*. 500p.

Records Chinese paintings from 399 collections worldwide; 7,120 items. Illus. consist of small half-tones, with attributions. *Class No:* 75.0(510)

Asia—South & South East

Bibliographies

[3641]

HINGORANI, R.P. Painting in South Asia: a bibliography. Delhi, Bhartya Publishing House, 1976. xxxi,253p.

Based on a *Bibliography of Indian Art* (Boston, Museum of Fine Arts, 1925).

The Hingorani bibliography is claimed to be the complete bibliography of painting in South Asia. The scope is wide as it includes background subjects such as history, epigraphy. It covers books and periodical articles on India, Pakistan, Nepal, Tibet and Sri Lanka. Manuscripts, unpublished theses and 20th century paintings have been included. In all, there are 19 sections with varied sub-arrangements. Within each further arrangement is by author. There are ten indexes.
Class No: 75.0(54+59)(01)

Canada

[3642]

NATIONAL GALLERY OF CANADA. Catalogue of the National Gallery of Canada: Canadian art. Hill, C.C. *and* Landry, P.B., *eds.* Chicago, Chicago University Press/ National Gallery of Canada, 1988. 500p. illus. £59.95. ISBN: 0226564568.

To be completed in 4 vols.

Volume one (A-F) records by artist works by the Canadian school. 1880-1980; about 6,700 items. Over 1,700 half-tone illustrations. *Class No:* 75.0(71)

[3643]

REID, D. A Concise history of Canadian painting. 2nd ed. Oxford, OUP, 1989. 432p. illus. £19.50. ISBN: 0195406648.

First published 1973.

Covers early 17th century to 1980. Biographical data and critical appraisals. 200 illustrations, 37 colour.
Class No: 75.0(71)

Biographies

[3644]

HARPER, J.R. Early painters and engravers in Canada. Ontario, University of Toronto Press, 1970. xv,376p. £23.30. ISBN: 0802016308.

Covers 4,000 artists born before 1867 or active before 1900. Alphabetical arrangement, giving biographical details, characteristic work, collections. Bibliography p.343-376.
Class No: 75.0(71)(092)

USA

[3645]

GERDTS, W.H., *ed.* Art across America: regional painting in America, 1710-1920. New York, Abbeville, 1990. 422,396, 396p. (3v.), illus. $495. ISBN: 0558590331.

The work of many authoritative contributors. State-by-state overview, with annotations on individual artists; excludes New York City, Boston & Philadelphia. 800 artists are included; cross-references; bibliographies at the end of each volume. *Class No:* 75.0(73)

[3646]

METROPOLITAN MUSEUM OF ART. New York. **[Catalogues of paintings].** New York, MMA.

American paintings. 1965-. v.1-.

A catalogue of French art. 1955-[67]. 3v. illus. maps.

Italian paintings. 1971-. *(Florentine School.* 1971; *Venetian School.* 1973; to be in 4v.).

Entries are arranged chronologically and data include biography, date, description and comment, provenance, medium, dimensions. Virtually all the paintings are illustrated and the volumes indexed. 'These catalogues meet the highest standards of modern scholarship' (Arntzen, E. and Rainwater, R. *Guide to the literature of art history* (1980), entry M300, on *Italian paintings*).
Class No: 75.0(73)

[3647]

NATIONAL MUSEUM OF AMERICAN ART. Washington. **Index of pre-1877 art exhibition catalogs.** Boston, G.K. Hall; 1986. 5v.

Includes over '1,000 rare catalogues of exhibitions held in the US and Canada up to the 1876 Centennial Exhibition. Indexed by artists, owner, medium, subject matter'. (*Art Libraries Journal* 13(1) 1988. p.12). *Class No:* 75.0(73)

Biographies

[3648]

DAWDY, D.O., *ed.* Artists of the American West: a biographical dictionary. Athens, OH, Ohio University Press, 1974-1985. 275,345,568p. (3v.). £24.; £21.60; $35. ISBN: 0804006075, v.1; 0804003521, v.2; 0804008515, v.3.

Also issued by Apollo Books (New York) in a 3-vol. set (0317548999; $100.).

Volume 1 (1974) is supplemented by volume 2 (1981); volume 3 (1985) concentrates on artists born before 1900.
Class No: 75.0(73)(092)

[3649]

GROCE, G.C. *and* **WALLACE, D.H. The New York Historical Society's Dictionary of artists in America 1564-1860.** London, Yale U.P. 1957. xxvii,759p. £62.95. ISBN: 0300005199.

Very comprehensive with essential bibliographical information. *Class No:* 75.0(73)(092)

[3650]
LESTER, P.D. The Biographical directory of Native American painters. New ed. Tulsa/London, University of Oklahoma Press, 1995. xvii,701p. ISBN: 0806199369.

Previous edition published 1968 as *American Indian painters* by J.S.King.

An important source, now fully updated; bibliography p687-701. *Class No:* 75.0(73)(092)

New Zealand

Biographies

[3651]
PLATTS, U. Nineteenth century New Zealand artists: a guide and handbook. Christchurch, NZ, Avon, 1979. 272p.,illus.

Alphabetical arrangement with some biographical & professional data. Entries range from 1 line to ½ page. Bibliography p.265-8. 66 plates containing 102 illustrations (14 colour). *Class No:* 75.0(931)(092)

Australia

Biographies

[3652]
SAYERS, A. Aboriginal artists of the nineteenth century. Melbourne/Oxford, Oxford University Press, 1996. 182p., illus. £25.00. ISBN: 0195539958.

Originally published 1994.

Important historical reference source, 24 pages of plates, and other colour and monochrome illustrations; bibliographical references. *Class No:* 75.0(94)(092)

Techniques

[3653]
HAYES, C., *ed*. The Complete guide to painting and drawing techniques and materials. New ed. Oxford, Phaidon, 1984. 224p.,illus. £11.95. ISBN: 0714823481.

A step-by-step guide in 17 chapters, including: 3. Oils; 4. Acrylics; 5. Tempera; 6. Fresco; 7. Exterior painting; 8. Water colour; 9. Gouache; 10. Pastels; 11. Charcoal; 12, Pen and Ink; 13. Pencil; 14. Airbrushing; 15. Drawing aids; 16. Printmaking; 17. Presentation and storage. Glossary. Manufacturers and suppliers. Analytical index, p. 216-22. Attractively produced (817 illus., of which 341 are in colour). *Class No:* 75.02

Materials & Paints

[3654]
FELLER, R.L., *ed*. Artists' pigments: a handbook of their history and characteristics. Cambridge, CUP, 1987. 300p. illus. £50. ISBN: 0521303745.

Monographs on ten pigments or groups of substances. Standard layout covers nomenclature, history, colour, permanence, compatibility, variations, inpurities, identification techniques, significant examples. 'Important addition to the literature' (*RSA Journal,* June 1988, p.517). *Class No:* 75.023

Glass Painting

Biographies

[3655]
THOMAS, B. *and* RICHARDSON, E., *eds*. Dictionary of master glass-painters. Newcastle-on-Tyne, Oriel Press, 1972. vi,122p., illus.

Painters, A-Z. Index of British counties, major cities and countries abroad; index of artists, architects and designers. Black-and-white illus. only. A standard reference work in its field. *Class No:* 75.023.1(092)

Water-colour Painting

[3656]
HARRISON, H. The Encyclopedia of watercolour techniques. London, Headline, 1990. 192p. illus. £14.95. ISBN: 0747202176.

Examines 40 techniques and gives easy directions with examples of the results. *Class No:* 75.023.2

Great Britain

[3657]
MALLALIEU, H.L. Dictionary of British watercolour artists up to 1920. 2nd ed. (vol.1). Woodbridge, Suffolk, Antique Collectors' Club, 1986 (reprinted 1997), 1979, 1990. 390,557,300p. (3v.), illus. £39.50; £29.95; £35. ISBN: 1851490256, v.1; 0902028634, v.2; 1851491112, v.3.

Volume one (2nd. ed.) lists over 6000 artists; bibliography; cross-references. Volume two gives 800 monochrome illustrations with dates, titles, sizes, commentary. Volume three has additional illustrations and guide to spotting fakes. Appendices include family trees. *Class No:* 75.023.2(410)

[3658]
ROYAL SOCIETY OF PAINTERS IN WATER-COLOURS. The Royal Watercolour Society: directory of artists, exhibits, and purchases: an Antique Collectors' Club research project. Woodbridge,Suffolk, Antique Collectors' Club, 1990-. 400p. £45.00. ISBN: 185149099x.

This first volume is entitled *The first fifty years 1805-1855.* Lists with annotations 17,000 watercolours exhibited at the annual shows. *Class No:* 75.023.2(410)

[3659]
VICTORIA AND ALBERT MUSEUM. London. **British watercolours in the Victoria and Albert Museum:** an illustrated summary catalogue of the National Collection. Lambourn, L. *and* Hamilton, J., *comps*. London, Sotheby Parke Bernet in association with the V. & A., 1980. xxi,455p.,illus. ISBN: 0856671118.

Earlier: Victoria and Albert Museum. *Catalogue of water colour painting by British artists and foreigners working in Great Britain* (Rev. ed. Board of Education, 1927. xiv636p. illus. *Supplement.* 1951).

The 1980 catalogue (p.1-431) lists over 5,600 works by *c.*1,600 artists. Data: title; painter; size; negative number; provenance. Appendix: Anonymous works. Bibliography, p.435. Topographic index; index of sitters; index of historical, Biblical, mythological and allegorical characters, subject and events; index of authors whose works are illustrated by the artists; index of donors. 2-5 black-and-white tiny illus. per page; 16p. of col.pl.

Also : *The National Collection of Watercolours in the Victoria and Albert Museum, on colour microfiche* (London,

....*(contd.)*
Ormond Publg. Co, 1982). comprising 6,557 paintings, complete with comprehensive indexes.
Class No: 75.023.2(410)

Ireland

[3660]
NATIONAL GALLERY OF IRELAND. Summary catalogue of drawings, watercolours and miniatures. Le Harivel, A., *ed*. Dublin, National Gallery of Ireland, 1984. xxviii,846p. illus. £40. ISBN: 0903162105.
Over 5000 items illustrated and described; eleven appendices, of which the last is an index to artists.
Class No: 75.023.2(415)

Periods & Styles

Prehistoric

[3661]
SIEVEKING, A. The Cave artists. London, Thames and Hudson, 1979. 221p. illus. maps. (*Ancient Peoples and Places, no. 93.*)
1. Early twentieth-century interest in Palaeolithic art: the establishment of its authenticity, age and chronology - 2. Present-day preoccupations with Palaeolithic art ... 5. Underground sanctuaries in Western France - 6/7 Pyrenees and Cantabria - 8. Palaeolithic art outside the Franco-Cantabrian region. Bibliography p.211-4. *Class No:* 75.031

Ancient World

[3662]
HEKLER, A. Greek and Roman portraits. London, Heinemann, 1912. xliii,335p., illus.
Reprinted New York, Hacker Art Books, 1973.
300 portraits reproduced. 'A major work on ancient art' (*The Papers of the Bibliographical Society of America*, v.67, 1973, p.489). *Class No:* 75.032

Asia

[3663]
STEIN, A. *and* **ANDREWS, F.H. Catalogue of wall painting from ancient shrines in central Asia and Sistan.** New Delhi, Cosmo Publications, 1987.
Reprint of 1933 edition.
Wall paintings catalogued and described in this volume were brought to India by Sir Aurel Stein from his two Central Asian expeditions for archaeological and geographical research extending over the periods 1906-1908 and 1913-1916. *Class No:* 75.032(5)

Mediaeval & Byzantine

England

[3664]
TRISTRAM, E.W. English medieval wall painting. Oxford, OUP for the Pilgrim Trust, 1944-50. xii,164,651p.,383 plates (3v.).
A new, illustrated edition of vol.1, edited by M. Bardswell was published in 1988 (Hacker Art Books; £71.50; ISBN: 0878173145).
1: *The twelfth century*. 1944. 2/3: *The thirteenth century*. 1950. A detailed, scholarly work that discusses technique and iconography, noting location of paintings, plus a full

....*(contd.)*
catalogue, with bibliography. V.2: Text; v.3: Plates (383 collotype plates, 12 in colour). 'An important work' (Arntzen, E., and Rainwater, R. *Guide to the literature of art history* (1980), entry M258). *Class No:* 75.033(420)

[3665]
TRISTRAM, E.W., *ed*. **English wall painting of the 14th century** ... with catalogue ... London, Routledge & Kegan Paul, 1955. xi,311p., illus.
Consists of text (pt.1), with bibliography, and catalogue (pt.2) with appendices. 'Concentrates on churches', the author having been involved in restoration of most of the works discussed (Arntzen, E., & Rainwater, R. *Guide to the literature of art history*, entry M259).
Class No: 75.033(420)

19th Century

[3666]
NORMAN, G. Nineteenth century painters and painting: a dictionary. London, Thames & Hudson, 1977. 240p. illus. £25. ISBN: 0500232490.
Introductory section with colour plates p.7-25. Over 700 A/Z entries on artists, movements, groups, institutions, societies. Bibliography p.233-9. Includes relatively obscure painters, but lacks a nationality index. *Class No:* 75.035

[3667]
PARKINSON, R. Catalogue of British oil paintings 1820-1860. London, HMSO/Victoria & Albert Museum, 1990. 200p. illus. £30. ISBN: 0112904637.
Reproduction with biographical notes, details of original commission, later history. About 500 pictures are included, half of the Museum's collection of this period.
Class No: 75.035

[3668]
WOOD, C. Victorian painters. 3rd.ed. Woodbridge, Suffolk, Antique Collectors' Club, 1995. 595,475p. (2v.) £35.00. per vol. (*Dictionary of British art, volume 4.*) ISBN: 1851491716, v.1; 1851491724, v.2.
First published 1971.
Vol 1: 11000 artists working 1837-1901. Alphabetical arrangement with brief information, titles of exhibited works. Includes many minor or obscure figures. Vol 2: 47 colour and 750 monochrome illustrations giving title, date, size, and location. *Class No:* 75.035

[3669]
WOOD, C. Victorian painting in oils and watercolour. Woodbridge, Suffolk, Antique Collectors' Club, 1996. 230p., illus. £35.00. ISBN: 1851492496.
Excellent scholarly survey that adds much extra detail to the foregoing item; over 100 colour illustrations further add to its importance. *Class No:* 75.035

20th Century

Bibliographies

[3670]
CUTUL, A.-M., *Ed*. **Twentieth-century European painting:** a guide to information sources. Detroit, Gale Research, 1980. xvi,520p. ISBN: 081031438x.
Annotated bibliography, in chapter form. Mainly on *c.*140 individual artists, ranging from Dali to Modigliani, the advent of Fauvism in 1905 taken as starting-point. Entries (largely English-language material) for basic items are asterisked: periodical articles excluded. Chapter headings

....*(contd.)*
include: General reference sources; General works relating to modern painting; Artists' writings, statements, interviews and studio visits: Aesthetics, philosophy, theory and techniques of modern painting; Histories, introductions and surveys of modern painting. Includes list of appropriate museums, galleries, special libraries, etc. Author, title and subject indexes. *Class No:* 75.036(01)

Encyclopaedias & Dictionaries

[3671]

Phaidon dictionary of twentieth-century art. 2nd ed. London, Phaidon, 1978. 420p.

First published 1973 as *Phaidon dictionary of modern art.*

40 contributors, covering painting, sculpture and architecture. Over 1,700 entries for 1,600 artists, Aaltonen ... Zwobada, plus over 140 groups of movements. Short bibliographies appended to many articles 'Picasso': 3½ columns, 5 references; 'Pop art': 1½ cols., 5 references; 'Expressionism': 1½ cols., 5 references). 'Much of the material here presented was originally written in German (*Foreword*). Includes European, Australian, Japanese and Israeli artists, as well as British and American.
Class No: 75.036(03)

Great Britain

Biographies

[3672]

SPALDING, F. *and* **COLLINS, J. Twentieth century painters and sculptors.** Woodbridge, Suffolk, Antique Collectors' Club, 1990. 484p. illus. £45. (*Dictionary of British art, volume 6.*) ISBN: 1851491066.

Contains biographical & professional information on some 7,000 artists, many still living. Covers all styles, schools, media. 450 excellent illustrations.
Class No: 75.036(410)(092)

[3673]

WATERS, G.M. Dictionary of British artists working 1900-1950. Eastbourne, Eastbourne Fine Arts, 1975-1976. 368,62p. (2v.), illus. £33. ISBN: 0902010050, v.1; 0902010069, v.2.

Alphabetical listing of over 5,500 artists, many minor or provincial. Brief details; volume 2 adds 1100 more, and updates volume 1. List of societies & groups. 228 pages of monochrome plates. *Class No:* 75.036(410)(092)

Impressionism

[3674]

DENVIR, B. Encyclopedia of Impressionism. London, Thames & Hudson, 1990. 312p. illus. £5.95. ISBN: 0500202397.

300 entries cover painters, critics, patrons, dealers, collectors, techniques, locations, cultural & social background. Chronology; gazetteer; good selection of representative illustrations. *Class No:* 75.036IMP

Surrealism

[3675]

PASSERON, R. Phaidon encyclopedia of Surrealism. London, Phaidon, 1978. 288p.,illus.

Original French as *Encyclopédie du Surréalisme* (1975).

Sections: Introduction (p.7-86: A short history; Pictorial Surrealism; Automatism; Oneirism/Pictorial Surrealism: erotics, politics and logic) - The precursors - The Surrealists (p.113-256). Glossary of terms and techniques. Groups; Reviews; Exhibitions. Notes, p.270-3. Bibliography (A-Z authors), p.274-5. Index of names. 415 illus. (164 in colour).
Class No: 75.036SUR

Painting Subjects

[3676]

DARS, C., ***ed.*** **Subject catalogue of paintings in public collections.** Volume one: London - National Gallery, Wallace Collection, Wellington Museum. London, Visual Arts Publishing, 1989. 1400p. £90. ISBN: 095141660x.

Descriptive listings by schools and artists p.1-741; listing by subjects p.742-1386. List of other names of people & artists. Topographical index. *Class No:* 75.04

[3677]

—DARS, C., *ed.* Subject catalogue of paintings in public collections. Volume two: the Tate Gallery Old Masters Collection. London, Visual Arts Publishing, 1990. 677p. ISBN: 0951416618.

Similarly arranged to volume one, but with the addition of a small monochrome illustration for each item.
Class No: 75.04

[3678]

HOOK, P. *and* **POLTIMORE, M. Popular nineteenth century painting:** a dictionary of European genre painters. Woodbridge, Suffolk, Antique Collectors' Club, 1986. 632p. illus. £45. ISBN: 1851490116.

Arranged by 31 genres (beauties, cats and dogs, monks etc.) dealing only with oil paintings of humans and animals. 1543 illustrations, 73 in colour. Bibliography; index of artists. *Class No:* 75.04

Portraits

Great Britain

[3679]

BAYNE-POWELL, R. Catalogue of portrait miniatures in the Fitzwilliam Museum, Cambridge. Cambridge, CUP, 1985. x,231p. illus. £60. ISBN: 0521267773.

Arranged alphabetically by artist or school; dates and brief biographical information. Each miniature is shown in monochrome, described, details of sitter. Bibliography; indexes. *Class No:* 75.041(410)

[3680]

NATIONAL PORTRAIT GALLERY. London. **Complete illustrated catalogue 1856-1979.** Yung, K.K., *comp.* London, NPG, 1981. 760p. illus. £29.95. ISBN: 0904017389.

Supersedes the *Concise Catalogue 1856-1969* (1970) and the *Concise Catalogue 1970-1976* (1977).

Arranged alphabetically by name of sitter; describes 8,000 portraits. Index of artists, engravers, photographers. Does not include the Contemporary Portraits Collection.
Class No: 75.041(410)

[3681]
ORMOND, R. *and* **ROGERS, M.,** ***ed*. Dictionary of British portraiture.** London, Batsford/National Portrait Gallery, 1979-81. 157,231,228,176p. (4v.). ISBN: 0713414685, v.1; 0713414707, v.2; 0713414723, v.3; 071341474x, v.4.

Vol.1 covers Middle Ages to the early Georgians; Vol.2 later Georgians and early Victorians; Vol.3 Victorians 1800-1860; vol.4 Twentieth century, born before 1900. The volumes list portraits in public galleries and institutions; arranged alphabetically by sitter with a list of known portraits in various media. Sitters name index in vol.4. 'Indispensible ... a very thorough guide' (*British Book News* Sept. 1982, p.563-4). *Class No:* 75.041(410)

[3682]
STEWART, B. *and* **CUTTEN, M. The Dictionary of portrait painters in Britain** up to 1920. Woodbridge, Suffolk, Antique Collectors' Club, 1997. 502p. £49.50. ISBN: 1851491732.

A/Z arrangement of 5,000 portraitists working in Britain from the early 16th to early 20th century are included. Recent research has brought to light much genealogical data which adds value to the information here. Some 400 illustrations - 75 plates in colour at the start of the volume, and one small monochrome per page. Each entry gives note of standard source in which further informatiuon can be found, and list of galleries where artist is represented. *Class No:* 75.041(410)

[3683]
STRONG, R., ***ed*. British portraits 1660-1960.** Woodbridge, Suffolk, Antique Collectors' Club, 1991. 420p., illus. £55. ISBN: 1851491074.

Expert contributors discuss seven major periods of British portrait painting. Detailed analysis of the work of key artists, styles, assistants, imitators. *Class No:* 75.041(410)

India

[3684]
ROHATGI, P. Portraits in the India Office Library and Records. London, British Library, 1983. 434p. £25. ISBN: 0712300155.

Lists *c.*5,600 portraits of men and women connected with India. 3 parts: individuals (whether single or in a group), A-Z; rulers of India and associated states, plus compatriots, under country; indexes. 'The strength of the collection is in its coverage of the British in India in the nineteenth and twentieth centuries' (*British books news*, November 1983, p.700). *Class No:* 75.041(540)

Animals

[3685]
BRIDSON, G. *and* **WHITE, J. Plant, animal and anatomical illustration in art and science.** Cirencester, St. Paul's Bibliographies, 1990. 464p., illus. £60. ISBN: 0906795818.

Lists primary level books, pattern books, and secondary historical, critical, bibliographical and biographical literature on natural history and human anatomical illustration. Over 7,500 references from 1700 to the present. Subject arrangement, subdivided into categories. Title, subject and name indexes. *Class No:* 75.042

[3686]
MITCHELL, S. The Dictionary of British equestrian artists. Woodbridge, Suffolk, Antique Collectors' Club, 1985. 517p. illus. £35. ISBN: 0907462421.

Introductory essay; pictorial, chronological chart of dress & saddlery; biographical dictionary of 870 artists 1600s to present day. Brief bibliography. *Class No:* 75.042

Historical Painting

[3687]
ROCHELLE, M. Historical art index, AD400-1650: people, places and events depicted. Jefferson, NC, McFarland, 1989. 217p. $45.00. ISBN: 0899504493.

Alphabetically arranged by subjects, mainly persons, with details of known illustrations and location. Includes portraits, paintings, woodcuts, miniatures, tapestries, engravings, but not seals & coins. Numerous cross-references; directory of collections, & bibliography. The very full descriptions of artwork may be of value in their own right. *Class No:* 75.044

USA

[3688]
DEAK, G.G. Picturing America 1497-1899: prints, maps, and drawings bearing on the New World discoveries and on the development of the territory that is now the United States. Princeton, NJ., Princeton University Press, 1988. 657p. (2v.), plates. $250. ISBN: 0691039992.

Chronological arrangement of descriptions and reproductions of 880 images of landscapes, seascapes, buildings, maps and views. Bibliography; indexes. 'Monumental survey ... substantial piece of scholarship'. (*Choice* 26,10. June 1989, p.1672). *Class No:* 75.044(73)

Land & Sea

[3689]
BROOK-HART, D. British nineteenth century marine painting. Woodbridge, Suffolk, Antique Collectors' Club, 1974. 370p. £45.00. ISBN: 0902028324.

Standard source for sea paintings. 250 illustrations, 32 in colour. *Class No:* 75.047

[3690]
BROOK-HART, D. Twentieth century British marine painting. Woodbridge, Suffolk, Antique Collectors' Club, 1981. 384p. £45.00. ISBN: 0902028901.

Companion volume to the above; 300 illustrations, 37 in colour. *Class No:* 75.047

[3691]
NATIONAL MARITIME MUSEUM. London. **Oil paintings in the National Maritime Museum:** a concise catalogue. Woodbridge, Antique Collectors' Club, 1988. 600p. illus. £45. ISBN: 1851490760.

Complete catalogue of paintings owned or on permanent loan. Over 2,000 illustrations, 56 in colour. Ten indexes to the 3000 entries. *Class No:* 75.047

[3692]
ROYAL SOCIETY OF MARINE ARTISTS. A Celebration of marine art: 50 years of the Royal Society of Marine Artists. London, Blandford, 1996. 176p., illus. £30.00. ISBN: 0713725648.

History of the Society, details of exhibitions and notable members. *Class No:* 75.047

Biographies

[3693]

ARCHIBALD, E.H.H. The Dictionary of sea painters. 3rd. ed. Woodbridge, Suffolk, Antique Collectors' Club, 1998. 576p. illus. £45.00. ISBN: 1851492690.

First published 1980.

Established as the classic source for this genre. Alphabetical discussion of 1200 painters; guide to dating pictures; specialist sections on flags, stems and sterns, coastal craft. Over 1000 illustrations, 60 in colour.

Class No: 75.047(092)

[3694]

BREWINGTON, D.E.R. Dictionary of marine artists. Salem, Mass., Peabody Museum/Mystic,. Conn., Seaport Museum, 1982. 431p. illus. $35. ISBN: 0913372242.

Lists 3,074 artists from sixteenth to twentieth centuries. Brief details; separate list of Chinese and Japanese (p.427-431). Illustrations few and poor quality.

Class No: 75.047(092)

[3695]

COCKETT, F.B. Early sea painters, 1660-1730. Woodbridge, Suffolk, Antique Collectors' Club, 1995. 142p., illus. £25.00. ISBN: 1851492305.

Comprehensive information and discussion of the group of artists working in England at this period, who followed the style and subject matter of the Van de Veldes. Mainly these were Dutch artists invited to settle in England by Charles II. Catalogues the known works of each painter, with notes on sources. Over 100 illustrations. *Class No:* 75.047(092)

Great Britain

[3696]

HEMMING, C. British landscape painters: a history and gazetteer. London, Gollancz, 1989. 224p. illus. £16.95. ISBN: 0575039574.

Historical section outlines developments and philosophies 1635-1980 (p.31-129); gazetteer briefly describes places and their associations with artists, groups, and paintings. References to over 450 artists. Index.

Class No: 75.047(410)

[3697]

Masters of landscape: the Norwich School of Artists 1803-1833. London, Stationery Office Publications, 1996. CD-ROM.

Interactive multimedia art history covers such artists as Crome, Cotman, Constable and many others. 250 images are available, and most are accompanied by an individual annotation. *Class No:* 75.047(410)

France

[3698]

HARAMBOURG, L. Dictionnaire des peintres paysagistes français au XIXe siècle. Paris, Le Bibliothèque des Arts, 1988. 360p. illus. FFr.984.

First published Switzerland: Ides & Calendes, 1985.

Alphabetical arrangement of over 3000 entries, with details of type of work, exhibitions, awards, locations etc. 898 monochrome illustrations and 32 colour plates. Bibliography. *Class No:* 75.047(44)

Still Life

[3699]

DUNTHORNE, G. Flower and fruit prints of the eighteenth and early nineteenth centuries: their history, makers, and uses, with a catalogue raisonné of the works in which they are found. New York, Da Capo, 1975. 275p. illus. £67.50. ISBN: 0306709589.

Facsimile of the 1938 edition.

Comprehensive guide; 82 colour illustrations.

Class No: 75.049.6

France

[3700]

HARDOUIN-FUGIER, E. *and* **GRAFE, E.,** ***eds*****. French flower painters of the nineteenth century:** a dictionary. London, Sotheby's,1989. 432p. illus. £55. ISBN: 085667348x.

Cover 3,500 artists; over 530 illustrations, 55 in colour. 'This beautifully produced dictionary ... will become a standard work of reference' (*Apollo* Nov.1989, p.357).

Class No: 75.049.6(44)

Miniature Painting

Biographies

[3701]

BRADLEY, J.W. A Dictionary of miniaturists, illuminators, calligraphers and copyists, with references to their works, and notices of their patrons, from the establishment of Christianity to the eighteenth century. London, Quaritch, 1887-89. 363,372,440p. (3v.).

International scope; entries range from a single line to several pages. Full entries give biographical and career data, description of range of work, lists of works. V.3 includes a list of additional names in an appendix pp.435-440.

Class No: 75.05(092)

Persia, Ancient

[3702]

TITLEY, N.M. Persian miniature painting and its influence on the art of Turkey and India; The British Library collections. London, British Library, 1983. 272p.,illus.

15 chapters: 2. Development of the Persian miniature in the early fourteenth century ... 5. The brilliance of Herat ... 11. Ottoman Turkey ... 13. Mughul India - 14. Methods and material - 15. Literature. Select bibliography, p.359-61 (author, A-Z). Index of manuscripts by location; general index (non-analytical). A well-produced quarto.

Class No: 75.05(355)

Great Britain

Biographies

[3703]

FOSKETT, D. A Dictionary of British miniature painters. London, Faber, 1972. 596,108p. (2v.), plates. ISBN: 0571082955, v.1; 0571097464, v.2.

Reprinted with the author's *Collecting miniatures* (1979) in one volume as *Miniatures: dictionary and guide* (Antique Collectors' Club, 1987).

Brief biographical details of 4,500 miniaturists 1520-1910. Entries give subjects, characteristics, signatures, important works. Bibliography p.592-6. Volume 2 contains the plates

.... *(contd.)*
and index. 'Information is neither invariably complete nor accurate' (*Royal Society of Arts Journal* v.137, no.5391, Feb. 1989, p.181). *Class No:* 75.05(410)(092)

[3704]
LONG, B.S. British miniaturists. London, Geoffrey Bles, 1929. xxxiii,475p. plates.

Lists miniaturists working 1520-1860, chiefly portrait painters. Biographical details, references, locations given. 32 monochrome plates. *Class No:* 75.05(410)(092)

Turkey

[3705]
TITLEY, N.M. Miniatures from Turkish manuscripts: a catalogue and subject index of paintings in the British Library and British Museum. London, British Library, 1982. 208p. illus. £45. ISBN: 0904654710.

Well produced, scholarly summary. *Class No:* 75.05(560)

76/77 Graphics & Photography

Graphic Arts

Abbreviations & Symbols

[3706]

ARNSTEIN, J. The International dictionary of graphic symbols. London, Kogan Page, 1983. 239p. illus. ISBN: 0850385784.

Alphabetical arrangement by subject (architecture, astrology, astronomy, biology, cartography, chemistry, etc.) with relevant symbols explained. Priority given to international practice, or US/UK practice.
Class No: 76(003)

[3707]

WALLIS, L.W. Dictionary of graphic arts abbreviations. London, Lund Humphries, 1986. 139p. £9.95. ISBN: 0853315000.

Over 5000 abbreviations and acronyms for organizations & associations, equipment, processes & technical terms.
Class No: 76(003)

Bibliographies

[3708]

BRIDSON, G.D.R. *and* **WAKEMAN, G.,** *eds.* **Printmaking and picture printing:** a bibliographical guide to artistic and industrial techniques in Britain, 1750-1900. Oxford, Plough Press, 1984. 250p. £30. ISBN: 0902813129.

The bibliography is in five sections - printmaking and picture printing in general, intaglio processes, relief block printing, planographic (lithographic) processes, photomechanical processes; list of periodicals consulted, and excellent indexes. *Class No:* 76(01)

[3709]

Graphic arts abstracts: a digest of scientific, technical and educational information for the graphic communications industries. Pittsburgh Graphic Arts Technical Foundation, 1947-. $90pa. ISSN: 10480293.

Bi-monthly; from 1989 issued as a part of *GATF World.*

About 120 indicative and informative abstracts per issue. 27 sections: Graphic arts: general - Management - In-plant printing - Education and training ... Typesetting and typography - Art and copy preparation ... Colour and colour printing ... Paper Ink ... Speciality printing - Packaging and converting - Science and technology. *Class No:* 76(01)

[3710]

Graphic arts bulletin. Atlanta, GA, Institute of Paper Science and Technology, 1954-. $400pa. ISSN: 00908207.

Monthly; incorporates *Graphic Arts Progress.* Previous title: *Graphic arts literature abstracts.*

Divided into subject areas; author and keyword indexes.
Class No: 76(01)

[3711]

LUDMAN, J. *and* **MASON, L. Fine print references:** a selected bibliography of print-related literature. New York, Kraus, 1982. 242p. $60. ISBN: 0527587281.

2,164 references arranged under 12 topic headings; indexes. *Class No:* 76(01)

[3712]

MASON, L., ***and others.*** **Old master print references:** a selected bibliography. New York, Kraus, 1986. 279p. $70. ISBN: 052762196x.

3,000 references to some 900 artists earlier in date than those in *Fine print references.* Citations from a wide range of sources; arranged alphabetically by artist, then chronologically. *Class No:* 76(01)

[3713]

MASON, L. *and* **LUDMAN, J.,** ***comps.*** **Print reference sources:** a select bibliography, eighteenth to twentieth centuries. 2nd ed. Millwood, NY, Kraus, 1979. xi,303p. $60. ISBN: 0527621900.

First published 1975.

About 6,000 references to some 1,800 artists, Abbé-Zom (Toulouse-Lautrec: 23 refs., chronologically arranged). Citations are to exhibition, museum and dealer catalogues, checklists, books and journal articles. 'An excellent source for *catalogues raisonnés* and similar documentation on prints by specific artists' (*Art Documentation* 1(5) Oct. 1982. p.163). *Class No:* 76(01)

[3714]

THOMSON, E.M., ***comp.*** **American graphic design:** a guide to the literature. Westport,CT, Greenwood Press, 1992. 282p. $55.00. ISBN: 0313287287.

Compiled in association with the American Institute of Graphic Arts; covers commercial art and graphic design. 18 sections - general reference then individual topics such as education, colour etc. Appendix of organizations.
Class No: 76(01)

Encyclopaedias & Dictionaries

[3715]

DALLEY, T., ***ed.*** **The Complete guide to illustration and design:** techniques and materials. New ed. Oxford, Phaidon, 1984. 224p.,illus.,tables. £14.95. ISBN: 0714823473.

2 parts: Illustration (Introduction. 1. Pencils and other point media; 2. Pen and ink; 3. Oils and other paint media; 4. Printmaking; 5. Technical illustration) - Graphic design (Introduction. 6. Design equipment; 7. Copying and photoprinting; 8. Design and typography; 9. Design procedures; 10. Design and photography; 11. Reproduction and printing). Glossary, p.208-213. Paper and sizes. Manufacturers and suppliers. Index, p.218-24. Step-by-step instruction, profusely illustrated (550 illus., 250 in colour), with descriptive captions. *Class No:* 76(03)

[3716]
GASCOIGNE, B. How to identify prints: a complete guide to manual and mechanical processes from woodcut to inkjet. London, Thames & Hudson, 1986. 208p. illus. £25. ISBN: 050023454x.

Three main sections: description and explanation of processes, keys to identification, reference (vocabulary, glossary, bibliography, index). 'This book is the best in the field' (*Choice* 24(9) May 1987, p.1386). *Class No:* 76(03)

[3717]
LIVINGSTON, A. Thames and Hudson encyclopedia of graphic design and designers. London, Thames and Hudson, 1992. 215p. £6.95. ISBN: 0500202591.

700 entries for terms and movements, advertising, corporate identity, posters, packaging, audio-visual, industrial. Subject index; cross-references; bibliography. 'Clearly written, informative, very well printed and gives an historical context in addition to a contemporary overview.' (*Reference reviews,* 7(2) 1993, p30.) *Class No:* 76(03)

[3718]
STEVENSON, G.A. Graphic arts encyclopedia. 3rd ed. New York, TAB Books, 1992. 624p. £52.00. ISBN: 0830625305.

First published 1968.

3,000 alphabetical entries cover terminology, technique, equipment, processes. Useful illustrations; bibliography. Lists US associations and societies, US and UK trade journals. *Class No:* 76(03)

Handbooks & Manuals

[3719]
BRISTOW, N. Screen-printing: design and technique. London, Batsford, 1990. 160p., illus. £19.95. ISBN: 0713458127.

Basic guide with chapters covering techniques from the simplest to the more advanced. *Class No:* 76(035)

[3720]
COTTON, B. The New guide to graphic design. London, Phaidon, 1990. 192p. illus. £16.95. ISBN: 0714826278.

Good overall guide to setting up in graphic design; principles, client relationships, studio organization, equipment, materials, case studies. Over 400 illustrations. *Class No:* 76(035)

[3721]
PORTER, T. *and* **GOODMAN, S. Manual of graphic techniques for architects, graphic designers, and artists.** New ed. London, Butterworth Architecture, 1988. 128p. per vol. (4v.), illus. £11.95 per vol. ISBN: 0408500123, v.1; 0408500077, v.2; 0408500089, v.3; 0408500093, v.4.

Copiously illustrated technical guide. *Class No:* 76(035)

Dictionaries

[3722]
GARLAND, K. Graphics, design and printing terms: an international dictionary. 2nd ed. London, Lund Humphries, 1988. 264p., illus. £16.95. ISBN: 085331523x.

First edition (1980) as the *Illustrated Graphics Glossary*.

Defines over 2,000 terms, with ample cross-references. US/UK usage discussed. Useful bibliography; over 300 illustrations. *Class No:* 76(038)

[3723]
GOLDMAN, P. Looking at prints, drawings and watercolours; a guide to technical terms. London, British Museum Publications, 1989. 64p. £7.50. ISBN: 0892361484.

Readable and authoritative list of terms, processes, materials, tools. Cross references and bibliography. *Class No:* 76(038)

Periodicals & Progress Reports

[3724]
Graphis: international journal of visual communication. Zurich, Graphis Press, 1944-. $108.00. ISSN: 00173452.

6 issues pa.; also an annual summary *Graphis Annual.* (00725528).

Excellently produced and illustrated; most issues include a small number of book reviews. *Class No:* 76(05)

[3725]
Print quarterly. London, Print Quarterly Publications, 1984-. £38pa. ISSN: 02658305.

Issued quarterly.

Scholarly journal covering the history of prints and printmaking from the 15th century to the present. Includes book reviews. 'The virtues of *PQ* lie not only in the consistent high standard and professionalism of its articles but in its ability to steer an independent course in a field particularly susceptible to commercial pressures'. (*TLS,* 9-15 June 1989; p.647). *Class No:* 76(05)

Yearbooks & Directories

[3726]
Gordon's print price annual. 20th.ed. Naples, FL, Gordon's Art Reference, Inc., 1997. 1340p.

This publisher has announced plans to relaunch related titles: *Lawrence's dealer print prices* is revived from 1997 (last issued in 1994); *Print price index* is suspended but should return in 1997; *Print price guide* is also to be re-launched.

CD-ROMs of the main title and two of the others mentioned here are to be available: *Gordon's print price annual* will cover 1986-1997; *Lawrence's* will cover 1992-1997; *Print price index* will also appear on CD-ROM.

Also Internet access; Website at <http://www.gordonart.com>

The main vol. lists sales A/Z by artist with full technical information; directory of auction houses. *Lawrence's* has 35,000 entries in its 1200 pages (CD-ROM will provide 200,000 prices); *Print price guide* covers 12,000 artists and has glossary, lexicon, directories, and bibliography; *Print price index* covers 40,000 artists arranged A/Z, with high standard of detail. *Class No:* 76(058)

[3727]
Graphis design 98. Pedersen, M., *ed.* New York, Graphis, Inc. 1997. 242p. ISBN: 1888001313.

Annual.

Showcase of international design; 600 examples of creative and innovative work - annual reports, brochures, packaging, other design products. Indexes of companies, creative directors, art directors, designers, artists, illustrators, photographers. *Class No:* 76(058)

[3728]

Sheppard's international directory of print and map sellers. 2nd ed. London, R Joseph, 1992. 448p. £24. ISBN: 187269909x.

Specialist dealers worldwide. *Class No:* 76(058)

[3729]

ZANETTA, J.E., ***ed.*** **Contemporary print portfolio:** a guide to prices, new editions and sources. Shawnee Mission, KS, Tirer, 1990-. 304p. $34.95. ISBN: 1878446002. ISSN: 10469087.

First issue of a biannual series.

Auction prices of the print market, obtained from publishers, galleries and dealers, and covering the previous three years in the US, Europe, & Japan. 4,000 prints listed, arranged by artist A/Z. Artist data, references and catalogues are noted. 100 monochrome illustrations. Bibliography; directory section. *Class No:* 76(058)

Histories

[3730]

BLUNT, W. The Art of botanical illustration. 4th ed. London, Collins, 1967. 304p. illus. (*New Naturalist Series.*) ISBN: 0002130025.

First published 1950.

Detailed & authoritative history covering major painters, etchers, engravers, schools, periodical & book sources. Further sources listed p.287-294. Index of names. *Class No:* 76(091)

[3731]

MEGGS, P. A History of graphic design. New ed. London, Viking, 1985. 511p.,illus. £37.50. ISBN: 0670807214.

Five sections in part one cover the evolution of graphic communications from ancient times to the invention of movable typography. Part 2 (4 sections) examines early typography in Europe, and design of the printed page. Part 3 (5 sections) discusses industrial revolution effects on printing. Part 4 (10 sections) concentrates on 20th century developments. Glossary p.492-496; bibliography p.492-502; 600 photographs & 400 line drawings. *Class No:* 76(091)

[3732]

SOUTER, N. ***and*** **SOUTER, T. Illustrator's source book:** 1850 to the present day. London, Macdonald Orbis, 1990. 319p., illus.

4 main periods - 1850/1899, 1900/1939, 1940/1969, and 1970/1990; alphabetical arrangement by illustrators' names, with marginal notes on the work shown. *Class No:* 76(091)

[3733]

WEILL, A. The Poster: a worldwide survey and history. Boston, G.K. Hall, 1985. 422p.

Major history 1469 to the present, with separate coverage of individuals. Bibliographies; good illustrations. *Class No:* 76(091)

Biographies

[3734]

WEINBERG, R.E. A Biographical dictionary of science fiction and fantasy artists. London, Greenwood Press, 1988. 352p. £40.95. ISBN: 0313243492.

Biographical and professional details of modern genre artists. *Class No:* 76(092)

[3735]

Who's who in graphic design. Zurich, Benteli-Werd Verlag, 1994. 597p., illus. ISBN: 3859321358.

Includes 300 designers from 46 countries, with over 1500 illustrations. A/Z by country Argentina-Zimbabwe; introductory commentary and individual designers - biographical and career information. Directory of professional organisations, journals by country, competitions, events. Parallel German and English text. *Class No:* 76(092)

[3736]

WILLIAMS, R. ***and*** **WILLIAMS, D. American screenprint artists 1932-1949.**

An appendix to the *Early history of the screen print* in *Print Quarterly* 3(4) December 1986, p.286-321 (Illus.).

Lists 213 artists with dates, location, lists of works. 18 colour illustrations. *Class No:* 76(092)

Great Britain

[3737]

LISTER, R. Prints and printmaking: a dictionary and handbook of the art in nineteenth-century Britain. London, Methuen, 1984. 385p., plates. ISBN: 0413401308.

Introductory chapters on lithography, wood-engraving, security-printing, steel engraving, etching. Glossary of techniques. Bibliography. Dictionary of engravers and others (p.105-385), giving dates, media, subjects etc. *Class No:* 76(410)

[3738]

MACKENZIE, I. British prints: dictionary and price guide. Rev.ed. Woodbridge, Suffolk, Antique Collectors' Club, 1998. 376p. illus. £39.50. ISBN: 1851492356.

First ed. 1987.

Brief biographical data, arranged A/Z, on over 2000 print-makers 1650-1950, with description of characteristic work, guide to market values. Comprehensive coverage includes 18th century mezzotints portraits, 19th century sporting aquatints and landscapes, 20th century etchings and lithographs. Identification advice. Over 500 monochrome illustrations, and 66 colour. Bibliography. *Class No:* 76(410)

Biographies

[3739]

HOUFE, S. The Dictionary of British book illustrators and caricaturists 1800-1914: with introductory chapters on the rise and progress of the art. 2nd. rev. ed. Woodbridge, Antique Collectors' Club, 1994. 350p. illus. £35.00. ISBN: 1851491937.

First published 1978; rev. ed. 1981.

Entries for 2,500 individuals from 15-20,000 books and periodicals. Scope and development of nineteenth century illustration; dictionary sequence. Lists schools of illustration, and specialist illustration. Bibliography; index; 300 monochrome illustrations. *Class No:* 76(410)(092)

London

[3740]

ADAMS, B. London illustrated 1604-1851: a survey and index of topographic books and their plates. London, Library Association, 1983. xxxiii,586p. illus. £75. ISBN: 0853657343.

Lists over 8250 engraved, etched or lithographic plates in 238 books and sets of prints published over 250 years.

....*(contd.)*
Entries are chronological by date of publication, with notes on publishing history, transcription of title-page, collation etc. Index to artists, engravers, architects, authors, book titles and select publishers. Chronological list of books xxv-xviii, topographical indexes. Select bibliography p.583-586.
Class No: 76(421)

Italy

Bibliographies

[3741]
KARPINSKI, C. Italian printmaking, fifteenth and sixteenth centuries: an annotated bibliography. Boston, G.K. Hall, 1987. 305p. $45. ISBN: 0816185565.
Sections cover general sources, histories, methods, publishing, iconography, use of prints, biographies (775 entries). List of collections; indexes. *Class No:* 76(450)(01)

Japan

[3742]
BLAKEMORE, F. Who's who in modern Japanese prints. New York, Weatherhill, 1989. 264p. illus. £9.95. ISBN: 0834801019.
Alphabetical list of 105 active Japanese print artists; index to over 400 printmakers. Profusely illustrated.
Class No: 76(52)

Bibliographies

[3743]
ABRAMS, L.E., *ed*. The History and practice of Japanese printmaking: a selectively annotated bibliography of English language material. London, Greenwood, 1984. 224p. £39.95. ISBN: 0313231885.
The literature of the Japanese woodblock print definitively explored. Listed in *Outstanding Academic Books 1984/85* (*Choice* 22,9. May 1985, p.1272). *Class No:* 76(52)(01)

USA

Biographies

[3744]
HORN, M., *ed*. Contemporary graphic artists. Detroit, Gale Research, 1986-1988. 272, 288, 269p. (3v). $180.00. ISSN: 08858462.
Particularly valuable for areas of work often omitted - cartoonists, animators, comic strip artists, illustrators, poster designers, computer graphic artists. Emphasis on modern American names, but some historical and foreign figures. 'An indispensible reference source'. (*Art Documentation*, 5(3), Fall 1986, p.138). *Class No:* 76(73)(092)

[3745]
WILLIAMS, L.B., *comp*. American printmakers, 1880-1945: an index to reproductions and biographical information. Metuchen,NJ, Scarecrow Press, 1993. 441p. $52.50. ISBN: 0810827867.
Indexes books and exhibition catalogues, biographical dictionaries etc. 3 parts: basic bibliography of 86 titles; index of artists with notes on specific monographs and works listed by title with date, medium etc. and citation to part 1; 370 illustrations listed by subject. *Class No:* 76(73)(092)

Woodcuts & Wood Engraving

Biographies

[3746]
BRETT, S. Engravers: a handbook for the nineties. Cambridge, Silent Books, 1987. 112p. illus. £8.95. ISBN: 1851830030.
Compiled for the Society of Wood Engravers.
Sections cover young artists, engravers born in the 1940's, mature work. List of names and addresses. 'Well produced and profusely illustrated' (*Print Quarterly* 5(2) June 1988, p.170). *Class No:* 761(092)

[3747]
ENGEN, R.K. Dictionary of Victorian wood engravers. Cambridge, Chadwyck-Healey, 1985. 320p. £60.00. ISBN: 0859641392.
Lists and evaluates work, with details of dates, partnerships, techniques, collections, signatures. Bibliographical notes and three major bibliographies.
Class No: 761(092)

Japan

[3748]
Ukiyo-e masterpieces in European collections. London, Serindia Publications, 1990. 248p. ISBN: 0870118846.
Catalogues the collections of Japanese woodblock prints and paintings (Ukiyo-e) in seven major European museums. .
Class No: 761(52)

Engraving & Etching

Biographies

[3749]
Bryan's Dictionary of painters and engravers. Williamson, G.C., *ed*. Port Washington, NY, Kennicat Press, 1964. 363,291,393,308,425p. (5v.), illus.
First published in 2 vols., 1816; subsequent editions 1849, 1884-9, 1903-4 (fourth edition, reprinted here).
Brief, authoritative entries; titles & location of work. A respected historical source. Monochrome plates bound in each volume. *Class No:* 762(092)

Great Britain

[3750]
BRITISH MUSEUM. Department of Prints and Drawings. **Catalogue of engraved British portraits** in the Department. London, British Museum, 1908-25. 6v.
V.1-4: A-Z; V.5: Groups; V.6: Supplement and index.
V.1-4 entries are arranged under sitter's name; brief bibliography. V.5, a classified catalogue of groups, has an index of individual portraits in those groups. V.6 supplements v.1-4 and indexes painters and engravers in v.1-5, with an appendix, - a list of cited books and periodicals containing portraits. *Class No:* 762(410)

Biographies

[3751]
ENGEN, R.K. Dictionary of Victorian engravers, print publishers and their works. Cambridge, Chadwyck-Healey, 1979. 245p. illus. ISBN: 085964054x.
Alphabetical list of engravers p.13-223; list of publishers, printers, and print-sellers p.227-245. 1000 entries in total. 39 monochrome illustrations. *Class No:* 762(410)(092)

[3752]

GUICHARD, K.M. British etchers, 1850-1940. Rev. ed. London, Robin Garton, 1981. 164p.,illus. £25. ISBN: 0906030099.

Biographies of over 400 etchers, arranged alphabetically, with 380 illustrations of their work. Handsomely produced. *Class No:* 762(410)(092)

[3753]

HUNNISETT, B. An Illustrated dictionary of British steel engravers. 2nd ed. Aldershot, Scolar Press, 1988. 224p. illus. £37.50. ISBN: 0859677400.

First published 1980.

Alphabetical list of 19th century engravers of original artwork for reproduction. 644 entries, giving name, dates, type of work, examples. 64 plates. *Class No:* 762(410)(092)

Canada

Biographies

[3754]

HARPER, J.R. Early painters and engravers in Canada. Ontario, University of Toronto Press, 1970. xv,376p. £23.30. ISBN: 0802016308.

Covers 4,000 artists born before 1867 or active before 1900. Alphabetical arrangement, giving biographical details, characteristic work, collections. Bibliography p.343-376. *Class No:* 762(71)(092)

Commercial Graphics

[3755]

SANDERS, N. Graphic designer's production handbook. Newton Abbot, David & Charles, 1984. 206p. illus. £10.95. ISBN: 0715385976.

Anglicized edition.

Covers 100 processes in three main categories: pre-press preparation, half-tone reproduction, printing and finishing operations. Each process is illustrated; written for graphic designers from the perspective of the printer. Index. *Class No:* 766

[3756]

SIMPSON, I., *ed*. The New guide to illustration. London, Phaidon, 1990. 192p. illus. £16.95. ISBN: 0714826286.

Aimed at professional illustrators and showing working practices and techniques. Includes computer-generated images. Glossary of technical terms, addresses of professional bodies, suppliers of materials. *Class No:* 766

Print Collections

[3757]

PARRY, P.J. *and* **CHIPMAN, K., *comps*. Print index.** Westport, CT, Greenwood Press, 1983. 310p.

Indexes over 2,000 prints appearing in 100 books. Index of subjects and titles. *Class No:* 769

[3758]

RIGGS, T.A., *comp*. The Print Council index to oeuvre-catalogues of prints by European and American artists. New York, Kraus, 1983. 834p. $120. ISBN: 0527753467.

Single alphabetical sequence of artists or publishers, including designers of posters, book-plates and book illustrators working by non-photomechanical methods. Each entry gives personal data, list of catalogues in chronological order of publication with notes on number of prints listed. Library locations indicated for rare items. Supplementary

.... (contd.)

sections cover nicknames and monograms. 'This massive work of reference is an invaluable aid to print scholarship' (*Print Quarterly* 2(1) March 1985. p.55-58). *Class No:* 769

Spain

[3759]

RIOS, E.P. Repertorio de grabados espanoles. Madrid, Ministerio de Cultura, 1981-83. 466,460,296p. (3v.), illus.

Handbook of Spanish prints in the Biblioteca Nacional, Madrid. Alphabetical arrangement of 12,000 items of 3,000 artists, including book illustrators. *Class No:* 769(460)

Photography

Bibliographies

[3760]

BLOCK, E.S. Photography: a survey of new reference sources. *Reference Services Review* 15(2) 1987. p.47-54.

Good narrative discussion with citations to 19 items. Arranged under headings - biography, dictionaries & encyclopedias, bibliographies, directories, catalogues, indexes. *Class No:* 77(01)

[3761]

BONI, A., *and others*. Photographic literature: international bibliographical guide to general and specialized literature on photographic processes, techniques, theory, chemistry, physics, apparatus, materials and applications, industry, history, biography, aesthetics, etc. New York, Morgan & Morgan 1962, 1972. xvi,335p. (Supplement: xv,535p.).

Supplement 1960-1970.

Covers over 12,000 books, pamphlets and journal articles (mainly English, French, and German) arranged under alphabetical subject headings. Emphasis on technical matters, but some coverage of individuals, history, aesthetics, bibliography and illustrated books. *Class No:* 77(01)

[3762]

Imaging abstracts. Leatherhead, PIRA, 1988-. £388pa. ISSN: 0896100x.

Published in conjunction with the Royal Photographic Society. Issued bi-monthly. Formerly *Photographic Abstracts* (*q.v.*). Available online from 1975, and on CD-ROM.

Abstracts and summaries from 100 international imaging trade and technical journals, reports and newspapers. Clear layout with prominent section heads; alerting service and individual searches available. *Class No:* 77(01)

[3763]

International photography index. Johnson, W.S., *ed.* Boston, G.K. Hall, 1983-. ISSN: 07371365.

Annual; first issue dated 1979.

A classed subject index of entries for books & periodicals on the creative, communications aspects, & history of photography. Covers over 100 journals. Personal name index; index to galleries & museums. *Class No:* 77(01)

[3764]

MOSS, M. Photography books index: a subject guide to photo anthologies. Metuchen, NJ., Scarecrow Press, 1980-85. xi,286,276p. (2v.). $45. ISBN: 0810812835, v.1; 081081773x, v.2.

Each volume has three parts: photographers, subjects, portraits of named individuals. *Class No:* 77(01)

[3765]

Photographic abstracts: abstracts of the world literature of the science, technology and application of photography. London, Royal Photographic Society. 1921-1987. ISSN: 00318701.

Originally monthly, later 6pa. From 1986 published by Pergamon Press, Oxford. From 1988 continues as *Imaging Abstracts* (*q.v.*).

1987 featured 4500 indicative abstracts and references to literature and patent specifications. 50 headings covering theory, accessories, processing, applications (*e.g.* radiography, aerial photography, cinematography). Annual & ten-yearly author, patent, and analytical subject indexes. *Class No:* 77(01)

[3766]

SENNETT, R.S. Photography and photographers to 1900: an annotated bibliography. New York, Garland, 1985. 134p. $30. ISBN: 0824087283.

409 annotated entries for 'influential' monographs published 1839-1940, including recent reprints. Alphabetical arrangement under five broad headings. Indexes. 'Recommended' (*Choice,* 23(9) May 1986, p:1380). *Class No:* 77(01)

Encyclopaedias & Dictionaries

[3767]

EDWARDS, M. Complete encyclopedia of photography. London, Multimedia Books, 1991. 191p. illus. ISBN: 1853750034.

Discusses equipment, films, cameras, lighting, darkroom practice, and photographic themes - portraits, still life, street life, sport etc. 250 good illustrations. *Class No:* 77(03)

[3768]

INTERNATIONAL CENTER OF PHOTOGRAPHY. Encyclopedia of photography. New York, Crown, 1984. 607p. illus. ISBN: 051755271x.

Entries cover technique, aesthetics, and biographical data for prominent photographers 1840-1940. Scholarly in approach. 1300 entries of which 350 are biographical. Appendices list other photographers (about 2000 with basic details); societies and associations; bibliography. Profusely illustrated. *Class No:* 77(03)

[3769]

LANGFORD, M. The Complete encyclopedia of photography. London, Ebury Press, 1982. 432p., illus., tables. £19.95. ISBN: 0852232292.

5 main sections: The art of photography - The techniques of photography (*e.g.* lighting) - Post-camera techniques (*e.g.* print making) - The specialized subject (*e.g.* medical and forensic photography) - Photographic styles (*e.g.* the documentary approach; surrealism). Step-by-step approach; boxed data in colour. Subject glossary, p.384-92; Glossary, p.393-421. Analytical index. Profusely illustrated; wide appeal. *Class No:* 77(03)

[3770]

STROEBEL, L. *and* **ZAKIA, R. The Focal encyclopedia of photography.** 3rd ed. London, Focal Press, 1993. 914p., illus. £75.00. ISBN: 0240800591.

First published 1956.

90 expert contributors provide a scholarly and comprehensive guide to all aspects - aesthetics, business practices, chemistry, light, optics etc. A/Z of terms, processes, individual names. Many charts, graphs, diagrams, photographs. 'It would be hard to imagine a more complete one-volume work. An essential purchase.' (*Choice,* 31(4) December 1993. p584.) *Class No:* 77(03)

Handbooks & Manuals

[3771]

BUNCHFIELD, J. *and* **JACOBS, M.** *and* **KOKRDA, K. Photography in focus.** 5th.ed. Lincolnwood, IL, NTC Publishing Group, 1997. 516p., illus. $27.95. ISBN: 0844257818.

Sections cover visual literacy, visual aspects of photography, cameras and basic functions, lenses, film and light, exposure, development, printing, image manipulations, digital imaging, lighting, finishing, presentation, storage. Brief history of photography p.465-500; bibliography p.503-516. *Class No:* 77(035)

[3772]

HEDGECOE, J. Complete guide to photography. London, Collins & Brown, 1990. 224p., illus. £15.95. ISBN: 1855850001.

Techniques and elements explained for all types of work - people, places, natural world, action, still-life. 70 practical projects are described in detail. Glossary of terms. 500 illustrations (400 in colour). *Class No:* 77(035)

[3773]

HEDGECOE, J. John Hedgecoe's new book of photography. London, Dorling Kindersley, 1994. 264p., illus. £19.99. ISBN: 0751301108.

Comprehensive general guide, with explanation of photographic terms, cameras, films, filters, exposure, lighting. *Class No:* 77(035)

[3774]

JACOBSON, R.E., ***and others.*** **Manual of photography.** 8th ed. London, Focal Press, 1988. 394p. illus., tables, diagrams. £25.00. ISBN: 0240512685.

Covers processes and principles, materials, colour chemistry, evaluation and faults. Formulae, diagrams etc. 361 illustrations. Comprehensive index. 'Essential ... its authority is in no doubt' (*Photographic Journal* August 1989, p.372). *Class No:* 77(035)

Yearbooks & Directories

[3775]

Directory of professional photography 1996. Chillingworth, J., *ed.* Macclesfield, McMillan Martin for the British Institute of Professional Photographers, 1996. 252p. ISBN: 1898340951.

Lists 3,000 qualified professional photographers and technicians. Buyers' guide. Lists of members UK & overseas. Directory of specializations. *Class No:* 77(058)

[3776]

Gordon's international photography price guide 1997. Naples, FL, Gordon's Art Reference, Inc., 1997. $65.00.

Available in print version and CD-ROM.

5000 entries covering sales worldwide. *Class No:* 77(058)

[3777]
Professional imaging directory 1996. 11th.ed. Bishop's Stortford, Cambridgeshire, MarketLink Publishing, 1995.

Entries for 1700 companies, almost all in the UK, covering many aspects of the imaging industry - producers, services, libraries, trade names, overseas agencies. Arranged under broad categories, giving basic contact data. *Class No:* 77(058)

Audio-Visual Materials

[3778]
COVERT, N., ***and others*****. Films and videos on photography.** New York, Program for Art on Film, 1990. 114p. £14.95. ISBN: 0870995731.

Produced by the Metropolitan Museum of Art/Getty Trust sponsored Program for Art on Film and the A/V Dept. of the Direction des Musées de France. Comprises two databases *Critical inventory of films on art* and *Base Audiart*. Arranged A/Z by title noting format, running time, technical credits, synopsis, reviews, awards. Subject & name indexes; list of distributors. Very valuable annotated source.
Class No: 77(086)

Histories

[3779]
GERNSHEIM, H. *and* **GERNSHEIM, A. The History of photography,** from the camera obscura to the beginning of the modern era. 3rd ed. London, Thames & Hudson, 1982/88. 280, 288p. (2v.) illus. £30.00 (v.1), £42.00 (v.2) ISBN: 0500540802, v.1; 0500973490, v.2.

First published by O.U.P. in 1955. Revised and reissued in 2 vols. - the *Origins of photography* and the *Rise of photography 1850-1880.*

Covers major stages in development; annotated bibliography, lists of journals, societies etc. 'The standard history and reference work on photography' (Arntzen & Rainwater, 1980, p.376). *Class No:* 77(091)

[3780]
JONES, B.E., ***ed*****. Encyclopaedia of early photography.** London, Bishopsgate Press, 1981. 572p. illus. £18.50. ISBN: 0900873442.

Originally published as *Encyclopaedia of photography* (Cassell, 1911).

Alphabetical arrangement of 2,500 entries covering terms, processes, materials, chemicals, equipment, optics, trade names, and significant figures, before 1900. 19 specialist contributors. *Class No:* 77(091)

[3781]
NEWHALL, B. History of photography, from 1839 to the present. Rev. 5th ed. London, Secker & Warburg, 1982. 319p., illus. ISBN: 0436305070.

First published 1937.

Considered one of the classic works in this field. Praised as a good, concise introduction, both 'readable' and 'engaging' (*Choice* February 1988). Illustrated with over 300 examples, newly selected for this edition. *Class No:* 77(091)

[3782]
ROSENBLUM, N. A World history of photography. 3rd.ed. New York, Abbeville, 1997. 696p. illus. £49.00. ISBN: 0789200287.

Thematic chapters cover the early years of photography, portraiture, landscape, photography as art, photojournalism, photography since 1950; profiles; cameras & processes. Glossary; bibliography; over 800 illustrations (80 in colour); index. *Class No:* 77(091)

[3783]
SZARKOWSKI, J. Photography until now. New York, Museum of Modern Art, 1990. 344p., illus. $60. ISBN: 0870705733.

Comprhensive history of photography, published to accompany a MOMA exhibition, & structured to mirror technical advances. Excellent illustrations.
Class No: 77(091)

Bibliographies

[3784]
JOHNSON, W.S. Nineteenth century photography: an annotated bibliography, 1839-1879. London, Mansell, 1990. 968p. £90. ISBN: 0720120896.

Excellent, comprehensive source to the world of photography in its early period. *Class No:* 77(091)(01)

[3785]
ROOSENS, L.P.J. *and* **SALU, L. History of photography:** a bibliography of books. London, Mansell, 1989, 1994, 1996. 446, 389, 448p. (3 vols.) £40, £60, £70. ISBN: 072012008x, v.1; 0720121523, v.2; 0720123100, v.3.

Volume 1 contains 7000 entries arranged alphabetically with cross-references, and covering books, exhibition catalogues, pamphlets and dissertations. 'As comprehensive as possible for sources published before 1914... an essential source' (*Choice* 27(8) April 1990. p.1305). Volume 2 contains 5250 entries and extends coverage to photographers born before 1936; a name index covers both volumes. Volume 3 continues the excellent coverage.
Class No: 77(091)(01)

Women

[3786]
ROSENBLUM, N. A History of women photographers. New York, Abrams, 1994. 356p., illus. £46.00. ISBN: 1558597611.

Arranged chronologically and geographically; examines the work of 240 photographers from the big names to the neglected. Mainly monochrome illustrations; biographical notes; brief bibliography. *Class No:* 77(091)-0055.2

Biographies

[3787]
BROWNE, T. *and* **PARTNOW, E.,** ***eds*****. Biographical encyclopedia of photographic artists and innovators.** London, Macmillan, 1983. 722p. ISBN: 0025175009.

Gives 2,000 names, living and dead, international coverage. Especially useful for the inclusion of less-well-known figures. Biographies p.3-684 with details of career, publications, locations, agents, etc. List of museums p.685-702, and photographic galleries p.703-721. 144 plates in centre section. *Class No:* 77(092)

[3788]

EDWARDS, G. International guide to nineteenth century photographers and their works. Boston, G.K. Hall, 1988. xvii, 591p. $50.00. ISBN: 0816189382.

Assembled from catalogues of auction houses and dealers, this list contains 4,000 names, of which 1,500 are American, with details of subjects, processes, locations. 'Landmark work for the field' (*Reference Books Bulletin*, June 1988). 'Users should be aware that it is not comprehensive' (*Art Libraries Journal*, 14(2)1989,p.45-47). *Class No:* 77(092)

[3789]

EVANS, M.M., *ed.* **Contemporary photographers.** 3rd.ed. Detroit/London, St.James Press, 1995. 1234p.,illus. £100.00. ISBN: 1558621903.

Worldwide survey which has established a good reputation; for this edition 140 new entries have been added, but those included in the 2nd.ed.(1987) and who have died or not added to their work are not featured here - the previous edition should therefore be retained. Entries give summary, artistic objectives, and an authoritative commentary; excellent coverage throughout the history of photography - classic names, contemporary figures, women, controversial persons. Nationality index. 'Serves as a definitive reference source for the next decade and well into the next century'.(*American reference books annual*, 1996. p429.) *Class No:* 77(092)

[3790]

Photographers on disc: an international index of photographers, exhibitions, and collections. Eskind, A.H., *ed.* Boston, G.K.Hall, 1996. CD-ROM. $495.00. ISBN: 0783815514.

80,000 listings of photographers, manufacturers and publishers giving nationality and affiliations, life dates, active periods, roles and annotations. 3500 exhibition histories 1839-1996 - mainly US and Western Europe. 595 institution records from museums, libraries, archives etc. Also 2000 bibliographic citations, not searchable directly but only as links from the other sections. *Class No:* 77(092)

Black Races

[3791]

THOMAS, D.W. An Illustrated bio-bibliography of black photographers, 1940-1988. New York, Garland, 1989. 483p. $85.00. ISBN: 082408389x.

Continues *Black Photographers 1840-1940* and concentrates on American blacks. A valuable work, although many entries are sparse. *Class No:* 77(092)(=96)

Great Britain

Bibliographies

[3792]

GERNSHEIM, H. Incunabula of British photography: a bibliography of British photographic literature 1839-1875, and British books illustrated with original photographs. London, Scolar Press, 1984. 160p. illus., facsims. £39.50. ISBN: 0859675789.

Three main sections cover 1200 titles; bibliography of books, newspapers, periodicals and magazines, bibliography of early British photographic literature; photographic journals, almanacs and annuals, non-photographic journals of relevance, important essays on photography. Appendices and indexes. 'A useful book for photographic historians, librarians, and student researchers' (*Photographic Journal*, November 1984, p.521). *Class No:* 77(410)(01)

Biographies

[3793]

PRITCHARD, M. A Directory of London photographers 1841-1908. Bushey, Herts., ALLM., 1986. 106p. illus. £6.95. ISBN: 0950678449.

Companion volumes cover Bath, Cardiff, Doncaster, Leeds, Leicester, Manchester, Oxford etc; part of Royal Photographic Society's Historical Group Survey.

Lists over 2500 photographers and firms active in the London area. Section on use of period trade directories. Alphabetical arrangement, with dates. Bibliography. *Class No:* 77(410)(092)

Microphotography

Yearbooks & Directories

[3794]

BAKER, G.G., *ed.* **Micrographics yearbook.** Windlesham, Surrey, G.G.Baker & Associates, 1997. 240p., illus. £20.00. ISBN: 0906635233. ISSN: 09679774.

Previously *Micrographics yearbook* (1981-1986), *Micrographics and optical recording buyers' guide* (1989-90), *Document image processing yearbook*(1991-1995).

Includes an opening section on micrographics - formats, production, COM, scanners, retrieval, etc., and directory sections on hardware, services, suppliers, associations, publications. Other chapters cover electronic image processing systems. Address list at end contains details of organisations and companies. *Class No:* 778.14(058)

Film & Television Photography

Dictionaries

[3795]

TAYLOR, R. Encyclopedia of animation techniques. Oxford, Focal Press, 1996. 176p., illus. ISBN: 0240514882.

Thorough reference source from a respected technical publisher. *Class No:* 778.5(038)

Video

[3796]

HEDGECOE, J. John Hedgecoe's camcorder basics. London, Collins & Brown, 1995. 160p., illus. £14.99. ISBN: 1855852179.

Very basic handbook for the beginner; well-written and sensible. *Class No:* 778.534

Yearbooks & Directories

[3797]

Billboard's international buyers' guide, of the music, record, tape industry. New York, BPI Communications Inc., 1958-. $83. ISSN: 00678600.

Lists video companies, retail suppliers, services (including organizations, libraries, schools). Directory of manufacturers and materials. *Class No:* 778.534(058)

Photographic Collections

[3798]

CEPIC directory 1998/99; a list of members: a practical guide to European agencies press and stock. Berlin, CEPIC, 1998. 244p. 25ecu.

CEPIC - Coordination of European Picture Agencies Press and Stock - was established in 1993 as a European Economic Interest Group within the CEC. Members are 10 national associations of picture agencies and libraries (BAPLA in the UK) representing 800 picture sources and 30,000 photographers. Class No: 779

[3799]

Electronic image safe service Hamburg, EISS, 1998-.

Website at <http://www.tg-online.com>

CEC-sponsored information and copyright-research database that will serve as a copyright registration and reference pool to protect visual assets and simplify trading between art buyers and image publishers. Operated by partners in the UK (PIRA), Germany, Austria and Switzerland. *Class No:* 779

[3800]

MUNZ, L.T. *and* **SLAUSON, N.G. Index to illustrations of living things** outside North America: where to find pictures of flora and fauna. Hamden, CT, Archon Books, 1981. 441p. £45.70. ISBN: 0208018573.

Indexes photographs, paintings and sketches of over 900 animals and plants worldwide. Index to illustrations p.19-306; code letters refer to 206 major sources mainly post-1963 (listed p.11-18). Scientific names index. Bibliography. *Class No:* 779

[3801]

THOMPSON, J.W. *and* **SLAUSON, N. Index to illustration of the natural world:** where to find pictures of living things in North America. Hamden, CT, Shoe String Press, 1983. 265p. £36.50. ISBN: 0208020381.

Reprint of 1977 edition.

Index to illustrations of flora and fauna in North America. *Class No:* 779

Handbooks & Manuals

[3802]

EVANS, H. *and* **EVANS, M.,** ***comps*****. Picture researcher's handbook:** an international guide to picture sources - and how to use them. 5th ed. London, Blueprint, 1992. xvii,516p. £39.00. ISBN: 0948905751.

1st ed. 1975.

Sources include picture libraries, general libraries, museums, commercial picture and press agencies, art galleries, archives and historical societies. In 4 sections: general; regional (material covering several countries); national (material relating to a particular country); specialist (subdivided in 11 subject categories). Entries give address, description of material held, stock size, research facilities, hours, loan procedures/fees etc. *Class No:* 779(035)

[3803]

Picture librarianship. Harrison, H.P., *ed.* London, Library Association Publishing, 1981. xii,542p. £40.00. ISBN: 0853659125.

Section 1: techniques and organizations (photographic sources p.35-54) selection, presentation & storage, arrangement & indexing, microforms, education & training. Section 2: case studies and surveys of picture libraries (26 divisions including the National Film Archive, art galleries and museums, public libraries, commercial libraries). Bibliography p.495-517; out-of-date in some aspects, but still a standard source. *Class No:* 779(035)

Great Britain

[3804]

EAKINS, R., ***ed.*** **Picture sources UK.** London, MacDonald, 1985. 474p. £45. ISBN: 0356100782.

Directory of over 1100 collections of photographs and prints. Arranged alphabetically by name of collection in categories, subject index, index of named collections. Each entry gives size, scope, subject coverage, access and condition of use, contact name. *Class No:* 779(410)

[3805]

McKEOWN, R. National directory of slide collections. London, British Library, 1990. viii,310p. (*British Library Information Guide, 12.*) ISBN: 0712332081. ISSN: 02691809.

Compiled from data collected in the *National Survey of Slide Collections* (BL Research Paper 67), and containing mainly non-commercial collections. Arranged in alphabetical name order, with subject and geographical indexes. Contains data on about 950 collections, giving size, coverage, access, facilities, charges, & contact name. *Class No:* 779(410)

[3806]

NAPLIB. Directory of aerial photographic collections in the United Kingdom. London, Aslib, 1993. 76p. £22.00. ISBN: 0851423043.

Produced in association with the National Association of Aerial Photographic Libraries (NAPLIB).

Introductory sections give details of the history, uses and copyright of aerial photographs; directory of 200 sources with symbols indicating type of photography, angle of view, coverage and availability. Post code location index. *Class No:* 779(410)

[3807]

WALL, J., ***comp*****. National photographic record:** directory of British photographic collections. London, Heinemann, 1977. 266p.

1,600 collections briefly described; subject arrangement, with indexes of owners, photographers, locations. *Class No:* 779(410)

Germany

[3808]

The Marburger index: guide to art in Germany. 2nd.ed. Munich, K.G.Saur, 1996. CD-ROM. DM2480. (Reductions for subscribers to the microfiche ed.) ISBN: 3598403402.

Edited by the Bildarchiv Foto Marburg at the University of Marburg, and many German museums, university departments and photo libraries.

The Index comprises 1,165,000 photographs, with an annual increase of 55,000 items. Text and catalogue, originally published 1977, has been issued on microfiche 1983-1990. CD-ROM version, to be re-issued annually, contains the text and catalogue and 21,000 images - more will be added as this becomes technically realistic. The holdings represented are photographs from the Bildarchiv Foto Marburg, the Rheinisches Bildarchiv Cologne, photo collections of various state departments, and after unification the collection of the Deutsche Fotothek in Dresden. Concentrates on German, especially Rhenish, art, conforms

.... *(contd.)*
to academic cataloguing standards, and gives access to 150,000 works of art. Topographical arrangement of photographs; access to artist database by name, genre, time period, location, patron etc. *Class No:* 779(430)

Asia—Near East

[3809]
GRANT, G. Middle Eastern photographic collections in the United Kingdom. London, Middle East Libraries Committee, 1989. 220p. £18.50. ISBN: 0948889039.
Full descriptions of holdings of specialized collections. *Class No:* 779(56)

USA

[3810]
BURGER, B.L., *comp*. Guide to the holdings of the Still Picture Branch of the National Archives. Atlanta, GA, National Archives Trust Fund, 1991. 176p., illus. $25.
Summary information on over 6 million prints, negatives, slides, posters etc., covering military, political, economic, social, and cultural history of the United States. Ranges from Civil War photographs to satellite images.
Class No: 779(73)

[3811]
Index to American photographic collections: compiled at the International Museum of Photography at George Eastman House. Eskind, A.H., *ed.* 3rd. enlarged ed. Boston, G.K.Hall, 1996. 1058p. £175.00. ISBN: 0783821492.
First published 1973 as *Photography: source and resource.* First ed. of this title published 1982; 2nd ed. 1990.
Derived from the Eastman House Interactive Catalog online database, this edition lists over 66,000 photographers and 585 collections. Two sections: collections listing arranged geographically within the USA gives contact and holdings data; photographers index A/Z with dates and references to collections. 'Monumental work prepared with great professional skill...the publisher is to be congratulated'.(*Reference reviews*, 10(6), 1996; p36.)
Class No: 779(73)

[3812]
MYERS, R., *comp*. Guide to archival materials of the Center for Creative Photography. Tucson, Arizona, University of Arizona, 1986. 128p. $25. ISBN: 0938262149.
Describes the 76 archive groups which form the CCP, and which document twentieth-century photographers, historians, and critics. Good description on scope and contents etc. Personal and corporate name indexes, chronological chart. 'The archives are one of the richest sources of original research material for the history of photography in the United States' (*Photographic Journal,* October 1987, p.467).
Class No: 779(73)

[3813]
New York theater 1919-1961. Cambridge, Chadwyck-Healey, 1987. 877 microfiche.
Copies of the 26,000 photographs in the Vandamm collection at the New York Public Library. Covers all productions, and includes alphabetical access to individual performers. Available as separate subject groups, musicals, etc. *Class No:* 779(73)

[3814]
SMITHSONIAN INSTITUTION. Guide to photographic collections at the Smithsonian Institution: Volume one: National Museum of American History.
O'Connor, D.V., *ed.* Washington, Smithsonian Institution Press, 1989. 351p. $29.95. ISBN: 0874749271.
The first of five projected volumes.
Details of 473 collections, totalling over 1 million photographs. Arranged by Museum divisions with details of access, usage etc. Detailed subject index. Section of selected photographs. *Class No:* 779(73)

78 Music

Music

Abbreviations & Symbols

[3815]

HOLST, I. ABC of music: a short practical guide to the basic essentials of rudiments, harmony, and form. Oxford, Oxford University Press, 1963. 200p., illus. £6.99. ISBN: 0193181031.

Re-issued 1996.

Classic introductory guide to written music, language and theory. Illustrated with musical examples.

Class No: 780(003)

[3816]

THOMSETT, M.C. Musical terms, symbols and theory: an illustrated dictionary. London; St. James Press, 1990. 277p. illus. £22. ISBN: 1558620540.

Comprises a glossary of terms; multi-language instrument guides; illustrated notation guide; scales, keys and chords.

Class No: 780(003)

Bibliographies

[3817]

BAVARIAN STATE LIBRARY. Catalogue of printed music. Munich, K.G.Saur, 1988. 7282p.(17v.) ISBN: 3598305605.

The collections of the Bayerische Staatsbibliothek comprise several private libraries and collections from monasteries assembled from 1558, and modern copyright deposits. All the material has been newly input for this catalogue, and is easy to consult. *Class No:* 780(01)

[3818]

BBC MUSIC LIBRARY. Catalogues. London, BBC, 1965-82. 13v. ISBN: 0563124784, 1982 set.

Series comprises: Chamber Music Catalogue (1965) Piano and Organ Catalogue (2v.; 1965) Song Catalogue (4v.; 1966) Choral and Opera Catalogue (2v.; 1967) Orchestral Catalogue (4v.; 1982). Reference guide to one of the world's largest collection of performing editions; over 300,000 entries in total. *Class No:* 780(01)

[3819]

BOSTON PUBLIC LIBRARY. Dictionary catalog of the music collection. Boston, G.K. Hall, 1972. 15617p. (20v.). Supplement 2681p. (4v.).

Supplement issued 1976.

450,000 cards representing 80,000 volumes; includes books, scores, parts, libretti, and periodicals.

Class No: 780(01)

[3820]

The British catalogue of music. London, Bowker-Saur, 1957-. £95pa. ISSN: 00681407.

Two interim issues and an annual cumulation each year; initially quarterly. Cumulation 1957-1985 published in 10 vols. (London, K.G. Saur, 1988). Available through BLAISE-LINE 1987-.

A record of new music published in the UK, foreign music available in the UK through a sole agent, music acquired from foreign publishers; based on receipts at the BL Copyright office. Classified section (now arranged by DDC 21; previously by a special BCM classification), title and composer index, subject index (arranged by musical forms).

Class No: 780(01)

[3821]

BRITISH LIBRARY. Books in the Hirsch Library, with supplementary list of music. London, BM, 1959. 542p.

11,500 entries under authors. Includes pamphlets, dealers' catalogues and opera libretti: most of the material was acquired in Germany 1897-1936. *Class No:* 780(01)

[3822]

BRITISH LIBRARY. Catalogue of manuscript music in the British Museum. Hughes-Hughes, A., *ed.* London. BM, 1906-09. 644,988,568p. (3v.).

Reprinted 1964-66. Supplement (1970) by P.J. Willetts covers acquisitions 1908-67.

Volumes cover sacred vocal music; secular vocal music; instrumental music, treatises, etc. Systematic arrangement with indexes. *Class No:* 780(01)

[3823]

BRITISH LIBRARY. Catalogue of printed music in the British Library. London, Munich, K.G. Saur, 1980-. 62v., and CD-ROMs. ISBN: 0862913004, set.

CD-ROM (1996 ed.) contains additional unpublished entries for 1981-1996, and corrections to the original material. (Bowker-Saur).

Over 1 million entries for 200,000 items; worldwide coverage, 1504-1980. Arranged by composer, or title if composer unknown; analytical entries for parts of larger works. Additionally, the CD-ROM contains the *Current music catalogue*, 135,000 entries for 1981-1996, and the *Supplement to the Catalogue of Printed Music*, a further 45,000 entries added after 1981. Access by composer, arranger, editor, title, keyword, series, publisher, instrument, voice, publication year etc. *Class No:* 780(01)

[3824]

BRITISH LIBRARY. Catalogue of printed music published between 1487 and 1800, now in the British Museum. Squire, W., *comp.* London, BM, 1912. 2v. (& 2 supplements).

Reprint available from Kraus Reprint. Supplement 1 included in vol.2. Supplement 2 issued 1940.

Arranged by composer and titles, including music published in periodicals. Supplemented in part by *Hand-list of music published in some British and foreign periodicals between 1787 and 1848, now in the British Museum.* (BM, 1965). *Class No:* 780(01)

[3825]

BRITISH LIBRARY. Catalogue of the King's Music Library. Squire, W., *ed.* London, BM, 1927-29. 3v.

Volume one contains the Handel manuscripts; volume two miscellaneous manuscripts; volume three (2 sections) covers printed music & music literature. *Class No:* 780(01)

[3826]

BRITISH LIBRARY. Music in the Hirsch Library. London, BM, 1951. 438p.

About 9,000 entries in 2 sections - pre 1800 and post 1800. *Books in the Hirsch Library* includes a supplement to this volume. *Class No:* 780(01)

[3827]

BROCKMAN, W.S. Music: a guide to the reference literature. Littleton, Col. Libraries Unlimited, 1988. 254p. $38.50. ISBN: 0872875261.

Contains some additional material not included in Duckles and Keller, 1988. *Class No:* 780(01)

[3828]

CRABTREE, P.D. Sourcebook for research in music. Indiana, Indiana University Press, 1993. 236p. $25.00 ISBN: 0253314763.

3000 titles are listed in a classified order; a few gaps are noted, but it is recommended as a serviceable guide for library collection assessment. (*Choice,* 31(8), April 1994, p1268.) *Class No:* 780(01)

[3829]

DUCKLES, V.H. *and* **KELLER, M.A. Music reference and research materials.** 5th ed. New York, Schirmer/London, Macmillan, 1997. 608p. $45.00. ISBN: 0028708210.

4th.ed. 1988; 4th.ed. revised 1994.

International coverage, including Asian sources; annotations mainly descriptive with some critical comment. Numbered entries arranged alphabetically within broad categories, in turn subdivided into narrower subject areas. Extensive, multi-access indexes. Previous eds. have been well-received but with some specific criticisms. *Class No:* 780(01)

[3830]

EITNER, R. Biographisch-bibliographisches Quellen-Lexikon der Musiker und Musikgelehrten der Christlichen Zeitrechnung bis sur mitte des neunzehnten Jahrhurderts. Graz, Akademische Druck und Verlagsanstalt, 1959. 11v.

Originally published Leipzig. 1900-1904.

A basic guide to musical sources from the Christian era to mid-nineteenth century; rendered obsolete in parts by World War II and being replaced progressively by RISM. (See entry below.) *Class No:* 780(01)

[3831]

International index to music periodicals. Cambridge, Chadwyck-Healey, 1996-. CD-ROM. £625.00. (single user). ISSN: 10876871.

CD-ROM updated quarterly; Internet access also available - details at: <http://www.chadwyck.co.uk>

Major new service, offering the contents of 400 music journals from 30 countries, with additional material from general news sources. Full texts of abstracts can be searched. All types of music are covered. Some 300,000 retrospective records are available from 1874. A thesaurus of 1000 terms is in use, which is claimed to produce consistent subject searching. *Class No:* 780(01)

[3832]

JACKSON, R. Performance practice, medieval to contemporary: a bibliographic guide. New York, Garland, 1988. 518p. $73.00. ISBN: 0824015126.

An extensive bibliography relating to points of style and technique. Good indexes. *Class No:* 780(01)

[3833]

KAHL, W. *and* **LUTHER, W.M.,** *eds.* **Repertorium der Musikwissenschaft:** Musikschrifttum, Denkmäler und Gesamtausgaben in Auswahl (1800-1950). Kassel & Basle, Bärenreiter, 1953. viii, 271p.

2,795 numbered entries, unannotated; locations in 62 German libraries, arranged by form of material in seventeen sections. Extensive indexes. *Class No:* 780(01)

[3834]

KRUMMEL, D.W., *ed.* **Bibliographical inventory to early music in Newberry Library, Chicago.** Boston, G.K. Hall, 1976. 587p.

Photolithographed catalogue entries for 10,000 items published before 1861. *Class No:* 780(01)

[3835]

LIBRARY OF CONGRESS. Music catalog. Washington,DC, Library of Congress, 1991-. $160 pa.

Issued semi-annually on CD-ROM. From 1953-1972 published as *Music and Phonorecords;* from 1973-1990 as *NUC music books, books on music and sound recordings.* Records form part of the RISM project; accessible via RLIN.

Bibliography of works including all music-related entries from the Library of Congress database, and pre-MARC records, and records for 12,000 librettos assembled by Albert Schatz and acquired by LC in 1908. Over 200,000 records are present. *Class No:* 780(01)

[3836]

MIXTER, K.E. General bibliography for music research. 3rd.ed. Warren, Michigan, Harmonie Park Press, 1996. 200p. ISBN: 0899901034.

1st.ed. 1964.

Sections (which consist of brief discussion followed by lists) cover basic research guides; bibliographies of bibliographies; national and trade bibliographies; dictionaries; encyclopedias; biographies and autobiographies; bibliographies; indexes and directories; vocal text sources; union lists and library catalogs. Index of names and titles. *Class No:* 780(01)

[3837]

Music index: a subject-author guide to current music periodical literature. Warren, Michigan, Harmonie Park Press, 1949-. ISSN: 00274348.

Monthly, cumulating annually. Publishers' previous name *Information Coordinators* (Detroit). Available on CD-ROM from 1991; first disc covered 1981-88; annual updates add a further year's data (UK agent: Cambridge, Chadwick Healey).

Alphabetical dictionary catalogue arrangement. Covers 350 periodicals, with an emphasis on US titles, and including several general publications. Recent CD-ROMs contain c400,000 citations. Content features jazz, popular and folk music as well as classical. Also includes obituaries, review of books & performances. Slow to appear, especially annual cumulations and CD-ROMs. *Class No:* 780(01)

[3838]

Music manuscripts after 1600: a thematic catalogue on CD-ROM. Munich, K.G. Saur, 1997. CD-ROM. DM 3980. ISBN: 3598403720.

Part of the RISM project; *see entry below for: Répertoire international des sources musicales,* series AII.
Class No: 780(01)

[3839]

Music research and information guides. New York, Garland, 1983-.

A valuable series of subject guide by specialist hands. Style and coverage varies; all are basically bibliographies, some annotated. Volumes include: 1. Opera (0824089995) 2. Latin American music (0824089340) 3. Dance (0824086767) 4. Popular music (0824086805) 5. Folk music in America (0824089359) 6. Art song (082408554x) 7. The blues (082408506x) 8. Chamber music (0824083466) 9. Performance practice (0824015126) 10. Piano information guide (0824077784) 11. Traditional music of Britain & Ireland (0824066235) 12. Polish music (0824046145) 13. Early American music 1620-1820 (0824041194).
Class No: 780(01)

[3840]

NEW YORK PUBLIC LIBRARY. Dictionary catalog of the music collection. 2nd ed. Boston, G.K. Hall, 1982-3. 44v.

First published 1964 (33v.), with supplements 1973 (10v.) and 1976.

750,000 cards covering all aspects of music and all formats; over 35,000 items not found in the first edition. *Bibliographic guide to music* (1976 onwards, issued annually) acts as a supplement. *Class No:* 780(01)

[3841]

PAZDIREK, F. Universal-Handbuch der Musikliteratur aller Zeiten und Völker. Hilversum, Knuf, 1967. 34v.

Originally published: Vienna, 1904-1910.

A major check-list, especially valuable for nineteenth century material. Half a million entries, arranged alphabetically by composers. International coverage.
Class No: 780(01)

[3842]

Répertoire international de la littérature musicale. RILM abstracts of music literature. Flushing, NY, RILM Center, City University of New York, 1967-.

Published quarterly; fourth quarterly issue is a cumulative author/subject index. Cumulative index to vols. 1-5 issued 1975. Available online (on OCLC's FirstSearch and EPIC), and on CD-ROM.

Main sections are reference & research materials; collected writings; historical musicology; ethnomusicology; instruments & voice; performance practice & notation; theory & analysis; pedagogy; other disciplines. International coverage - over 200 languages are present. Includes dissertations, and reviews. Abstracts are signed. Thorough indexing by name and subject. Database size is over 250,000 records. *Class No:* 780(01)

[3843]

Répertoire international de la presse musicale. Ann Arbor,MI, UMI, 1989-. 26 vols. to date. ISSN: 08966079.

RIPM is published under the auspices of the International Musicological Society and the International Association of Music Libraries, Archives and Documentation Centers.

Summaries and indexes to historically important periodical literature of the 18th, 19th and 20th centuries; English titles so far published include *Quarterly musical magazine and review* 1818-1823, *Harmonicon* 1823-1830, and *Musical times* 1842-. Other volumes cover major French, Dutch, German and Italian titles. *Class No:* 780(01)

[3844]

Répertoire international des sources musicales (RISM). Kassel, Basle, Bärenreiter (Series A & C); Munich, Henle Verlag (Series B), 1960-.

Published under the auspices of the International Musicological Society and the International Association of Music Libraries, Archives & Documentation Centres.

Series A covers composers; Series B subject or form; Series C is a directory of libraries.

A: Einzeldrucke von 1800. 1971. (9v.). Supplementary volume A-F, 1986. Series AII (Thematic catalogue of music manuscripts after 1600) has been issued on CD-ROM.

B.1: *Recueils imprimés, XVIe-XVIIe siècles.* Pt.1 *Liste chronologique,* 1960. B.2: *Recueils imprimés, XVIII siècle.* Pt.1. 1964. (Supplement in *Notes,* v.29, no.3, 1974). B.3: *The theory of music, from the Carolingian era up to 1400: a descriptive catalogue of manuscripts.* 1961-. (3v.). B.4: *Manuscripts of polyphonic music.* Pts.1-4. 1972. (Part 5 in preparation). B.5: *Tropen- und Sequenzenhandschriften.* Pts.1-4. 1964. B.6: *Ecrits imprimés concernant la musique.* Pts.1-2, 1971. B.7: *Handschriftlich überlieferte Leuten- und Gitarren tabulaturen...* 1978. B.8: *Das deutsche Kirchenlied.* pts.1-2. 1979-80. B.9: *Hebrew writings concerning music,* pts.1-2. 1975-80. B.10: *The theory of music in Arabic writings, c.900-1900.* 1979. B.11: *Ancient Greek music theory.* 1988. B.1, pt.1 is a chronological list of c.2,700 printed collections of 16-17th century music, a 'collection' being defined as any production containing the works of more than one composer. V.1, pt.2 is to list *incipits* of these collections. The series aims at recording all available bibliographies of musical works, writings about music and textbooks on music published up to 1800, with locations. Over 1,000 libraries in 30 countries are participating. When completed, RISM will displace Eitner's *Biographisch - bibliographisches Quellen-Lexikon* as a major location list.

For Series C, see entry at 780:061:026/027(058) headed *Directory of Music Research Libraries.* *Class No:* 780(01)

[3845]

SCHNAPPER, E.B., *ed.* **British union catalogue of early music,** printed before the year 1801. London, Butterworth, 1957. 2v.

Gives details of the holdings of over one hundred UK collections, in composer order with extensive index. Not confined to British music or British editions.
Class No: 780(01)

[3846]

STAATSBIBLIOTHEK ZU BERLIN. Musikhandschriften der Staatsbibliothek zu Berlin Preussischer Kulturbesitz: Die Bach-Sammlung. Munich, K.G. Saur, 1997. 1500 microfiche. DM 9980. ISBN: 3598344201.

Catalogue of an important collection of music manuscripts; over 80% of the surviving manuscripts by J.S.Bach and his sons are held in the collection. *Class No:* 780(01)

[3847]

TYRRELL, J. *and* **WISE, R. A Guide to international congress reports in musicology, 1900-1975.** London, Macmillan, 1979. xii, 353p. £45.00.

Chronological arrangement with detailed analytical subject index. *Class No:* 780(01)

[3848]
WOOD, D.A. Music in Harvard libraries: a catalogue of early printed music and books on music in the Houghton Library and the Eda Kuhn Loeb Music Library. Cambridge, Mass., Harvard University, 1980. xiv, 306p.

1,628 numbered entries arranged alphabetically under composers. *Class No:* 780(01)

Encyclopaedias & Dictionaries

[3849]
Algemene muziek encyclopedie. Robijns, J. *and* Zijlstra, M., *eds.* Haarlem, De Haan, 1979-84. 10v., illus.

Previous edition 1957-1972.

Generally short entries on all periods and forms of music, musicians, terms, instruments. Some longer articles on countries, styles, types of music have bibliographies. Vol.10 contains a glossary of terms and instrument names in several languages. Well illustrated. *Class No:* 780(03)

[3850]
BLOM, E. The New Everyman dictionary of music. Cummings, D., *comp.* 6th ed. London, Dent, 1988. 880p. £25.00. ISBN: 046003037x.

This new revision retains the high standard of its predecessors; over 1,500 new entries compared with the previous edition. *Class No:* 780(03)

[3851]
Brockhaus-Riemann-Musiklexikon. Dahlhaus, C. *and* Eggebrecht, H.H., *eds.* Wiesbaden, Brockhaus/Mainz, Schott, 1978-79. 2v., illus.

Covers types and styles of music, terms, instruments. Brief entries with bibliographies; German emphasis.
Class No: 780(03)

[3852]
Enciclopedia della musica. Milano, Rizzoli, 1972-74. 6v., illus.

Short entries covering all countries and periods of music. Biographies are included, and appendices to each volume give lists of composers' works. *Class No:* 780(03)

[3853]
HONEGGER, M. Dictionnaire de la musique - science de la musique. Paris, Bordas, 1976. 2,300p. (4v).

Two volumes cover *formes, techniques, instruments*, and two *les hommes et leurs oeuvres*.

About 160 contributors to *Formes* ... 'Sonate': nearly 10 columns (including 1 col. of bibliography). Cross-references. Prefatory general bibliography.

Les hommes ... consists of signed biographical sketches 'Debussy': over 6 columns (including 2 columns of bibliography); 3 ports. 'Britten': 1½ columns (½ column of bibliography); 1 port. Cross-references.

'An excellent reference tool' (Beaudiquez, M. & Bethery, A. *Ouvrages de réference pour les bibliothèques publiques*. Nouv. éd., 1978, entry 640). *Class No:* 780(03)

[3854]
KENNEDY, M. The Oxford dictionary of music. 2nd ed. Oxford, Oxford University Press, 1994. xv,985p. £25.00. ISBN: 0198691629.

Corrected revision issued 1997. First ed. 1985.

Thorough, low-priced and well produced, this edition adds 1000 new entries, and substantial amendments and corrections to the other 11,000 entries, including worklists and dates of composition. Compact layout is easy to read, but information is brief and abbreviated. Good coverage of jazz, light music, as well as classical. Includes composers, conductors, performers, musical terms and forms, named pieces, instruments, concert halls and opera houses, orchestras, publishers; small number of musical examples, no illustrations. *Class No:* 780(03)

[3855]
—KENNEDY, M. The Concise Oxford dictionary of music. 4th.ed. Oxford, Oxford University Press, 1996. 815p. £7.99. ISBN: 019280037x.

14,000 entries cover terms, composers, musicians, singers, orchestras, ballet, opera, instrumentalists. Fairly legible although 2-column layout is cramped.
Class No: 780(03)

[3856]
MOREHEAD, P.D. *and* **MacNEIL, A. New American dictionary of music.** New York, Dutton, 1991. 624p. ISBN: 052593345x.

10,000 brief definitions - classical, shows, popular music - covering performers, composers, groups etc. Glossary of terms in four languages. Considered to be less scholarly than others, but good for current performers and the US music scene. (*Reference books bulletin*, 15/11/94, p646.)
Class No: 780(03)

[3857]
Die Musik in Geschichte und Gegenwart. Allgemeine Enzklopädie der Musik. Blume, F., *ed.* Kassel & Basle, Bärenreiter, 1949-1986. 17v.

Supplements issued to update the main volumes. Reformatted India paper edition 1989. A revised ed. is in course of publication - scheduled date for completion is 2004.

The new revision will comprise 8 vols. Subject encyclopedia (scheduled 1994-1998), and 12 vols. Biographical encyclopedia (scheduled 1998-2004). Latest part traceable at present is Fascicle 3: Eng-Hamb. (?1995).

(This annotation refers to the existing 17v. set.) A work of international scholarship, directed more to the student than to the average inquirer. 'J.S. Bach' occupies columns 962-1047 of v.1, listing his works in congested, small type; bibliography, columns 1035-47; 24 illus., facsims, and autographs. (The same entry in *The New Grove*, v.1, p.785-840, has 21 sections of text, an admirably laid out table of works, p.818-36, and bibliography, p.837-40; 1 facsim, and 1 port.) The article 'Musikwissenschaft', v.9., cols. 1191-1219, has 4 main sections and a lengthy bibliography, cols. 1215-9. 'Zeitschriften' (cols. 1042-1187), mainly devoted to national lists of music periodicals (cols. 1050-1174), one of the largest listings of its kind, is now overshadowed by *The New Grove* contribution 'Periodicals', v.14, p.407-535. On the other hand MGGs article 'Intermezzo' in supplementary v.16, cols. 810-43 - omitted from v.6 - is a treatise, with 2 cols. of bibliography, compared to *The New Grove's* entry (v.9, p.269-72). A. Hughes (*Medieval music* (1974), p.9) finds MGG particularly valuable for its references to European dissertations. Illustrations are preferable to those in *The New Grove*; the latter scoring in its superior lay-out. Final volume is an index to the whole work (1986).
Class No: 780(03)

[3858]

New Grove dictionary of music and musicians. Sadie, S., *ed.* 6th ed. London, Macmillan, 1980. 20v. ISBN: 0333231112; 1561591742, pbk.

First published 1871-1889; several budget versions and paperback sets of the 6th.ed. have appeared. Corrected reprint issued 1995.

6th ed. is virtually a new work; '97% of the material has not been derived from former editions' (*Acta musicologica*, v.54, 1982, p.4) Of the 2,426 contributors, 34% are American, 20% British and 13% German. Its 22 million words compare strikingly with the 5th ed.'s 8 million. Of the 22,500 articles, 16,500 are biographical - chiefly on composers (*e.g.* 'Beethoven': 40p. of text; 24p. of lists of works and bibliography). 4,500 illus.; over 3,000 music examples; 9,000 cross-references (*e.g.* 'France', v.6, p.741-64: 28 cross-references), - compensating to some extent, for the lack of a general index. Leading features are: lengthy, signed and authoritative articles, prefaced by helpful outlines; and extensive work-lists and bibliographies (*e.g* J.S. Bach, v.1, p.785-840; works-list, p.818-36; bibliography, p.837-43. Dvorak, v.5, p.765-92; 14 sections; 8p. of works-list; 2½ columns of bibliography; 1 illus., 2 facsims., 3 ports., 8 musical examples). Also of importance for the librarian and musicologist/bibliographer: 'Bibliography of music', v.2, p.682-92; 'Periodicals', v.14, p.467-535 (*c.* 6,000 titles); 'Dictionaries and encyclopaedias', v.8, p.430-59; 'Libraries', v.10, p.719-821. *Class No:* 780(03)

[3859]

New Harvard dictionary of music. Randel, D.M., *comp.* Cambridge, Mass., & London: Belknap Press of Harvard University, 1986. xxi, 1024p. $37.50. ISBN: 0674615255.

Total revision of the 1969 edition by Apel.

Authoritative and respected, this edition is the work of nine advisers and seventy contributors. There are 6,000 entries, and musical examples, drawings and illustrations are featured. Coverage includes all countries and periods, from earliest times to jazz, rock etc., and styles, forms and instruments. There are no biographies. Major articles have brief bibliographies; bibliographical articles include *Dictionaries and Encyclopedias* p.226-230, and *Periodicals* p.625-628. *Class No:* 780(03)

[3860]

The New Oxford companion to music. Arnold, D., *ed.* Oxford, OUP, 1983. 2017p. (2v). £85.00. ISBN: 0193113163.

First published 1938; 10th ed. 1970 as *The Oxford companion to music*, by P.A. Scholes, which remains in print (1997).

The 1983 ed. has now acquired some weight, but one is still as likely to find the 1970 ed. in libraries and bookshops. 1983 ed. is the work of 90 contributors; 6,000 entries (of which over 2,000 define musical terms), 'Brahms'; 2½p. incl. port., music example, 4 references); 'Jazz'; 5½p., incl. 5 illus.; 'Broadcasting of music': 8p. incl. 4 illus., facsim; 'Electronic music intruments'; 4p., 3 illus.; 'Copyright': 7p. Longer articles are sectionalised, with list of headings (*e.g.* 'Ballet and theatrical dance': 17p.; 11 illus., but no bibliography; 'Records and reproduction': 12p., 7 illus., 4 references; 'Japanese music': 17½p., 8 illus., 6 music examples). Some inconsistency in provision of plot-synopses for operas. Over 1,500 illus., and music examples in all.

'In no way a successor to that curious, infuriating, but lovable compilation, the original *Oxford companion to music*.' Rather, 'a thorough, impersonal, dispassionate and

....*(contd.)*

accurate dictionary ... The most readily available source of information (*Brio*, v.20, no.3, Autumn/Winter 1983, p.61). *Class No:* 780(03)

[3861]

Penguin dictionary of music. 6th.ed. London, Penguin Books, 1997. 494p. £6.99. ISBN: 014051290x.

1996 ed. reprinted with minor revisions.

Includes opera, ballet, orchestral, solo, choral, chamber music; details of performers, composers, instrumentalists; terms; genres. Compact, reliable, and inexpensive. *Class No:* 780(03)

[3862]

REIMANN, H. Musik Lexikon. Gurlitt, W., *ed.* 12th ed. Mainz, Schott, 1959-1967 and 1972-1975. 5v.

First published 1882.

The 12th ed. consists of: v.1-2 *Personenteil* (A-K, L-Z) (1959-61), edited by W. Gurlitt, and v.3, *Sachteil*, begun by W. Gurlitt and completed by H.H. Eggebrecht (xv, 1087p.). The 2-v. biographical dictionary has closely-packed double columns and well-documented articles (*e.g.* 'Brahms': 8 columns, of which 1½ cols. list works by and material on Brahms). V.3, on subject aspects, has music examples but no illus. 'Bibliotheken' has notes on music libraries under countries; 'High fidelity';' 2/3p., with 8 lines of bibliography; 'Violinmusik', p.1041-5, has references up to 1965. The 2-v. biographical supplement (1972-75) includes living musicians and adds material on biographies in the parent work.

The fullest of the medium-sized music encyclopaedias 'remarkable for its scholarship, coverage and reliability' (*Notes*, v.36, no.4, June 1980, p.301). *Class No:* 780(03)

[3863]

SADIE, S. *and* **LATHAM, A.,** *eds.* **Grove concise dictionary of music.** London, Macmillan, 1994. 909p. £25.00. ISBN: 0333432363.

A revised and updated version of the 1988 edition; based on the *New Grove Dictionary of music and musicians*, 1980.

High standards of production and clear layout; mainly devoted to Western, classical music. Some 10,000 entries, but no bibliographic support, although work lists are included for major composers. *Class No:* 780(03)

[3864]

SLONIMSKY, N. Lectionary of music: an entertaining reference and reader's companion. London, Simon & Schuster, 1989. 532p. £17.95. ISBN: 0671653105.

Idiosyncratic but valuable guide, full of readable background information. *Class No:* 780(03)

[3865]

Sohlmans Musiklexikon. 2nd ed. Stockholm, Sohlmans Forlag, 1975-79. 5v., illus.

Previous edition 1948-52.

Signed articles covering all periods and countries, but strongest on Scandinavian material. Frequent bibliographies; index by broad topic in vol.5. *Class No:* 780(03)

[3866]

THOMSETT, M.C. Musical terms, symbols and theory: an illustrated dictionary. London; St. James Press, 1990. 277p. illus. £22. ISBN: 1558620540.

Comprises a glossary of terms; multi-language instrument guides; illustrated notation guide; scales, keys and chords. *Class No:* 780(03)

[3867]
WESTRUP, J., *and others*. Collins dictionary of music. Rev. ed. London, Collins, 1988. 576p. £5.75. ISBN: 0004343565.
A concise version of the *Collins Encyclopaedia of Music*.
Good coverage of modern musical figures, and revisions of articles on composers, instruments, terms, performers, critics, orchestras, etc. *Class No:* 780(03)

Dictionaries

[3868]
BAKER, T.A. A Dictionary of musical terms. 21st ed. New York, Scribner, 1980. 257p. $19.95.
First published 1895.
Over 9,000 terms, featuring all major western languages. *Class No:* 780(038)

[3869]
HEADINGTON, C. Illustrated dictionary of musical terms. London, Bodley Head, 1980. 160p. £11.95.
Defines over 800 terms with a good range of illustrations. *Class No:* 780(038)

[3870]
HILES, J. Dictionary of musical terms, phrases and abbreviations originating from Italian, French, German, English and other languages. Portsmouth, Bardon Enterprises, 1997. viii,349p. ISBN: 0952818418.
Revised ed. by W.B. Henshaw; previous ed. published by Brewer (1882).
12,500 entries; largely a historical curiosity but its thoroughness can offer items untraceable elsewhere. *Class No:* 780(038)

[3871]
KAUFMANN, W. Selected musical terms of non-western cultures: a notebook-glossary. Detroit, Harmonie Park, 1990. 806p. $75.00. ISBN: 0899900399.
12,000 terms are defined, generally in two or three sentences. Strong on India, less good on the rest of Asia and on Africa. Cross-references from variant spellings and romanizations. Bibliography of 320 items. *Class No:* 780(038)

[3872]
LEUCHTMANN, H. Wörterbuch Musik Dictionary of terms in music. 3rd ed. Munich, Saur, 1981. 560p. £27.50.
Some 20,000 terms in English and German. *Class No:* 780(038)

[3873]
STRAHLE, G. An Early music dictionary: musical terms from British sources 1500-1740. Cambridge, Cambridge University Press, 1995. 469p. £60.00. ISBN: 0521416884.
Covers Renaissance and Baroque periods, giving terms related to instruments, performance, theory, composition. Definitions are in chronological order under A/Z headwords. Based on lexicons, dictionaries, treatises, personal papers, manuscript sources of the period. Bibliography p.461-9. *Class No:* 780(038)

[3874]
Terminorum musicae index septem linguis redactus. [Polyglot dictionary of musical terms: German, English, French, Italian, Spanish, Hungarian, Russian.] Budapest, Akademai Kiadó, 1978. 798p. £48.00.
Includes a total of over 10,000 entries. Base language is German; Russian is in separate supplement. *Class No:* 780(038)

Theses

[3875]
ADKINS, C. *and* DICKINSON, A. Doctoral dissertations in musicology. 7th US ed.; 2nd international ed. Philadelphia, American Musicological Society/Basel, International Musicological Society, 1984. 545p.
Originally published 1952-1971 in five US editions; previous edition of this version published 1977 as *International index of dissertations and musicological works in progress.*
Over 6,500 titles included, of which two-thirds are North American. Listed by period, with sub-headings by subject. Author and subject indexes. *Class No:* 780(043)

Great Britain

[3876]
British music theses. Caldwell, J., *ed.* New York, Garland, 1980-. 52v. $4,000. (also available separately).
Reprints of theses from British Universities, presented during the 1980s. Individual volumes are priced at about $60., but many theses occupy two volumes. *Class No:* 780(043)(410)

French

[3877]
GRIBENSKI, J., *comp*. French language dissertations in music: an annotated bibliography. New York, Pendragon Press, 1979. 270p. $48.00.
Entries for 438 French, Swiss, Belgian and Canadian dissertations. 1883-1976. Subject index in French. *Class No:* 780(043)=40

Periodicals & Progress Reports

[3878]
Acta Musicologica. Basel, Bärenreiter, 1928-. £55pa. ISSN: 00016241.
Three issues pa.
Multi-lingual journal of the International Musicological Society; particularly valuable for reviews of new research. *Class No:* 780(05)

[3879]
Fontes artis musicae. Madison,WI, AR Editions, 1953- £35pa. ISSN: 00156191.
Issued quarterly.
The review journal of the International Association of Music Libraries, Archives, and Documentation Centres (IAML). Useful feature material, and authoritative book reviews, usually 2 or 3 per issue. *Class No:* 780(05)

[3880]
Music and letters. Fortune, N. *and* Whenham, J., *eds*. Oxford, University Press, 1920-. £62pa. ISSN: 00274224.
Quarterly.
Excellent source of book reviews; about half of each issue is devoted to reviews of new music and books (typically 25 substantial reviews per issue). *Class No:* 780(05)

[3881]
Music Library Association notes. Ochs, M., *ed.* Canton, MA, Music Library Association, 1942-. $80.00. ISSN: 00274380.
Quarterly. Previously *Notes.*
The Journal of the Music Library Association; excellent range and quality of book reviews in each issue, varying in

.... (contd.)
length from 350-1,500 words and sometimes totalling nearly 100 reviews. Also reviews of new music, and an excellent index of CD and record reviews. *Class No:* 780(05)

[3882]
Musical quarterly. Salzman, E., *ed.* New York, Oxford University Press, 1915-. $76.00. ISSN: 00274631.

Well respected, scholarly journal. Book reviews are a regular feature, and although few in number they are lengthy and authoritative. *Class No:* 780(05)

Periodicals

Bibliographies

[3883]
British union catalogue of music periodicals. Hodges, A., *comp and* McGill, R., *ed.* London: Library Association in association with IAML (UK), 1985. xxiv, 145p. ISBN: 0853655170.

Coverage includes UK and Eire up to mid 1984; an alphabetical list of periodicals with details of holdings in each location. Listing of libraries is coded in the same manner as RISM. *Class No:* 780(051)(01)

[3884]
FIDLER, L.M. *and* **JAMES, R.S.,** *eds.* **International music journals.** Westport, CT, Greenwood Press, 1990. 522p. $75. ISBN: 0313250049.

200 titles are discussed extensively; English-language titles represent both scholarly journals and those popular with performers & teachers. *Class No:* 780(051)(01)

[3885]
MEGGETT, J.M. Music periodical literature: an annotated bibliography of indexes and bibliographies. Metuchen, NJ, Scarecrow, 1978. 116p.

Remains valuable for historical coverage. Good indexes. *Class No:* 780(051)(01)

[3886]
ROBINSON, D. Music and dance periodicals: an international directory and guidebook. Voorheesville, NY, Peri Press, 1989. 395p. $65.00. ISBN: 096178444x.

Contains data on almost 2,000 annuals and journals, particularly in popular, folk and art music, and dance. All levels of material are included, but lists are not exhaustive. Subject arrangement, well indexed. 'A wealth of information, concisely and clearly presented' (*Choice*, Sept. 1989). *Class No:* 780(051)(01)

Yearbooks & Directories

[3887]
Billboard's international buyers' guide, of the music, record, tape industry. New York, BPI Communications Inc., 1958-. $83. ISSN: 00678600.

Lists music and video companies, retail suppliers, services (including organizations, libraries, schools). Directory of manufacturers and materials. *Class No:* 780(058)

[3888]
COTTERELL, L.E. Performance: business and law of entertainment. 3rd ed. London, Sweet and Maxwell, 1993. 719p. £14.95. ISBN: 0421471905.

Organization, business, and law relating to the performing arts; management, production, administration, contracts, agreements etc. Sections cover artists & directors, musicians, performer & mechanical media, performer & the

.... (contd.)
law, copyright, performance, licensing of places of entertainment, premises & people, agents. Index to collective agreements, and general index. *Class No:* 780(058)

[3889]
MBI world directory 1998. Scott, A., *ed.* London, Miller Freeman/Music Business International, 1997. 572p. £75.00. ISBN: 0862131804.

Annual.

Covers recording and video companies, music publishers, distributors, retail sector, artist managers, agents, promoters, venues, etc. Europe A/Z by country; North America; Latin America; Asia-Pacific; Africa and Middle East. Index of people; index of companies. *Class No:* 780(058)

[3890]
Showcase international music book. London, Showcase Publications. c500p. £35.00. ISSN: 00755451.

Annual; formerly *Kemp's international music book.*

Directory of concert & tour managers, broadcast & video services, recording facilities, sound equipment, trade etc. Mainly UK, with some international coverage in separate section. *Class No:* 780(058)

Quotations

[3891]
ABSE, D., *comp.* **The Music lover's literary companion.** London, Robson, 1990. 288p. illus. £8.99. ISBN: 0860516547.

Compilation of imaginative writing by authors and musicians. Covers all periods. *Class No:* 780(082.2)

[3892]
CROFTON, I., *comp and* **FRASER, D.,** *comp..* **A Dictionary of musical quotations.** London: Croom Helm, 1985. xii, 191p. £9.95. ISBN: 0709910355.

Contains 3,000 quotations, arranged into themes, such as definitions, opera, nationalism, atonality, and individual composers. Social, historical, technical, psychological angles, drawn from criticism, insights, invective, manifestos etc. Classical music is the largest area. A single alphabetical sequence, supported by cross-references, author index, and subject index of keywords. *Class No:* 780(082.2)

[3893]
WATSON, D., *ed.* **Chambers book of musical quotations.** London, Chambers, 1990. 256p. £12.95. ISBN: 0550210121.

Ranges widely from jazz, pop and folk to opera and orchestral music. An extertaining collection.
Class No: 780(082.2)

Festschriften

[3894]
GERBOTH, W. An Index to musical Festschriften and similar publications. New York, Norton, 1969. 188p.

Some 3,000 contributions from 500 volumes are listed, arranged by area and period. Detailed subject index.
Class No: 780(082.20)

Histories

[3895]

ABRAHAM, G. The Concise Oxford history of music. London, Oxford University Press, 1985. 990p., illus. £15.99. ISBN: 019284010x.

Originally published 1979; re-issued 1985.

Unrelated to the *New Oxford History of Music.* Five main sections - rise of West Asian & East Mediterranean music, ascendancy of Western Europe, ascendancy of Italy, ascendancy of Germany, fragmentation of tradition. Subdivided into 41 chapters, the structure being clearly set out in the contents pages. Further reading & recommended editions, arranged by main sections, p.864-912. Thorough index. *Class No:* 780(091)

[3896]

BESSLER, H. *and* **SCHNEIDER, M.,** *eds.* **Musikgeschichte in Bildern.** Leipzig, VEB Deutscher Verlag für Musick, 1961-.

Multi-volume work making slow progress.

A very detailed iconography, planned to cover all countries and all periods. Bibliographies, name and subject indexes. Current volumes are: Series 1 (Musikethnologie) Parts 1-4, 8-11; Series 2 (Musik des Altertums) Parts 1, 2, 4, 5, 7-9; Series 3 (Musik des Mittelalters und der Renaissance) Parts 2-5, 8, 9; Series 4 (Musik der Neuzeit) Parts 1-4, and Part 5 in preparation. *Class No:* 780(091)

[3897]

COOVER, J. Music at auction: Puttick and Simpson (of London) 1794-1971. Detroit, Harmonie Park, 1989. 528p. $55.00. (*Detroit Studies in Music Bibliography; no.60.*) ISBN: 0899900380.

Well produced listing of sales at a major auction house. Includes composer autographs, instruments, copyrights, books, portraits, letters etc. *Class No:* 780(091)

[3898]

GROUT, D. *and* **PALISCA, C. A History of Western music.** 5th ed. London, Norton, 1996. 862p. £25.00. ISBN: 0393969045.

A major, authoritative source; substantially revised; analyses of style, commentaries on developments, and chronologies within chapters are key features.
Class No: 780(091)

[3899]

JVC video anthology of world music and dance. Montpelier, VT. Rounder Records for Smithsonian/Folkways Records, [1989]. 30 videocassettes.

Authoritative series containing over 500 sequences shot in 100 countries; covers folk and classical music worldwide. Supervised by Japan's National Museum of Ethnology.
Class No: 780(091)

[3900]

The New Oxford history of music. London, Oxford University Press, 1997. 10v. £600.00. ISBN: 019816226x, (set.).

Re-issue of the 1954-1990 edition; originally as the *Oxford history of music* (1901-5; 6v.)

Volume titles and original publication dates are as follows:

1. *Ancient and Oriental music*; edited by E. Wellesz. 1957.

2. *Middle ages to 1300*; edited by R.L. Crocker and D. Hiley. 2nd ed. 1990.

3. *Ars Nova and the Renaissance, 1300-1540*; edited by A. Hughes and G. Abraham. 1960.

4. *The age of humanism, 1540-1630*; edited by G. Abraham. 1967.

....(*contd.*)

5. *Opera and church music, 1630-1750*; edited by A. Lewis and N. Fortune, 1975.

6. *Concert music, 1630-1750.* 1986.

7. *The age of enlightenment, 1745-1790*; edited by E. Wellesz and F.W. Steinfield. 1973.

8. *The age of Beethoven, 1790-1830*, by G. Abraham. 1982.

9. *Romanticism, 1830-1890*; edited by G. Abraham. 1990.

10. *The modern age, 1890-1960*; edited by M. Cooper. 1974.

11. *Chronological tables, bibliographies and index.*

The editor of each volume is assisted by specialists. V.2 has chapter bibliographies, footnotes, music examples and detailed indexes. While conceding that the then 4 new volumes stand favourably against all competition, *Library Journal* (v.93, no.8, 15 January 1968, p.1609-10) find that they are *isolated* music history and do not fulfil the stated objective - 'to present music ... as an art developing in constant association with every form of human culture and activity'. On v.10, *Music & letters* (v.56, no.2, April 1975, p.202) notes a 'prevailing tendency to survey rather than to excavate'. *Class No:* 780(091)

[3901]

RAEBURN, M. *and* **KENDALL, A.,** *eds.* **Heritage of music.** Oxford, OUP, 1989. 320, 320, 320, 334p. (4v). £95.00. ISBN: 019520493x.

Volumes are titled *Classical music and its origins, Romantic era, Nineteenth century legacy, Music in the twentieth century.* An essay format is used with independent chapters by 55 contributors, surveying developments and discussing themes. Biographies are restricted to major figures with others covered in short appendices to each volume. Scholarly standards are high; illustrations are lavish and well integrated. *Class No:* 780(091)

[3902]

STOLBA, K.M. The Development of western music: a history. Dubuque, IA, W.C.Brown, 1990. 966p., illus. ISBN: 0697001822.

26 chapters arranged chronologically: antiquity; early Christian; chant; liturgy; early Middle Ages etc. Comprehensive and attractively written. Bibliography p.895-925 (2-column) in chapter order. Index p.927-966 (3-column, very condensed.) *Class No:* 780(091)

Bibliographies

[3903]

KROHN, E.C., *comp.* **The History of music:** an index to the literature available in a selected group of musicological publications. St. Louis, Boston Music Co., 1958. 463p.

Reprint of 1952 publication.

6,000 unannotated entries, but valuable as an historical record of older material. *Class No:* 780(091)(01)

Biographies

[3904]

BAKER, T. Baker's biographical dictionary of musicians. Slonimsky, N., *ed.* 8th ed. New York, Schirmer, 1992. xlii, 2115p. £95.00. ISBN: 0028724151.

First published 1900. *Baker's biographical dictionary of 20th. musicians* is derived from this vol. (*See entry at:* 780(092)"19")

15,000 entries for composers, performers, critics, publishers, patrons, instrument makers, musicologists. Covers living as well as dead names; e.g. Mahler 4½

.... *(contd.)*
columns (career, works, bibliography covering one col.); John Lennon 1½ cols; Simon Rattle 1/3 col. A highly respected single-volume source. 'Slonimsky's idiosyncratic and witty writing and his candid opinions add spice to the careful, accurate (and sometimes quirky) facts he provides...this is a reference book one can read for pleasure.' (*Reference books bulletin,* 1/2/92, p1052.)
Class No: 780(092)

[3905]
—SLONIMSKY, N. The Concise Baker's biographical dictionary of musicians. New York, Schirmer, 1994. 1155p. £39.95. ISBN: 002872416x.

Based on *Baker's biographical dictionary of musicians,* 1992.

Half the size of the source volume, eliminating some less important categories of material. 4000 entries are short, but sound and well written. 'For sheer comprehensiveness, as well as value for money, the *Concise Baker* has long been hard to beat.' (*Reference reviews,* 8(5),1994. p34.)

Two further, smaller, derivatives have appeared: *Portable Baker's dictionary of music* (Schirmer/Macmillan, 1995; 350p; ISBN: 0028712250) and *Portable Baker's dictionary of musicians* (Schirmer/Macmillan, 1995; 293p; ISBN: 08255693942). *Class No:* 780(092)

[3906]
FETIS, F.J. Biographie universelle des musiciens et bibliographie générale de la musique. 2nd ed. Paris, Didot, 1867-70. 8v. in 4.

Reprinted Brussels, Culture and Civilization, 1964 (10v.) including a supplement which carries the entries up to the 1870s.

A historical curiosity, but very valuable and readable, featuring anecdotes, letters, etc. *Class No:* 780(092)

[3907]
GREENE, D.M. Greene's biographical encyclopaedia of composers. London: Collins, 1985. xl, 1348p. £30.00. ISBN: 0004343638.

Chronological listing of 2,400 composers, from earliest times to present day. Index at beginning of sequence; abundant cross references. Wide coverage, especially useful for less well-known. Entries combine biography, history and anecdote. *Class No:* 780(092)

[3908]
The Harvard biographical dictionary of music. Randel, D.M., *ed.* Cambridge, Mass., & London, Belknap Press of Harvard University, 1996. 1013p., illus. $39.95. ISBN: 0674372999.

5,500 entries, mainly Western concert/art music; each entry gives basic data and categorisation (pianist, composer, etc.), education and principal works. Longer entries may give a work list and bibliography. 18 contributors are named, but individual entries are not signed. Great variation in entry size; no cross-references. General bibliography of about 100 items. 'The articles in *Baker* are generally longer and the listing of works more extensive, but sources are not cited as they are in the *Harvard dictionary.*' (*Reference books bulletin,* 93(8), 1996; p749.) *Class No:* 780(092)

[3909]
JACOBS, A. The Penguin dictionary of musical performers: a biographical guide to significant interpreters of classical music - singers, solo instrumentalists, conductors, orchestras and string quartets - ranging from the seventeenth century to the present day. London, Viking Penguin, 1990. 240p. ISBN: 0670807559.

Designed as a companion to Jacobs *New Penguin dictionary of music,* 1977.

25,000 entries, each giving name, dates, nationality, brief biography and major works premiered. Founding dates for orchestras & quartets, also personnel and history. Index of composers. Some inconsistencies have been noted (*Choice,* February 1991. p.916). *Class No:* 780(092)

[3910]
MORTON, B. *and* **COLLINS, P. Contemporary composers.** London, St.James' Press, 1992. c1019p. £95.50. ISBN: 1558620850.

International coverage of 500 composers, mostly still living. Brief biography includes address and publisher; list of works with instrumentation, date, place and date of first performance; short evaluative essay; selective bibliographies and discographies. Appendix of publishers, music information centres, composers' organizations.
Class No: 780(092)

[3911]
SADIE, J.A., *ed.* **Companion to Baroque music.** London, Dent, 1990. 549p., illus. ISBN: 0460046020.

Principally of value for its biographies; covers 1600-1750 in a series of essays and aims to include 'every significant musician of the era' with an outline of works. Arranged geographically (countries of Europe and New World colonies); each section begins with a biographical dictionary. Cross-references and detailed chronology.
Class No: 780(092)

Bibliographies

[3912]
ADAMS, J.L., *comp.* **Musicians' autobiographies:** an annotated bibliography of writings available in English 1800-1980. London, McFarland, 1982. x,126p. ISBN: 0899500498.

Alphabetical, with brief notes; chronological & title indexes. *Class No:* 780(092)(01)

[3913]
BULL, S. Index to biographies of contemporary composers. Metuchen NJ, Scarecrow, 1964-1987. 854p. 3v. $62.50. ISBN: 0810819309.

First volume (1964) covers 1900-1950; second (1974) 1950-1960; this third volume (1987) includes 13,500 entries 1961 to 1986. International coverage; register of sources.
Class No: 780(092)(01)

[3914]
Composer resource manuals. New York, Garland, 1980-.

Volumes vary in size from 145 pages (De Falla) to over 900 (Beethoven).

An excellent series of volumes, each by a specialist compiler, and including a catalogue of works, biographical information, bibliography, collections and archives, letters, organizations, secondary sources, guide to research. Useful illustrations and good indexes.

Volumes include: 1. Schutz (0824093100) 2. Des Prez (0824093879) 3. Rachmaninoff (0824089960) 4. De Falla (0824087852) 5. Adams & Delibes (082409011x) 6. Nielson (0824085698) 7. Byrd (0824083881) 8. Gluck (0824084519)

....*(contd.)*
9. Frescobaldi (0824085558) 10. Foster (0824066405) 11. Bartok (0824077474) 12. Vivaldi (0824083865) 13. Ockeghem & Obrecht (0824083814) 14. Bloch (082407789x) 15. Wolf (0824084748) 16. Mozart (0824083474) 17. Rimsky-Korsakov (0824084667) 18. Purcell (0824077865) 19. Handel (0824084527) 20. Rameau (0824056450) 21. Vaughan Williams (0824077466) 22. Berlioz (0824046358) 23. Monteverdi (0824077431) 24. Weber (0824041186) 25. Lassus (0824009479) 26. Pergolesi (0824045955) 27. Debussy (0824057953) 28. Mahler (0824084837) 29. Liszt (0824083822) 30. Beethoven (0824088077). *Class No:* 780(092)(01)

[3915]

GREEN, R.D. Index to composer bibliographies. Detroit, Information Coordinators, 1985. 76p. (*Detroit Studies in Music Bibliography, 53.*) ISBN: 0899900259.

Composers are listed in alphabetical order; bibliographies in monograph format or from journals are featured, with very brief annotations. Index of authors, compilers, editors. *Class No:* 780(092)(01)

Black Races

[3916]

FLOYD, S.A. *and* **REISSER, M.J. Black music biography:** an annotated bibliography. White Plains, NY, Kraus International, 1987. 302p.

Documents black musicians of all types and all styles; covers 1850 to the present. Useful introduction.
Class No: 780(092)(=96)

[3917]

GRAY, J. Blacks in classical music: a bibliographical guide to composers, performers and ensembles. New York, Greenwood, 1988. 420p. $39.95. ISBN: 0313260567.

Three hundred entries spanning 1700-1980s. Gives biographical information, drawing on periodical, dissertation, and reference sources.
Class No: 780(092)(=96)

20th Century

[3918]

Contemporary musicians: profiles of the people in music. Rubiner, J. M., *ed.* Detroit, Gale Research, 1989-. £45.00. per vol. ISSN: 10442197.

Also available online.

Biannual volumes provide biographical and critical information on names from all types of popular music. Bibliographies and discographies are a valuable feature. Generally 80 - 100 entries per volume. Cumulative index at end of each vol. *Class No:* 780(092)"19"

[3919]

CUMMINGS, D. *and* **McINTIRE, D.,** *eds.* **International who's who in music and musician's directory 1996/97.** 15th ed. Cambridge, International Biographical Centre, 1996. 1,206p. £98.00. ISBN: 0948875224.

First published 1935. This vol. is now accompanied by "Volume 2" covering popular music, issued 1996; *see* entry at 785.19(092).

Biographical information on 8,000 contemporary composers, arrangers, soloists, conductors, managers etc. in the classical and light classical fields. Appendices list societies, schools, awards, orchestras, opera companies.
Class No: 780(092)"19"

[3920]

MORRIS, M. A Guide to twentieth-century composers. London, Methuen, 1996. xxvii,554p. £30.00. ISBN: 0413456013.

Arranged A/Z by country (Argentina - Yugoslavia) with introductory essay and detailed biographies. Style is discursive and brief, but adequate information is generally given - *eg. Arnold Bax* 6 columns with list of 'recommended works', bibliographic note (2 biographies); *Michael Nyman* 2 cols. Covers only the Western classical tradition. Index of names p.523-554. *Class No:* 780(092)"19"

[3921]

SLONIMSKY, N. Baker's biographical dictionary of twentieth century musicians. New York, Schirmer, 1997. 1595p. $75.00. ISBN: 0028712714.

Derived from *Baker's biographical dictionary of musicians*, 8th. ed., 1992.

500 entries, generally the same as in the source volume, but there is some new and updated material, and bibliographies have been revised to 1996.
Class No: 780(092)"19"

Women

[3922]

CLAGHORN, G. Women composers and songwriters: a concise biographical dictionary. Updated ed. Lanham, MD/ London, Scarecrow, 1996. vii,247p. £65.00. ISBN: 0810831309.

Previous ed. as *Women composers and hymnists*, 1984.

About 1000 entries arranged A/Z (Carrie B. Wilson Adams - Ellen Taafe Zwilch) with basic information: dates, one key work and a paragraph of commentary including principal compositions. *Class No:* 780(092)-0055.2

[3923]

COHEN, A.I. International encyclopedia of women composers. 2nd ed. New York, Books & Music USA, 1988. 1151p. (2v). $130.00. ISBN: 0961748524.

Over three times the size of the first edition; includes discographies. 'An impressive and valuable reference work' (*Choice*, Sept. 1988). Over 6,000 composers included from 72 countries, ranging from ancient times to the present.
Class No: 780(092)-0055.2

[3924]

FULLER, S. The Pandora guide to women composers: Britain and the United States 1629 - present. London, HarperCollins/Pandora, 1994. 368p., illus. £25.00. ISBN: 0044408978.

100 composers are included - probably too few to justify comprehensiveness - but the standard of the entries is high; biography, social mileau, career are covered in depth, with discursive commentary and note of major works in the text. Bibliography p.354-364. *Class No:* 780(092)-0055.2

[3925]

SADIE, J.A. *and* **SAMUEL, R.,** *eds.* **New Grove dictionary of women composers.** London, Macmillan, 1994. 548p., illus. £46.00. ISBN: 0333515986.

US ed. as *Norton/Grove dictionary of women composers,* 1995.

875 composers, writing in the Western classical tradition, are included; entries are revised and expanded to reflect new material researched since the publication of the parent volumes. Bibliographies are included; illustrations are small, monochrome, and few in number. 'Entries and their

....(contd.)
bibliographies tend to be brief and superficial...does not cover adequately the thousands of women composers'. (*Choice*, April 1996; p.1290.) *Class No:* 780(092)-0055.2

[3926]
Women composers through the ages. Schleifer, M.F. *and* Glickman, S., *eds.* New York, G.K. Hall/London, Prentice Hall International, 1996-. c375p. per vol. $100.00/£75.00. per vol. ISBN: 0816109265, v.1.

12 vols. are planned; vol 1 - composers born before 1599; vol.2 - 1600-1699; vol. 3 - 1700-1799; vols. 3-5 cover 1700-1799. 3 vols. will cover the 19th century; 4 vols. the 20th.

19 composers in the first vol. Entries are signed, arranged chronologically, and include a biographical essay, commentary on works, bibliography, texts and scores (at least one work is printed in full in a modern version for each name). Some entries have discographies. 'This will be a thoroughly valuable series when complete'. (*Reference reviews*, 10(6), 1996; p37-38.) *Class No:* 780(092)-0055.2

Bibliographies

[3927]
ERICSON, M.D. Women and music: a selective annotated bibliography on women and gender issues in music, 1987-1992. New York/London, G.K. Hall, 1996. xxii,400p. $100.00. ISBN: 0816105804.

1800 annotated citations for books, conference proceedings, newspaper articles, dissertations, online sources, videos, films. International coverage; categorised arrangement. Extends to popular music and Jazz, the music industry, and music education. *Class No:* 780(092)-0055.2(01)

Great Britain

Bibliographies

[3928]
PORTER, J. The Traditional music of Britain and Ireland. New York, Garland, 1989. 408p. $50. ISBN: 0824066235.

Annotated bibliography of 1,700 citations to significant publications over the last century. Concentrates on the music, not the song texts. Major part devoted to music collections and research publications.
Class No: 780(410)(01)

Handbooks & Manuals

[3929]
FORD, T. The Musician's handbook. 3rd ed. London: Rhinegold Publishing, 1996. xiii, 318p. £12.95. ISBN: 0946890676.

Guide to the profession in the UK; options for the professional musician; career development; financial consideration; insurance and related matters; legal concerns.
Class No: 780(410)(035)

Periodicals & Progress Reports

[3930]
Brio: journal of the United Kingdom Branch of the International Association of Music Libraries, Archives and Documentation Centres. Oxford, IAML (UK), 1964-. £22.50pa. ISSN: 00070173.

Issued twice per year.

Useful feature articles, listing of new publications received at the British Library Document Supply Centre (arranged in instrumental categories etc.), and a good selection of scholarly book reviews, supported by further short notices of new books. *Class No:* 780(410)(05)

Yearbooks & Directories

[3931]
British and international music yearbook. Carter, A., *ed.* London, Rhinegold Publishing. c700p. ISSN: 03065928.

Annual.

Basically a directory of the 'classical music industry'; orchestras, choirs, dance companies, instrumentalists, singers, conductors, concert halls, official organizations, artists & agents, venues, promoters (clubs, festivals etc). Also coverage of jazz and light music. Sections on early music, recording & broadcasting, competitions & scholarships, education, libraries, museums, marketing, suppliers & services. International section is brief (c125p.)
Class No: 780(410)(058)

[3932]
Early music yearbook. Cambridge, National Early Music Association. c300p. £13.00. ISSN: 09676619.

Annual.

Includes information sources, societies (UK and overseas), periodicals, performing material, record companies, concert promoters, agents, education, instrumental collections, fairs and exhibitions, dealers in books, records, music; buyers' guide. Register of individuals and groups in various category formats. *Class No:* 780(410)(058)

[3933]
INCORPORATED SOCIETY OF MUSICIANS. Yearbook and register of members. London, ISM. c160p. £32.00. ISSN: 09516220.

Annual.

Details of the Society, review of the year, and register of members arranged alphabetically, with regional index.
Class No: 780(410)(058)

[3934]
PERFORMING RIGHTS SOCIETY. Yearbook. London, PRS. c120p., illus. ISSN: 03090884.

Reviews activity, with statistics, revenue figures etc. Reference section gives details on membership, licensing procedures, new works, fees, tariffs, inspection, overseas arrangements. *Class No:* 780(410)(058)

Gazetteers

[3935]
NORRIS, G. A Musical gazetteer of Great Britain and Ireland. Newton Abbot, David and Charles 1981. 352p.

Over 3,000 entries, listing places where British musicians were born, and where they lived, worked or died. Areas: East Anglia (Cambridge 3½p.); Ireland, p.27-50; Greater London, p.51-134; The Midlands; The North-East; The North-West; Scotland, p.212-41; The South-East; Wales; The West country. 'Elgar': 32 references. Excludes foreign performers but includes foreign composers with connections. Name index (p.342-52), but no place-name index.
Class No: 780(410)(083.86)

Histories

[3936]

CALDWELL, J. The Oxford history of English music: volume 1 - from the beginnings to c.1715. Oxford, Oxford University Press, 1991. 650p. £60.00. ISBN: 0198161298.

A second volume is expected.

Chapters cover origins to 13th century, 13th/14th centuries, Power and Dunstable, 15th/16th centuries, Reformation, Elizabethan and Jacobean, secular music, instrumental music, Charles I; Commonwealth; Restoration, music under the later Stuarts. Extensive bibliography pp.616-657, including modern editions of music.
Class No: 780(410)(091)

[3937]

MATTHEWS, B., ***comp*****. The Royal Society of Musicians of Great Britain:** list of members 1738-1984. London, RSM, 1985. 253p. £14. ISBN: 095094811x.

Lists names alphabetically and chronologically, with dates of birth and death, and brief biographies. Especially valuable for the obscure; 'indispensable to the shelves of an academic library' (*Brio* 22(2) Autumn/Winter, 1985. p.69).
Class No: 780(410)(091)

Bibliographies

[3938]

MILLER, L. ***and*** **COHEN, A. Music in the Royal Society of London,** 1660-1806. Detroit: Information Co-ordinators, 1987. xv, 264p. $60.00. (*Detroit Studies in Music Bibliography, no. 56.*) ISBN: 0899900321.

A bibliographical catalogue of items on music in the Society's publication *Philosophical Transactions* and in nine manuscript collections held in the Society's archives. Divided into ten sections, with discussion in the introduction; subjects include acoustics, tuning, therapy, structure of instruments, etc. *Class No:* 780(410)(091)(01)

[3939]

PICKERING, J.M., ***ed*****. Music in the British Isles, 1700-1800:** a bibliography of literature. Edinburgh, Faculty of Music, 1990. 418p. £25. ISBN: 0951278517.

Useful historical source. *Class No:* 780(410)(091)(01)

Scotland

[3940]

SCOTTISH MUSIC INFORMATION CENTRE. Scottish music handbook - 1996. Glasgow, Scottish Music Information Centre, 1996. £12.99.

More needs to be done to improve coverage and extend the scope, but this is a useful handbook and deserves recognition. *Class No:* 780(411)

Ireland

[3941]

CONTEMPORARY MUSIC CENTRE. Irish composers 1995-96. 3rd.ed. Dublin, Contemporary Music Centre, 1995. 41p. (loose-leaf). ISBN: 1897996047.

Previous ed. 1994.

Brief career details, works-list; contact address.
Class No: 780(415)

[3942]

FLOOD, W.H.G. A History of Irish music. Dublin, Browne & Nolan, 1905. xiii, 357p.

The standard history, with list of collections, and good index. *Class No:* 780(415)

[3943]

MUSIC NETWORK. Irish music handbook: a comprehensive guide to music in Ireland, North and South. Dublin, Music Network, 1996. 271p. £14.95. ISBN: 0952878305.

Full of information; an excellent introduction to the musical scene. *Class No:* 780(415)

England

Bibliographies

[3944]

FORD, W.K. Music in England before 1800: a select bibliography. London, Library Association, 1967. xiv, 128p.

Annotated, scholarly bibliography of *c.*1,000 items. Valuable historically. *Class No:* 780(420)(01)

Biographies

[3945]

PULVER, J. A Biographical dictionary of old English music. London, Kegan Paul, 1927. xii, 537p.

Reprinted New York, Da Capo, 1973.

Covers period 1200-1695; cross references to variant spellings. Quotations; detailed analytical index.
Class No: 780(420)(092)

Wales

Histories

[3946]

Welsh music history /hanes cerddotiaeth cymru. Cardiff, University of Wales Press, 1996-. £15.00.pa. ISSN: 13620681.

Journal of the newly-established Centre for Advanced Welsh Music Studies; 2 issues per year.
Class No: 780(429)(091)

Biographies

[3947]

CLEAVER, E. Musicians of Wales: an account of the lives and work of the major musicians of Wales in the nineteenth and into the twentieth centuries. Ruthin, John Jones, 1968. 108p.

Original Welsh edition 1964 as *Gŵyn y Gân*.
Class No: 780(429)(092)

Germany

[3948]

Jahresverzeichnis der Musikalien und Musikschriften. Veröffentlichungen der DDR, der BDR und Westberlins, sowie deutschsprachige werke anderer Länder. Leipzig, F. Hofmeister (now VEB Friedrich Hofmeister Musikverlag) 1852-.

Annual.

Covers musical scores and musicology in German speaking countries. *Class No:* 780(430)

France

Bibliographies

[3949]
PIERRUSE, B. Catalogue général de l'édition musicale en France: livres, méthodes et partitions de musique sérieuse en vente. Paris, Editions Musicales Transatlantiques, 1984. xvi,458p. £48.

A valuable source for the French music publishing market, but now dated. *Class No:* 780(44)(01)

Italy

Bibliographies

[3950]
MISCHIATI, O. Indici, cataloghi e avvisi degli editiori e librai musicali italiani: dal 1591 al 1798. Florence, Olschki, 1984.

Lists and describes the contents of 67 indexes, catalogues and advertisements from 20 publishers and booksellers. Composer and short title index. *Class No:* 780(450)(01)

USSR

Biographies

[3951]
HO, A. *and* **FEOFANOV, D.,** *eds.* **Biographical dictionary of Russian/Soviet composers.** New York, Greenwood, 1989. 739p. $85. ISBN: 0313244855.

Over 30 distinguished contributors have provided material for this scholarly dictionary. More than 2,000 composers are featured, with worklists, discographies, and bibliographies. Includes those of Soviet birth who worked elsewhere. Introduction needs careful reading to get the most from the work. 'An extremely rich and excellent reference tool'. (*Choice* 27(8) April 1990, p.1296). *Class No:* 780(47)(092)

Greece

[3952]
WEST, M.L. Ancient Greek music. Oxford, Oxford University Press, 1992. 350p.,illus. £40.00. ISBN: 0198148976.

Principles, practice and historical development; defines its position at the interface between European and Afro-Asiatic cultures. Transcriptions of 30 surviving pieces.
Class No: 780(495)

China

Bibliographies

[3953]
LIEBERMAN, F. Chinese music: an annotated bibliography. 2nd ed. New York, Garland, 1979. 257p. $47. ISBN: 0824099222.

First published 1970 (New York Society for Asian Music).

Some 2,500 entries for Western material, with bibliography and discography. Indexes to serials and names.
Class No: 780(510)(01)

Japan

[3954]
SCHNEIDER, E.H. A History of Japanese music. Oxford, Oxford University Press, 1973. xviii, 720p. £24.00.

The authoritative western source; arranged in seven parts from earliest times to twentieth century, with extensive bibliography and indexes. *Class No:* 780(52)

Bibliographies

[3955]
TSUGE, G. Japanese music: an annotated bibliography. New York, Garland, 1984. 172p. $33. (*Garland Bibliographies in Ethnomusicology,* 2.) ISBN: 0824089952.

800 entries cover literature in English, French and German to the end of 1983. All types of publications are included. *Class No:* 780(52)(01)

India

[3956]
Encyclopaedia of Indian music with special reference to the Ragas. 2nd ed. Delhi, Sri Satguru Publications, 1986. 44,98,18p. (3v. in 1), illus. ISBN: 817030007x.

Especially valuable for its musical examples, and sections on the Ragas. *Class No:* 780(540)

[3957]
HOLRYDE, P. The Music of India. New York, Praeger, 1972. 290p.

An authentic and lucid account of classical Indian instrumental and vocal music. Chap. 1. The Hindu Background - Chap. 2. Ras Bhav: the feel of music - Chap. 3. Historical development and the growth of aesthetic principles. Chap. 4. The grammar of the Raag. Chap. 5. Memoria Technica - Chap. 6. A world for the vocalist - Chap. 7. Infinite variations on the theme. Text is followed by brief description of Indian instruments, glossary of terms, brief bibliography, and an index. *Class No:* 780(540)

[3958]
KAUFMANN, W. The Ragas of North India. Bloomington, Indiana University Press for the International Affairs Center, 1968. ix,625p. illus.

Detailed introduction & history; Ragas discussed by classification type, with musical examples. Bibliography.
Class No: 780(540)

[3959]
KAUFMANN, W. The Ragas of South India: a catalogue of scalar material. Bloomington, Indiana University Press, 1976. xxix,723p. ISBN: 0253395089.

Companion volume to the above; copious musical examples. *Class No:* 780(540)

Africa

[3960]
GRAHAM, R. Stern's guide to contemporary African music. London, Zwan/Off The Record Press, 1988. xii,315p. maps. ISBN: 1853050008.

Comprehensive guide to recorded African music; useful introductory survey, then arranged by country. Each entry gives a historical summary & current trends, and features traditional & contemporary music. *Class No:* 780(6)

South Africa

[3961]
MALAN, J.P., *ed*. South African music encyclopedia. Cape Town: OUP, 1979-1986. 458, 513, 381, 520p. (4v.). £63.00. ISBN: 0869655868; 0195702859; 0195703111.

Covers music of all races 1652-1960. Uneven in scope, but some entries are excellent with bibliographies. In volume two pp 265-508 there is an extensive feature on *indigenous musics*. *Class No:* 780(680)

Canada

[3962]
KALLMANN, H., *and others*. Encyclopedia of music in Canada. Toronto, University of Toronto Press, 1981. xxix, 1076p.

The work of 400 contributors, and regarded as comprehensive. *Class No:* 780(71)

Latin America

Biographies

[3963]
Latin American composers: a biographical dictionary. Ficher, M. *and* Schliefer, F. *and* Furmar, J.M., *eds*. Metuchen, NJ/London, Scarecrow, 1996. 440p. £53.20. ISBN: 0810831856.

Useful starting point, but a revised edition would be able to improve the quality of entries and expand coverage. Bibliography. *Class No:* 780(729.99)(092)

USA

Bibliographies

[3964]
JACKSON, R. United States music: sources of bibliography and collective biography. New York, Institute for Studies in American Music, 1973. 80p.

Important for folk music, blues, ragtime, jazz and twentieth century music; now dated but a useful record.
Class No: 780(73)(01)

[3965]
KRUMMEL, D.W. Bibliographical handbook of American music. Chicago, University of Illinois Press, 1988. 256p. $24.95. ISBN: 0252014502.

Four sections cover chronology, context, media and genres, and bibliographical forms. Entries numbered and annotated. *Class No:* 780(73)(01)

[3966]
WARNER, T.E. Periodical literature on American music 1620-1920; a classified bibliography with annotations. Warren, Mich., Harmonie Park Press, 1988. xli,644p. $60. (*Bibliographies in American Music, 12.*) ISBN: 0899900348.

Comprehensive in depth and coverage with a thorough subject index. Brief annotations where titles are not self-explanatory. *Class No:* 780(73)(01)

Encyclopaedias & Dictionaries

[3967]
HITCHCOCK, H.W. *and* SADIE, S., *eds*. New Grove dictionary of American music. London, Macmillan, 1986. 2600p. (4 vols.) £345.00. ISBN: 0943818362.

Covers all areas of musical life: composers, conductors, singers, virtuosi, orchestras, bands, opera houses,

.... *(contd.)*
instruments, cities, festivals, jazz, country music, rock, blues, film, choreography, patrons, critics, scholars, institutions, terminology. Over 5000 articles, supported by 700 photographs and over 2000 musical examples.
Class No: 780(73)(03)

[3968]
JABLONSKI, E. Encyclopedia of American music. New York: Doubleday, 1981. 629p. ISBN: 0385080883.

A chronological arrangement in seven major periods, from hymns of the Pilgrim Fathers to the present day; all types of music are included. Introductory sections are supported by some 1200 entries. Sometimes idiosyncratic, but an interesting approach. An appendix of recordings is provided on pp 579-592. *Class No:* 780(73)(03)

Yearbooks & Directories

[3969]
Music business handbook and career guide. Baskerville, D., *ed*. 6th.ed. Thousand Oaks, CA/London, Sage Publications, 1995. 588p. £28.00. ISBN: 0803971532.

Covers songwriting, publishing, copyright, licensing, unions, guilds, agents, managers, promoters, recording industry, broadcasting and film music, career planning, etc. Almost all information is US relevant only, but Canada is included (p.495-520). Appendices give ASCAP agreement drafts, copyright forms. Bibliography; glossary.
Class No: 780(73)(058)

[3970]
Musical America: international directory of the performing arts. New York, Musical America Publishing. c800p. $80.00. ISSN: 07357788.

Annual.

Feature articles of current interest, artist manager reports, US and Canadian listings - managers, orchestras, opera companies, choirs, dance companies, festivals, schools, awards, publishers, periodicals, record companies etc. Also an international section. Index by categories, and an index of names. *Class No:* 780(73)(058)

Histories

[3971]
CHASE, G. America's music: from the Pilgrims to the Present. 3rd ed. Chicago, Illinois University Press, 1986. 774p. $29.95. ISBN: 025200454x.

A good single-volume history, with excellent index and bibliography. Discographic essay useful.
Class No: 780(73)(091)

Biographies

[3972]
ANDERSON, E.R. Contemporary American composers: a biographical dictionary. 2nd ed. Boston, G.K. Hall, 1982. 578p. $60.00.

Includes over 4,500 names; especially useful for minor figures. Entries give extensive information.
Class No: 780(73)(092)

[3973]
BUTTERWORTH, N. A Dictionary of American composers. London, Garland, 1984. xi,423p. £48. ISBN: 0824093119.

Excludes light music and jazz, and songwriters. Useful for lesser known composers. *Class No:* 780(73)(092)

[3974]
Who's who in American music: classical. Cattell, J., *ed.* 2nd ed. New York: Bowker, 1985. xiii, 1200p. $125.00. ISBN: 0835220745.

Covers administrators, managers, composers, conductors, critics, directors, educators, instrumentalists, vocalists; 6,800 entries, included by invitation, not application. Indexes by geographical location and class of activity. Entries in alphabetical order, noting training, works, recordings, positions, teaching, awards. Bibliographies limited to three items; publications listed to a maximum of five. Agent's address given. *Class No:* 780(73)(092)

Jews

[3975]
NULMAN, M. Concise encyclopedia of Jewish music. New York, McGraw Hill, 1975. 276p. ISBN: 0070475466.

Over 500 entries with biographies and discussion of works. 150 illustrations. *Class No:* 780(=924)

Middle Ages

Dictionaries

[3976]
CARTER, H.N. A Dictionary of middle-English musical terms. Bloomington, Indiana University Press, 1961. xv, 655p.

Covers the period 1100-1500, and gives valuable illustrative quotations. *Class No:* 780"01/14"(038)

Renaissance

Dictionaries

[3977]
TINCTORIS, J. Dictionary of musical terms: an English translation. [Terminorum musicae diffinitorium.]
Parrish, C., *trans.* London, Collier Macmillan, 1963. 108p.
Originally compiled *c.*1475.

Essential for the understanding of renaissance music in theory and practice. *Class No:* 780"1095-1300"(038)

20th Century

Biographies

[3978]
Contemporary musicians: profiles of the people in music. Rubiner, J. M., *ed.* Detroit, Gale Research, 1989-. £45.00. per vol. ISSN: 10442197.
Also available online.

Biannual volumes provide biographical and critical information on names from all types of popular music. Bibliographies and discographies are a valuable feature. Generally 80 - 100 entries per volume. Cumulative index at the end of each vol. *Class No:* 780"19"(092)

Music Librarianship

[3979]
BRYANT, E.T. Music librarianship: a practical guide. 2nd ed. Metuchen NJ, London: Scarecrow Press, 1985. xiv, 449p. £17.50. ISBN: 0810817853.

Highly regarded, but now dated, this was an authoritative

....(contd.)
and comprehensive guide, covering administration, reference books, periodicals, cataloguing, classification, sound recordings. Bibliography pp423-442. *Class No:* 780:02

USA

[3980]
BRADLEY, C.J. American music librarianship. Westport, CT, Greenwood, 1990. 248p. $45. ISBN: 0313268207.

'A biographical and historical review of the musical situation' in US libraries; mainly detailing careers of 19th century librarians and the origins of the Music Library Association. *Class No:* 780:02(73)

Thesauri

[3981]
HARROLD, A. *and* LEA, G. Musaurus: music thesaurus. London, Music Press, 1991. £5. ISBN: 1873260008.

Comprehensive, structured & fully-indexed thesaurus for all aspects of music collections. *Class No:* 780:025.43

Music Librarianship

Music Libraries

[3982]
HARMONICA project.
Website at: <http://www.svb.nl/project harmonica/ harmonica.htm>

A European Union programme that started in 1996 and sought to map out the current state of the art in music libraries in three areas - cataloguing and indexing, user needs, and technologies. Two forums have been held (Athens, Amsterdam). The site also provides links to thousands of other music sites on the Web.
Class No: 780:061:026/027

[3983]
Music libraries online.
A project under the UK eLib programme. E-mail contact at: <mo.bains@uce.ac.uk>

MLO seeks to create a virtual union catalogue of the nine British music conservatoire libraries, using Z39.50. Options to extend to other music collections in universities, national and public libraries, and composer archives are being investigated. Also aims to coordinate acquisition policies and facilitate efficient interlending. Founded on principles stated in the 1994 'Library and information plan for music.' Current members of the project are: Birmingham Conservatoire (University of Central England), Royal Academy of Music, Royal Northern College of Music, Royal Scottish Academy of Music and Drama, and Trinity College of Music. These will be joined by The City of Leeds College of Music, Guildhall School of Music and Drama, Royal College of Music, and the Welsh College of Music and Drama in a second phase. *Class No:* 780:061:026/027

Yearbooks & Directories

[3984]
Directory of music research libraries, including contributions to RISM. Benton, R., *ed.* Kassel, Bärenreiter, 1967-. 5v.

Published under the auspices of the International Association of Music Libraries, Archives and Documentation Centres: Commission of Research Libraries.

Volume 1: (2nd ed. 1983) Canada & the US.

....(contd.)
(3761806841; 282p.). Volume 2: Thirteen European countries (1970) (Covers 784 libraries in Austria, Belgium, Denmark, Finland, E. & W. Germany, UK, Ireland, Luxembourg, Netherlands, Norway, Sweden, Switzerland). Volume 3: Spain, France, Italy, Portugal (1972; University of Iowa Press; republished by Bärenreiter, 1975). Volume 4: Australia, NZ, Japan, & Israel (1979). Volume 5: Czechoslovakia, Hungary, Poland, Yugoslavia (1985). Data: address; type and size of collection; lending library codes. Country index of libraries. Very favourably reviewed in *Brio*, Spring/Summer 1980, p.29. To be completed in 6v.
Class No: 780:061:026/027(058)

Great Britain

Yearbooks & Directories

[3985]
PENNEY, B. Music in British libraries: a directory of resources. 4th ed. London, Library Association, 1992. 112p. £37.00. ISBN: 0853657394.

Entries in alphabetical order of location giving details of collections of printed music and sound recordings in the UK. Coverage has been expanded from earlier editions to include university, polytechnic and college collections, music schools, cathedrals, private collections, in addition to public libraries. Standard range of data given. Indices by composer, collection names, etc. *Class No:* 780:061:026/027(410)(058)

USA

[3986]
BRADLEY, C.J., ***comp*****. Music collections in American libraries:** a chronology. Detroit: Information Co-ordinators, 1981. xiii, 249p. $22.00. (*Detroit Studies in Music Bibliography; no. 46.*) ISBN: 089990002x.

Discusses the resources of public and academic libraries in chronological order of establishment. First entry is 1731. Latest 1978. Details of special collections are given, and published catalogues. Bibliography, and a general index of names of institutions, libraries, and collections.
Class No: 780:061:026/027(73)

[3987]
KRUMMEL, D.W., ***and others*****. Resources of American musical history:** directory of source material from colonial times to World War ll. Urbana: University of Illinois, 1981. 463p. $47.50. ISBN: 0252008286.

Includes musical documents and collections, arranged by state alphabetically; limited coverage of Canadian and other locations. *Class No:* 780:061:026/027(73)

Music Education

Great Britain

Yearbooks & Directories

[3988]
British music education yearbook. 1997-1998. Carter, A., *ed.* 14th.ed. London: Rhinegold Publishing, 1997. xix, 667p. £14.00. ISBN: 0946890722. ISSN: 13538896.

Cover title now 'Music education yearbook.'

Covers resources for teachers, national and regional organisations, youth performance, examinations, schools, further and higher education, teacher training, jazz in education, suppliers and services. Includes classical and jazz, and popular music scene. Reference sections list periodicals with publisher details; libraries (p.631-41, categorised); books on specialist education.
Class No: 780:37(410)(058)

[3989]
INCORPORATED SOCIETY OF MUSICIANS. Register of professional private music teachers 1997/98. London, ISM, 1997. 128p. £16.00. ISSN: 09516239.

Directory by instrument in geographical groupings. A/Z index. *Class No:* 780:37(410)(058)

Music Publishing

[3990]
KRUMMEL, D.W., ***comp*****. Guide for dating early music:** a manual of bibliographical practices. London, Bärenreiter for IAML, 1974. 267p.

Systematic discussion of various ways of establishing the date of music editions published 1700-1860 (when dates were customarily omitted. Covers plate numbers, address, copyright notices, advertisements, characteristics of the physical document and mention of current events. Numerous examples; bibliographical references. Includes 'National reports'.

'Supplement to the *Guide for dating early printed music*', by D.W. Krummel (*Fontes artis musicae*, v.24, 1977, p.175-84). *Class No:* 780:655

[3991]
SADIE, S., ***ed*****. Music printing and publishing.** London, Macmillan Press, 1990. 450p. illus. £45. (*New Grove Handbooks in Musicology.*) ISBN: 0333470443.

Detailed and authoritative examination of the history of music publishing from the earliest period to the latest computerized methods. Full discussion of techniques and conventions. *Class No:* 780:655

Great Britain

[3992]
HUMPHRIES, C. ***and*** **SMITH, W.C. Music publishing in the British Isles,** from the earliest times to the middle of the nineteenth century: a dictionary of engravers, printers, publishers and music sellers. 2nd ed. Oxford, Blackwell, 1970. x, 390p.

First edition Cassell, 1954.

The dictionary section includes bibliographical references; also a general bibliography, p.43-48. Index of firms in places other than London; list of musical instrument makers and repairers. The 2nd ed. adds 137 new firms. Both eds. have 25 facsims. Vital for purpose of dating. 'Indispensable to libraries and researchers' (*British book news*, August 1970, p.636). *Class No:* 780:655(410)

Music Research

[3993]
PRUETT, J.W. ***and*** **SLAVENS, T.P. Research guide to musicology.** Chicago, ALA, 1985. 175p. $50. (*Sources of information in the Humanities, 4.*)

Two main sections: research & scholarship, & annotated list of basic sources. Bias against popular music. Subject index; author/title index. *Class No:* 780.001.5

[3994]
SPIESS, L.B. Historical musicology: a reference manual for research in music. Brooklyn, Institute of Medieval Music, 1963. xiii, 294p.

Of particular value for its record of out-of-print classics; some 2,000 unannotated items in six chronological sections. *Class No:* 780.001.5

Periods

Mediaeval Music

Bibliographies

[3995]
HUGHES, A. Medieval music. Toronto, University of Toronto Press, 1974. xii, 326p.

2,003 numbered entries. Sections: General reference works - General histories - Texts - Collections, editions - Philosophy and speculative literature - Notation - Rhythm - Technical matters - Music in everyday life - Iconography - Instruments - The Near East and Byzantium - Plainsong (p.476-714) - Tropes - Liturgical drama - Eastern Europe - Treatises. A very well annotated, scholarly and comprehensive bibliography. 'The value of this volume to musicologists is enormous' (*Choice*, v.12, no.4, June 1975, p.512). *Class No:* 780.033(01)

[3996]
SWITTEN, M.L. Music and literature in the Middle Ages: an annotated bibliography. New York, Garland, 1990. 351p. $45. (*Garland Medieval Bibliographies, no.4.*) ISBN: 0824047974.

Includes material on performance practice and styles, instruments, ensembles etc. Cites French, German, Italian material covering the 11th century to 1500. *Class No:* 780.033(01)

Published Music

Scores

[3997]
BBC MUSIC LIBRARY. Catalogues. London, BBC, 1965-82. 13v. ISBN: 0563124784, 1982 set.

Series comprises: Chamber Music Catalogue (1965) Piano and Organ Catalogue (2v.; 1965) Song Catalogue (4v.; 1966) Choral and Opera Catalogue (2v.; 1967) Orchestral Catalogue (4v.; 1982). Reference guide to one of the world's largest collection of performing editions; over 300,000 entries in total. *Class No:* 780.089.6

[3998]
The British catalogue of music. London, Bowker-Saur, 1957-. £95pa. ISSN: 00681407.

Two interim issues and an annual cumulation each year; initially quarterly. Cumulation 1957-1985 published in 10 vols. (London, K.G. Saur, 1988). Available through BLAISE-LINE 1987-.

A record of new music published in the UK, foreign music available in the UK through a sole agent, music acquired from foreign publishers; based on receipts at the BL Copyright office. Classified section (now arranged by DDC 21; previously by a special BCM classification), title and composer index, subject index (arranged by musical forms). *Class No:* 780.089.6

[3999]
CUNNINGHAM, W.P., *ed.* The Music locator. 3rd ed. New York, Resource Publications, 1984. $89.95. ISBN: 0893900486.

Indexes 12,500 vocal, choral and instrumental compositions by title, composer, category of music. Details of voicing given. *Class No:* 780.089.6

[4000]
DANIELS, D. Orchestral music: a handbook. 3rd.ed. Lanham, MD/London, Scarecrow, 1996. 611p. ISBN: 0810832283.

First ed. 1972.

Basic list of available music arranged A/Z by composer, indicating duration (total and each movement), parts required, publishers. Appendices list choral music, solo voice/instrumental music, orchestral music by instrumentation; organisations. Title index; publisher data. *Class No:* 780.089.6

[4001]
DAVIS, E., *ed.* A Basic music library: essential scores and sound recordings. 3rd.ed. Chicago/London, American Library Association, 1997. 665p. ISBN: 0838934617.

Selection and buying guide to 3000 scores and 7000 recordings. Chapters for scores are arranged: orchestral; chamber; solo instruments; vocal. (For sound recordings chapters *see entry at:* 789.90). *Class No:* 780.089.6

[4002]
MURRAY, S.E. Anthologies of music: an annotated index. Detroit: Information Co-ordinators, 1987. xxiii, 178. $75.00. (*Detroit Studies in Music Bibliography, no. 55.*) ISBN: 0899900313.

Indexes 33 historical anthologies, comprising 3,500 items by 600 composers, and including multi-volume sets and editions republished in different forms. Highly specialized anthologies are not included. Alphabetical arrangement, supported by *genre locator* to find examples of specific styles. *Class No:* 780.089.6

[4003]
Music in print. Philadelphia, PA, Musicdata,

Essential tool for the bibliographical control of printed music; many catalogues are issued, for example:*Orchestral music in print. Master index* (1994); *Master composer index*; *Master title index*; *Sacred choral music in print*; *Secular choral music in print*; *String music in print*; *Organ music in print*, etc.

New eds. of each of the titles are issued at intervals. *Class No:* 780.089.6

[4004]
NATIONAL FEDERATION OF MUSIC SOCIETIES. Catalogue of chamber music. London: NFMS, 1983. 66p. £5.00.

Arranged by ensemble headings, then alphabetically by composers. Covers works for 3-10 instruments, showing timings, details of movements, and publication data. *Class No:* 780.089.6

[4005]
NATIONAL FEDERATION OF MUSIC SOCIETIES. Catalogue of orchestral works 1976 and first supplement. London: NFMS, 1983. v.p. £3.00.

Reissue of the 1976 catalogue incorporating new sections.

Includes orchestral music, string orchestra music, concertos by instrument; new sections comprise new contents page and introduction, amendments to 1976 catalogue, supplement of new items, and a new section devoted to solo voice and orchestra. *Class No:* 780.089.6

[4006]

SALTONSTALL, C.D. *and* **SALTONSTALL, H. A New catalog of music for small orchestra.** 2nd ed. Clifton, N.J: European American Music Corporation, 1978. xxv, 323p. £28.00. ISBN: 0913574147.

First edition published 1940.

A very good, simple, compilation. The output of 200 publishers in 30 countries is covered, giving title, imprint, instrumentation and duration. *Class No:* 780.089.6

Composer's Works

[4007]

Bio-bibliographies in music. Westport, CT, Greenwood Press, 1988-. ISSN: 97426968.

Useful series of titles that give a concise biography for a composer, lists of works, bibliography, discography, efficient indexes.

Current titles include *Arthur Bliss* (1988); *Peter Maxwell Davies* (1995); *William Mathias* (1995); *Carl Ruggles* (1995); *William Thomas McKinley* (1995); *Michael Tippett* (1989). *Class No:* 780.089.8

[4008]

Composer resource manuals. New York, Garland, 1980-.

Volumes vary in size from 145 pages (De Falla) to over 900 (Beethoven).

An excellent series of volumes, each by a specialist compiler, and including a catalogue of works, biographical information, bibliography, collections and archives, letters, organizations, secondary sources, guide to research. Useful illustrations and good indexes.

Volumes include: 1. Schutz (0824093100) 2. Des Prez (0824093879) 3. Rachmaninoff (0824089960) 4. De Falla (0824087852) 5. Adams & Delibes (082409011x) 6. Nielson (0824085698) 7. Byrd (0824083881) 8. Gluck (0824084519) 9. Frescobaldi (0824085558) 10. Foster (0824066405) 11. Bartok (0824077474) 12. Vivaldi (0824083865) 13. Ockeghem & Obrecht (0824083814) 14. Bloch (082407789x) 15. Wolf (0824084748) 16. Mozart (0824083474) 17. Rimsky-Korsakov (0824084667) 18. Purcell (0824077865) 19. Handel (0824084527) 20. Rameau (0824056450) 21. Vaughan Williams (0824077466) 22. Berlioz (0824046358) 23. Monteverdi (0824077431) 24. Weber (0824041186) 25. Lassus (0824009479) 26. Pergolesi (0824045955) 27. Debussy (0824057953) 28. Mahler (0824084837) 29. Liszt (0824083822) 30. Beethoven (0824088077). *Class No:* 780.089.8

Bartók

[4009]

BOOSEY AND HAWKES. Béla Bartók: complete catalogue of his published works. London: Boosey & Hawkes, 1970. 40p. £5.00.

A chronological sequence with a classified index.
Class No: 780.089.8BAR

Bliss

[4010]

CRAGGS, S.R. Arthur Bliss: a source book. Aldershot, Scolar Press, 1996. xvii,366p £65.00. ISBN: 0859679403.

Detailed descriptions of manuscripts and correspondence, chronology; recordings, bibiography. Craggs has also produced a bio-bibliography of Bliss (*see series entry at 780.089.8*). *Class No:* 780.089.8BLI

Britten

[4011]

EVANS, J. *and* **REED, P.** *and* **WILSON, P.,** *eds.* **A Britten source book.** Aldeburgh, Suffolk, Britten-Pears Library, 1987. ix,328p. £35. ISBN: 0951193929.

A chronology of life and works which ' must become a standard reference for all future Britten scholars' (*Musical Times* vol. cxxx (1759) Sept. 1989 p.544-5). Bibliography covers 125 pages and includes ephemera and trivia. Full index of compositions. *Class No:* 780.089.8BRI

Bruckner

[4012]

GRASBERGER, R. Bruckner-Bibliographie bis 1974. Graz, Akademische Druck-u. Verlaganstalt, 1985. 296p. Sch.750.

Divided into 33 sections, each arranged A/Z by author, and supplemented by lists of Bruckner festivals, and journals cited. Author & subject indexes. *Class No:* 780.089.8BRU

Debussy

[4013]

ABRAVANEL, C. Claude Debussy: a bibliography. Detroit, Information Coordinators, 1972. 214p. (*Detroit Studies in Music Bibliography, 25.*)

Includes monograph reviews and dissertations.
Class No: 780.089.8DEB

Elgar

[4014]

CRAGGS, S.R. Edward Elgar: a source book. Aldershot, Scolar Press, 1995. 188p. £55.00. ISBN: 0859679209.

Chronologically arranged main entries with bibliographic information, performance details, publisher, date etc. Recordings; bibliography from late 1800s to the present.
Class No: 780.089.8ELG

Mahler

[4015]

NAMENWIRTH, S.M. Gustav Mahler: a critical bibliography. Wiesbaden, Harrassowitz, 1987. 3v. DM498. ISBN: 3447027312.

Massive, scholarly cumulation; volume three consists entirely of indexes. *Class No:* 780.089.8MAH

Maxwell Davies

[4016]

ARNOLD, J. Peter Maxwell Davies: the complete catalogue of published works. London: J. Arnold, 1981. 63p.

A classified arrangement. Includes dates of first performances. *Class No:* 780.089.8MAX

Palestrina

[4017]

HALL, A. Palestrina: an index to the Casimiri, Kalmus and Haberl editions. Philadelphia: Music Libraries Association, 1980. xiii, 82p. $18.00. ISBN: 0914954180.

Includes a table of volume contents of all editions, title index, and a classified guide. *Class No:* 780.089.8PAL

Shostakovich

[4018]

HULME, D.C. Dimitri Shostakovich: a catalogue, bibliography and discography. 2nd ed. Oxford, Clarendon Press, 1990. 480p. £45. ISBN: 0198162049.

First edition Kyle & Glen Music, 1982.

Entries include short descriptions of each composition, date, dedicatee, orchestration, duration, list of recordings, bibliographical references, location of autograph etc. Efficient indexes. *Class No:* 780.089.8SHO

Music Theory

Thematic Catalogues

Bibliographies

[4019]

BROOK, B.S. *and* **VIANO, R. Thematic catalogues in music:** an annotated bibliography. 2nd.ed. Stuyvesant, NY, Pendragon Press, 1997. xlviii,602p. ISBN: 091872886x.

First ed. 1972.

1,444 numbered, annotated entries, under composers A-Z. Symbols indicate 'in preparation', 'manuscript', 'literature', recommended title for library catalogues. Appendix A: Manuscript thematic catalogues before 1830 (p.503-7) - B. Printed thematic catalogues before 1830. (p.508-9) - C. Catalogue records for library catalogues. Index p.527-602. The most comprehensive bibliography of thematic catalogues. *Class No:* 781.973(01)

Albeniz

[4020]

BAYTELMAN, P. Isaac Albeniz: chronological list and thematic catalogue of his piano works. Detroit, Harmonie Park, 1993. 124p. $35.00 ISBN: 0899900674.

The catalogue is far from complete as so much is lost, but this is the product of thorough research. There is an up-to-date discography. *Class No:* 781.973ALB

Bach Family

[4021]

SCHMIEDER, W. Thematisch-systematisches Verzeichnis der musikalischen Werke von Johann Sebastian Bach. Bach-Werke-Verzeichnis (BWV). Leipzig, Breitkopf & Härtel, 1950. xii, 747p.

A revision is reported to be in progress.

Compositions are numbered 1-1,080, with a supplement, nos.1-189. Appendices: a chronological table, and a list of themes for the instrumental works. Title and name indexes. *Class No:* 781.973BAC

[4022]

SCHULZE, H.J., ***comp*** *and* **WOLFF, C.,** ***comp*****.. Bach Compendium:** analytisch - bibliographisches Repertorium der Werke J.S. Bachs. Frankfurt/Leipzig/Dresden: Peters, 1985. 419p. £54.00.

Abbreviated title is BC: this volume is the first of series 1 *Cantatas for the Sundays and Feast Days of the Liturgical Year* and the whole work will be in three series totalling about twenty volumes. Introductory list of libraries, synopsis, and bibliographies; works are listed with musical incipits, and at the end of the volume cross references to BWV are given. BC is more detailed than BWV, incorporates new research and aims to be totally comprehensive and systematic. *Class No:* 781.973BAC

[4023]

WOTQUEENNE, A. Thematisches Verzeichnis der Werke von Carl Philipp Emanuel Bach. Wiesbaden: Breitkopf & Härtel, 1964. 190p.

The standard, comprehensive guide.
Class No: 781.973BAC

Bax

[4024]

PARLETT, G., ***comp*****. Arnold Bax:** a catalogue of his music. London: Triad Press, 1972. 51p. £2.50.

Basically chronological with a classified listing. Adequate index. *Class No:* 781.973BAX

Beethoven

[4025]

DORFMÜLLER, K. Beiträge zur Beethoven - Bibliographie: Studien und Materialien zum Werkeverzeichnis von Kinsky-Halm. Munich: Henle, 1978. ix, 452p. £52.00. ISBN: 3873280280.

Scholarly articles and a general supplement to Kinsky. Incorporates indexes. *Class No:* 781.973BEE

[4026]

KINSKY, G. Das Werk Beethovens. Thematisch-bibliographisches Verzeichnis seiner sämtlichen vollendeten Kompositionen. Munich, Henle, 1955. xxii, 808p.

Completed, after Kinsky's death by Hans Halm.

Main sequence is by opus number. Appendix lists 205 unnumbered items. Entries include musical examples. Bibliography, appendices. Author and title indexes. *Class No:* 781.973BEE

[4027]

NOTTEBOHM, G. Ludwig van Beethoven: thematisches Verzeichnis. Weisbaden: Martin Sändig, 1969. 220p.

Reprint of the 1925 edition produced in Leipzig by Breitkopf and Härtel.

The reprint includes Emerich Kastner's *Bibliotheca Beethoveniana.*

The arrangement of the main work is by opus number, followed by unnumbered works. Adequately indexed. Kastner's work is arranged chronologically.
Class No: 781.973BEE

[4028]

—HESS, W. Verzeichnis der nicht in der Gesamtausgabe veröffentlichten Werke Ludwig van Beethovens. Weisbaden: Breitkopf & Härtel, 1957. 116p.

A classified arrangement of recent discoveries, to supplement Nottebohm. *Class No:* 781.973BEE

Berlioz

[4029]

HOLOMAN, D.K. Catalogue of the works of Hector Berlioz. Kassel, Bärenreiter, 1987. xlv,527p. DM396. ISBN: 3761804490.

Forms the final volume of the New Berlioz Edition (NBE) and represents years of research. Works are arranged chronologically and each entry gives the Holomon number, title, dedication, thematic index, details of instrumentation, reference to volume of NBE, and date of publication. Also includes a register of performances given in Berlioz's lifetime, and an appendix of works by opus number.
Class No: 781.973BER

[4030]
HOPKINSON, C. A Bibliography of the musical and literary works of Hector Berlioz 1803-1889. 2nd ed. Tunbridge Wells, Macnutt, 1980. xix, 230p. £32.00.
First published 1951 (Edinburgh Bibliographical Society).
Part 1: A note of Berlioz's earliest publications. Musical compositions, original and arrangements (p.6-162) - Part 2: Literary works (A-F; 70 works; full notes). Appendices A-G (A. Short-title list of works with opus numbers ... E. List of manuscripts, published and unpublished, with locations ... G. List of the principal biographical and critical works on Berlioz and his work). *Class No:* 781.973BER

Bliss

[4031]
FOREMAN, L. Arthur Bliss: catalogue of the complete works. London: Novello, 1980. 159p. £20.00. ISBN: 0853600694.
Principally a classified arrangement, supported by a chronological index. *Class No:* 781.973BLI

Brahms

[4032]
BRAUNSTEIN, J., *ed.* Thematic catalog of the collected works of Brahms. New York, Da Capo, 1973. 175p. $27.50.
First published by Omega Music Corporation, New York, 1956.
Sections: 1. Works with opus numbers - 2. Works without opus numbers - 3. Indices: (a) classified index (b) alphabetical index of titles and first lines of vocal works.
Class No: 781.973BRA

[4033]
McCORKLE, M.L. Johannes Brahms: thematisch bibliographisches Werkverzeichnis. Munich: Henle, 1984. lxxvii, 841p. £95.00. ISBN: 3873280418.
An extensive introduction leads into the main lists of works arranged by opus number, with miscellaneous sections. Copiously indexed. *Class No:* 781.973BRA

Britten

[4034]
BOOSEY AND HAWKES. Benjamin Britten: a complete catalogue of his works. London, Boosey & Hawkes, 1963. 47p.
A chronological list with classified index.
Class No: 781.973BRI

Buxtehude

[4035]
KARSTÄDT, G. Thematisch-systematisches Verzeichnis der musikalischen Werke von Dietrich Buxtehude. Wiesbaden: Breitkopf & Härtel, 1974. xvi, 245p. £16.00. ISBN: 376510065x.
A comprehensive survey in a classified arrangement.
Class No: 781.973BUX

Chopin

[4036]
BROWN, M.J.E. Chopin: an index of his works in chronological order. 2nd ed. New York, Da Capo, 1972. 214p.
First published London: Macmillan, 1960.
Mainly an index with music examples; appendices include a bibliography. Indexes by category, works by opus numbers and works without, general index.
Class No: 781.973CHO

[4037]
KOBYLAŃSKA, K. Frédéric Chopin: thematisch-bibliographisches Werkverzeichnis. Munich: Henle, 1979. xxii, 362p. £45.00. ISBN: 3873280299.
Works are arranged by opus number, followed by unpublished work, posthumous and miscellaneous compositions. There is a good index and extensive bibliography. *Class No:* 781.973CHO

Couperin

[4038]
CAUCHIE, M. Thematic index of the works of François Couperin. Monaco: Lyrebird Press, 1949. 133p..
Divided into published and unpublished works; chronologically arranged. *Class No:* 781.973COU

Debussy

[4039]
LESURE, F. Catalogue de l'oeuvre de Claude Debussy. Geneva: Minkoff, 1977. 167p. £15.00. ISBN: 2826606573.
A chronolgical arrangement with good indexes.
Class No: 781.973DEB

Delius

[4040]
THELFALL, R. Catalogue of the compositions of Frederick Delius: sources and references. London: Delius Trust, 1977. 206p. £10.00. ISBN: 0851620280.
A straightforward classified arrangement. Includes plates of some manuscripts. *Class No:* 781.973DEL

Dvořák

[4041]
BURGHAUSER, J. Antonin Dvořák Thematisches Verzeichnis mit Bibliographie und Übersicht des Leben und des Werkes. Kassell, Alkor-Edibon, 1960. 735p.
Also available in Czech edition.
Three main sections consist of the thematic catalogue, a bibliography, and survey of life and works. Various appendices and indexes. *Class No:* 781.973DVO

Geminiani

[4042]
CARERI, E. Francesco Geminiani (1687-1762): part 1 - life and works; part 2 - thematic catalogue. Oxford, Oxford University Press, 1993. 300p. £45. ISBN: 0198163002.
A well researched catalogue, likely to become the standard work on this composer. *Class No:* 781.973GEM

Grieg

[4043]

FOG, D. Grieg-Katalog. Copenhagen: Dan Fog, 1980. 143p. £8.70. ISBN: 8787099217.

A classified arrangement with index to titles and named persons. *Class No:* 781.973GRI

Gurney

[4044]

PILKINGTON, M. Gurney, Ireland, Quilter and Warlock. London, Duckworth, 1989. x,194p. £14.95p. ISBN: 0715622749.

An annotated list of the complete published song output of each composer. Appendices include notes on poetic sources, bibliography of standard editions, index of titles and first lines, index of poets, and an index by voice.
Class No: 781.973GUR

Handel

[4045]

BELL, A.C. Handel: chronological thematic catalogue. Darley, Grain-Aig Press, 1972. xii,452p.

Several useful appendices; indexes by librettists, titles, classified forms, first lines in English, French, German, Spanish & Italian. *Class No:* 781.973HAN

[4046]

EISEN, W. *and* **EISEN, M. Händel Handbuch.** Leipzig; VEB Deutscher Verlag, and Kassel; Bärenreiter, 1978-1986. 549, 800, 442. 621p. (4v). ISBN: 3761806108, v.1; 3761807155, v.2; 3761807163, v.3; 3761807171, v.4.

Volume 1 (1978) comprises an introduction and lists stage works; the second volume (1984) is a catalogue of vocal music, and volume 3 (1986) of instrumental music; volume 4 contains notes on documents and a scholarly biography (1985). The set will be completed with a fifth volume which is to be principally a bibliography. *Class No:* 781.973HAN

Haydn

[4047]

HOBOKEN, A. van, ***ed.*** **Joseph Haydn.** Thematisch-bibliographische Werkverzeichnis. Mainz, Schott, 1957-1978. 848, 602, 424p. (3v). ISBN: 3795700035.

A very detailed catalogue with bibliographies. Volume one (instrumental works) is divided into twenty sections; volume two covers vocal works, and three contains indexes to collections, and additions and corrections.
Class No: 781.973HAY

Holst

[4048]

HOLST, I. Thematic catalogue of Gustav Holst's music. London: Faber, 1974. xxviii, 285p. £10.00. ISBN: 057110004x.

A chronological arrangement, with adequate indexes and a useful bibliography. *Class No:* 781.973HOL

Ireland

[4049]

CRAGGS, S.R., ***comp.*** **John Ireland:** a catalogue, discography and bibliography. Oxford, Oxford University Press, 1993. 161p. £20. ISBN: 0198163177.

Exhaustive entries show great care and thoroughness; lists

.... (contd.)

of compositions arranged by category and alphabetically, lost and undated works, index of song titles etc.
Class No: 781.973IRE

[4050]

PILKINGTON, M. Gurney, Ireland, Quilter and Warlock. London, Duckworth, 1989. x,194p. £14.95p. ISBN: 0715622749.

An annotated list of the complete published song output of each composer. Appendices include notes on poetic sources, bibliography of standard editions, index of titles and first lines, index of poets, and an index by voice.
Class No: 781.973IRE

Lehar

[4051]

LEHAR MUSEUM. Bad Ischl. **Franz Lehar:** thematic index. London, Glocken Verlag, 1985. 182p. £18.

Compiled from existing printed editions, manuscripts and archive material housed in the Lehar Museum, Bad Ischl, Austria. Alphabetical, thematic and title index.
Class No: 781.973LEH

Marcello Family

[4052]

SELFRIDGE-FIELD, E. The Music of Benedetto and Alessandro Marcello: a thematic catalogue with commentary on the composers, repertory, and sources. Oxford, Oxford University Press, 1990. 517p. ISBN: 0193161265.

A meticulous work, exploring the complex source history of two important pre-Classical figures.
Class No: 781.973MAR

Monteverdi

[4053]

STATTKUS, M.H. Claudio Monteverdi: Verzeichnis der enhaltenen Werke. Bergkamen, Musikverlag Stattkus, 1985. xi,183p. Dm90.

Described as a small edition, and intended as a foretaste of a full thematic catalogue.

Two sections - printed collections and the 9 books of madrigals. Details of sources, arrangements, publishers, editors, anthologies etc. Bibliography and list of relevant libraries. *Class No:* 781.973MON

Mozart

[4054]

KING, A.H. A Mozart legacy: aspects of the British Library collections. London, British Library, 1984. 110p. illus. £11.50. ISBN: 0712300449.

An extremely important collection, rich in autographs and early editions; full list of materials with illustrations.
Class No: 781.973MOZ

[4055]

KÖCHEL, L.R. von. Chronologisch-thematisches Verzeichnis sämtlicher Tonwerke Wolfgang Amadé Mozarts. 7th ed. Weisbaden, Breitkopf & Härtel, 1965. cxliii, 1024p.

Compositions are numbered 1-626, with supplement. Köchel's indispensable authoritative thematic catalogue was published in 1862. Einstein's revision of 1937 was supplemented by a series of lists in *The Music review*, 1940-

....(contd.)
45. Entries, sometimes lengthy give data on first performance, autograph, relevant literature, etc., with music examples. Name and subject indexes.
Class No: 781.973MOZ

Paganini

[4056]

MORIETTI, M.R. *and* **SORRENTO, A. Catálogo tematico delle musiche di Niccolo Paganini.** Genova, Comune di Genova, 1983. xxvi,410p.

Six music sections - datable works, undated works, sketches, lost works, doubtful works, false attributions. Includes information on editions, history, first performances. Bibliography and indexes. *Class No:* 781.973PAG

Poulenc

[4057]

SCHMIDT, C.B. The Music of Francis Poulenc (1899-1963): a catalogue. Oxford, Clarendon Press, 1995. 608p. £65.00. ISBN: 0198163363.

Catalogue occupies p.1-512 with notes on first performance and other notable performances. Appendices list anthologies. Chronology; list of doubtful works. Bibliography p.538-553; indexes of titles, first vocal lines; general index. *Class No:* 781.973POU

Purcell

[4058]

ZIMMERMAN, F.B. Henry Purcell, 1659-1695: an analytical catalogue of his music. London, Macmillan, 1963. xxiv, 575p.

Thematic catalogue, p.1-404 (Sacred vocal works - Secular vocal works - Dramatic music - Instrumental music). 6 appendices (3. Manuscript sources, MS. nos.1-873; 5. Chronology). Indexes: 1. First lines, titles and sub-titles; 2. Instrumental forms and titles; 3. Authors, translations, paraphrasers, and sources of text; 4. General index. Well produced. *Class No:* 781.973PUR

[4059]

ZIMMERMAN, F.B. Henry Purcell: a guide to research. New York, Garland, 1989. 333p. $40. (*Garland Composer Resource Manuals, 18.*) ISBN: 0824077865.

Updates and corrects the author's 1963 *Analytical Catalogue*.

Highly recommended for its bibliographies, classified list of works, lists of editions etc. *Class No:* 781.973PUR

Quilter

[4060]

PILKINGTON, M. Gurney, Ireland, Quilter and Warlock. London, Duckworth, 1989. x,194p. £14.95p. ISBN: 0715622749.

An annotated list of the complete published song output of each composer. Appendices include notes on poetic sources, bibliography of standard editions, index of titles and first lines, index of poets, and an index by voice.
Class No: 781.973QUI

Rachmaninov

[4061]

THRELFALL, R. *and* **NORRIS, G. A Catalogue of the compositions of S. Rachmaninoff.** London, Scolar Press, 1982. 218p. £30. ISBN: 085967617x.

The catalogue is arranged by opus numbers, followed by works without numbers, and arrangements. Details of first performances and recordings are included.
Class No: 781.973RAC

Schoenberg

[4062]

RUFER, J. Works of Arnold Schoenberg: a catalogue of his compositions, writings and paintings. London; Faber. 1962. 214p. £12.00.

First published by Bärenreiter (Kassel) 1959.

Includes details of published works, followed by unpublished compositions, unfinished pieces, and sketches. Also contains details of non-musical activities; extensive descriptions and plates. *Class No:* 781.973SCH

Schubert

[4063]

DEUTSCH, O.E. Schubert: Thematisches Verzeichnis seiner Werke in chronologischer Folge. Kassell, Bärenreiter, 1978. xxiii, 712p. £70.00.

Revision of *Schubert: thematic catalogue of all his works, in chronological order*, by O.E. Deutsch and D.R. Wakeling (London, Dent, 1951). Thematic catalogue with numerous music examples, p.3-644 (dated works 1-965b; undated, 966-998). Appendices 1-3 (1. List of works of doubtful authorship and spurious items); 'Konkordanzen' 1-5 (1. Opus numbers). 6 indexes (general; location of MSS; migration of first editions; librettists; vocal music; instrumental music). The most obvious improvement on the 1951 ed. is 'the presentation of the thematic incipits and vastly superior information on autographs, early manuscripts and first edtions ... This revised edition is obviously essential for any well-equipped music library' (*Brio*, v.16, no.1, Spring 1979, p.20). *Class No:* 781.973SCH

[4064]

REED, J. The Schubert song companion. Manchester, Manchester U.P., 1984. xii,510p. £35. ISBN: 0719010934.

Alphabetical guide providing information on each of the 631 Lieder: date, key, translation, source of text, location of autograph. Critiques extend to several pages for the most significant cycles. Cross-referenced to other commentators; several appendices. *Class No:* 781.973SCH

Strauss Family

[4065]

WEINMANN, A. Verzeichnis sämtlicher Werke von Johann Strauss Vater und Sohn. Vienna: Krenn, 1955. 171p.

Two sections cover father and son; highly condensed layout, no musical examples. *Class No:* 781.973STR

Strauss

[4066]
ASOW, E.H.M. Richard Strauss: thematisches Verzeichnis. Vienna, Doblinger, 1959-1974. 1688p. (3v).

First two volumes cover works with opus numbers; third volume contains works without numbers; systematic, chronological and alphabetical indexes.
Class No: 781.973STR

Stravinsky

[4067]
CAESAR, C. Igor Stravinsky: a complete catalogue. San Francisco, Cal.: San Francisco Press, 1982. 66p. £3.95. ISBN: 0911302417.

Basic data in chronological order, showing durations, instrumentation, dates of first performances.
Class No: 781.973STR

Tchaikovsky

[4068]
JURGENSON, B. Catalogue thématique des oeuvres de P. Tschaikowsky. London: H. Baron, 1965. 168p. £30.00.

Reprint of original edition: Moscow; P. Jurgenson, 1897.

Lists compositions with opus numbers, followed by those without; includes theatrical works and posthumous items. Index to songs. *Class No:* 781.973TCH

Telemann

[4069]
RUHNKE, M., ***ed.*** **Georg Philipp Telemann:** Thematisch-systematisches verzeichnis seine Werke. Instrumentalwerke. Vol.1. Kassel, Bärenreiter, 1984. xi,246p. DM135.

Covers keyboard and lute music, works without continuo, and works for solo instrument with continuo. Thorough system of cross-references. 'Importance to Telemann scholars and editors is unquestionable' (*Music and Letters,* 66(3) July 1985, p.285-6). *Class No:* 781.973TEL

Vaughan Williams

[4070]
KENNEDY, M. A Catalogue of the works of Ralph Vaughan Williams. 2nd.ed. Oxford, Oxford University Press, 1996. xii, 322p. ISBN: 0198165846.

Chronological list of works; bibliography and discography. *Class No:* 781.973VAU

Vivaldi

[4071]
RYOM, P. Répertoire des oeuvres d'Antonio Vivaldi: les compositions instrumentales. Copenhagen: Engstrøm Sødring, 1986. lxxiii, 726p. £45.00. ISBN: 8787091194.

Based on Ryom's *Verzeichnis der Werke Antonio Vivaldis,* 2nd ed. 1980.

A full scale treatment, referring throughout to original documents; historical bias. *Class No:* 781.973VIV

[4072]
RYOM, P. Verzeichnis der Werke Antonio Vivaldis. 2nd ed. Leipzig: VEB Deutscher Verlag, 1980. 226p. £9.00.

First edition 1974, here revised and augmented.

Generally known as RV (Repetoire Vivaldi); deliberately condensed and concise, but aims to be totally comprehensive in coverage. *Class No:* 781.973VIV

Wagner

[4073]
KASTNER, E., ***comp.*** **Wagner-Catalog** Chronologisches Verzeichnis der von und über Richard Wagner erschienenen Schriften, Musikwerke etc. Hilversum, Frits Knuf, 1966. 181p.

Reprint of 1878 edition (Offenbach am Main).

A bibliography of works by and on Wagner, chronologically arranged. Name and subject index.
Class No: 781.973WAG

Walton

[4074]
CRAGGS, S.R. William Walton: a thematic catalogue of his musical works. Rev.ed. Oxford, Oxford University Press, 1990. 273p. ISBN: 0193154331.

Chronological arrangement; excellent introduction, clear layout. Efficiently indexed, and including a bibliography. Winner of the Library Association McColvin Medal for an outstanding reference book. *Class No:* 781.973WAL

Warlock

[4075]
PILKINGTON, M. Gurney, Ireland, Quilter and Warlock. London, Duckworth, 1989. x,194p. £14.95p. ISBN: 0715622749.

An annotated list of the complete published song output of each composer. Appendices include notes on poetic sources, bibliography of standard editions, index of titles and first lines, index of poets, and an index by voice.
Class No: 781.973WAR

Weber

[4076]
JÄHNS, F.W. Carl Maria Von Weber in seinem Werken: chronologisch thematisches Verzeichnis seiner sämtlichen Compositionen. Berlin: Robert Lienau, 1967. 476p. £127.00.

Reprint of original edition: Berlin; Schlesinger, 1871.

A chronological format, with good indexes.
Class No: 781.973WEB

Kinds of Music

Opera & Operettas

Bibliographies

[4077]
MARCO, G.A. Opera: a research and information guide. New York, Garland, 1984. 373p. $45. ISBN: 0824089995.

A selective list of 704 books, with concise annotations which concentrate on the presence of bibliographies and indexes. Opera singers are excluded, although there is some coverage of collective biographies. *Class No:* 782(01)

[4078]
PARSONS, C.H., ***comp.*** **An Opera bibliography.** Lewiston, NY/Lampeter, Edwin Mellen Press, 1995. ix,551p. ISBN: 0889464162.

A massive vol., which forms part of the *Mellen opera reference index.* (*see entry at:* 782(03)) *Class No:* 782(01)

Encyclopaedias & Dictionaries

[4079]

ANDERSON, J. Dictionary of opera. Rev.ed. London, Bloomsbury, 1998. 656p. £18.99. ISBN: 0747538743.

First ed. 1989 as the *Bloomsbury dictionary of opera and operetta.*

5000 entries: composers, singers, roles, conductors, critics, designers, arias, companies, terms, are included. Plot summaries; historical details; literary sources. Opera coverage is good; operetta - which does not include musical comedy - fills a gap in the literature. *Class No:* 782(03)

[4080]

GÄNZL, K. The Encyclopedia of musical theatre. New York, Schirmer, 1994. 1610p.(2v.) $150.00 ISBN: 0028714458.

2700 entries for performers, composers, writers and shows; also some producers, directors, choreographers and designers. Covers only text-based musicals - no opera, pantomimes or reviews. Includes UK, European, US, Australian and New Zealand material, of the 19th and 20th centuries. Basic biographies give lists of works; plot summaries and performance histories. Film adaptations are mentioned. In alphabetical order, with no cross-references, and no index. 'Although seemingly adequately researched, it is not written in a scholarly style...this is a must for music collections.' (*Reference books bulletin,* 1 September, 1994, p.68.) *Class No:* 782(03)

[4081]

GREEN, S. Encyclopedia of the musical film. New ed. New York, Oxford University Press, 1988. 352p. £9.95. (paper). ISBN: 0195054210.

Entries, A-Z, p.3-319. 'Wizard of Oz, The'; 2¾ columns (credits, cast, songs, history and synopsis, TV repeat, 2 references). 'Judy Garland': 1½ columns, with over ½p. list of parts played. 'Succinct information regarding the musical screen's most prominent individuals, productions, and songs. Though emphasis is on Hollywood output (including feature-length cartoons), British musical films and selected original television musicals are also covered' (*Preface*).
Class No: 782(03)

[4082]

HAMILTON, D. The Metropolitan Opera encyclopedia: a companion guide to the world of opera. New York, Simon & Schuster, 1987. 415p. $35.00. ISBN: 067161732x.

Covers 550 works, with synopses, biographies, glossary, and essays on specific aspects. Illustrated, with brief bibliographies. Highly rated (*Choice*, Feb. 1988).
Class No: 782(03)

[4083]

HOLDEN, A., ***ed.*** **The Penguin opera guide.** London, Penguin Books, 1997. 492p. £12.50. ISBN: 014051385x.

Previously issued 1995; abridged revision of the *Viking opera guide* (1993).

Covers 150 composers and 450 operas; arranged alphabetically by composer. 70 contributors have been involved. Entries include an assessment of the composer, plot summaries, musical analysis, edition and recording information, dates, premieres, cast requirements, orchestration. Indexes of librettists and titles.
Class No: 782(03)

[4084]

Kobbé's complete opera book. 11th ed. London, Bodley Head, 1997. xvii,1012p. illus. £45.00. ISBN: 0091814103.

First published 1922. Edited & revised by the Earl of Harewood.

Now a very substantial volume in a larger format, covers 500 operas, of which 200 are new to this edition. A/Z arrangement by composer, with synopses of plots, cast lists, performance histories, brief composer biographies. A thorough revision, with new illustrations and musical examples. *Class No:* 782(03)

[4085]

LARUE, C.S., ***ed.*** **International dictionary of opera.** Detroit, Gale, 1993. 1543p.(2v.) £175.00. ISBN: 1558620818.

1000 entries and 450 illustrations; contains biographies of composers, producers, designers etc, evaluative essays for individual operas, bibliographies for many entries.
Class No: 782(03)

[4086]

PARSONS, C.H., ***comp.*** **Mellen opera reference index.** Lewiston, NY/Lampeter, Edwin Mellen Press, 1986-. $139.00 per vol. on subscription. ISBN: 0889464014, v.1.

Planned as a 22 volume set.

A vast quantity of useful information is being assembled here. Vols. 1-4 (1986) cover *Opera composers and their works,* listing over 40,000 operas by composer, then chronologically, with brief but thorough information; vols.5-6 (1987) cover *Opera librettists and their work,* vols 7-8 (1989) *Opera premieres: a geographical index,* and vol. 9 (1989) *Opera subjects.* Vols 13-14 (1992) and 15-16 (1993) index the casts of opera premieres; vol. 17 (1995) is an opera bibliography. Overall a major series, with some inaccuracies apparent (*Choice* January 1990, p.776). A more recent review still notes several basic problems. (*Choice,* 31(6) February 1994, p.920.) *Class No:* 782(03)

[4087]

SADIE, S., ***ed.*** **New Grove dictionary of opera.** London, Macmillan, 1992. 5424p., illus. (4v.) £550.00. ISBN: 0935859926.

Paperback ed. 1998 (£149.00.)

1300 critics and scholars have contributed 11000 articles; 1800 operas are featured. Contents include performers, composers, opera houses, stagecraft, directors, librettists and literary sources, forms and terms, patrons, conductors. Appendices of role names and arias. 'Superlatives are lacking to describe this wonderful work.' (*Reference books bulletin,* 1 April, 1993, p.1452.) *Class No:* 782(03)

[4088]

STUDWELL, W.E. ***and*** **HAMILTON, D.A. Opera plot index.** New York, Garland, 1990. 480p. $47. ISBN: 0824046218.

Plots and descriptions of all types of opera, operettas, and musicals. Covers all periods. Arrangement is by title, indexed by composer. *Class No:* 782(03)

[4089]

WARRACK, J. ***and*** **WEST, E. The Oxford dictionary of opera.** Oxford, Oxford University Press, 1992. 782p. £27.50. ISBN: 0198691645.

4500 entries, covering terms and topics, cities, countries, operas, companies, houses, established names; some brief biographies; plot summaries. Informative, accurate and scholarly. 'Best such dictionary available.' (*Choice,* 30(8) April 1993, p1302.) *Class No:* 782(03)

[4090]
—WARRACK, J. The Concise Oxford dictionary of opera. 3rd.ed. Oxford, Oxford University Press, 1996. 571p. £8.99. ISBN: 0192800280.

3500 entries cover composers, singers, conductors, producers, designers, opera companies, festivals; plot summaries. *Class No:* 782.03

Dictionaries

[4091]
BARLOW, H. *and* **MORGENSTERN, S. A Dictionary of opera and song themes:** including cantatas, oratorios, lieder and art songs. 2nd. ed. London, Faber, 1983. 547p. £30.00. ISBN: 0571119999.

This ed. originally published by Crown (New York) 1976.

8,000 vocal themes arranged alphabetically by composer, title. Indexes by song title, first line, melody written in alphabetical notation. *Class No:* 782(038)

[4092]
PALLAY, S.G., ***comp*****. Cross index title guide to opera and operetta.** Westport, CT, Greenwood Press, 1989. 222p. $39.95. ISBN: 0313256225.

Vocal and instrumental themes identified from 1,400 works, from all periods. Popular titles and sub-titles, variant names, opening words are given and interlinked. *Class No:* 782(038)

Gazetteers

[4093]
TURNBULL, R. The Opera gazetteer. London, Trefoil, 1988. 244p. £14.95. ISBN: 086294080x.

Basic data and brief histories, repertoires of over 100 major opera houses worldwide. *Class No:* 782(083.86)

Concordances

[4094]
DIXON, G. The Gilbert and Sullivan concordance. New York, Garland, 1988. 1877p. (2v.). $197. ISBN: 0824085051.

Word index to the 14 Savoy operas 1871-1896. Context is given and location in the full text. *Class No:* 782(083.87)

Histories

[4095]
GROUT, D.J. A Short history of opera. 3rd ed. New York, Columbia University Press, 1988. xix,1120p. £44.00. ISBN: 0231061927.

First published 1947.

Six sections cover 16th, 17th, 18th, 19th centuries, Nationalism & opera, 20th century. Scholarly and authoritative; enormous bibliography p.731-825 arranged in chapter order. *Class No:* 782(091)

[4096]
LOEWENBERG, A. Annals of opera 1597-1940. Compiled from the original sources. 3rd ed. London, John Calder, 1978. xxvp. 1756 cols. £30. ISBN: 0714536571.

First published 1941.

4,000 operas discussed in chronological order, with details of dates & first performances. Indexes of titles, composers, librettists. General index. A major source. *Class No:* 782(091)

[4097]
PARKER, R., ***ed*****. The Oxford history of opera.** Oxford, Oxford University Press, 1996. 390p., illus. £11.99. ISBN: 0192840282.

Originally issued in 1994 as the *Oxford illustrated history of opera* - a hardback with lavish illustrations. (ISBN: 0198162820; £25.00.)

12 chapters trace the history from the 17th century to the present, including coverage of staging, singers, and opera as a social occasion. Concise, neat, and readable; thorough index; chapter bibliographies. Some plates are grouped at the centre. *Class No:* 782(091)

Biographies

Bibliographies

[4098]
COWDEN, R.H. Classical singers of the opera and recital stages: a bibliography of biographical materials. New York, Greenwood Press, 1994. 509p. $7500. ISBN: 0313293325.

Extends the coverage of *Concert and opera singers* (1986).

Good compilation of biographical data from scattered sources; now includes cross-references to variant forms of name, professional pseudonyms etc. *Class No:* 782(092)(01)

[4099]
COWDEN, R.H., ***comp*****. Concert and opera conductors:** a bibliography of biographical materials. Westport, CT, Greenwood Press, 1987. 301p. $35. ISBN: 0313256209.

A guide to sources of biographical information on 1250 major figures, from mid-nineteenth century to the present. *Class No:* 782(092)(01)

Great Britain

[4100]
ADAM, N., ***ed*****. Who's who in British opera.** Aldershot, Gower Publishing, 1993. 339p. £19.95. ISBN: 1859280447.

Covers active names only; includes foreign artists who regularly appear in the UK. Contents include singers, conductors, composers, instrumentalists, librettists, directors, designers, administrators, teachers and critics. 500 names in alphabetical order with personal and professional details and contact address. *Class No:* 782(092)(410)

Great Britain

[4101]
GÄNZL, K. The British musical theatre. London: Macmillan, 1986. x, 1196, ix, 1258p. (2v). ISBN: 0333419545, set.

First colume covers 1865-1914 in a chronological arrangement; introduction to each year, then details of productions, first-performance cast lists. Appendices of published music and recordings. Index covers composers, authors, librettists, lyricists, producers, directors, and theatres. Second volume similar, covers 1915-1984. Winner of the McColvin Medal 1987. *Class No:* 782(410)

England

Histories

[4102]

WHITE, E.W. A History of English opera. London, Faber, 1983. 472p. £30.00.

5 parts; 1. Tentative beginnings: 16th and 17th centuries - 2. Representations in the 17th century (culminating in Purcell) - 3. Serious operas, comic operas, masques, ballad operas, burlettas and pasticcios in the 18th century - 4. Romantic opera in the 19th century - 5. Laying permanent foundations: 20th century. 4 interludes and a postlude; summary and projection. Appendix: 'Rules and regulations of the Royal English Opera'. Well footnoted. 40 illus. Non-analytical index, p.443-72. Rich in anecdote and out-of-the-way information. *Class No:* 782(420)(091)

USA

[4103]

BORDMAN, G. American musical theatre: a chronicle. 2nd.ed. Oxford, Oxford University Press, 1992. viii,821p. £45. ISBN: 0195072421.

12 chapters. 1. Prologue: origins to 1866 ... 6. The birth of the modern musical, 1914-1921 ... 8. The golden age of the American musical, 1924-37 ... 10. The American musical as a conscious art form, 1942-1965 - 11. Exhaustion, 1965-1969. - 12. Full circle - new British trends 1969-90. For each musical: plot synopses; physical production, and principal statistics; biographies of actors, songwriters, librettists and producers. Examples of lyrics and dialogue. Appendix, - US provincial shows. Non-analytical indexes of shows and sources, songs and people. *Class No:* 782(73)

[4104]

ZIETZ, K.L. Opera companies and houses of the United States: a comprehensive illustrated reference. Jefferson, NC, McFarland, 1994. 336p., illus. $49.95. ISBN: 089950955x.

90 companies are included, from major city enterprises to fledgling companies in small conurbations. Arranged by state, then city. History of opera in each city is given, inaugural performances, staff, repertory, premieres. Illustrations show interiors and exteriors. Index of titles of operas, composers, artistic directors, companies' names. Bibliography. *Class No:* 782(73)

Chronologies

[4105]

FITZGERALD, G., *ed.* Annals of the Metropolitan Opera: the complete chronicle of performances and artists. Boston, G.K. Hall, 1990. 1,313p. (2v.), illus. $185. ISBN: 081618903x.

Vol. one contains a performance-by-performance record of 100 seasons, with introduction to each season, roster of artists, conductors, designers etc., and a chronological list with full cast details. Vol. two consists of tables showing career details of 5,000 individuals, through 21,872 events, & acts as a name index; an index at the end of v.2 guides to the relevant tables. *Class No:* 782(73)(090)

Sacred & Church Music

[4106]

DIEHL, K.S. Hymns and tunes: an index. Metuchen, NJ, Scarecrow, 1966.

Covers 78 Protestant hymnals with entries for 12,000 hymns by first line, author, composer, tune name, and opening notes. *Class No:* 783

[4107]

POULTNEY, D. Dictionary of western church music. Chicago, American Library Association, 1991. 234p. $40.00. ISBN: 0838905692.

Identifies and defines terms used in six Christian traditions - Roman Catholic, Anglican, Episcopalian, Lutheran, Methodist and Baptist. About 80 composers have entries; there are some musical examples. Uneven treatment is apparent in places. Appendices list church music publishers, societies, and periodicals. *Class No:* 783

[4108]

STUDWELL, W.E. Christmas carols: a reference guide. New York, Garland, 1984. 278p. $34. ISBN: 0824088999.

Provides information and historical notes on over 700 carols. *Class No:* 783

[4109]

TEMPERLEY, N. The Hymn tune index: a census of English-language hymn tunes in printed sources from 1535 to 1820. Oxford, Clarendon Press, 1997. 1,888p. (4v.) £300.00. ISBN: 0193111500.

A work of extraordinary thoroughness, which must be the standard souce for decades to come. Bibliographic references are given. *Class No:* 783

Bibliographies

[4110]

VON ENDE, R.C. Church music: an international bibliography. Metuchen, Scarecrow, 1980. xx, 453p. $22.50.

5,445 unannotated entries, involving *c.* 25 languages. 'The books included are principally those of the Western world and, to a considerable extent, of the Christian Church. Subject arrangement, Abbeys ... Yearbooks. Note group headings, *e.g.* 'Hymns and hymn tunes', 'Dictionaries, lexicons and glossaries', 'Personalities', 'National and/or Geographic entities'. Profuse cross-references.
Class No: 783(01)

Concordances

[4111]

McDORMAND, T.B. Judson concordance to hymns. New York, Judson, 1965.

First lines of 2,400 hymns are indexed by each word.
Class No: 783(083.87)

Histories

[4112]

BLUME, F., *and others*. Protestant church music: a history. London, Gollancz, 1975. 831p. £15.00.

A standard source, with extensive bibliography and musical examples. *Class No:* 783(091)

[4113]
PORTE, J. Encyclopédie des musiques sacrées. Paris, Editions Labergerie, 1968-1970. 3v.

1. *Le Sacré en Extrême-Ouest. Méditerranée. Afrique et Amérique.*

2. *Traditions chrétiennes, des premiers siécles aux cultes révolutionnaires.*

3. *Traditions chrétiennes (suite et fin), du Concordat à Vatican II.*

V.3 (682p.) has 112 contributors. France (p.69-198); the other countries of Europe, A-Z (p.199-336); England, (p.320-7, with bibliography and discography). Signed articles. No indexes, but detailed contents. A well-documented source-book. Some unevenness of treatment is noted in *Bulletin des bibliothèques de France*, v.20, no.8, August 1975, entry 1841. *Class No:* 783(091)

Biographies

[4114]
HUMPHREYS, M. Dictionary of composers for the Church in Great Britain and Ireland. London, Mansell, 1997. xiii,368p. £60.00. ISBN: 0720123305.

Authoritative and thorough; work-lists are given. Bibliography p.xi-xiii. *Class No:* 783(092)

Great Britain

[4115]
HOFMAN, M. *and* MOREHEN, J., *comps*. Latin music in British sources, *c.*1485-1610. London, Stainer & Bell, 1987. xiv,176p. £45. (*Early English Church Music, supplementary volume* 2.) ISBN: 0852496737.

Inventory of Latin works by British composers, with details of source. Checklists of Latin works by foreign composers available in British sources. First line index, and musical incipits of anonymous compositions.
Class No: 783(410)

England

[4116]
LONG, K. The Music of the English church. London, Hodder & Stoughton, 1991. 480p. £35. ISBN: 0340149620.

Explores the growth and development of the art of liturgical music, the circumstances of its writing and performance, and its place in a wider European culture.
Class No: 783(420)

[4117]
ROUTLEY, E. A Short history of English church music. Rev.ed. London, Mowbray, 1997. 146p., illus. ISBN: 0264674405.

Previous ed. 1977; this ed. has been expanded and revised by L. Dakers.

Useful and concise account, efficiently up-dated.
Class No: 783(420)

[4118]
TEMPERLEY, N. The Music of the English parish church. Cambridge, CUP, 1979. 447, 213p. (2v). £56.00.

'It tells what the music was like in English parish churches of different kinds at each period; traces the many changes in their music; and tries to explain why they occurred' (*Preface*, v.1). V.1 (10 chapters): 1. The significance of parish church music - 2. The Reformation era (1534-59) - 3. The establishment of Anglicanism (1559-1644) - 4. Commonwealth and Restoration (1644-1700) - 5. Urban parish church music (1600-1700) - 6. Country psalmody

....*(contd.)*
(1685-1830) - 7. Reform movements (1760-1830) - 8. The rediscovery of tradition - 9. The Victorian settlement (1850-1900) - 10. The twentieth century. Appendix 1: Collegiate parish churches and others endowed for church music; 2: Changing conditions in Sussex parish churches (1853-1976). Bibliography, p.359-415 (1. Manuscript sources; 2. Printed sources of music; 3. Other sources). Detailed, partly analytical index, p.416-47. V.2 consists largely of music examples (p.21-213). *Class No:* 783(420)

USA

Bibliographies

[4119]
DEVENNEY, D.P. Early American choral music: an annotated guide. Berkeley, Cal., Fallen Leaf Press, 1988. xxii,150p. $19.95. ISBN: 0914913093.

Late seventeenth and early nineteenth century works, covering both English-speaking Protestant and Moravian communities. Extensive indexes and an annotated bibliography with its own subject index.
Class No: 783(73)(01)

Tudor & Stuart Times

[4120]
DAY, T., *comp*. A Discography of Tudor church music. London, British Library, 1989. 317p., illus. ISBN: 0712305033.

Valuable introduction, followed by listings in chronological, composer, and performer order; attempts to list all commercial recordings, and the National Sound Archives' holdings of BBC Transcription Services discs and BBC Broadcast recordings. *Class No:* 783"1485-1760"

Liturgical Music

[4121]
WILSON, R.M. Anglican chant and chanting in England, Scotland and America 1660-1820. Oxford, Clarendon Press, 1996. xix,332p. £45.00. ISBN: 0198164246.

Standard history of chant outside the Catholic tradition; scholarly and comprehensive. Bibliography p.307-323.
Class No: 783.2

Gregorian Chant

[4122]
BRYDEN, J.P. *and* HUGHES, D.G., *comps*. An Index of Gregorian chant. Cambridge, Mass., Harvard University Press, 1969. 456, 353p. (2v).

Volume one is an alphabetical index, volume two a thematic index, to nineteen standard sources. Excludes Ambrosian chant. *Class No:* 783.5

[4123]
HILEY, D. Western plainchant: a handbook. Oxford, Oxford University Press, 1995. 760p., illus. £30.00. ISBN: 0198162898.

Traces the history of chant from the 8th century; all genres are covered, liturgical variants, notations. Repertory explored, with relationships between Gregorian, Old-Roman, Milanese, Spanish and other traditions considered. Important musicians and centres of composition are discussed. Illustrated with over 200 musical examples. *Class No:* 783.5

[4124]
WEBER, J.F., *comp*. A Gregorian Chant discography. Utica, NY, J.F. Weber, 1990. xxxv,380,424p. (2v.).
Vol. 1 includes recordings listed by company, with appendix of other types of chants; Vol.2 lists the chants by source, with indexes by performer and conductor. Bibliography p.xxxi-v. *Class No:* 783.5

Vocal Music

[4125]
BARLOW, H. *and* MORGENSTERN, S. A Dictionary of opera and song themes: including cantatas, oratorios, lieder and art songs. 2nd. ed. London, Faber, 1983. 547p. £30.00. ISBN: 0571119999.
This ed. originally published by Crown (New York) 1976.
8,000 vocal themes arranged alphabetically by composer, title. Indexes by song title, first line, melody written in alphabetical notation. *Class No:* 784

[4126]
DE CHARMS, D. *and* BREED, P.F. Songs in collections: an index. Detroit, Information Co-ordinators, 1966. $38.00. ISBN: 0911772537.
Covers collections published 1940-1957, and hence useful to supplement Sears'. Arranged in broad categories. *Class No:* 784

[4127]
JACOBS, D. Who wrote that song? New York, Betterway Publications, 1988. 415p. $29.95. ISBN: 1558701087.
Simple listings by year, composer, performer, group. Includes 11,000 songs by over 5,000 composers, and lists of award-winners. Amateurish appearance, but successful in use. *Class No:* 784

[4128]
LAX, R. *and* SMITH, F. The Great song thesaurus. 2nd ed. Oxford, OUP, 1988. 774p. £40.00. ISBN: 0195054083.
Includes over 11,000 songs published up to 1986. Extensive system of cross references; indexes by key word, key line, lyricists, subject, and category. Inventory of significant songs 1558-1986. *Class No:* 784

[4129]
LEIGH, R., *comp*. Index to song books: a title index to over 11,000 copies of almost 6,800 songs in 111 song books. New York, Da Capo, 1973. 242p. $29.50. ISBN: 0306705532.
Reprint of 1964 edition.
Covers publications 1933-1962, and thus supplements Sears' *Song Index*. *Class No:* 784

[4130]
PHILLIPS, L. Lieder line by line and word for word. Rev.ed. Oxford, Oxford University Press, 1996. 434p. £13.99. ISBN: 0198790171.
Previous ed. Duckworth, 1979.
Complete index to the works of almost all significant Lieder composers; text in English and German. *Class No:* 784

[4131]
SEARS, M.E., *ed*. Song index: an index to more than 12,000 songs in 177 song collections. New York, Shoe String, 1966.
Originally published 1926, with a supplement 1934.
Dictionary catalogue arrangement by title, composer, lyricist, first line. A much-respected standard source, but now largely superseded. *Class No:* 784

Bibliographies

[4132]
ANDERSON, K.H. Catalogue of sets of vocal music. 2nd ed. London, LASER, 1989. 2v. £46. ISBN: 0903764245.
Lists material available in public libraries in the London & South-East Library Region. Volume two contains indexes by composer, arranger, editor, titles. Reckoned sufficiently comprehensive to serve as a guide to published vocal music generally. *Class No:* 784(01)

[4133]
COFFIN, B. Singer's repertoire. 2nd ed. Metuchen, NJ, Scarecrow, 1960-1962. 5v. $100.00. ISBN: 0810801876.
7,500 classical solo songs arranged by voice range and song category. *Class No:* 784(01)

[4134]
ESPINA, N. Repertoire for the solo voice: a fully annotated guide to works for the solo voice published in modern editions and covering material from the thirteenth century to the present. Metuchen, NJ, Scarecrow, 1977. 2v. $70.00. ISBN: 0810809435.
Classified arrangement of over 10,000 titles, mainly classical; divided by country. Range and difficulty indicated. *Class No:* 784(01)

[4135]
GOLECKE, T. Literature for voice: index of songs in collections and source book for teachers of singing. Metuchen NJ, London: Scarecrow Press, 1984. 223p. $37.50. ISBN: 0810817020.
Indexes sixty collections and anthologies, showing range. Composer index, title index. Audio list pp173-179. Bibliography pp159-172. *Class No:* 784(01)

[4136]
LINCOLN, H.B. The Italian madrigal and related repertoires: indexes to printed collections, 1500-1600. London, Yale University Press. 1988. ix,1139p. £70. ISBN: 0300036833.
Composer arrangement with alphabetical list of titles and musical incipit of each part. Text incipit and RISM siglum of the source also given. Anonymous works listed at the end. *Class No:* 784(01)

[4137]
ROY, S. Art song: the secondary literature. *Choice*, December 1995; p.577-586.
Art song is defined as music for voice and written (rather than improvised) accompaniment, usually piano, set to texts of relatively high literary quality. The article discusses studies before 1980; bibliographic series; monographic song studies; German and Austrian song; French song; English song; American song; women, African Americans and art song; music and poetry; translations and pronunciation guides. *Class No:* 784(01)

[4138]
VILLAMIL, V.E. A Singer's guide to the American art song, 1870-1980. Metuchen,NJ, Scarecrow Press, 1993. 452p. $49.50. ISBN: 0810827743.
146 composer entries and various appendices, indexes and lists. Gives biographies and bibliographies. Useful to supplement Coffin. Review in *Choice* (31(1)June 1994, p1564.) notes many weaknesses but agrees that it fills a gap. *Class No:* 784(01)

England

[4139]

BANFIELD, S. Sensibility and English song: critical studies of the early twentieth century. Cambridge, CUP, 1989. xvii,619p. £19.50. ISBN: 052137944x.

Originally issued in 2v., 1985.

Includes lists of songs by 54 composers, arranged chronologically under each, and all indexed alphabetically in a 77 page, 3 column sequence. Composition and publication dates and text authors given. 'An excellent reference tool' (*Brio* 22(1) p.28-29). *Class No:* 784(420)

USA

[4140]

BLOOM, K. American song: the complete musical theatre companion. 2nd.ed. New York, Schirmer Books/London, Prentice Hall International, 1996. 2093p (2v.) $175.00. ISBN: 0028704843.

Previous ed. 1985.

Arranged A/Z by show title with performance data, personnel, source material, all songs, and commentary. No plot summaries. Adds 1800 musicals to those documented in the 1st.ed. Index to 70,000 songs and 27,000 people. *Class No:* 784(73)

[4141]

—BLOOM, K. Hollywood song: the complete film and musical companion. New York, Facts on File, 1995. 3v. $195.00. ISBN: 0816020027.

In the same style as the work above; arranged A/Z by film title. *Class No:* 784(73)

[4142]

EWEN, D. American songwriters. New York; H.W. Wilson, 1987. xi, 489p. £60.00. ISBN: 0824207440.

Includes 146 biographies of composers and lyricists, covering 150 years. Ranges over folk music, country and western, rock, jazz, tin-pan alley, R & B, minstrelsy, shows, film music. Performance histories of over 5,000 songs. Brief bibliographies. *Class No:* 784(73)

[4143]

HISCHAK, T.S. The American musical theatre song encyclopedia. Westport, CT, Greenwood Press, 1995. 543p. $59.95. ISBN: 0313294070.

Encyclopedia of songs from Broadway shows, covering 1866 to the 1993/94 season. Includes 1800 songs from over 500 musicals, with data on authors, original performers, dates, history of recordings, and description of each song. Index of titles, shows, authors, and performers. Glossary of terms, and a brief bibliography. *Class No:* 784(73)

[4144]

SUSKIN, S. Berlin, Kern, Rodgers, Hart, and Hammerstein: a complete song catalogue. Jefferson, NC, McFarland, 1990. 336p. $55. ISBN: 089950471x.

Includes all known songs, with production dates, publishers etc. Valuable bibliography appended. Indexed. *Class No:* 784(73)

Ballads

Bibliographies

[4145]

RICHMOND, W.E. Ballad scholarship: an annotated bibliography. New York and London, Garland, 1989. xxvii,356p. $38. (*Garland folklore bibliographies.*) ISBN: 0824089324.

.... *(contd.)*

A classified list of over 1,600 books and articles (most of them published in the 20th century) covering all aspects of ballard scholarship. 13 sections, of which E., 'Ballad theory', is the largest with 440 entries. Section D. lists 69 bibliographies and research tools. Concise evaluations. Author and subject indexes. *Class No:* 784.3(01)

Folk Songs

[4146]

The Oxford book of sea songs. Palmer, R., *ed.* Oxford, OUP, 1986. xxx,343p. illus. ISBN: 0192141597.

Useful introduction; 159 songs with sources noted. Bibliography; glossary of nautical terms; index of titles & first lines. *Class No:* 784.4

[4147]

SHAPIRO, N. *and* **POLLOCK, B.,** ***eds*****. Popular music: an annotated guide to American popular songs** , including introductory essays, lyricists and composers index, important performance index, awards index, and list of publishers. Detroit/London, Gale Research. ISSN: 0886442x.

Originally published as eight volumes by Adrian Press, 1964-1981 (vols. 1-6) and Gale Research (vols. 7-8). The series continues on an annual basis, and early volumes have been re-issued in a standard format. Coverage is now from 1920 to 1984 (vols 1-9) in 5 or 10 year steps, with a preliminary volume covering 1900-1919. Latest vol. published is that for 1993 (1994).

Described in the introduction as a 'selective, annotated list of the significant popular songs of our times.' Recent volumes index by title, composer and lyricist in a dictionary catalogue arrangement. Annotations are very brief. *Class No:* 784.4

[4148]

WHITE, M. You must remember this...: popular songwriters 1900-1980. London Warne, 1983. x,304p. £5.95. ISBN: 0723231877.

Alphabetical coverage of 130 songwriters, including major compositions. Indexes of titles, composers, lyricists, performers, shows and films. *Class No:* 784.4

Bibliographies

[4149]

BRUNNINGS, F.E. Folk song index: a comprehensive guide to the Florence E. Brunnings collection. New York, Garland, 1981. 357p. $91.00. ISBN: 082409462x.

Indexes over one thousand books and journals, and nearly 700 recordings, covering 50,000 songs. Arranged by title or first line, with cross references. *Class No:* 784.4(01)

[4150]

FERGUSON, G.L., ***comp*****. Song finder;** a title index to 32,000 popular songs in collections, 1854-1992. Westport, CT, Greenwood Press, 1995. 344p. $79.50. ISBN: 0313294704.

Indexes the contents of 621 songbooks; simple title index with cross -references. Probably one third of the songs, over two-thirds of the books, have not been indexed in any other source. The songbooks include theatre, folk, children's, African American, military, patriotic, pop, rock, country music, movie and TV themes, advertising jingles. A project of the State Library of Louisiana. *Class No:* 784.4(01)

[4151]
GOODFELLOW, W.D. SongCite: an index to popular songs. Hamden, CT, Garland, 1995. 433p. $60.00. ISBN: 0815320590.
Identifies 7000 popular songs published or republished in 248 music books since 1988. 350 compositions are listed as anonymous. *Class No:* 784.4(01)

[4152]
GREEN, J. The Green book of songs by subject: the thematic guide to popular music. 4th.ed. Nashville, TN, Professional Desk Reference, 1994. 725p. $64.95. ISBN: 0939735040.
Indexes 21,000 songs (mainly 1950 onwards) under 800 subject headings, based on keywords in the title or the subject of the song. Cross references. Information on performer, album and label is given to assist tracing recordings. A successful idea. *Class No:* 784.4(01)

[4153]
HAVLICE, P.P. Popular song index. Metuchen, NJ, Scarecrow, 1975-89. $175.00. ISBN: 081080820x.
Supplements have been published in 1978, 1984 and 1989.
The volumes cover collections of songs, both adult and childrens; title, first line, and chorus access. The third supplement contains 875 pages and adds 24,000 references to 181 anthologies published 1979-87. *Class No:* 784.4(01)

[4154]
POPSI: the popular song index. Boston Spa, British Library, 1990-. ISSN: 09585702.
Annual; printed version, microfiche edition and diskette.
Title index of songs in popular music anthologies held at BLDSC, 'from music hall to the current top ten'. Includes the contents of about 400 anthologies (BLDSC shelfmarks are given). Indexing on the database version allows for searching by single words or parts of titles.
Class No: 784.4(01)

Encyclopaedias & Dictionaries

[4155]
GAMMOND, P. The Oxford companion to popular music. Oxford, University Press, 1991. 204p. £25. ISBN: 0193113236.
Examines all aspects of Anglo-American popular music, from operetta to blues & folk. Includes historical material, performer and composer biographies, styles, instruments, songs, shows. *Class No:* 784.4(03)

[4156]
LOWE, L. Directory of popular music 1900-1980. 2nd ed. Droitwich, Worcs: Peterson Publishing Co, 1986. 1440p. £33.75. ISBN: 0904702022.
Arranged in nine sections comprising a chronological list followed by stage shows, films, directory of publishers, award winners, song contest winners. Novello award nominations, theme & signature tunes, title index.
Class No: 784.4(03)

[4157]
STAMBLER, I. *and* **LANDON, G. The Encyclopedia of folk, country and western music.** 2nd ed. New York, St. Martin's Press, 1983. 902p. $50.00.
400 entries, wide coverage; regarded as a standard source.
Class No: 784.4(03)

England

[4158]
DEAN-SMITH, M. A Guide to English folk song collections 1822-1952. Liverpool University Press in association with EFDSS, 1954. 120p.
Several hundred songs listed under title with variants and sources. *Class No:* 784.4(420)

Bibliographies

[4159]
ATKINSON, D. English folk song: an introductory bibliography based on the holdings of the Vaughan Williams Memorial Library of the English Folk Dance and Song Society. London, English Folk Dance and Song Society, 1996. 47p. ISBN: 0854181717.
Brief shelf-list of this important collection.
Class No: 784.4(420)(01)

[4160]
The Vaughan Williams Memorial Library Catalogue of the English Folk Dance and Song Society. London, Mansell, 1973. 783p. £25.00.
Re-issued on 14 microfiche 1975.
Covers acquisitions to 1971; about 17,000 entries in author and subject sequences. *Class No:* 784.4(420)(01)

Yearbooks & Directories

[4161]
BRITISH COUNTRY MUSIC ASSOCIATION. Yearbook. London, BCMA. c120p.
Directory section covers soloists, groups, instrumentalists etc. Also record companies and publishers. Large quantity of advertising. *Class No:* 784.4(420)(058)

[4162]
ENGLISH FOLK DANCE AND SONG SOCIETY. Folk directory London, EFDSS. c78p.
Annual.
Details of the Society, educational facilities, library. Classified directory section. Details of publishers, periodicals, organizations, festivals.
Class No: 784.4(420)(058)

USA

Bibliographies

[4163]
HORN, D. *and* **JACKSON, R. Literature of American music in books and folk music collections:** a fully annotated bibliography. Supplement 1. Metuchen, NJ, Scarecrow, 1988. 570p. $49.50. ISBN: 081081997x.
Basic volume published 1977.
A substantial supplement, more than doubling the number of titles listed in the basic volume. Over 2,000 titles, mainly in popular music fields. Classified arrangement.
Class No: 784.4(73)(01)

[4164]
MILLER, T.E. Folk music in America: a reference guide. New York, Garland, 1986. xx, 424p. $40.00. ISBN: 0824089359.
Annotated bibliographies, divided into nine chapters, each briefly introduced. Well indexed; good coverage of the popular press. 'An excellent starting point'. (*Reference Services Review* 17, March 1989). *Class No:* 784.4(73)(01)

[4165]
SCHUURSMA, A.B. Ethnomusicology research: a select annotated biliography. New York, Garland, 1992. 192p. $30.00. ISBN: 082405735x.

Covers 468 publications from 1960, on methods, theories, and approaches. In five categories - history, theory and method, fieldwork technique, musical analysis, related publications. English language material only; descriptive annotations of about 50 words each.
Class No: 784.4(73)(01)

Histories

[4166]
SANJEK, R. American popular music and its business: the first four hundred years. Oxford, OUP, 1988. 469, 482, 734p. (3v). £95.00. ISBN: 0195040287, v.1; 0195043103, v.2; 0195043111, v.3.

Concentrates on economic and business concerns, in classical and popular fields. Examines public concerts, religion, performing rights, recording industry, contracts, copyright, patronage, publishers etc. Excellent bibliographies. 'Unlikely to be superseded for many decades such is the range of scholarship and the depth and thoroughness of the examination.' (*Choice*, 1989, p.816).
Class No: 784.4(73)(091)

Children's Songs

[4167]
CUSHING, H.G., *comp*. Children's song index: an index to more than 22,000 songs in 189 collections. St. Clair Shores, MI, Scholarly Press; 1977. $125.00. ISBN: 0403072107.

Reprint of 1936 edition.

Dictionary catalogue arrangement featuring titles, first lines, composers, lyricists, and subjects. *Index to children's songs* updates this volume. *Class No:* 784.67

[4168]
PETERSON, C.S. *and* FENTON, A.D., *comps*. Index to children's songs: a title, first line, and subject index. New York, Wilson, 1979. 318p. $33.00. ISBN: 082420638x.

Continues Cushing's *Children's song index* and covers collections published 1909-1977. *Class No:* 784.67

National Anthems

[4169]
REED, W.L. *and* BRISTOW, M.J., *eds*. National anthems of the world. 9th ed. London, Cassell, 1997. 607p. £60.00. ISBN: 0304349259.

Over 195 nations listed alphabetically; gives piano score, notes on composer, lyricist, transliterations, translations into English. List of national days. *Class No:* 784.71

Instrumental Music

Bibliographies

[4170]
BROWN, H.M. Instrumental music printed before 1600: a bibliography. London, OUP, 1966. xi, 559p.

Chronological descriptive bibliography of all the volumes of instrumental music published between the 1480s and 1599 (p.9-435). Includes volumes 'known to have existed but now

....*(contd.)*

lost, as well as those still extant' (*Introduction*). List of works cited, p.441-69. 5 indexes: 1. List of libraries and their holdings - 2. Volumes described, arranged by types of notation - 3. Volumes described, arranged by performing medium - 4. Names - 5. First lines and titles (*c.*8,000 entries) - Scholarly, well produced. *Class No:* 785(01)

Orchestral Music

[4171]
ADEY, C. Orchestral performance: a guide for conductors and players. London, Faber, 1998. 868p. £25.00. ISBN: 0571177247.

An outstanding new title, covering fundamental principles; performance technique instrument by instrument; instilling quality of performance; the orchestra as a whole; general considerations and repertoire. Abundant musical examples.
Class No: 785.1

[4172]
ARONOWSKY, S. Performing times of orchestral works. London, Benn, 1959. xxix, 802p. £25.00.

15,000 works listed by composer; details of instrumentation, duration of each movement.
Class No: 785.1

[4173]
DEL MAR, N. A Companion to the orchestra. London, Faber, 1987. vii, 266p. £9.95. ISBN: 0571147356.

Covers all orchestral instruments, note values, terms, full cross references. Inexpensive ready reference guide.
Class No: 785.1

[4174]
PERONE, J.E., *comp*. Orchestration theory: a bibliography. Westport, CT/London, Greenwood Press, 1996. 183p., illus. $65.00. ISBN: 0313295964.

Lists articles and 300 books - mainly orchestration manuals, but also including monographs and theses dealing with orchestration practice. Covers the symphony orchestra, band, jazz ensemble, choral writing. Appendices include a chronological list of treatises. Cross referencing and indexing appear sound. *Class No:* 785.1

Abbreviations & Symbols

[4175]
READ, G. Thesaurus of orchestral devices. London, Pitman, 1953. xxi, 631p.

A lexicon of instrumentation, the references being to orchestral music published in minature form, 7 parts (71 chapters): The instruments of the orchestra - Woodwinds - Brass - Percussion - Keyboard instruments - Harp - Strings. List of publishers and of composers and their works. Indexes: notation; nomenclature; terminology, etc. Supplements standard works on orchestration. Well produced. *Class No:* 785.1(003)

Bibliographies

[4176]
British union catalogue of orchestral sets. 2nd ed. Boston Spa, British Library in cooperation with IAML/UK, 1987. £45.00. ISBN: 071232044x.

One supplement has been issued.

BUCOS lists orchestral sets held in 66 UK libraries. 10,000 entries are included with up to 35 holding libraries

.... *(contd.)*
listed for each set. Details given include composers, title, publishers, orchestration, duration, and the lending policy of each library. *Class No:* 785.1(01)

[4177]

NATIONAL FEDERATION OF MUSIC SOCIETIES. Catalogue of orchestral works 1976 and first supplement. London: NFMS, 1983. v.p. £3.00.

Reissue of the 1976 catalogue incorporating new sections.

Includes orchestral music, string orchestra music, concertos by instrument; new sections comprise new contents page and introduction, amendments to 1976 catalogue, supplement of new items, and a new section devoted to solo voice and orchestra. *Class No:* 785.1(01)

[4178]

RASMUSSEN, R.M. Recorded concert band music, 1950-1987: a selected, annotated listing. Jefferson, NC, McFarland, 1988. xi,442p. ISBN: 0899503187.

Brief survey, followed by the listing, arranged in composer order. Index includes composers, titles, groups, album titles, conductor, instruments etc.
Class No: 785.1(01)

Indexes

[4179]

PALLAY, S.G., ***comp*****. Cross index title guide to classical music.** New York, Greenwood, 1987. ix, 206p. $35.00. ISBN: 0313255318.

6,000 entries covering the works of 220 composers. Standard titles are given with popular and alternative variants. *Class No:* 785.1(014)

[4180]

RABSON, C. Orchestral excerpts: a comprehensive index. San Francisco, Fallen Leaf, 1993. 221p. $35.00. ISBN: 0914913263.

Indexes published orchestral excerpts by composer, then title, giving details of instrumentation and reference to sourcebooks. Cross lists of instruments. Very clear and usable. *Class No:* 785.1(014)

Histories

[4181]

KOURY, D.J. Orchestral performance practices in the nineteenth century: size, proportions and seating. New York, UMI, 1986. 427p. $65. ISBN: 083571649x.

A scholarly volume, regarded as an essential guide to the performance of nineteenth century music; illustrated with typical seating plans. *Class No:* 785.1(091)

[4182]

WHITWELL, D. The history and literature of the wind band and wind ensemble. Northbridge, CA, Winds, 1982-3. 9v. (ring bound). $335.

Volumes 1-5 cover the history of wind groups divided chronologically: pre-1500, renaissance, baroque, classical, nineteenth century. Volumes 6-9 consist of a catalogue of relevant music. The historical sections are arranged nationally and quote early sources. (Reviewed in *Brio* 22(1) p.25-27). *Class No:* 785.1(091)

Biographies

[4183]

COWDEN, R.H., ***comp*****. Concert and opera conductors:** a bibliography of biographical materials. Westport, CT, Greenwood Press, 1987. 301p. $35. ISBN: 0313256209.

A guide to sources of biographical information on 1250 major figures, from mid-nineteenth century to the present.
Class No: 785.1(092)

[4184]

COWDEN, R.H., ***comp*****. Instrumental virtuosi:** a bibliography of biographical materials. Westport, CT, Greenwood Press, 1989. 349p. $49.95. ISBN: 0313260753.

Three sections cover collected works on virtuosi, related collected works, and works on individual artists - some 1200 figures from all kinds of musical life. Useful appendices.
Class No: 785.1(092)

Symphonies

[4185]

LARUE, J. A Catalogue of eighteenth-century symphonies: volume one - thematic identifier. Bloomington, Indiana U.P., 1988. xvi,352p. $29.50. ISBN: 0253313635.

16,558 entries include many less well known composers. Incipits are represented by a combination of letter names and numerals; symphonies are listed in chromatically ascending order of key. Composers' surnames are preceded by a code referring to a full table of names. This volume was to be the first of three: the remaining two (still not published 1995) will reproduce the same data but substituting full thematic musical incipits. *Class No:* 785.11

Brass Bands

[4186]

TAYLOR, A.R. Brass bands. London, Granada, 1979. x,356p. illus. ISBN: 0246110821.

3 parts: 1. History of the brass band movement (up to the 1970s) - 2. Events and occasions (festivals, contests and championships) - 3. Appendices; 1. Contest results; 2. A brass band contest calendar; 3. Discography; 4. B.B.C radio broadcasting. 5 Salvation Army. Detailed, partly analytical index. No bibliography. *Class No:* 785.12

Bibliographies

[4187]

FASMAN, M.J. Brass bibliography: sources on the history, literature, pedagogy, performance and acoustics of brass instruments. Bloomington, Indiana, U.P. 1990. 488p. $37.50. ISBN: 0253321301.

Covers 1820-1988; classified arrangement. Described as 'very thorough' and 'indispensable' by *Choice* (October 1990. p.282) which also notes several problems of redundancy, typographical errors, and in the numbering and indexing of entries. *Class No:* 785.12(01)

Great Britain

Yearbooks & Directories

[4188]

Directory of British brass bands. Macclesfield, McMillan Martin for British Federation of Brass Bands. c110p.

Lists national organizations, associations, championships; contest calendar; area associations; directory of member bands. *Class No:* 785.12(410)(058)

Histories

[4189]

HERBERT, T., ***ed.*** **Bands:** the British brass band movement in the 19th and 20th centuries. Milton Keynes, Open University Press, 1990. 192p. £32.50. ISBN: 0335097022.

Also paperback (0335097030; £10.99).

Authoritative summary history, scholarly in approach and comprehensive. *Class No:* 785.12(410)(091)

[4190]

NEWSOME, R. Brass roots: a hundred years of brass bands and their music (1836-1936). Aldershot, Ashgate, 1997. 240p., illus. £35.00. ISBN: 1859281680.

Scholarly account, arranged chronologically; bibliographical references. *Class No:* 785.12(410)(091)

Jazz & Blues Music

Bibliographies

[4191]

GREGOR, C. *and* **MECKLENBERG, C.G.H. International jazz bibliography:** jazz books from 1919 to 1968. Strasbourg, P.H. Heitz, 1969. 198p.

Supplements issued 1971, and 1975 covering 1970-1973.

The original volume identifies 1,500 items - monographs, biographies, reference works, dissertations, and discographies published separately and as appendices. Supplements expand the coverage and fill gaps, and exceed the size of the original volume. Nine indexes.
Class No: 785.16(01)

[4192]

HEFELE, B. Jazz bibliography: an international bibliography of jazz, blues, spirituals, gospel and ragtime music. Munich, Saur, 1981. viii, 368p. £27.50.

6,600 unannotated entries in 28 sections (*e.g.* Periodicals - Bibliographies - Discographies - Reference Works (nos.549-647) - Background selected literature - Spirituals and gospel music - History of jazz - Jazz by country - Style of jazz - Ragtime - Sociology of jazz ... Dialectics of jazz - Jazz people (A-Z, nos.3933-6235) - Jazz organizations - Jazz clubs - Jazz in archives, libraries, museums - Jazz and tv, radio, and film - Jazz and phonograph records - Jazz instruments - Jazz and dance - Jazz in pictures. Index of persons, p.326-68, but no subject index.
Class No: 785.16(01)

[4193]

KENNINGTON, D. *and* **READ, D.L. The Literature of jazz:** a critical guide. 2nd ed. London, Library Association, 1980. xi, 236p. £9.50.

Library Association Fellowship thesis 1969.

9 chapters (each with biographical survey and bibliography): 1. The general background - 2. The blues - 3. The histories of jazz - 4. The lives of jazz musicians - 5. Analysis, theory and criticism - 6. Reference sources (p.133-62) - 7. Jazz education - 8. Jazz in novels, poetry, plays and films - 9. Jazz periodicals (p.189-202). Name and title indexes. Limited to publications in English up to 1979.
Class No: 785.16(01)

[4194]

MEADOWS, E.S. Jazz research and performance materials: a select annotated bibliography. 2nd.ed. Hamden, CT, Garland, 1995. 806p. £90.00. ISBN: 0815303734.

First ed. as *Jazz reference and research materials* (1981.)

2400 entries arranged in 16 subject/format chapters, mostly fully annotated but without ISBNs, series statements, or pagination cited. For this ed. the journal literature has been excluded - an unfortunate move. 300 jazz videos are cited with annotations. Definition of jazz is wide-ranging, but there is little coverage of non-US music.
Class No: 785.16(01)

Encyclopaedias & Dictionaries

[4195]

CARR, I. *and* **PRIESTLEY, B.** *and* **FAIRWEATHER, D. Jazz:** the essential companion. London, Paladin, 1989. 562p. £8.95. ISBN: 0135092744.

Published in US, by Prentice Hall, 1988.

1600 entries ranging over all types of jazz, from its origins to the present day; mainly biographical sketches with critical comments. Likely to become 'the standard one-volume reference source' (*Choice,* March 1989, p.1116).
Class No: 785.16(03)

[4196]

FEATHER, L. Encyclopedia of jazz. Rev. ed. London, Quartet Books, 1978. 527p., illus. £9.95. ISBN: 0704321734.

First published 1960; this edition doubles the size of the first, and incorporates material separately published in a series of yearbook supplements.

Includes 2,000 biographies, with discographies, addresses, over 200 photographs, occupying p.96-473; feature chapters include a chronology (52-59), histories of jazz on record (505-12), jazz organizations, record companies. Bibliography p.524-7. No index. *Class No:* 785.16(03)

[4197]

—FEATHER, L. Encyclopedia of jazz in the sixties. London, Quartet Books, 1978. 312p., illus. £9.95. ISBN: 0704321742.

First published 1966.

Similar arrangement to the base volume; over 1,100 biographies. *Class No:* 785.16(03)

[4198]

—FEATHER, L. *and* GITLER, I. Encyclopedia of jazz in the seventies. London, Quartet Books, 1978. 393p., illus. £9.95. ISBN: 0704321750.

A further 1,400 biographies. Guide to jazz films (p.382-6), recommended recordings 1966-75 (p.387-90) and a bibliography of books published 1966-75 (p.391-3).
Class No: 785.16(03)

[4199]

KERNFELD, B. New Grove dictionary of jazz. London, Macmillan, 1988. 670, 690p. (2v). £225.00. ISBN: 0333398467.

Budget-priced one-vol. reprint 1995 (ISBN: 0312113579; £25.00.) incorporates a small number of corrections..

Although based on the 1980 edition of *Grove*, up to 90% of the material is new. 4,500 entries from 250 contributors; articles signed; bibliographies and discographies. 'Difficult to convey the scope and importance' (*Choice* April, 1989. p.1310). *Class No:* 785.16(03)

[4200]
KINKLE, R.D. The Complete encyclopedia of popular music and jazz, 1900-1950. New Rochelle, Arlington House, 1974. 2644p. (4v). $75.00.

First volume examines music year by year; second and third have biographies, and the fourth comprises indexes and appendices. 28,000 song titles are indexed.
Class No: 785.16(03)

[4201]
McRAE, B. Jazz handbook. London: Longmans, 1987. 272p. £9.95. ISBN: 0582000920.

A chronological arrangement covering major musicians and groups, including 1,000 names. Entries give biography, critique, lineage, recordings; cross-references frequent. Glossary. Bibliography; full index in 'databank' section.
Class No: 785.16(03)

Histories

[4202]
GOTTLIEB, R., ***ed.*** **Reading jazz:** a gathering of autobiography, reportage and criticism from 1919 to now. London, Bloomsbury, 1997. 1068p. £20.00. ISBN: 0747533369.

3 sections: autobiographical excerpts by great names; reportage from an assortment of sources; criticism from far and wide. An excellent idea to provide an illuminating collection of insights into key figures from scattered sources.
Class No: 785.16(091)

[4203]
HASSE, J. Ragtime: its history, composers and music. London, Macmillan, 1985. 416p. illus. £27.50. (*Macmillan Popular Music Studies*.) ISBN: 0333405153.

Chapters by America's leading ragtime scholars, including history, biographies, interviews, annotated discography. Extensive bibliography. *Class No:* 785.16(091)

[4204]
OLIVER, P. Blues fell this morning: meaning and contents in the Blues. Rev. ed. Cambridge, CUP, 1990. 350p. illus. £30. ISBN: 0521374375.

First published 1962.

A seminal work, examining the complex meaning of Blues, and the variety of experiences expressed.

Oliver also wrote another classic title - *The Story of the Blues: the making of black music* (Barrie & Rockcliff, 1969) which has recently been revised and published in an updated edition (London, Pimlico, 1997. ISBN: 0712674926; 320p., illus; £12.50). *Class No:* 785.16(091)

Biographies

[4205]
CHILTON, J. Who's who of jazz. New ed. [?5th.ed.] London, Cassell, 1997. 370p. £15.99. ISBN: 0304339091.

1st ed. 1972; 4th.ed. 1985.

Wide coverage through all periods and generally comprehensive. Entries are brief but give adequate basic information. The new edition expands previous work, and the currency of the information is now a great advantage.
Class No: 785.16(092)

[4206]
FRIEDWALD, W. Jazz singing: America's great voices from Bessie Smith to bebop and beyond. New York, Scribner, 1990. 416p., illus. $29.95. ISBN: 0684185229.

Critical history and overview of jazz singers, and jazz-influenced pop singers; discusses all major figures in detail, but also brings in many secondary and minor names. Discography; bibliography; index. *Class No:* 785.16(092)

[4207]
HARRIS, S. Blues who's who: a biographical dictionary of blues singers. New Rochelle, NY, Arlington House, 1979. 775p.

Also available as a reprint from Da Capo Press, 1981.

A very good source in a difficult field; abundant cross-references link stage names. Lists compositions and critical comment, with lists of major appearances.
Class No: 785.16(092)

[4208]
LYONS, L. *and* **PERLO, D. Jazz portraits:** the lives and music of the essential jazz musicians. New York, Morrow, 1989. 544p. $22.95. ISBN: 068804946x.

Covers some 200 musicians; good glossary and bibliography. *Class No:* 785.16(092)

Bibliographies

[4209]
CARNER, G., ***comp.*** **Jazz performers:** an annotated bibliography of biographical materials. Westport, CT, Greenwood Press, 1990. 364p. $45. ISBN: 0313262500.

Main section is A/Z list with basic data, and bibliography, concentrating on biographical material but also including some works written by the performers. Author & subject indexes. Supplementary section of bibliographies relating to other figures - no index access to this material.
Class No: 785.16(092)(01)

Great Britain

Yearbooks & Directories

[4210]
WOOD, C., ***comp.*** **Jazz musicians guide** 1993. London, Jazz Services Ltd., 1993. c.1000p.(loose-leaf) £14.95. ISBN: 0951938010.

No further editions have appeared, but there is still some value in the original work. Directory sections include agents, festivals, record companies, studios, shops, venues, education, archives and libraries. Data on individual musicians is arranged regionally, and includes contact information. *Class No:* 785.16(410)(058)

Histories

[4211]
GODBOLT, J. A History of jazz in Britain, 1950-1970. London, Quartet Books, 1989. 337p., illus. £20. ISBN: 0704325268.

Companion to the author's earlier volume covering 1919-50 (Quartet Books, 1984).

Excellent synopsis of 20 busy years, including 'A flood of literature' (Chapter 13, dealing with small, specialist magazines, review sources etc.). Discography & bibliography, p.300-319. Index.
Class No: 785.16(410)(091)

Biographies

[4212]

CHILTON, J. Who's who of British jazz. London, Cassell, 1997. 370p. £25.00. ISBN: 0304339105.

850 career summaries from pre-1920 to the present. Each entry is about half-a-page; index of bandleaders mentioned in the text. A publication that seems to have been lacking for years, this is a notable new venture.
Class No: 785.16(410)(092)

Australia

[4213]

JOHNSON, B. The Oxford companion to Australian jazz. Oxford, OUP, 1988. 320p. £28.50. ISBN: 0195547918.

Presents historical overview from 1917; discusses major and lesser known figures, and influences. 'Meticulously detailed and thoroughly researched' (*Choice*. Sept. 1988).
Class No: 785.16(94)

Pop Music

[4214]

Billboard information network. New York, Billboard Publications.

Online database including charts appearing in the *Billboard* magazine, the weekly newspaper of rock, pop, country, and folk music. Provides market research data on recordings, videos, and entertainment software. Many derivative products, such as Bronson (below), *Billboard book of number 1 albums, Billboard book of top 40 hits, Billboard book of no.1 rhythm and blues hits*, etc.
Class No: 785.19

[4215]

BRONSON, F. The Billboard book of number one hits. 4th. ed. New York, Watson-Guptill/Billboard, 1997. 848p. £18.95. ISBN: 0823076415.

Listing of chart toppers; artist and song title indexes.
Class No: 785.19

[4216]

GAMBACCINI, P. *and* **RICE, J.** *and* **RICE, T. The Guinness book of British hit singles.** 11th ed. London, Guinness Publishing, 1997. 512p. illus. £13.00. ISBN: 085112027x.

Details of every hit single from 1952. Alphabetical index of names, title index. Miscellaneous information sections discuss specific trends and achievements. Contains information on 6000 artists and some 30,000 singles.
Class No: 785.19

[4217]

GARGAN, W. *and* **SHARMA, S. Find that tune.** New York, Neal Schuman, 1984-1988. $85.00. ISBN: 1555700209, 2v.

Index to rock, folk-rock, disco and soul music in collections. Includes useful performer index.
Class No: 785.19

[4218]

POLLOCK, B. Rock song index: essential information on the 7,500 most important songs of rock and roll. New York, Schirmer Books, 1997. 524p. $80.00. ISBN: 0028729687.

Arranged A/Z by performer, giving title, producer, album title, label, songwriter, and an annotation. Index of titles (but not of any other names.) *Class No:* 785.19

[4219]

POPSI: the popular song index. Boston Spa, British Library, 1990-. ISSN: 09585702.

Annual; printed version, microfiche edition and diskette.

Title index of songs in popular music anthologies held at BLDSC.

For fuller entry, and for other titles that are relevant to this topic, *see entries at:* 784.4 *and* 784.4(01). *Class No:* 785.19

[4220]

SHAPIRO, N. *and* **POLLOCK, B.,** *eds*. **Popular music: an annotated guide to American popular songs** , including introductory essays, lyricist and composers index, important performance index, awards index, and list of publishers. Detroit/London, Gale Research. ISSN: 0886442x.

Originally published as eight volumes by Adrian Press, 1964-1981 (vols. 1-6) and Gale Research (vols. 7-8). The series continues on an annual basis, and early vols. have been re-issued in a standard format. Now the series covers 1920-1984 (9 vols) in 5 or 10 year steps, with a preliminary vol. covering 1900-1919. Latest vol. is 1993 (1994).

Described in the introduction as a 'selective, annotated list of the significant popular songs of our times.' Recent volumes index by title, composer and lyricist in a dictionary catalogue arrangement. Annotations are very brief.
Class No: 785.19

Bibliographies

[4221]

FEEHAN, P. Researching rock'n'roll: a guide to reference sources. *Reference Services Review*; 15(2) 1987. p.91-93.

A brief treatment with annotations; headings are - encyclopedias, dictionaries, biographical dictionaries, almanacs, histories, collection development guides, bibliographies (general & subject), discographies.
Class No: 785.19(01)

[4222]

HAGGERTY, G. A Guide to popular music reference books: an annotated bibliography. Westport, CT, Greenwood Press, 1995. xv,210p. $59.95. ISBN: 0313296618.

Popular music is defined as 'styles that have developed measurable commercial success through recordings and live performances'. 400 entries to items published in the last 20 years, covering bibliographies, periodical indexes, indexes to printed and recorded music, dictionaries and encyclopedias, biographies, directories, discographies, yearbooks, etc. Single paragraph annotations. Appendices list individual discographies, individual bibliographies, and electronic resources (merely 6 items). *Class No:* 785.19(01)

[4223]

HOFFMANN, F. The Literature of rock, 1954-1978. Metuchen, NJ, Scarecrow, 1981. x, 337p. £12.25.

Annotated bibliography of rock literature, p.6-294. (21 sections: 1. Development of rock and roll out of its stylistic antecedents, 1954-56. 20. Power pop (1977-) - 21. Related topics, (*e.g.* Humor). Introductory brief historical survey of rock literature, p.1-5. Appendices: A. Annotated list of popular music festivals, p.295-304; B. A basic stock list of rock recordings. References, p.319-22. Detailed index, p.323-37. *Class No:* 785.19(01)

[4224]

—HOFFMANN, F. *and* COOPER, B.L. The Literature of rock, II, 1979-1983, with additional material for 1954-1978. Metuchen, N.J., Scarecrow, 1986. 1114p. $79.50. ISBN: 0810818213.

Arranged by categories of music, then in chronological sequence; sources include trade papers, underground press etc. *Class No:* 785.19(01)

[4225]

—HOFFMANN, F. *and* COOPER, B.L. The Literature of rock, III, 1984-1990, with additional material for the period 1954-1983. Metuchen, NJ, Scarecrow, 1995. xix,1003p. $94.55. ISBN: 081082762x.

Some 8000 bibliographical references under 26 main headings. Appendices include listings of the most frequently cited reference sources, and magazines/journals relevant to the field. *Class No:* 785.19(01)

[4226]

KREBS, G.M. Rock and roll reader's guide. New York, Billboard, 1997. 445p. $21.95. ISBN: 0823076024.

Annotated bibliography of books by and about rock stars. Reviews are quoted. 2 main sections: reference works/ themes/subjects; performers and groups (categorised into biography, criticism, pictorial etc.) *Class No:* 785.19(01)

[4227]

LEYSER, B.J. Rock stars/pop stars: a comprehensive bibliography, 1955-1994. Westport, CT, Greenwood Press, 1994. 302p. $59.95. ISBN: 0313294224.

Lists 3,600 books written about individual artists and groups; also related names - producers, managers, disc jockeys. Arranged A/Z by artist or group name, with subject, author and title indexes. Items under each entry are categorised (bibliography, discography, dictionary, etc). *Class No:* 785.19(01)

[4228]

McCOY, J. Rap music in the 1980s: a reference guide. Metuchen, NJ, Scarecrow Press, 1992. 260p. $32.50. ISBN: 0810826496.

1070 annotated articles from magazines such as *Billboard, Melody Maker, Rolling Stone, Village Voice,* covering performers, news stories, reviews. Discography of 76 albums - award winners, best sales etc. - with critical annotations. Good indexes, and plenty of cross-references. *Class No:* 785.19(01)

[4229]

Popular music studies: a select international bibliography. Shepherd, J., *comp.* London, Mansell, 1997. xxviii, 450p. ISBN: 0720123445.

Appears substantial and comprehensive; reviews awaited. *Class No:* 785.19(01)

[4230]

TAYLOR, P. Popular music since 1955: a critical guide to the literature. London, Mansell, 1985. 528p. £35. ISBN: 0720117275.

Examines over 1,800 books, periodicals, fanzines, pamphlets etc. with commentary on contents. Thoroughly indexed by author, title and subject. Glossary of popular music terms. *Class No:* 785.19(01)

Encyclopaedias & Dictionaries

[4231]

BARNARD, S. *and* **HARDY, P.** *and* **LAING, D. Encyclopaedia of rock.** London: MacDonald, 1987. 480p. £14.95. ISBN: 0356142744.

Based on *Encyclopaedia of Rock* 3v. Panther Books, 1976. A/Z list of soloists, groups, technicians, producers, styles, record companies. 1,500 entries; well-produced. Now obviously dated, but still a classic work. Largely superseded by Heatley, Larkin, and the *Rolling Stone* titles (*see entries below*). *Class No:* 785.19(03)

[4232]

COUNTRY MUSIC MAGAZINE. Comprehensive country music encyclopedia. London, Boxtree, 1995/New York, Times Books, 1994. 449p., illus. £16.99. ISBN: 075221697x, (UK); 0812922476, (US).

Based on *Country music encyclopedia* (1974) and *The illustrated history of country music* (Doubleday, 1979).

680 entries, mainly biographical but with some topics and features. No bibliography, discographies, index or cross references. McCloud's *Ultimate encyclopedia* (*see entry below*) is far more extensive. *Class No:* 785.19(03)

[4233]

GAMMOND, P. The Oxford companion to popular music. Oxford, University Press, 1991. 204p. £25. ISBN: 0193113236.

Examines all aspects of Anglo-American popular music, from operetta to blues & folk. Includes historical material, performer and composer biographies, styles, instruments, songs, shows. *Class No:* 785.19(03)

[4234]

HARDY, P. *and* **LAING, D. The Faber companion to twentieth century popular music.** London, Faber, 1990. 875p. £20. ISBN: 0571138373.

Definition of popular music is difficult: seems to specialise in jazz and rock but with omissions. Readable and well-designed; no general index. *Class No:* 785.19(03)

[4235]

HEATLEY, M., *ed.* **The Virgin encyclopedia of rock:** the world's most comprehensive illustrated rock reference. Rev.ed. London, Virgin Books, 1995. 304p., illus. £19.99. ISBN: 1852276665.

Previous ed. 1993.

History and criticism of rock music, with biographies of leading names. Bibliographic references. *Class No:* 785.19(03)

[4236]

KINKLE, R.D. The Complete encyclopedia of popular music and jazz, 1900-1950. New Rochelle, Arlington House, 1974. 2644p. (4v). $75.00.

First volume examines music year by year; second and third have biographies, and the fourth comprises indexes and appendices. 28,000 song titles are indexed. *Class No:* 785.19(03)

[4237]

LARKIN, C., *ed.* **The Guinness encyclopedia of popular music.** 2nd.ed. London, Guinness Publishing, 1995. 6v. ISBN: 0851126626.

Since this ed. was published, a link with Virgin Books has been developed and several derivative titles now carry the Virgin name (*see below*). A third ed. is expected late in 1998; this will be titled *The Virgin encyclopedia of popular music*, and will be in 8 vols.

Over 15,000 entries (each in the general range 150 - 3000 words) covering rock, jazz, blues, soul, country, reggae,

.... *(contd.)*

Latin, popular music of Africa and Asia. Includes performers, bands, writers, labels, shows, instruments, companies; history, discography and bibliography for topic entries. Extensive index, and a good general bibliography. Well received by critics, and the overall impression is of an excellent source.

A number of titles have been issued that are based on the *Encyclopedia*, such as *Virgin encyclopedia of sixties music, Virgin encyclopedia of seventies music, Virgin encyclopedia of eighties music, Virgin encyclopedia of indie and new wave, Virgin encyclopedia of country music, Virgin encyclopedia of blues, Virgin encyclopedia of r & b and soul.* *Class No:* 785.19(03)

[4238]

—LARKIN, C., *ed.* The Virgin encyclopedia of popular music; concise edition. London, Virgin Books, 1997. 1343p. £35.00. ISBN: 1852277459.

Based on *The Guinness encyclopedia of popular music* (1995).

An excellent single volume resource; 3000 entries, noting recordings using a star-rating system. Index of some 14,000 names. *Class No:* 785.19(03)

[4239]

LISSAUER, R. Encyclopedia of popular music in America: 1888 to the present. New York, Paragon House, 1991. 1600p. £95.00. ISBN: 1557780153.

Covers 19,000 songs (country, rock, standards, jazz, blues, shows, novelties) giving title, composer, lyricist, date, recording date, performer, brief history, awards won. Index to composers and lyricists, but not performers. *Class No:* 785.19(03)

[4240]

McCLOUD, B. The Ultimate encyclopedia of country music and its performers. New York, Pedigree/Berkley, 1995. 1132p., illus. $20.00. ISBN: 0399521445.

More than twice as many entries as the *Comprehensive country music encyclopedia* (*see entry above*), mainly biographical, but with discographies and bibliography. Also directory section. No index. *Class No:* 785.19(03)

[4241]

New Grove gospel, blues and jazz; with spirituals and ragtime. London, Macmillan, 1988. 395p. ISBN: 0333407857.

Based on material in the *New Grove Dictionary of music and musicians*, 1980.

Compact and authoritative, with good coverage, and notes of recordings. *Class No:* 785.19(03)

[4242]

The New Rolling Stone encyclopedia of rock and roll. Romanowski, P. *and* George-Warren, H., *eds.* Rev.ed. New York/London, Fireside, 1995. xvi,1120p., illus. £14.99. ISBN: 0684810441.

Previous ed. as *The Rolling Stone encyclopedia of rock and roll* (New York, Rolling Stone Press, 1983).

The *Rolling Stone* magazine is widely respected in its field; the 1983 encyclopedia enjoyed a similar status. *Class No:* 785.19(03)

[4243]

NITE, N.N. Rock on: the illustrated encyclopedia of rock'n'roll. New York, Harper & Row, 1978-85. 3v., illus.

Biographical sketches with discographies for performers and groups; volume titles are *Solid gold years* (2nd ed. 1982.); *modern years 1964-* (1978); *video revolution, 1979-84* (1985). *Class No:* 785.19(03)

[4244]

STAMBLER, I. Encyclopedia of pop, rock and soul. Rev. ed. New York, St. Martin's Press, 1989. 864p. $35.00. ISBN: 0312025734.

About 500 entries on mainstream rock and pop, but with brief coverage of less well known areas. Lengthy entries give good background data, recording information, and critical comment. *Class No:* 785.19(03)

Histories

[4245]

COHN, N. Awopbopaloobop alopbamboom: pop from the beginning. London, Minerva, 1996. xi,242p. £6.99. ISBN: 0749386533.

Originally published London, Paladin 1969, 1970.

Welcome re-issue of a classic early commentary; one of the first books on pop music to be widely and credibly reviewed. *Class No:* 785.19(091)

[4246]

HASSE, J. Ragtime: its history, composers and music. London, Macmillan, 1985. 416p. illus. £27.50. (*Macmillan Popular Music Studies.*) ISBN: 0333405153.

Chapters by America's leading ragtime scholars, including history, biographies, interviews, annotated discography. Extensive bibliography. *Class No:* 785.19(091)

[4247]

NITE, N.N. Rock on almanac: the first four decades of rock'n'roll; a chronology. New York, Harper, 1989. 528p. $27.95. ISBN: 0060960817.

A chronology covering the 1940s to 1980s; lacking in focus, but a useful compilation. *Class No:* 785.19(091)

[4248]

WHITE, M. You must remember this...: popular songwriters 1900-1980. London Warne, 1983. x,304p. £5.95. ISBN: 0723231877.

Alphabetical coverage of 130 songwriters, including major compositions. Indexes of titles, composers, lyricists, performers, shows and films. *Class No:* 785.19(091)

Biographies

[4249]

BIROSEK, P.J. The New Age music guide: profiles and recordings of 500 top New Age musicians. London, Collier-Macmillan, 1990. 288p. £20. ISBN: 0020416407.

Alphabetical arrangement by artist with discographies. Good coverage of small companies and obscure figures. Appendices describe New Age sub-genres and indicate relevant artists and companies. *Class No:* 785.19(092)

[4250]

HELANDER, B. The Rock who's who. 2nd.ed. New York, Schirmer/London, Prentice Hall International, 1996. xii,849p., illus. $65.00. ISBN: 0028710312.

Favourably noticed as a good source of biographical information; a substantial volume. Bibliography p.771-796. *Class No:* 785.19(092)

[4251]

REES, D. *and* **CRAMPTON, L. Rock movers and shakers.** Rev. ed. New York, ABC-Clio, 1991. 585p. ISBN: 0874366615.

A wealth of personal information and discographies, tour details, miscellaneous facts for some 700 performers active in the last 30 years. *Class No:* 785.19(092)

[4252]

SMITH, J. Off the record: an oral history of popular music. Fink, M., *ed.* London, Sidgwick & Jackson, 1989. 429p. £10.99. ISBN: 0283999144.

Covers 1938-88; interviews with 200 personalities (Artie Shaw, Dave Brubeck, Johnnie Ray, Tom Jones, Elton John, Billy Joel ...) who have become major names in popular music. Each interview covers 1-2 pages & includes musical and biographical aspects. Contents listed p.vii-ix, but no index. Useful for insights into otherwise hard-to-trace figures. *Class No:* 785.19(092)

[4253]

TYLER, S., *ed.* International who's who in music: volume two - popular music 1996/97. 1st.ed. Cambridge, International Biographical Centre, 1996. 735p. £95.00. ISBN: 0948875070.

Companion to Vol. 1 (15th.ed.) of similar title (*see entry at:* 780(092)"19")

Covers pop, rock, folk, jazz, country, blues etc. 5000 entries are biographical (p.1-627) giving date of birth, career, albums issued, Entries are brief (c.20 lines in 2-column format.) Also directory of record companies, management companies, agents and promoters, publishers, festivals and events, organisations (p.721-735; A/Z by country.) *Class No:* 785.19(092)

Chamber Music

[4254]

BERGER, M. Guide to chamber music. London: Hale, 1986. xix, 470p. £25.00. ISBN: 0709027281.

Fifty-five major composers surveyed, with details of biography and compositions. Limited coverage balanced by its readable style. *Class No:* 785.7

[4255]

COBBETT, W.W., *ed.* Cyclopedic survey of chamber music. 2nd ed. London, OUP, 1963. 3v.

First published 1929-39 (2v.).

V.1-2 (A-H, I-Z) are a reprint of the original ed., with its signed analyses of all important works in the repertoire, plus numerous music examples and lists of works, with publishers. Biographical entries are fairly full (*e.g.* J.S. Bach: v.1, p,81-111; 48 music examples; list of chamber music works).

V.3 (ix, 211p.) consists of updating surveys: 'European chamber music since 1929' (p.1-81) - 'Chamber music in Britain since 1929' (p.82-111) - 'Russian chamber music (p.123-51) - 'Chamber music in America' (p.152-93). Bibliography, p.194-200. Additions and corrections to dates in v.1-2, compiled by N. Slonimsky, p.201-9.

The standard work, being the only comprehensive survey of its field. *Class No:* 785.7

Bibliographies

[4256]

ALTMANN, W. Kammermusik - Catalog. Ein Verzeichnis von seit 1841 veröffentlichten Kammermusikwerken. 6th ed. Leipzig, Hofmeister, 1945. xii, 400p.

First published 1910. This edition reprinted 1967.

Comprehensive listing of 1841-1944 publications, grouped by combinations of instruments. *Class No:* 785.7(01)

[4257]

NATIONAL FEDERATION OF MUSIC SOCIETIES. Catalogue of chamber music. London: NFMS, 1983. 66p. £5.00.

Arranged by ensemble headings, then alphabetically by composers. Covers works for 3-10 instruments, showing timings, details of movements, and publication data.
Class No: 785.7(01)

[4258]

RIBEIRO, V.R. *and* **MARKEL, R. Chamber music:** an international guide to works and their instrumentation. New York, Facts on File, 1993. 352p. $45.00 ISBN: 0816022968.

7000 entries; 2 sections - Haydn/Mozart etc; Beethoven onwards (to 1992). Covers combinations of 3 to 20 instruments. Tabular format lists composers alphabetically, then works, year, key, duration, instrumentation. Quick reference index sorts out instruments and composers. 26 choices of instrumentation. 'A wonderful resource for professional chamber musicians, conductors, and program planners.' (*Reference books bulletin,* 15/9/93. p186/7.)
Class No: 785.7(01)

Musical Instruments

[4259]

JENKINS, J., *ed.* International directory of musical instrument collections. Buren (Netherlands), Knuf, 1977. 166p.

A directory of *c.*400 collections in some 100 countries. Data on each collection include hours and days of opening, number and type of instruments, date of acquisition; services, publications. Include instrument collections that are part of a more general museum, and also private collections.
Class No: 786/789

Bibliographies

[4260]

COOVER, J. Musical instrument collections: catalogues and cognate literature. Detroit, Information Co-ordinators, 1981. 464p. $25.00.

Section 1: Institutions and expositions (1712 entries, with index), p.31-259; 2. Private collections (entries 1713-2418, with index), p.261-408. Appendices: Some early inventories, to 1828; Expositions and exhibitions. 1878-1978. General index, p.427-62. Auctioneers, antiquarians and firms, p.463-4. *Class No:* 786/789(01)

Encyclopaedias & Dictionaries

[4261]

BAINES, A. The Oxford companion to musical instruments. Oxford, Oxford University Press, 1992. 404p. £25. ISBN: 0193113341.

Contains 2000 entries for Western and non-Western music, based largely on the 1983 *New Oxford companion to music.* Data on each instrument includes versions and translations of its name, material, tuning and range, method of performance, history. There are drawings and photographs, but no dimensions are given. Some brief bibliographies, and an index of instrument makers.
Class No: 786/789(03)

[4262]
Cambridge companions [to musical instruments]. Cambridge, Cambridge University Press, 1992-. £40.00 per vol. (Pbk. £14.95.)

The series presents the history and development of instruments, well and authoritatively written, and illustrated. A select bibliography is included.

Titles include *Cambridge companion to the violin* (1992), *Cambridge companion to the clarinet* (1995), *Cambridge companion to brass instruments* (1997).
Class No: 786/789(03)

[4263]
DEARLING, R., *ed.* **The Illustrated encyclopedia of musical instruments.** New York, Schirmer, 1996. 240p., illus. $75.00. ISBN: 0028646673.

Valuable mainly for the high quality of illustrations, which range from early paintings to photographs and drawings. Chapters include discussion of ensembles, non-Western instruments, and ancient and obsolete instruments. '*New Grove Dictionary of musical instruments* and the *Oxford Companion to musical instruments* provide more scholarly, detailed text in a straight alphabetical arrangement...but the colourful illustrations here and the informality of the arrangement provide a context for understanding broader meanings.' (*Reference books bulletin,* 93(9/10) 1997; p892/4.) *Class No:* 786/789(03)

[4264]
SADIE, S., *ed.* **New Grove dictionary of musical instruments.** London, Macmillan, 1984. 3v., illus. £250. ISBN: 0333378784.

Based on *New Grove* but with some significant revisions. Signed articles with bibliographies, illustrations and musical examples, cover Western instruments, makers, modern instruments, performing practice, and non-Western, and folk instruments. *Class No:* 786/789(03)

Histories

[4265]
GALPIN, F.W. Old English instruments of music: their history and character. 4th ed. London, Methuen, 1965. xxviii, 254p.

First published 1910.

A classic study, confined to musical instruments in use in England up to the end of the 18th century. Revision has been scrupulously confined to supplementary notes; updated references, p.xiii-xvii. Illus. include 56 plates, - also an improvement on previous eds. Analytical index.
Class No: 786/789(091)

[4266]
REMNANT, M. Musical instruments: an illustrated history from antiquity to the present. London, Batsford, 1990. 295p. illus. £19.95. ISBN: 0713451696.

Ten chapters covering families of instruments, and a final chapter on orchestration. A useful survey with 240 photographs. *Class No:* 786/789(091)

Great Britain

[4267]
BEVAN, C. Musical instrument collections in the British isles. London, Piccolo, 1990. 128p. £7.95. ISBN: 1872203108.

Details of the contents of 100 collections, with notes on access and facilities. Bibliographical references.
Class No: 786/789(410)

[4268]
VICTORIA AND ALBERT MUSEUM. London. **Catalogue of musical instruments in the Victoria and Albert Museum.** Schott, H., *ed and* Baines, A., *ed.*. 3rd. ed. London, A. & C. Black, 1998. 384p. illus. ISBN: 1851772502.

2nd. ed. was published in 2 vols. (vol 1 1985, vol 2 1968) by HMSO.

Part 1: keyboard instruments is edited by Schott; part 2: non-keyboard instruments by Baines. Detailed description of items in approximately chronological order; biographical notes on makers; bibliography; numerous excellent plates.
Class No: 786/789(410)

America — North

[4269]
MUSIC LIBRARY ASSOCIATION. A Survey of musical instrument collections in the United States and Canada. Lichtenwanger, W., *comp.* Ann Arbor, MLA, 1974. 137p.

Identifies 572 collections, of which 334 are based in institutions. Geographical arrangement, with a variety of indexes. *Class No:* 786/789(71+73)

Keyboard Instruments

[4270]
BOALCH, D.H. Makers of the harpsichord and clavichord 1440-1840. Mould, C., *ed.* 3rd.ed. Oxford, Clarendon Press, 1995. xxxii,788p. £80.00. ISBN: 019318429x.

Previous eds. 1956, 1974.

Completely revised and now divided into two parts. Part 1: makers listed alphabetically with biographical details, adding 500 not listed previously and updating entries for another 400. Part 2: Descriptions of more than 2000 surviving instruments. Geographical and chronological conspectus. New index of technical terms in seven languages. Bibliography p.749-780. *Class No:* 786

[4271]
CLINKSCALE, M.N. Makers of the piano, 1700-1820. Oxford, Oxford University Press, 1993. 403p. £45. ISBN: 0198163231.

Another volume is expected for 1820-1860.

With Boalch, will form a uniform, complete record of keyboard instruments 1440-1860. Biographical details of makers, dates, descriptions, locations, styles, collections. Comprehensive bibliography, which is in itself an important contribution to the literature. 'Excellent new source. Very highly recommended.' (*Choice,* 31(6)February 1994, p911.)
Class No: 786

Bibliographies

[4272]
GUSTAFSON, B. French harpsichord music of the seventeenth century: a thematic catalogue of the sources with commentary. Ann Arbor; UMI, 1977-1979. xlv, 394, 488, 380p. (3v). £45. ISBN: 0835710696.

The thematic catalogue is contained in volumes 2 and 3; the first volume consists of a lengthy introduction and extensive discussion of the sources. *Class No:* 786(01)

Histories

[4273]
APEL, W. The History of keyboard music to 1700. Bloomington, Indiana University Press, 1972. 878p. ISBN: 025313796x.

Originally as *Geschichte der orgel-und Klaviermusik* (Kassel, Barenreiter-Verlag, 1967).

4 parts (24 sections: 1. Clavier music before 1500 - 2. The sixteenth century - 3. The first half of the seventeenth century - 4. The second half of the seventeenth century (Germany ... Spain and Portugal). Notes, p.781-817. Bibliography, p.818-36. Analytical indexes of names, works, terms. *Class No:* 786(091)

[4274]
GORDON, S. A History of keyboard literature: music for the piano and its forerunners. New York, Schirmer Books/ London, Prentice Hall International, 1996. viii,566p. ISBN: 0028709659.

Useful and extensive bibliographical discussion of the development of keyboard music. *Class No:* 786(091)

[4275]
HARRIS, J.M. A History of music for harpsichord or piano and orchestra. Lanham, MD/London, Scarecrow, 1997. 464p. £66.00. ISBN: 0810832577.

History of the development of harpsichord composition, concerto innovation, the piano repertoire, the piano concerto. Bibliography. *Class No:* 786(091)

Piano

[4276]
CLINKSCALE, M.N. Makers of the piano, 1700-1820. Oxford, Oxford University Press, 1993. 403p. £45. ISBN: 0198163231.

See entry at 786. *Class No:* 786.2

[4277]
DUBAL, D. The Art of the piano: its performers, literature and recordings. New York, Summit Books, 1989. 480p. $40.00. ISBN: 0671492381.

Contents include biographies and assessments of major pianists, critical survey of piano literature with discography. A useful basic handbook. *Class No:* 786.2

[4278]
PALMIERI, R., *ed*. Encyclopedia of the piano. New York, Garland, 1996. xi,521p. $95.00. ISBN: 0815325827.

Originally published 1994 as *Encyclopedia of keyboard instruments. Vol. 1: piano.*

Signed articles offer concise definitions and lengthier treatments. Historical evolution is traced, with notable makers, companies, influential composers. Bibliographies follow many entries. Cross-references, and a good index.
Class No: 786.2

Bibliographies

[4279]
HINSON, M. Guide to the pianist's repertoire. 2nd ed. Bloomington, Indiana University Press, 1987. 856p. $47.50. ISBN: 0253326567.

Covers 1,800 composers, with information on keys, styles, publishers, duration, difficulty. Descriptive comments; revised and enlarged from first edition.
Class No: 786.2(01)

[4280]
HINSON, M. The Pianist's guide to transcriptions, arrangements, and paraphrases. Indiana, University Press, 1990. 159p. $22.50. ISBN: 0253327458.

Catalogue of arrangements with commentary on style, interpretation, technique. Related literature cited; full bibliographic details given. *Class No:* 786.2(01)

[4281]
METHUEN-CAMPBELL, J. Catalogue of recordings by classical pianists. Vol. 1: pianists born to 1872. Chipping Norton, Disco Epsom, 1984. 66p. ISBN: 0950992801.

Aims to include all released recordings. Brief biographical details with list of work arranged by composer. Details of matrix and recording numbers; no coverage of modern re-issues. *Class No:* 786.2(01)

[4282]
PALMIERI, R. Piano information guide: an aid to research. New York, Garland, 1989. 329p. $47.00. (*Music Research and Information Guide; no.10.*) ISBN: 0824077784.

Focuses primarily on the instrument, and offers annotated entries on 450 sources. Covers monograph and journal sources identified via OCLC etc. *Class No:* 786.2(01)

Glossaries

[4283]
SMITH, E. A pianist's glossary. London, Robert Hale, 1997. 96p. £6.99. ISBN: 0709061366.

Compact and concise, gives definitions for musical terms particularly applicable to the piano. *Class No:* 786.2(038.1)

Histories

[4284]
EHRLICH, C. The Piano: a history. 2nd. rev. ed. Oxford, OUP, 1989. 256p., illus. £25. (£9.95 pbk). ISBN: 0198161816.

First published 1976.

A scholarly study covering the earliest examples to the latest Japanese instruments. Includes details of technology, commerce, users. Appendices provide lists of makers from 1851, estimates of production, exotica. Bibliography.
Class No: 786.2(091)

Biographies

[4285]
LYLE, W. A Dictionary of pianists. New York, Schirmer/ Macmillan, 1984. 343p.

Gives information on 4,000 classical pianists from 1700's to the present. Alphabetical arrangement.
Class No: 786.2(092)

Organ

[4286]
SUMNER, W.L. The Organ: its evolution, principles of construction and use. 4th ed. London, Macdonald & Janes, 1973. xiv,603p. illus.

First published 1952.

3 sections (12 chapters): 1. History, to the present; 2, The organ: principles of construction; production of sound; tonal structure; organ mechanism and actions; 3, The study and use of the Organ. Appendices 1-5 (*e.g.* Organ specifications, - 144 well-known organs, their manuals, stops, etc. p.385-567). Bibliography, p.579-90 (A/Z, authors). Second

.... *(contd.)*

supplementary list of books for the 4th ed., p.591-2. Detailed index (analytical under towns, *e.g.* London, (2½ cols.), Oxford, Paris). 41 plates. *Class No:* 786.6

Bibliographies

[4287]

ARNOLD, C.R. Organ literature: a comprehensive survey. 3rd.ed. Metuchen, NJ, Scarecrow, 1995. 391,938p. (2v.) $97.50. ISBN: 0810829703.

Earlier eds. 1974, 1984.

Vol 1: historical survey from 1300 to the present (styles, periods, national schools; builders, treatises, maps, substantial bibliographies); vol.2 : biographical catalogue and list of works. *Class No:* 786.6(01)

Dictionaries

[4288]

IRWIN, S. Dictionary of pipe organ stops. 2nd ed. New York, Schirmer/Macmillan, 1983. 422p.

First published 1962.

Definitions, plates, charts, and various appendices. A bibliography is included. *Class No:* 786.6(038)

Great Britain

[4289]

BICKNELL, S. The History of the English organ. Cambridge, Cambridge University Press, 1996. 443p., illus. £40.00. ISBN: 0521550262.

Likely to become a standard work; covers instruments built in England between 900 AD and the present day. Significant instruments are described with information on builders, musical tastes of the period, liturgy, technical developments, links between companies. Illustrations show the instruments in their architectural settings.
Class No: 786.6(410)

[4290]

NORMAN, J. The Organs of Britain: an appreciation and gazetteer. London, David & Charles, 1984. 329p. illus. ISBN: 0715383132.

Excellent introductory sections, notes on builders, glossary of terms; gazetteer (p.145-320) by county then individual locations. Bibliography; index.
Class No: 786.6(410)

String Instruments

Bibliographies

[4291]

DODD, G. Thematic index of music for viol: third instalment. London, Viola de Gamba Society of Great Britain, 1984. 150p. £18.

In progress for 20 years, this series is now complete. Loose-leaf format; covers English and some foreign compositions, and is useful only if the composer is known. An index of incipits is under consideration.
Class No: 787(01)

[4292]

JAPE, M. Classical guitar music in print. New York, Musicdata, 1989. 443p. $95. ISBN: 0884780252.

International coverage, arranged into solos, concertos, studies etc. Indexes by composer, instrumentation, and series. Addresses of publishers. Two thematic indexes cover works by J.S. Bach and F. Tarrega. *Class No:* 787(01)

[4293]

McCUTCHEON, M.A. Guitar and vihuela: an annotated bibliography. New York, Pendragon, 1985. xlv,353p. $65. ISBN: 0918728282.

Thorough, extensive and accurate. *Class No:* 787(01)

[4294]

MARCAN, P. Music for solo violin unaccompanied: a performer's guide to the published literature of the seventeenth, eighteenth, nineteenth and twentieth century. High Wycombe, P. Marcan, 1983. ii,34p. ISBN: 0950421154.

Lists 600 items with annotations; arranged alphabetically within broad chronological categories. *Class No:* 787(01)

[4295]

MARKEVITCH, D. The Solo cello: a bibliography of the unaccompanied violoncello literature. New York, Fallen Leaf, 1989. 113p. $24.95. ISBN: 0914913123.

4 sections cover history of the instrument, cello as a solo instrument, survey of works, catalogue of published compositions - the last section being arranged alphabetically with full details of dates, publisher, etc. Useful appendices.
Class No: 787(01)

[4296]

REZITS, J., ***comp.*** **The guitarist's resource guide:** guitar music in print and books on the art of the guitar. Park Ridge, IL, Palma Music, 1983. 574p. £75.00. ISBN: 0849778026.

An extensive, international compilation with excellent coverage. Arrangement is by instrument combinations, solo, duo, etc. then by composer and title. Details are given of grade level, publisher and price. Includes also music for lute, mandolin and vihuela; details of books relating to these instruments are also listed. *Class No:* 787(01)

[4297]

SCHWARZ, W., ***comp.*** **Guitar bibliography:** an international listing of theoretical literature on classical guitar from the beginning to the present. Munich, Saur, 1984. xxxvii,257p. £29.50. ISBN: 3598105185.

Almost 5,000 items are included from monographs, reviews and theses. Divided by subject (history, technique, teaching etc.) and well indexed. *Class No:* 787(01)

Handbooks & Manuals

[4298]

STIMPSON, M., ***comp.*** **The Guitar: a guide for students and teachers.** Oxford, OUP, 1988. 284p. £25.00. ISBN: 0193174197.

Authoritative and readable, covers all aspects of learning and teaching. Appendices include data on publishers, technical points. *Class No:* 787(035)

Histories

[4299]

HAMMA, W. Geigenbauer der Deutschen Schule/ violin makers of the German school, from the 17th to the 19th century. Tutzing, Hans Schneider, 1986. xvi,519,591p. (2v.). ISBN: 3795204909, v.1; 3795204917, v.2.

Alphabetical list with brief biographies and descriptions; numerous & detailed illustrations. *Class No:* 787(091)

[4300]

HAMMA, W. Meister italienischer Geigenbaukunst. Hersching am Ammersee, Schuler Verlag, 1965. ISBN: 3779630575.

Based on F. Hamma's *Italian Violinmakers* (1931).

Alphabetical, with brief details; well illustrated.

Class No: 787(091)

[4301]

JALOVEC, K. Encyclopedia of violin makers. London, Hamlyn, 1968. 482, 399p. (2v).

Originally published in Czechoslovakia, 1965.

Aims 'to give a reasonably complete and up-to-date alphabetical source of information on the makers of stringed instruments, both bowed and plucked, on the instruments themselves, their characteristic properties, forms and conditions, on classical makers and especially on more recent makers and instruments' (*Foreword*). V.1 (A-K) has glossary, p.15-88; v.2 (L-Z) has an historical bibliography, p.393-7. 306 black-and-white illus. (many of labels, - 6 or more per page); 40 col. pl. illus. in v.1 include 'Some tools of a violin-maker' and 'Parts of a violin'. The definitive history of the craft. *Class No:* 787(091)

Wind Instruments

Bibliographies

[4302]

BEEBE, J.P. Music for unaccompanied solo bassoon: an annotated bibliography. Jefferson, NC, McFarland, 1990. 109p. £35. ISBN: 0899504639.

Includes 150 specific items, and transcriptions, adaptations. Indexed. *Class No:* 788(01)

[4303]

CANNON, R.D. A Bibliography of bagpipe music. Edinburgh, J. Donald, 1980. v, 295p. £15.00.

Covers five types of pipes (Union, Northumbrian, Scots Highlands, Irish War, Brien Boru Pipes). Aims to identify all music printed for each type, with history. *Class No:* 788(01)

[4304]

DAVIES, J.R., *comp*. Bibliography of the early clarinet. Brighton, Sussex, Clarinet & Saxophone Society, 1988. £150.

Covers a wide range of sources including dissertations and museum and exhibition catalogues. Clarinet tutors 1732-1845 are listed separately. Listing of national collections in several countries and access arrangements.

Class No: 788(01)

[4305]

FASMAN, M.J. Brass bibliography: sources on the history, literature, pedagogy, performance and acoustics of brass instruments. Bloomington, Indiana, U.P. 1990. 488p. $37.50. ISBN: 0253321301.

Covers 1820-1988; classified arrangement. Described as 'very thorough' and 'indispensable' by *Choice* (October

.... *(contd.)*

1990. p.282) which also notes several problems of redundancy, typographical errors, and in the numbering and indexing of entries. *Class No:* 788(01)

[4306]

SKEI, A., *comp*. Woodwind, brass and percussion instruments of the orchestra: a bibliographical guide. New York, Garland, 1985. 271p. $39. ISBN: 0824090217.

Arranged in 16 main sections - general and specialised discussion of each family is subdivided into sections dealing with specific instruments. Material includes acoustics, makers and performers, performance practice etc. Cross-references, and good indexes. *Class No:* 788(01)

[4307]

VESTER, F. Flute music of the eighteenth century: an annotated bibliography. Montreux, Musica Rara, 1985. 573p. £92.40. ISBN: 2950064604.

Arranged by composer, listing titles, instrumentation, original and current publishers. List of libraries holding copies. 'A vast and thorough compilation' (*Brio* 22(1) Spring/Summer 1985. p.41). *Class No:* 788(01)

[4308]

WHITWELL, D. The history and literature of the wind band and wind ensemble. Northbridge, CA, Winds, 1982-3. 9v. (ring bound). $335.

Volumes 1-5 cover the history of wind groups divided chronologically: pre-1500, renaissance, baroque, classical, nineteenth century. Volumes 6-9 consist of a catalogue of relevant music. The historical sections are arranged nationally and quote early sources. (Reviewed in *Brio* 22(1) p.25-27). *Class No:* 788(01)

Histories

[4309]

LANGWILL, L.G. An Index of musical wind-instrument makers. 6th ed. Edinburgh, Langwill, 1980. xiv, 331p. £13.50.

About 5,000 entries for makers, A-Z p.1-195 ('Boosey': 12½ lines; 'Metzler': 32½ lines; Adolphe Sax: 21 lines). Brief data include period of flourishing, career, references to sources and patents; present locations of surviving instruments. Bibliography, p.196-201. Appended: Collections and exhibitions. Selection of makers' marks. Introduction to list of makers. Addenda and corrigenda. List of wind instrument-makers under towns. List of makers whose places of work is unknown. 39 illus.

Class No: 788(091)

Percussion

[4310]

BECK, J.H. Encyclopedia of percussion. Hamden, CT, Garland, 1995. 436p., illus. $75.00. ISBN: 0824047885.

30 contributors have been involved in this work, which concentrates on the Western tradition, although there is some world coverage. 3 sections: A/Z list of instruments and terms; illustrations of instruments; articles on major instruments. Appendices of symbols; table of instrument names and other terms in English, French, German, Italian; select list of published writings on methods for percussion.

Class No: 789

[4311]

BLADES, J. Percussion instruments and their history. 4th ed. London, Kahn and Averill, 1993. 514p. illus. ISBN: 1871082366.

First published 1970.

International coverage, chapter bibliographies. Useful appendices including glossary of terms & additional bibliography & discography. *Class No:* 789

[4312]

BRINDLE, R.S. Contemporary percussion. Oxford, Oxford University Press, 1991. 224p. £14.95. ISBN: 0198162472.

Guide to modern instruments, discussing characteristics, and showing use through musical examples. *Class No:* 789

Bibliographies

[4313]

BAJZEK, D. Percussion: an annotated bibliography with special emphasis on contemporary notation and performance. Metuchen, NJ, Scarecrow, 1988. 185p. $18.50. ISBN: 0810821079.

Covers 1,400 books, dissertations and articles 1965-1985. Arranged into Western and non-Western areas, with good annotations; appendices include a bibliography, and journal lists. Index of authors, but no detailed subject index. *Class No:* 789(01)

[4314]

MEZA, F.A., ***comp.*** **Percussion discography:** an international compilation of solo and chamber percussion music. Westport, CT, Greenwood Press, 1990. 108p. $35. ISBN: 0313268673.

Includes recordings for which a written score is available; valuable as a repertory guide. Full details of company, performers etc. Excludes jazz & ethnic music. Appendices of companies & distributors; indexes of performers, titles. *Class No:* 789(01)

[4315]

SKEI, A., ***comp.*** **Woodwind, brass and percussion instruments of the orchestra:** a bibliographical guide. New York, Garland, 1985. 271p. $39. ISBN: 0824090217.

Arranged in 16 main sections - general and specialised discussion of each family is subdivided into sections dealing with specific instruments. Material includes acoustics, makers and performers, performance practice etc. Cross-references, and good indexes. *Class No:* 789(01)

Bells & Bellringing

[4316]

DOVE, R.H., ***comp.*** **Bellringer's guide to the church bells of Britain** and ringing peals of the world. 5th ed. Aldershot, Viggers, 1976. 198p.

List of towers containing five or more bells with data on rings, weight and pitch. *Class No:* 789.5

[4317]

JOHNSTON, R., ***and others.*** **An Atlas of bells.** Oxford, Blackwell, 1990. 150p. £25. ISBN: 0631151435.

International guide to locations of rings of bells. *Class No:* 789.5

Computer Music

[4318]

CARY, T. Dictionary of musical technology. Westport,CT, Greenwood Press, 1992. 542p. $79.95. ISBN: 0313286949.

Lucid style, suitable for the technician as well as the amateur. Important topics receive substantial length entries and diagrams. Extensive bibliography. *Class No:* 789.9:681.3

[4319]

DOBSON, R. Dictionary of electronic and computer music technology: instruments, terms, techniques. Oxford, Oxford University Press, 1992. 224p. £25. ISBN: 0193113449.

Mainly covers electronic instruments and allied technical features and processes. Not wholeheartedly recommended in review in *Choice*(30(7) March 1993, p1108.) *Class No:* 789.9:681.3

[4320]

WICK, R.L. The Literature of electronic and computer music: a basic library collection.

Bibliographic essay in *Choice,* vol.31, no.3.(November, 1993.) pp.411-420.

Good discussion of the literature from the early days to the present; 74 items are cited in the bibliography at the end of the paper. *Class No:* 789.9:681.3

Mechanical Musical Instruments

[4321]

BOWERS, Q.D. Encyclopedia of automatic musical instruments. Vestal, NY, Vestal Press, 1972. 1,008p.

Coverage: Cylinder music boxes - Disc music boxes - Player pianos - Coin-operated pianos - Orchestrions; Organettes; Player organs; Fairground organs. Dictionary of automatic music terms (p.945-81); bibliography (p.982). Index, p.983-1008. Many illus., including drawings of mechanisms. *Class No:* 789.9:681.82

Sound Recordings (Discography)

[4322]

Classical music CD listener's guide. Blumenthal, H. New York, Billboard Books, 1997. £9.95. ISBN: 0823082687.

Aims to offer 'the best' CD titles. One of a range of discographies from the *Billboard* database. *Class No:* 789.90

[4323]

CLOUGH, F.F. ***and*** **CUMING, G.J. The World's encyclopedia of recorded music.** Westport, CT, Greenwood Press, 1970. 890p.

Reprint of 1952 volume (published by Sidgwick & Jackson, London) and the first supplement. Second supplement (1953) covers 1951-52, and third supplement (1957) covers 1953-55.

Recordings from all countries are included in this monumental work, with good identifying data. No annotations, but renowned as a thorough and comprehensive, historical source. *Class No:* 789.90

[4324]

DANIELS, W.F., ***comp.*** **The American 45 and 78 r.p.m. record dating guide** 1940-1959. London, Greenwood Press, 1985. 157p. £37.50. ISBN: 0313242321.

Data on 93,000 recordings by 2,500 companies in the US. *Class No:* 789.90

[4325]

DAVIS, E., *ed*. A Basic music library: essential scores and sound recordings. 3rd.ed. Chicago/London, American Library Association, 1997. 665p. ISBN: 0838934617.

Selection and buying guide, covering 3000 musical scores and 7000 recordings. No annotations, but suitability for various sizes of library is indicated by asterisks. 33 discography chapters are grouped thus: Western classical music by period; traditional and popular music of the US; musicals and operettas; children's; folk music; Caribbean and Latin American; Europe (UK and Ireland, Western Europe, Eastern Europe). Non-Western covered briefly in 4 chapters p.513-558. Appendix of suppliers; indexes.
Class No: 789.90

[4326]

FAGAN, T. *and* **MORGAN, W.R.,** ***comps*. The Encyclopedic discography of Victor recordings:** pre-matrix series, the Consolidated Talking Machine Co., E.R. Johnson, and the Victor Talking Machine Co. London, Greenwood Press, 1983. 488p. £44.95. ISBN: 031323003x.

Lists all recordings of these companies in the very early twentieth century. *Class No:* 789.90

[4327]

The Gramophone classical catalogue. London, RED, 1953-. c.2000p. (master eds.). £79.00pa. ISSN: 03534890.

Published 1953 - 1995 by General Gramophone Publications Ltd (Harrow, Middx.) who continue to publish the *Gramophone* magazine. Master Editions published in December and June; ten monthly supplements are issued between these Editions. In US, Macmillan and Schirmer imprints have appeared on this catalogue. Now also available on CD-ROM, and online.

Regarded as an outstanding and authoritative source. Covers all formats (including minidiscs, laserdiscs, DATs, videos). The first section is divided into orchestral, chamber, instrumental, vocal & choral, stage works. Full details are given in each entry, including record company, manufacturers' code etc., and date of review in the *Gramophone* magazine. Index of manufacturers' names, labels, distributors, classical nicknames, abbreviations.
Class No: 789.90

[4328]

Gramophone classical good CD guide 1998. Pollard, C., *ed.* 11th ed. Harrow, General Gramophone Publications, 1997. 1332p. £15.99. ISBN: 0902470922.

First issued 1988. In US published by Music Sales Corp. (Chester, NY). Also available on CD-ROM.

Lists best buys on CD; narrative entries discuss the recording, and symbols indicate quality of performance, quality of sound, price range, period instruments, original review date in the *Gramophone* magazine. Efficient indexes.
Class No: 789.90

[4329]

MARCO, G.A., *ed*. Encyclopedia of recorded sound in the United States. New York/London, Garland, 1993. 910p. $125.00. ISBN: 0824047826.

Concentrates on the first 80 years, thus cuts off at a surprisingly early 1970. Technical definitions, information on record labels (probably the most useful part of the volume), periodicals (565 items, annotated), and miscellaneous topics. Some short biographies. Strange amalgam of 'facts' with basic data on some recording artists. Bibliography p.787-824. *Class No:* 789.90

[4330]

MUSIC MASTER. Master catalogue 1997.
Humphries, J., *ed.* London, Retail Entertainment Data (RED), 1996. c1500p. Also CD-ROM version. £150.00; CD-ROM £750.00. ISBN: 1900105047.

First published 1974. Annual. CD-ROM version from 1992. Standard service covers all forms of popular music, and there is a similar classical service. Both are available with a new release information service at extra cost. Discounts for taking both services.

Complete list of all singles, albums, cassettes, CDs and music videos available from British companies. A series of substantial derivatives is also published, including-

Heavy metal catalogue.
Music on video.
Films & shows catalogue.
Singles catalogue.
Jazz and blues catalogue.
Tracks catalogue.
CD catalogue.
Record catalogue.
Directory of popular music.
Country music catalogue.
Labels and distributors directory.
Price guide for record collectors.
Albums catalogue. *Class No:* 789.90

[4331]

The Penguin guide to compact discs and cassettes: 1996 edition. Greenfield, E. *and* Layton, R. *and* March, I. London, Penguin Books, 1996. xix,1580p. £18.00. ISBN: 0140513671.

Yearbook for 1997/98 (published 1997) updates the main volume. (699p.; ISBN: 0140513817; £13.99.)

Lists all recordings currently available with advice on interpretation, performance, recording quality, value for money. Composer arrangement with narrative discussion including the listings with manufacturers' catalogue numbers, star rating symbol. Sections also cover orchestral concerts, instrumental recitals, vocal & choral collections.
Class No: 789.90

[4332]

Penguin price guide for record and CD collectors. Hamlyn, N. London, Penguin Books, 1997. 1000p. £16.99. ISBN: 0140513914.

Contains valuations for 114,000 recordings.
Class No: 789.90

[4333]

RUPPLI, M. *and* **NOVITSKY, E. The Mercury labels:** a discography. Westport,CT, Greenwood Press, 1993. 5 vols. $395.00. ISBN: 0313273715.

Covers output from 1945 in four volumes, each with its own artist index. Volume 5 is an index volume. Blues, jazz and classical are included - a 'formidable task.' (*Choice,* 32(2) 1994, p.265.) *Class No:* 789.90

[4334]

—RUPPLI, M. The Decca labels: a discography. Westport, CT, Greenwood Press, 1996. c.6000p. (6v.) ISBN: 0313273707, set. ISSN: 0192334x.

Vols. cover: California sessions; Eastern and Southern sessions 1934-1942; Eastern sessions 1943-1956; Eastern sessions 1956-1973; country recordings, classical recordings and reissues; numerical listings and artists index.
Class No: 789.90

[4335]
Schwann CD. Chatsworth CA, ABC Consumer Magazines Inc, 1985-. $75pa.

Successor to the *Schwann Catalog* first issued in the early 1950s; from 1985-89 titled the *Schwann Compact Disc Catalog*. Issued monthly; a separately-published quarterly *Schwann Record & Tape Guide: Super Schwann* still appears for non-CD productions.

Currently lists some 20,000 items in each issue, divided by broad category (composers, pop/rock, jazz, musicals/ movies/TV shows, etc.). Date of first listing given, and expanded entries for new releases. Covers CDs, 3-inch CDs, LPs, cassettes, videodiscs, and digital audio tapes (DAT). *Class No:* 789.90

[4336]
SUTTON, A. Directory of American disc record brands and manufacturers, 1891-1943. Westport,CT, Greenwood Press, 1994. 282p. $65.00. ISBN: 0313292000.

Uses original sources - patents, court records, catalogues, discs themselves. Label directory of commercial and semi-private brands, and manufacturer directory of companies and individuals. An impressive amount of historical data. Appendix of phantom labels and corporate genealogies. Replaces B. Rust's *American record label book* (1978). *Class No:* 789.90

Bibliographies

[4337]
Bibliography of discographies. New York, Bowker, 1977-. 164,239,205p.(3v.). ISBN: 0835210235, v.1; 0835213420, v.2; 0835216837, v.3.

Planned in five volumes, of which only 3 appeared; volume 1 (1977) covers classical music 1925-1975; volume 2 (1981) jazz; volume 3 (1983) popular music, including rock, shows, country, bluegrass, film music, orchestral themes; volume 4 was to cover ethnic and folk music, and volume 5 general discographies. The *Journal of the Association for Recorded Sound Collections* supplements the volumes in its Bibliography of Discography feature.

Vol. 1. (M.H. Gray & G.D. Gibson) is arranged A/Z by personal names and subjects with an index covering editors, authors, series titles etc. Vol. 2. (D. Allen) is similarly arranged & contains over 3,000 items; Vol. 3. is arranged A/Z by names & LC subject headings, including entries for individual record labels. The index includes song titles. *Class No:* 789.90(01)

Reviews & Abstracts

[4338]
Billboard: international newsweekly of music and home entertainment. New York, BPI Communications, 1894-. ISSN: 00062510.

Issued weekly.

Reviews and news of new albums; classical, jazz, blues, dance, hits (UK & US), home videos; music charts. *Class No:* 789.90(048)

[4339]
Gramophone: review of new classical recordings. Harrow, Middx., General Gramophone Publications, 1923-. £34.00pa. ISSN: 0017310x.

Issued monthly. Reprints and microfilm available from UMI. *See entry at:* 789.90 for the *Gramophone classical catalogue* which provides an access route to the reviews in this periodical.

Reviews all major classical recordings released in the UK.

.... *(contd.)*

An outstanding and highly-respected source; includes over 200 reviews in each issue with initials of reviewers, each review being 500-700 words. *Class No:* 789.90(048)

[4340]
Music Library Association notes. Ochs, M., *ed.* Canton, MA, Music Library Association, 1942-. $80.00. ISSN: 00274380.

Quarterly. Previously *Notes.*

The Journal of the Music Library Association; excellent range and quality of book reviews in each issue, varying in length from 350-1,500 words, and sometimes totalling nearly 100 reviews. Also reviews of new music, and an excellent index of CD and record reviews. *Class No:* 789.90(048)

USSR

[4341]
BENNETT, J. Melodiya: a Soviet Russian L.P. discography. Westport, CT, Greenwood Press, 1981. xxii, 832p. $42.00. ISBN: 0313225966.

Arranged alphabetically by composer, then by artists, singers of the past, bel canto, pianists, composers playing their own works. Index of artists. Coverage begins in 1951. No annotations. *Class No:* 789.90(47)

India

[4342]
KINNEAR, M.S., ***comp.*** **A Discography of Hindustani and Karnatic music.** London, Greenwood Press, 1986. xviii,594p. £62.50. ISBN: 0313244790.

Details of 2,700 recordings of classical and semi-classical music; artists listed alphabetically with brief biographical details; index by melody and rhythm structure, and international index. *Class No:* 789.90(540)

Libraries

Great Britain

[4343]
BBC GRAMOPHONE LIBRARY. Gramophone library catalogue on CD-ROM. London, BBC, 1996. Set of 4 CDs.

Catalogue of an enormous and important collection; many items are unique. As a discographical source this is probably unequalled. *Class No:* 789.90:061:026/027(410)

[4344]
Directory of recorded sound resources in the United Kingdom. Weerasinghe, L., *comp.* London, British Library, 1989. xxii,173p. ISBN: 0712305025.

Includes libraries, museums, archives, record offices, learned societies, radio stations, business & industry, sound recording groups, private collections. Covers classical music, jazz & pop, dance & theatre, and other recorded materials; fuller details of the last category are given in the entry at 086.7. Details given include size, subject, access arrangements. 489 entries arranged by county. A/Z list p.xi-xvi; excellent index including subjects p.143-73. *Class No:* 789.90:061:026/027(410)

Opera

[4345]
BLYTH, A., ***ed*****. Opera on record.** London, Hutchinson, 1979-1983. 663p. (2v.); 399p. (vol.3). ISBN: 0091399807, v.1; 0091531209, v.2; 0091586208, v.3.

Discographies compiled by Malcolm Walker.

Chronological sections by 22 contributors; critical evaluation of over 5,000 recordings of 50 of the most popular operas. Although dated, it remains valuable for its meticulous editing & authoritative comment.

Class No: 789.90:782

[4346]
GÄNZL, K. Blackwell guide to the musical theatre on record. Oxford, Blackwell, 1990. 350p. £17.99. ISBN: 0631165177.

International coverage (British, US, French, Austrian, German recordings) and reliable in historical background. Written as a buyer's guide, comparing available recordings and suggesting a core collection. 'Highly recommended' (*Library Journal*, October 15, 1990, p.80).

Class No: 789.90:782

[4347]
GRUBER, P., ***ed*****. The Metropolitan Opera guide to recorded opera.** New York, Norton, 1993. 782p. $35.00. ISBN: 0393034445.

20 contributors (US and UK) make critical comparisons of every complete recording of 150 operas by 71 composers. 'It is by far the most thorough work of its kind, valuable for its coverage...and for the expansive performer index.'(*Choice*, 31(8),April 1994, p1274.) *Class No:* 789.90:782

[4348]
LYNCH, R.C., ***comp*****. Movie musicals on record:** a directory of recordings of motion picture musicals, 1927-1987. New York, Greenwood, 1989. 392p. $39.95. ISBN: 0313265402.

Lists commercial recordings with credits, casts etc. Chronological list of films; performer index, technical credit index, but no song index. Over 660 musicals included.

Class No: 789.90:782

Black Races

Biographies

[4349]
TURNER, P. Dictionary of Afro-American performers: 78 rpm and cylinder recordings of opera, choral music, and song, *c.*1900-1949. New York, Garland, 1990. 433p. $45. ISBN: 0824087364.

91 names are included, with extensive biographical summary, bibliographies, and detailed discographies.

Class No: 789.90:782(=96)(092)

Songs

[4350]
BAUER, R. The New catalogue of historical records, 1898-1908/9. 2nd ed. London, Sidgwick & Jackson, 1947. 494p.

'Record-listings of all internationally famous opera and concert singers known to have made lateral cut discs during the years, roughly from 1898 to 1908-09 ... (*Foreword*). The catalogue (performers, A-Z, p.15-477. Records of the Cappella Sistina, p.479 - Talking, p.481-2 - Instrumentation, p.483-7 - Complete operas, p.489-94.' Label identification (of leading companies). Supplemented to some extent, by *Le grandi voci*, edited by R. Celletti (*qv*).

Class No: 789.90:784

[4351]
BLYTH, A., ***ed*****. Song on record:** I. Lieder. Cambridge, Cambridge University Press, 1986. v, 357p. £19.50. ISBN: 0521268443.

Includes all major composers, and all frequently recorded items. Chapters devoted to composers, major cycles; meticulous detail. Cycle entries have discographies at beginning. *Class No:* 789.90:784

[4352]
Voices of the past: vocal recordings, 1898-1925. Lingfield, Surrey, Oakwood Press, 1957-. 11v.

Reprinted Greenwood Press, 1978.

1. *The English [HMV] catalogues,* by J.R. Bennett. 1957. 2. *The Italian [HMV] catalogues,* by J.R. Bennett, 1958. 3. *Supplement to 'Dischi fonotipia'.* 1958. 4. *The International Red Label catalogue of 'DB' and 'DA' His Master's Voice recordings, 1924-56,* by J.R. Bennett and E. Hughes. Book 1: DB (12"). 1961. 5. *The catalogue of 'D' and 'E' His Master's Voice recordings,* by Michael Smith. 1962. 6. *The International Red Label catalogue of 'DB' and 'DA' His Master's Voice recordings, 1924-56,* by J.R. Bennett and E. Hughes. Book 2: 'DA' (10"). 1963. 7. *The German Catalogues,* by J.R. Bennett and W. Wimmer. 1967.8. *Columbia Gramophone Co. Ltd. English celebrity issues,* by M. Smith and I. Cosens. 1970. 9. *A catalogue of vocal recordings from the 1898-1925 French catalogue of the Gramophone Company, Ltd.,* by J.R. Bennett. 1971. 10. *'Plum' label C series [12"], by M. Smith and P. Andrews. [Gramophone Co., Ltd. HMV recordings]. 1974. 11. A catalogue of the vocal recordings from the Russian catalogue of the Gramophone Company, Ltd. Obshchestvo Gramofon c Ogr. Otv. 1899-1915,* by J.R. Bennett. 1977. LP 1,2,3: *A label discography of long playing records.* Series 1-3. Oct. 1952 to Dec. 1962. 1975. 3v. (J.R. Bennett's *Dischi fonotipia: a golden treasury* [of vocal recordings] (Ipswich, Record Collector Shop) was published in 1953, and his *Catalogue of vocal recordings, 1898-1925* (new ed. London, Greenwood Press, xlvii, 238p.) in 1978.

Class No: 789.90:784

Biographies

[4353]
CELLETTI, R., ***ed*****. Le Grandi voci:** dizionario critico - bibliographico dei cantanti discografia operistica. Rome, Instituto per la Collaborazione Culturale, 1964. 1,044 cols.

21 contributors. A biographical dictionary of *c.*250 famous opera singers. A-Z, with full discography. Includes living singers. Signed articles (*e.g.* Galli Curci: cols. 307-11, incl, 3 cols. of discography). 'Opere complete e selezioni', cols. 921-1044, lists complete opera recordings and excerpts. 48 portraits. A classic in its day, but now very out-of-date.

Class No: 789.90:784(092)

Black Races

Biographies

[4354]
TURNER, P. Dictionary of Afro-American performers: 78 rpm and cylinder recordings of opera, choral music, and song, *c.*1900-1949. New York, Garland, 1990. 433p. $45. ISBN: 0824087364.

91 names are included, with extensive biographical summary, bibliographies, and detailed discographies.

Class No: 789.90:784(=96)(092)

Folk Music

[4355]
ARCHIVE OF AMERICAN FOLKSONG. Checklist of recorded songs in the English language in the Archive of American Folk Song to 1940. Washington, Library of Congress, 1942. 3v.

Volumes 1-2 are an alphabetical list; third volume is geographical index. *Class No:* 789.90:784.4

[4356]
DIXON, R. *and* **GODRICH, J. Blues and gospel records 1890-1943.** 4th.ed. Oxford, Clarendon Press, 1997. xlix,1370p. ISBN: 0198162391.

Previous ed. covered 1902-1943 (Chigwell, Essex: Storyville Publications, 1982).

Aims to include all known recordings to end of 1943; alphabetical by artists credits, with details, dates, matrix numbers, take numbers. Library of Congress Archive of Folk Song numbers, issue numbers; index of accompanists. Bibliography p.xvi-xxii. *Class No:* 789.90:784.4

Ireland

[4357]
SCHAEFFER, D.L., ***comp*****. Irish folk music:** a selected discography. Westport, CT., Greenwood Press, 1989. 180p. $39.95. ISBN: 0313253129.

Emphasis on current titles, arranged by principal artist. Full details are given, and indexes lead to specific artists, and song titles. Directory and glossary.
Class No: 789.90:784.4(415)

Africa

[4358]
STONE, R.M. *and* **GILLIS, F.J. African music and oral data:** a catalog of field recordings. 1902-1975. Bloomington, Indiana University Press, 1976. xiv, 412p.

An important record, though incomplete in many areas. Indexes to countries, culture groups, subjects.
Class No: 789.90:784.4(6)

Jazz

[4359]
CUSCUNA, M. *and* **RUPPLI, A.,** ***comps*****. The Blue Note label:** a discography. New York, Greenwood, 1988. 510p. $75.00. ISBN: 0313220182.

Blue Note was a key label in the history of jazz; this guide covers 1939 to 1969 and includes every recording in the heyday period. Index of artists. *Class No:* 789.90:785.16

[4360]
DIXON, R. *and* **GODRICH, J. Blues and gospel records 1890-1943.** 4th. ed. Oxford, Clarendon Press, 1997. xlix,1370p. ISBN: 0198162391.

Previous ed. covered 1902-1943 (Chigwell, Essex: Storyville Publications, 1982).

Aims to include all known recordings to end of 1943; alphabetical by artists credits, with details, dates, matrix numbers, take numbers. Library of Congress Archive of Folk Song numbers, issue numbers; index of accompanists. Bibliography p.xvi-xxii. *Class No:* 789.90:785.16

[4361]
Gramophone Jazz good CD guide. Shadwick, K., *ed.* 2nd.ed. Harrow, Gramophone Publications, 1997. 672p. £15.99. ISBN: 0902470795.

High standard of reviewing. *Class No:* 789.90:785.16

[4362]
HARRISON, M. *and* **FOX, C.** *and* **THACKER, E. The Essential jazz records:** volume 1 - Ragtime to swing. London, Mansell, 1984. £28. ISBN: 0720117429.

250 recordings listed with full discussions; for major figures representative recordings from different periods are recommended. Excellent index. *Class No:* 789.90:785.16

[4363]
Jazz CD listener's guide. Blumenthal, H. New York, Billboard Books, 1997. £9.95. ISBN: 0823076628.

Blumenthal has also compiled *Blues CD listener's guide* for Billboard (ISBN: 0823076105).

Selected recordings, from the *Billboard* database.
Class No: 789.90:785.16

[4364]
KERNFELD, B., ***ed*****. Blackwell guide to recorded jazz.** 2nd.ed. Oxford, Blackwell, 1995. xx,450p. £35.00. ISBN: 0631200754.

Previous ed. 1991.

Details of outstanding performances/recordings of all styles and periods, that would represent a basis for a comprehensive collection. Selection made by internationally renowned specialists. *Class No:* 789.90:785.16

[4365]
KERNFELD, B. *and* **RYE, H. Comprehensive discographies of jazz, blues and gospel.** *Notes*, 51(2), December 1994, p.510-547.

The first part of an outstanding detailed discussion and survey of historical and current sources for this difficult area. The second part appears in the March 1995 issue of *Notes*. *Class No:* 789.90:785.16

[4366]
LAIRD, R. Tantalizing tingles: a discography of early ragtime, Jazz and novelty syncopated piano recordings, 1889-1934. Westport, CT, Greenwood Press, 1995. 258p. $65.00. ISBN: 031329240x.

All non-classical recordings throughout the world from 1889 - discs, cylinders but not piano rolls. Solo, duets, trios, quartets, and piano with orchestra; many famous names are represented here. *Class No:* 789.90:785.16

[4367]
LORD, T. The Jazz discography. Vancouver/Redwood, NY, Lord Music Reference/Cadence Jazz Books, 1988-. 15 vols. to date. $55.00 per vol. ISBN: 1881993140, v.15.

At least 20 vols. are expected; vols. 1-15 cover A - Nelson.

A monumental series; alphabetically arranged by artist name. Very wide ranging, and including all known recordings, not just commercial releases, from 1898 to the present. Final volumes will contain artist and tune index, and supplements. 'Lord's work will be the single most important discography of jazz well into the 21st. century.' (*Choice*, 32(4), December 1994. p.577.) *Class No:* 789.90:785.16

[4368]
MUSIC MASTER. Jazz and blues catalogue. London, RED. c.800p. illus. £9.95.

Re-issued at regular intervals.

Jazz albums, cassettes, CDs, singles and music videos currently available; based on the Music Master *Master Catalogue (see* entry at 789.90). *Class No:* 789.90:785.16

[4369]

MusicHound blues: the essential album guide. Detroit/London, Visible Ink, 1997. 700p. £19.99. ISBN: 1578590302.

Companion title: *MusicHound Jazz: the essential album guide* (1997). *Class No:* 789.90:785.16

[4370]

OLIVER, P., *ed*. New Blackwell guide to recorded blues. New ed. Oxford, Blackwell, 1996. xiii,495p. £15.95. ISBN: 0631196390.

This ed. revised with assistance from J. Cowley.

Excellent introductory material on the history of blues, then arranged in 13 chronological chapters each presenting 10 essential recordings (with another 30 suggested). Bibliography (p.433-6) and index of names.
Class No: 789.90:785.16

[4371]

Penguin guide to jazz on CD. Cook, R. *and* Morton, B. 3rd.ed. London, Penguin Books, 1996. 1506p. £18.00. ISBN: 014051368x.

Knowledgeable; extensive and authoritative annotations.
Class No: 789.90:785.16

[4372]

RECORD INFORMATION SERVICES. Blues records, 1943-1970. Leadbetter, M., *and others*. London, Record Information Services [208 Stanstead Road, SE23 1DB], 1994. c1600p. (2v).

Bibliographical details are sparse, but the RIS guides provide valuable information. *Class No:* 789.90:785.16

[4373]

RICH, A. The Listener's guide to jazz. Poole, Blandford Press, 1980. 133p., illus. £4.95. ISBN: 0713711027.

10 chapters (New Orleans; Up the river; ragtime, stride & boogie-woogie; swing era; bop & post-bop; jazz singers; Ellington & Davis; foreign parts; new thing; fusion & beyond) featuring the best recordings of over 50 major names. Recordings are listed with extensive commentary.
Class No: 789.90:785.16

[4374]

RUST, B., *comp*. Jazz records 1897-1942. 4th ed. New Rochelle, Arlington House, 1978. xiv, 1,996p. (2v). $60.00. ISBN: 0870004042.

30,000 jazz recordings from 239 labels, mainly under artists' names. Indexes of songs and artists. Generally regarded as comprehensive. *Class No:* 789.90:785.16

[4375]

TUDOR, D. Popular music: an annotated guide to recordings. Littleton, CO, Libraries Unlimited, 1983. xxii, 647p. $45.00. ISBN: 0872873951.

Revision of the 1979 4 volume set entitled *Black music; contemporary popular music; grass roots music; jazz.*

Covers all recordings then available, including black music, folk, jazz, mainstream, popular religious, rock. Some lengthy annotations. Record numbers given: index of artists. List of periodicals p.632-633; bibliography p.615-630. Dated, but still of historical value. *Class No:* 789.90:785.16

Histories

[4376]

PRIESTLEY, B. Jazz on record: a history. London, Elm Tree Books, 1988. 210p. ISBN: 0241124409.

8 chapters covering recordings from the beginnings to .... *(contd.)* 'jazz & rock', 'collections, cassettes, & CDs'. Discography, p.188-201; bibliography p.202-3; index.
Class No: 789.90:785.16(091)

Women

[4377]

LEDER, J., *comp*. Women in jazz: a discography of instrumental music 1913-1968. London, Greenwood Press, 1986. 336p. £32.75. ISBN: 0313247900.

Two sections: individual names A/Z; chronological section of collective recordings. Full index.
Class No: 789.90:785.16-0055.2

Pop & Rock Music

[4378]

All music guide: the experts' guide to the best CDs, albums and tapes. Erlewine, M., *and others*. 3rd.ed. London, Miller Freeman, 1997. 1499p. £18.99. ISBN: 0879304235.

Contributions by 150 critics from reputable sources (such as *Billboard; Rolling Stone*) with reviews of 20,000 albums and 4000 artists, arranged in 20 categories: rock; rap; Blues; gospel; country; bluegrass; folk; Celtic; Cajun; world music; reggae; women's music; gay music; soundtracks; Christmas music; vocal; easy listening; new age; 20th century; avant-garde; Jazz. Entries give career details, brief biography, major albums, and star rating. *Class No:* 789.90:785.19

[4379]

BIANCO, D. Heat wave: the Motown fact book. Ann Arbor, Pierian Press, 1988. 524p. $49.50. ISBN: 0876502044.

Eight sections, including discography and indexes, cover 5,500 recordings 1959-1986. Full data supplied.
Class No: 789.90:785.19

[4380]

CHRISTGAU, R. Christgau's record guide: rock albums of the '80's. New York, Pantheon, 1990. 513p. $16.95. ISBN: 067973015x.

Review of 2,800 albums, based on a column in 'Village Voice'. Alphabetical arrangement by artist, with full details, date of release, reviewer's grading.
Class No: 789.90:785.19

[4381]

GAMBACCINI, P. *and* RICE, J. The Guinness book of British hit albums. 7th ed. London, Guinness Publications, 1996. 480p. illus. £12.99. ISBN: 0851126197.

Reviews albums issued 1958 onwards with statistical data; alphabetical list of every soloist and group that has featured in the Top 100. *Class No:* 789.90:785.19

[4382]

HOUNSOME, T. New rock records: a collectors' directory of rock albums and musicians. 3rd ed. Poole, Dorset, New York: Blandford Press, 1987. xii, 738p. £19.95. ISBN: 0713719524.

First published as *Rockmaster* 1978, and as *Rockrecord* 1979.

Covers 45,000 albums, 7,500 bands, and indexes names of 80,000 musicians. Alphabetical arrangement by group name; includes only basic data, no commentary.
Class No: 789.90:785.19

[4383]
Joel Whitburn's Top pop albums 1955-1996. 4th.ed. Menomonee Falls, WI, Record Research Inc., 1996. 1053p. ISBN: 0898201179.

Compiled from *Billboard* magazine pop album charts (based on sales figures); covers 19,000 albums from 4500 artists, divided into 4 sections: albums, soundtracks, top artists, top albums.

Related titles from the same source include: *Joel Whitburn's Top pop singles 1955-1993; Top pop singles CD guide; Pop hits 1955-1994; Top country singles 1944-1993.* *Class No:* 789.90:785.19

[4384]
KOCANDRLE, M. History of rock and roll: a selective discography. Boston, G.K. Hall, 1988. 297p. $40.00. ISBN: 0816189560.

Coverage wide, but sometimes idiosyncratic. Includes 12,000 recordings (without details) arranged under style headings then alphabetically. Historical approach. *Class No:* 789.90:785.19

[4385]
MusicHound Country: the essential album guide. Detroit/ London, Visible Ink, 1997. 1000p. £19.99. ISBN: 157819006x.

Presents a large amount of data; other titles from this source include *MusicHound R & B: the essential album guide* (1997). *Class No:* 789.90:785.19

[4386]
OSBORNE, J. Popular and rock records. 1948-1978. 2nd ed. Phoenix, O'Sullivan Woodside, 1978. 251p.

30,000 items on 45 rpm & 78 rpm recordings. Listed under performers or groups. Glossary; directory of US and foreign dealers. *Class No:* 789.90:785.19

[4387]
PRUTER, R., *ed.* **Blackwell guide to soul recordings.** Oxford, Blackwells, 1993. 453p. £17.50. ISBN: 063118595x.

A suggested core list of recordings, featuring the best work in the genre. Each of the 10 chapters offers 5 - 15 releases, with 30 supplementary sections. 7 specialist contributors; biographies are descriptive rather than critical. 'Excellent core discography of some 400 soul music recordings.' (*Choice,* 31(1) March 1994, p1088.) *Class No:* 789.90:785.19

[4388]
Rare record price guide 1997/98. 4th.ed. London, Record Collector Magazine/Diamond Publishing Group, 1997. 1440p. £19.95. ISBN: 0951555391.

Over 85,000 entries for 45s, EPs, LPs, CDs, cassettes, and 78s (UK commercial releases only); covers rock, pop, soul, punk, metal, indie, progressive, blues, country, folk, jazz. Arranged A/Z by artist; gives catalogue numbers and values for mint condition. Strong on the rare and collectable; minimum value £5. *Class No:* 789.90:785.19

[4389]
RASMUSSEN, R.M. Recorded concert band music, 1950-1987: a selected, annotated listing. Jefferson, NC, McFarland, 1988. xi,442p. ISBN: 0899503187.

Brief survey, followed by the listing, arranged in composer order. Index includes composers, titles, groups, album titles, conductor, instruments etc. *Class No:* 789.90:785.19

[4390]
RECORD INFORMATION SERVICES. Gospel records, 1943-1969. Hayes, C.J., *and others*. London, Record Information Services [208 Stanstead Road, SE23 1DB], 1993. 881p. (2v).

Bibliographical details are sparse, but the RIS guides are a valuable source. *Class No:* 789.90:785.19

[4391]
ROBBINS, I.A., *ed.* **The Trouser Press record guide:** the ultimate guide to alternative music. 4th.ed. New York, Macmillan/Collier, 1991. 800p. ISBN: 0020363613.

1600 entries, alphabetically arranged and signed, give data on some 2500 artists in fields such as rap, heavy metal, folk-rock, electronic etc. 'Important coverage of groups that lack commercial success and for whom it is difficult to find information.' (*Reference books bulletin,* 1/2/92, p1053/4.) *Class No:* 789.90:785.19

[4392]
RUST, B. *and* **FORBES, S. British dance bands on record,** 1911-1945, and supplement. Harrow, Middx., General Gramophone Publications, 1989. 1390,72p. ISBN: 0902470221.

First published 1987. Reprinted with corrections.

Arranged by main artist, with indexes by titles and artists. *Class No:* 789.90:785.19

[4393]
STRONG, M.C. The Great rock discography. 2nd.ed. Edinburgh, Canongate, 1995. 939p. £25.00. ISBN: 0862415624.

1st. ed. 1994.

Over 1000 entries; complete discographies for each person or group with brief biographies, dates of recordings, compilation details. The substantial A4 format in 2 columns contains an extraordinary quantity of information. *Class No:* 789.90:785.19

79 Entertainment & Leisure

Leisure

Dictionaries

[4394]

SMITH, S.L.J. Dictionary of concepts in recreation and leisure studies. Westport, CT, Greenwood Press, 1990. 372p. $56. ISBN: 0313252629.

Definition of terms such as 'national park', 'environment', 'holiday', 'wilderness'; entries discuss historical development of the term, different current opinions, suggested standard definition, and a bibliography usually of 10-30 scholarly sources. Cross-references; index.
Class No: 790(038)

Performing Arts

Bibliographies

[4395]

CLARKE, N.F. The Recreation and entertainment industries: an information sourcebook. Jefferson, NC, McFarland, 1990. 240p. $42.50. ISBN: 0899504647.

Provides information on 30 sectors in the industries; includes publications, databases, associations. Indexed.
Class No: 791/793(01)

[4396]

Performing arts books 1876-1981. New York, Bowker, 1981. 1656p. £165.00. ISBN: 0835213722.

50,000 titles listed under subject headings with author and title indexes. Covers dance, film, music, theatre, opera, television, radio, circus. Entries taken from *American Book Publishing Record;* also includes 3,000 serials titles under subject and title. *Class No:* 791/793(01)

[4397]

Performing arts resources. New York, Drama Book Specialists/Theatre Library Association, 1974-.

An annual publication sponsored by the Theatre Library Association, which aims to describe and discuss the holdings of major collections worldwide. Early volumes contain short essays by various hands on theatre, film, television and other popular entertainments (excluding dance and music) from the resources research angle (*e.g.* 'Reference works for film study', v.2., p.57-68). From volume 5, each volume concentrates on a single theme; latest vols. (17 and 18, 1994) are a chronological record of the New York Hippodrome. Detailed cumulative indexes (to v.1-3 in v.3; to v.4-5 in v.5). *Class No:* 791/793(01)

[4398]

SIMONS, L.K. The Performing arts: a guide to the reference literature. Littleton,CO, Libraries Unlimited, 1994. 230p. $42.00 ISBN: 0872879828.

Coverage is predominantly of theatre and dance, with a few fringe activities such as mime, puppetry, magic, and the circus. Details of 557 books, journals, electronic discussion groups, libraries and archives, and professional organizations. Nearly all the entries are for English language materials. Author/title, and subject indexes. 'The excellent and substantial annotations compare and contrast items and are the strong point of the volume.' *(Reference books bulletin,* July 1994.p1978) *Class No:* 791/793(01)

[4399]

WHALON, M.K. Performing arts research: a guide to information sources. Detroit, Gale Research, 1976. 296p. $68. ISBN: 0810313642.

Covers theatre, film, opera and dancing. 7 main form headings: guides; dictionaries, encyclopedias and handbooks; directories; play indexes and finding lists; sources for reviews of plays and motion pictures; bibliographies, indexes and abstracts; illustrative & audiovisual sources. Restricted to 700 sources. *Choice,* (v.14 July/August 1977, p.662) notes omissions.
Class No: 791/793(01)

[4400]

WILMETH, D.B. American and English popular entertainment: a guide to information sources. Detroit, Gale Research, 1979. 488p. $68. ISBN: 0810314541.

Part 1 examines sources on nineteenth century entertainments, Part 2 specific forms of entertainment-minstrel shows, vaudeville etc. and Part 3 the popular theatre. Some twentieth century coverage.
Class No: 791/793(01)

[4401]

WILMETH, D.B. Variety entertainment and outdoor amusements: a reference guide. Westport, CT, Greenwood Press, 1982. 242p. $39.95. ISBN: 0313214557.

Brings together many scattered sources; a useful adjunct to the previous item. Fuller details of contents in entry at 791.7(01) *Class No:* 791/793(01)

Encyclopaedias & Dictionaries

[4402]

Enciclopedia dello spettacolo. Rome, Maschere, 1954-62. 9v.

Supplement 1955-1965 published 1966 (Rome, Unione Editorale). Index volume 1968.

Comprehensive and copiously illustrated, covering all forms of presentation (circus, cinema, opera, ballet, theatre) with fully informative entries (in Italian) on authors, composers, designers etc. Contributors are acknowledged authorities. *Class No:* 791/793(03)

Handbooks & Manuals

[4403]

COTTERELL, L.E. Performance: business and law of entertainment. 3rd ed. London, Sweet and Maxwell, 1993. 719p. £14.95. ISBN: 0421471905.

Organization, business, and law relating to the performing arts; management, production, administration, contracts, agreements etc. Sections cover artists & directors, musicians, performer & mechanical media, performer & the law, copyright, performance, licensing of places of entertainment, premises & people, agents. Index to collective agreements, and general index. *Class No:* 791/793(035)

Reviews & Abstracts

[4404]

SALEM, J.M. A Guide to critical reviews. Metuchen, NJ, Scarecrow Press, 1991. 820p. ISBN: 081082387x.

Part of a five-volume set also covering drama and screenplay.

Vol. 2: The musical, 1909-1989. 2669 shows entered, mainly Broadway, but also some others; alphabetical by musical title citing reviews from popular magazines, and *New York Times*. Indexes by composer/ author/ lyricist, director/ designer/ choreographer, authors and titles of original works on which musicals have been based.
Class No: 791/793(048)

Periodicals & Progress Reports

[4405]

EDWARDS, C., *ed.* The World guide to performing art periodicals. London, British Centre of the International Theatre Institute/Unesco, 1982. 66p.

636 briefly annotated entries for periodicals from 51 countries. Argentina ... Zambia (United Kingdom: nos.400-462). Data: title, starting year, frequency, publisher's name and address, size, average pagination per issue, circulation, illus., price per issue and pa., etc.; brief description. (Coded data 1-18 are explained at the foot of each page, in either English or French.) Title index. Appended: Acronym index; Periodicals containing abstracts/bibliographies/play-texts, and a helpful 'Selective subject index to specialist periodicals' (Amateur theatre ... Third world theatre).
Class No: 791/793(05)

Awards & Prizes

[4406]

FRANKS, D. Entertainment awards: a music, cinema, theatre and broadcasting reference, 1928-1993. Jefferson NC, McFarland, 1996. 536p. $75.00. ISBN: 0786400315.

Arranged chronologically under the four categories of the title, lists 11,000 recipients of the Emmy, Peabody, Golden Globe, Grammy, Country Music Association, Pulitzer Prize, Oscar, New York Film Critics' and Drama Critics' Circle Awards, Tony, and Obie from the beginning of each award. Single page synopsis of the history of each award. Indexes of names, titles. *Class No:* 791/793(079.2)

[4407]

KAPLAN, M., *ed.* Variety presents: the complete book of major US show business awards. New York, Garland, 1985. 564p., illus. ISBN: 0824089197.

Earlier version 1982.

Lists winners of all categories (over 4,000) of Oscars 1927-83, Emmys 1948-83, Tonys 1947-83, Grammys 1958-83, Pulitzer Prize Plays 1917-83. Index of winners and nominees, titles. *Class No:* 791/793(079.2)

Biographies

[4408]

LA BEAU, T., *ed.* Theatre, film and television biographies master index: a consolidated guide to over 100,000 biographical sketches of persons living and dead, as they appear in over 40 of the principal biographical dictionaries devoted to the theatre, film and television. Detroit, Gale, 1979. xii,477p.

Entries, A.E. ... Stefan Zweig. Coverage: actors, actresses, directors, filmmakers, playwrights, lyricists, cinematographers, designers and others involved in these performing arts. Sources: over 40 biographical dictionaries and directories (largely US) devoted to the stage, screen, opera, popular music, radio and TV.
Class No: 791/793(092)

Great Britain

[4409]

British performing arts yearbook, 1998/9 : the complete guide to venues and performers. Barbour, S., *ed.* London, Rhinegold Publishing, 1998. 600p. £18.95. ISBN: 0946890811. ISSN: 09515208.

Covers England, Scotland, Wales, Isle of Man, Channel Islands, Northern Ireland. Details of venues (addresses etc., status, policy, administration, facilities, technical data, studios etc.) for London, and regionally with indexes by town, type of venue, audience capacity. Directory of companies and individual performers, management, orchestras, arts festivals, arts councils, suppliers and services, agents. *Class No:* 791/793(410)

Biographies

[4410]

Showcall: directory of the entertainment world. London, Stage Newspapers Ltd., 1973-. 2v. £20.00. ISSN: 02644150.

Issued annually.

Directory of artistes with details of accomplishments and agent contacts, managements, venues, services, suppliers, organizations. General and classified index.
Class No: 791/793(410)(092)

[4411]

Spotlight. Merrall, A., *ed.* London, Spotlight, 1923-. 3856p. (3v.), 3345p. (3v.). £140 (set). ISSN: 03090183, Actors volumes; 03089827, Actresses volumes.

First published 1923. Issued annually. CD-ROM available from 1993.

Volumes include agents, casting directors, choreographers, directors, theatre management, stage managers etc., then actors/actresses divided into 'leading', 'character', 'younger character', 'young'. All with photograph & agent details.

Supplementary volumes are issued covering *Afro-Asian artists*, and *Stunt performers and arrangers*.
Class No: 791/793(410)(092)

Ireland

[4412]

BARBOUR, S., *ed.* Irish performing arts yearbook, 1994 : the complete guide to venues and performers. London, Rhinegold Publishing, 1994. 112p. £6.00. ISBN: 0946890560.

Details of venues, agents, festivals, orchestras, etc.
Class No: 791/793(415)

America — North

[4413]

LEWIS, J.V., *ed.* Handel's National directory for the performing arts. 6th ed. New York, Bowker, 1992. 1800p. (2v). £215.00. ISBN: 0835232506.

First published 1973.

First volume covers organizations and facilities, the second educational institutions; arranged by state, with several indexes. Covers USA only.
Class No: 791/793(71+73)

[4414]

NEW YORK PUBLIC LIBRARY. Performing arts desk reference. New York, Macmillan, 1994. 585p. $35.00. ISBN: 0671799126.

One of a series of titles using the NYPL name, but compiled by freelance writers.

3 main sections: theatre, music, dance. Large quantities of current information, directory material, bibliographies. Clear contents page, and efficient index.
Class No: 791/793(71+73)

[4415]

SLIDE, A. *and* HANSON, P.K. Sourcebook for the performing arts: a directory of collections, resources, scholars, and critics in theatre, film and television. Westport, CT, Greenwood Press, 1988. 232p. £36.95. ISBN: 0313248729.

Contents include bookshops, journals & magazines, specialist publishers, organizations, US studios and production companies, TV networks etc.
Class No: 791/793(71+73)

[4416]

WASSERMAN, S.R. *and* O'BRIEN, J., *eds.* Lively arts information directory: a guide to the fields of music, dance, theatre, film, radio and television in the United States and Canada. 2nd ed. Detroit, Gale Research, 1985. xii, 1040p. $165.00. ISBN: 0810303213.

Provides factual details on over 9,000 organizations, agencies, associations, programs, publications, institutions, etc. Includes libraries and information centres.
Class No: 791/793(71+73)

Biographies

[4417]

Contemporary theatre, film and television. O'Donnell, M.M., *ed.* Detroit, Gale Research, 1983-. 450p.,illus.(vol.15 - 1996). £112.00. ISBN: 081039958x, vol.15. ISSN: 0749064x.

Until 1981 titled *Who's who in the Theatre*, issued in 17 editions from 1912.

Biographical and career information on currently popular figures, including performers, directors, writers, producers, designers, managers, choreographers, technicians, composers, dancers, critics. Entries vary in length from one column to several pages. Each volume contains about 700 entries, about one third of which have a photograph; obituaries are included, and revisions of previous entries. There are over 7000 names in the volumes of the present series. Heavy American emphasis.

Vol.6. contained a cumulative index for the series to that time and the seventeen editions of the previous title. Each volume now includes a cumulative index to the previous volumes in the series. *Class No:* 791/793(71+73)(092)

[4418]

LENTZ, H.M. Obituaries in the performing arts, 1994. Jefferson NC, McFarland, 1996. 197p.illus. £22.50. ISBN: 0786402539.

Similar volume covering 1995 also issued in 1996.

500 names included (600 in the 1995 volume) listed A/Z with dates and major credits, obituary date from major newspapers, cause of death. Some entries have monochrome photo. Wide definition, including cartoons, music, dance, theatre. *Class No:* 791/793(71+73)(092)

Black Races

Biographies

[4419]

MAPP, E. Directory of Blacks in the performing arts. 2nd ed. Metuchen, NJ, Scarecrow Press, 1990. 594p. $57.50.

First edition 1979.

Brief details on 1,100 performers; birth, death, education, prizes, performance credits, career data. Covers music, film, theatre, TV, radio, dance, directors, critics, and other categories. *Class No:* 791/793(=96)(092)

Libraries

[4420]

VEINSTEIN, A. *and* GOULDING, A.S. Performing arts libraries and museums of the world. 4th ed. Paris, CNRS, 1992. 740p.

Text in French and English; standard data arranged by country, then city. Index of persons, collections, places and institutions. *Class No:* 791/793:061:026/027

USA

[4421]

GEIST, C., *ed.* Directory of popular culture collections. Phoenix, AZ., Oryx Press, 1989. 234p. £39.95. ISBN: 0897743512.

Guide to US collections on TV, film, cartoons, pulp fiction, folklore, underground culture, humour etc. Organized with basic data and access details. Subject and collection name indexes. 'Many out-of-the-way collections and materials generally not catalogued' (*Choice* 27(1) Sept. 1989. p.78). *Class No:* 791/793:061:026/027(73)

Broadcasting & Radio

Bibliographies

[4422]

BLUM, E. *and* WILHOIT, F.G. Mass media bibliography: an annotated guide to books and journals for research and reference. 3rd.ed. Urbana, Univ. of Illinois Press, 1990. viii,344p. ISBN: 0252017064.

.... (contd.)

Previous editions 1972 and 1980 as *Basic books in the mass media.*

2,000 entries concentrate on theory, structure and research; annotations provided only for items published before 1987. Five chapters cover general communications, broadcasting, film, print media, advertising & public relations; four further chapters are arranged by type of source - bibliographies, directories, journals, indexes. Efficient indexes by author, title and subject. US bias and confined to English-language materials, but a good, standard source. *Class No:* 791.096(01)

[4423]

GREENFIELD, T.A. Radio: a reference guide. Westport, Greenwood, 1989. 185p. $39.95. ISBN: 0313222762.

A survey of research materials on radio; includes organizations and special collections; bibliography. American emphasis. *Class No:* 791.096(01)

[4424]

Information sources for the press and broadcast media. Eagle, S., *ed.* East Grinstead, Bowker-Saur, 1991. xiii,219p. £41.00. ISBN: 0862919002.

Contributions from end-users and information workers in the UK, USA, Germany and the Netherlands discuss the information needs of workers in broadcasting and the press, and how libraries respond. Reviews of practice and case studies. Good emphasis on electronic sources, but some chapters are anecdotal. *Class No:* 791.096(01)

[4425]

LANGHAM, J. *and* **CHRICHLEY, J.,** ***comps.*** **Radio research:** an annotated bibliography, 1975-1988. 2nd. ed. Aldershot, Gower, 1989. 357p. £35. ISBN: 0566071304.

First edition 1986.

Sections cover BBC research report summaries, IBA summaries, abstracts of other research on British radio in subject categories. Fourth part examines overseas work by country. Good indexes; thorough annotations.
Class No: 791.096(01)

[4426]

SKRETVEDT, R. *and* **YOUNG, J.R. The Nostalgia entertainment sourcebook:** the complete resource guide to classic movies, vintage music, old time radio, and theatre. Beverly Hills, Moonstone Press, 1991. 158p. $16.95. ISBN: 0940410257.

1100 entries from the pre-television era (1920s-1940s). Four subject divisions: music, movies, radio, theatre. Names and addresses of dealers, fan clubs, libraries, research centres, festivals, periodicals. Bibliography. 'The focus of this publication is on the obscure, the hard to locate, the unusual or forgotten materials of a bygone era.'(*Reference books bulletin,* September 1991,p88) *Class No:* 791.096(01)

Women

[4427]

Women and mass communications: an international annotated bibliography. Lent, J.A., *comp.* Westport,CT, Greenwood Press, 1991. xvii,481p. $85.00 ISBN: 0313265798.

Chapters cover various parts of the world, discussing media images of women, women as audience, women as practitioners - journalists, broadcasters, filmmakers etc. 3235 numbered entries; strong US bias. 'Excellent introduction briefly summarizes the literature and provides lists of journals selectively or thoroughly surveyed.' Also includes fugitive materials, conference papers, lists of

.... (contd.)

organizations. 'Only large-scale bibliography of its kind. Strongly recommended.' (*Choice,* July/August 1991. p1761)
Class No: 791.096(01)-0055.2

Dictionaries

[4428]

BOGNAR, D.K. International dictionary of broadcasting and film. London, Focal Press, 1995. 268p. £19.99. ISBN: 0240802128.

Mainly of interest for its international coverage; technical information is interspersed with lists of international news agencies, film festivals and awards, abbreviations for radio and television broadcasting systems in each country. Technical value limited by lack of illustrations.
Class No: 791.096(038)

[4429]

ELLMORE, R.T. NTC's mass media dictionary. Lincolnwood,IL, National Textbook Co., 1991. xi,668p. $39.95. ISBN: 0844231851.

20,000 terms defined from the fields of radio, film, television, books, newspapers, advertising, acting, graphic arts, lighting, printing, and public relations. Coverage gives technical terms, jargon and slang, acronyms and abbreviations. Alphabetical arrangement, with an abundance of cross references. Concise definitions are sometimes too condensed to make sense to the non-specialist. Weiner is fuller and clearer, but has fewer actual definitions.
Class No: 791.096(038)

[4430]

FIST, S. The Informatics handbook: a guide to multimedia communications and broadcasting. London, Chapman & Hall, 1996. 746p. £40.00. ISBN: 0412725304.

Covers techniques and concepts, and demands good technical knowledge; A/Z arrangement of terms with cross-references. Some overlap with Weiner (*see below*), but generally more computer orientated.
Class No: 791.096(038)

[4431]

PENNEY, E.F. The Facts on File dictionary of film and broadcast terms. New York, Facts on File, 1992. 257p. $29.95. ISBN: 0816019231.

Clear and concise definitions of broadcast formats, camera shots, general audio-visual matters, technical details, film theories, production staff and activities, networks, unions, etc. Major studios but no individuals are named. Reliable and thorough. *Class No:* 791.096(038)

[4432]

WEINER, R. Webster's New World dictionary of media and communications. Rev.ed. New York, Prentice Hall, 1996. 528p. ISBN: 0139697594.

32,000 entries include technical terms, abbreviations, jargon, awards in fields including performing arts, media, graphic arts, communications technology etc. New edition continues excellent coverage; cross references.
Class No: 791.096(038)

Theses

Bibliographies

[4433]

KITTROSS, J.M. A Bibliography of theses and dissertations in broadcasting, 1920-1973. Washington, DC, Broadcast Education Association, 1978. 238p.

Over 4,000 items from US universities listed by author name; keyword, and subject heading index.

Class No: 791.096(043)(01)

Periodicals & Progress Reports

[4434]

Journal of broadcasting and electronic media. Washington, DC, Broadcast Education Association, 1956-. $90.00. ISSN: 08838151.

Issued quarterly; previously titled *Journal of Broadcasting.*

Important, scholarly journal; book reviews are authoritative and perceptive (usually 4 or 5 per issue, each of about 1,000 words). *Class No:* 791.096(05)

Yearbooks & Directories

[4435]

AV market place: the complete business directory of audio, audiovisual, computer systems, film, video, programming, with industry yellow pages. New Providence,NJ, Bowker, 1969-. Annual. $139.95. ISSN: 10440445.

Title varies.

Primarily a directory of products, services and suppliers. Covers US and Canada only. 1994 ed. (xii,1467p.) lists 1,350 products and services from 7500 companies. Categories are revised to reflect new technologies - DAT, teleconferencing, etc. Lists associations, awards, festivals. Calendar of industry events; listing of reference books and periodicals. *Class No:* 791.096(058)

[4436]

BRITISH BROADCASTING CORPORATION. BBC annual report and accounts. London, BBC, 1928-.

Sections cover news, network TV, radio, policies, awards, World Service, education, religion, statistics.

Class No: 791.096(058)

[4437]

Broadcasting yearbook 1991. Washington, DC, Bowker/ Broadcasting Publications Inc., 1991. *c.*1008p. in sections. $115. ISBN: 0835231771.

Directory, mainly to the US scene: the Fifth Estate, radio, TV, cable, satellite, programming, advertising, technology, professional services. *Class No:* 791.096(058)

[4438]

COMMONWEALTH BROADCASTING ASSOCIATION. Handbook 1990/91. London, CBA, 1991. 144p.

Biennial.

Origins of the Association, details of conferences, charter, member organizations described. *Class No:* 791.096(058)

[4439]

MANN, R., *ed.* Blue book of British broadcasting. 24th.ed. London, Tellex Monitors Ltd, 1998. 438p. ISBN: 0952975424. ISSN: 09605142.

Annual.

Handbook of companies (with contact data, programmes, schedules) including the BBC, independent television, local independent radio, BBC local radio; regulations, standards, ...*(contd.)* satellite and cable, digital broadcasting. Indexes of organizations, contacts, radio and television programme titles. *Class No:* 791.096(058)

[4440]

MANN, R., *ed.* Burgundy book of European broadcasting 1997. London, Tellex Monitors Ltd, 1997. 653p. ISBN: 0952975416. ISSN: 13659677.

1st ed; intended to be annual.

Arranged A/Z by country giving details of companies and their programmes and schedules; covers radio, television, cable and satellite, digital broadcasting. Indexes by contact names, language, station name. *Class No:* 791.096(058)

[4441]

World radio TV handbook. Sennitt, A.G., *ed.* London, Billboard. c600p., illus., tables, maps.

Annual; first published 1947.

Main sections under continents and countries: names & addresses of broadcasting organizations, officials, transmitting stations (including frequencies, power, call signs (if used), music notations, and location when known). Long & medium-wave stations (by regions); short-wave stations of the world (by frequency). 'Listen to the world': a special feature section: world television, satellite broadcasts, equipment tests, software reviewed. The key technical publication for these subject areas. *Class No:* 791.096(058)

Great Britain

Bibliographies

[4442]

HIGGENS, G., *ed.* British broadcasting, 1922-82: a selected and annotated bibliography. London, BBC Data Publications, 1983. 279p. £15. ISBN: 0946358141.

1,213 numbered and briefly annotated entries for books and pamphlets. 30 sections; main headings: Broadcasting; Education; Engineering; External broadcasting; The Fourth Television Channel; General; Government publications; Organization policy; Personalities (A-Z); Pirate broadcasting; Production and programme making techniques; Programmes (11 subsections); Regional, local and community broadcasting; Relations with government. Appendices; 1. Periodicals, p.207-15; 2. BBC Engineering Division monographs; 3. BBC Lunchtime lectures. Index, to numbered sequence. 1-1213 only. 'Periodical articles have, with a few exceptions, been excluded, as these may well form the basis of a future publication' (*Preface*).

Class No: 791.096(410)(01)

[4443]

MacDONALD, B. Broadcasting in the United Kingdom: a guide to information sources. 2nd ed. London, Mansell, 1993. 316p. £50.00. ISBN: 0720120861.

Excellent, comprehensive survey; introductory history of broadcasting, then structure & organizations, including government bodies, councils, trade unions, professional associations, audience research groups, educational facilities, awards, festivals. Primary sources examined; printed & electronic sources by category (dictionaries, periodicals, abstracts, online etc.) each with annotations. Research sources; institutional sources (archives, libraries, museums). Further reading sections throughout; addresses quoted. Index. *Class No:* 791.096(410)(01)

Histories

[4444]

BRIGGS, A. The History of broadcasting in the United Kingdom. Oxford, OUP, 1961-79. 4v., illus.

1. *The birth of broadcasting*. 1961. xiii, 425p.
2. *The golden age of wireless*. 1965. xvi, 688p.
3. *The war of words*. 1970. xviii, [i], 766p.
4. *Sound and vision*. 1979. xiv, 1062p.

'I have had the fullest access to all surviving archives' (*Preface*, v.1). V.1 covers the period up to 1926, when the BBC was formed; numerous footnote references; 50 illus., 'Bibliographical note', p.407-9. V.2: 1927-39; 54 illus.; 'Bibliographical note', p.660-3. V.3 is a detailed, critical and well-documented account; 24 plates; 'Bibliographical note', p.727-32. V.4 reaches the passing of the Independent Television Act, 1955; 7 sections: 1. News, views and perspectives - 2. Politics - 3. Drama, features and variety - 4. Sounds of music - 5. Religion - 6. Education - 7. Sport. Numerous footnote references; 'Bibliographical note', p.1025-31. Each volume has its own analytical index.

An authoritative account, relating the history of broadcasting to that of British society during the period. 'Historians working on the cultural and political life after the Second World War will find it [v.4] to be a marvellously well-ordered source of indispensable information' (*TLS*, no.4001, 23 November 1979, p.30).
Class No: 791.096(410)(091)

[4445]

SCANNELL, P. *and* **CARDIFF, D. A Social history of British broadcasting.** Volume one 1922-1939: serving the nation. Oxford, Blackwell, 1991. £30.

Expected to continue into a four-volume set.

A major, authoritative examination of the BBC, seen from the social & political viewpoint. Concentrates on the production level, and analyses how one large audience was moulded from a large number of diverse interests. The problems of broadcasting v. politics recur repeatedly.
Class No: 791.096(410)(091)

USA

Histories

[4446]

BARNOUW, E.A. A History of broadcasting in the United States. Oxford, OUP, 1966-85. 3v., illus. £96. ISBN: 0195004744, v.1; 0195004752, v.2; 0195012593, v.3.

1. *A tower in Babel*. 1966. 344p.
2. *The golden web*. 1985. 398p.
3. *The image empire*. 1971. 402p.

Traces in v.1 the pre-1920 development of radio, its role in World War I and progress in the 1920s, up to the Depression of 1929. V.2 continues up to the 1950s, concentrating on the major broadcasting networks. V.3 covering 1953-69, concentrates 'on the emergence of television as a dominant force' (*RSR*,v.9, no.3,July/September 1981,p.37). Each volume has a bibliography and index. *Class No:* 791.096(73)(091)

Television

Bibliographies

[4447]

CASSATA, M. *and* **SKILL, T.D. Television:** a guide to the literature. Phoenix, AZ, Oryx Press, 1985. 160p. $36. ISBN: 0897741404.

Two part chapters - bibliographic essay, followed by listing of items. 460 items covered in all. 'The book achieves its purpose of providing an evaluative introduction to the best books about television'. (*Wilson Library Bulletin*, December, 1985. p.67). Subject index criticized as brief and selective. *Class No:* 791.097(01)

[4448]

FISHER, K.N. On the screen: a film, television, and video research guide. Littleton, CO, Libraries Unlimited, 1986. 209p. $35. ISBN: 0872874486.

English-language non-journal sources; 14 categories include bibliographies, dictionaries, encyclopedias, indexes, abstracts, databases etc. Separate lists for film and TV/video titles. Entries are annotated. Directory section lists research centres, archives, associations. Categorized by *Choice* as one of the outstanding reference books in 1988.
Class No: 791.097(01)

[4449]

SHIERS, G. Early television: a bibliographic guide to 1940. New York/London, Garland, 1997. xix,616p. £95.00. ISBN: 0824077822.

Useful and thorough compilation in a field otherwise poorly covered. *Class No:* 791.097(01)

Encyclopaedias & Dictionaries

[4450]

BROWN, L. Encyclopedia of television. 4th ed. Detroit, Gale, 1995. 800p. £33.00. ISBN: 0810389231.

1st ed 1977 as *New York Times encyclopedia of television.*

3000 entries cover developments in the industry, information on actors, producers, writers, programmes, companies, legal and regulatory issues, terms and concepts. US emphasis, but reasonable coverage of UK, Canada, Australia, France, Germany, Italy and Japan.
Class No: 791.097(03)

[4451]

DINTRONE, C.V. Television program master index: access to critical and historical information on 1002 shows in 341 books. Jefferson NC, McFarland, 1996. 133p. $36.50. ISBN: 0786401508.

Index to books about shows, scholarly and popular works, criticism and memoirs. Arranged A/Z by show title. Covers shows 1947-1995, but limited to books published in the 1980s and 1990s. Appendices for genre and class of people (such as ethnic groups.) *Class No:* 791.097(03)

[4452]

NEWCOMB, H., *ed.* **Encyclopedia of television.** Chicago/London, Fitzroy Dearborn in association with the Museum of Broadcast Communication, 1997. 1948p.(3v), illus. £225.00 ISBN: 1884964265.

The Museum's archive of radio and TV material led to the idea of an encyclopedia; A/Z coverage of shows, people, companies, programmes. Topics and analyses form a "map" of the development of the medium. 300 contributors; efficient 22p index at end of vol. 3. Good coverage of UK

....*(contd.)*
subjects as well as US - virtually nothing on other countries except national entry such as 'Brazil' (4 cols). Alan Bennett gets 6 cols. with photo and list of work; Jack Benny 4 cols, photo and work list. 'Brideshead Revisited' gets 4 cols and photo. Thus the work is idiosyncratic, but worthy none-the-less. Heavy US bias and several irritating shortcomings have been noted (*Library Association Record*, 100(6) June 1998, p321.) *Class No:* 791.097(03)

[4453]
SLIDE, A. The Television industry: a historical dictionary. Westport,CT, Greenwood Press, 1991 374p. $59.50. ISBN: 0313256349.
1000 entries for production companies, distributors, organizations, genres, technical and historical terms. Many entries have bibliographies. US emphasis, but international in scope. Name and programme indexes; general bibliography of reference books on television.
Class No: 791.097(03)

[4454]
TERRACE, V. Fifty years of television: a guide to series and plots, 1937-1988. Cranbury,NJ, Cornwall Books, 1991 864p. $29.95. ISBN: 0845348116.
4850 US programmes listed in categories (adventure, comedy, drama etc) with brief story-line summary, cast list, producer, date of broadcast, announcers, songs. Index of performers, but not of characters. *Class No:* 791.097(03)

Dictionaries

[4455]
OAKEY, V. Dictionary of film and television terms. New York, Barnes & Noble, 1983. 206p.
Concise definitions of business and technical terms, slang and jargon. *Class No:* 791.097(038)

[4456]
STEVENS, M., *comp*. International film, television and video acronyms. Westport,CT, Greenwood Press, 1993. 342p. $75.00. ISBN: 0313291233.
Single alphabetical sequence contains 1400 acronyms and abbreviations, and names of 2000 organizations, production, distribution and promotion companies, cable, satellite and television stations, institutes, events and festivals, information sources. Indexes by names, countries, subjects and themes. *Class No:* 791.097(038)

Periodicals & Progress Reports

[4457]
International index to television periodicals: an annotated guide. Moulds, M., *ed*. London, FIAF, 1983-.
Issued every 2 years.
Covers about 100 journals worldwide; four main sections - general subjects, individual programmes & films, biography, author index. Annotations are brief and descriptive only.
Class No: 791.097(05)

[4458]
SLIDE, A., *ed*. International film, radio and television journals. Westport, CT, Greenwood Press, 1985. 428p. $50.95. ISBN: 031323759x.
Detailed description of 200 titles, and brief information on a further 100. Includes evaluations, publication histories, index sources, locations. Appendix includes fan club journals, inhouse journals, and index by category and country. *Class No:* 791.097(05)

Yearbooks & Directories

[4459]
BRITISH FILM INSTITUTE. Film and television handbook. London, BFI. c400p., illus.
Annual.
Reviews UK cinema, examining production, distribution, exhibition, British films, TV programmes. Tables of statistics. Directory section includes archives & libraries, awards, bookshops, cinemas, courses, festivals, laboratories, publications, studios, etc. *Class No:* 791.097(058)

[4460]
International television and video almanac. Klain, J., *ed.* New York, Quigley Publishing. c800p. ISSN: 05390761.
Annual.
Extensive subject list leads to television year in review, statistics, awards, festivals, biographies of film & TV personalities (*c.*5,000 entries), services; television is covered through history, companies, programmes, stations, cable, advertising agencies, organizations, UK & Ireland industry, world market; home video covers statistics, companies, retailers, consumer & trade publications, services, market & distributors. *Class No:* 791.097(058)

[4461]
Kemp's film, television and video handbook. 1997. 41st.ed. London, Variety Media Publications. c1563p. ISSN: 13667068.
Issued annually from 1956; previous title *Film and television directory; International film and television yearbook*. Single vol. replaces earlier split vol. sets.
Also available on the Internet at Website <http://www.pkbaseline.com/kemps>
Production facilities guide with 43,000 entries from 54 countries. Directory of commercial services agencies, studios, music libraries, stock-shot libraries etc. Good coverage of Europe, UK, USA, Canada, Mexico, but 'rest of world' amalgamated in small section p1397-1550. Contact data, but no email addresses or Websites given.
Class No: 791.097(058)

[4462]
Screen International film and TV year book. Noble, P. *and* Roddick, N., *eds*. London, International Thomson Business Publishing. c600p., illus.
Annual.
General reference section lists UK top 100 films, US top 100, European organizations, obituaries. International section covers 52 countries listing agents, distributors, equipment suppliers, exhibitions, festivals, schools, laboratories, government and commercial organizations, production companies, PR, sales, publishers, studios, brief who's who, & market summary. Who's who (mainly UK), separately paginated, contains *c.*3,000 entries.
Class No: 791.097(058)

[4463]
World radio TV handbook. Sennitt, A.G., *ed.* London, Billboard. c600p., illus., tables, maps.
Annual; first published 1947.
Main sections under continents and countries: names & addresses of broadcasting organizations, officials, transmitting stations (including frequencies, power, call signs (if used), music notations, and location when known). Long & medium-wave stations (by regions); short-wave stations of the world (by frequency). 'Listen to the world': a special feature section: world television, satellite broadcasts, equipment tests, software reviewed. The key technical publication for these subject areas. *Class No:* 791.097(058)

Biographies

[4464]

PARISH, J.R. *and* **TERRACE, V. The Complete actors' television credits, 1948-88.** 2nd ed. Metuchen, NJ, Scarecrow Press, 1989-90. 518,389p. (2v.), illus. ISBN: 0810822040, v.1; 081082258x, v.2.

Volume 1 first issued 1973 and covered 1950-72; supplements 1973/76, 1977/81, 1982/85.

Volume 1 (actors) lists 1587 performers, quoting only television work in US; details of programme, date, company in chronological order. Volume 2 (actresses) lists 1739 names, & is similarly organized. *Class No:* 791.097(092)

[4465]

Who's who on television. New ed. London, Boxtree in association with TV Times, 1996. 280p., illus. £9.99. ISBN: 075221067x.

Previous ed. 1990.

Brief entries give credits and photograph for about 1,000 current names. 'Unforgetables' section lists great names no longer performing. Details of TV companies, agents, fan clubs. *Class No:* 791.097(092)

Black Races

[4466]

BOGLE, D. Blacks in American films and television: an encyclopedia. New York, Garland, 1988. 510p., illus. $50. ISBN: 0824087151.

Films arranged alphabetically by title; plot synopsis, characters, critical analyses, photographs. Profile section gives brief biographical sketches.
Class No: 791.097(092)(=96)

Women

Bibliographies

[4467]

HILL, G., ***and others*****. Black women in television:** an illustrated history and bibliography. New York, Garland, 1990. 168p., illus. $25. ISBN: 0824033396.

Covers books, articles, dissertations. Subdivision by topics, personalities. Brief annotations to the theses/ dissertations section. Indexes by author, subject, programme, film. *Class No:* 791.097(092)(=96)-0055.2(01)

Great Britain

[4468]

VAHAMAGI, T., ***ed*****. British television;** an illustrated guide. New ed. Oxford, Oxford University Press for the British Film Institute, 1996. 400p. illus. £30.00. ISBN: 0198159269.

Previous ed. 1994.

Authoritative and well-illustrated general guide; divided into decades, it traces history 1936 - 1992. Selection of 1100 programmes presented - plays, dramas, documentaries, variety shows, panel games etc. 'Each decade is introduced by an excellent survey of developments in the industry and the changing economic, social, and cultural trends affecting television.'(*Choice*, Sept. 1995, p92) which expresses disappointment with the tiny and squashed illustrations.
Class No: 791.097(410)

Histories

[4469]

SENDALL, B. *and* **POTTER, J. Independent television in Britain.** London, Macmillan, 1982-1990. 418,429,352,428p. (4v.). ISBN: 0333309413, v.1; 0333309421, v.2; 0333301956, v.3; 0333455436, v.4.

Volume 1 (Sendall): Origin & foundation, 1946-62.
Volume 2 (Sendall): Expansion & change, 1958-68.
Volume 3 (Potter): Politics & control, 1968-80.
Volume 4 (Potter): Companies and programmes, 1968-80.

The definitive history of independent TV; scholarly and comprehensive, with many references, and appendices giving the full texts of key documents etc. Fully indexed. Bibliography in vol. 4 (p.385-403) covers 1962-80.
Class No: 791.097(410)(091)

Films & Videos

Databases

[4470]

BRITISH FILM INSTITUTE. Film index international. Cambridge, Chadwyck-Healey, 1993-. CD-ROM. £1195.00 (base disc) + annual subscription.

Base disc (from 1930) and annual updates.

Based on the Summary of Information on Film and Television (SIFT) compiled by the British Film Institute since 1934; contains the key details of 90,000 entertainment films from all over the world and can be searched by title, date, director, cast. Plot summaries. References to over 400,000 periodical articles from 900 periodicals in 45 countries. Separate database of 38,000 personalities linked to the main sequence. From 1996 includes details of Oscars, BAFTAs, BFI awards, and the prize winners at Cannes, Berlin and Venice. *Class No:* 791.4(003.4)

[4471]

DEIVERT, B. *and* **HARRIES, D. Film and video on the Internet:** the top 500 sites. New York, Michael Wiese Productions, 1996. 255p. $26.95. ISBN: 094118854x.

Updates expected.

500 selected sites divided into 24 categories (actors, animation, etc). Entries give URL, rating, commentary. Sites range from serious research sources, new releases, 'cybershrines', and surveys. Appendix/cross-reference section lists all sites by provenance and intent (academic, professional, commercial-sponsored, entertainment etc). No overall index. *Class No:* 791.4(003.4)

[4472]

International film index on CD-ROM. Goble, A., *ed.* East Grinstead, Bowker Saur, 1996. CD-ROM. £850.00.

Contains coverage 1895-1995, featuring 245,000 film titles - from full-length features, to shorts, animations, TV documentaries etc. International, with 165 countries represented. Access to filmographies of some 185,000 actors and 35,000 directors. Hypertext links from film entries to filmographies. 'Details are spartan. There is no synopsis...no references to reviews...it does not give access by genre or subject' (*Information world review*, December 1996; p.61.), which notes that the range of search types is impressive and that it gives basic details of almost every film ever made. *Class No:* 791.4(003.4)

Bibliographies of Bibliographies

[4473]

WULFF, H., ***comp.*** **Bibliography of film bibliographies.** New York, K.G. Saur, 1987. 480p. $54. ISBN: 3598106300.

First two chapters list and describe general film bibliographies; seven further chapters cover topical bibliographies (*e.g.* history of cinema, film genres, national cinemas, etc.). The second part of the book repeats the pattern for items published in Eastern Europe. 1,200 items included with very brief annotations. German text.
Class No: 791.4(009)

Bibliographies

[4474]

AMERICAN FILM INSTITUTE. Catalog of motion pictures produced in the United States: feature films 1931-1940. Hanson, P.K., *ed.* Los Angeles, University of California Press, 1993. 3v. $185.00. ISBN: 0520079086.

Previous volumes cover 1911-1920 (1989), 1921-1930 (1971), 1960-69 (1976). In 1996, a two-vol. set covering 1893-1910 was published (Metuchen, NJ/London, Scarecrow Press; ISBN: 0810830213) edited by E. Savada and titled *Vol. A: Film beginnings, 1893-1910: a work in progress.*

Volumes 1 & 2 list 5,525 films with cast, credits, source, length, synopsis, review citations. Third volume contains 10 indexes (name, date, series, language, producer, genre, songwriters, location, source, subject) and a bibliography. The definitive work. *Class No:* 791.4(01)

[4475]

AUSTIN, B.A., ***ed.*** **The Film audience:** an international bibliography of research ... Metuchen, NJ, Scarecrow Press, 1983. 179p. £17.50. ISBN: 0810816229.

Excludes monographs; interesting journal-based bibliography examining cinema and its audience. Author arrangement A/Z with subject and title indexes.
Class No: 791.4(01)

[4476]

BOWLES, S.E. The Film anthologies index. Metuchen, NJ/ London, Scarecrow Press, 1994. 468p. $52.50. ISBN: 0810828960.

Indexes the contents of 716 English-language (and translated) books published between 1967 and 1993, and containing critical essays about film. Author index; index of names, subjects, phrases, keywords. Film reviews and monographs on specific persons are not included.
Class No: 791.4(01)

[4477]

BRITISH FILM INSTITUTE. Catalogue of the book library of the British Film Institute. Boston, G.K. Hall, 1975. 3v. $297. ISBN: 0816100047.

Supplement (2v.) issued 1983. ($240; 0816103887).

Reproduces catalogue cards; international coverage consisting of about 20,000 titles, of which 4,000 are film scripts. Vol.1: author catalogue, title catalogue A-F; vol.2: title catalogue G-Z, script catalogue, name index, film, title index; vol.3: subject catalogue & A/Z subject index.
Class No: 791.4(01)

[4478]

BURROWS, E., ***ed.*** **The British cinema source book:** BFI archive viewing copies and library materials. London, British Film Institute, 1995. xii, 216p., illus. ISBN: 0851704743.

Comprehensive listing of the BFI archive; a very valuable finding tool. *Class No:* 791.4(01)

[4479]

COSTELLO, T. International guide to literature on film. East Grinstead, Bowker-Saur, 1994. 416p. £65.00. ISBN: 0862915953.

Comprehensive, international, well-organized, meticulous source; lists 5200 works of imaginative literature which have been filmed, 1930-1990. Covers a wide range of authors, languages, forms of literature. *Class No:* 791.4(01)

[4480]

ELLIS, J.C. ***and*** **DERRY, C.** ***and*** **KERN, S. The Film book bibliography,** 1940-1975. Metuchen, NJ, Scarecrow Press, 1979. 752p. £40. ISBN: 0810811278.

5,500 English-language items arranged in a classified order with brief note on contents. Name and title indexes.
Class No: 791.4(01)

[4481]

FISHER, K.N. On the screen: a film, television, and video research guide. Littleton, CO, Libraries Unlimited, 1986. 209p. $35. ISBN: 0872874486.

English-language non-journal sources; 14 categories include bibliographies, dictionaries, encyclopedias, indexes, abstracts, databases etc. Separate lists for film and TV/video titles. Entries are annotated. Directory section lists research centres, archives, associations. Categorized by *Choice* as one of the outstanding reference books in 1988.
Class No: 791.4(01)

[4482]

GIFFORD, D., ***ed.*** **British film catalogue 1895-1985:** a reference guide. Newton Abbot, David & Charles, 1986. 1056p. £50.00. ISBN: 0715388355.

Originally published 1973 as *British Film Catalogue: 1895-1970.*

Chronological listing of British films, with standard descriptions, plot summaries, awards. *Class No:* 791.4(01)

[4483]

LIBRARY OF CONGRESS. National union catalog. Audiovisual materials. Washington, DC, Library of Congress, 1983-. Quarterly. $110 (US); $125 (elsewhere). ISSN: 07347669.

Issued on microfiche.

Earlier volumes entitled *Motion pictures and filmstrips* cover 1953-1972; *Films and other materials for projection* cover 1972-1979.

Includes films, video tapes, filmstrips, transparencies available in the US or Canada. Entries in register format (102 fiche October-December 1994), with name, title, series and subject indexes. *Class No:* 791.4(01)

[4484]

MANCHEL, F. Film study: an analytical bibliography. Rutherford,NJ, Farleigh Dickinson University Press, 1990. 4v. $55.00 per vol. ISBN: 083863186x; 0838634125; 0838634133; 0838634141.

Earlier edition as *Film study: a resource guide* (1974).

Expanded text includes longer annotations and comprehensive introductory essays. Numerous appendices and indexes. 'Excellent organization and thorough indexing make it a superb reference guide to a great variety of film topics.' (*Choice,* April 1991, p.1292.) *Class No:* 791.4(01)

[4485]

NATIONAL FILM ARCHIVE. London. **National Film Archive catalogue.** London, British Film Institute. 1980-. xv,808p., illus. (v.1). £15. ISBN: 0851701019.

An earlier series of catalogues was issued 1951-66. 1: *Silent news film, 1895-1933.* 1951. 2nd rev. ed., 1965. 310p. 2: *Silent non-fiction films, 1895-1934.* 1960. x, 195p. 3: *Silent fiction films, 1895-1930.* 1966. 326p.

Lists films by country of origin, then chronologically. Brief synopsis and other descriptive comments, indicating where research and fuller cataloguing have been undertaken. Title and subject indexes. To date, only non-fiction films have been covered. *Class No:* 791.4(01)

[4486]

REHRAUER, G. The Macmillan film bibliography: a critical guide to the literature of the motion picture. London, Macmillan, 1983. 1472p.(2v). £108. ISBN: 0026964007.

Rev. and expanded ed. of Rehrauer's *Cinema Booklist* (Metuchen, N.J., Scarecrow Press, 1972; suppts. 1974. 1977).

V.1 comprises, 6,762 annotated, evaluative entries for biographies, histories, reference works, directories, production handbooks and film scripts in English (inc. translations), published 1900-82; under titles A-Z. V.2 comprises 3 indexes: subject index (with detailed information, especially on films); author index; script index. 'Expensive, but worth the price. Highly recommended' (*RQ*, v.22, no.4, Summer 1983, p.426, which finds v.2 'A worthy reference tool in its own right'). *Class No:* 791.4(01)

[4487]

SKRETVEDT, R. *and* **YOUNG, J.R. The Nostalgia entertainment sourcebook:** the complete resource guide to classic movies, vintage music, old time radio and theatre. Beverly Hills, Moonstone Press, 1991 158p. $16.95. ISBN: 0940410257.

1100 entries from the pre-television era (1920s-1940s). Four subject divisions: music, movies, radio, theatre. Names and addresses of dealers, fan clubs, libraries, research centres, festivals, periodicals. Bibliography. 'The focus of this publication is on the obscure, the hard to locate, the unusual or forgotten material of a bygone era.'(*Reference books bulletin,* September 1991. p88.) *Class No:* 791.4(01)

[4488]

THEATER ARTS HISTORY. Los Angeles. **Motion pictures:** a catalog of books, periodicals, screenplays, television scripts and production stills. Boston, G.K. Hall, 1976. vi,776p. $65.

First published 1972.

The Library is based at the University of California. The catalogue contains 16,200 entries. 5 parts: 1. Authors (including personal papers, archives) - 2. 'Published screenplays' (under titles) - 3. 'Unpublished Screenplays (*c.*6,000) - 4. 'Television scripts' (over 3,000) - 5. 'Production stills' (including posters, programmes). Includes 'all titles in the 1st ed. plus retrospective and newly published works acquired through March 1976'.
Class No: 791.4(01)

[4489]

WORK PROJECTS ADMINISTRATION IN THE CITY OF NEW YORK. Writers' program. **The Film index:** a bibliography. New York, Krause International, 1988. 780p.(vol.1). $60 (v.1). ISBN: 0527293296, v.1.

Volume 1 originally published by H.W. Wilson 1941; volumes 2 & 3 published by Kraus, 1985 from material deposited at the Museum of Modern Art (MOMA) after the

....(contd.)
termination of the Administration in 1942.

Volume one *The film as art* is an annotated bibliography on history, technique and genre, based on holdings at MOMA and NYPL. Volume two is titled *The film as industry*, and three *The film in society*. Includes only material published before 1935. *Class No:* 791.4(01)

Indexes

[4490]

Annual index to motion picture credits. Woodward, B., *ed.* Beverley Hills, Academy of Motion Picture Arts & Sciences. c350p. ISSN: 01635123.

Issued annually, from mid-1930s; until 1978 titled *Screen Achievements Record Bulletin.*

Records credits to films open to entry for Academy Awards. 'Most reliable and complete source of information' (*Booklist*, Feb 1. 1989, p.922) especially for technical staff. Index to annual volumes 1976-87. *Class No:* 791.4(014)

Encyclopaedias & Dictionaries

[4491]

ALLAN, E., *ed.* **A Guide to world cinema:** covering 7,200 films of 1950-1984 including capsule reviews and stills from the programmes of the NFT, London. London, Whittet Books, 1985. vi, 682p. £75. ISBN: 0905483332.

Major films of UK, US, major European countries, Japan, Australia, etc. All types of film are included with basic data and brief commentary. Title arrangement with director index. *Class No:* 791.4(03)

[4492]

Cassell companion to cinema. London, Cassell, 1997. 617p. £25.00. ISBN: 0304349380.

Previous ed. (1995) as *Brewer's cinema: a phrase and fable dictionary.*

300 entries for films, people, terms, facts, trivia, anecdote; good for browsing and containing much fascinating material - but not an easy reference source for subject enquiries.
Class No: 791.4(03)

[4493]

DREW, B.A. Motion picture series and sequels a reference guide. New York, Garland, 1990. 412p. $50. ISBN: 0824042484.

Criticized for incompleteness, but valuable for its coverage of characters appearing in numerous films. (*Choice*. December 1990. p.607). *Class No:* 791.4(03)

[4494]

Encyclopedia of European cinema. Vincendeau, G., *ed.* London, Cassell/New York, Facts on File, 1995. xviii,475p., illus. £40.00. ISBN: 0304341649.

Eurocentric approach includes many unfamiliar names, and surveys of cinema that receive little attention. Performers, directors, producers and others with filmographies and career details; profiles of national film organisations, companies, studios. High standard of monochrome illustration; bibliography p.469-475. Index of films; index of subjects. *Class No:* 791.4(03)

[4495]

GIFFORD, D. Books and plays in films, 1896-1915. London, Mansell, 1990. 224p. £25. ISBN: 0720120802.

Covers US, UK, France, Germany, Italy, Australia, Canada, Japan, & Scandinavian countries; 850 films listed chronologically under author, being adaptations of novels, plays, poems, songs, opera, ballets, cartoon strips. A/Z list of titles relates to author sequence. *Class No:* 791.4(03)

[4496]

HALLIWELL, L. Halliwell's filmgoer's companion. 12th ed. London, HarperCollins, 1997. 514p. £16.99. ISBN: 0002557983.

General encyclopaedic guide to films; thorough, updated and extended. A/Z listing (p.1-450) of actors, actresses, directors, scriptwriters, editors, cinematographers, studios, themes, key films, technical terms. Symbols in the text indicate complete filmographies, outstanding figures, quotations. Top films 1980-1993 listed. Bibliography of some 700 items p.485-492; list of film guides on CD-ROM p.493-4. *Class No:* 791.4(03)

[4497]

HAYWARD, S. Key concepts in cinema studies. London, Routledge, 1996. 467p. £12.99. ISBN: 0415107199.

Discussion of major concepts - narrative, psychoanalysis, hegemony, etc., genres, production terms. Refreshing change from the people or techniques approaches. Concentrated and advanced content, extensively cross-referenced; bibliography. Katz (*see below*) covers some conceptual material, but with less depth. 'A welcome addition to the plethora of film encyclopedias.'(*Choice*,34(6), Feb. 1997; p944.) *Class No:* 791.4(03)

[4498]

HICKEN, M. *and* **BASKIN, E. Enser's filmed books and plays:** a list of books and plays from which films have been made, 1928-1991. 5th.ed. Aldershot, Ashgate, 1993. 986p. £45.00. ISBN: 1857420268.

6000 entries, of which 2000 are new to this edition; covers novels, plays, non-fiction, and some short stories. English and foreign language coverage; TV feature-length films, miniseries, and serials are included. 3 sections: film title index; author index; change of title index. Directory of production and distribution companies appended. 'Enser's is still the most comprehensive guide in its coverage of film adaptations of literature.'(*Reference books bulletin*, November 1993, p562.); the review notes some flaws and suggests some alternative and specialized titles.
Class No: 791.4(03)

[4499]

—LARSON, R.D. Films into books: an analytical bibliography of film novelisations Metuchen, NJ/London, Scarecrow Press, 1995. 610p. £62.50. ISBN: 0810829282.

A useful adjunct to Hicken; half of the volume is a bibliography of tie-ins, with access by title and author. The rest of the book is a discussion of novelisations, examination of 52 authors involved in novelisation, with references etc.
Class No: 791.4(03)

[4500]

KARSTEN, E. *and* **GROSS, D.E. From real life to reel life.** Metuchen,NJ, Scarecrow Press, 1993. 475p. $52.50. ISBN: 0810825910.

1000 films, English language or English subtitles, for cinema or television, which have a person's life as a subject. Arranged alphabetically by subject name; entries give title, *....(contd.)* date, producer, director, duration, cast, characters; no annotations. Indexes by title, performers, dates, subjects by occupations. Bibliography. *Class No:* 791.4(03)

[4501]

KATZ, E. The Macmillan international film encyclopedia. 2nd ed. London, Macmillan, 1996. 1496p. £35.00. ISBN: 0333616014.

First ed. 1979. US edition published 1994 as *The Film encyclopedia.*

Over 7000 entries in this highly recommended single-volume source; truly international with country overviews. Brief biographies and filmographies, definitions, technical processes, but no entries for individual films. For this edition many entries have been completely revised and new topics added. "The best single-volume film encyclopedia in the English language" (*Choice*, January 1995, p.752.)
Class No: 791.4(03)

[4502]

LIMBACHER, J.L. Haven't I seen you somewhere before? Remakes, sequels and series in motion pictures, videos and television, 1896-1990. Rev.ed. Ann Arbor, Pierian Press, 1991. 438p. ISBN: 0876502443.

First edition 1979.

3 sections: remakes (75% of total), sequels, series. Entries by title, with basic data giving year of release, distributor or other source. North American emphasis.
Class No: 791.4(03)

[4503]

LYON, C. *and* **VINSON, J.,** *eds.* **International dictionary of films and filmmakers.** 3rd ed. Detroit, Gale Research/ London, Routledge/Andover, St. James, 1996. 3600p. (4v.) £400.00 (set). ISBN: 1558621997, (set).

Scholarly team of advisers, consistent format; international but mainly western world. First volume examines significant films, second vol. covers 480 international directors, third vol. some 700 actors and actresses, fourth vol. writers and production artists; each vol. is indexed. Now illustrated with portraits and movie stills. *Class No:* 791.4(03)

[4504]

MAGILL, F.N., *ed.* **Magill's survey of cinema:** English-language films. Hanson, S.L. *and* Hanson, P.K., *eds.* Englewood Cliffs, NJ, Salem Press, 1980-1981. 10v. $500. ISBN: 0893562254, Series 1; 0893562300, Series 2.

First series published in 4v. 1980; second series 6v., 1981.

Entries for individual films give date of release, credits, principal cast, plot summary, and synopsis of criticism. Includes American, Canadian, British, Australian and Jamaican films (English-language only). Final volume of second series includes cumulative index of titles, directors, editors, performers. Chronological list of titles.
Class No: 791.4(03)

[4505]

MAGILL, F.N., *ed.* **Magill's survey of cinema:** foreign language films. Englewood Cliffs, NJ, Salem Press, 1966. 3000p.(8v.). £239.60. ISBN: 0893562432.

Extensive & authoritative; now rather dated.
Class No: 791.4(03)

[4506]

MAGILL, F.N., ***ed.*** **Magill's survey of cinema:** silent films. Englewood Cliffs, NJ., Salem Press, 1982. 1338p.(3v.). £150. ISBN: 0893562394.

Covers the years 1902-36 with signed articles on individual films. Introductory essays on history, technical developments. Indexes by title, directors, editors, actors, key technical names. *Class No:* 791.4(03)

[4507]

—MAGILL, F.N., *ed.* Magill's cinema annual. Englewood Cliffs, NJ, Salem Press, 1982-. 600p. £35. ISBN: 0893564095, 1990 vol.

Issued annually to form an update to *Magill's Survey*. International coverage with signed appraisal, reference to reviews, full details of cast and credits. Indexes of subjects, directors, performers, writers. *Class No:* 791.4(03)

[4508]

NASH, J. ***and*** **ROSS, S.R.,** ***eds*****. Motion picture guide.** Chicago, Cine Books, 1985-1987. 12 vols. $750.00. ISBN: 0933997000.

Outstanding reference work on English language films, including details of duration, cast, synopsis, critical evaluation, and reviews. Several excellent indexes. Over 25,000 entries. Ten volumes of text, and two index volumes; continued by *Motion Picture Guide Annual* (East Grinstead: Bowker Saur.) *Class No:* 791.4(03)

[4509]

New York Times encyclopedia of film. Brown, G., *ed.* New York, Times Books, 1984. 13v. $2,000.00. ISBN: 0812910591.

Collection of *New York Times* articles 1896-1974 on all aspects of cinema; final volume is an index to this enormous quantity of material. *Class No:* 791.4(03)

[4510]

NOWLAN, R. ***and*** **NOWLAN, G.W. Cinema sequels and remakes 1903-1987.** New York, McFarland, 1989. 954p. $75.00. ISBN: 0899503134.

Gives basic information and plot summary.
Class No: 791.4(03)

[4511]

NOWLAN, R. ***and*** **NOWLAN, G.W. The Films of the eighties:** a complete, qualitative filmography to over 3400 feature-length English language films, theatrical and video-only, released between January 1 1980 and December 31 1989. Jefferson,NC, McFarland, 1991. 852p. ISBN: 0899505600.

Alphabetical arrangement by title, giving year of release, production company, length, performers, characters, producer, brief description, note of awards. Good coverage - 'more recent films and more minor films than Halliwell.' (*Reference books bulletin,* October 1991. p462.)
Class No: 791.4(03)

[4512]

The Oxford companion to film. Bawden, L., *ed.* Oxford, OUP, 1976. 767p., illus.

50 contributors, 3,000 entries for performers, directors, key cinema industry figures, individual films, genres, technical terms, and brief examination of film in various countries. In need of revision in many respects, but still a valuable source. No bibliographies. *Class No:* 791.4(03)

[4513]

SADOUL, G. Dictionnaire des films. New ed. Paris, Microcosme/Seuil, 1982. 345p., illus.

First edition published 1965; reprinted with supplement 1978. English translation appeared 1972 (Univ. of California Press).

Lists films by title with credits summary, and critical commentary. International coverage; entries under French title with cross references from original. Index of directors. *Class No:* 791.4(03)

Dictionaries

[4514]

BEAVER, F.E. Dictionary of film terms: the aesthetic companion to film analysis. Rev.ed. New York, Twayne, 1994. 410p., illus. $29.95. ISBN: 080579333x.

Previous ed. 1983.

Alphabetical arrangement of definitions; several indexes, including topics by category (animation, editing, film types etc.), terms in context, and notable film titles. Aesthetic point of view leads to the effect of the idea described, not simply what it is. Monochrome stills illustrate visual and allusive content of terms. *Class No:* 791.4(038)

[4515]

CARLSON, V. Translation of film/video terms into French. Burbank, CA, Double C. 1984. 170p. $17.95. ISBN: 0943288002.

Also available in a 5 volume set with translation into German, Italian, Spanish and Japanese. (ISBN 0943288053).

Terms arranged by category; no definitions.
Class No: 791.4(038)

[4516]

CLASON, W.E. Dictionary of cinema, sound, and music; in six languages: English/American, French, Spanish, Italian, Dutch and German. Amsterdam, Elsevier, 1956. 948p.

Over three thousand entries: bibliography of dictionaries, glossaries, terminologies, is appended.
Class No: 791.4(038)

[4517]

KONIGSBERG, I. The Complete film dictionary. 2nd.ed. London, Bloomsbury, 1997. 469p., illus. £20.00. ISBN: 0747535930.

4,000 entries; comprehensive coverage of art forms, technical terms, industry topics. A well-respected source.
Class No: 791.4(038)

[4518]

PENNEY, E.F. The Facts on File dictionary of film and broadcast terms. New York, Facts on File, 1992. 257p. $29.95. ISBN: 0816019231.

Clear and concise definitions for broadcast formats, camera shots, general audio-visual matters, technical details, film theories, production staff and activities, networks, unions etc. Major studios, but no individuals are named. Reliable and thorough. *Class No:* 791.4(038)

[4519]

SINGLETON, R.S. Filmmaker's dictionary. Beverly Hills, CA, Lone Eagle, 1986. 188p. $12.95. ISBN: 0943728088.

1,500 film terms and slang concisely defined.
Class No: 791.4(038)

Reviews & Abstracts

[4520]

ALVAREZ, M.J. Index to motion pictures reviewed by *Variety*. 1907-1980. Metuchen, NJ, Scarecrow Press, 1982. 520p. $45. ISBN: 081081515x.

Arranged by titles, and including thousands of items from major films to 'shorts'. *Class No:* 791.4(048)

[4521]

Cahiers du cinéma. Paris, S. Toubiana, 1951-. £45pa. ISSN: 0008011x.

Issued monthly; index to previous year in January issues. English-language translation of articles from volumes covering 1951-1972 has been published (London, Routledge, 1996; editors J Hillier and N. Browne; ISBN: 0415150809; 3v. £150.00.)

Prestigious journal, international in scope although with emphasis on French work. New films are critically reviewed. *Class No:* 791.4(048)

[4522]

—Cahiers du cinéma - index. Paris, S. Toubiana, 1989. 152p. FFr140.

General index of articles from no. 200 (April 1968) to no. 339 (September 1987); 20 years of publication comprehensively listed under 18 category headings - Réalisateurs, films courts-métrages, auteurs, acteurs, producteurs, entretiens, tournages, festivals, théorie/esthétique, cinémas nationaux, technique, économie, cinéma et société, télevision/audiovisuel, livres/édition, vidéo, photo. *Class No:* 791.4(048)

[4523]

HANSON, P.K. *and* HANSON, S.L., *eds*. Film review index 1950-1985. Phoenix, Oryx, 1987. 416p. $67.50. ISBN: 0897743318.

Volume one covered 1882-1949.

Reviews from popular and technical periodicals of over 3,000 films. Rated as accurate and comprehensive on the basis of volume one (*American Reference Books Annual* 1988). *Class No:* 791.4(048)

[4524]

New York Times film reviews. New York, New York Times & Arno Press/Garland Press. ISSN: 03623688.

Issued biennially from 1913. A six volume cumulation covering 1913-1968 was published in 1970 (Arno Press), comprising 5v. of reviews; vol. 6 is appendix & index. 17 volumes covering 1913 - 1990 re-issued by Garland Press in 1992 (0815303505; $3200.00). The cumulations give reviews reprinted unaltered; the appendix gives corrections, omissions, awards. Index of titles, personal names, and companies. *Class No:* 791.4(048)

[4525]

Sight and sound. London, British Film Institute. 1932-. £36pa. ISSN: 00374806.

From May 1991 re-launched as a monthly, vol 1(1) (NS). Previously quarterly. Incorporates *Monthly film bulletin*.

In addition to feature articles, contains valuable book and film reviews. Film reviews cover 1-2 pages each and include full credits and stills. Video reviews give brief details and description of about 50 items. The publication aims to review "every new film and video". *Class No:* 791.4(048)

[4526]

Variety film reviews, 1907-. New York, R. R. Bowker/Reed Reference Publishing. ISBN: 0835235777, v. 23 (1993-94). ISSN: 08974373.

Series now continues biennially.

Complete reviews of all films until 1927, thereafter feature films only. International coverage, with reference to translated titles etc. Reviews are unabridged from the original appearance in *Variety*, and carry copious detail. A review of the 1993-94 ed. commented: '*Variety* reviews each of these 2900 entries with full credits; gives an assessment of the film's box office potential; and provides a worthy critique of the acting, directing, cinematography, and editing (or as their shorthand has it: thesping, helming, lensing, and cutting).' (*American reference books annual*, 1996; p.587) *Class No:* 791.4(048)

[4527]

Video rating guide for libraries. Blenz-Clucas, B., *ed.* Santa Barbara, ABC-Clio, 1995. $125.00. ISSN: 10453393.

CD-ROM cumulation covers 1990-1994. Supplements issued quarterly.

Reviews over 2,000 titles per year and indicates overall ratings (5 star - 1 star). Access by title, subject, price, top ratings, audience range etc. Reviewers are all librarians. Concentrates mainly on special-interest, educational, informational & children's material. *Class No:* 791.4(048)

Periodicals

[4528]

BRADY, A. *and* WALL, R. *and* WEINER, C.N. Union list of film periodicals: holdings of selected American collections. Westport, Conn., Greenwood Press, 1984. 352p. £35.25. ISBN: 0313237026.

Alphabetical arrangement by title, indicating title changes and detailed holdings. 35 major collections are included. *Class No:* 791.4(051)

[4529]

International index to film periodicals: an annotated guide. London, FIAF, 1973-. ISSN: 00000388.

Published annually. Various publishers 1973-77.

The work of film archives in Europe and the US, this project is coordinated by FIAF (International Federation of Film Archives). Indexes 97 periodicals; classified arrangement by general subjects, individual films, biography. Very brief descriptive annotations. Director index; author index. *Class No:* 791.4(051)

[4530]

LOUGHNEY, K. Film, television, and video periodicals: a comprehensive annotated list. New York, Garland, 1991. 431p. $50.00. ISBN: 082400647x.

900 journals - popular, technical, and scholarly; nearly all English language. Arrangment is by title, with bibliographic details, brief annotation (50 words), cross references from sub-titles, old titles, parallel titles etc. 8 indexes including country, genre, level, and annuals. *Class No:* 791.4(051)

[4531]

SLIDE, A., *ed*. International film, radio and television journals. Westport, CT, Greenwood Press, 1985. 428p. $50.95. ISBN: 031323759x.

Detailed description of 200 titles, and brief information on a further 100. Includes evaluations, publication histories, index sources, locations. Appendix includes fan club journals, in house journals, and index by category and country. *Class No:* 791.4(051)

Indexes

[4532]

Film literature index: a quarterly author-subject periodical index to the international literature of film. Albany, NY, Filmdex 1973-. $275 pa. ISSN: 00936758.

Quarterly, with annual cumulations.

Indexes some 300 periodicals worldwide, including television titles. Well organized, and with easy access. Book reviews are included. *Class No:* 791.4(051)(014)

Yearbooks & Directories

[4533]

Bowker's Complete video directory. Vol. one: entertainment; vol. two & three: education/special interest. New York, R. R. Bowker/Reed Reference Publishing. c4000p.(3v). £165.00.

Annual. Quarterly updates on CD-ROM.

41,000 currently-available titles listed in volume one; vols. 2 and 3 covering educational and special-interest videos contains a further 65,000 items. Alphabetical arrangement with annotation, genre, date, awards, plot summary, running time, cast, director, price and availability etc. Several indexes, including cast names, director, genre, series, format. Addresses of manufacturers and distributors. A review of the 1995 ed. noted "this edition has overcome all previous criticisms. It lists more titles than other current lists, and provides comprehensive indexing" (*American reference books annual* 1996; p406.) *Class No:* 791.4(058)

[4534]

COWIE, P., *ed.* Variety international film guide. London, Hamlyn. c400p., illus. £12.50.

Annual.

Reviews the industry in over 60 countries, with listings, statistics, and profiles of leading directors and performers. *Class No:* 791.4(058)

[4535]

ELLIOTT, J. Elliott's guide to home entertainment. 4th.ed. London, Aurum Press, 1997. 954p. £12.99. ISBN: 1854104853.

Wide coverage - about 10,500 entries (A/Z by title) - including films and feature-length dramas released in cinemas, on video, or on satellite or cable TV. Entries give credits, plot summary, critical comments, running time, format. Index of alternative titles and list of distributors. *Class No:* 791.4(058)

[4536]

FURTAW, J.C., *ed.* Video source book. 18th ed. Detroit, Gale, 1996. 4000p. (2 vols and supplement.) £210.00. ISBN: 081035778x. ISSN: 07480881.

Related to the *VideoHound multimedia* CD-ROM issued by Gale in 1994.

Entries give details of 76,000 videos in all areas of entertainment, feature films, rock videos, educational/instructional shorts, how-to videos, sports highlights, cartoons etc. Detail includes year of release, synopsis, running time, critical rating, distributor, price. Subject index uses 500 terms to categorize entries. Directors/cast members index. Includes items that are currently non-available. (Reviewed in *American reference books annual,* 1996; p.411.) *Class No:* 791.4(058)

[4537]

HALLIWELL, L. Halliwell's film and video guide. Walker, J., *ed.* 13th.ed. London, HarperCollins, 1997. xi,883p. illus. £19.99. ISBN: 000638868x.

First published 1977.

22,000 films and videos are arranged A/Z by titles (p.1-875), giving country of origin, year of release, running time, b & w/colour, production credit, alternative titles, synopsis, assessment, credits for writer, director, photographer, music. Principal cast listed; brief review quote for many entries; note on awards nominations. Lists of alternative titles, translated titles. Small number of illustrations are film stills. Clear 4-column layout; abbreviation symbols. Appendices list top-rated films by title, and by year of release. *Class No:* 791.4(058)

[4538]

International motion picture almanac. Klain, J., *ed.* New York, Quigley. c750p. ISSN: 00747084.

Annual; first published 1929.

Extensive contents list leads to year in review, statistics, awards, festivals, biographies, services, US government services, feature film releases, studio histories, theatre circuits, organizations, press, industry in UK & Ireland, Canada, world market. *Class No:* 791.4(058)

[4539]

International television and video almanac. Klain, J., *ed.* New York, Quigley Publishing. c800p. ISSN: 05390761.

Annual.

Extensive subject list leads to television year in review, statistics, awards, festivals, biographies of film & TV personalities (*c.*5,000 entries), services; television is covered through history, companies, programmes, stations, cable, advertising agencies, organizations, UK & Ireland industry, world market; home video covers statistics, companies, retailers, consumer & trade publications, services, market & distributors. *Class No:* 791.4(058)

[4540]

Kemp's film, television and video handbook. 1997. 41st.ed. London, Variety Media Publications, 1997. c1563p. ISSN: 13667068.

Issued annually from 1956; previous titles *Film and television directory; International film and television yearbook.* Single vol. replaces earlier split vol. sets.

Also available on the Internet at Website: <http://www.pkbaseline.com/kemps>

Production facilities guide with 43,000 entries from 54 countries. Directory of commercial services agencies, studios, music libraries, stock-shot libraries etc. Good coverage of Europe, UK, USA, Canada, Mexico, but 'rest of world' amalgamated in small section p1397-1550. Contact data but no email addresses or websites given. *Class No:* 791.4(058)

[4541]

MALTIN, L., *ed.* Movie and video guide: 1998 edition. London, Penguin Books, 1997. xxv,1620p. £8.99. ISBN: 0140269126.

Annual. First published 1969.

19,000 brief entries by title, new and old, with details of director, cast, plot, date, running time, and 'capsule review'. Symbol indicates availability on videocassette; star-rating feature. Double column pages, small typeface. Probably the best all-round value for general use; low-priced and comprehensive, but reviews are short and there is a US bias. *Class No:* 791.4(058)

[4542]

MILNE, T., *ed*. Time Out film guide. 6th ed. London, Penguin Books, 1997. 9xiv, 1170p. £13.99. ISBN: 0140265643.

Covers world cinema; includes 11,500 films arranged A/Z by title (p.1-990) giving brief details of director, cast, running time, video availability. Brief signed review - 200 contributors. Appendices by genre (Action & adventure, children's, comedies, documentaries, epics, fantasy, film noir, gangster, historical & costume, horror, musicals, S.F. thrillers, war, westerns) list titles and function as a category index. Also appendices of key foreign films, index of directors, general subject index. Good reputation for critical quality. *Class No:* 791.4(058)

[4543]

PITMAN, R. *and* **SWANSON, E. Video movies:** a core collection for libraries. Santa Barbara, ABC-Clio, 1990. 266p. £32.50. ISBN: 0874365775.

500 titles suggested (from a current total of 7,000 available). Annotated list with selection criteria noted; representative works of genre, and historical significance. Listed in alphabetical order, with additional listings by year of release, genre. Main emphasis is on general-release material; specialist European, independent, and third-world poorly represented. *Class No:* 791.4(058)

[4544]

Professional video international yearbook. Baker, S., *ed.* Croydon, Link House. ISSN: 02662256.

Annual.

International directory of products and services, covering equipment (aerials, cameras, erasers, lenses, mixers, satellite systems etc.), services (studios, transmitters) and standards. Interspersed are sections on jargon, reference sources (technical symbols & measurements). Address index.
Class No: 791.4(058)

[4545]

Screen International film and TV year book. Noble, P. *and* Roddick, N., *eds*. London, International Thomson Business Publishing. c600p., illus.

Annual.

General reference section lists UK top 100 films, US top 100, European organizations, obituaries. International section covers 52 countries listing agents, distributors, equipment suppliers, exhibitions, festivals, schools, laboratories, government and commercial organizations, production companies, PR, sales, publishers, studios, brief who's who, & market summary. Who's who (mainly UK), separately paginated, contains *c.*3,000 entries.
Class No: 791.4(058)

[4546]

SPEED, M.F. *and* **WILSON, J.C.,** ***eds*. Film review 1997-98** including video releases. London, Virgin Books, 1997. 192p., illus. £16.99. ISBN: 0753501082.

First published 1969/70.

Reference guide to the year's new films (July 1996-June 1997) A/Z in two sequences, with reviews, profiles, world film diary, obituaries, awards, festivals, and survey features. Well illustrated. Annotated 'bookshelf' section. Detailed index. *Class No:* 791.4(058)

[4547]

TOOKEY, C. The Critics' film guide. London, Boxtree, 1994. xxxiii,960p. £16.99. ISBN: 1852834153.

About 2000 films are included; the unique feature is that a range of comments is provided - good, bad, mixed - from several critics. Preliminary material has list of 'best' and 'worst' films, those under-rated, over-rated; director index.
Class No: 791.4(058)

[4548]

Variety's video directory plus. New York, R.R.Bowker/Reed Reference Publishing, 1991-. CD-ROM. £395.00 pa.

Issued quarterly; cumulates.

55,000 educational titles and 40,000 entertainment titles; searchable by 20 criteria, including title, performer, director, awards, distributor, year of production, language, etc. Full-text reviews from *Variety,* with several hundred added each year. *Class No:* 791.4(058)

[4549]

VideoHound's independent film guide. Sullivan, M., *ed.* Detroit, Visible Ink Press, 1998. 558p., illus. £12.99. ISBN: 1578590183.

Based on the VideoHound's *Golden retriever 1998* which has details on 22,000 movies. Several other derivatives of this database are also published by VideoHound.

Surveys 800 films made outside the Hollywood system; alphabetical arrangement by title. Indexes of cast members, directors, categories; distributor list. *Class No:* 791.4(058)

[4550]

The Virgin film guide. 6th.ed. London, Virgin Books, 1997. vi,857p. £16.99. ISBN: 0753501139.

Based on the Cine Books database; thus related to the *Motion picture guide* ed. by Nash & Ross; *See entry* at 791.4(03).

3,000 films; international coverage. Arranged A/Z by US release title; credits and brief summary; star ratings. Ranges over films from the 1930s to the present.
Class No: 791.4(058)

Awards & Prizes

[4551]

HAMMER, T.B. International film prizes: an encyclopedia. New York, Garland, 1991. 901p. $95.00. ISBN: 0824070992.

Identifies prizes awarded for films, actors, directors, and other associated persons in 42 countries, Argentina - Yugoslavia, and European Film Awards. In alphabetical order by country, including an overview of the industry, history of the award, and lists of prize-winners by year and category. 12000 entries in title index, with cross references to translated titles. (The index covers only feature films, although shorts and documentaries appear in the text.)
Class No: 791.4(079.2)

[4552]

MOWREY, P.C. Award winning films: a viewer's reference to 2700 acclaimed motion pictures. Jefferson,NC, McFarland, 1994. 544p. $35.00. ISBN: 0899507832.

Lists recipients of at least one major award, from 29 societies and festivals. Coverage from the silent era up to 1990. Arranged alphabetically by title with basic data given; indexes by studios and countries; actors, writers, directors; subject. *Class No:* 791.4(079.2)

[4553]

SHALE, R. Academy awards index: the complete categorical and chronological record. Westport,CT, Greenwood Press, 1993. 785p., illus. $75.00. ISBN: 0313277389.

Covers the awards made by the Academy of Motion Picture Arts and Sciences, 1927/28-1992, listing not just winners but all nominees in every category, including technical, special, and discontinued classes. Arranged chronologically and by category. Full index to persons and films; appendices. 'Truly comprehensive reference source.'(*Choice,* 31(9)1994, p.1420.)
Class No: 791.4(079.2)

Quotations

[4554]

NOWLAN, R. *and* **NOWLAN, G.W. Film quotations:** 11000 lines spoken on screen, arranged by subject and indexed. Jefferson,NC, McFarland, 1994. 745p. $75.00. ISBN: 0899507867.

900 subject headings with quotations arranged chronologically under each. Covers 1930s-1990s. Notes performers, release date, context; cross-references. Index of performers, movie titles. *Class No:* 791.4(082.2)

Histories

[4555]

The History of the cinema 1895-1940. Cambridge, Chadwyck-Healey, 1988. 3,900 microfiche. $14,250.00.

1,253 monographs and pamphlets selected by the eminent editorial team as key works in the history of the cinema; based on seven major collections including LC, MOMA, BFI, NYPL. Mainly English language, but some foreign titles. *Class No:* 791.4(091)

[4556]

JEANNE, R. *and* **FORD, C. Histoire encyclopédique du cinéma.** Paris, Laffont, 1970. 5v. in 6., illus.

Previous ed., 1947-62 (5v.).

1. *Histoire du cinéma français*, 1895-1929. 2v.
2. *Histoire du cinéma americain.*
3. *Histoire du cinéma parlant*, 1895-1929.
4. *Cinéma d'aujourd'hui.*
5. *Dictionnaire du cinéma universel.*

A detailed, well-illustrated international survey, v.5 in particular, being 'indispensable' (Beaudiquez, M., & Bethery, A. *Ouvrages de réference pour les bibliothèques publiques*, entry 665). *Class No:* 791.4(091)

[4557]

MITRY, J. Histoire du cinéma. Paris, Delarge, 1972-80. 5v.

1: *1895-1914.* 1972.
2: *1915-1925.* 1973.
3: *1923-1930.* 1973.
4: *1930-1940.* 1980.
5: *1940-1950.* 1980.

V.1-3 form a comprehensive survey of the silent film up to 1930 (v.1-2 were first published in 1967). Treatment is linked to types and schools. Index of names and film titles.
Class No: 791.4(091)

[4558]

NOWELL-SMITH, G. Oxford history of world cinema. Oxford, Oxford University Press, 1996. xxii,824p., illus. £30.00. (£19.99 paperback.) ISBN: 0198112572; 0198742428, Paperback.

Paperback ed. 1997.

Chronological arrangement; silent era (17 chapters); sound era 1930s-1960; sound era 1960 onwards. 90 contributors; major feature is the international approach. Essays and special sections are each accompanied by bibliographies. 4-column index p.785-821; general bibliography p.767-784 in 2 col. format - about 1000 items. 'Makes accessible a good, if otherwise inaccessible, contemporary film theory to the public in fairly understandable terms and with sections on every major film country from Turkey to Indonesia, it is an invaluable fund of information.' (*Independent*, 29 November 1996; p.7) *Class No:* 791.4(091)

[4559]

SADOUL, G. Histoire générale du cinéma. Paris, Editions Denoel, 1946-. 5v.

1. *L'invention du cinéma, 1832-97.* Rev. and enl. ed. 1973. 448p.
2. *Les pionniers du cinéma, 1897-1909.* 3rd ed. 1973. 572p.
3. *Le cinéma devient un art, 1909-20. (i)L'avant guerre.* 1951. 370p.
4. (ii). *La première guerre mondiale.* 1952. 546p.
5. Not published.
6. *Hollywood: la fin du muet, 1909-1929.* 1975. 582p.

The most comprehensive, scholarly and detailed history of the silent film. *Class No:* 791.4(091)

[4560]

SKLAR, R. Film: an international history of the medium. New York, Abrams, 1993. 560p. $49.50. ISBN: 0810933217.

Basic information on technology, social and artistic evolution, growth of the industry, and a selection of directors and titles. Critical evaluations; excellent illustrations. Not confined to the mainstream - many neglected fields, national cinemas, and independents are featured. *Class No:* 791.4(091)

[4561]

SLIDE, A. The International film industry: a historical dictionary. New York, Greenwood, 1989. 423p. $55.00. ISBN: 0313256357.

Alphabetical listings of countries, companies, associations, schools, archives, festivals, awards, genres, etc. Many major entries have bibliographies. *Class No:* 791.4(091)

Bibliographies

[4562]

HECHT, H. Pre-cinema history: an encyclopaedia and annotated bibliography of the moving image before 1896. East Grinstead, Bowker-Saur, 1993. 476p. £99.00. ISBN: 1857390563.

Published in association with the British Film Institute.

3700 entries covering 1321-1896; incorporating virtually every written source on the history of projection from the camera obscura to the magic lantern. Arranged in chronological order. *Class No:* 791.4(091)(01)

Biographies

[4563]
BALSKI, G. Directory of Eastern European film-makers and films, 1945-1991. Westport,CT, Greenwood Press, 1992. 546p. $79.50. ISBN: 0313282781.

Details of 400 Eastern European and old Soviet directors, giving brief biographies and lists of films directed or scripted. Comprehensive but without much real detail or background. Appendices include a film index, index of biographees by country, and a classified bibliography.
Class No: 791.4(092)

[4564]
BAUR, T. *and* **SCIVALLY, B.,** *comps.* **Special effects and stunts:** guide. Beverly Hills, Lone Eagle, 1989. 250p. $24.95. ISBN: 0943728312.

Directory of effects and stunts persons 'well-established & still active' with at least two feature film credits. Concentrates on films released since 1976; includes notable retired & deceased names. *Class No:* 791.4(092)

[4565]
BUSHNELL, B. Directors and their films: a comprehensive reference, 1895-1990. Jefferson,NC, McFarland, 1993. 1035p. $125.00. ISBN: 0899507662.

Basically just a two-way index, containing data on 108,000 films; international in scope, and including cartoons and alternative titles. The year of release is the only other information given, therefore this is a narrow and specialized work, but carries a huge amount of material.
Class No: 791.4(092)

[4566]
COREY, M. *and* **OCHOA, G. A Cast of thousands:** a compendium of who played what in film. New York, Facts on File, 1992. 2462p.(3v.) $245.00. ISBN: 0816024294.

10,000 films, mainly US sound films released between 1912 and 1981; selected from award winners, classics, popular successes, genre representatives, foreign, and silent. Entries give title, year of release, studio, director, cast (up to 15 names). Cross references for titles. Index of directors and actors. *Class No:* 791.4(092)

[4567]
HERBERT, S. *and* **McKERNEN, L.,** *eds.* **Who's who of Victorian cinema:** a worldwide survey. London, British Film Institute, 1996. ix, 178p., illus. £40.00. ISBN: 0851705391.

250 figures who 'collectively invented the cinema' - scientists, entrepreneurs, artists, politicians, photographers, reporters, showmen etc. International balance is claimed, although this is obviously limited at this stage. 23 film schools and archives have contributed information to this vol. which covers the period 1870 to 1901. Technical innovations are described. Bibliographic references occur throughout, and there is a select bibliography at the end. Indexes of names and devices. *Class No:* 791.4(092)

[4568]
International directory of cinematographers, set and costume designers in film. Krautz, A., *ed.* Munich, K.G. Saur, 1981-. 666p.(vol.6). £65 (v.6). ISBN: 3598214375, v.6.

In progress; published under the auspices of FIAF (International Federation of Film Archives).

Brief biographical data and list of films associated. Index of names and titles in each volume. Early volumes cover Germany (East & West), France, other Eastern European

.... *(contd.)*

countries. Vol.5 covers Scandinavia to 1984; vol.6 updates the set for the years 1978-84; vol.7 covers Italy to 1986.
Class No: 791.4(092)

[4569]
NOWLAN, R. *and* **NOWLAN, G.W. Movie characters of leading performers of the sound era.** Chicago, ALA, 1990. 396p. $47.50. ISBN: 0838904807.

450 actors & actresses and the characters portrayed, arranged alphabetically by performer with a paragraph of biographical information. Full details of the films involved are given. Criticized for high price, lack of photographs, and poor access as there are no indexes (*Booklist*, June 15, 1990. p.2032). *Class No:* 791.4(092)

[4570]
OLIVIERO, J. Motion picture players' credits: worldwide performers of 1967 through 1980 with filmography of their entire careers, 1905-1983. Jefferson,NC, McFarland, 1991. 1013p. $145.00. ISBN: 0899503152.

15,000 entries include performers in made-for-TV movies, TV series, shorts, documentaries and instructional films; also vocals, narrations, voice-overs. Coverage of minor players is good. 'Best listing of performance credits available.' (*Library Journal,* April 15, 1991. p.86.)
Class No: 791.4(092)

[4571]
PARISH, J.R. *and* **TERRACE, V. The Complete actors' television credits, 1948-88.** 2nd ed. Metuchen, NJ, Scarecrow Press, 1989-90. 518,389p. (2v.), illus. ISBN: 0810822040, v.1; 081082258x, v.2.

Volume 1 first issued 1973 and covered 1950-72; supplements 1973/76, 1977/81, 1982/85.

Volume 1 (actors) lists 1587 performers, quoting only television work in US; details of programme, date, company in chronological order. Volume 2 (actresses) lists 1739 names, & is similarly organized. *Class No:* 791.4(092)

[4572]
PICKARD, R. Who played who on the screen. London, Batsford, 1988. 300p. £17.95. ISBN: 0713456833.

Alphabetical reference guide to 800 screen characters, real and fictitious, with names of those who played them, and details of films. *Class No:* 791.4(092)

[4573]
PITTS, M.R. Famous movie detectives II. Metuchen,NJ, Scarecrow Press, 1991. 349p. $47.50. ISBN: 0810823454.

Volume I published 1979.

Covers literary detectives translated to movie, audio and television production; examines adaptation, discusses actors, explores plots. 14 major names (Holmes, Marple etc) then more limited coverage of 28 others. Critical comments and quotes, good illustrations, filmography at the end of each section. Extensive indexes. *Class No:* 791.4(092)

[4574]
RAGAN, D. Who's who in Hollywood: the largest cast of international film personalities ever assembled. New York, Facts on File, 1992. 1883p.(2v.) $135.00. ISBN: 0816020116.

Earlier edition in one volume, 1976/7.

Over 35,000 entries from 1893-1991; few cross-references, no illustrations, or index, but the sheer number of names makes this work useful. Basic details are given, but filmographies are not complete. *Class No:* 791.4(092)

[4575]

THOMSON, D. A Biographical dictionary of film. 3rd ed. London, Deutsch, 1994. 834p. £25.00. ISBN: 0233988599.

First published 1970; 2nd ed. 1975. Both earlier editions as *Biographical dictionary of cinema.*

Idiosyncratic and long out-of-print, this work has become a cult classic; about 1000 entries cover actors, directors, writers, producers. Opinionated and passionate, it is 'perverse, maddening, and compulsively readable...to be judged in terms of wit and ardour, rather than accuracy.' (Anthony Quinn, *Independent,* 7 January, 1995.) *Class No:* 791.4(092)

[4576]

TRUITT, E.M., *comp.* **Who was who on screen.** 3rd ed. New York, Bowker, 1983. 788p. £72.00. ISBN: 0835215784.

Lists over 13,000 names who died 1905-1981. Biographical details, awards, film credits. Includes only those who actually appeared on screen; no backroom names, writers or directors. *Class No:* 791.4(092)

[4577]

TULARD, J. Dictionnaire du cinéma. Paris, Laffont, 1982-4. 2v.

Volume 1: directors (biographical notes and filmographies). Volume 2: scriptwriters, actors, producers, designers, technical staff (divided by category). Index at end of v.2. *Class No:* 791.4(092)

[4578]

WAKEMAN, J. World film directors: volume one 1890-1945; volume two 1945-1985. New York, H.W. Wilson, 1987-89. 1247, 1205p. (2v). $175.00. ISBN: 0824207572, v.1; 0824207637, v.2.

Substantial entries comprising biography, filmography, analysis, and bibliography. 'The closest thing to a complete source that film buffs will find on the topic' (*Library Journal* April 15, 1989). *Class No:* 791.4(092)

Children

[4579]

DYE, D. Child and youth actors: filmographies of their entire careers 1914-85. New York, McFarland, 1988. 310p. $24.95. ISBN: 0899502474.

Coverage mainly US in alphabetical order; short bibliography, and useful index of film titles. *Class No:* 791.4(092)-0053

Women

[4580]

FOSTER, G.A. Women film directors: an international bio-critical dictionary. Westport, CT, Greenwood Press, 1995. 443p. $70.50. ISBN: 0313289727.

Covers women directors from 37 countries, from 1896 to the present. For each one there is a brief biography, discussion of important films, critical commentary, selected filmography and bibliography. *Class No:* 791.4(092)-0055.2

[4581]

KUHN, A., *ed* *and* **RADSTONE, S.,** *ed..* **The Women's companion to international film.** London, Virago, 1990. 500p. £10.99. ISBN: 1853810819.

US edition as *Women in film.* (NY: Ballantine/Fawcett.)

Feminist guide compiled by 80 international contributors. 600 entries cover all periods and countries from 1896; includes casts, technicians, critics, movements, festivals, studios. UK slant. *Class No:* 791.4(092)-0055.2

[4582]

SEGRAVE, K. *and* **MARTIN, L. The Continental actress:** European film stars of the postwar era - biographies, criticism, filmographies, bibliographies. Jefferson, NC, McFarland, 1990. 314p., illus. $35. ISBN: 0899505104.

41 actresses (including Bardot, Loren) receive entries of 3-10 pages each, with biography, English-language bibliography, list of films, and at least one photograph. Arranged by nationality (12 Italian, 2 Greek, 15 French, 6 German, 6 Scandinavian). Index of directors, critics etc. mentioned in the text. *Class No:* 791.4(092)-0055.2

Archives

[4583]

Film and television collections in Europe - the MAP-TV guide. Kirchner, D. London, Blueprint, 1995. 663p., illus. £75.00. ISBN: 1857130154.

MAP (Memory Archive Programme) is an initiative of the EU MEDIA Programme which exists to encourage film and TV research; based in Strasbourg.

Detailed guide to 1900 archives in 40 countries; listed A/Z by country. Entries give full details of the collection, formats, access, fees, copyright ownership, contact names. Also list of media organisations, researchers; bibliography. Indexes by local names, English translations, subject/keyword. *Class No:* 791.4(093.20)

[4584]

MAGLIOZZI, R.S., *comp.* **Treasures from the film archives:** a catalog of short silent films held by FIAF archives. Metuchen, NJ., Scarecrow, 1988. 834p. $62.50. ISBN: 081082180x.

Finding list of the holdings of 33 repositories, including Library of Congress and MOMA. Indexes by performer, director, title, series, production company; no commentary. *Class No:* 791.4(093.20)

Great Britain

[4585]

BRITISH FILM INSTITUTE. Film and television handbook. London, BFI. c400p., illus.

Annual.

Reviews UK cinema, examining production, distribution, exhibition, British films, TV programmes. Tables of statistics. Directory section includes archives & libraries, awards, bookshops, cinemas, courses, festivals, laboratories, publications, studios, etc. *Class No:* 791.4(410)

[4586]

British national film and video guide. London, British Library, 1995-. ISSN: 13570048.

Original title *British National film catalogue,* more recently *British National film and video catalogue,* issued by the British Film Institute from 1963. Issued quarterly with annual cumulations.

Details of all films and videos made available for screening to non-fee-paying audiences within the UK, such as colleges, businesses and special interest groups. Includes educational and training films, independent productions, documentaries, television programmes, & feature films. Classified subject arrangement with index. Full details given including plot summary/contents note, intended audience, distributors list. About 500 items are listed in each quarterly issue. *Class No:* 791.4(410)

[4587]
GIFFORD, D., ***ed.*** **British film catalogue 1895-1985:** a reference guide. Newton Abbot, David & Charles, 1986. 1056p. £50.00. ISBN: 0715388355.
Originally published 1973 as *British Film Catalogue: 1895-1970.*
Chronological listing of British films, with standard descriptions, plot summaries, awards. *Class No:* 791.4(410)

[4588]
WOOD, L., ***ed.*** **British films, 1971-1981.** London, British Film Institute, 1985. iii,154p., tables. £3.95. ISBN: 0851701493.
Companion vol. covers 1927-1939 (1986).
2 main sections: 2. British films released theatrically in the UK between 1971 and 1981 (title; registration no.; running time; director); 2. Films 'in production', 1971-1981 (title; studio locations; production company; director). Omissions: semi-commercial productions made/released on 16mm; films emanating from the independent movement which have a non-commercial basis; sponsored films; commercial films; 'anything under 52 minutes'. Prelims. include 'Major trends in the seventies', p.6-14, and 'Key events', p.15-21. Appended: 'Films made available by ACC' [Associated Communication Corpn.]; Statistics; Independent productions: sources of information; British television programmes.
Class No: 791.4(410)

Bibliographies

[4589]
BALLANTYNE, J., ***ed.*** **Researchers' guide to British newsreels.** London, British Universities Film & Video Council, 1983, 1988, 1993. 119,48,86p. (3v.). £11 per vol. ISBN: 0901299324, v.1; 090129957x, v.2; 0901299650, v.3.
Covers a wide array of pieces concerned with newsreel history - abstracts of articles, essays, etc.; in chronological order from 1901 by date of publication. Abstracts for each item (about 250 words). Indexes by subject. Appendices of newsreel organizations, libraries, archives, and documentation centres. Volume two updates coverage to 1987, and volume three to 1992. *Class No:* 791.4(410)(01)

Histories

[4590]
LOW, R. The History of British film. London, Routledge, 1997. 2444p. (7v.) £399.99. ISBN: 0415154510.
Originally published by Allen & Unwin between 1948 and 1985, as *The History of the British film:*
1896-1906, by R. Low and A.R. Manvell. (1948.)
1906-1914, by R. Low and A.R. Manvell. (1949.)
1914-1918, by R. Low. (1951.)
1918-1929, by R. Low. (1971.)
1929-1939: documentary and educational films of the 1930s. (1979.)
1929-1939: films of comment and persuasion of the 1930s. (1979.)
Film making in 1930s Britain. (1997)
Based upon research of the Historical Committee of the British Film Institute.
Covers both the film industry (production, distribution and exhibition) and the films themselves. Each volume carries a bibliography and list of British films of the period. Now recognised as a classic of history and of criticism; Low

....*(contd.)*
pioneered the interpretation of films within a context. This re-issue has an introduction by J. Richards.
Class No: 791.4(410)(091)

[4591]
SWANN, P. The British documentary film movement 1926-1946. Cambridge, CUP, 1980. 228p., illus. £25. (*Cambridge Studies in Film.*) ISBN: 0521334799.
A political and social history of an important and influential movement. *Class No:* 791.4(410)(091)

Biographies

[4592]
PALMER, S. British film actors' credits 1895-1987. Jefferson, NC, McFarland, 1988. 917p. £41.25. ISBN: 0899503160.
Lists 5,000 performers including old Commonwealth and foreign-born who worked in the UK. Sections cover silent 1895-1928, and sound 1929 onwards; usually three films is minimum entry requirement; brief details, chronological listing of films. No film title index. 'Exemplary piece of research' (*Choice,* January 1989).
Class No: 791.4(410)(092)

Germany

[4593]
HELT, R.C. West German cinema since 1945: a reference handbook. Metuchen, NJ, Scarecrow Press, 1987. 736p. $52.50. ISBN: 0810820536.
Covers feature-length films 1945-1985; plot synopsis and evaluation. Index to directors, and brief biographical sketches. Cross-references to titles in English. Bibliography of English-language titles. *Class No:* 791.4(430)

Bibliographies

[4594]
TRAUB, H. ***and*** **LAVIES, H.W. Das Deutsche Filmschrifttum:** Bibliographie der Bücher und Zeitschriften über das Filmwesen 1896-1939. Stuttgart, Hiersemann, 1980. 247,80p.
Reprint of original 1940 volume and supplement (1962) covering 1940-1960.
Monographs and journal material arranged in classified order with author and subject indexes. A major source, containing over 5,000 items. *Class No:* 791.4(430)(01)

France

[4595]
CHIRAT, R. Catalogue des films français de long métrage: films de fiction.
First collection covers 1919-29 (Toulouse, Cinémathèque de Toulouse, 1984).
Second collection covers 1929-39 (Bruxelles, Cinémathèque Royale, 2nd. ed., 1981).
Third collection covers 1940-50 (Luxembourg, Impr. Saint-Paul, 1981).
Each volume lists films alphabetically by title, with chronological and name indexes. Dates, technical credits, cast, plot summary, running time given. A major source for French cinema. *Class No:* 791.4(44)

Italy

[4596]
STEWART, J. Italian film: a who's who. Jefferson,NC, McFarland, 1994. 812p. $95.00. ISBN: 0899507611.

5000 actors, directors, writers, producers, and major technicians (Italian and non-Italian) involved in the Italian industry; gives brief biography and filmography. Index of titles. *Class No:* 791.4(450)

China

[4597]
CLARK, P. Chinese cinema: culture and politics since 1949. Cambridge, CUP, 1988. 243p. £25.00.

A reasonable summary, but not totally satisfactory. *Class No:* 791.4(510)

Japan

[4598]
BUEHRER, B.B. Japanese films: a filmography and commentary, 1921-1989. Jefferson, NC, McFarland, 1990. 328p., illus. $39.95. ISBN: 0899504582.

Discusses 89 films by 50 directors; includes obscure and well-known names, selected for importance in film history. Chronological arrangement; details include credits, cast list, plot summary, still. 29 page bibliography; glossary; index includes material from the text, glossary and bibliography. *Class No:* 791.4(52)

India

[4599]
NARWECKER, S., ***comp.*** **Directory of Indian film-makers and films.** Westport,CT, Greenwood Press, 1994. 500p. $85.00. ISBN: 0313292841.

383 directors from Hindi and regional cinemas, with filmographies for each; general and film title indexes (about 15000 entries). Sources used include published works and scattered inaccessible material. Selective, unannotated bibliography. 'Ambitiously conceived and broad-ranging work should be exceptionally useful.' (*Choice,* 32(1)1994. p74.) *Class No:* 791.4(540)

[4600]
RAJADHYAKSHA, A. ***and*** **WILLEMEN, P. Encyclopaedia of Indian cinema.** London, British Film Institute/New Delhi, Oxford University Press, 1994. 568p., illus. £35.00. ISBN: 0851704557.

Compiled in association with the National Film Archive of India.

Two large sections: dictionary (p.35-224) with 700 entries covering directors, actors, studios, writers, genres, movements etc; and films (p.225-460) with 1500 entries covering only titles selected as important. Summary of sources (p.13-15); chronicle (p.17-30). Multilingual bibliography of some 750 items (p.462-471); enormous index (p473-568; 4-column). *Class No:* 791.4(540)

[4601]
RANGOONWALLA, F. Indian filmography: silent and Hindu films, 1897-1969. Bombay, Viswanath Das, 1970. xx,471p.

Chronological directory of films produced in India 1897-1969. Also provides an index of Indian films. *Class No:* 791.4(540)

Africa

[4602]
PFAFF, F. Twenty-five Black African filmmakers: a critical study with filmography and bio-bibliography. Westport, CT, Greenwood Press, 1988. 344p. £40.95. ISBN: 0313246955.

Internationally respected names from 13 countries; good analysis and full index. *Class No:* 791.4(6)

[4603]
SCHMIDT, N.J. Sub-Saharan African films and filmmakers, 1987-1992: an annotated bibliography. London, Hans Zell, 1994. 468p. £48.00. ISBN: 187383621x.

Continues an earlier volume covering 1960-1987.

3000 entries, each with an annotation of 2 or 3 lines. Indexes by actors, titles, festivals, other personnel, country, and subject. Although such a work is a very difficult undertaking, this is an 'impressive attempt.' (*Reference reviews,* 9(1), 1995. p.34.) *Class No:* 791.4(6)

[4604]
SHIRI, K., ***comp.*** **Directory of African film-makers and films.** Westport,NJ, Greenwood Press, 1992. 194p. $79.50. ISBN: 0313287562.

259 filmmakers from 29 countries are included; several shortcomings are apparent, but literature in this area is very sparse. A particular failing is that 'it is an English language service in a field where 60% - 70% of the literature is in French.' (*Choice,* 30(7)1993, p1120.) *Class No:* 791.4(6)

USA

Histories

[4605]
FERNETT, G. American film studios: an historical encyclopedia. Jefferson, NC, McFarland, 1988. 295p. $35.00. ISBN: 0899502504.

Profiles of sixty studios. Early history outstanding, with a wealth of detail. *Class No:* 791.4(73)(091)

[4606]
SLIDE, A. The American film industry: a historical dictionary. Westport, CT, Greenwood Press, 1986. 431p. $50.00. ISBN: 0313246939.

Companies, series, terms, studios in the US industry are included. Many bibliographies. *Class No:* 791.4(73)(091)

Biographies

Jews

[4607]
LYMAN, D. Great Jews of stage and screen. Middle Village, NY, Jonathan David, 1987. 279p., illus. £19.95. ISBN: 0824603281.

100 biographical sketches ranging from ½page to four pages in length; career data and photograph. Second section gives much briefer entries for a further 200 names. Mainly US, but not entirely; indexes living and dead. *Class No:* 791.4(73)(092)(=924)

Black Races

[4608]

BOGLE, D. Blacks in American films and television: an encyclopedia. New York, Garland, 1988. 510p., illus. $50. ISBN: 0824087151.

Films arranged alphabetically by title; plot synopsis, characters, critical analyses, photographs. Profile section gives brief biographical sketches.

Class No: 791.4(73)(092)(=96)

New Zealand

Biographies

[4609]

PALMER, S. Who's who of Australian and New Zealand film actors: the sound era. Metuchen, NJ, Scarecrow Press, 1988. 179p. $22.50. ISBN: 0810820900.

Brief biographical notes with details of appearances.

Class No: 791.4(931)(092)

Australia

[4610]

MURRAY, S., *comp*. Australian film, 1978-1992: a survey of theatrical features. Oxford, Oxford University Press/ Melbourne, Australian Film Commission/Cinema Papers, 1994. 414p. $27.00. ISBN: 0195535847.

55 contributors cover all feature films, and technical and cast credits. Plot summaries and original evaluative appraisals. Bibliography. Index to names, titles, and organizations. *Class No:* 791.4(94)

Biographies

[4611]

PALMER, S. Who's who of Australian and New Zealand film actors: the sound era. Metuchen, NJ, Scarecrow Press, 1988. 179p. $22.50. ISBN: 0810820900.

Brief biographical notes with details of appearances.

Class No: 791.4(94)(092)

Research Methods

[4612]

MORGAN, J., *ed*. The Film researcher's handbook: a guide to sources in North America, South America, Asia, Australasia, and Africa. London, Blueprint, 1996. 572p. £50.00. ISBN: 0415151236.

International guide to film libraries and film collections outside Europe, including video and TV collections and national archives. Arranged by country and by subject, with annotations giving format of material held, fees, accessibility, opening hours, contact name. Several advisory features (copyright, contracts etc), and glossary.

Class No: 791.4:001.891

Thesauri

[4613]

YEE, M.M., *comp*. Moving image materials: genre terms. Washington, Library of Congress for American Film Institute, 1988. $20.00.

Well constructed and highly detailed thesaurus, featuring 190 terms building up into an extensive network of references. Intended for general collections; scope notes explain terms. *Class No:* 791.4:025.43

Film Libraries

[4614]

THORPE, F., *ed*. International directory of film and TV documentation centres. 3rd ed. Chicago, St. James Press, 1988. $45. ISBN: 0912289295.

Originally a publication of FIAF (International Federation of Film Archives).

Describes 104 sources worldwide with addresses, hours, access, size, facilities, holdings summary. Variable in data provided. *Class No:* 791.4:061:026/027

Great Britain

[4615]

BALLANTYNE, J., *ed*. Researcher's guide to British film and television collections. 4th ed. London, British Universities Film and Video Council, 1993. 226p. £18.95. ISBN: 0901299642.

Directory of resources arranged under broad categories and supported by excellent indexes. Useful and informative articles on many issues such as archives, research, franchises, copyright. Appendices include a directory to services in the Republic of Ireland, and a select bibliography of books, periodicals, and Acts of Parliament.

Class No: 791.4:061:026/027(410)

Gay People

[4616]

MURRAY, R. Images in the dark: an encyclopedia of gay and lesbian film and video. Philadelphia, PA, TLA Publications, 1994. 561p., illus. $19.95. ISBN: 1880707012.

Covers 200 gay, bisexual, and lesbian actors and directors, and entries for 3000 films and videos with gay themes. Also includes information on straight people who are popular in gay culture. Mainly US and UK emphasis. Annotations for films and videos are thorough, and give full information. *Class No:* 791.4-0055.3

Film Music

[4617]

ANDERSON, G.B., *comp*. Music for silent films 1894-1929: a guide. Washington, Library of Congress, 1989. 182p. $37.00. ISBN: 0844405809.

Covers two major collections held at the Library of Congress, the LC collection and the permanent loan collection from MOMA. Arranged alphabetically by film title with full details. Bibliography; appendix identifying other major collections. *Class No:* 791.43:78

[4618]

GREEN, S. Encyclopedia of the musical film. New ed. New York, Oxford University Press, 1988. 352p. £9.95. (paper). ISBN: 0195054210.

Entries, A-Z, p.3-319. 'Wizard of Oz, The'; 2¾ columns (credits, cast, songs, history and synopsis, TV repeat, 2 references). 'Judy Garland': 1½ columns, with over ½p. list of parts played. 'Succinct information regarding the musical screen's most prominent individuals, productions, and songs. Though emphasis is on Hollywood output (including feature-length cartoons), British musical films and selected original television musicals are also covered' (*Preface*).

Class No: 791.43:78

[4619]

HARRIS, S. Film, television and stage music on phonograph records: a discography. Jefferson, NC, McFarland, 1988. 445p. $49.95. ISBN: 0899502512.

Includes 12,000 American and British productions to the end of 1986. Brief annotations; alphabetical arrangement with composer index. *Class No:* 791.43:78

[4620]

—HARRIS, S. Film and television composers: an international discography 1920-1989. Jefferson, NC, McFarland, 1992. 302p. ISBN: 0899505538.

Sequel to the above, but now excluding stage music; 8000 entries, composed or adapted specifically. Title index. *Class No:* 791.43:78

[4621]

LIMBACHER, J.L. ***and*** **WRIGHT, H.S. Keeping score:** film and television music 1980-88 (with additional coverage 1921-1979). Metuchen,NJ, Scarecrow Press, 1991. 916p. ISBN: 0810824531.

Mainly devoted to film; not just a discography, it includes information on composers. Film and programme title index. *Class No:* 791.43:78

[4622]

MusicHound's soundtracks: music from the movies, Broadway and television. Detroit/London, Visible ink, 1997. 800p. £19.99. ISBN: 1578590256.

Straightforward discography, with brief reviews. *Class No:* 791.43:78

Bibliographies

[4623]

WESTCOTT, S.D., ***comp.*** **A Comprehensive bibliography of music for film and television.** Detroit, Information Coordinators, 1985. xix,432p. $60. (*Detroit Studies in Music Bibliography, 54.*) ISBN: 0899900275.

6,340 citations on the literature of film music; covers mainly US, Canadian and European sources in books, book reviews, journals, conference proceedings etc. Five sections examine history, composers, aesthetics, special topics, research. Full index. *Class No:* 791.43:78(01)

Biographies

[4624]

CRAGGS, S.R. Soundtracks: the international dictionary of composers for film. Aldershot, Ashgate, 1997. 180p. £35.00. ISBN: 1859281893.

Brief details and work-lists for significant film-music composers. *Class No:* 791.43:78(092)

Genres of Films

[4625]

GEHRING, D. Handbook of American film genres. New York, Greenwood, 1988. 405p. $55.00. ISBN: 0313247153.

Eighteen genres examined, with overview, bibliography and filmography. Mainly US but some European coverage. *Class No:* 791.43.0

[4626]

LOPEZ, D. Films by genre: 775 categories, styles, trends and movements defined, and with a filmography for each. Jefferson,NC, McFarland, 1993. 495p. $45.00. ISBN: 0899507808.

Covers from the silent era up to 1992; alphabetical arrangement by genre with brief descriptions, cross references, bibliographical references, and filmographies of selected, representative films with basic data - from *Abstract film* to *Zombie movie*. Name and title indexes. Mainstream, Western emphasis; distinctions between some of the categories seem artificially slight. *Class No:* 791.43.0

Animations

[4627]

HOFFER, T.W. Animation: a reference guide. Westport, CT, Greenwood Press, 1981. 448p. £35. ISBN: 0313210950.

6 bibliographical essays on animated motion pictures: 1. Introduction - 2. The historic outline - 3. Gateway to the animation literature - 4. Classes of animation and personalities - 5. Creating animation - 6. New directions. 7. appendices; Chronology; Major research centres; Sources for collectible animation art; Animated film on 8mm; Selected and annotated trade journal and popular press reports in animation, 1906-1979; Periodicals, newsletters, and irregular serials in English of animation interest (bibliography, p.362-72). Analytical index. 'A valuable guide to an uncharted area' (*Art documentation*, Summer 1982, p.127). *Class No:* 791.43.0ANI

[4628]

LENBURG, J. Encyclopedia of animated cartoons. Rev.ed. New York, Facts on File, 1991. 480p. £21.95. ISBN: 0816022526.

Covers animated films 'exhibited or broadcast in the US 1911-1990.' 6 sections: silent cartoons, theatrical sound cartoon series, television cartoon series, animated television specials, full-length animated features, award winners. Arranged alphabetically by title with indexes by subject, voice actors, producers and directors, animated characters. *Class No:* 791.43.0ANI

[4629]

TAYLOR, R. Encyclopedia of animation techniques. Oxford, Focal Press, 1996. 176p., illus. ISBN: 0240514882.

Thorough reference source from a respected technical publisher. *Class No:* 791.43.0ANI

Comedy films

[4630]

LANGMAN, L. Encyclopedia of American film comedy. New York, Garland, 1988. 639p. $60.00. ISBN: 0824084969.

Wide coverage of history, personalities, and entries for 150 films 1912-1984 which exemplify American humour. Filmography after each entry. No full index. *Class No:* 791.43.0COM

Film noir

[4631]

STEPHENS, M.L. Film noir: a comprehensive, illustrated reference to movies, terms and persons. Jefferson, NC/ London, McFarland, 1995. 424p., illus. $55.00. ISBN: 0899508022.

Brief essays (500-1000 words) on film noir titles, topics

....*(contd.)*
and personalities in a single A/Z sequence. Index to persons, films and subjects. Bibliography; monochrome illustrations.
Class No: 791.43.0FIL

Horror films

[4632]
HARDY, P., *ed.* Overlook film encyclopedia: horror. New York, Overlook Press, 1994. 496p. $50.00. ISBN: 087591518x.
Updates *Encyclopedia of horror movies* also edited by Hardy (Harper, 1986.)
Covers 1896-1992; entries give commentary and brief cast information. Lack of name index is a serious omission. International coverage; chronological arrangement.
Class No: 791.43.0HOR

[4633]
LENTZ, H.M. Science fiction, horror and fantasy film and television credits. Jefferson, NC/London, McFarland, 1984-1994. 2v., and 2 supplements. ISBN: 0899509274, Supplement 2.
Original 2v. set (1984), supplemented 1988 and 1994.
Vol.1 contains actors/actresses; directors and other major contributors. Vol. 2 contains film index and television index. Comprehensive and well-regarded. *Class No:* 791.43.0HOR

[4634]
NEWMAN, K., *ed.* The BFI companion to horror. London, Cassell, 1996. 352p., illus. ISBN: 0304332135.
Encyclopedic coverage; international scope.
Class No: 791.43.0HOR

[4635]
SENN, B. *and* JOHNSON, J. Fantastic cinema subject guide: a topical index to 2500 horror, science fiction and fantasy films. Jefferson,NC, McFarland, 1992. 682p. $45.00. ISBN: 089950681x.
Genres are divided into 81 subjects, then alphabetical listing by title with essential data and brief synopsis. Cross references; title index. Television films are not included.
Class No: 791.43.0HOR

[4636]
WILLIS, D.C. Horror and science fiction films 4. Metuchen, NJ/London, Scarecrow Press, 1997. 664p. £85.00. ISBN: 0810830558.
Extends coverage to end of 1994, and updates and corrects three earlier volumes. Vol. 3 was issued in 1984.
Over 1000 titles are listed; films included are theatrical or TV released in US or elsewhere. Critical annotations. Arranged A-Z order by title; list of alternative titles.
Class No: 791.43.0HOR

[4637]
WOLF, L. Horror: a connoisseur's guide to literature and film. New York/Oxford, Facts on File, 1989. 320p. $17.95. ISBN: 081602197x.
Adequate coverage of films; also includes novels, poems etc. Entries arranged A-Z by title with source details, plot summary and critical evaluation. Extensive bibliography.
Class No: 791.43.0HOR

Musicals

[4638]
BLOOM, K. Hollywood song: the complete film and musical companion. New York, Facts on File, 1995. 3v. $195.00. ISBN: 0816020027.
See entry at: 784(73). *Class No:* 791.43.0MUS

[4639]
GREEN, S. Encyclopedia of the musical film. New ed. New York, Oxford Universoty Press, 1988. 352p. £9.95. (paper). ISBN: 0195054210.
Entries, A-Z, p.3-319. 'Wizard of Oz, The'; 2¾ columns (credits, cast, songs, history and synopsis, TV repeat, 2 references). 'Judy Garland': 1½ columns, with over ½p. list of parts played. 'Succinct information regarding the musical screen's most prominent individuals, productions, and songs. Though emphasis is on Hollywood output (including feature-length cartoons), British musical films and selected original television musicals are also covered' (*Preface*).
Class No: 791.43.0MUS

Science fiction

[4640]
HARDY, P., *ed.* Overlook film encyclopedia: science fiction. Rev.ed. New York, Overlook Press, 1994. 478p. $50.00. ISBN: 0879515163.
First edition as *Aurum film encyclopedia*, 1984
1500 entries; many stills and monochrome photographs. Arranged chronologically by decades. Entries give basic data and annotations, making comparisons, describing themes, giving assessment. Statistics in appendices. Index covers film titles only. *Class No:* 791.43.0SCI

[4641]
LENTZ, H.M. Science fiction, horror and fantasy film and television credits. Jefferson, NC/London, McFarland, 1984-1994. 2v. and 2 supplements.
See annotation for this title at 791.43.0HOR.
Class No: 791.43.0SCI

[4642]
SENN, B. *and* JOHNSON, J. Fantastic cinema subject guide: a topical index to 2500 horror, science fiction and fantasy films. Jefferson,NC, McFarland, 1992. 682p. $45.00. ISBN: 089950681x.
Genres are divided into 81 subjects, then alphabetical listing by title with essential data, and brief synopsis. Cross references; title index. Television films are not included.
Class No: 791.43.0SCI

[4643]
WILLIS, D.C. Horror and science fiction films 4. Metuchen, NJ/London, Scarecrow Press, 1997. 664p. £85.00. ISBN: 0810830558.
Extends coverage to end of 1994, and updates and corrects three earlier volumes. Vol. 3 was issued in 1984.
Over 1000 titles are listed; films included are theatrical or TV releases in US or elsewhere. Critical annotations. Arranged A-Z order by title; list of alternative titles.
Class No: 791.43.0SCI

War films

[4644]
SHULL, M.S. *and* WILT, D.E. Hollywood war films, 1937-1945: an exhaustive filmography of American feature-length motion pictures relating to World War II. Jefferson, NC/London, McFarland, 1996. 482p., illus. £112.50. ISBN: 0786401451.

....(contd.)
Based on the files of the Office of War Information, entries give plot summary, release date, director, coding based on standard descriptors. Several appendices, two indexes, and an extensive bibliography.
Class No: 791.43.0WAR

Westerns

[4645]
BUSCOMBE, E., *ed.* The BFI Companion to the Western. Rev ed. London, Deutsch, 1993. 432p. £14.95 (paper). ISBN: 0233986189.
In addition to lists of films, provides excellent biographical and thematic essays, filmographies for actors, directors, scriptwriters etc., and an extensive historical background.
Class No: 791.43.0WES

[4646]
GARFIELD, B. Western films: a complete guide. New York, Da Capo, 1988. 400p., illus. £14.95. ISBN: 030680333x.
Descriptive opening chapters, then an A/Z title list of films (p.99-358) with data on credits, release date, cast, synopsis of plot, and brief appraisal. Includes about 1,500 films released in the US 1928-81. *Class No:* 791.43.0WES

[4647]
HARDY, P., *ed.* Overlook film encyclopedia: the Western. Rev.ed. New York, Overlook Press, 1995. 416p. $40.00. ISBN: 0879516259.
First edition as *Aurum film encyclopedia*, 1984.
1800 entries from the 1930s onwards; basic data is given with an annotation which makes comparisons, describes themes, offers an assessment. Index covers film titles only.
Class No: 791.43.0WES

[4648]
HOLLAND, T. B-Western actors encyclopedia: facts, photos and filmographies for more than 250 familiar faces. Jefferson, NC, McFarland, 1989. 493p. $40.00. ISBN: 0899503063.
Spans 1930-1953 and covers five categories: heroes, sidekicks, cowgirls, bad guys, and miscellaneous. Brief bibliography. *Class No:* 791.43.0WES

[4649]
LANGMAN, L. Guide to silent Westerns. Westport,CT, Greenwood Press, 1992. 577p. $75.00. ISBN: 031327858x.
Screen credits for over 5400 features, documentaries, shorts and serials issued 1890-1930. Coverage includes Indian tribes of the eastern seaboard, 1849 Gold Rush, early California and Mexico. In alphabetical order by title, with basic data including plot summary. Preface gives references to relevant film collections. *Class No:* 791.43.0WES

[4650]
LENTZ, H.M. Western and frontier film and television credits, 1903-1995. Jefferson, NC/London, McFarland, 1996. viii,1783p. (2v.) £157.50. ISBN: 0786401583.
Vol. 1 contains actors/actresses, and directors, producers, writers - each section A/Z with a complete list of credits, cross-referenced to the other sections. Vol. 2 contains film index, and television index. 'Excellent reference resource.' (*Reference books bulletin*, November 1, 1996; p.542.)
Class No: 791.43.0WES

Puppets

[4651]
BATCHELDER, M. The Puppet theatre handbook. Manchester, Educational Puppetry Institute, 1950. 295p., illus.
A concise treatise in 8 chapters (1. The Puppet theatre and its uses ... 6. Scenery, lighting, properties and special effects ... 8. Producing the puppet show). Bibliographies (by subjects), p.263-70. Appendices: Societies, organizations and firms; Puppet workshop equipment; Variety acts; Chapter references to the literature. *Class No:* 791.5

[4652]
CURRELL, D. Complete book of puppet theatre. London, Black, 1986. 352p.,illus. £20. ISBN: 0713624299.
Revised and expanded edition of the *Complete Book of Puppetry*.
Excellent all-round introduction, illustrated with photographs, performance diagrams etc. Suitable for novices, teachers, and experienced practitioners.
Class No: 791.5

[4653]
LEACH, R. The Punch and Judy show: history, tradition, and meaning. London, Batsford, 1985. 145p.,illus. £17.95. ISBN: 0713447842.
Unique, comprehensive history of the UK tradition; copiously illustrated and with numerous quotations.
Class No: 791.5

Bibliographies

[4654]
CROTHERS, J.F. The Puppeteer's library guide: the bibliographic index to the literature of the world's puppet theatre. Metuchen, NJ, Scarecrow, 1971-1983. 474,366p.(2v.). $32.50; 37.50. ISBN: 0810803194, v.1; 0810816113, v.2.
First volume concentrates on the historical background, including bibliographies of relevant material arranged by country; second volume examines puppets as an educational resource, and lists serials, monographs, theses etc. Originally planned as a six-volume set. *Class No:* 791.5(01)

Dictionaries

[4655]
PHILLPOT, A.R. Dictionary of puppetry. London, Macdonald, 1969. 291p., illus.
Covers technical terms, puppet matters, puppetry organizations. Title entry for books, plus annotations. Bibliography (grouped): p.287-91. *Class No:* 791.5(038)

Yearbooks & Directories

[4656]
Directory of professional puppeteers. Brooks, Z., *ed.* 8th ed. London, Puppet Centre Trust. 1990. 156p., illus.
Directory of UK practitioners; includes animations, performing companies, Punch & Judy professors, freelance operators, makers, workshop leaders, commercial suppliers. Regional listing; other puppetry organizations. Index.
Class No: 791.5(058)

Histories

[4657]

BÖHMER, G. Puppets through the ages: an illustrated history. London, Macdonald, 1971. 156p., illus.

First published Munich: Bruckmann, 1969.

Author was director of the Puppet Collection of the City of Munich, and the book is based on that collection. Introduction to European puppets, hand puppets, marionettes, rod puppets, paper theatre, non-European tradition, Asiatic shadow puppets. *Class No:* 791.5(091)

[4658]

JURKOWSKI, H. History of European puppetry from its origins to the end of the 19th century. Lewiston, NY/ Lampeter, Edwin Mellen, 1996. 426p. ISBN: 0773488030.

Good general survey; lengthy bibliography p.402-413. *Class No:* 791.5(091)

[4659]

SPEAIGHT, G. The History of the puppet theatre. 2nd ed. London, Hale, 1990. 366p. £19.95.

Ten chapters beginning with medieval mimes and tracing the history to the present day revival. Appendices list puppet shows in England, and plays performed by puppeteers in England. Extensive notes and references p.271-312. Index. *Class No:* 791.5(091)

Funfairs etc.

Bibliographies

[4660]

WILMETH, D.B. Variety entertainment and outdoor amusements: a reference guide. New York, Greenwood Press, 1982. xiii,242p. $39.95. ISBN: 0313214557.

Chapters on the circus, Wild West exhibition, dime museum, medicine and minstrel show, vaudeville, burlesque, the musical review and stage magic, each chapter with historical introduction and appended bibliography (*Choice*, v.20(8), April 1983, p.1116). *Class No:* 791.7(01)

Yearbooks & Directories

[4661]

Showman's directory. Godalming, Surrey, S. & J. Lance Publications. c400p. ISBN: 0946509476, (1998 ed.).

Annual.

Directory of UK contractors and services, entertainment, etc. Covers all types of public events - concerts, fun fairs, car rallies, country shows. Alphabetical index and chronological list of the year's shows, rallies, art shows, festivals, dog shows, Press, TV & radio contacts. Societies & organizations. *Class No:* 791.7(058)

Circuses

[4662]

RENEVEY, M.J., *ed.* Le Grand livre du cirque. Paris & Lausanne, Bibliothèque des Arts, 1977. 2v., illus.

16 contributors. V.1 (456p.) includes 19 sections on famous originators, such as Philip Astley (p.87-93; 13 illus.; 2 facsims.). Circuses in Soviet Union and Central Europe (p.296-327), and the American circus (p.346-385), among

....(contd.)

others. V.2 (sections 20-36) deal with equitation, pantomime, clowns, aerial artists, water and ice circuses and side-shows. Over 2,000 illus., in all. 'This is certainly the most ambitious work on the circus to have ever been published' (*TLS*, no.3988, 8 September 1978, p.988). *Class No:* 791.83

Bibliographies

[4663]

TOOLE-STOTT, R. Circus and allied arts: a world bibliography, 1500-1982 ... Derby, Harper & Sons, 1958-71. Vol.5 [1992] [London?], Circus Friends Association of Great Britain. 5v.,illus.

Based on the collection of the British Museum, Library of Congress, Bibliothèque Nationale and the Universiteitsbibliotheek Amsterdam. Vol.4 extends coverage to 1970, and vol.5 to 1982. Covers history and biography, technique, influences.

V.1 (1958,185p.) has 1,657 numbered entries on historical and biographical items. V.2 (1960,291p.) covers technicalities (acrobatics, equitation, etc.), freak exhibits, drama, literature, art and fiction; 2,745 entries. V.3 (392p., 34pl.) deals with juvenilia, reference works, circus dime novels, periodicals, etc. V.4 (335p.) has entries 9676-13086 in 3 parts (1. Books, etc; 2. Periodicals; 3. Appendices (*e.g.* Astley's amphitheatre), and includes errata and corrigenda to v.1-3. Vol.5 [ISBN: 1872904041] has 250p. Each volume carries an index. *Class No:* 791.83(01)

Histories

[4664]

OGDEN, T. Two hundred years of the American circus: from Aba-Daba to the Zoppe-Zavotta Troupe. New York, Facts on File, 1993. 462p. $50.00. ISBN: 0816026114.

In alphabetical order, this source comprises entries of 200-400 words giving details of performers, owners, terminology, animal acts and trainers, special equipment; there are numerous cross references, and about 100 monochrome photographs. There is an efficient index.'A unique and fascinating contribution, this is marred by poor quality paper and reproduction (especially the photographs and index) and by the use of sexist language.' (*Choice,* 31(7)1994. p1102) *Class No:* 791.83(091)

[4665]

SPEAIGHT, G. A History of the circus. London, Tantivy Press, 1980. 216p., illus.

6 parts (37 chapters); 1. The origins of circus - 2. The early years - 3. The circus in Britain in the 19th century - 4. The circus in America - 5. The golden age of the circus in Europe - 6. The circus in the 20th century. Appendix: Circus buildings in London, New York and Paris. Chapter notes, p.199-210. Non-analytical index of performers and proprietors. Defines circus as 'that entertainment of human bodily skills and trained animals that is presented in a ring of approximately 13 metres in diameter, with an audience grouped all around it' (*Introduction*). Russian circus: only 1 column. *Class No:* 791.83(091)

Biographies

[4666]

TURNER, J. Victorian arena: the performers. A dictionary of British circus biography. Formby, Lingdales Press, 1995. 141p., illus. £21.00. ISBN: 0950908460.

Described as v.1; a series is intended, with a future volume planned on *The Showmen.*

A/Z brief biographies of 1500 names, working in Britain, approximately in the Victorian period. Fascinating source; illustrations are decorative only. *Class No:* 791.83(092)

Bull Fights

[4667]

CONRAD, B. Barnaby Conrad's encyclopedia of bullfighting. London, Michael Joseph, 1962. xiv, 271p., illus.

Encyclopedia, p.1-256, including chart of 20th century matadors (p.142-59). 'The complete Reglamento taurino', p.256-69. Bibliography, p.271. *Class No:* 791.86

792 Theatre

Theatre

Bibliographies

[4668]
BAILEY, C.J. A Guide to reference and bibliography for theatre research. 2nd ed. Columbus, Ohio State University, 1983. 149p.

Annotated guide in two parts: first covers general reference tools and sources, the second examines special materials. Classified arrangement, with author/title index. *Class No:* 792.0(01)

[4669]
BAKER, B.M. Theatre and allied arts: a guide to books dealing with the history, criticism, and technic of the drama and theatre and related arts and crafts. New York, Blom. 1967. 536p. ISBN: 0405082304.

Originally published 1953 (H.W. Wilson).

Now mainly of historical value, but still regarded as a major source, covering over 6,000 books published between 1885 and 1945. *Class No:* 792.0(01)

[4670]
FRENCH'S THEATRE BOOKSHOP. London. **Parades.** London, Samuel French Ltd. gratis.

Issued at regular intervals.

Includes updates to guides to plays, musical plays, new books. Useful annotations for every item, details of cast requirements, staging etc. ISBN given for plays, but not for books. No publisher data. Regular booklists are also issued on acting; audition material; circus; magic; comedy; clowns & pantomime; costume; criticism; drama in education & drama training; elocution; make-up; mime; movement & dance; musical interest; production, stage management & lighting; puppetry; stagecraft & design; theatre; theatre biography; theatre history; writing, television & radio. *Class No:* 792.0(01)

[4671]
NEW YORK PUBLIC LIBRARY. Research Libraries. **Catalog of the theatre and drama collections.** Boston, Hall, 1967-1976. 51v. and supplements. ISBN: 081610106x.

The catalogue of a vast and comprehensive collection; Part 1 covers some 120,000 plays, published separately or in collections - fuller entry for this part at 82-2(01); Part 2 catalogues analytically some 24,000 books on the theatre. Part 3 covers 740,000 non book items - playbills, photographs etc. *Class No:* 792.0(01)

[4672]
SIMONS, L.K. The Performing arts: a guide to the reference literature. Littleton,CO, Libraries Unlimited, 1994. 230p. $42.00. ISBN: 0872879828.

Good coverage of theatre; see full entry at 791/793(01). *Class No:* 792.0(01)

[4673]
STRATMAN, C.J., ***and others*****. Restoration and eighteenth-century theatre research:** a bibliographical guide, 1900-1968. Carbondale, Ill. Southern Illinois Univ. Press, 1971. 822p. $25. ISBN: 0809304694.

Annotated bibliography of 6,500 items, under subject headings, A-Z. *Class No:* 792.0(01)

[4674]
THEATRE RESEARCH DATA CENTER. International bibliography of theatre. Ortolani, B., *ed.* New York, TRDC Brooklyn College, 1985-.

Annual volumes covering 1982 onwards, and international in coverage of countries and languages. Slow in appearance but potentially very important. The 1990/91 volume was published in 1995; 900 pages containing 6000 entries and 18000 subject references. Classified arrangement with geographical, chronological and author indexes. *Class No:* 792.0(01)

Encyclopaedias & Dictionaries

[4675]
BANHAM, M., ***ed.*** **The Cambridge guide to theatre.** 2nd.ed. Cambridge, CUP, 1995. 1233p. illus. £24.95. ISBN: 0521434378.

First ed. (1989) as *Cambridge guide to world theatre;* pbk.ed. 1992.

Encyclopaedic and international with bibliographies for major entries, and extensive cross referencing. Alphabetical arrangement covering history, stage, television, actors, directors etc. Illustrations are few and monochrome. All entries signed. Over 200 new entries in this ed. 'Enthusiastically recommended' (*Choice*, v33(6) p923, February 1996). *Class No:* 792.0(03)

[4676]
GRÖNING, K. ***and*** **KLEISS, W. Illustrated encyclopedia of world theatre.** London, Thames & Hudson, 1977. 319p.,illus.

Original ed. as *Friedrichs Theaterlexicon* (1969). English translation by Estella Schmid. Updated and expanded by M. Esslin.

2,000 cross-referenced entries, A-Z (Abbey Theatre ... Zuckmayer, Carl). 'Expressionism': 1 column, 3 references. 'USSR' 1½ columns; 3 references. Index of over 5,000 play titles and authors, 420 good illus. Continental European slant, a welcome corrective to the usual run of English-language theatre encyclopaedias. 'Will be extremely useful as a basic reference source on world theatre' (*RQ*, v.18, no.1, Fall 1978, p.95). *Class No:* 792.0(03)

[4677]
MAY, R.A. A Companion to the theatre: the Anglo-American stage from 1920. London, Lutterworth Press, 1973. 240p.,illus. ISBN: 0718819063.

Sections: Modern drama (names, A-Z; Eugene O'Neill; 12/3 cols.), p.15-70 - The World of Shakespeare and the classics. Some notable productions - A who's who of classical drama (actors, actresses, directors, etc., A-Z), p.78-146 - West End and Broadway: some stars, matin°ee

.... *(contd.)*
idols, major talents and popular favourites (A-Z), p.147-93 - The musical - Farce - Melodrama and murder - Theatre organizations, p.239-55 - British rep. - Impresarios and managers - Historians and long-running critics - Theatrical terms, p.273-83. Index: 1. Featured plays, productions, etc.; 2. People: a selective list. *Class No:* 792.0(03)

[4678]

The Oxford companion to the theatre. Hartnoll, P., *ed.* 4th ed. Oxford, OUP, 1983. x,934p.,illus. £32.50. ISBN: 0192115464.

First published 1951.

International in scope. 87 contributors. Entries, Abbey, Henry Eugene ... Zweig. Stefan. 'Theatre buildings'; 6 columns; 'Italy'; 15 cols; 'Comédie Française': 1 col.; 'Society for Theatre Research': ½col.; 'Broadway Theatre, New York': 1 col.; 'Theatre in the Round': 1 col.; 'Robson Flora': nearly 1 col. No entry made under 'Periodicals', and bibliographies are reserved for the appended, unannotated 'A guide to further reading', p.917-32 (reference works; general histories; Great Britain; Ireland; Europe; US; Asia; Dramatic forms; Technique of stagecraft; Acting; Theatre criticism). 96 plates. 'Miss Hartnoll is to be congratulated on the unabated excellence of the work she first launched in 1951' (*British book news*, January 1984. p.44).
Class No: 792.0(03)

[4679]

—The Concise Oxford companion to the theatre. Hartnoll, P., *ed and* Found, P., *ed.* 2nd.ed. Oxford, OUP, 1992. 568p. £25.00. ISBN: 0198661363.

Based on the fourth edition of the *Companion* (1983) with many deletions of minor theatres, actors now less popular, and with expanded, updated biographies. Individuals are included if their date of birth is earlier than 1952. The work is international, although UK and US material predominate; all aspects are covered - styles and techniques, staging, lighting, costume design etc. Numerous cross references; use of boldface type, asterisks and other symbols can make casual use confusing. *Class No:* 792.0(03)

[4680]

PICKERING, D. *and* **PACKARD, D.** *and* **SAVIDGE, C.,** *eds.* **Dictionary of theatre.** London, Sphere, 1988. 556p. ISBN: 0747400199.

US edition as *Facts on File Dictionary of the theatre*.

Brief entries on 5,000 actors, actresses, playwrights, directors, producers, plays, venues, genres, technical terms, organizations etc. For major plays the data includes first performance, plot summary, original cast.
Class No: 792.0(03)

[4681]

QUÉANT, G., *and others.* **Encyclopédie du théâtre contemporain.** Paris, Publications de France, 1957-59. 2v.,illus.

1: 1850-1914. 1957. 207p.

2: 1914-1950. [1959]. 213p.

A profusely illustrated record covering opera, ballet, variety, as well as literature and art, to some extent, in addition to the theatre proper. Many contributors. Footnote references; synoptic tables. Name indexes.
Class No: 792.0(03)

[4682]

RUBIN, D., *ed.* **The World encyclopedia of contemporary theatre.** Europe. New York/London, Routledge, 1994. 1052p, illus. $149.95. ISBN: 0415059283.

Second volume, subtitled 'Americas' appeared 1996 (ISBN: 0415059291; 627p.) Other vols. will cover Africa, Arab World, Asia, Oceana; Final vol. will be index and bibliography.

Projected six-volume work covering theatrical arts throughout the world from 1945; 150 countries are included. A project of the International Theatre Institute and other theatre institutes with support from UNESCO. Main entries are by country - Albania to Yugoslavia; each entry has twelve sections which include national background, structure of theatrical life (including variety, opera, ballet, circus, puppetry), artistic profile (companies, production etc.), design, space and architecture, training, criticism, scholarship and publishing, bibliography. Efficient index. Each entry contains some monochrome illustrations.
Class No: 792.0(03)

[4683]

THOMSON, P. *and* **SALGADO, G. The Everyman companion to the theatre.** London, Dent, 1985. 458p. £15. ISBN: 0460044249.

Brief alphabetically-arranged entries, including playwrights, actors, actresses, directors, buildings, companies, drama genres and movements. Accurate, concise source. *Class No:* 792.0(03)

Handbooks & Manuals

[4684]

MILES-BROWN, J. Acting. London, Peter Owen, 1990. 112p.,illus. £7.95. ISBN: 0720606322.

A basic textbook suitable for amateurs and drama students.
Class No: 792.0(035)

[4685]

TURNER, B., *ed.* **The Actor's handbook.** London, Bloomsbury. c400p.

Annual.

Lists drama schools, agents, theatres, critics, associations; useful, reasonably priced compilation. *Class No:* 792.0(035)

Dictionaries

[4686]

BOWMAN, W. *and* **BALL, R. Theatre language:** a dictionary of terms in English of the drama and stage, from medieval to modern times. New York, Theatre Arts, 1976. xii,428p. ISBN: 0878305513.

Paperback reprint of 1961 edition.

5,000 terms, technical terms being concisely defined. US-slanted, noting British variations. *Class No:* 792.0(038)

[4687]

DAVIS, P. Dictionnaire du théâtre: termes et concepts de l'analyse théâtrale. Paris, Editions Sociales, 1980. 482p.

Scholarly, documented articles on *c.*500 concepts (*e.g.* 'Catharsis', 'Brechtien', 'Comique', 'Sémiologie théâtrale'. Restricted to the Western theatre. Bibliography of 23p. Systematic index and a French-English-German lexicon. 'An important reference tool for theatre specialists' (*Modern drama*, no.4, December 1981, p.564).
Class No: 792.0(038)

[4688]

HODGSON, T. The Batsford dictionary of drama. London, Batsford; New York, New Amsterdam Books, 1988. 432p.,illus. £19.95. ISBN: 0713446935.

US title is *The Drama dictionary*.

'The main intention ... is to provide useful working definitions of terms used in the theatre and by theatre critics. It does not aim to provide exhaustive information about dramatists, plays, theatre companies and theatre buildings' (*Preface*). The 1,300 entries, arranged A-Z, are mainly brief (few run to a full page) and cover forms of drama, kinds of stage, acting terms, dramatic movements and styles, character types and dramatic structure. Entries are fully cross-referenced and most include suggestions for further reading, although there is no separate bibliography. 31 line drawings. *Class No:* 792.0(038)

[4689]

RAE, K. *and* **SOUTHERN, R.,** *eds*. **Lexique international de termes techniques de théâtre en huit langues ...** New York, Theatre Arts, 1968. 139p.

Originally published 1959 Elsevier, Amsterdam, for the International Theatre Institute.

637 technical base-terms in English, with equivalents (French, German, Italian, Spanish, Dutch, Swedish) across the double-page. Genders of foreign nouns are given. A/Z indexes: - German, Spanish, French, Italian, Dutch, Swedish, US (p.135-7, containing 'only those terms which differ in American usage from English use').
Class No: 792.0(038)

[4690]

TRAPIDO, J., ***and others*****. An International dictionary of theatre language.** Westport, CT, Greenwood Press, 1985. xxxvi,1032p. $99.50. ISBN: 0313229805.

Discusses 15,000 terms (English and foreign) from all periods. Abundant cross-references, and a good bibliography. *Class No:* 792.0(038)

[4691]

WHITE, R.K. An Annotated dictionary of technical, historical, and stylistic terms relating to theatre and drama: a handbook of dramaturgy. Lewiston, NY/Lampeter, Edwin Mellen, 1995. iii,254p. $69.95. ISBN: 0773488731.

Entries are illustrated with drawings and plans; useful bibliography p247-254. *Class No:* 792.0(038)

Reviews & Abstracts

[4692]

SAMPLES, G. How to locate reviews of plays and films: a bibliography of criticism from the beginnings to the present. Metuchen, NJ, Scarecrow Press, 1976. x,114p. $13. ISBN: 0810809141.

Plays (8 sections: Chronology of study guides; Review indexing sources; Newspaper indexes; Dramatic criticism checklists; Collected reviews of individual writers; Leading theatre periodicals; Leading reference guides; Play synopses and production controlling agencies) - Films (11 sections, somewhat similarly divided). Index, p.97-114.
Class No: 792.0(048)

Periodicals & Progress Reports

[4693]

Theatre notebook: journal of the history and technique of the British theatre. London, Society for Theatre Research, 1946-. £21.00. ISSN: 00405523.

Three issues pa. Indexes available for vols. 1-25 (1945-71) and 26-40 (1971-86).

Book reviews appear regularly. *Class No:* 792.0(05)

[4694]

Theatre record. Twickenham, I. Herbert, 1981-. *c.*64p. £95.00pa. ISSN: 09621792.

26 issues per year. From 1981-90 titled *London Theatre Record*.

London and UK regional productions reviewed (copies of newspaper and magazines reviews in full). Listing of current and future shows; schedules for London and UK regions.
Class No: 792.0(05)

[4695]

Theatre research international. Oxford, Oxford University Press for the International Federation for Theatre Research, 1958-. £54pa. ISSN: 03078833.

Three issues pa.

Major articles, and a large number of substantial, scholarly, book reviews (usually 10-15 per issue, 1,000 words in length). *Class No:* 792.0(05)

[4696]

Theatre world. Willis, J., *ed.* London, A.& C. Black. c300p., illus. £18.99. ISBN: 1557833230.

Annual.

Statistical and pictorial record of the Broadway and off-Broadway season, touring companies, and professional regional companies in the US. Cast lists, directors, authors, composers, song titles etc. Special section of biographical data, obituaries; lists of major drama awards.
Class No: 792.0(05)

French

[4697]

Revue d'histoire du théâtre. Paris, Society for Theatre History, 1948-. £55pa. ISSN: 00352373.

Quarterly.

Although concentrating on French theatre, there is good book review coverage (usually about 10 per issue, 1,000 words each) and lists of dissertations on theatre.
Class No: 792.0(05)=40

Periodicals

[4698]

STRATMAN, C.J. American theatrical periodicals, 1789-1967: a bibliographical guide. Durham, NC, Duke University Press, 1970. 133p.

Lists 700 serials, arranged chronologically with standard bibliographic data, and locations in 137 US, Canadian and British libraries. *Class No:* 792.0(051)

[4699]

STRATMAN, C.J. Britain's theatrical periodicals, 1720-1967: a bibliography. 2nd rev. ed. New York, NYPL, 1972. xiv,160p. $20. ISBN: 0871040344.

First edition 1962.

Brief bibliographical notes on 1,235 periodicals (1962 ed.: 674 titles), with *c.*150 British and US library locations. Chronological sequence. The 2nd ed., extends scope to the dance, ballet, vaudeville and magic. References, p.127-9. Detailed index, p.131-60. *Class No:* 792.0(051)

Yearbooks & Directories

[4700]
KULLMAN, C.H., ***ed and*** **YOUNG, W.C.,** ***ed.*****. Theatre companies of the world.** Westport,CT, Greenwood Press, 1986. 1024p.(2v). $95. ISBN: 0313214565.

An international listing of theatre companies, generally permanent and professional, but some part-time theatre groups are included. Full details given, including future plans. US is to be separately covered, so little emphasis in this volume. *Class No:* 792.0(058)

Quotations

[4701]
SNELL, G. The Book of theatre quotes: notes, quotes and anecdotes of the stage. London, Angus & Robertson, 1982. ix,195p.,illus.

Entries under 88 headings. Abbey Theatre ... W.B. Yeats. Each quotation (sometimes lengthy) has introductory remarks in bold. Appended credits. Detailed non-analytical index. Well illustrated. *Class No:* 792.0(082.2)

Portraits

[4702]
KERSLAKE, J.F., ***ed*****. Catalogue of theatrical portraits** in London public collections. London, Society for Theatre Research, 1961. xii,63p.

741 numbered entries; two sequences cover individual portraits, & group portraits. Index of artists; index of titles. *Class No:* 792.0(084.10)

Chronologies

[4703]
LONEY, G.M. Twentieth century theatre. New York, Facts on File, 1983. 521p.(2v.). $75. ISBN: 0871964635.

A chronological record 1900-1979 of British and American theatre; arranged by topic - premieres, revivals, debuts, productions etc., each chronologically listed within each year. Useful photographs, and an adequate index. *Class No:* 792.0(090)

Histories

[4704]
BERTHOLD, M. A History of world theater. New York, Ungar, 1972. x,735p.,illus.

Translated from *Weltgeschichte des Theater* (Stuttgart: Kröner).

Chapters are chronologically arranged, from 'The primitive theatre' to 'From naturalism to the present'. Bibliography, p.681-97 ('Standard works and dictionaries', then by chapters). Analytical index includes the many illus. (363 half-tones and 85 line-drawings). Useful background of social and anthropological influences. European emphasis. *Class No:* 792.0(091)

[4705]
BROCKETT, O.G. History of the theatre. 5th ed. Boston, Allyn & Bacon, 1987. x,768p.,illus. $30. ISBN: 0205104878.

First published 1968.

A careful and accurate single-volume summary; European emphasis, from earliest times to present. Bibliography, and good index. *Class No:* 792.0(091)

[4706]
BROWN, J.R., ***ed*****. The Oxford illustrated history of theatre.** Oxford, Oxford University Press, 1995. 582p. £13.99. ISBN: 0192880624.

Part 1: Ancient Greek theatre, Roman, early Africa and the Americas. Part 2: Europe to 1700. Part 3: Europe after 1700. Part 4: theatre in South Asia, East Asia, and South-east Asia. Distinguished team of specialist contributors examine role in society, varieties of form and production, interactions with other art froms. Also, they give weight to technical, practical and organisational issues. Good standard of colour and monochrome illustration. *Class No:* 792.0(091)

[4707]
FREEDLEY, G. ***and*** **REEVES, J. A History of the theatre.** Newly revised with a supplementary section. Rev. ed. New York, Crown Publishers, 1955. xvi,784p.,illus.

First published 1941.

A well-illustrated, well-documented survey of all aspects of the theatre, from the ancient Egyptian period to the present day. The supplementary section covers 1940-54. Bibliography, p.160-5. *Class No:* 792.0(091)

[4708]
IZENOUR, G.C. Theater design. 2nd.ed. London, Yale University Press, 1996. 666p., illus. £100.00. ISBN: 0300067755.

All aspect of planning and construction, and a history of theatre design from ancient times to the present. Structures, seating, acoustics, optimum conditions, etc. 900 illustrations and set of drawings. *Class No:* 792.0(091)

[4709]
KINDERMANN, H. Theatergeschichte Europas. Salzburg, Müller, 1957-74. 10v.,illus.

v.1: *Das Theater der Antike, und des Mittelalters*, 1957.
2: *Das Theater der Renaissance*, 1959.
3: *Das Theater der Barockzeit*, 1959.
4/5: *Von der Aufklärung zur Romantik*, 1961-62.
6: *Romantik*, 1964.
7: *Realismus*, 1965.
8: *Naturalismus und Impressionismus, pt.1: Deutschland, Österreich, Schweiz*, 1968.
9: *Naturalismus und Impressionismus, pt.2: Frankreich Rusland, England, Skandinavien*, 1970.
10: *Naturalismus und Impressionismus, pt.3: Holland, Belgien, Lettland, Litauen, Estland, Polen, Tschechoslowakei, Jugoslawien, Bulgarien, Ungarn, Rumänien, Italien, Spanien, Portugal, Turkei, Griechenland*, 1974.

Each volume has chapter notes and bibliographies (p.425-62, in v.7, subdivided by countries), plus a chronology and indexes (places; names of dramatists and titles of plays; subjects). V.10 includes an index to v.8-10 and a contents list of all 10v. *Class No:* 792.0(091)

[4710]
NICOLL, A. The Development of the theatre: a study of theatrical art, from the beginnings to the present day. 5th ed. London, Harrap, 1966. xix,292p.,illus.

First published 1927.

9 sections: 1. Introductory. Theatres of the Orient - 2. The Greek heritage ... 9. Theatres of the twentieth century. Appendix: The Dialogues of Leoni di Somi. Bibliography (p.279-83), - a valuable running commentary in 7 sections. Analytical index. 278 good illus. and ground plans of theatres. The standard general history of theatrical architecture and equipment. *Class No:* 792.0(091)

[4711]
The Revels history of drama in English. Potter, L., *and others, eds*. London, Methuen, 1975-83. 8v. illus.

Re-issued as a boxed set 1996. (London, Routledge. £495.00. ISBN: 0415143799.)

V.1 *Medieval drama*, by A.C. Cawley and others. 1983. xlviii, 348p. ISBN: 0416130208.

V.2 *1500-1576*, by N. Sanders and others. 1980. xxxvii, 290p. ISBN: 0416130305.

V.3 *1576-1613*, by J.L. Barroll and others. 1975. xxxiii, 526p. ISBN: 0416130402.

V.4 *1613-1640*, by P. Edwards and others. 1981. lvii, 337p. ISBN: 041613050x.

V.5 *1660-1750*, by J. Loftis and others. 1976. xxxi, 331p. ISBN: 0416130607.

V.6 *1750-1880*, by M.R. Booth and others. 1975. lxii, 304p. ISBN: 0416130704.

V.7 *1880 to the present day*, by H. Hunt and others. 1978. xlv, 298p. ISBN: 0416130801.

V.8 *American drama*, by T. Bogard and others. 1977. xliv, 324p. ISBN: 0416130909.

Each vol. has sections on the social and literary context; theatres and actors; and playwrights and plays; plus detailed chronological table of plays, theatrical events and historical events. Extensive chapter bibliographies with commentary. Well illustrated throughout. Index in each vol.
Class No: 792.0(091)

Bibliographies

[4712]
VINCE, R.W. Neoclassical theatre: a historiographical handbook. Westport, CT, Greenwood Press, 1988. 239p. $45. ISBN: 0313244456.

Continues similar work by Vince on *Renaissance Theatre* (1984) and *Ancient and Medieval Theatre* (1984).

An international examination of sources - texts, promptbooks, account books, playbills, biographies, portraits etc. Evaluation of major reference tools.
Class No: 792.0(091)(01)

Biographies

[4713]
BRYAN, G.B. Stage deaths: a biographical guide to international theatrical obituaries, 1850-1950. Westport,CT, Greenwood Press, 1991. 1354p.(2v.) ISBN: 0313275939.

Several thousand entries list actors, playwrights, producers, directors, opera stars, composers, designers and others connected with theatrical life. The selection is taken from British and US trade papers and books. Entries give stage name, real name, vital details, type of work done. Cross references link real names and stage names. Lists give locations of obituaries, details of biographies and autobiographies. *Class No:* 792.0(092)

[4714]
BRYAN, G.B., *comp*. Stage lives: a bibliography and index to theatrical biographies in English. Westport, CT., Greenwood Press, 1985. 368p. $75.00. ISBN: 0313245770.

Extends from classical times to the present day; international scope, but English-language material only. First part contains the bibliography (collective, individual & autobiographies) comprising some 2,800 items in total, the collective titles being briefly annotated. Index of biographees (p.179-329) and necrological annals. *Class No:* 792.0(092)

[4715]
FRICK, J.W. *and* VALLILLO, S.M. Theatrical directors: Westport,CT, Greenwood Press, 1994. 567p. $85.00. ISBN: 0313274789.

300 entries, international in scope but with a US emphasis. Each entry gives narrative synopsis (biography), assessment, influence, chronology, bibliography. *Class No:* 792.0(092)

[4716]
International dictionary of theatre. Hawkins-Dady, M., *ed*. Chicago and London, St. James Press, 1992-95. 3v. illus. £100.00 per vol. ISBN: 1558620974, vol. 3.

Vols 1 and 2 cover *Plays* and *Playwrights*; fuller entry for these volumes at 82-2(03).

Volume 3 covers actors, directors and designers; capsule biography, descriptions of roles and productions, bibliographic information, signed critical essay.
Class No: 792.0(092)

[4717]
LA BEAU, T., *ed*. Theatre, film and television biographies master index: a consolidated guide to over 100,000 biographical sketches of persons living and dead, as they appear in over 40 of the principal biographical dictionaries devoted to the theatre, film and television. Detroit, Gale, 1979. xii,477p.

Entries, A.E. ... Stefan Zweig. Coverage: actors, actresses, directors, filmmakers, playwrights, lyricists, cinematographers, designers and others involved in these performing arts. Sources: over 40 biographical dictionaries and directories (largely US) devoted to the stage, screen, opera, popular music, radio and TV. *Class No:* 792.0(092)

[4718]
MORLEY, S. The Great stage stars: distinguished theatrical careers of the past and present. London, Angus & Robertson, 1986. 520p.,illus. £15. ISBN: 0207149704.

Some 200 figures from the last 400 years, with an emphasis on the British stage. Good discussion with personal quotations and review comment. *Class No:* 792.0(092)

[4719]
WEARING, J.P. American and British theatrical biography: a directory. Metuchen, NJ, Scarecrow Press, 1979. v,1007p. $60. ISBN: 0810812010.

An index of *c*.50,000 persons covered in over 200 biographical sources. Data: name (with cross-references to stage names, pseudonyms, etc.), dates of birth and death, nationality, theatrical occupation(s) and source code for fuller biographical information. Sources indexed, p.1-10.
Class No: 792.0(092)

[4720]
Who was who in the theatre, 1912-1976; a biographical directory of actors, actresses, directors, playwrights, and producers from the English-speaking theatre, compiled from *Who's who in the theatre*, v.1-15(1912-1972). Detroit, Gale Research, 1978. 2643p.(4v.). £303. ISBN: 0810304068.

Persons dead or inactive by 1976; 41,000 entries from the first 15 volumes, excluding those carried over into the 16th volume. *Class No:* 792.0(092)

Jews

[4721]
LYMAN, D. Great Jews of stage and screen. Middle Village, NY, Jonathan David, 1987. 279p., illus. £19.95. ISBN: 0824603281.

100 biographical sketches ranging from ½page to four pages in length; career data and photograph. Second section

....*(contd.)*
gives much briefer entries for a further 200 names. Mainly US, but not entirely; indexes living and dead.
Class No: 792.0(092)(=924)

Great Britain

Bibliographies

[4722]
CAVANAGH, J. British theatre: a bibliography 1901-85. Romsey, Hants, Motley Press, 1989. 510p. £65. ISBN: 0900281014.

Published with the encouragement of the Society for Theatre Research. Shortlisted for the Besterman Medal 1990. Supplement 1986-1990 in preparation.

An excellent source, designed to follow on the work of Arnott and Robinson (1970). (*See* entry at 792.0(420)(01)). Theatre is taken to include dramatic theatre, opera, music hall, but not dance, mime, or puppetry. Cinema & television are generally omitted. Three main sections - theatre (general reference, government intervention, religion, theatre arts, history, theatre in London, out of London, companies, biography, criticism, pantomime, music hall, amateur theatre, teaching), - drama (history, biography & criticism), - music (in the dramatic theatre, opera, operetta, musical comedy). Over 9,000 items identified; some very brief annotations. Author and subject indexes.
Class No: 792.0(410)(01)

[4723]
LOEWENBURG, A., *comp.* **The Theatre of the British Isles,** excluding London: a bibliography. London, Society for Theatre Research, 1950. ix,75p.

Includes books, articles and MS. collections dealing with the British provincial theatre from earliest times to 1949. Entries are under places A-Z, and then chronologically. Supplements R.W. Lowe's *A bibliographical account of English theatrical literature* (*See* entry at 792.0(420)(01)), which lists mainly London items. *Class No:* 792.0(410)(01)

Yearbooks & Directories

[4724]
British theatre directory. Holland, A., *ed.* London, Richmond House. c650p.. ISSN: 03064107.

First published 1972; regular revisions.

Contents include details of theatres in London and provinces, concert venues, amateur theatres, arts centres (all with address, phone number, administration details, technical facilities), municipal arts and leisure departments, data on production companies, ballet & opera companies, orchestras, puppet theatres, circus etc.; lists of agents by speciality, directory of book and journal publishers, training & education facilities, advertisers' index.
Class No: 792.0(410)(058)

[4725]
British theatre yearbook. Lemmon, D., *ed.* 3rd ed. London, Deutsch, 1992. 376p.,illus. £25.00. ISBN: 0233987827.

Publishing pattern uncertain.

Divided into 6 main sections: theatres in London, National Theatre, Royal Shakespeare Company, outer-London theatres, regional, touring companies. Details of productions given with cast lists, reviews. Index of plays.
Class No: 792.0(410)(058)

[4726]
McGillivray's theatre guide. McGillivray, D., *ed.* London, Rebecca Books, 1994. 368p.,illus. £12.95. ISSN: 01425218.

Previous title *British alternative theatre directory.* First published 1979.

Contents: Alternative theatre companies - Young people's theatre - Puppet companies (data on each include policy; origins; subsidy; personnel; tours; audiences; equipment; productions; other activities; contact) - Venues (London, England, Scotland, Wales) - Arts Council and regional associations - Theatre organizations - National centres of the International Theatre Institute - Principal national festivals. Index to advertisers and photographs; Index to companies. Map and list of London fringe theatres.

Very full and clear details are provided, and coverage now extends to cabaret venues, film & video facilities.
Class No: 792.0(410)(058)

Scotland

[4727]
ARMSTRONG, N. The Edinburgh stage, 1715-1820: a bibliography. London, Library Association, 1969. 3v.

Thesis accepted for Fellowship of the Library Association, 1969.

Deals in turn with 7 premises used for productions of the professional stage during the period. 'Play index' (v.3, p.1-81), by authors and titles; 'Actor index' (p.82-442), by chapter and play-title. Appendix (p.443-70) lists some actors and actresses of the Edinburgh stage, with brief biographical details. Short bibliography. *Class No:* 792.0(411)

Ireland

[4728]
FITZ-SIMONS, C. The Irish theatre. London, Thames & Hudson, 1983. 202p.,illus. £14.95. ISBN: 0500013004.

Unique picture of theatre history from the Middle Ages to the contemporary Dublin scene. *Class No:* 792.0(415)

England

Bibliographies

[4729]
ARNOTT, J.F. *and* **ROBINSON, J.W. English theatre literature, 1559-1900:** a bibliography, incorporating R.W. Lowe's *A bibliographical account of English theatrical literature*, published in 1888. New York, Johnson Reprint/ London, Society for Theatre Research, 1970. xxii,486p.

4,506 numbered entries, with brief biographical notes; each edition of a work has a separate entry. 14 sections, including: Bibliography; General history; The London theatre; The theatre out of London; Biography (nos.2203-3691); Periodicals (nos.4068-4506). Excludes manuscripts, but has a guide to printed sources. Indexes; authors; short-titles; places of publication. References (abbreviated), p.xvii-xx. Awarded the LA's Besterman Medal for an outstanding bibliography/guide to the literature in 1970.
Class No: 792.0(420)(01)

[4730]

CONNOLLY, L.W. *and* **WEARING, J.P. English drama and theatre, 1800-1900:** a guide to information sources. Detroit, Gale Research, 1978. 508p.

Over 3,000 entries, mostly annotated. 10 chapters: Contemporary history and criticism - Modern history and criticism - Individual authors (110) - Bibliographies and reference works - Anthologies of plays - The theatres - Acting and management - The critics - Stage design, scenic art, and costume - Periodicals. Index. 'Used in conjuncture with J.F. Arnott & J.W. Robinson's English theatrical literature, 1559-1900(1970) & Allardyce Nicoll's handlists, this work should prove invaluable' (*Choice*, Spetember 1978, p.838). *Class No:* 792.0(420)(01)

[4731]

LOWE, R.W. A Bibliographical account of English theatrical literature from the earliest times to the present day. Detroit, Gale, 1966/Gordon Press, n.d. x,384p. $59.95. ISBN: 0879687355.

Originally published London, Nimmo, 1888.

Dictionary catalogue of books and pamphlets on actors and theatres. Chronological order under subjects; when the subject is a person, a short biographical sketch is added. Indispensable to students of theatre history.

Class No: 792.0(420)(01)

[4732]

STEVENS, D. English Renaissance theatre: a reference guide. Boston, G.K. Hall, 1982. 342p.

More than 1,650 annotated entries listing secondary scholarship published 1664-1979. Topics include playhouses, actors, companies, acting and acting styles, costumes, scenery, music, dance, staging, management, finance, censorship and audiences of the period. Purely literary studies, *e.g,*. of drama, are excluded. Full cross-references. *Class No:* 792.0(420)(01)

Chronologies

[4733]

FITZSIMMONS, L. *and* **McDONALD, A.W.,** *eds.* **The Yorkshire stage, 1766-1803:** a calendar of plays, together with cast lists for Tate Wilkinson's circuit of theatres. Metuchen, Scarecrow, 1989. 1097p. $87.50. ISBN: 0810821877.

A major scholarly effort, covering one of the most important eighteenth century circuits. Mainly based on material in the York Minster library.

Class No: 792.0(420)(090)

[4734]

MULLIN, M. *and* **MURIELLO, K.M.,** *comps.* **Theatre at Stratford-upon-Avon:** a catalogue-index to productions of the Shakespeare Memorial/Royal Shakespeare Theatre, 1879-1978. London, Library Association, 1980. 2v.

1: *Catalogue of productions*, xxxvi, 562p.

2: *Indexes and calendars*, xiv p., p.563-1038.

V.1 has 1,203 entries for plays, A-Z. Data; running number; title; data; playwright; director(s); designer(s); theatre actors; review. 'The Merchant of Venice', nos.583-629. V.2 has index to playwrights; index to theatre personnel; directors, designers, actors; index to reviewers. Calendar of productions, p.1015-38. Computer-generated. 'A major reference tool for modern Shakespeare production in this country' (*Library Review*, v.30, Spring 1981, p.54).

Class No: 792.0(420)(090)

Histories

[4735]

BENTLEY, G.E. The Jacobean and Caroline stage. Oxford, Clarendon Press, 1941-68. 7v. £50. ISBN: 0198116268.

1-2: *Dramatic companies and players*. 1941.

3-5: *Plays and playwrights*. 1955.

6: *Theatres*. 1968.

7: *Appendices to V.6. General index*. 1968.

Detailed histories of the period from the death of Shakespeare to the closing of the theatres in 1642. In v.3-5 arrangement is by playwright, A-Z. Entries include brief biographical data, a list of MSS, and important editions of plays, plus a bibliography of items on plays and their performance. V.6 deals with the histories of the theatres. Invaluable; serves as a continuation of E.K. Chamber's *Elizabethan stage* (*q.v.*). The 'General index' to v.1-7 covers p.129-390 of v.7. *Class No:* 792.0(420)(091)

[4736]

CHAMBERS, E.K. The Elizabethan stage. Oxford, Clarendon Press, 1923. 4v.,illus.

The 4v. deal with the Court and control of the stage; the companies and the playhouses; the staging at Court and in the theatres; the plays and their authors. V.4 ends with a consideration of anonymous works, appendices of original documents, and indexes. The standard work, although the chapters on the Elizabethan playhouse should be read in conjunction with later works on this subject.

Class No: 792.0(420)(091)

[4737]

TRUSSLER, S. The Cambridge illustrated history of British theatre. New York/Cambridge, Cambridge University Press, 1994. 404p. $39.95. ISBN: 0521419131.

Covers British theatre from the Roman period to 1990; generally each of the 22 chapters spans some 20 - 30 years. Emphasis on the performance aspects of theatre, with political and social background. Indexes of personal names, proper names, topics, titles; glossary; chronology; bibliographic essay. *Class No:* 792.0(420)(091)

[4738]

WICKHAM, G. Early English drama, 1300-1660. London, Routledge & Kegan Paul, 1959-81. 3v.,illus.

1: *1300 to 1576*. 1959. xliv, 428p.

2: *1574 to 1660*. 1963. Pt.2, 1965 (new ed. 1971. £5).

3: *Plays and their makers, to 1576* 1981. 357p. £14.50.

V.1 is in 3 books: 1. Open-air entertainments of the Middle Ages - 2. Indoor entertainments of the Middle Ages - 3. Mediaeval dramatic theory and practice. Valuable introductory survey of the literature, p.xxi-xliv. Lists of books and MSS., p.401-12. V.2, pt.1 has 2 books: 1. Regulating the theatre - 2. Emblems and images. Notes and sources; notes to illus. Lists of books and MSS., p.389-96. Many striking illus. Updates E.K. Chambers's *The mediaeval stage. (See* entry at 792.0"01/14").

Class No: 792.0(420)(091)

London

[4739]

HOWARD, D. London theatres and music halls, 1850-1950. London, Library Association, 1970. xiii,291p.,illus.

Part 1 is an A-Z systematically descriptive list (p.1-268) of 910 theatres, music halls and pleasure gardens, with bibliographies. Part 2, a bibliography of general works (bibliographies; official records and publications; select list of local newspapers; select list of theatrical periodicals; other publications. Part 3: Location of material; directory of

....(contd.)
collections. Name index of buildings. 'An extremely useful reference work for advanced students of the English stage or those involved with research in England' (*Choice*, v.10, no.576, July/August 1973, p.757). *Class No:* 792.0(421)

Chronologies

[4740]
The London stage, 1600-1800: a calendar of plays, entertainments and afterpieces, together with casts, box-receipts and contemporary comment. Carbondale, Ill., Southern Illinois Univ. Press, 1960-79. 5 parts in 11v.; index.

1: *1600-1700*; edited by W.B. van Lennep. 1966.
2: *1700-1729*; edited by E.L. Avery. 1960. 2v.
3: *1729-1747*; edited by A.L. Scouten. 1961. 2v.
4: *1747-1776*; edited by G.W. Stone, jr. 1962. 3v.
5: *1776-1800*; edited by C.B. Hogan.
Index to 'The London stage'. 1979. 939p.

A chronological listing of performances arranged day by day. Data on each play: cast, incidental comment (*e.g.* box receipts; whether dancing or singing included), and supporting references. Adequate cross-references. The computerised *Index* assembles 506,014 references under *c.*25,000 entries. 'References are to the date and theatre of the calendar entry' (*Introduction*). A very detailed source, with valuable introductory essays.
Class No: 792.0(421)(090)

[4741]
THEATRE MUSEUM. London. **Playbills and programmes from London theatres 1801-1900.** Cambridge, Chadwyck-Healey, 1987. 2,997 microfiche.

75 theatres are included, and the microfiche are available separately. For 25 largest theatres the collections range from 20 to 420 microfiche per theatre. Arranged in chronological order, and valuable for social and historical purposes as well as theatrical interest. *Class No:* 792.0(421)(090)

[4742]
WEARING, J.P. The London stage, 1900-1909: a calendar of plays and players. Metuchen, NJ, Scarecrow Press, 1981. 1202p.(2v.). $65. ISBN: 081081403x.

Lists 2,973 productions at 35 theatres; 95,810 performances, with accurate cast lists (often with changes during a production's run), production data, length of runs and details of where representative reviews may be found. Title and general indexes. *Class No:* 792.0(421)(090)

[4743]
—WEARING, J.P. The London stage, 1890-1899: a calendar of plays and players. Metuchen, NJ, Scarecrow Press, 1976. 1242p.(2v.). $69.50. ISBN: 0810809109.
Class No: 792.0(421)(090)

[4744]
—WEARING, J.P. The London stage, 1910-1919: a calendar of plays and players. Metuchen, NJ, Scarecrow Press, 1982. 1388p.(2v.). $79.50. ISBN: 0810815966.
Class No: 792.0(421)(090)

[4745]
—WEARING, J.P. The London stage, 1920-1929: a calendar of plays and players. Metuchen, NJ, Scarecrow Press, 1984. 1808p.(3v.). $97.50. ISBN: 0810817152.

Vol.1 covers 1920-24; vol.2 1925-29; vol.3 contains the index. *Class No:* 792.0(421)(090)

Biographies

[4746]
HIGHFILL, P.H. *and* **BURNIN, K.A.** *and* **LANGHANS, E.A. A Biographical dictionary of actors, actresses, musicians, dancers, managers, and other stage personnel in London 1660-1800** volume 16. Carbondale, South Illinois University Press, 1993. 375p. $60.00. ISBN: 0809318032.

Highly detailed and exhaustive, volume 16 completes the alphabetical sequence of this twenty-year project. The Theatre Library Association awarded the work a special citation after the publication of volume 6; there have been four grants from the National Endowment for the Humanities. Coverage is of everybody traceable who was in any way connected with performance. Well illustrated. 'Review opinion has moved from admiration...to awe.'(*Choice*, 31(6)1994, p.915) *Class No:* 792.0(421)(092)

Germany

Bibliographies

[4747]
PATTERSON, M. German theatre: a bibliography from the beginning to 1995. New York, G.K.Hall/Prentice Hall International, 1996. 887p. $240.00. ISBN: 0783816626.

17,500 citations, focussing on performance. Covers books, pamphlets and dissertations, but not journal articles. Categorised arrangement, but subject index is so broad that searching is clumsy. *Class No:* 792.0(430)(01)

Spain

Histories

[4748]
SHERGOLD, N.D. A History of the Spanish theatre, from medieval times to the end of the seventeenth century. Oxford, Clarendon Press, 1967. xxx,624p.,illlus.

Main chapters deal with buildings, stages, scenery, machines, actors and the like, especially for the 16th century and the literary development of the drama. Glossary of theatrical terms used before 1700, p.560-3. Sources and works cited, p.564-87. (A. Manuscripts (other than MS plays) - B. Texts of plays - C. Books and articles). Analytical index, p.589-624. A scholarly work, heavily footnoted. *Class No:* 792.0(460)(091)

Asia

Bibliographies

[4749]
BRANDON, J.R. *and* **WICHMANN, E.,** *eds.* **Asian theatre:** a study guide and annotated bibliography. Washington DC. American Theatre Association, 1980. 197p.

Arranged into geographical groups: Asia - Burma - Cambodia - China - India - Indonesia - Japan - Korea - Laos - Malaysia and Singapore - Nepal - Pakistan and Bangladesh - Philippines - Sri Lanka - Thailand - Tibet - Vietnam. Each group has an introduction and has subdivisions: History; Theory and practice; Plays; Audiovisual material. Descriptive annotations for books and articles, Restricted to English-language items. 'This excellent monograph, which meets a long-felt need' (*Choice*, v.18, no.8, April 1981, p.1067. *Class No:* 792.0(5)(01)

Japan

[4750]
BOWERS, F. Japanese theatre. Tokyo, Tuttle, 1975. 294p.,illus. £6.95. ISBN: 0804811318.

Comprehensive historical account, divided into chapters on origins, Noh, Kabuki, puppets, actors and playwrights, present scene. *Class No:* 792.0(52)

Africa

Bibliographies

[4751]
GRAY, J., ***comp.*** **Black theatre and performance:** a pan-African bibliography. Westport, Ct., Greenwood Press. 1990. 414p. $45. ISBN: 0313268754.

4,000 citations to journal articles, monographs, theses, audio and video sources, reviews. Includes US, European, and African publications. 3 main sections - cultural history and the arts; African theatre; black theatre & performance in the diaspora. An appendix lists by region individual names and theatre companies. Indexes of artistes, titles, authors, subjects. *Class No:* 792.0(6)(01)

Canada

Encyclopaedias & Dictionaries

[4752]
The Oxford companion to Canadian theatre. Benson, E. *and* Conolly, L.W., *eds.* Oxford, OUP, 1990. 662p.,illus. £30. ISBN: 0195406729.

703 signed articles on genres, theatres, companies, biographies of dramatists, directors, designers and major plays. Lengthy section (25,000 words) devoted to history of drama in English & French speaking Canada. General index of names; cross-references; bibliographies follow many entries. *Class No:* 792.0(71)(03)

USA

Bibliographies

[4753]
SILVESTER, R. United States theatre: a bibliography from the beginning to 1990. Romsey, Motley Press, 1993. 400p. £70.00. ISBN: 0900281030.

Companion to Cavanagh's *British theatre: a bibliography 1901-85* at 792.0(410)(01)

Contains 7464 items covering the English language theatre tradition and American Indian culture, but not other cultural traditions in the US. Journals articles are not included, but there is good coverage of theses. Author and subject indexes. *Class No:* 792.0(73)(01)

[4754]
WILMETH, D.B., ***ed.*** **The American stage to World War I:** a guide to information sources. Detroit, Gale Research, 1978. 296p. $68. ISBN: 0810313928.

Briefly annotated bibliography including general reference sources, bibliographies, indexes, histories, collections, individuals etc., mainly concentrating on entertainment, business, production, and not the literature of the stage. *Class No:* 792.0(73)(01)

Encyclopaedias & Dictionaries

[4755]
BORDMAN, G. The Oxford companion to American theatre. Oxford, OUP, 1985. 734p. £39.50. ISBN: 0195034430.

Biographies of authors, performers, composers, producers, directors etc., and forms of presentation. Good coverage of individual key works, and details of societies, organizations, journals etc. *Class No:* 792.0(73)(03)

[4756]
—BORDMAN, G. The Concise Oxford companion to American theatre. Oxford, OUP, 1987. 448p. £19.50. ISBN: 0195051211.

Based on the *Oxford Companion to American theatre* (1985). *Class No:* 792.0(73)(03)

[4757]
WILMETH, D.B. ***and*** **MILLER, T.L.,** ***eds.*** **The Cambridge guide to American theatre.** Rev.and expanded ed. Cambridge, Cambridge University Press, 1996 512p. £14.95. ISBN: 0521564441.

Previous ed. 1993.

'Comprehensive view of the history and present practice of the theatre in the United States.' Especially good on contemporary theatre. Several entries are revised and updated from the *Cambridge guide to world theatre*. Coverage includes circus, vaudeville, burlesque, folk festivals, gay/lesbian, African-American, Yiddish etc. Entries for actors, theatres, directors, professional schools, playwrights, companies, famous plays; also entries by topic, and by various major cities. Many entries have short bibliographies. Biographical index to 3000 names mentioned in the text, but no index of plays mentioned. 170 illustrations; 80 specialist contributors (entries are signed.) *Choice* (30(10),1993, p.1598) reviewing the earlier ed. notes there is an excellent general bibliography.
Class No: 792.0(73)(03)

Yearbooks & Directories

[4758]
LAWLISS, C. The New York theatre sourcebook: the ultimate guide to theatre in New York and environs. New York, Fireside, 1990. 367p. $12.95. ISBN: 0671688707.

Entries for 300 theatres; with address, phone numbers, seating capacity, disabled access, seating diagram, notes on history, famous performances, building design etc. Including parking and public transport details, adjacent restaurants etc. Notes on backstage tours; awards & prizes; glossary.
Class No: 792.0(73)(058)

[4759]
WANT, R.S., ***ed.*** **Want's Theatre directory** Washington,DC, Want Publishing Co. c140p.

Annual directory listing Broadway theatres, venues state-by-state in the US, Canada, and major theatres in London, Paris and Berlin. Gives details of touring productions, tours, venues, dates, current and long-running productions (with one-line descriptions), directors and principal cast lists. 'First-rate production' with several features to challenge other similar publications. *(Reference books bulletin,* Oct.1993. p388.) *Class No:* 792.0(73)(058)

Illustrations

[4760]

New York theater 1919-1961. Cambridge, Chadwyck-Healey, 1987. 877 microfiche.

Copies of the 26,000 photographs in the Vandamm collection at the New York Public Library. Covers all productions, and includes alphabetical access to individual performers. Available as separate subject groups, musicals, etc. *Class No:* 792.0(73)(084.1)

Portraits

[4761]

ODELL, G.C.D. Annals of the New York stage. New York, AMS, 1977. 15v.,illus. $1425 (set). ISBN: 0404078303.

Originally published Columbia U.P. 1927-49; v.1: To 1798 - v.2: 1798-1821 ... v.15: 1891-1894.

*c.*350 portraits and other illus. Full entry below at 792.0(73)(090). *Class No:* 792.0(73)(084.10)

[4762]

—Index to the portraits in Odell's *Annals of the New York stage*; transcribed from the file in the Theatre Collection at Princeton University. New York, American Society for Theatre Research, 1963. iv,179p.
Class No: 792.0(73)(084.10)

Chronologies

[4763]

BRONNER, E.J. The Encyclopedia of the American theatre, 1900-1975. London, Tantivy Press/New York, Barnes, 1980. 659p.,illus.

Data on over 2,000 plays produced on- and off-Broadway, 1900-75. The plays were written/adapted by American or Anglo-American authors. Titles A-Z, with appraisals. Excludes musicals. Appendices: 1. Theatre calendar (notable premières of the century: by months; by titles; leading perfomers); 2. Débuts: actors; 3. Débuts: playwrights; 4. The golden 100 ... 5. Statistical record (Broadway productions); 6. Awards (Pulitzer Prizes, etc.). Non-analytical index, p.587-659. *Class No:* 792.0(73)(090)

[4764]

LEITER, S. The Encyclopedia of the New York stage: 1940-1950. Westport, CT, Greenwood Press, 1992. 1299p. $196. ISBN: 0313275106.

Companion to similar volumes covering 1920-30 (1985), and 1930-40 (1989).

Productions chronicled, with details of production staff, star cast names, review quotations, and other data. Bibliography and indexes of names and titles.
Class No: 792.0(73)(090)

[4765]

ODELL, G.C.D. Annals of the New York stage. New York, AMS, 1977. 15v.,illus. $1425 (set). ISBN: 0404078303.

Originally published Columbia U.P. 1927-49; v.1: To 1798 - v.2: 1798-1821 ... v.15: 1891-1894.

A very detailed history of the stage in New York City. Thus, v.15 (xvii,1010p.) gives casts of plays, etc., of the period, plus historical background *c.*350 portraits and other illus., and an analytical index (as in the other volumes), p.847-1010. *Class No:* 792.0(73)(090)

Histories

[4766]

BORDMAN, G. American theatre: a chronicle of comedy and drama, 1914-1930. New York/London, Oxford University Press, 1995. 446p. £35.00. ISBN: 0195090780.

Second volume of a projected three-volume work; volume one appeared 1994 (ISBN: 0195037642; 793p.) and covers the years 1869-1914.

Clear style with personal insights; each season covered chronologically by opening date, with summaries of plays, critical commentaries, major characters and cast members. Background historical and cultural context. Appendices give history of each theatre mentioned; indexes of all titles and people. No coverage of musical theatre, which Bordman has dealt with elsewhere - see entry at 792.5(73)(091).
Class No: 792.0(73)(091)

[4767]

DURHAM, W.B., *ed.* American theatre companies, 1931-1986. Westport, CT, Greenwood Press, 1989. 596p. $95. ISBN: 0313253609.

Concludes a three-volume set; volume one covered 1749-1887, volume two 1888-1930.

Historical preface, biographies of 78 companies. Includes dates, locations, personnel, performers, repertory year-by-year. Bibliographies follow each entry. Indexes include personal names and play titles. *Class No:* 792.0(73)(091)

[4768]

WITHAM, B., *ed.* Theatre in the United States: a documentary history. Cambridge, Cambridge University Press, 1996. 450p. £65.00. ISBN: 0521308585.

The first volume covers 1750-1915, and is subtitled 'theatre in the colonies and the United States'.

First volume of a multi-part work; authoritative status is assured with the depth and quality of coverage.
Class No: 792.0(73)(091)

Biographies

[4769]

ARCHER, S.M., *ed.* American actors and actresses; a guide to information sources. Detroit, Gale Research, 1983. xxii,710p.

Pt.1 consists of annotated entries for general information sources. (*e.g.* encyclopedias, biographical dictionaries, bibliographies and indexes, histories). Pt.2, the larger part, is devoted to individual performers, (*c.*250), with bibliographical references. *Class No:* 792.0(73)(092)

Australia

[4770]

PARSONS, P., *ed.* Companion to theatre in Australia. Sydney, Currency Press/Cambridge, Cambridge University Press, 1995. 704p., illus. ISBN: 0521345286.

To the usual standard of other volumes from CUP, this provides a good general introduction; some illustrations; bibliographic references; index. *Class No:* 792.0(94)

Ancient Times

Histories

[4771]

BIEBER, M. The History of the Greek and Roman theater. 2nd ed. London, OUP, 1961. xvi,343p.,illus.

.... *(contd.)*
First published 1939.
15 chapters with copious footnote references; selected bibliography. *Class No:* 792.0"-"(091)

Middle Ages

[4772]
CHAMBERS, E.K. The Mediaeval stage. Oxford, Clarendon Press, 1903. 2v.
4 main sections: minstrelsy; folk drama; religious drama; interludes; also, bibliographies and appendices of original documents. The most comprehensive and authoritative account, from the collapse of the Roman civilization to the Tudor interludes. *Class No:* 792.0"01/14"

[4773]
VINCE, R.W. A Companion to the medieval theatre. Westport, CT, Greenwood, 1989. 420p. $75.00. ISBN: 0313246475.
Includes a bibliography and indexes of persons, places, plays and subjects. *Class No:* 792.0"01/14"

[4774]
WICKMAN, G. Mediaeval theatre. 3rd ed. Cambridge, CUP, 1987. 260p. £25.00. ISBN: 0521320690.
Well established as a standard source; extensive bibliography. *Class No:* 792.0"01/14"

Libraries

Great Britain

[4775]
HOWARD, D., ***comp.*** **Directory of theatre resources:** a guide to research collections and information services. 2nd ed. London, Library Association ISG and Society for Theatre Research, 1986. 144p. £10.50. ISBN: 0946347085.
Three hundred entries cover UK libraries of all types, and societies and associations. Basic data and brief descriptions; excellent layout, and good indexes.
Class No: 792.0:061:026/027(410)

America — North

[4776]
RACHOW, L.A., ***ed.*** **Theatre and performing arts collections.** New York, Haworth Press, 1981. 166p. $39.95. ISBN: 091772447x.
Confined to North American collections, but covering holdings related to all countries. Includes substantial collections on British theatre.
Class No: 792.0:061:026/027(71+73)

[4777]
YOUNG, W.C. American theatrical arts: a guide to manuscripts and special collections in the United States and Canada. Chicago, American Library Association, 1971. 176p.
Available as on-demand reprint from UMI.
A guide to 138 repositories and collections, arranged under states/provinces. Index of persons and subjects.
Class No: 792.0:061:026/027(71+73)

Theatre Technology

Bibliographies

[4778]
GAMBLE, W.B. The Development of scenic art and stage machinery: a list of references in the New York Public Library. Rev. ed. New York, NYPL, 1928. 231p.
Worldwide coverage of all periods. Classified arrangement, with name and subject indexes. Some items are annotated. Includes periodical articles and analytical references. An important bibliography, not superseded, although clearly only of historical value.
Class No: 792.02(01)

[4779]
—STOTTARD, R. Stage scenery, machinery and lighting: a guide to information sources. Detroit, Gale Research, 1977. xi, 274p.
Records 1621 items (including articles) published since Gamble's list. 3 parts (23 chapters): 1. General references (bibliographies and iconographies; dictionaries and encyclopedias; periodicals) - 2. Scenery and stage machinery (p.15-216) - 3. Stage lighting and projected scenery. Chapter 20 : manuals and textbooks. Author and subject indexes.
Class No: 792.02(01)

[4780]
HOWARD, J.Y. A Bibliography of theatre technology, acoustics and sound, lighting, properties and scenery. Westport, CT, Greenwood Press, 1982. 345p.
A convenient amalgamation of scattered materials, but compiled from secondary sources - leading to 'inaccuracies and omissions that mar an otherwise useful and well-organized work' (*RQ*, v.21, no.4, Summer 1982, p.423).
Class No: 792.02(01)

Handbooks & Manuals

[4781]
BOULANGER, N.C. *and* **LOUNSBURY, W.C. Theatre lighting from A to Z.** Seattle, Washington University Press, 1992. 197p.$24.95. ISBN: 0925972149.
An encyclopedia rather than a dictionary; designed for professional as well as amateur use. A North American bias is evident. Content emphasizes technical issues at the expense of historical; there are several drawings, detailed instructions, and illustrations of technique. 1200 entries and over 350 diagrams etc. The spiral binding is good for actual use, but less attractive to libraries. *Class No:* 792.02(035)

[4782]
IZENOUR, G.C. Theater technology. 2nd.ed. New Haven/ London, Yale University Press, 1996. 594p., illus. £100.00. ISBN: 0300067666.
Full-scale reference guide to theatre engineering and technology; discursive treatment, with almost 900 illustrations. Coverage appears to be thorough and up-to-date. *Class No:* 792.02(035)

[4783]
REID, F. The ABC of stage lighting. London, Black/New York, Drama Book, 1992. 129p. £9.95. ISBN: 0713636092.
An extensive treatment of the topic, comprising some 800 terms with useful illustrations. This is an essential adjunct to the author's *Stage lighting handbook.*
Class No: 792.02(035)

[4784]
REID, F. The Stage lighting handbook. 5th ed. London, A & C Black, 1996. 224p.,illus. £13.99. ISBN: 0713644362.
First edition 1976.
Considers various types of performances, indicating design, equipment etc. A thorough glossary, and index; the author's *ABC of stage lighting*,1992 is a helpful companion. *Class No:* 792.02(035)

[4785]
WALTERS, G. Stage lighting step-by-step. London, A.& C. Black,1997. 128., illus. £14.99. ISBN: 071364639x.
Comprehensive overall guide, with good illustrations. *Class No:* 792.02(035)

Production & Management

[4786]
HALNAUX, R., *ed.* Stage design throughout the world from 1970-1975. New York, Theatre Arts, 1976. 159p.,illus.
Previous volumes titled *Stage design throughout the world since 1935* (London, Harrap, 1957); - *since 1950* (Theatre Arts, 1963); - *since 1960* (Theatre Arts, 1973).
The 1970-1975 v. consists largely of illus. (p.17-152), arranged chronologically (Aeschylus ... Webber). Index to illustrations, listed under author and composers; directors, choreographers, designers and costume designers. 'Bibliographical references' (running commentary), p.158. *Class No:* 792.075

[4787]
REID, F. Theatre administration. London, Black, 1983. 176p.,illus. £8.95. ISBN: 0713623683.
A practical introduction with guidance on daily routines, adminstrative decisions, policy etc. Illustrated with diagrams and checklists. *Class No:* 792.075

[4788]
SCHNEIDER, D. The Art and craft of stage management. Fort Worth/London, Harcourt Brace, 1997. xvii,264p. £32.50. ISBN: 015503023x.
Well illustrated with plans, forms and templates. *Class No:* 792.075

[4789]
STUART, P. Theatre procedures and practice - or who does what in the theatre. London, Kemble Press, 1982. 130p. (spiral bound). £4.95. ISBN: 0906835119.
Basic handbook of terms, common practice etc. Intended as the simplest guide for students and amateurs. *Class No:* 792.075

Bibliographies

[4790]
WATTS, S., *comp.* Stagecraft and theatre. Penzance, Cornwall, Library Association Public Libraries Group, 1981. 24p. £1.10. (*Readers' Guide no.35.*) ISBN: 0853657041.
137 briefly annotated entries. 10 sections 1. History of the theatre - 2. Philosophy and aesthetics of theatre - 3. Theatre companies today - 4. Theatre management - 5. Theatre design - 6. Production - 7. Stage design - 8. Reference (nos.120-130) - 9. Periodicals - 10. Organizations. Experimental: Addendum. Author index. Annotations do not indicate presence of illus., bibliographies or indexes. A handy checklist. *Class No:* 792.075(01)

Handbooks & Manuals

[4791]
GRIFFITHS, T.R., *ed.* Stagecraft: the complete guide to theatrical practice. 2nd ed. London, Phaidon, 1990. 192p.,illus. £9.95. ISBN: 0714826448.
Previous edition 1982.
A practical guide to all aspects of production; includes stage management, direction, design, costumes, lighting, make-up, scenery building, props, administration. Well illustrated, with glossary and index. Intended for non-professional use. *Class No:* 792.075(035)

[4792]
JANS, M. Stage make-up techniques. New York, Players Press, 1993. 112p. $23.95. ISBN: 0887346219.
A primer of basic techniques, such as hairpieces, noses, prosthetics, wounds, animals, fantasy, clowns etc. Good for all amateurs and for children. High quality colour illustrations, showing lighting needs, temperature considerations. *Class No:* 792.075(035)

Ancient Greece

[4793]
WALTON, J.M. Living Greek theatre: a handbook of classical performance and modern production. New York, Greenwood, 1987. ix, 436p. $49.95. ISBN: 0313245975.
Examines the staging and performance of Greek drama, characteristics, conventions. Bibliography. *Class No:* 792.075(37)

Amateur Theatre

Yearbooks & Directories

[4794]
Amateur theatre yearbook, incorporating community theatre and training. Vance, C., *ed and* Hackworth-*Young, J., comp.*. St. Albans, Herts., Platform Publications. Annual.
Geographical listing of UK amateur theatre, community theatre, and theatrical training facilities. Details of publishers & publications for the performing arts, specialist bookshops, theatrical suppliers, back-up services etc. *Class No:* 792.077(058)

Musical Theatre

[4795]
BLOOM, K. American song: the complete musical theatre companion. 2nd.ed. New York, Schirmer Books/London, Prentice Hall International, 1996. 2093p. (2v.) $175.00. ISBN: 0028704843.
See entry at: 784(73). *Class No:* 792.5

[4796]
GÄNZL, K. The Encyclopedia of musical theatre. New York, Schirmer, 1994. 1610p.(2v.) $150.00 ISBN: 0028714458.
2700 entries for performers, composers, writers and shows; also some producers, directors, choreographers and designers. Text-based musicals only - no opera, pantomimes or reviews. Covers UK, Europe, US, Australia and New Zealand, 19th and 20th centuries. Basic biographies give lists of works; plot summaries and performance histories. Film adaptations are mentioned. In alphabetical order with

....(contd.)
no cross-references, and no index. 'Although seemingly adequately researched, it is not written in a scholarly style... this is a must for music collections.' (*Reference books bulletin,* 1 September, 1994, p.68.) *Class No:* 792.5

[4797]
HISCHAK, T.S. The American musical theatre song encyclopedia. Westport CT, Greenwood Press, 1995. 543p. $59.95. ISBN: 0313294070.
Encyclopedia of songs from broadway shows, covering 1866 to the 1993/94 season. Includes 1800 songs from over 500 musicals, with data on authors, original performers, dates, history of recordings, and description of each song. Index of titles, shows, authors, and performers. Glossary of terms, and a brief bibliography. *Class No:* 792.5

[4798]
HISCHAK, T.S. Stage it with music: an encyclopedic guide to the American musical theatre. Westport,CT, Greenwood Press, 1993. 341p. $45.00. ISBN: 0313287082.
910 short entries for shows, composers, lyricists, performers, institutions and genres. Good general bibliography; excellent index of other names mentioned in entries. Coverage is mainly US, but there are some UK figures. Biographical notes on individuals are especially useful. *Class No:* 792.5

[4799]
LEWINE, R. *and* **SIMON, A. Songs of the theater.** New York, Wilson, 1984. ix, 897p. £95.00. ISBN: 0824207068.
Lists 17,000 songs from 1,200 shows, mainly New York staged. Notes printed editions, and recordings, film and TV productions. *Class No:* 792.5

[4800]
SUSKIN, S. Berlin, Kern, Rodgers, Hart, and Hammerstein: a complete song catalogue. Jefferson, NC, McFarland, 1990. 336p. $55. ISBN: 089950471x.
Includes all known songs, with production dates, publishers etc. Valuable bibliography appended. Indexed. *Class No:* 792.5

USA

Histories

[4801]
BLOOM, K. Broadway: an encyclopedic guide to the history, people and places of Times Square. Oxford, Facts on File, 1990. 432p., illus. $45. ISBN: 0816012490.
Introductory history, then brief entries covering playwrights, composers, actors, producers, directors, restaurants, theatres (concise history of each one), jargon & slang, advertising etc. 'Essential for theatre collections' (*Library Journal*, November 1, 1990. p.80). *Class No:* 792.5(73)(091)

[4802]
BORDMAN, G. American musical theatre: a chronicle. 2nd.ed. Oxford, Oxford University Press, 1992. viii,821p. £45. ISBN: 0195072421.
12 chapters. 1. Prologue: origins to 1866 ... 6. The birth of the modern musical, 1914-1921 ... 8. The golden age of the American musical, 1924-37 ... 10. The American musical as a conscious art form, 1942-1965 - 11. Exhaustion 1965-1969 - 12.Full circle - new British trends 1969-90. For each musical: plot synopses; physical production, and principal statistics; biographies of actors, songwriters, librettists and producers. Examples of lyrics and dialogue.

....(contd.)
Appendix, - US provincial shows. Non-analytical indexes of shows and sources, songs and people. *Class No:* 792.5(73)(091)

[4803]
KRASKER, T. *and* **KIMBALL, R. Catalog of the American musical:** musicals of Irving Berlin, George & Ira Gershwin, Cole Porter, Richard Rodgers & Lorenz Hart. Washington, J.F. Kennedy Center, National Institute for Music Theater, 1988. 442p. $60.00. ISBN: 0961857501.
Scholarly project to identify and rescue original performance materials; this first phase surveys 75 works from 18 depositories, with standard data given. Index of 1,600 songs. *Class No:* 792.5(73)(091)

Music Hall & Pantomime

[4804]
PICKERING, D., *ed.* **Encyclopedia of pantomime.** Andover, Gale Research, 1993. 240p. £45.00. ISBN: 1873477457.
600 entries in alphabetical order; contains an enormous amount of information that is difficult to trace elsewhere, and makes fascinating browsing. Biographical entries are a particular strength. A short general bibliography is appended. *Class No:* 792.7

[4805]
SLIDE, A. Encyclopedia of vaudeville. Westport,CT, Greenwood Press, 1994. 605p. $75.00. ISBN: 0313280274.
500 entries 1800s-1930s, covering people, theatres, buildings, ballads, touring circuits, fires. Some reviews quoted; index of all names mentioned, and subject index. Bibliographies follow some entries. *Class No:* 792.7

Biographies

[4806]
SLIDE, A. The Vaudevillians: a dictionary of vaudeville performers. Westport, Conn., Arlington House, 1981. 172p.,illus.
Entries, A-Z, for more than 160 performers (*e.g.* The Duncan sisters, Mae West, Abbott and Costello, W.C. Fields). Includes the little-known as well as the more famous. Select general bibliography. 'This is a most helpful introductory work' (*Choice*, v.19, no.9, May 1982, p.1220). *Class No:* 792.7(092)

Great Britain

Bibliographies

[4807]
SENELICK, L., *and others*. **British music-hall,** 1840-1923: a bibliography and guide to sources, with an supplement on European music-hall. Hamden,CT, Shoe String Press, 1981. xviii,357p. $40. ISBN: 0208018409.
Very favourably reviewed in *Theatre Notebook* (v.36, no.3, 1982, p.137-8). *Class No:* 792.7(410)(01)

Biographies

[4808]

BUSBY, R. British music hall: an illustrated who's who from 1880 to the present day. London, Elek, 1976. 191p.,illus.

Who's who, A/Z, p.15-191. 'Marie Lloyd': 12/3p., 1 port.; 'Tony Hancock': 2 cols., 1 port. Includes entries for groups (*e.g.* Morecambe and Wise) and families. Preceded by 'Introduction: From pleasure gardens to variety', and list of terms. Fully illustrated. *Class No:* 792.7(410)(092)

Ballet

Bibliographies

[4809]

BALANCHINE, G. Choreography: a catalogue of works. New York, Eakins, 1983. 407p.

A closely annotated chronology of all 425 works by Balanchine, 1920-1982. 'One of the most significant dance books of the 20th century' (*Choice* v.20(11/12) July/August 1983, p.1572). *Class No:* 792.8(01)

[4810]

BOPP, M.S. Research in dance: a guide to the resources. Boston, G.K.Hall, 1994. 296p. $50.00. ISBN: 0816190658.

Covers major libraries and reference sources; 2 parts: details of 100 dance collections and archives mainly in the US and Canada; literature of dance - standard sources, serials, indexes, abstracts etc. Most material is recent, and English-language. Fully annotated. *Class No:* 792.8(01)

[4811]

BROWNMILLER, S.N. *and* **DICKINSON, D.C. The Literature of dance.** *Reference Services Review* 16(1-2) 1988. p.115-120.

Brief introduction, followed by annotated bibliography under headings - bibliographies, dictionaries & encyclopedias, ballet plot summaries, journals, histories, reviews, directories, indexes & abstracts, professional associations in the US. *Class No:* 792.8(01)

[4812]

NILES, D. *and* **LESLIE, S. A Bibliography of the dance collection** of Doris Niles and Serge Leslie.

Beaumont, C., *ed.* London, Beaumont (distributed by *Dancing Times*), 1966-81. 4v.

Author catalogue of *c.* 4,000 entries, v.3-4 mainly on 20th-century publications. Ballet is the main theme, although books on folk dancing, social dances and the like are included. Annotations often concern ballet music. Strong on French material. Each volume has a broad subject index. Headings include: Acrobats and gymnastics - Ancient and Classical dance - Autobiography, biography, memoirs - Ballets synopses, divertissements, operas and plays - Bibliography, catalogues, etc. - Correspondence - Criticism, essays & belles-lettres - Dance notations - Dance periodicals ... Dictionaries and encyclopedias ... Folk, national and ethnological dance ... Mime and pantomime - Music - Photographic records and illustrated books ... Tap dancing. *Class No:* 792.8(01)

[4813]

STUDWELL, W.E. *and* **HAMILTON, D.A. Ballet plot index:** a guide to locating plots and descriptions of ballets and associated materials. New York, Garland, 1988. 250p. $42. ISBN: 0824083857.

Detailed and informative. Voted an 'outstanding academic book 1989/90' by *Choice*. *Class No:* 792.8(01)

Encyclopaedias & Dictionaries

[4814]

BALANCHINE, G. *and* **MASON, F. Balanchine's festival of ballet.** London, W.H. Allen, 1978. xxv,838p.

First published 1954, as *Balanchine's Complete stories of the great ballets;* US revised edition under this title issued by Doubleday, 1977.

Part 1: 'Stories of the great ballets': scene-by-scene stories of 401 classic and contemporary ballets, A-Z by title. Parts 2-9: 2. How to enjoy a ballet - 3. A brief history of the ballet - 4. Chronology of significant events in the history of the ballet ... 6. Ballet for young children - 7. Careers in ballet - 8. Notes and comments on dancers, dancing and choreography - 9. Glossary (with line-drawings). Detailed, analytical index, p.689-805. 79 photographs. *Class No:* 792.8(03)

[4815]

BREMSER, M., *et al.* **International dictionary of ballet.** Detroit, St.James' Press, 1993. 1600p.(2v.) £175. ISBN: 1558620842.

750 entries, covering the ballet scene historically and internationally; emphasis on Russia, Europe and North America. Small number of key biographies in modern dance, but the majority of biographies are for dancers, choreographers, designers, composers, librettists, teachers. Good quantity of information and several monochrome photographs. Entries for ballets give details of first performance and all possible credits. The list of contributors is strong. Index of artists and companies. 'Excellent compendium of biographical and historical information on the art of ballet and its practitioners.' (*Reference books bulletin*, 15.1.94, p956-9.) *Class No:* 792.8(03)

[4816]

GRIGOROVICH, Y.N., *ed.* **Balet entsiklopediya.** Moscow, Izdat. Sovetskopediya, 1981. 623p.,illus.

International in scope, with entries for dancers ('Pavlova': *c.*1p. with 8 lines of bibliography, 4 illus.), ballets, composers, choreographers, companies, theatres ('Bolshoi' Theatre: p.82-88; bibliography of 23 lines, 13 illus.), and dance terms. Bibliography (12 sections), p.617-9. Numerous small illus., with line-drawings showing dance steps and positions. *Class No:* 792.8(03)

[4817]

KOEGLER, H. The Concise Oxford dictionary of ballet. 2nd ed. Oxford, OUP, 1982. 459p. £15. ISBN: 0193113252.

Original German edition *Friedrichs Ballettlexikon* 1972.

5,000 entries covering all aspects of ballet over 400 years: dancers, choreographers, designers, ballets, theatres, schools, companies, and technical terms. Small print; heavily abbreviated. *Class No:* 792.8(03)

[4818]
ROBERTSON, A. *and* **HUTERA, D. Dance handbook.** Boston, G.K. Hall, 1990. 278p., illus. $25. ISBN: 081619095x.

Confined to Western theatrical dance, the handbook contains entries for 200 major individuals, companies, choreographers, ballet and other dance works, arranged in chronological sections - romantic ballet, classical ballet, Ballets Russes, birth of modern dance, modern ballet, the dance explosion alternatives. Significance of items is explained, and links with related works. Sections contain glossaries, bibliographies, directories of journals, festivals etc. Indexes to persons, films, performances, terms.
Class No: 792.8(03)

[4819]
TERRY, W. Ballet guide: background, listings, credits, and descriptions of more than five hundred of the world's major ballets. New York, Dodd Mead, 1976. 388p.,illus.

Arranged alphabetically by title with details of choreographer, music, designer, dancers at first performance; important re-stagings etc. Glossary of terms.
Class No: 792.8(03)

Handbooks & Manuals

[4820]
WARREN, G.W. Classical ballet technique. Miami; South Florida University Press, 1990. 395p., illus. $85 (Pbk $39.95). ISBN: 0813008956; 0813009456, Pbk.

Excellent photographs illustrate essential elements & techniques; covers US, English, Soviet and continental variations. *Class No:* 792.8(035)

Dictionaries

[4821]
GRANT, G. Technical manual and dictionary of classical ballet. 3rd ed. New York, Dover, 1982. 139p.,illus.

First edition 1950.

Concise definitions of terms, illustrated with line drawings. *Class No:* 792.8(038)

[4822]
KERSLEY, L. *and* **SINCLAIR, J. A Dictionary of ballet terms.** 4th ed. London, A.& C. Black, 1997. 128p., illus. £8.99 ISBN: 0713647531.

Previous edition 1973.

Alphabetical arrangement of terms with explanations. Line drawings. *Class No:* 792.8(038)

[4823]
MARA, T. Language of ballet: a dictionary. Princeton, Princeton Book Co., 1987. vi, 120p. $18.95. ISBN: 0871271443.

Reprint of the 1966 edition.

Good definitions, particularly of technical terms, are a special feature of this concise, but authoritative volume on ballet terminology. *Class No:* 792.8(038)

[4824]
STUART, M. The Classic ballet: basic technique and terminology. London, Black, 1977. 243p.,illus.

Parts: General - Exercises at the bar - Exercises in the center - Allegro - Dance on pointes. Each of the main parts has an introduction, noting variant interpretations. Prefatory essay. 'The classic ballet; historical development', by Lincoln Kirstein. Accurate line-drawings; 118 plates, with captions noting definition, preparation, exercise, posture and muscular control. *Class No:* 792.8(038)

Yearbooks & Directories

[4825]
PARRY, J., *ed.* **World ballet and dance** 1990-91: an international yearbook. New York, Dance Books, 1990. 302p. ISBN: 1852730277.

Second publication in the series; four parts comprise: feature articles, dance archives, review of dance around the world, data on dance companies including repertory, associated schools. Contributors are of high calibre. 'International review of dance activities in a single resource ... the editors are to be congratulated' (*Choice* September 1991, p.72). *Class No:* 792.8(058)

Histories

[4826]
CLARKE, M. *and* **CRISP, C. Ballet: an illustrated history.** London, Black, 1973. 245p.,illus.

10 chapters (1. How it all began - 2. The age of reason and technique - 3. The Romantic movement - 4. Marius Petipa and the Imperial Russian Ballet - 5. Emigrés: Diaghilev and Pavlova (p.112-48) - 6. Bridging the gap; the baby ballerinas - 7. The building of British ballet - 8. America: two kinds of dancing - 9. Soviet ballet: Vaganova and her pupils - 10. Today's ballet [up to 1972]. Non-analytical index, p.237-45. 253 illus., the lengthy captions being a feature. *Class No:* 792.8(091)

[4827]
STEEN, J. History of ballet and modern dance. London, Hamlyn, 1982. 256p.,illus.

Arranged in four country groups: Italy, France, Russia (p.72-98), Great Britain (p.99-129), Australia and Canada - Denmark, Sweden, Finland, Norway - The Netherlands, Belgium - Austria, Germany, Czechoslovakia, Hungary, Poland, with biographical sketches of leading personalities, in each case. 'Modern dance', p.203-39. Chronology, 1480-1982. Non-analytical index. 70 illus., and ports.
Class No: 792.8(091)

Biographies

[4828]
COHEN-STRATYNER, B.N. Biographical dictionary of dance. London, Macmillan/New York, Schirmer, 1982. 970p. £75. ISBN: 0028702603.

Covers Europe and America from sixteenth century onwards; alphabetical listing of performers, choreographers, composers, designers, teachers, etc., giving standard data and career details and key roles. Includes all forms of dance from classical ballet, to variety shows. About 3,000 entries.
Class No: 792.8(092)

England

Bibliographies

[4829]
FORRESTER, F.S. Ballet in England: a bibliography and survey, *c.*1700-June 1966. London, Library Association, 1968. 224p.,illus.

Revision and expansion of a thesis for the Fellowship of the Library Association in 1966.

A painstakingly compiled bibliography of 664 annotated entries. 14 chapters (1. Publishing and bibliography - 2. Encyclopaedias, dictionaries and year-books ... 10. Design and costume - 11. Music - 12. Film and television - 13. Fiction - 14. Periodicals). Each chapter has an introduction;

....(contd.)
entries (which include periodical articles) appear chronologically. Appendix B: 'Guide to resources for further study' (libraries, etc.; p.193-200); C: Exhibitions (p.201-3). Detailed, partly analytical index of names, subjects and titles. Favourably reviewed in *Ballet today*, v.17, no.9, May/June 1968, p.31). *Class No:* 792.8(420)(01)

Histories

[4830]

BLAND, A. The Royal Ballet: the first fifty years. London, Threshold/Sotheby Parke Bernet, 1981. 320p.,illus. £17.95. ISBN: 0901366110.

Covers both the Royal Opera House and Sadler's Wells Theatre. Contents include A-Z list of dancers (with dates of earliest traceable date of appearance) and choreographers who have worked with either company, plus a chronology of their ballets. Also, each company's repertory, A/Z (data on production, revival, revision and new dancers) and chronology of production, plus an itinerary, conjointly, - providing a virtually complete record of performances. An important source. *Class No:* 792.8(420)(091)

[4831]

WOODCOCK, S. The Dancing Wells: the history of the Sadler's Wells Royal Ballet. London, Sinclair-Stevenson, 1990. 320p. £10.95. ISBN: 185619034x.

Excellent historical account from its founding in 1946 to its present national status. *Class No:* 792.8(420)(091)

Dancing

[4832]

MOORE, A. Ballroom dancing. 9th ed. London, A & C Black, 1986. 324p., illus. £9.95. ISBN: 0713627948.

First published 1936.

The standard textbook on technique; charts illustrate patterns and foot positions. 'An indispensable work for all dancers and teachers' (*Guardian* obituary of the author, March 9. 1991). Sections cover Quickstep, Waltz, Foxtrot, Tango, competitions, popular dances, novelty dances & games. *Class No:* 793.3

Bibliographies

[4833]

BEAUMONT, C. A Bibliography of dancing. New York, Blom/Ayer Co, 1964. $20. ISBN: 0405082479.

Reprint of 1929 edition, London: Dancing Times.

Annotated listing, based on the collection of the then British Museum Library. *Class No:* 793.3(01)

[4834]

BOPP, M.S. Research in dance: a guide to the resources. Boston, G.K.Hall, 1994. 296p. $50.00. ISBN: 0816190658.

Covers major libraries and reference sources, in 2 parts: details of 100 dance collections and archives, mainly in the US and Canada; literature of dance - standard sources, serials, indexes, abstracts etc. Material is generally recent and English-language; fully annotated. *Class No:* 793.3(01)

[4835]

FORBES, F.R. Dance: an annotated bibliography 1965-1982. New York, Garland, 1986. 280p. $39. ISBN: 0824086767.

1200 entries range over history, physiology, psychology, literature, and aesthetics. All forms of material included. *Class No:* 793.3(01)

[4836]

Index to dance periodicals, 1996. Boston, G.K.Hall, 1997. c500p. $205.00. ISBN: 0783820321.

Annual.

Comprehensive worldwide coverage. *Class No:* 793.3(01)

[4837]

MAGRIEL, P.D. A Bibliography of dancing: a list of books and articles on the dance and related subjects. New York, H.W. Wilson 1936. 229p.

Reprinted New York, Blom. 1966.

Cumulative supplements were issued covering years to 1940 (last, 4th supplement issued 1941).

Aims to be 'a comprehensive list of reference works on the dance in all its phases and of the arts definitely related to dancing' (*Preface*). About 1,000 items, one-third of them briefly annotated. Includes terms on folk dances and ballet. Locations for rare and out-of-print books. Detailed author and subject index. A major source. *Class No:* 793.3(01)

[4838]

NATIONAL RESOURCE CENTRE FOR DANCE. University of Surrey. **Dance current awareness bulletin.** Guildford, National Resource Centre for Dance, 1983-. 44p. (No. 34; Nov. 1994.) ISSN: 02656523.

Issued three times pa.

Arranged by broad subject; comprises an annotated index to dance journals, new books & all items received by NRCD, conference & events. Notes locations of book, film, video and performance reviews. *Class No:* 793.3(01)

[4839]

NEW YORK PUBLIC LIBRARY. Dance on disc: the complete dictionary catalog of the dance collection. Boston, G.K. Hall, 1992-. CD-ROM. $995.00.(Annual updates $495.00.)

Cumulation of the 10 volume Dictionary Catalog issued in 1974 and annual supplements *Bibliographic guide to dance.*

180,000 records; the Collection covers historical, theatrical, educational, religious and recreational aspects of the dance, and the material ranges from books, periodicals, playbills and letters to films, scrapbooks, tapes and notated dance scores. *Class No:* 793.3(01)

[4840]

PETERMANN, K. Tanzbibliographie. Leipzig, VEB Bibliographisches Institut, 1966-. 30 fascicles (in progress).

A 'second revision' in 3 vols. has been issued of the earlier sections (Munich: Saur, 1981/2).

A massive project to list all German language material on all forms of dance, including artistic, social, cultural aspects. Brief annotations and indication of locations. Classified arrangement, at present not supported by indexes. Slow progress, only about half the promised subject areas being so far included. *Class No:* 793.3(01)

[4841]

SIMONS, L.K. The Performing arts: a guide to the reference literature. Littleton,CO, Libraries Unlimited, 1994. 230p. $42.00. ISBN: 0872879828.

Good coverage of dance literature; see full entry at 791/793(01). *Class No:* 793.3(01)

Black Races

[4842]
ADAMCZYK, A.J. Black dance: an annotated bibliography. New York, Garland, 1989. 213p. $29.00. ISBN: 0824088085.

Covers the development of black dance from its African origins; mainly concentrates on the US in the last fifty years. *Class No:* 793.3(01)(=96)

Encyclopaedias & Dictionaries

[4843]
CHUJOY, A. *and* **MANCHESTER, P.W. The Dance encyclopedia.** Rev. ed. New York, Simon & Schuster, 1967. xii,992p.,illus.

First published 1949.

A very highly regarded standard source; 5,000 entries cover definitions, biographies, individual ballets with synopses. Especially strong on ballet, and on the American contribution. Chronology, and repertory lists included. *Class No:* 793.3(03)

[4844]
International encyclopedia of dance. Cohen, S.J., *ed.* Oxford, Oxford University Press, 1998 3072p.(6v.) illus. £750.00 ISBN: 019509462x.

Major new international source, covering over 1000 cultures and countries from ancient times to the present. Compilers are 600 experts from 50 countries. 2000 articles A/Z with photographs and drawings. Covers forms, music, costumes, history, performers, choreographers, dance as entertainment and popular culture, stage design, lighting, make-up, techniques, aesthetics, dance literature. Cross references and thorough index. *Class No:* 793.3(03)

[4845]
McDONAGH, D. The Complete guide to modern dance. New York, Doubleday, 1976. xv,534p.,illus.

Sections: The forerunners (*e.g.* Isadora Duncan) - The founders (*e.g.* Martha Graham) - In and out of the steps of the founders (p.121-274) - Freedom and new formalism - Freedom and formalism (second generation; names, A-Z). Chronology of significant dates and events in modern dance development. 'Further reading' (p.509-13; briefly annotated; includes periodical articles). Detailed, non-analytical index. Excellent illus. 'This is the only existing book that gives the subject matter (or stories) for modern dance' [as opposed to ballet] (*Choice*, v.13, no.10, December 1976, p.1274). *Class No:* 793.3(03)

[4846]
ROBERTSON, A. *and* **HUTERA, D. Dance handbook.** Boston, G.K. Hall, 1990. 278p., illus. $25. ISBN: 081619095x.

Confined to Western theatrical dance, the handbook contains entries for 200 major individuals, companies, choreographers, ballet and other dance works, arranged in chronological sections - romantic ballet, classical ballet, Ballets Russes, birth of modern dance, modern ballet, the dance explosion alternatives. Significance of items is explained, and links with related works. Sections contain glossaries, bibliographies, directories of journals, festivals etc. Indexes to persons, films, performances, terms. *Class No:* 793.3(03)

Dictionaries

[4847]
PRESTON-DUNLOP, V., *comp.* **Dance words.** Newark, NJ, Harwood Academy, 1995. 718p. $55.00 ISBN: 3718656019.

Words and phrases collected from books, programmes, classes, theses, workshops etc. Mainly current US and UK usage. Seven sections: 'domain', performers, movement, choreographic concepts, sound/space, events, research. Good bibliography *Class No:* 793.3(038)

[4848]
RAFFÉ, W.G. Dictionary of the dance. London, T. Yoseloff, 1975. 583p.,illus.

Reprint of the 1964 version.

Comprehensive and wide coverage; 3,000 terms are discussed. Folk and ethnic dance is particularly well treated. Bibliography from 1500 to the present. *Class No:* 793.3(038)

[4849]
SCHNEIDER, O. Tanz Lexikon. Wien, Verlag Bruder Hollinek, 1985. 620p. $50.

Specializes in European folk dances and national styles; biographies of major figures. Bibliographies follow some articles. *Class No:* 793.3(038)

Periodicals & Progress Reports

[4850]
Dance and dancers. London, Orpheus Publications. *c*48p., illus. ISSN: 00115983.

Issued monthly.

Includes performance reviews, new books, discs. Danceguide, national and international. *Class No:* 793.3(05)

[4851]
Dance research. Oxford, Oxford University Press, 1984-. 80p., illus.(v. 15, 1997). £46.00 pa. ISSN: 02642875.

Scholarly articles and reviews on all types of dance, including anthropological aspects. *Class No:* 793.3(05)

[4852]
Dancing times. London, Dancing Times Ltd., 1910-. *c.*100p., illus. ISSN: 0011605x.

Issued monthly. Incorporates *Ballet Annual* from 1964.

Includes many features and performance reviews; calendar section. A valuable feature is the list of new books and videos available. *Class No:* 793.3(05)

Periodicals

[4853]
BELKNAP, S.Y., *comp.* **Guide to dance periodicals:** an analytical index of articles and illustrations. Metuchen, NJ, Scarecrow Press, 1948-63. 10v.

Early volumes published by University of Florida Press. Initially 5-yearly, later biennial volumes.

Includes some 20 British journals indexed by subject and author. Very thorough work. *Class No:* 793.3(051)

Yearbooks & Directories

[4854]
Dancing yearbook 1998. Dearling, J., *ed.* 41st.ed. Brighton, International Dance Teachers Association, 1997. 152p. ISSN: 13689126.

Details of organizations, festivals, championships, teachers, rules, results. Bibliographies and journals listed. *Class No:* 793.3(058)

Histories

[4855]
CLARKE, M. *and* **CRISP, C. The History of the dance.** London, Orbis Publishing, 1981. 256p.,illus.

10 chapters: 1. Primitive & ancient dance - 2. Religious dance - 3. European folk dance - 4. Eastern dance - 5. Social dance - 6. Ballet de cour - 7/8. History of dance - 9. Modern dance - 10. Stage & Screen. Appendix: Notation, Chapter notes, p.246-7. Bibliography, p.248-9 (authors, A/Z). Index (*c*.2,000 entries), p.230-6. Over 250 illus., well-captioned. 'An encylopaedic survey of the dance in virtually all its known forms ... 'Highly readable' (*British book news*, June 1981, p.367-8). *Class No:* 793.3(091)

[4856]
LAYSON, J. *and* **ADSHEAD-LANSDALE, J.,** *eds.* **Dance history:** an introduction. 2nd.ed. London, Routledge, 1994. 320p., illus. £13.99. ISBN: 041509030x.

Paperback textbook that has gained a reputation as a self-contained introduction to dance history, with commentary on a number of topical issues. *Class No:* 793.3(091)

[4857]
SACHS, C. World history of the dance. New York, Norton, 1973. 224p.,illus.

First published in English in 1937, from a German original (1933) *Eine Weltgeschichten des Tanzes*.

Describes the development of dance in its social context from ancient times to the present; examines themes, forms and details of movements. References; detailed index.
Class No: 793.3(091)

[4858]
STEEN, J. History of ballet and modern dance. London, Hamlyn, 1982. 256p.,illus.

Arranged in four country groups: Italy, France, Russia (p.72-98), Great Britain (p.99-129), Australia and Canada - Denmark, Sweden, Finland, Norway - The Netherlands, Belgium - Austria, Germany, Czechoslovakia, Hungary, Poland, with biographical sketches of leading personalities, in each case. 'Modern dance', p.203-39. Chronology, 1480-1982. Non-analytical index. 70 illus., and ports.
Class No: 793.3(091)

Biographies

[4859]
COHEN-STRATYNER, B.N. Biographical dictionary of dance. London, Macmillan/New York, Schirmer, 1982. 970p. £75. ISBN: 0028702603.

Covers Europe and America from sixteenth century onwards; alphabetical listing of performers, choreographers, composers, designers, teachers, etc., giving standard data and career details and key roles. Includes all forms of dance from classical ballet, to variety shows. About 3,000 entries.
Class No: 793.3(092)

Great Britain

Yearbooks & Directories

[4860]
BRITISH COUNCIL OF BALLROOM DANCING. Directory of schools of ballroom dancing in Great Britain. London, BCBD, 1987. 30p.

Simple listing, arranged by county.
Class No: 793.3(410)(058)

India

Bibliographies

[4861]
KUPPUSWAMY, G. *and* **HARIHARAN, M. Indian music and dance literature:** a select bibliography. New Delhi, Biblia Impex, 1981. xv,156p.

Includes 800 books and about 3,000 journal articles in English and Tamil languages. Arranged A/Z by author.
Class No: 793.3(540)(01)

Dictionaries

[4862]
BOSE, M. Classical Indian dancing: a glossary. Calcutta, General Printers & Publishers, 1969. viii,216p., illus.

Devoted to the classification and explanation of technical terms used in Indian Classical dances.
Class No: 793.3(540)(038)

[4863]
KRISHNA, R.U.S. A Dictionary of Bharat Natya. Bombay, Orient Longman, 1980. 92p., illus. ISBN: 0861311558.

Briefly explains about 1,000 terms peculiar to the Indian dance style bringing out semantic differences and noting context. Key to pronunciation; line drawings.
Class No: 793.3(540)(038)

[4864]
MENON, K.P.S. A Dictionary of Kathakali. Bombay, Orient Longman, 1979. vi,80p., illus.

750 terms of this Indian dance form are explained and illustrated; uses classical and modern sources. Cross references and pronunciation aids are useful. Sometimes the English equivalents of terms are also given in parenthesis.
Class No: 793.3(540)(038)

Folk Dancing

Yearbooks & Directories

[4865]
ENGLISH FOLK DANCE AND SONG SOCIETY. Folk directory. London, EFDSS. c78p.

Annual.

Details of the Society, educational facilities, library. Classified directory section. Details of publishers, periodicals, organizations, festivals. *Class No:* 793.31(058)

Histories

[4866]
JVC video anthology of world music and dance. Montpelier, VT. Rounder Records for Smithsonian/Folkways Records, [1989]. 30 videocassettes.

Authoritative series containing over 500 sequences shot in 100 countries; covers folk and classical music worldwide. Supervised by Japan's National Museum of Ethnology.
Class No: 793.31(091)

Conjuring

[4867]

NELMS, H. Magic and showmanship: a handbook for conjurors. London, Dover Publications, 1969. 191p.,illus. £5.05. ISBN: 048622337x.

Manual of practical routines illustrated by over 200 line drawings. Aimed at the novice and amateur.
Class No: 793.8

Bibliographies

[4868]

COLEMAN, E. Magic: an information guide. New York, Greenwood Press, 1987. 200p. £32.75. ISBN: 0313213977.

A useful beginning in an area where there is little other material. *Class No:* 793.8(01)

[4869]

GILL, R. Magic as a performing art: a bibliography of conjuring. New York, Bowker, 1977. 252p.

Annotated entries for over 1,000 books and pamphlets on conjuring, published/reprinted since 1935. Focus is on readily available works in English or available in English. Subject, name and title indexes. 'The first basic annotated bibliography of performing-magic literature' (*Library journal*, v.102, no.9, 1 May 1977, p.1003).
Class No: 793.8(01)

Encyclopaedias & Dictionaries

[4870]

LAMB, G. Magic: illustrated dictionary. London, Kaye & Ward, 1979. 157p., illus.

About 500 entries and cross-references, including brief biographies (*e.g.* J.N. Maskelyne: ¾column). 'Some magic books for beginners'; 'Some standard magic books', p.156-7. 'Intended primarily for the reader who is interested in magical entertainment but has no expert knowledge of the subject' (*Preface*). Well illustrated. *Class No:* 793.8(03)

[4871]

WATERS, T.A. Encyclopedia of magic and magicians. Oxford, Facts on File, 1988. 372p., illus. £38.95. ISBN: 0816013497.

Also in paperback; (0816019819).

Alphabetical listing of technical terms (routines, effects) and 'performers and creators of magic past and present'. (Intro.). Cross-references; some entries have bibliographic notes. *Class No:* 793.8(03)

Histories

[4872]

CHRISTOPHER, M. The Illustrated history of magic. London, Robert Hale, 1975. 452p., illus. ISBN: 0709148143.

22 chapters covering the practice of magic from early times, to cinema & early TV performers. Significant names (*e.g.* Houdini) are the subject of individual chapters. Bibliography p.435-439. Index. *Class No:* 793.8(091)

[4873]

PRICE, D. Magic: a pictorial history of conjurors in the theatre. London, Cornwall Books, 1985. 551p., illus. £48. ISBN: 0845347381.

Well illustrated, narrative history, divided into 14 chapters from 16th/17th century to the mid-20th century. US emphasis, but coverage of major UK figures & scene. Bibliography p.539-41. Extensive index.
Class No: 793.8(091)

794/799 Games & Sport

Games & Sport

Bibliographies

[4874]

CLARKE, N.F. The Recreation and entertainment industries: an information sourcebook. Jefferson, NC, McFarland, 1990. 240p. $42.50. ISBN: 0899504647.

Provides information on 30 sectors in the industries; includes publications, databases, associations. Indexed. *Class No:* 794(01)

Histories

[4875]

BOTERMANS, J., ***and others*****. The World of games:** their origins and history. New York, Facts on File, 1989. 242p. $29.95. ISBN: 0816021848.

Details of 150 board, dice, card, domino, and activity games are featured. Well illustrated. Playing rules are included. *Class No:* 794(091)

Great Britain

[4876]

GOMME, A.B. Traditional games of England, Scotland, and Ireland; with tunes, singing-rhymes, and methods of playing ... London, Thames & Hudson, 1984. 1016p., illus. £9.50. ISBN: 0500273162.

Originally published London: Nutt (1894-98) in 2 vols.

Alphabetical arrangement; sources usually cited. Concentrates on children's games. *Class No:* 794(410)

[4877]

OPIE, I. ***and*** **OPIE, P. Children's games with things:** marbles, fivestones, throwing and catching, gambling, hopscotch, chucking and pitching, ball-bouncing, skipping, tops and tipcat. Oxford, Oxford University Press, 1997. xv,350p., illus. £18.99. ISBN: 0192159631.

Fascinating and authoritative account of children's games; the Opies have an international reputation for their knowledge in this field. *Class No:* 794(410)

Indoor Games

[4878]

BRANDRETH, G. Everyman's indoor games. London, Dent, 1981. 304p. diagrs. £10.50. ISBN: 0460044567.

Details of over 300 games, divided into categories (card games, dice games, paper & pencil games, etc.). Good index. *Class No:* 794.0

[4879]

CLARK, T.L. Dictionary of gambling and gaming. Cold Spring, NY, Lexik House, 1988. xxii, 263p. $48.00. ISBN: 0936368063.

Words, terms, phrases, quotations to demonstrate usage, references to OED. Good bibliography. *Class No:* 794.0

[4880]

SIFAKIS, C. Encyclopedia of gambling. Oxford, Facts on File, 1990. 340p.,illus. £26. ISBN: 0816016380.

Full explanations, with historical background, major figures, and some anecdotes. 'Comprehensive, accurate, and well-organized' (*Library Journal,* November 15,1989. p.82). Fascinating photographs; useful glossary; classified bibliography; name, title, subject index. *Class No:* 794.0

Laws

[4881]

MOREHEAD, A.H. ***and*** **MOTT-SMITH, G. Hoyle's rules of games.** 2nd.rev.ed. London, Plume (Penguin), 1983. 264p. £5.99. ISBN: 0452264162.

Concentrates on indoor games of skill and chance; covers 250 card and parlour games. Glossary of terms. *Class No:* 794.0(094.1)

Billiards & Snooker

[4882]

EVERTON, C., ***ed.*** **Embassy book of world snooker.** London, Bloomsbury, 1993. 192p. £14.99. ISBN: 0747516103.

Covers world professional snooker from the 1860s onwards; includes stories as well as facts. Profiles of stars of today, great matches, breaks, shots. Contains statistical data, diagrams and photographs. *Class No:* 794.0:796.382

[4883]

SHAMOS, M. Illustrated encyclopedia of billiards. New York, Lyons and Burford, 1993. 308p. $35.00. ISBN: 1558212191.

Alphabetical arrangement of 2500 terms, abbreviations and organizations; coverage includes pool and snooker. There are 200 illustrations. No biographies, but people mentioned in the text are included in an appended index. Another appendix lists the names of 400 billiard games. Addresses are given for most of the organizations. *Class No:* 794.0:796.382

Bibliographies

[4884]

CRAVEN, R.R. Billiards, bowling, table tennis, pinball and video games: a bibliographic guide. Westport, CT, Greenwood, 1983. 163p. £29.95. ISBN: 0313234620.

Mainly English-language materials, including journal articles. Associations also featured. Brief introductory essay to each of the five game sections. *Class No:* 794.0:796.382(01)

War Games

[4885]

DUNNINGAN, J.F. Complete wargames handbook: how to play, design, and find them. Rev.ed New York, Morrow/Quill, 1992. 288p. $12.95. ISBN: 0688103685.

Historical summary, and game reviews. Discusses use by the military, and possibilities for computer simulations. 'Clearly written, thoroughly researched, and well balanced.' (*Reference books bulletin,* December 1992, p643.)
Class No: 794.01:355

Chess

Bibliographies

[4886]

BETTS, D.A. Chess: an annotated bibliography of works published in the English language, 1850-1968. Boston, G.K. Hall, 1974. 659p.

Classified arrangement, with author, title, and subject indexes. *Class No:* 794.1(01)

[4887]

KONINKLIJKE BIBLIOTHEEK. Bibliotheca Van der Linde - Niemeijeriana; catalogue of the chess collection at the Royal Library, The Hague. The Hague, Royal Library, 1955. 342p.

Classified catalogue, with author index, of several important chess collections, particularly the two major collections named in the title. *Class No:* 794.1(01)

[4888]

LUSIS, A. Chess: an annotated bibliography, 1969-1988. London, Mansell, 1991. 320p. £55.00. ISBN: 0720120799.

Updates the volume by Betts, above; records more items in this twenty-year period than were contained in the original. 2601 items are noted, including materials from 600 chess periodicals. There are separate indexes by name, title, series, and by subject. *Class No:* 794.1(01)

Encyclopaedias & Dictionaries

[4889]

DIVINSKY, N. The Chess encyclopedia. New York, Facts on File, 1991. 247p. $35.00. ISBN: 0816026416.

Alphabetical arrangement, with index, covers technical terms, biographies, tournaments, 100 greatest games, diagrams, photographs of famous players. 'The definitive mathematical study of the strength of chess players through history'. Recommended (*Reference books bulletin,* August 1991, p2171), but the reviewer notes that the *Oxford companion to chess* 'includes about a third more entries, generally in fuller and more accessible narrative.'
Class No: 794.1(03)

[4890]

HOOPER, D. *and* **WHYLD, K. The Oxford companion to chess.** 2nd.ed Oxford, Oxford University Press, 1992. 483p., illus. £25.00. ISBN: 0198661649.

Paperback ed. published 1996. (ISBN: 0192800483; £12.99.)

2600 entries, greatly increased over the first edition. Includes terms, biographies of major players, openings, strategies, laws, regional variations, history, topics (*eg.* computers, chess in art, literature, theatre, film etc.) There is evidence of much new research and many new names. Features diagrams and photographs; cross references. Detailed discussion of 200 games. Well indexed; multi-language glossary; index to named openings and variations.

....*(contd.)*
'The new edition replaces its precursor as the best general reference.' (*Choice,* 30(8),1993. p.1296.)
Class No: 794.1(03)

[4891]

LEVY, D. *and* **O'CONNELL, K. The Oxford encyclopedia of chess games.** Oxford, OUP, 1981. 704p., illus., diagrs. ISBN: 0192175718.

Volume 1 covers 1485-1866; a second vol. was planned.

V.1 'includes all the recorded games played up to 1800, every game played in all major tournaments and matches from 1801, and every traceable game of each player who was at any time one of the two best players in the world' (*Introduction*). 4,000 games, arranged chronologically, 1499-1866. Introduction in English, Dutch, French, German, Russian, Czech and Swedish. Championship and elimination cross-tables. Bibliography, p.455-6. Opening, ending and players' indexes. *Class No:* 794.1(03)

Histories

[4892]

GOLOMBEK, H., *ed.* **A History of chess.** London, Batsford, 1977. 352p. illus., diagrs. £19.95. ISBN: 0713408782.

Thorough & readable history. Bibliography.
Class No: 794.1(091)

[4893]

MURRAY, H.J.R. A History of chess. Oxford, Clarendon Press, 1913. 900p., illus., diagrs.

The definitive work in the field, heavily footnoted. Part 1 covers Asian game, Part 2 the European. Excellent analytical index. *Class No:* 794.1(091)

Biographies

[4894]

HARTSTON, W. The Kings of chess: a history of chess traced through the lives of its greatest players. London, Pavilion, 1988. 202p., illus. £12.95. ISBN: 0907516785.

Covers the game from the earliest origins to the present by examination of the lives, playing styles, tournaments of major players. Well written text, with illustrations, and discussions of key games.

The same author has also compiled *The Guinness book of chess grandmasters* (London, Guinness Publishing, 1996) which covers much the same ground. (ISBN: 0851125549; £12.99.) *Class No:* 794.1(092)

Laws

[4895]

Official laws of chess, and other FIDE regulations. New ed. London, Batsford, 1989. 135p., tables. £8.99. ISBN: 0713462000.

First published 1985.

Official publication for the Féderation Internationale des Échecs; also includes Swiss system tournaments, and 5, 30, and 60 minute chess. *Class No:* 794.1(094.1)

Great Britain

[4896]

The Official chess yearbook Burgess, G., *ed.* London, British Chess Federation/Batsford. c200p. £9.99. ISBN: 0713478187, (1996).

Annual.

....*(contd.)*

Services and constitution of the Federation, championships and tournaments, results, useful feature articles, directory and calendar. *Class No:* 794.1(410)

Card Games

[4897]

MARKEY, K., ***comp*****. The Neal Schuman index to card games.** New York, Neal Schuman, 1990. 153p. £29.95. ISBN: 1555700527.

Offers only an index reference to 35 source volumes identified by 3-letter codes. Frustrating to use, but its coverage of 2,000 games makes it of some value for obscure games and variant names. *Class No:* 794.4

[4898]

PARLETT, D. The Oxford dictionary of card games. Oxford, Oxford University Press, 1996. 360p. £6.99. ISBN: 0198691734.

Re-issue of 1992 ed.

Broad coverage of all types of popular and classic games, including family and party games, patience, Tarot, 'unusual' games. *Class No:* 794.4

[4899]

PARLETT, D. The Penguin book of card games. Harmondsworth, Penguin Books, 1979. 474p. £5.99. ISBN: 0140463445.

Details of some 300 games divided into family categories (solo games, cribbage, casino games, rummy games etc.). Bibliography, glossary, and index. *Class No:* 794.4

Histories

[4900]

PARLETT, D. The Oxford guide to card games: a historical survey. Oxford, OUP, 1990. xii,361p., illus. £15. ISBN: 0192141651.

A source of information on the history and evolution of card games; does not cover rules, strategies, tactics. International coverage of all types of games. Excellent illustrations; useful appendices; glossary; full bibliographical notes; indexes. 'Authoritative and erudite, yet attractively written and interesting' (*Reference Reviews* 4(4) 1990, p.29). *Class No:* 794.4(091)

Bibliographies

[4901]

HARGRAVE, C.P. A History of playing cards and a bibliography of cards and gaming. New York, Dover, 1966. 468p., illus.

Originally published: London, Allen & Unwin. 1930.

Compiled from the collection of the United States Playing Card Company, Cincinnati. The bibliography occupies p.369-449. *Class No:* 794.4(091)(01)

Bridge

[4902]

DORMER, A. The New complete book of bridge. London, Gollancz in association with Peter Crawley, 1996. 448p. £14.99. ISBN: 0575060840.

A substantial and scholarly account in 24 chapters; two principal sections - the bidding, and the play.
Class No: 794.41

[4903]

FRANCIS, H.G., ***ed*****. The Official encyclopedia of bridge.** 4th ed. New York, Crown, 1984. 922p. illus.

First edition 1914.

Alphabetical arrangement of technical terms, procedures etc. Biographical section; statistics; bibliography. Authorized by the American Contract Bridge League. *Class No:* 794.41

[4904]

GOREN, C.H. Goren's bridge complete. Rev. ed. London, Stanley Paul, 1982. xiii,689p., illus. £9.95. ISBN: 0091492009.

Originally published 1977 (Barrie & Jenkin). Earlier edition 1958.

The 'Bible' of American contract bridge players.
Class No: 794.41

Bibliographies

[4905]

SACHEN, W.F. Bridge: a reference guide. New York, Garland, 1984. 171p. $18. ISBN: 0824090942.

A starting point for investigation of the literature.
Class No: 794.41(01)

Word Games

[4906]

AUGARDE, T. The Oxford A to Z of word games. Oxford, Oxford University Press, 1994. 249p. £12.99. ISBN: 0198661789.

Important current addition to the literature, covering new games of recent years as well as traditional material.
Class No: 795

[4907]

PARLETT, D. The Penguin book of word games. Harmondsworth, Middx., Penguin Books, 1982. 235p., illus.

Part 1: Spoken word games (*e.g.* Just a minute; Charades; Twenty questions) - Part 2: Written word games (*e.g.* Consequences; Scrabble; Anagrams). Data on each game: number of players; suitable age; whether serious or light-hearted. Postscripts. 'Acceptability of words games'; 'Some useful statistics for word-gamers' (*e.g.* letter-occurrence frequency), Solution to problems; Bibliography, p.230-1. Index, p.233-5. Over 100 games are described, with examples. *Class No:* 795

Sport

Databases

[4908]

SPORTS INFORMATION RESOURCE CENTRE. Ottawa. **SPORT database.** Gloucester, Ontario, SIRC, 1973-.

Online access; also a CD-ROM service titled *SPORT discus*.

A major database comprising some 450,000 citations and growing by 1500 items per month. A thesaurus of terms was issued in 1994 (*See entry at:* 796:025.43). 17 contributing countries. *Class No:* 796(003.4)

[4909]
Sports online. London, SPRITO and Mill House Internet Services, 1998-.
Website at <http://www.sportsonline.co.uk>
Designed, developed and managed by the UK National Training Organisation for Sport, Recreation and Allied Occupations (SPRITO), and supported by the Sports Councils, British Olympic Association, Central Council of Physical Recreation, and the National Coaching Foundation.
Provides a link to all existing sports Websites in the UK, and then internationally. Covers professional and amateur sports, statistics, equipment manufacturers and suppliers.
Class No: 796(003.4)

[4910]
Sportsweb. London, Intelligent Environments Group, 1998-.
Website at <http://www.thesportsweb.co.uk>
Electronic clearing house that offers clubs and other sporting bodies a means of linking up with sports professionals. Designed as a recruitment service for the Health and Leisure industries, and searchable by expertise, country, region. *Class No:* 796(003.4)

Bibliographies

[4911]
Leisure, recreation and tourism abstracts. Oxford, CAB International, 1975-. ISSN: 02611392.
Issued quarterly; Online access, and diskette.
Excellent coverage of the international journal literature. Arranged by broad subject; includes leisure, tourism, travel, sport, entertainment etc. *Class No:* 796(01)

[4912]
NATIONAL COACHING FOUNDATION. **Sporting update.** Leeds, UK, NCF, 1990-. £160.pa. (also available separately).
Quarterly abstracting service covering journals, reports, papers, & books. There are six titles at present. Sporting update - athletics (09584382); Sporting update - racket sports (09584404); Sporting update - health related fitness (09584412); Sporting update - teams (09584390); Sporting update - swimming (09584420); Coaching update (0953847x). *Class No:* 796(01)

[4913]
Physical education index. Cape Girardeau, MO, Ben Oak Publishing, 1978-. $175.00. ISSN: 01919202.
Quarterly, with the fourth part being an annual cumulation.
Wide ranging subject coverage of English-language materials; contains notes of biographies and obituaries, and a useful section on reviews of new books. Dance, health, physical therapy, recreation, sports, and sportsmedicine are included. *Class No:* 796(01)

[4914]
SHOEBRIDGE, M., *ed.* **Information sources in sport and leisure.** East Grinstead, Bowker-Saur, 1992. 345p. £55. ISBN: 0862919010.
Essay-type chapters cover databases, centres and libraries, abstracts and indexes, major journals, statistics, government sources (UK only), science and medicine, history and sociology, individual sports, Olympics, training and fitness, and coaching. The three final chapters concentrate on European, North American, and Australian sources.
Class No: 796(01)

[4915]
SPORTS COUNCIL INFORMATION CENTRE. **Scan:** selected new publications and articles. London, Sports Council, 1979-. 21p. (No. 106, December 1994.)
Generally issued four times pa.
Includes handbooks, yearbooks, annual reports and new monographs, in addition to journal articles. 3 parts cover periodical articles cited by journal title, reports & yearbooks etc. in alphabetical order, new publications arranged alphabetically by author's name. Brief abstracts are given.
Class No: 796(01)

[4916]
SPORTS DOCUMENTATION CENTRE. **Sports documentation monthly bulletin.** Birmingham, UK, Centre for Sports Science and History, 1972-. 41p. (vol.24 no.9; Sept.1994). £49.00. ISSN: 01421794.
Periodical articles, reports, conference papers are included; international coverage, English and foreign-language material. Arrangement is by broad subject headings; from 1987 (vol.17, no.1) abstracts are given for every item. Each monthly part includes a list of journals covered, and proceedings indexed. Author and subject indexes. *Class No:* 796(01)

[4917]
SPORTS INFORMATION RESOURCE CENTRE. Ottawa. **Sportsearch.** Gloucester, Ontario, SIRC, 1985-. ISSN: 0882553x.
Monthly coverage of some 300 mainly French & English-language journals, arranged by broad subject. Also includes book chapters and conference proceedings. From 1988 abstracts are included. *Class No:* 796(01)

Women

[4918]
SHOEBRIDGE, M. **Women in sport:** a select bibliography. London, Mansell, 1987. xi,231p. £28.50. ISBN: 0720118581.
Subject arrangement, (philosophy, history, disabled, sociological aspects etc.); covers books, with brief abstracts, conference proceedings, journal articles, & theses.
Class No: 796(01)-0055.2

Encyclopaedias & Dictionaries

[4919]
Encyclopedia of world sport from ancient times to the present. Levinson, D. *and* Christensen, K., *eds*. Oxford, ABC-Clio, 1997. 1317p.(3v.) £125.00. ISBN: 0874368197.
Worldwide, cross-cultural survey; topics include legal and medical aspects of sport, violence, rituals. Little critical attention - reviews awaited. *Class No:* 796(03)

[4920]
KENT, M. **The Oxford dictionary of sports science and medicine.** 2nd.ed. Oxford, Oxford University Press, 1998. xv,567p., illus. £19.95. ISBN: 0192628453.
A/Z arrangement of topics - injuries, conditions, anatomical details, drugs, treatments, etc. 2-column format with most entries receiving between 4 and 20 lines of text. Line drawings. Bibliography p.xi-xiv. *Class No:* 796(03)

[4921]
ZUMERCHIK, J., ***ed.*** **Encyclopedia of sports science.** New York, Macmillan, 1997. 943p. (2v.) $200.00.

2 sections: sports, and the body. Covers mechanics and scientific principles, individual sports and common concepts (*eg.* catching, throwing), anatomy, physiology, injuries. All articles are signed and have references and bibliographies. Good index, and network of cross-references.
Class No: 796(03)

Handbooks & Manuals

[4922]
CHALIP, L. ***and*** **JOHNSON, A.** ***and*** **STACHURA, L.,** ***eds.*** **National sports policies:** an international handbook. Westport, CT/London, Greenwood Press, 1996. xiv442p., illus. ISBN: 0313284814.

Examines activity around the world in a set of essays covering: Australia, Brazil, Canada, China (People's Republic), Communist bloc - 'the end of an era', Cuba, France, Germany, Hungary, India, Israel, Italy, Japan, Norway, Spain, UK, US. *Class No:* 796(035)

[4923]
PARKS, J.B. *and* **ZANGER, B.R.K.** *and* **QUARTERMAN, J.,** ***eds.*** **Contemporary sport management.** Champaign, IL/Leeds, Human Kinetics, 1998. 360p. £37.00. ISBN: 0873228367.

Textbook and reference manual for sports administrators and managers; 26 contributors. Discusses trends and challenges in the sport industry, application of management skills in diverse populations. References, case studies, publications, governing bodies, legal considerations.
Class No: 796(035)

Dictionaries

[4924]
CONSIDINE, T. The Language of sport. Oxford, Facts on File, 1983. 355p. £15. ISBN: 0871966530.

Definitions of over 5,000 terms, arranged alphabetically within groups by sport. Abundant cross-references, and a good index. *Class No:* 796(038)

[4925]
Dictionary of the sport and exercise sciences. Anshel, M.K., *ed.* Champaign, IL/Leeds, Human Kinetics, 1991. 176p. £16.50. ISBN: 0873223799.

3,000 terms are briefly defined; covers physical education, biomechanics, exercise physiology, motor control, motor development, motor learning, sport pedagogy, sport psychology, sport sociology. *Class No:* 796(038)

Periodicals & Progress Reports

[4926]
International journal of the history of sport. London, Cass, 1984-. £30.00pa. ISSN: 09523367.

3 issues pa. Previously *British Journal of Sports History.*

Covers social and historical aspects of sport, recreation and leisure; extensive book reviews (usually 8-10 per issue of about 1,000 words each), annual bibliography of new publications. *Class No:* 796(05)

Periodicals

[4927]
SPRIG directory of periodicals in sport and recreation. David Haynes Associates. 3rd.ed. Sheffield, Sport & Recreation Information Group, 1996. £35.00. (disk version £60.00.) ISBN: 1871787084.

Available in print or on disk.

900 journals worldwide are listed; holdings culled from 94 UK libraries. *Class No:* 796(051)

Yearbooks & Directories

[4928]
Information Please sports almanac. Meserole, M., *ed.* Boston, Houghton Mifflin. c850p., illus. ISSN: 10454980.

Reviews the preceding year, with a US bias; includes personalities, winners, statistics. *Class No:* 796(058)

[4929]
Sports illustrated's sports almanac. New York, Little Brown. c850p. £11.95. ISBN: 0316800082, 1998 vol.

Annual.

Packed with data on the standard range of popular sports - golf, tennis, track, baseball, basketball, football etc. US emphasis. *Class No:* 796(058)

Quotations

[4930]
JAMES, S., ***comp.*** **Chambers sporting quotations.** Edinburgh, Chambers, 1990. 250p. £5.99. ISBN: 055020489x.

Some 1,500 quotations, arranged under 110 headings (names of sports). Cross references; dates are given for each item and a brief citation of where it can be found.
Class No: 796(082.2)

[4931]
LIDDLE, B., ***comp.*** **Dictionary of sports quotations.** London, Routledge, 1987. 224p. £14.99. ISBN: 0710207859.

Broad topics form the basic arrangement; subject and author indexes. *Class No:* 796(082.2)

Official Records

[4932]
MATTHEWS, P. ***and*** **MORRISON, I. The Guinness encyclopedia of international sports records and results.** 4th. ed. London, Guinness Publishing, 1995. 416p., illus. £15.99. ISBN: 0851126863.

First edition 1987.

Introductory sections explain events. Entries arranged A/Z by sport (American football - yachting) give lists of winners, records, statistics. Covers national and world champions in over 100 sports. *Class No:* 796(093.2)

Laws

[4933]
DIAGRAM GROUP. Rules of the game: complete illustrated encyclopedia of all the sports of the world. Rev. ed. London, CollinsWillow, 1991. 320p., illus. £16.99. ISBN: 0002184001.

First edition 1974.

13 general categories of sport grouped (water, combat, etc.), with basic rules. Extensive use of drawings and

.... *(contd.)*
diagrams (over 2500 illustrations); a useful source, but treatment is limited in scope and omits strategies, variations. *Class No:* 796(094.1)

[4934]

The Sports rule book: essential rules for 54 sports. Hanlon, T., *ed.* Champaign, IL/Leeds, Human Kinetics, 1998. 372p, illus. $19.95. ISBN: 0880118075.

Fully detailed rules and procedures for 54 common sports, with clear explanations and well-drawn diagrams. Includes key terms, essential procedures, equipment regulations, signals, playing areas. *Class No:* 796(094.1)

Europe

Yearbooks & Directories

[4935]

GLANVILLE, M.P., ***ed.*** **Directory of European sports organizations.** Beckenham, CBD Research, 1992. 136p. £65.00. ISBN: 0900246561.

Lists governing bodies of sports in Europe; arranged alphabetically by title, with cross references from authorized translated versions. Two indexes: abbreviations/acronyms, subject/sport. 'For libraries that need an exhaustive listing...this is an outstanding resource.' (*Choice*, 30(6)1993, p938.) *Class No:* 796(4)(058)

Great Britain

Histories

[4936]

COX, R. Annual list of accessions of sporting manuscripts in repositories in the UK.

The list appears in vols. of the *Sports historian*, for example May 1994, p.105-7. *Class No:* 796(410)(091)

[4937]

COX, R. History of sport: a guide to the literature and sources of information. Frodsham, British Society of Sports History, 1994. 102p. £16.50. ISBN: 189801003x.

This vol. and the two items below appear to form part of a series intended to comprise five vols. in total; however they do not have a series title, nor do they originate from the same publisher.

Five sections: reference materials, secondary sources, primary sources, specialist sources, sources for specific associated topics such as sports fiction, sports costume etc. Well organized with excellent layout, index and network of cross references. There is a directory of organizations with full contact data, and a bibliography of over 100 items. *Class No:* 796(410)(091)

[4938]

COX, R. History of sport in Britain: a bibliography of historical publications 1800-1987. Manchester, University Press, 1990. 224p. £29.95. ISBN: 0719025923.

Includes 6,500 items-monographs, theses, journal articles, conference papers & reports. *Class No:* 796(410)(091)

[4939]

COX, R. Sport: a guide to historical sources in the UK. London, Sports Council, 1983. vii,61p. illus. £8.

Sections: National and special repositories (1-58, under counties) - Local record offices - Institutional archives of national sporting bodies and organizations - Select bibliography, p.51 (13 items) - Alphabetical list of repositories/governing bodies of sport. Data: name of repository/library/special collection; address; 'phone number; contact; hours open; records; additional information. Name and subject indexes. *Class No:* 796(410)(091)

USA

[4940]

WINDHAUSEN, J.D., ***ed.*** **Sports encyclopedia North America.** Gulf Breeze, FL, Academic International Press, 1987. Vols. 1-5; *c*250p. per vol. $34.95 per vol. ISBN: 0875690947, Set; 0685738523, Vol.1; 0685738531, Vol.2; 068573854x, Vol.3; 0685738558, Vol.4; 0685738566, Vol.5.

No further vols. can be traced after these first 5 in 1987.

SENA is intended to be a fifty-volume set, appearing over several years, with supplements to keep early material current. Lengthy scholarly articles, not intended for quick reference. Covers US and Canada, and includes all major teams, associations, competitions, etc. Bibliographies given. Review in *Choice* (April 1989) notes some unevenness but recommends the work. *Class No:* 796(73)

Yearbooks & Directories

[4941]

MORGAN, B.J., ***ed.*** **Sports fan's connection;** an all-sports-in-one directory to professional, collegiate, and Olympic organizations, events, and information sources. Detroit, Gale Research, 1992. 584p. ISBN: 0810379546.

Draws heavily on the *Encyclopedia of associations*, but also contains a wide variety of additional material, such as guides produced by *The Sporting News*. There are no results or data given, but indexing is good, so the value as a directory is excellent. *Class No:* 796(73)(058)

[4942]

Sports address bible: the comprehensive directory of sports addresses. Kobak, E., *ed.* Santa Monica, CA, Global Sports Productions. c350p. ISBN: 0961918152, 1994 vol.

Annual.

Reliable and extensive source for simple data. *Class No:* 796(73)(058)

Histories

[4943]

HICKOK, R. Encyclopedia of North American sports history. New York, Facts on File, 1992. 516p. ISBN: 0816020965.

Comprehensive source on US and Canada; covers all modern organized competitive sports. Arranged alphabetically in a clear and concise layout, with a good network of cross references. Many photographs and illustrations. Suggested further readings appear after major entries. Statistical material is well handled. *Class No:* 796(73)(091)

[4944]

LABLANC, M.L., *ed.* **Professional sports team histories.** Detroit, Gale, 1994. 4vols. $129.00. ISBN: 0810388588.

Team histories for the top professional sports in North America - baseball, basketball, football, hockey. Statistics, summaries and narrative histories up to 1992/93 season for every team in existence. *Class No:* 796(73)(091)

[4945]

Sports in North America: a documentary history. Menna, L. *and* Kirsh, G.B., *eds.* Gulf Breeze, FL, Academic International Press, 1992-. $75.00.per vol. ISBN: 0875691366, v.2.(1995); 0875691560, v.3.(1992); 0875691358, v.4.(1995).

Vols. 2, 3, and 4 have appeared to date.

The series is covering periods of US sporting history, based on annotated documents (which are reproduced in the vols.) with commentary on social background, external influences, urbanisation, transport, etc. Vol.4 covers 1860-1880. *Class No:* 796(73)(091)

Biographies

[4946]

Biographical dictionary of American sports. Porter, D.L., *ed.* Westport, CT, Greenwood Press, 1987-1989. 713,786,728,776p. (4v.).Supplement 1989-1992 (728p.) 1992. Supplement 1992-1995 (811p.) 1996. $90.00. per vol. ISBN: 0313237719, vol.1; 031325771x, vol.2; 0313262608, vol.3; 0313262619, vol.4; 0313267065, supplement 1989-1992; 0313284318, supplement 1992-1995.

Porter has also compiled *African-American sports greats: a biographical dictionary* (Greenwood Press, 1995; ISBN: 0313289875) in the same style.

Volumes cover baseball, football, outdoor sports, basketball and indoor sports; 200-900 word entries by specialist contributors cover living and dead names. Each volume contains about 500 names, many with brief bibliographies. Useful appendices. For index, see next entry. *Class No:* 796(73)(092)

[4947]

Cumulative index to the *Biographical dictionary of American sports*. Porter, D.L., *comp.* Westport,CT, Greenwood Press, 1993. 325p. $45.00. ISBN: 0313284350.

Covers the four main volumes of the parent work, and the first supplement. Lists persons, places, publications, topics, events, organizations in a single alphabetical sequence. Principal entries are italicized. *Class No:* 796(73)(092)

Women

[4948]

SPARHAWK, R.M., *comp.* **American women in sport, 1887-1987.** Metuchen, NJ, Scarecrow, 1989. 149p. $20. ISBN: 0810822059.

Chronological arrangement; includes bibliography and addresses of organizations. *Class No:* 796(73)(092)-0055.2

Australia

[4949]

VAMPLEW, W., *and others.* **The Oxford companion to Australian sport.** Melbourne, Oxford University Press for the Australian Society for Sports History, 1992. 430p. £25.00. ISBN: 0195532872.

Entries cover sports, people, locations, contests, topics such as literature, gender, sponsorship etc. A limited number of statistical tables and illustrations; detailed structure of cross references. Five editors and 250 contributors were involved, and entries are signed. There is a 30-page bibliography. *Class No:* 796(94)

Thesauri

[4950]

Sport thesaurus: the thesaurus of terminology used in the SPORT database. Stark, R.W., *and others.* Gloucester, Ontario, Sports Information Resource Centre, 1994. 297p. $115.00. ISBN: 0921817231.

7,500 keywords are listed, with broader, narrower and related terms. Cross references to preferred terms; scope notes. Includes many keywords from cognate areas (*eg* anatomy, medicine), event titles, proper names of teams, clubs and associations. *Class No:* 796:025.43

[4951]

WILMOT, C.E., *comp.* **Classification/thesaurus for sport and physical recreation** and allied topics. London, Sports Council, 1981. xii,185p. £50.

Five main categories: leisure facilities; leisure & society; properties, attributes & processes; disciplines & techniques; organization. *Class No:* 796:025.43

Olympic Games

[4952]

Chronicle of the Olympics: 1896-1996. Sutherland, M., *ed.* London, Dorling Kindersley, 1996. 312p., illus. £19.95. ISBN: 0751330132.

Each Games is covered in a chapter of description, with photographs and reproductions of posters. 4-5 pages are devoted to each Games, and there are over 750 photographs. Tables of statistics p.213-309. *Class No:* 796.032

[4953]

FINDLING, J.E. *and* **PELLE, K.D.,** *eds.* **Historical dictionary of the modern Olympic movement.** Westport, CT, Greenwood Press, 1996. 460p., illus. £75.00. ISBN: 0313284776.

Each Games discussed in a 5-page chapter - from 1896 (Winter from 1924). An exhaustive source. Bibliography; index. *Class No:* 796.032

[4954]

—BUCHANAN, I. *and* MALLON, B. Historical dictionary of the Olympic movement. Lanham, MD/London, Scarecrow Press, 1995. lxxv,247p., illus. £42.50.

Sharing almost the same title as the fore-going item, but offering a different perspective on the same information. Bibliography p189-207. *Class No:* 796.032

[4955]

GREENBERG, S. Olympics: facts and feats. London, Guinness Publishing, 1996. 256p. £13.99. ISBN: 0851126391.

Attractive presentation of results and records; intended for the general reader not the specialist in a particular sport. *Class No:* 796.032

[4956]

The Olympic century: the official 1st century history of the modern Olympic movement. Phillips, E. *and* Galford, E., *eds.* New York, Firefly, 1996-. c200p. per vol. $21.95 per vol. ISBN: 1888383089.

Announced as a 25 volume set that will include all the Games from ancient Olympiads to Atlanta 1996. Each vol. has 4 chapters - two on the summer Games, one on the

....(contd.)
winter, and a general account of the Olympic movement of the period. An appendix section gives full statistics, bibliography, and an index to that vol. A separate index to the set is expected. Profusely illustrated. *Class No:* 796.032

[4957]
WALLECHINSKY, D. The Complete book of the Olympics. London, Aurum Press, 1993. 763p. £12.95. ISBN: 1854101994.
Gives the final results of all previous Olympics, national medal totals, the rules and scoring used, number of events, competitors and countries. A useful retrospective source. *Class No:* 796.032

Bowls & Curling

Histories

[4958]
SMITH, D.B. Curling: an illustrated history. Edinburgh, John Donald, 1981. 232p.,illus. £15.00. ISBN: 085976074x.
23 sections: 2. Curling in history and literature ... 13. Curling in the New World ... 22. Curlers' jargon - 23. Curlers' library (60 items in chronological order), p.201-6. Appendix A: *'An account of the game of curling* (1811); B. *The Canadian curler's manual* (1840). Analytical index, p.227-32. The majority of the illus. are deliberately chosen to depict curling years ago. *Class No:* 796.2(091)

Basketball

[4959]
NATIONAL COLLEGIATE ATHLETIC ASSOCIATION. Official NCAA basketball. Kansas, NCAA/Chicago, Triumph Books. c750p. ISBN: 1880141469, 1994 vol.
Annual.
Directory of records, results, schedules for the season. *Class No:* 796.32

[4960]
The Official NBA basketball encyclopedia. Sachare, A., *ed.* 2nd.ed. New York, Random House/Villard, 1994. 842p., illus. $39.95. ISBN: 0679432930.
Historical narratives, coaches, referees, rules, hall of fame; over half the vol. is an 'all-time player directory' of every player who has participated in the NBA, BAA, or ABA. Name-subject index to the narrative sections. For fuller statistical data, the Sporting News' annual *Official NBA guide* is recommended. *Class No:* 796.32

[4961]
The Ultimate encyclopedia of basketball. Smith, R., *ed.* London, Hodder & Stoughton, 1996. 224p., illus. £19.99. ISBN: 0340681861.
Popular account, but useful for its good coverage and illustrations. *Class No:* 796.32

Soccer

Bibliographies

[4962]
SEDDON, P.J., *comp.* A Football compendium: a comprehensive guide to the literature of Association Football. London, British Library, 1995. 544p., illus. £60.00. ISBN: 0712310754.
5000 items arranged thematically in 14 chapters. Based on BL holdings and covering English, Scottish, Welsh and Irish

....(contd.)
football, with titles from 1865 to the end of 1994. Each chapter begins with an overview, and selective annotations indicate relative importance of titles cited. Includes topics such as 'football in literature', 'football and society'. Very thoroughly indexed. *Class No:* 796.332(01)

Encyclopaedias & Dictionaries

[4963]
The Guinness football encyclopedia. Hart, G., *ed.* 3rd.ed. London, Guinness Publishing, 1995. 222p., illus. £14.99. ISBN: 0851126642.
A good general source for history, clubs, major names. Single A/Z sequence of people, clubs, topics (*eg. Schoolboy football*). *Class No:* 796.332(03)

Yearbooks & Directories

[4964]
Rothmans football yearbook. Rollin, J., *ed.* London, Headline. c1100p., illus., tables. ISBN: 0747277389, 1998 vol.
Annual.
Details of clubs in Carling Premiership and Endsleigh Insurance Leagues (6 pages for each with photograph, records, statistics), general features on competitions, law, international and non-league clubs. Scottish, Welsh and Northern Ireland scene. European features. Directory section gives records, addresses, fixture lists. *Class No:* 796.332(058)

Histories

[4965]
BUTLER, B. The Official illustrated history of the F.A. Cup. London, Headline, 1996. 320p., illus. £25.00. ISBN: 0747217815.
Full and thorough account; impressive plates and numerous other illustrations. *Class No:* 796.332(091)

[4966]
BUTLER, B. Official illustrated history of the Football League 1888-1988. London, Queen Anne Press, 1987. 352p., illus. £16.95. ISBN: 0356150720.
Reprinted 1991.
Examines the League era by era in 5 or 10 year periods up to '1981- time for a change.' *Class No:* 796.332(091)

[4967]
FOOTBALL ASSOCIATION. The History of the Football Association. London, Naldrett Press for the FA, 1953. xii,692p., ports.
The official history, published for the 90th birthday of the FA. Lists members of international and cup-final teams, results of international matches, players who have gained international honours. Also traces development of FA laws. Analytical index. *Class No:* 796.332(091)

[4968]
FREDDI, C. The Complete book of the World Cup. London, CollinsWillow, 1998. 352p., illus. £14.99. ISBN: 0002188317.
Well designed and illustrated, covers every match played in the final stages from 1939. Prefers detail to narrative, and is therefore a valuable complement to *Glanville* below. *Class No:* 796.332(091)

[4969]

GLANVILLE, B. The Story of the World Cup. London, Faber, 1998. 382p. £9.99. ISBN: 0571190812.

First published after the 1974 finals and regularly updated. Compact and literate, with comprehensive coverage.
Class No: 796.332(091)

[4970]

MURRAY, B. Football: history of the world game. Aldershot, Scolar Press, 1994. 297p. £35.00. ISBN: 1859280919.

Covers early history, colonial period, Europe, Third World, New World, future trends. Chapter bibliographies.
Class No: 796.332(091)

Laws

[4971]

Soccer law illustrated. Lover, S. 3rd. rev. ed. London, Pelham, 1990. 128p., illus. £10.99. ISBN: 0720719992.

Officially approved and recommended by the Referees' Committeee of FIFA. Covers laws, match control, codes of conduct, duties of officials. 100 line drawings.
Class No: 796.332(094.1)

USA

Bibliographies

[4972]

SMITH, M.J., *comp*. Professional football; the official Pro Football Hall of Fame bibliography. Westport,CT, Greenwood Press, 1993. 414p. $75.00. ISBN: 031328928x.

15000 entries record English language materials 1900-1991; includes books, periodical articles, yearbooks, programmes, dissertations and theses, but not reviews or newspaper articles. 4 sections - reference works; general works, histories and special studies; professional leagues, teams and games; collective and individual biographies. Claimed to be the first guide that indexes basic football newsletters and magazines. *Class No:* 796.332(73)(01)

Rugby Football

[4973]

GRIFFITHS, J., *comp*. The Book of English international rugby 1871-1982. London, Collins, 1982. 496p., illus.

Contents: English international match summaries, 1871-1982, p.11-411 - English international rugby records, 1871-1982 (match records; season records; individual records, *e.g.* players' career records, p.458-89). Data on each match: venue; date; result; scoring; teams and clubs of players; description; name of referee. 70 historic photographs.
Class No: 796.333

Encyclopaedias & Dictionaries

[4974]

SOMMERVILLE, D. Encyclopedia of Rugby Union. London, Aurum Press, 1997. 192p., illus. £17.95. ISBN: 1854104810.

History; the game in various countries; competitions; tours; clubs; players; statistics. Abundant illustrations.
Class No: 796.333(03)

Yearbooks & Directories

[4975]

Rothmans Rugby League yearbook. Fletcher, R. *and* Howes, D. London, Headline Press. c450p.

Annual.

Details of clubs, records, cups, leagues, coaches, etc. British transfers, awards, attendances, referees, fixtures.
Class No: 796.333(058)

[4976]

Rothmans Rugby Union yearbook. Jones, S., *ed.* London, Headline Press. c450p., illus.

Annual.

International coverage: England, Scotland, Wales, Ireland, France, South Africa, Australia, New Zealand. Details of tours, people, results. Fixture list for forthcoming season. Includes youth, schools, colts, & women's game.
Class No: 796.333(058)

Racket Games

[4977]

ABERDARE, M.G.L.B. The Willis-Faber book of tennis and rackets. London, Stanley Paul, 1980. 368p. illus, tables. £25. ISBN: 009142710x.

3 parts: 1. Tennis (forerunner of lawn tennis): history; basic principles of play - 2. Rackets (forerunner of squash): history and prevalence - 3. Tennis and rackets: clubs (Aiken Tennis Club ... Winchester College, p.189-330). Championship records, p.335-52. Non-analytical index, p.355-68. *Class No:* 796.34

Tennis

Encyclopaedias & Dictionaries

[4978]

COLLINS, B. *and* HOLLANDER, Z., *eds*. Bud Collins' tennis encyclopedia. 3rd.ed Detroit/London, Visible Ink, 1997. 700p., illus., tables. £14.99. ISBN: 1578590000.

Previous ed. as *Bud Collins' modern encyclopedia of tennis*, (Gale Research, 1994.)

Includes the history of the game from 1874 and biographies of major players. Annual records of all major tournaments; glossary of terms; International Tennis Federation rules. *Class No:* 796.342(03)

Yearbooks & Directories

[4979]

BARRETT, J., *ed* World of tennis. 30th.ed. New York, Triumph Books/London, CollinsWillow, 1998. 544p. £12.99. ISBN: 0002188244.

Records the main tournaments and team competitions; reports on top players. Published on behalf of the International Tennis Federation. 9 sections: year in review, championships, tours, tournaments, circuits, international competitions, rankings, reference information, ITF data. Addresses for national associations. *Class No:* 796.342(058)

[4980]

PHILLIPS, D.J. Tennis sourcebook. Lanham, NJ/London, Scarecrow Press, 1995. xvi,530p. £66.00. ISBN: 0810830019.

Authoritative coverage of associations, history, regulations, periodicals and other publications.
Class No: 796.342(058)

Histories

[4981]
GILLMEISTER, H. Tennis: a cultural history. London, Cassell/Leicester University Press, 1997. 416p. illus. £60.00. ISBN: 0718501470.

Revision of a German original, published in 1990.

Scholarly history from the Middle Ages to 1914. Covers all European countries, and others worldwide in later periods. Illustrations include some from Mediaeval and Renaissance sources, and rare photographs from private collections. Bibliography. *Class No:* 796.342(091)

Badminton

Encyclopaedias & Dictionaries

[4982]
DAVIS, P. The Encyclopedia of badminton. London, Hale, 1987. 201p., illus. £12.95. ISBN: 0709027966.

Alphabetical arrangement of terms, competitions, venues, players, etc. Competition entries include lists of winners. Appendix gives official rules of the International Badminton Federation. *Class No:* 796.344(03)

Golf

Bibliographies

[4983]
KENNINGTON, D. The Sourcebook of golf; with an appendix on collecting golfiana. London, Library Association, 1981. vi,255p., illus. £15.

7 chapters (each with bibliography and occasional annotations): 1. The history of golf - 2. The golfers (bibliography, p.43-54, under authors/golfers, A-Z) - 3. How to play the game - 4. Essays, fiction and humour - 5. The golf business - 6. Reference sources (including encyclopaedias, dictionaries, statistical information, the rules of golf, bibliographic material and the golfing magazines) and periodical issues (p.167-90) - 7. Golfing organizations. Appendix 'Collecting golfiana', p.211-23. Title index; name and subject index. 'Highly recommended for all libraries with strong sports collections' (*Choice,* v.19,no.10, June 1982, p.1382). *Class No:* 796.352(01)

Dictionaries

[4984]
DAVIES, P. Davies' dictionary of golfing terms. New York, Simon & Schuster, 1980. 188p. illus. $13.95.

Accurate and careful source, using dated quotations to demonstrate developments of meanings.
Class No: 796.352(038)

Yearbooks & Directories

[4985]
The Golf majors records and yearbook 1998. Evans, A. London, Brassey's Sports, 1998. 377p. £12.99. ISBN: 1857532635.

Background sections; champions 1860-1997; full reports on 1997 majors; previews of 1998. Details of players 1860-1997, and records for the same period.
Class No: 796.352(058)

[4986]
McCORMACK, M.H. World of professional golf 1998. London, IMC, 1998. 702p., illus. £12.50. ISBN: 1878843206.

Annual.

Reviews events in the previous season, US Open, British Open, PGA, Ryder Cup, Dunhill, etc. Details of tours, winners. *Class No:* 796.352(058)

[4987]
Royal and Ancient golfer's handbook, 1997. 94th.ed. Basingstoke, Macmillan, 1997. 944p. £19.99. ISBN: 0333658914.

Annual.

Who's who of golf, results and records, calendar of international tournaments; directory of principal UK and European clubs. *Class No:* 796.352(058)

Hockey

Encyclopaedias & Dictionaries

[4988]
NHL Hockey: the official guide and record book, 1997-98. New York, Triumph Books, 1997. 448p., illus. $18.95. ISBN: 1572432268.

Official publication of the National Hockey League.

General guide to people, teams, events, technical terms. Includes history and background on all NHL terms.

Also from the same publisher: *NHL Hockey: official fan's guide 1997* (ISBN: 1572431571; 160p).
Class No: 796.355(03)

Baseball

[4989]
RILEY, J.A. The Baseball encyclopedia: the complete and official record of major league baseball. 10th.ed. New York, Macmillan, 1995. 2970p. $59.95. ISBN: 0028608151.

Also *Update 1997* (ISBN: 0028615123; $12.00).

The definitive work; team and player records, statistics, awards, special achievements, championships, etc. Introductory history; rules. *Class No:* 796.357

Bibliographies

[4990]
SMITH, M.J. Baseball: a comprehensive bibliography. Jefferson, NC, McFarland, 1986. 915p. £55. ISBN: 0899502229.

Substantial guide to the literature. *Class No:* 796.357(01)

[4991]
WALKER, D.E. *and* **LEE COOPER, B.,** ***comps*****. Baseball and American culture:** a thematic bibliography of over 4,500 works. Jefferson, NC, McFarland, 1995. 257p. $39.95. ISBN: 0786400498.

Covers material 1985-1993; useful for its ideas and wide scope (women in baseball, health hazards in baseball, etc) but depending too heavily on popular magazines and enthusiasts' accounts 'that are in no way distinctive for their treatment of baseball as a cultural phenomenon.' (*American reference books annual*, 1996; p325.)
Class No: 796.357(01)

Yearbooks & Directories

[4992]

Sporting News baseball guide 1998. New York, Sporting News, 1997. 608p. $15.95. ISBN: 0892045914.

Annual.

All the information relevant to the forthcoming season.

Also published is a companion vol. *Sporting News baseball register 1998* (ISBN: 0892045930; 624p; $15.95), which gives brief biographies and career summary of every major league player. *Class No:* 796.357(058)

Histories

[4993]

WARD, G.C. *and* **BURNS, K. Baseball:** an illustrated history. New York, Knopf, 1994. 512p. $60.00. ISBN: 0679404597.

9 chapters chronicle the game decade by decade; there are over 500 photographs. 'Impressionistic essays by various luminaries...are the only weak link.' 'With the exception of *The Baseball encyclopedia* there is no better one-volume history of this sport.' (*Reference books bulletin*, 90(21) July 1994, p1892.) *Class No:* 796.357(091)

Cricket

[4994]

FRINDALL, B. Wisden book of test cricket. London, Headline, 1995. 806,779p (2v.) £35.00.per vol. ISBN: 0747211175, V.1; 0747211183, v.2.

Major historical survey, based on the information archived in the annual volumes of *Wisden.* Vol.1 covers 1877-1977; vol.2 1977-1994. *Class No:* 796.358

Bibliographies

[4995]

PADWICK, E.W., *comp.* **A Bibliography of cricket.** 2nd ed. London, Library Association Publishing, 1985. 282,256p.(2v.) £16.50, £46.50. ISBN: 0853659028; 0853655286.

Second volume published in 1991, edited by Stephen Eley and Peter Griffiths.

Vol 1: Over 10,000 entries to the end of 1979; Thirty-two main sections covering all aspects of the game. Material from all relevant countries. Vol 2: 4000 entries covering 1980-1989. *Class No:* 796.358(01)

Encyclopaedias & Dictionaries

[4996]

RUNDELL, M. The Dictionary of cricket. 2nd.ed. Oxford, Oxford University Press, 1995. 214p., illus. £25.00. (Pbk. £6.99.) ISBN: 0198661983; 0192800442, pbk.

1100 terms arranged alphabetically; lengthy definitions are based on historical principles, and quote from many authoritative sources. Coverage of technical and legal aspects of the game. Line drawings. *Class No:* 796.358(03)

Yearbooks & Directories

[4997]

Wisden cricketers' almanac 1998. Wright, G., *ed.* 135th. ed. London, J. Wisden, 1998. 1472p., illus. £27.50. ISBN: 0947766456.

Scores & analysis for previous season; biographies, obituaries; laws of cricket. Absolutely comprehensive, the key publication for cricket enthusiasts. Index at front. *Class No:* 796.358(058)

[4998]

—BARNARD, D., *ed.* An Index to Wisden cricketers' almanack 1864-1984. London, Queen Anne Press, 1984. £17.50. ISBN: 0356102408.

Essential for historical study of cricket.
Class No: 796.358(058)

Histories

[4999]

ALTHAM, H.S. *and* **SWANTON, E.W. A History of cricket.** 5th ed. London, Allen & Unwin, 1962. 2v., illus.

First published 1926.

1: *From the beginnings to the First World War,* by H.S. Altham. 323p. 2.: *From the First World War to the present day* [1914-61], by E.W. Swanton. 334p. The standard history of cricket, v.1 (re-issue 1968) being of particular interest. Avowedly concerned with English and international cricket rather than cricket in other countries. Excellent final chapter by E.W. Swanton on cricket laws and their alteration. The 1st ed. of 1926 included a fine bibliography that is absent from later eds. *Class No:* 796.358(091)

[5000]

Test match grounds of the world. Jollands, T., *ed.* London, Collins Willow, 1990. 224p., illus. £14.95. ISBN: 0002182823.

7 contributors describe 62 grounds listed A/Z. History, anecdotes, summary of results at each ground.
Class No: 796.358(091)

Biographies

[5001]

BAILEY, P. *and* **THORN, P.** *and* **WYNNE-*THOMAS, P., comps.*** **Who's who of cricketers:** a complete who's who of all cricketers who have played first-class cricket in England, with full career records. London, Newnes Books in association with the Association of Cricket Statisticians, 1984. 1144p. £30. ISBN: 0600346927.

12,000 brief biographies, including members of touring sides. Earliest records start from 1801, but coverage in general is for the years 1864-1983. List of first class teams 1864-1983 (p.11); bibliography (p.6).
Class No: 796.358(092)

[5002]

The Cricketer's who's who 1998. Hawkes, C., *comp.* Harpenden, Queen Anne Press, 1998. 704p., illus. £12.99. ISBN: 1852915870.

Annual.

About 600 entries including all county players. Full personal details and a photograph with each entry.
Class No: 796.358(092)

[5003]

GREEN, B., *comp.* **Wisden book of obituaries:** obituaries from Wisden cricketers' almanack 1892-1985. London, Queen Anne Press, 1986. 1029p. £29.50. ISBN: 0356106403.

8,614 names are included: worldwide coverage. Entries range from 2-3 lines to 24 pages for W.G. Grace.
Class No: 796.358(092)

[5004]

MARTIN-JENKINS, C. The Complete who's who of test cricketers. 3rd ed. London, Macdonald/Queen Anne Press, 1987. 527p., illus. £16.95. ISBN: 0356144291.

Brief biographies of all players who have represented England, Australia, South Africa, West Indies, New Zealand, India, Pakistan, Sri Lanka over the last 100 years. Up-to-date to the end of 1986 season.
Class No: 796.358(092)

[5005]

MARTIN-JENKINS, C. World cricketers: a biographical dictionary. Oxford, Oxford University Press, 1996. xii,820p. £25.00. ISBN: 019210005x.

Full of fascinating facts and anecdotes; comprehensive coverage of players and other figures in cricket. Special sections on the nine Test nations, and information on players worldwide. *Class No:* 796.358(092)

Official Records

[5006]

FRINDALL, B., ***comps.*** **The Wisden book of cricket records.** 3rd ed. London, Headline Press, 1993. 690p. £35.00. ISBN: 0747207933.

First-class match records 1815-1985 - teams, individuals, partnerships, bowling, wicket-keeping, fielding. National cricket; test match records 1876/7 onwards.
Class No: 796.358(093.2)

Australia

[5007]

The Oxford companion to Australian cricket. Cashman, R., *and others*. Oxford, Oxford University Press, 1996. 600p., illus. £30.00. ISBN: 0195535758.

History, evolution, major players, records, statistics, role of cricket in Australian sporting tradition and culture, venues, clubs, associations, contests, trophies, etc. Six principal contributors and over 100 other experts have been involved; the work has been produced in association with the Australian Society for Sports History. Bibliography.
Class No: 796.358(94)

Athletics & Gymnastics

Track & Field Athletics

Bibliographies

[5008]

LOVESEY, P. ***and*** **McNAB, T. The Guide to British track and field literature,** 1275-1968. London, Athletics Arena, 1969. v,119p.

'A bibliography of athletics literature published in the United Kingdom', p.8-60. 'Appendix of foreign literature', p.61-62. Preceded by 'Some trends in the development of British athletics'. 890 items in all. Index of authors; index of titles; 'Guide to subject matter'; Addenda.
Class No: 796.42(01)

Yearbooks & Directories

[5009]

British athletics yearbook 1997. Mackay, D., *ed.* London, Kogan Page, 1997. 144p., illus. £12.99. ISBN: 0749422602.

Published in association with the British Athletic Federation.

Directory of the season ahead, results and reviews of previous year. *Class No:* 796.42(058)

[5010]

International Amateur Athletic Federation handbook 1998/99. Monaco, IAAF, 1998. 212p. £6.50.

Directory of events, organising bodies, associations etc.
Class No: 796.42(058)

[5011]

MATTHEWS, P., ***ed.*** **Athletics:** the international track and field annual 1998. London, SportsBooks Ltd. for the Association of Track & Field Statisticians, 1998. 608p. illus., tables. £14.95. ISBN: 1899807039.

Reviews the past year in detail; data on major championships, biographies of leading figures, records. Efficient indexes. *Class No:* 796.42(058)

[5012]

WHITTINGHAM, R. ***and*** **MATTHEWS, P.,** ***eds.*** **British athletics 1998:** statistical review of 1997, compiled by the National Union of Track Statisticians. Stockport, Umbra/ NUTC, 1998. 400p. £12.00. ISBN: 1898258066.

Totally comprehensive and reliable.
Class No: 796.42(058)

Histories

[5013]

QUERCETANI, R.L. A World history of track and field athletics 1864-1964. London, OUP, 1964. xxi,376p.,illus.

20 chapters, each devoted to a single sport; women's athletics not included. Bibliography. *Class No:* 796.42(091)

Biographies

[5014]

Who's who in world athletics, 1998. Watman, M., *ed.* Stanmore, Middx, Athletics International, 1998. 136p. £10.00. ISBN: 0952801124.

Biographies and statistics on 2500 leading track and field athletes. *Class No:* 796.42(092)

Outdoor Pursuits

Mountaineering

[5015]

GRAYDON, D. ***and*** **HANSON, K.,** ***eds.*** **Mountaineering:** the freedom of the hills. 6th.ed. Shrewsbury, Swan-Hill Press, 1997. 528p., illus. £16.95. ISBN: 1840370017.

Very comprehensive handbook of equipment, routes, survival techniques, procedures, tips. Soundly written and reliable. *Class No:* 796.52

[5016]

UNSWORTH, W. Encyclopedia of mountaineering. New ed. London, Hodder & Stoughton, 1992. 383p.,illus. £16.99. ISBN: 0340577444.

First edition 1975.

Over 1,000 entries for places, people, techniques, equipment, natural phenomena, miscellaneous/fringe topics. Alphabetical arrangement and numerous cross-references. British and Alpine emphasis. *Class No:* 796.52

Bibliographies

[5017]

NEATE, W.R. Mountaineering and its literature: a descriptive bibliography of selected works published in the English language, 1744-1976. Milnthorpe, Cumbria, Cicerone Press, 1978. 165p. £10. ISBN: 0902363182.

List of subject headings, leads to main sequence. Some annotations; useful summary tables (*e.g.* Alps, p.55-60) naming individual peaks, giving height, first recorded ascent, & references to books in the bibliography. Thorough but untidy in layout. *Class No:* 796.52(01)

Scotland

[5018]

BEARHOP, D.A., *ed.* Munro's tables of the 3000-feet mountains of Scotland, and other tables of lesser heights. New ed. Edinburgh, Scottish Mountaineering Trust, 1997. 167p., illus., tables. £15.95. ISBN: 0907521533.

First published 1891.

Summits arranged by district (3,000-feet; 2,500-feet), and 2,000-feet lowland hills. *Class No:* 796.52(411)

Cycling

[5019]

BALLANTINE, R. Richard's new bicycle book. Rev. ed. London, Pan, 1990. 363p., illus. £9.99. ISBN: 0330313150.

First edition 1975.

Recognized as an influential though idiosyncratic handbook for all cyclists. Part one covers history, equipment, selection of a machine, use for commuting, competitions, mountain-biking etc. Part two deals with maintenance in detail. Appendix of European cycle touring organizations. Illustrated with line drawings. *Class No:* 796.61

[5020]

LECCESE, M. *and* **PLEVIN, A. The Bicyclist's sourcebook:** the ultimate directory of cycling information. Rockville,MD, Woodbine House, 1991. 400p. $16.95. ISBN: 0933149417.

Covers topics such as clothing, nutrition, books, periodicals, manufacturers, racing, tours, safety. State-by-state guide to events, tracks, etc. Good advice, well-presented. *Class No:* 796.61

Bibliographies

[5021]

WILLIAMS, E. A Bibliography of cycling books. Birmingham, National Cycle Archive, 1993. 90p. £9.95. ISBN: 0952257718.

....*(contd.)*

A Cyclists' Touring Club project.

Books are presented in three lists - title, author, date. There are no annotations. *Class No:* 796.61(01)

Yearbooks & Directories

[5022]

Cycling yearbook 1997. Woodhead, L., *ed.* London, Kogan Page, 1997. 124p. £9.95. ISBN: 0749422610.

Published for the Cyclists' Touring Club.

Directory of events, reviews etc. Brief bibliography; index. *Class No:* 796.61(058)

[5023]

Mountain bikers almanac, 1996. Grant, P.W. *and* Langton, M., *eds.* Stateline, NV, Grant Wolf, 1995. 247p., illus. 5719.95. ISBN: 096476010x.

By enthusiasts, for enthusiasts; but some good information on history, equipment, records, who's who. Directory sections, glossary. *Class No:* 796.61(058)

Motor Sports

Motor Racing

[5024]

Formula 1 pocket annual 1998. Smith, B., *ed.* 4th.ed. London, Virgin Publishing, 1998. 240p. £4.99. ISBN: 075350295x.

Profiles of key figures, team directories, circuit directory for 1998. Review of 1997 and statistics; records section. *Class No:* 796.71

[5025]

GRIFFITHS, T.R. Grand Prix: the complete guide. London, Bloomsbury, 1997. 591p. £18.99. ISBN: 0747537488.

Full results 1950-1997; information on all drivers involved. Results and statistics for all constructors. *Class No:* 796.71

Biographies

[5026]

SMALL, S. The Guinness Grand Prix who's who. 2nd.ed. London, Guinness Publishing, 1996. 464p., illus. £17.95. ISBN: 0851126235.

Includes 10,000 race summaries and brief biographies for every Grand Prix driver from 1950. *Class No:* 796.71(092)

Combat Sports

Boxing

[5027]

BLEWETT, B. The A/Z of world boxing. London, Robson Books, 1996. 439p., illus. £22.95. ISBN: 1861050046.

Thorough and well-presented; covers people and topics. *Class No:* 796.83

[5028]

Hamlyn encyclopedia of boxing. Odd, G., *ed.* Rev. ed. London, Hamlyn, 1990. 224p., illus. £10.95. ISBN: 0600563847.

First edition 1983.

A/Z great boxers, with brief biographical and career details. Facts and figures including records, championships; glossary. *Class No:* 796.83

[5029]

The Ultimate encyclopedia of boxing. Mullan, H., *ed.* London, Hodder & Stoughton, 1996. 208p., illus. £19.99. ISBN: 0340674415.

Useful popular work; career details of major names in the sport. *Class No:* 796.83

Bibliographies

[5030]

HARTLEY, R.A. History and bibliography of boxing books: collector's guide to the history of pugilism. Alton, Hants., Nimrod, 1988. 349p., illus. £24. ISBN: 1852590742.

Valuable source in a sparsely-covered area. Short history of boxing literature (six chapters p.3-80). Bibliography contains 2113 items arranged A/Z by author with basic details and brief annotation. Title index.
Class No: 796.83(01)

Great Britain

Yearbooks & Directories

[5031]

British Boxing Board of Control yearbook, 1998. Hugman, B.J., *ed.* 14th ed. Harpenden, Lennard/Queen Anne Press, 1997. 312p., illus. £16.99. ISBN: 185291582x. ISSN: 13662228.

Annual survey of British professional boxing with reviews, careers, records, diary of fixtures. International, and amateur sections. Reviews of previous season, BBBC awards, champions from early 20th. century, records of current IBF, WBA, WBC, and WBO champions. Obituaries. Directory of promoters, managers, referees etc.
Class No: 796.83(410)(058)

Martial Arts

[5032]

CORCORAN, J. The Martial arts sourcebook: the complete reference to the most frequently sought information on the martial arts. London, HarperPerrenial, 1994. 434p. £13.99. ISBN: 0062732595.

Five sections: styles and practices of martial arts worldwide; famous martial artists; champions and competition results; films and videos; business directory including suppliers of equipment, specialist publishers.
Class No: 796.85

[5033]

DRAEGER, D.F. *and* **SMITH, R.W. Comprehensive Asian fighting arts.** Tokyo, Kodansha, 1982. 207p. illus. $19.95. ISBN: 0870114360.

Discusses the fighting arts in eleven countries. Bibliography. *Class No:* 796.85

Fencing

[5034]

EVANGELISTA, N. The Encyclopedia of the sword. Westport, CT, Greenwood Press, 1995. xxiv,690p., illus. $79.50. ISBN: 0313278962.

See entry at: 739.7(03); coverage of sporting aspects as well as the sword as object. *Class No:* 796.86

[5035]

MANLEY, A. Complete fencing. London, Hale, 1979. vii,311p., illus., diagrs. £11.95. ISBN: 0709176236.

Divided into three main sections covering basic information, the foil, advanced weapons. Appendices include bibliography and glossary. *Class No:* 796.86

[5036]

MORTON, E.D. The A-Z of fencing. Rev.ed. [S.l.], E.D.Morton, 1995. 312p. ISBN: 0952598108.

Previous ed. as *Martini A-Z of fencing*, 1988.

A comprehensive and valuable source; bibliography p310-312. *Class No:* 796.86

Winter Sports

Ice Skating

Yearbooks & Directories

[5037]

BERMAN, A. Skater's Edge sourcebook: ice skating resource guide. Kensington, MD, Skater's Edge, 1995. $39.95. ISBN: 0964302705.

Lists US rinks, books, videos, clubs, clothing, equipment, training centres; champions 1914-1994. Articles on fitting skates, choosing a coach etc. *Class No:* 796.91(058)

Skiing

Yearbooks & Directories

[5038]

Globalskiguide 98. London, Skier's Holiday Guide Club, 1997. 296p. £15.00. ISBN: 0951748157.

Described as 'the definitive guide to ski resorts worldwide.' Include good maps, plans, diagrams.
Class No: 796.93(058)

[5039]

Good skiing and snowboarding guide 1998. Hardy, P. *and* Eyston, F., *eds.* London, Which Books (Consumers' Association) in association with the Ski Club of Great Briain, 1997. 622p. ISBN: 0852026676.

Covers 500 resorts worldwide; summaries and maps. Resorts by country p.30-548 - Austria, France, Italy, Switzerland, North America, Best of Europe, Best of the World. Reference sections include Internet directory, safety, equipment, travel etc. *Class No:* 796.93(058)

Ice Hockey

[5040]

Ice hockey annual, 1997/98. Roberts, S. Brighton, Stewart Roberts, 1997. 208p. £9.95. ISBN: 0951508687.

Review of the previous season, directory of the next.
Class No: 796.96

Laws

[5041]
NATIONAL HOCKEY LEAGUE. Ice hockey rules in pictures. London, Columbus Books, 1989. 96p., illus. £2.95. ISBN: 0862879566.

Gives dimensions of ground, duties of officials, discusses equipment, strategy, signals. Illustrated with line drawings. Official rules in very small type p.79-96.
Class No: 796.96(094.1)

Water Sports

Boating & Sailing

[5042]
CUNLIFFE, T. The Complete yachtmaster; sailing, seamanship and navigation for the modern yacht skipper. 2nd.ed. London, Adlard Coles Nautical, 1997. 232p., illus., charts, maps, plans. £18.99. ISBN: 0713646578.

Previous ed. 1994.

Totally comprehensive handbook, covering all aspects of yachting. *Class No:* 797.1

[5043]
The Glenans manual of sailing. Davison, P., *trans.* Newton Abbott, David and Charles, 1992. 1129p., illus. £30.00. ISBN: 0715300164.

Translation of *Le Cours des Glenans,* Editions du Seuil, 1990/92; ISBN: 2020099632.

A very thorough production on the practice of sailing, the mechanics, boats, handling, meteorology, seascapes, navigation, cruising; includes useful addresses, brief bibliography, index, charts. *Class No:* 797.1

[5044]
JOHNSON, P. Encyclopedia of yachting. London, Dorling Kindersley, 1989. 352p., illus. £25. ISBN: 0863183662.

Covers origins, cruising, racing, America's Cup, inshore, Olympic, classes of craft, design, construction, equipment, sailing waters. Narrative format with adequate index. Glossary of terms. 600 excellent illustrations.
Class No: 797.1

[5045]
PERA, M. The Racing rules of sailing: a complete guide 1997-2000. 4th. ed. London, Adlard Coles Nautical, 1997. 256p., illus. £16.99. ISBN: 071364608x.

Previous ed. as *The Yacht racing rules.*

Rules, definitions, organisation and management, general requirements, rights of way, protests, appeals etc.
Class No: 797.1

Bibliographies

[5046]
TOY, E.W. Adventures afloat: a nautical bibliography. Metuchen, NJ, Scarecrow, 1988. 1193p. (2v.). $89.50. ISBN: 0810821893.

Annotated bibliography covering all aspects of sports boating, but concentrating on yachting. Vol.1 covers personal narratives, racing; vol.2 is devoted to sailing techniques & boat design. *Class No:* 797.1(01)

Dictionaries

[5047]
DEAR, I., *ed and* KEMP, P., *ed*.. An A-Z of sailing terms. 2nd.ed. Oxford, Oxford University Press, 1997. £7.99. ISBN: 019280068x.

Previous ed. (1987) as *The pocket Oxford guide to sailing terms.*

A basic, standard list of terms. Reliable, and up-to-date.
Class No: 797.1(038)

[5048]
ROUSMANIÈRE, J. Glossary of modern sailing terms. Rev. ed. London, Putnam, 1989. 132p., illus. £12.95. ISBN: 0399150056.

Useful illustrated glossary. *Class No:* 797.1(038)

[5049]
SCHULT, J., *ed*. The Sailing dictionary. London, Granada, 1981. 332p.,illus. £9.95. ISBN: 0229116191.

Translated from German original Segler-Lexicon.

Some 3,500 entries ranging from simple definitions to longer explanations of winds, tides etc. Cross-references; over 1,500 illustrations. *Class No:* 797.1(038)

[5050]
WEBB, B., *ed*. Yachtsman's 8-language dictionary: English, French, German, Dutch, Danish, Italian, Spanish, Portuguese. 3rd ed. London, Coles, 1983. 160p., diagrs.

Some 3,500 definitions systematically arranged.
Class No: 797.1(038)

Almanacs

[5051]
Macmillan Nautical almanac 1998, incorporating Reed's. London, Macmillan, 1998. 913p. £29.95. ISBN: 0333670965.

Previously *Reeds' Nautical almanac,* which had been published for over 60 years.

Notices to sailors, astronomy guide, navigation, passages, communications, tides, signals, weather, distress, harbours, marinas, first aid etc. The standard handbook for serious sailing. *Class No:* 797.1(059)

Canoeing

[5052]
Canoeing handbook: official handbook of the British Canoe Union. Rowe, R., *ed.* 2nd.ed., corrected. Nottingham, British Canoe Union, 1997. 549p. £15.96. ISBN: 0900082046.

Revision of the 1989 ed.

Standard source for canoe information.
Class No: 797.122

Bibliographies

[5053]
SKILLING, B.C. British canoeing literature, January 1866-January 1966. London, UMI, 1969. i,171p.

Library Association Fellowship thesis, 1967.

Subject guide, followed by detailed bibliography.
Class No: 797.122(01)

Rowing

Yearbooks & Directories

[5054]

British rowing almanack and Amateur Rowing Association yearbook, 1998. Osborne, K., *ed.* London, Amateur Rowing Association, 1998. 368p., illus. £18.50. ISSN: 00682446.

First published 1861.

Directory of clubs; list of statistics & records; calendar of events, tide-tables etc. *Class No:* 797.123(058)

Histories

[5055]

DODD, C. Story of world rowing. London, Stanley Paul, 1992. 468p., illus. £25.00. ISBN: 0091746108.

Chapters cover the origins, boats, coaches, development into a world sport. Glossary, chronology, further reading, index. *Class No:* 797.123(091)

Swimming & Diving

[5056]

WHITTEN, P. The Complete book of swimming. New York, Random House, 1994. 372p., illus. $16.00. ISBN: 0679746676.

Covers technique, strokes, training, organizations. Useful diagrams. *Class No:* 797.2

[5057]

WILKIE, D. *and* **JUBA, K. Handbook of swimming.** London, Pelham Books, 1990. 232p., illus. £12.99. ISBN: 0720719461.

First published in hardback 1986.

Includes material on history, equipment, principles, strokes, champions, records, organizations. *Class No:* 797.2

Animal Sports

Horsemanship

[5058]

RODDAM, J.H. Competitive riding. London, Prentice Hall, 1988. 208p. £15.00. ISBN: 0131551442.

Sections cover history and principles, management and training, fitness, movements, and the competitive scene. Excellent illustrations and diagrams. *Class No:* 798.2

[5059]

WATSON, J.N.P. A Concise guide to polo. London, Sportsmans Press, 1989. 80p., illus. £8.95. ISBN: 0948253339.

Discusses basic rules and positions, equipment etc. Brief history, and list of polo clubs in the main polo-playing countries. *Class No:* 798.2

Bibliographies

[5060]

GRIMSHAW, A. The Horse: a bibliography of British books, 1851-1976, with a narrative commentary on the role of the horse in British social history, as revealed by the contemporary literature. London, Library Association, 1982. xxxiv,474p., illus. £29.95. ISBN: 0853655332.

Originally a thesis, 1978.

....(contd.)

3,266 well-annotated entries. 6 period-sections: 1851-1886, 1887-1918, 1919-1945, 1946-1959, 1960-1969, 1970-1976. Each section has 4 subdivisions; Breeds and breeding; Horsemanship; Horse and arts; Generalia of the horse (encyclopedias, directories, yearbooks, compendia). Title and author indexes, but no subject index. Omits horse-racing. *Class No:* 798.2(01)

Handbooks & Manuals

[5061]

The Manual of equitation: the complete training of horse and rider. 3rd.ed. Addington, Bucks, Kenilworth Press in association with the British Horse Society, 1997. 140p., illus. £10.95. ISBN: 1872082386.

Reprint of the 1990 ed., which was issued as a paperback in 1992.

A standard and reliable source; two main sections - the rider, and the horse. *Class No:* 798.2(035)

[5062]

The Manual of horsemanship. Cooper, B., *ed.* 11th.ed. Kenilworth, Pony Club, 1997. 448p., illus. £13.95. ISBN: 0900226501.

Official manual of the Pony Club. Previous ed. 1993.

Sections cover the rider, the horse, training, jumping, care, saddlery, injuries and ailments. *Class No:* 798.2(035)

[5063]

SPOONER, G. Handbook of showing. 3rd. ed. London, J.A. Allen, 1990. 248p. £14.95. ISBN: 0851314856.

First edition 1968.

Opening section discusses qualities and defects. Detail of societies pp.73-132 with background information on their activities, and contact addresses. Sections on showing and judging, show organization, duties of officials.
Class No: 798.2(035)

Horse Racing

Bibliographies

[5064]

LODER, E.P. Bibliography of the history and organization of horse racing and thoroughbred breeding in Great Britain and Ireland: books published ... 1565-1973. London, Allen & Unwin, 1978. 352p. £25.

1,800 entries in classified order, each with brief annotation. Index of names & titles; subject index to the classification. *Class No:* 798.4(01)

Encyclopaedias & Dictionaries

[5065]

The Racegoers' encyclopedia. White, J., *comp.* Rev.ed. London, CollinsWillow, 1996. 256p., illus. £15.99. ISBN: 0002187604.

Previous ed. 1994.

Popular guide for the enthusiast; bibliography p.254; index. *Class No:* 798.4(03)

Yearbooks & Directories

[5066]

Chasers and hurdlers 1996/97. London, Timeform/Portway Press, 1997. 1007p. £62.00. ISBN: 0900599979.

Much of this information is also available on the Internet via the *Computer Timeform* service; Website: <http://www.timeform.com>

Statistics, champions, form summaries and rating symbols; .chasers and hurdlers p.25-937; promising horses; selected big races; characteristics of courses. *Class No:* 798.4(058)

[5067]

Ruff's guide to the turf, and Sporting Life annual. Oliver, K., *ed.* London, Sporting Life. c1800p. £55.00.

Annual.

Information, records, statistics - owners, trainers, jockeys, apprentices, breeders, horses, bloodstock. Also a directory section, including Rules of Racing. *Class No:* 798.4(058)

Greyhound Racing

[5068]

GENDERS, R. NGRC book of greyhound racing: a history of the sport completely revised and updated by the National Greyhound Racing Club. London, Pelham Books, 1990. 342p., illus., tables. £12.95. ISBN: 072071804x.

First edition published 1981 as *Encyclopaedia of greyhound racing.*

Entries cover courses, winners, associations. Bibliography pp. 330/1. *Class No:* 798.8

Yearbooks & Directories

[5069]

BETTS, B., ***comp.*** **Greyhounds annual.** London, Sporting Life. c150p., illus. £7.95.

Annual.

Includes track guides, records and statistics; background feature articles. *Class No:* 798.8(058)

[5070]

The NGRC greyhound racing yearbook. Lyndey, Gloucs., Ringpress. £9.99.

Annual; continues the *Daily Mail greyhound factfile.*

Records and results of the previous season; statistics; directory of the new season. *Class No:* 798.8(058)

Field Sports

Fishing

[5071]

BULLER, F. *and* **FALKUS, H. Freshwater fishing.** [3rd.ed.] London, Ebury Press, 1998. 525p., illus. £18.99. ISBN: 0091864518.

1st.ed. 1975; revised ed.1988.

Full and comprehensive coverage of fishes, tackle and equipment. *Class No:* 799.1

[5072]

FALKUS, H. Salmon fishing: a practical guide. London, Witherby, 1984. 448p. illus., diagrams. £20. ISBN: 0854931449.

A definitive guide to every aspect of the sport.
Class No: 799.1

[5073]

The Guinness book of game fishing. Currie, W.B. Rev. ed. Enfield, Guinness Superlatives, 1990. 239p., illus. £14.95. ISBN: 0851129099.

First edition 1980.

Extensive & handsome discussion of habitats; sections cover trout, sea trout, salmon, other game fish. Note on seasons. Index. *Class No:* 799.1

Encyclopaedias & Dictionaries

[5074]

CALABI, S. The Illustrated encyclopedia of fly-fishing: a complete A-Z of terminology, tackle and techniques. London, Holt, 1993. 336p. £25.00. ISBN: 0805019898.

500 entries cover terms, biographies, associations, techniques; many excellent illustrations. There are some very long and detailed entries (*eg* Knots - 12pages including line drawings.) Cross references for jargon and slang terms.
Class No: 799.1(03)

Handbooks & Manuals

[5075]

GREENHALGH, M. *and* **OVENDEN, D. The Complete fly-fisher's handbook.** London, Dorling Kindersley, 1998. 288p., illus. £25.00. ISBN: 0751304999.

Describes fishes' natural foods, with monthly guide to variations, and artificial flies; covers tying and presenting, tools and materials. Bibliography; index of flies.
Class No: 799.1(035)

[5076]

VEALL, M. Fishing flies and their plumage. London, Sportsmans Press, 1989. 127p., illus. £12.95. ISBN: 0948253398.

Introductory section leads to chapters discussing dressing flies, historical background, current scene - dry, wet, wet spiders, sea trout flies, lures, salmon flies, specials. Glossary of terms. *Class No:* 799.1(035)

Yearbooks & Directories

[5077]

GORAN, C. Classic fly-fishing waters of the world. Shrewsbury, Swan Hill Press, 1991. 167p. £19.95. ISBN: 1853104353.

This volume is of Swedish origin; it gives excellent geographical coverage of North and South America, Europe and the UK, New Zealand. Clear text and excellent colour photographs. There are 40 entries with full descriptions, including recommended flies and rods, licences, accommodation, species. Comprehensive index.
Class No: 799.1(058)

[5078]

Where to fish 1998-1999. Orton, D.A., *ed.* 86th ed. Beaminster, T. Harmsworth, 1998. 525p., illus., maps. £17.99. ISBN: 0948807415.

Annual.

Fishing stations in England, Wales, Scotland, Northern Ireland, Irish Republic. Club details. Fishing abroad (Africa, Australasia, US, Canada, Europe by country). Fish list; index. *Class No:* 799.1(058)

Great Britain

Encyclopaedias & Dictionaries

[5079]

PRICHARD, M., *ed*. Collins new encyclopedia of fishing in Britain and Ireland. Rev. ed. London, Collins, 1990. 212p., illus. £15.95. ISBN: 0002183544.

First edition 1977.

Specialist contributors cover coarse, game, sea fishing. Glossary of terms; knots. Handsomely produced with excellent illustrations, which are separately indexed.
Class No: 799.1(410)(03)

Hunting

[5080]

WATSON, J.N.P. British and Irish hunts and huntsmen. London, Batsford, 1982. 264,240p. (2v.), illus. £40. ISBN: 071342169x, v.1; 0713420936, v.2.

Each volume covers England, Wales, Scotland, Ireland by region, with history of each hunt. Maps, photographs, details of masters etc. *Class No:* 799.2

Shooting

[5081]

PETZAL, D.E., *ed*. Encyclopedia of sporting firearms. New York, Facts on File, 1991. 448p. $50.00. ISBN: 0816023050.

2200 entries assembled from 11 expert consulting editors; entries cover terminology, biographies of prominent individuals, manufacturers, histories of associations, game birds and animals, discussion of appropriate guns. Includes slang terms and acronyms. Cross references. Bibliography of 123 items 1882-1950. 'Highly recommended' (*Reference books bulletin*, July1991, p2066/8.) *Class No:* 799.3

USA

[5082]

Shooter's bible. Hackensack, NJ, Stoeger Publishing. c600p., illus.

Published annually.

Catalogue of firearms, with prices, and valuable background articles; useful for collectors, and hunters. Data on manufacturers, accessories, with an illustration of every item. Excellent bibliography, in subject categories. Directory sections list publishers, suppliers; index.
Class No: 799.3(73)

Archery

Bibliographies

[5083]

LAKE, F. *and* WRIGHT, H., *eds*. Bibliography of archery: an indexed catalogue of 5,000 articles, books, films, manuscripts, periodicals, theses ... Manchester, Simon Archery Foundation, 1974. xvii,501p. £15. ISBN: 0950319902.

9 sections (including 'Basic archery books'). Entries have bibliographical notes, plus American and British library locations. Select list of sources. Comprehensive index, arranged by countries as well as by subjects. A model bibliography of its kind. *Class No:* 799.32(01)

8.0 Languages & Linguistics

Bibliographies

[5084]

MODERN LANGUAGE ASSOCIATION OF AMERICA. MLA international bibliography of books and articles on the modern languages and literatures, 1921-. New York, MLA, 1922-. Annual.

The major English-language bibliography in its field. Known as *American bibliography* from 1921 to 1955, when it listed only writings by Americans on the literatures of various countries; then as *Annual bibliography*, 1956-62, with coverage extended to include foreign-language writers; present title since 1963.

In 5 parts since 1981: 1. *British Isles, British Commonwealth, English-Caribbean and American literatures* - 2. *European, Asian, African and Latin American literatures* - 3. *Linguistics* - 4. *General literature and related topics* - 5. *Folklore.* Since 1983 these have been published in 2 vols. with v.1 including the 5 parts and a document author index, and v.2 comprising a comprehensive subject index with many cross-references. Individual parts are available separately with their own author and subject indexes. The 1996 bibliography has nearly 48,000 entries gleaned from over 4,000 journals and series published worldwide.

Available online (via OCLC and Ovid) and on CD-ROM (distributed by Silver Platter), with records back to 1963. It is hoped that eventually the whole file back to 1921 will be available online. CD-ROM updated quarterly; online version updated 10 times per year. *Class No:* 8.0(01)

[5085]

The Year's work in modern language studies, 1929/30-. London, Oxford Univ. Press, 1931-35; Cambridge, Cambridge Univ. Press, 1936-63; London, Modern Humanities Research Association, 1964-. v.1-. Annual. ISSN: 00844152.

Annual bibliography, with running commentary, of studies in languages and literatures. V.57, *1995* (1996. x,1187p.) has sections for Latin, Romance, Celtic, Germanic, and Slavonic languages, with subdivisions by subject specialists on individual languages. Many thousands of studies cited. Indexes of names and subjects. *Class No:* 8.0(01)

Reviews & Abstracts

[5086]

Modern language review. London, Modern Humanities Research Association, 1905-. v.1, no.1-. Quarterly. ISSN: 00267937.

The official journal of the MHRA, noted for its lengthy, scholarly reviews of studies of language and literature. Each issue carries an average of 180 book reviews.
Class No: 8.0(048)

Periodicals

[5087]

MODERN LANGUAGE ASSOCIATION OF AMERICA. MLA directory of periodicals: a guide to journals and series in languages and literatures; complete international listings, 1978/79-. New York, MLA, 1979-. Triennial. ISSN: 01970380.

A companion to the *MLA international bibliography* (*q.v.*), providing information on over 3,000 journals and serials indexed there. Arranged A-Z by title, the entries include address, editor, date of first publication, ISSN, subscription information, indication of editorial content, and submission requirements for contributors. Indexes of subjects, sponsoring organizations, editorial personnel and languages. According to *Choice* (v.31(7), March 1994, p.1100), several titles are listed here which are omitted from *Ulrich's international periodicals directory* and *Serials directory*. A separate paperback vol. is produced which lists only those periodicals (1,300-plus) published in the Americas.
Class No: 8.0(051)

Language Teaching

Bibliographies

[5088]

CENTER FOR APPLIED LINGUISTICS, Washington, D.C. **Dictionary catalog of the Library of the Center for Applied Linguistics.** Boston, Hall, 1974. 4v. (Available on microfilm by request). $410. ISBN: 0816111146.

53,100 catalogue cards, covering the following subjects: the teaching of English as a second language, bilingual education, the teaching of African and Asian languages in the United States, the teaching of standard English to speakers of non-standard varieties, surveys of neglected languages, linguistic documentation, urban language, language acquisition, and American Indian language education policy. *Class No:* 80:372.88(01)

[5089]

CENTRE FOR INFORMATION ON LANGUAGE TEACHING AND RESEARCH. Foreign language testing. London, CILT, 1981. 112p. ISBN: 0903466325.

Supplement, 1981-87. 1988. 144p. ISBN: 0948003820

A bibliography in two parts with abstracts of major articles on testing published since 1966 and annotated list of books. Subject and author indexes. *Class No:* 80:372.88(01)

[5090]

CENTRE FOR INFORMATION ON LANGUAGE TEACHING AND RESEARCH. Vocabulary in a second language. Meara, P., *ed.* London, CILT, 1983-87. 2v.

V.1 *1960-1980.* 1983. 96p. ISBN: 090346654.

V.2 *1980-1985.* 1987. 96p. ISBN: 0948003863.

Lists and provides abstracts for published research in the

.... *(contd.)*
field of vocabulary and word-handling in a second language. Arranged A-Z by author, with subject index and glossary of terms in each vol. *Class No:* 80:372.88(01)

Handbooks & Manuals

[5091]
SMALLEY, A. *and* **MORRIS, D. The Modern language teacher's handbook.** 2nd ed. Cheltenham, Thornes, 1992. vii,296p. illus. £19.99 ISBN: 074871247x.

1st ed. London, Hutchinson, 1985, as *MLA modern language teacher's handbook.*

1. Survival in the classroom - 2. Running a modern languages department - 3. Beyond the school - 4. Reference section. Covers all aspects of language teaching, including National Curriculum, flexible learning techniques, assessment and information technology. Bibliography (4p.). *Class No:* 80:372.88(035)

Dictionaries

[5092]
CARTER, R. Keywords in language and literacy. London, Routledge, 1995. 192p. illus. £9.99. ISBN: 0415119294.

Defines and exemplifies terms, with the emphasis on concepts which have been the subject of recent debate, *e.g.* 'real books' and 'proper English'. Cross references and suggestions for further reading. *Class No:* 80:372.88(038)

[5093]
RICHARDS, J., *& others.* **Longman dictionary of language teaching and applied linguistics.** 2nd ed. Harlow, Longman, 1992. 448p. illus. £13.50. ISBN: 0582072441.

1st ed. 1985 as *Longman dictionary of applied linguistics.*

Defines and explains *c.*2,000 terms used in language teaching and learning. Entries include cross-references and suggestions for further reading. British and American pronunciation indicated for each term. Many new entries in this ed. *Class No:* 80:372.88(038)

Reviews & Abstracts

[5094]
Language teaching: the international abstracting journal for language teachers and applied linguists. Cambridge, Cambridge Univ. Press, 1968-. v.1, no.1-. Quarterly. ISSN: 02614448.

Produced jointly by the Centre for Information on Language Teaching and Research (CILT) and the British Council, English Language Division, and formerly known as *Language Teaching Abstracts* and *Language Teaching and Linguistics: Abstracts.*

Each issue carries over 130 abstracts, in English, in 2 main sections (1. Language learning and teaching - 2. Related research and language study) with sub-headings, plus 'a specially commissioned state-of-the-art survey article on an important aspect of language learning or teaching' (*e.g.* 'Residence abroad within language study' in the Jan. 1997 issue) with a full bibliography. Author and subject indexes in each issue, with annual cumulation in October issue. List of periodicals regularly scanned in each January issue: currently around 130. International coverage. *Class No:* 80:372.88(048)

Yearbooks & Directories

[5095]
Directory of language training and services for business: a guide to resources in further and higher education. Mellors, C., *& others, eds.* London, Routledge, 1993. 600p. £50. ISBN: 0415099986.

Lists 435 UK institutions providing language training and related services, *e.g.* translating and interpreting. Numbered entries, arranged A-Z by name of college, give full contact details, services and facilities. Index of 70 languages covered. Index of institutions by county. Information gathered by questionnaire and correct at start of academic year 1992-3. *Class No:* 80:372.88(058)

[5096]
ELT guide: the definitive guide to English language teaching worldwide. Lakin, P., *ed.* 7th ed. Douglas, Isle of Man, EFL Ltd., [1996?]. 216p. £9.95. ISBN: 0951457667.

A good-value directory of courses, training centres and employment opportunities, arranged in 6 chapters: 1. Becoming a teacher - 2. Further qualifications - 3. Finding a job - 4. World English - 5. Business English - 6. Reference section. Index of advertisers. *Class No:* 80:372.88(058)

[5097]
GARSON, J. The EARLS guide to language schools in Europe, 1995. London, Cassell, 1995. 320p. £18.99. ISBN: 0304345156.

Lists over 1,000 establishments belonging to the European Affiliation of Registered Language Schools, giving costs, contact names and location maps. Also lists further sources of information. *Class No:* 80:372.88(058)

[5098]
HAGEN, S. Vocational modern languages qualifications: a quick reference guide. London, CILT, 1995. 52p. £6.50. ISBN: 1874016437.

Outlines the main vocational and applied foreign language examination schemes on offer from UK examination bodies. Numbered entries for each exam give languages offered; aims of exam; levels of difficulty; age range; options available; vocational element; type of assessment; and relationship to National Language Standards. *Class No:* 80:372.88(058)

Teaching Materials

[5099]
CENTRE FOR INFORMATION ON LANGUAGE TEACHING AND RESEARCH. Teacher's handbooks. Buckby, M., *ed.* London, CILT, 1990-. no.1 - (in progress).

Series originally entitled *Resource guides for teachers.*

4 titles have so far appeared in this series which is 'designed to provide a wide range of directory and professional guidance in an easily accessible form to teachers of individual languages.' Handbooks include sections on managing teaching and learning; resources; bringing the country into the classroom; school travel and exchange visits; assessing progress; opportunities in higher and further education; professional development ; and useful addresses.

1. *Italian*, by J. Jackson. 1990. 68p. £8.50. ISBN: 0948003634.

2. *Urdu*, by S.B.C. Khan and M. Molteno. 1990. 80p. £6. ISBN: 094800309x.

3. *Russian*, by D. Rix and J. Macrae. 1991. 68p. £8.50.

....*(contd.)*
ISBN: 0948003693.

4. *Japanese*, by J. Jenkins. 1993. 80p. £8.50. ISBN: 1874016135. *Class No:* 80:372.88(072)

Languages

Bibliographies of Bibliographies

[5100]

Bibliography of bibliographies of the languages of the world: v.1, General and Indo-European languages of Europe. Troike, R.C., *ed.* Amsterdam, Benjamins, 1990. xxii,473p. Hfl.210. ISBN: 9027237433.

General section followed by 10 sections for language groups, with subsections for individual languages. 2,480 entries, the top 3 languages being German (196), Spanish (190) and English (163). Name and subject indexes.
Class No: 800(009)

Encyclopaedias

[5101]

CAMPBELL, G.L. Compendium of the world's languages. London, Routledge, 1991. 2v. (xxiv,1574p.). £150. ISBN: 0415029376.

V.1 *Abaza to Lusatian.*

V.2 *Maasai to Zuni.*

Contains clearly presented accounts of over 300 individual languages — covering their history, writing system, sound system and grammatical system — plus 20 language-families. Most languages are illustrated by a translation of the first 8 verses of St. John's Gospel. Details of 38 scripts appended. Bibliography (14p.). List of languages and cross-references.

'Covers considerably more ground than Comrie, and differs from Ruhlen in providing much more data on individual languages, though it nowhere approaches Ruhlen's completeness. Of the three, Campbell has the most thorough discussion of the extinct languages (such as Sumerian, Urartian and Elamite), a field ignored almost entirely by Comrie and handled indifferently by Ruhlen' (*TLS*, no.4628, Dec. 13, 1991, p.24).

Campbell's *Concise compendium of the world's languages* (1995. x,670p. £50. ISBN: 041511392x) features 100 major languages (based largely on numbers of contemporary speakers) the from the parent work, with representatives of all language families included. Many of the articles have been revised and the illustrative Gospel passages are retained. *Class No:* 800(031)

[5102]

CRYSTAL, D. The Cambridge encyclopedia of language. 2nd ed. Cambridge, Cambridge Univ. Press, 1997. vii,480p. illus. £45. ISBN: 0521550505.

1st ed. 1987.

The first attempt to cover the whole field of language in a single-volume encyclopedia is an unqualified success. A massive amount of information is organized in 11 chapters (called 'Parts'), which comprise 65 articles ('thematic sections') of between 2 and 20 pages, each of which is a self-contained presentation of a major theme in language study. The data is made accessible by means of a clearly presented table of contents, numerous cross-references and three indexes: languages, families, dialects and scripts; authors and personalities; topics. Attractively presented with

....*(contd.)*
many photographs, diagrams, maps and tables, and intelligent use of a variety of typefaces.

Appendices include: glossary of over 1,000 terms; lists of special symbols and abbreviations; table of the world's languages, indicating family, where spoken and by how many, bibliography (8p.) with the emphasis on recent publications. Main text contains many statistical tables which will be invaluable in reference work, *e.g.* speakers of English throughout the world, mother tongues of US citizens, letter and word frequency, most popular names, etc.

1st ed. was generously reviewed in *TLS* (no.4428, Feb. 12, 1988, p.166) and *Language Monthly* (no.52, Jan. 1988, p.16-17) and rightly so, considering it is essentially the work of a single author.

2nd ed. has been reset in full colour with a new typeface, allowing the redesign of several pages and the inclusion of new photographs and maps. Statistics and geopolitical data have been revised. *Class No:* 800(031)

[5103]

CRYSTAL, D. An Encyclopedic dictionary of language and languages. London, Blackwell, 1992. 428p. illus. £30. ISBN: 0631176527.

Not a dictionary of linguistics, but an ideal quick-reference tool with nearly 2,750 entries and *c.*5,000 cross-references, covering languages and 'the more popular and relevant concepts to do with languages.' These include major linguistic concepts and schools; core topics, such as grammar and phonetics; and terms from applied areas of language study, like lexicography and language teaching. Entries for individual languages and countries include useful facts and up-to-date statistics. Cartoons, a jargon-free style, and the omission of bibliographies emphasise that the work is aimed at a different audience from Crystal's *Cambridge encyclopedia of language* and *Dictionary of linguistics and phonetics (qq.v.)*. *Class No:* 800(031)

[5104]

—MATTHEWS, P.H. The Concise Oxford dictionary of linguistics. Oxford, Oxford Univ. Press, 1997. 410p. illus. £7.99. ISBN: 0192800086.

Over 3,000 entries, A-Z, on languages and language families, linguistic terms and concepts, and linguists. Brief explanations, examples and cross-references, but no bibliographies. *Class No:* 800(031)

[5105]

The Encyclopedia of language and linguistics. Asher, R.E. *and* Simpson, J.M.Y., *eds.* Oxford, Pergamon, 1994. 10v. illus. £1,860 ISBN: 0080359434.

The most comprehensive work in the field, with over 2,000 articles contributed by over 1,000 scholars (representing over 70 countries), under the supervision of 35 subject editors. Articles are arranged A-Z in vols. 1-9 and cover individual languages and countries and all aspects of linguistics, including peripheral areas like speech pathology, and aspects of related subjects such as anthropology and psychology. Biographical articles on over 400 key figures. Extensive cross-references. Bibliography with every article. V.10 includes glossary of over 3,000 technical terms (102p.); list of languages, with countries spoken and number of speakers (52p.); classified list of entries under 32 subject headings (31p.); list of contributors, with affiliations and titles of their articles; name index (81p.); and comprehensive, 3-level subject index (222p.).

TLS (no.4803, April 21, 1995, p.10-11) has reservations about the index and glossary, and wants to see more and

....*(contd.)*
fuller articles on individual languages: 'All in all, this is not yet a great encyclopaedia, but it at least has the makings of one.' *Class No:* 800(031)

[5106]

GUNNEMARK, E. Countries, people and their languages: a geolinguistic handbook. 3rd ed. Gothenburg, Gunnemark, 1991.

1st ed. 1983, as *What language do they speak? - a geolinguistic handbook*; 2nd ed. 1985.

A guide to the languages spoken in different countries. Main section arranged by country, with further sections on languages, scripts, classification, etc. Includes updated statistics of numbers of speakers. Bibliography. Indexes of terms and languages. 'A serious work of reference containing an enormous mass of details, figures and other information that would be difficult or impossible to obtain elsewhere' (*Language International*, v.4(1), 1992, p.40). *Class No:* 800(031)

[5107]

KATZNER, K. The Languages of the world. New. ed. London, Routledge, 1995. x,378p. £9.99. ISBN: 0415118093.

1st ed. 1977; rev. ed. 1986.

A handy guide in 3 sections: 1. Language families of the world (brief notes on 18 families, plus independent languages, artificial languages, pidgins and creoles) - 2. Individual languages (1-2p. on each of 200 languages, giving a passage from literature in native script, English translation, and notes on characteristics and status of the language, including number and distribution of current speakers) - 3. Country-by-country survey. Index of languages and families. Appears little changed from earlier eds. but still excellent value. *Class No:* 800(031)

[5108]

Les langues du monde, par un groupe de linguistes. Meillett, A. *and* Cohen, M., *eds.* Nouv. éd. Paris, Centre Nationale de la Recherche Scientifique, 1952. xliii,1294p. maps. (repr. Slatkine, 1981. 2v.). ISBN: 2051002541.

1st ed. 1924.

A major reference work, covering *c.*10,000 languages and dialects under language groups. Each language group has sections on classification, features, syntax, the various dialects, and a comprehensive bibliography. For individual languages: phonology; grammar; examples of phrases; morphology. Annotated bibliographies on language classification (19p.) and general linguistics (7p.). Index of languages (64p.). Accompanied by *Atlas des langues du monde* (21 folded maps in pocket). *Class No:* 800(031)

[5109]

—Les Langues dans le monde ancien et moderne. Perrot, J., *ed.* Paris, Centre Nationale de la Recherche Scientifique, 1981-89. [v.1-2] (in progress).

[V.1] *Les Langues de l'Afrique subsaharienne. Pidgins et créoles.* 1981. xii,691p. ISBN: 222017203.

[V.2] *Langues chamito-sémitiques.* 1989. 328p. ISBN: 2222040574.

A new survey which will eventually replace *Les Langues du monde.* The first vol. comprises detailed studies (all in French) of sub-Saharan languages (p.1-615) and of pidgins and creoles (p.621-672) by 26 international specialists. Many maps, tables and diagrams, plus extensive bibliographies. Index of languages and dialects. 12 coloured maps accompany the vol. in a portfolio. *Class No:* 800(031)

[5110]

The World's major languages. Comrie, B., *ed.* London, Routledge, 1987. xiii,1025p. illus. £85. ISBN: 0415045169.

50 essays (average 20p.) by 44 specialists on major languages and language groups, each one discussing the historical development of the language, its grammar, sound system and writing system, and sociological factors such as its use as a written or official language. Several maps and many tables. Selective bibliographies and lists of references follow each essay, but these concentrate on grammars and histories and do not include dictionaries. Over half of the essays (26) are devoted to Indo-European languages.

A lengthy review in *The Linguist* (v.27(2), Spring 1988, p.90-91) suggests that while the work will be 'indispensable in libraries, as it brings together much knowledge not easily available elsewhere', it does not supersede Meillet and Cohen's *Les Langues du monde*, which covers practically all languages, nor does it replace the language articles in the *New Encyclopaedia Britannica*, which provide fuller comparative and historical information, but it complements both of them.

4 regional selections from the main work are available, at £18.99 each, all ed. by B. Comrie and published by Routledge:

The Major languages of East and South-East Asia. 240p. ISBN: 0415047390.

The Major languages of Western Europe. 352p. ISBN: 0415047382.

The Major languages of Eastern Europe. 288p. ISBN: 041505771x.

The Major languages of South Asia, the Middle East and Africa. 336p. ISBN: 0415057728. *Class No:* 800(031)

Handbooks & Manuals

[5111]

ALLEN, C.G. A Manual of European languages for librarians. London & New York, Bowker, in association with the London School of Economics, 1975. xiii,803p.

Systematic treatment of the elements of 38 languages, arranged in linguistic groups (Germanic; Latin and the Romance languages; Celtic, Greek and Albanian; Slavonic; Baltic; Finno-Ugrian; Other languages: Maltese, Turkish, Basque, Esperanto). Data, plus examples, on the following points in nearly all the languages: general characteristics; bibliolinguistics; alphabet, phonetics, spelling; parts of speech; articles; numerals; word-formation. The section on Russian (p.394-426) includes 6 pages of tables of 'Cyrillic equivalents of Roman letters according to language'. A massive, unique and painstaking achievement. Winner of the Library Association's McColvin Medal, 1976.

New ed. due 1999 (ISBN: 18573924218).
Class No: 800(035)

[5112]

Cambridge language surveys. Allen, W.S., *ed.* Cambridge, Cambridge Univ. Press, 1980- (in progress).

A series which will eventually cover all the major language families of the world. Each vol. compares and contrasts the typological features of the languages covered, surveys their historical development and deals with current sociolinguistic issues. Intended for the student of linguistics or the general linguist, with no special knowledge of the languages concerned being assumed. Extensive bibliographies are a feature.

Titles published to date:

The Languages of Australia, by R.M.W. Dixon. 1980. ISBN: 0521223296.

....*(contd.)*

The Languages of the Soviet Union, by B. Comrie. 1981. ISBN: 0521232309.

Mesoamerican Indian languages, by J.A. Suárez. 1983. ISBN: 0521228344.

The Papuan languages of New Guinea, by W.A. Foley. 1986. £55. ISBN: 0521243556.

Chinese, by J. Norman. 1988. £50. ISBN: 0521228093.

Pidgins and creoles, by J. Holm. 1988-89. 2v. £47.90. ISBN: 0521271088(v.1); 0521359406(v.2).

The Languages of Japan, by M. Shibatani. 1990. £50. ISBN: 0521369185.

The Indo-Aryan languages, by C.P. Masica. 1991. £80. ISBN: 0521234204.

The Celtic languages, ed. by D. Macauley. 1992. £60. ISBN: 0521231272.

The Romance languages, by R. Posner. 1996. £45. ISBN: 0521236541. *Class No:* 800(035)

[5113]

HORVATH, B.M. *and* **VAUGHAN, P. Community languages: a handbook.** Clevedon, Avon, Multilingual Matters, 1991. x,276p. £39. ISBN: 1853590916.

Sociolinguistic profiles of 58 languages spoken by immigrants to English-speaking countries, covering functions, historical development, relationships to other languages, and social evaluation. Profiles average 4p. and are each followed by 5-10 references. *Class No:* 800(035)

[5114]

Routledge language family descriptions. London, Routledge, 1990- (in progress).

A series which provides comprehensive accounts of the members of the major language families in a consistent format which allows comparative study, both within vols. and across the series. Both historical and descriptive aspects are covered, including phonology, morphology, syntax, lexis, semantics, dialectology and sociolinguistics. Each vol. contains bibliographies, tables, maps, charts, glossary and detailed index.

Titles published to date:

The Celtic languages, ed. by M.J. Ball and G.E. Jones. 1993. xi,682p. £85. ISBN: 0415010357.

The Slavonic languages, ed. by B. Comrie and G.G. Corbett. 1993. xiii,1078p. £85. ISBN: 0415047552.

The Germanic languages, ed. by E. König and J. van der Auwera. 1994. xv,631p. £85. ISBN: 041505768x.

The Romance languages, by M. Harris and N. Vincent. 2nd ed. 1997. xii,500p. £65. ISBN: 0415164176.

The Uralic languages, ed. by D. Abondolo. 1998. 648p. £85. ISBN: 041508198x.

The Indo-European languages, ed. by A.G. Ramat and P. Ramat. 1998. 552p. £95. ISBN: 04156449x.

The Dravidian languages, ed. by S. Steever. 1998. 464p. £95. ISBN: 0415100232).

The Semitic languages, ed. by R. Hetzron. 1998. 592p. £125. (ISBN: 0415057671).

The Turkic languages, ed. by L. Johanson and E. Csato. 1998. 504p. £95. (ISBN: 0415082005). *Class No:* 800(035)

[5115]

VAN OSTERMANN, G.F. Manual of foreign languages for the use of librarians, research workers, editors, translators and printers. 4th ed., rev. and enl. New York, Central Book Co., 1952. 414p. illus.

3rd ed. Washington, D.C., Government Printing Office, 1936. The 4th ed. adds Estonian and tables of languages and monies of the world.

Some 130 languages and dialects are covered, the main

....*(contd.)*

sequence (A-Z), being followed by sections on American-Indian (p.295-334) and African languages (p.335-414), with native scripts where not Roman. For major languages, information is provided on the following points: alphabet (with pronunciation); capitalization; syllabification; abbreviations; accentuation; word formation; gender; articles; adjectives; nouns; pronouns; verbs; cardinal numbers; ordinal numbers; months; days; seasons; time; articles to be disregarded in filing. Some languages are sketchily treated. Thus, Arabic receives only 2p., not even the Arabic numerals being included. Selected library and bibliographical terms in 36 languages are given in the preliminaries.

Long overdue new ed. announced by Bowker-Saur for Spring 1999 (ISBN: 1857392418). *Class No:* 800(035)

Yearbooks & Directories

[5116]

Language industries atlas. Hearn, P.M. *and* Button, D.F., *eds.* Amsterdam & Washington, IOS Press, 1994. xviii,406p. $86.25. ISBN: 9051991487.

A new directory based on information collected by survey (and therefore not comprehensive) covering the US, Europe (especially EC countries) and Japan. Sections include: language organizations; standardization bodies; teaching and learning; language planning; research institutes; linguistic resources; conferences; amd publications. Indexes of titles and corporate names, countries, and abbbreviations.
Class No: 800(058)

[5117]

Language International world directory of sociolinguistic and language planning organizations. Domínguez, F. *and* López, N., *eds.* Amsterdam, Benjamins, 1995. xx,530p. Hfl.220. ISBN: 9027219516.

For each organization, provides full addresses and contact details, plus information on activities, programmes, publications, work in progress and future plans.

Cat. *Class No:* 800(058)

Maps & Atlases

[5118]

Atlas of the world's languages. Moseley, C. *and* Asher, R.E., *eds.* London, Routledge, 1993. viii,372p. 135 maps. £395. ISBN: 0415019257.

An ambitious attempt to map the locations of every living language on earth, including many that are on the point of extinction. Arranged in 8 regional sections, each edited by acknowledged experts, which include introductory article on the linguistic history of the area; detailed sociolinguistic and statistical data; exceptionally clear, full-colour maps with colour keys; and bibliography. Index of over 4,000 languages. Although 'there is no remotely comparable alternative' (*Reference Reviews*, v.9(1), 1995, p.19-20), this is for highly specialized collections only. According to *RQ* (v.34(2), Winter 1994, p.235-6), 'there are substantial errors in the North America subsection' which have been acknowledged by the publisher. *Class No:* 800(084.3)

[5119]

—The Atlas of languages: the origin and development of anguages throughout the world. Comrie, B., *& others, consultant eds*. New York, Facts on File, 1996; London, Bloomsbury, 1997. 224p. illus. £25. ISBN: 0816033889, US; 0747532311, UK.

Like De Agostini's *Atlas of literature* (*q.v.*), a misleadingly titled work of limited value for reference work, the maps being few (30-plus) in number. Explains the history and current distribution of the world's languages in 6 geographical chapters, plus 2 others on creoles and writing systems, the latter being the most detailed and useful. Lavishly illustrated with colour photographs of artefacts, manuscripts, monuments, etc., as well as tables and diagrams. Brief glossary and bibliography. Index. More an encyclopedia than an atlas and poor value in comparison with Crystal's *Cambridge encyclopedia of language*.
Class No: 800(084.3)

Europe

[5120]

POGARELL, R. Minority languages in Europe: a classified bibliography. Berlin, Mouton, 1983. vi,208p. DM.94. ISBN: 3110097834.

Over 2,400 numbered titles are listed A-Z by author/editor. No annotations, so good linguistic knowledge required as the titles are in a wide range of languages. Index 1 has languages, regions and states; Index 2 has keywords, *e.g.* bilingualism, interference, media. Compiler admits deficiences in coverage of Eastern Europe.
Class No: 800(4)

Great Britain

[5121]

Language in the British Isles. Trudgill, P., *ed.* Cambridge, Cambridge Univ. Press, 1984. xii,587p. ISBN: 0521240573.

A survey of the current linguistic situation in the British Isles, with 33 signed chapters (by 28 specialists) arranged in 4 sections: 1. English - 2. Celtic languages - 3. Other languages - 4. The Sociolinguistic situation. Each chapter has a bibliography. Particularly valuable for its coverage of languages and dialects on which there is little information generally available, *e.g.* Manx English; Channel Islands French; Orkney and Shetland Norn; Romani. Glossary (8p.). Indexes of topics and places. *Class No:* 800(410)

USA

[5122]

Language in the USA. Ferguson, C.A. *and* Heath, S.B., *eds.* Cambridge, Cambridge Univ. Press, 1981. xxxviii,592p. £85. ISBN: 0521298342.

Contains 23 specially-commissioned studies on the current language situation in the US, arranged in 4 sections: 1. American English - 2. Language before English (*e.g.* American Indian languages, New World Spanish) - 3. Languages after English (*e.g.* Slavic languages, Italian) - 4. Language in use (*e.g.* bilingualism, legal language). Has reference value for its statistical data, maps, tables, etc.; the notes on further reading following each essay; and the extensive bibliography (42p.). Glossary (7p.). Index. 29 contributors. *Class No:* 800(73)

Australia

[5123]

Language in Australia Romaine, S., *ed.* Cambridge, Cambridge Univ. Press, 1991. xviii,415p. ISBN: 0521327865.

'The purpose ... is to provide a comprehensive account of the present linguistic situation in Australia, primarily from a sociolinguistic perspective' (*Preface*). Historical introduction by the editor, followed by 25 essays by different contributors on aboriginal languages, pidgins and creoles, varieties of English, other European languages, and sociolinguistic issues. Many maps and tables. Substantial bibliography (28p.). Indexes of topics and place-names.
Class No: 800(94)

Translation & Translators

Bibliographies

[5124]

COLLECTIF DE L'ÉCOLE DE TRADUCTEURS ET D'INTERPRÈTES. Bibliographie du traducteur / Translator's bibliography. Ottawa, Les Presses de l'Université d'Ottawa, 1987. xiii,332p. ISBN: 2760301206.

Supersedes J. Delisle and L. Albert's *Guide bibliographique du traducteur, rédacteur et terminologue/ Bibliographic guide for translators, writers and terminologists* (Ottawa, 1979).

Lists over 2,000 books and articles in 6 sections: 1. Translation, interpretation, terminology - 2. French - 3. English - 4. Bilingual dictionaries - 5. Spanish - 6. Special dictionaries (90 subjects). Author index. New to this ed. are the section on Spanish and a major subsection on law dictionaries. *Class No:* 800:651.926(01)

Encyclopaedias & Dictionaries

[5125]

Routledge encyclopedia of translation studies. Baker, M., *ed.* London, Routledge, 1998. xviii,680p. £100. ISBN: 0415093805.

The first ever encyclopedia of translation studies is in 2 parts: Part 1, General, covers the conceptual framework of the discipline, with *c.*80 entries (average 3½p.) on central issues in translation theory (*e.g.* 'Equivalence'); terms which have a specific meaning in translation studies ('Paraphrase'); approaches to translation ('Semiotic approaches'); types of translation and interpreting ('Subtitling'); genres ('Poetry translation') and the translation of specific works ('Bible'). Part 2, History and traditions, has longer articles (average 9½p.) surveying the development of translation in 29 countries/regions. All entries are signed (over 90 contributors from 30 countries) and include cross-references and suggestions for further reading. Bibliography (56p.). Index. *Class No:* 800:651.926(03)

[5126]

—SHUTTLEWORTH, M. *and* COWIE, M. Dictionary of translation studies Manchester, St. Jerome, 1997. xvii,233p. £19.50. ISBN: 1900650037.

Over 300 entries on key terms and concepts (*e.g.* 'Equivalence', 'Refraction'), types of activity ('Signed language interpreting', 'Machine translation') and schools and approaches ('Leipzig school', 'Skopos theory'). Entries include definition, explanation, discussion of relevant viewpoints, and suggestions for further reading. Extensive bibliography. *Class No:* 800:651.926(03)

Handbooks & Manuals

[5127]

The Translator's handbook. Owens, R., *ed.* 3rd ed. London, Aslib, 1996. viii,328p. £38. ISBN: 0851423523.

1st ed. 1983; 2nd ed. 1989.

Completely revised under a new editor, with the following contributed chapters: 1. Introductory survey - 2. Training - 3. Careers - 4. Organisations for translators - 5. Working procedures, quality and quality assurance - 6. Providing quality and value - 7. Educating the client - 8. Raising the profile of translation and translators - 9. Operating in a mature market - 10. Basic tools of the trade - 11. Terminology management systems - 12. Machine translation - 13. New technology for translators. List of FIT members and associates. Index. *Class No:* 800:651.926(035)

Reviews & Abstracts

[5128]

Translation studies abstracts. Laviosa, S., *ed.* Manchester, St. Jerome, 1998-. v.1-. 2py.

Proclaimed by the publishers as the first abstracting service of its kind, this serial will cover all aspects of research within translation studies, including translation theory, interpreting, history of translation, corpus-based studies, literary translation, machine-aided translation, terminology, etc. Will include abstracts of articles from journals and collections, in a classified arrangement with author index. In addition, subscribers are promised an annual *Bibliography of translation studies.*
Class No: 800:651.926(048)

Yearbooks & Directories

[5129]

Directory of translators and translating agencies in the United Kingdom. Morris, P. *and* Weston, G., *eds.* 2nd ed. London, Bowker-Saur, 1990. viii,299p. ISBN: 0862912776.

1st ed. Beverley, Merton Press, 1987, as *Register of translators and translating agencies in the United Kingdom.*

1. Individual translators, A-Z, has over 750 entries giving name, professional qualifications, address, telephone, fax and E-mail numbers, languages covered, subject specialisms, availability of interpreting services and any other relevant information provided by the translator - 2. Agencies, A-Z, gives similar information for *c.*150 agencies - 3. Index of subject specialisms (Abrasives to Zoology via Footwear and Real Estate) - 4. Index of 55 languages (Afrikaans to Welsh via Faroese and Putonghua), further divided by geographical area - 5. Agencies translating most languages. Entries based on returns from a questionnaire distributed May 1989, with all entries from 1st ed. updated.

Very useful for business information services when first published, but does not appear to have been updated since 2nd ed. *Class No:* 800:651.926(058)

[5130]

INSTITUTE OF LINGUISTS. Directory: registers of translators, interpreters and tutors/trainers. London, The Institute, 1990-. Biennial.

Lists over *c.*6,500 fellows, members, and associates in 3 separate registers arranged by language and subject, followed by full A-Z list with addresses. Geographical index.
Class No: 800:651.926(058)

[5131]

INSTITUTE OF TRANSLATION AND INTERPRETING. Directory of translators and interpreters. London, ITI, 1989-. Annual. ISSN: 09612084.

Formerly known as *Index of members.*

1996 ed. (*c.*350p.) lists 1,442 members and associates of ITI, giving qualifications, full address, equipment available and languages and subjects covered. Separate indexes by language for translators and interpreters.
Class No: 800:651.926(058)

[5132]

Language International world directory of translation and interpreting schools. Harris, B., *comp.* Amsterdam, Benjamins, 1997. xii,238p. $95. ISBN: 9027219524.

Provides details on 243 courses worldwide, listing full addresses, names of teachers, languages taught, teaching methods, etc. *Class No:* 800:651.926(058)

Biographies

[5133]

VAN HOOF, H. Dictionnaire universel des traducteurs. Génève, Slatkine, 1993. ISBN: 2051012105.

Lists translators of all countries, from Plautus and Cicero to the present day. Most subjects are literary translators, but contemporary practitioners in commercial and technical fields are also included, as are teachers and theorists of translation. 'A glorious monument to a hundred generations of translators' (*Language International*, v.6(2), 1994, p.37-8.). *Class No:* 800:651.926(092)

Bilingualism

[5134]

Bibliographie internationale sur le bilinguisme / International bibliography on bilingualism. MacKey, W.F., *ed.* Québec, Presses de l'Université de Laval, 1972. xxviii,752p. (2nd ed. 1982. ISBN: 2763769918).

An author bibliography, 1940-70, of more than 11,000 unannotated items on bilingualism (*i.e.* primary bilingualism, not the bilingualism acquired through learning a second language). French and English indexes of languages, countries and subjects. *Class No:* 800.732

[5135]

International handbook of bilingual education. Paulston, C.B., *ed.* Westport, Conn., Greenwood, 1988. 614p. $135. ISBN: 0313244847.

Presents the basic facts about language and language families in the world and illustrates the range of possibilities of languages in contact. Much of the work is devoted to a series of 24 case studies of bilingualism/multilingualism within nation states, each containing suggestions for further reading. Glossary. Bibliographic essay. *Class No:* 800.732

Classification

[5136]

KLOSE, A. Languages of the world: a multilingual concordance of languages, dialects and language-families/ Sprachen der Welt: ein weltweiter Index der Sprachfamilien, Einzelsprachen und Dialekte, mit Angabe der Synonyma und fremdsprachigen Äquivalente. Munich and London, K.G. Saur, 1987. xlviii,410p. £125. ISBN: 359810443x.

The purpose is to 'identify languages and dialects, to classify them, and if necessary to determine the correct spelling' (*Introduction*). The work consists of a single sequence of names of languages and dialects, A-Z, with

.... *(contd.)*
synonyms cross-referenced. German forms of names are favoured, with English, French, and Russian (transliterated) forms also given. Does a similar job to the index of Voegelin and Voegelin (*q.v.*), but that work provides a lot more information on the languages. *Class No:* 800.8

[5137]

LYOVIN, A. An Introduction to the languages of the world. Oxford, Oxford Univ. Press, 1997. 510p. maps. £41.99. ISBN: 0195081153.

1. Classification of languages - 2. Classification of writing systems - 3. Languages of Europe - 4. Languages of Asia - 5. Languages of Oceania - 6. Native languages of the Americas - 7. Pidgins and creoles. *Class No:* 800.8

[5138]

RUHLEN, M. A Guide to the world's languages, vol. 1: Classification. London, Arnold, 1987. xxv,433p. maps. £49.95. ISBN: 0713165030.

The first of a 3-vol. set. Introductory chapter on principles and methods of genetic classification, followed by chapters on Europe, Africa, Asia, Oceania, America, and prospects for future research, each with appended bibliography. Final chapter is a complete classification of the world's 5,000 languages within 17 families and thousands of subgroups (104p.). Numerous lists, tables, figures, and maps. Indexes of personal names, language groups, and languages. Vols. 2 and 3 will cover language data and language universals. 'It is interesting to read, well-documented and thorough, and is useful as a work of reference' (*Modern Language Review,* v.85(1), Jan. 1990, p.124-25). *Class No:* 800.8

[5139]

VOEGELIN, C.F. *and* **VOEGELIN, F.M. Classification and index of the world's languages.** New York, Elsevier, 1977. 658p. ISBN: 0444001557.

'Based in part upon our earlier survey of the literature, *Languages of the world,* published as twenty separate numbers of the journal *Anthropological Linguistics* (1964-66)' (*Acknowledgements*).

Arranged by language groups, A-Z, then by 'genetic unit'. Under each unit are entries for individual languages, giving all spellings, names of dialects, geographical distribution, and numbers of speakers. List of references (25p.). Comprehensive index of names of groups, languages, dialects and tribes, with over 20,000 entries.
Class No: 800.8

Child Language

[5140]

The Handbook of child language. Fletcher, P. *and* MacWhinney, B., *eds.* London, Blackwell, 1995. x,786p. £70. (*Blackwell handbooks in linguistics.*) ISBN: 0631184058.

25 signed chapters (average 27p.), with numbered subsections, giving a comprehensive overview of current thinking on all aspects of child language development, plus a very comprehensive bibliography (88p.). Index.
Class No: 800.863

[5141]

HIGGINSON, R. *and* **MacWHINNEY, B. CHILDES/BIB:** an annotated bibliography of child language and language disorders. Hillsdale, NJ, Erlbaum, 1991. 1176p. $200. ISBN: 0805808590.

CHILDES stands for Child Language Data Exchange System.

Over 7,500 references to books and journal articles published over more than 100 years, covering not only language acquisition but also bilingualism, second languages, cognition, and atypical populations. Arranged by author with subject and author indexes. All entries have keyword annotations and many include lengthier abstracts.

1994 Supplement (693p. $125. ISBN: 0805814787) and *1997 Supplement* (680p. $150. ISBN: 0805824111) add a further 3,000 and 2,700 references respectively. Latest vol. includes a categorical listing of the complete set of keywords used in the bibliography.

Also available online (http://psyscope.psy.cmu.edu/childes). *Class No:* 800.863

Dialects

[5142]

Dialektologie: ein Handbuch zur deutschen und allgemeinen Dialektforschung. Besch, W., *and others, eds.* Berlin, de Gruyter, 1982-83. 2v. (xxxiv,1714p.). DM.1,155. (*Handbücher zur Sprach- und Kommunikationswissenschaft.*) ISBN: 3110059770, v.1; 3110095718, v.2.

102 signed chapters in 15 sections, offering a detailed survey of general and German dialectology. Well organized, with numbered paragraphs and numerous maps, charts and tables. Extensive chapter bibliographies. Index.
Class No: 800.87

Pidgin/Creole Languages

[5143]

A Bibliography of pidgin and creole languages. Reinecke, J.E., *and others, comps.* Honolulu, Univ. Press of Hawaii, 1975. lxxii,804p. ISBN: 082480306x.

Over 11,000 entries in 120 sections. First 2 sections cover bibliographies and collective works, then the rest are devoted to individual languages or groups of languages. Introduction to each section, then entries A-Z by author with concise annotations. 3 indexes: authors; Christian scriptures; anonymous titles. *Class No:* 800.88

[5144]

HOLM, J. Pidgins and creoles. Cambridge, Cambridge Univ. Press, 1988-89. 2v. (*Cambridge language surveys.*)

V.1 *Theory and structure.* 1988. xix,257p. £19.95. ISBN: 0521271088.

V.2 *Reference survey.* 1989. xxi,259-704p. £17.95. ISBN: 0521359406.

A very comprehensive, well-documented survey. V.1 has a comparative study of African and Caribbean creoles based on European languages, with chapters on lexicosemantics, phonology and syntax, plus a historical overview of theory.

V.2 provides a great deal of information on all known pidgins and creoles (about 100), grouped according to the language on which they are based (Portuguese, Spanish, Dutch, French, English, African languages, other languages). The section on each one discusses its salient linguistic features and presents a brief text with a morpheme-by-morpheme translation. Extensive bibliography (53p. in all) and index in each vol. 11 maps. *Class No:* 800.88

[5145]

TODD, L. Pidgins and creoles. 2nd ed. London, Routledge, 1990. x,117p. £12.99. ISBN: 0415053110.

1st ed. 1974.

A concise survey of English-based creoles in 6 chapters. Appendices include list of creoles with details of their geographical spread and 10 sample texts. Substantial bibliography (10p.). Index. *Class No:* 800.88

Artificial Languages

[5146]

ALBANI, P. *and* BUONARROTI, B. Aga Magera difure: dizionario delle lingue immaginarie. Bologna, Zanichelli, 1994. 478p. illus. ISBN: 8808095940.

An encyclopedia of artificial and imaginary languages and their creators. Bibliography (28p.). Cross-references but no index. *Class No:* 800.89

[5147]

Interlingua-English: a dictionary of the international language, prepared by the research staff of the (International Auxiliary Language) Association. Gode, A., *ed.* New York, Storm, 1951. (repr. New York, Ungar, 1971). lxiv,415p.

The first dictionary of Interlingua, a language based on words common to English and the Romance languages. The companion vol. is W.W. Bryne's *A Concise English-Interlingua dictionary* (New York, Storm, 1958. 84p.), with c.6,800 entries. *Class No:* 800.89

[5148]

LARGE, A. The Artificial language movement. London, Blackwell, 1985. x,239p. illus. (*The Language library*.) ISBN: 0631144978.

4 chapters on the history of artificial languages and 3 on their status in the contemporary world. Appendices include the 16 rules of Esperanto grammar and comparative texts in English and 5 artificial languages. References (16p.). Select bibliography (12p.). Index. *Class No:* 800.89

Esperanto

[5149]

BUTLER, M.C. Esperanto-English dictionary. London, British Esperanto Assoc., 1967. 450p. £9.60. ISBN: 0902756095.

The fullest Esperanto-English dictionary; based on E.A. Millidge's *The Esperanto-English dictionary* (1912; 5th ed., 1924) and replacing it. About 11,000 entries. Includes many idioms; terms are categorized. Officialized roots appear in capitals as entry words. Appendices cover proper names, place-names, personal names, etc. Preface has handy notes on formation of compound words, root endings, etc.
Class No: 800.892

[5150]

FORSTER, P.G. The Esperanto movement. The Hague, Mouton, 1982. xiv,413p. DM120. ISBN: 9027933995.

A revised version of a doctoral thesis, 'A Sociological study of the Esperanto movement', accepted by Hull University, 1977.

A very detailed study, with 9 chapters on the world Esperanto movement and 3 on Esperanto in Britain. Bibliographic references after each chapter. 51 tables of statistical information. Glossary (5p.). Classified bibliography (14p.). *Class No:* 800.892

[5151]

FULCHER, F. *and* LONG, B. English-Esperanto dictionary. 3rd ed. Rickmansworth, Herts., Esperanto Publishing Co., 1963 (repr. 1985. xvi,332p. £7.90.

1st ed. 1921.

Over 30,000 entry-words, with equivalents. Appended lists of proper names and neologisms. *Class No:* 800.892

[5152]

Plena ilustrita vortaro de Esperanto. Waringhien, G., *ed.* Represo de la tria eldono, kun suplemento. Paris, Sennacieca Asucio Tutmonda, 1987. xxxvii,1348p.

3rd ed. of a comprehensive Esperanto-Esperanto dictionary compiled by a large team of subject specialists. c.18,000 entry-words in main sequence, plus 500 in supplement, including many technical terms and proper names. Graphic symbols indicate the subject field to which each term belongs. Numerous illustrative sentences. Scientific tables. 30 Duden-style pages illustrating specialist vocabulary. *Class No:* 800.892

[5153]

WELLS, J.C. Concise Esperanto and English dictionary: Esperanto-English / English-Esperanto. Reprint of 1969 ed. London, Hodder, 1992. ix,419p. £9.99. (*Teach yourself books*.) ISBN: 0340583541.

Originally published London, English Univs. Press, 1969, as *The E.U.P. concise Esperanto and English dictionary*.

Has c.9000 entries in the first section and c.19,500 in the second. Based largely on the *Plena vortaro* (4th ed., with Supplement, 1954). Useful guide to pronunciation and summary of grammar (35p.). *Class No:* 800.892

Sign Language

[5154]

COSTELLO, E. Random House American Sign Language dictionary. New York, Random House, 1994. 1067p. $55. ISBN: 0394585801.

Defines and illustrates over 5,600 ASL signs, using high-quality drawings. *Class No:* 800.95

[5155]

Dictionary of British sign language / English, compiled for the British Deaf Association by the Deaf Studies Research Unit, University of Durham. Brien, D., *ed.* London, Faber, 1992. xxxiv,1084p. illus. £27.50. ISBN: 0571143466.

The main section (p.135-854) of this first major dictionary of British sign language has 1,800 numbered entries, with photographs on left-hand pages and detailed descriptions of how to make the signs, plus glosses, on the right. English-BSL index (p.856-1084). Detailed explanation of how to use the dictionary (26p.). Introductory essay on 'The Visual world of Britsh sign language' (133p.). 'This must surely be the definitive work in its field' (*Reference Reviews*, v.7(7), p.18). *Class No:* 800.95

[5156]

Sign now! Sunbury-on-Thames, Microbooks, 1997. CD-ROM £59.

Multimedia dictionary of British Sign Language on CD-ROM, with over 3,500 signs. Zoom, freeze, enlarge and slow video. Internet ready for connection to World Wide Web sites on hearing impairment.

Microbooks also publish *ISL dictionary* (£49), an Irish Sign Language dictionary on CD-ROM, also with over 3,500 signs. *Class No:* 800.95

[5157]

STERNBERG, M.L.A. American sign language: a comprehensive dictionary. New York, Harper & Row, 1981. 1192p. illus. $75. ISBN: 0317349864.

About 5,000 definitions of signs, supported by *c.*8,000 drawings. Many cross-references. Subject index, plus indexes to signs in France, Germany, Italy, Spain, Portugal, Russia and Japan. 1,285 references. The US system of sign language is closely allied to the European continental one-handed method, unlike the English two-handed system.

A CD-ROM version is now available as *The American sign language dictionary on CD-ROM* (New York, HarperCollins Interactive, 1994. $69.95. ISBN: 0062790153). It covers fewer words and phrases than the printed work (*c.*2,200), but has the advantage of showing hand movements and facial expressions by means of video which can be slowed down or speeded up to suit the user.
Class No: 800.95

[5158]

WORLD FEDERATION OF THE DEAF. Gestuno: international sign language of the deaf. Carlisle, British Deaf Assoc., 1975. unpaged. illus. £15. ISBN: 0950418706.

Illustrations of 1,470 sign-language gestures, arranged in subject categories with French and English parallel text and indexes in each language. *Class No:* 800.95

Linguistics

Bibliographies

[5159]

Analecta linguistica: informational bulletin of linguistics. Budapest, Akademiai Kiado, 1971-92. 22v. ISSN: 00448176.

A bibliographical bulletin which appeared twice yearly, with sections on linguistic monographs (subdivided by language groups), tables of contents of linguistic journals (with Slavic journals in good evidence), special linguistic bibliographies, and an index of authors. *Class No:* 801(01)

[5160]

BÁEZ SAN JOSÉ, V., *& others*. Bibliografía de lingüística general y española (1964-1990). Alcalá de Henares, Universidad de Alcalá, 1995-7. v.1-3 (in progress). ISBN: 848138965x.

A very comprehensive classified bibliography of recent studies in general and Spanish linguistics, which will comprise 5 vols. The first 3 vols. have 51,000 entries.
Class No: 801(01)

[5161]

BEARD, R. *and* **SZYMANEK, B. Bibliography of morphology, 1960-1985.** Amsterdam, Benjamins, 1988. xiv,193p. Hfl.68. ISBN: 9027237425.

*c.*2,200 entries, with the emphasis on synchronic works of theoretical interest by European and North American specialists. Indexed by subject and language.
Class No: 801(01)

[5162]

Bibliographie linguistique de l'année.../ Linguistic bibliography for the year ..., and supplement for previous years. Published by the Permanent International Committee of Linguists under the auspices of the International Council of Philosophy and Humanistic Studies. 1939/47-. Utrecht, Spectrum, 1949-77; The Hague, Martinus Nijhoff, 1978-87; Dordrecht, Kluwer, 1988-. Annual. ISSN: 03784592.

A bibliography supported by UNESCO and compiled by over 30 scholars worldwide. The bibliography for 1994 (1997. lxxxvi,1312p.) has 21,412 unannotated entries. Classified arrangement, with general sections followed by sections on language groups, subdivided by individual languages. Section and subsection headings in French and English. Author index. Detailed table of contents, but the lack of a comprehensive subject index is a drawback. Also available on CD-ROM. *Class No:* 801(01)

[5163]

Bibliographie Linguistischer Literatur (BLL)/ Bibliography of linguistic literature (BLL), 1978-. Frankfurt am Main, Klostermann, 1979-. v.4-. Annual.

Subtitle: *Bibliographie zur allgemein Linguistik und zur anglistischen, germanistischen und romanistischen Linguistik.*

Continues from *Bibliographie unselbständiger Literatur-Linguistik (BUL-L)*, of which 3 vols. were published, 1976-78, covering 1971-75, 1976, and 1977.

A comprehensive, classified bibliography, originally of non-monographic works, arranged in 4 main sections covering general, German, English, and Romance linguistics, with numerous subsections. V.18, *1992* (1994. xl,753p.) has 15,688 unannotated entries, including some supplementary material from earlier years. All section and subdivision headings are given in German and English. List of over 900 periodicals and 139 collective works exploited. Subject and name index. Author index.

Available online via STN International (http://www.cas.org/stn.html), with more than 201,000 citations by June 1998. Updated every second month with *c.*1,650 citations. *Class No:* 801(01)

[5164]

DEMILLER, A.L. Linguistics: a guide to the reference literature. Englewood, Colo., Libraries Unlimited, 1991. xvi,256p. £42.95. (*Reference sources in the humanities.*) ISBN: 0872876926.

Lists major reference sources published 1957-89 in 3 sections: 1. General linguistics - 2. Allied areas (*e.g.* sociolinguistics, psycholinguistics) - 3. Languages (*i.e.* works covering individual languages or groups of languages). 708 numbered entries with lengthy, evaluative annotations. Concentrates mainly on English-language sources, but includes some important material in French, German and Russian. Author index. *Class No:* 801(01)

[5165]

FERNÁNDEZ, M. Diglossia: a comprehensive bibliography, 1960-1990, and supplements. Amsterdam, Benjamins, 1993. lii,472p. Hfl.190. (*Library and information sources in linguistics.*) ISBN: 9027237492.

Nearly 3,000 entries, including several dozen pre-1960 items and a substantial number from 1990-92. 6 indexes: languages; diglossia in literature; historically oriented works; pedagogically oriented works; theoretical works; theses and dissertations. *Class No:* 801(01)

[5166]

Francis 524: Sciences du langage. Paris, Centre National de la Recherche Scientifique, 1947-. Quarterly. ISSN: 11573740.

Previous titles: ***Bulletin signalétique: Philosophie; sciences humaines; Bulletin signalétique, Sec. 21: Sociologie, sciences du langage; Bulletin signalétique 24: Sciences du langage; Bulletin signalétique 524: Sciences du langage.***

Present title since 1968, when it changed from an international abstracting service to a bibliography. Classified arrangement with author and subject indexes. Available online via QUESTEL and on CD-ROM. *Class No:* 801(01)

[5167]

HEWES, G.W. Language origins: a bibliography. 2nd, rev. and enl. ed. The Hague, Mouton, 1975. 2v. (xiv,890p.). ISBN: 9027934010.

1st ed. 1971.

Lists *c.*11,000 items from a wide range of disciplines (*e.g.* psychology, anatomy, anthropology) in addition to linguistics. Arranged by author, with detailed subject index (79p.). *Class No:* 801(01)

[5168]

KÖHLER, R. Bibliography of quantitative linguistics. Amsterdam, Benjamins, 1995. xlv,780p. Hfl.230. ISBN: 9027237514.

Lists over 6,500 titles (in many languages and from many countries) from all areas of quantitative linguistic research. Several indexes: authors; keywords in titles; subject headings; uncontrolled vocabulary; languages; and reviewed publications. *Class No:* 801(01)

[5169]

Kontaktlinguistik: ein internationales Handbuch zeitgenössischer Forschung. Goebl, H., *& others, eds.* Berlin & New York, de Gruyter, 1996-7. 2v. maps. (*Handbücher zur Sprach- und Kommunikationswissenschaft.*)

V.1 gives an overview, in 115 signed chapters, of the current state of international research on language contact. V.2 has 124 chapters on language pairs in contact in Europe (*e.g.* English-Welsh, Finnish-Swedish). Chapters are in German, French or English and are well organized with numbered paragraphs, charts and tables. Substantial bibliographies throughout. Comprehensive indexes of names and subjects. *Class No:* 801(01)

[5170]

NUYTS, J. *and* **VERSCHUEREN, J. A Comprehensive bibliography of pragmatics.** Amsterdam, Benjamins, 1987. 4v. (xi,2197p.). Hfl.630. ISBN: 902722031x.

*c.*13,000 entries under authors, A-Z, in vols. 2-4, with indexes of subjects, words, languages, and persons in v.1. *Class No:* 801(01)

Encyclopaedias

[5171]

An Encyclopaedia of language. Collinge, N.E., *ed.* London and New York, Routledge, 1990. xvii,1011p. illus. £90. ISBN: 0415020646.

Not to be confused with Crystal's *Cambridge encyclopaedia of language* (*q.v.*), this is a survey of the current state of the various branches of linguistics. 26 signed essays by 29 scholars are arranged in 3 sections: A. The Inner nature of language (phonetics, semantics, etc.) - B. The Larger province of language (psycholinguistics, sociolinguistics, etc.) - C. Special aspects of language (sign language, language geography, etc.). Essays average 37p. and each has a substantial bibliography. *English Today* (no. 24, Oct. 1990, p.57-9) suggests that the editor should have done more to ensure that the different contributions were 'more evenly authoritative and uniformly comprehensive.' Index of topics and technical terms. Index of names. *Class No:* 801(031)

[5172]

Encyclopedic dictionary of the sciences of language. Ducrot, O. *and* Todorov, T., *eds.* Baltimore, Md., Johns Hopkins Univ. Press, 1979; Oxford, Blackwell, 1981. xiii,380p. $18.95. ISBN: 0801828570, US.

First published Paris, Éditions du Seuil, 1972, as *Dictionnaire encyclopédique des sciences du langage*. This translation, by C. Porter, based on 2nd ed., 1973, with text and bibliography substantially updated.

Defines *c.*800 linguistic terms within some 50 topical essays which are grouped in 4 main sections covering schools, fields, methodological concepts, and descriptive concepts. Sectional annotated bibliography. Index of terms defined. Author index.

Review of English Studies (v.35(138), Summer 1984, p.214-15) notes 'a very pronounced bias towards structualism of a continental European type' and suggests that the book 'represents the state of the art around 1965 rather than 1981'.

New French ed. Paris, Éditions du Seuil, 1995, as *Nouveau dictionnaire encyclopédique des sciences du langage* by O. Ducrot and J.-M. Schaeffer (670p. 2020144379). 60 essays with bibliography after each subsection of each chapter. Many new terms defined. Indexes of terms and authors. *Class No:* 801(031)

[5173]

International encyclopedia of linguistics. Bright, W., *ed.* New York, Oxford Univ. Press, 1991. 4v. illus. maps. £295. ISBN: 0195051963.

A major reference work compiled by over 400 contributors (most of them based in North America), under the direction of 25 topic editors, and covering all aspects of contemporary linguistics. The 750 entries, which assume a basic competence in linguistics, are arranged A-Z and fall into 3 categories: lengthy, signed essays (up to 5,000 words) on major topics (*e.g.* Phonetics); shorter essays (also signed) on more specific topics and on languages or language families; and shorter, unsigned articles on minor languages. Most entries have bibliographies and those on languages and language families are followed by very useful 'language lists' giving geographical, statistical and sociolinguistic information. Well illustrated with maps, tables, charts, etc. Glossary of linguistic terms (76p.). Extensive cross-references, synoptic table of contents and detailed index (104p.) provide full access. 'A magnificent example of how a major work of reference that will be used by countless people over many years should be designed (*Language International*, v.4(6), 1992, p.40-41). *Class No:* 801(031)

[5174]

The Linguistics encyclopedia. Malmkjaer, K., *ed.* London, Routledge, 1991. xx,575p. illus. £75. ISBN: 0415029422.

Over 80 lengthy entries (average 6p.), by a team of 26 international specialists, on major and subsidiary areas of linguistic study, with applied linguistics (*e.g.* lexicography, speech therapy) particularly well covered. Entries are arranged A-Z, are extensively cross-referenced and followed by suggestions for further reading. Many are illustrated by diagrams and tables. Bibliography (39p.). Index. *Class No:* 801(031)

Handbooks & Manuals

[5175]

COULMAS, F., ***ed.*** **The Handbook of sociolinguistics.** London, Blackwell, 1996. 544p. £75. (*Blackwell handbooks in linguistics.*) ISBN: 0631193391.

28 newly-commissioned essays by international specialists, providing an up-to-date overview of this specialist branch of linguistics. 4 main parts: 1. Foundations - 2. Social dimensions of language - 3. Linguistic dimensions of society - 4. Applied issues. Extensive bibliography.

Class No: 801(035)

Dictionaries

[5176]

BUSSMANN, H., & ***others.*** **Routledge dictionary of language and linguistics.** London, Routledge, 1996. xxiv,530p. illus. £75. ISBN: 0415022258.

An adaptation by a team of over 30 scholars of Bussmann's *Lexikon der Sprachwissenschaft* (2nd ed. Stuttgart, 1990), with 2,500 entries (A-Z) for key terms, concepts and themes in over 30 subdisciplines of linguistics. Entries include definitions, cross-references, English examples and many suggestions for further reading. For major languages, lists of dictionaries, grammars, journals, bibliographies and histories are provided. Cumulative bibliography. 'One of the best one-volume linguistics dictionaries available' (*Choice*, v.34(4), Dec. 1996, p.587).

Class No: 801(038)

[5177]

CHALKER, S. ***and*** **WEINER, E.S.C. The Oxford dictionary of English grammar.** Oxford, Clarendon Press, 1994. x,448p. £6.99. ISBN: 0198613148.

Offers much wider coverage than the title suggests, listing and defining *c.*1,000 terms used in the study of grammar and other aspects of linguistics, such as phonetics, semantics and lexicology. Most entries include examples of language in use and some have quotations from grammar texts. Distinguishes between British and American uses of terms. List of over 150 works cited. Fully cross-referenced.

Class No: 801(038)

[5178]

CRYSTAL, D. A Dictionary of linguistics and phonetics. 4th ed. Oxford, Blackwell, 1997. xvii,426p. £50. ISBN: 0631200967.

1st ed. London, Deutsch, 1980, as *A First dictionary of linguistics and phonetics*; 3rd ed. Blackwell, 1991.

A well-established dictionary with over 1,400 main entries, covering a total of *c.*4,000 linguistic terms. Entries comprise definition, explanation and examples. Clearly laid out, with ample cross-references. 4th ed. incorporates new terms or senses which have developed during the 1990s, but the bibliography of standard textbooks has been dropped.

Class No: 801(038)

[5179]

Sprachwissenschaftliches Wörterbuch. Knobloch, J., *and others, eds.* Heidelberg, Winter, 1961-98. v.1, fasc.1 - v.2, fasc.3 (in progress).

A scholarly and well-documented dictionary of terms used in general and comparative linguistics, with the emphasis on German practice. Gives German equivalents for terms in other languages and equivalents in major languages for many German terms.

V.1 (in 11 fascicules, 1961-86) covers A-E.

Class No: 801(038)

[5180]

TRASK, R.L. A Dictionary of grammatical terms in linguistics. London, Routledge, 1993. ix,335p. £14.99 ISBN: 0415086280.

A specialized work intended primarily for students and teachers of linguistics, which concentrates exclusively on the terminology of grammar (mainly syntax, and to a lesser extent morphology). Lists 1,500 terms with pronunciation (IPA), definition and examples. Original sources are identified for many terms and further reading is suggested for the more important ones. Bibliography (25p.).

Class No: 801(038)

Reviews & Abstracts

[5181]

Linguistics abstracts. London, Blackwell, 1985-. v.1, no. 1-. Quarterly. ISSN: 02675498.

Covers the theory and practice of general linguistics, but not applied linguistics. Each issue has *c.*120 abstracts in a classified arrangement, with author and subject indexes. Cumulative indexes in 4th issue of each year. Over 140 periodicals analyzed. Also available online.

Class No: 801(048)

[5182]

Linguistics and language behavior abstracts (LLBA). San Diego, Calif., Sociological Abstracts Inc., 1967-. v.1, no.1-. 5py. ISSN: 08888027.

Vols. 1-18 (1967-84) entitled *Language and language behaviour abstracts.*

A leading abstracting journal in the field, covering 1,800 international periodicals in a wide range of disciplines, including anthropology, education, medicine, psychology and philosophy, as well as those devoted solely to linguistics. Also includes citations for monographs, reports, dissertations and book reviews.

V.32(1), Feb. 1998, has 2,078 abstracts under 29 subject headings with many subdivisions, followed by author index, source publication index and subject index, entries in the latter including brief abstracts of the abstracts. Bibliography of book reviews has 780 entries.

Available on CD-ROM from 1973 to the present and also available through the Internet Database Service from Cambridge Scientific Abstracts (contact sales@csa.com). The database contains over 225,000 records at June 1998, with over 12,000 added annually. *Class No:* 801(048)

Histories

[5183]

History of linguistics. Lepschy, G., *ed.* London, Longman, 1994- . V.1- (in progress).

Originally published in Italian, 1990, as *Storia della linguistica.*

V.1 *The Eastern traditions of linguistics.* 1994. xx,203p. £12.99. ISBN: 0582094895.

V.2 *Classical and medieval linguistics.* 1994. xx,380p. £46. ISBN: 0582094909.

V.3 *Renaissance and early modern Europe.* 1997. 256p. £40. ISBN: 0582094925.

V.4 *Nineteenth century linguistics.* 1998. 464p. £45. ISBN: 0582294770.

'A history of linguistic thought, rather than an account of the development of linguistic science' (*Introduction*), comprising signed, well-organized sections by 16 international scholars covering different societies and different periods. Comprehensive sectional bibliographies.

.... (contd.)
Index in each vol.

V.1 has sections on Chinese, Indian, Near Eastern, Hebrew and Arabic linguistics. V.2 covers Greek, Latin and medieval linguistics. *Class No:* 801(091)

[5184]
KOERNER, E.F.K. Western histories of linguistic thought: an annotated chronological bibliography, 1822-1976. Amsterdam, Benjamins, 1976. ix,113p. Hfl.63. (*Studies in the history of linguistics.*) ISBN: 9027209529.

Over 400 entries in 3 period divisions (1822-1915; 1916-61; 1962-76) plus Addenda. Author index.
Class No: 801(091)

[5185]
ROBINS, R.H. A Short history of linguistics. 4th ed. Harlow, Longman, 1997. 304p. £17.99. ISBN: 0582249945.

1st ed. 1967; 3rd ed. 1990.

A survey in 9 chapters from Ancient Greece to the present, with extensive lists of references and suggestions for further reading after each chapter. Index. 4th ed. has 2 new chapters replacing the previous one on the 20th century.
Class No: 801(091)

Biographies

[5186]
Lexicon grammaticorum: who's who in the history of world linguistics. Stammerjohann, H., *ed.* Tübingen, Niemeyer, 1996. xxvii,1047p. DM586. ISBN: 3484730188.

Biobibliographical entries by over 400 contributors on key linguistic scholars of all periods. Despite the title, living linguists are not included and the lack of indexes is disappointing. *Class No:* 801(092)

Dictionaries

Bibliographies

[5187]
Catalog of dictionaries, word books, and philological texts, 1440-1900: inventory of the Cordell Collection, Indiana State University. Vancil, D.E., *ed.* Westport, Conn., Greenwood, 1993. 448p. $85. (*Bibliographies and indexes in library & information science.*) ISBN: 0313287007.

Provides access to the world's largest collection of dictionaries, with over 5,100 pre-1901 titles and several thousand more from the 20th century. Interfiles foreign and English-language materials in main name sequence, with indexes of dates, languages and subjects.
Class No: 801.3(01)

[5188]
COLLISON, R.L. Dictionaries of English and foreign languages: a bibliographical guide to both general and technical dictionaries, with historical and explanatory notes and references. 2nd ed., rev. and enl. New York, Hafner, 1971. xvii,303p. ISBN: 0028431103.

1st ed. 1955, as *Dictionaries of foreign languages.*

About 2,000 items, based on the Univ. of California, Los Angeles, collections. Chapters 1-11 (p.1-181) deal with dictionaries by language groups, working from the more familiar (*e.g.* French, German) to the lesser known (*e.g.* African, Asian), with brief comments. Etymological, dialect, slang, period and bilingual language dictionaries are included. Chapter 12: Dictionaries of the English language, to 1753; 13. The modern English dictionary; 14: Dictionaries of the Celtic languages; 15: Dictionaries of

.... (contd.)
comparative philology. Unannotated list of technical dictionaries (p.227-60) and a general bibliography (p.261-63) are appended. Index of authors, subjects, languages, dialects, titles and sub-titles.

Collison's *A History of foreign dictionaries* (London, Deutsch, 1982. 214p. ISBN: 0233973109) has 14 chronological chapters, from the 4th century BC to 1980, brief chronology, bibliography (6p.), and detailed index.
Class No: 801.3(01)

[5189]
DALBY, A. A Guide to world language dictionaries. London, Library Assoc., 1998. 480p. £59.95. ISBN: 1856042510.

An ambitious attempt to provide 'a guide to the cream among language dictionaries, the ones that are of serious research use and are likely to remain so' (*Introduction*). Wisely sticks to *language* dictionaries, unlike Kabdebo (*q.v.*), and covers *c.*350 languages, A-Z. For each, the most important dictionaries are listed in numbered entries with full bibliographical details and evaluative comments. For many languages there are notes on history and distribution, and, where appropriate, a chart is included to show the script, transliteration and the alphabetical order used in dictionaries. For major languages, several dictionaries are listed (*e.g.* 28 for Arabic) under up to 7 subheadings: 1. Historical dictionaries - 2. The Modern standard - 3. Older periods - 4. Regional forms - 5. Slang and special vocabularies - 6. Etymological dictionaries - 7. Other works of interest. Covers language families as well as individual languages, with cross-references to family members and entries for comparative dictionaries and works on sub-groups. Index of personal names and book titles. A very impressive work which is likely to remain a valuable source for linguists and librarians for many years. *Class No:* 801.3(01)

[5190]
Dictionaries, encyclopedias and other word-related books. Brewer, A.M., *ed.* Detroit, Gale, 1988. 2v. ISBN: 0810304406.

1st ed. 1975; 3rd ed. 1982.

Provides reproductions of Library of Congress cards for *c.*35,000 titles. Main entry at 030(01). *Class No:* 801.3(01)

[5191]
GRANT & CUTLER LTD. Foreign language dictionaries: specialist and general, 1997-1998. London, Grant & Cutler, 1997. 152p.

A catalogue from the UK's largest foreign-language bookshop, listing *c.*1,000 specialist dictionaries between English and the main European languages under 50 subject headings. Also has sections on general dictionaries, business correspondence and translation. Some entries have brief annotations. Index of subjects and keywords.
Class No: 801.3(01)

[5192]
KABDEBO, T. *and* **ARMSTRONG, N. Dictionary of dictionaries** and eminent encyclopedias, comprising: dictionaries, encyclopedias and other selected wordbooks in English. 2nd ed. London, Bowker-Saur, 1997. vii,418p. £80. ISBN: 1857391039.

1st ed. 1992, by T. Kabdebo.

An unusual and potentially very useful work based on information amassed by one man over many years, in which 8,500 mainly English-language dictionaries and encyclopedic reference works (both current and historical) on a wide range of subjects are listed within 1,398 A-Z entries, under

....(contd.)

subjects, languages and, for certain major works, 'household names.' Some entries explain different types of dictionary and define terms used in lexicography. 400 headings are new for the 2nd ed., including 100 for additional languages, and over half the existing entries have been updated to include recent publications. The compilers say their aim is to present a 'practical reference tool' and that historical material makes up less than 12% of the titles listed. Indexes of keywords, authors and titles.

1st ed was described as 'a major landmark which you should hold in the same awe as you hold *Walford*' (*Reference Reviews* (v.7(3), 1993, p.7-8). *Walford* is not flattered, since Kabdebo's work must be used with extreme caution. As so often in a highly individual publication, the entries can be lively and readable, but the selection of material varies widely between subjects, being largely based on two Dublin libraries and the compilers' personal collections. Editing and indexing are improved but, sadly, many of the faults pointed out by reviewers of the 1st ed. (*e.g. Journal of Librarianship and Information Science*, v.25(3), Sept. 1993, p.160-1) have not been rectified and *Refer* (v.14(2), Spring/Summer 1998, p.7-8) finds several more: 'this is the work of an enthusiastic but inaccurate magpie'. *Class No:* 801.3(01)

[5193]

World dictionaries in print: a guide to general and subject dictionaries in world languages. New York, Bowker, 1983. xii,579p. $99.50. ISBN: 0835216152.

A product of Bowker's computerized database, which provides bibliographic details of 13,623 dictionaries. Full entries are found in the subject sequence under 5,854 Library of Congress subject headings. This is followed by indexes of titles, authors/editors/compilers, and languages, the latter grouping titles under 238 languages. Directory of publishers and distributors. Many of the dictionaries listed may no longer be 'in print', but this remains a valuable bibliography. *Class No:* 801.3(01)

Encyclopaedias

[5194]

Worterbücher: ein internationales Handbuch zur Lexicographie / Dictionaries: an international encyclopedia of lexicography. Hausmann, F.J., *and others, eds.* Berlin, de Gruyter, 1989-91. 3v. (lii,3355p.). $477.45. ISBN: 0899256678.

Covers all aspects of lexicography in 334 articles arranged in 38 chapters, including 114 articles on the lexicography of individual languages. Articles, by a huge team of contributors, are written in one of German, French and English, with all introductory and explanatory information in all 3 languages. Bibliography with each article, plus annotated bibliography of 130 dictionary bibliographies at end of v.3. Detailed contents table (18p.) plus subject and name indexes. *Class No:* 801.3(031)

Nicknames & Pseudonyms

[5195]

A Dictionary of names and nicknames Urdang, L., *ed.* Oxford, Oxford Univ. Press, 1991. viii,326p. ISBN: 0192828576.

A paperback reprint, with revisions, of *Names and nicknames of places and things* (London, Grafton, 1987).

Defines and explains the connotations of the names given to *c.*1,500 real, legendary and fictional locales and

....(contd.)

landmarks. Includes buildings, businesses, and some objects as well as places. Very thorough index.
Class No: 801.3:392.91

[5196]

FIRESTONE, B. Harrap's book of nicknames and their origins: a comprehensive guide to personal nicknames in the English-speaking world. London, Harrap, 1990. xii,371p. ISBN: 0245600191.

Lists over 5,000 nicknames for people of all periods. Concise entries include biographical details, information on the derivation of the nickname and cross-references. Brief bibliography (1p.). Full surname index (34p.).
Class No: 801.3:392.91

[5197]

Pseudonyms and nicknames dictionary. Mossman, J., *ed.* 3rd ed. Detroit, Gale, 1987. 2v. (2207p.). ISBN: 0810305410.

1st ed. 1980.

Lists over 80,000 pseudonyms and nicknames relating to over 55,000 individuals, both historical and contemporary, from all walks of life. Main entries under original name, giving assumed names, birth and death dates, nationality, occupation, and coded references to other sources of information. Cross-references provided under assumed names in the same sequence.

New pseudonyms and nicknames (1988. 306p. ISBN: 0810305488) is an inter-edition supplement with 9,000 additional nicknames and pseudonyms.
Class No: 801.3:392.91

[5198]

REES, N. *and* **NOBLE, V. A Who's who of nicknames.** London, Allen & Unwin, 1985. xiii,194p. ISBN: 0048271136.

Over 900 entries arranged A-Z by nickname, with index of real names. Gives popular-style explanations for the nicknames, mainly of people, with few references to sources. 12 generic entries in the sequence give lists of nicknames for people in particular groups *e.g.* gangsters, pop stars. Excludes nicknames of places.
Class No: 801.3:392.91

[5199]

SHARP, H.S. Handbook of geographical nicknames. Metuchen, N.J., Scarecrow, 1980. vii,153p. $29.50. ISBN: 0810812800.

Over 3,500 entries in a confusing single A-Z sequence of real names (in capitals) and nicknames (lower case). The latter are cross-referenced to the main entry, which appears under the real name and gives very brief details of location and a list of nicknames. *Class No:* 801.3:392.91

[5200]

SIFAKIS, C. The Dictionary of historic nicknames. New York, Facts on File, 1983. 584p. ISBN: 0871965615.

Provides information on over 7,500 nicknames from Egyptian pharaohs to contemporary politicans. A-Z arrangement with index by career/life-style (20p.).
Class No: 801.3:392.91

USA

[5201]

SHANKLE, G.E. American nicknames: their origin and significance. 2nd ed. New York, Wilson, 1955. vii,524p. $44. ISBN: 0824200047.

1st ed. 1937.

Over 2,300 proper-name entries interspersed with cross-references for nicknames. Main entries cover people, places, events, organizations, sports, teams, etc. and list all nicknames given to the subject along with a concise sketch describing their derivation. Detailed footnote references follow each entry. *Class No:* 801.3:392.91(73)

[5202]

Twentieth century American nicknames. Urdang, L., *ed.* New York, Wilson, 1979. 398p. $42. ISBN: 0824206428.

Lists over 4,000 nicknames for persons, places and events in a single A-Z sequence of nicknames and proper names. Entries for proper names identify the subject, give full legal name and birth and death dates for people, and list all relevant nicknames. Nickname entries refer to the proper names. *Class No:* 801.3:392.91(73)

Proper Names

[5203]

DICKSON, P. What do you call a person from ...? a dictionary of resident names. New York, Facts on File, 1990. 161p. ISBN: 0816019835.

Provides information on over 1,000 demonyms, *i.e.* the names given to people from particular places (*e.g.* 'Hoosier', 'Muscovite'). Most entries are brief, but some include extensive historical and geographical background.
Class No: 801.31

[5204]

DUNKLING, L. The Guinness book of names. 7th ed. Enfield, Guinness, 1995. 272p. illus. £11.99. ISBN: 0851126693.

1st ed. 1974; 6th ed. 1993.

Popular treatment of the whole field of name studies, with chapters devoted to place-names, first names, surnames, nicknames, street names, specialist groups of names (*e.g.* for pubs, ships, animals, houses, etc.) and name games, amongst other topics. Useful tables scattered throughout, especially those chronicling forename fashions in the UK since 1900. Bibliography of key reference works. Index of over 8,000 names. *Class No:* 801.31

[5205]

PAYTON, G. The Penguin dictionary of proper names. Paxton, J., *ed.* Rev. ed. London, Viking, 1991. viii,563p. £16.99. ISBN: 0670825735.

A long-awaited revision of *Payton's proper names* (London, Warne, 1969). An American version of the 1st ed. was published under the title *Webster's dictionary of proper names* (Springfield, Mass., Merriam, 1970), with many British-oriented entries dropped in favour of names more familiar to American users.

A dictionary of *c.*11,000 names which are regularly encountered in newspapers, literature, etc., including people and places (both real and fictional); titles of works of music, literature and art; historical events; ships, cars and planes; nicknames; political parties; religious groups; races and languages; sporting events; etc., etc. Entries contain brief explanatory notes and cross-references. 'A highly personal choice of names' (*Preface*) but nevertheless very useful.
Class No: 801.31

[5206]

Proper names master index: a comprehensive index of more than 200,000 proper names that appear as entries in standard reference works. Abate, F.R., *ed.* Detroit, Omnigraphics, 1994. 2v. $125. ISBN: 1558888373.

Identifies 200,000 proper names in over 60 widely held reference works, including general encyclopedias and dictionaries and companions to specific subjects, such as music, science, art and literature. Concentrates on *non-biographical* names, as historical personages can be found in other indexing sources, but covers a wide range of other names, *e.g.* song titles, battles, geographical locations, TV programmes, etc. Gives full bibliographical data for each reference work indexed, plus details of its coverage and arrangement. Before purchasing, librarians should remember that this work itself does not provide information about specific names and consider whether their staff really need an intermediary to direct them to standard reference sources.
Class No: 801.31

[5207]

ROBERT, P. Le Petit Robert 2: dictionnaire universel des noms propres, alphabétique et analogique. Nouv. éd. Paris, Robert, 1996. 1952p. illus. £42.

An abridgement of Robert's encyclopedic *Dictionnaire universel des noms propres, alphabétique et analogique* (4v.). First published 1974 and frequently revised and reprinted.

A dictionary of *c.*60,000 proper names from history, geography, art, literature and science. Numerous illustrations and maps. More detailed than the corresponding second part of the *Petit Larousse illustré. Class No:* 801.31

[5208]

ROOM, A. Cassell dictionary of proper names. Reprint of 1992 ed. London, Cassell, 1994. xxix,610p. £18.99. ISBN: 0304344478.

Originally published 1992, as *Brewer's dictionary of names.*

Over 8,000 entries, A-Z, explaining the origins of familiar names and proper nouns from a wide range of fields: places (the largest group of entries); forenames and surnames; mythological characters; days and months; trade names; sports clubs; musical pieces and pop groups; political movements; stars and constellations; buildings; and many more. Pronunciation guidance for difficult names. Worth a place alongside *The Penguin dictionary of proper names* (*q.v.*), because a work of this kind is essentially a personal selection and there is little overlap, although Room is usually stronger on etymology. Both are essential in small libraries which do not have a range of specialist dictionaries.
Class No: 801.31

[5209]

ROOM, A. Dictionary of translated names and titles. London, Routledge, 1986. xviii,460p. ISBN: 0710099533.

Lists over 4,000 well-known names and titles in English alphabetical order, followed by their equivalents in French, German, Italian, Spanish and Russian. This main sequence is numbered (1-4108) and followed by cross-indexes in the other 5 languages. Geographical names include countries, cities, seas, rivers, mountains and regions; personal names include historical personages, biblical, mythological and fictional characters, saints and popes. Titles cover works of art and literature, battles, treaties and international organizations. There is much additional information in the form of dates (for people, events and works) and locations

.... *(contd.)*
(for geographical features). An appendix lists 75 common personal forenames and their equivalents. Invaluable.
Class No: 801.31

[5210]
—ROOM, A. Literally entitled: a dictionary of the origins of the titles of over 1,300 major literary works of the nineteenth and twentieth centuries. Jefferson, N.C., McFarland, 1996. 249p. $48.50. ISBN: 0786401109.

Explains the origins of over 1,300 British and American literary works, mainly fiction and drama but including a few nonfiction titles. Arranged by title, the entries give author, publication date, explanation and source of title. If a title is a quotation, an excerpt sets it in context. Index of authors, titles and subjects. Bibliography of books on literary analysis. *Class No:* 801.31

[5211]
ROOM, A. The Naming of animals: an appellative reference to domestic, work and show animals, real and fictional. Jefferson, N.C., McFarland, 1993. xii,231p. $39.95. ISBN: 0899507956.

12 chapters on the types of names we give to animals, including generic, descriptive and pedigree names, and the names of famous animals in history, sport, mythology and fiction. The index lists 2,700 names mentioned in the text and specifies the type of animal concerned. Several useful appendices (not indexed), including lists of animals in the works of writers such as Scott, Dickens and Wodehouse, celebrity pets, and film titles which include animal names. Bibliography (4p.). As with so many of Room's works, a great deal of information has been assembled which is not readily available elsewhere. *Class No:* 801.31

Dictionaries

[5212]
ROOM, A. An Alphabetical guide to the language of name studies. Metuchen, N.J., Scarecrow, 1996. viii,123p. $34. ISBN: 0810831694.

Lists and defines over 660 specialist terms used in onomastics, with examples of usage and etymological notes. Appended glossary of Greek and Latin elements. Bibliography of related works. *Class No:* 801.31(038)

Ireland

[5213]
COGHLAN, R., *& others*. Book of Irish names: first, family and place names. New York, Sterling, 1989; Belfast, Appletree, 1990. 128p. illus. £5.95. ISBN: 086281247x, UK.

Combines *Pocket guide to Irish first names* (1985), *Pocket guide to Irish family names* (1985) and *Pocket guide to Irish place names* (1984). *Class No:* 801.31(415)

Germany

[5214]
BACH, A. Deutsche Namenkunde. Heidelberg, Winter, 1974-8 3v.

V.1 *Die Deutschen Personennamen*. 3rd ed. 1978. 2pts. (331+296p.).

V.2 *Die Deutschen Ortsnamen*. 1981. 2pts. (451+615p. 75 maps).

V.3 *Sachweiser und Namenregister*. 2nd ed. 1974.

Vols. 1-2 provide a systematic study of German personal and place names. In each case pt.1 deals with phonetics, form, syntax, formation and meaning; pt.2 with historical, geographical, sociological and psychological aspects. Both v.1 and v.2 have subject indexes. V.3 forms a detailed index. *Class No:* 801.31(430)

Portugal

[5215]
MACHADO, J.P. Dicionário onomástico etimológico da língua portuguesa. Lisboa, Confluência, 1984. 3v. (1503p.).

Lists 37,500 personal names and placenames, not only from Portugal, with etymologies and sources. List of sources (8p.). *Class No:* 801.31(469)

Japan

[5216]
O'NEILL, P.G. Japanese names: a comprehensive index by characters and readings. New York, Weatherhill; London, Phaidon, 1972. xvi,359p. £22.50. ISBN: 0834800608, US.

Covers 36,000 names in several categories (13,500 surnames, 11,000 personal names, 6,800 literary, historical and artistic names, 4,400 place names, and 300 Japanese era names) in 2 sequences; first in Japanese characters and second in romanized transcription, with radical appendix appended. Detailed, but clear, explanatory introduction.
Class No: 801.31(52)

Place Names

Worldwide

[5217]
ROOM, A. Dictionary of world place names derived from British names. London, Routledge, 1989. xvii,221p. maps. ISBN: 0415028116.

Over 1,300 place-names drawn from 6 major areas: United States, Canada, South Africa, Australia, New Zealand and Antarctica. Each entry provides a short account of the name's origin and the period in which it was named. Appendix 1. Categories of place-names (12p.) - 2. The Naming process. Bibliography (6p.).
Class No: 801.311(100)

[5218]
ROOM, A. Place-name changes, 1900-91. [2nd ed.] Metuchen, N.J., & London, Scarecrow, 1993. xxv,296p. $41.50. ISBN: 0810826003.

1st ed. 1979, as *Place name changes since 1900: a world gazetteer*.

A single A-Z sequence of main entries (names in current use) and cross-references (superseded names). Main entries give identification (town, country, etc.), location, former name(s) and year(s) of renaming, but there are no explanations of meanings of names nor of reasons for change. Covers *c.*4,600 places, many of them having changed their name more than once during this century. This edition includes numerous examples of reversion to original (usually pre-Communist) names. Appended list of official names of countries at 1st January, 1993. Enlarged and updated bibliography (7p.). *Class No:* 801.311(100)

[5219]

ROOM, A. Place-names of the world: origins and meanings of the names for over 5,000 natural features, countries, capitals, territories, cities and historic sites. Jefferson, N.C., McFarland, 1997. 441p. £58.50. ISBN: 0786401729.

Entries give name, brief description and location plus an account of the names's origin and meaning, with appropriate historical, topographical and biographical references. Glossaries, appendices and bibliography. Index.
Class No: 801.311(100)

[5220]

WILCOCKS, J. Countries and islands of the world: a guide to nomenclature. 2nd ed. London, Bingley, 1985. 132p. £20. ISBN: 0851573835.

1st ed. 1981.

'Compiled primarily for the use of librarians at reference desks' (*Introduction*), it lists in one A-Z sequence countries, islands, and states and provinces within the major federations. Main entry under the standard English-language form of the name (*e.g.* 'Crete') with cross-references from alternative and superseded forms (*e.g.* 'Kriti', 'Candia'). Notes on political status and name changes under main entries. Over 1,100 entries. *Class No:* 801.311(100)

Ancient Greece & Rome

[5221]

BELL, R.E. Place-names in classical mythology: Greece. Santa Barbara, Calif., ABC-Clio, 1988. 350p. $60. ISBN: 0874365074.

A companion to Bell's *Dictionary of classical mythology: symbols, attributes, and associations* (ABC-Clio, 1982). *c.*1,000 entries (in Latin spelling with modern name, where known, in parenthesis) recounting mythological events associated with specific places. List of modern place-names associated with ancient locations. Bibliography. 'A serious weakness is the lack of any map in the volume' (*Choice,* v.26(10), June 1989, p.1651-2). *Class No:* 801.311(37/38)

[5222]

GRANT, M. A Guide to the Ancient World: a dictionary of Classical place-names. New York, Wilson, 1986. 736p. illus. maps. $68. ISBN: 0824207424.

900 essays, arranged A-Z by place-name and ranging from 150 to 1,500 words, on the historical and mythological events associated with nations, cities, rivers, seas, battle-grounds and other sites. Entries also include geographical information, ancient and modern place-names and current archaeological information. 16p. of maps.
Class No: 801.311(37/38)

Great Britain

[5223]

FIELD, J. Place-names of Great Britain and Ireland. Newton Abbot, David & Charles; Totowa, N.J., Barnes & Noble, 1980. 208p. maps. £11.99. ISBN: 0715374397, UK; 0389201545, US.

Selective dictionary, for the general reader, of over 2,000 place-names, including all the largest towns, the counties and other administrative districts, and others chosen 'because the places are historically important or otherwise interesting' (*Introduction*). Entries give location, meaning, etymological and historical notes, and variant forms with dates. Glossary of common elements (7p.). Appendix lists post-1974 regions, counties, and districts. Bibliography (2p.).
Class No: 801.311(410)

[5224]

The Names of towns and cities in Britain. Nicolaisen, W.F.H., *ed.* London, Batsford, 1970. 215p. ISBN: 0713401133.

Explains the names of most English towns with a population of over 10,000, and Scottish and Welsh towns with over 5,000 inhabitants, in one A-Z sequence with a separate sequence of Greater London area names. Entries combine scholarly etymologies with readable historical and topographical notes. *Class No:* 801.311(410)

[5225]

ROOM, A. Bloomsbury dictionary of place-names in the British Isles. London, Bloomsbury, 1988. xxvi,414p. ISBN: 074750170x.

Origins and history of over 4,000 familiar place-names. Introduction discusses role and lore of place-names, sources, naming patterns, river names, etc. List of place-name elements (6p.). Bibliographical essay (6p.). *Reference Reviews* (v.3(1), March 1989, p.41) prefers *Concise Oxford dictionary of place names* for its more comprehensive coverage of specific areas, but commends the 'clear, jargon-free style' of the very informative entries.
Class No: 801.311(410)

[5226]

—ROOM, A. A Concise dictionary of modern place-names in Great Britain and Ireland. Oxford, Oxford Univ. Press, 1983. xliv,148p. ISBN: 0192819003.

Selective survey of over 1,000 post-1500 place names. Introduction explains problems of toponymic research and reviews topographical sources. Appendices on royal names (3p.) and seaside names (7p.). Bibliography (6p.).
Class No: 801.311(410)

[5227]

SPITTAL, J. *and* **FIELD, J. A Reader's guide to the place-names of the United Kingdom:** a bibliography of publications (1920-89) on the place-names of Great Britain and Northern Ireland, the Isle of Man and the Channel Islands. Stamford, Lincs., Watkins, 1990. xxi,341p. £30. ISBN: 1871615100.

Sections on each country are subdivided by topic, regional and county headings. Brief critical annotations for many entries. Useful introduction (40p.) on the history and development of place-name studies. Appendices cover older works on place-names, works on British place-names transferred abroad, and Arthurian place-names. Indexes of authors, *Festschriften*, and places. 'Without question the most comprehensive and scholarly bibliography on its subject' (*Reference Reviews*, v.6(1), 1992, p. 21-2)
Class No: 801.311(410)

Scotland

[5228]

DARTON, M. The Dictionary of place names in Scotland, and the elements that go to make them up. Rev. ed. Orpington, Dobby, 1994. vi,287p. £9.99. ISBN: 1858820111.

1st ed. Moffat, Lochar, 1990, as *The Dictionary of Scottish place names*.

5,000 entries, including rivers, mountains, lakes, etc. as well as habitations, with locations (modern district rather than historic county) and explanations (which the author admits are sometimes speculative). Brief introduction. 'An attractive addition at an affordable price, but does not supersede his predecessors' (*Reference Reviews*, v.5(2), 1991, p.18, on 1st ed.). *Class No:* 801.311(411)

[5229]

JOHNSTON, J.B. Place-names of Scotland. Reprint of 3rd ed. Bruceton Mills, W.V., Scotpress, 1988. xvi,335p. ISBN: 1559321911.

1st ed. Edinburgh, Douglas, 1892; 3rd ed. London, Murray, 1934.

An A-Z list of *c.*3,500 place-names (p.75-326), giving location, meaning and etymology. 5 introductory chapters on the different types of name: 1. Celtic - 2. Norse - 3. English - 4. Roman, Norman, and purely modern - 5. Ecclesiastical. Bibliography (1p.) and index to names not found alphabetically in the list. *Class No:* 801.311(411)

[5230]

MACKENZIE, W.C. Scottish place-names. London, Kegan, Paul, 1931. xi,320p.

Arranged in 10 mainly topographical chapters ('Rivers and burns', 'Isles and skerries', etc.) with extensive notes on specific places after each chapter giving variant forms and etymological notes. Index of *c.*2,200 names. Subject index. *Class No:* 801.311(411)

[5231]

NICOLAISEN, W.F.H. Scottish place-names: their study and significance. London, Batsford, 1976. xxviii,210p. maps. £10.99. ISBN: 071345234x.

A comprehensive survey in 9 chapters with an extensive bibliography (8p.), list of sources (5p.), and index of *c.*1,800 placenames mentioned in the text. 21 maps. *Class No:* 801.311(411)

[5232]

WATSON, W.J. The Celtic place-names of Scotland Reprint of 1926 ed. Edinburgh, Birlinn, 1993. xx,558p. £14.99. ISBN: 1874744068.

Originally published Edinburgh, Blackwood, 1926, as *The History of the Celtic place-names of Scotland, being the Rhind lectures on archaeology (expanded) delivered in 1916.*

15 thematic chapters. Index of *c.*4,600 places and tribes. Index of personal names. *Class No:* 801.311(411)

Ireland

[5233]

FLANAGAN, D. *and* **FLANAGAN, L. Irish place names.** Dublin, Gill & Macmillan, 1994. 271p. £7.99. ISBN: 071712066x.

First section is a list of *c.*450 root or stem words whch form the basis of most common Irish place names, with detailed explanations, many examples and 25 maps. Second section lists 3,000 names, giving county, derivation and meaning. *Class No:* 801.311(415)

[5234]

JOYCE, P.W. The Origin and history of Irish names of places. London, Longmans, Green, 1910-13. 3v.

Vols. 1-2 were originally published Dublin, Gill, 1869-71, and comprise a historical survey of Irish names, while v.3 is a dictionary of over 9,000 place-names in their Anglicized form, with location, Irish form, derivation and meaning. Alphabetical indexes to each chapter in vols. 1-2. *Class No:* 801.311(415)

[5235]

McMAHON, S. The Poolbeg book of Irish placenames. Dublin, Poolbeg Press; Chester Springs, Pa., Dufour, 1990. 113p. £3.99. ISBN: 1853710873.

Lists *c.*2,200 placenames under the 32 counties of Northern Ireland and the Irish Republic. Entries comprise current name, Gaelic name and meaning. Introduction includes list of name elements (5p.), arranged A-Z by Gaelic root word. *Class No:* 801.311(415)

[5236]

Ó CÍOBHÌN, B. Toponomia Hiberniae. Dublin, An Foras Duibhneach, 1978-85. v.1-4 (in progress). illus. maps.

1. *Barúntacht dhún Ciaráin thuaidh* (Barony of Dunkerron North). 1978. xxiii, 176p. ISBN: 0861280008.

2. *Paróiste chill Chrócháin* 1. (Kilcrohane parish). 1984. xv,165p. ISBN: 0861280024.

3. *Barúntacht dhún Ciaráin theas* (Barony of Dunkerron South). *Paróiste chill Chrócháin* 2. 1984. xviii,107p. ISBN: 0861280040.

4. *Paróiste an Teampaill nua* (Temple Parish). 1985. lxxii,136p. ISBN: 0861280067. Introduction (in English) to first 4 vols. (p. xix-lxxii) discusses scope of the work, nature of the material, editing, etc.

Detailed information presented throughout in the Irish language is derived from oral sources and from Ordnance Survey documents on Irish placenames *c.*1840. The whole work is expected to be completed in 25 vols. *Class No:* 801.311(415)

[5237]

ROOM, A. A Dictionary of Irish place-names. Rev. ed. Belfast, Appletree Press, 1994. 144p. £6.99. ISBN: 086281460x.

1st ed. 1986.

Over 3,000 names in Ulster and the Republic of Ireland, giving current English and Irish forms together with county and a geographical/historical annotation. Bibliography (2p.). 'There is no guide to pronunciation but the information in this short book should be sufficient to satisfy a passing curiosity or provide a useful first step to more thorough research' (*Reference Reviews,* v.2(3), September 1988, p.159, on 1st ed.). *Class No:* 801.311(415)

England

[5238]

CAMERON, K. English place-names. New [6th?] ed. London, Batsford, 1996. 256p. illus. maps. £16.99. ISBN: 0713473789.

1st ed. 1961; 5th ed. 1988.

A comprehensive survey in 20 chapters of all aspects of English place-name studies, with chapters devoted to the names of streets, roads, fields, woods and other topographical features as well as settlements. New ed. represents a substantial revision and includes a new chapter on modern place-names. Bibliography (4p.). Index of *c.*5,000 names cited. *Class No:* 801.311(420)

[5239]

EKWALL, E. The Concise Oxford dictionary of English place-names. 4th ed. Oxford, Oxford Univ. Press, 1960. li,546p. £25. ISBN: 0198691033.

1st ed. 1936; 3rd ed. 1947.

Recognized as the standard work in the field and has entries for over 10,000 place-names, giving the following information: county, historical forms with dates, authorities, comments on etymological development and likely meanings. Includes a valuable introduction with list of works

.... *(contd.)*
consulted (14p.). Incorporates many additions and corrections to 3rd ed.

Does not include many names originating after 1500, but these have been covered in recent works by A. Room.
Class No: 801.311(420)

[5240]
ENGLISH PLACE-NAME SOCIETY. [Survey of English place-names]. Cambridge, Cambridge Univ. Press (later Nottingham, English Place-Name Society), 1924-97. v.1-73 (in progress).

V.1, pt.1, *Introduction to the Survey of English Place-names* (1924); v.1, pt.2, *Chief elements used in English place-names* (1924); v.2, *Buckinghamshire* (1925); v.3, *Bedfordshire and Huntingdonshire* (1926); v.4, *Worcestershire* (1927); v.5, *The North Riding of Yorkshire* (1928); v.6-7, *Sussex* (1929-30); v.8-9, *Devon* (1931-32); v.10, *Northamptonshire* (1933); v.11, *Surrey* (1934); v.12, *Essex* (1935); v.13, *Warwickshire* (1936); v.14, *The East Riding of Yorkshire and York* (1937); v.15, *Hertfordshire* (1938); v.16, *Wiltshire* (1939); v.17, *Nottinghamshire* (1940); v.18, *Middlesex, apart from the City of London* (1942); v.19, *Cambridgeshire and The Isle of Ely* (1943); v.20-22, *Cumberland* (1950-52); v.23-24, *Oxfordshire* (1953-54); v.25-26, *English place-name elements* (1956); v.27-29, *Derbyshire* (1959); v.30-37, *The West Riding of Yorkshire* (1961-63); v.38-41, *Gloucestershire* (1964-65); v.42-43, *Westmorland* (1967); v.44-48 and v.54, *Cheshire* (1970-81); v.49-51, *Berkshire* (1973-76); v.52-53 and 59-60, *Dorset* (1977-89); v.55, *Staffordshire*, pt.1 (1984); v.56-57, *Cornish place-name elements* (1985); v.58, *Lincolnshire*, pt.1 (1985); v.61, *Norfolk*, pt.1 (1989); v.62-63, *Shropshire*, pt.1 (1990); v.64-66, *Lincolnshire* (1991-92); v.67-69, *Rutland* (1994); v.70, *Shropshire*, pt.2 (1995); v.71, *Lincolnshire*, pt.4 (1996); v.72 *Norfolk*, pt.2 (1996); v.73, *Lincolnshire*, pt.5 (1997).

The English Place-Name Society was formed in 1923 to carry out a survey of English place-names undertaken with the approval and encouragement of the British Academy. The Society publishes the results of the Survey county by county. Each volume contains a list of place-names arranged by hundred, with full notes on linguistic forms and derivations. Field names and street names are also analyzed. Entries bring to light valuable archaeological, historical and etymological evidence. Supplementary material is published by the Society in its annual *Journal*.
Class No: 801.311(420)

[5241]
MILLS, A.D. A Dictionary of English place-names. Oxford, Oxford Univ. Press, 1991. xxxii,388p. maps. ISBN: 0198691564.

Over 12,000 concise entries, giving modern county; most likely meaning and derivation of the name; a typical earlier form with date; and the name's spelling in Domesday Book if it occurs there. Includes rivers and coastal features as well as towns, villages, counties and districts. Glossary of name elements (7p.). Bibliography (3p.). Introductory essay (20p.) describes the development, formation and significance of place-names.

New ed. due mid-1998 (£7.99. ISBN: 0192800744).
Class No: 801.311(420)

[5242]
REANEY, P.H. The Origin of English place names. London, Routledge & Kegan Paul, 1960. x,277p. ISBN: 071020728x.

Comprehensive general survey with chapters on methodology, the various elements of English place-names (Celtic, English, Scandinavian, French, Latin), and specialised names (fields and streets). Bibliography arranged by chapter (4p.). Subject index and index of nearly 4,000 place-names (with county abbreviations) mentioned in the text. *Class No:* 801.311(420)

Wales

[5243]
CHARLES, B.G. Non-Celtic place-names in Wales. London, University College, 1938. xlvii,326p.

Considers, in the manner standardized by the English Place-Name Society, place-names of English, French, Flemish and Scandinavian origin, 'and these only when their history is known or old forms have been found for them' (*Preface*). Arranged by county, then by hundred. List of non-Celtic name elements (21p.). Index.
Class No: 801.311(429)

[5244]
A Gazetteer of Welsh place-names, prepared by the Language and Literature Committee of the Board of Celtic Studies in the University of Wales. Davies, E., *ed.* 3rd ed. Cardiff, Univ. of Wales Press, 1967 (repr. 1996). xxxvii,119p. £7.95. ISBN: 0708310389.

1st ed. 1957; 2nd ed. 1958.

A standard guide to the orthography of Welsh place-names, with *c.*4,800 entries giving an indication of the nature of each named feature, the civil parish and county in which it lies and a reference to the National Grid. Introduction in English and Welsh includes a guide to the pronunciation and meaning of major elements.

The Place-names of Wales by H.W. Owen (Cardiff, Univ. of Wales Press, 1998. 144p. £4.95. ISBN: 0708314589) is a handy paperback guide. *Class No:* 801.311(429)

Germany

[5245]
STURMFELS, W. *and* BISCHOF, H. Unsere Ortsnamen, im ABC erklärt nach Herkunft und Bedeutung. 3. verb. und stark erw. Aufl. Bonn, Dümmler, 1961. 359p. (4. Aufl. 1990).

A dictionary of place-names, giving information on origin and meaning. Includes entries for names outside Germany and the names of nations and peoples.
Class No: 801.311(430)

France

[5246]
DAUZAT, A. *and* ROSTAING, Ch. Dictionnaire étymologique des noms de lieux en France. 2e. éd. Paris, Guénégaud, 1979. 786p. Fr.180. ISBN: 2850230766.

The standard dictionary of French place-names with over 30,000 entries, giving department and derivation. List of sources.

Dauzat has also compiled *Dictionnaire étymologique des noms de rivières et de montagnes en France* (Paris, Klinksieck, 1978. x,233p. ISBN: 2252024070).

....*(contd.)*

See also A. Cherpillod's *Dictionnaire étymologique des noms géographiques* (2e. éd. Paris, Masson, 1991. 544p. Fr.383. ISBN: 2225822778). *Class No:* 801.311(44)

[5247]

NÈGRE, E. Toponymie générale de la France: etymologie de 35,000 noms de lieux. Genève, Droz, 1990-91. 3v. (1852p.).

In 7 chronological parts from pre-Celtic to modern French, with thematic sections within each part. Over 31,000 numbered entries, comprising placename, commune, department, etymology (dated source given) and meaning. Index in v.3. List of sources in v.1 (6p.). Compiler claims he has rectified many errors in Dauzat's dictionary.
Class No: 801.311(44)

Italy

[5248]

PELLEGRINI, G.B. Toponomastica italiana: 10,000 nomi di città, paesi, frazioni, regioni, contrade, fiumi, monti, spiegati nella loro origine e storia. Milano, Hoepli, 1990. 559p. ISBN: 8820318350.

8 chapters on different types of placenames, with 181 numbered subsections in which individual names are explained in detail. Glossary (2p.) Bibliography (27p.). Index of all words treated. 14 maps.
Class No: 801.311(450)

USSR

[5249]

ROOM, A. Place-names of Russia and the former Soviet Union: origins and meanings of the names for over 2,000 natural features, towns, regions and countries. Jefferson, N.C., McFarland, 1996. 288p. $58.50 ISBN: 0786400420.

Entries comprise transliterated name, Cyrillic form, location, origin and meaning, with historical, topographical and biographical references. *Class No:* 801.311(47)

Islamic World

[5250]

GROOM, N. A Dictionary of Arabic topography and placenames: a transliterated Arabic-English dictionary with an Arabic glossary of topographical words and placenames. Beirut, Librairie du Liban; London, Longman; New York, French & European, 1983. 369p. $95. ISBN: 058278381x, UK; 0828814589, US.

Lists and gives meanings of *c.*4,500 Arabic words which describe place and topographical features and which may be found in place-names. Bibliography (3p.).
Class No: 801.311(5.297)

Africa

[5251]

ROOM, A. African placenames: origins and meanings of the names for over 2,000 natural features, towns, cities, provinces and countries. Jefferson, N.C., McFarland, 1994. 235p. $49.95. ISBN: 0899509436.

Based on an unpublished dictionary of southern African placenames and has a preponderance of names from that part of the continent. Entries give meaning, date of naming and dates of any changes to the name. Appended lists of country

....*(contd.)*

names, independence dates, populations and official languages. Glossary of terms. Select bibliography of sources of general interest. *Class No:* 801.311(6)

South Africa

[5252]

NIENABER, P.J. Suid-Afrikaanse pleknaamwoordeboek, deel 1. Kaapstad, Suid-Afrikaanse Boeksentrum, 1963. 418p. (2nd ed. 1972).

The dictionary (p.147-403) has substantial accounts of *c.*1,000 place-names, and is preceded by a lengthy introduction (64p.) on the different types of name. List of name elements (31p.). Excellent bibliography (37p.).
Class No: 801.311(680)

[5253]

PETTMAN, C. South African place names, past and present. Reprint of 1931 ed. Johannesburg, Lowry, 1985. 238p. ISBN: 0947042016.

Originally published Queenstown, 1931, by 'The Queenstown Daily Representative'.

The standard study of South African place-names, with chapters on Bushman, Hottentot, Bantu, Portuguese, Dutch, French, English, and German names, and on names derived from flora and fauna. List of common name elements (6p.). Index of over 2,000 names mentioned.
Class No: 801.311(680)

[5254]

RAPER, P.E. Directory of Southern African place names. Johannesburg, Lowry, 1987. ix,368p. ISBN: 0947042067.

A semi-popular guide to the major place names: cities, towns, rivers, mountains, etc. Bibliography (12p.).
Class No: 801.311(680)

America — North

[5255]

Illustrated dictionary of place names: United States and Canada. Harder, K.B., *ed.* Reprint of 1976 ed. New York, Facts on File, 1986. 634p. illus. ISBN: 0816011435.

Originally published New York, Van Nostrand Reinhold, 1976.

Explains the names of *c.*15,000 places including cities, towns, provinces, states, counties, and natural features such as rivers, lakes and capes. Entries include variations of the name, and information about county and state capitals and emblems. All places whose name derives from the same source (*e.g.* the name of a president) are grouped within one entry. Bibliography (5p.). 200 illustrations.
Class No: 801.311(71+73)

[5256]

SEALOCK, R.B., ***and others*****. Bibliography of place-name literature: United States and Canada.** 3rd ed. Chicago, American Library Assoc., 1982. xii,435p. ISBN: 0838903606.

1st ed. 1948; 2nd ed. 1967.

Over 4,800 items in separate sequences for the US and Canada: general, gazetteers, and states and provinces alphabetically. Author and subject indexes. 'Although there has been an increase in the number of comprehensive guides to the origin and meaning of names in the states and provinces, the authors have found it necessary to include the many articles in little-known or ephemeral publications' (*Preface*). *Class No:* 801.311(71+73)

Canada

[5257]

RAYBURN, A. Dictionary of Canadian place names. Don Mills, Ont., Oxford Univ. Press, 1997. 480p. C$34.95. ISBN: 0195410866.

Explains the origins of the names of over 6,200 places, including cities, towns, villages, lakes, rivers, mountains, bays and other natural features. Entries include date of naming where known.

See also Rayburn's *Naming Canada: essays on place names from 'Canadian Geographic'* (Toronto, Univ. of Toronto Press, 1995. $C55. ISBN: 0802005691).
Class No: 801.311(71)

USA

[5258]

STEWART, G.R. A Concise dictionary of American place-names. Paperback reprint of 1970 ed. New York, Oxford Univ. Press, 1986. xl,550p. ISBN: 0195037251.

Originally published 1970 as *American place names: a concise and selective dictionary for the continental United States of America.*

A single A-Z sequence of *c.*12,000 entries for places in three categories: well-known places (the major cities, states, rivers, etc.), oft-repeated names, and unusual names, with names derived from persons and other 'obvious' names generally omitted. Entries give state (Zip-code), original language, meaning and, where appropriate, historical and nonscholarly etymological notes. Useful introduction (17p.) on the background to US names. Bibliography (7p.).
Class No: 801.311(73)

Australia

[5259]

REED, A.W. Aboriginal place names and their meanings. Sydney, Reed, 1967 (reprinted 1985). 144p. ISBN: 0730101274.

Place-names p.9-95. Appendix A. Word list (*i.e.* subject index) p.97-135 - B. Present-day names with earlier Aboriginal names p.136-144. *Class No:* 801.311(94)

[5260]

REED, A.W. Place-names of Australia. Sydney, Reed, 1973. 271p. A$12.95. ISBN: 0730100510.

A popular reference work listing *c.*2,500 names, giving state and brief notes on origins and history. Index of people mentioned. Index of aboriginal names.
Class No: 801.311(94)

Personal Names

Bibliographies

[5261]

LAWSON, E.D. Personal names and naming: an annotated bibliography. New York, Greenwood, 1987. xiii,185p. $59.95. (*Bibliographies and indexes in anthropology.*) ISBN: 0313238170.

A classified bibliography with 1,280 mainly English-language entries in 48 sections covering both family and given names. Very diverse coverage, with section headings including 'Graffiti and names', 'Obscenity and names' and 'Public health and names'. Author and subject indexes. Does not include material already recorded in E.C. Smith's *Personal names: a bibliography* (New York, NY Public Library, 1952) which has over 3,400 entries.

....(contd.)

Continued by Lawson's *More names and naming* (Westport, Conn., Greenwood, 1996. 320p. $75. ISBN: 0313285829) which has 2,200 citations for recent material.
Class No: 801.313(01)

Worldwide

[5262]

INGRAHAM, H. People's names: a cross-cultural reference guide to the proper use of over 40,000 personal and familial names in over 100 cultures. Jefferson, N.C., McFarland, 1997. 637p. $58.50. ISBN: 0786401877.

Covers both historical and contemporary cultures and for each group discusses rules for naming, use of family names (if any), gender specific names, and name order. Also provides for each culture a list of 50 'first' names and at least 100 family names. Index. *Class No:* 801.313(100)

Ancient Greece

[5263]

A Lexicon of Greek personal names. Fraser, P.M., *and others, eds.* Oxford, Clarendon Press, 1987-. v.1- (in progress).

V.1 *The Aegean Islands, Cyprus, Cyrenaica.* 1987. xxxv,489p. £75. ISBN: 0198642229.

V.2 *Attica.* 1994. 532p. £60. ISBN: 0198149905.

V.3 A *The Peloponnese, Western Greece, and Magna Graecia.* 1997. 530p. £65. ISBN: 0198152299.

The first 3 vols. in a projected 6-vol. work which aims to provide a list, with full itemized evidence, of personal names known from literature, inscriptions, papyri, vases, coins, and other objects, from earliest times to about the 7th century AD. *Class No:* 801.313(37)

Ireland

[5264]

Ó CORRÁIN, D. *and* **MAGUIRE, F. Irish names.** 2nd ed. Dublin, Lilliput Press, 1990. 188p. £5.95. ISBN: 0946640661.

1st ed. Dublin, Academy Press, 1981, as *Gaelic personal names.*

Almost 1,000 names extracted from medieval annals and histories. Index of variant forms. Note on sources.
Class No: 801.313(415)

Germany

[5265]

BAHLOW, H. Deutsches Namenlexikon: 15,000 Familien- und Vornamen nach Ursprung und Sinn erklärt. Bindlach, Gindrom, 1982. 576p. ISBN: 3811202944.

Lists forenames and surnames in one sequence, giving meaning, etymology and historical development.
Class No: 801.313(430)

France

[5266]

DAUZAT, A. Dictionnaire étymologique des noms de familles et prénoms de France. Morlet, M.-T., *ed.* Rev. ed. Paris, Larousse, 1985. 626p. Fr.110. ISBN: 2037300123.

1st ed. 1951.

A reprint of the 1st ed. (which contained *c.*15,000 entries,

....(*contd.*)
giving etymology, variants, meanings, and geographical distribution of surnames) with a supplement (22p.).
Class No: 801.313(44)

Russia in Asia

[5267]
BENSON, M. Dictionary of Russian personal names, with a revised guide to stress and morphology. [3rd ed.] Cambridge, Cambridge Univ. Press, 1992. xi,174p. £37.50. ISBN: 0521411653.

1st ed. Philadelphia, Pa., Univ. of Pennsylvania Press, 1964; 2nd ed. 1967.

Indicates stress in *c.*23,000 selected surnames, with a separate section listing names of famous people where stress differs from the accepted norm. Detailed notes on declension of surnames. List of the commonest given names and their diminutive forms. Selected bibliography (3p.).
Class No: 801.313(57)

Islamic World

[5268]
MALIK, Z.A. Muslim names and their meanings. Petaling Jaya, Selangor, Pelanduk Publications, 1985. xiii,123p. ISBN: 9679780198.

Contents include: Arabic alphabets and English equivalents; A General picture of Muslim names; Names of Allah; Names of Prophet Muhammad; Popular Muslim male names (transliteration, meaning, Arabic script), p.12-71; Popular Muslim female names, p.72-111; and Arabic equivalents of some Biblical names.
Class No: 801.313(5.297)

[5269]
SCHIMMEL, A. Islamic names. Edinburgh, Edinburgh Univ. Press, 1989. xii,137p. £17.50. ISBN: 0852245637.

6 chapters on different types of names. Bibliography (6p.). Glossary of technical terms (3p.). Index of *c.*2,500 personal names. Index of places, ethnic groups and languages.
Class No: 801.313(5.297)

Africa

[5270]
STEWART, J. 1001 African names: first and last names from the African continent. Secaucus, NJ, Citadel Press, 1997. vii,214p. £9.99. ISBN: 0806517379.

Introductory section on traditional naming practices and modern developments, followed by 1,001 forenames, A-Z, with separate lists for males and females under each letter. Entries include pronunciation, meaning and explanatory notes where required. Appended name charts (*e.g.* day or time of birth), list of surnames by country, and list of African languages and peoples. English language index to African names. List of periodicals (5p.) and bibliography (2p.). *Class No:* 801.313(6)

Forenames

[5271]
DUNKLING, L. *and* **GOSLING, W. Everyman's dictionary of first names.** London, Dent, 1983; New York, Facts on File, 1984. xvi,304p. 500.00/00 US title is *The Facts on File dictionary of first names.* ISBN: 0460030310, UK; 0871962748, US.

4,500 entries covering over 10,000 names which have been generally used in the English-speaking world over the last few centuries, with details of when they were most used and why. Tables list the top 50 first names for boys and girls in England and Wales 1925, 1950, 1965, 1975 and 1981, and in the US 1925, 1950, 1970 and 1982. Bibliography (3p.). *Class No:* 801.313.1

[5272]
DUNKLING, L. First names first. London, Dent, 1977; Detroit, Gale, 1982. 285p. illus. ISBN: 0460120255, UK; 0810301849, US.

22 chapters on all aspects of forenames in the English-speaking world. Includes useful tables of the most popular names in different countries and at different times. Bibliography (2p.). Index of nearly 4,000 names mentioned in the text.

For detailed information on the most popular forenames in England and Wales, see *First names: the definitive guide to popular names in England and Wales* (London, HMSO, 1995. £4.95. ISBN: 0116916338), which is based on 1994 registrations. *Class No:* 801.313.1

[5273]
HANKS, P. *and* **HODGES, F. A Dictionary of first names.** Oxford, Oxford Univ. Press, 1990. xxxvi,443p. £18.99. ISBN: 0192116517.

Main sequence covers names used in Britain, Europe and North America, tracing each name back to its linguistic root and listing pet and short forms, masculine and feminine forms, cognates, diminutives, and other variants. Highly readable entries include information about the fluctuations in popularity of individual names. Excellent introductory survey of naming practices in different countries, with bibliography. Supplementary sequences of names used in the Arab world (36p.) and the Indian subcontinent (57p.), each with introductory essay and bibliography. Covers *c.*7,000 names in all.

The authors have also produced *A Concise dictionary of first names* (Rev. ed. Oxford, Oxford Univ. Press, 1997. xii,308p. £4.99. ISBN: 0198600941) with *c.*3,000 entries, concentrating on the English-speaking world but including European names and forms that have become established in English. Appended lists of common Arabic, Russian, Indian, French, German, Italian and Spanish names (2,300 in all).
Class No: 801.313.1

[5274]
NAVARRO, Y. First name reverse dictionary: given names listed by meaning. Jefferson, N.C., McFarland, 1993. ix,206p. $29.95. ISBN: 0899507484.

Arranged by definition, A-Z, in separate sections for male and female names. Gives language of origin for each name plus variant forms, but no guide to pronunciation. Index of the 7,000 names included. Provides an alternative to conventional name listings, but of limited use and by no means comprehensive. *Class No:* 801.313.1

[5275]
ROOM, A. The Cassell dictionary of first names. London, Cassell, 1995. xiv,338p. £20. ISBN: 0304343986.

Over 2,000 entries, written in Room's usual informative style, giving language of origin, meaning, period adopted by English speakers, history and recent popularity, alternative forms, and examples of real and fictitious bearers of the name. *Class No:* 801.313.1

[5276]

WITHYCOMBE, E.G. The Oxford dictionary of English Christian names. 3rd ed. Oxford, Clarendon Press, 1977. xlvii,310p. £5.99. ISBN: 0192812130.

1st ed. 1945.

Includes names found in England since the 14th century, giving etymology, meaning, and earliest usage. Appendix: 'Some common words derived from Christian names'.

Class No: 801.313.1

Scotland

[5277]

DUNKLING, L. Scottish Christian names: an A-Z of first names. London, Johnston and Bacon, 1978. 151p. £1.95. ISBN: 071794249x.

Explains the origins of over 500 names and their variant and diminutive forms. Bibliography (3p.). Index.

Class No: 801.313.1(411)

Wales

[5278]

GRUFFUDD, H. Enwau i'r Cymry / Welsh personal names: 1,000 names for children. Talybont, Dyfed, Lolfa, 1980. 96p. £4.50. ISBN: 0904864995.

Translations and explanations. Brief bibliography.

Class No: 801.313.1(429)

USA

[5279]

STEWART, G.R. American given names: their origin and history in the context of the English language. New York, Oxford Univ. Press, 1979. viii,264p. £19.50. ISBN: 0195024656.

A historical sketch of the use of given names in the US (40p.) precedes the main sequence of names (Aaron-Zureel), which provides the following information: male/female, language of origin, meaning, and notes on usage and popularity. Cross-references. *Class No:* 801.313.1(73)

Hebrew

[5280]

KOLATCH, A.J. Complete dictionary of English and Hebrew first names. New York, Jonathan David, 1984. xxviii,488p. $25. ISBN: 0824602951.

A greatly enlarged version of *The Name Dictionary* (1967).

Over 11,000 main entries (4 times as many as 1st ed.) in 2 sequences, masculine and feminine, giving meaning and origin of each name. Hebrew names are transliterated, but the Hebrew script is also given. Introduction (17p.) on the history of names and the naming process. Subject index to Hebrew names.

Kolatch has also compiled *The New name dictionary: modern English and Hebrew names* (New York, J. David, 1989. 328p. $19.95. ISBN: 0824603311).

Class No: 801.313.1=924

Family Names

Worldwide

[5281]

HANKS, P. *and* HODGES, F. A Dictionary of surnames. Oxford, Oxford Univ. Press, 1988. liv,826p. £70. ISBN: 0192115928.

Some 10,000 entries, dealing with *c.*70,000 common surnames of the English-speaking world and Europe, selected after an international scrutiny of telephone directories. 'Each entry explains the linguistic origins of each surname, together with peculiarities of its history, current distribution, and other relevant facts' (*Introduction*). Introduction includes a lengthy and very authoritative section on the typology of surnames and a 'Survey of national and cultural groups of surnames'. Bibliography (2p.). Index (over 200p.) lists all names included, whether as main entry, variant or cognate. 'Immediately becomes the standard reference source for the information it contains' (*Booklist,* v.85 (21), July 1989, p.1882), its particular strength being the inclusion of so many European names.

Class No: 801.313.2(100)

Great Britain

[5282]

REANEY, P.H. A Dictionary of English surnames. 3rd ed., rev. Oxford, Oxford Univ. Press, 1997. 592p. £9.99. ISBN: 0198600925.

1st ed. London, Routledge, 1958, as *A Dictionary of British surnames*; 3rd ed., with corrections and additions by R.M. Wilson, 1991.

The standard work in the field, giving the meanings of over 16,000 names (4,000 added for this ed.) and their variants, together with early forms, sources and origins, plus notes on etymology. Lengthy, scholarly introduction (60p.) includes bibliographic details of sources and other works consulted. This revision adds a new Appendix by D. Hey, giving advice on tracing the origin of a family name (10p.).

'The change of title reflects a concentration on surnames of specifically English rather than Celtic origin which has become increasingly apparent in successive editions. As a rule, Scottish, Welsh and Irish names are only included when forms for them are found in English sources or when they coincide in form with specifically English surnames' (*Preface*). *Class No:* 801.313.2(410)

[5283]

—COTTLE, B. Penguin dictionary of surnames. 2nd ed. Harmondsworth, Penguin, 1978. 444p. £7.99. ISBN: 014051032x.

1st ed. 1967.

Has *c.*12,000 entries (8,000 in 1st ed.), assigning names to one of 4 broad classes (first-name, locality, occupation, nickname) and giving meaning, brief etymology and, occasionally, notes on current distribution. Useful introductory essay (17p.) and bibliography (2p.). More entries than Reaney and does not require specialist linguistic knowledge. *Class No:* 801.313.2(410)

[5284]

REANEY, P.H. The Origin of English surnames. London, Routledge & Kegan Paul, 1967 (reprinted in paperback 1980). xix,415p. maps. £10.99. ISBN: 0415059178.

A companion to the author's *Dictionary of British surnames,* it aims to give 'a general account of the development of English surnames, their classification, changes in pronunciation and spelling, and the gradual

....*(contd.)*
growth of hereditary family names' (*Preface*). 17 chapters with numerous subsections. Bibliography (3p.). Subject index and index of over 6,000 names treated in the text.
Class No: 801.313.2(410)

[5285]
—McKINLEY, R.A. A History of British surnames. London, Longman, 1990. viii,230p. £14.99. (*Approaches to local history*.) ISBN: 0582018692.

9 chapters including one on each of the 5 main types of name (locative, topographical, occupational, personal and nicknames). Advice on further reading (6p.) evaluates the major dictionaries and general works on surnames. Index of *c.*1,700 names mentioned in the text. Goes beyond the purely linguistic approach of Reaney, stressing the importance of historical, geographical, social and genealogical factors. The author was Director of the Survey of English Surnames at Leicester University for 22 years.
Class No: 801.313.2(410)

Scotland

[5286]
BLACK, G.F. The Surnames of Scotland; their origin, meaning and history. New York, New York Public Library, 1946 (repr. Edinburgh, Birlinn, 1996). lxxii,838p. £20. ISBN: 1874744831.

The standard dictionary of Scottish surnames has finally been published in the UK after being kept in print for many years by the NYPL, where Black worked. Covers *c.*8,000 names and contains much genealogical information. Sometimes cites conflicting opinions on etymology, even when these are considered to be erroneous. Glossary of obsolete or uncommon Scots words occurring in the dictionary. List of principal sources (*c.*350 titles).
Class No: 801.313.2(411)

[5287]
WHYTE, D. Scottish surnames and families. Edinburgh, Birlinn, 1995. 288p. £7.99. ISBN: 1874744394.

Lists 280 of the most common Scottish surnames, giving historical and geographical origins and substantial details of family histories. *Class No:* 801.313.2(411)

Ireland

[5288]
BELL, R. The Book of Ulster surnames. Belfast, Blackstaff Press, 1989. 304p. £9.99. ISBN: 0856406023.

Over 500 of the most common surnames in the Province: history; derivation; why name changed; what form it is today; name's famous bearers; where in Ulster it is most common. Glossary (4p.). Bibliography (2p.).
Class No: 801.313.2(415)

[5289]
DE BREFFNY, B. Irish family names: arms, origins, and locations. Dublin, Gill and Macmillan; New York, Norton, 1982. 192p. illus. maps. £9.95. ISBN: 071711225x, Ireland; 0393016129, US.

1. The counties of Ireland (topographical and historical notes, with details of family distribution) - 2. Map of Ireland showing locations of family names - 3. 1,000 Irish family names, A-Z, with many coats of arms in colour - 4. Index of additional names mentioned in the text. List of the 100 commonest surnames. Many colour illustrations.
Class No: 801.313.2(415)

[5290]
MacLYSAGHT, E. The Surnames of Ireland. 7th ed. Dublin, Irish Academic Press, 1989. 320p. maps. ISBN: 0716524414.

1st ed. 1964, as *Guide to Irish surnames;* 6th ed. 1985.

Lists over 4,000 Gaelic, Norman and Anglo-Irish surnames A-Z, giving linguistic derivation, the historical background and location of the Irish and Hiberno-Norman septs and families, and the date and place of settlement of Anglo-Irish families. Appendix 1. English and Scottish surnames in Ireland - 2. Notes on the simplification of Gaelic forms of Irish surnames. *Class No:* 801.313.2(415)

Wales

[5291]
MORGAN, T.J. *and* **MORGAN, P. Welsh surnames.** Cardiff, Univ. of Wales Press, 1985. 211p. £10.95. ISBN: 0708309364.

Based on Welsh, Latin and English texts, on parish registers and local histories. Lengthy introduction (31p.) explains the classification of Welsh surnames. Dictionary section has detailed information, including historical development and current distribution, for *c.*350 names and numerous variants. Likely to remain the standard work for many years. *Class No:* 801.313.2(429)

Germany

[5292]
GOTTSCHALD, M. Deutsche Namenkunde: unsere Familiennamen nach ihrer Entstehung und Bedeutung. 5. Aufl. Berlin, de Gruyter, 1982. 667p. DM.210. ISBN: 3110086182.

1st ed. 1931.

Over 18,000 entries. Lengthy, scholarly introduction (144p.) about name studies and types of names.
Class No: 801.313.2(430)

Italy

[5293]
FELICE, E. de. Dizionario dei nomi italiani: origine, etimologia, storia, diffusione e frequenza di oltre 18000 nomi. Milano, Mondadori, 1986. 410p. ISBN: 880428319x.

A dictionary of surnames with very informative entries, indicating variant forms, the number of people in Italy with the name, geographical distribution, etymology, and history. Index of all forms cited. *Class No:* 801.313.2(450)

Spain

[5294]
GOSNELL, C.F. Spanish personal names: principles governing their formation and use which may be presented as a help for catalogers and bibliographers. Reprint of 1938 ed. Detroit, Ethridge, 1971. x,112p.

First published New York, Wilson, 1938.

Primarily intended for librarians, but contains much useful information on the origin and evolution of Spanish names. Bibliography of sources (13p.). *Class No:* 801.313.2(460)

Japan

[5295]

HADAMITZKY, W. Japanese, Chinese and Korean surnames and how to read them: 125,947 Japanese, 594 Chinese, and 259 Korean surnames written with kanji as they appear in Japanese texts. München, Saur, 1998. 2v. DM596. ISBN: 359811334x.

V.1 *From characters to readings*. xxiv,1145p.

V.2 *From readings to characters*. v,405p.

V.1 is for looking up the pronunciations or transliterations of names given in kanji and uses the same kanji naming scheme as Hadamitzky and Spahn's *Japanese character dictionary* (*q.v.*). In v.2, all names are arranged A-Z according to their romanized spelling, using a slightly modified version of the Hepburn system.
Class No: 801.313.2(52)

Russia in Asia

[5296]

UNBEGAUN, B.O. Russian surnames. Oxford, Clarendon Press, 1972. xviii,529p.

A detailed study of both morphological and semantic aspects of Russian names, with 2 general chapters followed by 11 on different types of names. Index of over 10,000 names mentioned in the text. Index of name-endings. Extensive annotated bibliography (10p.).
Class No: 801.313.2(57)

South Africa

[5297]

PAMA, C. Die Groot Afrikaanse familienaamboek. Kaapstad, Human & Rousseau, 1983. 380p. illus. ISBN: 0798115610.

7 introductory sections, followed by dictionary, p.39-375. Bibliography (2p.). *Class No:* 801.313.2(680)

USA

[5298]

HOOK, J.N. Family names: how our surnames came to America. New York, Macmillan; London, Collier Macmillan, 1982. viii,388p. $8.95. ISBN: 0685462447.

An account of the evolution and development of American surnames arranged by ethnic group. Not compiled as a dictionary, but does highlight over 2,500 names.
Class No: 801.313.2(73)

[5299]

SMITH, E.C. New dictionary of American family names. New York, Harper & Row, 1973 (repr. Random House, 1988). 570p. $8.99. ISBN: 0517669544.

A new ed. of *Dictionary of American family names* (1957). Lists *c.*22,000 US surnames (a huge increase on earlier ed.) with brief notes on their origin and meaning but without detailed etymologies. *Class No:* 801.313.2(73)

Jews

[5300]

BEIDER, A. A Dictionary of Jewish surnames from the Russian Empire. Teaneck, N.J., Avotaynu, 1993. 760p. illus. $75. ISBN: 0962637335.

Lists 50,000 names and indicates for each the geographical district where it was found, according to early 20th-century records. Lengthy introduction (over 100p.) includes much useful information on the history and types of

.... *(contd.)*

Jewish surnames and lists the most common ones in the Russian Empire and the Soviet Union. 'A major contribution to onomastics, applied linguistics, and Jewish culture' (*Choice*, v.31(5), Jan. 1994, p. 747).

Beider has also compiled *A Dictionary of Jewish surnames from the Kingdom of Poland* (Avotaynu, 1996. 570p. illus. $69.50. ISBN: 0962637394), which covers 32,000 names in equally thorough fashion. *Class No:* 801.313.2(=924)

[5301]

GUGGENHEIMER, H.W. *and* **GUGGENHEIMER, E.H. Jewish family names and their origins:** an etymological dictionary. Hoboken, N.J., Ktav, 1992. 882p. $99.50. ISBN: 0881252972.

Detailed introductory survey, followed by etymologies for *c.*65,000 of the 75,000 names ever used by Jews worldwide. Related names grouped together.
Class No: 801.313.2(=924)

[5302]

KAGANOFF, B.C. A Dictionary of Jewish names and their history. New York, Schacken, 1977; London, Routledge, 1978. xiii,250p. $11.95. ISBN: 0805206434, US; 071008935x, UK.

A popular history of Jewish names in 11 chapters (120p.) followed by a dictionary of *c.*750 selected names, assigning them to one of 11 categories (patronymic, occupation, etc.) and giving information on origins, meanings, and variants. Bibliography (2p.). Index of nearly 4,000 names. Subject index. *Class No:* 801.313.2(=924)

Eponyms

[5303]

BEECHING, C.L. A Dictionary of eponyms. 3rd ed. London, Library Assoc., 1989. ix,218p. £30. ISBN: 0853655596.

1st ed. 1979; 2nd ed. 1983. Both published London, Clive Bingley.

511 eponyms arranged alphabetically from 'Aaron's beard' to 'Zwinglianism' and explained by short essays about the person behind the name. Concentrates on eponyms with interesting stories and generally excludes motor car names and examples from engineering, horticulture and botany. New entries for this ed. include 'Becquerel' and 'Listeria'. Subject index. *Class No:* 801.313.9

[5304]

Eponyms dictionaries index: a reference guide to persons, both real and imaginary, and the terms derived from their names, providing basic biographical identification and citing dictionaries, encyclopaedias, word books, journal articles, and other sources for additional information. Ruffner, J.A., *ed.* Detroit, Gale, 1977. 760p. ISBN: 0810306883.

About 20,000 eponym entries and 13,000 personal names on which they are based, in one sequence, A-Z. Over 500 biographical sources are cited in all. Fields include agriculture, anthropology, botany, chemistry, engineering and industry, fine arts, law, linguistics, mathematics, mythology, politics, religion, weaponry and zoology.

Supplement, no. 1, ed. by J. Mossman. 1984. 248p. $94. ISBN: 0810306891. *Class No:* 801.313.9

[5305]

FREEMAN, M.S. A New dictionary of eponyms. New York, Oxford Univ. Press, 1997. x,284p. £14.95. ISBN: 0195093542.

Gives quite lengthy (at least 200 words, often much more), anecdotal explanations of *c.*500 eponyms. No references to sources but 30 specialist dictionaries are listed at the end. *Class No:* 801.313.9

[5306]

MANSER, M.H. Dictionary of eponyms. London, Sphere, 1988. 307p. illus. ISBN: 0722163126.

Approx 1,000 eponyms are listed in a single A-Z sequence and explained in non-scholarly terms in this paperback. Concentrates on the more well-known eponyms in general use and includes brief biographical information. *Class No:* 801.313.9

[5307]

PARTRIDGE, E. Name into word: proper names that have become common property; a discursive dictionary. London, Secker & Warburg, 1949. xv,644p.

Entries on both eponyms and toponyms, *i.e.* words derived from personal and place names which have passed into common use in English. Explanatory notes, including biographical information. *Class No:* 801.313.9

Toponyms

[5308]

VINEY, N. A Dictionary of toponyms. London, Library Assoc., 1986. viii,103p. ISBN: 0853657475.

Over 500 entries for place names, with explanations of the words and phrases derived from each which have passed into the English language; more than one in many cases, *e.g.* 6 from Bath. *Class No:* 801.313.90

Multilingual Dictionaries

[5309]

Collins series 100 multilingual dictionary on CD-ROM. Worthing, HarperCollins Electronic Reference, 1997. CD-ROM. £29.99. ISBN: 0003712567.

Bilingual dictionaries of English with French, German, Italian and Spanish on a single CD-ROM. Over 75,000 references and 110,000 translations per dictionary pair. *Class No:* 801.323.9

[5310]

Elsevier dictionaries on CD-ROM. Amsterdam, Elsevier, 1997. CD-ROM. $750. ISBN: 0444827595.

A single disc containing 51 specialist technical dictionaries, most of them multilingual, *e.g. Elsevier's banking dictionary* gives terms in 7 languages. Dictionaries are grouped in 3 segments: Economics, business and finance (12 titles), Agriculture, food and animal sciences (17) and Engineering (26) and these can be purchased separately. The total number of terms is around 1,400,000, covering *c.*300,000 concepts. *Class No:* 801.323.9

[5311]

Harrap's CD-ROM multilingual dictionary database. London, Harrap; Lincolnwood, Ill., National Textbook Co., 1989. £88. ISBN: 0245600256, UK.

US title is *Languages of the world: multilingual dictionary database on CD-ROM*

18 dictionaries on one CD-ROM, giving access to over 7 million words in 12 languages: English, French, German, Spanish, Italian, Dutch, Danish, Finnish, Norwegian, Swedish, Japanese, and Chinese. The dictionaries include

....*(contd.)*

both general works (*e.g. Il Nuovo Ragazzini*) and specialist lexicons (*e.g. Sansyusha's dictionary of science and technology: English-German-Japanese*). 5 are Harrap publications. Updated according to dictionary revisions. Searching can be confined to a single dictionary or several dictionaries can be searched at once. *Class No:* 801.323.9

[5312]

Oxford 3-in-1 bilingual dictionary Oxford, Oxford Univ. Press, [1997?]. CD-ROM £120. ISBN: 0192683322.

Combines *The Oxford Hachette French dictionary*, *The Oxford Spanish dictionary* and *The Oxford Russian dictionary* (*qq.v.*) on a single disk. *Class No:* 801.323.9

[5313]

Visual dictionary: English, French, German, Spanish. Corbeil, J-C. *and* Archambault, A., *eds.* Oxford, Oxford Univ. Press, 1997. xxx,959p. illus. £19.99. ISBN: 0198631456.

Supersedes *The Facts on File visual dictionary* (New York, Facts on File, 1986; Oxford, Facts on File, 1988).

A British edition of a dictionary developed in Canada by scholars working in English and French and aimed at 'all persons who participate in one way or another in contemporary civilization and, as a consequence, need to know and use a great number of technical terms from a wide range of fields ... It is not designed only for specialists (*Introduction*). It comprises 3,500 labelled, full-colour illustrations, arranged thematically under 28 main headings (*e.g.* Weapons, Clothing) and covering 600 subjects, followed by indexes in 4 languages to the 20,000-plus terms illustrated. The pictures are of the highest quality and include detailed cutaways and cross-sections. Particularly useful for technological subjects. *Class No:* 801.323.9

Phonology

[5314]

The Handbook of phonetic sciences. Hardcastle, W.J. *and* Laver, J., *eds.* London, Blackwell, 1997. viii,904p. £90. (*Blackwell handbooks in linguistics.*) ISBN: 0631188487.

A comprehensive account of the state of current research, with 26 signed chapters by international experts. 5 sections: 1. Experimental phonetics - 2. Biological perspectives - 3. Models of speech production and perception - 4. Linguistic phonetics - 5. Speech technology. Bibliography (94p.). Index. *Class No:* 801.4

[5315]

The Handbook of phonological theory. Goldsmith, J.A., *ed.* London, Blackwell, 1995. xiv,986p. £75. (*Blackwell handbooks in linguistics..*) ISBN: 0631180621.

32 signed chapters (average 27p.), with numbered subsections, of which 22 describe the state of the art in the various specialisms within phonology (*e.g.* Stress Theory, Prosodic Morphology) and 8 review specific languages and language families which have been particularly important in recent phonological research. Comprehensive bibliography (76p.). Indexes of names, subjects and languages. *Class No:* 801.4

[5316]

LADEFOGED, P. *and* **MADDIESON, I. The Sounds of the world's languages.** London, Blackwell, 1995. 400p. illus. £50. ISBN: 0631198156.

An ambitious attempt to describe all the known ways in which the sounds of the world's languages differ. Chapters on each type of sound (fricatives, nasals, clicks, etc.) are illustrated with data drawn from nearly 400 languages and presented in numerous tables and diagrams.

CAT. *Class No:* 801.4

[5317]

PULLUM, G.K. *and* **LADUSAW, W.A. Phonetic symbol guide.** Chicago, Univ. of Chicago Press, 1986. xxx,266p. $35. ISBN: 0226685314.

Describes and explains the use of all phonetic symbols likely to be encountered in modern linguistic work, and also covers diacritical marks. Clearly presented entries include notes comparing usage under the European IPA tradition and the American tradition, the differences between these being explained in the introduction. Appendices include glossary of phonetic terminology, bibliography, and comparative charts of vowels and consonants. 'The book is unique. It is very competently done. The attention to detail is exemplary, as is the clarity of exposition' (*Journal of Linguistics*, v.24(2), Sept. 1988, p.570-71). *Class No:* 801.4

[5318]

TRASK, R.L. Dictionary of phonetics and phonology. London, Routledge, 1996. xii,424p. £15.99. ISBN: 0415112613.

Written for students of linguistics, applied linguistics and speech therapy, and defines over 2,000 terms. Entries include: pronunciation; notational devices and symbols; earliest sources of terms; suggestions for further reading; and usage guidance. Also includes an explanation of the most important theoretical approaches to phonology. Bibliography (30p.). *Class No:* 801.4

Semantics & Semiotics

[5319]

Encyclopedic dictionary of semiotics. Sebeok, T.A., *ed.* 2nd ed., rev. & updated. Berlin, Mouton de Gruyter, 1994. 3v. (xxi,1725p.). DM.738. ISBN: 3110142295.

1st ed. 1986.

V.1, *A-M;* v.2, *N-Z;* v.3, *Bibliography.*

Vols. 1-2 have 426 lengthy, signed articles, by 236 contributors from many countries, giving 3 types of information: the historical background and present usage of semiotic terms; biographical information on and assessment of the work of leading figures in semiotic studies; and exposition of the impact of semiotics on various disciplines. V.3 lists over 5,500 works under authors, A-Z, which are cited in the dictionary. 45 of the contributors submitted revisions for the 2nd ed.

For a beginner's guide, see V.M. Colapietro's *Glossary of semiotics* (New York, Paragon House, 1993. 212p. $19.95. ISBN: 1557785643). *Class No:* 801.54

[5320]

ESCHBACH, A. *and* **ESCHBACH-SZABÓ, V. Bibliography of semiotics, 1975-1985.** Amsterdam, J. Benjamins, 1986. 2v. (948p.). Hfl.404. ISBN: 9027237395.

Lists 10,839 books, articles, dissertations, conference proceedings, *Festschriften,* and reviews on the branch of linguistics dealing with signs and signalling systems.

....*(contd.)*

Arranged by author, A-Z, with no annotations. List of nearly 700 periodicals. Index of reviews and thorough index of subjects and names (165p.). *Class No:* 801.54

[5321]

GIPPER, H. *and* **SCHWARTZ, H. Bibliographisches Handbuch zur Sprachinhaltsforschung.** Köln, Westdeutscher Verlag, 1962-89. 2 pts. in 8v. (*Library and information sources in linguistics-16.*) ISSN: 01711105.

Pt. 1: *Schrifttum zur Sprachinhaltsforschung in alphabetischer Folge nach Verfassern mit Besprechungen und Inhaltsinweisen.* 1962-85. 4v.(32 fascicules. 4038p.). *Beiheft 1-2.* 1974-80.

Pt. 2: *Systematischer Teil (Register).* 1980-89. 4v.

Pt. 1 is a comprehensive bibliography of works in many languages on the semantic content of language. 30,744 entries arranged by author, A-Z, many with annotations and references to reviews. Pt. 2 is a series of index vols., including indexes to names, concepts, subjects and dictionaries. *Class No:* 801.54

[5322]

GORDON, W.T. Semantics: a bibliography, 1965-1978. Metuchen, N.J., Scarecrow, 1980. xiv,307p. ISBN: 0810813009.

3,326 entries, some with brief annotations, in 23 thematic sections listing books, articles, dissertations and conference papers in English, German, French, Italian, Spanish and Portuguese. Lexical index and author index. 'The most complete bibliography of semantics to date. No major works seem to have been omitted and few, if any, minor ones' (*Choice*, v.18(4), Dec. 1980. p.506).

Followed by *Semantics: a bibliography, 1979-85* (Scarecrow, 1987. 304p. ISBN: 0810820552), which has over 2,700 entries in a similar format, and *Semantics: a bibliography, 1986-91* (Scarecrow, 1992. ix,280p. $31. ISBN: 0810825988), which includes a glossary of specialist terms. *Class No:* 801.54

[5323]

The Handbook of contemporary semantic theory. Lappin, S., *ed.* London, Blackwell, 1996. xv,670p. £65. (*Blackwell handbooks in linguistics.*) ISBN: 0631187529.

22 signed chapters (average 28p.), with numbered subsections, providing a comprehensive overview of the central issues in contemporary semantic theory, plus a comprehensive bibliography (35p.). Index.

Class No: 801.54

[5324]

NÖTH, W. Handbook of semiotics. Bloomington, Ind., Indiana Univ. Press, 1990. 576p. $57.50. ISBN: 0253341205.

Covers the whole field of semiotics in 65 encyclopedic articles on the folowing main topics: signs; semiosis; language and language-based codes; schools and major figures; text semiotics; nonverbal communication; aesthetics and visual communication. Bibliography of nearly 3,000 titles. Indexes of names and terms. 'This is the most systematic discussion of semiotics yet published' (*Choice*, v.28(8), April 1991, p.1304). *Class No:* 801.54

802.0 English Language

English Language

Bibliographies of Bibliographies

[5325]

NORTHUP, C.S., *and others*. A Register of bibliographies of the English language and literature. New Haven, Conn., Yale Univ. Press; London, Oxford Univ. Press, 1925. xii,507p.

A fairly complete list of bibliographies up to 1922, covering a wider field than the title suggests. *c.*12,000 items, both separately published and in books, in 2 sections for general material and for individual authors and topics, A-Z. Detailed index. Superseded by Howard-Hill (*q.v.*) for literary bibliographies. *Class No:* 802.0(009)

Bibliographies

[5326]

ALSTON, R.C. A Bibliography of the English language, from the invention of printing to the year 1800: a systematic record of writings on English, and on other languages in English, based on the collections of the principal libraries in the world. Leeds, E.J. Arnold, 1965-87. 12v.

1. *English grammars written in English*. 1965.
2. *English grammars written in other languages; polyglot grammars and dictionaries*. 1967.
3. *Miscellaneous works dealing with various aspects of English; grammar; non-technical glossaries; theory of grammar*. 1971.
4. *Spelling*. 1967.
5. *The English dictionary*. 1966.
6. *Rhetoric; prosody; rhyme; pronunciation; elocution; phonetics*. 1969.
7. *Logic; philosophy; epistemology; universal language*. 1967.
8. *Short-hand*. 1966.
9. *Non-standard English; cant; dialect*. 1971.
10. *Education; teaching of languages*. 1972-73.
11. *Place and personal names*. 1977.
12. *Romance languages (grammars, dictionaries, glossaries, spelling, pronunciation)*. 1985-87. 2 pts.

Detailed descriptions, facsimiles, and library locations worldwide. 20 vols. planned. A corrected reprint of vols. 1-10 'reproduced from the author's annotated copy with corrections and additions to 1973, including cumulative indices' published 1974 in 1 vol. (1248p.) by Janus Press, Ilkley, Yorks. *Class No:* 802.0(01)

[5327]

Annual bibliography of English language and literature (ABELL), 1920-. London, Modern Humanities Research Assoc., 1921-. v.1-. ISSN: 00663786.

Earlier published by Cambridge Univ. Press for M.H.R.A.

V.70: *1995* (1997. xxix,1338p.) has 20,413 entries for books, pamphlets and periodical articles (from *c.*1,400 journals), as well as unpublished British and Irish theses,

....*(contd.)*

covering the English language and English, American and Commonwealth literature. English language section (p.105-201) has 1,577 entries under 10 main headings and numerous subheadings. Cross-references. Index of authors and subjects. Index of scholars. More comprehensive than *The Year's work in English studies* (*q.v.*), but not annotated.

Complete set of over 100,000 records, 1920-95, made available on CD-ROM in 1998 by Chadwyck-Healey, Cambridge. Also available on the Internet via their *Literature Online (LION)* subscription service (http://lion.chadwyck.co.uk). Subscribers can choose access extending back to 1920 or just to 1980. *Class No:* 802.0(01)

[5328]

The Year's work in English studies, 1919-. Oxford, Blackwell; Atlantic Highlands, N.J., Humanities Press, for The English Association, 1921-. v.1-. Annual. ISSN: 00844144.

Earlier published by Oxford Univ. Press and J. Murray.

V.76: *1995* (1998. lxxi,936p. £125) has 18 chapters in which subject specialists survey the year's output of books and articles (from over 950 journals) on the English language and English, American and Commonwealth literature. Chapter 1, English language (p.1-109), has 9 sections, with references to periodical articles in the text and over 150 books listed at the end of the chapter. Index of critics. Index of authors and subjects.

Special topic-based editions are announced for 1998 as *The English Association critical bibliographies*. These will comprise sets of volumes which include all references in this series to a particular period, subject or major author. The first three titles are:

A Critical bibliography of American literature studies, 1954-1994. 2984p. £425. ISBN: 0631209387.

A Critical bibliography of English language studies, 1940-1994. 1952p. £300. ISBN: 0631209425.

A Critical bibliography of twentieth-century English literature studies, 1954-1994. 2832p. £340. ISBN: 0631209409. *Class No:* 802.0(01)

Encyclopaedias & Dictionaries

[5329]

The Oxford companion to the English language. McArthur, T., *ed.* Oxford, Oxford Univ. Press, 1992. xxvii,1184p. £25. ISBN: 019214183x.

A major new reference work covering all aspects of the language, with over 4,000 entries in the usual *Oxford companion* double-column, A-Z arrangement, with cross-references and the welcome addition of a 33-page index of persons. Entries are signed (over 90 international contributors), vary in length from a few lines to 6p. on major topics, such as national literatures and the main varieties of English, and are each ascribed to one or more of 22 themes or topic areas. The full list of these themes, which include Geography (national and regional varieties); Biography (linguists, lexicographers, influential literary authors); Usage (contentious issues, usage guides); Education (theory and practice of teaching English); Media (publishing, journalism,

.... (contd.)

broadcasting); and Reference (dictionaries, thesauri), indicates the breadth of coverage. After the overview article for each theme all the entries within that topic are listed. Selective bibliographies follow the longer articles.

Difficult to fault the content, but maps, tables and illustrations would have increased accessibility. Nevertheless, excellent value and essential in both specialist and general collections.

The Oxford companion to the English language: abridged version (1996. 1074p. £14.99. ISBN: 0198631367) is a paperback with nearly 2,000 entries, concentrating on 5 key themes: grammar, usage, dialect, pronunciation and the history of English. *Class No:* 802.0(03)

Encyclopaedias

[5330]

CRYSTAL, D. The Cambridge encyclopedia of the English language. Cambridge, Cambridge Univ. Press, 1995. vii,489p. illus. £29.95. ISBN: 0521401798.

Comprehensive coverage of English worldwide in 6 main sections (1. The History of English - 2. English vocabulary - 3. English grammar - 4. Spoken and written English - 5. Using English - 6. Learning about English) containing 24 chapters and dozens of subsections. Beautifully presented, with illustrations on virtually every page (many in colour), numerous maps, charts and tables. Glossary (13p.). Bibliography (8p.). Addresses of journals and societies. Indexes of linguistic terms, authors and topics.

Another triumph for Crystal. 'As the work of one man, recalls Johnson in its ambition and scope ... I have been unable to think of a question his book cannot answer' (*TLS*, no.4831, Nov. 3, 1995, p.8), but not as easy to use for reference purposes as McArthur's dictionary-style *Oxford companion*. A good library will have both, alongside Crystal's other magnum opus, *The Cambridge encyclopedia of language* (*q.v.*). *Class No:* 802.0(031)

Reviews & Abstracts

[5331]

Abstracts of English studies. Boulder, Colo., National Council of Teachers of English (later Alberta, Univ. of Calgary Press), 1958-94. 37v. ISSN: 00013560.

See entry at 820-0(048). *Class No:* 802.0(048)

[5332]

Anglia: Zeitschrift für englische Phonologie. Halle (later Tübingen), Niemeyer, 1878-. v.1-. 2py. since 1983 (formerly annual). ISSN: 03405222.

A major periodical covering English language and literature, which carries *c.*200 lengthy book reviews each year. *Class No:* 802.0(048)

[5333]

—English and American studies in German: summaries of theses and monographs. A supplement to *Anglia*. 1968-. Tübingen, Niemeyer, 1969-. Annual. ISSN: 00710490.

Contains summaries in English of German-language studies of English and American language and literature, provided by the authors themselves. The vol. for 1992 (1993. xiii,191p.) has 91 summaries (1-2p. in length) in 4 sections (Language; English literature; American literature; Teaching of English) followed by 3 indexes: authors and editors; contributors to collectanea; authors and subjects treated. *Class No:* 802.0(048)

Histories

[5334]

BAUGH, A.C. *and* **CABLE, T. A History of the English language.** 4th ed. Englewood Cliffs, N.J., Prentice Hall; London, Routledge, 1993. xiv,444p. £14.99. ISBN: 0415093791, UK.

1st ed. 1951; 3rd ed. 1978.

Presents the historical development of English against the background of political, social and intellectual events. Includes a chapter on English in America. Extensive chapter bibliographies with evaluative commentary, plus footnote references. 11 chapters with numbered sections. Index. Changes for this ed. include a rewritten opening chapter on the place of English in the world; revised sections on Old English and Middle English syntax; expanded coverage of regional varieties of the language; and updated bibliographies. *Class No:* 802.0(091)

[5335]

The Cambridge history of the English language. Cambridge, Cambridge Univ. Press, 1992- . v.1- (in progress).

V.1 *The Beginnings to 1066*, ed. by R.M. Hogg. 1992. xxii,609p. £70. ISBN: 052126474x.

V.2 *1066-1478*, ed. by N.F. Blake. 1992. xxi,703p. £70. ISBN: 0521264758.

V.5 *English in Britain and overseas: origins and development*, ed. by R.W. Burchfield. 1994. xxiii,656p. £70. ISBN: 0521264782.

3 vols. have appeared so far of this projected 6-vol. set. Vols. 1 and 2 have 8 and 7 signed chapters respectively, with numbered subsections. V.5 has 10 chapters covering dialects of England and the English language in Scotland, Wales, Ireland, and the major Commonwealth countries. Each vol. has guide to further reading after each chapter; glossary of linguistic terms; substantial bibliography (over 40p. in each case); and comprehensive index. 'Certain to become a classic in the history of the English language' (*Choice*, v.30(9), May,1993, p.1460).

Vols. 3 and 4 (due 1998) will continue chronological coverage from the 1470s to the present and v.6 (due 1999) will deal with English in North America.

Class No: 802.0(091)

Origins

Anglo-Saxon

Bibliographies

[5336]

MITCHELL, B. A Critical bibliography of Old English syntax to the end of 1984, including addenda and corrigenda to *Old English syntax*. London, Blackwell, 1990. xxii,269p. £85. ISBN: 0631132759.

A bibliography of books, doctoral dissertations, articles, notes and reviews, to supplement Mitchell's 2-volume *Old English syntax* (Oxford, Clarendon Press, 1985). *c.*1,150 entries in chapters covering bibliographies; dictionaries; concordances and glossaries; grammars; general studies; and studies on the syntax of individual texts or authors. Annotations include references to reviews. Subject index and index of authors and reviewers. *Class No:* 802.0-022(01)

[5337]

Old English newsletter. Kalamazoo, Mich., Medieval Institute at Western Michigan Univ., for The Old English Division of the MLA, 1967-. v.1, no.1-. Quarterly. ISSN: 00301973.

See entry at 820-022(01). *Class No:* 802.0-022(01)

[5338]

TAJIMA, M. Old and Middle English language studies: a classified bibliography, 1923-1985. Amsterdam, Benjamins, 1988. xxxiii,391p. ISBN: 9027237328.

14 classified sections for linguistic topics (syntax, morphology, etc.), with 3 separate author sequences within each for general studies, Old English and Middle English. 3,913 entries plus references to reviews. Some brief annotations. Name index. International coverage, although Slavic and Japanese material is generally omitted.
Class No: 802.0-022(01)

Handbooks & Manuals

[5339]

PARTRIDGE, A.C. A Companion to Old and Middle English studies. London, Deutsch; Totowa, N.J., Barnes & Noble, 1982.

See entry at 820-022(035). *Class No:* 802.0-022(035)

Dictionaries

[5340]

BORDEN, A.R. A Comprehensive Old English dictionary. Washington, D.C., Univ. Press of America, 1982. vi,1606p. ISBN: 0819122548.

A simple listing of *c.*40,000 Anglo-Saxon words, giving part of speech (with gender indicated for nouns and class for verbs) and modern English equivalent. The author claims that he has included every word in the standard dictionaries (Bosworth, Hall, etc.) plus other words he has found in over 25 years of checking texts. *Class No:* 802.0-022(038)

[5341]

BOSWORTH, J. Anglo-Saxon dictionary, based on the manuscript collections of the late Joseph Bosworth, ed. and enl. by T.N. Toller. Oxford, Clarendon Press, 1882-98 (repr. 1972). xii,1302p. £160. ISBN: 0198631014.

— *Supplement*, by T.N. Toller. Oxford, Clarendon Press, 1908-21. 768p.

— *Enlarged addenda and corrigenda to the Supplement*, by A. Campbell. Oxford, Clarendon Press, 1972. viii,68p.

The *Supplement* and *Enlarged addenda* are now available in one vol. (£110. ISBN: 019863112x).

The standard dictionary of Old English. About 60,000 entries in all, with many illustrative quotations, drawn from manuscripts and printed sources. In the main volume sources are listed on p.iii-xii. In the *Supplement*, letters A-G occupy over half the volume, representing the revision and enlargement which T.N. Toller was not able to make in the main work. *Class No:* 802.0-022(038)

[5342]

Dictionary of Old English. Healey, A., *and others, eds.* Toronto, Pontifical Institute of Medieval Studies, for the Centre for Medieval Studies, Univ. of Toronto, 1986- (in progress).

Based on the computer-readable Old English corpus, which contains all surviving Old English texts written in England between 600 and 1150 AD.

Fascicles covering 5 (*a, æ, b, c, d, e*) out of 22 letters published by 1998. Entries contain translations, frequency counts for each word in the Corpus, citations for all words of 12 or fewer occurrences in the Corpus, and usage labels. Completed dictionary to be published in book form.

The Dictionary of Old English Corpus in electronic form (ISBN: 0472002775) is available as an online database via the World Wide Web, a site licence from the Univ. of Michigan Press costing $200 per year (enquiries to: site-

....*(contd.)*

licences@umich.edu). It contains around 3 million words of Old English and 2 million words of Latin. *Class No:* 802.0-022(038)

[5343]

English-Old English / Old English-English dictionary. Jember, G.K., *and others, eds.* Boulder, Colo., Westview Press, 1975. xxxiii,178p. ISBN: 0891580069.

Claims to be 'the first double-entry dictionary available to students of old English' (*Preface*). *c.*5,000 entries in each half. Introduction includes outline grammar and detailed notes on word formation and word order. *Class No:* 802.0-022(038)

[5344]

HALL, J.R.C. A Concise Anglo-Saxon dictionary. 4th ed., with a supplement by H.D. Merritt. Cambridge, Cambridge Univ. Press, 1960 (repr. Toronto, Univ. of Toronto Press, 1984). xv,432p. $19.95. ISBN: 0802065481.

1st ed. 1894; 3rd ed. 1931.

About 40,000 entries; aims to deal with all the words that occur in Anglo-Saxon poetry and prose. List of sources (7p.). It includes 12th-century words not in Bosworth and has references to Old English quotations in the *OED*. A standard dictionary for the non-specialist. The supplement covers 1,700 words. *Class No:* 802.0-022(038)

[5345]

POLLINGTON, S. Wordcraft: English / Old English dictionary and thesaurus. Pinner, Middx., Anglo-Saxon Books, 1993. 240p. £9.95. ISBN: 1898281025.

Provides Old English equivalents for common modern words in both dictionary and thesaurus formats. Thesaurus comprises thematic lists under subject headings and is cross-referenced to the dictionary. *Class No:* 802.0-022(038)

Theses

[5346]

PULSIANO, P. An Annotated bibliography of North American doctoral dissertations on Old English language and literature. East Lansing, Mich., Colleagues Press; Woodbridge, Boydell & Brewer, 1988. 336p. ISBN: 093719106x, UK.

Over 1,000 entries in 3 sections for general works, poetry, and prose, with a chronological arrangement within each. Entries include references to *Dissertation Abstracts International* and are fully cross-referenced. Subject and author indexes. *Class No:* 802.0-022(043)

Grammar

[5347]

HOGG, R.M. A Grammar of Old English: V.1 Phonology. Oxford, Blackwell, 1992. xii,355p. £55. ISBN: 063113672x.

A highly detailed study in 7 chapters with over 400 numbered subsections. Bibliography (15p.). Old English word index (36p.). Cross-references to the Toronto *Dictionary of Old English* project (*q.v.*). *Class No:* 802.0-022-5

Middle English Language

[5348]

LAING, M. Catalogue of sources for *A Linguistic atlas of early medieval English*. Cambridge, Brewer, 1993. x,186p. £35. ISBN: 0859913848.

A comprehensive inventory of English texts from the period *c.*1150-1300, the first stage in the creation of an atlas to complement *A Linguistic atlas of late medieval English* (*q.v.*), listing later versions of Old English texts and new compositions in early Middle English.

500 mss. listed by repository, A-Z, with date; contents; references to other sources of information; cross-references to other mss.; associations with people and places; number of hands; and language (*i.e.* provisional assessment of origin of English. Indexes of Middle English texts by author/title and incipit. Indexes of Old English, French and Latin texts. *Class No:* 802.0-023

[5349]

A Linguistic atlas of late medieval English. McIntosh, A., *and others*. Aberdeen, Aberdeen Univ. Press, 1986 (now available from The Mercat Press, Edinburgh). 4v. £335. ISBN: 0080324371.

V.1 *General introduction. Index of sources. Dot maps.* x,570p.

V.2 *Item maps.* xxiv,388p.

V.3 *Linguistic profiles.* xxiv,700p.

V.4 *County dictionary.* xxii,346p.

The product of nearly 35 years work at Edinburgh University. It covers England and (where possible) Wales in the period *c.*1350-1450, and comprises: an Index of Sources by repositories and by counties; a set of 'dot maps' for particular items; a more complex set of maps showing spellings and numbers for Linguistic Profiles; the Profiles themselves, giving the results of a 'questionnaire' applied to hundreds of scribes; and a dictionary giving forms for questionnaire items, county by county.

Packed with information (the Index of Sources is the largest list in existence of mss. containing Middle English), but 'dauntingly hard to use' (*TLS,* no.4413, Oct 30th., 1987, p.1200). *Guide to 'A Linguistic atlas of late medieval English'* (24p. £2.95. ISBN: 0080350763) has sample pages from all 4 vols. with explanations. *Class No:* 802.0-023

[5350]

Middle English dictionary. Kurath, H., *ed.* Ann Arbor, Mich., Univ. of Michigan Press, 1952-1998. pts. A1-U2 (in progress).

Covers the language of the period 1100-1475 and will eventually comprise *c.*13,000p. in some 10 vols. The bibliographical apparatus has been built up with the aid of the Middle English quotations collected for the *OED*. Entries include brief etymology (enabling reference to be made to other specialized dictionaries), variant forms, meanings (fine discriminations being avoided) and ample quotations in which regional and chronological variants are illustrated. Has reached 'unmightines' with pt. U2.

Plan and bibliography (xii,105p.) was published as a separate part in 1954, with *Supplement I* (v,36p.) appearing in 1984. *Class No:* 802.0-023

[5351]

STRATMANN, F.H. A Middle English dictionary, containing words used by writers from the twelfth to the fifteenth century. New ed., rearranged, rev. and enl. by H. Bradley. London, Oxford Univ. Press, 1891 (repr. 1963). xxiv,708p. £70. ISBN: 0198631065.

Over 20,000 entry-words, with etymology, meanings and references to selected texts. List of sources (8p.). Remains

.... *(contd.)*

the only comprehensive dictionary of Middle English in a completed form until Kurath's *Middle English dictionary* reaches an end.

For briefer coverage, see A.L. Mayhew and W.W. Skeat's *A Concise dictionary of Middle English, from AD1150 to 1580* (Oxford, Clarendon Press, 1888. xv,272p.). *Class No:* 802.0-023

Early Modern English Language

[5352]

HALLIWELL-PHILLIPPS, J.O. Dictionary of archaic and provincial words, obsolete phrases, proverbs, and ancient customs, from the XIVth century. 7th ed. London, Routledge, 1924. 2v. in 1.

First published 1847 and frequently reprinted without change.

30,000 entries, giving definition, provenance and often illustrative quotation. There is an introduction on English provincial dialects.

Supplemented by T.L.O. Davies's *A Supplementary English glossary* (London, Bell, 1881. 736p.). *Class No:* 802.0-024

[5353]

SKEAT, W.W. A Glossary of Tudor and Stuart words, especially from the dramatists, ed., with additions, by A.L. Mayhew. Oxford, Clarendon Press, 1914 (repr. New York, Franklin, 1968). xx,461p.

Lists *c.*7,000 words, giving modern English equivalents, quotations from literary works, with precise references, and explanatory notes where required. List of sources (10p.). *Class No:* 802.0-024

Usage

[5354]

British English for American readers: a dictionary of the language, customs, and places of British life and literature. Grote, D., *ed.* Westport, Conn., Greenwood, 1992. xv,709p. $95. ISBN: 0313278512.

Far more than a dictionary of British vocabulary, with explanations of a wide range of terms encountered in British books, films and TV programmes. Includes events, organizations, legal terms, titles, slang, animals, plants, foods, etc., with which Americans might not be familiar. Appendices include lists of monarchs and key historic dates; holidays and festivals; honours and initials; and military ranks. *Class No:* 802.0-06

[5355]

—SCHUR, N.W. British English, A to Zed. 3rd rev. ed. New York, Facts on File, 1987. xvi,477p. ISBN: 0816016356.

1st ed. published as *British self-taught: with comments in American,* New York, Macmillan, 1973; 2nd ed. as *English English,* Essex, Conn., Verbatim, 1980.

'... essentially a glossary of Briticisms for the guidance of Americans caught in the entrapment of a common language' (*Preface*). 5,000 British words and phrases are listed alphabetically with the American equivalent and a definition covering meaning and usage of the word and related terms. Index of American terms. Two very useful appendices. The first covers general differences between American and British English in 5 parts: syntax, pronunciation, spoken usage, punctuation and style, spelling. The second contains 13 glossaries and tables of financial terms, units of measure, musical notation, numbers, slang etc. Thorough and eminently readable. *Class No:* 802.0-06

[5356]

BRYSON, B. Troublesome words. 2nd ed. Harmondsworth, Penguin, 1987. 192p. £6.99. ISBN: 0140266402.

1st ed. London, Allen Lane, 1984, as *The Penguin dictionary of troublesome words*. Published in the US as *Facts on File dictionary of troublesome words* (New York, Facts on File, 1985. $22.95. ISBN: 0816019339).

A handy guide to usage which is 'mainly the product of questions encountered during the course of daily newspaper work' (*Introduction*). The A-Z sequence of words likely to cause problems is illustrated with questionable usages from leading British and American newspapers and magazines. The chatty entries use grammatical terms sparingly but there is a glossary of these. Bibliography (2p.) and useful appendix on punctuation (9p.). Author has worked as a journalist in the UK and US. *Class No:* 802.0-06

[5357]

Collins COBUILD English usage. Sinclair, J., *ed.* London, HarperCollins, 1992. xxii,808p. £11.50. ISBN: 0003702588.

Claims to be the first usage guide compiled from a large and representative corpus of English texts: the *Bank of English*, which contains 150,000 words. Over 2,000 entries, A-Z, for individual words; pairs of confusible words; groups of similar words; usage topics; and grammatical points. Entries include explanations and lots of real examples from the corpus. American variations are indicated. Glossary of grammar terms (7p.). Ideal for students of English as a second language. *Class No:* 802.0-06

[5358]

FOWLER, H.W. The New Fowler's modern English usage. Burchfield, R.W., *ed.* 3rd ed. Oxford, Clarendon Press, 1996. xxiii,864p. £16.99. ISBN: 0198691262.

1st ed. 1926, as *A Dictionary of modern English usage*; 2nd ed., rev. by Sir E. Gowers, 1965.

A complete rewrite, by a distinguished lexicographer from the *OED* stable, for one of the most respected guides to English usage, which attempts 'with the aid of quotational evidence drawn from identified sources, to guide readers to make sensible choices in linguistically controversial areas of words, meanings, grammatical constructions and pronunciations' (*Preface*). Over 3,000 entries, including definitions of literary terms as well as usage guidance. Burchfield has added hundreds of illustrative quotations from his personal database on grammar and usage, drawn from UK and US newspapers and periodicals and contemporary fiction from all over the English-speaking world. Pronunciation is now indicated by the universally accepted IPA rather than Fowler's respelling system.

A generally conservative guide which, nevertheless, recognizes when common sense should take precedence over hard and fast rules. 'Compared with the liberalism of other grammars, Burchfield's enlightened pedantry is a sheer joy to read and consult' (*The Independent*, Nov. 9, 1996).
Class No: 802.0-06

[5359]

—FOWLER, H.W. *and* FOWLER, F.G. The King's English. 3rd ed. Oxford, Clarendon Press, 1931 (repr. 1973). 383p. £6.99. ISBN: 0198813309.

Intended as an aid to literary composition. Pt. 1 has chapters entitled Vocabulary, Syntax, Airs and Graces (inversion, metaphor, etc.), and Punctuation. Pt. 2 has sections on euphony, the usage of quotation, grammar, meaning, ambiguity and style. Many examples of bad phraseology from newspapers and standard authors are cited throughout. *Class No:* 802.0-06

[5360]

The Good word guide. Manser, M.H., *ed.* 4th ed. London, Bloomsbury, 1997. xxi,292p. £16.99. ISBN: 0747534586.

1st ed. 1988 and 2nd ed. 1990, as *Bloomsbury good word guide*; 3rd ed. 1994, as *Bloomsbury guide to better English*.

A clearly laid out dictionary-style guide, with over 2,200 entries for words, word-elements, phrases, and grammatical points which can cause problems. Entries explain and illustrate, with generous use of quotations, and include details of American variants. Very up-to-date, with good coverage of 'buzzwords', *i.e.* words and phrases which are not necessarily new but which 'suddenly leap into fashionable prominence in the general language', such as 'leading edge' or 'downsizing'. 9 useful tables, including eponyms, countries and peoples, and nonsexist terms.
Class No: 802.0-06

[5361]

GOWERS, Sir E. The Complete plain words. 3rd ed., rev. by S. Greenbaum and J. Whitcut. London, H.M.S.O., 1986 (repr. Harmondsworth, Penguin, 1987). vii,288p. £7.99. ISBN: 0140511997.

1st ed. 1954, being an amalgamation and revision of Gowers' *Plain words* (1948) and *The ABC of plain words* (1951); 2nd ed., rev. by Sir B. Fraser, 1973.

'The main purpose of this book is to help officials in their use of written English as a tool of their trade' (*Prologue*) and has long been widely referred to in the Civil Service. Chapters 1-14 cover various aspects of English usage, with the emphasis on clarity of expression. Ch.15 discusses recent trends (*e.g.* objections to sexist language); ch.16 has 7 specimens of official writing, good and bad; and ch.17 has a checklist of words and phrases to be used with care. Many illustrative passages throughout, which have been updated by the revisers. Bibliography (2p.). Index of words, phrases and topics. *Class No:* 802.0-06

[5362]

GREENBAUM, S. *and* WHITCUT, J. Longman guide to English usage. Harlow, Longman, 1988 (repr. London, Penguin, 1996) xiv,786p. £8.99. ISBN: 0140513566.

An alphabetically-arranged guide with *c.*5,000 entries covering difficult words, grammatical problems, points of style, pronunciation, etc. Easy to use with clear page layout, full cross-references and a variety of typefaces. Addressed primarily to users of standard British English, but American usage is, nevertheless, well covered. *Class No:* 802.0-06

[5363]

HOWARD, G. The Good English guide: English usage in the 1990s. Basingstoke, Macmillan, 1993. xii,418p. £18.99. ISBN: 0333538676.

6,000 entries, A-Z, covering points of grammar, style, pronunciation, register, spelling, etc. Written in user-friendly style with plenty of examples. No citations, but lengthy list of writers whose works have been consulted. Concentrates on British usage, with occasional references to Amerian variations. *Class No:* 802.0-06

[5364]

Hutchinson dictionary of difficult words. Ayto, J., *ed.* [New ed.] Oxford, Helicon, 1993. 292p. £15.99. ISBN: 0091770793.

1st ed. by R. Hill as *Dictionary of difficult words* (London, Jarrolds, 1938).

Lists *c.*16,000 obscure words (1,000 new to this ed. while others have been dropped), giving pronunciation (IPA) and brief definition. 28 'grammar panels' are randomly inserted throughout the sequence, providing advice on difficult points

.... *(contd.)*

of grammar and usage.

L. Urdang's *Bloomsbury dictionary of difficult words* (London, Bloomsbury, 1993. iv,309p. £17.99. ISBN: 0747513430) is very similar, giving syllabification, pronunciation and definition for over 14,000 'obscure, exotic, complex, misunderstood and misused words' (*Preface*). Neither work provides etymologies and they add little to what can be gleaned from the standard dictionaries of English. *Class No:* 802.0-06

[5365]

MAGGIO, R. Talking about people: a guide to fair and accurate language. [3rd ed.] Phoenix, Ariz., Oryx Press, 1997. 448p. $27.50. ISBN: 1573560693.

1st ed. 1987, as *The Nonsexist word finder: a dictionary of gender-free usage*; 2nd ed. 1991, as *The Dictionary of bias-free usage: a guide to nondiscriminatory language*.

An easy-to-use guide for writers seeking to avoid discriminatory language, which has broadened its scope since the 1st ed. to go beyond terms believed to be prejudicial to women. The main dictionary section lists over 8,000 words and phrases which may be felt to be biased against people because of their race, age, sex, disability, sexual orientation, beliefs, etc. and suggests alternatives where possible. Goes over the top, however, when dealing with metaphors and figurative language: does anyone really believe that 'Achilles heel' and 'Scrooge' are sexist terms?

See also *Guidelines for bias-free writing* by M. Schwartz & the Task Force on Bias-Free Language of the Association of American University Presses (Bloomington, Ind., Indiana Univ. Press, 1995. 112p. $15. ISBN: 0253351022).
Class No: 802.0-06

[5366]

—MILLER, C. *and* SWIFT, K. The Handbook of non-sexist writing for writers, editors and speakers. 3rd British ed., rev. and updated London, Women's Press, 1995. 192p. illus. £6.99. ISBN: 0704344424.

1st ed. New York, Harper & Row, 1980; London, Women's Press, 1981. 2nd ed. 1988 and 1989.

A well-established, concise manual which contains numerous examples of sexism in writing with suggestions for nonsexist alternatives. Includes a thesaurus of nonsexist terms, mainly occupational. Reference notes for each chapter. Index. British edition has been suitably amended by The Women's Press.

The Women's Press also publishes *The A-Z of non-sexist language* by M. Doyle (1995. 128p. £6.99. ISBN: 0704344300), a dictionary of allegedly sexist words with non-sexist alternatives. *Class No:* 802.0-06

[5367]

MIKHAIL, E.H. The Cassell dictionary of appropriate adjectives. London, Cassell, 1994. viii,342p. £16.99. ISBN: 030434298x.

Attempts to help users of English to find the right adjective to fit a specific noun on a particular occasion: an almost impossible task. 4,000 nouns are treated and each is accompanied by a list (from a few to over 200) of adjectives that may be used, but as the adjectives are simply listed in what is described as a 'thematic' arrangement, without any indication of their meaning, users will often need to consult a conventional dictionary or thesaurus. Librarians are advised to spend their money on an extra one of these.
Class No: 802.0-06

[5368]

The Oxford guide to English usage. Weiner, E.S.C. *and* Delahunty, A., *comps*. 2nd ed. Oxford, Clarendon Press, 1993. xi,306p. £4.99. ISBN: 0192800248.

1st ed. 1983, comp. by E.S.C. Weiner.

Alphabetically-arranged entries in 4 sections (1. Word formation - 2. Pronunciation - 3. Vocabulary - 4. Grammar) with explanation, examples from modern writers, and recommendations, 'highlighting correct and acceptable standard British English'. Appendices include principles of punctuation and notes on English overseas. Subject and word indexes, the latter having *c.*4,600 entries. *Class No:* 802.0-06

[5369]

PARTRIDGE, E. Usage and abusage: a guide to good English. Whitcut, J., *ed.* New [7th] and completely rev. ed. London, Hamilton, 1994. viii,389p. £18.99. ISBN: 0241133017.

1st ed. 1942; 6th ed. 1965.

Similar in format to Fowler's *Modern English usage,* Partridge's aim being 'to supplement it and complement it, and yet to write a book that should be less Olympian and less austere' (*Foreword to 1st ed.*). Notable for its well-written long entries on topics like slang and vogue words, some of these having references to other reference books.

Whitcut has retained as much as possible of the original text, but has revised and updated the book to take account of three facts: (i) some of the usages Partridge condemned have come to be generally accepted; (ii) new topics (*e.g.* sexism) and problems have arisen; and (iii) the audience has changed and is now less likely to have had a classical education.
Class No: 802.0-06

[5370]

ROOM, A. Dictionary of confusing words and meanings. London, Routledge, 1985. 267p. ISBN: 0710206615.

A revised and enlarged amalgamation of *Room's dictionary of confusibles* (1979) and *Room's dictionary of distinguishables* (1981).

Explains approx. 3,000 words, in pairs and larger groups, which are frequently misused and confused, in a popular style similar to Urdang (*q.v.*). No index but cross-referenced throughout. *Class No:* 802.0-06

[5371]

—URDANG, L. Dictionary of differences. London, Bloomsbury; New York, Facts on File, 1988. 375p. $35. ISBN: 0747502684, UK; 081601650x, US.

US title is *The Dictionary of confusable words*.

Explains in short non-scholarly essays the distinctions between pairs (*e.g.* 'boat/ship') and sets (*e.g.* 'ass'/'donkey'/ 'mule'/'hinny'/'burro') of words which are commonly confused. Over 5,000 terms included in *c.*800 entries. Arranged A-Z by first term in group with all terms indexed and many cross-references. *Class No:* 802.0-06

[5372]

TODD, L. *and* HANCOCK, I. International English usage. London, Croom Helm, 1986. viii,520p. £35. ISBN: 0709943148.

Dictionary format, with a single A-Z sequence covering troublesome meanings, grammatical points and spellings (as in most usage guides), but also having entries for all countries/regions where English is the first language or an important second language, clearly explaining local phonology, vocabulary and grammar. Also articles on

....(contd.)
general linguistic topics such as transformational grammar and phonetics and some literary topics, *e.g.* parody and irony. *Class No:* 802.0-06

[5373]
Wired style: principles of English usage in the digital age. Hale, C., *ed.* San Francisco, HardWired, 1996. 158p. £12. ISBN: 1888869011.

A guide to online usage derived from the in-house style guide of the computer magazine *Wired*. 8 of the 10 chapters are specialized guides or glossaries for particular areas, such as acronyms ('FWIW') and colloquialisms ('spam').
Class No: 802.0-06

South Africa

[5374]
BEETON, D.R. *and* **DORNER, H. A Dictionary of English usage in Southern Africa.** Capetown, Oxford Univ. Press, 1975. xix,196p. ISBN: 0195700694.

*c.*6,000 entries covering local South African vocabulary and idiom; mistakes and problems, both characteristically South African and common to all English speakers; problems encountered by South Africans whose native tongue is not English; departures from standard English pronunciation characteristic of South Africa. Entries include symbols indicating language of origin of a term and its degree of acceptability, plus explanatory notes. Bibliography (3p.). *Class No:* 802.0-06(680)

USA

[5375]
COPPERUD, R.H. American usage and style: the consensus. New York, Van Nostrand Reinhold, 1970. vi,433p. $21.95. ISBN: 0422249068.

Revises, brings up to date, and consolidates 2 earlier works: *A Dictionary of usage and style* and *American usage: the consensus.*

*c.*3,500 entries, A-Z, in which the author, as well as offering his own advice, compares the judgements of 9 other usage guides and several general dictionaries. Bibliography of additional works consulted. *Class No:* 802.0-06(73)

[5376]
MAGER, N.H. *and* **MAGER, S.K. Prentice-Hall encyclopedic dictionary of English usage.** 2nd ed., rev. by J. Domini. New York, Prentice Hall, 1993. 427p. $27.95. ISBN: 0132768585.

1st ed. 1974.

A combination of usage guide and style manual with over 15,000 brief entries, A-Z, covering spelling, pronunciation, grammar, placenames, units of measurement, etc. Essentially a ready-reference tool for the writer rather than a guide through the more complex usage problems.
Class No: 802.0-06(73)

[5377]
MORRIS, W. *and* **MORRIS, M. Harper dictionary of contemporary usage.** 2nd ed. New York, Harper & Row, 1985. xxx,641p. ISBN: 006181606x.

1st ed. 1975.

Discursive entries on words and phrases, A-Z, many of them followed by the comments of members of a panel of writers (*e.g.* Isaac Asimov). These occupy space out of all proportion to their usefulness, with a brief entry often followed by a whole page of one-line quotations.
Class No: 802.0-06(73)

[5378]
RANDALL, B. Webster's New World guide to current American usage. New York, Simon & Schuster, 1988. xviii,420p. £12.95. ISBN: 0139478213.

Discursive entries, some of them running to several pages, on problematic words, phrases and topics. List of sources (24p.). Alphabetically arranged, but 'the quick reference value of the work, without an index, is dubious' (*Booklist*, v.85(6), Nov. 15, 1988). *Class No:* 802.0-06(73)

[5379]
Webster's dictionary of English usage. Gilman, E.W., *ed.* Springfield, Mass., Merriam-Webster, 1989. 12+978p. ISBN: 0877790329.

*c.*2,300 articles, A-Z, of varying length (up to a maximum of 4p.), which trace usage history and discuss contemporary usage. The entries include *c.*20,000 quotations (with details of author, source and date) from the vast Merriam-Webster files and also draw on the advice of some 275 other dictionaries and manuals. Introductory essay on the history of the study of English usage (5p.). Bibliography (5p.). 'It is likely to become the first choice for most users due to its authority, recency, readability, summarization of other advice, and generous number of illustrative quotations' (*Booklist*, v.86(2), Sept. 15, 1989, p.210). *English Today* (no. 26, April 1991, p.52-5) is even more effusive: 'It is the widest-ranging, most detailed, and most intelligent usage book ever made... No future work on the subject can afford to ignore the achievement of this book.'

Available on CD-ROM from Compton's NewMedia.
Class No: 802.0-06(73)

[5380]
WILSON, K.G. The Columbia guide to Standard American English. New York, Columbia Univ. Press, 1993. xv,482p. £25.50. ISBN: 023106988x.

Over 6,500 entries, A-Z, covering both grammatical and linguistic terms (bold upper case) and words, phrases and constructions which are frequently confused (bold lower case). Praised by reviewers for its clear style, treatment of spoken as well as written language, and awareness of and sensitivity to contemporary linguistic issues related to race and gender. Shorter entries than in *Webster's dictionary of English usage* because historical background is not explored, the emphasis being on *level* of usage in the context of 5 levels of Standard American speech and 3 levels of S.A. writing, which are described in the introduction. Cross-references and examples. Extensive bibliography of sources on the language (6p.). *Class No:* 802.0-06(73)

Australia

[5381]
HUDSON, N. Modern Australian usage. Melbourne, Oxford Univ. Press, 1993. viii,439p. £18.95 ISBN: 0195548604.

2,000 entries, A-Z, on confusible words, grammatical points, etc., with emphasis on Australian English. Entries are written in the style of Fowler, who the author acknowledges as a major inspiration, but are not prescriptive, the market being 'people who want to make up their own minds' (*Preface*). Many entries on publishing and typographical matters, the author being a professional editor. 'Much less a dictionary than a set of elegant factual essays set out under headwords' (*TLS*, no.4781, Nov. 18, 1994, p.8).

The Cambridge Australian English style guide, by P.

....(*contd.*)
Peters, (Cambridge, Cambridge Univ. Press, 1995. 862p. £55. ISBN: 0521434017) has over 2,500 alphabetical entries 11 line diagrams. *Class No:* 802.0-06(94)

English Slang

[5382]
AYTO, J. *and* **SIMPSON, J.A. The Oxford dictionary of modern slang.** Oxford, Oxford Univ. Press, 1992. vii,299p. £6.99. ISBN: 0192800078.

The first slang dictionary from OUP has over 5,000 entries, most of them taken from the 2nd ed. of the *OED* but also including 500 terms and meanings yet to appear in the parent work. Clearly presented entries consist of headword; part of speech; region, social group or discipline in which the term is prevalent; definition; period of usage (all have been current in the 20th century but many date from much earlier); and, in most cases, at least one illustrative example from a published source. Quotes are generally taken from the full *OED*, to which users are referred for bibliographical details of sources. Pronunciation (IPA) given in a few difficult cases. Etymology supplied where not self-evident. Offensive terms and meanings clearly indicated. North American and Commonwealth English well represented. *Class No:* 802.0-086

[5383]
DUNKLING, L. A Dictionary of epithets and terms of address. London, Routledge, 1990. 268p. £55. ISBN: 0415007615.

2,000 entries explaining terms used in English to address people both formally (*e.g.* 'sir', 'my lord') and informally (*e.g.* 'honey', 'love') plus generic entries for nicknames, religious vocatives, etc. Although based on thesis research, the entries are written in chatty style and include examples from some 500 novels. Excellent explanatory introduction (35p.) but no list of sources. *Class No:* 802.0-086

[5384]
FARMER, J.S. *and* **HENLEY, W.E. Slang and its analogues,** past and present. London, Routledge, 1890-1904. 7v. (repr. New York, Kraus. 3v.). $225. ISBN: 0527283002.

A monumental work, including thousands of quotations from the literature of the last 5 centuries. Entries include explanation, derivation, and synonyms in French, German, Italian and Spanish.

Only vols. 1 and 8 have appeared of a planned 8-vol. revised ed. to be published by University Books, New York (1966). V.1 is a reprint of the only vol. to be revised by the original compilers (1903-09) and v.8 is a study of French erotic slang (1896). *Class No:* 802.0-086

[5385]
FRANKLYN, J. A Dictionary of rhyming slang. 2nd ed. London, Routledge & Kegan Paul, 1961 (repr. 1975). xii,202p. £10.99. ISBN: 0415046025.

A dictionary of the rhyming slang of the London Cockney, with an introductory essay on the origins. The dictionary section (*c.*1,500 entries) states origin and date of currency, as well as an explanation of the phrase concerned. The slang terms are then grouped under such headings as 'abstract', 'amusements', 'animals', plus a list of meanings and examples (p.183-200) - verse and prose quotations - drawn not only from London but also from Ireland, America and Australia. *Class No:* 802.0-086

[5386]
—PUXLEY, R. Cockney rabbit: a Dick'n'Arry of rhyming slang. London, Robson, 1992. x,230p. £8.99. ISBN: 0860518272.

Over 2,000 entries with light-hearted explanations, followed by a reverse dictionary giving rhyming slang equivalents for 750 Standard English terms. Sticks to Cockney speech and adopts a more popular approach than Franklyn, with no attempts at dating and no references to printed sources, but useful for post-1960 coinings. *Class No:* 802.0-086

[5387]
GREEN, J. The Slang thesaurus. London, Elm Tree, 1986 (repr. Harmondsworth, Penguin, 1988). xiv,280p. £6.99. ISBN: 0140512055.

Groups nearly 16,000 slang terms from the English-speaking world into 516 numbered categories, under 13 major subject headings, in the style of *Roget's thesaurus.* Index (132p.) occupies almost as much space as the thesaurus proper. *Class No:* 802.0-086

[5388]
PARTRIDGE, E. A Dictionary of catch phrases: British and American, from the sixteenth century to the present. Beale, P., *ed.* 2nd ed. London, Routledge, 1985. xxv,384p. £17.99. ISBN: 041505916x.

1st ed. 1977.

Over 5,500 entries, of which 2,500 remain intact from the 1st ed., the rest being amended or completely new. As well as the catch phrases of entertainers there are a wide range of popular sayings, greetings, toasts, clichés, proverbs, euphemisms, similes, etc., all explained in a mixture of anecdote and scholarship. Most sources quoted are 20th century. A fine reference book, but a name index would have made it even better.

Shorter dictionary of catch phrases, by R. Fergusson (London, Routledge, 1994. 166p. £9.99. ISBN: 0415100518) is an abridged version of the 2nd ed., concentrating on phrases in current use, with some new phrases added. *c.*1,450 entries. *Class No:* 802.0-086

[5389]
PARTRIDGE, E. A Dictionary of slang and unconventional English: colloquialisms and catch phrases, fossilised jokes and puns, general nicknames, vulgarisms and such Americanisms as have been naturalised. Beale, P., *ed.* 8th ed. London, Routledge, 1984. xxix,1400p. £60. ISBN: 0415065682.

1st ed. 1937; 7th ed. 1970, in 2 vols.

Beale took over the editorship of this definitive work before Partridge's death in 1979 and has conflated the original text of the 1st ed. with all the subsequent addenda (which had appeared in a supplementary vol. in recent eds.), incorporated 5,000 new entries compiled by Partridge and over 1,000 of his own, and revised the whole. Some re-arrangement means that phrases are now entered under the term the user is most likely to turn to first. Entries comprise keyword, definition, register, dating, and sources, followed by editor's comments where appropriate. Approx. 55,000 entries in main sequence, plus Appendix of nearly 100 articles on particular topics, *e.g.* Nicknames, Back slang. *Class No:* 802.0-086

[5390]

—A Concise dictionary of slang and unconventional English. Beale, P., *ed.* London, Routledge, 1989. xxvi,534p. £17.99. ISBN: 0415063523.

Contains 'only terms known to have arisen in the Twentieth Century' (*Preface*), taken from the parent dictionary, plus *c.*1,500 new terms which have come to light in the 1980s, many of these concerned with drugs. *c.*15,000 entries, plus the Appendix from the main work. List of *c.*1,600 sources. *Class No:* 802.0-086

[5391]

—Shorter slang dictionary. Fergusson, R., *comp.* London, Routledge, 1994. 242p. £10.99 ISBN: 0415088666.

Brief entries on 5,000 contemporary slang expressions, most of them adapted from *DSUE* (8th ed. 1984) and the new material that first appeared in *A Concise DSUE* (1989), with some new entries for very recent coinings. Selection policy differs notably from that of Partridge's own *Smaller slang dictionary* (2nd ed. 1964), in that no terms are omitted on the grounds of offensiveness. *Class No:* 802.0-086

[5392]

PARTRIDGE, E. The Routledge dictionary of historical slang. Simpson, J., *ed.* London, Routledge & Kegan Paul, 1973. 1006p. £50. ISBN: 0710077610.

Nearly 50,000 entries drawn from *A Dictionary of slang and unconventional English,* covering words and expressions in use before World War 1. List of sources (3p.). Also available in paperback as *The Penguin dictionary of historical slang* (£14. ISBN: 014051046x).

Partridge has also compiled a number of specialized dictionaries of slang:

Slang, today and yesterday, with a short historical sketch and vocabularies of English, American and Australian slang (London, Routledge, 1933. 4th ed. 1970).

A Dictionary of Forces' slang, 1939-1945 (London, Secker & Warburg, 1948).

A Dictionary of the Underworld, British and American (London, Routledge, 1949. 3rd ed. 1968).

He has also edited Capt. F. Grose's *A Classical dictionary of the vulgar tongue* (London, Routledge, 1963), based on the text of the 3rd ed. of 1796, which is especially valuable for 18th-century colloquialisms. *Class No:* 802.0-086

[5393]

THORNE, T. Dictionary of contemporary slang. New ed. London, Bloomsbury, 1997 viii,440p. £18.99. ISBN: 074752856x.

1st ed., 1990, as *Bloomsbury dictionary of contemporary slang*.

Aims to describe the core of English language slang in use between 1950 and the mid-1990s and has entries for over 6,000 words and phrases likely to be encountered in contemporary literature, popular music, the media and conversation. Compiled in the UK, but the US, Australia and the Caribbean are well represented. Entries comprise: headword, variants, part of speech, regional label, definition(s), explanation if required, and illustrative sentences, some invented and others from fully referenced sources. Clear layout, with good use of typefaces.

Another source for recent terms is *The Macmillan dictionary of contemporary slang*, by J. Green (Basingstoke, Macmillan, 1995. xii,374p. £6.99. ISBN: 0333634071). This inexpensive paperback has *c.*14,000 entries and is an updated ed. of Green's *Dictionary of contemporary slang* (London, Pan. 1st ed. 1984; 2nd ed. 1992.).
Class No: 802.0-086

[5394]

TITELMAN, G.Y. Random House dictionary of popular proverbs and sayings. New York, Random House, 1996. xi,468p. £19.99. ISBN: 0679445544.

1,500 entries, mainly for proverbs but also including clichés, quotations and catchphrases. Entries give explanation, history, references to other dictionaries and, most notably, chronologically arranged quotations exemplifying the phrase itself and, in some cases, variants and papraphrases. These are all from American literary and media sources and usually include one early example and several from the 1980s and 1990s. A 5-star system is used to indicate frequency of phrases. *Class No:* 802.0-086

[5395]

WILKINSON, P.R. A Thesaurus of traditional English metaphors. London, Routledge, 1993. xiii,777p. £100. ISBN: 0415075238.

A highly idiosyncratic work, based on one man's personal collection of figurative language, including sayings, similes, proverbs, idioms, catchphrases and slang expressions, assembled over a lifetime of contact with the rural cultures of various regions of England and Scotland. Unique thematic arrangement, based on the rhyme 'Tinker, tailor, soldier, sailor', gives an idea of the folksy flavour of the work. Over 20,000 entries, providing meanings, derivations and geographical origins. Dates are provided in some cases, but there are few references to written sources. Indexes of themes (11p.) and keywords (275p.). A goldmine for language and folklore enthusiasts, but for reference library purposes there are less expensive and more thoroughly researched sources available. *Class No:* 802.0-086

Ireland

[5396]

SHARE, B. Slanguage: dictionary of slang and colloquial English in Ireland. Dublin, Gill & Macmillan, 1997. xx,325p. £35. ISBN: 0717123537.

Entries comprise headword; part of speech; etymology; geographical location (where confined to one area); meaning; and examples, using detailed quotations from literature, newspapers and periodicals. Covers Northern Ireland as well as the Republic. Bibliography (2p.). Appended list of over 60 racist epithets applied to Irish people by outsiders. *Class No:* 802.0-086(415)

USA

[5397]

LEWIN, E. *and* **LEWIN, A.E. The Thesaurus of slang:** 165,000 uncensored contemporary slang terms, common idioms, and colloquialisms, updated for the 1990's and arranged for quick and easy reference. Rev. ed. New York, Facts on File, 1994. 456p. $50. ISBN: 0816028982.

1st ed. 1988.

Over 12,000 standard English entry-words, A-Z, are followed by lists of synonymous slang terms used in the US (over 800 for 'drunk'). No definitions and, however abusive or offensive the slang terms may be, they are not discriminated. Cross-references. Bibliography of sources. 15,000 new terms added in this ed. *Class No:* 802.0-086(73)

[5398]

New dictionary of American slang. Chapman, R.L., *ed.* New York, Harper & Row, 1986; London, Macmillan, 1987. xxxvi,485p. $32.50. ISBN: 0061811572.

Based on Wentworth and Flexner's *Dictionary of American Slang* (New York, Crowell, 1960), which was enlarged and updated in 1967 and 1975.

An improvement on *DAS,* which is described by *English Today* (no.11, July 1987, p.41) as 'a lexicographic disaster', but not to be regarded as comparable to Partridge's monumental *Dictionary of slang and unconventional English* (*q.v.*), because it seldom gives even approximate dates for the appearance of particular terms, its illustrative quotations are undated, and it omits many etymologies that are by no means obvious. Over 17,000 entries (*c.*11,000 in *DAS*) with 'impact symbols' to denote vulgar and taboo terms. Fully cross-referenced. Drops *DAS*'s classified lists of slang terms.

Abridged paperback version published 1995, as *The Macmillan dictionary of American slang* (London, Macmillan. £8.99. ISBN: 0333634055). *Class No:* 802.0-086(73)

[5399]

Random House historical dictionary of American slang. Lighter, J.E., *ed.* New York, Random House, 1994-97. v.1-2 (in progress).

V.1 *A-G.* 1994. 1006p. $55. ISBN: 0394544277.

V.2 *H-O.* 1997. 736p. $65. ISBN: 067943464x.

The first dictionary of American slang to be completely based on accurately quoted and dated examples from written and spoken sources has been in preparation for over 20 years. Primary sources have been almost exclusively used in order to avoid repeating the mistakes of earlier slang dictionaries. V.1 has *c.*20,000 definitions, with illustrative quotations, chronologically arranged, from literary works, popular fiction, magazines, newspapers, films, TV programmes, songs and anonymous conversations. Field labels indicate in which sphere of activity terms are used and usage and status labels indicate whether they are regarded as vulgar, offensive, jocular, etc. Lengthy introductory essay on the history and significance of slang. Selected annotated bibliography of books and articles on American slang. Because coverage is historical, terms are included which were once regarded as slang, but which are now accepted as part of Standard English.

The last vol. will carry the full list of *c.*8,000 sources cited in the whole work. 'When completed, ... will be, without a doubt, the most definitive and scholarly treatment of American slang ever published' (*Reference Books Bulletin*, v.91(3), Oct. 1, 1994, p.352). *Class No:* 802.0-086(73)

[5400]

Thesaurus of American slang. Chapman, R.L., *ed.* New York, Harper & Row, 1989; London, Collins, 1990. 489p. $12.95. ISBN: 0062720104, US; 0004335503, UK.

17,000 synonyms drawn from the *New dictionary of American slang.* Each main entry gives part of speech, definition, usage examples (if appropriate) and numerous synonyms. Over 1,000 main entries, followed by index of synonyms and concepts. *Booklist* (v.86(12), Feb 15, 1990) strongly criticizes the lack of explanation of the work's compilation and organization and, especially, the very limited usage guidance in a potentially problematic area. *Class No:* 802.0-086(73)

Australia

[5401]

SIMES, G. A Dictionary of Australian underworld slang. Melbourne, Oxford Univ. Press, 1993. lxxviii,225p. illus. £27.50. ISBN: 0195534999.

A historically based dictionary of criminal slang from the first half of the 20th century, produced by interfiling edited versions of 2 glossaries originally compiled by prisoners in the 1940s and 1950s and adding explanatory notes plus illustrative quotations from written sources, many of which show the development of the terms in more recent decades. Scholarly introductory essay on the language and lexicography of crime (53p.). *Class No:* 802.0-086(94)

Dialects

[5402]

FISCHER, A. *and* **AMMAN, D. An Index to dialect maps of Great Britain.** Amsterdam, Benjamins, 1991. iv,150p. Hfl.79. ISBN: 9027248680.

Over 2,000 entries, listing the major dialect surveys of Britain and the numerous publications they have spawned. *Class No:* 802.0-087

[5403]

The Linguistic atlas of England. Orton, H., *and others, eds.* Atlantic Highlands, N.J., Humanities Press, 1977; London, Croom Helm, 1978 (repr. London, Routledge, 1996). 450p. £125. ISBN: 0415151295.

An interpretive presentation of selected linguistic facts elicited from Orton and Deith's *Survey of English dialects.* 249 phonological maps, 65 lexical maps, 83 morphological maps and 9 syntactical maps, with data from over 300 localities in 40 counties. 3 appendices: 1. Index to questions used in the 1957 questionnaire - 2. Notes on mapped lexical responses - 3. List of unmapped lexical responses. Index of mapped notions. *Class No:* 802.0-087

[5404]

—ANDERTON, P.M. A Structural atlas of the English dialects. London, Croom Helm, 1987. 153p. ISBN: 0709951167.

Based on the *Survey of English dialects,* and attempts to identify structural patterns in the sound systems of the dialects, and to identify some of the more prominent structural boundaries between dialect areas. 114 maps. Index of words by Middle English phoneme. *Class No:* 802.0-087

[5405]

—ORTON, H. *and* WRIGHT, N. A Word geography of England. London, Seminar Press, 1974. xv,302p. ISBN: 0127856080.

251 maps illustrating the regional distribution of dialect words and phrases, based on the *Survey of English dialects.* Introduction includes brief history of English vocabulary and analysis of the maps. Indexes of notions mapped and of words and phrases recorded. *Class No:* 802.0-087

[5406]

—UPTON, C. *and* WIDDOWSON, J.D.A. An Atlas of English dialects Oxford, Oxford Univ. Press, 1996. 216p. illus. £9.99. ISBN: 0198692749.

90 maps, based on the findings of the *Survey of English dialects*, are arranged in 3 groups (lexical, phonological and grammatical) with detailed commentaries on the linguistic, historical and cultural significance of words. Introductory essay sets the *Survey* in context. Thoroughly indexed. *Class No:* 802.0-087

[5407]

ORTON, H. *and* DIETH, E. Survey of English dialects. Leeds, E.J. Arnold, for the Univ. of Leeds, 1962-71. 12 pts.

Introduction. 1962. 112p.

V.1 *The Six northern counties and the Isle of Man.* 1962-63. 3 pts.

V.2 *The West Midland counties.* 1969-71. 3 pts.

V.3 *The East Midland counties and East Anglia.* 1969-70. 2 pts.

V.4 *The Southern counties.* 1967-68. 3 pts.

Presents the results of a survey carried out by field-workers, 1950-61, of the dialect 'normally spoken by elderly speakers of sixty years of age or over belonging to the same social class in rural communities, and in particular by those who were, or had formerly been, employed in farming' (*Introduction,* p.14). Introductory vol. includes list of over 300 localities (with map) and the questionnaire used.
Class No: 802.0-087

[5408]

—UPTON, C., *& others*. Survey of English dialects: the dictionary and grammar. London, Routledge, 1994. viii,506p. £90. ISBN: 0415020298.

A first — and very belated — attempt to present in dictionary form the material collected by *SED*. With over 18,000 entries, it is the first dialect dictionary to cover the whole country since Wright's (*q.v.*). However, it is not easy to use (an expert knowledge of phonetics is assumed) and can be fully exploited only in conjunction with the *SED*'s *Introduction* and 11 vols. of regional data. It must be stressed, too, that the language covered is limited to that of elderly country-dwellers in the mid-20th century. The grammar section makes up less 10% of the work and 'is not meant to be comprehensive' (*Introduction*). For specialist rather than general reference use. *Class No:* 802.0-087

[5409]

Real English: the grammar of English dialects in the British Isles. Milroy, J. *and* Milroy, L., *eds.* London, Longman, 1993. xvii,344p. £34. ISBN: 0582081777.

A substantial part of the book (p.245-339) is given over to 'A Directory of English dialect resources.' Arranged by region and county, it lists books, collections, recordings, research projects and societies, with 10p. on Yorkshire alone. *Class No:* 802.0-087

[5410]

WRIGHT, J. The English dialect dictionary. London, Frowde, 1898-1905 (repr. Oxford, Oxford Univ. Press, 1981). 6v. ISBN: 019580497x.

Subtitle: 'Being the complete vocabulary of all dialect words still in use, or known to have been in use during the last two hundred years; founded on the Publications of the English Dialect Society and on a large amount of material never before printed'.

Covers over 100,000 words and phrases from England, Scotland, Wales and Ireland. Each entry gives regions in which found and variations, pronunciation, illustrative quotations and etymology. V.6 includes a supplement of 179p., a bibliography of works quoted classified by area and indexed, and 'The English dialect grammar'.
Class No: 802.0-087

National Variants of English

Bibliographies

[5411]

VIERECK, W., *and others*. A Bibliography of writings on varieties of English, 1965-1983. Amsterdam, Benjamins, 1984. iv,319p. Hfl.100. (*Varieties of English around the world.*) ISBN: 9027248613.

1,278 unannotated entries arranged by author, A-Z, with indexes of regions and topics.

Continued by *A New Bibliography of writings on varieties of English, 1984-1992/93*, by B. Glauser, E.W. Schneider and M. Görlach (1994. 208p. Hfl.84. ISBN: 9027248664), which is in 4 parts, covering general studies, Britain and Ireland, the US and Canada, and the rest of the world.
Class No: 802.0-087.40(01)

Scotland

[5412]

Chambers Scots dictionary; serving as a glossary for Ramsay, Fergusson, Burns, Scott, Galt, minor poets, kailyard novelists, and a host of writers of the Scottish tongue. Warrack, A., *comp.* Edinburgh, Chambers, 1911 (regularly reprinted). xvii,717p. ISBN: 0550118012.

A concise record of Scots words in use since *c.*1650, with over 40,000 entries giving part of speech and meaning only. Introduction (11p.) and dialect map by W. Grant, editor of *The Scottish National Dictionary.* *Class No:* 802.0-087.41

[5413]

The Concise English-Scots dictionary. McLeod, I. *and* Cairns, P., *eds.* Edinburgh, Chambers, for the Scottish National Dictionary Association, 1993. xvii,302p. £12.99. ISBN: 0550118551.

The first comprehensive English-Scots dictionary (as opposed to brief glossary) concentrates on 20th-century Scots. Over 10,500 English entry-words with Scots equivalents of their different meanings. Entries include variant regional spellings and usages, idiomatic phrases, and cross-references to synonyms. Introductory guide to use includes notes on pronunciation. Maps of Scots dialect divisions and present and former counties. *Class No:* 802.0-087.41

[5414]

The Concise Scots dictionary. Robinson, M., *ed.* Aberdeen, Aberdeen Univ. Press, 1985 (repr. Edinburgh, Chambers) xli,820p. £19.99. ISBN: 0550118500.

An updated distillation of *The Scottish national dictionary* and *A Dictionary of the older Scottish tongue*, excluding illustrative quotations, rare items for which there is little evidence, obvious derivatives and Norse material from Shetland, Orkney and Caithness. A superbly laid-out introduction (33p.) gives a history of Scots, explains fully the relationship with the parent works and includes maps of dialect divisions and administrative regions. Approx. 25,000 entries, giving pronunciation, grammatical function, meaning, dating, geographical distribution and etymology.
Class No: 802.0-087.41

[5415]

—The Scots thesaurus. McLeod, I., *ed.* Edinburgh, Chambers (previously Aberdeen, Aberdeen Univ. Press), 1990. xx,536p. £19.99. ISBN: 0550118527.

Presents 20,000 words recorded in *The Concise Scots dictionary* underc.350 headings within 15 major subject groups. Words are listed A-Z within each section, with English definition and Scottish region/county if usage is restricted. Index (60p.). *Class No:* 802.0-087.41

[5416]

—STEVENSON, J.A.C. Scoor-oot: a dictionary of Scots words and phrases in current use. London, Athlone, 1989. 256p. £25.00. ISBN: 0485113732.

Defines approx. 850 words and phrases in popular style, with many illustrations from contemporary writing, newspapers and conversation. Words arranged in 15 sections relating to aspects of Scottish life. Bibliography (1p.). Index. *Class No:* 802.0-087.41

[5417]

Dictionary of the older Scottish tongue, from the twelfth century to the end of the seventeenth. Craigie, W.A., *and others, eds.* Oxford, Clarendon Press, 1931-95. Parts 1-44 (in progress). £40 per part; £150 per vol. ISBN: 0080306829.

Published in paperback parts, which then form volumes, and will eventually comprise 10 vols. Vols. 1-7 (pts. 1-41) cover 'A-R'. Pts. 1-29 originally published Chicago, Univ. of Chicago Press, and London, Oxford Univ. Press. Pts. 30-42 originally published Aberdeen, Aberdeen Univ. Press. Publication reverted to OUP with pt. 43.

'This dictionary is intended to exhibit and illustrate the whole range of the Older Scottish vocabulary, as preserved in literary, documentary, and other records, down to the year 1600, and to continue the history of the language down to 1700, so far as it does not coincide with the ordinary English usage of that century' (*Preface*).

Entries include variant forms, etymology, meanings, explanations of usage and numerous illustrative quotations, arranged chronologically. List of works quoted at the front of each vol. Craigie died in 1957 and the work is now edited by A.J. Aitken and others. *Class No:* 802.0-087.41

[5418]

The Edinburgh history of the Scots language. Jones, C., *ed.* Edinburgh, Edinburgh Univ. Press, 1997. 608p. £150. ISBN: 0748607544.

The first full-scale attempt to record the history of Scots, with extensive essays by a team of international scholars which provide 'a detailed and technical description of the syntax, phonology, morphology and vocabulary of the language' (*Publisher's catalogue*). 7 chapters on the language before 1700 and 5 on 1700 to the present, followed by chapters on the Scots-Gaelic interface and the Scots language in Ulster and Australia. *Class No:* 802.0-087.41

[5419]

The Linguistic atlas of Scotland: Scots section. Mather, J.Y. *and* Speitel, H.H., *eds.* London, Croom Helm, 1975-86. 3v. £195 per vol. ISBN: 085664160x, v.1; 0856641111, v.2; 0856647160, v.3.

Based on research into Scottish dialects carried out by The Linguistic Survey of Scotland at Edinburgh University and including Scots speech in Cumbria, Northumberland and Ulster. Vols. 1-2 cover word geography, with 180 maps for specific lexical items, regional lists in the latter part of each vol. and index to both in v.2. V.3 covers phonology, with

....(contd.)

175 maps for words and 120 for phonemes, and is the result of field research, whilst vols. 1-2 are based on questionnaires. *Class No:* 802.0-087.41

[5420]

The Scottish national dictionary; designed partly on regional lines and partly on historical principles, and containing all the Scottish words known to be in use since *c.*1700. Grant, W. *and* Murison, D.D., *eds.* Edinburgh, Scottish National Dictionary Assoc., 1931-76 (now available from Chambers). 10v. £850 the set. ISBN: 0080303617.

'The Scottish National Dictionary deals with (1) Scottish words in existence since *c.*1700: (a) in Scottish literature, (b) in public records, (c) in glossaries and in dictionaries, (d) in private collections, (e) in special interest dialect treatises; and (2) Scottish words gathered from the mouth of dialect speakers by competent observers' (*Introduction*).

Entries include variant spellings, meanings, status (*e.g.* literary, colloquial), pronunciation, illustrative quotations arranged by region, and etymology. List of works quoted at end of v.10 (38p.). Introduction to v.1 has 'Phonetic description of Scottish language and dialects' (48p.) with maps.

Compact ed. with reduced type size (magnifying glass supplied!) available in 2 vols. (£175. ISBN: 0080345182). *Class No:* 802.0-087.41

[5421]

—The Compact Scottish national dictionary. Grant, W. *and* Murison, D.D., *eds.* Aberdeen, Aberdeen Univ. Press, 1986 (now available from Chambers). 2v. £175 the set. ISBN: 0080345182.

Condenses the 5,000 pages of the 10-vol. *SND* into 1,264 pages, with 4 original pages reproduced on one page. *Class No:* 802.0-087.41

Northern Ireland

[5422]

A Concise Ulster dictionary. MacAfee, C.I., *ed.* Oxford, Oxford Univ. Press, 1996. xli,405p. illus. £9.99. ISBN: 0198600593.

'A record of non-standard English vocabulary that is used in traditional or dialectal speech' (in the 9 counties of the province of Ulster), mainly based on wordlists compiled in the late 19th and early 20th century. Entries for over 15,000 words and phrases, giving part of speech, meaning, etymology and geographical information. 200 illustrations. Scholarly introduction. Bibliography of sources (4p.). Of limited use for the contemporary language since 'apart from a few venerable examples, ... political terms, and certainly the argot of the current conflict, have been rigorously excluded' (*TLS*, no.4883, Nov. 1, 1996, p.10-11). *Class No:* 802.0-087.416

[5423]

TODD, L. Words apart: a dictionary of Northern Ireland English. Gerrard's Cross, Smythe; New York, Barnes & Noble, 1990. xv,260p. £19.50. ISBN: 086140338x, UK; 0389209163, US.

Introductory chapter on historical development (17p.), followed by dictionary of *c.*1,200 Northern Irish words and phrases, giving pronunciation, definition, etymology and illustrative sentences from 'live speech' recorded in Ulster. List of English words with N.I. equivalents. Selection of texts, both written and oral. Annotated bibliography (8p.). *Class No:* 802.0-087.416

Isle of Man

[5424]

MOORE, A.W. A Vocabulary of the Anglo-Manx dialect. London, Oxford Univ. Press, 1924. xii,206p.

Over 2,000 entries, giving pronunciation, definition, etymology (in the case of words from the Celtic Manx language), and examples of usage. *Class No:* 802.0-087.428.9

India

[5425]

NIHALANI, P., *and others*. Indian and British English: a handbook of usage and pronunciation. Delhi, Oxford Univ. Press, 1979. viii,260p. £4.95. ISBN: 0195624041.

Part One, Lexicon of Usage, lists some 1,000 items 'which are used in a distinctive manner by large numbers of educated Indian speakers of English' (*Introduction*) and explains how they differ from British English. Part Two, Dictionary of Pronunciation, prescribes pronunciation for approx. 2,000 words using as a model Educated Indian English rather than British Received Pronunciation. For Indian learners and teachers of English. *Class No:* 802.0-087.45

[5426]

YULE, H. Hobson-Jobson: a glossary of colloquial Anglo-Indian words and phrases, and of kindred terms, etymological, historical, geographical and discursive. Reprint of 1903 ed. London, Routledge & Kegan Paul, 1968. xlviii,1021p. ISBN: 0710028865.

1st ed. 1886; new ed., rev. by W. Crooke, 1903.

Still the standard work in its field, although something of a period piece, defining over 7,500 words and phrases and including citations from over 800 works. Due to be reprinted by Curzon Press, 1995, as *A Glossary of colloquial Anglo-Indian words and phrases* (£75. ISBN: 0700703217).

For more up-to-date coverage of Anglo-Indian vocabulary see I. Lewis's *Sahibs, nabobs and boxwallahs: a dictionary of the words of Anglo-India* (Oxford, Oxford Univ. Press, 1992. x,266p. £11.99. ISBN: 0195642236) and N.B. Hankin's *Hanklyn-janklin, or a stranger's rumble-tumble guide to some words, customs and quiddities, Indian and Indo-British* (New Delhi, Banyan, 265p. £19.95). *Class No:* 802.0-087.45

Africa

[5427]

DALGLISH, G.M. A Dictionary of Africanisms: contributions of Sub-Saharan Africa to the English language. Westport, Conn., Greenwood, 1982. xviii,203p. ISBN: 0313235856.

3,000 terms from African languages which have entered the general vocabulary of the English-speaking world or which are felt likely to do so because they are widely used by English speakers in Africa. Entries comprise headword, pronunciation (IPA), part of speech, definition, illustrative quote from a written source, and the source and history of the term. Appendix groups terms under 20 subject headings. *Class No:* 802.0-087.46

South Africa

[5428]

BRANFORD, J. *and* BRANFORD, W. A Dictionary of South African English. 4th ed. Cape Town, Oxford Univ. Press, 1991. xxxi,412p. £22.50. ISBN: 0195705955.

First published 1978; 3rd ed. 1987.

About 6,000 entries, including not only forms of English that are peculiarly South African, but also words absorbed from Afrikaans, native African languages and the local Malay, Indian and Jewish communities. Entries state pronunciation, part of speech, meaning(s) and etymology and are illustrated by often quite lengthy quotations from a wide variety of sources. The quotations make this scholarly reference work highly readable and many entries contain cross-references to quotations under other entries. Particularly long entries for 'boer', 'kaffir', 'kraal', 'veld' and their compounds. Clear introduction and pronunciation key; list of earliest recorded dates of selected items (2p.); list of word sources quoted, including individuals, newspapers and magazines (13p.). Bibliography (19p.).

4th ed. includes many quotations from sources previously banned and has more quotations from Black writers/ speakers. 'The flood of new material has necessitated some regrettable cuts in the earlier text, in order to make space for new entries' (*Introduction*). *Class No:* 802.0-087.468

[5429]

A Dictionary of South African English on historical principles. Silva, P., *ed.* Oxford, Oxford Univ. Press, 1996. 856p. £65. ISBN: 0198631537.

The long-awaited (25 years in the making) *OED*-style record of the English language in South Africa, with 8,000 entries in which definitions are supported by chronologically arranged quotations from the late 16th century to the present day. 47,000 quotations in all, from literature and the media. 'A wonderful achievement ... At long last, speakers of South African English have been given a work of reference commensurate with the rich, irreverent vigour of their language' (*The Independent*, Nov. 9, 1996, p.6). *Class No:* 802.0-087.468

Canada

[5430]

AVIS, W.S. *and* KINLOCH, A.M. Writings on Canadian English, 1792-1975: an annotated bibliography. Toronto, Fitzhenry & Whiteside, [1979]. 155p. ISBN: 088902121x.

Supersedes Avis's *A Bibliography of writings on Canadian English (1857-1965)* (Toronto, Gage, 1965), which had only 168 entries. The new bibliography lists 723 titles by author, A-Z, with concise, descriptive annotations. Index of co-authors. *Class No:* 802.0-087.471

[5431]

The Canadian Oxford dictionary. Barber, K., *ed.* Don Mills, Ont., Oxford Univ. Press, 1998. 1728p. C$39.95. ISBN: 019541120x.

A new dictionary announced by OUP which is not simply a list of Canadianisms, although it does contain over 2,000 distinctly Canadian words and meanings, but a general encyclopedic English desk dictionary with the emphasis on contemporary Canadian usage, spelling and pronunciation. 130,000 entries, including 5,000 biographical entries (over 800 on Canadians), 6,000 place names (over 1,200 of them Canadian, with all Canadian towns with more than 5,000 inhabitants featured) and 4,000 historical events. Definitions

....(contd.)
are supported by over 23,000 illustrative quotations from over 8,000 Canadian sources, including literary works, periodicals and newspapers. *Class No:* 802.0-087.471

[5432]
A Dictionary of Canadianisms on historical principles: produced by the Lexicographical Centre for Canadian English, University of Victoria, British Columbia. Avis, W.S., *ed.* Toronto, Gage, 1967. xxiii,927p. illus.

Over 10,000 entry-words, each being supported by dated evidence from printed sources, representing words originating in Canada, having a particular meaning there, or which are associated with an especially Canadian activity. Entries comprise headword, pronunciation (unusual words only), part of speech, etymology (if relevant), restrictive label (region, activity, etc.), definition, and quotations in chronological order. Many cross-references. Bibliography of sources and list of periodicals cited (47p.).

A Concise dictionary of Canadianisms, ed., by W.S. Avis and others, was published in 1973 (Toronto, Gage).

Avis has also edited (with others) the *Gage Canadian dictionary* (Toronto, Gage, 1983. 1313p. illus. ISBN: 077151980x), which claims to 'reflect the usage generally accepted by Canadians throughout the country' as regards spelling, pronunciation, vocabulary and style.
Class No: 802.0-087.471

[5433]
Dictionary of Prince Edward Island English. Pratt, T.K., *ed.* Toronto, Univ. of Toronto Press, 1988. xxxii,192p. $30. ISBN: 0802057810.

Similar in format to the *Dictionary of Newfoundland English,* with 873 entries for non-standard words used or once used on Prince Edward Island. Entries comprise headword, part of speech, variant forms, quotations from oral and written sources, and references to other dictionaries. Bibliography (12p.) and list of dictionaries (2p.). *Class No:* 802.0-087.471

[5434]
STORY, G.M., & *others.* **Dictionary of Newfoundland English.** 2nd ed. Toronto, Univ. of Toronto Press, 1990. 768p. £50. ISBN: 0802058876.

1st ed. 1982.

Records words which have originated in Newfoundland, those which have continued in use there after dying out elsewhere, and those which have a particular local meaning. Approx. 3,000 headwords, with entries which include part of speech, alternative forms, pronunciation (where local variation significant), notes on documentary evidence, etymology, definition, combinations, and quotations from printed and oral sources in chronological order. Clear layout and excellent scholarly, but readable, introduction. Bibliography of printed sources and lists of collectors and contributors. *Class No:* 802.0-087.471

Caribbean

[5435]
CASSIDY, F.G. *and* **LE PAGE, R.B. Dictionary of Jamaican English.** 2nd ed. Cambridge, Cambridge Univ. Press, 1980. lxiv,509p. £80. ISBN: 052122165x.

1st ed. 1967.

OED-style dictionary of words, meanings and pronunciations peculiar to Jamaica, originating there, or surviving there after being lost elsewhere. Entries give pronunciation, part of speech, etymology, definition and dated citations. Approx. 8,000 headwords. Bibliography of

....(contd.)
sources (12p.). Lengthy scholarly introduction.

2nd ed. adds information about usage elsewhere in the Caribbean to many entries and a Supplement with a further 380 entries. *Class No:* 802.0-087.472.9

[5436]
Dictionary of Caribbean English usage. Allsopp, R., *ed.* Oxford, Oxford Univ. Press, 1996. lxxviii,697p. £50. ISBN: 0198661525.

The first record of English usage in the entire Caribbean, which aims to provide 'as complete an inventory as practicable of the Caribbean environment and lifestyle as known and spoken in each territory but not recorded in the standard British and American desk dictionaries' (*Introduction*). Covers 18 territories and is based on information drawn from speech recordings and over 900 written sources, including Caribbean literature, reference works, magazines, newspapers and pamphlets. Entries include spelling variants, pronunciation, detailed definitions, etymology, regional differences and numerous illustrative quotations. Supplement lists Caribbean French and Spanish equivalents to selected items from the dictionary. Very detailed introduction. List of sources (71p.).
Class No: 802.0-087.472.9

[5437]
HOLM, J.A. *and* **SHILLING, A.W. Dictionary of Bahamian English.** Cold Spring, N.Y., Lexik House, 1982. 228p. maps. $42. ISBN: 0936368039.

Over 5,500 entries supported by quotations from written sources. *Class No:* 802.0-087.472.9

USA

Bibliographies

[5438]
BRENNI, V.J. American English: a bibliography. Philadelphia, Pa., Univ. of Pennsylvania Press, 1964 (repr. Westport, Conn., Greenwood, 1981). 221p. $35. ISBN: 0313233446.

1,496 numbered items in 9 sections: 1. General and historical - 2. Spelling - 3. Pronunciation - 4. Grammar, syntax and usage - 5. Dialects - 6. Slang - 7. Loan words - 8. Dictionaries - 9. Miscellaneous. Index of authors, subjects, etc. *Class No:* 802.0-087.473(01)

[5439]
McMILLAN, J.B. *and* **MONTGOMERY, M.B. Annotated bibliography of Southern American English.** Tuscaloosa, Ala., Univ. of Alabama Press, 1989. xii,444p. $32.95. ISBN: 0817304487.

1st ed. 1971.

A classified bibliography with over 2,800 entries (1,100 in 1st ed.), with descriptive annotations and cross-references. Author index. *Class No:* 802.0-087.473(01)

Dictionaries

[5440]
The American heritage dictionary. Morris, W., *ed.* 3rd ed. Boston, Houghton Mifflin, 1992. 2140p. illus. $45 ISBN: 0395448956.

1st ed. 1969; 2nd ed. 1982, as *The American heritage dictionary: 2nd college ed.*

An American desk dictionary with *c.*200,000 main entries, including 16,000 new to this ed., which reverts to the title and larger format of 1st ed. Syllabification indicated for

....(contd.)
headwords, plus pronunciation using the publisher's own symbols. Senses ordered according to frequency (commonest first), with illustrative examples and quotations from major writers in many cases. Etymologies for over 30,000 entries (no date of first use), with substantial 'word history' paragraphs for 400 terms of particular interest. 500 usage notes, including comments on contentious issues by contemporary writers. 900 synonym notes, with explanatory comments and illustrative phrases. 100 notes on regional variations. Abbreviations, acronyms, biographical and geographical entries are now part of the main sequence rather than listed separately. Extra material includes essays on the history of the English language and notes on Indo-European roots. A unique feature is the use of photographs among the 4,000 illustrations.

Regarded as a good dictionary for home and school use in the US because it takes a less scholarly approach than rivals like *Webster's ninth new collegiate dictionary*. 'Use of abbreviations within the prose of the definitions is almost nonexistent, which facilitates easy use' (*Booklist*, v.87(11), Feb. 1, 1991, p.1148).

Available from 1995 on CD-ROM, packaged with *Roget's II: the new thesaurus* (ISBN: 0395711460).
Class No: 802.0-087.473(038)

[5441]
—The American heritage college dictionary. 3rd ed. Boston, Houghton Mifflin, 1993. 1630p. illus. $18.45 ISBN: 0395669170.

2nd ed. 1982.

A desk dictionary based on the *AHD*, which, with 185,000 headwords, is not much smaller than the parent work. In order to retain so many entries, a smaller typeface has been used, illustrative sentences have been shortened, abbreviations used in etymologies, word histories dropped, and the number of illustrations reduced to 2,500. Most usage, regional and synonym notes have been retained, along with biographical and encyclopedic entries.
Class No: 802.0-087.473(038)

[5442]
CRAIGIE, W.A. *and* **HULBERT, J.R. A Dictionary of American English on historical principles,** compiled at the Univ. of Chicago. London, Oxford Univ. Press, 1936-44. 4v.

Compiled on the lines of the *OED*, to which it is complementary. All words (including names of plants, animals and institutions) of significance to the cultural life or linguistical usage of the US are included. Needless duplication with the *OED* is avoided: etymologies are given only for Americanisms and only the American meanings are given for words common to England and the US. No slang after 1875, no new words after 1900, nor quotations after 1925 are included. Bibliography of works cited, p.2529-2552. *Class No:* 802.0-087.473(038)

[5443]
Dictionary of American regional English. Cassidy, F.G., *ed.* Cambridge, Mass., The Belknap Press of Harvard Univ. Press, 1985-96. v.1-3 (in progress). $75 per vol.

V.1, *Introduction and A-C* (1985. clvi,903p. ISBN: 0674205111) contains a lengthy and detailed introduction to the *DARE* project and *c.*9,000 entries for regional words and phrases, with definitions, geographical distribution, and chronologically arranged quotations from written sources. Entries for certain terms include a computer-generated map of the US, with distribution of the term plotted from data compiled by a team of field workers, who conducted

....(contd.)
interviews with natives of 1,002 communities in 50 states during the period 1965-70. The text of their questionnaire and a list of informants (including details of community, age, education, occupation, sex and race) are included in the introduction.

Continued by v.2, *D-H* (1991. xv,1175p. ISBN: 067420512x) and v.3, *I-O* (1996. 960p. ISBN: 0674205197). A further 2 vols. are planned, but the project has already taken longer than the 10 years originally envisaged.

A.A. Metcalf and L. Von Schneidemesser have edited an *Index by region, usage and etymology* to vols. 1 and 2 for the American Dialect Society (Tuscaloosa, Ala., Univ. of Alabama Press, 1993. 208p. $16. ISBN: 0817306943).
Class No: 802.0-087.473(038)

[5444]
HENDRICKSON, R. Whistlin' Dixie: a dictionary of Southern expressions. New York, Facts on File, 1993. xxxi,251p. $24.95. ISBN: 0816021104.

The first in a projected 5-vol. series of dictionaries of US regional speech, aimed at the general rather than academic market. Defines and explains over 3,000 phrases of Southern origin, giving sources (newspapers, magazines, literary works, etc.) in many - but by no means all - cases. Lengthy introductory essay on Southern dialects. 'An entertaining and educational work...[but]...a disturbing feature is the unevenness of documentation' (*Reference Books Review*, Dec. 15, 1992, p.765). For a more scholarly approach, see *Dictionary of American regional English*. *Class No:* 802.0-087.473(038)

[5445]
—HENDRICKSON, R. Happy trails: a dictionary of Western expressions. New York, Facts on File, 1994. 274p. $24.95. ISBN: 0816021120.

A companion to *Whistlin' Dixie*, with a similar number of entries, most including quoted examples of usage and citing a source.

An alternative source is *Dictionary of the American West* by W. Blevins (New York, Facts on File, 1993. xiv,400p. illus. ISBN: 0816020310), which has *c.*3,500 entries, giving definitions and explanations (plus photographs in many cases) but no quotations. Many entries are unique to one or other of these dictionaries. Blevins includes a bibliography (4p.).

Other vols. by Hendrickson in Facts on File's *Dictionary of American regional expressions series* are:

Mountain range: a dictionary of expressions from Appalachia to the Ozarks. 1997. 176p. $24.95. ISBN: 0806021139.

Yankee talk: a dictionary of New England expressions. 1996. 272p. $24.95. ISBN: 0806021112. *Class No:* 802.0-087.473(038)

[5446]
HORNBY, A.S. *and* **RUSE, C. Oxford student's dictionary of American English.** 2nd ed. Oxford, Oxford Univ. Press, 1986. 752p. illus. ISBN: 0194311945.

1st ed. 1983.

An adaptation of the *Oxford student's dictionary of current English*, with some material from the *Oxford advanced learner's dictionary of current English*, listing 'the more usual words, compounds, and idomatic expressions that the learner is likely to hear in everyday conversation among educated Americans or to see written in letters, newspapers, and documents ... in the United States' (*Preface* to 1st ed.). Spelling and pronunciation are exclusively American.
Class No: 802.0-087.473(038)

[5447]

LEDERER, R.M. Colonial American English: words and phrases found in Colonial writing, now archaic, obscure, obsolete or whose meanings have changed. Essex, Conn., Verbatim, 1985. 267p. $24.95. ISBN: 0930454197.

Lists and briefly defines over 3,000 words and phrases used in America during the period 1608-1783. Illustrative quotations for most entries but sources not fully cited. Bibliography (6p.). Lists of entries by category (16 headings). *Class No:* 802.0-087.473(038)

[5448]

MATHEWS, M.M. A Dictionary of Americanisms on historical principles. Chicago, Univ. of Chicago Press; London, Oxford Univ. Press, 1951. 1946p.

Only words or expressions originating in the United States being entered, this work is of narrower scope than Craigie and Hulbert's *Dictionary of American English,* (London, Oxford Univ. Press, 1936-44. 4v.) though it does not have the latter's chronological limitations. Brief etymology, pronunciation in a modified IPA notation and illustrative quotations are given. Carefully chosen line-block illustrations in the text. Bibliography of works cited, p.1913-46.

An abridged version, entitled *Americanisms,* was published by Chicago Univ. Press in 1966 (304p.). *Class No:* 802.0-087.473(038)

[5449]

Merriam-Webster's collegiate dictionary. 10th ed. Springfield, Mass., Merriam-Webster, 1993. 1560p. illus. $21.95. ISBN: 0877797099.

1st ed. 1898, as *Webster's collegiate dictionary*; 9th ed. 1983, as *Webster's ninth new collegiate dictionary*.

A major American desk dictionary based on the extensive citation files (over 14 million examples) of Merriam-Webster. Claims to have nearly 160,000 entries and 211,000 definitions in this ed., supported by 35,000 verbal illustrations and illustrative quotations, 35,000 etymologies, 4,400 usage paragraphs and 700 line drawings. Entries give pronunciation (using a combination of IPA and Webster's symbols); etymology in most cases; date of first recorded instance (an unusual feature in a desk dictionary); and numbered definitions, the senses being ordered historically with the earliest first. Notes on usage and lists of synonyms follow some entries. Over 10,000 words or senses are new to this ed. The dictionary proper is followed by a great deal of useful supplementary material, including lists of abbreviations; foreign words and phrases; signs and symbols; biographical entries; geographical entries; and a handbook of style.

Available on CD-ROM as *Merriam-Webster's collegiate dictionary: deluxe electronic edition* ($69.95. ISBN: 0877794545), which also includes *Merriam-Webster's collegiate thesaurus*.

Can also be accessed on the Internet, free of charge, at http://www.m-w.com/netdict.htm *Class No:* 802.0-087.473(038)

[5450]

Random House Webster's college dictionary. Rev ed. New York, Random House, 1996. 1568p. illus. $23.95. ISBN: 0679438866.

1st ed. 1991, superseding *The Random House college dictionary* (1989).

Edited online from the computerized database of the unabridged *Random House dictionary of the English language* (2nd ed. 1987). Claims 180,000 entries, which include foreign words, abbreviations, 4,000 biographical

.... *(contd.)*

entries and 7,000 geographical names, all within the main sequence. Provides syllabification and pronunciation (modified IPA) for headwords, arranges senses by frequency (commonest first) and gives etymologies and (in some cases) illustrative sentences and lists of synonyms. 800 black and white illustrations. Appendices include 'A Guide for writers', with sample citation forms, and the introductory material includes an excellent user's manual. Rev. ed. has a supplementary list of 600 new terms. *Class No:* 802.0-087.473(038)

[5451]

Webster's New World college dictionary. Neufeldt, V. *and* Guralnik, D.B., *eds.* Reprint of 3rd ed. New York, Macmillan, 1996. xxvi,1574p. illus. £14.99. ISBN: 002860332x.

1st ed. Cleveland, Ohio, World Publishing Co., 1953; 2nd ed. 1970; this ed. first published New York, Simon & Schuster, 1988, as *Webster's New World dictionary of American English* (3rd college ed.).

Claims 170,000 entries, of which 20,000 are new to this ed. As the title suggests, strong attention is paid to words and meanings of American origin, including colloquial and slang terms, and some 11,000 Americanisms are marked by an asterisk. Entries give syllabification of headwords and guidance on end-of-line word division, and American pronunciation is indicated using the publisher's own system. Senses are arranged historically (earliest first) and coverage of etymology is particularly good, extending even to place names. Some entries have usage notes and synonym lists and there are over 650 line drawings. Abbreviations, foreign terms and proper names are treated in the main sequence. The list of colleges has been dropped, but the appended source documentation section has been expanded. Reviewers have welcomed the improved readability brought about by a change of typeface in this ed. Reprint includes corrections and several hundred new entries. *Class No:* 802.0-087.473(038)

Maps & Atlases

[5452]

CARVER, C.M. American regional dialects: a word geography. Ann Arbor, Mich., Univ. of Michigan Press, 1987. 416p. $34.50. ISBN: 0472100769.

Analyses data gathered for the *Dictionary of American regional English* and compares the results with works based on the *Linguistic atlas of the United States and Canada* project. Includes 92 maps and discusses *c.*1,500 lexical items. 'Indispensable to the study of American regional dialects today' (*Choice,* v.24(10), June 1987, p.1547-8). *Class No:* 802.0-087.473(084.3)

[5453]

Linguistic atlas of the Gulf States. Pederson, L., *and others, eds.* Athens, Ga., Univ. of Georgia Press, 1986-92. 7v.

V.1 1986. 384p. $60. ISBN: 0820307157.

V.2 *General index.* 1988. 400p. $60. ISBN: 0820309729.

V.3 *Technical index.* 1989. 464p. $60. ISBN: 0820311820.

V.4 *Regional matrix.* 1990. 552p, $65. ISBN: 0820312312.

V.5 *The Regional pattern.* 1991. 456p. $60. ISBN: 0820312762.

V.6 *Social matrix.* 1991. 400 maps. $65. ISBN: 0820313459.

V.7 *Social pattern.* 1992. 552p. $70. ISBN: 0820314471.

....*(contd.)*

Based on 1,118 field interviews carried out in Alabama, Arkansas, Florida, Georgia, Louisiana, Mississippi, Tennessee, and Texas. Also available in microform from UMI Research Collections.

Other comparable atlases are:

Linguistic atlas of the Upper Midwest, by H.B. Allen. Minneapolis, Univ. of Minnesota Press, 1973-76. 3v.

Linguistic atlas of New England, ed. by H. Kurath. Providence, R.I., Brown Univ., 1939-43. 3v. in 6.

Linguistic atlas of the Middle and South Atlantic States, ed. by R.I. McDavid and R.K. O'Cain. Chicago, Univ. of Chicago Press, 1980-. *Class No:* 802.0-087.473(084.3)

Histories

[5454]

DILLARD, J.L. A History of American English. London, Longman, 1992. xiv,258p. £18.99. (*Longman linguistics library.*) ISBN: 0582052963.

The first chronological, narrative account of the development of American English. 8 chapters followed by substantial bibliography (23p.). Index. *Class No:* 802.0-087.473(091)

[5455]

MENCKEN, H.L. The American language: an inquiry into the development of English in the United States. 4th ed. New York, Knopf; London, Kegan Paul, Trench, Trübner, 1936. xxix+769+xxixp. *Supplements 1-2.* New York, Knopf, 1945-48.

A well-documented historical survey, with chapters on pronunciation, spelling, the common speech, proper names and slang, plus an appendix on foreign dialects in the US. Indexes of words and phrases, and of proper names. The *Supplements* closely follow the plan of the original. Numerous footnote references.

An abridgement of the 4th ed., and its supplements, with annotations and new materials by R.I. McDavid, assisted by D.W. Maurer, appeared in 1963 (New York, Knopf, xxvi,778,cxxvip.). *Class No:* 802.0-087.473(091)

Black Races

[5456]

Juba to jive: a dictionary of African-American slang. Major, C., *ed.* New ed. London, Penguin, 1994. xxxv,548p. £9.99. ISBN: 014051306x.

1st ed. New York, International Publishers Co., 1970, as *Dictionary of Afro-American slang*.

Defines and dates nearly 7,000 slang words and phrases (over 3 times as many as 1st ed.), with examples of usage. Also indicates in which area(s) of the USA terms are prevalent and whether they are associated with a particular sphere of activity, *e.g.* jazz music, drug culture, etc. Cross-references between related terms. Citations to nearly 150 printed sources. Bibliography (26p.). *Class No:* 802.0-087.473(=96)

[5457]

—SMITHERMAN, G. Black talk: words and phrases from the Hood to the Amen Corner. Boston, Mass., Houghton, 1994. 242p. $17.95. ISBN: 0395674107.

According to *Reference Books Bulletin* (v. 91(2), Sept. 15, 1994, p.178), this is 'a somewhat less formal book than *Juba to jive*, and the language covered is more contemporary, with a strong emphasis on hip-hop culture.' Gives definitions and illustrative sentences, with regional and special group uses sometimes indicated. Sources are primarily oral; where scholarly works are cited, full bibliographical information is not supplied. *Class No:* 802.0-087.473(=96)

New Zealand

[5458]

The Dictionary of New Zealand English: a dictionary of New Zealandisms on historical principles. Orsman, H.W., *ed.* Oxford, Oxford Univ. Press, 1998. 982p. £90. ISBN: 0195583477.

The long-awaited (40 years in preparation) *OED*-style dictionary of New Zealand English, with 6,000 main headword entries and 9,300 separate subentries. Numerous chronologically arranged illustrative quotations from literature and the media. List of written sources. *Class No:* 802.0-087.493

Australia

[5459]

The Australian concise Oxford dictionary. Hughes, J., *& others, eds.* 2nd ed. Melbourne, Oxford Univ. Press, 1992. 1375p. ISBN: 0195534425.

1st ed. 1987, by G.W. Turner, based on 7th ed. of *COD*.

Computer-generated rather than the work of a single author like 1st ed., using data from the files of the *Concise Oxford dictionary* and *Australian national dictionary*. All words of purely British relevance are omitted. New introductory essay on 'The Present state of Australian usage' includes brief bibliography.

3rd ed. due 1998 (£25. ISBN: 0195506170) *Class No:* 802.0-087.494

[5460]

The Australian national dictionary: a dictionary of Australianisms on historical principles. Ramson, W.S., *ed.* Melbourne, Oxford Univ. Press, 1988. xv,814p. £50. ISBN: 0195547365.

OED-style dictionary of 10,000 Australianisms, which are defined as 'those words and meanings which have originated in Australia, which have a greater currency here than elsewhere, or which have a special significance in Australia because of their connection with an aspect of the history of the country' (*Introduction*). Approx. 6,000 main entries, comprising headword, pronunciation (International Phonetic Alphabet), part of speech, subject or restrictive label, variant spellings, etymology, definition, cross-references, variant forms and citations in chronological order. Combinations of which the headword is the main element are normally listed in a sub-section of the main entry. Over 60,000 dated and referenced quotations from 9,500 sources, the most frequently quoted being listed in the select bibliography (48p.). Map of 58 Aboriginal languages. 'Makes obsolete all earlier dictionaries of Australian English' (*Choice*, v.26(11/12), July/Aug. 1989, p.1806).

The Concise Australian national dictionary, ed. by J. Hughes (1993. 678p. £15.95. ISBN: 0195534336) contains all the words in the *AND*, with combinations and collocations, and gives definitions, etymologies and pronunciations, together with the earliest citation and at least one later one. *Class No:* 802.0-087.494

[5461]

—Australian words and their origins. Hughes, J., *ed.* Melbourne, Oxford Univ. Press, 1989. xiv,662p. £22.50. ISBN: 019553087x.

An abridged version of the *AND*, retaining the entire word list, including combinations and collocations, with definitions and etymologies but with much less illustrative material: the earliest citation and at least one other are given for each term. Will make an economical and perfectly adequate substitute for the parent work in smaller libraries.
Class No: 802.0-087.494

[5462]

Heinemann Australian dictionary, written and compiled in association with members of the academic staff of La Trobe University. White, L., *ed.* 4th ed. Richmond, Vic., Heinemann Educational, 1992. 1328p. A$18.95. ISBN: 0858596288.

1st ed. 1976.

Claims to be 'the first dictionary of its kind to be written in Australia, in *Australian* English' (*Preface*) and is aimed mainly at secondary school students. *c.*25,000 headwords, with pronunciation guide in some cases, part of speech, definition(s) written in Standard Australian, list of words in the same 'family', and etymology where appropriate. 4th ed. has 500 new words and usages. *Class No:* 802.0-087.494

[5463]

The Macquarie dictionary. Delbridge, A, *ed.* 2nd. ed. North Ryde, NSW, Macquarie Library, 1991. 2080p. A$49.95. ISBN: 0949757632.

1st ed. 1981.

'The first general reference dictionary ever to present a set of entries for a complete word list in which all the pronunciations, all the spellings, and all the definitions of meaning are taken from the use of English in Australia, and in which Australian English becomes the basis of comparison with other national varieties of English' (*Preface to 1st ed.*). The base dictionary is the *Encyclopedic world dictionary* (London, Hamlyn, 1971).

*c.*80,000 entries, comprising headword, pronunciation (IPA), part of speech, inflected forms, style label, numbered definitions, and etymology. 2nd ed. has 10,000 new words and phrases and includes encyclopedic entries for people and places. *Class No:* 802.0-087.494

[5464]

WILKES, G.A. A Dictionary of Australian colloquialisms. 4th ed. Sydney, Sydney Univ. Press; Oxford, Oxford Univ. Press, 1996. 432p. £12.99 ISBN: 019553798x.

1st ed. 1978; 3rd ed. 1991.

A revised and expanded ed. with over 2,500 words and phrases, including nearly 300 new ones. Entries are arranged by keyword, A-Z, and supported by chronologically arranged citations. Scholarly introduction.
Class No: 802.0-087.494

Jargon

[5465]

GREEN, J. Dictionary of jargon. London and New York, Routledge and Kegan Paul, 1987. xv,616p. ISBN: 0710099193.

A major expansion of *Newspeak: a dictionary of jargon* (Routledge and Kegan Paul, 1983).

Three times the size of its predecessor, with definitions of some 21,000 words, phrases, acronyms and abbreviations used in a wide variety of professions and occupations, as

....*(contd.)*
well as leisure activities like golf and surfing. List of sources includes over 200 books, newspapers and magazines.
Class No: 802.0-088

English as a Second Language

Databases

[5466]

COBUILD on CD-ROM. Worthing, HarperCollins Electronic Reference, 1994. £47. ISBN: 000371084x.

A single CD-ROM incorporating *Collins COBUILD English dictionary*, *Collins COBUILD English usage* and *Collins COBUILD English grammar*, plus a Word Bank containing 5 million words selected from the *Collins COBUILD Bank of English* corpus. Claims over 70,000 references and over 90,000 examples.

COBUILD English collocations on CD-ROM (1995. £47. ISBN: 0003710815), offers access to 10,000 headwords (the core vocabulary of English) and 140,000 collocations, with 2,600,000 examples showing collocations in use, taken from the *Bank of English* corpus.

COBUILDdirect is an on-line Internet service for accessing language data based on the Bank of English corpus, such as word frequency and distribution statistics (http://www.cobuild.collins.co.uk/direct-info.html).
Class No: 802.0-089(003.4)

Bibliographies

[5467]

CARRASQUILLO, A.L. Teaching English as a second language: a resource guide. New York, Garland, 1994. 219p. $35. (*Source books on education.*) ISBN: 0815308213.

Introduces theoretical approaches to ESL with chapters on learning styles, cultural diversity, etc., and includes programs, approaches, strategies, etc. List of references to books and periodical articles after each chapter. List of resources, with directory information, for ESL educators in the US. Subject and author indexes. *Class No:* 802.0-089(01)

[5468]

GOLDSTEIN, W.L. Teaching English as a second language: an annotated bibliography. New York, Garland, 1975-84. 2v. (218;323p.).

A classified listing, with 852 items in v.1 and over 900 in v.2. Author and keyword indexes. *Class No:* 802.0-089(01)

Dictionaries

[5469]

The BBC English dictionary. Sinclair, J., *ed.* London, BBC English & HarperCollins, 1992. xxxiv,1374p. £16.99 ISBN: 1854972693, BBC; 0003705544, HarperCollins.

Based on the English used by the BBC World Service, 1988-92, and compiled in association with the publishers of the *COBUILD* series, this dictionary takes a new approach to ESL lexicography by presenting each definition as a complete sentence. *c.*60,000 headwords and 70,000 definitions, with over 1,000 entries on people, places and events. These include every country in the world, its capital and at least one prominent person. Clearly set out with each headword, its pronunciation and inflected forms on a separate line, followed by numbered senses in separate paragraphs. For each sense there is a grammatical label;

.... *(contd.)*
definition; illustrative examples from radio broadcasts, newspapers and books; derivatives; stylistic information; and cross-references. *Class No:* 802.0-089(038)

[5470]

The BBI dictionary of English word combinations. Benson, M. *and* Benson, E. *and* Ilson, R., *comps*. 2nd, rev. ed Amsterdam, Benjamins, 1997. xl,386p. $38. ISBN: 9027221669, Europe; 1556195206, US.

1st ed. 1986, as *The BBI combinatory dictionary of English: a guide to word combinations*.

A unique dictionary which lists grammatical and lexical 'recurrent word combinations' (also called 'collocations') so that the non-native learner may know 'what goes with what' in English. No pronunciations or etymologies given, and often no definitions, as these are essentially common phrases (this is *not* a dictionary of idioms) but there are plenty of illustrative phrases and usage notes explain differences between American and British English. 90,000 collocations under 18,000 headwords (25% increase on 1st ed.). Lengthy, complex introduction. Title derives from the compilers' names. 1st ed. reviewed at length in *English Today,* no.19, July 1989, p.51-53. *Class No:* 802.0-089(038)

[5471]

The Cambridge international dictionary of English. Procter, P., *ed.* Cambridge, Cambridge Univ. Press, 1995. xviii,1774p. illus. £19.99. ISBN: 0521482364.

Cambridge's first venture into the ELT dictionary market has *c.*100,000 definitions written using a strictly controlled 2,000-word vocabulary. There are separate headwords for each distinct sense of a word (50,000 in all), with syllabification and pronunciation, followed by definition and phrases associated with that sense. Usage notes in boxes throughout the main sequence. Covers British, American and Australian English. Innovative features include an index (64p.) of 30,000 words used in illustrative phrases and 'false friend' information for 14 languages. Full list of words used in the defining vocabulary (6p.). *Class No:* 802.0-089(038)

[5472]

Collins COBUILD English dictionary. New ed. London, HarperCollins, 1996. 1951p. £20. ISBN: 0003750299.

1st ed. London, Collins, 1987, as *Collins COBUILD English language dictionary*.

A dictionary for learners and teachers of English, which is the result of research at Birmingham University, the acronym standing for Collins (CO) Birmingham University (BU) International Language Database (ILD).

75,000 entries, with each separate meaning of each word illustrated by a sentence taken from a 320-million word corpus of contemporary texts in order to demonstrate actual current usage. Great emphasis is placed on the 2-3,000 words regarded as the core vocabulary of English. Entries include pronunciation (IPA) with American variations. Marginal notes for each entry give word frequency count, grammatical classification, synonyms and antonyms. More detailed grammatical and semantic information is included in a separate column aimed at advanced users.
Class No: 802.0-089(038)

[5473]

HORNBY, A.S. The Oxford advanced learner's dictionary of current English. Crowther, J., *ed.* 5th ed. Oxford, Oxford Univ. Press, 1995 (repr. with corrections, 1997). x,1428p. illus. £18.55. ISBN: 0194314219.

1st ed. 1948, as *The Advanced learner's dictionary*. 4th ed. 1989.

The standard dictionary for students of English as a foreign language, with 63,000 headwords and derivatives, 11,600 idiomatic expressions, 90,000 illustrative phrases and many line drawings. Clearly laid out, making good use of different typefaces and symbols. Entries include pronunciation of headword (with US variants), grammatical information, usage notes in many cases, and cross-references. 5th ed. has 2,300 new words and meanings, and innovations include the use of the British National Corpus for examples, definitions rewritten using a 3,500-word defining vocabulary (listed as Appendix), and full colour pages with maps, geographical names and cultural information about the UK and USA. Appendices include lists of first names, military ranks and family relationships.

Also available on CD-ROM with over 500 interactive photos and 8,000 visual references, a single-user licence costing £69.99 (ISBN: 0194314677). *Class No:* 802.0-089(038)

[5474]

—The Oxford advanced learner's encyclopedic dictionary. Crowther, J., *ed.* Oxford, Oxford Univ. Press, 1992. xxxviii,1081p. illus. £20.95. ISBN: 0194313131.

Originally published as *The Oxford advanced learner's dictionary: encyclopedic edition.*

A greatly expanded version of *OALD*, specially compiled for students of English as a foreign or second language at university level. In a 3-column format, with 4,500 encyclopedic entries on people, places and events; over 90 articles on British life and institutions; 800 usage notes; wider coverage of specialist vocabulary, particularly from science and technology; maps of all countries; and nearly 600 photos and drawings. *Class No:* 802.0-089(038)

[5475]

Longman dictionary of contemporary English. 3rd ed. Harlow, Longman, 1995. xxii,1668+22p. illus. £18.95. ISBN: 0582237513.

1st ed. 1978; 2nd ed. 1987.

One of the best dictionaries for learners of English as a foreign language, with over 80,000 words and phrases, compounds always being treated as separate headwords. Definitions use a basic 2,000-word vocabulary and illustrative quotations are drawn from a computerized corpus. Over 2,300 words are illustrated and new to this ed. are 24p. of labelled, full colour illustrations. British and American pronunciation given, using IPA symbols. 3,000 most frequently used words are labelled. Supplementary material includes many usage notes and 8 tables, including geographical names, irregular verbs and list of words used in the defining vocabulary.

Longman lexicon of contemporary English by T. McArthur (Harlow, Longman, 1981. £25. ISBN: 0582556368) is the first ELT thesaurus and groups words under 130 subject headings, *e.g.* People and Family, Food and Drink, etc. Style and register are clearly explained and illustrative sentences are provided. Good coverage of American English. Alphabetical index. *Class No:* 802.0-089(038)

[5476]

—HEATON, J.B. *and* TURTON, N.D. Longman dictionary of common errors. 2nd ed. Harlow, Longman, 1996. vii,375p. £7.95. ISBN: 0582237521.

1st ed. 1987.

Aimed at foreign learners of English at intermediate level and above and based on errors found in Cambridge First Certificate papers. Over 2,500 errors arranged A-Z by keyword, with the correct version set out below in bold type and a clear, concise explanation. Examples are taken from the Longman Learners' Corpus and the British National Corpus. American and British differences included where appropriate. Glossary of grammatical terms (6p.) and checklist of common misspellings (2p.). Clearly presented and excellent value. *Class No:* 802.0-089(038)

[5477]

—Longman dictionary of American English. Harlow, Longman, 1997. 792p. £15.95. ISBN: 0801314097.

The only intermediate learners' dictionary to be based on American corpuses of natural written and spoken English. Over 44,000 words and phrases defined using the Longman Defining Vocabulary. Many idiomatic spoken phrases highlighted in boxes. Usage notes. *Class No:* 802.0-089(038)

[5478]

Longman dictionary of English language and culture. Summers, D., *ed.* Harlow, Longman, 1992. 31+1528+27p. illus. ISBN: 0582086752.

An encyclopedic dictionary for EFL students, with 80,000 standard entries for words and phrase and 15,000 'cultural' entries, covering people, places, literature, sport, entertainment, organizations, newspapers, companies, products, etc. Definitions written in the 2,000-word Longman Defining Vocabulary. Pronunciation (IPA) given for all headwords. Covers American as well as British language and culture. Over 500 black and white illustrations, plus 32p. of detailed, full-colour illustrations, *e.g.* scenes from literature, popular musicians, etc. Special feature pages give more details about aspects of British and American life, *e.g.* education, weddings, etc.

New ed. due mid-1998. *Class No:* 802.0-089(038)

[5479]

Longman language activator: the world's first production dictionary. Summers, D., *and others, eds.* Harlow, Longman, 1993. 34+1587+11p. £20.95. ISBN: 0582040922.

An innovative dictionary which aims to help students to find ways to express the different aspects of the basic ideas of the English language. The A-Z wordlist incorporates entries representing 1,052 key concepts (*e.g.* 'clever', 'big', 'walk') to which all other words are cross-referenced. These main entries include cross-references to similar concepts and lists of definitions (over 20 in many cases) written in the 2,000-word Longman Defining Vocabulary, with real illustrative sentences taken from the Longman Lancaster Corpus and other sources. Grammatical information is very clearly presented and equal coverage is given to both British and American English. Key concepts and defining vocabulary are listed after the main sequence. 'The ELT world at least will find the *Activator* a valuable challenge to preconceived ideas' (*English Today*, v.10(1), Jan. 1994, p.53-5). *Class No:* 802.0-089(038)

Spelling

[5480]

Collins English spelling dictionary. Shearer, T., *and others, eds.* Glasgow, HarperCollins, 1993. vii,662p. 5.99. ISBN: 0004336348.

The most extensive word-list available, with over 146,000 items including numerous proper (especially geographical) names. Uses colour to mark where words may be hyphenated at line-ends. US variants indicated.
Class No: 802.0-1

[5481]

The Oxford colour spelling dictionary. Waite, M., *ed.* 2nd ed. Oxford, Clarendon Press, 1995. xiv,624p. £6.99. ISBN: 0198600305.

1st ed. 1986, as *The Oxford spelling dictionary*, comp. by R.E. Allen.

A much expanded ed. with 158,000 entries, based on the vocabulary of the *Concise Oxford dictionary* (9th ed. 1995) and the *Oxford reference dictionary* (1995) and including over 30,000 names of people, places, companies, etc. Provides advice on word-division (for printing purposes) for each item. This ed. gives US as well as British spellings. Two-colour (blue and black) text gives extra clarity.
Class No: 802.0-1

Pronunciation

[5482]

BBC pronouncing dictionary of British names. Pointon, G.E., *ed.* Paperback reprint of 2nd ed. Oxford, Oxford Univ. Press, 1990. xxvii,274p. ISBN: 0192827456.

First published 1971, ed. by G.M. Miller; 2nd ed. 1983.

Lists over 20,000 family names, titles, place names, etc., in one A-Z sequence, giving pronunciation in both International Phonetic Alphabet and a modified version of conventional English spelling. Intended initially for use by BBC staff but now established as a standard reference source. *Class No:* 802.0-15

[5483]

JONES, D. English pronouncing dictionary. Roach, P. *and* Hartman, J., *eds.* 15th ed. Cambridge, Cambridge Univ. Press, 1997. xix,559p. illus. £19.95. ISBN: 0521452724.

First published 1917; 14th ed. 1977.

A.C. Gimson's 1977 ed. represented a very comprehensive revision of this standard work, but the new editors (one British and one North American) have gone further by including American terms and spellings, giving American as well as British pronunciations (IPA) for each word, and abandoning Received Pronunciation (RP) in favour of 'BBC English'. This is defined as 'the pronunciation of professional speakers employed by the BBC as newsreaders' and does not carry RP's connotations of high social class and privilege. A broadcasting model is also followed for American pronunciation. Over 18,000 new entries bring the total up to 80,000, including thousands of proper names. Syllable divisions have been restored for the benefit of foreign learners of English. Detailed notes on how to use the dictionary (15p.). *Class No:* 802.0-15

[5484]

WELLS, J.C. Longman pronunciation dictionary. Harlow, Longman, 1990. xxviii,802p. £24. ISBN: 0582964113.

Gives recommended British *and American* pronunciations plus variants (including those considered to be incorrect, clearly labelled) for 75,000 words, including technical vocabulary and many proper names, including acronyms and trade names. For British English, recommended

.... (contd.)
pronunciations are based on a modernized version of Received Pronunciation, and for American English on the accent known as General American. Transcription system is the same as that used in *Everyman's English pronouncing dictionary* (14th ed.) with a few minor variations. Usage notes on 33 important pronunciation features (*e.g.* elision, glottal stop, stress) are scattered through the dictionary in boxes.

Excellent use of colour, typefaces and symbols (typical of Longman language books) and good value for money. Particularly useful for students and teachers of English as a foreign language. *Class No:* 802.0-15

USA

[5485]

EHRLICH, E. *and* **HAND, R. NBC handbook of pronunciation.** 4th ed., rev. and updated. New York, Harper & Row, 1984 (repr. 1991). 539p. $10.95. ISBN: 0062730568.

1st ed. 1943, by J.F. Bender.

Lists over 21,000 commonly used words and proper names, indicating 'General American' pronunciation by means of 'a readily understandable respelling system' (*Preface*). *Class No:* 802.0-15(73)

[5486]

KENYON, J.S. *and* **KNOTT, T.A. A Pronouncing dictionary of American English.** [2nd ed.]. Springfield, Mass., Merriam-Webster, 1953. lvi,484p. $12.95. ISBN: 0877790477.

First published 1944.

The American equivalent of Jones's *Everyman's English pronouncing dictionary* (*q.v.*), its purpose is 'to show the pronunciation of cultivated colloquial English in the United States' (*Introduction*) using the alphabet of the International Phonetic Association (IPA). Approx. 39,000 entries, including many proper names. Lengthy explanatory introduction. *Class No:* 802.0-15(73)

[5487]

Pronouncing dictionary of proper names: pronunciations for more than 28,000 proper names, selected for currency, frequency, or difficulty of pronunciation. Bollard, J.K., *ed.* 2nd ed. Detroit, Omnigraphics, 1997. xxxv,1097p. $88. ISBN: 0780800982.

1st ed. 1993.

Covers a very wide range of people, places, products, companies and technical terms, with a strong emphasis on names from popular culture, *e.g.* musicians and actors. Usual American Pronunciation is given in a simplified respelling system, with a key at the foot of each page, and also in IPA. Both systems are explained in detail in the Introduction. Many of the names can be found elsewhere, but 'as a one-stop shopping guide there is no comparable reference tool' (*Choice*, v.31(5), Jan. 1994, p.760, on 1st ed.). 2nd ed. has over 5,000 new entries. *Class No:* 802.0-15(73)

Punctuation

[5488]

PARTRIDGE, E. You have a point there: a guide to punctuation and its allies, with a chapter on American practice by J.W. Clark. London, Hamilton, 1953 (repr. Routledge, 1990). x,230p. £10.99. ISBN: 0415050758.

10 chapters on punctuation proper, 9 on 'Allies and accessories' (capitals, italics, etc.), and 2 on 'Orchestration' (sentences, paragraphs, etc.), plus brief chapter on US practice (12p.). Appendix 1. lists other relevant works; Appendix 2. lists diacritics. Clearly laid out, with plenty of examples of usage. Subject index. *Class No:* 802.0-19

[5489]

TODD, L. Cassell guide to punctuation. London, Cassell, 1995. 128p. £8.99. ISBN: 0304344281.

1. Background (history and development of English punctuation) - 2. Dictionary (punctuation marks, A-Z, with explanation and examples of current usage) - 3. Punctuation in use (comparison of British, US and European usage; plus guidance on special contexts, *e.g.* correspondence, bibliographies). Index. *Class No:* 802.0-19

Dictionaries & Vocabularies

Bibliographies

[5490]

English language dictionaries, 1604-1900: the catalog of the Warren N. and Suzanne B. Cordell Collection. O'Neill, R.K., *comp.* New York and London, Greenwood, 1988. xxv,480p. $145. (*Bibliographies and indexes in library and information science.*) ISBN: 0313255229.

This catalogue of part of the dictionary collection at Indiana State University has 2,328 separate entries, representing virtually all the English dictionary titles known to have been published up to 1900. Arranged A-Z by author/compiler/editor, entries include publication statement, collation, brief descriptive notes where appropriate, provenance if known and references to bibliographical sources. Subject index (collection not confined to language dictionaries). *Class No:* 802.0-3(01)

[5491]

KISTER, K.F. Kister's best dictionaries for adults and young people: a comparative guide. Phoenix, Ariz., Oryx Press, 1992. 464p. $39.50. ISBN: 0897741919.

Supersedes Kister's *Dictionary buying guide* (New York, Bowker, 1977).

Reviews and evaluates 300 dictionaries, including electronic and CD-ROM versions. *Class No:* 802.0-3(01)

[5492]

LANDAU, S.I. Dictionaries: the art and craft of lexicography. New York, Scribner, 1984; Cambridge, Cambridge, Univ. Press, 1989. 416p. illus. £14.95. ISBN: 0684180960, US; 0521367255, UK.

Reviews the history of lexicography (with the emphasis on English), explains how dictionaries are compiled, and provides a very useful critical bibliography of the major English-language dictionaries worldwide (21p.). *Class No:* 802.0-3(01)

Illustrated Works

[5493]

Dorling Kindersley ultimate visual dictionary. Evans, J., *ed.* New ed. London, Dorling Kindersley, 1998. 640p. illus. £25. ISBN: 0751304875.

1st ed. 1994.

6,000 colour pictures (many of them photographs) on over 300 elegantly produced page-openings, with *c.*30,000 terms labelled. Thematically arranged in 14 sections, *e.g.* 'Human body', 'Music'. Index. Very strong on science and technology, with many detailed cutaways, but, as with similar works, very Eurocentric in approach. 1998 ed. has a

.... *(contd.)*
16-page preliminary section covering recent scientific and technological developments, *e.g.* interactive television.

Puts the older established *Duden* pictorial dictionaries, long associated with Oxford Univ. Press, firmly in the shade and it is significant that OUP has been working with DK on *The Dorling Kindersley illustrated Oxford English dictionary* (due late 1998. £30. ISBN: 0751311103) *Class No:* 802.0-3(0.025)

[5494]
The Oxford-Duden pictorial English dictionary. 2nd ed. Oxford, Clarendon Press, 1995. 812p. £11.99. ISBN: 0198613113.

1st ed. 1981.

Based on the *Bildwörterbuch der deutschen Sprache*, with 384 sets of labelled drawings, each covering the vocabulary of a particular subject, which identify *c.*28,000 objects or activities (1,500 new terms in this ed.). Alphabetical index of all terms follows the illustrations. The same drawings have been used by Oxford as the basis for a series of bilingual dictionaries and whilst some have been revised for this ed. many are looking dated. Particularly useful for technical and scientific subjects. *Class No:* 802.0-3(0.025)

Unabridged Dictionaries

[5495]
Random House Webster's unabridged dictionary Flexner, S.B., *and others, eds.* 2nd ed., rev. and updated. New York, Random House, 1997. 2550p. $59.95. ISBN: 0679458549.

1st ed. 1966; 2nd ed. 1987, as *The Random House unabridged dictionary of the English language*.

A single-vol. unabridged dictionary with over 315,000 entries (including biographical and geographical entries) in the main sequence) plus a great deal of encyclopedic information in its supplements. The basic format of the 1st ed. (which had *c.*260,000 entries) is retained, *i.e.* 3 columns per page, with entries in bold type and definitions in order of frequency from the commonest sense to archaic and obsolete meanings. Over 75,000 illustrative phrases have been specially created rather than drawn from printed sources. Entries include etymology (with approx. dates of entry into the language) and pronunciation, and many have appended synonym lists and notes on alternative pronunciations, usage, and regional variations. 2,400 black-and-white illustrations. This updated version of 2nd ed. is more compact and easier to use than its notoriously unwieldy predecesor. It has 1,000 new words and meanings in a separate 8-page section and 1,500 updated entries. Supplementary material includes various tables and maps, but the concise 2-way lexicons of French, Spanish, German and Italian, which added to the bulk of earlier printings, have very wisely been omitted.

Reviewing *RHD-2* at length, *Choice* (v.25(6), Feb. 1988, p.868-69) commends its 'relative comprehensiveness, currency, and clarity' but expects *Webster's Fourth,* when it eventually appears, to become the pre-eminent unabridged dictionary of American English.

Combined book and CD-ROM package published 1997 as *Random House Webster's unabridged dictionary and CD-ROM* ($75. ISBN: 0679458530). CD-ROM includes full vocabulary of dictionary (updated 2nd ed.), illustrations, maps and over 120,000 recorded pronunciations.
Class No: 802.0-30

[5496]
The Oxford English dictionary. Prepared by J.A. Simpson and E.S.C. Weiner. 2nd ed. Oxford, Clarendon Press, 1989. 20v. (21,728p.). £1,650. ISBN: 0198611862.

The definitive dictionary of the English language began life as the *New English dictionary on historical principles; founded mainly on the materials collected by the Philological Society,* ed. by Sir J.A.H. Murray, H. Bradley, Sir W.A. Craigie, and C.T. Onions, and issued in parts from Jan. 1884 to April 1928. This work is often referred to as *Murray's Dictionary* or *NED,* and includes 414,825 words and phrases.

The first edition of the *Oxford English dictionary* (a title which had been used on individual parts since July, 1895) was published in 1933 (12v. and suppl.), being 'a corrected reissue, with an introduction, supplement and bibliography' of *NED*. Cited as *OED*.

A Supplement to the Oxford English dictionary, ed. by R.W. Burchfield, was published over the period 1972-86 in 4 vols., subsuming the 1933 *Supplement,* and adding *c.*69,000 entries.

The 2nd ed. integrates the original 12-vol. *OED* and the 4-vol. *Supplement* into a single 20-vol. sequence, and incorporates a further 5,000 words and meanings which have been recorded since completion of the *Supplement*. It has 291,627 entries, defining over 500,000 words, supported by 2,435,671 quotations. Entries range from a single line to several pages, that for the verb 'set' taking *c.*60,000 words to explain its 430 senses and subsenses.

Statistics apart, *OED2* is mightily impressive. Each entry-word is followed by pronunciation (IPA replacing Murray's original system); part of speech; variant spellings arranged chronologically; detailed etymological history; and numbered senses, arranged chronologically, each one accompanied by a series of quotations (with precise references) illustrating the use of the term from its first known occurrence to the modern period. Early quotations are given in the original spelling. 'The collection of quotations ... remains the centre and the glory of this dictionary' (*Review of English Studies,* v.41(161), Feb. 1990, p.87). A staggering 33,150 are from Shakespeare, with Sir Walter Scott an unlikely, but distant, runner-up. Bibliography of sources (143p.) in v.20.

The CD-ROM version (£250. ISBN: 0198612605) contains 5,000 words more than the printed work and may be searched by etymology, definition, part of speech, topic, register, usage, frequency, and quotations (by date, author, work, and text). This is a powerful research tool, particularly for etymology, as well as a vast dictionary of quotations (over 1,800,000 entries).

The Compact Oxford English dictionary (New ed. 1991. 2416p. £195. ISBN: 0198612583) reproduces micrographically in a single vol. the complete text of the 20-vol. 2nd ed., with 9 pages of the original on each page. It is supplied in a slipcase with a magnifying glass.

A Guide to the Oxford English dictionary by D. L. Berg (Oxford, Oxford Univ. Press, 1991. 216p. ISBN: 0198691793) is supplied free with *The Compact OED* and also available separately at £12.95. In 2 sections, the first giving detailed explanations, with examples, of the component parts of entries, the second being an A-Z companion to the *OED*, with notes on its history, contributors and terminology, plus a chronology and a compendium of useful facts and figures. 'It is hard to imagine any user, however skilled, who would not learn something from this lucid and informative new tool' (*Jnl. of Librarianship and Information Science*, v.24(2), June, 1992, p.109). *Class No:* 802.0-30

[5497]

—The New Shorter Oxford English dictionary on historical principles. Brown, L., *ed.* [4th ed.]. Oxford, Clarendon Press, 1993. 2v. (xxvi,3801p.). £80. ISBN: 019861134x.

First published 1933, as *The Shorter Oxford English dictionary*; 3rd ed. 1944 (rev. and reset 1973).

'A replacement for the 3rd ed. of *SOED*, but not a direct revision of its text', the editors having returned to the *OED* itself and 'reabridged, conflated, revised, restructured, added and updated' (*Preface*). All entries have been rewritten, with a more chronological basis for the entry structure, *i.e.* senses within major semantic/grammatical units are arranged by period.

Entries include pronunciation (British Received Pronunciation represented by IPA); part of speech; century of entry into language; etymology; senses and definitions (with date ranges); and illustrative quotations. Dates are sometimes at variance with *OED* where earlier and later examples have been identified. Over 83,000 quotations, used primarily to illuminate semantic distinctions and exemplify grammatical constructions rather than etymological development. List of over 8,000 authors quoted, most of them contemporary.

Also available on CD-ROM at £49.99 (ISBN: 0192683020). *Class No:* 802.0-30

[5498]

—Oxford English dictionary additions series. Simpson, J.A. *and* Weiner, E.S.C., *eds.* Oxford, Oxford Univ. Press, 1993-97. v.1-3 (in progress). £25 (vols. 1-2); £30 (v.3).

3 vols. have appeared so far in this supplement to the 2nd ed. of the *OED*, whose style and format are followed in the entries. Each vol. has *c.*3,000 entries for new or newly researched words, and definitions, quotations and datings for new senses of existing words. Cumulative index in each vol. Unlike *Supplement* to 1st ed., each vol. covers the full alphabetical range, but within each one certain letters are more heavily represented, depending upon where recent work has been concentrated.

'What publication apart from the *Oxford English dictionary* could issue its rough drafts as separate books, in the confidence that they would sell extensively?' (*TLS*, no.4934, Oct. 24, 1997, p.8). *Class No:* 802.0-30

[5499]

Webster's third new international dictionary of the English language, unabridged. Gove, P.B., *ed.* Springfield, Mass., Merriam, 1961. 2662p. illus. £80. ISBN: 0877792011.

Webster's Dictionary first published 1828. *New international* first published 1909; 2nd ed. 1934, with later reissues including corrections.

Webster's Third (also known as *W3*) was published amid much controversy because it differed radically from its predecessors in adopting a descriptive rather than prescriptive approach, presenting the language as actually used and including, without qualification, many terms that might be regarded as vulgar or incorrect.

*c.*450,000 entries (a significant reduction from *W2's* 600,000), giving definitions in chronological order (earliest first); etymology; pronunciation (including regional variations), using the publisher's own (over-complicated) system; and illustrative quotations. There are over 200,000 of the latter, mainly from contemporary sources, but they are undated and citations are to author only. Abbreviations are included in the main sequence, but proper names are excluded, except as eponyms, and *W2's* biographical and geographical sections have been dropped. 3,000 illustrations.

Essential for contemporary American English, but most reviewers have advised libraries to retain *W2* for its comprehensive coverage of the language since Chaucer's day and its treatment of obsolete and rare words, foreign terms and proverbs, using a split-page layout. 'Some people who look to Merriam-Webster as the ultimate lexicographic authority refuse to use *W3*, preferring to rely instead on a cherished, dog-eared copy of the now long out-of-print *W2*' (*Wilson Library Bulletin,* v.62(6), Feb. 1988, p.40).

12,000 words: a supplement to 'Webster's Third new international dictionary' (1986. 212p. ISBN: 0877792070) lists new words and meanings which have become established since the publication of *W3*, with scientific and technical terms predominant.

Available on the Internet via Chadwyck-Healey's *Literature Online (LION)* subscription service (http://lion.chadwyck.co.uk), where it can be searched by headword, keyword, etymology, part of speech and author/quotation. *Class No:* 802.0-30

[5500]

World Book dictionary, 1990. Barnhart, C.L. *and* Barnhart, R.K., *eds.* Chicago, World Book, 1989. 2v. (2554p.). ISBN: 0716602903.

1st ed. 1963; frequently revised.

Designed for use with the *World Book encyclopedia* and therefore excludes biographical and geographical entries and very specialized terminology. Claims 225,000 definitions and 3,000 illustrations. Entries give syllabification of headword and pronunciation (modified IPA). Senses are ordered by frequency (commonest first), many illustrative examples are provided and etymologies are given. Some entries include usage notes and lists of synonyms. A wide range of supplementary material includes a history of the language; lists of prefixes and suffixes; forenames; notes on spelling, punctuation, etc.; and a guide to writing research papers. 'Unquestionably a best buy for libraries that serve patrons of all ages', according to *Booklist* (v.87(11), Feb. 1st, 1991, p.1149), which commends its currency, clear layout, and the consideration for younger readers shown in the writing of the definitions. *Class No:* 802.0-30

Desk Dictionaries

[5501]

The Chambers dictionary. Schwarz, C., *and others, eds.* Edinburgh, Chambers, 1993. xviii,2062p. £22.50. ISBN: 0550102558.

First published 1901. Frequently revised; latest previous revision 1988, as *Chambers English dictionary*. Earlier eds. had the title *Chambers twentieth-century dictionary*.

A dictionary popular for many years in the UK for the sheer size of its vocabulary (this ed. claims 215,000 references and 300,000 definitions); its coverage of dialect, regional (especially Scottish), archaic and literary words (from writers like Shakespeare, Milton and Spenser); and its occasional idiosyncratic definitions, *e.g.* 'eclair: a cake, long in shape, but short in duration'. The strong coverage of arcane vocabulary does not mean that neologisms are ignored, but American English is less well covered than in some of its rivals.

In order to save space, all words deriving from the same root are usually grouped ('nested') under one headword, with cross-references. Definitions are arranged in chronological order, oldest first, and illustrative phrases are not as common as in some comparable works (*e.g. Collins English dictionary*). Pronunciation is indicated by re-spelling and brief etymologies appear at the end of entries. 13

....*(contd.)*
appendices, including lists of forenames, abbreviations and foreign phrases. Essential for crossword puzzlers and players of word games.

Became available on CD-ROM in 1994 (£55. ISBN: 0550102604). New ed. due late 1998 (£25. ISBN: 055014000x). *Class No:* 802.0-300

[5502]

—Chambers 21st century dictionary. Robinson, M., *ed.* Edinburgh, Chambers, 1996. x,1654p. £16.99. ISBN: 0550105883.

Not to be confused with *The Chambers dictionary*, which used to be known as *Chambers twentieth-century dictionary*, this is a completely new product which claims to concentrate on 'the English people use and speak today'. It has far fewer entries than its stablemate (*c.*60,000, including abbreviations and acronyms), but is very easy to use with separate entries for virtually every term; IPA; clear etymologies; and highlighted lists of phrases and idioms after many phrasal verbs. Usage notes and other useful information (*e.g.* lists of French words and phrases) are found in boxes scattered throughout the dictionary. *Class No:* 802.0-300

[5503]

Chambers encyclopedic English dictionary. Allen, R., *ed.* Edinburgh, Chambers, 1994. illus. £30. ISBN: 0550110003.

Chambers enters the encyclopedic dictionary market with a work that is nearer to the encyclopedia end of the spectrum than its competitors from Collins and Oxford. Among the 70,000 entries are 5,000 concise biographies, 4,000 place-names, and 5,000 first names, literary characters, names of institutions, works of art and historical events. Over 1,000 annotated drawings, tables and maps, plus a 12-page set of world maps in colour. Available on CD-ROM at £39.99 (ISBN: 0550107525). *Class No:* 802.0-300

[5504]

Collins English dictionary. Makins, M., *and others, eds.* 3rd ed., updated. Glasgow, HarperCollins, 1994. xxvi,1791p. £25. ISBN: 0004706781.

1st ed. 1979; 2nd ed. 1986; 3rd ed. 1991.

Now firmly established as one of the leaders in the UK desk-dictionary field. This ed. has *c.*180,000 entries, including *c.*16,000 encyclopedic entries - enough to be useful, but not so many as to deflect from the dictionary's main purpose or to make it unwieldy. Coverage of science, technology, commerce and culture is strong and the English used outside the UK is very well represented and clearly labelled.

Derivatives and compounds are usually entered as separate headwords. Definitions are clearly written, and numbered, and the most common sense in current usage is placed first, with illustrative phrases and notes on usage in many cases. IPA is used for pronunciation and the etymologies which follow most entries include century of first recorded occurrence. Abbreviations are included in the main sequence. Biographical entries cover both historical and contemporary figures and include birth and death dates; geographical entries include population figures for towns, length for rivers, etc. Excellent explanatory notes on use of the dictionary (9p.) plus essays on the pronunciation of British English and the development of English as a world language. The more generous page-size adopted for 3rd ed. has allowed 14,500 new words and meanings to be incorporated without any loss of clarity.

Available on CD-ROM, with *Collins thesaurus in A-Z form* (*q.v.*), as *Collins electronic English dictionary and thesaurus* (£29.99. ISBN: 0004720814). *Class No:* 802.0-300

[5505]

Collins English dictionary and thesaurus Glasgow, HarperCollins, 1993. xxix,1378p. £25. ISBN: 0004702697.

105,000 dictionary entries and 325,000 synonyms and antonyms., but rather than being integrated as in *The Readers Digest Oxford*, they are presented in parallel text format on the same page. Dictionary entries are taken from *Collins concise English dictionary* and include pronunciation (adapted IPA), definitions, etymology, derivatives and usage notes. Introductory essay on the development of English as a world language (10p.). 13 appendices, including alphabets, collective nouns and foreign words and phrases.
Class No: 802.0-300

[5506]

Concise Oxford dictionary. Thompson, D., *ed.* 9th ed. Oxford, Oxford Univ. Press, 1995. xxi,1673p. £15.99. ISBN: 0198613199.

First published 1911, edited by H.W. and F.G. Fowler. 8th ed. 1990. Early eds. were entitled *The Concise Oxford dictionary of current English.*

8th ed. represented a complete revision and expansion of a standard British desk dictionary, based on the files used to produce the 2nd ed. of the *OED*. Overdue changes included adoption of IPA for pronunciation; systematic numbering of definitions (in order of comparative familiarity); use of continuous everyday prose for the definitions rather than 'telegraphese'; reduced use of symbols and abbreviations; and the provision of more information on grammar, inflection and usage; all of which made the dictionary easier to use. In terms of content, there was evidence of increased emphasis on currency as the criterion for selection and more attention was paid to derivatives, idioms, colloquialisms, and international varieties of English.

9th ed. is 14% bigger, claiming 140,000 meanings and 7,000 new words and senses, and has improved coverage of North American English and more scientific and technical terms. The improvements have continued: all compounds now have their own entry; etymologies are clearer, with fewer abbreviations; pronunciations have been revised to give a more up-to-date representation of the standard British accent. 16 appendices include lists of countries, UK counties and US states, the Greek and Russian alphabets, and a style guide.

Also available on CD-ROM, with sound, at £19.99 (ISBN: 0192684000). *Class No:* 802.0-300

[5507]

Longman dictionary of the English language. 2nd ed. Harlow, Longman, 1991. xxv,1890p. ISBN: 0582070384.

A dictionary noted for its comprehensive coverage of contemporary English throughout the world and for the extent and clarity of its advice on grammar and usage, the latter quality almost certainly a result of the publisher's long and successful involvement in the EFL field.

Nearly 100,000 headwords and over 220,000 definitions, most compounds being entered separately. Generous use is made of illustrative phrases taken from the publisher's own database and the Longman/Lancaster Corpus of representative 20th-century texts, the latter source providing direct quotations from named authors. Pronunciation is indicated by a simple re-spelling system and etymologies are provided.

For the 2nd ed., which includes *c.*6,000 new words and

....(contd.)
meanings, abbreviations have been absorbed into the main sequence; biographical and geographical entries have been expanded and also absorbed; and information on grammar, usage and the discrimination of synonyms is provided within 1,000 boxes scattered throughout the dictionary.
Class No: 802.0-300

[5508]
The Oxford dictionary and thesaurus. Tulloch, S., *ed.* Revised reprint. Oxford, Clarendon Press, 1997. xxiv,1892p. £22.99. ISBN: 0198601719.

First published 1993, as *The Reader's Digest Oxford wordfinder*. Reprinted 1995 with new title and 1997 in larger format. This ed. also published by Reader's Digest as *The Reader's Digest Oxford complete wordfinder*.

A very useful combination of dictionary and thesaurus, with a single sequence of integrated entries combining information from the *Concise Oxford dictionary* (8th ed. 1990) and *Oxford thesaurus* (1991). Claims 190,000 definitions and 300,000 synonyms. 23 appendices, including proverbs, alphabets, punctuation marks, nouns of assembly, and a history and chronology of English (8p.) taken from *The Oxford companion to the English language* (1992).
Class No: 802.0-300

[5509]
The Oxford English reference dictionary. Pearsall, J. *and* Trumble, B., *eds.* 2nd ed. Oxford, Oxford Univ. Press, 1996. xx,1765p. illus. maps. £25. ISBN: 0198600461.

1st ed. 1995, superseding *The Oxford encyclopedic English dictionary* (1991), which itself replaced *The Oxford reference dictionary* (1986).

190,000 dictionary definitions based on the *Concise Oxford dictionary* (8th ed. 1990), revised and updated with 3,000 new entries, plus 12,500 substantial encyclopedic entries of which 4,000 are biographical and 4,700 geographical (with population figures for countries and cities) and the rest come from science, history, arts, etc. Further encyclopedic information is appended in a 100-page section which includes chronologies of world events and scientific developments; lists of monarchs, prime ministers and presidents; tables of countries; alphabets; anatomical and architectural diagrams; and 16 coloured maps.
Class No: 802.0-300

[5510]
The Oxford large print dictionary. Pollard, E., *ed.* 2nd ed. Oxford, Oxford Univ. Press, 1995. 960p. £17.99. ISBN: 0198613229.

1st ed. 1989, ed. by J.M. Hawkins.

60,000 entries (5,000 new to this ed.), including 4,000 encyclopedic entries on people, places, and institutions, with usage notes and pronunciation guidance.

An alternative is *Collins large print dictionary* (Glasgow, HarperCollins, 1997. 992p. £16.99) with over 68,000 entries. *Class No:* 802.0-300

[5511]
—The New Merriam-Webster dictionary for large print users. Rev. ed. Boston, Hall, 1989. 1112p. ISBN: 081614754x.

1st ed. 1977.

Based on *The New Merriam-Webster dictionary,* with *c.*60,000 words. *Class No:* 802.0-300

Synonyms

[5512]
Bloomsbury thesaurus. Alexander, F., *ed.* 2nd ed. London, Bloomsbury, 1997. xiv,1201p. £20. ISBN: 0747532613.

1st ed. 1993.

A rarity among new thesauri, in that it embraces Roget's subject approach rather than an alphabetical one, but with a new classification scheme which is more relevant to contemporary English and allows better coverage of science and technology. 815 headwords in 23 sections, followed by lists of synonyms for each numbered sense and cross-references. Also includes vocabulary lists in boxes within the sequence, covering both common nouns (*e.g.* trees) and proper names (*e.g.* trade unions, composers). 130,000 terms in all, including American and Australian words (labelled). Alphabetical index (476p.). *Class No:* 802.0-314

[5513]
Chambers English thesaurus. Manser, M.H., *ed.* New ed. London, Chambers, 1997. vi,890p. £20. ISBN: 0550183086.

Supersedes *Chambers 20th century thesaurus* (1986) and *Chambers thesaurus* (1991).

An alphabetically arranged thesaurus with over 14,000 headwords. Lists of synonyms, grouped by register, for each sense of the headword, plus antonyms in many cases. Boxed usage notes for confusible pairs, *e.g.* 'censor' / 'censure'. Many panels with thematic lists, *e.g.* legal terms, parts of a church. *Class No:* 802.0-314

[5514]
—Collins thesaurus. Gilmour, L., *ed.* Glasgow, HarperCollins, 1995. ix,1070p. £25. ISBN: 0004704541.

Supersedes *Collins English thesaurus in A-Z form* (2nd ed. 1992), although the latter is still available on CD-ROM, bundled with *Collins English dictionary*, as *Collins electronic English dictionary & thesaurus* (£29.99. ISBN: 0004720814).

Similar in size and format to *The Chambers Thesaurus*, with *c.*340,000 synonyms, antonyms and related words (*e.g.* the adjective relating to a particular noun) listed under *c.*16,500 keywords. Particularly useful are the many lists of specialist vocabulary attached to certain keywords, *e.g.* under 'horse' are lists of breeds, types, colours, physical parts, tack, associated jobs, and horse-drawn vehicles. Appendices include foreign words and phrases.
Class No: 802.0-314

[5515]
GLAZIER, S. Random House word menu. New York, Random House, 1992. xxx,977p. $22. ISBN: 0679400303.

Another thematic thesaurus, but according to *Choice* (v.30(6), Feb. 1993, p.939), 'Glazier's well-conceived word classification scheme is a major improvement over Roget's outdated ... scheme.' 7 main classes (*e.g.* 'Nature,' 'Domestic Life') are divided in to 25 chapters with *c.*800 subsections. Around 75,000 entries in all, with part of speech and register label in many cases, but no guide to pronunciation. Easily accessible via detailed contents table and comprehensive index. *Class No:* 802.0-314

[5516]
Illustrated reverse dictionary. Kahn, J.E., *ed.* Pleasantville, NY, Reader's Digest Assoc., 1990. 608p. illus. $25. ISBN: 089577352x.

Aims to help readers find over 70,000 elusive words through a variety of access points, including synonyms, antonyms, definitions, associations and common phrases. 400 charts and colour illustrations scattered throughout the

....(contd.)
dictionary explain groups of related words (*e.g.* geographic terms, knots, trees) and are alphabetically indexed at the start of the work. *Class No:* 802.0-314

[5517]
—BERNSTEIN, T.M. Bernstein's reverse dictionary. 2nd ed., rev. by D. Grambs. New York, Times Books, 1988. 351p. £17.95. ISBN: 0812915933.

First ed. New York, Quadrangle, 1975; London, Routledge, 1976.

Nearly 16,000 definitions (an increase of 2,500 over first ed.), arranged A-Z by 'clue word' (*i.e.* keyword), lead to 'target words'. Has limited use because of inevitably subjective choice of clue words but contains some useful tables, *e.g.* creature terms, manias and phobias. *Class No:* 802.0-314

[5518]
KIPFER, B.A. Roget's 21st century thesaurus in dictionary form. New York, Dell, 1992; London, Hale, 1993. xi,978p. ISBN: 0709050801.

17,000 entry-words, A-Z, with definition and list of synonyms for each. 450,000 synonyms in total. Cross-references after each list to entry-words which cover similar concepts. Index of 837 *Roget*-style concepts. *Class No:* 802.0-314

[5519]
Longman synonym dictionary. Urdang, L., *ed.* Harlow, Longman, 1986. 1355p. ISBN: 0582893224.

Apparently a reprint of *The Synonym finder* (Emmaus, Pa., Rodale Press, 1978. ISBN: 0878572368), although this is not acknowledged in the book.

The largest thesaurus, with over 1,000,000 synonyms listed under over 20,000 entry-words, A-Z, and grouped according to different applications of the entry-word. Usage levels are indicated (slang, informal, etc.) and technical or specialized terms have field labels. *Class No:* 802.0-314

[5520]
LUTZ, W.D. The Cambridge thesaurus of American English. Cambridge, Cambridge Univ. Press, 1994. x,515p. £12.95. ISBN: 052141427x.

Records over 200,000 synonyms (and some antonyms) under alphabetically arranged entry terms. Very basic listings, with guidance on usage restricted to labelling of slang terms and others with restricted currency. Includes entries for phrasal verbs. *Class No:* 802.0-314

[5521]
MARCH, F.A. A Thesaurus dictionary of the English language. Reprint of 1911 ed. Detroit, Omnigraphics, 1994. xvi+1189+102p. $48. ISBN: 0780800117.

Originally published, Philadelphia, Historical Publishing Co., 1911.

Compiled by the foremost American linguist of the 19th century, this is a combination of standard dictionary and thesaurus. In the main A-Z sequence entry-words are defined very briefly, but cross-references lead to one or more of 400 semantic groups where related words are listed. These groupings are based on contrastive pairs (*e.g.* 'innocence-guilt' or 'health-sickness') and are placed in the sequence under the first word of the pair. They are complemented by numerous vocabulary groups which are listed under single entry-words throughout the dictionary. Many foreign words and phrases are included, as are literary quotations and allusions. Appended section on 'Our English speech' (102p.) includes notes on word-building, grammar, spelling and punctuation, and lists of forenames, American soubriquets

....(contd.)
and homonyms. Largely of historical interest, but also of value for contemporary enquiry work because of the vast store of linguistic and cultural knowledge March assembled. *Class No:* 802.0-314

[5522]
Merriam-Webster's dictionary of synonyms: a dictionary of discriminated synonyms, with antonyms and analogous and contrasted words. [2nd ed.]. Springfield, Mass., Merriam, 1968 (repr. 1984). 31+909p. £14.99. ISBN: 0877793417.

First published 1942 as *Webster's dictionary of synonyms*, this ed. being 'newly edited and entirely reset' and originally entitled *Webster's new dictionary of synonyms*.

One of the most useful dictionaries of synonyms because it explains the differences in meaning between related words, often at considerable length, and illustrates these differences with example sentences and quotations from literature. Over 7,000 main entries, A-Z, with many thousands of terms explained, and numerous cross-references. Entries also include lists of antonyms. List of authors quoted (23p.). *Class No:* 802.0-314

[5523]
—Cassell guide to related words. Hayakawa, S.I. *and* Ehrlich, E., *eds.* [New ed.] London, Cassell, 1994. xi,644p. £20. ISBN: 0304344826.

Appears to be a revision of Hayakawa's *Cassell thesaurus: comprehensive guide to synonymy and nuance* (1991), which was itself a reprint of *Cassell's modern guide to synonyms and related words (1971)* and substantially the same work as *Funk & Wagnall's modern guide to synonyms* (New York, 1968), with revisions made to reflect British usage. Paperback version available as *Guide to synonyms and related words* (London, Penguin, 1994. £8.99. ISBN: 0140513450).

Like *Webster's new dictionary,* has lengthy entries in which the different nuances of meaning between related words are explained and illustrated, although there are no literary quotations. Deals with *c.*6,000 terms under *c.*1,400 headwords, A-Z, with all the terms indexed. Lists of antonyms with each entry.

Discrimination also characterizes the much older, but still useful, *Crabb's English synonyms,* by G. Crabb, which was first published in 1816. A revised ed. appeared in 1916 (London, Routledge. 728p.) and has been frequently reprinted. *Class No:* 802.0-314

[5524]
The Oxford thesaurus, in A-Z form. Urdang, L., *ed.* 2nd ed. Oxford, Clarendon Press, 1997. 1088p. £22.99 ISBN: 0198600054.

1st ed. 1991, as *The Oxford thesaurus: an A-Z dictionary of synonyms.*

A major thesaurus which claims it lists over 500,000 synonyms and alternatives and 50,000 antonyms (new to this ed) under alphabetical headwords. Each entry includes lists of synonyms for each sense of the headword (commonest first), with an illustrative sentence for each sense-group and with words typical of a particular geographical or stylistic variety of English clearly labelled. The comprehensive index provides access to each occurrence of every term, whether as headword or synonym. Sample sentences are particularly noteworthy: 'lively, contemporary, natural and idiomatic, they are perhaps the most distinctive contribution made by this new work' (*Jnl. of Librarianship and Information Science*, v.26(1), March, 1994, p.35-7, on 1st ed.).

Oxford also publish *The Concise Oxford thesaurus*, comp. by B.J. Kirkpatrick (1995. viii,896p. £15.99. ISBN:

.... (contd.)
0198601263) with 350,000 synonyms and antonyms under 16,000 headwords, plus over 400 tables of specialist vocabulary. The text of this work, minus the tables and enlarged by 45%, forms *The Oxford large print thesaurus* (1997. xi,909p. £17.99. ISBN: 0198601298).
Class No: 802.0-314

[5525]
ROGET, P.M. Roget's thesaurus of English words and phrases. New ed., prepared by B. Kirkpatrick. Harlow, Longman, 1987. l, 1254p. ISBN: 0582893631.

1st ed. 1852, by Peter Mark Roget. Frequently revised; latest previous revision by S.M. Lloyd, 1982.

Roget's Thesaurus, one of the best-known of all English-language reference books, 'is essentially a collection of words and phrases classified according to underlying concepts and meanings' (*Preface*). Kirkpatrick has retained Roget's original scheme of grouping terms within 6 main 'classes' (1. Abstract relations - 2. Space - 3. Matter - 4. Intellect - 5. Volition - 6. Emotion, religion and morality), which are in turn subdivided into numbered 'sections', and 'heads'. The latter form the basic units of the book and there are 990 in this ed., compared with 1,000 in Roget's first ed. The 'heads' are divided into paragraphs, grouped according to part of speech and beginning with an italicized keyword. Within each paragraph, terms are grouped between semicolons according to meaning, context or stylistic level, and there are numerous cross-references to other 'heads'. An alphabetical index of *c.*45,000 terms provides access via references to head-numbers and keywords.

This ed. has over 11,000 new terms among its 250,000 words and phrases, and includes Roget's original introduction (14p.), instructions on use (4p.) and a detailed plan of classification (27p.). Although synonymous with thesauri, *Roget's* is by no means easy to use (still less to describe) and a simple alphabetical listing may often provide a quicker answer to a synonym enquiry.

Rev. and updated ed. due from Penguin late 1998 (ISBN: 0140277366). *Class No:* 802.0-314

[5526]
—ROGET, P.M. Collins Roget's international thesaurus. New ed. Glasgow, HarperCollins, 1997. 1080p. £22.99. ISBN: 000470455x, UK.

Arranged on the same general principles as the standard English eds., but expanded to include American words, phrases and colloquialisms. This ed. has over 258,000 words and phrases grouped into over 1,000 categories. Quotations are sometimes used to clarify nuances of meaning. Does not give antonyms, but includes useful wordlists, *e.g.* phobias. Index gives precise references to paragraphs.
Class No: 802.0-314

[5527]
Webster's collegiate thesaurus. Merriam-Webster Editorial Staff, *eds.* Springfield, Mass., Merriam-Webster, 1988. xxvi,868p. ISBN: 0877790698.

Apparently a reprint of the 1976 ed., which claimed to be 'the first totally new thesaurus in over 120 years'.

Simple A-Z arrangement of *c.*20,000 headwords, each followed by a definition (unusual in a thesaurus), an illustrative phrase, and separate lists of synonyms, related words (near-synonyms), antonyms, and contrasted words (near-antonyms). The material is mainly drawn from *Webster's third new international dictionary unabridged* (1961). *Class No:* 802.0-314

Euphemisms

[5528]
HOLDER, R.W. A Dictionary of euphemisms. [3rd ed.] Oxford, Oxford Univ. Press, 1995. xix,470p. £16.99. ISBN: 0198692757.

1st ed. Bath, Bath Univ. Press, 1987, as *A Dictionary of American and British euphemisms*; 2nd ed. London, Faber, 1989, as *The Faber dictionary of euphemisms*.

Lists over 5,000 euphemistic words and phrases, with definition and (in most cases) a quotation from a printed source. Entries are arranged A-Z by first word, with an exceptionally useful classified list (over 60 subject headings) appended. Bibliography of dictionaries and literary sources (9p.). *Class No:* 802.0-314.0

[5529]
NEAMAN, J.S. *and* **SILVER, C.G. Kind words:** a thesaurus of euphemisms. Rev. ed. New York, Facts on File, 1990. 371p. ISBN: 0816018960.

1st ed. 1983, published in UK by H. Hamilton as *A Dictionary of euphemisms.*

A thematically arranged reference work with over 4,000 terms explained within 11 chapters (9 in 1st ed.) on parts of the body, death, crime, sex, etc. Entries provide a history of the entry-term and lists of synonyms and related terms. Bibliography (10p.). Index.

New ed. shows little change apart from the addition of new chapters on health and occupations. *Class No:* 802.0-314.0

[5530]
RAWSON, H. Rawson's dictionary of euphemisms and other doubletalk: being a compilation of linguistic fig leaves and verbal flourishes for artful users of the English language. Rev. ed. New York, Crown, 1995. 463p. $25. ISBN: 0517702010.

1st ed. 1981, as *A Dictionary of euphemisms and other doubletalk.*

Considerably fewer entries than Holder (*q.v.*), with *c.*1,600 words and phrases defined, but the explanations are generally longer and written in an entertaining style. Most include quotations from printed sources, with reference to author, title and date. Arranged A-Z by first word, with many cross-references.

Rawson has also produced *Wicked words* (New York, Crown, 1989. 435p. $24.95. ISBN: 0517573342), a dictionary of 'curses, insults, put-downs, and other formerly unprintable terms' with *c.*1,000 entries. *Class No:* 802.0-314.0

Palindromes

[5531]
CHISM, S.J. From A to zotamorf: the dictionary of palindromes. Morristown, N.J., Word Ways Press, 1992. 173p. $35. ISBN: 0963515209.

An attempt to compile a complete list of English palindromes, with separate sections for single words, phrases/sentences, poems, and proper names. At least one source is cited for each example. Bibliography.
Class No: 802.0-316

Neologisms

[5532]

AYTO, J. The Longman register of new words. Harlow, Longman, 1989-90. 2v.

A record of new words (and new meanings for old ones) in the English language, based on the Longman Dictionary Database. V.1 (1989. 425p. ISBN: 0582037727) defines and explains 1,200 neologisms, illustrated by quotations from radio, TV, films, newspapers and magazines. V.2 (1990. 360p. ISBN: 0582063272) has over 1,000 entries. Sources are mainly British. Originally intended to be annual, but only 2 vols. have appeared. *Class No:* 802.0-316.1

[5533]

The Barnhart new-words concordance. Barnhart, D.K., *comp.* Cold Spring, New York, Lexik House, 1994. 704p. Loose-leaf. $65. ISBN: 0936368071.

Indexes over 28,000 words and phrases appearing in 8 British and American dictionaries of neologisms and *The Barnhart dictionary companion* (*q.v.*). Of limited use unless you have all the sources indexed and even then something of a luxury. *Class No:* 802.0-316.1

[5534]

Fifty years among the new words: a dictionary of neologisms, 1941-1991. Algeo, J., *ed.* Cambridge, Cambridge Univ. Press, 1991. 257p. £40. ISBN: 052141377x.

Reproduces in chronological order all the articles on neologisms which appeared over a 50-year period in *American Speech*, the journal of the American Dialect Society, in the regular feature entitled 'Among the new words.' An alphabetical index, with brief glosses, provides access to the detailed entries on *c.*3,700 words and phrases. Entries are generally fuller than those in dictionaries and include numerous quotations from American and British sources. Exemplary introductory essay by the editor on new-word formation (16p.). *Class No:* 802.0-316.1

[5535]

GREEN, J. New words: a dictionary of new words since 1960 Reprint of 1991 ed. London, Bloomsbury, 1994. xi,339p. £5.99. ISBN: 0747514569.

Originally published London, Bloomsbury, 1991, as *Neologisms: new words since 1960* and Rutland, Vt., Tuttle, 1992, as *Tuttle dictionary of new words since 1960*.

Nearly 2,700 entries, defining and explaining words and expressions which have recently entered mainstream British English. Gives date of first recorded appearance and, for most terms, an illustrative quotation from literature or the press. *Class No:* 802.0-316.1

[5536]

The Oxford dictionary of new words. Knowles, E. *and* Elliott, J., *eds.* New ed. Oxford, Oxford Univ. Press, 1997. ix,357p. £14.99. ISBN: 0198631529.

1st ed. 1991, comp. by S. Tulloch.

Provides information on *c.*2,000 words and phrases which have been in the news since 1980. The 750 lengthy entries include pronunciation (IPA), part of speech, alternative spellings, definition, etymology, an account of history and usage (including details of compounds, derivatives and related terms) and illustrative quotations, chronologically arranged, from 500 newspapers, magazines and works of fiction from the English-speaking world. Thoroughly cross-referenced. An excellent reference work, marred only by the largely incomprehensible graphic 'subject icons' attached to each headword, which have been inexplicably retained in the new ed. *Class No:* 802.0-316.1

[5537]

Third Barnhart dictionary of new English. Barnhart, R.K., *and others, eds.* New York, Wilson, 1990. 565p. $52. ISBN: 0824207963.

Supersedes *The Barnhart dictionary of new English since 1963* (Bronxville, N.Y., Barnhart/Harper & Row, 1973), which was published in the UK by Longman as *A Dictionary of new English, 1963-1972*, and *The Second Barnhart dictionary of new English* (1980), which included new terms appearing 1973-79.

Lists *c.*12,000 new words and phrases which have entered the vocabulary of the English-speaking world since *c.*1960, and new meanings for existing terms. Uses the same basic format as its predecessors, providing brief definitions, backed up by substantial quotations (with full bibliographical references); etymology where not obvious; date when the term became current; pronunciation (adapted IPA) for difficult words; and notes on usage, history, etc. Unfortunately, no indication is given as to how many entries have been retained from the earlier dictionaries and how many are new.

Updated by *The Barnhart Dictionary Companion* (New York, Springer-Verlag. Quarterly. ISSN: 07361122), which claims to be 'the only publication of its kind in the world devoted to updating general dictionaries'. *Class No:* 802.0-316.1

[5538]

THURNER, D. Portmanteau dictionary: blend words in the English language, including trademarks and brand names. Jefferson, N.C., McFarland, 1993. 174p. $29.95. ISBN: 0899506879.

Lists, defines and explains over 1,600 portmanteau words (*i.e.* words formed by fusing elements of two others, such as 'televangelist' and 'Oxbridge') which have been gleaned from over 80 sources, including the *OED*. Includes over 600 trade names, most of them American. An appendix groups the words under 42 subject headings. Bibliography of sources. *Class No:* 802.0-316.1

Loan Words

[5539]

BLISS, A. Dictionary of foreign words and phrases in current English. London, Routledge, 1966 (repr. 1983). x,389p. £13.99. ISBN: 0415059054.

More than 5,000 entries, giving original meanings, definition or translation, current usage, pronunciations, plurals, variant forms, etc., and, where possible, date of first introduction. Specific references to sources of quotations illustrating use. Much more than a dictionary, in that it discusses how to distinguish the foreign from the naturalized; how to deal with them grammatically; how they should be spelt or transliterated. A classified table shows when and what was borrowed. *Class No:* 802.0-316.3

[5540]

A Dictionary of foreign words and phrases. Tuleja, T., *ed.* New York, Macmillan, 1989; London, Hale, 1991. xiii,205p. £12.95. ISBN: 0026204207, US; 0709046626, UK.

American title is *Foreignisms: a dictionary of foreign expressions commonly (and not so commonly) used in English*.

A very selective compilation, with only *c.*540 entries in the main A-Z sequence but the entries are lengthier than is usual (up to half a page) and include details of the term's origin, meaning and pronunciation, and examples of its use.

.... *(contd.)*
11 useful supplementary lists, including ballet terms, musical terms, toasts, etc. Bibliography (21 items). Index of all terms covered in dictionary and lists (over 1,000). Subject index. *Class No:* 802.0-316.3

[5541]
EVANS, T.M. A Dictionary of Japanese loanwords. Westport, Conn., Greenwood, 1997. 248p. £47.50. ISBN: 0313287414.

Lists hundreds of borrowings from Japanese (the second most productive source of new loanwords to English) found in American publications 1964-95. Entries provide definition, pronunciation, variant spellings, etymological history and illustrative quotations. Bibliography. *Class No:* 802.0-316.3

[5542]
FENNELL, C.A.M. The Standard dictionary of anglicised words and phrases, edited for the Syndics of the University Press. Cambridge, Cambridge Univ. Press, 1964. xv,826p.

First published 1892.

Entries for over 13,000 loan words and phrases, stating accentuation and etymology, with examples of usage - as in *OED* - plus dates and sources. An asterisk before or on both sides of a word in an article implies that the form is unrecorded. Supplement, p.813-26. *Class No:* 802.0-316.3

[5543]
GUINAGH, K. Dictionary of foreign phrases and abbreviations. 3rd ed. New York, Wilson, 1982. xix,261p. $44. ISBN: 0824206754.

1st ed. 1965; 2nd ed. 1972.

3rd ed. adds 500 terms, making *c.*5,500 in all, with pronunciation guide, translation, and brief explanatory note where necessary. Sources cited for many entries. List of phrases by language (20, with Latin predominant). *Class No:* 802.0-316.3

[5544]
Le Mot juste: the Penguin dictionary of foreign terms and phrases. Ehrlich, E., *ed.* 3rd ed. New York, Harper & Row, 1987; London, Viking, 1988. xviii,423p. $20. ISBN: 0061815764, US; 067082092x, UK.

First published 1934 as the *Dictionary of foreign terms,* ed. by C.O.S. Mawson; 2nd ed., rev. and updated by C. Berlitz, New York, Crowell, 1975. This ed. reprinted in paperback, 1993, as *The Penguin dictionary of foreign terms and phrases* (£7.99. ISBN: 0140512942). US title is *The Harper dictionary of foreign terms.*

Lists and briefly defines over 15,000 foreign words and phrases likely to be encountered in American and English literature. There are many new entries in the 3rd ed., chiefly from Japanese, Russian and Modern Hebrew, and an index of English terms has been added. *Language International,* v.1(2), 1989, p.39-40, criticises the inadequate definitions and points out some serious omissions. *Class No:* 802.0-316.3

[5545]
The Oxford dictionary of foreign words and phrases. Speake, J., *ed.* Oxford, Oxford Univ. Press, 1997. xi,512p. £15.99. ISBN: 0198631596.

Lists 8,000 terms from over 40 languages. Entries give pronunciation (IPA), part of speech, language of origin, date of introduction into English, definition, usage notes and any other points of interest, with many including illustrative quotations. Appended lists of terms by language and century. Very impressive and particularly strong on 20th-century imports. *Class No:* 802.0-316.3

[5546]
PFEFFER, J.A. *and* **CANNON, G. German loanwords in English:** an historical dictionary. Cambridge, Cambridge Univ. Press, 1994. xxxiv,381p. £60. ISBN: 0521402549.

An updated, revised and greatly expanded English-language ed. of Pfeffer's *Deutsches Sprachgut im Wortschatz der Amerikaner und Engländer* (Tübingen, M. Niemayer, 1987).

Main sequence (220p.) lists over 5,380 terms which have been found in a survey of major English dictionaries, and gives first recorded date of German loan in English; semantic area; variant forms; etymology; first recorded date of German etymon; definition of English term; list of derivatives; plus grammatical comment in many cases. All terms are separately listed by semantic field and chronologically grouped within 50-year periods. Also includes nontechnical, discursive essays on the loan process. Appended list of 621 supplementary loanwords which are archaic, rarely used or in a state of transition. Also includes 2 detailed essays on linguistic and historical aspects of borrowing. 'This fine dictionary and its ... essays embody the highest standards of linguistic and historical scholarship' (*Reference Reviews*, v.9(7), 1995, p.24). *Class No:* 802.0-316.3

Homophones

[5547]
HOBBS, J.B. Homophones and homographs: an American dictionary. 2nd ed. Jefferson, N.C., McFarland, 1993. viii,302p. $29.95 ISBN: 089950776x.

1st ed. 1986.

Greatly expanded to include over 7,000 homophones (3,500 in 1st ed.) and 1,400 homographs (600 in 1st ed.) with definitions and cross-references. *Class No:* 802.0-317

[5548]
WILLIAMS, S.N. Dictionary of British and American homophones. London, Brookside Press, 1987. xii,503p. £25. ISBN: 0851730116.

Claims to be 'the first and only comprehensive dictionary' of its kind, listing 12,000 homophones in pairs and groups, A-Z. Entries include archaic, obsolete, dialect and slang words, and some proper names, and give pronunciation, variant spellings and definitions. *Class No:* 802.0-317

Idioms

[5549]
Collins COBUILD dictionary of idioms. Potter, E., *& others, eds.* London, HarperCollins, 1995. xvii,493p. £20. ISBN: 0003750302.

Some 4,400 British and US idioms arranged by keyword, A-Z, with clear definitions, usage notes and over 8,500 authentic examples from the Bank of English corpus. Frequency indicated. Index. A companion to the *Collins COBUILD dictionary of phrasal verbs* (*q.v.*).

Chambers dictionary of idioms, comp. by P. Hands (Edinburgh, Chambers, 1996. ix,404p. £7.99. ISBN: 0550107304) is similar in size and scope. *Class No:* 802.0-318

[5550]
COWIE, A.P., & *others*. Oxford dictionary of English idioms. New ed. Oxford, Oxford Univ. Press, 1993. lxiii,685p. £22.30 ISBN: 0194312860.

1st ed. 1983, as *Oxford dictionary of current idiomatic English, v.2, Phrase, clause and sentence idioms*.

14,000 entries under keyword, A-Z, tightly packed on each page and therefore difficult to access. Countless examples from contemporary literature and the media. Index of nouns, etc. used in head-phrases. Index of variant and derived forms. *Class No:* 802.0-318

[5551]
COWIE, A.P. *and* MACKIN, R. Oxford dictionary of phrasal verbs. New ed. Oxford, Oxford Univ. Press, 1993. xviii,517p. £20. ISBN: 0194312844.

1st ed. 1975, as *Oxford dictionary of current English: v.1, Verbs with prepositions and particles*.

A complete revision, with 1,000 new entries among the 11,000 verbs listed, including material from the *Oxford corpus of the English language*. Entries are arranged A-Z under keyword and list synonyms, antonyms and related verbs, after detailed explanations and usage notes. Extensive notes for users (66p.). List of sources (6p.). Index of nouns used in head-phrases. Index of nominalized forms.
Class No: 802.0-318

[5552]
—Cambridge international dictionary of phrasal verbs. Cambridge, Cambridge Univ. Press, 1997. xiii,381p. £20. ISBN: 0521562996.

Provides clear and simple explanations for EFL students of over 4,500 phrasal verbs, using a carefully controlled defining vocabulary, and includes detailed but uncomplicated information on grammar and collocation. Good coverage of American and Australian as well as British English.
Class No: 802.0-318

[5553]
—Collins COBUILD dictionary of phrasal verbs. Sinclair, J., *and others, eds*. London, HarperCollins, 1989. xx,492p. £20. ISBN: 000375023x.

Lists over 3,000 phrasal verbs, with 5,500 different meanings, under keywords, A-Z, and explains them clearly for EFL students, using over 12,000 authentic examples taken from the COBUILD database. Particle index (45p.) is a useful innovation. *Class No:* 802.0-318

[5554]
—COURTNEY, R. Longman dictionary of phrasal verbs. Harlow, Longman, 1983. 734p. £25. ISBN: 0582555302.

Over 12,000 entries, with separate numbered senses of each verb explained using a 2,000-word defining vocabulary and illustrated by 25,000 examples, many of them taken from contemporary literature and the press. Covers British and American usage, with regional variants clearly labelled.
Class No: 802.0-318

[5555]
FLAVELL, L. *and* FLAVELL, R. Dictionary of idioms and their origins. London, Kyle Cathie, 1992. vii,216p. £6.99. ISBN: 1856261298.

Examines only *c.*400 idioms, 'selected because they have a tale to tell' (*Introduction*), but has lengthy entries on each, comprising definition; explanation of origins and historical development; illustrative quotations (chronologically arranged) from contemporary literature and the press; and notes on usage. Arranged A-Z by keyword, with 22 thematic essays incorporated in the sequence. Index of other significant words. Bibliography (3p.). *Class No:* 802.0-318

[5556]
KJELLMER, G. A Dictionary of English collocations, based on the Brown Corpus. Oxford, Clarendon Press, 1994. 3v. (xliii,2241p.). ISBN: 0198239033.

A register of all collocations (*i.e.* groups of words which co-occur habitually) found in a major corpus of American English. Nearly 200,000 collocations, under keywords, with frequency statistics. Bibliography (3p.). For specialized linguistic research collections only. *Class No:* 802.0-318

[5557]
Longman dictionary of English idioms. Long, T.H., *and others, eds*. Harlow, Longman, 1979. xx,387p. £18.50. ISBN: 0582555248.

Lists and explains over 4,500 idioms and their derivatives under keywords, A-Z. All the definitions are written in a controlled vocabulary (listed on p.379-86) and the illustrative sentences are taken from contemporary written and spoken sources (written sources listed). Makes good use of a range of typefaces and symbols, all clearly explained in the introduction. *Class No:* 802.0-318

[5558]
PARTRIDGE, E. A Dictionary of clichés. 5th ed. London, Routledge, 1978. x,261p. ISBN: 0415065550.

1st ed. 1940; 4th ed. 1950.

Brief explanations of *c.*2,500 'outworn commonplaces' with dates but few sources. 50 new entries listed after main sequence, with dates only. *Class No:* 802.0-318

[5559]
—AMMER, C. The Methuen dictionary of clichés. London, Methuen; New York, Dutton, 1992. x,432p. £9.99. ISBN: 0413689905, UK; 0525933948, US.

US title is *Have a nice day - no problem!*

Lists nearly 3,000 hackneyed expressions A-Z by first important word and explains them in generally light-hearted style. Some fairly imprecise references to sources, but no bibliography. Keyword index. *Class No:* 802.0-318

[5560]
—KIRKPATRICK, B.J. Dictionary of clichés. London, Bloomsbury, 1996. xiv,207p. £18.99. ISBN: 0747520305.

Lists over 1,300 clichés, A-Z, explaining in chatty style their meaning, derivation and history, and in what context they are likely to be encountered. Examples of usage.
Class No: 802.0-318

[5561]
—ROGERS, J. The Dictionary of clichés. New York, Facts on File, 1985; London, Ward Lock, 1986. 290p. ISBN: 0816010102, US; 0706364964, UK.

Explains over 2,000 phrases in chatty entries which include references to written sources in most cases.
Class No: 802.0-318

[5562]
SEIDL, J. *and* MCMORDIE, W. English idioms and how to use them. 5th ed. Oxford, Oxford Univ. Press, 1988. 272p. ISBN: 0194327744.

1st ed. 1909, by W. McMordie; 4th ed. 1978.

A well-established reference book for students of English as a foreign language, which lists and explains idioms in chapters devoted to particular types of expression (*e.g.* 'idioms with the verb *to be*') rather than in a single dictionary sequence. Also includes a list of nearly 100 proverbs. Word and subject indexes. *Class No:* 802.0-318

USA

[5563]
MAKKAI, A., *and others*. A Dictionary of American idioms. 2nd rev. ed. New York, Barron's, 1988. 398p. $11.95. ISBN: 0812038991.

1st ed. 1975.

Lists over 5,000 of the commonest American idioms, all entries including definition, illustrative sentence, and a non-idiomatic paraphrase, and many including stylistic labels, etymology and notes on usage. Primarily useful for students and teachers of English as a second language.
Class No: 802.0-318(73)

[5564]
SPEARS, R.A. NTC's American idioms dictionary. Lincolnwood, Ill., National Textbook Co., 1987. xvi, 463p. $16.95. ISBN: 0844254525.

Defines over 8,000 idomatic expressions with at least 2 examples in each entry. Phrases arranged A-Z by first word (even when this is an article) with comprehensive key-word index to aid access. Clear typography, good layout and minimal use of specialist linguistic terms make this ideal for students of English as a foreign language. *Class No:* 802.0-318(73)

Grammar

[5565]
ALEXANDER, L.G. Longman English grammar. London, Longman, 1988. x,374p. £8.25 ISBN: 0582558921.

A superbly presented concise grammar of English as a foreign language. Clearly laid out with intelligent use of headings, numbered subsections and different typefaces. Appendix lists words and phrases which often cause difficulties for learners. Extensive cross references and comprehensive index make it a handy reference tool. Excellent value. *Class No:* 802.0-5

[5566]
Collins COBUILD English grammar. Sinclair, J., *ed.* Glasgow, HarperCollins, 1990. xxv,486p. £16. ISBN: 0003750256.

A comprehensive reference grammar for advanced students and teachers of English which has been developed from the COBUILD database. Exceptionally clearly presented in 10 chapters, with numbered paragraphs which contain numerous real examples of language in use. Very useful quick reference section appended (28p.). Full cross-referencing and thorough index. A distinctive feature is the inclusion of extensive lists of words which are used in particular constructions. 'Once again Collins COBUILD have scored a first, and ... moved the goalposts for the rest of us' (*English Today*, no.24, Oct. 1990, p.47-8 & 56-7).
Class No: 802.0-5

[5567]
EASTWOOD, J. Oxford guide to English grammar. Oxford, Oxford Univ. Press, 1994. ix,446p. ISBN: 0194313344.

A clearly arranged grammar for EFL students, with 40 chapters, 308 subsections and further numbered paragraphs. Plenty of examples and good use of headings and colour. Glossary (7p.). Comprehensive index (43p.).
Class No: 802.0-5

[5568]
GREENBAUM, S. The Oxford English grammar. Oxford, Oxford Univ. Press, 1996. xv,652p. £25. ISBN: 0198612508.

12 chapters with numbered sections and sub-sections containing numerous illustrative phrases, mostly taken from the International Corpus of English (*ICE*) at University College, London, and the *Wall Street Journal*. Based on standard British and American English, but also refers to non-standard varieties. Glossary (21p.). Detailed bibliographical notes by chapter. Index. *Class No:* 802.0-5

[5569]
JARVIE, G. Bloomsbury grammar guide. London, Bloomsbury, 1993. viii,216p. £15.99. ISBN: 0747538751.

First 2 chapters ('Words and phrases' and 'Sentences and clauses') occupy 40% of the book and provide a very accessible overview of English grammar. Further chapters go beyond grammar proper to cover word formation (useful lists of prefixes, suffixes and loanwords), punctuation, figures of speech and confusible words. Index. Clear presentation and lucid explanations make it ideal for school libraries. *Class No:* 802.0-5

[5570]
LEECH, G. An A-Z of English grammar and usage. London, Arnold, 1989 (repr. Harlow, Longman, 1996). xv,575p. illus. £9.85. ISBN: 0175560218.

Over 600 entries, arranged A-Z in one sequence and comprising 3 distinct types: common words which have a grammatical function ('of', 'should', etc.), grammatical terms, and language areas not usually covered in grammars (*e.g.* invitations, apologies, letter-writing). Clearly laid out and cross-referenced, with plenty of examples, many of them illustrated with cartoons, tables or diagrams. Ideal for non-native learners. *Class No:* 802.0-5

[5571]
QUIRK, R., *and others*. A Comprehensive grammar of the English language. Harlow, Longman, 1985. 1792p. £99.95. ISBN: 0582517346.

The largest and most detailed grammar available, clearly presented and illustrated with numerous vivid and up-to-date examples. Ch. 2 gives a general outline of the concepts and categories of English grammar; chs. 3-11 discuss sentence constituents in detail; chs. 12-19 deal with the more complex structure and discuss how constituents are arranged to form a message and how a whole text is constructed. Appendices cover word-formation, stress, rhythm, intonation, and punctuation. Detailed index.

Part or all of the same team (Quirk, Greenbaum, Leech and Svartvik) have produced the following shorter (but equally well arranged) grammars, all published by Longman:

A Student's grammar of the English language (1990. 528p. £25. ISBN: 0582075696).

A University grammar of English (1973. 496p. £22. ISBN: 0582552079).

A Grammar of contemporary English (1972. 1132p. £75. ISBN: 058252444x).

A Communicative grammar of English (2nd ed. 1994. 423p. £37.50. ISBN: 0582238277). *Class No:* 802.0-5

Etymology

[5572]

AYTO, J. Bloomsbury dictionary of word origins. London, Bloomsbury, 1990. 583p. ISBN: 0747507414.

Over 8,000 entries, representing 'the central core of English vocabulary' plus 'words whose etymology is intrinsically interesting' (*Introduction*). Gives date of first recorded use and a non-scholarly, often quite lengthy, narrative account of the word's history. Cross-references after most entries, since a primary aim is to 'uncover ... connections between elements of the English lexicon that have become obscured by centuries of linguistic change'. *Class No:* 802.0-54

[5573]

The Barnhart dictionary of etymology. Barnhart, R.K., *ed.* New York, Wilson, 1988. xxvii,1284p. $64. ISBN: 0824207459.

Over 30,000 entries written in a superbly accessible style, avoiding technical terminology and confusing abbreviations. Entries comprise headword, part of speech, brief definition, date of earliest recorded appearance and account of development through time. Particular attention paid to word elements, with entries for all living prefixes and suffixes. Based on contemporary American English and consequently has entries for many words not covered in the standard English etymological dictionaries.

Introductory essays on the history of English and on Proto-Germanic and Indo-European. Excellent annotated glossaries of language names and linguistic terms and of literary works cited. Bibliography (2p.). *Class No:* 802.0-54

[5574]

HENDRICKSON, R. The Encyclopedia of word and phrase origins. Rev. and exp. ed. New York, Facts on File, 1997. 768p. $65. ISBN: 0816032661.

1st ed. 1987.

Over 15,000 very readable narrative entries, of which 2,000 are new to this much expanded ed. Includes slang, proverbs, animal and plant names, place names, nicknames, historical expresions, foreign language expressions and quotations from literature. Scholarly sources are often quoted, but the author is not afraid to include wildly speculative theories about some etymologies.
Class No: 802.0-54

[5575]

—MORRIS, W. *and* MORRIS, M. Morris dictionary of word and phrase origins. 2nd ed. New York, Harper & Row, 1988. xiv,669p. $35. ISBN: 006015862x.

1st ed., 1977, was an amalgamation, with the addition of new material, of 3 vols. published 1962-71.

Explains common words and phrases in chatty style with few references to sources. 300 new entries in this ed., making *c.*3,000 in all, varying in length from one line to over a page. A-Z arrangement with thorough index.
Class No: 802.0-54

[5576]

KLEIN, E. A Comprehensive etymological dictionary of the English language. Single-volume reprint. Amsterdam, Elsevier, 1971. xxvi,844p. $208.75. ISBN: 0444409300.

Originally published in 2 vols., 1966-7.

About 45,000 entries. Gives full etymological analysis of the words treated, tracing them beyond the time of their introduction into the English language. Includes several hundred Tocharian references, and exact transliteration of Hebrew and Aramaic words, the compiler being a specialist in Semitic languages. Has many more entries than *The*

.... *(contd.)*
Oxford dictionary of English etymology (which is nevertheless adequate for most libraries) and is particularly valuable for its large number of scientific and technical terms and for personal and mythological names. *Class No:* 802.0-54

[5577]

The Oxford dictionary of English etymology. Onions, C.T., *and others, eds.* Oxford, Clarendon Press, 1966. xvi,1025p. £50. ISBN: 0198611129.

The standard etymological dictionary, with *c.*24,000 entries, the total number of words treated being over 38,000. Entries include the word's pronunciation, present meaning, century when first recorded in English and any developments in form and sense since then. Many entries for prefixes and suffixes. *Class No:* 802.0-54

[5578]

—The Concise Oxford dictionary of English etymology. Hoad, T.F., *ed.* Oxford, Clarendon Press, 1986. xvi,552p. £17.95. ISBN: 019861182x.

A handy compilation, based on *The Oxford dictionary of English etymology*, which treats *c.*17,000 words used in modern English. Each entry gives 'a concise statement of the route by which its headword entered the English language, together with, where appropriate, a brief account of its development in English' (*Introduction*). Century the word first recorded in English given in every case.
Class No: 802.0-54

[5579]

PARTRIDGE, E. Origins: an etymological dictionary of modern English. Reprint of 1966 ed. London, Routledge, 1990. xix,972p. £45. ISBN: 0415050774.

1st ed. 1958; 4th ed. 1966.

Provides etymologies for *c.*20,000 vocabulary items, often grouping related words together. Generally excludes scientific terms, dialect and slang, but includes many words in common use in the US and the Commonwealth. Main A-Z sequence is followed by one devoted to prefixes, suffixes and other compound-forming elements. Many cross-references. *Class No:* 802.0-54

[5580]

ROOM, A. Dictionary of changes in meaning. London, Routledge & Kegan Paul, 1986. 292p. ISBN: 0710203411.

Published 1992 in US by N.T.C. Publishing Group, as *NTC's dictionary of changes in meaning* (ISBN: 0844251364).

Traces changes in meaning for 1,342 common English words, the entries comprising a brief current definition, origin, and a narrative account of the word's development, with illustrative quotations from the *OED* and literary sources. Introductory essay on reasons for and categories of changes in meaning. Bibliography (2p.). *Class No:* 802.0-54

[5581]

—ROOM, A. A Dictionary of true etymologies. London, Routledge & Kegan Paul, 1986. ISBN: 0710203403.

Reprinted in US, 1991, as *NTC's dictionary of word origins* (Lincolnwood, Ill., National Textbook Co. 193p. ISBN: 0844251372.

Chatty entries (average 10 lines) on *c.*1,200 English words and phrases whose origins are not as their spelling would indicate or as is generally thought, *e.g.* 'Bombay duck', 'Sperm whale'. *Class No:* 802.0-54

[5582]
SHIPLEY, J.T. The Origins of English words: a discursive dictionary of Indo-European roots. Baltimore, Md., Johns Hopkins Univ. Press, 1984. xxxiv,636p. $50. ISBN: 0801830044.

Lengthy entries, arranged by Indo-European root, A-Z, with an index of *c.*18,000 English words discussed. Bibliography (2p.). *Class No:* 802.0-54

[5583]
SKEAT, W.W. An Etymological English dictionary. New (4th) ed., rev. and enl. Oxford, Clarendon Press, 1910 (repr. 1963). xliv,780p. £90. ISBN: 0198631049.

Original title was *An Etymological dictionary of the English language*.

A major specialized work. About 12,000 entries giving definition, scholarly discussion of etymology and references to texts. Appendices: lists of prefixes, suffixes, homonyms, doublets, Indo-Germanic roots, and distribution of words according to languages from which derived.

In Skeat's *A Concise etymological dictionary of the English language* (Rev. ed. Oxford, Clarendon Press, 1911. Repr. 1963. xv,664p. ISBN: 0198631057), compression has been achieved mainly by omitting the history of the use of words, given at some length in the larger work.
Class No: 802.0-54

[5584]
Webster's word histories. Merriam-Webster Editorial Staff, *eds*. Springfield, Mass., Merriam-Webster, 1989. 526p. £14.95. ISBN: 0877790485.

Entries for over 1,500 words with an 'interesting' history. Most give etymology only, with a cross-reference to one of 600 narrative 'stories'. Similar in style to the *Morris dictionary of word and phrase origins*, but according to *Choice* (v.27(10), June 1990, p.1664), there is 'surprisingly little duplication'. *Class No:* 802.0-54

Morphology

[5585]
MICHAELS, A. Suffix obsession: a dictionary of all words ending in annual, ennial, anthropy, archy, cracy, cide, culture, gamy, gon, hedron, lagnia, latry, theism, loquy, machy, mancy, mania, nym, phagous, vorous, phany, philia and phobia. Jefferson, N.C., McFarland, 1993. vii,189p. $32.50. ISBN: 0899506747.

Arranged A-Z by suffix. Defines words ending with common suffixes and gives other words with the same suffix that have related connotations. *Class No:* 802.0-55

[5586]
-Ologies and -isms: a thematic dictionary. Urdang, L., *and others, eds*. 3rd ed. Detroit, Gale, 1986. 795p. $99. ISBN: 0810311968.

1st ed. 1978; 2nd ed. 1981.

Lists and defines over 17,000 terms ending in '-ology', '-ism', '-ic', and '-phobia' under 430 subject headings. Alphabetical index of terms. Cross-references.
Class No: 802.0-55

[5587]
Prefixes; and other word-initial elements of English. Urdang, L., *ed*. Detroit, Gale, 1982. 533p. ISBN: 0810315483.

Explains the origins, meanings and applications of over 3,000 common and technical prefixes. Clearly laid out with many illustrative examples. *Class No:* 802.0-55

[5588]
—Suffixes; and other word-final elements of English. Urdang, L., *ed*. Detroit, Gale, 1982. ix,363p. ISBN: 0810311232.

Explains the origins, meanings and applications of 1,545 common and technical suffixes. *Class No:* 802.0-55

[5589]
ROBERTSON, J.G. Robertson's words for a modern age: a cross-reference of Latin and Greek elements. Eugene, Or., Senior Scribe, 1991. 256p. £24.95. ISBN: 0963091905.

A single-sequence dictionary of *c.* 3,000 Greek elements, Latin elements and English terms. Entries for Greek elements include English meaning, equivalent Latin element and a list of undefined English words which include that element. Entries for Latin elements are similarly arranged, whilst entries for English words have references to the relevant elements. 14 appendices, including list of animals with their Latin names and English terms for male, female, young, group, etc.; list of '-phobia' words (17p.); list of group names (5p.); and Latin and Greek expressions and abbreviations. 'Most useful, innovative, well produced, sensibly priced, in places charmingly idiosyncratic and quite definitely highly recommended' (*Reference Reviews*, v.7(3), 1993, p.20). *Class No:* 802.0-55

Prosody & Rhyme

[5590]
ESPY, W.R. Words to rhyme with: for poets and song writers. New York, Facts on File; London, Macmillan, 1986. xii,656p. $55. ISBN: 0816012377, US; 0333434269, UK.

Over 80,000 rhyming words, divided into 3 sets: single rhymes (accented on last syllable), double (accented on penultimate syllable) and triple (accented on prepenultimate syllable). Also contains a primer of prosody (52p.), glossary of 9,000 abstruse words and index of first lines of illustrative verses. *Class No:* 802.0-6

[5591]
FERGUSSON, R. The Penguin rhyming dictionary. London, Penguin, 1985. ix,530p. ISBN: 0140511369.

Rhyming words are presented in 555 phonetically arranged groups with subgroups. Index (240p.) lists over 50,000 words. *Class No:* 802.0-6

[5592]
WOOD, C. The Complete rhyming dictionary, revised: including the *Poet's craft book*. Bogus, R.J., *ed*. New York, Doubleday, 1991. 627p. $25. ISBN: 0385413505.

1st ed. 1936.

A revision of a long-established dictionary which gives single, double, and triple rhymes based on sound rather than spelling, with pronunciation, stress, and syllabification indicated for each word. Also includes practical advice for poets. *Class No:* 802.0-6

[5593]
YOUNG, S. The New comprehensive American rhyming dictionary. New York, Morrow, 1991. 622p. $24.95. ISBN: 068810360x.

Based on contemporary American pronunciation rather than spelling. Arranged by accented sounds that are divided into 5 vowel categories, each of which is further subdivided into long and short sounds. Often pairs single words with phrases to create rhyme and not afraid to include slang, colloquialisms and foreign terms. Over 50,000 entries.
Class No: 802.0-6

803 Germanic Languages

Germanic Languages

[5594]
Kurzer Grundriss der germanischen Philologie bis 1500. Schmitte, L.E., *ed.* Berlin, de Gruyter, 1970-71. 2v.
V.1 *Sprachgeschichte.* 1970. x,440p. $46. ISBN: 3110002604.
V.2 *Literaturgeschichte.* 1971. viii,665p. $56. ISBN: 3110064685.
V.1 has 10 signed essays by 9 specialists on the Germanic languages, each with a substantial bibliography.
Class No: 803.

[5595]
PAUL, H. Grundriss der germanischen Philologie, unter Mitwirkung zahlreicher Fachgelehrter, begründet von Hermann Paul. Berlin, de Gruyter, 1925-. v.1- (in progress).
A complete revision of Paul's *Grundriss,* which was first published 1891-93; 2nd ed. 1900-1909 (3v.); 3rd ed. 1911-16 (6v.).
A series of scholarly monographs on topics and periods in Germanic philology. *Class No:* 803.

Bibliographies

[5596]
McKAY, J.C. A Guide to Germanic reference grammars: the modern standard languages. Amsterdam, Benjamins, 1984. xviii,239p. Hfl.98. (*Library and information sources in linguistics.*) ISBN: 9027237360.
Describes and evaluates reference grammars and comprehensive works on the syntax of 11 Germanic languages, including Faroese, Frisian, and Yiddish. Most entries include references to book reviews. Separate chapter for each language. Bibliography (10p.). Index. Introductory survey of linguistic theories (53p.). *Class No:* 803.(01)

Theses

[5597]
Theses in Germanic studies: a catalogue of theses and dissertations in the field of Germanic studies (excluding English) approved for higher degrees in the universities of Great Britain and Ireland between 1903 and 1961. Norman, F., *ed.* London, Univ. of London, Institute of Germanic Studies, 1962. viii,46p. ISBN: 0854570152.
See entry at 830(043). *Class No:* 803.(043)

[5598]
UNIVERSITY OF LONDON. Institute of Germanic Studies. **Research in Germanic studies,** 1980/81-. London, The Institute, 1981-. Annual. ISSN: 00760803.
See entry at 830.(043). *Class No:* 803.(043)

German Language

Bibliographies

[5599]
Bibliographie der deutschen Sprach- und Literaturwissenschaft. Bd.1 (1945/53)-. Frankfurt am Main, Klostermann, 1957-. Annual.
As *Bibliographie der deutschen Literaturwissenschaft* until Bd.8 (1967-8).
See entry at 830(01). *Class No:* 803.0(01)

[5600]
Germanistik: internationales Referatenorgan mit bibliographischen Hinweisen. Tübingen, Niemeyer, 1960-. v.1-. Quarterly. ISSN: 00168912.
See entry at 830(01). *Class No:* 803.0(01)

[5601]
HANSEL, J. Bücherkunde für Germanisten: Studienausgabe. Tschakert, L., *ed.* 9., neubearb. Aufl. Berlin, E. Schmidt, 1992. 232p. ISBN: 3503030190.
1st ed. 1959, with the subtitle *Wie sammelt man das Schrifttum nach dem neuesten Forschungsstand?* 8th ed. 1983.
See entry at 830(035). *Class No:* 803.0(01)

[5602]
RICHARDSON, L.L. Introduction to library research in German studies: language, literature, and civilization. Boulder, Colo., Westview Press, 1984. xx,227p. ISBN: 0865311951.
Much of this handbook is devoted to the use of libraries and bibliographic searching techniques, but 251 major reference sources in German studies are evaluated. Index of authors, titles, and subjects. *Class No:* 803.0(01)

Encyclopaedias

[5603]
Kleine Enzyklopädie Deutsche Sprache. Fleischer, W., *and others, eds.* Leipzig, VEB Bibliographisches Institut, 1983. 724p. illus. maps.
A well-organized encyclopedia of the German language with a classified rather than alphabetical arrangement. 4 main sections and *c.*130 subsections containing a mass of detailed information, well illustrated by maps, tables and charts. Many cross-references using paragraph numbers. Bibliography (15p.). Index. *Class No:* 803.0(031)

[5604]
Lexikon der germanistischen Linguistik. Althaus, H.P., *and others, eds.* 2., vollständig neu bearb. und erw. Aufl. Tübingen, Niemeyer, 1980. xviii,870p. ISBN: 3484103930.
1st ed. 1973.
Contains 103 very detailed, signed chapters in 11 sections, 4 on general linguistics and 7 on German, each chapter having extensive bibliographies. Index.
Class No: 803.0(031)

Maps & Atlases

[5605]
KÖNIG, W. dtv-Atlas zur deutschen Sprache: Tafeln und Texte mit Mundart-Karten. 6.Aufl. München, Deutscher Taschenbuch, 1985. 250p. DM 19.90. ISBN: 3423030259.

1st ed. 1978.

A pocket-size volume which contains a remarkable amount of information on the history and current state of the German language. 140 colour illustrations, including many linguistic maps and charts. Bibliography has 380 items. Indexes of subjects, persons, and mapped terms.
Class No: 803.0(084.3)

[5606]
WENKER, G., ***and others*****. Deutscher Sprachatlas,** auf Grund des von Georg Wenker begründeten Sprachatlas des Deutschen Reichs und mit Einschluss von Luxemburg ... Marburg, Elwert, 1927-56. 27 Lfg.

Linguistic atlas of Germany, Austria and Switzerland. Accompanied by W. Mitzka's *Handbuch zum deutschen Sprachatlas* (Marburg, Elwert, 1952. 180p.).

Supplemented by:

Deutscher Sprachatlas: regionale Sprachatlanten, hrsg. vom. Forschungsinstitut für deutsche Sprache (Marburg, Elwert, 1962-) which is planned to comprise 60 vols. and:

Kleiner deutscher Sprachatlas (Tübingen, Niemeyer, 1984-) of which Bd. 1 is devoted to the pronunciation of consonants and Bd. 2 to vowels. *Class No:* 803.0(084.3)

Histories

[5607]
BACH, A. Geschichte der deutschen Sprache. 9., durchgesehene Aufl. Heidelberg, Quelle & Meyer, 1970 (repr. Wiesbaden, VMA-Verlag, 1985). 534p. maps.

1st ed. 1938.

A detailed history of the language in 12 chapters with 230 numbered sections, each of which has a substantial bibliography. Further bibliographies are appended (39p.). 23 maps. Subject index. *Class No:* 803.0(091)

[5608]
Sprachgeschichte: ein Handbuch zur Geschichte der deutschen Sprache und ihrer Erforschung. Besch, W., *and others, eds.* Berlin, de Gruyter, 1984-85. 2v. (xxxiii,2251p.). (*Handbücher zur Sprach- und Kommunikationswissenschaft.*) ISBN: 311007396x, v.1; 3110095904, v.2.

179 signed chapters on aspects of German historical linguistics. Well organized and extremely detailed, with numbered paragraphs, maps, charts and tables. All chapters have extensive bibliographies. Author and subject indexes.
Class No: 803.0(091)

[5609]
WELLS, C.J. German: a linguistic history to 1945. Oxford, Clarendon Press, 1985. xvi,591p. ISBN: 0198157959.

A detailed historical survey in 10 chapters, well illustrated with tables, maps and quotations. Select bibliography after each chapter. A wealth of references (p.436-88) and an extensive general bibliography (p.489-542). Index of names and general index of topics and places.
Class No: 803.0(091)

Origins

Old High German

[5610]
Althochdeutsches Wörterbuch. Karg-Gasterstädt, E. *and* Frings, T., *eds.* Berlin, Akademie-Verlag, 1952-95. v.1, fasc.1-v.4, fasc.14 (in progress).

A definitive dictionary of the German language as it was written from *c.*750-1050. Entries include grammatical information, later forms of the word, definitions, and examples of use from literary sources. Published in fascicules and likely to take many years to complete, v.4 covering *G-J*. A Latin-OHG index will be provided when the work is complete. *Class No:* 803.0-022

[5611]
SCHÜTZEICHEL, R. Althochdeutsches Wörterbuch. 4. Aufl. Tübingen, Niemeyer, 1989. 309p. ISBN: 3484106379.

A concise dictionary of Old High German, based on the main literary works of the period. Gives modern German equivalents for each word. *Class No:* 803.0-022

Middle High German

[5612]
BENECKE, G.F. Mittelhochdeutsches Wörterbuch. Leipzig, Hirzel, 1854-61. 3v.

The standard dictionary of Middle High German (*c.*1050-1500), arranged by etymological root with quotations from poetic sources.

Supplemented by M. von Lexer's *Mittelhochdeutsches Handwörterbuch* (Leipzig, Hirzel, 1872-78. 3v.), which is regularly reprinted. *Class No:* 803.0-023

[5613]
Wörterbuch der mittelhochdeutschen Urkundensprache, auf der Grundlage des Corpus der altdeutschen Originalkunden bis zum Jahr 1300. Kirschstein, B., *and others, eds.* Berlin, Schmidt, 1994-. Bd.1- (in progress). ISBN: 3503022473.

A scholarly dictionary based on a corpus of texts. Bd.1 (864p.) covers 'Ab-hinnen.' *Class No:* 803.0-023

Modern High German

[5614]
Frühneuhochdeutsches Wörterbuch. Anderson, R.R., *and others, eds.* Berlin, de Gruyter, 1986-. Bd.1- (in progress).

A scholarly dictionary of early New High German with numerous quotations from literature and references to other dictionaries and linguistic studies.

V.1 comprises 3 fascicules (1986-9): 1. Introduction - 2. List of sources (p.165-224) - 3. Bibliography of secondary literature (p.225-85), then the start of the dictionary, 'A'-'äpfelkern'. V.2 has a further 4 fascicules (1991-3), taking coverage to 'barmherzig'. Vols. 3,4 and 8 are also in progress. *Class No:* 803.0-024

[5615]
GRIMM, J. *and* **GRIMM, W. Deutsches Wörterbuch.** Leipzig, Hirzel, 1854-1960. 16v. (repr. München, Deutscher Taschenbuch, 1984. 33v.). DM.1200. ISBN: 3423059451.

The original design of this monumental dictionary was 'to give an exhaustive account of the words of the literary language (New High German) from about the end of the 15th century, including their earlier etymological and later history, with references to important dialectical words and forms; and to illustrate their use and history abundantly by

....(*contd.*)

quotations' (*Encyclopaedia Britannica,* 11th ed., v.8, p.189). Compared, on these principles, with the *New English dictionary,* the Grimm dictionary omits pronunciation and obsolete words and is less systematic and full in other respects, although later volumes show an improvement.

Quellenverzeichnis (1966-71. xp.,1094 cols.) is an alphabetical list of *c.*60,000 sources cited.

Deutches Wörterbuch von Jacob Grimm und Wilhelm Grimm, hrsg. von der Deutschen Akademie der Wissenschaften zu Berlin in Zusammenarbeit mit der Akademie der Wissenschaften zu Göttingen. Neubearbeitungen (Leipzig, Hirzel, 1965-) is a revised and expanded ed., incorporating the results of modern scholarship. Vols. 1 (*A*), 6 (*D*) and 7 (*E*) have been completed and vols. 2 and 8 are in progress.
Class No: 803.0-024

Usage

[5616]

BRIDGHAM, F. The Friendly German dictionary: a guide to German language, culture and society through faux amis, literary illustration and other diversions. London, Libris, 1996. xv,318p. £40. ISBN: 1870352653.

Explains differences of meaning between words which look similar in German and English, using examples from German periodicals and literary works. Entries are arranged within 10 thematic chapters (*e.g.* 'History and Politics', 'Food and Drink') and often include synonyms and cross-references. Distinctions between German, Austrian and Swiss German are noted, as are those between British and American English. Index of German keywords. *TLS* (no.4855, April 19, 1996) suggests that the dictionary is not all that 'friendly', in that the index which one has to consult first in order to locate an entry is not particularly comprehensive, but finds it 'instructive as well as entertaining'. *Class No:* 803.0-06

[5617]

Duden Stilwörterbuch der deutschen Sprache. Drosdowski, G., *ed.* 7., neubearb. und erw. Aufl. Mannheim, Bibliographisches Institut, 1988. 864p. (*Der Duden in 12 Bände - Bd.2.*) ISBN: 341120902x.

An alphabetical guide to usage, with *c.*10,500 entries for words which may cause difficulties. Questions of style, nuances of meaning, etc. are discussed at length and illustrated by exemplary phrases.

V.9 in the Duden series, *Richtiges und gutes Deutsch: Wörterbuch der Zweifelsfalle,* is also alphabetically arranged and deals with other aspects of usage, including punctuation, grammar and spelling. *Class No:* 803.0-06

[5618]

DURRELL, M. Using German: a guide to contemporary usage. Cambridge, Cambridge Univ. Press, 1992. xviii,270p. £40. ISBN: 0521420776.

5 main sections (1. Varieties of language - 2. Words and meanings - 3. Words and forms - 4. Grammar - 5. Syntax and word order) with many numbered subsections. Well organized and laid out, with good use of different typefaces and numerous examples. Glossary of linguistic terms (7p.). Easy access via detailed contents table, topic index and index of German words. *Class No:* 803.0-06

German Slang

[5619]

KÜPPER, H. Illustriertes Lexikon der deutschen Umgangssprache. Stuttgart, Klett, 1982-84. 8v. illus. ISBN: 312570300x.

Supersedes Küpper's *Wörterbuch der deutschen Umgangssprache* (3. Aufl. 1963-70. 6v.) and is much more convenient, having a single A-Z sequence whereas its predecessor had separate sequences for different types of slang. 120,000 entries, giving meanings, dates and regional distribution where appropriate. Index of people, places and subjects in each vol. 1,200 colour illustrations.
Class No: 803.0-086

[5620]

—KÜPPER, H. Pons Wörterbuch der deutsche Umgangssprache. Stuttgart, Klett, 1987. xii,959p. £45.95. ISBN: 3125706009.

A single-vol. dictionary with *c.*65,000 entries and extensive cross-references. Entries include details of regional or social origins of slang terms. *Class No:* 803.0-086

Dialects

[5621]

The Dialects of modern German: a linguistic survey. Russ, C.V.J. London, Routledge, 1990. xxiii,519p. maps. £50. ISBN: 0415003083.

15 regional chapters by specialists on German dialects of Germany, Austria, Luxemburg, Switzerland and Alsace, comprising in each case a discussion of the dialect's status in the region, a survey of the historical and geographical background, and a detailed description of the dialect, well illustrated with examples in IPA transcription, all of them with English translation. Extensive bibliographies after each chapter, but no index. 40 maps. *Class No:* 803.0-087

[5622]

Dialektologie: ein Handbuch zur deutschen und allgemeinen Dialektforschung. Besch, W., *and others, eds.* Berlin, de Gruyter, 1982-83. 2v. (xxxiv,1714p.). DM1,155. (*Handbücher zur Sprach- und Kommunikationswissenschaft.*) ISBN: 3110059770, v.1; 3110095718, v.2.

102 signed chapters in 15 sections, offering a detailed survey of general and German dialectology. Well organized, with numbered paragraphs and numerous maps, charts and tables. Extensive chapter bibliographies. Index.
Class No: 803.0-087

Austria

[5623]

EBNER, J. Wie sagt man in Österreich? Wörterbuch der österreichischen Besonderheiten. 2., neu bearb. und erw. Aufl. Mannheim, Bibliographisches Institut, 1980. 252p. (*Duden Taschenbücher - Bd.8.*) ISBN: 3411017945.

A concise dictionary of words used only in Austria and the adjacent regions and words which have a different meaning there. Entries include information on grammar and pronunciation, definition, and example of usage.
Class No: 803.0-087(436)

Yiddish

Bibliographies

[5624]

BRATKOWSKY, J.G. Yiddish linguistics: a multilingual bibliography. New York, Garland, 1988. xiv,407p. ISBN: 0824098048.

Lists 2,188 recent publications in 12 sections and many subsections, with entries grouped by language (1. English - 2. Yiddish - 3. Others) within each subsection. Includes references to reviews. List of bibliographies examined (8p.). Name index.

See also *Yiddish linguistics: a classified bilingual index to Yiddish serials and collections, 1913-1958*, by D.M. Bunis and A. Sunshine (New York, Garland, 1993. 216p. ISBN: 0824097580). *Class No:* 803.0-088(01)

Dictionaries

[5625]

GALVIN, H. *and* **TAMARKIN, S. The Yiddish dictionary sourcebook:** a transliterated guide to the Yiddish language. Hoboken, N.J., Ktav, 1986. x,317p. ISBN: 0870687153.

A popular introductory guide to Yiddish consisting mainly of a dictionary (English-Yiddish/Yiddish-English) of common words, giving English transliteration of the Yiddish, phonetic rendering of Yiddish pronunciation, and spelling in Yiddish using Hebrew characters. Appendices list popular expressions and proverbs. Introductory notes on history and grammar. Over 8,500 words and phrases covered.
Class No: 803.0-088(038)

[5626]

Groyser verterbukh fun der Yidisher shprakh / Great dictionary of the Yiddish language. Joffe, J.A. *and* Mark, Y., *eds*. New York, Yiddish Dictionary Committee, 1961- (in progress).

An unabridged, scholarly Yiddish-Yiddish dictionary of which the first 4 vols. appeared in 1961, 1966, 1971 and 1980. To be in 12 vols. Covers Yiddish from the earliest records to contemporary usage in various countries, and for each item gives spelling, pronunciation, Yiddish definitions, English and Hebrew glosses, examples of usage, citations tracing usage and changes in meaning over time, etymology, and information on geographical distribution.
Class No: 803.0-088(038)

[5627]

HARDUF, D.M. Transliterated English-Yiddish / Yiddish-English dictionary. Willowdale, Ontario, Harduf, 1991. 471+185p. £19.95. ISBN: 0920243223.

Over 11,500 English-Yiddish entries, comprising English headword, part of speech and gloss in Yiddish and transliterated form. Much shorter English-Yiddish section with *c.*5,500 entries. *Class No:* 803.0-088(038)

[5628]

HARKAVY, A. English-Yiddish / Yiddish-English dictionary. 22nd ed. New York, Hebrew Publishing Co., [195-?]. 2v. in 1 (viii,759p.; xvi,364p.).

A frequently reprinted dictionary, first published in the 1890s, with *c.*45,000 English-Yiddish entries and *c.*21,000 Yiddish-English. *Class No:* 803.0-088(038)

[5629]

HARKAVY, A. Yiddish-English-Hebrew dictionary. Reprint of the 1928 expanded 2nd ed. with a new introduction by D. Katz. New York, Schocken Books and the YIVO Institute for Jewish Research, 1988. xlv,583p. £24.99. ISBN: 0805240276.

1st ed. New York, The Author, 1925; 2nd ed. New York, Hebrew Publishing Co., 1928.

Complements Weinreich (*q.v.*), which prescribes normative, standard usage for modern Yiddish speakers, by providing the vocabulary of 19th and early-20th century literary works with their Hebrew equivalents, and is thus an important reference tool for students of Jewish history and literature. *c.*40,000 entries. *Class No:* 803.0-088(038)

[5630]

WEINREICH, U. Modern English-Yiddish, Yiddish-English dictionary. New York, YIVO Institute for Jewish Research and McGraw-Hill, 1968 (repr. New York, Schocken, 1977). xliii,790p. £27.99. ISBN: 0805205756.

A scholarly dictionary 'designed in the main for persons who have a firm grounding in English and at least a rudimentary command of Yiddish' (*Preface*). 'Destined to be a *vade mecum* for users of Yiddish for years to come' (*Library Journal*, v.93(20), Nov. 15, 1968, p.4282).
Class No: 803.0-088(038)

Maps & Atlases

[5631]

HERZOG, M., *and others*. **The Language and culture atlas of Ashkenazic Jewry.** Tübingen, Niemayer, 1992-4. v.1-2 (in progress).

V.1 *Historical and theoretical foundations*. 1992. xiv+136+8p. maps. ISBN: 348473013x.

V.2 *Research tools*. 1994. ISBN: 3484730048.

An ambitious attempt to produce a Yiddish dialect atlas of Eastern Europe after the Holocaust, based on a survey of 500 informants originating from as many locations and now dispersed. V.1 has a detailed introduction to the project and 81 small-scale maps. The full project is expected to comprise 10-11 vols. (with larger-scale maps) and a series of accompanying monographs and 'will not only portray the regionalization of the Yiddish language and its associated folk culture with hitherto unprecedented richness and precision, but will come to be regarded as an epoch-making contribution to structural dialect geography' (*TLS*, no.4698, April 16, 1993, p.13). *Class No:* 803.0-088(084.3)

Pronunciation

[5632]

Duden Aussprachewörterbuch: Wörterbuch der deutschen Standardaussprache. Mangold, M., *ed.* 3. Aufl. Mannheim, Bibliographisches Institut, 1990. 794p. (*Der Duden in 12 Bände - Bd.6.*) ISBN: 341120916x.

Phonetic transcriptions of German words (including those of foreign origin), using the International Phonetic Alphabet. Lengthy introductory survey of German pronunciation.
Class No: 803.0-15

Dictionaries & Vocabularies

Bibliographies

[5633]
KÜHN, P. Deutsche Wörterbucher: eine systematische Bibliographie. Tübingen, Niemeyer, 1978. x,266p. ISBN: 348410323x.

A classified bibliography of German dictionaries (general and specialized) and other word-related books. *c.*2,700 entries, including monolingual, bilingual and polyglot works. Author index. *Class No:* 803.0-3(01)

Synonyms

[5634]
BEATON, K.B. A Practical dictionary of German usage. Oxford, Clarendon Press, 1996. xvii,921p. £80. ISBN: 0198240023.

500 lengthy entries, arranged A-Z by English headword, focusing on words which cause difficulties for English speakers. Differs from its competitors in that each article defines and explains the different meanings of the English term before explaining in detail the usage of the German equivalents for each, with numerous illustrative examples. Very comprehensive, with, for instance, 6p. on 'put' dealing with 15 senses. Bibliography (2p.). Indexes of English and German terms. *Class No:* 803.0-314

[5635]
BULITTA, E. *and* **BULITTA, H. Wörterbuch der Synonyme und Antonyme.** 5. Aufl. Frankfurt am Main, Fischer Taschenbuch, 1994. 800p. £14.95. ISBN: 3596102243.

18,000 entries under keywords, A-Z, with 200,000 synonyms and antonyms listed separately in facing columns. *Class No:* 803.0-314

[5636]
FARRELL, R.B. Dictionary of German synonyms. 3rd ed. Cambridge, Cambridge Univ. Press, 1977. ix,414p. £19.95. ISBN: 0521290686.

1st ed. 1953; 2nd ed. 1971.

German synonyms are listed under *c.*900 *English* keywords, with explanations in English and many examples of usage, differences in meaning being very clearly delineated. Index of German words. *Class No:* 803.0-314

[5637]
WEHRLE, H. *and* **EGGERS, H. Deutscher Wortschatz:** ein Wegweiser zum treffenden Ausdruck. 15. Aufl. Stuttgart, Klett, 1989. xxxi,821p. £45. ISBN: 3129086102.

1st ed. 1880-81, as *Deutscher Wortschatz* by A. Schlessing.

The German counterpart to *Roget's Thesaurus*, with related words and phrases systematically arranged under 1,000 headings, followed by a comprehensive index (p.339-821) of *c.*65,000 terms. Words of foreign origin are clearly indicated, as are words whose use should be avoided. *Class No:* 803.0-314

Loan Words

[5638]
Duden: Das grosse Fremdwörterbuch - Herkunft und Bedeutung der Fremdwörter. Drosdowski, G., *ed.* Mannheim, Dudenverlag, 1994. 1557p. DM78. ISBN: 3411041617.

80,000 entries, giving pronunciation (IPA), meaning, etymology and usage. The scope is very wide, including

....*(contd.)*

technical terms, loanwords which are used only regionally, and 18th- and 19th-century terms which are important to the understanding of classical literature. Introductory essay on the history of loanwords in German. Index of 15,000 German words for which there are borrowed equivalents.

Duden Fremdwörterbuch CD-ROM (£26.95) has 50,000 entries and over 100,000 definitions. *Class No:* 803.0-316

[5639]
SCHULZ, H. Deutsches Fremdwörterbuch, begonnen von H. Schulz, fortgeführt von O. Basler, weitergeführt im Institut für deutsche Sprache. Berlin, de Gruyter, 1974-88. 7v.

Vols. 1-2 originally published 1913-42 (now reprinted).

A scholarly dictionary of loanwords, arranged A-Z in vols. 1-6, giving date of incorporation, definition, and explanation, supported by numerous quotations from literature, newspapers and periodicals, with precise references. V.7 has list of sources (224p.) and 5 indexes: words, A-Z; reverse index; chronological; language of origin; and word-types. *Class No:* 803.0-316

Idioms

[5640]
RÖHRICH, L. Lexikon der sprichwörtlichen Redensarten. Freiburg, Herder, 1994. 5v. illus. ISBN: 3451044005.

2-vol. ed. published 1973.

Gives meaning and origin of more than 10,000 phrases and expressions in colloquial German, grouped under 2,200 headwords, A-Z. Enlivened by over 600 illus. List of sources; index of topics. *Class No:* 803.0-318

[5641]
SCHEMANN, H. German dictionary of idioms. London, Routledge, 1996-7. 2v. £150.

V.1 *German-English dictionary of idioms*. 1996. 1280p. ISBN: 0415141990.

V.2 *English-German dictionary of idioms*. 1997. 560p. ISBN: 0415172543.

V.1 is a massive compilation with 33,000 headwords, giving for each expression the English equivalent, variants, contexts, and precise guidance on the degree of currency / rarity. V.2 has 15,000 headwords and provides similar information. *Class No:* 803.0-318

[5642]
SCHEMANN, H. Pons Synonymwörterbuch der deutschen Redensarten. Stuttgart, Klett, 1992. 464p. DM.128. ISBN: 3125707005.

Groups semantically-linked idiomatic expressions together and provides access via a keyword index. *Class No:* 803.0-318

[5643]
SPALDING, K. An Historical dictionary of German figurative usage. Oxford, Blackwell, 1952-98. Fasc. 1-59 (in progress). £30 per fasc.

Records figurative expressions, proverbs, quotations and other established phrases appearing in German literature since *c.*1750, with translations and explanations in English. Annotations illustrating use or change of meaning are often drawn from pre-1750 sources. A complete list of sources is planned for the conclusion of the work.

Vols. 1-5, covering 'A-Streiten', published in bound form in 1993 (£500. ISBN: 0631183965); the completed work will comprise 6 vols. *Class No:* 803.0-318

[5644]

TAYLOR, R.J. *and* **GOTTSCHALK, W. A German-English dictionary of idioms:** idiomatic and figurative German expressions with English translations. 4. Aufl. München, Hueber, 1983. 600p. ISBN: 3190062161.

1st ed. 1960.

Lists *c.*6,000 idiomatic expressions, A-Z, under the principal noun, and gives English (*i.e.* British) translation.
Class No: 803.0-318

Monoglot Dictionaries

[5645]

Brockhaus Wahrig deutsches Wörterbuch in sechs Bänden. Wahrig, G., *and others, eds.* Wiesbaden, Brockhaus, 1980-84. 6v. £60 per vol.

Based on Wahrig's *Deutsches Wörterbuch*, first published 1967; latest ed. 1975.

A major dictionary of contemporary German with 220,000 headwords and 555,000 definitions. Strong on scientific and technical terms, each of which is assigned to one of 180 categories. Syllabification is indicated in headwords and entries include numbered applications with examples of usage.

Der Brockhaus in einem Band (6. Aufl. 1994. 1120p. DM.49.80. ISBN: 3765316768) has 55,000 entries and 3,500 illustrations, most of them in colour. *Class No:* 803.0-323.1

[5646]

Duden. Das grosse Wörterbuch der deutschen Sprache in acht Bänden. Hrsg. und bearb. von Wissenschaftlichen Rat und den Mitarbeitern der Dudenredaktion unter Leitung von G. Drosdowski. 2. völlig neu bearb. und stark erw. Aufl. Mannheim, Dudenverlag, 1993-5. 8v. (4096p.). DM592. ISBN: 3411047321.

1st ed. in 6 vols., 1976-81.

A dictionary of the German language of the latter half of the 20th century, which is expected to have over 200,000 headwords in this completely revised 8-vol. ed. Colloquial usage is well covered, as are regional and national variations and technical terms. Also includes abbreviations, acronyms and some proper names. Entries give pronunciation, etymology (in many cases), definitions, compound and derivative forms, and include quotations from contemporary literature and the press. List of sources in v.1 (18p.). An excellent dictionary which is slightly let down by the use of a very small typeface and cramped page layout. Details of proposed spelling reforms in v.8 (24p.). *Class No:* 803.0-323.1

[5647]

Duden deutsches Universalwörterbuch. Drosdowski, G., *ed.* 3. neu bearb. und erw. Aufl. Mannheim, Dudenverlag, 1996. 1816p. £31.95. ISBN: 3411055030.

A dictionary of present-day German with over 120,000 headwords. Entries include examples of usage (150,000 in total) and a great deal of information on spelling, pronunciation, grammar, etymology and regional variations. Grammar supplement (34p.). This ed. takes account of the 1996 spelling reforms.

Available on CD-ROM alone (£32.95) or combined with *The Oxford-Duden German dictionary* (£49.95).
Class No: 803.0-323.1

[5648]

Der Duden in 12 Bänden. Mannheim, Bibliographisches Institut, 1958-. 12v. £16.50 per vol.

A well-established and reliable series of handbooks and dictionaries on various aspects of the German language, originally in 10v. under the title *Der grosse Duden in 10 Bände*. Revised editions appear regularly. Several of the works in the series are described individually under the appropriate heading.

1. *Die Deutsche Rechtschreibung*. 21. Aufl. 1996.
2. *Stilwörterbuch der deutschen Sprache*. 7. Aufl. 1988.
3. *Bildwörterbuch der deutschen Sprache*. 4. Aufl. 1992.
4. *Die Grammatik der deutschen Gegenwartssprache*. 5. Aufl. 1995.
5. *Fremdwörterbuch*. 6. Aufl. 1997.
6. *Das Aussprachewörterbuch*. 3. Aufl. 1990.
7. *Das Herkunftswörterbuch: Etymologie der deutschen Sprache*. 2. Aufl. 1989.
8. *Sinn- und sachverwandte Wörter: Wörterbuch der treffenden Ausdrucke*. 2. Aufl. 1986 (Neudruck 1997).
9. *Richtiges und gutes deutsch: Wörterbuch der sprachlichen Zweifelsfälle*. 4. Aufl. 1997.
10. *Bedeutungswörterbuch: Wortbildung und Wortschatz*. 2. Aufl. 1985.
11. *Redewendungen und sprichwörtliche Redensarten: Wörterbuch der deutschen Idiomatik*. 1992.
12. *Zitate und Aussprüche: Herkunft und aktueller Gebrauch*. 1993. *Class No:* 803.0-323.1

[5649]

Langenscheidts Grosswörterbuch Deutsch als Fremdsprache: das neue einsprachige Wörterbuch für Deutschlernende. Götz, D., *and others, eds.* Berlin, Langenscheidt, 1993. xxvi,1182p. illus. ISBN: 3468490003.

66,000 headwords with definitions specifically compiled with the needs of non-native users in mind. Over 2,000 usage notes and 30,000 illustrative phrases. Special attention paid to idiomatic and spoken German. Clear guide for users (18p.). A few line drawings. *Class No:* 803.0-323.1

[5650]

PAUL, H. Deutsches Wörterbuch. Henne, H., *and others, eds.* 9. vollständig neu bearb. Aufl. Tübingen, Niemeyer, 1992. xxxix,1130p. £42.95. ISBN: 3484106794.

1st ed. 1897. 8th ed. 1981.

A single-vol. monolingual dictionary with entries for *c.*11,000 basic words, often with lengthy discussion of their historical development supported by quotations from literary sources and references to other dictionaries and studies. List of sources (18p.). Subject index gives access to words derived from particular languages, used by certain authors, etc. *Class No:* 803.0-323.1

[5651]

WAHRIG, G. Deutsches Wörterbuch. 6. Aufl. Gütersloh, Bertelsmann, 1997. 1420p. £31.95. ISBN: 3577106778.

1st ed. 1975, being a revision of Wahrig's *Das grosse deutsche Wörterbuch* (1966).

A comprehensive desk dictionary with *c.*250,000 entries arranged in a 3-column format, plus a well-organized 90-page alphabetical guide to German grammar. Entries give clear definitions, etymologies (in some cases) and many examples of usage, and include numbered references to the grammar section. The vocabulary is contemporary and includes proper names, colloquialisms, and foreign terms. This ed. takes into account the German spelling reforms ratified in 1996.

.... *(contd.)*

Also available on CD-ROM from Deutscher Taschenbuch Verlag as *Wahrig Wörterbuch der deutschen Sprache* (DM49.90). *Class No:* 803.0-323.1

Illustrated Works

[5652]

Duden Bildwörterbuch der deutschen Sprache. Solf, K., *and others, eds.* 4. Aufl. Mannheim, Bibliographisches Institut, 1992. 785p. (*Der Duden in 12 Bände - Bd.3.*) ISBN: 3411040343.

The best known of all the pictorial dictionaries, in which 384 full-page labelled drawings illustrate the vocabulary of a wide range of subjects and activities. Word index has *c.*28,000 entries. Particularly useful for technical and scientific vocabulary. *Class No:* 803.0-323.1(0.025)

[5653]

Der Sprach-Brockhaus: deutsches Bildwörterbuch von A-Z. 9., neu bearb. und erw. Aufl. Wiesbaden, Brockhaus, 1984. 972p. illus. £24.95. ISBN: 3765303607.

1st ed. 1935.

A handy monolingual dictionary with over 80,000 entry-words, including technical terms, proper names and colloquialisms. Within the text are interspersed 515 sets of labelled line-drawings, illustrating 15,000 concepts, and lengthy explanatory notes on points of grammar and usage. *Class No:* 803.0-323.1(0.025)

Bilingual Dictionaries

[5654]

Collins German dictionary: German-English / English-German. Terrell, P., *and others, eds.* 3rd ed. Glasgow, HarperCollins; Stuttgart, Klett, 1997. xxv,1769p. £24.99. ISBN: 0004705807.

1st ed. 1980; 2nd ed. 1991.

Over 280,000 headwords and 460,000 translations, with the emphasis on *current* spoken and written language. Good coverage of US English and of Swiss, Austrian and East German varieties of German. Notable for its extensive and consistent use of style labels to indicate specific contexts and types of usage. 'Language in use' is a very useful thematically-arranged supplement (54p.) on the grammar of both languages. 3rd ed. has detailed supplement (21p.) on the 1996 spelling reforms, including wordlists showing old and new spellings. Exceptional value for money. *Class No:* 803.0-323.2

[5655]

—Collins German concise dictionary: German-English / English-German. Vennebusch, E. *and* Sawers, R., *eds.* 3rd ed. Glasgow, HarperCollins; Stuttgart, Klett, 1998. xxvi+1213+56p. £15.99. ISBN: 0004707095.

1st ed. 1987; 2nd ed. 1994.

Claims 150,000 references and 230,000 translations. This ed. has a new supplement (56p.) on self-expression in German, including many examples from the *Bank of English* and *Deutsche Textbörse* corpuses. Appended notes on 1996 spelling reforms (21p.). *Class No:* 803.0-323.2

[5656]

Harrap's standard German and English dictionary. Part one: German-English. Jones, T., *ed.* London, Harrap, 1963-74 (repr. Oxford, Oxford Univ. Press, 1977). v.1-3.

This dictionary was intended to be a definitive work, comparable to *Harrap's standard French dictionary* (*q.v.*), but although Oxford University Press took over the project in 1977 (and renamed it the *Oxford-Harrap standard German-English dictionary*) they have had to abandon publication. On the evidence of vols. 1-3 (covering the letters A-R), the dictionary would have been the most comprehensive available, with probably 100,000 German-English entries and countless examples of usage. *Class No:* 803.0-323.2

[5657]

Langenscheidt encyclopaedic Muret-Sanders German dictionary, based on the original work by E. Muret and D. Sanders. Springer, O., *ed.* Completely rev. ed. Berlin, Langenscheidt; London, Hodder & Stoughton, 1962-75 (repr. Langenscheidt, 1992). 4v.

Pt. 1 *English-German* (A-M, N-Z). 1962-63. 2v.(xxxvii,1844p.). £170.

Pt. 2 *German-English* (A-K, L-Z). 1974-75. 2v.(xxxvii,2024p.). £170.

With the demise of *Harrap's standard German and English dictionary, Muret-Sanders* is unrivalled as the most comprehensive bilingual dictionary. It has *c.*380,000 main entries, in a 3-column arrangement, with numerous compounds, derivatives and phrases. Entries include pronunciation guide (IPA) and numbered applications, with different styles and registers labelled. According to the *Preface,* 'American English is treated with the same degree of completeness and accuracy as British English' in terms of pronunciation, spelling and vocabulary. Appendices to each part include lists of abbreviations and proper names. *Class No:* 803.0-323.2

[5658]

—Langenscheidt condensed Muret-Sanders German dictionary: German-English / English-German. Messinger, H., *ed.* Berlin, Langenscheidt; London, Hodder & Stoughton, 1982-85 (repr. Langenscheidt, 1992). 2v. £65 per vol.

German-English. 1982. 1296p. ISBN: 3468970072.

English-German. 1985. 1199p. ISBN: 3468970064.

Based on the 4-vol. *Muret-Sanders,* but the 270,000 entries have not been simply lifted unaltered from that work. Many new terms have been added and existing entries have been revised where necessary. The abridged version retains the parent work's 3-column format and its clear presentation, using a variety of typefaces and style labels. Pronunciation is given for all headwords, including US variants in the English-German section. Appendices include lists of abbreviations and proper names. *Class No:* 803.0-323.2

[5659]

Oxford-Duden German dictionary: German-English / English-German. Scholze-Stubenrecht, W. *and* Sykes, J.B., *eds.* Rev. ed. Oxford, Clarendon Press, 1997. 1712p. £25. ISBN: 0198601301.

1st ed. 1990

The product of joint work by OUP and the Dudenverlag, claiming to be the first bilingual dictionary produced by a team based in *both* language areas. Claims 260,000 words and phrases with 450,000 translations. Entries are arranged in 3 rather cramped columns. Many illustrative phrases. Indicates regional usage of English in Britain and the US, and of German in Germany, Austria and Switzerland. Many useful appendices relating to both languages, including

....(*contd.*)
grammar, usage and letter-writing. Rev.ed. is essentially a reprint with a new Supplement (15p.) detailing the changes to the German spelling system ratified in 1996.
Also available on CD-ROM at £49.99 (ISBN: 0192683101). *Class No:* 803.0-323.2

[5660]
—The Concise Oxford-Duden German dictionary: English-German / German-English. Clark, M. *and* Thyen, O., *eds*. Rev. ed. Oxford, Clarendon Press, 1997. 1424p. £14.99. ISBN: 0198601336.
1st ed. 1991.
Claims 140,000 words and phrases and 240,000 translations. This ed. has appended notes (15p.) on the 1996 spelling reforms. *Class No:* 803.0-323.2

[5661]
The Oxford-Duden pictorial German & English dictionary. 2nd ed. Oxford, Clarendon Press, 1994. 677+96+95p. £25. ISBN: 0198645015.
1st ed. 1980, based on the 3rd, completely rev. ed. of the *Bildwörterbuch der deutschen Sprache,* published 1977 as v.3 of *Der Duden in 10 Bände*.
384 sets of line drawings and 6 colour plates illustrate the vocabulary of a wide range of subjects, with German and English terms for the numbered items and activities (over 29,000 in all) presented together on the same or a facing page. English terms are based on British usage with American variants noted. Alphabetical indexes in German and English.
The same illustrations have been used as the basis for a whole series of bilingual dictionaries. Reviewers have generally agreed that while they are exceptionally useful for technical and scientific subjects, their domestic scenes tend to reflect Western European (specifically German) life and some of the pictures look very dated. Whilst for this ed. vocabulary has been revised to reflect recent developments and 1,500 new items have been added, mainly in technological fields, sadly no attempt appears to have been made to update most of the illustrations. *Class No:* 803.0-323.2

Grammar

[5662]
Duden Grammatik der deutschen Gegenwartssprache. Drosdowski, G., *ed*. 5., völlig. neu bearb. und erw. Aufl. Mannheim, Bibliographisches Institut, 1984. 864p. £19.99. (*Der Duden in 12 Bänden - Bd.4.*) ISBN: 3411040459.
1st ed. 1959; 4th ed. 1984.
A thorough grammar for the advanced student, clearly arranged in 1,437 numbered sections. Many examples of usage. Detailed table of contents (10p.). Glossary (10p.). Bibliography (5p.). Word and subject index.
Class No: 803.0-5

[5663]
HAMMER, A.E. Hammer's German grammar and usage. Durrell, M., *ed*. 3rd ed. London, Arnold, 1996. xviii,542p. £19.99. ISBN: 034061451x.
1st ed. 1971; 2nd ed. 1991.
23 chapters, with numbered paragraphs containing countless examples. Layout and structure were totally revised to make 2nd ed. much more user-friendly and further improvements have been made for 3rd ed., which has a new section on the 1996 spelling reforms. Bibliography (6p.). Indexes of topics, German words and English words.

....(*contd.*)
See also *Modern German grammar: a practical guide*, by B. Dodd & others (London, Routledge, 1996. 504p. £45. ISBN: 0415098475). *Class No:* 803.0-5

Etymology

[5664]
Etymologisches Wörterbuch des Deutschen. Pfeiffer, W., *ed*. Rev. ed. München, Deutscher Taschenbuch-Verlag, 1995. xxvii,1665p. DM39. ISBN: 3423033584.
1st ed. Berlin, Akademie-Verlag, 1989.
Deals with *c.*21,600 words in over 8,000 entries arranged A-Z by keyword. Loanwords strongly represented. Entries give current meaning, date of first appearance in German, related forms in Germanic languages and many citations to sources. List of sources. Index of words. *Class No:* 803.0-54

[5665]
KLUGE, F. Etymologisches Wörterbuch der deutschen Sprache. Seebold, E., *ed*. 23. Aufl. Berlin, de Gruyter, 1995. lxiv,921p. DM.78. ISBN: 3110129221.
1st ed. 1883; 22nd ed. 1989.
The standard etymological dictionary, frequently revised and reprinted. 22nd ed. had an entirely new format which is retained in the expanded 23rd ed. Entries are arranged under 13,000 keywords with many citations to printed sources. Lengthy bibliography of sources. Glossary of specialist terminology. 'This work has long been, and will continue to be, the first step in the evaluation of the history and origin of any German word' (*The Linguist*, v.29(2), 1990, p.70).
V.7 of *Der Duden in 12 Bände* (*q.v.*) is a concise dictionary of German etymology. *Class No:* 803.0-54

[5666]
Trübners deutsches Wörterbuch; im Auftrag der Arbeitsgemeinschaft für deutsche Wortforschung. Götze, A., *and others, eds*. Berlin, de Gruyter, 1939-57. 8v. DM1,824. ISBN: 3110003198.
Intended as an abridged version of the Grimms' *Deutsches Wörterbuch* for home use. Particularly valuable for etymologies and historical surveys of the changing meanings of words. Lengthy entries followed by detailed references.
Class No: 803.0-54

Low German

[5667]
BUURMAN, O. Hochdeutsch-plattdeutsches Wörterbuch, auf der Grundlage ostfriesischer Mundart. Neumünster, Wachholtz, 1962-75. 12v.
A dictionary of Low German, based on the East Frisian dialect. Entries comprise standard German headword, Low German equivalent, and illustrative phrase(s). V.12 is an index of Low German words whose spelling is significantly different from the standard. *Class No:* 803.1

[5668]

Handbuch zur niederdeutschen Sprach- und Literaturwissenschaft. Cordes, G. *and* Möhn, D., *eds.* Berlin, E. Schmidt, 1983. xv,800p. ISBN: 3503016457.

32 lengthy, signed essays (by 21 contributors) on Low German language and literature, with a great deal of information organized in numbered paragraphs. Extensive chapter bibliographies. Index of authors and anonymous works. Subject index. *Class No:* 803.1

Frisian

[5669]

Wurdboek fan de Fryske taal / Woordenboek der Friese taal. van der Veen, K.F., *ed.* Leeuwarden, Fryske Akademy Ljouwert, 1984-94. v.1-11 (in progress).

The definitive Frisian-Dutch dictionary, which has reached the letter 'k' with v.11. Many *OED*-style quotations from literary sources. List of *c.*1,300 sources in v.1.

For everyday translation between Frisian and Dutch, see J.W. Zantema's *Frysk wurdboek* (1984-5. 2v.)
Class No: 803.92

Dutch

Bibliographies

[5670]

CLAES, F.M. *and* **BAKEMA, P. A Bibliography of Dutch dictionaries.** [2nd ed.] Tübingen, Niemeyer, 1995. xviii,377p. DM 196. ISBN: 3484309679.

1st ed. München, Kraus International, 1980, as *A Bibliography of Netherlandic dictionaries: Dutch-Flemish*, by F.M. Claes.

Lists 4,863 monolingual, bilingual, and polyglot dictionaries, including many on specialized subjects. A big increase over 1st ed., but the scope has been widened to include general encyclopedias and biographical dictionares. Brief annotations. Appended list of sources. Indexes.
Class No: 803.93(01)

Dictionaries

[5671]

BRUGGENCATE, K. ten. Engels woordenboek. Gerritsen, J. *and* Osselton, N.E., *eds.* Groningen, Wolters, 1986-90. 2v.

V.1 *Engels-Nederlands*. 20th ed. 1990. 1079p. £27.95.
v.2 *Nederlands-Engels*. 19th ed. 1986. 1004p. £27.95.

Regarded as the standard two-way Dutch and English dictionary before the appearance of Van Dale's pair of dictionaries in the mid-1980s. Obviously less comprehensive than *Van Dale*, with *c.*60,000 entry words in each vol., but strong on current idioms and clearly laid out. Does not give gender or pronunciation of Dutch words, being intended primarily for Dutch users. Frequently revised and reprinted.
Class No: 803.93(038)

[5672]

Cassell's Dutch dictionary. Coenders, H., *ed.* London, Cassell, 1995. 1472p. £45. ISBN: 0304337048.

An English edition of the 37th ed. of *Kramer's English-Dutch / Dutch-English dictionary*.

Over 18,000 English-Dutch entry-words and 21,000 Dutch-English, plus numerous compounds and phrases. Stress given for Dutch headwords and IPA pronunciation for English headwords. Includes neologisms, colloquialisms, proper names, and many technical terms. Dutch-English section includes many words and expressions used in northern Belgium. *Class No:* 803.93(038)

[5673]

DE COSTER, M. Woordenboek van jargon en slang. Amsterdam, Bakker, 1992. 631p. ISBN: 9035111281.

A classified list of nearly 8,000 jargon and slang terms with standard Dutch equivalents and explanations where necessary. 18 sections, A-Z. Bibliography (7p.). Index.
Class No: 803.93(038)

[5674]

JANSONIUS, H. Nieuw groot Nederlands-Engels woordenboek voor studie en pratijk. 2. druk. Leiden, Nederlandsche Uitgeversmaatschappij, 1972-73. 3v. (1917p.). £165. ISBN: 9061100321.

1st ed. 1950 (2v.); Supplement, 1959.

A comprehensive Dutch-English dictionary, now overtaken for sheer size by *Van Dale* but still valuable for its coverage of commercial and technical terms and very clear layout. *Class No:* 803.93(038)

[5675]

The Oxford-Duden pictorial Dutch & English dictionary. Oxford, Clarendon Press, 1986. 872p. ISBN: 0198641591.

See entry for *The Oxford-Duden pictorial German & English dictionary* (1980). Indexes in Dutch and English. Limitations exposed by a Dutch reviewer in *Modern Language Review*, v.83(4), Oct. 1988, p.1052-4.
Class No: 803.93(038)

[5676]

VAN DALE, J.H. Van Dale groot woordenboek der Nederlandse taal. Geerts, G. *and* Heestermans, H., *eds.* 12th ed. updated. Utrecht, Van Dale Lexicografie, 1995. 3v. £149.95.

1st ed. 1864; 12th ed. 1992.

About 180,000 entries, with new official spellings used in this updated reprint of 12th ed. For each entry-word, gives meaning, special forms, derivatives, usage in expressions, origins (if an unusual word), but not pronunciation. Exhaustive treatment of many verbs and prepositions. Appendices include Greek and Roman names, foreign phrases, and Biblical names. 12,000 new words and meanings in 12th ed. *Van Dale* has become the authoritative, practical source of information on all aspects of the Dutch language.

Van Dale groot woordenboek hedendaags Nederlands en synoniemen woordenboek (in die nieuwe spelling) is a CD-ROM combining a monlingual dictionary and thesaurus.
Class No: 803.93(038)

[5677]

Van Dale groot synoniemen woordenboek van Sterkenburg, P.G.J, *ed.* Utrecht, Van Dale, 1996. 1240p. £58.95.

The most extensive thesaurus available. New spellings used. *Class No:* 803.93(038)

[5678]
—BROUWERS, L. Het Juiste woord: standaard betekeniswoordenboek der Nederlandse taal. 7. druk Antwerpen, Standaard Uitgeverij, 1989. 1429p. ISBN: 9002181574.

1st ed. 1931.

A *Roget*-style thesaurus with synonyms and related words grouped under 1,000 headings. Index lists over 120,000 terms found in the thesaurus. A new edition was published in 1997 incorporating new spelling rules for Dutch.
Class No: 803.93(038)

[5679]
Van Dale groot woordenboek Engels-Nederlands. Martin, W. *and* Tops, G.A.J., *and others, eds.* 2. druk. Utrecht, Van Dale, 1989. 1654p. £65. ISBN: 9066481234.

1st ed. 1984.

Easily the most comprehensive English-Dutch dictionary available, with over 100,000 entries, including a great deal of technical vocabulary. Not easy to use at first because it employs a new, somewhat complicated, numerical code to distinguish between the various applications of each word and also labels words according to their frequency. The very small type-face is also inconvenient. Pronunciation given for all English headwords. Appendices include a compendium of English grammar (24p.) and a list of 776 English proverbs with translations. *Class No:* 803.93(038)

[5680]
Van Dale groot woordenboek Nederlands-Engels. Martin, W. *and* Tops, G.A.J., *and others, eds.* 2. druk. Utrecht, Van Dale, 1991. 1691p. £65. ISBN: 9066481277.

1st ed. 1986.

Similar in size and scope to the English-Dutch volume and, therefore, the fullest available dictionary of its kind. Uses the same numerical coding system. Packed with examples of usage, but does not give pronunciation for Dutch headwords. Appendices include compendium of English grammar (42p.) and lists of English words used in Dutch (4p.) and of 524 Dutch proverbs with translations.

This dictionary and its companion vol. are available on a single CD-ROM from Van Dale (£160).
Class No: 803.93(038)

[5681]
Woordenboek der Nederlandsche taal. 's-Gravenhage, Nijhoff, 1882-1995. 26v. Supplement, 1942-56.

The standard *OED*-style dictionary of the Dutch language, which has been appearing in fascicules for over a century, publication having been complicated by the introduction of spelling reforms in 1947. Entries include etymologies and numerous dated quotations. Probably the world's largest dictionary, with over 300,000 entries and 1.3 million citations. Available on CD-ROM from AND Electronic Publishing (ISBN: 9056490281).

List of sources in v.1, updated by *Bronnenlijst*, 1-2 (1953-66). *Class No:* 803.93(038)

Grammar

[5682]
DONALDSON, B.C. Dutch: a comprehensive grammar. London, Routledge, 1997. 376p. £50. (*Routledge grammars.*) ISBN: 0415154189.

Concentrates on the language used by contemporary native speakers and pays particular attention to areas of confusion and difficulty. Numerous examples. Numbered paragraphs and extensive index make access simple. Parallels with English are highlighted throughout. *Class No:* 803.93-5

Afrikaans Language

[5683]
BOSMAN, D., ***and others.*** **Tweetalige woordeboek:** Afrikaans-Engels / Engels-Afrikaans. 7. verbeterde uitg. Capetown, Tafelberg, 1967. xviii,1902p. (8. uitg. 1984). £29.50.

1st ed. 1931-36, in 2 vols.

A comprehensive bilingual dictionary with over 50,000 entry-words in each half. Many examples and idioms. The English word-list is based on the *Concise Oxford dictionary*. No pronunciation, but stress is marked. Lists of abbreviations after each section. *Class No:* 803.936

[5684]
Groot woordeboek: Afrikaans-Engels / Engels-Afrikaans. Kritzinger, M.S.B., *and others, comps.* 13. uitg. Pretoria, van Schaik, 1986. 1410p. £35. ISBN: 0627014917.

1st ed. 1926; 12th ed. 1981.

A comprehensive bilingual dictionary with *c.*40,000 entries in each section. Includes proper names.
Class No: 803.936

[5685]
Woordeboek van die Afrikaanse taal. Schoonees, P.C., *and others, eds.* Pretoria, Die Staatsdrukker, 1950-94. v.1-9 (in progress).

Spine title: *Die Afrikaanse woordeboek*.

An official dictionary, sponsored by the government, the Suid-Afrikaanse Akademie vir Wetenskap en Kuns, and the Univ. of Stellenbosch, which concentrates on words in current use, including scientific, botanical and technical terms.

Vols. 1-4 (*A-I*) have *c.*40,000 entries each, with line drawings and colour plates (*e.g.* of coats of arms, plants), but no etymologies. From v.5, the dictionary has changed significantly, the definitions now being supported by many quotations from literature, with precise references, and there are fewer illustrations. Consequently, there are fewer entries per vol. (*c.*15,000) and progress has slowed down, vols. 5-7 covering only *J-L*. V.7 has a detailed list of sources (22p.).
Class No: 803.936

Scandinavian Languages

Bibliographies

[5686]
HAUGEN, E. A Bibliography of Scandinavian dictionaries. White Plains, N.Y., Kraus International, 1984. xxii,387p. illus. ISBN: 0527388424.

Lists 2,527 monolingual, bilingual and polyglot dictionaries, published 1510-1980, with brief annotations. Includes many highly specialized items. Indexes of authors, languages, and subjects. *Class No:* 803.95(01)

[5687]
HAUGEN, E. A Bibliography of Scandinavian languages and linguistics, 1900-1970. Oslo, Universitetsforlaget, 1974. xix,527p. ISBN: 8200089975.

Nearly 6,000 entries arranged by author, A-Z, with alpha-numeric descriptors indicating languages and subjects covered. Subject index. A classified arrangement would have made reference considerably easier. *Class No:* 803.95(01)

[5688]

HAUGEN, E. *and* **MARKEY, T.L. The Scandinavian languages:** fifty years of linguistic research (1918-1968). The Hague, Mouton, 1972. 183p.

Survey chapters on Danish, Swedish, Norwegian, Faroese, Icelandic, and Pan-Scandinavian, followed by an extensive bibliography (52p.). *Class No:* 803.95(01)

Faeroese Language

[5689]

Faroese-English dictionary. Young, G.V.C. *and* Clewer, C.R., *comps.* Peel, I.O.M., Mansk-Svenska Publishing Co., 1985. 32+684p. £43.60. ISBN: 0907715222.

The first Faroese-English dictionary ever published is based on a consolidation of the Faroese-Danish *Ordabok* by M.A. Jacobsen and C. Matras (1961) and the supplement compiled by J.H.W. Poulsen (1974). *c.*27,000 entries, including phrases from Faroese folk-lore and proverbs. Introductory guide to pronunciation (23p.) by W.B. Lockwood. *Class No:* 803.958

Icelandic

Bibliographies

[5690]

BEKKER-NIELSEN, H. Old Norse-Icelandic studies: a select bibliography. Toronto, Univ. of Toronto Press, 1967; London, Oxford Univ. Press, 1968. 94p.

Over 700 entries, some with brief annotations, in 5 sections: 1. Introductory material (bibliographies, periodicals, collections, etc.) - 2. Study of language - 3. Literary history and criticism - 4. Texts (A-Z by title, listing editions, translations and studies) - 5. Background material. Index. *Class No:* 803.959(01)

[5691]

Bibliography of Old Norse-Icelandic studies, 1963-. Copenhagen, Munksgaard (subsequently The Royal Library), 1964-. Irregular. ISSN: 00677213.

Lists the year's editions of literary texts and books and articles on Old Norse language and literature and on medieval Norwegian and Icelandic history and related subjects. Arranged by author with subject index. Originally published annually, but the publications of 1981, 1982 and 1983 are treated in a single vol. published in 1988, which has 1,060 entries in 3 separate annual lists.
Class No: 803.959(01)

[5692]

CORNELL UNIVERSITY. Library. **Catalogue of the Icelandic Collection** bequeathed by William Fiske. Hermannsson, H., *comp.* Ithaca, N.Y., [The University], 1914-43 (repr. Cornell Univ. Press, 1960).

See entry at 839.59(01). *Class No:* 803.959(01)

Dictionaries

[5693]

CLEASBY, R. An Icelandic-English dictionary. 2nd ed., with a supplement by Sir W.A. Craigie. Oxford, Clarendon Press, 1957. xlv,833p. ISBN: 0198631030.

1st ed. 1874, initiated by Cleasby and subsequently revised, enlarged and completed by E. Vigfusson. 2nd ed. is a reprint with supplement (p.781-833).

A scholarly dictionary of classical Old Icelandic, giving .... *(contd.)* etymology, English translation and numerous quotations from literary works. Lengthy introduction includes list of sources and outline of grammar. *Class No:* 803.959(038)

[5694]

—ZOËGA, G.T. A Concise dictionary of Old Icelandic. Oxford, Clarendon Press, 1910 (repr. 1981). vii,551p. ISBN: 0198631081.

Includes 'all the words which the ordinary student of Icelandic is likely to meet with in the course of his reading' (*Preface*) and provides English translations.
Class No: 803.959(038)

[5695]

SIGURDSSON, A. Íslenzk-ensk ordabók. 4th ed. Reykjavik, Leiftur, 1983. 942p.

Over 60,000 modern Icelandic entry-words with English equivalents. Includes many colloquial phrases. Does not indicate pronunciation, gender or parts of speech. (New ed. 1994). *Class No:* 803.959(038)

[5696]

—HÓLMARSSON, S. *and* SANDERS, C. *and* TUCKER, J. Íslensk-ensk orðabók [Concise Icelandic-English dictionary.] Reykjavík, Iðunn, 1989. 536p. £50.

25,000 entries, with collocations and illustrative phrases. North American English used in definitions, with British variants noted. Guide to use in both languages (20p.). Notes on Icelandic grammar (17p.). *Class No:* 803.959(038)

[5697]

SÖRENSON, S. Ensk-íslensk orðabók: með alfræðilegu ívafi. Reykjavík, Örn og Örlygur, 1984. xxvii,1241p. illus.

Based on *The Thorndike Barnhart high school dictionary* (4th ed. 1965) and *Scott Foresman advanced dictionary* (1979).

Over 60,000 headwords, including encyclopedic entries: people, places, events, etc. All introductory material in Icelandic. *Class No:* 803.959(038)

[5698]

—BOGASON, S.Ö. Ensk-íslenzk ordabók / English-Icelandic dictionary. [2nd ed.]. Reykjavík, Isafoldarprentsmidja, 1966. 862p.

1st ed. 1952.

*c.*30,000 English entry-words, with pronunciation, and many phrases. (New ed. 1994). *Class No:* 803.959(038)

Norwegian

[5699]

Cappelens store engelsk-norsk ordbok. Svenkerud, H., *ed.* 2.utg. Oslo, Cappelen, 1988. xv,1302p. £95. ISBN: 8202108233.

1st ed. 1968.

A very comprehensive English-Norwegian dictionary, with *c.*160,000 headwords and 100,000 phrases. Includes proper names and abbreviations in main sequence. Intended for Norwegian users, giving pronunciation (IPA) of English headwords. 20,000 new entries in this ed. *Class No:* 803.96

[5700]

HAUGEN, E. Norwegian-English dictionary: a pronouncing and translating dictionary of modern Norwegian (bokmål and nynorsk). 4th ed. Oslo, Universitetsforlaget, 1996. 533p. £29.95 ISBN: 8200227227.

1st ed. 1965; 3rd ed. 1984.

Intended 'primarily as a tool for the learning of Norwegian by American students' (*Preface*) and claims to be the first such dictionary to include both forms of Norwegian, to give

....(contd.)

pronunciation of Norwegian words, and to label areas of usage and include quotations from Norwegian authors. Over 60,000 headwords with American English glosses. Lengthy introduction (34p.) including grammar, historical background and bibliography. *Class No:* 803.96

[5701]

KIRKEBY, W.A. English-Norwegian dictionary. Oslo, Norwegian Univ. Press, 1989 (distributed by Oxford Univ. Press). xv,810p. £36. ISBN: 8200182932.

*c.*40,000 entries, with pronunciation guide for English words and translation into *bokmål.* Many Americanisms included and extensive use of labels to indicate stylistic differences. Many illustrative phrases. *Class No:* 803.96

[5702]

KIRKEBY, W.A. Norsk-engelsk ordbok: stor utgave 2. utg. Oslo, Kunnskapsforlaget, 1986. xi,1373p. £65.10.

1st ed. 1979.

The largest Norwegian-English dictionary, with over 70,000 headwords. Detailed treatment of Norwegian compounds and prepositions. Rich in idioms. Where no short English parallel for a Norwegian term (*e.g.* legal) exists, English explanation is given. No pronunciation given. English-Norwegian vol. (2nd ed. 1996. iii,1317p. £65.10) also available. *Class No:* 803.96

[5703]

KNUDSEN, T. *and* **SOMMERFELT, A. Norsk riksmålsordbok.** 2. utg. Oslo, Kunnskapsforlaget, 1983. 4v.

1st ed. 1930-57 (2v.).

The standard monolingual dictionary of *riksmål* or *bokmål,* the Dano-Norwegian literary language. Many illustrative quotations. *Class No:* 803.96

[5704]

Norsk-engelsk ordbok. Slette, T., *ed.* Oslo, Det Norske Samlaget, 1977. xvi,1326p. ISBN: 8252106927.

A comprehensive *nynorsk*-English dictionary of both general and specialist vocabulary. Detailed introduction covers vocabulary, spelling, word forms, inflexion of nouns, strong and weak verbs, and Latin designations. 'Packed with accurate idioms and phrases, entries are well-structured, indicating gender, parts of speech and current usage' (*The Linguist*, v.29(1), 1990, p.34). *Class No:* 803.96

[5705]

Norsk ordbok: ordbok over det norske folkemålet og det nynorske skriftmålet. Hellevik, A., *ed.* Oslo, Det Norske Samlaget, 1966-. v.1-. (in progress).

V.1-2, 1966-78: A-Fluskin.

The official dictionary of *nynorsk* or *landsmål*, the modern language based on traditional Norwegian dialects rather than Danish. *Class No:* 803.96

[5706]

Norwegian dictionary: Norwegian-English / English-Norwegian. 2nd ed. London, Routledge, 1994. ix,553p. £15.99. ISBN: 0415108012.

1st ed. Oslo, Cappelens, 1990.

A paperback 2-way dictionary with *c.*9,000 headwords in each section. Good coverage of contemporary spoken language, with many idiomatic phrases. Pronunciation (IPA) given for all English entry-words and derivatives, but not for Norwegian terms. Supplementary notes on Norwegian pronunciation and grammar. *Class No:* 803.96

[5707]

TORVIK, I. *and* **GUNDERSEN, D. Ordliste for alle (bokmål).** 5. utg. Oslo, Universitetsforlaget, 1984.

A regularly updated vocabulary list, giving the prescribed forms as taught in schools and used by official bodies (CILT, *Norwegian,* 1986, p.19).

The equivalent prescriptive work for *nynorsk* is A. Hellevik's *Nynorsk ordliste* (Oslo, Det Norske Samlaget, 1985). *Class No:* 803.96

Grammar

[5708]

STRANDSKOGEN, Å.-B. *and* **STRANDSKOGEN, R. Norwegian: an essential grammar.** 2nd ed. London, Routledge, 1995. 202p. £12.99. ISBN: 0415109795.

This ed. originally published in Norway, 1989; 1st ed. 1986.

A grammar of contemporary *bokmål* written by Norwegians for non-Norwegians. Clearly presented in 13 main chapters with numerous subsections. Plenty of examples, with translations. Index. *Class No:* 803.96-5

Swedish

[5709]

DALIN, A.F. Svenska språkets synonymer. 7. uppl. Stockholm, Liber Förlag, 1971. 432p.

1st ed. 1870.

Related words are grouped in numbered sections, with meanings discriminated. Word index.

Another useful source is A. Strömberg's *Stora synonymordboken* (Borås, Strömbergs, 1979). *Class No:* 803.97

[5710]

Illustrerad svensk ordbok. Molde, B., *ed.* Stockholm, Natur och Kultur, 1982. 1917p. illus.

First published 1955. Frequently reprinted.

The standard household dictionary for Swedes, with *c.*200,000 words. 'The first recommendation for those needing a dictionary solely in Swedish' (Sather, L.S. and Swanson, A., *Sweden*, 1987, p.102). *Class No:* 803.97

[5711]

Norstedts stora engelsk-svenska ordbok. 2. uppl. Stockholm, Norstedts, 1993. v,1455p. £48.90. ISBN: 9119152221.

1st ed. Uppsala, Esselte Studium, 1980, as *Stora engelsk-svenska ordboken*, superseding Kärre's *Engelsk-svensk ordbok* (first published 1935), which was previously regarded as the standard work.

The largest available English-Swedish dictionary, with 129,000 words and phrases. Derivative forms are all entered separately rather than under the headword and numerous compounds and idioms from both British and American English are included. Stylistic values and specialist registers are clearly labelled. Pronunciation is indicated (IPA) for English headwords. 2nd ed. represents a complete revision and updating, with 10,000 new terms.

The companion work from the same publisher is *Norstedts stora svensk-engelska ordbok* (2nd ed. 1993. 1163p. £48.90. ISBN: 9119253729), which has also been thoroughly revised. Both dictionaries are available on a single CD-ROM at £145. *Class No:* 803.97

[5712]
Norstedts stora svenska ordbok. Stockholm, Norstedt, 1986. 1513p. £54.50. ISBN: 9119550723.

The standard general monolingual dictionary. 100,000 words and phrases in a single large-format vol. Pronunciation guidance given for recent loanwords.
Class No: 803.97

[5713]
ÖSTERGREN, O. Nusvensk ordbok. Stockholm, Wahlström & Wikstrand, 1919-72. 10v.

An important dictionary of modern Swedish, with *c.*50,000 entry words and many compounds, derivatives, and illustrative phrases. Entries include lists of synonyms. List of sources (170p.) in v.10. A 5-vol. edition was published in 1981. *Class No:* 803.97

[5714]
PETTI, V. *and* **PETTI, K. Collins-Norstedts Swedish dictionary:** English-Swedish / Swedish-English. 2nd ed. Stockholm, Norstedt; London, HarperCollins, 1993. xx,802p. £15.99. ISBN: 9119252420, Sweden; 0004707389, UK.

Swedish title is *Norstedts lilla engelska ordbok*

A compact, but very clearly presented, 2-way dictionary intended primarily for Swedish students of English. 24,000 Swedish-English entries, with nearly 10,000 examples and idioms. 20,000 English-Swedish entries with pronunciation (IPA) for headwords and over 16,000 phrases and illustrative sentences. American variants given. *Class No:* 803.97

[5715]
The Standard Swedish-English / English-Swedish dictionary. Petti, V., *ed.* Stockholm, Esselte Studium, 1983; London, Cassell, 1985. 758+480p. £45. ISBN: 0304340340, UK.

A merger of abridged versions of 2 major Swedish desk dictionaries, forming a handy 2-way dictionary with *c.*60,000 English-Swedish entries and 50,000 Swedish-English. The vocabulary here is now rather dated, the original dictionaries having been revised in the 1990s by Norstedts. *Class No:* 803.97

[5716]
SVENSKA AKADEMIEN. Ordbok öfver svenska språket. Lund, Gleerups, 1898-1993. v.1-31 (in progress).

The Swedish national dictionary, compiled on historical principles, giving etymology and profuse examples (with sources and dates) for each application of the words. Vols. 1-31 cover 'A-Stå'.

A list of sources (*Källförteckning*) appears in v.1 (24p.) and a supplement to this (206 cols.) was published separately in 1975.

For medieval Swedish, see K.F. Söderwall's *Ordbok öfver svenska medeltidsspråket* (Lund, Berlingska Boktryckeri, 1844-1918) and its supplements. *Class No:* 803.97

[5717]
Svenska Akademiens ordlista. Stockholm, Norstedts, 1986 (frequently updated). 680p. ISBN: 9118637221.

Explains and comments on Swedish vocabulary and gives detailed information on grammatical aspects such as declensions, conjugations and comparisons of adjectives, as well as phonological features such as stress and pronunciation. 120,000 words covered. *Class No:* 803.97

[5718]
Swedish dictionary: English-Swedish / Swedish-English. London, Routledge, 1995. 454+456p. £14.99. ISBN: 0415132444.

First published Stockholm, Prisma, 1993.

A compact 2-way dictionary with translations of 85,000 words and phrases. With a few exceptions, British spelling is used throughout.

Prisma publish a bigger 2-way dictionary in Sweden under the title *Prismas engelska ordbok*, with 140,000 translations, and this has been published in the US as *Prisma's modern Swedish-English and English-Swedish dictionary* (Minneapolis, Univ. of Minnesota Press, 1989. 622+613p. $69.95. ISBN: 081661734). *Class No:* 803.97

Grammar

[5719]
HOLMES, P. *and* **HINCHLIFFE, I. Swedish: a comprehensive grammar.** London, Routledge, 1994. ix,628p. £22.99. (*Routledge grammars.*) ISBN: 0415082080.

Very clearly arranged in 13 chapters with 1,310 numbered subsections. Numerous examples based on contemporary usage. Glossary of English linguistic terms (7p.). Bibliography (3p.). Index of Swedish and English keywords and grammatical concepts. Likely to remain the standard English-language grammar for a long time.
Class No: 803.97-5

Danish

[5720]
BRÜEL, S. *and* **NIELSEN, N.Å. Fremmedordbog** 11. udg. Copenhagen, Gyldendal, 1993. 677p. illus. ISBN: 8700149586.

1st ed. 1960.

A dictionary of loanwords with *c.*30,000 entries, giving spelling, inflection, pronunciation, etymology and definition. 1,000 new entries in this ed. *Class No:* 803.98

[5721]
Danish dictionary: English-Danish / Danish-English. Garde, A., *ed.* London, Routledge, 1995. xxv,684p. £15.99. ISBN: 0415108039.

Originally published Copenhagen, Gads, 1991.

*c.*26,000 entries in all, with many idioms and phrases. Pronunciation given for English headwords but not for Danish. Notes on Danish pronunciation and grammar (16p.) added for this English ed. *Class No:* 803.98

[5722]
DANSK SPROGNAEVN. Retskrivningsordbogen. København, Gyldendal, 1986 (repr. 1993). 622p. £11.95. ISBN: 8700913723.

The first official dictionary of Danish post-1848 orthography to appear since 1872. Pt. 1 lists Danish words (no definitions) in their officially approved forms, followed by inflected forms. Pt. 2 (p.509-614) is a guide to the alphabet, use of capitals, punctuation, etc. in 68 sections.
Class No: 803.98

[5723]
DANSKE SPROG- OG LITTERATURSELSKAB. Ordbog over det danske sprog, grundlagt af V. Dahlerup. København, Gyldendal, 1919-54. 27v.

The standard dictionary of the Danish language, including all words in use since 1700 plus some earlier ones. Dialect and foreign loanwords are also covered. Includes etymologies and illustrative quotations.

....*(contd.)*

The sources are fully listed in *Liste over forkortelser* ... (1956. 113p.).

A 5-vol. *Supplement* is in progress and is due to be completed by 2003. Vols. 1-2 (1993-4) cover A-Dozer. Detailed introduction to project in v.1 (38p.), plus bibliography (3p.) and list of sources (11p.).

For old Danish, the standard dictionary is O. Kalkar's *Ordbog til det aeldre danske Sprog, 1300-1700* (København, Thiele, 1881-1907. 4v.) with supplement (*Nachträge*, 1908-18) and list of sources (*Kilde-fortegnelse*, 1925).
Class No: 803.98

[5724]

HANSEN, P.M. Dansk udtaleordbog. København, Gyldendal, 1990. 761p. £29.50. (*Gydendals røde ordbøger.*)

Pronunciation dictionary using IPA symbols.
Class No: 803.98

[5725]

NIELSEN, B.K. Engelsk-dansk ordbog. 5. udg. (2. oplag) Copenhagen, Gyldendal, 1995. 1250p. £120.

1st ed. 1964.

A companion to Vinterberg and Bodelsen, with *c.*80,000 entry-words and translations for numerous derivatives, compounds and idioms. Pronunciation given for most of the English headwords. A very comprehensive dictionary, including Americanisms, scientific and technical terms, proper names and abbreviations. CD-ROM due 1998 (at £399). *Class No:* 803.98

[5726]

Politikens store nudansk ordbog. New ed. København, Politiken, 1996. 2v. (1394p.). £45.90.

1st ed. 1953.

The standard monolingual dictionary of modern Danish with *c.*60,000 entries, including foreign loanwords, place names and personal names. Gives spelling, inflection, meanings, etymology and synonyms. Also available on CD-ROM at £43. *Class No:* 803.98

[5727]

The Standard Danish-English / English-Danish dictionary. Axelsen, J., *ed.* Copenhagen, Gyldendal, 1984; New York, Holt, Rinehart & Winston; London, Cassell, 1986. 1235p. £47.50. ISBN: 0304340820.

*c.*65,000 entries in each section, covering 'the general contemporary vocabulary of the two languages, in addition to a large number of idioms and phrases, but it also includes a large selection of slang words, and technical terms from business, technology, and the arts and sciences' (*Preface*).
Class No: 803.98

[5728]

VINTERBERG, H. *and* **BODELSEN, C.A. Dansk-engelsk ordbog.** 3. udg. (3. oplag). Copenhagen, Gyldendal, 1990. 1472p. £120. ISBN: 8700258016.

1st ed. 1954-56; 2nd ed. 1966.

The most comprehensive Danish-English dictionary, with *c.*60,000 headwords and numerous examples of usage. Includes colloquial and obsolete meanings and many technical terms. Pronunciation not indicated for Danish headwords. 3-column format with small print. Also available on CD-ROM at £399. *Class No:* 803.98

[5729]

VINTERBERG, H. *and* **AXELSEN, J. Dansk-engelsk ordbog.** 10th ed. Copenhagen, Gyldendal, 1995. 1041p. £24.95.

A concise Danish-English dictionary, which has a companion *Engelsk-dansk ordbog* (1997. 724p. £19.95.).
Class No: 803.98

Grammar

[5730]

HOLMES, P., & *others.* **Danish: a comprehensive grammar.** London, Routledge, 1995. ix,628p. £18.99. (*Routledge grammars.*) ISBN: 0415082064.

Arranged like *Swedish: a comprehensive grammar* (*q.v.*), which Holmes co-authored, and equally impressive. 13 chapters with 1,315 numbered paragraphs, containing numerous examples of contemporary usage. Glossary of English grammatical terms (8p.). Bibliography (3p.). Thorough index. *Class No:* 803.98-5

Gothic

[5731]

KÖBLER, G. Gotisches Wörterbuch. Leiden, Brill, 1989. xlvi,716p. ISBN: 9004091289.

A scholarly dictionary with *c.*5,500 entries for Gothic words, with German and English glosses, etymology and references to sources. Intoductory essay, in German, on the origins and grammar of Gothic (28p.). Bibliography (5p.). Appended lists of Biblical names (22p.) and Gothic names (28p.). *Class No:* 803.99

[5732]

LECHMANN, W.P. A Gothic etymological dictionary. Leiden, Brill, 1986. xvii,712p. ISBN: 9004081763.

An English version of the 3rd ed. of S. Feist's standard work, *Vergleichendes Wörterbuch der Gotischen Sprache* (1939).

Entries include English gloss, references to sources, citations of cognates in Germanic and non-Germanic languages, and discussion of disputed etymologies and other linguistic problems. Word index with separate sequences for some 30 languages. Extensive bibliography (115p.).
Class No: 803.99

804 Romance Languages

Romance Languages

Bibliographies of Bibliographies

[5733]

BACH, K.F. *and* **PRICE, G. Romance linguistics and the Romance languages:** a bibliography of bibliographies. London, Grant and Cutler, 1977. 194p. £16.95. (*Research bibliographies and checklists.*) ISBN: 0729300552.

'... lists, with brief critical or descriptive notes, some 650 bibliographical items relating to Romance linguistics in general or to one or more of the individual Romance languages or dialects' (*Preface*). Arrangement follows the Romance section of *Bibliographie linguistique* (*q.v.*) with a first chapter on Romance linguistics in general, a second on Vulgar Latin and later chapters on each main language group working from west to east across Europe. Thoroughly annotated and cross-referenced. Index of names. Remarkable value for money. *Class No:* 804/806(009)

Bibliographies

[5734]

BAL, W. *and* **GERMAIN, J. Guide bibliographique de linguistique romane.** Louvain, Peeters, 1978. vi,267p. ISBN: 2801700991.

A selective, classified bibliography with over 2,500 unannotated entries. Detailed table of contents (11p.). Index of authors and titles.

Bal has also compiled (with others) *Bibliographie sélective de linguistique française et romane* (Paris, Duculot, 1991. 268p.) which is particularly strong on recent work and on some of the minor Romance languages like Occitan and Dalmatian. 'A much needed work, one that opens the doors to all modern works on the Romance languages' (*Language International*, v.4(2), 1992, p.39). *Class No:* 804/806(01)

[5735]

McKAY, J.C. A Guide to Romance reference grammars: the modern standard languages. Amsterdam, Benjamins, 1979. xviii,126p. Hfl.69 (*Library and information sources in linguistics.*) ISBN: 9027209979.

Describes and evaluates grammars and comprehensive works on the syntax of contemporary Catalan, French, Italian, Portuguese, Spanish, and Rumanian. Separate chapter for each language, with lengthy entries which include references to reviews. Introductory survey of linguistic theories (27p.). Bibliography (7p.). Index of technical terms and linguists. Index of authors and titles. *Class No:* 804/806(01)

[5736]

Romanische bibliographie, 1961/62-. Tübingen, Niemeyer, 1965-. Annual (formerly irregular). ISSN: 0080388x.

A continuation of the bibliographical supplement of *Zeitschrift für romanische Philologie, 1875/76-1960* (Halle, Niemeyer, 1877-1964).

An international, classified bibliography issued in 3 vols. for each year. In the bibliography for 1995 (published 1997) there are 13,316 unannotated entries, plus numerous references to book reviews. V.1 lists *Festschriften,* conference proceedings, general collections, etc., and has 4 indexes to the whole set for critics, reviewers, subjects, and authors as subjects. V.2 covers linguistics (4,221 entries) and v.3 literature (7,918 entries). Not indexed, but very clearly presented. *Class No:* 804/806(01)

[5737]

WEXLER, P. Judeo-Romance linguistics: a bibliography. New York, Garland, 1989. 200p. $29. ISBN: 0824045319.

According to Garland's catalogue, this bibliography is the first of its kind and is comprehensive through 1984. *Class No:* 804/806(01)

Encyclopaedias

[5738]

Lexikon der romanistischen Linguistik (LRL). Holtus, G., *and others, eds.* Tübingen, Niemeyer, 1988-. v.2(1), 2(2), 3, 4, 5(1), 5(2), 6(1), 6(2)-. (in progress). ISBN: 3484502509.

An encyclopedia of Romance linguistics which is scheduled to consist of 8 vols., of which v.4 was the first to appear in 1988. V.1 will be devoted to the history of the discipline of Romance philology and to methodology; v.2 will cover the history of the Romance family to the Renaissance; vols. 3-6 will deal with the history of individual languages since the Renaissance; v.7 will cover language contact and migration and the classification and typology of Romance languages; and v.8 will consist of bibliographies and indexes.

The vols. published so far are extremely impressive, offering clearly-structured essays by numerous specialists, often illustrated by maps and tables and always backed up by extensive bibliographies. V.5(1) (1990. xxii,894p.) is devoted entirely to French and has 47 such essays covering all aspects of the post-Renaissance history of the language. *Class No:* 804/806(031)

Dictionaries

[5739]

MEYER-LÜBKE, W. Romanisches etymologisches Wörterbuch. 6. unveränd. Aufl. Heidelberg, Winter, 1992. xxxiii,1204p. ISBN: 3825313948.

1st ed. 1911.

9,721 numbered entries, with many interpolations. Word index (p.815-1204) with separate sequences for Romance words and words from 15 non-Romance languages. *Class No:* 804/806(038)

French Language

Bibliographies

[5740]

BASSAN, F., *and others*. French language and literature: an annotated bibliography. [2nd ed.]. New York, Garland, 1989. xix,365p. $59. ISBN: 0824047982.

1st ed. 1976, as *An Annotated bibliography of French language and literature.*

1,253 entries (old ones revised and updated; new ones added, but many others omitted, leaving over 300 fewer than 1st ed.) in 3 parts and 20 chapters: 1. General bibliographies and reference works (287 items) - 2. General studies on the French language (55) - 3. Bibliographies and studies of literature (908, but individual authors not covered). Succinct descriptive annotations for all items. Largely confined to works in English and French 'which one can reasonably expect will be in an academic library, responsible for supporting a program of study in French language and literature' (*Preface*). Author-title index. A useful introductory handbook, although *French Studies* (v.45(2), April 1991, p.237) criticises 'the quirkiness of the selection' and suggests that 'the scholar will find the volume useful only outside his specialized field.' *Class No:* 804.0(01)

[5741]

Bulletin analytique de linguistique française. Paris, Didier, 1969-75; Klincksieck, 1976-. Quarterly. ISSN: 0007408x.

A comprehensive current bibliography covering books, articles and theses. Over 100 periodicals from several countries are examined. Each issue includes classified, annotated listings with several indexes (to authors, subjects, words, places, etc.). *Class No:* 804.0(01)

[5742]

OSBURN, C.B. Research and reference guide to French studies. 2nd ed. Metuchen, N.J., Scarecrow, 1981. xxxviii,532p. ISBN: 0810814404.

1st ed. 1968; *Supplement,* 1972.

Nearly 6,000 entries in 6 parts and 87 chapters: 1. French literature - 2. French language - 3. French language and literature outside France - 4. Romance philology and Occitan studies - 5. General background and related areas - 6. Scholars and critics. Far more entries than Bassan (*q.v.*) including many sources for individual authors, but without his annotations. Author and subject indexes.
Class No: 804.0(01)

Theses

[5743]

BARNWELL, H.T. *and* BARNWELL, J. Bibliography of theses on French language and literature deposited in university libraries of the United Kingdom (1905-1975). Society for French Studies, c/o Univ. of Bath, 1983. ix,72p.

Lists *c.*2,200 theses in 3 sections: 1. Linguistics and stylistics - 2. Literature and thought - 3. Studies of writers, anonymous works and historical or mythological persons or fictional characters. Sections 1 and 2 arranged by author and section 3 by name of person treated. No index. Incorporates (with some minor amendments) data from A.C. Taylor's bibliography (Oxford, Blackwell, 1964), which covered 1905-50, but keeps more strictly to linguistic and literary topics than Taylor and does not exclude published theses.
Class No: 804.0(043)

[5744]

Current research in French studies at universities in the United Kingdom and Ireland. 1969/70-. Glasgow, Society for French Studies, 1970-. Biennial. ISSN: 13509209.

Formerly known as Current research in French studies at universities and polytechnics in the United Kingdom and Ireland

V.23, *1995-96* (1996. x,139p. £10.50) has classified subject section (including non-literary and non-linguistic subjects) followed by list of studies of specific authors, artists, composers, etc., and of anonymous works. 3,100 projects listed. Index of researchers. *Class No:* 804.0(043)

Maps & Atlases

[5745]

Atlas linguistiques de la France par régions. Paris, Centre National de la Recherche Scientifique, 1939- (in progress).

A series of linguistic atlases, with usually several vols. covering a region. Areas covered so far include: *La Champagne et La Brie* (3v.); *L'Ouest* (3v.); *Jura et Alpes du Nord* (3v.); *Franche-Comté* (4v.); *L'Ile de France et L'Orléanais* (2v.); *Provence* (2v.); *Bretagne romane, L'Anjou et Maine* (2v.); *Le Centre* (3v.); *Normandie* (2v.); *Languedoc oriental* (3v.); *Lyonnais* (5v.); *Alsace*; *Pyrénées Orientales*; *Le Massif Central*; *La Gascogne*; *La Lorraine germanophone*; *L'Auvergne et Le Limousin* (3v.); *Lorraine romane*; *Languedoc occidental*(4v.).

The *Languedoc oriental* set (1981-86) has 980 maps on linguistic concepts, based on local informants' responses to a questionnaire. *Class No:* 804.0(084.3)

Histories

[5746]

BRUNOT, F. Histoire de la langue française des origines à nos jours. Nouv. éd. Paris, Colin, 1966-1979. 13v. in 22.

1st ed. 1905-53.

A monumental, well-documented history, tracing the development of the language against the social, political and literary setting. This edition comprises a reprint of the 1st ed. with the addition of a new preface and updated bibliographies, plus 2 new vols.(11 and 13).

P.F. Rickard's *A History of the French language* (2nd ed. London, Routledge, 1989. xii,179p. £11.99. ISBN: 041510887x) is a reliable, concise survey in English, with a bibliography and statistics on French speakers throughout the world. *Class No:* 804.0(091)

[5747]

Histoire de la langue française. Antoine, G. *and* Martin, R. Paris, Editions du CNRS, 1985-. v.1-. (in progress).

A continuation of Brunot's *Histoire*, which will comprise 4 vols., covering 1815-1880, 1880-1914, 1914-1945 and 1945-1985. The first 2 vols. to be published cover 1880-1914 (1985. 642p. Fr.405. ISBN: 2222035821) and 1914-1945 (1996. 1056. Fr.480), with classified bibliographies.
Class No: 804.0(091)

Usage

[5748]

BATCHELOR, R.E. *and* OFFORD, M.H. Using French: a guide to contemporary usage. 2nd ed. Cambridge, Cambridge Univ. Press, 1993. xii,276p. £37.50 ISBN: 052144361x.

1st ed. 1982, as *A Guide to contemporary French usage.*

3 main sections (Register; Vocabulary; Grammar) with

.... (contd.)

many numbered sections. Clearly laid out, with good use of headings, typefaces and tables, and numerous examples. Particularly good on synonyms. Detailed table of contents. Index of words and phrases covered in Vocabulary section.
Class No: 804.0-06

[5749]

COLIN, J.-P. Dictionnaire des difficultés du français. Nouv. éd Paris, Robert, 1993. xvi,623p. £17.75. ISBN: 2850362131.

1st ed. 1978

A single, A-Z sequence of words which may cause problems from the point of view of spelling, gender, meaning, usage, etc. Quotations from literature are used as illustrations. Appended guides to grammar and typography. Bibliography (4p.). Major revision for this ed.
Class No: 804.0-06

[5750]

GIRODET, J. Dictionnaire Bordas des pièges et difficultés de la langue française. Nouv. éd. Paris, Bordas, 1988. 896p. £19.40. ISBN: 2040209689.

1st ed. 1981, as *Dictionnaire du bon français*.

Words which present difficulties in respect of grammar, spelling, etc. are explained and exemplified. Appended notes on grammar (83p.). *Class No:* 804.0-06

[5751]

GRIEVE, J. A Dictionary of contemporary French connectors. London, Routledge, 1996. 544p. £45. ISBN: 0415135389.

The first guide to a difficult area for learners of French: words and phrases used as connectors. 200 such terms (*e.g.* 'en fait', 'or') are defined, discussed and illustrated by 2,000 examples from a wide range of contemporary sources.
Class No: 804.0-06

[5752]

HANSE, J. Nouveau dictionnaire des difficultés du français moderne. 3é ed. Paris, Duculot, 19994. 983p. £43.80. ISBN: 2801104221.

A greatly expanded and completely revised version of Hanse's *Dictionnaire des difficultés grammaticales et lexicologiques* (first published 1949).

Provides a comprehensive guide to French usage, with *c.*7,000 entries, A-Z, on problematic words and topics, covering spelling, pronunciation, grammar, syntax, style, register, semantics, regional variations, etc. Many exemplary phrases, including some quotations from literature. *Class No:* 804.0-06

[5753]

JOHNSON, S.M. Cassell guide to French officialese. London, Cassell, 1997. 160p. £12.99. ISBN: 030433815x.

Explains words and phrases which anyone spending any length of time in France needs to know but which are not always found in standard dictionaries. Nearly 2,500 entries, arranged by subject, in fields like employment, house purchase and renting, social services, education, health, justice, finance, local government, etc. Includes a selection of sample forms. Index of English terms. *Class No:* 804.0-06

[5754]

THODY, P. *and* **EVANS, H. Faux amis & key words:** a dictionary-guide to French language, culture and society through lookalikes and confusables. London, Athlone Press, 1985. 224p. £14.95. ISBN: 0485112434.

A guide to the pitfalls of French for English speakers, presented in popular style but reliable. Explanatory entries on *c.*500 words which are likely to be misinterpreted are arranged A-Z in 10 topical sections. Selective reading list (4p.). Index of headwords.

For more comprehensive coverage, see J. van Roey's *Dictionnaire des faux amis* (Paris, Duculot, 1988. xxxiii,792p. ISBN: 2801107654).

See also *NTC's dictionary of faux amis* by C.W.E. Kirk-Greene (Lincolnwood, Ill., NTC, 1990. v,197p. £8.95. ISBN: 0844215031), which has *c.*2800 entries.
Class No: 804.0-06

Slang

[5755]

CELLARD, J. *and* **REY, A. Dictionnaire du français non-conventionnel.** Nouv. éd. Paris, Hachette, 1991. 928p. Fr.280. ISBN: 2010162595.

1st ed. 1980.

A dictionary of *c.*5,000 colloquial, slang and jargon terms found in French literature. Entries give definition, quotations (with exact references to sources) and explanatory notes. Bibliography of literary works cited, most of them published since 1870. *Class No:* 804.0-086

[5756]

COLIN, J.-P., & ***others*. Dictionnaire de l'argot.** Nouv. éd. Paris, Larousse, 1992. xxvii,763p. £34.30. ISBN: 2033403335.

1st ed. 1990.

Over 6,500 slang terms, past and present, are explained and illustrated with over 8,000 quotations from literature, songs and the media. Etymologies provided. Index from standard French. List of sources (14p.). *Class No:* 804.0-086

[5757]

ESNAULT, G. Dictionnaire historique des argots français. Paris, Larousse, 1965. xvi,644p.

A scholarly dictionary of slang with *c.*7,500 entry-words. Gives definition, dated examples and (in most cases) etymology. *Class No:* 804.0-086

[5758]

MARKS, G.A. *and* **JOHNSON, C.B. Harrap's slang dictionary:** French-English / anglais-français. 2nd ed., rev. and ed. by H. Knox. Edinburgh, Harrap, 1993. xiv,701p. £12.99. ISBN: 0245604952.

First published under this title 1984, being a rev. ed. by J. Pratt of *Harrap's French and English dictionary of slang and colloquialisms* (1980).

Over 50,000 words and phrases in *c.*22,000 entries. Clearly laid out, with types of slang (rhyming, vulgar, Australian, etc.) indicated. A thesaurus of slang synonyms for key words asterisked in the text follows each A-Z section. *Class No:* 804.0-086

Dialects

Guernsey French

[5759]

DE GARIS, M. Dictiounnaire Angllais-Guernesiais. New ed., rev. and enl. Chichester, Phillimore, 1982. xxiii,291p. £25. ISBN: 0850334624.

1st ed. Guernsey, Société Guernesiaise, 1967.

A completely revised edition of the most comprehensive work on Guernsey French, with a new Guernesiais-English section added. As well as vocabulary, there is information on laws, customs and folklore. Local variants within the island are indicated. *Class No:* 804.0-087.41

Jersey French

[5760]

English-Jersey language vocabulary. Carré, A.L., *and others, comps*. Jersey, Don Balleine Trust, 1972. xv,80p.

Based entirely on Le Maistre's *Dictionnaire jersiais-français* and may be used as an English index to that work. Over 15,000 entries. *Class No:* 804.0-087.43

[5761]

LE MAISTRE, F. Dictionnaire jersiais-français, avec vocabulaire française-jersiais par A.L. Carré. Jersey, Don Balleine Trust, 1966. xxxiv,616p. £56.

The first full-scale dictionary of the Jersey language. Jersey-French section has nearly 20,000 entries, with numerous examples of usage. Second part lists over 14,000 French words and their Jersey equivalents. Lists of verb conjugations. *Class No:* 804.0-087.43

[5762]

LIDDICOAT, A. A Grammar of the Norman French of the Channel Islands: the dialects of Jersey and Sark. Berlin, Mouton de Gruyter, 1994. xii,452p. DM288. ISBN: 3110126311.

A study of phonology, syntax and lexicon based on spoken language data, which records both synchronic features of the dialects and their historical development. Includes a word list and selected texts transcribed into IPA. *Class No:* 804.0-087.43

Canadian French

[5763]

BÉLISLE, L.A. Dictionnaire nord-américain de la langue française. Ed. entièrement refondue. Montréal, Beauchemin, 1979. xiv,1196p. illus. ISBN: 2761600134.

Earlier eds. appeared under the title *Dictionnaire général de la langue française au Canada*.

Brief definitions and examples of French-Canadian usage. *Class No:* 804.0-087.471

[5764]

BERGERON, L. Dictionnaire de la langue québécoise. Montréal, VLB, 1980. 575p. $125. ISBN: 0828810923.

17,500 words and 5,500 expressions. *Supplément* (1981) adds 2,300 words and 500 expressions.

A condensed and adapted French-English version has been published as *The Québécois dictionary* (Toronto, Lorimer, 1982). *Class No:* 804.0-087.471

[5765]

Dictionnaire québécois d'aujourd'hui. Boulanger, J.-C., *ed.* Saint-Laurent, Québec, Dicorobert, 1992. xxxv,1269+343,lxiip. ISBN: 2980297801.

A *Robert*-style dictionary of Canadian French with 40,000 entries in the main sequence plus 12,000 proper names in a separate listing. Colour atlas and chronology of world history. *Class No:* 804.0-087.471

[5766]

DULONG, G. Bibliographie linguistique du Canada français. Québec, Presses de l'Université Laval, 1966. xxxii,166p.

1,054 entries chronologically arranged from 1691-1965, most of them annotated. List of cited journals (5p.). Indexes of authors and subjects. *Class No:* 804.0-087.471

[5767]

ROBINSON, S. *and* **SMITH, D. NTC's dictionary of Canadian French.** Lincolnwood, Ill., National Textbook Co., 1992. xii,292p. $14.95. ISBN: 0844214868.

Originally published Toronto, Anansi, 1984, as *Practical handbook of Quebec and Acadian French*.

A thematic dictionary with over 5,000 entries, A-Z, under 33 subject headings (*e.g.* Animaux, Temps). Arranged in 3 columns: words and phrases used in Quebec, but unknown or little used in France; standard French terms (if no French equivalent, an explanation in French is given); English translation. Appended notes on grammar and pronunciation of Quebec French, plus notes on Acadian French with list of local terms. Index. *Class No:* 804.0-087.471

Spelling

[5768]

JOUETTE, A. Dictionnaire d'orthographie et d'expression écrite . Paris, Robert, 1993. xxi,774p. Fr.195. ISBN: 2850362247.

Correct spellings for *c.*70,000 words, with pronunciation provided in difficult cases. Useful thematic entries in boxes throughout the sequence. *Class No:* 804.0-1

Pronunciation

[5769]

MARTINET, A. *and* **WALTER, H. Dictionnaire de la prononciation française dans son usage réel.** Paris, France-Expansion, 1973. 932p.

Gives International Phonetic Alphabet transcriptions of *c.*50,000 basic words, based on the pronunciation of 17 'informateurs', biographical details of whom are provided. *Class No:* 804.0-15

[5770]

WARNANT, L. Dictionnaire de la prononciation française dans sa norme actuelle. [4e. éd.]. Gembloux, Duculot, 1987. cxvii,988p. ISBN: 2801105813.

1st ed. 1962.

Gives the pronunciation of over 55,000 words and 24,000 proper names (French and foreign), in separate sequences, based on the speech of Parisians aged 20-50. Long introduction on general phonetics, including tables of phonetic elements of 24 languages. *Class No:* 804.0-15

Dictionaries & Vocabularies

Middle Ages

[5771]
Anglo-Norman dictionary. Rothwell, W., *and others, eds.* London, Modern Humanities Research Assoc., 1992. xxviii,889p. £250. ISBN: 0947623523.

A joint project by the MHRA and the Anglo-Norman Text Society, covering the vocabulary of texts in French used in Britain between the Norman Conquest and the late 15th century. It was published in 7 fascicles, 1977-92, and is now available in a single bound vol. Definitions and applications are fully supported by quotations. List of *c.*450 works quoted. *Class No:* 804.0-3"01/14"

[5772]
Dictionnaire étymologique de l'ancien français. Baldinger, K, *and others, eds.* Tübingen, Niemayer; Québec, Les Presses de l'Université Laval, 1974-. fasc. G1-10, H1- (in progress). ISBN: 3484503068.

Covers French vocabulary from *Les Serments de Strasbourg* (842) to mid-14th century and is expected to run to 4 or 5 1,000-page vols. 'G' complete in 10 fascicules, with detailed etymologies and references to sources, plus index vol. (1997).

Complément bibliographique by F. Möhren (1993. xix+637+47p.) lists texts and has a chronology, 842-1350. Indexes of authors, editors and manuscripts.
Class No: 804.0-3"01/14"

[5773]
GODEFROY, F.E. Dictionnaire de l'ancienne langue française et de tous ses dialectes du IXe au XVe siècle ... Paris, Vieweg, 1881-1902 (repr. Genève, Slatkine, 1983). 10v.

The basic work on old French, with a profusion of illustrative quotations. Vols. 9-10 are supplementary and include words which survive in modern French.
Class No: 804.0-3"01/14"

[5774]
GREIMAS, A.J. Dictionnaire de l'ancien français: le Moyen Age. [Nouv. éd.] Paris, Larousse, 1992. xxi,630p. £36.99. (*Trésors du français.*) ISBN: 2033403270.

1st ed. 1968.

About 12,000 entry-words from the *Chanson de Roland* to 1350, with citations for the word's first appearance in a literary work, etymology and illustrative quotations. List of sources (8p.). *Class No:* 804.0-3"01/14"

[5775]
TOBLER, A. *and* **LOMMATZSCH, E. Altfranzösisches Wörterbuch.** Berlin, Weidmann (later Wiesbaden, Steiner), 1925-93. 11v. ISBN: 3515029303.

An attempt to list all words used in the period 1100-1400, whether extinct or surviving, with special emphasis on the literary language. Indicates parallels in other Romance languages, giving history and examples of use of each word, with references to other studies. *Class No:* 804.0-3"01/14"

16th & 17th Centuries

[5776]
DUBOIS, J., *and others.* **Dictionnaire du français classique:** le XVIIe siecle. Paris, Larousse, 1992. 511p. Fr.200. (*Trésors du français.*) ISBN: 2033403289.

Earlier eds. as *Dictionnaire de la langue française classique.*

Over 5,000 entries for words from the classical literary texts of the 17th century, which have become obsolete or

.... *(contd.)*

whose meanings have changed. Illustrative quotations from Racine, Corneille, etc. Bibliography of sources.
Class No: 804.0-3"15/16"

[5777]
GREIMAS, A.J. *and* **KEANE, T.M. Dictionnaire du moyen français: français de la Renaissance.** Paris, Larousse, 1991. 600p. Fr.200. (*Trésors du français.*) ISBN: 203340322x.

Covers the vocabulary of texts from Froissart to Rabelais and Montaigne. *Class No:* 804.0-3"15/16"

[5778]
HUGUET, E. Dictionnaire de la langue française du seizième siècle. Paris, Champion (later Didier), 1925-67 (repr. Genève, Slatkine, 1982). 7v.

A dictionary of 16th-century words no longer in use or whose meanings have changed, profusely illustrated with quotations. Precise references to sources. *Class No:* 804.0-3"15/16"

Synonyms

[5779]
BATCHELOR, R.E. *and* **OFFORD, M.H. Using French synonyms.** Cambridge, Cambridge Univ. Press, 1993. vii,595p. £45. ISBN: 0521372771.

Follows the format of Batchelor's *Using Spanish synonyms* (*q.v.*), with synonyms grouped in 'semantic frames' and clearly explained and exemplified. Indexes of English and French terms, keyed to French frame titles.
Class No: 804.0-314

[5780]
BERTEAUD DU CHAZAUD, H. Dictionnaire des synonymes. Paris, Robert, 1994. x,768p. Fr.195. ISBN: 2850361933.

Very comprehensive coverage, with over 300,000 words and phrases grouped under *c.*30,000 entry words in a simple A-Z arrangement. 40,000 antonyms also included. Thoroughly cross-referenced. Bibliography (2p.).
Class No: 804.0-314

[5781]
The Cambridge French-English thesaurus. Lamy, M.-N., *ed.* Cambridge, Cambridge Univ. Press, 1998. xi,326p. £45. ISBN: 0521563488.

The first bilingual thesaurus of its kind has a classified arrangement with 14 main sections, 98 chapters and numbered subsections. For each concept it gives the usual French term, related words and synonyms, phrases, quotations and sayings - all with English equivalents. In many cases there are usage notes and warnings about "false friends". Indexes of French and English terms (8,000 of each) provide full access to this superb work.
Class No: 804.0-314

[5782]
GENOUVRIER, É., *and others.* **Nouveau dictionnaire des synonymes.** Nouv. éd. Paris, Larousse, 1992. 656p. Fr.140. ISBN: 2033409031.

1st ed. 1977.

Groups *c.*20,000 words under *c.*3,000 entry-words and illustrates meanings with exemplary sentences from current usage rather than direct quotes from literature. Makes good use of different type-faces. Cross-references and index.
Class No: 804.0-314

[5783]
Nouveau dictionnaire analogique. Niobey, G., *ed.* Nouv. éd. Paris, Larousse, 1991. viii,856p. illus. Fr.80. ISBN: 2037102011.

1st ed. 1979, superseding C. Maquet's *Dictionnaire analogique* (Larousse, 1936).

A very clearly presented thesaurus of related terms with *c.*15,000 words and phrases grouped below 2,000-plus keywords, A-Z. Uses an index rather than cluttering the sequence with cross-references. Etymologies provided for keywords. Includes some Duden-style labelled drawings.
Class No: 804.0-314

[5784]
Thésaurus Larousse: des idées aux mots, des mots aux idées. Péchoin, D., *ed.* 2e éd. Paris, Larousse, 1992. xxiv,1146p. £36.70. ISBN: 2033201481.

1st ed. 1991.

Roget-style thesaurus with synonyms grouped according to numbered senses under 873 headings. All terms listed in a 500-page index. *Class No:* 804.0-314

Loan Words

[5785]
REY-DEBOVE, J., *and others.* **Dictionnaire des anglicismes.** Nouv. éd. Paris, Robert, 1990. xix,1150p. Fr.179. (*Les Usuels du Robert.*) ISBN: 2850360279.

1st ed. 1980.

Lists *c.*10,000 English loanwords from 'aberration' to 'zoom', giving pronunciation, definition, date of introduction into French, quotation(s) and source. Bibliography has *c.*500 items. *Class No:* 804.0-316

Neologisms

[5786]
GILBERT, P. Dictionnaire des mots contemporains. Paris, Robert, 1980 (repr. 1985). xxv,739p. (*Les Usuels du Robert.*) ISBN: 2850360198.

Lists *c.*5,000 words which have entered the French language since 1960. Entries include definition, explanation, and dated quotations from periodicals, newspapers and books. Bibliography of sources (10p.). *Class No:* 804.0-316.1

Idioms

[5787]
BERNET, C. *and* **RÉZEAU, P. Dictionnaire du français parlé:** le monde des expressions familières. Paris, Seuil, 1989. 465p. ISBN: 2020109271.

A dictionary of contemporary, colloquial French with *c.*4,000 words and phrases listed under 800 headwords. Each term is defined and illustrated by a quotation from one of 500 books, newspapers and periodicals, which are listed in the bibliography. Index. *Class No:* 804.0-318

[5788]
HÉRAIL, R.J. *and* **LOVATT, E.A. Dictionary of modern colloquial French.** London, Routledge & Kegan Paul, 1984. xxi,327p. £10.99. ISBN: 0415058937.

8,000 entries for French colloquial terms with, wherever possible, 3 English definitions, 'the first register-keyed to the French, the second less colloquial, the third in what could be termed standard English' (*Preface*). Entries also include illustrative phrases, comments, anecdotes and historical information. No references to sources and no indication of pronunciation. *Class No:* 804.0-318

[5789]
REY, A. *and* **CHANTREAU, S. Dictionnaire des expressions et locutions.** Paris, Robert, 1993. xv,888p. £18.15. ISBN: 2850362158.

10,000 idiomatic phrases defined and explained, with date of first appearance, notes on evolution and a quote from literature in many cases. Arranged A-Z under keyword, with index of other significant words. Bibliography (12p.)
Class No: 804.0-318

Monoglot Dictionaries

[5790]
ACADÉMIE FRANÇAISE. Dictionnaire de l'Académie Française. 9e. éd. Paris, Imprimerie Nationale, 1986-90. fasc. 1-5. (in progress).

1st ed. 1694. 8th ed. 1932-35 (repr. Genève, Slatkine, 1979-82).

The very conservative 'official' dictionary of the language which has traditionally included few scientific, technical or foreign terms. Concerned only with words in current use and gives examples of usage, but not quotations as such. No etymologies. Fascicules 1-5 of the 9th ed. cover 'A-Encyclique'.

V.1 of 9th ed., *A-Enz*, published 1992 (834p. ISBN: 2110812494). *Class No:* 804.0-323.1

[5791]
Le Dictionnaire Hachette du français. Gatard, M., *ed.* Paris, Hachette, 1993. 1824p. ISBN: 2010188772.

A monolingual dictionary with 60,000 French words and 1,000 encyclopedic entries covering subjects like literature, art, history, law and science. An ideal companion to a bilingual dictionary, its layout allowing fuller descriptions of words.

The same publisher has produced the CD-ROM encyclopedic dictionary *Dictionnaire Hachette multimédia encyclopédique, 1998* (£56.95), with 80,000 entries, 4,500 high-definition full-screen images, 300 interactive maps, and hundreds of video clips, 3-D animations and audiorecordings. Includes links to the Internet, whence monthly updates can be updated. *Class No:* 804.0-323.1

[5792]
Grand dictionnaire Hachette encyclopédique. Nouv. éd. Paris, Hachette, 1994. 1620p. illus. maps. £44.99.

A relatively new encyclopedic dictionary (first published 1988), similar in scope to *Le Petit Larousse* but mixing general vocabulary and proper names in a single sequence of *c.*96,000 entries with 125,000 deinitions. Appended sections include lists of neologisms, anglicisms, verb conjugations and Nobel Prize winners. 3,500 illustrations. 295 maps.
Class No: 804.0-323.1

[5793]
Grand Larousse de la langue française. Guilbert, L., *and others, eds.* Paris, Larousse, 1971-78. 7v. (cxxviii,6729p.).

Covers the vocabulary of 19th- and 20th-century French, with scientific and technical terms very well represented. *c.*70,000 headwords, with pronunciation, etymology, date of first appearance, synonyms, antonyms, and quotations from literary sources. Throughout the dictionary, lengthy articles discussing concepts in grammar and linguistics are interspersed, giving it a secondary function as an encyclopedia of these subjects. V.7 has a bibliography of sources (97p.). *Class No:* 804.0-323.1

[5794]
Lexis: dictionnaire de la langue française. Dubois, J., *ed.* Nouv. éd. Paris, Larousse, 1992. xvi,2109p. illus. £38.95. ISBN: 2033202194.

1st ed. 1975

The best of the one-vol. Larousse language dictionaries, with *c.*76,000 entries and over 300,000 quotations and examples. Emphasises current vocabulary and is strong on scientific and technical terms. Includes Canadian, Belgian, Swiss and regional variants. Entries include etymology and date of first recorded use. Grammar summary appended (62p.). 90 plates with thematically-grouped illustrations.

Larousse have recently published a CD-ROM, *Dictionnaire Larousse de la langue française* (£13.95) which represents exceptional value for money, containing: *Dictionnaire de français* (50,000 entries), *Dictionnaire des synonymes* (400,000 synonyms), *Dictionnaire des analogies* and *Dictionnaire des citations* (10,000 quotations). *Class No:* 804.0-323.1

[5795]
MEL'ČUK, I., *and others.* **Dictionnaire explicatif et combinatoire du français contemporain.** Montréal, Les Presses de L'Université de Montréal, 1984-92. v.1-3 (in progress).

3 vols. have appeared so far of what the publishers claim is 'the first dictionary that provides the user with systematic and complete descriptions of each entry word.' Each entry has the same rigid structure, comprising a definition, a syntactic government pattern, a zone of lexical functions, and examples, the principal aim being to aid the user in finding out 'how to express X' rather than in understanding 'what X means.' 12 vols. are planned. *Class No:* 804.0-323.1

[5796]
Le Petit Larousse illustré, 1998. Paris, Larousse, 1997. 1784p. £34.99.

One of the most famous of all reference works, first published in 1856 and now appearing annually in a well-established format with 2 main sections: monolingual dictionary (59,000 headwords in this ed.) and encyclopedia (28,000 entries), giving brief biographical, historical and geographical data. Lists of classical and foreign quotations, plus French proverbs, divide the two sections. Over 3,800 colour illustrations and 289 maps. Also available on CD-ROM (£29.95).

The large-format ed. (£49.99. ISBN: 2033012980) has a supplement comprising world atlas, historical atlas and universal chronology. *Class No:* 804.0-323.1

[5797]
Le Petit Robert: dictionnaire alphabétique et analogique de la langue française. Rey-Debove, J. *and* Rey, A., *eds.* Nouv. éd. Paris, Robert; Glasgow, HarperCollins, 1994 (repr. with revisions 1995). xxxv,2551p. £55. ISBN: 2850363901, France; 0004705254, UK.

1st ed. 1967.

An abridgement of *Le Grand Robert*, forming one of the best single-vol. monolingual dictionaries available. Over 59,000 headwords, with pronunciation, style labels, etymology, quotations (from 500 classical and contemporary authors, plus periodicals and films), examples of use, synonyms and antonyms. This ed., effectively the 3rd, represents a major revision.

Also available on CD-ROM (£69.95. ISBN: 5639213014), with hypertext links connecting synonyms, antonyms and related words. *Class No:* 804.0-323.1

[5798]
ROBERT, P. Le Grand Robert de la langue française: dictionnaire alphabétique et analogique de la langue française. 2e. éd., entièrement revue et enrichie par A. Rey. Paris, Robert, 1985. 9v. £850. ISBN: 2850360996.

1st ed. 1951-64 (6v.); *Supplément*, 1970.

An outstanding dictionary, compiled on historical principles and giving comprehensive coverage of French from the 15th century to the present. Over 80,000 entries, showing etymology, pronunciation, analogies, synonyms and antonyms, and the history of the word's development. *c.*160,000 quotations, with precise references. Bibliography (49p.) in v.9 lists 2,000 featured authors and their works.

Available on CD-ROM as *Le Robert électronique* (£795. ISBN: 2850361089). *Class No:* 804.0-323.1

[5799]
Le Robert méthodique: dictionnaire méthodique du français actuel. Rey-Debove, J., *ed.* Nouv. éd., rev. et corr. Paris, Robert, 1985. xx,1617p. Fr.209. ISBN: 2850360899.

1st ed. 1982.

Groups over 34,000 words within entries for individual words or word-elements, and defines and explains them by means of numerous illustrative phrases. Makes good use of symbols and typefaces. An excellent tool for vocabulary development. *Class No:* 804.0-323.1

[5800]
Trésor de la langue française: dictionnaire de la langue du XIXe et du XXe siècle (1789-1960). Quémada, B. *and* Imbs, P., *eds.* Paris, Centre National de la Recherche Scientifique, 1972-94. 16v.

Originally planned as a very comprehensive historical dictionary of 19th- and 20th-century French, but the work's scope was reduced after 2 vols. in order to allow completion in *c.*15 vols. Entries comprise extended definition, quotations from texts (now much reduced), pronunciation, orthography, etymology, lengthy notes on history and usage, and references to other sources of information. *Class No:* 804.0-323.1

Bilingual Dictionaries

[5801]
Collins-Robert comprehensive French dictionary. Glasgow, HarperCollins, 1995. 2v. £35 per vol.

V.1 *French-English.* 1250p. ISBN: 0004702468.

V.2 *English-French.* 1250p. ISBN: 0004708962.

One of the largest bilingual dictionaries available, which claims over 400,000 references and 650,000 translations, plus a 20-page supplement of maps of French- and English-speaking countries and extensive thesauruses of the 2 languages. *Class No:* 804.0-323.2

[5802]
Collins-Robert French dictionary: French-English / English-French. Atkins, B.T., *and others, eds.* 5th ed. London, HarperCollins; Paris, Robert, 1998. xl+2081+62+45p. £23.99. ISBN: 0004705262.

1st ed. 1978; 4th ed. 1995.

An outstanding single-vol. bilingual dictionary resulting from collaboration between French and English lexicographers, which claims over 350,000 references. The emphasis is firmly on contemporary usage, with illustrative phrases taken from the 'Bank of English' and 'Banque de français moderne' corpuses. With each new ed. the layout and presentation has been improved and the 5th is no exception, as the structure of more complex entries has been simplified. The dictionary is particularly notable for its

....*(contd.)*
systematic use of labels and symbols to indicate style, register, etc.; *e.g.* 1 to 3 asterisks attached to a term, from slightly informal to taboo. Acronyms and abbreviations in main sequence. 'Language in use: a grammar of communication in French and English' forms a very useful appendix (62p.).

Also available on CD-ROM at £49.99 (ISBN: 0003710181).

Collins-Robert concise French dictionary: French-English / English-French (3rd ed. Glasgow, HarperCollins; Paris, Robert, 1996. xiii+551+72p. £15.99. ISBN: 0004707060) claims 133,000 references and 215,000 translations. New to 3rd ed. is an expanded supplement (72p.) incorporating a guide to business and social correspondence in French.
Class No: 804.0-323.2

[5803]

Larousse French dictionary: French-English / English-French. Carney, F., *and others, eds.* Unabridged ed. Paris, Larousse, 1994. xxi+924+viii+996p. £25. ISBN: 2034301005.

Claims to be the most comprehensive French bilingual dictionary available, with over 300,000 references and 500,000 translations, including extensive coverage of professional, technical and literary vocabulary and of Swiss, Belgian and Canadian French. Distinguished from its rivals by its thousands of encyclopedic and cultural entries covering politics, society, education, law, the arts and history, with further information in boxes on key 'culture-bound' terms: 'an important and highly commendable innovation' (*TLS*, no.4781, Nov. 18, 1994, p.12), although it necessitates the use of rather small print throughout . Pronunciation (IPA) given for all headwords. Abbreviations and acronyms in main sequence, which is arranged in 3 columns. 16p. of maps.

A single vol. of this size can be unwieldy, but a 2-vol. ed. is available (£35. ISBN: 203401300x).

CD-ROM version available as *Grand dictionnaire Larousse: anglais-français / français-anglais* (£33.80).
Class No: 804.0-323.2

[5804]

—Larousse standard French dictionary: French-English / English-French. Carney, F., *and others, eds.* Paris, Larousse, 1994. 1968p. £15.99. ISBN: 2034302508.

Derived from the unabridged *Larousse* and still very substantial, with over 220,000 references and 400,000 translations, including many encyclopedic and cultural entries. A distinctive feature of this ed. are special modules offering usage advice within the main sequence.

The desk dictionary in this series is *Larousse concise French dictionary* (1994. 1248p. £9.99. ISBN: 2034303008), with over 90,000 references and 120,000 translations.
Class No: 804.0-323.2

[5805]

MANSION, J.E. Harrap's standard French dictionary, rev. and ed. by D.M. and R.P.L. Ledésert. Rev. ed. London, Harrap, 1977-80. 4v. £40 per vol. ISBN: 0245509720, v.1; 0245509739, v.2; 0245518592, v.3; 0245518606, v.4.

Vols. 1-2, *French-English*; vols. 3-4, *English-French*.

French-English section first published 1934; English-French section first published 1939. Later published together as *Harrap's Standard French and English dictionary*.

A complete revision of a dictionary which has come to be regarded as the most comprehensive and authoritative of its kind and which the publishers claim is the largest bilingual reference work in existence. Nearly 250,000 headwords and

....*(contd.)*
over 500,000 references, embracing all aspects of modern spoken and written French, including technical terms, slang, neologisms, and the French of Canada, Belgium, etc. Numerous idiomatic phrases. Entries give pronunciation but not etymology. The English word-list includes many US and Commonwealth terms. Lists of abbreviations in vols. 2 and 4. *Class No:* 804.0-323.2

[5806]

—Harrap's shorter French dictionary: French-English / anglais-français. Goldie, J., *and others, eds.* New ed. Edinburgh, Chambers Harrap, 1996. xix+1118+76+64+984p. £30. ISBN: 024560524x.

1st ed. 1982.

A condensed version of *Harrap's Standard French and English dictionary,* which has been thoroughly revised and expanded.

Claims over 550,000 translations, including numerous compounds, phrases and idioms. Entries include pronunciation (IPA) in both sections, context indicators, style/register labels, and grammatical information. American English and Canadian French usage are well covered and clearly indicated. Appended sections on English grammar (76p.) and French grammar (64p.) have been revised and are linked to the dictionary by 1,400 cross-references.

Also available on CD-ROM at £39.99 (ISBN: 0245606165). *Class No:* 804.0-323.2

[5807]

The Oxford-Hachette French dictionary. Corréard, M.-H., *ed.* 2nd ed. Oxford, Oxford Univ. Press, 1997. lx,1949p. £28.99. ISBN: 0198600674.

1st ed. 1994.

A major rival for *Collins-Robert* which claims over 355,000 words and phrases and over 540,000 translations. The language, taken from large electronic text collections, is very up-to-date and the layout and typography are very attractive. Abbreviations, acronyms and proper names in main sequence. Pronunciation (IPA) given for all headwords, with US variations indicated. Clear guidance notes in both languages. Extra features include: notes on usage within numbered boxes (50 in each section - indexed and cross-referenced); guide to effective communication, including correspondence, telephone and e-mail (78p.); verb lists; maps. New to 2nd ed. is an extremely useful encyclopedic A-Z of contemporary France (20p.), covering geography, culture, media, politics, law, etc.

Also available on CD-ROM at £49.99 (ISBN: 0192683071).

The Concise Oxford-Hachette French dictionary, ed. by M.-H. Corréard and V.Grundy (1995. xxxviii,1447p. £15.99. ISBN: 0198643292) includes over 175,000 words and phrases and 270,000 translations and has a 58-page guide to correspondence. *Class No:* 804.0-323.2

Illustrated Works

[5808]

BRAGONNIER, R. *and* **FISHER, D. Le Whats what:** la première encyclopédie visuelle franco-anglaise. Nouv. éd. Paris, Mengès, 1983. xii,594p. ISBN: 2856201970.

1st ed. 1981, also published Maplewood, N.J., Hammond, as *What's what: a visual glossary of the physical world.*

Unusual for a pictorial dictionary in having many *photographs* as well as drawings, each labelled in French

.... *(contd.)*
and English. The illustrations are arranged in 12 subject categories and there are French and English (*i.e.* American) indexes of *c.*30,000 terms. *Class No:* 804.0-323.2(0.025)

[5809]
CORBEIL, J-C. *and* **ARCHAMBAULT, A. Harrap's visual French-English dictionary.** London, Harrap; New York, Facts on File, 1987. 924p. ISBN: 0245545964, UK; 0816015457, US.

US title is *The Facts on File English-French visual dictionary.*

Contains the 3,000-plus illustrations from *The Facts on File visual dictionary* (*q.v.*) with captions in English and French (the latter in blue). Separate indexes in English and French appear in 3 formats: general, thematic and specialized.

British users should note that unlike the *Facts on File visual dictionary* this has not been revised for the UK market but is a direct reproduction of the original Canadian edition, published under licence by Harrap. North American English therefore predominates, with British terms in italics, whilst the French is primarily Québecois/Canadian with European French variations alongside where appropriate.

Colour version published 1992 as *Le Visuel: dictionnaire thématique français-anglais* (New York, French & European. 928p. $115. ISBN: 0785980253).
Class No: 804.0-323.2(0.025)

[5810]
The Oxford-Duden pictorial French & English dictionary. 2nd ed. Oxford, Oxford Univ. Press, 1996. 880p. £27.99. ISBN: 0198645376.

1st ed. 1983.

See entry for *The Oxford-Duden pictorial German & English dictionary.* Indexes in French and English.
Class No: 804.0-323.2(0.025)

Grammar

[5811]
BYRNE, L.S.R. *and* **CHURCHILL, E.L. A Comprehensive French grammar.** Price, G., *ed.* 4th ed. Oxford, Blackwell, 1993. xv,584p. £12.99 (*Blackwell reference grammars.*) ISBN: 0631181652.

1st ed. 1950; 3rd ed. 1986.

A major revision of this standard English-language grammar was carried out by Price for the 3rd ed., with the 2-section division of the earlier eds. (basic rules followed by fuller explanations of difficult topics) abandoned and the word-lists dropped. All the information on a given topic can now be found in one place within the 715 numbered paragraphs. Further revisions effected for 4th ed. Numerous examples of usage, all with English translation. Index.

See also *Modern French grammar: a practical guide to grammar and usage*, by M. Lang & I. Perez (London, Routledge, 1996. 368p. £45. ISBN: 0415098513).
Class No: 804.0-5

[5812]
GREVISSE, M. *and* **GOOSSE, A.,** *ed.* **Le Bon usage:** grammaire française. 13e. éd. Paris, Duculot, 1993. 1800p. £52.50. ISBN: 2801110450.

1st ed. 1916; 12th ed. 1986.

The standard prescriptive grammar of French, which has 'attained monumental status and stature ... and reached almost legendary authority as the ultimate arbiter in matters of French grammar and usage' (*Modern Language Review*, v.83(1), Jan. 1988, p.184-86).

.... *(contd.)*
The 12th ed., the first to appear since Grevisse's death in 1980, represented a complete revision, with new terminology introduced, various items of grammar regrouped in accordance with modern practice, and most of the previous edition's many footnotes absorbed into the text. A phenomenal amount of detailed information is contained in over 1,100 numbered paragraphs, with numerous examples drawn from literature and contemporary usage. More attention is now paid to national and regional variations of French. Extensive bibliography and detailed index.
Class No: 804.0-5

Etymology

[5813]
BLOCH, O. *and* **WARTBURG, W. von. Dictionnaire étymologique de la langue française.** 10e. éd. Paris, Presses Universitaires de France, 1994. 720p. Fr.380. ISBN: 2130429149; 2130440657.

1st ed. 1942.

A scholarly etymological dictionary of contemporary French with over 10,000 entries. Considers words only in their basic meanings and gives dates of earliest appearance, historical information, and derivatives.

An alternative source is E. Baumgartner and P. Ménard's *Dictionnaire étymologique et historique de la langue française* (Paris, Le Livre de Poche, 1996. xvi,848p. ISBN: 2253130184). *Class No:* 804.0-54

[5814]
DAUZAT, A., & *others.* **Dictionnaire étymologique et historique du français.** Nouv. éd. Paris, Larousse, 1993. xlv,822p. Fr.200. (*Trésors du français.*) ISBN: 2033403297.

1st ed. 1964.

Over 20,000 entries, giving brief etymological information, date of first use, reference to source, and historical evolution. Bibliography of sources (6p.). Introductory essay on the history of the language. A major revision, with many new scientfic and tecnological terms.
Class No: 804.0-54

[5815]
Dictionnaire historique de la langue française: mille ans de la langue française. Rey, A., *ed.* Paris, Robert, 1993. 2v. Fr.920. ISBN: 2850361879.

A major new etymological dictionary published to mark 1,000 years of the French language. Each headword's history is described in great detail (but avoiding specialist language as far as possible), from the earliest sources to current usage. Lengthy, narrative entries include information on derivatives, figurative uses and phrases, with dates of first occurrences. A great achievement, making etymology accessible to the widest range of readers. *Class No:* 804.0-54

[5816]
PICOCHE, J. Dictionnaire étymologique du français. Paris, Robert, 1993. vii,619p. ISBN: 2850361941.

*c.*4,000 entries, with each word dated by century, its original sense explained and its variant forms listed.
Class No: 804.0-54

[5817]

WARTBURG, W. von. Französisches etymologisches Wörterbuch: eine Darstellung des galloromanischen Sprachschatzes. Bonn, Klopp; Basel, Helbing & Lichtenhahn, 1928- . v.1- . (in progress).

A comprehensive, scholarly etymological dictionary which is arranged by the orginal Vulgar Latin words and traces the historical development of all variant forms in great detail. Published in *Lieferungen*, numbered consecutively but forming parts of different volumes. At least 20 vols. have been completed, vols. 1-14 covering Latin-derived words, A-Z, and later vols. covering words from other languages.

Beiheft: Ortsnamenregister. Literaturverzeichnis. Übersichtskarte. (2. Aufl. Tübingen, Mohr, 1950. xiv, 135p.).

Supplement zur 2. Auflage des Bibliographischen Beiheftes. (Basel, Zbinden, 1957. 54p.). *Class No:* 804.0-54

Provençal

[5818]

LEVY, E. Petit dictionnaire provençal-français. 4th ed. Heidelberg, Winter, 1966. viii,387p.

A facsimile reprint of a dictionary first published 1909. About 20,000 medieval Provençal entry-words with French equivalents. *Class No:* 804.90

[5819]

MISTRAL, F. Lou Tresor dóu felibrige, ou Dictionnaire provençal-français; embrassant les divers dialectes de la langue d'oc moderne. Aix-en-Provence, Veuve Remondet-Aubin, 1879-87. 2v.

The standard dictionary of modern Provençal. *Class No:* 804.90

[5820]

RAYNOUARD, M. Lexique romane, ou Dictionnaire de la langue des troubadours. Paris, Silvestre, 1838-43. 6v.

The standard dictionary of medieval Provençal. Considerably supplemented by E. Levy's *Provenzalisches Supplement-Wörterbuch* (Leipzig, Reisland, 1894-1924. 8v.). *Class No:* 804.90

Catalan

[5821]

ALCOVER SUREDA, A.M. Diccionari català-valencià-balear: inventari lexical y etimològich... Palma de Mallorca, Alcover, 1930-62. 10v. illus.

A comprehensive dictionary of Catalan, as spoken and written in Valencia, Catalonia, the Balearics, and Sardinia. Entries include quotations, etymologies and regional variations. Bibliography of sources (37p.) in v.1. 2nd ed., updated and corrected, was published in 1964. *Class No:* 804.99

[5822]

Catalan dictionary: Catalan-English / English-Catalan. London, Routledge, 1994. xxxix+339+iii+269p. £19.99. ISBN: 0415108020.

Originally published Barcelona, Bibliograf, 1993.

18,000 entries in each section, plus many collocations and idiomatic phrases. Concentrates on words in common use, avoiding obsolete, slang and technical terms. Pronunciation (IPA) given for all headwords. Proper names, abbreviations and acronyms in main sequence. Catalan section also includes some words from Valencian, from North-Western

....*(contd.)*

Catalan and from Catalan spoken in Roussillon and the Balearic Islands. Summary of Catalan grammar (24p.). *Class No:* 804.99

[5823]

COROMINAS, J. Diccionari etimològic i complementari de la llengua catalana. Barcelona, Curial Edicions Catalanes, 1983-91. 9v. ISBN: 8472561739.

A scholarly etymological dictionary with lengthy, detailed entries which include numerous references to sources. *Class No:* 804.99

[5824]

Diccionari de la llengua catalana. Barcelona, Enciclopèdia Catalana, 1995. lvii,1908p. £34.95. ISBN: 8441224773.

A comprehensive single-vol. monolingual dictionary with *c.*50,000 entries. *Class No:* 804.99

[5825]

OLIVA, S. *and* **BUXTON, A. Diccionari anglès-català.** 2. ed. Barcelona, Enciclopèdia Catalana, 1985 (repr. 1991). 1109p. £21.95.

Has *c.*25,000 entries, with numerous idioms. The companion vol. is *Diccionari català-anglès* (1986. 842p. £21.95). *Class No:* 804.99

Italian Language

Bibliographies

[5826]

HALL, R.A. Bibliografia della linguistica italiana. 2. ed., riv. e aggiornata. Firenze, Sansoni, 1958. 3v.

1st ed. Baltimore, Md., Linguistic Soc. of America, 1941, as *Bibliography of Italian linguistics*.

Lists nearly 7,000 items published since *c.*1860 in 4 sections covering: history of the Italian language; description of the language; Italian dialectology; and history of Italian linguistics. V.3 has 5 indexes: authors and anonymous titles; localities and dialects; Italian words; etyma; and technical subjects.

Supplemented by: *Primo supplemento decennale (1956-1966)* (Firenze, Sansoni, 1969. 524p.), with nearly 2,500 items; *Secondo supplemento decennale (1966-76)* (Pisa, Giardini, 1980. 388p.), with *c.*3,500 items; *Terzo supplemento decennale* (Pisa, Giardini, 1988. xi,620p.), with over 6,000 items. *Class No:* 805.0(01)

[5827]

Letteratura italiana repertorio automatizzato (LIRA): CD-ROM bibliografico della lingua e della letteratura italiana, dal 1986 al 1995. Aschero, B., *ed.* Trieste, Alcione, 1996. CD-ROM.

See entry at 850(01). *Class No:* 805.0(01)

[5828]

MALATO, E., ***ed.*** **Bibliografia generale della lingua e della letteratura italiana (BiGLI),** v.1-. 1991-. Roma, Salerno Editrice, 1993-.

See entry at 850(01). *Class No:* 805.0(01)

[5829]

MULJAČIĆ, Ž. Scaffale italiano: avviamento bibliografico allo studio della lingua italiana. Scandicci, La Nuova Italia, 1991. 374p. ISBN: 8822109740.

Supersedes the author's *Introduzione allo studio della lingua italiana* (Torino, Einaudi, 1971).

Annotated entries on key works on topics in Italian linguistics, arranged in 22 chapters covering bibliographies, journals, grammar, dialect, etc., followed by a bibliography of 1,300 books and periodical articles. Includes non-Italian publications. Index of names, but no subject index. 'As a general bibliographical introduction to Italian linguistics, this book is second to none' (*Reference Reviews Europe Online*, 96-2/3-215). *Class No:* 805.0(01)

Histories

[5830]

MAIDEN, M. A Linguistic history of Italian. Cambridge, Cambridge Univ. Press, 1995. xviii,300p. £47. (*Longman linguistics library*.) ISBN: 0582059291.

1. Introduction - 2. History of the sound system - 3. Structural evolution of nouns, adjectives and verbs - 4. History of sentence structure - 5. Variation in modern Italian. Numbered subsections. Bibliography (12p.). Index. *Class No:* 805.0(091)

Usage

[5831]

BROWNE, V. Odd pairs & false friends: dizionario di false analogie e ambigue affinità fra inglese e italiano. Bologna, Zanichelli, 1987. 267p. £23.75. ISBN: 8808029468.

A very clearly presented dictionary of 'false friends', with over 1,000 entries for pairs of Italian and English words which can cause translation problems. Numerous examples of usage. English words used as entry-terms, with index of Italian words.

See also R. Ferguson's *Italian false friends* (Toronto, Univ. of Toronto Press, 1995. 138p. £15. ISBN: 0802069487). *Class No:* 805.0-06

[5832]

GABRIELLI, A. Dizionario linguistico moderno: guida pratica per scrivere e parlar bene. 5. ed. Verona, Mondadori, 1969. 1192p.

1st ed. 1956.

A practical manual of Italian usage comprising an alphabetical section covering stylistic and grammatical rules, neologisms, idiomatic and dialect phrases, etc., and a word-list indicating spelling, gender, and derivatives, which includes some proper names. *Class No:* 805.0-06

[5833]

PITTÀNO, G. Così si dice (e si scrive): dizionario grammaticale e degli usi della lingua italiana. Nuova ed., ampl. e riv. Bologna, Zanichelli, 1993. 381p.

1st ed. Milano, Rusconi, 1988, as *La Lingua italiana oggi*.

Alphabetically arranged entries for words which can cause difficulties in terms of spelling, usage, etc., interspersed with boxed articles (in many cases occupying a full page) on points of grammar and usage. *Class No:* 805.0-06

Dictionaries & Vocabularies

Synonyms

[5834]

CESANA, G. Dizionario ragionato dei sinonimi e dei contrari. 3. ed. Milano, De Vecchi, 1988. 779p.

Over 14,000 terms are covered in 1,958 lengthy, explanatory entries. Index of terms. *Class No:* 805.0-314

[5835]

COPPO, L. Dizionario dei sinonimi: vocabolario analogico della lingua italiana. Milano, Mondadori. ISBN: 8804331011.

20,000 headwords, each set in context with often copious examples of usage. *Class No:* 805.0-314

[5836]

GIOCONDI, M. Dizionario dei sinonimi e dei contrari. Firenze, Paradigma, 1988. 725p.

10,500 entries, with lengthy, clearly differentiated lists of synonyms and antonyms for each term. *Class No:* 805.0-314

[5837]

PITTÀNO, G. Sinonimi e contrari: dizionario fraseologico delle parole equivalenti, analoghe e contrarie. Bologna, Zanichelli, 1987. 863p. £32.95.

Over 34,000 entries, listing synonyms, antonyms and, in some cases, phrases containing the entry term. *Class No:* 805.0-314

Monoglot Dictionaries

[5838]

BATTAGLIA, S. Grande dizionario della lingua italiana. Torino, Unione Tipografico-Editrice Torinese, 1961-96. v.1-18 (in progress).

Vols. 1-18 cover 'A-Sikkhismo'.

A comprehensive, scholarly work, similar to the *OED*, with numerous quotations arranged chronologically but not dated. Cumulative fascicules, under the title *Indice degli autori citate*, provide precise bibliographic details of all the cited works. Entries include etymologies. Replaces *Dizionario della lingua italiana* by N. Tommaseo and B. Bellini (Turino, UTET, 1861-79. 4v. in 8). *Class No:* 805.0-323.1

[5839]

DEVOTO, G. *and* **OLI, G.C. Dizionario della lingua italiana.** Firenze, Le Monnier, 1995. 2196p. £46.95. ISBN: 8800510833.

The latest ed. of a regularly updated dictionary. Over 80,000 entry-words, with brief definitions, etymologies and examples of usage. No longer illustrated. Also available on CD-ROM (£95.50). *Class No:* 805.0-323.1

[5840]

GABRIELLI, A. Grande dizionario illustrato della lingua italiana. [Verona], Mondadori, 1989. 2v. (xv,4434p.). illus.

Claims 250,000 words and expressions, including abbreviations, neologisms, scientific terms, and archaic terms encountered in literary studies. Entries give syllabification, etymology (including century of acceptance) and many examples of usage. 40,000 quotations from 400 literary authors. Line drawings and colour plates. Appendices include terms for natives of Italian towns, Italian forenames (with etymology and explanation) and list of cited authors. *Class No:* 805.0-323.1

[5841]

Il Grande dizionario Garzanti della lingua italiana. Felici, L., *ed.* 2nd ed. Milano, Garzanti, 1993. xvii,2300p. £48.50.

Supersedes *Dizionario Garzanti della lingua italiana* (1965).

The largest single-vol. dictionary, with *c.*270,000 words, including many neologisms and foreign words. There are numerous Duden-style line drawings and many of the entries include etymologies. Appendices include 62 tables of specialist vocabulary and list of abbreviations.
Class No: 805.0-323.1

[5842]

Il Nuovo Zingarelli: vocabolario della lingua italiana. Dogliotti, M. *and* Rosiello, L., *eds.* 12. ed. Bologna, Zanichelli, 1993 (repr. 1998) 2144p. £56. ISBN: 8808000052.

1st ed. 1922; 11th ed. 1984.

Claims coverage of 134,000 words and 370,000 senses. Etymologies for 65,000 words. Over 6,000 quotations from literature. 4,500 line drawings and 420 colour illustrations. Appendices include lists of abbreviations, proper names and proverbs, and classified table of specialist vocabulary. 1998 reprint includes 400 new terms. Also available on CD-ROM (£61). *Class No:* 805.0-323.1

Bilingual Dictionaries

[5843]

The Cambridge Italian dictionary. Reynolds, B., *ed.* Cambridge, Cambridge Univ. Press, 1962-81. 2v.

V.1 *Italian-English.* 1962. xxxi,899p. ISBN: 0521060591.

V.2 *English-Italian.* 1981. xix,843p. ISBN: 0521087082.

V.1 has *c.*50,000 entry-words, including a great deal of vocabulary from specialist fields (*e.g.* music, technology, zoology), for which subject experts have provided definitions. Many obsolete words are also included.

V.2 has *c.*35,000 entries, the vocabulary being largely that of British English, with Americanisms only included if prevalent in the UK. Again, many specialist terms are included, making the dictionary particularly useful for translators.

Cambridge-Signorelli Italian-English / English-Italian dictionary, ed. by M. Pappini (Cambridge, Cambridge Univ. Press; Milan, Signorelli, 1986. 2276p. ISBN: 0521327024) is a single-vol. abridgement, adapted for Italian users.
Class No: 805.0-323.2

[5844]

The Collins-Sansoni Italian dictionary: English-Italian / Italian-English. Macchi, V., *ed.* 3rd ed. Firenze, Sansoni; London, Collins, 1988. 2277p. £40. ISBN: 0004335759.

1st ed. 1975; 2nd ed. 1981.

Claims over 240,000 references with a total of *c.*570,000 translations. Good coverage of contemporary idiomatic usage. Strong on neologisms, with 12,000 new entries collated since 2nd ed. Includes abbreviations and proper names. Pronunciation given for English headwords (IPA), with stress indicated for Italian. Like most Collins bilingual dictionaries, represents good value for money.

Collins Italian dictionary (1536p. £19.99. ISBN: 000470293x) is smaller but still very substantial, with over 160,000 references and 230,000 translations and a very useful 'Language in use' supplement. *Class No:* 805.0-323.2

[5845]

Harrap's shorter Italian dictionary / Il Nuovo Ragazzini. Ragazzini, G., *ed.* 2nd ed. Bologna, Zanichelli, 1988; London, Harrap, 1989. 2144p. £29.95. ISBN: 0245548378.

Supersedes Ragazzini's *Dizionario inglese-italiano/ italiano-inglese* (Bologna, Zanichelli, 1968).

A highly-regarded, up-to-date bilingual dictionary with over 60,000 entries in each section and numerous illustrative phrases and idioms. Includes proper names within the main sequences but also has appended lists. *Class No:* 805.0-323.2

[5846]

—RAGAZZINI, G. *and* BIAGI, A. Il Nuovo Ragazzini / Biagi concise: dizionario inglese e italiano. 2nd ed. Bologna, Zanichelli, 1986; Oxford, Oxford Univ. Press, 1993. 1,200p. £19.99. ISBN: 0198645074.

English title is *Concise Italian dictionary: English-Italian / Italian-English.*

Claims 120,000 references and 200,000 translations, but let down by tiny print. Both sections have appended lists of forenames, surnames, geographical names, abbreviations and proverbs. *Class No:* 805.0-323.2

[5847]

Il Nuovo dizionario Hazon Garzanti: inglese-italiano / italiano-inglese. Milano, Garzanti, 1990. xvi,2430p. £49.50. ISBN: 8811103215.

1st ed. 1961 as *Grande dizionario, inglese-italiano/ italiano-inglese.*

This long overdue revision puts Hazon back at the forefront of modern English-Italian dictionaries. Primarily intended for Italian users, it provides phonetic transcription for the English entries only. Noted for its comprehensiveness, reviewers suggesting that there is very little in other major dictionaries which is absent from *Hazon.* 135,000 headwords, including over 58,000 specialist terms. Includes *c.*2,000 quotations from literary sources.
Class No: 805.0-323.2

[5848]

The Oxford-Duden pictorial Italian & English dictionary. Oxford, Clarendon Press, 1995. 384+95p. illus. £25. ISBN: 0198645163.

See entry for *The Oxford-Duden pictorial German & English dictionary*. Indexes in Italian and English.
Class No: 805.0-323.2

[5849]

Sansoni-Harrap standard Italian and English dictionary. Macchi, V., *ed.* 2nd ed. Firenze, Sansoni; London, Harrap, 1970-76. 4v. £37.50 per vol. ISBN: 024559633x, v.1; 0245596348, v.2; 0245596356, v.3; 0245596364, v.4.

Pt.1 *Italian-English.* 1970-72. 2v.

Pt.2 *English-Italian.* 1973-76. 2v.

Claims to be the most comprehensive Italian and English dictionary ever compiled, with *c.*150,000 headwords in pt.1 and *c.*170,000 in pt.2, plus numerous phrases. Includes proper names, abbreviations, scientific and technical terms, neologisms, colloquialisms, slang, and regionalisms. Pronunciation indicated for English headwords (IPA). Stress given for Italian headwords, with value of e, o, s, and z. American and British English given equal treatment. All botanical and zoological terms accompanied by Latin name.
Class No: 805.0-323.2

[5850]

Scaffale elettronico-dizionari. Bologna, Zanichelli, 1989.

A CD-ROM which contains an Italian dictionary, an Italian thesaurus, an Italian style manual, an Italian-English dictionary, a dictionary of Italian-English false friends, an Italian-French dictionary, and a dictionary of Italian-French false friends. Software and interface: Microsoft Bookshelf. Information can be accessed using full-text searching, a table of contents, or specialized indexes. Integrated with most popular word processors. *Class No:* 805.0-323.2

Grammar

[5851]

PROUDFOOT, A. *and* **CARDO, F. Modern Italian grammar:** a practical guide. London, Routledge, 1997. 440p. £45. ISBN: 0415098491.

In 2 sections, the first covering traditional grammatical categories like word order, nouns, verbs, etc., with the second organized around language functions, such as expressing preferences or seeking information. Numerous examples, thorough cross-referencing and indexing. No prior knowledge of grammatical terms is assumed and a glossary is provided. The series includes similar titles on French, German and Spanish. *Class No:* 805.0-5

Etymology

[5852]

BATTISTI, C. *and* **ALESSIO, G. Dizionario etimologico italiano.** Firenze, Barbèra, 1950-57. 5v. (xxxi,4132p.).

A well-established etymological dictionary with *c.*80,000 entries, giving derivations from Latin, approximate date of introduction into Italian, variants and similarities in other languages, as well as definitions. Includes both contemporary and archaic literary terms, selected technical and foreign terms, outstanding dialect words, suffixes and prefixes. Examples are dated whenever possible.
Class No: 805.0-54

[5853]

CORTELAZZO, M. *and* **ZOLLI, P. Dizionario etimologico della lingua italiana.** Bologna, Zanichelli, 1979-88. 5v. (1470p.). £99.75.

Over 15,000 entries, with numerous quotations to support the etymologies. Bibliography of sources (13p.) appears in each vol. *Class No:* 805.0-54

[5854]

PFISTER, M. LEI: Lessico etimologico italiano. Wiesbaden, Reichert, 1979-98. fasc.1-57 (in progress).

A very scholarly etymological dictionary of the Italian language and its dialects. Entries include detailed references to sources and also citations to other dictionaries and linguistic studies. Fasc. 1-54 form vols. 1-5.

Supplemento bibliografico published 1991 (vi,271p. ISBN: 3882265051). *Class No:* 805.0-54

Rumanian

[5855]

ACADEMIA REPUBLICII SOCIALISTE ROMÂNIA. Dicţionarul explicativ al limbii române. Bucuresti, Editura Academiei Republicii Socialiste România, 1975. 1049p. illus.

*c.*60,000 entries. 'The most exhaustive one-volume monolingual dictionary of recent years. It incorporates many neologisms that have entered the language since the war and indicates stress but does not give phonetic transcriptions' (Deletant, A. and Deletant, D., *Romania*, 1985, p.126).
Class No: 805.90

[5856]

ACADEMIA REPUBLICII SOCIALISTE ROMÂNIA. Institutul de Lingvistică. **Dicţionar englez-român.** Leviţchi, L., *ed.* Bucureşti, Editura Academiei Republicii Socialiste România, 1974. xxxii,825p.

A very comprehensive English-Romanian dictionary, with *c.*120,000 entries. Intended for the use of Romanians, giving American and British pronunciation of English terms.
Class No: 805.90

[5857]

Dicţionarul limbii române. Bucureşti, 1906-44; 1965-83. v.1-11.

Vols. 1-11: A-Twist.

Vols. 1-4 and 3 fascicules of v.5 (covering A-Loj) were published 1906-44 by the Romanian Academy. Publication resumed in 1965 under the auspices of the Academia Republicii Populare Române and has reached v.11.

An authoritative, comprehensive dictionary of the Romanian language, compiled on historical principles with etymologies and examples of usage. The earlier vols. include French equivalents. *Class No:* 805.90

[5858]

LEVIŢCHI, L. Dicţionar român-englez. 3. ed. Bucureşti, Editura Ştiinţifică, 1973. 1085p.

1st ed. 1960.

30,000 entries. Intended primarily for Romanian students of English, but nevertheless useful for students of Romanian because so many idiomatic expressions are included.

A companion vol. is *Dicţionar englez-român*, by L. Leviţchi and A. Bantaş (Bucureşti, Editura Ştiinţifică, 1974. 1068p.). *Class No:* 805.90

[5859]

PANOVF, I. New Pocket Rumanian dictionary: Rumanian-English / English-Rumanian. New York, Hippocrene, 1983. 828p.

Originally published Bucharest, 1982.

Small in size, but contains *c.*30,000 entries and an extensive guide to Romanian grammar and pronunciation.
Class No: 805.90

[5860]

SCHÖNKRON, M. Rumanian-English and English-Rumanian dictionary, with an entirely new up-to-date supplement of new words, English-Rumanian, including important colloquial and technical terms and useful idioms. New York, Ungar, 1952 (repr. Hippocrene, 1991). xxiv+235+482+19p. £17.50. ISBN: 0870529862.

*c.*17,500 Rumanian-English entries and *c.*21,500 English-Rumanian entries. Supplement adds *c.*90 new words. 'Contains many anachronisms, with regard to both its vocabulary and its use of the now obsolete Romanian orthography of â for î. It is consequently of limited use to the student of the contemporary language' (Deletant, A. and Deletant, D., *Romania*, 1985, p.129). *Class No:* 805.90

Romansch

[5861]

SOCIETÀ RETORUMANTSCHA. Dicziunari rumantsch grischun ... . Pult, C., *and others, eds.* Cuoira, Bischofberger (later Winterthur, Stamparia Winterthur), 1939-93. fasc. 1-118 (in progress).

A scholarly dictionary of Romansh, with lengthy entries giving etymologies, quotations, references to sources, and explanations in German. Fascicules 1-118 cover 'A'-'ingrandir'. *Class No:* 805.99

[5862]

VELLEMAN, A. Dicziunari scurznieu de la lingua ladina. Abridged dictionary of the Ladin (or Romansh) language, with German, French and English translation, and numerous indications referring to topography and population. Samaden, Engadin Press, 1929. xlvii,928p.

A Romansh-German-French-English dictionary with over 15,000 entry-words, including many geographical names with descriptive annotations. *Class No:* 805.99

Spanish & Portuguese Languages

Theses

[5863]

CHATHAM, J.R., *and others*. Dissertations in Hispanic languages and literatures: an index of dissertations completed in the United States and Canada. Lexington, Ky., Univ. Press of Kentucky, 1970-81. 2v. (xiv,120p.;xi,162p.). ISBN: 0813111838, v.1; 0813114152, v.2.

V.1 lists 1,783 doctoral theses, completed 1876-1966, in a classified arrangement with a detailed author and subject index. Two main sections: Spain and Spanish America; Portugal and Brazil.

V.2 lists 3,527 theses, completed 1967-77, in a single A-Z author sequence, with 3 separate subject indexes for Catalan, Luso-Brazilian and Spanish/Spanish-American languages and literatures.

Updated annually in the May issue of the journal *Hispania.* (Greeley, Colo., American Assoc. of Teachers of Spanish and Portuguese. Quarterly. ISSN: 00182133).
Class No: 806.0+806.90(043)

[5864]

CHATHAM, J.R. *and* SCALES, S.M. Western European dissertations on the Hispanic and Luso-Brazilian languages and literatures: a retrospective index. Mississippi State Univ., Dept. of Foreign Languages, 1984. xiii,145p.

Lists over 6,000 dissertations by author, with thorough subject index. *Class No:* 806.0+806.90(043)

Spanish Language

Bibliographies

[5865]

BÁEZ SAN JOSÉ, V., & *others*. Bibliografía de lingüística general y española (1964-1990). Alcalá de Henares, Universidad de Alcalá, 1995-7. v.1-3 (in progress). ISBN: 848138965x.

A very comprehensive classified bibliography of recent studies in general and Spanish linguistics, which will comprise 5 vols. The first 3 vols. have 51,000 entries.
Class No: 806.0(01)

[5866]

BLEZNICK, D.W. A Sourcebook for Hispanic literature and language: a selected, annotated guide to Spanish, Spanish-American, and United States Hispanic bibliography, literature, linguistics, journals, and other source materials. 3rd ed. Lanham,Md., Scarecrow, 1995. x,310p. $60. ISBN: 0810829819.

See entry at 860(035). *Class No:* 806.0(01)

[5867]

NIEDEREHE, H.-J. Bibliografía cronológica de lingüística, la gramática y la lexicografía del español (BICRES), desde los comienzos hasta el año 1600. Amsterdam & Philadelphia, Pa., Benjamins, 1994. vi,457p. $110. (*Studies in the history of the language sciences.*) ISBN: 9027245630, Netherlands; 1556196121, US.

Lists over 1,000 titles chronologically, including Spanish grammars and dictionaries, histories of the language and studies of particular facets of its evolution. Bibliography of sources and studies (47p.). Several indexes, giving access by author, short title, place of production, printer, publisher and location. *Class No:* 806.0(01)

[5868]

Nueva revista de filología hispánica. México, Centro de Estudios Lingüísticos y Literarios, El Colegio de México, 1947-. v.1-. 2py. ISSN: 01850121.

Preceded by *Revista de filología hispánica,* v.1-8, 1936-46.

Each issue carries a classifed bibliography of current publications on Spanish language, literature and folklore. Those in v.43, 1995, have 2,380 entries, of which 17% are devoted to linguistic topics. The literature section includes thorough coverage of Spanish America and has subsections for numerous individual authors. *Class No:* 806.0(01)

[5869]

Revista de filología española. Madrid, Consejo Superior de Investigaciones Científicas, Instituto de Filología, 1914-. v.1-. 2py. ISSN: 02109174.

Regularly carries a classified bibliography of recent publications on Spanish language and literature. In v.76, 1996, the bibliography occupies 89p. and has 1,042 entries, divided equally between language and literature (including sections on many individual authors), with an author index. Includes the language and literature of Spanish America.
Class No: 806.0(01)

[5870]

SERÍS, H. Bibliografía de la lingüística española. Bogotá, Instituto Caro y Cuervo, 1964. lix,981p.

Items numbered 8,780-16,562, following on from the author's *Manual de bibliografía de la literatura española* (*q.v.*). The 7 main sections are: 1. Lingüística general - 2. Lingüística románica - 3. Lingüística española - 4. Lenguas peninsulares (catalán, valenciano, balear, gallego) - 5. Dialectos hispánicos - 6. El Español en América (A-Z by country) - 7. Enseñanza del español. Many entries annotated. References to book reviews. Detailed contents table and index of authors and subjects. The most comprehensive bibliography in the field.
Class No: 806.0(01)

[5871]

WOODBRIDGE, H.C. Guide to reference works for the study of the Spanish language and literature and Spanish American literature. 2nd ed. New York, Modern Language Assoc. of America, 1997. xvii,236p. $37.50. (*Selected bibliographies in language and literature.*) ISBN: 0873529677.

1st ed. 1987.

See entry at 860(035). *Class No:* 806.0(01)

Histories

[5872]

PENNY, R. A History of the Spanish language. Cambridge, Cambridge Univ. Press, 1991. xvi,319p. £15.95. ISBN: 0521397847.

The emphasis is on 'internal history' (*i.e.* historical grammar) but an introductory chapter surveys 'external history' or the circumstances in which Spanish has been spoken and written. 4 main chapters cover phonology, morpho-syntax, lexis and semantics, with numerous numbered sections and subsections. Detailed contents list makes arrangement clear. References (7p.). Indexes of Latin and Spanish words. Subject index. *Class No:* 806.0(091)

Usage

[5873]

BATCHELOR, R.E. *and* **POUNTAIN, C.J. Using Spanish:** a guide to contemporary usage. Cambridge, Cambridge Univ. Press, 1992. xvi,318p. £37.50. ISBN: 0521421233.

31 chapters, with numbered subsections, covering aspects of vocabulary and grammar which cause most difficulty to English speakers, taking account of differences between European and Latin American Spanish. Clearly presented, with good use of headings and tables and numerous examples. Index of Spanish words. Glossary of English grammatical terms. *Class No:* 806.0-06

[5874]

MOLINER, M. Diccionario de uso del español. Madrid, Gredos, 1984 (repr. 1994). 2v. (lvi+1446+1589p.) £94.95. ISBN: 8424913442.

Originally published 1966.

Over 40,000 headwords, with many examples of current usage and detailed explanatory notes. 'One of the most important of twentieth-century Spanish dictionaries' (Woodbridge, H.C., *Guide to reference works ...*, 1987, p.13). Also available on CD-ROM at £71.95.
Class No: 806.0-06

[5875]

SECO, M. Diccionario de dudas y dificultades de la lengua española. 9th ed. Madrid, Espasa Calpe, 1986. xxii,545p. £31.50. ISBN: 8423969487.

1st ed. 1961.

Dictionary of current Spanish usage (387p.) followed by 5 appendices: summary of Spanish grammar; tables of verb conjugations; list of words whose spelling may pose problems; abbreviations; punctuation and diacritics. Bibliography (19p.). Clearly laid out with excellent use of different type-faces, cross-references and tables.
Class No: 806.0-06

Mexican Spanish

[5876]

SANTAMARÍA, F.J. Diccionario de mejicanismos: razonado; comprobado con citas de autoridades; comparado con el de americanismos y con los vocabularios provinciales de los más distinguidos dicionaristas hispanamericanos. 4. ed., corr. y aum. Mejico, Porrua, 1983. xxiv,1207p.

1st ed. 1959.

Over 20,000 entries, including Mexican-Indian terms and Americanisms. Exact references provided for mention of words in other compilations. Many quotations, but these are in very small type. Bibliography of sources (25p.).
Class No: 806.0-087.72

Latin American Spanish

[5877]

Diccionario ejemplificado de chilenismos y de otros usos diferenciales del español de Chile. Pettorino, F.M., *and others, eds.* Valparaiso, Academia Superior de Ciencias Pedagógicas de Valparaiso, 1984-87. 4v. (xxi,4913p.).

A comprehensive, scholarly dictionary of Chilean Spanish, with *c.*50,000 entries which contain quotations from literature and references to other dictionaries and linguistic studies. Bibliography (30p.) in v.4. *Class No:* 806.0-087.8

[5878]

LIPSKI, J.M. Latin American Spanish. London, Longman, 1994. x,426p. £42.50. (*Longman linguistics library.*) ISBN: 0582087619.

5 chapters tracing the historical evolution of Latin American Spanish, followed by detailed descriptions of the dialects spoken in each of 19 countries, covering phonology, grammar and vocabulary. 65p. of references. Index. 'Will not easily be bettered or supplanted' (*Reference Reviews*, v.9(2), 1995, p.21-2). *Class No:* 806.0-087.8

[5879]

MORÍNIGO, M.A. Diccionario de americanismos. Barcelona, Muchnik Editores, 1966 (repr. Buenos Aires, 1985). 738p. ISBN: 8485501829.

A clearly laid-out dictionary of *c.*16,000 terms which have originated in Latin America or have different meanings there. Entries indicate the country/region where the terms are used. Substantial bibliography (46p.). *Class No:* 806.0-087.8

[5880]

SANTAMARÍA, F.J. Diccionario general de americanismos. México, Robredo, 1942. 3v.

A dictionary of words originating in America and accepted as part of the Spanish language there and of words from Spain which have particular meanings in Spanish America. Provides definitions, etymologies in many cases, and

.... *(contd.)*

indicates countries/regions where the term is used. Many botanical and zoological terms. The largest dictionary of its kind. *Class No:* 806.0-087.8

Dictionaries & Vocabularies

Bibliographies

[5881]

FABBRI, M. A Bibliography of Hispanic dictionaries: Catalan, Galician, Spanish, Spanish in Latin America and the Philippines. Imola, Galeati, 1979. 381p.

Lists *c.*3,500 general and technical dictionaries. Arranged by author, with author, language and subject indexes. *Class No:* 806.0-3(01)

Synonyms

[5882]

BATCHELOR, R.E. Using Spanish synonyms. Cambridge, Cambridge Univ. Press, 1994. viii,721p. £50. ISBN: 0521441609.

Claims to be the first guide to Spanish synonyms produced especially for English-speaking students of Spanish. Very clearly presented using a device called the 'semantic frame.' This is headed by a Spanish term and includes Spanish synonyms arranged by register (from formal to indecent) and then A-Z, with English translations, comments on usage, and illustrative Spanish phrases. *c.*900 frames in all, in A-Z order, with an average of 10 synonyms per frame. Good coverage of Latin American Spanish. Indexes of Spanish, English, Argentinian and Mexican terms, all keyed to Spanish frame headings. *Class No:* 806.0-314

[5883]

GILI GAYA, S. Vox diccionario de sinónimos. 9. ed. Barcelona, Bibliograf, 1983. xvi,357p.

Lists synonyms and also provides explanations of usage. Introduction includes evaluation of synonym dictionaries from the 18th to 20th centuries. *Class No:* 806.0-314

[5884]

ORTEGA CAVERO, D. Gran Sopena de sinónimos y asociación de ideas. Barcelona, Sopena, 1985. 2v. (xvii,1550p.). £51.50. ISBN: 8430310185.

Lists 870,000 synonyms and 84,000 antonyms under 37,500 entry-words. Lists of words used in specialist fields (*e.g.* nuclear energy, computing) are appended. *Class No:* 806.0-314

Idioms

[5885]

ALONSO PEDRAZ, M. Enciclopedia del idioma: diccionario histórico y moderno de la lengua español (siglos xii al xx) etimológico, tecnológico, regional y hispanoamericano. Madrid, Aguilar, 1958 (repr. 1984). 3v. (lxvii,4258p.). ISBN: 840327999x.

About 200,000 entries. In each case gives part of speech, country of origin, definition or equivalent, and example of use. Has drawn upon all the leading dictionaries since 1726. Includes proper names. Particularly valuable for regional and Latin-American words. *Class No:* 806.0-318

[5886]

RODRIGUES, L.J. *and* **BENET DE RODRIGUES, J. Harrap's dictionary of idioms: English-Spanish / Spanish-English.** London, Harrap, 1991. 466p. 14.99. ISBN: 024560054x.

Over 8,000 idioms from British and American English and Latin American and Castilian Spanish, some 60% of them in English-Spanish section. Entries under keywords, giving register label, translation and illustrative sentence. *Class No:* 806.0-318

Monoglot Dictionaries

[5887]

GARCÍA-PELAYO Y GROSS, R. Pequeño Larousse en color. Madrid, Itaca, 1988 (regularly reprinted). 1564p. illus. ISBN: 8477360006.

A deluxe ed. of *Pequeño Larousse ilustrado*, the Spanish version of *Le Petit Larousse illustré* (*q.v.*). Includes sequence of Latin and foreign phrases. *Class No:* 806.0-323.1

[5888]

Gran diccionario de la lengua española. Sánchez Pérez, A., *ed.* 7. ed. Madrid, SGEL, 1995. xv,1983p. £36.95. ISBN: 8471432994.

Over 60,000 entries, with definition, examples of usage from current language, pronunciation (adapted IPA) and lists of synonyms and antonyms. Includes common technical terms and Americanisms. Grammar summary (29p.). Designed primarily for freign learners. *Class No:* 806.0-323.1

[5889]

—Diccionario esencial Santillana de la lengua española. Madrid, Santillana, 1991. xv,1360p. illus. £14.99. ISBN: 8429434151.

Over 30,000 entries and 85,000 definitions, the entries including etymology, usage examples, synonyms and antonyms. Very clear layout with verb conjugations in boxes. Appended summary of grammar (35p.). *Class No:* 806.0-323.1

[5890]

MÜLLER, B. Diccionario del español medieval. Heidelberg, Winter, 1994- . Bd.1- (in progress). ISBN: 3825338797.

Covers the Spanish language up to *c.*1400, based on 500 texts (listed). Entries include etymology, quotes from texts and references to other sources (dictionaries, concordances, etc.). V.1 comprises 10 fascicules, published 1987-94, covering 'A-ademas.' *Class No:* 806.0-323.1

[5891]

REAL ACADEMIA ESPAÑOLA. Diccionario de la lengua española. 21. ed. Madrid, Espasa-Calpe, 1992. xxxi,1513p. £79.95. ISBN: 8423947777.

1st ed. 1726-39 in 6 vols.; 20th ed. 1984.

The authority for current Spanish usage, as well as for etymology. This ed. claims 83,500 entries, with 12,000 new words or senses. The different meanings and applications of words are noted, with many examples. Scientific and technical words in current use are included, as well as many Latin-American and Philippine words and phrases (their representation significantly increased in this ed.), but generally conservative in accepting new words. Also available on CD-ROM at £99.95. *Class No:* 806.0-323.1

[5892]

—REAL ACADEMIA ESPAÑOLA. Diccionario manual e ilustrado de la lengua española. 4. ed. Barcelona, Espasa-Calpe, 1989. 1666p. illus. ISBN: 8423959783.

Based on the Academy's *Diccionario de la lengua española* and enhanced with up-to-date technical terminology and slang. 4,000 illustrations, including labelled drawings. Special attention is given to Americanisms.
Class No: 806.0-323.1

[5893]

Vox diccionario general ilustrado de la lengua española. Alvar Ezquerra, M., *ed.* Nueva redacción. Barcelona, Bibliograf, 1987. xlv,1178p. illus. ISBN: 847153147x.

About 100,000 entries, including Americanisms and technical terms. Gives etymologies and synonyms. Fewer line-drawings than in the *Pequeño Larousse*. Lists of geographical terms and foreign phrases appended.
Class No: 806.0-323.1

Bilingual Dictionaries

[5894]

Collins Spanish dictionary: Spanish-English / English-Spanish. Álvarez García, T., *& others, eds.* 5th ed. Glasgow, HarperCollins; Barcelona, Grijalbo, 1997. xlv,1679p. £24.99. ISBN: 000471024x.

1st ed. 1971; 4th ed. 1996.

One of the best desk dictionaries, which claims over 230,000 references and 440,000 translations. Latin American Spanish and North American English usage well covered and clearly indicated. Many idioms. Style labels for all non-standard terms. Appendices include Spanish and English verbs; word formation in Spanish; numerals, weights and measures, etc.; and 'Language in use' (54p.) which comprises detailed notes on the grammar of communication in Spanish and English and is visually linked with the dictionary text. 5th ed. has over 5,000 new terms and senses, and innovations include clearer typography, language notes to aid translation, and encyclopedic entries in both sections on aspects of life and culture. Excellent value.
Class No: 806.0-323.2

[5895]

—Collins Spanish concise dictionary. 3rd ed. Glasgow, HarperCollins; Barcelona, Grijalbo, 1998. xx+1098+89p. £15.99. ISBN: 0004709659.

1st ed. 1985; 2nd ed. 1993.

Claims over 135,000 references and 220,000 translations. Comprehensive coverage of Latin American Spanish, including regional variations. User-friendly layout, with longer entries paragraphed for extra clarity. This ed. has new entries on Spanish life and culture and a 'Language Building' supplement (89p.) covering correspondence, translation, etc. and keyed to the main text.
Class No: 806.0-323.2

[5896]

Harrap concise Spanish dictionary: Spanish-English / English-Spanish. Blasco, J., *& others, eds.* Edinburgh, Chambers Harrap, 1998. xiv+457+xi+511p. £14.99. ISBN: 0245605673.

A very reasonably priced desk dictionary which claims 115,000 references and 160,000 translations. Includes Latin American terms, indicating country/region of use, and has good coverage of slang and idiomatic language. Up-to-date vocabulary includes Internet terminology. Table of Spanish verbs (16p.). *Class No:* 806.0-323.2

[5897]

Larousse Spanish dictionary: Spanish-English / English-Spanish. García-Pelayo, R., *and others, eds.* Unabridged ed. Paris, Larousse, 1994. 1592p. £25. ISBN: 2034302001.

Supersedes *Larousse gran diccionario, español-inglés* (1983).

Claims over 220,000 references and 400,000 translations, including wide-ranging coverage of literary, technical and professional vocabulary and of Latin American Spanish. Acronyms, abbreviations and proper names within main sequence, which is in 3 columns. Notes on grammmar and usage with many entries. Pronunciation (IPA) given for English headwords. Grammar and pronunciation supplement (34p.). 16p. of colour maps.

Larousse standard dictionary: Spanish-English / English-Spanish, ed. by E. De Moragas (Paris, Larousse, 1996. xxiii,665+xxii,717p. £15.99. ISBN: 2034302400) is a desk dictionary from the same stable, with 160,000 references and 260,000 translations. *Class No:* 806.0-323.2

[5898]

The Oxford Spanish dictionary: Spanish-English / English-Spanish. Galimberti Jarman, B. *and* Russell, R., *eds.* Oxford, Oxford Univ. Press, 1994. li,1829p. £24.99. ISBN: 0198645031.

A major new bilingual dictionary produced by a joint Spanish-UK team, which claims coverage of 275,000 words/phrases and over 450,000 translations. Entries in Spanish-English section include variant forms, field, style and regional labels (including Latin American countries), illustrative phrases, and cross-references. English-Spanish section includes pronunciation guidance (IPA) for headwords. American English spelling is used as the norm, with British forms indicated as variants. Abbreviations, acronyms and proper names in both sequences. Detailed guide for users (36p.). Appendices include guide to correspondence in both languages (28p.) and Spanish verb tables (19p.). 'A splendid piece of work, comprehensive and painstaking ... it will be indispensable to all serious Hispanists' (*TLS*, no.4781, Nov. 18, 1994, p.11).

Also available on CD-ROM at £49.99 (ISBN: 019268308x).

The Concise Oxford Spanish dictionary (1996. xxvi,1475p. £24.99. ISBN: 0198645236) claims over 170,000 words/phrases and 240,000 translations and has a 24-page supplement on correspondence in Spanish and English and appended verb tables. *Class No:* 806.0-323.2

[5899]

Simon and Schuster's international dictionary: English-Spanish / Spanish-English. de Gámez, T., *ed.* New York, Simon and Schuster, 1973. xviii,1605p. $55 ISBN: 0671212672.

One of the largest general bilingual dictionaries, with over 200,000 entries, including many scientific and technical terms. Strong on the Spanish of America and noted for its wealth of definitions, but regarded as weak on Spanish regional vocabulary. (2nd ed. 1997). *Class No:* 806.0-323.2

[5900]

University of Chicago Spanish dictionary: a new concise Spanish-English and English-Spanish dictionary of words and phrases basic to the written and spoken languages of today, plus a list of 500 Spanish idioms and sayings, with variants and English equivalents. Castillo, C. *and* Bond, O.F., *comps.* 4th ed., rev. and enl. by D.L. Canfield. Chicago, Univ. of Chicago Press, 1987. 475p. $19.95. ISBN: 0226104001.

1st ed. 1948; 3rd ed. 1977.

.... (contd.)

A handy desk dictionary 'compiled for the general use of the American learner of Spanish and the Spanish-speaking learner of English, with special reference to New World usages as found in the United States and Spanish America' (*Foreword*).

35,000 entry-words, with much new vocabulary in the 4th ed. Pronunciation given for all headwords. Very useful introductory sections to each part, both covering grammar and that to the first part including a history of the Spanish language in America.

An alternative source for American learners is *Random House Spanish-English / English-Spanish dictionary*, by M.H. Raventós, rev. and updated by D.L. Gold (New York, Random House, 1995. xxv,622p. £11.99. ISBN: 0679438971), which has over 60,000 entries.
Class No: 806.0-323.2

Illustrated Works

[5901]
CORBEIL, J-C. *and* **ARCHAMBAULT, A. The Facts on File English / Spanish visual dictionary.** New York, Facts on File, 1992. 924p. ISBN: 0816015465.

Contains the 3,000-plus illustrations from *The Facts on File visual dictionary* (*q.v.*) with captions in English (in black, with British English terms in italics) and Spanish (in blue). Index has general, thematic and specialized sections in both languages. *Class No:* 806.0-323.2(0.025)

[5902]
The Oxford-Duden pictorial Spanish & English dictionary. 2nd ed. Oxford, Clarendon Press, 1995. 884p. £25. ISBN: 0198645147.

1st ed. 1985.

See entry for *The Oxford-Duden pictorial German & English dictionary*. Includes variations from specific Spanish-American countries. Indexes in Spanish and English. *Class No:* 806.0-323.2(0.025)

Grammar

[5903]
BUTT, J. *and* **BENJAMIN, C. A New reference grammar of Spanish.** 2nd ed. London, Arnold; Lincolnwood, Ill., NTC, 1994. xiv,520p. £18.95. ISBN: 0340583908, UK; 0844270881, US.

1st ed. 1988.

A well-organized, clearly presented grammar for intermediate and advanced English-speaking students. 39 chapters with numbered paragraphs and abundant examples with translations. Bibliography (3p.). Index of English words. Index of Spanish words and grammatical points. For this ed. a larger format and clearer layout have been adopted, there are more Mexican examples and a greater effort has been made to avoid exclusively British usage in the translated examples.

See also *Modern Spanish grammar: a practical guide*, by J. Kattán-Ibarra and C.J. Pountain (London, Routledge, 1997. xxvii,496p. £45. ISBN: 0415098459), which has 73 chapters with numbered subsections including many examples. Glossary of grammatical terms (8p.). Index.
Class No: 806.0-5

[5904]
DE BRUYNE, J. *and* **POUNTAIN, C.J. A Comprehensive Spanish grammar.** Oxford, Blackwell, 1995. 624p. £50. (*Blackwell reference grammars.*) ISBN: 0631168036.

A clearly arranged grammar in 27 chapters, with bibliography, index verborum and index of topics. Good coverage throughout of Latin American Spanish.
Class No: 806.0-5

Etymology

[5905]
COROMINAS, J. *and* **PASCUAL, J.A. Diccionario crítico etimológico castellano e hispánico.** Madrid, Gredos, 1980-91. 6v. ISBN: 8424913620.

A greatly expanded and revised version of Corominas's *Diccionario crítico etimológico de la lengua castellana* (Berne, Francke, 1954-57. 4v.).

The most scholarly etymological dictionary, with numerous quotations from sources (listed on p.xxxvii-lxv of v.1) and lengthy commentary on the history of each word.
Class No: 806.0-54

[5906]
GÓMEZ DE SILVA, G. Elsevier's concise Spanish etymological dictionary. Amsterdam, Elsevier, 1985. xii,560p. $282.75. ISBN: 0444424407.

Gives the English equivalent and traces the history of 10,000 terms, including many personal and place names, prefixes and suffixes. Very expensive, but enthusiastically received by reviewers. *Class No:* 806.0-54

Portuguese Language

Bibliographies

[5907]
CHAMBERLAIN, B.J. Portuguese language and Luso-Brazilian literature: an annotated guide to selected reference works. New York, Modern Language Assoc. of America, 1989. xii,95p. $32. (*Selected bibliographies in language and literature.*) ISBN: 0873529561.

A classified, well-annotated guide, similar in style and format to Woodbridge's work on Spanish language and literature (*q.v.*). 538 entries in 4 main sections (Portuguese language; Portuguese literature; Brazilian literature; Luso-African and other Lusophone literatures) with numerous sub-sections. Index of authors, editors and compilers.
Class No: 806.90(01)

[5908]
FERREIRA, J. de Azevedo. Bibliografia selectiva da língua portuguesa. Lisboa, Instituto de Cultura e Língua Portuguesa, 1989. xvi,332p.

A classified bibliography, with 2,217 entries in 41 sections. Largely unannotated, but includes references to reviews. List of *c.*240 periodicals analyzed. Name index.
Class No: 806.90(01)

[5909]
NÚCLEO DE ESTUDOS DA LINGUÍSTICA CONTRASTIVA DA FACULDADE DE CIÊNCIAS SOCIAIS E HUMANAS DA UNIVERSIDADE NOVA DE LISBOA. Bibliografia de linguística portuguesa. [Lisboa], Litoral, [1987?]. 147p.

A classified bibliography of recent studies in Portuguese linguistics, with over 1,900 unannotated entries in 21 sections. List of over 200 periodicals and serials analyzed. No index. *Class No:* 806.90(01)

Dictionaries

[5910]
AZEVEDO, F.F. dos Santos. Dicionário analógico da língua portuguesa. Brasília, Coordenadora-Thesaurus, 1983. 685p.

'Arguably the best thesaurus of the Portuguese language' (Chamberlain, B.J., *Portuguese language and Luso-Brazilian literature*, 1989, p.14). *Class No:* 806.90(038)

[5911]
Collins Portuguese dictionary: English-Portuguese / Portuguese-English. Whitlam, J., *and others*. Glasgow, HarperCollins, 1991. xviii+382+367p. £11.99. ISBN: 0004332253.

A compact 2-way dictionary with 25-30,000 entries in each section (110,000 definitions claimed). Pronunciation given for all headwords. Covers both European and Brazilian Portuguese. *Class No:* 806.90(038)

[5912]
—NTC's compact Portuguese and English dictionary Lincolnwood, Ill., NTC, 1995. xix,792p. £16.95. ISBN: 0844246905.

A 2-way dictionary with 36,000 of the commonest words in the 2 languages, plus idioms and phrases. Pronunciation (IPA) and syllabification given for all headwords. *Class No:* 806.90(038)

[5913]
Dicionário prático ilustrado: o pequeno Larousse português. Novo enciclopédico luso-brasileiro. Seguier, J.J., *ed.* Ed. actualizada e aumentada par J. Lello e E. Lello. Porto, Lello, 1986. 2023p. illus.

1st ed. 1927.

Modelled on the *Petit Larousse* with 3 main sections: dictionary (*c.*10,000 entries), list of quotations, and encyclopedia. 6,000 line-drawings, over 100 plates, and many maps.

The Brazilian equivalent is *Pequeno dicionário enciclopédico Koogan Larousse*, ed. by A. Houaiss (Rio de Janeiro, Larousse, 1979. xx,1644p.). *Class No:* 806.90(038)

[5914]
MACHADO, J.P. Dicionário etimológico da língua portuguesa, com a mais antiga documentação escrita e conhecida de muitos dos vocábulos estudados. 3. ed. Lisboa, Confluência, 1978. 5v.

1st ed. 1952; 2nd ed. 1967.

The most authoritative etymological dictionary of Portuguese, with *c.*70,000 entries. *Class No:* 806.90(038)

[5915]
MORAIS SILVA, A. de. Grande dicionário da língua portuguesa. 10. ed., rev., corr., muito aumentada e actualizada. Lisboa, Confluência, 1949-59. 12v.

1st ed. 1789.

The Portuguese national dictionary, rich in quotations from literature. The dictionary occupies vols. 1-11, with v.12 including a summary of Portuguese grammar, lists of Latin and foreign terms, place-names, abbreviations, etc., and also details of the Acordo Ortográfico Luso-Brasileiro (1945), of which this edition takes account. Spine title is *Dicionario de Morais*. *Class No:* 806.90(038)

[5916]
Novo Michaelis dicionário ilustrado / The New Michaelis illustrated dictionary. Pietzschke, F., *ed.* São Paulo, Melhoramentos; Wiesbaden, Brockhaus, 1958-61 (frequently reprinted). 2v. £39.95 per vol.

Based on a dictionary originally published in 1893.

V.1 *English-Portuguese*. 45th ed. xxxiii,1151p.

V.2 *Portuguese-English* 43rd ed. li,1328p.

One of the best bilingual dictionaries available, with over 73,000 entries and over 4,000 Brockhaus-style illustrations in v.1. Many idiomatic phrases and technical terms. V.2 has over 78,000 entries and includes list of Portuguese abbreviations, verb conjugations, and table of weights and measures.

A concise edition is published as *Pequeno dicionário Michaelis* (São Paulo, Melhoramentos, 1988. xii,642p.). *Class No:* 806.90(038)

[5917]
The Oxford-Duden pictorial Portuguese-English dictionary. New ed. Oxford, Clarendon Press, 1992. 950p. £13.99. ISBN: 0198641826.

See entry for *The Oxford-Duden pictorial German & English dictionary*. Indexes in Portuguese and English. *Class No:* 806.90(038)

[5918]
TEXEIRA DE OLIVEIRA, M.M. Dicionário moderno português-inglês / Modern English-Portuguese dictionary. Lisboa, Gomes & Rodriques, 1984. 1304;909p.

The Portuguese-English section is one of the fullest of its kind and particularly rich in idioms. *Class No:* 806.90(038)

Brazilian Portuguese Language

Bibliographies

[5919]
DIETRICH, W. Bibliografia da língua portuguesa do Brasil. Tübingen, Narr, 1980. xxxii,292p. ISBN: 3878081200.

A comprehensive, classified bibliography, with 1,465 briefly annotated entries in 32 sections. List of *c.*240 periodicals and serials analyzed. Includes references to book reviews. Author index. *Class No:* 806.90-087.81(01)

Dictionaries

[5920]
AULETE, F.J.C. Dicionário contemporâneo da língua portuguesa Caldas Aulete. 3. ed. brasileira. Lisboa, Delta, 1974. 5v.

The 3rd Brazilian ed. of Aulete's dictionary, which was

.... *(contd.)*
first published in 1881. The 1st Brazilian ed. appeared in 1958, updated, revised and enlarged, with Brazilian terms, by H. Garcia. *Class No:* 806.90-087.81(038)

[5921]
CHAMBERLAIN, B.J. *and* **HARMON, R.M. A Dictionary of informal Portuguese,** with English index. Washington, D.C., Georgetown Univ. Press, 1983. xix,701p. $24.95. ISBN: 0878400915.

Lists 7,500 current Brazilian expressions, the entries including an indication of frequency of use, register, English definition, and a model sentence to illustrate usage. In the English index, Brazilian headwords are grouped under colloquial English headings. 'Over a third of the entries are widely used items that have never before appeared in other Portuguese-English bilingual dictionaries or even in Brazilian Portuguese dictionaries' (*Introduction*). Bibliography (3p.). *Class No:* 806.90-087.81(038)

[5922]
Dicionário inglês-português. Houaiss, A., *ed.* Rio de Janeiro, Record; New York, French & European, 1982. ix,927p. £46.50. ISBN: 8510165017, Brazil; 0828804923, US.

US title is *Webster's English-Portuguese dictionary*.

Over 100,000 entries, with the emphasis on Brazilian Portuguese. Many idiomatic phrases. Clearly-signalled explanatory entries for English prefixes and suffixes. *Class No:* 806.90-087.81(038)

[5923]
Dicionário multimédia Universal da língua portuguesa. São Paulo, Texto Editora, 1995. CD-ROM. £41.65.

A monolingual Brazilian dictionary on CD-ROM with over 93,000 entries. *Class No:* 806.90-087.81(038)

[5924]
FERREIRA, A.B. de Holanda. Novo dicionário da língua portuguesa. 2. ed. Rio de Janeiro, Nova Fronteira, 1986. xxiii,1838p.

1st ed. 1975.

A third larger than the 1st ed., with over 100,000 definitions, including many neologisms and slang terms. 'Perhaps the best dictionary of the Portuguese language available in a single volume' (Chamberlain, B.J., *Portuguese language and Luso-Brazilian literature*, 1989, p.13). *Class No:* 806.90-087.81(038)

[5925]
LIMA, H. da *and* **BARROSO, G. Pequeno dicionário brasileiro da língua portuguesa.** 11. ed., supervisionada e consideràvelmente aumentada por A.B. de H. Ferreira. Rio de Janeiro, Civilização Brasileira, 1968. xxxiii,1301p.

A standard single-vol. dictionary of Brazilian Portuguese, this ed. being 25% larger than its predecessor with *c.*97,000 entries. *Class No:* 806.90-087.81(038)

[5926]
NASCENTES, A. Dicionário da língua portuguesa. Rio de Janeiro, Block, 1988. 669p. ISBN: 8525803820.

An official dictionary of Brazilian Portuguese prepared for the Brazilian Academy of Letters, with *c.*100,000 entries. *Class No:* 806.90-087.81(038)

[5927]
Nôvo dicionário brasileiro Melhoramentos ilustrado. 6. ed., rev. São Paulo, Melhoramentos, 1970. 5v. illus.

1st ed. 1962-63 in 4 vols.

A popular dictionary of Brazilian Portuguese, with over 100,000 entries. *Class No:* 806.90-087.81(038)

[5928]
TAYLOR, J.L. Portuguese-English dictionary. Rev. ed. Stanford, Calif., Stanford Univ. Press; London, Harrap, 1970. xxii,662p. $39.50. ISBN: 0804704805, US; 0245572287, UK.

First published 1959.

Entries for *c.*60,000 Portuguese terms, giving English equivalent, synonyms, and (often) examples of usage. Follows official Brazilian orthography. Includes many technical terms, with usage labels. Appendix of Portuguese verb models. *Class No:* 806.90-087.81(038)

[5929]
VILLAR, M. Dicionário contrastivo luso-brasileiro: alguns lusismos, brasileirismos, regionalismos, expressões idiomáticas, ortografias, ortoépias, particularidades gramaticais, regenciais, fonêmicas, toponímia e outras pecularidades ou explicados. Rio de Janeiro, Guanabara, 1989. 318p. ISBN: 8527700921.

A contrastive dictionary of Portuguese and Brazilian usage, with *c.*7,500 entries in each of 2 sections: Portuguese-Brazilian and Brazilian-Portuguese. Bibliography (2p.). *Class No:* 806.90-087.81(038)

Grammar

[5930]
HUTCHINSON, A.P. *and* **LLOYD, J. Portuguese: an essential grammar.** London, Routledge, 1996. xiii,193p. £45. (*Routledge grammars.*) ISBN: 0415137071.

1. An essential grammar (11 chapters) - 2. Language functions (5) - 3. Brazilian variants (16). Arranged in short, numbered paragraphs which are largely free of jargon and concentrate on the language of contemporary native speakers in Portugal and other Lusophone countries. Numerous authentic examples with translations. Detailed contents list and thorough index provide full access. *Class No:* 806.90-5

Galician Language

[5931]
Diccionario normativo galego-castelán. Romero, H.M. *and* García Cancela, X., *eds.* Pontevedra, Galaxia, [1988?]. 996p. ISBN: 8471546418.

Galician-Spanish dictionary, with 35-40,000 entries. *Class No:* 806.99

807/808 Classical & Slavonic Languages

Classical Languages

Handbooks & Manuals

[5932]
JENKINS, F.W. Classical studies: a guide to the reference literature. Englewood, Colo., Libraries Unlimited, 1996. ix,263p. $43. (*Reference sources in the humanities.*) ISBN: 1563081105.

See entry at 870(035). *Class No:* 807(035)

Latin Language

Bibliographies

[5933]
COUSIN, J. Bibliographie de la langue latine, 1880-1948. Paris, Société d'Éditions 'Les Belles Lettres', 1951. xxiv,375p.

A classified bibliography with nearly 10,000 unannotated entries in 12 sections. Includes material in many languages. List of periodicals and other sources (8p.). Indexes of Latin words and Latin writers. *Class No:* 807.1(01)

Dictionaries

[5934]
ERNOUT, A. *and* **MEILLET, P.J.A. Dictionnaire étymologique de la langue latine:** histoire des mots. 4e. éd., rev., corr. et augm. d'un index. Paris, Klincksieck, 1959-60. 2v. in 1(xviii,820p.).

1st ed. 1932; 4th ed. issued with the assistance of the Centre National de la Recherche Scientifique. Corrected reprint published 1967.

A standard etymological dictionary, with *c.*7,000 entry-words. Index arranged by 25 language groups. List of sources (2p.). *Class No:* 807.1(038)

[5935]
—WALDE, A. Lateinisches etymologisches Wörterbuch. 3. neubearb. Aufl. von J.B. Hofmann. Heidelberg, Winter, 1938-54. 2v. *Register*. 1956. viii,287p.

1st ed. 1906.

Lays practically all its emphasis on the etymology of Latin words as related to Indo-European, giving the first appearance of each Latin word in the ancient documents, and stating whether it survived into the Romance period. Many Greek and other loan-words included. Derivatives listed under the primitives. The *Register*, compiled by Elsbeth Berger is arranged by language groups, first the Indo-Germanic group and then the non-Indo-Germanic group. The third part covers geographical names and surnames. *Class No:* 807.1(038)

[5936]
LEWIS, C.T. *and* **SHORT, C. Latin dictionary,** founded on Andrews' edition of Freund's Latin dictionary. Rev., enl. and in greater part rewritten. Oxford, Clarendon Press, 1879 (frequently reprinted). xiv,2019p. £90. ISBN: 0198642016.

Andrews' edition of Freund's dictionary was published in 1850.

The standard Latin-English dictionary for Latin up to *c.*1000AD and including patristic writings. About 60,000 entries, including proper and geographical names. Capital letters and figures (arabic and roman), in bold, introduce different meanings and applications of words. Very small type. Includes many quotations from classical authors, with adequate source references. List of authors and works cited, p.vii-xi.

C.T. Lewis's *Latin dictionary for schools*, first published 1889 (1204p.) is also frequently reprinted.
Class No: 807.1(038)

[5937]
Oxford Latin dictionary. Glare, P.G.W., *ed.* Oxford, Clarendon Press, 1982. 2150p. £200. ISBN: 0198642245.

Originally published in 8 fascicules, 1968-82.

About 40,000 Latin headwords, based on a collection of over one million quotations from literary, epigraphic and other sources, with exact references. Different meanings are numbered. Includes proper names. Brief etymological notes, with articles on the principal suffixes — an innovation in Latin lexicography. Covers the language from the earliest recorded word up to AD200, omitting patristic writings. Fasc. 1 includes a list of references ('Authors and works', p.ix-xx), and a 'Supplementary list of modern collections', p.xx-xxi. Aims to be 'a dictionary independent alike of Lewis & Short on the one hand and of the *Thesaurus linguae latinae* on the other ... and which aims to be approximately one-third longer than Lewis & Short'. Hailed by reviewers as a major work of modern scholarship.
Class No: 807.1(038)

[5938]
—The Pocket Oxford Latin dictionary: Latin-English / English-Latin. Morwood, J., *ed.* Oxford, Oxford Univ. Press, 1994. ix,357p. £9.99. ISBN: 019864227x.

Based on S.C. Woodhouse's *Latin dictionary* (1913), but taking into account recent philological advances. By no means as small as its name suggests, with over 60,000 entries including full grammatical information. Appended lists of historical, mythical and geographical names, plus summary of grammar (16p.). *Class No:* 807.1(038)

[5939]
SIMPSON, D.P. Cassell's Latin dictionary: Latin-English / English-Latin. [5th ed.]. London, Cassell, 1959 (frequently reprinted). xvii,883p. £25. ISBN: 0304522570.

1st ed. 1854. 4th ed. 1892. This ed. has also appeared under the title *Cassell's new Latin dictionary*.

A reliable dictionary of classical Latin for school and general use, with *c.*13,000 entry-words in each section, although the Latin-English section is twice as long, having detailed explanatory entries and citations for classical authors

.... *(contd.)*
(not exact references). The English-Latin section is intended chiefly as an aid to Latin prose composition.
Class No: 807.1(038)

[5940]
Thesaurus linguae latinae, editus auctoritate et consilio academiarum quinque germanicarum Berolinensis, Gottingensis, Lipsiensis, Monacensis, Vindobonensis. Leipzig, Teubner, 1900-. v.1- (in progress).

Vols. 1-9, *A-O*, completed (1900-81); v.10, *P*, in progress.

—*Supplementum: Nomina propria (Onomasticon).* Leipzig, Teubner, 1907-23. v.2-3, pt.2: C-DON.

—*Index librorum scriptorum inscriptionum ex quibus exempla adferuntur.* Leipzig, Teubner, 1904. 109p. *Supplementum* 1958. 13p.

The greatest and most important of modern historical dictionaries of the Latin language, prepared by the German universities of Berlin, Göttingen, Leipzig, Munich and Vienna. Illustrated by copious quotations from the classical authors (down to mid-2nd century AD), and planned to include every word (except the most familiar particles) used in their writings. Also cites other authors down to the end of the 6th century AD. *Class No:* 807.1(038)

Mediaeval Latin

Abbreviations & Symbols

[5941]
CAPELLI, A. Lexicon abbreviaturarum. Dizionario di abbreviature latine ed italiane. 6. ed. Milano, Hoepli, 1961. lxxiii,531p. £27.50.

6th ed. is a reprint of 3rd ed., 1929.

A-Z list of *c.*14,000 abbreviations, preceded by a valuable introduction on medieval abbreviations. List of signs relating to money, the calendar and measures, and epigraphic abbreviations. Bibliography (15p.).

Supplemented by A. Pelzer's *Abréviations latins mediévales. Supplément au 'Dizionario di abbreviature latine ed italiane' de Adriano Capelli* (Louvain, Publications Universitaires; Paris, Béatrice-Nauwelaerts, 1964. vi,86p. 2nd ed. 1966), which adds *c.*1,200 entries, based on Vatican Latin manuscripts. *Class No:* 807.33(003)

[5942]
MARTIN, C.T. The Record interpreter: a collection of abbreviations, Latin words and names used in English historical manuscripts and records. 2nd ed. London, Stevens, 1910. xv,464p. (repr. Chichester, Phillimore, 1982). £20. ISBN: 0850334659.

1st ed. 1892.

Useful handbook for the beginner in research on a medieval English subject. Abbreviations of Latin and French words, Latin forms of places, bishoprics, surnames and Christian names. As a glossary of Latin names is largely superseded by A. Souter's *A Glossary of later Latin (q.v.).*
Class No: 807.33(003)

Bibliographies

[5943]
STARNES, D.T. Renaissance dictionaries, English-Latin and Latin-English. Austin, Texas, Univ. of Texas Press, 1954. 427p. illus.

Examines 27 major 15th-, 16th- and 17th-century dictionaries, arranged chronologically by centuries. Compares texts of different editions and issues, with

.... *(contd.)*
numerous examples and facsimiles. Appendices include bibliography of references pertaining to the history of Latin-English lexicography and short-title list of Latin-English and English-Latin dictionaries (1500-*c.*1800) in American libraries, with locations. *Class No:* 807.33(01)

Handbooks & Manuals

[5944]
Medieval Latin: an introduction and bibliographical guide. Mantello, F.A.C. *and* Rigg, A.G., *eds.* Baltimore, Md., Catholic Univ. of America Press, 1996. xiv,774p. $54.95. ISBN: 0813208416.

A handbook to Latin language and literature of the period AD200-1500. Part 1 lists general research tools in printed and electronic form. Part 2 covers language, with introductions to a range of topics, (including orthography, syntax, lexicography and metrics), and essays on the Latin used in different fields, *e.g.* law, commerce, theology, science, etc. Part 3 covers literature, with introductory essays on various genres followed by lists of key texts, lexica and studies. *Class No:* 807.33(035)

Dictionaries

[5945]
ARNALDI, F. 'Latinitas italicae medii aevi inde ab a. CDLXXVI usque ad a. MXXII ...' In *Bulletin Du Cange*, v.10-34. Bruxelles, 1936-67. 4pts.

A dictionary of medieval Latin, covering the period 476-1022AD, which was published in fascicules within the *Bulletin Du Cange*.

Additions continue to appear in the *Bulletin*, *e.g.* v.44-45 (1985) has addenda to fasc.6, *Ha-In*. *Class No:* 807.33(038)

[5946]
Dictionary of medieval Latin from British sources, prepared by R.E. Latham (and others) under the direction of a committee appointed by the British Academy. London, Oxford Univ. Press, for the British Academy, 1975-97. fasc. 1-5 (in progress). £55 per fasc.

Fasc. 1: *A-B*. 1975. ISBN: 0197259480; fasc. 2: *C*. 1981. ISBN: 0197259685; fasc. 3: *D-E*. 1986. ISBN: 0197260233; fasc. 4: *F-G-H*. 1989. ISBN: 0197260829; fasc. 5: *I-L*. 1997. ISBN: 0197261485.

Aims 'to present a comprehensive picture of the Latin language current in Britain from the 6th to the 16th century' (*A note on editorial method*) to replace Du Cange. The vocabulary embraces three categories of material: Classical words used in their Classical meaning, by such British authors as Bede or in the Domesday Book; post-Classical words and usages (*e.g.* by the medieval Church); and words with an Anglo-Saxon, Anglo-Norman and other vernacular flavour. Extended quotations. 'In view of the project launched by the Royal Irish Academy for a Dictionary of Insular Celtic Latin, most Irish sources prior to 1200, together with certain Welsh sources, have been excluded'.

Bibliography of sources in fasc. 1 (30p.), with supplementary lists in later fascicules.
Class No: 807.33(038)

[5947]

DU CANGE, C. du Fresne. Glossarium mediae et infimae latinitatis ... auctum a monachis ordinis S. Benedicti; cum supplementis integris D.P. Carpentarii, Adelungii, aliorum, suisque digessit G.A.L. Henschel. Sequuntur Glossarium gallicum, tabulae, indices, auctorum et rerum, dissertationes. Ed. nova, aucta pluribus verbis aliorum scriptorum a L. Favre. Niort, L. Favre, 1883-87. 10v. illus. (repr. Graz, Akademische Druck- und Verlagsanstalt, 1954. 5v. £550).

Comprises Latin glossary, A-Z, in vols. 1-8, French glossary in v.9, and indexes in v.10.

The original *Glossarium* was published in Paris, 1678; 3 supplementary volumes were added by the Benedictines of St. Maur (Paris, 1733-36), and a further 4v. (Paris, 1766) by a Benedictine, P. Carpenter. G.A.L. Henschel's edition (7v.) appeared 1840-57.

With Du Cange's *Glossarium ad scriptores medi et infimae graecitatis* (*q.v.*), forms an indispensable aid to the student of history and literature of the Middle Ages. This medieval, Latin-Latin dictionary is characterized by its many quotations and exact references to sources.

Supplemented by C. Schmidt's *Petit supplément au Dictionnaire de Du Cange* (Strasbourg, Heitz, 1906. 71p.).

Additions and corrections to the glossary were published in *Bulletin Du Cange*, v.22, 1951, p.89-156.
Class No: 807.33(038)

[5948]

LATHAM, R.E. Revised medieval Latin word-list from British and Irish sources. Prepared under the direction of a committee appointed by the British Academy. London, Oxford Univ. Press, 1965. xxiii,524p. £22.50. ISBN: 0197258913.

Revision of *Medieval Latin word-list*, by J.H. Baxter and C. Johnson (1934 and revised reprints) which deal with *c.*20,000 words (excluding classical words unless their meanings have altered). About 40,000 entry-words and references, with English equivalents and dated citations (sources listed p.xxi-xxiii). Words are selected for inclusion 'in so far as they are non-classical either in form or in meaning' (*Introduction*), those in regular occurrence during the period being asterisked. *Class No:* 807.33(038)

[5949]

Mittellateinisches Wörterbuch bis zum Ausgehenden 13. Jahrhundert. In Gemeinschaft mit den Akademien der Wissenschaften zu Göttingen, Heidelberg, Leipzig, Wien und der Schweizerischen Geisteswissenschaftlichen Gesellschaft. Hrsg. von der Bayerische Akademie der Wissenschaften und der Deutschen Akademie der Wissenschaften zu Berlin. München, Beck, 1959-95. v.1-v.2, Lfg. 11 (in progress).

V.1: *A-B* (1959-67. viip. 1638 cols.).

A well-produced medieval Latin dictionary that covers the later period from the 7th century to the end of the 13th, and is thus complementary to *Thesaurus linguae latinae (q.v.)*. V.1 has *c.*15,000 entries, with exact references to sources.

Abkürzungs- und Quellenverzeichnisse (2. Aufl. 1996. 153p.) lists nearly 2,400 sources. *Class No:* 807.33(038)

[5950]

NIERMEYER, J.F. Mediae latinitatis lexicon minus: lexique latin médiéval-français / anglais; a medieval Latin-French / English dictionary. Leiden, Brill, 1976 (repr. 1993). 2v. £175.

Originally issued in 12 fascicules, 1954-76.

Has *c.*25,000 entries, with many cross-references for variants and profuse quotations from sources. Meanings are explained in French and English. Serves as a concise Du

.... *(contd.)*

Cange and continues from Souter's *Glossary* (which covers AD180-600) by concentrating on the period 550-1150.
Class No: 807.33(038)

[5951]

Novum glossarium mediae latinitatis ab anno DCCC usque ad annum MCC. Edendum curavit Consilium Academiarum Consociatarum. Blatt, F., *and others, eds.* Copenhagen, Munksgaard, 1957-. (in progress).

Vols. completed: *L* (1957); *M-N* (1959-60); *O* (1983). 3 fascicules of *P* published, 1985-89 (P-Passerulus).

Covers the language of authors active in the period AD800-1200, supplementing Du Cange. Very clearly presented, the entries giving French translations for separate, numbered applications of the Latin headwords supported by many quotations from literature.

Index scriptorum novus mediae latinitatis ab anno DCCC usque ad annum MCC qui afferuntur in Novo glossario ab Academiis Consociatis juris publici facto (Copenhagen, Munksgaard, 1973, xvii,246p.) lists the works of the medieval Latin writers cited in the *Novum glossarium*. Also includes extensive list of periodicals and collections.
Class No: 807.33(038)

[5952]

SOUTER, A. A Glossary of later Latin, to 600AD. Oxford, Clarendon Press, 1949. xxxii,454p.

Nearly 40,000 entries, covering the literature from AD180. This Latin-English glossary thus serves as a complement to the *Oxford Latin dictionary* (Classical Latin only, excluding Christian authors) and links up with the revised edition of Du Cange's *Glossarium mediae et infimae latinitatis*. It gives, where possible, Greek or Classical Latin equivalents, English translation and exact source. List of authors cited, p.vii-xxix; periodicals, p.xxx.
Class No: 807.33(038)

Greek Language

Bibliographies

[5953]

KESSELS, A.H.M. *and* **VERDENIUS, W.J. A Concise bibliography of Greek language and literature.** Apeldoorn, Administratief Centrum, 1979. vi,287p.

The 1st English ed. of a Dutch bibliography first published 1953 and intended for teachers and students of classics.

A classified, unannotated bibliography in 31 sections covering topics and individual writers, for whom editions, indexes, and studies are listed. Index. *Class No:* 807.5(01)

Dictionaries

[5954]

BUCK, C.D. *and* **PETERSEN, W. A Reverse index of Greek nouns and adjectives,** arranged by terminations with brief historical introductions. Chicago, Univ. of Chicago Press, 1945 (repr. Forestburgh, NY, Lubrecht & Cramer, 1983). xvii,756p. $128.70. ISBN: 3487032031.

More than 100,000 entries arranged in about 100 groups under main headings of vowel and diphthong stems, and nasal, liquid, labial, dental, guttural and palatal terminations in reverse alphabetical order within each group. Proper names mostly omitted. Covers literature, inscriptions, papyri, commentators, grammarians, and lexicographers up to the Byzantine age. *Class No:* 807.5(038)

[5955]
ESTIENNE, H. Thesaurus graecae linguae, ab Henrico Stephano constructus. Post editionem anglicam novis additamentis auctum, ordineque alphabetico digestum tertio ediderunt Carolus Benedictus Hase ... Gulielmus Dindorfus et Ludovicus Dindorfus. Paris, Didot, 1831-65 (repr. Graz, Akademische Druck- und Verlagsanstalt, 1954). 8v. in 9.

The original work was published in Geneva, 1572-73, in 5 folio vols. A London edition was published by Valpy, 1815-25.

Gives many quotations, with sources, and remains a very authoritative dictionary. *Class No:* 807.5(038)

[5956]
—SNELL, B. Lexikon des frühgriechischen Epos, begründet von B. Snell. Im Auftrag der Akademie der Wissenschaften in Göttingen, vorbereitet und herausgegeben vom Thesaurus Linguae Graecae. Göttingen, Vandenhoeck & Ruprecht, 1955-97. Lfg. 1-16 (in progress).

A new *Thesaurus graecae linguae,* covering the early Greek period up to, but not including, the works of Antimachos. Lfg. 1-9 (1955-78) form v.1. and Lfg. 10-14 form v.2. List of sources in Lfg. 1 (5p.). The work of many contributors. *Class No:* 807.5(038)

[5957]
FRISK, H. Griechisches etymologisches Wörterbuch. Heidelberg, Winter, 1954-72. 3v.

An authoritative etymological dictionary of Classical Greek, many of the entries running to more than a page. Etymologies are supported by references to *c.*3,000 sources, these being listed in v.1 (22p.). Many cross-references. Dictionary in vols. 1-2, v.3 containing supplement, word index and corrigenda. *Class No:* 807.5(038)

[5958]
—CHANTRAINE, P. Dictionnaire étymologique de la langue grecque: histoire des mots. Paris, Klincksieck, 1968-80. 4v.

French translations and detailed etymologies for over 6,000 words, with numerous references to literary sources. List of sources in v.1. Word index in over 20 languages in v.4. *Class No:* 807.5(038)

[5959]
LIDDELL, H.G. ***and*** **SCOTT, R. A Greek-English lexicon ... .** 9th ed., rev. and aug. throughout by H.S. Jones (and others); with revised Supplement, ed. by P.G.W. Glare. Oxford, Clarendon Press, 1995. 2378p. £100. ISBN: 0198642261.

1st ed. 1843. This ed. published in 10 pts., 1925-40. *Supplement* first published 1968.

The standard classical Greek-English dictionary, based on F. Passow's *Handwörterbuch der griechischen Sprache* (5th ed. Leipzig, Vogel, 1841-57. 2v. in 4). Etymological comment is deliberately reduced to a minimum; place names and many proper names are omitted, so that it is necessary to use Passow for this purpose. About 10,000 entries. Words beginning with the same element are usually grouped together. Latin and Semitic words in Greek form are included, but Byzantine and patristic literature is not covered, the dictionary limiting its period roughly to AD600. New words and new meanings are included in an Addendum. List of authors and works referred to precedes the dictionary.

The revised *Supplement* is a complete replacement for the 1968 ed. and is nearly twice its size, with over 20,000 entries. It adds words and forms from papyri and inscriptions discovered between 1940 and the 1990s and

.... (contd.)

includes numerous amendments and updatings to the main dictionary. *Supplement* may be purchased separately (320p. £50. ISBN: 0198642237). *Class No:* 807.5(038)

[5960]
—RENEHAN, R. Greek lexicographical notes: a critical supplement to the Greek-English lexicon of Liddell-Scott-Jones. Göttingen, Vandenhoeck & Ruprecht, 1975-82. 2v.

[First series], 1975. 208p. ISBN: 3525257295.

Second series. 1982. 143p. ISBN: 3525251726.

The 2 vols. comprise *c.*1,400 vocabulary entries which are either inadequately documented or non-existent in the 9th ed. (1940) of *A Greek-English lexicon. Class No:* 807.5(038)

[5961]
WOODHOUSE, S.C. English-Greek dictionary: a vocabulary of the Attic language. 2nd ed., with a supplement of proper names, including Greek equivalents for famous names in Roman history. London, Routledge, 1932 (frequently reprinted). viii,1029p. £70. ISBN: 0710023243.

1st ed. 1910.

20,000 entry-words in the main sequence, plus *c.*1,800 proper names in the supplement. Each Greek word preceded by 'P' or 'V' (or both) to indicate whether from a prose or verse writer. *Class No:* 807.5(038)

Histories

[5962]
HORROCKS, G. Greek: a history of the language and its speakers. Harlow, Longman, 1997. xxi,393p. £49. (*Longman linguistics library*.) ISBN: 0582031915.

Traces the development of the Greek language from the Mycenaean period to the present in 3 sections (Ancient Greek; Byzantium; from the Ottoman Empire to the European Union) and 17 chapters with numbered subsections. Narrative is supported by detailed summaries of key developments in checklist form, examinations of selected texts, and maps. Many quotations with transcription, gloss and translation. Detailed table of contents. Bibliography (15p.). Index. *Class No:* 807.5(091)

New Testament Greek

[5963]
BAUER, W. A Greek-English lexicon of the New Testament and other early Christian literature; a translation and adaptation of W. Bauer's *Griechisch-deutsches Wörterbuch zu den Schriften des Neuen Testaments und der übrigen urchristlichen Literatur* (4th ed. 1952) by W. F Arndt and F.W. Gingrich. 2nd ed., rev. and aug. from Bauer's 5th ed., 1958. Chicago, Cambridge Univ. of Chicago Press, 1979. 900p. £43.95. ISBN: 0226039323.

1st ed. Cambridge, Cambridge Univ. Press, 1957.

Gives exact references to sources, which include periodicals, collections and modern authors. List of sources (10p.). References to scholarly literature extend to late 1954.

J.R. Alsop's *An Index to the revised Bauer-Arndt-Gingrich Greek lexicon, second edition* (Grand Rapids, Mich., Zondervan, 1981. 525p. $22.99. ISBN: 0310440319) lists the entries in the order in which they appear in the New Testament, from Matthew to Revelation, with references to page numbers in the lexicon and English translations.
Class No: 807.7:225

[5964]

—GINGRICH, F.W. Shorter lexicon of the Greek New Testament. 2nd ed., rev. by F.W. Danker. Chicago, Univ. of Chicago Press, 1983. 221p. £19.95. ISBN: 0226136132.

1st ed. 1965.

An abridged, and slightly revised, version of Bauer, as translated by Arndt and Gingerich, with the emphasis 'on the bare meanings of words' (*Preface*). Some of the conclusions reached in the larger lexicon have been modified.
Class No: 807.7:225

Mediaeval & Byzantine

[5965]

DU CANGE, C. du Fresne. Glossarium ad scriptores mediae & infimae graecitatis ... réimp. du Collège de France. Paris, Geuthner, 1943. 1250p.

First published Lyon, 1688.

Remains one of the most authoritative reference works on medieval Greek. Includes many quotations, with precise references to sources. An appendix covers etymology.
Class No: 807.73

[5966]

A Patristic Greek lexicon. Lampe, G.W.H., *ed.* Oxford, Clarendon Press, 1968. 1616p. £190. ISBN: 019864213x.

Originally published in 5 fascicules, 1961-68.

The primary aim is 'to interpret the theological and ecclesiastical vocabulary of the Greek Christian authors from Clement of Rome to Theodore of Studium (*c.*AD200-400)' (*Preface*). Complementary to Liddell & Scott, which omits Patristic Greek. Numerous quotations. List of authors and works cited (35p.). *Class No:* 807.73

[5967]

SOPHOCLES, E.A. Greek lexicon of the Roman and Byzantine periods (from BC146 to AD1100). Thayer, J.H., *ed.* Memorial ed. New York, Scribner, 1887. xvi,1188p. (repr. New York, Ungar, 1957. 2v.).

1st ed. 1870.

Greek-English dictionary with *c.*45,000 entry-words and many quotations. Introductory survey of dialects, periods, grammar, etc. of the Greek language. List of authors cited (10p.). *Class No:* 807.73

Modern Greek

Dictionaries

[5968]

ANDRIOTIS, N.P. Etymologiko lexiko tis koinis noellinikis. Rev. ed. Thessaloniki, Univ. of Thessalonika, 1983. xxiv,443p. £18.

1st ed. 1951.

The standard etymological dictionary of literary and spoken demotic, with brief entries for *c.*22,000 words.
Class No: 807.74(038)

[5969]

Collins English-Greek dictionary. Glasgow, HarperCollins, 1997. xix,931p. £15.99. ISBN: 000433387x.

Claims over 60,000 references, including proper names and abbreviations. English phrases used as examples are drawn from the 'Bank of English' corpus.
Class No: 807.74(038)

[5970]

CRIGHTON, W. Mega ellinoanglikon lexikon / Great Greek-English dictionary. Athens, Eleftheroudakis, *c.*1988. 1681p. £38.75.

Covers both demotic and *katharevousa* (the written language until recently used by the state), with all explanatory material in Greek.

A companion vol. is G. Calfoglu's *Anglo-Greek dictionary* (Athens, privately printed, 1979. 1200p.).
Class No: 807.74(038)

[5971]

DEMETRAKOS, D.B. Mega lexikon tēs hēllenikēs glōssēs. Athens, Dēmētrakon, 1936-50. 9v.

A major monolingual dictionary, with *c.*200,000 entry words, covering both Classical and Modern Greek. Chronologically arranged examples. Extensive list of sources in v.1 (10p.).

Dēmētrakos's *Neon lexikon orthographikon kai hermēneutikon holēs tēs Hellēnikēs glōssēs* (Athens, Pergamēnai, 1959. 1526p.) is an abridged version.
Class No: 807.74(038)

[5972]

Hyper lexikon Stafylides, A.D., *and others, eds.* Athens, Stafylides, 1993. v,1358p. £89.60. ISBN: 9608525535.

A Greek-English / English-Greek dictionary which claims to be the most complete ever published, with *c.*60,000 entries, including proper names. *Class No:* 807.74(038)

[5973]

Langenscheidt's standard Greek dictionary, Greek-English / English-Greek. Magazis, G.A., *ed.* Berlin, Langenscheidt, 1989 (repr. 1992). 863p. £14.99. ISBN: 3468970625.

First published Athens, Efstathiadis, 1989, as *Efstathiadis English dictionary*.

A compact 2-way dictionary with *c.*50,000 entries, including many idiomatic expressions. Up-to-date vocabulary, with acronyms and abbreviations in main sequence. Intended primarily for Greek users, with phonetic transcriptions of all English headwords.
Class No: 807.74(038)

[5974]

Mega anglo-hellēnikon lexikon. Athens, Odysseus, [1962?] (available in UK from Zeno, London). 4v. £175. ISBN: 0900834536.

A comprehensive English-Greek dictionary, with *c.*80,000 entry-words including technical terms. Gives formal and demotic Greek equivalents of English terms. Many idioms and examples of usage. *Class No:* 807.74(038)

[5975]

NTC's new college Greek and English dictionary. Nathanail, P., *comp.* Lincolnwood, Ill., NTC, 1985 (repr. 1990). xviii,556p. £17.95. ISBN: 0844284823.

A 2-way dictionary of demotic Greek with over 50,000 entries, including many business and technical terms. Lists of geographical names (3p.) and Greek irregular verbs (13p.). *Class No:* 807.74(038)

[5976]

PRING, J.T. The Pocket Oxford Greek dictionary: English-Greek / Greek-English. Rev. ed. Oxford, Clarendon Press, 1995. 640p. £9.99. ISBN: 0198641966.

1st ed. published in 2 vols., 1982. Earlier printings of this ed. entitled *The Oxford dictionary of modern Greek.*

'Designed to meet the need for a compact, up-to-date dictionary suitable both for general reference and the language student' (*Preface*) and therefore concentrates on the vocabulary of everyday affairs and general literature. Claims

....*(contd.)*
67,000 words and phrases, with 82,000 translations. Many idioms and illustrative phrases included, with points of Greek style and usage explained in English. Uses the monotonic spelling system, now the most widely used in Greece. Appendices list place names, personal names and principal parts of Greek verbs. *Class No:* 807.74(038)

[5977]
'Proia' Lexikon tis neas ellinikis glossis. Athens, Dimitrakos, 1933 (repr. 1976). 3v.

The standard monolingual dictionary of Modern Greek, with over 75,000 words and many examples. Frequently reprinted but not revised, although reprints include a supplement first published *c.*1940. *Class No:* 807.74(038)

[5978]
STAVROPOULOS, D.N. *and* **HORNBY, A.S. The Oxford Greek-English learner's dictionary.** Oxford, Oxford Univ. Press, 1989. iv,1019p. illus. £19.99. ISBN: 0194311996.

Intended for Greek speakers (whereas Pring's dictionary is aimed at English speakers) and regarded as the best Greek-English dictionary available. 45,000 entries, with many examples of usage. Code numbers with inflected words refer to declension and conjugation tables.

The companion vol. is the same authors' *Oxford English-Greek learner's dictionary* (1977; repr. 1988. xxiv,839p. ISBN: 0194311473), which is based on Hornby's *Oxford advanced learner's dictionary of current English* with all the definitions and illustrative sentences adapted and translated into Modern Greek. Over 20,000 entry-words. Appended lists of abbreviations, geographical names, and classical names. All introductory material in Greek.
Class No: 807.74(038)

[5979]
Tegopoulos-Fytrakis Elliniko lexiko. New ed. Athens, Armonis, 1989. xvi,1005p. £35.

'A best-selling, compendious, up-to-date dictionary of demotic and katharevousa, with all interpretations and explanatory material in demotic' (*The Working languages of the European Community,* ed. by A.J. Walford, 1991, p.175). *Class No:* 807.74(038)

[5980]
VOSTANTZOGLOU, T. Antilexikon. 2nd ed. Athens, Domi, 1962. xxiv,1138p. £59.50.

'A voluminous thesaurus of Modern Greek by concepts (all in Greek); synonyms are distinguished from each other as far as possible by sub-headings' (*The Working languages of the European Community*, ed. by A.J. Walford, 1991, p.175).

Lexiko ton synonymon tis neoellinikis by K. Dangitsis (Athens, Vasiliou, 1986. xxii,489p.) is a smaller dictionary of synonyms, arranged A-Z by keywords.
Class No: 807.74(038)

Grammar

[5981]
Greek: a comprehensive grammar of the modern language. Holton, D., *& others, eds.* London, Routledge, 1997. xxi,519p. £50. (*Routledge grammars.*) ISBN: 0415100011.

3 main sections (1. The Sound and writing systems - 2. Morphology - 3. Syntax) with numbered chapters and subsections. Many up-to-date examples (with translations) are included: 'The form of the language described is primarily the usage of native Greek speakers living in the urban centres of Greece who have completed at least their compulsory secondary education' (*Preface*). Glossary of grammatical terms (13p.). Detailed contents list and extensive index. *Class No:* 807.74-5

Slavonic & Baltic Languages

[5982]
TERRY, G.M. East European languages and literatures: a subject and name index to articles in English-language journals, 1900-77. Oxford and Santa Barbara, Calif., Clio, 1978. xxv,275p. £26.50. ISBN: 0903450216.

Expanded version of an index published privately in 1976 for staff and students at Nottingham University.

Covers Slavic countries plus Finland, Baltic States, Hungary and Romania. Indexes over 9,500 articles from 800 journals in a single A-Z sequence of names and subjects.

Further vols. have been published by Astra Press, Nottingham, as follows: *1978-81, with articles in Festschriften, conference proceedings and collected papers, 1900-81.* 1982 (xxx,218p. ISBN: 0946134006); *1982-84.* 1985 (xviii,152p. ISBN: 0946134057); *1985-87.* 1988 (xviii,130p. ISBN: 0946134138); *1988-90.* 1991 (xxii,150p. £18. ISBN: 0946134251); *1991-93.* 1994 (xx,136p. £18. ISBN: 0946134391); *1994-96.* 1997 (xxii,138p. £18. ISBN: 0946134502). *Class No:* 808

Slavonic Languages

Bibliographies

[5983]
AKADEMIYA NAUK SSSR. Institut Russkogo Yazyka. **Slavyanskoe yazykoznanie:** bibliograficheskii ukazatel' literatury, izdannoi v SSSR s 1918 po 1960 gg. Moskva, [The Academy], 1963. 2v.

A classified bibliography of nearly 15,000 works published in the USSR, 1918-60, on Slavic linguistics.

Further vols. were published in 1969 (465p.) covering 1961-65, and in 1973 (447p.), covering 1966-70, adding over 20,000 items. *Class No:* 808.1(01)

[5984]
The American bibliography of Slavic and East European studies, 1968/69-. Stanford, Calif. (formerly Columbus, Ohio), American Assoc. for the Advancement of Slavic Studies, 1974-. Annual. ISSN: 00943770.

Succeeds *American bibliography of Russian and East European studies, 1955-66* (Bloomington, Ind., Indiana Univ. Press, 1957-67) and *1967* (Columbus, Ohio State Univ., 1972). Currently prepared for AAASS at the Univ. of Illinois, Urbana-Champaign.

An annual, classified list of US and Canadian publications in the field and of English-language studies published elsewhere. The bibliography for 1992 (1994. xviii,513p.) has 7,849 entries in 19 sections, of which 787 relate to literature and 143 to linguistics. Includes references for individual writers. Author index. *Class No:* 808.1(01)

[5985]
European bibliography of Soviet, East European and Slavonic studies, v.1, 1975-. Armand, M., *and others, eds.* Birmingham, Univ. of Birmingham, 1977-79; Paris, Institut d'Études Slaves, 1981-. Annual. ISSN: 1259458x.

See entry at 880(01). *Class No:* 808.1(01)

[5986]

LEWANSKI, R.C. A Bibliography of Slavic dictionaries. 2nd ed., rev. and enl. Bologna, Editrice Compositori/Istituto Informatico Italiano, 1972-73. 4v. (*World bibliography of dictionaries*.)

Lists over 11,000 monolingual, bilingual, and polyglot dictionaries. Polish in v.1, Russian in v.3, and 12 other Slavic languages in v.2, with supplementary listings for all languages in v.4. Indexes of authors, languages, and subjects in each vol. *Class No:* 808.1(01)

[5987]

Slavic studies: a guide to bibliographies, encyclopedias, and handbooks. Croucher, M., *ed.* Wilmington, Del., Scholarly Resources, 1993. 2v. $150. ISBN: 0842023747.

'Attempts to list major reference materials for Slavic studies in English, German, French and in any of the Slavic languages' (*Introduction*). 5,264 entries under Library of Congress headings in 8 sections: Area studies; Eastern Europe and Balkans; Bulgaria; Czechoslovakia; Poland; Soviet Union; Former Yugoslavia; General references. Language and literature sources listed in each section. Author and title indexes. *Class No:* 808.1(01)

[5988]

STANKIEWICZ, E. Grammars and dictionaries of the Slavic languages from the Middle Ages up to 1850: an annotated bibliography. Berlin, Mouton, 1984. xii,190p. illus. DM115. ISBN: 3110097788.

Arranged in separate sections for 10 languages, with author index and index of cities. Secondary bibliography (16p.), arranged by language. List of facsimiles and critical editions. *Class No:* 808.1(01)

[5989]

STANKIEWICZ, E. *and* **WORTH, D.S. A Selected bibliography of Slavic linguistics.** The Hague, Mouton, 1966-70. 2v.

A classified bibliography of mainly 20th-century studies, v.1 covering general studies, Old Church Slavonic and the South Slavic languages, and v.2 the West and East Slavic languages. Separate sections for individual languages are consistently divided by linguistic topics. *c.*16,000 entries. Name index in each vol. *Class No:* 808.1(01)

Handbooks & Manuals

[5990]

DE BRAY, R.G.A. Guide to the Slavonic languages. 3rd ed., rev. and expanded. Columbus, Ohio, Slavica, 1980. 3v.

1st ed. London, Dent, 1951; 2nd ed. 1969.

Pt. 1 *South Slavonic languages*. 399p. ISBN: 0893570605.

Pt. 2 *West Slavonic languages*. 483p. ISBN: 0893570613.

Pt. 3 *East Slavonic languages*. 254p. ISBN: 0893570621.

Separate sections on each of 12 languages, covering alphabet, pronunciation, dialects, characteristic features, morphology, and word order, and including representative literary texts. Bibliography of recommended dictionaries, grammars, and books on orthography and phonetics for each language, with the emphasis on works in English.
Class No: 808.1(035)

[5991]

HORÁLEK, K. An Introduction to the study of the Slavonic languages. Herrity, P., *trans. & ed.* Nottingham, Astra Press, 1992. 2v. £55. ISBN: 094613426x, v.1; 0946134340, v.2.

A translation of 2nd, amended and enlarged ed. of *Úvod do studia slovanských jazyků* (Praha, 1962). 1st ed. 1955).

A comprehensive and reliable introductory study. Topics covered include: Comparative historical linguistics; Indo-European; Proto-Slavonic; Early Slav tribes and kingdoms; Old Church Slavonic; Slavonic alphabets; Historical phonology, morphology and syntax of Slav languages; Lexicon; Development of literary languages; Characteristic features of individual Slav languages; History of comparative Slavonic linguistics to 1962. Expanded and updated bibliography has 1,800 entries. *Class No:* 808.1(035)

Standards

[5992]

BRITISH STANDARDS INSTITUTION. Transliteration of Cyrillic and Greek characters. London, BSI, 1983. 24p. £50.

BS 2979:1958 (1997).

1. British traditional-type system - 2. International system for modern Cyrillic - 3. Rule-of-thumb system for Greek, without special regard to phonetic peculiarities of Ancient or Modern Greek, in line with international practice.
Class No: 808.1(083.74)

Histories

[5993]

CARLTON, T.R. Introduction to the phonological history of the Slavic languages. Columbus, Ohio, Slavica, 1991. 462p. $24.95. ISBN: 0893572233.

9 chapters with many subdivisions, although these are not numbered. Particularly useful is ch.9: 'Summary of the major differences in the individual languages' based on a set of 21 questions applied to 12 languages. Appended table compares 200 basic vocabulary items in 15 languages. 14 dialect maps. 3 sets of parallel texts. Glossary of Slavic words used in the text, arranged by language (as in ch.9), with English translations (52p.). Bibliography (13p.). Index.
Class No: 808.1(091)

Russian Language

Bibliographies

[5994]

SCHALLER, H.W. Bibliographie zur russischen Sprache. Frankfurt am Main, Lang, 1980. 204p.

A classified bibliography with over 2,700 items. Author and subject indexes. *Class No:* 808.2(01)

[5995]

UNBEGAUN, B.O. A Bibliographical guide to the Russian language. Oxford, Clarendon Press, 1953. xii,174p.

1,043 items systematically arranged in 3 parts (General, Historical and Descriptive), 10 chapters, and numerous subsections. Russian titles and names in Cyrillic form only. Concise, evaluative annotations plus explanatory introductions to sections and running commentary. Fully cross-referenced. Index. *Class No:* 808.2(01)

Handbooks & Manuals

[5996]

An Introduction to Russian language and literature. Auty, R. *and* Obolensky, D., *eds*. Cambridge, Cambridge Univ. Press, 1977. xiii,300p. (*Companion to Russian studies, v.2.*) ISBN: 0521280397.

Chapters on Russian language (p.1-40) and Russian writing and printing (p.41-55) are followed by a history of the literature from AD1000 to 1975 in 5 chapters and a history of Russian theatre in 3 chapters. Each chapter is by an acknowledged specialist and is followed by extensive lists, with commentary, of recommended general studies and reference works, and of works by and about individual authors. Index. *Class No:* 808.2(035)

Histories

[5997]

VLASTO, A.P. A Linguistic history of Russia to the end of the eighteenth century. Oxford, Oxford Univ. Press, 1986. xx,408p. ISBN: 0198156626.

Separate chapters on phonology, morphology, syntax, vocabulary, dialects, and the spoken and written languages. Numbered paragraphs, tables and numerous examples. Index of words treated in vocabulary chapter (over 800 entries), but the lack of a general subject index is a drawback. Select bibliography. *Class No:* 808.2(091)

Usage

[5998]

OFFORD, D. Using Russian: a guide to contemporary usage. Cambridge, Cambridge Univ. Press, 1996. 436p. £40. ISBN: 0521451302.

A guide to Russian usage for those who have already acquired the basics of the language, paying special attention to those areas of grammar and vocabulary which cause most difficulty to English speakers. Well organized and easy to use, like the publisher's guides to French, German and Spanish in the same series. *Class No:* 808.2-06

Dialects

[5999]

FILIN, F.D. Slovar' russkikh narodnykh govorov. Leningrad, Nauka, 1965-74. 10v.

A dictionary of Russian national dialects. Extensive bibliography of manuscript and printed sources in v.1. *Class No:* 808.2-087

Dictionaries & Vocabularies

Bibliographies

[6000]

AKADEMIYA NAUK SSSR. Institut Russkogo Yazyka. **Slovari, izdannye v SSSR:** bibliograficheskii ukazatel', 1918-1962. Izhevskaya, M.G., *ed*. Moskva, Nauka, 1966. 232p.

A bibliography of Russian monolingual and bilingual dictionaries published in the USSR, with 4,052 entries systematically arranged by language and subject. Indexes of compilers and languages. *Class No:* 808.2-3(01)

[6001]

ZALEWSKI, W. Russian-English dictionaries with aids for translators: a selected bibliography. 2nd ed. New York, Russica, 1981. 101p. $12. ISBN: 089830041x.

1st ed. Stanford, Calif., Stanford Univ. Libraries, 1976.

An annotated list of postwar dictionaries, with particular emphasis on bilingual dictionaries of specialist subjects. *Class No:* 808.2-3(01)

Synonyms

[6002]

ALEKSANDROVA, Z.E. Slovar' sinonimov russkogo yazyka. 6. izd. Moskva, Russkii Yazyk, 1989. 494p.

1st ed. 1968.

Includes *c.*11,000 synonyms. *Class No:* 808.2-314

Loan Words

[6003]

PCHELINKA, V. Slovar' inostrannykh slov. Moskva, Russkii Yazyk, 1989. 622p.

19,000 foreign words adopted by the Russian language. *Class No:* 808.2-316.3

Idioms

[6004]

LUBENSKY, S. Random House Russian-English dictionary of idioms. New York, Random House, 1995. xxvii,1017p. £50. ISBN: 0679405801.

A major academic work which covers over 7,500 expressions, including idioms, set expressions and sayings. Entries comprise: the idiom in Russian; grammatical information; definition in English; usage notes; American English equivalents; illustrative examples (often lengthy) from Russian literature, with English translation; and etymological notes where these aid understanding. Bibliography of 235 literary sources and other dictionaries (14p.). Keyword index. *Class No:* 808.2-318

[6005]

—MERTVAGO, P. The Comparative Russian-English dictionary of Russian proverbs and sayings. New York, Hippocrene, 1995. viii,477p. £31.99. ISBN: 0781804248.

5,543 numbered entries comprising Russian phrase, literal translation, and comparison with English sayings where appropriate. The 1,900 most common Russian sayings are highlighted. Cross-references between sayings on related subjects. Bibliography (4p.). Keyword index of English proverbs for which there are Russian equivalents. *Class No:* 808.2-318

Monoglot Dictionaries

[6006]

AKADEMIYA NAUK SSSR. Institut Russkogo Yazyka. **Slovar' russkogo yazyka.** Evgen'eva, A., *ed*. 2. izd. Moskva, Izd-vo Russkii Yazyk, 1981. 4v. £85.

1st ed. 1957-61.

A general dictionary of the Russian language with the emphasis on current usage. Contains over 90,000 entries with detailed definitions and illustrative quotations from literary sources. Includes proper names. *Class No:* 808.2-323.1

[6007]

DAL', V.I. Tolkovyi slovar' zhivogo velikorusskogo yazyka. 4. izd. St. Petersburg, Wolf, 1913. 4v. (repr. Oxford, Pergamon, 1978. lxxxviii,700p.). ISBN: 0080235905.

A valuable pre-Revolutionary dictionary, which includes many dialect words, slang terms and colloquialisms. A facsimile reprint is in progress (Moskva, Russkii Yazyk, 1989-).

A similar work, based to some extent on Dal' is D.N. Ushakov's *Tolkovyi slovar' russkogo yazyka* (Moskva, 1938-40. 4v.). which categorizes words (literary, conversational, etc.) and indicates pronunciation, meaning and usage. Generally omits dialect words and technical terms.
Class No: 808.2-323.1

[6008]

OZHEGOV, S.I. Slovar' russkogo yazyka. 22. izd. Moskva, Russkii Yazyk, 1990. 928p. ISBN: 0569093007.

1st ed. 1949.

The standard one-vol. monolingual dictionary, regularly revised, with *c.*70,000 entries covering the basic vocabulary and indicating pronunciation, stress, grammatical agreements, and usage. *Class No:* 808.2-323.1

[6009]

ROSSIYSKAYA AKADEMIYA NAUK. Institut Russkogo Yazyka. **Slovar' sovremennego russkogo literaturnogo yazyka v 20 tomakh.** Moskva, Rossiyskaya Akademiya Nauk, 1990-94. v.1-6 (in progress). ISBN: 5200010683.

A dictionary of modern literary Russian (*i.e.* from the era of Pushkin to the present) which will supersede the Soviet Academy's 17-vol. work published 1950-65. Due to be completed in 20 vols. by the end of the century and expected to contain over 120,000 words.

Each vol. has *c.*15,000 entry-words, under which related words are grouped, philological background given, and meanings illustrated by quotations (with sources and dates) from literary, scientific and political works. Generally omits dialect and technical terms, but includes many foreign loanwords. Most entries include a reference section, showing the attribution of the word in earlier dictionaries, with a summary of its grammatical, word-forming, orthographical and orthoepic variants. Etymological information on words of foreign origin is also given.
Class No: 808.2-323.1

Bilingual Dictionaries

[6010]

BENSON, M. *and* BENSON, E. Russian-English dictionary of verbal collocations. Amsterdam, Benjamins, 1993. xviii,269p. £25. ISBN: 9027221278.

The work of 2 of the compilers of *The BBI combinatory dictionary of English* (*q.v.*), this dictionary lists *c.*20,000 verbal collocations used in contemporary Russian, under 4,600 main headings, and translates them, using corresponding English collocations whenever possible. Many illustrative examples from the Russian press. An invaluable aid to translators of both languages.
Class No: 808.2-323.2

[6011]

Bol'shoi anglo-russkii slovar'/ New English-Russian dictionary. Galperin, I.R. *and* Mednikova, E.M., *eds.* New ed. Moskva, Russkii Yazik, 1994. 3v. £69.95. ISBN: 5200084989.

1st ed. Moskva Sovetskaya Entsiklopediya, 1972. Supplement, 1980. Previous eds. in 2 vols., ed. by I.R. Galperin and E.M. Mednikova.

....*(contd.)*

The biggest English-Russian dictionary available, with *c.*150,000 entry-words. The emphasis is on current vocabulary, with many scientific and technical terms and idioms. Intended for Russians, with pronunciation given for English headwords, but the preface and introduction are in English and Russian. Supplement (now incorporated) lists *c.*12,000 new words and phrases. Appended lists of forenames, place names, and abbreviations. 'For sheer detail of coverage and range of usage, this work is almost unparalleled, and must long remain a true lodestar' (*Language Monthly*, April 1986, p.19, on an earlier ed.).
Class No: 808.2-323.2

[6012]

BROWN, N.J. Russian learners' dictionary: 10,000 words in frequency order. London, Routledge, 1996. 429p. £45. ISBN: 0415137918.

Takes the learner from a beginner's core vocabulary through to postgraduate level, with numbered entries comprising Russian headword and English translation, with usage examples for many terms (the first 600 all have these). Also includes information on stress and grammatical irregularities. Alphabetical index of headwords with English glosses. *Class No:* 808.2-323.2

[6013]

Elsevier's Russian-English dictionary. Macura, P., *comp.* Amsterdam, Elsevier, 1990. 4v. (xxxiv,3208p.). $389. ISBN: 044488467x.

A dictionary for translators, with *c.*240,000 entry words, many of them from specialized fields. Entries include a good deal of grammatical information, giving genitive case ending and gender for nouns and first and second person singular endings for verbs, with more if the verb is irregularly conjugated. Stress marked on Russian headwords.
Class No: 808.2-323.2

[6014]

KATZNER, K. English-Russian / Russian-English dictionary. Rev. ed. New York, Wiley, 1994. xv,1098p. £24.95. ISBN: 0471017078.

1st ed. 1984.

Claims to be the first full-size 2-way dictionary of Russian and English to be published in a single vol. and the first to be based on American English. 26,000 English-Russian entries and 40,000 Russian-English, with many illustrative sentences in the latter section. List of proper names (mainly geographical). Rev. ed. reflects post-Soviet language.
Class No: 808.2-323.2

[6015]

MARDER, S. A Supplementary Russian-English dictionary. Columbus, Ohio, Slavica, 1992. xv,522p. £24.50. ISBN: 0893572284.

29,000 entries, with the emphasis on vocabulary not covered by the established dictionaries, which it is intended to supplement rather than supplant. Strong on recent political, scientific and technological developments, especially computing, but jargon and highly specialized terms are avoided. Sources include contemporary literature, press, TV and films. Good coverage also given to spoken language, with many terms labelled to indicate that they belong to colloquial, slang or vulgar speech. Copious examples of usage, often in the form of short phrases or mini-dialogues. Abbreviations and acronyms in the main sequence. Primary stress shown in all polysyllabic words,

....(*contd.*)
with pronunciation indicated where not inferrable from the orthography (often words of foreign origin). Large page format. *Class No:* 808.2-323.2

[6016]

The Oxford Russian dictionary: Russian-English / English-Russian. Howlett, C., *ed.* Rev. ed. Oxford, Oxford Univ. Press, 1997. xvi,1340p. £30. ISBN: 0198601530.

1st ed. 1993, being an amalgamated, revised and updated ed. of *The Oxford English-Russian dictionary* (1984) and *The Oxford Russian-English dictionary* (2nd ed. 1984).

Over 180,000 words and phrases with 290,000 translations, including 5,000 new terms to bring the vocabulary up to date. Acronyms and abbreviations included. Coverage of American as well as British English and also regional Russian dialects. Numerous illustrative examples of current idioms and colloquial usage. Primarily intended for English speakers at college/university level, but all English headwords have been transcribed into IPA, enhancing its usefulness to native Russian speakers. Brief introductory guide for users (9p.).

Rev. ed. appears to include no new material, but according to the jacket blurb 'translations have been improved and updated where appropriate to reflect the most recent developments'.

Also available on CD-ROM at £49.99. (ISBN: 0192685589).

The Concise Oxford Russian dictionary (1996. 1040p. £19.99. ISBN: 0198643381) claims over 120,000 words and phrases with 190,000 translations. *Class No:* 808.2-323.2

[6017]

OZIEVA, A., *and others*. Collins Russian-English / English-Russian dictionary. Glasgow, HarperCollins, 1994. xxx+572+9+564+19p. £15.99. ISBN: 0004333888.

A major new dictionary of Russian which claims over 80,000 references and 115,000 translations, concentrating on contemporary written and spoken language with special emphasis on business and commerce. Numerous illustrative phrases. Style levels clearly marked. Stress indicated for all Russian headwords. 'Keywords' given special status, being highlighted and accompanied by notes on usage. Abbreviations, acronyms and proper names in main sequences. Introduction includes guide to pronunciation and grammar. *Class No:* 808.2-323.2

[6018]

RYAN, W.F. *and* NORMAN, P. The Penguin Russian dictionary. London, Viking, 1995. xxxi,1120p. ISBN: 067082836x.

A 2-way dictionary which claims 140,000 entries and derivatives, including slang and colloquialisms; commercial, legal, scientific and technical terms; abbreviations and acronyms; literary and archaic words; many proper names; and new post-Soviet terminology. Russian-English section includes grammatical information cross-referenced to introductory guide to Russian grammar (19p.). Stress on Russian words indicated throughout. Takes account of North American as well as British usage. A good dictionary marred by small format and consequent tiny typeface.
Class No: 808.2-323.2

[6019]

SMIRNITSKII, A.I. Russko-angliiski slovar' / Russian-English dictionary. 19. izd. (reprint) Moskva, Russki Yazyk, 1997. 768p. £19.95. ISBN: 5200024196.

1st ed. 1948.

30,000 entry-words, with 55,000 terms translated. Many idioms. Stress indicated on Russian words. List of geographical names. Notes on Russian grammar.
Class No: 808.2-323.2

[6020]

—MÜLLER, V.K. Anglo-russkii slovar' / English-Russian dictionary. New ed. Moskva, Russkii Yazyk, 1994. 880p. £19.95. ISBN: 5200021944.

1st ed. 1945.

A companion vol. to Smirnitskii, with over 50,000 entries. Pronunciation given for English headwords. Appended lists of forenames, place-names, and abbreviations.
Class No: 808.2-323.2

[6021]

WILSON, E.A.M. The Modern Russian dictionary for English speakers: English-Russian. Oxford, Pergamon; Moskva, Russkii Yazyk, 1982. 716p. £9.95. ISBN: 0080205542.

'The vocabulary comprises the words which the average educated man might want to use in speaking or writing Russian, including the simple technical terms in common use' (*Introduction*). Over 22,000 entry-words, with excellent coverage of idiomatic usage, the English being 'real and everyday, as it was conspicuously not in some earlier Soviet dictionaries' (*Language Monthly*, April 1986, p.19). Consequently, there are very extensive entries for verbs like 'be', 'get' and 'do', and for prepositions. Good use of stylistic and field labels. Stress indicated for Russian words and some grammatical information provided.
Class No: 808.2-323.2

Grammar

[6022]

AKADEMIYA NAUK SSSR. Institut Russkogo Yazyka. **Russkaya grammatika.** Moskva, Nauka, 1980. 2v. (783; 709p.).

A comprehensive, authoritative grammar from the Russian Academy, arranged in 3,194 numbered sections. Detailed table of contents in each vol. Bibliography (6p.). Indexes.
Class No: 808.2-5

[6023]

DAUM, E. *and* SCHENK, W. A Dictionary of Russian verbs: bases of inflection - aspects - regimen - stressing - meanings. 5th ed. New York, Hippocrene, 1995. 750p. £39.50. ISBN: 0781803713.

A translation of *Die russischen Verben*. 4th ed. Leipzig, VEB, 1988.

An extremely useful work with entries for *c.*20,000 verbs, A-Z, giving aspect, conjugation type, list of basic forms, syntactic regimen and English translation. Dictionary section is followed by an essay on the syntax and semantics of the verb in present-day Russian (p.697-750). *Class No:* 808.2-5

[6024]

WADE, T. A Comprehensive Russian grammar. Oxford, Blackwell, 1992. xxvi,582p. £18.50. (*Blackwell reference grammars.*) ISBN: 0631175024.

The first new reference grammar of Russian since the 1950s is very clearly organized in 10 chapters with 484 numbered sections and further subdivisions. Numerous examples from a wide range of contemporary Russian sources. Bibliography (6p.). Detailed table of contents (15p.), subject index and Russian word index. 'The most complete, accurate, and authoritative English-language reference grammar of Russian ever published' (*Choice*, v.29(10), June 1992, p.1552). *Class No:* 808.2-5

Etymology

[6025]

PREOBRAZHENSKII, A.G. Etymological dictionary of the Russian language. New York, Columbia Univ. Press, 1951. 3v. in 1.

A single-vol. reprint of an important work originally published in Moscow, vols. 1-2 appearing 1910-16 and v.2 in 1949. 'Each entry contains, in addition to examples for all the Slavic languages, comparative linguistic material drawn from other branches of the Indo-European family of languages' (*Introductory note*). Entries also include references to other dictionaries and linguistic studies, and to literary works in which the words are found.

T. Wade's *Russian etymological dictionary* (Bristol, Bristol Classical Press, 1996. 272p. £14.95. ISBN: 1853994146) provides systematic analysis of the derivations of 1,500 key words. *Class No:* 808.2-54

[6026]

VASMER, M. Russisches etymologisches Wörterbuch. Heidelberg, Winter, 1950-58. 3v.

A standard etymological dictionary, with *c.*17,000 entries, including proper names and dialect forms, all with precise references to sources. Bibliography of sources (33p. in v.1). Word index arranged in 32 sections for language groups, with subsections for individual languages.

Has been published in Russian as *Etimologicheskii slovar' russkogo yazyka* (Moskva, Progress Press, 1964-73. 4v.). *Class No:* 808.2-54

Byelorussian

[6027]

MARTYNAU, V., *ed.* **Etymalahichny slounik belaruskai movy.** Minsk, Navuka i Tekhnika, 1978-90. v.1-6 (in progress).

A scholarly etymological dictionary of the Belorussian language. *Class No:* 808.26

[6028]

USHKEVICH, A. *and* **ZEZULIN, A. Byelorussian-English / English-Byelorussian dictionary,** with complete phonetics. New York, Hippocrene, 1992. 290p. £8.99. ISBN: 0870521144.

6,500 entries, giving simple translations with no phrases. Pronunciation for all headwords. *Class No:* 808.26

Ukrainian

[6029]

AKADEMIYA NAUK URSR. Instytut Movoznavstva im. O.O. Potebni. **Slovnyk ukraïns'koi movy.**
Bilodid, I.K., *and others, eds.* Kyiv, Nauk. Dumka, 1970-80. 11v.

The Ukrainian Academy's scholarly monolingual dictionary of spoken and literary Ukrainian. Numerous illustrative quotations with precise references. List of sources (17p.) in v.1. *Class No:* 808.3

[6030]

ANDRUSYSHEN, C.H. *and* **KRETT, J.N. Ukrainian-English dictionary.** Toronto, Univ. of Toronto Press, for the Univ. of Saskatchewan, 1957 (paperback ed. 1981). xxix,1163p. £18. ISBN: 0802064213.

A comprehensive dictionary of *c.*130,000 words and phrases. Shows tonic stress on Ukrainian words and provides examples of usage. Includes proper names in main sequence. Uses the system of orthography accepted in 1928. *Class No:* 808.3

[6031]

BENYUKH, O. *and* **GALUSHKO, R. Hippocrene standard dictionary:** Ukrainian-English. New York, Hippocrene, 1994. xi,296p. £13.99. ISBN: 0781801893.

15,000 entries, with all Ukrainian words in both Cyrillic and transliterated form with pronunciation indicated. List of proper names (10p.). *Class No:* 808.3

[6032]

PODVEZ'KO, M.L. *and* **BALLA, M.I. Anhlo-ukraïns'kyi slovnyk** / English-Ukrainian dictionary. Kyiv, 'Radyans'ka shkola', 1974 (repr. Edmonton, Canadian Institute of Ukrainian Studies, 1993). 663p. £22.50. ISBN: 0920862624.

*c.*65,000 words. Appendices include lists of abbreviations, forenames and geographical names. Pronunciation given for English headwords.

The companion vol. is Podvez'ko's *Ukrains'ko-angliisky slovnyk* (2nd ed. 1989. 1011p. £35.50) with *c.*60,000 Ukrainian words and their English equivalents, including many idiomatic expressions, proverbs and phrases. Stress is marked for all Ukrainian words. *Class No:* 808.3

Polish Language

Dictionaries

[6033]

BULAS, K. *and* **WHITFIELD, F.J. The Kościuszko Foundation dictionary:** English-Polish / Polish-English. The Hague, Mouton, 1959-61. 2v. $54.75.

V.1 *English-Polish*. 1959. xii,1037p. ISBN: 9027909830.
V.2 *Polish-English*. 1961. xii,772p. ISBN: 9027909849.

A major bilingual dictionary, with *c.*50,000 entry-words in v.1 and *c.*40,000 in v.2. In the English-Polish section pronunciation is indicated for all headwords, with British and US practice differentiated. Proper names are included and coverage of slang (especially US) and colloquial usage is good. The vocabulary of v.2 is 'in principle restricted to twentieth-century standard Polish' (*Foreword*), with a few archaisms included. Provincialisms, specialist technical terms and loanwords are generally excluded. Pronunciation is given when not likely to be immediately evident to non-Poles. List of abbreviations appended. *Class No:* 808.4(038)

[6034]

Collins Polish dictionary. Fisiak, J., *ed.* Glasgow, HarperCollins; Warszawa, Polska Oficyna Wydawnicza, 1996. 2v. £30 the set. ISBN: 0004705297.

V.1 *English-Polish.* xvi,521p.

V.2 *Polish-English.* v+505+xiiip.

Claims over 80,000 references and 115,000 translations. Up-to-date vocabulary with business and commerce particularly well represented. Clear layout, good use of register labels and numerous illustrative phrases. Special attention is paid to 'keywords', which have boxed usage notes. Guide to Polish grammar (13p.) in v.2.
Class No: 808.4(038)

[6035]

POGONOWSKI, I.C. Hippocrene standard dictionary: Polish-English / English-Polish. Rev. ed. New York, Hippocrene, 1993. 682,xvip. £14.99. ISBN: 0781801834.

1st ed. 1979.

A handy 2-way dictionary with *c.*16,000 entries in each section. *Class No:* 808.4(038)

[6036]

POLSKA AKADEMIA NAUK. Słownik jezyka polskiego. Doroszewski, W., *ed.* Warszawa, Wiedza Powszechna, 1958-69. 11v.

The Polish Academy's official, scholarly dictionary. *c.*120,000 entries in vols.1-10, with many quotations from literary sources. V.11 is a supplement with *c.*8,000 entries. Bibliography of sources (81p.) in v.1.

The Academy's dictionary of Old Polish is *Słownik staropolski*, 9 vols. of which have been published (1953-87), covering A-Uzywowanie. 7 pts. of v.10 published, 1988-93. *Class No:* 808.4(038)

[6037]

SKORUPKA, S. Słownik frazeologiczny jezyka polskiego. Wyd. 2. Warszawa, Wiedza Powszechna, 1974. 2v.

1st ed. 1967-68.

A major dictionary of Polish idioms, phrases and collocations, with *c.*30,000 entry-words and numerous examples of usage. *Class No:* 808.4(038)

[6038]

Słownik jezyka polskiego. Szymczak, M., *and others, eds.* Rev. ed. Warszawa, Pánstwowe Wydawnictwo Naukowe, 1992. 3v. plus supplement (124p.) ISBN: 8301109025.

1st ed. 1978-81.

A major monolingual dictionary with *c.*80,000 entries, plus 4,000 in supplement.

A reliable single-vol. monolingual dictionary is *Mały słownik jezyka polskiego*, ed. by E. Sobol and others (New ed. Warszawa, PWN, 1993. xxvi,1181p. ISBN: 830111052x), with *c.*40,000 entries. *Class No:* 808.4(038)

[6039]

Słownik wyrazów obcych. Sobol, E., *and others, eds.* Warszawa, PWN, 1995. 1185p. ISBN: 8301114878.

Lists 30,000 loanwords in Polish, with meanings and etymologies. *Class No:* 808.4(038)

[6040]

STANISLAWSKI, J., *and others.* **Podreczny slownik angielsko-polski** / A Practical English-Polish dictionary. Wyd. 4. Warszawa, Wiedza Powszechna, 1981. xiv,913p. £30. ISBN: 8321402453.

1st ed. 1973.

A concise, reliable dictionary with *c.*50,000 words and phrases, covering both general vocabulary and some technical terms. Lists of abbreviations, geographical names and forenames.

.... *(contd.)*

A Practical Polish-English dictionary, by J. Stanislawski and M. Szercha (4th ed. Warszawa, Wiedza Powszechna, 1981. xvi,1036p. £30. ISBN: 8321401244) is similar in size and scope and has appended lists of geographical names and abbreviations. *Class No:* 808.4(038)

[6041]

STANISLAWSKI, J. Wielki slownik angielsko-polski, z suplementem. [Great English-Polish dictionary, supplemented.] Warszawa, Wiedza Powszechna, 1990. 2v. (xvi+692+715p.). £71.95. ISBN: 8321407609.

First published 1964 and frequently revised.

The most comprehensive English-Polish dictionary, with over 100,000 words and phrases, including many scientific and technical terms, plus dialect, colloquial, American and Commonwealth expressions. Entries give pronunciation of English headword and numbered applications. Appendices include lists of geographical names, forenames, literary characters, and abbreviations. This ed. has supplementary lists of new words and meanings in each vol., adding *c.*12,000 entries. *Class No:* 808.4(038)

[6042]

STANISLAWSKI, J. Wielki slownik polsko-angielski, z suplementem. [Great Polish-English dictionary, supplemented.] Warzsawa, Wiedza Powszechna, 1990. 2v. (xvi+800+928p.). £71.95. ISBN: 8321407595.

First published 1969 and frequently revised.

Like its counterpart, the leader in its field with *c.*180,000 Polish words, phrases and expressions, including technical and scientific terms, colloquial, dialectal and historical terms, and many idiomatic phrases. Makes good use of qualifying labels and different typefaces. Appendices include lists of geographical names and abbreviations, and a summary of Polish grammar (52p.).

This ed. has supplementary lists of new words and meanings in each vol., adding *c.*10,000 entries.
Class No: 808.4(038)

Czech

[6043]

ČESKÁ AKADEMIE VĚD A UMĚNI. Přiruční slovník jazyka českého. V Praze, Státní Pedagogické Nakl., 1935-57. 8v. in 9.

The Czech Academy's authoritative dictionary of the language, with illustrative quotations from literary sources. Over 130,000 entries.

A shorter work based on this dictionary is the Academy's *Slovník spisovného jazyka českého* (Praha, 1960-71, 4v.), with *c.*100,000 entries. *Class No:* 808.50

[6044]

HAIS, K. *and* **HODEK, B. Velký anglicko-český slovník /** Large English-Czech dictionary. 2 vyd. Praha, Academia, 1991-93. 4v. (2843p.). £99. ISBN: 802000064x.

1st ed. 1991-93 in 3 vols.

The most comprehensive English-Czech dictionary, with *c.*100,000 entries - the high figure due to the fact that each compound form has a separate entry. Entries comprise headword, pronunciation (IPA), numbered applications, and phrases. Usages specific to the US or UK are clearly labelled. Bibliography (3p.) Appended lists of place-names, personal names, and abbreviations. *Class No:* 808.50

[6045]
—POLDAUF, I. Velký česko-anglický slovník [Comprehensive Czech-English dictionary.] 3 vyd. Čelákovice, WD Publications, 1997. 1187p. £27.95. ISBN: 8090218032.

68,000 entries, with lots of compounds, derivatives and illustrative phrases. List of proper names (16p.). All introductory material in Czech, but includes abstract of Czech grammar (27p.) in English. *Class No:* 808.50

[6046]
MACHEK, V. Etymologický slovník jazyka českého. 3. vyd. Praha, Academia, 1971. 866p.

1st ed. 1957.

A scholarly etymological dictionary of Czech, with over 7,000 entries. Word index arranged in nearly 70 sections according to language of origin. *Class No:* 808.50

[6047]
PALA, K. *and* **VŠIANSKÝ, J. Slovník českých synonym.** [Praha], Nakladatelství Lidové Noviny, 1994. 437p. ISBN: 8071060593.

Lists synonyms for numbered senses of *c.*20,000 headwords, but does not offer guidance on usage. *Class No:* 808.50

[6048]
POLDAUF, I. Česko-anglický slovník, středního rozsahu / Czech-English dictionary, medium. [6. vyd.]. Praha, Státní Pedagogické Nákl., 1986. 1134p. £19.95. ISBN: 0569004047.

1st ed. 1959.

A standard Czech-English dictionary, which is aimed at both Czech and English users. *c.*30,000 entry-words, plus many idioms. Appended summary of Czech grammar in tables.

Poldauf's *English-Czech and Czech-English dictionary* (Praha, SPN, 1994. 1015p. £29.65) is a useful 2-way dictionary. *Class No:* 808.50

[6049]
—CAHA, J. *and* KRÁMSKÝ, J. Anglicko-český slovník / English-Czech dictionary. 5. vyd. Praha, Státní Pedagogické Nákl., 1982. 878p.

1st ed. 1960.

A companion volume to Poldauf, with *c.*30,000 entry-words. *Class No:* 808.50

[6050]
Slovník české frazeologie a idiomatikyi výrazy slovesné. Čermák, F. *and* Holub, J. *and* Hronek, J., *eds.* Praha, Academia Praha, 1994. 2v. ISBN: 802000503x.

A very detailed dictionary of idioms and verbal phrases, with explanations and examples plus translations into English, German, French and Russian. Phrases arranged under keywords, A-Z, with thorough index. *Class No:* 808.50

[6051]
—KROULÍK, B. *and* KROULÍKOVÁ, B. Anglicko-český slovník idiomů / English-Czech dictionary of idioms. Praha, Nakladatelství Svoboda-Libertas, 1993. 203p. £11.95. ISBN: 8020502343.

Lists many thousands of British and American idioms under 1,400 headwords and gives Czech translation. Includes literary and biblical quotations. *Class No:* 808.50

Slovak

[6052]
KONUŠ, J.J. Slovak-English phraseological dictionary. Passaic, N.J., Slovensky Katolicky Sokol, 1969. 1664p.

Despite the title, a standard dictionary with *c.*80,000 entries including proper names, compounds and idioms. Primarily intended for Slovaks living in the US. *Class No:* 808.54

[6053]
ŠIMKO, J. Anglicko-slovenský slovník / English-Slovak dictionary. 3. vyd. Bratislava, Slovenské Pedagogické Nakladatel'stvo, 1971. 1443p.

1st. ed. 1967.

Approx. 12,500 English entry-words (with pronunciation indicated) and many idioms and phrases. *Class No:* 808.54

[6054]
SLOVENSKÁ AKADÉMIA VIED. Ústav Slovenského Jazyka. **Slovník slovenského jazyka.** Peciar, Š., *ed.* Bratislava, Vydavtel'stvo Slovenskej Akadémie Vied, 1959-68. 6v.

The Slovak Academy's standard dictionary of the Slovak language, with over 100,000 words from literary sources in vols. 1-5. V.6 is a supplementary vol., with addenda and list of proper names. List of cited authors in each vol. *Class No:* 808.54

[6055]
VILIKOVSKÁ, J. *and* **VILIKOVSKÝ, P. Slovensko-anglický slovník** / Slovak-English dictionary. 4. vyd. Bratislava, SPN, 1991. 671p. £10.80.

1st ed. 1959.

Over 23,000 entry-words. *Class No:* 808.54

Serbo-Croat

Bibliographies

[6056]
FRANOLIĆ, B. A Bibliography of Croatian dictionaries. Paris, Nouvelles Editions Latines, 1985. 139p. illus. ISBN: 2723303020.

Lists 627 monolingual, bilingual and polyglot dictionaries, with brief annotations. Author, language and subject indexes. Some title-page facsimiles. *Class No:* 808.61/.62(01)

[6057]
GRUBIŠIĆ, V. Bibliography on the Croatian language. Norval, Ontario, HIŠAK-CSAC, 1987. iv,180p. ISBN: 0919817149.

A classified bibliography with *c.*2,300 unannotated entries in 15 sections. Author index. *Class No:* 808.61/.62(01)

[6058]
MILIVOJEVIĆ, D. *and* **MIHAILOVICH, V.D. A Bibliography of Yugoslav linguistics in English, 1900-1980** Columbus, Ohio, Slavica, 1990. 128p. $14.95. ISBN: 0893572136.

Attempts to include all English-language books, articles, reviews and dissertations written 1900-1980 on Yugoslav linguistics and the Serbo-Croat, Slovene and Macedonian languages. Nearly 1,200 entries arranged thematically, with individual languages as subdivisions. List of periodicals. Author index. *Class No:* 808.61/.62(01)

Dictionaries

[6059]

BENSON, M. English-SerboCroatian dictionary. 3rd ed. Cambridge, Cambridge Univ. Press, 1990. xlix,722p. £60. ISBN: 0521384966.

1st ed. Beograd, Prosveta, 1978; Philadelphia, Univ. of Pennsylvania Press, 1979; 2nd ed. Prosveta, 1984.

The most comprehensive and up-to-date dictionary of its kind, providing Serbo-Croatian equivalents for nearly 60,000 English headwords and 100,000 phrases and collocations. Provides phonetic transcription of both US and British pronunciations for all headwords and indicates differences in US and British usage. Includes scientific and technical terms. *Class No:* 808.61/.62(038)

[6060]

BENSON, M. SerboCroatian-English dictionary. 3rd ed. Cambridge, Cambridge Univ. Press, 1990. lxv,769p. £60. ISBN: 0521384958.

1st ed. Philadelphia, Pennsylvania Univ. Press, 1971; 2nd ed. Beograd, Prosveta, 1985.

Like Benson's *English-Serbocroatian dictionary,* a comprehensive and up-to-date work with *c.*60,000 headwords and *c.*100,000 compounds and phrases. Shows accents for all headwords and forms, and distinguishes between Eastern and Western variants of Serbo-Croat, as well as between US and British terms in the definitions. Detailed notes for users (33p.). Bibliography of sources (5p.). *Class No:* 808.61/.62(038)

[6061]

DRVODELIĆ, M. Hrvatsko-engleski rječnik / Croatian-English dictionary. 6. izd. Zagreb, Školska Knjiga, 1989. 847p.

1st ed. 1953, as *Hravtsko-engleski rječnik*; 5th ed. 1982.

Over 30,000 entries, with the emphasis on the Croatian variant of the language. *Class No:* 808.61/.62(038)

[6062]

FILIPOVIĆ, R., ***and others*****. Engelsko-hrvatski rječnik /** English-Croatian dictionary. 19. izd. Zagreb, Školska Knjiga, 1992. xviii,1435p. £27.50. ISBN: 8603008280.

1st ed. 1955.

A reliable and regularly revised English to Serbo-Croat dictionary, which emphasises the Croatian variant. Over 65,000 English entry-words, with pronunciation indicated, and many idioms. Appended lists of abbreviations and proper names. *Class No:* 808.61/.62(038)

[6063]

JUGOSLAVENSKA AKADEMIJA ZNANOSTI I UMJETNOSTI. Rječnik hrvatskoga ili srpskoga jezika. Daničič, U., *and others, eds*. Zagreb, Hartman, 1880-1976. 23v.

The Yugoslav Academy's standard and comprehensive monolingual dictionary. V.23 includes list of sources cited. *Class No:* 808.61/.62(038)

[6064]

The Oxford-Duden pictorial Serbo-Croat & English dictionary. Oxford, Clarendon Press, 1988. 854p. ISBN: 0198691653.

See entry for *The Oxford-Duden pictorial German & English dictionary* (1980). Uses the Croatian variant (Roman script) of Serbo-Croat which, according to *Choice* (v.26(9), May 1989, p.1498), 'will not pose problems for scientific and commercial uses, where the terms are more standardized' but is less useful for common household

....*(contd.)*

articles or clothing where the terms can vary from republic to republic and sometimes within. Indexes in Croatian and English. *Class No:* 808.61/.62(038)

Slovenian

[6065]

DERBYSHIRE, W.W. A Basic reference grammar of Slovene. Columbus, Ohio, Slavica, 1993. 154p. $16.95. ISBN: 0893572365.

The first grammar of Slovene to be produced for English speakers. Separate chapters on the major grammatical categories, with numerous examples of contemporary usage. Indexes of grammatical points and Slovene words. Bibliography of textbooks and dictionaries (3p.). List of grammatical terminology in Slovene. *Class No:* 808.63

[6066]

GRAD, A., ***and others*****. Veliki angleško-slovenski slovar.** Ljubljana, Državna Zalovba Slovenije, 1994 (distr. in UK by Oxford Univ. Press). xv,1377p. £85. ISBN: 8634108244.

*c.*80,000 English headwords (pronunciation indicated) plus numerous idioms and phrases. Appended list of proper names (35p.). Very high standard of production.

The companion vol. is *Slovensko-angleški slovar*, ed. by A.Grad and H.Leeming (1993. 827p. £62.50. ISBN: 86341098744), with *c.*25,000 entries. *Class No:* 808.63

[6067]

KOMAC, D. English-Slovene / Slovene-English modern dictionary. New York, Hippocrene, 1994. 935p. £22.99. ISBN: 0781802520.

Originally published Ljubljana, Cankarjeva Zalozba, 1993.

36,000 entries, with pronunciation given for English words. *Class No:* 808.63

[6068]

KOTNIK, J. Slovensko-angleški slovar / Slovene-English dictionary. 8. izd. Ljubljana, Državna Založba Slovenije, 1978 (repr. 1982). 831p.

1st ed. 1945.

Over 30,000 entry-words. Chiefly equivalents with some idioms and compounds. Appended lists of forenames, geographical names and proverbs.

The companion *Angleško-slovenski slovar* by R. Skerlj (6th ed. 1965. viii, 812p.) has a similar number of entries. *Class No:* 808.63

[6069]

Oxford-Duden-Cankarjeva Založba angleško-slovenski slikovni slovar. Berce, S., *and others, eds.* 2 izd. Oxford, Clarendon Press; Ljubljana, Cankarjeva Založba, 1989. 862p. £52.50. ISBN: 8636103738.

See entry for *The Oxford-Duden pictorial German & English dictionary* (1980). Indexes in English and Slovenian. *Class No:* 808.63

[6070]

Slovar slovenskega knjižnega jezika. Černelič, I., *and others, eds*. Ljubljana, Državna Založba Slovenije, 1970-91. 5v.

A major monolingual dictionary of the Slovenian literary language, with *c.*70,000 entries. Sequence of supplementary entries (20p.) at end of v.5 (20p.). *Class No:* 808.63

Bulgarian

[6071]
ATANASSOVA, T., ***and others.*** **Bulgarian-English dictionary.** 3rd. ed. Sofia, Nauka i Izkustvo, 1988. 2v. (1050p.). £42.

The fullest Bulgarian-English dictionary available, with over 40,000 entries. Many idioms and phrases.

The companion *English-Bulgarian dictionary* (3rd ed. 1985. 2v. £42.) is a very comprehensive dictionary, covering the English literary language from the 18th century to the present, with some dialect and slang words and technical terms of a general nature. Over 70,000 headwords, with pronunciation indicated, and numerous idioms and phrases. *Class No:* 808.67

[6072]
CHAKALOV, G., ***and others.*** **Bulgarsko-angliyski rechnik.** Sofia, Nauka i Izkustvo, 1961. 982p.

For many years the fullest Bulgarian-English dictionary, with *c.*35,000 entry-words. Now superseded by Atanassova, but still useful for its range of examples and marking of stress. Weak on coversational language and non-standard usage. Bibliography of sources. Lists of proper names and abbreviations.

The companion *Anglo-bulgarski rechnik* (Sofia, 1948. xvi,1229p.) has many idioms, colloquialisms and examples of usage. Appendices list place-names, proper names and abbreviations. *Class No:* 808.67

[6073]
CHOLOKOVA, K., ***and others.*** **Rechnik na bulgarskiya ezik.** Sofia, Bulgarskata Akademiya na Naukite, 1977-87. 5v.

The official dictionary of the Bulgarian Academy of Sciences. 'Promises to be the definitive monolingual dictionary of the Bulgarian language. Painstakingly researched, admirably documented and supplied with a rich variety of examples drawn from all levels of Bulgarian, past and present' (CILT, *Bulgarian*, 1983. p.15).
Class No: 808.67

[6074]
English-Bulgarian dictionary. Rankova, M, *and others, eds.* Sofia, Nauka i Izkustvo, 1987. 2v.(1086p.). £42.

A large-format dictionary, containing English and American variants with Bulgarian equivalents.
Class No: 808.67

[6075]
Rechnik na suvremmeniya bulgarski knizhoven ezik. Romanski, S., *and others, eds.* Sofia, Bulgarska Akademiya na Naukite, 1955-59. 3v.

The Bulgarian Academy's academic dictionary of the literary language, with many examples of usage from literary works. *Class No:* 808.67

[6076]
STANKOVA, E. ***and*** **HARLAKOVA, I. NTC's Bulgarian and English dictionary.** Lincolnwood, Ill., National Textbook Co., 1994. 288p. £8.95. ISBN: 0844249793.

10,000 entries in each section, with simple definitions and no idioms or illustrative phrases. Originally published in Bulgaria, so pronunciation indicated for English headwords. Stress of Bulgarian words is marked in both sections.
Class No: 808.67

Baltic Languages

Lithuanian

[6077]
Anglu-lietuviu kalbu žodynas. Laucka, A., *and others, eds.* 4th ed. Vilnius, Mokslas, 1992. 2v. £39.95.

1st ed. 1975; 3rd ed. 1986.

English-Lithuanian dictionary containing *c.*45,000 entries. Pronunciation given for English headwords. Many phrases and idioms. Lists of abbreviations and proper nouns.
Class No: 808.82

[6078]
PETERAITIS, V. Lietuviškai angliškas žodynas. 2. laida. [Chicago], Letuviskos Knygos Klubas, 1960 (repr. 1991). xv,586p. £42.50.

1st ed. 1948.

A Lithuanian-English dictionary, primarily intended for Lithuanians living in English-speaking countries.
Class No: 808.82

[6079]
PIESARSKAS, B. ***and*** **SVECEVIČIUS, B. Lietuvių-anglų kalbų žodynas.** [Vilnius?], JAV, 1991. 511p. £26.

A Lithuanian-English dictionary with *c.*15,000 entries and 27,000 translations in all. *Class No:* 808.82

[6080]
PIESARSKAS, B. ***and*** **SVECEVIČIUS, B. Lithuanian dictionary:** English-Lithuanian / Lithuanian-English. 2nd ed., with supplement London, Routledge, 1995. 799p. £50. ISBN: 0415128560.

1st ed. Vilnius, Žodynas, 1994.

The first dictionary of Lithuanian to be become generally available in the West for many years, with over 20,000 entries in each section. Supplementary section on Lithuanian orthography, pronunciation and grammar (48p.), by Prof. Ian Press of London University, includes select bibliography. Lists of geographical names (12p.).
Class No: 808.82

Latvian

[6081]
RAŠKEVIČS, J., ***and others.*** **Anglu-latviešu vārdnica /** English-Latvian dictionary. 4. izd. Riga, Avots, 1985. 819p.

Approx. 22,000 entries. Pronunciation given for English headwords. Appended lists of geographical names, personal names, and abbreviations. *Class No:* 808.83

[6082]
SOSĀRE, M. ***and*** **BIRZVALKA, I. Latvian-English / English-Latvian dictionary.** New York, Hippocrene, 1993. 286p. £14.75. ISBN: 0781800595.

16,000 entries, with pronunciation given for English headwords. *Class No:* 808.83

[6083]
TURKINA, E. Latviešu-anglu vārdnīca / Latvian-English dictionary. 4. izd. Riga, Avots, 1982. 638p. £44.95.

3rd ed. 1963.

Over 30,000 entry-words. Appendices include list of geographical names. *Class No:* 808.83

809 Oriental, African, etc. Languages

Asian Languages

[6084]

Languages of Asia and Africa. London, Routledge & Kegan Paul, 1981-82. 5v.

1. *The Swahili language;* 2. *The Panjabi language;* 3. *The Languages of South Asia;* 4. *The Polynesian languages;* 5. *The Hausa language.*

A series of detailed surveys translated from Russian. The vol. on South Asian languages has maps, bibliography (19p.), alphabet tables, and index of 350 language names. *Class No:* 809.0

[6085]

South-East Asia languages and literatures: a select guide. Herbert, P. *and* Milner, A., *eds.* Whiting Bay, Arran, Kiscadale Publications, 1988. x,182p. illus. £14.50. ISBN: 1870838106.

A quick-reference source and guide for newcomers to South-East Asian studies, compiled by members of the South-East Asia Library Group, with chapters on Burma, Thailand, Cambodia, Laos, Vietnam, Malaysia, Indonesia, The Philippines and Overseas Chinese. Chapters cover historical introduction; dating systems; languages and scripts; manuscripts; printing and development of the press; literature. Short references in the text, with full bibliographies after each chapter. Excellent value. *Class No:* 809.0

[6086]

Southeast Asian languages and literatures: a bibliographical guide to Burmese, Cambodian, Indonesian, Javanese, Malay, Minangkabau, Thai and Vietnamese. Kratz, E.U., *ed.* London, Tauris, 1996. xvi,455p. £65. ISBN: 1860641148.

A compilation by staff and students of London University's School of Oriental and African Studies, which updates and expands Herbert and Milner's guide. According to *Choice* (v.34(3), Nov. 1996, p.436), the Burmese section is excellent, but coverage of other languages is inconsistent and there are many typographical errors: 'Herbert and Milner, though more dated and also unindexed, is a better survey, more accessible and much more reasonably priced'. *Class No:* 809.0

Indo-European Languages

[6087]

BUCK, C.D. A Dictionary of selected synonyms in the principal Indo-European languages: a contribution to the history of ideas. Chicago, Univ. of Chicago Press, 1949; London, Cambridge Univ. Press, 1950 (repr. Forestburgh, NY, Lubrecht & Cramer, 1992). xvi,1188p. $174.20. ISBN: 3487057654.

A monumental work, arranged in 22 chapters for broad subjects (*e.g.* law, time, warfare) with further subdivisions

....*(contd.)*

for more specific concepts or objects. Under each term are listed synonyms from some 30 Indo-European languages, followed by detailed notes on their etymology and historical development. *Class No:* 809.1

[6088]

POKORNY, J. Indogermanisches etymologisches Wörterbuch. Berne, Francke, 1948-69. 2v. ISBN: 3317005262.

V.1 (iv,1183p.) comprises an etymological dictionary of the Indo-Germanic languages, citing authorities published up to 1947. V.2 (iv,465p.) includes corrigenda, abbreviations, bibliography and indexes.

See also A.J. Carnoy's *Dictionnaire étymologique du proto-indo-européen* (Louvain, Publications Universitaires, 1955. xii,223p.). *Class No:* 809.1

Indian Languages

[6089]

TURNER, R.L. A Comparative dictionary of the Indo-Aryan languages. London, Oxford Univ. Press, for the School of Oriental and African Studies, Univ. of London, 1960-71. 3v.

V.1 (xx,841p.) has *c.*50,000 Sanskrit headwords, followed by the forms assumed in some 50 languages and dialects of the Indo-Aryan family, with transliteration and English translation. Many quotations from literary sources.

V.2, *Indexes* (1969. ix,357p.) lists all the 140,000 words in the *Dictionary* according to language.

V.3, *Phonetic analysis* (1971. viii,235p.) covers *c.*1,500 sounds and sound-groups important to the phonetic history of Indo-Aryan languages. *Class No:* 809.11

Sanskrit

[6090]

EDGERTON, F. Buddhist hybrid Sanskrit grammar and dictionary. New Haven, Conn., Yale Univ. Press; London, Oxford Univ. Press, 1953 (repr. New York, French & European, 1987). 2v. $125. ISBN: 0828817812.

V.1, *Grammar.* xxx,239p; v.2, *Dictionary.* 627p.

V.1 includes a list of texts and other sources cited (2p.). V.2 has *c.*15,000 entry words, with English translations, quotations, and comments on usage, plus an index of Middle Indic words. *Class No:* 809.12

[6091]

An Encyclopaedic dictionary of Sanskrit on historical principles. Ghatage, A.M., *ed.* Poona, Deccan College Postgraduate and Research Institute, 1976-93. v.1, pt.1-v.4, pt.3 (in progress).

A scholarly dictionary which aims to be larger than those of Monier-Williams or Böhtlingk and Roth, and is based on 'an entirely new reading of the original texts and a fresh extraction of the material without relying on the earlier

.... (contd.)
lexicons' (*Preface*).

Issued in parts, with 3 parts forming a volume, and well illustrated with quotations. Some of the major entries extend to over 1,000 lines and include over 700 quotations. V.1, pt.1 lists the *c*.1,500 texts on which the dictionary is based and also provides a subject classification and chronology of the corpus. *Class No:* 809.12

[6092]
MacDONNELL, A.A. A Practical Sanskrit dictionary, with transliteration, accentuation and etymological analysis throughout. London, Oxford Univ. Press, 1924. xii,382p. £65. ISBN: 0198643039.

First published 1893, based on the monumental *Sanskrit-Wörterbuch* by O. von Böhtlingk and R. Roth (St. Petersburg, 1855-75. 7v.).

Aims 'to satisfy, within the compass of a comparatively handy volume, all the practial wants not only of learners of Sanskrit, but also of scholars for the purposes of ordinary reading' (*Preface*). Over 16,000 entries, giving Sanskrit form, transliterated form, English translation, derivatives, and compounds. Thorough coverage of Vedic literature, plus some selections from post-Vedic texts. *Class No:* 809.12

[6093]
MONIER-WILLIAMS, M. A Sanskrit-English dictionary, etymologically and philologically arranged, with special reference to cognate Indo-European languages. New ed., greatly enl. and improved, with the collaboration of E. Leumann, C. Cappeller (and others). Oxford, Clarendon Press, 1899 (regularly reprinted). xxxvi,1333p. £90. ISBN: 019864308x.

First published 1872, and, like Macdonnell (*q.v.*), is based on Böhtlingk and Roth's *Sanskrit-Wörterbuch*.

A comprehensive work, with etymologies and precise references to literary sources. Monier-Williams also compiled *A Dictionary, English and Sanskrit* (London, W.H. Allen, 1851; repr. Delhi, Motilal Banarsidass, 1992. £32.50. ISBN: 8120804546). *Class No:* 809.12

[6094]
SURYAKANTA. A Practical Vedic dictionary. Delhi, Oxford Univ. Press, 1981. xvii,750p. ISBN: 0195612981.

c.15,000 entries, defining almost all the words in the 4 Vedas in Hindi and English, the entries including many illustrative phrases. Claims to be the first comprehensive Vedic dictionary, earlier works covering either the whole field of Sanskrit literature (Vedic and classical) or the *Rigveda* alone. *Class No:* 809.12

Pali

[6095]
BUDDHADATTA, A.P. Concise Pali-English dictionary. Colombo, Colombo Apothecaries Soc., 1949 (repr. 1969). xii,281p.

A dictionary of modern Pali, giving Pali words in romanized form.

The companion *English-Pali dictionary* (Colombo, Pali Text Soc., 1955. 588p.) gives Pali equivalents of English words in Sinhalese script. *Class No:* 809.13

[6096]
CHILDERS, R.C. A Dictionary of the Pali language. London, Kegan Paul, Trench, Trübner, 1875 (repr. Kyoto, Rinsen Book Co., 1977).

'A dictionary which is old but still important as it gives some words and meanings (Canonical as well as medieval) missed by [Davids and Stede's] *PED*' (Warder, A.K., *Introduction to Pali*, 2nd ed., 1974, p.382).
Class No: 809.13

[6097]
DAVIDS, T.W.R. *and* STEDE, W. The Pali Text Society's Pali-English dictionary. Chipstead, Surrey, Pali Text Soc., 1921-25 (repr. 1972). xv,738p. £20. ISBN: 0860130592.

Originally issued in 8 parts.

A standard dictionary, although the compilers claim the work is entirely preliminary, there being many words of which the derivation is unknown. *c*.20,000 entry-words, with references to sources. *Class No:* 809.13

[6098]
TRENCKNER, V. A Critical Pali dictionary, begun by V. Trenckner; rev., continued, and ed. by D. Andersen (and others). Copenhagen, Munksgaard, for the Royal Danish Academy of Sciences and Letters, 1924-48; 1960-. v.1-. (in progress). ISBN: 8773041297.

A scholarly dictionary which is making slow progress. V.1 (11 pts.) and *Epilegomena* published 1924-48. Gives English definitions and references to sources. *Epilegomena* includes detailed bibliographies and lists of sources.

Publication resumed 1960, with 17 fascicules published 1960-88, forming v.2. First fasc. of v.3 published 1992. At least 9 more fascs. to come and not expected to be completed this century. *Class No:* 809.13

Punjabi (Panjabi)

[6099]
BAILEY, T.G. An English-Panjabi dictionary. Reprint of 1919 ed. Delhi, Ess Ess Publications, 1976. xvi,159p. £6.95. ISBN: 8185243220.

Originally published Calcutta, 1919, as *An English-Panjabi vocabulary*.

Gives transliterated Panjabi equivalents for *c*.5,800 English words and phrases. *Class No:* 809.142

[6100]
BHATIA, T.K. Punjabi: a cognitive-descriptive grammar. London, Routledge, 1993. xxxiv,423p. maps. £95. ISBN: 0415003202.

A very detailed, but clearly presented, grammar in 5 main chapters: 1. Syntax - 2. Morphology - 3. Phonology - 4. Ideophones and interjections - 5. Lexicon. Over 250 numbered subsections. Detailed table of contents. Bibliography (9p.). Index. *Class No:* 809.142

[6101]
SINGH, Maya. The Panjabi dictionary. Lahore, Munshi Gulab Singh, 1895 (repr. Patiala, Language Dept. 1972). 1221p. £29.95.

The largest Panjabi-English dictionary, but now very dated. Over 25,000 entries. *Class No:* 809.142

[6102]

WALIA, A.S. English-Punjabi dictionary (with meanings in English and Hindi also). New Delhi, Star Publications, 1992. 419p. illus. £14.90.

21,000 entries, comprising English headword, pronunciation, English definition, and translations into Punjabi and Hindi. A few unclear drawings.

Class No: 809.142

Hindi

[6103]

BAHRI, H. Comprehensive English-Hindi dictionary. Varanasi, Jnanamandal, 1974. 2v. £40.

First published 1960.

One of the largest English-Hindi dictionaries, with 100,000 English words and 50,000 phrases. Includes many scientific and technical terms, labelled as such in Hindi.

Class No: 809.143.2

[6104]

BAHRI, H. Learner's Hindi-English dictionary. Delhi, Rajpal, 1981 (repr. 1993). xix,758p. £17.50. ISBN: 8170280028.

10,500 Hindi entry-words followed by transliterated form, part of speech, meanings (in order of frequency), collocations, and idioms. Synonyms and antonyms are given in many cases. Classified word-lists appended.

Class No: 809.143.2

[6105]

Chambers English-Hindi dictionary. Awasthi, S. *and* Awasthi, I., *eds*. New Delhi, Allied Publishers, 1981 (repr. 1987). 1623p. £22.50. ISBN: 0550199802.

Over 45,000 entry-words, based on *Chambers English dictionary*, omitting archaic, obsolete and dialect words but including slang and colloquial forms. Many scientific and technical terms. 'Highly recommended to English-speaking learners of Hindi' by the CILT's Language and Culture Guide, *Hindi*, 1985. *Class No:* 809.143.2

[6106]

The Oxford Hindi-English dictionary. McGregor, R.S., *ed.* Oxford, Oxford Univ. Press, 1993. xx,1083p. £19.99. ISBN: 019864339x.

Based on a complete revision of J.T. Platts' *A Dictionary of Urdu, classical Hindi and English* (Lockwood, 1884), with the addition of new material to reflect 20th-century literary and spoken usage.

A major landmark in Hindi lexicography. 70,000 entries, with up to 12 components: 1. Headword in Devanāgari script - 2. Transliteration in Roman script - 3. Derivation - 4. Part of speech - 5. Phonemic transcription - 6. Subject label - 7. Linguistic label (*i.e.* variety of Hindi) - 8. Stylistic label - 9. Gloss - 10. Illustrative phrases (with translations) - 11. Compounds - 12. Run-on forms. List of sources.

Class No: 809.143.2

[6107]

PATHAK, R.C. Bhargava's standard illustrated dictionary of the Hindi language (Hindi-English ed.). Rev. ed. Varanasi, Bhargava, 1964. £12.95.

*c.*120,000 entry-words.

The companion vol. is *Bhargava's Standard illustrated dictionary of the English language (Anglo-Hindi ed.)* (12th ed. 1972. 1412p. £12.95.), with *c.*100,000 entries. Both dictionaries are frequently reprinted. *Class No:* 809.143.2

[6108]

A Practical Hindi-English dictionary. Chaturvedi, M. *and* Tiwari, B.N., *eds*. 2nd ed., rev. and enl. Delhi, National Publishing House, 1975. xvi,875p.

1st ed. 1970.

About 30,000 headwords, with actual pronunciation, part of speech, English equivalent, and compounds. Includes idioms, proverbs, and 'commonly prevalent technical or semi-technical terms' (*Preface*). 2nd ed. adds some mythological names, new technical terms, and dialect words.

Class No: 809.143.2

Urdu

[6109]

Ferozsons' English-Urdu dictionary: English words with their equivalents in Urdu. 4th ed. Lahore, Ferozsons, 1961. 910p.

About 30,000 entry-words, with *c.*50,000 words and phrases translated in total. *Class No:* 809.143.3

[6110]

Ferozsons' Urdu-English dictionary: a comprehensive dictionary of current vocabulary. Rev. ed. Lahore, Ferozsons, [1979?]. 831p. £13. ISBN: 9690005081.

1st ed. 1960.

About 30,000 entries, giving Urdu form, romanized form and English translation, with an indication of language of origin for each new headword.

A 2-way dictionary has been published as *Ferozsons' English-Urdu / Urdu-English dictionary* (1989. 1124p. £16. ISBN: 9690005103). *Class No:* 809.143.3

[6111]

HAQ, A. The Standard Urdu-English dictionary. Delhi, J.S. Sant Singh, [1978]. 831p.

An Indian edition of a work first published in Karachi in the 1930s and based on the then current ed. of *The Concise Oxford dictionary*. Still one of the most comprehensive dictionaries available, with *c.*20,000 entry-words and numerous phrases.

The companion vol. is Haq's *The Standard English-Urdu dictionary* (Delhi, J.S. Sant Singh. 1513;13;8p.) with *c.*30,000 entry-words. First published 1937.

Class No: 809.143.3

[6112]

MAHMUD, S. Urdu language and literature: a bibliography of sources in European languages. London, Mansell, 1992. xx,331p. £60. ISBN: 0720121434.

See entry at 891.43. *Class No:* 809.143.3

[6113]

PLATTS, J.T. A Dictionary of Urdu, classical Hindi and English. London, Oxford Univ. Press, 1965. viii,1259p. ISBN: 0198643098.

Photolitho reprint of the dictionary published by Lockwood in 1884.

About 50,000 entries, the headwords in Urdu script being preceded by an intial Roman letter to indicate the language from which the words originate (Sanskrit, Arabic, etc.). 'The only comprehensive Urdu-English dictionary that can be recommended without qualification' (CILT, *Urdu*, 1985, p.28). *Class No:* 809.143.3

Bengali

[6114]

BISWAS, S. Samsad Bengali-English dictionary. 2nd ed. Calcutta, Sahitya Samsad, 1982. 1278p. £14.

1st ed. 1968.

*c.*25,000 entry-words in Bengali script, plus numerous phrases.

Samsad English-Bengali dictionary (5th, rev. and enl. ed. 1980. xiv,1354p. £14.) has a similar number of entries. *Class No:* 809.144

[6115]

DEV, A.T. Students' favourite dictionary (English-to-Bengali). 28th ed. Calcutta, Dev Sahitya Kutir, 1977. x,1616p.

1st ed. 1934.

*c.*35,000 entry-words, plus compounds and phrases. Many appendices with miscellaneous information: dates, proverbs, biographies, etc.

There is a corresponding *Students' favourite dictionary (Bengali-English)* (27th ed. Calcutta, Dev Sahitya Kutir, 1978. x,1391p.). *Class No:* 809.144

Marathi

[6116]

SIRMOKADAM, M.S. The New standard dictionary: Marathi-English-Marathi. Bombay, Dhananjaya Balrishna Dhawale, 1970. 1281p.

Over 15,000 entries, comprising Marathi headword, language of origin, etymology, meanings in both English and Marathi, plus compound and derived forms. *Class No:* 809.146

Gujarati

[6117]

DESHPANDE, P.G. Universal English-Gujarati dictionary. Bombay, Oxford Univ. Press, 1988. 959p. £14.99. ISBN: 0195618289.

Provides Gujarati definitions for *c.*34,000 English words and phrases.

Deshpande's *Concise Gujarati dictionary* (Bombay, Oxford Univ. Press, 1986. 466p. £5.99. ISBN: 0195618270) translates *c.*15,000 English terms.

Deshpande has also compiled a *Gujarati-English dictionary* (Ahmadabad, University Book Production Board, 1974). *Class No:* 809.147

Sinhalese

[6118]

CARTER, C. A Sinhalese-English dictionary. Colombo, Baptist Missionary Soc., 1924 (repr. Colombo, Gunasena, 1965). x,806p.

Over 40,000 entry-words, plus appendix of over 4,000 botanical names.

Carter's *An English-Sinhalese dictionary* (first published Colombo, Skeen, 1891; 2nd ed. Colombo, Ceylon Observer Press, 1936. 535p.) was also reprinted by Gunasena in 1965. It has over 30,000 entry-words.

A Dictionary of the Sinhalese language, begun by the Ceylon Branch of the Royal Asiatic Society in 1935, had reached v.1, pt.15, by 1988. The current publisher is the Ministry of Cultural Affairs, Colombo. *Class No:* 809.148

Nepali

[6119]

COLLETT, N., & ***others*****. An English-Nepali-English dictionary.** Abingdon, printed by Burgess, 1994. ix,454p. £16.95. ISBN: 0950934526.

Produced primarily for use in the British Brigade of Gurkhas, but has few words of *solely* military nature. Nearly 16,000 entries in 2 sequences: English - Nepali (romanised) - Nepali, then the reverse. *Class No:* 809.149.3

[6120]

MEERENDONK, M. Basic Gurkhali dictionary. Folkestone, Bailey Bros. & Swinfen, 1986. 258p. £4.95. ISBN: 0561003300.

English-Gurkhali and Gurkhali-English sequences followed by a range of appendices: Nepali time, weights and measures, family relationships, grammar, numbers, and words common to both languages. All Gurkhali words romanized. *Class No:* 809.149.3

[6121]

TURNER, R.L. A Comparative and etymological dictionary of the Nepali language, with indexes of all words quoted from other Indo-Aryan languages. London, Kegan Paul, Trench, Trubner, 1931 (repr. with corrections 1965). xxiii,935p.

A comprehensive dictionary with over 20,000 Nepali headwords followed by transliterated form, English translation and etymology. Index of words arranged by language (*c.*90 sequences). *Class No:* 809.149.3

Iranian Languages

Persian Language

[6122]

ARYANPUR-KASHANI, A., ***and others*****. The New unabridged English-Persian dictionary.** Tehran, Amir-Kabir Publishing and Printing Institute, 1963-65. 5v. (6340p.). illus.

A comprehensive dictionary with detailed definitions, based on *Webster's International dictionary* and *The Shorter Oxford dictionary*. Includes much specialized terminology. *Class No:* 809.151

[6123]

BATENI, M.R. Farhang Moaser English-Persian dictionary. Tehran, Farhang Moaser, 1993. 996p. illus.

24,000 entries, plus list of geographical names (11p.). Line drawings. Aimed at Persian speakers, with introduction in Persian and pronunciation given for English terms. *Class No:* 809.151

[6124]

English-Persian dictionary. Haim, S., *ed.* New York, Hippocrene, 1993. 700p. £14.99. ISBN: 0781800560.

Originally published Tehran, Farhang Moaser, 1987.

40,000 entries. Hippocrene have also published Haim's companion *Persian-English dictionary* (1993. 709p. £14.99. ISBN: 0781800552). *Class No:* 809.151

[6125]

HAYYĪM, S. The Larger English-Persian dictionary, designed to give the Persian meanings of 80,000 words, idioms, phrases and proverbs in the English language, as well as the transliteration of difficult Persian words. Tehran, Bēroukhim, 1941-43 (repr. 1976). 2v.

An abridged version has been published as *The Shorter English-Persian dictionary* (3rd ed. Tehran, Bēroukhim, 1967). *Class No:* 809.151

[6126]

HAYYĪM, S. The New Persian-English dictionary, complete and modern, designed to give the English meanings of over 50,000 words, terms, idioms and proverbs in the Persian language, as well as the transliteration of the words in English characters. Together with a sufficient treatment of all the grammatical features of the Persian language. Tehran, Bēroukhim, 1934-36 (repr. 1975). 2v.

Hayyīm's *The Shorter Persian-English dictionary* (3rd ed. Tehran, Bēroukhim, 1963. xvi,814p.) is an abridgement with *c.*30,000 entry-words. *Class No:* 809.151

[6127]

MAHOOTIAN, S. Persian. London, Routledge, 1997. 408p. £95. (*Descriptive grammars.*) ISBN: 0415023114.

The first comprehensive grammar of Persian, providing detailed coverage of all aspects, including syntax, morphology and phonology. *Class No:* 809.151

[6128]

STEINGASS, F. A Comprehensive Persian-English dictionary, including the Arabic words and phrases to be met with in Persian literature, being Johnson's and Richardson's *Persian and Arabic dictionary,* revised, enlarged and entirely reconstructed. London, Kegan Paul, Trench, Trubner, 1892 (repr. Routledge, 1990). viii,1539p. £150. ISBN: 0415025435.

First published 1892.

Regarded as still the best dictionary for the classical Persian language. Arabic terms are given in Arabic script and in transliterated form. Over 30,000 entry-words. *Class No:* 809.151

Pahlavi

[6129]

MacKENZIE, D.N. A Concise Pahlavi dictionary. London, Oxford Univ. Press, 1971. xx,236p. ISBN: 0197135595.

A Pahlavi (*i.e.* Middle Persian) glossary, romanized, with English-Pahlavi index and Pahlavi key. *Class No:* 809.153

Kurdish

[6130]

McCARUS, E.N. A Kurdish-English dictionary: dialect of Sulaimania, Iraq. Ann Arbor, Mich., Univ. of Michigan Press, 1967. x,194p. $16. ISBN: 091679864x.

*c.*4,000 entry-words in Kurdish characters, with transliteration and English translation. Mainly literary language, but includes some idioms from the spoken language. *Class No:* 809.157

[6131]

WAHBY, T. *and* **EDMONDS, C.J. A Kurdish-English dictionary.** Oxford, Clarendon Press, 1966. xi,168p.

About 10,000 entry-words. 'The Kurdish of this dictionary is the standard language of belles-lettres, journalism, official and private correspondence, and formal speech as it has developed, on the basis of the Southern-Kirmanj dialect of Sulamani in Iraq, since 1918' (*Introduction*). Transliterated Kurdish terms with diacriticals. *Class No:* 809.157

Pashto (Pushto & Afghan)

[6132]

English-Pushto dictionary. 3rd ed. New Delhi, Publications India, 1989. 820p. £35. ISBN: 8185243107.

20,000 entries. *Class No:* 809.158

Celtic

Irish

Bibliographies

[6133]

BAUMGARTEN, R. Bibliography of Irish linguistics and literature, 1942-71. Dublin, Institute for Advanced Studies, 1986. xxiii,776p. £35. ISBN: 0901282812.

9,312 unannotated entries in a classified arrangement. 4 indexes: first lines of verse; words and proper names; authors; sources. *Class No:* 809.162(01)

[6134]

BEST, R.I. Bibliography of Irish philology and of printed Irish literature. New York, Johnson, 1970. xii,307p. ISBN: 0384131603.

See entries for this and its sequel at 891.62(01). *Class No:* 809.162(01)

[6135]

EDWARDS, J. The Irish language: an annotated bibliography of sociolinguistic publications, 1772-1982. New York, Garland, 1983. xviii,274p. ISBN: 0824092945.

810 entries arranged A-Z by author. Indexes of subjects and periodicals, plus chronological index. *Class No:* 809.162(01)

Dictionaries

[6136]

DINNEEN, P.S. An Irish-English dictionary, being a thesaurus of the words, phrases and idioms of the modern Irish language. New ed., rev. and greatly enl. Dublin, Irish Texts Society, 1992. xxx,1344p. £20. ISBN: 1870166000.

Reprint of 1934 ed. 1st ed. 1904.

A classic Irish-English dictionary, with comprehensive coverage of Irish phrases and idioms.

A complementary vol. is L.A.J. McKenna's *English-Irish dictionary* (Dublin, Stationery Office, 1935. xxii,1546p.). *Class No:* 809.162(038)

[6137]

English-Irish dictionary. De Bhaldraithe, T., *ed.* 11th printing, with terminological additions and corrections. [Dublin], An Roinn Oideachais, 1992. xii+864+25p. £22.50. ISBN: 1857910362.

First published 1959.

Companion vol. is *Irish-English dictionary* (1977. xii,1309p. £25.75).

Aims to provide romanized Irish equivalents for English words and phrases in common use. Not an exhaustive dictionary of the Irish language, because many thousands of words and phrases in use in the Gaeltacht are not the equivalents of common English. Primarily based on current Irish usage, but draws on the older literary language when necessary. Proper names are included. Over 35,000 entries. *Class No:* 809.162(038)

[6138]

Ó DÓNAILL, N. Foclóir Gaeilge-Béarla: Irish-English dictionary. Baile Átha Cliath, Oifig an tSoláthair, 1977 (repr. An Gúm, 1992.). xii,1309p. £25.95. ISBN: 1857910370.

A comprehensive Irish-English dictionary, which effectively supersedes Dinneen's *Irish-English dictionary* (New ed. Dublin, 1927). Over 45,000 entry-words, with numerous idiomatic phrases. Very clearly laid out, making good use of category labels and different typefaces. *Class No:* 809.162(038)

[6139]

ROYAL IRISH ACADEMY. Dublin. **Dictionary of the Irish language,** based mainly on Old and Middle Irish materials. Dublin, the Academy, 1913-76. 4v.

An incomplete but scholarly dictionary, compiled on historical principles, with numerous illustrative quotations. Comprises the 4 completed fascicules published 1913-57, under the title *Dictionary of the Irish language,* covering the letters D-F, and the parts published irregularly, 1939-76, under the title *Contributions to a Dictionary of the Irish language,* covering A-C and G-U.

A compact single-vol. ed. was published by the Academy in 1983 (632p.), with 4 photographically-reproduced and reduced pages of the original work on each page. *Class No:* 809.162(038)

[6140]

VENDRYES, J. Lexique étymologique de l'irlandais ancien. Dublin, Dublin Institute for Advanced Studies; Paris, Centre National de la Recherche Scientifique, 1959-. fasc. 1- (in progress).

Fascicules published to date cover A (1959); B (1980); C (1987); M,N,O,P (1961); R,S (1974); T,U (1978).

Gives French equivalent for each Irish word, followed by detailed etymology with precise references to sources. List of sources in *Avant-propos* to first fascicule (8p.). *Class No:* 809.162(038)

Maps & Atlases

[6141]

WAGNER, H. Linguistic atlas and survey of Irish dialects. Dublin, Dublin Institute for Advanced Studies, 1958-69. 4v.

V.1 *Introduction. 300 maps.* 1958. xviii,300p.

V.2 *The Dialects of Munster.* 1964. xix,306p.

V.3 *The Dialects of Connaught.* 1966. xvi,378p.

V.4 *The Dialects of Ulster and the Isle of Man. Specimens of Scottish Gaelic dialects. Phonetic texts of East Ulster Irish.* 1969. xx,303p.

Presents the results of a survey carried out at 88 Irish locations during the period 1949-56, plus (in v.4) a later

....*(contd.)*

survey at some Scottish locations. A questionnaire covering over 2,000 items was used. Details of locations and informants in v.1. *Class No:* 809.162(084.3)

Grammar

[6142]

Ó SIADHAIL, M. Modern Irish: grammatical structure and dialectal variation. Cambridge, Cambridge Univ. Press, 1989. xiv,369p. £18.95. ISBN: 0521425190.

3 main sections (phonology; morphology; syntax), with numbered subsections and paragraphs. Numerous examples from different dialects, with pronunciation given in adapted IPA. References (5p.). Index of Irish words. *Class No:* 809.162-5

Scots Gaelic

[6143]

DWELLY, E. The Illustrated Gaelic-English dictionary, containing every Gaelic word and meaning given in all previously published dictionaries, and a great many never in print before. To which is prefixed a concise Gaelic grammar. 11th ed. Glasgow, Gairm, 1994. xiv,1034p. illus. £19.95. ISBN: 0901771929.

First published in parts, 1901-11, as *Faclair gàidhlig le dealbahn.* The '11th ed.' is actually one of numerous reprints which have been published. Another recent version published Edinburgh, Berlinn, 1993 (£20. ISBN: 1874744432).

A comprehensive dictionary with *c.*30,000 headwords, their various meanings well illustrated by phrases. Great attention is paid to idioms and syntax. Appendix 1: Proper names; 2: Persons and places mentioned in old Gaelic folktales and poetry (from Armstrong's *Gaelic dictionary*). 675 illus.

Appendix to Dwelly's Illustrated Gaelic-English dictionary, ed. by D. Clyne and completed by D.S. Thomson (Glasgow, Gairm, 1991. 136p. £9.90. ISBN: 1871901081), has entries compiled by Dwelly but previously unpublished.

Gairm have also reprinted *A Gaelic grammar* by G. Calder (1996. xv,352p. £7.99. ISBN: 0901771341) which was originally published in 1923. *Class No:* 809.163

[6144]

MacKENZIE, J. English-Gaelic dictionary. Reprint of 1832 ed. Glasgow, Gairm, 1971. 267p.

Originally published 1832, as Part 2 of *A Pronouncing Gaelic dictionary* by N. Macalpine.

*c.*25,000 entries. *Class No:* 809.163

[6145]

MACLENNAN, M. Gaelic dictionary: Gaelic-English / English-Gaelic. Edinburgh, Mercat Press, 1979. xv,613p. £11.95. ISBN: 1873644116.

First published Edinburgh, Grant, 1925, as *A Pronouncing and etymological dictionary of the Gaelic language.* Based on N. MacAlpine's *A Pronouncing Gaelic dictionary* (*c.*1831).

About 20,000 entries in each half, chiefly equivalents of headwords and their compounds. *Class No:* 809.163

[6146]

OWEN, R.C. The Modern Gaelic-English dictionary / Am Faclair ur gaidhlig-beurla. Glasgow, Gairm, 1993. x,139p. £7.50 ISBN: 1871901294.

Intended for use alongside Thomson's dictionary. Provides full grammatical information and pronunciation guidance, including dialect variations in some cases. Appendix shows regular and irregular forms of Gaelic verbs, with meanings and examples. Chapters on personal names, surnames and placenames. *Class No:* 809.163

[6147]

—THOMSON, D.S. New English-Gaelic dictionary. 2nd rev. ed. Glasgow, Gairm, 1994. vii,241p. £8.95. ISBN: 1871901324.

1st ed. 1981.

A concise, all-purpose dictionary which adopts the new Gaelic spelling and claims to 'cut out the dead wood of earlier dictionaries.' *c.*17,000 English headwords with Gaelic equivalents, plus illustrative phrases in some cases. Draws on both literature and the spoken language. Extensively updated for 2nd ed., with over 1,000 new entries or glosses. *Class No:* 809.163

Manx

[6148]

CREGEEN, A. Fockleyr ny gaelgey: chaglit liorish. Ramsey, Isle of Man, Yn Cheshaght Ghailckagh, 1984. 188p. £9. ISBN: 1870029089.

A reprint of *A Dictionary of the Manks language, with the corresponding words or explanations in English,* first published Douglas, Quiggin, 1835.

Over 14,000 entries. *Class No:* 809.164

[6149]

FARGHER, D.C. Fargher's English-Manx dictionary. Stowell, B. *and* Faulds, I., *eds.* Douglas, Isle of Man, Shearwater Press, 1979. xvi,888p. £49.95. ISBN: 0904980235.

'It is largely a prescriptive work and not a descriptive one, [which] tries to provide some sort of basic standard upon which to build the modern Manx language of today and tomorrow' (*Preface*). *c.*50,000 entry-words and many phrases. *Class No:* 809.164

[6150]

KNEEN, J.J. English-Manx pronouncing dictionary. Reprint of 1938 ed., with corrections and a supplement by R.L. Thomson. Menston, Yorks., Scolar Press, for Yn Cheshaght Ghail, 1970. viii,113p. £15.75.

Originally published Douglas, Isle of Man, 'Mona's Herald', 1938.

6,000 entries in the reprinted dictionary, plus over 2,200 in the supplement. *Class No:* 809.164

Welsh

[6151]

AITCHISON, J. *and* **CARTER, H. A Geography of the Welsh language, 1961-1991.** Cardiff, Univ. of Wales Press, 1994. xi,130p. maps. £9.95. ISBN: 0708312365.

Updates, expands and re-evaluates findings contained in the same authors' *The Welsh language, 1961-1981: an interpretative atlas* (1985).

An extremely useful reference source, which examines language distributions in 1991 and relates them to changes that have taken place since 1961, using numerous maps and

....*(contd.)*

tables. Appended list of 908 census wards with numbers and percentages of Welsh speakers. Bibliography (5p.) *Class No:* 809.166

[6152]

Collins Spurrell pocket Welsh dictionary. Thorne, D.A., *& others, eds.* Rev. ed. Glasgow, HarperCollins, 1991. xii,372p. £6.99. ISBN: 000433549x.

Spurrell's Welsh-English dictionary first published Carmarthen, 1848. *Collins-Spurrell Welsh dictionary* first published London, Collins, 1960, ed. by H. Lewis.

A revision of a popular and well-established dictionary. Over 13,000 Welsh-English entries and over 14,000 English-Welsh. Lists of personal and place names. Notes on Welsh pronunciation. *Class No:* 809.166

[6153]

EVANS, H.M. Y Geiriadur Cymraeg cyfoes / The Dictionary of modern Welsh. Rev. ed. Abertawe, C. Davies, 1992. 611p. £9.99. ISBN: 0715407252.

1st ed. Llandybie, Hughes, 1982.

Welsh-English and English-Welsh sections, with *c.*21,000 entries in each, mainly equivalents. Pronunciation not indicated, but introduction includes detailed instructions (10p.) on the pronunciation of Welsh. Lists of personal names, place-names, and botanical and zoological terms follow each section. *Class No:* 809.166

[6154]

EVANS, H.M. *and* **THOMAS, W.O. Y Geiriadur mawr:** the complete Welsh-English/English-Welsh dictionary. 8th ed. Abertawe, C. Davies, 1987. 492+367p. £14.95. ISBN: 0715405438.

1st ed. 1958.

Far more than a revised and enlarged ed. of its predecessor, the *New Welsh dictionary* (1953), with the inclusion of many technical terms and also obsolete words. *c.*30,000 entries in Welsh-English section and *c.*20,000 in English-Welsh section, with terms new to this ed. appended to each section. *Class No:* 809.166

[6155]

Geiriadur prifysgol Cymru / A Dictionary of the Welsh language. Thomas, R.J., *and others, eds.* Caerdydd, Gwasg Prifysgol Cymru [Cardiff, Univ. of Wales Press], 1950-97. Pts.1-47 (in progress).

Published in fascicules, with parts 1-21 forming v.1, *A-FFYSUR* (1967. £45. ISBN: 0708305040) and parts 22-36 forming v.2, *G-LLYYS* (1987. £35. ISBN: 070830981x).

A scholarly dictionary of the Welsh language on *OED* lines, the entries including etymology, variant forms, Welsh meanings, English synonyms, and dated quotations from a range of sources. V.1 has *c.*45,000 entry-words and list of sources (16p.). The scope is 'all words in literary and colloquial use, a selection of the technical terms of the arts and sciences, and those obsolete or archaic words which have been in use at different periods in the development of the language' (*Preface*). *Class No:* 809.166

[6156]

Geiriadur termau [Dictionary of terms] Williams, J.L., *ed.* Cardiff, Univ. of Wales Press, 1973 (repr. in paperback 1991). xiv,544p. £7.95. ISBN: 0708309992.

English-Welsh, p.1-260; Welsh-English, p.263-544. About 3,000 headwords in each part. Contains terms required for the teaching of secondary school subjects to Advanced level and terms needed for business and administrative purposes. Based on previously published subject lists to which plural

....(contd.)
forms and guidance on gender have been added. Sponsored by the University of Wales School of Education.
Class No: 809.166

[6157]
Thesawrws cymraeg: y drysorfa eiriau. Swansea, Gwasg Pobl Cymru, 1993. 224p. £10.95. ISBN: 0952153602.

The first thesaurus of Welsh, with 40,000 synonyms and antonyms listed under 6,500 alphabetically arranged entry-words. *Class No:* 809.166

[6158]
The Welsh Academy English-Welsh dictionary. Griffiths, B. *and* Jones, D.G., *eds.* Reprint with minor emendations Cardiff, Univ. of Wales Press, 1997. lxxxii,1710p. 45. ISBN: 0708311865.

First published 1995.

The result of over 20 years work, this is the most comprehensive Engish-Welsh dictionary ever compiled. Based on the English-French half of *Harrap's shorter English and French dictionary* (1975), using the same conventions but with a much increased vocabulary which includes idioms, specialist terms, regional variations, personal and geographical names. Thousands of illustrative quotations. Notes on the morphology of Welsh (55p.). Bibliography of dictionaries and grammars of Welsh (2p.). 'Clears the field of any competitor' (*Choice*, v.33(10), June 1996, p.1616). *Class No:* 809.166

Grammar

[6159]
THORNE, D.A. A Comprehensive Welsh grammar. Oxford, Blackwell, 1993. x,491p. £55. (*Blackwell reference grammars.*) ISBN: 0631164073.

Very clearly presented in 7 main chapters with 421 numbered subsections and plenty of examples. Emphasis is on the modern spoken language. Appended glossary of easily confusible words (6p.) and list of proverbs (22p.). Classified bibliography (8p.). Index of subject headings and Welsh words, with references to section numbers. Claims to be the first comprehensive textbook of Welsh to have appeared for over 40 years. *Class No:* 809.166-5

[6160]
—KING, G. Modern Welsh: a comprehensive grammar. London, Routledge, 1993. viii,340p. £17.99. ISBN: 0415092698.

14 chapters with 530 numbered subsections, concentrating on contemporary spoken Welsh. Numerous examples. References (1p.). Index of English and Welsh words and grammatical terms, with references to section numbers. Available in paperback only. *Class No:* 809.166-5

Cornish

[6161]
BROWN, W. A Grammar of modern Cornish. Rev. ed. [Hayle], Cornish Language Board, 1993. 260p. £15.95. ISBN: 0907064094.

1st ed. 1984.

A chapter on each of the parts of speech, with frequent cross-references. General index plus separate index for verbs. Fully revised and converted to the new spelling system (*Kernewek Kemmyn*) adopted in 1987.
Class No: 809.167

[6162]
GEORGE, K. Gerlyver kernewek kemmyn: an gerlyver meur [Complete Cornish-English dictionary.] [Hayle], Cornish Language Board, 1993. 338p. ISBN: 0907064116.

A complete revision of R.M. Nance's prewar dictionary.

9,000 headwords, including all the words used in traditional Cornish texts plus modern terms which have come in to use since the language revival earlier this century. Entries include source and frequency of occurrence in texts, plus etymology and Welsh and Breton cognates. Uses revised system of spelling adopted by the Cornish Language Board in 1987. *Class No:* 809.167

[6163]
NANCE, R.M. A New Cornish-English and English-Cornish dictionary. Redruth, Dyllansow Truran, 1990. 209;109p. £10.95. ISBN: 1850220557.

A combined reprint of *A New Cornish-English dictionary* (St. Ives, Federation of Old Cornish Societies, 1938), with *c.*8,000 entries, and *An English-Cornish dictionary* (Marazion, F.O.C.S., 1952), with over 7,000 entries.
Class No: 809.167

Breton

[6164]
DELAPORTE, R. Elementary Breton-English dictionary. Cork, Cork Univ. Press, 1979. xviii,110p. £11.25. ISBN: 0902561162.

6,500 entries. The companion vol. is *Elementary English-Breton dictionary* (1990. xviii,179p. £12.75).
Class No: 809.168

[6165]
Dictionnaire breton: breton-français / français-breton. Helias, P.J., *ed.* Paris, Garnier, 1986. 816p. £36.95. ISBN: 2737002532.

A handy 2-way dictionary for current spoken Breton, with 15,000 Breton-French and 13,000 French-Breton entries. Grammar notes and lists of proper names.
Class No: 809.168

[6166]
FAVEREAU, F. Geriadur ar brezhoneg a-vreman: brezhoneg-galleg / galleg-brezhoneg. Morlaix, Skol Vreizh, 1993. xv,1357p. Fr.450. ISBN: 2903313652.

French title is *Dictionnaire du breton contemporain bilingue.*

Definitive dictionary of the contemporary language with nearly 50,000 Breton-French entries, giving pronunciation (IPA) and etymology for the headwords, and 40,000 French terms with Breton equivalents. Notes on Breton grammar (14p.). *Class No:* 809.168

[6167]
HEMON, R. Geriadur istorel ar brezhoneg / Dictionnaire historique du breton. Quimper, Preder, 1958-79. 36 pts. (3232p.).

A historical dictionary of Breton, with French translations and citations to literary sources which are listed in the final part (12p.). *Class No:* 809.168

[6168]
HEMON, R. Nouveau dictionnaire breton-français. 7e. éd, rev. et aug. Brest, Al Liamm, 1978 (repr. 1985). 848p. Fr.65. ISBN: 2736800060.

1st ed. 1947.

The standard learner's dictionary. Over 30,000 entry-words with French equivalents. Hemon has also compiled

.... *(contd.)*
Dictionnaire français-breton (Brest, Al Liamm, 1984. 420p.), a work first published in 1950 and frequently reprinted. *Class No:* 809.168

[6169]
PRESS, I. A Grammar of modern Breton. Berlin, Mouton de Gruyter, 1986. xiii,406p. £68.95. ISBN: 3110105799.
The first English-language grammar of Breton since 1948 has 4 main chapters on phonology, morphology, syntax, and word formation, with numbered subsections, following an introductory essay on the current state of the language. Appendices include a glossary of Breton grammatical terminology, maps, a short list of Breton literature, and 40p. of Breton texts. Select bibliography (14p.). Minimal index but detailed table of contents. *Class No:* 809.168

Basque Languages

[6170]
AULESTIA, G. *and* **WHITE, L. Basque-English dictionary.** Reno, Nev., Univ. of Nevada Press, 1989. 672p. £48. ISBN: 0874171261.
The first major Basque-English dictionary, the result of 10 years research, giving English equivalents for 50,000 words in 6 Basque dialects. Includes many Basque surnames and placenames. 42p. of information on the Basque language and grammar. *Class No:* 809.169

[6171]
AULESTIA, G. *and* **WHITE, L. English-Basque dictionary.** Reno, Nev., Univ. of Nevada Press, 1990. 16+397p. £45. ISBN: 0874171563.
25,000 English headwords with Basque equivalents in up to 6 dialects. Considerably smaller than the companion vol. since all dialectal variations can be included in one English entry. Bibliography of over 50 works consulted.
The authors have also produced a single-vol. 2-way dictionary based on these 2 works: *Basque-English / English-Basque pocket dictionary* (Reno, 1992. 600p. £15.99. ISBN: 0874171784). *Class No:* 809.169

[6172]
AZKUÉ, R.M. de. Diccionario vasco-español-francés. Reproduccíon facsímil de la edicíon príncipe, con un Apéndice. Bilbao, La Gran Enciclopedia Vasca, 1969. 2v.
First published 1905-6.
Basque-Spanish-French dictionary, with *c.*40,000 entries which include quotations from literary sources. List of sources in v.1 (3p.). Supplement adds over 5,000 new words with Spanish equivalents only. *Class No:* 809.169

[6173]
TRASK, R.L. The History of Basque. London, Routledge, 1997. xxii,458p. £75. ISBN: 0415131162.
Aims to 'present everything we know, believe and suspect about the origins and development of this famous but little-known language [and] to identify the numerous errors, misunderstandings, unsubstantiated hypotheses and outright fantasies which have grown up around Basque' (*Preface*). 6 chapters, with numbered subsections, covering the prehistory of Basque, including pronunciation, grammar and vocabulary; a lengthy account of the search for the language's relatives; a thumbnail sketch of the contemporary language; a summary of its typological features; and an external history. Extensive bibliography (15p.). Index.
Class No: 809.169

Armenian

[6174]
AROUTUNIAN, D. *and* **AROUTUNIAN, S. Hippocrene concise dictionary: Armenian-English / English-Armenian.** New York, Hippocrene, 1993. 378p. £10.50 ISBN: 0781801508.
Over 9,000 entries, simply comprising headword, pronunciation (compilers' own system), part of speech and gloss. *Class No:* 809.198.1

[6175]
KOUSHAKDJIAN, M. *and* **KHANTROUNI, D. Modern dictionary: English-Armenian / Armenian-English.** Beirut, Doniguian, 1976. 949;416p.
A combination of *English-Armenian modern dictionary* (2nd ed. 1976), with *c.*18,000 entry-words, and *Armenian-English modern dictionary* (1970) with *c.*16,000 entry-words. Armenian terms not transliterated.
Class No: 809.198.1

[6176]
KOUYOUMDJIAN, M.G. A Comprehensive Armenian-English dictionary. Cairo, Sahag-Mesrob Press; London, Safrastion, [1950]. iv,1159p.
About 80,000 modern Armenian entry-words, not transliterated, with English equivalents.
Class No: 809.198.1

[6177]
KOUYOUMDJIAN, M.G. A Comprehensive illustrated English-Armenian dictionary. Cairo, Sahag-Mesrob Press, [1961]. vii,1416p. illus.
Approx. 80,000 entries. Armenian characters are not transliterated. *Class No:* 809.198.1

Albanian

[6178]
DRIZARI, N. Albanian-English / English-Albanian dictionary. 2nd ed. New York, Ungar, 1957. vi,320p. £42.50. ISBN: 0804401306.
1st ed. 1934.
*c.*5,500 entry-words. Mostly equivalents. Pronunciation of Albanian not indicated. Separate entries for various verb forms. Short bibliography of sources. *Class No:* 809.198.3

[6179]
HYSA, R. Albanian-English dictionary. New York, Hippocrene, 1993. 510p. £13.50. ISBN: 0870520776.
Claims to be the only Albanian-English dictionary published in North America, but is a reprint of an Albanian publication with all introductory and explanatory material in Albanian. Over 20,00 entries, with many idiomatic expressions and illustrative sentences. No pronunciation guidance, *Class No:* 809.198.3

[6180]
HYSA, R. Hippocrene comprehensive dictionary: English-Albanian. New York, Hippocrene, 1997. 938p. £44.99. ISBN: 0781805104.
60,000 entries and 110,000 references, with numerous compounds, idioms and illustrative phrases. Primarily for Albanians, covering both US and British English, with the most frequently used English words treated in depth.
Class No: 809.198.3

[6181]
KICI, G. Albanian-English dictionary. [Washington, D.C.], G. Kici, 1976 (repr. 1991). 448p. $20. ISBN: 0686179048.

Aimed at students of literary Albanian, but also includes some scientific terms. Omits regionalisms. *c.*26,000 entry-words, with many idioms and illustrative phrases. Lists of abbreviations and geographical names. *Class No:* 809.198.3

[6182]
KICI, G. *and* **ALIKO, H. English-Albanian dictionary.** [Washington, D.C.], G. Kici, 1969 (repr. 1991). xi,627p. $20. ISBN: 0686049144.

Over 24,000 entry-words, with many idiomatic phrases. *Class No:* 809.198.3

[6183]
MANN, S.E. An English-Albanian dictionary. Cambridge, Canbridge Univ. Press, 1957. 434p.

'An attempt to express the essential vocabulary of the English literary language in modern literary Albanian' (*Preface*). Over 23,000 entry-words, with *c.*10,000 idiomatic phrases. Includes many bird and plant names, but excludes specialized scientific vocabulary. *Class No:* 809.198.3

[6184]
MANN, S.E. An Historical Albanian-English dictionary. London, Longmans, Green, 1948. ix,601p.

Originally published in 38 sections, 1938-48.

The standard dictionary, with over 40,000 entries. Bibliography (2p.).

L. Newmark's *Albanian-English dictionary*, announced for 1998 (Oxford, Oxford Univ. Press. 978p. ISBN: 0198643403) is likely to take over as the authoritative work. *Class No:* 809.198.3

Hittite

[6185]
CHICAGO. UNIVERSITY. Oriental Institute. **The Hittite dictionary of the Oriental Institute of the University of Chicago.** Güterbock, H.G. *and* Hoffner, H.A., *eds.* Chicago, The Institute, 1980-89. v.3, fasc.1-4; v.4, fasc.1-3 (in progress).

Follows the pattern of the Institute's *Assyrian dictionary* (*q.v.*), aiming 'to give complete coverage of the representative occurrences of each Hittite word' (*Preface*). Vols. 3 and 4 cover 'L-N' and 'P' respectively. *Class No:* 809.198.7

[6186]
PUHVEL, J. Hittite etymological dictionary. Berlin, Mouton de Gruyter, 1984-97. v.1-4 (in progress).

The first 3 vols. cover words beginning with A, E, I, H and K.

Another ongoing etymological dictionary is *Hethitisches etymologisches Glossar* by J. Tischler (Innsbruck, Institut für Sprachwissenschaft der Universität Innsbruck, 1983-), of which 2 of the 4 planned vols. have been completed, covering A-K and L-M. *Class No:* 809.198.7

Semitic

[6187]
A Basic bibliography for the study of the Semitic languages. Hospers, J.H., *ed.* Leiden, Brill, 1973-74. 2v.

V.1 has separate sections for languages or groups of languages, compiled by specialists, and a section on comparative Semitics. V.2 covers pre-classical, classical and modern literary Arabic, and modern Arabic dialects. About 10,000 unannotated entries, but no index. *Class No:* 809.2

Sumerian Language

[6188]
The Sumerian dictionary of the University Museum of the University of Pennsylvania. Sjöberg, Å.W., *ed.* Philadelphia, Pa., Babylonian Section of the Univ. Museum, 1984-92. v.1-2 (in progress). ISBN: 0934718636.

A scholarly dictionary arranged by presumed Sumerian word-unit (transliterated) with definitions and references to sources. List of bibliographical abbreviations in each vol. *Class No:* 809.211

Assyrian

[6189]
CHICAGO. UNIVERSITY. Oriental Institute. **The Assyrian dictionary of the Oriental Institute of the University of Chicago.** Gelb, I.J., *and others, eds.* Chicago, the Institute, 1956-89. v.1-11, 13, 15, 16, 17, 21 (in progress). ISBN: 0918986052.

Generally referred to as *CAD (Chicago Assyrian dictionary)*.

A scholarly dictionary, with transliterated entry-words, English translations and examples from literary texts. Precise references to sources. Not published in order, v.5(*E*) appearing first in 1956. The most recent, v.17 (*Š*), was published in 3 parts in 1989 and 1992 and has an updated, provisional list of over 800 bibliographical abbreviations. Complete references will appear in a later vol. *Class No:* 809.212

[6190]
SODEN, W. von. Akkadisches Handwörterbuch, unter Benutzung des lexikalischen Nachlasses von Bruno Meissner (1868-1947). Wiesbaden, Harrassowitz, 1965-81. 3v. (xvi,1592p.).

Romanized Akkadian headwords with German translation and numerous citations to sources, which are listed in v.1 (7p.). *Class No:* 809.212

Aramaic

[6191]
SOKOLOFF, M. A Dictionary of Jewish Palestinian Aramaic of the Byzantine period. Ramat-Gan, Israel, Bar Ilan Univ. Press, 1990. 823p. ISBN: 9652261017.

Claims to be 'the first attempt to treat in a comprehensive manner an individual dialect out of those which comprise the Rabbinic literature in its broadest sense (*Preface*). Over 7,000 entries, comprising lemma; part of speech; English gloss; etymology (showing relationships to Semitic cognates); documentation of morphological forms and semantic features (with numerous quotes from sources); and references to other studies. List of sources (10p.) and index of sources. *Class No:* 809.22

Syriac

[6192]

A Compendious Syriac dictionary, founded upon the *Thesaurus Syriacus* of R. Payne Smith. Smith, J. Payne (Mrs. Margoliouth), *ed.* Oxford, Clarendon Press, 1903. vii,626p. ISBN: 0198643071.

A Syriac-English dictionary, being an abridgement of R. Payne Smith's monumental *Thesaurus Syriacus* (Oxford, Clarendon Press, 1879-1901. 2v.). A *Supplement* to the larger work, collected and arranged by Mrs. Margoliouth, was published by Clarendon Press in 1927 (xx,346p.). The *Thesaurus* and *Supplement* were reprinted by G. Olms (Hildesheim) in 1981. *Class No:* 809.23

[6193]

GOSHEN-GOTTSTEIN, M.H. A Syriac-English glossary, with etymological notes. Based on Brockelmann's Syriac chrestomathy. Wiesbaden, Harrassowitz, 1970. x,95p.

A selective glossary with *c.*2,000 entries, for beginners who know neither German nor Latin. *Class No:* 809.23

Hebrew

Bibliographies

[6194]

WALDMAN, N.M. The Recent study of Hebrew: a survey of the literature with selected bibliography. Cincinnati, Ohio, Hebrew Union College Press/Eisenbrauns, 1990. 464p. $35. ISBN: 0878209085.

According to *Choice* (v.28(3), Nov. 1990, p. 495), this survey has 181p. of bibliography, listing *c.*3,700 items from *c.*1,350 authors. Covers Hebrew linguistic scholarship from the end of World War II to the mid-1980s.
Class No: 809.24(01)

Dictionaries

[6195]

ALCALAY, R. The Complete English-Hebrew dictionary. Tel Aviv, Massadah, 1959-61. 4v. (4270 cols.).

140,000 English words and expressions with Hebrew equivalents. Includes new words approved by the Hebrew Language Academy, all new words appearing in the *Reshumot* (Official Gazette), and new slang and colloquialisms; also cites numerous quotations from the Bible, proverbs, idioms, etc.

3-vol. edition published New York, Hemed Books, 1996 (ISBN: 9654481790). *Class No:* 809.24(038)

[6196]

—ALCALAY, R. The Complete Hebrew-English dictionary. Tel Aviv, Massadah, 1964-65. 4v. (2883 cols.).

About 100,000 entry-words. The English equivalents are accompanied by synonyms, and explanations, where considered necessary. Many idioms.

2-vol. edition published New York, Hemed Books, 1996 (ISBN: 9654481855). *Class No:* 809.24(038)

[6197]

BALTSAN, H. Webster's New World Hebrew dictionary: Hebrew-English / English-Hebrew. New York, Prentice Hall, 1992. xxx,827p. £27.95. ISBN: 0671889915.

Over 28,000 Hebrew-English entries, with the *transliterated* form used as the headword (although Hebrew form is also given) so that entries can be presented in conventional English A-Z order. Over 20,000 English-Hebrew entries. Very clear guide for users (22p.).
Class No: 809.24(038)

[6198]

BEN-YEHUDAH, E. Thesaurus totius Hebraitatis et veteris et recentioris. Berlin-Schöneberg, Langenscheidt; Jerusalem, Ben-Yehudah Hozaa-la'Or, 1908-59 (repr. New York, Yoseloff, 1960). 17v.

The authoritative dictionary for the literary language, for the development of Hebrew words and as a source book, because of its voluminous citations. Gives equivalents in English, French and German, with explanations in Hebrew. The basis for all modern dictionaries of Hebrew.
Class No: 809.24(038)

[6199]

CORBEIL, J-C. *and* **ARCHAMBAULT, A. Visual dictionary: English-Hebrew.** Jerusalem, CARTA, 1992. lix,723p. illus. ISBN: 9652201855.

Based on *The Facts on File visual dictionary* (*q.v.*), with Hebrew vocabulary by B. Sarel and R. Gherson. Detailed contents table and indexes in both languages. Bibliography (2p.). *Class No:* 809.24(038)

[6200]

The Dictionary of classical Hebrew. Clines, D.J.A., *ed.* Sheffield, Sheffield Academic Press, 1993-8. v.1-4 (in progress). £75 per vol.

A major project (described in detail in the introduction to v.1) to compile the first dictionary of the classical Hebrew language as a whole, going beyond the Bible to include Hebrew inscriptions, the Dead Sea Scrolls, Ben Sira and other texts down to *c.*200 CE. Except for the most common words, it will record every occurrence of each word in the extant classical literature. V.1 covers words beginning with *Aleph* and has 850 lengthy entries comprising headword, number of occurrences in corpus texts, part of speech, gloss, morphology, and semantic, syntagmatic and paradigmatic analysis. List of sources (37p.). Word frequency index. English-Hebrew index. 8 vols are envisaged.
Class No: 809.24(038)

[6201]

GESENIUS, H.F.W. A Hebrew and English lexicon of the Old Testament, with an Appendix containing the Biblical Aramaic. Brown, F., *and others, eds.* Oxford, Clarendon Press, 1907 (repr. with corrections, 1962). xix,1127p. £65. ISBN: 0198643012.

Based on Gesenius's lexicon, as translated by E. Robinson.

The standard Hebrew-English dictionary of Biblical Hebrew, and virtually a Hebrew concordance to the Old Testament. Often referred to as Brown-Driver-Briggs, after the English editors. *Class No:* 809.24(038)

[6202]

INBAL, S. User-friendly Hebrew-English dictionary. Jerusalem, Zack, 1988. 513p. £32.95. ISBN: 1870668170.

35,000 headwords in Hebrew script (no transliteration) with English gloss.

Companion work is *User-friendly English-Hebrew dictionary* (1988. 2v.). *Class No:* 809.24(038)

[6203]

KLEIN, E. A Comprehensive etymological dictionary of the Hebrew language for readers of English. New York, Macmillan; London, Collier Macmillan, 1987. xix,721p. $100. ISBN: 0029174317.

Provides etymologies for some 30,000 words from all periods of Hebrew, Biblical to contemporary, including loanwords from other languages. Entries comprise headword, part of speech, concise definition, etymology (clearly set out in brackets) and list of derivatives, most of

....*(contd.)*
which appear as separate entries. With the exception of the Hebrew terms, all information is in English. Useful notes on transliteration of Hebrew, Greek and Arabic.
Class No: 809.24(038)

[6204]
KOEHLER, L.H. *and* **BAUMGARTNER, W. Hebräisches und aramäisches Lexikon zum Alten Testament.** 3. Aufl., neu bearb. von W. Baumgartner, unter Mitarbeit von B. Hartmann und E.Y. Kutscher. Leiden, Brill, 1967-95. Lfg. 1-5 (in progress).

1st ed. Leiden, Brill, 1953, as *Lexicon in Veteris Testament libros: Wörterbuch zum hebräischen Alten Testament in deutscher und englischer Sprache / A Dictionary of the Old Testament in English and German* (lxvi,1138p.). *Supplementum.* 1958 (xl,227p.).

1st ed. had *c.*13,000 entry-words, giving German and English equivalents and quotations with precise references to sources. New ed. is completely revised and reset and incorporates the materials from the supplement, but *omits* the English translations. List of sources in Lfg. 1 (21p.).

The first 3 fascicles of a 4-part English version, trans. and ed. under the supervision of M.E.J. Richardson, have been published by Brill, 1994-6, under the title *The Hebrew and Aramaic lexicon of the Old Testament.* Fasc. 1 includes translations of the introductions to all previous eds.
Class No: 809.24(038)

[6205]
—HOLLADAY, W.L. A Concise Hebrew and Aramaic lexicon of the Old Testament, based upon the lexical work of L. Koehler and W. Baumgartner. Leiden, Brill, 1971. xix,425p.

An abridged English-language edition of Koehler and Baumgartner's *Lexicon*, based as far as possible on the 3rd ed. Omitted material includes: etymological material in cognate languages, bibliographical entries, citations to manuscript variations in the Hebrew text and conjectural emendations. *Class No:* 809.24(038)

[6206]
LAUDEN, E. *and* **WEINBACH, L. Multi dictionary:** bilingual learner's dictionary, Hebrew-Hebrew-English / English-Hebrew. Tel Aviv, A.D., 1993. 792+124p. ISBN: 965390003x.

Hebrew-English section has over 21,000 entries with simple definitions and examples from contemporary usage. English-Hebrew section gives simple equivalents and references to main dictionary. Appended thematic lists of specialist vocabulary, including animals and parts of the body. List of foreign words common to both languages (7p.). *Class No:* 809.24(038)

[6207]
The Oxford English-Hebrew dictionary, in collaboration with the Oxford Centre for Hebrew and Jewish Studies. Doniach, N.S. *and* Kahane, A., *eds.* Oxford, Oxford Univ. Press, 1996. xxii,1091p. £40. ISBN: 0198643225.

Over 50,000 entries, including idioms, phrases, slang, colloquialisms, scientific and technical terms. Attempts to cover and describe actual current Hebrew usage, so includes some terms rejected by linguistic purists (*e.g.* non-Semitic loanwords) which cannot be found in other dictionaries. English headwords have regional and field labels and many Hebrew glosses are complemented by usage notes in Hebrew. *Class No:* 809.24(038)

[6208]
ZILKHA, A. Modern Hebrew-English dictionary. New Haven, Conn., Yale Univ. Press, 1989. vi,305p. £32. (*Yale language series.*) ISBN: 0300046472.

Over 20,000 entries (just headword and English equivalent) covering the language of contemporary Israel, with special attention paid to the vocabulary of the media. Appendix lists over 300 common abbreviations.
Class No: 809.24(038)

Reviews & Abstracts

[6209]
Hebrew studies: a journal devoted to the Hebrew language and literature of all periods. Madison, Wis., National Assoc. of Professors of Hebrew, 1954-. Annual. ISSN: 01464094.

Formerly known as *Hebrew Abstracts.*

Includes brief abstracts of articles, books and periodicals on Hebrew published in all languages.
Class No: 809.24(048)

Histories

[6210]
SÁENZ-BADILLOS, A. A History of the Hebrew language. Elwolde, J., *trans.* Cambridge, Cambridge Univ. Press, 1993. xii,371p. £12.95. ISBN: 0521556341.

Originally published Sabadell, Editorial AUSA, 1988, as *Historia de la lengua hebrea.*

The Spanish original has been expanded and updated to form the most comprehensive extant history of Hebrew. 8 chapters with numbered subsections. Massive bibliography (67p.). Index. *Class No:* 809.24(091)

Grammar

[6211]
GLINERT, L. The Grammar of modern Hebrew. Cambridge, Cambridge Univ. Press, 1989. xxviii,580p. £80. ISBN: 0521256119.

A reference grammar of educated Israeli Hebrew in 42 chapters with numbered subsections. Clearly arranged, with detailed table of contents and numerous examples. Bibliography (8p.). Index.

Glinert has also produced a concise grammar for beginners: *Modern Hebrew: an essential grammar* (London, Routledge, 1994. 192p. £13.99. ISBN: 0415101905), with authentic examoples from newspapers, TV and conversations.

For classical Hebrew, see *A Practical grammar of classical Hebrew* by J. Weingreen (Oxford, Clarendon Press, 1959. xii,316p. £25. 0198154224).
Class No: 809.24-5

Maltese

[6212]
BUGEJA, P. Kelmet il-Malti. 3rd ed. Floriana, Associated News Ltd., 1988. xv,599p. £18.20.

1st ed. 1982; 2nd ed. 1984.

Maltese-English and English-Maltese dictionary, aimed at Maltese readers, with *c.*6,500 entry-words in the first section and *c.*7,500 in the second. *Class No:* 809.25

[6213]

BUSUTTIL, E.D. Kalepin (dizzjunarju): Ingliz-Malti. 3rd rev. ed. Valletta, Muscat, 1976. 542p.

1st ed. 1948; 2nd ed. 1968.

English-Maltese dictionary with *c.*37,500 entries.

Class No: 809.25

[6214]

BUSUTTIL, E.D. Kalepin (dizzjunarju): Malti-Ingliz. 6th ed. [Valetta?], Aquilina, 1981. 388p.

Maltese-English dictionary with *c.*31,000 entries, including some idioms. *Class No:* 809.25

Arabic

Bibliographies

[6215]

BAKALLA, M. Arabic linguistics: an introduction and bibliography. 2nd rev. ed. London, Mansell, 1983. lxx,741p. ISBN: 0720115833.

1st ed. 1975 as *Bibliography of Arab linguistics*.

5,500 entries covering books, articles and theses in 20 languages are arranged by author in 3 sections: General works, Occidental language items and Oriental language items. Most entries annotated. Analytical subject index plus name indexes for authors/editors, co-authors, reviewers and Arab authors. Forewords in English and Arabic discuss the history of Arabic linguistics and its current state in the US and UK. *Class No:* 809.27(01)

Dictionaries

[6216]

BA'ALBAKI, M. Al-Mawrid: a modern English-Arabic dictionary. Beirut, Dār al-'Ilim lil Malā-yīm, 1980. 1115;89p. illus. £44.95.

A comprehensive dictionary, designed for Arabic readers, with *c.*60,000 headwords. Includes lists of English proverbs with Arabic equivalents (95p.) and of English words of Arabic origin (16p.). Frequently updated, the latest ed. includes biographical entries with colour photographs.

The companion vol. is *Al-Mawrid: a modern Arabic-English dictionary* (6th ed. 1994. £38.95), with *c.*55,000 entries. *Class No:* 809.27(038)

[6217]

—KARMI, H.S. Al-Manar: an English-Arabic dictionary. 2nd, rev. ed. Beirut, Librairie du Liban; London, Longman, 1979. xii,903p. illus. ISBN: 0582761476.

1st ed. 1971.

Also for Arabic readers, but less full than Ba'albaki with *c.*40,000 English headwords and Arabic equivalents.

Class No: 809.27(038)

[6218]

BLACHÈRE, R., ***and others*****. Dictionnaire arabe-français-anglais** (langue classique et moderne). Paris, Maisonneuve et Larose, 1964-88. fasc. 1-46 (in progress). ISBN: 2706802723.

A dictionary of literary Arabic from the latter half of the 6th century to the present. V.1, fasc. 1 includes list of sources (10p.) and there are supplementary lists at the end of v.1 (7p.) and at the start of v.3 (8p.). 3 vols. completed, comprising fascicules 1-36. *Class No:* 809.27(038)

[6219]

DEUTSCHE MORGENLÄNDISCHE GESELLSCHAFT. Wörterbuch der klassischen arabischen Sprache. Ullmann, M., *ed.* Wiesbaden, Harrassowitz, 1957-. v.1, fasc.1- (in progress).

A major dictionary of pre-classical and classical Arabic which will take many years to complete. Entries are arranged by consonantal roots, with Arabic script followed by transliterated form, translations into German and English, and extensive references to sources. V.1 completed 1970; v.2, pt.1, 1989; v.2, pt.2, 1991.

Vorläufiges Literatur- und Abkürzungsverzeichnis zum zweiten Band (Wiesbaden, Harrassowitz, 1989. 62p.) is a detailed list of sources. *Class No:* 809.27(038)

[6220]

A Dictionary of Iraqi Arabic: English-Arabic. Clarity, B.E., *and others, eds.* Washington, D.C., Georgetown Univ. Press, 1964. 202p. £16.30.

About 8,000 entry-words, representing a basic vocabulary. Illustrative English sentences are based on everyday conversational usage.

The companion vol. is *A Dictionary of Iraqi Arabic: Arabic-English*, ed. by D.R. Woodhead and W. Beene (Washington, D.C., Georgetown Univ. Press, 1967. xii,509p. £23.50.). *Class No:* 809.27(038)

[6221]

ELIAS, E.A. ***and*** **ELIAS, E.E. Elias' Modern dictionary, English-Arabic.** 8th ed. Cairo, Elias, 1981. 912p. £24.95. ISBN: 9775028299.

1st ed. 1913.

A frequently reprinted dictionary with over 65,000 words. The companion vol. is *Elias' Modern dictionary, Arabic-English* (9th ed. Cairo, Elias, 1962. 870p. £29.95. ISBN: 9775028698) with a similar number of words.

Class No: 809.27(038)

[6222]

HINDS, M. ***and*** **BADAWI, E.-S. A Dictionary of Egyptian Arabic:** Arabic-English. Beirut, Librairie du Liban, 1986. 999p. £55. ISBN: 1853410039.

A dictionary of spoken Arabic. 'The compilers have organized their material in the traditional way under the ... root-forms in the cursive Arabic script, but the headwords entered under the root-forms are rendered phonetically and, in thousands of cases, the English definitions ... are accompanied by illustrative examples of the words' idiomatic use' (*TLS*, no.4424, Jan. 15, 1988, p.67).

Class No: 809.27(038)

[6223]

LANE, E.W. Arabic-English lexicon, derived from the best and most copious Eastern sources. In two books: the first containing all the classical words and significations commonly known to the learned among the Arabs; the second, those that are of rare occurrence and not commonly known. London, Williams & Norgate, 1863-93. 1v. in 8 pts. (3064p.). (repr. Cambridge, Islamic Text Soc., 1985. 2v.). £175. ISBN: 0946621039.

Book 2 was never published.

The standard dictionary of classical Arabic, with references to literary sources. *Class No:* 809.27(038)

[6224]

The Oxford English-Arabic dictionary of current usage. Doniach, N.S., *ed.* Oxford, Clarendon Press, 1972. xii,1392p. £45. ISBN: 0198643128.

About 40,000 headwords, the English word-list being based on the *Concise Oxford dictionary* and the *Oxford advanced learner's dictionary of current usage*. Includes both formal and colloquial terms and gives Arabic equivalents, indicating regional variations. Particularly valuable for its translations of English idioms and phrases. Intended for both Arabic- and English-speaking readers.

The Concise Oxford English-Arabic dictionary of current usage, ed. by N. Doniach and others (Oxford, Clarendon Press, 1982. x,461p. £14.99. ISBN: 0198643217), is a shortened and updated version. *Class No:* 809.27(038)

[6225]

WEHR, H. A Dictionary of modern written Arabic (Arabic-English). Cowan, J.H., *ed.* 4th ed., considerably enl. and amended. Wiesbaden, Harrassowitz, 1979 (repr. Ithaca, NY, Spoken Language Services Inc., 1994). xvii,1301p. £150. ISBN: 0879500034.

1st English ed., 1961, was a translated and enlarged version of *Arabisches Wörterbuch für die Schriftsprache der Gegenwart* (3. Aufl. 1958) and its *Supplement* (1959).

The standard dictionary for the modern written language, with *c.*100,000 entries including scientific and technical terms, neologisms, foreign loanwords, and colloquialisms. Entry-words are given in both Arabic and romanized script and arranged according to Arabic roots.
Class No: 809.27(038)

Standards

[6226]

BRITISH STANDARDS INSTITUTION. Transliteration of Arabic characters. London, BSI, 1983. 8p. £26.

BS 4280:1968 (1983).

Provides a system for the transliteration of Arabic consonants, vowels, diphthongs, and other conventional signs into the Roman alphabet. *Class No:* 809.27(083.74)

Amharic

[6227]

KANE, T.L. Amharic-English dictionary. Wiesbaden, Harrassowitz, 1990. 2v. (xxvi,2351p.). ISBN: 3447028718.

Basically a compilation of existing lexicons to form a comprehensive dictionary. Arranged by root and uses same transliteration system as Leslau's *Concise Amharic dictionary*. 115,000 words and phrases translated, with illustrative sentences in many cases. List of sources (5p.).
Class No: 809.28

[6228]

LESLAU, W. Concise Amharic dictionary: Amharic-English / English-Amharic. Wiesbaden, Harrassowitz, 1976. xiv,538p. £68.

Has *c.*7,500 Amharic-English entries and *c.*11,000 English-Amharic. Up-to-date vocabulary. Phonetic transcriptions are provided for Amharic terms in both sections. *Class No:* 809.28

[6229]

LESLAU, W. English-Amharic context dictionary. Wiesbaden, Harrassowitz, 1973. xviii,1503p. ISBN: 3447014822.

15,000 entries, comprising English term, Amharic equivalent, and English sentences using the word in its different meanings with Amharic translations. Amharic is not transliterated. English orthography and usage is that of the US. *Class No:* 809.28

Ge'ez

[6230]

LESLAU, W. Comparative dictionary of Ge'ez (Classical Ethiopic): Ge'ez-English / English-Ge'ez, with an index of Semitic roots. Wiesbaden, Harrassowitz, 1987. xlix,813p. ISBN: 3447025921.

Nearly 10,000 Ge'ez-English entries, including comparisons with Semitic and Ethiopic languages. 6,600 English-Ge'ez entries. Index of Semitic roots (49p.). Bibliography (13p.) *Class No:* 809.281

Hamitic

Ancient Egyptian

[6231]

BUDGE, E.A.T.W. An Egyptian hieroglyphic dictionary, with an index of English words, king list and geographical list, with indexes, list of hieroglyphic characters, Coptic and Semitic alphabets, etc. London, Murray, 1920 (repr. New York, Dover). 2v. (cliv,1314p.). £35.90. ISBN: 0486236153.

About 30,000 entries (transliterated form - hieroglyphic - English translation). List of *c.*60,000 English words (p.1067-1255), with references to page and column, making it a reverse index. List of authorities quoted or referred to, p.lxxv-xcvi; list of most frequently used hieroglyphic characters, p.xcvii-cxlvii. A monumental work.
Class No: 809.31

[6232]

A Dictionary of Late Egyptian. Lesko, L.H., *ed.* Berkeley, Calif., B.C. Scribe Publications, 1982-90. 5v.

A computer-produced dictionary covering the period of the 19th-21st Dynasties. *Class No:* 809.31

[6233]

ERMAN, A. *and* **GRAPOW, H. Wörterbuch der ägyptischen Sprache,** im Auftrage der Deutschen Akademien. 4. Aufl. Stuttgart, Kunst und Wissen, 1982. 7 Bde. und 5 Belegbde. ISBN: 3879530459.

A comprehensive German dictionary of Egyptian hieroglyphic and hieratic scripts, first published Leipzig, Hinrichs, 1926-31. Sources detailed separately in *Die Belegstellen*, ed. by H. Grapow and W. Erichsen and originally published Leipzig, Hinrichs, 1935-53.
Class No: 809.31

Coptic

[6234]
ČERNÝ, J. Coptic etymological dictionary. Cambridge, Cambridge Univ. Press, 1976. xxiv,408p. ISBN: 052107228x.

Lists and explains *c.*2,000 Coptic words whose etymology has been established with certainty or with a high degree of probability. Based on Crum's *Coptic dictionary*, which does not give etymologies, and adds some words discovered since the publication of that work. *Class No:* 809.32

[6235]
CRUM, W.E. A Coptic dictionary, compiled with the help of many scholars. Oxford, Clarendon Press, 1939 (repr. 1962). xxiv,953p. ISBN: 0198644043.

A Coptic-English dictionary with English, Greek, and Arabic indexes. Identifies over 3,300 independent words and numerous derivatives. Many illustrative quotations from Coptic texts. *Class No:* 809.32

Somali

[6236]
ABRAHAM, R.C. English-Somali dictionary. London, Univ. of London Press, 1967. 208p.

10-12,000 entry-words, with many cross-references, in 3-column layout. Tone-markings on Somali words. Numerous illustrative sentences. *Class No:* 809.351

[6237]
ABRAHAM, R.C. Somali-English dictionary. London, Univ. of London Press, 1964. xviii,332p.

Commissioned by the Government of the Republic of Somali. About 8,000 headwords with many illustrative phrases. Lengthy notes on grammar, stress and tone (73p.). *Class No:* 809.351

[6238]
English-Somali dictionary [Quaamuus ingiriisi-soomaali.] London, HAAN Associates, 1993. 272p. £15.95. ISBN: 1874209162.

First published in Somalia in the 1970s for students of English. *c.*5,600 entries in 3-column format: English word, English pronunciation, Somali meaning. *Class No:* 809.351

[6239]
KORSHEL, M. English-Somali / Somali-English dictionary. New Delhi, Star Publications, 1994 (distr. Hippocrene). 445p. £18.95. ISBN: 8186264000, India; 0781802695, US.

10,000 entries, compiled by a group of Somali teachers in India. Simple glosses with no guide to pronunciation. *Class No:* 809.351

[6240]
ZORC, R.D., *& others*. Somali-English dictionary, with English index. 3rd. ed. Kensington, Md., Dunwoody Press, 1993. 612p. £69.90.

1st ed. 1987, by V. Luling; 2nd ed. 1991.

Over 26,000 entries (1st ed. had 18,500), comprising headword, variant forms, part of speech and English gloss. Synonyms, antonyms and examples of usage given in some cases. Introductory notes on Somali grammar and pronunciation. Bibliography (1p.). *Class No:* 809.351

Turanian (Ural-Altaic)

Mongolic Languages

[6241]
BAWDEN, C. Mongolian-English dictionary. New York, Routledge, Chapman & Hall, 1992. 900p. £150. ISBN: 0710304390.

A dictionary, with English equivalents, of modern written Mongolian, in Cyrillic script and orthography, as used in the Mongolian People's Republic, which has been compiled on the basis of reading and excerpting current printed material, including books, newspapers, and popular and academic periodicals. Some short quotations from these sources are included. Tibetan originals of Tibetan loanwords are included wherever possible. *Class No:* 809.42

[6242]
HANGIN, J.G. A Concise English-Mongolian dictionary. Bloomington, Ind., Indiana Univ. Press, 1970 (repr. Richmond, Surrey, Curzon Press, 1997). 287p. £60. (*Uralic & Altaic series.*) ISBN: 0700708898.

About 10,000 English words with Mongolian equivalents. Some examples of usage. *Class No:* 809.42

[6243]
HANGIN, J.G., *& others*. A Modern Mongolian-English dictionary. Bloomington, Ind., Indiana Univ., Research Institute for Inner Asian Studies, 1986. (repr. Richmond, Surrey, Curzon Press, 1997). xxi,900p. £95. (*Uralic & Altaic series.*) ISBN: 0700709509.

40,000 entries (25,000 keywords plus 15,000 examples) based on the standard language of the Mongolian People's Republic, the aim being 'to enable its users to read current Mongolian newspapers, belles-lettres, and texts in the humanities and social sciences' (*Preface*). Keywords in Mongolian Cyrillic alphabetical order. Bibliography (6p.). List of Mongolian abbreviations (16p.). *Class No:* 809.42

[6244]
Mongolian-English dictionary. Lessing, F.D., *ed.* Berkeley, Calif., Univ. of California Press, 1960 (repr. Richmond, Surrey, Curzon Press, 1998). xv,1217p. £125. ISBN: 0700710434.

About 20,000 entry-words. 'Excluding the strictly archaic language, the dictionary contains the vocabulary of all periods from 1940 on, including the modern terminology developed since sovietization' (*Introduction*). Entries consist of romanized form, Mongolian characters, Russian equivalents and English meanings. Cyrillic index; index of ambiguous readings. Supplementary list of Buddhist terms. Select bibliography of dictionaries and grammars. *Class No:* 809.42

Turco-Tartar Languages

[6245]
ÖZTOPÇU, K., *& others*. Dictionary of Turkic languages. London, Routledge, 1996. xvi,361p. £50. ISBN: 0415141982.

2,000 English headwords are translated into each of the 8 Turkic languages: Turkish, Azerbaijani, Turkmen, Uzbek, Uighur, Kazakh, Kyrgyz and Tatar. Original script and Roman transliteration are provided for each language. Alphabetical index for each language. *Class No:* 809.43

Kazak

[6246]

SHNITNIKOV, B.N. Kazakh-English dictionary. The Hague, Mouton, 1966 (repr. Richmond, Surrey, Curzon Press, 1997). 301p. £65. (*Uralic & Altaic series.*)

The first Kazakh dictionary to be compiled outside the USSR, with *c.*20,000 entry-words (not transliterated) and English glosses. *Class No:* 809.434

Turkish

[6247]

Ingilizce-Türkçe Redhouse sözlügü / Redhouse English-Turkish dictionary. Avery, R., *and others, eds.* Istanbul, Redhouse; Washington, D.C., International Learning Systems, 1974 (repr. 1994). viii,1152p. £35. ISBN: 9754130604.

Based on *Revised Redhouse dictionary, English-Turkish* (1950) and *A Lexicon, English and Turkish* (1861), by J.W. Redhouse.

About 45,000 entry-words and 182,000 definitions. Includes technical terms, slang, colloquialisms, and idiomatic expressions. Pronunciation indicated for English entry-words, using a system based on the Turkish alphabet. The editors acknowledge in the Preface that the dictionary reflects their American point of view, but 'British usages in vocabulary, meanings, spelling and pronunciation have usually been noted'. *Class No:* 809.435

[6248]

Langenscheidt's standard Turkish-English / English-Turkish dictionary. Akdikmen, R., *comp.* 2nd ed. London, Harrap, 1990. 1350p. ISBN: 0245600507.

1st ed. London, Hodder, 1986.

A handy two-way dictionary with *c.*80,000 entries, reflecting contemporary vocabulary and including some technical and scientific terms. Many idioms. Pronunciation indicated for all English headwords and for difficult Turkish ones.

An alternative desk dictionary is *Redhouse büyük elsözlügü* [*The Larger Redhouse portable dictionary*] (Istanbul, Redhouse, 1997. xiv,570+x,853p. £35. ISBN: 975817603x), which is based on the big Redhouse dictionaries and *Webster's third new international dictionary of the English language*. *Class No:* 809.435

[6249]

The Oxford Turkish dictionary. Iz, F., *& others, comps.* Oxford, Oxford Univ. Press, 1993. xix,526,xvi,619p. £55. ISBN: 0198641907.

A one-vol. compilation of *The Oxford Turkish-English dictionary* (3rd ed. 1984) and *The Oxford English-Turkish dictionary* (2nd ed. 1978).

Turkish-English section has *c.*25,000 entry-words, including many everyday neologisms which have replaced loanwords from Arabic and Persian in recent decades, and much new scientific terminology based largely on Western European languages. Much idiomatic material. Includes cross-references to appropriate sections of G.L.Lewis's *Turkish grammar* (Oxford, 1967).

English—Turkish section has *c.* 27,000 entry-words, an increase of 50% over 1st ed., including basic scientific vocabulary, geographical and historical terms, and some American and Australian terms. Abbreviations in main sequence. *Class No:* 809.435

[6250]

—The Concise Oxford Turkish dictionary: Turkish-English / English-Turkish. Alderson, A.D. *and* Iz, F., *eds.* Oxford, Clarendon Press, 1959. xii,807p. ISBN: 0198641095.

Single-volume abridgement of the 1st eds. of the 2 works combined above, eliminating close synonyms, easily recognizable geographical and scientific terms, and many superseded Arabic and Persian forms. *Class No:* 809.435

[6251]

Redhouse yeni Türkçe-Ingilizce sözlük / New Redhouse Turkish-English dictionary. 12th ed. Istanbul, Redhouse, 1991. xxxii,1292p. £39. ISBN: 9754130221.

Based largely on Sir James Redhouse's *A Turkish and English lexicon* (1890).

A comprehensive dictionary with full coverage of Ottoman Turkish, plus dialectal and regional variants, as spoken during the past 200 years.

Redhouse cağdas Türkçe-Ingilizce sözlüğü (Istanbul, Redhouse, 1983. 455p.) is a concise dictionary of contemporary Turkish, with English equivalents based on American usage. *Class No:* 809.435

Grammar

[6252]

SWIFT, L.B. A Reference grammar of modern Turkish. Bloomington, Ind., Indiana Univ. Press, 1963 (repr. Richmond, Surrey, Curzon Press, 1997). 278p. £60. (*Uralic & Altaic series.*) ISBN: 0700708197.

450 numbered sections in 6 chapters: 1. Phonemics - 2. Morpho-phonemics - 3. Word formation - 4. Nominal inflection - 5. Predicate inflection - 6. Syntax. Appended sample analyses of typical sentences. Many examples with translations. Index.

See also J. Kornfilt's *Turkish* in the *Descriptive grammars* series (London, Routledge, 1997. 608p. £110. ISBN: 0415000106), which has many examples from different levels of vocabulary: contemporary and old, official and colloquial. *Class No:* 809.435-5

Azerbaijani

[6253]

AZIZBEKOV, Kh. Azerbaîdzhansko russkii slovar'. Baku, Azerbaîdzhanskoe Gosudarstvennoe Izdatel'stvo, 1985. 418p.

Azerbaijani-Russian dictionary with *c.*23,000 words. *Class No:* 809.436

Uzbek

[6254]

WATERSON, N. Uzbek-English dictionary. Oxford, Oxford Univ. Press, for the School of Oriental and African Studies, Univ. of London, 1980. xx,190p. £27.50. ISBN: 0197135978.

The first dictionary of its kind, it aims 'to cover the essential vocabulary of modern Uzbek' (*Introduction*). Nearly 10,000 headwords in unsuffixed form, with separate list of prefixes and suffixes. Uses Cyrillic script, but has notes on other writing systems. List of current abbreviations. *Class No:* 809.437

Finno-Ugrian Languages

Hungarian

[6255]

MAGAY, T. *and* **ORSZÁGH, L. A Concise Hungarian-English dictionary.** New ed. Oxford, Oxford Univ. Press; Budapest, Akadémiai Kiadó, 1990. 1152p. £30. ISBN: 0198641699.

The first completely revised ed. since 1959 of this standard concise dictionary contains over 30,000 new items, with translations for over 95,000 Hungarian words and phrases. Many illustrative sentences, including good coverage of US usage. Comprehensive and lucid explanatory notes for users (4p.). *Class No:* 809.451

[6256]

—ORSZÁGH, L. A Concise English-Hungarian dictionary. Oxford, Oxford Univ. Press; Budapest, Akadémiai Kiadó, 1990. 1052p. £30. ISBN: 0198641702.

A British edition of the 14th ed. of the standard concise dictionary, with *c.*40,000 entry-words and *c.*20,000 phrases drawn from comtemporary vocabulary. American usage well covered. Abbreviations and proper names included in main sequence. *Class No:* 809.451

[6257]

MAGYAR TUDOMÁNYOS AKADÉMIA. Nyelvtudományi Intézet. **A Magyar nyelv értelmezö szótára.** Budapest, Akademiai Kiadó, 1959-62. 7v.

The Hungarian Academy's authoritative dictionary of modern Hungarian, with numerous quotations from literary sources. *Class No:* 809.451

[6258]

ORSZÁGH, L. Angol-magyar szótár / English-Hungarian dictionary. 12. kiad. Budapest, Akadémiai Kiadó, 1995. 2v. (2318p.). £50. ISBN: 963056775x.

1st ed. 1960.

The most comprehensive English-Hungarian dictionary, with 110,000 entry-words and 150,000 idioms.

Also avalable on CD-Rom ($199. ISBN: 9630569639). *Class No:* 809.451

[6259]

—ORSZÁGH, L. Magyar-angol szótár / Hungarian-English dictionary. 11. kiad. Budapest, Akadémiai Kiadó, 1994. 2v. (xv,2159p.). £55. ISBN: 9630557991; 9630567784.

1st ed. 1960.

Like its companion vol., is the leader in its field with *c.*120,000 entry-words. Usually distinguishes between US and British usage. Noted for its accurate rendering of slang and colloquial phrases. List of abbreviations appended. *Class No:* 809.451

[6260]

The Oxford-Duden pictorial Hungarian & English dictionary. Oxford, Clarendon Press, 1994. 677+93p. ISBN: 0198645112.

See entry for *The Oxford-Duden pictorial German & English dictionary*. Hungarian and English indexes. *Class No:* 809.451

Finnish

[6261]

HURME, R., *& others*. Uusi suomi-englanti suursanakirja / Finnish-English general dictionary. Porvoo, Söderström, 1984. xxiv,1446p. £56 ISBN: 9510184357.

Regarded as the best large Finnish-English dictionary, with over 35,000 entry-words and numerous compounds and phrases. Primarily intended for Finnish speakers and takes account of both British and American English.

The companion vol. is *Englanti-suomi suursanakirja / English-Finnish general dictionary* by R. Hurme & others (3rd ed. Porvoo, Söderström, 1990. xx,1525p. £56. ISBN: 9510184349). Over 35,000 entries, with pronunciation given for English headwords. *Class No:* 809.454.1

[6262]

SUOMALAISEN KIRJALLISUUDEN SEURA. Nykysuomen sanakirja. Sadeniemi, M., *ed.* 6th ed. Porvoo, Söderström, 1978-89. 7v. ISBN: 9510027642.

A monolingual dictionary of modern Finnish, issued under the auspices of the Finnish Literary Society. Main A-Z sequence in vols. 1-3, followed by loanwords in v.4, slang, neologisms, abbreviations and geographical names in v.5, etymology in v.6 and synonyms in v.7. *Class No:* 809.454.1

[6263]

TUOMIKOSKI, A. *and* **SLÖÖR, A. Englantilais-suomalainen sanakirja** / English-Finnish dictionary. 6. painos. Helsinki, Suomalaisen Kirjallisuuden Seura, 1973. xiii,1100p.

1st ed. 1939.

The fullest English-Finnish dictionary, with numerous examples of usage and many idomatic phrases. *c.*30,000 English headwords, with pronunciation indicated. Appended lists of abbreviations and proper names. *Class No:* 809.454.1

[6264]

VIRTARANTA, P. Amerikansuomen sanakirja [Dictionary of American Finnish.] Turku, Siirtolaisuusinstituuti (Institute of Migration), 1992. 329p. illus. ISBN: 9519266437.

Based on a survey carried out 1965-80 of the language spoken by Finns who emigrated to North America pre-1930 and their descendants. 4,556 words listed. Details of 500 informants: date and place of birth; year of their (or their parent's) arrival in America; place and date of interview. English-Finnish index. *Class No:* 809.454.1

[6265]

WUOLLE, A. The Standard Finnish-English / English-Finnish dictionary. Eastbourne, Holt, Rinehart and Winston, 1986 (repr. London, Cassell, 1991). 1004p. £47.50. ISBN: 0304341428.

Originally published in 2 vols. Helsinki, Söderström, 1978 and 1981.

A well-established and frequently revised (this is the 6th ed.) concise dictionary made available in the UK for the first time. *c.*10,000 Finnish and 15,000 English headwords, with many examples of usage. *Class No:* 809.454.1

Grammar

[6266]

SULKALA, H. *and* **KARJALAINEN, M. Finnish.** London, Routledge, 1992. xv,426p. £85. (*Descriptive grammars.*) ISBN: 0415026431.

5 main chapters with numbered subsections: 1. Syntax - 2.

....*(contd.)*
Morphology - 3. Phonology - 4. Ideophones and interjections - 5. Lexicon. 1,612 numbered examples in ch.1 and 2. Bibliography (3p.). Index. *Class No:* 809.454.1-5

Estonian

[6267]
HARMS, R.T. Estonian grammar. Bloomington, Ind., Indiana Univ. Press, 1962 (repr. Richmond, Surrey, Curzon Press, 1997). 178p. £40. (*Uralic & Altaic series.*) ISBN: 070070812x.

11 chapters with numbered subsections in 4 main parts: 1. Phonemics - 2. Morphophonemics - 3. Morphemics - 4. Syntax. Bibliography. *Class No:* 809.454.5

[6268]
KYIV, K. *and* **BENYUCH, O. Estonian-English / English-Estonian dictionary.** New York, Hippocrene, 1992. xvii,180p. £10.50. ISBN: 0870520814.

A pocket dictionary with over 10,000 entries. Pronunciation indicated for all headwords. List of geographical names. *Class No:* 809.454.5

[6269]
SAAGPAKK, P.F. Eesti-inglise sõnaraamat / Estonian-English dictionary. New Haven, Conn., Yale Univ. Press, 1982. cxi,1180p. $195. (*Yale linguistics series.*) ISBN: 0300028490.

Claims to be the largest bilingual dictionary of Estonian ever compiled, with *c.*50,000 entries. Aimed at both Estonians learning English and students of Estonian language and literature. Introduction includes an English-language survey of Estonian grammar (51p.) and all headwords are cross-referenced to tables of inflection. *Class No:* 809.454.5

[6270]
SILVET, J. Eesti-inglise sõnaraamat / Estonian-English dictionary. 3rd ed. Tallinn, Valgus, 1989. 508p. £32.

1st ed. Toronto, Orto, 1965.

An Estonian-English dictionary with *c.*24,000 entry-words. List of geographical names appended. *Class No:* 809.454.5

[6271]
SILVET, J. Inglise-Eesti sõnaraamat. 3rd ed. Tallinn, Valgus, 1989. 2v. £49.50.

1st ed. 1938.

English-Estonian dictionary. Includes idioms and proper names. *Class No:* 809.454.5

Lappish

[6272]
NIELSEN, K. *and* **NESHEIM, A. Lappisk ordbok,** grunnet på dialektene i Polmak, Karasjok og Kautokeino / Lapp dictionary, based on the dialects of Polmak, Karasjok and Kautokeino. Oslo, Aschehoug; Cambridge, Mass., Harvard Univ. Press; London, Williams, 1932-63. 5v. (3200p.) illus. ISBN: 8200142019.

Vols. 1-3 (1932-38) comprise the alphabetical dictionary (Lapp-Norwegian-English), with *c.*25,000 entry-words and many examples of usage. V.4 (1956) groups words according to meaning and association in 552 groups. 584 illustrations. V.5 (1963) is a supplementary volume. *Class No:* 809.455

Caucasian

Georgian

[6273]
AKADEMIYA NAUK GRUZINSKOI, SSR, Tiflis. **Tolkovyi slovar' gruzinskogo yazyka** / Khartuli enis ganmartebithi lekhsikoni. Akhvlediani, G., *ed.* Tbilisi, 1950-64. 8v.

The Tbilisi Academy's reference dictionary of the Georgian language. *Class No:* 809.463.1

[6274]
ARONSON, H.I. Georgian: a reading grammar. Corrected ed. Columbus, Ohio, Slavica, 1990. 526p. $28.95 ISBN: 0893572071.

Originally published 1982; not rewritten or reset but many small additions have been made and misprints corrected in this limited edition reprint.

The first grammar of Georgian for beginners to be published in English, its aim is to allow the student to read literature (primarily scholarly) with the aid of a dictionary.

For a more comprehensive grammar, see B.G. Hewitt's *Georgian: a structural reference grammar* (Amsterdam, Benjamins, 1996. xviii,716p. £100. ISBN: 9027238022). Hewitt has also produced *Georgian: a learner's grammar* (London, Routledge, 1996. xi,483p. ISBN: 0415133246). *Class No:* 809.463.1

[6275]
CHERKESI, E. Georgian-English dictionary. Oxford, Printed for the Trustees of the Marjory Wardrop Fund, Univ. of Oxford, 1950. 275p.

'A first attempt to make the Georgian language and literature available to English students' (*Foreword*), which includes important ancient terms as well as modern Georgian. The *Russian-Georgian dictionary* by D. Chubinashvili (1886) was used as a standard book of reference. Over 12,000 entry-words. *Class No:* 809.463.1

[6276]
GVARDZHALADZE, T. *and* **GVARDZHALADZE, I. English-Georgian dictionary.** Tbilisi, State Publishing House, 1975. 1050p.

Over 30,000 entries. *Class No:* 809.463.1

Eskimo Language

[6277]
FORTESCUE, M., & *others.* **Comparative Eskimo dictionary,** with Aleut cognates. Fairbanks, Alaska Native Language Center, Univ. of Alaska, 1994. xx,614p. ISBN: 1555000517.

Groups related words from modern Eskimo languages in comparative sets with English equivalents. Very detailed entries. Bibliography (4p.). Indexes of 4 languages. Proto-form gloss index. *Class No:* 809.47

[6278]

THIBERT, A. Dictionary: English-Eskimo / Eskimo-English. Rev. ed. Ottawa, Canadian Research Centre for Anthropology, Saint Paul Univ., 1958. xi,180p.

1st ed. 1954.

Over 3,000 entries in each section plus 10 appendices, including numerals, placenames, parts of the body, clothing terms, etc. and notes on grammar. Useful bibliography of the Eskimo language (19 items). *Class No:* 809.47

Dravidian Languages

[6279]

BURROW, T. *and* **EMENEAU, M.B. A Dravidian etymological dictionary.** 2nd ed. Oxford, Clarendon Press, 1984. xli,853p. ISBN: 0198643268.

1st ed. 1961; *Supplement*, 1968.

Provides etymologies and English equivalents for words from 4 major languages (Tamil, Kannada, Malayalam, Telugu) and 14 minor ones. 2nd ed. incorporates the 4,572 entries from the 1st ed. and 889 from the *Supplement,* and adds new information. Language indexes (22 Dravidian and 18 non-Dravidian). Index of English meanings. Index of flora. Bibliography. *Class No:* 809.48

Tamil

[6280]

MADRAS UNIVERSITY. Tamil lexicon. Madras, Univ. of Madras, 1924-36. 6v. *Supplement*. 1938-39. 2v.

Issued in 24 pts., with various imprints, 1924-36.

The standard Tamil-English dictionary, providing transliteration and translation for over 100,000 Tamil words, including much specialist vocabulary. *Class No:* 809.481.1

[6281]

PILLAI, V.V. A Dictionary, Tamil and English (comprising chiefly High Tamil words). 6th ed., rev. and enl. with an appendix of modern scientific terms. Madras, Madras School Book and Literature Society, 1951. 706p.

1st ed. 1888.

Over 17,500 entries. *Class No:* 809.481.1

Telugu

[6282]

BROWN, C.P. Dictionary, English-Telugu. New Delhi, Asian Educational Services, 1980. xxvii,1367p. £19.90.

About 80,000 entries, including many idiomatic expressions. *Class No:* 809.483

[6283]

GWYNN, J.P.L. A Telugu-English dictionary. Delhi, Oxford Univ. Press, 1991. xxii,574p. £30. ISBN: 0195628632.

28,000 entries, with the vocabulary based on contemporary language and literature but incorporating forms from classical literature which have entered everyday language. Entries comprise headword in Telugu script, romanized form, part of speech, status or register label, meanings, examples of usage, and idiomatic expressions.

Gwynn is the joint author, with Bh. Krishnamurti, of *A Grammar of modern Telugu* (Delhi, Oxford Univ. Press, 1985. £25. ISBN: 0195616642). *Class No:* 809.483

Sino-Tibetan Languages

Chinese

Bibliographies

[6284]

CHIEN, D. Lexicography in China: bibliography of dictionaries and related literature. Exeter, Univ. of Exeter, 1986. 2v. in 1 (264p.). (*Exeter linguistic studies - 5.*) ISBN: 0859892638.

V.1 has over 1,000 references, with English translation, to the literature on Chinese lexicography published in China since 1949, arranged by author, A-Z, and annotated by means of 59 4-letter codes. List of nearly 200 periodicals.

V.2 is a classified bibliography of 630 monolingual, bilingual and polyglot dictionaries published in China in the same period. Annotations usually give the number of entries. *Class No:* 809.51(01)

[6285]

Chinese dictionaries: an extensive bibliography of dictionaries in Chinese and other languages. Chinese-English Translation Assistance Group, *eds.* Westport, Conn., Greenwood, 1982. xvi,448p. $115. ISBN: 0313235058.

Supersedes *A Compilation of Chinese dictionaries,* comp. and ed. by S. Hixson and J. Mathias (New Haven, Conn., Yale Univ. Press, 1975).

Lists over 2,700 monolingual, bilingual and polyglot dictionaries. Indexes of languages and titles. *Class No:* 809.51(01)

[6286]

YANG, P.F. Chinese lexicology and lexicography: a selected and classified bibliography. Hong Kong, Chinese Univ. Press, 1985. xlvi,361p. $53.50. ISBN: 9622013120.

4,165 entries in 7 sections with many subdivisions, titles in Chinese, Japanese, Russian and Latin being translated into English. Detailed contents table. List of Chinese and Japanese publishers and of 800 periodicals. Author index. *Class No:* 809.51(01)

[6287]

YANG, P.F. Chinese linguistics: a selected and classified bibliography. Hong Kong, Chinese University, 1974. xxvii,292p. $48.50. ISBN: 9622010202.

3,257 entries in 12 sections with numerous subsections. International coverage, with titles in Chinese, Japanese, Korean and Russian translated into English. Includes references to book reviews. Alphabetical author index, plus character index for oriental authors and Chinese names for western authors. *Class No:* 809.51(01)

Handbooks & Manuals

[6288]

MATTHIES, A. Transcription tables of Chinese and Japanese. München, K.G. Saur, 1989. 77p. DM58. ISBN: 3598107897.

Includes introduction in Chinese and English, dictionary section, and bilingual index using the Pinyin system. Appendices include a table for the conversion of the Chinese phonetic alphabet (Pinyin) to the Wade system and a table of Pinyin consonants and vowels with their corresponding international phonetic symbols. *Class No:* 809.51(035)

[6289]

SEYMOUR, N.N. How to identify Chinese characters. Metuchen, N.J., Scarecrow, 1989. xxxix,427p. $55.50. ISBN: 0810822784.

Presents a simple system of character identification, the Modified Stroke Count Method, whose primary goal is 'to enable non-Chinese readers to identify and transcribe Chinese characters into their Pinyin form' (*Foreword*) so that they have access to Chinese dictionaries.

The core of the book is ch.3, 'The Index of Modified Stroke Count' (p.59-160), which lists the 4,000 most frequently used characters, plus 1,600 variants, by total stroke count from 1 to 34. Ch.4 has Pinyin character index with English meanings. Appendix has Pinyin, Wade and Yale Romanization tables. *Class No:* 809.51(035)

Dictionaries

[6290]

ABC Chinese-English dictionary. Defrancis, J., *ed.* Honolulu, Univ. of Hawaii Press; Richmond, Surrey, Curzon Press, 1996. xix,897p. £25. ISBN: 0700705112, UK; 0824817443, US.

Claims to be the first strictly alphabetically ordered and Pinyin computerized dictionary, 'ABC' standing for 'alphabetically based computerized'. 71,300 entries, comprising transliterated headword, Chinese characters, part of speech and English gloss. *Class No:* 809.51(038)

[6291]

CORBEIL, J-C. *and* **LEE, M. The Facts on File English / Chinese dictionary.** New York, Facts on File, 1988. 823p. ISBN: 0816020434.

Contains the 3,000-plus illustrations from *The Facts on File visual dictionary* (*qv*) with captions in English and Chinese. General index in both languages, but lacks the thematic and specialized indexes of the original. English terms are based on North American usage. As with the Oxford-Duden series, the illustrations have not been amended to accommodate Chinese culture.
Class No: 809.51(038)

[6292]

—The Oxford-Duden pictorial Chinese & English dictionary. Simplified character ed. Hong Kong and Oxford, Oxford Univ. Press, 1989. 853p. £35. ISBN: 0195842030.

See entry for *The Oxford-Duden pictorial German & English dictionary*. Radical index in Chinese; alphabetical index in English. *Class No:* 809.51(038)

[6293]

HORNBY, A.S. The Oxford advanced learner's English-Chinese dictionary (simplified characters). 3rd ed. Hong Kong, Oxford Univ. Press, 1989. 1456p. £9.95. ISBN: 0195852958.

Based on *The Oxford advanced learner's dictionary of current English,* with definitions and examples of usage in English and Chinese and full coverage of American English. Pronunciation indicated using both the Jones and Kenyon & Knott phonetic systems.

Concise English-Chinese / Chinese-English dictionary (Hong Kong, Oxford Univ. Press, 1987. 606p. £6.95. ISBN: 0195840488) is a pocket 2-way dictionary ideal for learners of both English and Chinese. *Class No:* 809.51(038)

[6294]

HUANG, PO-FEI. Cantonese dictionary: Cantonese-English New Haven, Conn., Yale Univ. Press, 1970. xxi,489p. £60.

English-Cantonese section has *c.*20,000 entries, with many illustrative sentences. Cantonese-English section is arranged A-Z by romanized (Yale) form and Cantonese characters are given for each entry. *Class No:* 809.51(038)

[6295]

MATHEWS, R.H. Mathews' Chinese-English dictionary. Rev. American ed. Cambridge, Mass., Harvard Univ. Press, 1943. 1250p. $39.50. ISBN: 0674123506.

First published 1931, as *A Chinese dictionary, compiled for the China Inland Mission.*

For many years the standard reference source for both classical and modern Chinese, but now becoming rather dated. Over 100,000 entries under nearly 8,000 head characters, arranged A-Z by the Wade-Giles romanization system. *Class No:* 809.51(038)

[6296]

A New English-Chinese dictionary. Ge Chuan-gui, *and others, comps.* Rev. and enl. ed. Seattle, Univ. of Washington Press, 1988. 1770p. $19.95. ISBN: 0295966092.

1st ed. Hongkong, Joint Publishing Co., 1975.

Translates over 80,000 English and foreign words, including derivatives and compounds, and over 14,000 idioms and proverbs. Supplement includes over 4,000 new words, many of them scientific and technical terms, and words whose meanings have changed. Abbreviations and proper names in main sequence. 9 appendices, including list of British and American forenames. No transliteration.

The companion work is *A New Chinese-English dictionary*, ed. by Ding Guang-xun (Seattle, Univ. of Washington Press, 1986. 1448p. ISBN: 0295963360), with 4,600 Chinese characters and 36,000 phrases, arranged alphabetically by the Hanyu Pinyin system.
Class No: 809.51(038)

[6297]

The Pinyin Chinese-English dictionary. Wu Jingrong, *ed.* Reprint of 1979 ed. New York, Wiley, 1982. 976p. £53.95. ISBN: 0471867969.

Originally published Hong Kong, Commercial Press, and London, Pitman, 1979.

The work of over 50 compilers at the Beijing Foreign Languages Institute. 'Over 6,000 single-character entries, over 50,000 compound character entries and over 70,000 compound words, set phrases and examples' (*Foreword*). Emphasis on modern Chinese, but includes some common classical Chinese words, dialect words and proverbs. Arranged in Chinese phonetic alphabetical order, with radical index and phonetic index of syllables. 10 appendices, including geographical terms and conversion table to the Wade system. *Class No:* 809.51(038)

[6298]

YALE UNIVERSITY. Institute of Far Eastern Languages. **Dictionary of spoken Chinese.** New Haven, Conn., Yale Univ. Press, 1966. xxxix,1071p.

Authorized revision and expansion of the US War Dept.'s *Dictionary of spoken Chinese* (Washington, D.C., 1945).

Designed for students of colloquial Mandarin. Chinese-English section has over 2,000 characters, with many examples. English-Chinese section has *c.*2,500 entry-words with numerous phrases. Uses Yale system of romanization.

....(contd.)

'Restricted in content, but by far the best account of modern spoken Chinese grammar in action' (CILT, *Chinese,* 1986, p.33). *Class No:* 809.51(038)

Standards

[6299]

BRITISH STANDARDS INSTITUTION. Guide to the romanization of Chinese. London, BSI, 1989. 12p. £26.

BS 7014:1989, replacing PD 6483:1978.

Description and comparison of existing systems, particularly Wade-Giles and Pinyin, with comparative tables for these 2 systems in romanized form.
Class No: 809.51(083.74)

Histories

[6300]

RAMSEY, S.R. The Languages of China. Princeton, N.J., Princeton Univ. Press, 1987. xi,340p., maps. $52.50. ISBN: 0691066949.

Part I (p.3-154) is a history and description of the Chinese language in 8 chapters; Part II (p.157-291) describes the minority languages of China in 3 chapters, showing how they interrelate with each other and with Chinese. 'Written first and foremost with the educated general reader in mind' (*Preface*), but the narrative includes a mass of reference material set in smaller type, plus many charts and tables and some excellent maps. Detailed notes on sources for each chapter; general bibliography (10p.); bibliography for China's minority languages (8p.). Index.
Class No: 809.51(091)

Grammar

[6301]

MATTHEWS, S. *and* **YIP, V. Cantonese: a comprehensive grammar.** London, Routledge, 1994. xii,429p. £19.99. (*Routledge grammars.*) ISBN: 041508945x.

The first substantial English-language reference grammar of Cantonese. 21 chapters, with numbered subsections and many examples using modified Yale transcription system. Glossary of grammatical terms (7p.). Bibliography (4p.). Full contents table (8p.) and index. *Class No:* 809.51-5

[6302]

YIP PO-CHING *and* **RIMMINGTON, D. Chinese: an essential grammar.** London, Routledge, 1997. 240p. £45. (*Routledge grammars.*) ISBN: 0415135346.

A clear and concise reference guide to Mandarin arranged in short, readable sections and emphasising the language of contemporary native speakers. Numerous examples. Glossaries of grammatical terms and Chinese characters. Detailed contents list and thorough index provide easy access. *Class No:* 809.51-5

Thai

[6303]

McFARLAND, G.B. Thai-English Dictionary. Stanford, Calif., Stanford Univ. Press, 1944 (repr. 1969). xxii+1019+39p. $42.50. ISBN: 0804703833.

Originally published Bangkok, Times Press, 1941.

The classic Thai-English dictionary, giving headword in Thai script, romanized form and English translation. *c.*10,000 entry-words, with idioms and phrases, often accompanied by lengthy explanatory notes. List of the 1,000

....(contd.)

most frequently used words. Lists of birds, fishes, shells, flora, and snakes, arranged by Latin name with Thai translation and page reference. *Class No:* 809.523

[6304]

Thai-English student's dictionary. Haas, M., *and others, comps.* Kuala Lumpur and London, Oxford Univ. Press, 1964. xxix,638p. £21.95.

'Prepared especially to meet the needs of the American student who wishes to read Thai newspapers and other Thai source materials' (*Preface*). 20,000 entries in a single alphabetical sequence, including names of people and organizations, place names, and abbreviations. Entries comprise Thai spelling of headword, Roman phonemic transcription, part of speech, usage label, English definition, synonyms and antonyms, and examples of usage.
Class No: 809.523

Laotian

[6305]

KERR, A. Lao-English dictionary. Single-vol. reprint. Cheney, Wash., White Lotus, 1994. 1248p. £59.95. ISBN: 9748495698.

Originally published Washington, D.C., Catholic Univ. of America Press, 1972, in 2 vols. *Class No:* 809.525

[6306]

MARCUS, R. English-Lao / Lao-English dictionary. Rutland, Vt., Tuttle, 1970. 416p. £10.95. ISBN: 0804809097.

Pocket-sized dictionary with *c.*5,000 English-Lao entries and *c.*7,500 Lao-English. *Class No:* 809.525

Tibetan

[6307]

BUCK, S.H. Tibetan-English dictionary, with supplement. Washington, D.C., Catholic Univ. of America Press, 1969. xviii,833p. ISBN: 0813202698.

Aims 'to provide full accurate definitions of the vocabulary used in current publications in the Tibetan language, especially those appearing in Communist China' (*Introduction*). Also includes common colloquial terms and Buddhist terminology. *c.*16,000 entries. *Class No:* 809.541

[6308]

GOLDSTEIN, M.C. Tibetan-English dictionary of modern Tibetan. 2nd ed. Kathmandu, Ratna Pustak Bhandar, 1978; New York, French & European, 1987. 1234p. $75. ISBN: 082881760x.

1st ed. 1975.

Has *c.*40,000 entries, much of the vocabulary being drawn from contemporary newspapers and periodicals.

The companion vol. is Goldstein's *English-Tibetan dictionary of modern Tibetan* (Berkeley, Calif., Univ. of California Press, 1984. 600p. $60. ISBN: 0520051572), which emphasizes the spoken language. *Class No:* 809.541

[6309]

JÄSCHKE, H.A. Tibetan-English dictionary, with special reference to the prevailing dialects; to which is added an English-Tibetan vocabulary. Reprint of 1881 ed. London, Routledge, 1990. xxii,671p. £80. ISBN: 041505897x.

First published London, Trübner, 1882, being a revision of a Tibetan-German dictionary published 1871-76.

*c.*9,000 entry-words in Tibetan-English section (p.1-608), followed by English-Tibetan vocabulary (p.611-68). Many

....(*contd.*)
examples of usage. Paperback ed. announced by Curzon Press for 1998 (£30. ISBN: 070070681x).
Class No: 809.541

Japanese

Bibliographies

[6310]
YOSHIZAKI, Y. Studies in Japanese literature and language: a bibliography of English materials. Tokyo, Nichigai Associates, 1979. 451p.
A classified listing of books, periodical articles and dissertations in 3 sections: 1. Studies in Japanese literature - 2. Studies in Japanese language - 3. Materials for further information. Index of names and titles.
Class No: 809.56(01)

Dictionaries

[6311]
Basic Japanese-English dictionary. Reprint of Japanese ed. Oxford, Oxford Univ. Press, 1989. xvi,958p. £13.99. ISBN: 0198643284.
Originally published Tokyo, Bonjinsha, 1986.
A concise beginners' dictionary specially designed for English speakers (rather than for Japanese students of English) by The Japan Foundation and published under licence by Oxford Univ. Press. 2,873 entries in roman script, with standard Japanese script alongside, followed by example sentences, idioms and compounds. English translations clearly set out on opposite side of each page. Useful introduction to Japanese grammar appended (33p.).
Class No: 809.56(038)

[6312]
Collins-Shubun English-Japanese dictionary. London, Collins/Shubun International, 1993. 635p. £9.99. ISBN: 0004334051.
A handy, flexicover dictionary with 27,000 references and 38,000 definitions. The English is that of the US, but British differences are clearly indicated. Primarily intended for Japanese users, but includes an essay for English speakers on 'Understanding Japanese.' *Class No:* 809.56(038)

[6313]
Daijiten. Toyko, Heibonsha, 1974. 2v.
1st ed. 1934-36 (26v.); reduced-size repr. 1953-54 (13v.).
An encyclopedic 'great dictionary' of Japanese, with over 700,000 words, including modern, classical, dialect, and technical terms, plus personal and place names, literary titles, etc. *Class No:* 809.56(038)

[6314]
DE MENTE, B.L. NTC's dictionary of Japan's cultural code words. Lincolnwood, Ill., NTC, 1994. xvi,394p. £12.95. ISBN: 0844283150.
Defines and explains 230 quintessentially Japanese expressions crucial to understanding the country's culture, with around 1½p. on each. Also includes notes on 14 aspects of Japanese culture, *e.g.* 'Paying proper respect'.
Class No: 809.56(038)

[6315]
INOUE, J. Inoue's Japanese-English dictionary. 9th reprint of 1st Tuttle ed. of 1983 Rutland, Vt., & Tokyo, Tuttle, 1993. xi+926+28p. £17.99. ISBN: 0804814406.
Originally published 1926.
33,000 headwords listed by Romanized spelling (Hepburn), followed by *kanji* and *kana* equivalents, English definitions and illustrative phrases. Obviously of limited use for students of the contemporary language, but 'essential for reading and understanding Japan's classical and early modern literature' (*Reference Reviews*, v.8(3), 1994, p.21-2). *Class No:* 809.56(038)

[6316]
Kenkyusha's new English-Japanese dictionary, on bilingual principles. Koine, Y., *ed.* 5th ed. Tokyo, Kenkyusha, 1980. xxi,2477p. £195. ISBN: 0317593161.
1st ed. 1927.
Over 126,000 main entries, with Japanese terms not transliterated. Many phrases and compounds. Some line drawings. Appendix on the discrimination of synonyms (52p.). *Class No:* 809.56(038)

[6317]
Kenkyusha's new Japanese-English dictionary. Masuda, K., *ed.* 4th ed. Tokyo, Kenkyusha, 1974. xiii,2110p. £175. ISBN: 031759317x.
1st. ed. 1918; 3rd ed. 1954.
A comprehensive dictionary with *c.*80,000 entries, comprising transliterated form, Japanese characters, meaning, and phrases (in Japanese characters plus translation). *Class No:* 809.56(038)

[6318]
Kodansha's compact kanji guide: a new character dictionary for students and businessmen. Tokyo, Kodansha International, 1991. 928p. £29. ISBN: 4770015534.
A handy, flexicover dictionary that focuses on contemporary everyday usage. Text includes 1,945 *Joyo* (common use) characters, plus personal names, practical compounds and business terms. 3 indexes and character stroke order. *Class No:* 809.56(038)

[6319]
Merriam-Webster's Japanese-English learner's dictionary. Springfield, Mass., Merriam-Webster, 1993. 1121p. $27.95. ISBN: 0877791643.
Aimed at elementary and intermediate learners and concentrates on words encountered in everyday conversation. Each entry includes Japanese word in romanized form (modified Hepburn system), *furigana* and *kanji*, part of speech, and English definition. Most entries also include illustrative phrases and sentences in romanized and Japanese form and in English translation. Appended English-Japanese word-list and outline of Japanese grammar.
Class No: 809.56(038)

[6320]
NELSON, A.N.N. The New Nelson Japanese-English character dictionary. Haig, J.H., *ed.* 3rd ed. Rutland, Vt., & Tokyo, Tuttle, 1997. xi,1600p. $32.95. ISBN: 0804820368.
2nd ed. 1974.
7,107 numbered entries for characters (over 1,200 new to this ed.) with over 70,000 compounds. Arranged by radicals, with access improved in this ed. by the addition of the Universal Radical Index (32,000 entries), allowing look-up

.... (contd.)
not only by primary radical but by any radical in the character. 14 appendices, including Japanese and foreign geographical names. *Class No:* 809.56(038)

[6321]

NTC's new Japanese-English character dictionary. Halpern, J., *ed.* Lincolnwood, Ill., National Textbook Co., 1993. 226+1992p. $49.95. ISBN: 0844284343.

Originally published Tokyo, Kenkyusha, 1990, as *New Japanese-English character dictionary*.

4,421 character entries with core meaning, compounds, synonyms, usage notes, homophones and cross-references. 60,000 senses for 42,000 words and word elements. 3 indexes. 9 appendices, including 'How to write kanji' and the official Japanese government list of 1,006 basic characters ('Education Kanji') announced 1989. Well organized, with detailed guidance notes.
Class No: 809.56(038)

[6322]

The Oxford-Duden pictorial Japanese & English dictionary. Oxford, Clarendon Press, 1983. 864p. £13.99. ISBN: 0198601190.

See entry for *The Oxford-Duden pictorial German & English dictionary*. Indexes in Japanese and English.
Class No: 809.56(038)

[6323]

SPAHN, M. *and* **HADAMITZKY, W. Japanese character dictionary,** with compound lookup via any kanji. Tokyo, Nichigai Associates, 1989. xviii,1672p. ISBN: 4816908285.

47,000 entries (7,000 main character entries), with the emphasis on compounds and everyday expressions. Claims to be unique in that every compound is listed under each of its constituent characters. Arranged by radical, with alphabetical index of readings.

The same authors have produced *Kanji and kana: a handbook and dictionary of the Japanese writing system* (2nd ed. Rutland, Vt., Tuttle, 1996. 432p. £15.99. ISBN: 0804820775). *Class No:* 809.56(038)

[6324]

VANCE, T.J. Kodansha's romanized Japanese-English dictionary. Tokyo, Kodansha International, 1993. xxii,666p. £25. ISBN: 4770016034.

Unlike most Japanese-English dictionaries, this is designed for English speakers. Has a basic vocabulary of 16,000 words (with the emphasis on currency and frequency), of which 9,000 have separate entries. Headwords, compounds, derivatives and phrases are given in romanized Japanese (modified Hepburn system) and standard written Japanese. Speech register/level is labelled and there are ample illustrative sentences. Excellent introductory guide for users. 3 very useful appendices: verb conjugations, numerals and place names. 'Enthusiastically recommended to libraries at all levels' (*Reference Reviews*, v.8(2), 1994, p.17).
Class No: 809.56(038)

Standards

[6325]

BRITISH STANDARDS INSTITUTION. Specification for the romanization of Japanese. London, BSI, 1976. 16p. £20.

BS 4812:1972 (1976).

Sets out the standard Hepburn system for the romanization of Japanese, with explanatory notes, list of variants, and background information. *Class No:* 809.56(083.74)

Usage

[6326]

Effective Japanese usage guide: a concise explanation of frequently confused words and phrases. Tokyo, Kodansha, 1994. xiv,756p. £40. ISBN: 477001919x.

'Explains words and phrases that seem similar, but have very different uses' and illustrates their use by means of sample sentences, which are written in romanized Japanese and standard *Kanji* with English translations. 708 terms covered. 4 indexes. Introductory notes on how to use what is a complicated source. *Class No:* 809.56-06

Grammar

[6327]

MARTIN, S.E. A Reference grammar of Japanese. [Rev. ed.]. Rutland, Vt., Tuttle, 1988. 1198p. $69.95. ISBN: 080481550x.

1st ed. New Haven, Yale Univ. Press, 1975.

An extremely detailed grammar in 31 chapters with numbered subsections, using romanized Japanese throughout. Bibliography (8p.). Index of words, forms and technical terms (106p.). *Class No:* 809.56-5

Korean

[6328]

BRITISH STANDARDS INSTITUTION. Guide to the romanization of Korean. London, BSI, 1982. 52p. £66.

PD 6505:1982.

Describes written Korean and provides systems for transliteration (character-for-character) and phonetic romanization. *Class No:* 809.57

[6329]

GRANT, B.K. A Guide to Korean characters: reading and writing. *Hangŭl* and Hanja. 2nd rev. ed. Elizabeth, N.J., Hollym, 1982. 367p. $27.50. ISBN: 0930878132.

1st ed. 1979.

Lists the 1,800 basic characters in stroke-count order, from 1 to 26 strokes, with English definitions. Radical index and phonetic index. Appendices include Korean surnames, commonly abbreviated characters and easily confused characters. Selected bibliography (1p.). *Class No:* 809.57

[6330]

JONES, B.J. *and* **RHIE, G.S. NTC's compact Korean and English dictionary.** Lincolnwood, Ill., NTC, 1995. xvi,394p. £15.95. ISBN: 0844283614.

A 2-way dictionary covering *c.*20,000 of the most common words in the 2 languages. Korean entries in romanized form followed by Korean characters.
Class No: 809.57

[6331]

MARTIN, S.E., *and others*. **A Korean-English dictionary.** New Haven, Conn., Yale Univ. Press, 1967. xviii,1902p. ISBN: 0300007531.

Contains *c.*100,000 entry-words, with the emphasis on the basic native Korean vocabulary. Limited entries for Chinese loanwords and very few for European loans. Headwords in Korean script, followed by transliterated form, English translations, and illustrative phrases. Etymologies indicated where known. Notes on pronunciation provided where not predictable from spelling. Notes on Yale romanization plus table of 5 romanization systems. Guide to pronunciation (5p.). *Class No:* 809.57

[6332]

The New World comprehensive English-Korean dictionary. Seoul, Si-Sa-Yong-O-Sa Publishers, 1979. 2959p. illus.

Over 20,000 main entries, plus many compounds and phrases. No transliteration. Up to 4 illustrations (drawings and photographs) per page. *Class No:* 809.57

[6333]

The New World comprehensive Korean-English dictionary. Seoul, Si-Sa-Yong-O-Sa Publishers, 1979. xii,2519p.

*c.*100,000 entry-words, plus many compounds and phrases. *Class No:* 809.57

Grammar

[6334]

LEE, H.H.B. Korean grammar. Oxford, Oxford Univ. Press, 1989. xiii,216p. £32.50. ISBN: 0197136060.

A reference grammar of modern standard Korean in 7 chapters, with numbered sections and subsections. Numerous examples. 2-part bibliography, covering Korean and general linguistics (13p.). Detailed table of contents. Index of grammatical suffixes and endings. Subject index. *Class No:* 809.57-5

[6335]

MARTIN, S.E. A Reference grammar of Korean: a complete guide to the grammar and history of the Korean language. Rutland, Vt., Tuttle, 1992. x,1032p. £68. ISBN: 0804818878.

Part I is a detailed survey of the structure of contemporary Korean, in 12 chapters with numbered subsections. Part II (p.415-955) is a grammatical lexicon. Bibliography (7p.). Index to Part I. 9 appended lists, including surnames and placenames. *Class No:* 809.57-5

Burmese

[6336]

JUDSON, A. Judson's Burmese-English dictionary. Unabridged centenary ed., as rev. and enl. by R.C. Stevenson and edited by F.H. Eveleth. Rangoon, Baptist Board of Publications, 1953 (repr. 1969). viii,1123p.

First published Maulmain, American Mission Press, 1852, as *A Dictionary, Burmese and English.*

The standard Burmese-English dictionary prior to the commencement of Stewart and Dunn's opus (*q.v.*). Over 20,000 entry-words.

Judson has also compiled an *English and Burmese dictionary* (8th ed. Rangoon, American Baptist Mission Press, 1922. 928p.). *Class No:* 809.58

[6337]

STEWART, J.A. *and* **DUNN, C.W. Burmese-English dictionary.** London, Luzac (later School of Oriental and African Studies, Univ. of London), 1940-81. 6 pts.

A scholarly dictionary published initially under the auspices of the Univ. of Rangoon. The vocabulary is drawn from Burmese literature of all periods since its beginning in the 15th century and entries include etymologies and quotations. Extensive lists of sources. *Class No:* 809.58

Austroasiatic Languages

[6338]

HUFFMAN, F.E. Bibliography and index of mainland Southeast Asian languages and linguistics. New Haven, Conn., and London, Yale Univ. Press, 1986. xxxii,640p. £44. ISBN: 0300036795.

The compiler's 'very ambitious, not to say impossible, objective was to list everything ever written in any language about any language of mainland Southeast Asia' (*Introduction*). The result is a massive collection of 10,000 entries arranged A-Z by author, each followed by a brief descriptive annotation where content is not clear from the title and a list of reviews where applicable. The language and subject index includes alternative names, cross-references and an indication of major language group membership and is thus an important reference source in its own right, including, the compiler claims, the names of every language and dialect of the region (2,500-3,000 names). *Class No:* 809.59

Cambodian

[6339]

Cambodian-English dictionary. Headley, R.K., *and others, eds.* Washington, D.C., Catholic Univ. of America Press, 1977. 2v. (1495p.). ISBN: 0813205093.

Includes 'not only current literary and standard spoken forms of Khmer, but also archaic, obsolete, obsolescent, dialectal, and argot forms' (*Preface*). *Class No:* 809.596

[6340]

HUFFMAN, F.E. *and* **PROUM, I. English-Khmer dictionary.** New Haven, Conn., Yale Univ. Press, 1978. xix,690p. £48. ISBN: 0300022611.

Contains *c.*40,000 English entries and subentries, the aim being 'to provide a corpus of basic words and phrases which it would be useful for Western students of Khmer to know how to say (or write) in standard Khmer' (*Introduction*). A secondary objective is 'to provide the first comprehensive English-Khmer dictionary for Khmer students learning English', this being based on American English. Appendix has transcription system for standard Khmer and transliteration system for Khmer script. Bibliography (2p.). *Class No:* 809.596

[6341]

JACOB, J.M. A Concise Cambodian-English dictionary. London, Oxford Univ. Press, 1974. xxxiv,242p. ISBN: 0197135749.

Contains the basic vocabulary of modern spoken and written Cambodian. Over 6,000 entries, comprising headword in native characters, transcription, part of speech, English gloss and compounds. Some entries have commentary on variant spellings and pronunciations. Includes Indian loanwords. Introductory notes on pronunciation and grammar. Bibliography. *Class No:* 809.596

Vietnamese

[6342]

LÈ-BÁ-KHANH *and* **LÊ-BÁ-KÔNG. Vietnamese-English / English-Vietnamese dictionary.** Reprint of 1955 ed., with a supplement of new words, English-Vietnamese. New York, Hippocrene, 1991. 388+501p. £17.50. ISBN: 0870529242.

Originally published 1955 as *Standard pronouncing*

.... (contd.)

Vietnamese-English dictionary, with Standard pronouncing English-Vietnamese dictionary.

*c.*10,500 Vietnamese-English entries and *c.*14,500 English-Vietnamese, with a further 600 in the supplement. Vietnamese words are romanized. *Class No:* 809.597

[6343]

NGUYÊN-DÌNH-HÒA. Essential English-Vietnamese dictionary. Rutland, Vt., and Tokyo, Tuttle, 1983. xii,316p. £11.95. ISBN: 0804816611.

A dictionary which grew out of the glossary for the author's text book series, *Speak Vietnamese.* 16,000 entries. Romanised Vietnamese. *Class No:* 809.597

[6344]

NGUYÊN-DÌNH-HÒA. Vietnamese-English student dictionary. Rev. and enl. ed. Saigon, Vietnamese-American Assoc., 1967; Carbondale, Ill., Southern Illinois Univ. Press, 1971. xvi,674p.

1st ed. Saigon, Binh-Minh, 1959, as *Vietnamese-English dictionary*, being an enlargement of *Vietnamese-English vocabulary* (1954).

Over 20,000 romanized entry-words with English equivalents, plus some compounds and phrases. Includes guide to Vietnamese pronunciation, with regional variations.

NTC's Vietnamese-English dictionary (Lincolnwood, Ill., NTC, 1995. xiv,728p. £11.95. ISBN: 0844283576) appears to be a new ed. of the above dictionary. *Class No:* 809.597

[6345]

NGUYÊN-VĀN-KHÔN. English-Vietnamese dictionary. Saigon, Viet-Dang, 1955. viii,1741p.

Approx. 45,000 entry-words, with many idioms and compounds. Explanations given if no exact Vietnamese equivalent. *Class No:* 809.597

African Languages

Bibliographies

[6346]

African linguistic bibliographies. Rottland, F. *and* Vossen, R., *eds.* Hamburg, Buske (later Köln, Köppe), 1981- (in progress). ISSN: 07212488.

1. *Problems of linguistic communication in Africa,* by M. Reh. 1981. 230p. ISBN: 3871185094.

2. *Somali language and literature,* by M. Lamberti, 1986. 106p. ISBN: 3871187070.

3. *The Yoruba language: published works and dissertations, 1843-1986,* by L.O. Adewole, 1987. 182p. ISBN: 3871188425.

4. *Mande languages and linguistics,* by R. Kastenholz. 1988. 274p. ISBN: 3871188875.

5. *The Nubian languages,* by A. Jakobi and T. Kümmerle, 1993. x,135p. ISBN: 3927620351. *Class No:* 809.6(01)

[6347]

Bibliography of African languages. Meier, W., *ed.* Wiesbaden, Harrassowitz, 1984. lxxi,888p. ISBN: 3447024151.

A very thorough listing of over 14,000 works 'concerning the structure of individual languages as well as works dealing with the history, classification and geographical spread of linguistic phenomena, and the development of national and standard languages' (*Introduction*). Arranged A-Z by author, with 2 language indexes (*c.*2,000 languages listed), one to authors and one chronological. *Class No:* 809.6(01)

[6348]

HENDRIX, M.K. An International bibliography of African lexicons. Metuchen, N.J., Scarecrow, 1982. xxi,348p. $37. ISBN: 0810814781.

Lists 2,570 lexicons covering 600 languages and 200 dialects, each entry comprising author, title, publication details, and a brief annotation which usually indicates the languages covered and the direction of translation. 5 sections: 1. General - 2. Polyglot - 3. Special and classified - 4. Conversation and phrase books - 5. Periodical publications. Bibliography of 116 selected references. Index of languages and dialects. *Class No:* 809.6(01)

Handbooks & Manuals

[6349]

MANN, M. *and* **DALBY, D. A Thesaurus of African languages:** a classified and annotated inventory of the spoken languages of Africa, with an appendix on their written representation. London, Zell, 1987. 325p. £51. ISBN: 0905450248.

The main inventory (166p.) is followed by a directory of African states with notes on languages used there. Bibliography (43p.). Index of languages. 'Not an easy tool to use and not for beginners' (*Choice,* v.25(10), June 1988, p.1540).

Should be used in conjunction with Dalby's *Language map of Africa and the adjacent islands/Carte linguistique de l'Afrique et des îles avoisinantes* (Rev., bilingual ed. London, International African Institute, 1988. £40. ISBN: 295020970x), which uses the same classification scheme. *Class No:* 809.6(035)

Dictionaries

[6350]

South African multi-language dictionary and phrasebook: English, Afrikaans, Northern Sotho, Sesotho, Tswana, Xhosa, Zulu. Cape Town, Reader's Digest, 1991. 495p. illus. £38.50. ISBN: 0947008675.

5,000 words and 500 phrases in 7-column, 2-page layout, plus 20 colour illustrations labelled in all 7 languages. Basic grammar and pronunciation rules of each African language explained in English. *Class No:* 809.6(038)

Congo-Kordofan Languages

Bantu Group

[6351]

HANNAN, M. Standard Shona dictionary. 2nd ed. Salisbury, Rhodesia Literature Bureau, 1974. xxii,996p.

1st ed. 1959.

Over 45,000 Shona entry-words, with lexical tone, part of speech and English gloss. Index of English words used in definitions (238p.). *Class No:* 809.635

Kikuyu

[6352]

BARLOW, A.R. English-Kikuyu dictionary; ed. by T.G. Benson. Oxford, Clarendon Press, 1975. viii,332p. ISBN: 0198644078.

Nearly 10,000 entries. Follows the orthography used in Benson's *Kikuyu-English dictionary*. Started by Barlow, a missionary who died in 1965, and completed by Benson. *Class No:* 809.635.18

[6353]

Kikuyu-English dictionary. Benson, T.G., *ed.* Oxford, Clarendon Press, 1964. 1, 562p.

*c.*8,500 entry-words with many compounds and illustrations of usage. Introduction contains a detailed guide to the pronunciation indicators in the entries. *Class No:* 809.635.18

Swahili, Luganda, etc.

[6354]

INTER-TERRITORIAL LANGUAGE (SWAHILI) COMMITTEE TO THE EAST AFRICAN DEPENDENCIES. A Standard Swahili-English dictionary (founded on Madan's Swahili-English dictionary). Johnson, F., *ed.* London, Oxford Univ. Press, 1939. viii,548p. ISBN: 0198644035.

Still the most comprehensive dictionary of its kind. The companion vol. is *A Standard English-Swahili dictionary*, also based on Madan and prepared under Johnson's direction (London, Oxford Univ. Press, 1939. x,654p.; repr. New Delhi, Publications India, 1989. £15).

C.W. Rechenbach's *Swahili-English dictionary* (Washington D.C., Catholic Univ. of America Press, 1967. 641p.) is based on the above dictionary and includes much postwar vocabulary, including loanwords. *Class No:* 809.635.4

[6355]

Luganda-English dictionary, with an introduction on the tonal system by A. N. Tucker. Snoxall, R.A., *ed.* Oxford, Clarendon Press, 1967. xxxvi,357p.

*c.*10,000 entry words, arranged A-Z using the Standard Orthography recommended in 1947. Detailed introduction (23p.). *Class No:* 809.635.4

[6356]

MALAIKA, B. The Friendly Swahili-English dictionary 2nd ed. Arusha, Tanzania, Training Centre for Development Co-operation, 1994. xvi,206p. £19.95. ISBN: 8770286388.

1st ed. 1991.

13,300 entries (several hundred new in this ed.), giving part of speech and English gloss with 3,000 examples of current usage. *Class No:* 809.635.4

[6357]

PERROTT, D.V. Concise Swahili and English dictionary: Swahili-English / English-Swahili. Paperback reprint. Sevenoaks, Hodder and Stoughton, 1990. 184p. £6.99. (*Teach yourself books.*) ISBN: 0340546956.

Originally published 1965 as *The E.U.P. concise Swahili-English dictionary.*

Intended for use by both English and Swahili speakers, with *c.*4,500 Swahili-English entries and *c.*8,000 English-Swahili entries. Concise grammar of Swahili (15p.) and notes on pronunciation. *Class No:* 809.635.4

[6358]

SNOXALL, R.A. A Concise English-Swahili dictionary: Kamusi ya Kiingereza-Kiswahili. London, Oxford Univ. Press, 1958. xii,325p. illus. £5.99. ISBN: 0196393485.

Primarily intended for Swahili-speaking schoolchildren and modelled on *The English-reader's dictionary*, by A.S. Hornby and E.C. Parnwell (London, Oxford Univ. Press, 1952). *c.*8,000 entry-words, with some small illustrations in the text. List of common English prefixes and suffixes, with Swahili explanations. *Class No:* 809.635.4

Sotho

[6359]

CASALIS, A. English-Sotho vocabulary. 11th ed., rev. Morija, Basutoland Morija Sesuto Book Depot, 1950. iii,166p. £3.25.

About 11,000 entry-words, with Afrikaans words indicated and numerous examples of usage. *Class No:* 809.635.71

[6360]

MABILLE, A. *and* **DIETERLEN, H. Southern Sotho-English dictionary,** reclassified, rev. and enl. by R.A. Paroz. Morija, Basutoland, Morija Sesuto Book Depot, 1950. xvi,445p.

About 11,000 entry-words, with many idioms and grammar notes. *Class No:* 809.635.71

Xhosa, Zulu, etc.

[6361]

DOKE, C.M., ***and others.*** **English-Zulu / Zulu-English dictionary.** Johannesburg, Witwatersrand Univ. Press, 1992. xiv,572;vi,342p. £16.95. ISBN: 1868141608.

Includes in one vol. a reprint of *English-Zulu dictionary* (1958), with *c.*34,000 entries and an abridged version of *Zulu-English dictionary* (1948) with *c.*24,000 entries. *Class No:* 809.635.72

[6362]

DOKE, C.M. *and* **VILAKAZI, B.W. Zulu-English dictionary.** 2nd ed., rev. with addendum. Johannesburg, Witwatersrand Univ. Press. 1953. xxvi,918p. ISBN: 0854940278.

1st ed. 1948.

Over 27,000 entries, arranged A-Z under the initial stem of each word, with tone patterns indicated using a numerical system. Many idiomatic sentences and proverbs included, but proper names generally excluded. Useful introductory notes on Zulu grammar. *Class No:* 809.635.72

[6363]

FISCHER, A. English-Xhosa dictionary. Cape Town, Oxford Univ. Press, 1985. 738p. £20.95. ISBN: 0195702905.

15,000 main entries plus many derivatives. Plenty of illustrative phrases and sentences. Clearly laid out and easy to use. *Class No:* 809.635.72

Sudanic Languages

Ashanti, Yoruba etc.

[6364]

ABRAHAM, R.C. Dictionary of modern Yoruba. London, Univ. of London Press, 1958. xli,776p. illus.

'This dictionary covers every aspect of Yoruba civilization: it therefore includes countless idioms, current phrases, proverbs and riddles' (*Preface*). A Yoruba-English

.... (contd.)
dictionary, it includes proper names and provides the historical, religious and ethnological facts which form the background of the vocabulary. 62p. of line drawings appended, showing plants, animals, etc. with Yoruba and English terms. Pronunciation tones clearly indicated by symbols. *Class No:* 809.663

[6365]
A Dictionary of the Yoruba language. Reprint of 1937 ed. Oxford, Oxford Univ. Press, 1983. 461p. ISBN: 019575221x.

1st ed. Lagos, Church Missionary Society Bookshop, 1913; 2nd ed. 1937.

Part One, English-Yoruba, has *c.*15,000 entries and Part Two, Yoruba-English, has *c.*12,000. Lists of birds, plants and trees appended. *Class No:* 809.663

Hausa

[6366]
ABRAHAM, R.C. Dictionary of the Hausa language. 2nd ed. London, Univ. of London Press, 1962. xxvii,992p.

1st ed. Lagos, Govt. of Nigeria, by R.C. Abraham and M.M. Kano.

A Hausa-English dictionary with *c.*20,000 entries comprising headword (with pronunciation indicated), part of speech, English gloss and examples of usage. Preliminaries include a verb table which is referred to by index numbers in the dictionary. *Class No:* 809.668

[6367]
BARGERY, G.P. A Hausa-English dictionary and English-Hausa dictionary; compiled for the Government of Nigeria. London, Oxford Univ. Press, 1934. lv,1226p.

The Hausa-English section occupies p.1-1151 and has *c.*32,000 entries comprising headword, pronunciation guide, part of speech, English gloss and illustrative phrases. English-Hausa section has *c.*5,000 entries, simply listing English words and their Hausa equivalents. 'Compiler's introduction' includes detailed grammar notes and is preceded by 'Notes on the Hausa people and their language' by D. Westerman. *Class No:* 809.668

[6368]
NEWMAN, P. *and* **NEWMAN, R.M. Modern Hausa-English dictionary.** Ibadan, Oxford Univ. Press, 1977. xii,153p. £9.99. ISBN: 0195753038.

'Designed for native Hausa speakers who need guidance in matters of spelling, idiomatic usage, etc.' (*Preface*) as well as for new learners. Nearly 7,000 entries, with the emphasis on the vocabulary of everyday conversation and the contemporary media, comprising headword (pronunciation indicated), part of speech, English gloss and illustrative phrases. *Class No:* 809.668

[6369]
NEWMAN, R.M. An English-Hausa dictionary. New Haven, Conn., Yale Univ. Press, 1990. xxi,327p. £24. (*Yale language series.*) ISBN: 0300047029.

*c.*9,500 entries, giving the basic vocabulary needed for everyday use. Phrases and full sentences frequently used to illustrate Hausa usage. Includes loanwords from English and French. 6 appendices include Hausa pronoun paradigms and guides to pronunciation of personal and geographical names. Welcomed 'in spite of its flaws' by *TLS* (no.4543, April 27th,1990, p.451) as the first new English-Hausa dictionary for 25 years. *Class No:* 809.668

[6370]
Studies in Hausa language and linguistics: in honour of F.W. Parsons. Furniss, G. *and* Jaggar, P.J., *eds.* London, Kegan Paul International in association with the International African Institute, 1988. xxxi,282p. £55. ISBN: 0710302827.

Includes 'A Hausa language and linguistics bibliography 1976-86 (including supplementary material for other years)' by N. Awde, p.253-78. Lists *c.*480 items and supplements S. Baldi's *Systematic Hausa bibliography* (Rome, Istituto Italo-Africano, 1977), which is described in the Introduction to this collection as 'the most extensive bibliography of writing on Hausa linguistics and literature ... a most useful work but one which is not easy to obtain'. *Class No:* 809.668

Amerindian Languages

[6371]
SINGERMAN, R. Indigenous languages of the Americas: a bibliography of dissertations and theses. Metuchen, N.J., Scarecrow, 1996. 346p. $75. (*Native American bibliography series.*) ISBN: 0810830329.

Includes citations to over 1,600 dissertations and masters' theses from American, Canadian and British institutions. Arranged by language family with author, language, dialect and tribal indexes. *Class No:* 809.7/8

North Amerindian Languages

[6372]
PILLING, J.C. Bibliographies of American Indian languages. Washington, D.C., Government Printing Office, 1887-94. 9v. (repr. New York, AMS Press, 1973. 3v.). $125. ISBN: 0404073905.

The bibliographies cover the following languages: Algonquin, Athapascan, Chinookan, Eskimo, Iroquoian, Muskhogean, Salishan, Siouan, and Wakashan. *Class No:* 809.7

[6373]
—EVANS, G.E. *and* CLARK, J. North American Indian language materials, 1890-1965: an annotated bibliography of monographic works. Los Angeles, American Indian Studies Center, Univ. of California, 1980. 154p. $5. ISBN: 0935626158.

Supplements Pilling, listing dictionaries, grammars, and teaching materials relating to Native American languages spoken north of the Mexican border. Works are listed by author under each language. Index. *Class No:* 809.7

South Amerindian Languages

[6374]
TOVAR, A. *and* **LARRUCEA DE TOVAR, C. Catálogo de las lenguas de América del sur:** con clasificaciones, indicaciones tipológicas, bibliografía y mapas. Nueva ed., refundida. Madrid, Gredos, 1984. 632p. maps. ISBN: 8424909577.

1st ed. Buenos Aires, Sudamericana, 1961; *Supplemento*, Florencia, Consiglio Nazionale delle Ricerche, 1972.

A detailed survey, in Spanish, of the indigenous languages of South America. 27 chapters, followed by a very extensive bibliography (p.211-590). 6 maps. Index of *c.*2,500 languages and dialects. Includes a brief chapter on Spanish and Portuguese. For this ed., the work has been revised and updated and the supplement incorporated. *Class No:* 809.8

Australasian & Austronesian Languages

[6375]

Comparative Austronesian dictionary: an introduction to Austronesian studies. Tryon, D.T., *ed.* Berlin, Mouton de Gruyter, 1995. 4 pts. in 5v. (cii,3456p.) DM.1,220. ISBN: 3110127296.

The core of this mammoth work is a comparative wordlist (forming pts. 2-4) for 80 Austronesian languages, consisting of 1,200 items divided into 22 lexical or semantic domains. Detailed annotations for each form provide a wealth of synonyms and near-synonyms. Additional features include: 2 introductory essays on the Austronesian family; surveys of the phonology and morpho-syntax of each of the 80 languages; annotated A-Z list of all Austronesian languages, including major classificatory details, alternative names, numbers of speakers and their location; bibliography of Austronesian linguistics; and index of *c.*3,000 reconstructed Austronesian forms. *Class No:* 809.9

Indonesian

[6376]

ECHOLS, J.M. *and* **SHADILY, H. An English-Indonesian dictionary.** Ithaca, N.Y., and London, Cornell Univ. Press, 1975. xii,660p. £46.95. ISBN: 0801407281.

Prepared primarily for the use of Indonesians and 'attempts to embody a high percentage of the most common words and phrases in American English, with American orthography and pronunciation, along with the Indonesian equivalent' (*Preface*). *c.*21,000 entries. Many illustrative phrases. *Class No:* 809.92

[6377]

ECHOLS, J.M. *and* **SHADILY, H. An Indonesian-English dictionary.** 3rd ed., rev. and enlarged. Ithaca, NY., Cornell Univ. Press, 1989. 624p. £46.75. ISBN: 0801421276.

1st ed. 1961; 2nd ed. 1963.

The standard Indonesian dictionary, with many technical terms included and numerous illustrative phrases. Over 30,000 entries. *Class No:* 809.92

[6378]

Indonesian: a comprehensive grammar. London, Routledge, 1997. 416p. £19.99. (*Routledge grammars.*) ISBN: 0415155290.

Provides an exhaustive description of the language written in a clear, non-technical manner. Each level of the language is dealt with in a separate section, from words through phrases and clauses to sentences. Extensive cross-referencing and conprehensive index. *Class No:* 809.92

[6379]

KRAMER, A.L.N. *and* **KOEN, W. Tuttle's concise Indonesian dictionary:** English-Indonesian / Indonesian-English. 1st rev. ed. Rutland, Vt., Tuttle, 1993. 519p. £13.50. ISBN: 0804818649.

A revision by Koen of a dictionary by Kramer, published 1952 as *Van Goor's kamus inggeris ketjil.*

A compact, soft-cover dictionary with *c.*18,000 entries. Uses post-1972 Indonesian orthography. *Reference Reviews* (v.8(2), 1994, p.18) criticises 'utterly inadequate' pronunciation guidelines. *Class No:* 809.92

[6380]

SALIM, P. The Contemporary English-Indonesian dictionary. 4th, rev. ed. Jakarta, Modern English Press, 1989. xvii,2358p. illus.

1st ed. 1985.

Primarily intended for Indonesian students of English. 85,000 entry-words, 200,000 definitions and 30,000 phrases, including much specialized vocabulary. Some line drawings and photographs. *Class No:* 809.92

[6381]

SCHMIDGALL-TELLINGS, A.E. *and* **STEVENS, A.M. Contemporary Indonesian-English dictionary:** a supplement to the standard Indonesian dictionaries with particular concentration on new words, expressions, and meanings. Athens, Ohio Univ. Press, 1981. xv,388p. $39.95. ISBN: 0821404245.

Over 13,000 entries for words collected 'from recent newspapers, periodicals and scholarly publications written by Indonesians as well as from recorded conversations' (*Preface*). Many illustrative phrases and sentences. Supplements Echols and Shadily and is organized along similar lines. *Class No:* 809.92

Filipino

[6382]

ENGLISH, L.J. Tagalog-English dictionary. [Manila], Congregation of the Most Holy Redeemer, 1986. 1583p. ISBN: 971910550x.

16,000 headwords, 21,000 derivatives and 30,000 illustrative sentences. List of English loanwords in Tagalog (7p.).

L.J. English has also compiled *English-Tagalog dictionary* (Manila, Dept. of Education, 1965. 1211p.), with 14,000 main entries, 40,000 'nuances' and 30,000 illustrative sentences. *Class No:* 809.921

Malagasy

[6383]

RICHARDSON, J. A New Malagasy-English dictionary. Antananarivo, London Missionary Society, 1885 (repr. Gregg International, 1967). lix,832p. £125. ISBN: 0576116076.

24,000 entries, preceded by a very clear introduction (49p.) to the Malagasy language. *Class No:* 809.921.9

Malay

[6384]

Kamus dwibahasa: bahasa inggeris - bahasa malaysia. Kuala Lumpur, Dewan Bahasa Dan Pustaka, 1981. xv,1457p.

An English-Malay dictionary with *c.*30,000 entry-words and many illustrative sentences. *Class No:* 809.922.1

[6385]

Kamus inggeris-melayu dewan: an English-Malay dictionary. Salleh, D., *and others, eds.* Kuala Lumpur, Dewan Bahasa dan Pustaka, 1992. xxxviii,1945p. ISBN: 9836222820.

A very impressive dictionary which claims to be unique because 'it does not give *definitions* but instead provides Malay equivalents for each English word, phrase or idiom, based on context or usage' (*Preface*). 40,000 entries, with over 50,000 illustrative sentences. Mainly contemporary, everyday language, but also includes some technical and literary terms. *Class No:* 809.922.1

[6386]

SURYADINATA, L. Times comparative dictionary of Malay-Indonesian synonyms. Hassan, A., *ed.* Singapore, Times Books International, 1991. xvii,486p. 24.95. ISBN: 9812042156.

Explains the differences in usage between the 2 varieties of Malay spoken in Malaysia and Indonesia. 5,000 entries covering 4 groups (words with different spellings; words with different meanings; words with different usage; different words for the same concept) are under Bahasa Malaysian headwords and include detailed explanations and illustrative phrases. Cross-references from Bahasa Indonesian words. List of sources (3p.).
Class No: 809.922.1

[6387]

WINSTEDT, R.O. An Unabridged Malay-English dictionary. 5th ed. Kuala Lumpur, Marican, 1963. 390p.

1st ed. 1957.

Nearly 30,000 entry words, including scientific and technical vocabulary. Includes idioms, explanations, and language of origin of many terms.

The companion vol. is Winstedt's *An Unabridged English-Malay dictionary* (3rd ed. Singapore, Marican, 1958. 398p.).
Class No: 809.922.1

Javanese

[6388]

HORNE, E.C. Javanese-English dictionary. New Haven, Conn., and London, Yale Univ. Press, 1974. xl,728p. ISBN: 0300016891.

Over 20,000 entries, consisting of a root as citation form followed by derivatives and phrases (if any) plus English translation. Many illustrative sentences. Detailed introduction in 9 sections, including phonology, spelling and morphology. *Class No:* 809.922.2

Balinese

[6389]

BARBER, C.C. A Balinese-English dictionary. Aberdeen, Aberdeen Univ. Library, 1979. 2v. (ix,809p.). £40. ISBN: 0950532231.

Cover title is *Dictionary of Balinese-English*.

A translation to English and complete rearrangement of R. Van Eck's *Eerste proeve van een Balineesch-Hollandsch woordenboek* (Utrecht, 1876), supplemented from other more recent sources. Over 24,000 entries.
Class No: 809.922.3

Dayak

[6390]

RICHARDS, A. An Iban-English dictionary. Oxford, Clarendon Press, 1981. xxx,417p. ISBN: 019864325x.

Not merely a lexical dictionary, but a comprehensive reference work on the language of half the people of Sarawak. Over 11,000 entries, many of them containing detailed information about Iban daily life and occupations, rituals, myths and customs. Introduction includes notes on pronunciation and grammar, bibliography (7p.) and English-Iban index to major entries. *Class No:* 809.922.7

[6391]

SCOTT, N.C. A Dictionary of Sea Dyak. London, School of Oriental and African Studies, Univ. of London, 1956. xi,218p.

Nearly 10,000 entry-words, with pronunciation indicated. Many idioms. Introduction includes a scheme for the systematic spelling of Sea Dyak. *Class No:* 809.922.7

Oceanian (Melanesian & Polynesian)

Hawaiian

[6392]

ANDREWS, L. A Dictionary of the Hawaiian language, to which is appended an English-Hawaiian vocabulary and a chronological table of remarkable events. Reprint of 1865 ed., with a new introduction by T. Barrow. Rutland, Vt., Tuttle, 1974. x,559p. ISBN: 0804810877.

Originally published Honolulu, 1865.

The first major dictionary of the Hawaiian language and still an important source. *c.*15,000 entries for Hawaiian words, with English definitions. *Class No:* 809.923.0

[6393]

PUKUI, M.K. *and* **ELBERT, S.H. Hawaiian dictionary:** Hawaiian-English / English-Hawaiian. Rev. and enl. ed. Honolulu, Univ. of Hawaii Press, 1986. xxvi,572p. £28.45. ISBN: 0824807030.

Hawaiian-English dictionary first published 1957; 2nd ed. 1961; 3rd ed. 1965. *English-Hawaiian dictionary* first published 1964. Single-vol. ed. first published 1971.

A complete revision, with 3,000 new Hawaiian-English entries in a total of 29,000. Over 10,000 English-Hawaiian entries. Glossary of technical terms (2p.). List of sources (8p.). *Class No:* 809.923.0

Fijian

[6394]

CAPELL, A. A New Fijian dictionary. 3rd ed. Suva, Government Printer, 1968 (repr. 1984). viii,407p. £12.95.

1st ed. 1941; 2nd ed. 1957.

Fijian-English section (p.1-291) has *c.*6,000 entries with definitions and explanations. English-Fijian section (p.295-407) has *c.*5,500 entries with English word and Fijian equivalent only, and is intended more as an index to the first section than as a comprehensive dictionary.
Class No: 809.923.1

Maori & Samoan

[6395]

BAUER, W. Maori. London, Routledge, 1993. xxx,608p. £95. (*Descriptive grammars.*) ISBN: 0415022541.

A very detailed grammar in 5 main sections: 1. Syntax - 2. Morphology - 3. Phonology - 4. Ideophones and interjections - 5. Lexicon. Over 500 numbered sections and paragraphs, containing over 2,300 numbered examples with translations. Bibliography (5p.). Comprehensive table of contents (11p.). Index. *Class No:* 809.923.2

[6396]

BIGGS, B. The Complete English-Maori dictionary. Auckland, Auckland Univ. Press & Oxford Univ. Press, 1981. x,227p. NZ$29.95. ISBN: 1869400577, NZ; 0196479894, UK.

Over 15,000 headwords. Does not include examples of usage and should be used in conjunction with Williams.
Class No: 809.923.2

[6397]

BIGGS, B. English-Maori / Maori-English dictionary. Auckland, Auckland Univ. Press, 1990. 153p. £11.95. ISBN: 1869400569.

A handy 2-way dictionary with over 4,000 entries in each section. In the English-Maori section, 'an attempt has been made to indicate the part of speech of Maori words according to an explicit, systematic classification that has proved to be relevant to the language' according to the 5-page *Introduction*, which also includes a guide to pronunciation. Maori words derived from English are included. *Class No:* 809.923.2

[6398]

MILNER, G.B. Samoan dictionary: Samoan-English / English-Samoan. London, Oxford Univ. Press, 1966. li,465p.

Samoan-English section occupies 317p. and has *c.*6,000 entries arranged in A-Z order by base, with plenty of cross-references. Many illustrative sentences, including proverbial expressions. English-Samoan section (143p.) has *c.*8,500 brief entries with the emphasis on high-frequency English vocabulary. *Class No:* 809.923.2

[6399]

—Samoan reference grammar. Mosel, U. *and* Hovdhaugen, E., *eds*. Oslo, Scandinavian University Press, 1992. xxii,819p. £37.50. ISBN: 8200216683.

A comprehensive grammar in 2 main parts, the first covering the language's history and present status and offering general treatment of phonology, whilst the second comprises a detailed morpho-syntactic analyis. Bibliography (11p.). Index of grammatical terms. 'This mighty, innovative book is a *tour de force*' (*Reference Reviews*, v.7(6), 1993, p.19-20). *Class No:* 809.923.2

[6400]

RYAN, P.M. The Revised dictionary of modern Maori. [2nd ed]. Auckland, Heinemann, 1983 (repr. 1989). 139p. £12.75. ISBN: 0868635685.

First published 1974.

Maori-English and English-Maori. Over 12,000 concise entries, an increase of 1,000 over first ed. Separate reference section (16p.) includes notes on pronunciation and grammar and useful lists, *e.g.* days, months, names of countries, proverbs, etc. *Class No:* 809.923.2

[6401]

WILLIAMS, H.W. A Dictionary of the Maori language. 7th ed., rev. and augmented by the Advisory Committee on the Teaching of the Maori Language. Wellington, Government Printer, 1971 (repr. 1991). xl,499p. £19.95. ISBN: 1869560191.

1st ed. 1844; 6th ed. 1957.

The standard dictionary since first publication. *c.*12,500 headwords with part of speech, concise English translation and examples of use from Maori speech and writing. For some words no satisfactory translation can be given. Appendix lists words adopted from non-Polynesian sources. 2nd, 3rd and 4th eds. included an English-Maori section. *Class No:* 809.923.2

Australian Aboriginal

[6402]

DIXON, R.M.W., *& others*. Australian aboriginal words in English: their origin and meaning. Melbourne, Oxford Univ. Press, 1990. ix,255p. illus. £25. ISBN: 0195530993.

Introductory chapter on Australian languages (22p.) and notes on the major languages (37p.), followed by lists of over 400 aboriginal loanwords grouped under 12 main subject headings (*e.g.* Fauna, Implements). Entries give pronunciation, region of use, explanation, and quotations from literary sources to illustrate the word's use in English. Indexes of languages and loanwords. *Class No:* 809.951

[6403]

DIXON, R.M.W. The Languages of Australia. Cambridge, Cambridge Univ. Press, 1980. xxii,547p. maps. (*Cambridge language surveys*.) ISBN: 0521223296.

A comprehensive study of over 200 Aboriginal languages. 14 chapters, with numbered subdivisions, followed by notes and references (23p.); index of languages, which includes references to the major sources on each; glossary; and bibliography (19p.). General index. *Class No:* 809.951

Tongan

[6404]

CHURCHWARD, C.M. Tongan dictionary (Tongan-English and English-Tongan). London, Oxford Univ. Press, 1959. xiv,836p.

Tongan-English section (p.1-574) has 25-30,000 entries; no pronunciation is given. Enumerated applications. Many idioms and colloquialisms, but these are not translated. Frequent references to and quotations from sources listed on p.xxv. Appendix: 'Some of the more important words adopted from non-Polynesian sources'. *Class No:* 809.961.2

Tahitian

[6405]

ANDREWS, E. *and* ANDREWS, I.D. A Comparative dictionary of the Tahitian language: Tahitian-English, with an English-Tahitian finding list. Chicago, Chicago Academy of Science, 1944. xvi,253p.

Tahitian-English, p.1-195 (*c.*20,000 entries); English-Tahitian, p.197-253. List of sources (2p.). *Class No:* 809.962.11

82/89 Literature

Literature

Databases

[6406]

DiscLit: world authors. Twayne's *World authors* series and OCLC Subject Bibliographies on CD-ROM. Boston, Hall, 1994. $995. ISBN: 0783822049.

A CD-ROM with the full text of 146 vols. in Twayne's *World authors* series, providing critical analysis of authors active from Ancient Greece to the present, plus 200,000 entries from the OCLC Online Union Catalog. Separate CD-ROMs from the same publisher cover British and American authors. *Class No:* 82(003.4)

[6407]

DISCovering authors modules. Detroit, Gale, 1996. CD-ROM. £1,200. ISBN: 0810351048.

A single disc containing biographical and critical information on 1,260 authors in 6 databases: ***DISCovering multicultural authors***, ***DISCovering dramatists***, ***DISCovering novelists***, ***DISCovering poets***, ***DISCovering popular fiction*** and ***Genre authors***. Extended search options allow searching by author, ethnicity, gender, title, subject, time period or character. 3,500 suggested research and paper topics. Also includes ***Merriam-Webster's collegiate dictionary*** (10th ed. 1993). *Class No:* 82(003.4)

[6408]

—DISCovering authors: British edition. Detroit, Gale, 1995. CD-ROM £460. ISBN: 1873477414.

A CD-ROM with information on 330 classic and contemporary authors widely studied in the UK. By no means confined to British writers, with foreign authors included if regularly found on school and college syllabuses, *e.g.* Gide, Goethe, Hemingway, Racine. Contemporary figures include Fowles, Rushdie and Murdoch, whilst children's writers like Dahl and Garner are also present. Entries include the equivalent of *c.*60p. of information per author and comprise: pseudonyms; biography; awards and honours; full list of works; media adaptations; authorial statement (where available); 4-8 critical essays on key works and themes. Entries are accessible by: author name; subject/genre; title of work; literary character; personal data (*e.g.* birth/death dates); full data search.

Gale also produce a Canadian edition of this database (£460. ISBN: 0810399539). *Class No:* 82(003.4)

[6409]

Literature online (LION) Cambridge, Chadwyck-Healey, 1996. World Wide Web resource Subscription details from marketing@chadwyck.co.uk

URL: http://lion.chadwyck.co.uk

A large and expanding resource for English and American literature, which contains full-text databases, reference works and bibliographies and provides links to hundreds of other relevant websites, including discussion groups, author pages, research resources and journals. Annual subscription costs vary according to the number of databases chosen.

....*(contd.)*

Full-text databases include: *English poetry*, *English drama*, *Early English prose fiction*, *Editions and adaptations of Shakespeare*, *Eighteenth century fiction*, *American poetry* and *African American poetry*. These are also available separately on CD-ROM; see individual entries for details. Also included is the Authorized (King James) Version of the Bible.

Reference sources include: *Annual bibliography of English language and literature (ABELL)*, *Bibliography of American literature* and *Webster's third new international dictionary* (*qq.v.*).

A master index provides access by author or title keyword to all the material within *LION* as well as thousands of other literary websites. *Class No:* 82(003.4)

[6410]

Masterplots complete CD-ROM. Pasadena, Calif., Salem Press, 1997. CD-ROM. $750. ISBN: 0893562637.

Brings together the full texts of all 21 of the Salem Press *Masterplots* series, which contain over 12,000 articles in 80 vols. (see separate entries), plus both vols. of *Cyclopedia of literary characters* and of *Cyclopedia of world authors* (*qq.v.*). Main index is of titles, but can also be searched by author, locale, genre, subject and principal characters. Links are provided between a displayed entry and related material, *e.g.* from a literary work to its author and characters. To be updated every 12-18 months.

Other CD-ROMs available from Salem Press, containing selected *Masterplots* series, include *Masterplots definitive revised edition fiction CD-ROM*, *Masterplots II* and *Masterplots nonfiction, drama, poetry CD-ROM*.
Class No: 82(003.4)

Bibliographies of Bibliographies

[6411]

WORTMAN, W.A. A Guide to serial bibliographies for modern literatures. New York, Modern Language Assoc. of America, 1996. 333p. $37.50 ISBN: 0873529650.

1st ed. 1982

Lists comprehensive, classified, subject (African American Studies to Women's Studies) and author (Andersen to Zola) bibliographies, as well as periodical and citation indexes and abstracting services. Includes foreign-language sources, but gives preference to English and American. Over 1,200 annotated, evaluative entries, of which 270 are new in this ed., which has a larger typeface and improved layout. Appended list of sources from all sections which are also available online or on CD-ROM. Index. *Class No:* 82(009)

Bibliographies

[6412]

BALDENSPERGER, F. *and* **FRIEDERICH, W.P. Bibliography of comparative literature.** Chapel Hill, N.C., Univ. of North Carolina Press, 1950 (repr. New York, Russell & Russell, 1960). 701p.

*c.*35,000 references to books, periodicals and dissertations, arranged in 4 'books', of which nos. 1 and 3

....*(contd.)*
cover themes, motifs, genres, and international relations, and nos. 2 and 4 cover specific national literatures. 'Comprehensive in respect to its vast scope covering the world literature, the work is highly selective in the entries chosen for inclusion' (Blazek, R. and Aversa, E.S., *The Humanities*, 1988, p.282).

Yearbook of comparative and general literature (Bloomington, Ind., Indiana Univ. Press, 1952-. v.1-. Annual) carried an annual bibliography in vols. 1-19, which was designed to supplement Baldensberger and Friedrich. The last one covered publications of 1969. Thereafter carried an annual list of English translations from other languages until v.29 (1980). *Class No:* 82(01)

[6413]

Francis 523: Histoire et sciences de la littérature. Paris, Centre National de la Recherche Scientifique, 1947-. Quarterly. ISSN: 11573732.

Formerly known as *Bulletin signalétique 523*.

Indexes numerous periodicals and also covers conference proceedings, *Festschriften* and dissertations. International coverage. Also available online and on CD-ROM.
Class No: 82(01)

[6414]

Recent studies in myths and literature, 1970-1990: an annotated bibliography. Accardi, B., *and others, eds.* Westport, Conn., Greenwood, 1991. ix,251p. $59.95. ISBN: 0313275459.

7 chapters by different contributors, surveying over 1,000 English-language studies of myth in relation to the literature of different periods: 1. Theory and themes - 2. Classical literature - 3. English literature to 1660 - 4. British literature, 1660-1900 - 5. 20th-century British literature - 6. American literature to 1900 - 7. 20th-century American literature. Each section covers general studies and individual authors, A-Z, with substantial annotations. Author and subject indexes.
Class No: 82(01)

[6415]

The Whole story: 3000 years of sequels and sequences. Simkin, J.E., *ed.* Port Melbourne, Thorpe, 1996. 2v. (1198p.). £125. ISBN: 1875589260.

An impressive attempt to list all literary sequences from Greek drama to the present. The main sequence is arranged by sequel or sequence title and is indexed by author and title. Lists a total of 84,000 works by 12,500 authors in 17,000 series or sequences. Numerous cross-references and helpful annotations. Hailed by *Choice* (v.34(5), Jan. 1997, p.775) as the definitive work to date in English: 'Simkin on sequels and sequences joins that select list of reference works known forever by an individual's name'. *Class No:* 82(01)

18th & 19th Centuries

[6416]

The Romantic movement: a selective and critical bibliography. New York, Garland (later West Cornwall, Conn., Locust Hill Press), 1980-88. 8v.

Covers the years 1979-87 and is a continuation of the annual bibliography which formerly appeared in *ELH* (1937-49), then *Philological Quarterly* (1950-64), then *English Language Notes* (1965-79). 6 sections: general, English, French, German, Italian, and Spanish, with subsections including bibliographies, general criticism, and studies of individual authors. *Class No:* 82(01)"17/18"

[6417]

—The Romantic movement bibliography, 1936-1970: a master cumulation from *ELH, Philological Quarterly* and *English Language Notes.* Elkins, A.C. *and* Forstner, L.J., *eds.* Ann Arbor, Mich., Pierian Press, 1973. 7v. $290. ISBN: 0876500254.

Vols. 1-6 reprint the 35 annotated bibliographies from the 3 periodicals, with continuous paging. V.7 includes cumulative author, title, and subject indexes.
Class No: 82(01)"17/18"

20th Century

[6418]

POWNALL, D.E. Articles on twentieth-century literature: an annotated bibliography, 1954-70. New York, Kraus-Thomson, 1973-80. 7v. $630. ISBN: 0527721506.

An expanded cumulation of listings in the 'Current bibliography' section of the quarterly journal *Twentieth century literature*. Arranged by author (as subject), with 20,000 articles from nearly 400 journals cited. Excludes book reviews. Entries are numbered and cross-indexed in v.7. The periodical continued its coverage of current bibliography until 1981. *Class No:* 82(01)"19"

Women

[6419]

ALSTON, R.C. A Checklist of women writers, 1801-1900: fiction - verse - drama. London, British Library, 1990; Boston, Hall, 1991. 517p. £50. ISBN: 0712301828, UK; 0816172951, US.

Lists over 20,000 works by more than 2,000 women writers of the 19th century, many identified for the first time. Entries give author, title, date, place of publication and British Library shelfmark, with cross-references to pseudonyms, where known. *Class No:* 82(01)-0055.2

[6420]

BACKSCHEIDER, P., *and others.* **An Annotated bibliography of twentieth-century critical studies of women and literature, 1660-1800.** New York, Garland, 1977. x,287p. ISBN: 0824099346.

Lists 1,568 books and articles, published 1900-75, in 3 sections: 1. General studies - 2. Genre studies (including 6 major male authors) - 3. Individual women, A-Z (p.91-253). Concise, descriptive annotations. Indexes of women and critics. *Class No:* 82(01)-0055.2

[6421]

FENTON, J.R., *and others.* **Women writers: from page to screen.** Metuchen, N.J., Scarecrow, 1990. xiii,483p. ISBN: 0824085299.

Identifies over 2,200 feature films made in the UK or US, 1913-88, based on books (including nonfiction like *Out of Africa*) by *c.*800 women from several countries. Arranged by author, A-Z, then by book title, entries give film title, date of release, production company and distributor, but *not* details of director or leading actors. Indexes of film and book titles. Bibliography (8p.). *Class No:* 82(01)-0055.2

[6422]

MYERS, C.F. Women in literature: criticism of the Seventies. Metuchen, N.J., Scarecrow, 1976. 263p. ISBN: 0810808854.

Lists critical and biographical books and articles on *c.*300 women writers, A-Z.

More women in literature: criticism of the Seventies, by C. Fairbanks (Metuchen, N.J., Scarecrow, 1979. viii,457p.

....*(contd.)*
ISBN: 0810811936), adds citations for *c.*4,500 studies on over 1,000 writers from Sappho to the present. Neither vol. is indexed. *Class No:* 82(01)-0055.2

[6423]
Personal writings by women to 1900: a bibliography of American and British writers. Davis, G. *and* Joyce, B., *comps.* Norman, Okla., Univ. of Oklahoma Press; London, Mansell, 1989. xxi,294p. £75. (*Bibliographies of writings by American and British women to 1900.*) ISBN: 0806122064, US; 0720118859, UK.

The first in a projected series of bibliographies of women's literature, it covers autobiographies, letters, diaries and travel literature traced in a wide range of sources, including the National Union Catalog and the catalogue of the British Museum. Entries arranged A-Z by author give the woman's name, husband's name, nationality and dates, plus any pseudonyms, then basic bibliographic information about the book and an indication of source. 4,925 numbered entries in all, of which *c.*3,100 are actual citations, the rest being cross-references. Appendix lists authors chronologically by period. Subject index. *Choice* (v.27(5), Jan. 1990, p.766) advises caution because of 'numerous gaps, omissions and typographical errors'.
Class No: 82(01)-0055.2

[6424]
RESNICK, M. *and* **DE COURTIVRON, I. Women writers in translation:** an annotated bibliography, 1945-82. New Yok, Garland, 1984. xi,272p. ISBN: 0824093321.

Arranged in 10 sections for countries/regions, each having its own introduction explaining selection criteria. A-Z by author within each section with brief biographical notes followed by annotated lists of English translations published in the US, UK, Australia and Canada. Includes contributions to periodicals and anthologies as well as book-length works. Japanese is the only non-European language covered. Author index. *Class No:* 82(01)-0055.2

[6425]
SCHWARTZ, N.L. Articles on women writers: a bibliography. Santa Barbara, Calif., ABC-Clio, 1977. xx,236p. ISBN: 0874362520.

Includes citations to articles on over 600 women writing in English which were published in both scholarly and popular periodicals, 1960-75. Supplemented by *Articles on women writers, volume 2: 1976-1984* (1986. 304p. $65. ISBN: 0874364388), which covers over 1,000 writers.
Class No: 82(01)-0055.2

Gay People

[6426]
GRIER, B. The Lesbian in literature. 3rd ed. Tallahassee, Fla., Naiad Press, 1981. xxiv,168p. illus. ISBN: 0930044231.

1st ed. 1967; 2nd ed. 1975.

Lists *c.*7,000 books (mainly literary works) by lesbians or with significant lesbian content. Not annotated, but a coding system using letters and stars is used to rate the significance of every book listed. 16p. of photos of lesbian authors.
Class No: 82(01)-0055.3

[6427]
YOUNG, I. The Male homosexual in literature: a bibliography. 2nd ed. Metuchen, N.J., Scarecrow, 1982. 360p. ISBN: 081081529x.

1st ed. 1975.

Lists more than 4,000 English-language works of fiction, drama, poetry and autobiography having gay male characters or dealing with the subject of homosexuality. List of gay publishers. *Class No:* 82(01)-0055.3

Indexes

[6428]
Gale's literary index CDROM. Detroit, Gale, 1992- . £134 per annum. ISBN: 0810349531.

A combined index to 32 literary reference series (over 700 vols.) published by Gale, including *Contemporary authors*, *Dictionary of literary biography* and the *Literary criticism* series, which can be searched by author name (over 110,000 including pseudonyms) and title (150,000). A special feature of the software allows librarians to mark those series which are in their collection and to indicate their location, so that users will know which references are immediately available. Updated twice a year. *Class No:* 82(014)

[6429]
Twentieth-century literary movements index. Harris, L.L. *and* Henderson, H., *eds.* Detroit, Omnigraphics, 1991. 419p. $65. (*Literary movements reference series.*) ISBN: 1558883061.

Indexes references in 28 standard literary dictionaries, encyclopedias and handbooks (published 1959-88) to literary movements, schools, trends and ideologies. 1st section lists over 500 movements, A-Z, with references to sources and lists of associated individuals. 2nd part provides citations for *c.*3,000 people and gives their dates, nationality and the movement to which they are affiliated. References do not give page or vol. numbers, which can cause problems when turning to a source which is not alphabetically arranged, nor do they indicate the extent of the information provided. As with any index like this, users need to be careful as the best source may not have been indexed; this particularly applies here to enquiries about individuals, since strictly biographical reference works are not covered.
Class No: 82(014)

Encyclopaedias & Dictionaries

[6430]
BENET, W.R. Benet's reader's encyclopedia. Murphy, B., *ed.* 4th ed. New York, HarperCollins, 1996; London, Black, 1998. 1168p. £30. ISBN: 006270110x, US; 0713649852, UK.

1st ed. 1948; 2nd ed. 1965. Both have the title *The Reader's encyclopedia*, which is the title used for this ed. in the UK. 3rd ed. 1988.

A major literary companion which also contains much valuable information on other branches of the arts. Over 10,000 entries, arranged A-Z, including biographies of writers, artists and musicians; plot summaries of literary works; sketches of literary characters; explanations of biblical and classical allusions; and descriptions of literary schools, movements and terms. Now the work of numerous contributors (Benet died in 1950), with the scope considerably expanded in this ed. to give greater coverage to African American, Asian, African, Latin American and Eastern European literatures and to women's writing.
Class No: 82(03)

[6431]

Dictionnaire historique, thématique et technique des littératures: littératures française et étrangères, anciennes et modernes. Demougin, J., *ed.* Paris, Larousse, 1985-86. 2v. (xii,1862p.). illus. Fr.446 per vol. ISBN: 203508301x, v.1; 2035083028, v.2.

*c.*27,000 entries on authors, works, literary schools and movements, national literatures, genres, terms, periodicals, prizes, etc. Colour plates, thematically arranged. Over 300 contributors. Bibliographies of important secondary material which is currently available are provided for many of the entries but grouped alphabetically at the end of each vol., occupying 84p. in all. *Class No:* 82(03)

[6432]

Dictionnaire universel des littératures. Didier, B., *ed.* Paris, Presses Universitaires de France, 1994. 3v. (cxxviii,4393p.). illus. ISBN: 2130430139.

A hugely impressive compilation, the work of 45 sectional editors, each responsible for a national or regional literature, and numerous contributors. Each section has an introductory essay on the country/region, with a bibliography of general reference works, followed by signed entries on authors, genres, themes, etc., all with bibliographies. V.3 has the following useful lists: author entries by section; authors by period; linguistic entries; genre entries by section; anonymous works by section; themes and motifs; schools and movements. *Class No:* 82(03)

[6433]

GÓMEZ DE SILVA, G. Elsevier's international dictionary of literature and grammar. Amsterdam, Elsevier, 1991. xii,604p. $187.25. ISBN: 044488064x.

A strange mixture of entries on linguistic and literary terms and national literatures, which falls expensively between several stools. Entries on terms provide definitions, brief explanations and cross-references, while those on literatures are little more than chronological lists of key works, German literature, for example, being summarized in a mere 2p. Indexes of subjects, authors, and titles of anonymous works. Claims to be 'mainly intended for non-specialists' but is unlikely to find many with $170 to spare. *Class No:* 82(03)

[6434]

Kindlers neues Literaturlexikon. Jens, W., *ed.* München, Kindler, 1988-92. 20v. ISBN: 3463920344.

1st ed. Zurich, 1965-72 (7v.).

Whereas 1st ed. had entries for literary works arranged by title, this ed. covers authors, A-Z, in vols. 1-17, and anonymous and collective works, literary themes, and over 120 national literatures in vols. 18-20. Indexes of authors and titles in v.20. Over 50 contributors. Extensive bibliographies are a feature of the work. *TLS* (no.4515, Oct. 13, 1989, p.1136) regrets the dropping of the earlier edition's lavish illustrations, but welcomes the much improved treatment of poetry, the expanded coverage of Third World, Latin American, and women's literature, and the inclusion of some 2,000 contemporary authors. 'It will undoubtedly ... serve as the definitive reference work in its field for many years to come.' *Class No:* 82(03)

[6435]

LEEMING, D.A *and* **DROWNE, K.M. Encyclopedia of allegorical literature** Santa Barbara, Calif., and Oxford, ABC-CLIO, 1996. 275p. illus. £29.95. ISBN: 0874367816.

Entries on allegorical works from all periods and a wide range of literatures. Each entry is introduced in historical, geographical and cultural context and includes summary and extracts. Extensive cross-references. *Class No:* 82(03)

[6436]

Lexikon der Weltliteratur. Wilpert, G. von, *ed.* Stuttgart, Kröner, 1980-93. 2v.

V.1 *Biographisch-bibliographisches Handwörterbuch nach Autoren und anonymen Werken.* 3. Aufl. 1988. 1692p. ISBN: 3520807033.

V.2 *Hauptwerke der Weltliteratur in Charakteristiken und Kurzinterpretationen.* 3. Aufl. 1993. xviii,1569p. DM150. ISBN: 352080803x.

V.1 has over 10,000 entries on writers of the world, including primary and secondary bibliographies. V.2 has entries on over 4,000 literary works, A-Z by German title, providing analysis rather than summary. Author-title index, but no index of original titles. Lists of authors by nationality. *Class No:* 82(03)

[6437]

Der Literatur-Brockhaus. Habicht, W., *and others, eds.* Mannheim, Brockhaus, 1988. 3v. (2184p.) illus. ISBN: 376530400x.

Based on the literary entries in the *Brockhaus Enzyklopädie,* with the addition of *c.*200 specially written articles of varying length surveying national literatures. Well illustrated. 'Quite definitely the soundest medium-sized reference tool available at a price that the individual might just be able to afford' (*TLS*, no.4515, Oct. 13, 1989, p.1136).

A similar work is *Das Fischer-Lexikon Literatur*, ed. by U. Ricklefs (Frankfurt am Main, Fischer-Taschenbuch-Verlag, 1996. 3v.), which has lengthy signed entries by a large team of contributors on topics, A-Z. Selective bibliographies with all articles, with the emphahsis on key monographs. Fully indexed. *Class No:* 82(03)

[6438]

Merriam-Webster's encyclopedia of literature. Springfield, Mass., Merriam-Webster, 1995. 1236p. illus. $45. ISBN: 0877790426.

Over 10,000 entries including biographies of authors and critics, plot summaries, and articles on literary terms, characters, forms and genres. Entries include pronunciation and etymology where appropriate, but no bibliographies. Covers all periods and includes children's literature and genre fiction. 250 illustrations. *Class No:* 82(03)

[6439]

Neues Handbuch der Literaturwissenschaft. von See, K., *ed.* Wiesbaden, Athenaion (later AULA), 1978-97. v.1-25 (in progress).

An encyclopedia of world literature with each vol. covering a region, country or period; *e.g.* v.23, *Ostasiatische Literaturen* (1984. 459p. ISBN: 3891040717), has sections on Chinese, Korean, and Japanese literatures containing 25 signed chapters by specialists. Many illustrations. Quotations in German. Bibliographies after each chapter. Name index.

Reviewing v.6, *Europäisches Frühmittelalter* (1985), *Modern Language Review* (v.84(2), April 1989, p.424-6) describes the series as 'a major contribution to literary studies', a general feature of which is 'its presentation of

....(*contd.*)
literature less in a national continuity than in relation to the social and cultural setting of its own time'. Latest vol. to appear is v.5, *Orientalisches Mittelalter* (1990).
Class No: 82(03)

[6440]
Le Nouveau dictionnaire des oeuvres: de tous les temps et de tous les pays. de Roux, P., *ed.* Paris, Robert Laffont, 1994. 7v. Fr.1195. ISBN: 2221068874.

Supersedes *Dictionnaire des oeuvres de tous les temps et de tous les pays: littérature, philosophie, musique, sciences* (1962. 4v.)

Articles on 21,000 literary and other works from all countries, including writings on history, philosophy, art and science and also musical compositions. Arranged A-Z by title, entries include publication details, synopsis and commentary. V.7 has index of authors, who were born before 1951 or died before 1994. A companion to *Le Nouveau dictionnaire des auteurs* (*q.v.*). *Class No:* 82(03)

[6441]
The Reader's adviser: a layman's guide to literature. 14th ed. New York, Bowker, 1994. 6v. £435. ISBN: 0835233200.

Literary coverage in v.1, *The Best in reference works, British literature and American literature*, ed. by D. S. Kastan and E. Elliot (1512p. £90. ISBN: 0835233219), and v.2, *The Best in world literature*, ed. by R. DiYanni (1162p. £90. ISBN: 0835233227).

Also available on CD-ROM at £350 (ISBN:0835238490). Main entry for the set at 028. *Class No:* 82(03)

Europe

[6442]
Columbia dictionary of modern European literature. Bédé, J.A. *and* Edgerton, W.B., *eds.* 2nd ed., fully rev. and enl. New York, Columbia Univ. Press, 1980. xxi,895p. $205. ISBN: 0231037171.

1st ed. 1947.

Covers the 20th century and the latter part of the 19th, with over 1,800 signed biocritical articles on individual authors (brief bibliographies appended), plus survey articles on the national literatures (English excluded). The work of over 500 scholars. *Class No:* 82(03)(4)

20th Century

[6443]
Encyclopedia of world literature in the 20th century. Klein, L.S., *ed.* 2nd, rev. ed. New York, Ungar, 1981-84. 4v. $600.

1st ed. 1967-71 (3v.) by W.B. Fleischmann, plus *Supplement* (1975), based on *Lexikon der Weltliteratur* (Freiburg, 1960-61. 2v.).

A thorough revision, with all the retained entries updated and a more truly international coverage achieved. Consists mainly of signed biocritical entries on authors, with primary and secondary bibliographies and occasional critical excerpts appended, but there are also survey articles on national literatures and literary movements. Over 1,700 entries, A-Z, with separate index volume.

V.5, *Supplement and index*, ed. by S.R. Serafin and W.D. Glanze (New York, Continuum, 1993. 784p. $150. ISBN: 0826405711) adds over 400 biocritical articles (with bibliographies) on authors not previously covered, with Africa, Asia and Latin America well represented. In addition, there are 35 national-survey articles and 6 topical

....(*contd.*)
articles on recent trends such as deconstruction and postmodernism. Index of authors and subjects covers all 5 vols. *Class No:* 82(03)"19"

[6444]
The Oxford guide to contemporary writing. Sturrock, J., *ed.* Oxford, Oxford Univ. Press, 1996. x,492p. £20. ISBN: 0198182627.

Signed essays (average 16p.) by critics and academics on literary developments since 1960 in 28 regions (*e.g.* Arab countries, West Indies) and individual countries. Does not attempt to cover the whole world, concentrating on 'the literatures that seemed most likely to be of interest ... to English-language readers in the 1990s' (*Editor's introduction*). Many titles cited in essays, but lack of bibliographies limits reference value. Brief list of critical studies after each essay. Name index. *Class No:* 82(03)"19"

[6445]
SEYMOUR-SMITH, M. Macmillan guide to modern world literature. 3rd ed. London, Macmillan; New York, Bedrick, 1985. xxviii,1396p. ISBN: 0333334647, UK; 0872260003, US.

1st ed. London, Wolfe, 1973, as *Guide to modern world literature*, with US ed. as *Funk & Wagnall's Guide to modern world literature* (1973); 2nd ed. 1976. US title of 3rd ed. is *The New guide to modern world literature.*

Essays on the literature of 33 countries/regions of the world, with 1000s of individual writers and works discussed by a compiler who claims to have reading knowledge of 20 languages. Restricted to writers who were active after 1899. For each work discussed, a literal translation of the title and the original title with publication date are provided, plus title and date of any published English translation. Emphasis is on the major literatures (but it is nevertheless invaluable for minor literatures like Catalan) and on the first half of the 20th century. Index of authors, titles and movements. Select bibliography of reference sources and standard histories. A remarkable achievement which has been acclaimed by reviewers for its highly personal, often controversial, approach. *Class No:* 82(03)"19"

Women

[6446]
Bloomsbury guide to women's literature. Buck, C., *ed.* London, Bloomsbury; New York, Prentice Hall, 1992. xii,1171p. illus. ISBN: 074750895x, UK; 0136896219, US.

UK paperback version (1994) entitled *Women's literature A-Z* (£10.99. ISBN: 0747519536).

Essay section (p.1-243p.) has 37 signed essays on women's writing by area and period, with cross-references to the reference section, which has 5,000 entries, A-Z on authors, titles movements and topics. Recommendations for further reading after many entries. 40 contributors. International in scope. *Class No:* 82(03)-0055.2

[6447]
FISTER, B. Third world women's literatures: a dictionary and guide to materials in English. Westport, Conn., Greenwood, 1995. 408p. £67.50. ISBN: 0313289883.

Main A-Z sequence has entries for contemporary and historical writers, works and themes. 5 very useful appendices: list of authors by country; chronological list of authors; resources for research; anthologies; criticism. Index. *Class No:* 82(03)-0055.2

[6448]
Masterpieces of women's literature. Magill, F.N., *ed.* New York, HarperCollins, 1996. xi,594p. £30. ISBN: 006270138x.

175 signed articles (average 3p.), arranged A-Z by title, in the standard *Masterpieces* format: form and content; analysis; context; sources for further reading. 99 are on literary works, mostly chosen because they address women's issues directly and 76 cover non-fiction, including biography, history, literary criticism, politics, sociology, feminism, etc. Entries on novels and plays include lists of principal characters. Indexes of authors and titles.
Class No: 82(03)-0055.2

[6449]
Masterplots II: women's literature series. Magill, F.N., *ed.* Pasadena, Calif., Salem Press, 1995. 6v. $500. ISBN: 0893568988.

536 signed essays on works by women from 27 countries and all periods, including 159 nonfiction works (diaries, memoirs, social criticism, feminist theory, etc.) as well as literary writings. Entries are 4-5 pages in length, cover context, content and analysis, and make reference to other sources. Those on plays include character lists. Indexes of authors, titles, genres and countries. Over half of the works included are covered in other *Masterplots* series, but this set features new essays placing the works in the context of women's literature and the bibliographies have been updated. *Class No:* 82(03)-0055.2

Gay People

[6450]
The Gay and lesbian literary heritage: a reader's companion to the writers and their works, from Antiquity to the present. Summers, C.J., *ed.* New York, Holt, 1995; London, Bloomsbury, 1997. xiv,786p. £17.99. ISBN: 0805027165, US; 0747532958, UK.

Nearly 400 signed essays, with selective bibliographies of secondary, covering national and ethnic literatures, individual authors (over 200, not all of them gay), genres, movements and themes. For major national literatures, there are separate essays on different periods. Fully cross-referenced. Index of authors and subjects. Over 150 contributors. International in scope, but dominated by English-language literature. *Class No:* 82(03)-0055.3

Reviews & Abstracts

[6451]
Magill's literary annual, 1977-. Magill, F.N., *ed.* Englewood Cliffs, N.J., Salem Press, 1978-. Annual. ISSN: 01633058.

A successor to *Masterplots annual,* with 2 vols. published each year containing essay-reviews of 200 outstanding US publications of the previous year. Includes biography, history and current affairs, as well as literary works.
Class No: 82(048)

[6452]
Survey of contemporary literature. Magill, F.N., *ed.* Rev. ed. Englewood Cliffs, N.J., Salem Press, 1977. 12v. ISBN: 0893560502.

Contains updated reprints of 2,300 essay-reviews from *Masterplots annual,* 1954-76, which reviewed 100 outstanding US publications each year. Entries are arranged A-Z by title, with author index in v.12. *Class No:* 82(048)

Yearbooks & Directories

[6453]
Aslib directory of literary and historical collections in the UK. Reynard, K.W., *ed.* London, Aslib, 1993. 287p. £124. ISBN: 0851423094.

Lists 1,030 institutions holding rare, large or important collections of original manuscripts and other texts. Despite the title, not confined to literary and historical sources and includes collections relating to science and technology through the ages. Extensive author and subject indexes. For literary sources, the Library Association's directory offers much better value. *Class No:* 82(058)

[6454]
Dictionary of literary biography yearbook, 1980-. Detroit, Gale, 1981-. Annual. illus. £112 per vol.

Now in 2 main parts, articles on literary events of the year and lengthy obituaries, but prior to the 1988 vol. it contained new entries and updates of existing entries in the regular *DLB* series (*q.v.*). Also has lists of the year's award winners, a checklist of major publications in literary history and biography, and necrology. Cumulative index to all *DLB* vols. and yearbooks. *Class No:* 82(058)

[6455]
Directory of literary societies and author collections. Sheppard, R., *ed.* London, Library Assoc., 1994. viii,288p. £37.50. ISBN: 1856041131.

Based on a complete revision and updating of *The English Association handbook of societies and collections*, ed. by A.C Percival (London, Library Assoc., for The English Assoc., 1977) and Sheppard's own *Literary societies for bookmen* (Beckenham, Trigon Press, 1979).

Section 1 lists societies and organizations devoted to individual authors, literary figures, and characters, A-Z by surname, and special interest groups under generic headings (*e.g.* bibliography). Entries include aims, addresses, subscription details and publications. Section 2 lists notable literary collections in libraries, with separate sequences for public, academic and special libraries. Entries include addresses, contact names, brief details of collections and access arrangements. List of 30 key directories and bibliographic reference sources. Author and subject indexes.

Over 500 entries in total, including some US-based societies, although 'we have not ... attempted to cover Europe, America or the rest of the world in any depth' (*Introduction*). A very welcome but long overdue revision of an essential literary reference source; 17 years must not be allowed to elapse before the next ed. *Class No:* 82(058)

Awards & Prizes

[6456]
AUSTRALIA COUNCIL STAFF. **Australian literary awards and fellowships.** 2nd ed. Port Melbourne, Thorpe, 1993. 120p. £17. ISBN: 0909532885.

1st ed. 1991.

Provides details of eligibility criteria, entry procedures, prize money and contact addresses. Also lists past winners of major Australian, New Zealand, British, American, Canadian and international awards. *Class No:* 82(079.2)

[6457]
Foreign literary prizes: Romance and Germanic languages. Bufkin, E.C., *ed.* New York, Bowker, 1980. x,300p. ISBN: 0835212432.

Covers prizes awarded in 25 countries. Arranged by country, A-Z, giving details of each prize (history, conditions, etc.) and lists of prize winners which are complete through 1978. Excludes prizes for journalism and children's literature. N.B. Australia and New Zealand are included (presumably on the grounds that English is a Germanic language), but for UK, US and Canada, see *Literary and library prizes.* Select bibliography (2p.). Index of names. *Class No:* 82(079.2)

[6458]
Literary and library prizes. Weber, O.S., *ed.* 10th ed. New York, Bowker, 1980. viii,651p. ISBN: 0835212491.

1st ed. 1935, as *Famous literary prizes and their winners.*

4 sections, covering international, American, British, and Canadian prizes. For each award there is a brief history, details of the prize and its conditions, and list of winners up to 1979. Index of awards, recipients and donors, but not of books. Includes *c.*675 prizes and 10,000 winners.
Class No: 82(079.2)

[6459]
The Nobel Prize winners: literature. Magill, F.N., *ed.* Pasadena, Calif., Salem Press, 1988. 3v. illus. $210. ISBN: 0893565415.

Chronologically-arranged entries on 84 prizewinners, 1901-87, following a standard format. Each is preceded by a list of that year's laureates in other fields, a full page photograph of the subject, and the basic biographical facts, whilst the text of the entry comprises synopses of the presentation speech and the Nobel lecture, a biographical sketch, and evaluation of the writer's principal works. Bibliographies of primary and secondary literature are appended. Index of names and titles in v.3. Useful supplementary material includes a brief history of the Nobel Prize and an explanation of its selection procedures.
Class No: 82(079.2)

[6460]
—Nobel laureates in literature: a biographical dictionary. Katz, B.S. *and* Pribic, R., *eds.* New York, Garland, 1990. 473p. $95. ISBN: 0824057414.

Biocritical essays averaging 5p. on 85 laureates, 1901-88, are arranged A-Z and have brief bibliographies of primary and secondary material appended. Name index. Contains little information that cannot be found in standard biographical sources. *Class No:* 82(079.2)

[6461]
STRACHAN, A.E. Prizewinning literature: UK literary award winners. London, Library Assoc., 1989. xiii,267p. ISBN: 0853655588.

Lists the winners of 60 current awards based in the UK, giving bibliographic information and an indication of whether in print at June, 1989. Contact address provided for each award. Author index. Subject index to prizes. List of sources of information on other literary awards. Children's literature excluded. *Class No:* 82(079.2)

[6462]
—Guide to literary prizes, grants and awards in Britain and Ireland. Book Trust *and* Society of Authors, *comps.* 7th ed. London, Book Trust, in association with the Society of Authors, 1992. vi,55p. £3.95. ISBN: 0853534438.

1st ed. 1979, as *Guide to literary prizes*; 6th ed. 1990.

Lists awards A-Z by title, giving the address of the organizers, the scope of the award, the amount of money involved, and relevant dates. Category index.
Class No: 82(079.2)

Quotations

[6463]
ANDREWS, R. The Columbia dictionary of quotations. New York, Columbia Univ. Press, 1993. xii,1092p. $38. ISBN: 0231071949.

A thematically-arranged compilation of over 18,000 quotations, of which it is claimed that 11,000 have never previously appeared in a general quotations dictionary. 1,500 headings, A-Z, with quotes then arranged by author and supported by precise citational and contextual information. Cross-references and author index, but no keyword index. Strong on modern quotes, with a heavy American representation. Superbly produced and a welcome addition to an oversubscribed sector of the reference market.

Andrews has compiled a more selective work: *Famous lines: a Columbia dictionary of familiar quotations* (New York, Columbia, 1997. xxiii,625p. $29.95. 0231102186), which is also thematically arranged with 500 headings from Abandonment to Zoos. Precise citations (not only to first publication, but also to most accessible source) and some contextual notes. Author and keyword indexes.
Class No: 82(082.2)

[6464]
BARTLETT, J. Familiar quotations: a collection of passages, phrases and proverbs traced to their sources in ancient and modern literature. Kaplan, J., *ed.* 16th ed. Boston, Mass., Little, Brown, 1992. lvi,1405p. ISBN: 0316082775.

1st ed. 1855; 15th ed. 1980.

One of the standard collections, with over 22,500 quotations arranged by authors/speakers chronologically. 2,550 people are quoted in this ed., 340 for the first time; 245 quoted in 15th ed. have been dropped. Separate sections for anonymous quotations and those from the Bible, Koran, Book of Common Prayer, Buddhist and Sanskrit sources. Gives exact references (using printed sources wherever possible), with frequent footnotes for parallel usages and versions, interesting historical details, etc. Highly accurate, well researched, and exceptionally thoroughly indexed by authors and keywords. *Class No:* 82(082.2)

[6465]
Bloomsbury thematic dictionary of quotations. Daintith, J., *ed.* 3rd ed. London, Bloomsbury, 1997. 572p. £16.99. ISBN: 0747531161.

1st ed. 1988; 2nd ed. 1990.

Over 10,500 quotations listed under 750 subject headings, with key-word and name indexes. As well as traditional thematic categories ('love', 'death', etc.), the headings include topics of current interest, *e.g.* 'pollution', 'environment', 'human rights', and *types* of quotations, *e.g.* 'misquotations', 'epitaphs' and 'last words'. This ed. includes 650 new quotes from 200 additional authors/speakers. *Class No:* 82(082.2)

[6466]

Bloomsbury treasury of quotations. Daintith, J. *and* Stibbs, A., *eds*. London, Bloomsbury, 1994. xxxii,1054p. ISBN: 0747518130.

Over 20,000 quotations by 3,000 people in one A-Z sequence of thematic and biographical entries. The 450 biographical entries include notes about the person's life, quotations by and about him/her, and cross-references to other relevant entries. Citations are precisely dated and include chapter numbers where appropriate. Name and keyword indexes, the latter having 55,000 references.
Class No: 82(082.2)

[6467]

BOLLER, P.F. *and* GEORGE, J. They never said it: a book of fake quotes, misquotes, and misleading attributions. New York and Oxford, Oxford Univ. Press, 1989. xi,159p. ISBN: 0195055411.

Corrects over 200 misquotations and wrong attributions and explains how the mistakes arose. Arranged by (alleged) author with largely superfluous name index but no key to the phrases themselves. Sources cited for each entry.
Class No: 82(082.2)

[6468]

Chambers dictionary of quotations. Jones, A., *ed.* Edinburgh, Chambers, 1996. xii,1515p. £25. ISBN: 0550210199.

Yet another new quotations dictionary and it is not entirely clear how this one differs from its rivals, except that a quotation is said to have a better chance of selection if it 'throws light on the life and times of its author' (*Introduction*). Over 20,000 entries arranged A-Z by author (with an average of 4 lines of biographical data on each) and indexed by keyword. Citations to books usually give only title and date, although some have chapter numbers. Includes some foreign-language quotes in the original with English translation. Strong emphasis on contemporary quotations, but 30 by Margaret Thatcher seems excessive.
Class No: 82(082.2)

[6469]

Chronological dictionary of quotations. Wright, E., *ed.* Rev. ed. London, Bloomsbury, 1993. ix,448p. £17.99. ISBN: 0747514755.

1st ed. 1988, as *Who said what when: a chronological dictionary of quotations.*

Over 7,000 quotations arranged in 13 chapters from The Old Testament to The Post-war world, each chapter being divided into 4 sections: Politics, government and world events; Attitudes (further divided by up to 16 topics); Sayings of the time (apparently anything that does not fit in the previous sections); With hindsight (later sayings about the period). Keyword and name indexes. Useful for recent quotes, with 1,198 in the last chapter, including many from the 1980s, but otherwise dispensable. 25 compilers named.
Class No: 82(082.2)

[6470]

COHEN, J.M. *and* COHEN, M.J. The New Penguin dictionary of quotations. Rev. ed., repr. with minor revisions. London, Penguin, 1996. x,726p. £7.99. ISBN: 0140512446.

1st ed. 1960, as *The Penguin dictionary of quotations*; rev. ed. 1992.

A belated revision of a reliable reference source which is particularly strong in its coverage of quotations from literature. Over 14,000 entries (1st ed. had 12,000) under authors, A-Z, with thorough keyword index. Precision of citations varies disappointingly. Some quotations from foreign writers included with English translations.
Class No: 82(082.2)

[6471]

GROSS, J. The Oxford book of aphorisms. Oxford, Oxford Univ. Press, 1983. x,383p. £8.99. ISBN: 019282015x.

Arranged under 58 subject headings with entries attributed to author, title, and date. Includes translations, especially from French. Index of authors but not of keywords or topics. Over 3,000 entries. *Class No:* 82(082.2)

[6472]

—The Faber book of aphorisms. Auden, W.H. *and* Kronenberger, L., *eds*. London, Faber, 1970 (repr. 1988). x,405p. £8.99. ISBN: 0571095194.

Over 3,000 aphorisms by 450 authors, arranged under 16 broad subject headings with a few subheadings. Attributed to author only. Index of authors. *Class No:* 82(082.2)

[6473]

The Macmillan dictionary of quotations. New York, Macmillan, 1989. 736p. ISBN: 0025119311.

Lists *c.*20,000 quotations under 1,100 subject headings, with keyword and author indexes. Particularly useful for its biographical entries which include quotations by and about over 100 major figures. *Class No:* 82(082.2)

[6474]

Magill's quotations in context. Magill, F.N., *ed.* New York, Harper & Row, 1965 (now published by Salem Press). 2v. ISBN: 0893561320.

Lists *c.*2,000 quotations, A-Z by first word, setting each within a lengthier passage and explaining the context. Brief details of author and source. Author and keyword indexes.

Magill's quotations in context, 2nd series (New York, Harper, 1969. 2v. $75. ISBN: 0893561363) contains a further 1,500 quotations. *Class No:* 82(082.2)

[6475]

Metaphors dictionary. Sommer, E. *and* Weiss, D., *eds.* Detroit, Gale, 1995. 833p. £50. ISBN: 081039149x.

Lists over 6,500 metaphoric comparisons, in common use from ancient times to the present, under subject headings, arranged A-Z, and then by author/speaker. Entries include sources and, where appropriate, brief background notes and cross-references to related metaphors. Indexes of authors and subjects, but keyword index is lacking. Separate list of 600 metaphors from Shakespeare. Bibliography of book and periodical sources. Introductory essay on types of metaphor.
Class No: 82(082.2)

[6476]

O'CONNOR, G. First lines. London, Queen Anne Press/ Futura, 1988. 96p. illus. £2.99. ISBN: 0708842194.

Originally published Dublin, Wolfhound Press, 1985.

Light-hearted but nevertheless, useful collection of opening lines from over 300 works of English prose or foreign prose in translation. Arranged in 13 subject categories (*e.g.* Learning, Matchmaking) with indexes of first words and authors. *Class No:* 82(082.2)

[6477]

The Oxford book of humorous quotations. Sherrin, N., *ed.* Oxford, Oxford Univ. Press, 1995. xxiii,543p. £16.99. ISBN: 0192142445.

Nearly 5,000 quotations arranged under 150 subject headings from 'Actors and acting' to 'Youth'. Citations give author's birth and death dates and title and date of publication, with contextual notes in many cases. Author and keyword indexes. *Class No:* 82(082.2)

[6478]

The Oxford dictionary of literary quotations. Kemp, P., *ed.* Oxford, Oxford Univ. Press, 1997. xix,479p. £17.99. ISBN: 0198600569.

Over 4,000 quotations in 2 sections. 1. The Writer's World: 3,500 quotes by writers about aspects of literature and literary life under 120 subject headings - 2. Writers and their Works: 600 quotes about individual authors, British and foreign, from Amis to Yeats. Chronological arrangement within entries, with precise dates where known and publication details for quotes from books. Keyword and author indexes. *Class No:* 82(082.2)

[6479]

The Oxford dictionary of phrase, saying and quotation. Knowles, E., *ed.* Oxford, Oxford Univ. Press, 1997. xvii,694p. £18.99. ISBN: 0198662297.

A companion to *The Oxford dictionary of quotations*, which lists attributable quotations alongside anonymous proverbs, phrases, sayings and allusions, 'with the aim of illuminating the stock of figurative language for a given subject' (*Introduction*). Quotations are listed chronologically under 300 subject headings, from Absence to Youth, with author, publication and date, and followed by related phrases and sayings. Over 10,000 entries. Cross-references and keyword index but no index of authors/speakers. *Class No:* 82(082.2)

[6480]

The Oxford dictionary of quotations. Partington, A., *ed.* 4th ed., rev. Oxford, Oxford Univ. Press, 1996. 1104p. £25.00. ISBN: 0198600585.

1st ed. 1941; 4th ed. 1992.

The 3rd ed. represented a substantial revision, with only 60% of the 2nd ed. retained and as another major overhaul has taken place this time it is worth hanging on to this work's predecessors. It contains *c.*17,500 quotations, arranged under 2,500 authors, A-Z, with English literature particularly well represented. Lines from hymns and songs make a welcome return after being dropped from the 3rd ed., women are much better represented and coverage of non-English writers and speakers is greatly expanded. Citations are precise and explanatory notes are provided in some cases. Foreign quotations appear in the original with English translation. Birth and death dates and a brief description are given for each author. The keyword index has *c.*75,000 entries (in English only), keyed to page, item no., and abbreviated form of author's name.

The 1996 revision has new appendices covering sayings of the 90s (not indexed), popular misquotations, advertising slogans and mottos. It also provides expanded information on authors and more notes on individual quotes.

Available on a CDROM entitled *Oxford compendium 3.0* along with *The Oxford dictionary of modern quotations*, *Concise Oxford dictionary* and *Oxford thesaurus* (£39.99. ISBN: 0192684043).

The Concise Oxford dictionary of quotations (3rd ed., rev. 1997. 595p. £6.99. ISBN: 0192800701) is an abridged

....(contd.)

version, also edited by Partington, with *c.*9,000 quotations from 1,900 authors plus the new appendices. *Class No:* 82(082.2)

[6481]

POWELL, D. The Wisdom of the novel: a dictionary of quotations. New York, Garland, 1985. xvii,729p. ISBN: 0824090179.

Aims to rectify the neglect of novelists by the standard quotations dictionaries. Lists *c.*12,000 quotations from British and American novels, 1470-1900, by over 300 authors, under *c.*850 subject headings, A-Z. Index of authors and novels. Keyword index. References to chapter numbers. *Class No:* 82(082.2)

[6482]

REES, N. Cassell companion to quotations. London, Cassell, 1997. 640p. £25. ISBN: 0304348481.

A very selective collection which supersedes Rees's *Brewer's quotations* (London, Cassell, 1994) and, like it, concentrates on those quotations 'about which there is something to be said for their meaning to be properly appreciated' (*Preface*). Over 2,500 entries under authors, A-Z, with keyword index. Invaluable for reference work because of the emphasis on quotes which are actually sought and the amount of detailed contextual information provided on each one, including explanation of misquotations and misattributions and examples of the recycling of quotations in book, song and film titles. *Class No:* 82(082.2)

[6483]

Respectfully quoted: a dictionary of quotations requested from the Library of Congress. Platt, S., *ed.* Reprint of 1989 ed. Washington, D.C., Congressional Quarterly Inc., 1992. xxvi,520p. $29.95. ISBN: 0871876876.

First published Washington, D.C., Library of Congress, 1989, as *Respectfully quoted: a dictionary of quotations requested from the Congressional Research Service*.

Lists *c.*2,100 quotations which have been sought in the course of 75 years of quotation research in the Library of Congress. The quotations are mainly from the world of politics and are arranged by topic with exact references to printed sources. Indexes of subjects, authors and keywords. According to the publishers, almost half the quotations are not to be found in any other reference work. *Class No:* 82(082.2)

[6484]

ROOM, A. Bloomsbury dictionary of dedications. London, Bloomsbury, 1990; Boston, Tuttle, 1992. xiv,354p. ISBN: 0747505217, UK; 0804817782, US.

US title is *Tuttle dictionary of dedications*.

Lists over 1,500 dedications from published works, by no means all literary, with notes on the dedicator, the dedicatee and the circumstances of the dedication. Arranged A-Z by author, the great majority being British and American. Foreign-language dedications appear in translation, usually by the compiler. *Class No:* 82(082.2)

[6485]

RUFFIN, C.B. Last words: a dictionary of death bed quotations. Jefferson, N.C., McFarland, 1995. 261p. $39.95. ISBN: 0786400439.

2,033 entries arranged A-Z by speaker, with keyword index. Entries give dates, reputed last words and brief notes on circumstances of death. Impressive list of sources (26p.). Up to date, with some deaths from the 1990s (*e.g.* River Phoenix).

.... *(contd.)*

See also J. Green's *Famous last words* (London, Kyle Cathie, 1997. 160p. £9.99. ISBN: 1856262642).
Class No: 82(082.2)

[6486]
—O'KILL, B. Exit lines: famous (and not-so-famous) last words. Harlow, Longman, 1986. viii,184p. ISBN: 0582892236.

Essays (1½-2p.) on the last words - actual and alleged - and the circumstances in which they were spoken, of over 100 historical figures. A-Z arrangement by speaker but no index of phrases. Select bibliography (6p.).
Class No: 82(082.2)

[6487]
STEVENSON, B.E. The Home book of quotations, classical and modern. 10th ed., rev. New York, Dodd; London, Cassell, 1974 (repr. New York, Greenwich House, 1984). xliii,2816p.

1st ed. 1934. 10th ed. published in UK as *Stevenson's Book of quotations*.

One of the standard collections, along with Bartlett and *The Oxford dictionary*, but unlike them it has a subject arrangement. Over 50,000 quotations listed under subject headings, A-Z, often with further, more specific, subdivisions. Usually gives exact citation. Indexes of authors and keywords. 10th ed. has 2 appendices (27p.) which are separately indexed. *Class No:* 82(082.2)

[6488]
The Traveller's dictionary of quotation: who said what, about where? Yapp, P., *ed.* London, Routledge & Kegan Paul, 1983. xvi,1022p. ISBN: 0415027608.

Arranged A-Z under existing countries, plus supra-national entities in same sequence. Entry begins with general quotes, on the country and its peoples, then A-Z by place, finally chronological within place. Quotes on earth, sun, moon, universe etc. at end of book. Fictional quotes asterisked, dramatic quotes attributed to character. Attribution includes author, book, date, but not part of book. Quotes frequently lengthy (*e.g.* 34 lines from Wordsworth's *Prelude*). Indexes of places (including buildings) and peoples, and of persons quoted. Better for finding suitable extracts than identifying given quotes. Over 10,000 quotations. *Class No:* 82(082.2)

[6489]
WEAVER, B.L. Novel openers: first sentences of 11,000 fictional works, opically arranged with subject, keyword, author and title indexing. Jefferson, N.C., McFarland, 1995. 996p. $75. ISBN: 0786400501.

Should answer a lot of quiz questions.
Class No: 82(082.2)

[6490]
WILSTACH, F.J. Dictionary of similes. Reprint of 2nd ed. Detroit, Omnigraphics Inc., 1990. 536p. $45. ISBN: 0810343703; 1558888470.

1st ed. Boston, Little Brown, 1916; London, Harrap, 1917. 2nd ed. rev. and enl., Boston, Little Brown, 1924.

Over 19,000 similes arranged under some 4,600 subject headings (usually keywords). Over 1,400 authors represented but exact references not provided. Author index.
Class No: 82(082.2)

[6491]
—Similes dictionary. Sommer, E. *and* Sommer, M., *eds.* Detroit, Gale, 1988. xlviii,950p. £60. ISBN: 0810343614.

16,000 English-language similes from literature and other sources, including newspapers, films, TV and politics, arranged under 500 subject categories, with many cross-references, table of subject synonyms, and index of authors. Clearly the result of much work, but *Library Review* (v.38(2), 1989, p.64) is quite right in criticizing the 'mind-numbing banality' of many entries and in suggesting that 'the selection criteria would seem to require a considerable rethink' before any new edition is contemplated.
Class No: 82(082.2)

Databases

[6492]
The Columbia world of quotations on CD-ROM. Andrews, R., *& others, eds.* New York, Columbia Univ. Press, 1996. CD-ROM. $350. ISBN: 0231105185.

Over 65,000 quotations by 5,000 authors/speakers, which can be searched by author, title, keyword and subject (6,500 headings) and by author's gender, nationality, occupation, birthdate or century - or any combination of these. Provides detailed material on authors and much contextual information on the quotes. Includes far more quotations than all Columbia's printed collections combined.
Class No: 82(082.2)(003.4)

[6493]
Gale's quotations: who said what? Detroit, Gale, 1995. CD-ROM. £305. ISBN: 0810399881.

Over 117,000 quotations from a range of UK and US sources, accessible via subject, keyword, author name, author occupation, year, and any combination of these.
Class No: 82(082.2)(003.4)

Handbooks & Manuals

[6494]
SHIPPS, A.W. The Quote sleuth: a manual for the tracer of lost quotations. Champaign, Ill., Illinois Univ. Press, 1990. 194p. $24.95. ISBN: 0252016955.

Gives advice on quotation-hunting and evaluates a wide range of sources, including general quotations dictionaries, specialized and thematic compilations, single-author quotation books, and concordances. An annotated bibliography (63p.) lists all the works discussed in the text. Index. 'This book should not just be added to public and academic library reference collections but should also be read by reference librarians' (*Booklist*, v.86(20), June 15, 1990, p.2033). *Class No:* 82(082.2)(035)

Scotland

[6495]
CRAN, A. *and* **ROBERTSON, J. Dictionary of Scottish quotations.** Edinburgh, Mainstream, 1996. xv,431p. £20. ISBN: 1851588124.

Over 4,000 quotations arranged under 840 authors/speakers, A-Z, with contextual notes and citations to chapters. Most quotations are in English, but includes some in Gaelic with translation and some in Scots without. Subject and keyword indexes. *Class No:* 82(082.2)(411)

Ireland

[6496]

A Book of Irish quotations. McMahon, S., *comp.* Dublin, O'Brien Press, 1984. 231p. £5.95. ISBN: 0862780241.

Over 2,000 quotes by Irish people, arranged A-Z by author with a keyword index. Translation provided for all Gaelic quotes. Source and, in most cases, date with each quote. *Class No:* 82(082.2)(415)

Wales

[6497]

A Most peculiar people: quotations about Wales and the Welsh. Stephens, M., *ed.* Cardiff, Univ. of Wales Press, 1992. 186p. ISBN: 0708311687.

2,324 quotations arranged chronologically from 51BC (Julius Caesar) to 1990. Citations give title and date of publication. Index of nearly 700 authors/speakers. Subject index. *Class No:* 82(082.2)(429)

Canada

[6498]

Colombo's Canadian quotations. Colombo, J.R., *ed.* Edmonton, Hurtig, 1974. x,735p. ISBN: 0888300794.

'The largest dictionary of its kind ever published in Canada, the first to be based for the most part on primary sources' (*Preface*). 6,000 quotations arranged *Oxford dictionary*-style by contributor, A-Z, (2,500 names) with keyword index (20,000 entries). All quotations dated.

Supplemented by *Colombo's new Canadian quotations* (Edmonton, Hurtig, 1987. ISBN: 0888303092), which adds 4,000 quotations. *Class No:* 82(082.2)(71)

[6499]

HAMILTON, R.M. *and* **SHIELDS, D. The Dictionary of Canadian quotations and phrases.** Rev. and enl. ed. Toronto, McClelland & Stewart, 1979. 1063p. ISBN: 0771038461.

1st ed. 1952, as *Canadian quotations and phrases, literary and historical.*

Lists over 10,000 quotations under *c.*2,000 alphabetically-arranged subject headings, then chronologically within each section. List of subject headings with cross-references. Author index, but no index to keywords.
Class No: 82(082.2)(71)

USA

[6500]

CARRUTH, G. *and* **EHRLICH, E. The Harper book of American quotations.** New York, Harper & Row, 1988. 821p. ISBN: 0060159758.

Lists *c.*8,000 quotations by over 1,400 individuals under 264 subject headings, giving source and date. Index of authors, subjects, and some keywords.
Class No: 82(082.2)(73)

Australia

[6501]

The Dictionary of Australian quotations. Murray-*Smith, S., ed.* 2nd ed. Port Melbourne, Vic., Reed, 1992. 512p. A$29.95. ISBN: 186330147x.

1st ed. 1984.

Over 4,500 quotations by Australians or about Australia

....(contd.)

and the Australians. Arranged by author/speaker, with subject and keyword indexes. 1,000 new quotes in 2nd ed.
Class No: 82(082.2)(94)

Jews

[6502]

A Treasury of Jewish quotations. Baron, J.L., *ed.* Northvale, New Jersey, Aronson, 1985. 648p. $40. ISBN: 0876688946.

First published 1956.

Lists *c.*18,000 quotations from 2,500 years of Jewish literature, sacred and secular, under 1,004 subject headings, A-Z, and many subheadings. All quotations in English, with exact references to sources. Author index (with brief descriptions and dates) and subject index. Glossary of Hebrew and Yiddish terms. Bibliography (3p.).
Class No: 82(082.2)(=924)

Black Races

[6503]

KING, A. Quotations in black. Westport, Conn., Greenwood, 1981. 344p. $45. ISBN: 0313221286.

Quotations by over 200 Blacks, arranged chronologically by birth date. Separate sequence of proverbs from various countries. Author and subject/keyword indexes.

Supplemented by King's *Contemporary quotations in black* (Greenwood, 1997. 312p. illus. $39.95. ISBN: 0313291225), which lists over 1,000 quotations drawn from newspapers and magazines published 1990-1996 and includes photos of over 40 speakers. Arranged by author, A-Z, with author, keyword and subject indexes.
Class No: 82(082.2)(=96)

Amerindians, North

[6504]

American Indian quotations. Langer, H.J., *ed.* Westport, Conn., Greenwood, 1996. 260p. illus. $49.95. ISBN: 0313291217.

Nearly 800 quotations by Native Americans arranged chronologically by speaker, from the 16th century to the present, and indexed by author, subject/keyword and tribe. Source given for each quote (but no page numbers) with brief biographical notes on the speaker. Appended list of anonymous quotations, prayers and proverbs. Photographs of 22 speakers. *Class No:* 82(082.2)(=97)

Non-English

[6505]

COLLISON, R.L. *and* **COLLISON, M. Dictionary of foreign quotations.** New York, Facts on File; London, Macmillan, 1980. vii,407p.

Concentrates on modern rather than classical quotations, arranged A-Z by broad subject; within subject section arranged by language. Greek, Cyrillic scripts transliterated; Arabic in colloquial not classical form. Literal or well-known translation added. Index of authors and works (p.384-407) keyed to headwords. *Class No:* 82(082.2)=3/9

German

[6506]
BÜCHMANN, G. Geflügelte Worte: der klassische Zitatenschatz. Hofmann, W., *ed.* 40. Aufl. Frankfurt am Main, Ullstein, 1995. ix,613p. DM39.80. ISBN: 3550068298.

1st ed. 1864.

A scholarly quotations dictionary which provides a great deal of information on the background and sources of over 5,000 sayings, idioms, names, and allusions from many languages. Separate sections for the Bible, folklore, various languages and countries, and current affairs. Quotation in the original, with German translation, explanation, precise source citations and commentary. Name index. Keyword indexes in German, English, French, Italian, Spanish, Greek and Latin. *Class No:* 82(082.2)=30

[6507]
Reclams Zitaten-Lexikon. John, J., *ed.* Rev. ed. Stuttgart, Reclam, 1993. 581p. DM29.80. ISBN: 3150103916.

A dictionary of mainly literary German quotations which contains few quotes from contemporary popular culture and mass media. Arranged by keyword, A-Z, with index of authors, but lacks full keyword index.

Another source of German quotations is *Duden: Zitate und Aussprüche: Herkunft und aktueller Gebrauch* (Mannheim, Dudenverlag, 1993. 827p. DM34. ISBN: 3411041218) which forms part of *Der Duden in 12 Bände* (*q.v.*).
Class No: 82(082.2)=30

French

[6508]
Dictionnaire de citations françaises. Oster, P., *ed.* Paris, Robert, 1993. xiv,934p. Fr.240. ISBN: 2850361925.

Over 16,500 quotations under authors, arranged chronologically by birth-date. Subject and author indexes.
Class No: 82(082.2)=40

[6509]
DOURNON, J.-Y. Le Grand dictionnaire des citations françaises. Paris, Acropole, 1982. 906p. ISBN: 2714414427.

Lists *c.*10,000 quotations by French authors under 1,547 subject headings, but attributes them to author and title only. Author index. List of headings. Approx. half the quotations are from modern authors and half from classical writers.
Class No: 82(082.2)=40

[6510]
MATIGNON, J., *and others.* **Nouveau dictionnaire de citations françaises.** Paris, Hachette-Tchou, 1970. 1606p. illus.

16,241 numbered quotations, arranged chronologically by birth-date of author from Suger (1081) to Debray (1941). Subject index and alphabetical list of authors cited.
Class No: 82(082.2)=40

Italian

[6511]
FUMAGALLI, G. Chi l'ha detto? Tesoro di citazioni italiane e straniere, di origine letteraria e storica, ordinate e annotate. Milano, Hoepli, 1983. xxvi,848p. ISBN: 8820300923.

1st ed. 1894.

2,327 quotations under 85 subject headings, with exact references to sources and annotations which in some cases

.... *(contd.)*

run to several pages. Foreign quotes are mainly in Latin, French and English. Name index and index of quotations by first word only. *Class No:* 82(082.2)=50

Spanish

[6512]
VEGA, V. Diccionario ilustrado de frases célebres y citas literarias. Barcelona, Gili, 1952. xv,939p. illus.

Over 12,000 quotations, some of them lengthy, arranged by subjects, A-Z, with references to sources (not always exact) and explanatory notes. Includes foreign quotations, usually in the original with Spanish translation. Indexes of subjects, first words, names, and authors.
Class No: 82(082.2)=60

Classical Languages

[6513]
HARBOTTLE, T.B. Dictionary of quotations (classical). 3rd ed. London, Sonnenschein, 1906 (repr. New York, Ungar, 1958). 678p.

1st ed. 1897.

Separate Latin and Greek sections, the entries in each case being under first word of the original quotation with exact reference to source and English translation. Author index and 3 subject indexes: Latin, Greek and English. Appendix lists supplementary quotations which are not indexed.
Class No: 82(082.2)=7

Arabic

[6514]
FIELD, C.H.A. A Dictionary of oriental quotations (Arabic and Persian). London, Sonnenschein, 1911 (repr. New York, Gordon Press). ii,351p. $75. ISBN: 0849000432.

Quotations are aranged A-Z by first word of transliterated form and followed by a translation. Author index and brief index of keywords. *Class No:* 82(082.2)=927

20th Century

[6515]
ANDREWS, R. Cassell dictionary of contemporary quotations. London, Cassell, 1996. xvi,622p. £25. ISBN: 0304346403.

Lists *c.*7,000 quotations recorded since 1945 under 1,180 subject headings, Abortion to Yuppies. Strong on song lyrics. Precise citations, some with contextual notes. 1,825 authors/speakers represented. Keyword and author indexes.
Class No: 82(082.2)"19"

[6516]
COHEN, J.M. *and* **COHEN, M.J. The Penguin dictionary of twentieth-century quotations.** 3rd ed. London, Viking, 1993. viii,628p. £17.99. ISBN: 0670821659.

1st ed. 1971; 2nd ed. 1980, both as *The Penguin dictionary of modern quotations.*

Considerably larger than earlier eds., with over 8,500 quotations under authors, A-Z. Following a major change of policy, *all* 20th-century material from the compilers' *New Penguin dictionary of quotations* (1992) is now included, together with many additional quotes, whereas there was no overlap between previous eds. of these stable companions. Coverage is commendable, with plenty of advertizing slogans, somg lyrics, catchphrases, graffiti, etc. in addition to the usual literary and political quotes, but the precision of

.... *(contd.)*
the attributions, as in the parent work, varies rather alarmingly. Keyword index (208p.) Includes some foreign-language quotations in English translation.
Class No: 82(082.2)"19"

[6517]
MILSTED, D. The Guinness chronicle of the 20th century in quotations. Enfield, Guinness, 1996. 256p. £9.99. ISBN: 0851126065.

2,500 quotations, many of them not previously anthologized, arranged by year within chapters devoted to each decade of the century. Precise dates and detailed contextual information. Collections of quotations on major events are grouped within boxes in the annual sections, *e.g.* 20 quotes on the Falklands War within 1982. Index of names. Index of events and themes.
Class No: 82(082.2)"19"

[6518]
The Oxford dictionary of modern quotations. Augarde, T., *ed.* Oxford, Oxford Univ. Press, 1991. xi,371p. £6.99. ISBN: 0192830864.

Over 5,000 20th-century quotations, arranged A-Z by author with an index of keywords. Entries include exact references to sources. Foreign quotations appear in the original language followed by English translation. According to *Booklist* (v.87(17), May 1, 1991, p.1742) about half the people quoted are British.

Available on CD-ROM along with *The Oxford dictionary of modern quotations* (£49.99. 0192682482).
Class No: 82(082.2)"19"

[6519]
REES, N. Chambers dictionary of modern quotations. Edinburgh, Chambers, 1993. ix,405p. ISBN: 055021030x.

A revised version of *A Dictionary of twentieth century quotations* (London, Fontana Paperbacks, 1987).

2,500 quotations listed under author in an A-Z sequence, which also includes some specialist categories (*e.g.* Epitaphs, Slogans, Catchphrases). Index combines keywords, themes and subject terms. Includes common misquotations which are clearly marked and accompanied by a note of explanation. Particularly useful for quotations from films, TV, popular songs and advertising, which may not be in the standard larger dictionaries, and for the extra contextual information provided for many sayings, including alternative, variant and mistaken versions.
Class No: 82(082.2)"19"

[6520]
Simpson's contemporary quotations: the most notable quotes from 1950 to the present. Simpson, J.B., *ed.* Rev. ed. New York, HarperCollins, 1997. xiv,657p. $35. ISBN: 0062701371.

1st ed. under this title Boston, Houghton Mifflin, 1988, which itself updated *Contemporary quotations* (1964).

11,330 numbered quotations, with the emphasis on post-1988 sayings. US authors/speakers strongly represented. 3 sections (The World; Humankind; Communication and the Arts) and 55 subsections, with quotes arranged by authors under each heading. Indexes of authors, subjects and keylines (much less comprehensive than keywords). Citations to books give title and year only, but those to newspaper articles and speeches are more precise.
Class No: 82(082.2)"19"

Women

[6521]
MAGGIO, R. The Beacon book of quotations by women. Boston, Mass., Beacon Books, 1992. 390p. $25. ISBN: 0807067644.

Presents over 5,000 quotations under 800-plus subject headings, with name and subject indexes. Citations give source and first publication date only. *Class No:* 82(082.2)-0055.2

[6522]
The New quotable woman: from Eve to the Present Day. Partnow, E., *comp. & ed.* Rev. ed. New York, Facts on File, 1992; London, Headline, 1993. xxii,649p. $40. ISBN: 0816021341, US; 0747208638, UK.

An amalgamation, updating and complete revision of Partnow's *The Quotable woman: from Eve to 1799* (1985) and *The Quotable woman: 1800-1981* (1982).

Lists over 15,000 quotations by 2,540 women throughout history. Arranged chronologically by birthdate with indexes of names (including much biographical information) and subjects. Precise citations usually provided. A third of the quotes from previous eds. have been dropped, with 2,000 new ones added. 450 women are quoted for the first time in this ed. *Class No:* 82(082.2)-0055.2

[6523]
Women's words: the Columbia book of quotations by women. Biggs, M., *ed.* New York, Columbia Univ. Press, 1996. 501p. $24.95. ISBN: 0231079869.

3,000 quotations, primarily by Engish-speaking women from the past 2 centuries, arranged under 600+ subject headings with a 'source' (*i.e.* author/speaker) index. Many entries include biographical and contextual notes. *Choice* (v.34(5), Jan. 1997, p.765) is critical of the vague selection criteria and idiosyncratic subject headings, but 'considering that less than 1% of the quotes in ... Bartlett's *Familiar quotations* are by women, any addition to this field is welcome'. *Class No:* 82(082.2)-0055.2

Maps & Atlases

[6524]
The Atlas of literature. Bradbury, M., *ed.* London, De Agostini, 1996. 352p. illus. £25. ISBN: 1899883673.

A misleadingly titled book which is actually a collection of 80 chronologically arranged essays, by mainly literary writers, on various countries, regions and cities, in which the links between writing and place are explored, *e.g.* Melvyn Bragg on the Lake District of the Romantic poets. Lavishly illustrated with over 500 photographs and maps. Reference value is confined to the maps showing places with literary associations, few of which are allocated a full page, and lists of places to visit (museums, authors' homes, etc.) arranged by country with contact details and opening hours. Select bibliography of secondary sources by country. Index.
Class No: 82(084.3)

Chronologies

[6525]
BROWNSTONE, D. *and* FRANCK, I. Timeline of the arts and literature. New York, HarperCollins, 1994. 711p. $30. ISBN: 0062700693.

Literature is one of the 6 main categories in this chronology, the others being Visual Arts, Theater and Variety, Music and Dance, Film and Broadcasting, and World Events. 20,000 entries in all, ranging from prehistory

.... *(contd.)*
to 1992. Literary entries cover births and deaths of writers and publications of significant works. Personal name index, but no subject index. *Class No:* 82(090)

[6526]
Calendar of literary facts: a daily and yearly guide to noteworthy events in world literature from 1450 to the Present. Rogal, S.J., *ed.* Detroit, Gale, 1991. xii,877p. £55. ISBN: 0810329433.

First section is arranged by day, throughout the year, and gives birth and death dates for *c.*2,000 authors. Second section is a chronology from 1450 to 1989 with separate sections within each year for births, deaths, publications and events. List of 60 sources. Index of authors, titles and events. *Class No:* 82(090)

Histories

Gay People

[6527]
WOODS, G. A History of gay literature: the male tradition. New Haven, Conn. and London, Yale Univ. Press, 1998. 456p. illus. £25.95. ISBN: 0300072015.

Claims to be the first full account of male gay literature, across cultures and languages, from ancient times to the present. A narrative history in 32 chapters with many quotations. Bibliography (25p.). Index. *Class No:* 82(091)-0055.3

Biographies

[6528]
COMBS, R.E. *and* **OWEN, N.R. Authors:** critical and biographical references. 2nd ed. Metuchen, N.J., Scarecrow, 1993. 477p. $58. ISBN: 0810826798.

1st ed. 1971.

A finding tool for commentaries on the lives and works of authors, which analyzes 1,158 books (most of them US publications), excluding encyclopedic works and vols. devoted to a single author. 3,317 international authors treated, A-Z, with nearly 11,000 passages cited, more than doubling the coverage of the superseded ed. Goes beyond literature, perhaps unwisely, to include writers on philosophy, science, history, theology and other nonfiction subjects. Each passage cited is at least 6p. Not easy to use, but valuable for its coverage of minor authors on whom little has been written. *Class No:* 82(092)

[6529]
Contemporary authors: a bio-bibliographical guide to current writers in fiction, general nonfiction, poetry, journalism, drama, motion pictures, television, and other fields. Detroit, Gale, 1962-. £107 per vol. ISSN: 00107468.

V.1-159 (main series), 1962-97 (in progress). Individual physical vols. numbered as 4-vol. units from 1-4 to 97-100. Single numbering system begins with v.101.

First revision series. 1967-79. V.1-44 in 11 vols., representing an updating and cumulation of the corresponding vols. in the original series.

Permanent series. 1975-78. V.1-2, with entries for writers in the original series who have died or who have ceased publishing.

New revision series. 1981-97. V.1-62 (in progress). Whereas in the *First revision series,* whole vols. from the original series were updated, the *New revision series* vols. contain updated articles from a number of different vols. on active writers whose original entries require significant

.... *(contd.)*
revision.

The most comprehensive source of biographical information on writers of all kinds, which, because of its wide remit, may be considered as a general biographical source. There are entries for artists, biographers, musicians, theologians, scientists, politicians, film directors, journalists, etc., and although coverage is international, American representation is particularly strong. Each vol. has *c.*900 entries, arranged A-Z, with sections for personal and career data (including biography, address, memberships, awards, etc.); writings; work in progress; sidelights (review of career and critical reception, often including comments by the subject); and biographical/critical sources. Over 100,000 authors covered to date.

Cumulative indexes bound in even-numbered vols. of *CA*, up to and including v.126, which cover all *CA* series and also have references to other Gale biographical series (*DLB, CLC,* etc.). Since then, separate paperback cumulative index vols. have been supplied to subscribers with even-numbered vols. of *CA* and odd-numbered vols. of *New revision series.*

All *CA* series listed above, except *First revision series*, are available on a single CD-ROM (£665. ISBN: 0787615838), the equivalent of over 200 vols., providing information on 100,000 authors. Can be searched by subject/genre, author name, book title, personal data (birth/death dates, religion, etc.) or any combination of terms in a full text search. A very convenient source, but it should be noted that for authors who appear in more than 1 vol. (and there are many) the CD includes only the most recent 'full sketch' entry. Annual subscription includes semi-annual updates.

Also available online via the publisher's subscription service, GaleNet (details at http://www.gale.com).
Class No: 82(092)

[6530]
—Contemporary authors: autobiography series. Detroit, Gale. 1984-. v.1- (in progress). illus. £107 per vol. ISSN: 07480636.

Each vol. contains an original collection of 15-25 autobiographical essays written specially for the series by writers of all genres. Essays range from 10,000 to 15,000 words and are accompanied by photographs and followed by bibliographies of book-length works. Each vol. has cumulative index of authors and of subjects covered in the essays. By no means essential, as some very obscure writers have been included.

28 vols. published by end of 1997. *Class No:* 82(092)

[6531]
Contemporary popular writers. Mote, D., *ed.* Detroit and London, St. James Press, 1997. 528p. £90. ISBN: 1558622160.

Entries on 300 of today's most popular authors - not limited to novelists - giving (in familiar St. James style) biography, bibliography and a critical essay. Indexed by author, nationality, genre and title. *Class No:* 82(092)

[6532]
Cyclopedia of world authors. Magill, F.N. *and* Kohler, D., *eds.* Rev. ed. Englewood Cliffs, N.J., Salem Press, 1974. 3v. ISBN: 0893561258.

1st ed. 1958.

Entries on nearly 1,000 authors, giving place and date of birth and death, list of principal works, biocritical sketch (200-1,000 words), and references to biographical sources.

Supplemented by *Cyclopedia of world authors II* (1989. 4v. $300. ISBN: 0893565121), which has entries for 705 writers. 560 of them are new to this set and the remaining

....(*contd.*)
entries provide updated information on authors covered previously. Most of the writers included are English-language literary authors who have been active in the 20th-century. 'Most of the major contemporary writers one would expect to find are here' (*Reference Books Bulletin*, v.86(13), March 1, 1990), but some surprising omissions are noted (*e.g.* Ayckbourn, Heaney, Cela, Levertov). Index in v.4.

New 5-vol. ed. published 1997 ($350. ISBN: 0893564346). *Class No:* 82(092)

[6533]

Dictionary of literary biography. Detroit, Gale, 1978-98. v.1-188 (in progress). £112 per vol.

A major reference series, which has broadened its scope in recent vols. from British, American and Canadian writers to cover many of the world's major literatures. Each vol. contains lengthy, signed articles on the main authors of a particular genre or period, lavishly illustrated with photographs of the writer and his/her works, including manuscripts. The essays are 'career biographies, tracing the development of the author's canon and the evolution of his reputation' (*Plan of the series*), and all include primary and secondary bibliographies. Cumulative index in each vol.

Full subscription to the series is beyond the means of smaller libraries, but individual vols. should always be considered for purchase as they usually rank among the best sources in their field. These are listed in separate entries under national/regional literatures, *e.g.* vols. relating to Italian literature at 850(092).

Available online via the publisher's subscription service, GaleNet (details at http//:www.gale.com). All printed vols. due to be loaded by June 1998, with new vols. to be added quarterly thereafter. *Class No:* 82(092)

[6534]

KUNITZ, S.J. *and* **HAYCRAFT, H. World authors: 1900-1950.** Seymour-Smith, M. *and* Kimmens, A.C., *eds.* New York, Wilson, 1997. 4v. illus. $395. ISBN: 0824208994.

A complete (and long overdue) revision of S.J. Kunitz and H. Haycraft's *Twentieth-century authors: a biographical dictionary of modern literature* (New York, Wilson, 1942) and its *First supplement* (1955).

Biographical sketches of over 2,500 authors, from all countries, whose work has been published in English. The biographies have been rewritten in a more candid, contemporary style and entries also include critical commentary and up-to-date primary and secondary bibliographies. Some writers have been dropped and a few dozen added, but the focus is still predominantly on US and European writers. Autobiographical statements provided by the subjects for the original work have been retained.
Class No: 82(092)

[6535]

—World authors, 1950-1970: a companion volume to *Twentieth century authors.* Wakeman, J., *ed.* New York, Wilson, 1975. 1594p. illus. $95. ISBN: 0824204190.

Biocritical entries on 959 authors whose work is available in English and who gained attention between 1950 and 1970. Similar in style to *TCA*, but is more truly international in coverage as more translations have become available. Entries contributed by *c.*75 specialists, but not signed, with many of the authors covered having provided autobiographical articles. Supplemented by:

World authors, 1970-75, ed. by J. Wakeman (1980. 893p. $85. ISBN: 082420641x), with 348 new entries;

World authors, 1975-80, ed. by V. Colby (1985. 831p. $85. ISBN: 0824207157), with 379 entries;

....(*contd.*)
World authors 1980-85, ed. by V. Colby (1990. 1000p. $85. ISBN: 0824207971), with 320 entries.

World authors 1985-90, ed. by V. Colby (1995. 970p. $85. ISBN: 0824208757), with 345 entries.

Entries in the supplementary vols. are longer, varying from 1,500 to 6,000 words. *Class No:* 82(092)

[6536]

Larousse dictionary of writers. Goring, R., *ed.* Edinburgh, Larousse, 1994. ix,1070p. £25. ISBN: 0752300067.

Over 6,000 brief articles on writers from all periods and all countries. Entries are unsigned (38 contributors listed without details) and provide outline biographical information with an indication of major themes and some consideration of the most representative works. Cross-references to related entries. Bibliographical information is very limited, but one or two key biographies are cited for major writers. Mainly literary in scope, but some philosophers and psychological theorists are included. Strong coverage of writers of popular genre fiction. *Class No:* 82(092)

[6537]

Literary exile in the twentieth century: an analysis and biographical dictionary. Tucker, M., *ed.* Westport, Conn., Greenwood, 1991. xxiv,854p. $115. ISBN: 0313238707.

19 group articles for writers from a particular place or victims of a particular persecution (*e.g.* Soviet writers in exile, Holocaust writers) followed by entries on *c.*530 exiled writers, A-Z. Author entries average 1½p. (but as much as 9p. for major figures like Rushdie and Beckett) and include biography, critical analysis, list of works and selected secondary bibliography. General bibliography (8p.). Appended lists include: waves of exile by region; writers by country of departure; writers by country of arrival; writers by category of exile (political, religious, etc.). Index.
Class No: 82(092)

[6538]

Magill's survey of world literature. Magill, F.N., *ed.* New York, Marshall Cavendish, 1992. 6v. illus. £325. ISBN: 1854354825.

Provides information on 215 writers, of 30 nationalities (excluding Americans) from Aristotle to the present. Entries are arranged A-Z and include full-page portrait, biography, critical analysis, discussion of a few key works and selective bibliography of secondary sources, but no primary bibliography. Glossary in each vol. Author and title indexes in v.6. Combines elements of Magill's *Critical survey* and *Masterplots* series, duplicating much of their coverage, and seems to be aimed at US high school libraries. As both classical and popular writers are covered, selection is inevitably somewhat arbitrary and some major names are absent. *Class No:* 82(092)

[6539]

Major 20th-century writers: a selection of sketches from *Contemporary authors.* Ryan, B., *ed.* Detroit, Gale, 1991. 4v. £290. ISBN: 0810377667.

Another spin-off from *Contemporary authors* (*cf. Black writers* and *Hispanic writers*) offering libraries which cannot afford to subscribe to *CA* the opportunity to acquire comprehensive biobibliographical information on over 1,000 modern writers. Entries are arranged A-Z and concentrate on literary authors (including writers for children and genre fiction authors), although several philosophers (*e.g.* Russell, Freud), politicians (*e.g.* Kennedy, Churchill), critics (*e.g.* Frye, Leavis), journalists (*e.g.* Hunter S. Thompson, Malcolm Muggeridge) and other influential non-literary

....*(contd.)*

authors are also included. Entries follow the standard *CA* format and have been completely updated for this publication, with 40 newly-written articles which will appear in later *CA* vols. Coverage of British and European authors is better than is often the case in American literary reference works, a special effort having been made to cover the authors regularly studied in schools and colleges on both sides of the Atlantic. Nationality index (over 60 countries) and genre index. *Class No:* 82(092)

[6540]

Le Nouveau dictionnaire des auteurs: de tous les temps et de tous les pays. de Roux, P., *ed.* Paris, Robert Laffont, 1994. 3v. Fr.595. ISBN: 2221068882.

Supersedes *Dictionnaire biographique des auteurs de tous les temps et de tous les pays* (1957-8. 2v.).

Covers over 6,000 authors, A-Z, from all countries and all periods, including living writers born before 1951. Signed entries include biography, commentary on their works and complete primary bibliography. For major writers, selected quotations from their contemporaries are an additional feature. As well as literary writers, some musicians, artists and scientists are included. A companion to *Le Nouveau dictionnaire des oeuvres* (*q.v.*). *Class No:* 82(092)

[6541]

The Reader's companion to 20th century writers. Parker, P., *ed.* London, Fourth Estate, 1995. xvi,825p, £25. ISBN: 1857023323.

Brief biographies of 1,000 English-language literary authors, including writers of genre fiction but not of children's books, biography or criticism. Classified list of works with each entry, plus reference to a standard biography where available. Over 40 contributors, but entries are unsigned. Strong on the sort of gossipy detail normally lacking in biographical reference works: 'The book is so readable it is easy to forget what a comprehensive work of reference it is and what a prodigious feat of literary criticism' (*The Spectator*, Dec. 16/23, 1995, p.61-2). *Class No:* 82(092)

[6542]

Reference guide to world literature. Henderson, L., *ed.* 2nd ed. Detroit & London, St. James Press, 1995. 2v. $280. ISBN: 1558621954.

1st ed. 1984 as *Great foreign language writers*, ed. by J.Vincent and D. Kirkpatrick.

Entries on *c.*500 deceased writers (1st ed. had only 250) in languages other than English, from Ancient Times to the 20th century. Includes some nonfiction writers who have had an impact on imaginative literature, *e.g.* Nietzsche, Pascal, Plato. Usual St. James format: biography; complete list of works in all genres; select list of English-language critical studies; and signed critical essay. Also includes 500 articles on major individual works of literature. Title and nationality indexes. *Class No:* 82(092)

[6543]

—Contemporary world writers. Chevalier, T., *ed.* 2nd ed. Detroit & London, St. James Press, 1993. xiv,686p. $140. ISBN: 1558622004.

1st ed. 1984, as *Contemporary foreign language writers*, ed. by J. Vinson and D. Kirkpatrick.

Profiles over 340 living writers who use languages other than English (32 in all) and whose work has been translated. 102 are from western Europe, with a total of 60 countries represented. Signed entries (160 contributors) follow the

....*(contd.)*

same pattern as those in *Reference guide to world literature*, but there are no articles on individual works. Title index has nearly 9,000 entries. Nationality indexes. *Class No:* 82(092)

[6544]

World authors on CD-ROM. New York, Wilson, 1997.

A CD-ROM version of the *Wilson author series*, with 3 options:

World authors: 1950-present ($295) has 2,700 biographical sketches based in part on updated material from the 4 post-1950 *World authors* vols. plus *Spanish American authors: the twentieth century* (*q.v.*).

World authors: 1900-present ($495) adds the 4 pre-1950 *World authors* vols.

World authors: 800 B.C.-present ($595) adds *Greek and Latin authors: 800 B.C.-A.D. 1000*; *European authors: 1000-1900*; *British authors before 1800*; *British authors of the nineteenth century*; and *American authors: 1600-1900* (*qq.v.*) to give coverage of 10,000 writers.

Up to 150 authors are added to each database annually, the renewal fee being $95 in each case. *Class No:* 82(092)

[6545]

The Writers directory, 1998-2000. 13th ed. Detroit and London, St. James Press, 1997. x,1847p. £115. ISBN: 1558623604.

1st ed. 1971-72.

The latest ed. of this biennial publication provides biographical information on over 17,000 living writers (2,600 new for this ed.) who have published at least one full-length book in English. Entries comprise: name, pseudonyms, citizenship, year of birth, genres, past and present appointments, list of all published books, plus address where available. Index of writers by category is particularly useful for locating the nonfiction writers who make up over a third of all entrants. Obituaries section has entries for 480 writers who have died since the last ed. 'No other single source presents information on as wide a range of living fiction and nonfiction writers in so convenient and accessible form' (*Reference Reviews*, v.8(5), 1994, p.35, on 11th ed.). *Class No:* 82(092)

[6546]

—International authors and writers who's who. McIntire, D., *ed.* 15th ed. Cambridge, International Biographical Centre, 1997. 750p. £95. ISBN: 0948875720.

1st ed. 1934. 9th to 12th eds. incorporated *International who's who in poetry*, but this is now a separate publication once more.

Over 8,000 entries, dominated by British and American writers. Entries are based on information supplied by the writers and usually include the following data: place and date of birth, profession, education, major publications, honours, memberships, agent, and address. Appendices include lists of literary agents, literary organizations and awards, arranged by country in each case.

'A selection policy which is more truly international in character, and more rigorous in its approach to British media personalities who happen to have written the odd book, would render this work more authoritative and more reliably a reflection of its title' (*Reference Reviews*, v.8(4), 1994, p.37, on 13th ed.). *Class No:* 82(092)

Indexes

[6547]

Author biography master index. McNeil, B., *ed.* 5th ed. Detroit, Gale, 1997. 3v. (1813p.). £207. ISBN: 0787621439.

1st ed. 1978.

Indexes biographies of over 500,000 literary figures from all eras and countries. This ed. has over 1,230,000 citations (an increase of 220,000) to entries in 450 English-language reference works. Entries include author's birth and death dates and an indication of whether a portrait is available. Full bibliography of source works. *Class No:* 82(092)(014)

[6548]

HAVLICE, P.P. Index to literary biography. Metuchen, N.J., Scarecrow, 1975. 2v. (viii,1300p.). $95. ISBN: 0810807459.

Indexes entries on *c.*68,000 authors in 50 major biographical reference sources.

First supplement (1983. 2v. $89.50. ISBN: 081081613x) indexes biographies of *c.*53,000 authors in 57 reference works published 1969-81, and includes more non-western writers than its predecessor. *Class No:* 82(092)(014)

[6549]

Index to the *Wilson Authors Series*. Rev. ed. New York, Wilson, 1997. 120p. $27. ISBN: 0824209001.

Previous ed. 1991

Provides access to well over 10,000 biographical sketches in 21 reference sources. Includes birth and death dates and cross-references to variant forms of the names.
Class No: 82(092)(014)

Europe

[6550]

European authors, 1000-1900: a biographical dictionary of European literature. New York, Wilson, 1967. ix,1016p. $77. ISBN: 0824200136.

Biographical sketches of 967 authors from 31 different literatures. Appended bibliographies stress English translations and studies. *Class No:* 82(092)(4)

[6551]

European writers. Stade, G., *ed.* New York, Scribner, 1983-91. 14v. £802.95. ISBN: 0684192675.

V.1-2 *The Middle Ages and the Renaissance.* 1983.
V.3-4 *The Age of Reason and the Enlightenment.* 1984.
V.5-7 *The Romantic century.* 1985.
V.8-13 *The Twentieth century.* 1989-91.
V.14 *Index.* 1991.

Follows the same format as the publisher's *American writers* and *British writers* series, with a lengthy (*c.*15,000 words), signed critical essay on each author, followed by a select bibliography of primary and secondary literature. Entries are arranged chronologically by birth-date within each vol. 261 entries in all, the vols. on the 20th century covering over 120 writers, from Freud (born 1856) to Kundera (born 1929).

European writers: selected authors (New York, Scribner, 1993. 3v. $250. ISBN: 0684195836) contains 68 articles, taken direct from the main work, on the writers 'most often studied by high school students and undergraduates' and represents an affordable option for school libraries.

Also included on *The Scribner writers series on CD-ROM* (*q.v.*). *Class No:* 82(092)(4)

Black Races

[6552]

Black writers: a selection of sketches from *Contemporary authors.* Malinowski, S., *ed.* 2nd ed. Detroit, Gale, 1993. xxiv,619p. $95. ISBN: 0810377888.

1st ed. 1989

A one-volume compilation of entries from Gale's *Contemporary authors* series (*q.v.*) on over 400 Black (*i.e.* Afro-Caribbean) writers active during the twentieth century. 150 remain from the 1st ed. and have been updated, whilst 250 are new. Entries provide personal and career data, bibliographies, works in progress, references to sources of further information and a 'Sidelights' section, which includes the writer's critical reception. Includes many non-literary figures, *e.g.* Desmond Tutu, Marcus Garvey, Nelson Mandela, Martin Luther King. Most entries are for Americans, with some African and Caribbean Blacks included, but the omission of many British Blacks is disappointing. *Class No:* 82(092)(=96)

[6553]

Modern Black writers. Popkin, M., *ed.* New York, Ungar, 1978. xx,519p. $65. (*A Library of literary criticism.*) ISBN: 0804432589.

Contains excerpts from critical studies of 80 Black writers, A-Z, from 23 countries, 30 of the writers being American. Index of critics. Lists of authors by country and of works mentioned.

Supplement by S. Serafin published New York, Continuum, 1994. (544p. $75. ISBN: 0826406882).
Class No: 82(092)(=96)

[6554]

PAGE, J.A. *and* **ROH, J.M. Selected Black American, African, and Caribbean authors:** a bio-bibliography. Littleton, Colo., Libraries Unlimited, 1985. xiii,388p. ISBN: 0872874303.

A revision and enlargement of Page's *Selected Black American authors: an illustrated bio-bibliography* (Boston, Hall, 1977).

632 entries (453 in 1st ed.) based largely on questionnaires completed by the authors. Includes some non-literary authors (especially writers on religion and social affairs), giving biographical notes, list of writings (book-length works only), and references to biographical sources. Lists of writers by nationality and occupation. Bibliography of sources (10p.). Title index. *Class No:* 82(092)(=96)

Women

[6555]

An Encyclopedia of Continental women writers. Wilson, K.M., *ed.* New York, Garland; London, St. James Press, 1991. 2v. (xii,1389p.) $175. ISBN: 0824085477, US; 1558621512, UK.

From the same stable as *Encyclopedia of British women writers* (1988) but is able to provide more comprehensive coverage of its subject through the use of briefer essays. Some 270 scholars have contributed *c.*1,800 signed entries on writers from Ancient Greece to the present day, giving birth and death dates, languages and genres of the writings, biocritical essay, and lists of works (including English translations) and critical studies. Includes many women whose writings have yet to be translated into English and 'makes accessible information which is probably not currently available in UK libraries (*Public Library Jnl.*, v.7(1), 1992, p.26-27). Cross-references from alternative

.... *(contd.)*
names but, disappointingly (and contrary to the claims of the St. James Press catalogue), no indexes of languages (over 30 are represented) or nationalities. *Class No:* 82(092)-0055.2

[6556]
—Women writers of Great Britain and Europe: an encyclopedia. Wilson, K.M., *& others, eds.* New York, Garland, 1997. 571p. illus. $95. ISBN: 0815323433.

A selection of over 600 entries (revised and updated, but not rewritten) from the 2,000-plus in Garland's *An Encyclopedia of Continental women writers* and *An Encyclopedia of British women writers* (*qq.v.*). No index, but there are lists of authors by country and century and a list of pseudonyms and alternative names. Covers writers in over 30 languages. *Class No:* 82(092)-0055.2

[6557]
Feminist writers. Kester-Shelton, P., *ed.* Detroit & London, St. James Press, 1996. 641p. £100. ISBN: 1558622179.

Covers 293 women whose works are deemed to contain feminist themes, from Sappho to Beth Henley, in the standard St. James format: biography; list of writings; selected secondary bibliography; and signed critical essay on the major works. Includes writers on a wide variety of subjects (politics, sociology, history, etc.), but literary authors are also well represented, *e.g.* Margaret Atwood, George Sand). Appended list of 177 further femminist writers with brief annotations. Indexed by century, genre, themes and nationality. Title index of primary works. Very useful bibliography of publications on feminist writers (6p.) and directory of relevant organizations, periodicals, publishers and Internet resources. *Class No:* 82(092)-0055.2

Gay People

[6558]
Gay and lesbian literature. Malinowski, S., *ed.* Detroit & London, St. James Press, 1994-7. 2v. £76 per vol. ISBN: 1558621741, v.1; 1558622160, v.2.

Covers more than 400 mainly 20th-century literary and nonfiction writers, with inclusion based 'upon the gay and lesbian thematic content of a writer's work and not upon sexual identity' (*Preface*). Entries follow the familiar St. James format and include biographical information, lists of primary and secondary material, statement by the author (where available) and a signed critical essay. Introductory essays on gay and lesbian literature. Appended lists of relevant authors not featured; gay/lesbian literary awards; anthologies; and general critical studies. Indexes of names, nationalities, gender and subjects/genres.
Class No: 82(092)-0055.3

Manuscripts & Incunabula

[6559]
HUNTINGTON LIBRARY. Guide to literary manuscripts in the Huntington Library. San Marino, Calif., The Library, 1979. ix,539p. $35. ISBN: 0873281020.

A list of 125,000 items (mainly British and American) arranged by author, A-Z, with each manuscript categorized under one of 5 headings: verse, prose, letters, documents, other. *Class No:* 82(093)

Translations

[6560]
FARRAR, C.P. *and* **EVANS, A.P. Bibliography of English translations of medieval sources.** New York, Columbia Univ. Press; London, Oxford Univ. Press, 1946. xiv,534p.

Aims to include English translations published up to and during 1942 'of important literary sources produced during the period of Constantine the Great to the year 1500 within an area roughly inclusive of Europe, northern Africa and western Asia' (*Preface*). The main volume has almost 4,000 entries under authors, A-Z, with some title entries and subject headings. Data in each entry indicate *(a)* whether a given work has ever been translated; *(b)* whether an existing translation is adequate; *(c)* what relationship several translations of a given work bear to one another. Index of authors, editors, translators, titles, subjects, etc.

Supplemented by M.A.H. Ferguson's *Bibliography of English translations from medieval sources, 1943-1967* (New York, Columbia Univ. Press, 1974. 274p. $50. ISBN: 0231034350), which has 1,980 entries, similarly arranged and indexed. *Class No:* 82-03

[6561]
The Literatures of the world in English translation: a bibliography. New York, Ungar, 1967-70. 3v. in 4.

See separate entries for:
V.1 *The Greek and Latin literatures.* 1968. — at 870-03.
V.2 *The Slavic literatures.* 1967. — at 880(01).
V.3 *The Romance literatures.* 2 pts. 1970. — at 84.0.

Further vols. were planned on Celtic, Germanic and other European literatures, and on the literatures of Asia and Africa. *Class No:* 82-03

Digests & Abridgements

[6562]
HAYDN, H. *and* **FULLER, E. Thesaurus of book digests:** digests of the world's permanent writings from the ancient classics to current literature. New York, Crown, 1949 (repr. New York, Bonanza Books, 1968). 831p.

Very brief plot summaries, arranged A-Z by title, with indexes of authors and characters.

Continued by: *Thesaurus of book digests, 1950-1980*, by I. and A.D. Weiss (New York, Crown, 1980. 531p. $14.95. ISBN: 0517541750), which summarizes *c.*1,700 recent works of fiction and non-fiction. *Class No:* 82-05

[6563]
JOHN DAVIS WILLIAMS LIBRARY, UNIVERSITY OF MISSISSIPPI. Reference Dept. **Plot locator:** an index to summaries of fiction and nonfiction. New York, Garland, 1991. 704p. ISBN: 0815301456.

Indexes 82 sources, published 1902-90, which contain plot summaries of at least one page in length. Arranged by author, A-Z, then by individual work, with a title index. Covers plays and poems and certain nonfiction subjects, including history, philosophy, biography and politics. Duplicates C.K. Kolar's *Plot summary index* (2nd ed. Metuchen, N.J., Scarecrow, 1981) to a considerable extent, but does index several sources published in the 1980s.
Class No: 82-05

[6564]
Masterplots: 1,801 plot stories and critical evaluations from the world's finest literature. Magill, F.N., *& others, eds.* 2nd ed. Pasadena, Calif., Salem Press, 1996. 12v. $600. ISBN: 0893560847.

1st ed. 1976.

Plot summaries of works from 4000BC to the late 20th century, arranged A-Z by title and accompanied by biographical data on the author; details of setting and characters; review-essays of 400-1,000 words; and annotated bibliographies (a new feature in this ed.). Nonfiction works are included, as well as fiction, drama and poetry. 1st ed. had 2,010 entries, but many have been dropped for this revision as they are no longer on school/college curricula and 425 new titles brought in. These include *c.*75 works by Latin Americans, Asians and African Americans. All existing entries have been revised and updated. V.12 contains chronological, geographical, author and title indexes.

Some of the plot summaries for established classics originally appeared in 4 separate series under the title *Masterpieces of world literature in digest form* (New York, Harper, 1952-69).

Available on CD-ROM with all related series (See entry for *Masterplots complete CD-ROM*). *Class No:* 82-05

Stylistics

[6565]
BAILEY, R.W. *and* **BURTON, D.M. English stylistics:** a bibliography. Cambridge, Mass., M.I.T. Press, 1968. xxii,198p.

1. Bibliographical sources - 2. Language and style before 1900 (6 subsections for periods, listing major works and commentary, and general secondary sources) - 3. English stylistics in the 20th century (11 subsections). Most items annotated. 2 indexes: styles under scrutiny (*i.e.* authors) and critics. *Class No:* 82-08

[6566]
BENNETT, J.R. A Bibliography of stylistics and related criticism, 1967-1983. New York, Modern Language Assoc. of America, 1986. 405p. $37.50. ISBN: 0873521420.

Carries forward the work of Hatzfeld and Bailey and Burton (*qq.v.*) through 1983. 1,484 annotated entries in a classified arrangement which is clearly explained in the introductory matter. Many references to book reviews. Useful appended features include an annotated chronology from Saussure (1878) to Showalter (1985); a classification of critics by theory and method; and an annotated introductory reading list on stylistics. Indexes of terms, literary authors and anonymous works, critics as subjects, and critics as authors. *Class No:* 82-08

[6567]
HATZFELD, H. A Critical bibliography of the new stylistics applied to the Romance literatures. Chapel Hill, N.C., Univ. of North Carolina Press, 1953-66 (repr. New York, Johnson, 1971). 2v.

V.1 *1900-1952.* 1953. xxii,302p. ISBN: 0384217702.

V.2 *1953-1965.* 1966. 183p. ISBN: 0384217753.

Bibliographical survey of style investigation, with running commentary, listing general studies and studies of individual authors and works. Indexes of style investigators and of proper names, titles, stylistic terms, etc.

An expanded edition of v.1 has been published in Spanish as *Bibliografía crítica de la nueva estilística, aplicada a las literaturas románicas* (Madrid, Gredos, 1955. 660p.), and

....(contd.)

supplemented by Hatzfeld and Le Hir's *Essai de bibliographie critique de stylistique française et romane (1955-1960)* (Paris, Presses Universitaires de France, 1961. 313p.). *Class No:* 82-08

[6568]
WALES, K. A Dictionary of stylistics. Harlow, Longman, 1989. 504p. £22.99. ISBN: 0582031397.

Lengthy explanatory entries on over 600 specialist terms, with references to further sources of information. Confusing system of cross-references. Bibliography of *c.*500 sources. *Class No:* 82-08

Metaphor

[6569]
Metaphor: a bibliography of post-1970 publications. Van Noppen, J.P., *and others, comps.* Amsterdam, Benjamins, 1985. x,497p. Hfl.173. (*Library and information sources in linguistics.*) ISBN: 9027237379.

Follows W. Shibles' *Metaphor: an annotated bibliography* (Whitewater, Wis., Language Press, 1971). 4,193 entries, arranged by author with 4 indexes.

Continued by *Metaphor II: a classified bibliography of publications, 1985-90* (1990. 350p. Hfl.147. ISBN: 9027237468), with over 3,500 items. *Class No:* 82-080

Writing & Writing Techniques

Bibliographies

[6570]
HOWELL, J.B. Style manuals of the English-speaking world. Phoenix, Ariz., Oryx Press, 1983. 152p. $21. ISBN: 0897740890.

Lists the contents of 266 style manuals, identifies special features, and comments on the manuals' own bibliographic styles. Index of authors, titles, and subjects. *Class No:* 82-081(01)

[6571]
The Writer's advisor: a guide to books and articles about writing novels, short stories, poetry, dramatic scripts, screenplays, magazine articles, biographies, technical articles and books, as well as a guide to information about literary agents, marketing, and a wide range of legal and business materials of interest to full- and part-time writers. Alkire, L.G., *comp.* Detroit, Gale, 1985. xv,452p. $70. ISBN: 0810320932.

A bibliography covering, as the subtitle indicates, all aspects of creative writing. Nearly 800 books and over 3,000 periodical articles, most of them published between the late 1960s and 1984, are included under 34 headings, the books being described while the articles are merely listed. Indexes of authors, book titles, and subjects. Select lists of literary agents and writers' organizations. *Class No:* 82-081(01)

Encyclopaedias & Dictionaries

[6572]
The Oxford dictionary for writers and editors. Oxford English Dictionary Department, *comp.* Oxford, Oxford Univ. Press, 1981. xiv,448p. £9.99. ISBN: 0192129708.

Paperback reprints have appeared as *The Oxford writers' dictionary*.

Presents the house style of the Oxford Univ. Press, providing guidance, in a single A-Z sequence, on questions

....*(contd.)*
of usage, spelling, abbreviations, etc. Many proper names and foreign words and phrases included. *Class No:* 82-081(03)

[6573]

Writing A to Z: the terms, procedures, and facts of the writing business defined, explained, and put within reach. Polking, K., *and others, eds.* Cincinnati, Ohio, Writer's Digest, 1990. 545p. £12.95. ISBN: 0898794358.

A revised version of Polking's *Writer's encyclopedia* (1983) in which, according to *Reference Books Bulletin* (v.87(6), Nov. 15, 1990, p.683), the text of the 1,200 entries is virtually unchanged. 8 new charts and samples have been added to the original 63 and these are now scattered throughout the text rather than appended as before. Bibliography of sources. *Class No:* 82-081(03)

Handbooks & Manuals

[6574]

The Chicago manual of style, for authors, editors, and copywriters. 14th ed. Chicago, Univ. of Chicago Press, 1993. ix,921p. illus. $40. ISBN: 0226103897; 0226103897.

1st ed. 1906; 13th ed. 1982. First 12 eds. entitled *A Manual of style.*

Considered the standard reference tool in the US. 3 major sections (Bookmaking; Style; Production and printing), each with a detailed table of contents, covering all aspects of book production. The section on style makes up over half the book. Glossary of technical terms (29p.). Bibliography (9p.). Thorough index, with references to paragraph numbers. This ed. represents a major revision and expansion (nearly 200p. longer than previously) to accommodate changes in publishing practice since 1982, many of them brought about by the increased use of computer technology.

A more concise and very accessible American source is *Merriam-Webster's manual for writers and editors* (Springfield, Mass., Merriam-Webster, 1998. 424p. $17.95. ISBN: 087779622x), which is a revised ed. of *Webster's standard American style manual* (1985). *Class No:* 82-081(035)

[6575]

GIBALDI, J. MLA handbook for writers of research papers. 4th ed. New York, Modern Language Assoc. of America, 1995. xviii,293p. $13.50. ISBN: 0873525655.

1st ed. 1977; 3rd ed. 1988.

A comprehensive guide which covers research and writing, the format of the research paper, citations, etc. 4th ed. has new material on the use of electronic catalogues and online databases in research, the use of computers to compile bibliographies, and the citation of electronic publications, plus an expanded section on punctuation. Thorough index. *Class No:* 82-081(035)

[6576]

GIBALDI, J. MLA style manual and guide to scholarly publishing. 2nd ed. New York, Modern Language Assoc. of America, 1998. viii,343p. $25. ISBN: 0873526996.

1st ed. 1985, as *The MLA style manual.*

A standard guide for humanities scholars, which offers guidance on how to prepare a manuscript for submission. 2nd ed. begins with an expanded chapter on the publication process, from ms. to published work. Subsequent chapters cover legal issues, stylistic conventions, and the preparation of books, theses and dissertations. Gives a comprehensive presentation of MLA documentation style, including citation of electronic sources. Index. *Class No:* 82-081(035)

[6577]

KANE, T.S. The New Oxford guide to writing. New York, Oxford Univ. Press, 1988. viii,327p. £9.99. ISBN: 0195090594.

A practical guide for the American writer. 7 parts: 1. The Writing process - 2. The Essay - 3. The Expository paragraph - 4. The Sentence - 5. Diction - 6. Description and narration - 7. Punctuation. Illustrated by numerous examples of successful prose. Name and subject indexes. *Class No:* 82-081(035)

[6578]

The McGraw-Hill style manual: a concise guide for writers and editors. Longyear, M., *ed.* New York, McGraw-Hill, 1983. 256p. ISBN: 0070386765.

1. General standards - 2. Technical standards - 3. Grammar, usage and punctuation - 4. From manuscript to book. Bibliography (7p.). Good index and clear layout make this an ideal desk reference for the American writer. Particularly good on scientific writing. *Class No:* 82-081(035)

[6579]

MHRA style book: notes for authors, editors, and writers of theses. Maney, A.S. *and* Smallwood, R.L., *eds.* 5th ed. London, Modern Humanities Research Assoc., 1996. viii,100p. £5. ISBN: 0947623612.

1st ed. 1971; 4th ed. 1991.

A concise, inexpensive guide to writing and editing, which has been extensively revised in recent editions to take account of changes in printing technology and modern editorial practice. New sections have been added dealing with the preparation of indexes and book reviews, and several of the others expanded. *Class No:* 82-081(035)

[6580]

The New York Public Library writer's guide to style and usage. New York, HarperCollins, 1994. 838p. $35. ISBN: 0062700642.

A new guide for writers and editors which covers a wide range of subjects from usage, grammar and style to manuscript preparation, production and printing. The 18 contributors provide numerous illustrative examples in the text. Annotated bibliography of reference works. Subject index. A potential rival for *The Chicago manual,* 'this guide may attract a wider audience with its particular focus on the needs of writers and editors who have become directly involved in layout and production through computing technologies' (*Choice*, v.32(4), Dec. 1994, p.578). *Class No:* 82-081(035)

[6581]

Style manual for authors, editors and printers. 5th ed. Canberra, Australian Government Publishing Service, 1994. xi,468p. A$39.95. ISBN: 0644297700.

1st ed. 1966.

Originally published as a reference book for public servants, but now widely used in Australian publishing circles. 3 main sections: Writing and editing; Preparing copy for printing; Publishing and bookmaking. Appendices include lists of titles, honours and forms of address. Glossary, bibliography and index. All chapters updated for this ed., with particular attention paid to non-discriminatory language, proofreading, indexing, notes, references and bibliographies. *Class No:* 82-081(035)

[6582]

TURABIAN, K.L. A Manual for writers of term papers, theses and dissertations. 6th ed., rev. by J. Grossman and A. Bennett. Chicago, Univ. of Chicago Press, 1996. x,308p. illus. $27.50. ISBN: 0226816265.

1st ed. 1937; 5th ed. 1987.

A thorough revision of a long-established handbook, bringing it into line with *The Chicago manual of style* (14th ed. 1993) and recognizing the widespread use of computers for composition. 14 chapters, clearly divided into numbered paragraphs, dealing with abbreviations, punctuation, quotations, footnotes, bibliographies, illustrations, etc., and containing numerous examples. Select bibliography. Index. *Class No:* 82-081(035)

Yearbooks & Directories

[6583]

Novel and short story writer's market, 1989-. Cincinnati, Ohio, Writer's Digest, 1989-. Annual. ISSN: 08979812.

Succeeds *Fiction writer's market*, which appeared annually, 1981-88, and lists *c.*1,900 US markets for novels and short stories. Also includes articles on the writing and marketing of fiction. *Class No:* 82-081(058)

[6584]

Writers' and artists' yearbook, 1906-. A directory for writers, artists, playwrights, writers for film, radio and television, designers, illustrators and photographers London, Black, 1906- . Annual.

The 1998 ed. (vii,677p. £11.99. ISBN: 0713647213) has 15 sections and many subsections. Much of the book is a directory of UK and Irish newspapers, magazines, book publishers, radio and TV companies, literary agents, etc., with addresses and details of material accepted and payment rates. In addition there is a wide range of general information, with practical articles on finance, copyright, publishing practice, preparing material for publication, etc., which are regularly revised, plus lists of literary societies, awards, and prizes. Subject index. *Class No:* 82-081(058)

[6585]

The Writer's handbook. Turner, B., *ed.* London, Macmillan, 1987-. Annual.

A directory which claims to cover every possible market for writing, listing UK and Irish publishers; small presses; literary agents; national and regional newspapers; magazines; TV and radio companies; and film, video and theatre producers. Also lists professional associations; regional arts associations; libraries; literary prizes; writers' courses; and literature festivals. Selective lists of US and European publishers. Companies index and thorough subject index.

Differs from most directories in its inclusion of personal, often provocative, comments in many of its entries, based on the experience of professional writers, and in giving key contact names wherever possible. The 1998 ed. (1997. 742p. £12.99. ISBN: 033367538x), has over 5,000 entries and represents excellent value. *Class No:* 82-081(058)

[6586]

The Writer's handbook, 1936-. Boston, The Writer, 1936-. Annual. ISSN: 00842710.

The standard guide to American literary publishing, comprising articles on the technique of writing (often by well-known authors) and on the practicalities of getting published, followed by a market guide which provides relevant information on periodicals, book publishers, and

....(contd.)

other outlets such as radio and TV. Also lists literary prizes, grants and fellowships, and organizations for writers. Index to markets. *Class No:* 82-081(058)

[6587]

Writer's market: where and how to sell what you write Cincinnati, Ohio, Writer's Digest, 1922-. Annual. ISSN: 00842729.

A directory for writers hoping to get published in the US. 1995 ed. (999p.) includes entries for over 4,000 publishers and publications (700 of them new) in classified lists, giving addresses, contact names, editorial needs, pay rates, submission requirements, and tips from editors. Also contains practical advice on marketing manuscripts, tax, copyright, etc. and lists of author's agents and literary awards. Subject indexes to publishers and agents, and general index. *Class No:* 82-081(058)

Editing

[6588]

ANDERSON, D. A Guide to information sources for the preparation, editing and production of documents. Aldershot, Gower, 1989. xii,142p. £25. ISBN: 0566057433.

Deals with dictionaries, reference books, manuals and guidelines available in English, including the output of international bodies like Unesco and the International Organization for Standardization. Chronological arrangement from document writing through to final publication. Bibliography gives full details of 229 works covered in the text. Directory of useful addresses. Index. *Class No:* 82-083

[6589]

BUTCHER, J. Copy-editing: the Cambridge handbook for editors, authors and publishers. 3rd ed. Cambridge, Cambridge Univ. Press, 1992. xii,471p. illus. £27.95. ISBN: 0521400740.

1st ed. 1975; 2nd ed. 1981.

A detailed and definitive manual for those who prepare typescripts and illustrations for printing and publication, based on the practice of Cambridge Univ. Press. 15 chapters with numerous subsections, very clearly arranged. 13 appendices, including useful checklist of copy-editing. Glossary (18p.). Select bibliography (2p.). Index. Entirely revised and reset for this ed., with more examples, a fuller index and 5 new appendices. New sections include one on dealing with author-supplied typescripts on disk and, inevitably, one on avoiding bias and sexism. *Class No:* 82-083

Rhetoric & Oratory

[6590]

Eighteenth century British and American rhetoric and rhetoricians: critical studies and sources. Moran, M.G., *ed.* Westport, Conn., Greenwood, 1994. 328p. $85. ISBN: 0313279098.

Provides critical overviews of 33 major and minor figures in lengthy articles which include bibliographies of primary and secondary material. Bibliography of general sources on 18th-century rhetoric. Writers covered include Burke, Hume, Locke and Wollstonecraft. *Class No:* 82-085

[6591]

Encyclopedia of rhetoric and composition: communication from Ancient Times to the Information Age. Enos, T., *ed.* New York, Garland, 1996. 832p. $100. ISBN: 0824072006.

288 scholars have contributed articles on all aspects of rhetoric, including history (*e.g.* Liturgy, Marxist rhetoric), tools (Hyperbole, Metaphor) and practitioners (Derrida, Foucault), with coverage tailored to meet the needs of US teachers and students. Each entry is followed by a bibliography of key texts and recommended reading. Cross-references and comprehensive index. *Class No:* 82-085

[6592]

Historical rhetoric: an annotated bibliography of selected sources in English. Horner, W.B., *ed.* Boston, Hall, 1980. 294p. ISBN: 0816181918.

5 sections, by specialists, tracing the history of rhetoric from ancient Greece to the English-speaking world: Classical period; Middle Ages; Renaissance; 18th century; 19th century. Each has introductory survey followed by annotated lists of primary and secondary works. Index. *Class No:* 82-085

[6593]

LANHAM, R.A. A Handlist of rhetorical terms. 2nd ed. Berkeley, Calif., Univ. of California Press, 1991. 205p. $35. ISBN: 0520076680.

1st ed. 1969.

List of terms, A-Z, with definitions and examples. Bibliography of works cited. According to *Choice*, v.29(11/12), July/Aug. 1992, p.1658, the new ed. is 'vastly more readable' and has more, as well as more contemporary, examples. *Class No:* 82-085

[6594]

LAUSBERG, H. Handbook of literary rhetoric: a foundation for literary study. Orton, D.E. *and* Anderson, R.D., *eds.* Translation of 2nd ed. Leiden, Brill, 1998. 954p. $224. ISBN: 9004107053.

Originally published 1963, as *Handbuch der literarischen Rhetorik*; 2nd ed. 1973.

The first appearance in English of a work which enjoys unrivalled authority in its formal description of rhetorical techniques and which has for many years been a standard reference work in the field. Comprehensive bibliography. Detailed index. *Class No:* 82-085

[6595]

MURPHY, J.J. Medieval rhetoric: a select bibliography. 2nd ed. Toronto, Univ. of Toronto Press, 1989. xviii,198p. $37.50 (*Toronto medieval bibliographies.*) ISBN: 0802057500.

1st ed. 1971.

971 entries in 9 sections, covering subjects like letter-writing, poetics, grammar, and sermon theory, with key works annotated. Includes both primary and secondary sources. Appendix has list of 40 basic works in the field. Index.

Murphy has also compiled *Renaissance rhetoric: a short title catalog of works on rhetorical theory from the beginning of printing to AD1700, with special attention to the holdings of the Bodleian Library, Oxford* (New York, Garland, 1981. xv,353p. ISBN: 0824094875). *Class No:* 82-085

[6596]

PLETT, H.F. English Renaissance rhetoric and poetics: a systematic bibliography of primary and secondary sources. Leiden, Brill, 1995. 526p. $161.50. ISBN: 9004103430.

Claims to be the first comprehensive reference work on the subject and lists over 500 books on rhetoric and poetics published in the British Isles, 1479-1660, giving library call numbers and details of further historical and modern editions and relevant secondary literature. Also lists bibliographies and *c.*2,000 20th-century works on applied rhetoric and poetics. Indexes. *Class No:* 82-085

Literary Criticism

Bibliographies

[6597]

FROST, W. *and* **VALIQUETTE, M. Feminist literary criticism:** a bibliography of journal articles, 1975-1981. New York and London, Garland, 1988. xxiv,867p. ISBN: 0824077881.

Lists 1,947 articles from *c.*450 English-language periodicals. Entries are arranged in 6 major sections: Textual and contextual studies; Folklore and oral tradition; Interviews; Language and gender; Pedagogy and research; Theory; with the first section further divided by time period. Each entry comprises citation, set of key words indicating themes (often more than 10), explanatory note if necessary, and list of specific works/authors concerned, if any. Subject index, author/title index and index of critics.

Updated in part by *Feminist criticism of American women poets: an annotated bibliography, 1975-1993*, by L. Sakelliou-Schultz (New York, Garland, 1994. 384p. $54. ISBN: 0824070844). *Class No:* 82-09(01)

[6598]

—GELFAND, E.D. *and* HULES, V.T. French feminist criticism: women, language and literature; an annotated bibliography. New York and London, Garland, 1985. lii,318p. (*Garland bibliographies of modern critics and critical schools.*) ISBN: 082409252x.

'The bibliography lists not only the work of the most well-known and prolific theorists ... but all books, essays, and articles from the period 1970-1982 that concentrate on women and language, including work by feminist scholars in the United States who are participating in the elucidation of French feminist theory' (*Preface*). 555 entries with lengthy evaluative annotations. Appendix lists special periodical issues. Title and subject indexes. *Class No:* 82-09(01)

[6599]

—HUMM, M. An Annotated critical bibliography of feminist criticism. Brighton, Harvester; Boston, Hall, 1987. xi,240p. $40. ISBN: 071081061x, UK; 0816189374, US.

Includes a major section on feminist *literary* criticism (p.35-70), which lists 142 works on literature in general rather than on specific writers, arranged chronologically 1966-86. Brief annotations. Author and subject indexes. *Class No:* 82-09(01)

[6600]

Garland bibliographies of modern critics and critical schools. Cain, W.E., *ed.* New York, Garland, 1982-94. v.1-19, 21 (in progress).

V.1 *Eliseo Vivas*, by H.M. Curtler. 1982. 114p. ISBN: 0824093003.

V.2 *Arthur O. Lovejoy*, by D.J. Wilson. 1982. 240p. ISBN: 0824092570.

V.3 *John Crowe Ransom*, by T.D. Young. 1982. 213p.

....(*contd.*)
ISBN: 082409249x.

V.4 *Michael Foucault,* by M.P. Clark. 1983. 608p. ISBN: 0824092538.

V.5 *Elder Olson,* by J.L. Battersby. 1982. 327p. ISBN: 0824092546.

V.6 *Roland Barthes,* by S. Freedman and C.A. Taylor. 1981. 445p. ISBN: 0824092929.

V.7 *R.S. Crane,* by J.C. Sherwood. 1982. 129p. $53. ISBN: 0824092503.

V.8 *Sir William Empson,* by F. Day. 1982. 272p. ISBN: 0824092074.

V.9 *French feminist criticism,* by E.D. Gelfand and V.T. Hules. 1982. 380p. ISBN: 082409252x.

V.10 *Jacques Lacan,* by M. Clark. 1984. 2v. ISBN: 0824088484.

V.11 *R.G. Collingwood,* by D.S. Taylor. 1988. 296p. ISBN: 0824077970.

V.12 *F.R. and Q.D. Leavis,* by M. Kinch and others. 1988. 588p. $99. ISBN: 0824088948.

V.13 *Ernst Cassirer,* by W. Eggers and S. Mayer. 1983. 500p. $73. ISBN: 0824089928.

V.14 *Cleanth Brooks,* by J.M. Walsh. 1989. 478p. $66. ISBN: 0824049411.

V.15 *Edmund Wilson,* by F. Day. 300p. ISBN: 0824006895.

V.16 *Black aesthetic criticism,* by R. Martin. 250p. ISBN: 0824068904.

V.17 *Feminist criticism of American women poets, 1975-1993,* by L. Sakelliou-Schultz. 1994. 384p. $54. ISBN: 0824070844.

V.18 *Jacques Derrida,* by W.R. Schultz and L.L.B. Fried. 1992. 944p. $150. ISBN: 0824048725.

V.19 *Lionel Trilling,* by T.M. Leitch. 1992. 672p. $105. ISBN: 082407028x.

V.21 *Contemporary Canadian and US women of letters,* by T.M.F. Gerry. 1993. 312p. $49. ISBN: 0824069897.

A series of comprehensive, annotated bibliographies of the major modern critics. V.12, on the Leavises, lists 465 primary sources and nearly 1,700 secondary sources, with substantial, detailed abstracts, and has author, title and subject indexes. *Class No:* 82-09(01)

[6601]

Magill's bibliography of literary criticism: selected sources for the study of more than 2,500 outstanding works of western literature. Magill, F.N., *ed.* Englewood Cliffs, N.J., Salem Press, 1979. 4v. ISBN: 0893561886.

Over 36,000 citations to critical studies in books and periodicals of 2,546 works by 613 authors, with the emphasis on English-language criticism published in the 1960s and 1970s. A-Z arrangement by literary author, then by individual work. Covers western literature from *Gilgamesh* to 1978, with 12-25 citations per work. Title index in v.4. *Class No:* 82-09(01)

[6602]

MARSHALL, D.G. Contemporary critical theory: a selective bibliography. New York, MLA, 1993. 201p. $32. ISBN: 0873529634.

An annotated guide to key reference works and monographs, including works by and studies of major individual critics. Nearly 1,700 entries in 14 thematic sections. Cross-references. List of specialist journals. Author index. 'Marshall's book has no effective competition; it is one of the few reference works all academic libraries should have for literature studies' (*Choice*, v.31(6), Feb. 1994, p.917). *Class No:* 82-09(01)

[6603]

MILLER, J.M. French structuralism: an annotated bibliography. New York, Garland, 1981. xiii,553p.

*c.*5,500 entries in 3 sections covering general and introductory works; the applications of structuralism to various disciplines; and (likely to be most useful) works by and about 7 individuals: Althusser, Barthes, Derrida, Foucault, Lacan, Goldmann, and Lévi-Strauss. Includes much foreign-language material. Nonevaluative annotations. *Class No:* 82-09(01)

[6604]

Recent work in critical theory, 1989-1995: an annotated bibliography. Baker, W. *and* Womack, K., *eds.* Westport, Conn., Greenwood, 1996. 608p. £79.50. (*Bibliographies and indexes in world literature.*) ISBN: 0313294348.

1,876 entries for English-language monographs, essay collections and reference works, arranged in one general section and 6 on theoretical approaches. Annotations cite themes and list essays in collections. *Class No:* 82-09(01)

[6605]

Research in critical theory since 1965: a classified bibliography. Orr, L., *ed.* Westport, Conn., Greenwood, 1989. 480p. $85. (*Bibliographies and indexes in world literature.*) ISBN: 0313263884.

Lists 5,523 works (books, articles and dissertations) in English, French and German, published 1965-87. 12 sections, each covering a different approach to literary criticism (*e.g.* Semiotics, Feminist Criticism, Marxist Criticism, Structuralism, etc.) and some having sub-sections. Sectional indexes, plus a general index of subjects and theorists and a full author index. *Class No:* 82-09(01)

[6606]

The Year's work in critical and cultural theory, 1991-. Oxford, Blackwell, 1994-. v.1-. Annual. ISSN: 10774254.

Similar in style and format to *The Year's work in English studies* (*q.v.*). V.5, *1995*, (1998. viii,412p. £70) reviews over 300 titles in 21 chapters, each followed by a full book list. 2 main sections: 1. Critical theory - 2. Culture and communications. Scope goes far beyond literary criticism to include popular music, film and cultural policy. Index. *Class No:* 82-09(01)

Indexes

[6607]

WEINER, A.R. *and* **MEANS, S. Literary criticism index.** 2nd ed. Metuchen, N.J., Scarecrow, 1994. 580p. $66. ISBN: 0810826658.

1st ed. 1984.

Not a direct index to critical studies, but provides references to 146 bibliographies or checklists of criticism, *i.e.* the 86 covered in 1st ed. plus 60 additional works. Entries are arranged A-Z by literary author and refer to bibliographies which contain references to critical studies of his/her work: both general studies and criticism of individual works. Like all works of this kind, its usefulness is limited in libraries which do not hold a substantial number of the sources indexed. *Class No:* 82-09(014)

Encyclopaedias

[6608]

Critical survey of literary theory. Magill, F.N., *ed.* Englewood Cliffs, N.J., Salem Press, 1988. 4v. $300. ISBN: 0893563900.

Vols. 1-3 contain signed essays on over 250 critics and theorists, listing their works (including non-critical writings), assessing their career and influence, evaluating their writings, and listing selected secondary sources. Coverage is international and ranges from Aristotle to the 1980s. V.4 contains 12 essays on periods and schools of literary criticsm, glossary of critical terms, and index to the set. *Class No:* 82-09(031)

[6609]

Encyclopedia of contemporary literary theory: approaches, scholars, terms. Makaryk, I.R., *ed.* Toronto, Univ. of Toronto Press, 1993. xiv,656p. $150. ISBN: 0802059147.

A guide to 'the trends, tendencies and critics who have commanded attention over the past 50 years' (*Introduction*) in 3 separate A-Z sequences of double-column articles. Part I has 48 substantial essays (average nearly 5p.) on major schools of criticism; Part II assesses the work and influence of over 130 critics; Part III identifies and explains over 120 key terms. Substantial bibliography with each entry, but this leads to much wasteful repetition. Numerous cross-references but no index. 170 contributors, most of them Canadian. A lengthy review in *TLS* (no.4763, July 15, 1994, p.8-9) is critical of patchy bibliographies, inconsistencies between articles and, most disturbingly, lack of objectivity in the unquestioning coverage of the Franco-American schools of the 1960s and 'a remarkably coherent, collective ignoring of those writers who have dared to rock the boat.' *Class No:* 82-09(031)

[6610]

Encyclopedia of feminist literary theory. Kowaleski-Wallace, E., *ed.* New York, Garland, 1996. 472p. £69.95. ISBN: 0815308248.

Entries on topics, themes, schools, terms and critics, each accompanied by a bibliography. Emphasis throughout is on usage in the US and UK since the 1970s. Indexes of names, subjects, keywords and related topics. *Class No:* 82-09(031)

[6611]

Encyclopedia of literature and criticism. Coyle, M., *and others, eds.* London, Routledge, 1990. xix,1299p. £95. ISBN: 0415020654.

As with the same publisher's *Encyclopedia of language* (*q.v.*) the title is misleading. This is actually a collection of 90 essays (average length 14p.) reviewing 20th-century thinking on different aspects of the criticism of *English* literature. They cover genres, critical schools, book production, contexts (*e.g.* literature and music) and various national literatures in English, and each has a list of recommended further reading (only *c.*12 titles) and of works cited. 90 contributors. Index. *Class No:* 82-09(031)

[6612]

The Johns Hopkins guide to literary theory and criticism. Groden, M. *and* Kreiswirth, M., *eds.* Baltimore, Md., Johns Hopkins Univ. Press, 1994. xiii,775p. £45. ISBN: 0801845602.

A single sequence of 226 signed entries (average 3p.) on schools, movements, countries, historical periods, individual critics and influential figures from other disciplines (*e.g.* Chomsky, Freud). All entries have selective bibliographies

.... *(contd.)*

of primary and secondary material. The work of over 200 (mainly North American) scholars. Amply cross-referenced. Name and topic indexes. *Class No:* 82-09(031)

[6613]

SELDEN, R., *& others*. A Reader's guide to contemporary literary theory. 4th ed. Hemel Hempstead, Prentice Hall, 1997. 264p. £13.95. ISBN: 0134919521.

1st ed. 1985; 3rd ed. 1993. Previous eds. published by Harvester Wheatsheaf.

7 chapters on major schools (Marxism, feminism, postmodernism, etc., with subsections on individual critics and one on new developments. Substantial bibliographies (at least 2p.) after each chapter, listing basic texts, introductory studies and further reading. Index. *Class No:* 82-09(031)

[6614]

—HUMM, M. A Reader's guide to contemporary feminist literary criticism. Hemel Hempstead, Harvester Wheatsheaf, 1994. x,309p. £10.95. ISBN: 0745011942.

10 chapters on different schools, with subsections on individual critics. Bibliographies after each chapter list basic texts, introductory studies and further reading. Index. *Class No:* 82-09(031)

Excerpts

[6615]

Black literature criticism: excerpts from criticism of the most significant works of Black authors over the past 200 years. Draper, J.P., *ed.* Detroit, Gale, 1992. 3v. £211. ISBN: 0810379295.

A closed set in the same format as Gale's *Contemporary literary criticism* and similar series, from which over half of the entries have been extracted, the others having been specially compiled for *BLC*. 125 authors covered, from the 18th century to the present, 88 of them North American, 24 African and the rest from the Caribbean. As with the same publisher's *Black writers* (*q.v.*), no Britons are included. A-Z arrangement with indexes of authors, titles and nationalities. *Class No:* 82-09(082.200)

[6616]

Classical and medieval literature criticism. Detroit, Gale, 1988-. v.1- (in progress). illus. £107 per vol. ISSN: 08960011.

Covers authors active before 1400, including philosophers, scientists and political thinkers as well as literary writers, with each vol. carrying lengthy entries on 4-6 authors or works in the style of *Contemporary literary criticism*. V.1 exemplifies the truly international scope of the coverage, with entries on Apuleius, *Beowulf, La Chanson de Roland*, Homer's *Iliad, The Tale of Genji*, and *The Song of Igor's campaign*. Cumulative indexes, including author index to all of Gale's literary criticism series, in each vol.

23 vols. published by the end of 1997. *Class No:* 82-09(082.200)

[6617]

Contemporary literary criticism: excerpts from criticism of today's novelists, poets, playwrights, short story writers, scriptwriters, and other creative writers. Detroit, Gale, 1973- v.1- (in progress). illus. £107 per vol. ISSN: 00913421.

Each vol. contains selected, often lengthy, excerpts from criticism of a wide range of authors (as indicated by the subtitle), with English-language authors predominant. Entries are arranged A-Z, with excerpts appearing chronologically under each author, and also include a biocritical introduction to the author, photograph, list of principal works, and select

.... *(contd.)*
bibliography of further critical and biographical studies. Authors may be re-introduced in later vols. as new works become the subject of criticism. Title, author and nationality indexes in each vol. Softbound cumulative title index published annually.

103 vols. published by the end of 1997, covering over 4,000 authors. Recent vols. contain 8-12 author entries with many lengthy, excerpts, whereas earlier vols. had more entries (over 150 in some) with fewer excerpts.

A selection of entries relating to 150 major authors is available online via GaleNet as *Contemporary literary criticism select*. *Class No:* 82-09(082.200)

[6618]

Literature criticism from 1400 to 1800: excerpts from criticism of the works of fifteenth, sixteenth, seventeenth, and eighteenth-century novelists, poets, playwrights, philosophers, and other creative writers, from the first published critical appraisals to current evaluations. Detroit, Gale, 1984-. v.1- (in progress). illus. £107 per vol.

Early vols. followed the format of *Contemporary literary criticism*, with 7-9 authors covered in each, but later vols. are devoted to specific literary or historical topics, *e.g.* Renaissance Utopian literature, English mystery plays, etc. Excludes Shakespeare, for whom see Gale's *Shakespearean criticism* series. Cumulative author index to all Gale criticism series in each vol.

39 vols. published by the end of 1997. *Class No:* 82-09(082.200)

[6619]

Modern women writers. Robinson, L.S., *ed.* New York, Continuum, 1996. 4v. $400. ISBN: 0826408230.

Reprints critical writings on about 570 20th-century authors from a wide range of countries, including writers of popular genre fiction. Entries are arranged by author, A-Z, with the excerpts in chronological order. Includes some excerpts translated from foreign languages. Index of critics, but no index of nationality or language. *Class No:* 82-09(082.200)

[6620]

MOULTON, C.W. Library of literary criticism of English and American authors. Buffalo, Moulton, 1901-05 (repr. Gloucester, Mass., P. Smith, 1959). 8v. illus. $190. ISBN: 0844613185.

Entries on authors from 680-1904, containing brief biographical information followed by extracts, often lengthy, from critical studies. Exact references to sources.

Moulton's library of literary criticism of English and American authors through the beginning of the 20th century (New York, Ungar, 1966. 4v. $260. ISBN: 0804431906) is an abridged, revised, and updated version, ed. by M. Tucker, which includes excerpts from criticism published up to 1964. Some authors have been dropped and 11 new ones added. Index of critics in v.4. *Class No:* 82-09(082.200)

[6621]

—The Critical temper: a survey of modern criticism on English and American literature from the beginnings to the twentieth century. Tucker, M., *ed.* New York, Ungar, 1969-89. 5v. $75 per vol.

Supplements C.W. Moulton's *Library of literary criticism* (*q.v.*), providing excerpts from 20th-century critical studies of over 200 authors covered by that standard work. Vols. 1-3 (1969. ISBN: 0804433038) cover Old English to Shakespeare; Milton to Romantic literature; and Victorian and American literature respectively. V.4 (1979. 550p. ISBN: 0804433070) and v.5 (1989. 600p. ISBN: 0804404359) are supplementary vols. containing recent criticism on all periods and including some authors previously omitted. *Class No:* 82-09(082.200)

[6622]

The New Moulton's library of literary criticism: pre-twentieth century criticism of British and American literature to 1904. Bloom, H., *ed.* Broomall, Pa., Chelsea House, 1985-88. 11v. $770. (*Chelsea House library of literary criticism.*)

A thorough revision of C.W. Moulton's *Library of literary criticism* (*q.v.*), with some authors omitted and over 250 added. Contains excerpts from pre-1900 critical studies of over 550 authors, chronologically arranged in vols. 1-10 from *Beowulf* to Kate Chopin. Entries are longer than in the original series, the space allocated to each reflecting their reputation. V.11 contains index to critics, complete table of contents for the series, and bibliography of all separate publications by each author covered.

The Major authors edition of the New Moulton's Library (1985-88. 6v. $395. ISBN: 0877548145) reprints entries on 68 authors from Chaucer to Stephen Crane in vols. 1-5, with some additional critical material provided. Index and bibliography in v.6. *Class No:* 82-09(082.200)

[6623]

—The Critical perspective: twentieth-century criticism of British and American literature to 1904. Bloom, H., *ed.* Broomall, Pa., Chelsea House. 11v. $745. (*Chelsea House library of literary criticism.*) ISBN: 0877547890.

Excerpts from 20th-century criticism of 296 of the writers covered in *The New Moulton's Library*. Author entries arranged chronologically in vols. 1-10, with index and bibliography in v.11.

The Chelsea House literary criticism series is compared with Ungar's *Library of literary criticism* series in *Booklist*, v.85(11), Feb.1, 1989, p.917: 'Excerpts in the Ungar series are freely edited, while Bloom tries to retain the flavor of the original by making fewer changes ... Excerpts in the Ungar series are very brief while Bloom makes a point of offering complete texts as well as extracts'. The Chelsea House series also includes biographical essays and portraits. *Class No:* 82-09(082.200)

[6624]

Nineteenth-century literary criticism: excerpts from criticism of the works of novelists, poets, playwrights, short story writers, and other creative writers who lived between 1800 and 1900, from the first published critical appraisals to current evaluations. Detroit, Gale, 1981-. v.1- (in progress). illus. £107 per vol. ISSN: 07321864.

Covers 19th-century writers (around 10 per vol.) of all genres and nationalities following the well-established *Contemporary literary criticism* format. Scope extends beyond literary authors to include philosophers and writers on political, social and economic affairs. Every 4th vol. carries articles on topics that cannot be covered under the author approach.

Each vol. has cumulative author index to all Gale literary criticism series and cumulative title, author, nationality and topic indexes to *NCLC*.

64 vols. published by the end of 1997. *Class No:* 82-09(082.200)

[6625]

Twentieth-century literary criticism: excerpts from criticism of the works of novelists, poets, playwrights, short story writers, and other creative writers who died between 1900 and 1960, from the first published critical appraisals to current evaluations. Detroit, Gale, 1978-. v.1- (in progress). illus. £107 per vol. ISSN: 02768178.

Covers writers from the period immediately prior to *Contemporary literary criticism*, using that work's successful format. Recent vols. have included fewer author entries (8-12 per vol.) but more excerpts per author. Every 4th vol. carries articles on major literary topics and movements rather than specific authors.

Each vol. has cumulative author index to all Gale literary criticism series and cumulative title and nationality indexes to *TCLC*. 72 vols. published by the end of 1997.

Class No: 82-09(082.200)

[6626]

World literature criticism, 1500 to the present: a selection of major authors from Gale's literary criticism series. Draper, J.P., *ed.* Detroit, Gale, 1992. 6v. illus. £276. ISBN: 0810383616.

Selected from and organized like the various Gale series described above, this complete set is ideal for libraries with neither the space nor the budget to allow them to take the ongoing major series. Aimed primarily at high school and college libraries, with coverage focussed on the most frequently studied writers, especially 19th- and 20th-century figures. Entries on 231 authors (of which 33 are women), A-Z, with author, title and nationality indexes in v.6. 28 countries represented, although over half the featured writers are British or American. Up to 7 critical excerpts per author followed by very brief bibliography of further sources. Major media adaptations listed for selected authors.

Supplement (1997. 2v. illus. £96. ISBN: 0787616966) extends the coverage to important pre-Christian authors and influential writers from the 1st to 15th centuries, and adds more 20th-century authors whose works are being increasingly studied in the USA. Indexes to the full set.

Class No: 82-09(082.200)

Histories

[6627]

BALDICK, C. Criticism and literary theory from 1890 to the present. Harlow, Longman, 1996. 312p. £48. (*Longman literature in English.*) ISBN: 0582033810.

Covers British and American 20th-century criticism in 4 main chapters (1890-1918; 1918-1945; 1945-1968; post-1968) with numerous subsections on movements like modernism and feminism. Very useful reference section with bio-bibliographical notes on 50 major critics and recommendations for further reading. Chronology. Index.

Class No: 82-09(091)

[6628]

BLAMIRES, H. A History of literary criticism. Basingstoke, Macmillan, 1991. x,412p. (*Macmillan history of literature.*) ISBN: 0333517342.

A concise, well-organized history from the Classical Age to the present in 11 chapters, each with 4-7 subsections. Last chapter includes coverage of formalism, structuralism, feminism and Marxism. References (5p.). Bibliography (4p.). Chronology, 570BC-1988. Index. *Class No:* 82-09(091)

[6629]

The Cambridge history of literary criticism. Cambridge, Cambridge Univ. Press, 1989- . v.1- (in progress).

V.1 *Classical criticism*, ed. by G.A. Kennedy. 1989. xviii,378p. £15.95. ISBN: 0521317177.

V.4 *The Eighteenth century*, ed. by H.B. Nisbet & C. Rawson. 1997. 969p. £75. ISBN: 0521300096.

V.8 *From Formalism to Poststructuralism*, ed. by R. Selden. 1995. 495p. £50. ISBN: 0521300134.

A major series with 9 vols. planned. V.1 has 11 signed essays by 7 scholars, covering the Classical period up to *c.*AD325. Extensive bibliography of primary sources and modern scholarship (22p.). Index. Of v.8, *TLS* (no.4831, Nov. 3, p.14-15) states that 'the individual essays themselves are excellent and should becone required reading on the subjects represented'. *Class No:* 82-09(091)

[6630]

WELLEK, R. A History of modern criticism, 1750-1950. New Haven, Conn., Yale Univ. Press; London, Cape, 1955-93. 8v.

V.1 *The Later eighteenth century*. 1955. vii,358p.

V.2 *The Romantic age*. 1955. 459p.

V.3 *The Age of transition*. 1966. xvi,389p.

V.4 *The Later nineteenth century*. 1966. vi,671p.

V.5 *English criticism, 1900-1950*. 1986. 343p. £30. ISBN: 0300033788.

V.6 *American criticism, 1900-1950*. 1986. viii,345p. ISBN: 0300034865.

V.7 *German, Russian, and East European criticism, 1900-1950*. 1991. 476p. ISBN: 0300050399.

V.8 *French, Italian, and Spanish criticism, 1750-1950*. 1993. ix,369p. £30. ISBN: 0300054513.

A scholarly work which has been described as 'one of the great monuments of modern literary history' (*TLS*, no.4420, Dec. 18-24, 1987, p.1406). Chapters on critical schools and individual critics. Each vol. has extensive bibliographies, chronological table, and indexes of names and topics.

Class No: 82-09(091)

Biographies

[6631]

The A-Z guide to modern literary and cultural theorists. Sim, S., *ed.* Hemel Hempstead, Harvester Wheatsheaf, 1995. xiv,432p. £13.95. ISBN: 0133555534.

Signed essays of 1,500-2,000 words on 100 influential figures. Entries comprise biography; review of career, ideas and impact; list of main works; selective secondary bibliography (up to 6 items); and (if required) glossary of key terms used in the theorist's work. Index. *Class No:* 82-09(092)

[6632]

Contemporary literary critics. Borklund, E., *ed.* 2nd ed. London, St. James Press, 1982. 600p. £107. ISBN: 0912289333.

1st ed. 1977.

Entries on 124 British and American critics, comprising biographical notes, full list of publications, list of critical studies and a critical essay. Some entries include a statement by their subject. Unlike the rest of St. James's excellent *Contemporary writers* series, this is the work of a single scholar. *Class No:* 82-09(092)

Literary Themes & Motifs

[6633]

Companion to literary myths, heroes and archetypes. Brunel, P., *ed and* Allatson, W., *and others, trans*. London, Routledge, 1992. xvi,1223p. £35. ISBN: 0415133637.

Originally published Paris, Editions du Rocher, 1988, as *Dictionnaire des mythes littéraires*. New French ed. published Monaco, Editions du Rocher, 1994 (1504p. Fr.445. ISBN: 2268018253).

Over 120 signed essays (average 9½p., but ranging from 3 to 35p.) by members of a research team at the Centre de Recherche en Littérature Comparée, University of Paris IV, which trace the progress of a myth (or group of myths) through literature. Entries are aranged A-Z and fall into 4 main areas: the Cosmos (*e.g.* Apollo), the Psyche (Oedipus), Society (Utopias) and History/Politics (Dictators). Mythical places like Eden and Atlantis are featured, as are historical figures who have assumed heroic status, *e.g.* Joan of Arc. As well as western archetypes, myths from Africa, Asia and Latin America are analyzed. General bibliography, arranged by author, but no chapter or subject listings (24p.). The index is sadly inadequate for a work of this complexity, covering themes, mythical figures and topics but not authors and titles of cited works. *Class No:* 82-09.4

[6634]

DAEMMRICH, H.S. *and* **DAEMMRICH, I. Themen und Motive in der Literatur:** ein Handbuch. 2. Aufl. Tübingen, Francke, 1995. xxv,410p. ISBN: 3825280349.

1st ed. 1987.

Entries of varying length on over 175 themes and motifs, A-Z, explaining their characteristics, function and development. Many works cited, with bibliographies of further works and critical studies following each entry. Index added for 2nd ed.

1st ed. available in English from the same publisher as *Themes and motifs in western literature: a handbook* (1987. 255p. ISBN: 3772017908). *Class No:* 82-09.4

[6635]

Dictionary of literary themes and motifs. Seigneuret, J.C., *ed*. New York, Greenwood, 1988. 2v. (xxiii,1507p). $250. ISBN: 0313229430.

V.1 A-J; V.2 L-Z.

143 signed essays by 98 scholars on the major themes of literature. Limited to concrete and abstract common nouns (*e.g.* Death, City, Money, Utopia) and therefore no characters or places. Entries average 9½p. and comprise definition of headword, chronological survey of the theme's treatment, cross-references to related entries and brief bibliography (only 3 or 4 items). Cross-index of key words. Index of authors and titles cited. 'Some of the articles are authoritative ... but too many are not' (*Choice*, v.26(9), May 1989, p.1488). *Class No:* 82-09.4

[6636]

FRENZEL, E. Motive der Weltliteratur: ein Lexikon dichtungsgeschichtlicher Längsschnitte. 4. Aufl. Stuttgart, Kröner, 1992. xvi,907p. ISBN: 3520301040.

Lengthy essays (average 17p.) on 57 themes, A-Z, with select bibliographies of further studies appended. Index to the many authors and works cited. *Class No:* 82-09.4

Literary Allusions

[6637]

Allusions - cultural, literary, biblical and historical: a thematic dictionary. Urdang, L. *and* Ruffner, F.G., *eds*. 2nd ed. Detroit, Gale, 1986. 634p. ISBN: 0810318288.

1st ed. 1982.

8,700 entries (an increase of 25% on the 1st ed.) are arranged under 712 thematic categories, presented in A-Z order from Abandonment to Zodiac, via Baldness, Friendship and Usury. Under each numbered category heading are a series of allusions with very brief definitions and source references. These allusions are predominantly characters from history, literature and mythology (*e.g.* Rockefeller, Scrooge, Midas), but some places and events (*e.g.* Timbuktu, Boston Tea Party) are included. Index lists all allusions alphabetically. Bibliography of over 1,000 sources consulted.

Clearly the result of much research, but likely to be less useful than an alphabetical listing such as Grote's *Common knowledge* or *Brewer's dictionary of phrase and fable*.
Class No: 82-090.2

[6638]

BREWER, E.C. Brewer's dictionary of phrase and fable. Room, A., *ed*. 15th ed. London, Cassell, 1995. xviii,1182p. £25. ISBN: 0304345997.

1st ed. 1870; 14th ed. 1989.

Subtitle of 1894 ed.: 'giving the derivation, source or origin of common phrases, allusions and words that have a tale to tell'.

The core of Dr. Brewer's highly personal reference work remains, but the 1970 centenary ed. represented a complete revision. The 15th ed., (Room's first after several by I. Evans) has over 20,000 entries, including 1,000 new ones giving increased coverage of contemporary allusions and American literature and culture. All existing entries have been revised, with many completely rewritten. More details of quotation sources are provided and etymologies have been improved.

A work which is difficult to categorize, but which is invaluable for its coverage of phrases and adages (grouped under keywords), its lists (*e.g.* national anthems, patron saints), and for the fact that it contains an extraordinarily wide range of information within one volume.

Brewer's concise dictionary of phrase and fable, ed. by E.M. Kirkpatrick (2nd ed. London, Cassell, 1996. 1136p. £10.99. ISBN: 0304349011) is an abridgement, but nevertheless a substantial work with over 15,000 entries. Most of the quotations have been removed, as have words readily found in standard dictionaries, whilst many 20th-century references have been added. *Class No:* 82-090.2

[6639]

BREWER, E.C. The Reader's handbook of famous names in fiction, allusions, references, proverbs, plots, stories, and poems. New ed. London, Chatto, 1898 (repr. Detroit, Omnigraphics, 1966, in 3 vols.). viii,1501p. $85. ISBN: 1558882170.

1st ed. 1879.

A companion to *Brewer's dictionary* which is still valuable for its wide coverage. Over 14,000 entries. The 1898 ed. has 2 useful appendices (listing English and American authors and their works, and the dates of dramas and operas) which are omitted from some reprints, *e.g.* 1902, 1934.
Class No: 82-090.2

[6640]

Brewer's dictionary of twentieth century phrase and fable. Isaacs, A. *and* Law, J., *eds.* 3rd ed. London, Cassell, 1996. 662p. £25. ISBN: 0304349291.

1st ed. 1991; 2nd ed. 1994.

Extremely useful compilation of *c.*8,000 entries, in the style of the parent work, covering words and phrases entering the language since 1900. Includes slang terms, acronyms, idioms, catchphrases, quotations, jargon, neologisms and anecdotes; also many proper nouns, representing people, places, events and institutions to which allusion is often made. Details of sources not usually supplied, but the well-written entries nevertheless evince authority.

2nd ed. included over 100 new terms, *e.g.* 'Camillagate', 'ethnic cleansing', 'New World Order' and 'zoo television'. 3rd ed. adds a similar number and many existing entries have been revised and updated. *Class No:* 82-090.2

[6641]

A Dictionary of biblical tradition in English literature. Jeffrey, D.L., *ed.* Grand Rapids, Mich., Eerdmans; Leominster, Gracewing, 1992. xxxii,960p. £55. ISBN: 0802836348, US; 0852442246, UK.

An invaluable guide to the influence of the Bible on English literature, comprising nearly 1,000 signed articles (many of them running to several pages) on biblical people, places, quotations, allusions, motifs, etc. Major essays comprise 3 parts: details of the term's appearances in the Bible; interpretation of the term by early commentators and later exegetical writers; survey of its literary use and development, from the Middle Ages to the present, with examples drawn from English and world literature. Substantial bibliographies with most entries. A-Z arrangement with cross-references. 160 contributors. Extensive, annotated bibliographies appended (over 100p.) covering various aspects of biblical and literary scholarship. *Class No:* 82-090.2

[6642]

GROTE, D. Common knowledge: a reader's guide to literary allusions. New York, Greenwood, 1987. xv,437p. $65. ISBN: 0313257574.

'An attempt to present in one place the fundamental names in mythology, theater, literature, religion, history and popular culture that reasonably educated persons might be expected to know ...' (*Introduction*). Over 4,000 entries arranged A-Z (Aaron-Zuleika) - mainly for characters but with a few events, concepts and places (*e.g.* Crucifixion, Noble Savage, Zion) - designed to explain briefly with what trait, activity or type that name is usually associated. Sources are given, with dates, in most entries. Copious cross-references. No bibliography, but major sources are listed in the Introduction. Unlike some similar works, it includes contemporary allusions from film, TV and popular literature. *Class No:* 82-090.2

[6643]

REES, N. Phrases and sayings. London, Bloomsbury, 1997. x,531p. £14.99. ISBN: 0747531145.

A merger, revision and updating of 2 earlier works by Rees: *Bloomsbury dictionary of phrase and allusion* (1991) and *Bloomsbury dictionary of popular phrases* (1990), with over 3,000 chatty, informative entries on a wide range of sayings, including allusions, idioms, stock phrases, catchphrases, clichés, slogans, headlines, book/film/song titles, and nicknames. Gives explanation, history, dates and

.... *(contd.)*

sources, and is particularly strong on allusions from contemporary popular culture. Cross-references, but no index. *Class No:* 82-090.2

[6644]

URDANG, L. The Dictionary of numerical allusions. New York and Oxford, Facts on File, 1986. ix,324p. ISBN: 0816013004.

US title is *The Facts on File dictionary of numerical allusions.*

An ingenious reference book which explains over 1,300 numerical allusions encountered in literature, mythology, religion, music and many other fields. Arranged in ascending order from absolute zero to infinity, then alphabetically under each number, the bulk of the book (p.10-168) covering nos.1-12. Appendix lists Latin, French, Italian, Spanish and German numbers. Alphabetical index of terms. *Class No:* 82-090.2

Literary Terms

[6645]

ABRAMS, M.H. A Glossary of literary terms. 6th ed. New York, Harcourt Brace Jovanovich, 1993. 301p. £16.95. ISBN: 0030549825.

1st ed. 1941, by D.S. Norton and P. Rushton; 5th ed. 1988.

Organised as a series of *c.*200 succinct essays in A-Z order by the title word or phrase, with subsidiary or closely related terms discussed within the same essay and traceable via the general index. All essays are well illustrated and most have bibliographies.

For the 5th ed., all entries were rewritten and extra references and illustrations added, especially from American literature and from women and Black authors. The major change was the removal of the lengthy entries on schools of criticism from the Glossary, these now appearing in a separate section of 20 essays (average length 3p.) headed 'Modern theories of literature and criticism'. 6th ed. shows several new entries, further revision of existing ones and expanded bibliographies.

'For clarity, concision, and elegance Abrams has few peers and no superiors' (*Choice*, v.31(1), Sept. 1993, p.73). *Class No:* 82-090.3

[6646]

BALDICK, C. The Concise Oxford dictionary of literary terms. Oxford, Oxford Univ. Press, 1990. x,246p. £6.99. ISBN: 0192828932.

Does not attempt to cover all the terms used in literary studies but 'to clarify those thousand terms that are most likely to cause the student or general reader some doubt or bafflement' (*Preface*). Entries are arranged A-Z and include explanation of usage, derivatives (plurals, adjectival forms, etc.), pronunciation guide (where appropriate) and cross-references. Guide to further reading (2p.). *Class No:* 82-090.3

[6647]

BECKSON, K. *and* GANZ, A. Literary terms: a dictionary. 3rd ed., rev. and enl. New York, Noonday, 1989; London, Deutsch, 1990. 308p. £5.95. ISBN: 0374521778, US; 0233985611, UK.

1st ed. 1960, as *A Reader's guide to literary terms*; 2nd ed. 1975.

Defines over 1,000 terms with illustrative quotations or excerpts from literary works and, in many cases, references to sources of further information. Full-page entries on major

....*(contd.)*
concepts. New ed. has more cross-references, many expanded entries, and new entries for recent developments in literary criticism. Lists of terms grouped by subject are appended. *Class No:* 82-090.3

[6648]

The Columbia dictionary of modern literary and cultural criticism. Childers, J. *and* Hentzi, G., *eds.* New York, Columbia Univ. Press, 1995. xii,362p. $52. ISBN: 0231072422.

Claims to be the first dictionary to devote significant attention to the expanding field of cultural criticism. 450 entries (A-Z) on critical terms and schools, with those for terms focusing on their historical and cultural genesis, their contemporary usage, applications and primary critical exponents. Entries are cross-referenced and most include lists of key texts. General bibliography (27p.) Index of names. *TLS* (no.4831, Nov. 3, 1995, p.14) suggests that the editors have included too many currently fashionable, but probably transient, terms and concepts: 'Any future historian of late twentieth-century intellectual fashions will find it a godsend'. *Class No:* 82-090.3

[6649]

CUDDON, J.A. A Dictionary of literary terms and literary theory. 3rd ed. London, Blackwell, 1991. xviii,1051p. ISBN: 0631172149.

1st ed. 1977, as *A Dictionary of literary terms*; 2nd ed. 1979 (both published London, Deutsch; New York, Doubleday).

Nearly 3,000 entries (a substantial increase), varying considerably in length, which fall into 12 categories explained in the Preface, *e.g.* technical terms, genres, forms, schools and movements, concepts, etc. Entries include definition, explanation, etymology (where necessary) and examples, but no bibliographies, although there are references in some cases to definitive works on the subject. Fully cross-referenced. Many foreign-language terms. New ed. has expanded coverage of fiction genres (with lengthy lists of representative titles) and much new material on critical theory. 4th ed. due mid-1998 (£60. ISBN: 0631202714).

Also available in paperback as *The Penguin dictionary of literary terms and literary theory* (London, Penguin, 1992. £10.99. ISBN: 0140512276). *Class No:* 82-090.3

[6650]

DUPRIEZ, B. A Dictionary of literary devices.
Halsall, A.W., *trans. and adapt.* Toronto, Univ. of Toronto Press; Hemel Hempstead, Harvester Wheatsheaf, 1991. xx,545p. £45. ISBN: 0802027563, Canada; 0745010555, UK.

Originally published Paris, Union Générale des Editions, 1984, as *Gradus: les procédés littéraires (dictionnaire)*

'Aims to encourage the personal involvement that readers achieve with literary texts by increasing their understanding of rhetorical forms, and by helping them to produce their own readings' (*Introduction*). 4,000 entries, A-Z, for traditional literary figures, with definition, examples from literature, analogous terms, and commentary. Numerous cross-references. Examples are taken from an exceptionally wide range of sources, including TV, theatre and film as well as literature, and the translator has selected many new examples likely to be more familiar to English-speaking readers. Bibliography (21p.) in 2 parts: Critical studies and reference works; Literary works. Index. *Class No:* 82-090.3

[6651]

HARRIS, W.V. Dictionary of concepts in literary criticism and theory. Westport, Conn., Greenwood, 1992. xiv,444p. $85. (*Reference sources for the social sciences and humanities.*) ISBN: 0313259321.

Lengthy entries (average 6p.) on 70 fundamental concepts (*e.g.* Allegory, Tragedy), comprising statement of meaning; discursive history of origins and development, with full citations for all sources; and references to additional sources of information. Index of concepts and terms. Name index. *Class No:* 82-090.3

[6652]

HAWTHORN, J. A Glossary of contemporary literary theory. 2nd ed. London, Arnold, 1994. 352p. ISBN: 034060185x.

1st ed. 1992.

'Aims to provide the reader with sufficient information to enable him or her to make sense of those of the more common specialist terms used by recent [*i.e.* since 1970] literary critics or theorists which cannot be found in more general dictionaries or glossaries of literary terms' (*Using the Glossary*). Lengthy entries, often covering groups of related terms, with references to further reading. Extensive cross-referencing. 2nd ed. includes 50 new entries, plus revisions to existing entries and expanded bibliography.

3rd ed. due 1998 (£45. ISBN: 0340692219).

A Concise glossary of contemporary literary theory (2nd ed. 1994. xii,241p. £13.99. ISBN: 0340601876) omits some of the more general entries and abridges certain others. *Class No:* 82-090.3

[6653]

HOLMAN, C.H. *and* **HARMON, W. A Handbook to literature.** 7th ed. New York, Prentice Hall, 1996. 669p. $35. ISBN: 0132347822.

1st ed. 1936, by W.F. Thrall and A. Hibbard; 6th ed. 1992.

A well-established reference work which is basically a dictionary of literary terms, providing definitions of *c.*2,000 words and phrases encountered in the study of English and American literature and related fields like linguistics, classical studies, film and music. Entries vary from a couple of lines to several pages, are well cross-referenced and include references to sources. Also includes a chronology of literary history and lists of Nobel and Pulitzer Prize winners. Index of proper names. *Class No:* 82-090.3

[6654]

ORR, L. A Dictionary of critical theory. Westport, Conn., Greenwood, 1991. 488p. $85. ISBN: 0313235279.

Aimed at faculty and graduate students, defining terms from the perspective of literary critical use and providing references to mainly English-language sources. Includes terms that have appeared with great frequency in the indexes to anthologies of critical theory; terms that have appeared in the indexes to standard histories of criticism; schools of criticism; and key terms from foreign-language critical theory. Cross-references. Index of theorists. Complements Orr's *Research in critical theory since 1965: a classified bibliography* (*q.v.*).

Production severely criticized in *Choice* (v.29(9), May 1992, p.1372): 'The text suffers most annoyingly from messiness of punctuation, grammar, formatting, syntax, and argument: many misspellings, redundancies, wrong tenses, errors of agreement, inconsistencies of typefaces and diacritics, etc.' *Class No:* 82-090.3

[6655]

RUSE, C. *and* **HOPTON, M. Cassell dictionary of literary and language terms.** London, Cassell, 1992. 313p. ISBN: 0304319279.

Defines and explains over 1,600 terms encountered in the study of English literature and language and is aimed at A-level and first-year college/university students. Entries are clearly written and include numerous illustrative examples taken from commonly studied texts. Pronunciation guide to difficult words. Chronology of British and international literature. *Class No:* 82-090.3

German

[6656]

Metzler Literaturlexikon: Begriffe und Definitionen. Schweikle, G. *and* Schweikle, I., *eds*. 2. überarbeitete Aufl. Stuttgart, Metzler, 1990. 525p. ISBN: 3476006689.

1st ed. 1984.

Signed entries by over 50 contributors on *c.*3,000 terms, mainly from literature but also including a few from linguistics and publishing/book production. Gives etymologies, definitions and cross-references in highly informative, closely typed articles. Bibliography with each entry plus general bibliography (3p.). Classified list of entries. *Class No:* 82-090.3=30

[6657]

WILPERT, G. von. Sachwörterbuch der Literatur. 7., verb. und erw. Aufl. Stuttgart, Kröner, 1989. xi,1054p. ISBN: 3520231077.

1st ed. 1955; 6th ed. 1979.

A dictionary of over 4,000 literary terms, providing definition, examples, and many references to further sources. Thoroughly cross-referenced. *Class No:* 82-090.3=30

Spanish

[6658]

BAS, J. *and* **IWANAGA, G. Manual de términos literarios.** Lanham, Md., Univ. Press of America, 1987. 192p. $36. ISBN: 0819165492.

Defines briefly, with examples in some cases, approx. 1,100 terms commonly utilized in the study and analysis of Hispanic letters. Short bibliography (10 items). *Class No:* 82-090.3=60

Literary Characters

[6659]

AMOS, W. The Originals: who's really who in fiction. London, Cape, 1985. xx,614p. illus. ISBN: 0224023195.

Notes varying from 2 lines to over a page on nearly 3,000 characters said to have been based on real people. Entries are arranged A-Z by character and attempt 'to indicate the strength of the identification and the extent to which the character is based on the model' (*Foreword*). Like Bold and Giddings, Amos casts his net wider than fiction. 40 photographs of suspected 'originals'. Bibliography (11p.). Index of all real persons mentioned in the text. *Class No:* 82-090.6

[6660]

BOLD, A. *and* **GIDDINGS, R. Who was really who in fiction.** Harlow, Longman, 1987. ix,383p. ISBN: 0582892511.

Lengthy (at least 400 words), highly readable entries on over 600 literary characters thought to have been based on real people. Each entry includes a summary of the character's part in the literary work, an account of the original and, where appropriate, information about how the author came to use him/her. Arranged A-Z by character, with the main headings in the margin followed by author, title and date of book, name and dates of the original, and suggestions for further reading. Index cleverly uses different typefaces to distinguish titles, authors and originals.

Misleading title as the characters are by no means all from fiction; poetry, drama and opera are covered and there are also entries for a few eponyms (*e.g.* Martinet) and some literary places (*e.g.* Barchester). *Class No:* 82-090.6

[6661]

Cyclopedia of literary characters. Magill, F.N., *ed.* New York, Harper & Row, 1963. viii+1280+xiv+50p. ISBN: 0893561401.

Reprinted Englewood Cliffs, N.J., Salem Press, as *Masterplots cyclopedia of literary characters*.

Lists *c.*16,000 characters from 1,300 books of all countries and all periods. Arranged by title, A-Z, with all characters from each work identified and described. Lengthy analysis of major characters. Pronunciation indicated for many names. Indexes of authors and characters.

Cyclopedia of literary characters II (Englewood Cliffs, N.J., Salem Press. 1990. 4v. $300. ISBN: 0893565172) has entries for *c.*12,000 characters in over 1,400 works, arranged like the 1963 vol., but with generally lengthier comments on individual characters. Most of the works covered feature in the *Masterplots II* series.

New 5-vol. ed. due 1998 ($350. ISBN: 0893564389). *Class No:* 82-090.6

[6662]

Dictionary of American literary characters. Franklin, B., *ed.* New York, Facts on File, 1990. 560p. $75. ISBN: 0816019177.

Lists over 11,000 characters from American novels published 1789-1980, giving single-sentence description and reference to author and title. Main A-Z sequence is followed by list of series characters and index of nearly 400 authors, with lists of their novels and characters. *Class No:* 82-090.6

[6663]

—Major characters in American fiction. Salzman, J. *and* Wilkinson, P., *eds*. New York, Holt, 1994. 952p. $60. ISBN: 0805030603.

With nearly 1,600 entries, covers far fewer characters than Franklin, but provides more information in the form of biographical sketches by staff of the Center for American Cultural Studies at Columbia University. Arranged by character surname, entries give title, author and publication date of book followed by details of the character's life and its significance to the work. Cross-references to other entries. List of authors with references to characters and titles. List of titles with references to characters and authors. Includes some characters from classic stories for children. *Class No:* 82-090.6

[6664]

Dictionary of British literary characters: 18th- and 19th-century novels. Greenfield, J.R., *ed.* New York, Facts on File, 1993. 655p. $75. ISBN: 0816021791.

Lists over 11,500 characters, A-Z, from nearly 500 novels by 104 British authors, giving brief descriptions and information on their roles and relationships. Author index gives birth and death dates, titles and publication dates of works covered, and lists of characters for each novel. All major novelists are covered, plus many minor ones, with women writers well represented.

Companion vol. is *Dictionary of British literary characters: 20th-century novels* (New York, Facts on File, 1994. 583p. $75. ISBN: 0816021805), which covers 10,000 characters from 686 novels published 1900-80 and includes a title index to both vols. *Class No:* 82-090.6

[6665]

Dictionnaire des personnages littéraires et dramatiques de tous les temps et de tous les pays: poésie, théâtre, roman, musique. Nouv. éd. Paris, Robert Laffont, 1994. 1040p. illus. Fr.120. ISBN: 2221079426.

1st ed. 1960.

A companion vol. to *Le Nouveau dictionnaire des oeuvres* and *Le Nouveau dictionnaire des auteurs* (*qq.v.*), to which references are made, with signed articles by a large team of contributors on the major characters of world literature and music. *Class No:* 82-090.6

[6666]

FRENZEL, E. Stoffe der Weltliteratur: ein Lexikon dichtungsgeschichtlicher Längsschnitte. 8. Aufl. Stuttgart, Kröner, 1992. xvi,932p. ISBN: 3520300087.

Lengthy entries on over 300 characters, both historical (*e.g.* Cleopatra) and mythical (*e.g.* Orpheus) who regularly feature as motifs in literature. References to numerous authors and works. Bibliographies of further studies.
Class No: 82-090.6

[6667]

HARRIS, L.L. Characters in 20th-century literature. Detroit, Gale, 1990-5. 2v. £41.50 per vol. ISBN: 0810318474, v.1; 0810392038, v.2.

Misleading title as the books actually comprise a collection of synopses of representative works (novels, short stories and plays) by over 400 major writers, arranged A-Z by author with character and title indexes. Brief lists of further reading for each author. Over 2,000 characters mentioned but the selective approach to titles makes for serious omissions. Stronger on post-1960 literature. *Class No:* 82-090.6

[6668]

—HOWES, K.K. Characters in 19th-century literature. Detroit, Gale, 1993. x,597p. £41.50. ISBN: 0810383985.

Follows the same format as Harris' vol. on 20th-century literature, with synopses of nearly 200 works currently studied in US colleges and high schools, in which over 2,200 characters are discussed. Of the 100 writers represented most are British and American, but major European figures like Chekhov appear and an effort has been made to include some less well-known women and ethnic writers. Index of titles and characters. *Class No:* 82-090.6

[6669]

Larousse dictionary of literary characters. Goring, R., *ed.* Edinburgh, Larousse, 1994. xi,849p. £25. ISBN: 0752300016.

Coverage is confined to literature in English, with over 6,000 entries, A-Z, identifying the book(s) in which each character appears and giving a brief description, often including cross-references to other people. Index of authors, with their titles and characters listed. Concentrates on key personnel, sometimes only one major character from a work being included. Strong coverage of contemporary literature, including genre fiction. *Class No:* 82-090.6

[6670]

PRINGLE, D. Imaginary people: a who's who of fictional characters from the eighteenth century to the present day. 2nd ed. Aldershot, Scolar Press, 1996. x,296p. £29.50. ISBN: 1859281621.

1st ed. London, Grafton, as *Imaginary people: a who's who of modern fictional characters*.

Lists in A-Z order over 1,400 characters (including some animals) from modern literature (Robinson Crusoe is the earliest), opera, ballet, comics, songs, films, radio and TV, with the emphasis on those who 'have lived beyond the original source' (*Introduction*). Readable entries outline the character's 'career' through various media and include lists of 'sequels by other hands' in which authors other than the originator have used the character. Copious cross-references. 2nd ed. has over 100 new entries but illustrations have been dropped. Bibliography (10p.). Index of creators includes authors, cartoonists and songwriters. Particularly good for non-literary characters. *Class No:* 82-090.6

[6671]

RINTOUL, M.C. Dictionary of real people and places in fiction. London, Routledge, 1993. x,1184p. £100. ISBN: 0415059992.

Main sequence (839p.) lists over 4,000 real people and places (also animals, houses, organisations, etc.) found in over 1,000 English-language novels and short stories; provides biographical and explanatory notes; identifies fictional counterparts; lists their appearances in literature, with supporting quotations from sources such as diaries, letters, biographies and articles; and gives publication details of fictional works. 3 other finding aids are provided: list of literary authors with characters they have based on real people; index of fictional names; and index of titles of literary works. A highly personal compilation, based on the author's own reading, with some surprising omissions considering the price, *e.g.* Philip Larkin as Jim Dixon (*Lucky Jim*). Cheaper alternatives are available.
Class No: 82-090.6

[6672]

ROVIN, J. The Encyclopedia of monsters. New York, Facts on File, 1989. 400p. illus. $35. ISBN: 0816018243.

Information on over 1,000 monsters from literature and a wide range of media. Entries are arranged A-Z and include name and/or nickname, species, gender, size, biography, picture and comments. Appendix covers monstrous lands, planets and buildings. Over 240 illustrations. Index.

Rovin has also compiled *The Encyclopedia of super heroes* (1986. xi,443p. ISBN: 0816011680), *The Encyclopedia of super villains* (1987. ix,416p. ISBN: 0816018995) and *Adventure heroes: legendary characters from Odysseus to James Bond* (1994. 320p. $35. ISBN: 0816028818).
Class No: 82-090.6

[6673]
ROVIN, J. The Encyclopedia of super heroes. New York, Facts on File, 1986. xi,443p. illus. ISBN: 0816011680.

A-Z listing of over 1,200 heroes from literature, legend, TV, radio, films, comics and even video games. Entries give alter ego, first appearance (date and medium), occupation, costume, weapons, biography, quote and commentary. 5 appendices, including super hero teams and foreign (*i.e.* non-US) heroes. Index. Profusely illustrated, often in colour. *Class No:* 82-090.6

[6674]
ROVIN, J. The Encyclopedia of super villains. New York, Facts on File, 1987. ix,416p. illus. ISBN: 0816018995.

Dossiers on nearly 1,000 'baddies' presented in similar style to the above. Data includes real name, first appearance, costume, weapons, henchmen, biography and quote (a typical threat!). Dominated by US comic book characters. Appendix lists super villain teams. Index. 140 illustrations, with 32p. in colour. *Class No:* 82-090.6

[6675]
SEYMOUR-SMITH, M. The Dent dictionary of fictional characters. [4th ed.]. London, Dent, 1991. xv,598p. ISBN: 0460030353.

1st ed. 1963, by W. Freeman; 2nd ed. 1967; 3rd ed., 1973, rev. by F. Urquhart. All earlier eds. entitled *Everyman's dictionary of fictional characters.*

A thorough revision of a standard reference book, which now lists over 50,000 characters created by some 3,000 authors, giving brief descriptions with references to the works in which they appear. Main sequence is followed by a list of authors and works covered.

Seymour-Smith has retained Urquhart's additions while restoring some of the Victorians he dropped; omitted many characters from obscure works (especially plays) which Freeman originaly included; added many more from the works of Commonwealth, US and women writers; and introduced a selection from foreign-language works popular in translation. The larger format and improved layout make this ed. easier to use. *Class No:* 82-090.6

Women

[6676]
DREW, B.A. Heroines: a bibliography of women series characters in mystery, espionage, action, science fiction, fantasy, horror, western, romance and juvenile fiction. New York, Garland, 1989. 406p. $55. ISBN: 0824030478.

Main sequence is a list of *c.*1,200 women characters who feature in series, giving brief description of series, major characters, TV and film versions, and list of titles by year. Also author sequence, classified grouping of series by genre, and title index. *Class No:* 82-090.6-0055.2

[6677]
SWEENEY, P. Women in Southern literature: an index. Westport, Conn., Greenwood, 1986. xxiv,117p. $49.95. ISBN: 0313249725.

Lists 1,000 female characters, A-Z, from the literature of the Southern US, with brief description and reference to the work of drama or prose in which they appear. Lists of characters under 15 category headings (*e.g.* 'Spinsters', 'Black mammies') are appended. *Class No:* 82-090.6-0055.2

Literary Genres

Poetry

Databases

[6678]
Columbia Granger's world of poetry on CD-ROM. New York, Columbia Univ. Press, 1995. CD-ROM $695. ISBN: 0231101589.

The complete contents of *The Columbia Granger's index to poetry*, *The Columbia Granger's guide to poetry anthologies* and *The Columbia Granger's dictionary of poetry quotations* (*qq.v.*) on one CD-ROM. 135,000 poems by over 20,000 poets can be accessed by author, subject, title, first line, last line or keyword, or any combination of these. In addition, 10,000 well-known poems are available in full text, can be accessed by any word and, because they are out of copyright, may be downloaded or printed out, and there are 7,500 poetry quotations and evaluations of 700 anthologies. Call number customizing allows librarians to enter citations for anthologies in their own collections. *Class No:* 82-1(003.4)

[6679]
Poem finder. Great Neck, N.Y., Roth. World Wide Web resource. $600 per annum.

URL: http//www.poemfinder.com

The largest poetry database available, with 40,000 full-text poems and index entries for a further 550,000 poems. Poetry has been indexed in 2,500 anthologies, over 4,000 single-author collections, and 4,500 issues of over 100 different periodical titles. Search options include keyword, subject, author/translator, poem title, book title, first line and last line. Particularly strong on very recent (post-1985) poetry, although older material is not neglected. The 'Subject Navigator' facility provides enhanced subject access via over 7,000 headings arranged hierarchically. International in scope and continuously updated. *Class No:* 82-1(003.4)

Bibliographies

[6680]
ARTS COUNCIL OF GREAT BRITAIN. The Poetry Library of the Arts Council of Great Britain: short-title catalogue. Barker, J., *comp.* 6th ed., rev. and enlarged. London, The Council, 1981. 149p. ISBN: 0856353949.

1st ed 1953; 5th ed. 1973.

Claims to be the most comprehensive collection of modern poetry in English (including translations) from all countries. Lists books by over 3,000 poets, A-Z, and includes verse drama, children's verse, and pre-20th century poetry translated by modern poets. Entries give title, date and publisher for each work. *Class No:* 82-1(01)

[6681]
BROGAN, T.V.F. Verseform: a comparative bibliography. Baltimore, Md., Johns Hopkins Univ. Press, 1989. xv,122p. $30. ISBN: 0801833620.

Part 1 covers poetic structures, devices and forms, regardless of language, and Part 2 covers the verse systems of all major language groups, both Western and Eastern. Extensively cross-referenced. 'Another indispensable work-aid, after his monumental ... *English versification*' (*Modern Language Review,* v.86(2), April 1991, p.387). *Class No:* 82-1(01)

Indexes

[6682]

BREWTON, J.E. *and* **BREWTON, S.W. Index to children's poetry.** New York, Wilson, 1942. 966p. $63. ISBN: 0824200217.

Indexes 15,000 poems from 130 collections. *First supplement* (1954. 405p. $40. ISBN: 0824200225) indexes 7,000 poems from 66 collections published 1938-51; *Second supplement* (1965. 453p. $40. ISBN: 0824200233) indexes 8,000 poems from 85 collections published 1949-63. Titles, first lines, subjects and poets in a single A-Z sequence.

Further supplemented by *Index to poetry for children and young people, 1964-1969*, by J.E. Brewton and others (1972. 574p. $53. ISBN: 0824204352); ... *1970-1975* (1978. 471p. $53. ISBN: 0824206215); ... *1976-1981* (1983. 320p. $53. ISBN: 0824206819); ... *1982-1987* (1989. 392, xxxiip. $58. ISBN: 0824207734); and ... *1988-1992* (1994. 400p. $58. ISBN: 0824208617). These vols. index a total of 44,000 poems in 569 collections. *Class No:* 82-1(014)

[6683]

—AMERICAN LIBRARY ASSOCIATION. Subject index to poetry for children and young people. Sell, V., *and others, comps*. Chicago, A.L.A., 1957. 582p.

An alphabetical subject index to poems in 157 anthologies and collections. Supplemented by *Subject index to poetry for children and young people, 1957-1975,* by D.B.F. Smith and E.L. Andrews (1977. 1035p. $45. ISBN: 0838902421), which indexes a further 263 anthologies. *Class No:* 82-1(014)

[6684]

—MORRIS, H. The New Where's that poem? An index of poems for children; arranged by subject, with a bibliography of books of poetry. London, Blackwell, 1985. vii,264p. ISBN: 0631139427.

Supersedes *Where's that poem?* (1967. Rev. ed. 1974).

Indexes poems in 237 anthologies under *c*.800 subject headings from Aborigines to Zoos, the poems having been chosen with children aged 7 to 15 in mind. Annotated list of anthologies. Index of poets. *Class No:* 82-1(014)

[6685]

The Columbia Granger's index to poetry in anthologies. Frankovich, N., *ed.* 11th ed. New York, Columbia Univ. Press, 1997. 2150p. £190. ISBN: 0231110383.

1st ed. 1904, by E. Granger; 10th ed. 1994. 1st to 8th eds. entitled *Granger's index to poetry*. 9th and 10th eds. entitled *The Columbia Granger's index to poetry*.

An indispensable reference book which has provided access to the major British and American poetry anthologies since early in the century. As each ed. drops some anthologies in order to make way for new ones, it is worth retaining as many eds. as space allows, although standard anthologies are generally covered each time.

The 9th ed. broke new ground by indexing anthologies of English translations of foreign poetry and a major innovation in the 10th ed. was the introduction of last line indexing for 12,500 of the most frequently anthologized poems. In this ed. the main sequence of titles, first lines and last lines has entries for over 80,000 poems by 11,000 poets, keyed to abbreviations for over 400 anthologies, of which 150 are indexed here for the first time. The subject sequence lists poem titles and authors under over 3,500 headings and the author index lists each poet's titles. The list of anthologies gives publishing details and highlights key collections recommended for libraries with limited funds. *Class No:* 82-1(014)

[6686]

—The Columbia Granger's guide to poetry anthologies. Katz, W., *& others, eds.* 2nd ed. New York, Columbia Univ. Press, 1994. xxxiv,440p. $75. ISBN: 023110104x.

1st ed. 1991.

A much expanded ed. which provides critical annotations for over 800 anthologies indexed in the 7th, 8th, 9th and 10th eds. of *Granger's index*, plus some to be covered in the 11th. Entries are arranged in over 60 subject categories and include information on the arrangement of the poems, indexing, and the presence of notes, illustrations, etc. Index of subjects, editors/compilers/translators and anthology titles. List of 100 recommended anthologies. *Class No:* 82-1(014)

[6687]

—The Columbia Granger's index to poetry in collected and selected works. Frankovich, N., *ed.* New York, Columbia Univ. Press, 1998. 1952p. £180. ISBN: 0231107625.

Supplements the long-established *Granger's index* by providing access to many poems not included in anthologies. For example, 17 poems by T.S. Eliot which are not indexed in any ed. of *Granger's* are featured here. Indexes 55,000 poems by 251 poets in 275 collections. Title and first-line sequence followed by author and subject indexes, the latter being particularly useful as author collections do not usually have subject access. As well as major poets, many less well-known names are included as well as contemporary songwriters like Dylan and The Beatles. *Class No:* 82-1(014)

[6688]

GUY, P.A. Women's poetry index. Phoenix, Ariz., Oryx Press, 1985. xv,174p. $75. ISBN: 0897741730.

Indexes 51 anthologies of women's poetry not covered by Granger, by poet, title and first line. Index of poets gives birth and death dates and list of anthologies indicates those which contain biographical information. Includes some poems translated from foreign languages. *Class No:* 82-1(014)

[6689]

HOFFMAN, H.H. Hoffman's index to poetry: European and Latin American poetry in anthologies. Metuchen, N.J., Scarecrow, 1985. xiii,672p. ISBN: 0810818310.

A non-English language complement to *Granger's index,* which provides access to *c.*14,000 poems in Spanish, Portuguese, Provençal, German, Italian, Polish, Russian and Ukrainian, contained in over 100 anthologies available in British and American libraries. Author, title and first line indexes, the latter grouped by language. List of poets, grouped by language. List of anthologies, with those containing English translations asterisked. *Class No:* 82-1(014)

[6690]

Index of American periodical verse, 1971-. Metuchen, N.J., Scarecrow, 1973-. Annual. ISSN: 00909130.

Indexes poems published in nearly 300 English- and Spanish-language periodicals from the US, Canada and the Caribbean. The 24th annual vol. (1998. 672p. $69.50. ISBN: 0810833913) covers 1995 and has over 7,300 entries for individual poets and translators; more than 20,000 entries for specific poems; and the same number of title/first line entries. *Class No:* 82-1(014)

[6691]
KLINE, V. Last lines: an index to the last lines of poetry. New York, Facts on File, 1991. 2v. $145. ISBN: 0816012652.

A new index which complements *The Columbia Granger's index* (*q.v.*) by providing access to poetry in English via nearly 175,000 last lines. Covers 497 anthologies published between 1900 and 1987, of which 405 are indexed by the 8th ed. of *Granger's*. V.1 provides full bibliographic information and symbols for the anthologies, and indexes of last lines and titles; v.2 has indexes of authors and of keywords in last lines and titles. Keywords are not placed in context, so there is little point in searching under a common word like 'love' which gives references to over 1,800 poems. The author and keyword indexes do not contain location symbols, but these are less likely to be used than those in v.1. *Class No:* 82-1(014)

Encyclopaedias & Dictionaries

[6692]
Critical survey of poetry: English language series. Magill, F.N., *ed.* Rev. ed. Englewood Cliffs, N.J., Salem Press, 1992. 8v. $475. ISBN: 0893568341.

1st ed. 1982

Vols. 1-7 contain signed essays (average 10p.) on 368 poets, A-Z, of all periods. Entries include bibliographies of primary material (including major non-poetic works) and selected critical studies. V.8 includes 22 essays on the history of poetry and poetry criticism, and index to the set.

Critical survey of poetry: foreign-language series (1984. 5v. $275. ISBN: 0893563501) is similarly arranged. *Class No:* 82-1(03)

[6693]
DRURY, J. The Poetry dictionary. Cincinnati, Ohio, Story Press, 1995. 324p. £14.99. ISBN: 1884910041.

350 entries on poetic terms, forms, genres, devices, movements, etc. Notable for including whole poems in order to set examples in context. Index. *Class No:* 82-1(03)

[6694]
—PACKARD, W. The Poet's dictionary: a handbook of prosody and poetic terms. New York, Harper & Row, 1989. 221p. ISBN: 0060161302.

Defines and explains over 130 terms, A-Z, and provides many examples. Select bibliography. Instructions on how to submit a manuscript for publication are appended. 'Reliability and authenticity are hallmarks of this dictionary' (*Choice*, v.27(4), Dec. 1989, p.614). *Class No:* 82-1(03)

[6695]
Masterplots II: poetry series. Pasadena, Calif., Salem Press, 1992. 6v. $425. ISBN: 0893565849.

Signed articles (3-4pp.) on 760 poems by 275 authors, of all periods, writing in 10 languages. Entries are arranged A-Z by poem title and comprise 4 sections: quick-reference data (poet, type of poem, publishing history); overview of poem; notes on forms and devices, such as meter and imagery; and discussion of major themes. V.6 has annotated bibliography of general studies of poetry; bibliography on individual poets; and indexes of poets, titles and poem-types. Some major poems missing (*e.g.* 'The Rape of the lock') as they have already been covered in another *Masterplots* series. Yeats is the most represented writer (16 poems), followed by Shakespeare, Wordsworth and Wallace Stevens, with Baudelaire the leading foreign-language poet. *Class No:* 82-1(03)

[6696]
MORIER, H. Dictionnaire de poétique et de rhétorique. 4e. éd. Paris, Presses Universitaires de France, 1989. 1320p. illus. Fr.825. ISBN: 2130400973.

1st ed. 1961; 3rd ed. 1981.

Superbly presented dictionary of poetic terms, with numerous examples, illustrations, tables, and diagrams. Most entries occupy more than one page and many are considerably longer (*e.g.* 30p. on the sonnet). Bibliography (6p.). *Class No:* 82-1(03)

[6697]
MYERS, J. *and* **SIMMS, M. Longman dictionary of poetic terms.** Paperback reprint of 1985 ed. New York and London, Longman, 1989. xv,366p. ISBN: 0801303443.

First published as *Longman dictionary and handbook of poetry*, New York, 1985.

Aimed at both poets and students, to provide '(1) a catalogue of definitions, (2) a companion reader to traditional and contemporary poetry, and (3) a catalyst to the reader's own critical or creative writing' (*Preface*). 1,500 entries define terms relating to poetic techniques, devices, criticism, schools and movements, with ample illustrations and many cross-references. Within the single A-Z sequence are several lengthy essays on key terms, *e.g.* 9p. on Metaphor.

Appendix 1 classifies terms under 26 subject headings; Appendix 2 groups poetical devices under 6 headings; Appendix 3 is a selected bibliography, listing some 150 titles under 17 subject headings. *Class No:* 82-1(03)

[6698]
The New Princeton encyclopedia of poetry and poetics. Preminger, A. *and* Brogan, T.V.F., *eds.* New ed. Princeton, N.J., Princeton Univ. Press, 1993. xlvi,1383p. $150. ISBN: 0691032718.

1st ed. 1965, as *Encyclopedia of poetry and poetics*; enlarged ed. 1974, as *Princeton encyclopedia of poetry and poetics* (actually a reprint with supplement).

A welcome and overdue new ed. of a major reference work, with over 90% of the entries extensively revised, most major ones entirely rewritten and bibliographies and cross-references expanded. Over 1,000 entries, A-Z, ranging from 20 to more than 20,000 words and dealing with the history, theory, technique and criticism of poetry from earliest times to the present. The signed articles have been compiled by a team of over 200 scholars and most have bibliographies appended. A strong international flavour, with lengthy essays on the poetry of 106 nations. All quotations from non-English poetry have translations alongside. Still no name index and no entries for individual writers or works, but there are 162 new articles, including 'Feminist poetics' and 'Chicano poetry.' *Class No:* 82-1(03)

[6699]
—The New Princeton handbook of poetic terms. Brogan, T.V.F., *ed.* New ed. Princeton, N.J., Princeton Univ. Press, 1994. xv,339p. £32.50. ISBN: 0691036713.

1st ed. 1986, as *The Princeton handbook of poetic terms* by A. Preminger.

Nearly 200 entries, A-Z, selected from the *New Princeton encyclopedia,* on poetic genres, prosody, terminology, rhetorical figures, etc., concentrating on terms most commonly encountered in literary study. Bibliographies with entries, all updated since 1986. *Class No:* 82-1(03)

[6700]

—The Princeton handbook of multicultural poetries. Brogan, T.V.F., *ed.* Princeton, N.J., Princeton Univ. Press, 1996. 366p. £35. ISBN: 0691010897.

Another spin-off vol. from the *New Princeton encyclopedia*, comprising unchanged reprints of the articles on the poetry of 106 cultures in 92 national literatures. Sadly, the editor is taken to task by a reviewer in *Choice* (v.33(10), June 1996, p.1622) for daring in his Preface to criticise political correctness in the American academic world. *Class No:* 82-1(03)

Quotations

[6701]

The Columbia Granger's dictionary of poetry quotations. Hazen, E.P., *ed.* New York, Columbia Univ. Press, 1992. 1132p. $99. ISBN: 0231075464.

7,000 passages from the 4,000 most anthologized poems, according to *The Columbia Granger's index*, are arranged A-Z by poet and indexed by keyword and subject. References to 375 anthologies, using the same codes as the parent work. *Class No:* 82-1(082.2)

Excerpts

[6702]

Poetry criticism. Detroit, Gale, 1990-. v.1- (in progress). illus. £75 per vol.

A new series following the successful format of *Contemporary literary criticism* (*q.v.*). Concentrates mainly on English-language poets, although some major foreign poets whose work has been translated are also covered. 8-10 entries per vol., comprising biographical sketch, excerpts from critical analyses of major poems, and bibliography of further reading. Cumulative author, title and nationality indexes.

19 vols. published by the end of 1997. *Class No:* 82-1(082.200)

Sound Recordings & Tapes

[6703]

HOFFMAN, H.H. *and* **HOFFMAN, R.L. International index to recorded poetry.** New York, Wilson, 1983. xlvi,529p. ISBN: 0824206827.

Indexes over 1,700 recordings (on discs, tapes, cassettes and videos) of *c.*15,000 poems by *c.*2,300 poets. Separate sequences for authors, titles, first lines, and readers. Register of poets by language. List of recordings by manufacturer, with addresses. *Class No:* 82-1(086.7)

Histories

[6704]

GASPAROV, M.L. A History of European versification. Smith, G.S. *and* Holford-Stevens, L., *eds.* Oxford, Clarendon Press, 1996. 352p. £40. ISBN: 0198158793.

The first detailed history of European versification, examining poetry written in 30 languages from classical Greece and Rome to the present. Liberally illustrated with verse examples, both in the original language and in translation. *Class No:* 82-1(091)

Biographies

[6705]

Contemporary poets. Riggs, T., *ed.* 6th ed. Detroit and London, St. James Press, 1996. xxiii,1336p. $160. ISBN: 1558621911.

1st ed. 1970; 5th ed. 1991.

Entries on 779 English-language poets, comprising biographical notes, full list of publications, information about published bibliographies, manuscript locations, and critical studies, plus signed critical article by one of *c.*240 contributors. Many entries include comment by the subject. Title index gives name, date and author af all books mentioned in the text. 120 new entrants in this ed., which has a nationality index for the first time. 'Despite the inevitable omissions, no compilation of such magnitude for poets exists ... highly recommended wherever there is an interest in poets and poetry' (*RQ*, v.31(3), Spring 1992, p.435-6, on 5th ed.).

A separate vol. entitled *Contemporary women poets* (£69. ISBN: 0558623566) is due in 1998, with 250 entries.
Class No: 82-1(092)

[6706]

International who's who in poetry and poets' encyclopaedia. Cummings, D. *and* McIntire, D., *eds.* 8th ed. Cambridge, International Biographical Centre, 1997. 476p. £95. ISBN: 0948875372.

1st ed. 1959. 7th ed. 1993. Appeared as a separate publication in 5 eds. before 6th ed. was incorporated in 9th ed. of *International authors and writers who's who* (*q.v.*). Continued to be part of that work through its 10th-12th eds. but is now independent again.

Entries on *c.*4,000 poets, giving addresses, literary awards bestowed, and full career and education details. Appendices provide information on poetry prize winners, poets laureate, poetry publishers, magazines and societies. *Class No:* 82-1(092)

Drama

Bibliographies

[6707]

ADELMAN, I. *and* **DWORKIN, R. Modern drama:** a checklist of critical literature on 20th century plays. Metuchen, N.J., Scarecrow, 1967. xvii,370p.

A selective, unannotated bibliography with over 9,000 entries arranged under playwrights, A-Z. General studies are followed by studies of individual plays. *Class No:* 82-2(01)

[6708]

BREED, P.F. *and* **SNIDERMAN, F.M. Dramatic criticism index:** a bibliography of commentaries on playwrights from Ibsen to the Avant-Garde. Detroit, Gale, 1972. 1022p. ISBN: 0810310902.

Lists nearly 12,000 critical articles in English on over 300 playwrights, taken from *c.*630 books and over 200 periodicals. Largely confined to 20th-century writers. Arranged A-Z by playwright, with indexes of play titles and critics. List of books indexed. Not annotated. *Class No:* 82-2(01)

[6709]

BRITISH DRAMA LEAGUE. The Player's library: the catalogue of the library of the British Drama League. 2nd ed. London, Faber, 1950. xvi,1115p.

1st ed. 1930 as *The Player's library and bibliography of the theatre,* with supplement in 1934. Supplements to 2nd ed. issued in 1951 (128p.), 1954 (256p.) and 1956 (256p.).

Main sequence lists British and foreign plays by author, A-Z, and provides details of category, number of acts, cast, setting, period and costume. A classified list of books on the theatre follows (80p.). Title index of plays and author index of theatre books. *Third supplement* (1956) includes separate author list of French plays with title index. *Class No:* 82-2(01)

[6710]

CARPENTER, C.A. Modern drama scholarship and criticism, 1966-1980: an international bibliography. Toronto and London, Univ. of Toronto Press, 1986. xxxv,587p. £60. ISBN: 0802025498.

A classified, selective list of publications on world drama since Ibsen, with 27,300 entries in 13 major sections on the dramas of particular regions, with subsections for countries and further subdivisions for individual dramatists. Truly international in coverage, although confined to works in Roman-alphabet languages, and contains many items not included in the *MLA international bibliography*. Some brief annotations where titles are not clear. Thoroughly cross-referenced. 'A book to be unequivocally welcomed ... valuable and indispensable' (*Modern Language Review*, v.84(3), July 1989, p.706-7).

Continued by *Modern drama scholarship and criticism, 1981-1990: an international bibliography* (Toronto, 1996. 625p. £63.50. ISBN: 080200914x), which has 25,200 entries, including additions and corrections to the first vol. *Class No:* 82-2(01)

[6711]

COLEMAN, A. *and* **TYLER, G.R. Drama criticism.** Denver, Colo., Swallow Press, 1966-69. 2v.

V.1 *A Checklist of interpretation since 1940 of English and American plays*. 1966. 457p. ISBN: 0804000697.

V.2 *A Checklist of interpretation since 1940 of classical and continental plays*. 1969. 446p. ISBN: 0804005001.

Lists criticism in books and periodicals under dramatists, A-Z, then play titles. *Class No:* 82-2(01)

[6712]

Harrap's book of 1000 plays: a comprehensive guide to the most frequently performed plays. Fletcher, S. *and* Jopling, N., *comps.* London, Harrap; New York, Facts on File, 1989. 352p. ISBN: 0245547835, UK; 0816021228, US.

US title is *The Book of 1000 plays*.

Arranged A-Z by title, each entry comprising author, genre, date and place of first production, plot summary, and list of characters. Selection is based upon 4 criteria: longest runs in London and New York; most popular plays in British and American repertory theatre; most popular plays with British and American dramatic societies; most frequently studied plays in schools and colleges. Includes musicals and operettas. Author index. *Class No:* 82-2(01)

[6713]

—500 plays: plot outlines and production notes. Shank, T., *ed.* Rev. reprint of 1963 ed. New York, Drama Book Publishers, 1991. 450p. $15. ISBN: 0896761029.

Originally published New York, Crowell-Collier Press, 1963, as *A Digest of 500 plays*.

Actually summarizes 528 plays in 11 sections based on country and period, with plays listed chronologically within each. Production notes cover cast, scenery, costumes, etc. Entries are the work of 39 contributors, but unsigned. Author-title index. List of US and UK agents and publishers has been revised, but otherwise it is a straight reprint. *Class No:* 82-2(01)

[6714]

HECK, T.F. Commedia dell'arte: a guide to the primary and secondary literature. New York, Garland, 1988. 450p. ISBN: 0824066448.

808 entries in 11 sections, covering all manifestations of the *commedia dell'arte* in French, Italian and other languages. Lists books, articles, dissertations, source manuscripts, exhibition catalogues, and iconographic material, with objective abstracts. Indexes of primary and secondary titles, and of authors and subjects. *Class No:* 82-2(01)

[6715]

LEONARD, W.T. Theatre: stage to screen to television. Metuchen, N.J., Scarecrow, 1981. 2v. (vii,1804p.). $92.50. ISBN: 0810813742.

Lists, A-Z by title, 327 plays which have had US or UK film and TV versions up to 1979. Data: author; date; plot synopsis; history; critical reception; stage, screen and TV productions. Indexes of composers, lyricists, librettists and playwrights. Excludes Greek classics and Shakespeare. Includes musical, opera and ballet versions. *Class No:* 82-2(01)

[6716]

NEW YORK PUBLIC LIBRARY. Research Libraries. **Catalog of the theatre and drama collections,** part one: Drama collection. Boston, Hall, 1967. 12v. ISBN: 081610106x.

In 2 sections: *Author listing* and *Listing by cultural origin,* each comprising 6 vols. and including 120,000 and 115,000 photolithographed catalogue cards for plays in western languages and translations from other languages.

First supplement (1973. vii,503p. ISBN: 0816107459) continues both sections, listing all cataloged additions to the drama collection of printed plays through 1971. *c.*10,500 entries in 2 sequences. From 1972, all additions are included in the *Dictionary catalog of The Research Libraries,* a photo-composed, automated catalogue available by subscription from The New York Public Library. *Class No:* 82-2(01)

[6717]

PALMER, H.H. European drama criticism, 1900-1975. 2nd ed. Hamden, Conn., Shoe String; Folkestone, Dawson, 1977. vii,653p. ISBN: 0208015892, US; 0712907920, UK.

1st ed. 1968, by H.H. Palmer and A.J. Dyson, covered 1900-66. Supplements published 1970 and 1974.

Indexes books and periodicals in English and foreign languages and covers writers 'cited in drama histories as the outstanding playwrights of their respective countries and contemporary playwrights of international renown' (*Preface*). 2nd ed. cumulates original ed. and Supplements plus new material through 1975, giving *c.*17,000 unannotated references. Excludes Shakespeare. Arranged A-

.... *(contd.)*
Z by playwright, then by play, then by critic. Index of plays and playwrights. Lists of books (*c.*850) and journals (over 700) indexed. *Class No:* 82-2(01)

[6718]
SALEM, J.M. Drury's guide to best plays. 4th ed. Metuchen, N.J., Scarecrow, 1987. viii,480p. $47.50. ISBN: 0810819805.

1st ed. 1953 by F.K.W. Drury; 3rd ed. 1978 by J.M. Salem.

Aimed at play-givers, play-goers, play-readers and librarians, and provides information on *c.*1,500 non-musical, full-length plays in English. Arranged by author, giving title, date, publisher, citations to anthologies, synopsis, number of acts, cast, sets, and royalty details. Indexed by numbers of characters and by subjects. Lists of prize-winning plays and of most popular plays for amateur and school production. List of anthologies. *Class No:* 82-2(01)

[6719]
SALEM, J.M. A Guide to critical reviews, part III: foreign drama, 1909-1977. 2nd ed. Metuchen, N.J., Scarecrow, 1979. 448p. $40. ISBN: 0810812266.

1st ed. 1968.

Provides citations to reviews of productions found in popular US and Canadian periodicals and in the *New York Times*. Does not cover academic articles. Arranged by playwright with title index.

Companion volumes cover American drama, musicals, and screenplays. *Class No:* 82-2(01)

[6720]
STRATMAN, C.J. Bibliography of medieval drama. 2nd ed., rev. and enlarged. New York, Ungar, 1972. 2v. (xv,1035p.). ISBN: 0804432724.

1st ed. Berkeley, Calif., Univ. of California Press, 1954.

Over 9,000 entries (5,000 more than 1st ed.). General studies and *Festschriften* are followed by sections on the following dramas: Liturgical Latin, English, Byzantine, French, German, Italian. Low Countries, Spanish. Each regional section includes general critical studies, editions and criticism of individual plays. Detailed index. *Class No:* 82-2(01)

Indexes

[6721]
CONNOR, B.M. *and* **MOCHEDLOVER, H.G. Ottemiller's index to plays in collections:** an author and title index to plays appearing in collections published between 1900 and 1985. 7th ed., rev. and enlarged. Metuchen, N.J., Scarecrow, 1988. xi,564p. $52. ISBN: 0810820811.

1st ed. 1943, by J.H. Ottemiller; 6th ed. 1976, covering 1900-75.

Indexes 6,548 full-length plays (over 1,000 more than 6th ed.) by 2,555 authors from 1,350 collections (an increase of 251) published throughout the English-speaking world. Previous eds. were confined to US and UK publications. Main author sequence is followed by list of collections analyzed, with key to symbols, and title index.
Class No: 82-2(014)

[6722]
Cumulated dramatic index, 1909-1949: a cumulation of the F.W. Faxon Company's *Dramatic Index*. Faxon, F.W., *and others, eds.* Boston, Hall, 1965. 2v. $675. ISBN: 0816104026.

One A-Z sequence of over 300,000 entries, cumulated from 41 annual vols. of *Dramatic Index* (1910-52). Mainly subject entries, with additional headings for titles, playwrights, and major characters. Indexes over 150 US and British periodicals and is largely limited to English-language plays, with foreign plays covered only if for sale or copyrighted in the US. 3 appendices: 1. Author list of books about the drama (over 6,500 items) - 2. Title list of published play texts - 3. Author list of published play texts.
Class No: 82-2(014)

[6723]
The Drama scholar's index to plays and filmscripts: a guide to plays and filmscripts in selected anthologies, series and periodicals. Samples, G., *ed.* Metuchen, N.J., Scarecrow, 1974-1986. 3v. ISBN: 0810812495, v.2; 0810818698, v.3.

Entries are under playwrights with references from titles. What makes the *Index* unique is the inclusion of filmscripts of 18th- and 19th-century plays and of plays not in English. V.2 'goes back to the beginning of recorded literature and continues through 1977' (*Introduction*). V.3 extends coverage to 1985. *Class No:* 82-2(014)

[6724]
KARP, R.S. *and* **SCHLESSINGER, J.H. Plays for children and young adults:** an evaluative index and guide. New York, Garland, 1991. 580p. $78. ISBN: 0824061128.

Indexes over 3,500 plays, mainly American, published 1975-89 and suitable for performance to or by young people aged 5-18. Entries are arranged A-Z by title and include: author, audience grade level, evaluation, cast analysis, duration, number of acts, setting, brief plot summary, royalty information, and any special staging considerations. 5 indexes: author, grade level, cast size, subject, and playing time. 'Offers more extensive information about more current plays for youth than any other source' (*Reference Books Bulletin*, v.87(16), April 15, 1991, p.1667).

Continued by *Supplement 1, 1989-1994* (1996. 384p. $65. ISBN: 0815314930), with 2,158 entries. *Class No:* 82-2(014)

[6725]
KELLER, D.H. Index to plays in periodicals. Rev. and expanded ed. Metuchen, N.J., Scarecrow, 1979. xi,824p. $63. ISBN: 0810812088.

1st ed. 1971; *Supplement* 1973.

9,662 entries (cumulation of 1st ed. and *Supplement* plus 2,145 new entries) arranged A-Z by author. Entries give title, number of acts, type of play, and periodical citation. 267 periodicals indexed. Index of play titles.

Supplemented by *Index to plays in periodicals, 1977-1987* (Scarecrow, 1990. 391p. $47.50. ISBN: 0810822881), which indexes 4,605 plays in 104 periodicals. *Class No:* 82-2(014)

[6726]
Play index, 1949/52-. New York, Wilson, 1953-. ISSN: 05543037.

Play index, 1949-1952: an index to 2,616 plays in 1,138 volumes, ed. by D.H. West and D.M. Peake. 1953. 239p. $48.

Play index, 1953-1960: an index to 4,952 plays in 1,735 volumes, ed. by E.A. Fidell and D.M. Peake. 1963. 464p. $48.

....(contd.)

Play index, 1961-1967: an index to 4,793 plays, ed. by E.A. Fidell. 1968. 464p. $48.

Play index, 1968-1972: an index to 3,848 plays, ed. by E.A. Fidell. 1973. 403p. $48.

Play index, 1973-1977: an index to 3,878 plays, ed. by E.A. Fidell. 1978. 475p. $48.

Play index, 1978-1982: an index to 3,429 plays, ed. by J. Yaakov. 1983. 480p. $48.

Play index, 1983-1987: an index to 3,964 plays, ed. by J. Yaakov and J. Greenfieldt. 1988. 522p. $58.

Play index, 1988-1992: an index to 4,397 plays. 1993. 542p. $80.

Each vol. has 4 sections: 1. Main sequence of author, title and subject entries, A-Z, with main entries under author giving brief synopsis and details of acts and casts - 2. Cast analysis (groups of plays according to sex and number of cast) - 3. List of collections indexed, with bibliographical details - 4. Directory of publishers and distributors. Covers plays written in or translated into English, including plays for children. *Class No:* 82-2(014)

[6727]

TREFNY, B.R. *and* **PALMER, E.C. Index to children's plays in collections.** 3rd ed. Metuchen, N.J., Scarecrow, 1986. 124p. $23.50. ISBN: 0810818930.

1st ed. 1972; 2nd ed. 1977.

Indexes plays by author, title and subject. *Class No:* 82-2(014)

Encyclopaedias & Dictionaries

[6728]

Critical survey of drama: English language series. Magill, F.N., *ed.* Rev. ed. Englewood Cliffs, N.J., Salem Press, 1994. 7v. $425. ISBN: 0893568511.

1st ed. 1985 (6v.)

Critical essays, with bibliographies, on 240 British, American and Commonwealth dramatists from Marlowe to Caryl Churchill, in the standard *Critical survey* format (See entries on *Critical survey of poetry*, etc.). 22 new entries for contemporary figures in this ed., but existing entries are unchanged apart from slight updating of secondary bibliographies. V.7 includes 21 topical essays, list of dramatic terms and general bibliography.

Critical survey of drama: foreign language series (1986. 6v. $350. ISBN 089356382x) covers 197 playwrights from Aeschylus to the present day. *Class No:* 82-2(03)

[6729]

GREGOR, J. Der Schauspielführer: der Inhalt der wichtigsten zeitgenössischen Theaterstücke aus aller Welt. Dietrich, M. *and* Greisenegger, W., *eds.* Stuttgart, Hiersemann, 1953-96. v.1-16 (in progress). ISBN: 3777253057.

An encyclopedia of dramatic literature of the world, with the German-speaking countries very strongly represented. Vols. 1-5 cover specific countries and regions, but from v.8 onwards each vol. covers world drama in successive periods. Vols. 6 and 7 contain supplements to the preceding vols.

Information on each play includes: author, title, type of play, date of first publication, date and place of first performance, cast, brief critical annotation, and a fairly detailed plot summary. V.14, *Das Schauspiel von 1984 bis 1986* (1989. x,354p.) has signed entries (average 2½p.) by 46 international contributors on 131 plays from 33 countries (nos. 2,404-2,534 in the running sequence beginning in v.1), arranged A-Z by author. Indexes to this vol. by country, German title, and original title, plus author index to vols. 1-14. *Class No:* 82-2(03)

[6730]

GRIFFITHS, T.R. *and* **WODDIS, C. Bloomsbury theatre guide.** New ed. London, Bloomsbury, 1991. ix,466p. illus. ISBN: 0747509905.

1st ed. 1988.

Over 400 entries arranged A-Z, the majority being for dramatists with some for directors, theorists, theatre companies and types of drama. 'It concentrates on the writers, the plays and the companies you are actually likely to see in the theatre now, rather than those who get into theatre reference books because they have always been in theatre reference books' (*Introduction*) and is therefore especially good on contemporary British theatre, with women, ethnic minority and gay writers well represented. Entries on each writer comprise list of plays (not meant to be comprehensive), literary analysis and discussion of a key play. Excellent cross-referencing system, using margins, gives access to information on over 3,000 plays, playwrights and directors. Comprehensive index. *Class No:* 82-2(03)

[6731]

International dictionary of theatre. Hawkins-Dady, M., *ed.* Chicago & London, St. James Press, 1992-95. 3v. illus. £100 per vol.

V.1 *Plays*. 1992. xxviii,954p. ISBN: 1558620958.

V.2 *Playwrights*. 1994. xx,1218p. ISBN: 1558620966.

V.3 *Actors, directors, designers*. 1995. 830p. ISBN: 1558620974.

A major new reference work, covering theatre from Ancient Greece to the present, each vol. of which stands alone as a comprehensive source on its subject. V.1 covers 620 of the most performed plays in world theatre, the work of 350 dramatists, each entry comprising premiere information, details of English translations, lists of modern editions, selective bibliography of criticism published since mid-1960s, and a lengthy narrative and critical essay by a recognized expert. Entries are arranged A-Z by title and many are illustrated with photographs from recent or historic productions. Over 200 contributors.

V.2 profiles 485 playwrights in the well-established Gale/ St. James format: detailed biographical notes; complete list of plays, in original language and translation; details of nondramatic works; lists of bibliographies, biographies and recent critical studies; 1,000-word signed essay. Thorough cross-referencing between vols. Index of play titles. 215 contributors from a wide range of countries. *Class No:* 82-2(03)

[6732]

McGraw-Hill encyclopedia of world drama. Hochman, S., *ed.* 2nd ed. New York, McGraw-Hill, 1984. 5v. £385. ISBN: 0070791694.

1st ed. 1972 in 4 vols.

Contains *c.*2,500 lengthy entries (the work of numerous contributors), mainly on dramatists but also on dramatic genres and terms, and includes for the first time in this ed. survey articles on regional, national and ethnic-linguistic dramas. Author entries include: biography; critical analysis; synopses of major plays; play list, giving dates of writing, publication and first production, type, and number of acts; bibliography of primary works and selected criticism. A-Z arrangement, with general index of names, subjects and titles in v.5, plus glossary (48p.) and invaluable list of *c.*17,500

....(*contd.*)
play titles, which is keyed to authors and includes plays *not* discussed in the text. Profusely illustrated. *Class No:* 82-2(03)

[6733]
Masterplots II: drama series. Magill, F.N., *ed.* Englewood Cliffs, N.J., Salem Press, 1990. 4v. $365. ISBN: 0893564915.

Covers 327 plays by 148 20th-century authors, most of them written in English although some major foreign works (mainly French) are included. Signed entries are arranged A-Z by title, average 5p., and include brief details of authorship, setting, dates of first performance and publication, and list of main characters, followed by plot summary and critical evaluation, in which themes, dramatic devices, and contexts are discussed. References to a few sources of further information are appended. Author index. *Class No:* 82-2(03)

[6734]
The Reader's encyclopedia of world drama. Gassner, J. *and* Quinn, E., *eds.* New York, Crowell, 1969; London, Methuen, 1970. xi,1030p. illus. ISBN: 0416195407, UK.

*c.*2,000 signed articles by 95 scholars covering 'drama as literature, not as theatre' (*Preface*); therefore, there are entries for playwrights, plays, national dramas, genres and literary terms but not for actors, theatres, companies, etc. Most articles include suggestions for further reading. 350 illustrations. Appendix: 'Basic documents in dramatic theory' (94p.) has 24 chapters on dramatists and critics from Aristotle to Dürrenmatt. *Class No:* 82-2(03)

Yearbooks & Directories

[6735]
The Dramatist's bible. Delaplaine, A., *ed.* Chicago, St. James Press, 1989. 222p. ISBN: 0912289775.

A directory for aspiring American playwrights, which includes lists of theatres, publishers, agents, writers' organizations, competitions, grants, etc. 'Has a good selection of everything, but not an exhaustive list of anything' (*Choice*, v.27(4), Dec. 1989, p.606).

Similar information can be found in the less expensive *Dramatists sourcebook*, produced annually by the Theatre Communications Group since 1982 (ISSN: 07331606). *Class No:* 82-2(058)

Excerpts

[6736]
Drama criticism: criticism of the most significant and widely studied dramatic works form all the world's literatures. Detroit, Gale, 1991-. v.1- (in progess). £71 per vol.

Yet another series following the format of *Contemporary literary criticism* (*q.v.*). Each vol. has entries on 8-10 dramatists of all periods, comprising biographical sketch, list of major works, substantial excerpts from critical studies and production reviews, the author's own commentary where possible, and bibliography of further reading. Cumulative indexes.

7 vols. published by the end of 1997. *Class No:* 82-2(082.200)

[6737]
Major modern dramatists. Stein, R., *ed.* New York, Ungar, 1984-6. 2v. $150. (*Library of literary criticism.*) ISBN: 0804432880.

Provides substantial excerpts from critical writings, chronologically arranged, on the best-known post-Ibsen dramatists. V.1 covers 35 authors in 3 A-Z sequences: American; British and Irish; German, Austrian, Swiss. V.2 covers a further 35 authors in 5 sequences: Norwegian and Swedish (2 only); French and Belgian; Italian; Spanish; Russian, Czech, Hungarian and Polish. List of plays mentioned and index of critics in each vol. *Class No:* 82-2(082.200)

Sound Recordings & Tapes

[6738]
HOFFMAN, H.H. Recorded plays: indexes to dramatists, plays and actors. Chicago and London, American Library Assoc., 1985. ix,139p. ISBN: 0838904408.

Lists 1,844 recordings of 700 different plays on phonodiscs, audio cassettes or tapes, video and 16mm film. Arranged by author (284 names) with indexes of titles and actors. List of 270 recorded anthologies. Directory of recording companies. Includes many foreign-language recordings. *Class No:* 82-2(086.7)

Biographies

[6739]
Contemporary dramatists. Berney, K., *ed.* 5th ed. Chicago and London, St. James Press, 1993. xxv,843p. $140. ISBN: 1558621857.

1st ed. 1973; 4th ed. 1988.

Main A-Z sequence has entries for *c.*450 English-language dramatists (an increase of 70 over previous ed., with nearly 100 writers covered for the first time) comprising biographical notes; full list of publications; information about published bibliographies, critical studies and manuscript locations; signed critical article by one of 150 contributors; and further reading list. Supplements on screenwriters, radio and TV writers, musical librettists and theatre groups have been dropped for the 5th ed., which has been produced in a larger format, like other works in this series, and is consequently easier to use. Title index of all plays cited has over 13,000 entries with author and date and is a useful reference tool in its own right. *Class No:* 82-2(092)

[6740]
Contemporary women dramatists. Berney, K., *ed.* Detroit & London, St. James Press, 1994. xxi,335p. $50. ISBN: 1558622128.

Profiles 86 English-language playwrights from around the world who have been influential in postwar theatre. Entries conform to established St. James style: biography; full list of plays, including screen adaptations and those written for radio and TV; bibliography of writings in other genres; signed critical essay of up to 1,000 words. Also includes extended articles on 20 of the most significant postwar plays by women. Title index. *Class No:* 82-2(092)

Prose

[6741]
Encyclopedia of the essay. Chevalier, T., *ed.* London and Chicago, Fitzroy Dearborn, 1997. xxi,1002p. £95. ISBN: 1884964303.

The first reference work entirely devoted to the essay, covering the genre from Montaigne to the present. Signed articles by nearly 300 contributors on over 400 writers, plus geographical surveys and entries on important single essays. Also covers related genres like letters and sermons, and topics, *e.g.* Propaganda, Biography. Author entries include critical assessment, biographical data, selected primary bibliography and suggestions for further reading. Title index and general index. *Class No:* 82-3

Fiction

Bibliographies of Bibliographies

[6742]
HARTMAN, D.K. *and* **DROST, J. Themes and settings in fiction:** a bibliography of bibliographies. New York, Greenwood, 1988. xv,223p. $65. (*Bibliographies and indexes in world literature.*) ISBN: 031325866x.

1,412 entries for bibliographies published 1900-85, which deal with persons, places and themes in English-language adult fiction. A-Z arrangement by author, with subject index and joint-author index. *Class No:* 82-31(009)

Bibliographies

[6743]
ADELMAN, I. *and* **DWORKIN, R. The Contemporary novel:** a checklist of critical literature on the English language novel since 1945. 2nd ed. Lanham, Md., Scarecrow, 1997. 696p. 125. ISBN: 0810831031.

1st ed. 1972.

A selective, unannotated bibliography of critical studies in books and periodicals of over 200 novelists. Arranged A-Z by novelist, with critical studies for each listed by author. 1st ed. was restricted to British and American writers, but coverage has now been extended to English-language writers worldwide. Over 12,000 entries. List of books analyzed. *Class No:* 82-31(01)

[6744]
BAKER, E.A. *and* **PACKMAN, J. A Guide to the best fiction:** English and American, including translations from foreign languages. New and enl. ed. London, Routledge, 1932 (reprinted 1967). viii,634p.

1st ed. 1903 as *Descriptive guide to best fiction;* 2nd ed. 1913 as *A Guide to best fiction.*

'The object has been to supply as complete a list as might be of the most notable prose fiction in English, with as much characterization of the contents, nature, and style of each book as would go into a few lines of print' (*Preface*). 7,800 entries arranged A-Z by author (previous eds. were arranged by national groups with chronological subdivisions) with a single-sequence index of authors, titles, subjects, historical names and allusions, places, and characters. *Class No:* 82-31(01)

[6745]
Cumulated fiction index, 1945/1960-. London, Assoc. of Assistant Librarians, 1960-. Irregular.

The first vol. (also known as *Fiction index three* because it superseded *Fiction index 1,* covering 1945-53, and its 1957 supplement) listed over 25,000 works of fiction, including short story collections, under 3,000 subject headings. Compiled by G.B. Cotton and A. Glencross.

Supplementary vols. have appeared as follows:

Cumulated fiction index, 1960-1969, comp. by R.F. Smith (1970. xii,307p. ISBN: 090009205x).

... *1970-1974,* comp. by R.F. Smith and A.J. Gordon (1975. 192p. ISBN: 0900092246).

... *1975-1979,* comp. by M.E. Hicken (1980. viii,225p. ISBN: 0900092335).

... *1980-1989,* comp. by M.E. Hicken (1990. 495p. £30. ISBN: 0900092785).

... *1990-1994,* comp. by M.E. Hicken (1996. 269p. £20. ISBN: 1901353001).

Fiction index: a guide to works of fiction available during the year ... appears annually between cumulations. *Class No:* 82-31(01)

[6746]
Fiction, 1876-1983: a bibliography of United States editions. New York, Bowker, 1983. 2v. (3150p.). $99.50. ISBN: 0835217264.

Lists over 170,000 works of fiction from the databases of *Books in print* and *American book publishing record,* including novels, short stories, anthologies, and collections. V.1 contains classified author index, listing authors by country and period, and main A-Z author index. V.2 contains title index, which, like the author index, has full publishing information. *Class No:* 82-31(01)

[6747]
Fiction catalog. 13th ed. New York, Wilson, 1996. 1000p. $115. ISBN: 0824208943.

1st ed. 1908; 12th ed. 1991.

An annotated list of some 5,450 works of fiction in English, including some translations of major foreign-language authors, selected with the assistance of several American public librarians. Entries are arranged by author, A-Z, and give full bibliographic data, price, plot summary, extract from a review, and contents list in the case of short story collections. Includes out-of-print titles. Index gives access by title and subject, the latter feature being particularly valuable. Subscription includes 4 annual paperbound supplements which appear between the 5-yearly editions. *Class No:* 82-31(01)

[6748]
HICKEN, M. Sequels, volume I: Adult books. 11th ed. London, Assoc. of Assistant Librarians, 1995. 278p. £27.50. ISBN: 0900092912.

1st ed. 1922; 10th ed. 1991.

A well-established guide which lists novels in which the same characters appear; sequences of novels connected by theme; sequences of novels with a historical or geographical connection; and non-fiction (mainly autobiography) intended to be read in sequence. Arranged by author, A-Z, with index of series titles and characters. Out-of-print material is dropped from time to time, so older eds. are worth retaining. *Class No:* 82-31(01)

[6749]

—JACOB, M. *and* APPLE, H. To be continued: an annotated guide to sequels. Phoenix, Ariz., Oryx Press, 1995. 304p. £36.50. ISBN: 0897748425.

Lists in author order both in-print and out-of-print works of fiction 'featuring continuing themes, plots or characters in which there is a sense of development and passage of time' (*Publisher's catalogue*). *Class No:* 82-31(01)

[6750]

HUSBAND, J. *and* **HUSBAND, J.F. Sequels:** an annotated guide to novels in series. 3rd ed. Chicago, American Library Assoc., 1997. viii.688p. $70. ISBN: 0838906966.

1st ed. 1982; 2nd ed. 1990.

A much-expanded edition which claims to feature 33% more series than its predecessor. Like Hicken's similarly-titled work it is arranged by author, A-Z, but it differs in excluding nonfiction series and including scope notes for every author and a one-sentence plot summary for each novel listed. Indexes of titles and subjects, the latter including main characters. *Class No:* 82-31(01)

[6751]

KEARNEY, E.I. *and* **FITZGERALD, L.S. The Continental novel:** a checklist of criticism in English. Metuchen, N.J., Scarecrow, 1968-83. 2v.

V.1 *1900-1966.* 1968 (xiv,460p.). V.2 *1967-1980.* 1983 (xiv,496p. $35. ISBN 0810815982).

In 6 sections: French; Spanish and Portuguese; Italian; German; Scandinavian; Russian and East European. Arranged by novelist then by novel title within each section. No annotations. No index to either vol. *Class No:* 82-31(01)

[6752]

Modern fiction studies. West Lafayette, Ind., Purdue Univ., Dept. of English, 1955-. v.1, no.1-. Quarterly. ISSN: 00267724.

Often produces special numbers concerned with individual writers or particular topics (*e.g.* Fall 1996, *Gertrude Stein*). These usually include bibliographies, check-lists or review articles on recent publications.

A Cumulative index to 'Modern Fiction Studies' (1955-1984), volumes 1-30 (West Lafayette, Ind., M.F.S., 1985. 270p. ISBN: 0961580208) has separate sequences for subjects, authors, books reviewed, and reviewers.
Class No: 82-31(01)

Jews

[6753]

KEENOY, R. *and* **BROWN, S. The Babel guide to Jewish fiction.** London, Boulevard Books, 1998. 285p. £9.95. ISBN: 189946025x.

Provides original reviews by 21 specialists of 150 20th-century Jewish classics which are currently available in English. Each review is followed by a brief extract from the work in question. Appended database section (not easy to use) lists most of the 20th-century fiction which has been translated into English from Hebrew and Yiddish and published in the UK, US or Israel. Glossary of Hebrew and Yiddish terms (2p.). *Class No:* 82-31(01)(=924)

Women

[6754]

FUDERER, L.S. The female bildungsroman in English: an annotated bibliography of criticism. New York, Modern Language Assoc. of America, 1990. 47p. $10. ISBN: 0873529626.

Lists 133 studies (books, chapters, articles and dissertations) published 1972-87 on women's novels of adolescence and self-discovery. List of over 270 novels cited in the studies. Index of critics and authors. *Class No:* 82-31(01)-0055.2

[6755]

GRIMES, J., ***and others*****. Novels in English by women, 1891-1920:** a preliminary checklist. New York, Garland, 1981. xviii,805p. ISBN: 0824095227.

Computer-produced listing of over 15,000 novels by over 5,000 authors published in the UK and US. 3 alphabetical sequences: authors and their works, verified; anonymous and pseudonymous works; unverified references from periodicals and reviews. The annotations which accompany 75% of entries (usually plot summaries) have been criticised for inconsistency by reviewers, but are 'working notes not intended for publication' (*Preface*). *Class No:* 82-31(01)-0055.2

[6756]

—DAIMS, D. *and* GRIMES, J. Toward a feminist tradition: an annotated bibliography of novels in English by women, 1891-1920. New York, Garland, 1982. 905p. ISBN: 0824095235.

A selection of over 3,400 titles by 1,723 authors from the preceding checklist, in which the compilers have found evidence of a developing feminist fiction, *e.g.* novels featuring women in unconventional roles. Arranged A-Z by author with extracts from contemporary reviews.
Class No: 82-31(01)-0055.2

Gay People

[6757]

Out on the shelves: gay and lesbian fiction. Gay Interest Group of the Canadian Library Association, *comp.* [Ottawa], Canadian Library Association, 1982. 17p. ISBN: 0888021682.

Lists 11 anthologies, 50 lesbian novels, 51 gay men's novels, and 13 literary studies and bibliographies. Concise annotations. 'Does not presume to be a core list of the best gay or lesbian fiction, but rather a representative selection of titles currently available in print' (*Introduction*).
Class No: 82-31(01)-0055.3

Encyclopaedias & Dictionaries

[6758]

BIAGINI, M.K. A Handbook of contemporary fiction for public libraries and school libraries. Metuchen, N.J., Scarecrow, 1989. x,247p. $31. ISBN: 081082275x.

Aimed at librarians involved in book selection and reader guidance. Part 1, 'Popular fiction genres', has 9 sections, each with overview of the genre, list of reference and bibliographical sources, list of authors, A-Z, with their titles in date order (samples only for prolific writers). 1,158 authors covered. Part 2, 'Contemporary fiction', covers literary writing in 3 sections for Americans, Britons, and World authors by continent and country, in a similar format to Part 1. 327 authors covered. Extra information in some genre sections, *e.g.* lists of titles featuring a particular

.... *(contd.)*
detective/spy. Concentrates on postwar writing. Author index, but lack of title index is disappointing. *Class No:* 82-31(03)

[6759]
Critical survey of long fiction: English language series. Magill, F.N., *ed.* Rev. ed. Englewood Cliffs, N.J., Salem Press, 1991. 8v. $593.75. ISBN: 0893568252.

1st ed. 1983.

Vols. 1-7 contain entries on authors, A-Z, associated with the novel and novella, listing their works, discussing their achievements, analyzing major works, and listing selected secondary sources. V.8 includes background essays on the development of the 2 literary forms and an index to the set.

Critical survey of long fiction: foreign language series (1984. 5v. ISBN: 0893563692) is a similarly-arranged collection of critical essays on 182 foreign-language novelists. *Class No:* 82-31(03)

[6760]
HICKEN, M. *and* **PRYTHERCH, R. Now read on ...** a guide to contemporary popular fiction. 2nd ed. Aldershot, Scolar Press, 1994. 442p. £35. ISBN: 1859280080.

1st ed. 1990.

Provides brief biographical information and critical comment on over 350 English-language writers of popular fiction, together with lists of their publications and suggestions for further reading. Arranged in 20 categories, some of them difficult to differentiate, *e.g.* 'Family stories'/'The Saga'; 'Detective stories'/'Police work'. Does not cover westerns or light romantic novels and is dominated by British writers, which means that some public library favourites are omitted. Lists of literary award winners. Indexes of authors and of series and recurring characters. 2nd ed. includes 60 new authors and a new category, 'Women detectives.' *Class No:* 82-31(03)

[6761]
HINCKLEY, K. *and* **HINCKLEY, B. American best sellers:** a reader's guide to popular fiction. Bloomington, Ind., Indiana Univ. Press, 1989. 260p. $29.95. ISBN: 0253327288.

The core of the book is a listing (A-Z by author) of the 468 top fictional best sellers in the US, 1965-85, with biographical notes on the authors and brief plot summaries. Chapters on categories, characters, themes and trends include considerable statistical analysis. Appendices list award winners, pseudonyms, film versions and the best-sellers of each year. Bibliography (5p.) includes autobiographies by bestselling authors. *Class No:* 82-31(03)

[6762]
McLEISH, K. Bloomsbury good reading guide. New [*i.e.* 3rd] ed., completely rev. and updated. London, Bloomsbury, 1994. xiii,306p. £4.99. ISBN: 0747516812.

1st ed. 1988; 2nd ed. 1990.

'The bulk of the text is articles on some 350 authors, describing the kind of books they wrote, listing titles and suggesting books, by the same authors and by others, which might make interesting follow-ups' (*Introduction*). In addition, listed alphabetically alongside the author-articles, are over 90 'menus', *i.e.* subject lists of suggested reading varying from 'Action Thrillers' to 'Weepies', with 7-8 books per list. Restricted to prose fiction available in English and includes popular as well as literary novelists. Keep at the lending counter for the guidance of readers but treat the follow-up suggestions with caution as these are inevitably subjective. Author and title index.

.... *(contd.)*
3rd ed. has over 20 new entries and references to over 700 new titles, bringing the total number of books covered above 3,500. *Class No:* 82-31(03)

[6763]
Postmodern fiction: a bio-bibliographical guide. McCaffery, L., *ed.* New York, Greenwood, 1986. xxviii,604p. $89.50. (*Movements in the arts.*) ISBN: 0313241708.

Part I (p.5-244) has 15 signed 'overview articles' on the varieties of postmodern fiction and criticism, each followed by a selected bibliography. Part II contains signed entries on over 100 authors (Abish to Zelazny) averaging 2½p. and comprising biographical summary, critical assessment of major works and selected bibliography of primary and secondary sources. Selected bibliography of general postmodern criticism (7p.). Index. Notes on 88 contributors. *Class No:* 82-31(03)

[6764]
The Reader's companion to the twentieth-century novel. Parker, P., *ed.* London, Fourth Estate, & Oxford, Helicon, 1994. xxx,748p. £25. ISBN: 1857022092.

A very useful guide to modern fiction, comprising essays (average 750 words) on 750 novels by over 400 UK, US and Commonwealth writers. Arranged chronologically, 1900-93, the unsigned entries (38 contributors listed) provide plot summary and critical assessment and place the work in historical and biographical context. Over 150 entries include illustrative extracts. Genre fiction largely excluded, but a few key crime and espionage titles are covered, as are some seminal works for children. All Booker Prize winners are included. Brief biographies of all the authors follow the sequence of novels. List of major world events for each year. Author and title indexes and full list of contents provide easy access. *Class No:* 82-31(03)

[6765]
Der Romanführer: der Inhalt der Romane und Novellen der Weltliteratur. Olbrich, W., *and others, eds.* Stuttgart, Hiersemann, 1950-1996. v.1-32 (in progress).

A world digest of novels, with each vol. devoted to a country or region during a particular period; *e.g.* v.21, *Romanische Prosa aus dem Jahren 1973-1989* (1989. xii,358p.) lists 358 Romance-language novels by 258 authors in 8 sections for countries/regions. Entries give the author's place and date of birth and death, bibliographical details and classification of the novel, plot summary, and critical evaluation. Index of authors and titles. V.15 comprises an index (authors, titles, and subjects) to the first 14 vols.

Der Grosse Romanführer: 500 Hauptwerke der Weltliteratur; Inhalte, Themen, Personen, ed. by B. Gräf (Stuttgart, Hiersemann, 1996. xvi,760p. DM128. ISBN: 3777296244), is a single-vol. compilation of articles on 500 key titles. Selection is limited to works available in German translation and a restriction of one title per author leads to some surprising omissions. Index of authors and titles. *Class No:* 82-31(03)

[6766]
What do I read next? a reader's guide to current genre fiction. Barron, N., *and others, eds.* Detroit, Gale, 1991- . Annual.

An annual guide to genre fiction for librarians involved in readers advisory work, listing the year's US publications by author within sections for mysteries, science fiction, fantasy, horror, romance, and westerns. Entries include publication details; series name and number in series; description of

....(contd.)

main characters; time period and locale; references to up to 5 reviews; and list of similar works by the author and other writers. 8 indexes (author, title, series, character, character description, time period, geographic setting, and genre/sub-genre) provide full access. 1997 vol. (679p. ISBN: 078760058x) costs $84.

Available on CD-ROM from 1998 (£395. ISBN: 0787613630). The first release carries details of 63,000 titles, including standard and classic novels (and even some nonfiction works) in addition to genre fiction. Annual subscription includes quarterly updates.

The following genre-specific guides, with the same basic format as the parent work, have been published:

What do I read next? - multicultural literature. 1997. 800p. ISBN: 0787608149.

What historical novel do I read next? 1997. 2v. £96. ISBN: 0787603880.

What mystery do I read next? 1997. 545p. £61. ISBN: 0787615927.

What romance do I read next? 1997. 679p. £60.50. ISBN: 0787618675.

What western do I read next? 1998. 500p. £53. ISBN: 0787618659.

What fantastic fiction do I read next? 1998. 1679p. £68. ISBN: 0787618667. *Class No:* 82-31(03)

[6767]

—HERALD, D.T. Genreflecting: a guide to reading interests in genre fiction. 4th ed. Englewood, Colo., Libraries Unlimited, 1995. xxvi,367p. $38. ISBN: 156308354x.

1st ed. 1982 by B. Rosenberg; 3rd ed. 1991 by Rosenberg and Herald.

Chapters on 7 major genres (Western, Crime, Adventure, Romance, Science Fiction, Fantasy, Horror) with subgenres identified and described, major authors and works listed, and information on secondary literature, publishers, associations, conventions, films, periodicals, awards, etc. Indexes of genre authors and themes, and author-title index to secondary material. Does not aspire to exhaustive coverage, but is a useful readers' advisory tool. *Class No:* 82-31(03)

[6768]

WHISSEN, T.R. Classic cult fiction: a companion to popular cult fiction. Westport, Conn., Greenwood, 1992. 319p. $75. ISBN: 031326550x.

Essays on 50 novels which have attained cult status, from *The Sorrows of Young Werther* (1774) to *The Hitchhiker's guide to the Galaxy* (1979), with over half of them published since 1960. Entries average 5p.; are arranged by title; set the novel in its historical context; analyse major characters and themes; and include selective bibliography of critical studies. Long introductory essay on the history of the cult phemonenon; chronology of 83 major cult novels; list of first and current eds. of the 50 treated works; brief, annotated bibliography of general studies. Index lists authors and titles of the 50 novels and also themes treated in the Introduction, but does not cover topics discussed in the essays.
Class No: 82-31(03)

[6769]

Who else writes like? a readers' guide to fiction authors. Huse, R. *and* Huse, J., *eds.* 3rd ed. Loughborough, Library and Information Statistics Unit, Loughborough University, 1996. 312p. £18.95. ISBN: 0948848847.

1st ed. by P. Mann, 1985, as *A Readers' guide to fiction authors*; 2nd ed. 1993.

A tool for librarians faced with the question 'Who writes like my favourite author?'. Main A-Z list has over 1,200 of

....(contd.)

the most popular novelists, based on British Public Lending Right returns, with the names of up to 20 authors who normally write in a similar style, but should be used with care as there are no annnotations. Further lists of authors under 14 genre and sub-genre headings, *e.g.* crime writers are listed under 11 sub-genres with names of principal characters and detectives. Lists of winners of major British fiction awards since 1970. 3rd ed. has new section on writers of teenage fiction. *Class No:* 82-31(03)

Women

[6770]

WHEELER, K. A Guide to twentieth-century women novelists. Oxford, Blackwell, 1997. xiii,442p. £70. ISBN: 0631164936.

135 essays analyzing the narrative practices and stylistic devices of women novelists from the English-speaking world. Arranged in 4 chronological sections (1895-1925; 1918-45; 1944-75; 1970-95), each having 2 thematic essays followed by entries on authors, A-Z. 5th section has a chapter on feminist theory; a geographically arranged chapter on writers from the rest of the world; and a very useful bibliographic essay on research resources (10p.). Bibliography (79p.) lists secondary material on the 135 main writers, plus anthologies and general criticism. Index.
Class No: 82-31(03)-0055.2

Biographies

[6771]

Contemporary novelists. Brown, S.W., *ed.* 6th ed. Detroit and London, St. James Press, 1996. xxiv,1173p. £120. ISBN: 155862189x.

1st ed. 1972; 5th ed. 1991.

Entries on over 600 living English-language novelists, comprising biographical notes, full list of publications, information about published bibliographies and manuscript collections, plus a signed critical essay (800-1000 words) by one of a team of over 250 contributors. Title index of all novels mentioned, giving authors and dates. Index of authors by nationality. *Class No:* 82-31(092)

[6772]

Popular world fiction, 1900-present. Beacham, W. *and* Niemeyer, S., *eds.* Washington, D.C., Beacham, 1987. 4v. $189. ISBN: 0933833083.

A companion to *Beacham's Popular fiction in America* (*q.v.*), with signed entries on 176 authors, most of them British and American, but also including translated foreign authors, whose works have been popular in the US. Entries range from 7 to 10p. and concentrate on critical analysis rather than biography, with sections on publishing history, critical reception, and analysis of selected titles. Appended bibliographies list further works by the author and selected (up to 10) secondary sources. A-Z arrangement by author with title and author index in v.4 and lists of titles (by themes) and authors (by genre) in each vol.

By no means confined to writers of genre fiction, with literary writers like Conrad, Hemingway and Kafka included, but will be most valued for its coverage of the best-sellers. *Class No:* 82-31(092)

Women

[6773]

ROBINSON, D. Women novelists, 1891-1920: an index to biographical and autobiographical sources. New York, Garland, 1984. li,458p. ISBN: 0824089774.

A companion to *Novels in English by women, 1891-1920* and *Toward a feminist tradition (qq.v)*, it identifies English-language biographical and autobiographical works relating to 1,565 writers, most of them British and American. Includes individual and collective biographies, letters, diaries, obituaries and entries in reference works, but not periodical articles. 290 collective works indexed. Main A-Z sequence is followed by list of black writers (5 only) and national listings (24 countries). *Class No:* 82-31(092)-0055.2

Libraries

[6774]

A Guide to special fiction collections in libraries in the United Kingdom and the Republic of Ireland. Parry, D., *comp.* [Newcastle-upon-Tyne], LINC & CONARLS, 1992. 60p. £12.95. ISBN: 1873753047.

Lists collections in 171 academic, public and special libraries, including collections relating to specific authors, genres, periods and languages. Access arrangemants explained. Index of over 300 authors. Subject index. *Class No:* 82-31:061:026/027

Romantic Fiction

[6775]

JAEGLY, P.J. Romantic hearts: a personal reference for romance readers. 3rd ed. Lanham., Md., Scarecrow, 1997. 928p. illus. $62. ISBN: 0810830027.

Provides bibliographical information on over 10,000 titles from all types of romance fiction: historical, Gothic, Regency, contemporary, etc. Arranged by author with titles listed chronologically. Index of pseudonyms. *Class No:* 82-311

[6776]

Twentieth-century romance and historical writers. Vasudevan, A., *ed.* 3rd ed. Detroit & London, St. James Press, 1994. xx,890p. $140. ISBN: 1558621806.

1st ed. Detroit, Gale, 1982, as *Twentieth-century romance and gothic writers* (ed. J. Vinson); 2nd ed. St. James Press, 1990 (ed. L. Henderson).

Covers 539 writers, 100 of them new to 3rd ed. and several not automatically associated with genre fiction (*e.g.* Melvyn Bragg, Toni Morrison). Entries by over 140 contributors are arranged A-Z and comprise biographical notes; complete bibliography (including non-fiction works) with details of first UK and US editions; list of critical studies; manuscript locations; and signed critical essay of 800-1,000 words. New section in each entry covering film adaptations. All entries revised and updated. Reading list of over 100 general critical works. Title index has *c.*20,000 entries. Confined to English-language writers. *Class No:* 82-311

Crime Fiction

Bibliographies

[6777]

Australian crime fiction: a bibliography, 1857-1993. Loder, J., *ed.* Port Melbourne, Thorpe, 1994. 287p. A$55. ISBN: 1875589511.

Lists over 2,100 titles by more than 500 authors, giving full bibliographic details and a brief descriptive annotation. *Class No:* 82-312(01)

[6778]

BARZUN, J. *and* **TAYLOR, W.H. A Catalogue of crime:** being a reader's guide to the literature of mystery, detection and related genres. Rev. and enl. ed. New York, Harper & Row, 1989. xxxvi,952p. $50. ISBN: 0060157968.

1st ed. 1971.

A bibliography containing 5,045 entries (an increase of 1,570 over the 1st ed.) in 5 sections: novels; short stories, collections, anthologies, magazines, pastiches and plays; studies and histories of the genre, with lives of writers; true crime; and the literature of Sherlock Holmes. Entries comprise author's name, dates and pseudonyms; US publishing details; and a concise, highly personal, annotation. A-Z arrangement by author within each section, with author and title index which includes the names of true criminals under the heading 'Cases'. The section on supernatural fiction has been dropped for this ed., as has the subject index, while biographical data is almost entirely excluded because there are ample other sources. Has been criticized for not being absolutely comprehensive, but is clearly a personal selection and as such is valuable for its unique, often highly critical, annotations. *Class No:* 82-312(01)

[6779]

BREEN, J.L. What about murder? a guide to books about mystery and detective fiction. Metuchen, N.J., Scarecrow, 1981. xviii,157p. $25. ISBN: 0810814137.

Annotated entries on 239 secondary sources in 6 sections: histories; reference works; books on special subjects; collected essays and reviews; technical manuals; studies of individual authors. Index. Winner of the Edgar Allan Poe Award, 1981.

Continued by *What about murder? (1981-1991)*, also by Breen (1993. xi,376p. $41.50. ISBN: 0810826097), whose 565 entries testify to the greatly increased academic interest in the genre. Over 200 entries appear in a new section covering mystery anthologies with reference value. Evaluative, often lengthy, annotations by an obvious enthusiast. Index of authors, titles and series (115p.). *Class No:* 82-312(01)

[6780]

COX, J.R. Masters of mystery and detective fiction: an annotated bibliography. Englewood Cliffs, N.J., Salem Press, 1990 (later Sarecrow Press). 281p. $42. (*Magill bibliographies.*) ISBN: 0810828049.

Selective listings of biographical and critical studies for 74 authors, with the emphasis on sources which should be readily available in US libraries. 'Very useful ... as a beginning reference point for mystery fiction research' (*Choice*, v.27(10), June 1990, p.1648). *Class No:* 82-312(01)

[6781]

Crime fiction criticism: an annotated bibliography. Johnson, T.W., *and others, eds.* New York, Garland, 1981. xii,423p. ISBN: 0824094905.

1,810 items in 2 sections: general (reference works; books; dissertations; articles) and individual crime writers, A-Z. Surprisingly, the author with most citations is Dickens. Concise, descriptive annotations. Index of critics.

See also W. Albert's *Detective and mystery fiction: an international bibliography of secondary sources* (Madison, Ind., Brownstone, 1985. 800p. $62. ISBN: 094102802x). *Class No:* 82-312(01)

[6782]

Detective fiction: a collector's guide. Cooper, J. *and* Pike, B., *eds.* 2nd ed. Aldershot, Scolar Press, 1994. x,341p. illus. £39.50. ISBN: 0859679918.

1st ed. Taunton, Barn Owl Books, 1988.

Includes a checklist of the works of 157 of the most collected authors, listing all their novels and short story collections, with details of first eds., dust wrappers and series characters. 10 appendices, including lists of award winners, specialist dealers, journals and societies. 1st ed. concentrated on Golden Age authors and their successors, but more contemporary writers are covered this time. Colour illustrations of over 90 dust-wrappers and many more in black and white. *Class No:* 82-312(01)

[6783]

GREEN, J. *and* FINCH, J. Sleuths, sidekicks and stooges: an annotated bibliography of detectives, their assistants and their rivals in crime, mystery and adventure fiction, 1794-1995. Aldershot, Scolar Press, 1997. 868p. £70. ISBN: 1859281923.

7,000 entries from British and American fiction, arranged A-Z by detective. Entries give details of their colleagues and partners, bibliographical data on the books in which they appear, and biographical notes on authors. Indexes of sidekicks, protagonists, authors and titles. *Class No:* 82-312(01)

[6784]

HUBIN, A.J. Crime fiction II, 1749-1990: a comprehensive bibliography. [2nd ed.]. New York, Garland, 1994. 2v. $195. ISBN: 0824068912.

1st ed. 1979 as *Bibliography of crime fiction, 1749-1975*; *Supplement*, 1988, covering 1981-5.

An attempt to record all crime fiction (including gothic, suspense and spy novels) published in English in hardback and paperback, but omitting magazine and dime novels, children's fiction and anthologies. This ed. cumulates 1st ed. and *Supplement* and adds recent material.

Lists over 60,000 novels by author, A-Z, in v.1, with indexes of titles, series and settings in v.2. Author entries provide details of US and British publications and include citations to biographical reference sources. New features include a list of over 4,000 films, in all languages, based on crime novels, with details of studio, year of release, screenwriter and director (indexed), and a bibliographical listing of individual short stories included in over 4,000 collections. List of 4,500 series characters and the stories in which they appear. List of 340 settings with relevant titles. 'A comprehensive bibliography of primary works, far surpassing in coverage any similar title' (*Choice*, v.32(4), Dec. 1994, p.576). *Class No:* 82-312(01)

[6785]

LACHMAN, M. A Reader's guide to the American novel of detection. Boston, Hall, 1993. 435p. $45. (*Reader's guides to mystery novels.*) ISBN: 0816118035.

Lists over 1,300 novels by 166 US and Canadian authors, presenting series in chronological (rather than publication) order and including lists of characters, periods, settings, etc. Coverage confined to books featuring amateur detectives.

Other titles in the series, each covering over 1,000 works, are:

A Reader's guide to the private eye novel, by G.W. Niebuhr. 1993. 323p. $45. ISBN: 0816118027.

A Reader's guide to the classic British mystery, by S.P. Oleksiw. 1988. xiii,583p. $40. ISBN: 0816187878.

A Reader's guide to the police procedural, by J.A. Vicarel. 1995. 402p. $50. ISBN: 0816118019.

Class No: 82-312(01)

[6786]

MENENDEZ, A.J. The Subject is murder: a selective guide to mystery fiction. New York, Garland, 1986-90. 2v. ISBN: 0824086554, v.1; 0824025806, v.2.

Groups English-language crime novels under a wide range of subject headings (21 in v.1; 29 in v.2), but provides no further annotation other than brief bibliographical information. Author and title indexes. Appendix in v.2 ranks the most popular subjects. Over 5,900 works listed in all. *Class No:* 82-312(01)

[6787]

—MACKLER, T. Murder... by category: a subject guide to mystery fiction. Metuchen, N.J., Scarecrow, 1991. xiii,470p. $55.50. ISBN: 0810824639.

The work of a specialist bookseller, based on enquiries received from customers. Lists *c.*1,600 crime novels under 90 subject headings, from 'Academics' to 'Writers and their conventions', and provides bibliographic information with a brief synopsis. Strongly US-oriented and limited to titles in print. Appendices include brief lists of award winners and reference books and more substantial lists of female detectives and British women crime writers. Author index. *Class No:* 82-312(01)

Indexes

[6788]

CONTENTO, W. *and* GREENBERG, M.H. Index to crime and mystery anthologies. Boston, Hall, 1990. 736p. $60. ISBN: 0816186294.

Indexes over 1,000 post-1874 anthologies from the US, UK, Canada, and Australia, containing over 17,000 works by *c.*36,000 authors. Author and title sequences, but no subject index. Full bibliographic details and contents listing for each anthology. Excludes single-author collections. *Class No:* 82-312(014)

[6789]

OLDERR, S. Mystery index: subjects, settings, and sleuths of 10,000 titles. Chicago, American Library Assoc., 1987. 492p. $20. ISBN: 0838904610.

4 sections: 1. Main entry (author, US and UK titles, publication details, main characters) - 2. Title index - 3. Subject and setting index - 4. Character index. Largely confined to 20th-century hardback publications. *Class No:* 82-312(014)

Encyclopaedias & Dictionaries

[6790]
Critical survey of mystery and detective fiction. Magill, F.N., *ed.* Englewood Cliffs, N.J., Salem Press, 1989. 4v. $300. ISBN: 0893564869.

Covers 270 writers, A-Z, in vols. 1-3, the entries including place and date of birth, date of death, categorization within the genre, pseudonyms, details of series and characters, biocritical essay (*c.*2,500 words), bibliographies of crime fiction and other works, and brief list of secondary material. V.4 contains a glossary, indexes of plot types and characters, and author-title index. *Class No:* 82-312(03)

[6791]
Encyclopedia of mystery and detection. Steinbrunner, C. *and* Penzler, O., *eds.* Reprint of 1976 ed. San Diego, Harcourt Brace Jovanovich, 1984. 436p. illus. ISBN: 0156287870.

Originally published New York, McGraw-Hill; London, Routledge, 1976.

600 articles of which the majority cover authors, with others on detectives and criminals, and a few on topics (*e.g.* Television detectives, Pulp magazines). Checklists of books and films follow entries on major writers and characters. Over 300 illustrations, many of them from films. Definition of 'mystery' is wide as some gothic romance and adventure writers are included. *Class No:* 82-312(03)

[6792]
HAGEN, O.A. Who done it? a guide to detective, mystery and suspense fiction. New York, Bowker, 1969. xx,834p.

An author listing of over 50,000 US and British crime novels, 1841-1967, followed by a bibliographic guide to mystery fiction in 8 sections, including a list of novels by subject and details of mystery films and plays, awards and prizes, anthologies, and critical studies. Useful list of characters in crime fiction. Title index to the primary bibliography. *Class No:* 82-312(03)

[6793]
McLEISH, K. ***and*** **McLEISH, V. Bloomsbury good reading guide to murder, thrillers and crime fiction.** London, Bloomsbury, 1990. 224p. ISBN: 0747507325.

Deals with over 300 crime fiction authors, using the format used in the *Bloomsbury good reading guide* (*q.v.*). Includes a list of characters. *Class No:* 82-312(03)

Periodicals

[6794]
COOK, M.L. Mystery, detective, and espionage magazines. Westport, Conn., Greenwood, 1983. xxiv,793p. $105. (*Historical guides to the world's periodicals and newspapers.*) ISBN: 0313233101.

An A-Z listing, giving history, description of contents, details of editors, title changes, etc., and references to indexing sources. *Class No:* 82-312(051)

Biographies

[6795]
St. James guide to crime and mystery writers. Pederson, J.P., *ed.* 4th ed. Chicago & London, St. James Press, 1996. 1264p. £105. ISBN: 1558621784.

1st ed. New York, St. Martin's Press, 1980; 2nd ed. London, St. James Press, 1991. First 3 eds. entitled *Twentieth-century crime and mystery writers.*

Entries are arranged A-Z and cover 650 writers (mainly British and American, but including a few foreign writers

.... (contd.)

whose works are available in English), and comprise biographical notes, complete bibliography (including non-crime works), list of critical studies, manuscript locations, and signed critical essay. Guide to further reading. Comprehensive index of titles, with publication dates. Nationality index. 'In the world of crime and mystery fiction, this work is the Bible' (*Public Library Journal,* v.6(6), Nov/Dec. 1991. p.174-5, on 3rd ed.). *Class No:* 82-312(092)

Chandler

[6796]
BRUCCOLI, M.J. Raymond Chandler: a descriptive bibliography. Pittsburgh, Univ. of Pittsburgh Press, 1979. xv,146p. illus. $100. (*Pittsburgh series in bibliography.*) ISBN: 0822933829.

Section A. (106p.) lists and describes all Chandler's books and pamphlets, including collections. Further sections list contributions to books, magazines and newspapers, dust jacket blurbs for other authors and screenplays. Many reproductions of jackets and title pages. Index. *Class No:* 82-312CHA

Christie

[6797]
SOVA, D.B. Agatha Christie A to Z: the essential reference to her life and writings. New York, Facts on File, 1996. 416p. illus. $40. ISBN: 0816030189.

Over 2,500 cross-referenced entries covering works (including detailed synopsis, publishing history and descriptions of characters, but not the solutions to crimes!); film and TV productions; and Christie's friends, family and associates. 65 photographs. Chronology. Bibliography. Index. *Class No:* 82-312CHR

Doyle

[6798]
BUNSON, M.E. The Sherlock Holmes encyclopedia. London, Pavilion, 1995. xxi,326p. illus. £17.99. ISBN: 1857935020.

1,500 entries, A-Z, on all aspects of Holmes, including story synopses; characters; real and fictional places; methods of crime and detection; film, radio and TV adaptations; actors, etc. Over 100 illustrations, including maps, film stills and original drawings. 'Chronology of Sherlockiana, 1852-1987' (6p.). Appendices include list of films and list of Holmes societies. Unfortunately no sign of complete index mentioned in *Introduction*, but very impressive nevertheless. *Class No:* 82-312DOY

[6799]
DE WAAL, R.B. The World bibliography of Sherlock Holmes and Dr. Watson: a classified and annotated list of materials relating to their lives and adventures. New York, Bramhall House, 1974. xiv,526p. illus. ISBN: 0517217597.

Extraordinary compilation of all conceivable materials relating to Holmes. Lists all known book editions, including Braille, shorthand and foreign-language eds. (50 languages), plus films, musicals, plays, radio and TV broadcasts, recordings, parodies and memorials. 6,221 items in 10 sections and 29 subsections, with full annotations throughout. Critical studies included. Appendix has directory

....(contd.)

of collections and libraries and of Holmes societies worldwide. Indexes of personal names and of titles.
Class No: 82-312DOY

[6800]

—DE WAAL, R.B. The International Sherlock Holmes. Hamden, Conn., Archon; London, Mansell, 1980. 621p. ISBN: 0208017771, US; 0720116007, UK.

A further 6,135 entries in the same format as the *World bibliography*, covering material published 1971-78 and earlier items previously omitted. Updated directory of Holmes societies. *Class No:* 82-312DOY

[6801]

GREEN, R.L. *and* **GIBSON, J.M. A Bibliography of A. Conan Doyle.** Oxford, Clarendon Press, 1983 (reprinted with corrections, 1984). xvi,712p.illus. £62.50. (*Soho bibliographies.*) ISBN: 0198181906.

Exhaustive primary bibliography in 4 sections (works of fiction, including plays and poetry; miscellaneous works; minor contributions; periodical and newspaper contributions) plus list of biographical sources. Full descriptions with notes on publishing history. 8 appendices, including lists of UK, Continental, US and Canadian editions. Thorough index.
Class No: 82-312DOY

Hammett

[6802]

LAYMAN, R. Dashiell Hammett: a descriptive bibliography. Pittsburgh, Univ. of Pittsburgh Press, 1979. xiii,185p. illus. $100. (*Pittsburgh series in bibliography.*) ISBN: 0822933942.

Section A, Separate Publications (p.1-112), lists all editions in English of all books wholly or substantially by Hammett, with full descriptions. Other sections cover contributions to books, periodicals and newspapers, films and miscellaneous items. Appendices include lists of advertising copy and radio, TV and stage plays based on his work. Many title pages and jackets reproduced. Index.
Class No: 82-312HAM

Women

[6803]

DELLA CAVA, F.A. *and* **ENGEL, M.H. Female detectives in American novels:** a bibliography and analysis of serialized female sleuths. New York, Garland, 1993. xiv,157p. $30. ISBN: 0815312644.

Bibliographic entries for over 160 individual detectives discuss the character, identify the author and list stories in which the sleuth appears. Indexes of authors, book titles and detectives. Covers over 630 novels (by 147 authors) published in the US from the late 19th century to the 1990s. Useful introductory essay on the development of the female detective in American fiction. *Class No:* 82-312-0055.2

[6804]

Great women mystery writers: classic to contemporary. Klein, K.G., *ed.* Westport, Conn., Greenwood, 1994. xv,432p. $55. ISBN: 0313287708.

Signed entries, A-Z (average 3p.), on 117 writers from the mid-19th century to the 1990s (all but 15 of them British and American), giving biographical information; critical evaluation; recommendations of similar authors; complete list of crime fiction; and selective bibliography of criticism. Introductory historical study. Appendices include: award winners, mystery bookstores in North America, and lists of

....(contd.)

authors by category. Author/pseudonym index. Index of *c.*1,000 novel titles. 86 contributors, most of them women. Praised by *RQ* (v.34(3), Spring, 1995, p.395-6) for 'its scholarly tone, breadth of scope, [and] complete bibliographies of authors' works.' *Class No:* 82-312-0055.2

[6805]

NICHOLS, V. *and* **THOMPSON, S. Silk stalkings:** more women write of murder. [2nd ed.] Lanham, Md., Scarecrow, 1997. 704p. $49.95. ISBN: 081083393x.

1st ed. Black Lizard Books, 1988.

Provides a comprehensive survey of series characters created by women authors, 1867-1997. Master list is arranged by author and entries give series character, title in which they appear and publication dates. Chronology lists characters by date of introduction. List of pseudonyms. Character index. *Class No:* 82-312-0055.2

Spy Fiction

[6806]

McCORMICK, D. *and* **FLETCHER, K. Spy fiction:** a connoisseur's guide. New York, Facts on File, 1990. 352p. ISBN: 0816020981.

An updated and greatly expanded version of McCormick's *Who's who in spy fiction* (London, Elm Tree, 1977).

Introductory survey of the genre followed by entries for over 200 authors (mostly US and British), giving biographical notes, lists of titles (spy novels only), major characters, critical analysis, and details of film, TV, and radio adaptations. Biographies vary considerably in length. The dictionary section is followed by 8 essays on aspects of the genre. Appendix lists abbreviations and jargon used in spy fiction. Bibliography of sources. Index to pseudonyms, characters, subjects and themes. *Class No:* 82-314

[6807]

SMITH, M.J. *and* **WHITE, T. Cloak and dagger fiction:** an annotated guide to spy thrillers. 3rd ed. Westport, Conn., Greenwood, 1995. xl,849p. $99.50. (*Bibliographies and indexes in world literature.*) ISBN: 0313277001.

1st ed. Metuchen, N.J., Scarecrow, 1976, as *Cloak and dagger bibliography*; 2nd ed. Santa Barbara, Calif., ABC-CLIO, 1982.

Lists thousands of thrillers, by author, in 2 A-Z sequences (pre-1940 and 1940-onwards), with very brief plot summary for each but no evaluation. Appendices list pseudonyms, characters in series, and intelligence and terrorist organizations. Author and title indexes. New for this thoroughly revised ed. are a bibliography of recent critical studies in books and periodicals, 'Craft notes' by authors, and a glossary of espionage terms. *Class No:* 82-314

Science Fiction

Bibliographies

[6808]

BLEILER, E.F. Science-fiction, the early years: a full description of more than 3,000 science-fiction stories from earliest times to the appearance of the genre magazines in 1930, with author, title, and motif indexes. Kent, Ohio, Kent State Univ. Press, 1991. 998p. $75. ISBN: 0873384164.

Attempts to list all SF works published in English up to 1930. Arranged by author, with stories listed chronologically and summarized in some detail. Brief biographical notes on each author. Bibliography of background works. Date and magazine indexes, as well as those mentioned in subtitle. 'It

....*(contd.)*
is almost impossible to overstate the value of this work to any serious student of science fiction or popular culture' (*Choice*, v.28(10), June 1991, p.1611), although the quality of production is disappointing. *Class No:* 82-315(01)

[6809]

BURGESS, M. Reference guide to science fiction, fantasy and horror. Englewood, Colo., Libraries Unlimited, 1992. xvi,404p. $55. (*Reference sources in the humanities.*) ISBN: 087287611x.

Lists and evaluates over 550 key sources on 3 popular genres, in 29 sections covering the full range of reference materials, including bibliographies, encyclopedias, dictionaries, yearbooks, awards lists, magazine and anthology indexes, price guides, etc. Full bibliographic citations are provided, together with extensive annotations which point out both strengths and weaknesses. Core collection titles for different types of library listed by annotation number. Author, title and subject indexes. Warmly welcomed by reviewers: 'such an excellent example of how to organize and analyze materials that it should serve as a model' (*Booklist*, v.89(6), Nov. 15, 1992, p.628)
Class No: 82-315(01)

[6810]

CLARESON, T.D. Science fiction in America, 1870s-1930s: an annotated bibliography of primary sources. Westport, Conn., Greeenwood, 1984. xiv,305p. $69.50. ISBN: 0313231699.

Descriptive annotations, averaging 100 words, for 838 books, mainly by Americans but including some major British and European authors. A companion to Clareson's narrative history of the genre, *Some kind of paradise* (Greenwood, 1985). *Class No:* 82-315(01)

[6811]

CLARKE, I.F. Tale of the future from the beginning to the present day: a bibliography. 3rd ed. London, Library Assoc., 1978. xvi,357p. ISBN: 0853655502.

1st ed. 1961; 2nd ed. 1972.

Lists *c.*3,900 British publications chronologically, 1644-1976, with brief annotations. Author and title indexes. Complemented by Clarke's narrative survey, *The Pattern of expectation, 1644-2001* (London, Cape, 1979).
Class No: 82-315(01)

[6812]

COTTRILL, T., *and others*. Science fiction and fantasy series and sequels: a bibliography, vol.1: Books. New York, Garland, 1985. 432p. ISBN: 0824086716.

Lists *c.*1,160 series and over 6,600 books, mostly published in the 20th century. Arranged by author with title indexes of books and series. *Class No:* 82-315(01)

[6813]

PRINGLE, D. The Ultimate guide to science fiction: an A-Z of science fiction books by title. New ed. Aldershot, Scolar Press, 1994. 512p. £39.50. ISBN: 1859280714.

1st ed. London, Grafton, 1990.

3,500 entries, covering the most significant English-language adult works published up to the end of 1993. Entries are arranged by title and give the following information: date of first publication, star rating (0-4), classification, author's name and nationality, evaluation (including quotes from critics), and references to sequels, films, TV versions, etc. Author index. Excludes fantasy fiction. This ed. has over 500 new entries and older material has been revised. *Class No:* 82-315(01)

[6814]

REGINALD, R. Science fiction and fantasy literature: a checklist, 1700-1974, with *Contemporary science fiction authors II*. Detroit, Gale, 1979. 2v. £199. ISBN: 0810310511.

V.1 lists first eds. of 15,884 English-language works published 1700-1974, A-Z by author. Title and series indexes. V.2 is a biographical dictionary of 1,443 modern SF and fantasy writers. 'Likely to be the definitive bibliography for many years' (Barron, N., *Anatomy of wonder,* 1987, p.593), effectively superseding E.F. Bleiler's *Checklist of science-fiction and supernatural fiction* (Glen Rock, N.J., Fireball Books, 1978).

Supplemented by *Science fiction and fantasy literature, 1975-1991: a bibliography of science fiction, fantasy, and horror fiction books and nonfiction monographs* (Detroit, Gale, 1993. 1512p. £153. ISBN: 0810318253), which lists *c.*22,000 titles published in English, including some earlier works omitted from the earlier compilation. Indexes of titles, series and awards, but 'failure to provide subject access to bibliographic, biographical, critical, and other nonfiction works is a serious flaw'(*Booklist*, v.89(16), April 15, 1993, p.1538). *Class No:* 82-315(01)

[6815]

Science fiction, fantasy and horror, 1986-1991. Brown, C.N. *and* Contento, W., *eds.* Oakland, Calif., Locus Press, 1987-92. 6v.

An annual bibliography based on the monthly 'Books received' column of the American SF magazine *Locus*. The 1987 volume (1989. 417p. £34. ISBN: 0887362516) lists nearly 3,000 books from 530 publishers, plus nearly 5,800 shorter works. Author, title, and subject lists for books; author and title lists for stories; contents lists for anthologies and collections. Appendices include cinema reviews, necrology, awards, and directory of publishers.
Class No: 82-315(01)

[6816]

Science-fiction fantasy and horror reference: an annotated bibliography of works about literature and film. Justice, K.L., *ed.* Jefferson, NC, McFarland, 1989; London, St. James Press, 1990. xiii,226p. $45. ISBN: 089950406x, US; 1558620524, UK.

Lists and evaluates over 300 reference works in the genre and makes recommendations for library acquisition. Lengthy entries. Appendices include lists of critical and bibliographical book series and a core collection checklist. Indexes of subjects, titles, and authors/compilers.
Class No: 82-315(01)

[6817]

UNIVERSITY OF CALIFORNIA AT RIVERSIDE. Dictionary catalog of the J. Lloyd Eaton Collection of science fiction and fantasy literature. Boston, Hall, 1982. 3v. ISBN: 0816103798.

A dictionary catalogue with 42,000 cards, representing the largest collection of its kind. *c.*15,000 books and 4,500 magazine issues. Exceptional coverage for 1800-1950, including fringe areas like gothic, horror, and utopian literature. *Class No:* 82-315(01)

[6818]

Waterstone's guide to science fiction, fantasy and horror. Wake, P., *& others, eds.* Brentford, Waterstone's, 1998. 204p. illus. £3.99. ISBN: 0952740583.

A good-value guide to the best of these genres in print. Arranged by genre and sub-genre, with entries on individual authors, A-Z, including characterization of works and list of recommended titles. Not comprehensive, but useful for lending stock selection. Index of *c.*180 authors covered. *Class No:* 82-315(01)

Indexes

[6819]

CONTENTO, W. Index to science fiction anthologies and collections. Boston, Hall, 1978-84. 2v. (xii,608p.; xvi,503p.). ISBN: 081618092x, v.1; 0816185549, v.2.

First vol. indexes 12,000 English-language stories by 2,500 authors in 2,000 anthologies published to mid-1977. Author index, title index and full contents listing of each collection. Unattractively presented in capitals as photo-reduced printout in 2 cols., using many coded abbreviations for periodicals, publishers, etc.

Supplementary vol. indexes 1,017 anthologies, mostly published 1977-83 but including some omitted from v.1. Same format but better produced. *Class No:* 82-315(014)

[6820]

DAY, D.B. Index to the science fiction magazines, 1926-1950. Rev. ed. Boston, Hall, 1982. 289p.

1st ed. 1952.

Indexes 1,275 issues of 58 magazines (55 American, 3 British) by authors and titles. Checklist of issues of all the periodicals.

Continued by: *The MIT Science Fiction Society's index to the S-F magazines, 1951-1965* (Cambridge, Mass., 1966. 207p.); *Index to the science fiction magazines, 1966-1970* (West Hanover, Mass., New England Science Fiction Assoc., 1971. 82p.); and *The NESFA index to the science fiction magazines and original anthologies, 1971/72-.* (Cambridge, Mass., NESFA, 1973-. Annual. Latest title is *NESFA index to short science fiction.* *Class No:* 82-315(014)

[6821]

Science fiction and fantasy reference index, 1878-1985: an international author and subject index to history and criticism. Hall, H.W., *ed.* Detroit, Gale, 1987. 2v. (1460p.). ISBN: 0810321297.

2 sequences, providing 16,000 author citations and 27,000 subject citations to some 20,000 critical books, articles and essays. Continued by:

Science fiction and fantasy reference index, 1985-1991 (Englewood, Colo., Libraries Unlimited, 1993. 677p. $90. ISBN: 156308113x).

... *1992-1995* (1997. xxi,503p. $75. ISBN: 1563085275)

'Hall's compilations are major contributions to research because so much SF literature is fugitive and his subject indexing supports and promotes research in the genre' (*Choice*, v.31(4), Dec. 1993, p.590). *Class No:* 82-315(014)

[6822]

Science fiction book review index, 1923-1973. Hall, H.W., *ed.* Detroit, Gale, 1975. 438p.

Indexes nearly 14,000 reviews of *c.*6,900 books appearing in specialist SF magazines since 1923 and also in general reviewing journals since 1970. Full citations in author sequence. Title index. Directory of magazines indexed includes full bibliographic information and details of title changes, editors, etc.

.... *(contd.)*

Continued by *Science fiction book review index, 1974-1979* (1981. xxii,391p. ISBN: 0810311070), which lists 15,600 reviews of 6,220 books, and *Science fiction and fantasy book review index, 1980-1984* (1985. 761p. $195. ISBN: 0810316463), which has 13,800 citations for reviews in over 70 journals in its first part (p.1-345). The second part of this vol. cumulates the first 5 years of *Science fiction and fantasy research index* (1980-84), indexing over 4,700 books and articles by author and subject. *Class No:* 82-315(014)

Encyclopaedias & Dictionaries

[6823]

Anatomy of wonder: a critical guide to science fiction. Barron, N., *ed.* 4th ed. New Providence, N.J., Bowker, 1995. 912p. £52. ISBN: 0835236846.

1st ed. 1976; 3rd ed. 1987.

Part 1 covers primary literature, with 5 chapters tracing the history of the genre, from the earliest works to 1994, plus one on SF for young people. Part 2 deals with secondary literature and research aids, with 10 chapters on a wide range of topics, including reference works, histories, criticism, illustrations, magazines, awards, organizations and major collections. Every chapter is followed by a well annotated bibliography, with over 2,100 SF works listed and hundreds of research aids. Core collection titles asterisked. Indexes of authors, titles, series and themes. Coverage of foreign works not available in English has been dropped from this ed.

'It is informative, literate, comprehensive, and easy to use ... In the rapidly growing area of critical works pertaining to science fiction literature, this title ... stands out' (*RQ*, v.35(1), Fall 1995, p.129-30). *Class No:* 82-315(03)

[6824]

The Encyclopedia of science fiction. Clute, J. *and* Nicholls, P., *eds.* 2nd ed. New York, St. Martin's; London, Orbit, 1993. 1370p. £45. ISBN: 0312096186, US; 1857231244, UK.

1st ed. New York, Doubleday, 1979; London, Granada, 1980, as *The Science fiction encyclopedia.*

A very welcome revision and expansion of the definitive reference work on the genre. An international team of contributors has produced 4,360 signed entries (2,800 in 1st ed.), of which *c.*2,900 are for authors of science fiction, horror and fantasy, with the remainder covering a wide range of topics, including themes, terminology, films (544 titles), TV programmes (96), periodicals, specialist publishers, awards, critics, illustrators, library collections, and science fiction in 27 different countries. There are no separate entries for individual novels. Thoroughly cross-referenced. 'Scholarly, accurate, detailed, critical and interesting' (*TLS*, no.4722, Oct. 1, 1993, p.22).

Clute has also produced *Science fiction: the illustrated encyclopedia* (London, Dorling Kindersley, 1995. 312p. £25. ISBN: 0751302023). 'He is an intelligent and witty guide, and his excellent encyclopedia stimulates the mind as much as the eye' (*TLS*, no.4831, Nov. 3, 1995, p.13-4). *Class No:* 82-315(03)

[6825]

—The New encyclopedia of science fiction. Gunn, J., *ed.* London, Viking, 1989. xix,524p. illus. ISBN: 067081041x.

It should be noted that this is *not* a new edition of *The Science fiction encyclopedia* (New York, Doubleday, 1979; London, Granada, 1980).

Contains signed articles on over 500 writers and illustrators, over 250 films and 90 special topics, in a single A-Z sequence, with the topic headings listed separately and a checklist of film and TV entries. Over 200 illustrations, many in colour. Although most reviewers have praised the coverage of SF films, *TLS* (no.4490, 21st April, 1989, p.430) savages the standard of the author entries: 'Very simply, no user ... should take on trust any statement of fact contained in any author entry in this book.' *Class No:* 82-315(03)

[6826]

The Encyclopedia of science fiction and fantasy: a bibliographic survey of the fields of science fiction, fantasy and weird fiction through 1968. Tuck, D.H., *comp.* Chicago, Advent, 1974-82. 3v. $95 the set. ISBN: 0911682279.

Vols. 1-2 list authors A-Z, giving brief biographical notes and comprehensive lists of works, including contents listings for story collections. The sequence includes entries for magazines and newspapers which have published anthologies. Title index (52p.) in v.2.

V.3 has a range of miscellaneous listings, including: magazines, with checklists of issues; paperbacks, listed by author, publisher and title; pseudonyms; series and sequels. Ends with a general encyclopedic sequence of 270 entries for countries, films, TV shows and various topics. *Class No:* 82-315(03)

[6827]

GREEN, S.E. Contemporary science fiction, fantasy, and horror poetry: a resource guide and biographical directory. Westport, Conn., Greenwood, 1989. 216p. $49.95. ISBN: 0313263248.

A guide to a specialized area of SF, including details of magazines which publish poetry; a bibliography of genre anthologies and single-author collections; a biographical directory of poets; and a list of award-winners, 1978-88. General index and index of poem titles. *Class No:* 82-315(03)

[6828]

ROGOW, R. FutureSpeak: a fan's guide to the language of science fiction. New York, Paragon House, 1991. 408p. ISBN: 1557783470.

1,000 entries, mostly defining and explaining specialist terms, but there are also profiles of key works and notable personalities. Entries range from one sentence to half a page and are fully cross-referenced. 4 appendices, including addresses of publications and organizations and rules for the Hugo Awards. Bibliography. *Class No:* 82-315(03)

[6829]

—WOLFE, G.K. Critical terms for science fiction and fantasy: a glossary and guide to scholarship. Westport, Conn., Greenwood, 1986. 198p. $45. ISBN: 0313229813.

Entries on nearly 500 terms, ranging from brief definitions to short essays, with references to relevant works of fiction and secondary studies. Introductory essay on the development of SF criticism. *Class No:* 82-315(03)

[6830]

Survey of science fiction literature: five hundred 2,000-word essay reviews of world-famous science fiction novels with 2,500 bibliographical references. Magill, F.N., *ed.* Englewood Cliffs, N.J., Salem Press, 1979. 5v. ISBN: 0893561940.

Signed essays by *c.*130 contributors on works by 280 authors are arranged by title, preceded by details of first publication, setting and characters, and followed by references to reviews. A bibliographical supplement compiled by M.B. Tymn (1982. 183p.) lists more substantial critical studies. *Class No:* 82-315(03)

Reviews & Abstracts

[6831]

Science fiction and fantasy book review annual, 1988-. Collins, R.A. *and* Latham, R., *eds.* Westport, Conn., Greenwood, 1989-. Annual. ISSN: 1040192x.

The first vol. of this series contains more than 600 reviews by over 100 contributors, plus survey articles on the fantasy, horror, and SF genres in 1988, a review of the year's secondary literature, and lists of award winners. 'The reviews are crisp, informative, and intelligently critical, and may well represent the most comprehensive collection of reviews for a year of SF publishing ever available in one place' (*Choice*, v.26(10), June 1989, p.1667). No vols. have appeared since the one covering 1991 (1993. 896p. $115. ISBN: 0313283265). *Class No:* 82-315(048)

Periodicals

[6832]

Science fiction, fantasy and weird fiction magazines. Tymn, M.B. *and* Ashley, M., *eds.* Westport, Conn., Greenwood, 1985. xxx,970p. $105. (*Historical guides to the world's periodicals and newspapers.*) ISBN: 031321221x.

Main sequence lists magazines published since 1882 in the US, UK, Canada, and Australia, the entries providing a brief history; bibliography and sources of indexing; reprinting and publication information; and many cross-references. Other sections cover English-language anthologies; fanzines and scholarly journals; and foreign-language magazines (178 titles from 23 countries). *Class No:* 82-315(051)

Awards & Prizes

[6833]

GUILLEMETTE, A. The Best in science fiction: winners and nominees of the major awards in science fiction. Aldershot, Scolar Press; Brookfield, Vt., Ashgate, 1993. 379p. £25. ISBN: 1859280056.

A comprehensive guide to 17 major awards from the UK, US, Canada and Australia, in 5 sections: A. Awards, A-Z, with details of each one and lists of winners and nominees - B. Authors, A-Z, with references to first section - C. Titles, A-Z, keyed to first section - D. Winners only, by year - E. 'Best of the best' lists, by year, compiled using a weighting system to take account of the differing status of individual awards. *Class No:* 82-315(079.2)

[6834]

Reginald's science fiction and fantasy awards: a comprehensive guide to the awards and their winners. Mallett, D.F. *and* Reginald, R., *eds.* 2nd ed. San Bernardino, Calif., Borgo Press, 1991. 248p. $30 ISBN: 0893708267.

1st ed. 1981

First section lists awards from the US, UK, Ireland and Canada, explaining voting processes and listing winners. 2nd section lists foreign-language awards from many countries, including Japan and Russia. 3rd section lists non-genre awards (*e.g.* Oscars, Emmys) which have been won by SF and fantasy works. Appendices include lists of SF and fantasy conventions and statistical tables relating to award winners. Indexes of authors and award names.
Class No: 82-315(079.2)

Excerpts

[6835]

Modern mystery, fantasy and science fiction writers. Cassiday, B., *ed.* New York, Continuum, 1993. 673p. $75. (*Library of literary criticism.*) ISBN: 0826405738.

Reprints 6-12 excerpts from critical studies of 85 of the most popular writers in 3 genres. Highly selective, with some authors included who are not primarily associated with genre fiction, *e.g.* Hesse, Atwood. Biographical information confined to birth and death dates. Arranged A-Z by author, with index of critics. *Class No:* 82-315(082.200)

Chronologies

[6836]

RUDDICK, N. British science fiction: a chronology, 1478-1990. Westport, Conn., Greenwood, 1992. 250p. $69.50. (*Bibliographies and indexes in world literature.*) ISBN: 0313280029.

Lists biographical and publishing events since the year of the birth of Thomas More, author of *Utopia*, with people and works from film, radio and TV included after 1913. Indexes of authors, titles, and media. *Class No:* 82-315(090)

Biographies

[6837]

Reader's guide to twentieth-century science fiction. Fletcher, M.P., *ed.* Chicago, American Library Assoc., 1989. 673p. $30. ISBN: 0838905048.

Entries on over 130 major authors (mainly UK and US) average 5p. and include biography, survey of themes, summaries of key works, and selected secondary bibliography. Lists of award winners. Includes writers from recent subgenres like feminist SF and Cyberpunk.
Class No: 82-315(092)

[6838]

St. James guide to science-fiction writers. Pederson, J.P., *ed.* 4th ed. Detroit & London, St. James Press, 1996. xxiv,1175p. $140. ISBN: 1558621792.

1st ed. New York, St. Martin's Press, 1981; 3rd ed. Chicago & London, St. James Press, 1991. First 3 eds. entitled *Twentieth-century science-fiction writers*.

Entries by over 200 contributors are arranged A-Z, cover over 650 writers and comprise biographical notes; complete bibliography (including non-SF works); list of critical studies; details of published bibliographies and manuscript collections; plus a signed critical essay (800-1,000 words). Continues to focus on living, English-language writers, but

....(contd.)

this ed., which has over 50 new entries, includes important precursors of 20th-century science fiction, *e.g.* Mary Shelley. General bibliography (6p.). Complete title index to works mentioned, with over 6,000 entries giving author and publication date. Nationality index. *Class No:* 82-315(092)

[6839]

Science fiction writers: critical studies of the major authors from the early nineteenth century to the present day. Bleiler, E.F., *ed.* New York, Scribner, 1982. xv,623p. £69.95. ISBN: 0684167409.

Signed essays (average 8p.) on 76 authors by 26 scholars, providing biography, critical analysis of the fiction and the author's importance in the historical development of SF. Selected primary and secondary bibiography for each author. Apart from 3 (Verne, Capek, Lem) all are British or American. Index of authors and titles.

Also included on *The Scribner writers series on CD-ROM* (*q.v.*). *Class No:* 82-315(092)

Asimov

[6840]

GREEN, S.E. An Annotated bibliography of the Asimov Collection at Boston University. Westport, Conn., Greenwood, 1995. 168p. £49.50. (*Bibliographies and indexes in science fiction, fantasy and horror.*) ISBN: 0313288968.

Lists the contents of Asimov's personal book collection held in the Mulgar Library, with separate sections on his own works and those he owned by other writers. Arranged by genre within each chapter: novels, short stories, anthologies, nonfiction, poetry. Title index and general index. *Class No:* 82-315ASI

Verne

[6841]

TAVES, B. *and* **MICHALUK, S. The Jules Verne encyclopedia.** Lanham, Md., Scarecrow, 1996. xiii,257p. illus. £51.80. ISBN: 0810829614.

9 chapters on various aspects of the writer's life and works, including 'Philatelic tributes to Jules Verne' and 'Hollywood's Jules Verne'. Most useful for reference is ch.7, 'A Bibliographic and collecting guide' (107p.), which includes detailed descriptions of 67 US and British eds. Index. *Class No:* 82-315VER

Women

[6842]

SCHLOBIN, R.C. Urania's daughters: a checklist of women science fiction writers, 1692-1982. Mercer Island, Wash., Starmont, 1983 (repr. West Bridgford, Notts., Paupers' Press, 1990). 79p. £11.95. ISBN: 0916732568.

An expansion and revision of a checklist in *Extrapolation*, 23 (Spring 1982), which lists 375 authors and 830 novels, collections, and anthologies. Basic bibliographic information only. *Class No:* 82-315-0055.2

Short Stories

[6843]

BALDWIN, D. *and* **MORRIS, G.L. The Short story in English:** Britain and North America - an annotated bibliography. Metuchen, N.J., Scarecrow, 1994. xxi,349p. $47.50. (*Magill bibliographies.*) ISBN: 0810828340.

Lists critical and biographical studies relating to 50 19th- and 20th century writers of short stories from Britain, Ireland, Canada and the US, and includes studies of specific stories. Author selection based on inclusion in anthologies on US college curricula. Index of critics. 'Most British users ... will find that constant reference to North American sources restricts the bibliography's usefulness' (*Reference Reviews*, v.9(3), 1995, p.37-8). *Class No:* 82-32

[6844]

Critical survey of short fiction. Magill, F.N., *ed.* Rev. ed. Pasadena, Calif., Salem Press, 1993. 7v. $425. ISBN: 0893568430.

1st ed. 1981.

348 standardized entries (5-10p.) on major authors, which analyze their short fiction, detail their work in other genres, and provide biographical and bibliographical information. 65 are new to this ed., with most of the others revised. V.7 has 12 topical essays which provide a historical overview of the genre; chronology from 4000BC to AD1991; glossary; and index of authors, titles, terms and concepts. Includes writers from all periods and a variety of countries, many of them not normally considered primarily as writers of short fiction. *Class No:* 82-32

[6845]

Masterplots II: short story series. Magill, F.N., *ed.* Englewood Cliffs, N.J., Salem Press, 1986. 6v. $425. ISBN: 0893564613.

Covers over 700 short stories from all over the world. See entry on *Masterplots II: American fiction series* for format. *Class No:* 82-32

[6846]

Reference guide to short fiction. Watson, N., *ed.* Detroit & London, St. James Press, 1993. xxxii,1052p. $140. ISBN: 1558623345.

First section has entries on 325 authors, A-Z, giving biography, full primary bibliography (arranged by genre), secondary bibliography, and signed critical essay. Second section has signed articles on 400 important short stories from all periods in literary history. Chronological lists of authors and short stories. Bibliography of general critical studies and histories of the genre. Title index. *Class No:* 82-32

[6847]

Short story criticism. Detroit, Gale, 1988-. v.1- (in progress). illus. £80 per vol.

Covers short story writers of all nationalities and all periods, using the same format as Gale's *Contemporary literary criticism* series (*q.v.*). Each vol. covers 8-10 authors, the entries including critical introduction, list of major short story collections, excerpted criticism chronologically arranged, and additional bibliography of critical books and articles. Photographs of each author plus reproductions of title pages, dust jackets, etc. Cumulative author index in each vol. to all of Gale's literary criticism series and cumulative nationality and title indexes to the *SSC* series.

27 vols. published by the end of 1997. *Class No:* 82-32

[6848]

Short story index: an index to 60,000 stories in 4,320 collections. New York, Wilson, 1953. iv,1553p. $55. ISSN: 03609774.

Supersedes *Index to short stories* by I.T.E. Firkins (2nd ed. 1923) and its Supplements (1929 and 1936).

A single-sequence listing of stories by author, title, and subject. Includes translations of stories by foreign writers, but excludes stories for young children. List of collections indexed. Covers collections published 1900-49.

Supplements have been published covering the following periods: 1950-54 (1956. $65); 1955-58 (1960. $65); 1959-63 (1965. $65); 1964-68 (1969. $65); 1969-73 (1974. $65); 1974-78 (1979. $95); 1979-83 (1984. $105); 1984-88 (1989. $135) and 1989-93 (1994. $135). Over 162,000 stories have been indexed to date with coverage extended to selected periodicals in recent years. May be purchased on subscription with an annual vinyl-bound vol. received each year, to be replaced by the permanent clothbound cumulation after 5 years.

Short story index: collections indexed, 1900-1978 (1979. 349p. $45. ISBN: 0824206436) is an author/editor and title index to 8,400 collections. *Class No:* 82-32

[6849]

WALKER, W.S. Twentieth-century short story explication: explications 1900-1975, of short fiction since 1800. 3rd. ed. Hamden, Conn., Shoe String, 1977. viii,880p. $69.50. ISBN: 0208015701.

1st ed. 1961; 2nd ed. 1967.

Unannotated references to critical studies, arranged by short-story author then by title. Covers over 850 writers from 45 countries, the short story being defined as fiction of not more than 150p.

5 supplements to this ed. have been published, in 1980, 1984, 1987, 1989, and 1991. Prices range from $35 to $49.50 per vol. An index to the 3rd ed. and its supplements, ed. by W.S. Walker and B.K. Walker, was published in 1992 (280p. $47.50. ISBN: 0208023208), bringing the series to a close.

The first vol. of a new series, also by W.S. Walker, was published by Shoe String in 1993 (vi,366p. $49.50. ISBN: 0208023402) and lists 5,650 interpretations published in 1989 and 1990. Over 800 short story authors are cited, over 340 of them not covered in the first series. Includes a checklist of the 321 journals scanned. V.2 (1995. 295p. ISBN: 0208023704) covers 1991-2 and v.3 (1997. viii,347p. ISBN: 0208024190) covers 1993-4. Both are edited by W.M. Aycock. *Class No:* 82-32

Fantasy Fiction

Bibliographies

[6850]

SARGENT, L.T. British and American Utopian literature, 1516-1985: an annotated, chronological bibliography. New York, Garland, 1988. xix,559p. ISBN: 0824006941.

Lists 1,985 works of Utopian literature chronologically, with brief annotations and locations in *c.*150 US and British libraries. Author and title indexes. *Class No:* 82-34(01)

[6851]

SCHLOBIN, R.C. The Literature of fantasy: a comprehensive, annotated bibliography of modern fantasy fiction. New York, Garland, 1979. xxxv,425p. ISBN: 0824097572.

Claims to list 721 novels, 244 collections, 100 anthologies, 3,610 short stories, and 165 author bibliographies, with the emphasis on adult fantasy rather than supernatural/horror fiction. Arranged A-Z by fantasy authors. Concise annotations, often including evaluation. Index of authors, editors, translators, etc. Title index. *Class No:* 82-34(01)

Indexes

[6852]

ASHLEY, M. *and* **CONTENTO, W. Supernatural index:** a listing of fantasy, supernatural, occult, weird and horror anthologies. Westport, Conn., Greenwood, 1995. 952p. £175. (*Bibliographies and indexes in science fiction, fantasy and horror*.) ISBN: 0313240302.

The first index to all known English-language anthologies in these genres, with citations for 21,300 stories in over 2,100 collections published 1813-1994. Entries provide original publication sources for reprinted stories, including many from obscure magazines not previously indexed. Also included are pseudonyms and birth and death dates for over 7,700 authors. Citations can be accessed by editor, author, book title and story title. Full contents lists for each anthology. Hailed as a landmark work by several reviewers. *Class No:* 82-34(014)

Encyclopaedias & Dictionaries

[6853]

BLEILER, E.F. The Guide to supernatural fiction. Kent, Ohio, Kent State Univ. Press, 1983. ix,723p. ISBN: 0873382889.

The subtitle is an adequate précis: 'A full description of 1,775 books from 1750 to 1960, including ghost stories, weird fiction, stories of supernatural horror, fantasy, Gothic novels, occult fiction, and similar literature'. Entries include plot summaries, critical comments and notes on authors. Index of motifs and story types. *Class No:* 82-34(03)

[6854]

BOOKER, M.K. Dystopian literature: a theory and research guide. Westport, Conn., Greenwood, 1994. 424p. $79.50. ISBN: 0313291152.

Articles on 65 examples of dystopia (the opposite of utopia) in literature, in separate chapters covering fiction, drama and film. Entries include short bibliographies. Introductory essay. General bibliography. Index.

See also P.G. Hasack's *Utopian/Dystopian literature: a bibliography of literary criticism* (Metuchen, N.J., Scarecrow, 1994. 370p. $52.50. ISBN: 0810827522). *Class No:* 82-34(03)

[6855]

The Encyclopedia of fantasy. Clute, J. *and* Grant, J., *eds.* London, Orbit; New York, St. Martin's, 1997. xvi,1049p. £50. ISBN: 1857233689, UK; 0312158971, US.

Similar in format and quality to Clute and Nicholls' highly acclaimed *Encyclopedia of science fiction* (*q.v.*) and includes cross-references to that work. Over 4,000 signed entries, A-Z, covering all aspects of fantasy, not only in literature, but also in film, TV, opera, art and comics. Entries for authors, directors, works, series (*e.g.* 11p. on Tarzan films), genres, themes, characters, and regional and national literatures.

....*(contd.)*

Author entries include lists of works, with secondary sources for major writers. Over 70 contributors, but the editors are responsible for over half of the entries. *Class No:* 82-34(03)

[6856]

Fantasy literature: a reader's guide. Barron, N., *ed.* New York, Garland, 1990. 586p. $55. ISBN: 0824031482.

An outstanding guide to the genre, arranged on similar lines to Barron's definitive science fiction reference book, *Anatomy of wonder* (*q.v.*). Signed essays on periods in the development of fantasy (to 1811; 1812-1899; 1900-56); modern fantasy for adults; and modern fantasy for young adults — each followed by a critically annotated bibliography of key works. A section on research aids has 9 chapters covering reference works, author studies, magazines, fantasy on film and TV, library collections, etc. Recommended titles are asterisked. Many cross-references. Author, title and theme indexes. Over 1,700 works and studies evaluated. *Class No:* 82-34(03)

[6857]

—TYMN, M.B., *and others*. Fantasy literature: a core collection and reference guide. New York and London, Bowker, 1979. xiii,273p. ISBN: 0835214311.

The bulk of the book comprises 'a highly selective core list ... of more than 240 seminal works of high fantasy' (*Preface*), with extended annotations which include plot summary and critical evaluation. With one exception, all were written in English and published between 1854 and 1978. Part 2, Reference Aids, includes lists of reference books, periodicals, societies, awards and collections. Index. *Class No:* 82-34(03)

[6858]

SNODGRASS, M.E. Encyclopedia of Utopian literature. Santa Barbara, Calif., and Oxford, ABC-CLIO, 1995. xvi,644p. illus. £34.95 ISBN: 0874367573.

Covers Utopian (and Dystopian) literature of all periods, from Plato to Margaret Atwood, with entries on over 100 works, plus authors, themes, terms and characters, in a single A-Z sequence. Most entries average 1p., but there are a few longer ones on major themes, *e.g.* Heaven (15p.). Each entry has references to key primary and secondary sources. Bibliography of secondary material (29p.). Index. *Class No:* 82-34(03)

[6859]

Survey of modern fantasy literature. Magill, F.N., *ed.* Englewood Cliffs, N.J., Salem Press, 1983. 5v. ISBN: 0893564508.

Essay reviews of *c.*500 works from the last 200 years, including classics and modern works. Standard format articles (signed) giving author biographies, date published, type of work, description, list of characters, summary and (mostly) bibliographies. V.5 includes 19 topical essays, chronology from 1764 to 1981, annotated bibliography of secondary literature, list of anthologies, and detailed index. *Class No:* 82-34(03)

[6860]

ZIMBARO, V.P. Encyclopedia of apocalyptic literature. Santa Barbara, Calif., and Oxford, ABC-CLIO, 1996. xv,400p. illus. £29.95. ISBN: 0874368235.

Covers literature from a range of cultures which deals in some way with the end of the world, from the Book of Daniel to Kurt Vonnegut. Over 300 entries on writers (45), works (50), themes and characters. Appended lists of

....(contd.)
authors and works who have entries. Bibliographies of primary and secondary sources cited and of further reading. Cross-references. Index. *Class No:* 82-34(03)

Biographies

[6861]
St. James guide to fantasy writers. Pringle, D., *ed.* Detroit & London, St. James Press, 1996. xvi,711p. $140. ISBN: 1558622055.

A new addition to the well-established St. James series of biocritical reference works on genre writers. Covers over 400 authors of heroic fantasy, sword and sorcery, humorous fantasy, adult fairy tales and fables, plus some children's authors whose fantasies remain popular with adults. The emphasis is on 20th-century English-language writers, but some early pioneers of the genre are included. Entries follow the usual format of biographical notes, full list of publications, selected secondary bibliography and 1,000-word critical essay by an expert. Some entries include comments by the subject. 11 appended entries on foreign-language writers. General bibliography (2p.). Nationality index. Title index of all works mentioned, with authors and dates. Over 100 of the authors covered are also included in *St. James guide to science fiction writers* (*q.v.*), but with different critical essays. *Class No:* 82-34(092)

[6862]
Supernatural fiction writers: fantasy and horror. Bleiler, E.F., *ed.* New York, Scribner, 1985. 2v., xix,1169p. £131.95. ISBN: 0684178087.

Signed essays (average length 8p.) by 62 contributors on *c.*150 authors from Apuleius to the present day. Essays are arranged in 15 sections covering particular periods or countries and include biography, description and critical evaluation of major works, and assessment of historical significance. Selected primary and secondary bibliography for each author. Apart from 16, all authors are British or American. General bibliography (2p.). Index of authors and titles.

Also included on *The Scribner writers series on CD-ROM* (*q.v.*). *Class No:* 82-34(092)

Tolkien

[6863]
DAY, D. Tolkien: the illustrated encyclopedia. London, Mitchell Beazley; New York, Macmillan, 1991. 279p. illus. $29.95. ISBN: 0855339241, UK; 002533431x, US.

A guide to the world of Middle-Earth and the Undying Lands, with 500 entries arranged A-Z within 5 main chapters covering history, geography, sociology, natural history and biography. 200 colour illustrations. 20p. of maps and charts. Index of principal sources (*i.e.* Tolkien's works) plus general index.

Complementary works are *The Tolkien and Middle-Earth handbook* by C.Duriez (Tunbridge Wells, Monarch, 1992. 316p. £9.99. ISBN: 1854241184), which is an A-Z guide to Tolkien's life, thought and writings, with lengthy entries, and *The Complete guide to Middle-Earth* by R. Foster (London, HarperCollins, 1993. xii,441p. £6.99. ISBN: 0261102524), which is also alphabetically arranged and has entries, with book and page references, on all the characters in *The Hobbit*, *The Lord of the rings* and *The Silmarillion*. *Class No:* 82-34TOL

[6864]
HAMMOND, W.G. J.R.R. Tolkien: a descriptive bibliography. Winchester, St. Paul's Bibliographies, 1993. xiv,434p. £58. (*Winchester bibliographies of 20th century writers.*) ISBN: 1873040113.

Detailed coverage of Tolkien's output, including 68p. on *The Hobbit* and 95p. on *The Lord of the Rings*, providing full description, lists of variants and narrative publishing history. As well as Tolkien's books (which occupy over 75% of this work), Hammond lists contributions to books and periodicals, published letters, drawings, recordings, interviews, manuscripts, and translations into a wide range of languages. Index of names, titles and subjects. 'For a book of this length and detail there are remarkably few errors and inaccuracies' (*TLS*, no.4703, May 21, 1993, p.30.). *Class No:* 82-34TOL

[6865]
JOHNSON, J.A. J.R.R. Tolkien: six decades of criticism. Westport, Conn., Greenwood, 1986. viii,266p. $75. ISBN: 0313250057.

Arranged chronologically in 4 main sections: 1922-53; 1954-63; 1964-73; 1974-84. Each section has introductory essay, list of works by Tolkien arranged by title, and annnotated bibliography of criticism, organized by year, then by author. 95 primary items and 1,649 secondary items in all. Appendix lists organizations, societies and publications. Index of critics. Index of Tolkien's works and critical response to them, with some subject headings.
Class No: 82-34TOL

Horror Fiction

Bibliographies

[6866]
FISHER, B.F. The Gothic's Gothic: study aids to the tradition of the tale of terror. New York, Garland, 1988. 485p. ISBN: 0824087844.

An annotated bibliography of secondary sources on Gothic fiction from Horace Walpole to Stephen King. Part 1 lists 1,818 studies of 109 authors chronologically arranged. Part 2 has 796 entries under 28 subject headings. Indexes of critics, titles, and authors/artists/subjects. Generally compared unfavourably with Frank's *Guide to the Gothic* by reviewers because of shorter annotations and unclear criteria for inclusion. *Class No:* 82-35(01)

[6867]
FRANK, F.S. Gothic fiction: a master list of twentieth century criticism and research. Westport, Conn., Greenwood, 1988. xv,193p. $55. ISBN: 0313276714.

2,489 numbered items in 13 sections and many sub-sections, with the emphasis on English and American Gothic fiction, although French, German and other literatures are included. 24 major writers are allocated their own sub-section. Indexes of critics, authors and artists. No annotations. *Class No:* 82-35(01)

[6868]
FRANK, F.S. Guide to the Gothic: an annotated bibliography of criticism. Metuchen, N.J., Scarecrow, 1984-95. 2v. ISBN: 0810816695, v.1; 0810829681, v.2.

Has sections on English, Canadian, American, French and German Gothic literature, with subsections on individual writers. V.2 has over 1,500 entries from 1983-93, new studies of individual writers (including Stephen King) and a new section on anthologies of Gothic fiction. Index in each vol. *Class No:* 82-35(01)

[6869]

McNUTT, D.J. The Eighteenth-century Gothic novel: an annotated bibliography of criticism and selected texts. New York, Garland; Folkestone, Dawson, 1975. xxii,330p. ISBN: 0824010582, US; 0712906541, UK.

Over 1,000 entries, ranging from early reviews to modern scholarship, arranged in 7 general chapters (Bibliographies and research guides; Aesthetic background; Literary background; Psychological, social and scientific background; 18th century Gothic in general studies; Studies devoted to 18th century Gothic; The Gothic legacy) and 6 on key authors (Walpole, Reeve, Charlotte Smith, Radcliffe, Lewis and Beckford). Complete to 1971, with some material from 1972-4. Index. *Class No:* 82-35(01)

[6870]

SPECTOR, R.D. The English Gothic: a bibliographic guide to writers from Horace Walpole to Mary Shelley. Westport, Conn., Greenwood, 1984. xiii,269p. $59.95. ISBN: 0313225362.

Two general introductory chapters followed by 4 biographical and bibliographical essays on pairs of authors (Walpole and Reeve; Charlotte Smith and Radcliffe; Lewis and Beckford; Maturin and Shelley). Lists of references follow each chapter. Index. *Class No:* 82-35(01)

[6871]

TRACY, A.B. The Gothic novel, 1790-1830: plot summaries and index to motifs. Lexington, Ky., Univ. Press of Kentucky, 1981. 216p. $24. ISBN: 0813113970.

Plot summaries of 208 novels, arranged by author, A-Z. Index of motifs has *c.*200 headings. Index of characters has separate sequences for heroes, heroines, and villains/ villainesses. Title index. *Class No:* 82-35(01)

Encyclopaedias & Dictionaries

[6872]

FRANK, F.S. The First Gothics: a critical guide to the English Gothic novel. New York, Garland, 1987. xxxi,496p.illus. $60. ISBN: 0824085019.

'A highly selective survey of the English Gothic novel in its major phase' (*Preface*), with 500 entries arranged A-Z by author and giving bibliographical details of first eds. and modern reprints, classification (*i.e.,* type of Gothic), selective list of secondary material, and critical synopsis which often runs to more than a page. 3 appendices: 1. Glossary of Gothic terms (11p.) - 2. Selected bibliography of critical sources (6p.) - 3. Chronological list of titles, 1753-1832. Indexes of authors, titles and critics.

Frank has compiled a similar survey of 509 American Gothic novels from Charles Brockden Brown to Stephen King, under the title *Through the pale door: a guide to and through the American Gothic* (Westport, Conn., Greenwood, 1990. 338p. $55. ISBN: 0313259003). *Class No:* 82-35(03)

[6873]

Horror literature: a core collection and reference guide. Tymn, M.B., *ed.* New York and London, Bowker, 1981. xviii,559p. ISBN: 0835213412.

Part 1, Fiction, has 4 chronological chapters covering the period 1762-1980 and one on pulp magazines, while Part 2, Poetry, has a single chapter. Each chapter is followed by a well annotated bibliography, with over 1,100 works listed. Part 3, Reference Sources, comprises 6 invaluable annotated listings: Biography, Autobiography and Bibliography; Criticism, Indexes and General Reference; Periodicals; Societies and Organizations; Awards; Research Collections.

....(contd.)

Core collection titles asterisked, with separate checklist provided. Directory of publishers. Author and title index. *Class No:* 82-35(03)

[6874]

Horror literature: a reader's guide. Barron, N., *ed.* New York, Garland, 1990. 596p. $55. ISBN: 0824043472.

A companion to Barron's *Fantasy literature* (*q.v.*), with chapters on the following subjects appearing in the 'Research Aids' section of each book: fantasy and horror fiction in libraries; general reference books; fantastic art and illustration; fantasy and horror magazines; and library collections. Survey chapters cover the periods 1762-1824, 1825-96, 1897-1949, and 1950-1989, each with critically annotated bibliographies. Author, title, and theme indexes. *c.*1,500 works and studies evaluated. *Class No:* 82-35(03)

[6875]

MUSSELL, K. Women's gothic and romantic fiction: a reference guide. Westport, Conn., Greenwood, 1981. xix,157p. $47.95. (*American popular culture.*) ISBN: 0313214026.

6 chapters, including a history of the genres and a review of bibliographies and reference works. Appendix 1 lists collections and research facilities in the US. Appendix 2 is a selected chronology of authors and titles from 1740 (Samuel Richardson) to 1980 (Victoria Holt). Index. *Class No:* 82-35(03)

[6876]

WOLF, L. Horror: a connoisseur's guide to literature and film. New York, Facts on File, 1989. 320p. illus. ISBN: 081602197x.

Lists over 400 films, novels, poems and short stories produced since the mid-19th century. Entries are arranged A-Z by title and include all relevant source details, plot summary, and critical evaluation. Over 75 illustrations. *Class No:* 82-35(03)

Histories

[6877]

PUNTER, D. The Literature of terror: a history of Gothic fictions from 1765 to the present day. 2nd ed. Harlow, Longman, 1996. 2v. £15.99 per vol.

1st ed. 1980, in one vol.

V.1 *The Gothic tradition*. ix,237p. ISBN: 0582237149.

V.2 *The Modern Gothic*. x,234p. ISBN: 0582290554.

V.1 covers the period from 1765 to the Edwardian age in 8 chapters, with a new Appendix in 2nd ed. reviewing recent critical studies (8p.). V.2 covers the rest of the 20th century in a further 8, with new chapters on film and postwar fiction in this ed. Detailed, updated bibliographies and index in each vol. *Class No:* 82-35(091)

Western Fiction

[6878]

DREW, B.A., ***and others*. Western series and sequels:** a reference guide. New York, Garland, 1986. xvi,173p. ISBN: 0824086570.

A critical survey of the genre combined with a bibliography of 375 paperback Western series published in the US since 1933. Includes lists of titles in each series and biographical information on the authors. Index of *c.*3,500 titles. *Class No:* 82-36

[6879]
Encyclopedia of frontier and western fiction. Tuska, J. *and* Piekarski, V. New York, McGraw-Hill, 1983. xviii,365p. illus. ISBN: 0070655871.

Biographical entries for over 300 authors (mainly American, but with selected British and German writers), including mainstream authors (*e.g.* Steinbeck) who have contributed to the genre. Entries include lists of primary works (westerns only), derivative films and TV series, and book-length secondary works. *Class No:* 82-36

[6880]
Twentieth-century western writers. Sadler, G., *ed.* 2nd ed. Chicago & London, St. James Press, 1991. xxxii,848p. $140. ISBN: 0912289988.

1st ed. London, Macmillan, 1982, edited by J. Vinson.

Entries by a large team of contributors are arranged A-Z, cover 489 authors, and comprise biographical notes, primary bibliography, list of critical studies, details of published bibliographies and manuscript collections, plus a signed critical essay (800-1,000 words). 2nd ed. is published in a more readable format, with larger page- and type-size, and has entries on 150 new writers including 35 women. Essays on many writers previously included have been rewritten and biographies updated. Complete title index to all works mentioned. *Class No:* 82-36

Historical Fiction

[6881]
DICKINSON, A.T. Dickinson's American historical fiction. Gerhardstein, V.B., *ed.* 5th ed. Metuchen, N.J. Scarecrow, 1986. xvi,352p. $41.50. ISBN: 0810818671.

1st ed. 1958; 2nd ed. 1963; 3rd ed. 1971; all as *American historical fiction* by A.T. Dickinson. 4th ed. 1981, with new title.

Entries for 3,048 novels published 1917-84, plus some earlier publications now regarded as standard. Arranged by period from Colonial times to the present (12 sections), plus one section for family chronicles. Brief annotations place the works in historical perspective but do not make critical judgements. Author-title and subject indexes. *Class No:* 82-38

[6882]
HARTMAN, D.K. *and* **SAPP, G. Historical figures in fiction.** Phoenix, Ariz., Oryx, 1994. 352p. £35.95. ISBN: 0897747186.

Lists over 1,400 historical personages, A-Z, who appear as major characters in over 4,200 works of fiction. Entries include full name; birth and death dates; notes on profession and activities; and bibliographical details of relevant novels, including reading levels for juvenile and young adult books and lists of reviews. Indexes of authors, titles and professions. Most of the cited novels have been published during the last 50 years, but regularly reprinted classics of the genre are included. *Class No:* 82-38

[6883]
McGARRY, D.D. *and* **WHITE, S.H. World historical guide:** an annotated chronological, geographical, and topical list of selected historical novels. 2nd ed. Metuchen, N.J., Scarecrow, 1973. 650p.

1st ed. 1963, as *Historical fiction guide.*

Lists nearly 6,500 titles in English, including translations. Arranged by periods, then by countries. Author and title index. *Class No:* 82-38

[6884]
VANMETER, V.L. America in historical fiction: a bibliographic guide. Englewood, Colo., Libraries Unlimited, 1997. xvi,280p. $38.50. ISBN: 1563084961.

Aims to help teachers and students locate the best in classic and contemporary historical fiction. Arranged in major chronological divisions of US history, annotated entries include bibliographic information, time period, subject, location, research base (if known) and age group for which appropriate. Lists prequels and sequels. Extensive indexing. *Class No:* 82-38

War Fiction

[6885]
HAGER, P.E. *and* **TAYLOR, D. The Novels of World War I:** an annotated bibliography. New York, Garland, 1981. xvii,513p. ISBN: 0824094913.

Lists 895 adult and 370 junior novels in separate chronological sequences, 1914-1980, with lengthy annotations. Confined to novels written in English or available in translation. Author and title indexes. Bibliography of critical works (13p.).

The same authors have produced *The Novels of World War II: an annotated bibliography* (New York, Garland, 1992. 2v. ISBN: 0824056841), which lists 3,371 novels published in English, 1938-1990. Author and title indexes. *Class No:* 82-39

[6886]
MENENDEZ, A.J. Civil War novels: an annotated bibliography. New York, Garland, 1986. xii,174p. ISBN: 0824099338.

Lists over 1,000 novels on the American Civil War, written from shortly after the War to the present day, by author with a subject index which includes battles, persons, events, places, and themes. Book reviews are cited in the brief annotations. Title and subject indexes. Includes 120 stories for young people. *Class No:* 82-39

[6887]
PARIS, M. The Novels of World War Two: an annotated bibliography of World War Two fiction. London, Library Assoc., 1990. xii,184p. ISBN: 0853659184.

Lists over 2,000 novels published in English and in translation from 1939 to 1988 which have the War as their theme. Not confined to stories of combat. 1. Chronolgical list (author, title, publisher, brief indication of main theme) - 2. Subject index (lists novels under national headings then by branch of service and theatre of war) - 3. Author index - 4. Title index. *Class No:* 82-39

[6888]
SMITH, M.J. War story guide: an annotated bibliography of military fiction. Metuchen, N.J., Scarecrow, 1980. 437p. ISBN: 0810812819.

Lists over 3,900 fiction titles on wars from the earliest times to Vietnam. *Class No:* 82-39

Speeches

[6889]
American orators of the twentieth century: critical studies and sources. Duffy, B.K. *and* Ryan, H.R., *eds.* Westport, Conn., Greenwood, 1987. xxii,468p. $115. ISBN: 0313248435.

Essays on 58 political, social and religious figures, A-Z, averaging 7p. and including critical assessment of their oratorical style and role in history. Lists of information

....(contd.)
sources, including anthologies, critical studies and biographies, follow each essay. Glossary of rhetorical terms. Subject index and index of speeches and speakers. A companion vol. by the same editors, *American orators before 1900: critical studies and sources* (499p. $115. ISBN: 0313251290) was published by Greenwood in 1987.
Class No: 82-5

[6890]

Lend me your ears: great speeches in history. Safire, W., *ed.* Rev. and exp. ed. New York, Norton, 1997. 1055p. £30. ISBN: 0393040054.

1st ed. 1992.

200 outstanding speeches, from Demosthenes to Salman Rushdie, arranged under 13 subject headings. Introductory notes by the editor set each speech in historical context and analyze the techniques which give it force and effect. Index.

Another useful source is *The Penguin book of historic speeches*, ed. by B. McArthur (London, Viking, 1995. 544p. £20. ISBN: 0670848557). *Class No:* 82-5

[6891]

SUTTON, R.B. Speech index: an index to 259 collections of world famous orations and speeches for various occasions. 4th ed., rev. and enl. New York, Scarecrow, 1966. vii,947p. $76.50. ISBN: 0810801388.

Speeches found in books are indexed by orator, subject, and type of speech, in a single A-Z sequence. Covers collections in English, 1900-65, and includes all entries in 3 previous eds. published 1935, 1956, and 1962.

Supplement, 1966-1980, by C. Mitchell (Metuchen, N.J., Scarecrow, 1982. 466p. $68.50. ISBN: 0810815184), indexes over 130 recent collections, cumulating 2 earlier supplements (1966-70; 1971-75) and adding new material published 1975-80. *Class No:* 82-5

Satire & Humour

[6892]

EVANS, J.E. Comedy: an annotated bibliography of theory and criticism. Metuchen, N.J., Scarecrow, 1987. xxi, 397p. ISBN: 0810819872.

3,106 items published through 1984, either in English or later translated into English, are arranged in 4 sections: 1. Comic theory before 1900 (with 4 chronological sub-divisions) - 2. Comic theory after 1900 - 3. Comic literature (divided into national literatures) - 4. Related subjects, such as farce, satire, caricature, etc. Numbered items are arranged A-Z by author within each section or sub-section and given a brief annotation. All but 157 items are post-1900. Indexes of authors and subjects, plus 'see also' references throughout. Not confined to drama.
Class No: 82-7

[6893]

NILSEN, D.L.F. Humor scholarship: a research bibliography. Westport, Conn., Greenwood, 1993. 382p. $65. (*Bibliographies and indexes in popular culture.*) ISBN: 0313284415.

A selective listing in 10 sections: 1.The Individual - 2. Personal interactions - 3. Language play and rhetorical devices - 4. The Media - 5. National styles of humor - 6. Ethnicity - 7. Mythology and religion - 8. Maturity and education - 9. Humor theory - 10. Epistemology. Entries are not annotated, but essays outline trends and developments in 45 topical areas. Most of the cited works have been published since 1970. Appended lists of scholarly humor journals, publishers, organizations and academic courses.

....(contd.)
Nilsen has also compiled *Humor in American literature: an annotated bibliography* (New York, Garland, 1992. 580p. ISBN: 0824083954), which lists humorous, ironic and satirical books and studies of them. Chronological arrangement with name index. *Class No:* 82-7

Epics & Romances

[6894]

BRITISH MUSEUM. Department of Manuscripts. **Catalogue of romances in the Department of Manuscripts.** London, British Museum, 1883-1910 (repr. 1961-62). 3v.

V.1-2, by H.L.D. Ward; v.3, by J.A. Herbert.

V.1: Classical romances (the cycles of Troy, Alexander, etc.). British and English traditions (cycle of Arthur, etc.). French traditions (cycle of Charlemagne, etc.). Miscellaneous romances. Allegorical and didactic romances. Appendix.

V.2: Northern legends and tales. Eastern legends and tales. Aesopic fables. Reynard the fox. Visions of heaven and hell. Les Trois pèlerinages. Miracles of the Virgin. Appendix.

V.3: Exempla and moralized tales in prose. Exempla and moralized tales in verse. Collected tales. Appendix.

Authoritative; gives valuable background and bibliographical information on each item. Each volume carries an index table of mss. *Class No:* 82-90

[6895]

COLEMAN, A. Epic and romance criticism. New York, Watermill, 1973-74. 2v.

20,000 citations to English-language criticism, published 1940-73, arranged under titles of epics and romances. V.1 covers English and American epics and metrical romances, while v.2 covers classical and continental works.
Class No: 82-90

[6896]

JACKSON, G.M. Encyclopedia of traditional epics. Santa Barbara, Calif., and Oxford, ABC-CLIO, 1994. 732p. illus. $65. ISBN: 0874367247.

Entries (A-Z) on characters, themes and story lines from the world's epic literature. Appended lists of epics by region, period and sub-genre. Bibliography of both original sources and critical studies. Index. Particularly useful for information on less well-known epics, but *RQ* (v.34(4), Summer 1995, p.517), criticizes the all-encompassing selection policy which brings in literary stories not normally considered as traditional epics.

Jackson has also compiled a companion vol., the *Encyclopedia of literary epics* (ABC-CLIO, 1997. xv,660p. illus. $65. ISBN: 0874367735), which covers works by named authors of all periods and regions. Entries on works (including extracts), authors, genres, characters, terms, etc. Bibliography (16p.). *Class No:* 82-90

[6897]

SPENCE, L. A Dictionary of medieval romance and romance writers. London, Routledge; New York, Dutton, 1913 (repr. New York, Gordon Press). vi,395p. $200. ISBN: 0849000394.

Entries in one sequence for titles, characters, and authors, with detailed plot synopses under titles. Covers British, Celtic, and West European romances. Bibliography of standard studies of the romance (5p.). *Class No:* 82-90

Mottoes & Slogans

[6898]

Mottoes: a compilation of more than 9,000 mottoes from around the world and throughout history. Urdang, L. *and* Robbins, C.D., *eds.* Detroit, Gale, 1986. 1162p. ISBN: 0810320762.

Arranged A-Z by first word in 345 thematic categories. Data: language, English translation, family or institution. Indexes allow access by family, institution or individual associated with a particular motto. *Class No:* 82-98

[6899]

PINE, L.G. A Dictionary of mottoes. London, Routledge, 1983. xiii,303p. ISBN: 071009339x.

Explains the meaning and history of over 6,500 mottoes belonging to individuals, families, nations, cities, armed forces and corporate bodies. A-Z arrangement with separate list of Greek mottoes. Index. *Class No:* 82-98

[6900]

Slogans Urdang, L. *and* Robbins, C.D., *eds.* Detroit, Gale, 1984. 556p. ISBN: 0810315491.

See also N. Rees' *Dictionary of slogans: from 'Dig for victory' to 'Eat more fruit'* (2nd ed. London, HarperCollins, 1997. 288p. illus. £5.99. ISBN: 0004720423).

Over 6,000 slogans arranged in 126 categories, the majority from US commercial advertising. Most of the rest are political, *e.g.* over 400 from Presidential campaigns. A-Z index of slogans. Index of companies, products and people. *Class No:* 82-98

820 English Literature

English Literature

Databases

[6901]

Disclit: British authors. Twayne's *English authors* series and OCLC Subject Bibliographies on CD-ROM. Boston, Hall, 1992. $995. ISBN: 0816116601.

Provides the full texts of some 125 vols. in Twayne's series of critical studies of major writers together with over 100,000 bibliographical citations pertaining to authors covered in the series from the OCLC On-line Union Catalog. *Class No:* 820-0(003.4)

Bibliographies of Bibliographies

[6902]

HOWARD-HILL, T.H. Index to British literary bibliography. Oxford, Clarendon Press, 1969-. v.1-2, 4-6(in progress).

V.1 *Bibliography of British literary bibliographies*. 2nd ed. 1987. xxv,886p. £95. ISBN: 0198181841.

V.2 *Shakespearian bibliography and textual criticism*. 1971. 322p. See entry at 820-2SHA(01).

V.3 *British bibliography to 1890* (in preparation).

V.4-5 *British bibliography and textual criticism: a bibliography*. 1979. £85. ISBN: 0198181639. See entry at 01.0(01)(410).

V.6 *British literary bibliography and textual criticism, 1890-1969: an index*. 1980. £95. ISBN: 0198181809.

V.7 *British literary bibliography, 1970-1979*. 1992. xix,912p. £110. ISBN: 0198181833.

The 1st ed. of v.1 (1969) listed 5,219 bibliographies in English, published since 1890, on British writers active since 1475. Sections for period, regional, form/genre, and subject bibliographies, plus authors, A-Z, with nearly 3,000 items relating to *c*.1,500 individuals. Brief annotations with references to reviews. Index of names and subjects. The 2nd ed. has 1,860 new entries interpolated in the same sequence.

V.2 is dealt with under Shakespeare and vols. 4-5 under general British bibliographies. V.6 is an interim index to vols. 1-2 and 4-5, and includes corrections to vols. 4-5. V.7 is a supplementary work which continues the coverage of earlier vols.

'A vast and valuable undertaking' (*Review of English Studies*, v.41(161), Feb. 1990, p.104-5). *Class No:* 820-0(009)

[6903]

MELLOWN, E.W. A Descriptive catalogue of the bibliographies of 20th century British poets, novelists, and dramatists. 2nd ed., rev. and enl. Troy, N.Y., Whitston, 1978. xv,414p. $22.50. ISBN: 0878751378.

1st ed. 1972 as *A Descriptive catalogue of the bibliographies of twentieth-century British writers*.

Covers over 1,500 authors born after 1840 who published the larger part of their work in England after 1890. Includes Irish writers if born before 1920 or if published mainly in

....(*contd.*)

England, plus some Commonwealth writers. Cites primary and secondary bibliographies and entries in general works like *New Cambridge bibliography of English literature*. *Class No:* 820-0(009)

Bibliographies

[6904]

ALLIBONE, S.A. Critical dictionary of English literature and British and American authors, living and deceased, from the earliest accounts to the latter half of the nineteenth century; containing over 46,000 articles (authors), with forty indexes of subjects. Philadelphia, Lippincott, 1858 (repr. New York, Gordon Press). 3v. (3140p.). $300. ISBN: 087968965x.

Not always accurate, but still of value, since it often summarizes and gives lengthy excerpts from critical reviews, and assiduously records variant spellings of names.

Continued by J.F. Kirk's *Supplement ... containing over 37,000 articles (authors) and enumerating over 93,000 articles* (Philadelphia, Lippincott, 1891; repr. New York, Gordon Press. 2v. $200. ISBN: 0849011612). *Class No:* 820-0(01)

[6905]

The Annotated bibliography for English studies. Lisse, Swets & Zeitlinger, 1997. CDROM. £475 per annum.

A new bibliography which aims to provide guidance 'on what is worth reading in English studies' (a discipline which is interpreted very broadly to include cultural studies, media studies, women's studies, visual arts, etc.), by having a large team of scholars (450 worldwide) selecting and evaluating the important contributions in their subject fields. 'It is in this selectivity ... that its unique value lies' (*Computers and Texts*, no.15, Aug. 1997). Second release (Oct. 1997) comprises 18,800 records, averaging 200 words, in 4 main sections: Cultural Studies, Language Studies, Literary Studies and Film Studies. Searchable by keyword, author, period, language and title. To be updated twice a year with 4,000 new records and will be made available on the Internet in 1998 with monthly updates. *Class No:* 820-0(01)

[6906]

Annual bibliography of English language and literature (ABELL), 1920-. London, Modern Humanities Research Assoc., 1921-. v.1-. ISSN: 00663786.

Earlier published by Cambridge Univ. Press for M.H.R.A.

V.70: *1995* (1997. xxix,1338p.) has 20,413 entries for books, pamphlets and periodical articles (from *c*.1,400 journals), as well as unpublished British and Irish theses, covering the English language and English, American and Commonwealth literature. 1. *Festschriften* and other collections - 2. Bibliography (book production, publishing, etc.) - 3. Scholarly method - 4. Language, literature, and the computer - 5. Newspapers and other periodicals - 6. English language - 7. Traditional culture, folklore and folklife - 8. English literature (p.215-1228). Literature chapter has general section followed by sections on Old English, Middle

....(contd.)

English, and each century from 16th to 20th; each period-section has subsections for genres, followed by individual authors, A-Z. Cross-references. Index of authors and subjects. Index of scholars. More comprehensive than *The Year's work in English studies* (*q.v.*), but not annotated.

Complete set of over 100,000 records, 1920-95, made available on CD-ROM in 1998 by Chadwyck-Healey, Cambridge. Also available on the Internet via their *Literature Online (LION)* subscription service (http://lion.chadwyck.co.uk). Subscribers can choose access extending back to 1920 or just to 1980. *Class No:* 820-0(01)

[6907]

The New Cambridge bibliography of English literature. Watson, G., *and others, eds.* Cambridge, Cambridge Univ. Press, 1969-77. 5v. £300. ISBN: 052134378x.

1st ed. 1940, as *The Cambridge bibliography of English literature*(4v.). *Supplement*. 1957.

V.1 *600-1660*, ed. by G. Watson. 1974.
V.2 *1660-1800*, ed. by G. Watson. 1971.
V.3 *1800-1900*, ed. by G. Watson. 1969.
V.4 *1900-1950*, ed. by I.R. Willison. 1972.
V.5 *Index*, comp. by J.D. Pickles. 1977.

Designed to replace *CBEL*, following the same chronological arrangement with subdivisions within periods for literary forms and genres and author bibliographies (primary and secondary) for hundreds of major and minor figures. The main changes are as follows: coverage now extends to 1950; Commonwealth literatures are no longer covered (author listings now being confined to 'literary authors native to or mainly resident in the British Isles'); Celtic literature is excluded; some non-literary sections (*e.g.* those on political and social backgrounds) have been dropped, although others (*e.g.* travel, sport) have been retained.

V.4 has the following sections: 1. Introduction (covering general works and book production) - 2. Poetry - 3. The Novel - 4. Drama - 5. Prose (including critics, essayists, humorists, historians, philosophers, and writers on travel, theology, natural science, sport and the countryside) - 6. Newspapers and magazines. Skeleton index of primary authors and subject headings.

V.5 has a comprehensive single-sequence index of primary authors, subjects, anonymous titles, newspapers and periodicals, etc., with cross-references. *Class No:* 820-0(01)

[6908]

—The Shorter new Cambridge bibliography of English literature. Watson, G., *ed.* Cambridge, Cambridge Univ. Press, 1981. xivp.,1622 cols. £23.95. ISBN: 0521226007.

A concise edition of the *NCBEL*, with the same structure and retaining the primary material for all the major authors and some of the minor ones, whilst secondary entries have been reduced to only the most important studies. Coverage of bibliographies, literary histories, anthologies and critical surveys for particular periods has been retained, but certain marginal sections (*e.g.* book production and distribution) have been dropped. Index of primary authors.
Class No: 820-0(01)

[6909]

NEW YORK PUBLIC LIBRARY. Research Libraries. **Dictionary catalog of the Henry W. and Albert A. Berg Collection of English and American literature.** Boston, Hall, 1969. 5v. $535. ISBN: 0816108706.

The Berg Collection is one of America's most celebrated collections of first editions, rare books, autograph letters, and manuscripts. There are 20,000 printed items and 50,000

....(contd.)

manuscripts. Irving, Hawthorne, Emerson, Thoreau, and Whitman are represented in first editions as well as in manuscripts. For the following twentieth-century authors the collection is justly famous: Conrad, Hardy, Shaw, Woolf. The nineteenth century is represented by Dickens and Thackeray, Wordsworth, Coleridge, and Browning.

84,100 cards plus a further 15,800 cards in *First supplement* (1975. 757p. $120. ISBN: 0816100144) and 16,537 cards in *Second supplement* (1983. 1 reel of microfilm $165. ISBN: 0816114714), the latter covering items added 1976-81. *Class No:* 820-0(01)

[6910]

WISE, T.J. The Ashley Library: a catalogue of printed books, manuscripts and autograph letters collected by Thomas James Wise. London, printed for private circulation, 1922-36 (repr. London, Dawsons, 1971). 11v. (2,684p.). illus.

Full bibliographical descriptions (with notes) are given of some 2,000 items - first editions of English poets and dramatists, from Jacobean to modern times, but particularly of the 19th century. The index to v.1-9 appears at the end of v.9; the index to v.10-11 is at the end of v.11. Arrangement in v.1-8 is alphabetically by author; v.9 and v.10-11 have separate A-Z sequences. The Ashley Library is now in the British Library.

The 1971 reprint has a new preface by S. Nowell-Smith.
Class No: 820-0(01)

[6911]

The Year's work in English studies, 1919-. Oxford, Blackwell; Atlantic Highlands, N.J., Humanities Press, for The English Association, 1921-. v.1-. Annual. ISSN: 00844144.

Earlier published by Oxford Univ. Press and J. Murray.

V.76: *1995* (1998. lxxi,936p. £125) has 18 chapters in which subject specialists survey the year's output of books (1,100 titles evaluated) and articles (from over 950 journals) on the English language and English, American and Commonwealth literature. References to periodical articles in the text, with books listed at the end of each chapter. Chapters include: 1. English language - 2-14. English literature by period, from Old English to 20th century, with separate chapters devoted to Chaucer, Shakespeare and Milton - 15-16. American literature - 17. New literatures in English. Index of critics - 18. Bibliography and textual criticism. Index of authors and subjects.

Special topic-based editions are announced for 1998 as *The English Association critical bibliographies*. These will comprise sets of volumes which include all references in this series to a particular period, subject or major author. The first three titles are:

A Critical bibliography of American literature studies, 1954-1994. 2928p. ISBN: 0631209387.

A Critical bibliography of English language studies, 1940-1994. 1968p. ISBN: 0631209425.

A Critical bibliography of twentieth-century English literature studies, 1954-1994. 2832p. £340. ISBN: 0631209409. *Class No:* 820-0(01)

16th Century

[6912]

TANNENBAUM, S.A. *and* **TANNENBAUM, D.R. Elizabethan bibliographies.** New York, the Authors, 1937-50. 41v. plus supplements (repr. Port Washington, N.Y., Kennikat Press, 1967. 10v.).

....*(contd.)*

No.1, *Christopher Marlowe* (1937) and Suppl. 1-2 (1937-47); no.2, *Ben Jonson* (1938); no. 3, *Beaumont and Fletcher* (1938) and Suppl. (1946); no.4, *Philip Massinger* (1938); no.5, *George Chapman* (1938) and Suppl. (1946); no.6, *Thomas Heywood* (1939); no.7, *Thomas Dekker* (1939) and Suppl. (1945); no.8, *Robert Greene* (1939) and Suppl. (1945); no.9, *Shakspere's 'Macbeth'* (1939); no.10, *Shakspere's sonnets* (1940); no.11, *Thomas Lodge* (1940); no.12, *John Lyly* (1940); no.13, *Thomas Middleton* (1940); no.14, *John Marston* (1940); no.15, *George Peele* (1940); no.16, *Shakspere's 'King Lear'* (1940); no.17, *Shakspere's 'The Merchant of Venice'* (1941); no.20, *John Ford* (1941); no.21, *Thomas Nashe* (1941); no.22, *Michael Drayton* (1941); no.23, *Sir Philip Sidney* (1941); no.24, *Michael Eyquem de Montaigne* (1942); no.25, *Samuel Daniel* (1942); no. 26, *George Gascoigne* (1942); no.27, *Anthony Mundy, including the play of 'Sir Thomas Moore'*, (1942); no.28, *Shakspere's 'Othello'* (1943); no.29, *Shakspere's 'Troilus and Cressida'* (1943); nos.30-32, *Marie Stuart, Queen of Scots* (1944-46. 3v.); no.33, *Cyril Tourneur* (1946); no.34, *James Shirley* (1946); no.35, *George Herbert* (1946); no.36, *John Heywood* (1946); no.37, *Roger Ascham* (1946); no.38, *Thomas Randolph* (1946); no.39, *Nicholas Breton* (1947); no.40, *Robert Herrick* (1949); no.41, *Shakspere's 'Romeo and Juliet'* (1950).

Each bibliography has numbered entries for both primary and secondary material. *Class No:* 820-0(01)"15"

[6913]

—Elizabethan bibliographies. Supplements. Donovan, D., *and others, comps.* London, Nether Press, 1967-71. no.1-12, 15, 17-18.

No.1, *Thomas Middleton, John Webster* (1967); no.2, *Thomas Dekker, Thomas Heywood, Cyril Tourneur* (1967); no.3, *Robert Herrick, Ben Jonson, Thomas Randolph* (1968); no.4, *George Chapman, John Marston* (1968); no.5, *Robert Greene, Thomas Lodge, John Lyly, Thomas Nashe, George Peele* (1968); no.6, *Christopher Marlowe* (1968); no.7, *Samuel Daniel, Michael Drayton, Sir Philip Sidney* (1967); no.8, *Francis Beaumont, John Fletcher, Philip Massinger, John Ford, James Shirley* (1968); no.9, *Roger Ascham, George Gascoigne, John Heywood, Thomas Kyd, Anthony Munday* (1968); no.10, *Sir Thomas Browne, Robert Burton* (1968); no.11, *Traherne and the seventeenth-century Platonists* (1969); no.12, *Andrew Marvell (1969); no.15, Francis Bacon* (1968); no.17, *Sir Walter Raleigh* (1971); no.18, *John Evelyn, Samuel Pepys* (1971).

Chronological lists recording postwar research and updating the Tannenbaums' bibliographies. Some authors of the period not covered in the original series are included. *Class No:* 820-0(01)"15"

17th & 18th Centuries

[6914]

CRANE, R.S., ***and others*. English literature, 1660-1800:** a bibliography of modern studies, compiled for *Philological Quarterly*. Princeton, Princeton Univ. Press; London, Oxford Univ. Press, 1950-72. 6v.

Reprints of annual bibliographies in *Philological Quarterly*, 1926-70, including books and periodical articles. Each year's list is divided into 5 sections, whose contents vary but there is always one on individual authors. Annotations are frequent, the more important works being reviewed at some length. Name index in each vol.

Continued annually as 'English literature, 1660-1800', in *Philological Quarterly*, 1971-75, the last vol. covering publications of 1974, and thereafter as part of *The Eighteenth century: a current bibliography, 1975-*. (New York, AMS Press, 1977-. Annual. ISSN: 01610996), which covers a much wider range of subjects. *Class No:* 820-0(01)"16/17"

[6915]

SPECTOR, R.D. Backgrounds to Restoration and eighteenth-century English literature: an annotated bibliographic guide to modern scholarship. Westport, Conn., Greenwood, 1989. 553p. $99.50. ISBN: 0313240981.

Lists *c.*3,000 English-language studies published since the 1930s, in 12 sections for bibliographies and 11 broad subject areas. Entries are arranged A-Z by author within each section and indexed by author, but the lack of a subject index is a major drawback. 'The scholarship is here; access to it is most unsatisfactory' (*Choice*, v.26(11/12), July/Aug. 1989, p.1820). *Class No:* 820-0(01)"16/17"

17th Century

[6916]

DUGGAN, M.M. English literature and backgrounds, 1660-1700: a selective critical guide. New York, Garland, 1990. 2v. (658;564p.). $171. ISBN: 0824085027.

1. Background to literature (history, religion, music, etc.) - 2. General literary topics (bibliography, literary history, etc.) - 3. Special literary topics (*e.g.* women writers, foreign influences) - 4. Authors. Part 4 occupies nearly 900p. and covers 304 writers and other notable figures, listing bibliographies, editions, biographies and critical studies, but annotations are cursory: 'Comment on any particular work's importance is brief and limited at best' (*Choice*, v.28(1), Sept. 1990, p.74). *Class No:* 820-0(01)"16"

18th & 19th Centuries

[6917]

Literature of the Romantic period: a bibliographical guide. O'Neill, M., *ed.* Oxford, Clarendon Press, 1998. viii,408p. £40. ISBN: 0198711204.

18 signed bibliographical essays, of which one covers general studies of the period 1780-1830, 11 cover individual writers (Blake, Wordsworth, Coleridge, Byron, P.B. Shelley, Keats, Clare, Scott, Austen, Peacock and Mary Wollstonecraft Shelley) and 6 are devoted to genres or groups of minor writers. Each chapter is followed by a list of the texts and critical studies mentioned plus others of note. Index. *Class No:* 820-0(01)"17/18"

[6918]

WARD, W.S. Literary reviews in British periodicals: a bibliography, with a supplementary list of general (non-review) articles on literary subjects. New York, Garland, 1972-77. 4v.

1789-1797. 1979. 342p. ISBN: 0824097637.

1798-1820. 1972. 2v. (633p.). ISBN: 0824005120.

1821-1826. 1977. 301p. ISBN: 0824099389.

Each set lists reviews under the name of the author reviewed, then chronologically by publication date of the work concerned. *Class No:* 820-0(01)"17/18"

18th Century

[6919]

GLOCK, W.S. Eighteenth-century English literary studies: a bibliography. Metuchen, N.J., Scarecrow, 1984. xviii,847p. ISBN: 081081658x.

Lists critical books and articles published in the 50 years prior to publication on 25 major writers, with brief descriptive annotations. Critical editions are excluded. 'The fifty-year limit excludes much of the best and some of the essential criticism' (*Modern Language Review*, v.81(2), April 1986, p.425-6). *Class No:* 820-0(01)"17"

Victorian Age

[6920]

Annual bibliography of Victorian studies, 1976-. Chauduri, B., *& others, eds.* Edmonton, Alberta, LITIR Database, Univ. of Alberta, 1977-. Annual. ISSN: 02271400.

A computer-generated listing of books and periodical articles relating to various aspects of the Victorian period. Literature is strongly represented, with bibliographies for over 400 individual authors. Many references to reviews. Indexes of subjects (very detailed), authors, titles, and reviewers.

Cumulative vols. have appeared under the title *Comprehensive bibliography of Victorian studies,* for 1970-74 (1984), 1975-79 (1985), and 1980-84 (1985), and all three have been integrated to form *Cumulative bibliography of Victorian studies, 1970-1984* (1988. 2v.).

CD-ROM cumulation published 1996, as *Victorian database on CD-ROM, 1970-1995* ($995), with 60,000 items drawn from over 500 journals. Annual updates will add 2,500 records per annum. *Class No:* 820-0(01)"1837-1901"

[6921]

Bibliographies of studies in Victorian literature ...

...for the thirteen years 1932-1944, ed. by W.D. Templeman, Urbana, Ill., Univ. of Illinois Press, 1945 (x,450p.).

...for the ten years 1945-1954, ed. by A. Wright, Urbana, Ill., Univ. of Illinois Press, 1956 (vii,310p.).

...for the ten years 1955-1965, ed. by R.C. Slack, Urbana, Ill., Univ. of Illinois Press, 1967 (xvi,461p. ISBN: 0404180337).

...for the ten years 1965-1974, ed. by R.E. Freeman, New York, AMS, 1981 (xlv,876p. ISBN: 0404180329).

Each vol. consists of annual lists compiled by the Victorian Literature Group of the Modern Language Association of America, which originally appeared in the journals *Modern Philology* (up to 1956) and *Victorian Literature* (1957 onwards). Each list is in 4 sections: 1. Bibliographical material - 2. Economic, political, religious and social environment - 3. Movements of ideas and literary forms - 4. Individual authors (easily the biggest section). Some entries annotated. Reviews cited. Index of names and subjects in each vol. Entries have increased from 6,000 in the first vol. to 18,000 in the most recent and are not confined to literary studies.

Continued by *Victorian bibliography for ...,* appearing in the Summer issue of *Victorian Studies* (Bloomington, Indiana Univ., Quarterly). *Class No:* 820-0(01)"1837-1901"

[6922]

—Victorian studies. Bloomington, Ind., Program for Victorian Studies, Indiana Univ., 1956-. Quarterly. ISSN: 00425222.

Continues the annual bibliographies formerly published in *Modern Philology*. The bibliography for 1994 (in v.38(4), Summer 1995) has 6 sections, of which no.5 covers literary history, literary forms, and literary ideas (over 400 entries) and no.6 has bibliographies for well over 100 authors, A-Z, listing major new editions and biographical and critical studies. References to reviews are included. *Class No:* 820-0(01)"1837-1901"

20th Century

[6923]

DAVIES, A. An Annotated critical bibliography of modernism. Brighton, Harvester; Totowa, N.J., Barnes & Noble, 1982. xiv,261p. ISBN: 0710800312, UK.

216 entries on Modernism in general, arranged according to theory, genre, critical reception, and literary Modernism's relationship with other arts; followed by sections on W.B. Yeats (103 entries), Wyndham Lewis (47), D.H. Lawrence (167), and T.S. Eliot (128). Most useful for its general section and that on Lewis, the other writers being more comprehensively covered elsewhere. Indexes of critics and subjects. *Class No:* 820-0(01)"19"

[6924]

MARKET, L. The Bloomsbury Group: a reference guide. Boston, Hall, 1989. 325p. $45. ISBN: 0816189366.

An annotated bibliography of secondary sources, arranged chronologically from 1905 to 1987, then by author. Includes studies from a wide range of disciplines, including art criticism, philosophy and politics. Largely confined to English-language sources. Index of authors and subjects. *Class No:* 820-0(01)"19"

Women

[6925]

HORWITZ, B.J. British women writers, 1700-1850: an annotated bibliography of their works and works about them. Lanham, Md., Scarecrow, 1997. xiv,231p. £35.15. (*Magill bibliographies.*) ISBN: 0810833158.

A selective guide to 46 authors, including some little-known names as well as the major figures like Austen and the Brontës, which provides biographical information and lists accessible editions, recent bibliographies and key critical studies. Introductory chapters on British political events of the period and the history of women's writing. Author and subject indexes. *Class No:* 820-0(01)-0055.2

[6926]

Women and the literature of the seventeenth century: an annotated bibliography based on Wing's *Short-title Catalogue*. Smith, H.L. *and* Cardinale, S., *comps.* Westport, Conn., Greenwood, 1990. xxi,332p. $55. ISBN: 031322059x.

Lists 637 works by women and 973 works for and about women, with concise abstracts. List of women printers, publishers and booksellers. Chronological index. General index. Appended list of 183 works not seen. *Class No:* 820-0(01)-0055.2

Encyclopaedias & Dictionaries

[6927]

Bloomsbury guide to English literature. Wynne-Davies, M., *ed.* 2nd ed. London, Bloomsbury, 1995. xi,1102p. £25. ISBN: 0747522677.

1st ed 1990, published in USA as *Prentice-Hall guide to English literature.*

22 chronologically arranged, signed essays (average 16p.), outlining the development of major genres, are followed by an A-Z reference section with *c.*4,000 entries on authors (800+), works (1,000+), allusions, historical events and personages, literary terms, schools, movements and genres. Many cross-references between essay and reference sections. Author entries largely restricted to British-based writers. 28 contributors. For this ed. the number of essays has been increased by 10 and there are over 300 new reference entries, but illustrations and a chronology have been dropped.

A useful complement to the *Oxford companion* because of its coverage of contemporary writers and recent developments in criticism, but the omission of many names from the past means it should not be seen as a replacement. *Class No:* 820-0(03)

[6928]

OUSBY, I. The Cambridge guide to literature in English. [2nd ed.] Cambridge, Cambridge Univ. Press, 1993. 1055p. illus. £24.95. ISBN: 0521440866.

1st ed. 1988.

'Aims to provide a handy reference guide to the literature in English produced by all the various English-speaking cultures throughout the world' (*Editor's note*). Well over 4,000 entries, arranged A-Z, covering authors, major works, genres, literary movements, critical concepts, periodicals, theatres, awards, etc. Numerous cross-references. Over 300 illustrations. 100-plus contributors, although Ousby is assigned the status of author on the jacket and title-page. Like the *Bloomsbury guide,* it complements rather than replaces the *Oxford companion.* Coverage of contemporary writers, children's literature, Commonwealth literature and genre fiction is particularly strong but it lacks the *Oxford companion's* useful bibliographical notes. Warmly received by reviewers, in contrast to its disappointing predecessor, the *Cambridge guide to English literature* (1983), to which no reference is made in this work. Said to be completely revised and expanded for this ed., but no details provided in introductory notes regarding number of new entries, etc. *Class No:* 820-0(03)

[6929]

The Oxford companion to English literature. Drabble, M., *ed.* Revised reprint of 5th ed. Oxford, Oxford Univ. Press, 1995. xi,1171p. £25. ISBN: 0198662211.

1st ed. 1932, by Sir P. Harvey; 5th ed. 1985.

The 5th ed. represented a major revision of Harvey's standard work, with over 7,000 entries on authors, works, literary schools and movements, genres, terms, characters, and periodicals. All entries have been revised and updated, and many new ones added for authors previously omitted, contemporary authors, modern critics and critical schools, popular literary genres, and influential foreign authors, critics, artists, and composers. Omitted, however, are Harvey's many entries on allusions likely to be encountered in literature and on classical mythology, whilst the entries on classical authors have been very thoroughly revised, on account of the fact that 'fewer readers have the benefit of a classical education' (*Preface*), and their links with English literature are more strongly emphasized. Entries on major

....(*contd.*)

authors include references to selected biographical and critical studies. Thoroughly cross-referenced throughout. 1995 revision has 59 new entries on contemporary authors (*e.g.* Martin Amis, Salman Rushdie) and existing entries on living writers have been updated. New appendices include lists of winners of major literary prizes and chronology of literary and historical events, 1000-1994.

An indispensable reference book, which covers a far wider field than its title suggests, and is therefore particularly valuable in small libraries. *Class No:* 820-0(03)

[6930]

—The Concise Oxford companion to English literature. Drabble, M. *and* Stringer, J., *eds.* Rev. ed. Oxford, Oxford Univ. Press, 1996. 659p. £7.99. ISBN: 0192800396.

1st ed. 1987.

A paperback abridgement of the 5th ed. of the *Oxford companion*, containing over 5,000 entries. The editors 'have tried to prune rather than delete entries' (*Preface*) but have omitted references to many artists, musicians and foreign writers. Many plot summaries have been shortened but those on major works remain almost entirely intact. Rev. ed. has 60 new entries on contemporary authors. *Class No:* 820-0(03)

[6931]

Reference guide to English literature. Kirkpatrick, D.L., *ed.* 2nd ed. Detroit & London, St. James Press, 1991. 3v. $295. ISBN: 1558620788.

1st ed. published under the same title in a series of 8 vols. by St. James Press, 1984, and also included in Macmillan's 14-vol. series entitled *Great writers student library,* which also included 1st ed. of *Reference guide to American literature.*

Vols. 1-2, *Writers,* include entries (arranged A-Z) on nearly 900 UK, US and Commonwealth writers from Cynewulf to Rushdie. These comprise biographical notes; complete bibliography organized by genre; selected list of critical studies; and a signed critical essay by one of over 450 contributors. Most of the essays are straight reprints from the earlier ed. but biographical and bibliographical data has been updated. V.1 also contains 12 survey articles and general reading lists on the main genres and periods of English literature.

V.3, *Works,* is new to the 2nd ed. and comprises analytical essays (500-1000 words) on nearly 600 of the most important poems, stories, essays, novels and plays, and a complete title index to all 3 vols. *Class No:* 820-0(03)

16th & 17th Centuries

[6932]

RUOFF, J.E. Handbook of Elizabethan and Stuart literature. London, Macmillan, 1975. x,468p. ISBN: 0333191501.

Over 500 entries, A-Z, on writers (from More to Milton), works, literary movements, genres, and related subjects. Author entries include biography, review of works, assessment of importance, and selected bibliography of critical and biographical studies and of collected editions. Other entries also have bibliographies appended. Fully cross-referenced. *Class No:* 820-0(03)"15/16"

18th & 19th Centuries

[6933]

A Companion to Romanticism. Wu, D., *ed.* London, Blackwell, 1997. 560p. £75. (*Blackwell companions to literature and culture.*) ISBN: 0631198520.

8 introductory essays followed by 22 readings of key texts, a section on genres and modes, and 15 essays on issues and debates. The work of an international group of scholars. *Class No:* 820-0(03)"17/18"

[6934]

Encyclopedia of Romanticism: culture in Britain, 1780s-1830s. Dabundo, L., *ed.* New York, Garland; London, Routledge, 1992. xviii,662p. £95. ISBN: 0824069978, US; 0415081688, UK.

'Designed to survey the social, cultural and intellectual climate of English Romanticism' (*Preface*), with signed articles (by 140 contributors) on writers, critics, artists, architects and patrons, plus 'ideas, trends, fads and conventions.' Brief bibliography after each article. Index. *Class No:* 820-0(03)"17/18"

[6935]

A Handbook to English Romanticism. Raimond, J. *and* Watson, J.R., *eds.* Basingstoke, Macmillan; New York, St. Martin's Press, 1992. xix,326p. £7.99. ISBN: 0333607066, UK; 0312079141, US.

Over 80 essays (average 3½p.) by 29 British and French scholars on people, themes and events of the Romantic movement and on aspects of its cultural and historical background. Over 30 essays are about literary figures and contain mainly biographical information. Artists, philosophers and politicians are also covered. Index. *Class No:* 820-0(03)"17/18"

[6936]

Romanticism: the CD-ROM. Miall, D.S. *and* Wu, D., *eds.* London, Blackwell, 1997. CD-ROM. £395. ISBN: 0631199446.

A collection of fully linked texts and images which forms an invaluable resource for the study of Romanticism. Texts include canonical versions of key poems and other literary works as well as political documents, travel writing, articles from journals of the period and writings on history and aesthetics. 1,000 images, including paintings, scenes from the Lake District and the Alps, and maps of the travels of Romantic writers. Other useful features include a chronology of major literary and historical events and a biographical dictionary. Comprehensively indexed. *Class No:* 820-0(03)"17/18"

19th Century

[6937]

The 1890s: an encyclopedia of British literature, art, and culture. Cevasco, G.A., *ed.* New York, Garland, 1993. 714p. £150. ISBN: 0824025857.

Over 800 entries, A-Z, the majority being biographical studies of authors, artists, politicians, theologians and other influential figures. More than 100 significant books are individually treated and there are also articles on a wide range of cultural topics, schools and movements - with the emphasis on literature - and on important places and events. Short bibliographies with the articles. Cross-references and index. 'This handsome and nearly exhaustive guide ... [has] very few regrettable omissions' (*TLS*, no.4718, Sept. 3, 1993, p.20-21). *Class No:* 820-0(03)"18"

20th Century

[6938]

The Oxford companion to twentieth-century literature in English. Stringer, J., *ed.* Oxford, Oxford Univ. Press, 1996. xxi,751p. £25. ISBN: 0192122711.

Concise, unsigned entries (average 270 words, with major authors and topics allocated up to 1,000) on 2,400 authors and 400 works plus 650 on literary movements, genres, periodicals, etc. Lists of authors' works are very selective and only entries on major writers carry suggestions for further reading. Worldwide coverage with very broad subject scope, including a wide range of nonfiction authors such as journalists, biographers, philosophers, travel writers, etc., but children's writers are excluded. Appended lists of winners of Nobel, Booker and Pulitzer prizes. *Class No:* 820-0(03)"19"

Handbooks & Manuals

[6939]

BRACKEN, J.K. Reference works in British and American literature. Littleton, Colo., Libraries Unlimited, 1990-91. 2v. (*Reference sources in the humanities.*)

V.1 *English and American literature*. 1990. xii,252p. $45. ISBN: 0872876993.

V.2 *English and American writers*. 1991. xxiv,310p. $55. ISBN: 0872877000.

V.1 provides a very selective but thoroughly annotated guide to general reference sources, with 512 main entries and numerous sub-entries. V.2 is more useful for its thorough coverage of sources on 637 writers from Anglo-Saxon times to the present. Individual authors are not covered by Harner (*q.v.*) and Marcuse (*q.v.*) provides unannotated lists for only 69 major figures. Here, authors are arranged A-Z and for each are listed bibliographies, dictionaries/encyclopedic works, indexes/concordances, and current journals, giving a total of nearly 1,600 entries. Many other relevant works are cited in the evaluative annotations but, unfortunately, these cannot be traced via the author-title index, whose coverage is restricted to the numbered entries.

2nd ed. due mid-1998 (ISBN: 1563085186) *Class No:* 820-0(035)

[6940]

HARNER, J.L. Literary research guide: a guide to reference sources for the study of literatures in English and related topics. 2nd ed. New York, Modern Language Assoc. of America, 1993. vii,766p. $45. ISBN: 0873525582.

1st ed. 1989, superseding M. Patterson's *Literary research guide* (2nd ed. MLA, 1984).

21 chapters in 2 groups, the first describing general reference works such as biographical sources, guides to manuscripts, etc., and the second covering works on particular literatures in English. Annotations tend to be longer than Patterson's, describe and evaluate each work, occasionally cite reviews, and can be bluntly critical. The 'related topics' covered include children's literature, film and literature, and literary theory. Name, title and subject indexes. 2nd ed. adds works published since 1989, with half the remaining entries revised, making nearly 1,200 in all.

Some reviewers of 1st ed. suggested that as Harner states his opinions very vigorously users may sometimes feel the need to seek a second opinion, although *Choice* (v.31(1), Sept. 1993, p.82), reviewing 2nd ed., says 'his work can fairly claim to be the standard guide in the field.'

3rd ed. due 1998 (ISBN: 0873525736). *Class No:* 820-0(035)

[6941]

MARCUSE, M.J. A Reference guide for English studies. Berkeley, Calif., Univ. of California Press, 1990. lxxii,790p. $120. ISBN: 0520051610.

Provides bibliographical information and evaluative annotations on reference sources for all periods and genres of English and American literatures. Classified arrangement with thorough indexes (which occupy a quarter of the book) to authors, titles, and subjects. Over 2,700 entries in 24 sections, with over 10,000 titles listed. Current through 1985. Entries are of 3 types: full details of single works, with substantial annotations detailing scope, history, principles of inclusion, arrangement, etc. (2,500); lists of scholarly journals in particular fields (50); and unannotated lists of frequently recommended works on specific topics. Less likely to be critical than Harner (*q.v.*), but has similarly wide coverage, extending to folklore, film and women's studies. Contents table (30p.) includes short-form listing of every main entry. *Class No:* 820-0(035)

[6942]

Reader's guide to literature in English. Hawkins-*Dady, M., ed.* London and Chicago, Fitzroy Dearborn, 1996. xxxix,970p. £95. ISBN: 1884964206.

A slightly misleading title as this is not an encyclopedic guide to English-language writing like those published by Cambridge and St. James Press (see entries at 820-0(03)), but a handbook on *critical* sources. 573 signed bibliographical essays by nearly 250 contributors on the key works relating to 334 major writers plus movements, genres, literary theories, historical eras and regional traditions within the whole range of literature in English. Headings like 'Native American Literature', 'Travel Literature', 'Beat Generation', 'Aphra Behn' and 'Tom Stoppard' illustrate the scope. Coverage is very selective in some areas (*e.g.* under 'Old English Poetry' only 6 studies are evaluated) but 'at every random sampling the articles are taut, lucid and balanced' (*TLS*, no.4883, Nov. 1, 1996, p.12-13). A-Z arrangement by topic heading, with indexes of authors and themes and a particularly useful classified list of entries. This shows, for example, that there are over 80 entries relating to drama and 16 relating to Canadian literature, of which 11 are on individual writers. A very useful selection tool for librarians as well as a source for students and teachers.
Class No: 820-0(035)

Theses

[6943]

GABEL, G.U. *and* GABEL, G.R. Dissertations in English and American literature: theses accepted by Austrian, Swiss and French universities, 1875-1970. Hamburg, Gabel, 1977. 198p.

Lists 2,169 theses by period, with general studies and works on individual authors within each section. Indexes of authors and subjects.

Supplement, 1971-1975 (Köln, Gemini, 1982. 56p.) adds 418 theses.

The Gabels have also compiled *Catalogue of Austrian and Swiss dissertations (1875-1995) on English and American literatures* (Hürth, Gemini, 1997. 222p. ISBN: 392231378), which has 1892 unannotated entries, arranged broadly by period then by subject/author being treated. Subject and author indexes. *Class No:* 820-0(043)

[6944]

HOWARD, P.C. Theses in English literature, 1894-1970. Ann Arbor, Mich., Pierian Press, 1973. 387p.

Lists *c.*9,000 theses from American and foreign universities, according to the literary author covered. Author and subject indexes. *Class No:* 820-0(043)

[6945]

McNAMEE, L.F. Dissertations in English and American literature: theses accepted by American, British and German universities, 1865-1964. New York, Bowker, 1968. xi,1124p.

Computer-compiled listing of *c.*30,000 dissertations in 35 chapters, usually for literary periods or forms. Chaucer, Milton and Shakespeare are allocated full chapters while other writers have subsections. Index of major authors covered. Index of dissertation writers.

Supplement One (1969) and *Supplement Two* (1974) cover the period 1964-73. *Class No:* 820-0(043)

Reviews & Abstracts

[6946]

Abstracts of English studies. Boulder, Colo., National Council of Teachers of English (later Alberta, Univ. of Calgary Press), 1958-94. 37v. ISSN: 00013560.

A quarterly periodical which included abstracts of articles on the English language, English literature, American literature, and World literatures in English from 500 periodicals. Classified arrangement, with quarterly and annual indexes of names and subjects. Ceased publication 1994. *Class No:* 820-0(048)

[6947]

Anglia: Zeitschrift für englische Phonologie. Halle (later Tübingen), Niemeyer, 1878-. v.1-. 2py. since 1983 (formerly annual). ISSN: 03405222.

A major periodical covering English language and literature, which carries *c.*200 lengthy book reviews each year. *Class No:* 820-0(048)

[6948]

—English and American studies in German: summaries of theses and monographs. A supplement to *Anglia.* 1968-. Tübingen, Niemeyer, 1969-. Annual. ISSN: 00710490.

See entry at 802.0(048). *Class No:* 820-0(048)

Periodicals

[6949]

British literary magazines. Sullivan, A., *ed.* New York, Greenwood, 1983-6. 4v. (*Historical guides to the world's periodicals and newspapers.*) ISSN: 07425538.

V.1 *The Augustan Age and the Age of Johnson, 1698-1788* (1983. xxxi,427p. $85. ISBN: 031322871x).

V.2 *The Romantic Age, 1789-1836* (1983. xxv,491p. $85. ISBN: 0313228728).

V.3 *The Victorian and Edwardian Age, 1837-1913* (1984. xxvi,560p. $99.50. ISBN: 0313243352).

V.4 *The Modern Age, 1914-1984* (1986. xxx,628p. $115. ISBN: 0313243360).

From the same stable as Chielens' *American literary magazines* (*q.v.*) and uses the same format to profile 369 important literary magazines. Each vol. contains signed profiles, arranged A-Z by title, which average 5p. and are each followed by a list of information sources (selective bibliography, indexes, reprint editions and location sources) and publication history (title changes, volume and issue data, frequency of publication, publishers and editors). A variety

....(contd.)
of appendices list over 400 less important magazines with brief annotations. Each vol. has a chronology of social and literary events and literary magazines of its period, index and notes on contributors. Apart from 5 major titles, each magazine appears once only, in the volume covering the year it was first published. *Class No:* 820-0(051)

[6950]

WHITE, R.B. The English literary journal to 1900: a guide to information sources. Detroit, Gale, 1977. xiv,311p. ISBN: 081031228x.

Annotated bibliography of *c.*2,300 books, articles, and dissertations published since 1890. Sections for general studies are followed by sections for individual periodicals (A-Z), and people and places connected with them. Over 400 periodicals covered. Indexes of authors, periodicals, persons, and places. *Class No:* 820-0(051)

[6951]

—STANTON, M.N. English literary journals, 1900-1950: a guide to information sources. Detroit, Gale, 1982. 119p. ISBN: 0810313596.

Lists *c.*135 journals, giving publication dates, frequency, names of editors and notable contributors, and an indication of the nature of the contents. Bibliography of books and articles on literary journals (15p.). Index of authors and book titles. Index of journal titles, editors, and contributors. *Class No:* 820-0(051)

Excerpts

[6952]

Modern British literature. Temple, R.Z. *and* Tucker, M., *eds.* New York, Ungar, 1966-85. 5v. $375. (*A Library of literary criticism.*) ISBN: 0804432759, v.1-3; 0804432791, v.4; 080443140x, v.5.

Planned as a successor to Moulton's *Library of literary criticism* (*q.v.*) and similar in scope and format to D.N. Curley's *Modern American literature*. Comprises excerpts from critical studies of over 400 British and Commonwealth 20th-century authors, arranged chronologically under each author, in vols. 1-3, with cross-reference index and index of critics in v.3. Vols. 4 and 5 (1975-85) are supplementary vols., containing new material on some of the authors previously covered plus entries for extra authors. Primary bibliographies of the authors are also included. *Class No:* 820-0(082.200)

[6953]

Twentieth-century British literature. Bloom, H., *ed.* Broomall, Pa., Chelsea House, 1985-87. 6v. (*Chelsea House library of literary criticism.*) ISBN: 0877548080.

Lengthy critical excerpts on authors, A-Z in vols. 1-5, in the style of *The New Moulton's Library* (*q.v.*). V.6 contains index to critics, complete table of contents, and bibliographical supplement. *Class No:* 820-0(082.200)

Gazetteers

[6954]

OUSBY, I. Blue guide: literary Britain and Ireland. 2nd ed. London, Black; New York, Norton, 1990. £12.95. ISBN: 071363152x, UK; 0393304906, US.

1st ed. 1985.

Unlike most literary guide-books, this is arranged by writer rather than by place. 5 lengthy sections on Dickens, Hardy, Joyce, the Lake Poets, and Shakespeare (p.17-151), have detailed itineraries. *c.*180 writers are dealt with in briefer sections, arranged A-Z, in which reference is made to places in the course of biographical surveys. 37p. of maps. Indexes of Greater London locations and of other places. For 2nd ed., practical information (opening hours, telephone numbers, etc.) has been updated and new illustrations added. *Class No:* 820-0(083.86)

[6955]

The Oxford illustrated literary guide to Great Britain and Ireland. Eagle, D. *and* Stephens, M., *eds*. 2nd ed. Oxford, Oxford Univ. Press, 1992. vi,322p. illus. maps. ISBN: 0192129880.

First published 1977, as *The Oxford literary guide to the British Isles*, comp. and ed. by D. Eagle and H. Carnell; reprinted in paperback, with corrections, 1988. 1st ed. of this illustrated, large-format version published 1981. Paperback version currently available as *The Oxford literary guide to Great Britain and Ireland* (528p. £7.99. ISBN: 019283133x).

1,337 entries for places, A-Z, with details of their literary associations, followed by a list of 1,050 authors keyed to the main sequence. Place sequence includes useful cross-references from fictional names to real locations. Living writers continue to be excluded, but 137 new authors and 105 places have been added for this ed., with Scottish and Welsh representation increased. Corrections have been made to existing entries. Well illustrated throughout, including 32 colour plates. All places listed have references to the 13 appended maps. *Class No:* 820-0(083.86)

Chronologies

[6956]

Annals of English literature, 1475-1950: the principal publications of each year together with an alphabetical index of authors and their works. 2nd ed. Oxford, Clarendon Press, 1961. vi, 380p.

First published 1935, covering 1475-1925.

A chronological list of authors and titles of the main works published during each year. Parallel marginal columns give the dates of birth and death of authors, publication of newspapers, periodicals, translations, etc. and major historical events, including foreign ones. For the 2nd ed. numerous corrections have been made in the section covering 1475-1900, the section 1900-1925 has been completely reset and a new section covering 1925-1950 has been added. More Commonwealth and American authors have been included and the treatment of marginal entries, especially in French and German literature, has been improved. Detailed author index (85p.). *Class No:* 820-0(090)

[6957]

ROGAL, S.J. A Chronological outline of British literature. Westport, Conn., Greenwood, 1980. xv,342p. $42.95. ISBN: 0313214778.

Lists births, deaths, and literary events, 516-1979. Includes non-literary writers, *e.g.* philosophers, scientists, politicians, etc. Index of authors, anonymous titles, and events. *Class No:* 820-0(090)

[6958]

SMALLWOOD, P.J. A Concise chronology of English literature. London, Croom Helm, 1985. 220p. ISBN: 0709923627.

Separate unannotated lists, on facing pages, of literary and historical events from Chaucer to 1975. Index of authors. *Class No:* 820-0(090)

Histories

[6959]

The Cambridge history of English literature. Ward, A.W. *and* Waller, A.R., *eds*. Cambridge, Cambridge Univ. Press; New York, Putnam, 1907-27. 15v.

V.1 *From the beginnings to the Cycles of Romance.* V.2 *The End of the Middle Ages.* V.3 *Renascence and Reformation.* V.4 *Prose and poetry: Sir Thomas North to Michael Drayton.* V.5-6 *The Drama to 1642.* V.7 *Cavalier and Puritan.* V.8 *The Age of Dryden.* V.9 *From Steele and Addison to Pope and Swift.* V.10 *The Age of Johnson.* V.11 *The Period of the French Revolution.* V.12-14 *The Nineteenth century.* V.15 *Index.*

Each chapter is written by a specialist (as opposed to the *Oxford history*'s one volume per author) and there are very full chapter bibliographies, now superseded by the *Cambridge bibliography of English literature* and its successor. Covers English literature in the broadest sense and is still valuable for the minor genres; thus v.14 includes chapters headed 'Caricature and literature of sport' and 'The Literature of science'. Table of dates and name index in each vol. Reprints have appeared without the bibliographies.

Class No: 820-0(091)

[6960]

—SAMPSON, G. The Concise Cambridge history of English literature. 3rd ed., rev. throughout and with additional chapters on the literature of the United States of America and the mid-twentieth-century literature of the English-speaking world by R.C. Churchill. Cambridge, Cambridge Univ. Press, 1970. xiii,976p. £22.95. ISBN: 0521095816.

1st ed. 1941; 2nd ed. 1961.

16 chapters, of which the first 13 are based on the corresponding vols. of the parent work. Ch.14, 'Empire and After', covers the turn of the century, with strong emphasis on overseas literature, and the remaining chapters are referred to in the subtitle. Index largely confined to authors, with title entries for anonymous works. *Class No:* 820-0(091)

[6961]

A Literary history of England. Baugh, A.C., *ed.* 2nd ed. London, Routledge & Kegan Paul; New York, Appleton-Century-Crofts, 1967. xv+1796+lxxxp. $76. ISBN: 013537605x, US.

1st ed. 1950.

A reliable general history in 4 sections, each by a pair of scholars, covering the Middle Ages, the Renaissance, the Restoration and 18th century, and the 19th century and after. Numerous footnote references to standard editions and major biographical and critical studies. Extensive bibliographical supplement (188p.) arranged by chapter. Index to both text and bibliography. Available from Routledge in 4 vols. (£16.99 per vol.). *Class No:* 820-0(091)

[6962]

The New Pelican guide to English literature. Ford, B., *ed.* Harmondsworth, Penguin, 1982-88. 9v. in 10, plus *A Guide for readers*.

1st ed. 1954-64, as *The Pelican guide to English literature* (7v.).

V.1, pt. 1, *Medieval literature: Chaucer and the alliterative tradition*. 1982. 656p. ISBN: 0140222642.

V.1, pt. 2, *Medieval literature: the European inheritance*. 1983. 640p. ISBN: 01422273.

V.2 *The Age of Shakespeare*. 1982. 608p. ISBN: 014222650.

V.3 *From Donne to Marvell.* 1982. 432p. ISBN: 014222669.

....(*contd.*)

V.4 *From Dryden to Johnson*. 1982. 528p. ISBN: 014222677.

V.5 *From Blake to Byron*. 1982. 448p. ISBN 014222685.

V.6 *From Dickens to Hardy*. 1982. 528p. ISBN: 014222693.

V.7 *From James to Eliot*. 1983. 592p. ISBN: 014222707.

V.8 *The Present*. 1983. 624p. ISBN: 0140222715.

V.9 *American literature*. 1988. 816p. ISBN: 014225668.

Each vol. includes a survey of the social context of literature in the period concerned; a literary survey of the period; detailed studies of some of the chief writers and works; and an appendix comprising bio-bibliographies of the major authors and lists of further reading on the literature of the period and its background. Many specialists contribute chapters and sub-sections. Index in each vol. Individual vols. reprinted from time to time with updated bibliographies.

A Guide for readers (2nd ed. 1991. 566p. ISBN: 0140138161) brings together the appendices from vols. 1-8 and forms a handy bibliography of English literature.

Class No: 820-0(091)

[6963]

The Oxford history of English literature. Oxford, Clarendon Press, 1945-97. 15v.

V.1 *Middle English literature*, by J.A.W. Bennett; ed. and completed by D. Gray. 1986. xii,496p. ISBN: 0198122284.

V.2 *Chaucer and fifteenth-century verse and prose*, by H.S. Bennett. 1947. viii,327p. ISBN: 0198122292.

V.3 *Malory and fifteenth-century drama, lyrics, and ballads*, by E.K. Chambers. 1945. vi,248p. ISBN: 0198122306.

V.4 *Poetry and prose in the sixteenth century*, by C.S. Lewis. 1954. viii,696p. ISBN: 0198122314.

V.5 *English drama, 1485-1585*, by F.P Wilson; ed. with a bibliography by G.K. Hunter. 1969. 244p. ISBN: 0198122322.

V.6 *English drama, 1586-1642: the age of Shakespeare*, by G.K. Hunter 1997. vii,623p. £35. ISBN: 0198122136).

V.7 *The Early seventeenth century, 1600-1660: Jonson, Donne and Milton*, by D. Bush. 2nd ed. 1962. viii,680p. ISBN: 0198122330.

V.8 *Restoration literature, 1660-1700: Dryden, Bunyan and Pepys*, by J. Sutherland. 1969. vii,569p. ISBN: 0198122349.

V.9 *The Early eighteenth century, 1700-1740: Swift, Defoe and Pope*, by B. Dobrée. 1959. xii,701p. ISBN: 0198122357.

V.10 *The Age of Johnson, 1740-1789*, by J. Butt; ed. and completed by G. Carnall. 1979. vii,671p. ISBN: 0198122365.

V.11 *The Rise of the Romantics, 1789-1815: Wordsworth, Coleridge and Jane Austen*, by W.L. Renwick. 1963. viii,293p. ISBN: 0198122373.

V.12 *English literature, 1815-1832: Scott, Byron and Keats*, by I. Jack. 1963. xii,643p. ISBN: 0198122381.

V.13 *The Victorian novel*, by A. Horsman. 1991. vii,465p. ISBN: 0198122160.

V.14 *Victorian poetry, drama, and miscellaneous prose, 1832-1890*, by P. Turner. 1989. x,522p. ISBN: 019812239x.

V.15 *Writers of the early twentieth century: Hardy to Lawrence*, by J.I.M. Stewart. 1963. viii,704p. ISBN: 0198122403.

A standard history, many of whose vols. originally appeared under different titles and with different numbers. Each vol. is by a specialist, and has very extensive bibliographies. Like the *Cambridge history*, it interprets

....(contd.)
literature in the widest sense to include biography, history, travel writing, religious writing etc.

V.1, *Middle English literature,* is described as 'traditional literary scholarship and criticism at its best' by *Review of English Studies* (v.39(153), Feb. 1988, p.97-99), whose reviewer 'has to work hard to find fault'. *Class No:* 820-0(091)

[6964]
SANDERS, A. The Short Oxford history of English literature. Rev. ed. Oxford, Clarendon Press, 1996. 728p. £25. ISBN: 0198711573.

1st ed. 1994.

A single-vol. narrative history from Anglo-Saxon times to the 1990s, in 10 chapters, with subsections on major authors and schools, plus an introductory essay (15p.) on 'The Development of a canon of English literature'. Strong on modern literature (much of the book is devoted to the last 100 years) and has good coverage of women writers, Scottish, Irish and Welsh literature in English, and post-colonial writing. Chronology of literary works and historical events, 450-1991 (20p.). Index. Rev. ed. includes for the first time detailed guidance on further reading (39p.).
Class No: 820-0(091)

Biographies

[6965]
British authors before 1800: a biographical dictionary, complete in one volume with 650 biographies and 200 portraits. Kunitz, S.J. *and* Haycraft, H., *eds.* New York, Wilson, 1952. vi,584p. illus. $64. ISBN: 0824200063.

The biographies vary in length from 300 to 1,500 words and are followed by lists of works and selected secondary materials. Portraits accompany 220 of the longer biographies. *Class No:* 820-0(092)

[6966]
—British authors of the nineteenth century: complete in one volume with 1,000 biographies and 350 portraits. Kunitz, S.J. *and* Haycraft, H., *eds.* New York, Wilson, 1936. vi,677p. illus. $68. ISBN: 0824200071.

Similar in format to the above, with entries ranging between 100 and 2,500 words. Includes writers from Canada, Australia, South Africa, and New Zealand.
Class No: 820-0(092)

[6967]
Dictionary of literary biography. Detroit, Gale, 1978-98. v.1-188 (in progress). £112 per vol.

Titles relating to British literature:

10: *Modern British dramatists, 1900-1945.* (2 parts); 13: *British dramatists since World War II.* (2 parts); 14: *British novelists since 1960.* (2 parts); 15: *British novelists, 1930-1959.* (2 parts); 18: *Victorian novelists after 1885;* 19. *British poets, 1880-1914;* 20: *British poets, 1914-1945;* 21; *Victorian novelists before 1885;* 27: *Poets of Great Britain and Ireland, 1945-1960;* 32: *Victorian poets before 1850;* 34: *British novelists, 1890-1929: Traditionalists;* 35: *Victorian poets after 1850;* 36: *British novelists, 1890-1929: Modernists;* 39: *British novelists, 1660-1800.* (2 parts); 40: *Poets of Great Britain and Ireland since 1960.* (2 parts); 55: *Victorian prose writers before 1867;* 57: *Victorian prose writers after 1867;* 58: *Jacobean and Caroline dramatists;* 62: *Elizabethan dramatists;* 70: *British mystery writers, 1860-1919;* 77: *British mystery writers, 1920-1939;* 80: *Restoration and eighteenth-century dramatists,* First series; 84: *Restoration and eighteenth-century dramatists,* Second series; 87: *British mystery and thriller writers since 1940,* First series; 89: *Restoration and eighteenth-century dramatists,* Third series; 93: *British Romantic poets, 1789-1832,* First series; 95: *Eighteenth-century British poets,* First series; 96: *British Romantic poets, 1789-1832,* Second series; 98: *Modern British essayists,* First series; 100: *Modern British essayists,* Second series; 101: *British prose writers, 1660-1800,* First series; 104: *British prose writers, 1660-1800,* Second series; 106: *British literary publishing houses, 1820-1880*; 107: *British Romantic prose writers, 1789-1832,* First series; 109: *Eighteenth-century British poets,* Second series; 110: *British Romantic prose writers, 1789-1832,* Second series; 112: *British literary publishing houses, 1881-1965*; 116: *British Romantic*

For a description of series, see entry at 82(092).
Class No: 820-0(092)

[6968]
—Concise dictionary of British literary biography. Bruccoli, M.J. *and* Layman, R., *eds.* Detroit, Gale, 1991-2. 8v. illus. £383. ISBN: 0810379805.

V.1 *Writers of the Middle Ages and Renaissance before 1660.* ISBN: 0810379813.

V.2 *Writers of the Restoration and eighteenth century, 1660-1789.* ISBN: 0810379821.

V.3 *Writers of the Romantic period, 1789-1832.* ISBN: 081037983x.

V.4 *Victorian writers, 1832-1890.* ISBN: 0810379848.

V.5 *Late Victorian and Edwardian writers, 1890-1914.* ISBN: 0810379856.

V.6 *Modern writers, 1914-1945.* ISBN: 0810379864.

V.7 *Writers after World War II.* ISBN: 0810379872.

V.8 *Contemporary writers, 1960 to the present.* ISBN: 0810379880.

Each vol. covers 20-30 of the most widely studied English authors, using entire entries from the regular *DLB* series with some updating. Annotated bibliographies of sources of most interest to school and undergraduate students have been added. Each vol. has author index to whole set and v.8 has cumulative index to key people, places and titles.
Class No: 820-0(092)

[6969]
KAMM, A. Collins biographical dictionary of English literature. Glasgow, HarperCollins, 1993. xiv,528p. £25. ISBN: 000434572x.

A misleadingly titled work, as only just over half of its 1,576 entries cover British and Irish writers. Of the rest, 206 are on US authors, 292 on Commonwealth authors and 287 on writers of works in other languages which are widely read in English and/or have influenced the development of English literature. Entries are all based on a standard chronological format, incorporating details of the subject's major works, and end with a few references to further reading with the emphasis on generally accessible studies. Unlike most dictionaries of this kind, it is the work of a single author and some of the entries appeared in a slightly different format in Kamm's *A Dictionary of British and Irish authors* (Harlow, Longman, 1990). Includes many non-literary authors, such as biographers, historians, scientists, theologians, philosophers and travel writers

A revised US ed. (Blue Ridge Summit, Pa., Scarecrow, 1997. 632p. $60. ISBN: 0810833190) has the more accurate title, *Biographical companion to literature in English.*
Class No: 820-0(092)

[6970]

VRANA, S.A. Interviews and conversations with 20th-century authors writing in English: an index. Metuchen, N.J., Scarecrow, 1982-90. 3v.

Series I (1982. 259p. ISBN: 0810815427) lists over 3,500 interviews with *c.*1,600 mainly literary authors, published 1900-80 in US and foreign newspapers and periodicals (popular and literary) and in monographic sources. Arranged A-Z by author, with interviews listed chronologically for each. Index of interviewers.

Series II (1986. 328p. ISBN: 0810818477) lists nearly 6,000 interviews with over 1,100 authors published during the same period.

Series III (1990. 467p. $45. ISBN: 0810823527) records over 5,600 interviews with nearly 2,500 authors during 1981-85 plus addenda for 1900-80. *Class No:* 820-0(092)

16th Century

[6971]

Major Tudor authors: a bio-bibliographical critical sourcebook. Hager, A., *ed.* Westport, Conn., Greenwood, 1997. 528p. $95. ISBN: 0313294364.

Lengthy, signed entries on nearly 100 people who wrote between 1485 and 1603, comprising brief biography; discussion of major works and themes; review of critical reception; and bibliography of primary and secondary sources. Covers obvious major figures like Shakespeare, Spenser and Marlowe, but also many previously disregarded writers including a significant number of women. Index. *Class No:* 820-0(092)"15"

Women

[6972]

BELL, M., *and others.* A Biographical dictionary of English women writers, 1580-1720. Hemel Hempstead, Harvester Wheatsheaf; Boston, Hall, 1990. 240p. £19.95. ISBN: 0710809549, UK; 081611806x, US.

Entries on over 550 women are arranged A-Z and include birth and death dates, places of birth and residence, social status, religion, spouse's name and occupation, names of women associates, plus lists of works including modern reprints. Also includes essays on relevant subjects, *e.g.* prophetic writing, Quaker women, letters. *Class No:* 820-0(092)-0055.2

[6973]

BLAIN, V., *and others.* The Feminist companion to literature in English: women writers from the Middle Ages to the present. London, Batsford; New Haven, Conn., Yale Univ. Press, 1990. xvi,1231p. $55. ISBN: 0713458488, UK; 0300048548, US.

Over 2,700 biographical entries on women writers plus (in the same A-Z sequence) 65 topic entries for genres, events and institutions important in the development of women's writing (*e.g.* 'Suffrage', 'Gothic', 'Lesbian feminist criticism'). Author entries are not confined to literary writers, covering pamphleteers, diarists, travellers, etc.; are limited to *c.*500 words regardless of the status of the subject; and emphasize the conditions in which the women lived and wrote. Works are mentioned (with dates) and commented on in the author articles, but there are no separate entries for major works. Most author entries have references to other biographical sources. 58 contributors (all female) but entries are not signed and it is necessary to consult the Introduction to find out who covered which period or country. List of frequently cited works (4p.). Index of cross-references

....*(contd.)*

(pseudonyms, married names, etc.). Index of topic entries. Lists of writers by birth-date, in century, half-century, or quarter-century groups.

A lengthy review in *TLS* (no.4581, Jan. 18, 1991, p.8) suggests that the strictly feminist approach has led to some serious omissions: 'Women writers associated with male dominated movements, or working with men, or published by non-feminist avant-garde presses are less likely to be included'. *Class No:* 820-0(092)-0055.2

[6974]

A Dictionary of British and American women writers, 1660-1800. Todd, J., *ed.* London, Methuen, 1984; Totowa, N.J., Rowman & Allanheld, 1985. xxiv,344p. ISBN: 0416389503.

A-Z sequence of signed entries in essay form by *c.*100 contributors on almost 500 women writers from a wide variety of genres. The aim is 'to stimulate research into female literary history and to indicate the wealth and abundance of female writing' (*Preface*). Entries include biographical details (where available), lists of known works, short assessment of the work, and a statement of themes and major genres. Many illustrative quotations. Given the period covered British women naturally dominate, with only 68 Americans included. *Class No:* 820-0(092)-0055.2

[6975]

Dictionary of British women writers. Todd, J., *ed.* London, Routledge; New York, Continuum, 1989. xv,762p. ISBN: 0415036259, UK; 0804433348, US.

US title is *British women writers: a critical reference guide.*

Covers 447 British and Commonwealth writers from the Middle Ages (Julian of Norwich) to the present (Angela Carter) and includes writers on many non-literary subjects, *e.g.* cookery, religion, travel, history. Entries are arranged A-Z, unsigned, average 1½p., and include birth and death dates, pseudonyms if any, biographical sketch, discussion of key works and themes, list of works (selective for prolific writers) and a few critical references. Index. No indication of selection criteria, but there is a strong overlap with P. and J. Schlueter's *Encyclopedia of British women writers* (*q.v.*). 'Succinct, informative ... but by no means a complete guide to its subject' (*TLS*, no.4512, Sept. 22, 1989, p.1024). *Class No:* 820-0(092)-0055.2

[6976]

An Encyclopedia of British women writers. Schlueter, P. *and* Schlueter, J. New York, Garland; London, St. James Press, 1988. xvi,516p. $80 ISBN: 0824084497, US; 1558621180, UK.

Signed essays averaging 1,000 words by over 120 scholars on nearly 400 mainly literary writers, with contemporary writers particularly well represented. Includes Irish writers and Commonwealth writers who spent a long time in Britain (*e.g.* Katherine Mansfield, Ngaio Marsh). Entries comprise biographical notes, critical evaluation, comprehensive primary bibliography and selective secondary bibliography, including references to major biographical sources, *e.g. DNB.* Single-sequence index of names, pseudonyms and subjects. *Class No:* 820-0(092)-0055.2

[6977]

—Women writers of Great Britain and Europe: an encyclopedia. Wilson, K.M., *& others, eds.* New York, Garland, 1997. 571p. illus. $95. ISBN: 0815323433.

See entry at 82(092)-0055.2. *Class No:* 820-0(092)-0055.2

[6978]
SHATTOCK, J. The Oxford guide to British women writers. Oxford, Oxford Univ. Press, 1993. ix,492p. £19.95. ISBN: 0192141767.

Intended as a beginner's guide to women's writing, with entries on over 400 authors from the 14th century to the present, including non-literary writers, such as mystics, travellers and scientists, and some non-native writers who have been influential on the British literary scene, *e.g.* Sylvia Plath. Entries comprise brief biography, major works, critical reception and an assessment of her work, followed by suggestions (rarely more than a couple) for further reading. Some subject entries. Select bibliography of critical studies of women's writing (9p.). Reviewers have been critical of the selection policy, especially in regard to 20th-century writers *Class No:* 820-0(092)-0055.2

Manuscripts & Incunabula

[6979]
Index of English literary manuscripts. London, Mansell; New York, Bowker, 1980-. v.1- (in progress).

V.1 *1450-1625, Parts 1 and 2,* by P. Beal. 1980. 2 pts. (1258p.). £265. ISBN: 0720108071.

V.2 *1625-1700, Part 1, Behn-King,* by P. Beal. 1987. 616p. £225. ISBN: 0720118557.

V.2 *1625-1700, Part 2, Lee-Wycherley,* by P. Beal. 1993. 655p. £265. ISBN: 0720119979.

V.3 *1700-1800, Part 1, Addison-Fielding,* by M. Smith. 1986. 396p. £185. ISBN: 0720117798.

V.3 *1700-1800, Part 2, Gay-Phillips,* by M. Smith. 1989. 480p. £185. ISBN: 0720119987.

V.3 *1700-1800, Part 3, Pope-Steele,* by M. Smith and A. Lindsay. 1992. 480p. £185. ISBN: 0720120381.

V.3 *1700-1800, Part 4, Sterne-Young,* by A. Lindsay. 1997. xx,646p. £200. ISBN: 072012283x.

V.4 *1800-1900, Part 1, Arnold-Gissing,* by B. Rosenbaum and P. White. 1982. 864p. £195. ISBN: 0720115876.

V.4 *1800-1900, Part 2, Hardy-Lamb,* by B. Rosenbaum. 1990. 730p. £260. ISBN: 0720116600.

V.4 *1800-1900, Part 3, Landor-Patmore,* by B. Rosenbaum. 1993. 890p. £260. ISBN: 0720121531.

Aims 'to list and describe briefly the extant manuscripts of literary works by a select number of British and Irish authors who flourished between 1450 and 1900' (*General introduction*). The original intention was to include all authors listed in the *Concise Cambridge bibliography of English literature,* but 'the unexpectedly large numbers of papers of nineteenth century writers necessitated a severe restriction on the number of authors that could practicably be included' (*Preface* to v.4, pt. 2). Those omitted include A.E. Housman, Charles Kingsley, Thomas Hood and Leigh Hunt.

For each author, there is an introductory essay on the extent and distribution of existing manuscripts, followed by a descriptive listing of the manuscripts, arranged by genre, then A-Z by title, with details of locations including private collections. Includes corrected proofs, diaries, notebooks, marginalia, etc., but letters are excluded. V.5 will contain indexes to the whole set. Single author offprints are available from the publisher on request.

'No other single work has ever contributed so much to the study of the primary sources of English literature' (*Library Review,* v.29(4), Winter 1980, p.487-96). *Class No:* 820-0(093)

[6980]
Location register of twentieth-century English literary manuscripts and letters: a union list of papers of modern English, Irish, Scottish and Welsh authors in the British Isles. London, British Library; Boston, Hall, 1988. 2v. (x,1054p). £95. ISBN: 0712301461, UK; 0816189811, US.

A computer-generated listing of over 40,000 items relating to over 2,000 authors. Arranged in a triple-column layout, with mansucripts listed by title under each author followed by correspondence in date order. Entries include brief description, dates, name of owning or depository institution, call numbers and any access restrictions. Includes non-native authors who spent a long time in Britain (*e.g.* Tagore, Soyinka), popular as well as literary writers, and Victorians (*e.g.* Meredith, Ruskin) who lived beyond 1899. Reference is made to 'personalia' (photographs, tape recordings, etc.) as well as to the usual papers, and also (in notes at the head of author entries) to material held overseas. Appendix gives full addresses of all institutions listed.

The *Location register* is maintained as a computer-readable database on BLAISE-LOCAS. *Class No:* 820-0(093)

[6981]
—Location register of English literary manuscripts and letters: 18th and 19th centuries. Sutton, D., *ed.* London, British Library, 1995. 2v. £140. ISBN: 071230388x.

Covers over 1,500 authors in almost 35,000 entries and is comparable in size, range and house-style to the 20th-century *Location register*. *Class No:* 820-0(093)

Black Races

[6982]
DABYDEEN, D. *and* **WILSON-TAGOE, N. A Reader's guide to Westindian and Black British literature.** 2nd, rev. ed. London, Hansib Publishing, 1997. 190p. £8.95. ISBN: 187051842x.

1st ed. 1988, published jointly by Hansib and Rutherford Press.

'... outlines the history and development of the literatures, highlights their major themes, and suggests texts which best illustrate these themes for further reading' (*Foreword*). Aimed at teachers and specially prepared for the GCSE curriculum, but of some value as a reference tool in view of the limited material available in the field. Notes on the major texts at the end of each chapter. Select bibliography of secondary sources. Index of authors. *Class No:* 820-0(=96)

Old English Literature

Bibliographies

[6983]
BEALE, W.H. Old and Middle English poetry to 1500: a guide to information sources. Detroit, Gale, 1976. xxvi,454p. ISBN: 0810312476.

An annotated bibliography in 2 main period sections, listing texts, translations, commentaries, and critical studies in each. 411 Old English and 918 Middle English entries. Index of authors and titles of texts, modern editors and critics, and subjects. *Class No:* 820-022(01)

[6984]

BURNLEY, D. *and* TAJIMA, M. The Language of Middle English literature. Woodbridge, Brewer, 1994. viii,280p. £39.50. ISBN: 0859914054.

Lists and abstracts 1,335 works, published 1890-1990, in which linguistic analysis is used as an approach to the study of Middle English literature, but excludes studies of Chaucer. 3 sections: 1. Early Middle English literature - 2. Later Middle English literature - 3. Doctoral theses. Bibliography of works cited (5p.). Index of scholars and critics. Index of Middle English authors and works.
Class No: 820-022(01)

[6985]

GREENFIELD, S.B. *and* ROBINSON, F.C. A Bibliography of publications on Old English literature to the end of 1972. Toronto, Univ. of Toronto Press; Manchester, Univ. Press, 1980. xiii,437p. ISBN: 0802065058, US; 0719007739, UK.

The standard bibliography in the field, with 6,550 numbered items in 3 main sections (General works; Poetry; Prose) and over 200 sub-sections. Poetry and Prose sections have general works on the genres followed by material relating to individual authors and works. Includes book reviews. Some brief annotations. Many cross-references. Clear, detailed contents list and indexes of authors and subjects provide easy access. *Class No:* 820-022(01)

[6986]

HOLLIS, S. *and* WRIGHT, M. Old English prose of secular learning. Cambridge, Brewer, 1992. xi,383p. £39.50. (*Annotated bibliographies of Old and Middle English literature.*) ISBN: 0859913430.

The first vol. in a series designed to produce an annotated bibliography for every area of medieval English studies not already covered. 575 numbered entries in 5 sections: 1. Proverbs - 2. Dialogues - 3. Romance - 4. *Byrhtferth of Romsey* and *Computus* - 5. Magico-medical literature. Details of each text followed by lists of editions and commentaries, with lengthy annotations. Author and subject indexes. *Class No:* 820-022(01)

[6987]

Old English newsletter. Kalamazoo, Mich., Medieval Institute at Western Michigan Univ., for The Old English Division of the MLA, 1967-. v.1, no.1-. Quarterly. ISSN: 00301973.

Formerly published at Ohio State Univ. and the Center for Medieval and Early Renaissance Studies, SUNY.

Regularly carries bibliographies of the previous year's work in Old English studies. V.29(4), Summer 1996, has'Old English bibliography for 1995', with over 800 entries in 9 sections, mainly for language and literature but also covering history, archaeology and culture.
Class No: 820-022(01)

[6988]

QUINN, K.J. *and* QUINN, K.P. A Manual of Old English prose. New York, Garland, 1990. xviii,439p. ISBN: 0824090322.

A bibliography in 4 sections: 1. Manuscripts (lists all mss. containing Old English prose, arranged in the order established by Ker's *Catalogue*) - 2. Texts (lists all OE texts, except legal documents and works by Wulfstan and Aelfric) - 3. Editions (lists 535 eds. of the texts, excluding student readers and primers) - 4. Criticism (lists 1,030 books, articles and dissertations). Many cross-references, plus indexes of modern titles, manuscript titles, first lines and subjects. *Class No:* 820-022(01)

Handbooks & Manuals

[6989]

The Cambridge companion to Old English literature. Godden, M. *and* Lapidge, M., *eds*. Cambridge, Cambridge Univ. Press, 1991. xiii,298p. maps. £40. ISBN: 0521374383.

15 signed essays by specialists on various aspects of Anglo-Saxon (*e.g.* prose, verse, Biblical literature, the Old English language, etc.), each with references appended. Select bibliography, arranged according to chapters, with commentary (10p.). *Class No:* 820-022(035)

[6990]

PARTRIDGE, A.C. A Companion to Old and Middle English studies. London, Deutsch; Totowa, N.J., Barnes & Noble, 1982. xi,462p. ISBN: 0233974113, UK; 0389202878, US.

A historical, literary, and linguistic survey in 16 chapters, with chapter bibliographies (13p.). Index. *Class No:* 820-022(035)

Theses

[6991]

PULSIANO, P. An Annotated bibliography of North American doctoral dissertations on Old English language and literature. East Lansing, Mich., Colleagues Press; Woodbridge, Boydell & Brewer, 1988. 336p. ISBN: 093719106x, UK.

Over 1,000 entries in 3 sections for general works, poetry, and prose, with a chronological arrangement within each. Entries include references to *Dissertation Abstracts International* and are fully cross-referenced. Subject and author indexes. *Class No:* 820-022(043)

Histories

[6992]

ALEXANDER, M. Old English literature. London, Macmillan, 1983. xv,248p. illus. maps. (*Macmillan history of literature.*) ISBN: 0333269039.

A survey in 10 chapters which assumes 'little knowledge of this period ... and none of its language' (*Preface*). Numerous quotations in modern English translation. Select bibliography (4p.) of editions, translations, criticism and background material. Chronological table, 55BC-AD1154. Index. *Class No:* 820-022(091)

[6993]

GREENFIELD, S.B. *and* CALDER, D.G. A New critical history of Old English literature, with a survey of the Anglo-Latin background by M. Lapidge. [2nd ed.]. New York and London, New York Univ. Press, 1986. xiii,372p. illus. maps. £31.50. ISBN: 0814730027.

An extensively revised and updated edition of Greenfield's *A Critical history of Old English literature* (New York, 1965).

'The book is three things - a synopsis, a critical reading of texts, and a history of the criticism' (*Introduction*). Lapidge's background chapter is new to this ed., the space devoted to prose is tripled, and many texts are covered which were not in the first ed. Many quotations in modern English translation by the authors. The extensive bibliography (56p.), arranged A-Z by author and keyed to the numerous footnotes, includes many items that postdate the first ed. and is 'an extraordinarily helpful guide to the wealth of studies beyond' (*Modern Language Review,* v.83(3), July 1988, p.660-1). *Class No:* 820-022(091)

Beowulf

[6994]
A *Beowulf* handbook. Bjork, R.E. *and* Niles, J.D., *eds.* Lincoln, Nebr., Univ. of Nebraska Press; Exeter, Univ. of Exeter Press, 1997. x,468p. £40. (*Exeter medieval texts and studies.*) ISBN: 0803212372, US; 0859895432, UK.

Chapters by 16 contributors on various aspects of the work, *e.g.* 'Symbolism and allegory', 'Myth and history'. Each begins with a chronology of key books and articles on the topic, then gives a history of scholarly interest in the topic, a synthesis of present knowledge and an analysis of scholarly work that needs to be done. *Class No:* 820-022BEO

[6995]
SHORT, D.D. *Beowulf* scholarship: an annotated bibliography. New York, Garland, 1980. xvi,353p. (*Garland medieval bibliographies.*) ISBN: 0824095308.

A selective listing of 200 studies published 1705-1949, with brief annotations, followed by a virtually comprehensive bibliography for 1950-78 with over 900 well-annotated entries. Author and subject indexes.

Continued by *'Beowulf' scholarship: an annotated bibliography, 1979-1990* by H.J. Hasenfratz (New York, Garland, 1993. 424p. $70. ISBN: 0815300840), which has nearly 1,800 thoroughly annotated entries arranged by year and then by author. Subject and author indexes plus a line index. *Class No:* 820-022BEO

Middle English Literature

Bibliographies

[6996]
BROWN, C.F. *and* **ROBBINS, R.H. Index of Middle English verse.** New York, Columbia Univ. Press, for The Index Society, 1943. xx,785p.

Covers 4,365 poems, religious and secular, written in English before 1500. It supersedes C.F. Brown's *Register of Middle English religious and didactic verse* (1916-20. 2v.), which listed 2,273 poems. The entries, arranged A-Z by first lines, refer to manuscripts and critical studies in periodicals, etc. Subject and title index and location list of privately owned manuscripts. Continued by:. *Class No:* 820-023(01)

[6997]
—ROBBINS, R.H. *and* CUTLER, J.L. Supplement to the *Index of Middle English verse*. Lexington, Ky., Univ. of Kentucky Press, 1965. xxix,551p.

'Expands some 2,300 of the 4,365 entries in the original *Index* and adds some 1,500 new entries' (*Introduction*). Records changes in ownership and location of manuscripts and completes the entries for those items not available for inspection during the compilation of the original work.

A Manuscript index to the 'Index of Middle English verse' by R.Hamer (London, British Library, 1995. 64p. £18. ISBN: 0712303871) gives current locations for all mss. cited in *IMEV* and its *Supplement*.

For further citations for Middle English poetry, see W.A. Ringler's *Bibliography and index of English verse printed 1476-1558* (entry at 820-1(01)"1485-1760"). *Class No:* 820-023(01)

[6998]
Index of Middle English prose. Edwards, A.S.G., *& others, eds.* Cambridge, Brewer, 1984-95. v.1-11 (in progress). £25 - £45 per vol. ISSN: 02672472.

A record of all extant Middle English prose texts composed between *c.*1200 and *c.*1500 in both manuscript and printed form in medieval and post-medieval versions. Each vol. is a handlist describing the works in a particular collection or collections, as follows: v.1, Huntington Library; v.2, John Rylands University Library and Chetham's Library, Manchester; v.3, Digby Collection, Bodleian Library; v.4, Douce Collection, Bodleian Library; v.5, British Library, additional manuscripts, 10001-14000; v.6, Yorkshire libraries and archives; v.7, Parisian libraries; v.8, Oxford college libraries; v.9, Ashmole Collection, Bodleian Library; v.10, Scandinavian collections; v.11, Trinity College, Cambridge. Each handlist is indexed. *Class No:* 820-023(01)

[6999]
—LEWIS, R.E., *and others*. Index of printed Middle English prose. New York, Garland, 1985. xxxiii,362p. ISBN: 0824088395.

Lists 864 works, A-Z by first line, giving author, title, genre, date of composition, chronological list of all eds. up to 1982, and manuscript locations. General index, plus index of manuscript locations. *Class No:* 820-023(01)

[7000]
MODERN LANGUAGE ASSOCIATION OF AMERICA. Middle English Group. **A Manual of the writings in Middle English, 1050-1500.** Severs, J.B. *and* Hartung, A.E., *eds.* New Haven, Conn., Connecticut Academy of Arts and Sciences, 1967-93. v.1-9 (in progress). $49.95 per vol.

Based on *A Manual of the writings in Middle English, 1050-1400*, by J.E. Wells, and its Supplements, 1-9 (New Haven, Conn., Yale Univ. Press, 1916-51).

V.1 *Romances*. 1967.

V.2 *The Pearl poet. Wyclyf and his followers. Translations and paraphrases of the Bible, and commentaries. Saints' legends. Instructions for religious*. 1970.

V.3 *Dialogues, debates and catechisms. Thomas Hoccleve. Malory and Caxton*. 1972.

V.4 *Middle Scots writers. The Chaucerian apocrypha*. 1973.

V.5 *Dramatic pieces. Poems dealing with contemporary conditions*. 1975.

V.6 *Carols. Ballads. John Lydgate*. 1980.

V.7 *John Gower. Piers Plowman. Travel and geographical writings. Works of religious and philosophical instruction*. 1986.

V.8 *Chronicles and other historical writing*. 1989.

V.9 *Proverbs, precepts and monitory pieces. English mystical writings. Tales*. 1993.

A revision and expansion of Wells's *Manual*, with sections by specialists who provide the following information for each piece of literature: date; manuscripts; dialect of original work; sources; form and extent; content; commentary; summary of scholarly views; and extensive bibliography of manuscripts and critical studies. *Class No:* 820-023(01)

[7001]

RICE, J.A. Middle English romance: an annotated bibliography, 1955-1985. New York, Garland, 1987. xxxii,626p. ISBN: 0824088301.

Separate, classified sections for verse and prose romances, with general studies and collections followed by individual romances, A-Z by title, with editions from all periods and critical studies from 1955-85. Concise, nonevaluative annotations. Index of authors and editors. *Class No:* 820-023(01)

Handbooks & Manuals

[7002]

EDWARDS, A.S.G. Middle English prose: a critical guide to major authors and genres. New Brunswick, N.J., Rutgers Univ. Press, 1984. xii,452p. $60. ISBN: 0813510015.

18 chapters, each by a different scholar, devoted to individual writers, specific works or groups of works, and genres (*e.g.* sermons, history). Each chapter includes a survey of modern scholarship, suggestions for further research, and a bibliography of primary and secondary sources. Index. Although the value of the bibliographies varies considerably, 'it assembles an extensive range of useful information in lucid and scholarly fashion' (*Review of English Studies*, v.37(146), Aug. 1986, p.403-4).
Class No: 820-023(035)

Histories

[7003]

BARRON, W.R.J. English medieval romance. London, Longman, 1987. 288p. £17.99. (*Longman literature in English.*) ISBN: 0582492203.

A survey in 8 chapters, followed by chronology, 1066-1547, and extensive, classified bibliography (41p.) of editions and studies, with annotations. Index.
Class No: 820-023(091)

[7004]

BREWER, D. English Gothic literature. Basingstoke, Macmillan, 1993. xvi,315p. illus. (*Macmillan history of literature.*) ISBN: 0333271394.

A confusingly titled history of English literature during the period 1100-1500. 14 chapters on genres, major writers and works. Classified guide to further reading (3p.). Chronology, 1066-1497. Index. *Class No:* 820-023(091)

Langland

[7005]

COLAIANNE, A.J. ***Piers Plowman*****: an annotated bibliography of editions and criticism,** 1550-1977. New York, Garland, 1978. xi,195p. ISBN: 0824098226.

672 entries in 4 sections: 1. Biographical studies - 2. Editions and textual studies, selections and translations - 3. *Piers Plowman*: critical interpretation - 4. *Piers Plowman*: style, meter and language. Emphasis on 20th-century studies. Author and subject indexes. *Class No:* 820-023LAN

[7006]

DIMARCO, V. ***Piers Plowman*****: a reference guide.** Boston, Hall, 1982. xxviii,384p. ISBN: 0816183090.

Lists over 1,000 studies by year, 1395-1979, with substantial annotations. Index of authors, titles and subjects.
Class No: 820-023LAN

[7007]

PEARSALL, D. An Annotated critical bibliography of Langland. Hemel Hempstead, Harvester Wheatsheaf; Ann Arbor, Mich., Univ. of Michigan Press, 1990. xx,295p. ISBN: 0710809433, UK; 0472101854, US.

A guide to editions and translations of *Piers Plowman* and to 20th-century critical studies, arranged by subject. *Choice* (v.28(5), Jan. 1991, p.762) praises the 'critical selectivity, helpful topical arrangement, detailed and scholarly annotations, and thorough subject indexing'. Largely confined to English-language studies. Index of authors and subjects.

For up-to-date information on recent Langland scholarship, see the annual bibliographies in *The Yearbook of Langland Studies* (East Lansing, Mich., Colleagues Press, 1987-. ISSN: 08902917). *Class No:* 820-023LAN

English Poetry

Databases

[7008]

English poetry full-text database on CD-ROM. Cambridge, Chadwyck-Healey, 1994. World Wide Web resource Subscription details from marketing@chadwyck.co.uk

500.00/00$aPart of *Literature online (LION)* (*q.v.*). URL: http://lion.chadwyck.co.uk

A pioneering project, completed in 1994, to make available in digital form the complete English poetic canon fron Anglo-Saxon times to 1900. The bibliographic basis is the *New Cambridge bibliography of English literature* (1969-72) and the total corpus amounts to over 165,000 poems by more than 1,257 named British and Irish poets and many anonymous writers, drawn from *c.*4,500 printed sources. As well as poems, the database includes any accompanying text by the poet, *e.g.* dedications, notes, epigraphs, etc. Children's verse and pre-1800 translations into English verse are included. Exclusions include hymns published after 1800, pre-1900 poetry which was not published until the 20th century, and works in languages other than English. Verse dramas are also excluded, as these are covered by a separate project, *English drama: the full-text database* (*q.v.*). A full range of search options is available and searches can be made across the entire database or confined to individual poets, periods or genres/forms.

Also available on CD-ROM. *Class No:* 820-1(003.4)

[7009]

—English poetry plus on CD-ROM. Cambridge, Chadwyck-Healey, 1995. £495.

A multi-media CD-ROM offering a broad selection of the works of the best-known English-language poets of all periods, along with some works by lesser-known writers. Includes the full text of 5,000 poems by 275 poets, together with biographies, portraits, background illustrations and recorded readings. 200 of the poets are British, the rest coming from the USA and Commonwealth. Searching options include topic, period, genre/form, poet, first line, title and indivdual words. Ideal for school libraries.
Class No: 820-1(003.4)

Bibliographies of Bibliographies

[7010]

The Bibliography of contemporary British and Irish poetry, 1945-89: an annotated checklist. Glazier, L.P., *ed.* Westport, Conn., Greenwood, 1991. 175p. ISBN: 0887361684.

A comprehensive listing of bibliographies of postwar British and Irish poets, with annotations summarizing the content of each bibliography. *Class No:* 820-1(009)

Bibliographies

[7011]

ALEXANDER, H.S. American and British poetry: a guide to the criticism, 1925-1978. Athens, Ohio, Swallow Press; Manchester, Manchester Univ. Press, 1984. xii,486p. $55. ISBN: 0804008485.

Indexes critical studies appearing in books and periodicals. Covers poets from Spenser to Dickey and is arranged A-Z by poet, then by poem title. Excludes books about the poets themselves.

Continued by Alexander's *American and British poetry: a guide to the criticism, 1979-1990* (Swallow, 1996. 465p. $65. ISBN: 0804009880). *Class No:* 820-1(01)

[7012]

BROGAN, T.V.F. English versification, 1570-1980: a reference guide, with a global appendix. Baltimore, Md., Johns Hopkins Univ. Press, 1981. xxix,794p. ISBN: 0801825415.

Lists nearly 6,000 source materials with descriptive annotations. Sections include prose rhythm, classical sources, ballads and concrete poetry as well as syntax, metre, etc. Index of authors and poets. 'The most comprehensive bibliography of English versification yet attempted' (*Review of English Studies,* v.35(139), Autumn 1984, p.419-20. *Class No:* 820-1(01)

[7013]

First-line index of English poetry, 1500-1800, in manuscripts of the Bodleian Library, Oxford. Crum, M., *ed.* Oxford, Clarendon Press; New York, Index Committee of the M.L.A., 1969. 2v. (xi,1257p.). ISBN: 0199513236.

The *c.*23,000 entries include: first line in modernized spelling; last line of the usual version; author's name (if known); title; references to printed versions; list of Bodleian mss. in which the poem is found, with folio or page references. Indexes of authors and names mentioned. Index of references to composers and tunes. *Class No:* 820-1(01)

[7014]

MARCAN, P. Poetry themes: a bibliographical index to subject anthologies and related criticism in the English language, 1875-1975. London, Bingley; Hamden, Conn., Linnet, 1977. xvi,301p. ISBN: 0851572324, UK; 0208015450, US.

Lists 1,964 anthologies, including mixed prose and verse, which bring together material on one subject or a group of related subjects, under *c.*250 headings. Index of authors and compilers. Clear contents listing, but no subject index. Excludes subject-based collections by individual poets. *Class No:* 820-1(01)

[7015]

MARTINEZ, N.C., *& others.* Guide to British poetry explication. Boston, Hall, 1991-5. 4v.

V.1 *Old English - Medieval.* 1991. $65. ISBN: 0816189218

V.2 *Renaissance.* 1992. ISBN: 081618920x.

V.3 *Restoration - Romantic.* 1993. $65. ISBN: 081611997x.

V.4 *Victorian - Contemporary.* 1995. $50. ISBN: 0816189889.

A companion to *Guide to American poetry explication* (*q.v.*). The pair jointly supersede Kuntz and Martinez's *Poetry explication* (3rd ed. Boston, Hall, 1980) and provide greatly expanded coverage.

V.1 has citations for nearly 4,500 English-language studies of Old English and Medieval poems. V.3 has over 7,000 entries. Arrangement is by poet, then by title, then by critic. *Class No:* 820-1(01)

[7016]

UNIVERSITY OF CALIFORNIA. Davis. **Minor British poets, 1789-1918.** Davis, Calif., The Library, Univ. of California, 1983-86. 4v. illus.

V.1 *The Romantic period, 1789-1839.* 1983. 136p.

V.2 *The Early Victorian period, 1840-1869.* 1985. 170p.

V.3 *The Later Victorian period, 1870-1899.* 1986. 315p.

V.4 *The Edwardian period, 1900-1918.* 1984. 179p.

Lists over 10,000 titles in the University Library. Arranged A-Z by poet within each vol., with brief descriptive notes. Many of the works cannot be found anywhere else in the US. *Class No:* 820-1(01)

Tudor & Stuart Times

[7017]

GUTIERREZ, N.A. English historical poetry, 1476-1603: a bibliography. New York, Garland, 1983. xxvi,429p. ISBN: 0824091310.

Lists over 2,000 poems chronologically by the date of the event written about, giving author, title, first line, stanza description, Renaissance text locations, major modern reprints, and notes on content and historical background. Bibliography of works consulted (30p.). List of poems by date of composition. Indexes of authors and first lines. *Class No:* 820-1(01)"1485-1760"

[7018]

RINGLER, W.A. Bibliography and index of English verse printed 1476-1558. London, Mansell, 1989. 440p. £110. ISBN: 0720118921.

The bulk of the work comprises an index to Tudor verse, 1500-1558, but it also constitutes a companion to C.F. Brown and R.H. Robbins's *Index of Middle English verse* (1943) and its *Supplement* (1965), by providing extra citations for printed Middle English verse, 1476-1500. Bibliographies for books containing printed English verse, 1476-1500, and 1500-1558, are keyed to *Short Title Catalogue* numbers. 'This volume was done to exacting scholarly standards worthy of its predecessors' (*Choice,* v.27(1), Sept. 1989, p.90). *Class No:* 820-1(01)"1485-1760"

[7019]

—RINGLER, W.A. Index of English verse in manuscript, 1501-1558. London, Mansell, 1992. 344p. £110. ISBN: 0720120993.

Pt.1 is a descriptive bibliography of all mss. which contain English verse dateable within the period. Pt.2 is a first-line index of the poems, with full information on each, including author, title, length, verse-form, date, subject, genre, etc. Pt.3 is an index to Pt.2, divided into several categories, including burdens, refrains, poets, historical persons and events, subjects, titles, translations, etc. *Class No:* 820-1(01)"1485-1760"

17th & 18th Centuries

[7020]

MELL, D.C. English poetry, 1660-1800: a guide to information sources. Detroit, Gale, 1982. xviii,501p. ISBN: 0810312301.

General studies, in 4 sections, followed by bibliographies for 31 poets, A-Z, listing editions, correspondence, bibliographies, concordances, biography, and critical studies. Concise annotations. Index of authors, titles, and subjects. *Class No:* 820-1(01)"16/17"

17th Century

[7021]

ALLISON, A.F. Four metaphysical poets - George Herbert, Richard Crashaw, Henry Vaughan, Andrew Marvell: a bibliographical catalogue of the early editions of their poetry and prose (to the end of the 17th century). Folkestone, Dawsons, 1973. 134p. £15. (*Pall Mall bibliographies.*) ISBN: 0712905995.

Detailed bibliographical descriptions of every separate edition and issue, with 71 plates of title-page reproductions. Library locations listed. Index of printers and publishers. *Class No:* 820-1(01)"16"

[7022]

LULL, J. The Metaphysical poets: a chronology. New York, Macmillan, 1994. 240p. $45. ISBN: 081617251x.

Covers the lives and careers of Donne, Herbert, Crashaw, Marvell, Vaughan and Traherne, listing the known and probable activities of each poet year by year, 1572-1695. Annual entries also include major religious, political and social events. *Class No:* 820-1(01)"16"

18th & 19th Centuries

[7023]

The English Romantic poets: a review of research and criticism. Jordan, F., *ed.* 4th ed. New York, Modern Language Assoc. of America, 1985. xiii,765p. $50. ISBN: 0873522621.

1st ed. 1950; 3rd ed. 1972.

Bibliographic essays on the Romantic Movement in general, Wordsworth, Coleridge, Byron, Shelley and Keats, evaluating bibliographies, editions, biographies, and critical studies. Index of critics. Complements Houtchens' work on the Romantic poets and essayists. *Class No:* 820-1(01)"17/18"

[7024]

The English Romantic poets and essayists: a review of research and criticism. Houtchens, C.W. *and* Houtchens, L.H., *eds.* Rev. ed. New York, N.Y. Univ. Press, for M.L.A., 1966. xviii,395p.

1st ed. 1957.

Covers Blake, Lamb, Hazlitt, Scott, Southey, Campbell, Moore, Landor, Hunt, De Quincey, and Carlyle, with signed essays on each, surveying bibliographies, editions, biographies, and criticism. The Carlyle essay is new for the rev. ed. Index of critics. *Class No:* 820-1(01)"17/18"

18th Century

[7025]

FOXON, D.F. English verse, 1701-1750: a catalogue of separately printed poems, with notes on contemporary collected editions. London, Cambridge Univ. Press, 1975. 2v. ISBN: 0521081440.

V.1 *Catalogue*. 951p.; v.2 *Indexes*. 302p.

A short-title catalogue, arranged by author, with descriptive notes and library locations. Indexes of first lines, subjects, and imprints, plus chronological list of first editions. *Class No:* 820-1(01)"17"

[7026]

NOKES, D. *and* **BARRON, J. An Annotated critical bibliography of Augustan poetry.** Hemel Hempstead, Harvester Wheatsheaf; New York, St. Martin's Press, 1989. xi,158p. (*Annotated critical bibliographies.*) ISBN: 0710809727, UK; 0312019610, US.

A highly selective compilation whose principal aim is 'to guide student readers through the accumulated mass of secondary studies' (*Advice to the reader*). Part 1 has 100 general studies. Part 2 lists studies of 31 poets, A-Z. Author and subject indexes. Concentrates on 20th-century criticism. *Class No:* 820-1(01)"17"

19th Century

[7027]

Keats, Shelley, Byron, Hunt, and their circles; a bibliography: July 1, 1950 - June 30, 1962. Green, D.B. *and* Wilson, E.G., *eds.* Lincoln, Nebr., Univ. of Nebraska Press, 1964. ix,323p.

Reprints 12 annual bibliographies first published in the *Keats-Shelley Journal*, with a cumulative index, primarily of names. Each has *c.*500 items.

Continued by ... *a bibliography: July 1, 1962 - December 31, 1974*, ed. by R.A. Hartley (Lincoln, Nebr., 1978. 487p. ISBN: 0803209606), which includes the bibliographies in vols. 13-25 of the *Journal*. Index.

The *Keats-Shelley Journal* (Philadelphia, Pa., Dept. of English, Univ. of Pennsylvania, Keats-Shelley Assoc. of America. Annual. ISSN: 04534387) continues to publish a bibliography. That in v.39, 1990, has 415 items in 5 sections (General; Byron; Hazlitt and Hunt; Keats; Shelley) and is indexed. *Class No:* 820-1(01)"18"

[7028]

REIMAN, D.H. English Romantic poetry, 1800-1835: a guide to information sources. Detroit, Gale, 1979. xx,294p. ISBN: 081031231x.

Lists mainly modern studies on 5 major (Wordsworth, Coleridge, Byron, Shelley, Keats) and 12 minor poets. Includes concordances, bibliographies, editions, biography, and criticism. Also many general studies on Romanticism. Author, title, and subject indexes. *Class No:* 820-1(01)"18"

Victorian Age

[7029]
REILLY, C.W. Late Victorian poetry, 1880-1899: an annotated biobibliography. London, Mansell, 1994. xxi,577p. £70. ISBN: 0720120012.

Identifies nearly 3,000 British poets, A-Z, the entries including brief biographical data and lists of published works with bibliographical details and library where copy seen. Writings of major poets are not listed individually, but reference is made to the most authoritative bibliography. An invaluable source, however, for hundreds of minor poets. Index.

Further vols. are planned, covering 1840-59 and 1860-79. *Class No:* 820-1(01)"1837-1901"

[7030]
Victorian poetry: an annotated bibliography. Metuchen, N.J., Scarecrow, 1995. 261p. $34.50. (*Magill bibliographies.*) ISBN: 0810830086.

A selective bibliography, aimed at high school and college students, of recent secondary literature on over 80 of the most read and most taught poems by 14 poets. Coverage is restricted to books and chapters, but a select list of relevant periodicals is included. Author and subject indexes. *Class No:* 820-1(01)"1837-1901"

[7031]
The Victorian poets: a guide to research. Faverty, F.E., *ed.* 2nd ed. Cambridge, Mass., Harvard Univ. Press; London, Oxford Univ. Press, 1968. 433p. ISBN: 0674936604.

1st ed. 1956.

Bibliographical essays by specialists on Tennyson, the Brownings, Fitzgerald, Clough, Arnold, Swinburne, the Pre-Raphaelites, Hopkins, and the later Victorian poets, plus one on general materials. Analytical index. Similar in format to Stevenson's *Victorian fiction* and De Laura's *Victorian prose* (*qq.v.*). *Class No:* 820-1(01)"1837-1901"

20th Century

[7032]
ANDERSON, E.A. English poetry, 1900-1950: a guide to information sources. Detroit, Gale, 1982. xii,315p. ISBN: 081031360x.

Lists of general studies followed by bibliographies for 21 poets, including primary and secondary material. Author, title, and subject indexes. Most entries annotated. *Class No:* 820-1(01)"19"

[7033]
Contemporary poetry in America and England, 1950-1975: a guide to information sources. Gingerich, M.E. Detroit, Gale, 1983. xv,453p.

7 chapters listing general sources, followed by bibliographies for 131 poets, A-Z, the majority of them American, listing both primary and secondary literature. Author and title indexes. *Class No:* 820-1(01)"19"

[7034]
REILLY, C.W. English poetry of the First World War: a bibliography. London, Prior, 1978. xxxi,402p. ISBN: 0860431061.

Covers poetry on the theme of the War by British poets who experienced it and is 'confined to printed material in the form of book, pamphlet, card or broadside' (*Introduction*). Lists 131 anthologies, followed by over 3,100 works by over 1,600 individual poets. Library locations provided. Title index. Supplement lists war poets of other English-speaking nations. *Class No:* 820-1(01)"19"

[7035]
REILLY, C.W. English poetry of the Second World War: a biobibliography. London, Mansell, 1986. xxviii,393p. ISBN: 0720117933.

Lists works containing poetry on the theme of World War II written by British poets and published in the period 1939-80. Works by foreign nationals writing in English are included if they served in the British forces or had some other connection with the UK. Two main sections: Anthologies (87 listed), with index of compilers, editors, illustrators and writers of forewords, etc.; and Individual Authors (2,700), with title index. Brief biographical notes are provided on 75% of the poets listed and library locations are included. Winner of the Library Association's Besterman Medal for bibliography in 1986. *Class No:* 820-1(01)"19"

[7036]
SHIELDS, E.F. Contemporary English poetry: an annotated bibliography of criticism to 1980. New York, Garland, 1984. xix,238p. ISBN: 0824090160.

Lists 165 general critical works, followed by selected criticism of Davie, Gunn, Hill, Hughes, Larkin and Tomlinson. Includes books, chapters, articles and reviews, all in English. Substantial annotations. Author and subject indexes. Over 800 items in all. *Class No:* 820-1(01)"19"

Women

[7037]
DAVIS, G. *and* JOYCE, B. Poetry by women to 1900: a bibliography of American and British writers. London, Mansell: Toronto, Univ. of Toronto press, 1991. xxiv,340p. £75. (*Bibliographies of writings by American and British women to 1900.*) ISBN: 0720120160.

Lists just over 6,000 published vols. of poetry found in the BL's *General catalogue of printed books*, *The National union catalog*, the OCLC database and other standard sources. Numbered entries are arranged by author, A-Z, and include brief biographical notes as well as bibliographical information. Many early women writers used pseudonyms, so cross-references are supplied for all alternative names. Appended chronological list of writers. Subject index. *Class No:* 820-1(01)-0055.2

[7038]
JACKSON, J.R. de J. Romantic poetry by women: a bibliography, 1770-1835. Oxford, Clarendon Press, 1993. xxx,484p. £60. ISBN: 0198112394.

Based on the author's *Annals of English verse, 1770-1835: a preliminary survey of volumes published* (1985) and many other sources, this is an extremely thorough listing of the works of over 500 women who wrote at least one vol. of verse during the Romantic period. Arranged A-Z by poet, the entries include biographical notes and detailed bibliographical descriptions of each work, along with references to locations and other sources of information. Almost 2,600 works listed, including translations into English. 4 indexes: authors, titles, publishers and publishing locations. Detailed introduction (10p.). *Class No:* 820-1(01)-0055.2

Encyclopaedias & Dictionaries

[7039]
The Oxford companion to twentieth-century poetry in English. Hamilton, I., *ed.* Oxford, Oxford Univ. Press, 1994. xvi,602p. £27.50. ISBN: 0198661479.

Signed entries, ranging from a few lines to several pages, on 1,500 poets who have lived in the 20th century (even if

.... *(contd.)*
only very briefly, *e.g.* Stephen Crane) and have published at least one substantial collection, as well as on about 100 topics, movements, magazines, prizes and genres. The contributors include several poets (*e.g.* Heaney, Paulin, Ewart) and the emphasis is on critical appraisal, although biographical information is provided and some entries have brief bibliographies appended. *c.*550 of the poets covered are British and the same number are American. 200 are women and 100 are black. Selected list of anthologies. For no apparent reason, the crucial last two words of the title are omitted from both the front and spine of the dust-jacket, which may lead to some confusion in libraries. Otherwise, a hard book to fault. *Class No:* 820-1(03)

[7040]
SMITH, E. A Dictionary of classical reference in English poetry. Cambridge, Brewer; Totowa, N.J., Barnes & Noble, 1984. xii,308p. ISBN: 0859911446, UK; 0389204307, US.

A comprehensive listing of classical names and allusions, which covers over eighty of the most widely read English poets from Chaucer to the 20th century, listing all classical references in their works. First, entries by subject define the classical myths or stories attached to the character or event in question, giving the original sources; these are followed by a list of allusions in English poetry. The second part of the book is arranged by poet, listing each of his allusions with references to the main sequence. Can thus be used to compare the use of a particular myth by different poets or to survey one poet's use of classical allusions. *Class No:* 820-1(03)

Histories

[7041]
The Columbia history of British poetry. Woodring, C. *and* Shapiro, J., *eds.* New York, Columbia Univ. Press, 1994. xiv,732p. $63. ISBN: 0231078382.

26 signed chapters by distinguished (predominantly American) scholars on poetry written in Britain and Ireland from the Old English period to the present. Most chapters are devoted to periods, individual poets or groups of poets, and have brief lists of further reading. Brief biographical notes on poets and list of editions of each poet's works. Thorough index of names and titles. *Class No:* 820-1(091)

[7042]
CORCORAN, N. English poetry since 1940. Harlow, Longman, 1993. xvii,308p. £53. (*Longman literature in English.*) ISBN: 0582003237.

17 chapters in 5 sections, followed by substantial reference section: chronology, 1940-91; general bibliography (critical studies, reference works, bibliographies and anthologies); biobibliographical notes on nearly 60 poets. Index.
Class No: 820-1(091)

[7043]
COURTHOPE, W.J. A History of English poetry. London, Macmillan, 1895-1910. 6v.

The outstanding reference book on the subject, covering the whole of English poetry from the beginning down to the 20th century. Detailed analysis of contents prefaces each volume; some footnote references. Combined index at end of v.6. *Class No:* 820-1(091)

[7044]
PERKINS, D. A History of modern poetry. Cambridge, Mass., Harvard Univ. Press, 1976-87. 2v. $33 per vol.

V.1 *From the 1890s to the High Modernist mode.* 1976. xvi,623p. ISBN: 0674399455.

V.2 *Modernism and after.* 1987. xii,694p. ISBN: 0674399463.

A narrative history of English and American poetry, with sections on numerous individual poets and many quotations. Index in each vol. According to *World Literature Today* (v.62(1), Winter 1988, p.131), v.1 'has been widely acclaimed as the definitive work on the topic' and 'that definitiveness holds true for its sequel', but it lacks a bibliography. *Class No:* 820-1(091)

[7045]
The Routledge history of English poetry. Foakes, G., *ed.* London, Routledge & Kegan Paul, 1977-81. v. 1, 3, 4.

V.1 *Old English and Middle English poetry,* by D. Pearsall. 1977. xiv,352p. ISBN: 0710083963.

V.3 *Restoration and eighteenth century poetry, 1660-1780,* by E. Rothstein. 1981. xiv,242p. ISBN: 0710006608.

V.4 *Poetry of the Romantic period,* by J.R. de J. Jackson. 1980. xvi,334p. ISBN: 0710002890.

The first major history since Cowthorpe, but not completed. Very detailed surveys with many quotations. Each vol. has appended chronological table of principal verse published during the period covered, with annotations, the one in v.3 occupying 67p. References for each chapter. Index in each vol. *Class No:* 820-1(091)

Biographies

[7046]
SAUNDERS, J.W. A Biographical dictionary of renaissance poets and dramatists, 1520-1650. Brighton, Harvester; Totowa, N.J., Barnes & Noble, 1983. xxxiv,216p. ISBN: 0710803257, UK; 0389202717, US.

Biographical notes on 507 writers (only 12 women) arranged in one A-Z sequence. Lists important secondary material for major writers. Classified listing by occupation (18 headings). List of sources. Index. *Class No:* 820-1(092)

[7047]
The Victorian poets: an alphabetical compilation of the bio-critical introductions to the Victorian poets from A.H. Miles's *The Poets and poetry of the nineteenth century*. Fredeman, W.E., *ed.* New York, Garland, 1986. 3v. ISBN: 0824086317.

Reproduces the 428 bio-critical introductions in Miles's compilation, which was not only an important anthology of 19th-century poetry but also the only source of biographical information for many minor poets of the period.
Class No: 820-1(092)

Arnold

[7048]
MACHANN, C.J. The Essential Matthew Arnold: an annotated bibliography of major modern studies. Boston, Hall, 1993. 177p. $50. ISBN: 0816190879.

Lists 'the most significant contributions to ... Arnold criticism and scholarship' published 1900-91. 796 entries, thematically aranged, with annotations which summarize but rarely evaluate. Cross-references and indexes of authors, titles and topics. *Class No:* 820-1ARN

Auden

[7049]

BLOOMFIELD, B.C. *and* **MENDELSON, E. W.H. Auden: a bibliography, 1924-1969.** 2nd ed. Charlottesville, Va., Univ. Press of Virginia, 1972. xvi,420p. $35. ISBN: 0813903955.

1st ed. 1964 by B.C. Bloomfield, as *W.H. Auden: a bibliography; the early years through 1955.*

Section A. provides full description of first editions of 64 books and pamphlets by Auden. Section B. describes 115 books edited, translated or having contributions by Auden, and Section C. lists nearly 800 contributions to periodicals. 13 further sections cover the rest of his output, including interviews, letters, manuscripts, films and broadcasts. Appendix lists 577 secondary items. Index. *Class No:* 820-1AUD

[7050]

GINGERICH, M.E. W.H. Auden: a reference guide. Boston, Hall, 1977. xii,145p. ISBN: 0816178895.

Lists *c.*500 critical studies by year, 1931-76, with separate sections for books and shorter writings within each year. Concise annotations. Index of names, book titles and poem titles. *Class No:* 820-1AUD

Blake

[7051]

BENTLEY, G.E. Blake books: annotated catalogue of William Blake's writings in illuminated printing, in conventional typography and in manuscript, and reprints thereof, reproductions of his designs, books with his engravings, catalogues, books he owned and scholarly and critical works about him. Rev. ed. Oxford, Clarendon Press, 1977. xii,1079p. ISBN: 0198181515.

1st ed. by G.E. Bentley and M.K. Nurmi, 1964, as *A Blake bibliography.*

1. Editions of Blake's writings, comprehensively described - 2. Reproductions of drawings and paintings - 3. Commercial book engravings - 4. Catalogues and bibliographies - 5. Books owned by Blake - 6. Biography and criticism (2,300 items, A-Z by author). Addenda lists several hundred post-1972 publications. Aims to list everything written about Blake to 1863 and all significant material since then, and is almost 3 times larger than 1st ed. Index.

Continued by Bentley's *Blake books supplement: a bibliography of publications and discoveries about William Blake, 1971-1991* (Oxford, Clarendon Press, 1994. 720p. £75. ISBN: 019812354x). *Class No:* 820-1BLA

[7052]

DAMON, S.F. A Blake dictionary: the ideas and symbols of William Blake. Rev. ed. Hanover, N.H., Univ. Press of New England, for Brown Univ. Press, 1988. xxviii,532p. illus. $22. ISBN: 0874514363.

1st ed. Providence, R.I., Brown Univ. Press, 1965.

A paperback reprint of the original work, reduced in size from quarto to octavo, with the addition of an index, bibliography (6p.), and foreword. *c.*1,150 entries, explaining Blake's symbolism with references to Keynes's ed. of the complete writings (1957). *Class No:* 820-1BLA

[7053]

NATOLI, J.P. Twentieth century Blake criticism: Northrop Frye to the present. New York, Garland, 1982. xxvi,327p. ISBN: 0824093267.

An annotated, selective bibliography of 1,682 items in 11 sections, covering English-language criticism published 1947-80. Useful introductory survey to each section. Index of authors, titles, and subjects. *Class No:* 820-1BLA

The Brownings

[7054]

DONALDSON, S. Elizabeth Barrett Browning: an annotated bibliography of commentary and criticism, 1826-1990. Boston, Hall, 1993. 642p. $55. ISBN: 0816189102.

A comprehensive listing of secondary material in English, French and Italian, arranged by year and then by author. Includes dissertations. Index of Browning's works. Index of names and topics. *Class No:* 820-1BRO

[7055]

DREW, P. An Annotated critical bibliography of Robert Browning. Hemel Hempstead, Harvester Wheatsheaf, 1990. xxvii,106p. ISBN: 0710809093.

Brief list of primary texts, followed by coverage of bibliographical aids, biographical and critical studies (p.17-89), including studies of specific poems, and correspondence, with commentary throughout. Index of poems and general name index. All items have references to the bibliographies by Broughton (1953) and Peterson (1974) and the annual listings in *Browning Institute Studies.*
Class No: 820-1BRO

[7056]

Robert Browning: a bibliography, 1830-1950. Broughton, L.N., *and others, comps.* Reprint of 1953 ed. New York, Franklin, 1970. xiv,446p. (*Cornell studies in English.*) ISBN: 0833703811.

Originally published Ithaca, N.Y., Cornell Univ. Press, 1953.

A. Browning's writings (854 items in 7 subsections, including adaptations and translations) - B. Reference works (74) - C. Biography and criticism (4,940) - D. Calendar of letters (2,068) - E. Musical settings (419). Very comprehensive, but many items not annotated.
Class No: 820-1BRO

[7057]

—Browning Institute studies: an annual of Victorian literary and cultural history Princeton, N.J., The Institute, 1973- . Annual. ISSN: 00924725.

Carries annual bibliographies, using the same numbering system as Broughton. That in v.18, *1990* (1989), lists 67 items published in 1988 and is indexed. *Class No:* 820-1BRO

[7058]

—PETERSON, W.S. Robert and Elizabeth Barrett Browning: an annotated bibliography, 1951-1970. New York, The Browning Institute, 1974. xiii,209p. $27.50. ISBN: 0930252020.

Intended to fill the gap between Broughton *et al.* (1953) and the first annual Browning bibliography (for 1971) published in the 1973 vol. of *Browning Institute Studies. c.*1,350 briefly annotated entries in 3 sections: A. Primary works - B. Reference and bibliographical works and exhibitions - C. Biography, criticism and miscellanea. Cross-references to Broughton and *BIS*. Index of the Brownings' works. General index. *Class No:* 820-1BRO

Byron

[7059]

PAGE, N. A Byron chronology. Basingstoke, Macmillan; Boston, Hall, 1988. xi,117p. (*Macmillan author chronologies.*) ISBN: 0333399129, UK; 0816189528, US.

Recounts the main events of the poet's life, year by year and month by month. Biographical notes on the Byron circle (14p.). Select bibliography (2p.). Indexes of Byron's works, names, and topics. *Class No:* 820-1BYR

[7060]

SANTUCHO, O.J. George Gordon, Lord Byron: a comprehensive bibliography of secondary materials in English 1807-1974, with a critical review of research by C.T. Goode. Metuchen, N.J., Scarecrow, 1977. xiv,677p. ISBN: 0810809826.

Over 5,000 entries in 11 period sections. Index of critics.

Continued by C.T. Goode's *George Gordon, Lord Byron: a comprehensive annotated research bibliography of secondary materials in English, 1973-94* (Scarecrow, 1997. 624p. $95. ISBN: 0810831864), which has nearly 9,000 entries, indexed by author, poem and subject.
Class No: 820-1BYR

Chaucer

Bibliographies

[7061]

ALLEN, M. *and* **FISHER, J.H. The Essential Chaucer:** an annotated bibliography of major modern studies. London, Mansell; Boston, Hall, 1987. xiii,243p. ISBN: 0720119545, UK; 0816187398, US.

A guide to 20th century studies, based on the bibliography in Fisher's *The Complete poetry and prose of Geoffrey Chaucer* (New York, Holt Rinehart & Winston, 1982), updated to 1984 and annotated by Allen. 925 works are listed once each, alphabetically, under one of 29 subject headings or under the Chaucerian work they treat most directly. Annotations are mainly descriptive but contain some evaluation. Index. 'A most useful introduction to the maze of Chaucer scholarship' (*Choice,* v.25(7), March 1988, p.1061). *Class No:* 820-1CHA(01)

[7062]

BAIRD, L.Y. A Bibliography of Chaucer, 1964-1973. Boston, Hall, 1977. xxiv,287p. ISBN: 0816180059.

Continues the work of Griffith and Crawford (*qq.v.*) but much improved in organization with items numbered for cross-referencing purposes and separate author and subject indexes. Coverage is also improved with 6 new or expanded categories: *Festschriften* and collections; Foreign translations (12 languages); Literary and aesthetic backgrounds; Music background; Recordings, films and filmstrips; Musical settings and adaptations. 2,183 entries, some of them briefly annotated. *Class No:* 820-1CHA(01)

[7063]

BAIRD-LANGE, L.Y. *and* **SCHNUTTGEN, H. A Bibliography of Chaucer, 1974-1985.** Hamden, Conn., Archon; Cambridge, Brewer, 1988. lxxv,344p. ISBN: 0208021345, US; 0859912744, UK.

Generally follows the plan of Baird's *Bibliography of Chaucer, 1964-1973*, with the addition of 3 new categories: Facsimiles, Medieval women's studies and Pedagogy. 2,894 unannotated entries preceded by a comprehensive review of recent Chaucer scholarship (44p.). Author index, a thorough subject index and extensive cross-referencing make this excellent value. *Class No:* 820-1CHA(01)

[7064]

The Chaucer bibliographies. Colaianne, A.J. *and* Hahn, T., *eds.* Toronto, Univ. of Toronto Press, 1983-. v.1- (in progress).

V.1 *Chaucer's lyrics and 'Anelida and Arcite,'* by R.A. Peck. 1983. xx,226p. $40. ISBN: 0802024815.

V.2 *Chaucer's 'Romaunt of the Rose' and 'Boece', 'Treatise on the Astrolabe', 'Equatorie of the Planetis', lost works, and Chaucerian apocrypha,* by R.A. Peck. 1988. xviii,402p. $75. ISBN: 0802024939.

V.3 *Chaucer's 'General prologue to the Canterbury tales,'* by C.D. Eckhardt. 1990. 512p. $65. ISBN: 0802025927.

V.4 *Chaucer's 'Knight's Tale,'* by M. E. McAlpine. 1991. $85. liii,432p. ISBN: 0802059139.

Each vol. in this series is to be 'a comprehensive and self-contained reference guide to a single work or group of works, or to a major topic in Chaucer studies. The bibliographies will provide annotations to books, monographs, articles, dissertations, notes, and important reviews in all languages significant to modern Chaucer scholarship; where appropriate, editions will also be annotated' (*General editors' preface*).

V.2 has 742 entries, with substantial annotations and a thorough index. *Class No:* 820-1CHA(01)

[7065]

GRIFFITH, D.D. Bibliography of Chaucer, 1908-1953. Seattle, Univ. of Washington Press, 1955. xviii,398p.

Planned to supplement Hammond (*qv*) and incorporates the contents of the author's *A Bibliography of Chaucer, 1908-1924* (Seattle, Univ. of Washington Press, 1926).

*c.*3,100 entries under 20 headings, each section arranged A-Z by author. Includes editions and critical material. Some brief annotations and many references to reviews. Index.
Class No: 820-1CHA(01)

[7066]

—CRAWFORD, W.R. Bibliography of Chaucer, 1954-63. Seattle, Univ. of Washington Press, 1967. xliv, 144p. ISBN: 0295740272.

Supplements Griffith (*qv*) and follows, with minor exceptions, the same format. *c.*1,200 items. Lengthy introductory essay on 'New directions in Chaucer criticism' (37p.). Index. *Class No:* 820-1CHA(01)

[7067]

LEYERLE, J. *and* **QUICK, A. Chaucer: a bibliographical introduction.** Toronto, Univ. of Toronto Press, 1986. xx,321p. (*Toronto medieval bibliographies.*) ISBN: 0802064086.

Over 900 annotated entries, 'compiled primarily for readers relatively unfamiliar with the works of Chaucer and their context' (*Preface*), in 3 main sections: 1. Materials for the study of Chaucer's works - 2. Chaucer's works (editions; sources and analogues; critical studies) - 3. Backgrounds. Author index. Fully cross-referenced. Most items listed are in English, with a few essential French and German studies included. 'It fulfils its brief ... with clarity and intelligence ... but already has a slightly dated look about it' (*Review of English Studies,* v.38(152), Nov. 1987, p.540-1), coverage being complete only to 1979. *Class No:* 820-1CHA(01)

[7068]
SEYMOUR, M.C. A Catalogue of Chaucer manuscripts. Aldershot, Scolar Press, 1995-7. 2v.

V1 *Works before 'The Canterbury tales'.* 1995. 186p. £42.50. ISBN: 1859280560.

V.2 *The Canterbury tales.* 1997. 280p. £52.50. ISBN: 1859280579.

All existing mss. are described, in assumed order of composition, taking into account recent textual and linguistic scholarship. Indexes of mss. and of inscribed names and owners. *Class No:* 820-1CHA(01)

Encyclopaedias & Dictionaries

[7069]
A Chaucer glossary. Davis, N., *and others, comps.* Oxford, Clarendon Press, 1979. xx,185p. £11.99. ISBN: 0198111711.

'The primary aim ... is to explain the meanings of words and phrases in Chaucer's works which are used in ways unfamiliar in modern English, and to refer them to a number (necessarily limited) of typical instances' (*Introduction*). *c.*9,000 headwords, their spelling based on Skeat's 6-vol. edition (Oxford, 1894). References to texts based on Tatlock and Kennedy's *Concordance* (*qv*). Etymologies provided for each entry. Select list of *c.*350 proper names.
Class No: 820-1CHA(03)

[7070]
DE WEEVER, J. Chaucer name dictionary: a guide to astrological, biblical, historical, literary, and mythological names in the works of Geoffrey Chaucer. New York and London, Garland, 1988. xxi,451p. $65. ISBN: 0824083067.

Approx. 900 entries arranged A-Z by Chaucerian spelling, ranging in length from a few lines to 2p., and including the following elements: biographical information, explanation of Chaucer's use of the name, etymology, and bibliography of sources. Appendix has glossary of astronomical and astrological terms and 6 astrological maps. Excellent bibliography of recent modern editions of classicial and medieval texts and of secondary sources (46p.). Excludes place names, but 'generally superior in detail and convenience to all previous Chaucerian personal name dictionaries' (*Choice,* v.26(10), June 1989, p.1656).
Class No: 820-1CHA(03)

Concordances

[7071]
TATLOCK, J.S.P. *and* **KENNEDY, A.G. Concordance to the complete works of Geoffrey Chaucer** and to the *Romaunt of the Rose.* Washington, D.C., Carnegie Institution, 1927. xiv,1110p.

Based on the text of the Globe edition, 1898, on the grounds that it is more conservative than Skeat's edition and has sometimes utilized more manuscripts. Complete, except for nearly 150 very common words which are represented only by 'specimens'.

A. Oizumi has edited the definitive computerised work, *A Complete concordance to the works of Geoffrey Chaucer* (Hildesheim, Olms, 1991-2. 10v. DM398 per vol. ISBN: 3487094122) and is working on a supplementary 4-vol. series entitled *A Rhyme concordance to the works of Geoffrey Chaucer.* *Class No:* 820-1CHA(083.87)

Clare

[7072]
ESTERMANN, B. John Clare: an annotated primary and secondary bibliography. New York and London, Garland, 1985. xxviii,303p. ISBN: 0824087542.

Part 1 lists 174 works in 2 sections for those published separately and those in anthologies. Part 2 lists 880 secondary items by year, 1819-1984, then by author, with substantial annotations. Author and editor index. Subject index. *Class No:* 820-1CLA

Coleridge

[7073]
PURTON, V. A Coleridge chronology. Basingstoke, Macmillan, 1993. xix,193p. £52.50. ISBN: 0333460219.

Details the events of the writer's life, month by month and day by day. Supplemented by maps, family tree and 50 biographical sketches of the Coleridge circle. Index.
Class No: 820-1COL

[7074]
Samuel Taylor Coleridge: a selective bibliography of criticism, 1935-1977. Caskey, J.D. *and* Stapper, M.M., *comps.* Westport, Conn., and London, Greenwood, 1978. xvii,174p. $42.95. ISBN: 0313205647.

2,010 entries in 4 sections: Criticism of individual works; General criticism; Biography; Dissertations. Reviews cited for many individual items. Index.

See also *The Poetry of Samuel Taylor Coleridge: an annotated bibliography of criticism, 1935-70* by M.L.T. Milton (New York, Garland, 1981. xiv,251p. ISBN: 0824094514), which has only 445 entries but provides substantial annotations. *Class No:* 820-1COL

[7075]
Samuel Taylor Coleridge: an annotated bibliography of criticism and scholarship. Boston, Hall, 1976-83. 2v.

V.1 *1793-1899,* ed. by R. Haven and others, 1976. (xxviii,382p. ISBN: 0816178291). V.2 *1900-1939 (with additional entries for 1795-1899),* ed. by W.B. Crawford and others, 1983. (l, 812p. ISBN: 0816178666).

V.1 has over 1,900 items arranged by year then A-Z by author, with brief annotations. Author/title index. Index of proper names. Very complex subject index which requires explanatory notes. Index of parodies, satire, fictional portraits, etc.

V.2 has 800 new pre-1900 items and nearly 2,000 for 1900-1939, in the same format as v.1 but with much more substantial annotations. A lot of foreign material (21 languages). 7 indexes give complete access. A third vol. will continue the bibliography and include chronological lists of different types of material. *Class No:* 820-1COL

Cowper

[7076]
HARTLEY, L. William Cowper; the continuing revelation: an essay and a bibliography of Cowperian studies from 1895 to 1960. Chapel Hill, N.C., Univ. of North Carolina Press, 1960. x,159p.

The bibliography (p.75-152) has 1,028 annotated entries in 5 sections: 1. Bibliographical aids - 2. Editions and selections - 3. Biography - 4. Criticism - 5. Miscellaneous. Index. *Class No:* 820-1COW

[7077]

RUSSELL, N. A Bibliography of William Cowper to 1837. Oxford, Oxford Bibliographical Society, 1963. xxvi,339p. illus.

Over 500 items in 6 sections: A. Original works and translations - B. Works edited or reviewed by Cowper - C. Collected works - D. Biography and criticism of Cowper - E. Cowperiana - F. Iconography. Full descriptions throughout, with library locations. Appendix lists American eds. General index; index of printers and publishers; index of artists and engravers; index of individual poems. *Class No:* 820-1COW

Donne

[7078]

KEYNES, G. A Bibliography of Dr. John Donne, Dean of Saint Paul's. 4th ed. Oxford, Clarendon Press, 1973 (repr. Winchester, St. Paul's Bibliographies). xii,400p. illus. ISBN: 0906795222.

1st ed 1914; 3rd ed. 1958.

Full descriptive bibliography of Donne's prose works (68 items) and poetical works (124) with title-pages of all early editions reproduced in facsimile. Appendices include check-list of biography and criticism, 1594-1971. Indexes of libraries consulted and of printers and publishers, 1607-1719. General index. *Class No:* 820-1DON

[7079]

RAY, R.H. A John Donne companion. New York, Garland, 1990. 414p. ISBN: 0824045688.

The main part of the work, occupying 343p., is a dictionary with explanatory entries on Donne's works; persons and places of significance in his life and works; characters, allusions, and concepts in his works; words and phrases which may cause difficulty; associated writers; and relevant literary terms. Other sections include a chronology, a brief biography (9p.), and a selected bibliography (45p.), mainly of critical studies, which to some extent updates Roberts's compilations. *Class No:* 820-1DON

[7080]

ROBERTS, J.R. John Donne: an annotated bibliography of modern criticism. Columbia, Mo., Univ. of Missouri Press, 1973-82. 2v.

V.1 *1912-1967* (1973. 363p. $37.50. ISBN: 0826201369).

V.2 *1968-1978* (1982. 434p. $44. ISBN: 0826203647).

Entries are arranged by year, then by author, and have detailed descriptive annotations, often including quotations from the work in question. 1,280 items in v.1 and 1,044 in v.2. Each vol. has index of authors, editors and translators, subject index and index of Donne's works. Much foreign-language material included. *Class No:* 820-1DON

Dryden

[7081]

LATT, D.J. *and* **MONK, S.H. John Dryden: a survey and bibliography of critical studies, 1895-1974.** Minneapolis, Univ. of Minnesota Press, 1976. xv,199p. ISBN: 0816607745.

An updating of Monk's *John Dryden: a list of critical studies published from 1895 to 1948* (Minneapolis, 1950).

Over 2,800 entries (4 times as many as 1st ed.) in 9 sections, with numerous subsections for specific works. Much foreign-language material. New ed. adds dissertations from English, American, French and German universities. Brief annotations with some entries. Index of authors, names and titles. Topic index. *Class No:* 820-1DRY

[7082]

MACDONALD, H. John Dryden: a bibliography of early editions and of Drydeniana. Oxford, Clarendon Press, 1939. xiv,358p.

The aim was 'to include every edition of his writings published during his lifetime, and every contemporary book or pamphlet I have been able to trace in which he is praised, attacked, or alluded to' (*Preface*). Detailed descriptions of 334 items. Index. *Class No:* 820-1DRY

Eliot (T.S.)

[7083]

The Cambridge companion to T.S. Eliot. Moody, A.D., *ed.* Cambridge, Cambridge Univ. Press, 1994. xix,259p. £35. ISBN: 0521420806.

Essentially a collection of critical studies, but includes a very useful bibliographical essay, 'Eliot studies: a review and a select booklist' (15p.) by J.S.Brooker. Chronology (3p.). Index. *Class No:* 820-1ELI

[7084]

GALLUP, D. T.S. Eliot: a bibliography. Rev. ed. London, Faber, 1969. 414p. ISBN: 0571089283.

1st ed. 1952, itself an extension of *A Bibliographical checklist of the writings of T.S. Eliot* (1947).

7 sections, with full descriptive entries in those covering Eliot's books and pamphlets and his contributions to books and pamphlets. Other sections include translations (*c.*40 languages), musical settings and recordings. Comprehensive index of names and titles. *Class No:* 820-1ELI

[7085]

RICKS, B. T.S. Eliot: a bibliography of secondary works. Metuchen, N.J., Scarecrow, 1980. xxiii,366p. (*Scarecrow author bibliographies.*) ISBN: 0810812622.

A classified bibliography with over 4,300 entries, some of them briefly annotated. Topical index and index of critics.

For more recent material, see *T.S. Eliot, man and poet: v.2, annotated bibliography of Eliot criticism, 1977-86*, ed. by S.D.G. Knowles and S.A. Leonard (Orono, Me., National Poetry Foundation, Univ. of Maine, 1992. $45. ISBN: 0943373115). *Class No:* 820-1ELI

[7086]

The T.S. Eliot Collection of The University of Texas at Austin. Sackton, A., *comp.* Austin, Humanities Research Center, Univ. of Texas, 1975. 407p. illus. $25. ISBN: 0879590424.

Descriptive bibliography in 13 sections, with published material numbered as in Gallup. Full descriptions from Gallup not repeated as the aim is 'to describe distinctive features of the items held at Austin' (*Preface*). *Class No:* 820-1ELI

Graves

[7087]

BRYANT, H.B. Robert Graves: an annotated bibliography. New York, Garland, 1986. xvi,206p. ISBN: 0824085566.

Lists 351 primary sources in 6 sections, but most valuable for its classified listing of nearly 700 critical studies in 5 sections. Index. *Class No:* 820-1GRA

[7088]

HIGGINSON, F.H. A Bibliography of the writings of Robert Graves. 2nd ed., rev. by W.P. Williams. Winchester, St. Paul's Bibliographies, 1987. 354p. illus. ISBN: 0906795168.

1st ed. London, Vane, 1966.

Preserves and updates the first 3 sections from the 1st ed.: A. Books and pamphlets by Graves, alone or in collaboration, and works edited, translated or rewritten by him - B. Books containing contributions by Graves - C. Contributions to press and periodicals. Section D (Miscellanea) has become Appendix II and contains information about collections of manuscripts and printed books but omits non-print material. Section E (Selective bibliography of works about Graves) has been dropped and readers requiring secondary material are referred to Bryant (*q.v.*). Appendix I lists translations of selections of Graves' work and Addenda lists items seen late or noted from secondary sources. Well over 1,200 entries, an increase of 25% on the 1st ed., those in Sections A and B being descriptive. Index. 'An indispensable tool, meticulously compiled' (*TLS*, no.4437, April 15-21, 1988, p.434).
Class No: 820-1GRA

Gray

[7089]

McKENZIE, A.T. Thomas Gray: a reference guide. Boston, Hall, 1982. 334p. ISBN: 0816184518.

Lists critical studies chronologically since 1751. Indexed.
Class No: 820-1GRA

[7090]

NORTHUP, C.S. A Bibliography of Thomas Gray. New Haven, Yale Univ. Press; London, Oxford Univ. Press, 1917. xiii,296p. (*Cornell studies in English.*)

Aims 'to present a complete record of the editions..., together with a list of all the reviews, critical notices, and studies relating to him that have thus far appeared' (*Preface*). Nearly 2,000 items in 9 sections, plus Appendix (Undated editions) and Addenda. Index.

Supplemented by *A Bibliography of Thomas Gray, 1917-1951* by H.W. Starr (Philadelphia, Pa., Univ. of Pennsylvania Press, 1953. xii,152p.), which has 1,211 numbered entries plus interpolations. *Class No:* 820-1GRA

Herbert

[7091]

RAY, R.H. A George Herbert companion. New York, Garland, 1994. 240p. $39. ISBN: 0824048490.

A comprehensive guide to Herbert's life and works, the core of which is an A-Z sequence of entries which identify and explain poems, prose works, people, places, allusions, themes, concepts, and literary terms. Also includes a chronology, guide to research, and annotated bibliography of editions and key critical studies. *Class No:* 820-1HER

[7092]

ROBERTS, J.R. George Herbert: an annotated bibliography of modern criticism, 1905-1984. Rev. ed. Columbia, Mo., Univ. of Missouri Press, 1988. 433p. $42. ISBN: 0826204872.

1st ed. 1978, covering 1905-74.

Over 1,400 items arranged by year then by author, with lengthy, nonevaluative annotations often incorporating quotations from the work. Includes *c.*200 items published 1905-74 not in first ed. Many foreign-language items. Indexes of authors, subjects and Herbert's works. Excludes

....(contd.)

dissertations, but is nevertheless 'the best bibliography of Herbert scholarship now available' (*Choice,* v.26(8), April 1989, p.1312). *Class No:* 820-1HER

Herrick

[7093]

HAGEMAN, E.H. Robert Herrick: a reference guide. Boston, Hall, 1983. 245p.

An annotated, chronological list of secondary material, with indexes of authors, subjects, and poems.
Class No: 820-1HER

Hopkins

[7094]

DUNNE, T. Gerard Manley Hopkins: a comprehensive bibliography. Oxford, Oxford Univ. Press, 1976 (repr. Winchester, St. Paul's Bibliographies). xxvi,394p. ISBN: 0906795214.

1. Published writings by Hopkins (484 items, fully described, in 5 sections: poetry, prose, anthologies, translations, dubia) - 2. Writings about Hopkins in English (1,708 annotated entries in 7 sections) - 3. Writing about Hopkins in other languages (268 items) - 4. Notes on locations of source material. Index of authors, titles, names and subjects. *Class No:* 820-1HOP

[7095]

McDERMOTT, J. A Hopkins chronology. Basingstoke, Macmillan, 1996. 192p. £21.25. (*Macmillan author chronologies.*) ISBN: 0333661958.

Details the events of the writer's life, month by month and day by day and also provides notes on the religious and political background to his works and biographical notes on the Hopkins circle. Hopkins family tree. Chronology of poems. Select bibliography. Index. *Class No:* 820-1HOP

Housman

[7096]

CARTER, J. *and* **SPARROW, J. A.E. Housman: a bibliography.** 2nd ed. rev. by W. White. Godalming, St. Paul's Bibliographies, 1982. xvii,94p. ISBN: 0906795052.

1st ed. London, Hart-Davis, 1952, as *A.E. Housman: an annotated hand-list.*

140 items (only 49 in 1st ed.) in 7 sections: 1. Books and pamphlets - 2. Contributions to books - 3. Biographies - 4. Contributions to periodicals - 5. Periodicals containing original material (mainly letters) - 6. Books and pamphlets about Housman - 7. Translations. Full description of major book editions. *Class No:* 820-1HOU

Hughes

[7097]

SAGAR, K. *and* **TABOR, S. Ted Hughes: a bibliography, 1946-1980.** London, Mansell, 1983. xiv,260p. ISBN: 0720116546.

Sections A-I cover primary material, with full descriptive entries in A., Books, pamphlets and broadsides, and B., Contributions to books, etc. Includes translations, interviews, recordings and broadcasts. Section J. lists 124 books and articles about Hughes, but book reviews are listed within the appropriate primary entry. Index of names and

.... (contd.)

titles. Winner of the 1983 Besterman Medal for bibliography. 2nd ed. due mid-1998, covering 1946-95 (ISBN: 0720123372). *Class No:* 820-1HUG

Keats

[7098]

MacGILLIVRAY, J.R. Keats: a bibliography and reference guide, with an essay on Keats' reputation. Toronto, Univ. of Toronto Press, 1949 (reprinted with corrections, 1968). lxxxi,210p. £32.50. ISBN: 0802050042.

Lists Keats' published writings and significant secondary material published 1816-1946. Some brief annotations. Index. *Class No:* 820-1KEA

[7099]

PINION, F.B. A Keats chronology. Basingstoke, Macmillan, 1992. ix,174p. £52.50. ISBN: 0333552725.

Details the events of the writer's life, month by month and day by day. Also includes substantial biographical sketches of over 30 members of of Keats' circle. Bibliography of sources. 4 maps. General index and index of Keats' poems. *Class No:* 820-1KEA

[7100]

RHODES, J.W. Keats's major odes: an annotated bibliography of the criticism. Westport, Conn., Greenwood, 1984. 224p. $45. ISBN: 031323809x.

Over 900 entries, arranged by year, 1820-1980, then by author, with concise annotations. Lengthy introductory survey (34p.). Author and subject indexes. *Class No:* 820-1KEA

Larkin

[7101]

BLOOMFIELD, B.C. Philip Larkin: a bibliography, 1933-1976. London, Faber, 1979. 187p. £35. ISBN: 0571114474.

Section A. has descriptions of books and pamphlets by Larkin (p.17-57). 11 further sections include contributions to books and periodicals, interviews, recordings, published letters, translations, etc. Appendix lists 96 critical studies, including theses. Index. *Class No:* 820-1LAR

Marvell

[7102]

COLLINS, D.S. Andrew Marvell: a reference guide. Boston, Hall, 1981. xiv,450p. ISBN: 0816180172.

An annotated bibliography of secondary material, chronologically arranged from 1641 to 1980. 80% of the entries are for post-1950 publications and a third were published since 1970. Index. 'An indispensable work of reference' according to *Review of English Studies* (v.35(140), Winter 1984, p.542-3), with nothing of significance omitted. *Class No:* 820-1MAR

[7103]

RAY, R.H. An Andrew Marvell companion. New York, Garland, 1998. 224p. £34.95. ISBN: 0824062485.

A-Z entries on all aspects of Marvell's life and works, including people, places, characters, allusions, ideas, themes, relevant literary terms, and significant words and phrases found in the texts. Numerous cross-references. Chronology. Bibliography. *Class No:* 820-1MAR

Milton

[7104]

CAMPBELL, G. A Milton chronology. Basingstoke, Macmillan, 1997. 221p. £45. (*Macmillan author chronologies.*) ISBN: 0333633261.

Details the events of the writer's life, month by month and day by day, and 'in effect replaces, certainly in many cases corrects, the five volumes of *The Life records of John Milton* published by J.Milton French between 1949 and 1958' (*TLS*, no.4952, Feb. 27, 1998, p.6). Glossary of legal terms. Bibliography. Index. *Class No:* 820-1MIL

[7105]

KLEMP, P.J. The Essential Milton: an annotated bibliography of major modern studies. Boston, Hall, 1989. 474p. $50. ISBN: 0816187304.

Lists and describes over 1,000 English-language critical studies, published 1900-1987, in 3 main sections for general studies, poetry criticism and prose criticism, with subsections for specific works and themes. Substantial, nonevaluative annotations. Single index of authors, titles, and subjects. *Class No:* 820-1MIL

[7106]

A Milton encyclopedia. Hunter, W.B., *and others, eds.* Lewisburg, Pa., Bucknell Univ. Press; London, Associated Univ. Presses, 1978-84. 9v. $220. ISBN: 0686857429.

Vols. 1-8 have signed entries, A-Z, on people, places, works, and subjects, 'written for the general reader by specialists'. There are some bibliographic references in the articles, but full bibliographies had to be omitted because of pressure of space. However, v.9, published 4 years after the rest of the set, contains bibliographies as well as indexes of names, subjects and biblical allusions, and also some extra articles.

For specialist treatment of biblical influences on Milton, see S.J. Rogal's *Index to the biblical references, parallels and allusions in the poetry and prose of John Milton* (Lewiston, N.Y., Mellen, 1994. 356p. £49.95. ISBN: 0773423907). *Class No:* 820-1MIL

[7107]

STEVENS, D.H. Reference guide to Milton: from 1800 to the present day. Chicago, Univ. of Chicago Press, 1930. x,302p.

2,850 items, published 1800-1928, listed in 19 sections including editions and translations. Brief annotations and references to reviews. Index.

Supplemented by H.F. Fletcher's *Contributions to a Milton bibliography, 1800-1930* (Urbana, Ill., Univ. of Illinois Press, 1931. 166p.) with *c.*1,000 items, chronologically arranged, and continued by: *Class No:* 820-1MIL

[7108]

—HUCKABAY, C. John Milton: an annotated bibliography, 1929-68. Rev. ed. Pittsburgh, Duquesne Univ. Press, 1969. xv,392p.

1st ed. 1960, as *John Milton: a bibliographical supplement, 1929-1957.*

3,932 items (twice as many as 1st ed.) with brief annotations. Sections include bibliography, editions, translations, general criticism, criticism of individual works, and biography.

Continued by Huckaby's *John Milton: an annotated bibliography, 1968-1988* (Pittsburgh, Pa., Duquesne Univ. Press, 1996. 535p. $100. ISBN: 0820702722), which has over 4,500 entries, reflecting a huge growth in Milton scholarship. Annotations are more detailed compared with

....*(contd.)*
the earlier work and cross-references have been added. "No other Milton bibliography covers this period as comprehensively" (*Choice*, v.34(3), Nov. 1996, p.431).
Class No: 820-1MIL

Pope

[7109]
BERRY, R. A Pope chronology. Basingstoke, Macmillan; Boston, Hall, 1988. xiii, 221p. (*Macmillan author chronologies.*) ISBN: 0333399072, UK; 081618951x, US.

Presents the major events of the writer's life extremely clearly, year by year and month by month. Glossaries of principal persons and places mentioned. Short bibliography. Index of people, places, works and topics. *Class No:* 820-1POP

[7110]
KOWALK, W. Alexander Pope: an annotated bibliography of twentieth-century criticism, 1900-1979. Frankfurt, Lang, 1981. ix,371p. ISBN: 3820458816.

A classified listing with 1,975 items in 24 sections, several of them devoted to individual works by Pope. Concise annotations for titles which are not self-explanatory. Index of authors, titles and topics. *Class No:* 820-1POP

Shelley

[7111]
BRADLEY, J.L. A Shelley chronology. Basingstoke, Macmillan, 1993. xii,93p. £35. ISBN: 0333557700.

Details the events of the writer's life, month by month and day by day. Supplemented by biographical sketches of the Shelley circle. *Class No:* 820-1SHE

[7112]
DUNBAR, C. A Bibliography of Shelley studies, 1823-1950. New York, Garland; Folkestone, Dawson, 1976. lvii,320p. ISBN: 082409980x, US; 0712906746, UK.

3,238 items listed chronologically, with divisions within each year for periodical articles and books, plus Addenda with 33 further items. Combines entries from 10 bibliographies. Includes some major editions of Shelley's works. Index. *Class No:* 820-1SHE

Sidney

[7113]
STUMP, D.V., *& others*. Sir Philip Sidney: an annotated bibliography of texts and criticism (1554-1984). Boston, Hall, 1994. 834p. $75. ISBN: 0816182388.

A comprehensive listing of editions and translations of Sidney's works, plus biographies, bibliographies, correspondence, general criticism and studies of specific works. Substantial annotations. Cross-references. Indexes of authors, names and subjects. *Class No:* 820-1SID

Spenser

[7114]
CARPENTER, F.I. A Reference guide to Edmund Spenser. Chicago, Univ. of Chicago Press, 1923. vi,333p. illus.

A classified bibliography with sections on the life, works, criticism, influences and allusions, and topics. The more important items are annotated and there is some scattered commentary. Covers material from 1550 to the early 20th century. Index.

Continued by *Edmund Spenser: a bibliographical supplement*, by D.F. Atkinson (Baltimore, Md., Johns Hopkins Press; London, Oxford Univ. Press, 1937. xiv,242p.), which has *c.*1,650 items, similarly arranged, covering post-1923 material plus omissions from the earlier vol. Index. *Class No:* 820-1SPE

[7115]
MALEY, W. A Spenser chronology. Basingstoke, Macmillan, 1994. xv,120p. £55. ISBN: 0333537440.

Details the events of Spenser's life, month by month and day by day and claims to be the first serious attempt to map out in concrete detail all known facts concerning the poet.
Class No: 820-1SPE

[7116]
SIPPLE, W.L. Edmund Spenser, 1900-1936: a reference guide. Boston, Hall, 1984. xxxviii,244p. ISBN: 0816180075.

Lists *c.*1,400 critical studies by year, then by author, with annotations. Index of names, subjects and primary titles.
Class No: 820-1SPE

[7117]
—McNEIR, W.F. *and* PROVOST, F. Edmund Spenser: an annotated bibliography, 1937-1972. [2nd ed.]. New Jersey, Humanities Press; Sussex, Harvester Press, 1975. xxxi,490p. ISBN: 039100395x, US; 0855272473, UK.

1st ed. 1962, as *Annotated bibliography of Edmund Spenser, 1937-1960* (Pittsburgh, Pa., Duquesne Univ. Press).

Over 2,600 entries (1,200 in 1st ed.), in sections on life, works, general criticism, and individual works. Many dissertations included. References to reviews for post-1960 publications. Bibliography of sources, with 117 entries, and list of 350 serials. Concise, non-evaluative annotations. Thorough index of authors, editors, other persons, and 200 subject headings. *Class No:* 820-1SPE

[7118]
The Spenser encyclopedia. Hamilton, A.C., *ed.* Toronto, Univ. of Toronto Press; London, Routledge, 1990. xxi,858p. illus. £150. ISBN: 0802026761, US; 0415056373, UK.

Contains over 700 signed entries, A-Z, by over 400 contributors from 20 countries. Entries are of 3 types: essays on individual poems and on major biographical, historical and social issues; articles on particular topics; and articles on current work in Spenser studies, including his reputation in other countries. An extensive bibliography (21p.) includes all works cited more than once, whilst works cited only once are given full references in the reading list following the article in which they appear. Detailed subject index. Classified list of entries groups them under 22 broad headings. 'Without question, the book represents the nearest one could hope to approach to a one-volume comprehensive companion to Spenser' (*Reference Reviews*, v.5(2), 1991, p.33-4). *Class No:* 820-1SPE

Swinburne

[7119]
BEETZ, K.H. Algernon Charles Swinburne: a bibliography of secondary works, 1861-1980. Metuchen, N.J., Scarecrow, 1982. viii,227p. (*Scarecrow author bibliographies.*) ISBN: 0810815419.

Nearly 2,300 items chronologically arranged, with subject and author indexes. Some brief annotations. *Class No:* 820-1SWI

[7120]

WISE, T.J. A Bibliography of the writings in prose and verse of Algernon Charles Swinburne. London, printed for private circulation, 1919-20 (repr. London, Dawsons, 1966). 2v. illus.

6 parts: 1. Editiones principes (occupying v.1 and most of v.2) - 2. Contributions to periodical literature - 3. Collected editions - 4. Swinburneiana - 5. Works wrongly attributed to Swinburne - 6. Swinburne's unpublished writings. Notes and errata. Detailed descriptions. Many facsimiles.
Class No: 820-1SWI

Tennyson

[7121]

BAKER, A.E. A Tennyson dictionary: the characters and place-names contained in the poetical and dramatic works of the poet, alphabetically arranged and described with synopses of the poems and plays. London, Routledge; New York, Dutton, 1916 (repr. New York, Haskell, 1982). vii,296p. $75. ISBN: 083830706x.

2,040 entries, with separate sequences for the synopses and names. *Class No:* 820-1TEN

[7122]

PINION, F.B. A Tennyson chronology. Basingstoke, Macmillan, 1990. xiv,209p. £47.50. (*Macmillan author chronologies.*) ISBN: 0333460200.

Presents the major events of the writer's life extremely clearly, year by year and month by month. Biographical notes on persons of importance in Tennyson's life. 2 maps. Short bibliography. General index and index of poems and plays. *Class No:* 820-1TEN

[7123]

SHAW, M. An Annotated critical bibliography of Tennyson. Hemel Hempstead, Harvester Wheatsheaf; New York, St. Martin's, 1989. xiii,134p. (*Harvester annotated critical bibliographies.*) ISBN: 0710809697, UK; 0312019629, US.

426 items in 3 main sections: biography, bibliography and criticism. Each section further subdivided with entries arranged chronologically within subsections. For 'the keen undergraduate, the postgraduate beginning work on Tennyson, and the teacher' (*Advice to the Reader*). Subject index. Index of authors and editors. Index of poems and plays. Very selective. *Class No:* 820-1TEN

[7124]

WISE, T.J. A Bibliography of the writings of Alfred, Lord Tennyson. Single-vol. reprint. London, Dawsons, 1967. xv+363+vi+209p. illus.

Originally published London, for private circulation, 1908, in 2 vols.

1. Editiones principes (detailed descriptions) - 2. Contributions to periodicals - 3. Pirated issues - 4. Collated editions - 5. Complete volumes of biography and criticism - 6. Alphabetical list of poems, with references to poetry volumes and collected eds. *Class No:* 820-1TEN

Wordsworth

[7125]

BAUER, N.S. William Wordsworth: a reference guide to British criticism, 1793-1899. Boston, Hall; London, Prior, 1978. xii,467p. ISBN: 0816178283, US; 0860431703, UK.

*c.*2,500 items arranged by year with separate sections for books and shorter writings within each year. Does not

....(contd.)

include references in the daily press. Concise annotations. Index of names and titles, with subject headings under 'Wordsworth'. *Class No:* 820-1WOR

[7126]

HANLEY, K. An Annotated critical bibliography of William Wordsworth. London, Prentice-Hall, 1995. xii,329p. £70.95. ISBN: 0133553485.

A very selective bibliography with substantial annotations. 1. Editions and manuscripts (159 entries) - 2. Aids to research (55) - 3. Biographies and memoirs (26) - 4. Criticism (708). Covers 1798-1993. 3 indexes: Wordsworth's works; subjects and persons; authors and editors. *Class No:* 820-1WOR

[7127]

HEALEY, G.H. The Cornell Wordsworth Collection: a catalogue of books and manuscripts presented to the University by Mr. Victor Emmanuel. Ithaca, N.Y., Cornell Univ. Press; London, Oxford Univ. Press, 1957. xiv,458p. illus.

3,206 items in 10 sections: 1-2. Writings of Wordsworth in book form - 3. Writings in early periodicals - 4. Writings in early anthologies - 5. Wordsworthiana - 6. Coleridge - 7. The Lake District - 8. Books of associative interest - 9. Manuscripts - 10. Miscellaneous. Index. The first parts, which give full descriptions, represent the most satisfactory bibliography of the printed works. *Class No:* 820-1WOR

[7128]

JONES, M. *and* **KROEBER, K. Wordsworth scholarship and criticism, 1973-84:** an annotated bibliography, with selected criticism, 1809-1972. New York, Garland, 1985. xvi,316p. ISBN: 0824088409.

The core of the book is Section 5 (p.56-256), which lists, with annotations, critical material appearing 1973-84, *excluding* dissertations, foreign language materials and reprints. Preceded by a useful but 'radically selective' (*Introduction*) guide to standard research materials (texts, concordances, bibliography, biography) and a list of 84 important critical works published 1809-1972. Index of authors, editors and reviewers. Selective topic index.
Class No: 820-1WOR

[7129]

LOGAN, J.V. Wordsworthian criticism: a guide and bibliography. Columbus, Ohio State Univ. Press, 1947 (repr. New York, Gordian Press, 1974). xii,304p. $50. ISBN: 0877521719.

Part 1 (p.3-153) is a survey of Wordsworth criticism in 7 chapters: Part 2 is an annotated bibliography, listing 38 selected editions, 1849-1944, and 622 critical studies, 1850-1944. Detailed index of names and subjects. Index of titles.

Supplemented by: *Wordsworthian criticism, 1945-1964: an annotated bibliography*, by E.F. Henley and D.H. Stam (New York, N.Y. Public Library, 1965. 107p.), with 643 items, and *Wordsworthian criticism, 1964-1973*, by D.H. Stam (New York, 1974. 116p.), with 480 items.
Class No: 820-1WOR

[7130]

PINION, F.B. A Wordsworth chronology. Basingstoke, Macmillan; Boston, Hall, 1988. xx,255p. (*Macmillan author chronologies.*) ISBN: 0333388607, UK; 0816189501, US.

Presents the major events of the writer's life extremely clearly, year by year and month by month. Biographical sketches of persons of importance in Wordsworth's life.

....(contd.)

Bibliography of biographical sources. General index of people, places and topics and index of Wordsworth's works. 4 maps. *Class No:* 820-1WOR

English Ballads

[7131]

CARNELL, P.W. Ballads in the Charles Harding Firth Collection of the University of Sheffield: a descriptive catalogue with indexes. Sheffield, Centre for English Cultural Tradition and Language, Univ. of Sheffield, 1979. xvi,204p. illus. £3. ISBN: 090742600x.

Describes over 700 ballads in 7 vols., with many facsimiles. Indexes of titles, first lines, tunes, and printers. Bibliography of Firth's writings on the ballad. *Class No:* 820-14

[7132]

CARNELL, P.W. Broadside ballads and song-sheets from the Hewins MSS Collection in Sheffield University Library: a descriptive catalogue with indexes and notes. Sheffield, Sheffield Univ. Library and the Centre for English Cultural Tradition and Language, 1987. xvi,118p. illus.

Describes 220 items on 105 loose sheets, with many facsimiles. 9 indexes. Detailed notes (42p.) place the ballads in historical context. Select bibliography (4p.). *Class No:* 820-14

[7133]

Catalogue of the Pepys Library at Magdalene College, Cambridge, vol. II, Ballads. Weinstein, H., *ed.* Woodbridge, Boydell & Brewer, 1992-3. 2pts.

Pt.1 *Catalogue*. 1992. 494p. £130. ISBN: 0859913155.

Pt.2 *Indexes*. 1993. 320p. £120. ISBN: 0859913333.

Provides full bibliographical information on the largest surviving collection of English ballads printed in London in the 17th century, with indexes of first lines, tunes, titles, subjects and authors.

Brewer also publish a 5-vol. facsimile edition of the 4,000 ballads (£495. ISBN: 0859912566). *Class No:* 820-14

[7134]

CHILD, F.J. The English and Scottish popular ballads. Boston, Houghton; London, Stevens, 1882-98 (repr. New York, Dover, 1965). 5v.

The standard collection of ballads. Gives the text of 305 ballads in their different versions, with valuable introduction to each ballad. V.5 includes a glossary, index of published airs, index of titles, titles of collections, and an extensive bibliography (p.455-68).

The abridged, Cambridge ed. of Child, edited by H.C. Sargent and G.L. Kittredge (London, Nutt, 1905. xxxi, 729p.) is intended for the general reader, giving the text of almost all the ballads without the *apparatus criticus*. *Class No:* 820-14

[7135]

COFFIN, T.P. The British traditional ballad in North America. Rev. ed., with a supplement by R. de V. Renwick. Austin, Tex., Univ. of Texas Press, 1977. xvii,297p. $20. ISBN: 0292707193.

1st ed. Philadelphia, American Folklore Soc., 1950.

The aim is 'to offer a key to the published material on the Child ballad in America' (*Introduction*), the core of the book being a critical, bibliographical study of the ballads, arranged by Child number. Also includes general bibliography. Index of ballad titles. *Class No:* 820-14

[7136]

CRAWFORD, J.L.L., *26th Earl of*. Bibliotheca Lindesiana: catalogue of a collection of English ballads of the XVIIth and XVIIIth centuries, printed for the most part in black letter. [Aberdeen, Univ. Press], 1890 (repr. New York, Franklin, 1963). xviii,686p.

1,466 entries, arranged A-Z by first lines; index of titles, tunes, music, burdens and authors; list of printers, publishers and booksellers. An appendix lists first lines and titles of ballads in the Huth and Euing collections (the latter is now in Glasgow Univ. Library). *Class No:* 820-14

[7137]

RICHMOND, W.E. Ballad scholarship: an annotated bibliography. New York, Garland, 1989. xxvii,356p. (*Garland folklore bibliographies.*) ISBN: 0824089324.

See entry at 784.3(01). *Class No:* 820-14

English Sonnets

[7138]

DONOW, H.S. The Sonnet in England and America: a bibliography of criticism. Westport, Conn., Greenwood, 1982. xxii,477p. $59.95. ISBN: 0313213364.

Over 4,000 entries for critical studies published to mid-1981 on the sonnet and sonneteers from 1530 to 1900. General sections followed by sections on the Renaissance, Shakespeare, and periods. Index of poets, critics and subjects. *Class No:* 820-193

English Drama

Databases

[7139]

English drama: the full-text database. Cambridge, Chadwyck-Healey, 1996. World Wide Web resource Subscription details from marketing@chadwyck.co.uk

Part of *Literature online (LION)* (*q.v.*). URL: http://lion.chadwyck.co.uk

Combines the formerly separate *English verse drama* and *English prose drama* databases.

Aims to include all dramas by writers listed in the *New Cambridge bibliography of English literature* who were active before 1900, a corpus of over 4,000 works by 700 authors from the late 13th century onwards. The entire text of each drama is included, along with any accompanying text written by the original author and forming an integral part of the work, *e.g.* epigraphs, footnotes, etc. Bibliographic details, illustrations and errata lists are included from each of the editions used. Can be searched by keyword, play title, speaker, playwright, genre, period, gender, first performance date or publication date. Detailed user manual supplied.

Also available on CD-ROM. *Class No:* 820-2(003.4)

Bibliographies

[7140]

Bibliography of English printed tragedy, 1565-1900. Stratman, C.J., *ed.* Carbondale and Edwardsville, Southern Illinois Univ. Press, 1966. xx,843p.

Lists by author nearly 7,000 editions of 1,483 plays, of which 103 are anonymous and the rest are by 769 dramatists, with library locations and notes on sources, stage history, questions of authorship, etc. List of 285 anthologies. Chronological list of tragedies. Title index. Appendix lists extant manuscripts with locations. *Class No:* 820-2(01)

[7141]

English drama (excluding Shakespeare). Wells, S., *ed.* London, Oxford Univ. Press, 1975. viii,303p. £19.99. (*Select bibliographical guides.*) ISBN: 0198710348.

Bibliographic essays by different scholars, discussing editions, bibliographies, critical studies, etc. A general essay on the study of drama is followed by 16 (average length 17p.) covering periods, groups of dramatists and individuals. Classified list after each chapter gives bibliographical information on all works mentioned. *Class No:* 820-2(01)

[7142]

KAHRL, G.M. *and* **ANDERSON, D. The Garrick Collection of old English plays:** a catalogue with an historical introduction. London, British Library, 1982. xvi,320p. illus. £45. ISBN: 071230004x.

A history of the Garrick Collection (p.1-80), followed by an alphabetical author catalogue of 1,308 entries which include physical description. Title index and general index. *Class No:* 820-2(01)

[7143]

PENNINGER, F.E. English drama to 1660 (excluding Shakespeare): a guide to information sources. Detroit, Gale, 1976. xix,370p. ISBN: 0810312239.

Annotated bibliography of primary and secondary material, with the emphasis on book-length works published in English since 1950. Part 1 lists general works in 12 sections. Part 2 covers 35 individual dramatists. Over 1,700 entries. Index of authors, editors, anonymous titles, and a few selected topics. *Class No:* 820-2(01)

[7144]

Three centuries of English and American plays: a checklist. England: 1500-1800; United States: 1714-1830. Bergquist, G.W., *ed.* New York and London, Hafner, 1963. xii,281p. illus. ISBN: 0028412303.

Lists *c.*5,350 British and 250 American plays in one sequence of authors (main entry) and titles (including anonymous titles), giving the earliest extant edition available and later significant eds. References to the bibliographies by Greg and Woodward and McManaway (*qq.v.*). Title-page facsimiles for 34 plays. *Class No:* 820-2(01)

Middle Ages

[7145]

BERGER, S.E. Medieval English drama: an annotated bibliography of recent criticism. New York, Garland, 1990. xxii,500p. ISBN: 0824057902.

Lists *c.*2,000 items published since or not included in Stratman's *Bibliography of medieval drama* (*q.v.*), including books, articles, dissertations, editions and reviews. 'Although Berger's inclusiveness is impressive ... his organization leaves much to be desired' (*Choice*, v.28(1), Sept. 1990, p.68-9), a simple author listing having been adopted in preference to a classified arrangement. Includes much foreign-language material. Annotations provide nonevaluative summaries. Appendices list Cycle plays (Chester, York, etc.), plays by known authors, and anonymous late plays. Index of play titles, playwrights, characters, places, and topics. *Class No:* 820-2(01)"01/14"

[7146]

HOULE, P.J. The English morality and related drama: a bibliographical survey. Hamden, Conn., Archon, 1972. xviii,195p. ISBN: 0208012648.

For each of the 59 plays (A-Z), gives title, date, author (if known), editions, dramatis personae, no. of lines, plot summary, and brief comments with references to similar plays. Bibliography (8p.). Character index. *Class No:* 820-2(01)"01/14"

16th & 17th Centuries

[7147]

FLEAY, F.G. A Biographical chronicle of the English drama, 1559-1642. London, Reeves & Turner, 1891 (repr. New York, Franklin, 1962). 2v. (387;405p.). ISBN: 0833711512.

Under authors, A-Z. 'Under each name is given a list of the author's extant dramatic works in order of publication, followed by such particulars of his career as have any bearing on dramatic history, omitting information about the man personally which is unconnected with him as a writer' (*Introduction*). Appendices in v.2 list anonymous plays and masques, university plays, and translations. *Class No:* 820-2(01)"15/16"

[7148]

GREG, W.W. A Bibliography of the English printed drama to the Restoration. London, Bibliographical Society, 1939-59. 4v. illus.

V.1. *Stationers' records. Plays, to 1616: nos.1-349.* 1939.

V.2. *Plays, 1617-1689: nos.350-836. Latin plays. Lost plays.* 1951.

V.3. *Collections. Appendix. Reference lists.* 1957.

V.4. *Introduction. Additions. Corrections. Index of titles.* 1959.

Supersedes Greg's *A List of English plays written before 1643 and printed before 1700* (1900) and *A List of masques, pageants, etc.* (1902).

Aims to include all editions down to 1700 of all dramatic compilations written before the end of 1642 or printed before the beginning of 1660. Gives locations in British and American libraries. V.3 includes many useful lists including authors, dedications, companies, theatres, producers, printers, etc. V.4 explains the scope of the work in detail. *Class No:* 820-2(01)"15/16"

[7149]

Recent studies in English Renaissance drama. Logan, T.P. *and* Smith, D.S., *eds.* Lincoln, Nebr., Univ. of Nebraska Press, 1973-78. 4v.

[V.1] *The Predecessors of Shakespeare.* 1973. xiv,348p. ISBN: 0803207751.

[V.2] *The Popular school.* 1975. xiv,299p. ISBN: 0803208448.

[V.3] *The New intellectuals.* 1977. xiv,370p. ISBN: 0803208596.

[V.4] *The Later Jacobean and Caroline dramatists.* 1978. xvi,279p. ISBN: 0803228503.

Covers the period 1580-1642, each vol. having bibliographies by specialists on individual dramatists, listing editions and critical studies. Indexes of persons and plays. *Class No:* 820-2(01)"15/16"

[7150]

SALOMON, B. Critical analyses in English Renaissance drama: a bibliographic guide. 3rd. ed. New York, Garland, 1990. 288p. $38. ISBN: 0824071832.

1st ed. 1979; 2nd ed. 1985.

A selective, annotated list of modern English-language studies of plays by contemporaries of Shakespeare, plus anonymous plays and masques. Index of subjects and play titles. Author index. 936 entries, with key studies asterisked. *Class No:* 820-2(01)"15/16"

16th Century

[7151]

WHITE, D.I. Early English drama, *Everyman* to 1580: a reference guide. Boston, Hall, 1986. xx,289p. $55. ISBN: 0816183384.

Aims to provide 'a selective, though extensive, annotated bibliography of resources for the study of the drama of British playwrights during the period roughly from 1495 to 1580' (*Preface*). Lists 1,727 studies, published 1691-1982, in 4 sections: bibliographies, collections, general studies and studies of specific authors and plays (77 separate headings). Concise annotations. Index includes authors, titles and many subject headings. *Class No:* 820-2(01)"15"

17th & 18th Centuries

[7152]

LINK, F.M. English drama, 1660-1800: a guide to information sources. Detroit, Gale, 1976. xxii,374p. ISBN: 0810312247.

General studies in several sections (*e.g.* bibliography and reference; theatrical biography; dramatic theory, etc.), followed by bibliographical surveys for 155 dramatists, with biographical notes. Indexes of names and plays.
Class No: 820-2(01)"16/17"

17th Century

[7153]

ARMISTEAD, J.M. Four Restoration playwrights: a reference guide to Thomas Shadwell, Aphra Behn, Nathaniel Lee, and Thomas Otway. Boston, Hall, 1984. xxxvii,448p. ISBN: 0816182892.

Separate lists of critical studies of each writer, arranged chronologically from their lifetime to 1980. *c.*400 items on Shadwell, 260 on Behn, 360 on Lee and 500 on Otway, all well annotated, often with quotations. Single-sequence index. *Class No:* 820-2(01)"16"

[7154]

Caroline drama: a bibliographic history of criticism. Fordyce, R., *ed.* 2nd ed. New York, Hall, 1992. xix,332p. $55. ISBN: 0816118353.

1st ed. 1978.

1,602 annotated entries, mainly for critical works published since 1870, in 5 sections: General reference and bibliographies; Textual considerations; Caroline drama; Stage history; Individual studies and comprehensive works. Includes some foreign-language material. 3 indexes: subjects, critics, and plays and early sources.
Class No: 820-2(01)"16"

[7155]

CORBIN, P. *and* SEDGE, D. An Annotated critical bibliography of Jacobean and Caroline comedy (excluding Shakespeare). Hemel Hempstead, Harvester Wheatsheaf, 1988. xii,235p. (*Harvester annotated critical bibliographies.*) ISBN: 0710812760.

Aims to provide 'a selective survey of the most significant critical writing ...'(*Advice to the reader*). Over 700 entries in 13 sections (3 general and 10 on specific dramatists), with annotations varying from one line to one page. Many cross-references. Author index. *Class No:* 820-2(01)"16"

[7156]

LIDMAN, M.J. Studies in Jacobean drama, 1973-1984: an annotated bibliography. New York, Garland, 1986. viii,278p. ISBN: 0824087259.

A continuation of Logan and Smith's work. Lists 182 general studies, followed by bibliographies of Chapman, Dekker, Heywood, Tourneur, Marston, Middleton, Webster, Massinger, Ford, Brome, and Shirley, listing editions and critical studies for each. 877 entries in all. Index of critics. Confined to English-language studies. *Class No:* 820-2(01)"16"

[7157]

TAYLOR, T.J. Restoration drama: an annotated bibliography. Pasadena, Calif., Salem Press, 1989 (repr. Metuchen, N.J., Scarecrow). 156p. $42. (*Magill bibliographies.*) ISBN: 0810828081.

A selective bibliography designed as a starting point for the nonspecialist student. Over 500 items, arranged by dramatist, with annotations of up to 100 words. Subsections for individual plays under major dramatists. *Class No:* 820-2(01)"16"

[7158]

WOODWARD, G.L. *and* McMANAWAY, J.G. A Check list of English plays, 1641-1700. Chicago, Newberry Library, 1945. 155p.

Plays and masques are listed by author, A-Z, with US library locations. *Supplement* by F. Bowers (Charlottesville, Va., Univ. of Virginia, 1949. 22p.). *Class No:* 820-2(01)"16"

18th & 19th Centuries

[7159]

MACMILLAN, D. Catalogue of the Larpent plays in the Huntington Library. San Marino, Calif., [the Library], 1939. xv,442p.

2,399 numbered entries, arranged chronologically, 1737-1832, plus 103 unidentified items. Author and title indexes. John Larpent was the official Examiner, to whom plays designed to be performed on the stage in Great Britain had to be submitted for licence.

Continued by: *Catalogue of additions to the manuscripts: plays submitted to the Lord Chamberlain, 1824-1851* (London, British Museum, 1964. viii,359p.), covering additional mss., nos. 42865-43038. Author and title indexes. *Class No:* 820-2(01)"17/18"

19th Century

[7160]

CONNOLLY, L.W. *and* WEARING, J.P. English drama and theatre, 1800-1900: a guide to information sources. Detroit, Gale, 1978. xix,508p. ISBN: 0810312255.

An annotated bibliography with chapters on contemporary and modern criticism; individual authors; bibliographies and

.... *(contd.)*
reference works; anthologies; plus theatrical subjects such as acting and stage design. 110 playwrights are covered, with primary and secondary material listed. 3,234 entries in total. Index of names and subjects. *Class No:* 820-2(01)"18"

20th Century

[7161]

HARRIS, R.H. Modern drama in America and England, 1950-1970: a guide to information sources. Detroit, Gale, 1982. 606p. ISBN: 0810312182.

List of general bibliographies and selected critical studies, followed by bibliographies of primary and secondary material for 225 dramatists. Index of authors, titles and subjects. *Class No:* 820-2(01)"19"

[7162]

MIKHAIL, E.H. English drama, 1900 to 1950: a guide to information sources. Detroit, Gale, 1977. xiii,328p. ISBN: 0810312166.

2,504 briefly annotated entries. General studies in 4 sections (p.1-212), followed by bibliographies for *c.*80 dramatists, A-Z. Author, title, and subject indexes. *Class No:* 820-2(01)"19"

[7163]

Modern verse drama in English: an annotated bibliography. Wiggins, K.M., *ed.* Westport, Conn., Greenwood, 1994. xxvi,156p. $55. (*Bibliographies and indexes in world literature.*) ISBN: 0313289298.

Lists 547 verse plays (excluding musicals, librettos, operas and works written for children) published 1935-92 by *c.*230 dramatists. Arranged A-Z by author, entries include complete bibliographical and production information and plot summary. Introductory historical survey. List of works consulted (6p.). Title and subject indexes. International in scope. *Class No:* 820-2(01)"19"

Encyclopaedias & Dictionaries

[7164]

The Cambridge companion to English Renaissance drama. Braunmuller, A.R. *and* Hattaway, M., *eds.* Cambridge, Cambridge Univ. Press, 1990. xvi,456p. illus. £37.50. ISBN: 0521346576.

Chapters by 10 British and North American scholars on English drama, 1580-1642. 3 introductory chapters on theatres, dramaturgy, and the social, cultural and political background, are followed by surveys of various theatrical genres, *e.g.* burlesque, political drama, comedy, and tragedy. Chronological table lists plays first performed 1497-1642, with parallel lists of political and theatrical events (28p.). Bibliography of general studies (6p.), followed by very useful bibliographies of *c.*60 dramatists. Indexes of dramatists and play titles. *Class No:* 820-2(03)

[7165]

The Cambridge companion to medieval English theatre. Beadle, R., *ed.* Cambridge, Cambridge Univ. Press, 1994. xxii,372p. illus. £40. ISBN: 0521366704.

Chapters on each of the major regional cycles, the less well-known East Anglian and Cornish traditions, the morality drama and saints' plays; plus illustrated chapters on the performance of medieval plays, in their own time and in recent modern revivals. Reference section includes a guide to scholarship and criticism, extensive classified bibliography (492 items in 22 sections, with author index) and chronological table. *Class No:* 820-2(03)

Chronologies

[7166]

HARBAGE, A. Annals of English drama, 975-1700: an analytical record of all plays, extant or lost, chronologically arranged and indexed by authors, titles, dramatic companies, etc. 3rd ed., rev. by S.S. Wagonheim. London, Routledge, 1989. xix,375p. ISBN: 0415010993.

1st ed. 1940; 2nd ed., rev. by S. Schoenbaum, 1964.

An unannotated listing in tabular form which provides the following information: author, title, date of first performance, type of play (mask, tragedy, etc.), auspices of first production, earliest text, and latest modern edition. Supplementary lists of plays omitted from chronology because of uncertain date and identity. Indexes of English playwrights, English titles, foreign playwrights, foreign titles, and drama companies. List of theatres. List of extant play manuscripts with locations. 3rd ed. has over 1,000 'new entries, clarifications, corrections, and deletions' (*Preface*). *Class No:* 820-2(090)

Histories

[7167]

BEVIS, R.W. English drama: Restoration and eighteenth century, 1660-1789. London, Longman, 1988. £18.99. (*Longman literature in English.*) ISBN: 0582493935.

Includes a useful reference section (p.256-325), comprising chronology, general bibliography, and biobibliographical notes on *c.*70 dramatists, A-Z. Index. *Class No:* 820-2(091)

[7168]

CHOTHIA, J. English drama of the early modern period, 1890-1940 Harlow, Longman, 1996. 352p. £40.50. (*Longman literature in English.*) ISBN: 0582067383.

14 chapters, the first 4 setting the narrative context and considering the social and cultural changes happening in the period, with the remainder comprising closer readings of significant works and topics. Reference section includes general bibliography and bio-bibliographical notes on individual authors. Chronology. Index. *Class No:* 820-2(091)

[7169]

English drama, 1660-1700. Oxford, Clarendon Press, 1996. viii,503p. £65. ISBN: 0198119747.

Provides close critical studies (up to 5 pages on major works) on all surviving plays first written and professionally premiered in England during the period, placing the works in the context of influence, genre, history, religion and philosophy. 12 chapters, alternating comedy and tragedy. Bibliography of non-dramatic texts (13p.). Bibliography of plays: collected editions, individual eds. and anthologies. Index of plays. General index. 'No one planning to write papers or books on Restoration drama will ignore this work' (*Choice*, v.34(5), Jan. 1997, p.795). *Class No:* 820-2(091)

[7170]

INNES, C. Modern British drama, 1890-1990. Cambridge, Cambridge Univ. Press, 1992. xxiii,484p. £45. ISBN: 0521305365.

7 chapters, with subsections on individual dramatists and schools which are headed by checklists of major plays (title and date). Chronology of productions and historical events. Index. No secondary bbibliography. *Class No:* 820-2(091)

[7171]
NICOLL, A. British drama. 6th ed., rev. by J.C. Trewin. London, Harrap, 1978. vii,311p. illus. ISBN: 0245532315.

1st ed. 1925; 5th ed. 1962.

A general survey from the beginnings to the 1970s in 7 chapters with numerous subsections. Bibliography of playlists, general reference books and critical studies arranged by period (8p.). Index. *Class No:* 820-2(091)

[7172]
NICOLL, A. A History of English drama, 1660-1900. Cambridge, Cambridge Univ. Press, 1952-59. 6v.

V.1 *Restoration drama, 1660-1700.* 4th ed. 1952. viii,462p. ISBN: 0521058279.

V.2 *Early eighteenth century drama, 1700-1750.* 3rd ed. 1952. viii,468p. ISBN: 0521058287.

V.3 *Late eighteenth century drama, 1750-1800.* 2nd ed. 1952. vi,424p. ISBN: 0521058295.

V.4 *Early nineteenth century drama, 1800-1850.* 2nd ed. 1955. x,668p. ISBN: 0521058309.

V.5 *Late nineteenth century drama, 1850-1900.* 2nd ed. 1959. vi,901p. ISBN: 0521058317.

V.6 *A Short-title alphabetical catalogue of plays produced or printed in England from 1600 to 1900.* 1959. xii,565p. ISBN: 0521058325.

All volumes contain handlist of plays, plus date and place of first performance. Includes Italian operas and repertoire of French and Italian comedians presented in London in early 18th century.

V.6 is a guide to v.1-5, giving a title index of the plays in text and handlists, indicating authors (where known), date of original production or publication, and listing sub-titles and alternative titles. It adds titles and information not included in the separate handlists. *Class No:* 820-2(091)

[7173]
—NICOLL, A. English drama, 1900-1930: the beginnings of the modern period. Cambridge, Cambridge Univ. Press, 1973. x,1083p. ISBN: 0521084164.

6 chapters (1. The advent of the modern theatre - 2. The theatrical world - 3. The drama: influences, patterns and forms - 4. Popular entertainment: musicals, revues and melodramas - 5. The minority drama - 6. The 'general' drama (Barrie, Shaw, etc.). The 'Hand-list of plays, 1900-1930' occupies over half of the book, p.451-1053, and includes abbreviations for type of play, plus date. Index. *Class No:* 820-2(091)

[7174]
The Revels history of drama in English. Potter, L., *and others, eds.* London, Methuen, 1975-83. 8v. illus.

V.1 *Medieval drama*, by A.C. Cawley and others. 1983. xlviii,348p. ISBN: 0416130208.

V.2 *1500-1576*, by N. Sanders and others. 1980. xxxvii,290p. ISBN: 0416130305.

V.3 *1576-1613*, by J.L. Barroll and others. 1975. xxxiii,526p. ISBN: 0416130402.

V.4 *1613-1640*, by P. Edwards and others. 1981. lvii,337p. ISBN: 041613050x.

V.5 *1660-1750*, by J. Loftis and others. 1976. xxxi,331p. ISBN: 0416130607.

V.6 *1750-1880*, by M.R. Booth and others. 1975. lxii,304p. ISBN: 0416130704.

V.7 *1880 to the present day*, by H. Hunt and others. 1978. xlv,298p. ISBN: 0416130801.

V.8 *American drama*, by T. Bogard and others. 1977. xlix,324p. ISBN: 0416130909.

Each vol. has sections on the social and literary context; theatres and actors; and playwrights and plays; plus detailed

....*(contd.)*
chronological table of plays, theatrical events and historical events. Extensive chapter bibliographies with commentary. Well illustrated throughout. Index in each vol. Reissued as a boxed set by Routledge in 1996 (£495. ISBN: 0415143799). *Class No:* 820-2(091)

Biographies

[7175]
Contemporary British dramatists. Berney, K., *ed.* Detroit & London, St. James Press, 1994. xxi,886p. $60. ISBN: 1558622136.

Profiles 211 of the most influential playwrights since 1945. Entries conform to familiar St. James style: biography; full list of plays (including film, TV and radio productions); bibliography of works in other genres; signed critical essay of up to 1,000 words; and author's comments where available. Also includes articles on some of the most significant postwar plays. Title index. *Class No:* 820-2(092)

[7176]
DEMASTES, W.W. *and* **KELLY, K.E. British playwrights, 1880-1956:** a research and production sourcebook. Westport, Conn., Greenwood, 1996. xii,457p. $95. ISBN: 0313287589.

Lengthy, signed entries (average 12½p.) on 40 dramatists, from William Archer to Oscar Wilde, comprising: biography; list of major plays, premieres and significant revivals, with summary of critical response; list of additional plays, adaptations and productions; assessment of career, with reference to published evaluations in books, periodicals and dissertations; list of locations of unpublished material; select bibliography of published plays plus essays and articles on the theatre; select bibliography of secondary sources; and list of published bibliographies. Select general bibliography (3p.). Indexes of names and titles.

Followed by Demastes' *British playwrights, 1956-1995: a research and production sourcebook* (Greenwood, 1996. xi,502p. $95. ISBN: 0313287597), which treats 35 dramatists (John Arden to Snoo Wilson) in similar fashon. Demastes has edited similar vols. on American and Irish playwrights. *Class No:* 820-2(092)

Behn

[7177]
O'DONNELL, M.A. Aphra Behn: an annotated bibliography of primary and secondary sources. New York, Garland, 1986. xix,557p. ISBN: 0824089065.

First section (p.13-324) lists and fully describes 106 primary items. Second section lists 661 critical studies chronologically, 1666-1985. 8 appendices, including first-line index to poems. Indexes of names and of titles and subjects. *Class No:* 820-2BEH

Congreve

[7178]
BARTLETT, L. William Congreve: a reference guide. Boston, Hall, 1979. xxix,216p. ISBN: 081618142x.

Lists editions and critical studies by year, 1729-1977, then by author, with separate sections for books and shorter works within each year. Over 1,300 annotated entries. Index of authors and titles.

Continued by Bartlett's *William Congreve: an annotated*

.... (contd.)
bibliography, 1978-1994 (Blue Ridge Summit, Pa., Scarecrow, 1996. 120p. $29. ISBN: 081083166x).
Class No: 820-2CON

Farquhar

[7179]
JAMES, E.N. George Farquhar: a reference guide. Boston, Hall, 1986. xxiii, 112p. ISBN: 0816181829.

Annotated secondary bibliography arranged chronologically 1699-1979, then A-Z within each year. Approx. 470 entries, the great majority published post-1880. Includes some German items. Good introductory survey of Farquhar criticism (13p.). Index of authors and titles.
Class No: 820-2FAR

Ford

[7180]
TUCKER, K. A Bibliography of writings by and about John Ford and Cyril Tourneur. Boston, Hall, 1977. xix,134p. ISBN: 0816178348.

Lists 243 of Ford's works, by genre, and 548 secondary items, A-Z by author, with some brief annotations. Author/editor and title index for each dramatist. *Class No:* 820-2FOR

Goethe

[7181]
Goethes Werke auf CD-ROM. Cambridge, Chadwyck-Healey, [1996?]. CD-ROM. £3,950.

Contains the complete text of the 143-vol. Weimar edition, including illustrations. Also includes critical apparatus, notes and variants. Indexes of subjects and names. Interface in German and English. *Class No:* 820-2GOE

Heywood

[7182]
WENTWORTH, M. Thomas Heywood: a reference guide. Boston, Hall, 1986. xxxii, 315p. ISBN: 0816185751.

Nearly 1,250 works about Heywood are listed by year, 1808-1982, then A-Z within each year, with substantial descriptive annotations. Includes reviews of modern stage productions. Index of authors, titles and subjects.
Class No: 820-2HEY

Jonson

[7183]
BROCK, D.H. A Ben Jonson companion. Bloomington, Indiana Univ. Press; Brighton, Harvester, 1983. xii,307p. ISBN: 0253311594, US; 0710804385, UK.

Modelled on Halliday's *A Shakespeare companion* (*qv*), 'its primary purpose is to provide a convenient central reference and criticial resource for important and useful information and criticism on Jonson's life, works, times and critics' (*Preface*). Over 2,000 entries in one A-Z sequence covering works, characters, actors, historical figures, critics, allusions, etc. Selected classified bibliography (9p.). An invaluable handbook. *Class No:* 820-2JON

[7184]
JUDKINS, D.C. The Nondramatic works of Ben Jonson: a reference guide. Boston, Hall, 1982. xiii,260p. ISBN: 0816180369.

Lists over 1,600 secondary works by year, 1615-1978, then by author, with brief annotations. Name index.
Class No: 820-2JON

[7185]
LEHRMAN, W.D., *and others*. The Plays of Ben Jonson: a reference guide. Boston, Hall, 1980. xix,311p. ISBN: 0816181128.

Lists 1,264 secondary works published 1911-75, with concise, nonevaluative annotations, in 4 sections: Book-length studies and essay collections; Editions and studies of specific plays; Special topics (*e.g.* Jonson and Shakespeare); General topics. Appendix 1 lists 233 doctoral dissertations without annotation. Appendix 2 is a bibliography of sources. Author and subject indexes. Many cross-references.
Class No: 820-2JON

Marlowe

[7186]
BRANDT, B.E. Christopher Marlowe in the eighties: an annotated bibliography of Marlowe criticism from 1978 through 1989. West Cornwall, Conn., Locust Hill Press, 1992. 215p. ISBN: 0933951450.

Lists editions; bibliographies; concordances; critical and biographical studies (*c.*500 items); studies of individual plays and poems; and foreign-language criticism. Also includes 3 novels based on Marlowe's life. Includes dissertations but not book and production reviews. Highly specific subject index.

For earlier material, see K. Friedenreich's *Christopher Marlowe: an annotated bibliography of criticism since 1950* (Metuchen, N.J., Scarecrow, 1979. 166p. ISBN: 0810812398) and L.M. Chan's *Marlowe criticism: a bibliography* (Boston, Hall, 1978. xi,226p. ISBN: 0816178356). *Class No:* 820-2MAR

Marston

[7187]
TUCKER, K. John Marston: a reference guide. Boston, Hall, 1985. xxii, 204p. ISBN: 0816183554.

Lists 135 editions of Marston's works, 1633-1961, then approx. 1,100 secondary works, 1598-1981. Brief annotations but plenty of cross-references. Index of authors, editors, titles and subjects. *Class No:* 820-2MAR

Shakespeare

Databases

[7188]
Arden Shakespeare CD-ROM: texts and sources for Shakespeare studies. Bate, J., *consultant ed.* Walton-on-Thames, Nelson, 1998. CD-ROM £1,250. ISBN: 0174434707.

An integrated database which includes all 37 volumes of the acclaimed *Arden Shakespeare*, 2nd series (full texts of plays, introductions, notes, commentary, etc.); facsimile images of First Folio play texts and appropriate Early Quarto texts; select bibliography; Bullough's *Narrative and dramatic sources of Shakespeare* (*q.v.*); Abbott's *Shakespearean grammar*; Partridge's *Shakespeare's bawdy*; and Onions' *A Shakespeare glossary* (*q.v.*). Hypertext links

....(contd.)
enable speedy navigation between play texts, reference sources and secondary materials.

A review in *TLS* (no.4970, July 3, 1998, p.9) highlights a number of serious limitations (*e.g.* the 10 vols. of the *Arden* ed. updated since 1995 are not included; the bibliography does not refer to any work published in the last 20 years; it is difficult to search across different categories at the same time; and it is impossible to search the text and commentary simultaneously) and declares that 'its shortcomings should serve as a warning to editors and publishers preparing electronic books'. Some, but by no means all, of the criticisms are refuted by the publisher in a letter to the following week's issue of *TLS*. *Class No:* 820-2SHA(003.4)

[7189]
Editions and adaptations of Shakespeare (1591-1911). Cambridge, Chadwyck-Healey, 1997. World Wide Web resource Subscription details from marketing@chadwyck.co.uk

Part of *Literature online (LION)* (*q.v.*). URL: http://lion.chadwyck.co.uk

A database containing 11 major editions from the First Folio to the Cambridge edition of 1863-6; 24 separate contemporary printings of individual plays; selected apocrypha and related works; and over 100 adaptations, sequels and burlesques from the 17th century onwards. Searchable by keyword, edition, play/poem title, author, speaker and genre. Also available on CD-ROM at £2,500. *Class No:* 820-2SHA(003.4)

Bibliographies

[7190]
BIRMINGHAM SHAKESPEARE LIBRARY. A Shakespeare bibliography: the catalogue of the Birmingham Shakespeare Library. London, Mansell, 1971. 7v.

Over 100,000 entries, representing a collection of *c.*40,000 vols. Part 1 (vols.1-3) lists pre-1932 accessions from the original guard book catalogue and Part 2 (vols. 4-7) lists post-1932 accessions from the card catalogue. Each part has editions of the works followed by Shakespeariana, A-Z by author. Includes items in periodicals and collections, as well as separate publications. Index of editors, translators, illustrators and series for each part in vols. 3 and 7. *Class No:* 820-2SHA(01)

[7191]
CHAMPION, L.S. The Essential Shakespeare: an annotated bibliography of major modern studies. 2nd ed. Boston, Hall, 1993. 568p. $70. ISBN: 081617332x.

1st ed. 1986.

650 entries for the period 1984-91 have been added for this ed. and over 350 deleted, making a total of 1,807 for 1900-91. Descriptive annotations identify 'the most significant' 20th-century scholarship. General section followed by coverage of individual works, arranged by genre. 104 entries for *Hamlet*. Index of authors and play titles. *Class No:* 820-2SHA(01)

[7192]
EBISCH, W. *and* **SCHÜCKING, L.L. A Shakespeare bibliography.** Oxford, Clarendon Press, 1931. xviii,295p.

Part A, in 14 sections, is a classified, selective bibliography of Shakespearean studies covering Elizabethan literature, Shakespeare's life, personality, texts, sources, literary influence, stage and production of plays, literary taste in Shakespeare's time, civilization in Shakespeare's England and the Shakespeare-Bacon controversy. Part B deals with individual works of Shakespeare. Some brief annotations. Index of authors.

Continued by *Supplement for the years 1930-1935* (Oxford, 1937. vi,104p.). *Class No:* 820-2SHA(01)

[7193]
—SMITH, G.R. A Classified Shakespeare bibliography, 1936-1958. University Park, Pa., Pennsylvania State Univ. Press, 1963. lviii,784p.

Follows Ebisch and Schücking, with over 20,000 unannotated entries in a complicated classification system. Book entries include references to reviews. Detailed table of contents (35p.). *Class No:* 820-2SHA(01)

[7194]
FOLGER SHAKESPEARE LIBRARY, Washington, D.C. **Catalog of the Shakespeare collection.** Boston, Hall, 1972. 2v.

18,100 photolithographed catalogue cards, extracted from the *Catalog of printed books of the Folger Shakespeare Library* (Boston, Hall, 1970. 28v.). V.1 covers editions, translations, and selections and v.2 lists books about Shakespeare. One of the world's largest Shakespeare collections. The Library as a whole covers all aspects of British civilization in the 16th and 17th centuries, with drama and theatre particularly strongly represented.

Also relevant is the *Catalog of manuscripts of the Folger Shakespeare Library* (Boston, Hall, 1971. 3v.), with copies of 47,500 cards. *Class No:* 820-2SHA(01)

[7195]
Garland Shakespeare bibliographies. Godshalk, W.L., *ed.* New York, Garland, 1980-89. v.1-18, 20-23, 26 (in progress).

A series of extensive, annotated bibliographies of post-1940 criticism of individual plays. Thoroughly indexed, but 'of variable quality' according to S. Wells (*Shakespeare: a bibliographical guide*, 1990, p.2). Titles published so far:

V.1 *King Lear*, by L.S. Champion. 1980. 2pts. ISBN: 0824094980.

V.2 *Four plays ascribed to Shakespeare*, by G.H. Metz. 1981. 218p. ISBN: 0824094883.

V.3 *Cymbeline*, by H.E. Jacobs. 1982. 640p. ISBN: 0824092589.

V.4 *Henry V*, by J. Candido and C.R. Forker. 1980. ISBN: 0824093232.

V.5 *King Henry VI*, by J. Hinchcliffe. 1983. ISBN: 0824091159.

V.6 *Love's labor's lost*, by N.L. Harvey and A.K. Carey. 1982. 234p. ISBN: 0824092317.

V.7 *Hamlet in the 1950s*, by R.F. Robinson. 1982. 400p. ISBN: 0824091191.

V.8 *As you like it*, by J.L. Halio and B.C. Millard. 1983. 754p. ISBN: 0824090713.

V.9 *The Merchant of Venice*, by T. Wheeler. 1983. 408p. ISBN: 0824091140.

V.10 *Timon of Athens*, by J.J. Ruszkiewicz. 1982. 304p. ISBN: 0824091957.

V.11 *Richard III*, by J.A. Moore. 1983. 867p. ISBN: 0824091124.

V.12 *A Midsummer night's dream*, by D.A. Carroll and G.J. Williams. 1986. 680p. ISBN: 082409073x.

V.13 *Pericles*, by N. Michael. 1987. 320p. $29. ISBN: 0824091132.

V.14 *Richard II*, by J.A. Roberts. 1988. 2pts. ISBN: 0824085884.

V.15 *Henry VIII*, by L.M. Micheli. 1984. 476p. ISBN:

....(*contd.*)
0824088360.

V.16 *Two gentlemen of Verona*, by D. Pearson. 1988. 265p. ISBN: 0824056418.

V.17 *Coriolanus*, by A. Leggatt and L. Norem. 1989. 778p. ISBN: 0824089847.

V.18 *Hamlet in the 1960s*, by J.Dietrich. 1991. 773p. $112. ISBN: 0824089901.

V.20 *Othello*, by M.L. Mikesell and V.M. Vaughan. 1989. 979p. $120. ISBN: 0824027493.

V.21 *The Taming of the shrew*, by N.L. Harvey. 1994. 328p. $52. ISBN: 0824088921.

V.22 *Macbeth*, by T. Wheeler. 1989. 1030p. ISBN: 082408893x.

V.23 *King John*, by D.T. Curren-Aquino. 1993. 936p. $130. ISBN: 082406626x.

V.26 *Henry IV, Parts 1 & 2*, by C. Gira and A. Seeff. 1994. 616p. $96. ISBN: 0824070976. *Class No:* 820-2SHA(01)

[7196]

Shakespeare: a bibliographical guide. Wells, S., *ed.* 2nd ed. Oxford, Clarendon Press, 1990. x,431p. £50. ISBN: 0198710364.

1st ed. 1973.

'The aim is to provide a selectively critical guide to the best in Shakespeare scholarship and criticism' (*Introduction*). Comprises 19 bibliographic essays (9 of them entirely new, the rest revised) by distinguished scholars who 'have been encouraged to recommend the good rather than castigate the bad'. Ch.1, 'The Study of Shakespeare' by Wells, is a guide to general reference books, bibliographies, concordances, periodicals, etc., while the remaining chapters cover individual works, groups of works or particular aspects of Shakespearean studies. Each chapter is followed by a full bibliography of recommended works, but there is no index. *Class No:* 820-2SHA(01)

[7197]

Shakespeare index: an annotated bibliography of critical articles on the plays, 1959-1983. Sajdak, B.T., *ed.* München, Saur, 1992. 2v. (xxii,1765p.) DM.548. ISBN: 3598075820.

Gives full citations, plus summaries, for over 7,100 English-language articles in periodicals and other serial publications. Classified arrangement, with 48 chapters in 4 main groups: general studies; studies by period; studies by genre; studies of individual plays. Indexes of authors, characters, scenes and subjects. *Class No:* 820-2SHA(01)

[7198]

Shakespeare quarterly. Washington, Folger Shakespeare Library (previously New York, Shakespeare Assoc. Library), 1950-. 5py. ISSN: 00373222.

Carries an extensive 'World Shakespeare bibliography' in a special issue each year. The bibliography for 1994 appears as v.46(5), 1995, and has 4,752 entries in a classified sequence covering all aspects of Shakespeare scholarship and production. Includes references to book and theatre reviews. Indexes of authors, editors, etc.; actors, actresses, directors, etc.; dramatists, poets, musicians, etc.; and subjects. Over 70 contributors worldwide. *Class No:* 820-2SHA(01)

[7199]

—Shakespeare Jahrbuch. Berlin, Reimer, 1865-. v.1-. Annual. ISSN: 09455094.

Carried an annual bibliography from its inception until 1992. From 1965 to 1992, separate versions were published in East and West Germany under the titles *Shakespeare Jahrbuch* (Weimar, Böhlaus Nachfolger) and *Deutsche Shakespeare-Gesellschaft West Jahrbuch* (Bochum, Kamp). They were reunited in 1994 under the original title and the publisher now is Kamp. The West German yearbooks did not carry a bibliography but included lists of German Shakespeare productions, with references to reviews, and these are a feature of the current *Jahrbuch*. *Class No:* 820-2SHA(01)

[7200]

Shakespeare survey: an annual survey of Shakespearian study and production, v.1-. Cambridge, Cambridge Univ. Press, 1948-. Annual.

Each vol. carries scholarly articles on a particular theme, but, more significantly from a bibliographical point of view, there is a critical review of the year's contributions to Shakespeare studies. That in v.50 (1997. xi,300p. ISBN: 052159135x) occupies 54p. and has 3 sections on critical studies; Shakespeare's life, times, and stage; and editions and textual studies, each by a different specialist.
Class No: 820-2SHA(01)

[7201]

THOMPSON, A., *and others*. Which Shakespeare? - a guide to editions. Milton Keynes, Open Univ. Press, 1992. vi,197p. £75. ISBN: 0335090354.

A survey of eds. of the complete works, multi-vol. series, individual plays, and poems and sonnets, with breakdown of contents, critical assessment and consideration of suitability for different users. 'An admirable, definitive but very expensive work' (*English Today*, no.34, April 1993, p.60).
Class No: 820-2SHA(01)

[7202]

WOODBRIDGE, L. Shakespeare: a selective bibliography of modern criticism. West Cornwall, Conn., Locust Hill, 1988. xiv,266p. $20. ISBN: 0933951140.

2,460 unannotated citations in 10 main sections, with studies of individual plays and poems listed in the final section. Covers studies published 1900-1985, with major emphasis on recent publications. Name index. Small format and tiny print let down an otherwise useful compilation.

J. Rosenblum's *Shakespeare: an annotated bibliography* (Pasadena, Calif., Salem Press, 1992. 307p. $40. ISBN: 0893566764) is another selective, classified guide which concentrates on 20th-century criticism, including studies of individual plays. Author index. *Class No:* 820-2SHA(01)

[7203]

The World Shakespeare bibliography on CD-ROM: 1987-1994. Harner, J.L., *ed.* Cambridge, Cambridge Univ. Press, 1997. CD-ROM. £250. ISBN: 0521588863.

The second release of a major new resource for Shakespeare scholars, with over 24,000 annotated entries for material in 75 languages, based on the annual bibliographies in *Shakespeare Quarterly* (*q.v.*). Purchasers may be purchase this disk as a one-off or register for annual updates. The first release (1996) covered 1990-93 and the plan is to go 1 year forward and 3 years back annually, reaching 1900 eventually. 'It is a reference work for the very dedicated researcher' (*Multimedia Bookseller*, May, 1996, p.25).
Class No: 820-2SHA(01)

Encyclopaedias & Dictionaries

[7204]

BOYCE, C. Shakespeare A to Z: the essential reference to his plays, his poems, his life and times. New York, Facts on File, 1990. ix,742p. illus. $55. ISBN: 0816018057.

Over 2,000 entries covering plays, poems, fictional characters, Shakespeare's contemporaries and relatives, places, actors, directors, scholars, dramatic terms, etc. Play entries comprise synopsis, commentary, notes on sources and texts, and theatrical history. Select bibliography (4p.). Classified lists of entries. Deliberately avoids a scholarly approach, aiming towards 'the information and entertainment' of the student and general reader (*Preface*).
Class No: 820-2SHA(03)

[7205]

HALLIDAY, F.E. A Shakespeare companion, 1564-1964. 2nd ed. London, Duckworth; New York, Schocken, 1964. 569p. illus.

1st ed. 1952, as *A Shakespeare companion, 1550-1950.*

'A handbook not only to Shakespeare's life and works, to his friends and acquaintances, to his poems and plays, and their characters, but also to the Elizabethan-Jacobean theatre, the other dramatists who wrote for it, their most important plays, and the companies that performed them, and to the history up to the present day of Shakespeare's work, both on the stage and in the study, to his printers and publishers, players and producers, editors and adaptors, scholars and critics' (*Preface*). A mine of information in very compact form. Over 2,500 entries, alphabetically arranged. Classified bibliography (22p.). *Class No:* 820-2SHA(03)

[7206]

McLEISH, K. Shakespeare's characters: a Players Press guide. Studio City, Calif., Players Press, 1992. 252p. $39.95. ISBN: 0887346081.

A revision of *Longman guide to Shakespeare's characters: a who's who of Shakespeare* (Harlow, Longman, 1985).

Lists almost all the characters, A-Z, with descriptions and characterizations informally written and supported in some places by quotations. Also provides plot summaries of the plays. Cross-references to name variations, but no index.
Class No: 820-2SHA(03)

[7207]

Shakespeare: an illustrated dictionary. Wells, S., *ed.* Rev. ed. Oxford, Oxford Univ. Press, 1985. 224p. illus. ISBN: 0198710755.

1st ed. London, Kaye & Ward, 1978.

A concise dictionary with *c.*800 entries on Shakespeare's life, influences and works, and on associated theatres, companies, actors, critics, composers, etc. Many cross-references. Selective list of characters. Further reading (2p.). Numerous illustrations. New ed. due late 1998 (£7.99. ISBN: 0192800647). *Class No:* 820-2SHA(03)

[7208]

Shakespeare around the globe: a guide to notable postwar revivals. Leiter, S., *ed.* New York and London, Greenwood, 1986. xiii,972p. $155. ISBN: 0313237565.

Signed essays by over 70 contributors on 502 productions worldwide. Arranged under play titles, A-Z (all 38 plays covered), the essays include (as appropriate) details of director, designer, composer, translator, company, theatre, city and date; numbers of performances; abbreviated cast list; and a 500-word commentary, often citing critical reviews and other sources. A source list follows the group of essays on each play.

....(contd.)

Appendices include list of additional revivals (27p.) and geographical breakdown of productions (26 countries). Bibliography of selected books (4p.). Indexes of artists (*i.e.* actors, directors, composers, etc.), critics, and companies.
Class No: 820-2SHA(03)

[7209]

A Shakespeare encyclopaedia. Campbell, O.J. *and* Quinn, E.G., *eds.* London, Methuen; New York, Crowell, 1966. xviii,1014p. illus. ISBN: 0416951805.

US title is *The Reader's encyclopedia of Shakespeare.*

Over 2,700 entries arranged in a single A-Z sequence but falling into 7 main categories: Shakespeare the man; Shakespeare's works; Elizabethan life; Characters in the plays; Production; Scholarship and criticism; Documents. Longer articles are signed by one of the 66 contributors. Those on individual plays run to several pages and include notes on text, date and sources; plot synopsis; commentary; stage history; bibliography; and excerpts from selected criticism arranged chronologically. Appendices include chronology of events, 1552-1623 (8p.) and selected bibliography of criticism and works (32p.). Invaluable.
Class No: 820-2SHA(03)

[7210]

William Shakespeare: his world, his work, his influence. Andrews, J.F., *ed.* New York, Scribner, 1985. 3v. (xvii,954p.). illus. £190.95. ISBN: 0684178516.

60 essays (average 16p.), the 3 vols. covering respectively Shakespeare's world (the historical and cultural context), work (the life and works), and influence. Select bibliography follows each essay. Contributors include a wide range of writers, from academics (Stanley Wells) to authors (Anthony Burgess) and actors (John Gielgud). Index in v.3.
Class No: 820-2SHA(03)

Handbooks & Manuals

[7211]

BERGERON, D.M. *and* **DE SOUSA, G.U. Shakespeare: a study and research guide.** 3rd ed. Lawrence, Kan., Univ. Press of Kansas, 1995. 235p. £23.95. ISBN: 0700606920.

1st ed. 1975; 2nd ed. 1987.

First 2 chapters provide annotated citations to major critical studies and interpretation under various headings. 100 new books are covered in this ed. and there are new sections on cultural study, film and TV, and intellectual and political history. Third chapter provides advice on writing a paper and includes a model example. Very useful for the new student, but lacks subject index. *Class No:* 820-2SHA(035)

[7212]

The Cambridge companion to Shakespeare studies. Wells, S., *ed.* Cambridge, Cambridge Univ. Press, 1986. xi,329p. illus. £40. ISBN: 0521267374.

A successor to *Companion to Shakespeare studies* (1934) and *New companion to Shakespeare studies* (1971).

17 chapters by distinguished specialists on various aspects of Shakespeare scholarship, each with a reading list appended. Particularly valuable is ch. 17, 'Shakespeare reference books' by D. Mehl (p.303-315), in which key works are described and evaluated under 13 headings.
Class No: 820-2SHA(035)

[7213]
Narrative and dramatic sources of Shakespeare. Bullough, G., *ed.* London, Routledge & Kegan Paul, 1957-75 (repr 1996). 8v. illus. £599. ISBN: 0415143780.

Each vol. deals with a group of plays (*e.g.* v.5, *The Roman plays*), bringing together the major sources probably used by Shakespeare for plots and characters, plus similar works which he may have consulted. Foreign and Latin pieces are given in English translation, and whole works are reproduced whenever possible. Each vol. has a bibliography and an index to the introductory essays on each play.
Class No: 820-2SHA(035)

[7214]
Shakespeare for students. Scott, M., *ed.* Detroit, Gale, 1992-6. 2v. illus. £50 per vol. ISBN: 0810382474, v.1; 0787601578, v.2.

A very accessible guide for students to the 16 plays most often included in US high school and undergraduate courses. 50-75p. on each play (8 covered in each vol.), including introductory essay; plot summary; profiles of main characters; excerpts from critical studies on a range of topics and themes; selected bibliography of further studies; list of media adaptations. Illustrated with engravings, paintings and photographs. Shakespeare chronology and index of topics and characters in each vol. Glossary of terms in v.2.
Class No: 820-2SHA(035)

[7215]
WELLS, S. *and* **TAYLOR, G. William Shakespeare: a textual companion.** Oxford, Clarendon Press, 1987. x,671p. ISBN: 0198129149.

Written in conjunction with editorial work on the text of the *Complete Oxford Shakespeare* (published in modern- and original-spelling editions in 1986), the *Textual companion* has a chapter on each play, comprising: introductory essay; a series of textual notes, recording substantive departures from the control-text, press-variants in the early editions, discussions of emendations and of problems of modernization, and plausible alternative readings; a list of non-substantive changes made in the original-spelling texts (correction of misprints, etc.); a list of changes made to the lineation of the control-text; a letter-by-letter reprint of the stage directions of the control-text; and other material as appropriate. The definitive reference work on Shakespearean textual problems. *Class No:* 820-2SHA(035)

Glossaries

[7216]
ONIONS, C.T. A Shakespeare glossary. [3rd ed.] enl. and rev. throughout by R.D. Eagleson. Oxford, Clarendon Press, 1986. xvii,326p. £10.99. ISBN: 0198125216.

1st ed. 1911; 2nd ed. 1919 (Repr. with enl. addenda, 1963).

Onions was on the editorial staff of the *Oxford English dictionary* for 15 years and compiled the original *Glossary* with the aim of 'supplying definitions and illustrations of words or senses of words which are now obsolete or which survive only in archaic or provincial use, together with explanations of others involving allusions not generally familiar, and of proper names carrying with them some connotative signification or offering special interest or difficulty' (*Original preface*). Eagleson has revised the whole in the light of recent scholarship and improved the arrangement in several ways, with at least one citation from the Riverside edition (1974) now accompanying every definition. Approx. 10,000 entries. Bibliography (5p.). 'The

.... *(contd.)*
general scrupulousness of the book ... will safeguard our knowledge of the language of this period for years to come' (*Review of English Studies,* v.39(154), May 1988, p.291-2).
Class No: 820-2SHA(038.1)

[7217]
SCHMIDT, A. Shakespeare-lexicon: a complete dictionary of all the English words, phrases and constructions in the works of the poet. 6th ed. Berlin, De Gruyter, 1971. 2v. $193. ISBN: 3110022036.

1st ed. 1874-75.

Comparable to Onions' *Shakespeare glossary*, but much more extensive, covering the whole of Shakespeare's vocabulary. Provides definitions and references to the Globe edition. Appendices include a list of words and phrases from foreign languages. *Class No:* 820-2SHA(038.1)

[7218]
SHEWMAKER, E. Shakespeare's language: a glossary of unfamiliar words in his plays and poems. New York, Facts on File, 1996. 528p. $50. ISBN: 0816032769.

Defines over 15,000 terms, with a quote to set each in context. Includes geographical references, historical figures and foreign-language expressions. *Class No:* 820-2SHA(038.1)

[7219]
SPEVACK, M. A Shakespeare thesaurus. Hildesheim, Olms, 1993. xxvi,541p. DM98. ISBN: 3487097753.

A specialized work which attempts 'to describe the Shakespearean idiolect' by grouping the dramatist's words in 37 main categories (*e.g.* 'Animals') and 897 sub-categories (*e.g.* 'Dog'). Includes names of places and persons. Index. 'This thesaurus has tremendous potential, but it does need more analysis and some regrouping (*The Year in Reference, 1994*, p.160-2). *Class No:* 820-2SHA(038.1)

Quotations

[7220]
DE LOACH, C. The Quotable Shakespeare: a topical dictionary. Jefferson, N.C., McFarland, 1988. 544p. $43.50. ISBN: 0899503039.

6,516 quotations, based on the Riverside edition (Boston, Houghton Mifflin, 1974) are listed under *c.*1,200 subject headings, A-Z, with exact references to act, scene and line. The emphasis is less on plot, scene description, and characterization than on quotations that 'contain not only a philosophical axiom, a general truth or a fundamental principle' and which are 'immediately clear in meaning and capable of inspiring or delighting the reader'. Indexes of poem and play titles, characters, and topics (the latter with many cross-references), all keyed to entry numbers.
Class No: 820-2SHA(082.2)

[7221]
—MINER, M. *and* RAWSON, H. A Dictionary of quotations from Shakespeare: a topical guide to over 3,000 great passages from the plays, sonnets, and narrative poems. New York, Dutton, 1992; London, Penguin, 1995. xiv,368p. £6.99. ISBN: 0525934510, US; 0140513620, UK.

UK title is *The Penguin dictionary of quotations from Shakespeare*.

Based on the Signet Classic editions and arranged under 400 subject headings, with cross-references and keyword index. Has fewer entries than DeLoach, but provides more contextual information and is excellent value.
Class No: 820-2SHA(082.2)

[7222]

LAMB, G.F. Chambers Shakespeare quotations. Edinburgh, Chambers, 1992. ix,352p. £6.99. ISBN: 0550210261.

A thematic dictionary which lists 2,160 quotes (usually no more than 4 lines) under 197 subject headings. Citations give act and line number, speaker and, in some cases, the person addressed. Brief information on all characters mentioned is given in a separate dictionary sequence. List of 50 quotations written about Shakespeare and the stage, 1592-1992. Title index of works, with references to headings under which quotations occur. *Class No:* 820-2SHA(082.2)

[7223]

STEVENSON, B.E. Stevenson's book of Shakespeare quotations: being also a concordance and glossary of the unique words and phrases in the plays and poems. New York, Scribner; London, Cassell, 1938. xl, 2055p.

US title is *Home book of Shakespeare quotations*.

Based on the revised Globe edition (1911), with *c.*90,000 quotations arranged by subject, A-Z, and under each heading by poem/play title. The index and concordance (300p.) are unusually complete and refer to every occurrence of a word in the subject classification, with particular attention paid to words that occur only once. *Class No:* 820-2SHA(082.2)

Excerpts

[7224]

Shakespearean criticism: excerpts from the criticism of William Shakespeare's plays and poetry, from the first published appraisals to current evaluation. Detroit, Gale, 1984-. v.1- (in progress). illus. £112 per vol. ISSN: 08839123.

Vols. 1-10 each contain excerpts from critical studies, chronologically arranged, of 3-6 plays, in the familiar Gale format as used in *Contemporary literary criticism*, etc. Beginning with v.11, the series traced the history of the plays on stage and film. Since v.27, the approach has been thematic (*e.g.* v.39 covers 'Desire'), with the focus on post-1960 criticism. Annotated bibliographies. Cumulative indexes of artists and topics.

38 vols. published by the end of 1997. *Class No:* 820-2SHA(082.200)

Musical Adaptations

[7225]

A Shakespeare music catalogue. Gooch, B.N.S., *and others, eds.* Oxford, Clarendon Press, 1991. 5v. (xcv,2847p.).

V.1 *All's well that ends well - Love's labours lost.* £75. ISBN: 0198129416.

V.2 *Macbeth - The Taming of the shrew.* £75. ISBN: 0198129424.

V.3 *The Tempest - The Two noble kinsmen.* £68. ISBN: 0198129432.

V.4 *Indices.* £50. ISBN: 0198129440.

V.5 *Bibliography.* £45. ISBN: 0198129459.

Documents 20,000 pieces of music of all kinds, from songs to full operas, based on Shakespeare's dramatic works. Arranged by play in vols. 1-3, with 4 indexes in v.4: by first line and title; by musical title; by composer, arranger or editor; and by librettist or other writer. V.5 is a selected bibliography, separately indexed, with 2 preliminary sections on theatre music and song, the most comprehensive so far compiled, before the main sections on composers of Shakespeare music, which include much historical information which complements the entries in vols. 1-3.

....(contd.)

Acclaimed by reviewers: 'Undoubtedly one of the most important Shakespearean reference works published in our time' (*TLS*, no.4613, Aug. 30, 1991, p.14-5); 'Of its kind without peer ... Musical historians of every period and nation now have to hand an unrivalled source of up-to-date, detailed, concise information' (*Modern Language Review*, v.89(4), 1994, p.974-6). *Class No:* 820-2SHA(082.201)

Concordances

[7226]

BARTLETT, J. A Complete concordance to Shakespeare. Reprint of 1894 ed. London, Macmillan, 1990. 1918p. £175. ISBN: 0333042751.

Originally published 1894, as *A New and complete concordance or verbal index to words, phrases & passages in the dramatic works of Shakespeare with a supplementary concordance to the poems.*

Prepared from the 1875 Globe edition but revised and collated with the 1891 ed., for which it gives exact references to act, scene and line. Index words do not include articles but select examples of the verbs 'to do', 'to be', 'to have', etc. are included, as are many prepositions, pronouns, conjunctions, etc. *Class No:* 820-2SHA(083.87)

[7227]

SPEVACK, M. A Complete and systematic concordance to the works of Shakespeare. Hildesheim, 1968-80. 9v. DM.2,280. ISBN: 3487018179.

V.1 *Drama and character concordances to the folio comedies.*

V.2 *Drama and character concordances to the folio histories. Concordances to the non-dramatic works.*

V.3 *Drama and character concordances to the folio tragedies and 'Pericles', 'The Two noble kinsmen', 'Sir Thomas More'.*

V.4-6 *A Concordance to the complete works, A-Z; Appendices.*

V.7 *Concordances to stage directions and speech-prefixes.*

V.8 *Concordances to the 'bad' quartos and 'The Taming of a shrew' and 'The Troublesome reign of King John'.*

V.9 *Substantive variants.*

Aims 'to present, for the first time, a complete and accurate computer-generated concordance to all of Shakespeare' (*Preface*). Based on the Riverside edition, edited by G. Blakemore Evans (Boston, Houghton Mifflin, 1974), and indexes every word — nearly 885,000 in all. Appendices include a word-frequency index. *Class No:* 820-2SHA(083.87)

[7228]

—SPEVACK, M. The Harvard concordance to Shakespeare. Hildeshein, Olms; Cambridge, Mass., Harvard Univ. Press, 1973. ix,1600p. DM248. ISBN: 0674374754.

An abbreviated and slightly revised version of vols. 4-6 of Spevack's 9-vol. work. The most comprehensive single-vol. concordance, omitting only 43 of the most frequently used words. *Class No:* 820-2SHA(083.87)

Films

[7229]

ROTHWELL, K.S. *and* **MELZER, A.H. Shakespeare on screen:** an international filmography and videography. New York, Neal-Schuman, 1990; London, Mansell, 1991. 406p. £85. ISBN: 1555700497, US; 072012106x, UK.

Lists over 750 films and videos under play titles, A-Z, productions being arranged chronologically under each title

.... *(contd.)*
with country and year of release. Annotations include critical evaluation, references to reviews, and details of length, cast, production staff, etc. Annotated bibliography. Indexes of plays; series and genres; production dates; and names of actors, production staff, critics, etc. *Class No:* 820-2SHA(084.122)

Audio-Visual Materials

[7230]
As you like it: audiovisual Shakespeare. Grant, C., *ed.* Rev. ed. London, British Universities Film & Video Council, 1992. 124p. illus. £13.95. ISBN: 0901299634.

1st ed. as *Shakespeare: a list of audiovisual materials available in the UK.*

Lists 550 items available for hire or sale in the UK from 100 different distributors, including videos, films, slide sets, audiocassettes, computer programs and videodiscs. Fully annotated entries are arranged by play and include full-length performances, extracts and critical studies. There are also sections on acting and directing, social and cultural background, and theatre history. *Class No:* 820-2SHA(086)

Shaw

[7231]
LAURENCE, D.H. Bernard Shaw: a bibliography. Oxford, Clarendon Press, 1983. 2v. (xxiii,1058p.). (*Soho bibliographies.*) ISBN: 0198181795.

Extraordinarily comprehensive catalogue of Shaw's works. V.1 has 4 descriptive sections: Books and ephemeral publications; Rough proofs/Rehearsal copies; Contributions to books; Works edited by Shaw. V.2 has 9 sections: Contributions to periodicals and newspapers; Stereotyped postcards; Blurbs; Broadcasts; Recordings; Wraiths and strays; Manuscripts; Works on Shaw (357 items); Misattribution. Thorough index.

For secondary material, see J.P. Wearing's *G.B. Shaw: an annotated bibliography of writings about him, vol.1.* (De Kalb, Ill., Northern Illinois Univ. Press, 1986. xxi,562p. $55. ISBN: 0875801250), which has 3,676 entries. *Shaw: the annual of Bernard Shaw studies* (formerly *Shaw review.* Univ. Park, Pa., Pennsylvania State Univ. Press, 1951-. ISSN: 07415842) includes annual checklists. *Class No:* 820-2SHA

[7232]
WEINTRAUB, S. Bernard Shaw: a guide to research. Univ. Park, Pa., Pennsylvania State Univ. Press, 1992. 154p. $35. ISBN: 0271008318.

12 bibliographic essays surveying the key sources, including manuscripts, bibliographies, editions, biographies, general criticism, studies of specific works, and foreign-language criticism. Citations give author, title and date only. Indexes of authors, subjects and Shaw's works.

For Shaw quotations, see B.F. Dukore's *Not bloody likely, and other quotations from Bernard Shaw* (New York, Columbia Univ. Press, 1998. 224p. $19.95. ISBN: 0231104782). *Class No:* 820-2SHA

Sheridan

[7233]
DURANT, J.D. Richard Brinsley Sheridan: a reference guide. Boston, Hall, 1981. 312p. ISBN: 0816181462.

Annotated list of critical studies, 1816-1979, including reviews of stage productions. Index. *Class No:* 820-2SHE

Tourneur

[7234]
TUCKER, K. A Bibliography of writings by and about John Ford and Cyril Tourneur. Boston, Hall, 1977. xix,134p. ISBN: 0816178348.

Lists 75 of Tourneur's works, by genre, and 418 secondary items, A-Z by author, with some brief annotations. Author/editor and title index for each dramatist. *Class No:* 820-2TOU

Webster

[7235]
SCHUMAN, S. John Webster: a reference guide. Boston, Hall, 1985. xx, 280p. ISBN: 081618433x.

Lists chronologically approx. 1,700 works about Webster, 1602-1981, with annotations. A-Z arrangement within each year. Includes dissertations and some foreign-language items. Index of authors, titles and subjects. *Class No:* 820-2WEB

Wycherley

[7236]
McCARTHY, B.E. William Wycherley: a reference guide. Boston, Hall, 1985. xxxvi,195p. ISBN: 0816181845.

'The purpose ... is to list all editions of the works of William Wycherley from his first publication in 1669 to the present, and to list and annotate all works (and significant reprints) about him in books, articles, dissertations, and twentieth-century theater reviews' (*Preface*). Approx. 1,100 entries arranged by year, then A-Z within each year. Annotations are descriptive with some evaluation in the lengthy Introduction. Index of titles, authors and editors. *Class No:* 820-2WYC

Women

[7237]
DAVIS, G. *and* **JOYCE, B. Drama by women to 1900:** a bibliography of American and British writers. London, Mansell; Toronto, Univ. of Toronto Press, 1992. xxvi,189p. £75. (*Bibliographies of writings by American and British women to 1900.*) ISBN: 0720121027, UK; 0802027970, Canada.

A comprehensive listing based on major library catalogues (*BL, NUC*) and the OCLC database, plus drama dictionaries and bibliographies. Arranged A-Z, the 2,828 entries include author, life dates, play title and citation, including dates of publication or performance, and (in some cases) a brief descriptive statement. Appended lists of dramatists by chronological period and of actresses. Subject index and index of adaptations and translations. 'The camera-ready, two-column format is difficult to read and unattractive' (*Choice*, v.30(3), Nov. 1992, p.440). *Class No:* 820-2-0055.2

[7238]
Women playwrights in England, Ireland and Scotland, 1660-1823. Mann, D.D., *& others, eds.* Bloomington, Ind., Indiana Univ. Press, 1996. xiii,417p. £58.50. ISBN: 0253330874.

One A-Z sequence with entries for plays and playwrights. For the latter, entries comprise: biography; composition and publication history of plays; other literary works; main themes of plays; theatrical genres in which the writer excelled; select bibliography of primary and secondary material. Entries for works give: production history; plot

....(*contd.*)
synopsis; evaluation; comments on translations/adaptations if from foreign sources; and references to manuscripts, texts and modern eds. Appended checklist of playwrights and plays and chronological list of plays. Bibliography (5p.).
Class No: 820-2-0055.2

English Prose

Bibliographies

[7239]
HENINGER, S.K. English prose, prose fiction and criticism to 1660: a guide to information sources. Detroit, Gale, 1975. x,255p. ISBN: 0810312336.

Covers all types of prose written in English up to 1660, including religious, historical and scientific writings and translations of the Bible, arranged in 12 sections. 764 primary works are listed, with details of the best available modern editions, plus numerous bibliographies and works of criticism. Brief annotations. Author index, but no title or subject index. *Class No:* 820-3(01)

19th Century

[7240]
WILSON, H.W. *and* **HOEVELER, D.L. English prose and criticism in the nineteenth century:** a guide to information sources. Detroit, Gale, 1979. xx,437p. ISBN: 0810312352.

In 4 sections. 1. Basic surveys and reference works, including bibliographies, literary histories, anthologies; 2. Literary and cultural background; 3. Individual author bibliographies (34). 4. Guides and studies of 19th-century periodicals. Includes writers from a wide range of fields, including history (Macaulay), religion (Newman), science (Darwin) and travel (Burton). Author, title, and subject indexes. *Class No:* 820-3(01)"18"

Victorian Age

[7241]
Victorian prose: a guide to research. Delaura, D.J., *ed.* New York, Modern Language Assoc. of America, 1973. xvi,560p. $34.95. ISBN: 0873522508.

A collection of 12 bibliographical essays, complementary to L. Stevenson's *Victorian fiction* and F.E. Faverty's *Victorian poets.* 1. General materials - 2. Macaulay - 3. The Carlyles - 4. Newman - 5. Mill - 6. Ruskin - 7. Arnold - 8. Pater - 9. The Oxford Movement - 10. The Victorian churches - 11. The Critics - 12. The Unbelievers. Essays on individual authors have subsections covering bibliography, editions, biography, correspondence, criticism, etc. 13 contributors. Index of names. *Class No:* 820-3(01)"1837-1901"

20th Century

[7242]
BROWN, C.C. *and* **THESING, W.B. English prose and criticism, 1900-1950:** a guide to information sources. Detroit, Gale, 1983. xxi,553p. ISBN: 0810312360.

In 2 parts: 1. Generic and period studies, covering bibliographies, literary histories, biography and autobiography studies, essays and prose style, studies of literary criticism, travel writing; 2. Individual author bibliographies (37), listing their nonfictional prose and critical and biographical studies of them. Restricted to prose

....(*contd.*)
writers from the literary world, including critics, *e.g.* Connolly, Leavis, Empson. Author and title indexes.
Class No: 820-3(01)"19"

Histories

[7243]
FRASER, H. *and* **BROWN, D. English prose of the nineteenth century.** Harlow, Longman, 1997. £48. (*Longman literature in English.*) ISBN: 0582051371.

3 sections and 9 chapters: 1.1 Scientific writing - 1.2 Travel and exploration literature - 1.3 Social reportage - 2.1 Biography - 2.2 Autobiography - 2.3 Journals and letters - 3.1 Intellectual formations - 3.2 Writing and culture - 3.3 Criticism. Reference section includes general bibliography and bio-bibliographical notes on individual writers. Chronology. Index. *Class No:* 820-3(091)

Bunyan

[7244]
FORREST, J.F. *and* **GREAVES, R.L. John Bunyan: a reference guide.** Boston, Hall, 1982. 478p. ISBN: 0816182671.

An annotated, chronological bibliography of secondary material, which also includes details of major editions and reprints. *Class No:* 820-3BUN

Carlyle

[7245]
TARR, R.L. Thomas Carlyle: a bibliography of English-language criticism, 1824-1974. Charlottesville, Va., Univ. Press of Virginia, 1976. xi,295p. ISBN: 0813906954.

Over 3,000 items arranged by year with author and subject indexes. *Class No:* 820-3CAR

[7246]
TARR, R.L. Thomas Carlyle: a descriptive bibliography. Pittsburgh, Univ. of Pittsburgh Press, 1989; Oxford, Clarendon Press, 1990. xxi,543p. illus. $110. (*Pittsburgh series in bibliography.*) ISBN: 0822936070, US; 0198112122, UK.

Section A (400p.) lists and fully describes all printings of all Carlyle's books, pamphlets and broadsides up to 1880, together with reprints of first editions up to 1987. Further sections are: B. First book and pamphlet appearances - C. First contributions to journals and newspapers - D. Collected works - E. Miscellaneous collections - F. Material attributed to Carlyle - G. Jane Welsh Carlyle's publications. Appendices list Carlyle's unpublished writings and principal books about the Carlyles. Many title-page facsimiles. Index.
Class No: 820-3CAR

Goldsmith

[7247]
WOODS, S.H. Oliver Goldsmith: a reference guide. Boston, Hall, 1982. xxiii,208p. ISBN: 0816183392.

Annotated list of writing about Goldsmith's life and works, excluding his 'hack writing'. Arranged by year, 1759-1978, with separate annual sections for books and shorter writings. Includes major editions of Goldsmith's works and some foreign critical material. Index. Approx. 600 items.
Class No: 820-3GOL

Hazlitt

[7248]
HOUCK, J.A. William Hazlitt: a reference guide. Boston, Hall; London, Prior, 1977. xx,268p. ISBN: 0816178267, US; 0860430979, UK.

Lists critical material by year, 1805-1973, with separate sections for books and shorter writings within each year. Substantial nonevaluative annotations. Over 1,200 items. Index. *Class No:* 820-3HAZ

[7249]
KEYNES, G. Bibliography of William Hazlitt. 2nd rev. ed. Godalming, St. Paul's Bibliographies, 1981. 152p. illus. £12.00. ISBN: 090679501x.

1st ed. London, Nonesuch Press, 1931.

Full descriptive bibliography of Hazlitt's book editions (115 titles) and editions of selected essays and letters (30) plus checklist of 54 American editions. Title pages of all first editions reproduced as facsimiles. Index. *Class No:* 820-3HAZ

Hunt

[7250]
LULOFS, T.J. *and* **OSTROM, H. Leigh Hunt: a reference guide.** Boston, Hall, 1985. xix,264p. $55. ISBN: 0816183856.

Lists over 1,000 critical studies by year, 1800-1982, then by author, with descriptive annotations which often include a representative quotation. Index. *Class No:* 820-3HUN

Johnson

[7251]
CLIFFORD, J.L. *and* **GREENE, D.J. Samuel Johnson: a survey and bibliography of critical studies.** Minneapolis, Univ. of Minnesota Press, 1970. xvi,333p. ISBN: 0816605726.

Combines Clifford's *Johnsonian studies, 1887-1950* (Minneapolis, 1951) and Clifford and Greene's bibliography for 1950-1960 which appeared in *Johnsonian studies* (Cairo, 1962), with additions and corrections and 2 major extensions: recent studies, 1960-68, and studies published from Johnson's own lifetime to 1887. Nearly 4,000 items in 2 parts (general bibliography and bibliography of individual works) and 25 sections. Chronologically arranged within each section. Index of authors and subjects. *Class No:* 820-3JOH

[7252]
COURTNEY, W.P.A. *and* **SMITH, D.N. A Bibliography of Samuel Johnson,** with *Johnsonian bibliography,* a supplement to Courtney by R.W. Chapman with the collaboration of A.T. Hazen. Single-vol. reprint. Winchester, St. Paul's Bibliographies, 1984. 240p. illus. £33.50. ISBN: 0938768115.

Courtney's *Bibliography* originally published Oxford, Clarendon Press, 1915; Chapman's supplement originally published in the Oxford Bibliographical Society's *Proceedings and Papers,* v.5,pt.3, 1938, p.119-97.

Chronologically arranged descriptive bibliography with lengthy notes on each item, including references to pamphlets that were connected with Johnson's work and details of his associates. *Class No:* 820-3JOH

[7253]
PAGE, N. A Dr. Johnson chronology. Basingstoke, Macmillan; Boston, Hall, 1990. xv,136p. maps. £50. (*Macmillan author chronologies.*) ISBN: 0333459164, UK; 0816190917, US.

Presents the major events of the writer's life extremely clearly, year by year and month by month. List of the Johnson circle (11p.) with minimal biographical information. Select bibliography (3p.). Indexes to people, places and Johnson's works. *Class No:* 820-3JOH

[7254]
ROGERS, P. The Samuel Johnson encyclopedia. Westport, Conn., Greenwood, 1996. 520p. $85. ISBN: 0313294119.

Over 650 entries, A-Z, on every aspect of Johnson's life and career, including literary works, themes and concepts, and his family, associates and contemporaries. Detailed entries on works examine composition, publication and reception. Chronology. Bibliography. Cross-references and index. *Class No:* 820-3JOH

Lamb

[7255]
PRANCE, C.A. Companion to Charles Lamb: a guide to people and places, 1760-1847. London, Mansell, 1983. x,392p. ISBN: 0720116570.

An A-Z guide which lists Lamb's relations, friends and contemporaries; places, organizations and events with which he was connected; his editors and illustrators; and Lamb scholars and societies. Over 900 entries, of which 17% are for actors and other theatre people. Chronology of the Lambs, 1760-1891. Maps. 5 indexes for different types of entry. *Class No:* 820-3LAM

[7256]
ROFF, R. A Bibliography of the writings of Charles and Mary Lamb. Bronxville, N.Y., N.T. Smith, 1979. xv,292p., illus. ISBN: 0935164014.

A reprint of L.S. Livingston's descriptive collectors' bibliography (New York, Spoor, 1903) of first editions published to 1834 and his appendix on the works of the two John Lambs, plus a second appendix comprising a bibliography of periodical contributions compiled by J.C. Thomson. Many title page facsimiles. Index. *Class No:* 820-3LAM

Lawrence (T.E.)

[7257]
O'BRIEN, P.M. T.E. Lawrence: a bibliography. Winchester, St. Paul's Bibliographies; Boston, Hall, 1988. xii,724p. illus. ISBN: 0906795400, UK; 0816189455, US.

Part 1, The Lawrence canon, has 369 entries in 4 sections: A. Books, prefaces, introductions, translations, etc. - B. Periodical articles - C. Newspaper articles - D. Incidental works containing writings by Lawrence. Part 2, Biography and criticism, has 4,600 entries in 4 sections: E. Books about Lawrence - F. Incidental books containing references to Lawrence - G. Periodical articles - H. Newspaper articles. All books in *both* sections are described. Index of authors, titles, periodicals, newspapers and publishers. Likely to remain definitive, although the compiler admits that 'a supplement will be called for in the future' (*Preface*) to cover films, recorded materials and the many foreign language items he has been unable to locate. *Class No:* 820-3LAW

Lewis (C.S.)

[7258]
HOOPER, W. C.S. Lewis: a companion and guide London, HarperCollins, 1996. xvi,940p. £25. ISBN: 0006278000.

An impressive guide to Lewis's life and works, including concise biography (120p.), chronology (6p.), and accounts of all his writings, by genre, giving summary, history, background, analysis and critical reception. 'Key ideas' (63p.) duscusses themes, from Allegory to Thrills, Distrust of; 'Who's who' (127p.) has biographical notes on his family and circle; 'What's what' (193p.) explains significant places, events, oganizations, etc. Annotated bibliography of Lewis's works (83p.). Cross-references between sections. Index.

For secondary material, see *C.S. Lewis: an annotated checklist of writings about him and his works* by J.R. Christopher and J.K. Ostling (Kent, Ohio, Kent State Univ. Press, 1974) and *C.S. Lewis: a reference guide* (New York, Hall, 1993). *Class No:* 820-3LEW

Morris

[7259]
The Journal of The William Morris Society. London, William Morris Society, 1962-. 2py. ISSN: 00840254.

Includes a bibliographical supplement every 2 years. V.10(3), Autumn 1993, has 27p. of bibliography for 1990-91, with 189 annotated entries including editions, translations, critical studies, dissertations, and exhibition catalogues. Author index. *Class No:* 820-3MOR

[7260]
LATHAM, D. *and* **LATHAM, S. An Annotated critical bibliography of William Morris.** Hemel Hempstead, Harvester Wheatsheaf, 1990; New York, St. Martin's Press, 1991. 256p. £65. ISBN: 0710811535, UK; 0312056567, US.

A selective bibliography of critical studies in 8 main sections, with numerous subsections on specific works or particular aspects of Morris's activity. Index.
Class No: 820-3MOR

[7261]
SALMON, N. *and* **BARKER, D. The William Morris chronology.** Bristol, Thoemmes Press, 1996. 300p. £30. ISBN: 1855065053.

A very detailed day-by-day account of Morris's life which is 'by turns charming, evocative, useful and dull' (*TLS*, no.4883, Nov. 1, 1996). *Class No:* 820-3MOR

[7262]
WALSDORF, J.J. William Morris in private press and limited editions: a descriptive bibliography of books by and about William Morris, 1891-1981. Phoenix, Ariz., Oryx Press, 1983. xxvi,602p. illus. ISBN: 0897740416.

Part 1 lists and describes 53 Kelmscott Press titles, 1891-98. Part 2 covers 155 private press and limited eds., 1891-1981. Includes 70 full-page illustrations. *Class No:* 820-3MOR

Ruskin

[7263]
BRADLEY, J.L. A Ruskin chronology. Basingstoke, Macmillan, 1996. 144p. £37.50. (*Macmillan author chronologies.*) ISBN: 033363215x.

Details the events of the writer's life, month by month and day by day. Select bibliography. Index. *Class No:* 820-3RUS

[7264]
CATE, G.A. John Ruskin: a reference guide. Boston, Hall, 1988. 146p. $45. ISBN: 0816189080.

Lists secondary material chronologically, 1843-1987, including studies in French and German, with concise annotations. Index of authors and subjects. *Class No:* 820-3RUS

Swift

[7265]
LANDA, L.A. *and* **TOBIN, J.E. Jonathan Swift: a list of critical studies,** published from 1895 to 1945. Reprint of 1945 ed. New York, Octagon, 1975. 62p. ISBN: 0374947279.

Originally published New York, Cosmopolitan Science and Art Service Co., 1945.

573 items in 12 sections with cross-references. Index.
Class No: 820-3SWI

[7266]
—STATHIS, J.J. A Bibliography of Swift studies, 1945-1965. Nashville, Tenn., Vanderbilt Univ. Press, 1967. xi,110p. ISBN: 0826510957.

Follows Landa and Tobin, listing 659 items in 6 sections: 1. Bibliography, canon, editions - 2. Biography - 3. General criticism - 4. Poetry - 5. Prose writings (10 subsections) - 6. *Gulliver's travels.* Brief annotations, including references to reviews. Many cross-references. Index. *Class No:* 820-3SWI

[7267]
RODINO, R.H. Swift studies, 1965-1980: an annotated bibliography. New York, Garland, 1984. xl,252p. ISBN: 0824091973.

Follows Stathis, with 1,186 items in 6 similarly arranged sections. *Review of English Studies* (v.37(145), Feb. 1986, p.98-99) is scathing in its criticism of omissions, uneven annotations, and inadequate indexing. *Class No:* 820-3SWI

[7268]
TEERINK, H. A Bibliography of the writings of Jonathan Swift. 2nd ed., rev. and corr. by H. Teerink; ed. by A.H. Scouten. Philadelphia, Univ. of Pennsylvania Press, 1963. xviii,453p. illus.

1st ed. 1937.

1. Collected works - 2. Smaller collections - 3. *A Tale of a Tub*, etc. - 4. *Gulliver's Travels* - 5. Separate works - 6. Doubtful [works] - 7. Biography and criticism, 1709-1895. Lists all known editions of Swift's works to 1814, with full description of all important books and pamphlets. Different arrangement from first ed., but items retain their numbers and a key is provided. 12 title-page facsimiles. Index of titles. *Class No:* 820-3SWI

English Fiction

Databases

[7269]
Early English prose fiction (1500-1700): the full-text database. Cambridge, Chadwyck-Healey, 1997. World Wide Web resource Subscription details from marketing@chadwyck.co.uk

Part of *Literature online (LION)* (*q.v.*). URL: http://lion.chadwyck.co.uk

Contains the complete texts of 211 works of fiction, first editions being used in most cases. All prefatory matter and annotations by the author are included, as are bibliographic

.... (contd.)
details, illustrations and errata lists from the chosen editions. Translations and nonfiction prose works are excluded. Searchable by keyword, title, author and publication date. Also available on CD-ROM (£5,500. ISBN: 0859643344). 'With its superb help menu ... this database will present few obstacles for the undergraduate and will also serve specialists' (*Choice*, March 1998, p.1189).

Followed by *Eighteenth-century fiction (1700-1780)*, which is similarly organized and contains 77 complete works by writers from the British Isles. Includes 2 different eds. of *Clarissa*, *Pamela* and *Robinson Crusoe*. Additional search fields are genre and gender. Also available on CD-ROM (ISBN: 0859643239).

Eighteenth-century fiction (1700-1780) *Class No:* 820-31(003.4)

Bibliographies of Bibliographies

[7270]

GLAZIER, L.P. The Bibliography of contemporary British and Irish fiction, 1945-1989: an annotated checklist Westport, Conn., Greenwood, 1990. 200p. ISBN: 0887361692.

Records and describes bibliographical accounts of British and Irish writers. Annotated entries summarize the contents of each bibliography and allow the historical development of individual authors to be traced. *Class No:* 820-31(009)

Bibliographies

[7271]

BEENE, L.D. Guide to British prose explication: 19th & 20th centuries Boston, Hall, 1996. $70. ISBN: 0816119872.

Similarly arranged to Hall's *Guide to American poetry explication* (*q.v.*) and companion series. *Class No:* 820-31(01)

[7272]

The English novel: select bibliographical guide. Dyson, A.E., *ed.* Oxford, Oxford Univ. Press, 1974. x,372p. (*Select bibliographical guides.*) ISBN: 019871033x.

Bibliographical essays by different scholars on 20 major novelists, arranged chronologically from Bunyan to Joyce. Essays average 18p. and recommend the best texts, critical studies, biographies, bibliographies and background reading. Lists at the end of each chapter with full details of all works mentioned. *Class No:* 820-31(01)

[7273]

The English novel: twentieth century criticism. Chicago, Swallow Press, 1976-82. 2v.

V.1 *Defoe through Hardy*, ed. by R.J. Dunn. 1976. 202p. $20. ISBN: 080400742x.

V.2 *Twentieth-century novelists*, ed. by P. Schlueter and J. Schlueter. 1982. 380p. $35. ISBN: 0804004242.

Provides lists of general studies and criticism of individual novels, 45 authors being covered in v.1 and 80 in v.2. *Class No:* 820-31(01)

[7274]

LIBRARY OF CONGRESS. Author bibliography of English language fiction in the Library of Congress through 1950. Wright, R.G., *comp.* Boston, Hall, 1973. 8v. (6171p.). $870. ISBN: 0816109664.

Based on the Fiction Shelflist (PZ3) of the Library of Congress, this author bibliography includes all the works of English language fiction in the collection, from the beginning of these forms in the eighteenth century through works published in 1950. Arranged alphabetically by author under author's country of origin: US, UK, Ireland and Commonwealth. 133,000 entries.

Chronological bibliography of English language fiction ... (1974. ISBN: 0816111162. Available on microfilm by request. $870) has 131,000 entries, arranged by year of publication.

Title bibliography of English language fiction ... (1976. 9v. $875. ISBN: 0816100209) has over 132,000 entries, arranged by title. *Class No:* 820-31(01)

[7275]

PALMER, H.H. *and* **DYSON, A.J. English novel explication:** criticisms to 1972. Hamden, Conn., Shoe String, 1973. vi,329p. $24.50. ISBN: 0208013229.

Follows Bell and Baird, listing over 4,800 critical studies in 965 books and periodicals, published 1958-72. Lists of sources. Index of novelists and titles. Continued by:

English novel explication: supplement I, comp. by P.L. Abernethy and others, 1976 (vii,305p. $32.50. ISBN: 0208014640).

English novel explication: supplement II, through 1979, comp. by C.J. Kloesel, 1980 (332p. $35. ISBN: 0208017097).

English novel explication: supplement III, through 1984, comp. by C.J. Kloesel and L.F. Kloesel, 1986 (vi,533p. $57.50. ISBN: 0208020926).

English novel explication: supplement IV, comp. by C.J. Kloesel, 1990 (352p. $55. ISBN: 0208022317).

English novel explication: supplement V, comp. by C.J. Kloesel, 1994 (viii,431p. $59.50. ISBN: 0208023089). *Class No:* 820-31(01)

Tudor & Stuart Times

[7276]

ESDAILE, A. A List of English tales and prose romances printed before 1740. London, Bibliographical Society, 1912 (repr. New York, Franklin, 1971). xxxvi,329p. ISBN: 0833710680.

Part 1 covers 1475-1642 and part 2, 1643-1739. Includes translations of foreign works. Entries are arranged A-Z, by author and title, giving full titles and imprints with bibliographical notes. Indicates libraries in which the copy was seen and refers to bibliographies describing the work. *Class No:* 820-31(01)"1485-1760"

[7277]

—MISH, C.C. English prose fiction, 1600-1700: a chronological checklist. Charlottesville, Va., Bibliographical Society of the Univ. of Virginia, 1967. 110p.

Basically a chronological re-arrangement of the 17th-century material in Esdaile's *List of English tales*, with some titles added and some dropped because they cannot be described as fiction. Lists *c.*1,350 works by author within each year, with entry numbers from Wing or Pollard and Redgrave. Index. *Class No:* 820-31(01)"1485-1760"

16th & 17th Centuries

[7278]

HARNER, J.L. English Renaissance prose fiction, 1500-1660: an annotated bibliography of criticism (1800-1976). Boston, Hall, 1978. xxiv,556p. ISBN: 0816179964.

Lists 3,236 editions and studies in 4 main sections: bibliographies (52 entries); anthologies (21); general studies (365); and specific authors/translators/titles. The latter section covers over 170 writers and prose works. Index.

....(*contd.*)

A second vol. (1985. 244p. ISBN: 0816187096) covers studies published 1976-83 and a third (1992. $35. ISBN: 0816190887) covers 1984-90. 'The whole is executed with remarkable thoroughness, accuracy, and clarity' (*Modern Language Review*, v.83(3), July 1988, p.664-66).
Class No: 820-31(01)"15/16"

17th & 18th Centuries

[7279]

BEASLEY, J.C. English fiction, 1660-1800: a guide to information sources. Detroit, Gale, 1978. xvi,313p. ISBN: 0810312263.

Sections on general sources (bibliographies, histories, background material, etc.), followed by bibliographies for 29 authors, listing editions, correspondence, bibliographies, biographies, and criticism. 1,475 entries, most of them briefly annotated. Index of authors and titles.
Class No: 820-31(01)"16/17"

17th Century

[7280]

LETELLIER, R.I. The English novel, 1660-1700: an annotated bibliography. Westport, Conn., Greenwood, 1997. 488p. £67.95. (*Bibliographies and indexes in world literature.*) ISBN: 0313303681.

The first part presents overviews of existing bibliographies, anthologies and contextual studies on the early English novel. The second part includes alphabetically arranged sections for individual authors, listing editions and critical studies of specific works of fiction, with annotations. Chronological list of novels. Index of critics. Subject index.
Class No: 820-31(01)"16"

18th & 19th Centuries

[7281]

BLOCK, A. The English novel, 1740-1850: a catalogue including prose romances, short stories, and translation of foreign fiction. Reprint of 1961 ed. Westport, Conn., Greenwood, 1982. xv,349p. $75. ISBN: 0313232245.

1st ed. London, Grafton, 1939; Rev. ed. London, Dawsons, 1961.

Chronologically this continues Esdaile's *List of English tales...* (*q.v.*) but entries are not so full and lack bibliographical notes. *c.*7,700 entries, arranged A-Z by author (or title if anonymous). Title index. *Class No:* 820-31(01)"17/18"

[7282]

MAZZENO, L.W. The British novel, 1680-1832: an annotated bibliography. Lanham, Md., Scarecrow, 1996. 264p. $40. (*Magill bibliographies.*) ISBN: 0810832496.

Provides citations to 20th-century criticism of 20 major writers, including Austen, Beckford, Behn, Defoe, Johnson, Radcliffe, Scott, Mary Shelley and Horace Walpole. One chapter per novelist, with general criticism followed by studies of individual works. Author and subject indexes.
Class No: 820-31(01)"17/18"

18th Century

[7283]

HAHN, H.G. *and* **BEHM, C. The Eighteenth-century British novel and its background:** an annotated bibliography and guide to topics. Metuchen, N.J., Scarecrow, 1985. ix,392p. ISBN: 0810817861.

Lists 3,188 20th-century English-language publications in 6 sections: Bibliographies; Background studies; General criticism; Major novelists (5 individuals); Minor novelists (39); 'Near novelists' (Swift and Johnson). Very brief annotations. Topic index with over 800 headings. Index of critics. *Class No:* 820-31(01)"17"

[7284]

McBURNEY, W.H. A Check list of English prose fiction, 1700-1739. Cambridge, Mass., Harvard Univ. Press, 1960. x,154p.

Lists 391 titles, covering English prose fiction, translations into English and an appendix of dubious or unauthenticated works. Entry data include complete title and imprint, pagination and format, plus location in 14 British, American and French libraries of at least one extant copy. It does not include 'short character sketches, jest books, topical pamphlets, dialogues, chapbooks and fictional pieces in periodicals', or the many editions of *Gulliver's travels* and *Robinson Crusoe*. Bibliography (4p.). Thorough index of authors, titles, publishers, printers, etc. *Class No:* 820-31(01)"17"

[7285]

—BEASLEY, J.C. A Check list of prose fiction published in England, 1740-1749. Charlottesville, Va., Univ. Press of Virginia, for the Bibliographical Society of Virginia, 1972. xv,213p. ISBN: 0813904013.

Follows McBurney, listing 281 titles chronologically plus 19 unverified eds. of authentic works and 38 unauthenticated titles. Includes translations of foreign novels. Gives the location of at least one extant copy, usually in an American library. Bibliography (8p.). Index. *Class No:* 820-31(01)"17"

[7286]

ORR, L. A Catalogue checklist of English prose fiction, 1750-1800. Troy, N.Y., Whitston, 1979. 204p. $13.50. ISBN: 0878751718.

Follows Beasley, listing nearly 1,200 first editions published in London and giving locations. Indexes of authors and titles. *Class No:* 820-31(01)"17"

[7287]

RAVEN, J. British fiction 1750-1770: a chronological check-list of prose fiction printed in Britain and Ireland. Newark, Univ. of Delaware Press; London, Associated Univ. Presses, 1987. 349p. $50. ISBN: 0874133246.

Continues the work of McBurney and Beasley (*qq.v.*) listing 1,363 works of fiction, some of them lost, published 1750-1770 and including reprints of pre-1750 works. Annual lists are arranged A-Z by title for anonymous works, then by author. Entry data include, where possible, publication details, pagination, references to contemporary reviews, other editions of the work and locations of extant copies. Thorough introduction (42p.), with statistical tables, provides background to the period. *Class No:* 820-31(01)"17"

19th Century

[7288]
Nineteenth-century fiction: a bibliographical catalogue based on the collection formed by Robert Lee Wolff. Bruner, K., *ed.* New York, Garland, 1981-6. 5v. illus.

7,938 entries, four times as many as Sadleir (*q.v.*), including many American editions. Full descriptions, but 'where a title has already been described by Sadleir, mention is made only of significant variants, or of such matters as provenance which are necessarily peculiar to the Wolff copy' (*Publisher's note*). Includes many manuscript items, and letters relating to specific novels are transcribed in full.

A-Z author arrangement in vols.1-4, then A-Z by title. V.5 covers anonymous, pseudonymous and multiple-author fiction, annuals and periodicals, and has cumulative index. Many facsimiles. 'An indispensable tool ... it is unlikely that, until the far-off computerization of the British Library's nineteenth-century holdings, it will be superseded' (*TLS*, no.4372, Jan. 16, 1987, p.66). *Class No:* 820-31(01)"18"

[7289]
SADLEIR, M. XIX century fiction: a bibliographical record, based on his own collection. London, Constable; Los Angeles, California Univ. Press, 1951. 2v. illus.

Includes 'any novelist whose writing life was comprised within the limits of the nineteenth century' (*Explanatory guide*). Descriptive bibliography in 3 sections: 1. Alphabetical author list (v.1) - 2. Yellow-back collection - 3. 'Novelists' libraries', 'Standard novel' series, etc. Index of titles and authors in each vol. *Class No:* 820-31(01)"18"

Victorian Age

[7290]
MAZZENO, L.W. The Victorian novel: an annotated bibliography. Pasadena, Calif., Salem Press (later Scarecrow), 1989. 222p. $42. (*Magill bibliographies.*) ISBN: 0810828057.

Similar in format and scope to Mazzeno's *The British novel, 1680-1832* (*q.v.*), with selective listings for 13 regularly studied novelists, covering general studies and criticism of individual novels. *Class No:* 820-31(01)"1837-1901"

[7291]
Victorian fiction: a guide to research. Stevenson, L., *ed.* Reprint of 1964 ed. New York, Modern Language Assoc. of America, 1980. viii,440p. ISBN: 0873522583.

Originally published Cambridge, Mass., Harvard Univ. Press, 1964.

A chapter on general materials followed by bibliographical essays on the following novelists: Disraeli, Bulwer-Lytton, Dickens, Thackeray, Trollope, The Brontës, Gaskell, Kingsley, Collins, Reade, Eliot, Meredith, Hardy, Moore and Gissing. Each chapter surveys editions, biography, general criticism and criticism of specific works. Analytical index. The work of 13 scholars. *Class No:* 820-31(01)"1837-1901"

[7292]
—Victorian fiction: a second guide to research. Ford, G.H., *ed.* New York, Modern Language Assoc. of America, 1978. xxv,401p. $37.50. ISBN: 0873522540.

A sequel to Stevenson, updated to 1974, with additional chapters on R.L. Stevenson and Samuel Butler. Some pre-1962 items previously overlooked are included. 'Fresh emphasis' is given to 2 areas: 'the availability of mansucripts

....*(contd.)*
and the record of film versions of Victorian novels' (*Preface*). 16 contributors, 10 of them new to this vol. Index. *Class No:* 820-31(01)"1837-1901"

20th Century

[7293]
BUFKIN, E.C. The Twentieth-century novel in English: a checklist. 2nd ed. Athens, Ga., Univ. of Georgia Press, 1983. 192p. $25. ISBN: 0820306851.

1st ed. 1968.

An unannotated list of novels by major and minor English-language authors, regardless of nationality, arranged under authors, A-Z. *Class No:* 820-31(01)"19"

[7294]
CASSIS, A.F. The Twentieth-century English novel: an annotated bibliography of general criticism. New York, Garland, 1977. xxiii,413p. ISBN: 0824099427.

Over 2,800 titles listed in 4 sections: 1. Bibliographies and checklists (67 items) - 2A. Criticism: books (974) - 2B. Criticism: articles (1,553) - 3. Dissertations and theses (238). Author arrangement in each section with index of novelists discussed and index of 38 topics and themes. Excludes studies of popular and genre fiction and the short story. *Class No:* 820-31(01)"19"

[7295]
RICE, T.J. English fiction, 1900-1950: a guide to information sources. Detroit, Gale, 1979-83. 2v. ISBN: 0810312174, v.1; 081031505x, v.2.

Individual author bibliographies are arranged A-Z (v.1, Aldington-Huxley; v.2, Joyce-Woolf) and usually have 4 primary sections (fiction; miscellaneous writings, including poetry and drama; collected and selected works; letters) and 5 sections for secondary material (bibliographies; biographies; book-length criticism; general articles and chapters; studies of specific works). *c.*600 general studies are listed before the author bibliographies. Largely confined to English-language material. Author, title, and subject indexes. *Class No:* 820-31(01)"19"

[7296]
ROSA, A.F. *and* **ESCHHOLZ, P.A. Contemporary fiction in America and England, 1950-1970:** a guide to information sources. Detroit, Gale, 1976.

See entry at 820.73-31(01). *Class No:* 820-31(01)"19"

Encyclopaedias & Dictionaries

[7297]
Masterplots II: British and Commonwealth fiction series. Magill, F.N., *ed.* Englewood Cliffs, N.J., Salem Press, 1987. 4v. $365. ISBN: 0893564680.

Plot summaries and critical essays on works of British and Commonwealth fiction. See entry on *Masterplots II: American fiction series* for format. *Class No:* 820-31(03)

Victorian Age

[7298]
SUTHERLAND, J. The Longman companion to Victorian fiction. London, Longman, 1988; Stanford, Calif., Stanford Univ. Press, 1989. 696p. ISBN: 0582490413, UK; 0804715289, US.

US title is *The Stanford companion to Victorian fiction.*

1,606 entries, the work of one author, are arranged in a single A-Z sequence and break down as follows: 878

....(contd.)

novelists (566 men, 312 women), 554 novels, 47 periodicals, 63 publishers, 26 illustrators and 38 miscellaneous entries on literary genres and schools. Author profiles include references to entries in major biographical and bibliographical sources such as *DNB*. Appendices listing pseudonyms/proper names and maiden/married names, plus ample cross-references, make access simple.

Invaluable for minor writers and universally acclaimed by reviewers for both content and style. 'A remarkable achievement, an invaluable tool for understanding the Victorian literary milieu' (*TLS,* no.4504, July 28, 1989, p.817). *Class No:* 820-31(03)"1837-1901"

20th Century

[7299]

KEMP, S., & *others*. Edwardian fiction: an Oxford companion. Oxford, Oxford Univ. Press, 1997. xxxi,431p. £30. ISBN: 0198117604.

A single A-Z sequence with over 800 entries on authors (nearly half of them women) and 250 on literary works, plus articles on genres, periodicals and topics relevant to English fiction in the period 1900-14. *TLS* (no.4947, Jan. 23, 1998, p.25) finds some errors in the coverage of major writers and concludes that 'it is ... largely for its information on little-known and unknown writers that this *Companion* will be prized'. Chronology of literary and historical events, 1900-1914. Index of pseudonyms and name changes.
Class No: 820-31(03)"19"

Histories

[7300]

BAKER, E.A. The History of the English novel. London, Witherby, 1924-39 (repr. New York, Barnes & Noble, 1967). 10v.

From the beginnings, in the age of romance, to 1930. The definitive study of the English novel, based largely upon courses of lectures delivered at University College, London, on a doctoral thesis, and on reading done in preparing the various editions of the author's *Guide to the best fiction in English*. Each volume includes a reading list, a reference list of items dealt with, and an index.

Continued by L. Stevenson's *The History of the English novel, v.11: Yesterday and after* (New York, Barnes & Noble, 1967. 431p.), which covers novelists from H.G. Wells to John Braine. Bibliography (11p.). Index.
Class No: 820-31(091)

[7301]

The Columbia history of the British novel. Richetti, J., *ed.* New York, Columbia Univ. Press, 1994. xix,1064p. $73.50. ISBN: 0231078587.

39 signed chapters on novelists, groups of novelists, and themes (*e.g.* 'Imperialism and post-colonialism') from the 18th century to the present. Essentially a critical history, with no primary bibliography and only very selective secondary bibliographies (10-20 titles) after each chapter. Very brief biographical notes on major novelists (26p.) follow the narrative. Index. *Class No:* 820-31(091)

[7302]

PROBYN, C.T. English fiction of the eighteenth century, 1700-1789. London, Longman, 1987. xii,244p. £17.99. (*Longman literature in English.*) ISBN: 0582493692.

History of the early development of the English novel in seven chapters, followed by chronology of works of fiction, other literary works and historical events (22p.); general bibliographies on the period (9p.); notes on 18 individual authors, comprising brief outline of author's career and lists of biographies and critical works (20p.). Index.
Class No: 820-31(091)

[7303]

SALZMAN, P. English prose fiction, 1558-1700; a critical history. Oxford, Clarendon Press, 1985. xiii,391p. ISBN: 0198128738.

Combines a historical survey with a critical study of individual, representative texts. Includes a bibliography (28p.) which lists all known extant works of fiction from the period, including translations, with Elizabethan fiction arranged in one A-Z author sequence and 17th-century fiction in 25 generic categories. Index covers text and bibliography. *Class No:* 820-31(091)

[7304]

WHEELER, M. English fiction of the Victorian period, 1830-1890. 2nd ed. London, Longman, 1994. 352p. £15.99. (*Longman literature in English.*) ISBN: 0582088437.

1st ed. 1985.

4 main chapters cover pre- and Early Victorian, mid-century fiction, High Victorian fiction and Late Victorian fiction, with subsections on major writers and themes. Like the rest of this excellent series, includes a very useful reference section (over 60p.) comprising chronology, annotated general bibliography, and biobibliographical notes on individual authors, A-Z, which in 2nd ed. have been updated and extended to cover lesser-known writers. Chronology. Index. *Class No:* 820-31(091)

Austen

[7305]

GILSON, D. A Bibliography of Jane Austen. Reissue with new introduction. Winchester, St. Paul's Bibliographies, 1997. 920p. illus. £55. ISBN: 1873040377.

First published Oxford, Clarendon Press, 1982, in the *Soho bibliographies* series. Originally intended to be a 2nd ed., rev. and augmented, of Sir Geoffrey Keynes' *Jane Austen: a bibliography* (London, Nonesuch Press, 1929), but 'the extensiveness of the alterations and additions ... made it seem better to present this as a separate work' (*Preface*).

Definitive primary bibliography in 11 sections (A-L), including translations, dramatisations and continuations by other writers, plus a section on biography and criticism with over 1,800 annotated items. Explanatory introduction to each section. Appendix lists all editions, reprints and adaptations chronologically, 1811-1978. Many facsimiles. Very thorough index.

Reissue has new Introduction listing amendments to the original text, but it must be stressed that this is a *reprint* and not an updated ed., so the vast output of the Austen industry over the last 20 years has yet to be recorded.
Class No: 820-31AUS

[7306]

The Jane Austen handbook. Grey, J.D., *ed.* London, Athlone, 1986. xiii,511p. ISBN: 0485113015.

Includes 'A Dictionary of Jane Austen's life and works' by H.A. Bok (95p.), which lists both literary and historical people and places as well as allusions and quotations.
Class No: 820-31AUS

[7307]

PINION, F.B. A Jane Austen companion: a critical survey and reference book. London, Macmillan, 1973. xiii,342p. illus. £50. ISBN: 0333124898.

Reference section has dictionary of people and places in the fiction (107p.), glossary (9p.) and select annotated bibliography (19p.) of editions, biography and criticism.
Class No: 820-31AUS

[7308]

ROTH, B. *and* **WEINSHEIMER, J. An Annotated bibliography of Jane Austen studies,** 1952-1972. Charlottesville, Va., Univ. Press of Virginia for the Bibliographical Society of the Univ. of Virginia, 1973. xiii,272p. ISBN: 0813905443.

794 items, most published 1952-72 but including significant older material, in 3 sections: 1. Books, essays and articles - 2. Doctoral dissertations - 3. Mentions (*i.e.* in books not wholly devoted to Austen). Chronological arrangement in each section. Concise (max. 75 words) nonevaluative annotations. Indexes of authors, Austen titles, and topics.

Roth has compiled further vols. covering 1973-83 (Univ. Press of Virginia, 1985. 359p. $35. ISBN:0813910544) and 1984-94 (Ohio Univ. Press, 1996. 450p. $49.95. ISBN: 0821411675), the latter being the largest so far with 1,326 entries. *Class No:* 820-31AUS

Brontë family

[7309]

ALEXANDER, C. A Bibliography of the manuscripts of Charlotte Brontë. [Haworth], The Brontë Society; Westport, Conn., Greenwood, 1982. xx,205p. $65. ISBN: 0950582913, UK; 031327665x, US.

499 entries in separate sections for manuscript vols., prose, poetry, devoirs, and miscellaneous manuscripts. Descriptions and library locations. *Class No:* 820-31BRO

[7310]

BARCLAY, J.M. Emily Brontë criticism, 1900-1982: an annotated check list. Westport, Conn., Greenwood, 1984. xiii,162p. ISBN: 0313276676.

Update of *Emily Brontë criticism, 1900-1968: an annotated check list* (New York, Readex, 1974).

Arranged by author, A-Z, in 3 sections: Books and parts of books (425 items); Articles (528); Books and articles in foreign languages (68). Foreign material not annotated. Indexes to chapter, article and book titles. Chronological index. *Class No:* 820-31BRO

[7311]

CRUMP, R.W. Charlotte and Emily Brontë, 1846-1915: a reference guide. Boston, Hall, 1982. xvii,194p. $40. ISBN: 0816179530.

Annotated bibliography of secondary material arranged chronologically, then A-Z within each year. Over 900 entries. Index of authors, titles and genres (bibliography, biography, etc.). *Class No:* 820-31BRO

[7312]

CRUMP, R.W. Charlotte and Emily Brontë, 1916-1954: a reference guide. Boston, Hall, 1985. xvii,197p. ISBN: 0816186723.

Over 900 items in the same format as the previous vol. Appendix lists a further 11 items from the period 1846-1915.
Class No: 820-31BRO

[7313]

CRUMP, R.W. Charlotte and Emily Brontë, 1955-1983: a reference guide. Boston, Hall, 1986. xvii,319p. $40. ISBN: 0816187975.

Over 1,400 items in the same format as the previous vols. Appendix lists a further 6 items from the period 1916-54.
Class No: 820-31BRO

[7314]

PINION, F.B. A Brontë companion: literary assessment, background and reference. London, Macmillan, 1975. xiv,394p. illus. £52.50. ISBN: 0333144260.

Reference section comprises dictionary of people and places in the novels (85p.), glossary (5p.) and annotated select bibliography (16p.) of editions, biography and criticism. *Class No:* 820-31BRO

Conrad

[7315]

KNOWLES, O. An Annotated critical bibliography of Joseph Conrad. Hemel Hempstead, Harvester Wheatsheaf; New York, St. Martin's Press, 1992. lx,255p. £65. ISBN: 0710812655.

A very selective compilation, with only 598 entries in 21 sections. Includes coverage of specific novels. Indexes of authors, subjects and titles of Conrad's works.
Class No: 820-31CON

[7316]

KNOWLES, O. A Conrad chronology. Basingstoke, Macmillan; Boston, Hall, 1990. xix,165p. maps. £50. (*Macmillan author chronologies.*) ISBN: 033345913x, UK; 0816118396, US.

Chapters on Early Years (1857-73) and Sea Years (1874-93) followed by year-by-year and month-by-month listing of events in the writer's life, 1894-1924. Select Who's Who (22p.) has biographical notes on Conrad's circle. Glossary of locations and addresses (3p.). Select bibliography (2p.). Index of people, places and organizations. Subject index.
Class No: 820-31CON

[7317]

TEETS, B. Joseph Conrad: an annotated bibliography. New York, Garland, 1990. 786p. ISBN: 0824070372.

Supplements *Joseph Conrad: an annotated bibliography of writings about him,* ed. by B. Teets and H.E. Gerber (De Kalb, Ill., Northern Illinois Univ. Press, 1971. xii,671p. $55. ISBN: 0875800203).

The earlier work contained 1,977 entries covering the period 1895-1966. A further 762 entries for that period have been added, plus 1,389 published 1967-75. Arranged by year, then by author, with substantial abstracts. 5 indexes: authors; titles of secondary works; periodicals and newspapers; foreign languages (13); and primary titles.
Class No: 820-31CON

[7318]
WISE, T.J. A Bibliography of the writings of Joseph Conrad (1895-1921). 2nd ed., rev. and enl. London, printed for private circulation, 1921 (repr. London, Dawsons, 1964). xv,125p. illus.

1. Editiones principes (chronological order) - 2. Uncollected contributions to periodical literature - 3. Conradiana: complete volumes of biography and criticism (6 items only). No index. *Class No:* 820-31CON

Defoe

[7319]
HAMMOND, J.R. A Defoe companion. Lanham, Md., Barnes & Noble; Basingstoke, Macmillan, 1993. xi,151p. £52.50. (*Macmillan literary companions.*) ISBN: 0389210064, US; 0333513282, UK.

Mainly comprises essays on Defoe's life, achievements and works, but also includes a dictionary of his narrative works (5p.), key to characters and locations (13p.), list of film adaptations (1p.) and list of stories based on *Robinson Crusoe*. Select bibliography. Index. *Class No:* 820-31DEF

[7320]
LOVETT, R.W. ***Robinson Crusoe*: a bibliographical checklist of English-language editions (1719-1979).** Westport, Conn., Greenwood, 1991. 303p. $65. ISBN: 0313276951.

Lists and describes 1,198 separate eds., including abridgements and children's versions. Chronological arrangement with index of publishers. *Class No:* 820-31DEF

[7321]
MOORE, J.R. A Checklist of the writings of Daniel Defoe. 2nd ed. Hamden, Conn., Archon, 1971. xviii,281p. ISBN: 0208010866.

1st ed. Bloomington, Ind., Indiana Univ. Press, 1960.

1. Books, pamphlets, poems, and manuscripts - 2. Undated works published posthumously - 3. Periodicals. 2nd ed. has supplement with notes on many original entries plus 22 new items. *c.*570 items in all. Index of printers and booksellers and title index. *Class No:* 820-31DEF

[7322]
PETERSON, S. Daniel Defoe: a reference guide, 1731-1924. Boston, Hall, 1987. xxxiii,455p. $50. ISBN: 0816181578.

Lists over 1,500 works about Defoe chronologically then A-Z within each year, with substantial annotations. Includes items in 9 languages and several hundred introductions to editions of *Robinson Crusoe*. Author and title index; comprehensive subject index. *Class No:* 820-31DEF

Dickens

Bibliographies

[7323]
A Bibliography of Dickensian criticism, 1836-1975. Churchill, R.C., *ed.* New York, Garland; London, Macmillan, 1975. xiv,314p. ISBN: 0824010833, US; 0333191943, UK.

Classified bibliography in 6 sections: 1. Introduction (bibliographies, biographies, etc.) - 2. General criticism, 19th century - 3. General criticism, 20th century - 4. Criticism of particular works - 5. Aspects of Dickens (36 subject headings) - 6. Critical comparisons (with 65 other

....(*contd.*)
writers). Chronological arrangement in each section, with brief annotations and some illustrative quotations. Over 2,000 entries. Index of critics. *Class No:* 820-31DIC(01)

[7324]
BOLTON, H.P. Dickens dramatized. London, Mansell, 1987. xviii,501p. £120. ISBN: 0720118042.

An outstanding compilation of information about the dramatizations (including TV, radio and film versions) of Dickens's works, 1834-1984. Sections on each of the works, in chronological order, listing dramatizations, again chronologically, with 407 entries under *Oliver Twist* alone and over 3,000 in total. Index of playwrights, theatres, actors, producers, etc. 'A detailed, meticulous and quite fascinating work of reference' (*Library Review*, Winter 1987, p.295-6), and a worthy winner of the Besterman Medal for 1987. *Class No:* 820-31DIC(01)

[7325]
Dickens studies annual: essays on Victorian fiction. New York, AMS Press (earlier Carbondale and Edwardsville, Ill., Southern Illinois Univ. Press), 1970-. v.1-. Annual.

Carries narrative surveys of recent Dickens studies. That in v.21 (1992) covers 1990 publications, occupies 27p., and is followed by a list of over 100 books and articles mentioned. Studies of other Victorian novelists are also surveyed occasionally, the same vol. including a survey of Trollope studies, 1982-86 (31p.). *Class No:* 820-31DIC(01)

[7326]
FENSTERMAKER, J.J. Charles Dickens, 1940-1975: an analytical subject index to periodical criticism of the novels and Christmas books. Boston, Hall; London, Prior, 1979. xix,302p. ISBN: 0816180644, US; 0860432904, UK.

Indexes 1,100 articles in over 100 periodicals, under 17 major subject headings (*e.g.* 'Characters', 'Plot', 'Themes') with numerous subheadings. Separate sections for each novel, plus a general section and one for the Christmas novels. Appendices list selected books on Dickens and their reviews, and editions of his works, also with reviews, published 1940-75. Index of critics. *Class No:* 820-31DIC(01)

[7327]
Garland Dickens bibliographies. DeVries, D., *ed.* New York, Garland, 1981-93. v.1-12 (in progress).

V.1 *Our mutual friend*, by J. Brattin and B. Hornback. 1984. 220p. ISBN: 0824089863.

V.2 *Oliver Twist*, by D. Paroissien. 1986. 352p. ISBN: 0824091983.

V.3 *Hard times*, by S. Manning. 1984. 320p. $55. ISBN: 0824088956.

V.4 *Dickens's Christmas books, Christmas stories, and other fiction*, by R. Glancy. 1985. 640p. ISBN: 082408988x.

V.5 *Great expectations*, by G.J. Worth. 1986. 368p. ISBN: 0824088182.

V.6 *Barnaby Rudge*, by T.J. Rice. 1987. 351p. ISBN: 082408652x.

V.7 *Pickwick papers*, by E. Engel. 1990. 378p. $53. ISBN: 0824087666.

V.8 *David Copperfield*, by R.J. Dunn. 1981. 284p. ISBN: 0824093224.

V.9 *The Old curiosity shop*, by Paul and Priscilla Schlicke. 1988. 518p. ISBN: 0824085124.

V.10 *Martin Chuzzlewit*, by R.E. Lougy. 1990. 320p. $54. ISBN: 0824046080.

V.11 *The Mystery of Edwin Drood*, by D.R. Cox. 1991. 400p. ISBN: 0824085116.

.... *(contd.)*

V.12 *A Tale of two cities,* by R.F.Glancy. 1993. 264p. $45. ISBN: 0824070917.

A series of comprehensive, annotated bibliographies covering editions, manuscripts, adaptations, critical studies, etc. *Class No:* 820-31DIC(01)

Encyclopaedias & Dictionaries

[7328]

BENTLEY, N., & *others*. The Dickens index. Oxford, Oxford Univ. Press, 1988. xii,308p. ISBN: 0192827812.

Over 5,000 entries in a single A-Z sequence, covering all aspects of Dickens' oeuvre: his literary works (including periodical contributions), quotations, characters, allusions (listed separately and under cumulative headings such as 'Bible' and 'Shakespeare'), references to historical and contemporary events, obsolete words and phrases, places, and persons connected with his literary life, such as illustrators and publishers. Entries for works give basic bibliographical details of first publication. Most entries have references to the original work by chapter. Time chart of Dickens' life. Appendix on his journalism. ' ... the most comprehensive reference-book to the whole of Dickens ever to have appeared' (*TLS*, no.4481, April 17-23, 1989, p.173). *Class No:* 820-31DIC(03)

[7329]

The Charles Dickens encyclopedia. Hardwick, Michael *and* Hardwick, Mollie, *comps*. Reading, Osprey, 1973. xi,531p. ISBN: 0708848966.

A comprehensive reference work with the following sections: 1. Works (publication history and plot summary) - 2. People (2,000 characters, A-Z, with notes and illustrative quotations) - 3. Places (topography of Dickens's works and life) - 4. Time chart of his life and career, 1812-70 - 5. Dickens's circle (biographical notes on over 150 relatives and associates) - 6. Quotations (lengthy extracts, presented work by work) - 7. Index to quotations (*c.*3,000 keywords, names and subjects). General index. *Class No:* 820-31DIC(03)

[7330]

LEVIT, F. A Dickens glossary. New York, Garland, 1990. 450p. ISBN: 082405542x.

Lists *c.*2,700 words and phrases used by Dickens which may cause difficulties for readers, particularly those outside the UK. Each entry includes the full quotation containing the term and a reference to the source, as well as definition and explanation. *Class No:* 820-31DIC(03)

[7331]

NEWLIN, G. Every thing in Dickens: ideas and subjects discussed by Charles Dickens in his complete works - a topicon. Westport, Conn., Greenwood, 1996. 1168p. illus. £115. ISBN: 0313298742.

A remarkable compilation of over 860,000 words, which attempts to include every notable passage or short comment on the vast range of topics which interested Dickens. Extracts are arranged under 405 subject headings in 15 chapters, with titles like 'Industry and Government', 'London' and 'First and Last Things'. Each chapter has its own contents table, which constitutes a detailed index to the extracts and gives the source for each item. Exhaustive indexes to localities and to words and phrases. Over 50 illustrations. *Class No:* 820-31DIC(03)

[7332]

NEWLIN, G. Everyone in Dickens. Westport, Conn., Greenwood, 1995. 3v. illus. £250. ISBN: 0313295808.

V.1 *Plots, people and publishing particulars in the complete works, 1833-1849.* 896p.

V.2 *Plots, people and publishing particulars in the complete works, 1850-1870.* 928p.

V.3 *Characteristics and commentaries, tables and tabulations: a taxonomy*. 752p.

A massive assembly of data covering 13,143 people, real and fictitious, mentioned in 528 works by Dickens. Vols. 1 and 2 are arranged chronologically by work and present the characters in Dickens' own words with contemporary illustrations in many cases. V.3 has 12 detailed subject indexes to the character lists, plus numerous thematic lists and tables of, for example, frequently used names, given names, animal names, and parodic or allegorical names. Also studies of various aspects of Dickens' names, *e.g.* notable suffixes, name experiments, notable omissions, etc. plus essays on related topics such as orphanhood. A companion to *Everything in Dickens* (*q.v.*), the pair being the fruit of a lifetime's obsession *Class No:* 820-31DIC(03)

[7333]

—HAWES, D. Who's who in Dickens. London, Routledge, 1998. xxv,278p. illus. £45. ISBN: 0415136040.

A selective dictionary listing 1,650 people (plus a few animals) found in the fiction, essays and plays. Fuller entries for more important characters include limited critical comment and discussion of possible sources. Contemporary illustrations included for 40 major characters. References to chapters. *Class No:* 820-31DIC(03)

Chronologies

[7334]

PAGE, N. A Dickens chronology. Basingstoke, Macmillan; Boston, Hall, 1988. xiii,156p. £52.50. (*Macmillan author chronologies.*) ISBN: 0333388593, UK; 0816189498, US.

Details the main events of the writer's life, 1812-1870, year by year and month by month. Indexes of Dickens' works, people, and places. *Class No:* 820-31DIC(090)

Eliot (George)

[7335]

FULMER, C.M. George Eliot: a reference guide. Boston, Hall, 1977. xvi,247p. ISBN: 0816178593.

Lists over 1,200 secondary items published 1858-1971, the great majority having appeared since 1945. Substantial annotations. Indexes of Eliot's works, titles of secondary material, names of critics and subjects.

Supplemented by *George Eliot: a reference guide, 1972-1987*, by K.L. Pangallo (Boston, Hall, 1989. 320p. $40. ISBN: 0816189730), which includes many examples of feminist criticism in over 1,000 entries, chronologically arranged. Indexes of primary titles, authors, secondary titles, and subjects. *Class No:* 820-31ELI

[7336]

HANDS, T. A George Eliot chronology. Basingstoke, Macmillan; Boston, Hall, 1989. xiii,195p. £52.50. (*Macmillan author chronologies.*) ISBN: 033339836x, UK; 0816189838, US.

Presents the major events of the writer's life extremely clearly, year by year and month by month. Bibliography (5p.). Index of people, places, works and topics. *Class No:* 820-31ELI

[7337]

MUDGE, I.G. *and* **SEARS, M.E. A George Eliot dictionary:** the characters and scenes of the novels, stories and poems alphabetically arranged. Reprint of 1924 ed. Brooklyn, N.Y., Haskell, 1972. xlvii,260p. $75. ISBN: 0838313507.

Originally published London, Routledge, and New York, Wilson, 1924.

Main sequence (244p.) lists and identifies historical and fictitious people and places with chapter references and illustrative quotations. Also chronological list of Eliot's publications, synopses of plots and list of books mentioned in her works. Index of 'originals', *i.e.* real people and places which inspired fictional characters and locations.
Class No: 820-31ELI

Fielding

[7338]

HAHN, H.G. Henry Fielding: an annotated bibliography. Metuchen, N.J., Scarecrow, 1979. xiv,229p. (*Scarecrow author bibliographies.*) ISBN: 0810812126.

962 entries in 11 sections: editions and bibliography, general criticism, plays, 5 major novels, journalism, miscellaneous. Covers the period 1900-1978. Annotations 'reliable and useful' (*Choice*, v.16(10), Dec. 1979, p.1286), generally in the form of an abstract with some evaluation. Author and subject indexes. *Class No:* 820-31FIE

[7339]

MORRISSEY, L.J. Henry Fielding: a reference guide. Boston, Hall, 1980. 560p.

Writings by and about Fielding, 1755-1977, arranged by year in 2 sections: editions and book-length studies; shorter studies. Index to authors, Fielding's works and some topics.
Class No: 820-31FIE

Forster

[7340]

E.M. Forster: an annotated bibliography of writings about him. McDowell, F.P.W., *comp. and ed.* De Kalb, Ill., Northern Illinois Univ. Press, 1976. x,924p. $55. (*Annotated secondary bibliography series on English literature in transition, 1880-1920.*) ISBN: 0875800467.

1,913 numbered entries, arranged by year, 1905-1975, and chronologically within each year, covering material from a wide range of sources - including dissertations, letters to newspapers and entries in reference books - and from 10 languages. Each is abstracted and all major items receive the editor's critical comments in brackets. Checklist of Forster's works. Indexes of authors, titles of secondary works, periodicals and newspapers, foreign languages and primary titles. *Class No:* 820-31FOR

[7341]

KIRKPATRICK, B.J. A Bibliography of E.M. Forster. 2nd ed. Oxford, Clarendon Press, 1985. xvi,327p. illus. £60. (*Soho bibliographies.*) ISBN: 0198181914.

1st ed. 1965; 2nd (rev.) impression 1968. Both published London, Hart-Davis.

A. Books and pamphlets - B. Contributions to books and pamphlets - C. Contributions to periodicals and newspapers - D. Translations into foreign languages - E. Miscellaneous printed material - F. Audio-visual material - G. Manuscripts.

Completely revised and reset, with two new main sections (Audio-visual material and Manuscripts), several new subsections and additions to all original sections, making it 50% longer than the original edition. 'Indispensable to

....*(contd.)*

Forster scholars' (*Review of English Studies* v.38 (151), Aug. 1987, p.408-9), but no material *on* Forster, for which see McDowell. *Class No:* 820-31FOR

[7342]

STAPE, J.H. An E.M. Forster chronology. Basingstoke, Macmillan, 1993. xv,198p. £52.50. (*Macmillan author chronologies.*) ISBN: 0333545400.

Details the events of the writer's life, month by month and day by day, and also includes biographical notes on over 40 members of Forster's circle and list of locations and addresses. Select bibliography of biographical sources (2p.). 3 indexes: people and organizations; Forster's works; authors read by Forster. *Class No:* 820-31FOR

[7343]

SUMMERS, C.J. E.M. Forster: a guide to research. New York, Garland, 1991. xviii, 405p. ISBN: 0824046242.

Part 1., Primary Bibliography (p.3-13), has brief annotations but adds nothing to Kilpatrick. Part 2, Secondary Bibliography (p.17-372), has 12 sections covering bibliographies, biographies, general criticism and criticism of specific novels, short fiction and nonfiction, with substantial evaluative annotations. 1,245 entries. Author and subject indexes and index of Forster's works mentioned in annotations. Complements McDowell because of its classified arrangement and coverage of post-1975 criticism, but is more selective, omitting peripheral items.
Class No: 820-31FOR

Gaskell

[7344]

SELIG, R.L. Elizabeth Gaskell: a reference guide. Boston, Hall, 1977. xviii,431p. ISBN: 0816178135.

Annotated bibliography of *c.*1,600 secondary items arranged by year, 1848-1974, with separate sections for books and shorter writings within each year. Annotations are basically nonevaluative abstracts. Single-sequence index includes Gaskell titles, authors and titles of critical works, and selected subject headings. *Class No:* 820-31GAS

[7345]

WELCH, J. Elizabeth Gaskell: an annotated bibliography, 1929-1975. New York, Garland, 1977. xii,139p. ISBN: 0824099508.

Lists 237 articles, books and dissertations on Gaskell published since 1929, the year of publication of 2 bibliographies appended to the biographies by Sanders and Whitfield. Appendix 1 lists 78 editions of Gaskell's works published in the same period. Appendix 2 gives chronology of her life and works, 1810-66. Indexes of authors, Gaskell titles and subjects.

Continued by *Elizabeth Gaskell: an annotated bibliography of English-language sources, 1976-1991*, by N.S. Weyant (Metuchen, N.J., Scarecrow, 1994. 227p. $34. ISBN: 0810828901), which has 355 entries. *Class No:* 820-31GAS

Greene

[7346]

HOSKINS, R. Graham Greene: a character index and guide. New York, Garland, 1991. 512p. $66. ISBN: 0824041119.

Over 3,200 entries, covering not only characters but also placenames, historical and literary allusions, and significant

.... *(contd.)*
foreign phrases. Greene's works arranged chronologically, with entries A-Z under each title. Index. *Class No:* 820-31GRE

[7347]
WOBBE, R.A. Graham Greene: a bibliography and guide to research. New York, Garland, 1979. 440p. ISBN: 0910286442.

First editions described in detail, including drama. Lists a selection of 1,000 works about Greene and also broadcast interviews. 22p. of plates. Useful indexes, including books reviewed by Greene.

For more secondary material, see A.F. Cassis' *Graham Greene: an annotated bibliography of criticism* (Metuchen, NJ, Scarecrow, 1981. 423p. $39.50. ISBN: 0810814188). *Class No:* 820-31GRE

Hardy

Bibliographies

[7348]
DRAPER, R.P. *and* **RAY, M. An Annotated critical bibliography of Thomas Hardy.** Hemel Hempstead, Harvester Wheatsheaf, 1989. vi, 227p. (*Harvester annotated critical bibliographies.*) ISBN: 0710810105.

A selective survey of Hardy scholarship with the emphasis on recent output. 724 items in 15 sections, covering poetry, individual novels, short fiction and a range of general themes. Brief evaluative annotations with few cross-references. Indexes of authors, subjects and titles. *Class No:* 820-31HAR(01)

[7349]
PURDY, R.L. Thomas Hardy: a bibliographical study. Reprint of 1954 ed. Oxford, Oxford Univ. Press, 1978. 402p. plates. ISBN: 0198181310.

Originally published London, Oxford Univ. Press, 1954.

Comprehensive bibliography which gives 'a full and detailed description of every one of Hardy's books' (*Preface*). Locates and describes manuscripts and gives the publishing history and traces the development of texts through subsequent edtions.

Part I. Editiones principes - II. Collected editions - III. Uncollected contributions to books, periodicals and newspapers. Reprints and translations not included. *Class No:* 820-31HAR(01)

[7350]
SHERRICK, J. Thomas Hardy's major novels: an annotated bibliography. Lanham, Md., Scarecrow, 1997. 192p. $36. ISBN: 0810833824.

Evaluates a range of studies of Hardy's major novels. *Class No:* 820-31HAR(01)

[7351]
Thomas Hardy: an annotated bibliography of writings about him. Gerber, H.E. *and* Davis, W.E., *eds.* De Kalb, Ill., Northern Illinois Univ. Press, 1973-83. 2v. (841p.;735p.). $45; $50. (*Annotated secondary bibliography series on English literature in transition, 1880-1920.*) ISBN: 0875800394, v.1; 0875800912, v.2.

V.1 has 3,153 items arranged by year, 1871-1969, then by author, with substantial abstracts - particularly lengthy for less accessible material. Checklist of Hardy's works. 5 indexes: authors; titles of secondary works; periodicals and newspapers; foreign languages (10); primary titles.

V.2 covers 1970-78, with further material for 1871-1969. *Class No:* 820-31HAR(01)

Encyclopaedias & Dictionaries

[7352]
PINION, F.B. A Hardy companion: a guide to the works of Thomas Hardy and their background. London, Macmillan; New York, St. Martin's Press, 1968. xvii,555p. illus. maps. £57.50. ISBN: 0333072901.

The most useful feature of this guide is the 'Dictionary of people and places in Hardy's works' (p.225-520), but note that it does not include the historical characters of *The Dynasts* nor the numerous anonymous minor characters, for which see Saxelby. Preceded by summaries and appraisals of individual works and sections on Hardy's life and influences. Glossary (p.521-30); select bibliography (p.532-49) with annotations, especially for critical works on Hardy. List of manuscript locations. *Class No:* 820-31HAR(03)

[7353]
PINION, F.B. A Thomas Hardy dictionary, with maps and a chronology. Basingstoke, Macmillan, 1989. xv,322p. £17.99. ISBN: 0333576829.

Unlike Saxelby's earlier work with the same title, this is not a dictionary of characters and places but an attempt to help the reader cope with 'uncertainties and questions which could arise ... in the course of reading Hardy' (*Introductory notes*). Approx. 6,000 entries covering literary, classical and biblical allusions, archaic or dialect words, historical and contemporary events and personages, and members of Hardy's family and circle referred to in his work. Chronology of his life (12p.). 10 maps. *Class No:* 820-31HAR(03)

[7354]
SAXELBY, F.O. A Thomas Hardy dictionary: the characters and scenes of the novels and poems alphabetically arranged and described. Reprint of 1911 ed. Westport, Conn., Greenwood, 1980. lxxx,238p. maps. ISBN: 0313220786.

Originally published London, Routledge, 1911.

A comprehensive dictionary of people and places mentioned in Hardy's prose and early poetry with brief notes, preceded by a bibliography, which 'does not pretend to absolute completeness' (*Preface*), and synopses of the novels and stories. *Class No:* 820-31HAR(03)

Chronologies

[7355]
HANDS, T. A Hardy chronology. Basingstoke, Macmillan, 1992. xiii,227p. £55. (*Macmillan author chronologies.*) ISBN: 0333459148.

Details the events of the writer's life, month by month and day by day, based mainly on Florence Hardy's *The Life of Thomas Hardy* (1962) and his *Collected letters* (1978-88). List of principal sources. Thorough index. *Class No:* 820-31HAR(090)

Kipling

[7356]
LIVINGSTON, F.V. Bibliography of the works of Rudyard Kipling. New York, Wells, 1927 (repr. New York, Johnson, 1970). xviii,523p. illus.

504 editions listed and described, 1879-1926, plus list of collected eds. Title-page facsimiles.

Supplement (Cambridge, Mass., Harvard Univ. Press; London, Oxford Univ. Press, 1938. xvi,335p. illus.) continues the compilation to 1937 and also has additions and corrections to the original bibliography. Both vols. are very thoroughly indexed. *Class No:* 820-31KIP

[7357]

OREL, H. A Kipling chronology. Basingstoke, Macmillan; Boston, Hall, 1990. xiii,128p. £45. (*Macmillan author chronologies.*) ISBN: 0333459156, UK; 0816190909, US.

Presents the main events of the writer's life, year by year and month by month, 1865-1936. Biographical notes on *c.*75 of Kipling's associates. Select bibliography of secondary material (4p.). Index. *Class No:* 820-31KIP

[7358]

PAGE, N. A Kipling companion. London, Macmillan, 1984. xvii,202p. illus. (*Macmillan literary companions.*) ISBN: 0333315383.

A mixed bag of information on all aspects of Kipling's life and work, of which the largest and most useful sections are the two on his short stories, which comprise critical appraisal of the 21 collections and an alphabetical guide to nearly 200 individual stories. Also includes biographical notes on people associated with Kipling, notes on his novels, prose and verse, a filmography and select bibliography. Index. *Class No:* 820-31KIP

[7359]

STEWART, J.M. Rudyard Kipling: a bibliographical catalogue. Yeats, A.W., *ed.* Toronto, Dalhousie Univ. Press and Univ. of Toronto Press, 1959. xviii,673p. illus.

Based on and a partial checklist of the Stewart Kipling Collection in Dalhousie University. Two main sections deal with major works (700 items) and other works, and appendices cover items in sale catalogues; uncollected prose and verse; works in anthologies and readers; collected sets; musical settings; and unauthorized editions. Excludes translations. Entries are in chronological sequence as they appeared in the major editions of Kipling, thus showing the relationship of the many printings of Kipling's works. Incorporates many of the corrections and additions prepared by F.V. Livingston for a revised edition of her *Bibliography of the works of Rudyard Kipling* and its *Supplement*. Detailed index. *Class No:* 820-31KIP

[7360]

YOUNG, W.A. *and* **McGIVERING, J.H. A Kipling dictionary.** London, Macmillan; New York, St. Martin's Press, 1967. x,230p.

A completely revised and reset ed. of Young's *A Dictionary of the characters and scenes in the stories and poems of Rudyard Kipling, 1886-1911* (London, Routledge, 1911).

Over 4,000 entries for books, stories, poems, characters, places, and first lines of verse. Appendix 1 lists Kipling's books, with contents. Appendix 2 is a select secondary bibliography. *Class No:* 820-31KIP

Lawrence (D.H.)

[7361]

D.H. Lawrence: an annotated bibliography of writings about him. Cowan, J.C., *ed.* De Kalb, Ill., Northern Illinois Univ. Press, 1982-85. 2v. (xxvi,612p. ;xxxi,768p.). $45 per vol. (*Annotated secondary bibliography series on English literature in transition, 1880-1920.*) ISBN: 0875800777, v.1; 0875801056, v.2.

V.1 has 2,061 entries arranged by year, 1909-60, then by author, with abstracts. Checklist of Lawrence's works. 5 indexes: authors, titles of secondary works, periodicals and newspapers, foreign languages (11), primary titles.

V.2 adds entries for 2,566 items in 15 languages, published 1961-75, in the same format.

....*(contd.)*

D.H. Lawrence Review (Newark, Del., Univ. of Delaware, 1968-. 3 py. ISSN: 00114936) regularly includes bibliographical studies. *Class No:* 820-31LAW

[7362]

D.H. Lawrence review. Newark, Del., Univ. of Delaware (previously Fayetteville, Ark., Univ. of Arkansas), 1968-. v.1, no.1-. 3py.

Regularly includes bibliographies. V.23(2-3), Summer-Fall 1991, has a classified checklist of Lawrence scholarship for 1990 with 88 items in 7 sections. *Class No:* 820-31LAW

[7363]

POPLAWSKI, P. D.H. Lawrence: a reference companion. Westport, Conn., Greenwood, 1996. 744p. £79.50. ISBN: 031328637x.

90-page biographical overview followed by chapters on almost every text produced by Lawrence, excluding individual poems. These include history of composition and publication, who's who and summary. Third section includes a guide to Lawrence criticism and scholarship and a comprehensive listing of film adaptations and of criticism relating to them. Maps of Lawrence's travels. Chronology of his life and works. Bibliography of reference sources. Index. *Class No:* 820-31LAW

[7364]

PRESTON, P. A D.H. Lawrence chronology. Basingstoke, Macmillan, 1994. xxi,208p. £52.50. ISBN: 0333531337.

Details the events of the writer's life, month by month and day by day. Also offers details of his wide reading and relationships with contemporary figures. Bibliography. General index and index of Lawrence's works. 'A wealth of exact, detailed information' (*Choice*, v.32(7), March 1995, p.1090). *Class No:* 820-31LAW

[7365]

RICE, T.J. D.H. Lawrence: a guide to research. New York, Garland, 1983. xxiii,484p. ISBN: 0824091272.

A selective, annotated bibliography in 3 parts: 1. Primary bibliography, has 135 entries in 4 sections - 2. Secondary bibliography, has *c.*1,700 in 20 sections, of which 16 are devoted to specific works or groups of works - 3. Appendixes, lists 298 foreign-language studies plus a few study guides and unverified titles. The concise annotations aim for 'a balance between description and, in many cases, evaluation' (*Preface*). Thoroughly cross-referenced. Author, title and subject indexes. *Class No:* 820-31LAW

[7366]

ROBERTS, W. A Bibliography of D.H. Lawrence. 2nd ed. Cambridge, Cambridge Univ. Press, 1982. xvii,626p. illus. ISBN: 0521222958.

1st ed. London, Hart-Davis, 1963.

A. Books and periodicals (full descriptions of 1st eds. - 121 entries) - B. Contributions to books (85) - C. Contributions to periodicals (272) - D. Translations (29 languages) - E. Manuscripts (447 entries) - F. Books and pamphlets about Lawrence (242 entries). Retains the numbering from 1st ed., with interpolations. Index. *Class No:* 820-31LAW

Meredith

[7367]

COLLIE, M. George Meredith: a bibliography. Winchester, St. Paul's Bibliographies, 1974. 290p. $24. ISBN: 0906795230.

1. Novels and short stories - 2. Other prose - 3. Poems - 4. Collected editions - 5. Translations. '... the effective terminal date ... is 1924; the main entries contain references to editions and re-issues that appeared before that. Re-issues that have appeared since 1924 have not been enumerated; such publications are mentioned only when they have bibliographical or textual interest' (*Introduction*). Appendix lists all his publications chronologically, 1851-1970. Index.
Class No: 820-31MER

[7368]

OLMSTED, J.C. George Meredith: an annotated bibliography of criticism, 1925-1975. New York, Garland, 1978. xix,158p. ISBN: 0824098412.

Lists 586 secondary items chronologically with annotations. Includes American doctoral theses but omits newspaper articles and entries in reference works. Chronology of Meredith's life. Author, title and subject indexes. For earlier studies, see *A Bibliography of the writings in prose and verse of George Meredith, and Meredithiana* by M.B. Forman (London, Bibliographical Society, 1922-4. 2v. Repr. New York, Haskell House, 1971. $150. ISBN: 0838311148). *Class No:* 820-31MER

Orwell

[7369]

FENWICK, G. George Orwell: a bibliographical study. Folkestone, St. Paul's Bibliographies, 1998. 448p. illus. £55. (*Winchester bibliographies of 20th century writers.*) ISBN: 1873040059.

The first comprehensive bibliographical study of Orwell, with sections on first edition books, subsequent eds., variants, translations, and (where possible) unauthorized eds., giving full descriptions of all significant stages of publication. Further sections on books edited by Orwell, contributions to books and periodicals, published letters, poems, diaries, notebooks, radio programmes and fragments. *Class No:* 820-31ORW

[7370]

HAMMOND, J.R. A George Orwell companion: a guide to the novels, documentaries and essays. London, Macmillan, 1982. xii,278p. illus. ISBN: 0333286685.

Consists mainly of biographical and critical material, but useful for reference are: 'A George Orwell dictionary' (p.56-75), which is an A-Z guide to the books, essays and poems; 'Key to the characters and locations' (p.231-255); and the select, annotated bibliography (p.266-274). Index.
Class No: 820-31ORW

[7371]

MEYERS, J. *and* **MEYERS, V. George Orwell: an annotated bibliography of criticism.** New York, Garland, 1977. ix,132p. illus. ISBN: 0824099559.

A highly selective compilation of 500 entries, arranged A-Z by author with concise annotations. Excludes newpaper articles, reviews and dissertations. No index.
Class No: 820-31ORW

Richardson

[7372]

HANNAFORD, R.G. Samuel Richardson: an annotated bibliography of critical studies. New York, Garland, 1980. xxii,292p. ISBN: 0824095316.

1,460 concisely annotated entries in 6 main sections: 1. Richardson's works - 2. 18th-century criticism - 3. 19th-century criticism - 4. 20th-century criticism - 5. Richardson's influence and foreign reception - 6. Theses. Author and subject indexes.

An alternative source is S.W.R. Smith's *Samuel Richardson: a reference guide* (Boston, Hall, 1984. 425p. ISBN: 0816181705), which has chronologically-arranged, annotated entries for secondary material. *Class No:* 820-31RIC

[7373]

SALE, W.M. Samuel Richardson: a bibliographical record of his literary career with historical notes. New Haven, Yale Univ. Press; London, Oxford Univ. Press, 1936. xxiv,141p. illus.

Full descriptive bibliography in 3 sections: 1. Novels, edited works, pamphlets, books written in collaboration (53 items) - 2. Contributions to periodicals (5) - 3. Works inspired by the publication of Richardson's novels (32). Many title-page facsimiles. Index. *Class No:* 820-31RIC

Smollett

[7374]

CORDASCO, F. Tobias George Smollett: a bibliographical guide. New York, AMS Press, 1978. xiv,157p. $32.50. ISBN: 0404160182.

875 items in 8 sections: 1. General bibliography and reference guides (to 18th-century literature) - 2. Bibliographies (of Smollett) - 3. Texts - 4. Letters - 5. Biography and criticism - 6. Translations and the *Travels* - 7. Historical works and the Periodicals - 8. Miscellanea. Brief annotations. Index. *Class No:* 820-31SMO

[7375]

SPECTOR, R.D. Tobias Smollett: a reference guide. Boston, Hall, 1980. xiv,341p. ISBN: 0816179603.

Lists *c.*2,100 critical studies by year, 1746-1978, then by author, with brief nonevaluative annotations. Index. In his preface, the compiler suggests that Cordasco's bibliography is not entirely reliable. *Class No:* 820-31SMO

[7376]

WAGONER, M. Tobias Smollett: a checklist of editions of his works and an annotated secondary bibliography. New York, Garland, 1984. xvi,753p. ISBN: 0824090853.

Lists 752 primary items in 16 sections and nearly 2,800 secondary items in 17 sections. Concise annotations. Cut-off date: 1981. Author and subject indexes. *Class No:* 820-31SMO

Sterne

[7377]

HARTLEY, L. Laurence Sterne in the twentieth century: an essay and a bibliography of Sternean studies, 1900-1965. Corrected reprint of 1966 ed. Chapel Hill, N.C., Univ. of North Carolina Press, 1968. 207p.

First published 1966.

Lengthy introductory essay (72p.) followed by annotated bibliography in 7 sections 1. Bibliographical aids - 2. Editions and selections - 3. Biography - 4. Criticism - 5.

....(contd.)

Literary reputation - 6. Literary influences, affinities and imitations - 7. Miscellaneous. 1,178 succinctly annotated entries. Name index. *Class No:* 820-31STE

[7378]

—HARTLEY, L. Laurence Sterne: an annotated bibliography, 1965-77, with an introductory essay-review of the scholarship. Boston, Hall; London, Prior, 1978. x,103p. ISBN: 0816181675, US; 0860432041, UK.

Follows virtually the same format as Hartley's previous work, adding a further 409 items. Includes cross-references to the earlier vol. Name index. *Class No:* 820-31STE

Thackeray

[7379]

Annotations for the selected works of William Makepeace Thackeray: the complete novels, the major non-fictional prose, and selected shorter pieces. Harden, E.F., *ed.* New York, Garland, 1990. 2v. (653; 729p.). $180. ISBN: 0824031407.

Lists and explains historical, literary, topographical, religious, and other allusions in Thackeray's works, taking each work separately, in chronological order, and dealing with the allusions in the order they appear in the text. Index in v.2 to persons, periodicals, newspapers, subjects, and events. *Class No:* 820-31THA

[7380]

FLAMM, D. Thackeray's critics: an annotated bibliography of British and American criticism, 1836-1901. Chapel Hill, N.C., Univ. of North Carolina Press, 1966. 184p.

705 items, chronologically arranged, after a lengthy introduction (36p.). Key studies are asterisked. Index. *Class No:* 820-31THA

[7381]

—OLMSTED, J.C. Thackeray and his twentieth-century critics: an annotated bibliography, 1900-1975. New York, Garland, 1977. xxvi,249p. ISBN: 082409915x.

Lists 848 US and UK publications by year, then by author. Indexes of authors, Thackeray titles and subjects. *Class No:* 820-31THA

[7382]

GOLDFARB, S. William Makepeace Thackeray: an annotated bibliography, 1976-1987. New York, Garland, 1989. 175p. $34. ISBN: 0824012127.

Lists over 500 studies published since Olmsted's bibliography or omitted by him. Indexes of authors, subjects, primary titles, and Thackeray's characters. *Class No:* 820-31THA

[7383]

MUDGE, I.G. *and* **SEARS, M.E. A Thackeray dictionary:** the characters and scenes of the novels and short stories alphabetically arranged. London, Routledge; New York, Dutton, 1910. xlv,304p.

Entries include description (including appropriate quotations for major characters) and references to all chapters in which the person/place appears. Originals are identified only where there is certainty. Dictionary proper is preceded by synopses of Thackeray's fictional works. *Class No:* 820-31THA

Trollope

[7384]

MULLEN, R. *and* **MUNSON, J. The Penguin companion to Trollope.** London, Penguin, 1996. xxii,552p. £15. ISBN: 0140235582.

A single A-Z sequence with lengthy articles on 47 novels, 42 short stories and 14 nonfiction works, plus nearly 300 entries on people (real and fictitious), magazines, periodicals, publishers, topics, allusions, etc. Chronology (3p.) *Class No:* 820-31TRO

[7385]

OLMSTED, J.C. *and* **WELCH, J.E. The Reputation of Trollope:** an annotated bibliography, 1925-1975. New York and London, Garland, 1978. xxiii,212p. ISBN: 0824098854.

Lists 652 secondary items by year then by author, with annotations based on the critics' own words. Most of the items were published in the UK and US, but there are some from Australia, France, Germany and Italy. Reviews of major works are also listed. Indexes of authors, subjects and Trollope titles. *Class No:* 820-31TRO

[7386]

SADLEIR, M. Trollope: a bibliography; an analysis of the history and structure of the works of Anthony Trollope, and a general survey of the effect of original publishing conditions on a book's subsequent rarity. Reprint of 1928 ed., with *Addenda and corrigenda* (1934). Folkestone, Dawson, 1977. xvi,332p. illus. ISBN: 0712900500.

Originally published London, Constable, 1928.

Full descriptive bibliography of Trollope's books (83 items) plus listing of his contributions to periodicals and collected editions. Index. *Class No:* 820-31TRO

[7387]

TERRY, R.C. A Trollope chronology. Basingstoke, Macmillan, 1989. xxxiii,167p. (*Macmillan author chronologies.*) ISBN: 0333399145.

Presents the major events of the writer's life extremely clearly, year by year and month by month. Appendices include lists of Trollope's lectures and speeches, 1861-79, and contemporary reviews of his work. Indexes of names and places. *Class No:* 820-31TRO

Waugh

[7388]

PAGE, N. An Evelyn Waugh chronology. Basingstoke, Macmillan, 1997. 172p. £42.50. (*Macmillan author chronologies.*) ISBN: 0333638948.

Details the events of the writer's life, month by month and day by day, drawing on his letters, diaries and other sources. Biographical notes on the Waugh circle. Index. *Class No:* 820-31WAU

Wells

[7389]

SCHIECK, W.J. *and* **COX, J.R. H.G. Wells: a reference guide.** Boston, Hall, 1988. xxxiii,430p. $50. ISBN: 0816189463.

A massive compilation of critical works on Wells published 1895-1986. Over 3,000 entries arranged by year then A-Z within each year, including doctoral dissertations, letters to editors and introductions to editions of Wells's works. Annotations take the form of abstracts followed by compilers' critical remarks and cross-references. Index of authors, editors and translators but no titles or subjects.

....(*contd.*)
'Supplies, for the first time, a well-organized, well-edited summary of writing *about* Wells' (*Choice*, v.26(3), Nov.1988, p.468). *Class No:* 820-31WEL

[7390]
WELLS, G.H. The Works of H.G. Wells, 1887-1925: a bibliography, dictionary and subject index. London, Routledge; New York, Wilson, 1926. xxv,274p.

Descriptive bibliography (p.1-72) of Wells' works with several appendices, including list of *c.*60 critical studies. Dictionary (p.89-251) lists all volume, story and essay titles and names of chief characters, with notes and references. Subject index lists topics (including real people) in the works, keyed to entries in the Dictionary. *Class No:* 820-31WEL

Woolf

[7391]
BISHOP, E. A Virginia Woolf chronology. Basingstoke, Macmillan, 1989. xvii,268p. £52.50. (*Macmillan author chronologies.*) ISBN: 0333388550.

Presents the major events of the writer's life extremely clearly, year by year and month by month. Bibliography of sources. Name and title indexes. *Class No:* 820-31WOO

[7392]
HUSSEY, M. Virginia Woolf A to Z: a comprehensive reference for students, teachers, and common readers to her life, works, and critical reception. New York, Facts on File, 1995. 464p. illus. $50. ISBN: 0816030200.

Lively and accessible entries include biographical information; detailed synopses of all major and most minor works; an overview of the critical reception to each work; descriptions of all characters, both real and fictional, in the works; discussions of people associated with Woolf; and definitions of literary terms associated with her. 9 'family trees' illustrating the complicated relationships of the Bloomsbury Group. List of adaptations of Woolf's works. Chronology. Bibliography. Index. *Class No:* 820-31WOO

[7393]
KIRKPATRICK, B.J. *and* CLARKE, S.N. A Bibliography of Virginia Woolf. 4th ed. Oxford, Clarendon Press, 1997. 486p. illus. £70. (*Soho bibliographies.*) ISBN: 0198183836.

1st ed. 1957; 3rd ed. 1980. Previous eds. by Kirkpatrick alone.

7 sections: A. Books and pamphlets - AA. Composite editions - B. Contributions to books and pamphlets and books translated by Woolf - C. Contributions to periodicals and newspapers - D. Translations - E. Foreign editions in English and miscellaneous printed material - F. Letters - G. Manuscripts. Full descriptions in A. and B. Enormously expanded in this ed. by the inclusion of new items appearing since 1980, including 56 unsigned reviews in C. and 350 new translations in D. Index. *Class No:* 820-31WOO

[7394]
RICE, T.J. Virginia Woolf: a guide to research. New York, Garland, 1984. xix,258p. ISBN: 0824090845.

Primary bibliography in 4 sections (p.3-15), followed by secondary bibliography (p.19-213) in 20 sections, 9 of which are devoted to studies of individual works. Over 1,300 annotated entries, including 256 dissertations. Some foreign-language studies included. Indexes of authors, titles, subjects, and Woolf's works.

Woolf studies annual (New York, Pace Univ. Press, 1995-. v.1-) has a guide to special library collections which is updated each year. *Class No:* 820-31WOO

Satire & Humour

[7395]
Encyclopedia of British humorists: Geoffrey Chaucer to John Cleese. Gale, S.H., *ed.* New York, Garland, 1996. 2v. £125. ISBN: 0824059905.

206 lengthy, signed essays by 119 international scholars, covering all the usual suspects (Coward, Waugh, Wodehouse, etc.), plus many authors not primarily known for their humorous writing (*e.g.* Auden, Churchill, Forster). Each article includes biography, overview of the author's works, analysis of comic techniques, and bibliography of primary and secondary sources. Index of names and titles. Chronological index. List of pseudonyms. Index.
Class No: 820-7

[7396]
NILSEN, D.L.F. Humor in British literature, from the Middle Ages to the Restoration: a reference guide. Westport, Conn., Greenwood, 1997. 256p. $79.50. ISBN: 0313297061.

Introductory essay on the origins of British humour followed by separate chapters on humour in the literature of the Middle Ages and the 14th, 15th, 16th and 17th centuries. Each chapter contains an overview of the period, followed by chronologically arranged entries on individual authors, which discuss the role of humour in their work and include extensive bibliographies of modern studies. Index.

Followed by Nilsen's *Humor in eighteenth- and nineteenth-century British literature: a reference guide* (Westport, Conn., Greenwood, 1998. 312p. $75. ISBN: 0313297053). *Class No:* 820-7

Carroll

[7397]
GUILIANO, E. Lewis Carroll: an annotated international bibliography, 1960-77. Charlottesville, Va., Univ. Press of Virginia, 1980. viii,253p. ISBN: 0813908620.

Over 1,500 entries in 4 sections: A. Primary works (including translations into nearly 50 languages) - B. Reference and bibliographical works and exhibitions - C. Biography and criticism - D. Miscellaneous (including dramatic and pictorial adaptations). Concise nonevaluative annotations. Index.

R. Fordyce's *Lewis Carroll: a reference guide* (Boston, Hall, 1988. 160p. ISBN: 0816189250) is a selective, annotated bibliography of biographical and critical studies.
Class No: 820-7CAR

[7398]
JONES, J.E *and* GLADSTONE, J.F. The *Alice* companion: a guide to Lewis Carroll's *Alice* books. Basingstoke, Macmillan, 1998. xii,319p. illus. £25. ISBN: 0333673492.

Over 300 articles on characters, themes, jokes, film versions, associated people and places, etc. Cross-references. Select bibliography (10p.). Index.
Class No: 820-7CAR

[7399]
WILLIAMS, S.H. *and* MADAN, R.L. The Lewis Carroll handbook: being a new version of *A Handbook of the literature of the Rev. C.L. Dodgson*, revised and augmented by R.L. Green, now further revised by D. Crutch. [3rd ed.]. Folkestone, Dawson; Hamden, Conn., Archon, 1979. xix,340p. illus. ISBN: 0712909060, UK; 0208017801, US.

First published London, Oxford Univ. Press, 1931; 2nd rev. ed. 1962.

Part 1 is a descriptive bibliography of editions of Carroll's works, 1845-1898, and 'reprints of exceptional interest',

....(contd.)
1898-1978 (326 items). Part 2 lists ordinary editions, 1898-1978. Part 3 lists secondary material in 3 sections: Books and pamphlets; Periodical articles and book chapters; Miscellanea. Index. *Class No:* 820-7CAR

Wodehouse

[7400]
McILVAINE, E., ***and others.*** **P.G. Wodehouse: a comprehensive bibliography.** New York, J.H. Heineman; Detroit, Omnigraphics, 1990 (distr. in UK by Dawson). xlix,489p. illus. £75. ISBN: 087008125x.

A splendidly-produced bibliography, with fully descriptive entries in sections A-C covering novels and semi-autobiographical works, omnibus volumes, and published plays. Further sections cover periodicals; anthologies; translations (20 languages); published music; works about Wodehouse (283 items); stage and screen; named editions; imitations, parodies, etc.; manuscripts and archives; correspondence. Appended checklist of a major private collection and directory of societies, private collectors, dealers, exhibitions, and institutional collections. Index. Many illustrations, including 16 colour plates with photographs of 137 dust jackets. Likely to remain the definitive bibliography. *Class No:* 820-7WOD

Commonwealth Literature

Bibliographies

[7401]
Critical writings on Commonwealth literatures: a selective bibliography to 1970, with a list of theses and dissertations. New, W.H., *comp.* Univ. Park, Pa., Pennsylvania State Univ. Press, 1975. 333p. ISBN: 0271011661.

Arranged by country/region with research aids, general criticism and works on individual authors in each section. Separate national sequences for theses. 6,576 entries. Index of critics, editors and translators. *Class No:* 820.41-44(01)

[7402]
Journal of Commonwealth literature. London, Bowker-Saur (formerly Zell), 1965- . 3 per year (formerly 2 p.y.). ISSN: 00219894.

The third issue each year is wholly devoted to the 'Annual bibliography of Commonwealth literature' for the previous year. Arranged by region (Africa: East and Central; Africa: Western; Australia, with Papua New Guinea; Canada; India; Malaysia and Singapore; New Zealand, including South Pacific Islands; Sri Lanka; West Indies; with Pakistan and South Africa appended) with unannotated entries for primary and secondary material and a short introductory essay by the regional compiler. *Class No:* 820.41-44(01)

Encyclopaedias & Dictionaries

[7403]
Encyclopedia of post-colonial literatures in English. Benson, E. *and* Conolly, L.W., *eds.* London, Routledge, 1994. 2v. (xlix,1874p.) £165. ISBN: 0415051991.

A major work on the literature of 51 countries which are or were members of the British Commonwealth. Over 1,600 signed entries (by 574 contributors) in a single A-Z sequence, falling in to 4 groups: countries and regions; genres; major subjects; and individual writers. Genre entries can be particularly lengthy, *e.g.* 30,000 words on the novel in 18 separate entries relating to different countries and regions. Brief guides to further reading after most entries, but detailed bibliographies are not provided and there is no general bibliography. Full list of entries in each vol., plenty of cross-referencing and comprehensive index (nearly 200p.) of titles, names and subjects. 'Extremely useful for under-documented areas such as Aboriginal or Indigenous writing, or the literatures of the South Pacific' (*TLS*, no.4783, Dec. 2, 1994, p.24). *Class No:* 820.41-44(03)

[7404]
JAMES, T. English literature from the Third World. Harlow, Longman; Beirut, York Press, 1986. 207p. (*York handbooks.*) ISBN: 0582792770.

A handy, paperback guide to the many new national literatures written in English. Chapters on The Caribbean, Africa, The Indian subcontinent, Malaysia and Singapore, The Philippines, and Oceania, with notes on numerous individual authors and their works. Bibliography (25p.) covers general reference works, anthologies, periodicals and individual writers by region. Index. *Class No:* 820.41-44(03)

Excerpts

[7405]
Modern Commonwealth literature. Ferres, J.H. *and* Tucker, M., *eds.* New York, Ungar, 1977. xxiv,561p. $60. (*A Library of literary criticism.*) ISBN: 0804430802.

Excerpts from critical studies on 139 mainly English-language writers, although some French-Canadian and Indian-language writers are included. Arranged A-Z by author within separate sections for Africa (40 authors), Australia (27), Canada (31), Caribbean (6), Indian subcontinent (28), and New Zealand (7). Excerpts arranged chronologically under each author. Checklists of separately-published works by each author. Index of critics.
Class No: 820.41-44(082.200)

Biographies

[7406]
International literature in English: essays on the major writers. Ross, R.L., *ed.* New York, Garland; London, St. James Press, 1991. xvi,762p. $95. ISBN: 0824034376, US; 1558621628, UK.

Covers 60 writers (mainly novelists) from countries other than the UK and US. Signed entries by international scholars average 12p. and comprise brief biography, critical essay, list of works and annotated list of selected critical studies. General bibliography (7p.). Index. *Class No:* 820.41-44(092)

Libraries

[7407]
WARWICK, R. A Handbook of library holdings of Commonwealth literature: United Kingdom and Europe. 2nd rev. ed. Boston Spa, British Library Lending Division, 1977. 123p. ISBN: 0853501696.

1st ed. by G. Wilson (London, Commonwealth Institute, 1971) covered UK only.

Describes collections in over 60 libraries, arranged A-Z

.... (contd.)
by place-name in separate sections for UK and Europe. Indexes of libraries and subjects. *Class No:* 820.41-44:061:026/027

Scottish Literature

Bibliographies

[7408]
AITKEN, W.R. Scottish literature in English and Scots: a guide to information sources. Detroit, Gale, 1982. xxiv,421p. ISBN: 0810312492.

Lists 3,956 sources in 6 main sections: 1. General works - 2. Medieval-Renaissance - 3. 1660-1800 - 4. 1800-1900 - 5. 1900-1980 - 6. Popular and folk literature. Each section has many subdivisions, with the period sections each having bibliographies of works by and about individual authors, arranged chronologically by birth-date, as well as lists of general bibliographies, studies, histories and anthologies. Over 200 authors covered, with brief biographical notes in most cases. Some entries are briefly annotated. Author, title, and subject indexes. *Class No:* 820.411(01)

[7409]
SCHEPS, W. *and* **LOONEY, J.A. Middle Scots poets:** a reference guide to James I of Scotland, Robert Henryson, William Dunbar, and Gavin Douglas. Boston, Hall, 1986. xvi,292p. ISBN: 0816183562.

A list of general sources (12p.) is followed by chronologically-arranged, separate bibliographies of studies of the 4 poets, each preceded by a checklist of works. Over 1,300 entries for studies published 1521-1978, with concise, descriptive annotations. Separate indexes for each section. *Class No:* 820.411(01)

Indexes

[7410]
Scottish poetry index: an index to poetry and poetry-related material in Scottish literary magazines. Edinburgh, Scottish Poetry Library, 1994-. v.1- (in progress).

V.1 *Akros, 1965-1983*. 1994. 169p. ISBN: 0951622633.

V.2 *Verse, 1984-1995*. 1995. 120p. ISBN: 0951622641.

V.3 *Lines Review, 1952-1992*. 1995. 140p. ISBN: 095162265x.

V.4 *Chapman, 1970-1992*. 1996. 298p. 0951622668.

A project which aims to analyze the contents of 20 periodicals, building up a database which will eventually be made available electronically. Includes indexes of names, titles and subjects. *Class No:* 820.411(014)

Encyclopaedias & Dictionaries

[7411]
ROYLE, T. The Mainstream companion to Scottish literature. Rev. ed. Edinburgh, Mainstream, 1993. x,335p. £20. ISBN: 0333285085; 1851585834.

1st ed. London, Macmillan, 1983, as *The Macmillan companion to Scottish literature*.

Over 1,000 entries of which more than 600 are on writers (not confined to literary writers), the rest covering works, institutions, movements, historical events and personalities, publishing, folklore, etc. Bibliographies of primary and secondary material appended to all major author entries.

.... (contd.)
Fully cross-referenced. Includes references to Gaelic literature, but the author admits that these are limited. General bibliography (2p.). Rev. ed. has some new entries, including over 30 young writers who emerged during the 1980s, and all bibliographies have been updated. 'A vast improvement on the original ... remarkably comprehensive, accurate and up to date' (*Reference Reviews*, v.8(1), 1994, p.37-8). *Class No:* 820.411(03)

Gazetteers

[7412]
BOLD, A. Scotland: a literary guide. London, Routledge, 1989. ix,327p. ISBN: 0415007313.

Explains the literary associations of some 250 locations arranged alphabetically from Abbotsford to Yarrow Water, with notes on individual writers arranged chronologically under each geographical heading (over 40 under Edinburgh). The absence of maps and illustrations is very disappointing. Bibliography (1p.). Index of authors.
Class No: 820.411(083.86)

Histories

[7413]
BOLD, A. Modern Scottish literature. London, Longman, 1983. x,332p. ISBN: 0582490642.

Claims to be the first comprehensive account of the whole range of 20th-century Scottish literature. 3 parts (poetry, fiction, drama) and 56 chapters, most of which are devoted to individual authors. Many individual works and studies of authors cited in the text, with bibliographical details in references appended to each part. Index.
Class No: 820.411(091)

[7414]
The History of Scottish literature. Craig, C., *ed.* Aberdeen, Aberdeen Univ. Press, 1987-8 (now available from The Mercat Press, Edinburgh). 4v. £19.90 per vol.

V.1. *Origins to 1660*, ed. by R.D.S. Jack. ix,310p. ISBN: 0080350542.

V.2. *1660-1800*, ed. by A. Hook. ix,337p. ISBN: 0080350550.

V.3. *Nineteenth century*, ed. by D. Gifford. 471p. ISBN: 0080350569.

V.4. *Twentieth century*, ed. by C. Craig. xiv,399p. ISBN: 0080350577.

Essays by over 80 contributors on the major genres and movements of each period and on important individual writers. The 80 chapters average 17p. and include reading lists. Each vol. has editor's introduction, short general bibliography and index. A lengthy review in *TLS* (no.4465, 28th Oct. 1988, p.1198-9) suggests that over-hasty compilation has led to unfortunate choice of contributors, poor design, deficient bibliographies and inaccuracies, although a third of the essays are 'of a high standard'.
Class No: 820.411(091)

[7415]
LINDSAY, M. History of Scottish literature. Rev. ed. London, Hale, 1992. 511p. £15.95. ISBN: 0709048025.

1st ed. 1977.

Narrative history for the general reader. A chapter for each century from 15th to 20th, subdivided by genre, with an extra chapter in this ed. covering late 20th-century writing. Many quotations. Source notes for each chapter.

....(contd.)
Selective bibliography of general reference material, anthologies and criticism of individual authors (15p.). Index. *Class No:* 820.411(091)

[7416]
WALKER, M. Scottish literature since 1707. Harlow, Longman, 1997. £48. (*Longman literature in English.*) ISBN: 0582028930.

A cultural history in 12 chapters, followed by general bibliography and details of biographies, major works and criticism for major writers. Good coverage of women writers. Chronology. Index. *Class No:* 820.411(091)

[7417]
WATSON, R. The Literature of Scotland. Basingstoke, Macmillan, 1984. xiv,481p. illus. (*Macmillan history of literature.*) ISBN: 0333269233.

A comprehensive single-volume history from 'The Beginnings of Scotland' to the 1980s, which covers literature on Gaelic, Scots and English. 7 chapters (one up to 1400, then one for each century, 15th-20th) with numerous subsections, most of them devoted to individual authors. Many quotations. Short general bibliography (3p.). Chronology of literary and historical events, 500-1971. Index. *Class No:* 820.411(091)

Burns

[7418]
BOLD, A. A Burns companion. Basingstoke, Macmillan, 1991. xiv,447p. illus. £55. (*Macmillan literary companions.*) ISBN: 0333422708.

Mostly devoted to biography and criticism of Burns' works but includes the following reference sections: chronology (18p.); biographical notes on the Burns circle (41p.); topographical notes on places in his life and poems (14p.); glossary (8p.); select bibliography (9p.). *Class No:* 820.411BUR

[7419]
EGERER, J.W. A Bibliography of Robert Burns. Edinburgh, Oliver & Boyd, 1964. xiii,396p.

Comprehensive primary bibliography in 4 sections: Dated editions; Undated editions; Translations; Original material first published in periodicals. Editions published 1786-1802 described in full. Over 1,200 items. Indexes of proper names, titles and first lines. *Class No:* 820.411BUR

[7420]
GLASGOW DISTRICT LIBRARIES. The Mitchell Library. **Catalogue of Robert Burns Collection in the Mitchell Library, Glasgow.** Glasgow, Glasgow Corporation Public Libraries, 1959. vii,217p.

Lists over 3,500 volumes, both by and about Burns, in 30 sections. Index. Believed to be the largest Burns collection in the world. *Class No:* 820.411BUR

[7421]
LINDSAY, M. The Burns encyclopedia. 3rd ed., rev. and enl. London, Hale, 1980. xi,426p. illus. £12.99. ISBN: 0709057199.

1st ed. 1959; 2nd ed. 1970.

Over 1,000 entries (varying in length from a few lines to 17p.) on all aspects of Burns' life, circle and works, including individual poems and characters. 3rd ed. has some revisions plus Addenda (12p.) with 27 new entries. 16 illustrations, mainly portraits. Analytical index, but no bibliography. *Class No:* 820.411BUR

[7422]
MacKAY, J.A. Burns A-Z: the complete word finder. Darvel, Ayrshire, Alloway, 1990. 774p. £38.50. ISBN: 0906440513.

Originally conceived as a straight reprint, with supplement, of J.B. Reid's *A Complete word and phrase concordance to the poems and songs of Robert Burns* (Glasgow, Kerr and Richardson, 1889), this project has developed into a completely new index to Burns, compiled using computer technology and keyed to the Burns Federation's 1986 ed. of the complete works.

An index of titles and first lines is followed by a concordance, which lists all proper names, nouns, adjectives, verbs and adverbs, followed by the lines in which they occur. Over 12,000 key-words with over 60,000 quotations. Appendices list suppressed, cancelled, and variant lines, and dubious and spurious works.

See also *The Burns quotation book*, ed. by J. Lindsay and M. Lindsay (London, Hale, 1994. 192p. £9.99. ISBN: 0709052871). *Class No:* 820.411BUR

Scott

[7423]
BOLTON, H.P. Scott dramatized. London, Mansell, 1992. xiii,579p. £100. ISBN: 0720120608.

A companion to Bolton's monumental *Dickens dramatized* (*q.v.*). Arranged by Scott's works, chronologically, listing and describing in detail 4,881 productions on stage, screen, TV and radio. Full bibliographical information provided for over 250 published adaptations. Detailed index of names. 'An impressively thorough and painstakingly researched publication' (*Library Association Record*, v.95(1), Jan. 1993, p.42). *Class No:* 820.411SCO

[7424]
HUSBAND, M.F.A. A Dictionary of the characters in the Waverley novels of Sir Walter Scott. Reprint of 1910 ed. New York, Gordon Press, 1977. xvi,287p. $59.95. ISBN: 0849017246.

Originally published London, Routledge; New York, Dutton, 1910.

Lists 2,836 characters (including animals) with brief descriptions and references to the novels (but not to chapters) in which they appear.

For details of first editions, see *A Bibliography of the Waverley novels* by G. Worthington (London, Constable, 1931). *Class No:* 820.411SCO

[7425]
RUBENSTEIN, J. Sir Walter Scott: a reference guide. Boston, Hall; London, Prior, 1978. xxiii,344p. ISBN: 0816178682.

Lists secondary material by year, 1932-77, with separate author sequences for books and shorter works within each year. Concise annotations. Index of authors, titles and subjects. Over 1,500 items.

For more recent material, see Rubenstein's *Sir Walter Scott: an annotated bibliography of scholarship and criticism, 1975-1990* (Aberdeen, Assoc. for Scottish Literary Studies, Univ. of Aberdeen, 1994. 124p. £10. ISBN: 0948877251). *Class No:* 820.411SCO

[7426]
—CORSO, J.C. A Bibliography of Sir Walter Scott: a classified and annotated list of books and articles relating to his life and works, 1797-1940. Edinburgh, Oliver and Boyd, 1943. xvi,428p.

2,938 entries, with criticism by Scott's contemporaries listed more fully than modern works.
Class No: 820.411SCO

Stevenson

[7427]
HAMMOND, J.R. A Robert Louis Stevenson chronology. Basingstoke, Macmillan, 1996. 120p. £37.50. (*Macmillan author chronologies.*) ISBN: 0333638883.

Details the events of the writer's life, month by month and day by day. Separate chronology of principal works. List of sources. Index. *Class No:* 820.411STE

[7428]
HAMMOND, J.R. A Robert Louis Stevenson companion: a guide to the novels, essays and short stories. London, Macmillan, 1984. x,252p. illus. ISBN: 0333319060.

Includes dictionary of short stories and essays, keyed to vols. in the Tusitala Edition (14p.), and annotated list of characters and locations (26p.). Appendix lists film versions.
Class No: 820.411STE

[7429]
PRIDEAUX, W.F. A Bibliography of the works of Robert Louis Stevenson. 2nd rev. ed., edited and supplemented by Mrs. L.S. Livingston. London, Hollings, 1917. viii,401p. illus.

1st ed. 1903.

Full descriptive bibliography in 7 parts: 1. First editions and separate works - 2. Juvenilia - 3. Contributions to books - 4. Contributions to periodicals in prose - 5. Contributions to periodicals in verse - 6. Collected editions - 7. Selections from the works. Appendix lists biography and criticism in books, magazines and newspapers. Index.
Class No: 820.411STE

[7430]
SWEARINGEN, R.G. The Prose writings of Robert Louis Stevenson: a guide. Hamden, Conn., Shoe String; London, Macmillan, 1980. xxiii,217p. ISBN: 0208018263, US; 0333276523, UK.

Lists over 350 prose works, essays, novels, stories and plays chronologically from Stevenson's childhood in the 1850s to his death in 1894. In addition to bibliographical information there are extensive notes on the composition, revision and sources of the works, publication history and locations of all manuscripts. Thorough index.
Class No: 820.411STE

Women

[7431]
A History of Scottish women's writing. Gifford, D. *and* McMillan, D., *eds.* Edinburgh, Edinburgh Univ. Press, 1997. xxiv,716p. £50. ISBN: 0748607420.

The first comprehensive history of Scottish women's writing, covering poetry, drama, fiction, diaries, memoirs, biography and autobiography, didactic and polemical writing, popular literature and writing from the periodical press. Includes essays on individual writers and on groups and genres. According to the *Library Association Record*

.... (contd.)
(v.100(3), March 1998, p.150), 'the subject bibliographies are exceedingly useful' but 'there is a very scant index'.
Class No: 820.411-0055.2

Anglo-Irish Literature

Bibliographies

[7432]
Anglo-Irish literature: a review of research. Finneran, R.J., *ed.* New York, Modern Language Assoc. of America, 1976. xv,596p. ISBN: 0873522524.

Similar in format to the MLA's *Victorian poetry, Victorian prose,* and *Victorian fiction* (*qq.v.*), with signed, lengthy bibliographical essays on general studies, 19th-century writers, Wilde, Moore, Shaw, Yeats, Synge, Joyce, O'Casey, 4 Revival figures (Lady Gregory, A.E. Russell, St. John Gogarty, and James Stephens), and modern drama. Index.

Supplemented by *Recent research on Anglo-Irish writers* (New York, MLA, 1983. 361p. ISBN: 0873522591), which updates the chapters in the earlier work to 1980 and has new chapters on modern poetry and fiction.
Class No: 820.415(01)

[7433]
McKENNA, B. Irish literature, 1800-1875: a guide to information sources. Detroit, Gale, 1978. xvii,388p. ISBN: 0810312506.

Part 1, Background and research, lists *c.*350 anthologies, periodicals, general bibliographies, and critical studies. Part 2 has bibliographies of works and studies for *c.*120 authors, A-Z. Confined to English-language writers. Indexes of authors, titles, and subjects. *Class No:* 820.415(01)

Encyclopaedias & Dictionaries

[7434]
Dictionary of Irish literature. Hogan, R., *ed.* Rev. & exp. ed. Westport, Conn., Greenwood; London, Aldwych Press, 1997. 2v. (xx,1413p.). £99.50. ISBN: 0313291721, US; 0861721020, UK.

1st ed. 1979 in a single vol., with UK ed. published London, Macmillan, 1980, as *The Macmillan dictionary of Irish literature*.

The bulk of the dictionary is made up of signed biographical and critical essays, by *c.*150 contributors, on Irish authors who wrote mainly in the English language. Also has entries for some foreign authors who have made a lasting contribution to Irish literature and on a few general topics (*e.g.* folklore), plus literary institutions and publications. Entries range from 25 to 10,000 words, and include bibliographies of primary and secondary material. Introductory essays on Gaelic literature (46p.), contemporary literature in the Irish language (10p.) and on the history of Irish writing in English (10p.). Chronology of literary and historical events, 432-1996. Classified bibliography of secondary sources. Index.

Rev. ed. represents a considerable expansion, with 1,000 full entries and 200 short ones. Many new entries on writers who have emerged in the 1980s and 1990s as well as some who were previously omitted, whilst existing entries have been updated. *Class No:* 820.415(03)

[7435]
The Oxford companion to Irish literature. Welch, R., *ed.* Oxford, Clarendon Press, 1996. xxv,614p. £25. ISBN: 0198661584.

Over 2,000 entries, A-Z, on Irish- and English-language literature from the 4th century to the 1990s. Entries cover authors; works; movements; genres; institutions; historical and religious figures and events; mythology and folklore; and influential foreign writers. References to further reading in many entries. Extensively cross-referenced. Chronology of historical events (4p.). Select general bibliography (4p.). 2 maps. 160 contributors. 'It surpasses previous exercises of a similar nature in the richness of its detail and the ecumenism of its approach' (*TLS*, no.4855, April 19, 1996, p.10).
Class No: 820.415(03)

[7436]
WALL, R. A Dictionary and glossary for the Irish literary revival. Gerrard's Cross, Smythe, 1995. 137p. £14.95. ISBN: 0861403592.

Lists English colloquialisms and allusions and borrowings from Gaelic found in Anglo-Irish literary works from the period 1889-1939. Entries include definition, illustrative quotations and, where appropriate, notes on etymology and historical/cultural background. Pronunciation guide. List of works quoted and bibliography of secondary sources.
Class No: 820.415(03)

Theses

[7437]
Anglo-Irish literature: a bibliography of dissertations, 1873-1989. O'Malley, W.T., *ed.* Westport, Conn., Greenwood, 1990. xix,299p. $69.95. (*Bibliographies and indexes in world literature.*) ISBN: 0313273030.

Lists 4,359 dissertations from 355 universities in 27 countries. Most are arranged under Irish authors, A-Z, top subjects being Yeats (605) and Joyce (597). Also 161 general studies. List of sources (5p.). Author and subject indexes. *Class No:* 820.415(043)

Excerpts

[7438]
Modern Irish literature. Lane, D. *and* Lane, C.M., *eds.* New York, Ungar, 1988. xv,736p. $95. (*A Library of literary criticism.*) ISBN: 0804431442.

Substantial excerpts from works of criticism published 1900-1985 in the USA and UK about 87 twentieth century Irish writers (north and south) are arranged chronologically under each writer in one A-Z sequence. Very useful bibliographies for each writer list all major works, selected minor works and one published bibliography where available. Index to critics. Includes only one Irish-language writer: Pádraic Ó Conaire. *Class No:* 820.415(082.200)

Chronologies

[7439]
CAHALAN, J.M. Modern Irish literature and culture: a chronology. Boston, Hall, 1993. 474p. $45. ISBN: 0816172641.

See entry at 891.62(090). *Class No:* 820.415(090)

Histories

[7440]
DEANE, S. A Short history of Irish literature. London, Hutchinson; Notre Dame, Ind., Univ. of Notre Dame Press, 1986. 282p. $14.95. ISBN: 0091613604, UK; 0268017514, US.

After a chapter on the Gaelic background, surveys English-language writing in Ireland from 1690 to 1980. Select bibliography (6p.) of anthologies, bibliographies and background material, with numerous literary works mentioned in the text and chapter notes. Chronology of historical and literary events, 1550-1980. Index.
Class No: 820.415(091)

[7441]
JEFFARES, A.N. Anglo-Irish literature. London, Macmillan; Dublin, Gill and Macmillan, 1982. x,349p. illus. £14.99. (*Macmillan history of literature.*) ISBN: 0333269160, UK; 0717112381, Ireland.

Narrative history in 6 chapters: 3 general ones up to 1900 and one on each major genre for the 20th century. Numerous quotations. Brief appendices on Children's literature and Criticism and scholarship. Select bibliography of critical and background material. Chronological table of literary and historical events, 432-1980. Name index.
Class No: 820.415(091)

[7442]
McHUGH, R. *and* HARMON, M. Short history of Anglo-Irish literature: from its origins to the present day. Dublin, Wolfhound Press, 1981; New York, Barnes & Noble, 1982. 377p. illus. ISBN: 0905473523, Ireland; 0389203165, US.

Arranged in 5 period divisions, with 22 chapters. Bibliographies of texts and studies for each division are appended (32p.). Index. *Class No:* 820.415(091)

Biographies

[7443]
BRADY, A.M. *and* CLEEVE, B. A Biographical dictionary of Irish writers. [2nd ed.]. Mullingar, Lilliput Press; New York, St. Martin's Press, 1985. xii,388p. ISBN: 0946640033, Ireland; 0312078714, US.

1st ed. Cork, Mercier Press, 1967-71, as *Dictionary of Irish writers* (3v.) by B. Cleeve.

1,800 entries in 2 A-Z sequences: Writers in English and Writers in Irish and Latin. Includes many non-literary writers (*e.g.* politicians, theologians, historians, etc.) and gives strong emphasis to contemporary figures. Entries include biographical notes, critical comments and lists of principal works. *Class No:* 820.415(092)

[7444]
Modern Irish writers: a bio-critical sourcebook. Gonzalez, A.G., *ed.* Westport, Conn., Greenwood; London, Aldwych Press, 1997. 480p. £67.50. ISBN: 0313295573, US; 0861721055, UK.

Signed entries on 75 authors active since 1880, comprising biography; discussion of major works and themes; overview of critical reception; and bibliography of primary and secondary sources. Introductory essay reviews the growing body of scholarship on modern Irish literature. Extensive general bibliography. Particularly useful for its coverage of less familar writers and those who have come to prominence very recently. *Class No:* 820.415(092)

Anglo-Irish Poetry

[7445]

O'DONOGHUE, D.J. The Poets of Ireland: a biographical and bibliographical dictionary of Irish writers of English verse. Reprint of 1912 ed. New York, Johnson, 1970. iv,504p. ISBN: 0384429750.

Originally published Dublin, Figgis; London, Oxford Univ. Press, 1912. Has also been reprinted by Gordon Press and Gale.

Covers *c.*4,000 poets, A-Z, giving lists of works with biographical notes. As well as Irish natives, includes English poets who settled in Ireland. Appendix lists collections and anthologies of Irish verse, 1724-1912. *Class No:* 820.415-1

Yeats

[7446]

JOCHUM, K.P.S. W.B. Yeats: a classified bibliography of criticism, including additions to Allan Wade's *Bibliography of the writings of W.B. Yeats* and a section on the Irish literary and dramatic revival. 2nd ed. Urbana, Univ. of Illinois Press, 1990. 1192p. $75. ISBN: 0252017625.

1st ed. 1978.

Massive compilation of over 10,000 items, many of them briefly annotated. Superbly organized in 13 sections with numerous subsections. Numerous cross-references and 8 indexes provide complete access. Includes material from over 40 countries. Supersedes all previous bibliographies. Complete to 1986. *Class No:* 820.415-1YEA

[7447]

McCREADY, S. A William Butler Yeats encyclopedia. Westport, Conn., Greenwood; London, Aldwych Press, 1997. 512p. £69.50. ISBN: 0313283710, US; 0861721063, UK.

Chronology of Yeats' life followed by 1,000 entries, A-Z, on works, fictional characters, mythological figures, places, organizations, and real people known to Yeats or mentioned in his writings. Most entries include references to further reading. Select bibliography of primary and secondary sources. *Class No:* 820.415-1YEA

[7448]

WADE, A. A Bibliography of the writings of W.B. Yeats. 3rd ed. rev. and ed. by R.K. Alspach. London, Hart-Davis, 1968. 514p. illus. (*Soho bibliographies.*) ISBN: 024664138x.

1st ed. 1951; 2nd ed. 1958.

Sections 1 and 2 fully describe all first editions of books by Yeats and books edited by him or containing an introduction or other contribution by him. Further sections list his contributions to periodicals, translations of his works, and Japanese publications in English. Appendices include a list of *c.*120 books about Yeats. Index. *Class No:* 820.415-1YEA

[7449]

Yeats: an annual of critical and textual studies, 1983-. Ann Arbor, Mich., Univ. of Michigan Press (previously Ithaca, N.Y., Cornell Univ. Press), 1983-. v.1-. Annual. ISSN: 07426224.

Each vol. includes a bibliography of the year's scholarship on Yeats and reviews of recently published books.

Yeats annual (Basingstoke, Macmillan, 1982-. no. 1-. ISSN: 02787688) included bibliographies in early issues, but since no. 7 (1990) has merely listed books received. *Class No:* 820.415-1YEA

Anglo-Irish Drama

[7450]

MAXWELL, D.E.S. A Critical history of modern Irish drama, 1891-1980. Cambridge, Cambridge Univ. Press, 1984. xvii,250p. illus. ISBN: 0521295394.

A detailed survey in 10 chapters, followed by a select bibliography (15p.) of works and studies relating to 49 dramatists and of general studies. Chronology (6p.). Index. *Class No:* 820.415-2

[7451]

MIKHAIL, E.H. An Annotated bibliography of modern Irish drama, 1899-1970. [2nd ed.]. Troy, N.Y., Whitston, 1981. 300p. $20. ISBN: 0878752013.

An expanded verson of *A Bibliography of modern Irish drama, 1899-1970* (London, Macmillan, 1972).

1,775 secondary works, published 1899-1977, are listed in 6 sections: bibliographies, reference works, books, periodical articles, dissertations, library collections. *Class No:* 820.415-2

[7452]

MIKHAIL, E.H. Dissertations on Anglo-Irish drama: a bibliography of studies, 1870-1970. London, Macmillan, 1973. x,73p. ISBN: 0333150988.

Lists *c.*500 dissertations on 24 dramatists completed at universities in the UK, Ireland, US, Germany, France and Canada. Arranged by dramatist with indexes to authors and institutions. *Class No:* 820.415-2

[7453]

SCHRANK, B. *and* **DEMASTES, W.W. Irish playwrights, 1880-1995:** a research and production sourcebook. Westport, Conn., Greenwood, 1997. xii,454p. £75.95. ISBN: 0313288054.

Lengthy entries (average 12½p.) on 32 dramatists, comprising biographical sketch; major plays and significant revivals: theatrical reception; other plays; critical assessment of works; archival sources; primary and secondary bibliography; list of bibliographies. Select general bibliography (5p.). Indexes of names and titles. *Class No:* 820.415-2

Beckett

[7454]

ANDONIAN, C.C. Samuel Beckett: a reference guide. Boston, Hall, 1989. 754p. $60. ISBN: 0816185700.

Lists *c.*2,500 biographical and critical studies in English and French by year, 1931-84, then by author. Concise annotations, often including a quotation. Less important items are listed without annotation in the Appendix. Indexes of authors and subjects.

For further studies, see *Beckett criticism in German* by R. Breuer and others (München, Fink, 1986. 85p. ISBN: 3770523784). *Class No:* 820.415-2BEC

[7455]

FEDERMAN, R. *and* **FLETCHER, J. Samuel Beckett: his work and his critics;** an essay in bibliography. Berkeley, Calif., Univ. of California Press, 1970. xiii,383p. ISBN: 0520014758.

Part 1 is full descriptive bibliography of Beckett's works, grouped by language of composition and including unpublished material (618 items). Part 2 lists 2,500 critical studies in 10 sections with annotations for books and articles. 5 indexes: names; Beckett's works; subjects; periodicals and collections; publishers and printers. Very comprehensive, with material in several languages. *Class No:* 820.415-2BEC

O'Casey

[7456]

AYLING, R. *and* **DURKAN, M.J. Sean O'Casey: a bibliography.** London, Macmillan; Seattle, Univ. of Washington Press, 1978. xxiv,411p. illus. ISBN: 0333113489, UK; 029595566x, US.

Follows 'the Soho formula', listing O'Casey's works in 10 sections: Books; Contributions to books and pamphlets; Contributions to periodicals; Translations; Manuscripts and typescripts; Stage productions; Adaptations; Recordings; Broadcasts; Motion pictures. First section provides full description and cites selected reviews. Detailed index. *Class No:* 820.415-2OCA

[7457]

MIKHAIL, E.H. Sean O'Casey: a bibliography of criticism. London, Macmillan, 1972. xi,152p. ISBN: 0333131835.

*c.*2,500 unannotated entries in 3 sections: 1. Bibliographies - 2. Reviews of O'Casey's books - 3. Criticism, including film and stage reviews. Indexes of O'Casey's titles and of critics.

Mikhail has also compiled *Sean O'Casey and his critics: an annotated bibliography, 1916-1982* (Metuchen, N.J., Scarecrow, 1985. 362p. ISBN: 0810817470). *Class No:* 820.415-2OCA

[7458]

SCHRANK, B. Sean O'Casey: a research and production sourcebook. Westport, Conn., Greenwood, 1996. 312p. £59.95. (*Modern dramatists research and production sourcebooks.*) ISBN: 031327844x.

Provides plot summaries and critical overviews for all of O'Casey's 23 plays, with production credits for major performances. Primary bibliography. Annotated secondary bibliography including reviews. Introductory essay on O'Casey's career, the major themes of his works and the critical response to them. Author index. General index. *Class No:* 820.415-2OCA

Synge

[7459]

A J.M. Synge literary companion. Kopper, E.A., *ed.* Westport, Conn., Greenwood, 1988. 268p. $55. ISBN: 0313251738.

Essays by specialists on various aspects of Synge's writings. Reference value lies in the 'superb select bibliography' (*Choice*, v.26(7), March 1989, p.1158); detailed, annotated list of characters, locales and motifs; and the stage histories of Synge's plays. Index.

Kopper has also compiled *John Millington Synge: a reference guide* (Boston, Hall, 1979. xxix,199p. ISBN: 0816181993), which lists *c.*980 critical studies published 1900-77. *Class No:* 820.415-2SYN

[7460]

LEVITT, P. J.M. Synge: a bibliography of published criticism. Dublin, Irish Univ. Press, 1974. 224p. ISBN: 0716521555.

Largely unannotated listing which is complete to 1969. Part 1, Books and Periodicals, has 4 sections of general criticism followed by sections on individual books, plus 6 miscellaneous sections. Part 2 lists newspaper articles by place of publication (mainly in Ireland, UK and US) and includes some very obscure items. Nearly 4,000 entries. Index. Described by Kopper as 'an example of unblemished accuracy'. *Class No:* 820.415-2SYN

[7461]

MIKHAIL, E.H. J.M. Synge: a bibliography of criticism. Totowa, N.J., Rowman & Littlefield; London, Macmillan, 1975. xiii,214p. ISBN: 0333168291.

2,500 unannotated items in 3 main sections: Bibliographies; Books by Synge and their reviews; Criticism on Synge (6 subsections, including reviews of play productions). Index of Synge's works. Index of authors. Goes up to the end of 1971 and is described by Kopper as 'a model of completeness'. *Class No:* 820.415-2SYN

Wilde

[7462]

MASON, S. Bibliography of Oscar Wilde. Reprint of 1967 ed. New York, Haskell, 1972. 2v. (xxxix,605p.) illus. $150. ISBN: 0838313787.

1st ed. London, T. Werner Laurie, 1914; 'New ed'. (a reprint with some addenda) London, Rota, 1967.

Descriptive bibliography in 3 sections: 1. Periodical publications - 2. Works issued in book form - 3. Biographies, sketches, etc. Many facsimiles. Name index. *Class No:* 820.415-2WIL

[7463]

MIKOLYZK, T.A. Oscar Wilde: an annotated bibliography Westport, Conn., Greenwood, 1993. xiv,489p. £62.50. ISBN: 0313275971.

List of Wilde's works (43p.), followed by annotated bibliography of books, chapters, articles and dissertations on him. Over 3,300 secondary items cited in all. Indexes of authors, subjects and Wilde's works. Chronology of Wilde's life. *Class No:* 820.415-2WIL

[7464]

PAGE, N. An Oscar Wilde chronology. Basingstoke, Macmillan, 1991. x,105p. £50. (*Macmillan author chronologies.*) ISBN: 0333460073.

Details the events of the writer's life, month by month and day by day. Also includes biographical notes on nearly 100 members of Wilde's circle. Bibliography of sources (2p.). Indexes of persons and of Wilde's works.

For Wilde quotations, see K. Beckson's *I can resist everything except temptation, and other quotations from Oscar Wilde* (New York, Columbia Univ. Press, 1998. 224p. $19.95. ISBN: 0231104561). *Class No:* 820.415-2WIL

Anglo-Irish Fiction

[7465]

BROWN, S.J. Ireland in fiction: a guide to Irish novels, tales, romances and folk-lore. New ed. Dublin and London, Maunsel, 1919 (repr. Shannon, Irish Univ. Press, 1969). xx,362p. ISBN: 071650023x.

1st ed. 1915.

Lists 1,713 novels which deal with Ireland or the Irish abroad. Arranged A-Z by author, giving biographical notes on the novelist, bibliographical details of the novel, and plot summary. Many non-Irish writers included. Appendices include annotated bibliography of reference works, classified lists of novels, and subject index. *Class No:* 820.415-3

Joyce

[7466]

A Companion to Joyce studies. Bowen, Z.R. *and* Carens, J.F., *eds.* Westport, Conn., Greenwood, 1984. xiv,818p. £83.95. ISBN: 0313228329.

16 signed essays (average 48p.) on all aspects of Joyce's life and works, each followed by selected bibliographies. Ch.16, 'The History of Joyce criticism and scholarship', by S. Feshbach and W. Herman, is particularly useful, with a bibliography running to 13p. Appendix 1. Joyce's names - 2. Library collections of Joyce manuscripts. Index.
Class No: 820.415-3JOY

[7467]

DEMING, R.H. A Bibliography of James Joyce studies. 2nd ed., rev. and enl. Boston, Hall, 1978. xii,264p. ISBN: 0816179697.

1st ed. Lawrence, Kan., Univ. of Kansas Libraries, 1964.

5,885 mainly unannotated items (only 1,434 in 1st ed.) arranged in 3 main sections with numerous subsections: 1. Bibliographical, biographical and general treatments - 2. Studies of the separate works - 3. Uncategorized and unverified items. Three subsections new to this ed. are 'Reviews of Joyce's works', 'Dissertations' and 'Musical settings, theatrical productions, films, radio broadcasts, and recordings'. Index of authors, editors, translators and reviewers. *Class No:* 820.415-3JOY

[7468]

FARGNOLI, A.N. *and* **GILLESPIE, M.P. James Joyce A-Z:** an encyclopedic guide to his life and work. London, Bloomsbury; New York, Facts on File, 1995. 320p. illus. £25. ISBN: 0747524092, UK; 0816029040, US.

US title is: *James Joyce A-Z: the essential reference to his life and work.*

Over 800 entries on Joyce's works (including individual chapters in *Ulysses* and stories in *Dubliners*), characters, influences, associates, contemporaries and critics, plus publications and societies devoted to him. Chronology. Bibliography. Index. *Class No:* 820.415-3JOY

[7469]

RICE, T.J. James Joyce: a guide to research. New York, Garland, 1982. xxiii,390p. ISBN: 0824093836.

Brief primary bibliography, followed by secondary bibliography in separate sections for English- and foreign-language studies, with each listing general studies and those on specific works. Concise annotations. *c.*2,500 entries. Indexes of authors, titles and subjects. *Class No:* 820.415-3JOY

[7470]

SLOCUM, J.J. *and* **CAHOON, H. A Bibliography of James Joyce.** Reprint of 1953 ed. Westport, Conn., Greenwood, 1971. ix,195p. £39.95. (*Soho bibliographies.*) ISBN: 0837156394.

Originally published London, Hart-Davis, 1953.

Covers publication of Joyce's works up to 1950, with occasional subsequent additions. Full descriptions of all first editions, plus listing of contributions to books, pamphlets, periodicals and newspapers, and sections on translations, manuscripts and musical settings. Index of names, titles, periodicals and publishers. Approx 400 items.
Class No: 820.415-3JOY

Anglo-Irish Satire & Humour

[7471]

NILSEN, D.L.F. Humor in Irish literature: a reference guide. Westport, Conn., Greenwood, 1996. 248p. £51.95. ISBN: 0313295514.

A comprehensive guide to humour in Irish literature since the 16th century. Introductory essay on the nature of Irish humour is followed by chapters devoted to particular centuries. These include entries on individual authors, chronologically arranged, with an analysis of the humour in their works and a bibliography. Index of authors and subjects. *Class No:* 820.415-7

Anglo-Welsh Literature

[7472]

HARRIS, J. A Bibliographical guide to twenty-four modern Anglo-Welsh writers. Cardiff, Univ. of Wales Press, 1994. xi,387p. £20. ISBN: 0708312330.

Lists of Anglo-Welsh literary anthologies and general critical studies are followed by bibliographies of primary and secondary material for 24 20th-century writers. Nearly 6,000 entries, some of them briefly annotated but without evaluative comment. Alongside major figures like Dylan Thomas and Raymond Williams are several less well-known writers for whom this is the fullest available source.
Class No: 820.429

[7473]

JONES, G. *and* **ROWLANDS, J. Profiles:** a visitors' guide to writing in twentieth century Wales. Llandysul, Dyfed, Gomer Press, 1980. xxxi,382p. illus. £9.95. ISBN: 0850887135.

See entry at 891.66(092). *Class No:* 820.429

[7474]

MATHIAS, P. Anglo-Welsh literature: an illustrated history. Bridgend, Poetry Wales Press, 1986. 142p. illus. £5.95. ISBN: 0907476643.

An outline history in 18 chapters, from the 15th century to the 1980s, which was described by *World Literature Today* (V.62(1), Winter 1988, p.134) as 'a tremendous contribution to literary history and criticism.' 98 black-and-white illustrations. Useful bibliography (4p.). Index.
Class No: 820.429

[7475]

The Oxford companion to the literature of Wales. Stephens, M., *ed.* Oxford, Oxford, Univ. Press, 1986. xviii,682p. £29.50. ISBN: 0192115863.

See entry at 891.66(03). *Class No:* 820.429

Thomas (Dylan)

[7476]

DAVIES, J.A. A Reference companion to Dylan Thomas. Westport, Conn., Greenwood, 1998. 392p. $89.50. ISBN: 0313287740.

Chronological summary and 4 biographical chapters followed by overview of Thomas's works, including film scripts and broadcasts as well as poetry and prose. Further chapters survey the critical and scholarly response to his writings in Wales, England and North America. Selected bibliography of Thomas's works and key critical studies. Index. *Class No:* 820.429THO

[7477]

GASTON, G.M.A. Dylan Thomas: a reference guide. Boston, Hall, 1987. xi, 213p. $40. ISBN: 0816187797.

A selective, annotated bibliography of criticism in English, French and German published 1934-1985. Over 1,400 entries arranged by year, then A-Z within each year. Index of authors and titles with a few subject headings. *Choice*, v.25(7), March 1988, p.1064, points out some errors and omissions and advises caution. *Class No:* 820.429THO

[7478]

MAUD, R. *and* **GLOVER, A. Dylan Thomas in print:** a bibliographical history. London, Dent, 1970. xi,268p. ISBN: 0460078364.

5 sections: 1. Books, anthologies, theses (by year, 1934-68) - 2. Welsh periodicals and newspapers - 3. London, etc., periodicals and newspapers - 4. US and Canada periodicals and newspapers - 5. Foreign-language publications (15 languages). Each section includes entries for works by and about Thomas. Appendix covers 1969-71. Index.
Class No: 820.429THO

Asian Literature in English

Philippines

[7479]

VALEROS, F.B. *and* **VALEROS-GRUENBERG, E. Filipino writers in English:** a biographical and bibliographical directory. Quezon City, New Day, 1987. xii,236p. $15. ISBN: 971100285x.

Entries on *c.*650 writers, with information which has been gathered by questionnaire and interview.
Class No: 820.5(914)

[7480]

ZAPANTA-MANLAPAZ, E. *and* **ABAD, G.H. Index to Filipino poetry in English, 1905-1950.** Manila, National Book Store, 1988. xx,748p.

Indexes 16,000 poems by 900 poets in 270 sources, but provides access by *author* only with poems listed by title under each poet. *Class No:* 820.5(914)

Indian Literature in English

[7481]

SINGH, A., *and others.* **Indian literature in English, 1827-1979:** a guide to information sources. Detroit, Gale, 1981. xxii,631p. (*American literature, English literature and World literatures in English.*) ISBN: 0810312387.

Part 1 lists general sources under 4 main headings: Backgrounds; Reference works; Criticism and literary history; Anthologies. Part 2 lists primary and (where appropriate) secondary material for individual authors grouped by genre. A few brief annotations. Appendices list relevant journals and Indian publishers. Primary author index in genre groupings, plus general author and title indexes. Includes works written in Indian languages and translated into English by their author. *Class No:* 820.54

[7482]

WALSH, W. Indian literature in English. London, Longman, 1990. xi,219p. (*Longman literature in English.*) ISBN: 0582494796.

Narrative history in 5 chapters from the late 18th century to Salman Rushdie, plus a chapter on India in English fiction. Many quotations. Chronology of literary and historical events, 1583-1988 (9p.). Select bibliography (7p.). Very useful bio-bibliographical notes on 38 authors (12p.). Index. *Class No:* 820.54

[7483]

Writers of the Indian diaspora: a bio-bibliographical sourcebook. Nelson, E.S., *ed.* Westport, Conn., Greenwood, 1993. xix,468p. $99.50. ISBN: 0313279047.

Signed profiles (average 8p.) of 57 writers, in the standard Greenwood format: biography; major works and themes; critical reception; lists of works and critical studies. Includes Rushdie, Naipaul, Selvon, etc., but particularly useful for coverage of lesser-known writers. General bibliography (2p.). Index. *Class No:* 820.54

African Literature in English

Bibliographies

[7484]

LINDFORS, B. Black African literature in English: a guide to information sources. Detroit, Gale, 1979. xxx,482p. $68. (*American literature, English literature, and World literatures in English.*) ISBN: 0810312069.

Lists over 3,300 items in 2 sections: 1. Genre and Topical Studies and Reference Sources (26 sub-sections) - 2. Individual Authors (biographical and critical material on over 600 writers). Some brief annotations. Many cross-references. Author, title, subject and geographical indexes.

Continued by: *Black African literature in English: 1977-1981 supplement* (New York, Africana, 1986. xxx,382p. ISBN: 0841909628), which adds another 2,831 items; *Black African literature in English, 1982-1986* (London and New York, Zell, 1989. xxviii,444p. £63. ISBN: 0905450752), which adds a further 5,825; *Black African literature in English, 1987-1991* (London, Zell, 1995. 717p. £80. ISBN: 1873836163) with another 8,700-plus. Supplements follow the same format as the original and continue its numbering system. *Class No:* 820.6(01)

Nigeria

[7485]

A Bibliography of literary contributions to Nigerian periodicals, 1946-72. Lindfors, B., *ed.* Ibadan, Ibadan Univ. Press, 1975. 231p.

Lists over 4,100 contributions by over 1,200 authors to 177 periodicals. Includes material by non-Nigerian authors and English translations of articles originally written in other languages. *Class No:* 820.6(669)

Soyinka

[7486]

Wole Soyinka: a bibliography of primary and secondary sources. Gibbs, J., *and others, comps.* Westport, Conn., Greenwood, 1986. x,107p. $55. (*Bibliographies and indexes in Afro-American and African studies.*) ISBN: 0313239371.

....(contd.)

248 primary sources and 1,521 secondary sources listed in separate chronological sections. No annotations. Index of names and titles. Very favourably reviewed in *Research in African Literatures*, v.18(3), Fall 1987, p.379-81.
Class No: 820.6(669)SOY

Africa—East & Equatorial

[7487]

The Writing of East and Central Africa. Killam, G.D., *ed.* London, Heinemann, 1984. x,274p. $17.50. (*Studies in African literature.*) ISBN: 0435916718.

1. Countries: 6 chapters on Uganda, Kenya, Tanzania, Mauritius, Zambia and Zimbabwe - 2. Writers: 5 chapters on major authors - 3. Genres: 3 chapters on poetry, fiction and drama across the region. The chapters are signed by one of 13 contributors and several have very useful bibliographies, *e.g.* the Mauritius chapter has a checklist of works by 41 writers. Thorough analytical index.
Class No: 820.6(67)

Kenya

Ngugi

[7488]

SICHERMAN, C. Ngugi wa Thiong'o: a bibliography of primary and secondary sources, 1957-1987. London and New York, Zell, 1989. xx,249p. £40. (*Bibliographical research in African written literatures.*) ISBN: 090545071x.

Lists 637 primary sources in 3 sections: works in the original languages; manuscripts and unpublished material; translations (into 2 African and 22 non-African languages). Also 1,340 secondary sources, arranged by year then by author, including much foreign-language material. Some brief annotations. Author, title and subject indexes. The most comprehensive guide to Kenya's leading writer.
Class No: 820.6(676.2)NGU

Africa—Southern

[7489]

CHAPMAN, M. Southern African literatures. Harlow, Longman, 1996. xxxi,533p. £45. (*Longman literature in English.*) ISBN: 0582053064.

Covers literatures of South Africa, Zimbabwe, Zambia, Malawi, Angola, Mozambique and Namibia in 19 chapters arranged in 5 parts: 1. Oral tradition - 2. South Africa, 1652-1910 - 3. African or colonial literature, 1880s to 1960s - 4. Independence, Post-Independence - 5. South Africa, 1970-1995. Very useful reference section, comprising chronology of literary and historical events (32p.); bibliography of bibliographies, general critical studies, genre studies and periodicals; and biobibliographical notes on over 200 authors, A-Z. Index. *Class No:* 820.6(68)

[7490]

GRAY, S. Southern African literature: an introduction. Cape Town, Philip; London, Collings, 1979. 209p. illus. ISBN: 0908396082.

A history in 7 chapters of the English literature of South Africa, Lesotho, Botswana, Swaziland, Zimbabwe and Namibia. Biographical notes on 8 major authors. Select bibliography of works and background material (9p.). Index of authors, editors and critics. *Class No:* 820.6(68)

Zimbabwe

[7491]

VEIT-WILD, F. Teachers, preachers, non-believers: a social history of Zimbabwean literature. London, Zell; Harare, Baobab, 1992. xii,408p. illus. £52 ISBN: 1873836155, UK.

The first comprehensive study of the subject, covering literature in English and African languages. Includes bibliography (28p.) and list of over 200 writers published by 1987, with language breakdown. *Class No:* 820.6(689.1)

South African Literature in English

[7492]

BARNETT, U.A. A Vision of order: a study of Black South African literature in English (1914-1980). London, Sinclair Browne; Amherst, Mass., Univ. of Massachusetts Press, 1983. 336p. £32.50. ISBN: 086300007x, UK; 0870234064, US.

Chapter One (33p.) traces the history of Black writing and 6 subsequent chapters survey different genres: poetry, novel, short stories, autobiography, drama and critical writing. Excellent bibliography of primary and secondary works. Index. *Class No:* 820.680

[7493]

—SHAVA, P.V. A People's voice: Black South African writing in the twentieth century. London, Zed Books; Athens, Ohio Univ. Press, 1989. 179p. £29.95. ISBN: 0862326842, UK; 082140931x, US.

A history of Black literature from 1916, in 7 chapters, which emphasizes its political role. Good bibliography (10p.) of primary and secondary sources, many of the latter published in the 1970s and 1980s. Index. *Class No:* 820.680

[7494]

Companion to South African literature. Adey, D., *and others, comps.* Craighall, S.A., Donker, 1986. 220p. illus. ISBN: 086852039x.

A single A-Z sequence with entries for authors (450), works and journals, plus 39 'composite articles' on genres, themes and topics (*e.g.* Prison literature, Banned books). Author entries do not claim to provide full bibliographies but have lists of book-length studies appended. Essentially a guide to English-language writing, 1795-1986, but 'composite articles' cover Afrikaans and African-language literature. Some writers from neighbouring countries (Botswana, Lesotho, Swaziland, Zimbabwe) are included. Well illustrated. *Addendum* lists over 220 writers not covered in the main text, with lists of representative works.
Class No: 820.680

[7495]

DUBBELD, C.E. Reflecting apartheid; South African short stories in English with socio-political themes, 1960-1987: a select and annotated bibliography. Johannesburg, South African Institute of International Affairs, 1990. 337p. ISBN: 0908371837.

Lists anthologies and single-author story collections by year, then A-Z by author/anthology title. Entries include bibliographical details and library locations for the anthology, followed by synopses of each story and subject indexing terms. Summaries of major political events for each year. Introduction (19p.) gives historical overview. Bibliography of general sources (14p.). Author, title and subject indexes. *Class No:* 820.680

[7496]

GORMAN, G.E. The South African novel in English since 1950: an information and resource guide. Boston, Hall, 1978. xiv,238p. ISBN: 0816181780.

1. Survey of the literature and aspects of bibliographical control - 2. Guide to resources (critical essays on 8 types of material: bibliographies, periodicals, biographical dictionaries, etc.) - 3. Classified bibliography of all the works cited (35p.). Subject and author-title indexes. *Class No:* 820.680

[7497]

A Pilot bibliography of South African English literature from the beginnings to 1971. Beeton, D.R., *ed.* Pretoria, Univ. of South Africa, 1976. xii,104p. ISBN: 0869810723.

Aims 'to provide a representative listing of the most significant South African writings in English from the time of Lady Anne Barnard to the present day' (*Introduction*). General section (bibliographies, anthologies, journals, criticism, etc.) followed by *c.*200 individual authors, A-Z, with primary and secondary material listed. Lists of authors grouped by period and genre. Appendix lists 30 further names 'who would well bear further scrutiny.' Compiled by the Subject Reference Dept. of the Univ. of South Africa Library. *Class No:* 820.680

Gordimer

[7498]

Nadine Gordimer: a bibliography of primary and secondary sources, 1937-1992. Driver, D., *and others, comps.* London, Zell, 1994. xv,341p. £55. (*Bibliographical research in African literatures.*) ISBN: 1873836260.

Lists 717 primary works in 9 sections and 2,313 secondary sources in 7 sections, including reviews and theses. Chronological arrangement within sections, with 11 indexes providing full access. Largely unannotated. Biographical introduction by Driver plus chronology of Gordimer's life. *Class No:* 820.680GOR

820.7/.8 American Literature

North American Literature

Bibliographies

[7499]
COAN, O.T. *and* **LILLARD, R.G. America in fiction:** an annotated list of novels that interpret aspects of life in the United States, Canada and Mexico. 5th ed. Palo Alto, Calif., Pacific Books, 1967. viii,232p.

1st ed. 1941; 4th ed. 1956.

Lists of novels which illustrate various aspects of North American life are arranged under 7 main headings: Pioneering, Farm and village life, Industrial America, Politics and Institutions, Religion, Minority ethnic groups, Mexico. 'The lists are representative rather than exhaustive' (*Preface*). A-Z arrangement by author under each heading or sub-heading. Brief annotations. Author index. Most likely to be of use in school libraries. *Class No:* 820.71(01)

Biographies

[7500]
A Dictionary of North American authors deceased before 1950. Wallace, W.S., *comp.* Reprint of 1951 ed. Detroit, Gale, 1968. x,525p. ISBN: 0810331535.

Originally published Toronto, Ryerson Press, 1951.

25,000 brief entries for US and Canadian writers, giving full name, profession, place and date of birth and death, with references to 78 biographical dictionaries, histories of literature, encyclopedias, etc., for further information. Not confined to literary writers. *Class No:* 820.71(092)

[7501]
Who was who among North American authors, 1921-1939. Detroit, Gale, 1976. 2v. 1578p. ISBN: 0810310414.

Based on 7 editions of *Who's who among North American authors,* published 1921-39, containing 11,200 entries interfiled and photoreproduced. Foreword claims that 8,900 of the subjects are not listed in other standard reference guides, especially the journalists. Entries give occupation, place and date of birth, education, list of publications, offices held, addresses. 'Author' interpreted in the broadest sense, with many non-literary writers (scientists, academics, clerics, etc.) included. Cross-references for pseudonyms. *Class No:* 820.71(092)

Amerindians, North

[7502]
Dictionary of Native American literature. Wiget, A., *ed.* New York, Garland, 1994. 598p. $95. ISBN: 0815315600.

Over 40 substantial biographical and critical essays on Native Americans writing in English over the past 2 centuries, plus more than 20 topical articles to provide historical and cultural background. The entries are grouped by historical period (Native American oral literature; Indian writing to 1967; 1967 to the present), with each section having an introductory essay. Entries have been contributed by 52 members of the Association for the Study of American Indian Literature and include bibliographies of primary and secondary sources. Index of authors, titles, tribes and subjects. *Class No:* 820.71(=97)

[7503]
JACOBSON, A. Contemporary Native American literature: a selected and partially annotated bibliography. Metuchen, N.J., Scarecrow, 1977. xii,262p. ISBN: 081081031x.

Lists 2,024 literary works in English by native American authors, published 1960 to mid-1976. Includes Eskimo, Canadian and Mexican tribal writers as well as American Indians. 6 sections covering different genres, with poetry by far the largest (1,649 items). Lists of sources, periodicals and collections analyzed. Author index. Title and first line index. *Class No:* 820.71(=97)

[7504]
Native North American literature. Witalec, J., *ed.* Detroit, Gale, 1994. 706p. illus. £76. ISBN: 0810398982.

Similar in format to Gale's *Black literature criticism* and *Hispanic literature criticism* (*qq.v.*), with entries on 78 historical and contemporary figures in 2 sections covering oral and written literature. Entries comprise brief biography; list of major writings; lengthy excerpts from reviews and critical studies; and selective bibliography of secondary material. Many entries include excerpts from the subject's work and most have a photograph. Introductory essay gives an overview of the oral and written traditions. Title index and indexes of authors by tribe and genre. Very little overlap with other Gale reference works. *Class No:* 820.71(=97)

Women

[7505]
GERRY, T.M.F. Contemporary Canadian and US women of letters: an annotated bibliography. New York, Garland, 1993. 287p. $45. (*Garland bibliographies of modern critics and critical schools.*) ISBN: 0824069897.

Separate chapters on 16 women (slightly more Canadians than Americans) who have written both poetry and/or fiction and literary criticism and/or theory, and for whom there is no annotated bibliography available. Works are listed chronologically within each chapter. List of a further 18 women writers who have been accorded a major bibliography. *Class No:* 820.71-0055.2

Canadian Literature

Bibliographies

[7506]
The Annotated bibliography of Canada's major authors. Lecker, R. *and* David, J., *eds.* Downsview, Ontario, ECW Press, 1979-94. 8v. $C45 per vol. ISBN: 0920802087.

V.1 *Margaret Atwood (prose), Margaret Laurence, Hugh*

.... *(contd.)*
MacLennan, Mordecai Richler, and Gabrielle Roy. 1979. 263p.

V.2 *Leonard Cohen, Margaret Atwood (poetry), Archibald Lampman, E.J. Pratt, and Al Purdy*. 1980. 277p.

V.3 *Ernest Buckler, Robertson Davies, Raymond Knister, W.O. Mitchell, and Sinclair Ross*. 1981. 395p.

V.4 *Earle Birney, Dorothy Livesay, and F.R. Scott, and A.J.M. Smith,*. 1983. 370p.

V.5 *Morley Callaghan, Mavis Gallant, Hugh Hood, Alice Munro, and Ethel Wilson*. 1984. 480p.

V.6 *Margaret Avison, John Newlove, Michael Ondaatje, P.K. Page, Miriam Waddington, and Phyllis Webb*. 1985. 448p.

V.7 *Marian Engel, Anne Hébert, Robert Kroetsch, and Thomas Raddall*. 1987. 477p.

V.8 *Irving Layton, Dennis Lee, and D.C. Scott*. 1994. 576p.

4 vols. devoted to prose writers and 4 to poets, each containing discrete bibliographies, compiled by named specialists, of primary and secondary literature. Each bibliography is thoroughly annotated and has an index to critics. Good coverage of audio-visual materials. Many of the author bibliographies are available as individual reprints under the series title *Canadian author bibliographies*.

Choice (v.32(7), March 1995, p.1073) concludes that 'the series fails to meet its ambitious objective of surveying Canada's major French and English authors from the 19th and 20th centuries', as most of those covered are 20th century and English-Canadian and 20 important writers who were projected in v.1 are omitted. *Class No:* 820.72(01)

[7507]

Canadian literature: a quarterly of criticism and review. Vancouver, Univ. of British Columbia, 1959-. Quarterly. ISSN: 00084360.

From 1959-71, the Spring issue of this journal contained an annual checklist of books and critical articles, subdivided into English and French Canadian literature and further subdivided by form. In no.52, Spring 1972, p.7, the editor explains why the checklist has been discontinued and recommends the annual bibliography in *Journal of Commonwealth Literature* (*qv*) for English-Canadian books and that in *Livres et Auteurs Québecois* for French-Canadian books. *Class No:* 820.72(01)

[7508]

—An Index to the contents of the periodical *Canadian Literature*, nos. 1-102. Clever, G. *and* Zeber, C.S., *comps*. Ottawa, Tecumseh Press, 1984. 218p. ISBN: 091966203x.

Covers the years 1959-1984. Single sequence index of authors and topics. Book reviews indicated by asterisk.
Class No: 820.72(01)

[7509]

MOYLES, R.G. English-Canadian literature to 1900: a guide to information sources. Detroit, Gale, 1976. xii,346p. ISBN: 0810312220.

Slightly deceptive title as both primary and secondary material are included, with annotations. 7 sections: General reference guides; Literary histories and criticism; Anthologies; Major authors (12); Minor authors (36); Literature of exploration, travel and description; Selected nineteenth-century journals. Author and title indexes.
Class No: 820.72(01)

[7510]

WATTERS, R.E. A Checklist of Canadian literature and background materials, 1628-1960. 2nd ed. rev. and enlarged. Toronto, Univ. of Toronto Press, 1972. xxiv,1085p. ISBN: 0802018661.

1st ed. 1959, covering 1628-1950.

Lists about 16,000 titles (4,000 more than in 1st ed.) by 7,000 Canadian authors. Part 1 'attempts to record all known titles in the recognized forms of poetry, fiction and drama that were produced by English-speaking Canadians' (*Preface*), with authors listed A-Z under each literary form. Part 2 'is a more or less selective listing of books by Canadians which seem likely to be of value to anyone studying the literature or culture of Canada' (*Preface*), arranged in 7 sections: biography; essays and speeches; local history and description; religion and monarchy; social history; scholarship; travel and description. No annotations. Library locations. Index of anonymous titles. General index of names, initials and pseudonyms. A necessary companion to Klinck's *Literary history* (*q.v.*). *Class No:* 820.72(01)

Indexes

[7511]

Canadian literature index: a guide to periodicals and newspapers. Toronto, ECW Press, 1985-. Annual. C$195 per vol.

Indexes over 100 English- and French-language Canadian literary periodicals plus international journals which cover Canadian literature. Also covers literary book reviews and articles in major Canadian newspapers. In 2 sections: author index and subject index, the subject entries including lists of keywords which serve as annotations to the entry. Full subscription information, address and library location for each journal indexed. *Class No:* 820.72(014)

Encyclopaedias & Dictionaries

[7512]

The Oxford companion to Canadian literature. Toye, W., *ed*. Toronto and Oxford, Oxford Univ. Press, 1983. xx,843p. ISBN: 0195402839.

Supersedes the literary element of *The Oxford companion to Canadian history and literature* (1967) and its *Supplement* (1973).

By far the fullest single-volume guide to the subject, with 750 signed entries by 192 contributors. As well as the expected concise Oxford-style entries on writers and works, there are many lengthy contributions devoted to genres (*e.g.* nature writing, children's literature), regions (*e.g.* Newfoundland, The Maritimes) and ethnic minority literatures (*e.g.* Inuit, Ukrainian). Particularly good coverage of French-language writing and modern literature. Substantial bibliographies included in many entries. Extensive cross-references. 'Well presented and remarkably free from errors' (*Modern Language Review*, v.82(4), Oct. 1987, p.946-7). *Class No:* 820.72(03)

Theses

[7513]

GABEL, G.U. Canadian literature: an index to theses accepted by Canadian universities, 1925-1980. Cologne, Edition Gemini, 1984. 157p. ISBN: 3922331157.

Lists 1,531 theses in 2 sections. Part 1, Literary History, is subdivided into General Studies, Poetry, Fiction, Drama

.... *(contd.)*
and Periodicals; Part 2 lists theses on specific authors, arranged alphabetically. Indexes of thesis authors and subjects. *Class No:* 820.72(043)

Gazetteers

[7514]
MORITZ, A. *and* **MORITZ, T. The Oxford illustrated literary guide to Canada.** Toronto, Oxford Univ. Press, 1987. x,246p. illus. ISBN: 019540596x.

'More than 500 entries detail the literary associations of cities, towns, villages, hamlets, and even rivers and islands' (*Preface*). Arranged by province/territory (12 sections), then A-Z by locality within each section. Over 300 illustrations - mainly photographs of writers and their homes - but, disappointingly, no maps. Index of writers.
Class No: 820.72(083.86)

Histories

[7515]
KEITH, W.J. Canadian literature in English. London, Longman, 1985. xii,287p. (*Longman literature in English series.*) ISBN: 0582493080.

A critical survey of English-language literature in Canada from its earliest beginnings to the present day. Three useful appendices: Chronology of literary and historical events (26p.); General bibliography (5p.); Individual authors (34p. of biographical notes on 128 writers).
Class No: 820.72(091)

[7516]
Literary history of Canada: Canadian literature in English. Klinck, C.F., *ed.* 2nd ed. Toronto, Univ. of Toronto Press, 1976-90. 4v. ISBN: 0802022111, v.1; 0802022138, v.2; 0802022146, v.3; 0802056857, v.4.

1st ed. 1965.

Vols. 1 and 2 are a revised version of the single-vol. first ed., which went from earliest times to 1960, v.1 covering the years to 1920 and v.2 from 1920 to 1960. V.3 covers 1960-72 and v.4 (published separately in 1990 and ed. by W.H. New) from 1972 to 1984. 70 chapters in all, by over 40 scholars, treat literature in the broadest sense, to include scientific writing, folk song, religious literature, etc. Index of names and titles in each vol.

The bibliographical apparatus leaves something to be desired as the notes at the end of each vol. are 'brief and highly selective; they were appended only if the author of a chapter felt that they were essential. The entire omission of notes for certain other chapters means only that these contributors rely upon the reader to seek out the numerous sources recorded in bibliographies of Canadian literature' (*Introduction*). Klinck recommends Watters' *Checklist* (*q.v.*) as 'virtually a companion volume'. *Class No:* 820.72(091)

[7517]
NEW, W.H. A History of Canadian literature. Basingstoke, Macmillan Education, 1989. x,380p. illus. £14.99. (*Macmillan history of literature.*) ISBN: 0333413768.

Narrative account in 5 chapters, the first covering early literature, the rest taking the story on to 1867, 1922, 1959 and 1985 respectively. Chronological table of literary and historical events (64p.). Selective bibliography of booklength works arranged in 13 categories (8p.). Index.
Class No: 820.72(091)

Biographies

[7518]
Contemporary Canadian authors. Detroit, Gale, 1996. 496p. £96. ISBN: 1896413080.

Bio-bibliographical profiles of 203 literary authors, scriptwriters and journalists extracted from Gale's comprehensive *Contemporary authors* (*q.v.*) database.
Class No: 820.72(092)

[7519]
Dictionary of literary biography. Detroit, Gale, 1978-98. v.1-188 (in progress). £112 per vol.

The following vols., all ed. by W.H. New, give excellent coverage of Canadian literature:

V.53 *Canadian writers since 1960: first series.* 1986. 445p. ISBN: 0810317311.

V.60 *Canadian writers since 1960: second series.* 1987. 470p. ISBN: 0810317389.

V.68 *Canadian writers, 1920-1959: first series.* 1988. 417p. ISBN: 081031746x.

V.88 *Canadian writers, 1920-1959: second series.* 1989. 442p. ISBN: 0810345668.

V.92 *Canadian writers, 1890-1920.* 1990. 472p. ISBN: 0810345722.

V.99 *Canadian writers before 1890.* 1990. 434p. ISBN: 081034579x.

For a description of the series, see entry at 82(092).
Class No: 820.72(092)

[7520]
Profiles in Canadian literature. Heath, J.M., *ed.* Toronto, Dundurn Press, 1980-86. 6v. illus.

Signed profiles of 87 English- and French-language writers (mainly novelists and poets) of all periods. Entries are arranged chronologically within each vol., average 8p., and include the following components: portrait; critical essay, including quotations from the author's works; chronology; excerpts from the author's comments on his/her own works and from critical studies; selected bibliography of works and criticism. *Class No:* 820.72(092)

[7521]
STOUCK, D. Major Canadian authors: a critical introduction to Canadian literature in English. 2nd ed., rev. and expanded. Lincoln, Nebr., Univ. of Nebraska Press, 1988. xiv,330p. $25. ISBN: 080324195x.

1st ed. 1984.

Essays (average 16p.) on the life and writings of 18 authors, arranged chronologically from Thomas Haliburton to Margaret Atwood, the latter a new addition in 2nd ed. Selected primary bibliography appended to each essay, with major secondary works cited in footnotes. Brief notes on a further 60 authors. List of Governor General's Award winners. Brief general bibliography (2p.). Index. Full-page picture of each major writer. *Class No:* 820.72(092)

[7522]
Who's who in Canadian literature, 1983/1984-. Ripley, G.M. *and* Mercer, A.V., *eds.* Toronto, Reference Press, 1983-. Biennial.

A directory of over 1,000 living literary writers. Entries include place and date of birth, education, career, awards, address, work in progress, and list of works, the information being collected by questionnaire. Title index.
Class No: 820.72(092)

Canadian Poetry

[7523]

Canadian writers and their works: poetry series. Lecker, R., *& others, eds.* Toronto, ECW Press, 1987-95. 12v. illus. C$45-50 per vol.

Each vol. covers 4 or 5 writers, with lengthy signed essays by specialists providing detailed commentary on the author's life and times; review of his/her critical reception; discussion of works; and primary and secondary bibliographies. They are chronologically arranged, each with an introduction by G. Woodcock and its own index. A separate cumulated index is available (C$20. ISBN: 1550221434). The entries for individual authors are available in individual paperback editions under the series title *Canadian author studies*. *Class No:* 820.72-1

[7524]

McQUARRIE, J., ***and others*****. Index to Canadian poetry in English.** Toronto, Reference Press, 1984. 367p. ISBN: 091998102x.

Indexes *c.*7,000 poems in 51 anthologies which are likely to be found in Canadian and US libraries. Title and first-line sequence includes full references and is followed by subject and author indexes.

Another useful source is M. Fee's *Canadian poetry in selected English-language anthologies: an index and guide* (Halifax, Nova Scotia, Dalhousie Univ. Library, 1985. 257p. ISBN: 0770301835). *Class No:* 820.72-1

[7525]

STEVENS, P. Modern English-Canadian poetry: a guide to information sources. Detroit, Gale, 1978. xi,216p. ISBN: 0810312441.

Lists general sources on Canadian poetry and has bibliographies of primary and secondary material for 60 individual poets. Indexes of authors, titles, and subjects. *Class No:* 820.72-1

Canadian Drama

[7526]

The Brock bibliography of published Canadian plays in English, 1766-1978. Wagner, A., *ed.* Toronto, Playwrights Press, 1980. xi,375p. ISBN: 0887541577.

Lists 2,270 plays by author, A-Z, within separate sections for each century, giving publication information and details of scenes and casts. Includes French-Canadian plays translated into English. Title index. List of sources. *Class No:* 820.72-2

[7527]

Who's who in the Playwrights Union of Canada: directory of members. Boni, F., *comp.* Toronto, Playwrights Union of Canada, 1993. 248p. illus.

The Union's first directory carries details of 242 dramatists. Full-page entries include photograph, biography, list of plays, awards, professional affiliations and agent. List of a further 100 members not given a full entry. List of over 50 agencies.

The Playwrights Union also distributes *Who's who in the Writer's Union of Canada: a directory of members*, the 20th anniversary issue of which includes 700 short profiles written by the authors themselves. *Class No:* 820.72-2

Canadian Prose

[7528]

Canadian writers and their works: fiction series. Lecker, R., *& others, eds.* Toronto, ECW Press, 1982-95. 12v. illus. C$45-50 per vol.

A set organized on similar lines to the *Poetry series* (*q.v.*). A separate cumulative index is available (C$20. ISBN: 1550221426). *Class No:* 820.72-3

[7529]

HOY, H. Modern English-Canadian prose: a guide to information sources. Detroit, Gale, 1983. xxiv,605p. ISBN: 081031245x.

2 sections on general sources, followed by bibliographies for 68 fiction and 10 nonfiction authors, listing primary and secondary material including book reviews. Indexes of authors, titles, and subjects. *Class No:* 820.72-3

[7530]

WEISS, A. A Comprehensive bibliography of English-Canadian short stories, 1950-1983. Toronto, ECW Press, 1989. 973p. C$70. ISBN: 0920763677.

An attempt to record every short story written in English by a Canadian and first published 1950-83. Nearly 20,000 citations to over 14,000 stories by over 5,300 authors, which have appeared in periodicals and anthologies. Also cites appearances by Canadian stories in foreign publications. Arranged A-Z by author with a title index. *Class No:* 820.72-3

Atwood

[7531]

McCOMBS, J. ***and*** **PALMER, C.L. Margaret Atwood: a reference guide.** Boston, Hall, 1991. xxxi,735p. $60. ISBN: 0816189404.

Lists *c.*2,000 secondary items, including articles, book reviews, dissertations and interviews. Arranged by year, 1962-87, and by author within each year. Author and subject indexes. Palmer compiles an annual checklist of Atwood criticism which is published in the *Newsletter of the Margaret Atwood Society*. *Class No:* 820.72-3ATW

Caribbean Literature

Bibliographies

[7532]

ALLIS, J.B. West Indian literature: an index to criticism, 1930-1975. Boston, Hall, 1981. xxxvii,353p. ISBN: 0816182663.

Lists over 1,500 articles from North American, British and African periodicals, West Indian newspapers and magazines, and 5 collections of essays. 3 main sections: 1. Index of West Indian authors (general criticism of each followed by material on specific works) - 2. Index of critics and reviewers - 3. Index of general articles on West Indian literature (chronological list with annotations). Appendix lists 36 books on West Indian literature. Restricted to English-language literature. *Class No:* 820.729(01)

[7533]

FENWICK, M.J. Writers of the Caribbean and Central America: a bibliography. New York, Garland, 1992. 2v. $215. ISBN: 0824040104.

See entry at 860.7(01). *Class No:* 820.729(01)

Histories

[7534]

DABYDEEN, D. *and* **WILSON-TAGOE, N. A Reader's guide to Westindian and Black British literature.** 2nd, rev. ed. London, Hansib Publishing, 1997. 190p. £8.95. ISBN: 187051842x.

See entry at 820-0(=96). *Class No:* 820.729(091)

[7535]

A History of literature in the Caribbean. Amsterdam, Benjamins, 1994-. v.1, 3 (in progress). (*A Comparative history of literatures in European languages.*)

V.1 *Hispanic and Francophone regions* (1994. xviii,579p. $150. ISBN: 1556196016).

V.3 *Cross cultural studies* (1998. xviii,381p. $120. ISBN: 1556196032).

See entry at 860.7(729). *Class No:* 820.729(091)

[7536]

West Indian literature. King, B., *ed.* 2nd ed. London, Macmillan, 1995. viii,248p. £10.95. (*Macmillan new literature handbooks.*) ISBN: 0333594630.

1st ed. 1979.

19 chapters by 18 contributors. Introduction; 8 chapters of history; 10 chapters on individual writers, *viz.* Mittelholzer, Selvon, Lamming, Walcott, Naipaul, Harris, Rhys, Brathwaite, Lovelace and Rhone, the last 2 new for this ed. Index. *Class No:* 820.729(091)

Biographies

[7537]

Caribbean writers: a bio-bibliographical-critical encyclopedia. Herdeck, D.E., *and others, eds.* Washington, DC, Three Continents, 1979. xiv,943p. illus. $70. ISBN: 0914478745.

Covers all the islands plus Belize and the Guianas. Arranged in 4 'volumes' for English, French, Dutch and Spanish language writers, each including introductory essays, portraits of writers A-Z, and bibliographies of critical studies and anthologies. Author portraits range from single paragraphs to several pages for major names and include primary and secondary bibliographies. Over 2,000 mainly literary authors covered, with 15,000 works cited. 150 illustrations. Lists of authors by country and of those born outside the West Indies. *Class No:* 820.729(092)

[7538]

Dictionary of literary biography. Detroit, Gale, 1978-98. v.1-188 (in progress). £112 per vol.

The following titles cover Caribbean literature:

V.117 *Twentieth-century Caribbean and Black African writers, first series.* 1992.

V.125 *Twentieth-century Caribbean and Black African writers, second series.* 1993.

V.157 *Twentieth-century Caribbean and Black African writers, third series.* 1995.

For a description of the series, see entry at 82(092). *Class No:* 820.729(092)

[7539]

Fifty Caribbean writers: a bio-bibliographical critical sourcebook. Dance, D.C., *ed.* New York, Greenwood, 1986. xii,530p. $79.50. ISBN: 0313239398.

Follows the format successfully used by Greenwood Press in their bio-bibliographical sourcebooks on regional writers of the USA. (*Fifty Western writers*, etc.). Each entry is written by a named scholar, averages 10p. and comprises: biography, discussion of the subject's major works and themes, survey of critical reception, and bibliography of primary and secondary works. General bibliography (1p.), index and notes on the 35 contributors. Covers all the major Caribbean writers and provides the first extended studies of some less well-known names. *Class No:* 820.729(092)

Women

[7540]

Caribbean women novelists: an annotated critical bibliography. Paravisini-Gebert, L. *and Torres-Seda, O., eds.* Westport, Conn., Greenwood, 1993. 427p. $75. (*Bibliographies and indexes in world literature.*) ISBN: 0313283427.

Entries on 150 writers, A-Z, comprising biography, data on novels (including plot synopses), list of other works, and secondary bibliography. Articles range from less than a page to over 50 for Jean Rhys. List of general reference works. List of authors by country. Indexes of novel titles, critics and themes/keywords. Not restricted to English-language writers.

See also *Bibliography of women writers from the Caribbean, 1831-1986*, by B.F. Berrian and A. Broek (Washington, D.C., Three Continents, 1989. $25. ISBN: 0894106007). *Class No:* 820.729-0055.2

American Literature

Databases

[7541]

Disclit: American authors. Twayne's *United States authors* series and OCLC Subject Bibliographies on CD-ROM. Boston, Hall, 1991. $995. ISBN: 0816116504.

A CD-ROM with the full texts of 143 vols. in Twayne's well-known series of critical introductions to the lives and works of major authors, plus OCLC Electronic Publishing's subject bibliographies with over 120,000 citations relating to the same authors. 'The strength of *Disclit* lies in its ability to determine how various writers have treated a particular theme, to compare the works of two or more authors, or to trace the contributions of an author to a literary movement ... It supplements, but does not supplant, the *MLA international bibliography* on CD-ROM' (*Choice*, v.29(5), Jan. 1992, p.729-30). *Class No:* 820.73(003.4)

Bibliographies of Bibliographies

[7542]

NILON, C.H. Bibliography of bibliographies in American literature. New York, Bowker, 1970. xii,483p. ISBN: 0835202593.

Covers separately published bibliographies and those appearing within books and periodals. 6,463 entries (a few of them annotated) arranged in 4 sections: 1. Bibliography - 2. Authors (4 subsections for 17th, 18th, 19th and 20th centuries) - 3. Genre (Literary history and criticism, Drama, Fiction, Poetry) - 4. Ancillary (30 subjects arranged alphebtically from Almanacs to Travels). No cross-references but detailed index. *Class No:* 820.73(009)

Bibliographies

[7543]

American literary scholarship: an annual, 1968-. Durham, N.C., Duke Univ. Press, 1965-. Annual.

A survey of published research in American literature, consisting of signed bibliographic essays by scholars on major authors or groups of authors and on periods or genres. *ALS 1995* (1997. xxii,556p. ISBN: 0822319527) has 10 essays on authors and 12 thematic essays. Indexes of critics and of authors as subjects. A thoroughly reliable source for recent secondary material on American literature.
Class No: 820.73(01)

[7544]

American literature: a journal of literary history, criticism and biography. Durham, N.C., Duke Univ. Press, 1929-. Quarterly. ISSN: 00029831.

Until recently, each issue contained 'A Selected annotated list of current articles on American literature', in 2 sections: 'Selected articles' and 'Selected issues of journals'. Still very useful for journal issues devoted to one writer or topic and for its lengthy book reviews. *Class No:* 820.73(01)

[7545]

—MARSHALL, T.F. An Analytical index to *American Literature*, volumes I-XXX, March 1927-January 1959. Durham, N.C., Duke Univ. Press, 1963. vii,253p. $31.95. ISBN: 0822301148.

Comprises author-subject index (including writers as subjects) and book review index. Because of the comprehensive reviewing policy of the periodical during its early years, the *Index* is an almost complete bibliography of scholarly publications during this period.
Class No: 820.73(01)

[7546]

Articles on American literature, 1900-1950. Leary, L. Durham, N.C., Duke Univ. Press, 1954. xv, 437p.

A revision and expansion of *Articles on American literature appearing in current periodicals, 1920-1945* (1947).

About 10,000 entries in 2 alphabetical sequences: 1. Authors as subjects (p.3-330) - 2. Themes (26 headings from Almanacs to Theater). Authors of articles are not indexed. No annotations. Very little foreign-language material included. *Class No:* 820.73(01)

[7547]

Articles on American literature, 1950-1967. Leary, L., *comp., with the assistance of C. Bartholet and C. Roth.* Durham, N.C., Duke Univ. Press, 1970. xxi,751p. ISBN: 082231239x.

Continues the 1900-1950 bibliography, using as a basis the checklists of 'Articles on American literature appearing in current periodicals' in the quarterly *American Literature,* January 1951 - January 1968. Also includes pre-1950 articles omitted from the earlier volume and corrections of errors in that work. Similar format to the earlier volume, but includes more articles from foreign periodicals and claims to be more selective. About 20,000 entries.
Class No: 820.73(01)

[7548]

Articles on American literature, 1968-1975. Leary, L. *and* Auchard, J., *comps.* Durham, N.C., Duke Univ. Press, 1979. xxv, 745p. ISBN: 0822304325.

Supplements the previous 2 volumes and follows the same format. Includes numerous additions and corrections to the preceding volumes, particularly in the thematic sequence. Bibliographical essays are now marked with an asterisk.
Class No: 820.73(01)

[7549]

BLANCK, J. Bibliography of American literature, compiled for the Bibliographical Society of America. New Haven, Conn., Yale Univ. Press, 1955-91. 9v.

A selective bibliography of *c.*300 American authors from the beginning of the Federal period up to the early 20th century (anyone living beyond 1930 is excluded), which should eventually include some 35,000 items. Alphabetically arranged (Henry Adams to Elinor Wylie) giving all first eds. in date order with full collation, plus bibliographical references for each work. Also listed are variants, revised reprints, first appearances in books and pamphlets, etc., and selected biographical, bibliographical and critical material, but excluded are periodical and newspaper publications, translations, and volumes containing isolated correspondence. Gives US library locations. Appendix of initials, pseudonyms, and acronyms in each vol. Title page facsimiles.

Following Blanck's death, v.7 was edited by V.L. Smyers and M. Winship, and vols. 8 and 9 by M. Winship.

Also available on CD-ROM from Chadwyck-Healey, Ltd., Cambridge (£595. ISBN: 0898871905) and on the Internet via their *Literature Online (LION)* subscription service (http://lion.chadwyck.co.uk). The database can be searched by keyword, title keyword, imprint keyword, author, location of copy, publication date and entry number.
Class No: 820.73(01)

[7550]

Eight American authors: a review of research and criticism. Woodress, J.L., *ed.* Rev. ed. New York, Norton, 1971. xix, 392p. ISBN: 0393043509.

1st ed. New York, Modern Language Association of America, 1956, edited by F. Stovall; a bibliographical supplement by J.C. Matthews was published 1963.

Bibliographical essays by 8 scholars on Poe, Emerson, Hawthorne, Thoreau, Melville, Whitman, Twain and James, which evaluate published bibliographies, editions, biographies and critical studies of each author. Cut-off date is generally 1969. Bibliographical detail is disappointingly brief. Author index. *Class No:* 820.73(01)

[7551]

Fifteen American authors before 1900: bibliographical essays on research and criticism. Harbert, E.N. *and* Rees, R.A., *eds.* Rev. ed. Madison, Wis., Univ. of Wisconsin Press, 1984. 448p. $27.50. ISBN: 0299095908.

1st ed. 1971.

Bibliographical essays on pre-1900 writers not covered in J.L. Woodress' *Eight American authors* (*q.v.*), to which this work is similar in scope and format although with more complete bibliographical information. Writers surveyed: Adams, Bryant, Cooper, Stephen Crane, Dickinson, Edwards, Franklin, Holmes, Howells, Irving, Longfellow, Lowell, Norris, Taylor, and Whittier. Author index.
Class No: 820.73(01)

[7552]

First printings of American authors: contributions towards descriptive checklists. Bruccoli, M.J., *and others, eds.* Detroit, Gale, 1977-87. 5v. illus.

'... planned as a field guide for scholars, dealers, librarians, researchers, students and collectors. The rationale for this work is to identify the first American printings and the first English printings of books by selected American authors. The author selections are admittedly impressionistic, reflecting the editors' sense of collecting and scholarly interest ... A special effort has been made to include authors for whom no adequate bibliography or checklist is available' (*Introduction.*).

Each vol. has an A-Z sequence of checklists, compiled by numerous contributors, with a cumulative index in v.5. References to biographical and bibliographical studies at the end of some lists. Lavishly laid out with over 3,000 reproductions of title-pages and dust jackets, photos of some authors, and a great deal of blank space. Nearly 400 authors covered in all. *Class No:* 820.73(01)

[7553]

The French critical reception of African-American literature, from the beginnings to 1970: an annotated bibliography. Fabre, M., *& others, comps.* Westport, Conn., Greenwood, 1995. 328p. $75. (*Bibliographies and indexes in Afro-American and African studies.*) ISBN: 0313253684.

Covers the period 1844-1970, although most items were published after 1900. Mainly lists French critical articles on fiction writers, but some translations and original French publications of African-American literature are also included. Introductory essay surveys trends in French criticism. 3 indexes: authors and concepts; titles; periodicals. *Class No:* 820.73(01)

[7554]

HARVARD UNIVERSITY. Library. **American literature.** Cambridge, Mass., Harvard Univ. Press, 1970. 2v. $100. (*Widener Library shelflist - nos. 26-27.*) ISBN: 0674025350.

V.1 *Classification schedule. Classified listing by call number. Chronological listing.* xxi,631p.

V.2 *Author and title listing.* vi,632p.

Lists *c.*58,000 literary histories, anthologies, and works by and about individual authors. *Class No:* 820.73(01)

[7555]

PECK, D.R. American ethnic literatures: Native American, African American, Chicano/Latino, and Asian American writers and their backgrounds - an annotated bibliography. Englewood Cliffs, N.J., Salem Press, 1992 (later Scarecrow Press). 218p. $42. (*Magill bibliographies.*) ISBN: 0810827921.

4 introductory chapters covering general sources for students and teachers of ethnic literaures, followed by chapters on each of the 4 major ethnic literatures. These include annotated lists of anthologies, reference works, critical studies, journals, etc., plus unannotated lists of primary works by ethnic minority writers and a brief history of each literary tradition. Coverage limited to works in English, although some bilingual texts are included. Author index. 'A timely resource that addresses a need in this multicultural society' (*Booklist*, v.89(16), April 15, 1993, p.1531). *Class No:* 820.73(01)

[7556]

TURNER, A.K. Victorian criticism of American writers: a guide to British criticism of American writers in the leading British periodicals of the Victorian period, 1824-1900. San Bernadino, Calif., Borgo Press; West Bridgford, Notts., Paupers' Press, 1991. 456p. $49.95. ISBN: 089370816x, US; 0893709166, UK.

Presents critical studies from 47 sources and is arranged by journal in the style of *The Wellesley index to Victorian periodicals, 1824-1900.* Indexes provide access to individual American authors and titles. *Class No:* 820.73(01)

20th Century

[7557]

Contemporary authors: bibliographical series. Detroit, Gale, 1986-9. 3v. £99 per vol. ISSN: 08873070.

V.1 *American novelists.* 1986. xvii,431p.

V.2 *American poets.* 1986. xv,387p.

V.3 *American dramatists.* 1989. xvii,484p.

A companion to the main *CA* series, which is intended to provide a guide to the best critical studies about major postwar writers. Only 3 vols. have appeared, each treating 10 American authors. Entries are signed by specialists and comprise primary and secondary bibliographies and a lengthy, analytical bibliographical essay. Authors in v.1 include Baldwin, Bellow, Heller, Mailer and Updike. Cumulative indexes of authors and critics.
Class No: 820.73(01)"19"

[7558]

HICKEY, M. The Bohemian register: an annotated bibliography of the Beat literary movement. Metuchen, N.J., Scarecrow, 1990. 252p. illus. $34.50. ISBN: 0810823977.

Lists 56 general studies of the movement and 43 anthologies, then works by and about 63 Beat writers, A-Z, with over 700 titles covered. Also provides some biographical information. Selective list of little magazines. Poem and article title index; name, book title and subject index. *Class No:* 820.73(01)"19"

[7559]

Sixteen modern American authors: a survey of research and criticism. Bryer, J.R., *ed.* Rev. ed. Durham, N.C., Duke Univ. Press, 1974. xx,673p. ISBN: 0822302977.

First published 1969 as *Fifteen modern American authors.*

Modelled closely on Woodress' *Eight American authors* (*q.v.*), it includes bibliographical essays on Sherwood Anderson, Willa Cather, Hart Crane, Theodore Dreiser, T.S. Eliot, William Faulkner, F. Scott Fitzgerald, Robert Frost, Ernest Hemingway, Eugene O'Neill, Ezra Pound, E.A. Robinson, John Steinbeck, Wallace Stevens, Thomas Wolfe and - the new addition since 1969 - William Carlos Williams. The essays in the original ed. have been corrected and a supplement covering 1969-1972 added to each one. Author index.

Supplemented by ***Sixteen modern American authors, vol.2:*** *a survey of research and criticism since 1972* (Durham, N.C., Duke Univ Press, 1990. 810p. $60.50. ISBN: 0822309769). *Class No:* 820.73(01)"19"

[7560]
WITTMAN, S.M. Writing about Vietnam: a bibliography of the literature of the Vietnam conflict. Boston, Hall, 1989. xix,385p. $40. ISBN: 0816190836.

An annotated listing of novels, biographies, anthologies, drama, poetry, short stories, bibliographies, personal narratives, teaching materials, dissertations, theses, and secondary sources on the Vietnam War. 1,749 entries. Author and title indexes. *Class No:* 820.73(01)"19"

[7561]
—JASON, P.K. The Vietnam war in literature: an annotated bibliography of criticism. Englewood Cliffs, N.J., Salem Press, 1992 (later Scarecrow Press). xii,175p. $40. (*Magill bibliographies.*) ISBN: 0810827913.

Chapters on 69 authors of imaginative literature relating to the War, with annotated lists of major works and English-language critical studies. Also has chapters on general criticism and studies of particular genres: nonfiction, fiction, poetry, drama and film. *c.*500 items annotated in total. *Class No:* 820.73(01)"19"

[7562]
—NEWMAN, J.B., *& others*. Vietnam War literature: an annotated bibliography of imaginative works about Americans fighting in Vietnam. 3rd ed. Lanham, Md., Scarecrow, 1996. xi,667p. $68. ISBN: 0810831848.

1st ed. 1982; 2nd ed. 1988.

1,370 entries (over 600 new to this ed.) in 5 sections (novels, short stories, poetry, drama, and miscellaneous) with chronological arrangement within each section. Descriptive and evaluative annotations. Author and title indexes. *Class No:* 820.73(01)"19"

Encyclopaedias & Dictionaries

[7563]
American literary almanac: from 1608 to the present; an original compendium of facts and anecdotes about literary life in the United States of America. Rood, K.L., *ed.* New York, Facts on File, 1988. xi,427p. illus. ISBN: 0816015759.

' ... departs from the format of current almanacs - which are almost entirely given over to lists - and returns to the spirit of earlier American alamanacs' (*Foreword*) and is consequently more readable but less useful as a reference tool. 19 signed chapters by 10 contributors cover a wide range of literary topics. Contains some useful lists, *e.g.* last words of writers, burial places, title sources, pseudonyms, etc. Excellent bibliography of basic reference books. Nearly 200 illustrations. Index. *Class No:* 820.73(03)

[7564]
BURKE, W.J. *and* **HOWE, W.D. American authors and books,** 1640 to the present day. 3rd. rev. ed., rev. by I. and A. Weiss. New York, Crown, 1972. 719p. ISBN: 0517501392.

First published 1943; 2nd ed. 1962.

Aims 'to present the most useful facts about the writing, illustrating, editing, publishing, reviewing, collecting, selling and preservation of American books' (*Preface to 1st ed.*). 17,000 entries in one alphabetical sequence, covering authors, editors, publishers, titles of works, magazines (over 700), etc. Some subject headings, with many of those added in the rev. ed. having a distinctly Sixties flavour, *e.g.* 'Hippies', 'Pop poetry', 'Underground press'. Gives complete birth and death dates whereas the *Oxford companion* gives years only. *Class No:* 820.73(03)

[7565]
The Cambridge handbook of American literature. Salzman, J., *ed.* Cambridge, Cambridge Univ. Press, 1986. 286p. £25.95. ISBN: 0521307031.

750 entries which the editor hopes 'represent a core list of those writers, works and movements of which some knowledge is essential to all serious students of American literature' (*Preface*). The emphasis is on pure literature (with few entries on peripheral topics) and on information (with little critical comment). One A-Z sequence, with most of the entries on authors and works, clearly cross-referenced and followed by chronology and bibliography. *Review of English Studies* (v.39(153), Feb.1988, p.157-8) criticizes the plot summaries ('They are written in flat, uninspired prose and fail to say anything interesting about the topic in question') and suggests that 'more space could have been devoted to literary movements and trends'. *Class No:* 820.73(03)

[7566]
Handbook of American popular literature. Inge, M.T., *ed.* New York, Greenwood, 1988. x,408p. $57.95. ISBN: 0313254052.

15 signed bibliographic essays by 16 contributors about the main forms of popular literature: 1. Best sellers - 2. Big Little books - 3. Children's literature - 4. Comic books - 5. Detective and mystery novels - 6. Fantasy - 7. Gothic novels - 8. Historical fiction - 9. Popular history and biography - 10. Pulps and dime novels - 11. Romantic fiction - 12. Science fiction - 13. Verse and popular poetry - 14. Westerns - 15. Young adult fiction.

Essays average 25p. and comprise: historical survey of the genre; critical guide to reference works; discussion of research centres and collections; review of historical and critical writing on the genre; checklist of works cited and periodicals in the field. Index.

10 of the essays first appeared in Inge's *Handbook of American popular culture* (3v. Greenwood, 1978-81) and have been revised and updated; the other 5 were written especially for this book. *Class No:* 820.73(03)

[7567]
HART, J.D. The Oxford companion to American literature. Leininger, P.W., *ed.* 6th ed., rev. and enl. New York, Oxford Univ. Press, 1995. 880p. £35. ISBN: 0195065484.

First published 1941; 5th ed. 1983.

Of the 5,000 A-Z entries, over 2,000 are for authors (short biographies with bibliography and some critical comments) and 1,100 provide plot summaries of literary works, but also covered are fictional characters, literary schools and movements, literary awards, societies, magazines, etc., and there are numerous subject entries, ranging from 'Abolitionist' to 'Zuni Indians'. 6th ed. represents the most thorough revision so far, with 181 new entries and many others expanded and revised. Hart died in 1990 and the new editor has widened the scope of the work to include more women and writers from ethnic groups. Chronology of literary and historical events from 1577 to 1994. *Class No:* 820.73(03)

[7568]
Masterpieces of American literature. Magill, F.N., *ed.* New York, HarperCollins, 1993. xiii,626p. $40. ISBN: 0062700723.

199 articles, of which 162 cover specific titles and 37 are genre entries on the short stories, poetry or essays of individual authors. Provides quick-reference data and critical analysis in the sane format as Magill's *Masterpieces of Latino literature* (*q.v.*).

Magill has also produced a companion vol. *Masterpieces*

.... *(contd.)*
of African-American literature (New York, HarperCollins, 1992. 608p. $40. ISBN: 0062700669).
Class No: 820.73(03)

[7569]
Reference guide to American literature. Kirkpatrick, D.L., *ed.* 3rd ed. Detroit & London, St. James Press, 1994. 1202p. $140. ISBN: 1558623108.

No 1st ed. as such, but 2nd ed. (1987) was based on *American literature to 1900* and *20th century American literature*, both published New York, St. Martin's Press, and London, Macmillan, 1980.

The major part of the guide is a dictionary of over 400 authors, with entries providing biographical notes; complete list of publications; selected list of bibliographies and critical studies; and a signed critical essay by one of a long list of contributors. This is followed by a sequence of essays on 131 major works, a chronology of literary and historical events, and an index of works mentioned in the author entries. Introductory essays on the history of American literature have been expanded and updated.

This ed. features more African American writers than before and includes, for the first time, Asian, Hispanic and Native American writers. Coverage of women and gay writers is also expanded. *Class No:* 820.73(03)

Handbooks & Manuals

[7570]
FENSTER, V.K. Guide to American literature. Littleton, Colo., Libraries Unlimited, 1983. 243p. ISBN: 0872873730.

Part 1 lists general information sources, with brief annotations, and Part 2 comprises bibliographic essays on 100 authors regularly studied on literature courses. Index of authors, titles, and subjects. *Class No:* 820.73(035)

[7571]
GOHDES, C. *and* MAROVITZ, S.E. Bibliographical guide to the study of the literature of the USA. 5th ed., completely rev. and enl. Durham, N.C., Duke Univ. Press, 1984. xv,256p. ISBN: 0822305925.

1st ed. 1959; 4th ed. 1976. All previous eds. by C. Gohdes.

A well-established guide for the student of American literature. Arranged in 35 sections, the titles of which indicate the breadth of coverage, *e.g.* Newspapers, Psychology, Religion in the US, Racial and other minorities, Relations with other countries. Numbered entries arranged A-Z within sections and subsections, with brief but pertinent annotations. Indexes of subjects and authors/editors. Very useful appendix lists the principal biographies of 135 American authors. Many cross-references within annotations and at section ends.

5th ed. adds 850 revised eds. and new titles to give a total of 1,900 entries and has a new section entitled Women's Studies and several new subsections, including Computer Aids, Film and Literature, and Science Fiction and Utopian Writings. *Class No:* 820.73(035)

[7572]
KOSTER, D.N. American literature and language: a guide to information sources. Detroit, Gale, 1982. xiii,396p. ISBN: 0810312581.

A classified list of 149 general sources is followed by very selective, but well-annotated, bibliographies of critical studies on individual authors, A-Z, with the emphasis on recent publications. 1,885 items in total.
Class No: 820.73(035)

Theses

[7573]
HOWARD, P.C. Theses in American literature, 1896-1971. Ann Arbor, Mich., Pieran Press, 1973. 307p.

Lists *c.*7,000 theses from American and foreign universities, A-Z by literary authors covered. Indexes of thesis authors and subjects. *Class No:* 820.73(043)

[7574]
WOODRESS, J.L. Dissertations in American literature; 1891-1966. Newly rev. and enlarged ed., with the assistance of M. Koritz. Durham, N.C., Duke Univ. Press, 1968. xii,185p.

1st ed., 1957, covered 1891-1955; 2nd ed., 1962, was a reprint with a supplement covering 1956-61.

Completely reset, incorporating into the main work the supplement to the 1962 ed., plus new work published 1962-66. Lists 4,631 dissertations, including many from foreign universities, compiled from a wide range of sources. Two A-Z sequences: individual authors (2,846 items) and subjects. Index of dissertation authors. *Class No:* 820.73(043)

Periodicals

[7575]
American literary magazines: the eighteenth and nineteenth centuries. Chielens, E.E., *ed.* New York, Greenwood, 1986. xvi,503p. $75. (*Historical guides to the world's periodicals and newspapers.*) ISBN: 0313239851. ISSN: 07425538.

Profiles of 92 of the most important literary magazines founded before 1900 are arranged A-Z by title from *Aesthetic Papers* to *Yankee Doodle*. Profiles are signed, average 5p. and emphasize the literary aspects and importance of the magazines. Each is followed by a list of information sources (selective bibliography, indexes, reprint editions and location sources) and brief publication history (title changes, volume and issue data, frequency of publication, publishers and editors). Appendix A. lists some 100 minor literary magazines and non-literary magazines with literary contents, in chronological order with brief annotations. Appendix B. is a chronology of social and literary events and American literary magazines, 1774-1900. Index. Notes on 53 contributors. *Class No:* 820.73(051)

[7576]
—American literary magazines: the twentieth century. Chielens, E.E., *ed.* Westport, Conn., Greenwood, 1992. xii,474p. $105. ISBN: 031323986x.

Profiles of 76 major periodicals, with lengthy entries (average 6p.) following the same format as Chielens' work on 18th- and 19th-century titles. Appendices include: list of 100 minor magazines with brief notes (11p.); chronology of magazines and social and literary events, 1900-91 (30p.); details of important periodical collections in North America. 43 contributors. *Class No:* 820.73(051)

[7577]
CHIELENS, E.E. The Literary journal in America to 1900: a guide to information sources. Detroit, Gale, 1975. vi,197p. ISBN: 0810312395.

An annotated bibliography of writings about literary periodicals and personalities associated with them. Limited to periodicals which appeared no more frequently than once a week and no more infrequently than once a quarter. One section on each of the major regions (New England, Mid-Atlantic States, South, West) plus General studies, Bibliographies, and Background studies. 2 appendices: 'Literary material in non-literary periodicals' and 'Poe and

.... *(contd.)*
the American literary periodical'. Index of writers, critics and titles.

Continued by *The Literary journal in America, 1900-1950* (Detroit, Gale, 1977. viii,186p. ISBN: 0810312409), which has chapters on general literary periodicals, little magazines, regional literary periodicals, politically motivated literary periodicals, and academic quarterlies. Thoroughly indexed. *Class No:* 820.73(051)

[7578]
KRIBBS, J.K. An Annotated bibliography of American literary periodicals, 1741-1850. Boston, Hall, 1977. xvii,285p. ISBN: 0816179700.

Lists 940 journals by title, giving place of publication, dates of first and last issues, frequency, editor, publisher, library locations, contributors, and notes on contents. Chronological and geographical indexes, plus indexes of editors and publishers, names (literary figures), and titles of tales, novels and dramas. *Class No:* 820.73(051)

[7579]
The Literary index to American magazines, 1850-1900. Wells, D.A., *comp.* Westport, Conn., Greenwood, 1996. 441p. $85. ISBN: 0313298408.

Indexes 13 magazines (including *Atlantic Monthly* and *Harper's*) by author and 24 broad subjects (*e.g.* 'Drama', 'Women'). Entries for authors provide birth and death dates, nationality and genre; citations to articles about them in the magazines; and a list of their articles, poems and stories found there. Over 1,000 authors covered. 'On the critical points of usefulness and accuracy, this index is a winner' (*Choice*, v.34(5), Jan. 1997, p.777). *Class No:* 820.73(051)

Excerpts

[7580]
Modern American literature. Curley, D.N., *and others, eds.* 4th ed. New York, Ungar, 1969-85. 5v. $75 per vol.

Vols. 1-3 (1515p. ISBN: 0804430462) contain excerpts from critical studies of nearly 300 20th-century American authors, with full citations to the original sources and an index of critics in v.3.

V.4, *Supplement* (1976. 550p. ISBN: 0804430500) updates criticism of half the authors previously covered and includes excerpts on 49 new names. V.5, *Second supplement* (1985. 585p. ISBN: 0804432651), ed. by P. and J. Schlueter, updates v.1-4 and adds 11 new writers.

Index guide to 'Modern American literature' and 'Modern British literature' (New York, Ungar, 1988. 114p. ISBN: 0804430551) provides an index to the 838 authors covered in the 2 series and the 3,500 critics excerpted.
Class No: 820.73(082.200)

[7581]
Twentieth-century American literature. Bloom, H., *ed.* Broomall, Pa., Chelsea House, 1985-87. 8v. $535. (*Chelsea House library of literary criticism.*) ISBN: 0877548005.

Lengthy critical excerpts on authors, A-Z, in vols. 1-7, in the style of *The New Moulton's Library* (*q.v.*). V.8 contains index to critics, complete table of contents, and bibliographical supplement. *Class No:* 820.73(082.200)

Gazetteers

[7582]
EHRLICH, E. *and* **CARRUTH, G. The Oxford illustrated literary guide to the United States.** New York, Oxford Univ. Press, 1982. xiv, 464p. illus. ISBN: 0195031865.

Contains information about the literary associations of 1,586 localities. Arranged by region, then state, then locality, then individual writers A-Z within each locality. 1,527 writers mentioned, including many non-Americans. Indexes of places and writers. Illustrations on every page but maps disappointingly restricted to one per region, showing only the largest towns. *Class No:* 820.73(083.86)

Chronologies

[7583]
Annals of American literature, 1602-1983. Ludwig, R.M. *and* Nault, C.A., jr., *eds.* New York and Oxford, Oxford Univ. Press, 1986. ix,342p. £12.99. ISBN: 0195059190.

Modelled on *Annals of English literature 1475-1950* (*qv*). Year-by-year listings of major American literary works, with an indication of genre, are accompanied by parallel marginal lists of births and deaths of authors, the founding of newspapers and periodicals, major events in US and world history and important foreign publications. For major authors every well-known title is listed plus a selection of lesser works; for minor authors only the more influential publications are included. Reigning British monarchs appear as running heads from 1602-1774, to be replaced from 1789 on by US presidents. US census figures also appear as running heads at ten-yearly intervals from 1790 on. Comprehensive index (102p.) in the style of its English counterpart. *Class No:* 820.73(090)

[7584]
ROGAL, S.J. A Chronological outline of American literature. Westport, Conn., Greenwood, 1987. xiv,446p. $75. ISBN: 0313254710.

Covers the period from 1507 (the year when the term 'America' first appeared on a map) to 1986, listing significant births, deaths, events and literary works for each year. Very comprehensive from the literary standpoint in that many relatively minor writers and works are included, but very few non-literary events listed. Index of authors and events. *Wilson Library Bulletin* (Sept. 1987, p.89) strongly prefers Ludwig and Nault with this as 'a useful supplement'.
Class No: 820.73(090)

Histories

[7585]
American literature. Ford, B., *ed.* London, Penguin, 1988. xi,792p. £8.99. ISBN: 0140138153.

V.9 of *The New Pelican guide to English literature* (*qv*).

Handy paperback single-volume history with 38 chapters by 34 scholars, followed by selective bibliography (90p.) compiled by P. Davison. This has entries under 25 subject headings, followed by listings of primary and secondary material for over 170 major writers. Index.
Class No: 820.73(091)

[7586]

The Cambridge history of American literature. Bercovitch, S., *general ed.* Cambridge, Cambridge Univ. Press, 1994- . v.1- (in progress).

V.1 *1590-1820*. 1994. xiii,829p. £60. ISBN: 052130105x.

V.2 *Prose writing, 1820-1870*. 1995. 905p. £60. ISBN: 0521301068.

V.8 *Poetry and criticism, 1940-1995*. 1996. 557p. £50. ISBN: 0521497337.

A new history in 8 vols. which claims that unlike previous histories, which were 'either totalizing or encyclopedic,' it will offer 'a polyphony of large-scale narratives' and a flexible structure (*Introduction*), allowing, for example, some individual texts to be discussed within several narratives in one vol.

V.1 has 28 lengthy chapters in 5 major sections, a detailed chronology (72p.), and select bibliography of secondary sources (14p.). Index. *Class No:* 820.73(091)

[7587]

Columbia literary history of the United States. Elliott, E., *ed.* New York, Columbia Univ. Press, 1988. xxviii,1263p. $75. ISBN: 0231058128.

The first major history of American literature since that edited by Spiller and co. in 1948 is arranged in five parts (Beginnings to 1810; 1810-1865; 1865-1910; 1910-1945; 1945 to the present), each being the responsibility of one of five associate editors. Each part contains a general essay introducing the period and a number of signed essays on genres, movements and major figures. 85 essays in all by over 70 scholars. The decision not to include even a selective bibliography is a disappointment and footnotes have also been avoided, although a few essential sources are directly referred to in the essays. Index.

Given 'a modified welcome' by *TLS* (no.4440, May 6-12, 1988, p.497) in a lengthy review which criticises the widely varying quality of the essays; some are 'outstanding panoramic surveys' while others are 'very thin'.
Class No: 820.73(091)

[7588]

A History of American literature. Trent, W.P., *and others, eds.* Cambridge, Cambridge Univ. Press, 1918-21. 4v.

Described on title-page as 'Supplementary to *The Cambridge history of English literature*' and compiled on the same pattern as that work, *i.e.* chapters are by specialists and literature is interpreted in the broad sense, to include journalism, children's literature, early scientific works, song-writing, etc. Very extensive chapter bibliographies, which are brought together at the end of each volume, those in v.1 occupying 204p. Index of writers and works in each vol.
Class No: 820.73(091)

[7589]

Literary history of the United States. Spiller, R.E., *and others, eds.* 4th ed., rev. New York, Macmillan; London, Collier Macmillan, 1974. 2v. ISBN: 0026131609, v.1; 0026132109, v.2.

First published 1948(3v.); 3rd ed. 1963(2v.).

V.1 *History*. xxvi,1556p.

V.2 *Bibliography*. xxxviii,1466p.

V.1 covers the history of American literature in its broadest sense from Colonial times to the present day in 86 chapters by 60 contributors. Selective bibliography (41p). Index of writers, titles and subjects.

V.2 is the bibliography proper and comprises the original 1948 ed. (p.1-790) followed by a Supplement which was published separately in 1959 (p.793-1031) and the 1972 Supplement (p.1037-1375). Each of these has 4 main

....(contd.)
sections: 1. Guides to resources - 2. Literature and culture - 3. Movements and influences - 4. Individual authors. The bibliographies are in essay form and are, like the History, the work of numerous scholars. Combined table of contents and index of authors, titles and subjects.
Class No: 820.73(091)

Biographies

[7590]

American authors, 1600-1900: a biographical dictionary of American literature. Kunitz, S.J. *and* Haycraft, H., *eds.* New York, Wilson, 1938. vi,846p. illus. $76. ISBN: 0824200012.

Biographical sketches of almost 1,300 authors, none of them active at the time of publication, with 400 portraits. Concentrates on 'professional' men of letters but some politicians, orators, clergymen, etc. are included. Entries vary from 150 to 2,500 words and are followed by brief lists of principal works and selected crtical and biographical material. *Class No:* 820.73(092)

[7591]

American writers: a collection of literary biographies. Unger, L. *and* Litz, A.W., *eds.* New York, Scribner, 1974-91. 10v. £571.95 ISBN: 0684195941.

Vols. 1-4 comprise a collection of essays on 97 authors, A-Z, originally published in the series *University of Minnesota pamphlets on American writers*, which have been revised and updated. Essentially critical studies, with selected primary and secondary bibliographies. Vols. 5-10 cover writers not in the original series. Indexes in v.4 and each of the supplementary vols.

Also included on *The Scribner writers series on CD-ROM* (*q.v.*). *Class No:* 820.73(092)

[7592]

American writers before 1800: a biographical and critical dictionary. Levernier, J.A. *and* Wilmes, D.R., *eds.* Westport, Conn., Greenwood, 1984. 3v. (xxiii,1765p.). $295. ISBN: 0313222290.

Entries on 786 writers, each comprising list of works, biography, critical appraisal, and suggestions for further reading. Includes several non-literary writers and is particularly useful for minor figures. Appendices list writers by date of birth, place of birth, and main residence. Chronology and index. *c.*250 contributors. 'The entries are uneven but most are satisfactory' (*American Literature*, v.56(3), Oct. 1984, p.429). *Class No:* 820.73(092)

[7593]

Biographical dictionary of Transcendentalism. Mott, W.T., *ed.* Westport, Conn., Greenwood, 1996. 336p. $85. ISBN: 0313288364.

A comprehensive guide to the major and minor figures who shaped Transcendentalism in New England between 1830 and the Civil War, with entries on 204 writers, philosophers and theologians. Entries include biographical references. A short bibliographical essay identifies key general biographical sources on Transcendentalists. Index.

Mott has also edited *Encyclopedia of Transcendentalism* for Greenwood (1996. 320p. $79.50. ISBN: 0313299242), with 145 substantial entries on philosophies, religious movements, people, places, concepts, works and terms, and cross-references to the *Biographical dictionary*. Entries include bibliographies. Chronology. Index.
Class No: 820.73(092)

[7594]

Dictionary of literary biography. Detroit, Gale, 1978-98. v.1-188 (in progress). £112 per vol.

Titles relating to American literature:

1: *The American Renaissance in New England;* 2: *American novelists since World War II;* 3: *Antebellum writers in New York and the South;* 4: *American writers in Paris, 1920-1939;* 5: *American poets since World War II.* (2 parts); 6: *American novelists since World War II,* Second series; 7: *Twentieth-century American dramatists.* (2 parts); 8: *Twentieth-century American science-fiction writers.* (2 parts); 9: *American novelists, 1910-1945.* (3 parts); 11: *American humorists, 1800-1950.* (2 parts); 12: *American Realists and Naturalists;* 16: *The Beats: literary Bohemians in postwar America.* (2 parts); 17: *Twentieth-century American historians;* 22: *American writers for children, 1900-1960;* 23: *American newspaper journalists, 1873-1900;* 24: *American colonial writers, 1606-1734;* 25: *American newspaper journalists, 1901-1925;* 26: *American screenwriters*; 28: *Twentieth-century American-Jewish fiction writers;* 29: *American newspaper journalists, 1926-1950;* 30: *American historians, 1607-1865;* 31: *American Colonial writers, 1735-1781;* 33: *Afro-American fiction writers after 1955;* 37: *American writers of the Early Republic;* 38: *Afro-American writers after 1955: dramatists and prose writers;* 41: *Afro-American poets since 1955;* 42: *American writers for children before 1900;* 43: *American newspaper journalists, 1690-1872;* 44: *American screenwriters,* Second series; 45: *American poets, 1880-1945,* First series; 46: *American literary publishing houses, 1900-1980: trade and paperback;* 47: *American historians, 1866-1912;* 48: *American poets, 1880-1945,* Second series; 49: *American literary publishing houses, 1638-1899.* (2 parts); 50: *Afro-American writers before the Harlem Renaissance;* 51: *Afro-American writers from the Harlem Renaissance to 1940;* 52: *American writers for children since 1960: fiction;* 54:

For a description of series, see entry at 82(092).
Class No: 820.73(092)

[7595]

—Concise dictionary of American literary biography. Detroit, Gale, 1987-89. 6v. illus. £291. ISBN: 0810318180.

Colonization to the American Renaissance, 1640-1865. 1988. ISBN: 0810318199.

Realism, Naturalism and local color, 1865-1917. 1988. ISBN: 0810318210.

The Twenties, 1917-1929. 1989. ISBN: 0810318245.

The Age of maturity, 1929-1941. 1989. ISBN: 0810318202.

The New consciousness, 1941-1968. 1987. ISBN: 0810318229.

Broadening views, 1969-1988. 1989. ISBN: 0810308237.

Contains 200 entries for the authors most frequently studied in high school and college literature courses, selected from 2,300 American author entries in the regular *DLB* series (*q.v.*). Entries have been updated and expanded to include discussion of works published since the original entry was written and an annotated bibliography of secondary sources. *Class No:* 820.73(092)

[7596]

Dictionary of literary biography: documentary series. Detroit, Gale, 1982-97. v.1-16 (in progress). £112 per vol.

V.1 *Sherwood Anderson, Willa Cather, John Dos Passos, Theodore Dreiser, F. Scott Fitzgerald, Ernest Hemingway,* ed. by M.A. Van Antwerp. 1982. 423p. ISBN: 0810311127.

V.2 *James Gould Cozzens, James T. Farrell, William Faulkner, John O'Hara, John Steinbeck, Thomas Wolfe,*

.... *(contd.)*

Richard Wright, ed. by M.A. Van Antwerp. 1982. 479p. ISBN: 0810311143.

V.3 *Saul Bellow, Jack Kerouac, Norman Mailer, Vladimir Nabokov, John Updike, Kurt Vonnegut,* ed. by M. Bruccoli. 1983. 397p. ISBN: 0810311151.

V.4 *Tennessee Williams,* ed. by M.A. Van Antwerp and S. Johns. 1984. 436p. ISBN: 0810311135.

V.5 *American Transcendentalists,* ed. by J. Myerson. 1988. 437p. ISBN: 0810326396.

V.6 *Hardboiled mystery writers,* ed. by M.J. Bruccoli and R. Layman. 1989. 383p. ISBN: 0810327813.

V.7 *Modern American poets: James Dickey, Robert Frost, and Marianne Moore,* ed. by M. Bruccoli and R. Layman. 1990. 397p. ISBN: 08103727821.

V.8 *The Black Aesthetic movement,* ed. by J.L. Decker. 1991. 418p. ISBN: 0810375796.

V.9 *American writers of the Vietnam War: W.D. Erhart, Larry Heinemann, Tim O'Brien, Walter McDonald, John M. Del Vecchio,* ed. by R. Baughman. 1991. ISBN: 081037580x.

V.10 *The Bloomsbury Group,* ed. by E.L. Bishop. 1992. ISBN: 0810375818.

V.11 *American proletarian culture: the twenties and the thirties,* ed. by J.C. Suggs. 1993. ISBN: 081035542x.

V.12 *Southern women writers: Flannery O'Connor, Katherine Anne Porter, Eudora Welty,* ed. by M.A. Wimsatt and K.L. Rood. 1994.

V.13 *The House of Scribner, 1846-1904,* ed. by J. Delaney. 1996.

V.14 *Four women writers for children, 1868-1918,* ed. by C.C. Hunt. 1996.

V.15 *American expatriate writers: Paris in the Twenties,* ed. by M.J. Bruccoli and R.W. Trogdon. 1997. ISBN: 0787619310.

V.16 *The House of Scribner, 1905-1930,* ed. by J. Delaney. 1997.

Each vol. concentrates on the major figures of a particular literary period, movement, or genre. Individual author entries chronicle each writer's career through a selection of literary documents, including letters, notebook and diary entries, interviews, and contemporary book reviews. Entries are heavily illustrated, furnishing facsimiles of manuscripts and revised galley proofs, title pages and dust jackets, and pictures from the authors' lives. With the exception of v.10, coverage so far has been restricted to American literature. Each vol. has a cumulative index to all *DLB* vols. and yearbooks. *Class No:* 820.73(092)

[7597]

Magill's survey of American literature. Magill, F.N., *ed.* New York, Marshall Cavendish, 1991. 6v. £325. ISBN: 185435437x.

Provides information on 190 American writers from the 17th century to the present. Entries are arranged A-Z and include portrait, biographical notes, signed critical essay (up to 19p.) with analysis of key works, and selective secondary bibliography. Glossary of literary terms and author index in each vol. Title index in v.6. Authors have been selected to represent particular genres, periods or cultures and so, like *Magill's survey of world literature* (*q.v.*), 'although broad in scope, this work can not be called comprehensive' (*Choice,* v.29(9), May 1992, p.1370-2) *Class No:* 820.73(092)

[7598]

Who's who in writers, editors and poets (US and Canada): a biographical directory. Johnson, C., *ed.* 5th ed. Highland Park, Ill., December Press, 1994. 600p. $99. ISSN: 10498621.

1st ed. 1987, as *Who's who in US writers, editors and poets*; now appears biennially.

Contains information on *c.*10,000 writers from details supplied by the biographees. Entries include date and place of birth; family details; education; memberships; awards; political activities; military service; and address; but information on publications is limited. Includes journalists, biographers, translators, etc., as well as literary writers. Geographic index. *Class No:* 820.73(092)

Manuscripts & Incunabula

[7599]

American literary manuscripts: a checklist of holdings in academic, historical and public libraries, museums, and authors' homes in the United States. Robbins, J.A., *ed.* 2nd ed. Athens, Ga., Univ. of Georgia Press, 1977. liii,387p. ISBN: 0820304123.

1st ed. Austin, Univ. of Texas Press, 1960.

Lists the holdings of 600 libraries (1st ed. covered 273) of manuscripts of *c.*2,800 authors (1st ed. 2,350). Covers 'all major authors and a wide spectrum of minor authors through the nineteenth century' (*Preface*), with the 2nd ed. including 'a better representation of black authors and younger twentieth-century authors of growing reputation'. An appendix lists authors for whom no holdings were traced. Bibliography (10p.). *Class No:* 820.73(093)

Jews

[7600]

Handbook of American-Jewish literature: an analytical guide to topics, themes and sources. Fried, L., *ed.* New York, Greenwood, 1988. xii,539p. $89.50. ISBN: 0313245932.

'The purpose of this book is twofold: to acquaint the general reader with the major subjects and themes of American-Jewish literature, and to renew the scholar's familiarity with this material and its interpretation' (*Introduction*). It comprises 17 signed essays by distinguished scholars covering all aspects of American-Jewish letters since *c.*1880. Average length is 28p. and each has a bibliography and, if appropriate, suggestions for further reading. Select bibliography of European publications on American-Jewish fiction (4p.). Guide to selected reference materials and resources (4p.). Index. *Class No:* 820.73(=924)

[7601]

Jewish American women writers: a bio-bibliographical and critical sourcebook. Shapiro, A.R., *ed.* Westport, Conn., Greenwood, 1994. 557p. $99.50. ISBN: 0313284377.

Signed essays on 57 writers, most of them writing currently, in the established Greenwood format: biography, analysis of major themes, survey of criticism, bibliography of primary and secondary material. Introductory chapter on Jewish American women's writing and concluding survey of *c.*200 autobiographies. Glossary of Hebrew, Yiddish and Aramaic terms. General bibliography. Index of names and titles. *Class No:* 820.73(=924)

[7602]

NADEL, I.B. Jewish writers of North America: a guide to information sources. Detroit, Gale, 1981. xix,493p. ISBN: 0810314843.

List of general sources, subdivided by form and separated into American and Canadian, followed by bibliographies for poets (24 American; 15 Canadian), fiction writers (47 and 13), and dramatists (15 and 8). Appendix on Yiddish literature and checklists of additional writers. 3,291 entries in total. Indexes of authors, titles, and subjects. *Class No:* 820.73(=924)

Asian Races

[7603]

CHEUNG, K. *and* YOGI, S. Asian American literature: an annotated bibliography. New York, Modern Language Assoc. of America, 1988. 276p. $37.50. ISBN: 087352960x.

Covers creative and critical literature, written in or translated into English, by and about Asian Americans. Separate sections for primary and secondary material are subdivided by ethnic group (Chinese; Japanese; Filipino; Korean; South Asian; Vietnamese and Southeast Asian), and then by genre. 4 indexes: authors; critics; reviewers; editors, translators, and illustrators. *Class No:* 820.73(=95)

Black Races

[7604]

The Schomberg Center guide to Black literature, from the eighteenth century to the present. Valade, R.M., *ed.* Detroit, Gale, 1996. 545p. £57.50. ISBN: 0787602892.

A one-stop reference source on American and international Black literature, with biographical entries on over 500 writers, synopses of *c.*460 major works, and nearly 70 articles on literary topics, themes, events and characters. One A-Z sequence, with a comprehensive subject index. Chronology lists birth and death dates of writers, publication dates of key works and other significant events. Essay on the history of the Schomburg Center. *Class No:* 820.73(=96)

Bibliographies

[7605]

Black American writers: bibliographical essays. Inge, M.T., *and others, eds.* New York, St. Martin's; London, Macmillan, 1978. 2v.

V.1 *The Beginnings, through the Harlem Renaissance and Langston Hughes.* xi,217p. ISBN: 0312082606.

V.2 *Richard Wright, Ralph Ellison, James Baldwin and Amiri Baraka.* xi,187p. ISBN: 0312082959.

9 contributors have compiled essays which list and assess bibliographies, editions, manuscripts and letters, plus biography and criticism. 20 writers covered in v.1. Lacks title index but each vol. has name index. *Class No:* 820.73(=96)(01)

[7606]

GLIKIN, R. Black American women in literature: a bibliography, 1976 through 1987. Jefferson, N.C., McFarland, 1989. xii,251p. $47.50. ISBN: 0899503721.

Claims to be 'the only multi-genre bibliography on Black women authors that has citations for both original works and literary criticism' (*Preface*) and lists over 4,000 items relating to *c.*300 writers of poetry, drama, fiction, and essays. Arranged A-Z by author, with cross-references and author-title index. Appendices include bibliography of over

.... *(contd.)*
100 general works about Black women writers and lists of writers by genre. 'The strength of this work lies in its inclusion of many small literary and women's periodicals not indexed elsewhere' (*Booklist*, v.86(2), Sept.15, 1989, p.205), 80 titles having been searched.
Class No: 820.73(=96)(01)

[7607]
JORDAN, C.L. A Bibliographical guide to African-American women writers. Westport, Conn., Greenwood, 1993. xix,387p. $65. (*Bibliographies and indexes in Afro-American studies.*) ISBN: 0313276331.
Covers *c.*900 women, from the 18th century to the 1990s, who have written literary works in all genres as well as memoirs, diaries, etc. Entries are arranged A-Z and list primary and secondary material, but provide little biographical or contextual information. 'The only work that covers so vast an array of African American women writers' (*Choice*, v31(3), Nov. 1993, p.423).
Class No: 820.73(=96)(01)

[7608]
NEWBY, J.E. Black authors: a selected annotated bibliography. New York, Garland, 1990. 720p. ISBN: 0824033299.
A classified listing (using Library of Congress classification) of books and essays written by black Americans, 1773-1990. Also includes some works by African and Caribbean writers. Author and title indexes. Highly selective, but 'serves admirably as a beginning checklist for libraries with limited holdings by black American authors' (*Choice*, v.28(10), June 1991, p.1620).
Class No: 820.73(=96)(01)

[7609]
PEAVY, C.D. Afro-American literature and culture since World War II: a guide to information sources. Detroit, Gale, 1979. xiv,302p. ISBN: 0810312549.
Chapters on anthologies and bibliographies, followed by 26 subject sections (Civil Rights, Music, Black Muslims, etc.) listing books and periodical articles, then bibliographies for 56 authors, A-Z, which include primary and secondary material and interviews. Index. *Class No:* 820.73(=96)(01)

[7610]
PERRY, M. The Harlem Renaissance: an annotated bibliography and commentary. New York, Garland, 1982. xxxix,272p. ISBN: 0824093208.
913 entries in 8 sections, the one for authors (p.209-510) listing works by and studies of 19 individuals, A-Z. Other sections cover general studies, anthologies, library collections, and dissertations. Author and title indexes.
Class No: 820.73(=96)(01)

Encyclopaedias & Dictionaries

[7611]
The Harlem Renaissance: a historical dictionary for the era. Kellner, B., *ed.* Paperback reprint. New York, Methuen; London, Routledge & Kegan Paul, 1987. xliii,476p. illus. $16.95. ISBN: 0416016715, US; 0710214227, UK.
Originally published Westport, Conn., Greenwood, 1984.
Signed entries by 8 contributors on people, literary works, periodicals, newspapers, films, and topics related to the period 1917-35. Coverage extends to music, art, politics, etc., as well as literature. Most of the *c.*1,000 entries have references to other information sources. Appendices include: chronology of major events; bibliography of literary works;

.... *(contd.)*
list of plays by or about Black people; list of serial publications; and a slang glossary. Extensive bibliography of sources (17p.). Index. *Class No:* 820.73(=96)(03)

[7612]
Masterplots II: African-American literature series. Magill, F.N., *ed.* Pasadena, Calif., Salem Press, 1994. 3v. £237. ISBN: 0893565946.
266 entries in the standard *Masterplots* format covering major writings in all genres by African Americans. Includes some nonfiction, *e.g.* the speeches of Martin Luther King and Malcolm X. Women writers figure prominently. Thoroughly indexed. *Class No:* 820.73(=96)(03)

[7613]
The Oxford companion to African American literature. Andrews, W.L., *& others, eds.* New York, Oxford Univ. Press, 1997. xxvii,866p. £35. ISBN: 0195065107.
Signed entries by over 300 contributors on 400+ writers and 150+ literary works, plus characters, genres (long essays), societies, libraries, publishers, periodicals and a wide range of other related topics. Bibliographies with most entries, listing mainly biographies and critical studies. Includes coverage of some non-literary figures who are 'icons of black culture', *e.g.* Muhammad Ali, Marcus Garvey. Particularly useful 15-page essay on African American literary history. Cross-references and index. Excellent value. *Class No:* 820.73(=96)(03)

Histories

[7614]
JACKSON, B. A History of Afro-American literature, v.1: The Long beginning, 1746-1895. Baton Rouge, La., Louisiana State Univ. Press, 1989. 461p. $29.95. ISBN: 0807115118.
'The most exhaustive survey to date of African-American literary history' (*Choice*, v.27(5), Jan. 1990, p.797), although the 'rambling, digressive writing style' can be distracting. Includes a lengthy bibliographical essay.
Class No: 820.73(=96)(091)

[7615]
WHITLOW, R. Black American literature: a critical history with a 1,520-title bibliography of works written by and about Black Americans. Chicago, Nelson-Hall, 1973 (repr. Totowa, N.J., Littlefield, 1974). xv,287p. ISBN: 0822602784.
One chapter on folklore, followed by chapters for chronological periods since 1746 with subsections on individual authors. Bibliography (p.197-271) has 8 sections: poetry; autobiography; fiction; drama; folklore; anthologies; literary criticism and bibliography; social and historical comment. *Class No:* 820.73(=96)(091)

Biographies

[7616]
African American writers. Smith, V., *& others, eds.* New York, Scribner, 1991. 544p. $95 ISBN: 0684190583.
Complements Scribner's *American writers* series (*q.v.*), offering signed profiles of 33 authors from Phyllis Wheatley (born 1753) to Gloria Naylor. Entries range from 10 to 20p. and include biographical and critical information and selected bibliography of primary and secondary material. 8 of the subjects have been covered in *AW* and its supplements, but they are given new essays here with updated bibliographies. Chronology of significant events.

.... *(contd.)*
Index of authors, titles and topics.
Also included on *The Scribner writers series on CD-ROM* (*q.v.*). *Class No:* 820.73(=96)(092)

[7617]
Black writers: a selection of sketches from *Contemporary authors*. Malinowski, S., *ed.* 2nd ed. Detroit, Gale, 1993. xxiv,619p. $95. ISBN: 0810377888.
See entry at 82(092)(=96) *Class No:* 820.73(=96)(092)

[7618]
FOSTER, M.M.B. Southern Black creative writers, 1829-1953: biobibliographies. Westport, Conn., Greenwood, 1988. xvii,113p. $39.95. ISBN: 0313262071.
Information on 230 writers. 'Inclusion of lesser-known authors makes this volume useful' (*Choice*, v.26(5), Jan. 1989, p.782). *Class No:* 820.73(=96)(092)

[7619]
PAGE, J.A. *and* **ROH, J.M. Selected Black American, African, and Caribbean authors:** a bio-bibliography. Littleton, Colo., Libraries Unlimited, 1985. xiii,388p. ISBN: 0872874303.
A revision and enlargement of Page's *Selected Black American authors: an illustrated bio-bibliography* (Boston, Hall, 1977).
632 entries (453 in 1st ed.) based largely on questionnaires completed by the authors. Includes some non-literary authors (especially writers on religion and social affairs), giving biographical notes, list of writings (book-length works only), and references to biographical sources. Lists of writers by nationality and occupation. Bibliography of sources (10p.). Title index. *Class No:* 820.73(=96)(092)

[7620]
ROSES, L.E. *and* **RANDOLPH, R.E. The Harlem Renaissance and beyond:** literary biographies of 100 Black women writers, 1900-1945. Boston, Hall, 1990 (repr. Cambridge, Mass., Harvard Univ. Press, 1997). xxxiii,413p. illus. $12.50. ISBN: 0674372557.
Entries range from 1 to 12 pages, often include a photograph, and comprise biographical outline, critical survey of literary output, and selected primary and secondary bibliographies. Extensive bibliography of general studies. Appendices include lists of writers by genre, place, and chronological period. Title index to primary works. Particularly useful for lesser-known writers, including critics, historians, journalists, and editors, as well as literary authors. *Class No:* 820.73(=96)(092)

[7621]
RUSH, T.G., ***and others*****. Black American writers past and present:** a biographical and bibliographical dictionary. Metuchen, N.J., Scarecrow, 1975. 2v. (865p.). illus. $83.50. ISBN: 0810807858.
Entries for *c.*2,000 writers, from early 18th century to 1973. In most cases, a biographical sketch is followed by a bibliography of the author's works and a checklist of biographical and critical studies. General bibliography (60p.). Layout unclear. *Class No:* 820.73(=96)(092)

Amerindians, North

[7622]
COLONNESE, T. *and* **OWENS, L.D. American Indian novelists:** an annotated critical bibliography. New York, Garland, 1985. xvi,161p. ISBN: 082409199x.
Lists primary and secondary material for 21 authors.
Class No: 820.73(=97)

[7623]
LITTLEFIELD, D.F. *and* **PARINS, J.W. A Biobibliography of Native American writers, 1772-1924.** Metuchen, N.J., Scarecrow, 1981. xvii,343p. (*Native American bibliography series.*) ISBN: 0810814633.
Supplement published 1985 (350p. ISBN: 0810818027).
Includes works written in English by Native Americans, excluding those from Canada, from Colonial times to 1924, the year in which the American Indian was granted citizenship. Over 4,000 unannotated entries, many of them non-literary, including political essays and addresses, historical works, published letters and personal reminiscences. 111p. of biographical notes. Index of writers by tribal affiliation and subject index.
Class No: 820.73(=97)

[7624]
The Native American in American literature: a selectively annotated bibliography. Rock, R.O., *comp.* Westport, Conn., Greenwood, 1985. xix,211p. $59.95. (*Bibliographies and indexes in American literature.*) ISBN: 0313245509.
1,599 entries, a third of them annotated, arranged in three sections: I. Bibliographies - II. The Indian in literature (lists works which comment upon the treatment of the Indian as a character in American literature) - III. Native American literature (lists works by and about Indian authors and their literary products, concentrating on items not found in major bibliographies such as those by Marken or Littlefield and Parins (*qq.v*). Author and subject indexes.
See also *The Native American in long fiction: an annotated bibliography* by J. Beam & B. Branstad (Lanham, Md., Scarecrow, 1996. 384p. $56. ISBN: 0810830167), which seeks to identify all novel-length fictional works by and about Native Americans of the US published between the 1890s and 1990s, with citations to reviews.
Class No: 820.73(=97)

Immigrants

[7625]
New immigrant literatures in the United States: a sourcebook to our multicultural literary heritage. Knippling, A.S., *ed.* Westport, Conn., Greenwood, 1996. 408p. $75. ISBN: 0313289689.
Essays by 22 specialists on various ethnic groups (excluding African Americans) covering literary/cultural history; dominant concerns and major themes; main genres; key authors; and bibliography of primary and secondary sources. Among previously under-represented groups gaining inclusion are Pakistani Americans, Korean Americans and Arab Americans. 'One of the most comprehensive recent treatments of immigrant literature in the US' (*Choice*, v.34(4), Dec. 1996, p.592), but Hungarian, Russian and Vietnamese Americans are notable omissions. Selected general bibliography. Index. *Class No:* 820.73-0054.72

Women

[7626]
American women writers: a critical reference guide from Colonial times to the present. Mainiero, L., *ed.* New York, Ungar, 1979-82. 4v. $300.
V.1 *A-E.* 1979 (xlviii,601p. ISBN: 0804431515). V.2 *F-Le.* 1980 (xlii,575p. ISBN: 0804431523). V.3 *Li-R.* 1981 (xliii,522p. ISBN: 0804431531). V.4 *S-Z.* 1982 (xv,544p. ISBN: 0804431558).
Covers *c.*1,300 writers from a wide range of fields,

.... (contd.)
including children's literature, religion, history and politics as well as mainstream literature. Signed entries by a long list of contributors range from 400-5,000 words and include biographical notes (particularly good on names and pseudonyms), critical essay, primary bibliography and selected secondary bibliography. Index of names and subjects in v.4. Each vol. has list of *all* writers included, with ample cross-references.

V.5, *Supplement*, ed. by C.H. Green and M.G. Mason (New York, Continuum, 1993. 544p. $95. ISBN: 0826406033) has 145 new articles and 90 updates, with particularly good coverage of Black, Chicana and Asian-American writers. Index of authors and subjects.

Abridged ed. of vols. 1-4 published in one vol. (xxi,899p. $59.50) by Ungar in 1988; edited by L.L. Faust, with articles updated and revised where necessary and a few added. ISBN: 0804431574. *Class No:* 820.73-0055.2

[7627]

American women writers: bibliographical essays. Duke, M., *and others, eds.* Westport, Conn., Greenwood, 1983. xvi,434p. $49.95. ISBN: 0313221162.

14 signed essays by 20 scholars covering 24 writers in the style of *Eight American authors* (*q.v.*). Writers treated: Anne Bradstreet, Mary Rowlandson, Sarah Kemble Knight, Sarah Orne Jewett, Mary E. Wilkins Freeman, Mary N. Murfree, Kate Chopin, Edith Wharton, Gertrude Stein, Djuna Barnes, Anaïs Nin, Ellen Glasgow, Katherine Anne Porter, Eudora Welty, Flannery O'Connor, Carson McCullers, Zora Neale Hurston, Constance Rourke, Pearl Buck, Marjorie Kinnan Rawlings, Margaret Mitchell, Marianne Moore, Anne Sexton, Sylvia Plath. Index. *Class No:* 820.73-0055.2

[7628]

BARSTOW, J.M. One hundred years of American women writing: 1848-1948. Lanham, Md., Scarecrow, 1997. 352p. $42. (*Magill bibliographies.*) ISBN: 081083314x.

6 chapters group 66 authors under broad headings such as Late-Nineteenth Century Fiction Writers and African-American Women Writers. Each chapter begins with an introduction which sets the context, identifies general studies and relevant journals, and makes reference to writers not included yet worthy of note. For each featured writer there is a brief biographical note, a list of reissued editions and many annotated entries for critical studies in books and periodicals. Appended lists of selected women writers by birthdate and ethnicity. *Class No:* 820.73-0055.2

[7629]

DAVIS, C.J. *and* **WEST, K. Women writers in the United States:** a timeline of literary, cultural, and social history. New York, Oxford Univ. Press, 1996. 488p. $45. ISBN: 0195090535.

A chronology which was originally intended to be an addendum to *The Oxford companion to women's writing in the United States* (*q.v.*). 2 sections for each year: 'Texts' and 'Contexts', the former listing key publications (under authors) and the latter listing significant events. Coverage is not limited to literary authors and works, but includes a range of nonfiction, children's literature and songwriting. List of works consulted. Index surprisingly does not include titles of texts. *Class No:* 820.73-0055.2

[7630]

Modern American women writers. Showalter, E., *& others, eds.* New York, Scribner, 1991. 583p. £69.95. ISBN: 0684190575.

Paperback version published New York, Collier Books, 1993 (£9.95. 0020820259).

Complements Scribner's *American writers* series (*q.v.*), offering signed profiles of 41 women, from Frances Harper (born 1825) to Alice Walker. 22 of the subjects have also been covered in *AW* but by different contributors. Essays range from 10 to 20p. and include biography, critical analysis and bibliography. Index of authors, titles and subjects.

Also included on *The Scribner writers series on CD-ROM* (*q.v.*). *Class No:* 820.73-0055.2

[7631]

Nineteenth-century American women writers: a bio-bibliographical critical sourcebook. Knight, D.D., *ed.* Westport, Conn., Greenwood, 1997. 552p. £71.95. ISBN: 0313297134.

Covers 77 writers, including many now forgotten as well as the major names. Entries average 7p. and include biography; discussion of major works and themes; overview of critical reception; and bibliography of primary and secondary sources. General bibliography of major studies of 19th-century American writers. Index. *Class No:* 820.73-0055.2

[7632]

The Oxford companion to women's writing in the United States. Davidson, C.N. *and* Wagner-Martin, L., *eds.* New York, Oxford Univ. Press, 1994. 1021p. £35. ISBN: 0195066081.

Signed entries, ranging from a few lines to several pages, by over 500 contributors on topics and individual writers. Topical entries cover historical periods, events, ethnic groups, regions, genres, themes, critical schools, etc. 400 women, from Anne Bradstreet to present-day writers, are given an individual entry and many more are mentioned within articles. Timeline of US women's writing. Bibliography. Comprehensive index. Not confined to literary authors: 'What is unique about this volume is that it aims to explore the entire range of women's writing in a multidisciplinary framework' (*Booklist*, v.91(10), Jan. 15, 1995. p.962). *Class No:* 820.73-0055.2

Gay People

[7633]

Contemporary lesbian writers of the United States: a bio-bibliographical sourcebook. Pollack, S. *and* Knight, D.D., *eds.* Westport, Conn., Greenwood, 1993. xi,640p. $115. ISBN: 0313282153.

A companion vol. to E.S. Nelson's *Contemporary gay American novelists* (*q.v.*), profiling 100 writers of poetry, fiction and drama who have identified themselves as lesbians during the period 1970-92. Signed essays (4-8p.) comprise biography; discussion of major works and themes; overview of critical reception; and bibliography of primary and secondary material. Ethnic minority writers well represented. Appended lists of journals and of publishers of lesbian writing. Selective bibliography of nonfiction writing on lesbian issues (9p.). Index of titles, names and themes/genres. *Class No:* 820.73-0055.3

American Poetry

Databases

[7634]

American poetry: the full-text database. Cambridge, Chadwyck-Healey, 1996. World Wide Web resource Subscription details from marketing@chadwyck.co.uk

Part of *Literature online (LION)* (*q.v.*). URL: http://lion.chadwyck.co.uk

Aims to include the complete works of all major poets active before 1900, as listed in the *Bibliography of American literature* (New Haven, Conn., Yale Univ. Press, 1955-91), plus some works by additional poets, a corpus of over 40,000 poems by 200-plus writers. Verse dramas are included, but poems published only in periodicals are excluded, as are translations. Normally a single version of each poem appears, but exceptions have been made for significant revisions to major works, *e.g.* 5 eds. of Whitman's *Leaves of grass* are included. Searchable by keyword, first line / title keyword, poet, period and gender. Also available on CD-ROM at £6,000.

Supplemented by *American poetry* 2, an expanding database of 20th-century verse, which in April 1998 contained 10,000 poems drawn from 100 vols. by 94 poets. *Class No:* 820.73-1(003.4)

Bibliographies of Bibliographies

[7635]

McPHERON, W. Bibliography of contemporary American poetry, 1945-85. Westport, Conn., Greenwood, 1986. 72p. $42.95 ISBN: 0313277036.

A descriptive checklist of published bibliographies. The first part lists multiauthor sources, A-Z by compiler/editor, and the second part lists 122 single-author studies, A-Z by poet. *Class No:* 820.73-1(009)

Bibliographies

[7636]

BROWN UNIVERSITY. John Hay Library. **Catalog of broadsides of American verse in the Harris Collection of American poetry and plays.** Boston, Hall, 1987. 5v. $990. ISBN: 0816109842.

79,000 cards, newly recataloged to AACR standards, giving full access to 12,000 poems in broadside form dating from 1700 to the present. Includes the output of many small underground presses from the 1960s. Also available on microfilm ($715. ISBN: 0816114692). *Class No:* 820.73-1(01)

[7637]

BROWN UNIVERSITY. John Hay Library. **Dictionary catalog of the Harris Collection of American poetry and plays.** Boston, Hall, 1972. 13 reels of microfilm. ISBN: 0816114978.

Reproductions of 337,000 cards, covering 150,000 printed books and pamphlets in this very comprehensive collection of American, Canadian, and Mexican poetry and drama.

First supplement (1977. 3 reels of microfilm. ISBN: 0816114536) has a further 46,200 cards. *Class No:* 820.73-1(01)

[7638]

COOK, R.T. City Lights Books: a descriptive bibliography. Metuchen, N.J., Scarecrow, 1992. 361p. $41.50. ISBN: 0810826216.

Provides complete information on over 230 vols. of poetry published 1955-90 by Lawrence Ferlinghetti's City Lights Bookshop of San Francisco. 1,500 poets featured.
Class No: 820.73-1(01)

[7639]

DAVIS, L. *and* **IRWIN, R. Contemporary American poetry:** a checklist. Metuchen, N.J., Scarecrow, 1975. 183p. ISBN: 0810808323.

Lists 3,300 single-author collections published 1950-73.

Davis's *Contemporary American poetry: a checklist, second series, 1973-1983* (1985. 301p. $29.50. ISBN: 0810818299) lists a further 5,000 collections. Both vols. are arranged A-Z by poet. *Class No:* 820.73-1(01)

[7640]

Guide to American poetry explication. Boston, Hall, 1989. 2v.

V.1 *Colonial and nineteenth-century* by J. Ruppert. 252p. ISBN: 0816189196. $40.

V.2 *Modern and contemporary* by J.R. Leo. 546p. ISBN: 0816189188. $50.

The first 2 vols. of a 6-vol. set which supersedes J.M. Kuntz and N.C. Martinez's *Poetry explication: a checklist of interpretation since 1925 of British and American poems past and present* (3rd ed. Boston, Hall, 1980). A further 4 vols. cover British poetry under the title *A Guide to British poetry explication* (*q.v.*)

Arranged by poet, A-Z, then by poem, then by critic, and include references that were found in the 3 eds. of the earlier work plus new material published up to 1987. Both vols. contain references to many lesser-known poets and v.2 covers Canadian poets and many from minority groups, *e.g.* Native Americans, Hispanic Americans, gays, etc.
Class No: 820.73-1(01)

[7641]

JASON, P.K. Nineteenth-century American poetry: an annotated bibliography. Pasadena, Calif., Salem Press, 1989 (later Scarecrow Press). vii,257p. $42. (*Magill bibliographies.*.) ISBN: 0810828146.

A section of general studies followed by listings for 16 individual poets from Bryan to Dunbar. Very selective coverage of major poets like Poe and Whitman.
Class No: 820.73-1(01)

[7642]

POETS HOUSE STAFF. Directory of American poetry books. Wakefield, R.I., Asphodel, 1993. 159p. $8.95. ISBN: 1559210990.

The first ed. of what is intended to be an annual publication. Lists US poetry publishers, A-Z, with bibliographical details of their poetry books in print. Author/editor index and title index. Includes much material not included in standard sources. *Class No:* 820.73-1(01)

Indexes

[7643]

CASKEY, J.D. Index to poetry in popular periodicals, 1955-1959. Westport, Conn., Greenwood, 1984. xv,269p. $47.95. ISBN: 0313222274.

Indexes *c.*7,000 poems in 44 periodicals by title, first line, author, and subject. Followed by Caskey's *Index to poetry in*

.... *(contd.)*
popular periodicals, 1960-1964 (New York, Garland, 1988. 232p. $59.95. ISBN: 0313248109). *Class No:* 820.73-1(014)

[7644]
Index to poetry in periodicals: American poetic renaissance 1915-1919; an index of poets and poems published in American magazines and newspapers. Granger Book Co. Editorial Board, *ed.* New York, Roth, 1981. vii,221p. $49.99. ISBN: 0896092127.

122 periodicals indexed by author, but no title or first-line index. Continued by *Index to poetry in periodicals, 1920-1924* (1983. 178p. $49.99. ISBN: 0896092240), which covers 16,000 poems from 302 periodicals, and *Index to poetry in periodicals, 1925-1929* (1984. 290p. $49.99. ISBN: 0896092356). *Class No:* 820.73-1(014)

[7645]
Roth's American poetry annual, 1988-90. Great Neck, N.Y., Roth, 1989-91. 3v. ISSN: 10405461.

3 annual vols. have appeared, combining 3 formerly separate Roth publications, *American poetry index* (1981-86. 4v.), *Annual index to poetry in periodicals* (1984-86. 3v.), and *Annual survey of American poetry* (1985-86. 2v.), to form a single sourcebook. Contents include a survey of the previous year's poetry, with a selected anthology; an index to poetry in selected journals (108 in the 1989 vol.) and single-author collections; a list of poetry award winners; a bibliography of books and articles on poetry and poets; directories of grants, fellowships, organizations, newsletters, etc.; and a list of periodicals and publishers. *RQ* (v.30(1), Fall 1990, p.136-7) suggests that the work's importance lies in its combined author/title/first-line index, whose coverage of single-author collections is unique, whereas the information in its bibliography and directories is too selective.

For poetry in multi-author anthologies, see Roth's *Poetry index annual,* which remains a separate publication.
Class No: 820.73-1(014)

Encyclopaedias & Dictionaries

[7646]
MALKOFF, K. Crowell's handbook of contemporary American poetry. New York, Crowell, 1973. ix,338p. ISBN: 069022625x.

An introductory essay on the development of contemporary American poetry (43p.) is followed by biocritical essays on over 80 poets, schools and movements, with illustrative quotations and selective bibliographies. '... not primarily a compilation of facts. It is intended rather as a guide to the actual process of reading contemporary American poetry' (*Preface*). *Class No:* 820.73-1(03)

Histories

[7647]
The Columbia history of American poetry. Parini, J. *and* Millier, B.C., *eds.* New York, Columbia Univ. Press, 1994. xxxi,894p. $65. ISBN: 0231078366.

31 signed chapters by distinguished critics (including some active poets) on individual poets, groups, schools and movements. Most chapters have brief lists of further reading (rarely more than 12 titles), but there is no general bibliography. Comprehensive index (84p.) includes poem titles. *Class No:* 820.73-1(091)

[7648]
GRAY, R. American poetry of the twentieth century. London, Longman, 1990. xvi,424p. £19.99. (*Longman literature in English.*) ISBN: 0582494443.

A critical history in 6 chapters, plus a superb reference section comprising: chronology of literary and historical/cultural events, 1900-1985; annotated general bibliography (15p.); biographical notes on over 120 poets, with lists of major works and selected criticism. Index.
Class No: 820.73-1(091)

Black Races

[7649]
African-American poetry (1760-1900). Cambridge, Chadwyck-Healey, 1996. World Wide Web resource Subscription details from marketing@chadwyck.co.uk

Part of *Literature online (LION)* (*q.v.*). URL: http://lion.chadwyck.co.uk

A database whose contents are based on W.French's bibliography, *Afro-American poetry and drama, 1760-1975* (*q.v.*). Includes the complete text of nearly 3,000 poems (first editions normally), plus all additional authorial matter. Searchable by keyword, first line / title keyword, poet, period and gender. Also available on CD-ROM at £2,450.
Class No: 820.73-1(=96)

[7650]
CHAPMAN, D.H. Index to black poetry. Boston, Hall, 1974. xxii,541p.

Indexes 94 books and pamphlets by individual poets and 33 anthologies which contain *c.*5,000 poems by Black people and about the Black experience by poets of all races. Title/first line index, author index and subject index.
Class No: 820.73-1(=96)

[7651]
FRENCH, W.P., *and others*. Afro-American poetry and drama, 1760-1975: a guide to information sources. Detroit, Gale, 1979. 493p. ISBN: 0810312085.

Separate sections for poetry, 1760-1975, and drama, 1850-1975, each with annotated bibliography of general studies and bibliographies of individual authors, listing primary and secondary material. Appendix on folk songs, blues, and spirituals. Author, title, and subject indexes.
Class No: 820.73-1(=96)

[7652]
Index to poetry by Black American women. Chapman, D.H., *comp.* New York, Greenwood, 1986. xxiii,424p. $85. (*Bibliographies and indexes in Afro-American and African studies.*) ISBN: 0313251525.

Indexes over 4,000 poems by over 400 poets plus 185 anonymous poems (not necessarily by women), found in 83 anthologies and 120 books by individual poets. 3 alphabetical indexes: titles and first lines, authors, subjects (approx. 1,000 headings). Bibliographical details of all books indexed. A companion vol. on Black American male poets is planned. *Class No:* 820.73-1(=96)

[7653]
WAGNER, J. Black poets of the United States: from Laurence Dunbar to Langston Hughes. Urbana, Ill., Univ. of Illinois Press, 1973. xiii,563p. ISBN: 025200292x.

Originally published Paris, Librairie Istra, 1962, as *Les Poètes nègres des Etats-Unis.* This ed. translated by K. Douglas.

Comprehensive scholarly history of Black poetry from 1890 to 1940, with the lives and works of the poets studied in close connection. Major writers like McKay and Hughes

.... *(contd.)*
have their own chapters. Bibliographical appendix (24p.) lists general works on Black American literature, anthologies and works by and about the writers mentioned in the text, plus discography. Bibliographical supplement (9p.) by K. Kinnamon covers the decade between first publication and appearance of English translation. *Class No:* 820.73-1(=96)

Berryman

[7654]

ARPIN, G.Q. John Berryman: a reference guide. Boston, Hall, 1976. xii,158p. ISBN: 0816178046.

Lists secondary works by year, then by author, with separate sections for books and shorter writings within each year. Concise annotations. Index of authors and titles. *Class No:* 820.73-1BER

[7655]

STEFANIK, E.C. John Berryman: a descriptive bibliography. Pittsburgh, Pa., Univ. of Pittsburgh Press, 1974. xxix,285p. illus. $100. (*Pittsburgh series in bibliography*.) ISBN: 0822932814.

Section A provides very detailed descriptions of Berryman's separate publications. Sections B-H list contributions for books and periodicals, anthology items, interviews, recordings, dust-jacket blurbs, and poetry selections. Appended chronology of works and list of periodicals. Title-page facsimiles. Index. *Class No:* 820.73-1BER

Bishop

[7656]

MacMAHON, C. Elizabeth Bishop: a bibliography, 1927-1979. Charlottesville, Va., Univ. Press of Virginia, for The Bibliographical Society of the Univ. of Virginia, 1980. 227p. ISBN: 0813907837.

In 18 sections, largest of which is 'Separate publications', including physical description of every edition of each book. Other sections include contributions to periodicals, translation, phonorecordings, musical settings, etc. Appended list of unpublished poems. Index of names, titles and subjects. Includes facsimiles.

For secondary material, see D.E. Wyllie's *Elizabeth Bishop and Howard Nemerov: a reference guide* (Boston, Hall, 1983. 196p.). *Class No:* 820.73-1BIS

Bradstreet

[7657]

DOLLE, R. Anne Bradstreet: a reference guide. Boston, Hall, 1990. 145p. $40. ISBN: 0816189749.

Lists biographical and critical studies chronologically from 1650-1989, with concise, nonevaluative annotations. A lengthy introductory essay surveys Bradstreet's critical reception through the centuries. Index of authors and editors. Index of subjects, persons and titles. *Class No:* 820.73-1BRA

Crane (Hart)

[7658]

SCHWARTZ, J. *and* **SCHWEIK, R.C. Hart Crane: a descriptive bibliography.** Pittsburgh, Pa., Univ. of Pittsburgh Press, 1972. xxiv,168p. illus. (*Pittsburgh series in bibliography*.) ISBN: 0822932288.

Section A. provides full description of Crane's separate publications, with title-page facsimiles. Sections B-F list the remainder of his works, including translations and adaptations. Appended chronologies of his life and poems. Index. *Class No:* 820.73-1CRA

[7659]

SCHWARTZ, J. Hart Crane: a reference guide. Boston, Hall, 1983. xxiv,251p. ISBN: 0816184933.

An annotated list of 1,050 secondary sources. Chronological arrangement with index of authors and titles. *Class No:* 820.73-1CRA

Cummings

[7660]

ROTELLA, G.L. E.E. Cummings: a reference guide. Boston, Hall, 1979. xxxiv,212p. ISBN: 0816180792.

*c.*950 critical studies listed by year, 1922-77, then by author, with nonevaluative annotations. Some foreign-language material included. Index of authors, titles and subjects. *Class No:* 820.73-1CUM

Dickinson

[7661]

BOSWELL, J. Emily Dickinson: a bibliography of secondary sources, with selective annotations, 1890 through 1987. Jefferson, N.C., McFarland, 1990. xii,418p. $45. ISBN: 0899503683.

2,496 items with anonymous and initialed works (131 items) arranged chronologically, followed by the rest arranged A-Z by author. Substantial annotations for all except master's theses and newspaper articles. Largely confined to English-language material. Author, title and subject indexes. *Class No:* 820.73-1DIC

[7662]

DANDURAND, K. Dickinson scholarship: an annotated bibliography, 1969-1985. New York, Garland, 1988. xiv,203p. ISBN: 0824086414.

Lists 795 books, articles and dissertations in 3 sections, each arranged A-Z by author, with nonevaluative annotations. Some foreign-language material included. Indexes of poems, subjects, and authors. *Class No:* 820.73-1DIC

[7663]

DUCHAC, J. The Poems of Emily Dickinson: an annotated guide to commentary published in English, 1890-1977. Boston, Hall, 1979. 658p. ISBN: 0816178305.

Critical studies on individual poems are listed A-Z by first line of poem, then by year, then by author, with succinct annotations which often include a quotation. Poems keyed to Johnson's 1960 ed. Bibliography (36p.) has full references for all cited works. *c.*5,000 items in all.

Supplemented by *The Poems of Emily Dickinson: an annotated guide to commentary published in English, 1978-1989* (New York, Hall, 1993. 525p. $55. ISBN: 0816173524), which is similarly arranged and has 4,400 citations from 500 sources. *Class No:* 820.73-1DIC

[7664]

Emily Dickinson: an annotated bibliography; writings, scholarship, criticism and ana, 1850-1968. Buckingham, W.J., *ed.* Bloomington, Indiana Univ. Press. 1970. xii,322p. ISBN: 0253319471.

2,500 entries in 24 numbered sections, with the emphasis on 'scholarship, criticism and the history of Emily Dickinson's reputation' (*Preface*). Sections 3 and 4 cover the publication of Dickinson's poems and letters, but for detailed bibliographical description see Myerson. The remaining sections cover secondary material and are extremely comprehensive, including numerous foreign language items (*e.g.* 32 in Japanese), theses, recordings, broadcasts and films. A section headed 'Creative Tributes' lists 232 examples of drama and fiction based on her life, poems about her, musical settings of her work and portraits. Explication index by first lines; index of persons, periodicals and subjects. *Class No:* 820.73-1DIC

[7665]

An Emily Dickinson encyclopedia. Eberwein, J.D., *ed.* Westport, Conn., Greenwood, 1998. 416p. £67.95. ISBN: 0313297819.

Entries cover persons, places and institutions connected with Dickinson; cultural influences affecting her; stylistic aspects of her poetry; editorial and publication history; critical reception; modern responses to her in other art forms; and commentaries on a representative selection of her poems. Recommendations for further reading follow each entry. General bibliography of Dickinson scholarship. Chronology. Guide to major archival collections. Index of poems cited. General index. *Class No:* 820.73-1DIC

[7666]

MYERSON, J. Emily Dickinson: a descriptive bibliography. Pittsburgh, Pa., Univ. of Pittsburgh, 1984. xvii,209p. illus. $100. (*Pittsburgh series in bibliography.*) ISBN: 0822934914.

Thorough bibliography of writings by Dickinson through 1982 in 6 sections. Section A, Separate publications, describes in great detail all printings of all editions (p.1-89), with several title-pages reproduced. The other sections are: B. Miscellaneous collections; C. First book and pamphlet appearances; D. First-appearance contributions to magazines and newspapers; E. Material (falsely) attributed to Dickinson; F. Compiler's notes (on possible Japanese bilingual editions). Locations indicated in Sections A, B and C. Appendix lists principal works about Dickinson (2p.). Index to the poems by first lines. General index.
Class No: 820.73-1DIC

Frost

[7667]

CRANE, J.St.C. Robert Frost: a descriptive catalogue of books and manuscripts in the Clifton Waller Barrett Library, University of Virginia. Charlottesville, Va., Univ. Press of Virginia; London, Dawson, 1974. xxxv,280p. illus. ISBN: 0813905095, US; 0712906371, UK.

6 sections: A. Books and pamphlets (42 items) - B. Christmas cards (35) - C. First appearances of poetry in books and periodicals (51) - D. First appearances of prose (17) - E. Manuscripts (51) - F. Letters (48). Full description in A. and B. Index. *Class No:* 820.73-1FRO

[7668]

LENTRICCHIA, F. *and* LENTRICCHIA, M. Robert Frost: a bibliography, 1913-1974. Metuchen, N.J., Scarecrow, 1976. viii,238p. ISBN: 081080896x.

Primary material (122 items) in 4 sections, with major publications followed by records and films, letters and interviews, and library collections. Secondary material (1,042 items) in 8 sections without annotations. Appendices: 1. Bibliographical history of the poems (which also acts as index to first section) - 2. Selected anthologies - 3. Uncollected poems. Index of critics. *Class No:* 820.73-1FRO

[7669]

VAN EGMOND, P. The Critical reception of Robert Frost. Boston, Hall, 1974. xiv,319p. (*Research bibliographies in American literature.*) ISBN: 0816111057.

A bibliography in 12 sections, each chronologically arranged, containing 1,970 concisely annotated entries. Includes 95 foreign-language items. *Class No:* 820.73-1FRO

Ginsberg

[7670]

MORGAN, B. The Response to Allen Ginsberg, 1926-1994: a bibliography of secondary sources. Westport, Conn., Greenwood, 1996. 528p. $79.50. (*Bibliographies and indexes in American literature.*) ISBN: 0313295360.

Includes citations for *c.*6,500 biographical and critical studies and translations of Ginsberg's works. Translations are grouped by language (32), then by type of publication. Entries in all sections are arranged chronologically. Title and first line index. General index. *Class No:* 820.73-1GIN

[7671]

MORGAN, B. The Works of Allen Ginsberg, 1941-94: a descriptive bibliography. Westport, Conn., Greenwood, 1995. 480p. £67.50. (*Bibliographies and indexes in American literature.*) ISBN: 0313293899.

Over 10,000 entries in 8 sections: English-language books and pamphlets; broadsides; contributions to books; contributions to periodicals; publications that reproduce photos by Ginsberg; miscellaneous publications and ephemera; commercial recordings; film, radio and TV appearances. Chronological arrangement within each section. General index plus index of titles and first lines. Compiled with the cooperation and assistance of Ginsberg and his staff. 'Monumental' (*Choice*, v.33(1), Sept. 1995, p.86). For translations, see Morgan's bibliography of secondary material. *Class No:* 820.73-1GIN

Lowell

[7672]

AXELROD, S.G. *and* DEESE, H. Robert Lowell: a reference guide. Boston, Hall, 1982. xxxiii,445p. ISBN: 0816178143.

1,736 items arranged by year, 1943-1980, with separate sections for books and shorter writings within each year. Aims to include 'every book, dissertation, article, chapter, and review written in English about the poet' (*Preface*), but excludes foreign-language material. Substantial annotations. Index of names, with titles and topics under 'Lowell'.
Class No: 820.73-1LOW

Moore

[7673]

ABBOTT, C.S. Marianne Moore: a descriptive bibliography. Pittsburgh, Pa., Univ. of Pittsburgh Press, 1977. xiii,265p. $100. (*Pittsburgh series in bibliography.*) ISBN: 0822933195.

Full descriptive bibliography of Moore's works in 8 sections, including recordings and translations. Facsimiles of title pages and some dust-wrappers. Appendix lists principal works about her. Index of names and titles.
Class No: 820.73-1MOO

[7674]

ABBOTT, C.S. Marianne Moore: a reference guide. Boston, Hall, 1978. xvi,153p. ISBN: 081618061x.

Chronologically arranged list of writings about Moore, 1916-76, with abstracts. Index of names and titles with a few subject entries. *Class No:* 820.73-1MOO

Plath

[7675]

Sylvia Plath: a reference guide, 1973-88. Meyering, S.L., *ed.* Boston, Hall, 1990. 150p. $40. ISBN: 0816189293.

Lists and annotates all Plath scholarship in books, essays, reviews, letters, editorials, and personal reminiscences, published 1973-88. Appendix includes earlier works omitted from the Plath section of *Sylvia Plath and Anne Sexton: a reference guide*, by C. Northouse and T. Walsh (Boston, Hall, 1974), while reprints of items listed in the earlier bibliography are included in the main chronological sequence. Index of authors and titles. *Class No:* 820.73-1PLA

[7676]

TABOR, S. Sylvia Plath: an analytical bibliography. London, Mansell; Westport, Conn., Meckler, 1987. xvi,268p. £60. ISBN: 0720118301, UK.

A. Separate works by Plath - B. Contributions to books - C. Contributions to periodicals - D. Recordings - E. Broadcasts - F. Manuscripts - G. Works about Plath (931 items) - H. Translations (10 languages) - I. Adaptations. Full descriptions in A. and B. Chronology. Index. 'Unlikely to be equalled for its thoroughness and completeness' (*The Year's Work in English Studies,* v.67, 1986, p.643-4).
Class No: 820.73-1PLA

Pound

[7677]

GALLUP, D. Ezra Pound: a bibliography. Rev. ed. Charlottesville, Va., Univ. Press of Virginia; Godalming, St. Paul's Bibliographies, 1983. xiv,548p. £30. ISBN: 0906795079.

First ed. London, Hart-Davis, 1963, as *A Bibliography of Ezra Pound.*

A. Books and pamphlets by or translated by Pound (106 items) - B. Books and pamphlets edited or with contributions by Pound (126) - C. Contributions to periodicals (1,989) - D. Translations (246 items in 27 languages - E. Miscellanea, including musical settings and recordings. Full descriptions in A. and B. Thorough index. Full revision of 1st ed., but entry numbers for major works unchanged.
Class No: 820.73-1POU

[7678]

RICKS, B. Ezra Pound: a bibliography of secondary works. Metuchen, N.J., Scarecrow, 1986. xxii,281p. (*Scarecrow author bibliographies.*) ISBN: 0810818620.

Lists 3,696 items in 7 sections: biography; poetry and prose works; supplemental works; general criticism; interviews; letters; bibliography. Indexes of critics and topics. No annotations and no account of methodology, but 14p. list of periodical-title abbreviations, with numerous foreign titles, indicates that the net has been cast wide. 'One hopes for better alternatives in the future' (*ARBA,* 1987, p.452). *Class No:* 820.73-1POU

Stevens

[7679]

EDELSTEIN, J.M. Wallace Stevens: a descriptive bibliography. Pittsburgh, Pa., Univ. of Pittsburgh Press, 1973. xxiv,429p. illus. $100. (*Pittsburgh series in bibliography.*) ISBN: 0822932687.

Section A. provides full description of Stevens' books with title-page facsimiles. Sections B-G list further primary material, including translations, musical settings and recordings. Sections H-M list over 750 secondary items, including book reviews and dissertations. Index.
Class No: 820.73-1STE

[7680]

Wallace Stevens: an annotated secondary bibliography. Serio, J.N., *ed.* Pittsburgh, Pa., Univ. of Pittsburgh Press, 1994. $100. (*Pittsburgh series in bibliography.*) ISBN: 0822938367.

Lists 1,875 books, articles, dissertations and reviews published 1916-90. Chronological arrangement with indexes of authors, titles, journals and subjects. *Class No:* 820.73-1STE

Whitman

[7681]

MYERSON, J. Walt Whitman: a descriptive bibliography. Pittsburgh, Pa., Univ. of Pittsburgh Press, 1993. xxiv,1097p. illus. $250. (*Pittsburgh series in bibliography.*) ISBN: 0822937395.

Documents the numerous eds. and reprintings of *Leaves of grass* plus Whitman's other works, including individually published poems; newspaper and periodical articles; broadsides; circulars; and other prose works. Index shows the publishing history of poems in *Leaves of grass.* Bibliography of main works about Whitman (7p.). Index.
Class No: 820.73-1WHI

[7682]

Walt Whitman: a reference guide. Boston, Hall, 1981-82. 2v.

1838-1939, by S. Giantvalley. 1981. xxi,465p. ISBN: 0816178569.

1940-1975, by D.D. Kummings. 1982. xiv,264p. ISBN: 081617802x.

Annotated lists of critical and biographical studies arranged by year, then by author. 3,172 entries in the 2nd vol. Author and subject indexes in each vol.
Class No: 820.73-1WHI

Williams

[7683]
LARSON, K.A. A Guide to the poetry of William Carlos Williams. New York, Hall, 1995. xxii,182p. $50. (*Guides to 20th century poets.*) ISBN: 0816119864.

An annotated bibliography of critical studies in books and periodicals. Arranged A-Z by poem or collection title, then by critic. *Class No:* 820.73-1WIL

Women

[7684]
REARDON, J. *and* **THORSEN, K.A. Poetry by American women, 1900-1975:** a bibliography. Metuchen, N.J., Scarecrow, 1979. vii,624p. ISBN: 0810811731.

Lists *c.*5,500 poets, A-Z, who have had a least 1 vol. of verse published, with bibliographic details of their publications.

Continued by *Poetry by American women, 1975-1989: a bibliography*, by J. Reardon (1990. 242p. $31. ISBN: 0810823667), which lists chronologically 2,880 publications by 1,565 women. Title index in each vol. *Class No:* 820.73-1-0055.2

American Drama

Bibliographies

[7685]
American playwrights, 1880-1945: a research and production sourcebook. Demastes, W.W., *ed.* Westport, Conn., Greenwood, 1995. 494p. $85. ISBN: 0313286388.

Alphabetically arranged entries on 40 dramatists, comprising: biography; selected list of major plays, premieres and significant revivals; list of additional plays, adaptations and productions; critical assessment; locations of unpublished materials; primary and secondary bibliographies; list of bibliographies. Name and title indexes. Selected general bibliography of book-length studies of American drama of the period. Includes a significant number of previously ignored African-American and women playwrights. *Class No:* 820.73-2(01)

[7686]
American playwrights since 1945: a guide to scholarship, criticism, and performance. Kolin, P.C., *ed.* New York, Greenwood, 1989. xiii,595p. $99.50. ISBN: 0313255431.

Essays by different scholars describing the state of research on and the history of performances of 40 dramatists. Contributions average 14p. and are divided as follows: Assessment of reputation; Primary bibliography; Production history (including screen adaptations); Survey of secondary sources (a sub-divided, analytical account); Future research opportunities; Secondary sources cited (checklist). Name index. Play and screenplay index. Covers all the big names (Miller, Williams, Simon, etc.) but particularly useful for emerging writers. *Class No:* 820.73-2(01)

[7687]
EDDLEMAN, F.E. American drama criticism: interpretations, 1890-1977. 2nd ed. Hamden, Conn., Shoe String, 1979. viii,488p. $45 ISBN: 0208017135.

1st ed. 1967, by H.H. Palmer and A.J. Dyson, with *Supplements* in 1970 and 1976.

An unannotated listing of interpretations of American plays found in books and periodicals. Arranged by dramatist, then by play title. Continued by *Supplement I* (1984. 255p. $39.50. ISBN: 0208019782); *Supplement II* (1989. 269p. $47.50. ISBN: 0208021388) and *Supplement*

.... *(contd.)*
III (1992. ix,436p. $55. ISBN: 0208022708). Canadian and Caribbean playwrights are included if their plays have been staged in the US. *Class No:* 820.73-2(01)

[7688]
MESERVE, W.J. American drama to 1900: a guide to information sources. Detroit, Gale, 1980. 264p. ISBN: 0810313650.

General section (443 items) followed by bibliographies for 34 dramatists, A-Z. Nearly 1,500 items in all. Indexes of authors, titles, and subjects. *Class No:* 820.73-2(01)

[7689]
OTERO, R. Guide to American drama explication. New York, Hall, 1995. xxix,431p. $65. ISBN: 0816173516.

Similar to the publisher's *Guide to American poetry explication* series (*q.v.*), listing periodical articles and book-length critical studies published 1942-95. Arranged by playwright, A-Z, then by play title. List of sources with full bibliographical citations. *Class No:* 820.73-2(01)

[7690]
SALEM, J.M. A Guide to critical reviews, part 1: American drama, 1909-1982. 3rd ed. Metuchen, N.J., Scarecrow, 1984. 669p. $55. ISBN: 0810816903.

1st ed. 1966; 2nd ed. 1973, covering 1909-69.

Lists plays by title under American dramatists, A-Z, with citations for reviews in US and Canadian periodicals and the *New York Times*. Does not cite critical essays in scholarly journals. Index of play titles. *Class No:* 820.73-2(01)

[7691]
—MARKS, P. American literary and drama reviews: an index to late nineteenth-century periodicals. Boston, Hall, 1984. 313p. $57.50. ISBN: 0816184704.

Indexes reviews in 13 periodicals published 1880-1900, with separate sections for drama reviews (arranged by play title) and literary reviews (arranged by author of the book being reviewed). *Class No:* 820.73-2(01)

Encyclopaedias & Dictionaries

[7692]
LOVELL, J. Digests of great American plays: complete summaries of more than 100 plays from the beginnings to the present. New York, Crowell, 1961. xxiii,452p.

Entries are arranged chronologically from 1766 (Rogers) to 1959 (Hansberry) and include author, title, date, category, period, setting, list of characters, musical highlights, historical note, and plot summary, scene by scene. 12 appendices, including lists of titles, authors, songs, actors, themes and award-winners. *Class No:* 820.73-2(03)

Histories

[7693]
BERKOWITZ, G.M. American drama of the twentieth century. Harlow, Longman, 1992. ix,300p. £17.99. (*Longman literature in English.*) ISBN: 0582016010.

6 chapters covering 1890-1990, followed by very useful reference section: chronology of American drama, world drama and literary/historical/cultural events (59p.); general bibliography of reference works, histories and critical studies; biobibliographical notes on over 40 dramatists. Index. *Class No:* 820.73-2(091)

[7694]

BIGSBY, C.W.E. A Critical introduction to twentieth-century American drama. Cambridge, Cambridge Univ. Press, 1982-85. 3v. illus.

V.1 *1900-1940*. 1982. ix,342p. ISBN: 0521271169.

V.2 *Tennessee Williams. Arthur Miller. Edward Albee*. 1984. viii,355p. ISBN: 0521277175.

V.3 *Beyond Broadway*. 1985. x,485p. ISBN: 0521278961.

An authoritative survey, with select bibliographies and indexes in each vol. V.3 includes chapters on Black theatre, women's theatre and gay theatre. 'Their extensive, consistent, and coherent treatment of twentieth-century American drama makes these volumes worthy of becoming the standard critical introduction to the subject' (*American Literature*, v.58(2), May 1986, p.463-65).

Bigsby has also produced a one-vol. survey of postwar American drama: *Modern American drama, 1945-1990* (Cambridge, Cambridge Univ. Press, 1992. 372p. ISBN: 0521426677). *Class No:* 820.73-2(091)

[7695]

BOGARD, T., *and others*. The Revels history of drama in English, v.8, American drama. London, Methuen; New York, Barnes & Noble, 1978. li,368p. illus. ISBN: 0416130909.

A history of acting and the theatre as well as of dramatists and plays. 14 chapters. Extensive bibliography (with commentary) of critical studies (14p.). Chronological table of historical, theatrical, and literary events (38p.). Index.

Main entry for series at 820-2(091) *Class No:* 820.73-2(091)

[7696]

QUINN, A.H. A History of the American drama, from the beginning to the Civil War. 2nd ed. New York, Appleton-Century-Crofts, 1951. xvi,530p.

1st ed. 1923.

A narrative history in 12 chapters, followed by bibliographies of reference works, play collections, and critical studies (27p.), and a list of plays, 1665-1860, giving title, author, and places and dates of first publications and performances. Index.

Succeeded by *A History of the American drama, from the Civil War to the present day* (Rev. ed., New York, Appleton-Century-Crofts, 1936. xxv,432p. illus.), which has 24 chapters, general bibliography (10p.), and list of plays arranged by dramatist, A-Z, with reference to biographical and critical studies. Index. Both vols. reprinted New York, Irvington, 1982, at $44.50 each. *Class No:* 820.73-2(091)

Biographies

[7697]

Contemporary American dramatists. Berney, K., *ed.* Detroit & London, St. James Press, 1994. xxvi,771p. $60. ISBN: 1558622144.

Profiles 196 playwrights, A-Z, in standard St. James style, with biographical and bibliographical information and critical essay. Coverage confined to writers active since World War II, but includes those who have died. Also has entries on 30 of the most significant postwar US plays. Title index.
Class No: 820.73-2(092)

[7698]

National playwrights directory. Kaye, P.J., *ed.* 2nd ed. Waterford, Conn., Eugene O'Neill Theater Center, 1985. 507p. illus. $35. ISBN: 096051600x.

1st ed. Detroit, Gale, 1977.

Biographical information on *c.*500 US dramatists, including address, career and personal information, play titles, production details, script availability, etc., plus synopses of some plays. Based on questionnaires to the playwrights. Index of play titles. *Class No:* 820.73-2(092)

Black Races

[7699]

ARATA, E.S. *and* **ROTOLI, N.J. Black American playwrights, 1800 to the present:** a bibliography. Metuchen, N.J., Scarecrow, 1976. vii,295p. ISBN: 0810809125.

Arranged by playwright, A-Z, listing published and unpublished works with references to reviews and critical studies. Extensive bibliography of general studies (57p.). Title index.

Supplemented by *More black American playwrights: a bibliography* (1978. xiii,321p.), which includes 490 dramatists, of whom 190 were featured in the earlier vol.
Class No: 820.73-2(=96)

[7700]

PETERSON, B.L. Contemporary Black American playwrights and their plays: a biographical directory and dramatic index. New York, Greenwood, 1988. xxvi,625p. $79.50. ISBN: 0313251908.

A-Z listing of over 700 black playwrights (including radio, film and TV writers, musical theatre collaborators, etc.) resident and writing in the US between 1950 and 1985. Entries include biographical details and annotated lists of plays, with lengthy annotations for representative plays by major writers. Appendix A. lists another 100 playwrights whose scripts are located in special repositories. Appendix B. lists over 75 other playwrights known to have had work produced in the US since 1950. Extensive bibliography (20p.) lists libraries, anthologies, reference and critical books, dissertations and theses, periodicals. Title index. General index of theatrical names, organizations and awards. Particularly useful for unpublished writers.

A companion vol. appeared in 1990 entitled *Early Black American playwrights and dramatic writers: a biographical directory and catalog of plays, films, and broadcasting scripts* (298p. $75. ISBN: 0313266212). *Class No:* 820.73-2(=96)

Albee

[7701]

GIANTVALLEY, S. Edward Albee: a reference guide. Boston, Hall, 1987. xxix,459p. $50. ISBN: 0816187835.

Lists books, articles, reviews, interviews and dissertations published in the US since 1959, plus major foreign studies, with descriptive annotations. For more foreign material, see *Edward Albee at home and abroad: a bibliography*, by R.A. Amacher and M. Rule (New York, AMS Press, 1973. 95p. $29.50. ISBN : 0404079458), which covers 1958-68 and includes items from 15 countries. *Class No:* 820.73-2ALB

Miller

[7702]
FERRES, J.H. Arthur Miller: a reference guide. Boston, Hall, 1979. 225p. ISBN: 0816178224.

Lists studies of Miller by year, 1944-77, then by author, with annotations. Includes theatre reviews. Author and title index. *Class No:* 820.73-2MIL

[7703]
HAYASHI, T. An Index to Arthur Miller criticism. 2nd ed. Metuchen, N.J., Scarecrow, 1976. xiv,151p. ISBN: 0810809478.

Lists 110 items by Miller followed by 1,265 studies in 8 sections: books; essays; doctoral dissertations; masters' theses; interviews; periodical articles; newspaper articles; bibliographies. *Class No:* 820.73-2MIL

O'Neill

[7704]
ATKINSON, J.M. Eugene O'Neill: a descriptive bibliography. Pittsburgh, Pa., Univ. of Pittsburgh Press, 1974. xxiii,410p. illus. $90. (*Pittsburgh series in bibliography.*) ISBN: 0822932792.

Section A. (p.1-323) has full descriptions of all first printings of American first editions of the plays and of important later editions. Many title-page facsimiles. 5 further sections: Contributions to books and pamphlets; First appearances in newspapers and periodicals; Blurbs; Material quoted in catalogues; Plays in collections and anthologies. Appendix lists adaptations for film, radio, opera and musical comedy. Index. *Class No:* 820.73-2ONE

[7705]
RANALD, M.L. The Eugene O'Neill companion. Westport, Conn., Greenwood, 1984. xi,827p. $99.50. ISBN: 0313225516.

Approx. 1,200 entries in a single A-Z sequence covering plays, characters, theatrical companies, actors and other people associated with O'Neill. Entries for plays provide full synopsis, critical evaluation and production data. 3 appendices provide chronology of completed plays, list of film, musical, operatic and balletic adaptions, and assessment of his theory and practice of theatre. Bibliographic essay and listing (25p.). Index.
Class No: 820.73-2ONE

[7706]
SMITH, M. *and* **EATON, R. Eugene O'Neill: an annotated bibliography, 1973-1985.** New York, Garland, 1988. xvi,320p. $52. ISBN: 0824006917.

A classified bibliography, international in scope, including books, articles, dissertations, theatre productions and reviews, films, and radio and TV productions. Indexes of critics and play titles.

For earlier American criticism, see J.Y. Miller's *Eugene O'Neill and the American critic: a bibliographical checklist* (2nd ed. Hamden, Conn., Archon, 1974).
Class No: 820.73-2ONE

Wilder

[7707]
WALSH, C. Thornton Wilder: a reference guide, 1926-1990. Boston, Hall, 1993. 449p. $50. ISBN: 0816187908.

Lists English-language critical studies by year, then by author, with substantial annotations. Includes dissertations. Cross-references and indexes of authors and subjects.
Class No: 820.73-2WIL

Williams

[7708]
CRANDELL, G.W. Tennessee Williams: a descriptive bibliography. Pittsburgh, Pa., Univ. of Pittsburgh Press, 1995. 800p. illus. $195. (*Pittsburgh series in bibliography..*) ISBN: 0822937697.

Full descriptions of first editions in the usual comprehensive Pittsburgh style, including reproductions of dust jackets, title-pages, etc. Also includes details of translations and sound recordings. Index. *Class No:* 820.73-2WIL

[7709]
GUNN, D.W. Tennessee Williams: a bibliography. 2nd ed. Metuchen, N.J., Scarecrow, 1991. xxxii,436p. $59. (*Scarecrow author bibliographies.*) ISBN: 0810824957.

1st ed. 1980

A complete revision and updating to include primary and secondary material published up to 1991, bringing together all the material on each work, including production history, reviews, critical studies and dissertations. 9 sections: 1. Plays and screenplays - 2. Short stories and novels - 3. Poems and lyrics - 4. Occasional pieces, autobiography, letters - 5. Miscellaneous materials - 6. Biographical sources - 7. Manuscripts - 8. Translations and foreign-language productions (36 languages) - 9. Prior bibliographies. 3 indexes: Authors and directors; Musicians; Critics, reviewers, editors, interviewers and biographers. 'Remarkably good value and has no competitors' (*Reference Reviews*, v.7(2), 1993, p.38-9). *Class No:* 820.73-2WIL

Women

[7710]
American women playwrights, 1900-1930: a checklist. Bzowski, F.D., *comp.* Westport, Conn., Greenwood, 1992. 420p. $69.50. (*Bibliographies and indexes in women's studies.*) ISBN: 0313242380.

A bald list of dramatic writings of all kinds under authors, A-Z, giving year of publication or production if known. No index of titles or subjects. 'The value of this work lies in its wide scope rather than in exactness' (*Choice*, v.30(4), Dec. 1992, p.598). *Class No:* 820.73-2-0055.2

[7711]
COVEN, B. American women dramatists of the twentieth century: a bibliography. Metuchen, N.J., Scarecrow, 1982. 237p. ISBN: 0810815621.

Covers 133 women who have had at least one play successfully produced on the New York stage and who are deemed 'representative of other women playwrights writing at the same time' (*Introduction*). Lists plays, biographical and critical works and reviews, without annotation, for each writer. Selected general bibliography (5p.). Play-title index.
Class No: 820.73-2-0055.2

[7712]
GAVIN, C. American women playwrights, 1964-1989: a research guide and annotated bibliography. New York, Garland, 1993. 493p. $7 ISBN: 082403046x.

The core of the book lists 150 dramatists, A-Z, with details of selected plays, interviews, reviews and critical studies. Introductory bibliographic essay on studies of contemporary women playwrights and feminist theatre, followed by an annotated list of 110 key items. Over 4,200 entries in total. Index of critics, but no index of play titles. List of multicultural playwrights. *Class No:* 820.73-2-0055.2

[7713]

PETERSON, J.T. *and* **BENNETT, S. Women playwrights of diversity:** a bio-bibliographical sourcebook. Westport, Conn., Greenwood, 1997. 416p. $79.50. ISBN: 0313291799.

Covers 89 African-American, Asian-American, Latina and lesbian dramatists who have been active since 1970 and also has a few entries on minority theatre companies. Author entries are in the standard Greenwood format, comprising: biographical sketch; descriptions of individual works; production histories of plays; information on play availability; awards; and citations for reviews and criticism. Introductory essays on the 4 groups covered. Select bibliography of major critical studies. Appended lists of playwrights by cultural/ethnic group and of playwrights not included in the main part of the text. *Class No:* 820.73-2-0055.2

Gay People

[7714]

FURTADO, K. *and* **HELLNER, N. Gay and lesbian American plays:** an annotated bibliography. Metuchen, N.J., Scarecrow, 1993. 217p. $29. ISBN: 0810826895.

Lists, by author, nearly 700 plays with gay/lesbian themes or with major characters whose homosexuality is integral to the play's message. Entries include title; bibliographic citation (if the play has been anthologized); label ('comedy', 'musical', etc.); plot summary; numbers of acts and characters; details of first performance; and advice on acquisition. Title index has a subject coding system ('AIDS', 'coming out', etc.). Lists of agents, playwrights and theatres. Selective bibliography. 451 dramatists represented.
Class No: 820.73-2-0055.3

American Prose

Bibliographies

[7715]

YANNELLA, D. *and* **ROCH, J.H. American prose to 1820:** a guide to information sources. Detroit, Gale, 1979. xxii,653p. ISBN: 0810313618.

3 sections for general sources (p.1-160), followed by bibliographies for 83 authors, A-Z. Over 2,950 annotated entries. Index of authors, titles and subjects.

Continued by: *American prose and criticism, 1820-1900*, by E.H. Partridge (Detroit, Gale, 1983. 575p. ISBN: 0810312131) and *American prose and criticism, 1900-1950*, by P.A. Brier and A. Arthur (Detroit, Gale, 1981. xiii,242p. ISBN 081031214x), both of which list general sources for their period and have primary and secondary bibliographies for many individual authors and critics. *Class No:* 820.73-3(01)

Emerson

[7716]

Emerson: an annotated secondary bibliography. Burkholder, R.E. *and* Myerson, J., *eds.* Pittsburgh, Pa., Univ. of Pittsburgh Press, 1985. xiv,842p. $130. (*Pittsburgh series in bibliography*.) ISBN: 0822935023.

5,841 entries chronologically arranged, 1816-1979, with detailed, helpful annotations. Index of critics, topics and periodical titles.

Supplemented by the same compilers' *Ralph Waldo Emerson: an annotated bibliography of criticism, 1980-1991* (Westport, Conn., Greenwood, 1994. ix,234p. $69.50. ISBN: 0313291500), which has 1,055 entries.
Class No: 820.73-3EME

[7717]

MYERSON, J. Ralph Waldo Emerson: a descriptive bibliography. Pittsburgh, Pa., Pittsburgh Univ. Press, 1982. xviii,802p. illus. $110.00. (*Pittsburgh series in bibliography*.) ISBN: 0822934523.

9 sections: A. Separate publications - B. Collected editions - C. Miscellaneous collections - D. First book and pamphlet appearances - E. First-appearance contributions to magazines and newspapers - F. Books edited by Emerson - G. Reprinted material in books and pamphlets - H. Material attributed to Emerson - I. Compiler's notes. Appendix lists principal works about Emerson (3p.). Index. Lists all editions in English through 1980 and all foreign-language editions through 1882, with many title-page facsimiles.
Class No: 820.73-3EME

[7718]

VON FRANK, A.J. An Emerson chronology. Boston, Hall, 1994. 569p. $45. ISBN: 0816172668.

Thematic introductions for each year are followed by lists of events such as lectures, readings and visits, often illustrated by quotations and with references to biographies and other works where more information may be found. Biographical sketches of key figures in Emerson's circle. Index. *Class No:* 820.73-3EME

Thoreau

[7719]

BORST, R.R. Henry David Thoreau: a descriptive bibliography. Pittsburgh, Pa., Univ. of Pittsburgh Press, 1982. xvi,232p. illus. $100. (*Pittsburgh series in bibliography*.) ISBN: 0822934450.

Section A, Separate Publications (p.1-159), lists chronologically all printings of all editions in English to 1880 and selected reprints to 1980, with full descriptions. Other sections cover contributions to books, pamphlets, magazines and periodicals, collected works, and single-vol. collections. Illustrations of title pages and bindings. Index.
Class No: 820.73-3THO

[7720]

BORST, R.R. Henry David Thoreau: a reference guide, 1835-1899. Boston, Hall, 1987. xiii,147p. $40. ISBN: 081618822x.

An annotated bibliography of nineteenth century criticism with approx. 950 items arranged chronologically. The compiler has aimed to include all references made to Thoreau in print during his lifetime, but after his death (1862) only 'substantial statements about him' (*Preface*) are included. Index of authors and titles. *Class No:* 820.73-3THO

American Fiction

Bibliographies of Bibliographies

[7721]

The Bibliography of contemporary American fiction, 1945-1988: an annotated checklist. McPheron, W. *and* Sheppard, J., *eds.* Westport, Conn., Greenwood, 1989. 190p. $42.95. ISBN: 0313277028.

Lists and annotates 53 multi-author studies and 560 single-author studies, covering approx. 125 writers. Includes many

.... *(contd.)*
writers of popular genre fiction but no children's writers. Indexes to authors and subjects of bibliographies.
Class No: 820.73-31(009)

Bibliographies

[7722]
Facts on File bibliography of American fiction. Bruccoli, M.J. *and* Layman, R., *eds.* New York, Facts on File, 1991-94. 4v.

1588-1865, ed. by K.P. Ljungquist and J.S. Baughman. 1994. 352p. $85. ISBN: 0816021155.

1866-1918, ed. by J. Nagel and G.L. Nagel. 1993. 416p. $95. ISBN: 0816021163.

1919-1988, ed. by M.J. Bruccoli and J.S. Baughman. 1991. 2v. (704p.). ISBN: 0816026742.

The first segment of a projected 12-vol. bibliography of American literature, with further vols. planned to cover poetry, drama and nonfiction. Each vol. includes author entries, A-Z, which comprise concise headnotes on the author's style, critical reception, etc.; list of bibliographies, including those included in books and articles; lists of American first editions of all books, editions of letters and diaries, and complete editions of the works; details of manuscript collections and archives; and selective lists of secondary material, including concordances, biographies, interviews and critical studies. As well as author bibliographies, each vol. also has unannotated listings of reference works on American literature in general and on the period covered, chronology of American fiction and authors, and indexes.

The vol. for 1866-1918 covers *c.*150 authors and the set for 1919-88 covers *c.*220. The latter has good coverage of genre fiction and writers from ethnic minorities, but omits anyone born before 1941, *e.g.* Alice Walker. *Booklist*, v.88(9), Jan. 1, 1992, p.845, notes some other serious omissions, including Alison Lurie and Gore Vidal, but, nevertheless, 'this series is a significant undertaking and will be a necessary purchase for most [American] academic and large public libraries.' *Class No:* 820.73-31(01)

[7723]
—Essential bibliography of American fiction. Bruccoli, M.J. *and* Baughman, J.S., *eds.* New York, Facts on File, 1994- (in progress). $19.95 per vol.

Modern African American writers. 1994. xiv,92p. ISBN: 0816029989.

Modern women writers. 1994. xii,100p. ISBN: 0816030006.

Modern classic writers. 1994. xii,99p. ISBN: 0816030022.

A series based on the *Facts on File bibliography of American fiction* and aimed at high schools, community colleges and smaller public libraries. Each vol. covers 6-10 of the most widely studied authors in a particular fiction category and carries complete primary bibliographies with more selective listings of secondary material, plus a checklist of key reference sources on American fiction. Each entry in these first 3 vols. has been updated to the end of 1992. The vol. on African Americans includes a new entry on Alice Walker, who is not covered in the parent work.
Class No: 820.73-31(01)

[7724]
GERSTENBERGER, D.L. *and* **HENDRICK, G. The American novel, 1789-1959:** a checklist of twentieth-century criticism. Denver, Colo., Swallow Press, 1961. 333p.

Lists *c.*6,500 studies on authors, A-Z, with criticism of individual novels followed by general studies and bibliographies.

Continued by: *The American novel: a checklist of twentieth-century criticism on novels written since 1789, v.2: criticism written 1960-1968.* (Chicago, Swallow Press, 1970. vii,459p.), which has *c.*8,000 entries similarly arranged.
Class No: 820.73-31(01)

[7725]
KIRBY, D.K. American fiction to 1900: a guide to information sources. Detroit, Gale, 1975. xvii,296p. ISBN: 0810312107.

Section on general aids lists 84 handbooks, bibliographies, periodicals etc. and is followed by entries for 41 individual authors, listing principal works, collected works, letters, bibliographies, checklists, journals, biographies and critical studies. Brief annotations. Index of authors and titles. Highly selective, but useful for minor writers. *Class No:* 820.73-31(01)

[7726]
PARKER, P.L. Early American fiction: a reference guide. Boston, Hall, 1984. xx,197p. ISBN: 0816179999.

Lists *c.*500 secondary items on pre-1800 fiction. General section followed by sections on anonymous works and 27 individual authors. Chronological arrangement within each section. Concise annotations. Name index. Title and subject index. *Class No:* 820.73-31(01)

[7727]
WRIGHT, L.H. American fiction, 1774-1850: a contribution toward a bibliography. 2nd rev. ed. San Marino, Calif., Huntington Library, 1969. xviii,412p. ISBN: 0873280407.

1st ed. 1939; rev. ed. 1948.

Lists over 3,000 works of prose fiction, including 'fictitious biographies, travels, sketches, allegories, tract-like tales' (*Introduction*) as well as standard novels. Arranged A-Z by author, then by title, with brief biographical notes and American library locations. Chronological and title indexes. 143 new titles and many new editions added for this ed. Does not cover children's fiction. *Class No:* 820.73-31(01)

[7728]
—WRIGHT, L.H. American fiction, 1851-1875: a contribution toward a bibliography. Reprint with additions and corrections appended. San Marino, Calif., Huntington Library, 1965. xviii,438p. ISBN: 0873280415.

First published 1957.

Lists nearly 3,000 works by some 1,200 authors. Similar in scope and format to its predecessor, but without chronological index. *Class No:* 820.73-31(01)

[7729]
—WRIGHT, L.H. American fiction, 1876-1900: a contribution toward a bibliography. San Marino, Calif., Huntington Library, 1966. xix,683p. ISBN: 0873280423.

Lists nearly 6,200 titles. Known as 'Wright III' and follows the style of its immediate predecessor.
Class No: 820.73-31(01)

20th Century

[7730]

American fiction, 1901-25: a bibliography. Smith, G.D., *ed.* Cambridge, Cambridge Univ. Press, 1997. xviii,1038p. £80. ISBN: 0521434696.

Lists first printings of original fiction for adults in similar style to L.H. Wright's bibliographies of 19th-century American fiction (*qq.v.*). 15,000 entries arranged by author with bibliographical details, dates listed in *Library of Congress catalog of copyright entries* and *Publisher's weekly*, a note of British Library catalogue entry, and references to standard bibliographical sources which include additional descriptive information (52 of these are listed). Gives contents for story collections and anthologies. Indexes of titles, illustrators, publishers and pseudonyms. *Class No:* 820.73-31(01)"19"

[7731]

HANNA, A. A Mirror for the nation: an annotated bibliography of American social fiction, 1901-1950. New York and London, Garland, 1985. xiv,472p. ISBN: 0824087275.

Aims to include 'every title ... which describes, discusses, or reacts to life in these United States during the first half of this century' but 'literary quality has not been a criterion for inclusion' (*Introduction*). 3,943 items arranged A-Z by author with brief annotation indicating subject matter and geographical setting. Subject index (mainly places, but also themes, *e.g.* Marriage, Race problems). Title index. Index of illustrators. *Class No:* 820.73-31(01)"19"

[7732]

KELLMAN, S.G. The Modern American novel: an annotated bibliography. Pasadena, Calif., Salem Press, 1991 (later Scarecrow Press). 162p. $40. (*Magill bibliographies.*) ISBN: 0810827980.

An introductory and highly selective guide to studies of these early 20th-century novelists: Cather, Dos Passos, Dreiser, Faulkner, Fitzgerald, Glasgow, Hemingway, Hurston, Sinclair Lewis, London, Henry Roth, Steinbeck, West, Wilder and Wolfe. Index of critics. General section for each writer, followed by entries on individual novels. Index of critics. *Class No:* 820.73-31(01)"19"

[7733]

WOODRESS, J.L. American fiction, 1900-1950: a guide to information sources. Detroit, Gale, 1974. xxii,260p. ISBN: 0810312018.

Bibliography of general sources, followed by bibliographical essays on 44 individual novelists with references to bibliographies, editions, biographies and critical studies. Index. Preceded by Kirby and followed by Rosa and Eschholz. *Class No:* 820.73-31(01)"19"

[7734]

—ROSA, A.F. *and* ESCHHOLZ, P.A. Contemporary fiction in America and England, 1950-1970: a guide to information sources. Detroit, Gale, 1976. xxviii,454p. ISBN: 0810312190.

Brief list of general studies and reference works, followed by primary and secondary bibliographies for 136 authors (80 American and 56 British). Index. *Class No:* 820.73-31(01)"19"

Encyclopaedias & Dictionaries

[7735]

Beacham's encyclopedia of popular fiction. Beetz, K.H., *ed.* Osprey, Fla., Beacham, 1987. 11v. $495. ISBN: 0933833385.

Supersedes *Beacham's popular fiction in America, 1950-1986* (1987. 4v.) and supplementary vols.

Contains signed essays on novelists who are bestsellers in the US. Entries average 8p., are arranged A-Z by author, and include brief biographical details, review of publishing history and critical reception, and critical analysis of a few individual works in terms of social concerns, themes, characters, literary precedents, etc. Lists of additional sources follow each entry. Useful for coverage of truly popular authors, but literary authors who happen to be bestsellers (*e.g.* Alice Walker, William Styron) are covered better elsewhere. Very thoroughly indexed, including by social issues/problems. *Class No:* 820.73-31(03)

[7736]

Masterplots II: American fiction series. Magill, F.N., *ed.* Englewood Cliffs, N.J., Salem Press, 1986. 4v. $365. ISBN: 0893564567.

Covers over 360 20th-century works by 198 authors, of whom 34 are Latin Americans. In contrast to the original *Masterplots* series (1st ed.), which is not duplicated here, the signed entries now contain a shorter plot summary and a longer critical essay dealing with structure, characterization, themes, style, etc. A few references are made to other sources. Entries are arranged by title, with author index.

A 2-vol. *Supplement* published 1994 ($185. ISBN: 0893567191) includes more ethnic writers and writers exploring women's themes. Many of the works covered are from the 1980s and 1990s, but some neglected works from earlier periods are included. Incorporates cumulative index to whole series.

The *British and Commonwealth fiction series* (1987. 4v. ISBN: 0893564680) and *World fiction series* (1988. 4v. ISBN: 0893564737) are similar in format. *Class No:* 820.73-31(03)

Histories

[7737]

The Columbia history of the American novel. Elliott, E., *ed.* New York, Columbia Univ. Press, 1991. xviii,905p. $65. ISBN: 0231073607.

31 thematic chapters in 4 main sections covering the beginnings to the mid 19th century; late 19th century; early 20th century; and late 20th century, the latter section including one chapter each on Caribbean, Canadian and Latin American fiction. As a conventional biographical approach is eschewed in the text, brief biographies of some 200 novelists (3 per page on average) are appended, but these do not include lists of their works so reference value is limited. Select bibliography of critical studies (26p.). Thorough index (53p.). 36 contributors. *Class No:* 820.73-31(091)

[7738]

HILFER, T. American fiction since 1940. London, Longman, 1992. x,290p. £15.99. (*Longman literature in English.*) ISBN: 0582493501.

9 chapters on fictional genres and styles, with subsections on individual authors. Chronology (17p.). Classified and annotated bibliography of general studies (17p.).

.... *(contd.)*
Biobibliographical notes on individual novelists, listing major works and selected criticism (22p.). Index.
Class No: 820.73-31(091)

[7739]
LEE, B. American fiction, 1865-1940. London, Longman, 1987. xi,300p. £17.99. (*Longman literature in English.*) ISBN: 0582493161.

Part One, 1865-1900; Part Two, 1900-1940. Narrative literary history in 12 chapters, followed by chronology of fiction, other works and historical events (17p.); general bibliographies (9p.); and notes on individual novelists, covering biography, major works and selected criticism (21p.). Index. *Class No:* 820.73-31(091)

Jews

[7740]
Contemporary Jewish-American novelists: a bio-critical sourcebook. Shatkzy, J. *and* Taub, M., *eds.* Westport, Conn., Greenwood, 1997. 536p. £67.95. ISBN: 0313294623.

Covers 75 authors (Abish to Wouk) whose major works were largely written after World War II. Entries include biography; discussion of major works and themes; overview of critical reception; and bibliography of primary and secondary sources. Invaluable for coverage of less well-known and emerging writers. Introductory essay on postwar Jewish fiction. Select bibliography of general sources. Index.
Class No: 820.73-31(=924)

[7741]
CRONIN, G.L., *& others*. Jewish-American fiction writers: an annotated bibliography. New York, Garland, 1991. 1233p. $175. ISBN: 082401619x.

A comprehensive listing of primary and secondary sources (in English only) for 62 19th- and 20th-century authors, with descriptive abstracts for all secondary sources except book-length works. Omits major figures for whom individual bibliographies exist, *e.g.* Bellow, Malamud, Mailer, Roth. Introduction includes list of general studies.
Class No: 820.73-31(=924)

Black Races

[7742]
MARGOLIES, E. *and* BAKISH, D. Afro-American fiction, 1853-1976: a guide to information sources. Detroit, Gale, 1979. xviii,161p.

4 sections: 1. Checklist of 728 novels - 2. Bibliography of short stories and anthologies - 3. Secondary sources on 15 major authors - 4. Bibliographies and general studies. Chronology appended. Author, title, and subject indexes.
Class No: 820.73-31(=96)

[7743]
WERNER, C. Black American women novelists: an annotated bibliography. Englewood Cliffs, N.J., Salem Press, 1989 (later Scarecrow Press). 286p. $40. (*Magill bibliographies.*) ISBN: 0810827875.

Annotated lists of biographies and commentaries for 33 writers, plus an extensive annotated bibliography of general studies of the subject. 'Although the annotations are helpful, it is the 70-page introduction that is most impressive' (*Choice*, v.28(1), Sept. 1990, p.86). *Class No:* 820.73-31(=96)

Baldwin

[7744]
STANDLEY, F.L. *and* STANDLEY, N.V. James Baldwin: a reference guide. Boston, Hall, 1980. xv,310p. ISBN: 0816178445.

Lists *c.*900 critical studies by year, 1946-78, then A-Z by author, with substantial annotations in the form of abstracts. Includes dissertations and some foreign-language material. Checklist of Baldwin's writings (11p.). Index of authors, titles, names and subjects. *Class No:* 820.73-31BAL

Bellow

[7745]
CRONIN, G.L. *and* HALL, B.H. Saul Bellow: an annotated bibliography. 2nd ed. New York, Garland, 1987. xvii,312p. $52. ISBN: 0824094212.

Apparently a new ed. of *Saul Bellow: his works and his critics - an annotated international bibliography,* by M. Nault (Garland, 1977).

1,388 items covering primary and secondary material. Primary sources are not annotated, but include all editions of each work, including translations. Secondary sources are divided into 6 sections: bibliographies and checklists; books and monographs; special journal issues; biographical sources; criticism and reviews; doctoral dissertations. Only the criticism is annotated. Author and subject index.
Class No: 820.73-31BEL

Cather

[7746]
ARNOLD, M. Willa Cather: a reference guide. Boston, Hall, 1986. xxii,415p. $40. ISBN: 0816186545.

Comprehensive bibliography of writings about Cather arranged by year, 1895-1984, and A-Z by author within each year, with nonevaluative annotations. Over 2,100 entries, including many foreign items, a special effort having been made to find Japanese and Swedish criticism. Many cross-references, author index and excellent subject index.
Class No: 820.73-31CAT

[7747]
CRANE, J. Willa Cather: a bibliography. Lincoln, Nebr., Univ. of Nebraska Press, 1982. xxviii,412p. $50. ISBN: 0803214154.

Descriptive bibliography of Cather's works in 6 parts and 18 sections and sub-sections. 1. Books - 2. Poems - 3. Short fiction - 4. Articles, reviews and essays - 5. Translations - 6. Miscellany including Braille, large-type and recorded books, and adaptations for film and theatre. Locations given for pre-1920 publications. Detailed historical notes in Part 1, which occupies 224p. Over 1,100 items in all. Index.
Class No: 820.73-31CAT

[7748]
MARCH, J. A Reader's companion to the fiction of Willa Cather. Arnold, M., *ed.* Westport, Conn., Greenwood, 1993. 880p. $105. ISBN: 0313287678.

Contains several thousand entries (A-Z) on people, places and events (fictional and real) and on quotations, allusions, etc. in Cather's fiction. *Class No:* 820.73-31CAT

[7749]

A Reader's guide to the short stories of Willa Cather. Meyering, S.L., *ed.* New York, Hall, 1994. xvii,286p. $50. ISBN: 0816118345.

A chapter on each of Cather's 60-plus stories, giving publication history; background to composition; links with her other works (shared themes, etc.); overview of critical reception; and suggestions for further reading.
Class No: 820.73-31CAT

Crane (Stephen)

[7750]

STALLMAN, R.W. Stephen Crane: a critical bibliography. Ames, Ia., Iowa State Univ. Press, 1972. xxxxii,642p. ISBN: 0813803578.

A. Books and contributions to books - B. Miscellanea and curiosa - C. Published letters - D. Contemporary reviews and parodies - E. Writings of Crane arranged alphabetically by title - F. Writings biographical, bibliographical and critical about Crane, 1888-1970 (over 2,100 items). A, B and C are fully descriptive; D and F are annotated. Index.
Class No: 820.73-31CRA

[7751]

WERTHEIM, S. A Stephen Crane encyclopedia. Westport, Conn., Greenwood, 1998. 432p. $85. ISBN: 0313296928.

Contains hundreds of entries for Crane's family, friends and associates; educational institutions he attended; places where he lived; publishers and other employers; literary movements; plus his works of fiction, poetry and journalism. Many entries include citations for further reading. Chronology of Crane's life and works. Bibliography of key critical and biographical studies. Index. *Class No:* 820.73-31CRA

Faulkner

[7752]

BASSETT, J. William Faulkner: an annotated checklist of criticism. New York, David Lewis, 1972. xiii,551p.

5 sections: 1. Books on Faulkner - 2. Studies of individual novels - 3. Studies of short stories, poetry, and miscellaneous writings - 4. Topical studies - 5. Other material (including doctoral dissertations; British theses and dissertations). Index of critics. Over 5,000 entries, many of them unannotated despite the title. Confined to English-language material.

Continued by *Faulkner: an annotated checklist of recent criticism* (1983) and *Faulkner in the Eighties: an annotated critical bibliography* (Metuchen, N.J., Scarecrow, 1991. 334p. $37. ISBN: 081082485x) *Class No:* 820.73-31FAU

[7753]

RICKS, B. William Faulkner: a bibliography of secondary works. Metuchen, N.J., Scarecrow, 1980. xxvii,657p. $57. (*Scarecrow author bibliographies.*) ISBN: 0810813238.

Over 8,000 unannotated items in 4 sections: Biography; Works (subdivided by genre, then by individual works); General Criticism; Bibliography. Topical index and index of critics. *Class No:* 820.73-31FAU

[7754]

TUCK, D. Crowell's handbook of Faulkner. New York, Crowell; London, Chatto, 1964. xxvii,259p.

UK title is *A Handbook of Faulkner*.

Includes full synopsis of each novel with critical notes, précis of every published short story and dictionary of 172 characters. Index. *Class No:* 820.73-31FAU

Fitzgerald

[7755]

BRUCCOLI, M.J. F. Scott Fitzgerald: a descriptive bibliography. Rev. ed. Pittsburgh, Pa., Univ. of Pittsburgh Press, 1988. xix,479p. $100. (*Pittsburgh series in bibliography.*) ISBN: 0822935600.

1st ed. 1972; *Supplement* 1980.

Corrects and augments the original bibliography and its supplement, listing all printed items for which Fitzgerald's authorship can be established, with full descriptions of all editions of the novels, short stories and plays. Title page and jacket facsimiles. Index. 1st ed. was described as 'a model for all such studies' (*TLS,* no.3708, March 30, 1973, p.360).
Class No: 820.73-31FIT

[7756]

BRYER, J.R. The Critical reputation of F. Scott Fitzgerald: a bibliographical study. Hamden, Conn., Archon, 1967. xvii,434p. ISBN: 0208004122.

Over 2,100 annotated items in 6 sections: A. Reviews - B. Articles - C. Books and book sections - D. Foreign books and articles - E. Graduate research - F. Addenda. Appendices have chronology of Fitzgerald's life and checklist of first appearances of publications with contributions by him. Thorough index.

Continued by *Supplement one, through 1981* (Hamden, Conn., Archon, 1984. xvi,542p. $59.50. ISBN: 0208014896). *Class No:* 820.73-31FIT

[7757]

F. Scott Fitzgerald A-Z: the essential reference to his life and work. New York, Facts on File, 1998. 352p. illus. $45. ISBN: 0816031509.

Over 2,200 cross-referenced entries giving detailed synopses of all major and most minor works; an overview of the critical reception to each work; descriptions of all fictional and real characters in the works; and discussions of Fitzgerald's family and associates. Over 70 illustrations. Chronology. Bibliography. Index. *Class No:* 820.73-31FIT

[7758]

STANLEY, L.C. The Foreign critical reputation of F. Scott Fitzgerald: an analysis and annotated bibliography. Westport, Conn., Greenwood, 1980. xiii,276p. $59.95. ISBN: 0313214441.

Complements Bryer. Has a chapter for each of 5 major countries (France, Britain, Germany, Italy and Japan) comprising analysis of the critical responses, chronological list of translations, and annotated bibliography of criticism in books and periodicals and reviews of Fitzgerald's books. 6th chapter lists, with annotations, criticism from a further 11 countries. Index. *Class No:* 820.73-31FIT

Hawthorne

[7759]

BOSWELL, J. Nathaniel Hawthorne and the critics: a checklist of criticism, 1900-1978. Metuchen, N.J., Scarecrow, 1982. x,273p. ISBN: 0810814714.

2,816 items arranged A-Z by author, with a few brief annotations. Index of co-authors, editors and translators. Subject index. Includes some foreign-language items and major 19th-century material. *Class No:* 820.73-31HAW

[7760]

CLARK, C.E.F., *jr*. Nathaniel Hawthorne: a descriptive bibliography. Pittsburgh, Pa., Univ. of Pittsburgh Press, 1978. xxi,478p. illus. $100. (*Pittsburgh series in bibliography*.) ISBN: 0822933438.

Section A., Separate Publications (p.1-337), lists chronologically all printings of all editions in English to 1883 and selected reprints to 1975 with full description. Other sections cover collected works, contributions to books, magazines and newspapers, ephemera and prose and verse by or attributed to Hawthorne. Many title pages reproduced. Index. *Class No:* 820.73-31HAW

[7761]

GALE, R.L. A Nathaniel Hawthorne encyclopedia. Westport, Conn., Greenwood, 1991. xvii,583p. $79.50. ISBN: 0313268169.

1,500 entries, identifying all of Hawthorne's characters, summarizing the plots of his fiction and the substance of his essays, and introducing his relatives, friends and associates. *Class No:* 820.73-31HAW

[7762]

SCHARNHORST, G. Nathaniel Hawthorne: an annotated bibliography of comment and criticism before 1900. Metuchen, N.J., Scarecrow, 1988. xii,404p. $41.50. (*Scarecrow author bibliographies*.) ISBN: 0810821842.

2,586 items arranged by year, 1828-99, then by author, with brief annotations. Includes some French and German material. Index of names and titles of Hawthorne's works. *Class No:* 820.73-31HAW

Hemingway

[7763]

HANNEMAN, A. Ernest Hemingway: a comprehensive bibliography. Princeton, N.J. Princeton Univ. Press, 1967. 568p. ISBN: 0691060398.

Part 1 lists works in 6 sections: Books and pamphlets (full descriptions of first American and English editions); Contributions and first appearances in books and pamphlets; Contributions to newspapers and periodicals; Translations; Anthologies; Library holdings, published letters and ephemera. Part 2 lists secondary material in 2 sections, with annotations: Books (A-Z by author); Newspapers and periodical articles (chronological, 1918-65). Over 1,400 primary and over 2,000 secondary items. Appendix lists newspapers and periodicals cited. Index.

Supplement, 1975, (xii,393p. ISBN: 0691062846) adds some 600 primary and 1,500 secondary items published 1966-73, plus additions and amendments to first vol. 'The work is indeed definitive and basic' (*Library Journal*, v.100(19), 1st Nov. 1975, p.2036). *Class No:* 820.73-31HEM

[7764]

WAGNER, L.W. Ernest Hemingway: a reference guide. Boston, Hall, 1977. xix,363p. ISBN: 081617976x.

Lists *c.*1,900 critical studies by year, 1923-75, with separate sections for books and shorter writings within each year. Restricted to English-language material. Summary annotations. Index of critics and of Hemingway's titles.

K.A. Larson's *Ernest Hemingway: a reference guide, 1974-1989* (Boston, Hall, 1990. 318p. $50. ISBN: 0816189447) adds over 1,600 recent studies. *Class No:* 820.73-31HEM

Hurston

[7765]

DAVIS, R.P. Zora Neale Hurston: an annotated bibliography and reference guide. Westport, Conn., Greenwood, 1997. 224p. £51.95. (*Bibliographies and indexes in Afro-American and African studies*.) ISBN: 0313303878.

A comprehensive, classified listing of secondary materials, including books, dissertations, essays, articles, reviews, bibliographies and anthologies. Appended lists of media, Web sites and special library collections. Chronological list of Hurston's works. Author and subject indexes. *Class No:* 820.73-31HUR

James

[7766]

EDEL, L. *and* LAURENCE, D.L. A Bibliography of Henry James. 3rd ed., rev. with the assistance of J. Rambeau. Oxford, Clarendon Press, 1982. 428p. illus. ISBN: 0198181868.

1st ed. 1957; 2nd ed. 1961.

The standard primary bibliography. A. Original works - B. Contributions to books - C. Published letters - D. Contributions to periodicals - E. Translations - F. Miscellanea (including Braille editions, talking books and manuscripts). Over 1,100 entries. Many corrections and revisions in 3rd ed., but section on translations not updated. Index. *Class No:* 820.73-31JAM

[7767]

GALE, R.L. A Henry James encyclopedia. New York, Greenwood, 1989. xxi,791p. $135. ISBN: 0313258465.

Over 3,000 entries on James's works (giving plot summary and some critical evaluation), fictional characters and literary allusions and on his associates and relations. 12 appendices group entries under various headings, *e.g.* works by genre, writers influenced by James, friends of James, etc. Chronology of James's life. Bibliography. Some entries are short essays of up to 4,000 words. 'This brilliant, faultless, impeccably constructed work will maintain its status as an outstanding research tool' (*Choice*, v.27(3), Nov. 1989, p.460). *Class No:* 820.73-31JAM

[7768]

—A Companion to Henry James studies. Fogel, D.M., *ed.* Westport, Conn., Greenwood, 1993. xxii,545p. $89.50. ISBN: 0313257922.

Complement's Gale's encyclopedia with 20 essays on different aspects of James scholarship. Reference value lies in appended, annotated chronologies of James' principal publications in book form and of landmarks in James criticism, 1905-91. Index. *Class No:* 820.73-31JAM

[7769]

TAYLOR, L.J., *and others*. Henry James: a reference guide. Boston, Hall, 1979-91. 4v.

1866-1916, by L.J. Taylor (1982. xxvi,533p. $48.50. ISBN: 0816178747).

1917-1959, by K.P. McColgan (1979. xix,389p. $36.50. ISBN: 0816178518).

1960-1974, by D.M. Scura (1979. xx,490p. $46. ISBN: 081617850x).

1975-1987, by J.E. Funston (1991. 571p. $50. ISBN: 0816189536).

List writings about James by year, with one A-Z author sequence per year in v.1, and separate sequences for books and shorter writings in later vols. Strictly descriptive annotations throughout. Single-sequence index of authors,

.... *(contd.)*
titles, and subjects in each vol. Nearly 8,000 entries in total. 'Exhaustive, functional and reliable' (*Choice*, v.28(11/12), July/Aug. 1991, p.1758). *Class No:* 820.73-31JAM

Melville

[7770]
A Companion to Melville studies. Bryant, J., *ed.* New York, Greenwood, 1986. xxviii,906p. illus. $135. ISBN: 031323874x.

25 signed essays (average 33p.) by 26 contributors on all aspects of Melville's life and works, each including selected bibliographies. Particularly useful are ch.23, 'Melville in popular culture' by M.T. Inge, with a list of films, TV and radio programmes, comics, etc. and ch.25, 'Melville and the world of books' by G.T. Tanselle, with lists of major Melville editions and the principal research tools. General index. Index of authors cited. *Class No:* 820.73-31MEL

[7771]
GALE, R.L. A Herman Melville encyclopedia. Westport, Conn., Greenwood, 1995. 560p. $85. ISBN: 0313290113.

Contains hundreds of entries (arranged A-Z and varying from a few lines to several pages) on Melville's works and on both real and fictitious people and places associated with him. Entries on major subjects include bibliographies. Chronology of Melville's life. Index of names and titles. Bibliography of key works about Melville. Index. *Class No:* 820.73-31MEL

[7772]
HIGGINS, B. Herman Melville: a reference guide, 1931-1960. Boston, Hall, 1987. xvi,531p. $65. ISBN: 0816186715.

Lists over 1,900 critical works on Melville chronologically, with sections on books and shorter works within each year. Includes book reviews but omits dissertations and foreign-language material. Lengthy annotations. Subject and author indexes. Sequel to *Herman Melville: an annotated bibliography, Vol.1: 1846-1930 (1978. 421p. ISBN: 0816178437)*, although not clear from the title.

For dissertations, see J. Bryant's *Melville dissertations, 1924-1980: an annotated bibliography and subject index* (Westport, Conn., Greenwood, 1983. xxi,166p. $59.95. ISBN:0313238111). *Class No:* 820.73-31MEL

[7773]
KIER, K.E. Melville encyclopedia: the novels. Troy, N.Y., Whitston, 1990. 2v. (xxii,1220p.). $120. ISBN: 0878753265.

Lists and explains all the proper names (over 4,000) mentioned or alluded to in Melville's 9 novels, with references to chapters. V.2 includes list of quotations used by Melville (22p.) and glossary of nautical terms (25p.). Bibliography (19p.). *Class No:* 820.73-31MEL

Nabokov

[7774]
The Garland companion to Vladimir Nabokov. Alexandrov, V.E., *ed.* New York, Garland, 1994. 848p. £29.95. ISBN: 0815303548.

75 signed articles by 42 international contributors, covering his works, beliefs and artistic practices and his critical reception. Also includes chronology of Nabokov's life and works, primary and secondary bibliographies, and detailed index. *Class No:* 820.73-31NAB

Poe

[7775]
FRANK, F.S. *and* **MAGISTRALE, A. The Poe encyclopedia.** Westport, Conn., Greenwood, 1997. 480p. £71.50. ISBN: 0313277680.

Over 1,900 entries, A-Z, covering all aspects of Poe's life and career, including literary works, contemporaries, his known reading, and the wide range of subjects which interested him. Each entry has a bibliographical note giving the basis for the comment and suggesting sources for further reading, and those for individual works of fiction or poetry include a critical synopsis. Bibliography of key critical and biographical studies. Chronology. 3 indexes: critics, editors and other names; authors, artists and titles; themes, subjects and characters.

Complemented by *A Companion to Poe studies*, ed. by E.W. Carlson (Westport, Conn., Greenwood, 1996. 624p. $99.50. ISBN: 0313265062), which has 25 signed essays, 13 assessing specific literary works and the rest dealing with various aspects of Poe's life, thought, aesthetics and influence. Chapters include extensive documentation and there is a general bibliography of resources for Poe studies. *Class No:* 820.73-31POE

[7776]
HAMMOND, J.R. An Edgar Allan Poe chronology. Basingstoke, Macmillan, 1998. 136p. £37.50. (*Macmillan author chronologies.*) ISBN: 033369449x.

Details the events of the writer's life, month by month and day by day and also includes biographical notes on the Poe circle. Separate chronology of Poe's works. List of sources. Index of people, places and works. *Class No:* 820.73-31POE

[7777]
HYNEMAN, E.F. Edgar Allan Poe: an annotated bibliography of books and articles in English, 1827-1973. Boston, Hall, 1974. xv,335p. ISBN: 0816111049.

Lists over 2,400 critical works in 3 period categories: 1827-50, 1851-99 and 1900-73, the first 2 each having a single author sequence and the third being subdivided into 27 subject categories. Concise nonevaluative annotations with cross-references at the end of each section. Chronological and author indexes. *Class No:* 820.73-31POE

Steinbeck

[7778]
HAYASHI, T. A New Steinbeck bibliography, 1929-1971. Metuchen, N.J., Scarecrow, 1973. xix,225p. ISBN: 0810806479.

Part 1 lists 379 primary items in 13 sections, while Part 2 has 1,804 secondary items in 8 sections (including film reviews). A few entries have brief annotations. Index of authors, subjects and titles.

Continued by *A New Steinbeck bibliography, 1971-81* (Scarecrow, 1983. 169p. ISBN: 0810816105).

For details of other sources, see *Steinbeck bibliographies: an annotated guide*, by R.B. Harmon (Metuchen, N.J., Scarecrow, 1987. 145p. ISBN: 0810819635). *Class No:* 820.73-31STE

[7779]

John Steinbeck: an annotated guide to biographical sources. Harmon, R.B., *ed.* Lanham, Md., Scarecrow, 1996. 320p. illus. $55. ISBN: 0810831740.

Provides bibliographical and anecdotal information on a variety of media, including books, magazines, newspapers, films, audio recordings, dictionaries and encyclopedias. Includes detailed chronology of Steinbeck's life and photographs of the writer, his family and friends.
Class No: 820.73-31STE

Twain

[7780]

JOHNSON, M. A Bibliography of the works of Mark Twain, Samuel Langhorne Clemens: a list of first editions in book form and of first printings in periodicals and occasional publications of his varied literary activities. Reprint of 1935 ed. Westport, Conn., Greenwood, 1972. xiii,274p. ISBN: 0837156106.

1st ed. 1910; Rev. and enl. ed. 1935.

Lists and describes books chronologically, 1867-1935, followed by speeches, letters, contributions, broadsides, poems, plays and interviews. Thorough index.
Class No: 820.73-31TWA

[7781]

The Mark Twain encyclopedia. LeMaster, J.R. *and* Wilson, J.D., *eds.* New York, Garland, 1993. xxx,848p. £72. ISBN: 082407212x.

740 signed entries, A-Z, on all aspects of Twain's life and oeuvre: individual literary works; fictional characters and locales; family and associates; themes and attitudes; sources and influences; biographers and critics. Articles range in length from a few lines to several pages, but each has a selective bibliography and most are followed by useful cross-references. Chronology of Twain's life and posthumous publications. Genealogy of his family. Comprehensive index. 'This carefully conceived, meticulously edited, and admirably executed compendium could serve as a model for encyclopedias on individual authors' (*Booklist*, Oct. 15, 1993, p.474).

An alternative source is R.K. Rasmussen's *Mark Twain A to Z: the essential reference to his life and writings* (New York, Facts on File, 1995. 576p. illus. $45. ISBN: 0816028451), with 1,300 entries on Twain's works, characters, associates, publishers, etc., and places and events in his life. Chronology. Map of Twain's homes and travels in North America. Bibliography. Index.

For Twain quotations, see B. Collins' *When in doubt, tell the truth, and other quotations from Mark Twain* (New York, Columbia Univ. Press, 1998. 224p. $19.95. ISBN: 0231104987). *Class No:* 820.73-31TWA

[7782]

Mark Twain international: a bibliography and interpretation of his worldwide popularity. Rodney, R.M., *ed.* Westport, Conn., Greenwood, 1982. lxix,275p. $65 ISBN: 0313231354.

Covers some 5,000 editions of Twain's work, 1867-1980. Arranged geographically, 10 regions, then country, then title or subject (*e.g.* letters). Unique checklist of 52 countries, 72 languages. Includes statistical tables and introductory essay.
Class No: 820.73-31TWA

[7783]

TENNEY, T.A. Mark Twain: a reference guide. Boston, Hall,1977. xiv,443p. ISBN: 0818679662.

Lists 4,900 studies of Twain's works by year, 1858-1975, then by author, with separate sections for books and shorter writings within each year. Concise descriptive annotations. Index. *Class No:* 820.73-31TWA

Updike

[7784]

DE BELLIS, J. John Updike: a bibliography, 1967-1993. Westport, Conn., Greenwood, 1994. 360p. $59.95. (*Bibliographies and indexes in American literature.*) ISBN: 0313288615.

Lists 3,349 works by and about Updike. As well as standard items, primary material includes letters, interviews and unsigned periodical articles, and secondary material includes dissertations, parodies, caricatures and works in non-print media. Not annotated. Appended list of translations. Generous cross-references. Index.
Class No: 820.73-31UPD

Vonnegut

[7785]

LEEDS, M. The Vonnegut encyclopedia: an authorized compendium. Westport, Conn., Greenwood, 1994. 712p. $85. ISBN: 0313292302.

A comprehensive A-Z guide to characters, themes and images in Vonnegut's novels, short stories, plays and essays. Entries include extended quotations, each of which is precisely cited by page and line number of the first edition. Index. *Class No:* 820.73-31VON

Welty

[7786]

POLK, N. Eudora Welty: a bibliography of her work. Jackson, Miss., Univ. Press of Mississippi, 1993. xxi,517p. illus. $65. ISBN: 0878055665.

Detailed Pittsburgh-style descriptions of first editions of books in first section (including many illustrations), followed by briefer descriptions of other works. Detailed chronology of publishing history (49p.). Analytical index.

See also *The Welty Collection: a guide to the Eudora Welty manuscripts and documents at the Mississippi Department of Archives and History*, by S. Marrs (Jackson, Miss., Univ. Press of Mississippi, 1988. 244p. $32.50. ISBN: 0878053662), an annotated listing of a major collection of primary and secondary materials. *Class No:* 820.73-31WEL

Wharton

[7787]

GARRISON, S. Edith Wharton: a descriptive bibliography. Pittsburgh, Pa., Univ. of Pittsburgh Press, 1990. 514p. $100. (*Pittsburgh series in bibliography.*) ISBN: 0822936410.

Full descriptive listings, with library locations, of Wharton's books, pamphlets, and collections. Also provides bibliographic details of all titles up to 1986 in which any of Wharton's writings first appear and of her contributions to newspapers and periodicals. Index. 'The bibliographic scholarship reflected in this volume is most impeccable and complete' (*Choice*, v.28(9), May 1991, p.1456).
Class No: 820.73-31WHA

[7788]

LAUER, K.O. *and* **MURRAY, M.P. Edith Wharton: an annotated secondary bibliography.** New York, Garland, 1990. 528p. ISBN: 0824046366.

A classified listing of over 1,200 studies published 1897-1987 in English and other languages, with generous annotations. Indexes of authors, titles, subjects and works. Supersedes M. Springer's *Edith Wharton and Kate Chopin: a reference guide* (Boston, Hall, 1976) and 'will maintain its status as the major bibliographic study of Wharton' (*Choice*, v.28(2), Oct. 1990, p.285-6). *Class No:* 820.73-31WHA

Wolfe

[7789]

BASSETT, J.E. Thomas Wolfe: an annotated critical bibliography Lanham, Md., Scarecrow, 1996. 456p. $54.50. (*Scarecrow author bibliographies.*) ISBN: 0810831465.

5 sections covering books on Wolfe; reviews and critical articles on each of his 4 novels; reviews and articles on his other works; general studies; and other materials, including dissertations. 2,876 entries. Index of critics, but no subject index. Introductory history of Wolfe's critical reception.
Class No: 820.73-31WOL

[7790]

IDOL, J.L., ***jr*****. A Thomas Wolfe companion.** New York, Greenwood, 1987. xxii,205p. $55. ISBN: 0313238294.

A mixed bag of 'basic information about Wolfe's life, thought and art ... aimed more at beginning than experienced readers of Wolfe's writing' (*Preface*). Contains essays on his life, ideas and attitudes, the major themes of his works and his relationship with his editors and critics, but the main reference aids are: classified primary bibliography, including periodical pieces; surveys of the works and their critical reception; glossary of characters and places (not exhaustive); genealogical charts of 3 major fictional families. Appendix A. lists major special collections and other information sources. Appendix B. is an annotated bibliography of 89 secondary works. Index. *Class No:* 820.73-31WOL

[7791]

JOHNSTON, C. Thomas Wolfe: a descriptive bibliography. Pittsburgh, Pa., Univ. of Pittsburgh Press, 1987. xix,295p. illus. $100. (*Pittsburgh series in bibliography.*) ISBN: 0822935465.

Detailed descriptions of editions of Wolfe's full-length works in Section A. (p.1-207), including reproductions of title-pages, followed by lists of contributions to periodicals, etc. Index. *Class No:* 820.73-31WOL

Immigrants

[7792]

SIMONE, R. The Immigrant experience in American fiction: an annotated bibliography. Metuchen, NJ, Scarecrow, 1995. 230p. $41.50. ISBN: 0810829622.

Over 600 descriptive citations on 41 immigrant groups (from Armenian to Vietnamese), 6 combined groups (Asian, Hispanic, Jewish, Scandinavian, Slavic and West Indian) plus a category called 'The General Experience'. Covers adult and young adult novels, story collections, anthologies and secondary sources. *Class No:* 820.73-31-0054.72

Women

[7793]

CARTER, S. War and peace through women's eyes: a selective bibliography of twentieth-century American women's fiction. Westport, Conn., Greenwood, 1992. 336p. $65. (*Bibliographies and indexes in women's studies.*) ISBN: 0313277710.

Chapters on World War I, World War II, Vietnam and works that span more than one war or are not specific to any conflict. Each comprises overview of literature; annotated entries on novels and short fiction by women (including excerpts from the works and reviews); and references to bibliographical and critical sources. *Class No:* 820.73-31-0055.2

[7794]

WHITE, B.A. American women's fiction, 1790-1870: a reference guide. New York, Garland, 1990. xvii,294p. $45. ISBN: 0824066731.

Part 1 lists English-language sources of information on American women's fiction of the period, with descriptive annotations. Part 2 lists 328 women authors who published before 1870, giving full name, pseudonyms, birth and death dates, and references to the sources in Part 1. Indexes of authors, editors, topics, and pseudonyms. 'A valuable addition for finding information on these important but often neglected writers' (*Choice*, v.27(11/12), July/Aug. 1990, p.1811). *Class No:* 820.73-31-0055.2

Gay People

[7795]

Contemporary gay American novelists: a bio-bibliographical critical sourcebook. Nelson, E.S., *ed.* Westport, Conn., Greenwood, 1993. 456p. $79.50. ISBN: 0313280193.

Signed essays by 41 contributors on 57 gay men, including major figures like Baldwin, Burroughs and Capote and several as yet largely unknown names, although writers whose work is confined to erotic or pulp fiction are omitted. Entries comprise biography, discussion of major themes, review of critical reception, and bibliography of works and selected critical studies. General bibliography within introductory section. Appended list of small presses and selected journals. Index. *Class No:* 820.73-31-0055.3

[7796]

LEVIN, J. The Gay novel in America. New York, Garland, 1991. xiv,363p. $42. ISBN: 0824061489.

Claims to offer the only comprehensive account of the gay man as depicted in American fiction. Covers over 300 novels published 1888-1989. Author and title indexes.
Class No: 820.73-31-0055.3

Short Stories

[7797]

KENNEDY, T.E. Index to American short story award collections, 1970-1990. Boston, Hall, 1993. 116p. $40. ISBN: 0816118191.

Indexes stories in 7 award series, *e.g.* the Pushcart Prize. Contents listings for each vol. in each series, followed by author and title indexes for that series, but no overall index to the works covered. Useful for its coverage of story series outside the mainstream of American fiction.
Class No: 820.73-32

[7798]

Mothers and daughters in American short fiction: an annotated bibliography of twentieth-century women's literature. Carter, S., *comp.* Westport, Conn., Greenwood, 1993. xx,132p. $59.95. ISBN: 031328511x.

A thematically arranged listing of *c.*250 stories by women which explore the mother-daughter relationship. Annotations incorporate plot summary and critical analysis. Author, title and subject indexes. *Class No:* 820.73-32

[7799]

WEIXLMANN, J. American short-fiction criticism and scholarship, 1959-1977: a checklist. Athens, Ohio, Swallow Press/Ohio Univ. Press, 1982. xii,625p. ISBN: 0804003815.

Nearly 7,000 unannotated entries, relating to *c.*500 authors. General sections, with period subdivisions, followed by short-story writers, A-Z. List of over 300 serial publications indexed. *Class No:* 820.73-32

[7800]

WHITE, R.L. Index to *Best American short stories* and *O. Henry prize stories*. Boston, Hall, 1988. 183p. $38.50. ISBN: 0816189552.

Separate author indexes for each series, plus a combined title index. Introductory essays on the history and development of the series, which started in 1915 and 1919 respectively and have featured contributions by many of the key figures in 20th-century American fiction.
Class No: 820.73-32

Black Races

[7801]

The Afro-American short story: a comprehensive, annotated index with selected commentaries. Yancy, P.M., *comp.* Westport, Conn., Greenwood, 1986. xvi,171p. $49.95. (*Bibliographies and indexes in Afro-American and African studies.*) ISBN: 0313243557.

Covers 850 stories by approx 300 writers. Part 1 lists stories by year of publication, 1950-82, and A-Z by title within each year; Part 2 lists anthologies and collections A-Z by compiler with bibliographical details and lists of contents; Part 3 provides commentaries on over 100 selected stories (no indication of criteria for selection) and classifies them according to traditional genres (epic, comedy, etc.) and the accepted types of Afro-American literature (celebrative, militant, etc.). Author index is actually an annotated bibliography. Title index. Useful but confusing.
Class No: 820.73-32(=96)

American Satire & Humour

[7802]

Encyclopedia of American humorists. Gale, S.H., *ed.* New York, Garland, 1988. xviii, 557p. ISBN: 0824086449.

Essays by 78 scholars on 135 American and Canadian writers from Colonial times (Thomas Morton) to the present (Woody Allen). Average length is 3½p. and each comprises biography, literary analysis and bibliography of primary and secondary sources. Many previously neglected writers are covered. Index of authors and titles. *Class No:* 820.73-7

[7803]

Humor in America: a research guide to genres and topics. Mintz, L.E., *ed.* Westport, Conn., Greenwood, 1988. 251p. $59.95. ISBN: 0313245517.

Chapters by specialists on literary humour, comics, periodicals, film, broadcast humour, standup comedy, women's humour, racial/ethnic humour, and political humour, each one providing an overview of the genre and a bibliographic essay to facilitate further study. Concluding chapter on folklore methodology and American humour research. *Class No:* 820.73-7

American Regional Literature

Bibliographies

[7804]

ANDERSON, J.Q., *and others.* Southwestern American literature: a bibliography. Athens, Ohio, Swallow Press / Ohio Univ. Press, 1980. 445p. ISBN: 0804006830.

Covers writers from Arizona, New Mexico, Oklahoma and Texas, and includes primary and secondary materials. A 'treasure trove of obscure novelists, poets and dramatists' (*Choice*, v.18(4), Dec. 1980, p.512). *Class No:* 820.74(01)

[7805]

A Bibliographical guide to Midwestern literature. Nemanic, G., *ed.* Iowa City, Univ. of Iowa Press, 1981. xxiv, 380p. ISBN: 087745079x.

The work of nearly 100 contributors. Part 1, Subject Bibliographies, covers individual states and a wide range of themes, *e.g.* folklore, Indians, architecture. Part 2 has bibliographical information on 120 authors associated with the Midwest, the usual format being: short essay, checklist of major primary works, selective checklist of secondary sources ranging from 15 to 100 items according to status. Appendix A. lists 101 additional Midwestern writers; Appendix B. lists 101 additional fictional narratives set in the region. No index. *Class No:* 820.74(01)

[7806]

A Bibliographical guide to the study of Southern literature: with an appendix containing sixty-eight additional writers of the Colonial South, by J.A.L. Lemay. Rubin, L.D., *ed.* Baton Rouge, Louisiana State Univ. Press, 1969. xxiv,368p.

Part 1. (p.1-145) comprises 23 signed bibliographical essays on general topics (periods, genres, etc.). Part 2. (p.147-335) is a series of checklists of secondary materials on approx. 140 Southern authors, each compiled by a named scholar. Appendix has very brief checklists on 68 additional writers of the Colonial South. *Class No:* 820.74(01)

[7807]

—Southern literature, 1968-1975: a checklist of scholarship. Committee on Bibliography of the Society for the Study of Southern Literature, *comp.* Boston, Hall, 1978. xvi,271p. ISBN: 0816180512.

Continuation of L.D. Rubin's *A Bibliographical guide to the study of Southern literature*. Cumulates annotated entries from the annual bibliographies in Spring issues of *Mississippi Quarterly* and adds new items, cross-references and author index. Four chronological sections (Colonial, Antebellum, Postbellum, Contemporary) containing material on specific authors (A-Z in each section), followed by a short general section. *Class No:* 820.74(01)

[7808]

Contemporary Southern women fiction writers: an annotated bibliography. Reisman, R.M.C. *and* Canfield, C.J., *eds*. Metuchen, N.J., Scarecrow, 1994. 225p. $34.50. (*Magill bibliographies*.) ISBN: 0810828324.

A very selective bibliography of secondary material relating to 28 writers born in the South, ranging from 9 to 43 entries per subject with concise abstracts. Author index.

Companion vol. on *Contemporary Southern male fiction writers* due 1998 (ISBN: 0810831953), covering 39 authors active since 1970. *Class No:* 820.74(01)

[7809]

ETULAIN, R.W. A Bibliographical guide to the study of Western American literature. Lincoln, Univ. of Nebraska Press, 1982. xvii,317p. $35. ISBN: 080321801x.

5,030 unannotated entries. Bibliographies, anthologies, general works and special topics (*e.g.* Western films, Indian literature) are followed by checklists of secondary material on 350 individual writers. Largely confined to those who were born or lived to the west of the Mississippi, but also includes others who influenced Western literature, *e.g.* Irving, Crane, West. Major writers treated selectively. Author index. *Class No:* 820.74(01)

[7810]

SLOCUM, R.B. New England in fiction: an annotated bibliography. West Cornwall, Conn., Locust Hill Press, 1994. 2v. (xliv,980p.). $100. ISBN: 093395154x.

Lists 5,000 works of fiction set in New England, giving synopsis and, in some cases, critical evaluation and extracts from reviews. Indexes of subjects, titles and places. *Class No:* 820.74(01)

Periodicals

[7811]

Index to Southern periodicals. Riley, S.G., *comp*. Westport, Conn., Greenwood, 1986. 459p. $65. (*Historical guides to the world's periodicals and newspapers*.) ISBN: 0313245150.

An inventory of nearly 7,000 non-newspaper periodicals first published 1764 to 1984, a quarter of them before 1900.

Riley's *Magazines of the American South* (Greenwood, 1986. 359p. $59.95. ISBN: 0313243379) profiles *c*.90 of the major periodicals. *Class No:* 820.74(051)

Histories

[7812]

The History of Southern literature. Rubin, L.D., *and others, eds*. Baton Rouge, La., Louisiana State Univ. Press, 1985 (repr. 1990). xiv,626p. $16.95. ISBN: 0807116432.

Covers the period 1607-1982 in 4 main sections, each containing an introductory essay by one of the senior editors and signed chapters (mainly on individual authors) by contributing specialists. *American Literature* (v.58(2), May 1986, p.427-30) commends its judicious editing, consistently good critical writing, and factual accuracy ('almost entirely free of error'), but regrets the lack of a bibliography, which is only partially compensated for by M.T. Inge's brief essay (11p.) on 'The Study of Southern literature'. Index. *Class No:* 820.74(091)

Biographies

[7813]

Contemporary fiction writers of the South: a bio-bibliographical sourcebook. Flora, J.M. *and* Bain, R., *eds*. Westport, Conn., Greenwood, 1993. xiii,571p. $75. ISBN: 0313287643.

Signed essays on 49 writers active since World War I, comprising biography, analysis of style and themes, assessment of critical reception, and primary and secondary bibliographies. *Class No:* 820.74(092)

[7814]

—Contemporary poets, dramatists, essayists and novelists of the South: a bio-bibliographical sourcebook. Bain, R. *and* Flora, J.M., *eds*. Westport, Conn., Greenwood, 1994. 642p. $105. ISBN: 0313287651.

A companion to *Contemporary fiction writers of the South*, covering nearly 49 authors from all literary genres who have published at least 4 books and received significant critical attention. *Class No:* 820.74(092)

[7815]

Fifty Southern writers after 1900: a bio-bibliographical sourcebook. Flora, J.M. *and* Bain, R., *eds*. New York, Greenwood, 1987. xii,628p. $105. ISBN: 0313245193.

Arranged A-Z by author, each entry is written by a different, named scholar, averages 10 pages and comprises 5 parts: biographical sketch, discussion of the subject's major themes, survey of criticism, list of the subject's works and bibliography of selected criticism. Index of names and titles. Major authors like Faulkner and Williams will obviously be treated in more depth elsewhere, but invaluable for the lesser names. 'A most responsibly and effectively conceived, executed and edited guidebook that is important and semi-permanent' (*American Literature* v.59(4), Dec. 1987, p.716). *Class No:* 820.74(092)

[7816]

Fifty Southern writers before 1900: a bio-bibliographical sourcebook. Bain, R. *and* Flora, J.M., *eds*. New York, Greenwood, 1987. xii,601p. $99.50. ISBN: 0313245185.

A companion volume to *Fifty Southern writers after 1900*, arranged in the same way and, like it, most valuable for information on the minor names. Covers mainly 19th-century writers but includes 14 born before 1800, beginning with John Smith (1580-1631). *Class No:* 820.74(092)

[7817]

Fifty Western writers: a bio-bibliographical sourcebook. Erisman, F. *and* Etulain, R.W., *eds*. Westport, Conn., Greenwood, 1982. xiv,562p. $75. ISBN: 0313221677.

Ten-page essays by specialist contributors on writers associated with the American West: not merely writers of Westerns (*e.g.* Zane Grey, Luke Short, Ernest Haycox) but also literary authors such as Willa Cather, Jack London, Theodore Roethke and John Steinbeck. Each essay includes biography, discussion of major themes, survey of criticism, list of the subject's works and selective bibliography of criticism. Index of names and titles. *Class No:* 820.74(092)

[7818]

Southern writers: a biographical dictionary. Bain, R., *and others, eds*. Baton Rouge, Louisiana State Univ. Press, 1979. xxvii,515p. $18.95. ISBN: 0807103543.

A project of the Society for the Study of Southern Literature, it complements L.D. Rubin's *A Bibliographical guide to the study of Southern literature* (*q.v.*). Contains biographical sketches of 379 writers by 172 scholars. According to their importance, writers are allocated 1,000, 750, 500 or 300 words, with the majority (including most of

....*(contd.)*
the contemporary names) in the 300-word group. List of first printings of the writer's works after each sketch. Particularly useful for minor figures. *Class No:* 820.74(092)

Guyanese Literature in English

[7819]
McDOWELL, R.E. Bibliography of literature from Guyana. Arlington, Tex., Sable, 1975. xx,117p. ISBN: 0914832034.

Lists *c.*2,400 works under authors, A-Z, giving bibliographical details and categorization by 24 genre codes (mainly literary, but also includes travel writing, journalism, biography, etc.). Not confined to native Guyanese writings, but also includes works with Guyanese content by foreign writers. *Class No:* 820.881

820.9 Australasian Literature

Australasian & Oceanian Literature

[7820]

GOETZFRIDT, N.J. Indigenous literature of Oceania: a survey of criticism and interpretation. Westport, Conn., Greenwood, 1995. 368p. £67.50. (*Bibliographies and indexes in world literature.*) ISBN: 031329173x.

A detailed survey of the expanding amount of critical and interpretive material written about English-language imaginative literature produced by indigenous writers from the Pacific Islands, New Zealand and Australia. Entries are grouped in 4 geographical chapters and extensively annotated. Introductory essay on the evolution of Pacific literature. Bibliography. 3 indexes: titles and authors; critics; subjects. *Class No:* 820.90

New Zealand Literature

[7821]

ALCOCK, P. *and* **BROUGHTON, W. Three hundred years of New Zealand books,** being selected chronological listing and commentary, primarily but not solely literary, from Tasman to 1975. Palmerston North, NZ, Dept. of English, Massey Univ., 1990. [76p.]. NZ$27.50. ISBN: 0908665520.

Parallel lists for poetry, fiction, other writing, and events, the latter including periodical publications and biographical information about writers. Separate lists for drama and criticism & bibliography from 1956. No index.
Class No: 820.931

[7822]

BURNS, J. New Zealand novels and novelists, 1861-1979: an annotated bibliography. 2nd ed. London, Heinemann, 1981. 71p. ISBN: 0868633720.

1st ed. 1967, covering 1900-67.

Lists novels chronologically with brief notes on subject content. Includes works by expatriates and some with NZ interest by non-natives. Author and title indexes.
Class No: 820.931

[7823]

EVANS, P. The Penguin history of New Zealand literature. Auckland, Penguin, 1990. 287p. NZ$24.95. ISBN: 0140113711.

A narrative history from 1890 to 1983 in 12 chapters, with extensive bibliographical notes at the end of each. Index.
Class No: 820.931

[7824]

The Oxford history of New Zealand literature in English. Sturm, T., *ed.* Auckland, Oxford Univ. Press, 1991. xviii,748p. ISBN: 019558211x.

The most comprehensive work on the subject, with 9 signed thematic chapters: 1. Maori literature - 2. Non-fiction - 3. The Novel - 4. The short story - 5. Drama - 6. Poetry - 7. Children's literature - 8. Popular fiction - 9. Publishing,

.... *(contd.)*

patronage, literary magazines. Comprehensive, discursive bibliography (107p.) in 5 sections: 1. Bibliographies and reference works - 2. Literary history and criticism - 3. Anthologies - 4. Periodicals - 5. Authors, A-Z (primary and secondary material). References (25p.). Thorough index. The work of 11 contributors. *Class No:* 820.931

[7825]

THOMSON, J.E. New Zealand literature to 1977: a guide to information sources. Detroit, Gale, 1980. 272p. ISBN: 0810312468.

Section on general sources (bibliographies, anthologies, periodicals, etc.) followed by coverage of 31 individual authors. Includes references to several unpublished items.
Class No: 820.931

[7826]

WILLIAMS, M., & ***others*****. Post-colonial literatures in English: Southeast Asia, New Zealand, and the Pacific, 1970-1992.** Boston, Hall, 1996. 370p. $60. ISBN: 0816173532.

Intended to update W.H. New's *Critical writings on Commonwealth literature* (*q.v.*) and provides bibliographies for individual authors after introductory essays. Author and subject indexes. *Class No:* 820.931

Australian Literature

Databases

[7827]

AUSTLIT: the Australian literary database. Melbourne, Informit Electronic Publishing & Training, 1992. CD-ROM. £520 per annum.

A database for Australian literary studies which originated in a file of more than 50,000 index cards maintained by the School of English at the Australian Defence Force Academy (ADFA) and which has grown to the extent that in October 1995 it contained 500,000 individual references. Items indexed include literary works (single vols. and items in colllections and periodicals); film and TV scripts; critical studies; reviews of books, plays, films and TV programmes; biographical articles on literary figures; film, video and sound recordings of literary works; lists of award winners. Children's literature is excluded. Over 700 newspapers and journals indexed. Search fields include author, gender/ethnicity, title, genre, topic, etc. Updated 3 times per year.

Also available on the Internet via various subscription services, including AUSTPAC and TELNET.
Class No: 820.94(003.4)

Bibliographies

[7828]

ANDREWS, B.G. *and* **WILDE, W.H. Australian literature to 1900:** a guide to information sources. Detroit, Gale, 1980. 472p. ISBN: 0810312158.

Section on general sources followed by coverage of 66 individual authors. Also covers non-fiction prose writing and Australian English. Name and title indexes.
Class No: 820.94(01)

[7829]

Australian literary studies. St. Lucia, Univ. of Queensland, 1963-. 2 py. ISSN: 00049697.

May issue has included 'Annual bibliography of studies in Australian literature' since 1964, listing books, articles and reviews from the preceding year. In 2 sections: 'General' and 'Individual authors'. 'This bibliography is the most comprehensive and reliable guide to critical and scholarly writing on Australian authors and literary subjects and to the more important works on Australian literature' according to Lock and Lawson (*q.v.*).

'Research in progress in Australian Literature' is an extensive but not exhaustive listing which appears every 2 years in the October issue. *Class No:* 820.94(01)

[7830]

LEVER, R., *&* *others*. Post-colonial literatures in English: Australia, 1970-1992. Boston, Hall, 1996. 361p. $65. ISBN: 0816173753.

Intended to update W.H. New's *Critical writings on Commonwealth literature* (*q.v.*) and provides bibliographies for individual authors after introductory essays on genres. Author and subject indexes. *Class No:* 820.94(01)

[7831]

LOCK, F. *and* **LAWSON, A. Australian literature: a reference guide.** 2nd ed. Melbourne and Oxford, Oxford Univ. Press, 1980. xiv,120p. (*Australian bibliographies.*) ISBN: 0195542142.

1st ed. 1977.

417 annotated entries (an increase of 84 over 1st ed.) in 7 main sections: 1. Bibliographical aids - 2. Other reference sources - 3. Authors (reference sources for 48 individuals) - 4. Periodicals - 5. Library resources - 6. Literary studies (*i.e.* guides to general literary research) - 7. Organizations (new section in 2nd ed.). A very useful, compact guide.
Class No: 820.94(01)

[7832]

MILLER, E.M. Australian literature: a bibliography to 1938, extended to 1950. Rev. and extended ed., edited with a historical outline and descriptive commentaries by F.T. Macartney. Sydney and London, Angus and Robertson, 1956. x,503p.

First published Melbourne, Melbourne Univ. Press, 1940, as *Australian literature from its beginnings to 1935 ... with subsidiary entries to 1938*. 2 vols. (Reprinted with addendum of corrections and additions, Sydney, Sydney Univ. Press, 1975).

Covers *c.*5,000 authors (primarily literary), listing their works and providing biographical notes on the major names. Much easier to use than 1st ed. because of its A-Z rather than genre and chronological arrangement (indexes therefore dropped), but the elimination of much descriptive and critical material and the complete omission of certain categories of literature (*e.g.* children's) means that 1st ed. remains an important source. *Class No:* 820.94(01)

[7833]

ROSS, R.L. Australian literary criticism, 1945-1988: an annotated bibliography. New York, Garland, 1989. 375p. $62 ISBN: 082401510x.

Lists nearly 1,400 books and articles written in English, covering general topics, genres and 50 individual authors.
Class No: 820.94(01)

Encyclopaedias & Dictionaries

[7834]

WILDE, W.H., *and others*. The Oxford companion to Australian literature. 2nd ed. Melbourne and Oxford, Oxford Univ. Press, 1994. x,833p. £40. ISBN: 019553381x.

1st ed. 1986.

Over 3,000 entries covering authors (including many non-literary figures, such as historians, journalists and entertainers) and works; literary movements, awards and societies; publishers and libraries; influential foreign writers; and places, events and traditions crucial to Australian literature. Entries for major authors include lists of critical studies. Both *TLS* (no.4388, May 8th, 1987, p.499) and *Review of English Studies* (v.39 (154), May 1988, p.334-5) praise the subject entries (*e.g.* 'War Literature', 'Folk Song and Ballad', 'Criticism') and their meticulous cross-references.

2nd ed. has over 500 new entries, with the rest revised where necessary, and reflects the greater influence of writing by women and members of ethnic minority groups.
Class No: 820.94(03)

Periodicals

[7835]

STUART, L. Nineteenth century Australian periodicals: an annotated bibliography. Sydney, Hale & Iremonger, 1979. viii,200p. illus. ISBN: 0908094531.

Lists 449 periodicals 'which contain literary features in the form of essays, articles, fiction, poetry and minor literary items' (*Introduction*). Arranged A-Z by title, the entries contain a great deal of information, including place of publication, printer, publisher, proprietor, editor, frequency and dates of publication (including dates of title changes), library locations, categorization of contents, and any noted contributors and artists. Bibliography of sources (7p.). Index of printers, publishers, proprietors, editors, contributors, etc. *Class No:* 820.94(051)

Gazetteers

[7836]

The Oxford literary guide to Australia. Pierce, P., *ed., for the Association for the Study of Australian Literature*. Melbourne and London, Oxford Univ. Press, 1988. xvi,344p. illus. maps. £40. ISBN: 0195545923.

A guide to the literary associations of over 930 places in Australia and her territories. Sections on the 4 territories (Antarctica, Capital Territory, Norfolk Island, Northern Territory) and the 6 states, with localities listed A-Z within each section. 250 black and white photographs and 16 colour plates make this a most attractive book but it is also a serious work of scholarship, produced by 14 editors and numerous contributors. 8p. of maps include every locality mentioned in the text and are far superior to those in the equivalent guide to the USA. Index of over 400 authors, but no index of placenames. *Class No:* 820.94(083.86)

Chronologies

[7837]

Annals of Australian literature. Hooton, J. *and* Heseltine, H., *eds*. 2nd ed. Melbourne and Oxford, Oxford Univ. Press, 1993. viii,367p. £32.50. ISBN: 0195534751.

1st ed. 1970, by G. Johnston.

Similar in design to *Annals of English literature* (*q.v.*), consisting of annual lists of noteworthy books from 1789 to 1988, with a parallel column for each year listing births and deaths of authors and other literary events. Very thorough analytical index to both columns, which includes authors' birth and death dates. Includes activities of Australian writers abroad. *Class No:* 820.94(090)

Histories

[7838]

GOODWIN, K. A History of Australian literature. Basingstoke, Macmillan, 1986. xii,322p. illus. £15. (*Macmillan history of literature*.) ISBN: 0333364066.

Narrative history in 11 chapters, with strong emphasis on the 20th century. Select bibliography of background material and critical works (5p.). Chronology of literary and historical events, 1770-1984. *Class No:* 820.94(091)

[7839]

GREEN, H.M. A History of Australian literature, pure and applied: a critical review of all forms of literature produced in Australia from the first books published after the arrival of the First Fleet until 1950. 2nd ed., rev. by D. Green. Sydney and London, Angus & Robertson, 1984. 2v. (1543p.). £27.99 (v.1); £22.50 (v.2). ISBN: 0207138257, v.1; 0207142556, v.2.

First ed. 1961.

The most comprehensive history, which justifies its subtitle by including newspapers and magazines and writing on a whole range of subjects, including history, philosophy, science and the social sciences. Arranged in 4 period divisions: 1789-1850, 1850-1890, 1890-1923 and 1923-1950 (the latter occupying v.2), and 62 chapters devoted to particular genres. Many quotations and footnote references. Select list of reprints and new eds. of works discussed (17p.). Index in v.2.

2nd ed. does not take the survey beyond 1950, but a third vol. is planned for 1950-80. *Class No:* 820.94(091)

[7840]

The Literature of Australia. Dutton, G., *ed*. Rev. ed. Ringwood, Victoria, and Harmondsworth, Penguin, 1976. 612p. ISBN: 0140700080.

First ed. 1964.

A very handy paperback guide in 3 parts. Part 1 has a lengthy essay on 'The Social Setting' followed by histories of the major literary genres. Part 2 comprises critical essays (average 16p.) on 15 key authors. Part 3 is a selective bibliography (66p.) of general reference works and anthologies, and of primary and secondary material relating to over 50 authors, with biographical notes on each. Name index. The work of 23 contributors. *Class No:* 820.94(091)

[7841]

McLAREN, J. Australian literature: an historical introduction. Melbourne, Longman Cheshire, 1989. xix,272p. illus. A$31.50. ISBN: 0582712793.

From Aboriginal legends to the 1980s in a prologue and 15 chapters, with subsections on numerous individual authors and many quotations. Excellent annotated bibliography of general reference works and anthologies, and of primary and secondary material relevant to each

.... (contd.)

chapter. Index. Particularly useful for its coverage of contemporary writers and for its illustrations. *Class No:* 820.94(091)

[7842]

The Oxford history of Australian literature. Kramer, L., *ed*. Melbourne and Oxford, Oxford Univ. Press, 1981. vi,509p. ISBN: 0195505905.

Introduction by editor followed by chapters on fiction, drama and poetry by A. Mitchell, T. Sturm and V. Smith, and bibliography (62p.) in semi-narrative form by J. Hooton, subdivided as follows: Bibliographical and reference aids; General studies; Individual authors (71 names). Index to the text but not to bibliography. Does not cover non-fictional prose or popular literature. *Class No:* 820.94(091)

Biographies

[7843]

Who's who of Australian writers. 2nd ed. Port Melbourne, Thorpe, 1995. x,822p. £52. ISBN: 1875589201.

Published in association with the National Association for Australian Studies at Monash University, Melbourne. 1st ed. 1991.

Over 5,400 entries (200 new) for living writers of fiction, poetry, plays, and radio and TV scripts, as well as textbook and nonfiction authors. Information includes contact details; date and place of birth; awards and honours; publications; employment history; areas of specialization, etc. Includes 1,020 novelists and 1,070 writers of children's books. Comprehensive subject index. *Class No:* 820.94(092)

Women

[7844]

ADELAIDE, D. Australian women writers: a bibliographic guide. London, Pandora, 1988. xiv,208p. £14.95. (*Australian literary heritage*.) ISBN: 086358148x.

'Its purpose is to restore from the past those Australian women writers who have fallen into neglect and to provide a reference for contemporary women writers in the hopes of overcoming the same possibility' (*Introduction*). Biographical notes on 450 writers, arranged A-Z, followed by complete listings of their works, selected secondary bibliography and manuscript locations. Includes many journalists, historians, biographers, etc. as well as literary writers. *Class No:* 820.94-0055.2

[7845]

ADELAIDE, D. Bibliography of Australian women's literature, 1795-1990. Port Melbourne, Thorpe, 1991. 288p. £33. ISBN: 0909532907.

Provides full bibliographic citations for 11,560 works by 3,828 authors. Includes author checklists by genre. *Class No:* 820.94-0055.2

Australian Poetry

[7846]

Australian poets and their works: a reader's guide. Wilde, W.H., *ed*. Oxford, Oxford Univ. Press, 1996. 350p. £13.99. ISBN: 0195537696.

Assembles over 800 entries (updated where necessary) from *The Oxford companion to Australian literature* (*q.v.*) covering poets, poems, folk songs, prizes, journals and anthologies. Also includes some longer thematic articles. *Class No:* 820.94-1

[7847]

JAFFA, H.C. Modern Australian poetry, 1920-1970: a guide to information sources. Detroit, Gale, 1979. xviii,241p. ISBN: 0810312425.

4 sections on general sources but the bulk of the book is devoted to listings of primary and secondary material for individual poets. Also sections on schools, movements, etc. *Class No:* 820.94-1

[7848]

MURRAY, S. Bibliography of Australian poetry, 1935-1955. Port Melbourne, Thorpe, 1991. xii,274p. $A45. ISBN: 1875589007.

An annotated bibliography of all locatable vols. and pamphlets of poetry published over a 20-year period. 1,247 entries arranged by author, A-Z, with locations. Date and place indexes. The first of a series of Working Papers to be produced by the *Bibliography of Australian literature* project, which is ultimately expected to list some 35,000 titles by over 7,000 authors. *Class No:* 820.94-1

Australian Drama

[7849]

REES, L. A History of Australian drama. Sydney, Angus and Robertson, 1978-87. 2v. illus. ISBN: 0207138400, v.1; 020715354x, v.2.

V.1 *The Making of Australian drama: from the 1830s to the late 1960s*. 1978 (xii,435p. £10.75). A revised and expanded version of *Towards an Australian drama* (Sydney, 1953).

V.2 *Australian drama, 1970-85: a history and critical survey*. 1987 (vi,400p. £14.95). Expanded version of *Australian drama in the 1970s* (Sydney, 1978).

A comprehensive history of the genre. Chapters on individual writers and movements. Appendices include lists of plays published since 1936 (earlier works covered by Miller) and of radio and TV plays. Notes on theatres and companies. Select bibliography of critical studies. *Class No:* 820.94-2

Australian Fiction

[7850]

CLANCY, L. A Reader's guide to Australian fiction. Melbourne, Oxford Univ. Press, 1993. 382p. £15.95. ISBN: 0195546202.

A chronological account of the major Australian fiction writers from 1830 to the 1990s. Brief biographical information on the authors is accompanied by critical discussion of their work. *Class No:* 820.94-3

[7851]

DAY, A.G. Modern Australian prose, 1901-1975: a guide to information sources. Detroit, Gale, 1980. xix,462p. ISBN: 0810312433.

Covers fiction, selected nonfiction and drama, listing general sources and material on individual authors. Over 2,600 entries, many annotated. Author, title and subject indexes. *Class No:* 820.94-3

83 Germanic Literatures

German Literature

Bibliographies

[7852]

Bibliographie der deutschen Sprach- und Literaturwissenschaft. Bd.1 (1945/53)-. Frankfurt am Main, Klostermann, 1957-. Annual.

As *Bibliographie der deutschen Literaturwissenschaft* until Bd.8 (1967-8).

A comprehensive, unannotated bibliography of writings (including dissertations) on German language and literature. Bd.36: *1996* (1997. xxx,974p.) has 12,106 entries in 16 sections: 1. General - 2. Language - 3-16. Literature, by period, with subsections for genres and individual writers. List of over 800 periodicals surveyed. Name and subject indexes.

Cumulation from 1990 available on CD-ROM, with full-text searching capabilities. Updated annually.
Class No: 830(01)

[7853]

—KÖTTELWESCH, C. Bibliographisches Handbuch der deutschen Litteraturwissenschaft, 1945-1969. Frankfurt am Main, Klostermann, 1973-79. 3v.

V.1 *Von den Anfängen bis zur Romantik.* 1973. xxxii,xvi,2398 cols.

V.2 *1830 bis zur Gegenwart.* 1975. xliii,1995 cols. (This vol. extends coverage to 1972).

V.3 *Register.* 1979. xiv,1007 cols.

A select (but nevertheless very substantial) bibliography of primary and secondary literature, extracted from *Bibliographie der deutschen Sprach- und Literaturwissenschaft.* Lists *c.*100,000 items in a classified arrangement, including extensive bibliographies for many individual authors. V.3 has indexes of critics, authors as subjects, and topics. *Class No:* 830(01)

[7854]

Germanistik: internationales Referatenorgan mit bibliographischen Hinweisen. Tübingen, Niemeyer, 1960-. v.1-. Quarterly. ISSN: 00168912.

An international bibliography of books, articles, and dissertations on German language and literature. Books are usually given signed reviews, but periodical articles are not annotated. Classified arrangement, with annual name and subject indexes in part 4. V.36, 1995, has 6,106 entries in 34 sections. 'The most valuable source available to German scholars for keeping abreast of developments in the field' (Faulhaber and Goff, *German literature,* 1979, p.38).
Class No: 830(01)

[7855]

GOEDEKE, K. Grundriss zur Geschichte der deutschen Dichtung aus den Quellen. 2., ganz neu bearb. Aufl. Düsseldorf, Ehlermann, 1884-1953; Berlin, Akademie-Verlag, 1959-66. 15v.

1st ed. 1859-81.

V.1 *Das Mittelalter* [to 1515]. 1884.

V.2 *Das Reformationszeitalter* [1515-1600]. 1886.

V.3 *Vom dreissigjährigen bis zum siebenjährigen Kriege* [1600-1750]. 1887.

V.4-5 *Vom siebenjährigen bis zum Weltkriege* [1750-*c.*1800]. 1891-93.

V.6-7 *Zeit des Weltkrieges* [Romantic movement]. 1898-1900.

V.8-15 *Vom Weltfrieden bis zur französischen Revolution, 1830* [Late Romantic authors]. 1905-1966.

Further vols. are planned.

The most complete bibliography of German literature up to 1830. Bio-bibliographical entries, with critical comments on literary works and comprehensive lists of editions, translations, critical studies, etc. Each vol. has index, but access to the work has been greatly improved by the publication of H. Rambaldo's *Index zu Goedeke* (Nendeln, Liechtenstein, Kraus-Thomson, 1975. 393p.).

V.4 has appeared in a 3rd ed., issued in 5 parts (pts. 1-4, 1906-13, and pt.5, 1960). V.4, pt.5, is *Goethe-Bibliographie, 1912-1950* (997p.), by C. Diesch and P. Schlager, containing *c.*17,500 entries.

Deutsches Schriftstellerlexikon, 1830-1880: Goedekes Grundriss ... Fortführung, ed. by H. Jacob (Berlin, Akademie-Verlag, 1995- ,v.1-), continues where Goedeke leaves off, with extensive bibliographies of authors who were first published between 1830 and 1880 but excluding all others, even if the main body of their work falls within that period. V.1 (1995. 714p. DM248. ISBN: 3050021209) covers the letters 'A-B'. *Class No:* 830(01)

[7856]

—HIRSCHBERG, L. Der Taschengoedeke: Bibliographie deutscher Erstausgeben. Stuttgart, Deutscher Taschenbuch Verlag, 1990. 616p. DM.29.80. ISBN: 3423030267.

First published 1924.

Lists first editions of German literature from 1650 to the 1870s, with references to Goedeke. Some non-literary works included. Nearly 50,000 titles listed under 3,200 authors, A-Z.

The first editions listed have been made available on microfiche by K.G. Saur (München), 1990-94, under the title *Bibliothek der deutschen Literatur,* (ISBN: 3598500017, silver halide, $30,320; ISBN: 3598500009, diazo, $20,555). The full set comprises nearly 20,000 fiches. An index to the miocrofiche collection was published in 1994 (xv,584p. DM48. ISBN: 3598501005) and is free to subscribers of the completed edition. *Class No:* 830(01)

[7857]
Handbuch der Editionen: deutschsprachige Schriftsteller, Ausgang des 15. Jahrhunderts bis zur Gegenwart. Hagen, W., *and others, eds.* 2., unveränderte Aufl. München, Beck, 1981. 608p. ISBN: 3406041396.

First published Berlin, Volk und Wissen, 1979.

Detailed accounts of authoritative editions of the works of 239 key writers from 1480 to the present. A-Z arrangement. Notes on the editions include details of any textual commentary or other scholarly apparatus.
Class No: 830(01)

[7858]
Quellenlexikon zur deutschen Literaturgeschichte: Personal- und Einzelwerkbibliographien der internationalen Sekundärliteratur 1945-1990 zur deutschen Literatur von den Anfängen bis zur Gegenwart. Schmidt, H., *ed.* Duisburg, Verlag für Pädagogische Dokumentation, 1994-. v.1- (in progress).

V.1 *A-Bau.* 1994. 512p. DM198. ISBN: 3930551012.

An ambitious project which aims to record postwar critical studies on German writers of all periods. Includes bibliographies, articles in reference books, chapters in literary histories, periodical articles, etc. *Class No:* 830(01)

[7859]
SCHNEIDER, M. Deutsches Titelbuch: ein Hilfsmittel zum Nachweis von Verfassern deutscher Literaturwerke. 2., verb. und wesentlich verm. Aufl. Berlin, Paschke, 1927. viii,798p.

1st ed. 1907-9, as *Von wem ist das doch?*

Index of *c.*35,000 titles of literary works and first lines of poems in a single A-Z sequence, with date and author given. 19th-century works predominate. Index of authors and subjects. List of pseudonyms. Continued by:
Class No: 830(01)

[7860]
—AHNERT, H.-J. Deutsches Titelbuch 2; ein Hilfsmittel... 1915-1965, mit Nachträgen und Berichtigungen zum *Deutschen Titelbuch 1* für die Zeit von 1900 bis 1914. Berlin, Haude & Spener, 1966. xii,636p.

Over 20,000 entries, with each title followed by genre designation, author, and publication date. Unlike its predecessor, it is restricted to book titles - no poem titles or first lines. Keyword index. *Class No:* 830(01)

[7861]
SCHUMANN, A. Bibliographie zur deutschen Literaturgeschichtsschreibung, 1827-1945. München, Saur, 1994. xxxii,278p. DM.198. ISBN: 3598112297.

Lists and describes *c.*600 first editions of German-language works on German literary history. Later eds. are also listed, giving a total of *c.*1,950 entries. Author index includes detailed biographical notes. Further indexes give access via publisher, place, date and keyword.

A more comprehensive source is W. Fritsch-Rössler's *Bibliographie der deutschen Literaturgeschichten, mit Kommentar, Rezensionsangaben und Standortnachweisen* (Frankfurt am Main, Lang, 1994-). V.1, *1835-1899* (297p. ISBN: 363147055x), lists titles chronologically, with detailed descriptions, commentary and references to reviews.
Class No: 830(01)

[7862]
WILPERT, G. von *and* **GÜHRING, A. Erstausgaben deutscher Dichtung:** eine Bibliographie zur deutschen Literatur, 1600-1960. Stuttgart, Kröner, 1967. x,1468p.

Lists *c.*47,000 first editions of works by 1,360 authors, giving pagination and place and date of publication. Arranged A-Z by author, with chronological lists of works for each. Index of pseudonyms. *Class No:* 830(01)

17th & 18th Centuries

[7863]
Bibliographie zur deutschen Literaturgescichte des Barockzeitalters. Pyritz, H., *& others, eds.* Bern, Saur (previously Francke), 1985-94. 3v.

V.1 *Kultur- und Geistesgeschichte - Poetik - Gattungen - Traditionen - Beziehungen - Stoffe.* 1991. xxvii,738p. DM.320. ISBN: 3907820584.

V.2 *Dichter und Schriftsteller - Anonymes - Textsammlungen.* 1985. xxi,810p. DM.320. ISBN: 3907820622.

V.3 *Gesamtregister.* 1994. 220p. DM.248. ISBN: 3907820630.

A comprehensive bibliography with 9,033 numbered entries covering general background material (v.1) and studies of individual writers and works (v.2). V.3 has indexes of subjects, people and places.
Class No: 830(01)"16/17"

[7864]
DÜNNHAUPT, G. Personalbibliographie zu den Drucken des Barock. 2. Aufl. Stuttgart, Hiersemann, 1990-93. 6v. ISBN: 3777290122.

1st ed. 1980-81, as *Bibliographisches Handbuch der Barockliteratur* (3v.).

Descriptive bibliographies of the works of Baroque writers, A-Z, with lists of book-length critical studies and brief biographical notes. V.6 has several indexes, including names and pseudonyms; anonymous titles; publishers and booksellers. *Class No:* 830(01)"16/17"

[7865]
STIFTUNG WEIMARER KLASSIK. Herzogin Anna Amalia Bibliothek. **Internationale Bibliographie zur deutschen Klassik, 1750-1850:** Bibliographien und Kataloge der Herzogin Anna Amalia Bibliothek zu Weimar. Weimar, Nationale Forschungs- und Gedenkstätten der klassischen deutschen Dichtung, 1960-1993; München, Saur 1994-. v.1- (in progress). ISSN: 03235734.

Early vols. published in the periodical *Zeitschrift für deutsche Literaturgeschichte*; in book form since 1970.

The most complete and accurate bibliographical tool on the literature and history of the Classic and Romantic periods. V.39 (1994. 542p. ISBN: 3598233701) lists *c.*5,000 German and foreign publications from 1992, including studies of individual writers, sound recordings and translations of primary texts. *Class No:* 830(01)"16/17"

20th Century

[7866]
Deutschsprachige Exilliteratur seit 1933. Spalek, J.M., *and others, eds.* München, Saur, 1976-94. v.1-4 (in progress).

V.1 *Kalifornien.* 1976. 2v. (viii,1084p.). ISBN: 3907820444.

V.2 *New York.* 1989. 2v. (xxx,1817p.). ISBN: 3907820452.

V.3 *USA* (due 1998. ISBN: 3907820460).

V.4 *Bibliographien: Schriftsteller, Publizisten und*

.... *(contd.)*
Literaturwissenschaftler in den USA. 1994. 3v. (lix,2110p.). ISBN: 3907820479.

Detailed bibliographies of exiled German writers, not all of them literary authors. V.4 has entries for 225 writers, comprising review of state of bibliographical research; chronologically arranged primary bibliography; list of biographical and critical studies of the author; and list of reviews and studies of individual works.
Class No: 830(01)"19"

[7867]
Index Expressionismus; Bibliographie der Beiträge in den Zeitschriften und Jahrbüchern des literarischen Expressionismus, 1910-1925. Raabe, P., *ed.* Nendeln, Liechtenstein, Kraus-Thomson, 1972. 18v.

Indexes contributions to 100 periodicals and 5 yearbooks associated with the German Expressionist movement. 5 A-Z sequences: v.1-4, authors; v.5-9, subjects; v.10-14, serial titles (with full contents listings for each serial); v.15-16, article titles; v.17-18, genres. *Class No:* 830(01)"19"

[7868]
—RAABE, P. Die Autoren und Bücher des literarischen Expressionismus: ein bibliographisches Handbuch. Stuttgart, Metzler, 1985. xiv,1002p. illus. ISBN: 3476005755.

Part A., Lexikon, lists 347 German Expressionist authors, A-Z, giving biographical notes and lists of works. Part B., Repertorium, has a wide variety of useful lists, including authors grouped by birth-date, birth-place, etc.; books by genre, title, date, etc.; illustrators; posthumous works, etc. Part C., Übersichten, has book lists for 4 periods, each subdivided by genre. Index of illustrators and general name index. Superbly produced. *Class No:* 830(01)"19"

[7869]
KREWSON, M.B. Contemporary authors of the German-speaking countries of Europe: a selective bibliography Washington, D.C., Library of Congress, 1988. 306p. ISBN: 0844406139.

Lists the holdings of the Library of Congress pertaining to the major modern authors of East and West Germany, Austria and Switzerland. Separate sections for each country, with general reference sources followed by works by and about individual authors. *Class No:* 830(01)"19"

[7870]
WIESNER, H., *and others*. Bibliographie der Personalbibliographien zur deutschen Gegenwartsliteratur. München, Nymphenburger Verlagshandlung, 1970. 359p.

Provides primary and secondary bibliographies for some 500 20th-century German-language authors, in addition to biography, evaluations of research, and archival information. 'Excellent reference work' (Faulhaber, U.K. and Goff, P.B., *German literature*, 1979, p.56). *Class No:* 830(01)"19"

Nazi Germany

[7871]
STERNFELD, W. *and* TIEDEMANN, E. Deutsche Exil-Literatur, 1933-45: eine Bio-Bibliographie. 2. verb. und stark erw. Aufl. Heidelberg, Lambert Schneider, 1970. 606p.

1st ed. 1962.

Brief biographical notes on *c.*1,900 German exiles, with lists of their writings. Appended lists of series, anonyma and pseudonyma, almanacs, anthologies, periodicals, and publishers. *Class No:* 830(01)"1933-1945"

Encyclopaedias & Dictionaries

[7872]
Die Deutsche Literatur: biographisches und bibliographisches Lexikon. Roloff, H.-G., *ed.* Bern, Lang, 1985- (in progress). illus.

A massive, long-term project, with separate sections progressing simultaneously. Bd.1 of Reihe II, *1450-1620*, comprises 15 fascicles (1213p.) and is still on the letter 'A'. It includes very lengthy author entries with descriptive primary bibliographies and detailed classified bibliographies of secondary literature, with indexes of historic people, subjects, places, printers, places of publication, and libraries. Reihe III, *1620-1720*, IV, *1720-1830*, and VI, *1890-1990*, are also in progress. *Class No:* 830(03)

[7873]
The Feminist encyclopedia of German literature. Eigler, F. *and* Kord, S., *eds.* Westport, Conn., Greenwood, 1997. xiii,676p. £79.50. ISBN: 0313293139.

Over 500 signed entries, A-Z, but under 40 cover writers and even fewer are on literary works. The majority cover topics, such as literary periods and genres; critical approaches and theories; concepts and themes; female stereotypes; and organizations and archives relevant to women's literary studies. Brief bibliography with each entry. Appendix has list of all personal names with dates and references to all entries in which they appear. Index.
Class No: 830(03)

[7874]
GARLAND, H. *and* GARLAND, M. The Oxford companion to German literature. 3rd ed. Oxford, Oxford Univ. Press, 1997. x,951p. £45. ISBN: 0198158963.

1st ed. 1976; 2nd ed. 1986.

Aims 'to produce a Companion to the historical and cultural background to German literature as well as to the writers and works themselves' (*Preface to 1st ed.*). *c.*4,000 entries, in a single A-Z sequence of authors, works, literary movements, genres, events, places, etc. (but no characters), covering the literature of German-speaking countries since *c.*800AD. Brief bibliographies with some author entries. 3rd ed. brings coverage up to the mid-1990s, with 80 new entries and thorough revisions to 200 others, paying more attention to 20th-century literature and women writers.
Class No: 830(03)

[7875]
Hauptwerke der deutschen Literatur: über 1,000 Einzeldarstellungen und Interpretationen zu den Epochen der deutschen Literatur. Radler, R., *ed.* München, Kindler, 1994. 2v. DM39.80 per vol. ISBN: 3463402637.

1st ed. 1974, in 1 vol.

Bd.1 *Von den Anfängen bis zur Romantik.*

Bd.2 *Von Vormärz bis zur Gegenwartsliteratur.*

A compilation of selected articles from *Kindlers Literaturlexikon*, providing summaries of and commentaries on major German literary works. Arranged by period, then by author. Index of authors with their works, but no title index. *Class No:* 830(03)

[7876]
Literaturlexikon: Autoren und Werke deutscher Sprache. Killy, W., *ed.* München, Bertelsmann, 1988-94. 15v. illus. DM2,200.

A very impressive encyclopedia of German literature containing over 10,000 articles by more than 1,000 contributors. Vols. 1-12 have entries for authors and works, A-Z, each vol. having *c.*1,000 entries in 500p. Author entries include biography, some critical evaluation and

....*(contd.)*
selective primary and secondary bibliographies. Vols. 13-14 have *c*.300 lengthy articles on literary terms, periods, genres, movements, etc., plus book production and publishing, all with substantial bibliographies. V.15 has indexes of names, subjects and anonymous works. Many colour illustrations. *Class No:* 830(03)

[7877]
Reallexikon der deutschen Literaturgeschichte, begründet von Paul Merker und Wolfgang Stammler. Kohlschmidt, W., *and others, eds.* 2. Aufl. Berlin, de Gruyter, 1958-88. 5v.

1st ed. 1925-31 (4v.).

Issued in parts over a long period and comprising lengthy, signed articles on genres, periods, schools, movements and styles of German literature, but no entries on individual writers. Extensive bibliographies of primary and secondary material. Over 400 entries, A-Z, in vols. 1-4, with detailed subject index in v.5 (1988. xxviii,510p.). *Class No:* 830(03)

Handbooks & Manuals

[7878]
BLINN, H. Informationshandbuch deutsche Literaturwissenschaft. 3. Aufl. Frankfurt am Main, Fischer-Taschenbuch-Verlag, 1994. 490p. DM24.90. ISBN: 359612588x.

1st ed. 1982; 2nd ed. 1990.

A comprehensive and well-organized guide to library research in German literature and theatre and the German-language media. Over 2,400 annotated entries in separate sections covering reference sources, bibliographies, periodicals, collections, archives, literary societies, literary prizes, etc. Useful list of author bibliographies. Index. *Class No:* 830(035)

[7879]
FAULHABER, U.K. *and* **GOFF, P.B. German literature: an annotated reference guide.** New York, Garland, 1979. x,398p. ISBN: 0824098315.

Lists 2,046 information sources on German literature and related subjects (folklore, philosophy, etc.) in 13 sections. Pays particular attention to works in English and evaluates each one 'from the standpoint of quality, reliability, currency and usefulness' (*Preface*). Index of authors, titles and subjects. *Class No:* 830(035)

[7880]
HANSEL, J. Bücherkunde für Germanisten: Studienausgabe. Tschakert, L., *ed.* 9., neubearb. Aufl. Berlin, E. Schmidt, 1992. 232p. ISBN: 3503030190.

1st ed. 1959, with the subtitle *Wie sammelt man das Schrifttum nach dem neuesten Forschungsstand?* 8th ed. 1983.

A very useful annotated guide to the basic reference works and information sources in German language and literature. *c.*1,200 entries in 5 sections, covering general reference works; monographic subject bibliographies; serial bibliographies (specialized); serial bibliographies (general); and periodicals. Useful introductions to each section. Author-title and subject indexes. *Class No:* 830(035)

[7881]
RAABE, P., *and others*. **Einführung in die Bücherkunde zur deutschen Literaturwissenschaft.** 11. unveränd. Aufl. Stuttgart, Metzler, 1994. viii,148p. DM19.80. ISBN: 347611001x.

1st ed. 1961; 10th ed. 1989.

A practical, frequently-updated introduction to the key reference and bibliographic tools on German literature, describing them and explaining how to use them as well as giving bibliographic details. 462 entries in 11th ed. Index of authors and titles. *Class No:* 830(035)

[7882]
RICHARDSON, L.L. Introduction to library research in German studies: language, literature, and civilization. Boulder, Colo., Westview Press, 1984. xx,227p. ISBN: 0865311951.

Much of this handbook is devoted to the use of libraries and bibliographic searching techniques, but 251 major reference sources in German studies are evaluated. Index of authors, titles, and subjects. *Class No:* 830(035)

Theses

[7883]
GABEL, G.U. Verzeichnis französischer Dissertationen (1885-1990) zur deutschsprachigen Literatur vom Mittelalter bis zum 20. Jahrhundert. Hürth, Gemini, 1996. 144p. ISBN: 3922331416.

868 unannotated entries arranged by author in 7 sections covering general studies, the Middle Ages and the 16th to 20th centuries. Author and subject indexes. *Class No:* 830(043)

[7884]
Theses in Germanic studies: a catalogue of theses and dissertations in the field of Germanic studies (excluding English) approved for higher degrees in the universities of Great Britain and Ireland between 1903 and 1961. Norman, F., *ed.* London, Univ. of London, Institute of Germanic Studies, 1962. viii,46p. £5. ISBN: 0854570152.

Lists 455 theses by author, A-Z, giving title, degree awarded, university, and year. Subject index.

Continued by *Theses in Germanic studies, 1962-1967,* (1968. vi,18p. £1.25. ISBN: 0854570322); *1967-72* (1973. vi,18p. £1.20. ISBN: 0854570551); and *1972-77* (1980. £4.90); then by: *Class No:* 830(043)

[7885]
—UNIVERSITY OF LONDON. Institute of Germanic Studies. Research in Germanic studies, 1980/81-. London, The Institute, 1981-. Annual. ISSN: 02605929.

Known as *Theses in progress at British universities and other institutions of higher education* from 1970 to 1980.

The 1995-96 issue (1994. vii,95p.) has 4 classified lists: theses completed in 1995; theses in progress; work (*i.e.* books and contributions) published in 1995; work due to be published in 1995. Also available on the Internet (http://www.abdn.ac.uk/er042/) and the printed version is not likely to be produced for much longer. *Class No:* 830(043)

Periodicals

[7886]
DIETZEL, T. *and* **HÜGEL, H.-O. Deutsche literarische Zeitschriften, 1880-1945:** ein Repertorium. München, K.G. Saur, 1988. 5v. DM.880 ISBN: 3598106459.

Vols. 1-4 list 3,341 titles, A-Z. Detailed entries include publication dates, bibliographical details, categorization,

.... *(contd.)*
major contributors, etc. V.5 has indexes to editors, contributors, publishers, places, and subjects.

Continued by *Deutsche literarische Zeitschriften, 1945-1970: ein Repertorium*, ed. by B. Fischer and T. Dietzel (1992. 4v. DM.780. ISBN: 3598220006), which is similarly arranged, with 1,331 entries in vols. 1-3 and indexes in v.4. *Class No:* 830(051)

[7887]

ESTERMANN, A. Die Deutschen Literatur-Zeitschriften, 1850-1880. München, K.G. Saur, 1987-89. 6v. (lxx, 2954p.). DM.1,490. ISBN: 3598107080.

A comprehensive bibliography of literary periodicals, listing 2,953 titles in vols. 1-5 with indexes in v.6. Collations of each individual year, including publication details and notes on publishing history, follow an introduction providing a comprehensive review of all titles under which each periodical was published. Includes detailed information on proprietors, editors, publishers, printers, and contributors.

Preceded by *Die Deutschen Literatur-Zeitschriften, 1815-1850* (2. Aufl. 1990. 11v. DM.3,278. ISBN: 3598107234). *Class No:* 830(051)

[7888]

KUHLES, D. Deutsche literarische Zeitschriften von der Aufklärung bis zur Romantik: Bibliographie der kritischen Literatur von den Anfängen bis 1990. München, Saur, 1994. 2v. (lxiii,610p.). DM.360. ISBN: 3598111592.

Lists and describes *c.*3,000 critical studies of early German periodicals, including foreign-language publications. Classified arrangement with indexes of titles, names and subjects. *Class No:* 830(051)

Yearbooks & Directories

[7889]

Literarische Gesellschaften in Deutschland: ein Handbuch. Kussin, C., *comp.* [New ed.]. Berlin, Aufbau-Verlag, 1995. 390p. DM49.90. ISBN: 3351024355.

Previous ed. 1991.

Provides information (addresses, publications, museums, libraries, etc.) on 110 German literary societies, most of them devoted to specific authors. *Class No:* 830(058)

Excerpts

[7890]

Modern German literature. Domandi, A.K., *comp.* New York, Ungar, 1972. 2v. ISBN: 0804430756.

Excerpts from critical studies by over 700 critics on *c.*200 20th-century writers from Germany, Austria and Switzerland. Many excerpts translated from German for this work. Index of critics. *Class No:* 830(082.200)

Chronologies

[7891]

Annalen der deutschen Literatur. Berger, H.O., *ed.* 2., überarbeitete Aufl. Stuttgart, Metzler, 1971. 838p. ISBN: 347600029x.

1st ed. 1952.

An extremely detailed chronological survey from 200BC to 1900AD. 12 sections, in which specialists summarize the major works of each period. Summary table appended (50p.). Index of names, titles, and periodicals.
Class No: 830(090)

[7892]

FRENZEL, H.A. *and* **FRENZEL, E. Daten deutscher Dichtung:** Chronologischer Abriss der deutschen Literaturgeschichte von den Anfängen bis zur Gegenwart. München, Deutscher Taschenbuch, 1990. 2v. DM16.90 per vol. ISBN: 3423030038, v.1; 3423030046, v.2.

First published Köln, Kiepenheuer & Witsch, 1953. Regularly updated.

Annotated chronological lists of literary works within sections for the major periods of German literature since the 8th century. Lists of authors, with biographical notes. Author index. *Class No:* 830(090)

[7893]

MEID, V. Metzler-Literatur-Chronik: Werke deutschsprachiger Autoren. Stuttgart, Metzler, 1993. 724p. DM58. ISBN: 3476009416.

A literary history in the form of an annotated, chronological listing of 1,500 works of German literature from the 8th century to 1980. *Class No:* 830(090)

Histories

[7894]

BEUTIN, W., ***and others*****. A History of German literature,** from the beginnings to the present day. Krojzl, C., *trans.* 4th ed. London, Routledge, 1993. x,800p. £65. ISBN: 0415060346.

1st ed. 1979; this is an English translation of the 3rd ed. (Metzler, 1989) with an additional chapter on the early 1990s.

15 chronologically-arranged chapters by 9 authors. English translation given for all cited titles. Bibliography (13p.) of general studies, arranged by chapter. Index.
Class No: 830(091)

[7895]

The Cambridge history of German literature. Watanabe-O'Kelly, H., *ed.* Cambridge, Cambridge Univ. Press, 1997. xiii,613p. £65. ISBN: 0521434173.

A solid, narrative history from 750 to 1990 in 9 chapters, including one on East Germany, each by a different specialist. All titles and quotations translated. Select bibliography of secondary sources (76p.), arranged by chapter, 'aims to provide a starting point for the advanced undergraduate and the intelligent layperson' and lists some primary sources for the pre-1450 period. 'Even with its warts, ... the best single-volume history of the totality of German literature' (*TLS*, no.4950, Feb. 13, 1998, p.26).
Class No: 830(091)

[7896]

A Concise history of German literature to 1900. Vivian, K., *ed.* Columbia, S.C., Camden House, 1992. xi,345p. £40. ISBN: 1879751291.

12 chapters, each by a different scholar, on the major periods. All quotations in English translation. Further reading arranged by period (11p.). Index includes authors' birth and death dates. *Class No:* 830(091)

[7897]

Geschichte der deutschen Literatur von den Anfängen bis zur Gegenwart. Boor, H. de *and* Newald, R., *eds.* München, Beck, 1949-90. v.1-7, 12 (in progress).

V.1 *Die Deutsche Literatur von Karl dem Grossen bis zum Beginn der höfischen Dichtung (770-1170)*, by H. de Boor. 9. Aufl. 1979. viii,342p.

V.2 *Die Höfische Literatur: Vorbereitung, Blüte, Ausklang (1170-1250)*, by H. de Boor. 11. Aufl. 1991. x,494p.

V.3 *Die Deutsche Literatur im späten Mittelalter: Zerfall*

....*(contd.)*
und Neubeginn (1250-1400), by H. de Boor and I. Glier. 1973-87. 2 pts.

V.4 *Die Deutsche Literatur vom späten Mittelalter bis zum Barock (1370-1570)*, by H. Rupprich. 1973-94. 2 pts.

V.5 *Die Deutsche Literatur vom Späthumanismus zur Empfindsamkeit (1570-1750)*, by R. Newald. 6. Aufl. 1967. ix,592p.

V.6 *Aufklärung, Sturm und Drang, Frühe Klassik (1740-1789)*, by S.A. Jørgensen and others, 1990. xiii,665p.

V.7 *Die Deutsche Literatur zwischen Französischer Revolution und Restauration (1789-1830)*, by G. Schulz. 1983-89. 2 pts.

V.12 *Geschichte der deutschen Literatur von 1945 bis zur Gegenwart*, ed. by W. Barner. 1994. xxiv,1116p.

The standard multi-vol. history, the first part of which was originally published in 1949 but several of the earlier vols. have since appeared in revised eds. Each vol. comprises survey chapters chronologically arranged, extensive chapter bibliographies, chronological table and index.
Class No: 830(091)

[7898]
SAGARRA, E. *and* **SKRINE, P. A Companion to German literature,** from 1500 to the present. Oxford, Blackwell, 1997. xii,380p. £60. ISBN: 0631171223.

A history of the literature of the whole German-speaking area of Europe in 9 generically-structured narrative chapters. Good coverage of traditionally neglected women writers. Biographical index is a valuable reference source, with notes on 600 writers. General index. 6 maps. 'One of the great strengths ... is its emphasis on extra-literary forces, cultural, technological, linguistic, political, geographic' (*TLS*, no.4950, Feb. 13, 1998, p.26). *Class No:* 830(091)

Middle Ages

[7899]
BOSTOCK, J.K. A Handbook on Old High German literature. 2nd ed., rev. by K.C. King and D.R. McLintock. Oxford, Clarendon Press, 1976. xv,344p. maps. £47.50. ISBN: 0198153929.

1st ed. 1955.

A history of the vernacular literature of Germany from the 8th century to the 11th century, in 16 chapters with many bibliographical footnote references and quotations with translations. Appendix (25p.) on Old Saxon and Old High German metre. General bibliography of standard reference works (5p.). Index. *Class No:* 830(091)"01/14"

Biographies

[7900]
Dictionary of literary biography. Detroit, Gale, 1978-98. v.1-188 (in progress). £112 per vol.

The following vols. cover German literature:

V.56 *German fiction writers, 1914-1945*. 1987.

V.66 *German fiction writers, 1885-1913*. 1988.

V.69 *Contemporary German fiction writers: first series*. 1988.

V.75 *Contemporary German fiction writers: second series*. 1988.

V.90 *German writers in the Age of Goethe, 1786-1832: first series*. 1990.

V.94 *German writers in the Age of Goethe: Sturm und Drang to Classicism*. 1990.

V.97 *German writers from the Enlightenment to Sturm und Drang, 1720-1764*. 1990.

....*(contd.)*
V.118 *Twentieth-century German dramatists, 1889-1918*. 1992.

V.124 *Twentieth-century German dramatists, 1919-1992*. 1992.

V.129 *Nineteenth-century German writers, 1841-1900*. 1993.

V.133 *Nineteenth-century German writers to 1840*. 1993.

V.138 *German writers and works of the High Middle Ages, 1170-1280*. 1994.

V.148 *German writers and works of the Early Middle Ages, 800-1170*. 1994.

V.164 *German Baroque writers, 1580-1660*. 1996.

V.168 *German Baroque writers, 1661-1730*. 1996.

V.179 *German writers of the Renaissance and Reformation, 1280-1580*. 1997.

For a description of the series, see entry at 82(092).
Class No: 830(092)

[7901]
KOSCH, W. Deutsches Literatur-Lexikon: biographisches und bibliographisches Handbuch. Berger, B., *and others, eds*. 3., völlig neu bearb. Aufl. Bern, Francke (later Saur), 1968-1997. v.1-17. *Ergänzungsband* 1-5 (in progress). ISBN: 3907820002.

1st ed. 1927-30 (2v.); 2nd ed. 1947-58 (4v.).

Whereas earlier eds. contained entries for literary terms, place-names, allusions, etc., this is essentially a biobibliographical dictionary of German authors. The signed entries are arranged A-Z, have reached Siewert with v.17, and comprise outline biography (no commentary), comprehensive primary bibliography, and selected secondary bibliography. Includes non-literary writers, such as historians, theologians, philosophers, etc., and some anonymous works under titles. Over 5,000 entries per vol.

A supplementary series was launched in 1994, the first 5 vols. covering 'A - Lyser'.

Deutsches Literatur-Lexikon: Ausgabe in einem Band (Bern, Francke, 1963. 511p.) is a single-vol. abridgement of the 2nd ed., omitting most of the subject entries.
Class No: 830(092)

[7902]
Kürschners deutscher Literatur-Kalender. Berlin, de Gruyter, 1879-. Irregular.

A thorough who's who of German-language writers from Germany and other countries. Entries include address, biographical notes, prizes won, primary bibliography, and (in some cases) selected list of secondary works. Appendices list translators, publishers, periodicals, literary societies, prizes, etc. Also includes geographical index, necrology of recently deceased authors, and a calendar of birthdays. The *Literatur-Kalendar* was last published in 1988 (xx,1691p. ISBN: 3110109018).

K.G. Saur announce a microfiche edition for 1998, including all issues from no. 40 (1922) to no. 60 (1988) plus *Nekrolog*, 1936-1970, on *c*.240 fiches (DM2,400. ISBN: 3598337558). *Class No:* 830(092)

[7903]
—Kürschners deutscher Literatur-Kalender: Nekrolog, 1901-1935. Lüdtke, G., *ed*. Berlin, de Gruyter, 1936. 976 cols. ISBN: 3110044323.

A collection of biographies (with date and place of death added), reprinted from the *Literatur-Kalendar*, of *c*.3,700 authors who died 1901-35.

Continued by: ...*Nekrolog, 1936-1970*, hrsg. von W. Schuder (Berlin, 1973. 871p. ISBN: 3110043815).
Class No: 830(092)

[7904]

Metzler Autorenlexikon: deutschsprachige Dichter und Schriftsteller vom Mittelalter bis zur Gegenwart. Lutz, B., *ed.* 2. überarb. und erw. Aufl. Stuttgart, Metzler, 1994. 905p. illus. DM78. ISBN: 3476009122.

1st ed. 1986.

Signed entries (average 2p.) on *c.*450 authors (300 in 1st ed.) of all periods, giving place and date of birth and death, portrait, critical assessment, and references to a couple of biographical/critical studies. Bibliography of major reference works on German literature (2p.). Over 130 contributors. Name index. *Class No:* 830(092)

[7905]

WILPERT, G. von. Deutsches Dichterlexikon: biographisch-bibliographisches Handwörterbuch zur deutschen Literaturgeschichte. 3. erw. Aufl. Stuttgart, Kröner, 1988. 911p. ISBN: 3520288036.

1st ed. 1963; 2nd ed. 1976.

A compact biographical dictionary with over 3,000 entries on writers of all periods, comprising short biography, assessment of literary achievement, list of major works, and selective list of secondary works. Some title entries for key anonymous works. *Class No:* 830(092)

Middle Ages

[7906]

STAMMLER, W. Die Deutsche Literatur des Mittelalters: Verfasserlexikon. Ruh, K., *and others, eds.* 2., völlig neubearb. Aufl. Berlin, de Gruyter, 1977-1993. v.1-9 (in progress). ISBN: 3110037866.

1st ed. 1931-55 in 5 vols.

A bio-bibliographical dictionary of German writers from the 8th to 16th centuries. Includes some who wrote in Latin and many anonymous works, listed under title. Lengthy, signed entries comprise: biography, critical survey of the works, and extensive bibliographies of primary and secondary material. To be in 10 vols. Has reached Johannes Stetefeld with v.9, fasc.1. *Class No:* 830(092)"01/14"

20th Century

[7907]

Deutsche Dichter des 20. Jahrhunderts Steinecke, H., *ed.* Berlin, E. Schmidt, 1994. 912p. DM198. ISBN: 3503030735.

Lengthy articles on 60 authors, including biography, analysis of works and influence, political and social background, and bibliography. Selective bibliography of works on 20th-century German literature.
Class No: 830(092)"19"

[7908]

FURNESS, R. *and* **HUMBLE, M. A Companion to twentieth-century German literature.** 2nd ed. London, Routledge, 1997. 316p. £50. ISBN: 0415150566.

1st ed. 1991.

Provides information on over 400 writers from Germany, Austria and Switzerland. Entries are arranged A-Z and include critical comments on major works, but there are no references to translations or critical studies. German titles and quotations are not translated. Useful for coverage of minor writers, but very limited on the major figures. For 2nd ed. there are new entries on some East German writers and others have been updated to reflect reunification.
Class No: 830(092)"19"

[7909]

JÄGER, A. Schriftsteller aus der DDR: Ausbürgerungen und Übersiedlungen von 1961 bis 1989. Frankfurt am Main, Lang, 1995. 2v.

Auteronlexikon. xii,625p. DM148. ISBN: 3631486464.
Studie. 202p. DM65. ISBN: 363148643x.

Dictionary vol. has bio-bibliographical articles on *c.*100 authors who emigrated from East Germany after the building of the Berlin Wall, with detailed lists of primary and secondary material. Critical analysis is provided in a separate vol. 'This work ranks among the finest bio-bibliographical works ever done in German literary studies' (*Reference Reviews Europe Online*, 96-1-028)
Class No: 830(092)"19"

[7910]

Kritisches Lexikon zur deutschsprachigen Gegenwartsliteratur (KLG). Arnold, H.L., *ed.* München, Edition Text & Kritik, 1978-. v.1- (loose-leaf). ISBN: 3883770094.

Signed articles, ranging from 10 to 30 pages on postwar authors from Germany, Austria and Switzerland, comprising biography, critical survey of works, and extensive bibliographies of primary and secondary literature. Includes song-writers and film directors as well as literary authors. Loose-leaf format allows for regular revision. Over 450 authors covered in 10 vols. by 1997.
Class No: 830(092)"19"

[7911]

Neues Handbuch der deutschsprachigen Gegenwartsliteratur seit 1945, begründet von Hermann Kunisch. Moser, D.R., *ed.* München, Nymphenburger, 1990. 687p. ISBN: 3485035505.

Supersedes *Lexikon der deutschsprachigen Gegenwartsliteratur* (1987), which was a revised and updated single-vol. edition of Kunisch's *Handbuch der deutschen Gegenwartsliteratur* (1968-70. 3v.).

A dictionary of 592 20th-century authors, most of them literary writers but also including critics, theorists, and psychologists. Signed articles by over 200 contributors include biographical data, critical commentary on major works, and lists of works and bibliographies. Does not wholly supersede Kunisch's *Handbuch,* because that work also has articles on literary movements and genres and an annotated list of *c.*1,500 author bibliographies in v.3, but is particularly useful for its coverage of new writers. List of pseudonyms.

An 'updated' paperback ed. was published by Deutscher Taschen-Verlag in 1993 with the slightly amended title *Neues Handbuch der deutschen Gegenwartsliteratur seit 1945* (1226p. DM49. ISBN: 3423032960), but no new authors were added and the primary bibliographies were only minimally updated. *Class No:* 830(092)"19"

Manuscripts & Incunabula

[7912]

FRELS, W. Deutsche Dichterhandschriften von 1400 bis 1900. Leipzig, Hiersemann, 1934 (repr. 1970). xiv,382p. ISBN: 3777270172.

Lists manuscripts in libraries and archives in Germany, Austria, Switzerland, and Czechoslavakia. Separate lists by author, A-Z, and by location, A-Z. 'Very exhaustive compilation' (Faulhaber, U.K. and Goff, P.B., *German literature,* 1979, p.39). *Class No:* 830(093)

Institutions & Associations

[7913]

Literarische Gesellschaften in Deutschland: ein Handbuch mit Einzeldarstellungen in Texten und Bildern. Arnold, S., *ed.* Berlin, Argon, 1991. 319p. illus. ISBN: 3870241640.

57 literary societies profiled in essays averaging 4p. Directory section (59p.) provides a range of information on each society, including date of foundation, address, publications, library/archive details and membership numbers. *Class No:* 830:061:061.2

Women

[7914]

Deutsche Literatur von Frauen. Brinker-Gabler, G., *ed.* München, Beck, 1988. 2v. illus. ISBN: 3406328148, v.1; 3406330215, v.2.

V.1 *Von Mittelalter bis zum Ende des 18. Jahrhunderts.* 563p.

V.2 *19. und 20. Jahrhundert.* 591p.

A detailed history of German women's writing, with chapters by over 50 specialists. Extensive chapter bibliographies and references appended. Name index in each vol. *Class No:* 830-0055.2

[7915]

FRIEDRICHS, E. Die Deutschsprachigen Schriftstellerinnen des 18. und 19. Jahrhunderts: ein Lexikon. Stuttgart, Metzler, 1981. xxiii, 388p. (*Repertorien zur deutsche Literaturgeschichte - Bd.9.*) ISBN: 3476004562.

Lists *c.*4,000 women writers, A-Z, giving birth and death dates, biographical notes, and references to biographical sources. Cross-references from pseudonyms. Bibliography of over 400 sources. Name index. *Class No:* 830-0055.2

[7916]

Women writers of Germany, Austria, and Switzerland: an annotated bio-bibliographical guide. Frederiksen, E., *ed.* Westport, Conn., Greenwood, 1989. 323p. $59.95. ISBN: 031324989x.

Entries for 185 women writers from all periods, giving biographical sketch, critical evaluation, and list of works with summary and commentary. Chronological and geographical lists of authors appended. Bibliography of critical and biographical studies. Indexes to German and English titles.

An Encyclopedia of German women writers, 1900-1933: biographies and bibliographies with exemplary readings, ed. by B. Keith-Smith, (v1- ,1997-) is a new multi-vol. source announced by E. Mellen Press (Canada). 10 vols. published by mid-1998. *Class No:* 830-0055.2

German Literature in Translation

[7917]

KEENOY, R. *and* **MITCHELL, M. The Babel guide to German fiction in English translation** (Austria, Germany & Switzerland). London, Boulevard Books, 1997. 192p. illus. £8.95. ISBN: 1899460209.

Provides original reviews of 100 key 20th-century novels and short stories by writers from Germany, Austria and Switzerland, with excerpts, and lists all German fiction translated in the UK since 1950 (1500 titles). *Class No:* 830-03

[7918]

MORGAN, B.Q. A Critical bibliography of German literature in English translation, 1481-1927, with supplement embracing the years 1928-35. 2nd ed., completely rev. and greatly augmented. Stanford, Calif., Stanford Univ. Press; London, Oxford Univ. Press, 1938 (repr. without supplement, New York, Scarecrow, 1965). 690p.

1st ed. 1922.

Aims, with critical evaluations, to assist the scholar, reader, book buyer and librarian to make intelligent selections from the mass of published translations. A system of diacritical marks (asterisks, daggers and section marks) is used throughout. The main sequence (10,797 numbered titles) is supported by list A, Anonyma; list B, Bibliographies; list C, Collections, and the supplement. Locations in the British Museum and Library of Congress are given. Index of translators.

Continued by *Supplement embracing the years 1928-55* (New York, Scarecrow, 1965. vii,601p.), which incorporates the 1928-35 supplement and has *c.*9,000 entries. No longer assesses quality of translations and does not provide index of translators.

See also M.F. Smith's *A Selected bibliography of German literature in English translation, 1956-60: a second supplement to B.Q Morgan ...* (Metuchen, N.J., Scarecrow, 1972. 398p.), which includes translations of non-literary works, and *German literature in British magazines, 1750-1860,* ed. by B.Q. Morgan and A.R. Hohlfeld (Madison, Wis., Univ. of Wisconsin Press, 1949. v,364p.), which has over 5,500 entries, chronologically arranged.
Class No: 830-03

[7919]

O'NEILL, P. German literature in English translation: a select bibliography. Toronto, Univ. of Toronto Press, 1981. xii,242p. ISBN: 0802024092.

1,894 items arranged in 5 sections: General Collections, Before 1700, 18th, 19th and 20th centuries. Selection based on literary excellence and largely restricted to modern translations, with some reprints of established older ones. Entries arranged A-Z by author within sections, giving translated and original titles, translator and publication details. Translations in periodicals not included. Indexes of authors and translators. No annotations. *Class No:* 830-03

Yiddish Literature

[7920]

Leksikon fun der nayer yidisher literatur [Biographical dictionary of modern Yiddish literature] Niger, S., *and others, eds.* New York, Congress for Jewish Culture Inc., 1956-81. 8v.

Over 7,000 entries, all in Yiddish, for 19th- and 20th-century writers of many countries. Bibliographies with entries. *Class No:* 830-088

[7921]

LIPTZIN, S. A History of Yiddish literature. New York, J. David, 1972 (reprinted 1985). x,521p. $12.95. ISBN: 0824603079.

From the origins of Yiddish to the present in 24 chapters, with special emphasis on the contemporary period and including several chapters on Yiddish in different parts of the world. Numerous individual authors covered. Bibliography (7p.) of English-language reference material and translations of literary works. Detailed contents list. Index.
Class No: 830-088

[7922]

PRAGER, L. Yiddish literary and linguistic periodicals and miscellanies: a selective annotated bibliography. Darby, Pa., Norwood Editions, for The Assoc. for the Study of Jewish Languages, 1982. 271p.

Lists 386 periodicals by title (romanized form), with bibliographical details, highly personalized annotations ('I have not strained to achieve detached objectivity' - *Introduction*), and library locations in Israel and the US. Chronology, 1823-1979. Bibliography (7p.). Indexes of titles, editors, contributors, and places of publication. *Class No:* 830-088

German Poetry

[7923]

DÜHMERT, A. Von wem ist das Gedicht? Eine bibliographische Zusammenstellung aus 50 deutschsprachigen Anthologien. Berlin, Haude & Spener, 1969. viii,564p. ISBN: 3775900039.

An index to 50 anthologies of pre-20th century poetry published between the 1850s and 1960s, excluding Goethe, Schiller, and children's verse. Indexes of first lines, titles, poets, names and places. *Class No:* 830-1

[7924]

KUCHER, S. Bibliographie der deutschsprachigen Lyrikanthologien, 1840-1914. Schumann, A., *eds.* München, Saur, 1991. 2v. (xii,695p.). DM580. ISBN: 3598108389.

Provides full details of over 2,000 first editions of German verse anthologies and references to later eds. mean that over 5,000 titles are covered in total. Numerous indexes, giving access via title, publisher, place, year, theme, region, etc. *Class No:* 830-1

[7925]

PAULUS, R. *and* **STEULER, U. Bibliographie zur deutschen Lyrik nach 1945.** Frankfurt am Main, Athenaion, 1974. xi,157p. ISBN: 3761071949.

1,334 entries in sections for general studies, anthologies, and 9 individual poets: Bachmann, Bobrowski, Celan, Eich, Enzensberger, Heissenbüttel, Kaschnitz, Krolow, and Piontek. Includes primary and secondary materal. Author index. *Class No:* 830-1

Heine

[7926]

Heine-Jahrbuch Stuttgart, Metzler (formerly Hamburg, Hoffman & Campe), 1961-. Bd.1-, 1962-. ISSN: 04416554.

Carries annual bibliographies, *e.g. H-J 1996* includes a classified listing (16p.) of editions, translations and studies published 1994-95 *Class No:* 830-1HEI

[7927]

HÖHN, G. Heine-Handbuch: Zeit, Person, Werk. 2. Aufl. Stuttgart, Metzler, 1997. iv,570p. DM78. ISBN: 347601441x.

1st ed. 1987.

A revised and expanded version of an encyclopedic guide to Heine, based on the *Studienausgabe* edition of his works, ed. by K. Briegleb (Hanser, 1968-76). After a 40-page introductory section on aspects of Heine's life and times, there are lengthy articles on individual works, covering sources, history, themes, contemporary reception, etc. All entries have bibliographies. Bibliography of general studies. 3 indexes: names, subjects and Heine's works. *Class No:* 830-1HEI

[7928]

SAMMONS, J.L. Heinrich Heine: a selected critical bibliography of secondary literature, 1956-1980. New York, Garland, 1982. xviii,194p. ISBN: 0824092864.

977 concisely annotated items in 8 sections. Author/editor index and index of works and subjects. *Class No:* 830-1HEI

[7929]

WILHELM, G. Heine-Bibliographie. Weimar, Arion Verlag, 1960. 2v.

V.1 *Primärliteratur, 1817-1953.* xii,192p.

V.2 *Sekundärliteratur, 1822-1953.* 294p.

6,043 unannotated entries in all. V.1 (2,011 entries) covers German works (sections A-D) and translations, with name and title indexes and list of newspapers, periodicals, annuals, almanacks, etc. V.2 (4,032 items) covers general guides, life and work as a whole, individual biographies, ideas, and influence. Index of authors; index of subjects.

Continued by S. Seifert's *Heine-Bibliographie, 1954-1964* (Berlin and Weimar, Aufbau Verlag, 1968. xiv,396p.), which has 3,743 entries for both primary and secondary material, and *Heine-Bibliographie, 1965-1982,* by S. Seifert and A.A. Volgina (Aufbau, 1986. xiv,427p.), which adds a further 3,117 entries and has an extensive index of names, titles and subjects. 'Thorough, clearly-presented and authoritative' (*Modern Language Review,* v.83(4), Oct. 1988, p.1044-5). *Class No:* 830-1HEI

Herder

[7930]

STIFTUNG WEIMARER KLASSIK. Herzogin Anna Amalia Bibliothek. **Herder-Bibliographie, 1977-92.** Kuhles, D., *ed.* Stuttgart, Metzler, 1994. xii,360p. DM228. ISBN: 3476012476.

Follows *Herder-Bibliographie*, ed. by G. Günther & others (Berlin, Aufbau-Verlag, 1978. xi,643p.) and retains its classification scheme. Index of names, titles and subjects. *Class No:* 830-1HER

Hölderlin

[7931]

Internationale Hölderlin-Bibliographie (IHB): herausgegeben vom Hölderlin-Archiv der Württembergischen Landesbibliothek Stuttgart. Erste Ausgabe, 1804-1983. Kohler, M., *ed.* Stuttgart, Frommann-Holzboog, 1985. xv,756p. ISBN: 3772810004.

Lists 8,928 studies under subject headings, which include titles of poems, types of publications (biographies, bibliographies, etc.), names of real and fictional persons, and themes. Chronologically arranged under each heading. Index of critics. Lists of periodicals, anthologies, and Hölderlin editions. List of subject headings, with cross-references.

Continued by enormous biennial listings with the same title, each comprising 2 vols. respectively containing bibliographical citations and extensive indexes (ISSN: 01782142). Unfortunately, 'the work as a whole seems to be more the result of sorting by computer than of an intelligent organization of the material by expert (human) editors' (*Reference Reviews Europe Online*, 96-4-451, on the 1993/94 cumulation). *Class No:* 830-1HOL

Lessing

[7932]
Lessing-Bibliographie. Seifert, S., *ed.* Berlin and Weimar, Aufbau Verlag, 1973. x,858p.

Part 1 lists primary literature, including translations into 40 languages. Part 2 lists secondary material in 9 sections. Over 6,000 items. Name and subject index.

Continued by *Lessing-Bibliographie, 1971-1985,* ed. by D. Kuhles (Aufbau, 1988. x,473p.), which has 2,834 entries plus interpolations. 'For all serious research on Lessing, the present bibliography and its predecessor will remain indispensable' (*Modern Language Review,* v.85(3), July 1990, p.793). *Class No:* 830-1LES

Rilke

[7933]
Katalog der Rilke-Sammlung Richard von Mises. Obermüller, P. *and* Steiner, H., *eds.* Frankfurt am Main, Insel-Verlag, 1966. 431p.

The catalogue of this collection at the Houghton Library, Harvard University, forms an important Rilke bibliography. 943 works are listed and described in 7 sections, including translations into 31 languages, and 814 secondary items are listed in a further 6 sections. Indexes of names and titles. *Class No:* 830-1RIL

Schiller

[7934]
Schiller-Bibliographie, 1893-1958. Vulpius, W., *ed.* Weimar, Arion, 1959. xviii,569p.

7,202 entries (plus interpolations) in 10 sections, covering both primary and secondary literature. Some brief annotations. Name index.

Continued by: *Schiller-Bibliographie, 1959-63,* also ed. by Vulpius (Berlin, Aufbau, 1967), which has 1,907 entries; *Schiller-Bibliographie, 1964-74,* by P. Wersig; and by *Schiller-Bibliographie, 1975-85* (Aufbau, 1989. xiii,527p. ISBN: 3598072732), by R. Bärwinkel and others, which has *c.*3,500 entries. *Class No:* 830-1SCH

German Drama

[7935]
Bibliographia dramatica et dramaticorum: kommentierte Bibliographie der im ehemaligen deutschen Reichsgebiet gedruckten and gespielten Dramen des 18. Jahrhunderts nebst deren Bearbeitungen und Übersetzungen und ihrer Rezeption bis in die Gegenwart. Meyer, R., *ed.* Tübingen, Niemeyer, 1986-94. 7v.

1. Abteilung: *Werkausgaben. Sammlungen. Reihen.* 1986. 3v.

2. Abteilung: *Einzeltitel.* 1993-4. 4v.

A comprehensive, annotated bibliography of plays printed and performed in Germany in the 18th century. Pt.1 has lengthy introduction, followed by entries for over 400 authors, A-Z (not all German). Indexes of places, publishers, dedicatees and illustrators. Pt.2 lists individual plays chronologically by date of first documented performance, with details of casts, staging, locations, etc. *Class No:* 830-2

[7936]
GOETHE-INSTITUT. German plays in English translation: a stock-list of texts available in Goethe Institute Libraries. Stilkenboom, M., *ed.* London, Goethe-Institut, 1990. 85p. (loose-leaf).

Lists *c.*1,100 plays, with locations in the Goethe-Institut's: 44 libraries world-wide. Arranged by author, A-Z, then by German title. Entries give translator and publication details. *Class No:* 830-2

[7937]
HILL, C. *and* **LEY, R. The Drama of German expressionism:** a German-English bibliography. Chapel Hill, N.C., Univ. of North Carolina Press, 1960 (repr. New York, AMS Press). xii,211p. $27. ISBN: 0404509282.

4,011 unannotated entries, with a general section (682 items) followed by 16 sections for individual dramatists, A-Z, with listings for plays, translations, non-dramatic works, critical studies in German and English, and reviews. Indexes of authors and plays. *Class No:* 830-2

[7938]
RICHEL, V.C. The German stage, 1767-1890: a directory of playwrights and plays. New York, Greenwood, 1988. xiv,230p. $59.95. ISBN: 0313249903.

Lists over 800 playwrights, A-Z, giving dates and places of birth and death, references to biographical sources, and list of plays with the following data: type of play, number of acts, publication date, original language if adapted, and performance dates in 10 German and Austrian cities. Title index. *Class No:* 830-2

Brecht

[7939]
A Bertolt Brecht reference companion. Mews, S., *ed.* Westport, Conn., Greenwood, 1997. 448p. $95. ISBN: 0313292663.

17 signed chapters in 5 main sections covering most aspects of Brecht's work and influence: 1. Theory and practice of theater - 2. Poetry and prose fiction - 3. Film and music - 4. Marxism and feminism - 5. Translation, reception and appropriation. Reference guide to frequently cited works. Bibliography. Index. *Class No:* 830-2BRE

[7940]
SEIDEL, G. Bibliographie Bertolt Brecht. Titelverzeichnis, Bd. 1: Deutschsprachige Veröffentlichungen aus den Jahren 1913-1972. Werke von Brecht. Sammlungen. Dramatik. Berlin, Aufbau-Verlag, 1975. xxix,304p.

A very detailed bibliography of Brecht's plays in collections and separate editions. An undated *Interimistiche Register* (25p.) has also been published. *Class No:* 830-2BRE

Goethe

[7941]
Goethe-Handbuch: in vier Bänden. Witte, B., *ed.* [3. Aufl.]. Stuttgart, Metzler, 1996-. v.1- (in progress). illus. DM198 per vol.

1st ed. 1916-18 by J. Zeitler (2v.); 2nd ed. 1956-1961 by A. Zastrau (only 2 of the 4 planned vols. were published).

V.1 *Gedichte.* 1996. xviii,571p. ISBN: 3476014436

V.2 *Dramen.* 1996. x,553p. ISBN: 3476014444

A 4-vol. set which is due to be completed by the 250th anniversary of Goethe's birth in 1999 and which comprises a mixture of survey articles and analyses of specific works. Over 200 contributors. Indexes of works and personal names

....*(contd.)*
in each vol.

V.3 will cover prose and v.4 will include biographical information. 'Once completed, ... is sure to become an indispensable reference work not only for Goethe scholars, but also for researchers in other areas' (*Reference Reviews Europe Online*, 97-1/2-136). *Class No:* 830-2GOE

[7942]
PYRITZ, H. Goethe-Bibliographie. Raabe, P., *and others, eds.* Heidelberg, Winter, 1965-8. 2v. (xvi,829; xv,332p.).

A very thorough classified bibliography. V.1 was originally issued in parts, 1955-65, and has 10,700 entries in 14 sections, including primary and secondary material. Some brief annotations.

V.2 adds 2,489 items published 1955-64, in the same format, and has author index to both vols.

See also Goedeke's *Grundriss zur Geschichte der deutschen Dichtung aus den Quellen*, Bd.4, for an extensive Goethe bibliography. *Class No:* 830-2GOE

[7943]
—'Goethe-Bibliographie, 1970-', in *Goethe Jahrbuch*, v.89-. 1972-. Annual. ISSN: 03234207.

Each issue carries a classified international listing of editions and studies, with author index. Prior to 1972, annual bibliographies appeared in *Goethe: Neue Folge des Jahrbuchs der Goethe-Gesellschaft*, Bd. 1-33 (Weimar, Böhlaus, 1936-71).

'Goethe-Bibliographie, 1994', in *Goethe Jahrbuch, 1995*, has 67 primary and 838 secondary entries. *Class No:* 830-2GOE

Hauptmann

[7944]
HOEFERT, S. Internationale Bibliographie zum Werk Gerhart Hauptmanns. Berlin, E. Schmidt, 1986-89. 2v. ISBN: 3503022201, v.1; 3503022686, v.2.

V.1 (1986. 327p.) has 4,170 unannotated entries for primary material, including adaptations, translations into many languages, talks, interviews, and correspondence. Name index. V.2 (1989. 589p.) covers secondary literature. *Class No:* 830-2HAU

German Fiction

[7945]
EKE, N.O. *and* **OLASZ-EKE, D. Bibliographie der deutschen Roman, 1815-1830:** Standortnachweise, Rezensionen, Forschungsüberblick. München, Fink, 1994. 454p. ISBN: 3770528778.

Lists 1,582 novels under authors, A-Z, giving bibliographical details, locations and review citations. Indexes of authors, titles, publishers and libraries. *Class No:* 830-3

[7946]
O'PECKO, M.T. *and* **HOFSTETTER, E.O. The Twentieth-century German novel:** a bibliography of English-language criticism, 1945-1986. Metuchen, N.J., Scarecrow, 1989. v,810p. ISBN: 0810822628.

6,417 unannotated citations arranged by novelist, then by title (in German), after a short general section (222 items). Also includes full bibliographic information for each novel's first German ed. and lists available English translations. No index. *Class No:* 830-3

[7947]
Der Romanführer: der Inhalt der Romane und Novellen der Weltliteratur. Olbrich, W., *and others, eds.* Stuttgart, Hiersemann, 1950-96. v.1-32 (in progress). ISBN: 3777250015.

See entry at 82-31(03). Vols. 1-5, 13, 16, 18, 19, and 25-28 cover German fiction. *Class No:* 830-3

Böll

[7948]
Das Werk Heinrich Bölls: Bibliographie mit studien zum Frühwerk. Bellmann, W., *ed.* Opladen, Westdeutscher Verlag, 1995. 292p. DM48. ISBN: 3531126946.

An annotated bibliography in 5 sections covering belles lettres, letters to and from Böll, published interviews, works edited by Böll, and translations by Böll and his wife, Annemarie. Indexes of names and titles. Also includes 6 critical essays. *Class No:* 830-3BOL

Hesse

[7949]
Hermann Hesse - Personen und Schlüsselfiguren in seinem Leben: ein alphabetisches annotiertes Namensverzeichnis mit sämtlichen Fundstellen in seinen Werken und Briefen. Apel, U., *ed.* München, Saur, 1989. 2v. (xxii,1057p.) DM.448. ISBN: 3598108419.

Lists and explains *c.*5,000 people, with precise references to Hesse's works and letters. *Supplement* (1993. xxviii,512p. DM.228. ISBN: 3598111584). *Class No:* 830-3HES

[7950]
MILECK, J. Hermann Hesse: biography and bibliography. Berkeley, Calif., Univ. of California Press, 1977. 2v. (1402p.) illus. $95. ISBN: 0520027566.

Biography is confined to an introductory essay (108p.), the rest being a definitive primary bibliography in 11 sections followed by a list of critical studies (books, whole periodicals and theses only). 4 indexes: 1. Poetry book titles - 2. Prose titles - 3. Names - 4. Periodicals and newspapers. Poetry section of bibliography includes index of individual poem titles. *Class No:* 830-3HES

Kafka

[7951]
CAPUTO-MAYR, M.L. *and* **HERZ, J.M. Franz Kafka: eine kommentierte Bibliographie der Sekundärliteratur** (1955-1980, mit einem Nachtrag 1985). Bern, Francke, 1987. 692p. ISBN: 3317015691.

5 sections for bibliographies, anthologies, dissertations, articles, and books, plus addenda up to 1985, each arranged A-Z by author. References to book reviews. Subject index and index to Kafka's titles. 'A wonderfully comprehensive bibliography' (*Choice,* v.25(10), June 1988, p.1530). *Class No:* 830-3KAF

[7952]
CAPUTO-MAYR, M.L. *and* **HERZ, J.M. Franz Kafkas Werke:** eine Bibliographie der Primärliteratur (1908-1980). Bern, Francke, 1982. 94p. ISBN: 377201545x.

5 sections, covering collected works; collected novels; separate editions of novels; collections of short prose; and separately published short prose works. Translations into many languages included in each section. German and English title indexes. *Class No:* 830-3KAF

[7953]
FLORES, A. A Kafka bibliography, 1908-1976. New York, Gordian Press, 1976. 193p. $50. ISBN: 0877522065.
1. Primary works - 2. Secondary sources - 3. Biography and background - 4. Interpretative studies and commentaries. Part 1 includes translations. *Class No:* 830-3KAF

Mann

[7954]
Katalog der Thomas Mann Sammlung in der Universitätsbibliothek Düsseldorf. Gatterman, G., *ed.* Bern, Francke; München, Saur, 1991. 9v. DM.1,800. ISBN: 3317017708, Francke; 359822270x, Saur.
Catalogue of a major collection which houses nearly all first eds. up to 1934, one of the most extensive compilations of secondary literature and *c.*5,000 unpublished letters, a total of over 7,200 items. A-Z catalogue by title in vols. 1-6; subject catalogue in vols. 7-9. Disappointing format, with catalogue cards simply reproduced 10 to a page.
Class No: 830-3MAN

[7955]
POTEMPA, G. Thomas-Mann-Bibliographien zur Primärliteratur. Morsum/Sylt, Cicero-Presse, 1992. xvii,907p. DM440. ISBN: 3891200072.
The most comprehensive primary bibliography, superseding H. Burgin's *Das Werk Thomas Manns* (Frankfurt am Main, Fischer, 1959). Annotations provide information on manuscripts and early stages of Mann's works as well as printing history. Large collections of correspondence are included, but publications of individual letters are not. Thoroughly indexed. *Class No:* 830-3MAN

[7956]
Thomas-Mann-Handbuch. Koopmann, H., *ed.* 2. Aufl. Stuttgart, Kröner, 1995. xviii,1006p. DM69.80. ISBN: 3520828022.
1st ed. 1990.
Packs a colossal amount of information into 5 parts covering: Mann in his time; Literary and cultural history; Mann's literary oeuvre; Aesthetics; Literary criticism of Mann. Each part contains several signed essays, all with extensive bibliographies. Final single chapter on the history of research on Mann (45p.). Updated to include publications since 1990. Indexes of names, titles and subjects.
Class No: 830-3MAN

[7957]
Die Thomas-Mann-Literatur: Bibliographie der Kritik. Jonas, K.W., *ed.* Berlin, E. Schmidt, 1972-79; Frankfurt am Main, Klostermann, 1997-. v.1- (in progress)
V.1 *1896-1955*. 1972. 458p.
V.2 *1956-1975*. 1979. 719p.
V.3 *1976-1994*. 1997. xliii,614p. ISBN: 3465028473.
Lists critical studies by year, then A-Z by author. Around 18,000 entries in all so far, with indexes in each vol. to critics, Mann's titles, subjects, and periodicals. International coverage. *Class No:* 830-3MAN

Austrian Literature

[7958]
Dictionary of literary biography. Detroit, Gale, 1978-98. v.1-188 (in progress). £120 per vol.
The following vols., both edited by J. Hardin and D.G. Daviau, cover Austrian literature:
V.81 *Austrian fiction writers, 1875-1913*. 1989. 405p. ISBN: 0810345595.
V.85 *Austrian fiction writers, after 1914*. 1989. 394p. ISBN: 0810345633.
For a description of the series, see entry at 82(092).
Class No: 830-9436

[7959]
Geschichte der Literatur in Österreich: von den Anfängen bis zur Gegenwart. Zeman, H., *ed.* Graz, Akademische Druck- und Verlagsanstalt, 1994-. v.1- (in progress)
V.1 *Die Literatur des Früh- und Hochmittelalters in der Bistümern Passau, Salzburg, Brixen und Trient von den Anfängen bis zum Jahre 1273*, by F.P. Knapp. 1994. 666p. illus. ISBN: 320101611x.
The first in a planned 7-vol. history covers the period from *c.*1075 to 1273 and includes literature in Latin and Hebrew as well as German. Thorough bibliography (40p.). Index of authors and titles. *Class No:* 830-9436

[7960]
GIEBISCH, H. *and* **GUGITZ, G. Biobibliographisches Literaturlexikon Österreichs:** von den Anfängen bis zur Gegenwart. 2. Aufl. Wien, Hollinek, 1985. viii,517p. ISBN: 3851192133.
Lists over 6,000 German-language writers, A-Z, from the old Austro-Hungarian Empire and modern Austria. Entries give dates and places of birth and death, pseudonyms, biographical notes, list of works, and bibliography of secondary literature. Particularly useful for minor authors. Index of pseudonyms. *Class No:* 830-9436

[7961]
Hauptwerke der österreichischen Literatur: Einzeldarstellungen und Interpretationen. Fischer, E., *ed.* München, Kindler, 1997. xxvi,646p. DM49.80. ISBN: 3463403048.
Assembles the entries for Austrian authors and works from *Kindlers neues Literatur-Lexikon* (*q.v.*) in 8 literary-historical categories. *Class No:* 830-9436

[7962]
Katalog-Lexikon zur österreichischen literatur des 20. Jahrhunderts. Wien, IG Autoren-Autorensolidarität, 1995. 4v. ISBN: 3900419183.
Pt.1 *Autorinnen*. 2v.
Pt.2 *Lieferbare Titel*. 2v.
Pt.1 is an alphabetical *Who's who* of Austrian authors, giving date and place of birth, awards and memberships, biography and list of publications. Pt.2 lists books in print: 6,600 titles from Austrian publishers and 5,300 by Austrian authors published abroad. *Class No:* 830-9436

[7963]
Modern Austrian writing: literature and society after 1945. Best, A. *and* Wolfschütz, H., *eds.* London, Wolff; Totowa, N.J., Barnes & Noble, 1980. viii,307p. £12.50. ISBN: 0854960678, UK; 0389200387, US.
Includes biographical notes on . 26 authors, with bibliographies of works and critical studies (29p.), plus a general bibliography (3p.). *Class No:* 830-9436

[7964]
STOCK, K.F., ***and others*****. Personalbibliographien österreichischer Dichter und Schriftsteller;** von den Anfängen bis zur Gegenwart. Pullach bei München, Verlag Dokumentation, 1972. xxiii,703p.

Over 5,700 items. General reference works followed by works by and on authors, A-Z. Covers authors who were born or died in Austria and those who wrote in Austria or the area of the Austro-Hungarian empire. Index of authors and subjects.

Spin-off vols. on individual authors have been published, including:

Grillparzer-Bibliographien. 1991. 61p. ISBN: 390081807x.

Hofmannsthal-Bibliographien. 1992. 65p. ISBN: 3900818126.

Kafka-Bibliographien. 1991. vii,84p. ISBN: 3900818169.

All are published by Stock & Stock (Graz, Austria) and have annotated entries for bibliographies and key reference works, with an index of authors and titles. *Class No:* 830-9436

Swiss Literature

[7965]
Lexikon der schweizer Literaturen Walzer, P.-O., *ed.* Basel, Lenos, 1991. 520p. illus. ISBN: 3857872063.

Entries for *c.*500 authors of all periods, giving place and date of birth and death, photograph, brief critical article and quotation from his/her work. All Swiss languages covered, with lists of translations provided for many authors. 50 subject entries. Bibliography of general studies. Index of names and titles. Also available in French (published Lausanne, Editions de l'Aire) and Italian (Locarno, Dadò). *Class No:* 830-9494

[7966]
LINSMAYER, C. Literaturszene Schweiz: 157 Kurzporträts von Rousseau bis Gertrud Leutenegger. Zürich, Unionsverlag, 1989. 336p. illus. ISBN: 3293001521.

2-page biographical sketches of Swiss writers and foreign writers associated with Switzerland, chronologically arranged and indexed by name. Picture of each writer. *Class No:* 830-9494

[7967]
Schriftstellerinnen und Schriftsteller der Gegenwart/ Ecrivaines et écrivains d'aujourd'hui/Scrittici e scrittori d'oggi/Scripturas e scripturs da nos dis. Boulanger, G., *and others, eds.* Aarau, Sauerländer, 1988. x,286p. ISBN: 3794129334.

Supersedes *Schweizer Schriftsteller der Gegenwart* (Bern, Francke, 1962).

A dictionary of 1,600 living Swiss writers and foreign writers resident in Switzerland. Entries include address, biographical details and list of publications. Necrology appended, listing over 150 writers who have died since the publication of the earlier dictionary. *Class No:* 830-9494

[7968]
STUMP, D., ***& others*****. Deutschsprachige Schriftstellerinnen in der Schweiz, 1700-1945.** Zürich, Limmat-Verlag, 1994. 268p. SFr.48. ISBN: 3857912146.

The first bibliography to concentrate solely on women authors of German-speaking Switzerland, covering 923 writers and 4,500 publications. Includes some émigrés based in Switzerland. *Class No:* 830-9494

[7969]
Die Zeitgenössische Literatur der Schweiz. Gsteiger, M., *ed.* München, Kindler, 1974. 752p. illus. (*Kindlers Literaturgeschichte der Gegenwart.*) ISBN: 3463220040.

A survey of postwar Swiss literature, with a general introduction followed by signed chapters by specialists on German, French, Italian, and Romansch literatures. Biobibliographical notes on *c.*480 authors appended. Index. *Class No:* 830-9494

Dutch Literature

Bibliographies

[7970]
Bibliografie van de Nederlandse taal- en literatuurwetenschap. The Hague, Bureau voor de Bibliografie van de Nederlandistiek (BBN), 1975-. ISSN: 0045186x.

Annual publications are collected in triennial (originally quinquenial) vols., each vol. consisting of a systematic listing according to groups identified by decimal classification. Separate vols. have indexes of journals, subjects and authors. Includes works in Frisian. *Class No:* 839.3(01)

Encyclopaedias & Dictionaries

[7971]
Lexikon van literaire werken: besprekingen van Nederlandstalige literaire werken, 1900-heden. Anbeek van der Meijden, A.G.H., *and others. eds.* Groningen, Wolters-Noordhoff, 1989. 3v. (loose-leaf). ISBN: 9001032303.

Loose-leaf entries on 20th-century literary works are produced regularly, average 7p. per work, and comprise: background, synopsis, interpretation, evaluation, and list of critical studies. Arranged A-Z by author, with author and title indexes. *Class No:* 839.3(03)

[7972]
Winkler Prins lexicon van de Nederlandse letterkunde: auteurs, anonieme werken, periodieken. Lissens, R.F., *and others, eds.* Amsterdam, Elsevier, 1986. 477p. ISBN: 9010058689.

*c.*2,300 entries, A-Z, the great majority being for authors, with bibliographies of works and studies after each entry. Brief general bibliography of reference sources on Dutch literature. Index. *Class No:* 839.3(03)

Histories

[7973]
KNUVELDER, G.P.M. Handboek tot de Geschiedenis der Nederlandse Letterkunde. 7. druk. 's-Hertogenbosch, Malmberg, 1979-80. 4v. ISBN: 9020802410.

1st ed. 1948-53.

A comprehensive literary history, with v.1 going up to the

....(*contd.*)
Renaissance, v.2 covering 1567-1766, v.3 covering 1766-1875, and v.4 from 1876 onwards. Detailed bibliographical references in footnotes. Index of authors and titles in each vol. *Class No:* 839.3(091)

[7974]
MEIJER, R.P. Literature of the Low Countries: a short history of Dutch literature in the Netherlands and Belgium. 2nd ed. Cheltenham, Thornes; New York, Irvington, 1978. ix,402p. ISBN: 0859500993, UK; 0805734317, US.
1st ed. Assen, Van Gorcum, 1971.
Concise chronological narrative in 8 chapters from the 12th century to the 1970s. Quotations in Dutch with translations in footnotes. Select bibliography of works on Dutch literature in English, French and German (4p.). Index of names and titles. *Class No:* 839.3(091)

Biographies

[7975]
Kritisch lexicon van de Nederlandstalige literatur na 1945. Groningen, Wolters-Noordhoff; Brussel, Samsom, 1980-. 5v. (loose-leaf). ISBN: 9065003908.
A dictionary of contemporary Dutch authors, A-Z, with signed entries averaging 12p. and including biography, critical survey of works, and very thorough primary and secondary bibliographies. Over 400 writers covered. Loose-leaf format allows for regular updating.
Class No: 839.3(092)

[7976]
Lectuur-Repertorium. Auteurslijst bevattende 23,000 bio-bibliografische nota's en 3,000 portretten van auteurs behorende tot de Nederlandse en de algemene literatuur... 2. en definitieve uitg. Uitgave van het Algemeen Secretariaat voor Katholieke Boekerijen. Antwerpen, Vlaamsche Boekcentrale, 1952-4. 3v. illus. Supplements.
Supersedes 1st ed. (1932-6) and its 2 supplements (1939-46).
Biobibliographical notes on 23,000 Dutch authors and foreign authors whose works have been translated into Dutch. 2nd supplement to 2nd ed., covering 1952-66 (1969), has 27,000 biobibliographies and 1,500 portraits.
Class No: 839.3(092)

[7977]
Lexicon van de moderne Nederlandse literatuur. van Geelen, J., *and others, eds.* 2. druk. Amsterdam, Meulenhoff, 1981. 219p. illus.
1st ed. 1978.
A biobibliographical dictionary of 500 authors from the Netherlands, Belgium and Friesland. Includes photographs of several writers. *Class No:* 839.3(092)

[7978]
MOERMAN, J. Lexicon nederlandstalige auteurs. Utrecht, Spectrum, 1984. 272p. ISBN: 9027413770.
A compact biobibliographical dictionary of 1,400 Dutch and Flemish authors of all periods. *Class No:* 839.3(092)

[7979]
De Nederlandse en vlaamse auteurs: van middeleeuwen tot heden mit inbegrip van de friese auteurs van Bork, G.J. *and* Verkruijsse, P.J., *eds.* Weesp, De Haan, 1985. 670p. ISBN: 9022845656.
Entries for over 2,000 Dutch, Flemish and Frisian authors, giving biography and lists of primary and secondary materials. *Class No:* 839.3(092)

Flemish Literature

[7980]
ARENTS, P. Flemish writers translated (1830-1931): a bibliographical essay. The Hague, Nijhoff, 1931. 191p.
A classified list of translations into various languages. Indexes of authors, translators and illustrators.
Class No: 839.32

[7981]
ARENTS, P. De Vlaamse schrijvers in het Engels vertaald, 1481-1949. Gent, Erasmus, 1950. 466p.
A bibliography of translations from Flemish into English. Detailed bibliographical information, with locations of copies in American and European libraries. Entries are grouped under subject headings and include periodical articles. Appendices include a chronological list of books, an A-Z list of titles, an author index, places of publication, printers, a list of periodicals, etc. *Class No:* 839.32

[7982]
LISSENS, R.F. Flämische Literaturgeschichte des 19. und 20. Jahrhunderts. Köln, Böhlau Verlag, 1970. xviii,337p. illus. ISBN: 3412257702.
Originally published Brussels, Elsevier-Sequoia, 1967, as *De Vlaamse letterkunde van 1780 tot heden.*
A history of 19th- and 20th-century Flemish literature in 11 chapters. Bibliography of Dutch and German studies and anthologies (5p.). Name index. *Class No:* 839.32

Scandinavian Literature

Bibliographies

[7983]
AMERICAN-SCANDINAVIAN FOUNDATION. Index Nordicus: a cumulative index to English-language periodicals on Scandinavian studies. Kvamme, J., *comp.* Boston, Hall, 1980. 770p. $95. ISBN: 0816100802.
An index of the contents of 6 major journals from their origins up to 1976, including 2 which cover Scandinavian literature: *Scandinavian Studies* and *Scandinavica.* Access via subjects, titles, authors, and book reviewers.
Class No: 839.5(01)

[7984]
BUDD, J. Eight Scandinavian novelists: criticism and reviews in English. Westport, Conn., Greenwood, 1981. viii,180p. $99.50. ISBN: 0313228698.
1,163 entries for studies of Lie, Garborg, Lagerlöf, Hamsun, Undset, Lagerkvist, Moberg, and Laxness. Brief biography of each writer with list of major works. Index of critics, editors and translators. *Class No:* 839.5(01)

[7985]
Scandinavica: an international journal of Scandinavian studies. Norwich, Norvik Press, Univ. of East Anglia, 1962-. 2py. ISSN: 00365653.
Regularly carries select bibliographies of recent publications on Scandinavian studies and of literary works published in Scandinavia. *Class No:* 839.5(01)

Encyclopaedias & Dictionaries

[7986]

Dictionary of Scandinavian literature. Zuck, V., *ed.* New York, Greenwood, 1990. xi,792p. $115. ISBN: 0313214506.

A long-standing gap in literary reference coverage is filled by the appearance of this English-language dictionary of the literature of Scandinavia (including Finland), with *c.*700 signed entries (by some 120 contributors) on authors and subjects. Author entries range from 300 to 1,600 words and comprise biographical notes; analysis of major works; assessment of impact on the literary history of the writer's country; list of works (including English translations) and critical studies. Topical entries have 1,000-1,500 words and are followed by references to mainly English-language studies. Chronology, 400-1985. Bibliography of reference sources, periodicals, literary histories and anthologies for each country (16p.). Index of names, works, etc.
Class No: 839.5(03)

Handbooks & Manuals

[7987]

MUNCH-PETERSEN, E. Nordisk litteraturvidenskab: handbog til informationssongning. Esbo, Finland, NORDINFO, 1993. 212p. ISBN: 9514778308.

Evaluative annotations on 291 key reference works for the study of Scandinavian literature. Chapters are devoted to particular themes (*e.g.* history of language) or types of source (*e.g.* national bibliographies) and have sections on Scandinavia as a whole and each of its 5 countries. Indexes of authors, titles and publishers. *Class No:* 839.5(035)

Histories

[7988]

BLANKNER, F. The History of the Scandinavian literatures: a survey of the literatures of Norway, Sweden, Denmark, Iceland and Finland, from their origins to the present day, including Scandinavian-American authors and selected bibliographies. New York, Dial Press, 1938 (repr. Westport, Conn., Greenwood, 1975). xiv,407p. ISBN: 0837180368.

Sections on each of the national literatures, plus Swedish-American literature, Danish-American literature, etc., followed by selected bibliography (58p.) of books and articles on Scandinavian literature (with the emphasis on English-language studies) and English translations of the major works. Index. *Class No:* 839.5(091)

[7989]

Nordens litteratur. Brøndsted, M., *ed.* København, Gyldendal, 1972. 2v. ISBN: 8700286214.

V.1 ... *før 1860.* 428p.

V.2 ... *efter 1860.* 593p.

In 13 chapters for chronological periods, each divided into signed sections on the individual Scandinavian countries which are written in the language of that country. Bibliographies of literary histories and of translations from Finnish, Faroese, and Icelandic into the 3 major Scandinavian languages. Author index.
Class No: 839.5(091)

[7990]

ROSSEL, S.H. A History of Scandinavian literature, 1870-1980. Minneapolis, Univ. of Missouri Press, 1982. x,492p. (*The Nordic series; v.5.*) ISBN: 0816609063.

19 chapters, most devoted to a particular period in a particular country and divided into sections on 'outstanding authors who are considered to be characteristic of an epoch, a stylistic trend, or a social group' (*Preface*). Selective, classified bibliography (36p.) focuses mainly on works in English on the national literatures and individual authors. Index. *Class No:* 839.5(091)

Icelandic Literature

Bibliographies

[7991]

Bibliography of modern Icelandic literature in translation: including works written by Icelanders in other languages. Mitchell, P.M. *and* Ober, K.H., *comps.* Ithaca, N.Y., and London, Cornell Univ. Press, 1975. ix,317p. $69.50. (*Islandica; 40.*) ISBN: 0801408970.

Unannotated listing of translations of novels, stories, plays and poems that have appeared in book form or in periodicals up to 1970. Main sequence arranged A-Z by author; two short sequences for anthologies and anonymous works. Index of translators and editors. *Class No:* 839.59(01)

[7992]

Bibliography of Old Norse-Icelandic studies, 1963-. Copenhagen, Munksgaard (subsequently The Royal Library), 1964-. Irregular. ISSN: 00677213.

Lists the year's editions of literary texts and books and articles on Old Norse language and literature and on medieval Norwegian and Icelandic history and related subjects. Arranged by author with subject index. Originally published annually, but the publications of 1981, 1982 and 1983 are treated in a single vol. published in 1988, which has 1,060 entries in 3 separate annual lists.
Class No: 839.59(01)

[7993]

CORNELL UNIVERSITY. Library. **Catalogue of the Icelandic Collection** bequeathed by William Fiske. Hermannsson, H., *comp.* Ithaca, N.Y., [The University], 1914-43 (repr. Cornell Univ. Press, 1960). 3v.

The main volume (1914. xi,755p.) lists nearly 10,000 vols. and is supplemented by *Additions, 1913-26* (1927, ix,284p. repr. 1960) and *Additions, 1927-42* (1943. ix,295p. repr. 1960), bringing the total number of items to 21,830. Each vol. is arranged by author, with a subject index. The Collection includes editions and translations of Old Icelandic and Old Norse texts and books about them; works on the history, religion, culture, language, etc. of early Iceland and Scandinavia; works of modern Icelandic literature; and books on all aspects of modern Iceland.

Runic literature is listed separately in *Catalogue of Runic literature forming a part of the Icelandic Collection bequeathed by William Fiske,* also compiled by H. Hermannsson (Oxford, Univ. Press, 1917. viii,106p.).
Class No: 839.59(01)

[7994]
—Islandica: an annual relating to Iceland and the Fiske Icelandic Collection in Cornell University Library, v.1-36. Ithaca, N.Y., Cornell Univ. Library, 1908-53 (repr. N.Y., Kraus, 1966).

The following vols. are particularly useful for literary reference:

1. *Bibliography of the Icelandic sagas and minor tales.* 1908. 126p.

3. *Bibliography of the sagas of the kings of Norway and related sagas and tales.* 1910. 75p.

5. *Bibliography of the mythical-heroic sagas.* 1912. 73p.

6. *Icelandic authors of today.* 1913. xiv,69p.

9. *Icelandic books of the sixteenth century.* 1916. xii,72p.

11. *The Periodical literature of Iceland down to the year 1874.* 1918. 100p.

13. *Bibliography of the Eddas.* 1920. 95p.

14. *Icelandic books of the seventeenth century.* 1922. xiii,121p.

19. *Icelandic manuscripts.* 1929.

23. *Old Icelandic literature: a bibliographical essay.* 1933. 50p.

24. *The Sagas of Icelanders (Íslendinga sögur): a supplement to Bibliography of the Icelandic sagas and minor tales.* 1935. 113p.

26. *The Sagas of the kings and the mythical-heroic sagas: two bibliographical supplements.* 1937.

29. *Bibliographical notes.* 1942. 91p.

32-33. *History of Icelandic prose writers: 1800-1940,* by S. Einarsson. 1948. xiii,269p.

34. *History of Icelandic poets: 1800-1940,* by R. Beck. 1950. xi,247p.

Apart from nos. 32-34, all the above are by H. Hermannsson. Works in this series are now published occasionally rather than annually; see separate entries for nos. 40, 44 and 45. *Class No:* 839.59(01)

[7995]
FRY, D.K. Norse sagas translated into English: a bibliography. New York, AMS Press, 1980. xx,139p. $32.50. ISBN: 0404180167.

Lists all extant translations and the editions on which they are based. 154 sagas, arranged A-Z by Norse title, with detailed cross-references. Indexes of translators, editors, and other names. Bibliography of secondary works (8p.) and list of sagas in need of a reliable translation.
Class No: 839.59(01)

[7996]
KALINKE, M.E. *and* MITCHELL, P.M. Bibliography of Old Norse-Icelandic romances. Ithaca, N.Y., Cornell Univ. Press, 1985. xii,140p. $39.95. (*Islandica; 44.*) ISBN: 0801416817.

4 sections: 1. Catalogues and bibliographies - 2. Collections and anthologies - 3. General works - 4. Individual sagas, A-Z by title (p.18-134). For each saga, gives history, summary, manuscript locations, editions, translations and critical studies. Index of authors, editors, translators and reviewers. *Class No:* 839.59(01)

Histories

[7997]
EINARSSON, S. A History of Icelandic literature. New York, Johns Hopkins Press for The American-Scandinavian Foundation; London, Oxford Univ. Press, 1957. xii,409p.

Well-organized account in 22 chapters and numerous subsections covering 874 A.D. (Norse settlement of Iceland) to

....*(contd.)*
1955. Bio-bibliographical notes on many authors throughout. Substantial classified bibliography (7p.). Very thorough index of historical and fictitious persons, place names, titles of works, first lines, literary topics and folklore motifs.
Class No: 839.59(091)

[7998]
Old Norse-Icelandic literature: a critical guide. Clover, C.J. *and* Lindow, J., *eds.* Ithaca, N.Y., and London, Cornell Univ. Press, 1985. 387p. $39.95. (*Islandica; 45.*) ISBN: 0801417554.

Essays by 6 scholars on the major branches of the literature: Mythology, Eddic poetry, Skaldic poetry, Kings' sagas, Family sagas and Norse romance. The comprehensive, classified bibliographies following each essay (*e.g.* 30p. for Eddic poetry) make this an invaluable reference work. Indexes of texts and their authors, critics, and topics. *Class No:* 839.59(091)

Norwegian Literature

Bibliographies

[7999]
FET, J. New Norse literature in English translation, 1880-1982. Volda, Norway, Møreforskning/Møre og Romsdal Distrikthøgskule, 1985. 175p. ISBN: 8290155611.

Lists 683 translations from the nynorsk language, in 8 sections for different genres. Indexes of authors and translators, each with biographical notes. Index of poem titles and first lines of songs. List of works analyzed, with references to the entries. *Class No:* 839.6(01)

[8000]
Norsk litteraer årbok. Oslo, Det Norske Samlaget, 1966-. Annual. ISSN: 00781266.

Includes a yearly bibliography entitled 'Bibliografi over norsk litteraturforskning', classified under general topics, then writers, A-Z. *Class No:* 839.6(01)

[8001]
Norway. Lyngstad, S., *ed.* Whitestone, N.Y., Griffon House, 1983. 227p. $23. (*Reviews of national literature - 12.*) ISBN: 0918680174.

Signed essays on themes in Norwegian literature, including 'Bibliographical spectrum' by J. Hobermann (p.185-207), which surveys English-language works. (Sather, L.B., *Norway*, 1986). *Class No:* 839.6(01)

[8002]
ØKSNEVAD, R. Norsk litteraturhistorisk bibliografi, 1900-1945. Oslo, Gyldendal, 1951. 378p.

Lists books and articles on Norwegian literature, with a general section followed by sections on the 16th, 17th, 18th, 19th and 20th centuries. International coverage.

Continued by *Norsk litteraturhistorisk bibliografi, 1946-55* (Oslo, Gyldendal, 1958. 141p.), which is in turn continued by: Naess, H.S., *Norwegian literary bibliography, 1956-70* (Oslo, Universitetsforlaget, 1975. 128p.).
Class No: 839.6(01)

Histories

[8003]
BEYER, H. A History of Norwegian literature.
Haugen, E., *tr. and ed.* New York, N.Y. Univ. Press, for The American-Scandinavian Foundation, 1956. ix,370p. illus.

Translation of 1st ed. of Beyer's *Norsk litteratur historie*

.... *(contd.)*
(Oslo, 1952). Quotations in English. Footnote references to available translations. Bibliography (5p.) confined to English-language studies. Name and title indexes.

A 4th ed. of the original Norwegian work, by H. and E. Beyer, was published Oslo, Aschehoug, 1978.

See also *Modern Norwegian literature, 1860-1918,* by B.W. Downs (Cambridge, Cambridge Univ. Press, 1966. vii,276p.), which covers the 'classic' period of Norwegian literature. References to English translations in the text and to further reading in footnotes. Chapter bibliographies, with running commentary, are appended (8p.).
Class No: 839.6(091)

[8004]

BULL, F., *and others*. Norsk litteraturhistorie. 2. utg. Oslo, Aschehoug, 1957-63. 6v. illus.

1st ed. by F. Paasche and others, 1924-55 (6v.).

V.1 *Norges og Islands litteratur inntil utgangen av middelalderen.* 1957. 550p.

V.2 *Norges litteratur fra reformasjonen til 1814.* 1958. 538p.

V.3 ... *fra 1814 til 1850-årene.* 1959. 576p.

V.4 ... *fra Februarrevolusjonen til første verdenskrig.* 1960-63. 2pts. (800p.).

V.5 ... *fra 1880-årene til første verdenskrig.* 1961. 653p.

V.6 ... *fra 1914 til 1950-årene.* 1955.

A standard history, with each vol. written by a specialist. Each vol. has chapter bibliographies and name and subject index. N.B. V.6 is an unamended reprint of that in 1st ed., but a 2nd ed. of this vol., by P. Houm, was published separately in 1976. *Class No:* 839.6(091)

[8005]

DAHL, W. Norges litteratur. Oslo, Aschehoug, 1981-9. 3v. illus. ISBN: 8203105734.

V.1 *Tid og tekst 1814-1884.* 1981. 340p.

V.2 *Tid og tekst 1884-1935.* 1984. 430p.

V.3 *Tid og tekst 1935-1972, med et sluttkapitel om tekstere i 70- og 80-årene.* 1989. 375p.

A profusely illustrated history (many in colour) with many quotations, and biographies of major authors enclosed in boxes throughout the text. No bibliographies. Indexes to subjects and to names and titles in v.3. Invaluable for recent literature. *Class No:* 839.6(091)

[8006]

A History of Norwegian literature. Naess, H.S., *ed.* Lincoln, Nebr., Univ. of Nebraska Press, 1993. xviii,435p. illus. $55. (*Histories of Scandinavian literature.*) ISBN: 0803233175.

Signed chapters on chronological periods and on specialist genres (*e.g.* children's literature, women writers) in the style of Rossel's history of Danish literature in the same series (*q.v.*). Bibliography includes publications in English and Norwegian. Index. 'Highly recommended as an excellent comprehensive one-volume introduction in English to Norwegian literature within its historical context' (*Choice*, v.31(4), Dec. 1993, p.607). *Class No:* 839.6(091)

[8007]

Norges litteratur historie. Beyer, E., *ed.* Oslo, J.W. Cappelen, 1974-5. 6v. illus. ISBN: 8202030056.

V.1 *Fra runene til Norske selskab.* 623p.

V.2 *Fra Wegeland til Vinje.* 541p.

V.3 *Fra Ibsen til Garborg.* 591p.

V.4 *Fra Hamsun til Falkberget.* 687p.

V.5 *Mellomkrigstid.* 511p.

V.6 *Vår egen tid.* 528p.

.... *(contd.)*
A well-illustrated history with sections by specialists. V.6 has extensive bibliography (80p.), chronology, 400-1972, and cumulative index. *Class No:* 839.6(091)

Biographies

[8008]

DAHL, W. Nytt norsk forfatterleksikon. Oslo, Gyldendal, 1971. 267p. ISBN: 8205004773.

Lists *c.*650 authors, giving biography and lists of book-length works and selected criticism. Not confined to literary authors, but their biographies tend to be longer and include some critical evaluation. *Class No:* 839.6(092)

[8009]

HALVORSEN, J.B. Norsk forfatter-lexikon, 1814-1880. Kristiania, Norske Forlagsforening, 1885-1908. 6v.

A revision and expansion of *Norsk forfatterlexikon, 1814-1856,* by J.E. Kraft and C. Lange.

Biobibliographies of Norwegian authors, including details of their contributions to newspapers and periodicals and references to reviews of their work. For pre-1814 writers, see Ehrencron-Müller's *Forfatterlexikon* at 839.8(092).
Class No: 839.6(092)

Ibsen

[8010]

BRYAN, G.B. An Ibsen companion: a dictionary-guide to the life, works, and critical reception of Henrik Ibsen. Westport, Conn., Greenwood, 1984. xxix,437p. ISBN: 0313235066.

An invaluable one-stop guide to Ibsen, inspired by Halliday's *A Shakespeare companion* (*q.v.*), with entries on all aspects of the dramatist's life and work. These range from a couple of lines on a minor character (all speaking characters have an entry) to 11p. on *A Doll's house*. Articles on dramas include stage history (over 60 productions of *Hedda Gabler* listed), synopsis and structural analysis. Fully cross-referenced. Bibliographical references after most entries. Chronology of Ibsen's life (7p.). Appended list of early Ibsen translators (6p.). Selected classified bibliography (5p.). Index. *Class No:* 839.6IBS

[8011]

The Cambridge companion to Ibsen. McFarlane, J., *ed.* Cambridge, Cambridge Univ. Press, 1994. xxvi,271p. illus. £13.95. ISBN: 052142321x.

Primarily a collection of critical essays, but ch. 16, 'Works of reference' by S. Saari (9p.), is a useful bibliographical survey covering bibliographies, biographies, translations, concordances, dictionaries, critical studies and production histories. Also includes a chronology of Ibsen's life (7p.). *Class No:* 839.6IBS

[8012]

Contemporary approaches to Ibsen. Oslo, Universitetsforlaget (distr. Oxford Univ. Press), 1966-. v.1-. Biennial. ISSN: 00734365.

Carries 3-yearly bibliographies of Ibsen scholarship, *e.g.* vol.7 (1991) lists books, articles and reviews published 1987-90. *Class No:* 839.6IBS

Swedish Literature

Bibliographies

[8013]

HAGSTRÖM, T. Svensk litteraturhistorisk bibliografi intill år 1900. Uppsala, Svenska Litteratursällskapet, 1989. 629p. ISBN: 9187666014.

An annotated bibliography of books, articles and dissertations published before 1900 on Swedish literature. Over 10,300 items arranged according to historical periods, with subsections on numerous individual writers in which bibliographies, editions, and critical studies are listed. Thorough index. *Class No:* 839.7(01)

[8014]

—Svensk litteraturhistorisk bibliografi, 1880-. Uppsala, Svenska Litteratursällskapet, 1881-.

An annual, classified bibliography which appears as a supplement of *Samlaren: tidskrift för svensk litteraturvetenskaplig forskning* (ISSN: 03486133). Sections for bibliography, general studies, religious literature, folk literature, children's literature, and individual authors.

Svensk litteraturhistorisk bibliografi, 1900-1935 (Uppsala, 1939-50. 522p.) is a cumulation, issued in 6 parts and edited by J. Samzelius, of the annual bibliographies from *Samlaren.* *Class No:* 839.7(01)

[8015]

Litterära tidskrifter i Sverige, 1900-1970: en kommenterad bibliografi. Holmberg, C.-G., *ed.* Lund, Litteraturvetenskapliga Institutionen, 1975. 188p.

Lists 67 modern Swedish literary periodicals. 'A splendid little bibliography, extensively annotated' (Sather, L. and Swanson, A., *Sweden,* 1987, p.281). *Class No:* 839.7(01)

[8016]

Swedish plays in English translation, from Strindberg to the present. Engel, A.M. *and* Sonnermann, A., *eds.* 3rd ed. Stockholm, Swedish Institute, 1985. 24p.

According to L.S. Sather and A. Swanson (*Sweden,* 1987, p.279), over half the entries in this brief bibliography are for plays by Strindberg. Includes information on performance rights. *Class No:* 839.7(01)

Histories

[8017]

BRANDELL, G. *and* **STENKVIST, J. Svensk litteratur, 1870-1970.** Stockholm, Aldus, 1974-75. 3v. illus.

V.1 *Från 1870 till första världskriget.* 1970. 398p. ISBN: 9100398454.

V.2 *Från första världskriget till 1950.* 1975. 294p. ISBN: 9100398470.

V.3 *Den nyaste litteraturen.* 1975. 259p. ISBN: 9100398497.

A well-illustrated, author-based history of modern Swedish literature. Includes an excellent bibliography in v.3 (p.179-259), which is arranged by author, A-Z, giving biographical notes and lists of works and critical studies, and which also serves as an index. *Class No:* 839.7(091)

[8018]

—Aspects of modern Swedish literature. Scobbie, I., *ed.* Norwich, Norvik Press, 1988. vi,373p. £10.50. ISBN: 087004102x.

10 essays on Swedish literature since 1880, covering periods, movements and individual writers. Extensive bibliographies of works and studies with each essay, general bibliography (3p.), and very useful list of English translations of modern Swedish literary works (12p.). *Class No:* 839.7(091)

[8019]

GUSTAFSON, A. A History of Swedish literature. Minneapolis, Univ. of Minnesota Press for the American-Scandinavian Foundation, 1961. xv,708p. illus. ISBN: 0816602360.

Comprehensive history in 12 chapters from origins to 1950s. Quotations in English. Excellent bibliographic guide (77p.) has general section followed by surveys for the periods covered by each chapter. Selective list of English translations (15p.) with critical and explanatory notes. Index of names, titles and subjects. *Class No:* 839.7(091)

[8020]

A History of Swedish literature. Warme, L.G., *ed.* Lincoln, Nebr., Univ. of Nebraska Press, 1996. xvii,587p. £47.50. (*Histories of Scandinavian literature.*) ISBN: 0803247508.

7 chronological chapters from the earliest times to the present, plus chapters on women's writing and literature for children, each by a different specialist. Bibliography of English and Swedish critical studies. *Class No:* 839.7(091)

[8021]

Ny illustrerad svensk litteraturhistoria. Tigerstedt, E.N., *ed.* [2. uppl.]. Stockholm, Natur och Kultur, 1967. 4v. illus.

1st ed. 1955-58, in 5 vols. superseding *Illustrerad svensk litteraturhistoria* by H. Schück and K. Warburg (3. uppl., Stockholm, Geber, 1926-49. 8v.).

V.1, *Forntiden. Medeltiden. Vasatiden;* v.2, *Karolinska tiden. Frihetstiden. Gustavianska tiden;* v.3, *Romantiken. Liberalismen;* v.4, *Åttiotal. Nittiotal.*

Fem decennier av nittonhundratalet (Stockholm, Natur och Kultur, 1965-66. 2v.) by E.H. Linder, although not numbered in this series, is a revised and updated ed. of his *Fyra decennier av nittonhundratalet* (1958) which forms v.5 of 1st ed.

The standard literary history, with sections by specialists and extensive chapter bibliographies appended. Detailed index in each vol. Tigerstedt has also produced a single-vol. history, *Svensk litteraturhistoria* (Stockholm, Natur och Kultur, 1948; 3rd ed. 1969) which has thorough chapter bibliographies. *Class No:* 839.7(091)

[8022]

OLSSON, B. *and* **ALGULIN, I. Litteraturens historia i Sverige.** Stockholm, Norstedt, 1987. 605p. illus. ISBN: 9118730221.

A well-illustrated, narrative history in 11 chapters with numerous subsections. Biographical data on authors can be found (with portraits) in the margins throughout. Good bibliography (18p.) of critical studies (general and on specific authors) with running commentary. Name and title indexes. *Class No:* 839.7(091)

[8023]

Den Svenska litteraturen. Lönnroth, L. *and* Delblanc, S., *eds.* [Stockholm], Bonniers, 1987-90. 6v. illus.

V.1 *Från forntid till frihetstid, 800-1718.* 1987. 284p. ISBN: 9134508619.

V.2 *Upplysning och romantik, 1718-1830.* 1988. 320p. ISBN: 9134508627.

V.3 *De Liberala genombrotten, 1830-1890.* 1988. 319p. ISBN: 9134508635.

V.4 *Den Storsvenska generationen, 1890-1920.* 1989. 301p. ISBN: 9134508643.

....(*contd.*)

V.5 *Modernister och arbetardiktare, 1920-1950*. 1989. 319p. ISBN: 9134508651.

V.6 *Medieålderns litteratur, 1950-1985*. 1990. 320p. ISBN: 9134508678.

A profusely illustrated history (many in colour) with signed chapters by numerous specialists. Index in each vol. A bibliography is planned to appear in a separate vol.
Class No: 839.7(091)

Biographies

[8024]

RUNNQUIST, Å. Moderna svenska författare: en samblad översikt över svensk litteratur under fyra årtionden. 2. omarb., utökade uppl. Stockholm, Forum, 1967. 255p. illus.

1st ed. 1959.

A biographical dictionary of modern Swedish writers. Index of names and titles. *Class No:* 839.7(092)

[8025]

Svenskt författarlexikon, 1900-1940. Bibliografisk handbok till Sveriges moderna litteratur. Åhlén, B., *and others, eds.* Stockholm, Rabén & Sjögren, 1942. 3v. illus.

A biographical dictionary of Swedish authors, which includes lists of works and critical studies. V.3 is an index of titles.

Rabén & Sjögren have published further dictionaries covering the following periods: 1941-1950; 1951-1955; 1956-1960; 1961-1965; 1966-1970; and 1971-75. Editors vary. *Register 1941-1955* (1959) is a separate, cumulative title index. Vols. published since then each have a title index. Includes pictures of some authors.
Class No: 839.7(092)

[8026]

Svenskt litteraturlexikon. 2. utvidgade uppl. Lund, Gleerup, 1970. 643p.

1st ed. 1964.

Essentially a biographical dictionary of Swedish authors, although there are some entries defining and explaining literary terms. Longer articles are signed and include bibliographies. Index of titles mentioned in the biographies.
Class No: 839.7(092)

Danish Literature

Bibliographies

[8027]

BREDSDORFF, E. Danish literature in English translation, with a special Hans Christian Andersen supplement: a bibliography. Copenhagen, Munksgaard, 1950 (reprinted Westport, Conn., Greenwood, 1973). 198p. ISBN: 0837168678.

Attempts to give a complete list of translations from 1533 to the mid-20th century, including non-literary writers, *e.g.* Brahe, Kierkegaard. Also lists English books and articles *about* Danish literature. Supplement (74p.) lists books by and about Andersen. No annotations or index.
Class No: 839.8(01)

[8028]

—SCHROEDER, C.L. A Bibliography of Danish literature in English translation 1950-1980, with a selection of books about Denmark. Copenhagen, Det Danske Selskab, 1982. 197p. ISBN: 8774290444.

Continues Bredsdorff's work. 3 main sections: Authors (arranged A-Z), Genres (ballads, folk songs, folk tales, Faroese and Greenland literature) and Anthologies. Lists of secondary material in English are provided for genres and major authors. Books about Denmark listed under 34 subject headings. Over 5,000 entries. *Class No:* 839.8(01)

[8029]

BRYDER, M., *and others*. **75 yngre danske skonlitteraere forfattere:** en bibliografisk handbog. Copenhagen, Danmarks Biblioteksskole, 1981. 182p.

Lists works by and about 75 young contemporary writers A-Z. *Class No:* 839.8(01)

[8030]

JØRGENSEN, A. Contributions in foreign languages to Danish literary history, 1961-81: a bibliography. Ballerup, Bibliotekscentralens Forlag, 1982. 104p.

Lists contributions in non-Scandinavian languages to the literary history of Denmark from the Middle Ages to the present, with brief annotations (Miller, K.E., *Denmark*, 1987, p.123).

See also K.H. Ober's *Contributions in Dutch, English, Faroese, German, Icelandic, Italian, and Slavic languages to Danish literary history, 1925-1970* (Copenhagen, Det Kongelige Bibliotek, 1976. viii,32p.). *Class No:* 839.8(01)

[8031]

JØRGENSEN, A. Dansk litteraturhistorisk bibliografi, 1967-74. København, Akademisk Forlag, 1968-75. 8v.

A classified, annual bibliography which has been produced irregularly by different compilers and publishers since 1975 and which now appears long after the year covered. The volumes for 1975 and 1976-77 were published by Det Kongelige Bibliotek in 1985 and 1983 respectively and those for 1978 and 1979 by Danmarks Biblioteksskole. The latter (published 1987) has 965 entries, plus references to reviews, in sections for chronological periods and for Greenland and children's literature. Name index. *Class No:* 839.8(01)

[8032]

LINDTNER, N.C. Danske klassikere: en selectiv bibliografi. København, Danmarks Biblioteksskole, 1976. 200p.

A selective list of works by the major Danish writers.
Class No: 839.8(01)

Encyclopaedias & Dictionaries

[8033]

Litteraturhåndbogen. Hansen, I.F., *and others, eds.* 2. udg. Copenhagen, Gyldendal, 1985. 582p. illus. ISBN: 8700731765.

1st ed. 1981.

An extremely useful handbook in 3 main sections: 1. A literary history of Denmark (p.31-367), comprising 7 signed chapters on periods plus 2 on Faroese and Greenland literature - 2. A biographical dictionary of authors (p.371-508), with *c.*140 entries which include a portrait - 3. A dictionary of *c.*70 literary terms (p.511-77), giving lengthy explanations with examples. Index. *Class No:* 839.8(03)

Histories

[8034]

Dansk litteraturhistorie. Copenhagen, Gyldendal, 1983-5. 9v. illus. ISBN: 8701240315.

V.1, *800-1480;* v.2, *1480-1620;* v.3, *1620-1746;* v.4, *1746-1807;* v.5, *1807-1848;* v.6, *1848-1901;* v.7, *1901-1945;* v.8, *1945-1980;* v.9, *Notiser og register.*

The work of a collective of 47 writers. Many quotations and illustrations. Author index in each vol., while v.9 has cumulative indexes of names and titles, and of subjects. The bibliographical references in v.9 (p.11-157) are keyed to pages in the other vols. and rather difficult to use.
Class No: 839.8(091)

[8035]

Dansk litteraturhistorie. Traustedt, P.H., *ed.* 2. udg. Copenhagen, Politiken, 1976-77. 6v. illus. ISBN: 8756724713.

1st ed. 1965-66 (4v.).

V.1 *Fra runerne til Thomas Kingo.* 1976. 548p.

V.2 *Fra Ludwig Holberg til Carsten Hauch.* 1976. 653p.

V.3 *Fra Poul Møller til Søren Kierkegaard.* 1976. 576p.

V.4 *Fra Georg Brandes til Johannes V. Jensen.* 1977. 632p.

V.5 *Fra Tom Kristensen til Halfdan Rasmussen.* 1977. 522p.

V.6 *Fra Morten Nielsen til Kløvedal Reich.* 1977. 513p.

Each vol. is by 1 or 2 specialists and has an extensive bibliography of works and studies appended, covering numerous individual authors. Detailed table of contents in each vol. and cumulative indexes of names and titles in v.6.
Class No: 839.8(091)

[8036]

A History of Danish literature. Rossel, S.H., *ed.* Lincoln, Nebr., Univ. of Nebraska Press, 1992. xvi,709p. illus. $55. (*Histories of Scandinavian literature.*) ISBN: 080323886x.

7 chronological chapters from the Middle Ages to 1990, plus chapters on Faroese literature, women writers and children's literature, with sections on genres and subsections on individual writers. Quotations in translation. Bibliography, arranged by chapter, lists English-language studies, anthologies and translations of major works. Thorough index. 9 international contributors.
Class No: 839.8(091)

[8037]

MITCHELL, P.M. A History of Danish literature. 2nd, aug. ed. New York, Kraus-Thomson, 1971. 339p. illus. ISBN: 0527642002.

1st ed. Copenhagen, Gyldendal, 1957.

16 chapters from the earliest times to 1970, with ch.16 new for this ed. and minor changes to the other chapters. Quotations in English. Bibliography (5p.) of anthologies and critical works in English. Index of authors, translators and titles. *Class No:* 839.8(091)

[8038]

—BORUM, P. Danish literature: a short critical survey. Copenhagen, Det Danske Selskab, 1979. 141p. illus. $9.95. ISBN: 8774290304.

62p. on the first thousand years and 50p. on contemporary literature. Quotations accompanied by translations. Bibliography (12p.), based on the Royal Library, Copenhagen, of English-language literary histories and English translations of literary works. Index of Danish authors. *Class No:* 839.8(091)

Biographies

[8039]

Dansk skønlitteraert Forfatterleksikon, 1900-1950. Dahl, S., *and others, eds.* København, Grønholt Pedersen, 1959-64. 3v.

Bio-bibliographies of *c.*3,500 20th-century Danish writers of belles lettres. Excludes those who have only written children's books. In each case a brief biography is followed by a very detailed bibliography of writings by the author, listing even unprinted works (particularly of value for authors of revues and plays) and newspapers, periodicals and collected works to which the author has contributed, and a list of works on the author. *Class No:* 839.8(092)

[8040]

Danske digtere i det 20. århundrede. Brostrøm, T. *and* Winge, M., *eds.* Nyredigeret og nyskrevet udg. København, Gad, 1980-82. 5v. illus. ISBN: 8712174505.

1st ed. 1951 (2v.); 2nd ed. 1965-66 (3v.).

Lengthy signed biographical essays on Danish authors (30 entries per vol., chronologically arranged, and averaging 12p.). New to this ed., and increasing its usefulness for reference, are author bibliographies of works and studies in each vol. General bibliography in v.1. Cumulative indexes of names and titles in v.5. *Class No:* 839.8(092)

[8041]

EHRENCRON-MÜLLER, H. Forfatterlexikon omfattende Danmark, Norge og Island indtil 1814. København, Aschehoug, 1924-39. 12v. & Suppt. 2.

Vols. 1-9 comprise a biobibliographical dictionary, alphabetically arranged, plus *Supplement*; vols. 10-12 are a bibliography of Holberg's works; and *Supplement 2* has corrections and additions to all vols. Extensive list of writings for each author. For later Norwegian writers, see Halvorsen's *Norsk forfatterlexikon, 1814-1880* at 839.6(092). *Class No:* 839.8(092)

[8042]

—ERSLEW, T.H. Almindeligt Forfatter-Lexicon for Kongeriget Danmark med tilhørende bilande, fra 1814 til 1840. Kjøbenhavn, Forlagsforeningens Forlag, 1843-53. 3v.

A biobibliographical dictionary of Danish authors which follows Ehrencron-Müller and is continued by *Supplement ... indtil Udgangen of Aaret 1853* (Kjøbenhavn, 1858-68. 3v.).
Class No: 839.8(092)

[8043]

Vor tids Hvem-skrev-hvad, efter 1914. Sandvej, K., *ed.* 3rd ed. Copenhagen, Politiken, 1968. 2v.

Biographies in v.1 and lists of works in v.2. Includes foreign writers who have been translated into Danish.

Preceded by *Hvem skrev hvad før 1914* (2nd ed. Copenhagen, Politiken, 1961. 510p.) which covers pre-1914 writers of Denmark and other Scandinavian lands.
Class No: 839.8(092)

84 Romance Literatures

Romance Literatures

[8044]
The Romance literatures. Parks, G.B. *and* Temple, R.Z., *eds.* New York, Ungar, 1970. 2v. (*Literatures of the world in English translation.*) ISBN: 0804432392.

V.1 covers Catalan, Italian, Portuguese and Brazilian, Provençal, Rumanian, Spanish, and Spanish American literatures, while v.2 covers French. Chronological sections for each language, in which translations are listed by author, then by translated title. Detailed index with over 17,000 entries. *Class No:* 84.0

[8045]
Romanische bibliographie, 1961/62-. Tübingen, Niemeyer, 1965-. Annual (formerly irregular). ISSN: 0080388x.

A continuation of the bibliographical supplement of *Zeitschrift für romanische Philologie, 1875/76-1960* (Halle, Niemeyer, 1877-1964).

See entry at 804/806(01). *Class No:* 84.0

French Literature

Bibliographies

[8046]
Bibliographie der französischen Literaturwissenschaft, 1956/58-. Frankfurt am Main, Klostermann, 1960-. v.1-. Originally biennial; annual since v.7. ISSN: 05232465.

A companion to *Bibliographie der deutschen Sprach- und Literaturwissenschaft* (*q.v.*), listing books, articles and theses in sections devoted to chronological periods, plus one each on generalities and French literature outside France. V.34, *1996* (1997. 1031p.), has 14,245 unannotated entries and a list of *c.*700 periodicals analyzed. Name and subject indexes. Contents table and all headings in French.
Class No: 840(01)

[8047]
A Critical bibliography of French literature. Cabeen, D.C., *and others, eds.* Syracuse, N.Y., Syracuse Univ. Press, 1947-92. 6v. in 10.

V.1 *The Mediaeval period,* ed. by U.T. Holmes. 1947. xxvi,256p.; enl. ed. 1952.

V.2 *The Sixteenth century,* ed. by A.H. Schutz. 1956. xlii,365p.; rev. ed., ed. by R.C. La Charité, 1985. xxxii,847p. $95. ISBN: 0815623089.

V.3 *The Seventeenth century,* ed. by N. Edelman. 1961. xlii,638p. $45. ISBN: 0815620071.

V.3A *The Seventeeth century. Supplement,* ed. by H.G. Hall. 1983. xxviii,460p. $65. ISBN: 0815622759.

V.4 *The Eighteenth century,* ed. by G.R. Havens and D.F. Bond. 1951. xxx,411p. $45. ISBN: 081562008x. *Supplement,*ed. by R.A. Brooks. 1968. xxiv,283p. $45. ISBN: 0815620098.

....*(contd.)*

V.5 *The Nineteenth century,* ed. by D. Baguley. 1992. 2pts. (xxxvii,1488p.). $225. ISBN: 0815625669.

V.6 *The Twentieth century,* ed. by D.W. Alden and R. Brooks. 1980. 3pts. (lvii,2073p.). $150. ISBN: 081562204x.

An invaluable selective, evaluative bibliography, arranged by chronological periods, with each section contributed by a specialist who critically appraises books, dissertations and articles, and frequently cites reviews. Index in each vol.

It should be noted that the 'revised' ed. of v.2 (1985) actually represents a complete reappraisal by 38 scholars of French Renaissance studies. The Introduction states that 'it is an entirely new and comprehensive work', but that the first ed. (1956) should not be dismissed as many entries in the rev. ed. refer specifically by number to entries therein.

V.5 was finally compiled during the period 1987-91 after false starts in the 1950s and 1970s. It has 11,909 entries in 38 chapters, of which 26 are devoted to individual authors. Useful checklist of reference works on allied literatures (9p.).

The 3 parts of v.6, which contain nearly 18,000 entries, are: 1. *General subjects and principally the novel before 1940* - 2. *Poetry, theater, and criticism before 1940, and essay* - 3. *All genres since 1940. Index.* *Class No:* 840(01)

[8048]
MAHAFFEY, D. A Concise bibliography of French literature. London, Bowker, 1975. xxvii,286p. ISBN: 0859350088.

Provides short-title descriptions of the major works of French literature written since 1100 by some 450 authors, giving dates of publication, notes on standard English translations and recommended critical studies. 6 period sections (A-Z by author within each period), preceded by a general section listing bibliographies, anthologies, literary histories, etc. Index of authors. *Class No:* 840(01)

[8049]
RANCOEUR, R. Bibliographie de la littérature française du Moyen Âge à nos jours, 1953-80. Paris, Colin, 1953-81. 28v.

Earlier titles were: 1953-61, *Bibliographie littéraire;* 1962-65, *Bibliographie de la littérature française moderne (XVIe - XXe siècles).*

An annual bibliography of editions and studies, which ceased publication with the vol. for 1980 (published 1981) which contained 7,525 citations. General sections followed by period sections. Author and subject indexes. Since 1981 has appeared regularly in *Revue d'histoire littéraire de la France* (Paris, Colin. 6 py. ISSN: 00352411).
Class No: 840(01)

[8050]
Research bibliographies and checklists. Deyermond, A.D., *and others, eds.* London, Grant & Cutler, 1971-.

Titles on French literature: 1. Little, R. *Saint-John Perse: a bibliography for students of his poetry*. 1971. 76p. £10.75. *Supplement No.1.* 1976. 88p. £10.75. *Supplement No.2.* 1982. 58p. £9.25 - 2 Sheringham, M. *André Breton: a bibliography*. 1972. 120p. £11.50. *Supplement No.1, 1972-*

....(contd.)
1989. 1992. 147p. £19.50 - 4. Hoy, P. *Julien Gracq: essai de bibliographie*. 1973. 101p. £11.50 - 5. Little, J.P. *Simone Weil: a bibliography*. 1973. 91p. £10.75. *Supplement No. 1*. 1979. 80p. £10.75 - 6. de Labriolle, J. *Claudel and the English-speaking world: a critical bibliography*. 1973p. 173p. £16.95 - 7. Scott, J.W. *Madame de Lafayette: a selective critical bibliography*. 1974. 76p. £10.75 - 8. Wright, B. *Eugène Fromentin: a bibliography*. 1973. 63p. £9.25 - 9. Wells, M.B. *Du Bellay: a bibliography*. 1974. 113p. £11.50 - 10. Bradby, D. *Adamov*. 1975. 77p. £10.75 - 15. Duggan, J.J. *A Guide to studies on the 'Chanson de Roland'*. 1976. 136p. £14.50 - 16. Bishop, M. *Pierre Reverdy: a bibliography*. 1976. 1976. £10.75 - 17. Kelly, D. *Chrétien de Troyes: an analytical bibliography*. 1976. 176p. £16.95 - 18. Rees, M. *French authors on Spain, 1800-1850: a checklist*. 1977. 123p. £14.50 - 21. Burgess, G.S. *Marie de France: an analytical bibliography*. 1977. 124p. £14.50. *Supplement No.1*. 1986. 76p. £10.75. *Supplement No.2*. 1997. 168p. £14.95 - 24. Hare, G. *Alphonse Daudet: a critical bibliography. I. Primary material*. 1978. 121p. £14.50. *II. Secondary material*. 1979. 185p. £16.95 - 25. Geoghegan, C. *Louis Aragon: esai de bibliographie. I. Œuvres, Tome 1 (1918-1959)*. 1979. 140p. £14.50. *I. Œuvres, Tome 2 (1960-1977)*. 1979. 144p. £14.50 - 26. Lowe, D.K. *Benjamin Constant: an annotated bibliography of critical editions and studies (1946-1978)*. 1979. 140p. £14.50 - 27. Mason, B. *Michel Butor: a checklist*. 1979. 98p. £11.50 - 28. Shirt, D.J. *T* *Class No:* 840(01)

[8051]
THOMAS, D.H. A Checklist of editions of major French authors in Oxford libraries, 1526-1800. Oxford, Voltaire Foundation, 1986. xiv,243p. £42 ISBN: 0729403475.

Lists *c.*2,850 editions of works by 50 authors found in 45 academic libraries. Gives brief descriptions and locations. Omits works written in Latin. A supplement appears in v.266 of *Studies on Voltaire* (Oxford, Voltaire Foundation, 1989). *Class No:* 840(01)

Middle Ages

[8052]
BOSSUAT, R. Manuel bibliographique de la littérature française du Moyen Âge: suivi des suppléments de 1949-1953 et 1954-1960. Single-volume reprint. Gex, Slatkine, 1986. xxiv+638+150+132p. ISBN: 205100739x.

Main work originally published Melun, 1951; supplements published Paris, 1955 and 1961.

Lists, with brief introductory notes, principal editions, translations, adaptations, and critical studies, in 2 main sections: 'L'Ancien français' and 'Le Moyen français'. Index of authors, titles and critics. Over 8,000 entries for material in French and other western European languages. *Class No:* 840(01)"01/14"

[8053]
—VIEILLIARD, F. *and* MONFRIN, J. Manuel bibliographique de la littérature française du Moyen Âge de Robert Bossuat: troisième supplément (1960-1980). Paris, CNRS, 1986-91. 2v.

V.1 *Les Origines. Les Légendes épiques. Le Roman courtois*. 1986. xii,392p.

V.2 *L'Ancien français (Chapitres IV à IX); Le Moyen français*. 1991. 742p.

The first vol. of the 3rd supplement to Bossuat's manual has 4,217 entries, independently numbered rather than continuing the original sequence. The original classification

....(contd.)
is retained with very few modifications. Concise annotations.

V.2 has 4,396 entries and cumulative indexes to the original work and to all 3 supplements. Detailed list of contents. 'The qualities for which this monumental work is well-known: its clarity, its convenience, the exhaustiveness of its documentation, and the judiciousness of its selection ... are even more apparent in the *Third Supplement* than in the original *Manual*' (*Modern Language Review*, v.89(2), 1994, p.469-70). *Class No:* 840(01)"01/14"

16th & 17th Centuries

[8054]
ARBOUR, R. L'Ère baroque en France: répertoire chronologique des éditions de textes littéraires. Genève, Droz, 1977-85. 4v. in 5.

V.1-2 *1585-1615*. 1977; v.3 *1616-1628*. 1979; v.4 *1629-1643*. 1980; v.5 *Supplément, 1585-1643*. 1985.

Lists literature in French; in Latin by French writers; in foreign languages published in France; translations of French literature into foreign languages; and French translations of foreign works. Arranged by year, then A-Z by author/anonymous title, giving library locations in France and abroad. Over 21,600 entries in all. Indexes of names, editors, places of publication, and pseudonyms in each vol. *Supplément* includes additions and amendments to earlier vols. *Class No:* 840(01)"15/16"

[8055]
CIORANESCU, A. Bibliographie de la littérature française du seizième siècle. Paris, Klinksieck, 1959 (repr. Genève, Slatkine, 1975). xiv,745p.

In 2 parts, covering generalities (p.3-73) and individual authors, A-Z (p.78-696), the latter part including works by and about the authors. Over 22,100 unannotated items, published up to 1950. Single index of names, anonymous titles and subjects. Interprets literature widely, to include science, theology, etc., but Cioranescu's bibliographies of later periods omit these marginal areas.
Class No: 840(01)"15/16"

[8056]
—CIORANESCU, A. Bibliographie de la littérature française du dix-septième siècle. Paris, Centre National de la Recherche Scientifique, 1965-6. 3v. (xiv,2231p.).

Over 67,400 unannotated entries, similarly arranged to those in the author's 16th-century bibliography, with generalities followed by individual authors, A-Z. Cut-off date: 1960. Separate indexes of authors, illustrators, pseudonyms, and subjects. *Class No:* 840(01)"15/16"

[8057]
French XVII: an annual descriptive bibliography of French seventeenth century studies. No. 27-. 1978-. Fort Collins, Colo., Colorado State Univ., for Seventeenth Century French Division of Modern Language Assoc. of America, 1979. Annual. ISSN: 01919199.

Preceded by *French III: bibliography of French seventeenth century studies,* nos. 1-26, 1952/53-1977 (Bloomington, Ind., Indiana Univ., 1953-78, for French Group III, MLA).

Lists books and articles in 5 sections: 1. Bibliography, linguistics and history of the book - 2. Artistic, political and social background - 3. Philosophy, science and religion - 4. Literary history and criticism -5. Authors and personages (A-Z). Brief annotations and citations to reviews. Since 1981, it has included details of research in progress.
Class No: 840(01)"15/16"

18th Century

[8058]
CIORANESCU, A. Bibliographie de la littérature française du dix-huitième siècle. Paris, Centre National de la Recherche Scientifique, 1969. 3v. (vii,2137p.).

Similar in format to the author's earlier bibliographies, with over 27,000 unannotated entries on general topics and individual authors, and separate indexes for authors, illustrators, pseudonyms, and subjects. Cut-off date: 1960.
Class No: 840(01)"17"

[8059]
CONLON, P.M. Le Siècle des lumières: bibliographie chronologique. Genève, Droz, 1983-1997. v.1-17 (in progress). (*Histoire des idées et critique littéraire.*)

A bibliography of 18th-century French literature, arranged by year (starting 1716), then by author or anonymous title. Each vol. covers 5 or 6 years and has *c.*4,500 entries, giving bibliographical details and locations in 150 European and North American libraries. Has reached 1775 with v.17. 'The whole work continues to win unmitigated admiration for its indefatigably erudite author' (*French Studies*, v.45(3), July 1991, p.321). *Class No:* 840(01)"17"

19th & 20th Centuries

[8060]
French VII bibliography: critical and biographical references for the study of contemporary French literature. Vols. 1-4 (nos. 1-20). New York, Stechert-Hafner (later French Institute), 1949-69. Annual. 4v.

An unannotated bibliography of books and articles, compiled by the Bibliography Committee for French VII of the MLA, covering general subjects in a classified arrangement, author-subjects (A-Z), and cinema. Thoroughly cross-referenced. Includes references to reviews of books, plays and films. Indexes of critics and of authors as subjects. Over 65,000 items in all. Continued by *French XX bibliography*. *Class No:* 840(01)"18/19"

[8061]
French XX bibliography: critical and biographical references for French literature since 1885. V.5, no.1-. 1968-. Alden, D.W., *and others, eds.* New York, French Institute, 1970-85; Selinsgrove, Pa., Susquehanna Univ. Press, and London, Associated Univ. Presses, 1986-. Annual. ISSN: 00850888.

Follows *French VII*, whose numbering it continued, starting with item no. 65,343, until the end of v.5 (issue no. 25) with item no. 102,455. Each issue is now individually numbered, v.10, no. 3 (issue no. 48), 1993, having 12,063 entries. Each issue covers the previous year's publications and incorporates new entries to complete the information for earlier years. Cross-referencing continues to be very thorough. *Class No:* 840(01)"18/19"

[8062]
TALVART, H. *and* **PLACE, J. Bibliographie des auteurs modernes de langue française (1801-1975).** Paris, Chronique des Lettres Françaises, 1928-76. v.1-22. (in progress).

Bio-bibliographies of leading 19th- and 20th-century authors, each vol. including material published up to the year of its publication with title-page details varying accordingly; *e.g.* v.1 covers 1801-1927; v.22, 1801-1975 (latest vol., taking the A-Z sequence to Morgan). Arranged by author, with entries including brief biography, list of works, and selected list of biographical and critical studies.

Vols. 16-17 comprise a title index of works covered in vols. 1-15 (up to Mirbeau). V.22 (1976) includes an index of illustrators of works mentioned in vols. 1-22.
Class No: 840(01)"18/19"

[8063]
THIEME, H.P. Bibliographie de la littérature française de 1800 à 1930. Paris, Droz, 1933 (repr. Genève, Slatkine, 1983). 3v. in 2 (2370p.). ISBN: 2051004781.

1st ed. 1907.

Vols. 1-2 comprise unannotated primary and secondary bibliographies for *c.*2,000 authors, A-Z. V.3 is a classified list of books and articles on French literature, language and culture.

Supplemented by Dreher, S. and Rolli, M., *Bibliographie de la littérature française, 1930-1939* (Genève, Droz, 1948-9; repr. Genève, Slatkine, 1976. xviii,438p.) and by Drevet, M.L., *Bibliographie de la littérature française, 1940-1949* (Genève, Droz, 1954-5; repr. Genève, Slatkine, 1979. xvi,644p.), which follow the same format and add new material on the authors covered in Thieme's first 2 vols. Both include lists of pseudonyms.
Class No: 840(01)"18/19"

Encyclopaedias & Dictionaries

[8064]
BOUTY, M. Dictionnaire des oeuvres et des thèmes de la littérature française. Nouv. éd., rev. et aug. Paris, Hachette-Classiques, 1991. 447p. Fr.89. ISBN: 2010165837.

1st ed. 1972.

An analysis of major French works and an index to their themes. Part 1 lists works by title, A-Z, and Part 2 lists themes, A-Z, with references to relevant works.
Class No: 840(03)

[8065]
Dictionnaire des grandes oeuvres de la littérature française. Mitterand, H., *ed.* Paris, Robert, 1992. 706p. Fr.200. ISBN: 2850361968.

Entries on *c.*1,200 works, published 1040-1990, are arranged A-Z by author and include summary, analysis, review of critical reception, and bibliographies of editions and studies. Indexes of authors and titles (over 6,000 mentioned). *Class No:* 840(03)

[8066]
Dictionnaire des lettres françaises. Grente, G., *ed.* Paris, Fayard, 1951-96. 5v. in 7.

V.1 *Le Moyen Âge.* 2nd ed. 1994. lxi,1506p. ISBN: 221359340x.

V.2 *Le Seizième siècle.* 1951. xxv,718p.

V.3 *Le Dix-septième siècle.* 2nd ed. 1996. lxiv,1278p. ISBN: 221359435x.

V.4 *Le Dix-huitième siècle.* 2nd ed. 1995. lxvi,1371p. ISBN: 2213595437.

V.5 *Le Dix-neuvième siècle.* 1971-2. 2v.

Each vol. has a general survey of the period concerned, with bibliography, followed by signed articles, A-Z, on authors, literary works, themes, institutions and genres. Major authors are treated at length (*e.g.* 21p. on Voltaire in v.4) with a detailed biographical account followed by an extensive bibliography of works and studies. List of thematic articles at end of each vol.

New ed. of v.1 represents a major expansion and revision to reflect changes in research emphasis over 3 decades. 80%

....(contd.)
of the entries have been revised and all have been updated bibliographically. New eds. of vols. 3 and 4 show fewer changes. *Class No:* 840(03)

[8067]
Dictionnaire des littératures de langue française. Beaumarchais, J.-P. de, *& others, eds.* 3e éd. Paris, Bordas, 1994. 4v. (3120p.). illus. Fr.1800.
1st ed. 1984, in 3 vols.; 2nd ed. 1987.
Covers French literature from the 9th century to the present, with over 2,300 signed articles, arranged A-Z, on authors (1,900), anonymous works, literary reviews, and French-language literatures of other countries. Entries on major authors are very comprehensive, including survey of life and works (with extremely useful chronological tables), critical commentary, plot synopses of key works, and bibliography. Illustrations (350 in colour) are grouped thematically and indexed in v.4, which also has index of 21,000 titles cited in the text, index of literary terms, and lists of Academy members and literary prize-winners.
Class No: 840(03)

[8068]
Dictionnaire des œuvres littéraires de langue française. Beaumarchais, J.-P. de *and* Couty, D., *eds.* Paris, Bordas, 1994. 4v. (2360p.). illus. Fr.1800.
Signed articles of up to 5 pages, by almost 100 specialists, on *c.*3,700 literary works, 45% of them published since 1900. Entries set the work's first appearance in context and provide synopsis, critical analysis, and details of available editions, but no references to secondary sources. Many colour illustrations. Cross references. Author index. Also available on CD-ROM from Liris Interactive.
Class No: 840(03)

[8069]
DOLBOW, S.W. Dictionary of modern French literature: from the Age of Reason through Realism. New York, Greenwood, 1986. x,365p. $69.50. ISBN: 0313237840.
Nearly 300 entries, arranged A-Z, covering the major writers, works, and literary movements of the period 1715-1880. Bibliographies appended to each entry are largely confined to books and articles published in English, 1980-85. Plenty of cross-references. Appendix A lists historical and literary events and B groups entries by subject matter or period. Index. A companion vol. will cover 1880 to the present. *Class No:* 840(03)

[8070]
LEMAÎTRE, H. Dictionnaire Bordas de littérature française. Nouv. éd. Paris, Bordas, 1994. xi,915p. Fr.149. ISBN: 204019682x.
Formerly known as *Dictionnaire Bordas de littérature française et francophone*.
Over 1,300 entries for authors, giving biography, critical analysis and list of published works; 800 major works summarized and 300 entries for literary movements, genres and terms. Index of works. *Class No:* 840(03)

[8071]
LEVI, A. Guide to French literature. Detroit & London, St. James Press, 1992-4. 2v. $250. ISBN: 155862161x.
[V.1] *Beginnings to 1789*. 1994. xlvi,1111p.
[V.2] *1789 to the Present*. 1992. xiii,884p.
326 scholarly essays (average 5 large-format pages., with some as long as 20,000 words) by a single author, most of them on writers, providing detailed biography, critical evaluation of all major works, plot summaries and bibliographies of primary and secondary materials. 21

....(contd.)
topical entries on literary movements, groups, publications and controversies. Each vol. has chronology, title index and comprehensive general index (173p. in v.1; 110p. in v.2), which includes additional concise entries on authors and subjects not covered in the body of the text. Title index is an extremely valuable quick-reference source, giving author and date for each work (over 7,000 titles listed in v.2).
Class No: 840(03)

[8072]
The New Oxford companion to literature in French. France, P., *ed.* Oxford, Clarendon Press, 1995. xlix,865p. £35. ISBN: 0198661258.
A long-awaited replacement for Harvey & Heseltine's *Oxford companion to French literature* (1959), but claims to be not so much a revised ed. as a 'new and completely reconceived work', the amended title indicating that French literature from outside France is now included. Other areas given greater coverage include critical theory, genre fiction and women's writing.
Over 3,000 signed entries, A-Z, on authors, works and subjects, with brief bibliographies after author entries. A list of subject entries is provided and it includes genres, schools, movements, institutions, national literatures, other languages and foreign influences, and relevant topics from linguistics, history, politics, religion and the arts. Very useful entries on Dictionaries, Bibliographies, and Histories of French literature. 130 contributors. *Class No:* 840(03)

[8073]
ROUCH, A. *and* CLAVREUIL, G. Littératures nationales d'écriture française; Afrique noire, Caraïbes, Océan Indien: histoire littéraire et anthologie. Paris, Bordas, 1986. 512p. illus. ISBN: 2040165703.
Chapters on 21 countries, A-Z, plus brief notes on 7 more. Outline of each country's literary history is followed by entries on authors, A-Z, giving brief biography, survey of literary output, list of works, and excerpt from a key work. 155 authors fully treated with many more mentioned in the histories. Bibliography of general studies (2p.). Index of authors. *Class No:* 840(03)

20th Century

[8074]
Dictionnaire des oeuvres du XXe siècle: littérature française et francophone. Mitterand, H., *ed.* Paris, Robert, 1995. 621p. Fr.240. ISBN: 285036262x.
Entries on 1,500 literary works and 50 journals, plus 73 overview articles on movements, genres and topics. Entries on works give author, genre, first publication date, brief synopsis and analysis, and list of in-print editions and selected critical studies. Chronology of cultural and political events. Indexes of authors and titles. *Class No:* 840(03)"19"

Handbooks & Manuals

[8075]
BASSAN, F., *and others*. French language and literature: an annotated bibliography. [2nd ed.]. New York, Garland, 1989. xix,365p. $59. ISBN: 0824047982.
See entry at 804.0(01). *Class No:* 840(035)

[8076]

BEUGNOT, B. *and* **MOUREAUX, J.M. Manuel bibliographique des études littéraires,** les bases de l'histoire littéraire, les voies nouvelles de l'analyse critique. Paris, Nathan, 1982. 479p. ISBN: 2091905143.

A handbook for graduate students of French literature, in 3 sections covering basic research tools, the main fields of research, and new areas of research (*e.g.* French literature outside France). 3,400 entries, with the emphasis on recent publications, arranged by subject, then chronologically. Name and subject indexes. *Class No:* 840(035)

[8077]

KEMPTON, R. French literature: an annotated guide to selected bibliographies. New York, Modern Language Assoc. of America, 1981. xii,42p. $10. ISBN: 0873529510.

The annotations in this very selective listing are instructive, often evaluative, and include references to other relevant titles. 'An excellent introductory guide to library research for advanced students' (Bassan, F., and others, *French language and literature*, 1989, p.9).
Class No: 840(035)

[8078]

OSBURN, C.B. Research and reference guide to French studies. 2nd ed. Metuchen, N.J., Scarecrow, 1981. xxxviii,532p. ISBN: 0810814404.

1st ed. 1968; *Supplement,* 1972.

Nearly 6,000 entries in 6 parts and 87 chapters: 1. French literature - 2. French language - 3. French language and literature outside France - 4. Romance philology and Occitan studies - 5. General background and related areas - 6. Scholars and critics. Far more entries than Bassan (*q.v.*) including many sources for individual authors, but without his annotations. Author and subject indexes.
Class No: 840(035)

Theses

[8079]

BARNWELL, H.T. *and* **BARNWELL, J. Bibliography of theses on French language and literature deposited in university libraries of the United Kingdom (1905-1975).** Society for French Studies, c/o Univ. of Bath, 1983. ix,72p.

See entry at 804.0(043). *Class No:* 840(043)

[8080]

Current research in French studies at universities in the United Kingdom and Ireland. 1969/70-. Glasgow, Society for French Studies, 1970-. Biennial. ISSN: 13509209.

See entry at 804.0(043). *Class No:* 840(043)

[8081]

GABEL, G.U. Répertoire bibliographique des thèses françaises (1885-1975) concernant la littérature française des origines à nos jours. Köln, Gemini, 1984. 336p. ISBN: 3922331114.

4,100 items, of which 2,365 are devoted to 19th- and 20th-century literature. Arranged in chronological sections, with a general subsection followed by individual authors, A-Z. Indexes of thesis-writers and of topics.

Gabel has also compiled (with G.R. Gabel) *La Littérature française: bibliographie des thèses de doctorat soutenues devant les universités autrichiennes et suisses, 1885-1975* (Köln, Gemini, 1981. 130p. ISBN: 3922331017), which lists 1,475 theses in period sections. Name and subject indexes.
Class No: 840(043)

Periodicals

[8082]

PLACE, J.M. *and* **VASSEUR, A. Bibliographie des revues et journaux littéraires des XIXe et XXe siècles.** Paris, Éditions de la Chronique des Lettres Françaises, 1973-7. 3v.

Vols. 1-2 list chronologically periodicals which first appeared 1840-1899, giving a history of each work, a facsimile of the first cover, details of major contributors, complete contents listing for each issue, and much other useful information. V.3 covers the period 1916-25 and has index of names. *Class No:* 840(051)

Excerpts

[8083]

Modern French literature. Popkin, D. *and* Popkin, M., *eds.* New York, Ungar, 1977. 2v. (xxiii,597p.; xvii,590p.). (*A Library of literary criticism.*) ISBN: 0804432562.

Excerpts from critical writings on 168 20th-century authors. All excerpts in English, many of them specially translated by the editors. Arranged A-Z, with index of critics in v.2. List of non-French authors by country (13 countries).
Class No: 840(082.200)

Gazetteers

[8084]

Guide littéraire de la France. Paris, Hachette, 1964. xxii,836p. illus. maps.

A guide to localities with literary connections, arranged in 6 sections for the major regions with 128 itineraries. Masses of detailed information, as expected from a work in the *Guides bleus* series. Indexes of Paris streets, towns, and writers. *Class No:* 840(083.86)

Histories

[8085]

BIRKETT, J. *and* **KEARNS, J. Guide to French literature:** from early modern to postmodern. Basingstoke, Macmillan, 1997. x,361p. £45. ISBN: 0333428536.

A slightly misleading title, in that this is a history of French literature since the Renaissance. 9 chapters with many subsections. Detailed bibliographical references (all secondary material) arranged by chapter (34p.). More coverage of women's writing and Francophone literature outside France than in traditional histories. Index.
Class No: 840(091)

[8086]

BRUNEL, P., *and others.* **Histoire de la littérature française.** Nouv. éd., augm. Paris, Bordas, 1986. 2v. Fr.220.

1st ed. 1977.

V.1 *Du Moyen Âge au XVIIIe siècle.* 381p. ISBN: 2040166548.

V.2 *XIXe et XXe siècles.* 416p. ISBN: 2040166564.

New ed. includes Black African literature, updated bibliographies and a chronology of francophone literatures, 1945-85. *Class No:* 840(091)

[8087]

Histoire littéraire de la France. Abraham, P. *and* Desnée, R., *eds*. Nouv. éd. Paris, Messidor-Éds. Sociales, 1987. 6v.

V.1, *Des origines à 1600.* 659p. ISBN: 2209059283; v.2, *1600-1715.* 492p. ISBN: 2209019362; v.3, *1715-1789.* 624p. ISBN: 2209059291; v.4, *1789-1848.* 588p. ISBN: 2209059305; v.5, *1848-1913.* 814p. ISBN: 2209052459; v.6, *De 1913 à nos jours.* 920p. ISBN: 2209054400.

The work of many specialists. Each vol. has bibliography of general studies; primary and secondary bibliographies for individual authors; name index; and very detailed chronological tables of literary, historical and cultural events. The bibliography in v.6 (57p.) includes sections on French literature outside France. *Class No:* 840(091)

[8088]

Histoire littéraire de la France: ouvrage commencé par des religieux bénédictins de la Congrégation de Saint Maur, et continué par des membres de l'Institut (Académie des Inscriptions et Belles-Lettres). Paris, Imprimerie Nationale, 1733-1981. v.1-41 (in progress).

An extremely detailed history, which has not yet got beyond the 14th century. Comprises lengthy, signed contributions, mainly on individual authors, with bibliographical references. Indexes to groups of vols. are occasionally included, *e.g.* v.38 has index to vols. 33-38.
Class No: 840(091)

[8089]

LANSON, G. Histoire de la littérature française: remaniée et complétée par la période 1850-1950 par P. Tuffrau. Paris, Hachette, 1952. (repr. 1986). xviii,1441p. Fr.180. ISBN: 2010118154.

The standard single-vol. history, first published 1894 with many subsequent editions. Footnotes include biographical and bibliographical data. Lengthy chronological table appended. Index of names. Detailed contents table.
Class No: 840(091)

[8090]

Littérature française. Pichois, C., *ed.* Paris, Arthaud, 1968-79. 16v. illus.

V.1-2 *Le Moyen Âge,* by J.C. Payen and D. Poirion. 1970-71.

V.3-5 *La Renaissance,* by Y. Giraud and others. 1972-74.

V.6-8 *L'Âge classique,* by A. Adam and others. 1968-71.

V.9-11 *Le XVIIIe siècle,* by J. Erhrard and others. 1974-77.

V.12-14 *Le Romantisme,* by M. Milner and others. 1968-79.

V.15-16 *Le XXe siècle,* by P. Walzer and G. Brée. 1975-78.

Studies of literary movements and major writers, followed in each vol. by a directory of authors of the period, with biographies and extensive bibliographies of works and criticism. There are also chapter bibliographies and each vol. has a synoptic chart listing literary, historical and cultural events.

A 9-vol. set, *Littérature française/Poche,* was produced by the same publisher, 1984-86, under Pichois' editorship. Each vol. has dictionary of authors, bibliographies, and chronologies. *Class No:* 840(091)

[8091]

A New history of French literature. Hollier, D., *ed.* Cambridge, Mass., Harvard Univ. Press, 1989. xxv,1150p. illus. £19.95. ISBN: 0674615662.

165 signed essays by different (mainly American) contributors are arranged chronologically from 778 to 1985, each headed by a date and a headline, 'evoking an event, which specifies not so much the essay's content as its chronological point of departure' (*Introduction*). Essays range from 1,500 to 4,000 words and cover genres, individual books, literary movements, periods, etc. but none are devoted to specific authors. English title given for each French work mentioned and all quotations in English. Bibliography after each essay. Chronology (13p.). Map. Index.

Well received in a lengthy review in *TLS* (no.4531, Feb. 2, 1990, p.107-8) but 'not to be thought of as an exhaustive reference book.' *Class No:* 840(091)

[8092]

WORTH-STYLIANOU, V., ***ed.*** **Cassell guide to literature in French.** London, Cassell, 1996. 288p. £50. ISBN: 0304331945.

A misleadingly titled work which is actually a history of French literature from the Middle Ages to the 1990s. Chapters on 8 major periods, plus one on Francophone literatures and one on French thought since 1940. Chronology. Index. 8 contributors. Strong on women's writing. *Class No:* 840(091)

20th Century

[8093]

BOISDEFFRE, P. de. Histoire de la littérature de langue française des années 1930 aux années 1980. Nouv. éd., entièrement refondue. Paris, Perrin, 1985. 2v. ISBN: 226200370x.

V.1 *Roman et théâtre.* 1390p.

V.2 *Poésie et idées. Dictionnaire des auteurs.* 1254p.
Class No: 840(091)"19"

[8094]

BRÉE, G. Twentieth-century French literature.
Guiney, L., *tr.* Chicago and London, Univ. of Chicago Press, 1983. viii,390p. $30. ISBN: 0226071952.

Originally published Paris, 1978, as v.16 of Arthaud's *Littérature française* series, under the title *Le XXe siècle II: 1920-1970.*

Particularly useful for its dictionary of authors (58p.), which provides biobibliographical data on *c.*150 writers; list of literary journals and reviews (4p.); and bibliography (10p.). Index. *Class No:* 840(091)"19"

Biographies

[8095]

Dictionary of literary biography. Detroit, Gale, 1978-98. v.1-188 (in progress). £112 per vol.

The following vols., all edited by C.S. Brosman, cover French literature:

V.65 *French novelists, 1900-1930.* 1988.

V.72 *French novelists, 1930-1960.* 1988.

V.83 *French novelists since 1960.* 1989.

V.119 *Nineteenth-century French fiction writers: Romanticism and Realism, 1800-1860.* 1992.

V.123 *Nineteenth-century French fiction writers: Naturalism and beyond, 1860-1900.* 1992.

For a description of the series, see entry at 82(092).
Class No: 840(092)

[8096]

GARCIN, J. Le Dictionnaire: littérature française contemporaine. Paris, Bourin, 1988. 452p. Fr.150. ISBN: 287686021x.

Entries on 250 authors written in the third person *by the authors themselves,* describing and explaining their work. Bibliographies of works appended. *Class No:* 840(092)

[8097]

JOURDAIN, G. *and* **FAVRE, Y.-A. Dictionnaire des auteurs de langue française.** Paris, Garnier, 1980. 437p. Fr.100. ISBN: 2705002944.

Entries on *c.*1,200 authors from the Middle Ages to the 1970s, with good coverage of writers based outside France. Gives date and place of birth and death, with brief biography including titles and dates of works. *Class No:* 840(092)

Women

[8098]

French women writers. Sartori, E.M. *and* Zimmerman, D. W., *eds.* Lincoln, Neb., Univ. of Nebraska Press, 1994. xxiii,632p. $25. ISBN: 0803292244.

Originally published New York, Greenwood, 1991, as *French women writers: a bio-bibliographical source book.*

Lengthy, signed articles on over 50 writers, A-Z, from all periods, comprising biography, discussion of major themes and survey of critical reactions. Each is followed by bibliographies of primary works, English translations and selected critical studies, with more information provided for lesser-known writers. Additional chapter on medieval women troubadours. Chronology 'situating women writers in French history' (23p.). List of authors by birth-date. Title and subject indexes. *Class No:* 840(092)-0055.2

French Literature in Translation

[8099]

KEENOY, R., *& others.* The Babel guide to French fiction in English translation. London, Boulevard Books, 1996. 256p. £9.95. ISBN: 1899460101.

Provides 150 original reviews of key 20th-century French fiction titles, with excerpts, and lists all English translations of French fiction published since 1950, including works by Francophone writers of many countries. *Class No:* 840-03

French Poetry

Bibliographies

[8100]

COLEMAN, K. Guide to French poetry explication. New York, Hall, 1993. 593p. $55. ISBN: 0816190755.

Lists English- and French-language criticism published 1960-90. Arranged by poet, A-Z, then by individual poem, with studies listed (without annotation) under each poem. Coverage extends to French-language poets from Canada, Africa and the Caribbean. Index of critics. List of sources. 'In the guide's simplicity lies its strength' (*Choice*, v.31(3), Nov. 1993, p.426). *Class No:* 840-1(01)

[8101]

LACHÈVRE, F. Bibliographie des recueils collectifs de poésies du XVIe siècle (du'Jardin de plaisance', 1502, aux 'Recueils de Toussaint du Bray', 1609). Paris, Champion, 1922 (repr. Genève, Slatkine, 1967). 613p.

Describes the contents of 16th-century verse collections and provides attributions for many anonymous works. Chronologically arranged, with title index to collections and indexes of names and pseudonyms. *Class No:* 840-1(01)

[8102]

—LACHÈVRE, F. Bibliographie des recueils collectifs de poésies publiées de 1597 à 1700. Paris, Leclerc, 1901-05 (repr. Genève, Slatkine, 1967). 4v.

V.1, *1597-1635;* v.2, *1636-1661;* v.3, *1662-1700;* v.4, *Supplément (additions, corrections, tables générales).*

Describes contents of 17th-century verse collections (arranged chronologically), with bio-bibliographies of poets and attributions for anonymous poems. Several useful indexes in v.4, to poets, editors, titles of collections, etc.

Supplemented by Lachèvre's *Les Recueils collectifs de poésies libres et satiriques publiés depuis 1600 jusqu'à la mort de Théophile (1626). Bibliographie de ces recueils et bio-bibliographie des auteurs qui y figurent* (Paris, Champion, 1914-22). *Class No:* 840-1(01)

[8103]

LINKER, R.W. A Bibliography of Old French lyrics. University, Miss., Romance Monographs Inc., 1979. 401p. $52. ISBN: 8449928095.

Based on a reworking and updating of the material in G. Raynaud's *Bibliographie des chansonniers français* (Paris, 1884).

The first part lists bibliographies of manuscripts, anthologies of lyrics, critical studies, etc., while the second part is a bibliography of the lyrics themselves, arranged by lyrist (264 names), then by initial word, with 1,751 anonymous poems listed separately by first word. Cross-index of Raynaud's and Linker's numbers.

See also *The Lyrics of the Trouvères: a research guide (1970-1990),* by E. Doss-Quinby (New York, Garland, 1993. 278p. ISBN: 0815300859). *Class No:* 840-1(01)

Encyclopaedias & Dictionaries

[8104]

CHARPENTREAU, J. *and* **GEORGES, J. Dictionnaire des poètes et de la poésie.** Paris, Gallimard, 1983. 427p. illus. ISBN: 2070510190.

*c.*400 entries, A-Z, mainly for individual poets and comprising picture, biography, principal works, and a short extract. Some entries on poetic movements. *Class No:* 840-1(03)

[8105]

FLUTRE, L.-F. Table des noms propres avec toutes leurs variantes figurant dans les romans du Moyen Âge; écrits en français ou en provençal et actuellement publiés ou analysés. Poitiers, Centre d'Études Supérieures de Civilisation Médiévale, 1962. xvi,324p.

Lists proper names found in medieval romances, with separate sections for personal and geographical (including ethnic) names. *c.*12,000 main entries, with citations to 220 texts. Bibliography of sources. *Class No:* 840-1(03)

[8106]

—LANGLOIS, E. Table des noms propres de toute nature compris dans les chansons de geste imprimées. Paris, Bouillon, 1904 (repr. New York, Franklin, 1971). xx,674p. ISBN: 0833742116.

Lists personal and geographical names in a single A-Z sequence. Over 6,000 main entries. Bibliography of *c.*100 texts cited in the dictionary. *Class No:* 840-1(03)

[8107]

—WEST, G.D. An Index of proper names in French Arthurian verse romances, 1150-1300. Toronto, Univ. of Toronto Press, 1969. xxv,168p. ISBN: 0802052266.

*c.*2,500 entries, giving variant forms of the name, explanatory notes, exact citations to texts, and (occasionally) references to critical studies. Bibliography (11p.).

West has also compiled *An Index to proper names in French Arthurian prose romances* (Toronto, 1978. xxix,312p. ISBN: 0802053882), which is equally well presented and has bibliography of texts and studies (16p.). *Class No:* 840-1(03)

[8108]

RUCK, E.H. An Index of themes and motifs in twelfth-century French Arthurian poetry. Woodbridge, Boydell & Brewer, 1991. 208p. £39.50. ISBN: 085991335x.

Analyzes not only the recognized literary themes (*e.g.* the Unspelling Quest, the Faithless Wife), but also everyday motifs such as weaponry. Covers all 4 Tristan poems, all the works of Chrétien de Troyes and several other poems. *Class No:* 840-1(03)

Histories

[8109]

SABATIER, R. Histoire de la poésie française. Paris, A. Michel, 1975-88. 6v. in 9.

Volumes on the Middle Ages, 16th, 17th, 18th, 19th, and 20th centuries, the 19th having 2 parts and the 20th 3 parts. A comprehensive history, with sections on hundreds of poets with quotations and lists of works. Each vol. has index and detailed contents table. Includes French poets from outside France. *Class No:* 840-1(091)

Mallarmé

[8110]

MORRIS, D.H. Stéphane Mallarmé: twentieth century criticism (1901-1971). University, Miss., Romance Monographs Inc., 1977. 208p. ISBN: 8439964234.

1,077 items chronologically arranged, most of them briefly annotated. Index of authors, editors and translators, and subject index.

Supplemented by *Stéphane Mallarmé: twentieth-century criticism (1972-79)* (1989. 97p. $22. ISBN: 8459927172), which adds 358 recent items and includes a decade-by-decade summary of Mallarmé scholarship. *Class No:* 840-1MAL

Valéry

[8111]

ARNOLD, A.J. Paul Valéry and his critics: a bibliography. French-language criticism, 1890-1927. Charlottesville, Va., Univ. of Virginia Press, 1970. (repr. New York, Haskell, 1972). xxii,617p. $68.95. ISBN: 0838315909.

1,969 briefly annotated entries, arranged chronologically. Title index. *Class No:* 840-1VAL

[8112]

KARAISKAKIS, G. *and* CHAPON, F. Bibliographie des oeuvres de Paul Valéry, publiées de 1889 à 1965. Paris, Blaizot, 1976. xl,575p.

Fully descriptive listing with 475 entries chronologically arranged. Title index. *Class No:* 840-1VAL

Villon

[8113]

PECKHAM, R.D. François Villon: a bibliography. New York, Garland, 1990. xx,534p. $69. (*Garland medieval bibliographies.*) ISBN: 0824045300.

Over 2,000 entries in 8 sections, covering documentary sources of biographical data; textual sources of Villon's work; editions; translations; general and topical studies; line, section and poem studies; works inspired by Villon; reviews and abstracts. Covers works published mid-15th century to 1985 in 25 languages. Largely unannotated, but fully cross-referenced. Index of authors, editors and translators. Subject index. The compiler provides updates in the journal *Fifteenth-century studies*.

See also *François Villon: Bibliographie und Materialen, 1489-1988*, ed. by R. Sturm (München, Saur, 1990. 2v. ISBN: 3598108923), of which v.1 (344p. illus.) is a bibliography of 1,895 editions and studies, arranged by year, with indexes of authors, translators, illustrators, publishers and countries. *Class No:* 840-1VIL

French Drama

[8114]

BRADBY, D. Modern French drama, 1940-1990. 2nd ed. Cambridge, Cambridge Univ. Press, 1991. 336p. illus. ISBN: 0521402719.

1st ed. 1984, as *Modern French drama, 1940-1980*

A thorough history, illustrated with production photographs. Quotations in English. Bibliography lists the works of over 60 dramatists, A-Z, and of numerous critics and theatre historians. Historical table of the productions cited gives date, author, title, director and theatre. Index. *Class No:* 840-2

[8115]

LANCASTER, H.C. A History of French dramatic literature in the seventeenth century. Baltimore, Johns Hopkins Press, 1929-42 (repr. New York, Gordian Press, 1966). 5v. in 9. $450. ISBN: 0877520607.

Part 1: *The Pre-classical period, 1610-1634.* 2v.
Part 2: *The Period of Corneille, 1635-1651.* 2v.
Part 3: *The Period of Molière, 1652-1672.* 2v.
Part 4: *The Period of Racine, 1673-1700.* 2v.
Part 5: *Recapitulation, 1610-1700.* 235p.

A comprehensive history of the golden age of French drama, with detailed bibliographic information in footnote references. The second vol. of each part has a list of plays first acted during the period covered, with date and place of first performance, and an index. Part 5 has cumulative indexes of subjects, plays and names. *Class No:* 840-2

[8116]

LEWICKA, H. Bibliographie du théâtre profane français des XVe et XVIe siècles. 2e éd., rev. et aug. Paris, Éditions du Centre National de la Recherche Scientifique, 1980. 181p. ISBN: 2222023424.

1st ed. 1972.

A classified bibliography of 1,826 studies in 14 sections, briefly annotated. Indexes of places; dramatists and play titles; and modern editors and critics. *Class No:* 840-2

[8117]

WICKS, C.B. The Parisian stage: alphabetical indexes of plays and authors. University, Ala., Univ. of Alabama Press, 1950-79. 5v.

V.1, *1800-1815.* 1950; v.2, *1816-1830.* 1953; v.3, *1831-1850.* 1961; v.4, *1851-1875,* 1967; v.5, *1876-1900.* 1979.

Lists nearly 32,000 plays presented in Paris, based on information in contemporary newspapers. Each vol. has A-Z list by title plus author index, with cumulative author index in v.5. Entries state title and sub-title, type of play, number of acts, whether in prose or verse, real names of authors, theatre and date of Paris première. *Class No:* 840-2

Anouilh

[8118]

KELLY, K.W. Jean Anouilh: an annotated bibliography. Metuchen, N.J., Scarecrow, 1973. viii,132p. ISBN: 0810805936.

Ch. 3 lists 38 full-length studies by author with annotations and ch. 4 lists 278 shorter studies without annotation. Ch. 5 lists Anouilh's plays A-Z by title, giving editions, translations, plot summary, details of first productions in Paris, London and New York, and lists of critical works in date order. Ch. 6 lists Anouilh's other works, including screenplays and ballets. 936 entries in all. Index of critics. *Class No:* 840-2ANO

Beaumarchais

[8119]

MORTON, B.N. *and* **SPINELLI, D.C. Beaumarchais: a bibliography.** Ann Arbor, Mich., Olivia and Hill Press, 1988. xxiii,374p. ISBN: 0934034087.

2,058 entries covering both primary and secondary material published since 1767. Includes translations, parodies, imitations, satires, adaptations, music, and a survey (nearly 250 entries) of the long series of controversies and litigation to which the dramatist was prone. Locations indicated wherever possible. Manuscripts excluded. 880 entries for biographical and critical studies are concisely annotated. Author index. *Class No:* 840-2BEA

Corneille

[8120]

PICOT, E. Bibliographie cornélienne; ou, Description raisonnée de toutes les éditions des oeuvres de Pierre Corneille, des imitations ou traductions qui en ont été faites, et des ouvrages relatifs à Corneille et à ses écrits. Reprint of 1876 ed. Millwood, N.Y., Kraus, 1990. xv,552p. ISBN: 0811538192.

Originally published Paris, Fontaine, 1876.

1,585 annotated items in 21 sections, with full descriptive entries for the major works. Index of printers and publishers, and general index.

Supplemented by *Additions à la 'Bibliographie cornélienne'* by P. Le Verdier and E. Pelay (Rouen, Lestringant; Paris, Rahir, 1908. xi,251p.) which was reprinted by Van Bekhoven (Holland) in 1968.

For more recent critical studies, see A. Ritter's *Bibliographie zu Pierre Corneille, von 1958 bis 1983* (Erfstadt, Lukassen, 1983. iii,229p. ISBN: 3923769067), which is chronologically arranged with author and subject indexes. *Class No:* 840-2COR

Hugo

[8121]

DOYLE, R.L. Victor Hugo's drama: an annotated bibliography, 1900-1980. Westport, Conn., Greenwood, 1981. x,217p. $55. ISBN: 0313228841.

826 entries in 3 sections: editions and translations; general studies; criticism of individual plays. Critical annotations. Author and subject indexes. *Class No:* 840-2HUG

[8122]

VAN TIEGHEM, P. Dictionnaire de Victor Hugo. Paris, Larousse, 1970. 256p. illus. maps.

Entries for Hugo's works and for his family and associates. Chronology of Hugo's life and works (31p.). List of his poems by title or first-line, with sources and dates. Bibliography (6p.). *Class No:* 840-2HUG

Molière

[8123]

GUIBERT, A.-J. Bibliographie des oeuvres de Molière publiées au XVIIe siècle. Paris, Centre National de la Recherche Scientifique, 1961 (repr. 1978). 2v. Fr.262. ISBN: 2222005698.

Fully descriptive listing in 8 sections, covering separate editions of plays, collected works, poems, etc., with bibliographic notes. 2 supplements (1965 and 1971) add descriptions of editions previously omitted, and library locations and further bibliographic references for items in the original work. *Class No:* 840-2MOL

[8124]

SAINTONGE, P. *and* **CHRIST, R.W. Fifty years of Molière studies:** a bibliography, 1892-1941. Baltimore, Md., Johns Hopkins Press; London, Oxford Univ. Press, 1942. 313p.

4 main sections (1. Biography - 2. Criticism - 3. Criticism of specific plays - 4. Miscellanea) with numerous subsections. 4 appendices: 1. French eds. since 1933 - 2. American eds. - 3. Translations and adaptations - 4. Records of performances. 3,316 entries, some briefly annotated. Index of authors, editors and translators.

Continued in 'Thirty years of Molière studies: a bibliography, 1942-1971' by P. Saintonge in *Molière and the commonwealth of letters: patrimony and posterity,* ed. by R. Johnson *et al.* (Jackson, Miss., Univ. Press of Mississippi, 1975. ISBN: 0878050590). *Class No:* 840-2MOL

Racine

[8125]

GUIBERT, A.-J. Bibliographie des oeuvres de Jean Racine publiées au XVIIe siècle et oeuvres posthumes. Paris, Éditions du Centre National de la Recherche Scientifique, 1968. 318p. illus.

Fully descriptive bibliography in 3 sections covering original editions of the separate plays and reprints of them up to 1700; collected editions; and miscellaneous works in verse and prose. Title-page facsimiles.

For secondary material, see E.E. Williams's *Racine depuis 1885; bibliographie raisonnée des livres, articles, comptes-rendus critiques relatifs à la vie et l'oeuvre de Jean Racine* (Baltimore, Md., Johns Hopkins Press, 1940. 279p.). *Class No:* 840-2RAC

Women

[8126]

French women playwrights before the twentieth century: a checklist. Beach, C., *ed.* Westport, Conn., Greenwood, 1994. 264p. £51.95. (*Bibliographies and indexes in women's studies.*) ISBN: 0313291748.

Lists nearly 3,000 plays by over 400 women from the 16th to 19th centuries, giving brief biographical data plus performance, publication and availability information (including library locations) for the plays. Index.

Continued by Beach's *French women playwrights of the twentieth century: a checklist* (Greenwood. 1996. 515p. $79.50. ISBN: 0313291756), which is similarly organized and lists a further 2,000 plays. Title index and bibliography. *Class No:* 840-2-0055.2

French Prose

[8127]

WOLEDGE, B. Bibliographie des romans et nouvelles en prose française antérieurs à 1500. Genève, Droz, 1954 (repr. 1975). 180p.

Lists 190 prose works by author or anonymous title, with notes on manuscripts, sources, old and modern editions, and critical studies. Several indexes, covering manuscript locations, printers, patrons, etc.

Supplément, 1954-73 (1975. 139p.) lists further works published on the topic and corrects some of the original entries. *Class No:* 840-3

Diderot

[8128]

SPEAR, F. Bibliographie de Diderot: répertoire analytique international. Génève, Droz, 1980-88. 2v. (*Histoire des idées et critique littéraire, vols. 187 and 264.*)

V.1 (lviii,902p.) lists 3,967 biographical and critical studies in 10 sections with numerous subsections. Brief annotations and references to reviews. Truly international in scope. Author index.

V.2 (xxviii,218p.) adds 1,877 items published 1976-86, and has amendments to v.1. *Class No:* 840-3DID

Montaigne

[8129]

CLIVE, H.P. Bibliographie annotée des ouvrages relatifs à Montaigne publiés entre 1976 et 1985, avec un complément de la bibliographie de Pierre Bonnet. Paris, Champion, 1990. 251p. Fr.352. ISBN: 205101101x.

Lists *c.*1,000 studies, A-Z by author, with notes on content and references to reviews. Over 300 periodicals surveyed. Cross-references and subject index. Follows P. Bonnet's *Bibliographie méthodique et analytique des ouvrages et documents relatifs à Montaigne, jusqu'à 1975* (Paris, Slatkine, 1983. 594p.) and includes over 200 items he missed. *Class No:* 840-3MON

Rousseau

[8130]

Dictionnaire de Jean-Jacques Rousseau. Trousson, R. *and* Eigeldinger, F., *eds.* Paris, Champion, 1996. 961p. Fr.480. ISBN: 2852036045.

*c.*700 signed entries of which over 200 are on themes/topics in Rousseau's oeuvre and the rest cover specific works and people and places in his life. Brief bibliographies with each entry. Also gives locations for manuscripts.

....(contd.)

A Rousseau dictionary by N.J.H. Dent (London, Blackwell, 1992. vii,279p. £17.50. ISBN: 0631175695) has some 100 lengthy entries (average 2¼p.) covering Rousseau's ideas and works plus miscellaneous background information. List of sources after each article. Good classified bibliography of primary and secondary material (25p.). Biographical introduction (12p.). Chronology (5p.). Index. Main focus is on Rousseau's philosophy, with the *Dictionnaire* better suited to literary collections.
Class No: 840-3ROU

[8131]

McEACHERN, J.-A. E. Bibliography of the writings of Jean Jacques Rousseau to 1800. Oxford, Voltaire Foundation, 1989-93. v.1-2 (in progress).

V.1 *Julie, ou la Nouvelle Héloïse.* 1993. ix,814p. ill. £114. ISBN: 0729403785.

V.2 *Emile, ou de l'education.* 1989. ix,473p. ill. £68. ISBN: 0729403793.

A major scholarly project whose aim is 'to give an historical account of the printing and publication of the first edition of each of Rousseau's works, and to provide full descriptions of all the editions of his writings published in the eighteenth century, both in French and in other languages' (*Prospectus*). In contrast to earlier bibliographies, it is not based mainly on particular collections in France and Switzerland and, as a result, many previously unrecorded editions and variants are identified. Descriptions are extremely detailed. Each vol. contains a list of over 100 libraries visited.

8 vols. are planned, the last one to contain a complete set of cross-references to enable readers to trace all publications of any given work. *Class No:* 840-3ROU

[8132]

ROGGERONE, G.A. *and* **VERGINE, P.I. Bibliografia degli studi su Rousseau, 1941-1990.** Lecce, Milella, 1992. 1385p. ISBN: 8870482243.

Lists 6,000 secondary studies published since 1941, thus supplementing A. Schinz's *Etat présent des travaux sur J.-J. Rousseau* (Paris, 1941). Annotated throughout. Appended list of Rousseau editions and translations published 1950-90 supplements J. Sénelier's *Bibliographie générale des oeuvres de Jean-Jacques Rousseau* (Paris, 1950). *Class No:* 840-3ROU

Voltaire

[8133]

BARR, M.M.H. A Century of Voltaire study: a bibliography of writings on Voltaire, 1825-1925. New York, Institute of French Studies, 1929 (repr. New York, Franklin, 1972). xxiii,123p.

1,494 unannotated entries in 7 sections, with numerous subsections. Index of proper names.

Continued by *Quarante années d'études voltairiennes: bibliographie analytique des livres et articles sur Voltaire, 1926-1965* (Paris, Colin, 1968. viii,212p.), which lists 2,184 items in a wide range of languages. Many items annotated. Index. *Class No:* 840-3VOL

[8134]
—SPEAR, F. Bibliographie analytique des écrits relatifs à Voltaire, 1966-1990. Oxford, Voltaire Foundation, 1992. xxix,493p. £56. ISBN: 0729404439.

A classified bibliography listing 3,546 recently published studies in 9 general sections and sections on individual works. Brief annotations. Indexes of names and subjects.
Class No: 840-3VOL

[8135]
BENGESCO, G. Voltaire: bibliographie de ses oeuvres. Paris, Perrin, 1882-89. 4v.

A confusingly arranged, but exhaustive, bibliography of Voltaire's prodigious output. Indexed by J. Malcolm in *Table de la bibliographie de Voltaire par Bengesco* (Genève, Institut et Musée Voltaire, 1953. 127p.), which lists titles of works and first lines of poems. *Class No:* 840-3VOL

[8136]
Dictionnaire Voltaire: les oeuvres, les thèmes, les personnages, les lieux. Trousson, R., *& others, eds.* Paris, Hachette, 1994. v,281p. Fr.150. ISBN: 2012351166.

Signed articles by 54 contributors, mainly on Voltaire's works but also covering people, places, genres, themes and topics. Selective bibliography after many, but not all, entries. General index and index of Voltaire's works.
Class No: 840-3VOL

French Fiction

[8137]
DAWSON, R.L. Additions to the bibliographies of French prose fiction, 1618-1806. Oxford, Voltaire Foundation, 1985. xxi,397p. £66. (*Studies on Voltaire and the eighteenth century.*) ISBN: 0729403270.

247 entries, almost exclusively for works in the author's private collection, to supplement the bibliographies compiled by Jones (1939), Lever (1976) and Martin *et al* (1977) (See separate entries). *Class No:* 840-31

[8138]
GODENNE, R. Bibliographie critique de la nouvelle de langue française (1940-1985). Genève, Droz, 1989. 392p.

1,200 authors, A-Z, with annotated lists of their novellas. Appendices include chronological list of commentaries on the novella, with quotations, and lists of award winners. Select bibliography of critical studies.

Continued by *Premier supplément* (1992. 282p.), which goes up to 1990 and adds some earlier material.
Class No: 840-31

[8139]
HICKS, B.E. Plots and characters in classic French fiction. Hamden, Conn., Shoe String Press, 1981. 253p. $36. ISBN: 0208017038.

Covers 32 novels from *La Princesse de Clèves* (1678) to *Germinal* (1885). Plot summaries plus lists of characters with brief notes. *Class No:* 840-31

[8140]
JONES, S.P. A List of French prose fiction from 1700 to 1750. New York, Wilson, 1939. xxxii,150p.

An annotated list of *c.*950 works arranged by year, then A-Z by author, giving library locations. Index of authors, titles, pseudonyms, etc. *Class No:* 840-31

[8141]
—MARTIN, A., *and others.* Bibliographie du genre romanesque français, 1751-1800. London, Mansell; Paris, France Expansion, 1977. lxxii,529p. illus. ISBN: 0720103797, UK; 222900650, France.

Follows Jones in scope, but also includes French translations of foreign fiction and new editions of earlier works. Lists *c.*6,750 works by year, then A-Z by author, with a separate section for reprints within each year. Entries include notes on form and content, variant editions, serializations, and library locations. Index of authors and titles. *Class No:* 840-31

[8142]
LEVER, M. La Fiction narrative en prose au XVIIe siècle: répertoire bibliographique du genre romanesque en France (1600-1700). Paris, Éditions du Centre National de la Recherche Scientifique, 1976. 645p. ISBN: 2222018757.

Lists over 1,200 novels A-Z by title, providing full bibliographic information, references to later editions, library locations, and attributions for anonymous works. Author index (including pseudonyms), plus lists of people, places and nationalities mentioned in titles, and of foreign authors translated into French. Chronological list. Bibliography (3p.).

Transcends R.C. Williams' *A Bibliography of the 17th-century novel in France* (New York, Century Press, 1931) and R.W. Baldner's revision of it, *Bibliography of seventeenth-century French prose fiction* (New York, MLA, 1967). *Class No:* 840-31

Balzac

[8143]
LOTTE, F. Dictionnaire biographique des personnages fictifs de 'La Comédie humaine'. Paris, Corti, 1952. xxxiii,676p.

Notes on over 6,000 characters from Balzac's great novel cycle, with references to the works in which they appear.
Class No: 840-31BAL

[8144]
—LONGAUD, F. Dictionnaire de Balzac. Paris, Larousse, 1969. 256p.

800 entries for Balzac's works, literary periodicals, fictional characters, and real people and places associated with him. Chronology, bibliography (2p.) and maps, plus many illustrations. *Class No:* 840-31BAL

[8145]
ROYCE, W.H. A Balzac bibliography: writings relative to the life and works of Honoré de Balzac. Chicago, Univ. of Chicago Press, 1929-30 (repr. New York, Gordon Press). 2v. $69.95. ISBN: 0879686995.

V.1 (xvii,464p.) has 4,010 entries in separate sections for book and periodical material, each arranged A-Z by author. Brief annotations. V.2 (xi,190p.) comprises an index to periodicals cited in the second part of v.1 and an elaborate topical index (Part 1, Balzac's life; Part 2, Balzac's works) to the whole bibliography. *Class No:* 840-31BAL

Camus

[8146]
Camus: a bibliography. Roeming, R.F., *comp. and ed.* Madison, Wis., Univ. of Wisconsin Press 1968. xii,298p.

Lists 741 works by Camus, including many translations, and 2,691 secondary items from over 50 countries. No

.... (contd.)
annotations. Indexes of authors and journals and chronological index, all divided by country and language.
Class No: 840-31CAM

[8147]
FITCH, B.T. Albert Camus: essai de bibliographie des études en langue française, 1937-1970. 3e éd. Paris, Minard, 1972. [480p.].

1st ed. 1965; 2nd ed. 1970.

A checklist arranged by year, then by author, with some brief annotations and cross-references. Includes amendments to entries in earlier eds. Indexes of authors and periodical titles. *Class No:* 840-31CAM

de Beauvoir

[8148]
BENNETT, J. *and* **HOCHMANN, G. Simone de Beauvoir: an annotated bibliography.** New York, Garland, 1988. xx,474p. $77. ISBN: 0824066316.

Lists 1,600 items published 1940-86 in 6 sections: 1. General criticism - 2. Interviews - 3. Theses - 4. Book reviews: works by de Beauvoir - 5. Book reviews: biography and criticism - 6. Obituaries. Includes material in the 5 major European languages. Chronology of her life (4p.). Index of authors and named persons. 'No other bibliography attempts to be as comprehensive in time and breadth' (*Choice,* v.26(11/12), July/Aug. 1989, p.1806).
Class No: 840-31DEB

Flaubert

[8149]
COLWELL, D.J. Bibliographie des études sur G. Flaubert. Egham, Runnymede Books, 1988-90. 4v.

1837-1920. 1989. 192p. ISBN: 1870725050
1921-1959. 1988. 240p. ISBN: 1870725018.
1960-1982. 1988. 344p. ISBN: 1870725034.
1983-1988. 1990. 150p. ISBN: 1870725077.

A very comprehensive bibliography arranged chronologically. For each year major editions of Flaubert's works are listed, followed by critical and biographical studies A-Z by author. Indexes of authors and subjects in each vol. The *1960-1982* vol. has an additional index of Flaubert's works and correspondence and a list of 58 studies of interest to the general reader. Includes studies in several languages. No annotations. *Class No:* 840-31FLA

[8150]
DUMESNIL, R. *and* **DEMOREST, D.L. Bibliographie de Gustave Flaubert.** Paris, Giraud-Badin, 1937. 360p.

Descriptive bibliography of editions of individual works, with lengthy commentary on each. *Class No:* 840-31FLA

Genet

[8151]
WEBB, R.C. *and* **WEBB, S.A. Jean Genet and his critics:** an annotated bibliography, 1943-1980. Metuchen, N.J., Scarecrow, 1982. xii,600p. (*Scarecrow author bibliographies.*) ISBN: 0810815125.

1,790 annotated items in 10 sections and 2 appendices, including many theatre reviews and newspaper articles. Covers mainly French and English criticism, with one section devoted to criticism in other languages (271 items). Name index. *Class No:* 840-31GEN

Gide

[8152]
BROSMAN, C.S. An Annotated bibliography of criticism on André Gide, 1973-1988. New York, Garland, 1990. xxii,327p. $53. ISBN: 0824079736.

Continues the Gide bibliography in *A Critical bibliography of French literature,* v.6 (*q.v.*), listing recent editions of texts and correspondence, and critical studies in European languages and Japanese. Includes references to book reviews. 1,272 entries. Author and subject indexes.
Class No: 840-31GID

[8153]
COTNAM, J. Bibliographie chronologique de l'oeuvre d'André Gide (1889-1973). Boston, Hall, 1974. x,604p.

1,233 items arranged chronologically, with separate sections within each year for articles, books, prefaces, and letters. Index. *Class No:* 840-31GID

[8154]
NAVILLE, A. Bibliographie des écrits d'André Gide de 1891 jusqu' à sa mort. Reprint of 1949 ed. plus *Complément bibliographique* for 1949-52. New York, Franklin, 1971. 237p. ISBN: 0833725033.

Originally published Pairs, Matarasso, 1949.

Descriptive bibliography of Gide's works, followed by lists of translations (by Gide and of his works) and of secondary material (6 sections). Lists of dedicatees, editors and illustrators. *Class No:* 840-31GID

Malraux

[8155]
ROMEISER, J.B. André Malraux: a reference guide, 1940-1990. Boston, Hall, 1994. 370p. $45. ISBN: 0816190712.

Lists over 1,300 studies published in the UK, US, France, Germany and Spain. Arranged by year, then by author within each year. Concise annotations. Indexes. Introductory survey of Malraux's life and critical reception.
Class No: 840-31MAL

Maupassant

[8156]
ARTINIAN, R.W. *and* **ARTINIAN, A. Maupassant criticism:** a centennial bibliography, 1880-1979. Jefferson, N.C., McFarland, 1982. xxii,178p. ISBN: 0899500463.

An expansion of A. Artinian's bibliography in *Maupassant criticism in France, 1880-1940* (New York, King's Crown Press, 1941).

An unannotated checklist, chronologically arranged, of *c.*3,000 studies, preceded by an annotated, select bibliography of Maupassant editions and key critical works (8p.). Index of critics. *Class No:* 840-31MAU

Proust

[8157]
GRAHAM, V.E. Bibliographie des études sur Proust et son oeuvre. Genève, Droz, 1976. 237p.

Lists 2,274 studies, by author, in a single sequence with subject index. Separate list of collections of essays and special editions of periodicals devoted to Proust. Cut-off date: 1972. *Class No:* 840-31PRO

[8158]
KILMARTIN, T. A Guide to Proust. London, Chatto & Windus, 1984. viii,193p. ISBN: 0701126361.

An index to *Remembrance of things past,* with 4 sequences for fictional characters, real or historical persons, places (both real and fictional), and themes. Keyed to Kilmartin's 3-vol. revision of Scott Moncrieff's translation (Chatto & Windus, 1981). *Class No:* 840-31PRO

[8159]
STOCK, J.C. Marcel Proust: a reference guide, 1950-1970. Boston, Hall, 1991. xxiv,565p. $47.50. ISBN: 0816189870.

Lists 1,350 books, chapters, articles and dissertations published in English, French and German. Detailed annotations. Author and subject indexes. *Class No:* 840-31PRO

[8160]
TAYLOR, E.R. Marcel Proust and his contexts: a critical bibliography of English-language scholarship. New York, Garland, 1981. xvii,235p. ISBN: 0824093550.

1,393 entries, most of them briefly annotated, in 6 sections with 8 subsections on themes in Proust's works. Subject and author indexes. Includes works translated into English. *Class No:* 840-31PRO

Rabelais

[8161]
BRAUNROT, B. François Rabelais: a reference guide, 1950-1990. New York, Hall, 1994. 438p. $50. ISBN: 0816190798.

A selective, annotated bibliography of secondary material, arranged by year and then by author. Includes American dissertations and new editions of Rabelais' works. Author and subject indexes. *Class No:* 840-31RAB

[8162]
RAWLES, S. *and* **SCREECH, M.A. A New Rabelais bibliography:** editions of Rabelais before 1626. Genève, Droz, 1987. xvi,691p. (*Études Rabelaisiennes. Tome 20.*)

Comprehensive descriptions of 148 editions, with bibliographical notes and library locations. Many facsimiles. Indexes of editions, and of printers and booksellers. 'Both a worthy example of the descriptive bibliographer's art and an essential reference tool for the Rabelais scholar' (*Library Association Record,* v.90(10), Oct. 1988, p.590). *Class No:* 840-31RAB

Sartre

[8163]
CONTAT, M. *and* **RYBALKA, M. Les Écrits de Sartre:** chronologie, bibliographie commentée. Paris, Gallimard, 1970. 788p.

Chronology of Sartre's life, 1904-69, followed by chronologically arranged bibliography of his works, 1923-69, with substantial annotations and extracts. 'Chers amis, votre travail est remarquable' (*Lettre-préface* by Sartre). *Class No:* 840-31SAR

[8164]
CONTAT, M. *and* **RYBALKA, M. Sartre: bibliographie, 1980-1992.** Paris, CNRS; Bowling Green Ohio, Philosophy and Documentation Center, Bowling Green State Univ., 1993. 247p. ISBN: 2271051142, France.

6,000 entries arranged by year, with editions followed by secondary material. Separate list of theses. Indexes of names and Sartre's works. *Class No:* 840-31SAR

[8165]
LAPOINTE, F.H. Jean-Paul Sartre and his critics: an international bibliography (1938-1980). 2nd ed. Bowling Green, Ohio, Bowling Green State Univ. Press, 1981. 697p. ISBN: 0912632445.

1st ed. 1975.

11,000 unannotated entries (more than double those in 1st ed.) in 12 sections. Author and subject indexes.

For theses, see G.U. Gabel's *Sartre: a comprehensive bibliography of international theses and dissertations, 1950-1985* (Hürth-Efferen, Edition Gemini, 1990. ISBN: 3922331300). *Class No:* 840-31SAR

[8166]
WILLCOCKS, R. Jean-Paul Sartre: a bibliography of international criticism. Edmonton, Univ. of Alberta Press, 1975. xxi,767p. ISBN: 0888640129.

A classified listing with 8 sections and over 80 subsections. Over 8,000 entries, many of them briefly annotated. Author index. *Class No:* 840-31SAR

Stendhal

[8167]
CORDIER, H. Bibliographie stendhalienne. Paris, Champion, 1914. xiv,416p. illus.

First part describes Stendhal's works (293 entries). Second part lists 459 books and articles on Stendhal. Name and title index. Title-page facsimiles.

Supplemented by irregular publications with the same title published Grenoble, Arthaud, 1945-55, and Lausanne, Éditions du Grand Chêne, 1958-75. *Class No:* 840-31STE

[8168]
MICHEL, F. Stendhal fichier / Fichier stendhalien. Fabre, J., *and others, eds.* Boston, Hall, 1964. 3v. $330. ISBN: 0816105839.

Over 14,500 entries, A-Z, from a unique card-file compiled by a great Stendhal scholar, covering all aspects of Stendhal's life, works and milieu. Entries for names of people and places (real and fictitious), allusions, words needing explanation, themes, etc., with detailed references to texts. *Class No:* 840-31STE

Zola

[8169]
BAGULEY, D. Bibliographie de la critique sur Émile Zola, 1864-1970. Toronto, Univ. of Toronto Press, 1977-82. 2v.

V.1 *1864-1970.* 1976. 689p. ISBN: 0802053696.

V.2 *1971-1980.* 1982. 235p. ISBN: 0802024564.

8,713 briefly annotated items, arranged by year, then by author, plus supplement in v.2 with a further 600 items for 1864-1970, and 247 unpublished theses. Subject and name indexes. International coverage. *Class No:* 840-31ZOL

[8170]
PATTERSON, J.G. A Zola dictionary: the characters of the Rougon-Macquart novels of Émile Zola, with a biographical and critical introduction, synopses of the plots, bibliographical note, map, genealogy, etc. London, Routledge; New York, Dutton, 1912 (often reprinted). xl,232p.

Main A-Z sequence of over 1,000 characters is followed by brief list of geographical locations. *Class No:* 840-31ZOL

Belgian Literature

[8171]
Alphabet des lettres belges de langue française. Bruxelles, Association pour la Promotion des Lettres belges de langue française, 1982. 311p. illus.

A history of Belgian literature (p.11-202), then a dictionary of 182 authors, with biography, brief analysis, and select primary and secondary bibliographies.
Class No: 840.493

[8172]
CHARLIER, G. *and* **HANSE, J. Histoire illustrée des lettres françaises de Belgique.** Bruxelles, La Renaissance du Livre, 1958. vii,656p. illus.

Profusely illustrated history with 59 chapters contributed by 31 specialists. Chapter bibliographies. Index of authors and anonymous titles. *Class No:* 840.493

[8173]
CULOT, J.-M. Bibliographie des écrivains français de Belgique (1881-1960). Bruxelles, Palais des Académies, 1958-89. v.1-5 (in progress).

Arranged A-Z by author, following a bibliography (65p.) of general literary histories, critical studies, anthologies and collections in v.1. Under each author are listed works (chronologically arranged), translations, contributions to journals, works in other languages, and secondary material.
Class No: 840.493

[8174]
FRICKX, R. *and* **TROUSSON, R. Lettres françaises de Belgique:** dictionnaire des oeuvres Paris, Duculot, 1988-94. 4v. ISBN: 2801107824.

V.1 *Le Roman*. 1988, 539p.
V.2 *La Poésie*. 1988. 607p.
V.3 *Le Théâtre. L'Essai*. 1989. 484p.
V.4 *1981-1990*. 1994. 376p.

Signed entries for over 3,000 literary works, published 1830-1980, are arranged A-Z by title within vols. 1-3 and comprise synopsis, brief critical evaluation, and bibliography of critical studies. V.4 adds *c.*800 works (from all genres) published in the 1980s, plus some omissions from earlier vols. Each vol. has author index and index of titles which are not entry-terms. General bibliography in v.3(4p.).
Class No: 840.493

[8175]
MALLINSON, V. Modern Belgian literature, 1830-1960. London, Heinemann, 1966. 205p.

A history in 10 chapters, covering both French and Flemish writings, with many subsections on individual authors. Many quotations in the original language. Select bibliography (15 items). Index. *Class No:* 840.493

African-French Literature

[8176]
BLAIR, D.S. African literature in French: a history of creative writing in French from West and Equatorial Africa. Cambridge, Cambridge Univ. Press, 1976 (reprinted in paperback 1981). xx,348p. ISBN: 0521284031.

Introductory chapter followed by chapters on each genre: oral literature, drama, poetry, fiction. Numerous subsections on individual writers are headed by lists of their original works and available translations. Bibliography (16p.) arranged by chapter with good annotations. Index.
Class No: 840.96

[8177]
CORNEVIN, R. Littératures d'Afrique noire de langue française. Paris, Presses Universitaires de France, 1976. 273p.

7 chapters with numbered subsections. Ch.7 has sections on 20 national literatures, in some cases further subdivided by genre. Extensive bibliographical notes throughout, plus appended bibliographical essay (16p.) on general sources. Index of authors, journals, countries and cities.
Class No: 840.96

[8178]
DÉJEUX, J. Dictionnaire des auteurs maghrébins de langue française. Paris, Karthala, 1984. 404p. Fr.140. ISBN: 2865370852.

Lists authors, A-Z, in separate sections for Algeria (1880-1982), Morocco (1920-82), and Tunisia (1900-82), giving brief biographical notes and lists of works. Includes non-literary writers. *Class No:* 840.96

[8179]
Dictionnaire des oeuvres littéraires négro-africaines de langue française, des origines à 1978. Kom, A., *ed.* Québec, Naaman; Paris, Agencie de Coopération Culturelle et Technique, 1983. 672p. ISBN: 2890402428.

Signed articles by 93 scholars from 20 countries on *c.*650 literary works by Black African French-language authors. Arranged A-Z by title, giving plot summary, critical analysis, and bibliographical details of 1st ed. Most entries have 500-1,000 words, but those for major works have up to 2,000. Covers all literary genres, plus songs and screenplays. Indexes of African authors (giving year and country of birth) and of genres. *Class No:* 840.96

[8180]
MÉRAND, P. *and* **DABLA, S. Guide de littérature africaine de langue française.** Paris, L'Harmattan, 1979. 219p.

Annotated bibliography of francophone African writing, arranged A-Z by author, with over 1,000 entries. Lists of authors by country. Lists of winners of literary prizes. Introductory historical survey. Index of authors and titles.
Class No: 840.96

[8181]
NKASHAMA, P.N. Dictionnaire des oeuvres littéraires africaines de langue française. Ivry-sur-Seine, Editions Nouvelles du Sud, 1994. 745p. Fr.300. ISBN: 2879310938.

Arranged by genre, then by author, then chronologically by title. Entries give author's nationality, year of birth and list of titles with notes on content, but no references to secondary sources. North Africa is excluded. Indexes of authors and titles. *Class No:* 840.96

[8182]
RADIO FRANCE INTERNATIONALE, PARIS. Centre de Documentation Africaine. **Bibliographie des auteurs africains de langue française.** Baratte-Eno Belinga, T., *and others, eds.* 4th ed. Paris, Nathan, 1979. vi,245p.

3rd ed. 1972.

2,303 entries (nearly twice as many as 3rd ed.) for 1,170 authors. Covers literary history, criticism, bibliographies, etc. as well as creative writing. Excludes periodical literature. New categories include translations and sound recordings. Arranged by country with indexes of authors, editors, discs and cassettes.

For secondary material, see A. Cherchari's *Réception de*

....(contd.)
la littérature africaine d'expression française jusqu'en 1970: essai de bibliographie (Silex, 1982. 116p. Fr.80. ISBN: 2903871094). *Class No:* 840.96

Algeria

[8183]
DÉJEUX, J. Bibliographie méthodique et critique de la littérature algérienne de langue française, 1945-1977. Alger, Société Nationale d'Édition et de Diffusion, 1979. 307p.
Annotated bibliography with separate sections for pre- and post-independence literature. *Class No:* 840.96(65)

Ivory Coast

[8184]
BONNEAU, R. Écrivains, cinéastes et artistes ivoiriens: aperçu bio-bibliographique. Dakar, Nouvelles Editions Africaines, 1973. 176p.
Of the 80-plus entries, most are for writers. Information comprises biography (compiled from personal interview), photograph, primary bibliography and list of critical studies. *Class No:* 840.96(666.8)

Benin

[8185]
HUANNOU, A. La Littérature béninoise de langue française, des origines à nos jours. Paris, Karthala-A.C.C.T., 1984. 327p. ISBN: 2865371050.
A history of the literature of Benin (formerly Dahomey) in 17 chapters, with an excellent bibliography (25p.) of literary works, periodicals, and critical and historical studies. Chronology, 1862-1982. Index of authors, titles and subjects. *Class No:* 840.96(668.2)

Cameroon

[8186]
BARATTE-ENO BELINGA, T. Écrivains, cinéastes et artistes camerounais: biobibliographie. Yaoundé, Ministère de l'Information et de la Culture, 1978. 217p.
93 entries, arranged A-Z, of which 46 are for authors and 16 for journalists and critics. *Class No:* 840.96(671.1)

[8187]
ZIMMER, W. Répertoire du théâtre camerounais. Paris, Harmattan, 1986. 120p. ISBN: 2858026154.
Lists 712 plays under authors, A-Z. Title index. *Class No:* 840.96(671.1)

Mauritian Literature

[8188]
PROSPER, J.P. Histoire de la littérature mauricienne de langue française. Ile Maurice, Editions de l'Océan indien, 1978. 345p.
12 chapters, with subsections on individual authors. Numerous quotations. Appended list of authors, with biographical notes and lists of works. *Class No:* 840.969

Canadian French Literature

Bibliographies

[8189]
BOIVIN, A. Le Conte québécois au XIXe siècle: essai de bibliographie critique et analytique. Montréal, Fides, 1975. xxii,385p. ISBN: 0775505579.
Lists 1,138 stories by author, A-Z, with plot summary and references to sources and critical studies. Bibliography of general studies and reference works (8p.). Lists of periodicals and story collections. *Class No:* 840.971(01)

[8190]
CANTIN, P., ***and others*****. Bibliographie de la critique de la littérature québécoise dans les revues des XIXe et XXe siècles.** Ottawa, Centre de Recherche en Civilisation Canadienne-Française, 1979. 5v.
General studies in v.1, followed by studies of individual authors, A-Z, in vols. 2-5.
For more recent criticism, see *Bibliographie de la critique de la littérature québécoise et canadienne-française dans les revues canadiennes (1974-1978)*, by R. Dionne and P. Cantin (Ottawa, Presses de l'Université d'Ottawa, 1988) and the same authors' *Bibliographie de la critique de la littérature québécoise et canadienne-française dans les revues canadiennes (1979-82)* (1991). *Class No:* 840.971(01)

[8191]
HAYNE, D.M. ***and*** **TIROL, M. Bibliographie critique du roman canadien-français, 1837-1900.** Toronto, Univ. of Toronto Press, 1968. viii,144p.
1,150 briefly annotated entries for editions, translations and studies of French-language fiction. 43 authors covered. Index. *Class No:* 840.971(01)

[8192]
—DROLET, A. Bibliographie du roman canadien français, 1900-1950. Québec, Presses Universitaires de Laval, 1955. 125p.
Lists 886 French-language novels by author, with title index. Bibliography of general sources on the French-Canadian novel (4p.). *Class No:* 840.971(01)

[8193]
KANDIUK, M. French-Canadian authors: a bibliography of their works and of English-language criticism. Metuchen, N.J., Scarecrow, 1990. xii,222p. ISBN: 0810823624.
Claims to be the first bibliography devoted to English-language criticism of French-Canadian authors and covers 36 novelists, poets and dramatists who have work available in English translation. Secondary sources listed include dissertations and book reviews. Indexes of critics and editors. *Class No:* 840.971(01)

[8194]
RINFRET, E.G. Le Théâtre canadien d'expression française: répertoire analytique des origines à nos jours. [Montréal], Leméac, 1975-8. 4v. ISBN: 0776194089.
Vols. 1-3 list plays of all periods under authors, A-Z, giving substantial information, including category, number of acts, setting, cast, plot summary, dates of publication and first performance, and library locations. V.4 has a separate author sequence for TV plays, 1952-73, plus title index for the whole set and chronological list of the TV plays. Very clearly presented. *Class No:* 840.971(01)

[8195]
TOUGAS, G. A Checklist of printed materials relating to French-Canadian literature, 1763-1968. 2nd ed. Vancouver, Univ. of British Columbia Press, 1973. xvi,174p. ISBN: 0774800070.
1st ed. 1958.
More than 2,800 titles, representing the Univ. of British Columbia's holdings in the field. Arranged under authors A-Z, with an appended list of material on them. Includes translations, parliamentary oratory, travellers' chronicles and folklore. Also - in the 1973 ed. - periodicals, bibliographies and theses. *Class No:* 840.971(01)

Encyclopaedias & Dictionaries

[8196]
Dictionnaire des oeuvres littéraires du Québec. Lemire, M., *ed.* Montréal, Fides, 1978-94 6v.
V.1 *Des origines à 1900.* 1978.
V.2 *1900 à 1939.* 1980.
V.3 *1940 à 1959.* 1982.
V.4 *1960 à 1969.* 1984.
V.5 *1970 à 1975.* 1987.
V.6 *1976 à 1980.* 1994.
Each vol. lists works A-Z by title, with author index, and has general and author bibliographies for the period concerned. *Class No:* 840.971(03)

Handbooks & Manuals

[8197]
FORTIN, M., *& others*. Guide de la littérature québécoise. Québec, Boréal, 1988. 156p. ISBN: 2890522482.
A selective guide to resources with *c.*400 annotated entries in 7 sections, including dictionaries, bibliographies and studies. One section lists libraries, archives and literary organizations. Author index. *Class No:* 840.971(035)

Histories

[8198]
Histoire de la littérature française de Québec. Grandpré, P. de, *ed.* Montréal, Beauchemin, 1967-9. 4v. illus.
V.1 *1534-1900.* 1967 (rev. reprint 1971.). 368p.
V.2 *1900-1945.* 1968. 390p.
V.3 *1945 à nos jours - la poésie.* 1969. 407p.
V.4 *Roman, théâtre, histoire, journalisme, essai, critique (de 1945 à nos jours).* 1969 (rev. reprint 1973). 428p.
Lavishly illustrated history, consisting mainly of biobibliographical entries by specialists on authors, with substantial excerpts from their works. Includes non-literary writers. Bibliography of general studies and reference works in v.4 (11p.). Index of names and titles in each vol.
Class No: 840.971(091)

[8199]
TOUGAS, G. History of French-Canadian literature. 2nd ed., trans. A.L. Cook. Toronto, Ryerson Press, 1966. ix,301p.
1st ed. 1960; 2nd ed. originally published Paris, Presses Universitaires de France, 1964, as *Histoire de la littérature canadienne-française.*
Chapters on periods (1845-65; 1865-99; 1900-39; Contemporary) have subsections on genres and individual authors. Extensive chapter notes include bibliographies. Index of authors and titles. *Class No:* 840.971(091)

Biographies

[8200]
HAMEL, R., *and others*. Dictionnaire des auteurs de langue française en Amérique du Nord. Montréal, Fides, 1989. xxvi,1364p. illus. ISBN: 2762114756.
Supersedes the same authors' *Dictionnaire pratique des auteurs québécois* (1976) and broadens the scope to include US-based writers. Entries for over 1,600 authors of all periods, comprising biography, critical evaluation, and primary and secondary bibliography, plus photograph in many cases. Very useful bibliography of general reference sources (6p.). Includes non-literary authors.
Class No: 840.971(092)

Provençal Literature

[8201]
GAUTHIER, J.D. French XX bibliography. Provençal supplement, no.1. Tussing, R.-E., *ed.* New York, French Institute-Alliance Française and the Camargo Foundation, 1976. xxv,111p.
1,968 unannotated entries covering Provençal literature since its 19th-century revival. In the same format as the parent work, except that coverage starts as early as 1850. Part 1, General subjects, has 7 subsections. Part 2, Author-subjects, has 2 A-Z sequences of studies of authors, one for Le Midi Provençal and one for western areas of southern France. *Class No:* 849

[8202]
PILLET, A. Bibliographie der Troubadours. Carstens, H., *ed.* Halle, Niemeyer, 1933 (repr. New York, Franklin, 1968). xliv,518p. ISBN: 0833727710.
Lists 460 troubadours, A-Z, followed by over 250 anonymous works, giving details of poems, editions and manuscripts. Many references to secondary sources. Rhyme index.
2 vols. of a projected 6-vol. index of troubadours' rhymes, based on critical editions and keyed to this bibliography, have appeared under the title *Rimario trobadorico provenzale*, ed. by P.G. Beltrami and others (Pisa, Pacini, 1988-). *Class No:* 849

[8203]
TAYLOR, R.A. La Littérature occitane du Moyen Age: bibliographie sélective et critique. Toronto, Univ. of Toronto Press, 1977. xv,166p. $32.50. (*Toronto medieval bibliographies.*) ISBN: 0802054072.
885 entries, concisely annotated (in French) in 5 sections, covering reference works; critical studies; the lyric poetry of the troubadours: texts and studies (over 80 poets, A-Z); other literary genres; and material on related subjects, *e.g.* Catalan literature. Index. *Class No:* 849

[8204]
ZUFFEREY, F. Bibliographie des poètes provençaux des XIVe et XVe siècles. Genève, Droz, 1981. 91p.
Lists manuscripts, editions, and studies relating to 14th- and 15th-century poets. *Class No:* 849

Catalan Literature

[8205]

Bibliography of Old Catalan texts. Concheff, B.J. Madison, Wis., Hispanic Seminary of Medieval Studies, 1985. xi,177p. $15. ISBN: 094226066x.

Known as *BOOCT* and a companion to *Bibliography of Old Spanish texts (BOOST) (q.v.).* Lists 1,470 pre-1500 texts with library locations. 9 indexes provide total access. *Class No:* 849.9

[8206]

Diccionari de la literatura catalana. Molas, J. *and* Massot i Muntaner, J., *eds.* Barcelona, Edicions 62, 1979. 763p. ISBN: 8429715509.

Over 3,000 signed entries, in Catalan, on authors, anoymous works, literary characters, literary terms, movements, etc., including some lengthy essays on genres, with secondary bibliographies appended. Over 80 contributors. *Class No:* 849.9

[8207]

Double minorities of Spain: a bio-bibliographical guide to women writers of the Catalan, Galician and Basque countries. McNerney, K. *and* Enríquez de Salamanca, C., *eds.* New York, MLA, 1994. 421p. ISBN: 0873523970.

Covers 421 Catalan women, 31 Galicians and 20 Basques in a single A-Z sequence. Signed entries by over 40 contributors comprise biography, assessment of major works, lists of publications and translations and (where applicable) secondary sources. Chronological list of authors. General bibliography (10p.). *Class No:* 849.9

[8208]

Història de la literatura catalana. Riquer, M. de, *and others, eds.* Barcelona, Ariel, 1964-88. 11v. illus. ISBN: 8434476002.

Splendidly produced history in 2 parts: *Part Antiga* (v.1-4, ed. by M. de Riquer) and *Part Moderna* (v.5-6, ed. by A. Comas, and v.7-11, ed. by J. Molas).

Each vol. comprises lengthy, signed essays by several scholars on genres, periods, authors, etc., with numerous quotations and bibliographical notes. Sumptuously illustrated throughout (many in colour), with index of illustrations in each vol. Detailed tables of contents provide access to each vol. and there is a cumulative index of names and titles (174p.) in v.11, with a separate index of periodical titles.

See also A.M. Espadaler's *Història de la literatura catalana* (Barcelona, Barcanova, 1993. 316p.). *Class No:* 849.9

[8209]

RIBERA LLOPIS, J.M. Literaturas catalana, gallega y vasca. Madrid, Playor, 1982. 236p. (*Lectura critica de la literatura española.*) ISBN: 843590296x.

For each literature (Catalan, Galician, Basque) provides critical essays on major writers, commentaries on 2 key texts, and select bibliography of primary and secondary material. Lacks index. *Class No:* 849.9

[8210]

TERRY, A. Catalan literature. London, Benn; New York, Barnes & Noble, 1972. xix,136p. (*A Literary history of Spain.*) ISBN: 0510322999, UK; 0064968103, US.

Narrative history in 4 main sections: 1. Medieval and Early Renaissance - 2. Decadence and enlightenment - 3. The Nineteenth century - 4. The Twentieth century. Literal translations of all quotations provided in notes at ends of sections. Select bibliography (5p.). Index. *Class No:* 849.9

[8211]

VERDAGUER, P. Histoire de la littérature catalane. Barcelona, Barcino, 1981. 379p.

Well-organized history in 3 main parts (Le Moyen Âge; La Décadence; Le XIXe et Le XXe siècles) and numerous sub-sections, many of them comprising bio-bibliographical notes on individual writers. Author index and detailed table of contents. *Class No:* 849.9

Italian Literature

Databases

[8212]

LIZ: Letteratura Italiana Zanichelli 3rd ed. Bologna, Zanichelli, 1997. CD-ROM £280.
1st ed. 1993.

Contains the full text of 770 works of Italian literature by authors of all periods, from Francesco d'Assisi to contemporary writers. Text in Latin or Italian, with interface and accompanying booklet in Italian. Comprehensive search facilities. *Class No:* 850(003.4)

Bibliographies

[8213]

Bibliografia generale della lingua e della letteratura italiana (BiGLI), v.1-. 1991- Malato, E., *ed.* Roma, Salerno Editrice, 1993-. Annual.

A new, annual bibliography of the type which already exists for most other major European languages and which should 'fill a gaping void in the bibliographic organization of Italian language and literature' (*Western European Specialists Section Newsletter*, v.18(2), Spring 1995, p.4). Lists texts and studies (including references to reviews), with signed abstracts by an international team of nearly 70 scholars. Aims to be selective for contemporary literary texts and their commentary, but exhaustive for earlier periods. V.4, *1994*, has 16,500 entries and is in 2 parts, with general and linguistic material followed by literary citations, by century, in pt.1. Indexes of authors, editors, publishers and subjects in pt.2. List of *c.*2,500 periodicals scanned. A CD-ROM version is planned. *Class No:* 850(01)

[8214]

—Letteratura italiana repertorio automatizzato (LIRA): CD-ROM bibliografico della lingua e della letteratura italiana, dal 1986 al 1995. Aschero, B., *ed.* Trieste, Alcione, 1996. CD-ROM.

A CD-ROM index to studies of Italian language and literature, based on *Letteratura italiana, aggiornamento bibliografico* (Trieste, Alcione, 1991-. ISSN: 11210753), which is known as *LIAB.* Worldwide coverage, providng citations for books (including primary texts if accompanied by critical apparatus), chapters, articles and reviews. Indexes Italian newspapers and news magazines as well as

.... *(contd.)*
specialized literary journals and is thus very strong on 20th-century literature, but coverage of linguistics is inferior to that of *BiGLI* *Class No:* 850(01)

[8215]
La Rassegna della letteratura italiana. Firenze, Le Lettere (previously Sansoni), 1893- . 2py. ISSN: 00339423.

Each issue includes 'Rassegna bibliografica', a bibliography of recent editions and studies, arranged by period, which has lengthy annotations and occupies half the journal. *Class No:* 850(01)

[8216]
Repertorio bibliografico della letteratura italiana, 1943-1947, a cura della Facoltà di Magistero di Roma. Bosco, U., *ed.* Firenze, Sansoni, 1969. 138p.

Lists nearly 4,500 studies, A-Z by critic, with subject index. Not annotated. Follows Prezzolini (*q.v.*) and is in turn followed by: *Class No:* 850(01)

[8217]
—Repertorio bibliografico della letteratura italiana, a cura della Facoltà di Magistero di Roma. Bosco, U., *ed.* Firenze, Sansoni, 1953-60. 2v.

V.1 covers 1948-9 and lists nearly 4,500 critical studies, while v.2 has over 16,700 entries from 1950-53. Each vol. arranged A-Z by critic, with subject index. Not annotated. *Class No:* 850(01)

[8218]
Repertorio bibliografico della storia e della critica della letteratura italiana dal 1902 al 1932, preparato nella Casa Italiana della Columbia University... Prezzolini, G., *ed.* Roma, Edizioni Roma, 1937-9. 2v.

Annotated lists of literary works and critical studies, arranged by Italian authors and literary subjects (*e.g.* 'Futurismo'), in a single sequence (v.1, A-L; v.2, M-Z). Cumulative index and list of subject entries in v.2.

Supplemented by *Repertorio bibliografico della storia e della critica della letteratura italiana dal 1933 al 1942* (New York, Vanni, 1946-8. 2v.), which has the same basic format. Followed by Bosco's compilations (*qq.v.*). *Class No:* 850(01)

Encyclopaedias & Dictionaries

[8219]
Dictionary of Italian literature. Bondanella, P., *& others, eds.* Rev. ed. Westport, Conn., Greenwood: London, Cassell, 1996. xiv,716p. £35. ISBN: 0313277451, US; 0304338419, UK.

UK title is *Cassell dictionary of Italian literature*. 1st ed. 1979, published in UK by Macmillan as *The Macmillan dictionary of Italian literature*.

Nearly 400 signed entries (38 new ones and the rest updated), mainly for writers, but also for forms and genres, literary movements and schools, and topics like art, film, feminism, etc., each with a bibliography which is aimed at the reader with little or no knowledge of Italian. All Italian titles mentioned in entries are translated and full details of English translations are provided. Brief list of key reference aids. Chronology of literary and historical events, 1071-1995. Lists of entries by subject matter or period. Thorough index. *Class No:* 850(03)

[8220]
Dizionario critico della letteratura italiana. Branca, V., *ed.* 2. ed. Torino, Unione Tipografico-Editrice Torinese, 1986. 4v. illus. ISBN: 8802040184.

1st ed. 1974 in 3 vols.

Lengthy, signed articles (*e.g.* 7p. on Calvino, 17p. on Boccaccio) by over 200 contributors, mainly on authors but also on literary topics and movements, in a single A-Z sequence, with extensive bibliographies of primary and secondary material appended. Index of names (124p.) in v.4. *Class No:* 850(03)

[8221]
Dizionario critico della letteratura italiana del Novecento. Ghidetti, E. *and* Luti, G., *eds.* Roma, Editori Riuniti, 1997. 940p. ISBN: 8835941326.

A guide to 20th-century Italian literature, with entries by 33 contributors on authors, journals, literary movements, etc., with women writers well represented. All entries have substantial bibliographies. 'Offers depth of information and analysis rarely found in other shorter literary dictionaries or "companion" guides' (*Reference Reviews Europe Online*, 97-3/4-314).

An alternative source is *Dizionario della letteratura italiana del Novecento*, ed. by A. Asor Rosa (Torino, Einaudi, 1992). *Class No:* 850(03)

[8222]
Dizionario della letteratura italiana. Bonora, E., *ed.* Milano, Rizzoli, 1977. 2v. (lviii,724p.).

Handy small-format literary encyclopedia in 5 parts: 1. Introductory essay on literary studies (p.xi-lviii) - 2. Dictionary of authors and literary movements, with selective secondary bibliographies (p.1-590) - 3. Dictionary of major literary works (p.593-648) - 4. Dictionary of literary terms (p.651-661) - 5. Chronology (p.665-724). *Class No:* 850(03)

[8223]
Dizionario della letteratura italiana contemporanea. Ronconi, E., *ed.* Firenze, Vallecchi, 1973. 2v.

V.1 *Movimenti letterari. Scrittori.* 829p. V.2 *Repertorio.* 705p.

V.1 has introductory essay on 20th-century Italian literary movements (43p.) followed by dictionary of *c.*1,000 authors, giving biographical notes, some critical evaluation, and lists of main works and selected critical studies. V.2 has 50 lengthy appreciations of major authors, with extracts from critical studies (*e.g.* 28p. on Moravia). *Class No:* 850(03)

[8224]
Dizionario enciclopedico della letteratura italiana. Petronio, G., *ed.* Bari, Laterza; Roma, UNEDI, 1966-70. 6v. illus.

Vols. 1-5 contain unsigned articles, A-Z, on Italian authors; foreign authors who have influenced Italian literature; patrons of Italian literature (popes, monarchs, etc.); literary movements, organizations and libraries; periodicals; and literary and critical terms. Bibliographies appended to articles. V.6 (v,549p.) contains addenda (17p.) and extensive indexes of names and works, the latter with *c.*36,000 entries. 20 contributors. *Class No:* 850(03)

[8225]

The Feminist encyclopedia of Italian literature. Russell, R., *ed.* Westport, Conn., Greenwood, 1997. 416p. £63.50. ISBN: 0313294356.

Covers Italian literature by both male and female writers of all periods. Entries on authors discuss how they have shaped the image of women in Italian literature and how feminist criticism has responded to their works. Other entries cover literary schools and movements; genres and forms; figures and types; and many other topics. All entries are signed, summarize the relationship of the topic to feminist thought and include a brief bibliography. Selected general bibliography. Index. *Class No:* 850(03)

Handbooks & Manuals

[8226]

Guida allo studio della letteratura italiana. Pasquini, E., *ed.* Bologna, Società Editrice il Mulino, 1985. 516p. £22.55. ISBN: 8815009361.

16 signed bibliographical surveys by different specialists; 8 in the first part covering general materials, genres, and aspects of literary criticism, and 8 in the second part on periods of literary history. References at end of each chapter. Lacks index.

L'Italianistisca: introduzione allo studio della letteratura e della lingua italiana, ed. by B. Squarotti (Torino, UTET Libreria, 1993. 420p. ISBN: 8877502096) is a similar guide but its coverage extends to the language. 12 contributed chapters, each followed by a bibliography.
Class No: 850(035)

[8227]

PUPPO, M. *and* **BARONI, G. Manuale critico-bibliografico per lo studio della letteratura italiana.** 4th ed. Torino, Società Editrice Internazionale, 1994. 594p. ISBN: 8805023027.

1st ed. 1954. Edition numbering refers to major revisions, the previous one being in 1972; this is actually the 15th different ed. to appear. All previous eds. by Puppo alone.

Parts 1-4 comprise surveys of scholarship on literary topics, with bibliographies appended. Part 5 contains invaluable essays (average 6p.) on major authors, chronologically arranged, each with primary and secondary bibliography. 7 new authors have been added for this ed., including Calvino, Montale and Svevo. An author index has been added, but there is still no title index. 'This is the best, most current and comprehensive of introductions to Italian literary bibliography' (*Reference Reviews Europe Online*, 96-2/3-269). *Class No:* 850(035)

Histories

[8228]

The Cambridge history of Italian literature. Brand, P. *and* Pertile, L., *eds.* Cambridge, Cambridge Univ. Press, 1996. xxxv,701p. £70. ISBN: 0521434920.

The first substantial history to appear in English for many years is arranged in 11 parts and 44 chapters by an international team of 19 scholars. Translations provided for all quotations. Includes opera in coverage of theatre history. Bibliography (67p.) arranged by chapter, giving major primary and secondary sources. Chronology of literary, political and cultural events, 1050-1994. Index. 'The emphasis falls on providing clear, succinct exposition, with interpretation and commentary of the sort that will win the consent of the professionals and provide valid orientation for the student. It is a modern conservative approach. The idea

....(contd.)

of a tradition is not questioned, and what lies outside it is largely marginalized' (*TLS*, no.4950, Feb. 13, 1998, p.28).
Class No: 850(091)

[8229]

La Letteratura italiana: storia e testi. Muscetta, C., *ed.* Bari, Laterza, 1970-80. 10v. in 20. illus.

V.1 *Il Duecento;* v.2 *Il Trecento;* v.3 *Il Quattrocento;* v.4 *Il Cinquecento;* v.5 *Il Seicento;* v.6 *Il Settecento;* v.7 *Il Primo ottocento;* v.8 *Il Secondo ottocento;* v.9 *Il Novecento;* v.10 *L'Età presente.* 2 parts per vol.

Multi-volume, multi-contributor reference work of the kind beloved of Italian publishers, combining literary history with textual commentary and close readings of key passages by specialists. Extensive bibliographies with each section. Each vol. has index of names and titles and index of extracts, while the final vol. has cumulative author/title and subject indexes (343p.). *Class No:* 850(091)

[8230]

Storia della letteratura italiana. Cecchi, E. *and* Sapegno, N., *eds.* Milano, Garzanti, 1965-69. 9v. illus.

V.1, *Le Origini e il duecento;* v.2, *Il Trecento;* v.3, *Il Quattrocento e l'Ariosto;* v.4, *Il Cinquecento;* v.5, *Il Seicento;* v.6, *Il Settecento;* v.7, *L'Ottocento;* v.8, *Dall'ottocento al novecento;* v.9, *Il Novecento.*

Chapters by specialists, with extensive chapter bibliographies and footnotes. Fully illustrated; *e.g.* v.1 has 218 illustrations, of which 64 are in colour. Many quotations. Cumulative index of names in v.9.

A new ed. of v.9, *Il Novecento,* was published in 1987 in 2 vols. (702p.;1061p.), ed. by N. Sapegno. It comprises 15 lengthy chapters, a bibliography of general studies (10p.), and a dictionary of authors (163p.) which gives biographical notes and bibliographies of works and studies.
Class No: 850(091)

[8231]

Storia letteraria d'Italia. Balduino, A., *ed.* Padova, La Nuova Libraria Editrice; Milano, Vallardi, 1942-. 11v.

1st ed. 1880-1913.

V.1, *Le Origini,* by C. Leonardi; v.2, *Il Duecento,* by M. Picone; v.3, *Dante,* by A. Vallone; v.4, *Storia della critica dantesca dal XIV al XX secolo,* by A. Vallone; v.5, *Il Trecento,* by N. Sapegno; v.6, *Il Quattrocento,* by V. Rossi; v.7 *Il Cinquecento,* by G. Toffanin; v.8, *Il Seicento,* by M. Capucci and C. Jannaco; v.9, *Il Settecento,* by G. Natali; v.10, *L'Ottocento,* by R. Assunto and others; v.11, *Il Novecento,* by A. Galletti.

These volumes are in a state of continuous revision or rewriting. Chapter bibliographies are extensive and each vol. is indexed. *Class No:* 850(091)

[8232]

WILKINS, E.H. A History of Italian literature. 2nd ed., rev. by T.G. Bergin. Cambridge, Mass., Harvard Univ. Press, 1974. xi,570p. map. ISBN: 0674397010.

1st ed. 1954.

Covers 1200 to the present in 53 chapters, many of them devoted to individual writers. Quotations in English translation. List of additional writers not treated in main text. Bibliography of English translations and English-language works on the literature (20p.). Chronology of literary and historical events. Index. *Class No:* 850(091)

[8233]
—WHITFIELD, J.H. A Short history of Italian literature. 2nd ed., with a new chapter from 1922 to the present by J.R. Woodhouse. Manchester, Manchester Univ. Press, 1980. 335p. ISBN: 0719007828.

1st ed. Harmondsworth, Penguin, 1960.

Narrative history in 16 chapters, with select bibliography of general reference works and studies (4p.). Index.
Class No: 850(091)

Biographies

[8234]
Dictionary of literary biography. Detroit, Gale, 1978-98. v.1-188 (in progress). £112 per vol.

The following vols. cover Italian literature:

V.114 *Twentieth-century Italian poets, first series.* 1992.

V.128 *Twentieth-century Italian poets, second series.* 1993.

V.177 *Italian novelists since World War II, 1945-1965.* 1997.

For a description of the series, see entry at 82(092).
Class No: 850(092)

[8235]
Dizionario degli scrittori italiani d'oggi. 2. ed. Cosenza, Pellegrini, 1975. 240p. illus.

1st ed. 1969.

Concise biobibliographical articles on modern Italian writers. Includes some updated entries from 1st ed., but most of the entries are new. *Class No:* 850(092)

[8236]
Letteratura italiana. Milano, Marzorati, 1956-74. 19v. illus.

Comprises 5 sets, made up as follows:

Le Correnti. 2v. 1956; *I Maggiori. 2v. 1956. I Minori.* 4v. 1961-2; *I Contemporanei.* 6v. 1963-74. *I Critici.* 5v. 1969.

Apart from the first 2 vols., which deal with general works and literary periods, this is essentially a biobibliographical encyclopedia, comprising lengthy, signed articles on Italian authors and critics, each with bibliographies appended. Cumulative indexes in the final vol. of each set. The work of numerous scholars. *Class No:* 850(092)

Women

[8237]
CLEIS, F. Ermiza e le altre: il percorso della scrittura femminile nella Svizzera italiana con bibliografia degli scritti e biografie delle autrici. Torino, Rosenberg & Sellier, 1993. 412p. ISBN: 8870115577.

A guide to Italian-language writing by Swiss women, comprising historical survey (50p.), bibliography of books and articles, brief biographies and name index.
Class No: 850-0055.2

[8238]
Italian women writers: a bio-bibliographical sourcebook. Russell, R., *ed.* Westport, Conn., Greenwood, 1994. 520p. £75.95. ISBN: 0313283478.

Signed profiles of 51 writers from the 14th century to the present, compiled in standard Greenwood format: biography and literary career; themes of major works; critical reception; bibliography of primary works, English translations and critical studies. *Class No:* 850-0055.2

Italian Literature in Translation

[8239]
KEENOY, R., *and others*. The Babel guide to Italian fiction in English translation. London, Boulevard, 1995. 176p. illus. £7.95 ISBN: 1899460004.

The first of a series of guides to foreign literature in translation, which is intended eventually to cover all major national literatures and is aimed at readers, students and teachers of world literature, librarians and booksellers. Includes 150 reviews of key books by 20th-century Italian authors, with excerpts and pictures of the writers, and provides a complete list of Italian fiction translated into English since 1945 (over 600 titles) with publication details. Enthusiastically received by reviewers. *Class No:* 850-03

[8240]
SHIELDS, N.C. Italian translations in America. New York, Institute of French Studies, 1931 (repr. New York, Gordon Press). x,410p. $59.95. ISBN: 0849004292.

1,383 translations of Italian works arranged chronologically, 1751-1928, with bibliographical notes and library locations. List of reference works quoted (3p.). Thorough index. *Class No:* 850-03

Italian Poetry

[8241]
CUCCHI, M. Dizionario della poesia italiana: i poeti di ogni tempo, la metrica, i gruppi e le tendenze. Milano, Mondadori, 1983. viii,419p.

Main sequence has entries for *c.*750 poets, A-Z, giving biographical information and some critical commentary with references to works. Appendix contains dictionary of terms (24p.) encountered in the study of Italian metrics.
Class No: 850-1

[8242]
JONES, F.J. The Modern Italian lyric. Cardiff, Univ. of Wales Press, 1986. 643p. ISBN: 070830902x.

An enlarged and revised English version of *La Poesia italiana contemporanea* (Firenze, 1975).

A study of the development of the modern Italian lyric in the first half of the 20th century, covering 3 major schools: crepuscularism, futurism and hermeticism. Substantial bibliography (35p.), listing the works of 10 poets treated and general studies of the period. Index. *Class No:* 850-1

[8243]
Libri di poesia. Pantani, I., *ed.* Milano, Bibliografica, 1996. xxiii,488p. (*Biblia: La Biblioteca de libro Italiano antico.*)

The first vol. in a massive project to compile a short-title catalogue of books published in Italy or in Italian, 1465-1600. 20 vols. are planned and this one has entries for 5,270 books of poetry, with short annotations describing the poetic form or providing content information, plus details of major Italian libraries which have verified the bibliographic record. 4 indexes: dates; secondary authors; printers, typographers and booksellers; place of publication. *Class No:* 850-1

Ariosto

[8244]
FATINI, G. Bibliografia della critica ariostea (1510-1956). Firenze, Le Monnier, 1958. xv,723p.

3,624 numbered entries (plus interpolations), chronologically arranged, with subject and name indexes.
Class No: 850-1ARI

[8245]

RODINI, R.J. *and* **DI MARIA, S. Ludovico Ariosto:** an annotated bibliography of criticism, 1956-80. Columbia, Mo., Univ. of Missouri Press, 1984. xii,270p. $32. ISBN: 0826204457.

Follows Fatini's monumental work, listing 930 recent studies. Arranged A-Z by author, with subject index and index of Ariosto's works cited. *Class No:* 850-1ARI

Dante

[8246]

The Cambridge companion to Dante. Jacoff, R., *ed.* Cambridge, Cambridge Univ. Press, 1993. xx,270p. £37.50. ISBN: 0521417481.

15 essays on different aspects of Dante's life and works, all with bibliography. Selective general bibliography. Chronology. Index. *Class No:* 850-1DAN

[8247]

Dante studies. Albany, NY, State Univ. of New York Press for The Dante Society of America, 1881-. Annual. ISSN: 00702862.

Former title (until 1980) was *Dante Society of America: annual report with accompanying papers.*

Carries annual American bibliographies, *e.g. DS 1994* has 'American Dante bibliography for 1993' (38p.), an annotated listing of translations, studies and reviews published in the US. *Class No:* 850-1DAN

[8248]

Enciclopedia dantesca. Bosco, U., *and others, eds.* Roma, Istituto della Enciclopedia Italiana, 1970-78. 6v. illus.

All you ever wanted to know about Dante ... and then some. Vols. 1-5 comprise a single A-Z sequence of signed entries for Italian and foreign words found in Dante's works (with examples from the texts and discussion of forms and meanings); proper names (historical and fictional people and places, cultural and religious movements, etc.) referred to in the text or relevant to the study of Dante; ancient and modern Dante scholars (lengthy profiles). Most entries have bibliographies.

V.6 has biography of Dante (59p.); articles on many aspects of his language and style; bibliography of his works and critical studies (118p.); and, finally, the text of Dante's works (375p.). Superbly produced. *Class No:* 850-1DAN

[8249]

ESPOSITO, E. Bibliografica analitica degli scritti su Dante, 1950-70. Firenze, Olschki, 1990. 4v. ISBN: 8822237242.

An annotated bibliography of secondary literature with 9,180 entries. Over 1,600 journals have been scanned. Entries include summary of contents, critical commentary and references to reviews. Thoroughly indexed in v.4. Continues a series of bibliographies published in Italy, usually in specialist journals. 'The definitive Dante bibliography for the period' (*Reference Reviews Europe Online*, 96-2/3-276). *Class No:* 850-1DAN

[8250]

TOYNBEE, P. A Dictionary of proper names and notable matters in the works of Dante. [2nd ed.] rev. by C.S. Singleton. Oxford, Clarendon Press, 1968. xxiv,722p. maps. ISBN: 0198153562.

First published 1898.

A complete revision and updating of Toynbee's *magnum opus*, taking into account 20th century Dante scholarship. References are to the Società Dantesca Italiana's *Le Opere di Dante* (2nd ed., 1960). Bibliography (9p.). Appended genealogical and chronological tables and maps.

.... (contd.)

An abridged ed. was issued as *A Concise dictionary of proper names and notable matters in the works of Dante* (Oxford, Clarendon Press, 1914) and reprinted by Phaeton (New York) in 1968 (ISBN: 0877530408). *Class No:* 850-1DAN

Petrarch

[8251]

FUCILLA, J.G. Oltre un cinquantennio di scritti sul Petrarca (1916-1973). Padova, Editrice Antenore, 1982. xviii,331p.

Lists over 3,800 modern studies of Petrarch in 23 sections. Appended is a supplement (24p.) to Fowler's catalogue of the Cornell Univ. Petrarch Collection. *Class No:* 850-1PET

Italian Drama

[8252]

FOLGER SHAKESPEARE LIBRARY, Washington, D.C. **Italian plays (1500-1700) in the Folger Library:** a bibliography, with introduction by L. G. Clubb. Firenze, Olschki, 1968. xlvi,267p. illus.

890 items with brief bibliographical descriptions. Arranged A-Z by author with title index. Lists of basic reference works and of sources cited. *Class No:* 850-2

[8253]

TORONTO UNIVERSITY. Library. **Catalogue of Italian plays, 1500-1700,** in the Library of the University of Toronto. Corrigan, B., *comp.* Toronto, Univ. of Toronto Press, 1961. xvii,134p. illus.

About 500 briefly annotated entries, arranged A-Z by author with title index and list of Italian printers. Supplements have been published in *Renaissance News*, v.16, 1963, p.298-307, and v.19, 1966, p.219-28. *Class No:* 850-2

Pirandello

[8254]

A Companion to Pirandello studies. DiGaetani, J.L., *ed.* Westport, Conn., Greenwood, 1991. xxviii,443p. $105. ISBN: 0313257140.

27 essays on the life, works and influence of Pirandello. Appendices include a very useful classified bibliography (19p.) by M.G. D'Aponte, listing editions, English translations, critical books, articles and dissertations. Index. *Class No:* 850-2PIR

Italian Fiction

[8255]

The New Italian novel. Barański, Z.G. *and* Pertile, L., *eds.* Edinburgh, Edinburgh Univ. Press, 1993. vi,261p. £14.95. (*Writers of Italy.*) ISBN: 0748609180.

Signed critical studies (average 17p.) on 15 contemporary novelists, with bibliographies of works (including translations) and critical studies. Index. *Class No:* 850-31

[8256]
PACIFICI, S. The Modern Italian novel. Carbondale and Edwardsville, Ill., Southern Illinois Univ. Press, 1967-79. 3v.
V.1 *From Manzoni to Svevo.* 1967. vii,199p.
V.2 *From Capuana to Tozzi.* 1973. xiii,188p.
V.3 *From Pea to Moravia.* 1979. xiii,273p.
A history of 19th- and 20th-century Italian fiction, with most chapters devoted to one novelist. Bibliographical essays on each novelist and detailed index at end of each vol.
Class No: 850-31

Boccaccio

[8257]
CONSOLI, J.P. Giovanni Boccaccio: an annotated bibliography. New York, Garland, 1992. xiv,484p. $65. (*Garland medieval bibliographies.*.) ISBN: 0824031474.
A classified listing of *c.*1,500 books, articles and dissertations published 1939-86. Includes material in English, Italian, French and German. Author and subject indexes. *Class No:* 850-31BOC

[8258]
Studi sul Boccaccio Firenze, Le Lettere (previously Sansoni), 1963-. v.1-. Annual.
Carries bibliographical updates in each vol. That in v.24, 1996, lists 196 studies. *Class No:* 850-31BOC

[8259]
STYCH, F.S. Boccaccio in English: a bibliography of editions, adaptations and criticism. Westport, Conn., Greenwood, 1995. 280p. £63.50. (*Bibliographies and indexes in world literature.*) ISBN: 0313289670.
1. Editions of the works - 2. Adaptations and parallels - 3. Criticism and references. Annotated entries chronologically arranged within each section. 7 indexes provide full access.
Class No: 850-31BOC

Rumanian Literature

[8260]
ACADEMIA REPUBLICII POPULARE ROMÎNE. Istoria literaturii romîne. Bucureşti, Editura Academiei Republicii Populare Romîne, 1964-73. 3v. illus.
V.1 *Folclorul. Literatura romînă în perioada feudală (1400-1780).* 1964. (2nd ed. 1970).
V.2 *De la şcoala ardeleană la junimea.* 1968.
V.3 *Epica marilor clasici.* 1973.
Official history of Rumanian literature, with sectional bibliographies, general bibliographies, and indexes of names and titles in each vol. *Class No:* 859

[8261]
—PIRU, A. Istoria literaturii române. Bucureşti, Editura Didactică şi Pedagogică, 1970-71. 2v. illus.
V.1 *Perioada veche.* 3rd ed. 1971. 416p.
V.2 *Epoca premodernă.* 2nd ed. 1970. 484p.
Chapters largely devoted to individual authors, with bibliographies appended. General bibliography in each vol., but no index. *Class No:* 859

[8262]
BĂLAN, I.D. A Concise history of Rumanian literature. Bucureşti, Editura ştiinţifică şi enciclopedică, 1981. 119p.
A history comprising biographical articles on Romanian authors, arranged chronologically and often including translated passages from their work. 'A balanced introduction to the principal figures of Romanian literature and the anonymous masterpieces of Romanian oral literature' (Deletant, A. and Deletant, D., *Romania,* 1985, p.132), but lacks bibliography. *Class No:* 859

[8263]
—MUNTEANO, B. Modern Roumanian literature.
Sprietsma, C., *tr.* Bucureşti, Editura Cuvântul, 1943. 322p.
Originally published in French as *Littérature roumaine* (Paris, Éditions du Sagittaire, 1938). 'Still the only intelligible history of Romanian literature in English' (Deletant, A. and Deletant, D., *Romania,* 1985, p.135), but does not begin until the mid-19th century. *Class No:* 859

[8264]
BIBLIOTECA CENTRALĂ UNIVERSITARĂ BUCUREŞTI. Literatura română: ghid bibliografic. Vol.1, Surse. Bucureşti, La Biblioteca, 1979. xii,715p.
A comprehensive guide to information sources on Romanian literature, with special sections on German and Hungarian literature in Romania. Includes a dictionary of literary terms, with references to a lengthy bibliography of works on literary theory and stylistics (105p.). 4 indexes: names; periodicals; literary terms; libraries and cultural institutions. *Class No:* 859

[8265]
—ACADEMIA REPUBLICII POPULARE ROMÎNE. Biblioteca. Bibliografia literaturii romîne, 1948-60.
Vianu, T., *ed.* Editura Academiei Republicii Populare Romîne, 1965. xxiii,1123p.
Short general bibliography (p.1-24), followed by primary and secondary bibliographies of *c.*400 Romanian authors, A-Z. Index of names. *Class No:* 859

[8266]
Dictionarul literaturii române de la origini pînâ la 1900. Bucureşti, Editura Academici Republicii Socialiste România, 1979. 976p. illus.
Entries on authors, literary movements and organizations, periodicals, etc., with substantial bibliographies.
Class No: 859

[8267]
Literatura română i dicţionar cronologic Chiţimia, I.C., *ed.* Bucureşti, Editura ştiinţifică şi enciclopedică, 1979. 862p.
A chronology of Romanian literature from the 6th century to 1979, listing births, deaths and literary events. Bibliography (5p.). Index of authors and anonymous titles.
Class No: 859

Spanish & Portuguese Literature

Encyclopaedias & Dictionaries

[8268]
Dictionary of the literature of the Iberian peninsula. Bleiberg, G., *& others, eds.* Westport, Conn., Greenwood, 1993. 2v. (xxi,1806p.). $195. ISBN: 031321302x.
Updates and makes available to English-speaking users the material in *Diccionario de literatura española* by G.

.... *(contd.)*
Bleiberg and J. Marías (4th ed. Madrid, 1972), but whereas the original work concentrated solely on literature in Spanish, including that of the Americas, this dictionary covers the literature of Iberia, with Catalan, Galician and Portuguese replacing Spanish American literature. Many late 20th-century writers have been added.

Signed entries by over 140 scholars range from a few lines to several pages and cover writers, movements, genres, themes and terms. Most literary titles cited are followed by either details of a published translation or a literal rendering of the original. All entries include bibliographies, with those for individual authors listing primary works, translations and secondary sources. Ample cross-references. A welcome English-language source, with much-improved coverage of women's writing, but coverage of Portuguese literature, especially pre-20th century is disappointing. Comprehensive index (64p.). *Class No:* 860+869(03)

Theses

[8269]

CHATHAM, J.R., ***and others*****. Dissertations in Hispanic languages and literatures:** an index of dissertations completed in the United States and Canada. Lexington, Ky., Univ. Press of Kentucky, 1970-81. 2v. ISBN: 0813111838, v.1; 0813114152, v.2.

See entry at 806.0+806.90(043).
Class No: 860+869(043)

[8270]

CHATHAM, J.R. ***and*** **SCALES, S.M. Western European dissertations on the Hispanic and Luso-Brazilian languages and literatures:** a retrospective index. Mississippi State Univ., Dept. of Foreign Languages, 1984. xiii,145p.

Lists over 6,000 dissertations by author, with thorough subject index. *Class No:* 860+869(043)

Excerpts

[8271]

Hispanic literature criticism. Krstovic, J., *ed.* Detroit, Gale, 1994. 2v. illus. £146. ISBN: 0810391457.

Reprints excerpts from selected critical studies of 72 Hispanic writers (only 11 of them from Spain and Portugal, with 42 from Latin America and 19 from the USA) from the last 100 years. Entries include portrait, biographical details, chronology of principal works (with translations where available), chronologically arranged excerpts with full bibliographical citations, and recomendations for further reading. Many of the excerpts have been taken from vols. in Gale's *Literary criticism* series, but 23 of the authors covered here are not represented in those series. Indexes of authors, titles and nationalities.
Class No: 860+869(082.200)

[8272]

Modern Spanish and Portuguese literatures. Schneider, M.J. *and* Stern, I., *eds.* New York, Continuum, 1988. xxxii,615p. $85. (*A Library of literary criticism.*) ISBN: 0804432805.

Presents lengthy excerpts from critical writings about 80 20th-century authors writing in Spanish, Catalan, Galician and Portuguese, with some excerpts newly translated by the editors. Two A-Z sequences (Spain and Portugal) with criticism arranged chronologically under each author. Nearly 800 excerpts in all. Lists of works mentioned (including

.... *(contd.)*
English translations) constitute useful primary bibliographies for the authors concerned. Index to critics.
Class No: 860+869(082.200)

Biographies

[8273]

Diccionario de autores iberoamericanos. Shimose, P., *ed.* Madrid, Instituto de Cooperacíon Iberoamericana, 1982. 459p.

Short, signed biographies, with lists of principal works, of authors born between 1880 and 1930. Includes Spanish, Catalan, Galician, Basque, Spanish-American, Portuguese, Brazilian and Chicano writers. 7 contributors.
Class No: 860+869(092)

Spanish Literature

Bibliographies of Bibliographies

[8274]

ZUBATSKY, D. Spanish, Catalan and Galician literary authors of the twentieth century: an annotated guide to bibliographies. Metuchen, N.J., Scarecrow, 1992. 184p. $29. ISBN: 081082518x.

A major revision and expansion of an article which appeared in *Hispania* 61, Oct. 1978. Covers over 500 authors, A-Z, including linguists, historians, critics and journalists as well as literary figures. Includes bibliographies found in periodicals, dissertations and *Festschriften*, in addition to standard reference works. Not all entries are annotated.

For earlier material, see Zubatsky's *Spanish, Catalan and Galician literary authors of the eighteenth and nineteenth centuries: an annotated guide to bibliographies* (Metuchen, N.J., Scarecrow, 1995. 166p. $26.50. ISBN: 0810829479).
Class No: 860(009)

Bibliographies

[8275]

Nueva revista de filología hispánica. México, Centro de Estudios Lingüísticos y Literarios, El Colegio de México, 1947-. v.1-. 2py. ISSN: 01850121.

Preceded by *Revista de filología hispánica,* v.1-8, 1936-46.

See entry at 806.0(01). *Class No:* 860(01)

[8276]

Research bibliographies and checklists. Deyermond, A.D., *and others, eds.* London, Grant & Cutler, 1971-.

Titles on Spanish literature:

3. Sharrer, H.L. *A Critical Bibliography of Hispanic Arthurian Material. I. Texts: the prose romance cycles.* 1977. 55p. £9.25.

11. Aquila, A.J. *Alonso de Ercillà y Zúñiga: a basic bibliography*. 1975. 96p. £11.50.

12. Griffin, N. *Jesuit School drama: a checklist of critical literature*. 1976. 54p. £9.25. *Supplement No.1*. 1986. 219p. £21.50.

13. Crosby, J.O. *Guía bibliográfica para el estudio crítico de Quevedo*. 1976. 136p. £14.50.

14. Smith, P. *Vicente Blasco Ibáñez: an annotated*

....*(contd.)*
bibliography. 1976. 124p. £14.50.

19. Snow, J.T. *The Poetry of Alfonso X: a critical bibliography*. 1977. 140p. £14.50.

20. Hitchcock, R. *The Kharjas: a critical bibliography*. 1977. 68p. £9.25. *Supplement no.1*. 1996. 95p. £12.95.

23. Eisenberg, D. *Castilian romances of chivalry in the sixteenth century: a bibliography*. 1979. 112p. £11.50.

29. McGaha, M.D. *The Theatre in Madrid during the Second Republic: a checklist*. 1979. 105p. £11.50.

32. Bergman, H.E. and Szmuk, S.E. *A Catalogue of Comedias sueltas in the New York Public Library. I. A-H*. 1980. £14.50. *II. I-Z*. 1981. £16.95.

33. Best, M. *Ramón Pérez de Ayala: an annotated bibliography of criticism*. 1980. 81p. £10.75.

41. Whinnom, K. *The Spanish sentimental romance 1440-1550: a critical bibliography*. 1983. 85p. £10.75.

46. Valis, N.M. *Leopoldo Alas (Clarín): an annotated bibliography*. 1986. 279p. £22.50.

47. Faulhaber, C.B. *Libros y bibliotecas en la Esapaña medieval: una bibliografía de fuentes impresas*. 1987. 213p.

51. Freire Lopez, A.M. *Poesia popular durante la Guerra de la Independencia española (1808-1814)*. 1993. 203p. £22.50. *Class No:* 860(01)

[8277]

Revista de filología española. Madrid, Consejo Superior de Investigaciones Cientificas, Instituto de Filología, 1914-. v.1-. 2py. ISSN: 02109174.

See entry at 806.0(01). *Class No:* 860(01)

[8278]

Revista de literatura. Madrid, Consejo Superior de Investigaciones Científicas, Instituto de Filología, 1952-. v.1-. 2py.

Each issue carries a classified bibliography of editions and studies. That in v.57(113), Jan-June 1995, has over 1,700 items, most of them devoted to individual authors. Coverage includes colonial Spanish American authors, but post-independence Spanish Americans are excluded.
Class No: 860(01)

[8279]

SIMÓN DÍAZ, J. Bibliografía de la literatura hispánica. Madrid, Consejo Superior de Investigaciones Cientificas, Instituto 'Miguel de Cervantes' de Filologia Hispánica, 1950-94. v.1-16 (in progress). ISBN: 8400052021.

V.1 has sections on Castilian, Catalan, Galician and Basque literature, covering general works such as histories of literature, collections of texts, anthologies, etc. V.2 also lists general works, including bibliographies and biographical dictionaries. V.3 (2 parts) covers the Middle Ages and v.4 the Golden Age. Individual bibliographies for Golden Age writers begin in v.4 and continue through v.16, having reached Pazos. The series is in a state of continuous revision, with some vols. now in their 2nd or 3rd ed.

An extremely thorough bibliography of all the Hispanic literatures (including that of pre-independence America), covering books, periodical articles and theses. Annotations are occasional and brief, but reviews are cited and locations (usually in Spanish libraries) listed wherever possible. Comprehensive indexes (names, first lines, subjects, libraries, etc.) in each vol. provide complete access.
Class No: 860(01)

[8280]

SIMÓN DÍAZ, J. Manual de bibliografía de la literatura española. 3rd ed., refundida, corr. y aum. Madrid, Gredos, 1980. 1156p. ISBN: 8424900235.

1st ed. 1963.

Selective, unannotated bibliography (not an abridgement of the author's multi-volume work *Bibliografía de la literatura hispánica*) of nearly 27,000 items. General section followed by chronological sections covering Middle Ages, Golden Age, 18th, 19th, and 20th centuries, listing general works followed by works by and about specific authors. Excellent name and subject indexes. *Class No:* 860(01)

Middle Ages

[8281]

Bibliography of Old Spanish texts. Faulhaber, C.B., *and others, comps*. 3rd ed. Madison, Wis., Hispanic Seminary of Medieval Studies, 1984. xxxiii,341p. ISBN: 0942260430.

1st ed. 1975; 2nd ed. 1977.

Created as a preliminary process in the compilation of a computer-based *Dictionary of the Old Spanish Language (DOSL)*, the bibliography (*BOOST*) is essentially a citational lexicon reflecting Old Spanish word usage as manifested by surviving pre-1501 manuscripts and books. 3rd ed. provides full citations for 3,378 items, arranged A-Z by location. 11 indexes, including author, title and language, provide complete access. *Class No:* 860(01)"01/14"

16th & 17th Centuries

[8282]

MOSELEY, W.W., *and others*. Spanish literature, 1500-1700: a bibliography of Golden Age studies in Spanish and English, 1925-80. Westport, Conn., Greenwood, 1984. lxiii,765p. $115. ISBN: 0313214913.

Over 11,000 entries, with lists of general and genre studies followed by bibliographies of studies of nearly 300 individual authors and anonymous works, A-Z, the latter section occupying 60% of the book. Index of critics, subject index, and index of Golden Age authors and anonymous works. Lists of periodicals and *Festschriften* analyzed.
Class No: 860(01)"15/16"

18th Century

[8283]

AGUILAR PIÑAL, F. Bibliografía de autores españoles del siglo XVIII. Madrid, Consejo Superior de Investigaciones Cientificas, Instituto 'Miguel de Cervantes', 1981-95. 8v. ISBN: 8400053176.

Arranged by author, A-Z, with 5-6,000 numbered items in each vol. Each author entry has brief biographical notes followed by lists of manuscripts, editions and translations, with library locations. Each vol. has indexes of names, subjects, places, titles of theatrical works, and imprints (by town). *Class No:* 860(01)"17"

Encyclopaedias & Dictionaries

[8284]

Diccionario de literatura española e hispanoamericana. Gullón, R., *ed*. Madrid, Alianza, 1993. 2v. (xiv,1081p.). ISBN: 842065292x.

Signed entries by *c.*160 contributors are mainly on authors, giving place and date of birth and death, concise review of career and list of works, with secondary bibliography in most cases. *c.*120 longer topical entries on

.... *(contd.)*
movements, periods and genres, all with bibliographies, but no articles on national literatures. One of these lists winners of various literary awards. Title index (232p.) has *c.*28,000 entries. *Class No:* 860(03)

[8285]
The Oxford companion to Spanish literature. Ward, P., *ed.* Oxford, Clarendon Press, 1978. viii,629p. ISBN: 0198661142.

Approx. 3,000 entries in one A-Z sequence, mainly for authors (not limited to literary writers) and works, but also for literary institutions, movements, terms and styles. Covers Spanish-American literature and also non-Spanish literature of Spain: Basque, Catalan, Galician. Rather more bibliographical information included than is traditional in *Oxford companions*, rather less on historical and political background, with references to other sources at the end of most author entries. Must be due for an update.
Class No: 860(03)

Handbooks & Manuals

[8286]
BLEZNICK, D.W. A Sourcebook for Hispanic literature and language: a selected, annotated guide to Spanish, Spanish-American, and United States Hispanic bibliography, literature, linguistics, journals, and other source materials. 3rd ed. Lanham, Md., Scarecrow, 1995. x,310p. $60. ISBN: 0810829819.

1st ed. Philadelphia, Pa., Temple Univ. Press, 1974; 2nd ed. Scarecrow, 1983.

Lists 1,519 sources in 15 sections, with brief annotations. New entries account for some 40% of the text in this ed., but coverage of anthologies has been dropped. Author and title indexes. *Class No:* 860(035)

[8287]
FOSTER, D.W. *and* **FOSTER, V.R. Manual of Hispanic bibliography.** 2nd ed., rev. and expanded. New York, Garland, 1977. xv,329p. ISBN: 0824098889.

1st ed. Seattle, Univ. of Washington Press, 1970.

'An attempt at providing Spanish and Spanish-American literary scholars with a comprehensive bibliographical guide to primary and important secondary sources of investigation' (*Introduction*). 1,050 well-annotated entries (an increase of 30% over 1st ed.) in 4 main sections, covering general bibliographies, Spanish literature, Spanish-American literature, and Spanish-American national bibliographies. Author and short-title indexes. *Class No:* 860(035)

[8288]
JAURALDE POU, P. Manual de investigación literaria (guía bibliográfica para el estudio de la literatura española). Madrid, Gredos, 1981. 416p.

Nearly 2,000 items in 22 sections, including general bibliographies, literary histories, dictionaries and anthologies, and materials relating to specific periods. Most entries annotated. Author index. No subject index, but table of contents is detailed. *Class No:* 860(035)

[8289]
WOODBRIDGE, H.C. Guide to reference works for the study of the Spanish language and literature and Spanish American literature. 2nd ed. New York, Modern Language Assoc. of America, 1997. xvii,236p. $37.50. (*Selected bibliographies in language and literature.*) ISBN: 0873529677.

1st ed. 1987, being a greatly enlarged version of Woodbridge's *Spanish and Spanish-American literature: an*

.... *(contd.)*
annotated guide to selected bibliographies (New York, MLA, 1983).

1,230 well-annotated entries (an increase of over 300 on 1st ed.) on reference works published since 1950, confined in general 'to the latest and best sources available' (*Introduction*). Excellent classified arrangement, clearly demonstrated in the table of contents, based on 4 main sections: 1. The Spanish of Spain - 2. American Spanish - 3. Spanish literature of Europe - 4. Spanish literature of the western hemisphere. Index of authors, editors, compilers and translators. Index of authors as subjects. Title index.
Class No: 860(035)

Chronologies

[8290]
VIÑA LISTE, J.M., *and others.* **Cronologia de la literatura española.** Madrid, Cátedra, 1991-. v.1-. (in progress)

V.1 *Edad Media.* 1991. 468p.

V.3 *Siglo XVIII y XIX.* 1992. 1051p.

Highly detailed chronologies of Spanish literature. V.1 lists 1,072 works and has title and subject indexes and a separate chronology of historical events. V.3 lists thousands of works under 240 authors. Vols. 2 and 4 are to cover the Golden Age and the 20th century. *Class No:* 860(090)

Histories

[8291]
ALBORG ESCARTÍ, J.L. Historia de la literatura española. 2. ed. ampliada. Madrid, Gredos, 1982-86. 4v.

1st ed. 1966-80.

V.1 *Edad media y renacimiento.* 1986. 1082p.

V.2 *Época barroca.* 1983. 966p.

V.3 *Siglo XVIII.* 1985. 980p.

V.4 *El Romanticismo.* 1982. 934p.

Extensive footnote references, giving details of editions and material on authors. Author and title index in each vol.
Class No: 860(091)

[8292]
CHANDLER, R.E. *and* **SCHWARTZ, K. A New history of Spanish literature.** Rev. ed. Baton Rouge, La., Louisiana State Univ. Press, 1991. xv,437p. $45. ISBN: 0807116998.

1st ed. 1961.

Introductory chapter on Spanish history, culture and literature, followed by 5 chapters which each cover a genre (epic poetry, drama, fiction, lyric poetry, nonfiction prose) from its origins to 1990. Classified bibliography of full-length studies (29p. in 1st ed.) appears to have been dropped. Index. *Class No:* 860(091)

[8293]
DIAZ-PLAJA, G. Historia general de las literaturas hispánicas. Barcelona, Barna, 1949-67. 6v. in 7. illus.

V.1 *Desde les origenes hasta 1400.* 1949.

V.2 *Pre-renacimiento y renacimiento.* 1951.

V.3 *Renacimiento y barroco.* 1953.

V.4 (2 pts.) *Siglos XVIII y XIX.* 1956.

V.5 *Post-romanticismo y modernismo.* 1958.

V.6 *Literatura contemporanea* (Barcelona, Vergara, 1967).

Resembles *Cambridge history of English literature* in scope and style, with each chapter written by a specialist and accompanied by an extensive bibliography. Coverage includes literatures in other languages of Spain (*e.g.* Basque, Catalan), Spanish-American literature, and literatures of other Spanish-speaking countries (*e.g.* Philippines).

....(*contd.*)

A History of Spanish literature (New York, N.Y. Univ. Press, 1971. xxii,374p. ISBN: 0814717756) is a translation by H.A. Harter of a single-vol. history by Diaz-Plaja. It contains extensive quotations and a bibliography of English translations of classic Spanish drama, poetry and prose. *Class No:* 860(091)

[8294]

Historia y crítica de la literatura española. Rico, F., *ed.* Barcelona, Crítica, 1980-92. 9v.

V.1 *Edad media.* 1980.
V.2 *Siglos de oro: renacimento.* 1980.
V.3 *Siglos de oro: barroco.* 1983.
V.4 *Ilustración y neoclasicismo.* 1983.
V.5 *Romanticismo y realismo.* 1982.
V.6 *Modernismo y 98.* 1980.
V.7 *Época contemporánea: 1914-1939.* 1984.
V.8 *Época contemporánea: 1939-1980.* 1980.
V.9 *Los Nuevas nombres: 1975-1990.* 1992.

A detailed history comprising signed chapters and subsections by a large team of scholars. Comprehensive primary and secondary bibliographies. Index in each vol. Supplementary vols. have been published during the 1990s to accompany vols. 1-7, each one a substantial work in its own right. *Class No:* 860(091)

[8295]

VALBUENA PRAT, A. Historia de la literatura española. 9. ed., ampliada y puesta al día por M. del Pilar Palomo. Barcelona, Gili, 1981-3. 6v. ISBN: 8425210712.

V.1 *Edad media.* xv,599p.
V.2 *Renacimiento.* viii,531p.
V.3 *Siglo XVII.* xii,831p.
V.4 *Siglo XVIII. Romanticismo.* vii,422p.
V.5 *Del realismo al vanguardismo.* viii,495p.
V.6 *Época contemporánea.* x,975p.

A very comprehensive history, with many quotations and extensive footnote references. Indexes of authors and works in each vol. *Class No:* 860(091)

Biographies

[8296]

Dictionary of literary biography. Detroit, Gale, 1978-98. v.1-188 (in progress). £112 per vol.

The following vols. cover Spanish literature:

V.108 *Twentieth-century Spanish poets, first series.* 1991.
V.134 *Twentieth-century Spanish poets, second series.* 1994.

For a description of the series, see entry at 82(092). *Class No:* 860(092)

[8297]

Hispanic writers: a selection of sketches from *Contemporary authors.* Ryan, B., *ed.* Detroit, Gale, 1991. xxvi,514p. £73. ISBN: 0810376881.

See entry at 860.7(092). *Class No:* 860(092)

[8298]

Quién es quién en las letras españolas. 3. ed. Madrid, Instituto Nacional del Libro Español, 1979. 495p. ISBN: 8485635051.

1st ed. 1969; 2nd ed. 1973.

Provides biographical information on some 2,000 writers, including address, date and place of birth, and career details. Publications listed. Not confined to literary writers. Superfluous index. *Class No:* 860(092)

Women

[8299]

WALDMAN, G.F., *eds.* Spanish women writers: a bio-bibliographical source book. Levine, L.G. *and* Marson, E.E. Westport, Conn., Greenwood, 1993. 596p. $95. ISBN: 0313268231.

Covers 50 women from the 14th century to the present, 27 of them born since 1900. Signed entries (average 11p.) in a standard format comprising biography, analysis of major themes, survey of criticism and bibliography. Selected general bibliography. Appended list of 30 of the authors' works available in translation. Title and subject indexes. 'Clearly fills a bibliographic gap in Spanish literature for both newer writers and established authors revisited' (*RQ*, v.33(4), Summer 1994, p.566). *Class No:* 860-0055.2

[8300]

Women writers of Spain: an annotated bio-bibliographical guide. Galerstein, C.L., *ed. (non-Castilian materials ed. by K. McNerney).* New York, Greenwood, 1986. xxi,389p. £38.50. (*Bibliographies and indexes in women's studies.*) ISBN: 0313249652.

300 entries by 79 contributors are arranged A-Z and provide biographical data and an alphabetical list of major works with annotations, in most cases, which aim to 'evaluate the contribution made by each author and her work to the development of a particular genre and to the literary representation of the historical period in which whe wrote' (*Preface*). Confined to creative literary writers, with the emphasis on the feminist movement. 4 appendices: 1. Chronological list of authors - 2. Authors in Catalan - 3. Authors in Galician - 4. Translated titles. Title index.

For critical analysis, see *Contemporary women writers of Spain* by J. Pérez (Boston, Twayne, 1988. 226p. $26.95. ISBN: 080578229x), in which over 300 works are examined. *Class No:* 860-0055.2

Spanish Literature in Translation

[8301]

ALLISON, A.F. English translations from the Spanish and Portuguese to the year 1700: an annotated catalogue of the extant printed versions (excluding dramatic versions). Folkestone, Dawsons, 1974. 224p. ISBN: 071290641x.

Arranged by author, with biographical notes preceding extended short-title entries for translated works and references to sources. Includes translations published separately and as part of larger works. Index of translators, with biographical notes. Subject index. English title index. By no means confined to literary works. *Class No:* 860-03

[8302]

RUDDER, R.S. The Literature of Spain in English translation: a bibliography. New York, Ungar, 1975. ix,637p. ISBN: 0804432619.

Very comprehensive listing, arranged by literary period (6 sections) then by author. As well as pure literature it includes 'essays and works of history that either have literary merit or have influenced literature' (*Preface*). Not confined to Spanish, but includes translations from Basque, Catalan, Valencian, Galician, Mozarabic and Latin. Original titles provided wherever possible. List of frequently cited anthologies. Indexes of authors and of anonymous works. *Class No:* 860-03

Spanish Poetry

[8303]
DOMINGUEZ CAPPARÓS, J. Diccionario de métrica española. Madrid, Paraninfo, 1985. 200p.

Defines and explains technical terms in Spanish metrics, with examples. *Class No:* 860-1

[8304]
DUTTON, B., ***and others.*** **Catálogo-índice de la poesía cancioneril del siglo XV.** Madison, Wis., Seminary of Medieval Studies, 1982. 2v. (xv,285;291p.). ISBN: 0942260252.

V.1 contains the catalogue of manuscripts and printed works and an index of first lines. V.2 has 9 specialized indexes, covering authors, titles, languages, etc., a general index, and a select bibliography. *Class No:* 860-1

[8305]
Quién es quién en poesía. Lenguas de España. Ruiz de Torres, J., *and others, eds.* Madrid, Asociación Prometeo de Poesía, 1985. 1v. (loose-leaf). ISBN: 8439848897.

Provides biographical information on 400 poets (186 Spanish, 159 Spanish-American, 42 Catalan and 13 Galician), and refers to anthologies where their works may be found. *Class No:* 860-1

[8306]
RODRÍGUEZ-MOÑINO, A. Manual bibliográfico de cancioneros y romanceros. Askins, A.L.-F., *ed.* Madrid, Castalia, 1973-8. 4v.

Essentially two 2-vol. sets, with vols. 1-2 describing 250 16th-century works and vols. 3-4 describing 256 from the 17th century. Each set has several indexes, covering book titles, first lines, names, places, etc. *Class No:* 860-1

[8307]
STEUNOU, J. ***and*** **KNAPP, L. Bibliografía de los cancioneros castellanos del siglo xv y repertorio de sus géneros poéticos.** Paris, Centre National de la Recherche Scientifique, 1975-78. 2v. (800p.; xvi,632p.). ISBN: 2222017165, v.1; 2222022010, v.2.

A computer-generated bibliography of 15th-century *cancioneros*. V.1 lists 90 sources (*i.e.* manuscripts and early eds.) with details of their contents and has an author index. V.2 lists poems by first line and by author. A proposed third vol. was to have classified the poems by subject. *Class No:* 860-1

Jiménez

[8308]
CAMPOAMOR GONZÁLES, A. Bibliografía general de Juan Ramón Jiménez. Madrid, Taurus, 1983. 724p.

Comprehensive, classified bibliography which lists over 9,000 items of primary and secondary literature. Includes radio and TV broadcasts, musical settings, and iconography. *Class No:* 860-1JIM

Spanish Drama

[8309]
BAINTON, A.J.C. ***Comedias sueltas*** **in Cambridge University Library:** a descriptive catalogue. Cambridge, The Univ. Library, 1977 (repr. Cambridge Univ. Press, 1980). xvi,281p. ISBN: 0521238498.

919 items, fully described. Arranged A-Z by title, with indexes of authors, printers, and booksellers. *Class No:* 860-2

[8310]
BOYER, M.V. The Texas collection of ***comedias sueltas*****:** a descriptive bibliography. Boston, Hall, 1978. 620p. ISBN: 0816181179.

Describes over 1,100 pre-1835 editions of *c.*750 different plays held at the Univ. of Texas at Austin. Anonymous titles, A-Z, followed by author listing. *Class No:* 860-2

[8311]
FERNÁNDEZ GÓMEZ, J.F. Catálogo de entremeses y sainetes del siglo XVIII. Oviedo, Instituto Feijóo de Estudios del Siglo XVIII, 1993. 758p. ISBN: 8460614786.

Lists over 2,000 minor 18th-century dramas and provides the following information: known performances; adaptations; manuscripts and printings; locations; bibliographical commentary and citations. Biographical notes on dramatists. Index. *Class No:* 860-2

[8312]
GRISMER, R.L. Bibliography of the drama of Spain and Spanish America. Minneapolis, Minn., Burgess-Beckwith, 1967. 2v. (xix,231p.; xxiv,231p.).

About 7,000 entries arranged by author (v.1: A-L; v.2: M-Z). Includes reviews of published plays. *Class No:* 860-2

[8313]
McCREADY, W.T. Bibliografía temática de estudios sobre el teatro español antiguo. Toronto, Univ. of Toronto Press, 1966. xix,445p.

Lists nearly 4,000 books and articles published 1850-1950 on early Spanish theatre, in 2 parts: 1. Período formativo (beginnings to Juan de la Cueva); 2. Período aureosecular (Lope de Vega to José de Cañizares). Some entries annotated. Author index. *Class No:* 860-2

[8314]
REICHENBERGER, K. ***and*** **REICHENBERGER, R. Das Spanische Drama im Goldenen Zeitalter:** ein bibliographisches Handbuch. [El Teatro español en los Siglos de Oro: inventario de bibliografías.] Kassel, Reichenberger, 1989. xiv,319p. ISBN: 3923593724.

Lists 1,482 sources of information on Golden Age drama in 7 sections, including one on specific authors and one on library catalogues. Many entries annotated. Indexes of subjects, modern authors, and libraries. Very thorough. *Class No:* 860-2

Calderón de la Barca

[8315]
Calderón de la Barca studies, 1951-1969: a critical survey and annotated bibliography. Parker, J.H. *and* Fox, A.M., *eds.* Toronto, Univ. of Toronto Press, 1971. xiii,274p.

The work of 11 compilers. Critical survey, p.3-23. The annotated bibliography consists of 'Editions' and 'Studies', in both cases subdivided into general and individual works. Index of authors, translators and critics. *Class No:* 860-2CAL

[8316]
REICHENBERGER, K. ***and*** **REICHENBERGER, R. Bibliographisches Handbuch der Calderón-Forschung/** Manual bibliográfico calderoniano. Kassel, Thiele & Schwarz, 1979-. To be in 3 vols.

V.1, *Die Calderón-Texte und ihre Überlieferung / Los Textos de Calderón y su transmisión* (1979. xiii,832p. ISBN: 3878160232), has over 3,300 entries in 8 sections, covering Calderón's works. V.2 is to cover critical studies.

V.3, *Bibliographische Beschreibungen / Descripciones*

....*(contd.)*
bibliográficas (1981. xiii,838p. ISBN: 3878160380), is mainly devoted to descriptions of *sueltas.* Additions and corrections to v.1 and title index to vols. 1 and 3.
Class No: 860-2CAL

García Lorca

[8317]
García Lorca. Colecchia, F., *ed.* New York, Garland, 1979-82. 2v.

V.1 *A Selectively annotated bibliography of criticism.* 1979. xxii,313p. ISBN: 0824098005.

V.2 *An Annotated primary bibliography.* 1982. xxiv,281p. ISBN: 0824094964.

The work of an MLA committee of some 40 compilers. V.1 has nearly 1,900 entries; v.2 has *c.*1,300 entries.
Class No: 860-2GAR

Lope de Vega

[8318]
GRISMER, R.L. Bibliography of Lope de Vega: books, essays, articles, and other studies on the life of Lope de Vega, his works and his imitators. Minneapolis, Minn., Burgess-Beckwith, 1965-6. (repr. New York, Kraus, 1977). 2v. (iii,174p.; viii,154p.). ISBN: 052736195x.

V.1 lists, without annotation, over 3,000 books, essays, articles and reviews on Lope de Vega in a single A-Z author sequence. V.2 lists his works A-Z by title. Index of names in each vol. *Class No:* 860-2LOP

[8319]
PARKER, J.H. *and* **FOX, A.M. Lope de Vega studies, 1937-1962:** a critical survey and annotated bibliography. Toronto, Univ. of Toronto Press, 1964. xi,201p.

Critical survey, 1937-61 (19p.), followed by bibliography in 2 sections, for editions and studies, each subdivided by genre. Survey and bibliography for 1962 appended (p.181-210). No index. *Class No:* 860-2LOP

Spanish Fiction

[8320]
CALIMANO, I.E. Index to Spanish-language short stories in anthologies. Albuquerque, N.M., SALALM Secreteriat, Univ. of New Mexico, 1994. 332p. $52.95. ISBN: 091761741x.

Analyzes the contents of over 200 anthologies published since 1979 in Spain, Spanish America and the USA. Main sequence is author index, with additional indexes of titles and countries. Does not cover English translations.
Class No: 860-31

[8321]
The Contemporary Spanish novel: an annotated, critical bibliography, 1936-1994. Amell, S., *ed.* Westport, Conn., Greenwood, 1996. 288p. $75. (*Bibliographies and indexes in world literature.*) ISBN: 0313247846.

Lists and evaluates 211 critical books and 667 periodical articles in separarate sections, with annotations running to 150-250 words. Does not include studies of individual novelists and works. Most of the studies covered are in Spanish or English, but some works in Catalan, French, Galician and Italian are included. Author and title indexes.
Class No: 860-31

[8322]
FERRERAS, J.I. Catálogo de novelas y novelistas españoles del siglo XIX. Madrid, Cátedra, 1979. 454p.

2,158 entries, A-Z, for authors and anonymous titles, giving brief biographical notes and chronological list of titles for each author. List of sources (7p.) includes libraries, collections, reference works, etc. *Class No:* 860-31

[8323]
LAURENTI, J.L. Bibliografía de la literatura picaresca: desde sus orígenes hasta el presente. [A Bibliography of picaresque literature: from its origins to the present.] Metuchen, N.J., Scarecrow, 1973 (repr. New York, AMS Press, 1981). xviii,262p. $32.50. ISBN: 0404180191.

Lists editions, translations and studies of 19 novels, plus general studies and anthologies, 2,439 entries. Index of names.

Suplemento (New York, AMS, 1981. xxxi,163p. $32.50. ISBN: 0404180183) adds material published 1973-8, plus some omitted from the main work. 1,009 entries.
Class No: 860-31

[8324]
LAURENTI, J.L. Catálogo bibliográfico de la literatura picaresca, siglos XVI-XX. Kassel, Reichenberger, 1988. xi,605p. ISBN: 3928064029.

A classified bibliography with 4,509 entries in 27 sections. 20 sections cover specific works of fiction, listing editions, translations and studies, with 7 sections listing general sources. Indexes of names, subjects and abbreviated periodical titles. *Class No:* 860-31

[8325]
RICAPITO, J.V. Bibliografía razonada y anotada de las obras maestras de la picaresca española. Madrid, Castalia, 1980. 613p.

General section of material on the Spanish picaresque novel followed by sections devoted to *La Vida de Lazarillo de Tormes, Guzmán de Alfarache* and *Vida del Buscón.* Substantial annotations. Thoroughly cross-referenced. Detailed table of contents (7p.) and index. 'The finest bibliography yet compiled on this genre by a scholar in the field' (Woodbridge, H.C., *Guide to reference works...,* 1987, p.53). *Class No:* 860-31

Cervantes

[8326]
BARCELONA. Biblioteca Central. **Catálogo de la Colección Cervantina.** Givanel Mas, J. *and* Plaza Escudero, L.M., *eds.* Barcelona, 1941-64. 5v.

V.1 *Años 1590-1785.* 1941. V.2 *Años 1786-1854.* 1943. V.3 *Años 1855-1890.* 1947. V.4 *Años 1891-1915.* 1959. V.5 *Años 1916-1930.* 1964.

3,727 entries, chronologically arranged and fully described. *Class No:* 860-31CER

[8327]
'Bibliografía cervantina', in *Anales cervantinos.* Madrid, Consejo Superior de Investigaciones Científicas, Instituto de Filología, 1951-. Annual.

A classified list of recent Cervantes studies, with substantial annotations. That in v.31, *1993* (1993), has 103 entries in 10 sections. *Class No:* 860-31CER

[8328]

DRAKE, D.B. Cervantes' *Novelas ejemplares*: a selectively annotated bibliography. 2nd ed., rev. and exp. New York, Garland, 1981. xxiv,218p. ISBN: 0824094735.

A classified list of 554 studies, with author and subject indexes. *Class No:* 860-31CER

[8329]

DRAKE, D.B. Don Quijote (1894-70): a selective annotated bibliography. Chapel Hill, N.C., Univ. of North Carolina, Dept. of Romance Languages, 1974 (v.1) and Miami, Universal, 1978 (v.2). 2v. (267p.;269p.). ISBN: 0884389383, v.1; 0897291867, v.2.

These 2 vols. list 321 and 339 studies respectively of *Don Quixote,* with substantial annotations. Cumulative subject index in v.2.

Supplemented by *Don Quijote in world literature: a selective annotated bibliography* (New York, Garland, 1980. 272p. ISBN: 0824095421) and *Don Quijote (1894-1970): a selective annotated bibliography (v.4, extended to 1979)* (Lincoln, Neb., Society of Spanish and Spanish-American Studies, 1984. 214p. $35. ISBN: 0892950269).
Class No: 860-31CER

[8330]

FORD, J.D.M. *and* **LANSING, R. Cervantes:** a tentative bibliography of his works and of the bibliographical and critical material concerning him. Cambridge, Mass., Harvard Univ. Press, 1931 (repr. Wakefield, N.H., Longwood, 1977). xii,239p. ISBN: 0893414549.

About 6,000 entries in 15 sections, of which nos. 1-7 list primary material (including translations into 40 languages) and nos. 8-15 secondary material. Brief annotations. Lacks index. *Class No:* 860-31CER

[8331]

GRISMER, R.L. Cervantes: a bibliography. Books, essays, articles and other studies on the life of Cervantes, his works, and his imitators. Reprint. Millwood, N.Y., Kraus, 1980. 2v. (183p.;233p.). ISBN: 0527362018.

V.1 originally published New York, Wilson, 1946; v.2 originally published Minneapolis, Minn., Burgess-Beckwith, 1963.

Each vol. lists *c.*4,000 items A-Z by author, without annotation. V.1 has index of names and subjects.
Class No: 860-31CER

[8332]

RIUS Y DE LLOSELLAS, L. Bibliografía crítica de las obras de Miguel de Cervantes Saavedra. Madrid, Murillo, 1895-1904 (repr. New York, Franklin, 1970). 3v. illus. ISBN: 0833730053.

V.1 is a descriptive bibliography of Cervantes' works, with 1,112 entries. V.2 is a secondary bibliography, with 814 annotated items in 6 sections. V.3 has miscellaneous material in 20 sections, including lengthy excerpts from critical studies. *Class No:* 860-31CER

Pérez Galdós

[8333]

HERNÁNDEZ SUÁREZ, M. Bibliografía de Galdós. Las Palmas, Excm. Cabildo Insular de Gran Canaria, 1972. xiv,553p. illus.

Classified bibliography of Galdós' works in 16 sections, with full descriptions and many title-page facsimiles. Detailed contents table (9p.). *Class No:* 860-31PER

[8334]

PERCIVAL, A. Galdós and his critics. Toronto, Univ. of Toronto Press, 1985. ix,537p. $45. ISBN: 0802056016.

A survey of criticism in 5 chapters, followed by references (p.345-482) and selected bibliography of critical studies (p.483-504). Index of Galdosian works and characters cited. General index. *Class No:* 860-31PER

[8335]

WOODBRIDGE, H.C. Benito Pérez Galdós: a selective annotated bibliography. Metuchen, N.J., Scarecrow, 1975. xi,321p. ISBN: 0810808005.

Lists *c.*500 biographical and critical studies under broad subject headings. Author, title and subject indexes.
Class No: 860-31PER

Spanish-American Literature

Bibliographies of Bibliographies

[8336]

BRYANT, S.M. A Selective bibliography of bibliographies of Hispanic American literature. 2nd ed., greatly expanded and rev. Austin, Univ. of Texas, Inst. of Latin American Studies, 1976. x,100p. ISBN: 0292775229.

1st ed. published by Pan American Union as 'Basic bibliography', no.3 (Washington, 1966).

Lists 662 bibliographies (374 in 1st ed.) by author. About two-thirds are devoted to individual writers. Brief annotations. Index includes all persons mentioned plus some subject headings. *Class No:* 860.7(009)

[8337]

ZUBATSKY, D. Latin American literary authors: an annotated guide to bibliographies. Metuchen, N.J., Scarecrow, 1986. ix,332p. ISBN: 0810819007.

Lists bibliographies of over 600 Spanish American and Brazilian authors appearing in books, periodicals, dissertations, and *Festschrift* volumes. A-Z arrangement by author, followed by lists of additional biobibliographic sources by country/region. *Class No:* 860.7(009)

Bibliographies

[8338]

FENWICK, M.J. Writers of the Caribbean and Central America: a bibliography. New York, Garland, 1992. 2v. $215. ISBN: 0824040104.

A wide-ranging compilation which covers literature in 4 major languages (Spanish, English, French, Dutch) and 2 minor ones (Papiamento and French Creole) from several countries, including the Caribbean states, Colombia, Venezuela, Guyana, Guiane and Suriname. Entries for over 10,000 authors (nearly 6,500 writing in Spanish and over 1,300 in English) are arranged by country and include basic biographical data, chronological lists of works, and references to appearances in anthologies and periodicals. 'A wonderful tour de force with no comparable single rival for so large a chunk of Western Hemisphere literature' (*Choice*, v.29(11/12), July/Aug. 1992, p.1655). *Class No:* 860.7(01)

[8339]

Handbook of Latin American studies: a selective and annotated guide to recent publications ... Vols. 1-13 (1935-47), Cambridge, Mass., Harvard Univ. Press, 1936-51; Vols. 14-40 (1948-74), Gainesville, Fla., Univ. of Florida Press, 1951-78; Vols. 41-, Austin, Tex., Univ. of Texas Press, 1979-. Annual. ISSN: 00729833.

Annotated subject bibliography in humanities and social sciences since 1935. Since 1964, the 2 major branches have been covered in separate volumes published in alternate years; *e.g.* no.52, *Humanities*, 1992, has nearly 2,000 entries for language and literature. Subject and author indexes in each vol. Also available on CD-ROM (ISBN: 0292746903) with full-text search facilities.
Class No: 860.7(01)

[8340]

RELA, W. A Bibliographical guide to Spanish American literature: twentieth century sources. New York and London, Greenwood, 1988. xiv,381p. $65. (*Bibliographies and indexes in world literature.*) ISBN: 0313258619.

1,884 annotated entries in 4 sections (Bibliographies; Dictionaries; History and Criticism; Anthologies), each section having general items followed by subsections on the 14 national literatures, arranged A-Z, with further subdivision by genre in most cases. Author index. Confined to books and excludes works on individual authors.

Essentially a selective integration of Rela's mammoth *Guía bibliográfica de la literatura hispanoamericana desde el siglo XIX hasta 1970* (*q.v.*) and *Spanish American literature: a selected bibliography... 1970-1980* (East Lansing, Mich., Michigan State Univ., 1982) with the addition of material from the 1980s. *Class No:* 860.7(01)

[8341]

RELA, W. Guía bibliográfica de la literatura hispanoamericana desde el siglo XIX hasta 1970. Buenos Aires, Casa Pardo, 1971. 613p.

6,023 unannotated entries arranged in groups: general, national and personal bibliographies; general and national literary histories; general history and criticism; criticism of individual writers; general, national and individual anthologies; biography; dictionaries; miscellanea. Name index. *Class No:* 860.7(01)

Encyclopaedias & Dictionaries

[8342]

Handbook of Latin American literature. Foster, D.W., *comp.* 2nd ed. New York, Garland, 1992. 799p. $95.00. ISBN: 0815303432.

1st ed. 1987

Signed essays in English (several of them translated) on the national literatures of all Latin American countries, including French and Creole Haiti and Portuguese Brazil, with the emphasis on the internal coherence of each national tradition. Important literary works are cited in the text and each essay is followed by a short, annotated bibliography of literary histories and surveys relating to that country. Bibliography of material on Latin America in general. Revised, expanded and updated, the 2nd ed. has new articles on film, paraliterature and the literature of Hispanic groups in the US. Index of names. *Class No:* 860.7(03)

[8343]

Latin American literature in the 20th century: a guide. Klein, L.S., *ed.* New York, Ungar, 1985; Harpenden, Oldcastle, 1988. x,278p. ISBN: 0948353155, UK.

Handy guide based on Ungar's 5-vol. *Encyclopedia of world literature in the 20th century,* rev. ed., 1981-84 (*qv*). All entries on Mexico, Brazil, and the Spanish-speaking countries of Central and South America and the Caribbean are reproduced with some minor revisions and corrections, but unfortunately not updated. 13 national/regional surveys are arranged A-Z, each followed by articles on the major authors (92 in all). Appendix has articles on Afro-Cubanism, Magic Realism and Modernism. All articles/surveys are signed and include bibliographies. Index to author articles.
Class No: 860.7(03)

[8344]

Masterpieces of Latino literature. Magill, F.N., *ed.* New York, HarperCollins, 1994. 655p. $45. ISBN: 0062701061.

A guide to major works written by 105 authors of Latino descent from North, Central and South America. 140 articles on individual works and 33 on genres (*e.g.* 'The Essays of Jorge Luis Borges'). Title entries follow a standard format: quick-reference notes on author, type of work, type of plot, locale, and dates of first publication and first English translation; descripton of principal characters; plot summary (*c.*700 words); 600-word analysis; and 500 words on critical context. Genre entries comprise quick-reference notes and 2,500-word essay. A good introductory source, but 'its limitations in terms of the authors it includes and its formulaic approach make it inadequate for serious study' (*Booklist*, v.91(7), Dec. 1, 1994, p.707). Indexes of authors and titles. *Class No:* 860.7(03)

[8345]

SMITH, V., *ed.* Encyclopedia of Latin American literature. London, Fitzroy Dearborn, 1997. xxii,926p. £95. ISBN: 1884964184.

Around 400 lengthy, signed articles by *c.*170 contributors on authors, works and topics in a single A-Z sequence. Most entries are of around 1,500 words, but there are lengthy survey articles (up to 10,000 words) on the literature of individual countries, of the Colonial period, and of ethnic minorities, including Hispanic communities in the USA. Author entries comprise critical essay; biographical notes; select primary bibliography; further reading; and details of bibliographies and interviews. Other entries also have substantial lists of further reading. Title index with authors and dates. General index. Coverage extends to the Francophone Caribbean.

'In a reference work as ambitious as this which aims to compress an immensely rich literary universe into slightly less than a thousand pages, the primary challenge is to identify what is truly important. It is one which the editor and her colleagues have met with genuine distinction' (*TLS*, no.4950, Feb. 13, 1998, p. 27-8). *Class No:* 860.7(03)

Excerpts

[8346]

Modern Latin American literature. Foster, D.W. *and* Foster, V.R., *eds.* New York, Ungar, 1975. 2v. $120. (*A Library of literary criticism.*) ISBN: 0804431396.

Presents a selection of international critical commentary on 137 20th-century writers from 16 countries, including Brazil. Half the excerpts are translated from Spanish or Portuguese. Of the rest, most are by English-speaking critics, but there are translations from French, German, Italian and Swedish

.... *(contd.)*
sources. Arranged A-Z by author, with index to critics in v.2. Lists of works mentioned at end of each vol.
Class No: 860.7(082.200)

Histories

[8347]
BELLINI, G. Historia de la literatura hispanoamericana. Madrid, Castalia, 1985. ix,814p. ISBN: 8470394487.

An expanded and much updated version of Bellini's *La Letteratura ispanoamericana* (Milan, 1970), the index of authors' names having grown by 50%. 19 chapters, with many subsections on specific countries, genres, authors, etc. Bibliography (29p.). Name and title indexes. 'It is indispensable', according to *Modern Language Review* (v.82(3), July 1987, p.768-9), which praises its accuracy and up-to-dateness. *Class No:* 860.7(091)

[8348]
Cambridge history of Latin American literature. Gonzalez Echevarria, R. *and* Pupo-Walker, E., *eds.* Cambridge, Cambridge Univ. Press, 1996. 3v. £175. ISBN: 0521482402.

V.1 *Discovery to Modernism.* 690p.

V.2 *The Twentieth century.* 639p.

V.3 *Brazilian literature. Bibliographies.* 858p.

The most comprehensive history ever, with 52 signed chapters covering all of Latin America, plus Spanish writing in the USA, from pre-Columbian times to the present. V.1 goes up to the end of the 19th century and v.2 to 1990, with chapters on genres and subsections on individual writers. V.3 has 17 chapters on Brazilian literature plus comprehensive bibliographies which occupy 455p. These include a bibliography of general bibliographies by H.C. Woodbridge (43p.) and annotated listings of primary and secondary literature for each chapter. Index in each vol.
Class No: 860.7(091)

[8349]
FRANCO, J. An Introduction to Spanish-American literature. 3rd ed. Cambridge, Cambridge Univ. Press, 1994. xii,390p. £37.50. ISBN: 0521444799.

1st ed. 1969; 2nd ed. 1975.

Highly readable, concise survey in 11 chapters. Quotations in Spanish with footnote translations. Substantial reading lists for each chapter, giving texts, translations and background material. Final chapters revised for 3rd ed. and bibliographies updated. Author index. *Class No:* 860.7(091)

[8350]
GOIC, C. Historia y crítica de la literatura hispanoamericana. Barcelona, Editorial Crítica, 1988-91. 3v. £23.95 per vol.

V.1 *Época colonial.* 1988. 599p. ISBN: 847423350x.

V.2 *Del romanticismo al modernismo.* 1991. 771p. ISBN: 8474234824.

V.3 *Época contemporánea.* 1988. 692p. ISBN: 8474233682.

Lengthy chapters on literary genres and individual authors, with extensive bibliographies and extracts from critical studies. Index in each vol. *Class No:* 860.7(091)

[8351]
GROSSMANN, R. Historia y problemas de la literatura latinoamericana. Madrid, Revista de Occidente, 1972. 758p.

Originally published München, Hueber, 1969, as *Geschichte und Probleme der Lateinamerikanischen Literatur.*

Extremely well-organized history in 4 parts, 25 chapters, and numerous subsections, which are clearly explained in the contents table. Substantial classified bibliography (55p.) in 2 sections, covering Latin America in general and the various national literatures. Index of names and titles.
Class No: 860.7(091)

[8352]
Historia de la literatura hispanoamericana. Íñigo Madrigal, L., *ed.* Madrid, Cátedra, 1982-87. v.1-2 (in progress).

V.1 *Epoca colonial.* 1982. 434p. ISBN: 843760334x.

V.2 *Del neoclasicismo al modernismo.* 1987. 749p. ISBN: 8437606438.

Signed chapters (average 20p. in v.1; 12p. in v.2), by numerous contributors, on periods, genres, movements, and individual writers, with substantial bibliographies appended. Chronology, author index and title index in each vol. Well illustrated throughout. V.2 stops at 1918. A third vol. is planned for the 20th century. *Class No:* 860.7(091)

Biographies

[8353]
ALBOUKREK, A. *and* **HERRERA, E. Diccionario de escritores hispanoamericanos del siglo XVI al siglo XX.** Buenos Aires, Larousse, 1992. viii,306p. ISBN: 9505389043.

Brief articles on 309 writers (including Brazilians), providing biographical information, critical appraisal, and selective listing of representative works. No coverage of secondary literature. *Class No:* 860.7(092)

[8354]
BECCO, H.J. Diccionario de literatura hispano-americana: autores. Buenos Aires, Huemul, 1984. 313p. illus.

Covers authors from Juan de Castellanos to the present, giving biographical information and lists of their works. Includes pictures of some authors. 'An extremely useful manual' (Woodbridge, H.C., *Guide to reference works ...*, 1987, p.103). *Class No:* 860.7(092)

[8355]
Dictionary of literary biography. Detroit, Gale, 1978-98. v.1-188 (in progress). £112 per vol.

The following vols. cover Latin American literature:

V.113 *Modern Latin-American fiction writers, first series.* 1992.

V.145 *Modern Latin-American fiction writers, second series.* 1994.

For a description of the series, see entry at 82(092).
Class No: 860.7(092)

[8356]
FLORES, A. Spanish American authors: the twentieth century. New York, Wilson, 1992. 915p. $100. ISBN: 0824208064.

A new, and very welcome, addition to the *Wilson authors series*, covering 331 novelists and poets from Central and South America, Puerto Rico and the Caribbean. Entries vary in length (as much as 8p. on major writers like Neruda) and include biographical information, critical analysis, comprehensive list of works (including English translations)

....*(contd.)*
and secondary bibliography. Many authors (*e.g.* Isabel Allende) prepared autobiographical sketches, to which supplementary material has been added by 100 contributors. 'A monumental contribution to research on Latin American literature' (*Choice*, v.30(9), May 1993, p.1440), with many of the subjects profiled in an English-language reference work for the first time. *Class No:* 860.7(092)

[8357]

Hispanic writers: a selection of sketches from *Contemporary authors*. Ryan, B., *ed.* Detroit, Gale, 1991. xxvi,514p. £73. ISBN: 0810376881.

A single-volume compilation of entries from Gale's *Contemporary authors* series (*q.v.*) on over 400 20th-century Hispanic writers, most of them from the US and 20 countries of Hispanic America, but including 'a limited number of authors from Spain who have influenced the literature of the New World' (*Introduction*). 40% of the entries have been taken from *CA* and updated; the rest were written specially for this work and many will appear later in *CA*. Entries provide personal and career data, bibliographies, works in progress, references to biographical and critical sources, and a review of the author's critical reception. Includes some non-literary figures, *e.g.* Ché Guevara, Joan Baez, Luis Buñuel. Nationality index. *Class No:* 860.7(092)

[8358]

Latin American writers. Solé, C.A., *ed.* New York, Scribner's, 1989. 3v. ISBN: 068418463x.

Substantial essays on 176 authors (149 writing in Spanish and 27 from Brazil) are arranged chronologically by birthdate, from 1474 to the 20th century, and include brief biography, survey of output (including plot summaries of major works and quotations in the original language and/or English), and bibliography of first eds., modern eds., translations, biographies, critical studies, and bibliographies. Chronological table of literary and historical events. General index, list of writers by country, and alphabetical index of writers partly compensate for the inconvenience of the chronological arrangement.

Also included on *The Scribner writers series on CD-ROM* (*q.v.*). *Class No:* 860.7(092)

Caribbean

[8359]

A History of literature in the Caribbean. Arnold, A.J., *& others, eds.* Amsterdam, Benjamins, 1994-. v.1, 3 (in progress). (*A Comparative history of literatures in European languages.*)

V.1 *Hispanic and Francophone regions* (1994. xviii,579p. $150. ISBN: 1556196016).

V.3 *Cross cultural studies* (1998. xviii,381p. $120. ISBN: 1556196032).

The first history to cover the literature of the entire Caribbean, (the continental littoral as well as the islands) as one cultural region, rather than treating the literatures of particular languages separately. V.3 is arranged in 9 thematic and methodological sections and among the wide variety of topics covered are the origins of Creole literatures and the history of racial inequality in Caribbean colonization. Index of names. The work of a team of over 30 specialists. *Class No:* 860.7(729)

USA

[8360]

Biographical dictionary of Hispanic literature in the United States: the literature of Puerto Ricans, Cuban Americans, and other Hispanic writers. Kanellos, N., *ed.* New York, Greenwood, 1989. 357p. $75. ISBN: 0313244650.

Provides information on 50 Hispanic writers based in the US, whose works are published, distributed and studied in Spanish, English, or both, primarily in the US and Puerto Rico. Entries average 6p. and include biography, major themes, survey of criticism, and primary and secondary bibliographies. General bibliography. Index. *Class No:* 860.7(73)

[8361]

Chicano literature: a reference guide. Martínez, J.A. *and* Lomelí, F.A., *eds.* Westport, Conn., Greenwood, 1985. xiv,492p. $79.50. ISBN: 0313236917.

Approx. 45 signed essays (average length 10p.) in one A-Z sequence treat the major authors, themes and genres (*e.g.* Children's literature, Mexican literature), each having a selected bibliography. 4 appendices: A. Galarza, Muro and Quinn (3 writers heavily influenced by Chicano literature) - B. Chronology - C. Glossary - D. Bibliography of general works (2p.). Index. *Class No:* 860.7(73)

[8362]

EGER, E.N. A Bibliography of criticism of contemporary Chicano literature. Berkeley, Calif., Univ. of California Chicano Studies Library, 1982. xxi,295p. $16.50. ISBN: 0685056538.

Lists nearly 2,200 books, articles, reviews and dissertations (both general and relating to specific authors), mostly published since 1960. 'An erudite bibliographical handbook of paramount importance' (*RQ,* v.22(1), Fall 1982, p.90). *Class No:* 860.7(73)

Jews

[8363]

Jewish writers of Latin America: a dictionary. Lockhart, D.B., *ed.* New York, Garland, 1997. 618p. $75. ISBN: 0815314957.

Signed entries by 50 scholars from the US, Latin America and Israel on 118 authors, providing biographical information and a critical summary of their works. Argentina, Brazil and Mexico have the greatest representation but writers from 7 other countries are included. *Class No:* 860.7(=924)

Black Races

[8364]

JACKSON, R.L. The Afro-Spanish American author: an annotated bibliography of criticism. New York, Garland, 1980. xix,129p. ISBN: 0824095294.

562 annotated entries for general bibliographies, general studies, anthologies, and works by and about 25 individual authors from 10 countries. Index of critics.

Supplemented by *The Afro-Spanish American author II: the 1980s; an annotated bibliography of recent criticism* (West Cornwall, Conn., Locust Hill, 1989. 154p. $25. ISBN: 0933951264), which includes material on 67 authors from 12 countries. *Class No:* 860.7(=96)

Women

[8365]

CORTINA, L.E.R. Spanish-American women writers: a bibliographical research checklist. New York, Garland, 1983. xi,292p. ISBN: 0824092473.

Lists nearly 2,000 authors, from 19 countries, by country then A-Z, giving brief biographical information and lists of works. Does not include Spanish-language writers from the US. Should be used with caution as many of the entries are incomplete, but 'will be extremely useful for scholars in the field who need a starting place for further investigation' (*Tulsa Studies in Women's Literature,* v.4(1), Spring 1985, p.151-2). *Class No:* 860.7-0055.2

[8366]

CYPESS, S.M., *&* *others*. Women authors of modern Hispanic South America: a bibliography of literary criticism and interpretation. Metuchen, N.J., Scarecrow, 1989. 168p. $24. ISBN: 0810822636.

Lists references to critical studies of 169 writers, including monographs, essays, periodical articles and dissertations. *Class No:* 860.7-0055.2

[8367]

LEONARD, K.S. Index to translated short fiction by Latin American women in English language anthologies. Westport, Conn., Greenwood, 1997. 136p. $65. (*Bibliographies and indexes in women's studies.*) ISBN: 0313300461.

Indexes 165 anthologies, published 1938-96, by author, country and title. Provides full bibliographical details and contents for each collection. Appended list of bibliographies of Latin American literature in translation. *Class No:* 860.7-0055.2

[8368]

—CORVALÁN, G.N.V. Latin American women writers in English translation: a bibliography. Los Angeles, California State Univ., Latin American Studies Center, 1980. iv,109p.

Covers 282 women writers whose works have been translated into English or about whom there are English-language studies available. *Class No:* 860.7-0055.2

[8369]

Women writers of Spanish America: an annotated bio-bibliographical guide. Marting, D.E., *ed.* New York, Greenwood, 1987. xvi,448p. $85. (*Bibliographies and indexes in women's studies.*) ISBN: 0313249695.

A companion vol. to *Women writers of Spain* (*q.v.*) but less consistent in approach, with many authors and works merely listed without annotation. Approx. 1,200 entries by 72 contributors are arranged A-Z and cover literary authors who write principally in Spanish and who were born or have lived most of their lives in Spanish America, plus those of Spanish-American background born or living in the USA. 5 useful appendices: 1. Partially annotated list of anthologies - 2. Authors born before 1900 - 3. Classified list of authors by country - 4. Dramatists - 5. Translations and bilingual editions.

Followed by *Spanish American women writers: a bio-bibliographical source book* (New York, Greenwood, 1990. 645p. $85. ISBN: 0313251940), which, according to *Choice* (v.28(4), Dec. 1990, p.616) 'does more than improve on its predecessor', providing information on the lives and works of 50 major writers. Appended essays cover Indian women writers of Spanish America and Latina writers of the US. *Class No:* 860.7-0055.2

Gay People

[8370]

Latin American writers on gay and lesbian themes: a bio-critical sourcebook. Foster, D.W., *ed.* Westport, Conn., Greenwood, 1994. 495p. $85 ISBN: 0313284792.

130 entries, A-Z, on Latin American (including Chicano) authors who are openly gay or lesbian or who have treated gay or lesbian themes in their work. Articles include biography, critical evaluation and bibliography of major works and criticism. Author, title and subject indexes. *Class No:* 860.7-0055.3

Spanish American Literature in Translation

[8371]

Index to anthologies of Latin American literature in English translation. Freudenthal, J.R. *and* Freudenthal, P.M., *eds.* Boston, Hall, 1977. xxxvi,199p. ISBN: 0816178615.

Indexes writings by 1,122 Spanish-American and Brazilian authors in 116 anthologies. Arranged A-Z by author, then by genre. Indexes of translators and countries. Annotated bibliographies of anthologies covered and of further reading. Original titles not given. *Class No:* 860.7-03

[8372]

SHAW, B.A. Latin American literature in English translation: an annotated bibliography. New York, New York Univ. Press, 1976. x,144p. ISBN: 0814777627.

1. Spanish American literature - 2. Brazilian literature - 3. Non-Hispanic literature of the Caribbean Islands and Guyanas - 4. Indian literature and Spanish chronicles of the New World. 624 entries arranged in the 3 main sections by genre, then by country. Indexes by author, English title, original title, and country.

Continued by *Latin American literature in English, 1975-1978,* Supplement to *Review* (Center for Inter-American Relations) 24, 1979, which has 111 entries arranged A-Z by author. *Class No:* 860.7-03

[8373]

WILSON, J. An A to Z of Latin American literature in translation. London, Institute of Latin American Studies, 1989. 96p. ISBN: 090114567x.

Lists 650 published translations by 256 authors, A-Z, from both Spanish- and Portuguese-speaking countries. Appendix has list of 118 anthologies. Bibliography of sources. *Class No:* 860.7-03

Spanish-American Poetry

[8374]

HOFFMAN, H.H. Hoffman's index to poetry: European and Latin American poetry in anthologies. Metuchen, N.J., Scarecrow, 1985. xiii,672p. ISBN: 0810818310.

See entry at 82-1(014). *Class No:* 860.7-1

[8375]

SEFAMI, J. Contemporary Spanish American poets: a bibliography of primary and secondary sources. Westport, Conn., Greenwood, 1992. 272p. $59.95. (*Bibliographies and indexes in world literature.*) ISBN: 0313278806.

Entries on 86 poets born 1910-52, listing poetic works; compilations and anthologies; works in other genres; bibliographies and critical studies. Bibliography of general studies, including sections on individual countries. List of poets by birth date. Index of critics. *Class No:* 860.7-1

Spanish-American Drama

[8376]

ALLEN, R.F. Teatro hispanoamericano: una bibliografía anotada. Boston, Hall, 1987. 633p. $55. ISBN: 0816183953.

Over 2,000 entries for individual plays, anthologies, collections, plays in periodicals, and screenplays. Annotations (in Spanish) provide plot summary, critical evaluation (with reference to source), and library locations. *Class No:* 860.7-2

[8377]

HOFFMAN, H.H. Latin American play index. Metuchen, N.J., Scarecrow, 1983-4. 2v.

V.1 *1920-1962.* iv,147p. $20. ISBN: 0810816717.

V.2 *1962-1980.* iv,131p. $20. ISBN: 0810816334.

Provides data on 3,300 plays by over 1,000 dramatists. Covers plays written in Spanish, Portuguese and French, and appearing in 4 formats: stand-alone works, parts of single-author collections, parts of multi-author anthologies, and parts of periodicals. Arranged A-Z by author, with title index and lists of collections, anthologies and periodicals indexed. *Class No:* 860.7-2

[8378]

LYDAY, L.F. *and* **WOODYARD, G.W. A Bibliography of Latin American theater criticism, 1940-1974.** Austin, Tex., Univ of Texas, Inst. of Latin American Studies, 1976. xviii,243p. ISBN: 0292707177.

2,360 items, many of them annotated, arranged A-Z by author with subject index.

C.A. Carpenter adds a further 97 items in 'Latin American theater criticism, 1966-1974: some addenda to Lyday and Woodyard', in *Revista interamericana de bibliografía,* 30 (1980), p.246-53. *Class No:* 860.7-2

[8379]

NEGLIA, E. *and* **ORDAZ, L. Repertorio selecto del teatro hispanoamericano contemporáneo.** 2. ed., rev. y ampl. Tempe, Ariz., Center for Latin American Studies, Arizona State Univ., 1980. xix,110p. ISBN: 0879180420.

1st ed. Caracas, 1974.

General sources followed by chronological lists of dramas by individual playwrights, grouped by country, with bibliographical information for published works. Lists of bibliographies and anthologies. Author index. Not annotated and rather selective, concentrating on the major dramatists. *Class No:* 860.7-2

[8380]

TORO, F. de *and* **ROSTER, P. Bibliografía del teatro hispanoamericano contemporáneo (1900-1980).** Frankfurt, Vervuert, 1985. 2v.

V.1, *Libros originales,* has 6,952 items in 3 sections: A. Revistas, libros, colecciones - B. Antologías - C. Traducciones. V.2, *Crítica,* has 3,132 items in 3 sections: A. Análisis - B. Bibliografías - C. Miscelánea. 'Finest and fullest bibliography of twentieth-century Spanish American theater' (Woodbridge, H.C., *Guide to reference works ...,* 1987, p.108), but lacks index. *Class No:* 860.7-2

Spanish-American Fiction

Bibliographies

[8381]

BECCO, H.J. *and* **FOSTER, D.W. La Nueva narrativa hispanoamericana:** bibliografía. Buenos Aires, Pardo, 1976. 226p.

An unannotated list of 2,257 items on the 'new' novel and

.... *(contd.)*

short story, including general studies, studies relating to particular countries, and works, translations and criticism of 25 leading authors. *Class No:* 860.7-3(01)

[8382]

BROWER, K.H. Contemporary Latin American fiction: an annotated bibliography. Englewood Cliffs, N.J., Salem Press, 1989 (later Scarecrow Press). 218p. $42. (*Magill bibliographies.*) ISBN: 0810828103.

A very selective guide, aimed at high school and undergraduate students, to English-language criticism of the major Latin American novelists. *Class No:* 860.7-3(01)

[8383]

COLL, E. Indice informativo de la novela hispanoamericana. Río Pedras, Universidad de Puerto Rico, 1974-1992. v.1-5 (in progress). ISBN: 0847720055.

V.1 *Las Antillas.* 1974. V.2 *Centroamerica.* 1977. V.3 *Venezuela.* 1978. V.4 *Colombia.* 1979. V.5 *El Altiplano (Bolivia, Ecuador, Perú).* 1992.

V.1 covers Puerto Rica, Cuba and the Dominican Republic. V.2 covers Costa Rica, El Salvador, Guatemala, Honduras, Nicaragua, and Panama. Arranged A-Z by author within each country, with biographical notes, lists of works, and references to secondary sources. *Class No:* 860.7-3(01)

[8384]

FOSTER, D.W. The 20th century Spanish-American novel: a bibliographic guide. Metuchen, N.J., Scarecrow, 1975. vii,227p. ISBN: 0810808714.

'Our goal here has been, first, to provide ... a working bibliography on the criticism pertaining to the 56 Spanish-American novelists most commonly studied in the US, in Europe and in Latin America' (*Introduction*). Lists of general bibliographies, periodical indexes and monographic studies are followed by sections on 56 writers, with between 6 and 158 entries per individual. These include bibliographies, critical books and essays, but exclude theses, dissertations and short reviews. No annotations. Index of critics. *Class No:* 860.7-3(01)

[8385]

The Latin American short story: an annotated guide to anthologies and criticism. Balderston, D., *ed.* Westport, Conn., Greenwood, 1992. 576p. $79.50. (*Bibliographies and indexes in world literature.*) ISBN: 031327360x.

Part I cites 1,302 anthologies in Spanish, Portuguese or English translation, listing authors and story titles in each collection. Part II is an annotated bibliography of 376 critical studies. Each section covers Latin America in general, regions, and 20 countries, A-Z. 4 indexes; short story authors; critics; titles of anthologies and studies; and themes. No index of story titles. *Class No:* 860.7-3(01)

[8386]

OCAMPO, A.M. Novelistas iberoamericanos contemporáneos: obras y bibliografía crítica. México, UNAM, 1971-81. 6v.

V.1 is a bibliography of general works on the contemporary novel, with a list of cited periodicals. Vols. 2-6 cover authors, A-Z, giving nationality, dates, and lists of works and critical studies. *Class No:* 860.7-3(01)

Encyclopaedias & Dictionaries

[8387]
Masterplots II: American fiction series. Magill, F.N., *ed.* Englewood Cliffs, N.J., Salem Press, 1986. 4v. $365. ISBN: 0893564567.

34 of the 198 authors treated are from Latin America. See main entry at 820.73-31(03). *Class No:* 860.7-3(03)

Histories

[8388]
ALEGRÍA, F. Nuevo historia de la novela hispanoamericana. Hanover, N.H., Ediciones del Norte, 1986. iv,460p. $22.50. ISBN: 0910061297.

Completely revised version of the author's *Historia de la novela hispanoamericana,* 4th ed., Mexico, Andrea, 1974.

History of the Spanish-American novel in three major sections (origins to 1900, twentieth century and the 1960's), each subdivided by type of novel rather than geographically and including sections on over 100 major novelists. Brief bibliography (8p.). Name index. 'Likely to become a standard reference work on the Latin American novel for many years to come' according to *World Literature Today* (v.61(2), Spring 1987, p.427-8), which praises the move away from encyclopedic coverage towards more detailed discussion of key novels. *Class No:* 860.7-3(091)

[8389]
SCHWARTZ, K. A New history of Spanish American fiction. Coral Gables, Fla., Univ. of Miami Press, 1972. 2v.

V.1 *From Colonial times to the Mexican Revolution and beyond.* 1972. xii,436p. ISBN: 087024227x.

V.2 *Social concern, universalism and the new novel.* 1971. x,445p. ISBN: 0870242288.

A narrative history which concentrates on the novel rather than shorter fictional forms, with hundreds of works discussed. Many references. Extensive bibliographies in each vol. (59p. and 52p.) of critical studies - general, then by country and author. Indexes of authors and titles in each vol. *Class No:* 860.7-3(091)

Guatemalan Literature

[8390]
ALBIZÚREZ PALMA, F. Diccionario de autores guatemaltecos. Guatemala, Tipografía Nacional, 1984. 96p.

Biographical notes on Guatemalan writers with lists of their publications (with dates), but no references to critical studies. *Class No:* 860.728.1

Nicaraguan Literature

[8391]
ARELLANO, J.E. Panorama de la literatura nicaragüense. 3rd ed. Managua, Nacionales, 1977. 195p.

A history of Nicaraguan literature which includes a useful general bibliography (80 items), and a list of works by and about 30 Nicaraguan authors (28p.). *Class No:* 860.728.5

Costa Rican Literature

[8392]
KARGLEDER, M. *and* **MORY, W.H. Bibliografía selectiva de la literatura costarricense.** San José, Costa Rica, 1978. 109p.

Covers 1869 to 1976. Does not list works included in anthologies and periodicals unless they have also been published separately. *Class No:* 860.728.6

Cuban Literature

[8393]
Dictionary of twentieth-century Cuban literature. Martínez, J.A., *ed.* New York, Greenwood, 1990. 537p. $85. ISBN: 0313251851.

A biobibliographical dictionary of 113 authors, including exiles, with entries which provide biography, critical evaluation, and bibliography of primary and secondary materials. Also includes information on 45 critics, essays on the major genres, information on literary journals, and general bibliography. Index. 'Should be the first choice as a reference guide to writers in Cuba or in exile therefrom' (*Choice,* v.27(10), June 1990, p.1648).
Class No: 860.729.1

[8394]
FOSTER, D.W. Cuban literature: a research guide. New York, Garland, 1985. 522p. ISBN: 0824089030.

Classified bibliography of general material, followed by listings for 98 individual authors, A-Z. Index of critics.
Class No: 860.729.1

[8395]
INSTITUTO DE LITERATURA Y LINGÜÍSTICA DE LA ACADEMIA DE CIENCIAS DE CUBA. Diccionario de la literatura cubana. La Habana, Letras Cubanas, 1980-84. 2v. (1132p.). illus.

Over 3,000 entries for authors, periodicals, genres, movements and organizations. Author entries include biographical information and primary and secondary bibliographies. General bibliography (6p.) at end of v.2. Woodbridge (*Guide to reference works* ... 1987, p.128) notes political bias (*e.g.* no entry for Cabrera Infante), but admits this is 'an indispensable source'.
Class No: 860.729.1

[8396]
MARATOS, D.C. *and* **HILL, M.D. Escritores de la diáspora cubana:** manual biobibliográfica. [Cuban exile writers: a biobibliographic handbook.] Metuchen, N.J., Scarecrow, 1986. xi,391p. ISBN: 0810818787.

Bilingual compilation on 420 writers exiled from Cuba since 1959, plus some remaining there whose work has been published abroad. Over 1,400 titles listed without annotation. Biographical information based on responses to questionnaire and therefore variable. Title index.
Class No: 860.729.1

Dominican Literature

[8397]
OLIVERA, O. Bibliografía de la literatura dominicana (1960-1982). Lincoln, Nebr., Society of Spanish and Spanish-American Studies, 1985. 86p. $18. ISBN: 0892950277.

Nearly 1,200 entries, arranged mainly by literary genre. Includes critical studies of Dominican authors. Name index. *Class No:* 860.729.3

Mexican Literature

[8398]
Dictionary of Mexican literature. Cortés, E., *ed.* Westport, Conn., Greenwood, 1992. xliii,768p. $105. ISBN: 0313262713.

545 signed entries (by 40 contributors) ranging from 1p. to 16p., virtually all of them biographical, with the emphasis on 20th-century writers. Each comprises biographical sketch, list of works, and substantial bibliography of critical studies. 11 topical entries. English translation given for all cited titles. Valuable introductory essay (19p.) giving 'Overview of Mexican letters and literature.' General bibliography (13p.). Index. *Class No:* 860.972

[8399]
FORSTER, M.H. An Index to Mexican literary periodicals. New York, Scarecrow, 1966. 276p.

Lists by author 4,036 articles from journals which began and completed publication during the period 1920 to 1960. Subject index. *Class No:* 860.972

[8400]
FOSTER, D.W. Mexican literature: a bibliography of secondary sources. 2nd ed. Metuchen, N.J., Scarecrow, 1992. xi,686p. $76. ISBN: 0810825481.

1st ed. 1981.

A greatly expanded and updated version of a very useful source. Part I has general references in 28 sections. Part II covers *c.*80 authors (50 in 1st ed.) from the 16th century to the present, with fewer than 20 citations in some cases but over 540 for Octavio Paz. No annotations. Index of critics. *Class No:* 860.972

[8401]
HOFFMAN, H.H. Cuento mexicano index. Newport Beach, Calif., Headway, 1978. 599p.

An index to 7,230 short stories by 400 Mexican authors in 674 anthologies published since 1945. *Class No:* 860.972

[8402]
Mexican literature: a history. Foster, D.W., *ed.* Austin, Tex., Univ. of Texas Press, 1994. x,458p. $50. ISBN: 0292724829.

A collection of essays by specialists, surveying over 500 years of Mexican literature from a sociocultural perspective. Topics covered include Pre-Columbian indigenous writing, Colonial literature, Romanticism, Nineteenth-century prose fiction, Modernism, Major twentieth-century genres (narrative, poetry, theater), Literary criticism, and Literary journals. Annotated bibliography of key critical studies and reference sources with each chapter. Index. *Class No:* 860.972

[8403]
MONTERDE GARCÍA ICAZBALCETA, F. Bibliografía de teatro en México. México, Impr. de la Secretaría de Relaciones Exteriores, 1933 (repr. New York, Franklin, 1970). lxxx,649p.

In 4 sections, covering original works by Mexicans and foreigners resident in Mexico; translations and adaptations; foreign drama published in Mexico or with a Mexican theme; works containing studies of Mexican theatre and dramatists. *Class No:* 860.972

[8404]
—LAMB, R.S. Mexican theater of the twentieth century: bibliography and study. 2nd ed. Claremont, Calif., Ocelot Press, 1975. 143p. $8.95. ISBN: 091243418x.

Introductory essay (12p.) followed by bibliography (arranged by author) of plays, bibliography of critical studies, and list of relevant Mexican magazines and newspapers. *Class No:* 860.972

Puerto-Rican Literature

[8405]
HILL, M.D. *and* SCHLEIFER, H.B. Puerto Rican authors: a biobibliographic handbook. Metuchen, N.J., Scarecrow, 1974. x,267p. ISBN: 0810806819.

Gives brief biographical information on 251 authors, arranged A-Z, plus lists of their works with annotations for major titles. Indexes of topics, historical periods, and titles. Bilingual throughout. *Class No:* 860.9729

[8406]
MANRIQUE CABRERA, F. Historia de la literatura puertorriqueña. Río Pedras, Cultural, 1977. 384p.

1st ed. 1969.

Chapters devoted to periods from the 16th century to the present, with subsections on genres. General bibliography (2p.). Many bibliographical references after each chapter. Index. *Class No:* 860.9729

[8407]
Puerto Rican literature: a bibliography of secondary sources. Foster, D.W., *comp.* Westport, Conn., Greenwood, 1982. xxiii,232p. $49.95. ISBN: 0313234191.

23 general sections (572 entries) are followed by bibliographies for 80 individual authors with between 5 and 277 entries per section. No annotations. Index to authors of critical works. *Class No:* 860.9729

[8408]
RIVERA DE ALVAREZ, J. Diccionario de literatura puertorriqueña. 2. ed., rev. y aumentada. San Juan, Instituto de Cultura Puetorriqueña, 1970-74. 2v. in 3.

1st ed. 1955 in one vol.

V.1 is a history of Puerto Rican literature; v.2 (in 2 parts) is a dictionary, with entries for authors, literary movements, etc. Selective general bibliography in v.1 and bibliographies within entries in v.2. *Class No:* 860.9729

Argentine Literature

[8409]
FARES, G. *and* **HERMANN, E. Escritoras argentinas contemporaneas.** Frankfurt am Main, Lang, 1993. xi,255p. DM100. (*Univ. of Texas studies in contemporary Spanish American fiction.*) ISBN: 0820420964.

Profiles of 13 women writers, with portrait, biography, bibliography, interview and lengthy excerpts from works. General bibliography on Latin American women's literature (15p.). *Class No:* 860.982

[8410]
FOSTER, D.W. Argentine literature: a research guide. 2nd ed., rev. and exp. New York, Garland, 1982. xliii,778p. ISBN: 0824093976.

1st ed. 1970, by D.W. and V.R. Foster, as *Research guide to Argentine literature.*

General references in 30 sections followed by listings for 73 authors, giving bibliographies, critical monographs and dissertations, and critical essays for each, with the emphasis on material likely to be accessible in the US and Latin America. Index of critics. 2nd ed. shows very considerable expansion. *Class No:* 860.982

[8411]
Historia de la literatura argentina. Arrieta, R.A., *ed.* Buenos Aires, Peuser, 1958-1960. 6v. illus.

The work of 14 specialists. Chronological account in vols. 1-4 from Colonial Times to 1950; v.5 covers folklore; v.6 covers historiography and bibliography. Chapters have bibliographies of varying length. Index of authors and titles in v.6. *Class No:* 860.982

[8412]
LICHTBLAU, M.I. The Argentine novel: an annotated bibliography. Lanham, Md., Scarecrow, 1997. 1136p. $99.50. ISBN: 0810832429.

A comprehensive listing, from 1788 to 1990. Where possible, all editions of each novel are cited, as well as translations into foreign languages, and citations are followed by one or more critical commentaries or select bibliographies of additional studies on the work or its author. *Class No:* 860.982

[8413]
ORGANBIDE, P. *and* **YAHNI, R. Enciclopedia de la literatura argentina.** Buenos Aires, Sudamericana, 1970. 639p.

Biographical information and critical comments on Argentine authors provided by 19 contributors. Many entries include concise bibliographies of secondary material. A few topic entries. *Class No:* 860.982

Borges

[8414]
FISHBURN, E. *and* **HUGHES, P. A Dictionary of Borges.** London, Duckworth, 1990. xiv,270p. £25. ISBN: 0715621548.

Over 1,200 concise entries explaining the allusions (to people, places, literature, folklore, mythology, etc.) that are characteristic of Borges' fiction. *Class No:* 860.982BOR

[8415]
FOSTER, D.W. Jorge Luis Borges: an annotated primary and secondary bibliography. New York, Garland, 1984. xlvi,328p. ISBN: 0824090756.

In 16 sections, the first listing Borges' works (119 items), the rest listing secondary material of all kinds (1,100 items). Annotations are both descriptive and evaluative. Index of original titles of the works. Index of critics, translators and illustrators. Well cross-referenced. *Class No:* 860.982BOR

Chilean Literature

[8416]
FOSTER, D.W. Chilean literature: a working bibliography of secondary sources. Boston, Hall, 1978. xxii,236p. ISBN: 0816181802.

Part 1., General References, has 28 sections covering genres, periods and special topics (*e.g.* Women authors); Part 2., Authors, lists bibliographic and critical material on 46 individuals. 2,777 entries in all (500 on Neruda). No annotations. Index of critics. *Class No:* 860.983

[8417]
ROMAN-LAGUNAS, J. The Chilean novel: a critical study of secondary sources and a bibliography. Metuchen, N.J., Scarecrow, 1995. 578p. $89.50. ISBN: 0810828685.

Includes bibliographical information on 60 Chilean novelists as well as a comprehensive annotated bibliography of secondary sources on the Chilean novel.
Class No: 860.983

[8418]
SZMULEWICZ, E. Diccionario de la literatura chilena. 2nd ed. Santiago, Bello, 1984. xviii,494p.

Biobibliographical information which 'must be used with extreme caution', according to Woodbridge, H.C., *Guide to reference works...,* 1987, p.121. *Class No:* 860.983

Neruda

[8419]
WOODBRIDGE, H.C. *and* **ZUBATSKY, D. Pablo Neruda: an annotated bibliography of biographical and critical studies.** New York, Garland, 1988. 629p. ISBN: 0824087321.

Over 2,300 annotated entries for material in a wide range of languages. Annotations are descriptive and often include quotations. Indexes of titles and of authors, editors, translators, etc. *Class No:* 860.983NER

Bolivian Literature

[8420]
CÁCERES ROMERO, A. Nueva historia de la literatura boliviana. La Paz, Amigos del Libro, 1987-90. v.1-2 (in progress).

V.1 *Literaturas aborígenes; aimara, quecha, callawaya, guaraní.* 1987. 405p.

V.2 *Literatura colonial.* 1990. 426p.

2 more vols. are planned, under the titles *Literatura de la independencia y del siglo XIX* and *Literatura boliviana del siglo XX.* *Class No:* 860.984

[8421]
GUZMÁN, A. Biografías de la literatura boliviana: biografía, evaluación, bibliografía. Cochabamba, Amigos del Libro, 1982. 307p.

Biographical sketches of authors born between 1520 and 1925, arranged chronologically by year of birth and including primary bibliographies. *Class No:* 860.984

[8422]
ORTEGA, J. *and* **CÁCERES ROMERO, A. Diccionario de la literatura boliviana.** La Paz, Amigos del Libro, 1977. 337p.

A dictionary of Bolivian authors, giving brief biography, list of works, bibliography of criticism and, in some cases, critical evaluation. Covers 1825 to the present. *Class No:* 860.984

Peruvian Literature

[8423]
ARRIOLA GRANDE, M. Diccionario literario del Perú: nomenclatura por autores. 2. ed. Lima, Universo, 1983. 2v. illus.

Biographical information on Peruvian writers, living and dead, with some critical evaluation. A-Z arrangement. Includes some non-Peruvians who have lived in the country and written about its literature and history. *Class No:* 860.985

[8424]
FOSTER, D.W. Peruvian literature: a bibliography of secondary sources. Westport, Conn., Greenwood, 1981. xxix,324p. $59.95. ISBN: 0313230978.

General references in 24 sections for genres, themes, etc., followed by references for 38 authors, A-Z, including 523 on C. Vallejo and 288 on M. Vargas Llosa. *c.*4,500 unannotated entries. Index of critics. *Class No:* 860.985

[8425]
HIGGINS, J. A History of Peruvian literature. Liverpool, Cairns, 1987. xiv,379p. £35. (*Liverpool monographs in Hispanic studies.*) ISBN: 0905205359.

Covers literature in Spanish and Quechua (the language of the indigenous population) from the Renaissance onwards, with two-thirds of the book devoted to the twentieth century. 6p. of general bibliography plus bibliographies for each cited author in footnotes throughout the text. These include works and critical material and except in the case of major authors are comprehensive. Indexes of authors and works plus a short glossary. All quotations are accompanied by an English translation. 'A necessary and trustworthy guide' (*TLS*, no.4405, Sept. 4-11, 1987, p.961). *Class No:* 860.985

Colombian Literature

[8426]
ORJUELA, H.H. Fuentes generales para el estudio de la literatura colombiana: guia bibliográfica. Bogotá, Instituto Caro y Cuervo, 1968. xl,863p.

Comprehensive, partially annotated bibliography in 12 main sections: General bibliographies; Library catalogues; Dictionaries of literature; Biographies; Anthologies; Literary history and criticism; Literary periods and movements; Genres; Folklore and popular literature; Religious literature; Translations; Press and journalism. Usually gives locations in Colombian and US libraries. Name index and clear list of contents. *Class No:* 860.986

[8427]
—ORJUELA, H.H. Bibliografía del teatro colombiano. Bogotá, Instituto Caro y Cuervo, 1974. xxvii, 312p.

A bibliography of Colombian plays, briefly annotated, followed by 'Secciones complementarias' (68p.), listing works on Colombian and Spanish American theatre, and theatre in general. Colombian and US library locations. Index of play titles.

Additions and corrections appear in Gonzalez Cajiao, F., *Materiales para una historia del teatro en Colombia* (Bogotá, Instituto Colombiano de Cultura, 1978). *Class No:* 860.986

[8428]
—ORJUELA, H.H. Bibliografía de la poesía colombiana. Bogotá, Instituto Caro y Cuervo, 1971. xii,486p.

Lists books and pamphlets by Colombian poets, including translations from other languages. Colombian and foreign library locations. *Class No:* 860.986

[8429]
PORRAS COLLANTES, E. Bibliografía de la novela en Colombia. Con notas de contenido y crítica de las obras y guías de comentarios sobre los autores. Bogotá, Instituto Caro y Cuervo, 1976. xix,888p.

Bibliographical information on 2,326 novels published up to 1974, including details of translations, notes on contents and references to critical studies. Colombian and foreign library locations. Arranged A-Z by author, with title index, chronological index, and list of pseudonyms. *Class No:* 860.986

[8430]
SÁNCHEZ LÓPEZ, L.M. Diccionario de escritores colombianos. 3. ed., rev. y aum. Bogotà, Plaza y Janes, 1985. 903p. illus. ISBN: 8449957087.

1st ed. 1978; 2nd ed. 1982.

Very brief entries on *c.*12,000 Colombian writers of all periods; as little as 1 or 2 lines in many cases. Birth and death dates often lacking, but works listed for major authors. List of pseudonyms. *Class No:* 860.986

García Márquez

[8431]
FAU, M.E. Gabriel García Márquez: an annotated bibliography, 1947-1979. Westport, Conn., Greenwood, 1980. x,198p. $55. ISBN: 031322224x.

Part 1 lists 110 works, including translations. Part 2 lists over 1,300 secondary sources, including book reviews and interviews. Brief annotations for major critical works. Author index.

Supplemented by *Bibliographic guide to Gabriel García Márquez, 1979-1985* by M.E. Fau and N. Sfeir de González (Greenwood, 1986. xvii,181p. $69.50. ISBN: 0313252483), which adds 200 primary and 950 secondary sources, and *Bibliographic guide to Gabriel García Márquez, 1986-1992* by N. Sfeir de González (Greenwood, 1994. 430p. $89.50. ISBN: 0313288321), which includes dissertations for the first time. *Class No:* 860.986GAR

Ecuadorian Literature

[8432]
BARRIGA LÓPEZ, F. *and* **BARRIGA LÓPEZ, L. Diccionario de la literatura ecuatoriana.** 2. ed., corr. y aum. Guayaquil, Cultura Ecuatoriana, Nucleo del Guayas, 1980. 5v.

Basically a dictionary of authors, with some articles on literary societies and cultural organizations. Lists authors' works with dates and sometimes cites critics, but no bibliography of critical studies. *Class No:* 860.986.6

[8433]
LUZURIAGA, G. Bibliografía del teatro ecuatoriano, 1900-1980. Quito, Cultura Ecuatoriana, 1984. 131p.

1. General reference works on Ecuadorian literature and drama - 2. Bibliography of plays published or performed since 1900 (A-Z by author) - 3. Bibliography of critical studies on the drama of the period and on individual playwrights. *Class No:* 860.986.6

Venezuelan Literature

[8434]
BECCO, H.J. Fuentes para el estudio de la literatura venezolana. Caracas, Centauro, 1978. 2v.

A classified bibliography of nearly 1,900 sources, including bibliographies, biographies, literary histories, critical studies, anthologies, periodical indexes, etc. Well indexed. *Class No:* 860.987

[8435]
—ROJAS UZCÁTEGUI, J. *and* CARDOZO, L. Bibliografía del teatro venezolano. Mérida, Univ. de Los Andes, Facultad de Humanidades y Educación, Instituto de Investigaciones, 1980. 199p.

The core of the book is a list, by author, of plays published 1801 to 1978. Appendices list unpublished plays and those for which little information is available; operas and musicals; and translations. Chronology of Venezuelan theatre. Title index. Bibliography of critical studies.
Class No: 860.987

[8436]
—SAMBRANO URDANETA, O. Contribución a una bibliografía general de la poesía venezolana en el siglo XX. Caracas, Univ. Central de Venezuela, Facultad de Humanidades y Educación, Escuela de Letras, 1979. 367p.

The section on individual poets and their works lists over 2,000 poems by 747 poets. Other sections list reference works, anthologies and critical studies. Chronology of Venezuelan poetry. Title index. *Class No:* 860.987

[8437]
Diccionario general de literatura venezolana (autores). Mérida, Univ. de Los Andes, Centro de Investigaciones Literarias, Facultad de Humanidades y Educación, 1974. xiv,829p.

Provides biographical information, critical evaluation and primary and secondary bibliographies for Venezuelan authors and non-native authors working there or writing about the country. 'It should be an indispensable guide to students of Venezuelan literature' according to H.C.

.... *(contd.)*
Woodbridge (*Guide to reference works ...*, 1987, p.154), who considers this one of the finest works of its kind produced in Spanish America. *Class No:* 860.987

[8438]
MEDINA, J.R. Ochenta años de literatura venezolana, 1900-1980. Caracas, Monte Avila, 1980. 473p.

A history (p.7-335) followed by chronological lists of prose works and poetry and a bibliography of 185 critical studies and 80 anthologies. Name index. *Class No:* 860.987

Uruguayan Literature

[8439]
RELA, W. Diccionario de escritores uruguayos. Montevideo, Ediciones de la Plaza, 1986. 397p.

Covers Uruguayan writers of all periods, giving biographical information, critical evaluation, and bibliographies of works and secondary sources.
Class No: 860.989.9

[8440]
RELA, W. Fuentes para el estudio de la literatura uruguaya, 1835-1968. Classified bibliography of 930 unannotated items, including bibliographies, literary histories, and anthologies. Author index. Montevideo, Banda Oriental, 1969. 134p.

See also Rela's *Uruguayan literature: a selective bibliographical guide* (Tempe, Ariz., Arizona State Univ., Center for Latin American Studies, 1986. 85p. ISBN: 0879180609). *Class No:* 860.989.9

[8441]
WELCH, T.L. Bibliografía de la literatura uruguaya. Washington, D.C., Secretaría general, Organización de los Estados Americanos, 1985. xii,502p.

A catalogue of Uruguayan literature in the Columbus Memorial Library, Washington, D.C., listing over 9,000 literary works and critical and historical studies, by author, with name and title indexes. *Class No:* 860.989.9

[8442]
—ENGLEKIRK, J.E. *and* RAMOS, M.M. La Narrativa uruguaya: estudio crítico-bibliográfico. Berkeley, Calif., Univ. of California Press, 1967 (repr. San Bernardino, Calif., Borgo Press, 1983). 338p. ISBN: 0893707929.

Lists 525 novels and *c.*7,000 short stories by 265 authors, giving bibliographical information, library locations (Spain, Uruguay and US) and, in many cases, excerpts from critical studies. *Class No:* 860.989.9

Galician Literature

[8443]
VARELA, A.T. Literatura gallega. Madrid, Taurus, 1988. 280p.

A wide-ranging survey written in Spanish. Reviewed at length in *World Literature Today,* v.63(2), Spring 1989, p.296-7. *Class No:* 860.99

Portuguese Literature

Bibliographies

[8444]
KUNOFF, H. Portuguese literature from its origins to 1990: a bibliography based on the collections at Indiana University. Metuchen, NJ, Scarecrow, 1994. ix,497p. $52. ISBN: 0810828448.

The largest bibliography of Portuguese literature published in the US, with over 8,000 titles organized according to Library of Congress classification in the following chapters: 1. Bibliography - 2. History and criticism - 3. Collections - 4. Individual authors (over 400p.) - 5. Provincial, local, colonial - 6. Serials. Disappointing lack of indexes.
Class No: 869(01)

[8445]
MOISÉS, M. Bibliografia da literatura portuguesa. São Paulo, Saraiva-Univ. de São Paulo, 1968. xx,383p.

General section followed by 9 chronological sections (1198-1960s), plus one on overseas literature. Each section has brief list of general studies and is then subdivided into genres and individual authors (primary and secondary material). Not annotated. Name index. *Class No:* 869(01)

Encyclopaedias & Dictionaries

[8446]
Biblos enciclopédia Verbo das literaturas de língua portuguesa. Cardoso Bernardes, J.E., *& others, eds.* Lisboa, Verbo, 1995-7. v.1-2 (in progress).

3,500 signed entries (A-Z) in each vol., mainly on writers but also covering topics, periodicals, genres and national literatures of Lusophone countries. Bibliographies with all entries. First 2 vols. cover 'A-Le'. *Class No:* 869(03)

[8447]
Dicionário da literatura medieval galega e portuguesa. Lanciani, G. *and* Taviani, G., *eds.* Lisboa, Caminho, 1993. 698p. illus. ISBN: 9722108719.

*c.*700 lengthy, signed articles, by nearly 100 contributors, on all aspects of medieval literature: people, works, topics, etc. Bibliographies after each entry. Cross-references, but no index. Colour plates. *Class No:* 869(03)

[8448]
Dicionário de literatura: literatura portuguesa; literatura brasileira; literatura galega; estilística literária. Coelho, J do P., *ed.* 3rd ed. Porto, Figueirinhas, 1978 (repr. 1994). 5v. (1526p.). illus. ISBN: 972661032x.

1st ed. 1960, under the title *Dicionário das literaturas portuguesa, galega e brasileira.*

Signed articles by 45 contributors on authors, works, journals, topics, characters, periods, movements, genres, and regions of Portuguese, Brazilian and Galician literatures. Bibliographies after most articles. Copiously illustrated. Arranged A-Z in vols. 1-4, with indexes of authors and titles in v.5, but this ed. can also be found in 3 vols.
Class No: 869(03)

[8449]
Dicionário de literatura portuguesa. Machado, A.M., *ed.* Lisboa, Presença, 1996. 567p. £33.75. ISBN: 972232084x.

Signed entries by 70 contributors on *c.*1,000 authors in one sequence (496p.) and on genres, periods and movements in another (57p.). Selective bibliographies with all entries.
Class No: 869(03)

Handbooks & Manuals

[8450]
CHAMBERLAIN, B.J. Portuguese language and Luso-Brazilian literature: an annotated guide to selected reference works. New York, Modern Language Assoc. of America, 1989. xii,95p. $32. (*Selected bibliographies in language and literature.*) ISBN: 0873529561.

A classified, well-annotated guide, similar in style and format to Woodbridge's work on Spanish language and literature (*q.v.*). 538 entries in 4 main sections (Portuguese language; Portuguese literature; Brazilian literature; Luso-African and other Lusophone literatures) with numerous sub-sections. Index of authors, editors and compilers.
Class No: 869(035)

Histories

[8451]
BELL, A.F.G. Portuguese literature. Oxford, Oxford Univ. Press, 1922 (repr. 1970). 395p.

General history in 6 period divisions: 1185-1325; 1325-1521; 1502-80; 1580-1706; 1706-1816; 1816-1910. Appendix 1. Literature of the People - 2. The Galician Revival. Select bibliography (20p.) of texts and critical works has been added by B. Vidigal for the reprint and includes a section on contemporary writing.
Class No: 869(091)

[8452]
FORJAZ DE SAMPAIO, A., *and others*. História de literatura portuguesa ilustrada. Paris, Aillaud & Bertrand, 1929-42. 4v. illus.

A profusely illustrated history (some of the plates and facsimiles being in colour) with many quotations and footnote references, and substantial chapter bibliographies. Limited coverage of 20th-century literature. No index, but table of contents is detailed. *Class No:* 869(091)

[8453]
SARAIVA, A.J. *and* **LOPES, Ó. História da literatura portuguesa.** 14th ed., corr. e actualizada. Pôrto, Pôrto Editôra, 1987. 1223p.

Comprehensive single-vol. history in 6 sections corresponding to the major periods of literary history, further divided into 45 chapters, each with bibliography. Name index. Regularly updated. *Class No:* 869(091)

Biographies

[8454]
BRINCHES, V. Dicionário biobibliográfico luso-brasileiro. Rio de Janeiro, Editôra Fundo de Cultura, 1965. 509p.

Covers *c.*200 Portuguese and a similar number of Brazilian authors in separate A-Z sequences, preceded by brief notes on literary institutions and movements.
Class No: 869(092)

[8455]
Dicionário cronológico de autores portugueses, v.1. Lisboa, E., *ed.* Mem Martins, Europa-América, 1985. 530p. ISBN: 9721006408.

The first vol. of a projected 3-vol. set has entries for over 800 writers born 1200-1800, arranged in chronological sequences within major period divisions. Entries comprise biographical notes and lists of principal works. Name index.
Class No: 869(092)

[8456]

MOISÉS, M. A literatura portuguesa moderna: guia biográfico, crítico e bibliográfico. São Paulo, Cultrix, 1973. 202p.

A biobibliographical dictionary compiled by 11 contributors and covering 20th-century authors. Some entries for literary movements and topics. *Class No:* 869(092)

[8457]

Quem é quem na literatura portugêsa. Machado, A.M., *ed.* Lisboa, Dom Quixote, 1979. 260p. illus. ISBN: 9722005871.

2 A-Z sequences for pre- and post-1900 writers. Entries include date and place of birth and death, review of career and list of principal works. Covers approx. 900 authors. Many photographs. *Class No:* 869(092)

Africa

[8458]

CHABAL, P., & ***others*****. The Postcolonial literature of Lusophone Africa.** London, Hurst, 1996. vi,314p. £14.95. ISBN: 1850652503.

Lengthy, signed chapters on the literatures of Mozambique, Angola, Guinea-Bissau, Cape Verde, and Sao Tomé and Príncipe, plus one on oral literature and popular culture in the latter region. Bibliography (25p.) lists principal Portuguese- and English-language literary and critical works from and about Lusophone Africa published since 1974, including anthologies, general studies and criticism of individual authors. Index. *Class No:* 869(6)

[8459]

GOMES, A. ***and*** **CAVACAS, F. Dicionário de autores de literaturas africanas de língua portuguesa.** Lisboa, Caminho, 1997. 454p. ISBN: 9722111558.

A *Who's who*-style dictionary which is not confined to living authors. Entries give country; genre; birth and death dates; education; career; chronological list of works; translations; anthologies in which included; prizes; and quotation from a critical review. List of anthologies, with bibliographical information (7p.). Lists of authors by country. Bibliography of studies of Lusophone African literature (23p.). Name index. *Class No:* 869(6)

[8460]

MOSER, G. ***and*** **FERREIRA, M. A New bibliography of the Lusophone literatures of Africa.** 2nd ed., completely rev. and exp. London, Zell, 1993. 432p. £55. ISBN: 1873836856.

1st ed. Lisboa, Nacional-Moeda, 1983, as *Bibliografia das literaturas africanas de expressão portuguesa*, being essentially an updated and expanded bilingual version of Moser's *A Tentative Portuguese-African bibliography* (University Park, Pa., Pennsylvania State Univ. Libraries, 1970).

Separate sections for the 5 main regions of Portuguese Africa (Angola, Cape Verde, Guinea-Bissau, Mozambique, and São Tomé & Principe), with 3 subsections for each: oral literature; creative writing; literary history and criticism. Regional introductions and chronologies have been dropped for this ed., as have lists of periodical articles, but biographical notes on authors native to or resident in Africa have been expanded and updated, and an introductory essay on the social history of Africa's Lusophone literatures has been added. Annotations are now all in English. Indexes of authors and titles.

The authors are right to admit that the new ed. is 'less pleasing to the eye' (*Preface*), with no illustrations, a 2-

.... *(contd.)*

column computer-printout layout, cluttered pages and type fonts which are far from reader-friendly, but it is 'meticulously compiled, and jam-packed with highly elusive facts and figures' (*Reference Reviews*, v.8(4), 1994, p.41). *Class No:* 869(6)

Pessoa

[8461]

BLANCO, J. Fernando Pessoa: esboço de uma bibliografia. Lisboa, Imprensa Nacional - Casa da Moeda, Centro de Estudos Pessoanos, 1983. 482p.

An extensive bibliography in 3 sections: 1. Bibliografia activa (Pessoa's works, 1912-82) - 2. Bibliografia passiva (over 1,300 studies in 14 sections) - 3. Traduções (translations into 17 languages). Detailed table of contents. *Class No:* 869PES

Portuguese Literature in Translation

[8462]

KEENOY, R. ***and*** **TREECE, D. The Babel guide to the fiction of Portugal, Brazil and Africa in English translation.** London, Boulevard Books, 1995. 164p. illus. £7.95. ISBN: 1899460055.

Provides original reviews of over 70 key 20th-century Portuguese-language novels and short stories, with brief excerpts, plus longer review-essays on major figures like Pessoa and Lispector. Also lists all post-1945 English translations with publication details. Particularly strong on Brazilian and African fiction. *Class No:* 869-03

Brazilian Literature

Bibliographies

[8463]

Bibliografia de dramaturgia brasileira. São Paulo, Escola de Comunicações e Artes da U. de São Paulo; Associação Museu Lasar Segall, 1981-3. 2v.

A list of over 3,000 plays arranged by author (v.1, A-M; v.2, N-Z) with details of acts and casts, library locations, and bibliographical information. Title indexes in each vol. *Class No:* 869.981(01)

[8464]

CARPEAUX, O.M. Pequena bibliografia crítica da literatura brasileira. Nova edição [*i.e.* 4th ed.] com um apêndice de Assis Brasil, incluindo 47 novos escritores. Rio de Janeiro, Edições de Ouro, [1979?]. 470p.

1st ed. 1951; 3rd ed. 1964.

Over 3,500 entries arranged in 38 sections (8 general, followed by 30 chronological sections from colonial times to the present). Lists of main works by and about individual authors but minimal biographical and critical data. Essentially the same as 3rd ed. with the addition of the appendix of new writers. Name index. *Class No:* 869.981(01)

[8465]

FOSTER, D.W. *and* **RELA, W. Brazilian literature: a research bibliography.** New York, Garland, 1990. 426p. $62. ISBN: 0824034422.

General studies (arranged under 11 subject headings) are followed by bibliographies for many individual authors. *Choice* (v.28(4), Dec. 1990, p.608) regrets several omissions, particularly of women writers, but 'for those authors included, this is now the *first* recourse'. Author index. *Class No:* 869.981(01)

[8466]

GOMES, C.M. O conto brasileiro e sua crítica. Bibliografia (1841-1974). Rio de Janeiro, Biblioteca Nacional, 1977. 2v. (xxi,654p.).

Supersedes the author's *Bibliografia do conto brasileiro* (1968-69. 2v.), which covered 1841-1967.

Bibliography of the Brazilian short story with entries for over 2,800 works and 2,250 critical studies and reviews. Arranged A-Z by story-writer, with index of titles and critics. List of periodicals. Bibliography of 191 anthologies appended. *Class No:* 869.981(01)

Encyclopaedias & Dictionaries

[8467]

Dictionary of Brazilian literature. Stern, I., *ed.* New York, Greenwood, 1988. l, 402p. $85. ISBN: 0313249326.

300 signed entries, arranged A-Z, 'covering the most significant writers, literary schools, and related cultural movements in Brazilian literary history, with an emphasis on twentieth-century and very contemporary figures' (*Preface*). Author entries include citations for major works and are followed by bibliography of selected additional works, translations and criticism, the latter comprising primarily English-language sources where available. Introductory essay with general bibliography (14p.); map; chronology of historical and literary events (11p.); glossary of Brazilian words (1p.). Index. 46 contributors. *Class No:* 869.981(03)

[8468]

MENEZES, R. de. Dicionário literário brasileiro. 2. ed., rev., aum. e atualizada. Rio de Janeiro, Livros Técnicos e Científicos, 1978. xix,803p.

1st ed. São Paulo, Saraiva, 1969, in 5 vols. with illustrations.

An excellent source of biographical information with entries on *c.*3,800 authors. Bibliographies of primary and secondary materials with each entry. Separate A-Z sequence (69p.) of articles on literary movements, schools and institutions, also with bibliographies. List of pseudonyms. Select general bibliography (3p.). *Class No:* 869.981(03)

[8469]

—Pequeno dicionário da literatura brasileira. Paes, J.P. *and* Moisés, M., *eds.* 2nd ed., rev. e amp. São Paulo, Cultrix, 1980. 462p.

1st ed. 1967.

Signed articles by 31 contributors, mainly on authors (over 350 covered) but also on literary works, movements, periods, genres, etc. Bibliographies with each entry. Author and title indexes. *Class No:* 869.981(03)

Histories

[8470]

COUTINHO, A. A Literatura no Brasil. 2. ed. Rio de Janeiro, Sul-Americana, 1968-71. 6v.

1st ed. 1955-59, in 4 vols.

V.1 *Introduções. Barroco. Neoclassicismo. Arcadismo.* V.2 *Romantismo.* V.3 *Realismo. Naturalismo. Parnasianismo.* V.4 *Simbolismo. Impressionismo. Transição.* V.5 *Modernismo.* V.6 *Teatro. Conto. Crônica. A Nova Literatura.*

Thorough history with bibliographical footnotes throughout. V.6 has general bibliography (60p.), details of contributors, index of names, titles and subjects, and contents listing for the set. *Class No:* 869.981(091)

[8471]

—COUTINHO, A. An Introduction to literature in Brazil. New York, Columbia Univ. Press, 1969. xii,326p. ISBN: 0231029934.

A translation by G. Rabassa of the introductions supplied by Coutinho for the various sections of his multi-volume history. Copious notes and references. Bibliography (16p.). Name index. Described by the translator as a 'history of the history of Brazilian literature' (*Preface*).
Class No: 869.981(091)

[8472]

MOISÉS, M. História da literatura brasileira. São Paulo, Cultrix/EDUSP, 1985-9. 5v.

V.1 *Origens. Barroco. Arcadismo.* 2. ed. 1989; v.2 *Romantismo.* 2. ed. 1989; v.3 *Realismo.* 2. ed. 1989; v.4 *Simbolismo.* 2. ed. 1988. v.5. *Modernismo (1922-actualide).* 1989.

A bio-bibliographical history, with subsections on hundreds of authors giving lists of works and some critical evaluation. Bibliographies of critical studies (general and on specific authors) at end of each vol. *Class No:* 869.981(091)

Biographies

[8473]

BRASIL, A. Dicionário prático de literatura brasileira. Rio de Janeiro, Edições de Ouro, 1979. 324p. illus.

About 300 entries on Brazilian writers of all periods, comprising biographical notes, list of works, brief critical commentary, and - in most cases - a portrait. Arranged A-Z by *first* name. Bibliography of general studies of Brazilian literature (4p.). *Class No:* 869.981(092)

[8474]

FOSTER, D.W. *and* **REIS, R. A Dictionary of contemporary Brazilian authors.** Tempe, Ariz., Center for Latin American Studies, Arizona State Univ., 1981. 152p. $5. ISBN: 087918051x.

Bio-critical articles on approx. 300 authors by 35 contributors, with the emphasis on younger writers. Entries are 'more critical than biographic in nature' (*Introduction*) and are followed by lists of principal works. Entries originally written in Portuguese have been translated into English. *Class No:* 869.981(092)

[8475]

HULET, C.L. Brazilian literature. Washington, D.C., Georgetown Univ. Press, 1974-5. 3v. ISBN: 0878400362, v.1; 0878400370, v.2; 0878400397, v.3.

A chronologically arranged anthology (v.1, 1500-1800; v.2, 1880-1920; v.3, 1920-60) which includes a brief biography, critical commentary, and a substantial

.... *(contd.)*
bibliography of critical studies for each of the 100-plus authors represented. Index of authors and extensive general bibliography in each vol. *Class No:* 869.981(092)

87 Classical Literature

Classical Literature

Bibliographies

[8476]

L'Année philologique: bibliographie critique et analytique de l'antiquité gréco-latine, 1924/26-. Paris, Société d'Édition 'Les Belles Lettres', 1928-. Annual. ISSN: 01846949.

A classified current bibliography which follows Marouzeau's *Dix années de bibliographie classique* (*q.v.*). Each vol. includes additional references to previous years.

V.64, *1993* (1996. xxxix,1242p.) has 16,005 entries, many of them annotated, in 2 parts. Authors and texts (6,726 entries, A-Z by author) are followed by a classified listing with 10 sections, covering literature, linguistics, law, history, etc. Indexes of collections, personal names, place names and authors. *Class No:* 870(01)

[8477]

—The Year's work in classical studies, 1906-47; edited for the Council of the Classical Association by W.H.D. Rouse and others. London, Murray, 1907-20; Bristol, Arrowsmith, 1921-50. 34v.

The volume for 1945-47 (v.34) edited by M. Platnauer (1950. xvi,102p.) was the final issue. While its scope was decidedly more restricted than that of *L'Année philologique* and similar compilations, *The Year's work* was truly international. Each chapter was written by a specialist.
Class No: 870(01)

[8478]

ENGELMANN, W. Bibliotheca scriptorum classicorum. 8. Aufl. umfassend die Literatur von 1700 bis 1878. Neu bearb. von E. Preuss. Leipzig, Engelmann, 1880-82. 2v.

V.1 *Scriptores graeci.* 1880. vii,802p.

V.2 *Scriptores latini.* 1882. iv,771p.

Standard bibliography of works of classical authors, translations, and works about those authors. Continued in:
Class No: 870(01)

[8479]

—KLUSSMAN, B. Bibliotheca scriptorum classicorum et graecorum et latinorum. Die Literatur von 1878 bis 1896 einschliesslich umfassend. Leipzig, Riesland, 1909-13. 2v. in 4.

Similar arrangement to Engelmann, with separate vols. for Greek and Latin literature. *Class No:* 870(01)

[8480]

—LAMBRINO, S. Bibliographie de l'antiquité classique, 1896-1914. Premier partie: Auteurs et textes. Paris, Belles Lettres, 1951. xvi,761p. ISBN: 2251903003.

Follows Klussmann chronologically with the same arrangement as Marouzeau's first vol. (*q.v.*), listing *c.*30,000 editions, translations and critical studies. A second vol. was to have covered *Matières et disciplines.* Not restricted to literature, but covers all aspects of Greek and Latin culture. *Class No:* 870(01)

[8481]

—MAROUZEAU, J. Dix années de bibliographie classique. Bibliographie critique et analytique de l'antiquité gréco-latine pour la période 1914-24. Paris, Belles Lettres, 1927-28 (repr. New York, Franklin, 1969). 2v. (xvi,1286p.). ISBN: 0833722441.

V.1 *Auteurs et textes.* V.2 *Matières et disciplines.*

Follows Lambrino and has similarly wide coverage. For publications after 1924, see *L'Année philologique.*
Class No: 870(01)

[8482]

GWINUP, T. *and* **DICKINSON, F. Greek and Roman authors:** a checklist of criticism. 2nd ed. Metuchen, N.J., Scarecrow, 1982. xii,280p. ISBN: 0810815281.

1st ed. 1973.

Lists nearly 4,000 critical works (books and periodical articles) in English on 70 writers, with the emphasis on recent publications. One A-Z sequence of Classical authors, further divided by general criticism and criticism of specific works. Bibliography of general works on Classical literature (11p.). *Class No:* 870(01)

[8483]

Lustrum: internationale Forschungsberichte aus dem Bereich des klassischen Altertums, 1956-. Göttingen, Vandenhoeck & Ruprecht, 1957-. v.1-. Annual. ISSN: 00247421.

Contains extensive subject bibliographies. V.34, *1992* (1994. 390p.) largely consists of a bibliography of Plato, 1985-90, listing over 1,500 critical studies, editions, translations and commentaries, with a detailed subject index. Also has addenda to earlier Plato bibliographies covering 1950-57, 1958-75, 1975-80 and 1980-85. *Class No:* 870(01)

[8484]

SIENKEWICZ, T.J. The Classic epic: an annotated bibliography. Englewood Cliffs, N.J., Salem Press, 1991 (later Scarecrow Press). 265p. $40. (*Magill bibliographies.*) ISBN: 0810828111.

A selective list of source materials for the study of the epic, including material on the historical background; biographies; plot summaries; character studies; and analyses of individual works and passages. Limited to books and chapters, with periodical articles excluded. Author index.
Class No: 870(01)

[8485]

WHITAKER, G. A Bibliographical guide to classical studies. Hildesheim & New York, Olms-Weidmann, 1997- . v.1- (in progress)

A classified listing of monographs, published 1873-1980, which is expected to run to 9 vols. The first 2 vols. have 6,532 entries covering general material, literary studies, and authors from Accius to Fulgentius. The descriptive entries include contents listings and cross-references, but no evaluation. Vols. 3 and 4 will cover more authors, v. 5 will cover language, vols. 6 and 7 will deal with a range of subjects including art, music, politics and philosophy. The final vol. will list periodicals and include indexes to the set.
Class No: 870(01)

Encyclopaedias & Dictionaries

[8486]

FEDER, L. The Handbook of classical literature. London, Barker; New York, Crowell, 1964. viii,448p. maps.

US title is *Crowell's handbook of classical literature.*

A single A-Z sequence of over 900 entries for authors, works, and mythological and historical people and places. Entries for literary works (*e.g.* 24p. on *The Iliad*) include list of translations, background (historical, religious, social and mythical), synopsis, and commentary. *Class No:* 870(03)

[8487]

The Oxford companion to classical literature. Howatson, M.C., *ed.* 2nd ed. Oxford, Oxford Univ. Press, 1989. vii,615p. maps. £30. ISBN: 0198661215.

1st ed. 1937, by Sir P. Harvey.

A long-awaited revision and expansion of Harvey's work, which no longer assumes a knowledge of Greek and Latin on the part of the reader. Approx. 3,000 entries covering authors, works, characters, literary forms and the historical, political and religious background basic to an understanding of the classics. Ample cross-references. Chronological table of historical and literary events from 2200BC to AD529. 6 maps.

The Concise Oxford companion to classical literature, ed. by Howatson and I. Chilvers (1993. 582p. £9.99. ISBN: 0192827081) has accounts of the lives and works of key authors, plot summaries, entries on genres and major characters, and some background information. With translations of all Greek and Latin words, it is ideal for school libraries. *Class No:* 870(03)

[8488]

WELLINGTON, J.S. Dictionary of bibliographic abbreviations found in the scholarship of classical studies and related disciplines. Westport, Conn., Greenwood, 1983. xv,393p. $85. ISBN: 0313235236.

Lists *c.*11,000 abbreviations of journals, series, and standard works met in all areas of classical studies. One A-Z list, plus separate lists for Cyrillic and Greek characters, with references to a separate section which has bibliographic details of all the works listed. *Class No:* 870(03)

Handbooks & Manuals

[8489]

JENKINS, F.W. Classical studies: a guide to the reference literature. Englewood, Colo., Libraries Unlimited, 1996. ix,263p. $43. (*Reference sources in the humanities.*) ISBN: 1563081105.

Lists and evaluates over 700 information sources across the whole field of classical studies and contains much of interest to literary researchers. Part 1, Bibliographical Resources, has chapters on general bibliographies; indexes and abstracts; review journals; topical bibliographies; bibliographies of 39 individual writers; and library catalogues. Part 2, Information Resources, has chapters on general and specialized dictionaries; biographical sources; geographical sources; Greek and Latin language; primary sources in translation; periodicals; directories; and Internet resources. Part 3, Organizations, lists research centres and professional associations. Detailed contents table. Author/title and subject indexes. 'A wonderful reference and collection development tool' (*Booklist*, v.92(17), May 1996, p.1520). *Class No:* 870(035)

Theses

[8490]

Bulletin of the Institute of Classical Studies. London, the Institute, 1954-. Annual. ISSN: 00760730.

Regularly carries information on research in progress for higher degrees in classical studies at universities in Great Britain and Ireland. *Class No:* 870(043)

[8491]

Catalogus dissertationum philologicarum classicarum. Zusammengestellt von der Zentralstelle für Dissertationen und Programme der Buchhandlung Gustav Fock. Editio 2. et 3. Leipzig, Fock, 1910-37 (repr. New York, Johnson Reprint Corp., 1963). iii+652+176p.

A facsimile reprint of the 2nd ed., listing *c.*27,400 studies on classical philology and archaeology, and the 3rd ed., which lists commentaries on Greek and Latin literature, 1911-36, plus a selection of earlier material. Index of names. *Class No:* 870(043)

[8492]

THOMPSON, L.S. Bibliography of dissertations in classical studies. Hamden, Conn., Shoe String Press, 1976. viii,296p. ISBN: 0208014578.

Updates *A Bibliography of American doctoral dissertations in classical studies and related fields* (1968).

Covers American doctoral theses, 1964-72, and British masters and doctoral theses, 1950-72. Cumulative index to this and earlier vol. *Class No:* 870(043)

Reviews & Abstracts

[8493]

The Classical review. Oxford, Oxford Univ. Press, for the Classical Association, 1887-. 2py. ISSN: 0009840x.

Publishes lengthy reviews of new publications from all countries on classical studies. V.46(2), 1996, of the new series (v.111 of full series) carries reviews of over 100 books, concise notices of a further 40, and a list of over 400 books received. General index and index locorum.

Indexes to the first series and to vols. 1-36 of the new series are available from The Classical Association. *Class No:* 870(048)

Histories

[8494]

DIHLE, A. Greek and Latin literature of the Roman Empire, from Augustus to Justinian. Malzahn, M., *trans.* London, Routledge, 1994. vii,647p. £50. ISBN: 0415063671.

German ed. originally published München, Beck, 1989.

A detailed, narrative history in 7 chronological sections, comprising 59 chapters with numbered subsections. Bibliography lists 604 critical studies. Index. *Class No:* 870(091)

[8495]

PFEIFFER, R. History of classical scholarship. Oxford, Clarendon Press, 1968-76. 2v.

V.1 *From the beginnings to the end of the Hellenistic Age.* 1968. xviii,311p. £35. ISBN: 0198143427.

V.2 *From 1300 to 1850.* 1976. ix,214p. £42. ISBN: 0198143648.

A narrative survey of the field, with many footnote bibliographical references. Index in each vol. A third vol., bringing the history in to the 20th century, has yet to appear. *Class No:* 870(091)

[8496]

SANDYS, J.E. History of classical scholarship. Cambridge, Cambridge Univ. Press, 1903-8. 3v. (1629p.).

V.1 *From the sixth century BC to the end of the Middle Ages.* 1903 (2nd ed. 1906; 3rd ed. 1921).

V.2 *From the revival of learning to the end of the eighteenth century in Italy, France, England and the Netherlands.* 1908.

V.3 *The Eighteenth century in Germany and the nineteenth century in Europe and the United States of America.* 1908.

'Even though out of date in many respects, this standard work will always remain an indispensable reference book ... a catalogue of classical scholars, century by century, nation by nation, and book by book' (Pfeiffer, R. *History of classical scholarship,* v.1, p.viii). *Class No:* 870(091)

[8497]

WILAMOWITZ-MOELLENDORFF, U. von. History of classical scholarship. Lloyd-Jones, H., *ed.* London, Duckworth, 1982. xxxii,189p. £25. ISBN: 0715609769.

Originally published as *Geschichte der Philologie* (Teubner Verlag, 1921; rev. ed. 1927).

An English translation by A. Harris of the standard short history of the subject, with additional notes by H. Lloyd-Jones which explain allusions, correct factual errors, and mention relevant modern works. Numerous footnote references plus select bibliography (3p.). Index. *Class No:* 870(091)

Biographies

[8498]

Ancient writers: Greece and Rome. Luce, T.J., *ed.* New York, Scribner's, 1982. 2v. (1148p.). $130. ISBN: 0684165953.

47 essays by 46 specialists on over 50 writers (either individually or in pairs) arranged chronologically, v.1 covering Homer to Caesar and v.2 Lucretius to Ammianus Marcellinus. Essays include biographical information but primarily assess the subject's contemporary impact and historic significance. Each has bibliography of texts, translations, commentaries and critical studies. Chronological table. Index in v.2.

Also included on *The Scribner writers series on CD-ROM* (*q.v.*). *Class No:* 870(092)

[8499]

Classical scholarship: a biographical encyclopedia. Briggs, W.W. *and* Calder, W.M., *eds.* New York, Garland, 1990. xxiv,534p. illus. $80. ISBN: 0824084489.

Signed biographical essays (average 10-11p.) on 50 influential scholars, A-Z, with a picture of each and primary and secondary bibliographies. Chronological list of scholars by birth-date, 1729-1908. 43 contributors. *Class No:* 870(092)

[8500]

—Biographical dictionary of North American classicists. Briggs, W.W., *ed.* Westport, Conn., Greenwood, 1994. 880p. $115. ISBN: 0313245606.

Profiles of *c.*600 scholars, including basic biographical and professional information, narrative career summary and bibliography. Lengthy essays on the history of classical scholarship in the US and Canada precede the biographical entries. Appended chronological table and general bibliography. Index. Excludes archaeologists. *Class No:* 870(092)

[8501]

GRANT, M. Greek and Latin authors, 800BC-AD1000. New York, Wilson, 1980. xiv,490p. illus. $68. ISBN: 0824206401.

A biographical dictionary with entries for 376 authors, giving an account of the life, description of and commentary on the works, discussion of the writer's influence on later works, and select bibliography of editions, translations and studies. Appendix A. lists 16 works of doubtful attribution. Appendix B. groups authors by century. *Class No:* 870(092)

Classical Literature in Translation

[8502]

The Greek and Latin literatures. Parks, G.B. *and* Temple, R.Z., *eds.* New York, Ungar, 1968. xix,442p. (*The Literatures of the world in English translation.*)

Aims 'to list all translations of reasonable length, even early ones', including all forms of literature, 'both imaginative literature (belles lettres) together with its history and criticism, and the literature of thought' (*Plan of the book*). Main sections deal with Greek and Latin literatures in periods, sub-divided by authors A-Z. Includes general background material, and also Byzantine, neo-Latin and modern authors translated into French, German and Spanish, as well as into English. Index of authors and anonymous works, but not of editors and translators. *Class No:* 870-03

[8503]

GREEN, A.M.W. Classics in translation: a selective bibliography, 1930-76. 2nd ed. Cardiff, Univ. College, Dept. of Classics, 1976. 48p. ISBN: 0901426695.

1st ed. 1974.

Covers Greek literature to AD300 and Latin to AD450, listing translations published since 1930, but is highly selective. For earlier translations, see F.S. Smith. *Class No:* 870-03

[8504]

SMITH, F.S. The Classics in translation: an annotated guide to the best translations of the Greek and Latin classics into English. London and New York, Scribner, 1930 (repr. New York, Franklin, 1968). 307p. ISBN: 0833732951.

'No Greek or Latin author has been omitted whose name appears in the standard literary histories and whose works have been translated into English' (*Introduction*). Translations published up to 1929 are included. Asterisks and double asterisks provide some evaluation; the occasional annotations are usually quotations. *Class No:* 870-03

Classical Drama

[8505]

FORMAN, R.J. Classical Greek and Roman drama: an annotated bibliography. Englewood Cliffs, N.J., Salem Press, 1989. 239p. $40. ISBN: 0893566594.

General section followed by chapters on 9 individual dramatists in which translations, commentaries and critical studies are listed. Index of authors and editors. 'A worthwhile reference source for anyone who deals with this subject matter at a basic level' (*Choice,* v.27(9), May 1990, p.1472-4). *Class No:* 870-2

[8506]
HARSH, P.W. A Handbook of classical drama. Stanford, Calif., Stanford Univ. Press; London, Oxford Univ. Press, 1944. xii,526p. $62.50. ISBN: 0804703809.

In 5 sections (1. Greek tragedy - 2. Old comedy - 3. New comedy - 4. Roman comedy - 5. Roman tragedy), with the more important plays treated in some detail under author headings. A critical discussion follows the factual material and is concerned primarily with dramatic technique. It is assumed that the reader is well acquainted with the play. An extensive bibliography (p.497-511) lists texts in the original language and in English translation. Recommended translations are starred. Bibliographies, histories and critical studies of classical drama also listed. Thorough index. *Class No:* 870-2

[8507]
HATHORN, R.Y. The Handbook of classical drama. New York, Crowell; London, Barker, 1967. 350p. maps.

Over 2,000 entries, in a single A-Z sequence, for dramatists, individual plays, dramatic forms and terms, and for real and mythological characters and places mentioned in the plays. Entries for plays include details of translations, notes on history and scenes, plot summary, and brief commentary. *Class No:* 870-2

Latin Literature

Databases

[8508]
Patrologia latina database. Cambridge, Chadwyck-Healey, 1994-5. 5 CD-ROMs. £27,000.

An ambitious project which will make available the complete text (including prefatory material and critical apparatus) of the *Patrologia latina* compiled by the 19th-century ecclesiastical publisher, Jacques-Paul Migne. It comprises 217 quarto vols. of texts and 4 vols. of indexes, all major and minor Latin authors are included, and their works cover theology, philosophy, history and literature. Can be searched on any word or combination of words, and searches can be made across the entire database or restricted to a single author or work, or any group of these. Published in 5 releases, with the final one due Nov. 1995. Detailed user manual suplied. *Class No:* 871(003.4)

Bibliographies

[8509]
QUELLET, H. Bibliographia indicum, lexicorum et concordantiarum auctorum Latinorum / Répertoire bibliographique des index, lexiques et concordances des auteurs latins. Hildesheim, G. Olms, 1980. xiii,262p. ISBN: 3487070146.

Nearly 1,100 annotated entries for concordances and indexes, arranged A-Z by Latin author, then chronologically. *Class No:* 871(01)

[8510]
SCHWEIGER, F.L. Handbuch der classischen Bibliographie. Reprint of 1834 ed. Bryn Mawr, Pa., Scholasticus Press, 1993. 1350p. $175.

Originally published Leipzig, 1834.

An important source of information on Latin classics, listing almost every edition published from the first printed books to 1830. Describes collected editions, individual works and translations into German, French, English and Scandinavian languages. *Class No:* 871(01)

Histories

[8511]
ALBRECHT, M. von. Geschichte der römischen Literatur: von Andronicus bis Boëthius, mit Berücksichtigung ihrer Bedeutung für die Neuzeit. 2. Aufl. München, Saur, 1994. 2v. DM.248. ISBN: 3598111983.

1st ed. Bern, Francke, 1992.

4 lengthy chapters on periods, with sections on poetry and prose and subsections on individual authors. Extensive bibliographies throughout. List of abbreviations for cited books and periodicals (22p.). Index of names and subjects. Superbly organized throughout. *Class No:* 871(091)

[8512]
The Cambridge history of Classical literature, vol.2: Latin literature. Kenney, E.J. *and* Clausen, W.V., *eds.* Cambridge, Cambridge Univ. Press, 1982. xviii,973p. plates. £90. ISBN: 0521210437.

42 signed chapters arranged in 7 parts: Readers and Critics; Early Republic; Late Republic; The Age of Augustus; Early Principate; Later Principate; Epilogue. The essays concentrate on discussion of the literary texts, with material relating to biography, chronology and bibliography presented mainly in the very thorough 'Appendix of Authors and Works' (137p.). Another appendix (4p.) covers metrics. Bibliography of works cited in the text (19p.). Index. *Class No:* 871(091)

[8513]
CONTE, G.B. Latin literature: a history. Fowler, D.P. *and* Most, G.W., *eds.* Baltimore, Md., Johns Hopkins Univ. Press, 1994. 896p. £45. ISBN: 0801846382.

First published 1987; trans. by J.B. Solodow.

Covers a 1,000-year period from the origins of Latin as a written language to the early Middle Ages, in 5 main parts: 1. The Early and Middle Republics - 2. The Late Republic - 3. The Age of Augustus - 4. The Early Empire - 5. The Late Empire. Separate sections on all the major writers. Updated bibliographies after each chapter. Chronological tables of both Greek and Roman history and culture. Glossary of rhetorical terms. 'This excellent volume should easily eclipse any of the standard histories of Latin literature now in print' (*Choice*, v.32(3), Nov. 1994, p.448). *Class No:* 871(091)

[8514]
SCHANZ, M. Geschichte der römischen Literatur, bis zum Gesetzgebungswerk des Kaisers Justinian. Hosius, C., *ed.* München, Beck, 1914-35. 4v. in 5.

V.1 *Die römische Literatur in der Zeit der Republik.* 4.Aufl. xiv,654p.

V.2 *Die römische Literatur in der Zeit der Monarchie bis auf Hadrian.* 4.Aufl. xvii,886p.

V.3 *Die Zeit von Hadrian 117 bis auf Constantin 324.* 3.Aufl. xvi,473p.

V.4 *Die römische Literatur von Constantin bis zum Gesetzgebungswerk Justinians.* 2.Aufl. 1914-20. 2 pts. (xv,572p.; xvi,681p.).

The standard history, going up to the 6th century. Detailed and well documented. Index to complete work in v.4. *Class No:* 871(091)

Mediaeval Latin Literature

Bibliographies

[8515]

Catalogus translationum et commentariorum; Medieval and Renaissance Latin translations and commentaries: annotated lists and guides. Kristeller, P.O., *and others, eds.* Washington, D.C., Catholic Univ. of America Press, 1960-92. v.1-7 (in progress).

Aims to 'list and describe the Latin translations of ancient Greek authors and the Latin commentaries on ancient Latin (and Greek) authors up to the year 1600' (*Preface*). V.1 has a bibliography of general reference works and catalogues of printed editions and manuscripts, and a list of extant Greek and Latin authors (76p.). Thereafter, the work consists of signed articles by specialists on individual authors in no particular order. These can be lengthy, *e.g.* v.7 (1992. xxi,356p.) covers only 5 authors (4 Greek, 1 Latin) in 292p. V.7 also has indexes of manuscripts and of translators and commentators for that vol., plus index of ancient authors treated in vols.1-7 and contents tables for each vol.
Class No: 871-023(01)

[8516]

LAPIDGE, M. *and* **SHARPE, R. A Bibliography of Celtic-Latin literature, 400-1200.** Dublin, Royal Irish Academy, 1985. xii,361p. £19.50. ISBN: 0901714437.

An attempt to list all Latin texts which were composed in Celtic-speaking areas or by native Celtic speakers during the period 400-1200. 1,317 entries in 7 sections: 5 geographical and 2 for authors of possible or disputed Celtic origin. Each section has separate A-Z sequences for named authors and anonymous titles, and entries give bibliographical details of manuscripts, printed editions, listings in reference works, and comments in secondary literature. Index.
Class No: 871-023(01)

Encyclopaedias & Dictionaries

[8517]

IJSEWIJN, J. Companion to neo-Latin studies, pt.1: History and diffusion of neo-Latin literature. New ed. Leuven-Louvain, Leuven Univ. Press & Peeters Press, 1990. xii,370p. ISBN: 906186366x, Leuven; 9068312243, Peeters.

1st ed. Amsterdam and Oxford, North-Holland, 1977, in 1 vol.

Covers 'all writings in Latin since the dawn of humanism in Italy from about 1300AD down to our own time' (*Preface*). Sections on over 30 countries and regions, with bibliographies. 5 indexes, including names, places, genres and themes. A second vol. will 'discuss divers genres, linguistic, stylistic, metrical, editorial, and bibliographical problems' and will include bibliographies of individual authors. *Class No:* 871-023(03)

Handbooks & Manuals

[8518]

Medieval Latin: an introduction and bibliographical guide. Mantello, F.A.C. *and* Rigg, A.G., *eds.* Baltimore, Md., Catholic Univ. of America Press, 1996. xiv,774p. $54.95. ISBN: 0813208416.

See entry at 807.33(035). *Class No:* 871-023(035)

Histories

[8519]

BRUNHÖLZL, F. Geschichte der lateinischen Literatur des Mittelalters. München, Fink, 1975-90. 2v.

V.1 *Von Cassiodor bis zum Ausklang der karolingischen Erneuerung*. 1975. x,594p. ISBN: 3770511131.

V.2 *Die Zwischenzeit vom Ausgang des karolingischen Zeitalters bis zur Mitte des elften Jahrhunderts.* 1992. 672p. ISBN: 3770526147.

A scholarly history with extensive bibliographies (70p. in v.1) and indexes. *Class No:* 871-023(091)

[8520]

LAPIDGE, M. Anglo-Latin literature, 900-1066. London, Hambledon Press, 1993. xiv,506p. illus. £45. ISBN: 1852850124.

A collection of 16 essays from earlier publications. Much bibliographical data provided in footnotes, with additional notes appended (23p.) to update the information. Quotations in Latin. Index.

Lapidge's *Anglo-Latin literature, 600-899* (London, Hambleton Press, 1997. 520p. £45. ISBN: 1852850116) has 17 essays and is similarly organized. *Class No:* 871-023(091)

[8521]

MANITIUS, M. Geschichte der lateinischen Literatur des Mittelalters. München, Beck, 1911-31. 3v.

V.1 *Von Justinian bis zur Mitte des zehnten Jahrhunderts.* 1911.

V.2 *Von der Mitte des zehnten Jahrhunderts bis zum Ausbruch des Kampfes zwischen Kirche und Staat.* 1923.

V.3 *Vom Ausbruch des Kirchenstreites bis zum Ende des zwölften Jahrhunderts.* 1931.

The standard history for the medieval period, following on from Schanz's *Geschichte der römischen Literatur* (*q.v.*). Each volume is closely sub-divided, with subsection bibliographies; copious footnotes; chronology. Detailed, analytical index to each volume; v.3 has indexes of geographical names and index of personal names and subjects. *Class No:* 871-023(091)

[8522]

RIGG, A.G. A History of Anglo-Latin literature, 1066-1422. Cambridge, Cambridge Univ. Press, 1992. xviii,414p. £70. ISBN: 0521415942.

A chronological history with quotations in Latin with English translations in verse or prose. Anglo-Latin metres are explained and exemplified in an Appendix.
Class No: 871-023(091)

Latin Poetry

Catullus

[8523]

HOLOKA, J.P. Gaius Valerius Catullus: a systematic bibliography. New York, Garland, 1985. xx,324p. $68. ISBN: 0824088972.

Classified arrangement, with over 3,000 entries for items published 1878-1981. Author index. *Class No:* 871-1CAT

[8524]

McCARREN, V.P. A Critical concordance to Catullus. Leiden, Brill, 1977. 210p. ISBN: 9004052240.

A computer-produced keyword-in-context concordance based on R.A.B. Mynors' ed. (1958) in the 'Oxford Classical Texts' series, but including variant readings.
Class No: 871-1CAT

Horace

[8525]

ECHEGOYEN, J.-J.I. Concordantia Horatiana / A Concordance to Horace. Hildesheim and New York, Olms-Wiedmann, 1990. iv,594p. $128.70. ISBN: 3487093626.

Based on the Shackleton Bailey edition (Stuttgart, Teubner, 1985) and uses the keyword-in-context format which has become standard after Packard's *Concordance of Livy* (*q.v.*). *Class No:* 871-1HOR

Lucretius

[8526]

GORDON, C.A. A Bibliography of Lucretius. 2nd ed. Winchester, St. Paul's Bibliographies, 1985. vii,323p. illus. ISBN: 0906795060.

1st ed. London, Hart-Davis, 1962. 2nd ed. is a reprint of the author's annotated copy with the addition of an introduction (7p.) and bibliographical notes (2p.) by E.J. Kenney.

1. Text editions - 2. Annotated editions - 3. Pocket editions - 4. Translations (23 languages) - 5. Illustrated editions - 6. Selections and extracts - 7. Ghosts. European and American library locations. Appendices include list of 49 manuscripts. Chronological list of editions and translations. Index. *Class No:* 871-1LUC

Ovid

[8527]

DEFERRARI, R.J., *and others*. A Concordance of Ovid. Washington, D.C., Catholic Univ. of America Press, 1939 (repr. Hildesheim, G. Olms, 1968). ix,2220p. ISBN: 0317938541.

A massive compilation, combining concordance and index verborum, based exclusively on the Teubner ed. of Ovid (1911-32). *Class No:* 871-1OVI

[8528]

PARATORE, E. Bibliografia Ovidiana. Sulmona, Comitato per le Celebrazioni del Bimillenario, 1958. 169p.

About 2,500 entries, arranged chronologically within separate sections for incunabula, editions, translations, dissertations, critical studies, articles and dictionaries. No index. *Class No:* 871-1OVI

Vergil

[8529]

Enciclopedia virgiliana. Della Corte, F., *ed.* Roma, Istituto della Enciclopedia Italiana, 1984-90. 5v. illus.

A lavishly illustrated reference work modelled on the superb *Enciclopedia dantesca* (*q.v.*), with a single A-Z sequence of lengthy, signed articles (*c.*1,000 per vol.) on words encountered in Vergil's works (not the complete vocabulary, but the more important words culturally, historically and poetically) and on people and places (real and fictitious) associated with Vergil. The entries contain detailed references to the works and most have extensive bibliographies. Numerous contributors. *Class No:* 871-1VER

[8530]

WARWICK, H.H. A Vergil concordance. Minneapolis, Univ. of Minnesota Press, 1975. 982p. ISBN: 0816607370.

A keyword-in-context concordance based on R.A.B. Mynors' 'Oxford Classical Texts' edition (Oxford, Clarendon Press, 1969).

For a modern computer-generated concordance, see *Concordantia Vergiliana* ed. by M. Wacht (Hildesheim, Olms, 1996. 2v. DM298. ISBN: 3487098482). *Class No:* 871-1VER

Latin Drama

Terence

[8531]

McGLYNN, P. Lexicon Terentianum. London, Blackie, 1963-67. 2v. (xvi,455p.; x,315p.).

Records and sets in context every example of every word in the six plays and notes manuscript variants. Includes explanatory notes from ancient and modern commentators and conjectures from learned periodicals. Scholarly and well-produced. Entirely in Latin. *Class No:* 871-2TER

Latin Prose

Cicero

[8532]

ABBOTT, K.M., *and others*. Index verborum in Ciceronis Rhetorica; necnon incerti auctoris libros Ad Herennium. Urbana, Ill., Univ. of Illinois Press, 1964. xxi,1160p.

Based on the editions of Cicero's *Rhetorica* by A.S. Wilkins, *De inventione* by E. Stroebel, and *Ad Herennium* (2nd ed.) by F. Marx. Also includes bibliography of critical materials (6p.). *Class No:* 871-3CIC

[8533]

OLDFATHER, W.A., *and others*. Index verborum Ciceronis Epistularum. Urbana, Ill., Univ. of Illinois Press, 1938. 583p.

Index to *Epistulae*, based on L.C. Purser's 'Oxford Classical Texts' edition (1901-3). *Class No:* 871-3CIC

[8534]

SPAETH, J.W. Index verborum Ciceronis Poeticorum fragmentorum. Urbana, Ill., Univ. of Illinois Press, 1955. vii,130p.

Based on Baehrens' text of the verse fragments, contained in his *Poetae Latini minores* (v.1, 1879) and *Fragmenta poetarum Romanorum* (1886). *Class No:* 871-3CIC

Livy

[8535]

PACKARD, D.W. A Concordance to Livy. Cambridge, Mass., Harvard Univ. Press; London, Oxford Univ. Press, 1968. 4v. (5400p.). $275. ISBN: 0674158903, US.

Computer-produced keyword-in-context index of 505,000 words. Based on printed texts (Oxford and Teubner) without including manuscript variants. *Class No:* 871-3LIV

Seneca

[8536]

MOTTO, A.L. *and* **CLARK, J.R. Seneca: a critical bibliography, 1900-1980:** scholarship on his life, thought, prose and influence. Amsterdam, Hakkert, 1989. 372p. ISBN: 9025609597.

1,759 annotated entries in 10 sections: 1. Bibliographies - 2. Indices and concordances - 3. Editions, translations and commentaries - 4. Manuscript studies - 5. Textual criticism - 6. Life, works and philosophy - 7. Studies of individual prose works - 8. Language and style - 9. Source studies - 10. Seneca's influence. Author index. *Class No:* 871-3SEN

Tacitus

[8537]

Concordantia Tacitea [A Concordance to Tacitus] Blackman, D.R. *and* Betts, G.G., *eds*. Hildesheim, Olms-Weidmann, 1986. 2v. (1923p.). ISBN: 3487077493.

A computer-produced keyword-in-context concordance, based on the Teubner editions of Tacitus. *Class No:* 871-3TAC

Greek Literature

Bibliographies

[8538]

KESSELS, A.H.M. *and* **VERDENIUS, W.J. A Concise bibliography of Greek language and literature.** Apeldoorn, Administratief Centrum, 1979. vi,287p.

The 1st English ed. of a Dutch bibliography first published 1953 and intended for teachers and students of classics.

A classified, unannotated bibliography in 31 sections covering topics and individual writers, for whom editions, indexes, and studies are listed. Index. *Class No:* 875(01)

[8539]

Thesaurus linguae graecae: canon of Greek authors and their works. Berkowitz, L. *and* Squitier, K.A., *eds*. 3rd ed. New York, Oxford Univ. Press, 1990. 544p. £37.99. ISBN: 0195060377.

1st ed. 1977; 2nd ed. 1986.

A register of all known ancient Greek works from Homer to AD400 as stored in the computerized database of the *Thesaurus linguae graecae*. The database, with *c*.61 million words of text from over 700 literary works, is available on a CD-ROM with the title *TLG CD-ROM 'C'* from Thesaurus Linguae Graecae Project in the US and L.I.S. Information in Europe. *Class No:* 875(01)

Handbooks & Manuals

[8540]

ROSE, H.J. A Handbook of Greek literature, from Homer to the Age of Lucian. Repr. of 4th ed. with minor corrections. London, Methuen; New York, Dutton, 1961. ix,458p. ISBN: 0416681905.

1st ed. 1934; 4th ed. 1951.

13 chapters on all aspects of Greek literature, except for Christian and Jewish literature. Detailed bibliographic references in footnotes plus general bibliography (6p.) of texts and studies. Index has all names in transliterated and Greek forms, with pronunciation indicated.
Class No: 875(035)

Histories

[8541]

The Cambridge history of Classical literature, vol 1: Greek literature. Easterling, P.E. *and* Knox, B.M.W., *eds*. Cambridge, Cambridge Univ. Press, 1985. xv,936p. plates. £90. ISBN: 0521210429.

21 chapters by several named scholars are arranged in broadly chronological order from Homer to the 3rd century A.D. As in the companion vol. on Latin literature (*qv*) these are followed by the 'Appendix of Authors and Works' (172p.), which provides biographical and bibliographical material on all the major writers. Further appendix on metrics (7p.) and bibliography of works cited in the text (19p.). Index. *Class No:* 875(091)

[8542]

CROISET, A. *and* **CROISET, M. Histoire de la littérature grecque.** 4th ed. Paris, 1928-47. 5v.

First published 1887-99. Vols.2-4 are photographic reproductions of vols.2-4 of 3rd ed.; v.5 is reproduction of v.5 of 1st ed.

V.1 *Homère. La Poésie cyclique. Hésiode.*

V.2 *Lyricisme. Premiers prosateurs. Hérodote.*

V.3 *Période attique. Tragédie. Comédie. Genres sécondaires.*

V.4 *Période attique. Éloquence. Histoire. Philosophie.*

V.5 *Période alexandrine. Période romaine.*

A detailed survey with copious footnotes. General index in v.5. Many bibliographies.

Abridged history of Greek literature, a translation by G.F. Heffelbower of a single-vol. work by Croiset and Croiset, is published by AMS Press ($32.50. ISBN: 0404018572). *Class No:* 875(091)

[8543]

DE ROMILLY, J. A Short history of Greek literature. Doherty, L., *trans*. Chicago, Univ. of Chicago Press, 1985. xii,293p. ISBN: 0226143112.

Originally published Paris, Presses Universitaires de France, 1980, as *Précis de littérature grecque*.

10 chronologically arranged chapters, with subsections on major writers. Chronology (18p.). Bibliography (23p) specially compiled for English ed., listing basic reference works, general studies, editions, translations, lexicons, and studies of individual writers and works. *Class No:* 875(091)

[8544]

DIHLE, A. A History of Greek literature, from Homer to the Hellenistic Period. Krojzl, C., *trans*. London, Routledge, 1994. x,332p. £40. ISBN: 0415086205.

German ed. originally published München, Beck, 1991.

A narrative history in 25 chapters forming 4 main sections: 1. Archaic literature - 2. Classical literature of the 5th century B.C. - 3. Classical literature of the 4th century B.C. - 4. Hellenistic literature. Bibliographical notes arranged by chapter (12p.). Index. *Class No:* 875(091)

[8545]

LESKY, A. A History of Greek literature. 2nd ed., trans. by J. Willis and C. de Heer. London, Methuen, 1966; New York, Crowell, 1976 (repr. London, Duckworth, 1997). xxiii,921p. £25. ISBN: 0715627619.

1st ed. Bern, Francke, 1957-8, as *Geschichte der griechischen Literatur;* 2nd ed. 1963.

A comprehensive, scholarly history from the beginnings to the Empire in 7 chapters, with numerous subsections for genres and individual writers. Many footnote references,

....*(contd.)*
with thorough bibliographies for each subsection. Index. Omits Christian and Jewish Greek literature.
Class No: 875(091)

[8546]
SCHMID, W. *and* **STÄHLIN, O. Geschichte der griechischen Literatur.** München, Beck, 1929-48. 1v. (5 pts.).
V.1, covering the classical period, replaces v.1 of *Geschichte der griechischen Literatur* by Wilhelm von Christ (6th ed., 1912-24, 2v. in 3). A detailed and well-documented survey.
V.2 of von Christ's *Geschichte,* on the post-classical period up to AD530, is still authoritative.
Class No: 875(091)

Biographies

[8547]
Dictionary of literary biography. Detroit, Gale, 1978-98. v.1-188 (in progress). £112 per vol.
The following vol. covers Greek literature:
V.176 *Ancient Greek authors*, ed. by W.W. Briggs. 1997.
For a description of the series, see entry at 82(092).
Class No: 875(092)

Greek Literature in Translation

[8548]
FOSTER, F.M.K. English translations from the Greek: a bibliographical survey. New York, Columbia Univ. Press, 1918 (repr. New York, AMS Press). xxix,146p. $15. ISBN: 0404025412.
Lists English and American translations, 1476-1917, under the original authors, A-Z. Index of translators.
Class No: 875-03

Greek Poetry

[8549]
FATOUROS, G. Index verborum zu frühgriechischen Lyrik. Heidelberg, Winter, 1966. xxii,415p.
Includes Anacreon, Sappho and Pindar. Texts used: Diehl, E. *Anthologia lyrica graeca* (Leipzig, 1954); Loebel, E., and Page, D. *Poetarum Lesbiorum fragmenta* (Oxford, 1955); *Poetae melici Graeci,* edited by D.L. Page (Oxford, 1962), etc. *Class No:* 875-1

[8550]
TRYPANIS, C.A. Greek poetry from Homer to Seferis. London, Faber, 1981; Chicago, Univ. of Chicago Press, 1982. 896p. $50. ISBN: 0571083463, UK; 0226813169, US.
A comprehensive survey of ancient and modern Greek poetry in 5 parts and 28 chapters, with subsections on numerous individual poets and types of poetry. Notes, p.705-786. Extensive classified bibliography (p.789-885) of texts, anthologies and studies. Index of poets.
Class No: 875-1

Homer

[8551]
AUTENREITH, G. Homeric dictionary. Keep, R.P., *tr.* Reprint of 1896 ed. London, Macmillan, 1896 (repr. London, Duckworth, 1994). 368p. illus. £10.95. ISBN: 0715617737.
Originally published in German. English ed. first published London, Macmillan, 1896, as *An Homeric dictionary for use in colleges and schools*.
Based on the small Teubner ed. of the *Iliad* and *Odyssey,* edited by Dindorf. Interspersed with line drawings.
Class No: 875-1HOM

[8552]
DUNBAR, H. A Complete concordance to the Odyssey and Hymns of Homer. Marzullo, B., *ed.* New ed., completely rev. and enl. Hildesheim, G. Olms, 1962. 398p.
1st ed. Oxford, Clarendon Press, 1880.
Compiled from Ameis's ed. of the *Odyssey* (1874) and from Baumeister's ed. of *Hymns, Epigrams, etc., commonly attributed to Homer* (1874).
Olms published a computer concordance by J.R. Tebben to the van Thiel ed. of the *Odyssey* in 1994, under the title *Concordantia Homerica I: Odyssea* (2v. DM248. ISBN: 3487097834). *Class No:* 875-1HOM

[8553]
PACKARD, D.W. *and* **MEYERS, T. A Bibliography of Homeric scholarship:** preliminary edition, 1930-1970. Malibu, Calif., Undena, 1974. vi,183p. ISBN: 0890030057.
A cumulation of the yearly listings for Homer in *L'Année philologique* (*q.v.*), with many of the entries corrected or expanded. *c.*3,750 entries in one author sequence, with a detailed subject index which includes Homeric words and specific passages from the *Iliad* and *Odyssey*.
Class No: 875-1HOM

[8554]
PRENDERGAST, G.L. A Complete concordance to the Iliad of Homer. Marzullo, B., *ed.* New ed., completely rev. and enl. Hildesheim, G. Olms, 1962. vii,427p.
1st ed. London, Longmans, Green, 1875.
Compiled from Priestley's ed. of Heyne's *Homer* (1834).
Class No: 875-1HOM

[8555]
WACE, A.J.B. *and* **STUBBINGS, F.H. A Companion to Homer.** London, Macmillan, 1962. xxix,595p. illus.
Part 1., 'The Homeric poems and their authorship', has 7 signed chapters on metre, style, language, etc. Part 2., 'The Picture and the record', has 16 chapters on the geographical, historical and cultural background to Homer's writing. Notes appended to chapters. Index of passages of Homer cited in the text; general index; index of Greek words. The work of 16 scholars. *Class No:* 875-1HOM

Pindar

[8556]
GERBER, D.E. A Bibliography of Pindar, 1513-1966. Cleveland, Ohio, the Press of Case Western Reserve Univ., for the American Philological Assoc., 1969. xv,160p.
Lists texts, translations and commentaries, plus critical studies. Arranged in 30 sections. No index. *Class No:* 875-1PIN

Greek Drama

[8557]
BROWN, A. A New companion to Greek tragedy. London, Croom Helm; New York, Barnes and Noble, 1983. 209p. illus. ISBN: 0709906609, UK; 0389203890, US.
An A-Z sequence of *c.*600 concise entries, covering all mythical and geographical names occurring in 15 major plays; technical terms used in the criticism of Greek tragedy;

....(contd.)
and relevant aspects of Greek life, religion and theatre. Select bibliography of English translations and critical studies. *Class No:* 875-2

[8558]
FERGUSON, J. A Companion to Greek tragedy. Austin, Tex., Univ. of Texas Press, 1972. xi,623p. ISBN: 0292710003.

General introduction to Greek theatre (25p.) followed by sections on Aeschylus, Sophocles and Euripides, including biographical sketch and analysis of the plays (average 12p. per play). Many quotations in translation. Glossary of Greek terms (3p.). Bibliography of general works on Greek theatre and of editions, translations, commentaries and studies of the individual dramatists and plays. Index. *Class No:* 875-2

Aeschylus

[8559]
ITALIE, G. Index Aeschyleus. Editio Altera, correcta et aucta, curavit S.L. Radt. Leiden, Brill, 1964. xii,345p.

1st ed. 1955.

Preface surveys previous indexes. Entries give contexts. Well produced. *Class No:* 875-2AES

[8560]
WARTELLE, A. Bibliographie historique et critique d'Eschyle et de la tragédie grecque, 1518-1974. Paris, Belles Lettres, 1978. xvi,685p. ISBN: 2251325735.

Chronologically arranged listing of editions and translations of Aeschylus, plus critical studies on him and general studies of Greek tragedy. Indexes of authors, subjects, editions and translations. *Class No:* 875-2AES

Aristophanes

[8561]
DUNBAR, H. A Complete concordance to the comedies and fragments of Aristophanes. New ed., completely rev. and enl. by B. Marzullo. Hildesheim and New York, G. Olms, 1973. 382p. ISBN: 348705017x.

1st ed. Oxford, Clarendon Press, 1883.

A reprint of the 1st ed. with marginal notes leading to corrections in an appendix (26p.). Introduction explains the methodology. Based on Dindorf's ed. of the comedies (Oxford, 1835) and Meineke's ed. of the fragments (Berlin, 1840). *Class No:* 875-2ARI

[8562]
TODD, O.J. Index Aristophaneus. Cambridge, Mass., Harvard Univ. Press, 1932 (repr. Hildesheim, G. Olms, 1962). ix,275p. ISBN: 3487054132.

Based on the text of F.W. Hall and W.M. Geldart (2nd ed., Oxford, Clarendon Press, 1906-7). Preface in Latin. Index of word forms; no contexts. *Class No:* 875-2ARI

Euripides

[8563]
ALLEN, J.T. *and* **ITALIE, G. A Concordance to Euripides.** Berkeley, Calif., Univ. of Caliornia Press; London, Cambridge Univ. Press, 1954. xi,686p.

Based 'upon the best texts from Kirchhoff's to those of Murray and of Méridier, Parmentier, and Grégoire' (*Introduction*). *Class No:* 875-2EUR

Sophocles

[8564]
ELLENDT, F.T. Lexicon Sophocleum, adhibitis veterum interpretum explicationibus, grammaticorum notationibus, recentiorum doctorum commentariis. Ed. altera emendata. Curavit Hermannus Genthe. Berlin, Borntraeger, 1874 (repr. Hildesheim, Olms, 1958). 812p.

1st ed. 1834-5 (2v.). An English version appeared in 1841 (Oxford) as *A Lexicon to Sophocles, principally abridged and translated from Ellendt.*

See also Ellendt's *Index commentationum Sophoclearum* ... (Berlin, Borntraeger, 1874. 134p.). *Class No:* 875-2SOP

Greek Prose

[8565]
The Greek novel, AD1-1985. Beaton, R., *ed.* London, Croom Helm, 1988. xi,229p. ISBN: 0709950934.

A survey in 3 parts arranged in reverse order (1. From Independence to the 1980s - 2. From the Middle Ages to the 18th century - 3. The Birth of the novel in Greek antiquity) and comprising 21 signed chapters by different specialists. Many quotations, mostly in translation. Notes and references appended to each chapter. Index. *Class No:* 875-3

Modern Greek Literature

Bibliographies

[8566]
PHILIPPIDES, D.M.L. Census of modern Greek literature: checklist of English-language sources useful in the study of modern Greek literature (1824-1987). New Haven, Conn., Modern Greek Studies Assoc., 1990. 248p. ISBN: 0912105011.

An unannotated, classified listing of translations, anthologies, bibliographies, periodicals, histories and critical studies. Includes works by and about individual authors. Index of authors, critics, editors and translators.
Class No: 877(01)

Histories

[8567]
BEATON, R. An Introduction to modern Greek literature. Oxford, Clarendon Press, 1994. xiii,426p. £42.50. ISBN: 0198158599.

Updates Dimaras and Politis (*qq.v.*), with good coverage of recent developments, including the establishment of demotic as Greece's official language, the increasing importance of popular music in literary culture, and the emergence of Marxist writers. 5 chronological chapters from 1821 to 1992 plus a final chapter on te modern Greek language. Quotations in Greek with translation by the author. Bibliographic notes (2p.). List of translations (6p.). References give full bibliographical details of all cited sources, primary and secondary (25p.). General index and index of Greek titles. Omits drama, but 'for the 19th and 20th centuries, and especially for post-war prose, ... will assuredly become a standard resource' (*TLS*, no.4780, Nov. 11, 1994, p.25).

Rev. paperback ed. due late 1998 (ISBN: 0198159749).
Class No: 877(091)

[8568]

DIMARAS, C. Th. A History of modern Greek literature. Albany, N.Y., State Univ. of New York Press; London, Univ. of London Press, 1972. xvii,539p. ISBN: 0340171790, UK.

Translation of 4th ed. of the standard Greek history.

From the 9th century to mid-20th century in 9 chapters, with 29 subsections, plus Supplement. Many quotations in English translation. Select bibliography (8p.). Index. 'Marred by an unsatisfactory translation, but still provides a useful overview' (Clogg, M.J. and Clogg, R., *Greece*, 1980, p.153). *Class No:* 877(091)

[8569]

POLITIS, L. A History of modern Greek literature. Oxford, Clarendon Press, 1973. xi,338p. ISBN: 0198157215.

Part 1 covers 11th to 18th centuries in 5 chapters; Part 2 covers 19th and 20th centuries in 12 chapters. Quotations in English in the text with originals in Appendix. Chronological tables of literary and historical events. Selected bibliography of general works, texts and critical studies (22p.). Index. *Class No:* 877(091)

88 Slavonic Literatures

Slavonic Literatures

Bibliographies

[8570]

The American bibliography of Slavic and East European studies, 1968/69-. Stanford, Calif. (formerly Columbus, Ohio), American Assoc. for the Advancement of Slavic Studies, 1974-. Annual. ISSN: 00943770.

See entry at 808.1(01). *Class No:* 880(01)

[8571]

European bibliography of Soviet, East European and Slavonic studies, v.1, 1975-. Armand, M., *and others, eds.* Birmingham, Univ. of Birmingham, 1977-79; Paris, Institut d'Études Slaves, 1981-. Annual. ISSN: 1259458x.

Covers the formerly Communist countries of Eastern Europe (excluding East Germany), with particular emphasis on the social sciences and arts, listing books, articles and scholarly reviews published in the UK, France, West Germany, Belgium, Austria, the Netherlands, Finland, and Switzerland. Arranged by country, then by subject, with numerous individual writers covered in the literature sections. Author index.

V.18, *1992* (1996. xxxvii,447p.), has 9,981 entries, of which over 1,700 relate to literature and over 400 to linguistics. List of *c.*1,700 periodicals searched.
Class No: 880(01)

[8572]

LEWANSKI, R.C. The Slavic literatures. New York, New York Public Library and Ungar, 1967. 630p. (*The Literatures of the world in English translation.*) ISBN: 0804431450.

Lists translations of Slavic belles-lettres either published separately or included in anthologies and periodicals up to 1960. Arranged by language, then by author, with a preliminary section on general anthologies. Index of authors and translated titles, but not of original titles.
Class No: 880(01)

[8573]

Slavic studies: a guide to bibliographies, encyclopedias, and handbooks. Croucher, M., *ed.* Wilmington, Del., Scholarly Resources, 1993. 2v. $150. ISBN: 0842023747.

See entry at 808.1(01). *Class No:* 880(01)

[8574]

TERRY, G.M. East European languages and literatures: a subject and name index to articles in English-language journals, 1900-77. Oxford and Santa Barbara, Calif., Clio, 1978. xxv,275p. £26.50. ISBN: 0903450216.

See entry at 808. *Class No:* 880(01)

[8575]

WYTRZENS, G. Bibliographische Einführung in das Studium der slavischen Literaturen. Frankfurt am Main, Klostermann, 1972. xii,348p.

Over 5,000 items in 106 sections. Three main parts: A. Literaturwissenschaft und Literaturgeschichte (1-22) - B. Hilfs- und Grenzwissenschaften (23-32) - C. Bibliographie (33-100). Supplement. Name index. Includes periodical articles, but publishers of books are not stated. Entries for outstanding items are asterisked. Comprehensive.

Supplemented by *Bibliographie der literarwissenschaftlichen Slawistik, 1970-80* (1982. 348p.), which adds a further 5,000 items. Both vols. cover all the Slavic literatures and include works in Western European and Slavic languages. *Class No:* 880(01)

Encyclopaedias & Dictionaries

[8576]

The Everyman companion to East European literature. Pynsent, R.B. *and* Kanikova, S.I., *eds.* London, Dent; New York, HarperCollins, 1993. xiv,605p. £25. ISBN: 046087201x, UK; 0062700073, US.

US title is *Reader's encyclopedia of East European literature.*

For the purposes of this major new reference work, 'Eastern Europe indicates those linguistic areas or nation-states which were or considered themselves oppressed by ... one of the four great European continental empires (Austrian, Prussian, Ottoman and Russian)' (*Preface*). Authors who wrote in the 'imperial' languages (German, Turkish, Russian) are therefore omitted, as are those (*e.g.* Conrad) who chose one of the Western languages as their medium of literary expression.

Main sequence has signed entries by 24 specialists (most of them British) on 800 writers, many of whom have never before been written about in English, giving biographical information and brief descriptions of their works. List of published English translations after each entry, plus advice on further reading which is limited to 3 items (in English, French, German or Italian) on a single author or work. A further sequence (45p.) has articles on anonymous, collective and oral-tradition texts (Bible, hagiography, etc.), each genre being subdivided by country. Particularly useful are brief histories (average 2½p.), of 22 literatures: Albanian, Armenian, Bulgarian, Byelorussian, Croatian, Czech, Estonian, Finnish, Georgian, Greek, Hungarian, Latvian, Lithuanian, Macedonian, Polish, Roumanian, Serbian, Slovak, Slovene, Sorbian, Ukrainian, and Yiddish. Lists of authors (with dates) by language. Index of anonymous works. General index of names and subjects.
Class No: 880(03)

Excerpts

[8577]

Modern Slavic literatures. Mihailovich, V.D., *and others, comps.* New York, Ungar, 1972-76. 2v. $65. (*A Library of literary criticism.*) ISBN: 0804431760.

V.1 *Russian literature* (xii,424p.). V.2 *Bulgarian, Czechoslovak, Polish, Ukrainian and Yugoslav literatures* (xvi,720p.).

V.1 has excerpts from criticism on 69 20th-century authors, arranged A-Z, concentrating on those whose work is available in translation. Criticism is arranged chronologically under each author and is mainly from the US and UK, with some Russian and European critics included.

V.2 covers 196 authors in separate sections (with different editors) for each literature. Most of the criticism excerpted is by Slavic scholars and is here translated for the first time, but there are also excerpts from English-language and European critics. A proposed section on Byelorussian literature had to be omitted for lack of critical material. Both vols. cover émigré authors. Index to critics in each vol.

Class No: 880(082.200)

Biographies

[8578]

Dictionary of literary biography. Detroit, Gale, 1978-98. v.1-188 (in progress). £112 per vol.

The following vols. cover Slavonic literature:

V.147 *South Slavic writers before World War II*, ed. by V.D. Mihailovich. 1994.

V.181 *South Slavic writers after World War II*, ed. by V.D. Mihailovich. 1997.

For a description of the series, see entry at 82(092).

Class No: 880(092)

Russian Literature

Bibliographies of Bibliographies

[8579]

KANDEL', B.L., *and others*. Russkaya khudozhestvennaya literatura i literaturovedenie: ukazatel' spravochno-bibliograficheskikh posobii s kontsa XVIII veka po 1974 god. Moskva, Kniga, 1976. 494p.

A classified list of bibliographies of literature and literary criticism from the end of the 18th century to 1974. 2,522 entries, including many on individual authors. Index.

Class No: 882(009)

[8580]

ZENKOVSKY, S.A. *and* ARMBRUSTER, D.L. A Guide to the bibliographies of Russian literature. Nashville, Tenn., Vanderbilt Univ. Press, 1970. ix,62p. ISBN: 0826511600.

Lists 331 items, with a general section followed by sections devoted to periods and genres. Author index.

Class No: 882(009)

Bibliographies

[8581]

AKADEMIYA NAUK SSSR. Bibliografiya sovetskikh russkikh rabot po literature XI-XVII vv. za 1917-1957 gg. Moskva, Izd-vo Akademii Nauk, 1961. 434p.

A bibliography of Soviet works on the literature of the 11th-17th centuries, chronologically arranged by year of

....(contd.)

publication, 1917-57. Index of proper names (authors of literary works, translators and critics) and subject index which includes titles of Old Russian writings.

Class No: 882(01)

[8582]

FOMIN, A.G. Putevoditel' po bibliografii, biobibliografii, istoriografii, khronologii i entsiklopedii literatury; sistematicheskii, annotirovannyi ukazatel' russkikh knig i zhurnal'nykh rabot, napechatannykh v 1736-1932 gg. Leningrad, Goslitizdat, 1934. (repr. New York, Johnson, 1966). 335p. ISBN: 0384163505.

Title translates literally as 'A Guide to the bibliography, bio-bibliography, historiography, chronology and encyclopaedias of literature; a systematic, annotated list of Russian books and periodical articles printed 1736-1932'. Fully annotated and still an invaluable guide to Russian language reference materials on the period concerned.

Class No: 882(01)

[8583]

HARVARD UNIVERSITY. Library. **The Kilgour Collection of Russian literature,** 1750-1920, with notes on early books and manuscripts of the 16th and 17th centuries. Cambridge, Mass., Harvard Univ. Press, 1959. 1v. (unpaged). illus. ISBN: 0674503503.

A catalogue of 1,348 first editions of Russian literary works with title-pages reproduced in facsimile and bibliographic notes to aid identification and comparison of editions. Appendices include reproductions of book-plates, labels and stamps. *Class No:* 882(01)

[8584]

Introduction to reference works. Zalewski, W., *comp.* Stanford Univ. Library. World Wide Web resource

URL: http//www-sul.stanford.edu/depts/hasrg/slavic/3refint.html

This freely accessible bibliography of reference sources on Russian studies has a very comprehensive literature section, with over 200 key works listed, often with annotations.

Class No: 882(01)

[8585]

KUZNEROVA, Z.I., *and others*. Literatura i folklor narodov SSSR: ukazatel' otecestuennyh bibliograficeskih posobii i spravocnyh izdanij 1926-1970. Moskva, Kniga, 1975. 237p.

Annotated index of fundamental bibliographic aids, dictionaries of writers and biographical reference works, dictionaries of pseudonyms, descriptions of literary archives, accounts of writers and literary life of the republics. Subject index and thematic catalogue. *Class No:* 882(01)

[8586]

MATSUEV, N.I. Khudozhestvennaya literatura, russkaya i perevodnaya: bibliografiya 1917/25-1938/53. Moskva, Gos. Izd-vo Khudozh. Lit-ry, 1926-59. 6v.

Bibliography of Russian literature and of literature translated into Russian from any language. Vols. 1-4 cover 1917-37. Vols. 5-6 coincide with the establishment of *Sovetskaya khudozhestvennaya literatura i kritika* (*q.v.*) and thus cover only current editions and studies of pre-Soviet authors, and foreign literature translated into Russian, 1938-53. *Class No:* 882(01)

[8587]

MOSCOW. PUBLICHNAYA BIBLIOTEKA. Russkie pisateli vtoroi poloviny XIX nachala XX vv. (do 1917 goda); rekomendatel'nyi ukazatel' literatury. Moskva, 1958-63. 3v.

An annotated bibliography of recommended editions of the major writers of the period 1850-1917 and of critical works about them. Preceded by *Russkie pisateli XVIII veka* (1954) and *Russki pisateli pervoi poloviny XIX veka* (1951), covering the 18th century and 1800-1849 respectively.
Class No: 882(01)

[8588]

SIMMONS, J.S.G. Russian bibliography, libraries and archives: a selective list of bibliographical references for students of Russian history, literature, political, social and philosophical thought, theology and linguistics. Twickenham, Middx., A.C. Hall, 1973. xviii,76p. ISBN: 090199703x.

Chapter on literary bibliography has 114 unannotated entries in 7 sections: 1. Bibliographies of bibliographies - 2. Methodology, historiography - 3. Literary encyclopaedias - 4. Literary biographical reference works - 5. General and retrospective bibliographies - 6. Current bibliographies - 7. Special periods and topics (including children's literature, science fiction, and literary periodicals). Appendix 1. provides a helpful comparative table of Russian transliteration. Author and title indexes, each with Cyrillic and Roman sections. UK and US library locations.
Class No: 882(01)

[8589]

Sovetskaya khudozhestvennaya literatura i kritika: bibliografiya, 1938/48-1964/65. Matsuev, N.I., *ed.* Moskva, Sovetskii Pisatel, 1952-72. 9v.

Current bibliography of Soviet literature and criticism. V.1 (1952) covers output for 1938-48; v.2 (1953) covers 1949-51. Biennial thereafter. Includes literatures of ethnic groups of the USSR as translated into Russian. *Class No:* 882(01)

18th Century

[8590]

AKADEMIYA NAUK SSSR. Institut Russkoi Literatury. **Istoriya russkoi literatury XVIII veka:** bibliograficheskii ukazatel'. Stepanov, V.P. *and* Stennik, Yu.V., *comps.* Leningrad, Nauka, 1968. 500p.

Primary and secondary bibliography of 18th-century Russian literature. *Class No:* 882(01)"17"

[8591]

CROSS, A.G. *and* **SMITH, G.S. Eighteenth century Russian literature, culture and thought:** a bibliography of English-language scholarship and translations. Newtonville, Mass., Oriental Research Partners, 1984. xv,130p. ISBN: 0892503343.

1,303 unannotated entries in 14 sections, the last one listing translations and critical studies of *c.*50 individual authors, A-Z (p.38-101). 5 indexes: dissertations, critics, translators, names, and subjects. *Class No:* 882(01)"17"

19th & 20th Centuries

[8592]

AKADEMIYA NAUK SSSR. Institut Russkoi Literatury. **Istoriya russkoi literatury kontsa XIX nachala XX veka;** bibliograficheskii ukazatel'. Muratova, K.D., *ed.* Leningrad, Izd-vo Akademii Nauk SSSR, 1963. 516p.

A bibliography (12,247 items) on Russian literature at the

....(*contd.*)

end of the 19th century and beginning of the 20th. Similarly arranged to Muratova's 19th-century bibliography, listing publications up to 1962. Soviet literature is dealt with in greater detail. *Class No:* 882(01)"18/19"

19th Century

[8593]

AKADEMIYA NAUK SSSR. Institut Russkoi Literatury. **Istoriya russkoi literatury XIX veka;** bibliograficheskii ukazatel'. Muratova, K.D., *ed.* Leningrad, Izd-vo Akademii Nauk SSSR, 1962. 996p.

A bibliography (19,596 numbered items) on Russian literature in the 19th century. The first part covers aspects of the history of Russian literature, criticism and journalism. The second consists of 300 author bibliographies (material by and on). Lists items published up to January 1959. Subject (partly analytical) and name indexes.
Class No: 882(01)"18"

[8594]

PROFFER, C. *and* **MEYER, R. Nineteenth-century Russian literature in English:** a bibliography of criticism and translations. Ann Arbor, Mich., Ardis, 1990. 188p. $49.50. ISBN: 0882339435.

Lists English-language works on 19th-century Russian literature in general and works by and about 69 individual authors published up to 1986. Necessarily selective for major writers, but invaluable for lesser known names. Largely unannotated. *Class No:* 882(01)"18"

20th Century

[8595]

AKADEMIYA NAUK SSSR. Fundamental'naya Biblioteka Obschchestvennykh Nauk. **Sovetskoe literaturovedenie i kritika:** Russkaya sovetskaya literatura (obshchie raboty); knigi i stat'i 1917-1962 godov. Bibliograficheskii ukazatel'. Moskva, Nauka, 1966. 586p.

An annotated, systematically arranged bibliography of over 10,700 books and articles, published 1917-62, containing critical and historical studies of Soviet literature in general. Excludes material on individual writers. Thorough index.

Supplements, ed. by A. Blazer and others, covering 1963-67 (1970. 180p.), 1968-70 (1975. 397p.), and 1971-73 (1979. 460p.), add a further 21,000 items.
Class No: 882(01)"19"

[8596]

FOSTER, L.A. Bibliography of Russian émigré literature, 1918-1968. Boston, Hall, 1970. 2v. (lvii,1374p.).

17,000 entries, registering works written in Russian as well as those translated into Russian, and featuring items published in literary journals, collections and anthologies, as well as those in book form. Main entries arranged according to Cyrillic alphabet. Library locations.
Class No: 882(01)"19"

[8597]

Ten bibliographies of 20th century Russian literature. Moody, F., *ed.* Ann Arbor, Mich., Ardis, 1977. 175p. ISBN: 0882332511.

9 bibliographies of individual authors plus one on Russian versification, 1958-72. 8 of the bibliographies were originally published in *Russian Literature Triquarterly.*

....(contd.)
Authors covered: Kuprin, Annenskii, Blok, Evreinov, Mayakovsky, Grin, Aksenov, Akhmadulina, Brodsky.
Class No: 882(01)"19"

[8598]
WOLL, J. Soviet dissident literature: a critical guide. Boston, Hall, 1983. xlviii,241p. ISBN: 081618626x.

Rev. ed. of *Soviet unofficial literature - samizdat* (1978).

Annotated bibliography of 1,300 'samizdat' works published in the West up to January, 1982. Arranged by author, A-Z, with subject index. *Class No:* 882(01)"19"

Encyclopaedias & Dictionaries

[8599]
Handbook of Russian literature. Terras, V., *ed.* New Haven, Conn., and London, Yale Univ. Press, 1985 (repr. in paperback, 1990). xix,558p. £19.95. ISBN: 0300048688.

Approx. 1,000 signed entries by 106 (mainly American) scholars are arranged A-Z and cover authors, journalists and critics; literary movements and schools; periodicals and publishing houses; genres, styles and themes; and literary and historical terms. Titles of Russian works are given in translation, usually followed by Russian title in parentheses, and names are given in their familiar English spelling. Brief bibliographies appended to most articles are intended 'to give the reader a head start, no more' (*Preface*) and are largely restricted to material in Russian and English. Excellent classified general bibliography (7p.). Ample cross-references and thorough index. The best single-volume source available, it is 'unlikely to be surpassed for a long time...[and] deserves to be acquired by libraries everywhere' (*Modern Language Review*, v.82(1), Jan. 1987, p.264-5).
Class No: 882(03)

[8600]
KASACK, W. Dictionary of Russian literature since 1917. New York, Columbia Univ. Press, 1988. xvi,502p. $73. ISBN: 0231052421.

Translation and amalgamation of Kasack's *Lexikon der russischen Literatur ab 1917* (Stuttgart, Kröner, 1976) and its supplement, *Ergänzungsband* (Munich, Sagner, 1986), by M. Carlson and J.T. Hedges, with bibliographical revision by R. Atack.

706 entries covering the whole field of Russian (not merely Soviet) literature since the Revolution, are arranged A-Z by transliterated names. 619 author entries comprise biographical sketch, critical evaluation of works and selected bibliography of works and criticism. 87 subject entries cover journals, associations, literary movements and topics essential to an understanding of modern Russian literature, *e.g.* Emigration, Censorship, Gulag. Indexes of names and subjects. List of place name changes. Numerous cross-references. The original 1976 ed. was praised for its 'authoritative, comprehensive and nonideological coverage' (*World Literature Today,* v.51(1), Winter, 1977, p.637-8).
Class No: 882(03)

[8601]
Literaturnaya entsiklopediya. Lebedev-Polyanski, I.M. *and* Nusinov, I.M., *eds.* Moskva, Khudozhestvennaya Literatura, 1929-39 (repr. Ann Arbor, Mich., J.W. Edwards for American Council of Learned Societies, 1948). v.1-9, 11.

A comprehensive Marxist-Leninist encyclopedia of world literature, with a strong emphasis on the USSR. Valuable bibliographies. In 1991, Sagner (München) published 'the only existing and by chance preserved makeup copy of the prohibited and up to now missing tenth volume' (*Preface*), which includes an important and lengthy entry on Russian literature (columns 88-397). It is slightly damaged in places and contains numerous proofmarks; a few columns and several illustrations are missing. *Class No:* 882(03)

[8602]
—Kratkaya literaturnaya entsiklopediya. Surkov, A.A., *ed.* Moskva, Sovetskaya Entsiklopediya, 1962-78. 9v.

A 'concise' encyclopedia covering world literature from a Soviet perspective, with good coverage of Soviet Russian literature and of ethnic groups within the USSR. Bibliographies appended to articles. Subject and name index to the set in v.9. Launched during the Khrushchev era to replace *Literaturnaya entsiklopediya.* 'With all its deficiencies and gaps, it is a valuable source of biographical and bibliographical information' (Struve, G., *Russian literature under Lenin and Stalin,* 1971, p.412).
Class No: 882(03)

[8603]
The Modern encyclopedia of Russian and Soviet literature (including non-Russian and émigré literatures). Weber, H.B., *ed.* Gulf Breeze, Fla., Academic International Press, 1977-. v.1-9 (in progress?). ISBN: 0318593068.

A multi-volume work which had only reached the letter 'H' with the publication of v.9 in 1989 (since when no more have appeared) consisting of articles by numerous contributors, both Soviet and Western, on writers, works, movements, genres, subjects, periodicals, etc. By no means confined to pure literature, 'the encyclopedia strives, ultimately, to arrive at a cultural profile of Russia and the Soviet Union, as revealed in Russian literature, in the many other national Soviet literatures, and in their literary traditions and literary history' (*From the editor*). Several entries have been taken from authoritative Russian sources and translated, and almost all have bibliographies. Vols. 1-8 ed. by Weber; v.9 ed. by G.J. Gutsche.

Modern Language Review (v.84(1), Jan. 1989, p.269-70) points out some strange omissions from v.8, criticises the lack of cross-references and concludes that 'the gap between intention and achievement is such that it cannot be unreservedly recommended'. *Class No:* 882(03)

[8604]
Reference guide to Russian literature. Cornwell, N., *ed.* London, Fitzroy Dearborn, 1998. xl,972p. £95. ISBN: 1884964109.

Signed essays, by a 150-strong international team of scholars, on 273 writers and 293 major works, preceded by 13 substantial survey articles on periods, topics and genres. Author entries comprise 1,000-word critical essay, biographical notes, and bibliography of works and critical studies. For major writers, there are separate essays on key works (*e.g.* 8 of Chekhov's works are covered), not always by the author of the biographical entry. General bibliography of anthologies and English-language criticism (7p.). Chronological list of writers. Title index with authors and dates. *Class No:* 882(03)

Handbooks & Manuals

[8605]
An Introduction to Russian language and literature. Auty, R. *and* Obolensky, D., *eds.* Cambridge, Cambridge Univ. Press, 1977. xiii,300p. (*Companion to Russian studies, v.2.*) ISBN: 0521280397.

See entry at 808.2(035). *Class No:* 882(035)

Histories

[8606]

AKADEMIYA NAUK SSSR. Institut Russkoi Literatury. **Istoriya russkoi literatury.** Moskva, Izd-vo Akademiya Nauk SSR, 1941-56. 10v. in 13.

The official Soviet history of Russian literature from the beginnings in the 11th century to 1917. Vols. 5-10 deal with the 19th and early 20th centuries. Chapters contributed by numerous specialist scholars. Includes quotations and portraits. Footnote references, but no general bibliography or critical apparatus. *Class No:* 882(091)

[8607]

The Cambridge history of Russian literature. Moser, C.A., *ed.* Rev. ed. Cambridge, Cambridge Univ. Press, 1992. x,709p. £60. ISBN: 0521415543.

1st ed. 1989.

Narrative history from 988 to 1980 in 10 chapters by different scholars. The 2 chapters on the Soviet era treat literature published within and outside the Soviet Union equally. Bibliography (36p.) of secondary works in book form, with the emphasis on 20th-century publications. 'Thoroughly traditional in approach and form, the volume offers a solid introduction to its subject matter' (*Choice*, v.28(1), Sept. 1990, p.122, on 1st. ed.). However, a lengthy review in *Modern Language Review* (v.86(2), April 1991, p.536-541) is critical of the traditional approach ('This weighty volume is completely uninformed by the developments that have taken place in critical theory during the last twenty years') and asserts that the bibliography 'contains an unacceptably high proportion of outdated works'.

Rev. ed. adds a chapter on 'Russian literature in the 1980s' (20p.) and includes some corrections. Bibliography updated through 1990. *Class No:* 882(091)

[8608]

Histoire de la littérature russe: . Etkind, E., *and others, eds.* Paris, Fayard, 1987-. v.1- (in progress).

V.1 *Des Origines aux Lumières*. 1992. 895p. ISBN: 2213019851.

V.3 *Le XIXe siècle: l'époque de Pouchkine et de Gogol.* 1996. 1100p. ISBN: 221301986x.

V.4 *Le XXe siècle: l'Age d'argent*. 1987. 782p. ISBN: 2213018928.

V.5 *Le XXe siècle: la Révolution et les années vingt*. 1988. 1003p. ISBN: 2213019606.

V.6 *Le XXe siècle: gels et dégels*. 1990. 1090p. ISBN: 2213019509.

The first vol. to appear (v.4) of this projected 7-vol. history covers 1890-1915 in a series of essays on movements, genres, subperiods and individual authors. 'Volume 1 augurs well for the prodigious enterprise which it inaugurates. It affords ... an impressive amount of information grounded in up-to-date research and a significant body of critical insight' (*World Literature Today*, v.62(4), Autumn 1988, p.680-1). The work of an international team of scholars. *Class No:* 882(091)

[8609]

TERRAS, V. A History of Russian literature. New Haven, Conn., Yale Univ. Press, 1991. x,654p. $28. ISBN: 0300059345.

A chronological account from the 11th century to the Soviet period in 9 chapters, with a brief epilogue covering recent developments. 'Addressed to Western readers, this history tries to present Russian literature as it was perceived by Russian readers' (*Preface*). Footnote references. Select bibliography of English-language reference works,

....*(contd.)*

anthologies and histories (4p.). Index.

'To embrace the thousand-year history of Russian literature in one volume is a mighty task and one which Victor Terras has accomplished in style ... the book's minor shortcomings are overshadowed by its numerous merits: its accuracy, keenness of observation, subtle comments, vivid quotations, erudition' (*TLS*, no.4666, Sept. 4, 1992, p.3-4). *Class No:* 882(091)

17th Century

[8610]

BROWN, W.E. A History of seventeenth-century Russian literature. Ann Arbor, Mich., Ardis, 1980. 182p. illus. ISBN: 0882333437.

5 chapters on prose genres (medieval type); prose genres (modern type); popular oral verse in contact with written literature; learned or bookish poetry; and drama. Many extracts in English. Bibliography (2p.). Index.
Class No: 882(091)"16"

18th Century

[8611]

BROWN, W.E. A History of eighteenth-century Russian literature. Ann Arbor, Mich., Ardis, 1980. 659p. illus. ISBN: 0882333410.

4 parts and 12 chapters, with subsections for individual writers and works. Quotations in English. Good bibliography of anthologies, bibliographies, general studies, and studies of 35 individual authors (20p.). Index.
Class No: 882(091)"17"

19th Century

[8612]

BROWN, W.E. A History of Russian literature of the Romantic period Ann Arbor, Mich., Ardis, 1986. 4v. (1590p.). illus. ISBN: 0882339389.

Massive compilation covering the period 1800-1840, to follow Brown's single-volume histories of 17th and 18th century Russian literature. Essentially traditional in approach, the author contending that 'a poet's or an artist's work is the only thing about him that matters'.

Many illustrative quotations translated by the author. Selected bibliography (7p.). Index in each vol. *TLS* (no.4421, Dec. 25, 1987, p.1442) states that 'a whole galaxy of secondary figures have received their due as never before in English' but criticizes the poor coverage of women writers. *Class No:* 882(091)"18"

[8613]

TSCHIZEWSKIJ, D. History of nineteenth-century Russian literature. Zenkovsky, S.A., *ed.* Reprint of 1974 ed. New York, Greenwood, 1986. 498p. $85. ISBN: 0313252742.

Originally published München, 1964-67, as *Russische Literaturgeschichte des 19. Jahrhunderts* (2v.). This English translation by R.N. Porter first published Nashville, Tenn., Vanderbilt Univ. Press, 1974 (2v.).

A clearly structured history with chapters on literary movements and major writers and numerous subsections. Many quotations, both in Russian and English. Substantial bibliography, completely revised by the editor to cater for English-speaking readers. *Class No:* 882(091)"18"

20th Century

[8614]

AKADEMIYA NAUK SSSR. Istoriya russkoy sovetskoy literatury. Dementyev, A., *ed.* 2nd ed. Moskva, Akademiya Nauk SSSR, 1967-71. 4v.

1st ed. 1958-61, in 3 vols.

The Soviet Academy's official history of Soviet Russian literature. Each vol. covers a chronological period and has a general introductory survey; articles on special topics; a series of monographs on individual writers written by specialist scholars; surveys of journalism, literary criticism and international relations; and a detailed chronology of literary events. *Class No:* 882(091)"19"

[8615]

BROWN, E.J. Russian literature since the Revolution. 3rd ed., rev. and enlarged. Cambridge, Mass., Harvard Univ. Press, 1982. viii,413p. ISBN: 0674782038.

1st ed. 1963; 2nd ed. 1969.

Comprehensive critical history from 1917 to the early 1980s in 16 chapters with numerous subsections, many of them devoted to individual writers. Includes émigré literature. All quotations in English translation. Select bibliography of critical studies (3p.). Index.

Class No: 882(091)"19"

[8616]

STRUVE, G. Russian literature under Lenin and Stalin, 1917-1953. Norman, Okla., Univ. of Oklahoma Press, 1971. xvi,454p. ISBN: 0806109319.

A 'considerably revised version' (*Foreword*) of *Soviet Russian Literature: 1917-1950* (1951).

A comprehensive account in 8 parts (7 for chronological periods, plus Conclusion), with 30 chapters and numerous subsections on individual writers and movements. Many quotations in English translation. Substantial bibliography (37p.) in 5 sections: 1. Books cited in footnotes - 2. Biographical, bibliographical and other reference works - 3. General background works in English about Russia - 4. Works about Soviet literature - 5. Soviet literature in English translation. Index. *Class No:* 882(091)"19"

[8617]

—BROWN, D. Soviet Russian literature since Stalin. Cambridge, Cambridge Univ. Press, 1978. 394p. ISBN: 052121694x.

Covers the period from 1953 to the mid-1970s in 14 chapters, relating the literature to cultural, ideological, social and political developments. Quotations in translation. Select bibliography (4p.). Index. *Class No:* 882(091)"19"

Biographies

[8618]

Dictionary of literary biography. Detroit, Gale, 1978-98. v.1-188 (in progress). £112 per vol.

The following vol. covers Russian literature:

V.150 *Early modern Russian writers: late seventeenth and eighteenth centuries*, ed. by M.C. Levitt. 1995.

For a description of the series, see entry at 82(092).

Class No: 882(092)

[8619]

LENINGRAD. Publichnaya Biblioteka. **Russkie sovetskie pisateli-prozaiki:** bio-bibliograficheskii ukazatel'. Akimov, V.M., *and others, eds.* Leningrad, 1959-72. 7v.

Biobibliographical information on prose writers of the Soviet period, each contribution having 1-2 pages of biography and a substantial bibliography of books, articles, dissertations, film scripts, dramatizations, etc.

Class No: 882(092)

[8620]

MATSUEV, N.I. Russkie sovetskie pisateli: materialy dlya biograficheskogo slovarya, 1917-1967. Moskva, Sovetskie Pisatel, 1981. 254p.

Very brief entries on nearly 5,000 Soviet writers.

Class No: 882(092)

[8621]

STEVANOVIC, B. *and* **WERTSMAN, V. Free voices in Russian literature, 1950s-1980s:** a bio-bibliographical guide. Sumerkin, A., *ed.* New York, Russica, 1987. 510p. $87.50. ISBN: 0898300908.

Lists over 900 writers whose works have been first published in the West (in either books or journals) during the period 1957-85. Entries comprise biography and a list of publications. List of authors, with birth and death dates. Selected list of émigré periodicals, serial editions and almanacs. Not just a guide to *dissident* literature, 'the value ... lies in the variety of authors included' (*Choice,* v.25(5), Jan. 1988, p.752). *Class No:* 882(092)

Women

[8622]

Dictionary of Russian women writers. Ledkovsky, M., *& others, eds.* Westport, Conn., Greenwood, 1994. xli,869p. $155. ISBN: 0313262659.

Signed essays (often running to several pages) on 448 writers, comprising biography, critical analysis, primary bibliography (including translations) and secondary bibliography. List of works cited, arranged by language and type. Introductory history of Russian women's writing (15p.) with bibliographical notes. Chronology of writers' birth dates, 1714-1967. Chronology of literary and historical events, 1759-1991. List of over 100 contributors. Index.

Class No: 882-0055.2

[8623]

KELLY, C. A History of Russian women's writing, 1820-1992 Oxford, Clarendon Press, 1994. xii,497p. £15.99. ISBN: 0198159641.

A companion to the author's *Anthology of Russian women's writing* (OUP, 1994). 4 chronological sections (1820-80; 1881-1917; 1917-53; 1954-92) comprising 18 chapters, of which 13 relate to individual writers. Quotations in Russian with the author's English translation. Substantial bibliography (37p.) of reference sources, critical studies, anthologies, and works by individual women. General index and index of women writers. The author adopts a modernist and feminist position and 'makes no pretence of objectivity' (*TLS*, no.4773, Sept. 23, 1994, p.26). *Class No:* 882-0055.2

Russian Literature in Translation

[8624]

Bibliography of Russian literature in English translation, to 1945. Line, M.B., *and others, eds.* London, Methuen, 1972. 170p.

Reprints together Line's *A Bibliography of Russian literature in English translation, to 1900* (London, Library Assoc., 1963) and A. Ettlinger and J.M. Gladstone's *Russian literature, theatre and art: a bibliography of works, published 1900-45* (London, Hutchinson, 1946).

Over 2,000 entries. *Class No:* 882-03

[8625]

GIBIAN, G. Soviet Russian literature in English; a checklist bibliography: a selective bibliography of Soviet Russian literary works in English and books in English about Soviet Russian literature. Ithaca, N.Y., Center for International Studies, Cornell Univ., 1967. vi,118p.

Covers 33 individual authors as well as general materials on Soviet literature. Author bibliographies compiled by 12 specialists, with annotations varying considerably in length. *Class No:* 882-03

Russian Poetry

[8626]

BRISTOL, E. A History of Russian poetry. New York, Oxford Univ. Press, 1991. ix,354p. £32.50. ISBN: 0195046595.

17 chapters in 7 chronological sections, with subsections on specific poets and schools. Quotations in English translation by the author. Chapter bibliographies list anthologies, general studies, editions and studies (in English and Russian) of individual poets. Glossary (2p.). Chronology (2p.). Index. *Class No:* 882-1

[8627]

Russkie sovetskie pisateli. Poety. Biobibliograficheskii ukazatel'. Moskva, Kniga, 1977-91. v.1-15.

A biobibliographical dictionary of Russian poets, with vols. 1-14 covering Avramenko to Mayakovsky. Entries include very extensive bibliographies of primary and secondary literature. Index in each vol.

Title changed to *Russkie pisateli. Poety. (Sovetskii period): bibliograficheskii ukazatel'* with v.16 (1991). Vols. 16-19 published St. Petersburg, 1991-5. *Class No:* 882-1

Akhmatova

[8628]

TERRY, G.M. Anna Akhmatova in English: a bibliography, 1889-1966-1989. Nottingham, Astra Press, 1989. 24p. £3.25. ISBN: 0946134146.

Lists translations of Akhmatova's works and English-language studies. 172 entries. Name index. *Class No:* 882-1AKH

Lermontov

[8629]

Bibliografiya literatury o M. Ju. Lermontove, 1917-77. Miller, O.V., *ed.* Leningrad, Nauka, 1980. 515p.

Lists nearly 7,000 Russian-language studies chronologically. Index of authors, periodical titles, Lermontov's works, and subjects. *Class No:* 882-1LER

Pasternak

[8630]

SENDICH, M. Boris Pasternak: a reference guide. Boston, Hall, 1994. 376p. $50. ISBN: 0816189927.

Lists over 500 works by Pasternak (including translations of Western literary works) and over 1,400 studies, most of them in English or Russian although other languages are represented. Covers the period 1913-90. Well annotated. Author and subject indexes. Introductory survey of Pasternak's critical reception. *Class No:* 882-1PAS

Pushkin

[8631]

AKADEMIYA NAUK SSSR. Bibliografiya proizvedenii A.S. Pushkina 1949 yubileinyi god. Moskva, Izd-vo Akademiya Nauk SSR, 1951. 566p.

A bibliography of Pushkin's works published to mark the 150th anniversary of his birth. 3,857 numbered entries, systematically arranged, with 5 indexes. *Class No:* 882-1PUS

[8632]

SHAW, J.T. Pushkin: a concordance to the poetry. Columbus, Ohio, Slavica, 1985. 2v. $99.95. ISBN: 089357130x.

Based on the most authoritative and complete ed. of Pushkin's works, the so-called 'large Academy' ed. Lists alphabetically all the Cyrillic word forms (except for 11 common function words) found in all the basic texts of all the poetry, giving for each: number of times it occurs; number of lines in which it is used; poem-and line location; and the complete line in which the form occurs. Supplemented by several special tables (*e.g.* Hyphenated words; Lines containing Latin-Alphabet words) and prints the stress for all 42,433 endwords. *Class No:* 882-1PUS

[8633]

ZAITSEVA, V.V., *and others*. Bibliografiya proizvedenii A.S. Pushkina i literatury o nem, 1937-1948. Moskva, Izdat. Akademiya Nauk SSSR, 1963. 747p.

7,012 numbered entries for material by and on Pushkin, closely subdivided. Lists translations of works into various languages of the Soviet Union. Indexes of authors, subjects, titles, etc. *Class No:* 882-1PUS

Russian Drama

[8634]

KARLINSKY, S. Russian drama from its beginnings to the age of Pushkin. Berkeley, Calif., Univ. of California Press, 1985. 357p. $47.50. ISBN: 0520052374.

A history of early Russian drama in 10 chapters, with subsections on individual authors and works. Quotations in the original with translation. Footnote references, but no general bibliography. Indexes of names and play titles. *Class No:* 882-2

Chekhov

[8635]

A Chekhov companion. Clyman, T.W., *ed.* Westport, Conn., Greenwood, 1985. ix,347p. $75. ISBN: 031323423x.

17 signed essays by Chekhov scholars on all aspects of his life and work, each with bibliographical notes. Particularly useful are: ch.11 'Chekhov at home: Russian criticism'; ch.12 'Chekhov abroad: Western criticism'; ch.13 'Chekhov on stage' (with list of noteworthy productions); ch.14

.... *(contd.)*

'Chekhov into film' (with annotated selective filmography); and ch.17 'Chekhov in English' (selective bibliography of translations). Selected classified bibliography (21p.) by L. Poliakiewicz concentrates on post-1960 critical works. Index. *Class No:* 882-2CHE

[8636]

LANTZ, K.A. Anton Chekhov: a reference guide to literature. Boston, Hall, 1985. xlvi,287p. ISBN: 0816187010.

Lists and annotates 1,200 works of criticism by year, 1886-1983, with A-Z arrangement within each year. 'Items were chosen to give a representative sampling of the development of critical attitudes to Chekhov' (*Preface*), with the emphasis on more recent material and English-language titles, although items in French, German and Russian are also included. Checklist of Chekhov's writings, 1880-1904. Index of authors, titles and selected subjects.

See also C.W. Meister's *Chekhov bibliography: works in English by and about Anton Chekhov; American, British and Canadian performances* (Jefferson, N.C., McFarland, 1985. 190p. $39.95. ISBN: 0899501540) and *Chekhov criticism, 1880 through 1986* (Jefferson, N.C., McFarland, 1988. x,350p. $47.50. ISBN: 0899503551). *Class No:* 882-2CHE

Russian Fiction

[8637]

AKADEMIYA NAUK SSSR. Biblioteka. **Sovetskii roman, ego teoriya i istoriya:** bibliograficheskii ukazatel', 1917-1964. Leningrad, Sostavila N.A. Groznova, 1966. 257p.

1,161 numbered entries, with concise annotations, on the theory and history of the Soviet novel. Arranged by authors, A-Z, under individual years. Author index. *Class No:* 882-31

[8638]

BERRY, T.E. Plots and characters in major Russian fiction. Hamden, Conn., Archon, 1977-8. 2v. ISBN: 0208015841, v.1; 0208016015, v.2.

Pushkin, Lermontov, Turgenev and Tolstoy in v.1; Gogol, Goncharov and Dostoevsky in v.2. Each vol. in 2 parts: 1. Plot synopses A-Z by novel title, each followed by character list; 2. Characters (historical and fictional), A-Z, from all the novels, with brief notes. *Class No:* 882-31

[8639]

The Russian novel from Pushkin to Pasternak. Garrard, J., *ed.* New Haven, Conn., Yale Univ. Press, 1983. xii,300p. $42. ISBN: 0300029357.

12 critical essays by American and European scholars, followed by a chronology of Russian novels and novelists, 1763-1981, and a list of recommended translations (3p.). Index. *Class No:* 882-31

[8640]

The Russian short story: a critical history. Moser, C.A., *ed.* Boston, Twayne, 1986. xxiv,232p. $22.95. ISBN: 0805793607.

Introductory essay by the editor followed by 4 on specific periods, 1830-1980, by specialists, in which over 100 writers are discussed. Neglects émigré writers but has excellent annotated bibliography (24p.) of anthologies of stories in Russian and in English translation, and of critical studies. Chronology. Index. *Class No:* 882-31

Bulgakov

[8641]

TERRY, G.M. Mikhail Bulgakov in English: a bibliography, 1891-1991. Nottingham, Astra Press, 1991. 32p. £3.75. ISBN: 0946134243.

Lists English translations of Bulgakov's works plus articles, books and dissertations about him in English. 220 unannotated entries. Name index. *Class No:* 882-31BUL

Dostoevsky

[8642]

CHAPPLE, R. A Dostoevsky dictionary. Ann Arbor, Mich., Ardis, 1983. 511p. ISBN: 0882336169.

Arranged by work, based on the Soviet 30-vol. ed., listing for each one characters and literary allusions, A-Z, with explanatory notes and cross-references. Main entries for characters are under full name, with references from alternative forms. *Class No:* 882-31DOS

[8643]

LEATHERBARROW, W.J. Feodor Dostoevsky: a reference guide. Boston, Hall, 1990. xxxviii,317p. $40. ISBN: 0816189412.

Lists *c.*1,200 sources by year, 1846-1988, with the emphasis on recent Russian- and English-language publications, although studies in several other languages are included. Concise, nonevaluative annotations. Checklist of Dostoevsky's works. Indexes of authors and subjects.

For an annual checklist of criticism, see *Dostoevsky Studies* (Knoxville, Tenn., Univ. of Tennessee, Dept. of Germanic and Slavic Languages, 1980-.), the bulletin of the International Dostoevsky Society. *Class No:* 882-31DOS

Gogol

[8644]

FRANTZ, P.E. Gogol: a bibliography Ann Arbor, Mich., Ardis, 1989. 360p. $35. ISBN: 0882338099.

The publishers claim this is the most comprehensive bibliography of works by and about Gogol, with *c.*8,000 entries. Most are for Russian- and English-language publications, but material in a wide range of other languages is also included. *Class No:* 882-31GOG

Gorky

[8645]

CLOWES, E.W. Maksim Gorky: a reference guide. Boston, Hall, 1987. xxvii,226p. $40. ISBN: 0816187223.

The first English-language research bibliography, it attempts to redress Soviet bias in Gorky criticism by omitting 'the hundreds of Soviet reviews, scholarly articles and books that merely repeat established patterns of interpretation' (*Preface*) and by including European and American sources and Russian émigré publications. Approx. 1,100 annotated entries arranged by year, 1898-1986, then A-Z within each year. Checklist of Gorky's major works, 1892-1941 (Russian texts only). Author and subject indexes. '... the most valuable reference work on Gorky currently available in any language' (*Modern Language Review*, v.84(2), April 1989, p.537). *Class No:* 882-31GOR

[8646]

TERRY, G.M. Maxim Gorky in English: a bibliography. 2nd ed. Nottingham, Astra Press, 1992. 44p. £5. ISBN: 0946134324.

1st ed. 1985, as *Maxim Gorky in English: a bibliography, 1868-1936-1986.*

Lists translations of Gorky's works plus English-language critical studies and dissertations. Over 500 entries. *Class No:* 882-31GOR

Solzhenitsyn

[8647]

FIENE, D.M. Alexander Solzhenitsyn: an international bibliography of writings by and about him. Ann Arbor, Mich., Ardis, 1973. xix,148p. ISBN: 088233042x.

2,465 entries, covering the period 1962-73. Lists works in Russian and in translation, biographies, criticism and reviews. Index of names.

Updated by M. Nicholson's 'Solzhenitsyn in 1976: a bibliographical reorientation', in *Russian Literature Triquarterly,* no.143, Winter 1976, p.462-82. For further updates, see *Solzhenitsyn Studies: a quarterly survey* (Univ. of Lancaster, 1980-.). *Class No:* 882-31SOL

Tolstoy

[8648]

Bibliografiya literatury o L.N. Tolstoi, 1917-1958. Shelyapina, N.G., *and others, eds.* Moskva, Izdat. Vsesoyuznaya Knizhnoi Palaty, 1960. 792p.

A bibliography of literature on Leo Tolstoi. Three main sections: 1. Lenin and Tolstoi - 2. Biographical (p.45-654; 5,094 numbered and annotated items in annual lists, 1917-58) - 3. Bibliographical. *Class No:* 882-31TOL

[8649]

Bibliografiya proizvedenii L.N. Tolstogo. Zaidenshnur, E.E., *and others, eds.* Moskva, Izd-vo Akademii Nauk SSSR, 1955. 295p.

A bibliography of editions of Tolstoy's works: 1. Editions in Russian, published 1928-53 (1,319 items) - 2. Translations in 61 non-Russian languages of the Soviet Union, 1917-53 (730 items). Three indexes. *Class No:* 882-31TOL

[8650]

EGAN, D.R. *and* **EGAN, M.A. Leo Tolstoy: an annotated bibliography of English-language sources to 1978.** Metuchen, N.J., Scarecrow, 1979. xxxv,267p. (*Scarecrow author bibliographies.*) ISBN: 0810812320.

2,054 items in 10 sections, each subdivided as follows: books; essays and chapters; introductions; periodical articles; dissertations. Fiction section (p.56-141) has 766 entries. Other sections are thematic, *e.g.* Philosophy, Education, Religion. Indexes of authors and subjects. Over 400 periodicals cited. *Class No:* 882-31TOL

Turgenev

[8651]

ŽEKULIN, N.G. Turgenev: a bibliography of books 1843-1982 by and about Ivan Turgenev. With a check-list of Canadian library holdings. Calgary, Alberta, Univ. of Calgary Press, 1985. 221p. ISBN: 0919813151.

The first international bibliography, superseding the Soviet Academy's *Bibliografiya literatury o I.S. Turgeneve: 1918-1967* (Leningrad, 1970) and the New York Public Library's *Turgenev in English* (New York, 1962). Main sequence

....*(contd.)*

arranged by year, followed by 3 appendices: Canadian library holdings; chronological list of translations into English, French and German; and unpublished Canadian academic theses since 1960. Indexes include: names, titles of Turgenev's works, and languages of translation. 'Should be a standard work for years to come' (*Modern Language Review,* v.82(4), Oct. 1987, p.1049). *Class No:* 882-31TUR

Byelorussian Literature

[8652]

MCMILLIN, A.B. Die Literatur der Weissrussen: a history of Byelorussian literature from its origins to the present day. Giessen, W. Schmitz, 1977. 447p.

19 chapters from the 12th century. Bibliography (32p.) arranged by chapter. *Class No:* 882.6

Ukrainian Literature

[8653]

ČYŽEVS'KYJ, D. A History of Ukrainian literature, (from the 11th to the end of the 19th century), with an overview of the twentieth century. 2nd ed. Englewood, Colo., Ukrainian Academic Press, 1997. xvi,815p. $75. ISBN: 1563085224.

Originally published 1956, as *Istoriia ukrains'koi literatury vid pochatkiv do doby realizmu.* 1st English ed. 1975.

The first comprehensive survey in English, with 14 chapters covering periods and many subsections for genres. Chapter bibliographies appended (19p.). 2nd ed. has extra chapter by G.S.N. Luckyj (original author died 1977) on 20th-century literature, with slight revisions to earlier chapters. Extensive index of names and titles. *Class No:* 883

[8654]

Istoriia ukrains'koi literatury. Kyryliuk, I.P., *ed.* Ky'iv, 'Naukova dumka', 1968-71. 8v. in 9. illus.

The 'official' history of Ukrainian literature by the (Soviet) Ukrainian Academy, from the origins to 1967. Some bibliographical references in footnotes, but no general bibliography. Index in each vol. *Class No:* 883

[8655]

TARNAWSKY, M. Ukrainian literature in English: books and pamphlets, 1890-1965 - an annotated bibliography. Edmonton, Canadian Institute of Ukrainian Studies, Univ. of Alberta, 1988. 296p.

91 entries by author, A-Z, with lengthy annotations including lists of contents. Indexes of authors, editors, translators and subjects, plus chronological index.

Complemented by the same author's *Ukrainian literature in English: articles in journals and collections, 1840-1965 - an annotated bibliography* (Edmonton, 1992. xii,176p.) which has 791 entries with shorter annotations. *Class No:* 883

[8656]

Ukrains'ki pys'mennyky: biobibliohrafichnyi slovnyk. Bilets'kyi, O.I., *ed.* Kiev, Derzh. Vyd-vo Khudozh. Lit-ry, 1960-65. 5v.

Detailed biobibliographical coverage of Ukrainian writers, and also Byelorussian and Old Russian literature. V.1 covers 11th-18th centuries; vols. 2-3 the 19th and early 20th centuries; and v.3 the Soviet period. *Class No:* 883

Polish Literature

Bibliographies

[8657]
STARNAWSKI, J. Warsztat bibliograficzny historyka literatury polskiej (na tle dyscyplin pokrewnych). Wyd. 3. Warszawa, Państwowe Wydawnictwo Naukowe, 1982. 525p. ISBN: 830103842x.

1st ed. 1957; 2nd ed. 1971.

Title translates as 'A Working bibliography of Polish literary history (and related disciplines)'. Very comprehensive bibliographic essays, with references to 1000s of information sources and critical works. Name index. *Class No:* 884(01)

Encyclopaedias & Dictionaries

[8658]
Dictionary of Polish literature. Czerwinski, E.J., *ed.* Westport, Conn., Greenwood, 1994. 512p. £67.95. ISBN: 0313262225.

The first English-language guide to Polish literature, with entries (unsigned) on authors, works, periods and organizations. Lists of primary and secondary sources with entries, plus general bibliography. Index. *Class No:* 884(03)

[8659]
Słownik literatury polskiej XX wieku. Brodzka, A., *and others, eds.* Wrocław, Zakład Narodowy im Ossolińskich, 1993. 1432p. ISBN: 8304039427.

A dictionary of Polish literature, 1890-1980, with signed, lengthy (many over 10p.) entries, A-Z, covering genres, themes, topics, terms, schools and movements, but *not* individual writers. Bibliography with each entry. Name and subject indexes. *Class No:* 884(03)

Histories

[8660]
KRZYZANOWSKI, J. A History of Polish literature. Ronowicz, D., *tr.* Warszawa, PWN-Polish Scientific Publishers, 1978. vii,807p. 68 plates. ISBN: 0569126428.

Originally published Warszawa, 1972, as *Dzieje literatury Polskiej od początków do czasów najnowszych.*

From the Middle Ages to 1939 in 8 chapters with over 80 subsections. Bibliography (67p.) lists general works on Polish culture and literature followed by general studies, collections and texts relating to each chapter, and primary and secondary material for individual writers. List of book-length English translations (14p.). Index.
Class No: 884(091)

[8661]
MILOSZ, C. The History of Polish literature. 2nd ed. Berkeley, Calif., and London, Univ. of California Press, 1983. xix,583p. plates. $42.50. ISBN: 0520044657.

1st ed. 1969.

Definitive history by the 1980 Nobel Prize winner. 11 chapters on the main periods, with sub-sections on particular genres, movements and individual writers. All quotations are accompanied by translations. Substantial bibliography (17p.). Index of names and titles.

2nd ed. is reproduction of original ed. with the addition of an epilogue (7p.) covering the late 1960s and 1970s and an updated bibliography. *Class No:* 884(091)

Biographies

[8662]
Bibliografia literatury polskiej, 'Nowy Korbut'. Budzyk, K., *and others, eds.* Warzawa, Państwowy Instytut Wydawniczy, 1963-81. v.1-9, 12-17.

'The New Korbut' comprises extensive biobibliographies of Polish writers, compiled by many specialist contributors.
Class No: 884(092)

[8663]
CZACHOWSKIEJ, J. Współcześni polscy pisarze i badacze literatury i słownik biobibliograficzny. Szałagan, A., *eds.* Warszawa, Wydawnictwa Szkolne i Pedagogiczne, 1994-. v.1- (in progress). ISBN: 8302054445.

A biographical dictionary of contemporary writers and literary scholars which is scheduled to comprise 7 vols., the first 2 covering letters 'A-F'. Over 400 entries in each vol., with primary and secondary bibliographies.
Class No: 884(092)

[8664]
KORBUT, G. Literatura polska od poczatków do wojny światowej. Wyd.2., powiekszo. Warszawa, Sklad Glówny w Kasie im. Mianowskiego, 1929-31. 4v.

1st ed. 1917-21 in 3 vols.

Polish literature from its beginnings to World War One. Coverage of the volumes is as follows: 1. 10th-17th centuries - 2. 1700-1820 - 3. 1820-63 - 4. 1864-1914. Includes bio-bibliographies. *Class No:* 884(092)

[8665]
Słownik wspólczesnych pisarzy polskich. Korzeniewska, E., *and others, eds.* Warszawa, Państwowe Wydawnictwo Naukowe, 1963-66. 4v.

Follows Korbut, providing biobibliographical information on 20th-century writers. V.4 is index volume.

Continued by *Słownik wspólczesnych pisarzy polskich: seria II,* ed. by J. Czachowskiej, from the same publisher, 1977-80 (3v.), which covers contemporary writers not in the first set. *Class No:* 884(092)

Polish Literature in Translation

[8666]
COLEMAN, M.M. Polish literature in English translation: a bibliography. Cheshire, Conn., Cherry Hill Books, 1963. 180p.

Lists translations of literary works from the 16th century to 1960. Arranged A-Z by author with index of translators.

See also *Bibliography of Polish literature in English translation,* ed. by S.S. Birkenmayer and Z. Folejewski (3rd ed. New York, Kosciuszko Foundation, 1978. ISBN: 0917004116). *Class No:* 884-03

[8667]
MACIUSZKO, J.J. The Polish short story in English: a guide and critical bibliography. Detroit, Wayne State Univ. Press, 1968. 473p.

Bibliography of translations, p.55-332, under authors A-Z (brief literary career; plots of short stories; bibliographical details of books or periodical articles in which short stories appeared). 6 appendices, including list of anthologies, etc.; periodicals referred to; list of translators and their translations. Bibliography (6p.); index of authors.
Class No: 884-03

[8668]

RYLL, L. *and* **WILGAT, J. Polska literatura w przekladach:** bibliografia 1945-1970. Warszawa, Agencja Autorska, 1972. 369p.

Supersedes Wilgat's *Literatura polska w świecie; bibliografia przekladów, 1945-1961* (Warszawa, PEN Club, 1965).

Lists translations of Polish literary works published since 1945, including those found in anthologies. Indexes of authors, editors and translators, and of countries of publication. *Class No:* 884-03

[8669]

TABORSKI, B. Polish plays in English translations: a bibliography. New York, Polish Institute of Arts and Sciences in America, 1968. 79p. $3.50. ISBN: 0940962349.

Arranged by playwright in 3 sections: 1. Classic - 2. Modern Poland - 3. Abroad. Entries include brief biography of writer, plot summaries of plays, and details of casts and sets. Supplement lists books and articles in English on Polish drama in general and on individual writers. Index of dramatists. *Class No:* 884-03

Czech Literature

[8670]

Dějiny české literatury. Mukařovský, J., *ed.* Praha, Nakl. Ceskoslovenské Akademie Ved., 1959-61. 3v.

The 'official' history of Czech literature, published by the (Soviet) Czechoslovak Academy of Sciences and covering 1785-1900. A fourth vol. on the 20th century has never materialized. *Class No:* 885

[8671]

KOVTUN, G.J. Czech and Slovak literature in English: a bibliography. 2nd ed. Washington, D.C., Library of Congress, 1988. viii,152p. ISBN: 0844405787.

1st ed. 1984.

Lists translations into English and English-language studies of the 2 literatures in 5 sections: A. Anthologies (prose and poetry) - B. Anthologies (folklore) - C. General history and criticism - D. Czech authors, A-Z (233 authors) - E. Slovak authors, A-Z (93). US library locations given. Index of authors, editors and critics; index of translators. *Class No:* 885

[8672]

KUNC, J. Slovník českých spisovatelů beletristů, 1945-1956. Praha, Státní Pedagogické Nakl., 1957. 483p.

A biographical dictionary of 478 Czech literary writers. Continues the author's *Slovník soudobých českých spisovatelů; krásné písemnictví v letech 1918-45* (Praha, Orbis, 1945-46. 2v. illus.). *Class No:* 885

[8673]

MĚŠŤAN, A. Česká literatura 1785-1985. Toronto, Sixty-Eight, 1987. 458p.

A heavily revised Czech version of *Geschichte der tschechischen Literatur im 19. und 20. Jahrhundert* (Köln, Böhlau, 1984).

A history of Czech literature which gives equal weight to official and unofficial publications and concentrates mainly on the 20th century. The original, German-language edition has 4 sections on the literature of Bohemian and Moravian Germans, but these have now been omitted. Name index. Warmly welcomed by *World Literature Today* (v.62(4), Autumn 1988, p.685) as 'a nontendentious, interesting, and

.... *(contd.)*

informative reference work which is also the first to encompass all segments of recent Czech literature: official, *samizdat*, and exile'. *Class No:* 885

[8674]

NOVAK, A. Czech literature: ed. with a supplement by W.E. Harkins. Kussi, P., *tr.* Ann Arbor, Mich., Michigan Slavic Publications, 1976. ix,375p. $15. ISBN: 0930042646.

Originally published 1945 as *Stručné dějiny literatury české*.

A translation of the last of several versions of Novak's narrative history. Supplement (22p.) covers 1945-74. *Class No:* 885

Slovak Literature

[8675]

PETRO, P. A History of Slovak literature Montreal, McGill-Queen's Univ. Press, 1995; Liverpool, Liverpool Univ. Press, 1996. 176p. £25. ISBN: 0773513116, US; 0853238804, UK.

A detailed history from the 9th century to the present, which includes translations of passages from key works, many appearing in English for the first time. Bibliography of sources in English and other languages. Index. 'No significant Slovak writer or literary event escapes mention in this highly readable narrative' (*Choice*, v.33(10), June 1996, p.1650). *Class No:* 885.4

Yugoslav Literature

[8676]

BARAC, A. A History of Yugoslav literature. Ann Arbor, Mich., Slavic Publications [1972?]. 266p. $15. ISBN: 0930042190.

Well-organized history in 8 main chapters, each having several sub-sections covering the different nations. Bio-bibliographical notes included on many writers. 'The literature from 1918 down to the present has been given brief treatment, only mentioning trends, and introducing one representative writer of each of the several nations whose literature is dealt with' (*Note*). Name index. *Class No:* 886.1

[8677]

Jugoslovenski književni leksikon Popov, R., *ed.* 2 izd. Novi Sad, Matica Srpska, 1984. 923p. illus.

Signed entries on over 3,500 writers, giving short biography and primary and secondary bibliographies, plus portraits in some cases. *Class No:* 886.1

[8678]

Leksikon pisaca Jugoslavije. Bokov, Ž., *ed.* [Novi Sad], Matica Srpska, 1972-87. v. 1-3 (in progress). illus.

Vols. 1-3 cover A-Lj.

A biobibliographical dictionary of Yugoslav writers of all periods, which is the work of many contributors. Each vol. has *c.*700p. and *c.*1,400 entries, which include extensive primary and secondary bibliographies. Photographs of many writers. *Class No:* 886.1

[8679]
MIHAILOVICH, V.D. *and* **MATEJIC, M. A Comprehensive bibliography of Yugoslav literature in English, 1593-1980.** [2nd ed.]. Columbus, Ohio, Slavica, 1984. xii,586p. $29.95. ISBN: 0893571369.

1st ed. 1976, entitled *Yugoslav literature in English: a bibliography of translations and criticism (1821-1975).*

Lives up to its title, with 5,255 entries covering all the literatures of Yugoslavia. Part 1, Translations, has sections on folk literature and individual authors. Part 2 lists criticism under 4 headings: Entries in reference works; Books and articles; Reviews; Dissertations. Easy access via 4 indexes: English titles; original titles; periodicals and newspapers; subjects and names. The planned 5-yearly updates 'will be eagerly awaited and welcomed by all in the field' (*Modern Language Review,* v.81(1), Jan. 1986, p.272).

First supplement (1989. 338p. $18.95. ISBN: 0893571881) and *Second supplement* (1992. 301p. $19.95. ISBN: 0893572306) are similarly arranged and cover 1981-85 and 1986-90 respectively. *Class No:* 886.1

[8680]
SLODNJAK, A. Geschichte der slowenischen Literatur. Berlin, de Gruyter, 1958. viii,363p. DM158. ISBN: 3110056946.

A scholarly work which is 'the only substantial history of Slovenian literature ... available in a western language' (Horton, J.J., *Yugoslavia,* 1977, p.141). Index of authors. *Class No:* 886.1

[8681]
TERRY, G.M. A Bibliography of Macedonian studies. Nottingham, Nottingham Univ. Library, 1975. xi,121p.

Literature section (p.86-103) has 275 unannotated entries in 5 subsections: bibliographies and reference aids; history and criticism; individual authors; anthologies; folk literature. Name index and geographical index. *Class No:* 886.1

Bulgarian Literature

[8682]
MANNING, C.A. *and* **SMAL-STOCKI, R. The History of modern Bulgarian literature.** Reprint of 1960 ed. New York, Greenwood, 1974. 198p. ISBN: 0837161304.

Originally published New York, Bookman Associates, 1960.

From the 18th century to the Communist period, with some historical background, in 12 chapters. Selections of Bulgarian poetry in translation (20p.). Bibliography (2p.). Index. *Class No:* 886.7

[8683]
MATEJIC, M., ***and others.*** **A Biobibliographical handbook of Bulgarian authors.** Black, K.L., *ed.* Columbus, Ohio, Slavica, 1981. 347p. illus. $17.95 ISBN: 0893570915.

Covers 88 authors chronologically in 5 periods from 580 to the present, giving biographical sketch and bibliography of works and critical studies (in English and Bulgarian). Some entries have photographs. Lacks index.
Class No: 886.7

[8684]
MOSER, C.A. A History of Bulgarian literature, 865-1944. The Hague, Mouton, 1972. 282p. $58.70. ISBN: 9027920087.

5 chapters: 1. Old Bulgarian literature (9th-18th centuries) - 2. The Bulgarian renaissance (1762-1878) - 3. The Post-liberation epoch (1878-1896) - 4. The Age of modernism and individualism (1896-1917) - 5. From war to war (1917-1944). Bibliography (18p.) of mainly western-language material, aranged by chapter and listing general sources and studies of individual writers. Index. *Class No:* 886.7

Baltic Literatures

[8685]
Baltic drama: a handbook and bibliography. Straumanis, A., *ed.* Prospect Heights, Ill., Waveland Press, 1981. xiv,705p. $44.95. ISBN: 0917974638.

Sections on Estonia, Latvia and Lithuania, each comprising overview, biographies of dramatists, A-Z, and annotated bibliographies of dramatists (5,349 entries in all). Classified bibliography of background material and critical studies (15p.). Author and title indexes. *Class No:* 888

[8686]
Latviešu rakstniecība biogrāfijās. Hausmanis, V., *and others, eds.* Riga, Latvijas Enciklopēdija, 1992. 413p. illus. ISBN: 5899600349.

A dictionary of Latvian writers with over 1,600 signed entries, which include biography, list of works and secondary bibliography. Photographs with many entries. Chronological list of birth dates, 1550-1966. Lists of birth and burial places. *Class No:* 888

[8687]
Lietuvių egzodo literatūra, 1945-1990. Bradūnas, K. *and* Šilbajoris, R., *eds.* Chicago, Lituanistikos Institutas, 1992. 861p. illus.

A history of postwar Lithuanian literature with substantial bibliographies. Index. *Class No:* 888

[8688]
RUBULIS, A. Baltic literature: a survey of Finnish, Estonian, Latvian, and Lithuanian literatures. Notre Dame, Ind., Univ. of Notre Dame Press, 1970. xv,215p.

Separate sections for each national literature comprising introduction to the ethnic characteristics of their respective folklores and the origins of their written literatures, followed by discussion of the main literary movements and major individual authors. Many quotations in English translation. Bibliography (3p.). Lacks index. *Class No:* 888

89 Oriental, African, etc. Literature

Oriental Literature

Bibliographies

[8689]

ANDERSON, G.L. Asian literature in English: a guide to information sources. Detroit, Gale, 1981. 336p. ISBN: 0810313626.

A bibliography of translations into English of Asian-language literary works and of English-language studies of those works. Covers China, Japan, Korea, Burma, Cambodia, Indonesia, Laos, Malaysia, Singapore, Thailand, Vietnam, Mongolia, Tibet and Turkey. Over 2,200 entries. For India, see A. Singh's *Indian literature in English* in the same series. *Class No:* 890(01)

[8690]

JENNER, P.N. Southeast Asian literatures in translation: a preliminary bibliography. Honolulu, Univ. Press of Hawaii, 1973. xvi,198p. ISBN: 0824802616.

Lists 3,690 translations (mainly into English and French, with some into Dutch and German) in 10 sections: 1. Burma - 2. Cambodia - 3. Champa - 4. Indonesia - 5. Laos - 6. Malaysia and Singapore - 7. Philippines - 8. Thailand - 9. Vietnam - 10. Regional and general works. Subdivisions within each national section for genres, folk literature, etc. *Class No:* 890(01)

[8691]

Southeast Asian languages and literatures: a bibliographical guide to Burmese, Cambodian, Indonesian, Javanese, Malay, Minangkabau, Thai and Vietnamese. Kratz, E.U., *ed.* London, Tauris, 1996. xvi,455p. £65. ISBN: 1860641148.

See entry at 809.0. *Class No:* 890(01)

Encyclopaedias & Dictionaries

[8692]

Dictionary of Oriental literatures. Průšek, J., *ed.* London, Allen & Unwin; New York, Basic Books, 1974. 3v.

V.1 *East Asia*, ed. by Z. Slupski (xxiii,226p. ISBN: 0048900044). V.2 *South and South-east Asia*, ed. by D. Zbavitel (xv,191p. ISBN: 0048900052). V.3 *West Asia and North Africa*, ed. by J. Becka (xvii,213p. ISBN: 0048900060).

2,000 concise, signed articles by over 150 scholars from many countries. Most entries give biographical information and critical evaluation on individual writers from classical to modern times and many have brief bibliographies appended. Other entries cover literary terms, genres, schools, movements, etc. Lists of entries at the end of each vol., grouped according to national literatures. N.B. Vol.3 includes the Arab countries of North Africa. *Class No:* 890(03)

[8693]

Far Eastern literatures in the 20th century: a guide. Klein, L.S., *ed.* New York, Ungar, 1986; Harpenden, Oldcastle, 1988. ix,195p. $12.95. ISBN: 0804463522, US; 0948353171, UK.

Handy guide based on Ungar's 5-vol. *Encyclopedia of world literature in the 20th century,* rev. ed., 1981-84 (*qv*). All entries on the literatures of East and Southeast Asia plus the major Pacific islands (Fiji, Western Samoa and Papua New Guinea) are reproduced with some minor revisions and corrections, but unfortunately not updated. 15 national/regional surveys are arranged A-Z, with 9 followed by articles on the major authors (60 in all). All articles and surveys are signed and include bibliographies. Index to author articles. *Class No:* 890(03)

[8694]

A Guide to Eastern literatures. Lang, D.M., *ed.* London, Weidenfeld and Nicolson; New York, Praeger, 1971. x,501p. ISBN: 0297002740, UK.

Signed chapters by 19 contributors on 15 literatures of the Middle and Far East, comprising outline of historical background, survey of major trends and literary movements, and biographical directory of key writers which includes details of English translations. Select bibliography of critical and background material appended to each chapter. Index. *Class No:* 890(03)

[8695]

South-East Asia languages and literatures: a select guide Herbert, P. *and* Milner, A., *eds.* Whiting Bay, Arran, Kiscadale Publications, 1988. x,182p. illus. £14.50. ISBN: 1870838106.

See entry at 809.0. *Class No:* 890(03)

Indian Literature

[8696]

DAS, S.K. A History of Indian literature, v.8: 1800-1900, Western impact - Indian response. New Delhi, Sahitya Akademi, 1991. xiii,815p. £14.95. ISBN: 8172010060.

The only one of a projected 10-vol set to be published so far. 15 chapters on genres and themes, with numbered subsections. Classified bibliography of secondary sources (15p.). Detailed chronology of literary events, 1800-1910, covering births, deaths and publications in 23 languages, with annotations. Indexes of names, titles, subjects and organizations. *Class No:* 891.1

[8697]

Encyclopaedia of Indian literature. Datta, A., *ed and* Lal, M., *eds..* New Delhi, Sahitya Akademi (distributed in US by South Asia Books), 1987-94. 6v.

Aims to cover the growth and development of Indian literature in 22 languages. Signed entries on authors (born up to 1947), genres, movements and works are arranged A-Z, in vols. 1-5, with supplementary entries and index in v.6. Some entries have short bibliographies. *Choice* (v.26(8),

.... (contd.)

April 1989, p.1304, and v.27(3), Nov. 1989, p.458) notes some serious omissions, but nevertheless welcomes 'a scholarly, authoritative reference work'. *Class No:* 891.1

[8698]

GARG, G.R. International encyclopaedia of Indian literature. Delhi, Mittal Publications (distributed in US by South Asia Books), 1988-91. v.1-8 (in progress). ISBN: 8170990270.

1st ed. of v.1 published New York, Humanities Press, 1983.

Coverage is as follows: v.1 (2nd ed.). Sanskrit, Pali, Prakrit, Apabhramsa - 2. Tamil - 3. Assamese - 4. Kannada - 5. Telugu - 6. Malayalam. 7. Urdu - 8. Sindhi. Further volumes are expected covering other languages. Basically one A-Z sequence of authors and titles in each vol. *Choice* (v.27(3), Nov. 1989, p.460) makes some strong criticisms (lack of indexes; lack of systematic transliteration system; patchy coverage of some languages; uneven standard of entries) and compares it unfavourably with Datta's *Encyclopaedia*. However, vols. 7 and 8 (both published 1991) do have indexes. *Class No:* 891.1

[8699]

GONDA, J. History of Indian literature. Wiesbaden, Harrassowitz, 1973-. v.1,fasc.1- (in progress).

V.1 *Veda and Upanishads.*

V.2 *Epics and Sanskrit religious literature.*

V.3 *Classical Sanskrit literature.*

V.4-6 *Scientific and technical literature.*

V.7-9 *Modern Indo-Aryan literature.*

V.10 *Dravidian literatures.*

Each vol. is made up of a number of fascicules which cover the history of a particular aspect of Indian literature or the literature of one of the Indian languages in great detail, with many bibliographical references. 'All these volumes are significant improvements on the volumes on regional literatures of India published by the Sahitya Akademi' (Gupta, B. and Kharbas, D.S., *India*, 1984, p.160). Examples of regional histories are: v.10, fasc.1, *Tamil literature*, by K.V. Zvelebil (viii,316p.), and v.8, fasc.4, *Kashmiri literature*, by B.D. Kachru (114p.).
Class No: 891.1

[8700]

Handbook of twentieth-century literatures of India. Natarajan, N., *ed.* Westport, Conn., Greenwood, 1996. 448p. $85. ISBN: 0313287783.

Signed chapters on the literatures of 12 languages and regions (Assamese, Bengali, English, Gujarati, Hindi, Kannada, Malayalam, Marathi, Punjabi, Tamil, Telugu, Urdu) covering trends, genres, themes, etc. and including extensive bibliographies of primary works. Some chapters cite key secondary sources. 5 further chapters on special topics (*e.g.* film) and sub-cultural literatures. List of general sources. Index. *Class No:* 891.1

Sanskrit Literature

[8701]

BANERJI, S.C. Companion to Sanskrit literature. 2nd ed. Delhi, Motilal, 1989. xviii,810p. £32. ISBN: 812080063x.

1st ed. 1971.

A very useful encyclopedic work, with sections on authors, works, characters, technical terms, geographical names, and the principal figures in myths and legends. Entries for literary works have references to editions and translations. 16 appendices (4 added for 2nd ed.), including a classified list of Sanskrit works and a select, classified bibliography of western-language studies (24p.).
Class No: 891.2

[8702]

BHATTACHARJI, S. History of classical Sanskrit literature. Hyderabad, Orient Longman, 1993. vi,351p. £17.95. ISBN: 0863112420.

From 3rd century BC to 16th century AD, in 5 chapters covering the major periods with subsections on key writers. Notes after each chapter. Bibliography of critical books and articles (8p.). Index. *Class No:* 891.2

[8703]

KEITH, A.B. A History of Sanskrit literature. Oxford, Clarendon Press, 1928 (repr. India, Motilal Banarsidass, 1993). xxxvi,575p. £15. ISBN: 8120809793.

A scholarly history of purely classical Sanskrit literature in 3 sections (1. The Language - 2. Belles-lettres and poetics - 3. Scientific literature) and 27 chapters, with numerous subsections. Quotations in the original and in translation. Many footnote references. English and Sanskrit indexes. Does not cover Vedic literature or the epic histories and dramas. *Class No:* 891.2

[8704]

MANI, V. Puranic encyclopedia: a comprehensive dictionary with special reference to the epic and puranic literature. 4th ed. Columbia, Mo., South Asia Books, 1975. 922p. ISBN: 0842608222.

1st ed. 1964, in Malayalam.

Over 5,000 entries (some occupying several pages) on characters, episodes, places, etc., with references to the texts. Genealogical tables appended. A very impressive compilation. *Class No:* 891.2

[8705]

WINTERNITZ, M. A History of Indian literature. Delhi, Motilal Banarsidass (distr. by South Asia Books), 1981-5. 3v.

Originally published Leipzig, Amelang, 1908-22, as *Geschichte der indischen Litteratur* (3v.). Earlier English ed. published Calcutta, Univ. of Calcutta, 1933-67.

V.1 *Vedic period.* 1981. £12.50. ISBN: 8120802640.

V.2 *Buddhist literature and Jaina literature.* 1983. £15. ISBN: 8120802659.

V.3, pt.1 *Classical Sanskrit literature;* pt. 2 *Scientific literature.* 1985. ISBN: 8120800567.

The most complete treatment in English of Sanskrit literature. *Class No:* 891.2

Pali Literature

[8706]

LAW, B.C. A History of Pali literature. London, Kegan Paul, Trench, Trubner & Co., 1933. 2v. (xxviii,689p.).

9 lengthy chapters. Appendix 1. Historical and geographical references in the Pali pitakas - 2. Pali tracts in the inscriptions. Index. *Class No:* 891.3

[8707]

VON HINUBER, O. A Handbook of Pali literature. Berlin & New York, de Gruyter, 1996. xiii,257p. DM195. (*Indian philology and South Asian studies, v.2.*) ISBN: 3110149923.

450 sections covering various texts of the *Tipitaka* and other Pali texts. Entries include discussion of the text's structure and composition history, an indication of its age, and lists of commentaries, editions, translations and key secondary sources. Detailed bibliography (11p.).
Class No: 891.3

Modern Indian Literature

[8708]

Contemporary Indian literature: a symposium. 2nd ed., rev. and enl. New Delhi, Sahitya Akademi, 1959. 338p.

1st ed. 1957.

Signed essays (average 20p.) on 16 literatures of India, giving the background of each language, a short account of the growth of its literature, and a survey of recent trends. Bibliography of English-language studies appended. Still useful for literatures in languages like Kannada, Kashmiri and Marathi, on which there are few other sources.
Class No: 891.4

[8709]

Who's who of Indian writers. Rao, S.B., *ed.* [2nd ed.]. New Delhi, Sahitya Akademi, 1983. 731p.

1st ed. 1961.

Provides biographical and bibliographical data on nearly 6,000 living writers in 22 languages, including English, based on information supplied by the biographees.
Class No: 891.4

Urdu Literature

[8710]

MAHMUD, S. Urdu language and literature: a bibliography of sources in European languages. London, Mansell, 1992. xx,331p. £60. ISBN: 0720121434.

Easily the most comprehensive work in its field, with 3,545 numbered entries under the following headings: Works of reference; Language; General literature; Poetry; Prose; Drama; Dastan (adaptations and translations from Persian). The latter sections are mainly arranged by literary author, with *c.*270 individuals covered. Author index. Despite the title, there are very few non-English works listed. 'Unlikely to be superseded for many years' (*New Library World*, v.94(1108), 1993, p.10). *Class No:* 891.43

[8711]

MATTHEWS, D.J., *and others*. Urdu literature. London, Third World Foundation for Social and Economic Studies, and Urdu Markaz, 1985. x,139p. ISBN: 0907962300.

A concise survey for the general reader of the history of the literature, with accounts of the major writers. Quotations in translation. Useful bibliography (3p.). Glossary of Urdu literary terms. Index. *Class No:* 891.43

[8712]

RUSSELL, R. The Pursuit of Urdu literature: a select history. London, Zed Books, 1992. 285p. £39.95. ISBN: 1856490289.

14 chapters in 3 main sections: Classical poetry (18th to mid-19th century); Literature in reaction to British rule (1857-1922); Literature and the people (1920s and onwards). Quotations in Urdu with translations. Notes and references (18p.). A highly personal account but nonetheless useful, especially for bibliographic essay offering suggestions for further reading (6p.) and bibliography of Russell's writings on Urdu, 1950-88 (4p.). *Class No:* 891.43

[8713]

SADIQ, M. A History of Urdu literature. 2nd ed., rev. and enl. Delhi, Oxford Univ. Press, 1984. xv,652p. ISBN: 0195615581.

1st ed. 1964.

A critical survey from the early 17th century to the present. Quotations in Urdu and English. References and notes. Index. 2nd ed. contains many revisions and much new material on post-Iqbal literature. *Class No:* 891.43

Bengali Literature

[8714]

GHOSH, D. Translations of Bengali works into English: a bibliography. London, Mansell, 1986. xii,264p. ISBN: 0720118093.

Lists over 700 books and period articles published since the early 19th century. Arranged in 16 subject categories (most of them literary), then by author, with brief annotations and library locations, mainly in the UK. Author and title indexes. *Class No:* 891.44

[8715]

GHOSH, J.C. Bengali literature. Reprint of 1948 ed. London, Curzon Press, 1976. 198p. ISBN: 0700700978.

Originally published London, Oxford Univ. Press, 1948.

A history to 1900 with an additional chapter devoted to Tagore. Quotations in English. Lacks bibliography. Index.
Class No: 891.44

[8716]

SEN, S. History of Bengali literature. Rev. ed. New Delhi, Sahitya Akademi, 1971. xii,394p.

1st ed. 1960.

From the beginnings to the death of Tagore (1941). Quotations in English translation with original texts in Appendix. Bibliography (5p.). *Class No:* 891.44

Tagore

[8717]

HENN, K. Rabindranath Tagore: a bibliography. Metuchen, N.J., The American Theological Library Assoc. and Scarecrow Press, 1985. xvii,331p. ISBN: 081081790x.

Lists works in English by and about Tagore. Part I has 1,719 items by Tagore arranged under 19 genre headings; Part II has 1,969 items about Tagore published up to 1982, including dissertations and theses, in 6 sections. Books about Tagore are briefly annotated (400 items). Name and subject indexes. *Class No:* 891.44TAG

Sinhalese Literature

[8718]
GODAKUMBURA, C.E. Sinhalese Literature. Colombo, Colombo Apothecaries' Co. Ltd., 1955. xiv,376p.

A survey in 27 chapters. Numerous quotations with English translations. Bibliography (2p.). Index of Sinhalese titles. Name and subject indexes. *Class No:* 891.48

Nepali Literature

[8719]
PRADHAN, K. A History of Nepali literature. New Delhi, Sahitya Akademi, 1984 (distr. in US by South Asia Books). 240p. $10. ISBN: 0836414500.

'Not a scholarly conspectus, it only gives a rapid account of a few major tendencies' (*Preface*). 14 chapters. Quotations in Nepali with translation. Select bibliography of studies in English and Nepali. Pronunciation chart. Index. *Class No:* 891.493

Persian Literature

[8720]
ARBERRY, A.J. Classical Persian literature. London, Allen & Unwin, 1958. 464p.

From the beginnings (9th century) to the death of Jami (1492) in 16 chapters, with many quotations, all in English. Chapter bibliographies (7p.). Index. *Class No:* 891.5

[8721]
BROWNE, E.G. A Literary history of Persia. Cambridge, Cambridge Univ. Press, 1928. 4v. illus.

Originally published 1902-24; vols.1-2 by Fisher Unwin, vols.3-4 by Cambridge Univ. Press.

V.1 *From the earliest times until Firdawsí.* ISBN: 0521043441.

V.2 *From Firdawsí to Sa'dí.* ISBN: 052104345x.

V.3 *The Tartar dominion (1265-1502).* ISBN: 0521043468.

V.4 *Modern times (1500-1924).* ISBN: 0521043476.

The standard history, it contains many original quotations with English translations and biographies of poets and prose-writers. Numerous detailed footnote references. Analytical index in each vol.

Reprint announced by Curzon Press for Spring 1998 (4v. £295. ISBN: 070070406x). *Class No:* 891.5

[8722]
KAMSHAD, H. Modern Persian prose literature. Cambridge, Cambridge Univ. Press, 1966. xiv,226p. ISBN: 0521054648.

Part 1 is a history from the late 19th century to the 1960s in 13 chapters. Part 2 is a study of Sādiq Hidāyat in 9 chapters. All quotations in English translation. List of Hidāyat's works (7p.) and general bibliography (9p.). Index. Accompanied by *A Modern Persian prose reader*, 1968 (258p. ISBN: 0521070775). *Class No:* 891.5

[8723]
Persian literature. Yarshalter, E., *ed.* [New York], Bibliotheca Persica, 1988. xi,562p. (*Columbia lectures on Iranian studies.*) ISBN: 0887062636.

6 main sections, comprising 25 signed chapters (23 contributors) based on a series of lectures given at Columbia University: 1. Introductory survey - 2. Pre-Islamic literatures - 3. Classical period - 4. Contemporary literature of Iran - 5. Persian literature outside Iran - 6. Translation of Persian literature. Quotations in English. Very useful classified, annotated bibliography of Persian literature in translation. Index of names, titles, subjects and technical terms. *Class No:* 891.5

[8724]
RYPKA, J., *and others*. History of Iranian literature. Jahn, K., *ed.* Enl. and rev. ed. Dordrecht, Reidel, 1968. xxvii,928p. map. $158. ISBN: 9027701431.

First published Prague, 1956, as *Dějiny perské a tadžicke literatury*. For the English ed., sections have been revised, enlarged and updated.

A scholarly history from a Marxist perspective. 8 sections, each by a specialist, devoted to different periods and branches of the literature. Selected bibliography (111p.) by sections, plus sectional notes and references. Detailed index. *Class No:* 891.5

Celtic Literatures

[8725]
BROMWICH, R. Medieval Celtic literature: a select bibliography. Toronto, Univ. of Toronto Press, 1974. 109p. (*Toronto medieval bibliographies.*)

Annotated entries for over 500 books and articles in 5 sections: 1. Introductory materials - 2. Language - 3. Literary history and criticism - 4. Texts and translations - 5. Background materials. *Class No:* 891.6

[8726]
HARVARD UNIVERSITY. Library. **Celtic literatures.** Classification schedule. Classified listing by call number. Chronological listing. Author and title listing. Cambridge, Mass., Harvard Univ. Press, 1970. viii,192p. (*Widener Library shelflist, no.25.*) ISBN: 0674104803.

Covers Irish, Welsh, Gaelic, Cornish, Manx, Breton and Gaulish literatures and includes non-literary texts. 8,000 titles: 5,500 in Celtic languages, 700 in English, the rest in other languages. *Class No:* 891.6

Irish Literature

Bibliographies

[8727]
BAUMGARTEN, R. Bibliography of Irish linguistics and literature, 1942-71. Dublin, Institute for Advanced Studies, 1986. xxiii,776p. £35. ISBN: 0901282812.

9,312 unannotated entries in a classified arrangement. 4 indexes: first lines of verse; words and proper names; authors; sources. *Class No:* 891.62(01)

[8728]
BEST, R.I. Bibliography of Irish philology and of printed Irish literature. Rev. ed. Dublin, Institute for Advanced Studies, 1992. xii,339p. £25. ISBN: 1855001594.

1st ed. Dublin, National Library of Ireland, 1913.

About 4,000 entries, of which 75% are in the literature section, most of them annotated. Detailed index.
Class No: 891.62(01)

[8729]
—BEST, R.I. Bibliography of Irish philology and manuscript literature: publications, 1913-1941. Dublin, Dublin Institute for Advanced Studies, 1942. x,251p.

2,441 numbered entries, of which 1,456 relate to literature. Annotations include analysis of contents. Indexes of Irish words and first lines of poems, plus general index.
Class No: 891.62(01)

[8730]
A Bibliography of modern Irish and Anglo-Irish literature. Kersnowski, F., *ed.* Dublin, Trinity Univ., 1976. 156p.

Concentrates on writers of the Irish literary renaissance, arranged A-Z with data on writer's creative work, biography, autobiography, travel, criticism (except in periodicals), and major works about him/her. Long list of background titles in Preface. *Class No:* 891.62(01)

Encyclopaedias & Dictionaries

[8731]
Dictionary of Irish literature. Hogan, R., *ed.* Rev. & exp. ed. Westport, Conn., Greenwood; London, Aldwych Press, 1997. 2v. (xx,1413p.). £99.50. ISBN: 0313291721, US; 0861721020, UK.

See entry at 820.415(03). *Class No:* 891.62(03)

[8732]
The Oxford companion to Irish literature. Welch, R., *ed.* Oxford, Oxford Univ. Press, 1996. xxv,614p. £25. ISBN: 0198661584.

See entry at 820.415(03). *Class No:* 891.62(03)

Chronologies

[8733]
CAHALAN, J.M. Modern Irish literature and culture: a chronology. Boston, Hall, 1993. 374p. $45. ISBN: 0816172641.

Covers 1601-1992, with only major events recorded for the early part of the period and then separate entries for each year from 1858 in which literary events and works (in both Irish and English) are listed along with developments in other cultural fields, *e.g.* education, art and the Irish language. Particularly good coverage of newspapers and periodicals. Biographical notes on 37 key literary and historical figures. Bibliography of secondary works. Thorough index. *Class No:* 891.62(090)

Histories

[8734]
HYDE, D. A Literary history of Ireland: from earliest times to the present day. New ed., with introduction by B. Ó Cuív. London, Benn; New York, Barnes & Noble, 1967. xlii,654p.

First published London, Fisher Unwin, 1899.

A pioneering work in 44 chapters, with many (often lengthy) quotations in translation. Analytical index. New ed.

.... *(contd.)*
has bibliography of 20th-century studies of Irish literature, but, according to the new introduction, none has superseded Hyde's work. *Class No:* 891.62(091)

[8735]
WILLIAMS, J.E.C. *and* **FORD, P.K. The Irish literary tradition.** Cardiff, Univ. of Wales Press, 1997. xii,355p. illus. £19.95. ISBN: 0708311652.

Originally written in Welsh by Williams and published 1958 as *Traddodiad llenyddol iwerddon.*

A history of literature in the Irish language since the 5th century, which has been extensively revised and updated for publication in English. Final chapter offers critical appraisals of the work of recent and contemporary Irish writers. Numerous references to primary and secondary sources.
Class No: 891.62(091)

Biographies

[8736]
BRADY, A.M. *and* **CLEEVE, B. A Biographical dictionary of Irish writers.** [2nd ed.]. Mullingar, Lilliput Press; New York, St. Martin's Press, 1985. xii,388p. ISBN: 0946640033, Ireland; 0312078714, US.

See entry at 820.415(092). *Class No:* 891.62(092)

[8737]
Modern Irish writers: a bio-critical sourcebook. Gonzalez, A.G., *ed.* Westport, Conn., Greenwood; London, Aldwych Press, 1997. 480p. £67.50. ISBN: 0313295573, US; 0861721055, UK.

See entry at 820.415(092). *Class No:* 891.62(092)

Welsh Literature

Bibliographies

[8738]
JONES, E.J.L. *and* **LEWIS, H. Mynegai i farddoniaeth y llawysgrifau.** Cardiff, Univ. of Wales Press, 1928. iv,392p. ISBN: 0708302548.

An index to Welsh poetry found in the principal collections of manuscripts relating to Wales.
Class No: 891.66(01)

[8739]
Llyfryddiaeth llenyddiaeth gymraeg. Parry, T. *and* Morgan, M., *eds.* Cardiff, Univ. of Wales Press, 1976. xxiii,313p. £8.50. ISBN: 0708306314.

A well-organized, classified bibliography of studies of Welsh literature. Nearly 6,000 unannotated entries in 12 sections with numerous subdivisions. Many individual authors treated. Index.

Followed by *Llyfryddiaeth llenyddiaeth gymraeg, Cyfrol 2: 1976-1986*, by G.O. Watts (1993. xx,286p. £14.95. ISBN: 070831161x). *Class No:* 891.66(01)

Encyclopaedias & Dictionaries

[8740]
JONES, R.M. Llenyddiaeth Gymraeg, 1936-72. Llandybie, C. Davies, 1975. 463p. ISBN: 071540198x.

Essays in Welsh on 65 authors and topics, with short chapter bibliographies. Name and title indexes.

Preceded by *Llenyddiaeth Gymraeg, 1902-1936* (Llandybie, Gyhoeddiadau Barddas, 1987. 581p.), which has 51 essays. No bibliographies, but many works are cited in the essays. Name index. *Class No:* 891.66(03)

[8741]

The Oxford companion to the literature of Wales. Stephens, M., *ed.* Oxford, Oxford Univ. Press, 1986. xviii,682p. £29.50. ISBN: 0192115863.

Covers literature in Welsh and English from the 6th century to the present. Over 2,800 entries, of which 1,200 are for writers, the majority of them users of the Welsh language and by no means all literary authors. No one born after 1950 is included. Entries for major writers carry substantial bibliographical notes. Other entries cover historical figures (royalty, politicians, sportsmen, clerics, etc.); literary movements, genres and periodicals; myths, legends and folklore; places and events of literary significance; and all aspects of Welsh culture, *e.g.* 'Rugby', 'Methodism', 'Nationalism'. Many cross-references. Chronology of Welsh history, AD43-1985 (8p.). 222 contributors listed, but entries not signed. 'A reliable and indispensable reference-book ... its factual material invariably accurate and up to date' (*Modern Language Review,* v.83(3), July 1988, p.713-5).

A Welsh-language edition, *Cydymaith i Lenyddiaeth Cymru* (New ed. Cardiff, Univ. of Wales Press, 1997. xiii,831p. £27.50. ISBN: 0708309151), has more and lengthier articles on the traditional rules of poetic art. A revised and expanded ed. of the English-language version is announced by the Univ. of Wales Press for late 1998, under the title *A New companion to the literature of Wales* (£27.50. ISBN: 0708313833) *Class No:* 891.66(03)

Histories

[8742]

A Guide to Welsh literature. Jarman, A.O.H., *& others, eds.* Swansea, C. Davies (later Cardiff, Univ.of Wales Press), 1976-. v.1- (in progress).

V.1. 2nd, rev. ed. 1992. 302p. illus. £10.95. ISBN: 0708311431.

V.2. 2nd, rev. ed. 1997. x,375p. £14.95. ISBN: 0708314392.

V.3. 1997. x,293p. £14.95. ISBN: 0708314007.

V.6. 1998. ix,308p. £14.95. ISBN: 0708314244.

1st eds. of vols. 1 and 2 published 1976 and 1979.

4 vols. have appeared so far of a projected 6-vol. set, which aims 'to outline the history and development of Welsh literature from its beginnings in the sixth century to the present day' (*Preface*). V.1 covers 6th to 13th centuries; v.2 continues to 1550 and v.3 to 1700; v.6 deals with the 20th century. Almost all quotations are in English translation. Bibliographies after each chapter. Index in each vol. *Class No:* 891.66(091)

[8743]

PARRY, T. A History of Welsh literature; translated from the Welsh by H. Idris Bell. Oxford, Clarendon Press, 1955. xii,534p.

Originally published 1944 as *Hanes llenyddiaeth Gymraeg hyd 1900* (Reprinted 1979 by Univ. of Wales Press. ISBN: 0708307280).

Comprehensive survey from the 6th century to 1900, to which the translator has added an appendix (125p.) on the 20th century and many footnotes on technical terms, geographical names and allusions likely to confuse non-Welsh readers. All quotations have been translated. The original's comprehensive bibliography is replaced by brief notes on a selection of English-language publications. Author and subject indexes. *Class No:* 891.66(091)

Biographies

[8744]

JONES, G. *and* **ROWLANDS, J. Profiles:** a visitors' guide to writing in twentieth century Wales. Llandysul, Dyfed, Gomer Press, 1980. xxxi,382p. illus. £9.95. ISBN: 0850887135.

Biographical and critical sketches (average length 5½p.) on 28 Welsh language and 29 English language writers active in the 20th century, with brief notes on many more in each category. Bibliographies and photographs for most of the major writers. Glossary. Bibliographical notes (3p.) on anthologies and critical material in English.
Class No: 891.66(092)

Cornish Literature

[8745]

MURDOCH, B. Cornish literature. Cambridge, Brewer, 1993. ix,174p. £29.50. ISBN: 0859913643.

Aims 'to place the literature of Cornish into a broad literary context for the general reader' (*Preface*). 6 chapters followed by an excellent classified bibliography (19p.). Index. *Class No:* 891.67

Albanian Literature

[8746]

ELSIE, R. Dictionary of Albanian literature. New York, Greenwood, 1986. viii,170p. $49.95. ISBN: 031325186x.

A welcome guide to a little-known literature, containing over 500 entries on writers and literature-related topics, including basic biographical and bibliographical data. Translations provided for all titles mentioned. Bibliography of general sources (3p.). Index. *Class No:* 891.983

[8747]

ELSIE, R. History of Albanian literature. Boulder, Colo., Social Science Monographs, 1995 (distr. by Columbia Univ. Press). 2v. illus. $66.50. (*East European monographs.*) ISBN: 088033276x.

The first comprehensive history of Albanian literature, including coverage of Kosovo and the Italo-Albanian communities of Calabria and Sicily and of 20th-century writers who were persecuted for ideological reasons. Bibliographical references. Index. *Class No:* 891.983

[8748]

Historia e letërsisë shqiptare. Shuteriqi, D.S., *ed.* Tiranë, Akademia e Shkencave e RPS të Shqipërisë, 1983. 629p. 30 lekë.

An improved and much-expanded version of a two-volume history of Albanian literature which appeared in 1959 and 1965, which has been compiled by a team of scholars from the Institute of Linguistics and Literature of the Albanian Academy of Sciences. 3 sections cover old Albanian literature, the Rilindja or national renaissance, and the 1912-39 period. Selective bibliography. Index of authors and works.

'From the Marxist-Leninist view at least, [a] definitive history of Albanian literature indispensable as a basic reference for all Albanologists' (*World Literature Today,* v.59(3), Summer, 1985, p.473). *Class No:* 891.983

Hebrew Literature

Bibliographies

[8749]

GOELL, Y. Bibliography of modern Hebrew literature in translation. Jerusalem, Executive of the World Zionist Organization, Youth and Hechalutz Dept., and Israel Universities Press, 1968. vii; 110; 22p. ISBN: 0878551875.

Lists *c.*7,500 translations from the post-*Haskalah* period (*i.e.* since 1880) in 7 sections: General anthologies; poetry; prose; drama; essays, criticism and miscellaneous; children's poetry; children's prose. Indexes of authors and translators. List of periodicals. Hebrew index of authors and titles. Based almost entirely on the holdings of the Jewish National and University Library in Jerusalem. *Class No:* 892.4(01)

[8750]

GOELL, Y. Bibliography of modern Hebrew literature in translation. Tel Aviv, Institute for the Translation of Hebrew Literature, 1975. 117p.

Lists translations by language, then by genre, with the emphasis on separate publications. Indexes of Hebrew authors and of translators, editors, etc. *Class No:* 892.4(01)

[8751]

—Bibliography of modern Hebrew literature in translation, 1972/76-1984. Goldberg, I., *ed.* Ramat Gan, Institute for the Translation of Hebrew Literature, 1979-85. 7v. ISSN: 0334309x.

Contains citations to translations of Hebrew literature into world languages, and includes references to book reviews and critical studies of recent Hebrew publications. Also provides bio-critical material on Hebrew writers.

Continued by *New series* (ISSN: 9334309x), which began in 1988 (covering 1985-6) and is now annual. Arranged by language, A-Z, then by genre, entries include author and title in Roman and Hebrew characters, bibliographical details, name of translator and subject of work. Indexes of authors, Hebrew titles, translated titles and translators. V.7-8, *1991-92* (1996. xii,731p.), lists nearly 4,000 translations in 23 languages. *Class No:* 892.4(01)

[8752]

SCHWAB, M. Index of articles relative to Jewish history and literature, published in periodicals from 1665 to 1900. Augmented ed. New York, Ktav, 1972. xvi,539; 409-613p. ISBN: 087068163x.

First published as *Répertoire des articles relatifs à l'histoire et la littérature juives* ... (Paris, Geuthner, 1914-23).

An author index of articles in 90 periodicals (only 7 in English; the majority are in French, German and Hebrew). Text in Hebrew and English. Subject index.
Class No: 892.4(01)

Reviews & Abstracts

[8753]

Hebrew studies: a journal devoted to the Hebrew language and literature of all periods. Madison, Wis., National Assoc. of Professors of Hebrew, 1954-. Annual. ISSN: 01464094.

Formerly known as *Hebrew Abstracts.*

Includes brief abstracts of articles, books and periodicals on Hebrew published in all languages. *Class No:* 892.4(048)

Histories

[8754]

KRAVITZ, N. 3000 years of Hebrew literature; from the earliest time through the 20th century. Athens, Ohio, Swallow Press, 1971; London, W.H. Allen, 1973. xviii,586p. maps. ISBN: 0804005052, US; 049011415, UK.

15 chapters with numerous subsections, most of them devoted to individual writers. Covers a wide range of literature, including theology, philosophy, science, etc. Many quotations in English translation. Appendix A. lists important dates in Jewish history; B. lists *c.*70 writers not covered in the text. Bibliography (7p.). Index.
Class No: 892.4(091)

[8755]

WAXMAN, M. A History of Jewish literature. 2nd ed. New York and London, Yoseloff, 1960. 5v. in 6. maps.

1st ed. in 4 vols. as *A History of Jewish literature from the close of the Bible to our own days* (New York, Bloch, 1930-41); v.2 and v.4 appeared in enlarged and corrected eds., 1943-7.

V.1 *From the close of the canon to the end of the twelfth century.* xvi,539p.

V.2 *From the twelfth century to the middle of the eighteenth century.* xiii,712p.

V.3 *From the middle of the eighteenth century to 1880.* xii,767p.

V.4 *From 1880 to 1935.* 2pts. (xv,1312p.).

V.5 *From 1935 to 1960.* 361p.

Covers literature in the widest sense, including theology, philosophy, history, biography, etc., with chapters devoted to genres and periods. Chapter bibliographies at the end of each vol. Index to whole set in v.5. *Class No:* 892.4(091)

[8756]

ZINBERG, I. A History of Jewish literature. Martin, B., *tr. and ed.* Cleveland, Ohio, The Press of Case Western Reserve Univ. (vols. 1-3); Cincinnati, Ohio, Hebrew Union College / New York, Ktav (vols. 4-12), 1972-78. 12v. $315. ISBN: 068553636x.

Originally written in Yiddish and published Vilna, 1929-37, in 8 vols. as *Di Geshikhte fun der Literatur bay Yidn.*

From the beginnings in 10th-century Spain to the end of the Haskalah period in 19th-century Russia, covering not only pure literature but also theology, philosophy, folklore, science, etc. Many quotations in English translation. Detailed bibliographical notes, glossary and index at end of each vol. *Class No:* 892.4(091)

Arabic Literature

Bibliographies

[8757]

ALTOMA, S.J. Modern Arabic literature: a bibliography of articles, books, dissertations, and translations in English. Bloomington, Ind., Indiana Univ. Press, 1975. 73p. (*Asian Studies Research Institute occasional papers - 3.*)

A classified list of *c.*850 items. Author index.
Class No: 892.7(01)

[8758]

ALTOMA, S.J. Modern Arabic poetry in English translation: a bibliography. [Riyadh?], The King Fahd School of Translation, 1993. 177p. $20. ISBN: 9981953105.

Lists over 2,000 poems (most of them published after 1950) by 350 poets. Arranged by poet, A-Z, then by (English) poem title, entries give name of translator and citation for book or journal of publication. Lists of cited bibliographies, anthologies and periodicals. 'A valuable and unique work' (*Choice*, v.31(8), April 1994, p.1267).
Class No: 892.7(01)

[8759]

ANDERSON, M. Arabic materials in English translation: a bibliography of works from the pre-Islamic period to 1977. Boston, Hall, 1980. xiii,249p. ISBN: 0816179549.

Over 1,600 entries in 10 categories, of which 2 (p.150-207) cover classical and modern literature, the rest covering music, philosophy, Islam, etc. Concise annotations. Index of authors, translators, and titles. *Class No:* 892.7(01)

Encyclopaedias & Dictionaries

[8760]

Encyclopedia of Arabic literature. Meisami, J.S. *and* Starkey, P., *eds.* London, Routledge, 1998. 2v. £175. ISBN: 0415068088.

Over 1,300 signed entries on authors, works, journals, genres and key concepts in Arabic literature. Covers the classical (pre-Islamic to 1258), transitional (1258-1798) and modern periods, without geographical limitation, including writers in Arabic in North and South America, medieval Spain and Sicily, Persia and Turkey. Entries are followed by selective secondary bibliographies and biographical entries include references to major works and translations. Chronological tables of dynasties. Fully indexed.
Class No: 892.7(03)

Excerpts

[8761]

Modern Arabic literature. Allen, R., *comp. and ed.* New York, Ungar, 1987. xxxiii,370p. $75. (*A Library of literary criticism.*) ISBN: 0804430241.

Presents substantial excerpts from literary criticism on about 71 writers from Algeria, Egypt, Iraq, Lebanon, Palestine, Sudan, Syria and Tunisia, many of them translated from Arabic by the editor. Single A-Z sequence of writers, with excerpts arranged chronologically under each one. Bibliography of works mentioned lists full-length books by each author and available English translations. Index to critics. *Class No:* 892.7(082.200)

Histories

[8762]

BADAWI, M.M. Early Arabic drama. Cambridge, Cambridge, Univ. Press, 1988. 148p. £37.50. ISBN: 0521344271.

'An attempt to trace the development of Arabic drama from its beginnings in the middle of the nineteenth century until it reached its maturity in the second and third decades of the twentieth century' (*Introduction*), in 4 chapters with subsections on the major dramatists. Quotations in English. Index.

Followed by *Modern Arabic drama in Egypt* (Cambridge, Cambridge Univ. Press, 1987. ix,246p. £37.50. ISBN: 0521242223), which covers the 1930s to the 1980s.
Class No: 892.7(091)

[8763]

BADAWI, M.M. A Short history of modern Arabic literature. Oxford, Clarendon Press, 1993. ix,314p. £50. ISBN: 0198265425.

7 chapters in 3 main sections, covering poetry, prose fiction and drama since the mid-19th century. Selective, classified bibliography (13p.) of works in European languages (mainly English), including background material, general criticism, and translations and studies of specific writers. Described by *TLS* (no.4738, Jan. 21, 1994, as 'infinitely better informed' than Haywood's history (*q.v.*), but presents, nevertheless, 'an unfocused and incomplete picture of the modern Arabic literary tradition.'
Class No: 892.7(091)

[8764]

—HAYWOOD, J.A. Modern Arabic literature, 1800-1970: an introduction, with extracts in translation. London, Lund Humphries, 1971. xiii,306p. ISBN: 0853314675.

A survey in 4 chapters, with subsections on specific countries and genres and 12 lengthy extracts in English. References (13p.). Glossary (5p.). Useful bibliography of studies in 6 languages (4p.). *Class No:* 892.7(091)

[8765]

BROCKELMANN, C. Geschichte der arabischen Litteratur. 2nd ed. Leiden, Brill, 1943-9. 2v.

1st ed. Weimar (later Berlin), Felber, 1898-1902. Supplementary vols. 1-3, Leiden, Brill, 1937-42.

A standard reference work comprising a series of bio-bibliographical summaries. Lists manuscripts as well as printed editions. *Class No:* 892.7(091)

[8766]

BRUGMAN, J. An Introduction to the history of modern Arabic literature in Egypt. Leiden, Brill, 1984. xiv,439p. (*Studies in Arabic literature.*) ISBN: 9004071725.

From 1800 to 1950 in 12 chapters, with numbered subsections on genres and individual writers. Primary bibliographies for major figures. Bibliography of critical studies in Arabic and European languages (15p.).
Class No: 892.7(091)

[8767]

The Cambridge history of Arabic literature. Cambridge, Cambridge Univ. Press, 1983- (in progress). £75 per vol.

Arabic literature to the end of the Umayyad period, ed. by A.F.L. Beeston and others. 1983. xvi,547p. ISBN: 0521240158.

'Abbasid belles-lettres, ed. by J. Ashtiany and others. 1990. xv,517p. ISBN: 0521240166.

Religion, learning and science in the Abbasid period, ed. by M.J.L. Young and others. 1990. xxi,587p. ISBN: 0521327636.

Modern Arabic literature, ed. by M.M. Badawi. 1993. xi,571p. ISBN: 0521331978.

Each unnumbered vol. contains several signed essays by international scholars. Many quotations in English translation. 1st vol. has extremely useful bibliography of translations of the Koran into European languages (19p.); latest vol. has comprehensive bibliography of primary and secondary works (58p.). Glossary of Arabic terms and index in each vol.

A lengthy review of the latest vol. in *TLS* (no.4715, Aug.13, 1993, p.7-8) suggests that the series to date has

.... (contd.)
been 'uneven in content and coverage, with gaps, overlaps and a mixed bag of styles and appproaches.'
Class No: 892.7(091)

[8768]
GIBB, H.A.R. Arabic literature: an introduction. 2nd rev. ed. Oxford, Oxford Univ. Press, 1963. xi,182p.
1st ed. 1926.
A survey for the non-specialist, with a chapter on the Arabic language followed by 5 chapters on the main literary periods from AD500 to 1800. Bibliography by chapters (11p.) is a useful select list of reference books and translations in English and other Western languages. 3 indexes: literary genres; authors and titles; place-names, peoples and religions. *Class No:* 892.7(091)

[8769]
HUART, C. A History of Arabic literature. Reprint of 1903 ed. London, Darf, 1987. vii,478p. £26. ISBN: 1850771782.
Originally published, London, Heinemann, 1903.
Remains an important history, containing much biographical information on individual writers within its 12 chapters. Classified bibliography (4p.). Index.
Class No: 892.7(091)

[8770]
NICHOLSON, R.A. A Literary history of the Arabs. London, Fisher Unwin, 1907 (reprinted Richmond, Surrey, Curzon Press, 1995). xxxi,500p. £35. ISBN: 070070261x.
Regarded as the standard history in English until the arrival of *The Cambridge history,* it covers religion, philology, science and culture as well as literature, and is particularly strong on poetry. Many quotations in English translation. Footnote references. Classified, selective bibliography (10p.) of studies by European authors. Index.
Class No: 892.7(091)

Egyptian Literature

[8771]
LICHTHEIM, M. Ancient Egyptian literature: a book of readings. Berkeley, Calif., Univ. of California Press, 1973-80. 3v. $13 per vol.
V.1 *The Old and Middle Kingdoms.* 1973. (xxi,245p. ISBN: 0520028996). V.2 *The New Kingdom.* 1976. (xiv,239p. ISBN: 0520036158). V.3 *The Late period.* 1980. (xiv,228p. ISBN: 0520040201).
Collections of texts in translation, including monumental inscriptions and works written on papyrus, with introduction and detailed notes. Each vol. has chronology and 6 indexes: divinities, monarchs, personal names, geographical and ethnical terms, Egyptian words, and topics. *Class No:* 893.1

Coptic Literature

[8772]
KAMMERER, W., ***and others*****. A Coptic bibliography.** Ann Arbor, Mich., Univ. of Michigan, 1950. xv,205p.
Classified list of over 3,700 books and articles on all aspects of Coptic history and culture, including literature and philology. The entries are drawn from a wide range of countries and many are annotated. Author index.
Class No: 893.2

Mongolian Literature

[8773]
HEISSIG, W. Geschichte der mongolischen Literatur. Wiesbaden, Harrassowitz, 1972. 2v. (xix,969p.).
V.1 *19. Jahrhundert bis zum Beginn des 20. Jahrhunderts.* V.2 *20. Jahrhundert bis zum Einfluss moderner Ideen.*
18 chapters covering the period *c.*1850-*c.*1932, with numerous quotations and footnotes. Bibliography (20p.). Indexes of Mongolian titles, German titles, literary genres, place-names, and authors. *Class No:* 894.21

Turkish Literature

[8774]
BOMBACI, A. Histoire de la littérature turque. Melikoff, I., *tr.* Paris, Librairie C. Klincksieck, 1968. 431p.
Originally published Milan, Nuova Accademia Editrice, 1956, as *Storia della letteratura turca.*
A history in 6 parts from the origins in pre-Islamic Turkey to the early 20th century. 'The most comprehensive study of Turkish literature ever written in the West' (Güçlü, M., *Turkey,* 1981, p.214). *Class No:* 894.35

[8775]
MITLER, L. Contemporary Turkish writers: a critical biobibliography of leading writers in the Turkish Republican period up to 1980. Bloomington, Ind., Research Institute for Inner Asian Studies, 1988 (repr. Richmond, Surrey, Curzon Press, 1997). 325p. £75. (*Uralic & Altaic series.*) ISBN: 0700709460.
An A-Z listing of authors active since 1923, giving pseudonyms, subject areas, birth and death dates, biographical notes, critical evaluation, and list of works which includes translations of all Turkish titles. Some entries include translated passages from the writer's works. Glossary. List of literary award winners. Select bibliography of European-language works on Turkish literature. 'The only work on modern Turkish writers in a Western language' (*Choice,* v.26(5), Jan. 1989, p.786). *Class No:* 894.35

[8776]
MITLER, L. Ottoman Turkish writers: a bibliographical dictionary of significant figures in pre-Republican Turkish literature. New York, Lang, 1988. xvii,203p. $31.50. ISBN: 0820406333.
Covers *c.*100 authors, giving biographical sketch, critical comment on major works, brief translated extract, and lists of works and critical studies. *Class No:* 894.35

Hungarian Literature

Bibliographies

[8777]
CZIGÁNY, M. Hungarian literature in English translation published in Great Britain, 1830-1968: a bibliography. London, Szepsi Csombor Literary Circle, 1969. 117p. ISBN: 0950045616.
250 numbered entries, with British Museum press marks and other locations, notes on Hungarian editions and

.... (contd.)
references to reviews. Bibliography of translations (items 67-250) is preceded by bibliography of books and articles in English on Hungarian literature. Chronological index and name index. *Class No:* 894.511(01)

[8778]
A Magyar irodalom és irodalomtudomány bibliográfiája, 1971/75-. Budapest, Országos Széchényi Könyvtár, 1989-. Annual. ISSN: 01341464.
Classified bibliography of the year's work in Hungarian literature, with author index. Latest vol. published 1993, covering 1987, has 10,000 entries, including studies of individual writers. *Class No:* 894.511(01)

[8779]
A Magyar irodalomtörténet bibliográfiája. Vargha, K., *ed.* Budapet, Akadémiai Kiadó, 1972-. v.1- (in progress). ISBN: 9630503069.
V.1 *1772-ig*. 1972. 638p.
V.2 *1772-1849*. 1975. 925p.
V.3 *1849-1905* (general, plus individual writers, A-G). 1990. 774p.
V.6 *1905-1945* (writers, A-K). 1982. 959p.
V.7 *1905-1945* (writers, L-Z). 1989. 789p.
V.8 *1945-1970* (writers A-Z). 1991. 488p.
A comprehensive bibliographical handbook on the history of Hungarian literature, produced by the Hungarian Academy of Sciences. Each vol. has detailed contents table and extensive name index. To be in 8 vols. V.4 will cover 1849-1905 (authors, H-Z) and v.5 will cover 1905-1970 (general material). *Class No:* 894.511(01)

[8780]
TEZLA, A. An Introductory bibliography to the study of Hungarian literature. Cambridge, Mass., Harvard Univ. Press, 1964. xxvi,290p. $27.50. ISBN: 0674463501.
Part One, Secondary Sources, lists 774 items in 12 sections with excellent annotations. Part Two, Primary Sources, has 2 sections, listing anthologies and selected editions of the works of 101 major authors. Locations in US and European libraries provided. 3 appendices list periodicals, dictionaries and libraries. Index of sources in non-Hungarian languages. Name index. Superbly organized. *Class No:* 894.511(01)

[8781]
—TEZLA, A. Hungarian authors: a bibliographical handbook. Cambridge, Mass., Belknap Press of Harvard Univ. Press, 1970. xxviii,792p. $70. ISBN: 0674426509.
An extension of Tezla's *An introductory bibliography to the study of Hungarian literature* (Cambridge, Mass., Harvard Univ. Press, 1964. xxvi,290p. ISBN: 0674463501), which aims at a complete record of first editions, an extensive list of later editions and a selection of the major bibliographical, biographical and critical works for 162 authors. Two A-Z sequences for authors 1450-1945 and 1945-present. Biographical notes on each author. Library locations for most items. Appendix A. updates the *Introductory bibliography* with material published 1960-65; B. lists literary awards, societies, newspapers and periodicals mentioned in biographical notes; C. lists periodicals from which articles are cited; D. lists authors by literary period; E. lists libraries. Name index. Fine annotations throughout. Over 4,600 entries in all. *Class No:* 894.511(01)

Encyclopaedias & Dictionaries

[8782]
GYULA, B. Nyugati magyar irodalmi lexikon és bibliográfia. Budapest, Hitel, 1992. 826p. ISBN: 9630418592.
Biographical entries on authors, A-Z (p.19-409), followed by classified bibliography (p.413-781) of Hungarian works published in western countries both in translation and in Hungarian. Index of authors. *Class No:* 894.511(03)

[8783]
Magyar irodalmi lexikon. Benedek, M., *ed.* Budapest, Akadémiai Kiadó, 1963-5. 3v.
An encyclopedia of Hungarian literature, with entries mainly on writers but also covering periodicals, literary terms, etc. *Class No:* 894.511(03)

Histories

[8784]
CZIGÁNY, L. The Oxford history of Hungarian literature: from the earliest times to the present. Oxford, Clarendon Press, 1984. x,582p. ISBN: 0198157819.
25 chapters, of which 18 cover the 19th and 20th centuries. Major authors and works discussed in detail, with quotations in translation. Special attention paid to literary relations with Britain and the USA and good coverage of émigré writers. Annotated bibliography (46p.). Glossary of Hungarian literary and geographical terms (17p.). 'The comprehensive index ... adds to the general usefulness of what is likely to remain a standard work' (*Modern Language Review*, v.82(1), January, 1987, p.270-272). *Class No:* 894.511(091)

[8785]
A History of Hungarian literature. Klaniczay, T., *ed.* Budapest, Corvina, 1982. 572p. plates. ISBN: 9631315428.
An 'official' history in 10 main sections and over 60 chapters. Sub-sections on numerous individual authors. Quotations in translation. Selected bibliography (52p.) in 2 parts: reference material on Hungarian literature and individual writers, and Hungarian literature in English translation. Name index. *Class No:* 894.511(091)

[8786]
A Magyar irodalom története. Sötér, I., *ed.* Budapest, Akadémiai Kiadó, 1964-66. 6v.
A Marxist history of the literature, compiled in the Institute for Literary History of the Hungarian Academy of Sciences. The 6 vols. cover the following periods: to 1600; 1600-1772; 1772-1849; 1849-1905; 1905-1919; 1919 to the 1960s. *Class No:* 894.511(091)

[8787]
PINTÉR, J. A Magyar irodalomtörténete: tudományos rendszerezés. Budapest, Magyar Irodalom történeti Társaság, 1930-41. 8v.
Comprehensive scholarly history of Hungarian literature with general bibliography in v.1 and bibliographies appended to chapters. *Class No:* 894.511(091)

Finnish Literature

[8788]
AHOKAS, J. A History of Finnish literature. Bloomington, Ind., Indiana Univ. Research Center for the Language Sciences, for the American-Scandinavian Foundation, 1973 (repr. Richmond, Surrey, Curzon Press, 1997). ix,568p. £95. (*Uralic & Altaic series.*) ISBN: 0700708723.

Arranged by period, with notes on individual authors and works. Index of names and titles.

The Univ. of Nebraska Press announce *A History of Finland's literature* ($60. ISBN: 0803241895), by G.C. Schoolfield, for 1998 in their *Histories of Scandinavian literature* series. *Class No:* 894.541

[8789]
HALTSONEN, S. *and* **PURANEN, R. Kaunokirjallisuutemme käännöksiä:** bibliografinen luettelo suomenkielisen kaunokirjallisuude käännöksistä. Helsinki, Suomalaisen Kirjallisuuden Seura, 1979. 150p.

A revised and expanded ed. of a bibliography by Haltsonen published in 1961.

Lists over 1,800 translations of Finnish novels, short stories, poetry and plays into 38 languages.
Class No: 894.541

[8790]
Suomalaisia kirjailijoita 1500-luvulta nykypäiviin. Rantala, R., *ed.* Keuruu, Otava, 1994. 224p. ISBN: 951112854x.

A concise dictionary of over 700 Finnish writers active since 1500. Entries give place and date of birth and death, brief biography and list of works. List of award winners. Title index with *c.*8,000 entries. *Class No:* 894.541

[8791]
Suomen kirjailijat / Finlands författare / Writers in Finland. Launonen, H., *and others, eds.* Helsinki, Suomalaisen Kirjallisuuden Seura, 1981-93. 3v. ISSN: 03551768.

1809-1916. 1993. 954p.
1917-1944. 1981. 616p.
1945-1980. 1985. 871p.

Each vol. contains biobibliographical articles on authors, with extensive lists of primary and secondary sources. Some non-literary writers (biographers, philosophers, etc.) are covered and many entries include photographs. Title index in each vol. *Class No:* 894.541

[8792]
Suomen kirjallisuus. Helsinki, Suomalaisen Kirjallisuuden Seura & Otava, 1963-70. 8v.

The most complete account of Finnish literature available, covering the subject both thematically and chronologically. The companion anthology is *Suomen kirjallisuuden antologia* (Helsinki, Otava, 1963-75. 8v.). *Class No:* 894.541

Estonian Literature

[8793]
Eesti kirjanduse biograafiline leksikon. Nirk, E. *and* Sogel, E., *eds*. Tallinn, Eesti Raamat, 1975. 463p. illus.

A dictionary of *c.*500 Estonian authors. Entries include biography, survey of works and a photograph in many cases, with a secondary bibliography appended. *Class No:* 894.545

[8794]
MAGI, A. Estonian literature: an outline. Eliaser, E., *tr.* Stockholm, The Baltic Humanitarian Association, 1968. 109p.

Originally written in Estonian.

A historical survey in 9 chapters, with appendices on Soviet literature in Estonia and exile literature. Biobibliographical notes on authors, A-Z (9p.). Chronological table. Index. *Class No:* 894.545

[8795]
MAUER, M. Eesti kirjandus võõrkeeltes: bibliograafianimestik. Tallinn, 1978.

A bibliography of Estonian literature in translation, including anthologies and the works of individual authors.
Class No: 894.545

[8796]
NIRK, R. Estonian literature: historical survey with biobibliographical appendix. Hone, A.R. *and* Mutt, O., *tr.* 2nd ed. Tallinn, Perioodika, 1987. 416p. illus. ISBN: 0828537720.

1st ed. 1970.

Two-thirds of the survey is devoted to the 20th century. Bibliography of Estonian literature in English (7p.). Still not entirely free of Soviet control (very little coverage of émigré writers) but nevertheless 'in many ways more sensible than the five-volume official academic history of Estonian literature' (*World Literature Today,* v.62(3), Summer 1988, p.482-3). *Class No:* 894.545

Georgian Literature

[8797]
RAYFIELD, D. The Literature of Georgia: a history. Oxford, Oxford Univ. Press, 1995. 376p. £45. ISBN: 0198151918.

The first comprehensive English-language history, from the first religious texts of the 5th century, through the medieval 'golden age', to the diverse literature of the 20th century. *Class No:* 894.631

Tamil & Malayalam Literature

[8798]
CHAITANYA, K. A History of Malayalam literature. New Delhi, Orient Longman, 1971; Port Washington, N.Y., Associated Faculty Press, 1979. xii,596p.

A narrative history in 14 chapters. 360 passages quoted in English translation, with the originals appended. Index.
Class No: 894.8

[8799]
GEORGE, K.M. A survey of Malayalam literature. Bombay, Asia Publishing House, 1968. xii,354p.

A history in 17 chapters, with translations of 12 poems and 8 short stories appended. Pronunciation guide. Glossary. Bibliography (3p.). Index. *Class No:* 894.8

[8800]

JESUDASAN, C. *and* **JESUDASAN, H. A History of Tamil literature.** Calcutta, Y.M.C.A. Publishing House, 1961. xiv,305p.

Arranged by periods up to 1960. Bibliography (3p.). Index of authors and titles. *Class No:* 894.8

[8801]

THANI NAYAGAM, X.S. A Reference guide to Tamil studies: books. Kuala Lumpur, Univ. of Malaya Press, 1966. viii,122p.

Lists over 1,300 books available in many western languages. 14 sections, of which one covers translations and summaries of texts (131 items) and another the history of literature and literary criticism (71). Some brief annotations. Author index. *Class No:* 894.8

[8802]

ZVELEBIL, K.V. Lexicon of Tamil literature. Leiden, Brill, 1995. xxiv,782p. (*Handbuch der Orientalistik.*) ISBN: 9004100725.

Over 4,000 entries on authors, works, scholars, institutions, literary terms, forms and genres. Many cross-references. Based on cards gathered during research for a detailed history of Tamil literature which has not materialised. *Class No:* 894.8

Chinese Literature

Bibliographies

[8803]

GIBBS, D.A. *and* **LI, Y. A Bibliography of studies and translations of modern Chinese literature, 1918-1942.** Cambridge, Mass., East Asian Research Center, Harvard Univ., 1975. 239p. ISBN: 0674071115.

In 3 sections, the first 2 listing Western-language sources and general studies of the literature. Part 3 is main section, listing all known Western studies and English translations of the works of individual authors. 3 appendices list conference papers, unpublished works and Chinese sources. No annotations. Index to translators and authors of studies. *Class No:* 895.1(01)

[8804]

HINRUP, H.J. An Index to *Chinese Literature*, 1951-1976. London, Curzon Press, 1978. 231p. ISBN: 0700701222.

An index to a periodical published in Peking. Classified sequence has 4,203 entries in 10 parts with subsections. Parts 1-3 cover contemporary literature, classical literature, and theatre, and have 2,461 entries. The rest cover culture, art, history, etc. Also A-Z index of authors, artists and anonymous titles. *Class No:* 895.1(01)

[8805]

LI, Tien-Yi. The History of Chinese literature: a selected bibliography. 2nd ed. New Haven, Conn., Far Eastern Publications, Yale Univ., 1970. 98p. ISBN: 0887100309.

1st ed. 1968.

A classified, unannotated bibliography of books on classical and modern Chinese literature written in Chinese, English, French, and Japanese. Includes translations of literary works, anthologies, bibliographies, glossaries, biographical dictionaries and other reference works. *Class No:* 895.1(01)

[8806]

LYNN, R.J. Chinese literature: a draft bibliography in Western European languages. Canberra, Faculty of Asian Studies, in association with Australian National Univ. Press, 1979. 102p.

An unannotated, classified listing of all Western-language studies and translations (including dissertations) in monograph form that were known to the compiler as of mid-1979. Detailed table of contents. Index of authors, translators and other names. *Class No:* 895.1(01)

Encyclopaedias & Dictionaries

[8807]

The Indiana companion to traditional Chinese literature. Nienhauser, W.H., *and others, eds.* Bloomington, Ind., Indiana Univ. Press, 1985. xlii,1052p. £60. ISBN: 0253329833.

Covers literature up to 1911 and is the work of 200 contributors, who have produced 10 survey essays on the major types of literature and over 500 signed articles on authors, works, genres, literary movements, etc. Selective bibliographies of editions, translations and studies with each entry. General bibliography (10p.). Indexes of names, titles and subjects. 'A stunning example of what careful coordination of effort and painstaking editorial supervision can achieve; ... a work that far surpasses anything now available' (*Choice*, v.23 (11/12), July/Aug. 1986, p.656-8). *Class No:* 895.1(03)

[8808]

A Selective guide to Chinese literature, 1900-1949. Malmqvist, N.G.D., *and others, eds.* Leiden, Brill, 1988-90. 4v. £169.

V.1 *The Novel,* ed. by M. Doleželová-Velingerová. 1988. xvii,238p. ISBN: 9004078800.

V.2 *The Short story,* ed. by Z. Slupski. 1988. xiii,300p. ISBN: 9004078819.

V.3 *The Poem,* ed. by L. Haft. 1989. xi,301p. ISBN: 9004089608.

V.4 *The Drama,* ed. by B. Eberstein. 1990. xi,347p. ISBN: 9004090983.

The work of over 100 scholars from 16 countries, this series is intended to 'facilitate the first stage of research for anyone interested in 20th century Chinese literature' (*Preface*). Each vol. has an introductory essay and general bibliography, followed by signed entries for *c.*100 major works. These are arranged A-Z by author (romanized name) and include bibliographical details of 1st ed., synopsis, commentary, and lists of critical studies and translations into European languages. Author index and index of journals, publishers and literary series. *Class No:* 895.1(03)

Histories

[8809]

CH'EN, Shou-Yi. Chinese literature: a historical introduction. New York, Ronald Press, 1961. xii,665p.

The fullest treatment in English 'but has many factual errors, repetitions, misprints, and problems in interpretation' (Yang, W.L.Y., *Classical Chinese fiction,* 1978, p.139). Particularly strong on the historical background to Chinese literature and contains many translations of representative works. *Class No:* 895.1(091)

[8810]

—LIU, Wu-Chi. An Introduction to Chinese literature. Bloomington, Ind., Indiana Univ. Press, 1966. (repr. Westport, Conn., Greenwood). xii,321p. $75. ISBN: 0313267030.

Not a comprehensive history, but a survey of the major developments written for the general reader. Contains many extracts of key works in English translation. Select bibliography, chronology and glossary.
Class No: 895.1(091)

[8811]

GILES, H.A. A History of Chinese literature. Reprint of 1901 ed., with a supplement on the modern period by Wu-Chi Liu. New York, Ungar, 1967. viii,448p.

Originally published London, Heinemann, 1901.

Now outdated, this first history of Chinese literature, although written by a Westerner, reflects traditional Chinese views of literature. Arranged in 8 'books', each devoted to a period or dynasty, and 28 chapters, it covers BC600-AD1900. Quotations in English. Bibliographical note (2p.). Index. Supplement covers 20th-century literature.
Class No: 895.1(091)

[8812]

LAI MING. A History of Chinese literature. London, Cassell, 1964. xi,439p.

From the Yin Dynasty (12th century BC) to the 1930s in 17 chapters. 'More than two-thirds of the book is devoted to the presentation of the lives of outstanding literary figures and their works, which generally speaking are arranged as the second and third sections of each chapter, while the first section ... depicts the background or trends leading to the flowering of each genre' (*Introduction*). Many lengthy quotations in English translation. Bibliography (3p.). Table of dynasties. Index. *Class No:* 895.1(091)

Biographies

[8813]

CHEN, C.K.H. A Biographical and bibliographical dictionary of Chinese authors. Hanover, N.H., Oriental Society, 1971. xiv,703.

Over 2,000 entries for writers of all periods, compiled from the Chinese Author Information Cards issued by the Oriental Society. Arranged A-Z by romanized form of name, giving dates, birth place, family details, pseudonyms and list of works.

Supplement (1976. 2v.) covers another 3,700 writers.
Class No: 895.1(092)

Chinese Poetry

[8814]

FUNG, S.S.K. *and* **LAI, S.T. 25 T'ang poets:** index to English translations. Hong Kong, Chinese Univ. Press; Seattle, Univ. of Washington Press, 1984. xxviii,696p. illus. ISBN: 9622012973, Hong Kong; 0295961554, US.

Arranged by poet, A-Z, then by poem title. Over 4,000 entries, giving Romanized title, Chinese title, Chinese first line, translator, bibliographical details of translation, and English first line. Bibliography lists *c.*220 anthologies analyzed. Indexes of English first lines and of translators.
Class No: 895.1-1

[8815]

LYNN, R.J. Guide to Chinese poetry and drama. 2nd ed. Boston, Hall, 1984. xxii,200p. ISBN: 0816186332.

1st ed. 1973, by R.B. Bailey.

31 entries from 1st ed. have been deleted and 137 new ones added, giving 221 entries for English-language studies and translations, arranged as follows: poetry, nos. 1-138; drama, 139-207; general, 208-221. Substantial annotations. Index of critics and translators. *Class No:* 895.1-1

[8816]

WONG, Kai-chee, *and others.* **A Research guide to English translations of Chinese verse** (Han dynasty to T'ang dynasty). Hong Kong, Chinese Univ. Press; Seattle, Univ. of Washington Press, 1977. xii,368p. ISBN: 9622011411, Hong Kong; 0295957425, US.

Lists translations of over 2,900 poems, giving translator's name and bibliographical details. Arranged by poet, then by title, according to the order in 2 Chinese anthologies. 5 indexes: English titles; English first lines; names of poets in Chinese by stroke-count; transliterated names of poets, A-Z; translators. *Class No:* 895.1-1

Chinese Drama

[8817]

LOPEZ, M.D. Chinese drama: an annotated bibliography of commentary, criticism, and plays in English translation. Metuchen, N.J., Scarecrow, 1991. viii,525p. $62.50. ISBN: 0810823470.

Part I has 1,395 entries in over 60 sections, under 4 main headings: 1. Background and development - 2. Components of Chinese theatre - 3. Comparisons with other national theatres - 4. Overseas Chinese theatre. Part II lists 1,929 translated plays by title. Name index to each part. Largely unannotated, despite the title. *Class No:* 895.1-2

Chinese Fiction

[8818]

BERRY, M. Chinese classic novels: an annotated bibliography of chiefly English-language studies. New York, Garland, 1988. xvi,302p. ISBN: 0824066332.

Lists 118 general studies then 378 translations and critical studies of the 6 acknowledged classic novels. Largely confined to post-1955 publications. *c.*400 entries. Indexes of authors and titles. 'The annotations are brisk, comprehensive, and opinionated' (*Choice,* v.26(4), Dec. 1988, p.621-2). *Class No:* 895.1-3

[8819]

HSIA, C.T. A History of modern Chinese fiction. 2nd ed. New Haven, Conn., and London, Yale Univ. Press, 1971. xvi,701p. ISBN: 0300014627.

1st ed. 1961. 2nd ed. is a corrected reprint with Epilogue.

From 1917 to 1957 in 19 chapters, with Epilogue covering Communist fiction since 1958. All quotations in English translation. Notes (47p.) have detailed bibliographic information. Glossary of Chinese names, titles and terms (31p.). Bibliography (42p.) lists general studies, anthologies, magazines, and primary and secondary material for major authors. Analytical index. *Class No:* 895.1-3

[8820]

LI, Tien-Yi. Chinese fiction: a bibliography of books and articles in Chinese and English. New Haven, Conn., Far Eastern Publications, Yale Univ., 1968. xiv,356p. ISBN: 0887100171.

An unannotated, selective listing of reference works, critical studies, and English translations of works of fiction. Includes many general studies on Chinese literature.
Class No: 895.1-3

[8821]

Modern Chinese fiction: a guide to its study and appreciation; essays and bibliographies. Yang, W.L.Y. *and* Mao, N.K., *eds.* Boston, Hall, 1981. xxii,288p. ISBN: 0816181136.

Follows the same format as the earlier *Classical Chinese fiction (q.v.)*, with essays surveying modern (*i.e.*, post-1917) fiction (p.3-92) followed by annotated bibliography of general sources in Chinese literature (187 items) and of modern Chinese fiction (766 items), which lists English translations of nearly 100 authors, including many from Taiwan. Index of authors and translators. *Class No:* 895.1-3

[8822]

PAPER, J.D. Guide to Chinese prose. 2nd ed. Boston, Hall, 1984. xx,149p. ISBN: 0816186219.

1st ed. 1973.

Lists 196 English translations and studies of Chinese prose works in 9 sections with lengthy annotations. Glossary. Bibliography (3p.). Index of authors, editors, translators, and titles. *Class No:* 895.1-3

[8823]

TSAI, M. Contemporary Chinese novels and short stories, 1949-1974: an annotated bibliography. Cambridge, Mass., Council on East Asian Studies, Harvard Univ. (distributed by Harvard Univ. Press), 1979. xvi,408p. $30. (*Harvard East Asian monographs.*) ISBN: 0674166817.

Lists 455 authors A-Z according to Wade-Giles romanization, giving biographical notes in many cases and details of their works. Titles given in romanization and Chinese characters, followed by English translation, publishing details and brief synopsis. Includes fiction published in periodicals. Indexes of authors, titles and subjects. *Class No:* 895.1-3

[8824]

YANG, W.L.Y., *and others*. Classical Chinese fiction: a guide to its study and appreciation; essays and bibliographies. Boston, Hall; London, Prior, 1978. xxvi,302p. ISBN: 0816178099, US; 0860431460, UK.

9 essays (p.9-116) provide an introduction to the major novels and short stories. These are followed by an annotated bibliography of general sources in Chinese literature (272 items) and of Classical Chinese fiction, with the emphasis on recent translations and studies in English (632). Some French and German material included. Glossary of Chinese authors, titles and terms. Index. *Class No:* 895.1-3

Japanese Literature

Bibliographies

[8825]

INADA, H.I. Bibliography of translations from the Japanese into western languages: from the 16th century to 1912. Tokyo, Sophia Univ., 1971. viii,112p.

439 entries arranged by year, then A-Z by translator, and including author, title and date of original, and comments on historical importance of translation. Bibliography (5p.). Indexes of authors, translators, original titles (romanized), and subjects. *Class No:* 895.6(01)

[8826]

Japanese history: a guide to survey histories. pt.2: Literature. Fukuda, N., *ed.* Ann Arbor, Mich., Center for Japanese Studies, Univ. of Michigan, 1986. xxii,139p. $15. ISBN: 0939512254.

An annotated list of Japanese-language studies of Japanese literature published 1955-82. Arranged by historical period with subject subdivisions. Author and title indexes.
Class No: 895.6(01)

[8827]

Japanese literature in foreign languages, 1945-1990. Japan P.E.N. Club, *comp.* [Tokyo], Japan Book Publishers Assoc., 1990. v,383p.

A bibliography of Japanese literature in translation and of foreign-language books, articles, and dissertations on Japanese literature. Lists over 13,000 works under 4,153 authors/anonymous titles. Entries for translations include title, language, translator, publication details, and original title in romanized form.

For pre-1945 translations, see the P.E.N. Club's *Japanese literature in European languages: a bibliography* (2nd ed. Tokyo, 1961. xii,98p.) and its *Supplement* (1964. 8p.), which have *c.*1,750 entries. *Class No:* 895.6(01)

[8828]

—Modern Japanese literature in translation: a bibliography. The International House of Japan Library, *comp.* Tokyo, Kodansha International, 1979. 311p. ISBN: 0870113399.

Author listing of translations of fiction, poetry, drama and prose, including those in periodicals and anthologies, based on the collections of Japanese and 19 foreign libraries. Entries comprise original title (with romanized and Japanese version), translated title, translator, publisher, date and pagination. Over 1,300 authors covered. Indexes of titles and translators. *Class No:* 895.6(01)

[8829]

Kokubungaku nenkan. [Bibliography of research in Japanese literature.] Tokyo, Kokubungaku Kenkyu Shiryokan, 1979-. Annual.

Comprises 2 classified bibliographies, the first covering journal articles, the second books with annotations and a title index. Author index to both parts. Preceded by *Kokubungaku kenkuyu bunken motoruku* (1965-78).
Class No: 895.6(01)

[8830]

TEIJI, I. Kokubungaku kenkyu shomoku kaidai. Tokyo, Tokyo Daigaku Shuppankai, 1982. 739p.

A classified, annotated bibliography of *c.*2,400 works on literary studies from the Meiji period to 1980. Title index.
Class No: 895.6(01)

[8831]

YOSHIZAKI, Y. Studies in Japanese literature and language: a bibliography of English materials. Tokyo, Nichigai Associates, 1979. 451p.

A classified listing of books, periodical articles and dissertations in 3 sections: 1. Studies in Japanese literature - 2. Studies in Japanese language - 3. Materials for further information. Index of names and titles. *Class No:* 895.6(01)

Encyclopaedias & Dictionaries

[8832]

KOKUSAI BUNKA SHINKOKAI. Introduction to contemporary Japanese literature: synopses of major works. Tokyo, K.B.S., 1939-72. 3v.

V.1 (1939. xlii,485p.) has synopses of 84 works, published 1902-35 by 69 writers, chronologically arranged, plus commentary and biography. Index of authors, titles, and literary movements.

V.2 (1959. xxxix,296p.) covers 71 works published 1936-55, plus 10 pre-1936 works previously omitted, and includes photographs of the writers. Index.

V.3 (1972. lv,313p.) has a different format, with entries for 72 authors, A-Z, comprising biographical sketch and synopsis of one major work, but for 15 authors whose works have been translated into English there is only biography. Appendix has primary bibliographies for each author.
Class No: 895.6(03)

[8833]

Nihon kindai bungaku daijiten. Tokyo, Kodansha, 1977-8. 6v.

The standard encyclopedia of modern Japanese literature. Vols. 1-3 comprise a biographical dictionary of over 5,100 writers; v.4 is a dictionary of historical issues, literary terms, associations, etc.; v.5 is a dictionary of periodicals; and v.6 contains indexes.

V.1-3 have been revised and published as a single-vol. biographical dictionary, *Nihon kindai bungaku daijiten kijoban* (1984), with *c.*5,600 entries. *Class No:* 895.6(03)

[8834]

Nihon koten bungaku daijiten. Tokyo, Iwanami Shoten, 1983-5. 6v.

The standard encyclopedia of classical Japanese literature and related fields, *e.g.* religion, art, etc. *c.*13,000 signed entries on people, works, events, etc., with bibliographies. V.6 contains index.

Nihon koten bungaku daijiten kan'yakuban (1986) is a single-vol. abridgement with *c.*4,000 entries.
Class No: 895.6(03)

[8835]

The Princeton companion to classical Japanese literature. Miner, E., *and others, eds.* Princeton, N.J., Princeton Univ. Press, 1985. xxi,570p. illus. $24.95. ISBN: 0691008256.

Definitive handbook to Japanese literature from its beginnings to 1868 in 10 parts. Part 3 (127p.) is a dictionary of major authors (325 entries) and works (110). Other useful features include a brief history (60p.), chronologies, glossary of literary terms, and lists of placenames, ranks and offices. Well-illustrated sections on theatre, architecture, costume and armour. Comprehensive index and extensive cross-referencing. Bibliography (5p.). *Class No:* 895.6(03)

[8836]

RIMER, J.T. A Reader's guide to Japanese literature: from the eighth century to the present. Tokyo and New York, Kodansha International, 1988. 208p. £13.50. ISBN: 087011896x.

Describes 20 classical and 30 modern literary works (average length of essays is 3p.) and lists English translations of the work concerned and of other works by the same author. Annotated bibliography of general studies, anthologies and studies of individual authors (4p.). Index. 'An excellent guide for the uninitiated' (*Choice,* v.26(7), March 1989, p.1130). *Class No:* 895.6(03)

[8837]

Shincho nihon bungaku jiten. Tokyo, Shinchosha, 1988. 1348;408p.

A single-volume dictionary of Japanese literature.
Class No: 895.6(03)

Histories

[8838]

KATO, S. A History of Japanese literature. London, Macmillan; Tenterden, Norbury, 1979-83. 3v. £135. ISBN: 0333362675.

V.1 *The First thousand years,* trans. D. Chibbett. 1979. xxvi,319p.

V.2 *The Years of isolation,* trans. D. Sanderson. 1983. xx,230p.

V.3 *The Modern years,* trans. D. Sanderson. 1983. xvii,307p.

Narrative history from 7th century to the 1970s. Quotations in English. Each vol. has glossary of terms, brief bibliographical notes and index.

Abridged single-vol. ed. published Richmond, Surrey, Japan Library, 1997, as *A History of Japanese literature: from the Man'ōyshū to modern times* (ix,400p. £17.99. ISBN: 1873410484). *Class No:* 895.6(091)

[8839]

KEENE, D. Dawn to the west: Japanese literature of the modern era. New York, Holt, Rinehart & Winston, 1984. 2v. $100. ISBN: 0030628148, v.1; 0030628164, v.2.

V.1, *Fiction;* v.2, *Poetry, drama, criticism.*

Covers Japanese literature since the Meiji Restoration of 1868, with references and bibliography after each chapter. Glossary, selected list of English translations and index in each volume.

Preceded by *World within walls: Japanese literature of the pre-modern era, 1600-1867* (London, Secker, 1976. xiii,606p. ISBN: 0436232669), in 2 parts (1600-1770 and 1770-1867) with 22 chapters on genres. Chapter bibliographies. Summaries of 6 plays appended. Glossary (10p.). Index. *Class No:* 895.6(091)

[8840]

KONISHI, J. A History of Japanese literature. Miner, E., *ed.* Princeton, N.J., Princeton Univ. Press, 1984-. v.1- (in progress).

Originally published Tokyo, 1985-7, as *Nihon bungei shi* (5v.).

V.1 *The Archaic and Ancient Ages,* trans. A. Gatten and N. Teele, 1984 (xx,475p. ISBN: 0691101469).

V.2 *The Early Middle Ages,* trans. A. Gatten, 1986 (xv,461p. ISBN: 0691066558).

V.3 *The High Middle Ages,* trans. A. Gatten and M. Harbison, 1991 (xix,654p. ISBN: 0691066566).

The first 3 vols. to appear in English of a comprehensive 5-vol. history which is primarily concerned with the

....(*contd.*)
technical aspects of the literature (original title literally means 'A History of Japanese literary art'). Romanized Japanese quotations have parallel English translations. Each vol. has chronological table, select bibliography of editions and critical material in Japanese and other languages, and index.

TLS (no.4419, Dec. 11, 1987, p.1382) commends Konishi's international perspective and transcendence of parochial barriers: 'He ... sets Japanese literature in the broad context of East Asian literary history, something not systematically attempted in Western accounts before.'
Class No: 895.6(091)

Biographies

[8841]
Biographical dictionary of Japanese literature. Hisamatsu, S., *ed.* Tokyo, Kodansha International, 1976. 437p. ISBN: 0870112538.

320 entries in 5 period divisions, placing the writers in their literary and historical context and including translated extracts. Diagram of Japanese literary schools. Glossary of literary terms. Bibliography. Index. *Class No:* 895.6(092)

[8842]
Dictionary of literary biography. Detroit, Gale, 1978-98. v.1-188 (in progress). £112 per vol.

The following vols. cover Japanese literature:

V.180 *Japanese fiction writers, 1868-1945*, ed. by V.C. Gessel. 1997.

V.182 *Japanese fiction writers since World War II*, ed. by V.C. Gessel. 1997.

For a description of the series, see entry at 82(092).
Class No: 895.6(092)

[8843]
Gendai Nihon shippitsusha daijiten. [Contemporary writers of Japan.] Keitaro, A., *and others, eds.* Tokyo, Nichigai Asoshietsu, 1984. 5v.

Followed by *Gendai Nihon shippitsusha daijiten, 1977/82*, ed. by K. Jun'ichiro and others (5v.). The two sets provide biographical information on *c.*18,000 writers from the humanities and social sciences. Entries include lists of publications and secondary literature. *Class No:* 895.6(092)

Women

[8844]
Japanese women writers: a bio-critical sourcebook. Mulhern, C.I., *ed.* Westport, Conn., Greenwood, 1994. 552p. £79.50. ISBN: 0313254869.

Profiles (6-9 pages) of 58 writers of all periods since the 9th century, comprising biography, literary career, analysis of major works, and bibliography. Includes some diarists and film and TV scriptwriters as well as literary authors.
Class No: 895.6-0055.2

[8845]
MAMOLA, C.Z. Japanese women writers in English translation: an annotated bibliography. New York, Garland, 1989-92. 2v.

V.1 (1989. xxix,469p. ISBN: 0824030486) is in 3 sections: writings of the Heian period (794-1185) (13 items); 19th- and 20th-century fiction (209); 19th- and 20th-century nonfiction (361). A-Z arrangement by author within each section, with substantial, descriptive annotations and biographical notes.

V.2 (1992. xxvii,452p. $77. ISBN: 0824070771) is the

....(*contd.*)
result of a search through 35 major bibliographies, including *The Bibliography of Asian studies*, 1941-86, and has 4 sections: fiction (87 items); nonfiction (413); specialized works (837); dissertations (48). Index in each vol.
Class No: 895.6-0055.2

[8846]
SCHIERBECK, S. Japanese women novelists in the 20th century. Copenhagen, Museum Tusculanum, 1994. 378p. illus. £30. ISBN: 8772892684.

Supersedes Schierbeck's *Postwar Japanese women writers: an up-to-date bibliography with biographical sketches* (Copenhagen, East Asian Institute, Univ. of Copenhagen, 1989).

Profiles 104 writers who have received major literary prizes, 1900-93. Entries include photograph, biographical notes, critical evaluation, and lists of selected works and English translations. *Class No:* 895.6-0055.2

Japanese Poetry

[8847]
RIMER, J.T. *and* **MORRELL, R.E. Guide to Japanese poetry.** 2nd ed. Boston, Hall, 1984. xxiii,189p. ISBN: 0816186065.

1st ed. 1975.

A bibliography of translations, anthologies, histories, critical studies, etc., preceded by a historical and bibliographical outline. 264 entries with detailed annotations. Index. *Class No:* 895.6-1

Japanese Drama

[8848]
PRONKO, L.C. Guide to Japanese drama. 2nd ed. Boston, Hall, 1984. xviii,149p. ISBN: 0816186316.

1st ed. 1973.

A bibliography of English translations of Japanese plays and of English-language historical and critical studies, preceded by a valuable introductory essay on Japanese theatre. 105 entries with lengthy annotations. Chronology and list of further reading. Index of authors, editors, translators and titles. *Class No:* 895.6-2

Japanese Fiction

[8849]
LEWELL, J. Modern Japanese novelists: a biographical dictionary. Tokyo, Kodansha, 1993. xii,497p. £45. ISBN: 4770016492.

Profiles of 57 writers, the earliest born 1859. Entries average 8p. although major writers are given greater coverage (*e.g.* 20p. on Mishima), and include photograph, biography, critical analysis, and bibliography of translations and critical studies. Annotated list of 17 general English-language studies. Glossary (12p.). *Class No:* 895.6-3

[8850]
MARKS, A.H. *and* **BORT, B.D. Guide to Japanese prose.** 2nd ed. Boston, Hall, 1984. xviii,186p. ISBN: 0816186308.

1st ed. 1975.

An annotated bibliography of Japanese prose available in English translation, giving plot summaries and critical evaluation. Arranged in 2 sections, for pre-Meiji literature (up to 1867) and Meiji literature onwards (1868 to the present), and chronologically within each section. 174 entries, plus selected bibliography of critical studies (10p.).

....(contd.)
Introductory essay (18p.) places the works reviewed in a historical context. Index of authors, editors, translators and titles. *Class No:* 895.6-3

[8851]
MORRISON, J.W. Modern Japanese fiction. Salt Lake City, Univ. of Utah Press, 1955 (reprinted Westport, Conn., Greenwood, 1975). xiii,230p. ISBN: 0837180538.
A critical and historical survey in 8 chapters with a useful selected list of 70 authors and their works (titles romanized and translated) appended. Bibliography (17p.) of European-language studies and translations. *Class No:* 895.6-3

Korean Literature

[8852]
Han'guk munhak tae sajŏn. [An Encyclopaedia of the Korean literature.] Seoul, Munwŏn'gak, 1973. 1390p. illus.
Over 5,000 entries in several sequences. Photographs of many authors. Indexes. *Class No:* 895.7

[8853]
KIM DONGUK. History of Korean literature.
Hurvitz, L., *tr.* Tokyo, Centre for East Asian Cultural Studies, 1980. xi,321p.
Intended for Japanese readers and originally published by the Japan Broadcast Publishing Co., 1974, as *Chosen bungaku-shi.*
4 main sections (1. Ancient literature - 2. Medieval literature - 3. Early modern literature - 4. Modern literature) with subsections on genres and major works. Quotations in English. No index or bibliography, but the appended 'History of the study of Korean literature' (26p.) has many references to sources. *Class No:* 895.7

[8854]
LEE, P.H. Korean literature: topics and themes. Tucson, Ariz., Univ. of Arizona Press, for the Assoc. for Asian Studies, 1965. x,141p.
Basically a history of Korean vernacular verse and prose in 12 chapters, each with a bibliography of 'the most important books, articles and translations which have appeared by 1963' (*Preface*). Many quotations in translation. Chronology (9p.), glossary, and index. *Class No:* 895.7

[8855]
Synopses of Korean novels: reader's guide to Korean literature. Seoul, Korean National Commission for UNESCO, [197-?]. 100p.
Introductory essays on the Korean classical novel and trends in modern Korean fiction, followed by summaries (1p. each) of 40 classical and 40 modern novels.
Class No: 895.7

Cambodian Literature

[8856]
JACOB, J.M. The Traditional literature of Cambodia: a preliminary guide. Oxford, Oxford Univ. Press, 1996. 294p. £32.50. (*London Oriental series.*) ISBN: 0197136125.
The first book in English to cover the classical period of the 16th to 19th centuries, with chapters on each of the 10 genres followed by detailed A-Z inventories of authors,

....(contd.)
texts, translations and studies. 'A template for what should become a series of guides to Asia's national literatures' (*Choice*, v.34(2), Nov. 1996, p.451). *Class No:* 895.96

Vietnamese Literature

[8857]
DURAND, M.M. *and* **NGUYEN TRAN HUAN. An Introduction to Vietnamese literature.** Hawke, D.M., *tr.* New York, Columbia Univ. Press, 1985. xiii,213p. $36. ISBN: 0231058527.
Originally published in French in 1969. This ed. has extra sections in 2 chapters covering 1969-75.
13 chapters tracing the development of the literature from earliest times to 1975. Quotations in English translation. Very useful bibliography of general sources and French and English translations of Vietnamese literary works (9p.). Index. *Class No:* 895.97

African Literature

Bibliographies

[8858]
JAHN, J. *and* **DRESSLER, C.P. Bibliography of creative African writing.** Nendeln, Liechtenstein, Kraus-Thomson, 1971. xl,446p. maps. ISBN: 0527451509.
Covers creative literature written in all languages in Black Africa and published in book form or performed on stage. Plays published in journals included, but not poems and stories. General section (bibliographies, periodicals, criticism, anthologies) followed by 4 regional sections (Western, Central, Eastern, Austral), with each having subsections for secondary literature, anthologies, and works of individual authors. Introductory material in English, French and German. General index plus indexes to books in African languages, translations and countries. Over 2,800 unannotated entries.
Supersedes Jahn's *A Bibliography of Neo-African literature from Africa, America and the Caribbean* (New York, Praeger; London, Deutsch, 1965) - which was not restricted to Africa proper and was thus unable to include secondary material - and the supplements to its African section later compiled by P. Páricsy. *Class No:* 896(01)

[8859]
LIMB, P. *and* **VOLET, J.-M. Bibliography of African literatures.** Metuchen, N.J., Scarecrow, 1996. 456p. $55. (*Scarecrow area bibliographies.*) ISBN: 0810831449.
Arranged by language and focuses primarily on literatures in English and French, with works in Portuguese, Arabic, and various indigenous African languages also included. Also lists general bibliographies, anthologies and critical studies. Introduction includes historical notes and bibliographical essay. Author, gender and country indexes.
Class No: 896(01)

[8860]

MANN, M. *and* **SANDERS, V. A Bibliography of African language texts** in the collections of the School of Oriental and African Studies, University of London, to 1963. London, Zell, in association with SOAS, 1994. xviii,429p. £72. (*Documentary research in African literatures.*) ISBN: 1873836317.

Lists 7,770 published titles in over 300 languages, excluding Afrikaans, Arabic and Classical Ethiopic. Numbered entries arranged by language, A-Z, then by title, giving author, date, source reference and library/archive call mark. Extensive cross-references. Religious material produced by missions is predominant. List of 368 sources. Indexes of titles, authors and languages. Lists of languages by country and linguistic group. *Class No:* 896(01)

[8861]

Research in African literatures. Bloomington, Ind., Indiana Univ. Press (formerly Austin, Tex., Univ. of Texas Press), 1970-. Quarterly. ISSN: 00345210.

Regularly carries bibliographies and also includes reports on recent research, university literature programmes, library and archival resources, dissertations and conferences. *Class No:* 896(01)

[8862]

SCHEUB, H. African oral narratives, proverbs, riddles, poetry and song: an annotated bibliography. Boston, Hall, 1977. 393p. (*Bibliographies and guides in African studies.*) ISBN: 0816180342.

A rev. and enl. ed. of *Bibliography of African oral narratives* (Madison, Wis., Univ. of Wisconsin, 1971).

*c.*2,800 entries for books and periodical articles, most of them annotated. *Class No:* 896(01)

[8863]

—GÖRÖG, V. Littérature orale d'Afrique noire: bibliographie analytique. Paris, Maisonneuve et Larosse, 1981. 394p. ISBN: 2706808195.

Lists 2,780 books and articles by author, A-Z, plus 103 theses, with concise, descriptive annotations. International coverage, but all titles not in French or English are translated into French. Ethno-linguistic and subject indexes. *Class No:* 896(01)

Encyclopaedias & Dictionaries

[8864]

African literatures in the 20th century: a guide. Klein, L.S., *ed.* New York, Ungar, 1986; Harpenden, Oldcastle, 1988. x,245p. £10.99. ISBN: 080446362x, US; 0948353163, UK.

Handy guide based on Ungar's 5-vol. *Encyclopedia of world literature in the 20th century,* rev. ed., 1981-84 (*qv*). All entries on African literatures (of whatever language) are reproduced with some minor revisions and corrections, but unfortunately not updated. 38 national surveys are arranged A-Z by country, with 16 followed by articles on the major authors (43 in all). Extra article on Negritude included. All surveys and articles are signed and include bibliographies. Index to author articles. *Class No:* 896(03)

[8865]

Literatures in Afrian languages: theoretical issues and sample surveys. Andrzejewski, B.W., *and others, eds.* Warszawa, Wiedza Powszechna; Cambridge, Cambridge Univ. Press, 1985. 672p. £65. ISBN: 0521256461.

18 signed essays on individual literatures or groups of literatures by 14 international scholars, accompanied by biographical notes on writers and extensive bibliographies; *e.g.* 'Somali literature' has notes on over 70 writers and 8p. of bibliograpy. Title conceals a very useful reference work. *Class No:* 896(03)

[8866]

A New reader's guide to African literature. Zell, H.M., *and others, eds.* 2nd ed., completely rev. and expanded. London, Heinemann; New York, Holmes and Meier, 1983. xvi,553p. illus. $45.95. (*Studies in African literature.*) ISBN: 0435919997, UK; 0841906394, US.

First published 1971 as *A Reader's guide to African literature.*

Comprehensive guide to literature by Black authors from south of the Sahara writing in English, French and Portuguese. General bibliography (125p.) in 5 sections. (Bibliographies and reference works; General criticism; Criticism of individual authors; Collections; Folklore and oral tradition), followed by primary bibliographies for individual authors from 43 countries grouped by language and region, with over 3,000 titles (a vast increase over first ed.) listed and annotated. Selective bibliography of children's literature (21p.). List of relevant magazines (16p.). Biographical sketches (average 1½p.) of 95 authors, 50 of them new to this ed., many with photographs. Directory of specialist booksellers and publishers and libraries with African collections. Index of authors, editors, critics and journal titles. Indispensable in its field. *Class No:* 896(03)

[8867]

SUNKULI, L.O. *and* **MIRUKA, S.O. A Dictionary of oral literature.** Nairobi, Heinemann, 1990. xii,132p. £8.50. ISBN: 9966465073.

The first attempt to define, standardize and systemize the growing vocabulary used in the academic study of oral literature. 400 entries, with examples and illustrations taken mainly from Kenya. Bibliography (5p.). *Class No:* 896(03)

Histories

[8868]

DATHORNE, O.R. African literature in the twentieth century. Minneapolis, Minn., Univ. of Minnesota Press, 1974; London, Heinemann, 1976. xx,387p. ISBN: 081660769, US; 0435890565, UK.

An abridged version of *The Black mind: a history of African literature* (1974), which covered all periods.

9 chapters covering indigenous, French, Portuguese, and English literatures in the 20th century. Chapter references (18p.). Bibliography (13p.) of bibliographies, journals, anthologies, and general studies, plus the works of selected writers which are available in English. *Class No:* 896(091)

[8869]

European-language writing in Sub-Saharan Africa. Gérard, A., *ed.* Budapest, Akadémiai Kiadó, 1986. 2v. (1289p.). Hfl.260. (*A Comparative history of literatures in European languages.*) ISBN: 9630538326.

A comprehensive survey by over 60 scholars from 25 countries, which is arranged in 4 chronologically-ordered parts, 18 chapters, and numerous subsections devoted to individual writers, countries and genres. Bibliographical

.... (contd.)

essay by the editor (19p.). Index. 'If one tries to find omissions, one will try in vain' (*World Literature Today*, v.62(1), Winter 1988, p.168). *Class No:* 896(091)

[8870]

GÉRARD, A. African language literatures: an introduction to the literary history of Sub-Saharan Africa. London, Longman, 1981. xv,398p. maps. ISBN: 058264352x.

Comprehensive survey of over 50 literatures in 3 major sections (The Saba inheritance; The Legacy of Islam; The Impact of the West) and 11 chapters, with subsections on specific countries and languages. Notes and references (45p.) contain much bibliographic information. Index. *Class No:* 896(091)

[8871]

GÉRARD, A. Four African literatures: Xhosa, Sotho, Zulu, Amharic. Berkeley, Calif., and London, Univ. of California Press, 1971. 458p. maps. ISBN: 0520017889.

Scholarly historical survey of each of the literatures. References (31p.). Bibliography (34p.) of sources and studies. Index. *Class No:* 896(091)

[8872]

KLÍMA, V., ***and others*****. Black Africa:** literature and language. Dordrecht, Holland, and Boston, Reidel, 1976. 310p. ISBN: 9027705313.

A modified and enlarged English version of *Literatura černé Afriky* (Prague, 1972).

A survey of Sub-Saharan literature with signed chapters by the 3 authors on the various literatures and regions, and subsections on individual countries and writers. Bibliography (10p.). Index of persons. Index of African languages and dialects. *Class No:* 896(091)

Biographies

[8873]

African writers. Cox, C.B., *ed.* New York, Scribner, 1997. 2v. (xxxi,936p.). $220. ISBN: 0684196514.

Provides signed profiles of 65 authors (9 women) who came from or lived much of their lives in Africa in the late 19th and 20th centuries and who have written in English, French, Portuguese, Arabic and indigenous African languages. 17 countries represented. Entries average 13p. and include biography, critical analysis of works and selected bibliography of primary and secondary material. Chronology of African history, 1830-1996. Comprehensive index. *Class No:* 896(092)

[8874]

Dictionary of literary biography. Detroit, Gale, 1978-98. v.1-188 (in progress). £112 per vol.

The following vols. cover African literature:

V.117 *Twentieth-century Caribbean and Black African writers, first series*. 1992.

V.125 *Twentieth-century Caribbean and Black African writers, second series*. 1993.

V.157 *Twentieth-century Caribbean and Black African writers, third series*. 1995.

For a description of the series, see entry at 82(092). *Class No:* 896(092)

[8875]

HERDECK, D.E. African authors: a companion to Black African writing. Volume 1: 1300-1973. Washington, D.C., Black Orpheus Press, 1973. x,605p. illus. maps. $70. ISBN: 0810300761.

Provides information on 594 authors from Sub-Saharan Africa (plus Malagasy and Mauritius) writing in 37 African languages, Afrikaans and the major West European languages. One A-Z sequence of entries, which comprise biographical notes, critical comments and lists of writings, with secondary bibliography for major figures. 16 appendices include lists of authors by category and language, lists of journals and publishers, and bibliographies of critical studies and anthologies. *Class No:* 896(092)

[8876]

JAHN, J., ***and others*****. Who's who in African literature:** biographies, works, commentaries. Tübingen, Erdmann, for the Deutsche Afrika Gesellschaft, 1972. 406p. illus.

Covers over 400 modern sub-Saharan authors writing in African or European languages. Indexes of languages and countries. Bibliographies provided, but for full details readers are referred to Jahn and Dressler's *Bibliography of creative African writing* (*q.v.*). Many photographs. *Class No:* 896(092)

[8877]

Postcolonial African writers: a bio-bibliographical critical sourcebook. Parekh, P.N., *ed and* Jagne, S.F., *eds.*. Westport, Conn., Greenwood; London, Fitzroy Dearborn, 1998. 560p. £55. ISBN: 0313290563, US; 157958053x, UK.

Lengthy, signed essays on 60 authors (Achebe to Tutuola), most of whom write in English or French. Entries follow the standard Greenwood format: biography: discussion of key works and themes; overview of critical reception; primary and secondary bibliographies. Introductory essay on postcolonial criticism and African writing. Select general bibliography of critical studies. Index. *Class No:* 896(092)

Ghana

[8878]

Ghanaian literatures. Priebe, R.K., *ed.* New York, Greenwood, 1988. x,300p. $55. ISBN: 0313264384.

18 essays on different genres, followed by a classified bibliography compiled by Priebe, of over 200 critical studies in books and periodicals. *Class No:* 896(667)

Women

[8879]

BERRIAN, B. Bibliography of African women writers and journalists (Ancient Egypt-1984). Washington, D.C., Three Continents Press, 1985. xii,279p. $25. ISBN: 0894102265.

Sections for 8 genres, plus bibliographies, interviews, biographies and critical studies. A-Z by author within each section. Not annotated. 9 appendices, including groups of writers by country and genre. Author index. *Class No:* 896-0055.2

Amerindians, North—Literature

[8880]
Dictionary of Native American literature. Wiget, A., *ed.* New York, Garland, 1994. 598p. $95. ISBN: 0815315600.
See entry at 820.71(=97). *Class No:* 897

[8881]
JACOBSON, A. Contemporary Native American literature: a selective and partially annotated bibliography. Metuchen, N.J., Scarecrow, 1977. xii,262p. ISBN: 081081031x.
See entry at 820.71(=97). *Class No:* 897

[8882]
Native North American literature. Witalec, J., *ed.* Detroit, Gale, 1994. 706p. illus. £76. ISBN: 0810398982.
See entry at 820.71(=97). *Class No:* 897

[8883]
RUOFF, A.L.B. American Indian literatures: an introduction, bibliographic review, and selected bibliography. New York, Modern Language Assoc. of America, 1990. viii,200p. $45. ISBN: 0873521919.

Introductory section surveys oral literature, autobiography, and written literature since the 18th century. Bibliographic review comprises essays on bibliographies and research guides; anthologies and collections; and scholarship and criticism. Classified bibliography lists all works mentioned plus additional material. List of significant dates. Index of people, events, and subjects. 'This scholarly volume is the most comprehensive introduction currently available to the genres and major authors of native American oral and written literature' (*Booklist*, v.87(13), March 1, 1991, p.1419).

See also J.P. Miska's *Ethnic and Native Canadian literature: a bibliography* (Toronto, Toronto Univ. Press, 1990. xv,445p. ISBN: 0802058523). *Class No:* 897

Indonesian Literature

[8884]
KRATZ, E.U. A Bibliography of Indonesian literature in journals: drama, prose, poetry. Yogyakarta, Indonesia, Gadjah Mada Univ. Press, 1988. x,901p. ISBN: 9794201081.

Lists over 27,000 articles by 5,500 authors appearing in 113 Indonesian-language periodicals, 1922-82 (61% poetry, 38% prose, 1% drama). Arranged A-Z by author, with title indexes for each genre. Appendices include lists of libraries consulted and journals analyzed. *Class No:* 899.2

[8885]
TEEUW, A. Modern Indonesian literature. The Hague, Nijhoff, 1967. xv,308p., illus.

In 2 parts, covering pre- and post-war literature. 2 bibliographies, one giving details of Indonesian literary works and the other of references cited in the text. Many quotations in translation. Detailed index. *Class No:* 899.2

Filipino Literature

[8886]
MELLA, C.T. Directory of Filipino writers, past & present. Manila, CTM, 1974. viii,256p. illus.

Biographical notes on *c.*660 writers, A-Z, usually accompanied by a photograph. List of award winners appended. *Class No:* 899.21

Javanese Literature

[8887]
PIGEAUD, T.G.T. Literature of Java: catalogue raisonné of Javanese manuscripts in the library of the University of Leiden and other public collections in The Netherlands. The Hague, Nijhoff, 1967-80. 4v. illus. maps.

V.1 *Synopsis of Javanese literature, 900-1900AD*. 1967. xx,325p.

V.2 *Descriptive lists of Javanese manuscripts in the Library of the University of Leiden and other public collections in The Netherlands*. 1968. xv,972p.

V.3 *Illustrations and facsimiles of manuscripts, maps, addenda, and a general index of names and subjects*. 1970. xvii,441p.

V.4 *Supplement*. 1980. xxiii,390p. (published by Leiden Univ. Press).

Supplement describes post-1970 acquisitions and has additions to the bibliography of books on Javanese literature in v.1. Index. *Class No:* 899.22

Malayan Literature

[8888]
HUSSEIN, I. The Study of traditional Malay literature, with a selected bibliography. Kuala Lumpur, Dewan Bahasa dan Pustaka, Kementerian Pelajaran Malaysia, 1974. 75p.

A critical account of the study of traditional Malay literature, followed by a select bibliography of works, translations and studies. *Class No:* 899.221

[8889]
SALMON, C. Literature in Malay by the Chinese of Indonesia: a provisional annotated bibliography. Paris, Éditions de la Maison des Sciences de l'Homme, 1981. 588p. illus. ISBN: 0835705927.

Lists 3,005 titles by 806 writers and gives library locations. Lengthy introduction (143p.) surveying the history of this literature. Also includes biographical information on writers, lists of literary reviews, translations from Chinese and western languages, and a bibliography of studies of Chinese Malay literature. *Class No:* 899.221

[8890]
WINSTEDT, R.O. A History of classical Malay literature. Reprint of 2nd ed. Kuala Lumpur, Oxford Univ. Press, 1969. x,323p.

First published in *Journal of the Malayan Branch of the Royal Asiatic Society,* v.31, pt.3, no.183, 1939; 2nd ed. 1961.

....(contd.)

Standard history in 13 chapters with extensive bibliography (12p.). Appendix gives outlines of 12 Malay Hikayat. *Class No:* 899.221

Author / Title Index

The index reference is to the running number given to each item. The running numbers are in one sequence throughout the volume and can be found at the top right-hand corner of the entry for each item.

This index is of authors and titles in one sequence. The names of the authors are printed in bold type. Where works are jointly authored, only the first name is indexed. All books and periodicals listed or mentioned in the text, except where cited as the source of review quotations or for purposes of comparison, are entered under the headings given. All entries in *Walford* have title entries in the index; where the main heading in *Walford* is under title, added entries to the index have usually been made for an editor or compiler.

Filing is word by word, with groups of initials counted as single words. Since *Walford* uses only initials and not forenames it may occasionally happen that titles by different authors with the same surname and initials are found grouped together.

The arrangement of entries under an author is alphabetically by title. To save space, most sub-titles have been omitted, and many lengthy titles have been shortened.

Subject Index

The index reference is to the running number given to each item. The running numbers are in one sequence throughout the volume and can be found at the top right-hand corner of the entry for each item.

The index is computer generated, thus terms for the index have been largely derived from the headings and sub-headings used throughout *Walford*, but many other entries have been added, including synonyms, inverted headings, and cross-references. Some form headings such as 'Bibliographies', 'Dictionaries', etc., are omitted as leading to too great a bulk.

The arrangement of the index is alphabetical and filing is word by word, with groups of initials counted as single words. Under each main heading printed in bold type in the index will be found a resumé of all the subject terms used under that heading and the numbers of the items to which they refer. Similarly, under each narrower sub-heading there is a list of terms used. Where the term in the index needs to be qualified by the broader term of which it is a sub-division, then the broader term is given in square brackets, *e.g.* **Africa** [Folk Music] or [Theatre].

Online and Database Services Index

The index reference is to the running number given to each item. The running numbers are in one sequence throughout the volume and can be found at the top right hand corner of the entry for each item. This index is of authors and titles in one sequence. The names of authors are printed in bold type. Filing is word by word with groups of initials counted as single words.

The titles appearing in this index have been published as electronic databases. The databases are available on subscription as online database services, or in CD-ROM or disk formats. An indication of the names of some of the hosts from whom the online databases are available is given in the text.